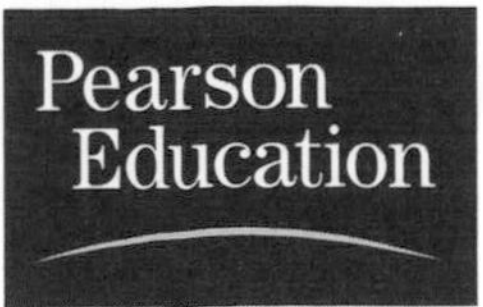

PEARSON EDUCATION
SECONDARY GROUP

1 Lake Street
Upper Saddle River, NJ 07458
201-236-5401…781-455-1309
Fax: 201-236-5553…781-433-8425
E-Mail: marty.smith@phschool.com

Martha G. Smith
President
Pearson Education
Secondary Group

To the Teacher:

As a former social studies teacher, I cannot imagine a more important time to be a social studies educator.

Since the terrorist attacks on New York City and Washington, D.C., on September 11, 2001, you have served at the front line of efforts to understand the causes and effects of those momentous events. In the social studies classroom, you have helped your students understand our nation's heritage of unity and determination in times of crisis. You have had the opportunity to instill in your students the core values of democracy, free enterprise, and the rule of law. Your students have probably explored concepts of freedom and justice, through primary sources from the Declaration of Independence to the "I Have a Dream" speech, and the rights and responsibilities of citizenship, through the Constitution of the United States. They may be learning and applying critical thinking skills as well—debating, for example, the benefits and challenges of living in an open and tolerant society.

As a social studies educator, you can help your students master the fundamentals of history, geography, civics, and economics, providing a context within which to analyze current events. With your guidance, this knowledge can inform and encourage young people's participation in the democratic process.

Today more than ever, you play a crucial role in the maturing of responsible citizens. You help create tomorrow's leaders—the future defenders of America's freedoms, as defined by one President during another time of great crisis:

> *"In the future days which we seek to make secure, we look forward to a world founded upon four essential human freedoms. The first is freedom of speech and expression—everywhere in the world. The second is freedom of every person to worship God in his own way—everywhere in the world. The third is freedom from want . . . everywhere in the world. The fourth is freedom from fear . . . anywhere in the world."*
>
> —President Franklin Delano Roosevelt
> State of the Union Address, January 6, 1941

Sincerely,

Martha G. Smith

TEACHER'S EDITION

IN ASSOCIATION WITH
American Heritage®

PRENTICE HALL

AMERICA

PATHWAYS TO THE PRESENT

MODERN AMERICAN HISTORY

Andrew Cayton
Elisabeth Israels Perry
Linda Reed
Allan M. Winkler

Prentice Hall

Needham, Massachusetts
Upper Saddle River, New Jersey
Glenview, Illinois

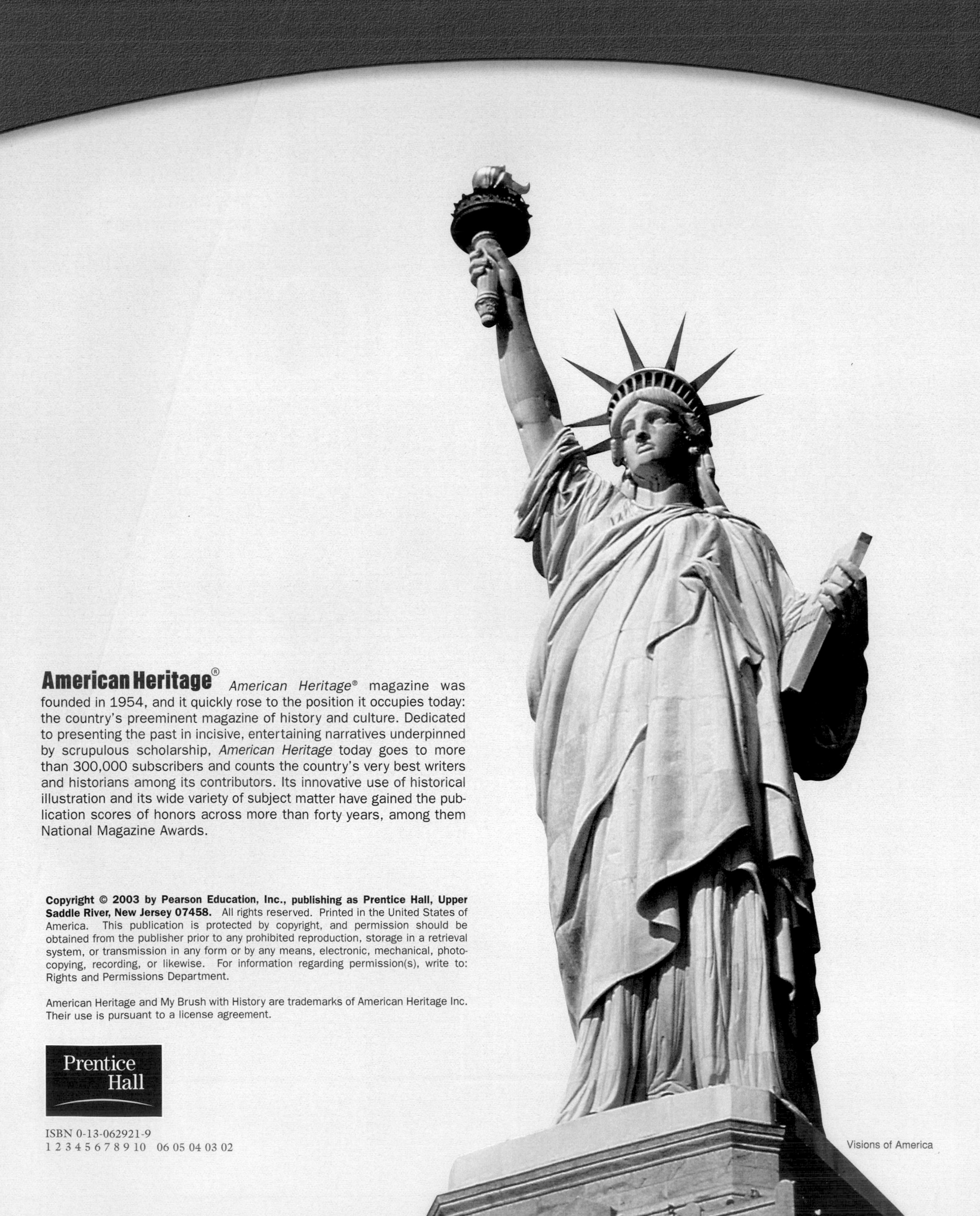

American Heritage® *American Heritage®* magazine was founded in 1954, and it quickly rose to the position it occupies today: the country's preeminent magazine of history and culture. Dedicated to presenting the past in incisive, entertaining narratives underpinned by scrupulous scholarship, *American Heritage* today goes to more than 300,000 subscribers and counts the country's very best writers and historians among its contributors. Its innovative use of historical illustration and its wide variety of subject matter have gained the publication scores of honors across more than forty years, among them National Magazine Awards.

Prentice Hall

ISBN 0-13-062921-9
1 2 3 4 5 6 7 8 9 10 06 05 04 03 02

Visions of America

Contents

Teacher's Edition

Student Edition

Inspire students with the rich story of America.

Modern American History Edition

Student Edition
Teacher's Edition

Classroom Resources

Teaching Resources
- Program Overview
- Pacing Charts
- Learning Styles Lesson Plans
- Unit Books
  - Section Quizzes
  - Chapter Tests
  - Chapter Summaries
  - American Pathways Activities
  - History's Lasting Impact
  - Answer Key
- American Pathways Posters (10)
- Skills for Life
- Guided Reading and Review
- Learning with Documents
- Great Debates in American History
- Biography, Literature, and Comparing Primary Sources
- Geography and History
- Constitution Study Guide
- Constitution Study Guide Teacher's Guide
- Guide to the Essentials (English)
- Guide to the Essentials (Spanish)
- Guide to the Essentials (Teacher's Edition)
- Nystrom Atlas of Our Country

Guided Reading and Review Workbook (English)
Guided Reading and Review Workbook (Spanish)
Guided Reading and Review Workbook Teacher's Edition (English)
Guided Reading and Review Workbook Teacher's Edition (Spanish)
Color Transparencies with Lesson Suggestions
- American Photos
- Fine Art
- Time Lines
- Cause-and-Effect
- The Way it Works
- American Diversity
- Political Cartoons
- Historical Maps

Section Reading Support Transparency System
Perspectives: Readings in American History
Classroom Literature Library
American History Block Scheduling Support File
American History Historical Outline Map
Brief Review in U.S. History and Government
Brief Review in U.S. History and Government Answer Key
Humanities Pack

Assessment

Prentice Hall Assessment System
- Program Assessment
  - Chapter Tests with ExamView® Test Bank CD-ROM
  - Document-Based Assessment
  - Alternative Assessment Handbook
- Test Prep
  - *Diagnose and Prescribe*
    - Diagnostic Tests for High School Social Studies Skills
  - *Review and Reteach*
    - Review Book for United States History
  - *Practice and Assess*
    - Test Prep Book for United States History
    - Test-taking Strategies with Transparencies for High School
    - Test-taking Strategies Posters

ExamView® Test Bank CD-ROM

Technology

Prentice Hall Presentation Pro CD-ROM
Resource Pro® CD-ROM
Modern American History Edition on Audio CD
Sounds of an Era Audio CD
Exploring Primary Sources in U.S. History CD-ROM
Interactive Constitution CD-ROM
Social Studies Skills Tutor CD-ROM
American Heritage® My Brush with History™
- Video Program
  - Videotapes (4) with Teacher's Guide

United States History Video Collection
- Videotapes with Teacher's Guide

iText®
Companion Web site

PH SuccessNet

Program Highlights:

- In-depth, balanced content makes history accessible for all students.
- Built-in reading strategies help students master content.
- Special features and technology develop social studies skills.
- Ongoing, embedded assessment prepare students for high-stakes exit tests.
- Association with **American Heritage**® brings the excitement of the nation's premier American history magazine right into the classroom.

Teach history in exciting new ways through our exclusive association with American Heritage®.

American Heritage® magazine was founded in 1954, and it quickly rose to the position it occupies today: the country's preeminent magazine of history and culture. Dedicated to presenting the past in entertaining narratives underpinned by scrupulous scholarship, *American Heritage* today goes to more than 300,000 subscribers and counts the country's very best writers and historians among its contributors. We have partnered to combine the best of their content with ours so you can teach history in exciting new ways.

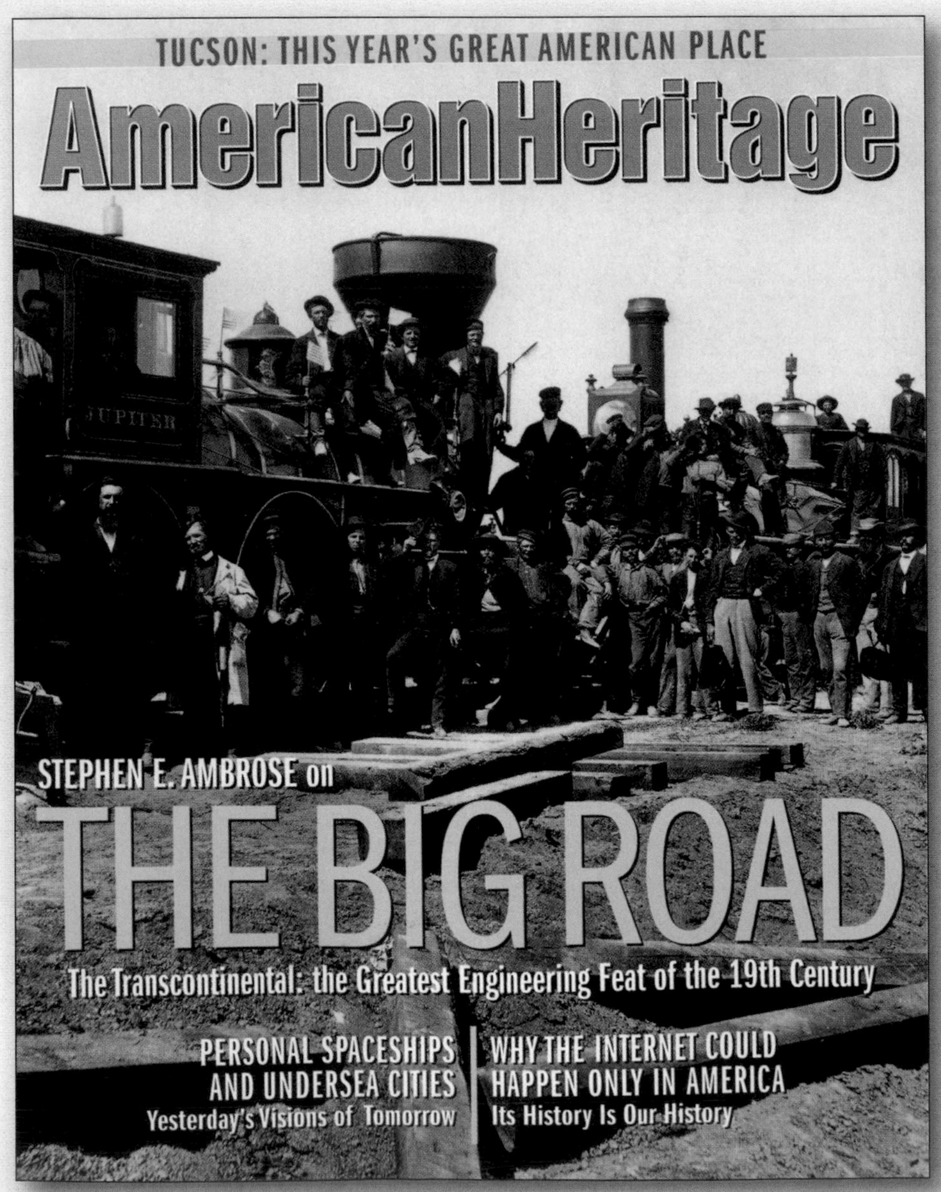

American Heritage magazine features compelling accounts and historical scholarship that add a whole new dimension to the way your students perceive their American history studies.

AmericanHeritage

MY BRUSH WITH **HISTORY**

by DAVID CONYNGHAM

A Civil War Soldier's Story

One day soldiers from North and South are shooting at each other engaged in a life and death struggle, the next they're trading coffee and conversation. Though it sounds too strange to be true, the following eyewitness account, selected by the editors of *American Heritage* magazine, describes just such a scene. The account is written by David Conynham, an officer in the army of William T. Sherman and a journalist. As you read the following excerpt, think about why such "private truces" might have taken place.

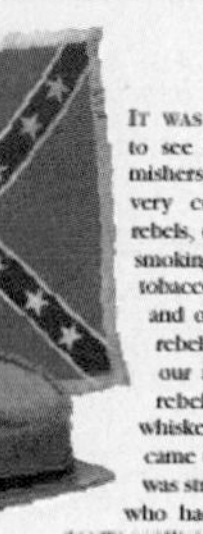

It was no unusual thing to see our pickets and skirmishers enjoying themselves very comfortably with the rebels, drinking bad whiskey, smoking and chewing worse tobacco, and trading coffee and other little articles. The rebels had no coffee, and our men plenty, while the rebels had plenty of whiskey; so they very soon came to an understanding. It was strange to see these men, who had been just pitted in deadly conflict, trading, and bantering, and chatting, as if they were the best friends in the world. They discussed a battle with the same gusto they would a cock-fight, or horse-race, and made inquiries about their friends, as to who was killed, and who not, in the Friends that have been separated for years have met in this way. Brothers who parted to try their fortune have often met on the picket line, or on the battle-field.

In those improvised truces, the best possible faith was observed by the men. These truces were brought about chiefly in the following manner. A rebel, who was heartily tired of his crippled position in his pit, would call out, "I say, Yank!"

"Well, Johnny Reb," would echo from another hole or tree.

"I'm going to put out my head; don't shoot."

"Well, I won't."

The reb would pop up his head; the Yank would do the same.

"Hain't you got any coffee, Johnny?"

"Na'r a bit, but plenty of rot-gut.

"All right; we'll have a trade."

They would meet, while several others would

402

My Brush with History™

Based on the popular *American Heritage* magazine feature, this engaging student edition feature presents eyewitness accounts of ordinary Americans and extraordinary events.

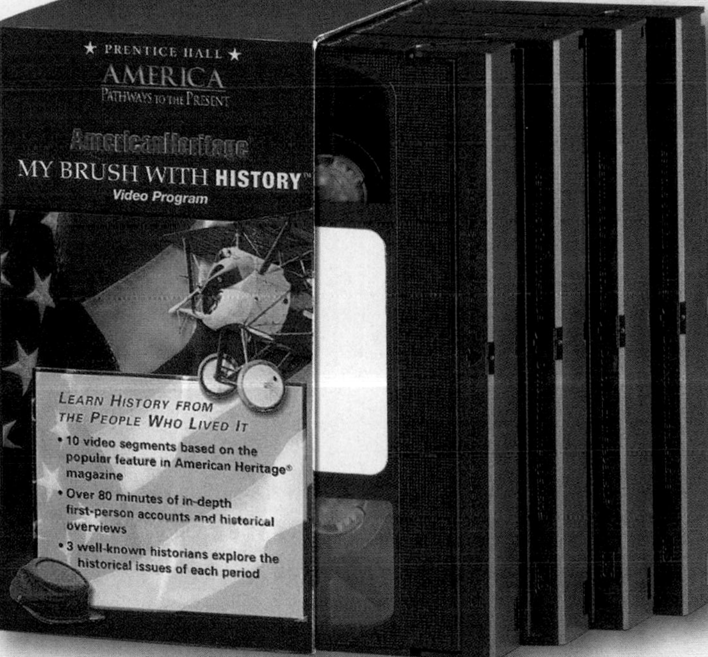

From the Archives of
AmericanHeritage®

Ending the War to End All Wars

In 1921, three years after the end of the Great War, Americans dealt with some unfinished business from that conflict. On November 8, President Warren Harding signed a joint resolution to end the war. Then, three days later on November 11, the remains of an unknown American soldier, exhumed from a French grave, were buried in Washington, D.C. Military men from all nations paid tribute with medals, ribbons, and decorations, including a Native American who laid a coup stick and war bonnet on the bier. In a moving address, Harding asked the American people to give of their influence and strength "...to put mankind on a little higher plane, exulting and exalting, with war's distressing and depressing tragedies barred from the state of righteous civilization." Source: Frederic D. Schwarz, "The Time Machine," *American Heritage* magazine, November 1996.

READING CHECK
The Allies were vehemently opposed to some aspects of Wilson's program, and lacked enthusiasm for the Fourteen Points as a whole. Clemenceau, Lloyd George, and Orlando were determined to extract reparations and territory from the defeated nations. The Allies also defied Wilson by insisting that Germany accept guilt for starting the war.

Point-of-Use Teaching Notes

Point-of-use teaching notes from *American Heritage* magazines and books are woven throughout the Teacher's Edition to give you background information for vitalizing classroom lectures and discussions.

American Heritage® My Brush with History™ Video Program

This brand-new video program extends the My Brush with History™ feature in the student edition. In-depth, first-person accounts, historical overviews, and interviews with well-known historians, provide a dramatic context for understanding larger events in American history.

But I'm Not a Reading Teacher!

Few people choose to be social studies teachers in order to focus on reading. Yet a significant number of today's students lack reading proficiency. Without it, they cannot access the wealth of social studies content they need to absorb from textbooks, primary sources, literature, and more. When students can't read well, they don't read and won't read.

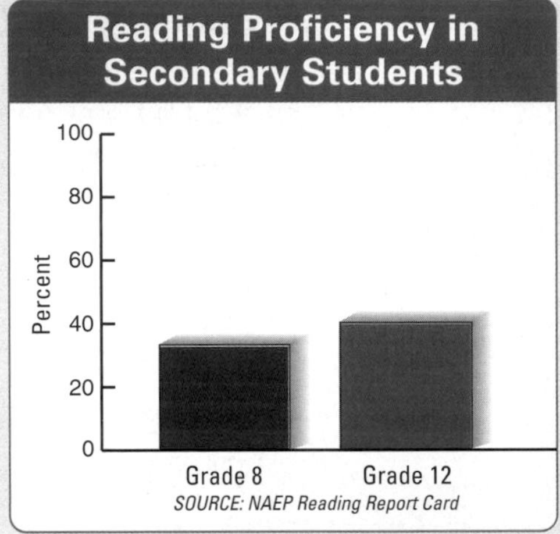

Best Practices in Reading

Instead of plunging in and plodding through a section, students need a plan of action, a strategy. Best practices for teaching reading in social studies focus on **comprehension strategies**—teaching students what to do *before reading, during reading,* and *after reading.*

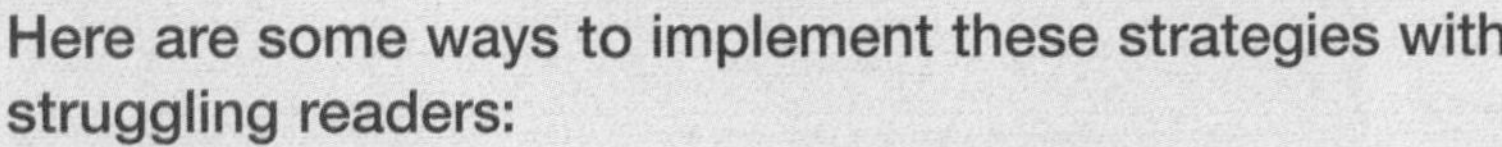

Here are some ways to implement these strategies with struggling readers:

Before Reading Both teacher and student preparations precede reading.

- Use an anecdote, photo, artifact, or audio to set the scene.
- Display a map or other visual aid to encourage students to identify what they already know and to make predictions to apply this knowledge to a new situation.
- Model for students how to look at pictures, captions, and headings in order to predict what they will be learning.

During Reading Student-directed, individual activities take place during reading. Providing guided practice will help students develop these habits.

- Show students how to take notes, using graphic organizers that match the type of information they are reading. For example, use a Venn diagram for comparing and contrasting, a flowchart for sequencing, and a concept web for finding main idea and supporting details.
- Teach students to ask themselves questions as they read.
- Demonstrate for students how to make connections between what they read and what they already know.

After Reading Both student-directed and teacher-directed activities can follow reading.

- Conduct a sample self-check for students—"What have I learned?"
- Teach students to ask themselves, "How does this relate to what I already know?"
- Demonstrate both formal and informal assessments that students will encounter.

Reading success happens when students can construct meaning from information.

Comprehension Strategies

Before Reading

- Activate prior knowledge
- Build needed prior knowledge
- Focus attention
- Set purpose for reading
- Make predictions

During Reading

- Confirm predictions
- Read and self-monitor
- Take notes and ask questions

After Reading

- Recall information
- Respond to new learning
- Extend and transfer new learning
- Assess reading success

Prentice Hall Support Throughout the Program

The structure of each Prentice Hall program embeds the development of solid reading skills in the Student Edition. Each section of the text starts with suggestions to the student for *before reading* and *during reading*.

At the end of each section, students will find opportunities to recall and apply information and construct meaning from it.

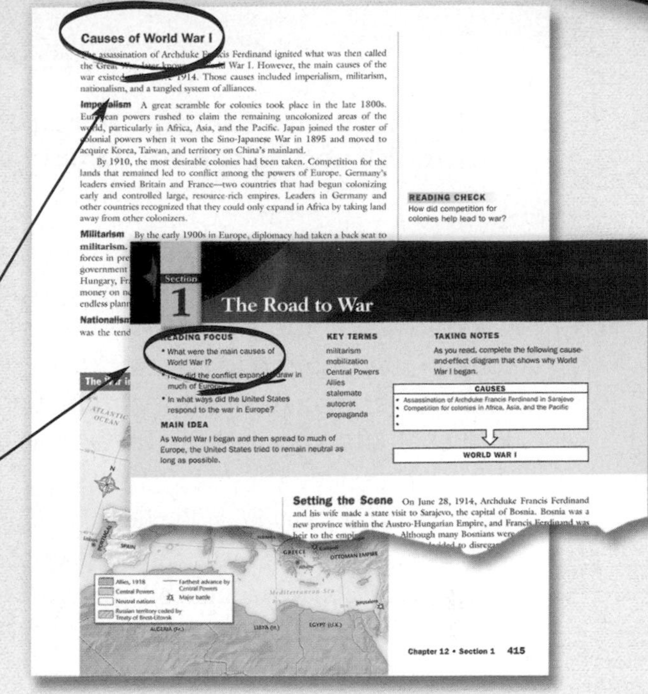
Causes of World War I

Section 1 The Road to War

READING FOCUS

- What were the main causes of World War I?
- In what ways did the United States respond to the war in Europe?

MAIN IDEA

As World War I began and then spread to much of Europe, the United States tried to remain neutral as long as possible.

KEY TERMS

militarism
mobilization
Central Powers
Allies
stalemate
autocrat
propaganda

TAKING NOTES

As you read, complete the following cause-and-effect diagram that shows why World War I began.

CAUSES

- Assassination of Archduke Francis Ferdinand in Sarajevo
- Competition for colonies in Africa, Asia, and the Pacific

WORLD WAR I

READING CHECK

How did competition for colonies help lead to war?

Chapter 12 • Section 1 415

Notice that the *Reading Focus* questions align with the subheadings in the section.

Teacher's Edition

Additional reading strategies as well as ways to customize instruction for less proficient readers and English language learners give you focused strategies to improve students' comprehension.

CUSTOMIZE FOR ...

ESL

Have students read the material under the heading "Causes of World War I." Then have them use the map on this page titled "The War in Europe, 1914–1918" to explain the causes of the war in their own words.

TEST PREPARATION

Have students reread the section "Causes of World War I" on this page and then answer the question below.

Which of the below is an example of nationalism?

A The desire of a powerful nation to expand by seizing control of a smaller nation.

B The growth of a nation's military power in the interest of waging war.

(C) The longing of an ethnic minority for independence.

D The decision by a government to remain neutral in wartime.

CAPTION ANSWERS

Map Skills The Allies, because the Central Powers were nearly surrounded by enemy nations.

Chapter 12 Section 1 • **415**

Section Reading Support Transparency System

Every section of the text has a companion reading support transparency that delivers the main points through a graphic organizer.

Transparency 12.1
Causes Chart

Chapter 12, Section 1

CAUSES

- Assassination of Archduke Francis Ferdinand in Sarajevo
- Competition for colonies in Africa, Asia, and the Pacific
- Nationalists seek independence for expansion for their homelands
- Alliances require major powers to take sides in small regional conflicts

WORLD WAR I

Guide to the Essentials

Look in the Teaching Resources box for the Guide to the Essentials in both English and Spanish. Students use this book to review and master new content through summaries written below grade level.

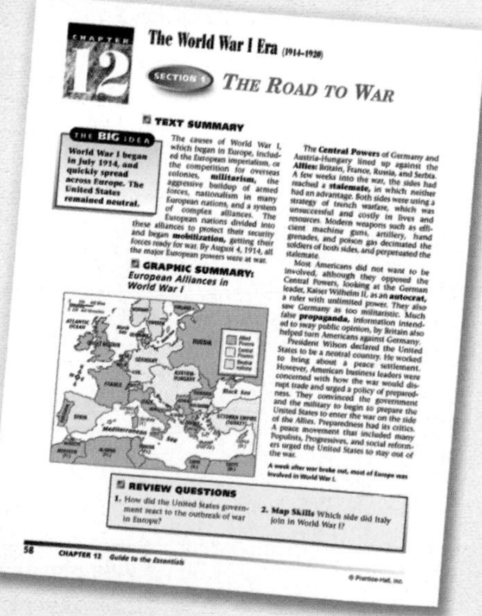
CHAPTER 12 The World War I Era (1914–1920)

SECTION 1 THE ROAD TO WAR

TEXT SUMMARY

THE BIG IDEA

World War I began in July 1914, and quickly spread across Europe. The United States remained neutral.

The causes of World War I, which began in Europe, included the European imperialism, or the competition for overseas colonies, **militarism,** the aggressive buildup of armed forces, nationalism in many European nations, and a system of complex alliances. The European nations divided into these alliances to protect their security and began **mobilization,** getting their forces ready for war. By August 4, 1914, all the major European powers were at war.

The **Central Powers** of Germany and Austria-Hungary lined up against the **Allies:** Britain, France, Russia, and Serbia. A few weeks into the war, the sides had reached a **stalemate,** in which neither had an advantage. Both sides were using a strategy of trench warfare, which was unsuccessful and costly in lives and resources. Modern weapons such as efficient machine guns, artillery, hand grenades, and poison gas decimated the soldiers of both sides, and perpetuated the stalemate.

Most Americans did not want to be involved, although they opposed the Central Powers, looking at the German leader, Kaiser Wilhelm II, as an **autocrat,** a ruler with unlimited power. They also saw Germany as too militaristic. Much false **propaganda,** information intended to sway public opinion, by Britain also helped turn Americans against Germany.

President Wilson declared the United States to be a neutral country. He worked to bring about a peace settlement. However, American business leaders were concerned with how the war would disrupt trade and urged a policy of preparedness. They convinced the government and the military to begin to prepare the United States to enter the war on the side of the Allies. Preparedness had its critics. A peace movement that included many Populists, Progressives, and social reformers urged the United States to stay out of the war.

GRAPHIC SUMMARY: European Alliances in World War I

A week after war broke out, most of Europe was involved in World War I.

REVIEW QUESTIONS

1. How did the United States government react to the outbreak of war in Europe?

2. **Map Skills** Which side did Italy join in World War I?

58 CHAPTER 12 Guide to the Essentials

© Prentice-Hall, Inc.

Student Edition on Audio

Auditory learners, less proficient readers, and English language learners can benefit from listening to the book on CD as they read the text.

Why Should I Teach Skills?

"Give a man a fish, and he eats for a day. Teach a man to fish and he eats for a lifetime."

— Anonymous

Following this advice, if we present our students with only content, we are, in essence, giving them the fish. If we are to prepare students for life, we need to teach the skills needed to make sense out of the increasing volume of information in the world. To help students become lifelong learners, we need to develop their abilities to question, read, analyze, interpret, and evaluate information, as well as to communicate their ideas to others.

Because these skills lie at the heart of understanding social studies, they need to be embedded in content instruction. Think of social studies content as having three levels: facts, concepts, and enduring understandings or "big ideas." Skills development is essential for comprehension at each level, as in this example.

Topic: Colonization

	Example	Skill
Facts	Location of colonies	Map reading
Concepts	Migration	Cause and effect
Big Ideas	People make choices to meet needs	Problem-solving

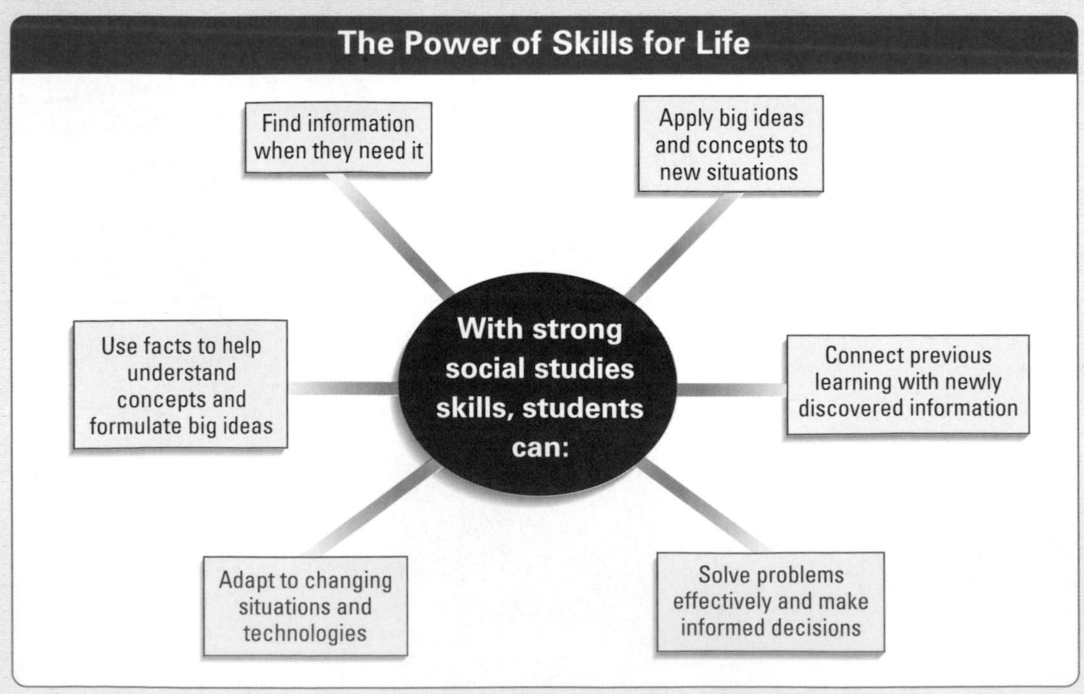

The Power of Skills for Life
Find information when they need it
Apply big ideas and concepts to new situations
With strong social studies skills, students can:
Use facts to help understand concepts and formulate big ideas
Connect previous learning with newly discovered information
Adapt to changing situations and technologies
Solve problems effectively and make informed decisions

Best Practices in Skills Integration

These guidelines will help you to embed skills development within content instruction.

1. **Plan each unit around an enduring understanding or big idea.** For example, if the unit you are about to teach is The Early Republic, 1789–1825, the big idea might be "new institutions face many challenges to their existence."

2. **Develop each lesson around the facts, concepts, the big idea, and the skills students need to be able to connect the content to the big idea.** For part of a lesson on foreign relations, you might want to focus on the Embargo Act and its impact.

Topic: Foreign Relations		
	Example	**Skill**
Facts	Economic impact of Embargo Act	Graph reading
Concepts	Supply and demand	Cause and effect
Big Ideas	New institutions face many challenges to their existence	Synthesizing information

3. **Teach skills that are new or that add another level of complexity to a previously mastered skill.** Follow the elements of good skill instruction:
   - Set a purpose for using the skill.
   - Present the steps to follow.
   - Model the process for using the skill.
   - Guide practice and provide feedback.
   - Apply to a prompt such as a picture, map, or reading passage.

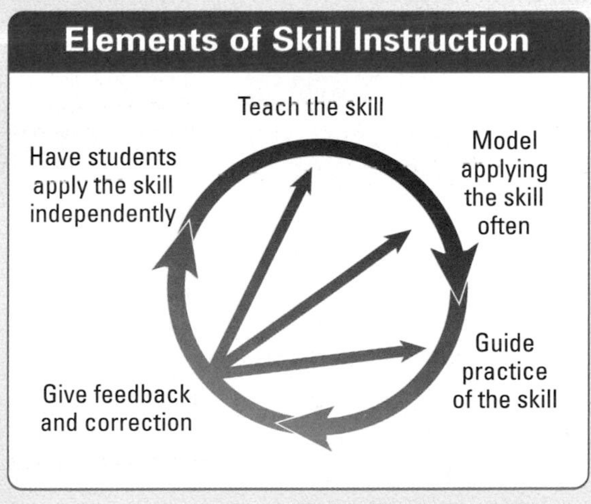
Elements of Skill Instruction
Teach the skill
Model applying the skill often
Guide practice of the skill
Give feedback and correction
Have students apply the skill independently

4. **Reinforce skills whenever possible.** Ask critical thinking questions about maps, photos, graphs, charts, and primary sources.

5. **Assess both content and skills mastery regularly.** It is important to determine whether students are remembering important information, but equally important to determine whether they are internalizing skills as lifelong learners.

6. **Include skills in big projects.** Give students opportunities to combine their thinking and research abilities at least several times a year.

Prentice Hall Support for Skills

Skills mastery means developing habits of mind that enable us to turn information into meaning. To achieve mastery, students need both instruction and continuous reinforcement— many, many opportunities to practice and apply skills in new situations. Every Prentice Hall social studies program contains a wealth of resources to build skills for life.

Skills pages in the Student Edition provide three-step instruction strategy.

Learn

Practice

Apply

Using Cross-Sectional Maps

SKILLS FOR LIFE

It is sometimes helpful to use more than one type of map to understand a particular piece of land. Physical-political maps show the land as if viewed from above, revealing distances across the surface. Cross-sectional maps show how the land would look if viewed from the side; they indicate the heights of mountains and valleys. The cross-sectional map below shows the changes in elevation along the route of the first transcontinental railroad. These changes posed a great challenge to workers building the railroad between 1862 and 1869.

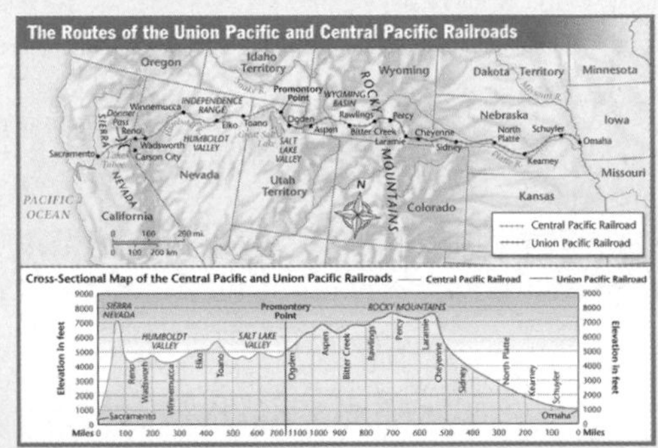

LEARN THE SKILL

Use the following steps to analyze a cross-sectional map:

1. **Study the region shown on both maps.** Compare the area covered and the elements shown on each map. Find several points that appear on both maps, and notice how they are depicted on each map.
2. **Analyze the information shown on the cross-sectional map.** Notice how changes in elevation are shown on the map (in this case, as the rising and falling of the green and red lines). Study the scale on the map, and notice both the distance covered across land and the elevation.
3. **Draw conclusions about the places or events depicted on the maps.** Use what you learn from both maps to better understand the landforms and the human activity in that area.

PRACTICE THE SKILL

Answer the following questions:

1. **(a)** Which landforms on the physical-political map correspond to those on the cross-sectional map? Which landforms appear on only one map? **(b)** Does the cross-sectional map show the same land area as the physical-political map? Explain. **(c)** Does the cross-sectional map cover the same east-west distance as the physical-political map? Explain.
2. **(a)** What were the highest and lowest elevations of each railroad route? **(b)** Which 100-mile section on each route had the sharpest changes? **(c)** Which 100-mile section on each route had the most gradual changes? **(d)** How long was each route?
3. **(a)** How do the length and elevation changes of the two routes compare? **(b)** Which railroad workers faced the greatest challenge at the start of the project: those working east from Sacramento, or those working west from Omaha? Explain. **(c)** Which workers faced the greatest overall challenge? Explain.

APPLY THE SKILL

See the Chapter Review and Assessment for another opportunity to apply this skill.

236 Chapter 6 • *The Expansion of American Industry*

Teaching suggestions accompany skills lessons and reinforcement activities.

Using Cross-Sectional Maps

Focus Students compare the data provided in a cross-sectional map with that in a physical-political map.

Instruct To be sure students understand the information presented in the cross-sectional map, ask them to identify the locations on the map at elevation 1,000 feet and 7,000 feet. Have them indicate the elevation at Bitter Creek. Ask students to think about some other useful subjects for cross-sectional maps. *(The ocean floor, rivers, and other waterways.)*

Extend See the Skills for Life activity in the Resource Directory below.

Skills reinforcement appears in all caption questions.

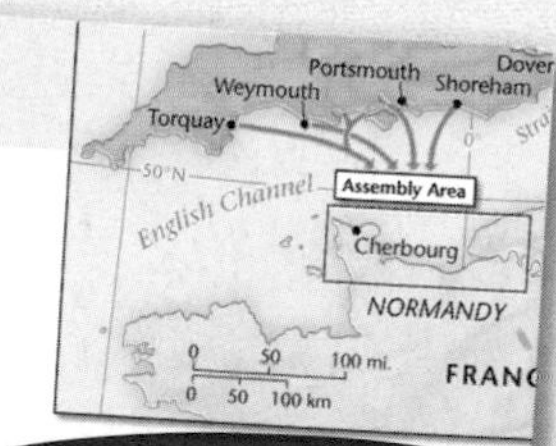

MAP SKILLS Allied troops began the liberation of Western Europe on the beaches of Normandy on June 6, 1944. **Movement** *Cite evidence to show that the Allies carefully planned most aspects of the invasion.*

Social Studies Skills Tutor CD-ROM provides two levels of interactive instruction and practice in 20 core social studies skills.

The Prentice Hall Vertical Alignment System

Mastery also requires that students learn skills at increasing levels of complexity as they progress through school. Prentice Hall takes the guesswork out of aligning skills instruction by developing 20 core social studies skills with increasing difficulty from grade to grade in every Prentice Hall program.

Here you see how three Prentice Hall programs build and elaborate the skill of analyzing graphic data.

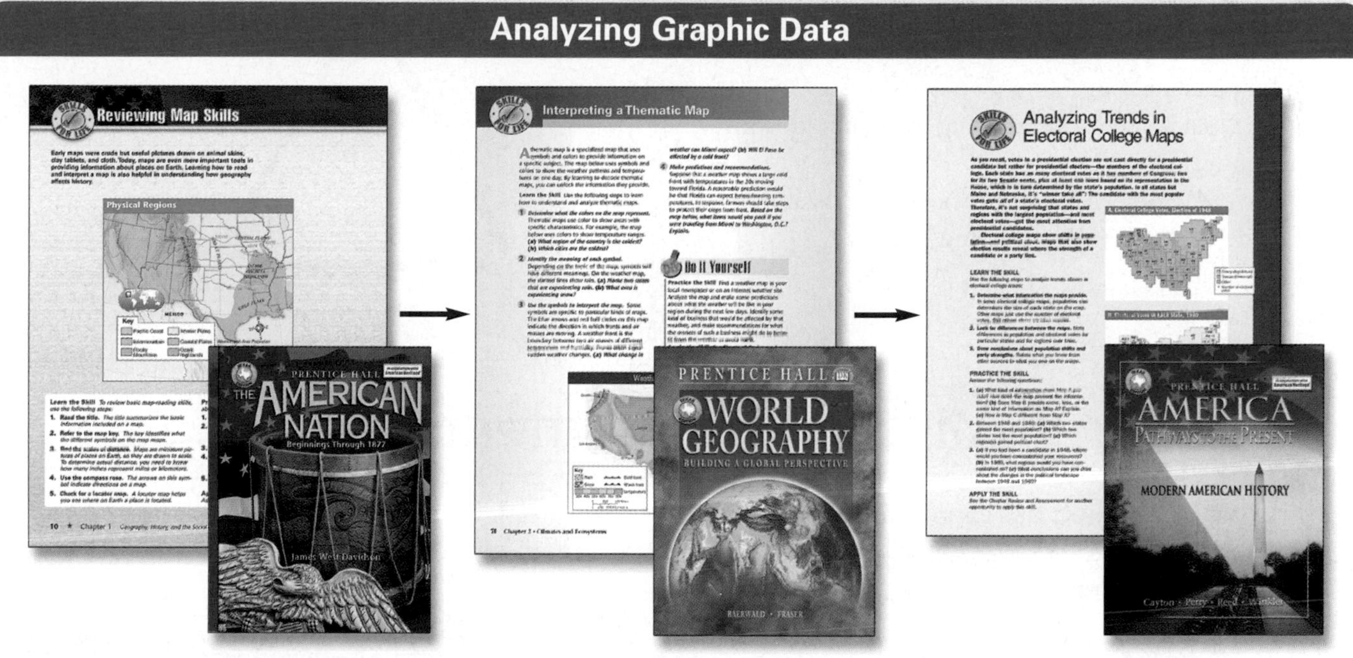

The 20 Core Social Studies Skills

1.	Using the Cartographer's Tools	**11.**	Comparing and Contrasting
2.	Using Special Purpose Maps	**12.**	Analyzing Primary Sources
3.	Analyzing Graphic Data	**13.**	Recognizing Bias and Propaganda
4.	Analyzing Images	**14.**	Identifying Frame of Reference and Point of View
5.	Identifying Main Ideas/Summarizing	**15.**	Decision-making
6.	Sequencing	**16.**	Problem-solving
7.	Identifying Cause & Effect/ Making Predictions	**17.**	Using Reliable Information
8.	Drawing Inferences and Conclusions	**18.**	Transferring Information from One Medium to Another
9.	Making Valid Generalizations	**19.**	Synthesizing Information
10.	Distinguishing Fact & Opinion	**20.**	Supporting a Position

Should I Teach to the Test?

The increasing importance of state standards and student accountability leads many teachers to wonder whether they must limit their classes to the content of high-stakes exams. While based on state standards and student needs, a truly effective social studies program requires alignment of curriculum, instruction, and assessment. When each of these elements dovetails with the others, *all* instruction prepares students for assessment based on curriculum objectives.

In an aligned system, both teacher and student know what is expected. There are no secrets or surprises. To ensure alignment:

- Teach the objectives in your standards to the specified level of understanding.
- Make sure that students know what they should learn before you teach.
- Test those same objectives as precisely as possible to the same depth of understanding that the standards require.

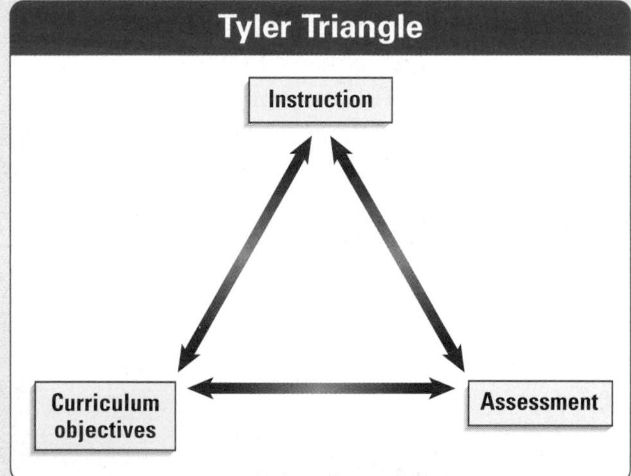

Constructing Aligned Assessments

The principle of aligning assessment questions to curriculum objectives and instruction needs to be applied for both standardized tests and teacher-created exams.

At the state level

To create assessments based on state standards, test writers dissect the objectives for the pieces of appropriate content and the thinking level required of the student. Test questions are written, reviewed, piloted, reviewed once again, and placed in testing banks.

At the classroom level

While state tests occur perhaps once a year, teachers must use an ongoing system of testing to measure student learning throughout the year. Teachers need to plan instruction and assessment simultaneously, with both of them based on the state curriculum objectives.

Best Practices in Assessment

Good assessment is part of an integrated cycle that is repeated throughout the school year. Following the principle of alignment, good assessment grows out of preparation that begins long before any test is administered and leads to improvements in teaching and learning long after the test. Here are some ways to integrate ongoing assessment into instruction:

Assessment Techniques	
Diagnose and Prescribe Evaluate student abilities at the beginning of the year.	The best way to know whether students are ready for the difficulty level you intend to use is to give a diagnostic test when school opens. Students will not know the content you are about to teach them, but they should bring with them a number of social studies skills that they will apply to new content. Evaluate student facility in these areas: • Map and globe skills • Critical thinking and reading • Graph and chart skills • Communications
Plan and Align Plan instruction to align with assessment.	• Examine objectives carefully. • Choose learning activities that require more than a knowledge level (or memorized level) from students. • Test students on all of the objectives, omitting none. Do not test information not contained in an objective. • Test skill development at the same time you assess content. • Integrate skill and content questions so that students must use what they know and combine it with new information that they gather. • Test students' understanding of the objectives on many levels of thinking.
Review and Reteach Weave ongoing review into aligned instruction and assessment.	One quick and easy way to check how much students remember from one unit to the next is to include some review questions on each of your tests. • Find ways to connect new learning to previous learning as you put your lessons together. This previous learning could come from units previously studied during the same year or from content studied in other courses. • Choose review questions that are aligned to your current lessons.
Practice and Assess Apply assessment results to improve teaching and learning.	• Use individual student information for tutoring and devising individualized plans for improvement. • Use whole-class data to determine if your teaching was aligned to the assessment. If many students missed an item, it was probably not aligned to your instruction and intent. Make changes when you teach this unit again. • Use review data on both individuals and the whole class to make a list of those objectives with which students may have difficulty on an end-of-year test.

Prentice Hall Assessment System

The Prentice Hall Assessment System provides comprehensive support for both program content assessment and preparation for high-stakes standardized tests.

Program Assessment

Use the Chapter Tests to assess core content for every chapter.

Develop your own customized tests and practice worksheets with the ExamView® Test Bank CD-ROM, selecting from hundreds of test questions and using the word-processing and editing capabilities. Create online tests and study guides and receive instant feedback on student progress.

Prepare students for document-based questions by evaluating, analyzing, and interpreting primary and secondary sources.

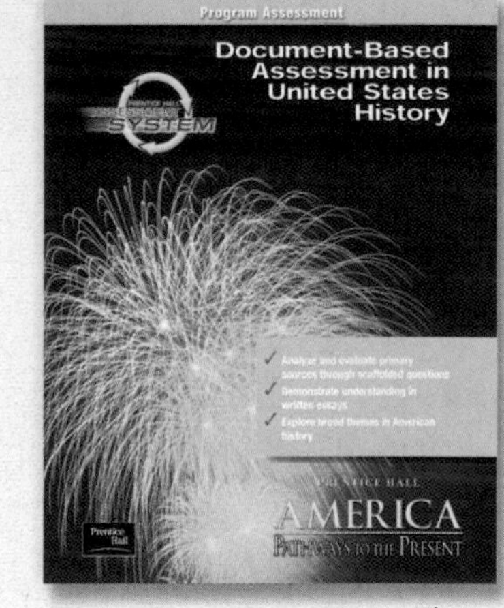

Use a variety of assessment options to evaluate students' performance, such as activity-based assessment or portfolio assessment.

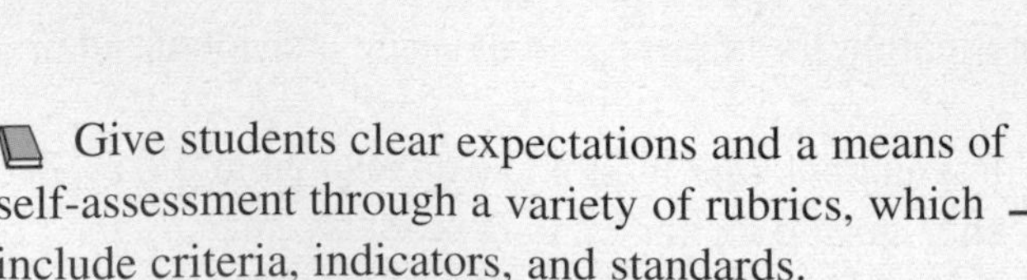

Give students clear expectations and a means of self-assessment through a variety of rubrics, which include criteria, indicators, and standards.

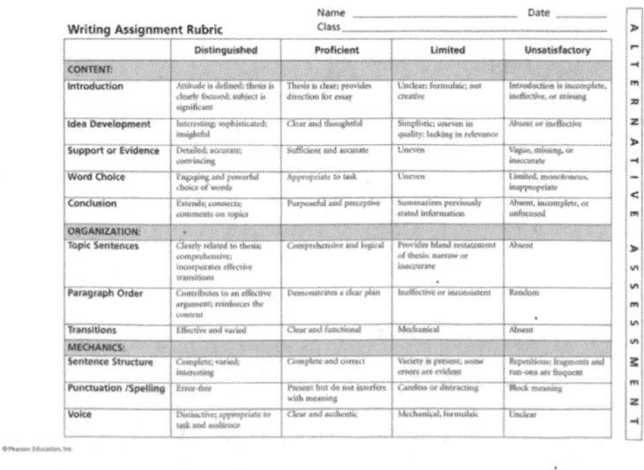

8 • Alternative Assessment

Name ______ Date ______
Class ______

Writing Assignment Rubric

	Distinguished	Proficient	Limited	Unsatisfactory
CONTENT:				
Introduction	Attitude is defined; thesis is clearly focused; subject is significant	Thesis is clear; provides direction for essay	Unclear; formulaic; not creative	Introduction is incomplete, ineffective, or missing
Idea Development	Interesting; sophisticated; insightful	Clear and thoughtful	Simplistic; uneven in quality; lacking in relevance	Absent or ineffective
Support or Evidence	Detailed; accurate; convincing	Sufficient and accurate	Uneven	Vague, missing, or inaccurate
Word Choice	Engaging and powerful choice of words	Appropriate to task	Uneven	Limited, monotonous, inappropriate
Conclusion	Extends; connects; comments on topics	Purposeful and perceptive	Summarizes previously stated information	Absent, incomplete, or unfocused
ORGANIZATION:				
Topic Sentences	Clearly related to thesis; comprehensive; incorporates effective transitions	Comprehensive and logical	Provides bland restatement of thesis; narrow or inaccurate	Absent
Paragraph Order	Contributes to an effective argument; reinforces the content	Demonstrates a clear plan	Ineffective or inconsistent	Random
Transitions	Effective and varied	Clear and functional	Mechanical	Absent
MECHANICS:				
Sentence Structure	Complete; varied; interesting	Complete and correct	Variety is present; some errors are evident	Repetitious; fragments and run-ons are frequent
Punctuation /Spelling	Error-free	Present but do not interfere with meaning	Careless or distracting	Block meaning
Voice	Distinctive; appropriate to task and audience	Clear and authentic	Mechanical, formulaic	Unclear

ALTERNATIVE ASSESSMENT

© Pearson Education, Inc.

Standardized Test Preparation

Prentice Hall Assessment System gives you the tools to help your students succeed on standardized tests, from the beginning of the year to the culminating high-stakes exam.

Diagnose and Prescribe

- Profile student skills with Diagnostic Tests A & B.
- Address student needs with program resources correlated to diagnostic test questions.

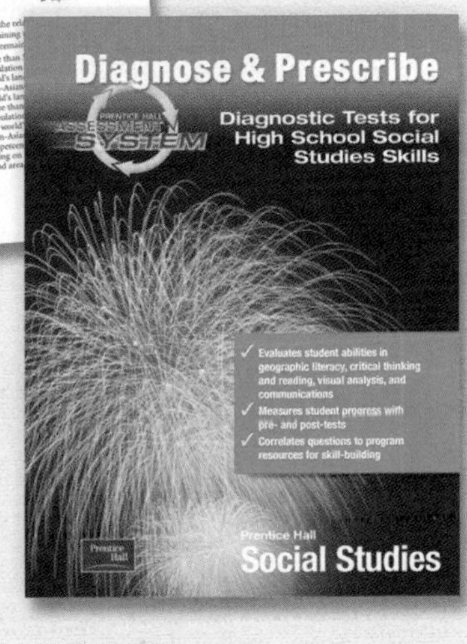

Review and Reteach

- Provide cumulative content review with unit-level questions and study sheets.

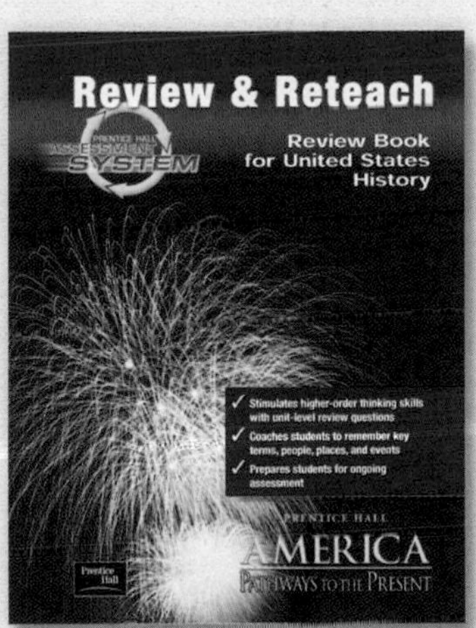

Practice and Assess

- Build assessment skills using Test-Taking Strategies With Transparencies.

Reinforce assessment skills with Test-Taking Posters.

- Develop students' test-taking skills and improve their scores on standardized tests with the Test Preparation Workbook.

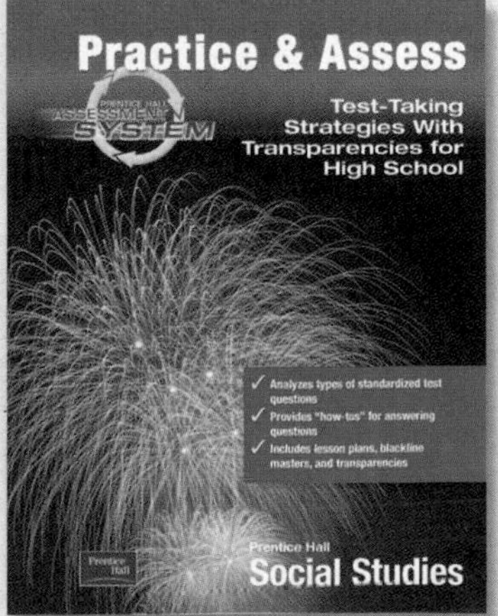

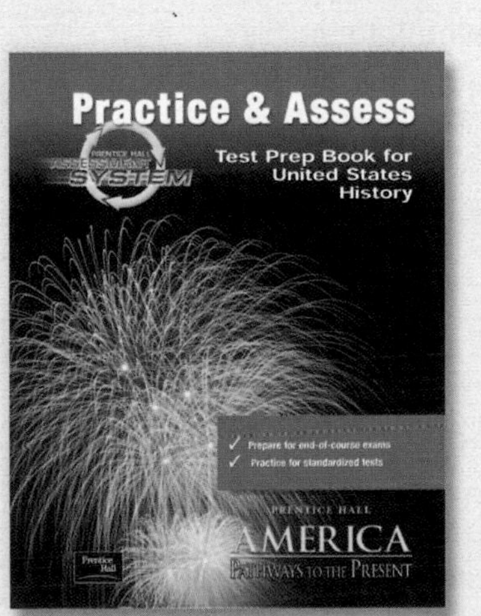

How Am I Doing?

Paired with the demand for high student achievement has come the drive for greater teacher accountability. More and more states and districts are establishing standards for teaching and new systems of teacher evaluation.

The Texas Essential Knowledge and Skills have changed the focus from what the teacher will do to what students will be able to do. As a result, student success emerges as the most critical measure of teaching—the teacher has not taught if students have not learned. The goal is the learner-centered class, alive with critical thinking, problem-solving activities, collaborative learning, projects, and investigations. The Professional Development and Appraisal System (PDAS) and local teacher appraisals apply the essential components of active, learner-centered instruction in their criteria.

Prentice Hall social studies programs provide a variety of ways to support learner-centered instruction. Below you will find a guide to program resources to help you address criteria commonly found in teacher evaluations.

Common Criteria	Where to Look for Support
Active, successful student participation in the learning process	• Structured reading support • Activities at section and chapter levels • Group and individual activities
Learner-centered instruction	• Critical-thinking questions in every caption • Technology for students: Social Studies Skills Tutor CD-ROM, Interactive Constitution CD-ROM, www.phschool.com, Exploring Primary Sources in U.S. History CD-ROM, • Customize For... in TE
Evaluation and feedback on student progress	• Section and chapter assessments in student edition • Diagnostic tests and correlations to program resources in Prentice Hall Assessment System • ExamView® Test Bank CD-ROM
Management of student discipline, instructional strategies, time, and materials	• TE lesson plans • Pacing charts • Chapter interleaf • Resource Pro® CD-ROM
Professional communications	• Letters to families • Resource Pro® CD-ROM
Professional development	• eTeach • PHSuccessNet • www.phschool.com/Texas • Skylight Professional Development services at www.skylightedu.com
Compliance with policies, operating procedures, and requirements	• Resource Pro® CD-ROM
Improvement of academic performance of all students	• Prentice Hall Assessment System

Texas Essential Knowledge and Skills Correlation

***Note:* Entries with a page number preceded by *TE* refer to the Teacher's Edition; *iText* indicates the interactive text.**

1. History. The student understands traditional historical points of reference in U.S. history from 1877 to the present. The student is expected to:		
(A) identify the major eras in U.S. history from 1877 to the present and describe their defining characteristics	**major eras in U.S. history,** 290–315, 316, 383–407, 408, 461–464, 474, 511–523,	530; TE: 459
(B) apply absolute and relative chronology through the sequencing of significant individuals, events, and time periods	**sequencing of significant individuals,** TE: 508 **events,** 336, 356, 371, 574, 579, 608, 656, 727, 812, 817, 850; TE: 357, 380, 396, 403, 508, 581, 609, 636, 653, 717, 739, 752, 772, 813, 835 **time periods,** TE: 508	**Chapter Time Lines,** 2–3, 38–39, 104–105, 154–155, 198–199, 224–225, 256–257, 288–289, 318–319, 350– 351, 380–381, 412–413, 450–451, 478–479, 506–507, 534–535, 566–567, 592–59, 634–635, 666–667, 696–697, 734–735, 762–763, 790–791, 824–825, 862–863, 892–893
(C) explain the significance of the following dates: 1898, 1914-1918, 1929, 1941-1945, and 1957	**1898,** 350, 359–361; TE: 357 **1914-1918,** 412–413, 414–418, 437 **1929,** 506, 508–512; TE: 506	**1941-1945,** 592–593; TE: 592 **1957,** 635, 660–661, 667, 668; TE: 666
2. History. The student understands the political, economic, and social changes in the United States from 1877 to 1898. The student is expected to:		
(A) analyze political issues such as Indian policies, the growth of political machines, and civil service reform	**Indian policies,** 261, 262, 263, 264, 265–267, 284; TE: 261, 263, 264, 265	**growth of political machines,** 308–309, 316 **civil service reform,** 292–293, 296; TE: 291
(B) analyze economic issues such as industrialization, the growth of railroads, the growth of labor unions, farm issues, and the rise of big business	**industrialization,** 243–246, 254; TE: 233, 237, 244 **growth of railroads,** 226, 230–233, 235, 254; TE: 225, 230, 231, 232 **growth of labor unions,** 247, 248–253, 254, 385, 387; TE: 247, 248, 250, 251,	252, 385, 394 **farm issues,** 268, 272–275, 276, 277–282, 285; TE: 273, 274, 277, 278, 280, **rise of big business,** 237–242, 254; TE: 237, 238
(C) analyze social issues such as the treatment of minorities, child labor, growth of cities, and problems of immigration	**treatment of minorities,** 301, 302, 314, 315, 323–325, 332–335; TE: 247 **child labor,** 243, 245, 246, 254; TE: 243 **growth of cities,** 304, 305–309, 316, 331; TE: 304, 305, 306	**problems of immigration,** 297–303, 314, 315, 316, 321; TE: 240, 243, 297, 298, 299, 300, 301
3. History. Students understand the emergence of the United States as a world power between 1898 and 1920. The student is expected to:		
(A) explain why significant events and individuals, including the Spanish-American War, U.S. expansionism, Henry Cabot Lodge, Alfred Thayer Mahan, and Theodore Roosevelt, moved the United States into a position of a world power	**Spanish-American War,** 357–361, 364; TE: 358, 361 **U.S. expansionism,** 352–356, 376; TE: 360 **Henry Cabot Lodge,** 352, 356, 376; TE: 353	**Alfred Thayer Mahan,** 350, 355, 376; TE: 376 **Theodore Roosevelt,** 351, 360, 366, 367, 368–370, 371, 376, 377; TE: 360, 367, 369, 399
(B) identify the reasons for U.S. involvement in World War I, including unrestricted submarine warfare	**reasons for U.S. involvement in World War I,** 418–419, 421–424, 442; TE: 422	**including unrestricted submarine warfare** 421–423, 424, 442, 443; TE: 421, 422, 423

(C) analyze significant events such as the battle of Argonne Forest and the impact of significant individuals including John J. Pershing during World War I	**significant events,** 427, 428, 429, 430, 431, 442; TE: 428 **battle of Argonne Forest,** 427; TE: 428	**John J. Pershing,** 425, 426, 427, 442; TE: 427 **other significant individuals,** 427, 428, 429, 431; TE: 427
(D) analyze major issues raised by U.S. involvement in World War I, Wilson's Fourteen Points, and the Treaty of Versailles	**analyze major issues raised by U.S. involvement in World War I,** 432–433, 434–436, 440–441, 442; TE: 425, 426, 433 **Wilson's Fourteen Points,** 437–438, 441,	442; TE: 438, 439 **Treaty of Versailles,** 437, 439–440, 441, 442; TE: 438
4. History. The student understands the effects of reform and third party movements on American society. The student is expected to:		
(A) evaluate the impact of Progressive Era reforms including initiative, referendum, recall, and the passage of the 16th and 17th amendments	**Progressive Era reforms,** 384, 387, 389–395, 403–407, 408; TE: 382, 383, 389, 390, 393, 398, 403 **initiative,** 392, 395	**referendum,** 392; TE: 392 **recall,** 392 **16th amendment,** 395 **17th amendment,** 395
(B) evaluate the impact of reform leaders such as Susan B. Anthony, W.E.B. DuBois, and Robert LaFollette on American society	**reform leaders,** 324–325, 382, 384, 385, 386, 387, 389, 393, 394, 399, 403, 404; TE: 385, 392, 393, 394, 397, 398, 399, 401, 404	**Susan B. Anthony,** 403–404, 407; TE: 404 **W.E.B. DuBois,** 324–325; TE: 324 **Robert LaFollette,** 393; TE: 393
(C) evaluate the impact of third parties and their candidates such as Eugene Debs, H. Ross Perot, and George Wallace	**impact of third parties,** 281–282, 396, 398–399, 402; TE: 396, 398, 399 **Eugene Debs,** 250–251, 253, 399; TE: 399	**H. Ross Perot,** 894–895, 897–898 **George Wallace,** 811
5. History. The student understands significant individuals, events, and issues of the 1920s. The student is expected to:		
(A) analyze causes and effects of significant issues such as immigration, the Red Scare, Prohibition, and the changing role of women	**immigration,** 297–303, 316, 911–912, 917 **Red Scare,** 480, 481–483, 489, 502, 503; TE: 480, 482 **Prohibition,** 467–469, 473, 474; TE: 467, 468	**changing role of women,** 337–341, 342, 453–454, 458, 474; TE: 337, 338, 403, 452, 453
(B) analyze the impact of significant individuals such as Clarence Darrow, William Jennings Bryan, Henry Ford, and Charles A. Lindbergh	**Clarence Darrow,** 470–471, 473; TE: 471 **William Jennings Bryan,** 282, 372, 470–471, 473; TE: 471	**Henry Ford,** 491, 493–496, 497, 502; TE: 494 **Charles A. Lindbergh,** 456–457, 458; TE: 456, 457
6. History. The student understands the impact of significant national and international decisions and conflicts from World War II and the Cold War to the present on the United States. The student is expected to:		
(A) identify reasons for U.S. involvement in World War II, including the growth of dictatorships and the attack on Pearl Harbor	**reasons for U.S. involvement in World War II,** 568–574, 585, 586–589, 590; TE: 568, 572, 576, 577, 586, 587, 601, 614 **including the growth of dictatorships,**	568–574, 576–578; TE: 568, 569, 571, 586 **attack on Pearl Harbor,** 585, 588–589, 590; TE: 585, 586, 588, 601, 614

(B) analyze major issues and events of World War II such as fighting the war on multiple fronts, the interment of Japanese-Americans, the Holocaust, the battle of Midway, the invasion of Normandy, and the development of and Harry Truman's decision to use the atomic bomb	**major issues and events of World War II,** 594–599, 600–608, 609–613, 614–621, 622–629, 630–631 **fighting the war on multiple fronts,** 600–608, 614–621; TE: 600 **interment of Japanese-Americans,** 623, 626–628, 629; TE: 624 **Holocaust,** 609–613, 630, 631; TE: 610, 611, 612	**battle of Midway,** 617, 621, 630; TE: 592, 600, 616, 617 **invasion of Normandy,** 605–606, 608, 630; TE: 600, 601 **development of and Harry Truman's decision to use the atomic bomb,** 620–621, 630; TE: 614, 615
(C) explain the roles played by significant military leaders during World War II, including Omar Bradley, Dwight Eisenhower, Douglas MacArthur, George Marshall, and George Patton	**Omar Bradley,** 607; TE: 604 **Dwight Eisenhower,** 602, 605; TE: 604 **Douglas MacArthur,** 614; TE: 604	**George Marshall,** 605 **George Patton,** 602
(E) analyze the conflicts in Korea and Vietnam and describe their domestic and international effects	**Korea,** 652–656, 662; TE: 652, 653, 654 **Vietnam,** 759, 790–791, 792–796, 798–804, 805–811, 812–817, 818–819; TE:	754, 790, 791, 792, 793, 794, 795, 798, 799, 801, 802, 803, 805, 806, 808, 810, 812, 813, 815, 816
(F) describe the impact of the GI Bill, the election of 1948, McCarthyism, and Sputnik I	**GI Bill,** 668, 672–673, 674, 688; TE: 672 **election of 1948,** 682–684, 688; TE: 680, 681	**McCarthyism,** 657–658, 661, 662; TE: 657, 658, 659 **Sputnik I,** 660, 661
(D) describe U.S. responses to Soviet aggression after World War II, including the Truman Doctrine, the Marshall Plan, the North Atlantic Treaty Organization, and the Berlin airlift	**U.S. responses to Soviet aggression after World War II,** 635–642, 644–648, 651, 662; TE: 636, 637, 638, 640, 644, 645, 647, 648, 657, 751 **Truman Doctrine,** 636, 641–642, 662, 663; TE: 636	**Marshall Plan,** 644–645, 651, 663; TE: 636, 639, 646 **North Atlantic Treaty Organization,** 644, 647–648, 651, 662; TE: 636, 647 **Berlin airlift,** 644, 645–647, 662; TE: 636, 646
(G) analyze the reasons for the Western victory in the Cold War and the challenges of changing relationships among nations	**Western victory in the Cold War,** 883–885, 887, 888; TE: 882	**challenges of changing relationships among nations,** 882, 885–887, 888, 903–910, 918; TE: 873, 882, 904
(H) identify the origins of major domestic and foreign policy issues currently facing the United States	**origins of major domestic policy issues currently facing the United States,** 896, 900, 911–917, 918	**foreign policy issues currently facing the United States,** 885, 887, 900–901, 903–910, 916, 918; TE: 654
7. History. The student understands the impact of the American civil rights movement. The student is expected to:		
(A) trace the historical development of the civil rights movement in the 18th, 19th, and 20th centuries, including the 13th, 14th, and 15th amendments	**civil rights movement in the 18th, 19th, and 20th centuries,** 206–211, 471–473, 474, 623–625, 630, 682, 696–697, 698–703, 704–708, 709–714, 716– 721, 722– 727, 728–729, 877–878; TE: 218, 471, 472, 517, 572, 596, 682, 698–703, 705, 706, 707, 709–713, 716–720, 722–726	**13th amendment,** 155, 190–191, 194, 198, 222; TE: 213 **14th amendment,** 198, 207, 220, 221, 222; TE: 207, 210 **15th amendment,** 198, 209, 210, 220, 221, 222; TE: 210

(B) identify significant leaders of the civil rights movement, including Martin Luther King, Jr.	**significant leaders of the civil rights movement,** 472–473, 624, 698–703, 704–708, 709–714, 716–721, 722–727, 728; TE: 700, 702, 705, 706, 707, 709, 719,	720, 722, 723, 724 **Martin Luther King, Jr.,** 697, 701–702, 706–707, 716, 718, 725–726, 728; TE: 705, 706, 719, 720, 726, 807
8. Geography. The student uses geographic tools to collect, analyze, and interpret data. The student is expected to:		
(A) create thematic maps, graphs, charts, models, and databases representing various aspects of the United States	**maps,** 255; TE: 10, 11, 17, 31, 113, 118, 161, 231, 270, 297, 366, 398, 428, 430, 457, 494, 585, 603, 607, 614, 720 **graphs,** 342, 901; TE: 270, 405, 455, 500 **charts,** 254, 284, 297, 316, 342, 382, 408, 452, 467, 474, 501, 502, 513, 553, 585, 662, 760, 805, 818, 826, 858, 876, 888,	894, 903; TE: 114, 215, 617 **Cause/Effect Chart,** 106, 116, 206, 352, 376, 414, 480, 508, 530, 652, 792, 838; TE: 270, 668, 792 **models,** TE: 270 **databases,** TE: 270
(B) pose and answer questions about geographic distributions and patterns shown on maps, graphs, charts, models, and databases	**maps,** 10, 15, 22, 27, 32, 41, 42, 47, 92, 95, 97, 98, 108, 109, 136, 138, 141, 161, 162, 171, 180, 183, 188, 208, 223, 255, 264, 269, 271, 281, 296, 360, 363, 367, 370, 377, 399, 400, 407, 415, 416, 427, 440, 455, 456, 457, 515, 529, 541, 569, 572, 577, 583, 588, 601, 606, 612, 616, 646, 654, 659, 673, 700, 711, 737, 752, 754,	793, 802, 811, 813, 883, 899, 906, 909; TE: 10, 391, 430, 456, 457, 493, 494, 601, 619, 673, 710, 753 **graphs,** 130, 134, 214, 244, 255, 277, 299, 317, 355, 487, 672, 677, 774, 816 **charts,** 266, 272, 274, 784 **models/diagrams,** 428, 494–495 **databases,** TE: 912
(C) evaluate government efforts, including the Civil Rights Act of 1964, to achieve equality in the United States	**government efforts,** 206–211, 219, 702–703, 716–721, 728; TE: 700, 703, 716–720	**Civil Rights Act of 1964,** 716, 718–720, 728; TE: 218, 716, 717
(D) identify changes in the United States that have resulted from the civil rights movement such as increased participation of minorities in the political process	**changes in the United States that have resulted from the civil rights movement,** 727, 729, 764–766, 769, 770, 771–776, 786, 911–914; TE: 766	**increased participation of minorities in the political process,** 721, 727; TE: 699
9. Geography. The student understands the impact of geographic factors on major events. The student is expected to:		
(A) analyze the effects of physical and human geographic factors on major events including the building of the Panama Canal	258–260, 269–274, 305–306, 366–367, 395, 514–515, 518; TE: 8, 17, 110, 111, 113, 133, 170, 180, 183, 234, 259, 360, 363, 366, 367, 368, 373, 391, 428, 430,	493, 494, 500, 515, 558, 577, 587, 594, 783, 834 **Focus on Geography,** 55, 131, 179, 306, 440, 514, 540
(B) identify and explain reasons for changes in political boundaries such as those resulting from statehood and international conflicts	**statehood,** TE: 354, 363, 373, 884	**international conflicts,** 637, 653; TE: 354, 362, 884
10. Geography. The student understands the effects of migration and immigration on American society. The student is expected to:		
(A) analyze the effects of changing demographic patterns resulting from migration within the United States	**migration within the United States,** 258–261, 284, 304–309, 452, 454–456,	672–674; TE: 133, 259, 305, 453, 455, 456, 494, 667, 673, 681

(B) analyze the effects of changing demographic patterns resulting from immigration to the United States	**immigration to the United States,** 243, 246, 284, 297–303, 455, 458, 487, 747,	772, 774, 911–912, 913–914; TE: 302, 313, 391
(D) predict the effects of selected contemporary legislation on the roles of state and federal governments	**contemporary legislation,** 870–873, 877–878, 880, 895–897	
11. Geography. The student understands the relationship between population growth and modernization on the physical environment. The student is expected to:		
(A) identify the effects of population growth and distribution and predict future effects on the physical environment	**population growth,** 297–303, 304–309, 454–456, 672–674, 912, 914–915; TE: 306, 363, 456, 673	
(B) trace the development of the conservation of natural resources, including the establishment of the National Park System and efforts of private nonprofit organizations	**conservation of natural resources,** 275, 391, 395, 538–539, 781–785, 786, 853, 866, 872	
12. Economics. The student understands domestic and foreign issues related to U.S. economic growth from the 1870s to 1920. The student is expected to:		
(A) analyze the relationship between private property rights and the settlement of the Great Plains	**private property rights and the settlement of the Great Plains,** 258–259, 260, 284; TE: 266	
(B) compare the purpose of the Interstate Commerce Commission with its performance over time	**the Interstate Commerce Commission,** 281, 284, 295, 394, 398, 712, 853, 871	
(C) describe the impact of the Sherman Antitrust Act on businesses	**Sherman Antitrust Act,** 242, 253, 254, 394, 916–917; TE: 237, 240	
(D) analyze the effects of economic policies including the Open Door Policy and Dollar Diplomacy on U.S. Diplomacy	**Open Door Policy,** 364, 376 **Dollar Diplomacy,** 366, 370, 371, 376	
(E) describe the economic effects of international military conflicts, including the Spanish-American War and World War I, on the United States	**international military conflicts,** 595–599, 816; TE: 373, 401 **Spanish-American War,** 359–361; TE: 357	**World War I,** 421–423, 426, 432–434, 436, 439, 440–441, 442; TE: 418
13. Economics. The student understands significant economic developments between World War I and World War II. The student is expected to:		
(A) analyze causes of economic growth and prosperity in the 1920s.	**economic growth and prosperity in the 1920s,** 491–497, 498–499, 502; TE: 481,	492, 498, 515
(B) analyze the causes of the Great Depression, including the decline in worldwide trade, the stock market crash, and bank failures	**causes of the Great Depression,** 499–501, 508–512, 530; TE: 508, 509, 525, 526	

(C) analyze the effects of the Great Depression on the U.S. economy and government	**effects of the Great Depression,** 513–518, 520–523, 524–529, 530; TE: 510, 525, 546
(D) evaluate the effectiveness of New Deal measures in ending the Great Depression	**New Deal measures in ending the Great Depression,** 527–528, 536–544, 545–551, 560; TE: 538, 558, 537
(E) analyze how various New Deal agencies and programs such as the Federal Deposit Insurance Corporation, the Securities and Exchange Commission, and Social Security continue to affect the lives of U.S. citizens	**New Deal programs,** 540–541, 543, 544, 558–559; TE: 538, 539, 540, 547, 554 **Federal Deposit Insurance Corporation,** 558 **Securities and Exchange Commission,** 558 **Social Security,** 557, 559
14. Economics. The student understands the economic effects of World War II, the Cold War, and increased worldwide competition on contemporary society. The student is expected to:	
(A) describe the economic effects of World War II on the home front, including rationing, female employment, and the end of the Great Depression	**home front,** 594, 595–597, 598–599; TE: 594 **rationing,** 598; TE: 594 **female employment,** 595, 623, 628–629; TE: 594 **end of the Great Depression,** 596–597, 630; TE: 594, 597
(B) identify the causes and effects of prosperity in the 1950s	**causes and effects of prosperity in the 1950s,** 668–674, 688; TE: 668, 669
(C) describe the impact of the Cold War on the business cycle and defense spending	**impact of the Cold War,** 656; TE: 644
(D) identify actions of government and the private sector to expand economic opportunities to all citizens	**government,** 624, 625, 626, 628–629, 671–672, 719, 720, 746; TE: 743, 870 **private sector,** 492, 773; TE: 870
(E) describe the dynamic relationship between U.S. international trade policies and the U.S. free enterprise system	**international trade policies,** 908–910, 918; TE: 278, 355, 903
15. Government. The student understands changes in the role of government over time. The student is expected to:	
(A) evaluate the impact of New Deal legislation on the historical roles of state and federal governments	**impact of New Deal legislation,** 550, 557, 558–559; TE: 537, 538, 539, 546, 547, 553
(B) explain the impact of significant international events such as World War I and World War II on changes in the role of the federal government	**World War I,** 433–436, 438, 440–441; TE: 423 **World War II,** 595–597, 627, 636–639, 641–642, 644–647
(C) evaluate the effects of political incidents such as Teapot Dome and Watergate on the views of U.S. citizens concerning the role of the federal government	**political incidents,** 809–810, 813, 880, 897–898, 899; TE: 488 **Teapot Dome,** 488, 489, 502 **Watergate,** 838–844, 858; TE: 839, 840–844

Standard	Correlation	
16. Government. The student understands the changing relationship among the three branches of the federal government. The student is expected to:		
(A) evaluate the impact of events, including the Gulf of Tonkin Resolution and the War Powers Act, on the relationship between the legislative and executive branches of government	**impact of New Deal legislation,** 550, 557, 558–559; TE: 537, 538, 539, 546, 547, 553	
(B) evaluate the impact of events, including Franklin Roosevelt's attempt to increase the number of U.S. Supreme Court justices, on the relationship among the legislative, executive, and judicial branches of government	**impact of events,** 560, 683–684, 699–701, 718–721, 745–749, 841–843, 880, 897, 898, 899	**Franklin Roosevelt's attempt to increase the number of U.S. Supreme Court justices,** 546, 551
17. Government. The student understands the impact of constitutional issues on American society in the 20th century. The student is expected to:		
(A) analyze the effects of 20th-century landmark U.S. Supreme Court decisions such as Brown v. Board of Education, Regents of the University of California v. Bakke, and Reynolds v. Sims	**Brown v. Board of Education,** 698, 699–703, 728, 867; TE: 700	**Regents of the University of California v. Bakke,** 854–855 **Reynolds v. Sims,** 749
(B) analyze reasons for the adoption of 20th-century constitutional amendments	**constitutional amendments,** 394, 395, 399, 404–407, 453, 455, 467, 468, 473, 522, 523, 527, 536, 683–684, 686, 721,	733, 739, 806; TE: 790
18. Citizenship. The student understands efforts to expand the democratic process. The student is expected to:		
(A) identify and analyze methods of expanding the right to participate in the democratic process, including lobbying, protesting, court decisions, and amendments to the U.S. Constitution	**expanding the right to participate,** 716–721, 728, 912; TE: 700, 701 **lobbying,** 405, 407; TE: 403 **protesting,** 407, 716, 720–721; TE: 403	**court decisions,** 694, 748, 749, 899 **amendments to the U.S. Constitution,** 404–407; TE: 403
(B) evaluate various means of achieving equality of political rights, including the 19th, 24th, and 26th amendments	**equality of political rights,** 341, 403–404, 716–721, 728, 912 **19th amendment,** 394, 404–407, 453, 454,	732; TE: 403 **24th amendment,** 720, 721, 739 **26th amendment,** 733, 806
(C) explain how participation in the democratic process reflects our national identity	**participation in the democratic process,** 404–407, 454, 472, 698–703, 704–708, 709–714, 716–721, 764–769, 770–776,	777–780, 781–785, 865–868, 912; TE: 392, 404
19. Citizenship. The student understands the importance of effective leadership in a democratic society. The student is expected to:		
(A) describe the qualities of effective leadership	**leadership,** 389–390, 395, 407, 473, 685; TE: 190, 680, 681, 700, 826 **American Biography,** 21, 91, 164, 210, 239,	263, 265, 308, 324, 359, 404, 431, 462, 496, 517, 542, 582, 605, 624, 655, 676, 706, 727, 749, 773, 794, 833, 843, 878, 915

(B) evaluate the contributions of significant political and social leaders in the United States such as Andrew Carnegie, Shirley Chisholm, and Franklin D. Roosevelt	**Andrew Carnegie,** 238–239, 254; TE: 239 **Shirley Chisholm,** 727, 767–768, 769 **Franklin D. Roosevelt,** 536–539, 544; TE: 601 **American Biography and Presidents,** 21, 91, 164, 210, 239, 263, 265, 308, 324, 359, 404, 431, 462, 496, 517, 542, 582, 605, 624, 655, 676, 706, 727, 749, 773, 794, 833, 843, 878, 915; TE: 29, 61, 92, 93, 95, 97, 111, 124, 137, 138, 139, 141, 142, 158,	164, 170, 181, 182, 184, 202, 208, 215, 220, 231, 233, 245, 250, 252, 272, 273, 275, 281, 293, 294, 295, 308, 312, 323, 330, 338, 360, 362, 370, 393, 394, 399, 405, 434, 470, 482, 484, 486, 488, 495, 522, 526, 538, 541, 542, 549, 572, 573, 602, 650, 660, 682, 684, 700, 702, 707, 719, 747, 756, 767, 775, 779, 784, 794, 800, 802, 841, 842, 848, 865, 878, 884, 896, 897
(C) identify the contributions of Texans who have been President of the United States	**contributions of Texans,** 685–686, 718–721, 728, 744–747, 760, 882–887,	888; TE: 680, 744, 747, 883
20. Culture. The student understands the relationship between the arts and the times during which they were created The student is expected to:		
(A) describe how the characteristics and issues of various eras in U.S. history have been reflected in works of art, music, and literature such as the paintings of Georgia O'Keeffe, rock and roll, and John Steinbeck's The Grapes of Wrath	**works of art,** 463, 558, 778; TE: 271, 463, 480, 553 **music,** 330–331, 461–463, 678–679, 705, 717, 777, 779–780, 801; TE: 230, 359, 385, 461, 463, 524, 553, 705, 738 **literature,** 330, 463–464, 465, 474, 678, 679; TE: 118, 400, 463, 464, 553, 556, 659, 677, 766, 767	**paintings of Georgia O'Keeffe,** 463 **rock and roll,** 678–679 **John Steinbeck's The Grapes of Wrath,** 556; TE: 556 **Viewing Fine Art,** 25, 40, 48, 212, 374, 516, 574
(B) describe the impact of significant examples of cultural movements in art, music, and literature on American society, including the Harlem Renaissance	**impact of significant examples of cultural movements in art,** 463, 778; TE: 460 **music,** 330–331, 459, 461–464, 678–679, 717, 777, 779–780; TE: 230, 461, 462, 678, 676	**literature,** 275–276, 330, 463–464, 678, 679; TE: 463 **Harlem Renaissance,** 464–465; TE: 460, 461, 462, 464
(C) identify examples of American art, music, and literature that transcend American culture and convey universal themes	**art,** 778 **music,** 461–462, 547, 705, 717, 779–780, 801; TE: 385, 678 **literature,** 678, 679; TE: 896	
(D) analyze the relationship between culture and the economy and identify examples such as the impact of the entertainment industry on the U.S. economy	**culture and the economy,** 244, 327, 328, 329, 669–670, 678–679, 811; TE: 6, 160, 162, 339, 496	
(E) identify the impact of popular American culture on the rest of the world	**impact of popular American culture,** 275–276, 331, 461–463, 678–679, 779; TE: 328, 330, 459, 460, 557	
21. Culture. The student understands how people from various groups, including racial, ethnic, and religious groups, adapt to life in the United States and contribute to our national identity. The student is expected to:		
(A) explain actions taken by people from racial, ethnic, and religious groups to expand economic opportunities and political rights in American society	**racial,** 332, 335–336, 623–625, 630, 698, 702, 703, 706, 716, 771–773, 843; TE: 263, 333, 361, 405, 427, 440, 461, 557, 700, 701, 706, 707	**ethnic,** 771–776, 771; TE: 360, 374, 543, 772, 773, 774 **religious groups,** 470–471, 676, 723, 867–869

(B) explain efforts of the Americanization movement to assimilate immigrants into American culture	**Americanization movement,** 321–322, 325, 678–679	
(C) analyze how the contributions of various racial, ethnic, and religious groups have helped to shape the national identity	**racial,** 323, 547, 698, 703, 706, 892–893, 911–914; TE: 30, 45, 172, 173, 203, 215, 231, 261, 264, 334, 623, 843, 914 **ethnic,** 263, 771–776, 911–194; TE: 181,	184, 240, 265, 306, 360, 374, 623, 773, 914 **religious groups,** 867–868; TE: 311, 623, 914
(D) identify the political, social, and economic contributions of women to American society	**reform leaders,** 324–325, 382, 384, 385, 386, 387, 389, 393, 394, 399, 403, 404; TE: 385, 392, 393, 394, 397, 398, 399, 401, 404	**Susan B. Anthony,** 403–404, 407; TE: 404 **W.E.B. DuBois,** 324–325; TE: 324 **Robert LaFollette,** 393; TE: 393
22. Science, technology, and society. The student understands the impact of science and technology on the economic development of the United States. The student is expected to:		
(A) explain the effects of scientific discoveries and technological innovations such as electric power, the telegraph and telephone, petroleum-based products, medical vaccinations, and computers on the development of the United States	**scientific discoveries and technological innovations,** 233–234, 274, 276, 493–494, 686, 824, 831, 853–854, 915–916; TE: 269, 340, 359, 417, 557, 810 **electric power,** 226, 228–229; TE: 227, 228 **telegraph,** 226, 229–230, 235; TE: 227	**telephone,** 226, 230; TE: 227, 340 **petroleum-based products,** 228; TE: 227 **medical vaccinations,** 671, 674; TE: 307, 499 **computers,** 230, 235, 254, 670–671, 915–916
(B) explain how technological innovations in areas such as space exploration have led to other innovations that affect daily life and standard of living	**scientific discoveries and technological innovations,** 226–235, 274, 493–494, 824, 831, 853–854, 915–916; TE: 417, 669 **agriculture,** 274; TE: 268	**military,** 421–423; TE: 159, 417, 578, 596, 603, 618, 671, 801, 873 **medicine,** 671, 674; TE: 307, 499
(C) analyze the impact of technological innovations on the nature of work, the American labor movement, and business	**nature of work,** 229, 243–246, 493–494; TE: 227, 269, 274, 392, 493–494, 669, 783 **American labor movement,** 248–253; TE: 227, 251, 493, 783	**business,** 226, 229, 232–233, 235, 493–494, 497, 918; TE: 227, 232, 359, 493, 669, 783
23. Science, technology, and society. The student understands the influence of scientific discoveries and technological innovations on daily life in the United States. The student is expected to:		
(A) analyze how scientific discoveries and technological innovations, including those in transportation and communication, have changed the standard of living in the United States	**standard of living,** 235, 243–246, 274, 307, 491–493, 668, 669–674, 688; TE: 673 **transportation,** 230–233; TE: 290	**communication,** 229–230, 669–670, 688, 911, 915–916; TE: 459, 668
(B) explain how technological innovations in areas such as space exploration have led to other innovations that affect daily life and standard of living	**daily life,** 497, 669–671; TE: 357, 641 **standard of living,** 669–671	

24. Social studies skills. The student applies critical thinking skills to organize and use information acquired from a variety of sources including electronic technology. The student is expected to:		
(A) locate and use primary and secondary sources such as computer software, databases, media and news services, biographies, interviews, and artifacts to acquire information about the United States	**CD-ROM,** 255, 285, 317, 343, 377, 409, 475, 503, 531, 561, 591, 631, 663, 689, 729, 761, 787, 819, 859, 889, 919; TE: 515 **iText,** 254, 284, 342, 376, 408, 474, 502, 530, 560, 590, 630, 662, 688, 728, 760, 786, 818, 858, 888, 918 **net,** 235, 242, 246, 260, 267, 276, 282, 303, 309, 315, 331, 336, 341, 356, 364, 371, 375, 387, 407, 465, 489, 518, 529, 544, 559, 599,	608, 621, 629, 642, 651, 656, 661, 679, 686, 689, 703, 708, 714, 721, 727, 741, 750, 759, 769, 776, 780, 785, 796, 804, 811, 817, 831, 837, 844, 850, 857, 875, 881, 887, 901 **Analyzing Political Cartoons and Analyzing Primary Sources,** 35, 101, 147, 195, 223, 255, 285, 317, 343, 377, 409, 443, 475, 503, 531, 561, 591, 631, 663, 689, 729, 761, 787, 819, 859, 889, 919; TE: 515, 516
(B) analyze information by sequencing, categorizing, identifying cause-and-effect relationships, comparing, contrasting, finding the main idea, summarizing, making generalizations and predictions, and drawing inferences and conclusions	**sequencing,** 336, 356, 371, 574, 579, 608, 656, 727, 812, 817, 835, 850; TE: 357, 396, 403, 508, 581, 609, 636, 653, 717, 736, 739, 752, 772, 813 **categorizing,** 389 **identifying cause-and-effect relationships,** 12, 16, 34, 173, 252, 284, 296, 341, 356, 386, 408, 414, 423, 426, 501, 512, 589, 630, 656, 663, 688, 702, 721, 785, 801, 842, 868, 888, 891; Cause/Effect Chart, 106, 116, 206, 352, 376, 414, 480, 508, 530, 652, 792, 838; TE: 230, 389 **comparing/contrasting,** 34, 100, 125, 194, 212, 235, 242, 253, 254, 266, 305, 316, 325, 364, 368, 371, 402, 408, 458, 461, 465, 485, 495, 497, 512, 514, 523, 544, 551, 574, 590, 599, 608, 620, 621, 648, 671, 672, 677, 679, 686, 688, 703, 712, 723, 741, 760, 765, 776, 778, 786, 811, 857, 858, 884; TE: 233, 470, 481, 516, 712, 802, 865 **finding the main idea,** 33, 146, 185, 222, 232, 243, 247, 342, 374, 376, 396, 442, 489, 508, 518, 560, 590, 613, 651, 662, 688, 722, 724, 726, 786, 794, 837, 840, 852, 856, 858, 875, 897, 902, 910; TE: 719, 783	**summarizing,** 134, 384, 405, 497, 662, 729; TE: 581, 719 **making generalizations and predictions,** 13, 58, 100, 165, 194, 216, 316, 399, 442, 473, 586, 590, 611, 630, 662, 760, 818, 847, 850, 899, 917, 918, 919; TE: 13, 572, 636, 812 **drawing inferences,** 40, 43, 57, 90, 96, 111, 121, 126, 128, 142, 144, 157, 181, 192, 200, 204, 205, 214, 224, 251, 260, 280, 290, 298, 303, 309, 315, 316, 331, 333, 356, 361, 391, 397, 407, 422, 425, 428, 436, 437, 441, 442, 452, 463, 470, 474, 480, 486, 513, 518, 520, 527, 531, 536, 537, 548, 555, 570, 576, 587, 598, 614, 629, 641, 642, 650, 671, 755, 759, 760, 775, 793, 804, 808, 815, 818, 831, 838, 850, 917, 918 **drawing conclusions,** 6, 26, 33, 46, 106, 163, 190, 192, 206, 211, 213, 221, 229, 240, 254, 274, 277, 282, 284, 302, 303, 307, 323, 329, 334, 340, 376, 406, 408, 454, 474, 492, 522, 530, 538, 572, 573, 578, 584, 596, 637, 642, 645, 651, 656, 657, 668, 708, 760, 796, 800, 817, 818, 830, 837, 849, 855, 858, 875, 876, 880, 888, 907, 910
(C) explain and apply different methods that historians use to interpret the past, including the use of primary and secondary sources, points of view, frames of reference, and historical context	**different methods that historians use to interpret the past,** 144, 205, 216, 235, 279, 331, 336, 364, 377, 387, 402, 407, 409, 436, 441, 529, 544, 561, 574, 599, 621, 631, 642, 663, 686, 703, 708; TE: 9, 32, 57, 111, 263, 270, 273, 281, 293, 302, 334, 355, 369, 401, 405, 416, 433, 455, 471, 486, 515, 516, 539, 550, 598, 615, 646, 658, 711, 726, 737, 740, 867 **Comparing Historian's Viewpoints,** 354, 483, 549, 639, 749	**Identifying/Comparing Points of View,** 176, 211, 222, 309, 314, 438, 474, 502, 560, 818 **Review and Assessment,** 34–35, 100–101, 146–147, 194–195, 222–223, 254–255, 284–285, 316–317, 342–343, 376–377, 408–409, 442–443, 474–475, 502–503, 530–531, 560–561, 590–591, 630–631, 662–663, 688–689, 728–729, 760–761, 786–787, 818–819, 858–859, 888–889, 918–919

(D) use the process of historical inquiry to research, interpret, and use multiple sources of evidence	**process of historical inquiry,** 23, 35, 101, 115, 144, 147, 176, 195, 205, 211, 260, 285, 315, 325, 356, 364, 371, 387, 407, 409, 419, 431, 436, 441, 465, 489, 497, 501, 518, 544, 551, 574, 621, 631, 642, 679, 686, 703, 727, 729, 776; TE: 13, 32, 48, 57, 60, 93, 95, 96, 109, 111, 120, 121, 137, 174, 181, 184, 202, 240, 250, 265, 270, 272, 281, 293, 300, 307, 314, 323, 330, 334, 335, 329, 355, 363, 368, 369, 392, 393, 401, 404, 406, 416, 433, 435, 439, 452, 455, 457, 471, 472, 499, 500, 515, 516, 539, 540, 541, 542, 549, 550, 597, 605, 611, 615, 618, 646, 649, 658, 671, 681, 683, 684, 706, 711, 712, 723, 737, 746, 758, 772, 810, 815, 829, 841, 867, 884, 898 **Comparing Historian's Viewpoints,** 354, 483, 549, 639, 749
(E) evaluate the validity of a source based on language, corroboration with other sources, and information about the author	**evaluate the validity of a source,** 529, 551, 561, 589, 599, 689, 703, 721, 729, 769, 796, 868, 875
(F) identify bias in written, oral, and visual material	**bias,** 12, 316, 342, 385, 432, 502, 524, 627, 629, 674, 767, 787, 811, 831; TE: 658, 814
(G) support a point of view on a social studies issue or event	**support a point of view,** 185, 193, 195, 205, 211, 223, 242, 253, 325, 343, 356, 364, 371, 377, 387, 407, 473, 475, 501, 503, 551, 559, 561, 584, 591, 629, 642, 651, 663, 714, 727, 750, 769, 780, 796, 831, 837, 844, 875, 887, 910; TE: 90, 124, 183, 224, 335, 361, 372, 377, 390, 401, 435, 484, 511, 517, 547, 570, 711, 880
(H) use appropriate mathematical skills to interpret social studies information such as maps and graphs	**mathematical skills,** 125, 299, 355, 367, 531, 618, 689, 873, 899; TE: 60, 119, 133, 169, 220, 273, 300, 234, 251, 297, 355, 405, 452, 455, 496, 500, 509, 646, 681, 710, 810 **Interpreting Graphs,** 128, 130, 134, 175, 192, 214, 218, 244, 293, 299, 322, 355, 485, 487, 511, 554, 656, 672, 677, 739, 746, 765, 774, 816, 828, 848, 871, 874, 875, 912
25. Social studies skills. The student communicates in written, oral, and visual forms. The student is expected to:	
(A) use social studies terminology correctly	**key terms,** 4, 14, 24, 40, 54, 89, 106, 116, 126, 135, 156, 166, 178, 186, 200, 206, 212, 218, 226, 237, 243, 247, 258, 261, 268, 277, 290, 297, 304, 311, 320, 327, 332, 337, 352, 357, 366, 372, 382, 389, 396, 403, 414, 421, 425, 432, 437, 452, 459, 467, 491, 498, 508, 513, 520, 524, 536, 545, 553, 568, 575, 581, 585, 594, 600, 609, 614, 623, 636, 644, 652, 657, 668, 675, 680, 698, 704, 709, 716, 722, 736, 743, 751, 764, 771, 777, 781, 792, 799, 805, 812, 826, 832, 838, 846, 864, 870, 876, 882, 894, 902, 911 **Review and Assessment,** 34, 100, 146, 194, 222, 254, 284, 316, 342, 376, 408, 442, 474, 502, 530, 560, 590, 630, 662, 688, 728, 760, 786, 818, 858, 888, 918
(B) use standard grammar, spelling, sentence structure, and punctuation	**Section Assessment: Writing Activities,** 12, 23, 33, 49, 64, 98, 115, 144, 165, 176, 185, 193, 205, 211, 216, 221, 235, 242, 246, 247, 253, 260, 267, 276, 282, 295, 303, 309, 341, 356, 364, 371, 387, 395, 402, 419, 424, 431, 436, 441, 458, 465, 473, 489, 497, 501, 512, 518, 523, 529, 544, 551, 559, 574, 584, 589, 599, 608, 613, 621, 642, 651, 661, 674, 679, 686, 703, 708, 714, 727, 741, 750, 759, 769, 776, 780, 785, 796, 804, 811, 817, 831, 837, 844, 850, 857, 868, 875, 881, 901, 910, 917 **Review and Assessment,** 35, 101, 147, 195, 223, 255, 285, 317, 343, 377, 409, 443, 475, 503, 531, 561, 591, 631, 663, 689, 729, 761, 787, 819, 859, 889, 919

(C) transfer information from one medium to another, including written to visual and statistical to written or visual, using computer software as appropriate	**transfer information from one medium to another,** 125, 205, 267, 315, 375, 409, 424, 436, 441, 465, 473, 501, 523, 579, 656, 708, 714, 727, 749, 750, 759, 769, 859,	881, 887; TE: 17, 111, 120, 233, 385, 404, 405, 406, 428, 429, 433, 440, 471, 496, 499, 500, 516, 526, 527, 558, 646, 723
(D) create written, oral, and visual presentations of social studies information	**writing,** 12, 23, 33, 49, 64, 98, 115, 144, 165, 176, 185, 193, 205, 211, 216, 221, 235, 242, 246, 247, 253, 260, 267, 276, 282, 295, 303, 309, 341, 356, 364, 371, 387, 395, 402, 419, 424, 431, 436, 441, 458, 465, 473, 489, 497, 501, 512, 518, 523, 529, 544, 551, 559, 574, 584, 589, 599, 608, 613, 621, 642, 651, 661, 674, 679, 686, 703, 708, 714, 727, 741, 750, 759, 769, 776, 780, 785, 796, 804, 811, 817, 831, 837, 844, 850, 857, 868, 875, 881, 901, 910, 917; TE: 28, 32, 56, 58, 94, 111, 113, 121, 164, 180, 184, 192, 203, 207, 226, 229, 250, 270, 301, 308, 334, 362, 363, 384, 390, 392, 397, 401, 416, 433, 437, 439, 472, 484, 487, 511, 514, 517, 539, 549, 570, 573, 582, 588, 612, 615, 641, 654, 669, 711, 767, 774, 800, 808, 843, 899 **Writing to Learn,** 35, 101, 147, 195, 223, 255, 285, 317, 343, 377, 409, 443, 475, 503, 531, 561, 591, 631, 663, 689, 729, 761, 787, 819, 859, 889, 919TE: 270, 363, 472, 494, 654, 671, 723, 738, 746, 773, 906, 914	**oral,** 101, 193, 228, 265, 272, 274, 329, 340, 363, 472, 488, 542, 50, 640, 723, 738, 746, 878, 881, 887, 906, 907, 914; TE: 41, 42, 44, 46, 47, 57, 63, 99, 109, 119, 124, 137, 167, 168, 170, 171, 172, 173, 174, 181, 187, 188, 189, 208, 209, 214, 228, 230, 245, 249, 258, 263, 264, 265, 272, 279, 280, 281, 294, 295, 335, 359, 361, 363, 365, 385, 390, 417, 426, 435, 439, 440, 462, 469, 471, 472, 482, 485, 487, 510, 515, 528, 539, 542, 547, 550, 555, 569, 571, 572, 578, 583, 588, 598, 627, 628, 640, 648, 649, 707, 723, 745, 748, 803, 816, 829, 880, 900 **visual,** 205, 211, 260, 315, 331, 375, 424, 465, 473, 501, 656, 749, 759, 901; TE: 28, 62, 90, 91, 93, 99, 111, 113, 120, 143, 273, 301, 306, 323, 328, 369, 392, 404, 405, 406, 422, 428, 429, 433, 440, 457, 470, 493, 495, 496, 499, 500, 516, 522, 526, 540, 548, 558, 571, 576, 582, 606, 607, 611, 617, 638, 646, 656, 677, 700, 713, 723, 749, 758, 768, 802, 809, 810, 834, 855, 872, 878, 913
26. Social studies skills. The student uses problem-solving and decision-making skills, working independently and with others, in a variety of settings. The student is expected to:		
(A) use a problem-solving process to identify a problem, gather information, list and consider options, consider advantages and disadvantages, choose and implement a solution, and evaluate the effectiveness of the solution	**problem-solving process,** 35, 101, 147, 195, 260, 285, 407, 424, 443, 631, 703, 857, 859, 875, 901; TE: 9, 17, 637, 702, 832	
(B) use a decision-making process to identify a situation that requires a decision, gather information, identify options, predict consequences, and take action to implement a decision	**decision-making process,** 101, 364, 442, 473, 475, 589, 591, 631, 859, 875, 881, 887, 889, 901, 910, 917; TE: 9, 583	

IN ASSOCIATION WITH
American Heritage®

PRENTICE HALL

AMERICA

PATHWAYS TO THE PRESENT

MODERN AMERICAN HISTORY

Andrew Cayton

Elisabeth Israels Perry

Linda Reed

Allan M. Winkler

Prentice Hall

Needham, Massachusetts
Upper Saddle River, New Jersey
Glenview, Illinois

About the Authors

Andrew Cayton, Ph.D. Andrew Cayton is Distinguished Professor of History at Miami University in Oxford, Ohio. He received his B.A. in History from the University of Virginia and his M.A. and Ph.D. in American history from Brown University. A specialist in the history of the Early Republic and the Midwest, Dr. Cayton is the author of several books and articles, including *Frontier Indiana, Contact Points: American Frontiers from the Mohwk Valley to the Mississippi, The American Midwest: Essays in Regional History,* and *So Many Possibilities: A History of Ohio.* In 1999, Cayton was the John Adams Visiting Professor of American Studies at Leiden University in the Netherlands.

Elisabeth Israels Perry, Ph.D. Elisabeth Israels Perry holds the John Francis Bannon Endowed Chair in History at Saint Louis University in St. Louis, Missouri. She received her Ph.D. in history from the University of California at Los Angeles. Dr. Perry's period of specialization is the late nineteenth and early twentieth centuries. Her greatest scholarly interests are in women's political history and issues of citizenship and identity in U.S. history. She is the author of *Belle Moskowitz: Feminine Politics and the Exercise of Power in the Age of Alfred E. Smith* and *Women in Action: Rebels and Reformers, 1920–1980.* Since 1987, she has directed five NEH Summer Seminars for Secondary School Teachers.

Linda Reed, Ph.D. Linda Reed is Associate Professor of History at the University of Houston. For nine years she directed the African American Studies Program. She received her B.S. from Alabama A & M University, her M.A. from the University of Alabama, and her Ph.D. from Indiana University. Dr. Reed's specialization is twentieth-century African American history, particularly the modern-day civil rights era. She is the author of *Simple Decency and Common Sense: The Conference Movement, 1938-1963* and co-editor of *"We Specialize in the Wholly Impossible": A Reader in Black Women's History.*

Allan M. Winkler, Ph.D. Allan M. Winkler is Distinguished Professor of History at Miami University in Ohio. He has also taught at Yale University and the University of Oregon and, for one year each, at the University of Helsinki in Finland, the University of Amsterdam in The Netherlands, and the University of Nairobi in Kenya. A prize-winning teacher, he is the author of seven books, including *The Politics of Propaganda: The Office of War Information, 1942–1945; Home Front U.S.A.: America during World War II;* and *Life Under a Cloud: American Anxiety About the Atom.*

American Heritage® *American Heritage®* magazine was founded in 1954, and it quickly rose to the position it occupies today: the country's preeminent magazine of history and culture. Dedicated to presenting the past in incisive, entertaining narratives underpinned by scrupulous scholarship, *American Heritage* today goes to more than 300,000 subscribers and counts the country's very best writers and historians among its contributors. Its innovative use of historical illustration and its wide variety of subject matter have gained the publication scores of honors across more than forty years, among them National Magazine Awards.

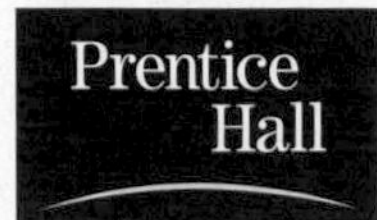

ISBN 0-13-062916-2
1 2 3 4 5 6 7 8 9 10 06 05 04 03 02

Program Reviewers

HISTORIAN REVIEWERS

William Childs
Department of History
Ohio State University
Columbus, Ohio

Donald L. Fixico
Department of History
Western Michigan University
Kalamazoo, Michigan

George Forgie
Department of History
University of Texas at Austin
Austin, Texas

Mario Garcia
Department of History
University of California at Santa Barbara
Santa Barbara, California

Gerald Gill
Department of History
Tufts University
Medford, Massachusetts

Huping Ling
Division of Social Science
Truman State University
Kirksville, Missouri

Roy Rosenzweig
Department of History
George Mason University
Fairfax, Virginia

Susan Smulyan
Department of American Civilization
Brown University
Providence, Rhode Island

TEACHER REVIEWERS

Suzanne P. Brock
Vestavia Hills High School
Birmingham, Alabama

Debra Brown
Eisenhower High School
Houston, Texas

Stephen Bullick
Mt. Lebanon School District
Pittsburgh, Pennsylvania

Alfred B. Cate, Jr.
Central High School,
Memphis City Schools
Memphis, Tennessee

Janet K. Chandler
Hamilton Southeastern High School
Fishers, Indiana

Lee Chase
Chesterfield County Public Schools
Chesterfield County, Virginia

Vern Cobb
Okemos High School
Okemos, Michigan

Joyce Dixon Cooper
Sunset High School
Dallas I.S.D.
Dallas, Texas

Michael Jerry DaDurka
David Starr Jordan High School (LBUSD)
Long Beach, California

Mike Ferguson
Hebron High School
Lewisville, Texas

Robert Hasty
Lawrence Central High School
Indianapolis, Indiana

Robert C. McAdams
East Burke High School
Icard, North Carolina

Lawrence Moaton
Memphis City Schools
Memphis, Tennessee

Dr. Brent Muirhead
South Forsyth High School
Cumming, Georgia

Keith Denny Olmsted
Amon Carter Riverside High School
Fort Worth I.S.D.
Fort Worth, Texas

Debbie W. Powers
Fulton County
Atlanta, Georgia

Betsy Schmidt
Round Rock I.S.D.
Round Rock, Texas

Walter T. Thurnau
Southwestern Central High School
Jamestown, New York

Kevin Wheeler
Lamar High School
Houston, Texas

Barry Wilmoth
Lamar High School
Arlington, Texas

Judy Heckendorf Wood
Parkway West High School
Ballwin, Missouri

CONTENT CONSULTANTS

Senior Consultant
T. R. Fehrenbach
San Antonio, Texas
author, *Lone Star*

Senior Consultant
Herman Viola
Falls Church, Virginia
Curator emeritus,
Smithsonian Institution

Curriculum and Assessment Specialist
Jan Moberley
Dallas, Texas

Reading Consultant
Dr. Bonnie Armbruster
Professor of Education
University of Illinois at Urbana-Champaign
Urbana, Illinois

Constitution Consultant
William A. McClenaghan
Department of Political Science
Oregon State University
Beaverton, Oregon
author, *Magruder's American Government*

Internet Consultant
Brent Muirhead
Teacher, Social Studies Department
South Forsyth High School
Cumming, Georgia

Holocaust Consultant
Marjorie B. Green
Director, Educational Policy & Programs
Anti-Defamation League
Los Angeles, California

PROGRAM ADVISORS

Pat Easterbrook
Social Studies Consultant
Cary, North Carolina

Michal Howden
Social Studies Consultant
Zionsville, Indiana

Kathy Lewis
Social Studies Consultant
Fort Worth, Texas

Rick Moulden
Social Studies Consultant
Federal Way, Washington

Sharon Pope
Social Studies Consultant
Houston, Texas

Joe Wieczorek
Social Studies Consultant
Baltimore, Maryland

Table of Contents

Unit 3: The United States on the Brink of Change, 1890–1920 348

The New York Times. EXTRA

LUSITANIA SUNK BY A SUBMARINE, PROBABLY 1,260 DEAD; TWICE TORPEDOED OFF IRISH COAST; SINKS IN 15 MINUTES; CAPT. TURNER SAVED, FROHMAN AND VANDERBILT MISSING; WASHINGTON BELIEVES THAT A GRAVE CRISIS IS AT HAND

Unit 4: Boom Times to Hard Times, 1920–1938 448

Mar. 4, 1933
THE NEW YORKER
Price 15 cents

THIS IS ONE RABBIT THAT NEVER FAILED ME!
SPENDING
OLD RELIABLE!

Unit 5: Hot and Cold War, 1931–1960 564

The BUCK STOPS here!

Unit 6: A Period of Turmoil and Change, 1950–1975 694

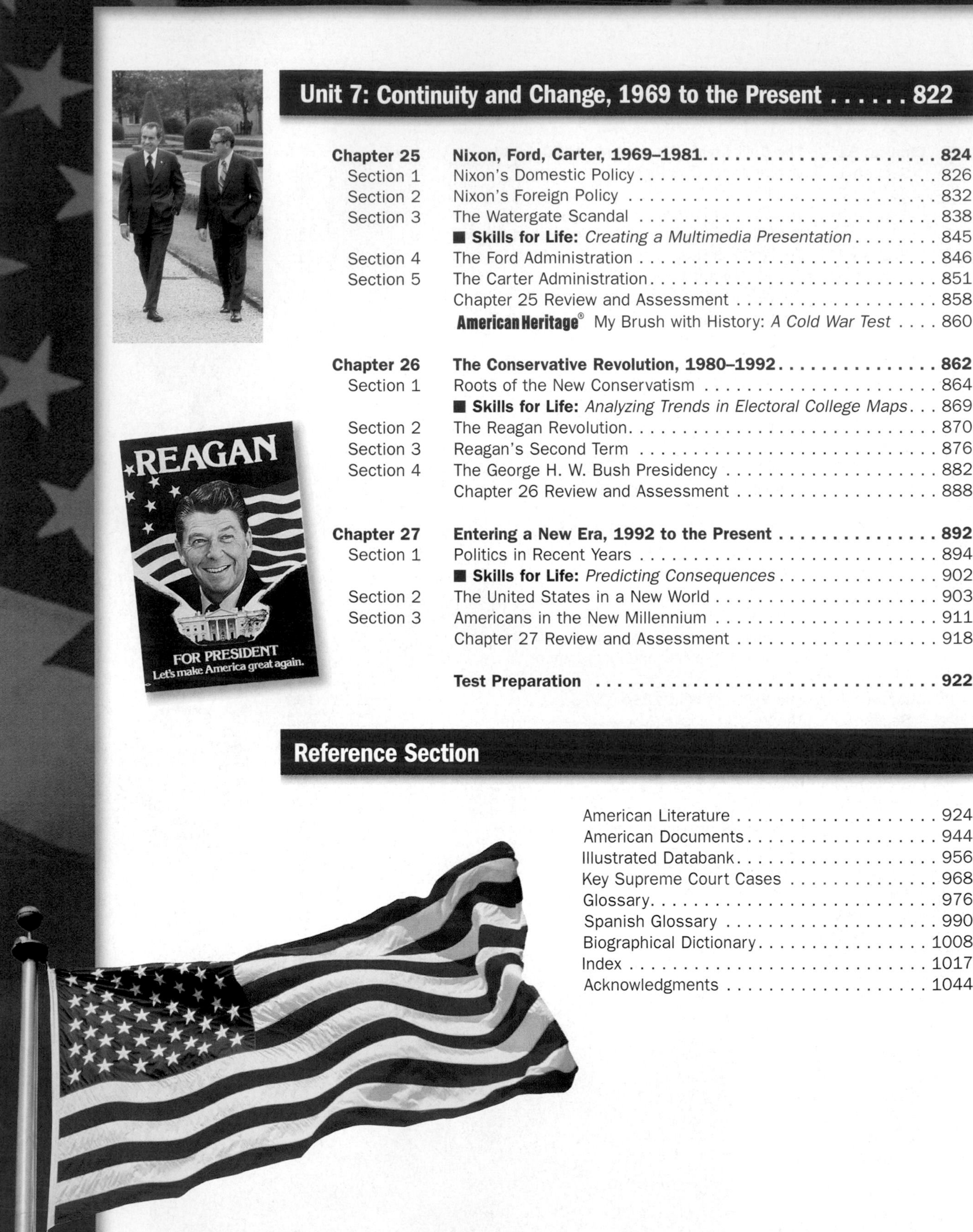

Unit 7: Continuity and Change, 1969 to the Present 822

Reference Section

American Pathways

Thematic time tables clarify connections between events across time

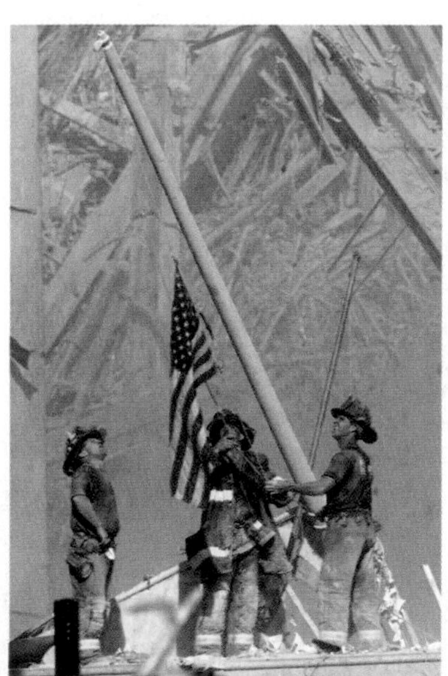

AmericanHeritage® MY BRUSH WITH HISTORY™

Eyewitness accounts from *American Heritage* magazine of ordinary Americans and extraordinary events

Geography & History

An in-depth look at the links between geography and history

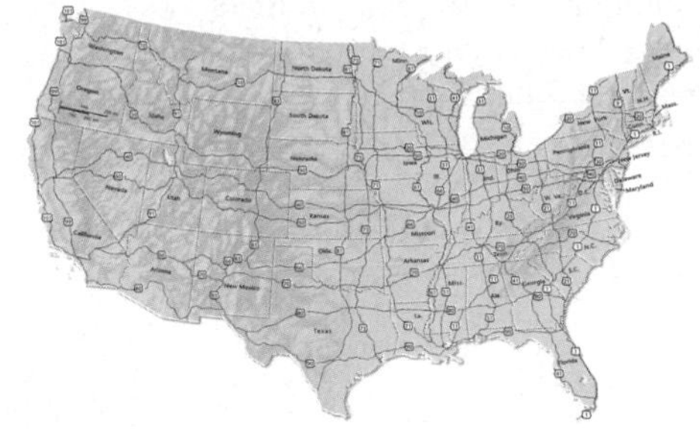

TEST PREPARATION

Practice questions to help prepare for classroom exams and standardized assessment

Step-by-step lessons to learn and practice important skills

Focus on ...

CITIZENSHIP

CULTURE

DAILY LIFE

ECONOMICS

GEOGRAPHY

GOVERNMENT

TECHNOLOGY

WORLD EVENTS

COMPARING PRIMARY SOURCES

Primary source quotations on controversial issues of the period

COMPARING HISTORIANS' VIEWPOINTS

Respected historians debate events in our nation's history

American BIOGRAPHIES

Profiles describing the lives and accomplishments of prominent Americans

NOTABLE PRESIDENTS

Biographies of some of the most highly respected Presidents

Links between events of the chapter and present-day issues

Key Documents

Primary Sources

Maps

Charts, Graphs, and Tables

American Pathways

Much of what you learn about American history can be better understood if you view events as part of a larger pattern. The themes described below and the American Pathways features throughout this book can help you identify the larger patterns and see the connections between events across time.

***Take It to the NET:* Creating a Study Guide** As you complete your course in American history, you can use the American Pathways features and the printable worksheets available at **www.phschool.com** to create your own thematic study guides.

▶ History

Fighting for Freedom and Democracy

Throughout the nation's history, Americans have risked their lives to protect their freedoms and to fight for democracy both at home and abroad. Use the American Pathways feature on pages 410–411 to help you trace specific events in the struggle to protect and defend these cherished ideals.

A cannon used in the Battle of Gettysburg

▶ Geography

The Expansion of the United States

Through a series of treaties, purchases, and warfare, the United States has grown from a small country bordering the Atlantic Ocean to one that stretches from the Atlantic to the Pacific, as well as north to Alaska and west to Hawaii. This vast territory has provided American citizens with many natural resources. Use the American Pathways feature on pages 148–149 to help you trace specific events in the expansion of the United States.

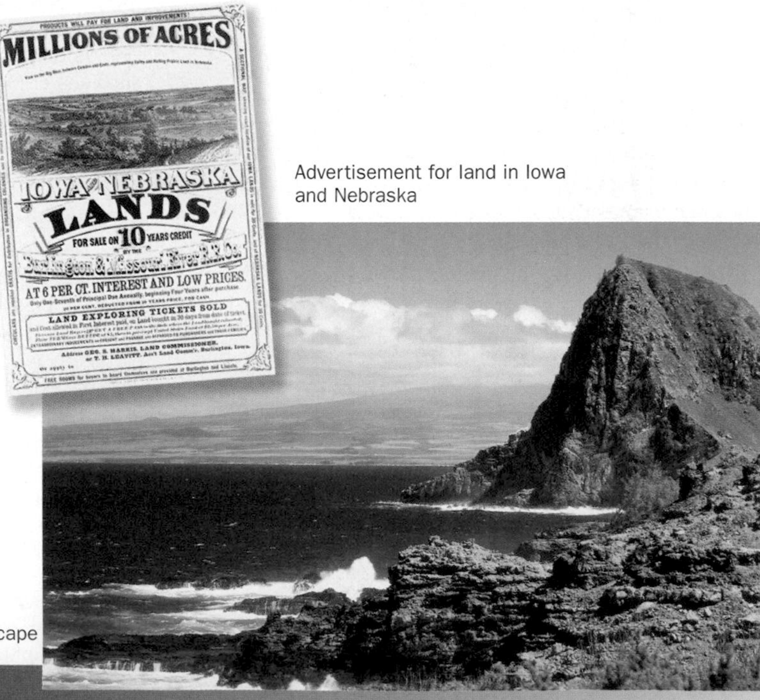

Advertisement for land in Iowa and Nebraska

A Hawaiian landscape

▶ Economics

Free Enterprise and the American Economy

The combination of abundant natural resources, an economic system that encourages individual initiative, and a political system that ensures private property rights has allowed hard-working Americans to build a strong and prosperous American economy. Use the American Pathways feature on pages 920–921 to help you trace specific events in the unfolding of our nation's economy.

Currency from the Free Banking Era, 1837–1863

Thurgood Marshall (center) outside the U.S. Supreme Court

▶ Government

Federalism and States' Rights

The Framers of the Constitution based the American system of government on federalism, the sharing of power between the national, or federal, government and state governments. Throughout the nation's history, Americans have debated exactly which powers belong to the federal government and which belong to the states. Use the American Pathways feature on pages 196–197 to help you trace specific events in this ongoing debate.

Two women protesting child labor

▶ Citizenship

Expanding Civil Rights

The United States was founded on such ideals as equality and democratic representation. Throughout American history many groups, including women and African Americans, have fought for and won important civil rights. Use the American Pathways feature on pages 732–733 to trace the events surrounding various groups' struggles for civil rights.

An American suffragette

Dr. Martin Luther King, Jr.

▶ Culture

The Arts in America

In every period of their history, Americans have expressed their views in forms such as art, literature, films, and music. Use the American Pathways feature on pages 476–477 to help identify major contributions to the arts throughout American history.

Louis Armstrong's Hot Five jazz band and record labels from the 1920s

▶ Science and Technology

American Innovation in Technology

Innovations in science and technology have had an enormous impact on our nation's economy, standard of living, and quality of life. Use the American Pathways feature on pages 664–665 to identify important American inventions from the telephone to the microchip.

A textile mill label from Lowell, Massachusetts

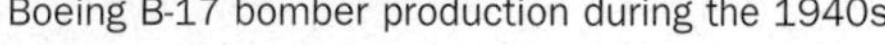

Boeing B-17 bomber production during the 1940s

An implantable replacement heart

The Five Geographic Themes

Like history, geography can be divided into themes. Geographers use five themes, described below, to organize their study of the world. You will find these themes in the captions that accompany the maps in this textbook. In addition, a Geography and History feature in each unit explores one of the themes in greater depth.

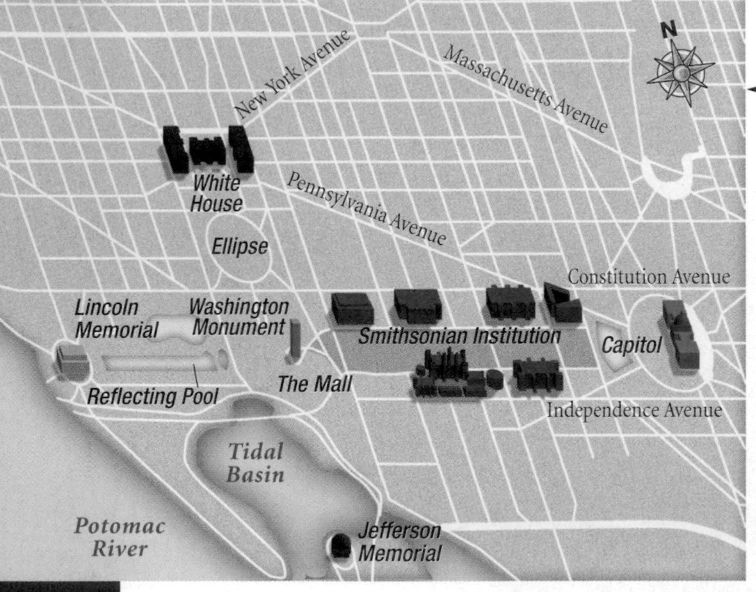

Location

The most basic of the geographic themes, location tells where a place is. Location can be expressed in two ways. Absolute location describes a place's position on the globe as determined by latitude and longitude. Relative location describes a place's position in relation to other places. While each place can have only one absolute location, its relative location can be expressed in a number of ways. For example, the relative location of the Smithsonian Institution can be described as "west of the Capitol," "at the Mall," or "east of the Washington Monument."

Place

Place describes the characteristics that make a location distinctive. There are two kinds of characteristics. Physical characteristics include landforms, vegetation, and climate. Human characteristics include the culture, economy, and government of the people who live in a place. Each place in the United States—indeed, on Earth—has a unique combination of physical and human characteristics.

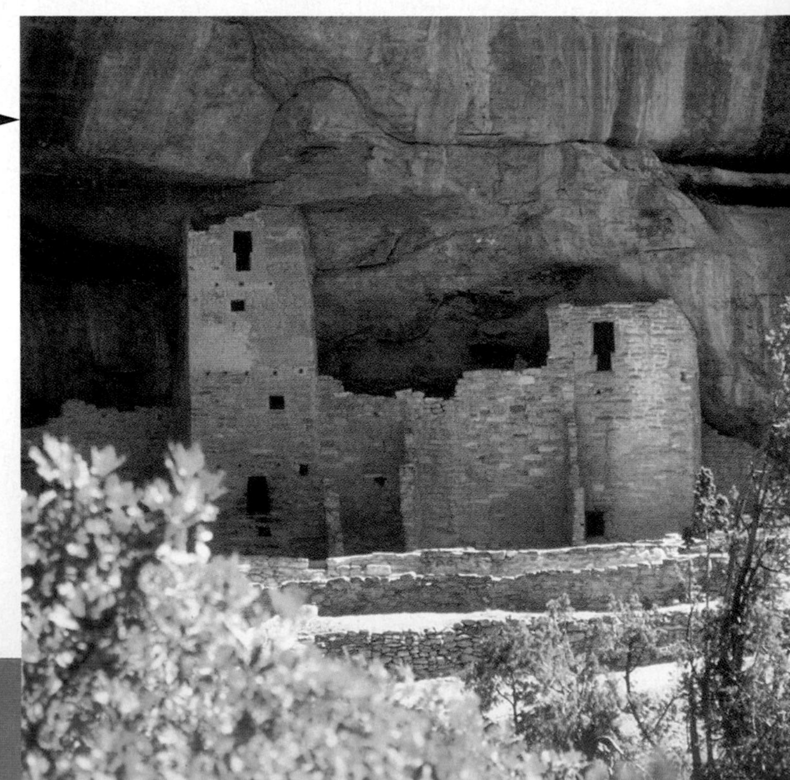

Movement

People, goods, and ideas regularly travel from one place to another. Examples from American history include the continuing immigration of new Americans, the westward migration of Americans through the 1800s, and the spread of American ideals of individual liberty through the world following the American Revolution. Today's advances in communication and transportation make movement easier and more common than ever.

Regions

A region is any group of places with at least one common characteristic. Regions can be any size, and a single place can belong to several different regions. The city of San Diego, for example, is part of California (a political region), the Sunbelt (a demographic region), and the Pacific Rim (an economic region).

Human-Environment Interaction

Human-environment interaction explores the ways in which people use and modify their environment. The Brooklyn Bridge, the coal mines of West Virginia, the wheat fields of the Plains states, Hoover Dam—all are examples of Americans modifying their environment in order to produce or extract needed resources or to make movement more efficient.

Use This Book for Success

You can use this book as a tool to master United States history. Spend a few minutes to become familiar with the way the book is set up and learn how it can help you succeed in understanding the rich story of America.

Read for Content Mastery

Before You Read The sections in this book begin with Reading Focus questions. These questions point out important ideas in the section. Another helpful aid is the Taking Notes exercise at the beginning of each section. It will help you take notes as you read.

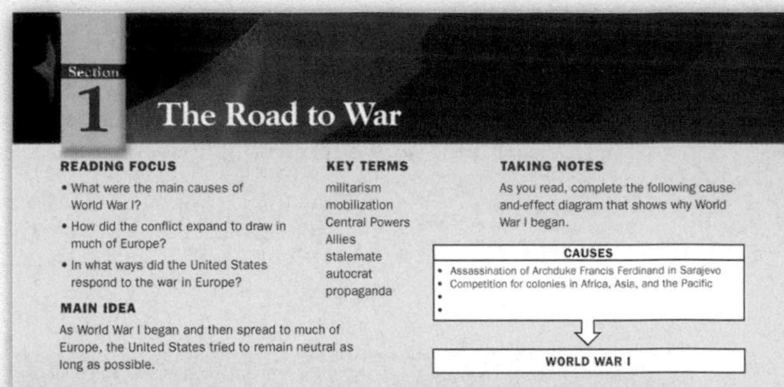

Section 1 The Road to War

READING FOCUS
- What were the main causes of World War I?
- How did the conflict expand to draw in much of Europe?
- In what ways did the United States respond to the war in Europe?

MAIN IDEA
As World War I began and then spread to much of Europe, the United States tried to remain neutral as long as possible.

KEY TERMS
militarism
mobilization
Central Powers
Allies
stalemate
autocrat
propaganda

TAKING NOTES
As you read, complete the following cause-and-effect diagram that shows why World War I began.

CAUSES
- Assassination of Archduke Francis Ferdinand in Sarajevo
- Competition for colonies in Africa, Asia, and the Pacific

WORLD WAR I

As You Read Asking questions will help you gather evidence and gain knowledge. Suppose you are reading about World War I. Here are some questions you might ask: What events led up to the start of the war? What effect would improved weapons have upon the war? Questions like these can be found in the margins of this book and are labeled "Reading Check." Use these questions to strengthen your understanding of new material.

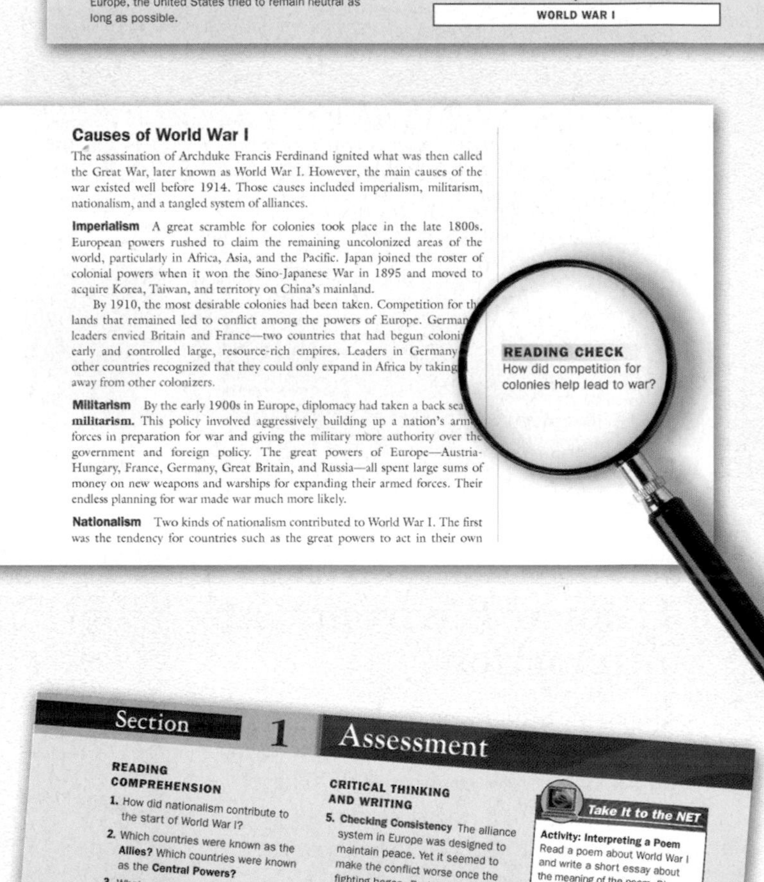

Causes of World War I

The assassination of Archduke Francis Ferdinand ignited what was then called the Great War, later known as World War I. However, the main causes of the war existed well before 1914. Those causes included imperialism, militarism, nationalism, and a tangled system of alliances.

Imperialism A great scramble for colonies took place in the late 1800s. European powers rushed to claim the remaining uncolonized areas of the world, particularly in Africa, Asia, and the Pacific. Japan joined the roster of colonial powers when it won the Sino-Japanese War in 1895 and moved to acquire Korea, Taiwan, and territory on China's mainland.

By 1910, the most desirable colonies had been taken. Competition for th lands that remained led to conflict among the powers of Europe. Germa leaders envied Britain and France—two countries that had begun coloni early and controlled large, resource-rich empires. Leaders in Germany other countries recognized that they could only expand in Africa by taking away from other colonizers.

Militarism By the early 1900s in Europe, diplomacy had taken a back sea **militarism.** This policy involved aggressively building up a nation's arm forces in preparation for war and giving the military more authority over th government and foreign policy. The great powers of Europe—Austria-Hungary, France, Germany, Great Britain, and Russia—all spent large sums of money on new weapons and warships for expanding their armed forces. Their endless planning for war made war much more likely.

Nationalism Two kinds of nationalism contributed to World War I. The first was the tendency for countries such as the great powers to act in their own

READING CHECK
How did competition for colonies help lead to war?

After You Read The questions in the Section Assessment will help you understand what you read. Use these questions to assess yourself. Were your predictions on target? Did you find answers to your questions? Demonstrate your understanding by completing the activity.

Section 1 Assessment

READING COMPREHENSION
1. How did nationalism contribute to the start of World War I?
2. Which countries were known as the **Allies?** Which countries were known as the **Central Powers?**
3. What were two causes of the **stalemate** in the West?
4. What was the main reason that the United States stayed neutral at the start of World War I?

CRITICAL THINKING AND WRITING
5. **Checking Consistency** The alliance system in Europe was designed to maintain peace. Yet it seemed to make the conflict worse once the fighting began. Explain the apparent inconsistency.
6. **Writing to Persuade** Write an essay in which you express your support for the preparedness movement. Persuade your readers that the United States had no choice but to be ready to go to war.

Take It to the NET
Activity: Interpreting a Poem
Read a poem about World War I and write a short essay about the meaning of the poem. Discuss how the writer felt about the war. What symbols does the writer use? Use the links provided in the *America: Pathways to the Present* area of the following Web site for help in completing this activity.
www.phschool.com

Chapter 12 • Section 1 419

Develop Your Skills

Each chapter has a Skills for Life exercise. Use these exercises to learn and practice Social Studies skills. These skills will help you be successful in studying United States history. Complete the Skills Assessment at the end of every chapter to apply the skills you have learned.

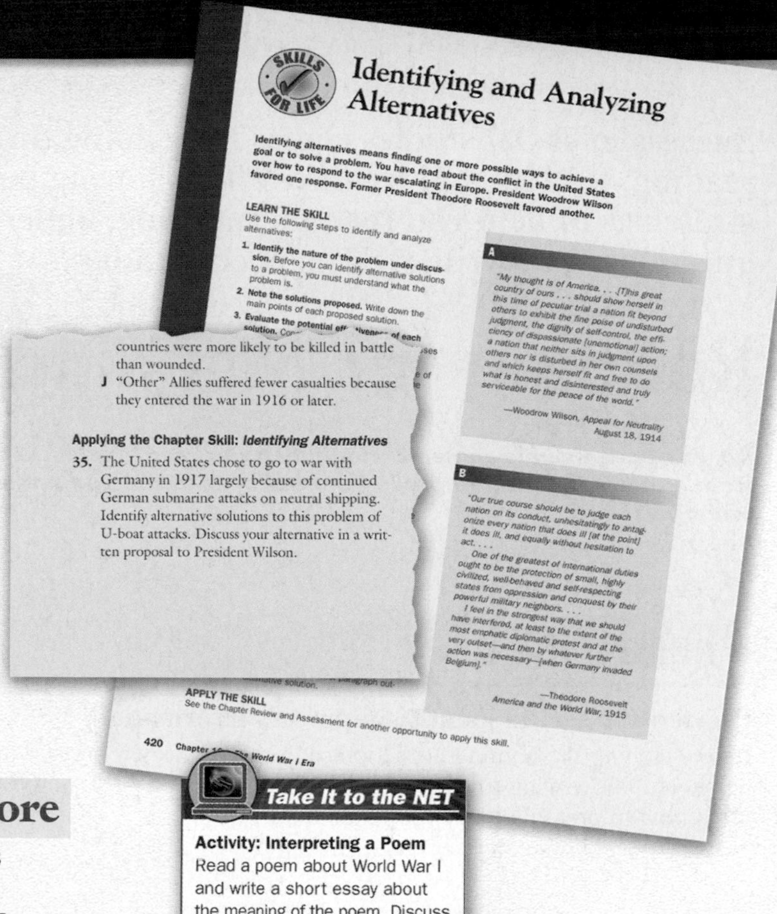

SKILLS FOR LIFE

Identifying and Analyzing Alternatives

Identifying alternatives means finding one or more possible ways to achieve a goal or to solve a problem. You have read about the conflict in the United States over how to respond to the war escalating in Europe. President Woodrow Wilson favored one response. Former President Theodore Roosevelt favored another.

LEARN THE SKILL
Use the following steps to identify and analyze alternatives:

1. **Identify the nature of the problem under discussion.** Before you can identify alternative solutions to a problem, you must understand what the problem is.
2. **Note the solutions proposed.** Write down the main points of each proposed solution.
3. **Evaluate the potential eff**...**iveness of each solution.** ...

countries were more likely to be killed in battle than wounded.
J "Other" Allies suffered fewer casualties because they entered the war in 1916 or later.

Applying the Chapter Skill: *Identifying Alternatives*
35. The United States chose to go to war with Germany in 1917 largely because of continued German submarine attacks on neutral shipping. Identify alternative solutions to this problem of U-boat attacks. Discuss your alternative in a written proposal to President Wilson.

A
"My thought is of America . . . [T]his great country of ours . . . should show herself in this time of peculiar trial a nation fit beyond others to exhibit the fine poise of undisturbed judgment, the dignity of self-control, the efficiency of dispassionate [unemotional] action; a nation that neither sits in judgment upon others nor is disturbed in her own counsels and which keeps herself fit and free to do what is honest and disinterested and truly serviceable for the peace of the world."
—Woodrow Wilson, *Appeal for Neutrality* August 18, 1914

B
"Our true course should be to judge each nation on its conduct, unhesitatingly to antagonize every nation that does ill [at the point] it does ill, and equally without hesitation to act. . . .
One of the greatest of international duties ought to be the protection of small, highly civilized, well-behaved and self-respecting states from oppression and conquest by their powerful military neighbors. . . .
I feel in the strongest way that we should have interfered, at least to the extent of the most emphatic diplomatic protest and at the very outset—and then by whatever further action was necessary—[when Germany invaded Belgium]."
—Theodore Roosevelt *America and the World War*, 1915

APPLY THE SKILL
See the Chapter Review and Assessment for another opportunity to apply this skill.

420 Chapter ... The World War I Era

Use the Internet to Explore

At the click of a mouse, the Internet offers you access to a wealth of United States history resources. Use the Take It to the Net activities to research and learn more about key events and themes in United States History. At the Pathways Companion Web site you will find virtual field trips, interactive self-tests, and dozens of links to historical sites online.

Take It to the NET

Activity: Interpreting a Poem
Read a poem about World War I and write a short essay about the meaning of the poem. Discuss how the writer felt about the war. What symbols does the writer use? Use the links provided in the *America: Pathways to the Present* area of the following Web site for help in completing this activity.
www.phschool.com

Prepare for Tests

This book helps you prepare for tests. Start by answering the questions at the end of every section and chapter. Go to **www.phschool.com** at the end of each chapter to take the practice Self-Test. Then, use the Test Preparation pages at the end of the unit to check yourself further.

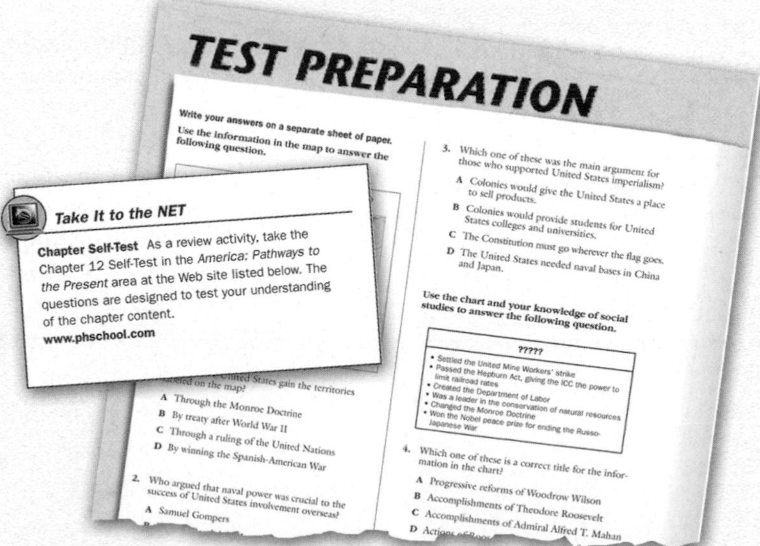

TEST PREPARATION

Write your answers on a separate sheet of paper.
Use the information in the map to answer the following question.

...United States gain the territories ...ed on the map?
A Through the Monroe Doctrine
B By treaty after World War II
C Through a ruling of the United Nations
D By winning the Spanish-American War

2. Who argued that naval power was crucial to the success of United States involvement overseas?
A Samuel Gompers

3. Which one of these was the main argument for those who supported United States imperialism?
A Colonies would give the United States a place to sell products.
B Colonies would provide students for United States colleges and universities.
C The Constitution must go wherever the flag goes.
D The United States needed naval bases in China and Japan.

Use the chart and your knowledge of social studies to answer the following question.

?????
• Settled the United Mine Workers' strike • Passed the Hepburn Act, giving the ICC the power to limit railroad rates • Created the Department of Labor • Was a leader in the conservation of natural resources • Changed the Monroe Doctrine • Won the Nobel peace prize for ending the Russo-Japanese War

4. Which one of these is a correct title for the information in the chart?
A Progressive reforms of Woodrow Wilson
B Accomplishments of Theodore Roosevelt
C Accomplishments of Admiral Alfred T. Mahan
D Actions of...

Take It to the NET
Chapter Self-Test As a review activity, take the Chapter 12 Self-Test in the *America: Pathways to the Present* area at the Web site listed below. The questions are designed to test your understanding of the chapter content.
www.phschool.com

Student Success Handbook

Success in social studies comes from doing three things well—reading, testing, and writing. The following pages present strategies to help you read for meaning, understand test questions, and write well for social studies.

Reading for Meaning

Do you have trouble remembering what you read? Here are some tips from experts that will improve your ability to recall and understand what you read:

▶ Before You Read

Preview the text to identify important information.

Like watching the coming attractions at a movie theater, previewing the text helps you know what to expect. Study the questions and strategies below to learn how to preview what you read.

Ask yourself these questions:	Use these strategies to find the answers:
• What is the text about?	Read the headings, subheadings, and captions. Study the photos, maps, tables, or graphs.
• What do I already know about the topic?	Read the questions at the end of the text to see if you can answer any of them.
• What is the purpose of the text?	Turn the headings into *who, what, when, where, why,* or *how* questions. This will help you decide if the text compares things, tells a chain of events, or explains causes and effects.

▶ As You Read

Organize information in a way that helps you see meaningful connections or relationships.

Taking notes as you read will improve your understanding. Use graphic organizers like the ones below to record the information you read. Study these descriptions and examples to learn how to create each type of organizer.

Sequencing

A **flowchart** helps you see how one event led to another. It can also display the steps in a process.

Use a flowchart if the text—

- tells about a chain of events.
- explains a method of doing something.

TIP▶ List the events or steps in order.

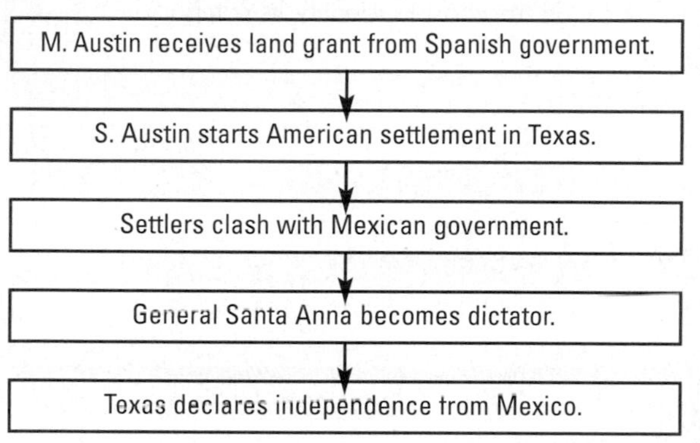
M. Austin receives land grant from Spanish government.
S. Austin starts American settlement in Texas.
Settlers clash with Mexican government.
General Santa Anna becomes dictator.
Texas declares independence from Mexico.

Comparing and Contrasting

A **Venn diagram** displays similarities and differences.

Use a Venn diagram if the text—

- compares and contrasts two individuals, groups, places, things, or events.

TIP▶ Label the outside section of each circle and list differences.
Label the shared section and list similarities.

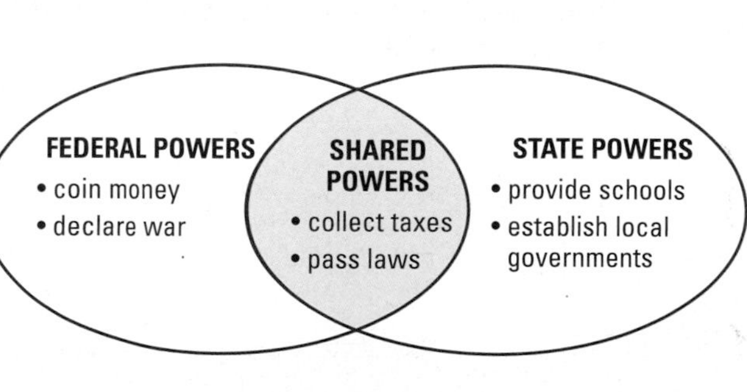
FEDERAL POWERS
• coin money
• declare war
SHARED POWERS
• collect taxes
• pass laws
STATE POWERS
• provide schools
• establish local governments

▶ As You Read *(continued)*

Categorizing Information

A **chart** organizes information in categories.

Use a chart if the text—

- lists similar facts about several places or things.
- presents characteristics of different groups.

TIP▶ Write an appropriate heading for each column in the chart to identify its category.

COLONY	FOUNDED	LEADERS
Massachusetts	1620	William Bradford John Winthrop
New Hampshire	1623	John Wentworth
Connecticut	1636	Thomas Hooker
Rhode Island	1636	Roger Williams

Identifying Main Ideas and Details

A **concept web** helps you understand relationships among ideas.

Use a concept web if the text—

- provides examples to support a main idea.
- links several ideas to a main topic.

TIP▶ Write the main idea in the largest circle. Write details in smaller circles and draw lines to show relationships.

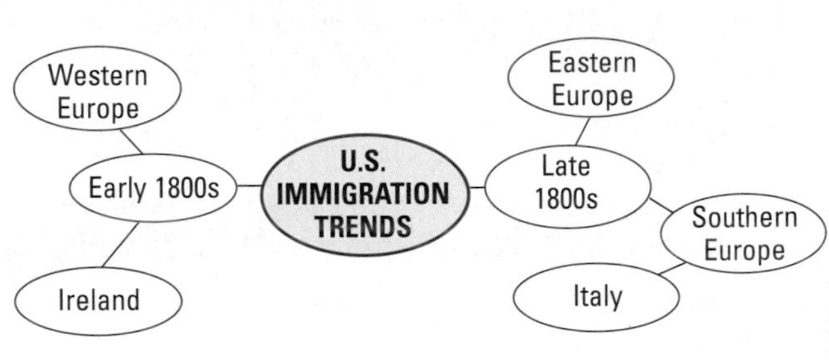

Organizing Information

An **outline** provides an overview, or a kind of blueprint for reading.

Use an outline to organize ideas—

- according to their importance.
- according to the order in which they are presented.

TIP▶ Use Roman numerals for main ideas, capital letters for secondary ideas, and Arabic numerals for supporting details.

I. Differences Between the North and the South
- **A.** Views on slavery
  - **1.** Northern abolitionists
  - **2.** Southern slave owners
- **B.** Economies
  - **1.** Northern manufacturing
  - **2.** Southern agriculture

Identifying Cause and Effect

A **cause-and-effect** diagram shows the relationship between what happened (effect) and the reason why it happened (cause).

Use a cause-and-effect diagram if the text—

- lists one or more causes for an event.
- lists one or more results of an event.

TIP▶ Label causes and effects. Draw arrows to indicate how ideas are related.

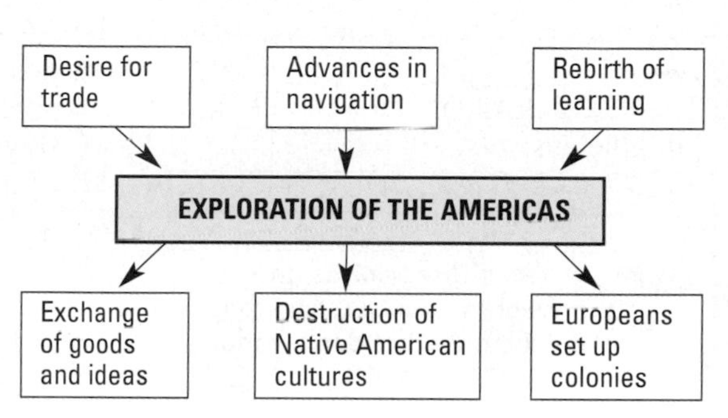

▶ After You Read

Test yourself to find out what you learned from reading the text.
Go back to the questions you asked yourself before you read the text. You should be able to give more complete answers to these questions:

- What is the text about?
- What is the purpose of the text?

You should also be able to make connections between the new information you learned from the text and what you already knew about the topic.

Study your graphic organizer. Use this information as the *answers.* Make up a meaningful *question* about each piece of information.

Taking Tests

Do you panic at the thought of taking a standardized test? Here are some tips that most test developers recommend to help you achieve good scores.

▶ Multiple-Choice Questions

Read each part of a multiple-choice question to make sure you understand what is being asked.

Many tests are made up of multiple-choice questions. Some multiple-choice items are **direct questions.** They are complete sentences followed by possible answers, called distractors.

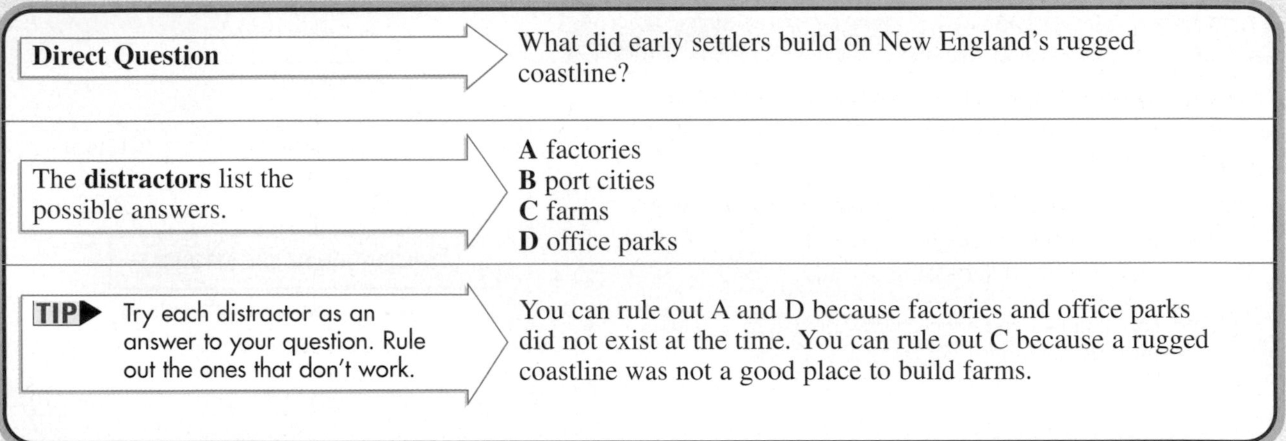

Direct Question
What did early settlers build on New England's rugged coastline?
The distractors list the possible answers.
A factories
B port cities
C farms
D office parks
TIP▶ Try each distractor as an answer to your question. Rule out the ones that don't work.
You can rule out A and D because factories and office parks did not exist at the time. You can rule out C because a rugged coastline was not a good place to build farms.

Other multiple-choice questions are **incomplete sentences** that you are to finish. They are followed by possible answers.

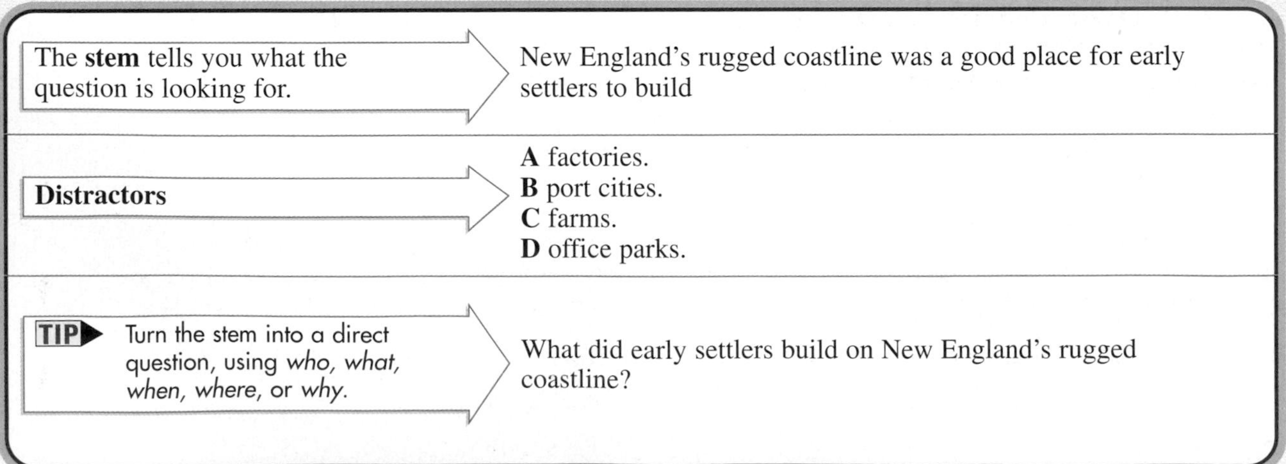

The stem tells you what the question is looking for.
New England's rugged coastline was a good place for early settlers to build
Distractors
A factories.
B port cities.
C farms.
D office parks.
TIP▶ Turn the stem into a direct question, using who, what, when, where, or why.
What did early settlers build on New England's rugged coastline?

▶ What's Being Tested?

Identify the type of question you are being asked.

Social studies tests often ask questions that involve reading comprehension. Other questions may require you to gather or interpret information from a map, graph, or chart. The following strategies will help you answer different kinds of questions.

Reading Comprehension Questions

What to do:	How to do it:
1. Determine the content and organization of the selection.	Read the **title.** Skim the selection. Look for key words that indicate time, cause-and-effect, or comparison.
2. Analyze the questions. Do they ask you to *recall facts?*	Look for **key words** in the stem: According to the selection . . . The selection states that . . .
Do they ask you to *make judgments?*	The main idea of the selection is . . . The author would likely agree that . . .
3. Read the selection.	Read quickly. Keep the questions in mind.
4. Answer the questions.	Try out each distractor and choose the best answer. Refer back to the selection if necessary.

Example:

The Dust Bowl During the 1930s, an area of the southern Great Plains became known as the "Dust Bowl." Climate and farming methods combined to cause one of the worst environmental disasters in United States history. As a result of a severe drought, the soil was dry. When farmers plowed the land, they removed the prairie grasses that held the soil in place. When strong winds swept the region, the soil was easily eroded and carried hundreds of miles away. A series of destructive duststorms brought economic ruin to farmers.

What caused the soil to become dry?
A strong winds
B plowing
C drought
D high temperatures

TIP▶ The key words as a result tell why the soil was dry.

(The correct answer is C.)

▶ What's Being Tested? *(continued)*

Map Questions

What to do:	How to do it:
1. Determine what kind of information is presented on the map.	Read the map **title.** It will indicate the purpose of the map. Study the **map key.** It will explain the symbols used on the map. Look at the **scale.** It will help you calculate distance between places on the map.
2. Read the question. Determine which component on the map will help you find the answer.	Look for **key words** in the stem. About how far . . . [use the scale] What crops were grown in . . . [use the map key]
3. Look at the map and answer the question in your own words.	Do not read the distractors yet.
4. Choose the best answer.	Decide which distractor agrees with the answer you determined from the map.

Example

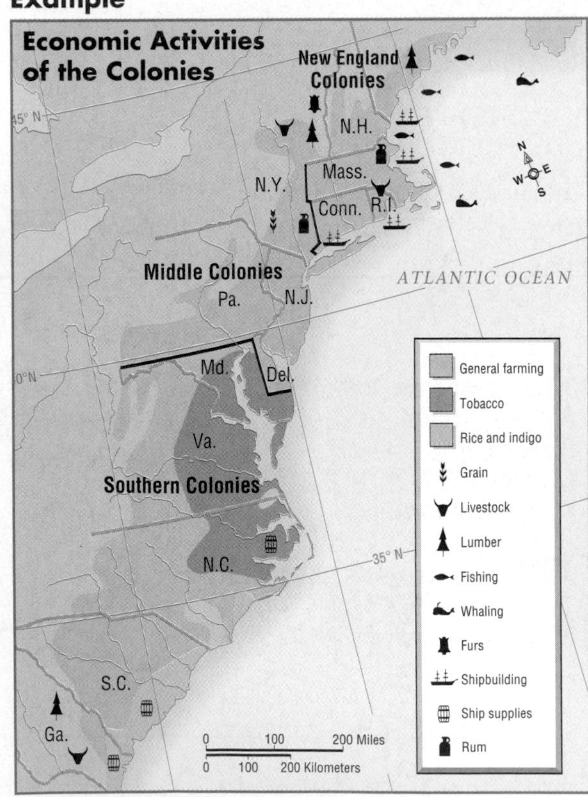

Which of the southern colonies produced ship supplies, tobacco, rice, and indigo?

A New Jersey
B North Carolina
C Virginia
D South Carolina

TIP▶ Read the labels and the key to understand the map.

(The correct answer is B.)

Graph Questions

What to do:	How to do it:
1. Determine the purpose of the graph.	Read the graph **title.** It indicates what the graph represents.
2. Determine what information on the graph will help you find the answer.	Read the **labels** on the graph or on the key. They tell the units of measurement used by the graph.
3. Choose the best answer.	Decide which distractor agrees with the answer you determined from the graph.

Example

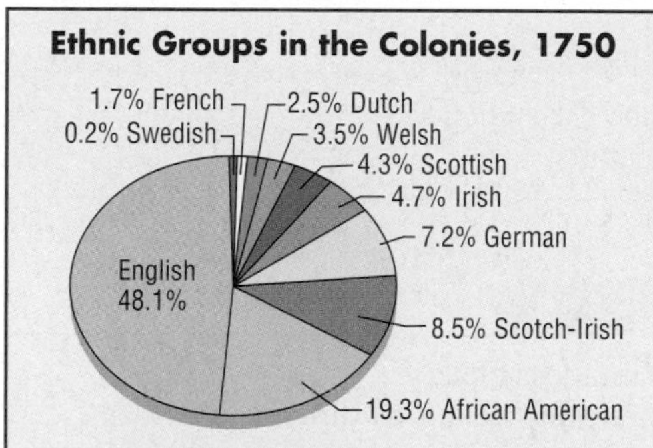

A **circle graph** shows the relationship of parts to the whole in terms of percentages.

After the English, the next largest ethnic group in the colonies was
A French. **C** German.
B Irish. **D** African American.

TIP Compare the percentages listed in the labels.

(The correct answer is D.)

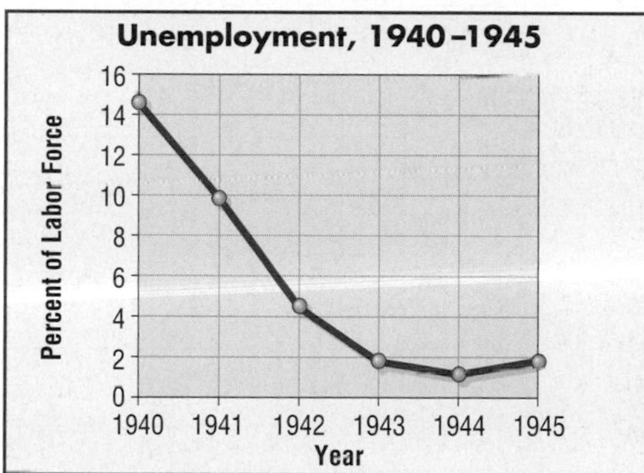

A **line graph** shows a pattern or change over time by the direction of the line.

Between 1940 and 1943, unemployment
A decreased a little. **C** stayed about the same.
B decreased greatly. **D** increased a little.

TIP Compare the vertical distance between the two points on the line graph.

(The correct answer is B.)

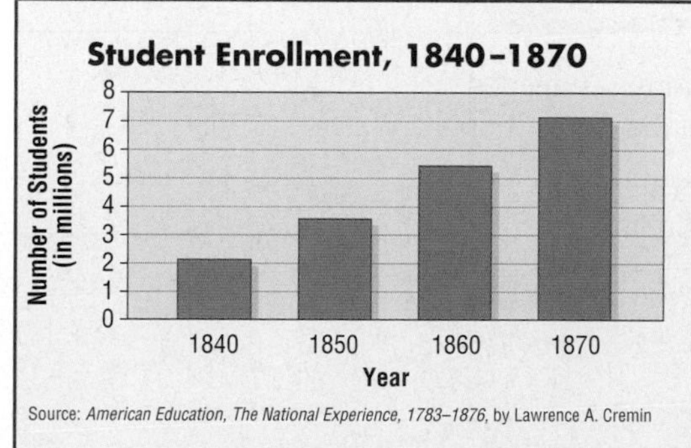

Source: *American Education, The National Experience, 1783–1876*, by Lawrence A. Cremin

A **bar graph** compares differences in quantity by showing bars of different lengths.

Between 1850 and 1860, school enrollment increased by about
A 1 million. **C** 3 million.
B 2 million. **D** 4 million.

TIP Compare the heights of the bars to find the difference.

(The correct answer is B.)

Writing for Social Studies

When you face a writing assignment, do you think, "How will I ever get through this?" Here are some tips to guide you through any writing project from start to finish.

▶ The Writing Process

Follow each step of the writing process to communicate effectively.

Step 1. Prewrite

- Establish the purpose.
- Define the topic.
- Determine the audience.
- Gather details.

Step 2. Draft

- Organize information logically in an outline or graphic organizer.
- Write an introduction, body, and conclusion.
- State main ideas clearly.
- Include relevant details to support your ideas.

Step 3. Revise

- Edit for clarity of ideas and elaboration.

Step 4. Proofread

- Correct any errors in spelling, grammar, and punctuation.

Step 5. Publish and Present

- Copy text neatly by hand, or use a typewriter or word processor.
- Illustrate as needed.
- Create a cover if appropriate.

▶ Types of Writing for Social Studies

Identify the purpose for your writing.

Each type of writing assignment has a specific purpose, and each purpose needs a different plan for development. The following descriptions and examples will help you identify the three purposes for social studies writing. The lists of steps will help you plan your writing.

Writing to Inform

Purpose: to present facts or ideas

Example

During the 1960s, research indicated the dangers of the insecticide DDT. It killed insects but also had long-term effects. When birds and fish ate poisoned insects, DDT built up in their fatty tissue. The poison also showed up in human beings who ate birds and fish contaminated by DDT.

TIP▶ Look for these **key terms** in the assignment: explain, describe, report, narrate

How to get started:

- Determine the topic you will write about.
- Write a topic sentence that tells the main idea.
- List all the ideas you can think of that are related to the topic.
- Arrange the ideas in logical order.

Writing to Persuade

Purpose: to influence someone

Example

Teaching computer skills in the classroom uses time that could be spent teaching students how to think for themselves or how to interact with others. Students who can reason well, express themselves clearly, and get along with other people will be better prepared for life than those who can use a computer.

Look for these **key terms** in the assignment: convince, argue, request

How to get started:

- Make sure you understand the problem or issue clearly.
- Determine your position.
- List evidence to support your arguments.
- Predict opposing views.
- List evidence you can use to overcome the opposing arguments.

Writing to Provide Historical Interpretation

Purpose: to present the perspective of someone in a different era

Example

The crossing took a week, but the steamship voyage was hard. We were cramped in steerage with hundreds of others. At last we saw the huge statue of the lady with the torch. In the reception center, my mother held my hand while the doctor examined me. Then, my father showed our papers to the official, and we collected our bags. I was scared as we headed off to find a home in our new country.

TIP▶ Look for these **key terms** in the assignment: go back in time, create, suppose that, if you were

How to get started:

- Study the events or issues of the time period you will write about.
- Consider how these events or issues might have affected different people at the time.
- Choose a person whose views you would like to present.
- Identify the thoughts and feelings this person might have experienced.

Unit 1

Introducing the Unit

Beginnings to 1861 In this unit, students will learn about the settlement and colonization of North America by European emigrants, and the growth of those colonies. They will then find out about the path America took to establish independence from colonial rule. Finally, they will explore the adventures and challenges of establishing a new nation, ending with the wrenching crisis that led to the Civil War.

Using Historical Evidence

Direct students' attention to the painting on these pages. It depicts George Washington presiding over the Constitutional Convention held in Philadelphia, Pennsylvania, between May and September 1787. Discuss with students the fact that the successful establishment of the United States was by no means certain. In 1783 Washington declared, "something must be done, or the fabric must fall, for it is certainly tottering." He urged a meeting to revise the country's original Articles of Confederation.

Though he sought a way to retire from public life, at the meeting Washington was chosen to be the first President of the United States, an honor he never sought, but an obligation that he discharged with his customary sense of duty. Discuss with students Washington's desire to see the Revolution he helped achieve result in a stable, unified country combined with his desire to see his own task completed and to retire to a private life.

eTeach

Be sure to check out this month's online discussion with a Master Teacher. Go to **www.phschool.com**.

Review Unit 1

Beginnings to 1861

"I always consider the settlement of America with reverence and wonder, as the opening of a grand scene and design in providence. . . ."

John Adams
Notes for "A Dissertation on the Canon and Feudal Law," 1765

This painting by Howard Chandler Christy shows George Washington presiding over the Constitutional Convention in Philadelphia, Pennsylvania, in 1787. ▶

RESOURCE DIRECTORY

Teaching Resources

Units 1/2 booklet
- American Pathways Activity, pp. 34–35
- History's Lasting Impact, pp. 36–37

Geography and History booklet, pp. 2–7

Other Print Resources

Prentice Hall Assessment System
- Document-Based Assessment

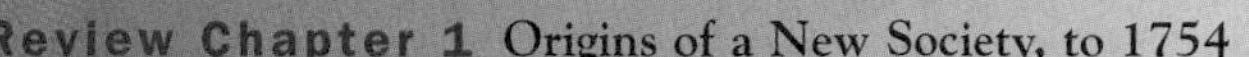

RESOURCE DIRECTORY

Technology

Color Transparencies *Historical Maps,* A1, A2, A3, A4, A5, A6, A7, A8, A9, A10, A11, A12, A13, A14, A15, A16, A17, A18, A19, A55, A56, A60; *Political Cartoons,* B1, B2, B3, B4; *Time Lines,* C1, C2, C3, C4; *Cause-and-Effect Charts,* D1, D2, D3, D4; *Fine Art,* E1, E2, E3, E4, E5, E6, E7; *American Photo,* F1, F2, F3; *American Diversity,* G1, G2, G3, G4, G5, G6, G7, G8; *The Way It Works,* H1, H2, H3, H4, H5, H6, H7

Section Reading Support Transparencies

Prentice Hall United States History Video Collection™ Volume 1, *Three Worlds Meet;* Volume 2, *The Era of Colonization (1585–1763);* Volume 3, *Slavery and Freedom;* Volume 4, *The American Revolution;* Volume 5, *A New Nation;* Volume 6, *Expansionism;* Volume 7, *Democracy and Reform;* Volume 8, *Causes of the Civil War;* Volume 11, *Industrialization and Urbanization*

Companion Web site, www.phschool.com

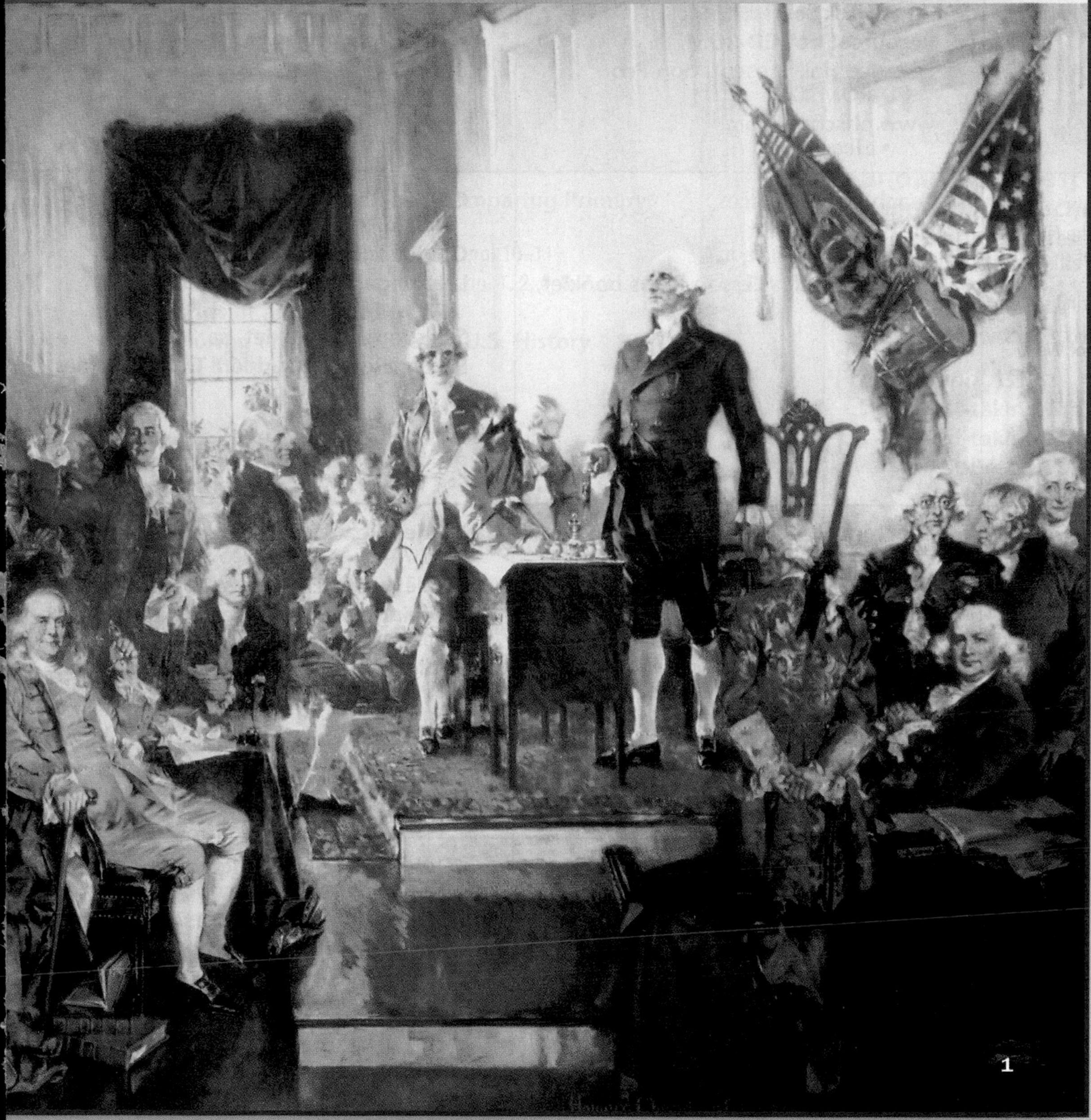

TECHNOLOGY CENTER

Take It to the NET

Prentice Hall School Web site offers student-appropriate Internet activities and links that extend core content. Visit us at the Social Studies area. **www.phschool.com**

AmericanHeritage®

My Brush with History™ Video Program This new video series lets your students learn history from the people who lived it.

RESOURCE PRO®

Teaching Resources on CD-ROM offer lesson-planning flexibility, test-generation capability, and resource manageability.

- **PRESENTATION PRO CD-ROM** Provides you with multimedia lecture notes for each chapter.
- **SOCIAL STUDIES SKILLS TUTOR CD-ROM** Provides interactive practice in Geographic Literacy, Critical Thinking and Reading, Visual Analysis, and Communications.
- **INTERACTIVE CONSTITUTION CD-ROM** Exploring active citizenship and civic responsibilities, this CD-ROM shows students how the Constitution affects their lives today.
- **EXPLORING PRIMARY SOURCES IN U.S. HISTORY CD-ROM** This interactive exploration of primary sources allows students to analyze and to evaluate writing and images from American history.
- **GUIDED READING AUDIOTAPES**
- **STUDENT EDITION ON AUDIO CD**
- **SOUNDS OF AN ERA AUDIO CD** Bring the sounds of American history to life in the classroom with music, speeches, poetry, interviews, and news reports.

Don't miss the exclusive interactive version of this textbook on the Web and on CD-ROM.

Chapter 1

Origins of a New Society

(To 1754)

Introducing the Chapter

Five hundred years ago, frequent contact began among Native Americans, Europeans, and West Africans on the shores of North America. This contact grew as more and more European explorers established settlements on the continent. Eventually, colonies were established that quickly destroyed most Native American settlements and established a new way of life in North America.

Time Line Activity

To provide students with practice in using the time line, ask questions such as these:

1. What significant religious event began in 1517? *(The Reformation)*
2. Which settlement was established first, Jamestown or Quebec? *(Jamestown)*
3. What revolt temporarily drove Spanish settlers from New Mexico? *(The Pueblo Revolt of 1680)*

Review Chapter 1

Origins of a New Society, To 1754

A modern replica of one of Columbus's ships

The signing of the Mayflower Compact

American Events

- **1492** Columbus sails to the Americas.
- **1565** The Spanish establish St. Augustine, in present-day Florida.
- **1570–1600** The Iroquois League, a confederation of Native American nations, is formed.
- **1607** The English establish Jamestown, Virginia.
- **1620** Pilgrims establish Plymouth Colony in present-day Massachusetts.

1475 · 1525 · 1575 · 1625

World Events

- **1500** European slave raids begin in Africa.
- **1517** The Reformation begins.
- **1608** Samuel de Champlain establishes Quebec, New France.

eTeach

Be sure to check out this month's online discussion with a Master Teacher. Go to **www.phschool.com**.

RESOURCE DIRECTORY

Teaching Resources

Pacing Charts booklet
Block Scheduling booklet, pp. 13–14
Units 1/2 booklet
- Chapter Summary, p. 3

Technology

Guided Reading Audiotapes (English/Spanish), Ch. 1
Student Edition on Audio CD, Ch. 1
Prentice Hall Presentation Pro CD-ROM, Ch. 1
Resource Pro® CD-ROM
Social Studies Skills Tutor CD-ROM
Companion Web site, www.phschool.com

Native American Culture Groups and Subsistence Areas, *circa* 1500

Primary subsistence areas

- Acorn
- Balance of animal and wild plant foods
- Buffalo, Large game
- Caribou, Moose
- Fish
- Game, Maize
- Maize
- Maize, River subsistence
- Sea mammals
- Tapioca
- Wild plants, Maize
- Wild plants, Small game

TO BE SOLD,
A CARGO
of
Ninety-Four
Prime, Healthy
NEGROES,
consisting of
Thirty-nine Men, Fifteen Boys, Twenty-four Women, and Sixteen Girls.
Just arrived,
in the Brigantine Dembia, Francis Bare, Master, from Sierra Leon, by
David & John Deas.

A bell from a Spanish mission

1640s–1670s Virginia and Maryland pass a series of laws codifying the practice of enslaving African Americans.

1664 The English take New Amsterdam from the Dutch and rename it New York.

1680 The Pueblo Revolt in New Mexico temporarily drives the Spanish from the area.

1730s The Great Awakening, a religious revival sparked by Jonathan Edwards, begins in New England and spreads throughout the colonies.

1675 · 1725 · 1775

1689 England's Glorious Revolution brings William and Mary to the throne and produces a bill of rights.

Native American Culture Groups and Subsistence Areas, *circa* 1500

Activating Prior Knowledge What was the primary subsistence of the Cochimi? *(Wild plants and small game)*

Previewing Ask the students to examine the map and determine whether the Hopi were farmers or nomads. *(Because maize was their primary subsistence, it is obvious they were farmers.)*

BACKGROUND
About the Pictures

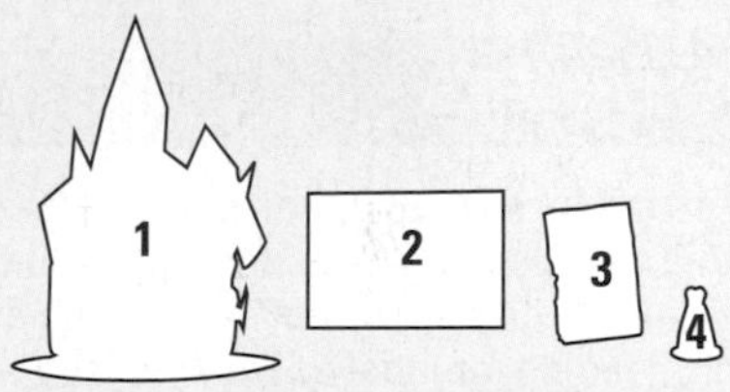

1. Though there is still dispute over the exact location of where Columbus first landed, he never actually set foot on North American soil, and to his dying day never admitted to discovering new land.
2. Painting by E. Morgan of the signing of the Mayflower Compact. The document was created to prevent the passengers from leaving the group to begin their own settlement and was signed by 41 of the male passengers.
3. Many states had laws preventing slaves from going on ships, leaving their town without written permission, or owning various kinds of property.
4. After the Pueblo Revolt, the Pueblo leader, Popé, tried to rid his tribes of anything related to Christianity or the Spanish culture.

Don't miss the exclusive interactive version of this textbook on the Web and on CD-ROM.

BIBLIOGRAPHY

For the Teacher

Boorstin, Daniel. ***The Americans, The Colonial Experience (A Caravelle Edition).*** Random House, 1964. (First book in a trilogy. An interpretation of how the habits of colonial America have shaped American life today.)

Thornton, John. ***Africa and Africans in the Making of the Atlantic World, 1400–1680.*** Cambridge University Press, 1998. (A careful analysis of this aspect of Western history.)

For the Student

Colonial America. C.A.I. Software. Video. (Narrated by eminent historian Henry Steele Commager. Focuses on the Pilgrims' search for freedom of religion.)

Hawthorne, Nathaniel. ***The Scarlet Letter.*** Silver Burdett Classics, 1985. (A famous novel that draws on sin and guilt in Puritan New England.)

Section 1

The Atlantic World

Section Objectives

1. Learn about the characteristics of the Native American world before the arrival of Columbus.
2. See what life was like in Europe during the Middle Ages and the Renaissance.
3. Discover what traditional societies of West Africa were like.
4. Find out how Columbus's voyages led to the birth of the Atlantic World.

Bellringer

Warm-Up Activity Ask students to name any Native American groups that are familiar to them from movies, television, reading, or local influences (such as geographical names). Ask them to recall any facts they know about the group, such as its location or way of life. Can students list the major nations of Western Europe today? Which do they think were important in the 1400s? Finally, ask students to list as many facts as they can about the continent of Africa.

Activating Prior Knowledge What do students already know about the conflicts and difficulties that arose between Native American people and European settlers?

Reading Strategy

Before students read, have them make a list of questions they might ask about the contact between Native Americans and Europeans, and between Europeans and West Africans. As they read the section, have students fill in the answers to their questions.

Section 1

The Atlantic World

READING FOCUS

- What were the characteristics of the Native American world before the arrival of Columbus?
- What was life like in Europe during the Middle Ages and the Renaissance?
- What were the traditional societies of West Africa like?
- How did Columbus's voyages lead to the birth of the Atlantic World?

MAIN IDEA

Columbus's voyages to the Americas brought together and reshaped the differing cultures of the Americas, Europe, and West Africa.

KEY TERMS

migration
nomad
clan
barter
middle class
monarch
Magna Carta
Columbian Exchange
plantation

TAKING NOTES

Copy the chart below. As you read, use the boxes to describe the three cultures before Columbus's voyages took place.

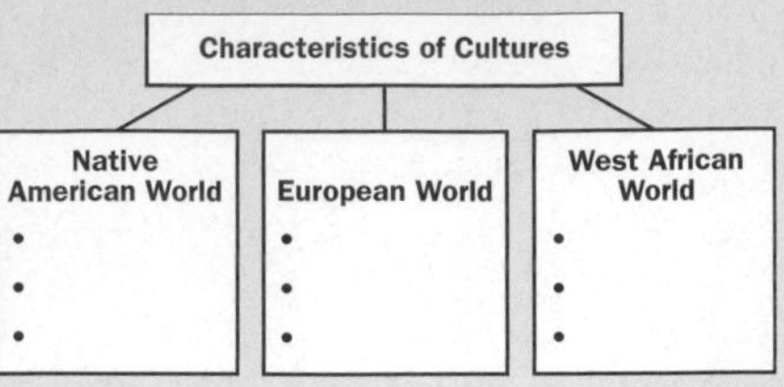

Setting the Scene A few hours after midnight on the morning of October 12, 1492, a sailor named Rodrigo de Triana spotted land. His ship, the *Pinta,* was part of an expedition authorized by Spain to find a water route to "the Indies" (India, China, and other Asian lands). The sailors thought they had reached their goal. Actually they were somewhere in the Caribbean Sea, probably approaching the island now called San Salvador. The source of their confusion was that Christopher Columbus, the expedition's leader, had underestimated the size of the earth. Columbus had probably realized his error, for he repeatedly misled the crew about the distance they had sailed. About two months after they had set sail, Columbus reported that the crew had lost patience, and that he encouraged them by "representing the profits they were about to acquire." He added that "having come so far, they had nothing to do but continue on to the Indies, till with the help of our Lord, they should arrive there." Two days later they sighted land.

This nineteenth-century American painting shows Columbus coming ashore in the Americas.

Columbus was not the first European to reach the Americas. About 500 years earlier, Norsemen led by Leif Ericson had most likely sailed along the North American coast and probably stopped occasionally in present-day Maine and Newfoundland, Canada. Columbus's voyage had far greater importance, however, because of the explorers, conquerors, and settlers who followed him to the Western Hemisphere. Through Columbus, the separate parts of the Atlantic World—the Americas, Europe, and West Africa—became permanently linked. This would change forever the histories of the peoples on these continents.

The Native American World

Today's Native Americans, or Indians, are descendants of the first people to live in the Americas. Many

RESOURCE DIRECTORY

Teaching Resources

Learning Styles Lesson Plans booklet, pp. 4–5
Guided Reading and Review booklet, pp. 3–6

Other Print Resources

Historical Outline Map Book *Hunters Reach America,* p. 1; *Physical Regions of the United States,* p. 2; *Native American Cultures,* p. 4

Technology

Section Reading Support Transparencies
Guided Reading Audiotapes (English/Spanish), Ch. 1
Student Edition on Audio CD, Ch. 1
Color Transparencies *Historical Maps,* A1; *Fine Art,* E1, E2; *American Diversity,* G1; *The Way It Works,* H1
Sounds of an Era Audio CD *Ely S. Parker on the Iroquois Constitution* (time: one minute, 45 seconds)
Prentice Hall United States Video Collection™ Volume 1, *Three Worlds Meet*
Prentice Hall Presentation Pro CD-ROM, Ch. 1
Companion Web site, www.phschool.com

thousands of years ago, those first Americans arrived as part of a **migration,** or movement of people for the purpose of settling in a new place. They reached the Americas from Asia, most experts believe, by crossing what is now called the Bering Strait, a waterway off Alaska's west coast. During the last Ice Age, glaciers trapped much of the earth's ocean water in ice, causing sea levels to drop and exposing a "land bridge" that experts believe Asians crossed to reach North America.

Gradually the human population spread from the Arctic Circle to the southernmost tip of South America. Over thousands of years, Native American societies living in different regions developed a variety of distinct languages and cultures.

VIEWING HISTORY This 1754 engraving shows a multifamily dwelling typical of the Nootka people of the Northwest Coast. **Analyzing Visual Information** *How does the engraving show the importance of fish in the Nootka diet?*

Native Peoples Across North America The North American continent varies greatly from region to region, and Native Americans adapted their ways of life to fit their local environments. The Inuit and Aleut peoples, for example, lived in the far north, on the coastal edges of North America. They were skilled at hunting on ice and snow. Other northern peoples, such as the Koyukon and Ingalik, were **nomads.** That is, they moved their homes regularly in search of food.

Native Americans of the Northwest Coast took advantage of the rich ocean fishing grounds nearby. In the Southwest, groups such as the Hopi and the Zuñi developed farming methods to suit their dry environment. Other southwestern groups, such as the Apache, were nomadic. In the center of the continent, Plains Indians traveled great distances on foot, hunting vast herds of buffalo that fulfilled many of their needs, from food to clothing to shelter.

In the Northeast, Indian peoples gathered wild plants and grew corn and other crops. They also hunted game such as deer, bear, and moose in the vast woodlands of the region. Native Americans of the Southeast included the Natchez, who settled the lower Mississippi River. Natchez towns included as many as several thousand inhabitants, who often built magnificent temples on raised mounds of earth.

Shared Customs and Beliefs Despite their cultural differences, Native American peoples had much in common. For example, many Native American societies were organized by kinship, or family relationships, rather than by social classes or by wealth or age. Individuals relied on their kin, or family, to fulfill many of their social needs, such as child care and education. Kinship groups were organized by clans. A **clan** is made up of groups of families who share a common ancestor.

Native American groups had similar religious beliefs. Indian peoples believed that the most powerful forces in the world are spiritual, and they followed traditional religious practices, or rituals, that recognized the power of these forces. Failure to perform these rituals, they believed, would cause disasters such as invasions, disease, or bad harvests. To preserve their beliefs and customs, Native Americans relied on oral history, or passing traditions from generation to generation by word of mouth. Elders told stories, sang songs, and provided instructions for ceremonies to young people, who later passed this knowledge on to their own children.

Trading Patterns Native American trading routes crisscrossed North America. For example, the Inuit traded copper from the Copper River in

Focus on GOVERNMENT

The Iroquois League Also called the Iroquois Confederacy or the Five Nations, the Iroquois League was a confederation of five tribes (Mohawk, Oneida, Onandaga, Cayuga, and Seneca) centered in present-day New York State. When the Tuscarora joined in 1722, it became known as the Six Nations.

According to tradition, the League was formed between 1570 and 1600 to put an end to constant warfare among the tribes and to provide a united force to withstand invasion. The League was governed by a council made up of clan and village chiefs. Voting in the council was by tribe, and a unanimous vote was required to declare war. The Iroquois were extremely successful in war, and subdued many of the neighboring tribes.

Following colonial settlement, the Iroquois traded beaver for firearms with the Europeans, and became important in the rivalry between French and British colonists. The confederacy was officially recognized by the British in 1722, and survived for more than 200 years.

Lesson Plan

Focus Explain that the Native American world included a diversity of peoples. Across the continent, these peoples established kinship groups, traded, and shared religious beliefs and ceremonies. Explain further that Europeans in the 1400s were ready to expand and explore. Finally, tell students that the first interactions between European and African cultures came in the 1400s along the coast of West Africa, where great kingdoms had prosperous, complex cultures. Have students think about what those cultures were like and what factors influenced their contact with European cultures.

Instruct Point out that the Atlantic World was based on elements from Native American, European, and West African cultures, although historically it appears that the Europeans were dominant. Ask students to suggest ways in which the other cultures influenced and contributed to the interchange.

Assess/Reteach Ask students if they could possibly imagine what America would be like today without the mixture of cultures that exists here.

Activity
Connecting with Culture

Have students create a chart that allows them to compare visually the Native American groups in different regions using these criteria: social organization and kinship patterns, food supply, religious beliefs and observations, trading patterns. **(Visual/Spatial)**

Customize for ...
Gifted and Talented

Much of what we know about earlier Native American cultures comes from the work of archaeologists and anthropologists. Have students choose one Native American group—perhaps one with a connection to your community—and find out what has been discovered about its history and way of life. What is its status today?

Caption Answers

Viewing History Racks of fish are suspended from the ceiling, hung on drying racks; the people around the fire are probably cooking fish.

ACTIVITY
Connecting with Culture

Have students discuss the difference between the Native American and the European views toward land. Why did Native peoples feel so strongly about not owning land? Why did the Europeans want to own land in a new country? Why is this difference in attitude an important factor in understanding future clashes between the cultures? **(Verbal/Linguistic)**

BACKGROUND
Navajo Language

Changes in the language of the Navajo people dramatically demonstrate how culture and environment interact. The Navajos once lived in eastern Alaska, where they adapted to snow and cold by gathering wild food and hunting. Later they migrated to the more temperate Southwest, where they grew corn as a basic food. The Navajos chose the corn plant as a symbol of life and incorporated it into their religious beliefs and creation stories. Because they needed a word for seed, they adapted their old word for snowflake.

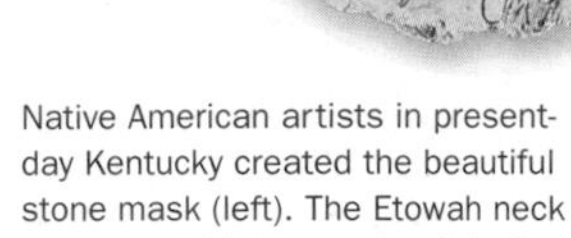

Native American artists in present-day Kentucky created the beautiful stone mask (left). The Etowah neck ornament (right) is made of shell.

southern Alaska for sharks' teeth collected by people living in coastal Washington. The Mohave of the Great Basin carried out **barter,** or trade, with people on the California coast, and then traded the coastal goods to the Pueblo in present-day Arizona.

Attitudes Toward the Land One item that Native Americans never traded was land. In their view, the land could not be owned. They believed that people had a right to use land or to allow others to use it, but buying or selling land was unthinkable. Land, like all of nature, deserved respect. The Europeans who arrived in North America in the 1400s, however, had quite a different idea about land ownership. They frequently did not understand Indian attitudes and interpreted Native American references to land use to mean land ownership.

The European World

The voyages that brought Columbus and other Europeans to the Americas were a sign of Europe's rebirth. Between about A.D. 500 and 1300, a time known as the Middle Ages, or medieval period, Europeans had been too busy dealing with internal problems to give much thought to the world beyond their own continent.

The Early Middle Ages The early part of the Middle Ages, roughly 500 to 1000, was marked by instability. Germanic tribes such as the Franks surged across the borders of the former Roman Empire. From the north, fierce Viking warriors came to loot and burn villages. In the south, the powerful Muslim empire spread from its birthplace in Arabia across North Africa and into what is now Spain. (The Muslim empire had arisen in the 600s, based on a new religion, Islam, inspired by the teachings of the prophet Muhammad.)

To protect themselves from these threats, Europeans created a political and economic system known as feudalism. Under feudalism, a powerful noble, or lord, divided his large landholdings among lesser lords. In return, they owed him military service and other favors. Peasants called serfs farmed the lord's manor, or estate, and gave him a portion of the harvest. They received his shelter and protection in return. Born into lifetime servitude, serfs had no education and knew little about the world outside the manor, which they were forbidden to leave.

The manor system produced everything a feudal society needed to survive. As a result, the trade links that had tied Europe to foreign lands during the Roman Empire largely died out.

VIEWING HISTORY Asian spices were sold to Europeans in medieval marketplaces like this. **Drawing Conclusions** *What can you learn about medieval life from this marketplace?*

The Power of the Church The Roman Catholic Church governed the spiritual life and daily activities of medieval Christians, both rich and poor. The head of the Church, the pope, claimed authority over emperors and kings, and often appointed them. The clergy, or Church officials who were authorized to perform religious ceremonies, often owned their own manors. Much of the clergy's power came from the fact that they were virtually the only educated people in medieval Europe. They alone could study the Bible and other holy writings of Christianity, so they controlled how the faith was communicated to the people. Christians were expected to obey Church authority completely.

After Muslims from Turkey seized Jerusalem, a city holy to both Christians and Muslims, the Church organized a series of military campaigns to retake the city. These holy

CAPTION ANSWERS

Viewing History A wide variety of goods—including textiles, metal wares, and shoes—were available in small stalls in large marketplaces. Men did much of the "shopping" for these goods. The architecture of this period features elaborately cut stone blocks and vaulted archways. The predominant style of clothing worn by men seems to have been a sort of kilt.

RESOURCE DIRECTORY

Teaching Resources

Learning with Documents booklet (Key Documents) *Magna Carta,* p. 74

Biography, Literature, and Comparing Primary Sources booklet (Literature) *The Koran,* p. 40

Other Print Resources

Nystrom *Atlas of Our Country* *The Americas Before Columbus,* pp. 10–11

Technology

Color Transparencies *Time Lines,* C1

RESOURCE PRO® **Literature Activity** *"Corn Mother,"* found on Resource Pro, uses a Penobscot folk tale to portray the Native American view of land use.

wars, which took place between 1096 and 1291, were called the Crusades. The Crusaders failed to establish permanent Christian control of Jerusalem, but they did increase Europeans' awareness of the world beyond their borders. Returning home to Europe, Crusaders brought spices, fabrics, and other Asian goods they had looted in war. Europeans quickly developed a taste for these items, which helped revive Europe's trade with the outside world.

Signs of Change Meanwhile, Europe's economy had entered a period of new growth. New farming methods increased food supplies, which in turn led to population growth. More people, including runaway serfs, began moving to towns and cities that were growing up along trade routes. The growth of cities and trade in Europe created a new **middle class** of merchants, traders, and artisans who made and sold goods to the manors. It also revived the use of money, which had declined in the early part of the Middle Ages. Finally, it contributed to the eventual breakdown of the feudal system.

Europe's growing wealth also increased the power of **monarchs,** or those who rule over territories or states. Monarchs attracted the loyalty of the new middle class by protecting trade routes and keeping the peace. Strong monarchs sometimes clashed with one another. In 1066, the Duke of Normandy, who ruled a region in present-day France, conquered England. This event, called the Norman Conquest, led to a gradual blending of French and Anglo-Saxon cultures that became part of the English and American heritage.

Monarchs also clashed with their own nobles, sometimes over a king's attempts to impose heavy taxes. In 1215, England's King John, a weak and insensitive leader, was forced by his nobles to sign a document granting them various legal rights. That document, the **Magna Carta** or "Great Charter," not only shaped British government but also became the foundation for future American ideals of liberty and justice. One clause declared:

> "*No freeman shall be arrested or imprisoned or dispossessed or . . . in any way harmed . . . except by the lawful judgment of his peers or by the law of the land.*"
>
> —Magna Carta, 1215

Ambitious rulers such as King John also came into conflict with the Church. For a time, strong popes prevailed in these struggles, but by the 1200s, monarchies were growing stronger as papal supremacy declined.

The Renaissance Begins The 1300s in Italy signaled the beginning of a new era for Europe. Called the Renaissance, a French word meaning "rebirth," it was a time of enormous creativity and rapid change. The Renaissance spread throughout western Europe and peaked in the 1500s. It was a quest for knowledge in nearly every field of study, including art, literature, science, and philosophy.

Freed from the rigid thinking of the medieval past, Renaissance thinkers and artists rediscovered the art and learning of ancient Greece and Rome and of Muslim culture. They used reason and experimentation to explore the physical world and the individual's place in it. This philosophy is called humanism.

Focus on WORLD EVENTS

Marco Polo Europeans learned about Asia not only from the Crusaders, but also from a fascinating account of China written by Marco Polo. Born in the mid-1200s to a wealthy family of traders, Polo grew up in the Italian city of Venice. In 1271, when Polo was still a teenager, he left with his father and uncle on an overland journey to China. Their caravan is shown in the illustration below. They remained in China for more than 15 years. During this time, Polo saw many parts of that vast country while conducting business for China's emperor, Kublai Khan.

Polo returned to Italy in 1295, but he soon was briefly imprisoned in Genoa, a city that was a rival of Venice. There he dictated the story of his travels to a fellow prisoner. The book, commonly known as *The Travels of Marco Polo*, was a huge hit in Italy. Its descriptions of the wonders of Asia sent European merchants scrambling to set up trading missions to the East.

ACTIVITY
Connecting with Government

Tell students to research the Magna Carta. Suggest that they use library resources or go online to gather information about this important document. After students finish their research, have them write a short essay summarizing what they have learned about the Magna Carta and its influence on the United States government. **(Verbal/ Linguistic)**

BACKGROUND
Connections to Today

Jerusalem remains a battleground for Jews, Christians, and Palestinian Muslims—all claiming this holy spot to be their spiritual home. It is important to remember that Mecca in Saudi Arabia is the holy city for all Muslims. Jerusalem is being contested by Israelis and Palestinians. Israelis and Palestinians both feel strongly that Jerusalem should be their capital city. The most hotly debated section in Jerusalem is the Old City, where Jews and Muslims both lay claim to the Temple Mount, the site of an ancient Jewish temple and two of Islam's holiest mosques.

CUSTOMIZE FOR ...
Less Proficient Readers

Tell students that in this section they will read about the early interactions among the three cultures of the Atlantic World. As they read, have them take notes on how these interactions affected the people of each of the three cultures.

ACTIVITY
Connecting with Government

Ask students to choose one person who was important in European history at this time and prepare his or her biography. They may choose either a person mentioned in the chapter, such as Leonardo da Vinci or Queen Isabella, or another influential figure. **(Verbal/Linguistic)**

BACKGROUND
Geography in History

During the Middle Ages, spices from Southeast Asia traveled overland to the Mediterranean, where Italian merchants monopolized sales to Europe. Wealth from trade allowed Italian cities to sponsor the great artists and architects of the Renaissance. When the Portuguese rounded the Cape of Good Hope in 1488, they challenged the Italian monopoly. Lost income contributed to Italy's decline, and the great Renaissance centers of the 1500s were regions that profited from new trade routes. The Netherlands was a particularly big winner in this regard.

Focus on CULTURE

The Renaissance Man The idea of the Renaissance is embodied in what we now call the Renaissance man, the person who is skilled and knowledgeable in all the arts and sciences. This concept came from Leon Battista Alberti (1404–1472), who said that "a man can do all things if he will."

Today, Leonardo da Vinci (1452–1519) is regarded as the ultimate Renaissance man. He was a painter, sculptor, architect, and musician. His *Mona Lisa* (right) still fascinates viewers. In addition, Leonardo was a scientist and engineer; some of his inventions, such as a type of helicopter (below), were centuries ahead of their time. In his notebooks, Leonardo combined a spirit of scientific inquiry with extraordinary powers of observation and artistic skill. He studied anatomy in order to be a better sculptor—even dissecting corpses to view the muscles, skeleton, and organs—thus making contributions to both art and science.

The most admired art works of the Italian Renaissance, such as Michelangelo's sculpture of David and his paintings in the Sistine Chapel, and Leonardo da Vinci's *Mona Lisa,* depicted human beings and their emotions realistically.

The Renaissance Spreads North Eventually, the Renaissance spread northward from its Italian birthplace. By the late 1500s, it had reached much of Europe. Among the artists of this Northern Renaissance was the English playwright and poet William Shakespeare, generally regarded as the most gifted writer in history.

The works of writers like Shakespeare became available to many more Europeans thanks to the invention of the printing press. In 1455, Johann Gutenberg used a process involving movable metal type to produce a Bible. This invention set off a communications revolution over the next century, as some 200 million books came off European printing presses.

A large number of these books were Bibles, which now circulated among a wider audience. The printing revolution came at a time when critics, angry at corruption among the clergy, were calling for Church reform. In 1517, this criticism flared into a revolt known as the Reformation. A German monk named Martin Luther claimed that the Bible, not the Church, was the true authority in spiritual matters. Luther's followers called themselves Protestants because they protested Church authority.

The Rise of Nations During the Renaissance, government by local nobles and the Church gradually declined. Instead, monarchs began to combine smaller areas into the larger nation-states we know today. For the first time, Europeans began thinking of themselves as citizens of nations, such as France, England, or Portugal.

The young nations soon started competing for the highly profitable Asian trade, which had become important after the Crusades. In 1400, the only way to reach Asia was still by land, since Europeans did not have the technology to explore the faster sea route without becoming hopelessly lost. With the help of instruments developed by Renaissance scientists, however, long-range sea travel finally became possible. Sailors could use a compass to determine direction when neither the coastline nor the sun was visible. In addition, the astrolabe and the quadrant allowed ship captains to find their location far from visible land.

In 1418, Prince Henry of Portugal established a school for mariners. His seamen developed the final tool necessary for long-range voyages: the caravel, a ship that could sail against the wind as well as with it. In 1488, a navigator trained at this school, Bartolomeu Dias, sailed around the southern tip of Africa, the Cape of Good Hope. Nine years later, another Portuguese mariner, Vasco da Gama, sailed from Portugal to India. The first sea route from Europe to Asia was now open.

Portugal had a competitor, however. In 1469, two strong Christian monarchs, Queen Isabella of Castile and King Ferdinand of Aragon, were married, uniting their kingdoms into the nation of Spain. They launched a successful campaign to drive the Muslim empire out of Spain. Queen Isabella also wanted to surpass Portugal in the race to explore new sea routes, and to bring Christianity to

RESOURCE DIRECTORY

Teaching Resources

Learning with Documents booklet (Visual Learning Activity) *Mapmakers,* p. 40

Biography, Literature, and Comparing Primary Sources booklet (Biography) *Isabella I, Queen of Castille,* p. 6

Other Print Resources

Historical Outline Map Book *To India by Sea,* p. 6; *Voyages of Discovery,* p. 8

Technology

Sounds of an Era Audio CD *Olaudah Equiano on West Africa* (time: 45 seconds)

new lands. So, as her ships dropped anchor along the west coast of Africa, they carried not only trade goods but Christian missionaries as well.

The West African World

Europeans and Africans had first met in ancient times, when a wide trading network of land and sea routes thrived throughout the Mediterranean region. Much of this contact stopped during the Middle Ages, but it resumed during the Renaissance. European traders began to trade salt for gold from North African middlemen, who obtained it from their trading partners in the interior of West Africa. Europeans wanted to get around these middlemen and go directly to the sources of gold. This was the prize for which Portugal and Spain competed in the 1400s as their ships explored Africa's Atlantic coast.

READING CHECK
Why did exploration by European mariners increase during this time?

Early relations between Europeans and West Africans were mostly peaceful. Portugal established trade ties with wealthy coastal kingdoms that produced much of the gold. The Portuguese built a string of forts along the coast for their ships to load and unload trade goods. Africans ran the trading operations and set their own prices. The Netherlands, France, and England soon launched expeditions to the region to set up similar trade arrangements.

West African Geography and Cultures Like other peoples, West Africans adapted their culture to their geographic surroundings. Rain forests covered a large band of coastal land in the south. Some of the continent's earliest societies evolved in this resource-rich region, where people hunted, fished, mined, and farmed the land.

Farther north lay a wide expanse of savanna, or tropical grassland with scattered trees, where nomadic peoples hunted and raised livestock. Merchants did a brisk business obtaining gold and other goods from the forest regions and trading them to merchants in the north. The deserts of West Africa remained largely uninhabited. But scattered towns did arise at major watering holes, where camel caravans loaded with trade goods stopped to rest.

As in the Americas, West African societies were organized according to kinship groups. Often, all residents of a town or a city belonged to kinship groups that had a common ancestor. This type of organization is called a lineage. African lineage groups provided the types of support that clans did for Native Americans.

West Africans generally shared certain religious beliefs. They worshipped a Supreme Being, as well as many lesser gods and goddesses, or spirits. These spirits were thought to inhabit everything in the natural world, from animals to trees to stones. Humans also were thought to be living spirits both before and after death. Africans appealed to the spirits of their ancestors for help in their daily lives. Information about religious beliefs, as well as family stories and laws, were handed down from generation to generation through oral tradition. As in the Americas, oral histories gave kinship groups a sense of identity.

Kingdoms and Trade Several well-established kingdoms ruled parts of West Africa for centuries. One was Benin, which arose in the late 1200s in the coastal forest. Artists left a record of their society in a series of bronze plaques that once decorated the palace of the king, or Oba. A European traveler who had visited the capital of Benin observed: "This city is about a league [three miles] long from gate to gate; it has no wall but is surrounded by a large moat, very wide and deep, which suffices for its defense. . . . Its houses are made of mud walls covered with palm leaves." The streets of Benin were wide and clean, and they led to a grand palace.

Gold from the forest regions of West Africa was traded to other parts of Africa and to Europeans. This gold pendant was made by the Baule people.

ACTIVITY
Connecting with Geography and Culture

This activity might take place over several class periods: Divide the class into groups of four. Three students will do research as "experts"; the fourth student will act as the recorder/spokesperson. Have each group choose one of the following European states in this period: Portugal, France, England, Castille and Aragon, Holy Roman Empire, and Naples. Three students in each group should research the government, economy, and culture of the chosen kingdom. The fourth person in the group should collect the data, record it on a chart, and present it in class. **(Verbal/Linguistic; Visual/Spatial)**

BACKGROUND
Biography

Between 1480 and 1780, European voyagers explored all the seas in the world except for the polar regions, giving this period the name "Age of Discovery." In Spain's search for new land and markets, Vasco Nuñez de Balboa (1475–1519) became the first European to see the Pacific Ocean. Balboa came to the Americas in 1500 and settled on Hispania. Later he traveled to what is now Panama. Looking for gold, in 1513 Balboa led an expedition across the Isthmus of Panama to the western coast, where he climbed a mountain ridge and saw the great ocean. He named it *Mar del Sur* (the Sea of the South), since he thought it was south of Asia. In fact, it was near the site of the present-day Panama Canal.

READING CHECK
To facilitate direct trade and avoid going through middlemen was the immediate goal. Ocean travel was greatly aided by Renaissance innovations, such as improved navigational instruments and the caravel type of sailing ship.

CUSTOMIZE FOR ...
ESL

Point out that a variety of different factors motivated and made possible the voyages of discovery that brought Europeans to the Americas. Ask students to take note of each of these factors as they read the section and to notice how the factors interacted.

ACTIVITY
Connecting with Geography

To help students better understand trade in West Africa, have them trace the route of a trader going from Benin to Songhai to North Africa. Have them use the map on this page to answer these questions: What direction will the trader travel from Benin to Songhai? About how far is it from the city of Benin to Timbuktu? From Timbuktu to Fez in North Africa? What kind of terrain will the trader have to cross? **(Logical/Mathematical; Visual/Spatial)**

BACKGROUND
Art History

For centuries, West African craftsmen have fashioned evocative masks out of materials like wood and gold. Scary, cheerful, or impassive, these masks are not only decorative, but serve a variety of purposes such as worship and the warding off of dangerous spirits. See Hugh Honor and John Fleming, *The Visual Arts: A History,* Prentice Hall, 1986.

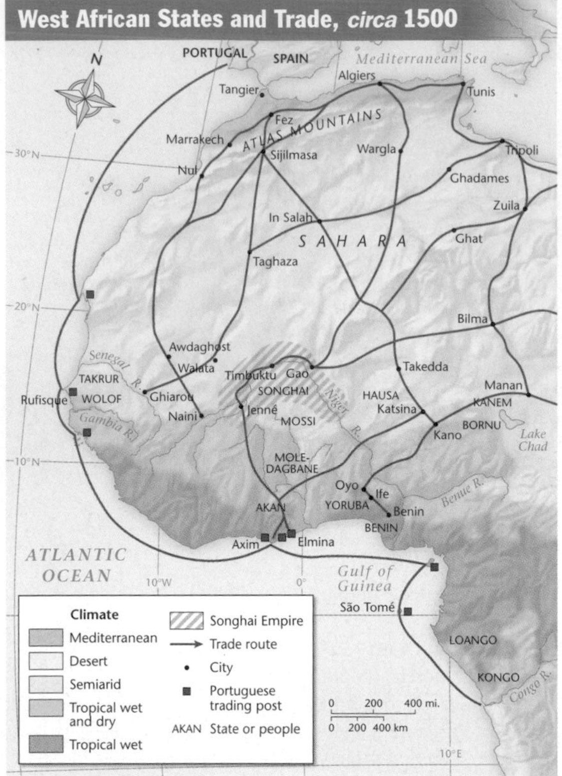

MAP SKILLS By 1500, extensive trade routes crisscrossed West Africa. **Movement** *Why do you think the Portuguese established their trading posts along Africa's west coast?*

Benin's wealth came from trade. The kingdom produced goods such as palm oil, ivory, and beautiful woods. Some of the finest artwork of the time came from Benin, especially sculpted heads created in a unique style. Before long, sculptors added figures with beards and helmets. These figures represented the Portuguese. A strong Oba had come to the throne in 1481, and had established friendly and profitable relations with the Portuguese.

Farther east, between the coastal rain forest region and the Sahara, the Songhai empire thrived from 1464 to 1590. Songhai's best-known monarch, Askia Muhammad, created a complex government with separate departments for defense, banking, and farming. A bureaucracy of paid officials enforced laws, collected taxes, negotiated with other nations, and kept the peace. Many trade caravans passed through Songhai—and paid heavy fees to do so.

Songhai's capital, Timbuktu, was a center of learning. Most of Timbuktu's scholars (like those in medieval Europe) studied religion. In Timbuktu, that religion was Islam, which had reached West Africa around 1050 through trade and by invasion from the north. Askia Muhammad, a devout Muslim, had made Songhai a Muslim empire. Yet most people, especially outside the cities, still followed traditional African beliefs.

Slavery in Africa Africans, like Europeans, believed in the private ownership of goods and property. Yet they differed from Europeans in their attitudes toward land and people. In Europe, land was scarce and thus very valuable. In Africa, labor was often valued more than land. The power of leaders was determined by the number of people they ruled, not the amount of land they controlled. Growing kingdoms such as Benin and Songhai needed increasing numbers of workers. As in many other societies, slaves provided the labor.

The most likely people to be enslaved in Africa were those who had been cut off from their lineage. Most slaves had probably been captured in war, although many were kidnapped in slave raids carried out by rival ethnic groups. Africans' concept of slavery differed from slavery as it developed in the Americas. In Africa, slaves became adopted members of the kinship group that enslaved them. They could marry into a lineage, even into the high ranks of society, and move out of their slave role. Children of slaves were not presumed to be born into slavery. Finally, slaves carried out a variety of roles, working as soldiers and administrators as well as laborers.

In the 1500s, Europeans began to exchange valuable goods, such as guns, for slaves sold by coastal societies such as Benin. Both sides profited greatly. The Africans obtained advanced technology, and the Europeans obtained labor for use in large farming operations in the Americas and elsewhere. As time wore on, however, Europeans demanded more and more slaves. Those who resisted dealing in the human cargo became themselves the victims of bloody slave raids.

CAPTION ANSWERS

Map Skills The Portuguese chose water routes for their African trade because they were excellent sailors and because travel across the Sahara from Portugal was extremely difficult.

RESOURCE DIRECTORY

Teaching Resources

Learning with Documents booklet (Primary Source Activity) *Europeans Encounter Native Americans,* p. 6

Biography, Literature, and Comparing Primary Sources booklet (Comparing Primary Sources) *On Celebrating Columbus Day,* p. 97

Sounds of an Era Audio CD *"Letter to the Spanish Crown," Christopher Columbus* (time: 30 seconds)

Other Print Resources

Historical Outline Map Book *Columbus Reaches America,* p. 7

Technology

RESOURCE PRO® **Biography** *Askia Muhammad,* found on Resource Pro, profiles the brilliant ruler of the West African kingdom of Songhai. **Visual Learning Activity** *Slave Factories,* found on Resource Pro, helps students understand slavery through illustration. **Primary Source Activity** *The Portuguese in Africa,* found on Resource Pro, uses a chronicle written in the mid-1400s to present the reasons Portugal explored West Africa.

Exploring Primary Sources in U.S. History CD-ROM *The Log of Christopher Columbus*

The Birth of the Atlantic World

In January 1492, Spain's Queen Isabella and King Ferdinand authorized the Italian-born mariner Christopher Columbus to make contact with the people of "the lands of India." Much to his pleasure, they made him "High Admiral of the Ocean Sea and . . . Governor of the islands and continent which I should discover," as Columbus wrote later.

The Voyages of Columbus Columbus's commission appealed to his ambition, but the Spanish nobles and clergy also had reasons for wanting his voyage to succeed:

1. Columbus hoped to enrich his family and to gain honor and fame. He also planned to conquer non-Christian lands and convert their peoples to Christianity. Like many people of the time, he believed that other cultures and religions were inferior to his own, and he felt that God wanted him to bring Christianity to other lands.
2. Columbus's royal patrons shared his desire to spread Christianity, but they had economic motives as well. Muslims controlled the overland trade routes connecting Europe and Asia. Europeans wanted to bypass the Muslims and trade directly for eastern spices and herbs.
3. Portuguese sailors had found an eastern route to India by sailing around Africa. If the Spanish could find an easier, western route, they might gain an advantage in their rivalry with Portugal.

Shortly before sunrise on August 3, 1492, three ships under Columbus's command set sail from Spain. The *Niña, Pinta,* and *Santa Maria* reached the Americas roughly two months later. The Spanish received a warm welcome from the first Native Americans they met, the Tainos. Columbus collected the gifts given him by the Tainos—and took others by force—before returning to Spain. He also took back with him some Native Americans, whom he called "Indians" because he thought he had reached the Indies.

Upon his return to Spain, Columbus received the honors he had sought, including the governorship of present-day Hispaniola, an island in the Caribbean. Eventually, he made four voyages to the Americas. Columbus proved to be a far better admiral than governor. The Spanish settlers on Hispaniola complained to the Spanish government of harsh and unfair treatment. Columbus lost his governorship, as well as his prestige at court. And despite increasing evidence that he had found a new continent, he clung to his claim that he had reached the Indies. In 1506, Columbus died a disappointed man, never knowing how much he had changed the course of history.

The Impact of Columbus's Voyages Others, however, realized the importance of Columbus's findings. Beginning in 1497, the Italian seaman Amerigo Vespucci made several voyages along the coast of South America. He suggested that it might be a continent previously unknown to Europeans, "what we may rightly call a New World." In 1507, the German mapmaker Martin Waldseemüller read Vespucci's account and printed the first map showing the "New World" as separate from Asia. Waldseemüller named the unfamiliar lands "America," after Vespucci.

Columbus's voyages changed far more than maps. They also launched a new era of transatlantic trade known as the **Columbian Exchange.** European ships returned with exciting new foods from the Americas. The potato quickly became the new food of Europe's poor, helping to save them from famine. In return, Europeans brought to the Americas crops such as wheat, and domestic

Sounds of an Era

Listen to Columbus's description of his first voyage and other sounds from the era of exploration of the Americas.

Christopher Columbus was born Cristoforo Colombo in the Italian city of Genoa in 1451. His father was a merchant and worked in the wool industry, and his mother was the daughter of a wool weaver. Columbus wrote volumes about his voyages, yet we know little about his early life.

ACTIVITY
Connecting with Geography

Ask students to trace an outline map of the world and draw lines to represent interactions among the three cultures of the Atlantic World. Have them use symbols or icons to show the major interactions: food and crops, animals, diseases, slaves, gold, and silver. **(Visual/Spatial)**

BACKGROUND
The Taino

One of the least understood of Native American cultures was also the first that Columbus encountered when his ships reached the Caribbean—the Taino (TIE no). Within decades of that encounter, the Taino had almost disappeared, and so had their homes, craftworks, and tools, which decomposed quickly in the tropical climate. Then, in the 1980s, fishermen noticed wooden carvings along the edge of a lagoon on Cuba's northern coast. When archaeologists investigated, they found the remains of a whole Taino village, which had apparently been covered with silt when seas rose slightly in the 1700s. Archaeologists say the site offers the first real evidence of what Taino villages were like.

CUSTOMIZE FOR ...
Less Proficient Writers

Have students write *Forest Kingdoms* and *Songhai* as headings on a piece of paper. Ask them to write details under each heading to support the statement that the West African kingdoms were rich and well-organized.

TEST PREPARATION

Have students read the section "The Impact of Columbus's Voyages" on this page and then answer the question below.

What is the meaning of "Columbian Exchange"?

Ⓐ Europeans exchanged food and culture with natives of the Atlantic World.

B Europeans brought slaves to the Atlantic World and brought back produce.

C Natives whom Columbus encountered on his voyages changed places with Europeans.

D Columbus exchanged sailors and ships with other explorers.

Section 1 Assessment

Reading Comprehension

1. (a) Clans extended the family structure, allowing individuals to rely on their kin to fulfill their social needs, like child care and education.
(b) Lineage groups provided the same kind of support for Africans as clans did for Native Americans.
2. The growing wealth in Europe led to the development of a middle class, which, in turn, increased the power of monarchs. Monarchs attracted the loyalty of the new middle class by protecting trade routes and keeping the peace.
3. A time of enormous creativity beginning in the1300s that spread throughout Europe. It was a quest for, and an advance in, knowledge in nearly every field of study, including art, literature, science, and philosophy.
4. A new era of transatlantic trade launched by Columbus's voyages.

Critical Thinking and Writing

5. Beliefs that other cultures were inferior motivated European conquests; Europeans felt they must convert non-Christians, a tenet of their belief systems.
6. (a) The North American continent varied greatly from region to region, so Native Americans adapted their ways of life to fit their local environments.
(b) The two countries competed to explore sea routes, seeking gold and trade. The fact that Spain and Portugal share a common border in Europe probably increased the competitive nature of each country's leaders in regard to overseas exploration.
(c) Songhai's location made it an ideal trading region for goods traveling between the resource-rich coastal forests and North African traders in the Sahara. The government levied fees on travelers who wished to pass through Songhai territory.

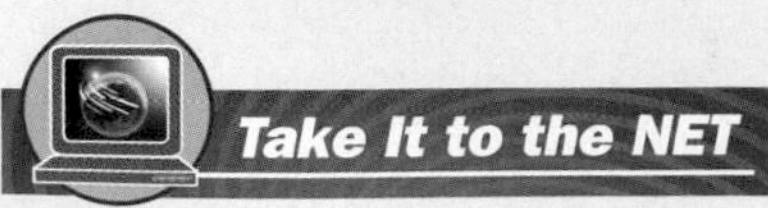

Tables will vary, but should include the potato and its importance, as well as other key crops and their impact.

Caption Answers

Viewing History They had never been exposed and hadn't developed immunity.

animals such as the cow and the horse. They also brought firearms and the wheel and axle. Finally, Europeans introduced their culture to the Americas, including European laws, languages, and customs.

One European import, however, caused immense suffering among Native Americans: disease. Explorers and soldiers infected the native populations with smallpox, typhus, measles, and other deadly diseases to which the Indians had not developed resistance. These diseases spread rapidly along the extensive Native American trade network, killing hundreds of thousands and weakening the social structure of Native American cultures.

Meanwhile, Europeans saw the New World as a source of wealth. Rival nations all wanted to gain land in the Americas. Resenting Spain's claim to the whole Western Hemisphere, Portugal sent a complaint to the pope. In 1494, at the urging of Pope Alexander, Portugal signed the Treaty of Tordesillas. It drew an imaginary line around the world called the Line of Demarcation. Spain was to rule over lands west of the line, including most of the Americas. Portugal would receive the rest, including Brazil. To this day, people in most of South America speak Spanish, but the language of Brazil is Portuguese.

VIEWING HISTORY A Native American in Mexico drew this picture of a smallpox victim being comforted by a healer. The squiggle near the healer's mouth represents spoken words. **Recognizing Cause and Effect** *Why do you think smallpox did so much damage to Indian populations throughout the Americas?*

Slave Labor in the Americas To produce the American foods that brought a high price in Europe, Portugal and Spain established large farms called **plantations.** At first, soldiers forced Native Americans to work on the plantations. Unaccustomed to that type of work and weakened by disease, these slaves did not provide a reliable labor force. Europeans then turned to West Africa.

The European settlers' enormous need for labor transformed the West African slave trade into an industry. Historians still debate the number of Africans who were abducted from their homeland and taken to the Americas, but it appears that some 9–11 million people were enslaved. Even such huge numbers, though, cannot portray the full horror of slavery. Slaves were regarded as mere property and were treated no better than farm animals. In the Americas, slavery was a lifetime sentence from which there was no escape. And in West Africa, the loss of many young and healthy people to the slave trade had a damaging effect on society for many years to come.

Section 1 Assessment

READING COMPREHENSION

1. (a) How were **clans** important in Native American societies? (b) How was lineage important in West African societies?
2. How were the rise of the **middle class** and the increased power of **monarchs** related?
3. What was the Renaissance?
4. What was the **Columbian Exchange?**

CRITICAL THINKING AND WRITING

5. **Recognizing Bias** What beliefs influenced Europeans' views of themselves and other cultures? How did these beliefs affect their actions?
6. **Writing to Inform** Explain how geography contributed to (a) the diversity of Native American peoples, (b) the rivalry between Spain and Portugal, and (c) the wealth of Songhai.

Take It to the NET

Activity: Creating a Table Read about the Columbian Exchange. Create a table showing the impact of the American foods that first arrived in Europe at this time. Use the links provided in the *America: Pathways to the Present* area of the following Web site for help in completing this activity.
www.phschool.com

RESOURCE DIRECTORY

Teaching Resources

Units 1/2 booklet
- Section 1 Quiz, p. 4

Guide to the Essentials
- Section 1 Summary, p. 5

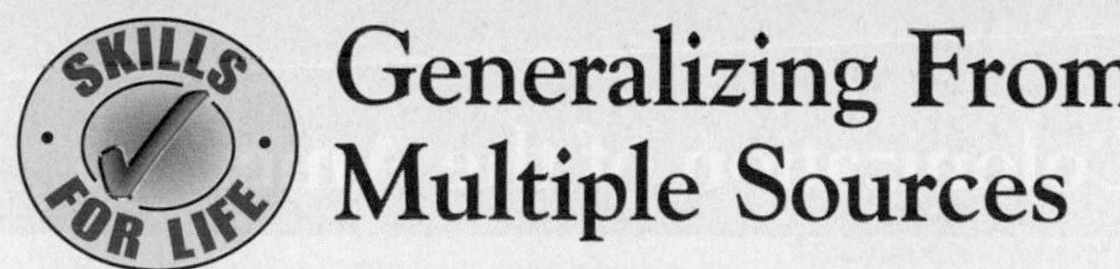

Generalizing From Multiple Sources

A generalization is a broad statement based on multiple examples or facts, often from various sources. Valid generalizations are useful for summing up information, but "sweeping generalizations"—those that are too broad and do not allow for exceptions—can be misleading. For example, you might generalize from your experience that *most* dogs like to be petted. But believing that *all* dogs *always* like to be petted could get you into serious trouble.

The time line and the quotation below relate to Christopher Columbus's effort to find financial backing for his first voyage. Friar Marchena, mentioned in the letter, was a priest whom Columbus had met in Spain.

1484 Columbus presents his proposal to King John II of Portugal.

1485 After a panel of experts reviews Columbus's calculations about the size of the earth and the ocean, they advise King John against supporting the venture.

1486 Columbus is summoned to the court of Ferdinand and Isabella of Spain.

1487 or 1488 Isabella's advisors recommend rejection of Columbus's proposal, again based on his calculations.

1490–1491 Columbus and his brother request backing from the Italians, English, and French. All their requests are rejected.

1492 Columbus again appears before Queen Isabella; again, her advisors reject his proposal, this time based on financial considerations. Before he reaches home, however, Columbus is overtaken by a messenger from the queen. She has reconsidered and agrees to finance the voyage.

1480 · 1485 · 1490 · 1495

Letter to the Spanish Monarchs

"Your majesties know that I spent seven years in the court pestering you for this; never in the whole time was there found a pilot, nor a sailor, nor a mariner, nor a philosopher, nor an expert in any other science who did not state that my enterprise was false, so I never found support from anyone, save father Friar Antonio de Marchena, beyond that of eternal God."

—Christopher Columbus, *circa* 1501

LEARN THE SKILL

Use the following steps to make generalizations:

1. **Identify the main ideas of each source.** Consider both the information and the time period.
2. **List relevant facts.** Determine which facts in the sources support each main idea. You may find that some facts are not relevant to your topic.
3. **Find a common element.** Look for general trends, or a common thread, in the ideas stated in the sources. Also look for patterns or trends in the details and facts.
4. **Make a generalization.** "Add up" the facts and ideas in your sources to make a general statement. Be sure that you can support your generalization with facts and that it is not too broad. Valid generalizations often include words such as *many, most, often, usually, some, few,* and *sometimes.* Faulty generalizations may include words such as *all, none, always, never,* and *every.*

PRACTICE THE SKILL

Answer the following questions:

1. **(a)** What is the main idea of the time line? How do you know? **(b)** What time period does it cover? **(c)** What is the main idea of the excerpt? **(d)** What time period does the excerpt refer to?
2. **(a)** How many facts does the time line present to support its main idea? **(b)** What are two of those facts? **(c)** Describe how Columbus supports his main idea. **(d)** Is this support reliable? Explain.
3. **(a)** What main idea do both sources share? **(b)** How does the time line support the quotation and vice versa? In other words, what is the benefit of having these two kinds of sources?
4. What valid generalizations can you make about **(a)** Columbus, **(b)** his contemporaries, and **(c)** monarchs in the late 1400s?

APPLY THE SKILL

See the Chapter Review and Assessment for another opportunity to apply this skill.

Generalizing From Multiple Sources

Focus Students learn to draw conclusions by identifying the main ideas of various sources, listing relevant facts, and finding a common element that enables them to make a generalization.

Instruct Ask students what type of evidence they would need to create a general statement about an event in history. How much evidence is necessary? What would they do if the evidence is contradictory? *(Research each source's reliability; find evidence that corroborates a point of view.)* Ask students to use the material on this page to write a brief essay on all of Columbus's efforts to get funded. Ask them to include quotes from Columbus.

Extend See the Skills for Life activity in the Resource Directory below.

ANSWERS

Practice the Skill

1. **(a)** That Columbus persisted in trying to get backing for his first voyage even though, until 1492, each petition he made was rejected. **(b)** The years 1480–1495. **(c)** That Columbus persisted in his effort to gain backing, despite years of disappointment. **(d)** The period 1485–1492.
2. **(a)** Eight. **(b)** Students should name two of the following: presenting proposal to King John; King John's rejection; appearance at Spanish court; rejection by Spanish monarchs (1487 or 1488); requests to Italians, English, and French rejected; another rejection by Queen Isabella's advisers; Isabella's final agreement to finance voyage. **(c)** By noting all of the types of people who did not support it. **(d)** Students may note that this support would be hard to verify.
3. **(a)** Columbus's petition was rejected many times over several years. **(b)** Both show that Columbus appealed for backing over a seven-year period. The time line provides specific times and places.
4. **(a)** Columbus was persistent. **(b)** His contemporaries were cautious. **(c)** They relied on experts but were capable of independent decisions, as well.

RESOURCE DIRECTORY

Teaching Resources
Skills for Life booklet, pp. 3–5

Technology
Social Studies Skills Tutor CD-ROM
Interactive Practice in
- Geographic Literacy
- Critical Thinking and Reading
- Visual Analysis
- Communications

ACTIVITY

Connecting with Geography

Have students create a fact file on each of the following explorers: Ponce de León, Balboa, Magellan, Cortés, Pizarro, Cabeza de Vaca, Estevanico, Coronado, and de Soto. Fact files should include each explorer's nationality and summarize what he accomplished. **(Verbal/Linguistic)**

From the Archives of AmericanHeritage®

Cabot Drops By

On June 24, 1497, the Genoa-born English mariner John Cabot became the first European since Viking days to set foot in North America, when he landed on what is now called Newfoundland. At least, that's the story. In actuality, an event resembling Cabot's voyage did take place in 1497, but virtually every detail is subject to question. Cabot left no written record of his journey, and the few surviving secondhand sources contradict one another. Even the basic biographical facts are skimpy. Cabot's point of disembarkation elicits the most controversy. Based on a few scraps of maddeningly vague description, historians have located the site everywhere from Labrador down to Maine, with Newfoundland the most popular choice. Source: Frederic D. Schwarz, "The Time Machine," *American Heritage®* magazine, May/June 1997.

Focus on ECONOMICS

Riches From America The Spanish came to the Americas seeking gold, and they found it—in staggering amounts. They found vast silver resources as well. The average value of precious metal that was shipped back to Spain each year jumped from about 1 million pesos in the period of 1526–1530 to more than 35 million pesos during 1591–1595.

The flow of so much American gold and silver into Spain, however, helped cause inflation. Since precious metal was used as money, an increase in the precious metal supply caused an increase in the money supply as well. That, in turn, led to inflation, or higher prices: more pesos in circulation meant each peso was worth less, so each peso could buy fewer goods than previously. Prices in Spain increased three- to five-fold during the 1500s.

Because the Spanish and Native Americans lived together on the same land, in time a population arose that was a mixture of both peoples. They were called *mestizos,* which is Spanish for "mixed."

The Spanish Push North

Cortés and Pizarro strengthened Spain's grip on Mexico and Peru. Other conquistadors explored the southern parts of what would become the United States.

For example, the Spaniard Alvar Núñez Cabeza de Vaca and an enslaved African named Estevanico were part of an expedition that was shipwrecked in 1528 near present-day Galveston, Texas. With two other survivors, they wandered through the Gulf Coast region for eight years before being rescued. Estevanico later traveled into the American Southwest in search of seven golden cities that were rumored to exist there. Francisco Vásquez de Coronado, too, searched for the fabled golden cities. Between 1540 and 1542, he traveled through present-day Texas and pushed north as far as Kansas. In 1539, Hernán de Soto landed in Florida and traveled westward. He and his men were probably the first Spaniards to cross the Mississippi River.

Forts for Defense The regions explored by Cabeza de Vaca, Estevanico, de Soto, and others did not seem to offer much in riches or farming possibilities. For this reason, few of the approximately 450,000 Spanish immigrants to the Americas before 1650 settled in the lands that are now the United States.

As a result, the Spanish government tried to encourage settlement in certain neglected regions, such as the Southeast Coast. The Spanish built bases in Florida to protect their ships carrying silver and gold from Cuba to Spain. St. Augustine is the only Florida settlement that still survives. In the Southwest, the conquistador Juan de Oñate and several hundred settlers claimed an area they called New Mexico in 1598. (Spanish New Mexico included parts of present-day Arizona and Texas.) Finally, the Spanish began to consider settlements in California in the hopes of keeping their European rivals out of the region. Major efforts to colonize this region, however, did not begin until the 1700s.

Missionaries The Spanish settlements that eventually dotted the South and West were forts, or presidios, most of them occupied by a few soldiers. The survival of these Spanish outposts was due not to the soldiers, but to the hard work of a few dozen Catholic missionaries. **Missionaries** are people who are sent out by their church to teach people their religion. In North America, the missionaries converted Native Americans to Christianity and established dozens of missions—headquarters where the missionaries lived and worked.

Resistance to the Spanish Some Native Americans fiercely resisted the Spanish, but much of this resistance was disorganized. In New Mexico, however, the Pueblo people united in what is called the Pueblo Revolt of 1680. By the 1670s, widespread sickness and drought had reduced the Pueblo population. Seeking to reverse this decline, the Pueblo began to return to their traditional religious practices, which the Spanish had tried to stamp out. In August of 1680, inspired by a religious leader named Popé, the Pueblo people in New Mexico rose up and drove the Spanish out of Santa Fe. Years passed before the Spanish were able to return and rebuild. Similar Native American rebellions also occurred in Florida.

VIEWING HISTORY This painting of a missionary pierced by a lance depicts the Pueblo Revolt of 1680. **Recognizing Cause and Effect** *What caused the Pueblo Revolt?*

CAPTION ANSWERS

Viewing History The Catholic missionaries who accompanied Spanish troops had forced Native Americans to convert to Christianity. When drought and disease reduced their population, the Pueblo wanted to return to their traditional religious practices. The religious leader Popé led the Pueblo in a revolt against the Spanish.

RESOURCE DIRECTORY

Other Print Resources

American History Block Scheduling Support *Settling the New World,* found in the Forging a New Nation folder, includes interdisciplinary lesson suggestions and activities for Geography and History, Primary Sources, Biography, and Literature.

Nystrom *Atlas of Our Country* *Early European Exploration,* pp. 12–13; *Colonies in the South and West,* pp. 18–19

Historical Outline Map Book *The First English Settlements,* p. 14

Technology

Color Transparencies *Political Cartoons,* B1

Sounds of an Era Audio CD *The First Voyage Made to the Coasts of America, Roger Barlowe* (time: one minute, 30 seconds)

RESOURCE PRO® **Biography** *Popé, Medicine Man of the Pueblos,* found on Resource Pro, illustrates Pueblo attachment to ancient beliefs and traditions.

RESOURCE PRO® **Literature** *Determining Relevance: Native American Words,* found on Resource Pro, helps students apply this skill by making a chart of Native American words.

English Colonization

In the race to take advantage of the opportunities in the Americas, the Spanish were soon far ahead. Among the other European nations, England was the most determined and, in time, the most successful.

English Explorers Several explorers sailed to the Americas for England before the 1600s. Although none discovered fabulous riches as the Spanish had, they did greatly expand England's knowledge of the North American coast.

John Cabot was the first known explorer sailing for the English to cross the Atlantic. He may have reached present-day Newfoundland, Canada, in 1497. Sir Martin Frobisher made three voyages across the Atlantic Ocean in the 1500s. Like Cabot, he was searching for the Northwest Passage, a trade route to Asia that would go past or through the continent of North America. Henry Hudson explored for both the English and the Dutch. On his third voyage, in 1609, he sailed 150 miles (240 km) up the river later named for him in present-day New York. When he realized that it was not the Northwest Passage, he turned back.

Sir Francis Drake was the most famous of England's "sea dogs," or privateers. (A privateer is a privately owned ship, or the captain of such a ship, hired by a government to attack foreign ships.) Elizabeth I, the Protestant queen of England from 1558 to 1603, authorized the sea dogs to attack the ships of Catholic Spain. Drake's raids on St. Augustine and other Spanish port cities in the Americas severely weakened the finances of the Spanish empire. Earlier, during his 1577–1580 voyage around the world, Drake had made his way into San Francisco Bay and along the Pacific coast of present-day Canada.

England's Sir Francis Drake became the first sea captain to sail his own ship around the globe.

The Roanoke Disaster By Drake's time, the English had decided that they, like the Spanish, should have American colonies. They had several reasons:

1. Privateers were sailing far from England in search of riches. They wanted a base in the Americas from which they could attack Spanish ships and cities.
2. Europeans were still convinced that they could find a Northwest Passage through the Americas. When they did find such a passage, they reasoned, they would need supply stations in North America for their ships.
3. English merchants also wanted new markets. Some hoped that a growing population in the colonies would someday become buyers of English cloth and other products.
4. Some English people thought the Americas would be a good place to send those who could not find work or homes in England.

With these reasons in mind, the sea dog Sir Walter Raleigh tried twice to start a colony on Roanoke Island, off the coast of present-day North Carolina. Raleigh's first attempt, in 1585, ended when the starving settlers abandoned the colony and returned home. Two years later, there was a second attempt, and how it ended remains a mystery to this day. In 1590, a supply expedition from England found only empty buildings at the settlement. On a doorpost was carved the only clue to the settlers' fate—the word *Croatoan,* an early form of the name of a nearby Native American group. Whether the settlers joined the Indians, or fought them and were defeated, is not known.

READING CHECK
Why was the Roanoke colony settled, and what happened to it?

The Jamestown Settlement In 1606, several Englishmen made plans to establish another colony. They first had to obtain a **charter,** or certificate of permission, from the king. The charter allowed them to form what is now called a joint-stock company—a company funded and run by a group of investors who share the company's profits and losses. In 1607, the Virginia

ACTIVITY
Connecting with Geography

Have small groups of students select one of the explorers mentioned on this page. Tell each group to research their explorer and present an oral report summarizing what they have learned. Encourage students to create visual aids, such as maps showing the routes that their explorer took. **(Verbal/ Linguistic)**

BACKGROUND
Recent Scholarship

The struggles of the early settlers at Jamestown are well documented. Now geographers David Stahle, Malcolm Cleaveland, Dennis Blanton, Matthew Therrell, and David Gay, writing in *Science,* offer evidence that there is an additional reason the settlers suffered so. They believe the colonists were the victims of one of North America's most devastating droughts. Using tree ring data, the geographers propose that the settlers landed in the driest seven-year period in over 700 years. If true, the drought would add another compelling reason why the Roanoke Colony became the Lost Colony and why the first permanent English colony almost failed.

READING CHECK
Great Britain wished to compete with Spain by establishing British colonies in North America. It was hoped that these would provide the following: bases from which British ships could attack Spanish nationals in the New World; new markets for British goods; havens for Great Britain's unemployed citizens; and replenishment stations for British explorers. The first group of Roanoke settlers returned to England. The second group disappeared with hardly a trace.

ACTIVITY

Connecting with Culture

Ask students to write an advertisement designed to attract young English men and women to migrate to the Virginia Colony. Students should review the section "English Colonization" before deciding how best to "sell" Virginia to the English. **(Visual/Spatial)**

From the Archives of

American Heritage®

The Jamestown Massacre

The Powhatan Indians and the Jamestown settlers mingled freely. In fact, the Powhatans often ate and slept in the settlers' houses and borrowed their possessions, even firearms. So when Jamestown and its surrounding plantations began to stir that fateful Good Friday morning, the presence of Indian guests and traders drew no particular attention. Then, at the pre-arranged hour of eight o'clock, Indians throughout the widely spaced settlements suddenly attacked their hosts with clubs, tomahawks, and the settlers' own fowling pieces. Others descended from the woods to join the slaughter and cut off escape routes. Most of the outlying settlements were destroyed. Only a timely warning from a Christianized Indian saved the town of Jamestown from complete destruction. Source: Frederic D. Schwarz, "The Time Machine," *American Heritage®* magazine, February 1997.

Company sent about a hundred colonists to Virginia, the region that Raleigh had reached and named two decades earlier. The settlers called their new village Jamestown in honor of their king, James I.

Jamestown nearly failed, for several reasons. First, most of the settlers were not used to doing the hard work required to start a settlement. Many had come to get rich quickly, so they ignored the daily tasks necessary for their survival and instead searched feverishly for gold. Second, the village was little better than a swamp swarming with disease-bearing mosquitoes. Lastly, the colony suffered from poor leadership. The settlers squabbled about minor matters even when they were in danger of starving. In early 1608, however, a brave and experienced soldier named John Smith emerged as a strong leader. Smith warned the settlers:

> *"You must obey this now for a law, that he that will not work shall not eat . . . for the labors of thirty or forty honest and industrious men shall not be consumed to maintain a hundred and fifty idle loiterers."*
>
> —John Smith

Unfortunately for the colonists, Smith soon left the Virginia colony because of an injury. The colony suffered from starvation and sickness for its first ten years. One particularly difficult period from October 1609 to March 1610 was remembered as the "Starving Time." Only the food and water provided by Native Americans kept the colonists alive.

King James made Virginia a royal colony in 1624 and appointed a governor to lead it. Beginning in 1619, Virginia also had a legislature, or lawmaking assembly made up of representatives from the colony. Although no one understood it in these terms at the time, this legislature, called the House of Burgesses, was the first example of limited self-government in the English colonies.

Growing Tobacco During the difficult early years, one thing—tobacco—saved the Virginia colonists from failing completely. This plant was native to the Western Hemisphere but unknown in Europe. In 1613, colonist John Rolfe shipped some tobacco to Europe, where it quickly became popular. Soon tobacco was the basis of the colony's economy. In order to cash in on the tobacco boom, settlers carved out plantations on the banks of the James, York, Rappahannock, and Potomac rivers, and along the shores of Chesapeake Bay. They established their plantations close to waterways, so that they could grow and transport their tobacco more easily.

Labor for Plantations Planters, as owners of these plantations were called, needed laborers to work their tobacco fields. One way to obtain these laborers was to promise them land when they arrived in the colony. Over time, the custom developed of giving each "head," or person who came to the colony, the right to fifty acres of land.

Many people, however, did not have the money for the voyage. To pay for the crossing, they became **indentured servants.** These people had to work for a master for a period of time, usually seven years, under a contract called an indenture. In return for their work, their master paid the cost of their voyage to Virginia and gave them food and shelter.

Historians estimate that between 100,000 and 150,000 men and women came as servants to work in the fields of Virginia and Maryland during the

VIEWING HISTORY This indentured servant is bundling and packing dried tobacco leaves. **Determining Relevance** *What was the relationship of tobacco to the need for inexpensive labor, such as indentured servants or slaves?*

CAPTION ANSWERS

Viewing History Producing tobacco was labor-intensive, and both slaves and indentured servants provided labor that was cheap enough to allow tobacco planters to make a profit.

RESOURCE DIRECTORY

Teaching Resources

Biography, Literature, and Comparing Primary Sources booklet (Comparing Primary Sources) *On Life in Jamestown,* p. 99

Biography, Literature, and Comparing Primary Sources booklet (Literature) *The Fate of an Indentured Servant,* p. 41

Learning with Documents booklet (Primary Source Activity) *Cultural Clashes in the Virginia Colony,* p. 7

Learning with Documents booklet (Key Documents) *The Mayflower Compact,* p. 75

Other Print Resources

Historical Outline Map Book *The French Explore North America,* p. 12; *The New England Colonies,* p. 16

Technology

Color Transparencies *Cause-and-Effect Charts,* D1; *American Diversity,* F1

RESOURCE PRO® **Primary Source Activity** *Native American Customs,* found on Resource Pro, uses an excerpt from settler John Lawson's *History of North Carolina* to enhance students' understanding of Native American traditions.

1600s. Most of them were 18 to 22 years of age, unmarried, and poor. Among Virginia's indentured servants were some Africans, the first to settle in the present-day United States. The first group of about 20 Africans arrived in 1619, and their numbers remained small.

Pushing West As the population of Virginia increased, settlers pushed farther west in search of new farmland, causing clashes with the Native American inhabitants. These clashes led, in turn, to Bacon's Rebellion which showed that the frontier settlers were unwilling to tolerate a government that was not concerned about their interests.

The French in North America

The English were not the only Europeans interested in the East Coast of North America. The French, too, had been exploring the region for decades, in search of trading opportunities.

French Explorers One early French expedition was led by Giovanni da Verrazano, an Italian who sailed for the French from 1523–1524. Searching for the Northwest Passage, he explored the coast of North America from present-day North Carolina to Newfoundland, and entered New York harbor. Jacques Cartier made three voyages to Canada (1534–1542). On the basis of Cartier's explorations, the French king claimed a region called New France. It included not only the land covered by present-day Canada, but also parts of what is now the northern United States.

In 1608, Samuel de Champlain founded the first successful French colony in North America at Quebec in present-day Canada. Champlain also mapped the Atlantic shores as far as Massachusetts, and traveled inland to present-day Lake Huron and Lake Champlain.

The Fur Trade The French discovered that a product from North America, fur, could be sold for great gain in Europe. Clothing made from the skins of deer, beaver, and other animals became highly fashionable in Europe in the 1600s. Native Americans trapped these animals, collected their furs, and traded them to the French. The fur trade determined the shape of New France. By the late 1600s, it was a long, narrow colony stretching far into the interior of Canada, along the St. Lawrence River and the Great Lakes. New France clung to the waterways because, as in Virginia, water was vital for transporting goods.

English Colonies in New England

While the French were building the fur trade in New France, the English were beginning new colonies along the Atlantic Coast. Known as New England, this region included land that became the states of Connecticut, Rhode Island, Massachusetts, Vermont, New Hampshire, and Maine.

Plymouth Colony The first successful colony in New England was the result of religious conflicts in England. In 1534, England's King Henry VIII had broken with the Catholic Church and had founded the Anglican Church, England's national church. Some of the English, however, complained that the Anglican Church continued too many Catholic practices and traditions. Because they wanted what they considered a "purer" kind of church, they were called **Puritans.** Some Puritans started separate churches of their

Focus on GOVERNMENT

Bacon's Rebellion Nathaniel Bacon arrived in Virginia from England when high taxes, low tobacco prices, and privileges dispensed by Governor William Berkeley were already causing resentment in the colony. In the west, there was the added problem of fighting between Indians and frontier settlers. Governor Berkeley refused to raise troops to defend the settlers against Indian raids. Although he was Berkeley's cousin, a planter, and a member of the governor's council, Bacon sympathized with the frontiersmen.

In 1676, Bacon raised an army to fight the Native Americans. Angry that Bacon was acting without his permission, Berkeley declared him a rebel and gathered an army to stop him. Bacon's supporters then charged that Berkeley had failed to protect the western settlers and that those settlers had too little voice in colonial government. Bacon's forces attacked and burned Jamestown. For a time, they controlled nearly all of Virginia. When Bacon died suddenly in October 1676, the rebellion collapsed.

Wampum belts, like this Iroquois example, served as currency in trade between Native Americans and Europeans.

BACKGROUND
Biography

Samuel de Champlain (1567–1635) was born in a small fishing village in France. Like other explorers of his day, Champlain hoped to find a passage to the Indies and import Christianity to the New World. On April 5, 1608, Champlain sailed from France on an expedition designed to establish a colony in Canada. He arrived in the St. Lawrence River on June 3. By July 3 Champlain had started to build the city of Quebec. Champlain and his men drew inspiration from French architecture as they built three wooden buildings surrounded by a moat with a drawbridge. During the winter, all of the Frenchmen became sick with scurvy. By the time spring came, only eight of the 24 Frenchmen had survived. Champlain, however, was one of the lucky ones. He went on to live another 26 years.

ACTIVITY
Connecting with History and Conflict

Have pairs of students improvise a debate between William Berkeley and Nathaniel Bacon about Bacon's reasons for rebelling and his plans for the western lands of the colony. Each pair of students should take a point and illustrate it through argument. **(Verbal/Linguistic)**

ACTIVITY
Connecting with Government

Engage students in a discussion about William Bradford's idea of self-government. How does Bradford's idea differ from the European monarchies that were in place at the time? Why would a self-governing system appeal to the Puritans? Why would such a system not be attractive? How is this concept reflected in our current government? **(Verbal/Linguistic)**

BACKGROUND
Geography in History

The journey taken by Pilgrims from England to the coast of North America was much longer than we sometimes remember. Members of the English Separatists Church, some of whom would later be the first English settlers of Massachusetts, first left Great Britain in 1609 and sailed to the Netherlands. They stayed for a decade before they began to formulate a plan for founding a colony in the New World. It is worth noting, too, that they were not the only persecuted religious minority to seek refuge in the Netherlands. Jews whose ancestors had been persecuted in, and exiled from, Spain were present in the Netherlands, as well.

own and were called Separatists. Both Puritans and Separatists were persecuted, or attacked because of their beliefs.

One group of Separatists, those who came to be called the Pilgrims, decided to make a new home in North America, where they hoped they would be free to worship as they wished. In 1620, a group of roughly 100 Pilgrims sailed to New England on the *Mayflower*. As the ship neared shore, some non-Separatists on board threatened to go off and live by themselves. Afraid that the group would break up, the Pilgrims made a compact, or agreement, called the **Mayflower Compact.** In it, the settlers agreed to obey all of their government's laws. As they put it:

VIEWING HISTORY The Pilgrims signed the Mayflower Compact while still aboard ship. **Determining Relevance** *How do you think this agreement helped the Pilgrims survive their initial hardships and eventually prosper?*

KEY DOCUMENTS

> *"We . . . do . . . combine ourselves together into a civil body politic, for our better ordering and preservation . . . and . . . to . . . frame such just and equal laws . . . as shall be thought most [fitting] and convenient for the general good of the colony, unto which we promise all due . . . obedience."*
>
> —The Mayflower Compact

The compact kept the Pilgrims together. It also showed that the Pilgrims expected to decide for themselves how they would be governed. One of the men who drew up the Mayflower Compact, William Bradford, went on to be elected governor of the colony 30 times between 1621 and 1656. He helped create a form of government in which the people guided their own affairs. Later this concept of self-government would become one of the founding principles of the United States.

The Pilgrims settled near a harbor, and named their colony Plymouth after the English port from which they had sailed. Like the Jamestown settlers, the Pilgrims endured tremendous hardships. Half of them died in the first winter alone. The next summer, the colonists had the help of a Native American, Squanto, who taught them how to plant corn. Their plentiful harvest of corn led the settlers to hold a great feast of thanksgiving in the fall of 1621.

The Massachusetts Bay Colony In 1630, a thousand English settlers braved a voyage across the Atlantic to found the Massachusetts Bay Colony, just a few miles north of Plymouth. These were the first of a flood of colonists who came to New England in a movement called the Great Migration. By 1643, the Massachusetts Bay Colony had grown to roughly 20,000 people living in 20 towns, including its capital, Boston.

Many of these new settlers were Puritans hoping to live where they could worship as they wished. They did not, however, believe in **religious tolerance**—the idea that people of different religions should live in peace together. They had no desire to live among people who held beliefs different from their own. By law, everyone in the Massachusetts Bay Colony had to attend the Puritan Church and pay taxes to support it.

The Puritans believed that they were creating a new, pure society to serve the will of God. John Winthrop, a founder of the colony and later its governor, summarized the colonists' goals in 1630. To succeed, he said, "We must be knit together in this work, as one man. We must . . . make others' condition our own. . . . For we must consider that we shall be as a city on a hill. The eyes of all people are upon us." Winthrop voiced a belief that many on board the ship, and

CAPTION ANSWERS

Viewing History It ensured that everyone would work together for the benefit of the colony as a whole.

RESOURCE DIRECTORY

Teaching Resources

Learning with Documents booklet (Visual Learning Activity) *A Lasting Stereotype,* p. 41

Other Print Resources

Nystrom *Atlas of Our Country* *Colonies in the North and East,* pp. 14–15

Technology

Sounds of an Era Audio CD *"A Modell of Christian Charity," John Winthrop* (time: two minutes)

Exploring Primary Sources in U.S. History CD-ROM *Fundamental Orders of 1639; Mayflower Compact*

many Americans since that time, have shared: America would be an example to people throughout the world.

The Puritans worked hard, not only for themselves but also for the common good. Each new town, for example, allotted a "common," or tract of land to be used by all. The colony was successful; children born in Massachusetts could be expected to live at least twice as long as children born in early Virginia. By 1700, New England was home to more than 93,000 people living fairly comfortable lives.

Yet life in the Puritans' "city on a hill" had its dark moments. In 1692, several girls and young women in Salem, Massachusetts, accused three townspeople of being witches. In the public uproar that followed, neighbors fearfully accused one another of dealing with the devil. As a result of the Salem witch trials, the Massachusetts authorities ordered 20 men and women to die by hanging. After a few months, however, the community regained its balance, and the trials and hangings came to an end.

Some historians believe that the witch trials reflected the colonists' fears about political changes taking place at the time. The year before the trials, England's new monarchs, William and Mary, had joined the Massachusetts Bay Colony and the Plymouth Colony into one. They were now a single royal colony, known as Massachusetts.

Other New England Colonies As the population of New England increased, farmland in Massachusetts grew scarce. Some Puritans were given permission to establish new communities. In the mid-1630s, for example, the Puritan minister Thomas Hooker led a group of settlers from Massachusetts to Connecticut. Similarly, settlements in Maine and New Hampshire were populated by Puritans. New Hampshire became a separate colony in 1680. Maine was part of Massachusetts until it became a separate state in 1820.

Other people left Massachusetts because of religious conflicts with the colony's Puritan leaders. In 1635, for example, Roger Williams, a Separatist minister, was banished from Massachusetts. The next year he started a settlement called Providence, which later joined with several other Separatist communities to become the self-governing colony of Rhode Island. Roger Williams's colony was remarkable because it guaranteed religious tolerance to all settlers.

War With the Indians English settlers pushed Native Americans out of their homelands during the 1600s, sparking several wars between the two groups. As one sachem, or Native American leader, explained:

> "*Our fathers had plenty of deer and skins, our plains were full of deer, as also our woods, and of turkies, and our coves full of fish and fowl. But these English having gotten our land, they with scythes cut down the grass, and with axes fell the trees; their cows and horses eat the grass, and their hogs spoil our clam banks, and we shall be starved.*"
>
> —Miantonomo, 1642

The bloodiest of the wars between the English settlers and the Indians was called King Philip's War after King Philip (or Metacom), a leader of the Algonquin peoples of New England. In 1675, Metacom united Indian groups from Rhode Island to Maine in an attempt to drive out the English once and for all. He and his

American BIOGRAPHY

Anne Hutchinson
1591–1643

Although Anne Hutchinson and her family moved from England to Boston to escape religious persecution and to join the community of Puritans living there, Hutchinson did not accept Puritan authority. She believed that it was wrong to obey the church if by doing so, a person felt he or she was disobeying God. Her home soon became a center for colonists who wanted to think for themselves. Critics of John Winthrop and the Massachusetts government gathered there, as did women who wanted to study the Bible.

The Puritan authorities called Hutchinson to trial in November 1637 to explain her actions. She skillfully defended herself with references to the law and the Bible. Still, the judges rejected her claim that her own beliefs about God could override the authority of Puritan laws and leaders. The court declared Hutchinson "unfit for society" and banished her from the colony.

Early the next year, the Hutchinsons settled in present-day Rhode Island. After the death of her husband, Anne Hutchinson and her children settled on Long Island Sound in New York where most of them were killed by Indians in 1643.

ACTIVITY
Connecting with Citizenship

Have students conduct a debate on whether John Winthrop's image of a "city on a hill" is still relevant today. Do other countries perceive the United States to be a model of good citizenship? What recent actions and events support the idea that we are still that city on a hill? What actions or events contradict that notion? Have each team gather to draw up a list of key points to prove its position. After the debate, invite non-participants to discuss which team was more persuasive, and why. **(Verbal/Linguistic)**

BACKGROUND
Salem Witch Trials

Accusations of witchcraft in the town of Salem were used to punish people who deviated from the established social norms. Historian John Demos, in a study of witchcraft in colonial New England, found that women accused of being witches were most likely to be middle-aged (40 to 60), married but without children, of low social status, and involved in medical care such as midwifery.

TEST PREPARATION

Have students review the material on this page about the Salem witch trials and then answer the question below.

Which is a fact from the passage?

A The devil took control of several girls and young women in Salem.

(B) Accused townspeople were put on trial to determine if they were witches.

C The Puritans formed an ideal community in Salem.

D In 1692 three townspeople in Salem practiced witchcraft.

ACTIVITY
Connecting with History and Conflict

The new settlers' choice of primary occupation and industry influenced their relationship with Native Americans. For example, because the French were fur trappers, they experienced fewer conflicts with Native Americans than did the English, whose agricultural settlement interrupted the Native American way of life. Have small groups of students choose an industry to be introduced into their community and list three ways it would alter their present way of life. **(Verbal/Linguistic)**

BACKGROUND
Connections to Today

By 1675 tuberculosis and smallpox had reduced the southern New England population of Native Americans to about 20,000—against the approximately 50,000 settlers who had displaced them. This put the Native Americans at a disadvantage before King Philip's War had even begun. In fact, one present-day writer regards King Philip's defeat as "America's first war of ethnic cleansing." Today, there are approximately 12,000 Wampanoags living in Massachusetts—many on Cape Cod and on the Gay Head reservation on Martha's Vineyard, an island off the coast of Cape Cod.

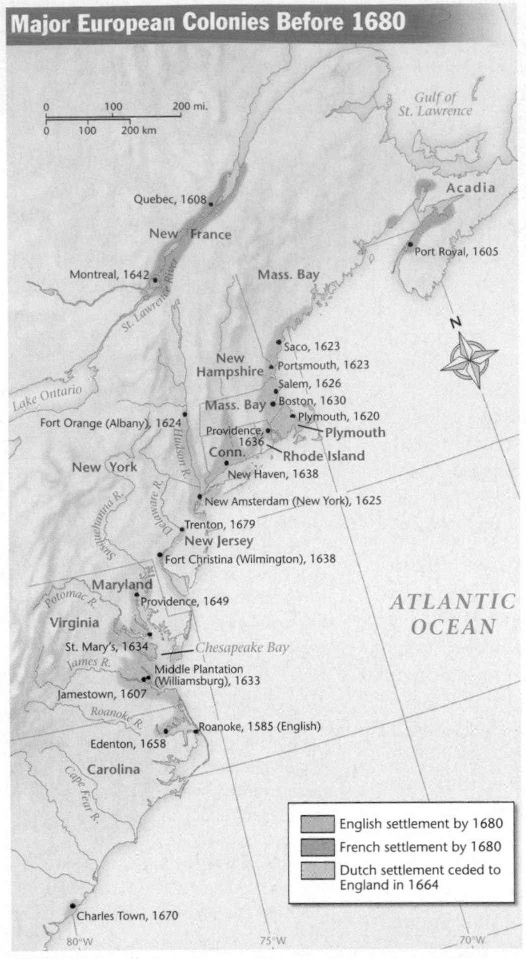

MAP SKILLS Both the French and the Dutch were more interested in the fur trade than they were in establishing permanent settlements. **Location** *How does the resulting settlement pattern of the French and Dutch differ from that of the English?*

warriors destroyed 112 English towns, attacked 52 others, and killed about 600 settlers. The English struck back, killing or wounding about 4,000 Native Americans. By the war's end, Metacom was dead and the English conquest of the region was nearly complete. But Metacom and his allies had dealt New England settlers a severe blow from which they would not fully recover until the early 1700s.

The Middle Colonies

The colonies to the south of New England, called the Middle Colonies, included New York, New Jersey, Pennsylvania, and Delaware. They developed differently from the colonies in New England, in part because their settlers came from a variety of countries.

New York New York began in 1624 as the Dutch colony of New Netherland, in the Hudson and Delaware river valleys. (The Dutch came from Holland, also called the Netherlands.) The heart of the colony was the trading station of New Amsterdam, founded at the mouth of the Hudson River in 1625. The settlers built up a prosperous fur trade with Europe, and sold crops to other colonies. New Amsterdam became a port where the Dutch, Swedes, French, Germans, English and many others carried on peaceful business together. Some 18 different languages were spoken in its streets. Religious tolerance was a firm rule. The town even boasted the first synagogue, or house of Jewish worship, on the North American continent.

The prosperity of New Netherland attracted England's interest. In 1664, the English king, Charles II, declared that the entire region of the Dutch colonies belonged to his brother, the Duke of York. When the duke sent ships and soldiers to New Amsterdam to back up his claim, the Dutch were forced to give up New Netherland to the English, who renamed it New York.

The Other Middle Colonies The colony of New York was a **proprietary colony**—a colony granted by a king or queen to an individual or group who could make laws and rule it as they wished. (*Proprietor* means "owner.") The other Middle Colonies were also proprietary.

New Jersey was originally part of the Duke of York's charter. He transferred certain lands over to two English noblemen, and these lands were divided into East Jersey and West Jersey. In 1702, East and West Jersey became a single royal colony called New Jersey. Delaware began as a Swedish colony in 1638. The Dutch captured it from the Swedes, and then the Duke of York captured it from the Dutch. In 1682, he turned it over to the Englishman William Penn, who allowed Delaware to become a separate colony in 1704.

William Penn also owned the colony of Pennsylvania, which he established on land he had received from King Charles II in 1681. Like the Puritans, Penn saw his colony as a "Holy Experiment." Unlike the Puritans, he wanted to establish a society that practiced religious tolerance. Many of the colonists, like Penn himself, were Quakers, members of a Protestant group that had suffered

CAPTION ANSWERS

Map Skills The French and Dutch settlements follow rivers, while the English settled along the coast.

RESOURCE DIRECTORY

Teaching Resources

Units 1/2 booklet
- Section 2 Quiz, p. 5

Guide to the Essentials
- Section 2 Summary, p. 6

Other Print Resources

Historical Outline Map Book *The Middle Colonies,* p. 17; *The Southern Colonies,* p. 18

persecution in England. Quakers believed firmly that all people should be treated as equals. Pennsylvania also attracted many non-Quaker settlers.

The Southern Colonies

In addition to Virginia, the Southern Colonies included Maryland, the Carolinas, and Georgia. All began as proprietary colonies.

Maryland Maryland was first settled in 1634. It was created as a haven for Roman Catholics being persecuted in England, but Puritans outnumbered the Catholics from the very beginning. Therefore, the Maryland Toleration Act was passed to protect Catholics from persecution in the colony. This law was part of a general trend toward religious tolerance in the English colonies. The act was severely limited, however, in that it did not provide protection for non-Christians.

The planters of Maryland, like those in Virginia, grew prosperous during the 1600s by growing tobacco. And like the Virginians, they began to use enslaved Africans to work their fields. The Africans were brought to the colonies by slave traders. By 1704, roughly 15,000 of the 90,000 people in the two colonies were African slaves.

The royal charter of North Carolina, 1663, includes the likeness of King Charles II.

The Carolinas King Charles II gave ownership of a region known as Carolina to a group of English noblemen in 1663. It was first split into North and South Carolina in 1691. In 1721, South Carolina became a royal colony. North Carolina became a royal colony in 1729. Both colonies thrived on tobacco profits and trade with Native Americans.

Georgia Although Georgia was set up like a proprietary colony in 1732, it was actually managed not by owners but by trustees. A trustee is someone entrusted to manage a business. The trustees, led by James Oglethorpe, wanted to create a haven for people who had been jailed in England because they could not pay their debts. At first, Oglethorpe and the trustees ruled Georgia strictly, barring slavery and liquor. Although Catholics could not live in Georgia, all Protestants were permitted. Gradually, however, the colonists forced the trustees to change their rules. Settlers were allowed to use and sell liquor, and enslaved Africans were brought in to work the land. After 20 years, the trustees gave their charter back to the king, and Georgia became a royal colony.

Section 2 Assessment

READING COMPREHENSION

1. What is a **colony?**
2. How was tobacco important to Virginia?
3. Why did each of these groups come to the Americas: (a) **missionaries,** (b) **Puritans,** and (c) **indentured servants?**
4. What is the importance of the **Mayflower Compact?**

CRITICAL THINKING AND WRITING

5. **Synthesizing Information** What role did religion play in the settlement of the Americas? How did religious tolerance—or the lack of it—affect the American colonies?
6. **Writing an Introduction** Write the introduction to an essay about the origins of the principle of self-government in the American colonies.

Take It to the NET

Activity: Writing an Ad Investigate the history of Jamestown. Then create a British newspaper advertisement that would have been used to lure settlers to the colony. Use the links provided in the *America: Pathways to the Present* area of the following Web site for help in completing this activity.
www.phschool.com

Section 2 Assessment

Reading Comprehension

1. An area settled by immigrants who continue to be ruled by their parent country.
2. During the early, difficult times, the growing of tobacco, which was native to the Western Hemisphere but unknown in Europe, allowed Virginia to revitalize its economy.
3. (a) To convert Indians to Christianity. (b) They sought a place where they could be free to practice a strict and "pure" form of Protestantism. (c) People looking for a new opportunity who could not afford the transatlantic voyage often became indentured servants to pay for their crossing.
4. The Mayflower Compact kept the Pilgrims together, united, and showed that they expected to decide for themselves how they would be governed.

Critical Thinking and Writing

5. Spanish missionaries wished to spread the Christian religion by converting Native Americans. Other colonists sought to escape religious persecution. As colonies were established, lack of religious tolerance in some of them led to the banishing of some settlers, which in turn led to the settling of more colonies with greater religious tolerance. This created homogeneous, as well as diverse, colonies.
6. Introductions will vary, but should be supported with facts from the section and include a description of the Mayflower Compact and the desire for religious freedom.

Take It to the NET

Ads will vary, but should highlight the positive aspects of life in the colony in order to attract settlers, and emphasize ways that the colony is more appealing than life in Britain.

Section 3
Growth of the American Colonies

Section Objectives

1. Read about England's colonial policies.
2. Learn about the origins of self-government in the colonies.
3. Find out about the economic and social systems that developed in the colonies.
4. Learn about what lives of African Americans were like in the different colonies.
5. Discover the tensions that were caused by westward expansion and religious revivals.

Bellringer

Warm-Up Activity Ask students to define the term *empire* as broadly as they can. Encourage students to think about why a country would want an empire. What obligations and responsibilities does an empire bring with it?

Activating Prior Knowledge Have students consider the reasons the first English settlers came to America. Many were seeking to flee English systems and authority. In what ways would this put these settlers in opposition to an increasingly controlling English presence?

Reading Strategy

Have students skim the section and use the heads and subheads to create an outline. As they read, have them fill in supporting evidence under each head.

Section 3 Growth of the American Colonies

READING FOCUS

- What were England's colonial policies?
- What were the origins of self-government in the colonies?
- What kinds of economies and social systems developed in the colonies?
- What were the lives of African Americans like in the different colonies?
- What tensions were caused by westward expansion and religious revivals?

KEY TERMS

mercantilism
balance of trade
triangular trade
Middle Passage
immigrant
Great Awakening

TAKING NOTES

Copy the web diagram below. As you read, fill in the circles with the reasons that the English colonies prospered during the mid-1600s and early 1700s.

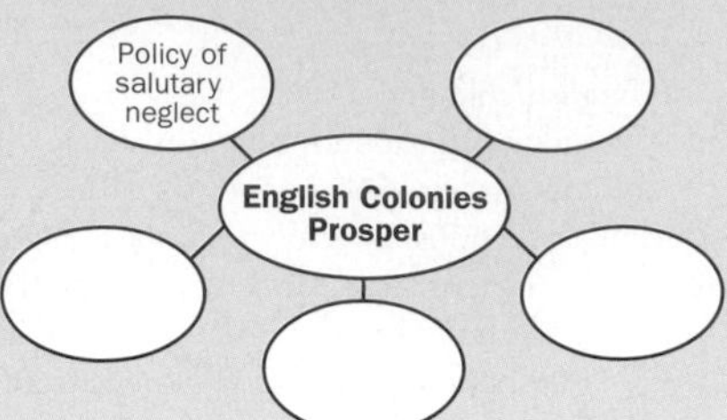

MAIN IDEA

The English colonies developed diverse economies and prospered with little direct interference from England. Meanwhile, enslaved African Americans often suffered brutal treatment, and tensions developed with the French and Native Americans.

Young Benjamin Franklin is shown above, working as a printer's apprentice. A view of Philadelphia in approximately 1720 is shown below.

Setting the Scene Not quite 18 years old, and not very clean after a journey of several days, Benjamin Franklin arrived in the city of Philadelphia in October 1723. He had one dollar in his pocket. Franklin had quarreled with his brother (who was also his boss) and had left his home city of Boston to seek his fortune. He was determined to get ahead by improving himself. Franklin began by assembling a list of 13 virtues, including such qualities as temperance, frugality, and industry. He then set out to live by them. Each week, he decided, he would try to make one of the virtues part of his daily life. At the end of 13 weeks, he would repeat the cycle.

Although he did not succeed in mastering his virtues, Franklin did become America's best-known promoter of them. "Time is money"; "God helps them that helps themselves"; "Early to bed, early to rise, makes a man healthy, wealthy, and wise"—these and other famous sayings were published by Franklin. They helped convince American colonists of the economic opportunity available to them. According to Franklin, through hard work and clean living, a person from a humble background could prosper, maybe even become rich. In reality, this opportunity did not extend to all; enslaved African Americans in particular were excluded. Still, thanks to the labor of the colonists and the abundant resources of North America, England's American colonies grew in wealth, power, and self-confidence.

24

RESOURCE DIRECTORY

Teaching Resources
Learning Styles Lesson Plans booklet, pp. 8–9
Guided Reading and Review booklet, pp. 11–14

Other Print Resources
Nystrom *Atlas of Our Country* *Colonies in the North and East,* pp. 14–15

Technology
Section Reading Support Transparencies
Guided Reading Audiotapes (English/Spanish), Ch. 1
Student Edition on Audio CD, Ch. 1
Sounds of an Era Audio CD *The Autobiography of Benjamin Franklin* (time: one minute, 30 seconds)
Color Transparencies *Historical Maps,* A4
RESOURCE PRO® **Biography** *Hannah Callowhill Penn,* found on Resource Pro, profiles the wife of Pennsylvania's founder, William Penn.
Prentice Hall United States History Video Collection™ Volume 2, *The Era of Colonization (1585–1763)*
Prentice Hall Presentation Pro CD-ROM, Ch. 1
Social Studies Skills Tutor CD-ROM
Companion Web site, www.phschool.com

England's Colonial Policies

In the late 1600s and early 1700s, England prized its cluster of colonies on the Atlantic coast of North America for two reasons: The colonies supplied England with food and raw materials, and they bought large amounts of English goods. What's more, the colonists were, in general, loyal to their parent country. Thus, England got what it wanted from its colonies—raw materials and a place to sell its goods—by leaving them alone.

Mercantilism England's economic relationship with its colonies was based on a theory adopted by several western European nations in the 1600s. Called **mercantilism,** this theory held that a country should try to get and keep as much bullion, or gold and silver, as possible. The more gold and silver a country had, argued mercantilists, the wealthier and more powerful it would be.

For countries without sources of gold and silver like the mines Spain controlled in the Americas, the only way to obtain more bullion was through trade. If a country sold more goods to other countries than it bought from them, it would end up with more bullion. In other words, a country's **balance of trade,** or the difference in value between imports and exports, should show more exports than imports.

Mercantilists believed that a nation should have colonies where it could buy raw materials and sell products. The colonies should not be allowed to sell products to other nations or even to engage in manufacturing. The right to make goods for sale should be reserved exclusively for the parent country, since manufacturing was a major source of profit. What's more, to maintain control over trade and to increase profits, the parent country should require its colonies to use its ships for transporting their raw materials.

English rulers came to realize that the American colonies could provide raw materials such as tobacco, furs, and perhaps gold for England to sell to other countries. Furthermore, if the colonies had to buy England's manufactured goods, this exchange would greatly improve England's balance of trade. English leaders, therefore, set out to have as many colonies as possible, and to control colonial trade in order to provide the maximum profit to England.

Controlling Colonial Trade In 1660, England's King Charles II approved a stronger version of a previous law called the Navigation Act. Along with other legislation, the Navigation Act tightened control over colonial trade. The new laws required the colonies to sell certain goods, including sugar, tobacco, and cotton, only to England. Moreover, if colonists wanted to sell anything to other countries, they had to take the crop or product to England first and pay a duty, or a tax, on it. They also had to use English ships for all their trade.

During the next two decades, England tried in several ways to tighten its control over the colonies. This effort peaked in 1686, when King James II attempted to take direct control over New York and the New England colonies by creating the Dominion of New England. This action abolished colonial legislatures within the Dominion and replaced them with a governor and a council appointed by the king.

Colonists up and down the Atlantic seaboard deeply resented the king's grab for power. They resented, too, the actions of Edmund Andros, whom James II had appointed governor of the Dominion. Andros collected taxes without the approval of the king or the colonists, and demanded payment of an annual land tax. He also declared a policy of religious tolerance, or respect for different religious beliefs. The Puritans saw these actions as blows to their freedom from English influence and their control over local religious matters.

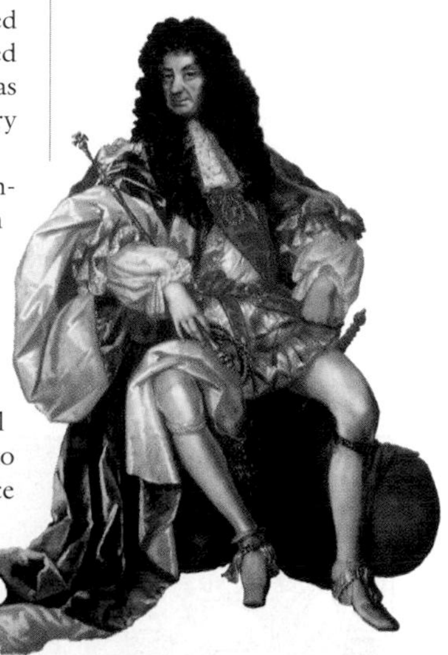

VIEWING FINE ART This painting of Charles II hangs in the National Portrait Gallery, London. **Analyzing Visual Information** *What do you think the artist wanted to convey about the monarchy in general and about Charles II in particular? Explain.*

Lesson Plan

Focus Explain to students that the years before 1754 were a defining period for the American colonies. Varied landforms and climate, a steady stream of immigrants from different regions of the world, and England's policy of salutary neglect gave rise to a future hallmark of America: diversity of belief, economy, and people.

Instruct Discuss with students the ways in which a spirit of independence spread among the colonists during this period. The colonists sought not just independence from England, but also from each other. In what ways does that spirit persist in America today?

Assess/Reteach In what ways did the English colonies operate as a direct outgrowth of the English political system? In what ways did they operate differently?

Activity

Student Portfolio

You may wish to have students add the following to their portfolios: Ask students to prepare an illustrated report about the different styles of housing that developed in each of the three colonial regions. Reports should include information about the houses of the wealthy as well as those of ordinary citizens. Students may want to include information on the effect of climate on architecture in each of the regions. **(Visual/Spatial; Verbal/Linguistic)**

Customize for ...

ESL

Have students write the main heading and subheadings of the section on a piece of paper. Then have them fill in details about the British empire and the American colonies as they read the section.

Caption Answers

Viewing Fine Art The artist was probably trying to convey the grandeur, wealth, and power (scepter) of the monarchy, and the dignity and imposing character of Charles II.

ACTIVITY

Connecting with History and Conflict

Tell students to create an artistic expression in response to the quotation by Olaudah Equiano. Students may choose to write a poem or make a collage, drawing, or painting. Encourage students to think about how it must have felt to be separated from their siblings, against their will. After students complete their artistic responses, have them share them with the class. Invite volunteers to explain how their creation reflects Equiano's experience. **(Visual/Spatial)**

ACTIVITY

Connecting with Culture

Tell students to write a position paper on one of the following topics: attending school or being home-schooled during the colonial era. Suggest that before they begin writing, students consider the pros and cons of each form of education. They might also address the fact that schools were predominant in New England, while home schooling was more prevalent in the South. **(Verbal/Linguistic)**

BACKGROUND

Recent Scholarship

In *The Many-Headed Hydra,* authors Peter Linebaugh and Marcus Rediker identify Olaudah Equiano as the "African sailor." However, one critic, David Brion Davis, refutes their claim, arguing that Equiano named Carolina as his birthplace when he was baptized in England in 1759. In a separate document, Equiano was listed as "an able seaman, aged 28, and born in South Carolina." Apparently, the claim that Equiano was born in Africa originated in oral tradition. Davis says that Catherine Obianju Acholonu is responsible for claiming Equiano's African descent. Scholars reject the authenticity of her claim.

Focus on CITIZENSHIP

The Trial of Peter Zenger At the age of 13, John Peter Zenger emigrated from Germany to New York where he became indentured to a printer. After establishing his own printing business, in 1733 he launched the *New York Weekly Journal*, which often contained articles critical of the Royal Governor of New York. These criticisms led to Zenger's arrest for libel. Although he had not written the articles, Zenger was legally responsible for the contents of the paper he published.

After ten months in prison, Zenger was finally brought to trial in 1735. His attorney was Andrew Hamilton, who had also begun his life in America as an indentured servant but was now Speaker of the Philadelphia Assembly. Hamilton argued that the controversial articles were true and therefore could not be considered libelous. He further claimed that it was the duty of a publication to print the truth. Over the objections of the judges, Hamilton appealed to the jurors directly, and they found Zenger not guilty. The trial of Peter Zenger established truth as a defense against libel, and was a landmark victory for freedom of the press in the English colonies.

was Benjamin Franklin, who published several newspapers and magazines, as well as *Poor Richard's Almanac*, which was printed annually from 1732 to 1757. (An almanac is a book containing information such as calendars, weather predictions, proverbs, and advice.)

In colonial America, women juggled a number of duties that contributed to the well-being of their households and of the community. Women managed the tasks that kept a household operating, such as cooking, gardening, washing, cleaning, weaving cloth, and sewing. They supported one another by helping in childbirth and sharing equipment and tools. Women did not have political equality with men, however. Laws prevented them from voting, holding office, or serving on a jury. While many boys lacked the opportunity for schooling, young girls generally were not allowed to go to school—they were expected to learn everything they needed to know from their mothers at home.

During colonial times, most children received very little formal education. New England was an exception. Because the Puritans believed that everyone should be able to read the Bible, Massachusetts and Connecticut passed legislation in 1647 requiring communities to support local schools. As a result, literacy rates were higher in New England than anywhere else in British North America. Outside New England, if there were no schools in the area, parents taught their children at home. In the Southern Colonies, plantation owners often hired private instructors to teach their children.

Colonial colleges were primarily training grounds for ministers and lawyers; generally only the very wealthy attended. Up until the 1740s, there were only three colleges in the colonies, Harvard in Massachusetts (established in 1636), William and Mary in Virginia (1693), and Yale in Connecticut (1701).

African Americans in the Colonies

Not counting Native Americans, about one out of every five people living in British North America by the middle of the 1700s was of African descent. Most of these African Americans were enslaved.

One Person's Story As in the case of all immigrants, the experiences of African Americans in the colonies varied depending on where they lived. Yet the stories of Africans, uprooted from their homeland and sold into slavery, had many elements in common. One African who later told his story was Olaudah Equiano.

Born around 1745 in the country of Benin, Equiano was kidnapped at age 10. He was enslaved to a series of African masters, then sold and put aboard a British slave ship bound for the Americas. During the **Middle Passage,** Equiano witnessed many terrible scenes of suffering and cruelty. (The Middle Passage was one leg of the triangular trade between the Americas, Europe, and Africa. The term is also used to refer to the forced transport of slaves from Africa to the Americas.)

Equiano's ship finally arrived in the West Indies, where the Africans were sold at a public auction. Most went to work—and die—in the sugar plantations of the West Indies. Equiano noted that the sale separated families, leaving people grief-stricken and alone:

Olaudah Equiano described the horrors of slavery from firsthand knowledge.

> "*In this manner, without scruple [concern], are relations and friends separated, most of them never to see each other again. I remember . . . there were several brothers who, in the sale, were sold in different lots; and it was very moving on this occasion to see and hear their*

RESOURCE DIRECTORY

Teaching Resources

Biography, Literature, and Comparing Primary Sources booklet (Literature) *As Poor Richard Says,* p. 42

Learning with Documents booklet (Primary Source Activity) *A Marriage Agreement,* p. 8

Learning with Documents booklet (Visual Learning Activity) *The First American Schoolbook,* p. 42

Technology

Color Transparencies *Fine Art,* E3; *The Way It Works,* H2

RESOURCE PRO® Critical Thinking Activity *Identifying Central Issues: The Status of Colonial Women,* found on Resource Pro, enhances students' understanding of complex issues through summarizing excerpts from colonial authors.

Prentice Hall United States History Video Collection™ Volume 3, *Slavery and Freedom* *cries at parting. O, ye nominal Christians [Christians in name only]! might not an African ask you, Learned you this from your God, who says unto you, Do unto all men as you would men should do unto you?"*

—Olaudah Equiano

VIEWING HISTORY This scene aboard a slave ship was painted by an eyewitness in 1846. **Analyzing Visual Information** *What does this painting add to your knowledge of the slave trade?*

Slavery in the Colonies On the coastal plain of South Carolina and Georgia, called the low country, rice and indigo were grown most efficiently on large plantations with many slaves. High temperatures and dangerous diseases made life particularly difficult for the enslaved workers there, and they labored under especially brutal conditions. African Americans made up the majority of the population in South Carolina and Georgia. Wealthy planters often chose to spend most of their time away from their isolated estates, so slaves generally had regular contact with only a handful of white colonists.

In Virginia and Maryland, slaves made up a minority rather than a majority of the population, and relatively few of them had come directly from Africa. Slaves in these colonies performed many kinds of work. Cultivating tobacco, the major crop, did not take as much time as growing rice, so slaveowners put enslaved African Americans to work at other tasks. This led to more regular contact between African Americans and European Americans. The result was greater integration of European American and African American cultures than in South Carolina and Georgia. In the latter half of the 1700s, slaves in Virginia and Maryland blended the customs of African and European origin in everything from food and clothing to religion.

Some male slaves in Virginia even worked away from plantations as artisans or laborers in Richmond and other towns. As long as they sent back part of their wages to the plantations, they lived fairly independently of their owner's control. They were, however, still subject to harsh laws that controlled what they could do. In addition, their children were born enslaved.

About 400,000 African Americans lived in the Southern Colonies by the late 1700s. In contrast, there were only about 50,000 African Americans in the New England and Middle Colonies combined. These colonies had a more diverse economy, and their farms were much smaller than those in the Southern Colonies and did not require as many slaves for field work. It was more common to find slaves in this region working in the cities as cooks, housekeepers, or personal servants. Male slaves often worked in manufacturing and trade or as skilled artisans. They also worked in the forests as lumberjacks. Because shipbuilding and shipping were major economic activities, some African American men worked along the seacoast. As dockworkers, merchant sailors, fishermen, whalers, and privateers, they contributed to the growth of the Atlantic economy.

READING CHECK How did slavery develop in the various colonies?

Slave Laws and Revolts Laws controlling the lives of slaves varied from region to region. Every colony passed its own slave laws, and revised them over time. Generally, slaves could not go aboard ships or ferries or leave their town limits without a written pass. Crimes for slaves ranged from owning hogs and carrying canes to disturbing the peace and striking a white person. Punishments included whipping, banishment to the West Indies, and death. Many of these laws also applied to free African Americans and to Native Americans.

BACKGROUND — Biography

Paul Cuffe (1759–1817), the son of an ex-slave father and a Native American mother, went to sea at the age of 16. He became a successful ship owner, hiring only African American crews. Cuffe, who joined the Quakers in 1808, became convinced that African Americans should resettle in Africa. In 1811 he took the first African American recruits to Africa.

BACKGROUND — Recent Scholarship

Because slave women were banned from practicing a craft or from taking on supervisory roles, they did a greater share of the fieldwork than men. Many field gangs were led by women, who had no choice but to perform increasingly heavy and boring work. In an essay entitled "Rethinking Early American Slavery" (in *Inequality in Early America*), Philip D. Morgan writes that since male slaves could not own land or marry legally, there was probably some measure of equality among slave men and women. Many slave women raised children without the help of men, who tended to run away more often. Morgan says that by necessity, slave women became self-reliant and self-sufficient.

READING CHECK

In the South, due to the large plantations, slavery developed to provide an agricultural labor source. In the North, slaves were used in more diverse ways: as labor on smaller farms, as household servants, as artisans, and even on ships.

CUSTOMIZE FOR ...

Less Proficient Writers

Have students restate in their own words the quotation from Olaudah Equiano that starts on the bottom of the previous page.

TEST PREPARATION

Have students review the quote by Olaudah Equiano that starts on the previous page and then complete the sentence below.

The main thrust of Olaudah Equiano's quotation is that—

- **A** people in the American colonies were not very religious.
- **B** slavery is wrong.
- **C** families were cruelly separated by slavery.
- **(D)** those who would be slaveholders should treat others as they themselves would wish to be treated.

CAPTION ANSWERS

Viewing History Answers will vary, but students should note the crowded conditions, the darkness of the hold, the emaciation of the slaves, and the fact that they were "stored" among barrels and kegs as though they were also merely cargo.

The Gullah Language and Culture

In the 1700s, owners of rice plantations in the Sea Islands off the South Carolina and Georgia coasts imported slaves from West African rice-growing regions, including present-day Sierra Leone. The Sea Islands could be reached only by boat, and white planters did not want to live there. Thus, these isolated enslaved Africans were able to preserve their distinctive culture, as shown in the batik *Dawn to Dusk* by Frances Johnson.

The Gullah language that developed among these slaves and their descendants is a mixture of English and West African languages. For example, the Gullah "Dey fa go shum," is "They went to see her" in English.

When new roads linked the islands to the mainland in the 1960s, it was feared that the Gullah culture would die out. Today, however, there is renewed interest in preserving the Gullah language, and festivals celebrate Gullah storytelling, crafts, and cuisine.

Do you think it is important to record and preserve distinctive historic dialects such as the Gullah language? Why or why not?

Laws restricting the movement of slaves made organizing slave rebellions extremely difficult. Because slaves could not travel or meet freely, they had only limited contact with slaves in other areas. A few early slave revolts are documented. In 1739, several dozen slaves near Charleston, South Carolina, killed more than 20 whites in what is known as the Stono Rebellion. The slaves burned an armory and began to march toward Spanish Florida, where a small colony of runaway slaves lived. Armed planters captured and killed the rebels. In New York City, brutal laws that were passed to control African Americans also led to rebellions.

More commonly, African Americans resisted slavery indirectly, by such acts as pretending to misunderstand orders or faking illness. While these actions could not give them freedom, they did grant the slaves a small degree of control over their own lives. In addition, strong African kinship networks helped people survive slavery and also helped preserve their traditions.

Sounds of an Era

Listen to a Gullah storyteller and other sounds relating to colonial life.

Free Blacks Not until after the American Revolution did the free black population in the Northern and Southern Colonies grow significantly. Some slave laws discouraged people from freeing slaves. Owners had to get permission from the legislature before they could do so. Some laws demanded that freed slaves leave a colony within six months of gaining freedom. Despite the obstacles, those slaves who earned money as artisans or laborers had the possibility of saving enough to purchase their freedom.

Free African Americans did much of the same kind of work as enslaved African Americans. They were, however, probably worse off materially. Free blacks often endured poorer living conditions and more severe discrimination than slaves who were identified with specific white households. The rights of free blacks were also limited: they could not vote, testify in court against whites, or marry whites. Nevertheless, they valued their freedom far above material conditions.

ACTIVITY
Connecting with Economics

Engage students in a discussion about the economics of slavery. Why did landowners want slaves? How did owning slaves work to their advantage? Could colonial landowners have managed their farms without the help of slaves? **(Verbal/Linguistic)**

BACKGROUND
A Diverse Nation

By the late eighteenth century, slaves were coming from many different African groups, such as Tehlbo, Ashanti, and Yoruba societies on the African west coast. Most African cultural and religious practices died out in the American colonies because Europeans felt threatened by the prospect of a cohesive African community. While much of the African culture was lost, certain traditions survived, such as those involving magic, healing, and burial. Despite many obstacles, Africans managed to forge relationships, raise families, and create a culture that bridged Old World traditions with New World experiences.

CAPTION ANSWERS

Fast Forward to Today Answers will vary. Some students may feel that it is essential to keep old dialects alive in order to preserve the diversity of American life. Others may feel that a dialect cannot be "preserved"; it will either survive or vanish on its own according to its level of usage in a society.

RESOURCE DIRECTORY

Teaching Resources

Biography, Literature, and Comparing Primary Sources booklet (Comparing Primary Sources) *On Expansion into Native American Lands*, p. 101

Other Print Resources

Nystrom *Atlas of Our Country* *Early Expansion of the United States*, pp. 20–21

Historical Outline Map Book *The Thirteen Colonies*, p. 15; *North America in 1753*, p. 20

Technology

Color Transparencies *American Diversity*, G2

Sounds of an Era Audio CD *Gullah Storyteller Janie Hunter* (time: 30 seconds)

Emerging Tensions in the Colonies

By the mid-1700s, 13 prosperous British colonies hugged the Atlantic Coast. Colonial settlers had transformed the Atlantic colonies into a world of thriving farms, towns, and plantations. The success of the colonies came at a price, however. The growth of the colonies, both in population and territory, raised new issues in colonial life.

Western Expansion In the mid-1700s, the colonial population increased rapidly, almost doubling every 25 years, as the birth rate grew faster than the death rate. The colonies also experienced a growth in the number of **immigrants,** or people who enter a new country to settle. While colonists continued to come from England, they also began to arrive from Ireland and Germany. Those people immigrating from Ireland were often called Scotch-Irish, because they had originally come from Scotland. As the population grew, the colonists began to feel crowded, especially in the smaller colonies of New England.

According to English custom, fathers tried to provide their sons with some land of their own. New Englanders now found it increasingly difficult to do so. Maintaining a family required about 45 acres, and since colonists were having many children, there was simply not enough fertile land to go around.

Clearly the colonies could not continue to flourish if forced to remain confined to the land along the Atlantic Ocean. By the mid-1700s, European settlers were moving into the interior of North America. Scotch-Irish and Germans settled central Pennsylvania and the Shenandoah Valley of Virginia. Farther to the north, colonists spread into the Mohawk River valley in New York and into the Connecticut River valley in present-day Vermont. In southern Pennsylvania and the Carolinas, settlements sprang up as far west as the Appalachian Mountains. In a few cases, settlers pushed through the Appalachians and began cultivating land in Indian territory.

Tensions With the French and Native Americans The colonists' desire for more land raised tensions between the new settlers and those groups who already lived on the land—the French and the Indians. In the Ohio and Susquehanna River valleys, Native American groups, including the Delaware, the Shawnee, and the Huron, were moving west, too. As white settlers migrated into Native American territory, they forced the local Indians to relocate into lands already occupied by other Native American groups.

The French as well as the Native Americans were alarmed by the steady migration of the English settlers. In 1749, disturbed by the expansion of British trading posts in the Ohio Valley, the French sent defenders to strengthen the settlement of Detroit and to seize the Ohio Valley. Tensions continued to rise in the summer of 1752 when the French built Fort Presque Isle (where Erie, Pennsylvania, is now located) and attacked and killed the defenders of an English trading post in the valley.

COMPARING PRIMARY SOURCES
Expansion Into Native American Lands

Colonial efforts to purchase Native American lands in Pennsylvania created a difference of opinion.

Analyzing Viewpoints According to each speaker, what gives the land its value? How does each speaker characterize the actions and motives of the other? Do you think either or both are justified in their opinions? Explain your reasoning.

Opposed to Expansion

"We know our Lands are now more valuable. The white People think we do not know their Value; but we are sensible [aware] that the Land is everlasting, and the few Goods we receive for it are soon worn out and gone. . . . Besides, we are not well used [treated] with respect to the lands still unsold by us. Your people daily settle on these lands, and spoil our hunting. . . . Your horses and cows have eaten the grass our deer used to feed on."

—Canasatego, Iroquois leader, July 7, 1742

In Favor of Expansion

"It is very true that lands are of late becoming more valuable; but what rises their value? Is it not entirely owning to the industry and labor used by the white people in their cultivation and improvement? Had not they come among you, these lands would have been of no use to you, any further than to maintain you. . . . The value of the land is no more than it is worth in money."

—Governor George Thomas of Pennsylvania, July 7, 1742

ACTIVITY
Connecting with Geography

Have students make maps showing the growth that occurred during the mid-1700s. Tell students to label the colonies and indicate which ones experienced large growth. Also have students locate various immigrant groups in the appropriate colonies. **(Visual/Spatial)**

BACKGROUND
Geography in History

By the mid-1700s, standards for leisure and recreation had relaxed. The severe morality of the early Puritan era gave way to a more diversified culture and more relaxed attitudes. By 1730 there were more than 250 incorporated towns in New England. While Boston and Newport were the most important cities, there were numerous others, including Portsmouth, Salem, Springfield, Providence, New London, New Haven, and Hartford. As these urban centers grew, they replaced the Puritan village, and in so doing, they offered a wide variety of churches, taverns, and forms of leisure and entertainment.

CUSTOMIZE FOR ...
Less Proficient Readers

Read aloud the first paragraph of the section "Emerging Tensions in the Colonies." Then have students write down two major issues that they feel might have been sources of tension. When they have finished, have them test their predictions against the text.

ACTIVITY
Connecting with Culture

Tell students to write a short report detailing the religious history of your state. As students do their research, they should consider the following questions. When your state was first settled, which religious group or groups were predominant? What kind of conflicts emerged between different religious groups? How has the religious makeup of your state changed over the years? What is the religious makeup of your state now? **(Verbal/Linguistic)**

BACKGROUND
A Diverse Nation

Small but stable Jewish communities emerged during the 1690s. There were almost 100 Jews living in New York by 1695. By 1770 there were about 250 Jewish families in the colonies, most living in Newport, New York City, Philadelphia, and Charleston. While most Jews were merchants and shopkeepers, a small number were artisans. Colonial Jews chose to stay in cities in order to keep their small communities intact. Although Jews faced discrimination from town officials, they managed to build a small synagogue in New York City in 1728. In Newport in 1763, the small Jewish community built what is now the nation's oldest synagogue.

British, French, and Indians in the Ohio River Valley, 1754

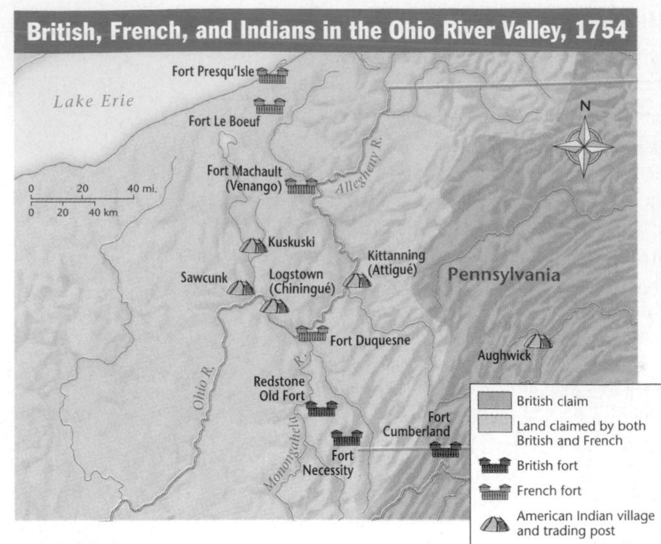

MAP SKILLS As English colonists pushed west, they came into conflict with both the French and the Indians. **Location** *Which British forts are in disputed territory?*

By the early 1750s, it was clear that some kind of explosion was rapidly approaching. The most likely setting was the western part of present-day Pennsylvania. There, the interests of the colonies of Pennsylvania and Virginia came into conflict with those of the Native Americans and the French. Whoever controlled the area where the Allegheny and Monongahela rivers meet to form the Ohio River could dominate the entire region. This was, in other words, an area worth fighting for.

Religious Tensions While tensions built along the outer edges of the British colonies, unrest was also increasing within them. Nowhere was this more obvious than in colonial religious life.

While the British colonies were overwhelmingly Protestant (aside from a small number of Jews in cities and some Catholics in Maryland), no single group of Protestants was more powerful than any other. Southern planters and northern merchants and professionals tended to belong to the Church of England. Most New Englanders were either Congregationalists or Presbyterians. Quakers were strong in Pennsylvania, as were Lutherans and Mennonites, while the Dutch Reformed Church thrived in the colony of New York.

In the early 1700s, many ministers, especially Congregationalists, believed that the colonists had fallen away from the faith of their Puritan ancestors. In the 1730s and 1740s, they led a series of revivals designed to renew religious enthusiasm and commitment. Known today as the **Great Awakening,** this revival of religious feeling was not a single event that began or ended at one specific time, nor did it take place in every colony. Most historians date the beginning of the Great Awakening to the great explosion of religious feeling that arose in the 1730s in response to the preaching of Jonathan Edwards, a Massachusetts minister.

News of Edwards's success spread throughout the colonies and even to Britain. It encouraged other ministers to increase their efforts to energize their followers. These ministers sought to remind people of the power of God and, at least in the beginning, to remind them of the authority of their ministers as well. In a well-known fiery sermon, "Sinners in the Hands of an Angry God," Edwards gave his congregation a terrifying picture of their situation:

> "*O sinner! Consider the fearful danger you are in: it is a great furnace of wrath, a wide and bottomless pit, full of the fire of wrath, that you are held over in the hand of that God, whose wrath is provoked and incensed as much against you, as against many of the damned in hell. You hang by a slender thread.*"
>
> —Jonathan Edwards

Edwards would eventually be eclipsed in popularity by George Whitefield, a young English minister who toured the colonies seven times between 1738 and 1770. Whitefield's tour of New England in 1740 was a great triumph. In

CAPTION ANSWERS

Map Skills Redstone Old Fort and Fort Necessity

RESOURCE DIRECTORY

Teaching Resources

Units 1/2 booklet
- Section 3 Quiz, p. 6
- Chapter 1 Test, pp. 7, 10

Guide to the Essentials
- Section 3 Summary, p. 7
- Chapter 1 Test, p. 8

Biography, Literature, and Comparing Primary Sources booklet (Biography) *Jonathan Edwards,* p. 8

Other Print Resources

American History Block Scheduling Support *Reviving Religion: The Great Awakening,* found in the Forging a New Nation folder, includes interdisciplinary lesson suggestions and activities for Geography and History, Primary Sources, Biography, and Literature.

Chapter Tests with ExamView® Test Bank CD-ROM, Ch. 1

Technology

Sounds of an Era Audio CD *"Sinners in the Hands of an Angry God," Jonathan Edwards* (time: one minute, 50 seconds)

RESOURCE PRO® **Primary Source Activity** *The Great Awakening*

ExamView® Test Bank CD-ROM, Ch.1

Social Studies Skills Tutor CD-ROM

Boston, he preached to vast crowds packed into churches. Later, he held open-air meetings at which thousands of listeners could hear his ringing sermons.

Effects of the Great Awakening As time went on, the Great Awakening did more than revive people's religious convictions. It energized them to speak for themselves and to rely less on the traditional authority of ministers and books.

In some areas, the Great Awakening was led by ministers in established congregations. But many people flocked instead to revival leaders, such as Whitefield, who were itinerant, or traveling, preachers. If welcomed by the local minister, the itinerants would preach inside the church as a "visiting minister." If unwelcome, they preached in fields and barns to anyone who would come to hear their sermons. These ministers, some of whom had received little formal education, preached that anyone could have a personal relationship with Jesus. The infinitely great power of God did not put Him beyond the reach of ordinary people, they argued. Faith and sincerity, rather than wealth or education, were the major requirements needed to understand the Gospel.

One sign of the new religious independence brought about by the Great Awakening was the shift of many New Englanders to the Baptist faith in the 1740s and 1750s. In the South, both the Baptist and, later, the Methodist Churches drew new followers. The appeal of these two churches lay in their powerful, emotional ceremonies and their celebration of ordinary people. While some churches grew, others split when only part of the congregation embraced the new emotionalism. Some of these splinter groups were more tolerant of dissent, or difference of opinion, than the organizations from which they had split. This helped make religion in the colonies more democratic.

Although it was a religious movement, the Great Awakening had long-term social and political effects. Methodists and Baptists tended to be people at the middle or bottom of colonial society. When they claimed that individuals could act on their own faith and not rely on a minister or other authority, they were indirectly attacking the idea that some people are better than others. Such talk of equality would, in time, have revolutionary consequences.

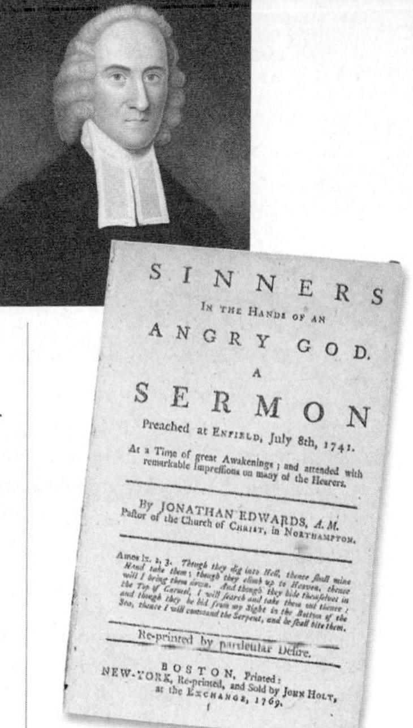

SINNERS

In the Hands of an

ANGRY GOD.

A

SERMON

Preached at Enfield, July 8th, 1741.

At a Time of great Awakenings; and attended with remarkable Impressions on many of the Hearers.

By JONATHAN EDWARDS, A.M.
Pastor of the Church of Christ, in Northampton.

Re-printed by particular Desire.

BOSTON, Printed;
NEW-YORK, Re-printed, and Sold by John Holt, at the Exchange, 1769.

VIEWING HISTORY Jonathan Edwards, shown above, declared, "The bow of God's wrath is bent, and the arrow made ready on the string" in the sermon shown here. **Drawing Conclusions** *Why do you think so many people responded to this kind of preaching in the 1700s?*

Section 3 Assessment

READING COMPREHENSION

1. (a) What is **mercantilism?** (b) According to this theory, what kind of **balance of trade** is desirable?
2. What kinds of economies developed in the Southern, Middle, and New England Colonies?
3. What part did the **Middle Passage** play in the **triangular trade?**
4. What was the **Great Awakening?**

CRITICAL THINKING AND WRITING

5. **Identifying Central Issues** What situations, events, and policies began to lead toward a demand for self-government in the colonies?
6. **Writing a Letter** It is the mid-1700s, and you are moving west from one of the English colonies. Write a letter to a friend back home explaining why you are moving.

Take It to the NET

Activity: Writing a Poem
Research the Gullah language and the people who speak it. Write a poem or a song about the Gullah. Try using the Gullah language in all or part of your poem. Use the links provided in the *America: Pathways to the Present* area of the following Web site for help in completing this activity.
www.phschool.com

Section 3 Assessment

Reading Comprehension

1. (a) A theory that a country should get and keep as much gold and silver as possible. (b) One that shows more exports than imports.
2. Southern Colonies' economies were based on growing labor-intensive staple crops; Middle Colonies' economies were a mixture of farming and commerce; New England Colonies depended on long-distance trade.
3. It was one leg of the triangular trade that was used to bring enslaved Africans to the West Indies.
4. A revival of intense religious feeling in America during the 1730s and 1740s.

Critical Thinking and Writing

5. Answers will vary but may include descriptions of: the evolving power of colonial legislatures; policy of salutory neglect; tradition of self-government that British settlers were accustomed to; the effects of the Great Awakening.
6. Letters will vary, but should be supported with facts from the section.

Take It to the NET

Answers will vary, but should demonstrate a familiarity with the Gullah language and culture.

Caption Answers

Viewing History Answers will vary, but students should note the emotional nature of the preaching as well as the new sense that individuals—regardless of class or education—could be in control of their own religious responses and destiny and were able to communicate directly with God.

Chapter 1 Review and Assessment

creating a CHAPTER SUMMARY

Copy the web diagram (right) on a piece of paper. Complete it by adding examples of the development of self-government in the English colonies. Include English as well as colonial events. Add circles as needed.

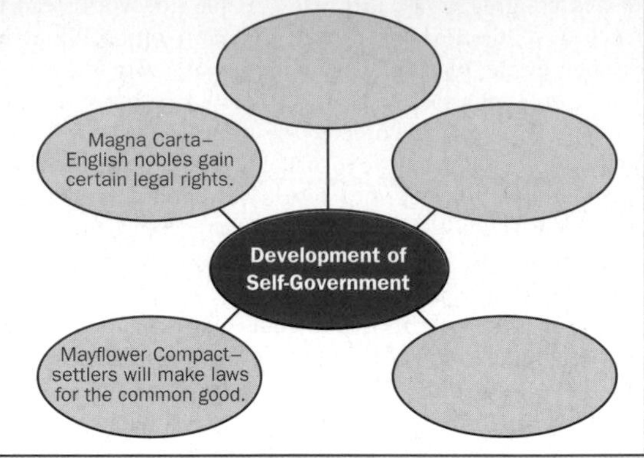

iTEXT

For additional review and enrichment activities, see the interactive version of *America: Pathways to the Present*, available on the Web and on CD-ROM.

★ Reviewing Key Terms

For each of the terms below, write a sentence explaining how it relates to the creation of a new American society.

1. migration
2. clan
3. monarch
4. Columbian Exchange
5. colony
6. Mayflower Compact
7. religious tolerance
8. triangular trade
9. Middle Passage
10. Great Awakening

★ Reviewing Main Ideas

11. What are three characteristics shared by Native American cultures? (Section 1)
12. How did the Renaissance change Europe? (Section 1)
13. Describe one of the wealthy West African kingdoms of the 1400s. (Section 1)
14. How did Columbus's voyages affect Europe, West Africa, and the Native Americans? (Section 1)
15. What are three reasons the Spanish explored and settled in the Americas? (Section 2)
16. Describe the early years of (a) the Jamestown colony and (b) the first two settlements in Massachusetts. (Section 2)
17. How did the English acquire New York? (Section 2)
18. What was the policy of salutary neglect? (Section 3)
19. What kinds of economies developed in the different colonies? (Section 3)
20. Why did dependence on slave labor increase in the Southern Colonies? (Section 3)

★ Critical Thinking

21. **Demonstrating Reasoned Judgment** European nations competed first to find a sea route to Asia and later to conquer and settle the Americas. Do you think this competition was beneficial or harmful to the development of the Atlantic World? Explain your answer.
22. **Making Comparisons** Compare the ways that religion contributed to the founding of Spain's American colonies and the New England Colonies.
23. **Recognizing Ideologies** How was the European settlers' treatment of Native Americans and Africans similar? What do these actions tell you about the worldview of those Europeans?
24. **Recognizing Cause and Effect** How did geography help to determine the economies and social customs of the English colonies?
25. **Determining Relevance** Choose three events in English and colonial history that would later lead to the colonists' insistence on self-government, and explain their significance.

34 **Chapter 1 • *Origins of a New Society***

Reviewing Key Terms

Students should refer to the definitions of key terms in the chapter to write sentences that show an understanding of life in the Atlantic region and the Americas prior to 1754.

Reviewing Main Ideas

11. Sample answer: similar religious beliefs, kinship structure, and a reliance upon oral history.
12. It was a shift from the rigid beliefs of the church to a time of rediscovery of ancient cultures; explorations both geographical and in science, logic, and the arts; the advent of the printing press; and the development of nation-states.
13. Sample answer: Benin arose in the late 1200s; mud-and-leaf houses; wide, clean streets leading to the grand palace; wealth came from trade; led by a strong king.
14. Europe: Led to the establishment of colonies, the search for precious metals, Columbian Exchange, trade, foods that helped save Europeans from famine; West Africa: European settlers' need for labor transformed the West African slave trade into an industry, damaging West African society for many years to come; Native Americans: Hundreds of thousands killed by diseases brought by explorers, weakening the structure of Native American cultures.
15. Spread Christian religion, gain wealth, and win glory.
16. (a) Most settlers were not used to doing the hard work required; they focused on searching for gold rather than the upkeep needed for daily life; the village was located in an unhealthy area; the colony's survival owed much to the strong leadership of John Smith. (b) Separatists sought a place to worship freely and moved to Plymouth, abiding by the Mayflower Compact to keep them united; half died in the first winter. The Massachusetts Bay Colony was a successful Puritan community that expanded through hard work.
17. In 1664 Charles II declared that the region belonged to his brother, the Duke of York. The Dutch were forced to give the area to the English, who renamed it New York.

Creating a Chapter Summary

Magna Carta—English nobles gain certain legal rights.
Desire for economic independence
Diverse colonial economies
Development of Self-Government
Mayflower Compact—settlers will make laws for the common good.
Property rights
Desire for religious freedom

★ Skills Assessment

Analyzing Political Cartoons ▶

26. The topic of this modern-day cartoon is the current debate over immigration to the United States.
(a) Who does the man in the center represent?
(b) Who do the people on the left represent?
(c) Who does the man on the right represent?

27. (a) What historical events does the cartoonist want viewers to recall? (b) What point is the cartoonist making? (c) Do you agree or disagree with this view?

Analyzing Primary Sources

Columbus wrote to the Spanish monarchs, describing the first Native Americans the Spanish met. Read the excerpt from his letter, and answer the questions that follow.

> *"They are so ingenuous [innocent] and free with all they have, that no one would believe it who has not seen it; of anything that they possess, if it be asked of them, they never say no; on the contrary, they invite you to share it and show as much love as if their hearts went with it."*
>
> —Letter from Columbus to the Spanish monarchs, 1493

28. Which statement best represents the meaning of the quotation?
- **A** The Tainos are innocent, generous, and cooperative.
- **B** The Tainos loved the Europeans.
- **C** The Tainos are loving but possessive.
- **D** The Tainos are just like the Spanish.

29. What conclusion do you think the king and queen probably drew from Columbus's description?
- **F** The Tainos should be treated the same way they treated Columbus.
- **G** Spain should leave the area and not come back.
- **H** The Tainos would provide no resistance to Spanish conquest.
- **J** The Tainos must be wiped out.

Applying the Chapter Skill: *Generalizing from Multiple Sources*

30. Review the Skills for Life page and the chapter text about Columbus to make a new generalization about Columbus or the Spanish monarchs.

ACTIVITIES

Writing to LEARN

Writing to Learn
The First Amendment to the Constitution of the United States guarantees people the right to practice their religion as they wish. Which early American colonies set precedents for such a guarantee? What were their reasons for doing so? Which colonies did not favor religious tolerance? What were their reasons? How did their views of religious tolerance affect the development of these colonies?

Primary Source CD-ROM

Working With Primary Sources Find additional information on the origins of a new society in the Americas on the *Exploring Primary Sources in U.S. History CD-ROM* and use the selection(s) provided to complete the Chapter 1 primary source activity located in the *America: Pathways to the Present* area of the following Web site.
www.phschool.com

Take It to the NET

Chapter Self-Test As a review activity, take the Chapter 1 Self-Test in the *America: Pathways to the Present* area at the Web site listed below. The questions are designed to test your understanding of the chapter content.
www.phschool.com

18. The British policy of leaving their colonies alone, rarely enforcing trade regulations.
19. Economies based on growing staple crops in the Southern Colonies, farming and commerce in the Middle Colonies, and long-distance trade in the New England Colonies.
20. In South Carolina and Georgia, rice and indigo were grown most efficiently on large plantations that required many slaves.

Critical Thinking

21. Answers will vary but should be supported with facts from the section.
22. The Spanish sought to convert the Native Americans to Christianity. In New England there was no interest in converting the natives; settlers there simply desired to worship free from interference.
23. Europeans made use of both Native Americans and Africans as slaves. Europeans believed that other cultures were inferior.
24. Most commerce took place on water; temperature and land determined what crops could be grown and who would supply the labor; location determined the number and frequency of traders passing through and thus affected the success of commerce. The custom of slavery developed in parts of the South where crops needed to be grown on large plantations that required many laborers.
25. Answers will vary but may include and describe the effects of the Magna Carta, the Mayflower Compact, salutory neglect, and the Great Awakening.

Skills Assessment

26. (a) An Anglo-Saxon.
(b) Mexican Americans.
(c) A Native American.
27. (a) The displacement of Native Americans by European settlers. (b) Everyone immigrated to America at some point in history, so complaints about "illegal" immigrants are hypocritical. (c) Answers should show an understanding of the issues raised in the cartoon and in this chapter.
28. A
29. H
30. Columbus seems to have owed his success at least as much to his perseverance as a lobbyist as to his navigational skills. He spent years appealing to the monarchs of Portugal and Spain before receiving the needed financial backing.

ANSWERS TO ACTIVITIES

Writing to LEARN

Answers will vary. Colonies setting precedents for religious freedom include Rhode Island, New York, Pennsylvania, Maryland (partial), and Georgia (partial). Colonies setting precedents for religious intolerance include Massachusetts.

Primary Source CD-ROM

Direct students to the additional primary sources that can be found on the *Exploring Primary Sources in U.S. History CD-ROM.*

Take It to the NET

Additional support materials and activities for Chapter 1 of *America: Pathways to the Present* can be found in the Social Studies area at the Prentice Hall School Web site. **www.phschool.com**

Colonial Settlements

Focus Review with students the priorities that were in the minds of colonial people when they established their settlements. What factors were foremost in the settlers' minds? How does the basic layout of a town like Sudbury reflect colonial priorities?

Instruct Explain to students that settlers in the new world of America brought ideas with them from their original countries. Among the most important was the notion of how a settlement should be set up. Yet, each new settlement also needed to take into consideration geographical factors, such as landforms, access to available water, proximity to established roads, and other factors. Ask students to list the general factors that would influence the establishment of a settlement in colonial New England. Then have them do library research to see how those factors were taken into consideration in the settlements of towns such as Andover, Dedham, and Watertown, Massachusetts.

Extend Have students do library research to find out about the dwellings of Wampanoag Indians, the native neighbors of Pilgrim settlers at Plymouth. How were they similar to the Pilgrims' houses? How were they different? In what ways were the Wampanoag houses more suited to the elements than the Pilgrim houses? In what ways did both types of structures draw upon available materials for their construction?

Geography & History

Colonial Settlements

Most early colonial settlements, particularly those in New England, consisted of tight clusters of houses, usually centered on a single church, or meetinghouse. Settlements often shared a mill where grain was ground. Near the center of many New England towns were commons, or commonly owned pastures, that were open to all townspeople. These shared spaces and institutions reflected the close-knit community spirit found in many early settlements.

Sudbury, Massachusetts, 1656

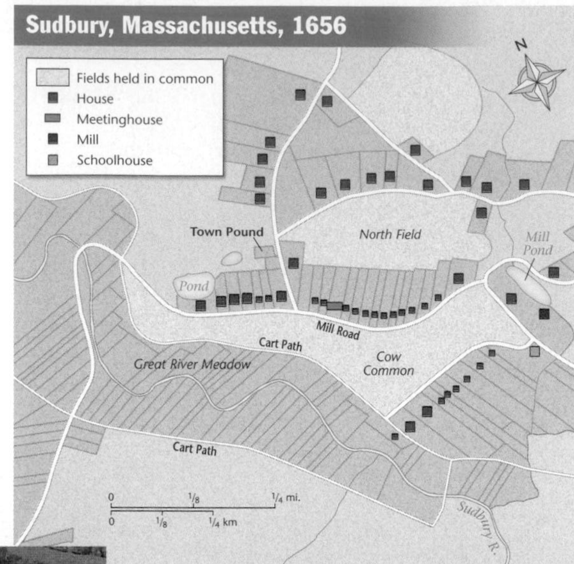

Geographic Connection How did the layout of colonial Sudbury, Massachusetts, reflect its physical geography and cultural values?

A Familiar Pattern
In many ways, these early settlements resembled villages where the settlers might have lived in England. This modern view of an English village shows a striking similarity in layout to colonial Sudbury.

Geographic Connection How is the geography of this English village similar to the geography of colonial Sudbury?

Reminders of Home
Colonial settlers not only patterned their settlements after villages in their homeland, they also brought treasured possessions with them. This chest was carried from England to Plymouth, Massachusetts, on the *Mayflower.*

36

Answers

1. The Sudbury settlement occupied a site between rich bottomlands along the Sudbury River and a smaller stream that could be harnessed to power a mill. It appears that the residents of colonial Sudbury were expected to farm large plots of land as a communal group, rather than as individuals farming their own land.

RESOURCE DIRECTORY

Teaching Resources
Geography and History booklet, pp. 2–3

Other Print Resources
Nystrom *Atlas of Our Country* *Colonies in the North and East,* pp. 14–15

Technology
Prentice Hall United States History Video Collection™ Volume 2, *The Era of Colonization*

Early Homes

In their first years in North America, settlers had to make do with small houses made of local wood with thatched (straw) roofs. These houses at Plimoth Plantation in Plymouth, Massachusetts, are part of a modern reconstruction of the first permanent English settlement in New England.

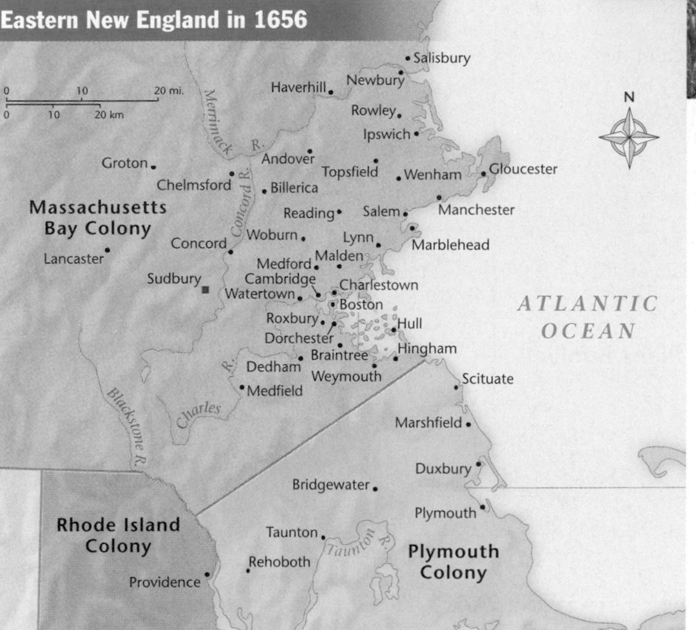

The Colonial Frontier

This map shows the towns that existed near Sudbury when it was first settled. As you can see, Sudbury was near the edge of the area already settled by the English. Tightly clustered villages may have given English settlers a sense of security at the edge of a vast wilderness inhabited by peoples with different customs.

Geographic Connection **Where were most of the settlements in eastern New England located in 1656?**

A Culture Takes Root

As a new generation came of age, colonists abandoned some of the traditions of the old country to develop their own new regional cultures. This meetinghouse shows the elegant building style that gradually replaced the crude structures of the first settlers across New England. An increasingly self-confident population gathered in meetinghouses like this one to hear native-born preachers such as Cotton Mather, pictured here.

Answers

2. In both colonial Sudbury and the English village, the clustering of many houses so close together reflects a strong community spirit, and the positioning of a house of worship at the center of each settlement reflects the importance of religion to the residents of each community. Both settlements appear to be surrounded by arable land.
3. Most settlements were located along or near the Atlantic coast. Those that were inland tended to lie along major rivers. Also, many settlements were clustered around Boston.

Chapter 2 Planning Guide

Resource Manager

	Core Instruction	Reading/Skills
Chapter-Level Resources **TEKS** 24(D), 25(A), 25(C), 25(D)	Teaching Resources • Pacing Charts booklet • Block Scheduling booklet **Resource Pro® CD-ROM,** Ch. 2 **Prentice Hall Presentation Pro CD-ROM, Ch. 2** **www.phschool.com** • eTeach	**Guided Reading Audiotapes (English/Spanish)** **Student Edition on Audio CD,** Ch. 2 **Social Studies Skills Tutor CD-ROM** **Color Transparencies,** A7, A8, A9, A10, A11, A12, A55, A60, B2, B3, C2, D2, E4, E5
1 The Road to Independence 1. Discover the importance of the French and Indian War. 2. See what issues led to the Revolution. 3. Find out why the shots fired at Lexington and Concord were "heard round the world." 4. Study the political ideas that led to the Declaration of Independence. 5. Learn how colonists fought for and won independence. **TEKS** 8(B), 24(A), 24(B), 24(G)	Teaching Resources **Units 1/2 booklet** • Section 1 Quiz, p. 14 **Learning Styles Lesson Plans booklet,** pp. 10–11	**Guided Reading and Review booklet,** pp. 15–19 **Guide to the Essentials,** p. 9 **Learning with Documents booklet,** pp. 43, 76 **Section Reading Support Transparencies**
2 The Constitution of the United States 1. See how the early government of the United States was structured by the Articles of Confederation. 2. Learn about the type of government structure set up by the Framers at the Constitutional Convention. 3. See how the Federalists won the battle over ratification. 4. Discover how Washington's administration set precedents for the new nation and provided for the capital city. **TEKS** 24(B), 25(B)	Teaching Resources **Units 1/2 booklet** • Section 2 Quiz, p. 15 **Learning Styles Lesson Plans booklet,** pp. 12–13	**Guided Reading and Review booklet,** pp. 20–23 **Guide to the Essentials,** p. 10 **Learning with Documents booklet,** pp. 10, 44, 77 **Section Reading Support Transparencies**
3 The Origins of American Politics 1. Find out how the issue of liberty versus order divided Americans in the 1790s. 2. See what controversies marked the presidency of John Adams. 3. Discover the significance of the election of 1800. 4. Learn how Jefferson's administration changed the nation. 5. Read about the importance of the War of 1812. **TEKS** 8(B), 19(A), 19(B), 24(A), 24(G), 25(B)	Teaching Resources **Units 1/2 booklet** • Section 3 Quiz, p. 16 **Learning Styles Lesson Plans booklet,** pp. 14–15	**Guided Reading and Review booklet,** pp. 24–28 **Guide to the Essentials,** p. 11 **Learning with Documents booklet,** pp. 11, 45, 78 **Skills for Life booklet,** pp. 6–8 **Section Reading Support Transparencies**

Enrichment/Pre-AP

Prentice Hall United States History Video Collection™
www.phschool.com
- Section Activities, Virtual Field Trip, Chapter Activities, Current Events Online

Biography, Literature, and Comparing Primary Sources booklet, pp. 10, 43, 103–104
American History Block Scheduling Support
Historical Outline Map Book, pp. 21, 22, 23, 24
Sounds of an Era Audio CD
Exploring Primary Sources in U.S. History CD-ROM

Biography, Literature, and Comparing Primary Sources booklet, pp. 10, 44, 105
American History Block Scheduling Support
Nystrom *Atlas of Our Country*, pp. 20–21
Historical Outline Map Book, p. 28
Sounds of an Era Audio CD
Exploring Primary Sources in U.S. History CD-ROM

Biography, Literature, and Comparing Primary Sources booklet, pp. 11, 45–46, 107
American History Block Scheduling Support
Nystrom *Atlas of Our Country*, pp. 20–21
Historical Outline Map Book, pp. 29–30, 31–32
Sounds of an Era Audio CD
Exploring Primary Sources in U.S. History CD-ROM
American Pathways Thematic Posters

Assessment

Core Assessment
ExamView® Test Bank, Ch. 2
ExamView® Test Bank CD-ROM, Ch. 2

Standardized Test Preparation
Diagnose and Prescribe
Diagnostic Tests for High School Social Studies Skills

Review and Reteach
Review Book for U.S. History

Practice and Assess
Test-taking Strategies With Transparencies
Test-taking Strategies Posters
Test Prep Book for U.S. History
Alternative Assessment Handbook
Document-Based Assessment

Teaching Resources
Units 1/2 booklet
- Section Quizzes, pp. 14–16
- Chapter Tests, pp. 17, 20

www.phschool.com Ch. 2 Self-Test

AmericanHeritage Resources

From the Archives of American Heritage®, pp. 43, 92, 93, 97
AmericanHeritage® My Brush with History™ Videotapes
www.americanheritage.com

Don't miss the exclusive interactive version of this textbook on the Web and on CD-ROM.

Chapter 2

Balancing Liberty and Order

(1753–1820)

INTRODUCING THE CHAPTER

The American Revolution was more than a war for independence. The struggle reflected the development of a unique American identity that was fueled by colonists' personal definitions of democracy and equality. After the war, a group of powerful men succeeded in writing and winning approval of the federal Constitution and in establishing a strong central government. In the years following ratification of the Constitution, American leaders fought passionately over the formation of the new government.

TIME LINE ACTIVITY

To provide students with practice in using the time line, ask questions such as these:

1. In what year did the Seven Years' War begin? *(1756)*
2. Where and in what year did the Constitutional Convention take place? *(In Philadelphia, in 1787)*
3. What action caused the size of the nation to double in 1803? *(The Louisiana Purchase)*

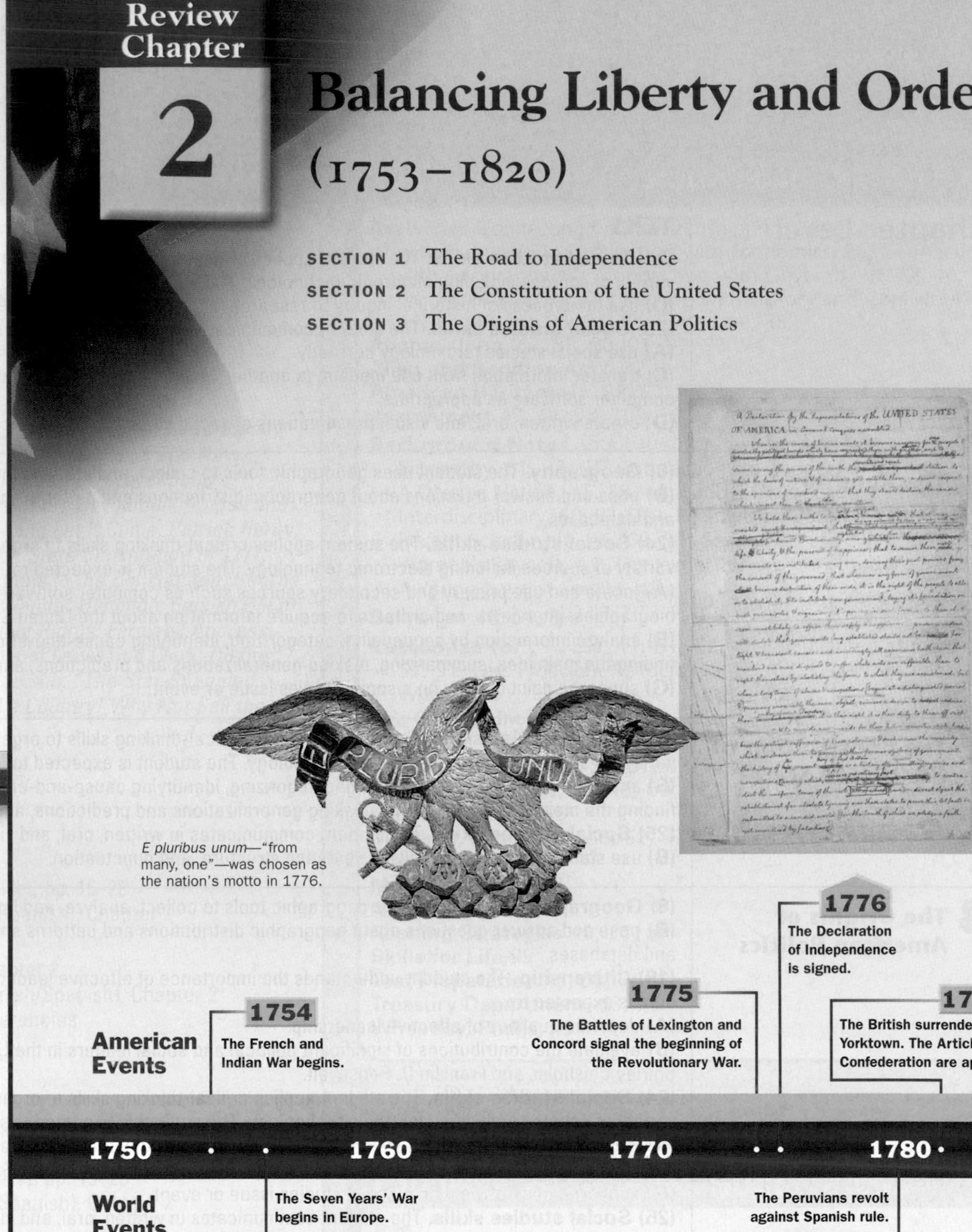

Review Chapter 2

Balancing Liberty and Order

(1753–1820)

E pluribus unum—"from many, one"—was chosen as the nation's motto in 1776.

E PLURIBUS UNUM
American Events
1754 The French and Indian War begins.
1775 The Battles of Lexington and Concord signal the beginning of the Revolutionary War.
1776 The Declaration of Independence is signed.
1781 The British surrender at Yorktown. The Articles of Confederation are approved.
1750
1760
1770
1780
World Events
1756 The Seven Years' War begins in Europe.
1780 The Peruvians revolt against Spanish rule.

eTeach

Be sure to check out this month's online discussion with a Master Teacher. Go to **www.phschool.com**.

RESOURCE DIRECTORY

Teaching Resources

Pacing Charts booklet
Block Scheduling booklet, pp. 15–16
Units 1/2 booklet
- Chapter Summary, p. 13

Technology

Guided Reading Audiotapes (English/Spanish), Ch. 2
Student Edition on Audio CD, Ch. 2
Prentice Hall United States History Video Collection™ Volume 4, *The American Revolution*
Prentice Hall Presentation Pro® CD-ROM
Resource Pro® CD-ROM
Social Studies Skills Tutor CD-ROM
Companion Web site, www.phschool.com

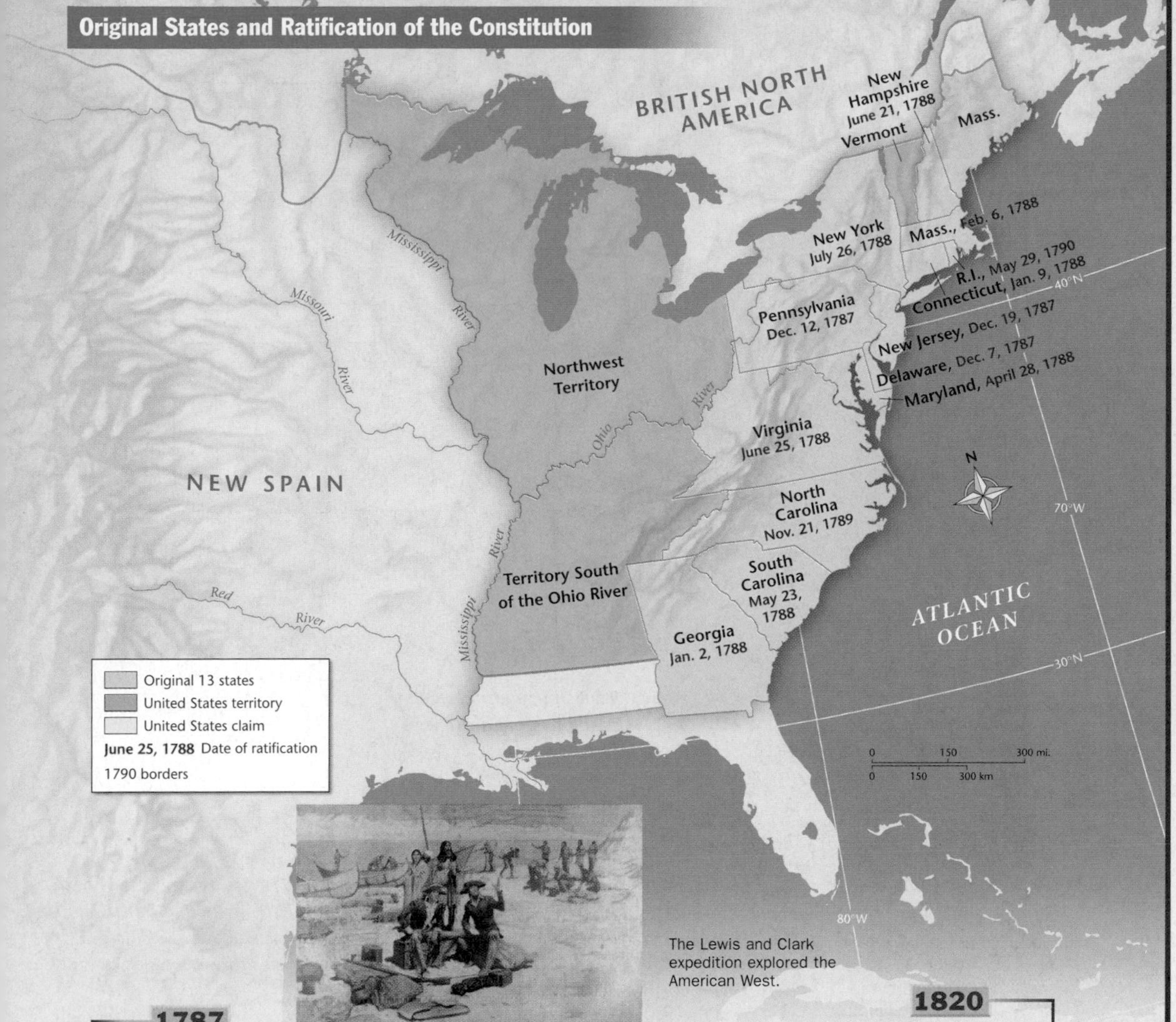

Original States and Ratification of the Constitution

BRITISH NORTH AMERICA

New Hampshire June 21, 1788

Vermont

Mass.

New York July 26, 1788

Mass., Feb. 6, 1788

R.I., May 29, 1790

Connecticut, Jan. 9, 1788

Pennsylvania Dec. 12, 1787

New Jersey, Dec. 19, 1787

Delaware, Dec. 7, 1787

Maryland, April 28, 1788

Northwest Territory

Virginia June 25, 1788

North Carolina Nov. 21, 1789

South Carolina May 23, 1788

Georgia Jan. 2, 1788

Territory South of the Ohio River

NEW SPAIN

ATLANTIC OCEAN

Mississippi River, Missouri River, Ohio River, Red River

40°N, 30°N, 70°W, 80°W

0 150 300 mi.

0 150 300 km

Original 13 states

United States territory

United States claim

June 25, 1788 Date of ratification

1790 borders

The Lewis and Clark expedition explored the American West.

1787 The Constitutional Convention meets in Philadelphia and draws up the Constitution of the United States.

1791 Ten amendments, which will become known as the Bill of Rights, are added to the Constitution.

1803 The Louisiana Purchase doubles the size of the nation.

1812 The War of 1812 between the United States and Britain begins.

1820 Congress agrees to the Missouri Compromise, which keeps the balance of free and slave states and prohibits slavery north of 36°30′ N latitude.

George Washington 1789–1797 | John Adams 1797–1801 | Thomas Jefferson 1801–1809 | James Madison 1809–1817 | James Monroe 1817–1825

1790 | 1800 | 1810 | 1820

1789 The French Revolution begins.

1804 Haiti wins independence from France.

Original States and Ratification of the Constitution

Activating Prior Knowledge Which of the original states was the last to ratify the Constitution? *(Rhode Island)*

Previewing Ask students why they think some states ratified the Constitution later than others did. *(Many people feared that the Constitution granted the President king-like powers and wished to prevent the government from becoming a monarchy by prolonging the ratification process.)*

BACKGROUND
About the Pictures

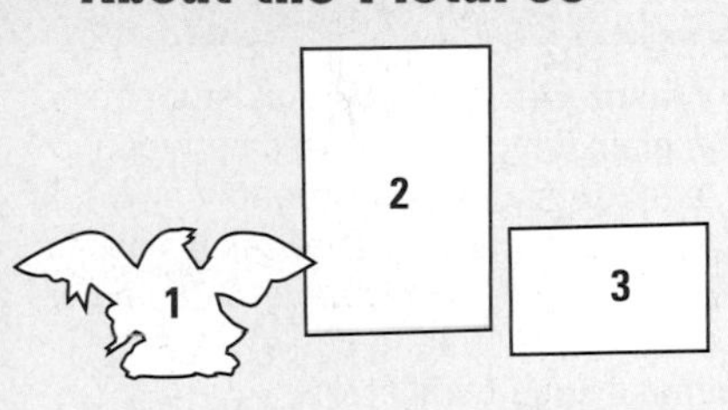

1. Pierre du Simitierre, a consultant and artist, recommended this motto at the first Great Seal Committee.
2. Primarily written by Thomas Jefferson, the Declaration of Independence was signed by 56 men from the 13 original colonies.
3. Though Meriwether Lewis and William Clark are widely acknowledged for their exploits in the West, it is estimated that the expedition included about 40 people.

BIBLIOGRAPHY

For the Teacher

Boorstin, D. ***The Lost World of Thomas Jefferson.*** University of Chicago Press, 1993. (An acclaimed re-creation of the Jeffersonian world view.)

Grant, Linda. ***Founding Mothers: Women in America in the Revolutionary Era.*** Houghton Mifflin, 1975. (Narrative accounts of women's contributions during the revolutionary period.)

Lessons on the Federalist Papers: Supplement to High School Courses in American History, Government and Civics. Organization of American Historians, 1987. (Core concepts from ***The Federalist.***)

For the Student

Hamilton, Alexander, et al. ***The Federalist.*** Mentor, 1999. (Eighty-five letters written in support of the Constitution at the time of its creation. One of the most important books in American history.)

Jefferson, Thomas. ***The Portable Thomas Jefferson.*** Viking, 1997. (Essential documents penned by one of this country's most influential leaders.)

Legguth, A. J. ***Patriots: The Men Who Started the American Revolution.*** Simon & Schuster, 1988. (Well-illustrated biographical sketches of some of the most important figures of the Revolution.)

Don't miss the exclusive interactive version of this textbook on the Web and on CD-ROM.

Section Objectives

1. Discover the importance of the French and Indian War.
2. See what issues led to the Revolution.
3. Find out why the shots fired at Lexington and Concord were "heard round the world."
4. Study the political ideas that led to the Declaration of Independence.
5. Learn how colonists fought for and won independence.

Bellringer

Warm-Up Activity Ask students to explain why relationships between teenagers and their parents can be difficult. Tell students this was similar to the relationship between the colonies and Britain. What types of issues cause such conflict?

Activating Prior Knowledge Can students name some key events or figures in the American Revolution? Ask them if they know the significance of the following people: Paul Revere, Patrick Henry, Thomas Paine.

Reading Strategy

As students read this section, have them create an outline of the major events leading to the outbreak of the Revolutionary War.

Section 1 The Road to Independence

READING FOCUS

- What was the importance of the French and Indian War?
- What issues led to the Revolution?
- Why were the shots fired at Lexington and Concord "heard round the world"?
- What political ideas led to the Declaration of Independence?
- How did the colonists fight for and win independence?

MAIN IDEA

Ideas about equality and self-government, as well as grievances against the British, led to the outbreak of the Revolutionary War, in which the American colonies won their independence from Britain.

KEY TERMS

French and Indian War
boycott
Boston Massacre
First Continental Congress
Battles of Lexington and Concord
Revolutionary War
Declaration of Independence
patriotism

TAKING NOTES

Copy the flowchart below. As you read, fill in the ideas and events that led to the American colonists declaring and winning their independence.

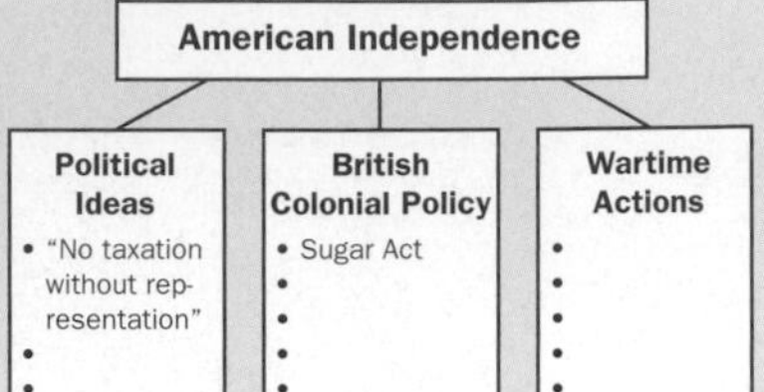

Setting the Scene

> *Listen, my children, and you shall hear*
> *Of the midnight ride of Paul Revere,*
> *On the eighteenth of April, in Seventy-Five;*
> *Hardly a man is now alive*
> *Who remembers that famous day and year. . . .*
>
> —Henry Wadsworth Longfellow, "Paul Revere's Ride"

VIEWING FINE ART This depiction of Paul Revere's famous ride was done in the naïve, or folk art, style. **Drawing Inferences** *What idea do you think the artist wanted to convey?*

Through Longfellow's famous poem, generations of young Americans have learned about the start of this nation's struggle for independence. On that night of April 18, 1775, Revere and other colonists warned the Massachusetts countryside of the approach of British soldiers. The next morning, colonial militia fought the British at Lexington and Concord.

The confrontations at Lexington and Concord were indeed the beginning of the Revolutionary War. Yet they also marked an ending—the end of a series of disagreements that drove Britain and its colonies further and further apart. For more than a decade, the two sides had argued over issues related to taxation and trade. Strangely, these issues arose in part from a tremendous victory for Britain and the colonies over a common enemy: France.

The French and Indian War

The rivalry among European nations for control of North America began soon after they started to explore and colonize the continent. While English colonists built their settlements along the eastern seacoast during the 1600s, the French explored farther inland—and claimed a vast region stretching all the way to the Rocky Mountains. Conflict erupted because the English claimed some of this territory also. An unsuccessful attempt by the English colonists of Virginia to take a French fort at the forks of the Ohio River in 1754 marked the beginning

Resource Directory

Teaching Resources

Learning Styles Lesson Plans booklet, pp. 10–11
Guided Reading and Review booklet, pp. 15–19
Biography, Literature, and Comparing Primary Sources booklet (Literature) *Laying Siege to Quebec,* p. 43
Learning with Documents booklet (Primary Source Activity) *Braddock's Defeat,* p. 9

Other Print Resources

Historical Outline Map Book *The French and Indian War,* p. 21

Technology

Section Reading Support Transparencies
Guided Reading Audiotapes (English/Spanish), Ch. 2
Student Edition on Audio CD, Ch. 2
Color Transparencies *Historical Maps,* A6
Prentice Hall Presentation Pro® CD-ROM, Ch. 2
Companion Web site, www.phschool.com

Caption Answers

Viewing Fine Art Answers will vary, but might mention that the illustration conveys a sense of the urgency of Revere's mission.

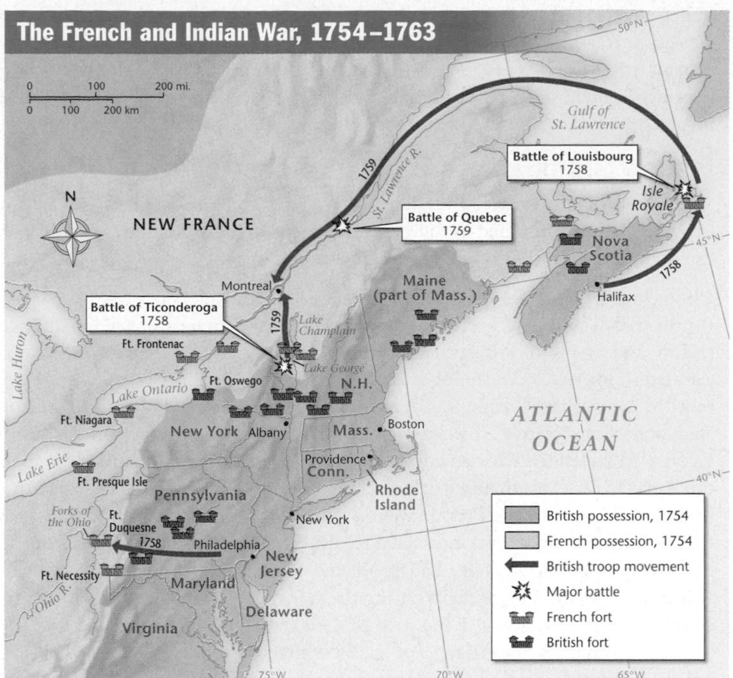

MAP SKILLS The three main thrusts of British strategy are shown here. **Movement** *How did waterways play a role in British strategy?*

of the **French and Indian War,** so-called because the British and their American colonists fought against the French and their Indian allies.

In June 1754, delegates from seven English colonies convened at Albany, New York, to work out a unified war effort in the northern colonies. Benjamin Franklin, a Pennsylvania delegate, offered an ambitious plan for a permanent union of the colonies. Named the Albany Plan of Union, it called for a grand council of delegates from each colony, elected by their colonial legislatures. Although the colonies rejected the plan, it did provide a model for the later government of the United States.

At first the war went poorly for the British. In 1758, however, British troops began to overwhelm French and Indian forces, and the French retreated into New France, or present-day Canada. The Iroquois, who had cleverly been playing each side against the other, now decided that the French cause was hopeless, and switched their support to the British.

In 1759, the British invaded New France. Their capture of Quebec proved to be the turning point of the war and led to more British victories in New France. In 1763, representatives of Great Britain, France, and France's ally Spain signed the Treaty of Paris, which ended the French and Indian War. In the treaty, France turned New France over to Britain and surrendered its claim to all lands east of the Mississippi River. The only exception was the city of New Orleans, which France had given to Spain in a secret treaty the year before. The British returned Cuba, captured during the war, to Spain in exchange for Florida.

Despite the victory, the French and Indian War seriously strained relations between Britain and the American colonists. The British thought the colonists did not provide enough support for the long and costly war that Britain had fought to protect them. For their part, the colonists were shocked by the weakness of British

READING CHECK
List the important events of the French and Indian War.

LESSON PLAN

Focus Explain that the French and Indian War showed the colonists that they had their own, distinctly American identity. Ask students to describe that identity. The French and Indian War left Great Britain in debt, which led to an increase in taxes on the colonists. This move was fiercely fought and eventually led to the War for Independence. Many leaders came forward from amongst the colonists. These leaders spoke eloquently of freedom and an American identity.

Instruct Review the growing change in the relationship between the colonists and the British, beginning with the French and Indian War and continuing through the many acts of taxation. Ask why the passage of the Stamp Act was significant. You might want to discuss how the ideas that fueled the War for Independence also helped create a new society.

Assess/Reteach Ask students to reflect on the ways that the beliefs expressed in the Declaration of Independence—that people were born equal and could rule themselves—took a passionate hold on colonial thinking, and ultimately led to the American Revolution.

READING CHECK
1754: unsuccessful attempt by English colonists of Virginia to take a French fort on the Ohio River; 1758: British troops began to overwhelm French and Indian forces, French retreated into Canada, Iroquois switched their support to the British; 1759: British invaded Canada, captured Quebec, the turning point in the war; 1763: Treaty of Paris was signed, ending the war.

CUSTOMIZE FOR ...

ESL

Have students make a list of unfamiliar words and phrases as they read Section 1. Then divide students into groups to help decipher the words on each other's lists. Help them use context clues and dictionaries to find the meaning of words and phrases with which they are having trouble.

CAPTION ANSWERS

Map Skills The British used waterways as routes of invasion into New France (Canada): The Atlantic Ocean toward Isle Royale; the Gulf of St. Lawrence and the St. Lawrence River to Quebec and Montreal; and lakes George and Champlain to Montreal.

ACTIVITY
Connecting with History and Conflict

This activity may take place over several class periods: Divide the class into groups of six to eight students. In order to show how the French and Indian War brought the British and the colonists into contact with one another, have students enact a discussion in a tavern on a given topic from the viewpoint of either British soldiers or colonists. Possible topics include life in the colonies, British mercantile policy, or the French and Indian War. **(Verbal/Linguistic)**

BACKGROUND
Art History

The 1759 capture of Quebec inspired Benjamin West's 1771 painting *The Death of General Wolfe.* While European soldiers were usually painted in Roman togas and armor, West's subjects wore contemporary British uniforms, and the artist included a pensive Indian crouching at Wolfe's feet. King George III complained, but West replied that modern clothing was an appropriate choice "in a region of the world unknown to the Greeks and Romans."

ACTIVITY
Connecting with Government

To demonstrate the British policy of forcing the colonists to share in the cost of running the colonies (and the colonists' reaction to it), have students list their most cherished privileges at home. Responses may include using the phone, driving the family car, watching TV, and so on. Then announce that students will be taxed for such privileges. Divide the class into two groups—parents (Tories) and students (colonists). Have the groups informally debate this new taxation policy. **(Verbal/Linguistic)**

military tactics. They demanded to be led by colonial officers, which the British viewed as treason. Moreover, now that the French no longer held present-day Canada or the area west of the Appalachian Mountains, the colonists saw no reason why they should not expand and prosper on their own, without British help. These feelings would deepen the split between Britain and its colonies.

Issues Leading to the Revolution

At the end of the French and Indian War, British colonists believed they had every right to be regarded as full-fledged citizens of a great empire. The British, however, had no intention of treating their colonists as equals.

Changing British Policy As the French and Indian War drew to a close, British traders and land speculators showed increased interest in the Great Lakes region and the Ohio River valley. Native Americans in these areas became alarmed, and in 1763 a number of Indian peoples in the Great Lakes region rebelled against the British. Europeans named the uprising Pontiac's Rebellion, after one of the Native American leaders. To help restore peace, Britain's King George III issued the Proclamation of 1763. This order closed the region west of the Appalachian Mountains to all settlement by colonists. The area, which had just been given up by the French, was placed under the control of the British military. Nevertheless, colonists continued to move west into the forbidden territory.

The British, meanwhile, had problems of their own—financial problems. Britain had acquired huge debts during the war, and Parliament now felt that the colonists should pay some of the costs of their own government and defense.

The passage of the Sugar Act in 1764 marked the start of a new British policy designed to raise more income from the colonies. To enforce this tax and others, Parliament issued a flurry of rules. For example, smuggling cases were now to be tried in British, rather than colonial, courts. Under British law, such cases were decided by a judge alone, not by a jury. In addition, judges received a commission on all illegal cargoes and fines, which encouraged them to find

MAP SKILLS The French and Indian War drastically changed the political map and political future of North America. **Regions** *How did the relative size of European land claims in North America change between 1754 and 1763?*

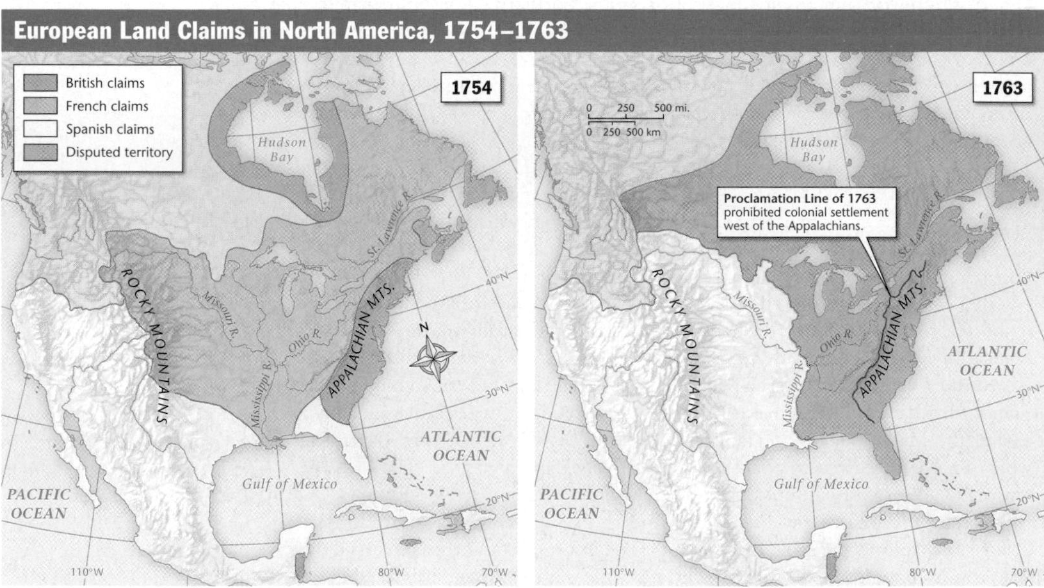

RESOURCE DIRECTORY

Teaching Resources

Learning with Documents booklet (Visual Learning Activity) *Boycotting Tea,* p. 43

Other Print Resources

Historical Outline Map Book *North America in 1763,* p. 22

Technology

RESOURCE PRO® **Biography** *Pontiac,* found on Resource Pro, profiles the chief of the Ottawa who headed a Native American confederation to stop the spread of the British colonies.

RESOURCE PRO® **Visual Learning Activity** *The American Rattlesnake,* found on Resource Pro, uses a cartoon depicting the rebellious colonies as a rattlesnake to emphasize the seriousness and strength of the colonists' position.

Exploring Primary Sources in U.S. History CD-ROM *The Bloody Massacre, 1770*

CAPTION ANSWERS

Map Skills British territory got much larger, the French lost a great deal of territory, including Canada, and Spanish territory decreased overall.

accused smugglers guilty. The Quartering Act of 1765 required the colonies to provide housing and supplies for the British troops who remained in America after the French and Indian War. Although colonists complained about these British changes, most went along with them.

The Stamp Act Crisis In March 1765, the British Parliament passed the Stamp Act. This law placed a tax on newspapers, legal documents, and most other printed materials. An official government stamp had to appear on these materials to show the tax had been paid. The Stamp Act marked the first time that the British government had taxed the colonists for the clear purpose of raising money. While the Sugar Act was really a way to raise money, too, it had been presented to the American colonists as a way to regulate trade. The colonists' reaction against the Stamp Act was widespread and extreme.

In October 1765, delegates from nine colonies held what became known as the Stamp Act Congress. The main organizer of the meeting was James Otis of Massachusetts. As early as 1761, Otis had claimed that Britain had no right to force laws on the colonies because the colonists had no representatives in the British Parliament. In 1764, he had used the same "no taxation without representation" argument to protest the Sugar Act. Otis and other delegates now made this argument again in petitions, or letters, they sent to the king and Parliament. Colonists should have the same rights and liberties that the people of Great Britain enjoyed, the delegates argued.

In addition, colonial merchants and others organized a **boycott** of British goods. (A boycott is a refusal to buy certain products or use certain services.) Groups known as the Sons of Liberty and the Daughters of Liberty sprang up to enforce the boycott and to resist British policies in other ways. By November 1765, when the Stamp Act was to take effect, most stamp distributors had resigned or fled, leaving no one to sell the stamps. In Britain, merchants also protested as the colonists' boycott threatened their profitable trade with America. Parliament repealed the Stamp Act in March 1766.

Rising Tensions in the Colonies The colonists celebrated wildly when news arrived that the Stamp Act had been repealed. Yet on the very day the Stamp Act was abolished, Parliament passed the Declaratory Act. This measure stated that Parliament had the authority to make laws that applied to the colonists "in all cases whatsoever."

In 1767, Parliament reasserted this authority by passing the Townshend Acts, which placed duties on certain imported goods, including glass and tea. The protests and violence began again. Trade duties were just as unacceptable to the colonists as direct taxes. Either way, the colonists were being taxed without their consent. Either way, Britain would use this money for the salaries of royal governors in America, who then would not have to turn to the colonial legislatures for their pay. This change would weaken the legislatures and undermine self-government in the colonies.

The growing hostility between the colonists and the British soon erupted into violence. In Boston, on the evening of March 5, 1770, an unruly crowd threatened a squad of British soldiers. The soldiers opened fire, leaving an African American named Crispus Attucks and four other colonists dead or dying in the snow. The incident, which became known as the **Boston Massacre,** added to an already tense situation.

Colonists who poured their tea from this pot demonstrated their resistance to the Stamp Act.

VIEWING HISTORY Paul Revere created this engraving of the Boston Massacre to arouse anger toward the British. **Drawing Inferences** *(a) Why do you think Revere depicted this aspect of the incident? (b) What part of the event might a British artist have chosen? Explain your reasoning.*

From the Archives of
AmericanHeritage®

The *Gaspée* Incident

On June 9, 1772, the British revenue schooner *Gaspée* ran aground in Rhode Island's Narragansett Bay while chasing a suspected smuggler. Word quickly spread among the merchants, sailors, and smugglers of nearby Providence, who, like all Rhode Islanders, hated anything to do with duties and tariffs. That evening John Brown, a wealthy merchant, rounded up about a hundred men. Shortly after midnight they piled into longboats and rowed out to the *Gaspée*. The Providence men boarded the ship and set it on fire. When the king decreed that anyone implicated in the attack would be taken to Britain for trial, rage over this violation of the right to a trial by one's peers spread through all the colonies. In March 1773 Virginia's House of Burgesses, angered over the flagrant attack upon "American liberty," established the first Committee of Correspondence. Similar committees sprang up in the other colonies to circulate information and coordinate responses. The *Gaspée* incident brought America another step closer to open revolt. Source: Frederic D. Schwarz, "The Time Machine," *American Heritage®* magazine, May/June 1997.

CUSTOMIZE FOR ...

Less Proficient Readers

Tell students that by 1770, growing numbers of Americans were convinced that British politicians were engaged in nothing less than a deliberate plot to rob them of their personal independence through taxation. As they read, students should list and briefly describe specific British actions that led so many Americans to feel this way.

Caption Answers

Viewing History (a) Possible answer: To show the British as evil, firing on civilians. The civilians appear to be unarmed and helpless. (b) Possible answer: A British artist might have shown the mob attacking and taunting the British soldiers in order to imply that the British exercised restraint for as long as possible.

ACTIVITY
Connecting with History and Conflict

Have students reenact a session of the First Continental Congress. Tell students to discuss which colonies they will represent. Try to have each colony represented by at least one student. Then have students prepare for the session by thinking and reading about some of the issues that were raised at the gathering. **(Verbal/Linguistic)**

BACKGROUND
Women's Boycott

Women played a central role in the movement to boycott British goods. Instead of tea, Patriot women served coffee and herbal brews. Refusing to buy British cotton, they dressed themselves and their families in homespun. At times women took more direct action. One Boston man described a "Female Riot" in which a large mob of women attacked a merchant who was overcharging for coffee, "and demanded the Keys to his Store, which he refusing to deliver, they immediately placed him in a Cart and threatened to Cart him out of Town."

Focus on CITIZENSHIP

"Remember the Ladies" Women were shut out of public debate in the 1700s, even when the subject of debate was how to create a free nation. Yet Abigail Adams made sure her voice was heard. To her husband, John, a member of the Continental Congress and later President of the United States, Abigail wrote in March 1776: "I long to hear that you have declared an independency—and by the way in the new Code of Laws which I suppose it will be necessary for you to make I desire you would Remember the Ladies, and be more generous and favorable to them than your ancestors. Do not put such unlimited power into the hands of the Husbands. Remember all Men would be tyrants if they could."

Abigail did not suggest that women be allowed to vote, an idea that was far too radical for that era. Instead, she urged that women be given greater opportunities for education.

Soon after the Boston Massacre, Parliament canceled the Townshend taxes. It kept only the duty on tea as a reminder of its authority over the colonies. While life in the colonies generally quieted down, some colonists continued to organize. In 1772, Samuel Adams, James Otis, and other Bostonians formed a Committee of Correspondence to coordinate resistance throughout the colonies. By 1774, nearly all the colonies had such committees.

In May 1773, Parliament passed the Tea Act, which gave the British East India Company the right to sell its tea in America without paying the normal taxes. Colonists had been smuggling much of their tea in order to avoid paying these taxes. The Tea Act would make the British East India Company's tea even less expensive than smuggled tea, thereby driving the American tea merchants out of business. Colonists, especially tea merchants, protested, and several colonial port cities refused to let ships carrying the tea dock in their harbors. On the night of December 16, 1773, a group of colonists disguised as Indians boarded three tea ships in Boston and threw the tea into the harbor. This act of protest became known as the Boston Tea Party.

To punish Boston and all of Massachusetts, in the spring of 1774, Parliament passed a series of harsh measures known as the Coercive Acts. The colonists labeled these laws the Intolerable Acts.

The First Continental Congress Committees of Correspondence in several colonies called for a meeting to plan a united response to the Intolerable Acts. On September 5, 1774, the **First Continental Congress** convened in Philadelphia. The 56 delegates (including George Washington, Patrick Henry, Samuel Adams, and John Jay) came from every colony but Georgia, and they had a wide range of viewpoints. The First Continental Congress agreed to boycott English goods, and called on the people of all the English colonies to arm themselves and form militias. At the same time, the delegates made a direct appeal to the king:

KEY DOCUMENTS

> *"The foundation of English liberty, and of all free government, is a right of the people to participate in their legislative council: and as the English colonists are not represented, and . . . cannot properly be represented in the British parliament, they are entitled to a free and exclusive power of legislation in their several provincial legislatures, where their right of representation can alone be preserved."*
>
> —Declaration and Resolves of the First Continental Congress, 1774

On October 26, the Congress ended, though its members vowed to meet again in the spring if the crisis was not resolved. However, George III remained stubborn and firm. On November 18, he wrote, "The New England colonies are in a state of rebellion, blows must decide."

The Shot Heard Round the World

The Americans that King George labeled "rebels" (they called themselves *Patriots*) followed the advice of the First Continental Congress. Massachusetts Patriots formed militias and began to gather guns and ammunition. A major stockpile of weapons was stored in Concord, a town about 20 miles from Boston.

Late at night on April 18, 1775, some 800 British troops moved out of Boston and marched toward Concord with orders to seize these supplies.

RESOURCE DIRECTORY

Teaching Resources

Learning with Documents booklet (Key Documents) *Patrick Henry, Speech to the Virginia Provincial Convention,* p. 76

Other Print Resources

American History Block Scheduling Support *To Arms! The Revolution Begins,* found in the Forging a New Nation folder.

Historical Outline Map Book *Lexington and Concord,* p. 23

Technology

Color Transparencies *Historical Maps,* A7

Sounds of an Era Audio CD *Patrick Henry; Battle of Lexington and Concord*

Exploring Primary Sources in U.S. History CD-ROM *Common Sense, Thomas Paine; The New American Man, Michel-Guillaume Jean de Crevecoeur; Correspondence on the Progress of the Revolution, Abigail and John Adams; War Is Inevitable—and Let It Come!, Patrick Henry*

RESOURCE PRO® **Literature Activity** *Common Sense* uses excerpts from Thomas Paine's famous pamphlet.

Boston Patriots learned of the plan and sent Paul Revere, William Dawes, and Dr. Samuel Prescott on horseback through the countryside to alert Patriot leaders. When the main British force reached Lexington, just east of Concord, they encountered 70 armed militia, known as minutemen, blocking their path on the village green. Someone—no one knows who—fired a shot. The troops fired a volley into the militia. Within minutes, eight Americans lay dead on the green and another ten were wounded. The British then marched on to Concord, where they destroyed some of the militia's supplies.

As the British troops returned to Boston, thousands of Patriots gathered along the road to shoot at them from behind trees and stone walls. When the **Battles of Lexington and Concord** were over, what had seemed an easy British victory at dawn had turned into a costly defeat. More than one fourth of the British soldiers had been killed or wounded. The **Revolutionary War,** which became a war for American independence from Britain, had begun.

Just days before this fateful clash, Patrick Henry had warned his fellow Virginians to prepare for what was soon to come:

> "*Gentlemen may cry, 'Peace! Peace!'—but there is no peace. . . . The next gale that sweeps from the north will bring to our ears the clash of resounding arms! . . . Is life so dear, or peace so sweet, as to be purchased at the price of chains and slavery? Forbid it, Almighty God! I know not what course others may take; but as for me, give me liberty or give me death!*"
>
> —Patrick Henry

Ralph Waldo Emerson noted the significance of the Battles of Lexington and Concord in his famous poem "Concord Hymn": "Here once the embattled farmers stood, / And fired the shot heard round the world." The American Revolution would prove momentous not just for the participants but for the entire world.

Revolutionary Ideas

On one level, the American Revolution was a struggle for power between the American colonists and Great Britain over who would rule the colonies. However, the Revolution was also a struggle over ideas. The colonists were rethinking the proper relationship between citizens and their government.

Common Sense Both levels of the Revolution were addressed in Thomas Paine's pamphlet *Common Sense,* which appeared in Philadelphia in January 1776. Paine's message to the colonists was blunt:

> KEY DOCUMENTS "*The period of debate is closed. Arms as the last resource decide the contest. . . . Every thing that is right or natural pleads for separation. The blood of the slain, the weeping voice of nature cries, 'TIS TIME TO PART.*"
>
> —*Common Sense*, 1776

Within a year some 25 editions of *Common Sense* were sold. The pamphlet convinced many readers, including those who had favored a peaceful settlement of differences with Britain, to support a complete break instead.

The Declaration of Independence *Common Sense* appeared while the Second Continental Congress was meeting in Philadelphia. Delegates included Benjamin Franklin, John Hancock, and Thomas Jefferson. In June 1776, the

This statue at the Old North Bridge in Concord, Massachusetts, honors the minutemen—those "embattled farmers" who "fired the shot heard round the world."

ACTIVITY
Connecting with Citizenship

Invite students to hold an informal debate as it might have occurred in the 1770s over the question of whether or not people are capable of self-rule. Suggest that students assume the roles of an artisan, farmer, African American, woman, gentleman member of the "leisure" class, British supporter, or other individual from the revolutionary period. Have students research to prepare for their role in the debate. **(Verbal/Linguistic)**

BACKGROUND
A Diverse Nation

African American writer and poet Phillis Wheatley was brought to Boston on a slave ship in 1761 while still a child. A prodigy, she studied English, Latin, the Bible, and poetry; she published her first poem at the age of 14. Wheatley was a Patriot, admired by Washington, Franklin, and Hancock, and she wrote several poems on patriotic themes. Her only book of poems, however, *Poems on Various Subjects, Moral and Religious,* published in England in 1773, was decidedly apolitical.

TEST PREPARATION

Have students read the passage from *Common Sense* on this page and then answer the question below.

What does Thomas Paine mean when he writes "Arms as the last resource decide the contest"?

A Whichever side has more weapons will win the coming war.

(B) To resolve the situation with the British, it will eventually be necessary to fight.

C It will be necessary for the Patriots to obtain guns.

D The British are not listening to the colonists.

ACTIVITY
Connecting with Government

Have small groups of students discuss some of the concepts behind the Declaration of Independence. Encourage students to consider Jefferson's idea that people have the right to change or overthrow the government if it doesn't serve their best interests. Tell students also to discuss the idea that ordinary citizens have a strong voice in their government. Have students think about how this notion differs from the governments of other countries during the eighteenth century. **(Verbal/Linguistic)**

BACKGROUND
Recent Scholarship

The concept of revolution is often associated with violence, instability, and repression. But as Gordon S. Wood demonstrates in his Pulitzer Prize–winning *The Radicalism of the American Revolution,* the American Revolution transformed a monarchical society into the democratic, capitalist society in which we now live. The most radical thing about it was the creation of a nation whose success depended not on the judgments of kings and aristocrats, but on the active participation of millions of ordinary citizens. Wood's book is a reminder of the revolutionary significance of these three simple words: "We the People."

Congress decided it was time for the colonies to cut their ties with Britain. They appointed a committee to prepare a statement of the reasons for the separation—a **Declaration of Independence**—and chose Thomas Jefferson to draft it. (See the full text of the Declaration on the pages following this section.)

Jefferson's political ideas had been influenced by the Enlightenment, an eighteenth-century movement that emphasized science and reason as the keys to improving society. He also drew ideas from earlier political thinkers, such as the Englishman John Locke. Locke believed that people had natural rights—rights that belonged to them simply because they were human, not because kings or governments had granted them these rights. According to Locke's theory, people formed governments to protect their natural rights. If a government failed to act in the best interests of the people it governed, the people had the right to revolt and replace the government with a new one.

In the Declaration, Jefferson also stated that all people have inalienable rights, and that they have a right to change or overthrow a government that does not serve their best interests. He then listed the wrongs, or "repeated injuries," the colonists believed had been committed by the British king in an effort to establish "an absolute Tyranny." Therefore, Jefferson concluded, "these United Colonies are, and of Right ought to be Free and Independent States."

On July 4, the date now celebrated as Independence Day, delegates from 12 colonies approved the Declaration. Jefferson's document did much more than declare a nation's independence. It also defined the basic principles on which American government and society would rest. The United States would be a nation in which ordinary citizens would have a strong voice in their own government.

Fighting the Revolutionary War

By the time the Declaration of Independence was issued, Britain and the American colonists had been fighting for more than a year. The early military action centered in Boston.

VIEWING HISTORY This eight pence colonial note is from an engraving made by Paul Revere. **Drawing Conclusions** *Why do you think Revere shows the minuteman holding both a sword and the Magna Carta?*

The Siege of Boston Following the clashes at Lexington and Concord in April 1775, as many as 20,000 armed Patriots surrounded Boston and prevented the 6,000 British troops led by General Thomas Gage from quickly crushing the rebellion. The Patriots then turned their attention to gathering badly needed military equipment. In May, the Vermont militia's capture of Fort Ticonderoga in northern New York provided the Patriots with cannons and other supplies.

In June 1775, the Americans occupied two hills north of Boston. After two failed attempts, British troops succeeded in taking this strategic high ground. Their victory in the Battle of Bunker Hill came at a tremendous cost, however. Nearly 1,100 of 2,400 British soldiers had been killed or wounded. Patriot casualties—persons killed, wounded, or missing—amounted to around 400.

In January 1776, George Washington, whom the Congress had named commanding general of the Patriot forces, placed the cannons that had arrived from Fort Ticonderoga on Dorchester Heights. From there he could shell the British forces in Boston and the British ships in Boston harbor. The British could no longer defend their position and abandoned Boston in March 1776.

Strengths and Weaknesses Britain's main strength was its well-equipped, disciplined, and trained army. In addition, the British navy, the world's finest, provided support by transporting and landing troops and by protecting supply lines at sea. The British also received help from a number of sources. John Adams estimated that about one third of all colonists were Patriots; another third were Loyalists, or Tories as the Patriots called them; and the remaining third of

CAPTION ANSWERS

Viewing History Possible answer: The Magna Carta represents the rights of the colonists as English subjects; the sword shows that the colonists were willing to use arms to retain these rights.

RESOURCE DIRECTORY

Teaching Resources
Biography, Literature, and Comparing Primary Sources booklet (Comparing Primary Sources) *On Rule by the People,* pp. 103–104

Other Print Resources
Historical Outline Map Book *The Revolutionary War: An Overview,* p. 24

Technology
Color Transparencies *Fine Art,* E4
Exploring Primary Sources in U.S. History CD-ROM *Declaration of Independence*

Sounds of an Era Audio CD *The Declaration of Independence* (time: three minutes)

RESOURCE PRO® **Critical Thinking Activity** *Checking Consistency: Lexington and Concord,* found on Resource Pro, helps students apply this skill by comparing accounts of the battles.

RESOURCE PRO® **Primary Source Activity** *War Diary of Margaret Hill Morris,* found on Resource Pro, profiles a colonial woman's reactions to the advance of British troops.

Americans were neutral in the war. Although Adams's estimate of Loyalists was probably high, roughly 50,000 Loyalists fought with the British army. Some African Americans, largely in the South, also helped Great Britain. The British promised freedom to all slaves who served their cause. Additional help came from Native Americans. Most Indian nations believed an American victory would be harmful to their interests. In addition, the British hired about 30,000 mercenaries, or foreign soldiers who fight for pay. They were called "Hessians" because most of their officers came from the German province of Hesse.

The British also had their problems, however. Many British citizens resented paying taxes to fight the war and sympathized with the Americans. British troops had to fight in hostile territory, and British commanders resisted adapting their tactics to conditions in America.

British weaknesses were, of course, American strengths. Patriot forces were fighting on their own territory, and many of their officers were familiar with the tactics that had worked in the French and Indian War. Even with the British promise of freedom, more African Americans served the Patriot cause than supported the British. Washington's army had some all-black units, but more often, African Americans served in white units.

On the other hand, for much of the war, the Americans lacked a well-supplied, stable, and effective fighting force. The Continental Congress lacked the power to force states to provide troops, money, and supplies. Experienced soldiers, their time of service up, would simply head home. Washington never could be sure how many troops he would have.

Fighting in the North In the summer of 1776, British and German troops under General William Howe drove Washington's poorly trained and poorly equipped army out of New York City and into Pennsylvania. A young Patriot officer named Nathan Hale, who had volunteered to spy on the British, was

READING CHECK
What were British strengths during the Revolutionary War?

MAP SKILLS Fighting shifted south during the latter part of the war. **Movement** *How was General Washington able to trap the British at Yorktown?*

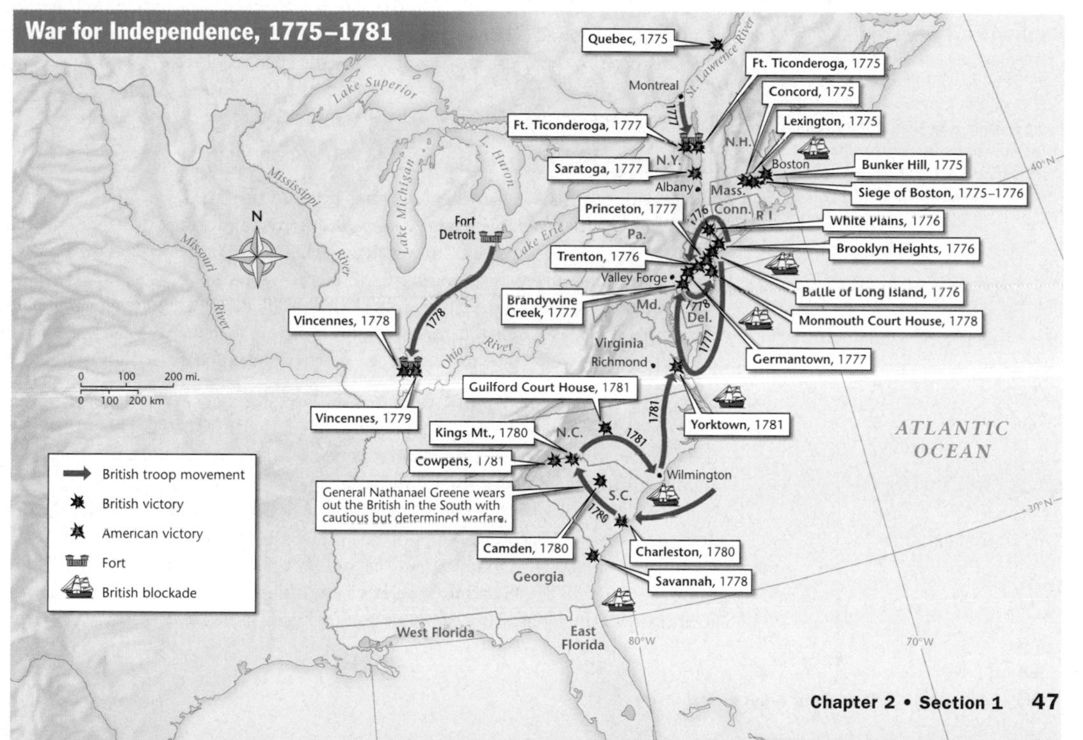

ACTIVITY
Connecting with History and Conflict

Tell students to debate the positions taken by colonists during the Revolutionary War. Assign one third of the class to represent the Patriots, one third to represent the Loyalists, and one third to remain neutral. Have students present their arguments clearly, stating why they maintain their position. **(Verbal/Linguistic)**

BACKGROUND
The Real Battle of Bunker Hill

The first major conflict of the Revolutionary War, and one that has become synonymous with the fight for American independence, is the Battle of Bunker Hill. The battle, however, was actually fought a few thousand feet away from Bunker Hill, at a mound known as Breed's Hill. Though colonial officers were ordered to fortify Bunker Hill against possible British attack in an effort to control Boston Harbor, they, for reasons still unknown, fortified Breed's Hill. Today, Breed's Hill is known as Bunker Hill, and the original site of Bunker Hill has homes built on it.

READING CHECK

In June 1775 Americans occupied two hills north of Boston. British troops finally captured these hills after two failed attempts, and with high casualties. When cannons arrived in 1776 from Fort Ticonderoga, Patriots were able to shell the British forces both in the city and in Boston harbor. This forced the British to abandon Boston.

CAPTION ANSWERS

Map Skills The British were trapped on a peninsula. Washington's force of American and French troops attacked Cornwallis by land while the French navy prevented British reinforcements from arriving by sea.

CUSTOMIZE FOR ...
Gifted and Talented

Have students analyze why the Revolution can be considered "a people's war." Why did so many different kinds of people become involved? What might African Americans have hoped to gain by participating in it? Why do you suppose many Americans sided with the British?

ACTIVITY

Connecting with History and Conflict

Have students research the role of either the Marquis de Lafayette or General von Steuben in the Revolutionary War. Ask them to review either man's background and his contribution to the war effort. **(Verbal/Linguistic)**

BACKGROUND

A Young Loyalist Speaks

The Journal of Nicholas Cresswell, 1774–1777 chronicles the travels of a young English Loyalist who said of Trenton: "Six weeks ago . . . [the Americans thought] all was gone, all was lost. But now the scale is turned and Washington's name is extolled to the clouds. Alexander, Pompey, and Hannibal were but pygmy Generals, in comparison with the magnanimous Washington. Poor General Howe is ridiculed in all companies and all my countrymen abused. I am obliged to hear this daily and dare not speak a word in their favor. It is the Hessians that has caused this, curse the scoundrel that first thought of sending them here."

caught. About to be hanged, he is said to have declared, "I only regret that I have but one life to lose for my country." Not all of Washington's soldiers felt that way, however. Many troops deserted, and by the winter of 1776, the entire Patriot cause seemed on the point of collapse.

Desperate times call for heroic measures, and Washington and his troops met the challenge. On Christmas night of 1776, Patriot troops were ferried across the ice-choked Delaware River in small boats. Early the next morning they surprised a force of Hessians in Trenton, New Jersey. Nearly the entire Hessian force was captured in the Battle of Trenton. The next month, a similar attack on nearby Princeton was also successful. These victories greatly boosted Patriot morale and convinced more Americans to support the Patriot cause.

In June 1777, General John Burgoyne led a British force from present-day Canada to northern New York in an effort to cut New England off from the rest of the colonies. At first, the Americans retreated, but at the same time the Continental Army and Patriot militias were assembling to confront the invaders. In mid-September the Americans won a series of victories around Saratoga, New York. Finally, on October 17, 1777, surrounded by a force now much larger than his own, Burgoyne surrendered his army. The Battle of Saratoga was the biggest American victory yet, and it marked the turning point of the war.

VIEWING FINE ART *George Washington Crossing the Delaware* by Emanuel Gottlieb Leutze is one of the most famous American paintings. **Analyzing Visual Information** *(a) How does the artist show the hardships of the crossing? (b) How does he indicate its heroism?*

Help From Abroad Meanwhile, the Americans had been seeking help from France, and the victory at Saratoga finally convinced the French that the Americans had a real chance of winning the war. The alliance with France, signed on February 6, 1778, meant not only more supplies, but loans of money, French troops, and a navy. Even before France officially entered the war, the Marquis de Lafayette, a French nobleman, had volunteered his help to the Patriot cause. So, too, had Polish military engineer Thaddeus Kosciusko and German Baron Friedrich von Steuben.

Winning Independence

In the end, the British lost their colonies because the Americans had the determination to outlast their rulers. George Washington understood this better than anyone. He never gave up, no matter what the hardships. For example, Washington and his troops endured the harsh winter of 1777–1778 at Valley Forge, Pennsylvania, huddled in huts with few blankets, ragged clothing, and almost no food. Washington reported to Congress that nearly one third of his 10,000 soldiers were unfit for duty because they lacked coats or shoes.

Victories in the West and South By late summer 1778, Patriot militia, with the help of French settlers, had captured all the British posts in present-day Indiana and Illinois. The American recapture of the fort at Vincennes strengthened the Patriots' claim to the Ohio River valley.

In 1779, the focus of the war shifted to the South, where the British hoped to draw on Loyalist sympathies. Supported by the Royal Navy, British forces seized Savannah, Georgia, in December 1778, and then Charleston, South Carolina, in May 1780. By 1781, General Charles Cornwallis had managed to set up camp at Yorktown, on a peninsula between the York and James rivers, and was waiting

CAPTION ANSWERS

Viewing Fine Art (a) The overcrowded boat, the ice in the river, stormy conditions, the uniforms (except for Washington's) look ragged. (b) The proud bearing of General Washington, the flag, the troops struggling to get the boat through the ice in spite of all the obstacles.

RESOURCE DIRECTORY

Teaching Resources

Units 1/2 booklet
- Section 1 Quiz, p. 14

Guide to the Essentials
- Section 1 Summary, p. 9

Biography, Literature, and Comparing Primary Sources booklet (Biography) *Deborah Sampson Garrett,* p. 10

Other Print Resources

Color Transparencies *Cause-and-Effect Charts,* D2; *Fine Art,* E5

Historical Outline Map Book *The Revolutionary War in the Northeast, The Revolutionary War in the West,* and *The Revolutionary War in the South,* pp. 25–27

Technology

Sounds of an Era Audio CD *Champ Clark on Valley Forge* (time: one minute, 15 seconds); *Sylvanus Woods and Lieutenant Barker on Revolutionary War* (time: one minute, 45 seconds)

for the Royal Navy to arrive with reinforcements. Lafayette's troops blocked an overland escape from the peninsula.

Washington immediately recognized the opportunity to deal the British a fatal blow at Yorktown. He quickly moved a combined American-French force south from New York while the French fleet set up a blockade off the Virginia coast. When Washington's troops arrived to reinforce Lafayette, the Battle of Yorktown began. Cornwallis now faced an army more than twice the size of his own, blocking his escape from the peninsula. The French fleet prevented him from being reinforced or removed by sea. Escape was impossible. On October 19, 1781, Cornwallis surrendered to Washington.

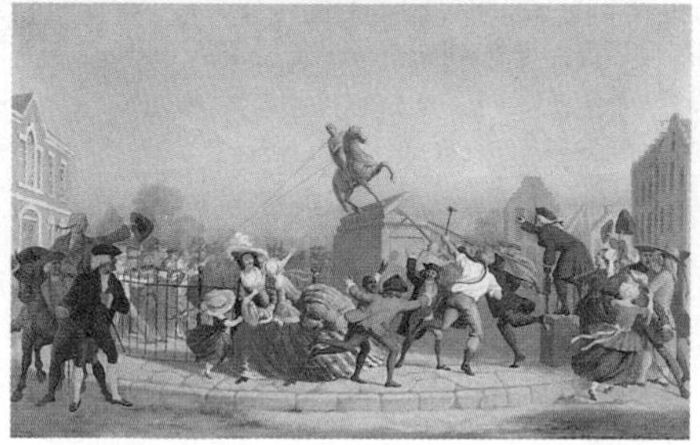

American colonists pull down a statue of King George III.

The Treaty of Paris In September 1783, the Treaty of Paris officially ended the Revolutionary War. In the treaty, Great Britain recognized the independence of the United States of America. The treaty also set the northern border between the United States and British Canada, and made the Mississippi River the boundary between the new United States and Spanish territory to the west, assuring the right to navigation on the river to both American and British citizens. Florida was returned to Spain, and the border between Florida and the United States was set.

The Impact of the Revolution The Revolution did more than establish American independence. It also helped inspire Americans' **patriotism,** or love of their country. Patriotism is the passion that inspires a person to serve his or her country, either in defending it from invasion or protecting its rights and maintaining its laws and institutions. People who had made sacrifices during the Revolution, and especially those whose friends or relatives had given their lives in it, best understood the value of the freedom their country had earned.

The Revolution also spread the idea of liberty, at home and abroad. Jefferson's assertion that "all men are created equal" was a radical concept in a world that had long accepted the idea of human inequality. Jefferson, like most members of the Continental Congress, probably had no thought of applying this principle to people other than white men. However, he had set in motion a powerful idea that no one could long control. Over the next two centuries many groups in the United States, such as women and African Americans, would demand and win greater equality. At the same time, the principles for which the Patriots fought would also inspire people around the world—a process that continues to this day.

Section 1 Assessment

READING COMPREHENSION

1. What was the purpose of the colonists' **boycott** in 1765?
2. Describe the **First Continental Congress.**
3. Why were the **Battles of Lexington and Concord** important?
4. How did the **Revolutionary War** lead eventually to American **patriotism?**

CRITICAL THINKING AND WRITING

5. **Determining Relevance** How did the French and Indian War help set the stage for the American Revolution?
6. **Writing a News Story** It is 1776, and you are a journalist covering the Second Continental Congress. Write a story about the creation of the Declaration of Independence.

Take It to the NET

Activity: Writing an Editorial
Choose either the Patriot or Loyalist point of view, and write an editorial about one key battle for a newspaper of the time. Use the links provided in the *America: Pathways to the Present* area of the following Web site for help in completing this activity.
www.phschool.com

Section 1 Assessment

Reading Comprehension

1. To resist British policies, especially the imposition of taxes without allowing the colonists to be represented in the British parliament.
2. Fifty-six delegates convened from every colony, except Georgia, in Philadelphia from September 5 to October 26, 1774, to plan a united response to the Intolerable Acts. They agreed to boycott English goods, called on the people of all the English colonies to form militias, and appealed to the king in their Declaration of Resolves.
3. They signified the beginning of the Revolutionary War, a conflict that would have worldwide significance.
4. In defending their country from invasion and protecting its rights, laws and institutions, Americans began to have a different kind of feeling toward their country. Through making sacrifices and losing friends or relatives in the war, people began to truly understand the value of the freedom their country had earned.

Critical Thinking and Writing

5. It strained relations between Britain and the American colonists, weakening colonists' loyalty to Britain; the British thought the colonists did not provide enough support for the long and costly war that Britain had fought to protect them; colonists desired to expand and prosper without the aid of Britain.
6. Answers will vary, but should be supported with facts from the section.

Take It to the NET

Editorials should focus on a critical battle of the American Revolution, such as the Battles of Lexington and Concord, or the Battle of Saratoga, and should describe the battle from either the Patriot or the Loyalist point of view.

Focus Write the following quotation on the chalkboard: "We must all hang together, or assuredly we will all hang separately." Explain that Benjamin Franklin spoke these words at the signing of the Declaration of Independence. Ask students what they think Franklin meant.

Instruct Explain how the ideals that inspired the American Revolution are embodied in the Declaration of Independence. Have students read the first paragraph of the Declaration and explain its purpose. Why was the Declaration such a revolutionary document in its time? How does it define basic principles upon which American society is based? Ask a volunteer to read from "We hold these truths to be self-evident" to ". . . effect their safety and happiness." Discuss why this section forms the heart of the Declaration.

Close The Declaration describes the basic rights on which the nation was founded, the wrongs committed by Britain, and the colonists' intentions to cut ties with Britain. The men who signed it made a brave commitment to pursue revolutionary ideals regarding human rights.

The Declaration *of* INDEPENDENCE

In Congress, July 4, 1776

THE UNANIMOUS DECLARATION OF THE THIRTEEN UNITED STATES OF AMERICA,

When in the Course of human events, it becomes necessary for one people to dissolve the political bands which have connected them with another, and to assume among the Powers of the earth, the separate and equal station to which the Laws of Nature and of Nature's God entitle them, a decent respect to the opinions of mankind requires that they should declare the causes which impel them to the separation.

We hold these truths to be self-evident, that all men are created equal, that they are endowed by their Creator with certain unalienable Rights, that among these are Life, Liberty and the pursuit of Happiness. That to secure these rights, Governments are instituted among Men, deriving their just powers from the consent of the governed, That whenever any Form of Government becomes destructive of these ends, it is the Right of the People to alter or to abolish it, and to institute new Government, laying its foundation on such principles and organizing its powers in such form, as to them shall seem most likely to effect their Safety and Happiness. Prudence, indeed, will dictate that Governments long established should not be changed for light and transient causes; and accordingly all experience hath shown, that mankind are more disposed to suffer, while evils are sufferable, than to right themselves by abolishing the forms to which they are accustomed. But when a long train of abuses and usurpations, pursuing invariably the same Object evinces a design to reduce them under absolute Despotism, it is their right, it is their duty, to throw off such Government, and to provide new Guards for their future security.—Such has been the patient sufferance of these Colonies; and such is now the necessity which constrains them to alter their former Systems of Government. The history of the present King of Great Britain is a history of repeated injuries and usurpations, all having in direct object the establishment of an absolute Tyranny over these States. To prove this, let Facts be submitted to a candid world.

He has refused his Assent to Laws, the most wholesome and necessary for the public good.

He has forbidden his Governors to pass Laws of immediate and pressing importance, unless suspended in their operation till his Assent should be obtained; and when so suspended, he has utterly neglected to attend to them.

He has refused to pass other Laws for the accommodation of large districts of people, unless those people would relinquish the right of Representation in the Legislature, a right inestimable to them and formidable to tyrants only.

He has called together legislative bodies at places unusual, uncomfortable, and distant from the depository of their Public Records, for the sole purpose of fatiguing them into compliance with his measures.

RESOURCE DIRECTORY

Teaching Resources

Biography, Literature and Comparing Primary Sources booklet (Comparing Primary Sources)
On Rule by the People, p. 103

Technology

Prentice Hall United States History Video Collection™ Volume 4, *The American Revolution*

He has dissolved Representative Houses repeatedly, for opposing with manly firmness his invasions on the rights of the people.

He has refused for a long time, after such dissolutions, to cause others to be elected; whereby the Legislative powers, incapable of Annihilation, have returned to the People at large for their exercise; the State remaining in the mean time exposed to all the dangers of invasions from without, and convulsions within.

He has endeavored to prevent the population of these States; for that purpose obstructing the Laws for Naturalization of Foreigners; refusing to pass others to encourage their migration hither, and raising the conditions of new Appropriations of Lands.

He has obstructed the Administration of Justice, by refusing his Assent to Laws for establishing Judiciary powers.

He has made Judges dependent on his Will alone for the tenure of their offices, and the amount and payment of their salaries.

He has erected a multitude of New Offices, and sent hither swarms of Officers to harass our people and eat out their substance.

He has kept among us in time of peace, Standing Armies, without the Consent of our legislature.

He has affected to render the Military independent of and superior to the Civil power.

He has combined with others to subject us to a jurisdiction foreign to our constitutions, and unacknowledged by our laws; giving his Assent to their Acts of pretended Legislation:

For Quartering large bodies of armed troops among us:

For protecting them, by a mock Trial, from Punishment for any Murders which they should commit on the Inhabitants of these States:

For cutting off our Trade with all parts of the world:

For imposing Taxes on us without our Consent:

For depriving us in many cases, of the benefits of Trial by Jury:

For transporting us beyond Seas to be tried for pretended offenses:

For abolishing the free System of English Laws in a neighbouring Province, establishing therein an Arbitrary government, and enlarging its Boundaries so as to render it at once an example and fit instrument for introducing the same absolute rule into these Colonies:

For taking away our Charters, abolishing our most valuable Laws, and altering fundamentally the Forms of our Governments;

For suspending our own Legislature, and declaring themselves invested with Power to legislate for us in all cases whatsoever.

He has abdicated Government here, by declaring us out of his Protection, and waging War against us.

He has plundered our seas, ravaged our Coasts, burned our towns, and destroyed the lives of our people.

He is at this time transporting large Armies of foreign mercenaries to compleat the works of death, desolation and tyranny, already begun with circumstances of Cruelty and perfidy scarcely paralleled in the most barbarous ages, and totally unworthy the Head of a civilized nation.

He has constrained our fellow Citizens taken Captive on the high Seas to bear Arms against their Country, to become the executioners of their friends and Brethren, or to fall themselves by their Hands.

He has excited domestic insurrections amongst us, and has endeavored to bring on the inhabitants of our frontiers the merciless Indian Savages, whose known rule of warfare, is an undistinguished destruction of all ages, sexes, and conditions.

CUSTOMIZE FOR ...

Gifted and Talented

Have students research the ideas of John Locke and the English tradition of government. Then ask students to correlate these ideas with specific ideas in the Declaration. They may present the results of their project in essay or chart form.

CUSTOMIZE FOR ...

ESL

Ask students to make a list of sentences from the Declaration that they find challenging. Have them work together to restate the sentences in their own words.

CUSTOMIZE FOR ...

Less Proficient Readers

Have students draw cartoons representing main ideas from the Declaration. Have them share their cartoons with the class and explain their meaning. You may want to collect their cartoons in a class political cartoon booklet.

CUSTOMIZE FOR ...

Less Proficient Writers

Ask students to select a passage from the Declaration and have them write the passage in their own words.

The Declaration *of* INDEPENDENCE

Vocabulary
Answers should reflect an understanding of the words selected.

Comprehension

1. That all men are created equal, and all are endowed by their Creator with certain rights.
2. Life, liberty, and the pursuit of happiness.
3. The consent of the governed.
4. The people may change or abolish the government.
5. King George III.
6. The phrase "imposing taxes on us without our consent."
7. Powers to declare war, conclude peace, contract alliances, and establish commerce.
8. New Hampshire, Massachusetts Bay, Rhode Island, Connecticut, New York, New Jersey, Delaware, Maryland, Virginia, Pennsylvania, North Carolina, South Carolina, and Georgia.

Critical Thinking

1. Judges were likely to favor the king over the colonists in court.
2. "When in the Course of human events"; "We hold these truths to be self-evident"; "The history of the present King of Great Britain is a history of repeated injuries and usurpations"; "We, therefore, the Representatives of the United States of America."
3. No. Many of the signers, including Thomas Jefferson, owned slaves and were unwilling to extend these basic rights to African Americans. Laws limited the rights of women and Native Americans, who were denied the right to live and govern themselves on their own land.
4. The Declaration accuses King George of encouraging "merciless Indian Savages" to attack colonists on the frontier. Colonists considered Native Americans to be barbarians who attacked indiscriminately.
5. The Declaration claims that the colonists had petitioned the King many times.

In every stage of these Oppressions We have Petitioned for Redress in the most humble terms. Our repeated Petitions have been answered only by repeated injury. A Prince, whose character is thus marked by every act which may define a Tyrant, is unfit to be the ruler of a free People.

Nor have We been wanting in attentions to our British brethren. We have warned them from time to time of attempts by their legislature to extend an unwarrantable jurisdiction over us. We have reminded them of the circumstances of our emigration and settlement here. We have appealed to their native justice and magnanimity, and we have conjured them by the ties of our common kindred to disavow these usurpations, which, would inevitably interrupt our connections and correspondence. They too have been deaf to the voice of Justice and of consanguinity. We must, therefore, acquiesce in the necessity, which denounces our Separation, and hold them, as we hold the rest of mankind, Enemies in War, in Peace Friends.

We, therefore, the Representatives of the United States of America, in General Congress, Assembled, appealing to the Supreme Judge of the world for the rectitude of our intentions, do, in the Name, and by the Authority of the good People of these Colonies, solemnly publish and declare, That these United Colonies are, and of Right ought to be Free and Independent States; that they are Absolved from all Allegiance to the British Crown, and that all political connection between them and the State of Great Britain, is and ought to be totally dissolved, and that as Free and Independent States, they have full Power to levy War, conclude Peace, contract Alliances, establish Commerce, and to do all other Acts and Things which Independent States may of right do. And for the support of this Declaration, with a firm reliance on the protection of Divine Providence, we mutually pledge to each other our Lives, our Fortunes and our sacred Honor.

JOHN HANCOCK
President of the Continental Congress 1775–1777

NEW HAMPSHIRE
Josiah Bartlett
William Whipple
Matthew Thornton

MASSACHUSETTS BAY
Samuel Adams
John Adams
Robert Treat Paine
Elbridge Gerry

RHODE ISLAND
Stephen Hopkins
William Ellery

CONNECTICUT
Roger Sherman
Samuel Huntington
William Williams
Oliver Wolcott

NEW YORK
William Floyd
Philip Livingston
Francis Lewis
Lewis Morris

NEW JERSEY
Richard Stockton
John Witherspoon
Francis Hopkinson
John Hart
Abraham Clark

DELAWARE
Caesar Rodney
George Read
Thomas McKean

MARYLAND
Samuel Chase
William Paca
Thomas Stone
Charles Carroll of Carrollton

VIRGINIA
George Wythe
Richard Henry Lee
Thomas Jefferson
Benjamin Harrison
Thomas Nelson, Jr.
Francis Lightfoot Lee
Carter Braxton

PENNSYLVANIA
Robert Morris
Benjamin Rush
Benjamin Franklin
John Morton
George Clymer
James Smith
George Taylor
James Wilson
George Ross

NORTH CAROLINA
William Hooper
Joseph Hewes
John Penn

SOUTH CAROLINA
Edward Rutledge
Thomas Heyward, Jr.
Thomas Lynch, Jr.
Arthur Middleton

GEORGIA
Button Gwinnett
Lyman Hall
George Walton

Reviewing the Declaration

Vocabulary

Choose ten words in the Declaration with which you are unfamiliar. Look them up in the dictionary. Then, on a piece of paper, copy the sentence in the Declaration in which each unfamiliar word is used, and after the sentence write the definition of the unfamiliar word.

Comprehension

1. Which truths in the second paragraph are "self-evident"?
2. Name the three unalienable rights listed in the Declaration.
3. From what source do governments derive their "just powers"?
4. What right do people have when their government becomes destructive?
5. In the series of paragraphs beginning, "He has refused his Assent," to whom does the word "He" refer?
6. Which phrase in the Declaration expresses the colonists' opposition to taxation without representation?
7. According to the Declaration, what powers does the United States have "as Free and Independent States"?
8. List the colonies that the signers of the Declaration represented.

Critical Thinking

1. **Cause and Effect** Why do you think the colonists were unhappy with the fact that their judges' salaries were paid by the king?
2. **Drawing Conclusions** As Section 1 of this chapter explains, the Declaration was divided into four parts. Write down the first phrase of each of those four parts.
3. **Identifying Assumptions** Do you think that the statement "all men are created equal" was intended to apply to all human beings? Explain your reasoning.
4. **Recognizing Bias** What reference do you see to Native Americans? What attitudes toward Native Americans does this express?
5. **Drawing Conclusions** What evidence is there that the colonists had already unsuccessfully voiced concerns to the King?

Issues Past and Present

1. Write a letter to the Continental Congress from the perspective of a woman or an African American who has just read the Declaration in 1776. In your letter, comment on the Declaration's statement that "all men are created equal" and also express your attitude toward American independence.
2. What evidence in the Declaration is there of religious faith? How do you think this religious faith influenced the ideals expressed in the Declaration?
3. Examine the unalienable rights of individuals as stated in the Declaration. Do you think these rights are upheld today? Give examples to support your answer.

Analyzing Political Cartoons

1. This cartoon was published in 1779. (a) Read the caption and identify the horse. (b) Who is the master being thrown? (c) How do you know?
2. Examine the figure on the horse. (a) What is he holding? (b) What does it represent?
3. What is the cartoonist's overall message?

THE HORSE AMERICA, throwing his Master.

REVIEWING THE DECLARATION

Issues Past and Present

1. Answers will vary. Women may discuss the use of "men" in the quote. An African American might read "all men are created equal" and hope that American independence would bring freedom.
2. It asserts that the right to life, liberty, and the pursuit of happiness comes from God. The signatories put their trust in "the protection of Divine Providence."
3. Answers may mention current issues such as censorship, children's rights, religion, gun control, abortion, or the death penalty.

Analyzing Political Cartoons

1. (a) America. (b) King George. (c) Britain was America's master, and the rider is dressed like King George.
2. (a) A whip made of swords, bayonets, and axes. (b) The British Army.
3. Because Britain used force to control the colonies, Americans became angry and tried to throw off British control.

Section 2
The Constitution of the United States

Section Objectives

1. See how the early government of the United States was structured by the Articles of Confederation.
2. Learn about the type of government structure set up by the Framers at the Constitutional Convention.
3. See how the Federalists won the battle over ratification.
4. Discover how Washington's administration set precedents for the new nation and provided for the capital city.

Bellringer

Warm-Up Activity Ask students on what occasions, or for what reasons, people turn to the federal government. Why do people expect the federal government to help after large-scale disasters? Discuss the differences between a dictatorship and a democracy, including the pros and cons of each.

Activating Prior Knowledge Ask students to state what they know about the United States Constitution and its creation. In what ways has the Constitution been modified since it was written?

Reading Strategy

As students read this section, have them list the arguments for and against the Articles of Confederation.

Background
Global Connections

After the success of the American Revolution, many British people blamed King George III, whose irascible nature and inability to compromise, they felt, provoked the American colonies to rebel. Also, the aftermath of the war with America left the British economy severely strained. Within a few years, however, the British economy greatly improved, as trade with the United States became a more lucrative enterprise than it had ever been with the American colonies.

Section 2

The Constitution of the United States

READING FOCUS

- How was the early government of the United States structured by the Articles of Confederation?
- What type of government structure did the Framers set up at the Constitutional Convention?
- How did the Federalists win the battle over ratification?
- How did Washington's administration set precedents for the new nation and provide for a new capital city?

KEY TERMS

Articles of Confederation
democracy
republic
United States Constitution
federal system of government
separation of powers
checks and balances
Federalists
anti-Federalists
Bill of Rights
administration

TAKING NOTES

Copy the chart below. As you read, list the problems of the Articles of Confederation and the ways in which the Constitution addressed them.

Problems of the Articles of Confederation	Solutions Provided by the Constitution
Government lacked the power to tax.	Congress has the power to tax.

MAIN IDEA

Some prominent Americans felt that the Articles of Confederation did not provide a strong enough national government. A new plan of government, the Constitution, was drafted at the Constitutional Convention. It was ratified after the promise was made to add a Bill of Rights.

This painting shows George Washington saying farewell to his officers after resigning his commission.

Setting the Scene On December 23, 1783, George Washington performed perhaps the most important act of his life: he voluntarily gave up power. The triumphant general was easily the country's most popular and best-known figure. Now that the Revolutionary War was over, many people expected him to move into a new role as head of the new nation, maybe even its king.

Washington, though, had other plans. Having helped Americans win their freedom from a king, he believed that the nation did not need another supreme ruler. In an act that stunned the world, he gave up his commission as commander of the American army and headed home to his estate at Mount Vernon, Virginia, to retire.

Early Government

Americans now faced a new challenge. Could they enjoy their hard-won freedoms without a strong, unified, national government? Could they keep their new liberty and maintain order at the same time? In short, what kind of government should a free people have?

The Continental Congress that had approved the Declaration of Independence in 1776 was simply a loose collection of delegates from 13 separate states. Almost no one wanted a powerful national government. Most people regarded Congress as only a wartime necessity.

Americans at that time generally thought of themselves as citizens of individual states, not of a nation. In fact, when referring to the United States, most Americans wrote "the United States *are*" (plural) rather than "the United States *is*" (singular) as people do today. They believed that the country as a whole

RESOURCE DIRECTORY

Teaching Resources
Learning Styles Lesson Plans booklet, pp. 12–13
Guided Reading and Review booklet, pp. 20–23
Biography, Literature, and Comparing Primary Sources booklet (Comparing Primary Sources) *On the United States as an Independent Nation,* p. 105

Other Print Resources
Historical Outline Map Book *North America in 1783,* p. 28

Technology
Section Reading Support Transparencies
Guided Reading Audiotapes (English/Spanish), Ch. 2
Student Edition on Audio CD, Ch. 2
Exploring Primary Sources in U.S. History CD-ROM *N.Y. State Constitution of 1777; Articles of Confederation*
Prentice Hall Presentation Pro® CD-ROM, Ch. 2
Companion Web site, www.phschool.com

was less important than its 13 parts. It was not a nation as much as it was a confederation, an alliance of separate governments that work together.

State Constitutions During the Revolution and immediately afterward, state governments had more power than the national government of the United States. The individual state constitutions, which created and described the state governments, were thus the primary forms of government in the new nation. Most of these constitutions were established during the Revolution, well before the United States adopted the federal Constitution. State constitutions were also important as models and inspiration for the later national documents. Pennsylvania's constitution of 1776, for example, introduced bold new ideas about democratic government. It gave voting rights to all white men 21 years of age or older who paid taxes. Thus, that state became the first to open the voting process to ordinary people, not just wealthy gentlemen.

The Articles of Confederation In 1777, the Continental Congress adopted a set of laws to govern the United States. These laws were called the **Articles of Confederation.** Approved in 1781, the Articles established a limited national government. Most of the political power lay with the states.

The national government created by the Articles had only one branch: a legislature, or Congress, made up of delegates from the states. The Congress carried out both legislative duties (making the laws) and executive functions (carrying out, or enforcing, the laws). The Articles did not create a judicial branch for the national government; each state maintained its own court system.

The Congress set up by the Articles differed in several other ways from today's Congress. For example, while it could declare war and borrow money, it lacked the power to tax. To carry out its tasks, Congress had to petition the states for money. It had no power to force the states to do its will. What's more, under the Articles, each of the 13 states had only 1 vote in Congress. Passage of any measure involving money required 9 votes out of the 13, not just a simple majority of 7. Changes in the Articles themselves could be made only if all 13 states agreed. These provisions made it difficult for the national government to get things done—which was just what some Americans wanted. But, as time went on, other Americans became dissatisfied with this weak form of government.

After fighting a war to gain independence from what they regarded as a tyrannical king and Parliament, Americans generally agreed that their new nation should be a **democracy,** or government by the people. Specifically, they favored the creation of a **republic,** a government run by the people through their elected representatives. Yet Americans held widely differing views on how much influence ordinary citizens should have in the governing of the republic. This division became clear as objections to the Articles began to surface.

One set of objections arose out of the economic problems of the new nation. By 1786, three years after the Revolution, the nation still had a debt of about $50 million, an unthinkably huge sum at that time. State governments and the national government had borrowed money from foreign countries and from their own citizens to pay for the war. Some state governments had even printed cheap paper money to help their citizens pay off their loans. This created economic chaos. Desperate for money, states with

Focus on GEOGRAPHY

Who Owns the West? Although the Articles of Confederation were signed in 1777, they were not ratified until 1781 because of a disagreement among the states over western lands. Seven of the 13 states had claims to land west of the Appalachian Mountains. Most of these claims rested on states' colonial charters, some of which had granted states ownership of lands westward to the "South Sea."

The six states without western land claims argued that all such lands should become the property of the entire nation. The states with claims wrote their response into the Articles of Confederation, which declared that no state should be deprived of territory for the benefit of the United States. Furious, one state without a claim—Maryland—refused to ratify the Articles until 1781. Finally, though, the states with western claims gave them up, and the Articles were ratified.

LESSON PLAN

Focus Explain that the years after the American Revolution were difficult ones for the new United States, which was disorganized and suffered from economic and political problems. Explain that delegates to the Constitutional Convention struggled over how much power to leave with the states and how much to give the national government.

Instruct Review the ideas that fueled the American Revolution. Have students explain how the United States government before 1788 reflected these ideas. Explain that crafting a lasting national government was an arduous process of debate and compromise. Ask why compromise was so important to the success of the convention.

Assess/Reteach Ask students to discuss why it was so important to take as many viewpoints as possible into account when crafting the Constitution. Ask for examples that demonstrate how this system of "checks and balances" is still part of American government.

CUSTOMIZE FOR ...

Less Proficient Readers

Have students read the section's main headings. Then ask students to write a question about each heading and to look for the answers to their questions as they read.

ACTIVITY

Connecting with Citizenship

Have students create a work of art that expresses their feelings about the importance of the Bill of Rights. Encourage students to concentrate on one or two aspects of the Bill of Rights. Students may make a drawing, collage, or painting to represent their response. **(Visual/ Spatial)**

BACKGROUND

Recent Scholarship

Alexander Hamilton, John Jay, and James Madison all played very important roles in the ratification of the Constitution. Historian Richard B. Morris's work *Witnesses at the Creation: Hamilton, Madison, Jay and the Constitution* focuses on how ratification was not certain at the time and how these three men set aside their differences to work collaboratively for what Madison called "the instrument that would decide forever the fate of republican government." Morris studied correspondence, notes, memoranda, diaries, pamphlets, and newspapers to focus on the role of the trio in the ratification of the Constitution, the document that Morris believes is the mortar that binds Americans together.

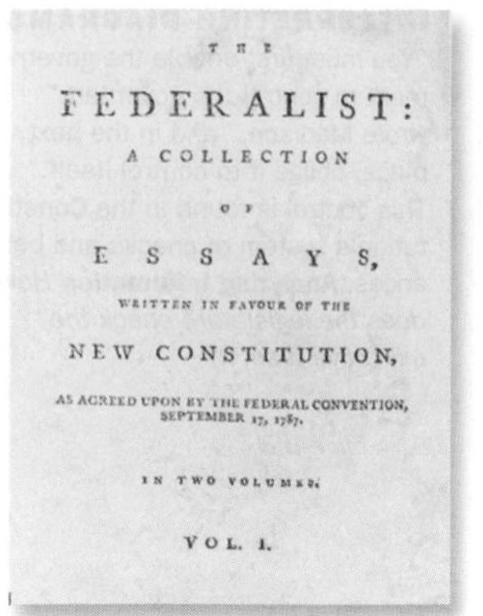
THE FEDERALIST: A COLLECTION OF ESSAYS, WRITTEN IN FAVOUR OF THE NEW CONSTITUTION, AS AGREED UPON BY THE FEDERAL CONVENTION, SEPTEMBER 17, 1787. IN TWO VOLUMES. VOL. I.

The essays in *The Federalist* are still quoted today.

a series of 85 essays called *The Federalist.* These articles appeared in New York City newspapers in 1787 and 1788 under the pen name *Publius.*

The *Federalist* essays are perhaps the most sophisticated explanation of the new American political system ever written. They emphasize the separation of powers and the system of checks and balances as protections against tyranny.

The anti-Federalists rallied behind the leadership of older revolutionary figures, such as Patrick Henry of Virginia. Most anti-Federalists saw the Constitution as a betrayal of the American Revolution. A President would be nothing but a king, they warned. Had American patriots fought and died to create yet another government to tax them and tell them what to do?

While the Federalists feared the people more than government, the anti-Federalists feared government more than the people. Many anti-Federalists objected to the lack of a bill of rights in the new Constitution, since it did not expressly protect such basic liberties as freedom of speech, the press, and religion, or the right to a fair trial.

The Constitution was officially submitted to the states for approval on September 28, 1787. From the start, the Federalists had several advantages in their campaign to promote it. First, they drew on the widespread feeling that the Articles of Confederation had serious flaws. They were also united around a specific plan—the Constitution. The anti-Federalists, in contrast, were united only in their opposition to the Constitution, and had no constructive plan of their own to offer. In addition, the Federalists were a well-organized national group in regular contact with one another. The anti-Federalists tended to be local and state politicians who could not coordinate their activities on the national level.

Finally, the Federalists had the support of George Washington. People were more willing to accept the idea of a stronger government and a powerful executive because they assumed Washington would be the first President.

In June 1788, New Hampshire became the ninth and final state needed to ratify the Constitution. Yet everyone knew that the new nation would not succeed without the backing of the heavily populated states of Virginia and New York. Loud debates and quiet maneuvers during the summer of 1788 produced narrow Federalist victories in both these states. In May 1790, Rhode Island became the last of the original 13 states to approve the new government.

The Bill of Rights In a number of states, Federalists won the battle over ratification only because they had offered to support several amendments to the Constitution designed to protect citizens' rights. In September 1789, Congress proposed 12 such amendments. The states ratified ten of the amendments, and they took effect on December 15, 1791. These first ten amendments are known today as the **Bill of Rights.**

INTERPRETING POLITICAL CARTOONS This cartoon shows the individual states as pillars. Nine states had to approve the new Constitution before it became law. **Synthesizing Information** *What is the message of the words that appear above the pillars?*

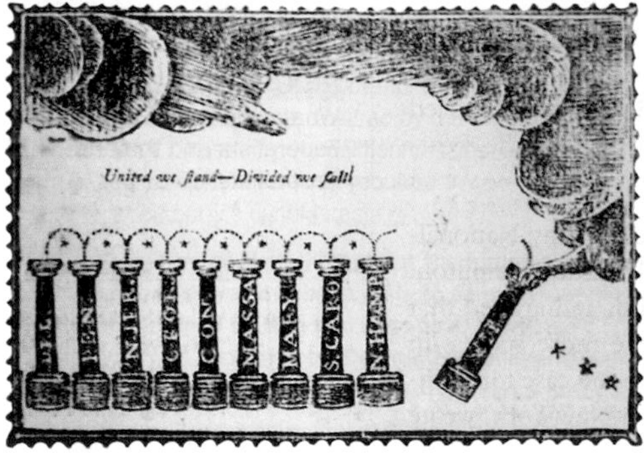
United we stand—Divided we fall!

Most Federalists saw no need for these amendments. In *The Federalist,* No. 84, Hamilton quoted the Preamble of the Constitution to claim that "the people surrender nothing" under the new system. That is, they keep all the power. "Here is a better recognition of popular rights" than any added list of rights, he argued.

In contrast, Thomas Jefferson (who also favored the Constitution) insisted that it include a Bill of Rights. "A bill of rights is what the people are entitled to against every government on earth," he wrote Madison. Facing overwhelming pressure for the Bill of Rights, the Federalists gave in. This compromise led them to victory.

CAPTION ANSWERS

Interpreting Political Cartoons That the future of the nation depends on the ratification of the Constitution.

RESOURCE DIRECTORY

Teaching Resources

Learning with Documents booklet (Key Documents) *The Federalist,* no. 71, p. 77

Learning with Documents booklet (Visual Learning Activity) *The First United States Coins,* p. 44

Other Print Resources

American History Block Scheduling Support *The Birth of the Constitution: The Philadelphia Convention* and *Taking Sides: The Creation of Political Parties,* found in the Forging a New Nation folder, include interdisciplinary lesson suggestions and activities for Geography and History, Primary Sources, Biography, and Literature.

Technology

Color Transparencies *Historical Maps,* A8; *Political Cartoons,* B3

Sounds of an Era Audio CD *The Federalist, No. 51, James Madison* (time: one minute, 15 seconds)

Exploring Primary Sources in U.S. History CD-ROM *English Bill of Rights; U.S. Constitution: The Bill of Rights*

Washington Becomes President

On April 30, 1789, a crowd of thousands surrounded Federal Hall, an elegant building on New York City's Wall Street that served as the temporary home of the new government. Those within earshot listened as George Washington repeated the oath of office of President of the United States and kissed a Bible. The crowd then roared its approval.

READING CHECK
Where was Washington sworn in as President?

Washington had been elected in early 1789 by a unanimous vote of the new electoral college. (*Unanimous* means having the agreement of everyone.) Massachusetts patriot John Adams, a leading Federalist, became Vice President.

Immediately, President Washington began selecting his Cabinet, the officials who head the major departments of the executive branch. Besides running their own agencies, Cabinet officers advise the President. Washington called on two of the nation's most respected patriots, Thomas Jefferson and Alexander Hamilton, to fill his most crucial Cabinet posts.

Jefferson was a logical choice to head the Department of State because he had just spent several years serving as ambassador to France, the closest ally of the United States. Alexander Hamilton, the new head of the Department of the Treasury, was a brilliant man who had served as private secretary to General Washington during the Revolution. Now Hamilton headed the government's largest department. In contrast to Jefferson, Hamilton believed that governmental power, properly used, could accomplish great things.

Despite the strong contrasts between Jefferson and Hamilton, the first months, even years, of the new government went fairly smoothly. The economic problems brought on by the war eased, and the adoption of the Constitution gave the nation much-needed stability.

NOTABLE PRESIDENTS
George Washington

1st President
1789–1797

"The basis of our political systems is the right of the people to make and to alter their Constitutions of Government."

—Farewell Address, 1796

George Washington was not only the nation's first President, but also the person for whom the office was created. A former Virginia planter and surveyor, he had fought in the French and Indian War and had led the Continental Army during the Revolution. His leadership in the fight for independence made him the nation's leading public figure.

Washington was famous, too, for his honesty, dignity, and self-control. In 1787, the Framers of the Constitution were confident that he could be trusted with the enormous powers of the presidency. Washington's dignity and restraint as President eased many people's fears about the new government.

Washington could not, however, make the new government universally popular. Many Americans distrusted strong government, Hamilton's economic plans, and Washington's pro-British foreign policy. Convinced that Washington was leading the nation away from the ideals of the Revolution, they rallied behind Thomas Jefferson. Saddened that he could not prevent factions, Washington refused to run for a third term in 1796.

When Washington died, however, Americans joined together to honor his steadfast service to the nation, first as a general fighting a difficult war and later as a President seeking a workable balance between order and liberty.

Connecting to Today

Do you believe that dignity and restraint are as important for American Presidents today as they were in Washington's era? Explain your answer.

Take It to the NET **Biography** To read more about George Washington, visit the links provided in the *America: Pathways to the Present* area of the following Web site. **www.phschool.com**

ACTIVITY
Connecting with Government

Tell students to learn more about either the State Department or the Treasury Department. As students prepare to do their research, tell them to think about the following questions: What is the primary function of this department? What kinds of actions does the head of the department do to get the job done? How has the role of the department changed over time? Has it become more or less important? Name a few outstanding people who have headed the department. **(Verbal/Linguistic)**

BACKGROUND
A Diverse Nation

George Washington had ambivalent feelings toward slavery. After the end of the Revolutionary War, Washington expressed his regrets about the institution of slavery. His experiences during the war had proven to him that African Americans were just as dedicated and courageous as their white counterparts. Though Washington did not liberate the 250 slaves that he owned upon his return to his home in Mount Vernon, he did free these slaves in his will.

READING CHECK
At Federal Hall in New York City.

CUSTOMIZE FOR ...
Less Proficient Readers

Ask students to write the following headings on a piece of paper: *Powerful Government, Democratic Government.* Then have them list examples under each heading as they read the section.

Section 2 Assessment

Reading Comprehension

1. (a) A government by the people. (b) A government run by the people through their elected representatives. (c) A system in which power is shared between state and national authorities.
2. Separation of powers gives each branch of government its own area of authority, but gives no one branch complete power over the government. The system of checks and balances gives each branch the power to stop the other branches in certain ways, in order to prevent misuse of power by any one branch.
3. Federalists: favored the Constitution and wanted the strong national government the Constitution provided. Anti-Federalists: opposed the Constitution, believing that it posed a threat to state governments and to the rights of individuals.
4. The first ten amendments to the Constitution.

Critical Thinking and Writing

5. Sample answers: Fact: The Articles created a weak national government, giving most powers to the states. Opinion: Such a system did not give the national government enough authority. Thus, the Articles needed to be replaced, not simply amended.
6. Opinions will vary, but should be supported with facts from the section in order to persuade the reader of the student's viewpoint.

Sample answer: James Madison might have written a diary entry detailing the debate between the Virginia and New Jersey plans, which ended in the Great Compromise.

This 1792 engraving is based on L'Enfant's plan for Washington, D.C.

Washington knew that his every decision, every action, and every inaction as President would establish a precedent for how to govern. (A precedent is something done or said that becomes an example, rule, or tradition to be followed.) He worked to establish a tone of dignity in his term of office, or **administration.** (*Administration* can also refer to the members and agencies of the executive branch as a whole.) His own appearance and personality helped. More than six feet tall, Washington made an impressive figure. By nature he was solemn, reserved, and very formal.

Throughout his first term, Washington remained a popular figure, and in 1792 he won unanimous reelection. Reluctantly, he accepted. As you will read, though, his second administration would be marked by criticism and controversy.

Planning a Capital City

A new nation needed a new capital, one that could equal the beauty and stature of Europe's grand capital cities. The Residence Act of 1790 specified that the capital would be a 10-square-mile stretch of land on the Potomac River along the Maryland-Virginia border. At Jefferson's suggestion, Washington appointed Benjamin Banneker, an African American mathematician and inventor, to the commission to survey the city. Pierre-Charles L'Enfant, a French artist and architect who had fought for the United States during the Revolution, developed the plan for a spacious capital with broad streets laid out in an elegant, European-style pattern. The federal government moved to the new District of Columbia in 1800, decades before the plan was fully realized.

Today, Washington, D.C., with its great boulevards, marble buildings in the Roman style, and public monuments, is the most visible legacy of the Federalists' grand plans for the United States. It was meant to display the power and dignity of the new federal government that they had fought to build.

Section 2 Assessment

READING COMPREHENSION

1. What kind of government is (a) a **democracy,** (b) a **republic,** and (c) a **federal system of government?**
2. Explain how the **separation of powers** and the system of **checks and balances** affect government power.
3. What were the views of the **Federalists** and the **anti-Federalists?**
4. What is the **Bill of Rights?**

CRITICAL THINKING AND WRITING

5. **Distinguishing Fact From Opinion** Write two major facts about the kind of government set up by the Articles of Confederation. Then write an opinion about each of those facts.
6. **Writing a Letter to the Editor** It is 1787, and you are strongly in favor of (or strongly opposed to) ratification of the Constitution. Write a short letter to the editor expressing your views.

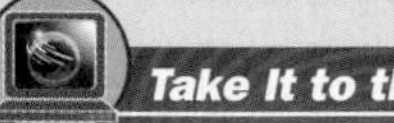

Activity: Writing a Diary Entry
Learn more about the delegates to the Constitutional Convention. Write a diary entry that one delegate might have written while attending the Convention. Use the links provided in the *America: Pathways to the Present* area at the following Web site for help in completing this activity.
www.phschool.com

RESOURCE DIRECTORY

Teaching Resources

Units 1/2 booklet
- Section 2 Quiz, p. 15

Guide to the Essentials
- Section 2 Summary, p. 10

Biography, Literature, and Comparing Primary Sources booklet (Biography) *Pierre Charles L'Enfant,* p. 10

Technology

RESOURCE PRO® **Primary Source Activity** *A Department of Peace,* found on Resource Pro, helps demonstrate the ideals people had for the development of their new country.

RESOURCE PRO® **Visual Learning Activity** *A Portrait of a President,* found on Resource Pro, uses a 1789 print of George Washington to illustrate some images and ideals prevalent at the time.

RESOURCE PRO® **Primary Source Activity** *Meeting President and Mrs. Washington,* found on Resource Pro, provides a personal viewpoint on George and Martha Washington.

The Constitution of the United States

THE SIX BASIC PRINCIPLES

The classic textbook *Magruder's American Government* outlines the six basic principles of the Constitution. Below is a description of these principles:

1 Popular Sovereignty

The Preamble to the Constitution begins with the bold phrase, "We the people . . ." These words announce that in the United States, the people are sovereign. The government receives its power from the people and can govern only with their consent.

2 Limited Government

Because the people are the ultimate source of all government power, the government has only as much authority as the people give it. Government's power is thus limited. Much of the Constitution, in fact, consists of specific limitations on government power.

3 Separation of Powers

Government power is not only limited, but also divided. The Constitution assigns certain powers to each of the three branches: the legislative (Congress), executive (President), and judicial (federal courts). This separation of government's powers was intended to prevent the misuse of power.

4 Checks and Balances

The system of checks and balances gives each of the three branches of government the ability to restrain the other two. Such a system makes government less efficient but also less likely to trample on the rights of citizens.

5 Judicial Review

Who decides whether an act of government violates the Constitution? Historically, the courts have filled this function. The principle of judicial review means that federal courts have the power to review acts of the federal government and to cancel any acts that are unconstitutional, or violate a provision in the Constitution.

6 Federalism

A federal system of government is one in which power is divided between a central government and smaller governments. This sharing of powers is intended to ensure that the central government is powerful enough to be effective, yet not so powerful as to threaten states or individuals.

Focus Ask students to describe their student government. Is there a constitution? If so, what is its purpose? What is the procedure for making changes? If there is no constitution, would the student government benefit from one? Why or why not? Explain that student governments and other organizations often use the Constitution of the United States as a model.

Instruct Review the issues that divided Federalists and anti-Federalists. Discuss how the Constitution preserves popular sovereignty and limits the powers of government while avoiding the weaknesses of the Articles of Confederation. On the chalkboard, write the Six Basic Principles of the Constitution that are listed on this page. Ask students to explain each one in their own words. Then ask them to find examples of each principle within the Constitution.

Discuss how the Bill of Rights protects Americans' basic rights. Ask students to make a list of examples of the rights that are protected in their own lives.

Close The Constitution provides a broad explanation of the limits of government, based on six basic principles. It has protected the rights of Americans for more than 200 years.

RESOURCE DIRECTORY

Teaching Resources
Constitution Study Guide

Other Print Resources
American History Block Scheduling Support Checks and Balances: The Rise of the American Judiciary, found in the Forging a New Nation folder, includes interdisciplinary lesson suggestions and activities for Geography and History, Primary Sources, Biography, and Literature.

Technology
Prentice Hall United States History Video Collection™ Volume 5, *A New Nation*
Interactive Constitution CD-ROM

The Constitution of the United States

CUSTOMIZE FOR ...
Gifted and Talented
Have students research one amendment to the Constitution and give a report to the class on the importance of the amendment and its impact on American society.

CUSTOMIZE FOR ...
ESL
Ask a volunteer to read the Preamble to the Constitution aloud. Then have students paraphrase the Preamble in their own words.

CUSTOMIZE FOR ...
Less Proficient Readers
Help students to begin reading the Constitution by having volunteers read the first several sections and clauses aloud, then read the appropriate paraphrase found in the Commentary. Point out that students can look to the Commentary to help them understand the reading.

CUSTOMIZE FOR ...
Less Proficient Writers
Invite students to choose an amendment to the Constitution that is meaningful to them, and invite them to write a few paragraphs about why they feel that amendment is important.

PARTS OF THE CONSTITUTION

Preamble

ARTICLE I	**LEGISLATIVE BRANCH**
Section 1	Legislative Powers; The Congress
Section 2	House of Representatives
Section 3	Senate
Section 4	Elections and Meetings
Section 5	Legislative Proceedings
Section 6	Compensation, Immunities, and Disabilities of Members
Section 7	Revenue Bills, President's Veto
Section 8	Powers of Congress
Section 9	Powers Denied to Congress
Section 10	Powers Denied to the States
ARTICLE II	**EXECUTIVE BRANCH**
Section 1	President and Vice President
Section 2	Powers of the President
Section 3	Duties of the President
Section 4	Impeachment
ARTICLE III	**JUDICIAL BRANCH**
Section 1	Courts, Terms of Office
Section 2	Jurisdiction
Section 3	Treason
ARTICLE IV	**RELATIONS AMONG THE STATES**
Section 1	Full Faith and Credit
Section 2	Privileges and Immunities of Citizens
Section 3	New States and Territories
Section 4	Protection Afforded to States by the Nation
ARTICLE V	**PROVISIONS FOR AMENDMENT**
ARTICLE VI	**NATIONAL DEBTS, SUPREMACY OF NATIONAL LAW, OATH**
ARTICLE VII	**RATIFICATION OF CONSTITUTION**
AMENDMENTS	

A Note on the Text of the Constitution
The complete text of the Constitution, including amendments, appears on the pages that follow. Portions of the Constitution altered by later amendments or that no longer apply have been crossed out. Commentary appears in the outside column of each page.

PREAMBLE

We the People of the United States, in Order to form a more perfect Union, establish Justice, insure domestic Tranquility, provide for the common defence, promote the general Welfare, and secure the Blessings of Liberty to ourselves and our Posterity, do ordain and establish this Constitution for the United States of America.

The Preamble states the broad purposes the Constitution is intended to serve—to establish a government that provides for greater cooperation among the States, ensures justice and peace, provides for defense against foreign enemies, promotes the general well-being of the people, and secures liberty now and in the future. The phrase *We the People* emphasizes the twin concepts of popular sovereignty and of representative government.

Article I.

Section 1.

All legislative Powers herein granted shall be vested in a Congress of the United States, which shall consist of a Senate and House of Representatives.

LEGISLATIVE BRANCH

Section 1. Legislative Power; Congress

Congress, the nation's lawmaking body, is bicameral in form; that is, it is composed of two houses: the Senate and the House of Representatives. The Framers of the Constitution purposely separated the lawmaking power from the power to enforce the laws (Article II, the Executive Branch) and the power to interpret them (Article III, the Judicial Branch). This system of separation of powers is supplemented by a system of checks and balances; that is, in several provisions the Constitution gives to each of the three branches various powers with which it may restrain the actions of the other two branches.

Section 2.

1. The House of Representatives shall be composed of Members chosen every second Year by the People of the several States, and the Electors in each State shall have the Qualifications requisite for Electors of the most numerous Branch of the State Legislature.

2. No Person shall be a Representative who shall not have attained to the age of twenty-five Years, and been seven Years a Citizen of the United States, and who shall not, when elected, be an Inhabitant of that State in which he shall be chosen.

3. Representatives ~~and direct Taxes~~* shall be apportioned among the several States which may be included within this Union, according to their respective Numbers, ~~which shall be determined by adding to the whole Number of free Persons, including those bound to Service for a Term of Years and excluding Indians not taxed, three fifths of all other Persons.~~ The actual Enumeration shall be made within three Years after the first Meeting of the Congress of the United States, and within every subsequent term of ten Years, in such Manner as they shall by Law direct. The Number of Representatives shall not exceed one for every thirty Thousand, but each State shall have at Least one Representative; and, until such enumeration shall be made, the State of New Hampshire shall be entitled to choose three, Massachusetts eight, Rhode Island and Providence Plantations one, Connecticut five, New York

*The black lines indicate portions of the Constitution altered by subsequent amendments to the document.

Section 2. House of Representatives

Clause 1. Election Electors means voters. Members of the House of Representatives are elected every two years. Each State must permit the same persons to vote for United States representatives as it permits to vote for the members of the larger house of its own legislature. The 17th Amendment (1913) extends this requirement to the qualification of voters for United States senators.

Clause 2. Qualifications A member of the House of Representatives must be at least 25 years old, an American citizen for seven years, and a resident of the State he or she represents. In addition, political custom requires that a representative also reside in the district from which he or she is elected.

Clause 3. Apportionment The number of representatives each State is entitled to is based on its population, which is counted every 10 years in the census. Congress reapportions the seats among the States after each census. In the Reapportionment Act of 1929, Congress fixed the permanent size of the House at 435 members with each State having at least one representative. Today there is one House seat for approximately every 650,000 persons in the population.

The words "three-fifths of all other persons" referred to slaves and reflected the Three-Fifths Compromise reached by the Framers at Philadelphia in 1787; the phrase was made obsolete, was in effect repealed, by the 13th Amendment in 1865.

Clause 4. Vacancies The executive authority refers to the governor of a State. If a member leaves office or dies before the expiration of his or her term, the governor is to call a special election to fill the vacancy.

Clause 5. Officers; impeachment The House elects a Speaker, customarily chosen from the majority party in the House. Impeachment means accusation. The House has the exclusive power to impeach, or accuse, civil officers; the Senate (Article I, Section 3, Clause 6) has the exclusive power to try those impeached by the House.

Section 3. Senate

Clause 1. Composition, election, term Each State has two senators. Each serves for six years and has one vote. Originally, senators were not elected directly by the people, but by each State's legislature. The 17th Amendment, added in 1913, provides for the popular election of senators.

Clause 2. Classification The senators elected in 1788 were divided into three groups so that the Senate could become a "continuing body." One-third of the Senate's seats are up for election every two years.

The 17th Amendment provides that a Senate vacancy is to be filled at a special election called by the governor; State law may also permit the governor to appoint a successor to serve until that election is held.

Clause 3. Qualifications A senator must be at least 30 years old, a citizen for at least nine years, and a resident of the State from which elected.

Clause 4. Presiding officer The Vice President presides over the Senate, but may vote only to break a tie.

Clause 5. Other officers The Senate chooses its own officers, including a president pro tempore to preside when the Vice President is not there.

Clause 6. Impeachment trials The Senate conducts the trials of those officials impeached by the House. The Vice President presides unless the President is on trial, in which case the Chief Justice of the United States does so. A conviction requires the votes of two-thirds of the senators present.

No President has ever been convicted. In 1868 the House voted eleven articles of impeachment against

six, New Jersey four, Pennsylvania eight, Delaware one, Maryland six, Virginia ten, North Carolina five, South Carolina five, and Georgia three.

4. When vacancies happen in the Representation from any State, the Executive Authority thereof shall issue Writs of Election to fill such Vacancies.

5. The House of Representatives shall choose their Speaker and other Officers; and shall have the sole Power of Impeachment.

Section 3.

1. The Senate of the United States shall be composed of two Senators from each State ~~chosen by the Legislature thereof~~ for six Years; and each Senator shall have one Vote.

2. Immediately after they shall be assembled in Consequences of the first Election, they shall be divided, as equally as may be, into three Classes. The Seats of the Senators of the first Class shall be vacated at the Expiration of the second Year; of the second Class, at the Expiration of the fourth Year; and of the third Class, at the Expiration of the sixth Year; so that one-third may be chosen every second Year; ~~and if Vacancies happen by Resignation, or otherwise, during the Recess of the Legislature of any State, the Executive thereof may make temporary Appointments until the next Meeting of the Legislature, which shall then fill such Vacancies.~~

3. No Person shall be a Senator who shall not have attained to the Age of thirty Years, and been nine Years a Citizen of the United States, and who shall not, when elected, be an Inhabitant of that State for which he shall be chosen.

4. The Vice President of the United States shall be President of the Senate but shall have no Vote, unless they be equally divided.

5. The Senate shall choose their other Officers, and also a President pro tempore, in the Absence of the Vice President, or when he shall exercise the Office of President of the United States.

6. The Senate shall have the sole Power to try all Impeachments. When sitting for that Purpose, they shall be on Oath or Affirmation. When the President of the United States is tried, the Chief Justice shall preside: And no Person shall be convicted without the Concurrence of two thirds of the Members present.

7. Judgment in Cases of Impeachment shall not extend further than to removal from Office, and disqualification to hold and enjoy any Office of honor, Trust, or Profit under the United States: but the Party convicted shall nevertheless be liable and subject to Indictment, Trial, Judgment and Punishment, according to Law.

Section 4.

1. The Times, Places and Manner of holding Elections for Senators and Representatives, shall be prescribed in each State by the Legislature thereof; but the Congress may at any time by law make or alter such Regulations, except as to the Places of choosing Senators.

2. The Congress shall assemble at least once in every Year, and such Meeting shall be on the first Monday in December, unless they shall by Law appoint a different Day.

Section 5.

1. Each House shall be the Judge of the Elections, Returns and Qualifications of its own Members, and a Majority of each shall constitute a Quorum to do Business; but a smaller Number may adjourn from day to day, and may be authorized to compel the Attendance of absent Members, in such Manner, and under such Penalties, as each House may provide.

2. Each House may determine the Rules of its Proceedings, punish its Members for disorderly Behavior, and, with the Concurrence of two thirds, expel a Member.

3. Each House shall keep a Journal of its Proceedings, and from time to time publish the same, excepting such Parts as may in their Judgment require Secrecy; and the Yeas and Nays of the Members of either House on any question shall, at the Desire of one fifth of those Present, be entered on the Journal.

4. Neither House, during the Session of Congress, shall, without the Consent of the other, adjourn for more than three days, nor to any other Place than that in which the two Houses shall be sitting.

President Andrew Johnson, but the Senate fell one vote short of convicting him. In 1974 President Richard M. Nixon resigned the presidency in the face of almost certain impeachment by the House. The House brought two articles of impeachment against President Bill Clinton in late 1998. Neither charge was supported by even a simple majority vote in the Senate, on February 12, 1999.

Clause 7. Penalty on conviction The punishment of an official convicted in an impeachment case has always been removal from office. The Senate can also bar a convicted person from ever holding any federal office, but it is not required to do so. A convicted person can also be tried and punished in a regular court for any crime involved in the impeachment case.

Section 4. Elections and Meetings

Clause 1. Election In 1842 Congress required that representatives be elected from districts within each State with more than one seat in the House. The districts in each State are drawn by that State's legislature. Seven States now have only one seat in the House: Alaska, Delaware, Montana, North Dakota, South Dakota, Vermont, and Wyoming. The 1842 law also directed that representatives be elected in each State on the same day: the Tuesday after the first Monday in November of every even-numbered year. In 1914 Congress also set that same date for the election of senators.

Clause 2. Sessions Congress must meet at least once a year. The 20th Amendment (1933) changed the opening date to January 3.

Section 5. Legislative Proceedings

Clause 1. Admission of members; quorum In 1969 the Supreme Court held that the House cannot exclude any member-elect who satisfies the qualifications set out in Article I, Section 2, Clause 2.

A majority in the House (218 members) or Senate (51) constitutes a quorum. In practice, both houses often proceed with less than a quorum present. However, any member may raise a point of order (demand a "quorum call"). If a roll call then reveals less than a majority of the members present, that chamber must either adjourn or the sergeant at arms must be ordered to round up absent members.

Clause 2. Rules Each house has adopted detailed rules to guide its proceedings. Each house may discipline members for unacceptable conduct; expulsion requires a two-thirds vote.

Clause 3. Record Each house must keep and publish a record of its meetings. The *Congressional Record* is published for every day that either house of Congress is in session, and provides a written record of all that is said and done on the floor of each house each session.

Clause 4. Adjournment Once in session, neither house may suspend (recess) its work for more than three days without the approval of the other house. Both houses must always meet in the same location.

UNITED STATES CONSTITUTION

Section 6. Compensation, Immunities, and Disabilities of Members

Clause 1. Salaries; immunities Each house sets its members' salaries, paid by the United States; the 27th Amendment (1992) modified this pay-setting power. This provision establishes "legislative immunity." The purpose of this immunity is to allow members to speak and debate freely in Congress itself. Treason is strictly defined in Article III, Section 3. A felony is any serious crime. A breach of the peace is any indictable offense less than treason or a felony; this exemption from arrest is of little real importance today.

Clause 2. Restrictions on office holding No sitting member of either house may be appointed to an office in the executive or in the judicial branch if that position was created or its salary was increased during that member's current elected term. The second part of this clause—forbidding any person serving in either the executive or the judicial branch from also serving in Congress—reinforces the principle of separation of powers.

Section 7. Revenue Bills, President's Veto

Clause 1. Revenue bills All bills that raise money must originate in the House. However, the Senate has the power to amend any revenue bill sent to it from the lower house.

Clause 2. Enactment of laws; veto Once both houses have passed a bill, it must be sent to the President. The President may (1) sign the bill, thus making it law; (2) veto the bill, whereupon it must be returned to the house in which it originated; or (3) allow the bill to become law without signature, by not acting upon it within 10 days of its receipt from Congress, not counting Sundays. The President has a fourth option at the end of a congressional session: If he does not act on a measure within 10 days, and Congress adjourns during that period, the bill dies; the "pocket veto" has been applied to it. A presidential veto may be overridden by a two-thirds vote in each house.

Clause 3. Other measures This clause refers to joint resolutions, measures Congress often passes to deal with unusual, temporary, or ceremonial matters. A joint resolution passed by Congress and signed by the President has the force of law, just as a bill does. As a matter of custom, a joint resolution proposing an amendment to the Constitution is not submitted to the President for signature

Section 6.

1. The Senators and Representatives shall receive a Compensation for their Services, to be ascertained by Law, and paid out of the Treasury of the United States. They shall in all Cases, except Treason, Felony, and Breach of the Peace, be privileged from Arrest during their Attendance at the Session of their respective Houses, and in going to and returning from the same; and for any Speech or Debate in either House, they shall not be questioned in any other Place.

2. No Senator or Representative shall, during the Time for which he was elected, be appointed to any civil Office under the Authority of the United States, which shall have been created, or the Emoluments whereof shall have been increased during such time; and no Person holding any Office under the United States, shall be a Member of either House during his Continuance in Office.

Section 7.

1. All Bills for raising Revenue shall originate in the House of Representatives; but the Senate may propose or concur with amendments as on other Bills.

2. Every Bill which shall have passed the House of Representatives and the Senate, shall, before it become a law, be presented to the President of the United States: If he approve, he shall sign it, but if not he shall return it, with his Objections to that House in which it shall have originated, who shall enter the Objections at large on their Journal, and proceed to reconsider it. If after such Reconsideration two thirds of the House shall agree to pass the Bill, it shall be sent, together with the Objections, to the other House, by which it shall likewise be reconsidered, and if approved by two thirds of that House, it shall become a Law. But in all such Cases the Votes of both Houses shall be determined by Yeas and Nays, and the Names of the Persons voting for and against the Bill shall be entered on the Journal of each House respectively. If any Bill shall not be returned by the President within ten Days (Sunday excepted) after it shall have been presented to him, the Same shall be a law, in like Manner as if he had signed it, unless the Congress by their Adjournment, prevent its Return, in which Case it shall not be a Law.

3. Every Order, Resolution, or Vote to which the Concurrence of the Senate and House of Representatives may be necessary (except on a question of adjournment) shall be presented to the President of the United States; and before the Same shall take Effect, shall be approved by him, or, being disapproved by him, shall be repassed by two thirds of the Senate and House of Representatives, according to the Rules and Limitations prescribed in the Case of a Bill.

Section 8.

The Congress shall have Power

1. To lay and collect Taxes, Duties, Imposts and Excises to pay the Debts and provide for the common Defence and general Welfare of the United States; but all Duties, Imposts and Excises, shall be uniform throughout the United States;

2. To borrow Money on the credit of the United States;

3. To regulate Commerce with foreign Nations, and among the several States, and with the Indian Tribes;

4. To establish an uniform Rule of Naturalization, and uniform Laws on the subject of Bankruptcies throughout the United States;

5. To coin Money, regulate the Value thereof, and of foreign Coin, and fix the Standard of Weights and Measures;

6. To provide for the Punishment of counterfeiting the Securities and current Coin of the United States;

7. To establish Post Offices and post Roads;

8. To promote the Progress of Science and useful Arts, by securing, for limited Times to Authors and Inventors the exclusive Right to their respective Writings and Discoveries;

9. To constitute Tribunals inferior to the supreme Court;

10. To define and punish Piracies and Felonies committed on the high Seas, and Offences against the Law of nations;

11. To declare War, grant Letters of Marque and Reprisal, and make Rules concerning Captures on Land and Water;

or veto. Concurrent and simple resolutions do not have the force of law and, therefore, are not submitted to the President.

Section 8. Powers of Congress

Clause 1. The 18 separate clauses in this section set out 27 of the many expressed powers the Constitution grants to Congress. In this clause Congress is given the power to levy and provide for the collection of various kinds of taxes, in order to finance the operations of the government. All federal taxes must be levied at the same rates throughout the country.

Clause 2. Congress has power to borrow money to help finance the government. Federal borrowing is most often done through the sale of bonds on which interest is paid. The Constitution does not limit the amount the government may borrow.

Clause 3. This clause, the Commerce Clause, gives Congress the power to regulate both foreign and interstate trade. Much of what Congress does, it does on the basis of its commerce power.

Clause 4. Congress has the exclusive power to determine how aliens may become citizens of the United States. Congress may also pass laws relating to bankruptcy.

Clause 5. Congress has the power to establish and require the use of uniform gauges of time, distance, weight, volume, area, and the like.

Clause 6. Congress has the power to make it a federal crime to falsify the coins, paper money, bonds, stamps, and the like of the United States.

Clause 7. Congress has the power to provide for and regulate the transportation and delivery of mail; "post offices" are those buildings and other places where mail is deposited for dispatch; "post roads" include all routes over or upon which mail is carried.

Clause 8. Congress has the power to provide for copyrights and patents. A copyright gives an author or composer the exclusive right to control the reproduction, publication, and sale of literary, musical, or other creative work. A patent gives a person the exclusive right to control the manufacture or sale of his or her invention.

Clause 9. Congress has the power to create the lower federal courts, all of the several federal courts that function beneath the Supreme Court.

Clause 10. Congress has the power to prohibit, as a federal crime: (1) certain acts committed outside the territorial jurisdiction of the United States, and (2) the commission within the United States of any wrong against any nation with which we are at peace.

Clause 11. Only Congress can declare war. However, the President, as commander in chief of the armed forces (Article II, Section 2, Clause 1), can make war without such a formal declaration. Letters of marque and reprisal are commissions authorizing private persons to outfit vessels (privateers) to capture and destroy enemy ships in time of war; they were forbidden in international law by the Declaration of Paris of 1856, and the United States has honored the ban since the Civil War.

Clauses 12 and 13. Congress has the power to provide for and maintain the nation's armed forces. It established the air force as an independent element of the armed forces in 1947, an exercise of its inherent powers in foreign relations and national defense. The two-year limit on spending for the army insures civilian control of the military.

Clause 14. Today these rules are set out in a lengthy, oft-amended law, the Uniform Code of Military Justice, passed by Congress in 1950.

Clauses 15 and 16. In the National Defense Act of 1916, Congress made each State's militia (volunteer army) a part of the National Guard. Today, Congress and the States cooperate in its maintenance. Ordinarily, each State's National Guard is under the command of that State's governor; but Congress has given the President the power to call any or all of those units into federal service when necessary.

Clause 17. In 1791 Congress accepted land grants from Maryland and Virginia and established the District of Columbia for the nation's capital. Assuming Virginia's grant would never be needed, Congress returned it in 1846. Today, the elected government of the District's 69 square miles operates under the authority of Congress. Congress also has the power to acquire other lands from the States for various federal purposes.

Clause 18. This is the Necessary and Proper Clause, also often called the Elastic Clause. It is the constitutional basis for the many and far-reaching implied powers of the Federal Government.

Section 9. Powers Denied to Congress

Clause 1. The phrase "such persons" referred to slaves. This provision was part of the Commerce Compromise, one of the bargains struck in the writing of the Constitution. Congress outlawed the slave trade in 1808.

Clause 2. A writ of habeas corpus, the "great writ of liberty," is a court order directing a sheriff, warden, or other public officer, or a private person, who is detaining another to "produce the body" of the one being held in order that the legality of the detention may be determined by the court.

Clause 3. A bill of attainder is a legislative act that inflicts punishment without a judicial trial. See Article I, Section 10, and Article III, Section 3, Clause 2. An *ex post facto* law is

12. To raise and support Armies; but no Appropriation of Money to that Use shall be for a longer Term than two Years;

13. To provide and maintain a Navy;

14. To make Rules for the Government and Regulation of the land and naval Forces;

15. To provide for calling forth the Militia to execute the Laws of the Union, suppress Insurrections and repel Invasions;

16. To provide for organizing, arming, and disciplining the Militia, and for governing such Part of them as may be employed in the Service of the United States, reserving to the States respectively the Appointment of the Officers, and the Authority of training the Militia according to the discipline prescribed by Congress;

17. To exercise exclusive Legislation in all Cases whatsoever, over such District (not exceeding ten Miles square) as may, by Cession of Particular States, and the Acceptance of Congress, become the Seat of the Government of the United States, and to exercise like Authority over all Places purchased by the Consent of the Legislature of the State in which the Same shall be, for the Erection of Forts, Magazines, Arsenals, Dockyards and other needful Buildings;—And

18. To make all Laws which shall be necessary and proper for carrying into Execution the foregoing Powers and all other Powers vested by this Constitution in the Government of the United States, or in any Department or Officer thereof.

Section 9.

1. The Migration or Importation of such Persons as any of the States now existing shall think proper to admit, shall not be prohibited by the Congress prior to the Year one thousand eight hundred and eight, but a Tax or duty may be imposed on such Importation, not exceeding ten dollars for each Person.

2. The Privilege of the Writ of Habeas Corpus shall not be suspended, unless when in Cases of Rebellion or Invasion the public safety may require it.

3. No Bill of Attainder or ex post facto Law shall be passed.

4. No Capitation, ~~or other direct, Tax~~ shall be laid, unless in Proportion to the Census of Enumeration hereinbefore directed to be taken.

5. No Tax or Duty shall be laid on Articles exported from any State.

6. No Preference shall be given by any Regulation of Commerce or Revenue to the Ports of one State over those of another: nor shall Vessels bound to, or from, one State, be obliged to enter, clear or pay Duties in another.

7. No Money shall be drawn from the Treasury, but in Consequence of Appropriations made by Law; and a regular Statement and Account of the Receipts and Expenditures of all public Money shall be published from time to time.

8. No Title of Nobility shall be granted by the United States: And no Person holding any Office of Profit or Trust under them, shall, without the Consent of the Congress, accept of any present, Emolument, Office, or Title, of any kind whatever, from any King, Prince, or foreign State.

Section 10.

1. No State shall enter into any Treaty, Alliance, or Confederation; grant Letters of Marque and Reprisal; coin Money; emit Bills of Credit; make any Thing but gold and silver Coin a Tender in Payment of Debts; pass any Bill of Attainder, ex post facto Law, or Law impairing the Obligation of Contracts, or grant any Title of Nobility.

2. No State shall, without the Consent of the Congress, lay any Imposts or Duties on Imports or Exports, except what may be absolutely necessary for executing its inspection Laws; and the net Produce of all Duties and Imposts, laid by any State on Imports or Exports, shall be for the Use of the Treasury of the United States; and all such Laws shall be subject to the Revision and Control of the Congress.

3. No State shall, without the Consent of Congress, lay any Duty of Tonnage, keep Troops, or Ships of War in time of Peace, enter into any Agreement or Compact with another State, or with a foreign Power, or engage in War, unless actually invaded, or in such imminent Danger as will not admit of delay.

any criminal law that operates retroactively to the disadvantage of the accused. See Article I, Section 10.

Clause 4. A capitation tax is literally a "head tax," a tax levied on each person in the population. A direct tax is one paid directly to the government by the taxpayer—for example, an income or a property tax; an indirect tax is one paid to another private party who then pays it to the government—for example, a sales tax. This provision was modified by the 16th Amendment (1913), giving Congress the power to levy "taxes on incomes, from whatever source derived."

Clause 5. This provision was a part of the Commerce Compromise made by the Framers in 1787. Congress has the power to tax imported goods, however.

Clause 6. All ports within the United States must be treated alike by Congress as it exercises its taxing and commerce powers. Congress cannot tax goods sent by water from one State to another, nor may it give the ports of one State any legal advantage over those of another.

Clause 7. This clause gives Congress its vastly important "power of the purse," a major check on presidential power. Federal money can be spent only in those amounts and for those purposes expressly authorized by an act of Congress. All federal income and spending must be accounted for, regularly and publicly.

Clause 8. This provision, preventing the establishment of a nobility, reflects the principle that "all men are created equal." It was also intended to discourage foreign attempts to bribe or otherwise corrupt officers of the government.

Section 10. Powers Denied to the States

Clause 1. The States are not sovereign governments and so cannot make agreements or otherwise negotiate with foreign states; the power to conduct foreign relations is an exclusive power of the National Government. The power to coin money is also an exclusive power of the National Government. Several powers forbidden to the National Government are here also forbidden to the States.

Clause 2. This provision relates to foreign, not interstate, commerce. Only Congress, not the States, can tax imports; and the States are, like Congress, forbidden the power to tax exports.

Clause 3. A duty of tonnage is a tax laid on ships according to their cargo capacity. Each State has a constitutional right to provide for and maintain a militia; but no State may keep a standing army or navy. The several restrictions here prevent the States from assuming powers that the Constitution elsewhere grants to the National Government.

EXECUTIVE BRANCH

Section 1. President and Vice President

Clause 1. Executive power, term This clause gives to the President the very broad "executive power," the power to enforce the laws and otherwise administer the public policies of the United States. It also sets the length of the presidential (and vice-presidential) term of office; see the 22nd Amendment (1951), which places a limit on presidential (but not vice-presidential) tenure.

Clause 2. Electoral college This clause establishes the "electoral college," although the Constitution does not use that term. It is a body of presidential electors chosen in each State, and it selects the President and Vice President every four years. The number of electors chosen in each State equals the number of senators and representatives that State has in Congress.

Clause 3. Election of President and Vice President This clause was replaced by the 12th Amendment in 1804.

Clause 4. Date Congress has set the date for the choosing of electors as the Tuesday after the first Monday in November every fourth year, and for the casting of electoral votes as the Monday after the second Wednesday in December of that year.

Clause 5. Qualifications The President must have been born a citizen of the United States, be at least 35 years old,

Article II

Section 1.

1. The executive Power shall be vested in a President of the United States of America. He shall hold his Office during the Term of four Years, and, together with the Vice President, chosen for the same Term, be elected as follows:

2. Each State shall appoint, in such Manner as the Legislature thereof may direct, a Number of Electors, equal to the whole Number of Senators and Representatives to which the State may be entitled in the Congress: but no Senator or Representative, or Person holding an Office of Trust or Profit, under the United States, shall be appointed an Elector.

3. ~~The Electors shall meet in their respective States, and vote by Ballot for two Persons, of whom one at least shall not be an Inhabitant of the same State with themselves. And they shall make a List of all the Persons voted for, and of the Number of Votes for each; which List they shall sign and certify, and transmit sealed to the Seat of the Government of the United States, directed to the President of the Senate. The President of the Senate shall, in the Presence of the Senate and House of Representatives, open all the Certificates, and the Votes shall then be counted. The Person having the greatest Number of Votes shall be the President, if such Number be a majority of the whole Number of Electors appointed; and if there be more than one who have such Majority, and have an equal Number of Votes, then, the House of Representatives shall immediately choose by Ballot one of them for President; and if no Person have a Majority, then from the five highest on the List the said House shall in like Manner choose the President. But in choosing the President, the Votes shall be taken by States, the Representatives from each State having one Vote; a quorum for this Purpose shall consist of a Member or Members from two thirds of the States, and a Majority of all the States shall be necessary to a Choice. In every Case, after the Choice of the President, the Person having the greatest Number of Votes of the Electors shall be the Vice President. But if there should remain two or more who have equal Votes, the Senate shall choose from them by Ballot the Vice President.~~

4. The Congress may determine the Time of choosing the Electors, and the Day on which they shall give their Votes; which Day shall be the same throughout the United States.

5. No Person except a natural born Citizen, or a Citizen of the United States, at the time of the Adoption of this

Constitution, shall be eligible to the Office of President; neither shall any person be eligible to that Office who shall not have attained to the Age of thirty-five Years, and been fourteen Years a Resident within the United States.

6. ~~In Case of the Removal of the President from Office, or of his Death, Resignation, or Inability to discharge the Powers and Duties of the said Office, the Same shall devolve on the Vice President,~~ and the Congress may by Law provide for the Case of Removal, Death, Resignation or Inability, both of the President and Vice President, declaring what Officer shall then act as President, and such Officer shall act accordingly, until the Disability be removed, or a President shall be elected.

7. The President shall, at stated Times, receive for his Services, a Compensation, which shall neither be increased nor diminished during the Period for which he shall have been elected, and he shall not receive within that Period any other Emolument from the United States, or any of them.

8. Before he enter on the Execution of his Office, he shall take the following Oath or Affirmation:
"I do solemnly swear (or affirm) that I will faithfully execute the Office of President of the United States, and will to the best of my Ability, preserve, protect and defend the Constitution of the United States."

Section 2.

1. The President shall be Commander in Chief of the Army and Navy of the United States, and of the Militia of the several States, when called into the actual Service of the United States; he may require the Opinion, in writing, of the principal Officer in each of the executive Departments, upon any Subject relating to the Duties of their respective Offices, and he shall have Power to Grant Reprieves and Pardons for Offences against the United States, except in Cases of Impeachment.

2. He shall have Power, by and with the Advice and Consent of the Senate, to make Treaties, provided two thirds of the Senators present concur; and he shall nominate, and by and with the Advice and Consent of the Senate, shall appoint Ambassadors, other public Ministers and Consuls, Judges of the supreme Court, and all other Officers of the United States, whose Appointments are not herein otherwise provided for, and which shall be established by Law: but the Congress may by Law vest the Appointment of such

and have been a resident of the United States for at least 14 years.

Clause 6. Vacancy This clause was modified by the 25th Amendment (1967), which provides expressly for the succession of the Vice President, for the filling of a vacancy in the Vice Presidency, and for the determination of presidential inability.

Clause 7. Compensation The President now receives a salary of $400,000 and a taxable expense account of $50,000 a year. Those amounts cannot be changed during a presidential term; thus, Congress cannot use the President's compensation as a bargaining tool to influence executive decisions. The phrase "any other emolument" means, in effect, any valuable gift; it does not mean that the President cannot be provided with such benefits of office as the White House, extensive staff assistance, and much else.

Clause 8. Oath of office The chief justice of the United States regularly administers this oath or affirmation, but any judicial officer may do so. Thus, Calvin Coolidge was sworn into office in 1923 by his father, a justice of the peace in Vermont.

Section 2. President's Powers and Duties

Clause 1. Military, civil powers The President, a civilian, heads the nation's armed forces, a key element in the Constitution's insistence on civilian control of the military. The President's power to "require the opinion, in writing" provides the constitutional basis for the cabinet. The President's power to grant reprieves and pardons, the power of clemency, extends only to federal cases.

Clause 2. Treaties, appointments The President has the sole power to make treaties; to become effective, a treaty must be approved by a two-thirds vote in the Senate. In practice, the President can also make executive agreements with foreign governments; these pacts, which are frequently made and usually deal with routine matters, do not require Senate consent. The President appoints the principal officers of the executive branch and all federal judges; the "inferior officers" are those who hold lesser posts.

Clause 3. Recess appointments When the Senate is not in session, appointments that require Senate consent can be made by the President on a temporary basis, as "recess appointments."

Section 3. President's Powers and Duties

The President delivers a State of the Union Message to Congress soon after that body convenes each year. That message is delivered to the nation's lawmakers and, importantly, to the American people, as well. It is shortly followed by the proposed federal budget and an economic report; and the President may send special messages to Congress at any time. In all of these communications, Congress is urged to take those actions the Chief Executive finds to be in the national interest. The President also has the power: to call special sessions of Congress; to adjourn Congress if its two houses cannot agree for that purpose; to receive the diplomatic representatives of other governments; to insure the proper execution of all federal laws; and to empower federal officers to hold their posts and perform their duties.

Section 4. Impeachment

The Constitution outlines the impeachment process in Article I, Section 2, Clause 5 and in Section 3, Clauses 6 and 7.

JUDICIAL BRANCH

Section 1. Courts, Terms of Office

The judicial power conferred here is the power of federal courts to hear and decide cases, disputes between the government and individuals and between private persons (parties). The Constitution creates only the Supreme Court of the United States; it gives to Congress the power to establish other, lower federal courts (Article I, Section 8, Clause 9) and to fix the size of the Supreme Court. The words "during good behavior" mean, in effect, for life.

Section 2. Jurisdiction

Clause 1. Cases to be heard This clause sets out the jurisdiction of the federal courts; that is, it identifies those cases that may be tried in those courts. The federal courts can hear and decide—have jurisdiction over—a case depending on either the subject matter or the parties involved in that case. The jurisdiction of the federal courts in cases involving States was substantially restricted by the 11th Amendment in 1795.

inferior Officers, as they think proper, in the President alone, in the Courts of Law, or in the Heads of Departments.

3. The President shall have Power to fill up all Vacancies that may happen during the Recess of the Senate, by granting Commissions which shall expire at the End of their next Session.

Section 3.

He shall from time to time give to the Congress Information of the State of the Union, and recommend to their Consideration such Measures as he shall judge necessary and expedient; he may, on extraordinary Occasions, convene both Houses, or either of them, and in Case of Disagreement between them, with Respect to the Time of Adjournment, he may adjourn them to such Time as he shall think proper; he shall receive Ambassadors and other public Ministers; he shall take Care that the Laws be faithfully executed, and shall Commission all the Officers of the United States.

Section 4.

The President, Vice President and all Civil Officers of the United States, shall be removed from Office on Impeachment for and Conviction of, Treason, Bribery, or other high Crimes and Misdemeanors.

Article III

Section 1.

The judicial Power of the United States, shall be vested in one supreme Court, and in such inferior Courts as the Congress may from time to time ordain and establish. The Judges, both of the supreme and inferior Courts, shall hold their Offices during good Behavior, and shall, at stated Times, receive for their Services, a Compensation, which shall not be diminished during their Continuance in Office.

Section 2.

1. The judicial Power shall extend to all Cases, in Law and Equity, arising under this Constitution, the Laws of the United States, and Treaties made, or which shall be made, under their Authority;— to all Cases affecting Ambassadors, other public ministers, and Consuls;— to all Cases of Admiralty and maritime Jurisdiction;— to Controversies to which the United States shall be a Party;— to Controversies between two or more States;— ~~between a State and Citizens of another State;—~~ between Citizens of different States;—

between Citizens of the same State claiming Lands under Grants of different States, ~~and between a State, or the Citizens thereof, and foreign States, Citizens, or Subjects.~~

2. In all Cases affecting Ambassadors, other public Ministers and Consuls, and those in which a State shall be a Party, the supreme Court shall have original Jurisdiction. In all the other Cases before mentioned, the supreme Court shall have appellate Jurisdiction, both as to Law and Fact, with such Exceptions, and under such Regulations as the Congress shall make.

3. The trial of all Crimes, except in Cases of Impeachment, shall be by Jury; and such Trial shall be held in the State where the said Crimes shall have been committed; but when not committed within any State, the Trial shall be at such Place or Places as the Congress may by Law have directed.

Section 3.

1. Treason against the United States shall consist only in levying War against them, or in adhering to their Enemies, giving them Aid and Comfort. No Person shall be convicted of Treason unless on the Testimony of two Witnesses to the same overt Act, or on Confession in open Court.

2. The Congress shall have Power to declare the Punishment of Treason, but no Attainder of Treason shall work Corruption of Blood, or Forfeiture except during the Life of the Person attainted.

Article IV

Section 1.

Full Faith and Credit shall be given in each State to the public Acts, Records, and judicial Proceedings of every other State. And the Congress may by general Laws prescribe the Manner in which such Acts, Records and Proceedings shall be proved, and the Effect thereof.

Section 2.

1. The Citizens of each State shall be entitled to all Privileges and Immunities of Citizens in the several States.

Clause 2. Supreme Court jurisdiction Original jurisdiction refers to the power of a court to hear a case in the first instance, not on appeal from a lower court. Appellate jurisdiction refers to a court's power to hear a case on appeal from a lower court, from the court in which the case was originally tried. This clause gives the Supreme Court both original and appellate jurisdiction. However, nearly all of the cases the High Court hears are brought to it on appeal from the lower federal courts and the highest State courts.

Clause 3. Jury trial in criminal cases A person accused of a federal crime is guaranteed the right to trial by jury in a federal court in the State where the crime was committed; see the 5th and 6th amendments. The right to trial by jury in serious criminal cases in the State courts is guaranteed by the 6th and 14th amendments.

Section 3. Treason

Clause 1. Definition Treason is the only crime defined in the Constitution. The Framers intended the very specific definition here to prevent the loose use of the charge of treason—for example, against persons who criticize the government. Treason can be committed only in time of war and only by a citizen or a resident alien.

Clause 2. Punishment Congress has provided that the punishment that a federal court may impose on a convicted traitor may range from a minimum of five years in prison and/or a $10,000 fine to a maximum of death; no person convicted of treason has ever been executed by the United States. No legal punishment can be imposed on the family or descendants of a convicted traitor. Congress has also made it a crime for any person (in either peace or wartime) to commit espionage or sabotage, to attempt to overthrow the government by force, or to conspire to do any of these things.

RELATIONS AMONG THE STATES

Section 1. Full Faith and Credit

Each State must recognize the validity of the laws, public records, and court decisions of every other State.

Section 2. Privileges and Immunities of Citizens

Clause 1. Residents of other States In effect, this clause means that no State may discriminate against the residents of other States; that is, a State's laws cannot draw unreasonable distinctions between its own residents and those of any of the other States. See Section 1 of the 14th Amendment.

Attest: William Jackson,
SECRETARY
George Washington,
PRESIDENT AND DEPUTY
FROM VIRGINIA

NEW HAMPSHIRE
John Langdon
Nicholas Gilman

MASSACHUSETTS
Nathaniel Gorham
Rufus King

CONNECTICUT
William Samuel Johnson
Roger Sherman

NEW YORK
Alexander Hamilton

NEW JERSEY
William Livingston
David Brearley
William Paterson
Jonathan Dayton

PENNSYLVANIA
Benjamin Franklin
Thomas Mifflin
Robert Morris
George Clymer
Thomas Fitzsimons
Jared Ingersoll
James Wilson
Gouverneur Morris

DELAWARE
George Read
Gunning Bedford, Jr.
John Dickinson
Richard Bassett
Jacob Broom

MARYLAND
James McHenry
Dan of St. Thomas
Jennifer
Daniel Carroll

VIRGINIA
John Blair
James Madison, Jr.

NORTH CAROLINA
William Blount
Richard Dobbs Spaight
Hugh Williamson

SOUTH CAROLINA
John Rutledge
Charles Cotesworth
Pinckney
Charles Pinckney
Pierce Butler

GEORGIA
William Few
Abraham Baldwin

The first 10 amendments, the Bill of Rights, were each proposed by Congress on September 25, 1789, and ratified by the necessary three-fourths of the States on December 15, 1791. These amendments were originally intended to restrict the National Government—not the States. However, the Supreme Court has several times held that most of their provisions also apply to the States, through the 14th Amendment's Due Process Clause.

1st Amendment. Freedom of Religion, Speech, Press, Assembly, and Petition

The 1st Amendment sets out five basic liberties: The guarantee of freedom of religion is both a protection of religious thought and practice and a command of separation of church and state. The guarantees of freedom of speech and press assure to all persons a right to speak, publish, and otherwise express their views. The guarantees of the rights of assembly and petition protect the right to join with others in public meetings, political parties, interest groups, and other associations to discuss public affairs and influence public policy. None of these rights is guaranteed in absolute terms, however; like all other civil rights guarantees, each of them may be exercised only with regard to the rights of all other persons.

2nd Amendment. Bearing Arms

Each State has the right to maintain a militia, an armed force for its own protection—today, the National Guard. The National Government and the States can and do regulate the private possession and use of firearms.

3rd Amendment. Quartering of Troops

This amendment was intended to prevent what had been common British practice in the colonial period; see the Declaration of Independence. This provision is of virtually no importance today.

4th Amendment. Searches and Seizures

The basic rule laid down by the 4th Amendment is this: Police officers have no general right to search for or seize evidence or seize (arrest) persons. Except in particular circumstances, they

AMENDMENTS

1st Amendment.

Congress shall make no law respecting an establishment of religion, or prohibiting the free exercise thereof, or abridging the freedom of speech, or of the press; or the right of the people peaceably to assemble, and to petition the Government for a redress of grievances.

2nd Amendment.

A well-regulated Militia being necessary to the security of a free State, the right of the people to keep and bear Arms, shall not be infringed.

3rd Amendment.

No Soldier shall, in time of peace be quartered in any house, without the consent of the Owner, nor, in time of war, but in a manner to be prescribed by law.

4th Amendment.

The right of the people to be secure in their persons, houses, papers, and effects, against unreasonable searches and seizures, shall not be violated, and no Warrants shall issue, but upon probable cause, supported by Oath or affirmation, and particularly describing the place to be searched, and the persons or things to be seized.

5th Amendment.

No person shall be held to answer for a capital, or otherwise infamous crime, unless on a presentment or indictment of a Grand Jury, except in cases arising in the land or naval forces, or in the Militia, when in actual service in time of War, or public danger; nor shall any person be subject for the same offence to be twice put in jeopardy of life or limb; nor shall be compelled in any criminal case to be a witness against himself, nor be deprived of life, liberty, or property, without due process of law; nor shall private property be taken for public use, without just compensation.

6th Amendment.

In all criminal prosecutions, the accused shall enjoy the right to a speedy and public trial, by an impartial jury of the State and district wherein the crime shall have been committed, which district shall have been previously ascertained by law, and to be informed of the nature and cause of the accusation; to be confronted with the witnesses against him; to have compulsory process for obtaining witnesses in his favor, and to have the Assistance of Counsel for his defence.

7th Amendment.

In Suits at common law, where the value in controversy shall exceed twenty dollars, the right of trial by jury shall be preserved, and no fact tried by a jury, shall be otherwise re-examined in any Court of the United States, than according to the rules of the common law.

8th Amendment.

Excessive bail shall not be required, nor excessive fines imposed, nor cruel and unusual punishment inflicted.

9th Amendment.

The enumeration in the Constitution, of certain rights, shall not be construed to deny or disparage others retained by the people.

must have a proper warrant (a court order) obtained with probable cause (on reasonable grounds). This guarantee is reinforced by the exclusionary rule, developed by the Supreme Court: Evidence gained as the result of an unlawful search or seizure cannot be used at the court trial of the person from whom it was seized.

5th Amendment. Criminal Proceedings; Due Process; Eminent Domain

A person can be tried for a serious federal crime only if he or she has been indicted (charged, accused of that crime) by a grand jury. No one may be subjected to double jeopardy—that is, tried twice for the same crime. All persons are protected against self-incrimination; no person can be legally compelled to answer any question in any governmental proceeding if that answer could lead to that person's prosecution. The 5th Amendment's Due Process Clause prohibits unfair, arbitrary actions by the Federal Government; a like prohibition is set out against the States in the 14th Amendment. Government may take private property for a legitimate public purpose; but when it exercises that power of eminent domain, it must pay a fair price for the property seized.

6th Amendment. Criminal Proceedings

A person accused of crime has the right to be tried in court without undue delay and by an impartial jury; see Article III, Section 2, Clause 3. The defendant must be informed of the charge upon which he or she is to be tried, has the right to cross-examine hostile witnesses, and has the right to require the testimony of favorable witnesses. The defendant also has the right to be represented by an attorney at every stage in the criminal process.

7th Amendment. Civil Trials

This amendment applies only to civil cases heard in federal courts. A civil case does not involve criminal matters; it is a dispute between private parties or between the government and a private party. The right to trial by jury is guaranteed in any civil case in a federal court if the amount of money involved in that case exceeds $20 (most cases today involve a much larger sum); that right may be waived (relinquished, put aside) if both parties agree to a bench trial (a trial by a judge, without a jury).

8th Amendment. Punishment for Crimes

Bail is the sum of money that a person accused of crime may be required to post (deposit with the court) as a guarantee that he or she will appear in court at the proper time. The amount of bail required and/or a fine imposed as punishment must bear a reasonable relationship to the seriousness of the crime involved in the case. The prohibition of cruel and unusual punishment forbids any punishment judged to be too harsh, too severe for the crime for which it is imposed.

9th Amendment. Unenumerated Rights

The fact that the Constitution sets out many civil rights guarantees, expressly provides for many protections against government, does not mean that there are not other rights also held by the people.

10th Amendment. Powers Reserved to the States

This amendment identifies the area of power that may be exercised by the States. All of those powers the Constitution does not grant to the National Government, and at the same time does not forbid to the States, belong to each of the States, or to the people of each State.

11th Amendment. Suits Against States

Proposed by Congress March 4, 1794; ratified February 7, 1795, but official announcement of the ratification was delayed until January 8, 1798. This amendment repealed part of Article III, Section 2, Clause 1. No State may be sued in a federal court by a resident of another State or of a foreign country; the Supreme Court has long held that this provision also means that a State cannot be sued in a federal court by a foreign country or, more importantly, even by one of its own residents.

12th Amendment. Election of President and Vice President

Proposed by Congress December 9, 1803; ratified June 15, 1804. This amendment replaced Article II, Section 1, Clause 3. Originally, each elector cast two ballots, each for a different person for President. The person with the largest number of electoral votes, provided that number was a majority of the electors, was to become President; the person with the second highest number was to become Vice President. This arrangement produced an electoral vote tie between Thomas Jefferson and Aaron Burr in 1800; the House finally chose Jefferson as President in 1801. The 12th Amendment separated the balloting for President and Vice President; each elector now casts one ballot for someone as President and a second ballot for another person as Vice President. Note that the 20th Amendment changed the date set here (March 4) to January 20, and that the 23rd Amendment (1961) provides for electors from the District of Columbia. This amendment also provides that the Vice President must meet the same qualifications as those set out for the President in Article II, Section 1, Clause 5.

10th Amendment.

The powers not delegated to the United States by the Constitution, nor prohibited by it to the States, are reserved to the States respectively, or to the people.

11th Amendment.

The Judicial power of the United States shall not be construed to extend to any suit in law or equity, commenced or prosecuted against one of the United States by Citizens of another State, or by Citizens or Subjects of any Foreign State.

12th Amendment.

The Electors shall meet in their respective States and vote by ballot for President and Vice President, one of whom, at least, shall not be an inhabitant of the same State with themselves; they shall name in their ballots the person voted for as President, and in distinct ballots the person voted for as Vice President, and they shall make distinct lists of all persons voted for as President, and of all persons voted for as Vice President, and of the number of votes for each, which lists they shall sign and certify, and transmit sealed to the seat of the government of the United States, directed to the President of the Senate;— The President of the Senate shall, in the presence of the Senate and the House of Representatives, open all the certificates and the votes shall then be counted;— the person having the greatest Number of votes for President shall be the President, if such number be a majority of the whole number of Electors appointed; and if no person have such a majority, then, from the persons having the highest numbers not exceeding three on the list of those voted for as President, the House of Representatives shall choose immediately, by ballot, the President. But in choosing the President, the votes shall be taken by States, the representation from each State having one vote; a quorum for this purpose shall consist of a member or members from two thirds of the States, and a majority of all the States shall be necessary to a choice. And if the House of Representatives shall not choose a President whenever the right of choice shall devolve upon them, before the fourth day of March next following, then the Vice President shall act as President, as in case of death or other constitutional disability of the President. The person having the greatest number of votes as Vice President, shall be the Vice President, if such number be a majority of the whole number of Electors appointed, and if no person have a majority, then from the two highest numbers on the list, the Senate shall choose the Vice President; a quorum for the purpose shall consist of two thirds of the whole number of Senators, a majority of the whole number shall be necessary to a choice. But no person constitutionally ineligible to the office of President shall be eligible to that of Vice-President of the United States.

13th Amendment.

Section 1. Neither slavery nor involuntary servitude, except as a punishment for crime whereof the party shall have been duly convicted, shall exist within the United States, or any place subject to their jurisdiction.

Section 2. Congress shall have power to enforce this article by appropriate legislation.

13th Amendment. Slavery and Involuntary Servitude

Proposed by Congress January 31, 1865; ratified December 6, 1865. This amendment forbids slavery in the United States and in any area under its control. It also forbids other forms of forced labor, except punishments for crime; but some forms of compulsory service are not prohibited—for example, service on juries or in the armed forces. Section 2 gives to Congress the power to carry out the provisions of Section 1 of this amendment.

14th Amendment.

Section 1. All persons born or naturalized in the United States and subject to the jurisdiction thereof, are citizens of the United States and of the State wherein they reside. No State shall make or enforce any law which shall abridge the privileges or immunities of citizens of the United States; nor shall any State deprive any person of life, liberty, or property, without due process of law; nor deny to any person within its jurisdiction the equal protection of the laws.

14th Amendment. Rights of Citizens

Proposed by Congress June 13, 1866; ratified July 9, 1868. Section 1 defines citizenship. It provides for the acquisition of United States citizenship by birth or by naturalization. Citizenship at birth is determined according to the principle of *jus soli*—"the law of the soil," where born; naturalization is the legal process by which one acquires a new citizenship at some time after birth. Under certain circumstances, citizenship can also be gained at birth abroad, according to the principle of *jus sanguinis*—"the law of the blood," to whom born. This section also contains two major civil rights provisions: the Due Process Clause forbids a State (and its local governments) to act in any unfair or arbitrary way; the Equal Protection Clause forbids a State (and its local governments) to discriminate against, draw unreasonable distinctions between, persons.

Most of the rights set out against the National Government in the first eight amendments have been extended against the States (and their local governments) through Supreme Court decisions involving the 14th Amendment's Due Process Clause.

Section 2. Representatives shall be apportioned among the several States according to their respective numbers, counting the whole number of persons in each State, excluding Indians not taxed. But when the right to vote at any election for the choice of electors for President and Vice President of the United States, Representatives in Congress, the Executive and Judicial officers of a State, or the members of the Legislature thereof, is denied to any of the male inhabitants of such State, being twenty-one years of age and citizens of the United States, or in any way abridged, except for participation in rebellion, or other crime, the basis of representation therein shall be reduced in the proportion which the number of such male citizens shall bear to the whole number of male citizens twenty-one years of age in such State.

The first sentence here replaced Article I, Section 2, Clause 3, the Three-Fifths Compromise provision. Essentially, all persons in the United States are counted in each decennial census, the basis for the distribution of House seats. The balance of this section has never been enforced and is generally thought to be obsolete.

Section 3. No person shall be a Senator or Representative in Congress, or elector of President and

This section limited the President's power to pardon those persons who had led the Confederacy during the Civil War. Congress finally removed this disability in 1898.

Vice President, or hold any office, civil or military, under the United States, or under any State, who, having previously taken an oath, as a member of Congress, or as an officer of the United States, or as a member of any State legislature, or as an executive or judicial officer of any State, to support the Constitution of the United States, shall have engaged in insurrection or rebellion against the same, or given aid or comfort to the enemies thereof. But Congress may, by a vote of two thirds of each House, remove such disability.

Section 4 also dealt with matters directly related to the Civil War. It reaffirmed the public debt of the United States; but it invalidated, prohibited payment of, any debt contracted by the Confederate States and also prohibited any compensation of former slave owners.

Section 4. The validity of the public debt of the United States, authorized by law, including debts incurred for payment of pensions and bounties for services in suppressing insurrection or rebellion, shall not be questioned. But neither the United States nor any State shall assume or pay any debt or obligation incurred in aid of insurrection or rebellion against the United States, or any claim for the loss or emancipation of any slave; but all such debts, obligations and claims shall be held illegal and void.

Section 5. The Congress shall have power to enforce, by appropriate legislation, the provisions of this article.

15th Amendment. Right to Vote—Race, Color, Servitude

Proposed by Congress February 26, 1869; ratified February 3, 1870. The phrase "previous condition of servitude" refers to slavery. Note that this amendment does not guarantee the right to vote to African Americans, or to anyone else. Instead, it forbids the States from discriminating against any person on the grounds of his "race, color, or previous condition of servitude" in the setting of suffrage qualifications.

15th Amendment.

Section 1. The right of citizens of the United States to vote shall not be denied or abridged by the United States or by any State on account of race, color, or previous condition of servitude.

Section 2. The Congress shall have power to enforce this article by appropriate legislation.

16th Amendment. Income Tax

Proposed by Congress July 12, 1909; ratified February 3, 1913. This amendment modified two provisions in Article I, Section 2, Clause 3, and Section 9, Clause 4. It gives to Congress the power to levy an income tax, a direct tax, without regard to the populations of any of the States.

16th Amendment.

The Congress shall have power to lay and collect taxes on incomes, from whatever source derived, without apportionment among the several States, and without regard to any census or enumeration.

17th Amendment. Popular Election of Senators

Proposed by Congress May 13, 1912; ratified April 8, 1913. This amendment repealed those portions of Article I, Section 3, Clauses 1 and 2 relating to the election of senators. Senators are now elected by the voters in each State. If a vacancy occurs, the governor of the State involved must call an election to fill the seat; the governor may appoint a senator to serve until the next election, if the State's legislature has authorized that step.

17th Amendment.

The Senate of the United States shall be composed of two Senators from each State, elected by the people thereof, for six years; and each Senator shall have one vote. The electors in each State shall have the qualifications requisite for electors of the most numerous branch of the State legislatures.

When vacancies happen in the representation of any State in the Senate, the executive authority of such State shall issue writs of election to fill such vacancies: *Provided,* That the legislature of any State may empower the executive thereof to make temporary appointments until the people fill the vacancies by election as the legislature may direct.

This amendment shall not be so construed as to

affect the election or term of any Senator chosen before it becomes valid as part of the Constitution.

18th Amendment.

~~**Section 1.** After one year from the ratification of this article the manufacture, sale, or transportation of intoxicating liquors within, the importation thereof into, or the exportation thereof from the United States and all territory subject to the jurisdiction thereof for beverage purposes is hereby prohibited.~~

~~**Section 2.** The Congress and the several States shall have concurrent power to enforce this article by appropriate legislation.~~

~~**Section 3.** This article shall be inoperative unless it shall have been ratified as an amendment to the Constitution by the legislatures of the several States, as provided in the Constitution, within seven years of the date of the submission hereof to the States by Congress.~~

18th Amendment. Prohibition of Intoxicating Liquors

Proposed by Congress December 18, 1917; ratified January 16, 1919. This amendment outlawed the making, selling, transporting, importing, or exporting of alcoholic beverages in the United States. It was repealed in its entirety by the 21st Amendment in 1933.

19th Amendment.

The right of citizens of the United States to vote shall not be denied or abridged by the United States or by any State on account of sex.

Congress shall have power to enforce this article by appropriate legislation.

19th Amendment. Equal Suffrage—Sex

Proposed by Congress June 4, 1919; ratified August 18, 1920. No person can be denied the right to vote in any election in the United States on account of his or her sex.

20th Amendment.

Section 1. The terms of the President and Vice President shall end at noon on the 20th day of January, and the terms of Senators and Representatives at noon on the 3d day of January, of the years in which such terms would have ended if this article had not been ratified; and the terms of their successors shall then begin.

Section 2. The Congress shall assemble at least once in every year, and such meeting shall begin at noon on the 3d day of January, unless they shall by law appoint a different day.

20th Amendment. Commencement of Terms; Sessions of Congress; Death or Disqualification of President-Elect

Proposed by Congress March 2, 1932; ratified January 23, 1933. The provisions of Sections 1 and 2 relating to Congress modified Article I, Section 4, Clause 2, and those provisions relating to the President, the 12th Amendment. The date on which the President and Vice President now take office was moved from March 4 to January 20. Similarly, the members of Congress now begin their terms on January 3. The 20th Amendment is sometimes called the "Lame Duck Amendment" because it shortened the period of time a member of Congress who was defeated for reelection (a "lame duck") remains in office.

Section 3. If, at the time fixed for the beginning of the term of the President, the President elect shall have died, the Vice President elect shall become President. If a President shall not have been chosen before the time fixed for the beginning of his term, or if the President-elect shall have failed to qualify, then the Vice President elect shall act as President until a President shall have qualified; and the Congress may by law provide for the case wherein neither a President elect nor a Vice President elect shall have qualified, declaring who shall then act as President, or the manner in which one who is to act shall be selected, and such

This section deals with certain possibilities that were not covered by the presidential selection provisions of either Article II or the 12th Amendment. To this point, none of these situations has occurred. Note that there is neither a President-elect nor a Vice President-elect until the electoral votes have been counted by Congress, or, if the electoral college cannot decide the matter, the House has chosen a President or the Senate has chosen a Vice President.

person shall act accordingly until a President or Vice President shall have qualified.

Congress has not in fact ever passed such a law. See Section 2 of the 25th Amendment, regarding a vacancy in the vice presidency; that provision could some day have an impact here.

Section 4. The Congress may by law provide for the case of the death of any of the persons from whom the House of Representatives may choose a President whenever the right of choice shall have devolved upon them, and for the case of the death of any of the persons from whom the Senate may choose a Vice President whenever the right of choice shall have devolved upon them.

Section 5 set the date on which this amendment came into force.

Section 5. Sections 1 and 2 shall take effect on the 15th day of October following the ratification of this article.

Section 6 placed a time limit on the ratification process; note that a similar provision was written into the 18th, 21st, and 22nd amendments.

Section 6. This article shall be inoperative unless it shall have been ratified as an amendment to the Constitution by the legislatures of three fourths of the several States within seven years from the date of its submission.

21st Amendment. Repeal of 18th Amendment

Proposed by Congress February 20, 1933; ratified December 5, 1933. This amendment repealed all of the 18th Amendment. Section 2 modifies the scope of the Federal Government's commerce power set out in Article I, Section 8, Clause 3; it gives to each State the power to regulate the transportation or importation and the distribution or use of intoxicating liquors in ways that would be unconstitutional in the case of any other commodity. The 21st Amendment is the only amendment Congress has thus far submitted to the States for ratification by conventions.

21st Amendment.

Section 1. The eighteenth article of amendment to the Constitution of the United States is hereby repealed.

Section 2. The transportation or importation into any State, Territory, or possession of the United States for delivery or use therein of intoxicating liquors, in violation of the laws thereof, is hereby prohibited.

Section 3. This article shall be inoperative unless it shall have been ratified as an amendment to the Constitution by conventions in the several States, as provided in the Constitution, within seven years from the date of the submission hereof to the States by the Congress.

22nd Amendment. Presidential Tenure

Proposed by Congress March 24, 1947; ratified February 27, 1951. This amendment modified Article II, Section I, Clause 1. It stipulates that no President may serve more than two elected terms. But a President who has succeeded to the office beyond the midpoint in a term to which another President was originally elected may serve for more than eight years. In any case, however, a President may not serve more than 10 years. Prior to Franklin Roosevelt, who was elected to four terms, no President had served more than two full terms in office.

22nd Amendment.

Section 1. No person shall be elected to the office of the President more than twice, and no person who has held the office of President, or acted as President, for more than two years of a term to which some other person was elected President shall be elected to the office of the President more than once. But this Article shall not apply to any person holding the office of President, when this Article was proposed by the Congress, and shall not prevent any person who may be holding the office of President, or acting as President, during the term within which this Article becomes operative from holding the office of President or acting as President during the remainder of such term.

Section 2. This article shall be inoperative unless it shall have been ratified as an amendment to the Constitution by the legislatures of three fourths of the several states within seven years from the date of its submission to the States by the Congress.

23rd Amendment.

Section 1. The District constituting the seat of Government of the United States shall appoint in such manner as the Congress may direct:

A number of electors of President and Vice President equal to the whole number of Senators and Representatives in Congress to which the District would be entitled if it were a State, but in no event more than the least populous State; they shall be in addition to those appointed by the States, they shall be considered, for the purposes of the election of President and Vice President, to be electors appointed by a State; and they shall meet in the District and perform such duties as provided by the twelfth article of amendment.

Section 2. The Congress shall have power to enforce this article by appropriate legislation.

23rd Amendment. Presidential Electors for the District of Columbia

Proposed by Congress June 16, 1960; ratified March 29, 1961. This amendment modified Article II, Section I, Clause 2 and the 12th Amendment. It included the voters of the District of Columbia in the presidential electorate; and provides that the District is to have the same number of electors as the least populous State—three electors—but no more than that number.

24th Amendment.

Section 1. The right of citizens of the United States to vote in any primary or other election for President or Vice President, for electors for President or Vice President, or for Senator or Representative in Congress, shall not be denied or abridged by the United States or any State by reason of failure to pay any poll tax or other tax.

Section 2. The Congress shall have power to enforce this article by appropriate legislation.

24th Amendment. Right to Vote in Federal Elections—Tax Payment

Proposed by Congress September 14, 1962; ratified January 23, 1964. This amendment outlawed the payment of any tax as a condition for taking part in the nomination or election of any federal officeholder.

25th Amendment.

Section 1. In case of the removal of the President from office or of his death or resignation, the Vice President shall become President.

Section 2. Whenever there is a vacancy in the office of the Vice President, the President shall nominate a Vice President who shall take office upon confirmation by a majority vote of both Houses of Congress.

Section 3. Whenever the President transmits to the President *pro tempore* of the Senate and the Speaker of the House of Representatives his written declaration

25th Amendment. Presidential Succession, Vice Presidential Vacancy, Presidential Inability

Proposed by Congress July 6, 1965; ratified February 10, 1967. Section 1 revised the imprecise provision on presidential succession in Article II, Section 1, Clause 6. It wrote into the Constitution the precedent set by Vice President John Tyler, who became President on the death of William Henry Harrison in 1841.

Section 2 provides for the filling of a vacancy in the office of Vice President. Prior to its adoption, the office had been vacant on 16 occasions and had remained unfilled for the remainder of each term involved. When Spiro Agnew resigned the office in 1973, President Nixon selected Gerald Ford in accord with this provision; and, when President Nixon resigned in 1974, Gerald Ford became President and then chose Nelson Rockefeller as Vice President.

This section created a procedure for determining if a President is so incapacitated that he cannot perform the powers and duties of his office.

that he is unable to discharge the powers and duties of his office, and until he transmits to them a written declaration to the contrary, such powers and duties shall be discharged by the Vice President as Acting President.

Section 4 deals with the circumstance in which a President will not be able to determine the fact of incapacity. To this point, Congress has not established the "such other body" referred to here. This section contains the only typographical error in the Constitution; in its second paragraph, the word "department" should in fact read "departments."

Section 4. Whenever the Vice President and a majority of either the principal officers of the executive departments or of such other body as Congress may by law provide, transmit to the President *pro tempore* of the Senate and the Speaker of the House of Representatives their written declaration that the President is unable to discharge the powers and duties of his office, the Vice President shall immediately assume the powers and duties of the office as Acting President.

Thereafter, when the President transmits to the President *pro tempore* of the Senate and the Speaker of the House of Representatives his written declaration that no inability exists, he shall resume the powers and duties of his office unless the Vice President and a majority of either the principal officers of the executive department or of such other body as Congress may by law provide, transmit within four days to the President *pro tempore* of the Senate and the Speaker of the House of Representatives their written declaration that the President is unable to discharge the powers and duties of his office. Thereupon Congress shall decide the issue, assembling within forty-eight hours for that purpose if not in session. If the Congress, within twenty-one days after receipt of the latter written declaration, or, if Congress is not in session, within twenty-one days after Congress is required to assemble, determines by two-thirds vote of both Houses that the President is unable to discharge the powers and duties of his office, the Vice President shall continue to discharge the same as Acting President; otherwise, the President shall resume the powers and duties of his office.

26th Amendment. Right to Vote—Age

Proposed by Congress March 23, 1971; ratified July 1, 1971. This amendment provides that the minimum age for voting in any election in the United States cannot be more than 18 years. (A State may set a minimum voting age of less than 18, however.)

26th Amendment.

Section 1. The right of citizens of the United States, who are eighteen years of age or older, to vote shall not be denied or abridged by the United States or by any State on account of age.

Section 2. The Congress shall have the power to enforce this article by appropriate legislation.

27th Amendment. Congressional Pay

Proposed by Congress September 25, 1789; ratified May 7, 1992. This amendment modified Article I, Section 6, Clause 1. It limits Congress's power to fix the salaries of its members—by delaying the effectiveness of any increase in that pay until after the next regular congressional election.

27th Amendment.

No law varying the compensation for the services of the Senators and Representatives, shall take effect, until an election of Representatives shall have intervened.

Section
3 The Origins of American Politics

READING FOCUS

- How did the issue of liberty versus order divide Americans in the 1790s?
- What controversies marked the presidency of John Adams?
- What was the significance of the election of 1800?
- How did Jefferson's administration change the nation?
- Why was the War of 1812 important?

KEY TERMS

strict construction
loose construction
political party
Marbury v. *Madison*
judicial review
Louisiana Purchase
embargo
War of 1812
depression
Missouri Compromise

TAKING NOTES

Copy the chart below. As you read, fill in the major events that occurred during each presidency.

President	Major Events
Washington	• National government assumes states' debts. • Congress creates a tariff on imported goods. •
Adams	
Jefferson	
Madison	
Monroe	

MAIN IDEA

The debate over liberty versus order led to the development of political parties. The nation peacefully transferred power from one party to another, continued to expand westward, and again went to war with Britain.

Setting the Scene Early in the morning of July 11, 1804, two of the nation's most powerful men faced each other on the dueling grounds of Weehawken, New Jersey. One was Aaron Burr, Vice President of the United States. The other was Alexander Hamilton, former Secretary of the Treasury. Each man fired his dueling pistol, and Hamilton was hit in the stomach. He died the next day.

Burr and Hamilton had been political adversaries and bitter personal enemies for years. Yet their duel was much more than personal. It also symbolized the deep political divisions that had opened up in the young United States.

Liberty vs. Order in the 1790s

The debate over the proper role of government did not end when Americans gained a new Constitution and a new government in the late 1780s. In fact, it continued through Washington's administration and beyond.

Hamilton's Economic Program As Secretary of the Treasury under Washington, Hamilton was a keen supporter of strong national power. He had little faith in the people. In his view, the government should take an active role in directing the development of the American economy.

In 1790, Congress approved Hamilton's plan for the national government to take on the debts acquired by the states during the Revolution. The vote was controversial. Southern states did not want to be responsible for northern debts. Yet Hamilton managed to win their support through a deal: If southern states would back Hamilton's debt plan, Hamilton promised northern support for locating the nation's capital in the South. Thus, in 1790, Congress approved both the debt plan and a plan to locate the capital on the banks of the Potomac River.

Hamilton's debt plan was controversial for another reason: the federal government already had a huge debt of about $50 million. To satisfy the concerns of the creditors (the banks and individuals that had lent this money), Hamilton

In 1800, Alexander Hamilton (lower photo) privately circulated a letter critical of President John Adams, a member of his own party. Aaron Burr (upper photo) obtained a copy and had it published, thus embarrassing Hamilton and causing a breach in the Federalist Party.

Section 3
The Origins of American Politics

Section Objectives

1. Find out how the issue of liberty versus order divided Americans in the 1790s.
2. See what controversies marked the presidency of John Adams.
3. Discover the significance of the election of 1800.
4. Learn how Jefferson's administration changed the nation.
5. Read about the importance of the War of 1812.

Bellringer

Warm-Up Activity Ask students if they consider themselves to be Republicans, Democrats, Independents, or members of another political party. Have them define the different goals of these parties.

Have students consider the decision process they went through as they identified their own political affiliation. Can they imagine a circumstance in which they might change their minds about this?

Activating Prior Knowledge Ask students to rate (on a scale of 1–5, with 1 being the lowest possible score) the importance of the following conditions to presidential campaigns: honesty, length, relevance of issues raised during the campaign.

Reading Strategy

As students read this section, have them create an outline of the major headings and write main idea statements for each heading.

RESOURCE DIRECTORY

Teaching Resources
Learning Styles Lesson Plans booklet, pp. 14–15
Guided Reading and Review booklet, pp. 24–28

Lesson Plan

Focus As the Federalists tried to institute their vision of government, their opponents created a new political party to stop them. This led to a bitter and raucous election in 1800, and eventually to the peaceful transfer of power from the Federalists to the Jeffersonians. Once in office, Thomas Jefferson sought both to limit the size of government and to expand the role of President. A few years later, the establishment of the new country was challenged by the War of 1812.

Instruct Explain that Jefferson called the election of 1800 "as real a revolution in the principles of our government as that of 1776 was in its form."

Discuss the steps Jefferson took to limit the role of government and why they were almost guaranteed to make him popular with voters. Ask students to state in their own words Jefferson's dilemma concerning the Louisiana Purchase.

Finally, ask students to create a time line of major events in the War of 1812. Then have them write newspaper headlines on why the Battle of New Orleans unified the country and restored patriotism.

Assess/Reteach Ask students to summarize some ways in which Jefferson's presidency differed from those of his Federalist predecessors, Washington and Adams. Can they define what is meant by "Jeffersonian Democracy"?

Activity
Connecting with History and Conflict

Assign volunteers one of the following roles: a farmer from western Pennsylvania, a French revolutionary, a Dutch banker, John Adams, John Marshall, the wife of a Virginia tobacco planter, a wealthy Boston merchant, or a tavern keeper from upper New York State. Ask students to state their point of view (Federalist or Jeffersonian), giving two reasons in support of their chosen party. **(Verbal/Linguistic; Logical/Mathematical)**

Caption Answers

Viewing History That government agents were corrupt, taking bribes in the form of the very whiskey that was supposed to be taxed.

outlined a specific budget and set up a regular payment plan. Two measures would help raise money to pay off the debts: a tariff—a tax on imported goods—that Congress had created in 1789, and a tax on whiskey passed in 1791.

Hamilton put some of the money raised by these two taxes into a special fund. From that fund, the government paid its creditors interest—an extra sum of money that borrowers pay creditors in return for a loan. To handle these complicated financial matters, Congress again followed Hamilton's lead and established the Bank of the United States in 1791.

Opposition to Hamilton Many Americans objected to the federal government's interference in local and state affairs. They also disliked Hamilton's new taxes. These policies reminded them of British actions toward the colonies in the 1760s. To opponents, the Federalist program, combined with the elegant style of Washington's presidency, suggested a return to aristocracy and monarchy. Many people saw this as an all-out assault on the hard-won liberty of the American people.

Secretary of State Jefferson was particularly opposed to Hamilton's plans. President Washington usually sided with Hamilton, and Jefferson increasingly found himself a minority voice in the President's Cabinet. At the end of 1793, Jefferson resigned as Secretary of State.

Jefferson and Hamilton represented two ways of looking at government and human nature, and two ways of interpreting the Constitution. Jefferson favored a **strict construction,** or interpretation, of the Constitution. That is, he believed that the government should not do anything—such as start a national bank—that the Constitution did not specifically say it could do. Hamilton preferred a **loose construction.** He thought the government could do anything that the Constitution did not say it could *not* do. The differences between the two men went deeper than this, however. Jefferson had more faith in the people than in their government. To him, Hamilton was betraying the ideals of the American Revolution.

VIEWING HISTORY This drawing protesting federal economic plans was done about the time of the Whiskey Rebellion. It shows a government agent collecting taxes—in the form of two kegs of whiskey. **Drawing Inferences** *What is the message of the drawing?*

Declaring Neutrality The outbreak of a war between Britain and France put the United States in a difficult position. The nation could not afford to offend the British, whose navy dominated the oceans. Few people, however, wanted to abandon the French, who had helped Americans during the Revolutionary War. What's more, some Americans, Thomas Jefferson included, viewed the French Revolution of 1789 as an extension of the American Revolution, and therefore favored the French over the British.

The most sensible strategy was to remain neutral, or not to take either side. Thus in April 1793, after his reelection as President, Washington issued a Proclamation of Neutrality.

The Whiskey Rebellion Meanwhile, resistance to Hamilton's economic program grew. In western Pennsylvania and other frontier areas, many people refused to pay the tax on whiskey. Whiskey was critically important to the frontier economy because it was one of the only corn products that could be transported to market without spoiling. In 1794, western Pennsylvania appeared to be in a state of rebellion against the tax. The Whiskey Rebellion followed the tradition of opposition to the Stamp Act and Shays' Rebellion. The rebels closed courts and attacked tax collectors.

President Washington and Secretary Hamilton saw the rebellion as an opportunity to demonstrate the power of the federal government. In the summer of 1794, Washington gathered an army of more than 12,000 men. General "Light Horse Harry" Lee, accompanied by Hamilton, led the army to the Pittsburgh

Resource Directory

Technology

Color Transparencies *Historical Maps,* A55

Sounds of an Era Audio CD *Farewell Address, George Washington* (time: one minute, 15 seconds)

Exploring Primary Sources in U.S. History CD-ROM *Farewell Address, George Washington*

Resource Pro® Critical Thinking Activity *Recognizing Bias: The Seeds of Nationalism,* found on Resource Pro, helps students apply the skill by analyzing a patriotic song written in the 1800s.

area. The rebellion soon dissolved. Washington's tough response had demonstrated that the young American government was committed to enforcing its laws.

Jay's Treaty Also in 1794, the debate over American neutrality between Great Britain and France rose to a fever pitch. Washington and Hamilton believed that the long-term interests of the United States lay with Britain. Therefore Washington sent Chief Justice John Jay to London to negotiate an agreement with the British. In the agreement, called Jay's Treaty, Britain agreed to leave the forts it occupied in the Northwest Territory. (In the Treaty of Paris of 1783, Britain had promised to leave these forts, but had not fully done so.) Other provisions encouraged the expansion of trade between the two nations. Jay was unable, however, to convince the British to end their practice of stopping American ships on the high seas and searching them for British subjects.

Jay's Treaty unleashed a storm of controversy throughout the United States. Many saw it as a sellout to the hated British. Although Congress ratified the treaty in 1795, the Federalists had lost the support of a great many Americans.

Political Parties As early as 1793, artisans and professional men were forming what were called Democratic Societies to oppose the Federalists. Meanwhile, Jefferson and various state leaders were furiously promoting resistance to the Federalists in letters to one another. Historians call these critics Jeffersonian Republicans. They, along with the Federalists, were the first political parties in the United States. A **political party** is a group of people who seek to win elections and hold public office in order to control government policy and programs.

President Washington was opposed to political parties. He was also dismayed over the way in which events in the United States and abroad had divided Americans. By the end of his second term, Washington was eager for retirement. In the midst of criticism from the Jeffersonian Republicans, he chose not to run for a third term. Instead, Vice President John Adams ran for President against Thomas Jefferson in 1796. Adams, a Federalist, gained a majority of electoral votes and was elected President. Because Jefferson finished second in the electoral vote race, Jefferson became the new Vice President under the election system established by the Constitution. Thus the President and the Vice President were of different political parties.

In his Farewell Address of 1796, Washington warned against competing political parties:

KEY DOCUMENTS

> *"[A system of political parties] agitates the Community with ill-founded jealousies and false alarms, kindles the animosity of one part against another, [and] foments [stirs up] occasional riot and insurrection."*
>
> —George Washington, Farewell Address, 1796

John Adams would painfully discover the truth of these words.

The Presidency of John Adams

Despite having served as a leader during the American Revolution and as Vice President for eight years, John Adams lacked the prestige of George Washington. As President, Adams faced the difficult task of trying to govern a young country in which party differences were growing wider and wider.

BIOGRAPHY

John Adams
1735–1826

It was John Adams who nominated George Washington to lead American forces during the Revolutionary War and Thomas Jefferson to write the Declaration of Independence—two brilliant contributions to American independence. Adams is better known for opposing British taxes, being a delegate to both Continental Congresses, and signing the Declaration of Independence. Even so, he served as defense counsel for British soldiers involved in the Boston Massacre, insisting on defending their legal rights at the expense of his own popularity.

In 1796, Adams had the difficult task of succeeding the revered Washington as President. He unwisely kept on Washington's "Hamiltonian" Cabinet, and quarreled with his old friend, Vice President Jefferson. Many years after Adams's loss to Jefferson in the 1800 election, the two friends reconciled and began a long correspondence, which continued until their deaths on the same day, July 4, 1826.

ACTIVITY
Connecting with Culture

Engage students in a discussion about the concept and practice of political parties within a democracy. Ask students to think about the following questions: How does a two-party system allow for greater debate on issues? How does a third party affect the two-party system? What are the advantages and disadvantages of a strong third party? How can the presence of a strong third party challenge affect the outcome of a presidential election? **(Verbal/Linguistic)**

BACKGROUND
Interdisciplinary

The federal government may manipulate money in order to produce a desired economic effect within the American economy. In the 1790s the government sought to pay off war debts from the Revolution completely; by assuming the debts of the states, it aimed to restore national credit, create wealth, and promote new business. During the Great Depression the government, following Keynesian economics, purposely ran up large deficits to get money into circulation, promote private spending, and hasten the return of prosperity.

BACKGROUND
Recent Scholarship

John Adams, David McCullough's biography of our second president, takes a close look at the sometimes acrimonious relationship between Adams and Thomas Jefferson. McCullough writes that these two men were polar opposites—Adams the son of a farmer, Jefferson the son of an aristocratic slave owner. Despite their differences, these two men shared an unshakable commitment to their country. Although they became bitter enemies during their fight for the presidency in 1800, years later Adams and Jefferson renewed their friendship. Amazingly, both men died on July 4, 1826.

CUSTOMIZE FOR ...
Gifted and Talented

Tell students that in 1969 President Nixon announced a policy that he called the "New Federalism." Ask students to write a description, based on what they have learned about Federalist beliefs and programs, of what such a policy might entail. Students might also research and report on the "New Federalism."

Adams also faced the threat of war with France. The French were angry about Jay's Treaty with the British and began seizing American ships in French harbors. In an effort to avoid war, Adams sent officials to Paris to negotiate with the revolutionary government.

The XYZ Affair Once in Paris, the American officials were met by secret agents sent by the French foreign minister. These agents were later identified only as X, Y, and Z. The French agents demanded a bribe of $250,000 and a loan to the French of $10 million before the Americans would even be allowed to see the French foreign minister. Although such a request was common practice in European diplomacy, it outraged Americans and became known as the XYZ Affair.

Refusing to pay the bribe, the American diplomats quickly returned home. They were met with public cries of patriotism, war, and defiance against the French. The slogan "Millions for defense, but not one cent for tribute [bribery]" rang out in the United States. By 1798, France and the United States were fighting an undeclared war. Both sides fired on and seized each other's ships.

The Alien and Sedition Acts The Federalists took advantage of the war crisis to push important new measures through Congress. One measure increased the size of the army. Another, the Alien and Sedition Acts of 1798, proved more controversial. The Sedition Act made it against the law to criticize government officials unless all charges could be proven. The Federalists used the Sedition Act to silence Republican opposition.

Thomas Jefferson and James Madison believed that the Sedition Act violated the constitutional protection of freedom of speech. They responded to the Alien and Sedition Acts with the Virginia and Kentucky resolutions, adopted by the legislatures of those states. According to these resolutions, if a state decided that a law was unconstitutional, it could declare that law "null and void" within the state. This principle of nullification remained untested. Neither Virginia nor Kentucky tried to enforce the resolutions. Still, their defiance of federal power was clear.

The Election of 1800

Tensions between Federalists and Jeffersonian Republicans continued to grow during the late 1790s. As the presidential election of 1800 loomed, many people believed that the future of the nation was at stake. Would the nation tilt toward what Jefferson called "the Spirit of 1776" and the idea of liberty found in the Declaration of Independence? Or would the nation choose the Spirit of 1787, with an emphasis on order as stated in the Constitution?

The campaign of 1800 was truly nasty. Jeffersonian newspapers accused Adams of being a monarchist, which was a terrible insult at the time. Federalists, on the other hand, asserted that Jefferson was a godless man who would lead the United States into chaos.

Jefferson won the popular vote. Both he and Aaron Burr, who had run as the Republicans' vice presidential candidate, received more electoral votes than the Federalist Adams. However, since Jefferson and Burr had the same number of electoral votes, the House of Representatives was required to choose between them. It was Hamilton's opposition to Burr that

MAP SKILLS The election of 1800 revealed the nation's political divisions. **Place** *How does this map show the regional differences in the nation in 1800?*

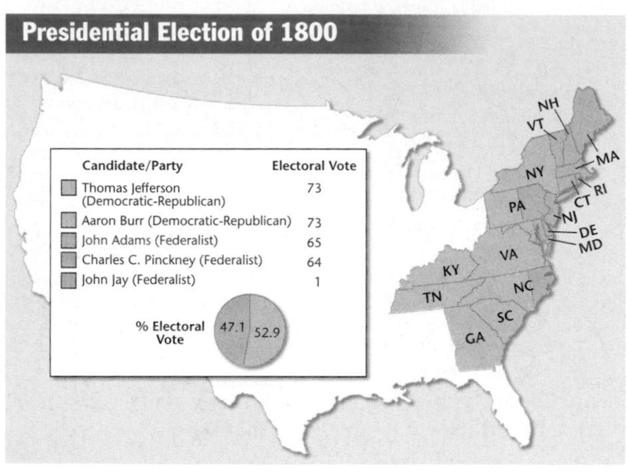

Activity
Connecting with Government

Have students discuss the merits of the Alien and Sedition Acts of 1798. Why did the Federalists act to protect government officials? Were these acts politically motivated? Why or why not? Do you think that these acts violated the constitutional protection of freedom of speech? Would such acts ever win approval today? Why or why not? **(Verbal/Linguistic)**

From the Archives of
American Heritage®

About the Presidents

John Adams (1797–1801) took office under difficult circumstances. In the first place, he succeeded the Father of Our Country—a tough act to follow. Then he made the mistake of keeping Washington's "Hamiltonian" Cabinet. Conflict between Adams and Hamilton, also a Federalist, marred the whole administration. Finally, Adams was saddled with a Vice President who led the opposition. At first, Adams hoped to work effectively with Thomas Jefferson, but a gap developed between them. During hostilities with France, Jefferson refused to go to France as a special envoy. Their differences grew wider over the issues of nullification and the Alien and Sedition Acts. By the end of Adams's term, the two men weren't even speaking. Source: David Jacobs, "John Adams," *The American Heritage® Pictorial History of the Presidents of the United States,* vol. 1, 1968.

Caption Answers

Map Skills The Democratic-Republicans received the most votes from people in the South.

Resource Directory

Other Print Resources

Color Transparencies *Time Lines,* C2

American History Block Scheduling Support *Taking Sides: The Creation of American Political Parties,* found in the Forging a New Nation folder, includes interdisciplinary lesson suggestions and activities for Geography and History, Primary Sources, Biography, and Literature.

finally broke the six-day stalemate and led to the election of Jefferson as the third President of the United States. Hamilton's role in his defeat was just one of a series of grievances that Burr held against Hamilton in their longstanding feud.

READING CHECK
Describe the election of 1800.

Why Adams Lost In a way, John Adams's defeat was an unfair judgment of his abilities. Adams was devoted to public service and, some historians believe, one of the nation's most honorable Presidents. Rising above Federalist hostility to France, he had sent a second diplomatic mission to that country in 1799. This mission had cooled tensions between the United States and France considerably. Like most decisive Presidents, however, Adams had failed to quiet his critics and had angered many of his supporters.

Why Jefferson Won By 1800, Thomas Jefferson was the clear leader of those who preferred local to national government. Jefferson and his followers believed it was better to risk too much liberty than to suffer from too much government. Jefferson always denied that he was a politician. He never saw himself as working to build a permanent political party. Nevertheless, that is exactly what he did.

Jefferson Takes Office

On March 4, 1801, Thomas Jefferson took the oath of office. Whether they stood for individual liberty or a strong central government, Americans had proved that they could transfer power from one party to another—and do it peacefully. Jefferson understood that his administration would not succeed, nor the nation survive, unless Americans were willing to disagree peacefully. As he stated at his inauguration:

NOTABLE PRESIDENTS
Thomas Jefferson

"We hold these truths to be self-evident; that all men are created equal."

—Declaration of Independence

Thomas Jefferson had impressive qualifications for the presidency. The Virginia-born planter and lawyer had not only drafted the Declaration of Independence, but had served as ambassador to France, Secretary of State, and Vice President. Jefferson promised a more democratic government, one that would leave most decisions in the hands of the people.

During his successful first term, Jefferson trimmed the federal government's size and cost, and acted as President in a simple, democratic manner. When given the chance to buy Louisiana from France, he did so, thereby doubling the size of the nation. On the other hand, although he feared the power of federal judges, who were appointed for life, Jefferson failed to limit the federal courts.

Jefferson's second term was less successful. His embargo of 1807, which halted trade with European nations until they promised to stop harassing American ships, was a disaster. Americans ignored the embargo, and it was repealed before a disappointed Jefferson left office in 1809.

In his time, Jefferson's commitment to equality among white men, as well as his opposition to slavery, were brave and radical ideas. Today, Jefferson remains a puzzle for historians: the author of some of the most eloquent words ever written about human freedom was himself the owner of slaves.

3rd President 1801–1809

Connecting to Today
Explain a current issue in which one or both sides might use the famous phrase "all men are created equal" to support their case.

Take It to the NET **Biography** To read more about Thomas Jefferson, visit the links provided in the *America: Pathways to the Present* area of the following Web site. **www.phschool.com**

ACTIVITY
Connecting with History and Conflict

Tell students to research the contentious battle for the presidency in 1800. Suggest that students explore Hamilton's role, Jefferson's appeal to the electorate, and Adams's response to his defeat. Have small groups present their findings, and discuss why this complex election proved to be a fierce battle of personalities. **(Verbal/Linguistic)**

BACKGROUND
Biography

Although Thomas Jefferson (1743–1826) was not a strong public speaker, this tall, reserved man was an eloquent writer who made important contributions to the Declaration of Independence, among many other important American documents. He authored the famous phrase stating ". . . that all men are created equal, that among their inalienable rights are life, liberty, and the pursuit of happiness." Jefferson worked hard to ensure that the new country would protect individual rights, freedom of the press, and religious freedom. In addition, he was a successful scientist, architect, and agriculturist.

From the Archives of **American Heritage®**

What Made the Government Grow?

In the early years of the federal government, the Treasury Department was the largest of the federal departments. By 1801, 78 people worked in the Washington, D.C., office and 1,615 others worked in the field, collecting taxes and import duties. Source: Bernard A. Weisberger, "What Made the Government Grow?" *American Heritage®* magazine, September 1997.

CUSTOMIZE FOR ...
Less Proficient Writers

Ask students to find five or more words in the section that are new to them. Have them define the words by using context clues or by looking them up in a dictionary. Have them use each of the new words in a sentence.

READING CHECK
Following a nasty campaign, Jefferson won the popular vote over Adams. However, since Jefferson and Burr had the same number of electoral votes, the House of Representatives was required to choose between them. After a stalemate, Hamilton's influence was instrumental in Jefferson's election.

ACTIVITY
Connecting with Citizenship

Have students write an essay stating whether they think Presidents should be able to make last-minute decisions before leaving office. Tell students to consider some of the following issues: a President's desire to have a lasting impact; a President's wish to bestow favors on those who have supported the presidency; a President's potential abuse of office. When students complete their essays, have volunteers read theirs aloud. **(Verbal/Linguistic)**

BACKGROUND
Connections to Today

While outgoing President John Adams made last-minute judicial appointments that proved controversial, President Bill Clinton ended his term with a series of pardons that caused public outrage. The most controversial pardon was that of fugitive financier Marc Rich. When the media revealed that Rich's estranged wife had made large contributions to the Clinton campaign, the public responded angrily.

Focus on GEOGRAPHY

The Lewis and Clark Expedition President Thomas Jefferson appointed Meriwether Lewis and William Clark to lead an expedition to explore the Louisiana Territory. The Lewis and Clark expedition—some 40 men and Lewis's Newfoundland dog—began in the spring of 1804. Its goals were to search for river routes to the western ocean, make contact with the Native Americans living in the territory, and gather information about the region's natural resources. To help in this task, the expedition hired a French-Canadian fur trapper and his wife Sacajawea, a Shoshone Indian, as interpreters. The expedition reached the Pacific Ocean late in 1805 and returned to St. Louis in September 1806.

The expedition encountered a wide range of wild creatures. Clark reported seeing a massive herd of some 10,000 buffalo. Grizzly bears sent the men scurrying up a tree. Lewis and Clark's detailed journals, maps, and drawings provided President Jefferson and a curious American public with extensive information about the new American West.

KEY DOCUMENTS *"We are all republicans—we are all federalists. If there be any among us who would wish to dissolve this Union or to change its republican form, let them stand undisturbed as monuments of the safety with which error [difference] of opinion may be tolerated where reason is left free to combat it."*

—Thomas Jefferson, First Inaugural Address, 1801

Reducing Government Jefferson entered office with a straightforward agenda, or list of things that he wanted to accomplish. His goal was to reduce the influence of the national government in the lives of the American people.

Together with Congress, Jefferson reduced taxes and severely cut the size of the federal bureaucracy—the departments and workers that make up the federal government. He also slashed the size of the army from 12,000 soldiers to only 3,000. Jefferson, however, did not intend to undo all the acts of the Federalists. For example, he let the Bank of the United States continue to function, knowing that its 20-year term would run out in 1811. These aspects of Jefferson's program made him an extremely popular President during his first term, and he easily won reelection in 1804.

Marbury* v. *Madison Jefferson's first term was not without controversy, however. That controversy involved the judicial branch, particularly the Supreme Court.

Near the end of the administration of President John Adams, Congress had passed the Judiciary Act of 1801, which increased the number of federal judges. Adams filled the new judicial posts just before leaving office. These last-minute appointments, known as the midnight judges, angered Jefferson, who believed that he had the right to appoint judges from his own party. Included as one of Adams's last-minute acts was the appointment of John Marshall, a long-time Federalist, as Chief Justice (the leading judge of the Supreme Court). This appointment was to have far-reaching effects—beginning with the historic case of ***Marbury* v. *Madison*** (1803).

This case arose when Jefferson tried to block the activities of Federalist judges. Just before he left office, Adams had appointed William Marbury as justice of the peace for the District of Columbia. But Secretary of State James Madison, under orders from Jefferson, never delivered the official papers giving Marbury his authority. Marbury sued Madison, demanding that the Supreme Court order the Secretary of State to let him take his office. According to the Judiciary Act of 1789, the Court had the power to give such an order.

Marshall ruled against Marbury, declaring that it was against the Constitution for the Supreme Court to give this order to the executive branch. In other words, Marshall declared part of the Judiciary Act of 1789 unconstitutional—the first time a federal court had been so bold.

The Court's ruling was a victory for Jefferson. Yet in a much larger sense it was a victory for the Supreme Court, for it established the power of **judicial review.** This is the power of federal courts to review state laws and state court decisions to determine if they are in keeping with the federal Constitution. Judicial review also allows federal courts to decide whether laws passed by Congress are constitutional.

RESOURCE DIRECTORY

Other Print Resources

American History Block Scheduling Support *Checks and Balances: The Rise of the American Judiciary,* found in the Forging a New Nation folder, includes interdisciplinary lesson suggestions and activities for Geography and History, Primary Sources, Biography, and Literature.

Nystrom *Atlas of Our Country* *Early Expansion of the United States,* pp. 20–21

Historical Outline Map Book *Western Land Claims* and *Exploring the Louisiana Purchase,* pp. 29–30

Technology

Color Transparencies *Historical Maps,* A9, A10, A60

Exploring Primary Sources in U.S. History CD-ROM *The Journals of Lewis and Clark*

RESOURCE PRO® **Visual Learning Activity** *Honoring Thomas Jefferson,* found on Resource Pro, features a picture of Jefferson's burial monument, which shows the achievements for which he wanted to be remembered.

The Louisiana Purchase As a strict constructionist, Jefferson opposed the development of a strong central government. In issues concerning American expansion west of the Appalachians, however, Jefferson used the power and money of the national government as boldly as the Federalists had ever dared.

In 1803, Jefferson sent James Monroe to Paris to buy the city of New Orleans, a port important to American farmers, from France. Napoleon offered instead to sell *all* of the French claims known as Louisiana. Jefferson overcame his doubts about the constitutionality of purchasing foreign lands and the expenditure of $15 million of public funds, and urged Congress to approve the sale. With the stroke of a pen, the **Louisiana Purchase** dramatically increased both the national debt and the size of the United States.

Congress also agreed to finance an expedition to explore the area included in the Louisiana Purchase. The Lewis and Clark expedition, which set out in 1804 and returned in 1806, reached all the way to the Pacific Ocean. Additional information about the West was gathered by Zebulon Pike, who traveled as far west as the Rockies and then south into Spanish-held territory.

Jefferson's Foreign Policy Jay's Treaty, under which the United States had remained at peace with Great Britain since 1795, expired in 1805. By then, Europeans were back at war with each other. Both British and French warships began harassing American trading ships. The British also kidnapped American sailors to serve in their navy. Although Jefferson was outraged by these acts, he rejected the use of force, in part because of the small size of the American navy. Instead, he convinced Congress to pass the Embargo Act of 1807, which outlawed almost all trade with foreign countries. (An **embargo** is a restriction on trade.)

The embargo did not severely injure its intended targets, Britain and France. It did, however, hurt Americans who made their living through trade, and it also ruined Jefferson's second term. While he was able to see his friend and Secretary of State, James Madison, elected President in 1808, the nation's third President retired to his home at Monticello an unpopular figure.

Chief Justice John Marshall was instrumental in determining how the Constitution would be interpreted by future generations.

MAP SKILLS Lewis and Clark not only reached the Pacific Ocean but also had to make their way back to St. Louis. **Movement** *What do you think were the most difficult obstacles they faced? Explain your reasoning.*

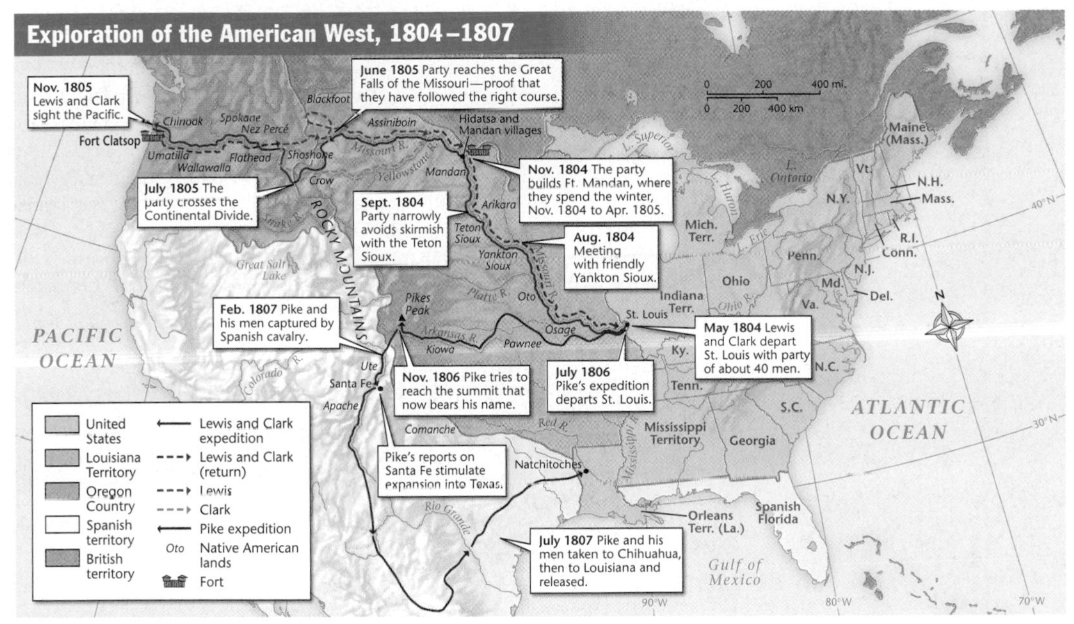

Exploration of the American West, 1804–1807
Nov. 1805 Lewis and Clark sight the Pacific.
June 1805 Party reaches the Great Falls of the Missouri—proof that they have followed the right course.
July 1805 The party crosses the Continental Divide.
Sept. 1804 Party narrowly avoids skirmish with the Teton Sioux.
Nov. 1804 The party builds Ft. Mandan, where they spend the winter, Nov. 1804 to Apr. 1805.
Aug. 1804 Meeting with friendly Yankton Sioux.
Feb. 1807 Pike and his men captured by Spanish cavalry.
May 1804 Lewis and Clark depart St. Louis with party of about 40 men.
Nov. 1806 Pike tries to reach the summit that now bears his name.
July 1806 Pike's expedition departs St. Louis.
Pike's reports on Santa Fe stimulate expansion into Texas.
July 1807 Pike and his men taken to Chihuahua, then to Louisiana and released.
Fort Clatsop
Chinook
Spokane
Nez Percé
Blackfoot
Assiniboin
Hidatsa and Mandan villages
Umatilla
Wallawalla
Flathead
Shoshone
Crow
Mandan
Arikara
Teton Sioux
Yankton Sioux
Oto
Osage
Pawnee
Kiowa
Ute
Apache
Comanche
Great Salt Lake
ROCKY MOUNTAINS
Pikes Peak
Santa Fe
St. Louis
Natchitoches
Orleans Terr. (La.)
Spanish Florida
Mississippi Territory
Georgia
Tenn.
Ky.
Indiana Terr.
Ohio
Mich. Terr.
Penn.
N.Y.
Vt.
N.H.
Mass.
Maine (Mass.)
R.I.
Conn.
N.J.
Del.
Md.
Va.
N.C.
S.C.
PACIFIC OCEAN
ATLANTIC OCEAN
Gulf of Mexico
0 200 400 mi.
0 200 400 km
United States
Louisiana Territory
Oregon Country
Spanish territory
British territory
Lewis and Clark expedition
Lewis and Clark (return)
Lewis
Clark
Pike expedition
Oto Native American lands
Fort

ACTIVITY

Connecting with History and Conflict

Throughout history, the U.S. government has used trade embargoes to send a message to an unfriendly nation. These political acts always have economic consequences. Have students learn about some of the countries, such as Cuba, Iraq, and Afghanistan, that have been targets of recent U.S. embargoes. Tell students to find out about the effects of these trade embargoes. When they finish their research, engage students in a discussion about what they have learned. **(Verbal/Linguistic)**

BACKGROUND

Biography

Chief Justice John Marshall (1755–1835) was licensed to practice law by his cousin Thomas Jefferson. But Marshall, stating a firm belief in "a more efficient and better organized general government," embarked upon a lifelong crusade against the Jeffersonian cause of states' rights. One hundred years after his death, a scholar said that Marshall "embodied in his career clear proof that ours is a government of men, not laws."

TEST PREPARATION

Have students read the section about the Louisiana Purchase on this page, and then answer the question below.

What was the original goal of the expedition of Lewis and Clark?

A To discover new Indian tribes in western lands.
B To find the shortest route to the Pacific Ocean.
(C) To explore the land included in the Louisiana Purchase.
D To claim more territory for the United States.

CAPTION ANSWERS

Map Skills Answers will vary, but may include rivers and mountains; winter weather; wild animals; hostile Native Americans; the very length of the journey; and continual need for supplies.

ACTIVITY
Connecting with History and Conflict

Tell students to research some of the underlying causes of the War of 1812, such as the conflict between Napoleon and Great Britain. Have students learn about the reasons for this conflict. Ask students to find out why the United States was caught in the conflict and how we became entangled in the war. **(Verbal/Linguistic)**

BACKGROUND
Connections to Today

An intense spirit of nationalism ensued after both the American Revolution and the War of 1812. This unifying spirit, which usually accompanies times of conflict, was conspicuously absent during the Vietnam War in the 1960s and 1970s. Many citizens protested openly against the war on a grand scale, and many refused to join the armed forces.

ACTIVITY
Connecting with Economics

War can take its toll—both emotionally and economically. But while the War of 1812 weakened the nation's economy, some wars, such as World War II, actually provide economic stimulus. Discuss with students ways in which war can mobilize the country. Suggest they consider the boost to war-related industries, and the resulting jobs, both for civilians and those in combat. Encourage students to consider some of the other economic effects of war. **(Verbal/Linguistic)**

The War of 1812

Trouble between the United States and Britain was not limited to the high seas. It was also the result of Britain's encouragement of Native American resistance to American settlement of the West.

VIEWING HISTORY The Shawnee prophet Tenskwatawa urged his followers to return to traditional Native American ways and reject all European values. **Drawing Inferences** *Why do you think his message appealed to Native Americans at this time?*

Native American Resistance At the beginning of the 1800s, Native Americans found their power greatly reduced. In the early 1790s, many Indian groups had joined together to fight American expansion to the west. After some early success, they suffered a series of crushing defeats. They were forced to accept the loss of the southern two thirds of Ohio and to recognize that the Ohio River was no longer a permanent boundary between their lands and the lands of American settlers.

In 1808, two important Native American leaders made another attempt to stop westward expansion. The Shawnee prophet Tenskwatawa established Prophetstown on the Wabash River (near present-day Lafayette, Indiana). There, he began to show an increasingly warlike attitude toward the United States. In 1810, Tenskwatawa's older brother, Tecumseh, and several dozen warriors met with Governor William Henry Harrison of the Indiana Territory to complain that whites were buying Native American lands without the approval of all Native Americans who lived there. Instead of resolving the issue, the meeting led to a battle between Tenskwatawa's warriors and Harrison's militia. Neither side won the Battle of Tippecanoe, but the confrontation shattered Native American morale. Within a few days, Harrison burned an abandoned Prophetstown to the ground.

War With Britain When Native Americans increased their attacks against settlers who were moving onto their lands, most Americans believed that the Indians were being encouraged and armed by the British. In Congress, calls for war against Britain came from members who represented the interests of western farmers. In June 1812, President Madison asked Congress to declare war against the British. Congress approved, and the **War of 1812** began.

In many ways, the declaration of war was a foolhardy action. The United States had only a small army and navy, and no offers of help from foreign countries. Nevertheless, American troops invaded British-held Canada—and were beaten by the British in the summer of 1812. Meanwhile, the British used their superior sea power to blockade the American coast and strangle American trade. Then, in 1814, a British fleet sailed up Chesapeake Bay and landed about 4,000 troops, who marched on Washington, D.C. On August 24, 1814, the enemy entered the American capital and started fires that consumed the city. Even the Capitol and the White House were gutted by flames, and President Madison and his wife were forced to flee.

The British troops next moved toward Baltimore. An American named Francis Scott Key witnessed an all-night British bombardment of Fort McHenry, at the entrance to Baltimore harbor, and wrote this testimony to the Americans' determination:

> *"And the rocket's red glare,*
> *the bombs bursting in air*
> *Gave proof through the night*
> *that our flag was still there.*
> *O say, does that Star-Spangled*
> *Banner yet wave*
> *O'er the land of the free*
> *and the home of the brave?"*
>
> —Francis Scott Key, "The Star-Spangled Banner"

CAPTION ANSWERS

Viewing History Answers will vary, but may include the Native Americans' recent losses and feelings of helplessness and hostility toward the white settlers who were taking their land and threatening their way of life.

RESOURCE DIRECTORY

Teaching Resources

Learning with Documents booklet *Native American Politics,* p. 11; *"The Present State of Our Country,"* p. 45; *"The Star-Spangled Banner,"* p. 78

Biography, Literature, and Comparing Primary Sources booklet *For and Against the War of 1812,* p. 107; *William Henry Harrison,* p. 11; *An Illustrious Career,* pp. 45–46

Other Print Resources

American History Block Scheduling Support *Proud to Be American: A New Spirit of Nationalism,* found in the Forging a New Nation folder.

Historical Outline Map Book *Land Acquired from Native Americans to 1810* and *The War of 1812,* pp. 31–32

Technology

Color Transparencies *Historical Maps,* A11

Exploring Primary Sources in U.S. History CD-ROM *On the Burning of Washington, Dolly Madison; "The Star-Spangled Banner," Francis Scott Key; Sell a Country! Why Not Sell the Air?, Tecumseh*

RESOURCE PRO® **Biography** *Francis Scott Key,* profiles the man who wrote "The Star-Spangled Banner."

The "star-spangled banner" did indeed still wave over the fort, and American forces were able to turn back the enemy.

Not all Americans felt as patriotic about the War of 1812 as did Francis Scott Key. "Mr. Madison's War," others bitterly called it, while pointing to the harm it had done to the country. The national treasury was empty, the Capitol lay in ruins, and the British blockade had brought trade to a standstill. In December 1814, New Englanders sent delegates to a meeting in Hartford, Connecticut, to consider the possibility of leaving the nation. In the end, the Hartford Convention called only for constitutional amendments to increase New England's political power.

Meanwhile, both the British and the Americans had recognized that this was a war no one wanted. On December 24, 1814, representatives of the two nations signed the Treaty of Ghent, ending the War of 1812.

Before news of the treaty reached the warring armies, however, a British force tried to capture New Orleans. General Andrew Jackson and soldiers and volunteers from all over the Mississippi Valley successfully defended the city. The British suffered more than 2,000 casualties; the Americans, fewer than two dozen. The Battle of New Orleans was a remarkable victory for the United States. It allowed Americans to end an unhappy war on a powerful, positive note. The battle also made Andrew Jackson a national hero.

Postwar Issues

In 1815, the United States entered a period of growth and prosperity. Republican James Monroe of Virginia, easily won election as the fifth President of the

MAP SKILLS Although the United States considered the War of 1812 a victory over Britain, in the end neither side gained nor lost any territory. **Movement** *Why was the British naval blockade such a threat?*

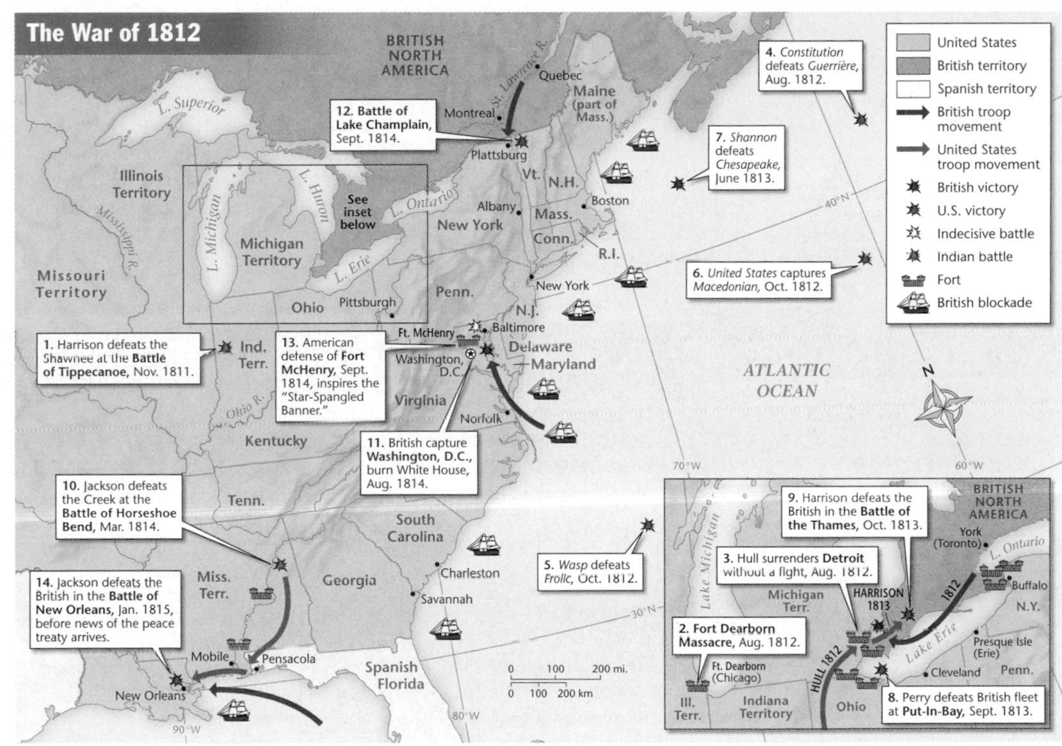

From the Archives of

AmericanHeritage®

About the Presidents

James Madison (1809–1817) understood clearly that Americans were divided about waging a war with Britain. But he had already tried diplomacy, embargo, and threats. American ships and seamen were still being harassed. The war vote in Congress reflected the nation's disunity—79 to 49 in the House, 19 to 13 in the Senate. Not surprisingly, Congress was slow to approve funds for fighting the war. And though the frontier states were united in the war effort, the New England states refused to be involved. In fact, the Treaty of Ghent settled few of the issues that started the war. But the President's prestige was enhanced for standing up to the world's strongest empire. Source: Vincent Buranelli, "James Madison," *The American Heritage® Pictorial History of the Presidents of the United States,* vol. 1, 1968.

From the Archives of

AmericanHeritage®

About the Presidents

When James Monroe (1817–1825) became President, the United States was growing rapidly. Americans were already looking at the Pacific Ocean as their eventual border in the West. The question of north-south boundaries was less clear, however. In 1817 Monroe sent negotiators to London to settle the northern border with Canada. The Convention of 1818 set the 49th parallel as the boundary as far as the Rockies. Beyond the Rockies Americans and Canadians would share equally in the Oregon Territory. Source: David Jacobs, "James Monroe," *The American Heritage® Pictorial History of the United States,* vol. 1, 1968.

Caption Answers

Map Skills It not only threatened the United States economy, but it also allowed British troops access to Washington, D.C.

Section 3 Assessment

Reading Comprehension

1. Strict construction is an interpretation of the Constitution that supports the belief that the government should not do anything that the Constitution does not specifically say it could do. Loose construction is the interpretation of the Constitution that suggests that the government could do anything that the Constitution does not forbid.
2. The Supreme Court declared part of the Judiciary Act of 1789 unconstitutional, and thus established the power of judicial review.
3. Sample answer: It provided a port important to American farmers and dramatically increased the size of the United States.
4. An 1820 agreement calling for the admission of Missouri as a slave state and Maine as a free state, and outlawing slavery in future states to be created north of 36° 30° N latitude.

Critical Thinking and Writing

5. Political parties arose out of the support and opposition provoked by the Federalist program. Jeffersonian Republicans is the name given to the party that consisted of those in the 1790s who opposed such things as Hamilton's budget plan and the taxes the plan would entail. Such measures seemed intrusive and heavy-handed to the Jeffersonian Republicans. The Federalists can be said to date back further, at least as early as the writing of the essays contained in *The Federalist.* A strong national government was a consistent theme of the Federalists.
6. Answers will vary, but should include: Increased: Louisiana Purchase; Decreased: reduced taxes and cut the size of the federal bureaucracy. Explanations should be convincing and should be supported with material from the section.

Invite students to take a Virtual Field Trip at **www.phschool.com**

Caption Answers

Map Skills (a) New free states. (b) It would affect representation in the House of Representatives and ultimately affect manpower during the Civil War.

MAP SKILLS The Missouri Compromise kept the *number* of free and slave states even. **Regions** *(a) Which would cover more land under the Compromise: areas that permitted slavery or those that did not? (b) Why might this difference prove important?*

United States in 1816. Monroe and the Republican Party dominated American politics, as the Federalists faded out of existence.

Banks and the Economy Congress, in an attempt to deal with financial problems resulting from the war, created the Second Bank of the United States in 1816. (The first national bank had dissolved in 1811.) Encouraged by abundant credit and federal land laws, Americans began moving westward at an incredible rate. Meanwhile, American trade with Europe boomed.

Then, in 1819, the United States experienced the first great **depression,** or severe economic downturn, in its history. Known as the Panic of 1819, it began across the Atlantic when London banks demanded that banks in the United States pay money owed to them. American banks in turn demanded the money that they had loaned to the American public. Many of the Americans who had borrowed too much in the days of easy loans after 1815 were financially ruined.

The Missouri Compromise While the economy would eventually rebound from the depression, another problem that year would pose a greater long-term danger. In 1819, Congress began debating the admission of Missouri as a state. The underlying issue was slavery. Several members of Congress from the North objected to admitting Missouri as a slave state. They were not simply concerned about the liberty of African Americans; they worried that another slave state would increase the power of the South in the Senate. Southern members of Congress replied that the federal government had no business dictating to states what they could and could not do.

After months of bitter debate, in 1820 Congress reached what is now called the **Missouri Compromise.** Slavery would be permitted in Missouri; at the same time, Maine was carved out of northern Massachusetts and admitted to the Union as a free (nonslave) state. This arrangement kept the balance in the Senate between slave and free states. Furthermore, Congress agreed that as the United States expanded westward, states north of 36° 30′ N latitude would be free states.

Section 3 Assessment

READING COMPREHENSION

1. Explain the difference between **strict construction** and **loose construction** of the Constitution.
2. What was the importance of ***Marbury* v. *Madison?***
3. Give two reasons why the **Louisiana Purchase** was important.
4. What was the **Missouri Compromise?**

CRITICAL THINKING AND WRITING

5. **Determining Relevance** How did the continuing American debate over liberty versus order lead to the development of political parties?
6. **Writing a List** Make two lists to show how Jefferson both reduced and increased the power of the national government. Briefly explain each example in your lists.

Take It to the NET

Activity: Virtual Field Trip Learn more about the Lewis and Clark expedition by visiting an online exhibit that focuses on their journey. Use the links provided in the *America: Pathways to the Present* area of the following Web site for help in completing this activity.
www.phschool.com

RESOURCE DIRECTORY

Teaching Resources

Units 1/2 booklet
- Section 3 Quiz, p. 16
- Chapter 2 Test, pp. 17, 20

Guide to the Essentials
- Section 3 Summary, p. 11
- Chapter 2 Test, p. 12

Other Print Resources

Chapter Tests with ExamView® Test Bank CD-ROM, Ch. 2

Technology

Color Transparencies *Historical Maps,* A12
ExamView® Test Bank CD-ROM, Ch. 2
Social Studies Skills Tutor CD-ROM

Creating an Oral or Visual Presentation

How can you make a historical event come alive for an audience? One way is to synthesize several kinds of sources to create an oral or visual presentation. Suppose your topic is the burning of Washington, D.C., by the British in 1814. Although there are no photographs or recordings of the event, you can show maps, diagrams, paintings, and drawings, or you can read aloud from primary sources such as newspaper accounts, letters, and journals. The author of Source A below was a captain in a British regiment that burned the White House. Source B was written in the White House by the First Lady.

LEARN THE SKILL

Use the following steps to create an oral or visual presentation:

1. **Explore a variety of sources.** Use a reliable secondary source for general information. Consider the topic: Are there likely to be letters or diaries? What visual depictions might be useful?
2. **Select and evaluate your sources.** Knowing the background of a writer or the source of a map helps you evaluate the information. For balance, try to select sources representing different points of view. Also vary the types of sources.
3. **Draw conclusions.** Determine the main points of each source. Combine different pieces of information to present and support your conclusions.
4. **Give life to your presentation.** Read excerpts from primary sources aloud as though you were the historical person who wrote them, show a variety of illustrations depicting the event, or combine oral and visual presentations for a more dramatic effect.

PRACTICE THE SKILL

Answer the following questions:

1. **(a)** Are Sources A and B primary or secondary sources? **(b)** How can you tell? **(c)** Taken together, do your sources represent one side of the War of 1812, or both sides?
2. **(a)** What information do you get from Source A that you would not get from the American side? **(b)** Do you think that this information is reliable? Explain. **(c)** What information do you get from Source B that you could not get from a newspaper account? **(d)** Evaluate Dolley Madison's reaction to the event.
3. **(a)** What is the main point of each excerpt? **(b)** Use what you already know and these sources to draw one or more conclusions about this event.
4. **(a)** What parts of each excerpt might make a good dramatic reading? **(b)** How might you use visuals in your presentation?

APPLY THE SKILL

See the Chapter Review and Assessment for another opportunity to apply this skill.

A

"[W]e entered Washington for the barbarous purpose of destroying the city. Admiral Cockburn would have burnt the whole, but [General] Ross would only consent to the burning of the public buildings. I had no objection to burn arsenals, dockyards . . . etc., but well do I recollect that . . . we were horrified at the order to burn the elegant Houses of Parliament [the Capitol] and the President's house. . . . I shall never forget the destructive majesty of the flames as the torches were applied to beds, curtains, etc."

—Harry Smith, *Various Anecdotes and Events of My Life*, 1846 (published 1901)

B

"Dear Sister—
My husband left me yesterday morning to join General Winder. . . .
Three o'clock.—Will you believe it, my sister? We have had a battle, or skirmish, near Bladensburg, and here I am still, within sound of the cannon! Mr. Madison comes not. May God protect us! . . . Our kind friend, Mr. Carroll, has come to hasten my departure, and in a very bad humor [mood] with me, because I insist on waiting until the large picture of General Washington is secured, and it requires to be unscrewed from the wall. This process was found too tedious for these perilous moments; I have ordered the frame to be broken, and the canvas taken out. It is done! and the precious portrait placed in the hands of two gentlemen from New York, for safe keeping. And now, dear sister, I must leave this house, or the retreating army will make me a prisoner in it. . . . When I shall again write to you, or where I shall be tomorrow, I cannot tell!"

—Dolley Madison, August 23–24, 1814

RESOURCE DIRECTORY

Teaching Resources
Skills for Life booklet, pp. 6–8

Technology
Social Studies Skills Tutor CD-ROM
Interactive Practice in
- Geographic Literacy
- Critical Thinking and Reading
- Visual Analysis
- Communications

SKILLS FOR LIFE

Creating an Oral or Visual Presentation

Focus Students learn how to use a variety of elements, including maps and primary sources, to build a presentation re-creating a historical event.

Instruct Ask students how they would recreate a historical event that took place in an era before photography or television. Remind them that in a situation such as a war, it might be necessary to use primary source documents and eyewitness accounts.

Have volunteers read the excerpts on the page. Then hold a class discussion on words or phrases that indicate the perspective of Dolley Madison and Harry Smith.

Extend See the Skills for Life activity in the Resource Directory below.

ANSWERS

Practice the Skill

1. **(a)** They are primary sources. **(b)** Each is in the first person, describing events as they occurred. **(c)** Both sides.
2. **(a)** The British soldier was horrified at being asked to burn the Capitol and the White House. **(b)** Possible answer: It is reliable, insofar as it represents one person's perspective, written many years later. **(c)** Possible answer: Dolley Madison's feelings. **(d)** She seems to have remained calm and resourceful in the face of danger.
3. **(a)** Excerpt A: That some British soldiers in the War of 1812 were reluctant to destroy Washington, D.C. Excerpt B: That Dolley Madison gave less thought to her own safety than to preserving an important painting. **(b)** Possible answer: The destruction of Washington, D.C., by British forces was a terrifying event, and the First Lady came close to being captured by the British.
4. **(a)** Excerpt A: The description of flames engulfing the house. Excerpt B: Madison ordering the portrait to be taken. **(b)** Answers will vary, but students should include the portrait of George Washington.

Reviewing Key Terms

Students should refer to the definitions of key terms in the chapter to write sentences that show an understanding of the major events and characters central to the birth of the United States.

Reviewing Main Ideas

11. Possible answers: To prevent further war with the Indians and to resolve Britain's financial problems; or that the British had incurred heavy debts fighting the French and Indian War and so began to tax the colonists more heavily to pay those debts.

12. Answers will vary, but should include the assertion of inalienable rights and the right to change or overthrow a government that does not serve the best interests of its citizens.

13. French and Spanish aid, in the form of money, supplies, troops, ships and military expertise, enabled the Americans to fight the British effectively.

14. Sample answers: It created a government with only one branch, Congress had to petition the states for money, changes could only occur to the Articles if all 13 states were in agreement.

15. Sample answer: The Great Compromise; created a legislative branch made up of two houses: the Senate and the House of Representatives. In the Senate, each state would be represented equally, whereas the number of representatives each state could send to the House was to be determined by that state's population.

16. This system gives each branch of the federal government the power to stop the other branches in certain ways, preventing misuse of power by any one branch of government.

17. In his plan, the national government assumed the debts of the states, focused the national government on the economy, and transferred some power from states to the national government.

18. Jefferson was a leader of those who preferred local government; he had faith in the ability of the people to behave properly with only a limited, rather than an overly intrusive, federal government.

Chapter 2 Review and Assessment

creating a CHAPTER SUMMARY

Copy the chart (right) on a piece of paper. Complete it by adding other important events and documents, and explain how each one affected the balance between liberty and order.

For additional review and enrichment activities, see the interactive version of *America: Pathways to the Present*, available on the Web and on CD-ROM.

Balance Between Liberty and Order

Event/Document	Effect
Boston Tea Party	This illegal protest against unfair taxes favored liberty over order.
Declaration of Independence	
British surrender at Yorktown	

★ Reviewing Key Terms

For each of the terms below, write a sentence explaining how it relates to the Revolution and the early years of the nation.

1. boycott
2. First Continental Congress
3. Battles of Lexington and Concord
4. patriotism
5. republic
6. separation of powers
7. Bill of Rights
8. administration
9. strict construction
10. embargo

★ Reviewing Main Ideas

11. Why did British colonial policies change after 1763? (Section 1)
12. What reasons for independence are given in the Declaration of Independence? (Section 1)
13. Why was foreign aid important to the Patriot cause during the Revolution? (Section 1)
14. What were three weaknesses of the Articles of Confederation? (Section 2)
15. Describe one compromise reached at the Constitutional Convention. (Section 2)
16. Explain the system of checks and balances. (Section 2)
17. What was the importance of Hamilton's debt plan? (Section 3)
18. Why did Jefferson win the election of 1800? (Section 3)
19. What was the importance of (a) *Marbury* v. *Madison* and (b) the Louisiana Purchase? (Section 3)
20. What were the causes of the War of 1812? (Section 3)

★ Critical Thinking

21. **Determining Relevance** Why were the Battles of Lexington and Concord important? In what sense were these shots "heard round the world"?
22. **Making Comparisons** Compare the views of the Federalists and anti-Federalists regarding ratification of the Constitution.
23. **Predicting Consequences** What do you think might have happened if the government had not put down the Whiskey Rebellion? Explain your answer.
24. **Demonstrating Reasoned Judgment** Do you think the development of political parties in the young United States was beneficial or harmful? Explain your answer.
25. **Recognizing Ideologies** (a) What did passage of the Sedition Act show about the Federalists' position regarding the balance of liberty and order? (b) How did the Virginia and Kentucky Resolutions demonstrate an opposing ideology?

Creating a Chapter Summary

Balance Between Liberty and Order

Event/Document	Effect
Boston Tea Party	This illegal protest against unfair taxes favored liberty over order.
Declaration of Independence	This bold statement in defiance of the British government favored liberty over order.
British surrender at Yorktown	The end of the Revolutionary War was a triumph for liberty and heralded the return of order.

★ Skills Assessment

Analyzing Political Cartoons ▶

26. This cartoon by Benjamin Franklin appeared in several variations during the American Revolution. (a) What do the segments of the snake represent? (b) How does the cartoonist convey this meaning?
27. What is the message of the cartoon?
28. What makes this an effective cartoon?

Analyzing Primary Sources

Reread the Preamble to the Constitution in Section 2 of this chapter, and then answer the questions below.

29. What is the importance of the opening phrase, "We the People"?
    - **A** It shows that the Constitution is replacing the Articles of Confederation.
    - **B** It shows that in the United States, it is the people who govern.
    - **C** It shows that the United States will have a bicameral legislature.
    - **D** It shows that everyone who lives in the United States will be able to vote.
30. Why were the Framers attempting to "form a more perfect Union"?
    - **F** Under the Articles of Confederation, the national government had little power to resolve problems among the states.
    - **G** Smaller states tried to leave the Union because they feared a strong national government.
    - **H** Shays' Rebellion had shown Americans that their national government was too powerful.
    - **J** The Articles of Confederation did not give people enough say in their government.

Applying the Chapter Skill: *Creating an Oral or Visual Presentation*

31. Prepare an oral presentation about either George Washington or Thomas Jefferson. Use visual aids to add interest to your presentation.

ACTIVITIES

Writing to LEARN

Writing an Opinion
Thomas Jefferson and his supporters believed that a Bill of Rights was absolutely crucial to the protection of liberty. Do you think their conclusion has proven to be correct? Use examples from history or from current events to show your reasoning.

Primary Source CD-ROM

Working With Primary Sources Find additional information on the American Revolution and the early years of the republic on the *Exploring Primary Sources in U.S. History CD-ROM.* Use the selections provided to complete the Chapter 2 primary source activity located in the *America: Pathways to the Present* area of the following Web site.
www.phschool.com

Take It to the NET

Chapter Self-Test As a review activity, take the Chapter 2 Self-Test in the *America: Pathways to the Present* area at the Web site listed below. The questions are designed to test your understanding of the chapter content.
www.phschool.com

ANSWERS TO ACTIVITIES

Writing to LEARN

Essays will vary, but should demonstrate an understanding of Jefferson's ideas and be supported with specific examples and quotes where applicable.

Primary Source CD-ROM

Direct students to the additional primary sources that can be found on the *Exploring Primary Sources in U.S. History CD-ROM.*

Take It to the NET

Additional support materials and activities for Chapter 2 of *America: Pathways to the Present* can be found in the Social Studies area at the Prentice Hall School Web site. **www.phschool.com**

19. (a) It established the practice of judicial review. (b) It greatly expanded the size of the United States.
20. Continuing trouble between the U.S. and Britain, and the fact that Americans felt it was due to Britain's encouragement that Native Americans were resistant to American settlement of the West.

CRITICAL THINKING

21. The battles marked the beginning of the Revolutionary War. Because of the impact the Revolutionary War was to have on the future of the United States, and the world.
22. Federalists: stressed the weaknesses of the Articles of Confederation and argued that the new government based on the Constitution would have more success in dealing with the difficulties facing the nation; emphasized the separation of powers and the system of checks and balances. Anti-Federalists: saw the Constitution as a betrayal of the American Revolution; felt that a President would be just like a king; objected to the lack of a bill of rights in the new Constitution.
23. Answers will vary, but students should try to define the proper role of the new federal government.
24. Answers will vary, but should demonstrate an understanding of the benefits as well as the limitations of political parties.
25. (a) They favored order over liberty. (b) The resolutions suggested that liberty could only be protected if a state had the right to refuse to adhere to a federal law deemed by that state's government to be unconstitutional.

SKILLS ASSESSMENT

26. (a) The Thirteen Colonies. (b) Each segment is labeled with the initial(s) of a state or a region.
27. The colonies must unite in order to survive.
28. The imagery is easy to understand, but it makes a powerful impression.
29. B
30. F
31. Students' presentations should provide an accurate representation of either Washington or Jefferson, while also reflecting each student's views about their subject.

Diary of a Wartime Winter

Focus Have students find the meaning of each of these words in a dictionary before they begin to read: *acquaintance, conjectured, prophesy, procure.* Explain that Israel Putnam was an American general from Connecticut. Ask them to think, as they read, about the advantages of fighting on one's home soil.

Instruct Review the account of the battles at Trenton and Princeton in the textbook. Discuss details that make this a factual, objective account of the battle. Then discuss how the information provided in the diary entries differs from the description in the chapter. Ask volunteers for words and phrases describing the point of view of the diary entries. *(Personal, emotional)*

Analyzing the Document Have students explain how the diary entries enhance their understanding of the Revolution.

Use this additional question to generate class discussion:

Critical Thinking: Making Inferences How does Margaret Hill Morris regard Count Donop? Give evidence from the document to support your answer. *(At first, Morris resents Donop for ignoring her town's request to remain neutral, but later she comes to respect him. After his death, Morris observes that the Hessians "have lost a brave and humane commander.")*

AmericanHeritage®

MY BRUSH WITH **HISTORY**™

by MARGARET HILL MORRIS

Diary of a Wartime Winter

Fought in the towns and farms of the American colonies, the battles of the American Revolution dominated the lives not only of soldiers but of the unlucky civilians who lived nearby. The editors of *American Heritage* magazine have selected entries from the diary of Margaret Hill Morris. Morris lived in New Jersey, site of the Battle of Princeton and other battles.

December 22, 1776: It is said Putnam with 1,000 men [600 New Jersey militia and Virginia artillerymen] are at Mount Holly. All the women removed from the town, except one widow of our acquaintance. This evening we hear the sound of much hammering at Bristol, and it is conjectured that a fortification is carrying on there. More cannon are said to be planted on the island. We hear this afternoon that the gentlemen who went last to the Count Donop [Col. Carl von Donop, Hessian] with a request that our town might be allowed to remain a neutral one, are returned, and report that he had too many affairs of greater consequence in hand to attend to them, or give an answer. I think we don't like the Count quite so well today as we did yesterday. . . .

We hear this afternoon that our officers are afraid their men will not fight and wish they may all run home again. A peaceable man ventured to prophesy today that if the war is continued through the winter, the British troops will be scared at the sight of our men, for as they never fought with naked men, the novelty of it will terrify them and make them retreat faster than they advanced to meet them; for he says, from the present appearance of our ragged troops, he thinks it probable they will not have clothes to cover them a month or two hence. . . .

The Death of General Mercer at the Battle of Princeton, January 3, 1777, *by John Trumbull*

Dec. 29: This morning the soldiers at the next house prepared to depart, and as they passed my door, they stopped to bless and thank me for the food I sent them, which I received, not as my due, but as belonging to my Master who had reached a morsel to them by my hands. A great number of soldiers are in town today. Another company took possession of the next house when the first left it. The inhabitants are

102

RESOURCE DIRECTORY

Technology

AmericanHeritage® My Brush with History™ Videotapes *Diary of a Wartime Winter*

TEST PREPARATION

Have students use the excerpt on these pages to answer the following question.

From what you have read, which statement best describes Margaret Hill Morris?

A She hates the enemy soldiers who were captured.
(B) She is deeply compassionate.
C She despairs at humankind.
D She is prejudiced against soldiers.

much straitened for bread to supply the soldiers and firewood to keep them warm. This seems to be only one of the many calamities of war.

Dec. 30: A number of poor soldiers sick and wounded brought into town today, and lodged in the court-house; some of them in private houses. Today I hear several of our town's men have agreed to procure wood for the soldiers; but they found it was attended with considerable difficulty, as most of the wagons usually employed to bring in wood were pressed to take the soldiers' baggage.

Dec. 31: We have been told of an engagement between the two armies, in which it was said the English had 400 taken prisoners, and 300 killed and wounded. The report of the evening contradicts the above intelligence, and there is no certain account of a battle.

The Start of a New Year

January 1, 1777: This New Year's day has not been ushered in with the usual ceremonies and rejoicing; indeed, I believe it will be the beginning of a sorrowful year to very many people. Yet the flatterer—hope—bids me look forward with confidence and trust in Him who can bring order out of this great confusion. I do not hear that any messengers have been in town from the camp.

Jan. 3: This morning between 8 and 9 o'clock we heard very distinctly a heavy firing of cannon. The sound came from toward Trenton. About noon a number of [American] soldiers, upwards of 1,000, came into town in great confusion with baggage and some cannon. From these soldiers we learn there was a smart engagement yesterday at Trenton, and that they left them engaged near Trenton Mill, but were not able to say which side was victorious. . . .

Several of those who lodged in Col. Cox's house last week returned tonight, and asked for the key, which I gave them. At about bedtime I went into the next house to see if the fires were safe, and my heart was melted with compassion to see such a number of my fellow creatures lying like swine on the floor, fast asleep, and many of them without even a blanket to cover them. It seems very strange to me that such a number should be allowed to come from the camp at the very time of the engagements, and I shrewdly suspect they have run away—for they can give no account why they came, nor where they are to march next.

Jan. 4: The accounts hourly coming in are so contradictory and various that we know not which to give credit to. We have heard our people have gained another victory [Battle of Princeton], that the English are fleeing before them, some at Brunswick, some at Princeton. We hear today that Sharp Delany, Anthony Morris, and others of the Philadelphia militia are killed, and that the Count Donop is numbered with the dead; if so, the Hessians have lost a brave and humane commander. The prisoners taken by our troops are sent to Lancaster jail. A number of sick and wounded were brought into town—calls upon us to extend a hand of charity towards them. Several of my soldiers left the next house, and returned to the place from whence they came. Upon my questioning them pretty close, I brought several to confess they had run away, being scared at the heavy firing on the 3rd. There were several innocent looking lads among them, and I sympathised with their mothers when I saw them preparing to return to the army.

Source: *Weathering the Storm: Women of the American Revolution* by Elizabeth Evan, Scribner's, 1975.

Understanding Primary Sources

1. What is a "flatterer"?
2. Why, given her situation, does Morris refer to hope as a "flatterer"?

American Heritage® MY BRUSH WITH **HISTORY**™ Videotapes

For more information about the Revolutionary War, view "Diary of a Wartime Winter."

103

CUSTOMIZE FOR ...

Gifted and Talented

Have students write three diary entries for a soldier garrisoned in Morris's town. Entries should be set between December 22, 1776, and January 4, 1777.

CUSTOMIZE FOR ...

ESL

Students may need help with the following words and phrases:

a fortification is carrying on soldiers are building military defenses
canteen a container for water
straitened for lacking sufficient supplies of
smart engagement brisk battle
hand of charity help and kindness

CUSTOMIZE FOR ...

Less Proficient Readers

As students read the selection, write these topics on the chalkboard: *Preparations at Mount Holly, Challenges of Lodging Soldiers, A Funny Prophesy, A False Rumor,* and *The Soldiers' Confession.* Have students make a two-column chart titled *Margaret Hill Morris Diary.* In the first column, have students write the topics listed on the chalkboard. In the second column, have them write details from the document to explain each topic.

CUSTOMIZE FOR ...

Less Proficient Writers

Have students read the entry for January 3. It describes events that took place at intervals during an eventful day. Have students list the events in chronological order, using as much specific information as they can gather from the passage.

Answers

1. A flatterer is one who pays false compliments or gives false encouragement to another.
2. Although hope gives her encouragement, she has difficulty believing in it because wartime is so grim.

Chapter 3 Planning Guide
Resource Manager

	CORE INSTRUCTION	READING/SKILLS
Chapter-Level Resources **TEKS** 25(A), 25(C), 25(D)	Teaching Resources • Pacing Charts booklet • Block Scheduling booklet **Resource Pro® CD-ROM, Ch. 3** **Prentice Hall Presentation Pro CD-ROM,** Ch. 3 **www.phschool.com** • eTeach	**Guided Reading Audiotapes (English/Spanish)** **Student Edition on Audio CD,** Ch. 2 **Social Studies Skills Tutor CD-ROM** **Color Transparencies,** A13, A14, A15, A16, A17, A18, A19, A60, C3, C4, D3, D4, E6, E7, F3, G3, G4, G5, G8, H5, H6, H7
1 Life in the New Nation 1. Find out how America expanded, and discover how the United States gained Texas and the Oregon Country. 2. See how a spirit of improvement, the Industrial Revolution, and new transportation and communication affected development. 3. Learn about the Second Great Awakening and African American worship. **TEKS** 22(A), 24(A), 24(H)	Teaching Resources **Units 1/2 booklet** • Section 1 Quiz, p. 24 **Learning Styles Lesson Plans booklet,** pp. 16–17	**Guided Reading and Review booklet,** pp. 29–31 **Guide to the Essentials,** p. 13 **Learning with Documents booklet,** pp. 12, 46 **Section Reading Support Transparencies**
2 The Market Revolution 1. Learn about the economy in the early 1800s. 2. Find out about events of the early 1800s that reflected the rise of nationalism in America. 3. Discover how new opposition parties arose. 4. See what issues shaped the presidency of Andrew Jackson. **TEKS** 24(A), 24(D), 25(B)	Teaching Resources **Units 1/2 booklet** • Section 2 Quiz, p. 25 **Learning Styles Lesson Plans booklet,** pp. 32–36	**Guided Reading and Review booklet,** pp. 17–18 **Guide to the Essentials,** p. 14 **Learning with Documents booklet,** pp. 13, 47, 79 **Section Reading Support Transparencies**
3 Religion and Reform 1. See how religion and philosophy affected the growing American reform movement. 2. Learn about reform movements that emerged in the early 1800s. 3. Find out how the antislavery movement arose and grew. 4. Discover the ways in which women's roles changed in the early 1800s. 5. Read about factors that caused growing social divisions in America. **TEKS** 24(G), 24(H)	Teaching Resources **Units 1/2 booklet** • Section 3 Quiz, p. 26 **Learning Styles Lesson Plans booklet,** pp. 20–21	**Guided Reading and Review booklet,** pp. 37–40 **Guide to the Essentials,** p. 15 **Learning with Documents booklet,** pp. 14, 48, 80 **Section Reading Support Transparencies**
4 The Coming of the Civil War 1. Read about how U.S. expansion to the Pacific affected slavery in the territories. 2. Find out what changes in political parties occurred in the 1850s. 3. See how North-South tensions worsened in the 1850s. 4. Discover the issues that dominated the Lincoln-Douglas debates. 5. Learn about events that finally divided the nation and led to war. **TEKS** 24(C), 24(D), 24(G)	Teaching Resources **Units 1/2 booklet** • Section 4 Quiz, p. 27 **Learning Styles Lesson Plans booklet,** pp. 22–23	**Guided Reading and Review booklet,** pp. 41–45 **Guide to the Essentials,** p. 16 **Learning with Documents booklet,** pp. 15, 49 **Skills for Life booklet,** pp. 9–12 **Section Reading Support Transparencies**

Enrichment/Pre-AP

Prentice Hall United States History Video Collection™
www.phschool.com
- Section Activities, Virtual Field Trip, Chapter Activities, Current Events Online

Biography, Literature, and Comparing Primary Sources booklet, pp. 12, 13, 47, 109
American History Block Scheduling Support
Historical Outline Map Book, pp. 33, 38, 39, 40
Sounds of an Era Audio CD
Exploring Primary Sources in U.S. History CD-ROM

Biography, Literature, and Comparing Primary Sources booklet, p. 111
American History Block Scheduling Support
Nystrom *Atlas of Our Country,* pp. 26–27, 49
Historical Outline Map Book, pp. 34, 36, 37, 44
Sounds of an Era Audio CD
Exploring Primary Sources in U.S. History CD-ROM

Biography, Literature, and Comparing Primary Sources booklet, pp. 4, 50, 113
American History Block Scheduling Support
Nystrom *Atlas of Our Country,* pp. 24–25, 26–27
Sounds of an Era Audio CD
Exploring Primary Sources in U.S. History CD-ROM

Biography, Literature, and Comparing Primary Sources booklet, pp. 15, 51, 115
American History Block Scheduling Support
Nystrom *Atlas of Our Country,* pp. 26–27, 28–30
Historical Outline Map Book, pp. 41, 42, 46, 47, 48
Sounds of an Era Audio CD
Exploring Primary Sources in U.S. History CD-ROM
American Pathways Thematic Posters

Assessment

Core Assessment
ExamView® Test Bank, Ch. 3
ExamView® Test Bank CD-ROM, Ch. 3
Standardized Test Preparation

Diagnose and Prescribe
Diagnostic Tests for High School Social Studies Skills

Review and Reteach
Review Book for U.S. History

Practice and Assess
Test-taking Strategies With Transparencies
Test-taking Strategies Posters
Test Prep Book for U.S. History
Alternative Assessment Handbook
Document-Based Assessment
Teaching Resources

Teaching Resources
Units 1/2 booklet
- Section Quizzes, pp. 24–27
- Chapter Tests, pp. 28, 31

www.phschool.com Ch. 3 Self-Test

AmericanHeritage Resources

From the Archives of American Heritage®, pp. 112, 118, 121, 123, 124, 130, 139, 141, 142
AmericanHeritage® My Brush with History™ Videotapes
www.americanheritage.com

Don't miss the exclusive interactive version of this textbook on the Web and on CD-ROM.

Chapter 3 Planning Guide
In Your Classroom

Customize for Individual Needs

Gifted and Talented

Teacher's Edition
- Customize for Gifted and Talented, pp. 133, 139

Teaching Resources
- Biography, Literature, and Comparing Primary Sources booklet, pp. 4, 12, 13, 15, 47, 50, 51, 109, 111, 113, 115

Technology
- Exploring Primary Sources in U.S. History CD-ROM *Letter from the Alamo, Lt. Col. Comd't. William Barrett Travis; A Description of Factory Life in 1846; Monroe Doctrine; Our Federal Union: It Must Be Preserved, Andrew Jackson; Audubon and His Journals: My Style of Drawing Birds, John James Audubon; Civil Disobedience, Henry David Thoreau; Meaning of July Fourth for the Negro, Frederick Douglass; First Issue of the Liberator, William Lloyd Garrison; Seneca Falls Declaration of Sentiments; A Frontier Lady, Sarah Royce; Uncle Tom's Cabin, Harriet Beecher Stowe; Dred Scott v. Sandford*

ESL

Teacher's Edition
- Customize for ESL, pp. 113, 117, 119, 127

Teaching Resources
- Guided Reading and Review booklet, pp. 29–45
- Guide to the Essentials (English/Spanish), Chapter 3

Technology
- Student Edition on Audio CD, Chapter 3
- Guided Reading Audiotapes (English/Spanish), Chapter 3
- Section Reading Support Transparencies

Less Proficient Readers

Teacher's Edition
- Customize for Less Proficient Readers, pp. 111, 115, 137, 143

Teaching Resources
- Guided Reading and Review booklet, pp. 29–45
- Guide to the Essentials (English/Spanish), Chapter 3

Technology
- Student Edition on Audio CD, Chapter 3
- Guided Reading Audiotapes (English/Spanish), Chapter 3
- Section Reading Support Transparencies

Less Proficient Writers

Teacher's Edition
- Customize for Less Proficient Writers, p. 131

Teaching Resources
- Guided Reading and Review booklet, pp. 29–45
- Guide to the Essentials (English/Spanish), Chapter 3

Technology
- Student Edition on Audio CD, Chapter 3
- Guided Reading Audiotapes (English/Spanish), Chapter 3
- Section Reading Support Transparencies

Teacher's Edition Index

Chapter 3 – Pacing Suggestions

For 90-minute Blocks

- Teach sections 1,2,3 and 4 using Transparencies A13, A14, A15, A16, A17, A18, A19, A60, C3, C4, D3, D4, E6, E7, F3, G3, G4, G5, G8, H5, H6, and H7, and the Recent Scholarship notes on pages 108 and 132 for class discussions.

Running Out of Time?

If you are running short on time to cover this chapter, consider the following options:

- Use the Prentice Hall Presentation Pro CD-ROM to create an outline for this chapter.
- Use the Section Summaries for Chapter 3, from **Guide to the Essentials (English/Spanish).**

TEKS Correlation

Chapter-Level	TEKS
	(25) Social studies skills. The student communicates in written, oral, and visual forms. The student is expected to: **(A)** use social studies terminology correctly. **(C)** transfer information from one medium to another, including written to visual and statistical to written or visual, using computer software as appropriate. **(D)** create written, oral, and visual presentations of social studies information.
1 Life in the New Nation	**(22) Science, technology, and society.** The student understands the impact of science and technology on the economic development of the United States. The student is expected to: **(A)** explain the effects of scientific discoveries and technological innovations such as electric power, the telegraph and telephone, petroleum-based products, medical vaccinations, and computers on the development of the United States. **(24) Social studies skills.** The student applies critical-thinking skills to organize and use information acquired from a variety of sources including electronic technology. The student is expected to: **(A)** locate and use primary and secondary sources such as computer software, databases, media and news services, biographies, interviews, and artifacts to acquire information about the United States. **(H)** use appropriate mathematical skills to interpret social studies information such as maps and graphs.
2 The Market Revolution	**(24) Social studies skills.** The student applies critical-thinking skills to organize and use information acquired from variety of sources including electronic technology. The student is expected to: **(A)** locate and use primary and secondary sources such as computer software, databases, media and news services, biographies, interviews, and artifacts to acquire information about the United States. **(D)** use the process of historical inquiry to research, interpret, and use multiple sources of evidence. **(25) Social studies skills.** The student communicates in written, oral, and visual forms. The student is expected to: **(B)** use standard grammar, spelling, sentence structure, and punctuation.
3 Religion and Reform	**(24) Social studies skills.** The student applies critical-thinking skills to organize and use information acquired from a variety of sources including electronic technology. The student is expected to: **(G)** support a point of view on a social studies issue or event. **(H)** use appropriate mathematical skills to interpret social studies information such as maps and graphs.
4 The Coming of the Civil War	**(24) Social studies skills.** The student applies critical-thinking skills to organize and use information acquired from a variety of sources including electronic technology. The student is expected to: **(C)** explain and apply different methods that historians use to interpret the past, including the use of primary and secondary sources, points of view, frames of reference, and historical context. **(D)** use the process of historical inquiry to research, interpret, and use multiple sources of evidence. **(G)** support a point of view on a social studies issue or event.

Chapter 3

An Emerging New Nation

(1783–1861)

Introducing the Chapter

Nineteenth-century America was characterized by movement and change. It was a time of dramatic population growth and new technology, a period of migration and settlement. Americans responded to the changes in society by putting greater reliance on material progress and religious salvation. Yet the fierce divisions between north and south were causing a growing alienation between the two regions as bitter arguments over slavery reached the boiling point.

Time Line Activity

To provide students with practice in using the time line, ask questions such as these:

1. What was the status of child labor in Britain in 1802? *(Children were not allowed to work more than 12 hours a day.)*
2. When did W. L. Garrison establish the American Anti-Slavery Society? *(In 1833)*
3. Who was President at the end of the Mexican War? *(James K. Polk)*

Review Chapter 3

An Emerging New Nation (1783–1861)

Covered wagons heading west

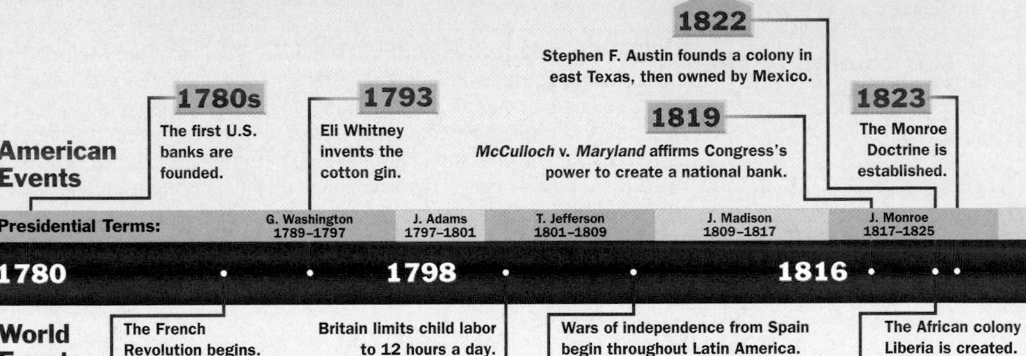

1822
Stephen F. Austin founds a colony in east Texas, then owned by Mexico.
1780s
The first U.S. banks are founded.
1793
Eli Whitney invents the cotton gin.
1819
McCulloch v. Maryland affirms Congress's power to create a national bank.
1823
The Monroe Doctrine is established.
American Events
Presidential Terms:
G. Washington 1789–1797
J. Adams 1797–1801
T. Jefferson 1801–1809
J. Madison 1809–1817
J. Monroe 1817–1825
1780
1798
1816
World Events
The French Revolution begins.
1789
Britain limits child labor to 12 hours a day.
1802
Wars of independence from Spain begin throughout Latin America.
1808
The African colony of Liberia is created.
1822

eTeach

Be sure to check out this month's online discussion with a Master Teacher. Go to **www.phschool.com**.

Resource Directory

Teaching Resources

Pacing Charts booklet

Block Scheduling booklet, pp. 16–18

Units 1/2 booklet

- Chapter Summary, p. 23

Technology

Guided Reading Audiotapes (English/Spanish), Ch. 3

Student Edition on Audio CD, Ch. 3

Prentice Hall United States History Video Collection™ Volume 5, *A New Nation;* Volume 6, *Expansionism;* Volume 7, *Democracy and Reform;* Volume 8, *Causes of the Civil War*

Prentice Hall Presentation Pro CD-ROM, Ch. 3

Resource Pro® CD-ROM

Social Studies Skills Tutor CD-ROM

Companion Web site, www.phschool.com

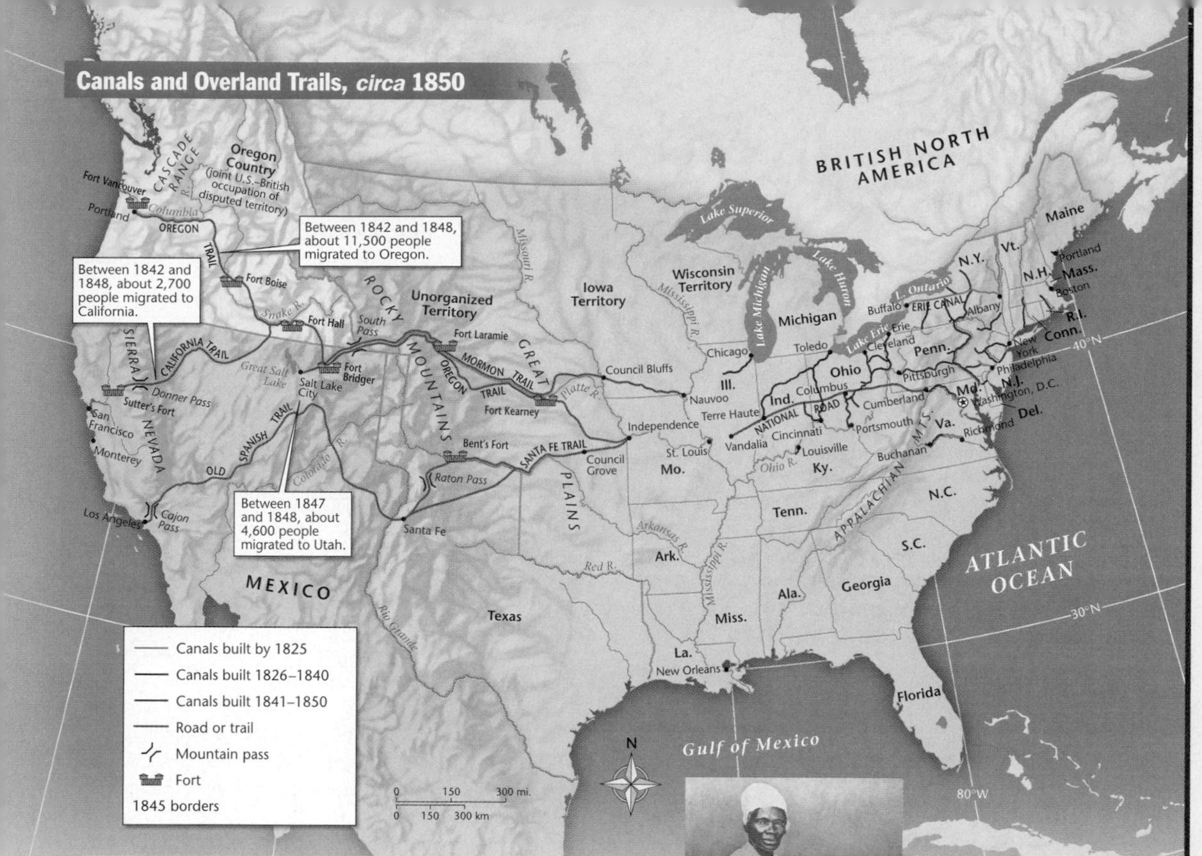

Canals and Overland Trails, *circa* 1850

Between 1842 and 1848, about 11,500 people migrated to Oregon.

Between 1842 and 1848, about 2,700 people migrated to California.

Between 1847 and 1848, about 4,600 people migrated to Utah.

Oregon Country (Joint U.S.–British occupation of disputed territory)

- Canals built by 1825
- Canals built 1826–1840
- Canals built 1841–1850
- Road or trail
- Mountain pass
- Fort
- 1845 borders

Abolitionist Sojourner Truth

1833	1848	1850	1860	1861
W. L. Garrison founds the American Anti-Slavery Society.	The Mexican War ends; U.S. gains Texas, New Mexico, and California.	The Compromise of 1850 addresses slavery in new U.S. territories.	South Carolina leads secession of the Lower South from the Union.	The Confederate States of America is formed. The first shots of the Civil War are fired.

J.Q. Adams 1825–1829 | A. Jackson 1829–1837 | Van Buren 1837–1841 | Harrison 1841 | J. Tyler 1841–45 | J. Polk 1845–1849 | Taylor '49–50 | Fillmore '50–53 | F. Pierce 1853–57 | J. Buchanan 1857–1861 | A. Lincoln 1861–1865 | A. Johnson 1865–1869

1834 • 1852 • 1870

1839	1845	1859
Opium War between Britain and China begins.	Irish potato famine begins.	War for unification of the Italian peninsula begins.

Canals and Overland Trails, *circa* 1850

Activating Prior Knowledge When was the Erie Canal built? *(By 1825)*

Previewing Ask students what purposes they think the canals served. *(They facilitated the transportation of both people and goods between places that were previously more difficult to access.)*

BACKGROUND
About the Pictures

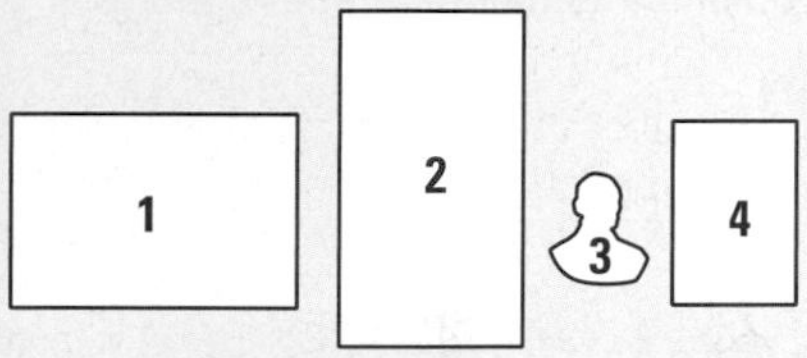

1 2  4

1. Pioneers often traveled in wagon trains like the one shown in this photograph. The wagon trains, which could include up to 100 wagons, were typically caravans of Conestoga wagons carrying both people and goods.
2. Stephen F. Austin was a prominent figure in the battle between the United States and Mexico over the possession of Texas.
3. William Lloyd Garrison used his journal, *The Liberator,* as a platform for his antislavery sentiments.
4. Born Isabella Van Wagener, Sojourner Truth was the daughter of slaves who became an advocate for abolition and women's rights.

BIBLIOGRAPHY

For the Teacher

Blockson, Charles L. ***The Underground Railroad: First Person Narratives of Escape to Freedom in the North.*** Prentice Hall, 1987. (Including accounts of Tubman, Douglass, and Truth.)

Landes, David. ***The Unbound Prometheus: Technological Change and Industrial Development in Western Europe from 1750 to the Present.*** Cambridge University Press, 1990.

Lerner, Gerda. ***Black Women in White America: A Documentary History.*** Vintage, 1972. (Collection of primary and secondary source accounts.)

For the Student

Fitzgerald, Frances. ***Cities on a Hill.*** Simon & Schuster, 1986. (Compact history of America's utopian communities.)

Colt, Margaret Louise. ***Andrew Jackson.*** Grey Castle, 1990. (A biography of the seventh President.)

Ehle, John. ***Trail of Tears: The Rise and Fall of the Cherokee Nation.*** Anchor, 1988. (Compact account of the forced removal of the Cherokee.)

Styron, William. ***The Confessions of Nat Turner.*** Vintage, 1993. (A blending of fact and fiction on the famous slave uprising.)

Don't miss the exclusive interactive version of this textbook on the Web and on CD-ROM.

Section 1 Life in the New Nation

Section Objectives

1. Find out how America's growing and young population spurred territorial expansion, and discover how the United States gained Texas and the Oregon Country.
2. See how a spirit of improvement, along with the Industrial Revolution and new transportation and communication, affected the nation's development.
3. Discover the key characteristics of the Second Great Awakening and of African American worship.

Bellringer

Warm-Up Activity Tell students that in 1810 only one seventh of the American population of 7.2 million lived west of the Alleghenies; by 1840, more than one third of the 17.2 million Americans lived there. Have them consider the impact of such rapid population growth.

Activating Prior Knowledge Ask students to list some of the impacts of a surge in population and the resettlement of citizens in new areas. Ask students to consider the impact from several perspectives, such as economics, family life, a sense of connectedness, impact on native populations, and so forth.

Reading Strategy

Have students skim the section and create an outline using the headings and subheadings. As they read, have them fill in their outlines using supporting evidence from the section.

Caption Answers

Viewing History Sample answer: advantages—avoided travel over the hills and mountains; disadvantages—narrow and twisting roads over which to drive wagons, water barriers, easy targets for attack by enemies.

Section 1 Life in the New Nation

READING FOCUS

- How did America's growing and young population spur territorial expansion, and how did the United States gain Texas and the Oregon Country?
- How did a spirit of improvement, along with the Industrial Revolution and new transportation and communication, affect the nation's development?
- What were the key characteristics of the Second Great Awakening and of African American worship?

KEY TERMS

Adams-Onís Treaty
republican virtues
Industrial Revolution
interchangeable parts
cotton gin
Second Great Awakening
denomination
spirituals

TAKING NOTES

As you read, complete the following chart to show causes and effects of westward expansion in the early 1800s.

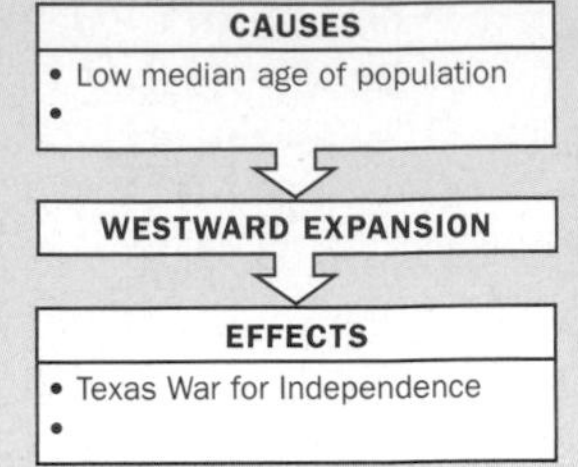

MAIN IDEA

In the early 1800s, the nation expanded south and westward. Innovations in industry brought great social change. A revival of religion resulted in new American forms of worship.

Setting the Scene Americans were moving west into new lands in the late 1700s and early 1800s. One of them, Daniel Boone, became a symbol of the personal qualities needed to explore and settle those lands: courage, practical know-how, and bottomless determination.

After spending several years exploring present-day Kentucky, Boone was hired in 1775 to cut the Wilderness Road through the Cumberland Gap, a low spot in the Appalachian Mountains. This road began in eastern Tennessee and ended in what is now Louisville, Kentucky. It became the main route to the lands west of the Appalachians for countless Americans, including Boone's own family.

During the American Revolution, Boone was captured by the Shawnee, who were allies of Britain. A few months later, Boone escaped to warn colonists of a coming attack by the British and Native Americans, which the colonists repelled.

After the war, Boone became a leading citizen of the Ohio Valley. He was a member of the Kentucky legislature as well as a hunter and a trapper. Moving west with the growing nation, he migrated to Missouri in 1799. When he died there in 1820, his fame as a bold and tough pioneer had spread across the nation.

VIEWING HISTORY The Cumberland Gap—the 1700s' equivalent of a new superhighway—opened the way westward for explorers and settlers. **Drawing Conclusions** *Using evidence from this picture, draw conclusions about the advantages and challenges of traveling through the Cumberland Gap.*

RESOURCE DIRECTORY

Teaching Resources
Learning Styles Lesson Plans booklet, pp. 16–17
Guided Reading and Review booklet, pp. 29–31

Other Print Resources
American History Block Scheduling Support *No Neighbors for Miles: The Northwest Territory,* found in the Forging a New Nation folder, includes interdisciplinary lesson suggestions and activities for Geography and History, Primary Sources, Biography, and Literature.
Historical Outline Map Book *Trails to the West,* p. 40

Technology
Section Reading Support Transparencies
Guided Reading Audiotapes (English/Spanish), Ch. 3
Student Edition on Audio CD, Ch. 3
Color Transparencies *American Photo,* F3
Sounds of an Era Audio CD *Morris Birkbeck on America Moving Westward* (time: 50 seconds)
Prentice Hall Presentation Pro CD-ROM, Ch. 3
Companion Web site, www.phschool.com

America's Population: Growing and Young

The westward surge of people symbolized by Daniel Boone was partly the result of a rapidly growing population. In 1780, about 2.7 million people lived in the original 13 states. By 1830, the population had grown to 12 million people in 24 states. Most of the growth came from an astonishing increase in the number of children born to each family. Between 1800 and 1849, the average American woman had about five children.

The large number of children meant that most of the population was young. The median age of Americans in 1820 was about 17. That is, half of the population was under the age of 17, and half was over that age. Young couples dreamed of working hard to make a good future. The place to make those dreams come true, many felt, was the area west of the Appalachian Mountains, a region known as trans-Appalachia.

Territorial Expansion

In the late 1780s, only a few hundred white Americans lived north of the Ohio River. By 1830, there were hundreds of thousands of Americans living in the region, which by then consisted of Michigan Territory and three new states: Ohio, Indiana, and Illinois.

Life on the Frontier Most of the settlers in this region had traveled down the river from western Pennsylvania and Virginia, or northward from Kentucky and Tennessee. Entire families made the long and difficult journey, as an English traveler crossing the Appalachians in the spring of 1817 described:

> "*Old America seems to be breaking up and moving westward. We are seldom out of sight, as we travel on this grand track towards the Ohio, of family groups behind and before us, some [intending to go] to a particular spot, close to a brother perhaps, or [to] a friend who has gone before and reported well of the country.*"
>
> —Morris Birkbeck

In the Northwest Territory, north of the Ohio River, slavery had been forbidden by the Northwest Ordinance of 1787. Supposedly, African Americans who gained their freedom could live in this region. Yet many settlers north of the Ohio did not want free African Americans in their states. In particular, they feared that blacks would compete for land and jobs. Therefore they made laws to discourage African Americans from moving in.

Focus on TECHNOLOGY

The Log Cabin One reason so many Americans left their homes and migrated westward may have been that they knew it would not be very difficult to build a new shelter. The typical log cabin took only a few days to build and required no expensive nails or spikes. (The builder cut notches in the logs to fit them together.) In fact, a pioneer could build a log cabin with no tools except an axe, and could even build a small cabin without help.

Many log cabins had only one room, with blankets or sheets hung from the ceiling to provide a bit of privacy. Glass windows were rare, since glass was both costly and difficult to transport. For floors, some cabins used wooden boards; others simply used packed earth.

Families generally saw their cabins as temporary homes while they cleared the surrounding fields for farming. In time, many built larger, more comfortable homes.

107

Lesson Plan

Focus To many Americans the Revolution seemed to mark a new era of experimentation and invention. Ask students what kinds of social change this new attitude brought about.

Instruct Point out that the ideas of rapid change, progress, and improvement of humankind are concepts most Americans take for granted today. This was not always the case, but with the coming of the Industrial Revolution, a sense of new possibilities began to take hold among the nation's citizens. Discuss what caused this change in people's thinking. How did society's values change? What was the connection between changes in people's attitudes and changes in technology?

Assess/Reteach Ask students to compare the surge in economic growth in the time of the Industrial Revolution with the era of economic growth experienced in the United States in the 1990s. How were the two eras similar? How were they different?

Activity: Connecting with Geography

Direct pairs of students to locate, or provide them with, a small-scale topographical map that shows the Cumberland Gap and the surrounding area. Have the students study the map, conduct research, and then make a presentation about the Gap. Their presentation should identify the Cumberland Gap, describe it, and explain why it became an avenue to the lands west of the Appalachians. **(Visual/Spatial)**

Activity
Connecting with Geography

Ask students why people began to move west after 1790. What were the motives of whites who moved westward? How did slavery complicate this migration? Why did Native Americans move west? **(Verbal/Linguistic)**

Background
Recent Scholarship

We sometimes think of westward expansion as a movement of individuals. Recent scholars, including John Mack Faragher in *Daniel Boone: The Life and Legend of an American Pioneer,* emphasize the importance of family in frontier life. Americans often migrated in groups and depended on each other for assistance. Boone was a successful pioneer in Kentucky in the late 1700s for reasons that went beyond his individual hunting and scouting skills. Just as significant were the contributions of his wife, Rebecca; his relatives; and his neighbors, including Native Americans, with whom Boone had much in common.

READING CHECK
Jackson invaded Florida while Spain was preoccupied by rebellions in South America, and as a result of the 1819 Adams-Onís Treaty, Spain lost Florida.

MAP SKILLS Native Americans were forced farther and farther west as wagon trains of settlers moved into Indian lands. Some Native American groups went peacefully; others, such as the Seminoles, fought relocation as long as they could. The Seminole people battled United States troops well into the 1840s.
Movement *Who were some of the last groups to lose their land by 1850?*

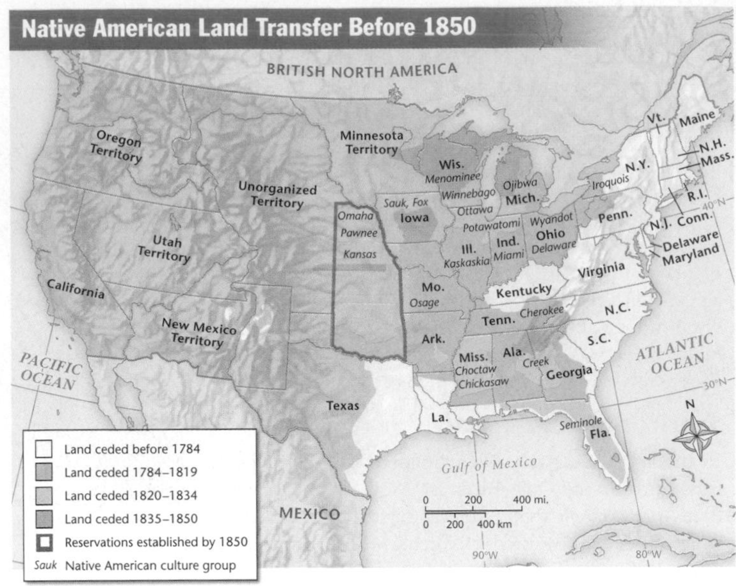

From the South, an estimated 98,000 southern slaves moved west with their owners between 1790 and 1810. Thousands more African Americans were brought directly from Africa or the West Indies.

Native Americans gradually lost their land to the United States government in one treaty after another. As they lost their homelands, Indians were forced to make long, dangerous journeys to areas west of the Mississippi River.

Expansion Into Florida Thousands of settlers also flocked to the newly acquired land of Florida. Under the Pinckney Treaty of 1795, the southern boundary of the United States had been set at 31° N latitude, leaving Florida firmly in Spanish hands. However, Spain and the United States also agreed to control the Native Americans living within each country's territories and to prevent them from attacking the other country's territory.

During the 1810s, Spain was distracted by rebellions in its South American colonies and therefore paid little attention to its two colonies of East and West Florida. The Seminoles, a Native American group living in the Floridas, took advantage of the loose control and stepped up their raids on settlers in southern Georgia. The Seminoles also angered American officials by allowing escaped slaves to live among them.

Jackson and Florida The general in charge of protecting the settlers was the tough veteran of the War of 1812, Andrew Jackson. When told to put an end to the attacks, Jackson did so, by invading Florida.

READING CHECK
How was the United States able to gain possession of Florida?

Within a few weeks Jackson claimed possession of the entire western part of the territory. Spain was outraged, and Congress threatened to condemn Jackson. Most Americans, however, applauded Jackson's move.

President Monroe and his Secretary of State, John Quincy Adams, decided to make the best of the situation. Refusing to apologize for Jackson's actions, Adams accused Spain of breaking the Pinckney Treaty by failing to control the Seminoles.

Spain reluctantly agreed to accept the loss of Florida. In 1819, Spain and the United States agreed on what has since been called the Transcontinental

Caption Answers

Map Skills The Creek, Cherokee, Menominee, Ojibwa, Sauk, and Fox.

RESOURCE DIRECTORY

Teaching Resources
Biography, Literature, and Comparing Primary Sources booklet (Literature) *The Pioneers,* p. 47
Biography, Literature, and Comparing Primary Sources booklet (Comparing Primary Sources) *Peace and Friendship,* p. 109

Other Print Resources
Historical Outline Map Book *Oregon County,* p. 38

Technology
Color Transparencies *Historical Maps,* A15, A16; *American Diversity,* G3
RESOURCE PRO® **Critical Thinking Activity** *Making Comparisons: Population Boom,* found on Resource Pro, allows students to apply this skill by analyzing census data from 1790 to 1830.
Exploring Primary Sources in U.S. History CD-ROM *Letter from the Alamo, Lt. Col. Comd't. William Barrett Travis*

Treaty, or the **Adams-Onís Treaty.** In the treaty, Spain gave up Florida, as well as its long-held claim on the Pacific Northwest. Now for the first time, the United States stretched from the Atlantic to the Pacific Ocean.

The Adams-Onís Treaty also fixed the boundary between the Louisiana Purchase and Spanish territory in the West. To settle the dispute over this boundary, the United States agreed to give up its claims to a huge territory in what is now the southwestern United States, including part of Texas.

Texas and Oregon Country

The United States government assumed that the lands of the Louisiana Purchase, which were located west of the Mississippi River, would remain part of "Indian Country." Thousands of Americans had other ideas.

Mexico and Texas Mexico, which had won independence from Spain in 1821, encouraged trade with the United States. In 1822, Stephen F. Austin, a former member of the Missouri Territorial legislature, founded a colony of several hundred families in east Texas, in northern Mexico. By 1824, some 2,000 immigrants were living in Austin's colony. By 1835 their numbers exceeded 30,000.

As their numbers swelled, these Americans demanded more political control. In particular, they wanted slavery to be guaranteed under Mexican law. The newcomers called for the same rights from the Mexican government that they had possessed in the United States.

The Texas War for Independence When General Antonio López de Santa Anna declared himself dictator of Mexico and stripped Texas of its rights of self-government, Texans became united in the cause of independence. In November 1835, these independence-minded settlers clashed with Mexican troops, beginning the Texas War for Independence.

Santa Anna led an army across the Rio Grande to subdue the rebellion. In February 1836, the Mexicans reached the Alamo, a walled mission in San Antonio that was occupied by Texans. Led by William Travis and James Bowie, the Texans hoped to slow the general's advance long enough to allow their fellow rebels to assemble an army. Under siege by a vastly larger Mexican force, Travis vowed "to sustain myself as long as possible and die like a soldier who never forgets what is due to his own honor or that of his country."

The courageous Texans inflicted heavy casualties, but the Mexicans eventually overwhelmed the Alamo and killed most of those inside. Two weeks later, Santa Anna ordered the killing of more than 300 Texan prisoners at Goliad. These two events enraged and energized Texans to mighty actions for their cause.

On March 2, 1836, the rebels formally declared the founding of an independent Republic of Texas. The following month, a Texan force led by Sam Houston and

MAP SKILLS After a stinging defeat at the Alamo, Texans led by Sam Houston (below) finally overcame the army of General Antonio López de Santa Anna at the Battle of San Jacinto. **Place** *Why was it crucial that Santa Anna be stopped at that point?*

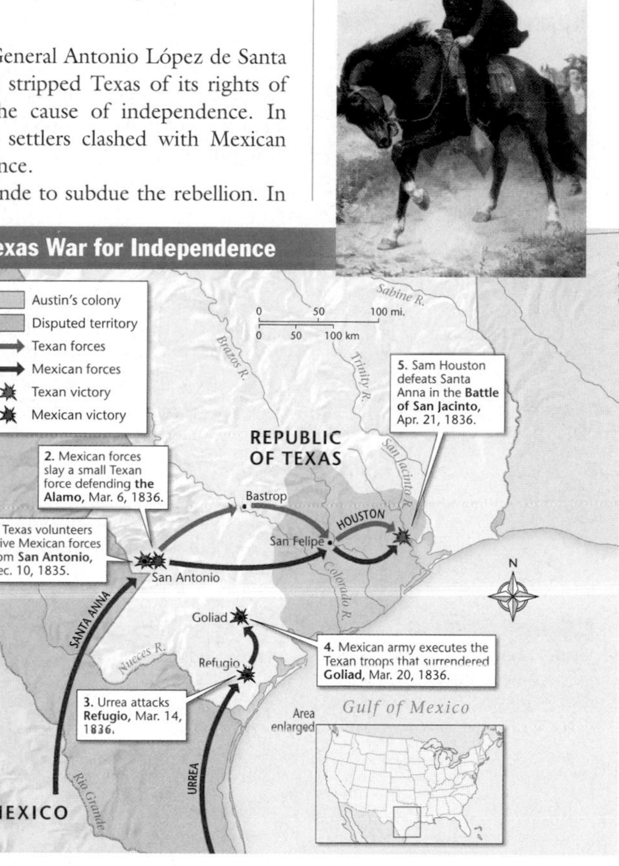

ACTIVITY
Connecting with History and Conflict

Have students conduct research to locate the text of William Travis's famous "Victory or Death" letter, in which he pleaded for reinforcements at the Alamo. Have a volunteer provide a dramatic reading of the short but powerful letter to the class. **(Bodily/Kinesthetic)**

BACKGROUND
Connections to Today

The Alamo still stands, and it is "remembered" today by more people than William Travis and James Bowie could ever have imagined. More than 2.5 million people visit the Alamo every year. What most people think of as "The Alamo" is actually an old mission that is just part of a four-acre complex. The complex is owned by the state of Texas and operated by the Daughters of the Republic of Texas. Many visitors are surprised to find the Alamo—in their imagination, a dusty, run-down building in the middle of the Texas wilderness—standing smack in the middle of bustling downtown San Antonio, population: approximately one million.

TEST PREPARATION

Have students reread the section "Texas and Oregon Country" and answer the question below.

What was the origin of the name of Austin, Texas?

A Austin was named after George Austin, an American cavalryman.

B Austin was named after James Austin, an American cattleman.

Ⓒ Austin was named after Stephen Austin, who led the first large group of American settlers into Texas.

D Austin was a Mexican who lived in America.

CAPTION ANSWERS

Map Skills A win by Santa Anna at that point would have given him control of most of Austin's colony.

ACTIVITY
Connecting with Citizenship

Have small groups of students cooperate to make a table of the "republican virtues." Each row in the table should represent one of the virtues, and the column headings should read: *Name of Virtue, Definition, Why Important for the Republic,* and *Example of Virtue in Action.* Have the students use their work as a springboard for a discussion, touching on whether the virtues listed are sufficient, whether they should be taught in schools today, and if so, how they should be taught. **(Visual/Spatial)**

BACKGROUND
Geography in History

The Oregon Trail remained a popular route for many more years. By the year 1869—the year the Transcontinental Railroad was completed—350,000 people had traveled the route. Not everyone who attempted the trail completed it, however. Some 20,000 people—men, women, and children—lost their lives while trying to reach their dreams of life out west.

READING CHECK

It was felt that schools should impart values such as thrift, hard work, and community service in addition to academics. These values would help Americans to peacefully govern their young nation.

shouting "Remember the Alamo!" routed Mexican troops at the San Jacinto River. The Texans captured Santa Anna and forced him to sign a treaty recognizing the Republic of Texas. In the fall of 1836, the citizens of Texas elected Sam Houston as their first president.

The Oregon Country Far to the north of Texas, other Americans in the early 1820s were headed for a vast territory known as the Oregon Country, which stretched from northern California to the southern border of Alaska. In 1818, the United States and Britain signed a treaty agreeing to joint occupation of the Oregon Country.

Some of the first Americans to arrive were fur traders. Other newcomers were missionaries sent by churches back East to convert Native Americans to Christianity.

Starting in 1843, organized wagon trains carried masses of migrants to Oregon along Indian trails. Groups met at a small town in western Missouri called Independence. From there they began the 2,000-mile journey across the Great Plains and the Rocky Mountains along the Oregon Trail. Most came in search of land or trading opportunities.

By 1845, more than 5,000 Americans had migrated to the Oregon Country. In the Treaty of 1846, the United States and Great Britain agreed to divide the Oregon Country along the 49th parallel (line of latitude).

A historic marker along the Oregon Trail

The Spirit of Improvement

Migrating westward was one way that Americans tried to make their lives better, but it was hardly the only one. The need to survive and the hope of making a profit led Americans in every part of the country to invent and innovate, or find new ways of doing things. This spirit of improvement partly reflects the ideals of the Enlightenment.

Improvement Through Education Americans believed that the general condition of humankind could be improved through education. In 1790, educator Noah Webster wrote:

> "*Americans, unshackle your minds, and act like independent beings. . . . You have an empire to raise and support by your exertions, and a national character to establish and extend by your wisdom and virtues. To effect these great objects, it is necessary to [build] a broad system of education.*"
>
> —Noah Webster

Webster's primary contribution to American education was the first major dictionary of American English.

Many state constitutions encouraged free public education for all children. Even though few state governments actually provided free education in those early years, academies, or private high schools, often filled the gap.

Many Americans wanted their schools not just to teach academic subjects but to develop character by promoting certain virtues. The virtues the American people would need to govern themselves in the new republic were called **republican virtues.** They included self-reliance, industry, frugality, harmony, and the sacrifice of individual needs for the good of the community.

READING CHECK
What "republican virtues" did some Americans seek to promote? Why?

The Role of Women In the early 1800s, Americans began to look to women to set the standard for republican virtues. After all, they reasoned, women were mothers, wives, and sometimes teachers. Thus women had a powerful influence on the men who would vote in, and govern, the nation. If

RESOURCE DIRECTORY

Teaching Resources
Biography, Literature, and Comparing Primary Sources booklet (Biography) *Brigham Young,* p. 12
Learning with Documents booklet (Primary Source Activity) *The American Spirit,* p. 12

Other Print Resources
Historical Outline Map Book *Independence for Texas,* p. 39

Technology
Color Transparencies *Cause-and-Effect Charts,* D4

women had such virtues as honesty, self-restraint, and discipline, they could teach these qualities to men.

To serve as examples of these virtues, however, women had to learn them first. In the late 1700s, the vast majority of schools were for boys only. As people began to see the value of educating girls, many academies added "female departments" to help girls become "republican women." A republican woman was one who had the virtues that would help her contribute to the success of the republic. Women were far from achieving equality, but people were now beginning to think about the importance of women in the life of the republic.

The Industrial Revolution

Americans pursued profit with the same energy with which they pursued self-improvement. As the young republic expanded, Americans developed and profited from a variety of inventions that produced goods and materials faster and more cheaply.

Many of the inventions grew out of what is now known as the **Industrial Revolution.** This revolution was an ongoing effort over many decades to increase production by using machines powered by sources other than humans or animals. Several key British inventions sparked the Industrial Revolution in the 1700s. Among these was James Watt's steam engine, which harnessed the tremendous force given off by expanding steam.

The British jealously guarded all knowledge of their new technology. Anyone who knew about the design of these machines was forbidden to emigrate, or move out of the country.

New Technology Comes to America Britain's secrets and its technological lead were spoiled by a man named Samuel Slater, who emigrated to the United States in 1789 after working in Britain's advanced textile industry. Working in a clothier's shop in Pawtucket, Rhode Island, Slater reproduced the complicated machinery of the British mills in 1790. Slater and his partners went on to establish the nation's first successful textile mill, in 1793.

The Industrial Revolution in America

Date	Inventor	Invention or Innovation
1787	John Fitch	The first American steamboat
1790	Samuel Slater	Machinery for first U.S. textile mill
1793	Eli Whitney	The cotton gin
1795	Robert Fulton	The steam shovel (for digging canals)
1798	Eli Whitney	Mass production of muskets with standard measures and interchangeable parts
1807	Robert Fulton	The *Clermont*, the first commercially successful steamboat
1814	Frances C. Lowell	The first completely mechanized cotton mill
1820	William Underwood	The first U.S. canning factory
1826	Samuel Morey	An internal combustion engine
1828	Joseph Henry	The electromagnet

INTERPRETING CHARTS
The Industrial Revolution brought American advances in engineering, medicine, science agriculture, and technology. In fact, the word *technology* was coined in 1829.
Drawing Inferences *What aspects of American life did many of these advances affect?*

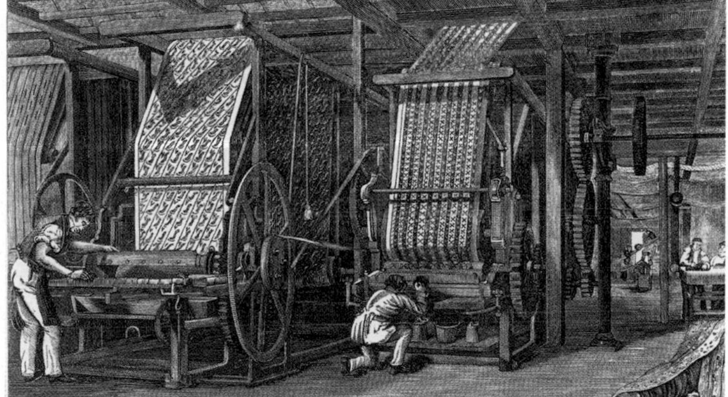

This woodcut shows two men operating machinery in an early textile mill. The machines are printing long sheets of a fabric called calico.

ACTIVITY
Connecting with Science and Technology

This activity may take place over more than one class period: Divide the class into groups of four to six students. Ask students to produce a chapter of a book that describes American inventors of the 1700s and 1800s. Students should illustrate the invention as well as provide a brief description of its effects on society. An example is Eli Whitney and his cotton gin. Groups should consult encyclopedias, the Internet, and other reference materials. **(Verbal/Linguistic; Visual/Spatial)**

BACKGROUND
Biography

Emma Willard (1787–1870), a champion of women's rights, proposed "A Plan for Improving Female Education" in 1819 to widen women's access to knowledge and to end misconceptions about the ability of women to handle such "masculine" subjects as mathematics and philosophy. She put her plan into action in 1821 when she founded the Troy Female Seminary, one of the first women's colleges in the United States.

BACKGROUND
Geography in History

Key to the progress and success of the Industrial Revolution was the revolution in power sources. The steam engine played a vital role, of course, but also important was the power of moving water. The new factories and mills were typically powered by waterwheels. So many waterwheels were turned by the water of the Merrimack River in New England that it was nicknamed "the hardest working river in the world."

CUSTOMIZE FOR ...
Less Proficient Readers

Have students skim the section and read each of the headings and subheadings. Ask students to turn each heading into a question. Then have students jot down, as they read, answers to the questions they have created.

CAPTION ANSWERS

Interpreting Charts Answers include: travel, manufacturing, farming.

BACKGROUND
Interdisciplinary

Eli Whitney, famous for inventing interchangeable parts and the cotton gin, made another important contribution to the American economy. He pioneered, in fulfilling his contract with the government to make guns, the use of the division of labor in which individual workers repeatedly perform just one part of a manufacturing process. This, combined with interchangeable parts, marks the key elements of mass production, which would soon change the world.

From the Archives of
American Heritage®

Up the River

On April 23, 1823, the riverboat *Virginia* steamed out of St. Louis with a few passengers and a cargo of military supplies bound for Fort St. Anthony, an army post on the site of the present-day St. Paul, Minnesota. Its departure marked the first time a steamboat was going to travel up the Mississippi River as far as the river was navigable for large vessels. The low-pressure steam engine employed by Robert Fulton in his famous *Clermont* had been of little use against the powerful currents, treacherous rapids, islands, and shoals that characterized western rivers like the upper Mississippi, so a new type of engine with much higher pressure had to be developed. Although *Virginia's* voyage was slow, it proved that a steamboat could conquer the upper Mississippi. Before long a fleet of steamers was carrying lead, furs, and grain down the Mississippi and settlers up it. Source: Frederic D. Schwarz, "The Time Machine," *American Heritage®* magazine, April 1998.

Others soon copied Slater's methods. By 1814, there were about 240 mills operating in the United States, most of them in Pennsylvania, New York, and New England.

Eli Whitney and Interchangeable Parts Although the Industrial Revolution began in Great Britain, American inventors were not far behind. In 1798, Eli Whitney signed a contract with the federal government to make 10,000 guns in a little over two years. It was a bold promise. In those days, a gunmaker made parts for one gun at a time. The process took weeks, because each part fit only one gun.

Whitney realized that if all the parts were made exactly alike, they could be used on any of the guns. The gunmaker could assemble the parts rapidly, which would translate into higher production and greater profit. In fact, it took Whitney more than ten years to make the guns, and he had trouble making indentical parts. But he worked hard on his new system, and other inventors later perfected what is now called the system of **interchangeable parts,** in which all parts are made to an exact standard.

The Cotton Gin

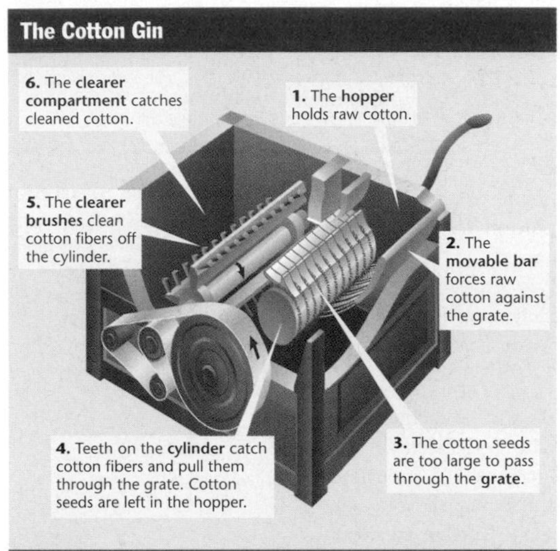
6. The clearer compartment catches cleaned cotton.
1. The hopper holds raw cotton.
5. The clearer brushes clean cotton fibers off the cylinder.
2. The movable bar forces raw cotton against the grate.
4. Teeth on the cylinder catch cotton fibers and pull them through the grate. Cotton seeds are left in the hopper.
3. The cotton seeds are too large to pass through the grate.

INTERPRETING DIAGRAMS
By hand, a worker could clean (remove the seeds from) only one pound of cotton per day. However, with a hand-operated gin like the one shown here, a worker could clean 50 pounds of cotton per day. **Determining Relevance** *How did the invention of the cotton gin lead to the expansion of slavery?*

The Cotton Gin While visiting a Georgia plantation in 1793, Whitney noted the time and effort needed to clean cotton seeds from the cotton fibers. Working by hand, a laborer could only clean one pound of cotton per day. Whitney devised a solution to the problem: the **cotton gin,** a machine that separates the seeds from raw cotton fibers. (The word *gin* means an "engine" or "machine.") With a gin operated by water power, one worker could now clean 1,000 pounds per day.

Whitney's invention had several important effects. Profit per pound of cotton skyrocketed, and with it the amount of cotton planted for harvest. United States cotton exports rose 6,000 percent between 1790 and 1815. Many southern planters began to depend on cotton as their only major crop, because it was so profitable. Planters began looking for new land where they could grow ever larger crops of cotton. They bought up and quickly settled large areas in Alabama, Mississippi, Louisiana, and finally Texas. These planters bought more enslaved Africans to work on the new and expanded cotton plantations. The enslaved population of the South more than doubled between 1790 and 1820, rising from 700,000 to 1.5 million.

The cotton gin helped keep the southern states a land of slavery and of farming, while the northern states became a land of free labor and of industry. In time, these fundamental differences between North and South would help lead to civil war.

Transportation and Communication

The Industrial Revolution was not the only "revolution" of the early 1800s in the United States. New technologies and new building projects produced a revolution in transportation.

Steam Power Although James Watt had first used his steam engine to make textiles, American inventor Robert Fulton proved it could also be used to power a ship. His steamboat *Clermont* chugged up the Hudson River in 1807, demonstrating that a steamboat could travel against the current. Before long, hundreds of steamboats were plying the rivers of America's West. Steam power

CAPTION ANSWERS

Interpreting Diagrams The cotton gin could clean cotton in large amounts, which allowed farmers to put increasing amounts of farmland into cotton production. The use of field slaves therefore increased dramatically.

RESOURCE DIRECTORY

Teaching Resources
Biography, Literature, and Comparing Primary Sources booklet (Biography) *Catherine Littlefield Greene,* p. 13

Other Print Resources
American Heritage Block Scheduling Support *On the Job: Industrialism in America,* found in the Expansion, Reconstruction, and Immigration folder, includes interdisciplinary lesson suggestions and activities for Geography and History, Primary Sources, Biography, and Literature.
Historical Outline Map Book *Transportation to the West,* p. 33

Technology
Color Transparencies *Historical Maps,* A14; *Fine Art,* E7; *American Diversity,* G4, G5; *The Way It Works,* H5, H6

RESOURCE PRO® **Literature Activity** *The Natural World,* found on Resource Pro, uses William Cullen Bryant's "Inscription for the Entrance to a Wood" to reveal how this poet and journalist viewed nature.

RESOURCE PRO® **Biography** *Anne Newport Royall,* found on Resource Pro, profiles the woman considered to be the first American journalist.

made it possible for western farmers and southern planters to ship their goods to markets around the world.

Canals Since waterways were the cheapest way to carry goods, American innovators built artificial waterways, or canals. By 1840, the nation had some 3,000 miles of canals.

The best known of these canals, and the one that had the greatest impact, was the Erie Canal, which opened in 1825. Built by the state of New York, this 363-mile waterway connected the Hudson River with Lake Erie. People and goods could now travel easily between the Atlantic Coast and the Great Lakes. The Erie Canal thus speeded the development of the entire Great Lakes region. Farmers of that area could now ship their products to markets as far away as New York City and beyond.

Roads Although canal building boomed in the young republic, it did not match road building. At first, roadbuilders had simply carved routes out of forests, throwing down the cut trees to surface the roadway. These roads were neither fast nor durable. The National, or Cumberland Road was built to last. Financed by the federal government, construction began in Cumberland, Maryland, in 1811. By the 1830s it had reached Columbus, Ohio, and later continued westward. Most of the new roads were privately built. Companies constructed highways and made a profit by collecting tolls.

Railroads Several inventors in England and the United States adapted James Watt's steam engine technology to build a steam locomotive—a self-propelled vehicle used for pulling railroad cars. In 1828, construction on the first American railroad began in Baltimore, Maryland. It came to be known as the Baltimore and Ohio (B & O) line. By 1840, the nation had more than 3,300 miles of track on several different lines, more than any other country in the world.

Along with the revolution in transportation came advances in communication. The federal government led the way by greatly expanding its postal service. Regular mail delivery helped create a national network of information in the form of newspapers, magazines, and books.

By the 1820s, more than 500 newspapers and magazines of all sorts were being published daily in the United States. Advances in education had increased the nation's literacy rate. Newspapers and magazines now made information available to large numbers of people. Improved communication and the free exchange of ideas helped tie together the different parts of the country.

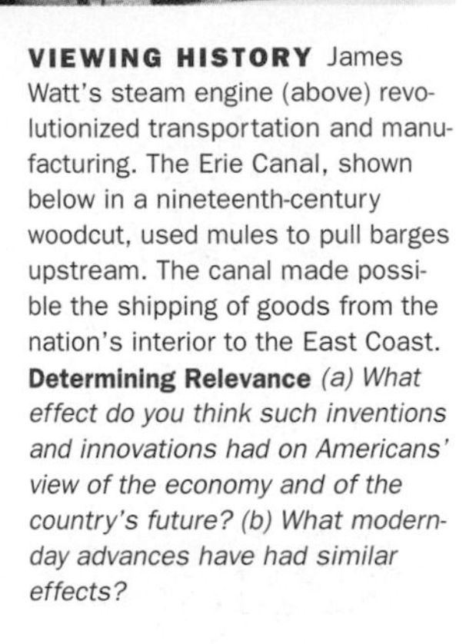

VIEWING HISTORY James Watt's steam engine (above) revolutionized transportation and manufacturing. The Erie Canal, shown below in a nineteenth-century woodcut, used mules to pull barges upstream. The canal made possible the shipping of goods from the nation's interior to the East Coast. **Determining Relevance** *(a) What effect do you think such inventions and innovations had on Americans' view of the economy and of the country's future? (b) What modern-day advances have had similar effects?*

ACTIVITY
Connecting with Geography

Assign students the task of writing a brief report entitled "The Erie Canal Today." The reports should identify how the canal is currently used, where it runs, who maintains it, and so on. Encourage the students to illustrate the report with photographs or a map. Consider directing the students to share their reports with the class. **(Verbal/Linguistic)**

BACKGROUND
Geography in History

Although the early trains solved some problems, they created many of their own. Routes were frequently unfenced or single-tracked, leading trains to collide with livestock or each other. Wood-burning locomotives threw out sparks that set fire to passengers' clothing and nearby forests. Some trains even included a car stuffed with cotton to protect passengers from locomotive explosions. Train travel became safe and viable only with the introduction of closed cars and new safety devices in the 1850s.

CUSTOMIZE FOR ...
ESL

Have each student create a poster entitled "New Types of Transportation." Posters should use text and drawings to illustrate how these types of transportation helped America prosper.

CAPTION ANSWERS

Viewing History Sample answers: (a) They created a spirit of optimism about the economy and the country's opportunities for growth and prosperity. (b) Innovations in electronics, computer technology, space technology.

ACTIVITY
Connecting with Geography

Constant migration turned the early Republic into a nation of strangers. To ease their loneliness, many Americans turned to church and social organizations to establish relationships, social contact, and a sense of community. To demonstrate the importance of community and social relationships, have students identify the communities of which they feel a part. These could be neighborhoods, schools, religious groups, clubs, or their town or city. Ask what needs are filled by their community and what qualities members have in common. The information might be recorded on a class chart. **(Verbal/Linguistic)**

BACKGROUND
Marriage in the 1800s

For women in the 1800s, marriage meant the loss of their legal rights. When feminist Lucy Stone agreed to marry Harry Blackwell in 1865, the following protest against the existing marriage laws was read at their wedding: "We protest . . . against those laws which give to the husband:

(1) The custody of the wife's person.

(2) The exclusive control and guardianship of their children.

(3) The sole ownership of her personal [property], and use of her real estate."

VIEWING HISTORY From a makeshift pulpit, a speaker addresses a large crowd at a revival meeting. **Analyzing Visual Information** *How does the artist depict the atmosphere of this meeting?*

The Second Great Awakening

The 1790 census showed that only about 1 out of 10 Americans was a member of a church. Yet in the early 1800s, the pressures of a changing society led many people to renew their religious faith. The great religious movement of the early 1800s is known as the **Second Great Awakening.** Like the Great Awakening of the 1730s and 1740s, it took place among Protestant Christians.

The Second Great Awakening was democratic. Anyone, rich or poor, could win salvation if he or she chose to do so. Generally, the congregation, or the people of the church, was seen as more significant than its ministers.

One common feature of the Second Great Awakening was the revival. This was a gathering at which people were "revived," or brought back to a religious life, by listening to preachers and accepting belief in Jesus Christ. Revivals were also called camp meetings because they were often held outdoors in temporary shelters such as tents.

New Denominations Partly as a result of the Second Great Awakening, during the early 1800s several Protestant **denominations,** or religious subgroups, experienced rapid growth. The United States soon had a greater variety of Christian denominations than any other nation.

One of the fastest-growing denominations was the Baptists. Unlike other denominations, which tend to baptize people as infants, Baptists believe that only those who were old enough to understand Christian beliefs should be baptized. (Baptism is a Christian ceremony by which a person is made a member of the church.) By 1850, Baptists were the nation's second-largest denomination.

Another denomination that gained many new members was the Methodists. The Methodists spread their message through a system of traveling ministers called circuit riders. Traveling on horseback in sweeping routes or "circuits" through the wilderness, these circuit riders won many new members. By 1850, the Methodists had become the largest Protestant denomination in the United States.

The Unitarians likewise gained strength during the Second Great Awakening. (Unitarianism is not an evangelical faith. The name *Unitarian* comes from the belief that God is a unity. Many other Christian groups believe that God is a trinity, or made up of three parts.) Unitarians believe that Jesus Christ was a human messenger of God, not divine himself. They see God not as a stern judge but as a loving father.

Focus on CULTURE

Awaiting the Advent Many ministers believed that America was leading the world into the millennium, or Earth's final thousand years of glory before the biblical Day of Judgment. They looked for signs of the coming event in everyday life.

Vermont farmer William Miller declared that Jesus Christ would return to the world in 1843. This return was called the Advent, or Second Coming. Miller preached that only those who believed in the Advent would be saved and go to heaven. He estimated that his followers, called Millerites, numbered from 50,000 to 100,000.

While the Advent did not arrive in 1843, Millerites continued to await Jesus' return. In the 1860s, they formed several churches, including the Seventh-day Adventist Church, which exists today.

CAPTION ANSWERS

Viewing History The atmosphere appears to be informal, probably friendly and respectful. Some people are paying rapt attention to the speaker, while others chat on the side.

RESOURCE DIRECTORY

Teaching Resources

Learning with Documents booklet (Visual Learning Activity) *"Do They Miss Me at Home?"* p. 46

Units 1/2 booklet
- Section 1 Quiz, p. 24

Guide to the Essentials
- Section 1 Summary, p. 13

Technology

Color Transparencies *American Diversity,* G8

Sounds of an Era Audio CD *"Sacred Harp,"* 1942 recording (time: one minute); *"Free at Last"* (time: 45 seconds)

RESOURCE PRO® **Visual Learning Activity** *"Married Mum?"* found on Resource Pro, uses a humorous cartoon to describe lifestyles on the western frontier during the 1780s.

Unitarianism took root not on the frontier, like other new denominations, but in New England.

Another region of great activity during the Second Great Awakening was central New York State. Here, in 1830, Joseph Smith published *The Book of Mormon.* The book foretold that God would soon restore a truer, simpler church, free of ministers. This was to take place not in the faraway Holy Land but in North America. Smith started a religion based on the book. He called it the Church of Jesus Christ of Latter-day Saints. In time, people began calling members of the church Mormons.

Women were extremely active in the Second Great Awakening. In part this may have reflected the loneliness and unhappiness of many women on the frontier. They worked together to help widows and orphans, to spread the Christian religion, or to improve conditions for mothers.

African American women preachers, such as Juliann Jane Tillman, found a voice within the African Methodist Episcopal Church (AME).

African American Worship

In the 1700s and early 1800s, Methodist and other evangelical churches included whites and blacks. As African Americans joined Christian churches, black and white religious traditions blended together. One example is the call-and-response method of worship, in which the congregation responds together to a statement made by one member. This is a feature of both older Protestant worship and African music.

Both white and black Christians also sang **spirituals,** or folk hymns. African American singers, however, often focused on themes that held a double meaning. For example, in the Bible, the Jewish people, called Israelites, had been kept in slavery under Egypt's pharaoh, or ruler, and were led out of Egypt to freedom by Moses. African Americans made this story a symbol for winning both spiritual salvation and freedom from physical slavery.

African Americans sometimes felt unwelcome in white-dominated churches. The tensions between whites and blacks increased as African Americans became more assertive about sharing in democratic liberty.

In several cities, African Americans started their own churches. In 1816, for example, 16 congregations joined to form the African Methodist Episcopal Church (AME). By 1831, the AME had 86 churches with about 8,000 members.

Section 1 Assessment

READING COMPREHENSION

1. Why was the population young and growing in the early 1800s?
2. Trace the causes and effects of (a) the westward migration of Native Americans; (b) the independence of Texas; (c) the **Adams-Onís Treaty.**
3. Name three inventions or innovations that changed early American life.
4. What new religious **denominations** arose during the **Second Great Awakening?**

CRITICAL THINKING AND WRITING

5. **Determining Relevance** How was the spirit of improvement related to the Industrial Revolution?
6. **Writing to Describe** Write an essay describing the changing role of American women as seen in (a) the call for republican virtues and (b) the Second Great Awakening.

Take It to the NET

Activity: Writing a Magazine Article Research the Erie Canal and write the introduction and outline for a magazine article on the canal's history and impact on America. Use the links provided in the *America: Pathways to the Present* area of the following Web site for help in completing this activity.
www.phschool.com

CUSTOMIZE FOR ...

Less Proficient Readers

During the Second Great Awakening, events such as revival meetings attracted large numbers of people searching for meaning. Ask students to describe the feelings an American might have experienced attending a revival meeting for the first time.

Section 1 Assessment

Reading Comprehension

1. Between 1800 and 1849, the average American woman had about five children, causing a population boom and a dramatic decrease in the median age.
2. (a) Causes: forced to move west by treaties imposed by the United States as white settlers moved into Native Americans' land; effects: deterioration of Native American culture and population decrease due to diseases spread by whites. (b) Causes: Mexico put an end to autonomous self-government in Texas, Americans in Texas worried that their individual liberties might be further restricted (particularly the right to own slaves), the Texas War for Independence; effects: eventual annexation of Texas by the United States. (c) Causes: Jackson's invasion of Florida while Spain was preoccupied by rebellions in South America; effects: Spain lost Florida and its claim in the Pacific Northwest, U.S. stretched from Atlantic to Pacific.
3. Answers might include: steamboat, cotton gin, steam shovel, interchangeable parts, mechanized cotton mill, canning factory, internal combustion engine, or electromagnet.
4. Baptists, Methodists, Unitarians.

Critical Thinking and Writing

5. The Industrial Revolution was a manifestation of the spirit of improvement tenets of profit, improvement, and efficiency.
6. Essays may include: (a) Americans began to look to women to set the standard for republican virtues. It was hoped that education might enable women to pass on these virtues to their husbands, children, and others. (b) The rigors of pioneer life meant that women had to labor just as hard as did men. (c) Women recruited fellow Christians and aided mothers, orphans, and widows.

Answers should provide a thorough summary of the canal's history, examining its social, political, and economic influence.

Section 2 The Market Revolution

Section Objectives

1. Learn about ways the economy expanded in the early 1800s and see how the northern and southern economies differed.
2. Find out about events of the early 1800s that reflected the rise of nationalism in America.
3. Discover how new opposition parties arose.
4. See what issues shaped the presidency of Andrew Jackson.

Bellringer

Warm-Up Activity Explain to students that during the first half of the 1800s, expanding markets and thriving industries and business transformed American life. The Market Revolution, as this transformation was called, made the making of money the chief goal of most Americans.

Activating Prior Knowledge Ask students to consider whether or not the roots of our current culture, with its emphasis on material goods, might have its origins in the Market Economy.

Reading Strategy

Have students refer back to the Main Idea from time to time and list details from the section that support it.

Section 2 The Market Revolution

READING FOCUS

- How did the economy expand in the early 1800s, and how did the northern and southern economies differ?
- What events of the early 1800s reflect the rise of nationalism in America?
- How did new opposition parties arise?
- What issues shaped the presidency of Andrew Jackson?

MAIN IDEA

In the early 1800s, manufacturing and banking expanded the U.S. economy. A sense of unified nationhood took hold, but growing regional differences began to challenge that unity.

KEY TERMS

Market Revolution
manufacturing
free enterprise system
capital
industrialization
strike
labor union
Monroe Doctrine
nullify
states' rights
secede
Trail of Tears

TAKING NOTES

As you read, complete the following chart to show causes and effects of the Market Revolution.

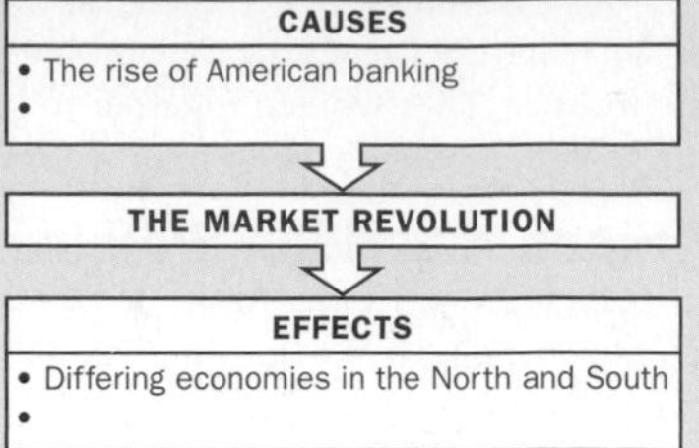

CAUSES
• The rise of American banking
•
THE MARKET REVOLUTION
EFFECTS
• Differing economies in the North and South
•

Setting the Scene On July 4, 1826, Americans celebrated the fiftieth anniversary of the Declaration of Independence with parades, cannon salutes, and speeches. It was a day to remember the achievements of the men and women who had won this nation's freedom.

Only after the celebrations were finished did many Americans learn that two of the greatest of those men, Thomas Jefferson and John Adams, had died that very day. Their deaths reminded Americans that the Revolutionary generation, for all its accomplishments, was now passing into history.

Not only were the men and women of the Revolutionary generation leaving the scene. The world they had lived in was disappearing as well.

This cast metal weathervane, a symbol of American patriotism, dates to about 1800.

An Expanding Economy

In the decades after the War of 1812, the American economy soared. While the United States remained mostly a nation of farmers, a new generation of Americans began buying and selling goods, borrowing and circulating money, and creating wealth. This change in the way Americans made, bought, and sold goods is known as the **Market Revolution.**

The Rise of Manufacturing The Market Revolution was fueled by the American genius for invention, which resulted in new and better ways to make and transport goods. Farmers started putting more and more frontier lands into the production of crops such as wheat and corn. Land in New England could then be put to other uses, such as **manufacturing,** or the making of products by machinery. The region's fast-moving rivers supplied power to the new machines in factories that sprang up in the early 1800s.

In 1813, a group of businessmen led by a Boston merchant named Francis Cabot Lowell built a factory in Waltham, Massachusetts, to manufacture textiles. Lowell's was the first truly centralized textile factory in the world. That is, all

RESOURCE DIRECTORY

Teaching Resources

Learning Styles Lesson Plans booklet, pp. 32–36
Guided Reading and Review booklet, pp. 17–18

Other Print Resources

American History Block Scheduling Support *On the Job: Industrialism in America,* found in the Expansion, Reconstruction, and Immigration folder, includes interdisciplinary lesson suggestions and activities for Geography and History, Primary Sources, Biography, and Literature.

Technology

RESOURCE PRO® **Literature Activity** *Preacher to the World,* found on Resource Pro, features excerpts from the journals of Ralph Waldo Emerson to give students a glimpse of other reactions to American materialism.
Section Reading Support Transparencies
Guided Reading Audiotapes (English/Spanish), Ch. 3
Student Edition on Audio CD, Ch. 3
Prentice Hall Presentation Pro CD-ROM, Ch. 3
Companion Web site, www.phschool.com

the tasks involved in making a product (in this case, cloth) were carried out in one place.

From the 1820s through the 1840s, manufacturing industries arose in New England and spread across the Northeast and parts of the Northwest Territory, such as the Ohio River valley. Manufacturing would soon become the backbone of the North's economy.

READING CHECK
What factors led to the rise in manufacturing?

The Free Enterprise System The changes of the Market Revolution were based on a **free enterprise system.** This is an economic system characterized by private or corporate ownership of capital goods; investments that are determined by private decision rather than by state control; and determined in a free market. In a free enterprise economy, most property is owned by private individuals and companies. The operation of supply and demand decides how goods are produced and distributed. This system, also called capitalism, rewards people who can find better, faster, and more efficient ways of running their businesses. It encourages the creation of new industries, jobs, and wealth.

Generally these new jobs were located outside the home. In the past, most Americans had worked in the home or around the farm, making the food, clothing, and shelter they needed. Now more people began working in factories for a specific number of hours each day and for a certain amount of money.

As products became available and people worked for money, Americans began to shop. The relatively simple homes of the 1700s gave way to much more decorated homes in the 1800s.

The Rise of the Banking Industry The Market Revolution could not have happened without large amounts of **capital,** or wealth that can be invested to produce goods and make money. Businesses used capital to buy land or to invest in money-making projects. Banks provided this capital.

The first real banks in the United States appeared in the 1780s and 1790s. By the 1830s, hundreds of new banks had been established.

Generally, a group of private investors would obtain a charter from the state to start a bank. The bank made money by charging interest for the loans it made. It made these loans using the money that customers deposited in the bank for safekeeping. Banks thus helped the economy grow by providing the money that businesses needed to expand.

However, banks often made bad loans to people who could not pay them back. Since (unlike today) the government did not require banks to keep a certain amount of cash on hand, banks sometimes lacked the cash to give to depositors who wanted to withdraw money. Customers would panic, rushing to the banks to get their money out before the banks went broke. As a result, the American economy experienced wild booms followed by panics, bank failures, and depressions.

As this bank note shows, people began earning a living outside the home in the early 1800s.

Bank Notes The most common form of money in the early 1800s was the bank note, a piece of paper that banks issued to their customers. Similar to modern-day checks, bank notes were promises to pay specie (coins, mainly of gold or silver) on demand.

Because banks simply printed more bank notes whenever they needed money, the value of this money was unpredictable. A $100 bank note could be worth anything from $50 to $200 in specie, depending on the time and place its owner tried to cash it.

Lesson Plan

Focus The American economy underwent a fundamental change at the beginning of the 1800s. Ask how this change affected American life. Explain that most of the South's economy centered on commercial agriculture, while the North's economy centered on manufacturing and urban growth.

Instruct Discuss the changes brought about by the Market Revolution in the North and in the South. Ask how farmers in the Northwest contributed to the growth of cities in the Northeast. Ask how agriculture differed in the North and South. In what ways were southern planters and farmers as capitalistic as their northern counterparts?

Ask students to analyze the role that enslaved people played in the southern economy. Would southern commercial agriculture have been possible without slavery?

Have students analyze the plight of factory and mill workers in northern cities in the first half of the 1800s. Why did they feel powerless to change their working conditions?

Assess/Reteach In both the southern and the northern economies, society was divided into strata according to wealth. Slaves and many impoverished workers were victimized by being forced to meet the production requirements of the Market Economy. Can students see some ways in which northern factory workers were oppressed? How did their oppression differ from that experienced by slaves in the South?

READING CHECK
As more frontier land was being used to produce wheat and corn, land in New England could be put to other uses; for example, the region's rivers supplied power to the new machines that supported the growth of manufacturing.

CUSTOMIZE FOR ...

ESL

Ask students to skim the section, noting any unfamiliar words. Help them define these words using context clues or a dictionary.

ACTIVITY
Connecting with Geography

Have students color and label outline maps of the United States to identify the North, the South, and the old Northwest. **(Visual/Spatial)**

From the Archives of
AmericanHeritage®

Cooper's Coup

In February 1823 James Fenimore Cooper published *The Pioneers,* which sold over 3,500 copies the first day it went on sale. It became so popular that it would be translated and read around the world. *The Pioneers* introduced America's first great fictional character, Natty Bumppo. Bumppo, also known as Leatherstocking for his deerskin breeches, is an aging frontiersman who has spent decades living off the wilderness until America's burgeoning population begins to encroach on his ways. Bumppo complains about losing his shooting and fishing playground to the settlers' farms. By shunning the settlers' "wasty ways," he sounds an early warning against the American tendency to confuse abundance with inexhaustibility. The popularity of *The Pioneers* led Cooper to write a series of novels called *The Leatherstocking Tales* in which Bumppo was the star. Source: Frederic D. Schwarz, "The Time Machine," *American Heritage®* magazine, February/March, 1998.

INTERPRETING DIAGRAMS New England mill builders adopted a system of belts to harness river power. On the first floor cotton was combed; on the second floor, it was spun into thread; on the third, thread was woven into cloth; and on the fourth, the cloth was dressed, or finished. **Determining Relevance** *What effect did geography have on the location of a mill?*

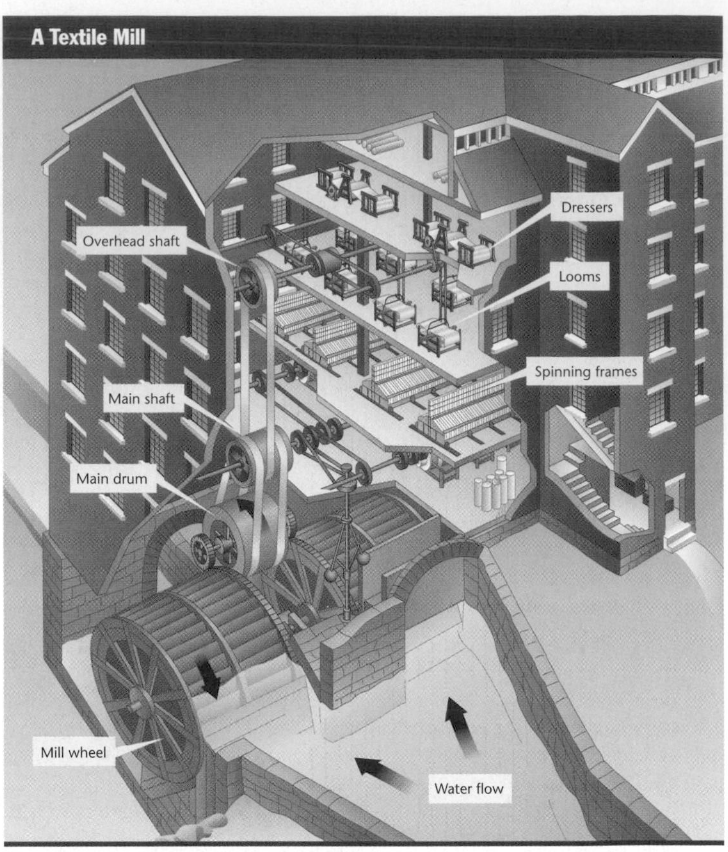

Despite such economic growing pains, banks were essential to economic expansion. While different areas of the country grew at different rates, the United States as a whole achieved a new level of prosperity.

The Northern Economy

In the early 1800s, Americans became more aware that their nation had distinct regions or sections. The two main sections during this period were the North and the South.

One part of the North was the region north and west of the Ohio River, which historians call the Old Northwest. It included land that is now Ohio, Indiana, Illinois, Michigan, Wisconsin, and part of Minnesota. The other part was the Northeast, composed of New England and the states of New York, New Jersey, and Pennsylvania.

Northwest Farming, Northeast Industry The fertile fields of the Old Northwest were ideal for growing corn, wheat, and other grains. Grains could be sold or turned into other products. Many specialized businesses arose to handle the processing, transport, and selling of farm products.

Although most people in the Northeast still lived on farms, many others now worked in factories in urban areas. As more people came to the cities to

CAPTION ANSWERS

Interpreting Diagrams Mills needed to be located near a good source of continuous, strongly flowing water.

RESOURCE DIRECTORY

Other Print Resources

Nystrom *Atlas of Our Country* *A Divided Nation,* pp. 26–27

Historical Outline Map Book *The Northern States,* p. 43; *The Southern States,* p. 44

Technology

Color Transparencies *The Way It Works,* H7

RESOURCE PRO® **Primary Source Activity** *New England Mill Women,* found on Resource Pro, helps students examine the pros and cons of factory life.

RESOURCE PRO® **Biography** *Sarah Todd Astor,* found on Resource Pro, profiles Sarah Todd Astor and John Jacob Astor, a couple who exemplified the Market Revolution.

Exploring Primary Sources in U.S. History CD-ROM *A Description of Factory Life in 1846*

work, the Northeast's population density, or the number of people living within a given space, rose as well. Between 1810 and 1840, the number of Americans living in cities jumped from about 6 percent of the total population to 12 percent. Much of that growth was in the Northeast.

Industrialization, or the growth of industry, increased rapidly. The mill town of Lowell, Massachusetts, founded in 1826, would become a booming industrial center. The Lowell mills hired young, unmarried women from New England farms to run the spinning and weaving machines. Women mill workers usually lived in boardinghouses established by the mill owners. Six days a week, twelve hours a day, they tended the machines. In the evening they might attend lectures or classes, or gather in sewing or reading circles.

The Rise of Labor Unions The Lowell mills treated their employees much better than did other early industries. Most factory owners paid their employees little and did not provide benefits such as housing or food. Meanwhile, workers saw owners grow rich while they labored long hours for low wages. Workers had only one real weapon: a **strike,** or work stoppage. From 1834 through 1836, more than 150 strikes took place in the United States.

In 1834, workers also organized the first national labor union, the National Trades Union (NTU). A **labor union** is an organization of workers formed to protect their interests, usually by negotiating to resolve issues such as wages and working conditions. Close to 300,000 people joined the NTU or other labor unions in the 1830s, a large number for that period.

These early unions soon died out, however. Factory owners obtained court rulings that outlawed labor organizations. Workers were also hard hit by the economic depressions of 1837 and 1839, which caused higher unemployment and lower wages.

The Southern Economy

The South consisted of 6 of the original 13 states: Delaware, Maryland, Virginia (including what would become West Virginia), North Carolina, South Carolina, and Georgia. It also included newer states carved out of lands south of the Ohio River that stretched from the Appalachian Mountains to the Mississippi River: Kentucky, Tennessee, Alabama, Mississippi, Louisiana, and Arkansas.

A Rural Economy While urban centers developed in the North, the South remained mostly a rural region of farms and countryside. Farmers enjoyed fertile soil, plentiful rain, and 200 to 290 frost-free days a year in which to grow crops.

The primary southern crop was cotton. Virginia and North Carolina were mainly tobacco states. Sugar and rice crops thrived in hot, wet places such as South Carolina. Kentucky developed a varied rural economy that included the breeding of thoroughbred horses.

This print shows workers loading and unloading cotton shipments at the port city of New Orleans in 1883.

The Slavery System By 1804, all the northern states had either banned slavery or passed laws to end it gradually. The Constitution specified that Congress could not end the slave trade before 1808. In that year, Congress banned further importing of slaves.

Within the South, however, the slave trade increased sharply for the next half century due to population growth among people already enslaved. By

Activity
Connecting with History and Conflict

Divide the class into groups of four. Have one student in each group assume the role of a worker who is trying to persuade his coworkers to strike, while the other students role-play the following: a male worker with a large family and a sick wife at home; an unmarried woman with no children; a woman with a large family and no husband; and a young, unmarried male. Ask students to explain their reasons for wanting or not wanting to strike. **(Logical/Mathematical)**

Background
The Flour Riot

Desperate economic conditions in New York City, where 50,000 people—about one third of the working population—were unemployed, resulted in the Flour Riot of 1837. The New York *Commercial Register* reported, "Barrels of flour, by dozens, fifties and hundreds were tumbled into the street . . . thrown in rapid succession from the windows . . . [And] numbers of women were . . . filling . . . their aprons, with flour, and making off with it."

Background
Interdisciplinary

One sign of the Market Revolution was the expansion of invention and innovation during the time. The U.S. Patent Office was established during this period, in 1836. During its first quarter century, it issued tens of thousands of patents, at the rate of about four a day, every day.

Customize for ...
ESL

Have each student create a poster entitled "Economies of the North and South." Posters should use text and drawings to illustrate how the two economies differed.

Test Preparation

Have students read the section on "The Southern Economy" and then answer the question below.

What sustained the economy of Kentucky?

- **A** Cotton
- **B** Tobacco
- **C** Sugar and rice
- **(D)** A varied economy, including horse breeding

ACTIVITY
Connecting with Citizenship

Have students conduct research in order to write one-page reports on the differences between the concept of *nationalism* and the concept of *patriotism.* To give students a better understanding of both, discuss the differences between the two terms and writing ideas in class. **(Verbal/Linguistic)**

ACTIVITY
Connecting with Culture

The "southern gentleman" was characterized by a unique style of behavior called chivalry, after the medieval code of knights and ladies. Ask students to work in groups to research this southern tradition. Have them write and produce a short skit. **(Verbal/Linguistic; Bodily/Kinesthetic)**

BACKGROUND
Interdisciplinary

When Nat Turner led his rebellion, there were about two million slaves living in the United States—approximately one out of every six people in the country.

COMPARING PRIMARY SOURCES

Slavery

The issue of slavery opened up a bitter divide between the North and the South. The writers below present viewpoints on whether enslaved people wished to remain in slavery.

Analyzing Viewpoints Compare the main arguments made by the two writers.

In Support of Slavery

"A merrier being does not exist on the face of the globe than the Negro slave of the United States. They are happy and contented, and the master is much less cruel than is generally imagined. Why then . . . should we attempt to disturb his contentment by planting in his mind a vain and indefinite desire for liberty—something which he cannot understand?"

—Professor Thomas R. Dew, speech to the Virginia legislature, 1832

In Opposition to Slavery

"I thank God I am not property now, but am regarded as a man like yourself. . . . You may perhaps think hard of us for running away from slavery, but as for myself, I have but one apology to make for it, which is this: I have only to regret that I did not start at any early period."

—Henry Bibb, who escaped from slavery with his family, in a letter to his former master, 1844

1860, African American slaves made up more than half of the population of South Carolina and of Mississippi, as well as two fifths of the population in several other states.

Slave Revolts Only a small percentage of slaves managed to escape captivity or to win their freedom. Rebellions, especially on a large scale, stood little chance of success.

One attempt at a revolt was made by a former slave named Denmark Vesey. In 1822, he laid plans for the most ambitious slave revolt in American history. In a conspiracy that reportedly involved hundreds or even thousands of rebels, Vesey plotted to seize the city of Charleston. He was betrayed by some of his followers, however, and troops smashed the rebellion before it could get started. Thirty-five African Americans, including Vesey, were hanged.

Nine years later, Nat Turner, an African American preacher, carried out a violent uprising known as Turner's Rebellion. He led up to 70 slaves in raids on white families in southeastern Virginia. In attacks on four plantations, the rebels killed some 57 white people.

Eventually, local militia captured most of the rebels. The state of Virginia hanged about 20 of the slaves, including Turner. Crowds of frightened, angry whites rioted, killing about a hundred African Americans who had had no part in the revolt. Some southern states reacted to the Vesey and Turner rebellions by tightening restrictions on slaves.

The Rise of Nationalism

Eventually, the economic differences between the North and South would place great strains on the nation's unity. In the 1820s, though, the nation seemed to be pulling closer together. Americans began thinking of themselves as belonging to a country under a national government, instead of an association of states under separate governments. Reflecting this shift, a new generation of American leaders sought to exercise the powers of the federal government to unite the country.

Nationalism at Home After the War of 1812, the nation was weary of conflict. It adopted new nationalist policies to resolve political struggles at home and abroad. In domestic affairs, the Supreme Court under Chief Justice John Marshall made decisions in three key areas that strengthened the federal government's role in the economy.

The first decision supported the national bank. The Constitution did not specifically grant the federal government the right to charter a national bank. In 1819, the Supreme Court considered a case involving Maryland's attempt to wipe out the bank by levying heavy taxes on it. Maryland's action challenged Congress's authority to create such an institution. In *McCulloch* v. *Maryland,* Chief Justice Marshall ruled that Congress did have the authority to charter the bank. He based his argument on Article I, Section 8, which states that Congress

RESOURCE DIRECTORY

Teaching Resources

Learning with Documents booklet (Key Documents) *The Monroe Doctrine,* p. 79

Biography, Literature, and Comparing Primary Sources booklet (Literature) *The Confessions of Nat Turner,* p. 49

Other Print Resources

Nystrom *Atlas of Our Country* *A Divided Nation,* pp. 26–27

Technology

Color Transparencies *Time Lines,* C3

RESOURCE PRO® **Critical Thinking Activity** *Making Comparisons,* found on Resource Pro, helps students summarize the differences between the economies of the North and South.

RESOURCE PRO® **Critical Thinking Activity** *Identifying Alternatives: Reacting to Slave Uprisings,* found on Resource Pro, allows students to apply this skill by assuming the role of a Virginia legislator after Turner's Rebellion.

Exploring Primary Sources in U.S. History CD-ROM *Monroe Doctrine*

Nationalist Supreme Court Decisions, 1819–1824		
Case	**Issues**	**Outcomes**
McCulloch v. *Maryland* (1819)	Does the government have the power to create a national bank? Do states have the right to tax institutions created by the federal government?	Reinforced (1) the doctrine of implied powers and (2) the principle of the power of the national government over state governments.
Dartmouth College v. *Woodward* (1819)	Was Dartmouth's contract protected by the Constitution? Was New Hampshire interfering with the contract?	Prevented state interference in business contracts. Gave stability to the economy by encouraging growth of corporations.
Gibbons v. *Ogden* (1824)	Who has the power to regulate navigation, the states or the federal government?	Established the federal government's right to regulate all aspects of interstate commerce.

INTERPRETING CHARTS The Supreme Court under Chief Justice John Marshall made several decisions that greatly increased the authority of the federal government. **Drawing Inferences** *How do these decisions reflect the shift toward nationalism?*

has the right "to make all laws necessary and proper" for carrying out the powers granted it under the Constitution.

An 1819 ruling protected the legality of contracts. The Court barred New Hampshire from changing the charter of Dartmouth College. The college had been chartered during colonial times. In *Dartmouth College* v. *Woodward,* the Court ruled that states cannot interfere in such contracts. The long-term effect of the ruling was to protect business contracts, providing further stability to the economy.

In the 1824 case *Gibbons* v. *Ogden,* Chief Justice Marshall declared that states could not regulate commerce on interstate waterways. A man named Aaron Ogden had purchased a state license giving him exclusive rights to operate a New York–New Jersey steamboat line. When a competitor, Thomas Gibbons, started a business on the same route, Ogden sued him. Gibbons said he operated under federal license. Gibbons's victory gave the federal government authority over all types of interstate business.

Nationalism Abroad At the same time, American Presidents strengthened the nation's foreign policy. The new policies took shape under the leadership of President James Monroe and his Secretary of State, John Quincy Adams, the son of Abigail and John Adams.

In foreign policy, one of Monroe's main concerns was to ease tensions with Great Britain. In 1817, the United States and Britain signed the Rush-Bagot Agreement, in which both sides agreed to reduce the number of warships in the Great Lakes region. The following year, the two countries agreed to extend the northern border of the United States westward along 49° N latitude from the Great Lakes to the Rocky Mountains.

A second concern for Monroe was that European countries might resume their efforts to colonize the Western Hemisphere. Monroe spelled out American policy on these urgent matters in an address to Congress on December 2, 1823. The speech established a policy that has been followed to some degree by every President since Monroe. The **Monroe Doctrine,** as it is called, had four main parts. First, the United States would not get involved in the internal affairs of European

Focus on CULTURE

Democracy in America One of the most influential books ever written about America was authored by a Frenchman. Alexis de Tocqueville wrote *Democracy in America* after spending nine months in the United States in 1831.

Tocqueville was struck by "the general equality of condition among the people." Compared to Europe, America had fewer very rich or very poor people and more who were in between. Also, Americans did not regard a wealthy person as being better than anyone else.

Yet equality had its drawbacks, Tocqueville warned. He knew of "no country in which there is so little . . . real freedom of discussion," since few Americans dared to disagree with the majority. Still, he hoped that Europeans would some day enjoy the liberty and equality he found in the United States.

BACKGROUND
Geography in History

Britain adapted easily to the Monroe Doctrine. Britain's strategy was to make economic gains in the Western Hemisphere without the trouble of colonies. Investors built railroads and plantations in developing countries to grow crops for Europe, and in turn Latin Americans bought manufactured goods such as clothing and ships from Britain. This strategy meant that the British could control a country's economy without paying for defense or government, and without stepping on the toes of the young United States.

From the Archives of American Heritage®

About the Presidents

John Quincy Adams (1825–1829) favored justice for Native Americans, denouncing the "crying sins for which we are answerable before a higher jurisdiction." He asked Congress to give the Native Americans territory in the West and to guarantee their rights. But Andrew Jackson's treatment of Native Americans in Florida reflected the popular attitude: evict and exterminate. Congress defeated Adams's request. Source: David Jacobs, "John Quincy Adams," *The American Heritage® Pictorial History of the Presidents of the United States,* vol. 1, 1968.

CAPTION ANSWERS

Interpreting Charts Sample answer: The decisions strengthened the powers of the federal government over state governments, while also clarifying the lines of authority.

ACTIVITY
Connecting with Citizenship

Have a student locate several of Alexis de Tocqueville's more remarkable statements about America and Americans (using a book of quotations) and share them with the class. Ask students to comment on each one: Do de Tocqueville's observations still hold true today? **(Verbal/ Linguistic)**

BACKGROUND
Connections to Today

Andrew Jackson's Tennessee plantation was named "The Hermitage," and it stands today much as it did when Jackson lived there. Visitors can enjoy the garden (which is planted in the way it was during Jackson's time) and tour the impressive house. Behind Jackson's huge home visitors can see the remains of tiny, 20-feet by 20-feet cabins. Each was home to a whole family of people: slaves owned by the seventh President.

READING CHECK

President Monroe "threw down the gauntlet" by declaring that any European effort to take over a nation in the Western Hemisphere would be construed as an act of war by the United States. This was a daring policy because it offered a direct challenge to European powers at a time when the young United States had not yet fully established itself as a world power.

countries nor take sides in wars among them. Second, America recognized the existing colonies and states in the Western Hemisphere and would not interfere with them. Third, America would not permit further colonization of the Western Hemisphere. Fourth, America would view any attempt by a European power to control any nation in the Western Hemisphere as a hostile action.

As President Monroe stated:

READING CHECK
Why was the Monroe Doctrine a bold diplomatic move?

> *"Our policy in regard to Europe . . . is, not to interfere in the internal concerns of any of its powers. . . . It is impossible that the allied [European] powers should extend their political system to any portion of either [the North American or South American] continent without endangering our peace and happiness. . . ."*
>
> —The Monroe Doctrine speech by President James Monroe to Congress, December 2, 1823

The Rise of Opposition Parties

The elections of 1824 and 1828 were bitter battles. Yet out of these disputes arose new political parties that offered clear choices to voters.

The Election of 1824 In 1824, for the first time no presidential candidate could boast of having been a leader during the Revolution. Challenging John Quincy Adams were the brilliant political leader Henry Clay of Kentucky and war hero General Andrew Jackson of Tennessee.

Clay, former Speaker of the House and United States senator from Kentucky, was energetic and charming, with a magnificent gift for speech making. Andrew Jackson had served in the Senate in the 1790s and was a wealthy plantation owner near Nashville, Tennessee. His victories in the War of 1812 and his attacks on the Seminole Indians in Florida had won him widespread popularity.

In the 1824 election, Jackson won the most popular votes, but none of the candidates received the required majority of electoral college votes. Thus in February 1825, as the Constitution required, the House of Representatives voted to decide the election. Clay managed to swing Kentucky's votes to Adams to give him the victory. Just days later, Adams made Clay his Secretary of State. Furious Jackson supporters charged that Adams and Clay had made a "corrupt bargain" to deny Jackson the presidency.

New Political Parties Emerge At every turn, Jackson's supporters in Congress blocked Adams' plans for public improvements and protective tariffs. Meanwhile Jackson prepared for the coming election—and for revenge.

This first photograph of an American President shows John Quincy Adams—son of President John Adams and his wife, Abigail—in the 1840s.

Supporters of Adams and Clay adopted a new name: the National Republicans. They believed they were true to the Jeffersonian spirit of improvement. Jackson's followers called themselves Democrats. (Historians refer to them as Jacksonian Democrats.) They believed they were true to Jefferson's ideal of limited government.

Unlike most previous elections, the 1828 campaign offered voters a choice between candidates of sharply differing views. Jackson trounced Adams, winning 178 electoral votes to Adams's 83.

French writer Alexis de Tocqueville visited the United States three years later, in 1831. In his book, *Democracy in America,* he noted that "liberty is

RESOURCE DIRECTORY

Teaching Resources
Learning with Documents booklet (Primary Source Activity) *President Jackson's Inauguration,* p. 13
Learning with Documents booklet (Visual Learning Activity) *The Jackson Ticket,* p. 47

Other Print Resources
Historical Outline Map Book *The United States in 1824,* p. 34; *Election of 1828,* p. 36
Nystrom *Atlas of our Country* *The Second Wave of Immigration,* pp. 24–25

Technology
Color Transparencies *Political Cartoons,* B4; *American Photo,* F2
Exploring Primary Sources in U.S. History CD-ROM *The Sovereignty of the People in America, Alexis de Tocqueville; Debate Over Nullification, Daniel Webster and John C. Calhoun*

generally born in stormy weather, growing with difficulty amid civil discords, and only when it is already old does one see the blessings it has brought." The rise of opposition parties in America would indeed produce "discords." But the party system would stir healthy debates and strengthen the democratic process.

The Presidency of Andrew Jackson

The rise of Andrew Jackson signaled several changes in American politics. Jackson was the first President from west of the Appalachian Mountains. He also came to the presidency not through party politics but on a wave of popular support. State laws requiring voters to be property holders had been repealed in the previous decade, and new states such as Indiana and Maine allowed all white adult men to vote. The votes cast for President tripled between 1824 and 1828, from roughly 356,000 to more than 1.1 million.

The Spoils System For many years, newly elected officials had given government jobs to friends and supporters. Although he did not originate this practice, known as patronage, Andrew Jackson made it official when he took office. However, during his eight years as President, Jackson actually removed fewer than one fifth of presidential appointees and other federal office holders and replaced them with Jacksonian Democrats. Patronage under Jackson became known as the *spoils system*. In this case, the spoils, or loot taken from a conquered enemy, were jobs for party supporters.

Jackson defended the spoils system on the grounds that any intelligent person could be a competent public official. He also argued that "rotation in office" would prevent a small group of wealthy, well-connected people from controlling the government.

Limited Government Jackson shared the beliefs of Americans who feared the power of the federal government. He attacked politicians whom he considered corrupt and laws that he thought would limit people's liberty. He used his veto power to restrict federal activity as much as possible, rejecting more acts of Congress than the six previous Presidents combined.

The Tariff Crisis While Jackson sought to limit federal power, he did not shy away from strong federal action when he thought it necessary. In 1828, Congress had passed a high tariff to discourage foreign imports and encourage American manufacturing. The tariff benefited the industrial North but forced southerners to pay higher prices for manufactured goods. They called the import tax the "Tariff of Abominations." (*Abomination* refers to something especially horrible or monstrous.)

The tariff prompted South Carolina to declare that states had the right to judge when the federal government had exceeded its authority. The state maintained that in such cases, states could **nullify**, or reject, federal laws they judged to be unconstitutional.

South Carolina's nullification threat was based on a strict interpretation of states' rights. **States' rights** are the powers that the Constitution neither gives to the federal government nor denies to the states. The concept of states' rights is based on the constitutional principle of divided sovereignty between the federal government and the state government. In other words, each has its own powers that the other cannot take away.

The strict interpretation of states' rights that South Carolina endorsed is what some people call *state sovereignty*. The theory of state sovereignty maintains

A navy ship bore this figurehead of Andrew Jackson in 1834.

ACTIVITY
Connecting with Citizenship

Share with students the following names given Andrew Jackson, and have them explain how each one reflects Jackson as an individual, Jackson as a public figure, or both: General Andrew Jackson; Hero of the Battle of New Orleans; Hero of the Common Man; King Andrew; Old Hickory; Self-Made Man; President Andrew Jackson. **(Verbal/Linguistic)**

BACKGROUND
Connections to Government

The United States of the early nineteenth century was shaped by Andrew Jackson in a way that few other eras in the history of the country have been shaped by an individual. So influential was Jackson during this watershed period of U.S. history that the era is known to historians today as the "Age of Jackson."

From the Archives of
AmericanHeritage®

About the Presidents

Andrew Jackson (1829–1835) embodied the American dream. Born poor, his successes were won by strength, will, effort, and conviction. After his victory in the War of 1812, Jackson became America's greatest hero since George Washington. But Washington had been a gentleman-hero. Jackson was one of the "common people"—a backwoodsman. Source: Saul Braun, "Andrew Jackson," *The American Heritage® Pictorial History of the Presidents of the United States,* vol. 1, 1968.

TEST PREPARATION

Have students read the passage on the previous page by James Monroe and then complete the sentence below.

Monroe clearly felt that European powers—

A should help Americans when needed.
B should be closely involved in North and South American politics.
(C) should not attempt to control any North or South American country.
D should be ready to colonize more territories if needed.

ACTIVITY

Connecting with History and Conflict

Organize two teams to debate the following resolution: "Resolved: The Indian Removal Act was a good law." One team will support the resolution, and the other will oppose it. Each team will make a presentation supporting its position, and then make a brief rebuttal attacking their opponents' position. Allow the teams time to cross-examine each other. Conclude with a discussion about U.S. government treatment of Native Americans and how it is viewed in the U.S. today. **(Verbal/Linguistic; Logical/Mathematical)**

From the Archives of

American Heritage®

About the Presidents

Martin Van Buren (1837–1841) faced the Panic of 1837 just days after his inauguration. "The less government interferes with private pursuits the better for the general prosperity," he said. Van Buren pressed Congress for an independent treasury to deal with the nation's finances. But the permanent independent treasury he hoped for was not established until 1846. Source: Wilson Sullivan, "Martin Van Buren," *The American Heritage® Pictorial History of the Presidents,* vol. 1, 1968.

When William Henry Harrison (1841) ran for President, a Baltimore, Maryland, newspaper insulted his lack of intellectual depth. They said he'd be content with a log cabin and a barrel of hard cider. The Whigs turned the insult to their advantage by giving out log cabin songbooks and cider. Although the Whigs ignored real issues, their "log cabin" campaign won Harrison the presidency. Source: David Jacobs, "William Henry Harrison," *The American Heritage®* Pictorial History of the Presidents, vol. 1, 1968.

CAPTION ANSWERS

Viewing History Answers might include: People and animals are loaded down with all the belongings they can carry. The landscape is dry and sparse, unlike their homelands. The tone suggests gloom and weariness.

Sounds of an Era

Listen to reenactments of Native American history and Andrew Jackson on the bank war (next page), as well as other sounds from the early 1800s.

that because states created the federal government, they have the right to nullify its acts and even to **secede,** or withdraw, from the Union if they wish to do so. In 1832, after the passage of yet another tariff, South Carolina declared the tariffs null and void, and threatened to secede if its nullification was not respected.

An enraged Jackson believed the state was defying the will of the people. At his urging, in 1833 Congress passed the Force Bill, which required South Carolina to collect the tariff. Jackson threatened to send 50,000 federal troops to enforce the law.

The crisis eased when Congress reduced some of the import duties and South Carolina canceled its nullification act. Yet in an act of continued defiance, the state nullified the Force Bill at the same time.

Indian Relocation In the 1820s, wealthy plantation owners were buying up much of the best cotton-farming land in the South. Large and small planters alike wanted to expand westward into Native American lands. The Cherokee, Creek, Choctaw, Chickasaw, and Seminole peoples lived on about 100 million acres of fertile land in western parts of the Carolinas and in Georgia, Florida, Alabama, Mississippi, and Tennessee.

In 1830, Jackson encouraged Congress's passage of the Indian Removal Act, which authorized him to give Native Americans land in parts of the Louisiana Purchase in exchange for lands taken from them in the East.

In all, Jackson forcibly relocated about 100,000 members of the Five Tribes. For their 100 million acres of largely cultivated land, the Native Americans received about 32 million acres of prairie land in what is now Oklahoma.

In 1832, the Cherokees brought their case to the Supreme Court through a missionary from Vermont, Samuel Austin Worcester. In *Worcester* v. *Georgia,* Chief Justice John Marshall ruled that Georgia had no authority over Cherokee territory. Georgia, however, simply ignored the ruling, and Jackson backed the state. "John Marshall has made his decision. Now let him enforce it!" Jackson is said to have declared. Of course, the Court had no power to enforce its decisions.

In 1838, the United States Army rounded up more than 15,000 Cherokees. In a nightmare journey that the Cherokees called the **Trail of Tears,**

VIEWING HISTORY Jackson claimed that his Indian removal policy would "place a dense and civilized population in large tracts of country now occupied by a few savage hunters." **Analyzing Visual Information** *In this painting of the* Trail of Tears, *what difficulties does the artist suggest the displaced Indians faced under Jackson's policy?*

RESOURCE DIRECTORY

Teaching Resources

Units 1/2 booklet
- Section 2 Quiz, p. 25

Guide to the Essentials
- Section 2 Summary, p. 14

Biography, Literature, and Comparing Primary Sources booklet (Comparing Primary Sources) *On* Worcester *v.* Georgia, p. 111

Other Print Resources

American Heritage Block Scheduling Support *The Trail of Tears: Native Americans During the Jackson Presidency,* found in the Expansion, Reconstruction, and Immigration folder.

Historical Outline Map Book *Indian Removal,* 1830–1842, p. 37

Technology

Sounds of an Era Audio CD *Andrew Jackson on the Bank of the United States* (time: one minute); *Elias Boudinot on Indian History* (time: one minute)

RESOURCE PRO® **Visual Learning Activity** *The Presidential Election of 1840*

Exploring Primary Sources in U.S. History CD-ROM *Our Federal Union: It Must Be Preserved, Andrew Jackson* men, women, and children, most on foot, began a 116-day forced march westward. One out of every four Cherokees died of cold or disease on the journey.

INTERPRETING CARTOONS
In this cartoon, Andrew Jackson drags Henry Clay behind him as he attacks the monster national bank. **Analyzing Visual Information** *How does the artist suggest that the danger is imaginary?*

The Bank War Like many Americans, Jackson saw the Bank of the United States as a "monster" institution controlled by a small group of wealthy easterners. He blamed it for the Panic of 1819 and the hard times that had followed.

Under its charter, the Bank of the United States could only operate until 1836, unless Congress issued it a new charter. Supporters of the bank decided to recharter it four years early, in 1832. If Jackson vetoed the charter, Jackson's opponents planned to use that veto against him in the 1832 election. Jackson vetoed the bill anyway.

Jackson then won reelection in 1832 by a huge margin, defeating National Republican Henry Clay. In the process, a distinct two-party system was reestablished, consisting of Jackson's Democratic Party and the National Republicans. Later the National Republicans would take the name Whigs, after the party in the British parliament that had opposed the king in the 1700s. These American Whigs saw themselves as defenders of liberty against an executive so powerful they dubbed him "King Andrew I."

Jackson's Successors In frail health, Jackson chose not to run for a third term in 1836. The next President, Martin Van Buren, whom Jackson had supported as a candidate, was not as popular as the general had been.

Weakened by panics in 1837 and 1839, the economy remained in poor shape in the 1840 election year. The Whig candidate, military hero William Henry Harrison, defeated Van Buren, only to be defeated himself by illness. Just one month after taking office, he died of pneumonia. Vice President John Tyler, who took over as President, was more of a Jacksonian Democrat than a Whig, and his term was largely one of fruitless quarreling between the parties.

Section 2 Assessment

READING COMPREHENSION

1. Describe the effects of **manufacturing** and **capital** on the U.S. economy.
2. How did America's **free enterprise system** affect the growing **Market Revolution?**
3. What two new political parties emerged in the 1820s, and how did their views differ?
4. How did President Jackson react to the tariff and Indian crises?

CRITICAL THINKING AND WRITING

5. **Making Comparisons** Compare the types of labor upon which economic activity was based in the North and in the South. How was labor a difficult issue in both regions?
6. **Writing to Inform** Trace the rise of nationalism in the early 1800s, and then explain how that sense of national unity yielded to regional rivalries.

Take It to the NET

Activity: Creating a Graph
Research census data to learn how America's demographics and economy changed in the early 1800s. Using a variable of your choice, create a bar graph measuring the changes from 1800 to 1840. Use the links provided in the *America: Pathways to the Present* area of the following Web site for help in completing this activity.
www.phschool.com

Section 2 Assessment

Reading Comprehension

1. Manufacturing made more goods available, so money became more widely used. For the first time, those who produced the goods were not the people who used them. Capital allowed investment, which brought about economic expansion.
2. The free enterprise system encouraged the creation of new industries that came to be known as the Market Revolution.
3. Republicans who supported the Jeffersonian spirit of improvement, and Democrats, who supported Jefferson's ideal of limited government.
4. In both cases, he exerted federal control, threatening use of federal power to compel South Carolina to cancel nullification and using federal force to relocate Indians.

Critical Thinking and Writing

5. Northern economic activity was based primarily on farming and industry. Industry workers often worked long hours for little pay in poor conditions, and labor unions developed in response. Southern land was ideal for cotton farming, increasing the use of slave labor, around which revolts and controversy developed.
6. Answers will vary, but students may mention Supreme Court decisions strengthening the federal government, improvement projects funded by the federal government, a feeling of unity amongst citizens from different states, and the Monroe Doctrine as evidence of the rise of nationalism in the 1820s. The later destruction of national unity can be traced to the disparity in wealth between the North and the South, the role of political parties, and (especially) slavery.

Take It to the NET

Variables may include the number of slaves, the number of whites, or perhaps the total number of people engaged in agriculture. Graphs should indicate how the chosen variable changed over time.

Caption Answers

Interpreting Cartoons Answers should note that the "monster" bank is represented as a many-headed hydra—an imaginary creature.

Section 3 Religion and Reform

Section Objectives

1. See how religion and philosophy affected the growing American reform movement.
2. Learn about reform movements that emerged in the early 1800s.
3. Find out how the antislavery movement arose and grew.
4. Discover the ways in which women's roles changed in the early 1800s.
5. Read about factors that caused growing social divisions in America.

Bellringer

Warm-Up Activity Ask students to describe their ideal society. Would it have rules and standards? If so, what kind? What kinds of values might it seek to promote among its members?

Activating Prior Knowledge Ask students if they are familiar with these terms: *abolitionism, suffrage, transcendentalism.* Can they offer simple definitions of those terms?

Reading Strategy

Have students make a list of all the headings in the text of this section. As they read, have them write down one important factor under each heading.

Section 3 Religion and Reform

READING FOCUS

- How did religion and philosophy affect the growing American reform movement?
- What reform movements emerged in the early 1800s?
- How did the antislavery movement arise and grow?
- In what ways did women's roles change in the early 1800s?
- What factors caused growing social divisions in America?

KEY TERMS

transcendentalism
temperance movement
abstinence
utopian community
abolitionist movement
Underground Railroad
Seneca Falls Convention
suffrage
discrimination

TAKING NOTES

Copy the web diagram below. As you read, fill in the blank circles with types of reform movements and their leaders. Add more circles if needed.

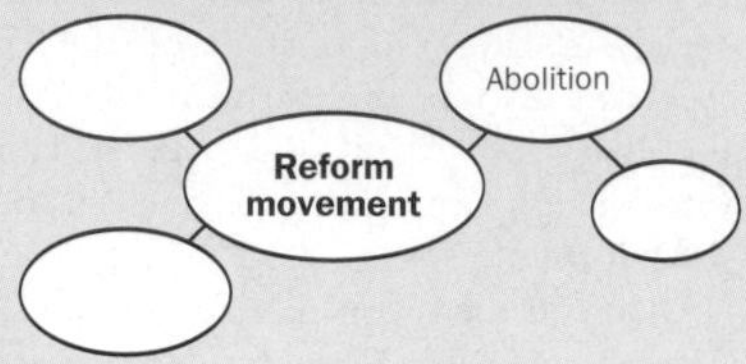

MAIN IDEA

Powerful reform movements arose in the early 1800s. They transformed society and produced regional and ethnic tensions.

Setting the Scene In 1688, a group of Mennonites, a Christian sect of German immigrants, passed a resolution that stated:

> "*There is a saying, that we should do to all men like as we will be done ourselves; making no difference of what generation, descent, or colour they are. And those who steal or rob men, and those who buy or purchase them, are they not all alike?*"
>
> —Resolutions of Germantown Mennonites, 1688

This resolution, the earliest known protest against slavery in the colonies, shows the deep roots that reform movements have in American history. It also serves as an example of the strong ties that have existed between religious faith and social reform.

In the early decades of the 1800s, America's young cities experienced growing pains such as poverty, alcoholism, illiteracy, overcrowded housing, poor healthcare, abuse of women, and declining moral values. Because these growing pains occurred first in the urban North, it was there that powerful reform movements to address these problems first took hold.

VIEWING HISTORY After a string of personal tragedies, including a failed engagement in 1840 and the loss of his brother in 1842, Henry David Thoreau sought a quieter life at Walden Pond (below) in Massachusetts. **Drawing Inferences** *From what you know about economic and social trends taking place in the Northeast during this time, how might Thoreau's life at Walden Pond have represented a contrast from those trends?*

Caption Answers

Viewing History Sample answer: Thoreau's quiet, self-sufficient life at Walden Pond contrasted with the increasing pace of life elsewhere—in crowded cities, manufacturing industries, marketplaces, and banks.

RESOURCE DIRECTORY

Teaching Resources
Learning Styles Lesson Plans booklet, pp. 20–21
Guided Reading and Review booklet, pp. 37–40

Technology
Color Transparencies *Fine Art,* E6
RESOURCE PRO® **Critical Thinking Activity** *Recognizing Ideologies: Transcendentalism,* found on Resource Pro, helps students identify a writer's point of view by analyzing an excerpt from Henry David Thoreau's "Higher Laws."
Section Reading Support Transparencies
Guided Reading Audiotapes (English/Spanish), Ch. 3
Student Edition on Audio CD, Ch. 3
Sounds of an Era Audio CD *"Self-Reliance," Ralph Waldo Emerson* (time: one minute, 30 seconds)
Exploring Primary Sources in U.S. History CD-ROM *Audubon and His Journals: My Style of Drawing Birds, John James Audubon; Civil Disobedience, Henry David Thoreau*
Prentice Hall Presentation Pro CD-ROM, Ch. 3
Companion Web site, www.phschool.com

The Roots of Reform: Religion and Philosophy

The reform movement was rooted largely in religious faith. Most reformers based their arguments on Protestant principles. Their faith gave them purpose and courage. In addition, philosophers who rejected traditional religion strongly influenced the reform movement.

Protestant Revivalists The democratic principles of the Second Great Awakening stirred the reform movements of the 1830s and 1840s. The central figure in the revivalist movement was Charles Grandison Finney. His commonsense sermons emphasized individuals' power to reform themselves. Lyman Beecher, another major revivalist, warned that the country was threatened by the ". . . diversity of local interests, the power of selfishness, and the fury of sectional jealousy and hate." Beecher taught in simple terms that good people would make a good country.

The Transcendentalists The reform movement also drew inspiration from a group of philosophers and writers who rejected traditional religion. The group, centered in Concord, Massachusetts, founded a philosophical movement known as **transcendentalism.** (To *transcend* means to "rise above.") Transcendentalism taught that spiritual discovery and insight would lead a person to truths more profound than could be reached through reason.

In writings and lectures from about 1830 to 1855, transcendentalists declared that humans are naturally good. They rejected outward rituals and group worship in favor of private, inward searching. They urged people to be self-reliant and to have the courage to act on their own beliefs.

Transcendentalist Henry David Thoreau

Emerson and Thoreau The leader of the Transcendental movement was Ralph Waldo Emerson (1803–1882), a lecturer and writer who became one of America's greatest thinkers. From his home in Concord, Emerson helped launch what historians call an "American renaissance" in literature. Like other transcendentalists, Emerson supported various reform causes and urged others to do so. "What is man born for," Emerson wrote, "but to be a Reformer. . . ?" Emerson's work attracted a generation of young thinkers and writers.

Just down the road from the town of Concord is a pine forest surrounding a small pond. This serene setting produced one of the best-known works of American literature: *Walden, or Life in the Woods.* Its author was a friend and neighbor of Emerson's, Henry David Thoreau (1817–1862), who would become an equally renowned figure among the New England transcendentalists.

In 1845, Thoreau built a small cabin for himself at Walden Pond and spent the next two years in a mostly solitary life of thinking, reading, writing, and observing nature. *Walden* describes Thoreau's experiment in living simply:

Lesson Plan

Focus The young republic sped through rapid social change in the early 1800s—change that brought not only new benefits but also new regional and cultural tensions. Many Americans were concerned about the problems that accompanied the growth and development of the United States. Ask students how Americans reacted to these problems.

Instruct Explain that although both Protestant reformers and transcendentalists believed that people were responsible for their own destiny, their beliefs differed in other ways. Discuss the ways in which the two groups' spiritual beliefs differed. Abolitionism and suffrage were two movements that also grew in this era of reform and reexamination. Ask students to describe the ways these movements are connected to religious reforms and the core beliefs of transcendentalism.

Assess/Reteach Ask students to discuss the ways in which religious reform gave power to movements designed to bring equality to all people.

Activity: Connecting with Citizenship

Have students write journal entries in which they explore and seek to answer this question: Is participating in a social reform movement the duty of every American citizen? **(Verbal/Linguistic)**

Customize for ... ESL

Write the word *reform* on the chalkboard. Have students look the word up in the dictionary. Then ask two volunteers to perform a brief skit to illustrate its meaning.

ACTIVITY
Connecting with Government

This activity may take place over more than one class period: Divide class into groups of three students. One member of each group represents the transcendentalists, another represents the temperance movement, and the third is an education reformer. Their task is to start a new political party called the Reform party. Have them draft a document stating their key positions and goals. **(Verbal/ Linguistic)**

BACKGROUND
Art History

Shakers led a simple life dedicated to hard work and personal discipline. Influenced by this philosophy, Shaker craftsmen produced basic, well-engineered furniture for their villages. Their neighbors appreciated the elegance and strength of the Shaker style, and in 1790 the village of New Lebanon, New York, became the first of many to manufacture chairs for commercial sale. Shaker chairs, tables, and boxes have become prized collector's items.

> *"Why should we be in such desperate haste to succeed, and in such desperate enterprises? If a man does not keep pace with his companions, perhaps it is because he hears a different drummer. Let him step to the music which he hears, however measured or far away."*
>
> —Henry David Thoreau, *Walden*, 1854

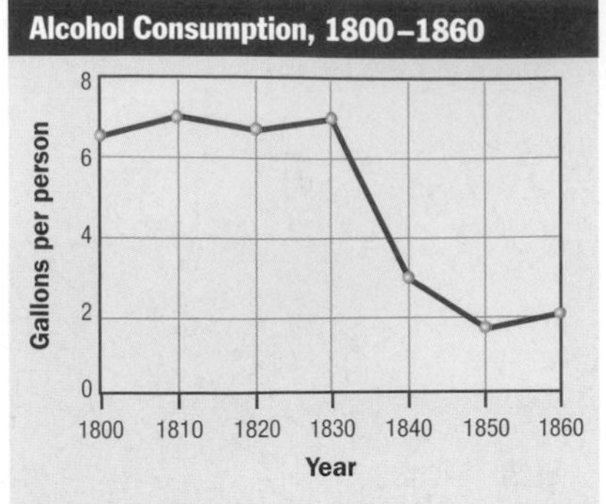

INTERPRETING GRAPHS
Temperance societies relied primarily on persuasion to discourage drinking. **Drawing Inferences** *Based on information in this graph, how successful was the temperance movement? Explain.*

Reform Movements

Whatever their religious or philosophical approaches, reformers set out to profoundly change American society. In a few short decades, they made considerable progress.

The Temperance Movement The first and most widespread of the reform efforts of the early 1800s was the **temperance movement,** a campaign to eliminate alcohol consumption.

In the early 1800s, Americans were consuming more alcoholic beverages per person than at any other time in the country's history. Reformers opposed alcohol consumption because it tended to make people lose control. Women reformers in particular saw drinking as a threat to family life.

Between 1815 and the 1840s, thousands of local temperance societies were formed. Members urged people to take pledges to practice abstinence from drinking alcohol. **Abstinence** means refraining from doing something.

In 1851, Maine became the first state to ban the manufacture and sale of all alcoholic beverages. Although several other states passed similar laws around this time, the protests of brewers, distillers, and other citizens soon led to the repeal of most of these laws. Still, between the 1830s and the 1860s, U.S. alcohol consumption dropped dramatically.

Public Education The geography of the mid-Atlantic and southern states, where people tended to live on isolated farms, discouraged the building of schools. Even in New England, where colonial laws had required towns to provide elementary schools, support for public education had declined. But in the 1820s, many working-class and middle-class citizens began to demand tax-supported public schools.

A leading pioneer of education reform was Horace Mann. His achievements in Massachusetts encouraged reformers in other states. By the 1850s, most northern states had free public elementary schools.

Free public schools were less common in the South and in urban areas in general. Girls often were discouraged from attending or were taught only to read and write. Schools also frequently excluded free black students or placed them in separate, inferior schools. Higher education was even more limited. Some private colleges admitted a small number of African American students, and a handful of black colleges were founded during this period. Several other private colleges were coeducational. For the most part, however, only white male students were welcome at most universities.

Dorothea Dix

Reforming Prisons In the early 1800s, many states built prisons rather than punish criminals by branding them or putting them on display in public stocks. The hope was that prisoners would use their time in jail to reflect on their sins and become law-abiding citizens. But when Boston schoolteacher Dorothea Dix visited a Massachusetts jail in 1841, she discovered men and women, young

CAPTION ANSWERS

Interpreting Graphs Highly successful, with consumption dropping from about 7 gallons per person per year in 1830 to a low of less than 2 gallons per person per year in 1850.

RESOURCE DIRECTORY

Teaching Resources

Biography, Literature, and Comparing Primary Sources booklet (Comparing Primary Sources) *On Property in Utopian Communities,* p. 113

Learning with Documents booklet (Visual Learning Activity) *Countrymen in Chains,* p. 48

Technology

RESOURCE PRO® Primary Source Activity *Protecting Society's Outcasts,* found on Resource Pro, highlights the inhumane treatment of prisoners and the mentally ill through an excerpt from Dorthea Dix's testimony to the Massachusetts legislature.

Sounds of an Era Audio CD *The Narrative of the Life of an American Slave, Frederick Douglass* (time: one minute); *Dorothea Dix on Asylum Reform* (time: 50 seconds)

and old, sane and insane, first-time offenders and hardened criminals, all crowded together in shocking conditions.

Dix then spent two years visiting every prison in Massachusetts. She persuaded the state to improve prisons and create separate facilities for the mentally ill. Dix's efforts led 15 other states to build mental hospitals.

Utopian Communities While most reformers worked to improve society at large, some formed **utopian communities,** small societies dedicated to perfection in social and political conditions. In the first half of the 1800s, more than 100 utopian communities arose in the United States.

Among the most famous was New Harmony, Indiana, founded in 1825 by Scottish industrialist and social reformer Robert Owen. Owen envisioned a town in which well-educated and hard-working people would share property in common and live in harmony. Like most of the utopias, however, New Harmony fell victim to laziness, selfishness, and quarreling.

Most utopian communities were religiously oriented. One example was the Shakers, an offshoot of the Quakers, who established their first community at New Lebanon, New York, in 1787. The Shakers strived to lead lives of productive labor, moral perfection, and equality among women and men.

READING CHECK
What successes and failures did reform movements have?

The Antislavery Movement

The **abolitionist movement,** or the movement to end slavery, was started by a group of free African Americans and whites. During the late 1700s, several antislavery societies formed in the North, while abolitionist newspapers appeared in both the North and the South. From 1774 to 1807, every state north of Maryland passed laws that gradually abolished slavery. All importing of slaves to the United States ended in 1808.

The Colonization of Liberia In the early 1800s, some abolitionists favored colonization, a program to send free blacks and emancipated (freed) slaves to Africa. Convinced that African Americans would never receive equal treatment in U.S. society, these antislavery advocates founded the American Colonization Society in 1817. To pursue its plan, the society established the West African country of Liberia (its name taken from *liberty*) in 1822.

White supporters of colonization did not all believe in racial equality. Many were eager to send African Americans out of the country. Some southern

VIEWING HISTORY Abolitionist Frederick Douglass is shown here speaking at an antislavery meeting. **Formulating Questions** *Write down four or five questions you might have wanted to ask Douglass if you had attended this meeting.*

ACTIVITY
Connecting with Culture

Share with students what one historian wrote about the utopian community at New Harmony, Indiana: "[New Harmony's] legacy was not a place or a plan but a reformist outlook that made its way into American political thought." Challenge students to explain what this statement means. **(Verbal/Linguistic)**

BACKGROUND
Interdisciplinary

The colonization of Liberia was supported by the most prominent slaveholders of the day, among them John C. Calhoun, Henry Clay, and Andrew Jackson. Ironically, they supported the freedom Liberia would offer as a way to ensure the existence of slavery in the United States: They feared a large population of free black people would threaten the institution of slavery.

READING CHECK

Successes: temperance societies formed, several states outlawed alcoholic beverages, alcohol consumption dropped dramatically; development of free public elementary schools in the North, expansion of higher education, development of mental hospitals. Failures: repeal of temperance laws; lack of free public schools in the South; girls discouraged from attending schools; black students discouraged from attending or placed in separate, inferior, schools.

TEST PREPARATION

Have students read the quotation by Thoreau on the previous page and then complete the statement below.

By "desperate enterprises," Thoreau means—

A pursuits that are destined to fail.
(B) attempts to achieve success and keep up with others.
C actions that are attempted too hastily.
D pursuits motivated by desperation.

CAPTION ANSWERS

Viewing History Sample questions: How has your life changed since you became free? Have you ever lost contact with a slave relative because that person was sold? What do you think is the best strategy for abolishing slavery? Do you think the United States can abolish slavery without erupting into war? What will happen to enslaved people once they become free?

BACKGROUND
Geography in History

While some slaves escaped to the North, others were sent southward from Virginia and Maryland. Two centuries of tobacco farming had worn out Virginia's soil, and plantations there sold many of their slaves to estates in the deep South where laborers were needed. A common punishment for slaves who tried to revolt or escape was to be "sold South," where the climate was hotter and free territory too far away to encourage runaways.

From the Archives of
AmericanHeritage®

Out of Africa!

On December 1, 1822, in what is now Monrovia, Liberia, three dozen former American slaves desperately fought off an armed assault by 1,000 native-born Africans determined to reclaim their land. In 1821 the American Colonization Society had forced a local king at gunpoint to deed them a 130-mile strip of coastland in return for a few cartloads of hardware and household goods (including place settings for twelve, complete with wineglasses). Ever since, his subjects had been waiting for a chance to expel the interlopers. When fever had killed or weakened a sufficient number, they struck. Some of the warriors carried spears. Others bore large-caliber muskets, which they loaded with foot-long copper and iron slugs for close-range use. But the settlers had artillery, which made up for their numerical disadvantage. Despite repeated attacks, the colony continued for three more decades until the Civil War made it irrelevant. By that time, a mere 15,000 blacks had been resettled. Source: Frederic D. Schwarz, "The Time Machine," *American Heritage®* magazine, Dec. 1997.

CAPTION ANSWERS

Interpreting Graphs The enslaved population.

Free and Enslaved Black Populations, 1820–1860

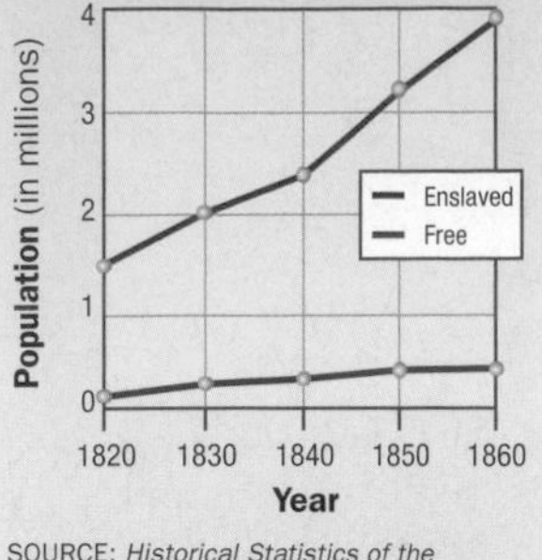

SOURCE: *Historical Statistics of the United States, Colonial Times to 1970*

INTERPRETING GRAPHS
The population of both free and enslaved African Americans rose in the first half of the 1800s. **Analyzing Visual Information** *Which population rose more rapidly?*

planters backed colonization as a way to eliminate the threat of free blacks who might encourage slaves to revolt.

The colonization plan offended most African Americans. They wanted to improve their lives in their homeland, the United States, not on a faraway continent. By 1831, only about 1,400 free blacks and former slaves had migrated to Liberia.

William Lloyd Garrison One of the most famous of the radical abolitionists was a white Bostonian named William Lloyd Garrison. In 1831, Garrison began publishing *The Liberator,* an antislavery newspaper supported largely by free African Americans. Garrison denounced moderation in the fight against slavery:

> "*I do not wish to think, or speak, or write, with moderation. . . . I am in earnest—I will not equivocate—I will not excuse—I will not retreat a single inch—AND I WILL BE HEARD.*"
>
> —William Lloyd Garrison, in the first issue of *The Liberator*, 1831

In 1833, with the support of both white and African American abolitionists, Garrison founded the American Anti-Slavery Society. As the decade progressed, more middle-class white northerners began to support the immediate end of slavery. By 1835, the American Anti-Slavery Society had some 1,000 local chapters with roughly 150,000 members.

Frederick Douglass The nation's most influential African American abolitionist was Frederick Douglass. Born into slavery, Douglass escaped north and became an agent of the American Anti-Slavery Society.

In 1845, Douglass published his autobiography, *Life and Times of Frederick Douglass,* which sold thousands of copies. Douglass's speeches in the United States and Great Britain convinced many people of the evils of slavery. Douglass also published an abolitionist newspaper, the *North Star.*

Sounds of an Era

Listen to reenactments of passages from Frederick Douglass, Dorothea Dix, Ralph Waldo Emerson, and other sounds from the reform era.

Divisions Among Abolitionists While abolitionists shared a common goal, divisions appeared within the movement. One of the first splits occurred over women's participation in the American Anti-Slavery Society. At the time, Americans in general did not approve of women's involvement in political gatherings. When Garrison insisted that female abolitionists be allowed to speak at antislavery meetings, some members resigned in protest.

Women who became prominent in the abolition movement included two white sisters from South Carolina named Sarah and Angelina Grimké, as well as Sojourner Truth, an African American and former slave. Truth took that name because she believed her life's mission was to sojourn, or "travel up and down the land," preaching the truth about God at revival meetings.

Another source of tension among abolitionists was political action. Garrison believed that the Constitution supported slavery. Thus, he reasoned, attempting to win emancipation by passing new laws would be pointless, because any such laws would be unconstitutional.

Abolitionists who disagreed with Garrison formed the Liberty Party in 1840. The Liberty Party received only a fraction of the presidential vote in 1840 and in 1844. Yet it drew off enough support from the Whig Party in such key states as Ohio and New York to give the 1844 election to James K. Polk, a Democrat.

The Underground Railroad Risking arrest, and sometimes risking their lives, abolitionists created the **Underground Railroad,** a network of escape routes that

RESOURCE DIRECTORY

Other Print Resources

American History Block Scheduling Support *"Come Along to Freedom": The Underground Railroad,* found in the Expansion, Reconstruction, and Immigration folder, includes interdisciplinary lesson suggestions and activities for Geography and History, Primary Sources, Biography, and Literature.

Nystrom *Atlas of Our Country* *A Divided Nation,* pp. 26–27

Technology

Color Transparencies *Historical Maps,* A17

Sounds of an Era Audio CD *"Fourth of July Speech,"* Frederick Douglass (time: one minute, 30 seconds)

RESOURCE PRO® **Biography** *William Lloyd Garrison* profiles the man known as the conscience of the abolitionist movement.

RESOURCE PRO® **Literature Activity** *Life as a Freeman* presents a passage from *Narrative of the Life of Frederick Douglass.*

Exploring Primary Sources in U.S. History CD-ROM *Meaning of July Fourth for the Negro, Frederick Douglass; First Issue of the* Liberator, *William Lloyd Garrison*

provided protection and transportation for slaves fleeing north to freedom. The term *railroad* referred to the paths that African Americans traveled, either on foot or in wagons, across the North-South border and finally into Canada, where slave-hunters could not go. *Underground* meant that the operation was carried out in secret, usually on dark nights in deep woods. Men and women known as conductors acted as guides. They opened their homes to the fugitives and gave them money, supplies, and medical attention. Historians' estimates of the number of slaves rescued vary widely, from about 40,000 to 100,000.

The most famous conductor was a courageous former slave named Harriet Tubman, who herself had escaped from a plantation in Maryland in 1849 and fled north on the Underground Railroad. Tubman (shown in the photo below) returned just the next year to rescue family members and lead them to safety. Thereafter, she made frequent trips to the South, rescuing more than 300 slaves and gaining the nickname "the Black Moses."

Resistance to Abolitionism In the decades before the Civil War, most white Americans viewed abolitionism as a radical idea, even in the North. White workers and labor leaders feared competition from escaped slaves willing to work for lower wages. Most Northerners, including some who opposed slavery, did not want African Americans living in their communities.

Opposition to the abolitionists eventually became violent. The most brutal act occurred in Alton, Illinois, where Elijah P. Lovejoy edited a Presbyterian weekly newspaper. In his editorials, Lovejoy denounced slavery and called for gradual emancipation. Opponents repeatedly destroyed his printing presses, but each time Lovejoy resumed publication. On the night of November 7, 1837, rioters again attacked the building. Lovejoy, trying to defend it, was shot and killed.

Most white Southerners were outraged by the criticisms that the antislavery movement leveled at slavery. In 1836, Southerners in Congress succeeded in passing the so-called gag rule, which for the next eight years prohibited antislavery petitions from being read or acted upon in the House. Abolitionists pointed to the gag rule as proof that slavery threatened the rights of all Americans, white as well as black.

Women's Changing Roles

As industrialization and urbanization took hold in the United States, women (especially in the North) felt the impact. Many lower-class women took jobs in factories. Middle-class women, however, were freed from chores such as growing their own food and making clothes, as more products appeared on store shelves.

Private and Public Roles Most people believed that women should remain in the home. Middle-class women were expected to raise and educate their children, entertain guests, serve their husbands, do community service, and engage in at-home activities such as needlework and quilting. In this division of labor, men engaged in public activities such as politics, law, and public speaking. Most people would have been shocked at the idea of women doing these things.

Although some women defied these limits, they still faced strict legal restrictions. For example, the law denied women the right to vote. In most

Focus on GEOGRAPHY

A Path to Freedom People escaping slavery knew that freedom lay to the north, in the free northern states or in Canada. With no maps to guide them, they followed the North Star. More detailed instructions came in the form of a song passed secretly among some slaves, called "Follow the Drinking Gourd":

"When the sun comes back
and the first quail calls,
Follow the Drinking Gourd.
For the old man is waiting
for to carry you to freedom,
If you follow the Drinking Gourd. . . ."

The "Drinking Gourd" is the Big Dipper, which points to the North Star. The first line of the song tells slaves to leave in the winter, when the sun is higher in the sky and quail have migrated to the South. This will give them time to reach the Ohio River by the following winter and cross it on foot over the ice. The "old man" is a man named Peg Leg Joe, who taught slaves the escape route described in the song.

ACTIVITY
Connecting with Geography

Challenge students to locate the direction north by using the "Drinking Gourd" (The Big Dipper) to find the "North Star" (Polaris). Explain that the line formed by the two stars that form the outer side of the Big Dipper's cup points directly toward Polaris (in the direction "up" from the cup). Polaris is about five times the distance from the top of the cup as the distance between the two stars that make up the outer side of the cup. Have students report to the class how easy or difficult it was for them to find the direction north by "following the drinking gourd." **(Bodily/ Kinesthetic)**

BACKGROUND
Biography

Harriet Tubman (1821–1913) was one of 11 children born into slavery. She ran away to the North alone, later saying, "There was no one to welcome me to the land of freedom. I was a stranger in a strange land." By the beginning of the Civil War in 1861, Tubman had escorted more than 300 slaves to freedom, including her brothers, sisters, and parents. Then, as a scout for the Union army, she helped free more than 750 slaves. In 1896, Tubman founded the National Association of Colored Women.

CUSTOMIZE FOR ...
Less Proficient Writers

Have students list the main reasons people supported or opposed the abolition of slavery. Have them identify whether each reason was primarily moral or economic.

ACTIVITY
Connecting with Culture

The public and private spheres were clearly demarcated in the early 1800s. Women in particular were excluded from participating in the public sphere. To help students understand the concept of cultural spheres, ask students of the same gender to sit in circle groupings. Have each "sphere" list five activities in which they participate but the members of the other "sphere" do not. **(Verbal/Linguistic)**

BACKGROUND
Recent Scholarship

Women dominated the antislavery movement. Historians have long known about white women who took up the cause in alliance with their demands for equal rights. More recently, they have begun to write about the important roles played by the large community of free women of color. *Shirley J. Yee's Black Women Abolitionists: A Study in Activism, 1828–1860* illuminates the contributions of African American women and reminds us that free blacks had to deal with racism and inequalities even among radical opponents of slavery.

states, married women could not own property or make a will. Despite the increasing number of women working outside the home, women generally could not keep the money they earned. Instead they had to turn it over to a husband or father.

As more women became educated, however, they grew eager to apply their knowledge and skills beyond the home. They also became increasingly dissatisfied with the laws and attitudes that prohibited them from doing so.

The religious revivals and reform movements of the early 1800s heightened women's sense of their potential and power. Women played a prominent role in nearly every avenue of reform, from temperance to abolition. For some women, participation in a reform movement was a first, satisfying taste of the world outside the family.

Fighting for Abolition Women who participated in the abolition movement saw parallels between the plight of enslaved African Americans and the status of women. Neither group could vote or hold office, for instance. Both were denied the full rights of American citizens.

Women writers had an enormous influence on public opinion about slavery. Harriet Beecher Stowe opened the eyes of many northerners with her 1852 abolitionist novel *Uncle Tom's Cabin.* Harriet Ann Jacobs authored the 1861 book *Incidents in the Life of a Slave Girl.* Sojourner Truth could not read or write, but she dictated her experiences to an author to produce *The Narrative of Sojourner Truth.*

A Convention for Women's Rights In 1848, Lucretia Mott and Elizabeth Cady Stanton organized the first women's rights convention in United States history. It took place in Stanton's hometown of Seneca Falls, New York.

At the **Seneca Falls Convention,** Stanton herself wrote and presented a historic set of resolutions called a Declaration of Sentiments. The document echoed the language of the Declaration of Independence:

> "*The history of mankind is a history of repeated injuries and usurpations [seizure of power] on the part of man toward woman, . . . [to establish] absolute tyranny over her. . . . [B]ecause women do feel themselves aggrieved, oppressed, and fraudulently deprived of their most sacred moral rights, we insist that they have immediate admission to all the rights and privileges which belong to them as citizens of the United States.*"
>
> —Elizabeth Cady Stanton, Declaration of Sentiments, 1848

The convention passed resolutions protesting the lack of legal and political rights for women and urging women to demand these rights. One controversial resolution called for women's **suffrage,** or the right to vote. This resolution subjected the convention to considerable public criticism.

The Seneca Falls Convention did not trigger an avalanche of support for women's rights. Most Americans still believed that women should influence public affairs indirectly, through their work in the home. Yet it did mark the beginning of the organized movement for women's rights and women's suffrage in the United States.

Elizabeth Cady Stanton was a key organizer of the Seneca Falls Convention on women's rights in 1848.

RESOURCE DIRECTORY

Teaching Resources

Learning with Documents booklet (Primary Source Activity) *Plantation Life,* p. 14

Learning with Documents booklet (Key Documents) *Seneca Falls Declaration,* p. 80

Biography, Literature, and Comparing Primary Sources booklet (Literature) *A First-Hand Account of the Potato Famine,* p. 50

Biography, Literature, and Comparing Primary Sources booklet (Biography) *Maria Mitchell,* p. 4

Other Print Resources

American History Block Scheduling Support *The Reformers: A Struggle for Women's Rights,* found in the Prosperity, Depression, and War folder.

Nystrom *Atlas of Our Country* *The Second Wave of Immigration,* pp. 24–25

Technology

Sounds of an Era Audio CD *"Ain't I a Woman?"* Sojourner Truth (time: one minute, 40 seconds)

Exploring Primary Sources in U.S. History CD-ROM *Seneca Falls Declaration of Sentiments*

The Role of African American Women For most African American women, the abolition of slavery was a more pressing issue than women's rights. The abolitionist and former slave Sojourner Truth was an exception. In 1852, she told a convention of white women in Akron, Ohio:

> "*I have as much muscle as any man, and can do as much work as any man. . . . I can carry as much as any man, and can eat as much too . . . I have heard the Bible and have learned that Eve caused man to sin. Well, if woman upset the world, do give her a chance to set it right side up again.*"
>
> —Speech by Sojourner Truth, 1852

Growing Social Divisions

Early reform movements often did as much to divide American society as improve it. One reason was that the nation was becoming more diverse. Immigrants came from a variety of European cultures. The North and the South were becoming more distinct. Differences among working people and wealthier Americans were widening. Some segments of this diverse population did not share the reformers' vision of America.

Rising Immigration The economic changes of the early 1800s created a growing demand for cheap labor in factories and in the building of canals and railroad lines. Immigration rose accordingly. The number of immigrants arriving in the United States skyrocketed from about 129,000 in the 1820s to some 2.8 million in the 1850s. Nearly all of these new arrivals settled in the North and West, because the use of slave labor in the South offered few job opportunities.

Almost all of the immigrants to the United States from 1820 to 1860 came from northern Europe, especially Ireland and Germany. Irish immigration soared in the mid-1840s when a famine struck Ireland. Irish men filled manual labor jobs in factories or on canals or railroads. Irish communities in northern cities grew steadily, and Irish Americans became a potent political force.

Many Germans came to America seeking political freedom after a series of failed rebellions across Europe in 1848. Most Germans bought up large tracts of farmland in the Midwest, especially in Wisconsin and Missouri. Many also settled in Texas, making up 5 percent of the state's population by 1850. German artisans and intellectuals tended to settle in northern cities such as New York, Chicago, and Milwaukee.

Focus on WORLD EVENTS

The Irish Potato Famine The Irish potato famine began in 1845, when a fungus from North America destroyed much of Ireland's potato crop. Harvests over the next few years were no better. Because the potato was a staple crop, especially for the poor, loss of the crop caused a terrible famine.

The British government, which ruled Ireland, provided some aid to its desperate people. Still, Ireland continued to export food to Britain because the Irish lacked the money to buy it for themselves.

More than 1 million Irish (out of a population of less than 9 million) died from starvation or related diseases. Up to 1.5 million more Irish emigrated to places such as the United States or Britain. Many settled in Boston, New York, and other northeastern cities.

Immigration to the United States, 1821–1860

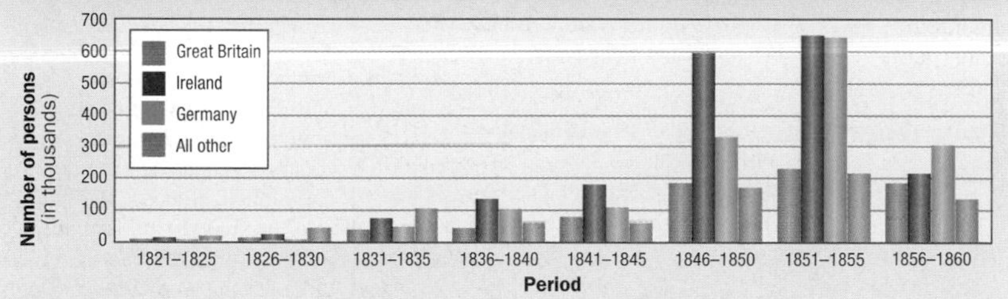

SOURCE: *Historical Statistics of the United States, Colonial Times to 1970*

INTERPRETING GRAPHS The graph at left tracks the largest immigrant groups from the 1820s to 1860. **Analyzing Visual Information** *(a) When did immigration surge? (b) During that period, from which country did the most immigrants arrive?*

ACTIVITY
Connecting with Culture

Refer students to this sentence under "Rising Immigration" in their textbooks: "The number of immigrants arriving in the United States skyrocketed from about 129,000 in the 1820s to some 2.8 million in the 1850s." Have students use these figures to calculate: (1) the percentage increase in immigration during this time period, and (2) the average number of immigrants that arrived each month during the 1840s and during the 1860s. **(Logical/Mathematical)**

BACKGROUND
Geography in History

One heritage of German immigration to the United States is scores of American toponyms (place names). Today, areas that were settled by German immigrants still have predominately German names for towns and counties. Examples include the Germantown section of Philadelphia; New Braunfels, Texas; and the town of Womelsdorf in southeastern Pennsylvania.

CUSTOMIZE FOR ...
Gifted and Talented

Some reformers of the time believed that the role of women in the home was crucial to the nation's welfare. Have students discuss how feminists might have responded to this argument.

Section 3 Assessment

Reading Comprehension

1. Transcendentalism grew out of a rejection of traditional religion. The temperance movement was a response to the concern that alcohol was causing people to lose control and threatening family life. Some reformers wanted to form their own small societies in an attempt to achieve perfect social and political conditions.
2. Sample answers: Operated the Underground Railroad; funded American Anti-Slavery Society; attacked slavery in print (*Uncle Tom's Cabin* is a prime example of abolitionist writing).
3. (a) To attain the rights and privileges that belonged to women as citizens of the United States, in particular the right to vote. (b) Lower-class women took factory jobs, while middle-class women were freed from chores as more products appeared in stores. Women became active in reform movements in response to the social and legal restrictions they faced.
4. Southerners resented abolitionists' efforts to prevent the spread of slavery and to shelter escaped slaves. They were disturbed by the charge that slaveholders were immoral. Calls for public schools and equal rights for women upset southerners who saw these demands as suggestions that they did not properly care for their families. Many southerners depended on children for farm labor and saw no reason to disrupt traditional family roles.

Critical Thinking and Writing

5. Answers should succinctly summarize the motives, aims, and results of the reformer selected.
6. Answers will vary, but should discuss: opposition from both northerners and southerners, splits within the movement, the role of women in the antislavery movement, political action, and interpreting the Constitution.

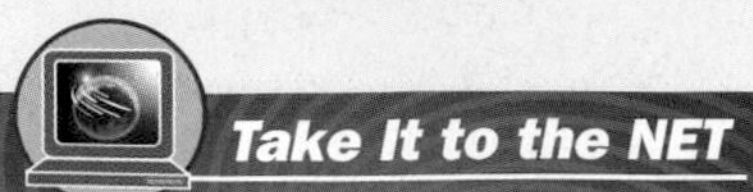

Take It to the NET

Lists will vary, but may include food, water, extra clothes, or a disguise.

Caption Answers

Interpreting Graphs (a) 1846 through 1855; (b) Ireland

INTERPRETING POLITICAL CARTOONS The cartoon above shows Irish immigrants arriving in a ship depicted as a poorhouse. **Recognizing Bias** *What is the message of the cartoon? What details reflect the cartoonist's view?*

Tensions Over Immigration Irish and German immigrants often faced **discrimination,** the unequal treatment of a group of people because of their nationality, race, sex, or religion. The Irish arrived just as new, struggling labor unions were striking for better wages and working conditions. The Irish would work for lower wages, so companies used them as strike breakers. In addition, many Protestants disapproved of the Roman Catholic religion to which many of the immigrants belonged.

In 1843, anti-immigrant citizens formed the American Republican Party, which favored requiring immigrants to live in the United States for 21 years before being eligible for citizenship. The following year, Irish Catholics attacked American Republicans who were attempting to vote in Philadelphia's Irish districts. This led to riots in which dozens of people were killed.

North-South Tensions Reform movements increased ill will between the North and the South as well. Southerners bitterly resented abolitionists' efforts to prevent the spread of slavery and to shelter escaped slaves. They felt stung by the charge that slaveholders were immoral.

As the abolition movement intensified, it produced deep rifts in the Methodist and Baptist churches. After the Methodist Church demanded in 1842 that one of its southern bishops free his slaves, churches in the slaveholding states left the national organization. They then formed the Methodist Episcopal Church South, which endorsed slavery. The Baptist Church also splintered, as about 300 churches withdrew in 1845 to form the proslavery Southern Baptist Convention.

Reformers' calls for public schools and equal rights for women further offended many white Southerners, who saw these demands as suggestions that they did not properly care for their families. In the South, where personal honor was particularly important, such suggestions provoked outrage. The call for public schools disturbed many Southerners who depended on their children for farm labor.

Most of the South remained untouched by the social turmoil that came with urbanization and industrialization in the North. Thus, Southerners saw no need to reform their society. Families held fast to their traditional family roles.

Section 3 Assessment

READING COMPREHENSION

1. What led to the growth of **transcendentalism,** the **temperance movement,** and **utopian communities?**
2. What tactics did the abolitionist movement use to combat slavery?
3. Describe (a) the goals of the **Seneca Falls Convention** and (b) changes in the role of women in the early 1800s.
4. Why did reform movements offend many Southerners?

CRITICAL THINKING AND WRITING

5. **Summarizing Information** Choose a reformer mentioned in this section and outline his or her motives, specific goals, and any successes and/or failures.
6. **Writing a News Story** As a reporter for an abolitionist newspaper, describe the challenges faced by antislavery activists. Use examples to illustrate your main points.

Take It to the NET

Activity: Recreating History
Find out what escaping slaves took with them on the Underground Railroad. Prepare a list of items you would have taken on that journey. Remember, you could only take what you could carry long distances. Use the links provided in the *America: Pathways to the Present* area of the following Web site for help in completing this activity.
www.phschool.com

RESOURCE DIRECTORY

Teaching Resources

Units 1/2 booklet
- Section 3 Quiz, p. 26

Guide to the Essentials
- Section 3 Summary, p. 15

Section 4

The Coming of the Civil War

READING FOCUS

- How did U.S. expansion to the Pacific affect slavery in the territories?
- What changes in political parties occurred in the 1850s?
- How did North-South tensions worsen in the 1850s?
- What issues dominated the Lincoln-Douglas debates?
- What events finally divided the nation and led to war?

KEY TERMS

manifest destiny
annex
Mexican War
Compromise of 1850
prejudice
Kansas-Nebraska Act
nativism
Border States
Confederate States of America

TAKING NOTES

As you read, complete this table listing the major government policies affecting Native Americans in the West and the outcomes of those policies. Add as many rows as needed to finish the table.

Major Events of the 1840s and 1850s	Results or Effects
Mexican War	U.S. gains Texas, New Mexico, and California

MAIN IDEA

Westward expansion ignited conflicts over slavery in the territories. After Lincoln's election as President, Southern states left the Union. A crisis at Fort Sumter, South Carolina, triggered the first shots of war.

Setting the Scene On March 4, 1861, Abraham Lincoln took the presidential oath of office. In his Inaugural Address, Lincoln spoke directly to Southerners. He stated, "In your hands, my dissatisfied fellow-countrymen, and not in mine, is the momentous issue of civil war." Lincoln concluded with this plea:

> "*We must not be enemies. Though passion may have strained, it must not break our bonds of affection. The mystic chords of memory, stretching from every battlefield and patriot grave to every living heart . . . will yet swell the chorus of the Union when again touched, as surely they will be, by the better angels of our nature.*"
>
> —Abraham Lincoln, First Inaugural Address, 1861

Expanding to the Pacific

Westward expansion helped make slavery a difficult issue to solve. Migration from the United States into western territories surged in the 1830s and 1840s. That started some Americans dreaming of an empire stretching from the Atlantic to the Pacific. The United States, they believed, had a divine mission to spread liberty across the continent. A New York journalist named John L. O'Sullivan captured this sense of mission when he wrote that it was the nation's **manifest destiny**, or undeniable fate, to possess the entire continent.

Annexation of Texas As you read in Section 1, Texas won independence from Mexico in 1836. Later, the Republic of Texas voted to be annexed by the United States. To **annex** means to "join" or "attach." Most Southerners and Democrats supported the annexation of Texas, since it would increase the number of slave states. Northerners and Whigs generally opposed annexation for the same reason.

A rare full-length photograph of Abraham Lincoln, 1860

135

Section 4

The Coming of the Civil War

SECTION OBJECTIVES

1. Read about how U.S. expansion to the Pacific affected slavery in the territories.
2. Find out what changes in political parties occurred in the 1850s.
3. See how North-South tensions worsened in the 1850s.
4. Discover the issues that dominated the Lincoln-Douglas debates.
5. Learn about events that finally divided the nation and led to war.

BELLRINGER

Warm-Up Activity Ask students how they might feel if their school administration decided to make changes, such as denying open campus privileges, in order to make the school "safer." Describe the kind of reception such "reformers" might get.

Activating Prior Knowledge Ask students to describe the ways in which the reform movements of the 1840s led to a deepening rift between the North and the South by the 1850s.

READING STRATEGY

As students read this section, ask them to make notes on the beliefs and traditions of groups of Americans mentioned. Then ask them to note what the groups have in common, and how they differ.

ACTIVITY

Connecting with History and Conflict

Point out to students that the synonymous phrase given in their textbooks for *manifest destiny* is "undeniable fate." Have them come up with several other phrases that also capture the meaning and spirit of manifest destiny (they can be more than two words long). Record salient ideas on the board. **(Verbal/Linguistic)**

RESOURCE DIRECTORY

Teaching Resources

Learning Styles Lesson Plans booklet, pp. 22–23
Guided Reading and Review booklet, pp. 41–45

Other Print Resources

Historical Outline Map Book *Growth of the United States to 1853,* p. 42

Technology

Section Reading Support Transparencies
Guided Reading Audiotapes (English/Spanish), Ch. 3
Student Edition on Audio CD, Ch. 3
Sounds of an Era Audio CD *Walt Whitman on America* (time: 45 seconds)
Prentice Hall Presentation Pro CD-ROM, Ch. 3
Companion Web site, www.phschool.com

LESSON PLAN

Focus As the United States grew increasingly diverse, some segments of society deeply resented middle-class reformers. Can students state some possible reasons for this? In the 1850s, differences between the North and the South increasingly divided the two regions. Ask what these key differences between the North and the South were.

Instruct Review the economies of the North and the South. Ask students to compare the two regions in terms of their economic and material differences. Discuss the way in which slavery divided the North and the South. Ask why so many Northerners found slavery morally offensive. Why did Southerners accuse Northerners of hypocrisy regarding slavery?

Assess/Reteach Considering the seriousness of the growing rift between the North and the South, can students think of any way it would have been possible to avoid secession?

The Mexican War, 1846–1848

Oregon Country
ROCKY MTS.
Unorganized Territory
UNITED STATES
Wis. Terr.
Iowa
Ill.
Mo.
Ark.
La.
Texas
MEXICO
PACIFIC OCEAN
Gulf of Mexico
San Francisco
San Diego
Santa Fe
Fort Leavenworth
Nueces R.
Rio Grande
Corpus Christi
Mazatlán
SANTA ANNA
Tampico
1. Palo Alto May 8, 1846
2. Bear Flag Revolt June 14, 1846
3. Monterey occupied July 7, 1846
4. Santa Fe occupied Aug. 18, 1846
5. Monterrey Sept. 20–25, 1846
6. San Pasqual Dec. 6, 1846
7. El Brazito Dec. 25, 1846
8. San Gabriel Jan. 8, 1847
9. Buena Vista Feb. 22–23, 1847
10. Sacramento Feb. 28, 1847
11. Veracruz Mar. 27, 1847
12. Cerro Gordo Apr. 18, 1847
13. Chapultepec Sept. 13, 1847
14. Mexico City entered Sept. 14, 1847
Disputed territory
American forces
Mexican forces
American victory
Mexican victory
Fort
0 150 300 mi.
0 150 300 km
90°W
100°W
20°N

MAP SKILLS Many Americans, including President Polk, viewed the Mexican War as an opportunity to expand America's borders across the continent. The painting below heroically depicts General Winfield Scott and his men at the siege of Veracruz (see map) in 1847. **Movement** *What information on this map can you use to predict who won the war?*

In 1843, Mexican leader Santa Anna warned that annexation would be "equivalent to a declaration of war against the Mexican Republic." Despite this warning, President John Tyler signed a treaty of annexation with Texas in April 1844. Two months later, the Whig-controlled Senate defeated the treaty.

Later that year, Democrat James K. Polk, a strong advocate of expansion, won the presidency. Before Polk even took office, Congress reversed itself and approved annexation. In December 1845, after Texas voters added their approval, Texas became the twenty-eighth state in the Union.

War With Mexico Even if the United States could persuade Mexico to accept the annexation, a dispute about the southern boundary of Texas remained an explosive issue. The United States claimed that the Rio Grande was the official American-Mexican border. Mexico claimed that the Nueces River, located quite a few miles farther north, was the border.

Polk, though, wanted much more from Mexico than just Texas. Polk had dreams of acquiring the entire territory stretching from Texas to the Pacific. He sent a representative to Mexico City in November 1845 with an offer to buy New Mexico and California. The Mexican government refused to meet with the representative.

Polk then ordered more than 3,000 American troops under General Zachary Taylor into the disputed area of southern Texas. Mexican troops engaged in a skirmish with Taylor's forces in late April 1846. Expressing outrage at the loss of "American blood on American soil," Polk pushed for a declaration of war. Despite some opposition, Congress gave it to him on May 13, 1846, and the **Mexican War** was declared.

American troops soon took the offensive. An expedition under Captain John C. Frémont moved into California, where a group of American settlers

CAPTION ANSWERS

Map Skills The map shows the Mexicans becoming trapped in isolated pockets where opportunities for escape were limited. The map also indicates that the American forces enjoyed a much greater freedom of movement than did the Mexican troops.

RESOURCE DIRECTORY

Other Print Resources

American History Block Scheduling Support *Along the Oregon Trail,* found in the Expansion, Reconstruction, and Immigration folder.

Historical Outline Map Book *War with Mexico, 1846–1848,* p. 41

Technology

Color Transparencies *Historical Maps,* A13, A18; *Cause-and-Effect Charts,* D3

Sounds of an Era Audio CD *John Quinney, Leader of the Mohicans* (time: one minute, 45 seconds), *"Sovinir de Porto Rico,"* Louis Moreau Gottschalk

RESOURCE PRO® **Visual Learning Activity** *Living Dead in Califor-nee* uses a cartoon to illustrate the fate of some who sought gold in the California Gold Rush.

RESOURCE PRO® **Biography** *Kamiakin* profiles the influential Native American chief during the time the Native American groups of the Northwest were being forced off their land and onto reservations.

Exploring Primary Sources in U.S. History CD-ROM *A Frontier Lady, Sarah Royce*

had already proclaimed an independent Republic of California. The settlers' flag pictured a grizzly bear and a single star, so the uprising became known as the Bear Flag Revolt. Frémont assumed control of the rebel forces and then drove the Mexican army out of northern California.

Another American force crossed into New Mexico. Meeting little resistance, it marched west to California to join Frémont. By January 1847, the United States had taken control of the territories of New Mexico and California.

Meanwhile, General Taylor had taken the war into Mexico, forcing Santa Anna to abandon the northeastern part of the country. Even worse for the Mexicans, General Winfield Scott captured the port city of Veracruz and marched his army of 10,000 men toward Mexico City. After fierce fighting, Scott defeated Santa Anna's forces and captured the Mexican capital on September 14, bringing the war to an end.

The Treaty of Guadalupe Hidalgo, signed on February 2, 1848, ended the war. Under its harsh terms, Mexico gave up its claim to Texas and recognized the Rio Grande as the southern border of Texas. Mexico also gave up New Mexico and California, which together made up more than two fifths of its territory. The United States paid Mexico $15 million.

In 1853, Mexico sold 30,000 square miles of what is now southern New Mexico and Arizona to the United States for $10 million. This land was known as the Gadsden Purchase. The 1846 division of Oregon, the Treaty of Guadalupe Hidalgo, and the Gadsden Purchase established the present-day boundaries of the continental United States.

The California Gold Rush Even as the United States was acquiring California from Mexico, Americans were starting to pour into the territory. In January 1848, gold was discovered in California. Word of the gold strike quickly spread throughout the country, and the California Gold Rush began.

California's population jumped from 14,000 residents in 1848 to 200,000 by 1852, as Americans—mostly unmarried men—rushed west. Immigrants, too, headed for California. By 1852, about 10 percent of Californians were Chinese. Chinese immigrants mainly labored in mines and as servants.

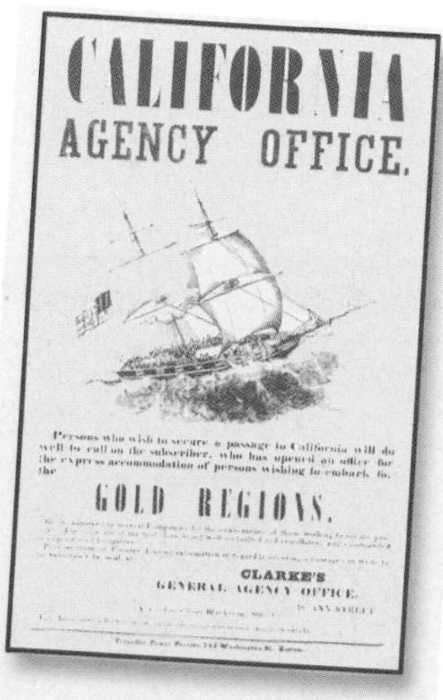

Posters such as this, circulated by land dealers and other entrepreneurs in California, lured eager prospectors with visions of a gleaming land of gold.

Indians and Western Migration Until the Mexican War, the United States had proclaimed all land west of the 95th meridian, or line of longitude, to be Indian Country. The migration of thousands of settlers into Indian Country, therefore, posed a problem. By the 1850s, the government increasingly saw the answer to that problem in the creation of reservations, or areas that the government sets aside for Native Americans who have lost their homelands. Many Native Americans refused to be herded onto reservations and fought to preserve their way of life.

Slavery in the Territories

A central issue facing Congress in the 1840s and 1850s was whether to allow slavery in the territories acquired from Mexico. In the short run, the Missouri Compromise of 1820 had maintained the balance in the Senate between slave and free states. The compromise did not, however, settle the issue of whether slavery would be legal in the western territories.

In 1846, the Wilmot Proviso came before Congress. The bill stated that slavery would not be permitted in any of the territory acquired from Mexico. Several times Congress rejected it, but Northerners continued to urge its approval.

ACTIVITY
Connecting with Culture

Probably the best-known writer to describe the California Gold Rush was Bret Harte. Have students research the work of this writer and read one of his short stories depicting life during the Gold Rush, for example, "The Luck of Roaring Camp." **(Verbal/Linguistic)**

BACKGROUND
Biography

Though relatively few of his stories were successful, Bret Harte (1836–1902) played an important role in creating a vivid, lasting portrait of the "Old West." Harte's stories, filled with intriguing characters and expressive dialogue, provided much of post–Civil War America with its first glimpse into Western life.

CUSTOMIZE FOR ...
Less Proficient Readers

Have students read the section's main headings and then write a question based on each, filling in the answers as they read.

ACTIVITY
Connecting with History and Conflict

Ask students to research the various opinions that made up the Compromise of 1850. Have them select an individual, such as Daniel Webster, who favored the Northern viewpoint, or one such as John C. Calhoun, who favored the Southern viewpoint. Then tell students to list three or four points made by this individual that helped support his or her point of view. **(Verbal/Linguistic)**

BACKGROUND
Biography

Henry Clay was terrified of a country split over the issue of slavery. In arguing for the Compromise of 1850, he said, "I implore, as the best blessing which heaven can bestow me on earth, that if the direful and sad event of the dissolution of the Union shall happen, I may not survive to behold the sad and heart-rending spectacle." Clay received this dubious blessing when he passed away, just two years later.

ACTIVITY
Connecting with Culture

In 1852 the publication of *Uncle Tom's Cabin* ignited the antislavery movement. The author, Harriet Beecher Stowe, created one character who evoked sympathy and a contrasting, despicable character. To help students understand both sides of the slavery issue, divide the class into small groups. Ask each group to develop a theme for a book and create two main characters who would evoke the reader's sympathies toward the South. **(Verbal/Linguistic)**

MAP SKILLS The painting at right depicts Senator Henry Clay leading a debate over the Compromise of 1850. Clay warned that a failure to compromise would lead to "furious" and "bloody" war. The compromise that resulted is shown in the map below. **Region** *What issues did the Compromise of 1850 attempt to address?*

The Compromise of 1850

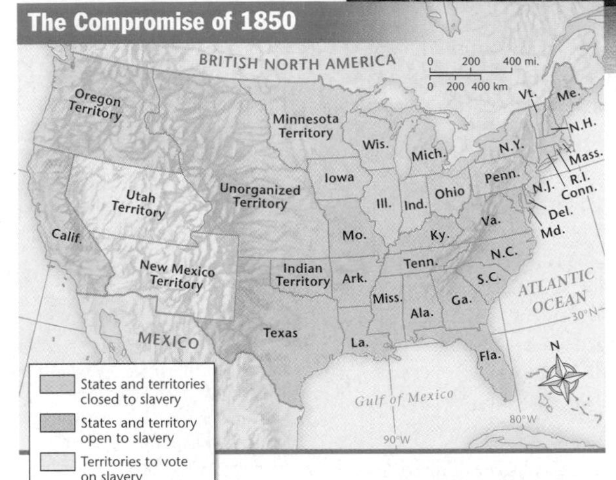

The Compromise of 1850 In 1849, the thousands of Americans who had rushed into California during the Gold Rush requested that California be admitted to the United States as a free state. This change would upset the fragile balance between free and slave states in the Senate.

Henry Clay of Kentucky proposed a plan that would become known as the **Compromise of 1850.** Seeking a middle ground on the slavery debate, Clay proposed five separate laws, two of which favored the North and two of which favored the South:

1. Congress would admit California into the Union as a free state.
2. The people of the New Mexico and Utah territories would decide for themselves whether to allow slavery.
3. Congress would abolish the sale of enslaved people in Washington, D.C.
4. Slavery itself would remain legal in Washington, D.C.
5. A Fugitive Slave Act would order all citizens of the United States to assist in the return of escaped slaves and would deny a jury trial to escaped slaves.

Debating the Compromise South Carolina's John C. Calhoun expressed the view of the South. The "great and primary" cause of the crisis, he said, was that the North now had "the exclusive power of controlling the Government" due to its larger population, which gave it more seats in the House and more votes in the electoral college.

Surprisingly, Daniel Webster of Massachusetts, who had opposed the extension of slavery, backed Clay's compromise. Webster argued that slavery would never be practical in New Mexico and that it was a constitutional duty to return fugitive slaves. Northern abolitionists and many of Webster's long-time supporters were furious.

Congress eventually passed the Compromise of 1850. Yet it brought only a brief period of calm.

Sounds of an Era

Listen to John C. Calhoun on the Compromise of 1850 and other sounds from the pre–Civil War era.

CAPTION ANSWERS

Map Skills The issues of whether newly acquired states and territories would be slave or free; how to deal with slavery in Washington, D.C.; and the fate of fugitive slaves.

RESOURCE DIRECTORY

Teaching Resources

Biography, Literature, and Comparing Primary Sources (Literature) *An Abolitionist Bestseller,* p. 51

Learning with Documents booklet (Visual Learning Activity) *The Annexation of Texas,* p. 49

Other Print Resources

Historical Outline Map Book *The Compromise of 1850,* p. 46; *Kansas-Nebraska Act, 1854,* p. 47

Technology

Color Transparencies *Historical Maps,* A19, A60

Sounds of an Era Audio CD *John C. Calhoun for the Compromise of 1850* (time: one minute, 45 seconds)

RESOURCE PRO® Literature Activity *"A Poem in Defense of Slavery,"* found on Resource Pro, illustrates some of the arguments that were used in defense of slavery.

Exploring Primary Sources in U.S. History CD-ROM *Uncle Tom's Cabin, Harriet Beecher Stowe*

Differences Between North and South By the 1850s, many white Northerners had come to believe that slavery violated the basic principles of the United States and of the Christian religion. They did not necessarily believe that blacks and whites were equal. Many, in fact, were deeply prejudiced against African Americans. (A **prejudice** is an unreasonable, usually unfavorable, opinion of another group that is not based on fact.) Nevertheless, these people saw slavery as an evil that could not be tolerated.

The most popular antislavery statement of the period was a novel published in 1852 by Harriet Beecher Stowe, called *Uncle Tom's Cabin.* Through Stowe's novel, many northern readers saw the evils of slavery for the first time.

Many Southerners saw *Uncle Tom's Cabin* as a book of insulting lies. Most planters took a personal interest in the well-being of their slaves, they claimed, while Northern industrialists took no responsibility for their workers.

Yet the differences between North and South went deeper than attitudes toward slavery. The North was becoming still more urban, still more industrial than the South. In 1860, the North had 110,000 factories, compared to 20,000 in the South, and produced more than $1.6 billion worth of goods, compared to the South's $155 million. The North's population was more than twice as large as the South's.

New technology had a heavier impact on the North than on the South. For example, in 1860, the North had 70 percent of the nation's railroad track. The telegraph, developed by Samuel F. B. Morse in 1844, also was more widely used in the North. The telegraph allowed people to send messages over wire by using a code of short and long pulses of electricity.

Economic Advantages of the North and South

	Northern States	Southern States
Agriculture		
Corn (bushels)	✓446 million	280 million
Wheat (bushels)	✓132 million	31 million
Oats (bushels)	✓150 million	20 million
Cotton (bales)	4 thousand	✓5 million
Tobacco (pounds)	✓229 million	199 million
Rice (pounds)	50 thousand	✓187 million
Finance		
Bank Deposits	✓$207 million	$47 million
Specie	✓$56 million	$27 million
Livestock		
Horses	✓4.2 million	1.7 million
Donkeys and Mules	300 thousand	✓800 thousand
Milk Cows	✓5.7 million	2.7 million
Beef Cattle	6.6 million	✓7 million
Sheep	✓16 million	5 million
Swine	✓16.3 million	15.5 million
Manufacturing		
Number of Factories	✓110.1 thousand	20.6 thousand
Number of Workers	✓1.17 million	111 thousand
Value of Products	✓$1.62 billion	$155 million
Population	✓21.5 million	9 million
Railroad Mileage	✓21.7 thousand miles	9 thousand miles

SOURCE: *The American Heritage Picture History of the Civil War*

INTERPRETING CHARTS The economic contrasts between the North and South were sharp, as this chart demonstrates. **Analyzing Visual Information** *Summarize the types of advantages held by the North and by the South.*

The Kansas-Nebraska Act In January 1854, Senator Stephen Douglas of Illinois introduced the **Kansas-Nebraska Act,** which called for the creation of two new territories, Kansas and Nebraska. It also stated that the people in these territories would be permitted to decide whether slavery would be allowed there, a principle known as popular sovereignty. Since both Kansas and Nebraska lay north of 36° 30′ N, which the Missouri Compromise had set as the boundary between slave and free states, Douglas basically was calling for repeal of the Missouri Compromise.

Douglas knew his proposal would please Southerners. After all, it raised the possibility that Kansas and Nebraska might become slave states. He also thought that Northerners would assume that slavery would never take hold on the Great Plains (where cotton could not grow) and thus would back his proposal. Congress passed the Kansas-Nebraska Act, angering northern Democrats.

Changes in Political Parties

The continuing debate over slavery contributed to a breakdown of the party system during the early 1850s. By the end of the 1850s, the Whig Party had

BACKGROUND

Biography

Harriet Beecher Stowe (1811–1896), author of *Uncle Tom's Cabin,* lived in the shadow of two famous men in her family—her father, the Calvinist minister Lyman Beecher, and her brother Henry Ward Beecher, an outspoken and well-known clergyman and orator. Her father wrote to a friend, "Hattie is a genius. I would give a hundred dollars if she was a boy."

From the Archives of

AmericanHeritage®

About the Presidents

Zachary Taylor (1849–1850) proved to be a strong-willed President. This surprised many people, as the twelfth President had never before held political office. He was a slave owner, but he wanted to stop the spread of slavery. He proposed to admit California and New Mexico to the Union, knowing that both would apply as free states. Furthermore, Taylor promised to put down any southern rebellion with force. He also appeared ready to veto a congressional compromise, supported by northern Whigs. Only after Taylor's death did the Compromise of 1850 become law. Source: Michael Harwood, "Zachary Taylor," *The American Heritage® Pictorial History of the United States,* vol. 1, 1968.

CUSTOMIZE FOR ...

Gifted and Talented

Ask students to write a paragraph summarizing how the failure of politicians to solve the important issues of the day led to the rise of new political parties in the 1850s.

CAPTION ANSWERS

Interpreting Charts The North held advantages in finance, industry, population, and railroads; the South, in certain areas of agriculture and livestock.

ACTIVITY
Student Portfolio

You may wish to have students place this activity in their portfolios: Have students write brief essays entitled "Growing Tension" in which they attempt to capture and convey the "spirit of times" of the 1850s, focusing on the growing tensions between North and South. Students should refer to particular historical events in their essays. **(Verbal/Linguistic)**

BACKGROUND
Art History

Photographer Matthew Brady (1823–1896), the son of Irish immigrants, is best known for his "on the spot" studies of the Civil War. But in 1844, when he opened a studio in New York City, he was well known for his portraits of celebrities. In 1850, Brady published a portfolio entitled *Gallery of Illustrious Americans,* containing studies of Henry Clay and Daniel Webster and a portrait of John C. Calhoun. During his career, Brady photographed several Presidents including Zachary Taylor and Abraham Lincoln, the latter proved to be Brady's favorite study.

ACTIVITY
Connecting with History and Conflict

Ask students to review Lincoln's famous "A house divided against itself cannot stand" statement shown on this page. Then have them rewrite the statement in their own words. **(Verbal/Linguistic)**

largely disappeared. Many northern Whigs abandoned the party because they were unhappy with its leaders' support of compromise on slavery.

Another issue that brought down the Whigs was the rise of the American Party, or the Know-Nothings. Its members promoted **nativism,** a movement to ensure that native-born Americans receive better treatment than immigrants. Nativism arose in response to a surge in immigration: Between 1846 and 1854, close to 3 million Europeans had arrived in the United States.

In 1849, fear about immigrants led to the formation of a secret nativist society called the Order of the Star-Spangled Banner. Members replied to questions about the organization with the answer, "I know nothing."

In 1854, nativists went public by forming the American Party, which became known as the Know-Nothings. It opposed Irish Catholic candidates and sought laws requiring immigrants to wait longer before they could become citizens.

Also in 1854, a group of antislavery Northerners launched a new Republican Party, the direct ancestor of today's Republican Party. Its members dedicated themselves to stopping the "Slave Power," or the South.

Focus on GOVERNMENT

Violence in the Capitol In 1856, violence over slavery even reached the United States Capitol. Senator Charles Sumner of Massachusetts, a powerful opponent of slavery, made a speech bitterly attacking Southerners for forcing slavery on Kansas. His speech included bold insults against Senator Andrew Butler of South Carolina. The speech angered Preston Brooks, a House member who was also Butler's nephew. Two days after Sumner's speech, Brooks approached Sumner at his Senate desk and began beating him with his cane.

Sumner survived the caning but never returned to full health. Brooks resigned his House seat and was immediately reelected. People across the South voiced their support for Brooks. One Southerner sent him a cane inscribed with the words "Hit him again." Northerners were outraged by Brooks's action and the support he received.

Worsening Tensions

Neither the Compromise of 1850 nor the Kansas-Nebraska Act brought North and South into a workable compromise over slavery. Events in the mid-1850s only worsened the situation.

"Bleeding Kansas" Under the Kansas-Nebraska Act, voters in Kansas would decide whether to become a free state or slave state. Antislavery groups in the Northeast sent more than a thousand New Englanders, known as free-soilers, to settle in Kansas to fight against slavery. Meanwhile, many proslavery settlers crossed into Kansas to vote illegally in territorial elections. By 1855, Kansas had an antislavery capital at Topeka and a proslavery capital at Lecompton. In 1856, tensions in Kansas escalated into violent raids and counter-raids that won the territory the grim nickname of "Bleeding Kansas."

The Election of 1856 In the 1856 presidential campaign, Democratic candidate James Buchanan supported the Compromise of 1850 and the Kansas-Nebraska Act. Republican John C. Frémont declared the federal government's right to restrict slavery in the territories and called for the admission of Kansas as a free state.

Buchanan won the election and pledged to his supporters in the South that he would stop "the agitation of the slavery issue" in the North. Buchanan hoped that the Supreme Court would use its power to resolve the issue for good.

The Dred Scott Decision In March 1857, the Supreme Court handed down one of the most controversial decisions in its history, *Scott* v. *Sandford.* The case had started when Dred Scott, an enslaved man living in Missouri, had filed suit against his owner. Scott argued that because he and his wife, Harriet, had once lived in states and territories where slavery was illegal, the couple was in fact free.

The Court under Chief Justice Roger Taney ruled 7 to 2 against Scott. The justices held that Scott, and therefore all slaves, were not citizens and therefore had no right to sue in court. The Court also ruled that living in a free territory

RESOURCE DIRECTORY

Teaching Resources

Biography, Literature, and Comparing Primary Sources booklet (Comparing Primary Sources) *On the Southern Secession,* p. 115

Other Print Resources

Nystrom *Atlas of Our Country* *A Divided Nation,* pp. 26–27

Technology

RESOURCE PRO® **Visual Learning Activity** *Anthony Burns and the Fugitive Slave Law,* found on Resource Pro, features contemporary sketches depicting the escape of Anthony Burns and his subsequent return to slavery as a result of the Fugitive Slave Act of 1850.

RESOURCE PRO® **Primary Source Activity** *Lincoln-Douglas Senate Campaign,* found on Resource Pro, presents a passage from Gustave Koerner's impressions of the Lincoln-Douglas debates to demonstrate the differences between the two candidates.

Exploring Primary Sources in U.S. History CD-ROM *Dred Scott* v. *Sandford*

for a time had not made Scott free. Most important, the Court found that Congress had no power to ban slavery anywhere, including the territories, because slaves were private property. Antislavery forces were horrified by the Dred Scott decision.

The Lecompton Constitution In the fall of 1857, a small proslavery group in Kansas elected members to a convention to write their own constitution, which was required to attain statehood. Most Kansans were opposed to slavery and refused even to vote on the proslavery Lecompton constitution. The attempt to gain statehood failed, and for the time being, Kansas remained a territory where slavery was legal according to the Dred Scott decision. In reality, however, the free-soiler majority prohibited it.

"Bleeding Kansas," 1856

MAP SKILLS Outsiders from slave and free states tried to influence the political future of Kansas. In one election, some 5,000 proslavery Missourians crossed the border to vote. About four times as many votes were cast as there were registered Kansas voters. In violent clashes, some 200 people died. **Location** *(a) About how far did proslavery supporters from Kansas City, Missouri, have to travel to participate in the actions against abolitionists in Lawrence, Kansas? (b) About how far apart were the two Kansas capitals, and what effect might that have had on political tensions?*

The Lincoln-Douglas Debates

In 1858, Senator Stephen Douglas ran for reelection against a relatively unknown Republican, Abraham Lincoln. Born in Kentucky in 1809, Lincoln had studied law and worked at various jobs, including postmaster and rail splitter. In 1837, he settled in Springfield, Illinois, where he practiced law. He served one term in Congress in the 1840s.

Lincoln and Douglas conducted seven highly publicized debates on the issue of slavery in the territories. The debates highlighted two important principles in American government, majority rule and minority rights. Douglas supported popular sovereignty on issues including slavery. Lincoln did not believe that a majority should have the power to deny a minority of their rights to life, liberty, and the pursuit of happiness. Thus he opposed the extension of slavery to the territories. However, Lincoln did not propose forbidding slavery in the South because he thought the federal government did not have the power to do so. He hoped that if slavery were confined to the states in which it already existed, it would eventually die out.

In a now-famous speech, Lincoln foresaw the confrontation that the country would soon face over slavery. He stated:

> “*A house divided against itself cannot stand. I believe this government cannot endure, permanently half slave and half free. I do not expect the Union to be dissolved—I do not expect the house to fall—but I do expect it will cease to be divided. It will become all one thing, or all the other.*”
>
> —Abraham Lincoln, speech in Springfield, Illinois, June 1858

READING CHECK
Describe the outcome(s) of the Lincoln-Douglas debates.

Douglas won the election. Nevertheless, Lincoln earned a reputation for eloquence and moral commitment in the campaign that would serve him well just two years later.

A Nation Divided

Lincoln's "house divided" continued to be torn apart by violence. Furthermore, Lincoln himself would become the political issue that finally brought the house down.

From the Archives of
AmericanHeritage®

About the Presidents

Millard Fillmore (1850–1853) took advantage of the brief period of calm following the Compromise of 1850. He secured grants for railroad construction in the West and, by promoting a good neighbor policy, he sought to open new markets abroad. To the south, his efforts led to railroad links with Mexico and negotiations to cut a canal through Nicaragua. In the Pacific, his letters urging trade helped to break down barriers. But Fillmore's accomplishments abroad came at the expense of long-term domestic tranquility. The issue of slavery continued to simmer and get worse.

Franklin Pierce (1853–1857) threw his support behind the Kansas-Nebraska Act. He helped to bring enough Democratic dissenters in line to win its passage. At the time, he believed he had won a great victory, but the Kansas-Nebraska Act proved to be the great tragedy of the administration. First, it cost him control of the Democratic Party. Then, it cost the Democrats the control of the House. Source: David Jacobs, "Millard Fillmore"; Martin Luray, "Franklin Pierce," *The American Heritage® Pictorial History of the United States,* vol. 1, 1968.

READING CHECK
Douglas won the election, and Lincoln became known as an eloquent speaker who was in support of placing limits on slavery.

TEST PREPARATION

Have students read the excerpt about the American Party on the previous page and then complete the statement below.

From the passage, you can infer that the only people the Know-Nothings welcomed, besides Protestants born in the United States were—

A Catholic immigrants.
(B) naturalized Protestant immigrants.
C naturalized Catholic immigrants.
D immigrants who were neither Protestant nor Catholic.

CAPTION ANSWERS

Map Skills (a) Approximately 40 miles; (b) Slightly less than 20 miles. Their close proximity may have heightened tensions in the struggle for power in Kansas.

John Brown's Raid On October 16, 1859, the former Kansas raider John Brown and a small group of men attacked the federal arsenal at Harpers Ferry, Virginia. (An arsenal is a place where weapons are made or stored.) Brown and his followers hoped to seize the weapons and give them to enslaved people to start a slave uprising.

United States troops under the command of Colonel Robert E. Lee cornered and defeated Brown's men. Convicted of treason, Brown was sentenced to be hanged. Just before his execution, he wrote a note that would prove to be all too accurate:

> "*I John Brown am now quite certain that the crimes of this guilty land will never be purged away; but with Blood.*"
>
> —John Brown

Northerners hailed Brown as a martyr to the cause of justice and celebrated him in song. Southerners denounced him as a tool of Republican abolitionists. In short, Brown's raid only deepened the divisions between North and South.

The Election of 1860 As 1860 began, it was clear that most Northerners would not accept leadership by a Southerner. Southerners would not accept a leader from the ranks of the antislavery Republicans in the North. A presidential election was looming. Could the Union survive it?

INTERPRETING CARTOONS This cartoon shows Abraham Lincoln defeating his opponents in the 1860 election. In this baseball metaphor, Lincoln uses an iron rail to score a "home run," while his complaining opponents have only wooden baseball bats. **Drawing Inferences** *(a) What might the iron rail represent? (b) What overall point do you think the cartoonist is making?*

The Democratic Party met in Charleston, South Carolina, in April 1860 to nominate its candidate for President. Divided between Southern Democrats who wanted to protect slavery in the territories and Northern Democrats who stood by popular sovereignty, the party broke in two. Delegates from eight southern states left the convention and agreed to meet separately to nominate their own candidate.

Southern Democrats eventually chose John C. Breckinridge, who was committed to expanding slavery in the territories. Northern Democrats nominated Stephen Douglas of Illinois, who supported popular sovereignty.

In the meantime, moderate Southerners who had belonged to the Whig and American parties met in Baltimore to form their own new party. These Southerners, along with a few politicians from the **Border States** (Delaware, Maryland, Kentucky, and Missouri), formed the Constitutional Union Party. They chose John Bell of Tennessee, a moderate slaveholder, as their presidential nominee.

When the Republican Party convened in Chicago, it nominated Abraham Lincoln. Although he was little-known outside Illinois, Lincoln combined a firm stance against the spread of slavery with moderate views on slavery itself.

The November election made absolutely clear that there were no longer any national political parties. In the South, the race was between Bell and Breckinridge. (Lincoln's name did not even appear on many southern ballots.) In the North, voters chose between Lincoln and Douglas. Lincoln won every free state except New Jersey, which he split with Douglas. Breckinridge, meanwhile, won North Carolina, Arkansas, Delaware, Maryland, and the states of the Lower South—Texas, Louisiana, Mississippi, Alabama, Florida, Georgia, and South Carolina. Bell carried Tennessee, Kentucky, and Virginia. Douglas took Missouri.

ACTIVITY
Connecting with Government

This activity may take place over several class periods: Divide the class into groups of four to six students. To help students understand that the primary consideration for presidential candidates in 1860 was how to win in a divided nation, have them select a candidate from this election and develop a political campaign for him. **(Verbal/Linguistic; Logical/Mathematical)**

BACKGROUND
Biography

John Brown was as eloquent as he was passionate. In court, he said, "Had I so interfered [on] behalf of the rich, the powerful, the intelligent, the so-called great . . . every man in this court would have deemed it an act worthy of reward rather than punishment." On the way to his hanging, riding on his own coffin on a wagon, he remarked, "This *is* a beautiful country."

From the Archives of
American Heritage®

About the Presidents

James Buchanan (1857–1861) called for help from Congress at the end of his term. Southern states were pulling away from the Union. Southerners were also capturing forts and arsenals all over the South. Buchanan did not believe he had the power by law to declare war against a state. Instead, he hoped for a legal solution from Congress: an amendment to the Constitution guaranteeing slavery in states that wanted it. Source: Michael Harwood, "James Buchanan," *The American Heritage® Pictorial History of the United States,* vol. 1, 1968.

CAPTION ANSWERS

Interpreting Cartoons (a) Possible answers: superior strength; the industrial North. (b) Because opposition parties were split, they were at a competitive disadvantage to Lincoln's support from the Republican Party.

RESOURCE DIRECTORY

Teaching Resources

Learning with Documents booklet (Primary Source Activity) *An Interview with John Brown,* p. 15

Other Print Resources

Nystrom *Atlas of Our Country* *Settling the West,* pp. 28–29

Historical Outline Map Book *Election of 1860,* p. 48

Technology

Color Transparencies *Time Lines,* C4

Lincoln captured the presidency without winning a single electoral vote in the South. While gaining only 39 percent of the popular vote, Lincoln had won 180 electoral votes—the majority he needed to win. His was a decisive victory, but a sectional one.

The Lower South Secedes Southerners were outraged that a President could be elected without any southern electoral votes. The government of the nation, it seemed, had passed completely out of their hands. Wrote an Augusta, Georgia, newspaper editor:

> “*[The Republican Party] stands forth today, hideous, revolting, loathsome, a menace not only to the Union of these states, but to Society, to Liberty, and to Law.*”
>
> —Augusta, Georgia, newspaper editor

Southern supporters of slavery called for the South to secede, or withdraw, from the Union. They argued that since the states had voluntarily joined the United States, they also could choose to leave it.

South Carolina left the Union officially on December 20, 1860. Over the next few weeks, six other states of the Lower South did the same. In early February 1861, delegates from the seven states met in Montgomery, Alabama. There they created a new nation, the **Confederate States of America,** also called the Confederacy. Jefferson Davis of Mississippi was elected its president.

The outgoing President, Buchanan, believed that secession was illegal but said he would not try to prevent it by force. Senator John J. Crittenden of Kentucky proposed a last-minute compromise by which slavery would be recognized in territories south of 36° 30' N. President-elect Lincoln opposed the plan, however, and convinced the Senate to reject it.

Other Americans proposed that the seceding states be allowed to go in peace. Many opposed this option, especially those who believed strongly in the Union. How could the United States continue to function as a country if its members could come and go as they pleased?

The government's response was in the hands of Abraham Lincoln, who took office in March 1861. Lincoln believed secession was wrong. He also was strongly committed to stopping the

Fast Forward to Today

Fort Sumter

Fort Sumter, South Carolina, was a symbol of national unity that President Lincoln wished to protect. Instead, the fort became the flash point that ripped apart the Union.

Construction of the fort, on an artificial island at the entrance to the Charleston Harbor, had begun in 1829. One Charleston newspaper described it in 1860 as a "most perfect specimen of civil and military engineering." But the structure was still incomplete and partially unprotected when it came under fire in 1861. Because the fort was built to protect the city from attack by sea, its 60 guns faced outward—not toward the Confederate outposts onshore that shelled the fort, severely damaging it.

On April 14, 1865, four years to the day that Major General Robert Anderson had surrendered the fort, the aging commander returned to raise the American flag above the fort.

In 1948, Fort Sumter was designated as a national monument. Today, tour boats take visitors on a harbor cruise out to the island and back to Charleston, a city whose antebellum charm and history attracts visitors from around the world.

Why was Fort Sumter a flash point in tensions between the North and South?

ACTIVITY
Connecting with History and Conflict

Ask students to design a handbill recruiting soldiers for either the Confederate or the Union army. **(Visual/Spatial; Verbal/Linguistic)**

BACKGROUND
Interdisciplinary

The Confederate States of America crafted a constitution that, in many ways, paralleled the United States Constitution. One important difference: It gave more power to the states, and less to the central government. Another difference: It required that "the institution of Negro slavery, as it now exists in the Confederate states, shall be recognized and protected."

CUSTOMIZE FOR ...
Less Proficient Readers

Have students reread the Augusta, Georgia, newspaper editor's quote on this page. Then have students discuss what event the editor was writing about and why the editor felt this way.

CAPTION ANSWERS

Fast Forward to Today The fort was Federal property, but it lay in the heart of the Confederacy. If the South allowed the Federal troops there to be resupplied, it would signify the continued existence of Federal power in the South. However, attacking the fort was a direct revolt against the Federal government.

Section 4 Assessment

Reading Comprehension

1. The belief that it was the fate of the U.S. to possess the entire continent led to the annexation of Texas. A boundary dispute and President Polk's desire to acquire more territory led to the start of the Mexican War.
2. Neither addressed all the issues at hand, so at best they offered temporary solutions.
3. Nativism arose in response to a surge in immigration and helped bring about a secret nativist society called the Order of the Star-Spangled Banner. Out of this grew the American Party, which became known as the Know Nothings. They pushed for anti-immigrant legislation and worked to defeat Irish Catholic candidates.
4. Southern outrage that Lincoln had been elected without any southern electoral votes led to the secession of the South and the creation of a new nation: the Confederate States of America. Lincoln believed that secession was wrong and was committed to stopping the expansion of slavery. He did not want war, but the Confederate attack on Fort Sumter left Lincoln with no choice but to call for volunteers to put down the rebellion.

Critical Thinking and Writing

5. Texans would become "southerners" if Texas joined the Union. Southerners supported the admission of Texas into the Union because it would add one more slave state to the South's representation in the U.S. Congress.
6. Students should choose figures whose views are strongly in opposition to each other, and clearly compare and contrast their ideas.

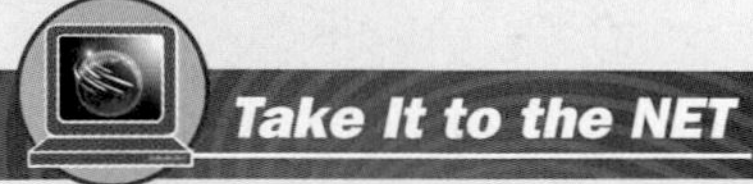

Take It to the NET

Possible answers include examining the Kansas-Nebraska Act or *Dred Scott* v. *Sanford*, and should give a detailed analysis of the language and ideas of the chosen topic.

Caption Answers

Viewing History The North: patriotism; preservation of the Union and of liberty; duty of "All Able Bodied Men"; urgency. The South: protection of home soil; opposition to abolition; protecting southerners' values, economy, and way of life; duty to the Confederacy.

VIEWING HISTORY Civil War recruitment posters from the North (left) and South (right) urge their citizens to join the military. **Recognizing Ideologies** *To what emotions and beliefs do these posters appeal?*

expansion of slavery. Yet he did not want to be the one to start a civil war.

The War Starts In January of 1861, prior to Lincoln's inauguration, a federal ship had been sent to supply Fort Sumter, a federal fort in the harbor of Charleston, South Carolina. Confederate forces had fired on the ship, forcing it to withdraw. Now federal soldiers under the command of Major Robert Anderson were running out of supplies. If Lincoln did not resupply the fort, it would have to be abandoned to the Confederates.

Lincoln struggled over a decision. To fight to keep the fort, or even to send new troops there, might make him responsible for starting the war. Yet to abandon the fort would mean acknowledging the authority of the Confederate government. He chose a middle course.

On April 6, Lincoln told the governor of South Carolina that he was sending food, but no soldiers or arms, to Fort Sumter. On April 10, before supplies could arrive, Confederate President Davis ordered General P.G.T. Beauregard to demand that Fort Sumter surrender. If Anderson refused, Beauregard was to take it by force. Anderson did refuse, and on April 12, 1861, Beauregard opened fire on the fort. After a 24-hour bombardment, Anderson surrendered Fort Sumter to Confederate troops on April 14.

By firing on federal property, the Confederate states had committed an act of open rebellion. As the defender of the Constitution, Lincoln had no choice but to respond. When he called for volunteers, Southerners saw his action as an act of war against them. The Upper South states of Virginia, North Carolina, Tennessee, and Arkansas now joined the Lower South in the Confederacy. For the time being, the four Border States remained uncommitted to either side.

The fighting at Fort Sumter in April 1861 proved that the division between the North and South could not be settled peacefully. Now a new question was raised: Could the Union be restored by force?

Section 4 Assessment

READING COMPREHENSION

1. How did **manifest destiny** lead the United States to **annex** Texas and fight the **Mexican War?**
2. Why did the **Compromise of 1850** and the **Kansas-Nebraska Act** fail to settle the slavery issue?
3. What trends led to the rise of **nativism,** and how did it influence party politics?
4. What events led to the creation of the **Confederate States of America** and to the outbreak of civil war?

CRITICAL THINKING AND WRITING

5. **Drawing Inferences** (a) What benefits did Texas gain by joining the Union? (b) What did it give up by becoming a state?
6. **Writing to Inform** Choose two major figures in this section who represent opposing views on slavery. Write a comparison of their views, goals, and tactics.

Take It to the NET

Activity: Analyzing Primary Sources Select an act of Congress or a Supreme Court ruling in this section. Read the document and analyze its main goals or message. Cite wording from the document in your analysis. Use the links provided in the *America: Pathways to the Present* area of the following Web site for help in completing this activity.
www.phschool.com

RESOURCE DIRECTORY

Teaching Resources

Units 1/2 booklet
- Section 4 Quiz, p. 27
- Chapter 3 Test, pp. 28, 31

Guide to the Essentials
- Section 4 Summary, p. 16
- Chapter 3 Test, p. 17

Biography, Literature, and Comparing Primary Sources booklet (Biography) *General P.G.T. Beauregard,* p. 15

Other Print Resources

Chapter Tests with ExamView® Test Bank CD-ROM, Ch. 3

Technology

ExamView® Test Bank CD-ROM, Ch. 3
Social Studies Skills Tutor CD-ROM

Analyzing Political Speeches

The goal of political speeches has always been to persuade listeners to take a particular view. Speeches can also serve as valuable evidence about historical figures and events. Political speakers use a variety of techniques. Sometimes they appeal to the listener's self-interest: "What I propose will make your life better." Sometimes they appeal to social conscience: "What I propose will benefit the community (or the nation, or the world)." Political speeches often appeal to patriotism.

Part of a speech Henry Clay made during the Senate debate over the Compromise of 1850 is shown below.

LEARN THE SKILL

Use the following steps to analyze political speeches:

1. **Identify the main topic of the speech and the speaker's position, or stand, on the issue.** Recall what you already know about the speaker, his or her political ideas, and the circumstances of the speech. Skim through the speech to get a general idea of its topic and purpose.
2. **Analyze the persuasive techniques the speaker uses.** Political speakers appeal to both the hearts and minds of their listeners. Evaluate the speaker's persuasiveness and how he or she achieves it. Be sure to consider the speaker's audience.
3. **Study the speech for clues about the historical period.** Look for hints about events and how people felt about those events, as well as the style of speeches at that time.

PRACTICE THE SKILL

Answer the following questions:

1. **(a)** Who is Henry Clay? Who is the audience for this speech? **(b)** What is the main topic of the speech? **(c)** What evidence in the speech tells you that Clay believes the compromise will work? **(d)** What is Clay's stand on the measure?
2. **(a)** What does Clay tell his listeners to "disregard" and "forget"? **(b)** Where in the speech does he appeal to reason? **(c)** Where in the speech does he appeal to patriotism? **(d)** How well do Clay's techniques suit his audience? **(e)** How would you evaluate the persuasiveness of this speech?
3. **(a)** Based on the speech, do you think that people in 1850 regarded the tensions between the North and the South as somewhat serious or very serious? Explain. **(b)** What does the excerpt tell you about the style of speeches during that period?

"I believe from the bottom of my soul that this measure is the reunion of the Union. And now let us disregard all resentments, all passions, all petty jealousies, all personal desires, all love of place, all hungering after the gilded crumbs which fall from the table of power. Let us forget popular fears, from whatever quarter they may spring. Let us . . . think alone of our God, our country, our conscience, and our glorious Union; that Union without which we shall be torn into hostile fragments, and sooner or later become the victims of military despotism, or foreign domination. . . .

What is an individual man? An atom, almost invisible without a magnifying glass—a mere speck upon the surface of the immense universe—not a second in time, compared to immeasurable, never-beginning, and never-ending eternity; a drop of water in the great deep, which evaporates and is borne off by the winds; a grain of sand, which is soon gathered to the dust from which it sprung. Shall a being so small, so petty, so fleeting, so evanescent [quick to disappear], oppose itself to the onward march of a great nation? . . . Let us look at our country and our cause; elevate ourselves to the dignity of pure and disinterested patriots, wise and enlightened statesmen, and save our country from all impending dangers. . . . What are we—what is any man worth who is not ready and willing to sacrifice himself for the benefit of his country when it is necessary?"

—Henry Clay, United States Senator from Kentucky

APPLY THE SKILL

See the Chapter Review and Assessment for another opportunity to apply this skill.

Analyzing Political Speeches

Focus Students analyze a speech as evidence of the politics, issues, and language style of a historical period.

Instruct Explain that political speeches are a useful tool in a government where politicians' success is based on the ability to win popular support for their views. Henry Clay, a popular politician, was one of the greatest orators of his time and was venerated for his speeches.

Have a volunteer read the excerpt aloud. Then ask students to identify elements that make it extraordinary. How does Clay use language to affect the listener?

Extend See the Skills for Life activity in the Resource Directory below.

ANSWERS

Practice the Skill

1. **(a)** Henry Clay is a United States senator from Kentucky. His audience is the U.S. Senate. **(b)** The Compromise of 1850. **(c)** Clay says that "this measure is the reunion of the Union." **(d)** That "our country and our cause" should come before individual concerns.
2. **(a)** "[A]ll resentments, all passions and petty jealousies, all personal desires, all love of place, all hungering after . . . power [and] popular fears." **(b)** He warns that the nation may become the victim of domination by a foreign power if it is disunified. **(c)** He invokes God, country, conscience, and the Union at the beginning, and at the very end he urges patriotism, asking the senators to be willing to sacrifice themselves for their country. **(d)** Very well, as the senators are likely to be swayed by appeals to patriotism and the importance of the Union. **(e)** Possible answer: Clay's appeal to both emotion and reason is very persuasive.
3. **(a)** Clay's speech has an urgent tone, and he reflected concerns shared by the people that sectional conflict was very serious. **(b)** That speakers used very flowery and poetic language and often exaggerated for effect.

RESOURCE DIRECTORY

Teaching Resources

Skills for Life booklet, pp. 9–12

Technology

Social Studies Skills Tutor CD-ROM

Interactive Practice in
- Geographic Literacy
- Critical Thinking and Reading
- Visual Analysis
- Communications

Chapter 3 Review and Assessment

creating a CHAPTER SUMMARY

Copy the chart (right) on a piece of paper and complete it by adding information about changes in early America. Some entries have been completed for you as examples.

Type of Change	Effects on the North	Effects on the South
Westward expansion		
Market Revolution		
Reform movements		
Conflicts over slavery		

For additional review and enrichment activities, see the interactive version of *America: Pathways to the Present*, available on the Web and on CD-ROM.

★ Reviewing Key Terms

For each of the terms below, write a sentence explaining how it relates to the growth of the United States from the late 1700s through the mid-1800s.

1. republican virtues
2. interchangeable parts
3. denomination
4. Market Revolution
5. free enterprise system
6. Monroe Doctrine
7. Trail of Tears
8. temperance movement
9. utopian communities
10. Seneca Falls Convention
11. suffrage
12. manifest destiny
13. Kansas-Nebraska Act
14. Confederate States of America

★ Reviewing Main Ideas

15. (a) How did the Industrial Revolution come to the United States? (b) How did it affect America's society and economy? (Section 1)
16. What attracted Americans to the Second Great Awakening? (Section 1)
17. What events led to Texas' independence and statehood? (Section 1)
18. How did economic growth in the North and in the South differ in terms of (a) major products and (b) the use of labor? (Section 2)
19. Give examples of nationalism in the early 1800s. (Section 2)
20. Explain President Jackson's response to the tariff crisis. (Section 2)
21. What were the main beliefs and goals of the transcendentalists? (Section 3)
22. How did the Underground Railroad operate? (Section 3)
23. Why was the Compromise of 1850 a failure? (Section 4)
24. Why did Lincoln's election prompt the secession of southern states? (Section 4)

★ Critical Thinking

25. **Determining Relevance** How did the invention of the cotton gin ultimately affect (a) North-South relations; (b) the slave trade; (c) Native Americans?
26. **Identifying Alternatives** With southern states seizing Indian lands illegally and white settlers pouring into these areas, how did President Jackson respond? How else might he have responded?
27. **Expressing Problems Clearly** Explain why the addition of Mexico's northern territories caused problems for the United States.
28. **Identifying Central Issues** Summarize the key issue in the dispute over Fort Sumter that led the United States into civil war.

Chapter 3

Reviewing Key Terms

Students should refer to the definitions of key terms in the chapter to write sentences that show an understanding of the changes taking place in American society between 1783 and 1861.

Reviewing Main Ideas

15. (a) Samuel Slater's re-creation of British textile machinery in the U.S. increased production and inspired American inventions. (b) Advancements in technology, communication, and transportation brought people closer together and expanded the economy.
16. The democratic nature of the movement and the movement's promise of meaning and community.
17. The desire for more political control and the right to own slaves led to Texas independence. Texans later voted to accept U.S. annexation.
18. (a) North: manufacturing products and the ability to build large pieces of machinery; South: farming of cotton and other cash crops. (b) North: used poorly paid and treated labor in factories and mills; South: largely dependent upon slave labor.
19. Supreme Court decisions supporting federal commerce control, improvement projects, Monroe Doctrine.
20. Jackson urged Congress to pass the Force Bill, which required South Carolina to pay the Tariff of 1832 and threatened force if the state did not comply.
21. That spiritual discovery and insight would lead people to deeper truths. Urged people to be self-reliant.
22. A network of escape routes provided protection and transportation for slaves fleeing north. Men and women known as conductors acted as guides.
23. Because it inflamed, rather than quelled, passions on both sides. Southerners were disappointed to see California admitted to the Union as a free state. Northerners were opposed to the Fugitive Slave Act.
24. Lincoln was an antislavery President. The South no longer felt it had a voice in government.

Creating a Chapter Summary

Type of Change	Effects on the North	Effects on the South
Westward expansion	Expanded number of free states and territories	Expanded number of slave-holding states
Market Revolution	Growth of cities Increased immigration	Increased emphasis on rural economy
Reform movements	Growth of influence of groups concerned with temperance, public education, prison reform, abolition	Not much involvement with these movements; opposition to growth of abolition movement
Conflicts over slavery	Brief calm after Compromise of 1850 Anger over Kansas-Nebraska Act Opposition to Dred Scott decision Support for John Brown's raid	Brief calm after Compromise of 1850 Satisfaction with Kansas-Nebraska Act Support for Dred Scott decision Opposition to John Brown's raid

★ Skills Assessment

Analyzing Political Cartoons ▶

29. This cartoon is titled "King Andrew the First." (a) Who is "King Andrew"? (b) What is he holding in his left hand? (c) What is he standing on?

30. The other document on the floor is labeled "Internal Improvements" and "U.S. Bank." The book in the foreground is labeled "Judiciary of the United States." To what do these items refer?

Analyzing Data

Refer to the chart entitled "Free and Enslaved Black Population, 1820–1860" in Section 3 to answer these questions:

31. From 1820 to 1860, the enslaved black population increased by roughly how many people?
   A 4 million
   B 1 million
   C 1.5 million
   D 2.5 million

32. In 1860, how many times larger was the enslaved population than the free population?
   F two times
   G five times
   H eight times
   J eleven times

Applying the Chapter Skill: *Analyzing Political Speeches*

33. (a) Summarize the excerpt below. (b) What techniques does Webster use to appeal to his audience?

> "*When my eyes shall be turned to behold, for the last time, the sun in heaven, may I not see him shining on the broken and dishonored fragments of a once glorious Union. . . . Nor those . . . words of delusion and folly, Liberty first and Union afterwards . . . [but instead] Liberty and Union, now and forever, one and inseparable.*"
>
> —Senator Daniel Webster of Massachusetts

ACTIVITIES

Writing to LEARN

Writing an Opinion
Write a newspaper column that identifies a problem—economic, social, or political—that divided Americans in the decades preceding the Civil War. Explain both sides of the issue, and then state your own opinion. Support your opinion with clear reasoning and historical facts.

Primary Source CD-ROM

Working With Primary Sources Find additional information on the early United States on the *Exploring Primary Sources in U.S. History CD-ROM* and use the selection(s) provided to complete the Chapter 3 primary source activity located in the *America: Pathways to the Present* area of the following Web site.
www.phschool.com

Take It to the NET

Chapter Self-Test As a review activity, take the Chapter 3 Self-Test in the *America: Pathways to the Present* area at the Web site listed below. The questions are designed to test your understanding of the chapter content.
www.phschool.com

CRITICAL THINKING

25. (a) It was largely responsible for the growth of slavery as profits from cotton grew. This poisoned North-South relations. (b) The demand for slave labor increased. (c) As more prime agricultural land in the South was taken over for cotton farming, Native Americans were forced out.

26. He supported the Indian Removal Act and ignored the Supreme Court's ruling in favor of the Cherokee. Jackson might instead have sent troops to protect Native Americans, or he might have ensured better compensation for them and safer conditions for their removal.

27. It aggravated the slavery issue, as a decision had to be made whether new territories would be slave or free states. Though new bills addressed the problem, the issue remained unresolved.

28. Federal soldiers stationed at the fort were running out of supplies. Lincoln could either abandon the fort to the Confederates or risk a conflict even by simply sending new supplies. He decided to send food, but no soldiers or arms. The Confederate president, however, demanded surrender of the fort's garrison. Confederate forces opened fire on the fort. By firing on federal property, Confederate states had committed an act of rebellion, leaving Lincoln no choice but to respond with military action.

29. (a) Andrew Jackson. (b) A paper saying "veto." (c) The U.S. Constitution.

SKILLS ASSESSMENT

30. Jackson vetoed the rechartering of the National Bank and money for internal improvements. The book on the floor is a reminder that Jackson ignored the Court in its ruling that opposed Cherokee relocation.

31. D

32. H

33. (a) Webster is pleading for the North and the South to become reconciled. He appeals to Southerners to put the national interest ahead of states' rights. (b) He appeals to the patriotism and the religious beliefs of his audience. He also reminds his audience that he is getting older and that a younger generation is going to have the responsibility of maintaining the Union.

ANSWERS TO ACTIVITIES

Writing to LEARN

Answers will vary, but may include an examination of how the reform movement deepened hostilities between the North and the South.

Primary Source CD-ROM

Direct students to the additional primary sources that can be found on the *Exploring Primary Sources in U.S. History CD-ROM.*

Take It to the NET

Additional support materials and activities for Chapter 3 of *America: Pathways to the Present* can be found in the Social Studies area at the Prentice Hall School Web site. **www.phschool.com**

The Expansion of the United States

Focus From the late eighteenth century until the end of the nineteenth century, the United States steadily pushed its borders outward. As the East Coast became populated, people moved westward. By the mid-nineteenth century, the United States had acquired territory in Mexico, and by the end of the century, the United States had purchased Alaska and annexed Hawaii.

Instruct Tell students to read the text, and study the map and photos telling about "The Expansion of the United States." Ask them to think about the various reasons why Americans continued to explore and settle unknown regions. Suggest that students discuss the American desire to seek new frontiers.

Extend Have students choose a geographic region of the country. Then tell them to find out when that area was settled and by whom. Encourage students to write up their findings in a short report.

American Pathways

GEOGRAPHY

The Expansion of the United States

From its start as 13 former British colonies along the Atlantic Coast, the United States expanded steadily westward. Explorers, trappers, and settlers pushed across the Appalachian Mountains, the Great Plains, and the Rocky Mountains all the way to the Pacific Coast and beyond. Through more than a century of treaties, purchases, and warfare, the nation grew to its present size.

1 **Establishing the Original States**

1607–1776 In the 1600s and 1700s, a mix of English, Dutch, Swedes, Germans, enslaved Africans, and others settled in colonies along the Atlantic Coast. These colonies later united to seek their indepen-dence from Great Britain and establish a new nation.

E pluribus unum—"from many, one"—was chosen as the nation's motto in 1776 (right).

Crossing the Appalachians

1775–1830 As the population along the Atlantic Coast grew, Americans moved west to settle in the region between the Appalachian Mountains and the Mississippi River.

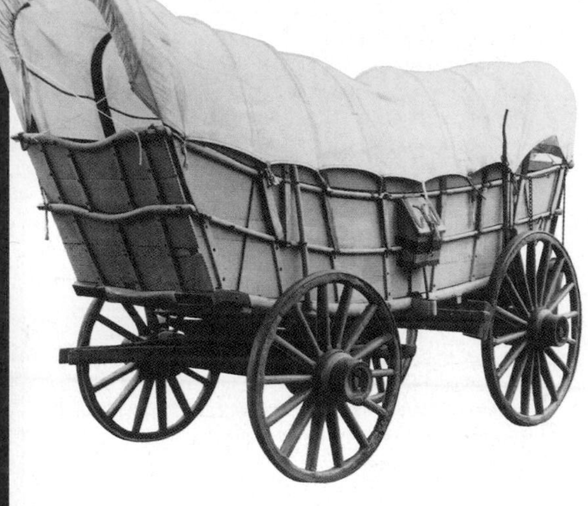

Covered wagons (left) carried settlers westward.

Moving Beyond the Mississippi

1803–1846 The Louisiana Purchase nearly doubled the size of the United States and gave Americans full control of the Mississippi River. Several groups explored the region in the early 1800s, but new settlements there remained sparse for many years. Most migrants who crossed the Mississippi in the mid-1800s had one goal in mind—reaching Oregon.

An advertisement for land in Iowa and Nebraska (above)

RESOURCE DIRECTORY

Teaching Resources

Units 1/2 booklet

- American Pathways Activity, pp. 34–35

American Pathways Thematic Posters

Technology

Companion Web site, www.phschool.com

Territorial Expansion From 1763

CANADA
MEXICO
ATLANTIC OCEAN
Gulf of Mexico
RUSSIA
WA OR CA ID NV MT WY UT AZ CO NM ND SD NE KS OK TX MN IA MO AR LA WI IL MI IN OH KY TN MS AL GA FL SC NC VA WV PA NY VT NH ME MA CT RI NJ DE MD DC AK HI
Proclamation of 1763
Treaty of Paris, 1783
Louisiana Purchase, 1803
West Florida annexation, 1810, 1813
East Florida ceded by Spain, 1819
Ceded by Britain, 1818, 1842
Texas annexation, 1845
Oregon Country, 1846
Ceded by Mexico, 1848
Gadsden Purchase, 1853
Purchased from Russia, 1867
Annexed, 1898
Present-day state borders

4 Capturing Mexican Territory

1821–1853 During this period, Americans obtained Mexico's northern territories mainly through warfare. By 1853, they had established the boundaries of the continental United States as we now know them, fulfilling what many called the nation's "manifest destiny."

5 Acquiring Alaska and Hawaii

1867–1898 The United States expanded beyond its continental borders in the period following the Civil War, first with the purchase of Alaska in 1867 and later with the annexation of Hawaii in 1898.

A Hawaiian landscape (right)

6 Remaining a Mobile Society

1890–Present Streams of settlers moving west reflected the mobility of American society. Even after the nation's frontier ceased to exist, Americans continued to migrate, usually in search of a better life.

Continuity and Change

1. What circumstances drove Americans to leave their homes and settle in new places?
2. **Map Skills** What lands were included in the Gadsden Purchase in 1853?

Take It to the NET: Creating a Study Guide
Print and complete the study guide for this topic found in the *America: Pathways to the Present* area of the following Web site. **www.phschool.com**

American Pathways

Take It to the NET

Students can print the American Pathways thematic study guide for this topic at the Prentice Hall School Web site, or you can provide students with copies of the study guide, which is found in the Units 1/2 booklet, the American Pathways Activity, pages 34–35. Students should use their texts to fill in a one-sentence description for each event on the study guide. When completed for each of the American Pathways topics, the thematic study guides will aid students in preparing for an end-of-course exam.

Answers

1. Answers will vary. Students may suggest that Americans left their homes in order to take advantage of new lands that became available as the nation expanded in size, or to find jobs and a better quality of life.
2. The Gadsden Purchase included lands in southern New Mexico and southern Arizona.

TEST PREPARATION

Use this sample exam to help your students prepare for standardized tests.

Tips for Test Taking

You might want to remind your students of the following:

1. Read the directions carefully.
2. Read each question carefully.
3. For multiple choice questions, try to answer the question before you look at the choices. Read all the choices. Then, eliminate those that are absolutely incorrect.
4. For short answer questions, be sure to answer the question completely if there is more than one part.
5. Answer the easy questions first. Then, go back to the ones that will take more time.
6. Pace yourself. Be sure to set aside enough time for the writing questions.

TEST PREPARATION

Write your answers on a separate sheet of paper.

1. Before the Europeans arrived in North America, which one of the following was never traded by the Native Americans?

   A Land
   B Fish
   C Minerals
   D Tools

2. Which of the following products was the first successful cash crop in the Jamestown Colony?

   A Fur
   B Tobacco
   C Wheat
   D Fish

Use the chart and your knowledge of social studies to answer the following question.

Early American Colonies
• Connecticut • Maryland • Massachusetts Bay • Plymouth • Rhode Island

3. What common experience did all of these colonies share?

   A All had farming on plantations.
   B All had economies based on tobacco.
   C All were established for religious reasons.
   D All were created to block Spanish expansion.

4. In the mid-1700s, Baptist and Methodist churches in North America increased their membership as a result of the

   A growth of American nationalism.
   B mercantilist policies of the British.
   C French and Indian War.
   D Great Awakening.

5. How was the Stamp Act different from all previous British laws for the colonies?

   A Its purpose was to raise money.
   B It applied only to cities along the coast.
   C It was supported by the French government.
   D It required each colony to create a post office.

6. Why was the Patriot victory at the Battle of Saratoga in the American Revolution a turning point in the war?

   A It caused the Native Americans in the Ohio Valley to join the Patriots.
   B It permitted George Washington to move his troops into Boston.
   C It guaranteed the Patriots control of the Atlantic Ocean.
   D It convinced the French government to aid the Patriots.

> **"It is . . . the duty of the judicial department to say what the law is."**
>
> —*Marbury* v. *Madison*, 1803

7. The *Marbury* decision by the United States Supreme Court is the basis for

   A implied powers.
   B a federal system of government.
   C separation of powers.
   D judicial review.

150

Diagnose and Prescribe
- Profile student skills with Diagnostic Tests A&B.
- Address student needs with program materials correlated to test questions.

Review and Reteach
- Provide cumulative content review with the Review Book.

Practice and Assess
- Build test-taking skills with Test-taking Strategies With Transparencies.

Use the information in the graph to answer the following question.

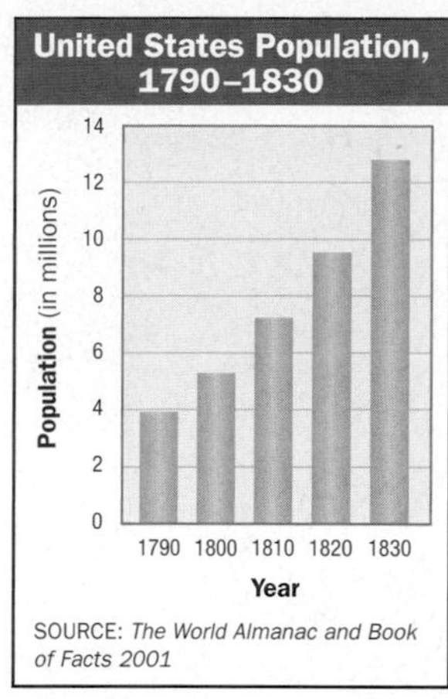

8. The population trend shown in the bar graph was caused by

A immigration from Europe.

B a high birth rate.

C migration from farms to cities.

D conquering lands with many people.

9. Which one of the following statements about the Southern Colonies is correct?

A Their economy was based on staple crops.

B They were the center of American commerce and trade.

C Most people lived on small, family-owned farms.

D Most of the people came from Great Britain.

> **". . . that the American continents, by the free and independent condition which they have assumed and maintain, are henceforth not to be considered as subject for future colonization by any European power. . . ."**
>
> *—President James Monroe, Seventh annual message to Congress, December 2, 1823*

10. This quotation is the basis for the

A *Gibbons* v. *Ogden* (1824) decision.

B Adams-Onís Treaty.

C Monroe Doctrine.

D Missouri Compromise.

11. On the Underground Railroad, freedom came at the final destination

A by the Great Lakes.

B across the Ohio River.

C in Massachusetts or Rhode Island.

D in Canada.

Writing Practice

12. Describe the motives Columbus had for making his voyages.

13. Describe the effect of Eli Whitney's cotton gin on the United States.

14. Explain the economic differences between the Northern and Southern states preceding the Civil War.

1. A
2. B
3. C
4. D
5. A
6. D
7. D
8. B
9. A
10. C
11. D
12. Columbus sought honor and fame; he wanted to convert people of non-Christian lands to Christianity; he hoped to please his financial backers who sought wealth from new trade routes; and he endeavored to represent his country in its economic competition with Portugal.
13. Profit per pound of cotton skyrocketed, and with it the amount of cotton planted for harvest. This increase in production led to the economic growth of the South and a vast increase in the amount of Southern land under cultivation. These changes caused a corresponding increase in and reliance upon slavery. This issue, in turn, led to the U.S. Civil War.
14. By 1860 nine of the country's ten largest cities were located in the North. Railroads and improved communications nourished the booming industries of the North.

Unit 2

Introducing the Unit

Building a Powerful Nation (1850–1915) This unit covers a dramatic period in American history. It begins with the searing national trauma of the Civil War, continues with the painful Reconstruction period, and moves into the dynamic era of industrial expansion. A chapter on the settlement of the American West depicts events that took place as America settled the new frontier west of the Mississippi River. Further settlement is demonstrated by a look at the period of massive immigration that took place at the end of the nineteenth century. Finally, the unit depicts the state of the nation at the beginning of the twentieth century, a time of rapid growth, invention, and activity.

Using Historical Evidence

Direct students' attention to the photograph on these pages. Discuss with them the likely impressions of the group who have come out to view the progress of the Transcontinental Railroad. Can students imagine what it must have been like to contemplate, for the first time, the opportunity to travel the vast distance from one end of the country to the other in the comfort, convenience, and relative safety of a rail car?

Ask students to consider what types of new opportunities in business, government, and cultural life might be made possible thanks to reliable rail travel. How did this capability change the United States?

Unit 2 Building a Powerful Nation (1850–1915)

"Up to our own day American history has been in a large degree the history of the colonization of the Great West. The existence of an area of free land, its continuous recession, and the advance of American settlement westward, explain American development."

Frederick Jackson Turner, 1893

An excursion party, awed by the new technologies of the era, stops to be photographed at Devil's Gate Bridge in Utah. ▶

152

RESOURCE DIRECTORY

Teaching Resources

Units 1/2 booklet
- American Pathways Activity, pp. 104–105
- History's Lasting Impact, pp. 106–107

Geography and History booklet, pp. 8–11

Other Print Resources

Prentice Hall Assessment System
- Document-Based Assessment

eTeach

Be sure to check out this month's online discussion with a Master Teacher. Go to **www.phschool.com**.

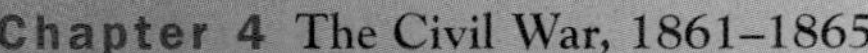

153

TECHNOLOGY CENTER

Take It to the NET

Prentice Hall School Web site offers student-appropriate Internet activities and links that extend core content. Visit us at the Social Studies area. **www.phschool.com**

AmericanHeritage®

My Brush with History™ Video Program This new video series lets your students learn history from the people who lived it.

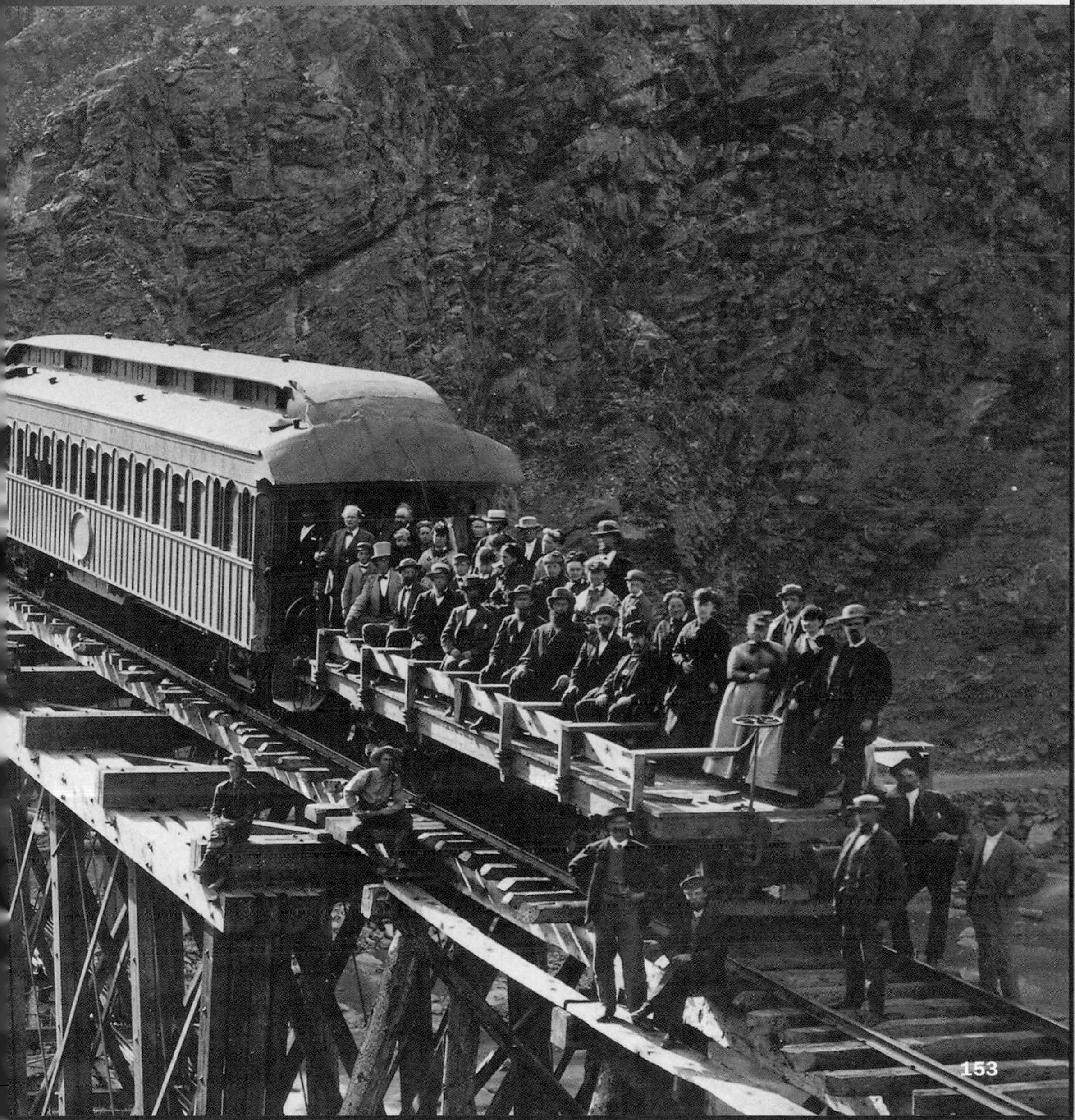

RESOURCE PRO®

Teaching Resources on CD-ROM offer lesson-planning flexibility, test-generation capability, and resource manageability.

- **Presentation Pro CD-ROM** Provides you with multimedia lecture notes for each chapter.
- **Social Studies Skills Tutor CD-ROM** Provides interactive practice in Geographic Literacy, Critical Thinking and Reading, Visual Analysis, and Communications.
- **Interactive Constitution CD-ROM** Exploring active citizenship and civic responsibilities, this CD-ROM shows students how the Constitution affects their lives today.
- **Exploring Primary Sources in U.S. History CD-ROM** This interactive exploration of primary sources allows students to analyze and to evaluate writing and images from American history.
- **Guided Reading Audiotapes**
- **Student Edition on Audio CD**
- **Sounds of an Era Audio CD** Bring the sounds of American history to life in the classroom with music, speeches, poetry, interviews, and news reports.

Don't miss the exclusive interactive version of this textbook on the Web and on CD-ROM.

RESOURCE DIRECTORY

Technology

Color Transparencies *Historical Maps,* A20, A21, A22, A23, A24, A25, A26, A58, A60; *Political Cartoons,* B5, B6, B7, B8; *Cause-and-Effect Charts,* D5, D6; *Fine Art,* E8, E9, E10, E11, E12, E13, E14, E15; *American Photo,* F4, F5; *American Diversity,* G9, G10; *The Way It Works,* H8, H9, H10, H11, H12, H13, H14

Section Reading Support Transparencies

Prentice Hall United States History Video Collection™ Volume 9, *The Civil War;* Volume 10, *Reconstruction and Segregation (1865–1910);* Volume 11, *Industrialization and Urbanization;* Volume 12, *Immigration and Cultural Change*

Companion Web site, www.phschool.com

Chapter 4 Planning Guide

Resource Manager

	Core Instruction	Reading/Skills
Chapter-Level Resources **TEKS** 8(B), 24(A), 24(B), 24(D), 25(C), 25(D)	Teaching Resources • Pacing Charts booklet • Block Scheduling booklet **Resource Pro® CD-ROM,** Ch. 4 **Prentice Hall Presentation Pro CD-ROM,** Ch. 4 **www.phschool.com** • eTeach	**Guided Reading Audiotapes (English/Spanish)** **Student Edition on Audio CD,** Ch. 4 **Social Studies Skills Tutor CD-ROM** **Color Transparencies,** A20, A21, A22, A23, A24, D5, E8, E9, F4, H8
1 From Bull Run to Antietam 1. Understand the significance of the First Battle of Bull Run. 2. Find out how the North and the South prepared for war. 3. Learn why the battles in the West were important. 4. Discover the outcome of each of the battles in the East in 1862. **TEKS** 24(H), 25(A)	Teaching Resources **Units 1/2 booklet** • Section 1 Quiz, p. 39	**Guided Reading and Review booklet,** p. 46 **Guide to the Essentials,** p. 18 **Section Reading Support Transparencies**
2 Life Behind the Lines 1. Learn how wartime politics affected the Confederate and Union governments. 2. Discover how the Emancipation Proclamation affected both the North and the South. 3. Find out the causes and effects of African Americans' joining the Union army. 4. List the kinds of hardships that befell the North and the South during the war. **TEKS** 24(C), 24(G)	Teaching Resources **Units 1/2 booklet** • Section 2 Quiz, p. 40	**Guided Reading and Review booklet,** p. 47 **Guide to the Essentials,** p. 19 **Learning with Documents booklet,** p. 81 **Skills for Life booklet,** p. 13 **Section Reading Support Transparencies**
3 The Tide of War Turns 1. Identify the importance of Lee's victories at Fredericksburg and Chancellorsville. 2. Describe how the battles of Gettysburg and Vicksburg turned the tide of the war. 3. Find out why 1863 was a pivotal year in the Civil War. 4. Interpret the message of the Gettysburg Address. **TEKS** 24(H), 25(B)	Teaching Resources **Units 1/2 booklet** • Section 3 Quiz, p. 41 **Learning Styles Lesson Plans booklet,** p. 24	**Guided Reading and Review booklet,** p. 48 **Guide to the Essentials,** p. 20 **Learning with Documents booklet,** p. 16 **Section Reading Support Transparencies**
4 Devastation and New Freedom 1. Determine General Grant's strategy for defeating the South and how he and General Sherman implemented it. 2. Outline the issues and results of the election of 1864. 3. Explain how the South was finally defeated on the battlefield. 4. State how and why John Wilkes Booth assassinated President Lincoln. **TEKS** 24(G), 24(H), 25(B)	Teaching Resources **Units 1/2 booklet** • Section 4 Quiz, p. 42 **Learning Styles Lesson Plans booklet,** p. 25	**Guided Reading and Review booklet,** p. 49 **Guide to the Essentials,** p. 21 **Learning with Documents booklet,** p. 50 **Section Reading Support Transparencies**

Enrichment/Pre-AP

Prentice Hall United States History Video Collection™
www.phschool.com
- Section Activities, Virtual Field Trip, Chapter Activities, Current Events Online

Biography, Literature, and Comparing Primary Sources booklet, pp. 16, 117
Historical Outline Map Book, pp. 49, 50, 51
Sounds of an Era Audio CD
Exploring Primary Sources in U.S. History CD-ROM

American History Block Scheduling Support
Historical Outline Map Book, pp. 43, 44
Exploring Primary Sources in U.S. History CD-ROM

Nystrom *Atlas of Our Country,* pp. 26–27
Historical Outline Map Book, p. 50
Sounds of an Era Audio CD
Exploring Primary Sources in U.S. History CD-ROM

Historical Outline Map Book, p. 52
Exploring Primary Sources in U.S. History CD-ROM
American Pathways Thematic Posters

Assessment

Prentice Hall Assessment System

Core Assessment

ExamView® Test Bank, Ch. 4
ExamView® Test Bank CD-ROM, Ch. 4

Standardized Test Preparation

Diagnose and Prescribe

Diagnostic Tests for High School Social Studies Skills

Review and Reteach

Review Book for U.S. History

Practice and Assess

Test-taking Strategies With Transparencies
Test-taking Strategies Posters
Test Prep Book for U.S. History
Alternative Assessment Handbook
Document-Based Assessment

Teaching Resources

Units 1/2 booklet
- Section Quizzes, pp. 39–42
- Chapter Tests, pp. 43, 46

www.phschool.com Ch. 4 Self-Test

AmericanHeritage Resources

From the Archives of American Heritage®, pp. 160, 170
AmericanHeritage® My Brush with History™ Videotapes
www.americanheritage.com

Don't miss the exclusive interactive version of this textbook on the Web and on CD-ROM.

Chapter 4 Planning Guide

In Your Classroom

Customize for Individual Needs

Gifted and Talented

Teacher's Edition
- Customize for Gifted and Talented, p. 677

Teaching Resources
- Biography, Literature, and Comparing Primary Sources booklet, pp. 16, 55, 117

Technology
- Exploring Primary Sources in U.S. History CD-ROM *A Diary from Dixie, Mary Chesnut; Civil War Photograph, Mathew Brady; Beat! Beat! Drums!, Walt Whitman; The Education of Henry Adams: Foes or Friends, Henry Adams; Emancipation Proclamation; Gettysburg Address, Abraham Lincoln; In the Wilderness, Thomas J. Halsey; Second Inaugural Address, Abraham Lincoln*

ESL

Teacher's Edition
- Customize for ESL, p. 669

Teaching Resources
- Guided Reading and Review booklet, pp. 46–49
- Guide to the Essentials (English/Spanish), Chapter 4

Technology
- Student Edition on Audio CD, Chapter 4
- Guided Reading Audiotapes (English/Spanish), Chapter 4
- Section Reading Support Transparencies

Less Proficient Readers

Teacher's Edition
- Customize for Less Proficient Readers, p. 673

Teaching Resources
- Guided Reading and Review booklet, pp. 46–49
- Guide to the Essentials (English/Spanish), Chapter 4

Technology
- Student Edition on Audio CD, Chapter 4
- Guided Reading Audiotapes (English/Spanish), Chapter 4
- Section Reading Support Transparencies

Less Proficient Writers

Teacher's Edition
- Customize for Less Proficient Writers, p. 683

Teaching Resources
- Guided Reading and Review booklet, pp. 46–49
- Guide to the Essentials (English/Spanish), Chapter 4

Technology
- Student Edition on Audio CD, Chapter 4
- Guided Reading Audiotapes (English/Spanish), Chapter 4
- Section Reading Support Transparencies

Teacher's Edition Index

Chapter 4 – Pacing Suggestions

For 90-minute Blocks

- Teach sections 1, 3, and 4 using Transparencies A20, A21, A22, A23, A24, D5, E8, E9, F4, and H8, and the Recent Scholarship notes on pages 158, 164, 174, and 191 for class discussions.

Running Out of Time?

If you are running short on time to cover this chapter, consider the following options:

- Use the Prentice Hall Presentation Pro CD-ROM to create an outline for this chapter.
- Use the Section Summaries for Chapter 4, from **Guide to the Essentials (English/Spanish).**

TEKS Correlation

Chapter-Level	TEKS
	(8) Geography. The student uses geographic tools to collect, analyze, and interpret data. The student is expected to: **(B)** pose and answer questions about geographic distributions and patterns shown on maps, graphs, charts, models, and databases. **(24) Social studies skills.** The student applies critical-thinking skills to organize and use information acquired from a variety of sources, including electronic technology. The student is expected to: **(A)** locate and use primary and secondary sources such as computer software, databases, media and news services, biographies, interviews, and artifacts to acquire information about the United States. **(B)** analyze information by sequencing, categorizing, identifying cause-and-effect relationships, comparing, contrasting, finding the main idea, summarizing, making generalizations and predictions, and drawing inferences and conclusions. **(D)** use the process of historical inquiry to research, interpret, and use multiple sources of evidence. **(25) Social studies skills.** The student communicates in written, oral, and visual forms. The student is expected to: **(C)** transfer information from one medium to another, including written to visual and statistical to written or visual, using computer software as appropriate. **(D)** create written, oral, and visual presentations of social studies information.
1 From Bull Run to Antietam	**(24) Social studies skills.** The student applies critical-thinking skills to organize and use information acquired from a variety of sources, including electronic technology. The student is expected to: **(H)** use appropriate mathematical skills to interpret social studies information such as maps and graphs. **(25) Social studies skills.** The student communicates in written, oral, and visual forms. The student is expected to: **(A)** use social studies terminology correctly.
2 Life Behind the Lines	**(24) Social studies skills.** The student applies critical-thinking skills to organize and use information acquired from a variety of sources, including electronic technology. The student is expected to: **(C)** explain and apply different methods that historians use to interpret the past, including the use of primary and secondary sources, points of view, frames of reference, and historical context. **(G)** support a point of view on a social studies issue or event.
3 The Tide of the War Turns	**(24) Social studies skills.** The student applies critical-thinking skills to organize and use information acquired from a variety of sources, including electronic technology. The student is expected to: **(H)** use appropriate mathematical skills to interpret social studies information such as maps and graphs. **(25) Social studies skills.** The student communicates in written, oral, and visual forms. The student is expected to: **(B)** use standard grammar, spelling, sentence structure, and punctuation.
4 Devastation and New Freedom	**(24) Social studies skills.** The student applies critical-thinking skills to organize and use information acquired from a variety of sources, including electronic technology. The student is expected to: **(G)** support a point of view on a social studies issue or event. **(H)** use appropriate mathematical skills to interpret social studies information such as maps and graphs. **(25) Social studies skills.** The student communicates in written, oral, and visual forms. The student is expected to: **(B)** use standard grammar, spelling, sentence structure, and punctuation.

Chapter 4

The Civil War

(1861–1865)

Introducing the Chapter

"The Civil War," wrote historian Page Smith, "took place because the southern states felt that they could no longer tolerate their status as members of the Union." After the bloodiest war in the western world in the nineteenth century, enslaved African Americans gained their freedom, while the federal government became a strong force in citizens' lives.

Time Line Activity

To provide students with practice in using the time line, ask questions such as these:

1. What event marked the beginning of the Civil War? *(The firing on Fort Sumter by Confederate forces)*
2. Why was the Union victory at Gettysburg hard on both the Union and the Conferacy? *(There were huge losses on both sides, for the winners as well as the losers.)*
3. If the Union forces were winning in 1864, why did Sherman continue his destructive march through the Deep South? *(To help end the war quickly)*

Chapter 4

The Civil War (1861–1865)

The Battle of Missionary Ridge, Tennessee

Civil War cannon

American Events

1861 The Confederate attack on Fort Sumter in April signals the start of the Civil War. The South wins the First Battle of Bull Run (Manassas).

1862 After the Battle of Antietam in September, the Confederate army under the command of General Robert E. Lee retreats into Virginia. In December, the Confederates defeat a Union army at Fredericksburg.

1863 The Emancipation Proclamation takes effect on January 1. In July, both sides suffer huge losses in the Union victory at Gettysburg. The Union gains control of the Mississippi River.

Presidential Terms: Abraham Lincoln 1861–1865

1861 — 1862 — 1863

World Events

1861 Czar Alexander II emancipates Russian serfs.

1862 Otto von Bismarck becomes prime minister of Prussia.

1863 French emperor Napoleon III sets up the Austrian Archduke Maximilian as the emperor of Mexico.

eTeach

Be sure to check out this month's online discussion with a Master Teacher. Go to **www.phschool.com**.

RESOURCE DIRECTORY

Teaching Resources

Pacing Charts booklet
Block Scheduling booklet, p. 18
Units 1/2 booklet
- Chapter Summary, p. 38

Technology

Guided Reading Audiotapes (English/Spanish), Ch. 4
Student Edition on Audio CD, Ch. 4
Sounds of an Era Audio CD *Senator Robert Toombs on Secession,* 1960s recording (time: 30 seconds); *Former Slave Fountain Hughes,* 1941 recording (time: 20 seconds); *"When Johnny Comes Marching Home Again"* (time: 40 seconds)
Prentice Hall United States History Video Collection™ Volume 9, *The Civil War*
Prentice Hall Presentation Pro CD-ROM, Ch. 4
Resource Pro® CD-ROM
Social Studies Skills Tutor CD-ROM
Companion Web site, www.phschool.com

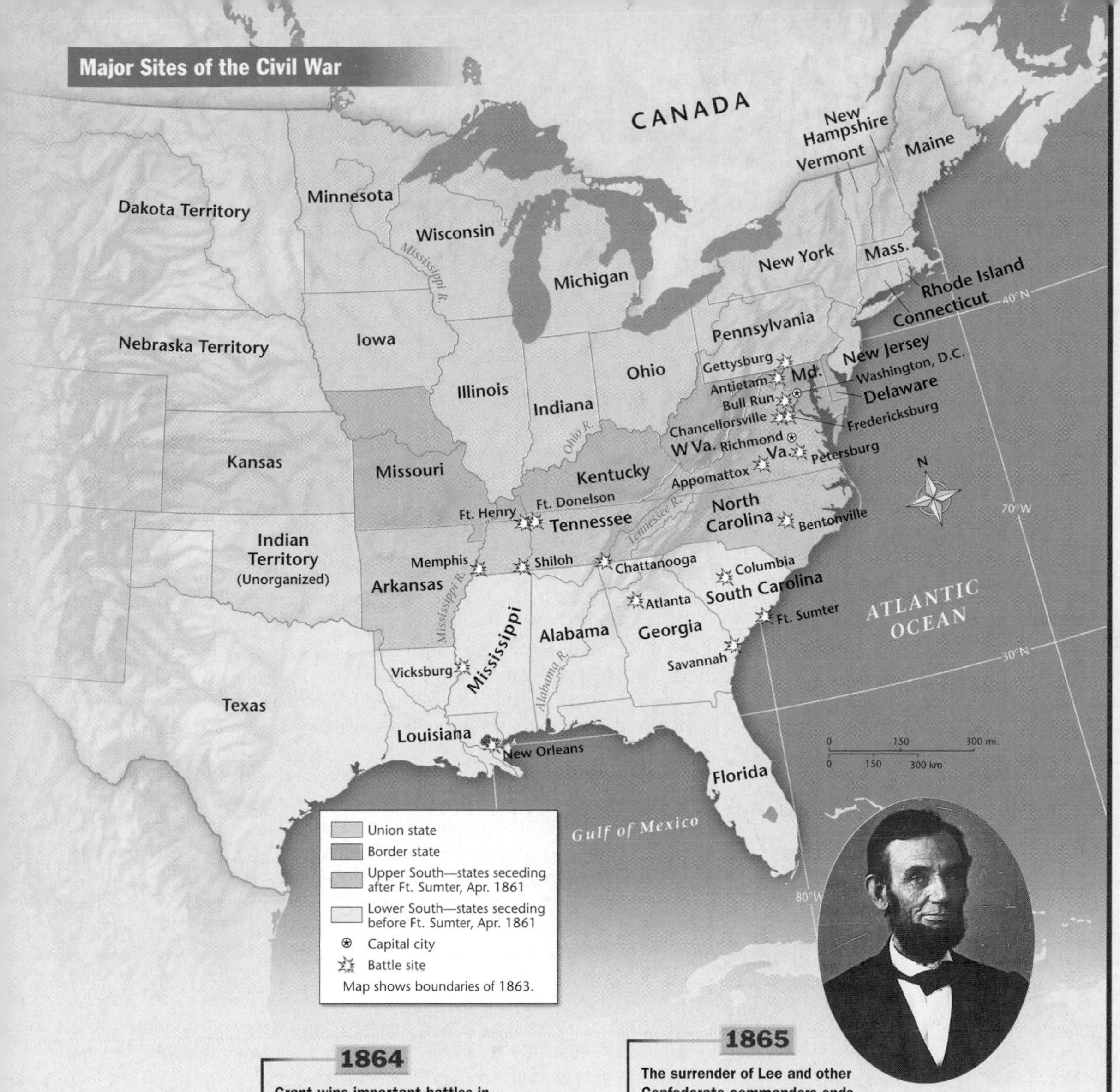

Major Sites of the Civil War

Union state
Border state
Upper South—states seceding after Ft. Sumter, Apr. 1861
Lower South—states seceding before Ft. Sumter, Apr. 1861
Capital city
Battle site
Map shows boundaries of 1863.

Abraham Lincoln

1864

Grant wins important battles in Virginia; Sherman captures Atlanta and begins his march to the sea. Lincoln wins reelection.

1865

The surrender of Lee and other Confederate commanders ends the Civil War. Ratification of the Thirteenth Amendment abolishes slavery.

Andrew Johnson 1865–1869

1864 1865 1866

After 14 years, the Chinese government finally crushes the Taiping Rebellion.

1864

Work begins on the first undersea transatlantic telegraph cable.

1865

Major Sites of the Civil War

Activating Prior Knowledge Were most of the battle sites in the Union states or the Confederate states? *(In the Confederate states)*

Previewing How did this affect the Confederate war effort? *(The multiple battles on Confederate sites made it more difficult for the Confederate forces by lowering morale, putting the South in the position of defense rather than offense, and making it possible for Union forces to destroy Southern supplies and supply routes.)*

BACKGROUND
About the Pictures

1. This painting by American painter Douglas Volk depicts Union soldiers attacking during the Battle of

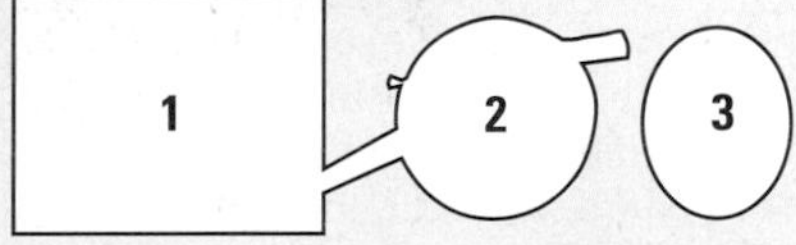

Missionary Ridge.

2. Cannons such as this one of the Napoleon variety were used to devastating and deadly effect by both sides during the Civil War.
3. Portrait of Abraham Lincoln, United States President from 1861 to 1865. Lincoln, who served as President during the Civil War, was shot by an assassin on April 14, 1865, and died the next day without regaining consciousness.

BIBLIOGRAPHY

For the Teacher

Chesnut, Mary Boykin. ***A Diary from Dixie.*** Random House Value Publishing, 1997. (Observations of the war from the Southern point of view.)

Quarles, Benjamin. ***The Negro in the Civil War.*** De Capo Press, 1989. (The role of African Americans in the Civil War.)

Garry Wills. ***Lincoln at Gettysburg: The Words That Remade America.*** Touchstone, 1993. (Pulitzer Prize–winning examination of the Gettysburg Address.)

For the Student

Crane, Stephen. ***The Red Badge of Courage.*** Washington Square Press, 1996. (Classic novel of a Union soldier in the face of enemy fire; originally published in 1895.)

The Civil War, PBS Video. (Acclaimed, multipart series that combines scholarly analysis and primary sources.)

Don't miss the exclusive interactive version of this textbook on the Web and on CD-ROM.

Section 1
From Bull Run to Antietam

Section Objectives

1. Understand the significance of the First Battle of Bull Run.
2. Find out how the North and the South prepared for war.
3. Learn why the battles in the West were important.
4. Discover the outcome of each of the battles in the East in 1862.

Bellringer

Warm-Up Activity Tell students that at the start of the Civil War, many Northerners expected the war to be over quickly. Some even called it "the six months' war." Write the words *new tactics* and *new technology* on the chalkboard. Ask students to predict how these two factors changed Northerners' expectations.

Activating Prior Knowledge In what ways did the debate over states' rights lead to the Civil War? Does the debate over states' rights versus the governing power of the federal government continue to this day?

Reading Strategy

Ask students to reread the Main Idea shown on this page. Then, have them rewrite it as a question. As they read, have them take notes about events that help answer the question.

Activity
Student Portfolio

You may wish to have students add the following to their portfolios: Ask students to write two letters home, one from a Union soldier and one from a Confederate soldier. The Union letter should describe the military strategies of naval blockades. The Confederate letter should describe the military strategy of waging a war of attrition. **(Verbal/Linguistic)**

Section 1

From Bull Run to Antietam

READING FOCUS

- What was the significance of the First Battle of Bull Run?
- How did the North and the South prepare for war?
- Why were the battles in the West important?
- What was the outcome of each of the battles in the East in 1862?

MAIN IDEA

Bloody fighting during the first two years of the Civil War made it clear to both North and South that the struggle would be long and difficult.

KEY TERMS

Civil War
First Battle of Bull Run
casualty
war of attrition
shell
canister
Battle of Shiloh
Battle of Antietam

TAKING NOTES

Copy the chart below. As you read this section, fill in the advantages of each side at the start of the Civil War. Also include the battles each side won.

Advantages/Battles Won	
North	South
More railroad track	First Battle of Bull Run

Setting the Scene The first shots fired on Fort Sumter, South Carolina, in April 1861 signaled the start of the nation's **Civil War**—the war between the Union states of the North and the Confederate states of the South. At the outbreak of hostilities, neither side would have predicted that the war would last four long years. As a matter of fact, in many places in the South, people were both jubilant and defiant. In her memoir, Sallie Hunt, who was a child at the time, recalled the mood in Richmond, Virginia:

> "*One spring day in April, 1861, all Richmond was astir. Schools were broken up, and knots of excited men gathered at every street corner. Sumter had been fired upon, and Lincoln had ordered the men of Virginia to rush upon their brethren of the South and put the rebellion down. Now 'the die was cast,' our lot was with theirs, and come weal [well-being] or woe, we would fight for independence. . . . [O]ur hearts swelled with pride to think we could say to our tyrants: 'Thus far shalt thou come, and no further.'*"
>
> —Sallie Hunt

Women on both sides contributed to the war effort by sewing uniforms and other supplies. This Southern woman is making caps.

In response to the call to "put the rebellion down," Virginia seceded from the Union. By May 1861, the Upper South (Virginia, North Carolina, Tennessee, and Arkansas) had joined the Confederacy, and the Confederate capital had been moved from Montgomery, Alabama, to Richmond, Virginia. In July, some 35,000 Northern volunteers were training in Washington, D.C., just 100 miles away. "Forward to Richmond!" urged a headline in the *New York Tribune*. Many Northerners believed that capturing the Confederate capital would bring a quick end to the Civil War.

The First Battle of Bull Run

General Irvin McDowell, commander of the Union troops, was not yet ready to fight. He felt that he needed more time to prepare even though most of his troops had volunteered for just 90 days and their term of service was nearly over. "This is not an army," McDowell told the President. "It will take a long

Resource Directory

Teaching Resources

Guided Reading and Review booklet, p. 46
Biography, Literature, and Comparing Primary Sources booklet (Literature) *The First Battle of Bull Run,* p. 55

Other Print Resources

Historical Outline Map Book *Choosing Sides,* p. 49

Technology

Section Reading Support Transparencies
Guided Reading Audiotapes (English/Spanish), Ch. 4
Student Edition on Audio CD, Ch. 4
Color Transparencies *Cause-and-Effect Charts,* D5; *Fine Art,* E8
Exploring Primary Sources in U.S. History CD-ROM *A Diary from Dixie, Mary Chesnut*
Exploring Primary Sources in U.S. History CD-ROM *Civil War Photograph, Mathew Brady*
Prentice Hall Presentation Pro CD-ROM, Ch. 4
Companion Web site, www.phschool.com

time to make an army." Despite this warning, Lincoln ordered his general into action.

On July 16, McDowell marched his poorly prepared army into Virginia. His objective was the town of Manassas, an important railroad junction southwest of Washington. Opposing him was a smaller Confederate force under General P.G.T. Beauregard, the officer who had captured Fort Sumter. The Confederates were camped along Bull Run, a stream that passed about four miles north of Manassas.

It took the Union army nearly four days to march the 25 miles to Manassas. Lack of training and discipline contributed to the soldiers' slow pace. As McDowell later explained, "They stopped every moment to pick blackberries or get water. . . . They would not keep in the ranks, order as much as you pleased." Meanwhile, Beauregard had no trouble keeping track of McDowell's progress. Accompanying the troops was a huge crowd of reporters, politicians, and other civilians from Washington, planning to picnic and watch the battle. They got a rude surprise.

McDowell's delays had allowed Beauregard to strengthen his army. Some 11,000 additional Confederate troops had been packed into freight cars and sped to the scene. (This was the first time in history that troops were moved by train.) When McDowell finally attacked on July 21, he faced a force nearly the size of his own army. But beyond the Confederate lines lay the road to the Confederate capital at Richmond.

After hours of hard fighting, the Union soldiers appeared to be winning. Their slow advance pushed the Southerners back. However, some Virginia soldiers commanded by General Thomas Jackson refused to give up. Seeing Jackson's men holding firm, another Confederate officer rallied his retreating troops, shouting: "Look! There is Jackson standing like a stone wall! Rally

VIEWING HISTORY This portrait of members of the U.S. Signal Corps is by the famous photographer Mathew Brady. **Making Inferences** *Judging by their expressions, what do these men think of their role in the Civil War?*

COMPARING PRIMARY SOURCES

The Aims of the Civil War

Throughout the years of quarreling between North and South, Southerners protested repeatedly that Northerners were trampling on their rights, including the right to own slaves as property.

Analyzing Viewpoints How did the war aims of each side reflect their quarrel, as described above?

The Aims of the South

"We have vainly endeavored to secure tranquillity and obtain respect for the rights to which we were entitled . . . . If . . . the integrity of our territory and jurisdiction [legal authority] be assailed [attacked], it will but remain for us, with firm resolve, to appeal to arms."

—*President Jefferson Davis, Inaugural Address, February 18, 1861*

The Aims of the North

"This war is not waged upon our part in any spirit of oppression, nor for any purpose of conquest or subjugation, nor purpose of overthrowing or interfering with the rights or established institutions of those [seceding] States, but to defend and maintain the supremacy of the Constitution and to preserve the Union."

—*House of Representatives, Crittenden Resolution, July 25, 1861*

LESSON PLAN

Focus In the first two years of the Civil War, Union forces tried unsuccessfully to capture the Confederate capital. They did succeed, however, in blockading the coasts of the South and seizing control of the river valleys of its midwestern states.

Instruct Discuss with students how the expectations of both sides were called into question in the early days of the war. Why did the Union want to capture the Confederate capital? How did the First Battle of Bull Run affect those calling for a short war? Ask students to discuss the tactics of the war. How did tactics lag behind technology? What caused the lag?

Assess/Reteach Have students create a time line of major events in the first years of the Civil War. Have them suggest an answer to the question: By the end of 1862, which side was in a stronger position, the North or the South?

CUSTOMIZE FOR ...

ESL

Ask students to write the following column headings on a piece of paper: *Union Tactics, Confederate Tactics, Union Victories, Confederate Victories.* As they read, have them fill in details from the text in the appropriate column.

CAPTION ANSWERS

Viewing History Students may note that the men look serious and seem to sense the importance of their role.

BACKGROUND
Recent Scholarship

Feared and revered Confederate general Thomas Jackson earned his nickname Stonewall at the First Battle of Bull Run. Confederate General Bee, attempting to rally his men in a sea of swirling chaos, shouted out, "There is Jackson, standing like a stone wall!" At the time, most people assumed that Bee was praising Jackson for his courage and steadfastness. Immediately after the war, however, some Jackson critics offered another interpretation: they contended that Bee wanted Jackson to advance and that his comment was filled with disdain and dismay. James I. Robertson, Jr., in *Stonewall Jackson: The Man, the Soldier, the Legend,* attempts to put that interpretation to rest. Robertson acknowledges that we may never truly know (as Bee was killed that day), but he offers evidence to support the idea that Bee was praising Jackson and his stand.

BACKGROUND
Biography

Mary Boykin Chesnut (1823–1886) is the best known of the Confederate women diarists. A member of a prominent political family, she was the wife of James Chesnut, Jr., a wealthy senator, and her social circle included President Jefferson Davis. The time in which she lived was one of upheaval for the entire country, but she limited her observations to what was going on around her. It was her eye for daily life under wartime conditions that makes her diary so valuable. In July 1861 she wrote: "They brought me a Yankee soldier's portfolio from the battlefield. . . . One might shed tears over some of the letters. Women, wives and mothers, are the same everywhere."

Focus on GOVERNMENT

West Virginia Statehood As early as 1776, there were divisions between the eastern and western parts of Virginia. Pioneers lived in the west, where both culture and geography discouraged slavery. Wealthy planters in the east depended on slave labor. Tax laws and the restriction of suffrage to men of property benefited the east and caused resentment in the west, where there was already talk of forming a separate state.

The Civil War only added to these differences. Western delegates walked out of Virginia's Secession Convention in April 1861, declaring secession an illegal attempt to overthrow the federal government. They formed a "Restored Government." In October, 39 western counties approved formation of a new Unionist state, and the Restored Government gave its permission. Congress approved West Virginia's entry into the Union on June 20, 1863, on the condition of gradual emancipation of slaves in the region.

behind the Virginians!" The Union advance was stopped, and "Stonewall" Jackson had earned his famous nickname.

Tired and discouraged, the Union forces began to fall back in late afternoon. Then a trainload of fresh Confederate troops arrived and launched a counterattack. The orderly Union retreat fell apart. Hundreds of soldiers dropped their weapons and ran north. They stampeded into the sightseers who had followed them to the battlefield. As the army disintegrated, soldiers and civilians were caught in a tangle of carriages, wagons, and horses on the narrow road. Terrified that the Confederate troops would catch them, they ran headlong for the safety of Washington, D.C. The Confederates, however, were too disorganized and exhausted to pursue the Union army.

The first major battle of the Civil War was over. It became known as the **First Battle of Bull Run,** because the following year another bloody battle occurred at almost exactly the same site. In the South, this engagement was known as the First Battle of Manassas. The First Battle of Bull Run was not a huge action. About 35,000 troops were involved on each side. The Union suffered about 2,900 **casualties,** the military term for those killed, wounded, captured, or missing in action. Confederate casualties were fewer than 2,000. Later battles would prove much more costly.

Preparing for War

Bull Run caused some Americans on both sides to suspect that winning the war might not be so easy. "The fat is in the fire now," wrote President Lincoln's private secretary. "The preparations for the war will be continued with increased vigor by the Government." Congress quickly authorized the President to raise a million three-year volunteers. In Richmond, a clerk in the Confederate War Department began to worry, "We are resting on our oars, while the enemy is drilling and equipping 500,000 or 600,000 men."

Strengths of the North and the South In several respects, the North was much better prepared for war than was the South. The North had more than twice as much railroad track as the South. This made the movement of troops, food, and supplies quicker and easier in the North. There were also more than twice as many factories in the North, so the Union was better able to produce the guns, ammunition, shoes, and other items needed for its army. The North's economy was well balanced between farming and industry, and the North had far more money in its banks than the South.

What's more, the North already had a functioning government and a small army and navy. Most importantly, two thirds of the nation's population lived in Union states. This made more men available to the Union army, while at the same time allowing for a sufficient labor force to remain behind for farm and factory work.

The Confederates had some advantages, too. Because most of the nation's military colleges were in the South, a majority of the nation's trained officers were Southerners, and they sided with the Confederacy. In addition, the Southern army did not need to initiate any military action to win the war. All they needed to do was maintain a defensive position and keep from being beaten. In contrast, to restore unity to the nation, the North would have to attack and conquer the South. Southerners had an additional advantage: they felt that they were fighting to preserve their way of life and, they believed, their right to self-government.

RESOURCE DIRECTORY

Teaching Resources

Biography, Literature, and Comparing Primary Sources booklet (Comparing Primary Sources)
On the Purpose of the Civil War, p. 117

Technology

Color Transparencies *American Photo,* F4

Patriotism was also important in the North. And there were strongly held beliefs about slavery. The abolitionist Harriet Beecher Stowe responded to the Union call to arms by writing, "This is a cause to die for, and—thanks be to God!—our young men embrace it." There were other reasons that people on both sides were eager to fight. Some enlisted for the adventure, and feared that the war would be over before they got a chance to participate.

Union Military Strategies After the fall of Fort Sumter, President Lincoln ordered a naval blockade of the seceded states. By shutting down the South's ports along the Atlantic Coast and the Gulf of Mexico, Lincoln hoped to keep the South from shipping its cotton to Europe. He also wanted to prevent Southerners from importing the manufactured goods they needed.

Lincoln's blockade was part of a strategy developed by General Winfield Scott, the hero of the Mexican War and commander of all U.S. troops in 1861. Scott realized that it would take a long time to raise and train an army that was big enough and strong enough to invade the South successfully. Instead, he proposed to choke off the Confederacy with the blockade and to use troops and gunboats to gain control of the Mississippi River, thus cutting the Confederacy in two. Scott believed these measures would pressure the South to seek peace and would restore the nation without a bloody war.

Northern newspapers sneered at Scott's strategy. They scornfully named it the Anaconda Plan, after a type of snake that coils around its victims and crushes them to death. Despite the Union defeat at Bull Run, political pressure for action and a quick victory remained strong in 1861. This public clamor for results led to several more attempts to capture Richmond. Seizing the Confederate capital was another important strategic goal of the Union.

Confederate War Strategies The South's basic war plan was to prepare and wait. Many Southerners hoped that Lincoln would let them go in peace. "All we ask is to be let alone," announced Confederate president Jefferson Davis, shortly after secession. He planned for a defensive war.

Southern strategy called for a **war of attrition.** In this type of war, one side inflicts continuous losses on the enemy in order to wear down its strength.

READING CHECK
What were the most important strengths of the North and the South?

Northern Advantages	Southern Advantages
Population 21.5 million N 9 million S	**Leadership** Seven of the nation's eight military colleges were in the South; most officers sided with the Confederacy.
Railroad Mileage 21,700 miles N 9,000 miles S	**Military Tactics** Because the South was defending its borders, its army needed only to repel Northern advances rather than initiate military action.
Number of Factories 110,100 N 20,600 S	**Morale** Many Southerners were eager to fight, considering the war a struggle for their way of life.

INTERPRETING DIAGRAMS
This diagram shows the advantages that the North and the South had at the start of the Civil War. **Analyzing Information** *The North and the South had different kinds of advantages. Explain the differences.*

BACKGROUND
Geography in History

Many Civil War battles have two names, one Northern and one Southern. The names given by the North tend to connect a battle with a physical feature near the battlefield, such as the stream Bull Run. Southerners usually named a battle after the nearest town; they called this one the First Battle of Manassas.

BACKGROUND
Global Connections

One of the most popular forms of ammunition during the Civil War was the Minié ball. A French army officer named Claude-Etienne Minié invented the Minié ball in 1849. This self-cleaning cylindrical bullet had a hollow base and had four times the range of the musket. Soldiers could fire many rounds with a Minié-ball rifle before having to clean the barrel. The use of the Minié ball sped the pace of war. Its use was one of the factors responsible for the high casualties on Civil War battlefields.

READING CHECK
The North had more people, industry, railroad track, governing experience, and money. The South did not need to win, only to survive. Qualified officer candidates were available in large numbers for the Confederate armies.

TEST PREPARATION

Have students read the first paragraph under the heading "Preparing for War" on the previous page, and then answer the question below.

After the First Battle of Bull Run, Lincoln's private secretary wrote, "The fat is in the fire now." What did he mean by that?

A There would not be enough food for the Union Army.
B The war would soon consume a tremendous amount of resources.
C The war would soon be over.
(D) The war might not be over for a long time.

CAPTION ANSWERS

Interpreting Diagrams The North's advantages were in manpower to fight the war and to keep the economy going at home, and in supplies and transportation. Southern armies had strong leadership and high morale. The South could fight a defensive war.

ACTIVITY
Connecting with Economics

Tell students to research the role of cotton in the Civil War. Students might look into the large number of slaves who worked in the cotton fields. (In 1793 there were nearly 700,000 slaves working in the cotton fields. By 1860 the number had soared to almost 4 million.) How did the war impact the cotton industry? **(Logical/Mathematical)**

BACKGROUND
Interdisciplinary

Hot-air balloons, first employed in warfare by France in 1794, were used by American balloonist Thaddeus Lowe to provide the Union army with information on Confederate troop movements. Lowe conducted the first airborne operation of the recently invented telegraph. He also brought aloft cameras, which were just coming into popular use, to provide panoramic shots of military positions.

From the Archives of
AmericanHeritage®

Wartime Medicine

Injured Civil War soldiers could have benefited from modern medical expertise, but the knowledge simply wasn't there at the time. Surgeons, for example, thought it was a good sign if pus formed at the site of the wound; they called it "laudable pus." In fact, pus generally indicated a bacterial infection that would eventually kill the soldier. Source: Bruce Catton, *The American Heritage® Picture History of the Civil War,* 1960.

Southerners counted on their forces being able to turn back Union attacks until Northerners lost the will to fight. However, this strategy did not take into account the North's tremendous advantage in resources. In the end, it was the North that waged a successful war of attrition against the South.

Southern strategy in another area also backfired. The South produced some 75 percent of the world's cotton, much of it supplying the textile mills of Great Britain and France. However, Confederate leaders convinced most Southern planters to stop exporting cotton. They believed that the sudden loss of Southern cotton would cause British and French industrial leaders to pressure their governments to help the South gain its independence in exchange for restoring the flow of cotton. Instead, the Europeans turned to India and Egypt for their cotton. By the time Southerners recognized the failure of this strategy, the Union blockade had become so effective that little cotton could get out. With no income from cotton exports, the South could not earn the money it needed to buy guns and maintain its armies.

Tactics and Technology For generations, European commanders had fought battles by concentrating their forces, assaulting a position, and driving the enemy away. The cannons and muskets they used were neither accurate nor capable of repeating fire very rapidly. Generals relied on masses of charging troops to overwhelm the enemy. Most Civil War generals had been trained in these methods, and had seen them work well in the Mexican War.

The newer bullets (at right) were far more accurate than round musket balls like the one shown wedged in a soldier's shoulder plate.

By the time of the Civil War, however, gun makers knew that bullet-shaped ammunition drifted less as it flew through the air than a round ball, the older type of ammunition. They had also learned that rifling, a spiral groove cut on the inside of a gun barrel, would make a fired bullet pick up spin, causing it to travel farther and straighter. Older muskets, which had no rifling, were accurate only to about 100 yards. Bullets fired from rifles, as the new guns were called, hit targets at 500 yards. In addition, they could be reloaded and fired much faster than muskets.

Improvements in artillery were just as deadly. Instead of relying only on iron cannon balls, gunners could now fire **shells,** devices that exploded in the air or when they hit something. Artillery often fired **canister,** a special type of shell filled with bullets. This turned cannons into giant shotguns. Thousands of soldiers went to their deaths by following orders to cross open fields against such weapons. Commanders on both sides, however, were slow to recognize that these traditional strategies exposed their troops to slaughter.

War in the West

After the disaster at Bull Run, President Lincoln named General George McClellan to build and command a new army. While McClellan was involved with this task, Union forces in the West invaded the Confederacy. The states of Arkansas, Louisiana, Mississippi, and Tennessee held the key to control of the Mississippi River, which ran through the heart of the Confederacy. The fighting in these four states is generally referred to as the "war in the West."

The most successful Union forces in the West were led by General Ulysses S. Grant. After the fall of Fort Sumter, Grant's success at organizing and training a group of Illinois volunteers caused Lincoln to promote him from colonel to general. He was assigned to command the Union forces based in Paducah, Kentucky, where the Ohio and Tennessee rivers meet.

RESOURCE DIRECTORY

Technology

RESOURCE PRO® **Visual Learning Activity** *A British View of the Civil War,* found on Resource Pro, depicts European hopes for the war in a political cartoon.

RESOURCE PRO® **Literature Activity** *Diary from Dixie,* found on Resource Pro, features excerpts from the diary of Mary Boykin Chesnut to describe life in the war-torn South.

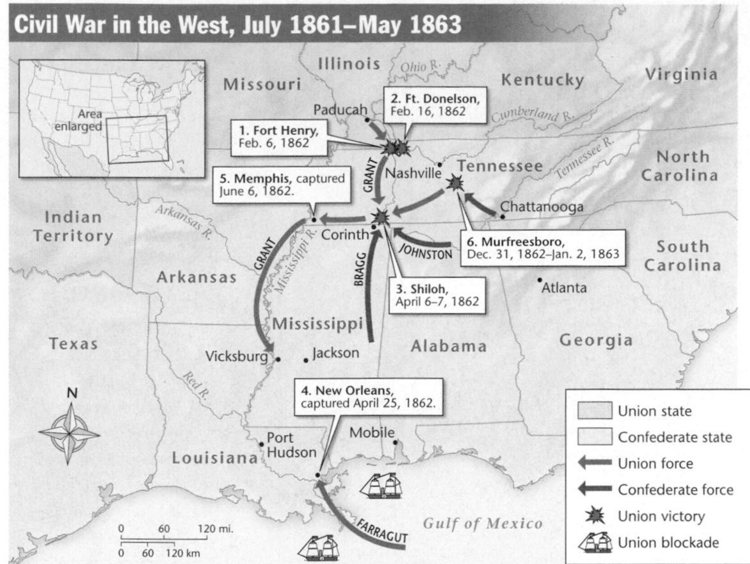

MAP SKILLS Union generals in the West focused their attention on the Mississippi River. "That Mississippi ruins us, if lost," worried Southern observer Mary Chesnut in 1862. **Place** *What two key cities on the Mississippi had the Union captured by the summer of 1862?*

Forts Henry and Donelson In February 1862, Grant advanced south along the Tennessee River with more than 15,000 troops and several gunboats. Powered by steam and built to navigate shallow bodies of water, these gunboats were basically small floating forts fitted with cannons. Grant's objectives were Fort Henry and Fort Donelson, located just over the border in the Confederate state of Tennessee. The forts protected the Tennessee and Cumberland rivers, important water routes into the western Confederacy.

On February 6 the Union gunboats pounded Fort Henry into surrender before Grant's troops arrived. The general then marched his army east and attacked Fort Donelson on the Cumberland River. Following three days of shelling by the gunboats, Fort Donelson also gave up.

The battles caused a sensation in both the North and the South. Northerners rejoiced that at last the Union had an important victory. Southerners worried that loss of the forts exposed much of the region to attack. Indeed, Nashville soon fell to another Union army. Meanwhile, Grant and some 42,000 soldiers pushed farther south along the Tennessee River to threaten Mississippi and Alabama.

The Battle of Shiloh In late March, Grant's army advanced toward Corinth, Mississippi, an important railroad center near the Tennessee-Mississippi border. Confederate general Albert Sidney Johnston gathered troops from throughout the region to halt the Union advance. By the time Grant's forces approached, Johnston had assembled an army of about 40,000 to oppose them. Grant, however, stopped at Pittsburg Landing, Tennessee, a small river town about 20 miles north of Corinth. Here he waited for more Union troops that General Don Carlos Buell was bringing from Nashville. Johnston decided to launch an attack against Grant's army before the Union force got any larger.

General Grant's demand for the "unconditional and immediate surrender" of Fort Donelson earned him the nickname "Unconditional Surrender Grant."

Background

A Diverse Nation

Soldiers on both sides of the war came from a variety of different ethnic groups. Some ethnic groups formed their own fighting units. On the Union side, there were several all-German regiments. About 10,000 Americans of Spanish descent participated in the Civil War, on both the Union and Confederate sides. Many recent Irish immigrants fought in the war, primarily on the Union side, since most Irish immigrants had settled in the North. The 39th New York Infantry Regiment was known as the Garibaldi Guard for the many Italian soldiers in its ranks.

Activity

Connecting with Geography

Have small groups work together to draw a large map showing the area in which Fort Henry and Fort Donelson were located. Tell students to identify the major geographical features—such as the Tennessee River, the Cumberland River, and the states of Tennessee, Mississippi, and Alabama. Ask students to describe the military actions, taken in sequential order. **(Visual/Spatial)**

Customize For ...

Gifted and Talented

Ask students to research evidence to support the view that the differences between the North and the South were so great that these two regions were really distinct nations within the United States.

Caption Answers

Map Skills Memphis and New Orleans.

Activity
Connecting with Economics

Have groups of students research the economic effect of the Civil War on civilians. How was everyday civilian life affected by the war? Why were there food shortages, especially in the South, and how did people cope? What was the impact of paper and metal shortages in the South? What did people do for work? **(Logical/Mathematical)**

Background
Interdisciplinary

The men who risked their lives in the conflicts of the Civil War were a highly literate group. Throughout the war, they read newspapers, voted in state and national elections, and wrote letters home. Many soldiers, both Union and Confederate, kept journals recounting their experiences in the war. Because their letters and journals were not subject to censorship, Civil War soldiers wrote freely about a broad range of issues associated with their war experience. Much of what we know and understand about the war comes from the diaries of these men.

READING CHECK

Union and Confederate armies clashed near Pittsburgh Landing in southern Tennessee in April 1862. Grant's Union troops prevailed and won an important Union victory on the second day. The battle was extremely bloody and hinted that this war would be a war of total destruction.

MAP SKILLS McClellan's extreme caution was his own worst enemy. "No one but McClellan would have hesitated to attack," said Confederate general Joseph Johnston during McClellan's slow advance toward Richmond before the Seven Days' Battles. **Movement** *What action did Lee take following the Seven Days' Battles?*

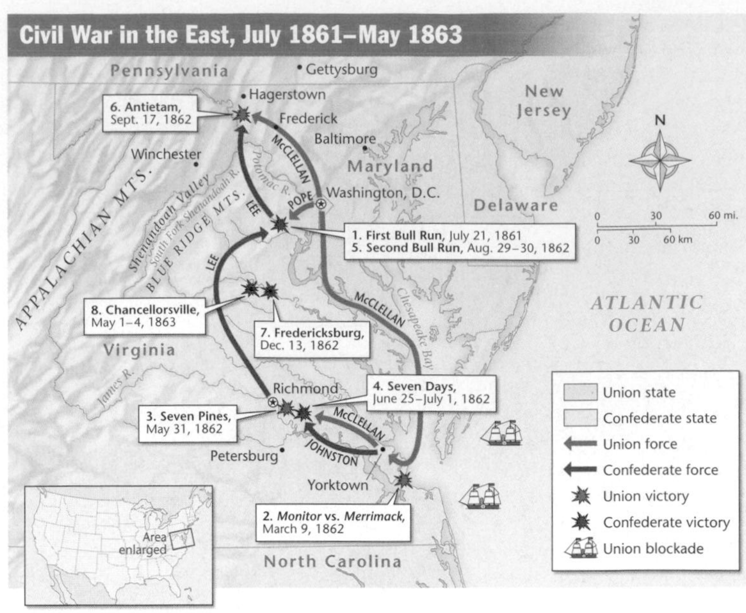

On April 6, 1862, Johnston's forces surprised some of Grant's troops, who were camped at Shiloh Church outside Pittsburg Landing. Fighting quickly spread along a battle line six miles long. By the end of the first day of the **Battle of Shiloh,** the Southerners had driven the Union forces back, nearly into the Tennessee River. That night, some of Grant's officers advised a retreat before the Confederates could renew their attack the next day. "Retreat?" Grant scoffed. "No. I propose to attack at daylight and whip them."

Fortunately for Grant, Buell's troops arrived during the night. The next day, Union forces counter-attacked and defeated Johnston's army. However, the cost to both sides was very high. The Union suffered more than 13,000 casualties, the Confederates nearly 11,000. General Johnston was among the Confederate dead.

READING CHECK Briefly describe the Battle of Shiloh.

Shiloh was the bloodiest single battle that had taken place on the North American continent to that time. It shattered any remaining illusions either side had about the glory of war, and it destroyed Northern hopes that the Confederacy would soon be defeated.

Action on the Mississippi While Grant advanced into the Confederacy from the north, Union forces were also moving up the Mississippi River from the Gulf of Mexico. In late April 1862, a naval squadron commanded by David Farragut fought its way past two forts in the Louisiana swamps to force the surrender of New Orleans. Pushing upriver, Farragut soon captured Baton Rouge, Louisiana, and Natchez, Mississippi. In her diary, Southerner Mary Chesnut voiced her concerns about the Confederate losses: "Battle after battle—disaster after disaster . . . Are we not cut in two? . . . The reality is hideous."

On June 6, the Union navy seized Memphis, Tennessee. Only two major posts on the Mississippi River now remained in Confederate hands. These were Vicksburg, Mississippi, and Port Hudson, Louisiana. If Northern forces could

Caption Answers

Map Skills He moved northward across Virginia into Maryland.

RESOURCE DIRECTORY

Teaching Resources

Biography, Literature, and Comparing Primary Sources booklet (Biography) *General Robert E. Lee,* p. 16

Other Print Resources

Historical Outline Map Book *The Civil War in the East,* p. 51

Technology

Color Transparencies *The Way It Works,* H8

RESOURCE PRO® **Critical Thinking Activity** *Recognizing Bias: Six Months on the Potomac,* found on Resource Pro, helps students practice identifying points of view and bias with an 1862 cartoon of General McClellan and his Confederate counterpart encamped along the Potomac.

Sounds of an Era Audio CD *"The Iron Merrimack"* (time: about one minute)

find some way to capture them, the entire Mississippi River valley would finally be under Union control. The Confederacy would be split into two parts.

War in the East

While the Union army marched through the western Confederacy, Union warships maintained the blockade of Virginia's coast. The Confederates, however, had developed a secret weapon with which to fight the blockade. In early March 1862, a Confederate ship that resembled a floating barn roof steamed out of the James River. When the Union warships guarding the mouth of the river opened fire on the strange-looking vessel, their cannon shots bounced off it like rubber balls. In hours, the Confederate vessel destroyed or heavily damaged three of the most powerful ships in the Union navy.

The *Monitor* and the *Merrimack* Southerners had created the strange-looking vessel by bolting iron plates to an old wooden steamship called the *Merrimack*. (Although the ship was renamed the *Virginia*, it is still called the *Merrimack* in most historical accounts.) The Union's wooden navy was no match for this powerful ironclad warship. Northern leaders feared the new weapon might soon break apart the entire blockade.

Fortunately for the Union, early reports of the Confederates' work on the *Merrimack* had reached the North, and President Lincoln had ordered construction of a similar Union warship. It was made entirely of iron and was rushed to completion in about 100 days. Named the *Monitor*, it looked like a tin can on a raft.

On March 9, the *Monitor* arrived off the Virginia coast to confront the Confederate ironclad. Neither ship was able to do serious damage to the other. After several hours of fighting, the *Merrimack* finally withdrew. The two ships never met again. The Confederates blew up the *Merrimack* at its base in Norfolk, Virginia, in May 1862, rather than let it fall into Union hands. The following December, the *Monitor* sank in a storm. Their one encounter, however, changed the history of warfare. In a single day, the wooden navies of the world became obsolete.

VIEWING HISTORY At the center of this painting, the *Merrimack* and the *Monitor* exchange shots at close range. The *Minnesota*, which the *Monitor* was ordered to protect, sits grounded at right. **Drawing Conclusions** *How did this single battle of the ironclads make traditional wooden warships like the* Minnesota *obsolete?*

The Peninsular Campaign When Union general George McClellan landed troops near Norfolk in May 1862, he was launching the North's second attempt to capture Richmond. At 36 years old, McClellan was young for a commanding general. However, he was an outstanding organizer, an excellent strategist, and was well liked by his troops. McClellan's great weakness was that he was very cautious and never seemed quite ready to fight. This irritated Lincoln and other Northern leaders, who were impatient to avenge the Union's defeat at Bull Run.

In March 1862, McClellan finally ordered the Army of the Potomac out of Washington. Because he thought that marching to Manassas again would be a mistake, he transported some 100,000 soldiers by boat to a peninsula southeast of Richmond. As the Union troops moved up the peninsula, they encountered some 15,000 Southerners at Yorktown, Virginia, about 60 miles from the Confederate capital.

Although the Confederate force was much smaller than his own, McClellan asked for more troops. Lincoln dispatched a stern message to his general:

ACTIVITY
Connecting with History and Conflict

Ask students to correct each of the following incorrect statements.

- The First Battle of Bull Run was a Union victory that fed the notion that the war could be won quickly.
- The Confederacy planned an offensive war against the Union.
- By 1863 the Union was clearly on its way to winning the war. **(Verbal/Linguistic)**

BACKGROUND
Biography

The Civil War divided the nation in very cruel ways. First Lady Mary Todd Lincoln had four brothers and three brothers-in-law fighting on the Confederate side. Already a controversial figure, accused of extravagance and mental instability, Mrs. Lincoln was also alleged to be a rebel spy. Such rumors led President Lincoln to state: "I, of my own knowledge, know that it is untrue that any of my family hold treasonable communication with the enemy."

CUSTOMIZE FOR ...
Less Proficient Readers

Have students read about the *Monitor* and the *Merrimack* under the heading "War in the East." Have them list the events that ultimately led to a new kind of warship. Explain why wooden ships had become obsolete.

CAPTION ANSWERS

Viewing History The battle showed that ironclads could easily destroy wooden battleships and yet not be damaged by them. Only another ironclad could withstand an attack by an ironclad.

ACTIVITY
Connecting with Citizenship

Tell students to consider the fact that the Confederates lost more than 20,000 soldiers in the Seven Days' Battles. Then have them imagine that they are among the surviving Confederate soldiers. Ask them to write a poem, song, or journal entry reflecting on their recent experience. Encourage students to ponder how it would feel to lose so many of their comrades so quickly. **(Verbal/Linguistic)**

BACKGROUND
Recent Scholarship

Thousands of female nurses tended to the many thousands of soldiers wounded in Civil War battles. However, as historian Elizabeth Leonard documents in *Yankee Women: Gender Battles in the Civil War*, women were not always treated civilly by the male doctors with whom they worked. Mary Walker was the first female physician working for the Union forces. Despite her qualifications and the desperate need for doctors, Walker fought for years for a surgeon's commission.

American BIOGRAPHY

Robert E. Lee 1807–1870

A warm and charming Southern gentleman, Robert E. Lee came from an old and distinguished Virginia family. Among his relatives were two signers of the Declaration of Independence. In 1829, Lee graduated second in his class from West Point. Later he was recognized for outstanding service in the Mexican War.

When the Southern states seceded, Lincoln offered Lee the command of Union forces. Although he was opposed to slavery and secession, Lee refused, explaining "I cannot raise my hand against my birthplace, my home, my children." Instead, he resigned from the army and became the top military advisor to Confederate president Jefferson Davis. In May 1862, he took command of the Army of Northern Virginia, a post he held for the rest of the war. As a commander, Lee earned the loyalty and trust of his troops. Stonewall Jackson declared, "I would follow him onto the battlefield blindfolded."

> "*It is indispensable to you that you strike a blow. . . . The country will not fail to note—is now noting—that the present hesitation to move upon an entrenched enemy is but the story of Manassas repeated. . . . I have never written you . . . in greater kindness of feeling than now. . . . But you must act.*"
>
> —President Lincoln

McClellan, however, did not act. He waited outside Yorktown for about a month. When he finally advanced, the defenders abandoned their positions and retreated toward Richmond. On May 31, as McClellan's army neared the capital, the Southerners suddenly turned and attacked. Although the North claimed victory at the Battle of Seven Pines, both sides suffered heavy casualties. Among the wounded was the Confederate commander, General Joseph Johnston. Command of his army now fell to Robert E. Lee. Like all great generals, Lee believed in good training and planning. However, he also understood that victory sometimes depends on the willingness to take chances.

The South Attacks

With McClellan's forces still threatening Richmond, Lee had his opportunity to take a chance. In early June he divided his 55,000-man army, sending several thousand troops to strengthen Stonewall Jackson's forces in western Virginia. The Seven Pines battle had cut McClellan's army to about 80,000 soldiers. Lee was gambling that the overly cautious McClellan, who was awaiting reinforcements, would not attack Richmond before the Confederates could act.

General Jackson then began a brilliant act of deception: He pretended to prepare for an attack on Washington. Lincoln responded by canceling the order for McClellan's additional troops, keeping them in Washington to protect the Union capital. Jackson then slipped away to join Lee outside Richmond. In late June their combined forces attacked McClellan's larger army in a series of encounters called the Seven Days' Battles. Although the Confederates lost more than 20,000 soldiers, 4,000 more than the Union, McClellan decided to retreat.

The Second Battle of Bull Run After McClellan's failure, Lincoln turned to General John Pope, who was organizing a new army outside Washington. The President ordered McClellan's troops back to Washington and put Pope in overall command. Lee knew that he must draw Pope's army into battle before McClellan's soldiers arrived and made the size of the Union force overwhelming.

Again, Lee divided his army. In late August he sent Jackson's troops north in a sweeping movement around Pope's position. After marching 50 miles in two days, they struck behind Pope's army and destroyed some of his supplies, which were stored at Manassas. Enraged, Pope ordered his 62,000 soldiers into action to smash Jackson. On August 29, while Pope's force was engaged, Lee also attacked it with the main body of the Confederate army.

The battle was fought on virtually the same ground where McDowell had been defeated the year before. And Pope's Union troops met the same fate at this Second Battle of Bull Run. After Pope's defeat, McClellan was returned to

RESOURCE DIRECTORY

Teaching Resources

Units 1/2 booklet
- Section 1 Quiz, p. 39

Guide to the Essentials
- Section 1 Summary, p. 18

Other Print Resources

Historical Outline Map Book *Major Battles of the Civil War*, p. 50

Technology

Exploring Primary Sources in U.S. History CD-ROM *Beat! Beat! Drums!, Walt Whitman*

command. "We must use what tools we have," Lincoln said in defense of his decision. "If he can't fight himself, he excels in making others ready to fight."

The Battle of Antietam With Richmond no longer threatened, Lee decided that the time had come to invade the North. He hoped that a victory on Union soil would arouse European support for the South and turn Northern public opinion against the war. So, in early September 1862, Lee's army bypassed the Union troops guarding Washington and slipped into western Maryland. McClellan had no idea where the Confederates were. Then one of his soldiers found a copy of Lee's orders wrapped around some cigars near an abandoned Confederate camp. Now that he knew the enemy's strategy, McClellan crowed, "If I cannot whip Bobbie Lee, I will be willing to go home."

True to his nature, however, McClellan delayed some 16 hours before ordering his troops after Lee. This gave the Confederate general, who had learned that his plans were in enemy hands, time to prepare for the Union attack. The two armies met at Antietam Creek near Sharpsburg, Maryland, on September 17. Lee had about 40,000 troops, McClellan over 75,000, with nearly 25,000 more in reserve.

VIEWING HISTORY This painting depicts two great Confederate generals: Robert E. Lee, left, and Stonewall Jackson. **Drawing Conclusions** *How does the artist show which general is in command?*

Union troops attacked throughout the day, suffering heavy losses. In the first three hours of fighting, some 12,000 soldiers from both sides were killed or wounded. By day's end Union casualties had grown to over 12,000. Lee's nearly 14,000 casualties amounted to more than a third of his army. The next day the battered Confederates retreated back into Virginia. Lincoln telegraphed McClellan, "Destroy the rebel army if possible." But the ever-cautious general did not take advantage of his opportunity to destroy Lee's army.

The **Battle of Antietam** became the bloodiest day of the Civil War. "God grant these things may soon end and peace be restored," wrote a Pennsylvania soldier after the battle. "Of this war I am heartily sick and tired."

Section 1 Assessment

READING COMPREHENSION

1. Which side won the **First Battle of Bull Run?** Why?
2. What were the effects of the invention of new kinds of rifles, bullets, **shells,** and **canister?**
3. Briefly describe the war strategies of the North and the South.
4. Briefly describe the **Battle of Shiloh** and the **Battle of Antietam.**

CRITICAL THINKING AND WRITING

5. **Predicting Consequences** Choose one early Civil War battle that demonstrated the result of a lost opportunity, and describe what might have happened if a different decision had been made.
6. **Writing an Outline** Write an outline for a newspaper editorial of May 1861 in which you will argue why either the North or the South will easily win the Civil War.

Take It to the NET

Virtual Field Trip Visit the site of the Battle of Antietam, and view photos and paintings from the time of the battle and "tour" the park through current photos. Use the links provided in the *America: Pathways to the Present* area of the following Web site for help in completing this activity.
www.phschool.com

Section 1 Assessment

Reading Comprehension

1. The Confederacy, because of Jackson's stoic leadership, and the arrival of fresh troops just as the Union army was beginning to fall back.
2. They turned the tactic of attacking a position with massed troops into an act of slaughter.
3. North: implement Anaconda Plan by blockading the South and gaining control of the Mississippi river; seize Richmond. South: fight a war of attrition; apply pressure on Great Britain and France to help by stopping cotton exports.
4. Battle of Shiloh: Johnston's Confederates surprised some of Grant's troops, causing retreat. Buell's troops arrived during the night; Union forces counterattacked and won. Bloodiest battle to date; Johnston killed. Battle of Antietam: Lee decided to invade the North; Union discovered Lee's orders, delayed battle; both sides suffered great losses. Confederates retreated; Union victory. Bloodiest battle of Civil War.

Critical Thinking and Writing

5. Students should choose a battle, such as the Peninsular Campaign, and examine the leadership and strategies used, then analyze the outcome and the variables that could have been changed to alter results.
6. Answers may include a discussion of leadership, skilled troops, manpower, and geography.

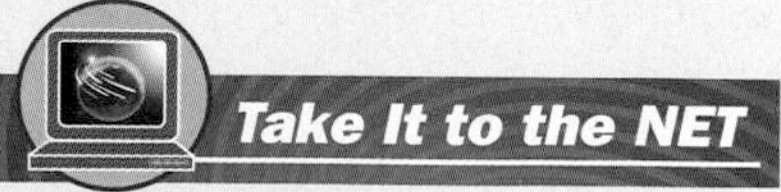

Take It to the NET

Invite students to take a Virtual Field Trip at **www.phschool.com**

CAPTION ANSWERS

Viewing History Lee's gesture indicates he is giving a command. Lee's head is also higher than Jackson's, and he has a white horse and is in sunlight.

Section 2
Life Behind the Lines

Section Objectives

1. Learn how wartime politics affected the Confederate and Union governments.
2. Discover how the Emancipation Proclamation affected both the North and the South.
3. Find out the causes and effects of African Americans' joining the Union army.
4. List the kinds of hardships that befell the North and the South during the war.

Bellringer

Warm-Up Activity Ask students to think about how the power of the federal government in the United States changed during the nation's first century. Ask them to consider the effects of war on the power of government.

Activating Prior Knowledge How did the Civil War affect the United States' relationships with England and France? Ask students to list reasons why France and England might choose to support either the Union or the Confederacy.

Reading Strategy

Have students list some possible solutions to the problems that the Confederate and Union governments faced during the war. As they read, have them take specific notes on how both sides actually responded.

Section 2
Life Behind the Lines

READING FOCUS

- How did wartime politics affect the Confederate and Union governments?
- How did the Emancipation Proclamation affect both the North and the South?
- What were the causes and effects of African Americans joining the Union army?
- What kinds of hardships befell the North and the South during the war?

MAIN IDEA

The Union and the Confederacy struggled to raise and support their armies and to provide for the well-being of their citizens. The Emancipation Proclamation had a profound effect on both those efforts.

KEY TERMS

draft
recognition
greenback
Copperhead
martial law
writ of *habeas corpus*
Emancipation Proclamation
contraband

TAKING NOTES

As you read, prepare an outline of the first part of this section. Use Roman numerals for the first two major headings, capital letters for subheads, and numbers for supporting details. Include responses to problems as shown in the sample below.

I. Politics in the South
A. Mobilizing for War
1. Not enough soldiers to fight/Lee calls for draft.
2. ______
B. ______
1. ______
2. ______

Setting the Scene By early 1862, the "picnic" atmosphere evident at the beginning of the First Battle of Bull Run was gone. It was clear that the war was going to be neither quick nor easy, and that the resources of both sides would be severely strained. The South, for example, faced a crisis of manpower. As Grant moved toward Mississippi and McClellan's army threatened Richmond, many Confederate soldiers neared the end of their enlistments. Few seemed ready to reenlist. "If I live this twelve months out, I intend to try mighty hard to keep out [of the army]," pledged one Virginia soldier. A young Wisconsin boy who had run away to join the Union Army also had second thoughts:

> *"I want to say, as we lay there and the shells were flying all over us, my thoughts went back to my home, and I thought what a foolish boy I was to run away and get into such a mess as I was in. I would have been glad to have seen my father coming after me."*
>
> —Elisha Stockwell

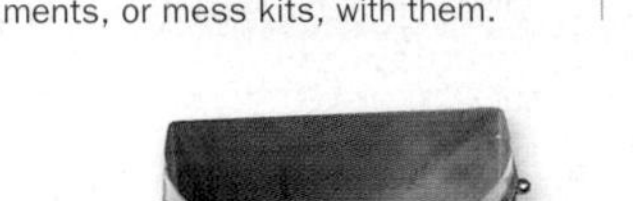

Soldiers carried their eating implements, or mess kits, with them.

Politics in the South

While both sides had to deal with the practical and political problems of a long and costly war, the South had a further difficulty. The branches and powers of the Confederate government were similar to those of the government of the United States. However, the framers of the Confederate constitution had made certain that it recognized states' rights and slavery—two of the main reasons for the South's secession from the Union. These two issues caused problems for the South throughout the war.

Like the government of the North, the Confederate government had to persuade individual citizens to sacrifice their

RESOURCE DIRECTORY

Teaching Resources
Guided Reading and Review booklet, p. 47

Other Print Resources
Historical Outline Map Book *The Southern States,* p. 44

Technology
Section Reading Support Transparencies
Guided Reading Audiotapes (English/Spanish), Ch. 4
Student Edition on Audio CD, Ch. 4
Prentice Hall Presentation Pro CD-ROM, Ch. 4
Companion Web site, www.phschool.com

personal interests for the common good. In addition, Confederate leaders had to find a way to build Southerners' loyalty to their new government. Furthermore, because the South had fewer resources than the North, its war effort depended more on making the best possible use of the resources it had. Since the Southern state governments were strong and sometimes fiercely independent, meeting these objectives would sometimes prove difficult.

Mobilizing for War Fearing the war would be lost if there were not enough soldiers to fight, General Lee called for a **draft**, or required military service. Opponents of strong central government claimed that a draft violated the principles of states' rights that the South was fighting for. A Texas senator disagreed:

> "*Cease this child's play. . . . The enemy are in some portions of almost every state in the Confederacy . . . We need a large army. How are you going to get it? . . . No man has any individual rights, which come into conflict with the welfare of the country.*"
>
> —Senator Louis Wigfall

In April 1862, the Confederate congress passed a draft law requiring three years of military service for white men ages 18 to 35. This automatically extended the service of all volunteers for two more years. After the horrible losses at Antietam, the upper age for the draft became 45. Later it was raised again to 50. The Confederate government also took charge of the South's economy. It determined how much wool, cotton, and leather should be produced, and seized control of Southern railroads from private owners. Farmers were required to contribute one tenth of their produce to the war effort.

To help raise money for the war, the Confederate congress imposed a tax on personal incomes. The Confederate government also authorized the army to seize male slaves for military labor. Though they were paid a monthly fee for borrowed slaves, planters resented this practice because it disrupted work on their plantations.

The Impact of States' Rights Not all of the mobilization efforts described above were successful. A fierce commitment to states' rights worked against the Confederate government and harmed the war effort in many ways. You will recall that the national government under the Articles of Confederation had suffered similar difficulties, and was replaced by the Constitution when Americans of that time felt the need for a stronger central government. Many Americans, especially in the South, had continued to champion states' rights—both under the United States Constitution and under the new Confederacy. The governor of Georgia put it this way:

> "*I entered into this revolution . . . to sustain the rights of the states . . . and I am still a rebel . . . no matter who may be in power.*"
>
> —Governor Joseph Brown

Many Southerners shared the governor's point of view. Local authorities sometimes refused to cooperate with draft officials. Whole counties in some states were ruled by armed bands of draft-dodgers and deserters. It is estimated that perhaps one quarter of Confederate men eligible for the draft failed to cooperate.

Focus on WORLD EVENTS

Britain and France While Britain and France had often been rivals and military foes, during the period preceding the American Civil War they had become allies. The two nations had fought on the same side in the Crimean War (1854–1856), and in 1860, Napoleon III of France had negotiated a treaty with Britain to lower tariffs levied on goods traded between them. What's more, by 1864, the German leader Bismarck was changing the balance of power in Europe and posing a threat to France.

LESSON PLAN

Focus The Civil War brought many changes to Northerners and Southerners. The national governments of both sides grew in power. How did the war affect African Americans?

Instruct Discuss the strengths and weaknesses of the Confederate government. List the ways the federal government increased its power during the war. Was Lincoln justified in taking on extraordinary powers to keep the Border States in the Union?

Assess/Reteach Based on what they are learning in the section, ask students to identify the following changes in the federal government as temporary or permanent.

- A draft law supplied troops for the army.
- Congress passed new tax laws, including a federal tax on income.
- Congress created a national currency.
- The President suspended the writ of *habeas corpus.*
- The President shut down newspapers that disagreed with his policies.

ACTIVITY
Connecting with Citizenship

The Confederacy could not rely on its own political unity due to its commitment to individual states' rights. Some believe that this attitude led to the defeat of the South. To help students understand the Unionist and Confederate beliefs about the structure of a nation, divide the class into small groups. Each group member should give an example of one situation in his or her life in which pooling resources was more beneficial than doing something alone, and one in which it was not. **(Verbal/Linguistic)**

CUSTOMIZE FOR ...
Less Proficient Readers

Ask students to turn each of the section's headings and subheadings into a question. Have them then skim the text to answer these questions before reading the section.

ACTIVITY
Connecting with Government

Divide the class into two groups. One group will represent those who opposed the Confederate draft law of 1862, and the other will represent the Confederate congress. Let students brainstorm in their groups and list reasons why their views are correct. Have a volunteer from each group represent the group's position. **(Verbal/Linguistic)**

BACKGROUND
A Diverse Nation

Antislavery activities grew in the Border States in anticipation of emancipation. For example, Wisconsin infantryman Stanley Lathrop wrote from northern Arkansas: "We are the first Federal troops who have ever been in this part of the state. Almost all the rich plantation owners have fled as usual, and their Negroes are beginning to come to us. . . . Colonel Daniels says he did not persuade them to run away and he will not return them as the Fugitive Slave law privilege of habeas corpus etc. are suspended."

VIEWING FINE ART After operating for about 21 months, the Confederate privateer *Alabama* was finally sunk by the U.S.S. *Kearsarge* off the coast of France, as shown in this 1864 painting by Edouard Manet. **Determining Relevance** *Why was the South's ability to capture Union merchant vessels important to the Confederacy?*

"If we are defeated," warned an Atlanta newspaper, "it will be by the people at home."

Seeking Help From Europe Although the Union blockade effectively prevented Southern cotton from reaching Great Britain and France, Southerners continued to hope for British and French intervention in the war. In May 1861, the Confederate government sent representatives to both nations. Even though the Confederacy failed to gain **recognition,** or official acceptance as an independent nation, it did receive some help. Great Britain agreed to allow its ports to be used to build Confederate privateers. One of these vessels, the *Alabama,* captured more than 60 Northern merchant ships. In all, 11 British-built Confederate privateers forced most Union shipping from the high seas for much of the war.

Formal recognition of the Confederacy did seem possible for a time in 1862. Napoleon III, the ruler of France, had sent troops into Mexico, trying to rebuild a French empire in the Americas. He welcomed the idea of an independent Confederate States of America on Mexico's northern border. However, France would not openly support the Confederacy without Great Britain's cooperation.

British opinion about the war was divided. Some leaders clearly sympathized with the Southerners. Many believed an independent South would be a better market for British products. However, there was also strong antislavery feeling in Britain, and there were those who did not want to come to the aid of a slave-owning nation. Others questioned whether the Confederacy would be able to win the war. The British government adopted a wait-and-see attitude. To get foreign help, the South would first have to prove itself on the battlefield.

Politics in the North

After early losses to Confederate forces, President Lincoln and his government had to convince some Northern citizens that maintaining the Union was worth the sacrifices they were being asked to make. As in the South, efforts focused on raising troops and uniting the nation behind the war effort. In addition, the federal government found itself facing international crises as it worked to strengthen civilian support for the war.

Tensions With Great Britain British talks with the South aroused tensions between Great Britain and the United States. Late in 1861, Confederate president Davis again sent two representatives from the Confederacy to England and France. After evading the Union blockade, John Slidell and James Mason boarded the British mail ship *Trent* and steamed for Europe.

Soon a Union warship stopped the *Trent* in international waters, removed the two Confederate officials, and brought them to the United States. An outraged British government sent troops to Canada and threatened war unless Slidell and Mason were freed. President Lincoln ordered their release. "One war at a time," he said.

CAPTION ANSWERS

Viewing Fine Art The capture of Union merchant vessels by Southern privateers limited the Union's ability to earn money through trade and get supplies from abroad.

RESOURCE DIRECTORY

Other Print Resources

American History Block Scheduling Support *Experiences of the Civil War Soldier,* found in the Expansion, Reconstruction, and Immigration folder, includes interdisciplinary lesson suggestions and activities for Geography and History, Primary Sources, Biography, and Literature.

Historical Outline Map Book *The Northern States,* p. 43

Technology

Exploring Primary Sources in U.S. History CD-ROM *The Education of Henry Adams: Foes or Friends, Henry Adams*

The Union vigorously protested Great Britain's support of the Confederacy. Lincoln demanded $19 billion compensation from Great Britain for damages done by the privateers built in British ports, and for other British actions on the South's behalf. This demand strained relations between the United States and Great Britain for nearly a decade after the war.

READING CHECK What caused tension between the Union and Great Britain?

Republicans in Control With Southern Democrats out of the United States Congress, Republican lawmakers had little opposition. The Civil War Congresses thus became among the most active in American history. Republicans were able to pass a number of laws during the war that would have a lasting impact, even well after the South rejoined the Union.

For example, Southerners had long opposed building a rail line across the Great Plains. It was first proposed by Illinois senator Stephen Douglas in the early 1850s, in part to benefit Chicago by linking that city to the West. In July 1862, however, Congress passed the Pacific Railroad Act with little resistance. The law allowed the federal government to give land and money to companies for construction of a railroad line from Nebraska to the Pacific Coast. The Homestead Act, passed in the same year, offered free government land to people willing to settle on it.

The disappearance of Southern opposition also allowed Congress to raise tariff rates. The tariff became more a device to protect Northern industries than to provide revenue for the government. Union leaders turned to other means to raise money for the war.

Financial Measures In 1861, the Republican-controlled Congress passed the first federal tax on income in American history. It collected 3 percent of the income of people earning more than $600 a year but less than $10,000, which is the equivalent of about $11,000 to $180,000 today. Those making more than $10,000 per year were taxed at 5 percent. The Internal Revenue Act of 1862 imposed taxes on items such as liquor, tobacco, medicine, and newspaper ads. Nearly all of these taxes ended when the war was over.

During the war, Congress also reformed the nation's banking system. Since 1832, when President Jackson vetoed the recharter of the Second Bank of the United States, Americans had relied on state banks. In 1862, Congress passed an act that created a national currency, called **greenbacks** because of their color. This paper money was not backed by gold, but was declared by Congress to be acceptable for legal payment of all public and private debts.

Opposition to the War Like the South, the North instituted a draft in order to raise troops for what now looked like a longer, more difficult war. And like the Southern law, this March 1863 measure allowed the wealthy to buy their way out of military service. Riots broke out in the North after the draft law was passed. Mobs of whites in New York City vented their rage at the draft in July 1863. More than 100 people died during four days of destruction. At least 11 of the dead were African Americans, who seemed to be targeted by the rioters.

There was political opposition to the war as well. Although the Democrats remaining in Congress were too few to have much power, one group raised their voices in protest against the war. This group was nicknamed **Copperheads,** after a type of poisonous snake. These Democrats warned that Republican policies would bring a flood of freed slaves to the North. What's more, they predicted that these freed slaves

Focus on GOVERNMENT

Civil War Conscription The Civil War marked the first time that conscription, or the draft, was instituted in the United States. Both sides used it to raise troops, and both sides used it unfairly. In the South, owners of 20 or more slaves were excused from serving. A Northerner could pay the government $300 to avoid service. In both the Union and the Confederacy, wealthy men could hire substitutes to fight in their place. No wonder many angry Southerners called the conflict "a rich man's war and a poor man's fight."

ACTIVITY
Connecting with Today

The first income tax was levied during the Civil War. But it did not remain in place for very long. Have students research the history of the income tax in the United States to discover when it was abandoned following the Civil War, when it started up again, and so forth. Can students list the reasons why federal taxes were levied and then rescinded at certain times? How does the 5–10 percent tax rate of the Civil War era compare with tax brackets today? **(Logical/Mathematical)**

BACKGROUND
Interdisciplinary

The term *Copperhead* was first used by James Gordon Bennett, editor of the *New York Herald,* on July 20, 1861. He compared a group opposed to the Civil War to copperhead snakes, which strike savagely without warning. "A rattlesnake rattles, a viper hisses, an adder spits, a black snake whistles, a water snake blows, but a copperhead just sneaks," he wrote.

READING CHECK The Confederacy found sympathy in Great Britain. The Lincoln administration was enraged that Great Britain built privateers, such as the *Alabama,* for the Confederacy. The *Trent* episode greatly angered the government of Great Britain.

TEST PREPARATION

Have students reread the section titled "Seeking Help from Europe" on the previous page and then answer the question below.

Which of the following does not belong?

- Ⓐ Napoleon III supported the Union cause.
- **B** Napoleon III supported the Confederate cause in the Civil War.
- **C** France's effort to gain control of Mexico would be helped by an independent Confederate States of America.
- **D** Great Britain was sympathetic in some ways with the Confederacy.

ACTIVITY
Connecting with Government

Divide students into small discussion groups. Have each group discuss the pros and cons of preserving the Union. Why was Lincoln so determined to keep the nation intact? What kinds of problems would the country have faced if Lincoln's convictions had been weaker? **(Verbal/Linguistic)**

BACKGROUND
Geography in History

Maryland was an important state during the Civil War for several reasons. In addition to being on the brink of seceding, Maryland was geographically significant because of its proximity to Washington. Confederate General Stonewall Jackson wanted to capture a Northern city, such as Baltimore or Philadelphia. Baltimore was appealing because it was where all the Northern railways merged. Jackson hoped to block the railroads that delivered food and supplies to Washington. However, General Lee ultimately rejected Jackson's strategy.

From the Archives of
American Heritage®

About the Presidents

Abraham Lincoln (1861–1865) faced a multitude of problems in 1862. McClellan, his difficult general, was only one. On the one hand, abolitionists called for a total war on slavery. On the other, defeatists said that peace was more important than the Union. Lincoln's Cabinet was divided, too. Many members had personal ambitions. (Secretary Seward, for example, had challenged Lincoln's experience and authority.) Desertions from the army were constant. To make matters worse, Lincoln faced terrible personal grief: the death of his 11-year-old son, Willie. Source: Wilson Sullivan, "Abraham Lincoln," *The American Heritage® Pictorial History of the Presidents of the United States,* vol. 1, 1968.

would take jobs away from whites. Radical Copperheads also tried to persuade Union soldiers to desert the army, and they urged other Northerners to resist the draft.

Emergency Wartime Actions Like the government of the Confederacy, the United States government exercised great power during the Civil War. To silence the Copperheads and other opponents of the war, Lincoln resorted to extreme measures. He used the army to shut down opposition newspapers and denied others the use of the mails.

The border states provided a special set of problems. Four of them were slave states that remained—at least for the moment—in the Union. Because of their locations, the continued loyalty of Delaware, Maryland, Missouri, and Kentucky was critical to the North. Lincoln considered Delaware, where few citizens held slaves, to be secure. In nearby Maryland, however, support for secession was strong. In September 1861, Lincoln ordered that all "disloyal" members of the Maryland state legislature be arrested. This action prevented a vote on secession and assured that Washington would not be surrounded by the Confederacy.

The Union needed the loyalty of Kentucky and Missouri in order to keep control of the Ohio and Mississippi rivers. In Missouri, Lincoln supported an uprising aimed at overthrowing the pro-Confederate state government. To secure Kentucky, he put the state under **martial law** for part of the war. This is emergency rule by military authorities, during which some Bill of Rights

NOTABLE PRESIDENTS
Abraham Lincoln

"A house divided against itself cannot stand."
—Speech in 1858

Abraham Lincoln entered the White House with little experience in national politics. Before being elected in 1860, he had been a successful lawyer in Illinois and a one-term member of Congress. Nothing, however, could have prepared him for the extraordinary challenges he would face as President.

Lincoln confronted crises on every side. Southern states began seceding from the Union even before he took office. The border states had to be kept in the Union. Many Northerners who opposed secession did not want to fight the South, and white Northerners disagreed among themselves about slavery.

Lincoln's actions as President all pointed toward one goal: preserve the Union. He changed commanding generals again and again in a desperate search for one who could defeat the Confederate army. He suppressed freedom of speech and assembly. He issued the Emancipation Proclamation to free the slaves living behind Confederate lines, and in 1863 he called upon free blacks to join the Union army.

Along with his commitment to preserve the Union, Lincoln's greatest strengths were his sense of compassion and his ability to express powerful ideas in simple yet moving language. In fact, his words have come to help define the Civil War, from his warning that "A house divided against itself cannot stand" to his hope in 1865 that Americans would face the future "with malice toward none, with charity for all." Lincoln did not live to work for the compassionate peace he favored, but he had done more than any other single person to preserve the Union at its time of greatest danger.

16th President
1861–1865

Connecting to Today
How important is it that a President be able to rally people behind a cause?

Take It to the NET **Biography** To read more about Abraham Lincoln, visit the links provided in the *America: Pathways to the Present* area at the following Web site. **www.phschool.com**

RESOURCE DIRECTORY

Teaching Resources
Learning with Documents booklet (Key Documents) *The Emancipation Proclamation,* p. xx

Technology
RESOURCE PRO® **Biography** *Mary Elizabeth Bowser,* found on Resource Pro, profiles a former slave and important spy for the Union.
Exploring Primary Sources in U.S. History CD-ROM *Emancipation Proclamation*

guarantees are suspended. Although Jefferson Davis imposed martial law on parts of the Confederacy, Lincoln is the only United States President ever to exercise this power.

In some places Lincoln suspended the ***writ of habeas corpus.*** This is a legal protection requiring that a court determine if a person is lawfully imprisoned. Without it, people can be held in jail for indefinite periods even though they are not charged with a crime. The Constitution allows suspension of the writ of *habeas corpus* during a rebellion.

More than 13,000 Americans who objected to the Union government's policies were imprisoned without trial during the Civil War. They included newspaper editors and elected state officials, plus Southern sympathizers and some who actually did aid the Confederacy. Most Northerners approved of Lincoln's actions as necessary to restore the Union.

Extent of the Emancipation Proclamation, 1863

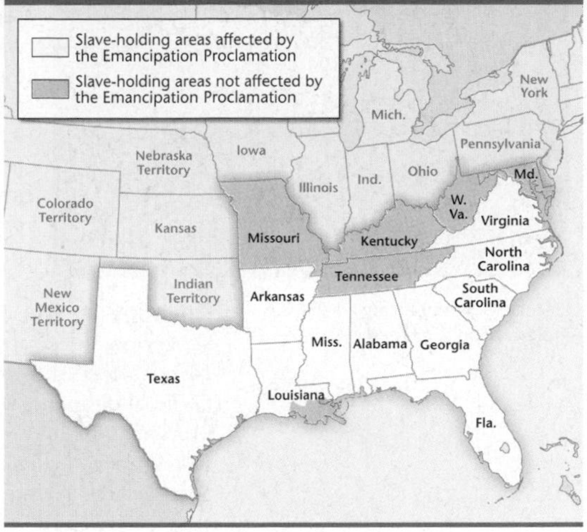

MAP SKILLS This map shows where the Emancipation Proclamation actually freed the slaves. The state of Tennessee and small areas of Virginia and Louisiana were parts of the Confederacy occupied by Union troops, so they were no longer "in rebellion." **Region** *Where could the emancipation of slaves be enforced? Explain. Why was the Emancipation Proclamation important anyway?*

Emancipation and the War

While the Copperheads attacked Lincoln for making war on the South, abolitionists and others attacked him for not making the military action a war to end slavery. As the Union's battlefield casualties mounted, many Northerners began to question whether it was enough to simply restore the nation. Some, including a group in the Republican Party called the Radical Republicans, thought that the Confederacy should be punished for causing so much suffering. No punishment could be worse, the Radical Republicans argued, than freeing the slaveholders' "property."

Lincoln and Slavery At first, the President resisted pressure to make the abolition of slavery a goal of the war. He insisted that under the Constitution he was bound only to preserve and protect the Union. Lincoln explained this view in a letter to Horace Greeley, an abolitionist newspaper editor:

> "*My paramount object in this struggle is to save the Union, and is not to either save or to destroy slavery. If I could save the Union without freeing any slave, I would do it, and if I could save the Union by freeing all the slaves, I would do it; and if I could save it by freeing some and leaving others alone, I would also do that.*"
>
> —President Lincoln

Although Lincoln personally opposed slavery, he did not believe that he had the legal authority to abolish it. He also worried about the effect such an action would have on the loyalty of the border states. However, Lincoln recognized the importance of slavery to the South's war effort. Every slave working in a field or in a factory freed a white Southerner to shoot at Union soldiers. Gradually, Lincoln came to regard ending slavery as one more strategy for winning the war.

The Emancipation Proclamation In the fall of 1862, as Lee retreated south from Antietam, Lincoln proclaimed that on January 1, 1863, slaves in areas of rebellion against the government would be free. Then, on New Year's Day, 1863, he issued the final **Emancipation Proclamation:**

ACTIVITY
Connecting with Government

Have students analyze the following statement by Viscount Palmerston, a contemporary British observer, that in the Emancipation Proclamation, Lincoln attempted "to abolish slavery where he was without power to do so, while protecting it where he had power to destroy it." Ask students to explain and then agree or disagree with the statement. Did Lincoln accomplish his purpose with the Emancipation Proclamation? **(Verbal/Linguistic)**

BACKGROUND
Interdisciplinary

American poet Walt Whitman (1819–1892), best known for *Leaves of Grass,* volunteered as a hospital nurse in Washington from 1862 until 1865. He also worked as a clerk in the Department of the Interior, but was dismissed from that job because of claims that *Leaves of Grass* was immoral. Whitman wrote two volumes of poetry inspired by the Civil War, *Drum-Taps* and *Sequel to Drum-Taps.* Students may be interested in reading Whitman's poems about Lincoln: "When Lilacs Last in the Dooryard Bloom'd" and "O Captain! My Captain!"

CUSTOMIZE FOR ...
Gifted and Talented

Have students copy the following statement: "The Civil War forever changed the relationship between Americans and their government and gave a new meaning to American citizenship." After reading the section, have them discuss and analyze reasons to support this statement.

CAPTION ANSWERS

Map Skills It could not really be enforced since it applied only to areas under Confederate control. However, it had an important psychological effect: it rallied support of antislavery Northerners; it ended any real chance that France or Britain (where the abolition movement was strong) would recognize the Confederacy, and it caused resentment in the South. It also encouraged slaves to run away and join the Union army.

ACTIVITY
Connecting with Culture

Tell students that the signing of the Emancipation Proclamation put an end to the need for the Underground Railroad. Although this secret network had provided an escape for thousands of slaves, many others had been captured and in some cases tortured or killed along the way. The risk of escape and the hope for freedom inspired music. Have students research the spiritual music that was sung as an expression of these feelings. **(Musical/Rhythmic)**

BACKGROUND
A Diverse Nation

When African American soldiers joined the Union army, they were paid only $7 a month, compared to the $13 a month paid other soldiers. James Gooding, an African American soldier, wrote to President Lincoln, "We have done a soldier's duty. Why can't we have a soldier's pay?"

Lincoln reads the Emancipation Proclamation to his cabinet.

KEY DOCUMENTS *"I, Abraham Lincoln, President of the United States, by virtue of the power in me vested as Commander-in-Chief, of the Army and Navy of the United States in time of actual armed rebellion against the authority and government of the United States, and as a fit and necessary war measure for suppressing said rebellion . . . do order and declare that all persons held as slaves within said designated States, and parts of States, are and henceforward shall be free. . . ."*

—President Lincoln, January 1863

Reaction to the Proclamation The decree had little direct impact on slavery because it applied only to places that were under Confederate control. Nevertheless, it was condemned in the South and debated in the North. Some abolitionists criticized Lincoln for not having gone far enough. The proclamation did nothing to free people enslaved in the border states, nor did it free slaves living in Confederate areas controlled by Union forces. Other Northerners, fearing that freed people coming north would cause unemployment, criticized even this limited action. After Lincoln's September announcement, the Democratic Party made gains in the congressional elections of November 1862.

The response of black Northerners was much more positive. "We shout for joy that we live to record this righteous decree," abolitionist Frederick Douglass exclaimed. Even if the proclamation brought no immediate end to slavery, it promised, through the word *henceforward,* that an enslaved people would be free when the North won the war.

Perhaps the most significant reaction occurred in Europe. The abolition movement was strong in England. The Emancipation Proclamation, coupled with news of Lee's defeat at Antietam, ended any real chance that France and Great Britain would intervene in the war.

African Americans Join the War

The Emancipation Proclamation had two immediate effects. It inspired Southern slaves who heard about it to free themselves by escaping to the protection of Union troops. It also encouraged African Americans to join the Union army.

The Contraband Issue Union troops had been making gains in the South. Southern slaveholders sometimes fled with their slaves when the Union army approached. Frequently, however, slaves remained behind or escaped to the safety of nearby Union forces. Believing they had no choice, some Union officers gave these slaves back to slaveholders who demanded the return of their "property."

Early in the war, Union general Benjamin Butler devised a legal argument that allowed the Union army to free escaped slaves they captured. It was generally accepted that, during war, one side's possessions could be seized by its enemy. Called **contraband,** these captured items then became the property of the enemy government. Butler maintained that if slaves were property then they could be considered contraband of war. The Union government, as their new owner, could then let the slaves go.

At first, the army employed these freed African Americans to build fortifications, drive wagons, and perform other noncombat jobs. After the Emancipation Proclamation, however, many former slaves enlisted to fight the Confederacy.

African American Soldiers When the Civil War began, black volunteers were not allowed to join the Union army. In July 1862, following McClellan's defeats in Virginia, Congress authorized Lincoln to accept African Americans into the military. Several months later, Lincoln made the announcement in the Emancipation Proclamation.

Given this encouragement, African Americans rushed to join the fight. By 1865, nearly 180,000 African Americans had enlisted in the Union army. More than half were black Southerners who had been freed from slavery by the fighting. For these soldiers, fighting to help free others who were still enslaved held special meaning. Many African Americans viewed the chance to fight against slavery as a milestone in their history. In total, African Americans composed almost 10 percent of the troops who served the North during the war.

On warships, black and white sailors served together. African American soldiers, however, served in all-black regiments under the command of white officers. Until June 1864, African Americans earned less pay than white soldiers.

In July 1863, an African American regiment earned a place in history at Fort Wagner, a stronghold that protected the harbor at Charleston, South Carolina. On July 18, the 54th Massachusetts Infantry, commanded by Colonel Robert Gould Shaw, led the attack on the fort. The regiment's charge across a narrow spit of sand cost it nearly half its men. Sergeant William Carney, the first African American to earn the Congressional Medal of Honor, was among the survivors. So were Frederick Douglass's two sons, one of whom wrote this in a letter to his sweetheart:

VIEWING HISTORY Over the course of the Civil War, nearly 180,000 African Americans wore the Union uniform. **Recognizing Cause and Effect** *How did the Emancipation Proclamation change the role of African Americans in the military?*

> "*I have been in two fights . . . The last was desperate. [W]e charged that terrible battery on Morris Island known as Fort Wagner. . . . I escaped unhurt. . . . Should I fall in the next fight killed or wounded I hope I fall with my face to the foe. . . . Remember if I die I die in a good cause. . . .*"
>
> —Lewis Douglass

The actions of the 54th Massachusetts demonstrated what Lewis's father, Frederick Douglass, wrote in his newspaper the following month:

> "*Once let a black man get upon his person the brass letters, U.S.; let him get an eagle on his button, and a musket on his shoulder and bullets in his pocket, and there is no power on earth which can deny that he has earned the right to citizenship.*"
>
> —Frederick Douglass

The Hardships of War

The Emancipation Proclamation and the welcoming of black troops into the Union army drastically changed the culture and the economy in the South. First, these developments prompted thousands of slaves to escape to freedom. Some who remained on plantations resisted the continuation of slavery by not

ACTIVITY
Connecting with History and Conflict

Tell students to imagine that they are African American soldiers from the South who recently joined the Union effort. Have each student write a letter home telling about the experience. Suggest that students write about how it feels to be fighting against the Confederacy. Encourage students also to consider some of the negative aspects of the experience, such as getting less pay than their white counterparts. **(Verbal/Linguistic)**

BACKGROUND
Connections to Today

Students can see the story of the 54th Massachusetts Regiment retold in the film *Glory.* The film, which won three Academy Awards in 1989, also won praise for its attention to historical detail. Historian Peter Burchard wrote: "It took great heart . . . to tell the story of the 54th as it is told in *Glory*—from the point of view of the regiment's rank and file."

TEST PREPARATION

Have students reread the two quotes on this page and then answer the question below.

How did African Americans view the chance to fight on the side of the Union in the Civil War?

A They resisted having to go to war.
(B) They were proud to be able to fight for a cause they believed in.
C They were indifferent to the outcome of the war.
D They preferred to fight on the Confederate side.

CAPTION ANSWERS

Viewing History It encouraged freed African Americans to volunteer to serve in the Union army as combat soldiers.

ACTIVITY
Connecting with Economics

Have students role-play a group of Southern women who are responsible for keeping their households running during the war. Tell them that their discussion should mirror some of the concerns that Southern women faced—food shortages, lack of supplies to make repairs to their homes, the need to earn money while also keeping their children safe. Encourage students to come up with creative yet realistic solutions to some of their problems. **(Bodily/Kinesthetic)**

BACKGROUND
Recent Scholarship

In *Civil War Stories,* historian Catherine Clinton examines the effects of the Civil War on women and children. Because of the immense number of men slaughtered on the battlefields, many Americans lost sons and brothers. The war also resulted in a tremendous loss of husbands and fathers. More children became orphans during the Civil War than at any other time during the nineteenth century. Numerous orphanages, many affiliated with religious organizations, sprang up during this time to address the problem.

doing their work or by destroying farm equipment. These developments hurt the Confederacy in two ways. They depleted or weakened the South's labor force, and they provided the North with even greater numerical advantages in the war effort.

The war produced drastic changes in the lives of both Northerners and Southerners. With the majority of men off fighting, women on both sides took on new responsibilities. Wives and mothers lived with the fear that every day could bring news of the loss of a loved one. In addition, both sides faced labor shortages, inflation, and other economic problems. By 1863, however, it was clear that the North's greater resources were allowing it to meet these challenges, while the South could not.

The Southern Economy Among the problems the Confederacy faced during the war was a food shortage. Invading armies disrupted the South's food-growing regions as well as its production of cotton. In parts of the South not threatened by Union forces, the Confederate draft pulled large numbers of white males out of rural areas. Southern women worked the land, oversaw slaves, and tried to keep farms and plantations operating. However, food production declined in the South as the war progressed.

Many planters made the problem worse by resisting the central government's pleas to shift from raising cotton to growing food crops. While cotton piled up in warehouses due to the Union blockade, food riots erupted in Southern cities. The worst of these occurred in Richmond, where nearly 1,000 women looted bakeries and other shops in April 1863.

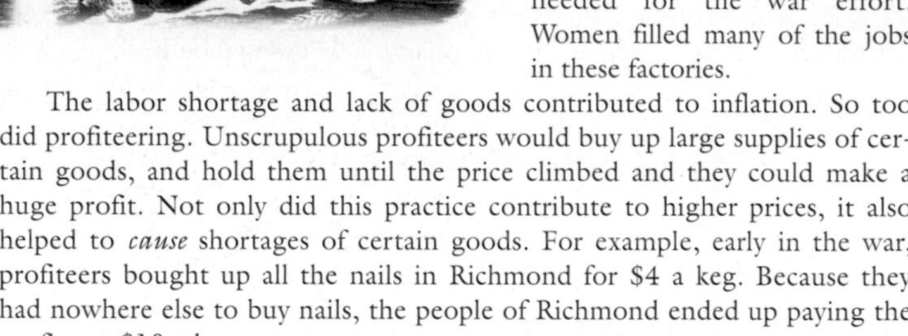

INTERPRETING POLITICAL CARTOONS This cartoon was published in a Northern newspaper. At left, Southern women urge their men to go off to war. The panel on the right shows the bread riots resulting from the war. **Recognizing Ideologies** *What is the cartoonist saying about the women's responsibility for their plight?*

Although the Confederacy was never able to provide all the manufactured goods its army needed, Southern industry grew during the war. The Confederate government supervised construction of factories to make railroad track, guns and ammunition, and many other items needed for the war effort. Women filled many of the jobs in these factories.

The labor shortage and lack of goods contributed to inflation. So too did profiteering. Unscrupulous profiteers would buy up large supplies of certain goods, and hold them until the price climbed and they could make a huge profit. Not only did this practice contribute to higher prices, it also helped to *cause* shortages of certain goods. For example, early in the war, profiteers bought up all the nails in Richmond for $4 a keg. Because they had nowhere else to buy nails, the people of Richmond ended up paying the profiteers $10 a keg.

The hardships at home increased desertions in the Confederate army. Some soldiers returned home to work their farms and help provide for their wives and children. "We are poor men and are willing to defend our country but our families [come] first," a Mississippi soldier declared.

CAPTION ANSWERS

Interpreting Political Cartoons The cartoonist is blaming the women for their plight: if they hadn't urged their men to fight this war and supported secession, they would not be hungry now. There is a sense of "you got what you deserved."

The Northern Economy In the North, the war hurt industries that depended heavily on Southern markets or Southern cotton. However, most Northern industries boomed. Unlike the Confederacy, the North had the farms and factories to produce nearly everything its army and civilian population needed. War-related industries fared especially well. Philip Armour made a fortune packaging pork to feed Union soldiers. Samuel Colt ran his factory night and day producing guns for the army.

As in the South, when men went off to war, women filled critical jobs in factories and on farms. Many factory owners preferred women employees because they could be paid less than male workers. This hiring practice kept wages down overall. Prices rose faster than pay during the war.

A few manufacturers made their profits even greater by selling the Union government inferior products: rusty rifles, boats that leaked, hats that dissolved in the rain. Uniforms made from compressed rags quickly fell apart. The soles came off some boots after a few miles of marching. Like the Southern profiteers, these manufacturers took shameful advantage of the needs of their countrymen.

Prison Camps Captured Confederate soldiers were sent to prison camps throughout the North, including Point Lookout in Maryland and Camp Chase in Ohio. The Ohio Penitentiary also housed some Confederate prisoners. The South's prison camps were located wherever there was room. Andersonville, its most notorious camp, was in a field in Georgia. Richmond's Libby Prison was a converted tobacco warehouse.

The North and the South generally treated their prisoners about the same. In most cases officers received better treatment than other prisoners. Andersonville was the exception. Built to hold 10,000 men, it eventually confined nearly 35,000 Northerners in a fenced, 26-acre open area. About 100 prisoners a day died, usually of starvation or exposure. The camp's commander was the only Confederate to be tried for war crimes after the South's defeat. He was convicted and hanged.

Medical Care While soldiers faced miserable conditions in prison camps, life was not much better in the battle camps. Health and medical conditions on both sides were frightful. About one in four Civil War soldiers did not survive the war, but it was disease that killed many of them. Poor nutrition and contaminated food led to dysentery and typhoid fever. Malaria, spread by mosquitoes, was also a killer. Many soldiers died of pneumonia.

A Union soldier was three times more likely to die in camp or in a hospital than he was to be killed on the battlefield. In fact, about one in five Union soldiers wounded in battle later died from their wounds. While most doctors were aware of the relationship between cleanliness and infection, they did not know how to sterilize their equipment. Surgeons sometimes went for days without even washing their instruments.

On both sides, thousands of women volunteered to care for the sick and wounded. Government clerk Clara Barton quit her job in order to provide supplies and first aid to Union troops in camp and during battle. Known to soldiers as the "angel of the battlefield," Barton continued her service after the war by founding the American Red Cross. Mental health reformer Dorothea Dix volunteered to organize and head the Union army's nursing corps. Nursing was a difficult task, as the following letter shows:

Focus on ECONOMICS

Inflation in the South As the war dragged on and Union armies advanced into the South, shortages and the falling value of Confederate currency caused almost unbelievable inflation. Inflation is a steady increase in prices over time. Even by late 1862, a bag of salt that had cost $2 before the war was selling for $60 in some places. Southerner Rose Frye remembered the price of calico going from 50 cents to $20 per yard, and paying $125 for shoes.

Another way to look at inflation is to compare the value of Confederate currency to $100 worth of gold as shown in this graph.

ACTIVITY
Connecting with History and Conflict

Conditions were grim not only for captured and wounded soldiers, but for just about everyone involved in the Civil War. Have groups of students discuss their own perceptions of the Civil War experience. Ask them to consider why movies, TV shows, and documentaries don't generally show soldiers as thin, starving, and clothed in ripped uniforms. **(Verbal/Linguistic)**

BACKGROUND
A Diverse Nation

Soldiers fighting for the Confederacy were more likely to die in battle than their Union counterparts. Between 37 and 39 percent of Confederate men were killed in battle, whereas 17.5 percent of Union soldiers died on the battlefield. Estimates indicate that between 750,000 and 850,000 men served on the Confederate side. At least 258,000 of them died during the war. While 94,000 died on the battlefield, 164,000 died from disease. On the Union side, about 2.2 million men served during the war. About 360,000 Union soldiers died during the war, 110,100 in battle and the rest from disease or accidents.

CUSTOMIZE FOR ...
ESL

To help students understand the main idea of the section, have them list the effects of the Emancipation Proclamation on the Union's efforts to raise and support an army and on the Confederacy's efforts to raise and support an army.

Section 2 Assessment

Reading Comprehension

1. Southern draft laws required: three years of military service for white men ages 18 to 35; extended service of all volunteers for two more years; upper age for draft eventually extended to 50; owners of 20 or more slaves were excused. North instituted similar laws, and Northerners could pay the government to avoid service. In both North and South, wealthy men could hire substitutes to fight in their place.
2. Copperheads were Democrats who believed that Republican policies would bring freed slaves to the North, taking jobs away from whites. They tried to persuade Union soldiers to desert the army and urged other Northerners to resist the draft.
3. Lincoln used martial law, suspending some Bill of Rights guarantees, to ensure that Kentucky would remain loyal to the Union. The suspension of the writ of habeas corpus imprisoned, without trial, those who objected to the Union government's policies during the war.
4. Lincoln recognized the importance of slavery to the South's war effort, and came to regard ending slavery as another strategy to end the war.

Critical Thinking and Writing

5. Wigfall's: Allegiance to welfare and preservation of the nation and the ideals on which it was founded.
6. Students' lists should highlight: Southern slaves freed themselves by escaping to the protection of Union troops; encouraged African Americans to join the Union army.

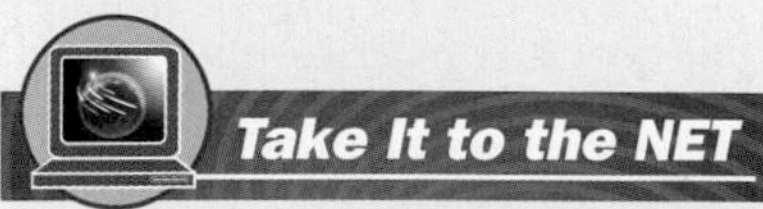

Answers will vary. Students should note that the branches and powers of the government were similar in both documents, but the Confederate constitution recognized states' rights and slavery.

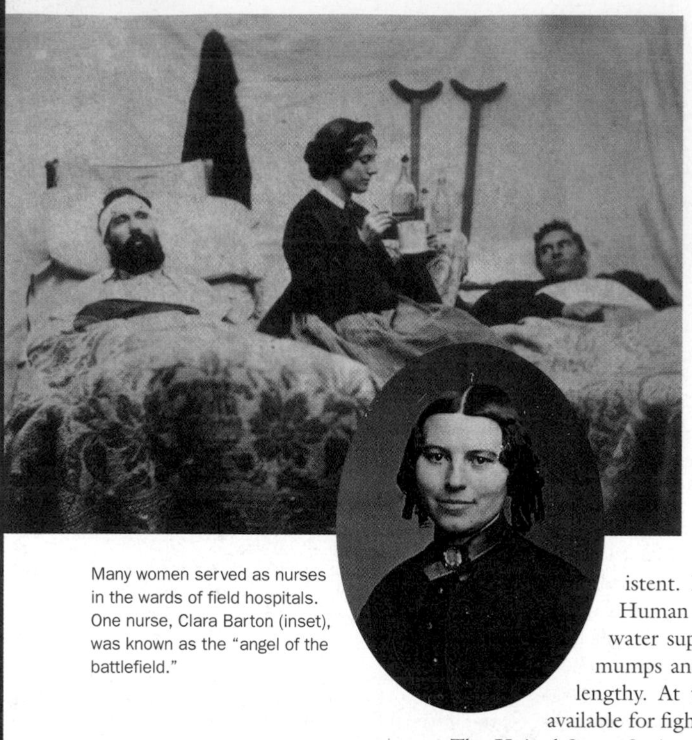

Many women served as nurses in the wards of field hospitals. One nurse, Clara Barton (inset), was known as the "angel of the battlefield."

"I am very tired tonight; I have been in the field all day. There are no words in the English language to express the sufferings I witnessed today. The men lie on the ground; their clothes have been cut off them to dress their wounds; they . . . have nothing but hardtack to eat. . . . [F]our surgeons, none of whom were idle for fifteen minutes at a time, were busy all day amputating legs and arms. . . . I would get on first rate if they would not ask me to write to their wives; that I cannot do without crying, which is not pleasant to either party."

—Cornelia Hancock

Some 4,000 women served as nurses for the Northern army. By the end of the war, nursing was no longer only a man's profession.

Sanitation in most army camps was nonexistent. Rubbish and rotting food littered the ground. Human waste and heaps of animal manure polluted water supplies. Epidemics of contagious diseases, such as mumps and measles, swept through camps. Sick lists were lengthy. At times only half the troops in a regiment were available for fighting.

The United States Sanitary Commission, created in June 1861, attempted to combat these problems. Thousands of volunteers, mostly women, inspected army hospitals and camps. They organized cleanups and provided advice about controlling infection, disease prevention, sewage disposal, and nutrition. Despite these and similar Confederate efforts, about twice as many soldiers on each side died from disease as from enemy gunfire.

Section 2 Assessment

READING COMPREHENSION

1. Describe the **draft** laws in the North and the South.
2. Who were the **Copperheads?**
3. How were **martial law** and the suspension of the **writ of *habeas corpus*** used to stifle dissent?
4. Why did Lincoln decide to issue the **Emancipation Proclamation?**

CRITICAL THINKING AND WRITING

5. **Comparing Points of View** Compare the quotes from Senator Louis Wigfall and Governor Joseph Brown. Given the measures President Lincoln used during the war, which position do you think he would have favored?
6. **Writing a List** Make a list of the effects of the Emancipation Proclamation in both the North and the South. Underline the two most important effects.

Take It to the NET

Activity: Making a Chart Read the constitutions of the United States and the Confederacy. Make a chart showing three important similarities and three important differences between the documents. Use the links provided in the *America: Pathways to the Present* area of the following Web site for help in completing this activity.
www.phschool.com

RESOURCE DIRECTORY

Teaching Resources
Units 1/2 booklet
- Section 2 Quiz, p. 40

Guide to the Essentials
- Section 2 Summary, p. 19

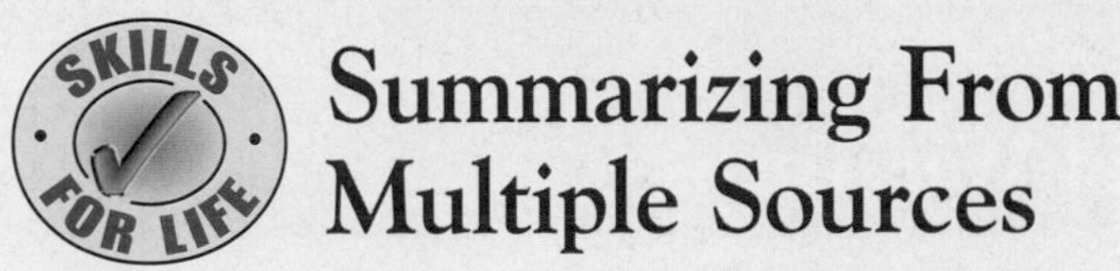

Summarizing From Multiple Sources

When you are doing research, you will often find two or more sources with information about one topic. Combining the main ideas of these sources into a single summary can provide a more complete picture of events than either source could alone. You can also use each source to test the reliability of the others: if the sources do not seem to agree, you should do further research to find out which ones provide the most reliable information.

In February 1865, General Sherman's army began marching through South Carolina, sparing little in its path. Dr. Samuel McGill, a resident of the state, made entries in his diary as the army advanced. Ten years later, in his memoirs, General Sherman would recall his own thinking at the time.

LEARN THE SKILL

Use the following steps to summarize from multiple sources:

1. **Find the main idea of each source.** Sometimes the main idea is stated by the writer, often in the first sentence of a paragraph. In other cases, you may have to use your judgment to identify the main idea from the details in the source.
2. **Identify supporting details in each source.** These include any facts, reasons, explanations, examples, or descriptions that helped you find each main idea.
3. **Write a summary of each source.** State or restate its main idea in your own words.
4. **Create a summary based on the main ideas of all the sources.** Use your own words to tie the sources' main ideas together. If possible, include a supporting detail from each source.

PRACTICE THE SKILL

Answer the following questions:

1. **(a)** Which sentence in Source A states the main idea of the two diary entries? **(b)** Which sentence in Source B provides the main idea of that excerpt?
2. **(a)** What actions are described in Source A? **(b)** How do they support the writer's sense of the mood of the people? **(c)** In Source B, what is the "power" that Sherman planned to use? **(d)** What was Sherman ready to do in order to use it?
3. **(a)** State the main idea of Source A in your own words. **(b)** State the main idea of Source B in your own words.
4. **(a)** What historical event links McGill's diary entries with the excerpt from Sherman's memoirs? **(b)** Do the two sources contradict or complement each other? Explain. **(c)** Drawing information from both sources, describe what happened in the Williamsburg District in 1865 and why it happened.

APPLY THE SKILL

See the Chapter Review and Assessment for another opportunity to apply this skill.

A

February 28, 1865: *"All is gloom and uncertainty, and preparations are being made for the worst. Furniture and provisions are hidden against pending raids. . . . It is feared famine will possess the land; our army is demoralized and the people panic stricken. . . . The power to do [act] has left us. . . . To fight longer seems to be madness; to submit tamely is dishonor."*

March 1, 1865: *"The whole country is in the wildest commotion and many are fleeing to the woods with their wives and daughters, while a few have gone to meet the advance and to give battle."*

—From the diary of Dr. Samuel McGill, Williamsburg District, South Carolina

B

"My aim then was, to whip the rebels, to humble their pride, to follow them to their inmost recesses [their inner selves], and make them fear and dread us. . . . It was to me manifest [obvious] that the soldiers and people of the South entertained a . . . fear of our . . . men. . . . [T]his was a power, and I intended to utilize it. . . . and therefore on them should fall the scourge of war in its worst form."

—William Tecumseh Sherman, *Memoirs, Vol. 2*, 1875

Summarizing From Multiple Sources

Focus Students recognize that an effective way to reconstruct a historical event is to gather sources that recreate the event from various perspectives.

Instruct Ask volunteers to read statements A and B to the class. Divide the class into two groups. Have one group analyze statement A and another group analyze statement B. What are some key words in each that reflect the writer's perspective? *(Statement A: "gloom, uncertainty, famine, demoralized, panic stricken"; Statement B: "whip, humble, fear, dread, the scourge of war.")* How would students characterize the writer's perspective in each statement?

Extend See the Skills for Life activity in the Resource Directory below.

ANSWERS

Practice the Skill

1. **(a)** "All is gloom and uncertainty, and preparations are being made for the worst." **(b)** "My aim then was, to whip the rebels, to humble their pride, to follow them to their inmost recesses [their inner selves], and make them fear or dread us. . . ."
2. **(a)** Furniture and provisions being hidden; people fleeing; a few going to the front to fight. **(b)** The actions show fear, confusion, and desperation. **(c)** Fear. **(d)** He was prepared to be as destructive as possible.
3. **(a)** Possible answer: Residents are terrified of the approaching Union army, hiding their belongings, and running away. **(b)** Possible answer: General Sherman plans to show no mercy to the "rebels" and to use fear as a weapon.
4. **(a)** General Sherman's march through the Williamsburg district of South Carolina. **(b)** Complement: the events in excerpt A allow excerpt B to become a reality. **(c)** Sherman's strategy of instilling fear worked. As his army advanced, panicked residents scattered and hid.

RESOURCE DIRECTORY

Teaching Resources
Skills for Life booklet, p. 13

Technology
Social Studies Skills Tutor CD-ROM
Interactive Practice in
- Geographic Literacy
- Critical Thinking and Reading
- Visual Analysis
- Communications

Section 3
The Tide of War Turns

Section Objectives

1. Identify the importance of Lee's victories at Fredericksburg and Chancellorsville.
2. Describe how the Battles of Gettysburg and Vicksburg turned the tide of the war.
3. Find out why 1863 was a pivotal year in the Civil War.
4. Interpret the message of the Gettysburg Address.

Bellringer

Warm-Up Activity Ask students if they can remember being without electricity for any length of time. If so, ask them to describe how they spent that time. Then ask them how that experience would compare to living in a cave for several months while an enemy army shelled their city.

Activating Prior Knowledge Photography was a new tool used widely for the first time during the Civil War. Can students state some impacts of this new technology? What would it have been like for the general public to be able to see real-life battle scenes, often for the first time? How did photography help generals make their battle plans?

Reading Strategy

Ask students to write the headings *Gettysburg* and *Vicksburg* on a sheet of paper and take notes about each battle as they read. When they have finished reading the section, ask them to write briefly about why each battle was important in turning the tide of the war.

Section 3

The Tide of War Turns

READING FOCUS

- What was the importance of Lee's victories at Fredericksburg and Chancellorsville?
- How did the Battles of Gettysburg and Vicksburg turn the tide of the war?
- Why was 1863 a pivotal year?
- What is the message of the Gettysburg Address?

MAIN IDEA

Despite Southern victories at Fredericksburg and Chancellorsville, the tide of war turned in the summer of 1863, when the North won at Gettysburg and Vicksburg.

KEY TERMS

Battle of Fredericksburg
Battle of Chancellorsville
Battle of Gettysburg
Pickett's Charge
siege
Gettysburg Address

TAKING NOTES

As you read, complete the following chart. For each battle, fill in the important officers, tell which side won, and write what you consider the most important reason for that side's victory.

Major Battles of 1863			
Battle	Union Officer	Confederate Officer	Victor/Why
Fredericksburg	Burnside	Lee	South/Burnside crossed right in front of Lee's army; kept charging into gunfire.

Drummer boys were a vital part of the armies of both the North and the South.

Setting the Scene Civil War battles were noisy and smoky. Cannons boomed, rifles fired, men shouted, and the battlefield was wreathed in a haze of gunfire and dust. How did commanders communicate with their troops in this chaos? How did soldiers know when to advance, when to retreat, or even where their units were located? In the early years of the Civil War, it was the sound of the drumbeat that communicated orders. For that reason, drummer boys—usually only 12 to 16 years old—were so important that they were often purposely fired on by the enemy, and hundreds were killed in battle. One drummer boy who was wounded in action at Vicksburg received the Medal of Honor. Another boy described his experience this way:

> *"A cannon ball came bouncing across the corn field, kicking up dirt and dust each time it struck the earth. Many of the men in our company took shelter behind a stone wall, but I stood where I was and never stopped drumming. An officer came by on horseback and chastised the men, saying 'this boy puts you all to shame. Get up and move forward.' . . . Even when the fighting was at its fiercest and I was frightened, I stood straight and did as I was ordered. . . . I felt I had to be a good example for the others."*
>
> —A Civil War drummer boy

Victories for General Lee

The Emancipation Proclamation may have renewed enthusiasm for the war among some Northerners, but the war still had to be won in the din and dust of the battlefield. When General George McClellan delayed in following up on his victory over Robert E. Lee at the Battle of Antietam, Lincoln again removed McClellan from command and replaced him with General Ambrose Burnside in November 1862. Sadly for Lincoln, Burnside was better known for his thick whiskers, the origin of the term "sideburns," than for his skills as a military strategist. He soon proved that his poor reputation was justified.

RESOURCE DIRECTORY

Teaching Resources
Guided Reading and Review booklet, p. 48
Learning Styles Lesson Plans booklet, p. 24

Other Print Resources
Nystrom *Atlas of Our Country* *A Divided Nation,* pp. 26–27

Technology
Section Reading Support Transparencies
Guided Reading Audiotapes (English/Spanish), Ch. 4
Student Edition on Audio CD, Ch. 4
Prentice Hall Presentation Pro CD-ROM, Ch. 4
Companion Web site, www.phschool.com

The Battle of Fredericksburg Knowing that McClellan had been fired for being too cautious, Burnside quickly advanced into Virginia. His plan was simple—to march his army of some 122,000 men straight toward Richmond. In response, Lee massed his army of nearly 79,000 at Fredericksburg, Virginia, on the south bank of the Rappahannock River. Lee spread his troops along a ridge called Marye's Heights, behind and overlooking the town.

Incredibly, instead of crossing the river out of range of the Confederate artillery, Burnside decided to cross directly in front of Lee's forces. "The enemy will be more surprised [by this move]," he explained. Lee was surprised—by the poor strategy of Burnside's plan.

Union troops poured across the river on specially constructed bridges and occupied the town. Lee let them cross. He knew that his artillery had the area well covered. Lee believed that if Burnside's army attacked, the Confederate forces could easily deal it a crushing defeat.

On December 13, 1862, the **Battle of Fredericksburg** began. Throughout the day Burnside ordered charge after charge into the Confederate gunfire. Some Union army units lost more than half their men. When the fighting ceased at nightfall, the Union had suffered nearly 13,000 casualties. Confederate losses were just over 5,000. A demoralized Burnside soon asked to be relieved of his command.

The Battle of Chancellorsville After accepting Burnside's resignation, a worried Lincoln turned to yet another general, Joseph "Fighting Joe" Hooker. General Hooker's plan was to move the Union army around Fredericksburg and attack the Confederates' strong defenses from behind. "May God have mercy on General Lee, for I will have none," Fighting Joe promised.

In late April 1863, Hooker put his plan into action. Leaving about a third of his 115,000-man army outside Fredericksburg, he marched the rest of his troops several miles upriver and slipped across the Rappahannock. Lee soon became aware of Hooker's actions. Confederate cavalry commanded by General J.E.B. "Jeb" Stuart discovered Hooker's force camped about ten miles west of Fredericksburg, near a road crossing called Chancellorsville.

Dividing his forces, Lee sent more than 40,000 Confederate soldiers westward to meet Hooker. About 10,000 troops remained in Fredericksburg. Lee ordered them to build many fires at night, so the enemy across the river would not realize that most of the army was gone.

The **Battle of Chancellorsville** began on May 1, 1863. When the Union troops started their march toward Fredericksburg, they suddenly saw Lee's army in front of them. After a brief clash, Fighting Joe ordered them to pull back into the thick woods and build defenses. The next day, when the Confederates did not attack, Hooker assumed they were in retreat. Instead, Lee had daringly divided his forces a second time. He sent General Stonewall Jackson and 26,000 men on a 12-mile march around the Union army for a late-afternoon attack on its right side. The movement of Jackson's troops was concealed by heavy woods that covered the area.

Again, Hooker was taken by surprise. The only warning was a wave of rabbits and deer that poured into the Union camp moments ahead of the Confederate charge. If darkness had not halted his attack, Jackson would have crushed the Union army. That night, Jackson and some other officers left the Confederate camp to scout the Union positions for a renewed attack. As they returned in

Focus on GEOGRAPHY

The Shenandoah Valley One of Stonewall Jackson's deadliest weapons was a detailed map of the Shenandoah Valley, a corridor about 150 miles long and 25 miles wide between the Blue Ridge Mountains and the Allegheníes. Southern armies were able to travel north through the Valley. Although forested, its slopes were not too steep or rocky for troops on foot or horseback, and the main road through the center of the Valley allowed even Robert E. Lee's large army to travel rapidly. What's more, the many gaps in the Blue Ridge Mountains and the pro-Confederate population permitted Southern forces to duck easily in and out of the Valley. However, Union forces that ventured there were harassed by armed raiders. Finally, the Shenandoah's splendid pastures and crops also supplied the Confederate Army with a much-needed source of food.

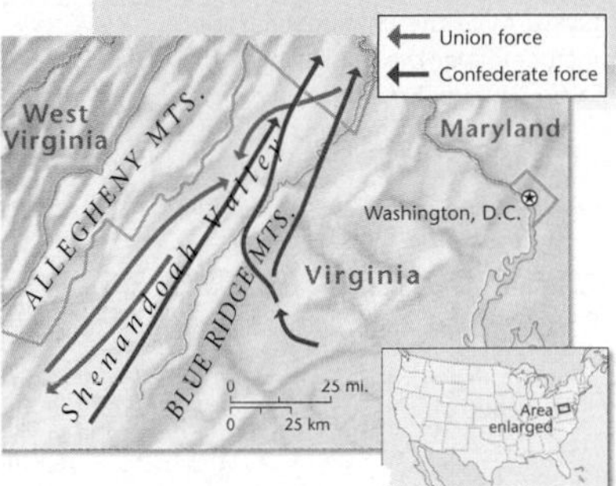

LESSON PLAN

Focus Explain that the turning point of the war came in 1863 with the battles of Vicksburg and Gettysburg. Ask why those battles were so important.

Instruct The capture of Vicksburg was part of the Anaconda Plan, by which the Union intended to divide and squeeze the Confederacy. Tell students that Lincoln said, "Vicksburg is the key. The war cannot be brought to a close until the key is in our pocket." Tell students that General Lee hoped that invading Pennsylvania might encourage foreign countries to recognize and assist the Confederacy and might also dishearten Northern civilians.

Assess/Reteach Have students create a fact file on each of the following battles: Fredericksburg, Chancellorsville, Gettysburg, and Vicksburg. Fact files should include the significance of the battle and a brief summary of what took place.

ACTIVITY

Connecting with Geography

Have students use a map to explain why Vicksburg was so critical to Union strategy. Ask students to trace Lee's route to Gettysburg. **(Visual/Spatial)**

CUSTOMIZE FOR ...

Less Proficient Readers

To reinforce the reading material and aid comprehension, have students construct a battlefield time line listing the battles in this section in chronological order. On the time lines, students should include each battle's location and victor.

the darkness, some Confederate soldiers mistook them for enemies and opened fire. Three bullets hit Jackson, one shattering his left arm so badly that it had to be amputated.

On May 3, with Stuart now leading Jackson's command, the Confederate army completed its victory. On May 5, Hooker's badly beaten troops withdrew back across the river. Chancellorsville was Lee's most brilliant victory, but it was also his most costly one. On May 10, Jackson died of complications from his wounds. Stonewall Jackson was probably Lee's most brilliant general. His popularity with the troops was exceeded only by Lee's. His death deprived Lee of a man he called his "strong right arm."

The Battle of Gettysburg

The crushing defeats at Fredericksburg and Chancellorsville were the low point of the war for the Union. The mood in Washington was dark. Rumors swept the capital that Lincoln would resign as President. Some Northern leaders began to talk seriously of making peace with the South. "If there is a worse place than Hell," Lincoln said, "I am in it."

In June 1863, Lee marched his forces northward. The Union blockade and the South's lack of resources were beginning to weaken his army. With all the fighting in Virginia, supplies there had become scarce. Lee hoped to find some in Pennsylvania. More importantly, he hoped that a major Confederate victory on Northern soil would finally push the Union into giving up the war.

As Lincoln prepared to replace Hooker, the Union army moved north, too, staying between the Confederates and Washington. On July 1, some Confederate troops entered the town of Gettysburg, Pennsylvania. Many of them were barefoot, and a supply of shoes was rumored to be stored in the town. There the Confederates encountered a unit of Union cavalry and a fight developed. From this skirmish grew the greatest battle ever fought in North America, the three-day **Battle of Gettysburg.**

MAP SKILLS The Battle of Gettysburg was fought over three days. Notice the changes in troop positions over the course of the battle. **Human-Environment Interaction** *How did each side attempt to use the terrain to gain an advantage?*

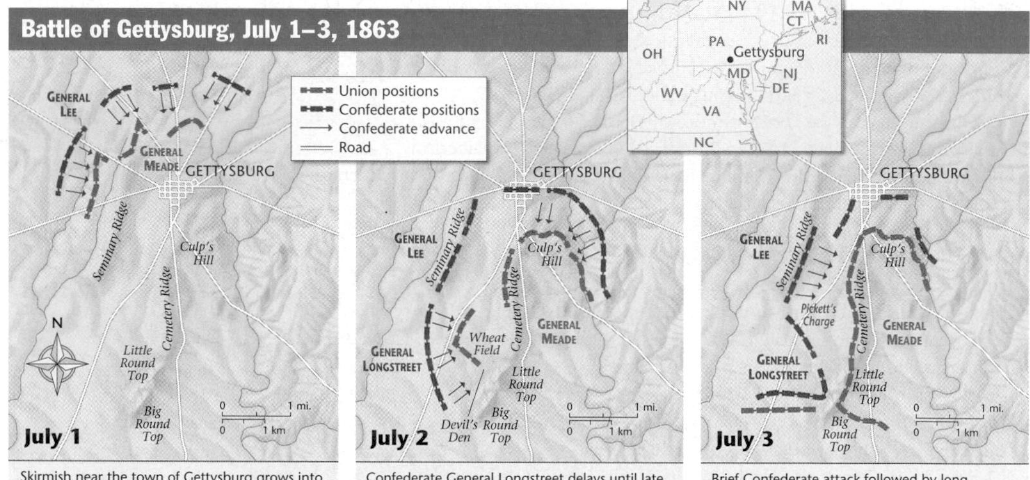

Skirmish near the town of Gettysburg grows into a full-scale battle. Confederates push Union troops south; armies gather on both sides. Lee orders an attack on Union position at Cemetery Ridge for the next morning.

Confederate General Longstreet delays until late afternoon to attack southern end of Union line, giving Union a chance to bring reinforcements. Maine unit defends Union position at Little Round Top; Union lines remain intact.

Brief Confederate attack followed by long artillery exchange. Thinking his army has destroyed enemy's guns, Lee orders direct infantry attack known as Pickett's Charge. Union is ready with artillery barrage; Confederates prepare to retreat into Virginia.

ACTIVITY
Connecting with History and Conflict

The Battle of Gettysburg was brutal and hard-fought. No soldier who was present and survived would ever have forgotten that day. Ask students to choose a portion of the Battle of Gettysburg to research in depth. Then, have them choose to view that portion of the battle from the perspective of a member of the Union or Confederate army. Have them write an "eyewitness account" of the experience in the form of a letter home to family. **(Verbal/Linguistic)**

BACKGROUND
Geography in History

Roads and railways were poor in the Upper South, so rivers played an important role in the Union planning. Armies covered the most ground in the west, where north-south rivers like the Mississippi and the Tennessee offered an easy route into the Confederacy. In Virginia, however, most rivers flow east from the Appalachians into the Atlantic Ocean. These formed a natural defense for the Confederate troops, since the Union army had to stop to build pontoon bridges across the wider rivers.

CAPTION ANSWERS

Map Skills The Confederacy attempted to gain high ground to fire down on the enemy; the Union assumed a defensive position on a ridge, forcing the Confederates to attack.

RESOURCE DIRECTORY

Other Print Resources

Historical Outline Map Book *Major Battles of the Civil War,* p. 50

Technology

Color Transparencies *Historical Maps,* A22

July 1, 1863 Hearing the gunfire coming from Gettysburg, units of both armies rushed to the scene. At first, the Confederates outnumbered the Union forces. Fighting through the day, they pushed the Northerners back onto some hills south of town. Meanwhile, troops on both sides continued to gather. Among the Union soldiers to arrive that night was General George Meade, the new head of the Union army. He had been in command for less than a week.

VIEWING HISTORY This lithograph shows part of the Battle of Gettysburg. **Drawing Inferences** *What can you tell about the military tactics of the battle from the picture?*

Each army took up positions on a series of hills. Their lines stretched from the outskirts of town, in a southerly direction, for about four miles. The center of the Union line was a long hill called Cemetery Ridge. Another series of hills, called Seminary Ridge, was the center of the Confederate position. Between these two ridges was a large field several hundred yards wide.

That evening, Lee discussed his battle plan with General James Longstreet, his second-in-command since the death of Stonewall Jackson. Having won the day's fighting, and fresh from his victory at Chancellorsville, Lee's confidence was high. He proposed to continue the battle the next day. Longstreet advised against attacking such a strong Union position, but Lee had made up his mind. "The enemy is there," said Lee, pointing to Cemetery Ridge, "and I am going to attack him there." He ordered Longstreet to lead an attack on the southern end of the Union line the next morning.

July 2, 1863 Although a graduate of West Point, Longstreet preferred more peaceful endeavors. An accountant, he wanted to be in charge of the Confederate army's payroll. Lee made him a field commander instead. "Longstreet is a very good fighter when he . . . gets everything ready," Lee said of him, "but he is so slow."

On this second day of the battle, Longstreet was not ready to attack until about 4:00 P.M. His delays gave Meade the chance to bring up reinforcements. The battle raged into the early evening. Heavy fighting occurred in a peach orchard, a wheat field, and a mass of boulders known locally as the Devil's Den.

At one point, some Alabama soldiers noticed that one of the hills in the Union position, called Little Round Top, was almost undefended. They rushed to capture the hill. From it, Confederate artillery could have bombarded the Union lines. However, Union commanders also had noticed that Little Round Top was vulnerable. About 350 Maine soldiers under Colonel Joshua Chamberlain, a college professor before the war, were ordered to defend the position. They arrived on the hill just before the Alabamans' assault and then held off repeated attacks until they ran out of ammunition. Unwilling to give up, Chamberlain ordered a bayonet charge. The surprised Confederates retreated back down the hill. The Maine soldiers' heroic act likely saved the Union army from defeat. At the end of the day, the Union lines remained intact.

READING CHECK
Describe the battle for Little Round Top.

July 3, 1863 The third day of battle began with a brief Confederate attack on the north end of the Union line. Then the battlefield fell quiet. Finally, in the early afternoon, about 150 Confederate cannons began the heaviest artillery barrage of the war. Some Union generals thought the firing might be to protect a Confederate retreat. They were wrong. Lee had decided to risk everything on an infantry charge against the center of the Union position. As he had two days before, Longstreet opposed such a direct attack. Again Lee overruled him.

ACTIVITY
Connecting with Citizenship

Ask students to deliver a brief monologue on the celebration of July 4, 1863, by one of the following figures: a formerly enslaved African American, a citizen of Vicksburg, or a Union soldier. Have students choose their character, do research to prepare the monologue, and present the monologue in front of the class. **(Verbal/Linguistic)**

BACKGROUND
Biography

Cuban-born artist Federico Fernández Cavada served as a captain and engineer in the Union army. Sent aloft in hot-air balloons near the battle lines, Cavada sketched from the air what he could see of Confederate troop movements until he was captured at the Battle of Gettysburg. In 1864 Cavada published *Libby Life,* an account of his cruel treatment in a Confederate prison.

READING CHECK
Confederate troops rushed up the slope of the Little Round Top, a lightly defended hill which was an important part of the Union line. A small group of Union reinforcements arrived just in time to defend the Little Round Top. Their spirited defense caused the Confederate troops to fall back.

TEST PREPARATION

Have students read the text under the heading "July 1, 1863" on this page and then answer the question below.

Which event occurred on the evening of July 1, 1863?

- **A** General Longstreet decided to attack Cemetery Ridge.
- **B** General George Meade arrived to command the Confederate army.
- **C** General Longstreet suggested attacking Cemetery Ridge, but General Lee disagreed.
- **(D)** General Lee ordered General Longstreet to attack Cemetery Ridge.

CAPTION ANSWERS

Viewing History Foot soldiers charged across open fields in an effort to overwhelm the enemy but suffered terrible casualties. Officers on horseback directed the battle from behind the lines.

Activity
Student Portfolio

You may wish to have students add the following to their portfolios: Ask students to speculate about what might have happened if General Meade had pursued Lee's forces after the Battle of Gettysburg. Ask students to create a time line showing events from Gettysburg to the end of the war under those circumstances. **(Visual/Spatial)**

Background
Biography

Much criticized after the failure of Pickett's Charge, General George Pickett was thought by some to be a coward. Even so, Robert E. Lee kept Pickett in command of his division. Just eight days before Lee surrendered at Appomattox in April 1865, Pickett's division was nearly destroyed in battle while he attended a picnic.

Photography and War

The Civil War was the first American conflict to be photographed. Mathew Brady and his team of photographers showed its grim realities to great effect.

The Vietnam War was the first to "invade" American homes via television, and the nightly news footage from Vietnam helped turn American public opinion against the war.

During the 1991 Gulf War, CNN's Peter Arnett actually broadcast *live* from Baghdad, Iraq, as American bombs fell on the city.

***?* Which of these images has the most impact on you, the viewer? Why? What do you learn about war from these images?**

After a two-hour artillery duel, the Union guns stopped returning fire. Thinking that the Confederate artillery had destroyed the enemy's guns, Longstreet reluctantly ordered the direct attack. Actually, the Union artillery commander had ceased fire only to save ammunition. Now, however, Northern soldiers on Cemetery Ridge saw nearly 15,000 Confederates, formed in a line a mile long and three rows deep, coming toward them.

Although this event is known in history as **Pickett's Charge,** General George Pickett was only one of three Southern commanders on the field that day. Each led an infantry division of about 5,000 men. As the Confederates marched across about a mile of open ground between the two ridges, the Union artillery resumed firing. Hundreds of canister shells rained down on the approaching soldiers, tearing huge gaps in their ranks. When the Southern troops closed to within about 200 yards of the Union lines, Northern soldiers poured rifle fire into those who remained standing.

Only a few hundred Confederates reached the Union lines—at a bend in a stone wall that became known as the Angle. A survivor described the fighting:

> *"Men fire into each other's faces, not five feet apart. There are bayonet-thrusts, sabre-strokes, pistol-shots; . . . men going down on their hands and knees, spinning round like tops, throwing out their arms, falling; legless, armless, headless. There are ghastly heaps of dead men."*
>
> —Soldier at Gettysburg

In about 30 minutes it was over. Scarcely half the Confederate force returned to Seminary Ridge. Lee ordered Pickett to reform his division in case Meade counterattacked. "General Lee, I have no division," Pickett replied.

Pickett's Charge ended the bloodiest battle of the Civil War. Losses on both sides were staggering. The Union army of about 85,000 suffered over 23,000

Caption Answers

Fast Forward to Today Answers will vary, but student explanations should include impact of the reality of war and the death it brings.

Resource Directory
Technology
Color Transparencies *Historical Maps,* A23

casualties. Of some 75,000 Southerners, about 28,000 were casualties. For the second time, Lee had lost more than a third of his army. The next day, July 4, the Confederates began their retreat back to Virginia.

Vicksburg

While armies clashed in the East, a Union force in the West struggled to capture the city of Vicksburg, Mississippi. Only this stronghold and a fortress at Port Hudson, Louisiana, stood in the way of the Union's complete control of the Mississippi River. Vicksburg seemed safe from attack. It sat on a bluff, high above a sharp bend in the river. From this bluff, Confederate artillery could lob shells at any Union ships that approached the city. In addition, much of Vicksburg was surrounded by swamps. The only approach to the city over dry land was from the east, and Confederate forces held that territory.

Grant Attacks The Union general who faced these difficult challenges was Ulysses S. Grant. Between December 1862 and April 1863, he made several attempts either to capture or to bypass the city. First, he sent General William Tecumseh Sherman and several thousand troops in an unsuccessful attack on Vicksburg from the north. Next he had his army dig a canal across the bend in the river, so Union boats could bypass the city's guns. However, the canal turned out to be too shallow. Then he tried to attack from the north by sending gunboats down another river. This too failed.

An attempt to approach the city through a swampy backwater called Steele's Bayou nearly ended in disaster. The Confederates cut down trees to slow the Union boats and fired on them from shore. Finally, Sherman's troops had to come and rescue the fleet.

By mid-April 1863, the ground had dried out enough for Grant to try a daring plan. He marched his army down the Louisiana side of the river and crossed into Mississippi south of Vicksburg. Then he moved east and attacked Jackson, the state capital. This maneuver

MAP SKILLS Lincoln called capturing Vicksburg "the key" to winning the war. Jefferson Davis considered the city to be "the nailhead that holds the South's two halves together." **Movement** *(a) Trace Grant's route on the map and explain the strategy behind it. (b) According to the painting, what made the attempt to attack the city by gunboat so difficult?*

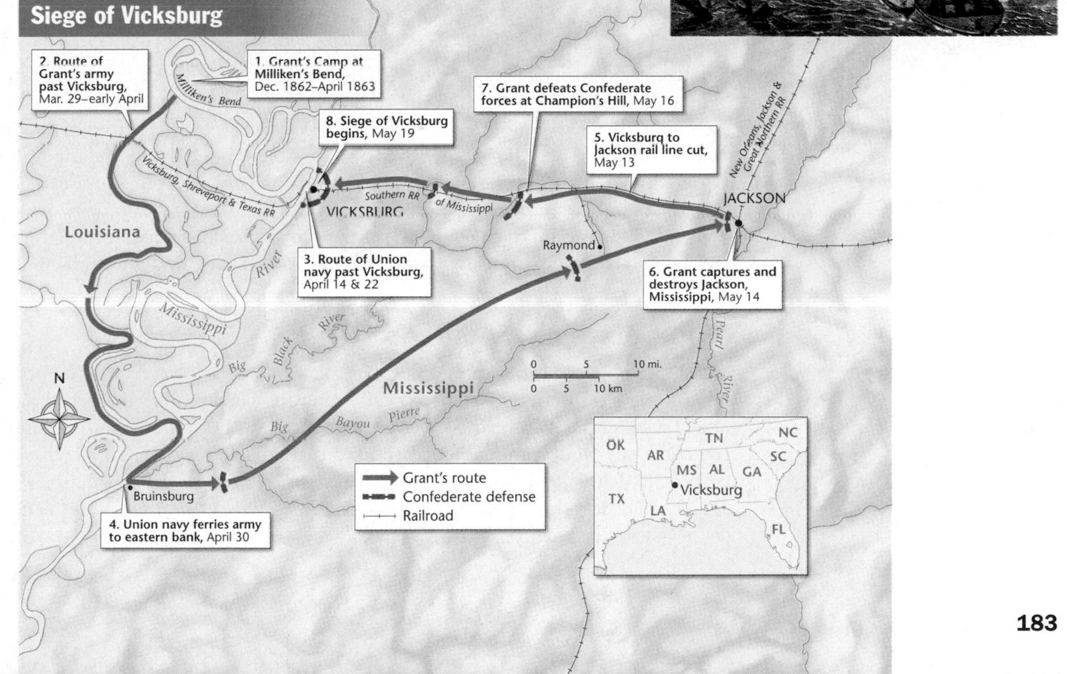

ACTIVITY

Connecting with History and Conflict

Ask students to agree or disagree with this statement by Sir Basil Liddell Hart, an English military authority and biographer of Sherman: "Loss of hope is worse than loss of men and land. It was the moral effect, above all, which made Vicksburg the great turning point of the war." Have students discuss whether they think Liddell Hart's statement correctly describes the results of the siege of Vicksburg. Why or why not? **(Verbal/Linguistic)**

BACKGROUND

Geography in History

Throughout the Civil War, it had been a goal of the Union army to gain control of the Mississippi River. Just as steadfastly, the Confederate army fought to hold on to this vital waterway. Finally in 1863, the superior arms, ships, and equipment of the Union army made control of the Mississippi within reach. With the fall of Vicksburg, Abraham Lincoln, who had worked on a Mississippi River flatboat when he was young, announced that "the Father of Waters flows unvexed to the sea." With this important territorial gain, the triumph of the Union began to seem inevitable.

TEST PREPARATION

Have students reread the first paragraph under the section "Vicksburg" on this page and then answer the question below.

Which of the following statements is correct?

(A) Vicksburg was key to the Union's control of the Mississippi River.

B Vicksburg was always held by Union troops, but at great cost.

C Confederates were hesitant to defend Vicksburg, as it was very vulnerable.

D Union forces totally surrounded Vicksburg and were placing it under siege.

CAPTION ANSWERS

Map Skills (a) Because of the terrain, Grant chose to pass south of Vicksburg and then attack the city from the east, after first taking Jackson, Mississippi. By destroying Jackson and cutting its rail line to Vicksburg, Grant cut Vicksburg off from incoming supplies, enabling him to conduct a siege of Vicksburg. (b) The boats had to pass right under enemy guns. The enemy could also clog the river with flaming debris.

ACTIVITY
Student Portfolio

You may wish to have students add the following to their portfolios: Have students research the shelling of Sarajevo, Bosnia-Herzegovina, in the Bosnian war that began in 1992. Ask them to compare the shelling to the siege of Vicksburg. Then have them write two newspaper reports, one from a reporter on the scene in Sarajevo and one from a reporter on the scene in Vicksburg. **(Verbal/Linguistic)**

BACKGROUND
Biography

An immigrant from Germany to the United States at the age of 6, Thomas Nast (1840–1902) began his drawing career at the age of 15 when he worked for Frank Leslie's *Illustrated Newspaper.* By age 18 he was drawing for *Harper's Weekly,* one of the most widely circulated sources of news and information of the day. He became one of the first specialists in the art of political cartooning, and used his pen to help rouse sentiment for his strong antislavery, pro-Union point of view. Two of his cartoons, "After the Battle," published in 1862, and "Emancipation," published in 1863, had so much impact in support of the Union cause that President Lincoln called him "our best recruiting sergeant."

Focus on DAILY LIFE

Life Underground A young mother described living in a cave during the siege of Vicksburg: "Our new habitation was an excavation made in the earth, a cave in the shape of a T. In one of the wings my bed fitted; the other I used as a kind of a dressing room. In this the earth had been cut down a foot or two below the floor of the main cave. I could stand erect here and when tired of sitting in other portions of my residence, I bowed myself into it and stood impassively resting at full height. Our quarters were close indeed, yet I was more comfortable than I expected I could have been under the earth.

"We were safe at least from fragments of shell—and they were flying in all directions—though no one seemed to think our cave any protection should a mortar shell happen to fall directly on top of the ground above us."

—Mary Ann Loughborough

drew out the Confederate forces from Vicksburg, commanded by General John Pemberton, to help defend the capital. Before they could arrive, Grant captured the city of Jackson. Then he turned his troops west to fight Pemberton.

On May 16, the two armies clashed at Champion's Hill, halfway between Jackson and Vicksburg. Although Grant won the battle, he could not trap Pemberton's army. The Confederates were able to retreat back to Vicksburg's fortifications. In late May, after two more unsuccessful attacks, Grant began a **siege,** a tactic in which an enemy is surrounded and starved in order to make it surrender.

The Siege of Vicksburg When Union cannons opened fire on Vicksburg from land and water, a bombardment began that would average 2,800 shells a day. For more than a month, the citizens of Vicksburg endured a nearly constant pounding from some 300 guns. The constant schedule of shelling took over everyday life.

To avoid being killed by the shells falling on their homes, residents dug caves in hillsides, some complete with furniture and attended by slaves. "It was living like plant roots," one cave dweller said. As the siege dragged on, residents and soldiers alike were reduced to eating horses, mules, and dogs. Rats appeared for sale in the city's butcher shops.

By late June, Confederate soldiers' daily rations were down to one biscuit and one piece of bacon per day. On July 4, some 30,000 Confederate troops marched out of Vicksburg and laid down their arms. Pemberton thought he could negotiate the best terms for the surrender on the day that celebrated the Union's independence.

The Importance of 1863

For the North, 1863 had begun disastrously. However, the Fourth of July, 1863, was for some the most joyous Independence Day since the first one 87 years earlier. For the first time, thousands of former slaves could truly celebrate American independence. The holiday marked the turning point of the Civil War.

In the West, Vicksburg was in Union hands. For a time, the people of that city had been sustained by the hope that President Jefferson Davis would send some of Lee's troops to rescue them. But Lee had no reinforcements to spare. His weakened army had begun its retreat into Virginia; it would never again seriously threaten Union soil. Four days later, Port Hudson surrendered to Union forces. The Mississippi River was now in Union hands, cutting the Confederacy in two. "The Father of Waters again goes unvexed [undisturbed] to the sea," announced Lincoln in Washington, D.C.

In Richmond there began to be serious talk of making peace. Although the war would continue for nearly two years more, for the first time the end seemed in sight.

The Gettysburg Address

Sounds of an Era

Listen to the Gettysburg Address and other sounds from the Civil War era.

On November 19, 1863, some 15,000 people gathered at Gettysburg. The occasion was the dedication of a cemetery to honor the Union soldiers who had died there just four months before. The featured guest was Edward Everett of Massachusetts, the most famous public speaker of the time. President Lincoln was invited to deliver "a few appropriate remarks" to help fill out the program.

Everett delivered a grand crowd-pleasing speech that lasted two hours. Then it was the President's turn to speak. In his raspy, high-pitched voice,

RESOURCE DIRECTORY

Teaching Resources

Units 1/2 booklet
- Section 3 Quiz, p. 41

Guide to the Essentials
- Section 3 Summary, p. 20

Learning with Documents booklet (Primary Source Activity) *The Gettysburg Address,* p. 16

Technology

Sounds of an Era Audio CD *"The Gettysburg Address"* (time: almost three minutes)

Exploring Primary Sources in U.S. History CD-ROM *Gettysburg Address, Abraham Lincoln*

Lincoln delivered his remarks, which became known as the **Gettysburg Address.** In a short, two-minute speech he eloquently reminded listeners of the North's reason for fighting the Civil War: to preserve a young country unmatched by any other country in history in its commitment to the principles of freedom, equality, and self-government:

> KEY DOCUMENTS
>
> *"Fourscore and seven years ago our fathers brought forth on this continent, a new nation, conceived in Liberty, and dedicated to the proposition that all men are created equal.*
>
> *Now we are engaged in a great civil war, testing whether that nation, or any nation so conceived and so dedicated, can long endure. . . .*
>
> *It is for us the living, rather, to be dedicated here to the unfinished work which they who fought here have thus far so nobly advanced. It is rather for us to be here dedicated to the great task remaining before us—that from these honored dead we take increased devotion to that cause for which they gave the last full measure of devotion—that we here highly resolve that these dead shall not have died in vain—that this nation, under God, shall have a new birth of freedom—and that government of the people, by the people, for the people, shall not perish from the earth."*
>
> —Lincoln's Gettysburg Address, November 19, 1863

VIEWING HISTORY "In times like the present," Lincoln said, "men should utter nothing for which they would not willingly be responsible through time. . . ." **Identifying Central Issues** *How do Lincoln's words at Gettysburg represent the noblest goals of the Union cause?*

In 1863, most Americans did not pay much attention to Lincoln's speech. Some thought it was too short and too simple. Lincoln's fellow speaker, Edward Everett, was an exception. He wrote to Lincoln the next day, "I wish I could flatter myself that I had come as near to the central idea of the occasion in two hours as you did in two minutes." Future generations have agreed with Everett. The Gettysburg Address has become one of the best-loved and most-quoted speeches in English. It expresses simply and eloquently both grief at the terrible cost of the war and the reasons for renewed efforts to preserve the Union and the noble principles for which it stands.

Section 3 Assessment

READING COMPREHENSION

1. Briefly describe the **Battle of Fredericksburg** and the **Battle of Chancellorsville.**
2. Why was the **Battle of Gettysburg** a turning point in the war?
3. What were three effects of Grant's **siege** of Vicksburg?
4. Summarize the main points of the **Gettysburg Address.**

CRITICAL THINKING AND WRITING

5. **Determining Relevance** How did the superior manpower of the North and its greater ability to produce both crops and manufactured goods begin to affect the war in 1863?
6. **Writing to Persuade** Which do you think was a more significant turning point: Vicksburg or Gettysburg? Write the opening paragraph of a persuasive essay supporting your choice.

Take It to the NET

Activity: Writing an Ad Read more about the equipment and clothing that Civil War soldiers typically carried, and create an advertisement aimed at selling these items to the soldiers. Use the links provided in the *America: Pathways to the Present* area of the following Web site for help in completing this activity. **www.phschool.com**

CUSTOMIZE FOR ...

Gifted and Talented

Ask students to respond to the following statement by Josiah Gorgas, the chief of Confederate ordnance in 1863: "One brief month ago we were apparently at the point of success. Lee was in Pennsylvania. . . . Vicksburg seemed to laugh all Grant's efforts to scorn. . . . Yesterday we rode on the pinnacle of success—today absolute ruin seems to be our portion." Students should explain why Union victories at Vicksburg and Gettysburg meant ruin for the Confederacy.

Section 3 Assessment

Reading Comprehension

1. Battle of Fredericksburg: In an attempt to surprise the Confederacy, Burnside approached Lee's troops directly. Union losses extremely heavy. Confederate victory, Burnside demoralized. Battle of Chancellorsville: General Hooker led the Union, Lee became aware of Hooker's plan and strategically divided and subdivided troops, resulting in a Confederate victory.
2. It defined how each side would be able to operate thereafter. The North had now seized the initiative in the east. After Gettysburg, Lee was restricted to operating defensively within the South.
3. The siege caused Confederate residents to move into underground dwellings, reduced supplies and soldiers' rations, and ultimately forced a surrender.
4. It summarized the North's reasons for fighting the Civil War: to preserve the country's commitment to the principles of freedom, equality, and self-government.

Critical Thinking and Writing

5. Union blockade and South's lack of resources began to weaken the Confederate army. Union had a large pool of new recruits, and could sustain farming, manufacturing, and fighting. Confederate troops were depleted.
6. Essays should use facts from the section to persuade readers of their point.

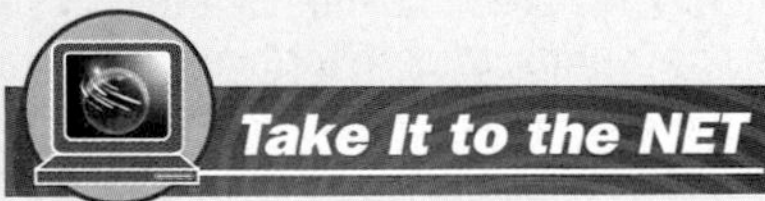

Take It to the NET

Sample answer: Soldiers could buy a better mess kit, containing more than the standard knife, fork, cup, and plate.

Caption Answers

Viewing History They stress the importance of the nation. Lincoln's primary goal in the war was to preserve the nation by any means necessary.

Section 4
Devastation and New Freedom

Section Objectives

1. Determine General Grant's strategy for defeating the South and how he and General Sherman implemented it.
2. Outline the issues and results of the election of 1864.
3. Explain how the South was finally defeated on the battlefield.
4. State how and why John Wilkes Booth assassinated President Lincoln.

Bellringer

Warm-Up Activity Ask students to think about what it means to surrender. Have them describe the feeling of giving up a fight. How does it feel to win a long-fought struggle?

Activating Prior Knowledge The submarine was used for the first time in the Civil War, when the Confederate-operated submarine *Hunley* sneaked up on and sank the Union ship *Housatonic.* Ask students to imagine and describe the impact of such an unexpected surprise attack from a completely new type of weapon.

Reading Strategy

Lincoln ended his Second Inaugural Address with these words: "With malice towards none; with charity for all; with firmness in the right, as God gives us to see the right, let us strive on to finish with work we are in; to bind up the nation's wounds; to care for him who shall have borne the battle, and for his widow, and his orphan—to do all which may achieve and cherish a just and lasting peace, among ourselves, and with all nations." As students read about the end of the Civil War, ask them to consider ways in which Lincoln's words were an attempt to help the nation begin the process of reconciliation.

Section 4

Devastation and New Freedom

READING FOCUS

- What was General Grant's strategy for defeating the South, and how did he and General Sherman implement it?
- What were the issues and results of the election of 1864?
- How was the South finally defeated on the battlefield?
- How and why did John Wilkes Booth assassinate President Lincoln?

KEY TERMS

Battle of the Wilderness
Battle of Spotsylvania
Battle of Cold Harbor
Thirteenth Amendment
guerrilla

TAKING NOTES

Copy this flowchart. As you read, fill in the boxes with some of the important events that led to the surrender of the South.

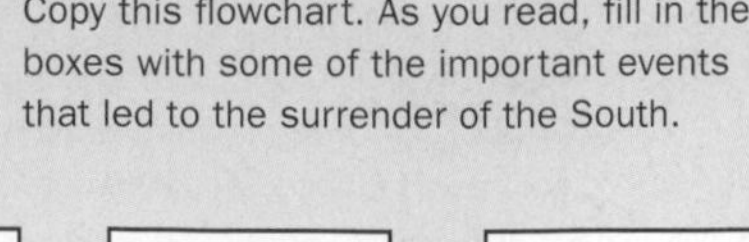

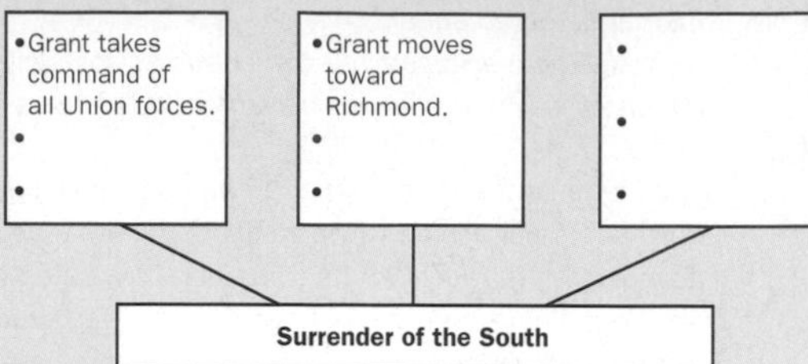

MAIN IDEA

After years of fighting, countless casualties, and considerable devastation, the South finally surrendered in April 1865.

Setting the Scene In April 1865 the city of Richmond, which had welcomed the war with such enthusiasm four years earlier, was a very different place. The war was nearly over, and both the Confederate government and its army abandoned the city. While many Southern cities, towns, and farms were set ablaze by conquering Union armies, the fires in the Confederate capital were set by retreating Southern troops in an effort to keep stored provisions from falling into the hands of the enemy. One Union soldier described the scene as he approached the city:

Retreating Confederate troops and citizens flee their burning capital.

> "*[I] looked down upon the grandest and most appalling sight that my eyes ever beheld. Richmond was literally a sea of flame, out of which the church steeples could be seen protruding here and there, while over all hung a canopy of dense black smoke, lighted up now and then by the bursting shells from the numerous arsenals scattered throughout the city. . . . The spacious capitol grounds afforded the only spot of refuge, and these were crowded with women and children, bearing in their arms and upon their heads their most cherished possessions.*"
>
> —R. B. Prescott

While there was certainly much destruction and misery, there were also pockets of rejoicing. African Americans joyously welcomed Union troops. Prescott went on to say that the freed slaves "hailed our appearance with the most extravagant expressions of joy. . . . 'God bless you' and 'Thank God, the Yankees have come' resounded on every side."

Grant Takes Command

At the beginning of 1864, the Confederates still hoped to keep the Union forces out of Richmond. Their war strategy was a simple one—to hold on. They knew that the North would have a presidential election in November. If the war dragged on and casualties mounted, some Southerners felt that Northern voters

Resource Directory

Teaching Resources

Guided Reading and Review booklet, p. 49
Learning Styles Lesson Plans booklet, p. 25

Technology

Section Reading Support Transparencies
Guided Reading Audiotapes (English/Spanish), Ch. 4
Student Edition on Audio CD, Ch. 4
Color Transparencies *Historical Maps,* A20, A21, A24
Exploring Primary Sources in U.S. History CD-ROM *In the Wilderness, Thomas J. Halsey*
Prentice Hall Presentation Pro CD-ROM, Ch. 4
Companion Web site, www.phschool.com

might replace Lincoln with a President willing to grant the South its independence. "If we can only subsist," wrote a Confederate official, "we may have peace."

At the same time, President Lincoln understood that his chances for reelection in 1864 depended on the Union's success on the battlefield. In March he summoned Ulysses S. Grant to Washington and gave him command of all Union forces. Grant's plan was to confront and crush the Confederate army and end the war before the November election.

Placing General William Tecumseh Sherman in charge in the West, Grant remained in the East to battle General Lee. He realized that Lee was running short of men and supplies. Grant now proposed to use the North's superiority in population and industry to wear down the Confederates. He ordered Sherman to do the same in the West.

Battle of the Wilderness In early May 1864, Grant moved south across the Rapidan River in Virginia with a force of some 115,000 men. Lee had about 64,000 troops. The Union army headed directly toward Richmond. Grant knew that to stop the Union advance, Lee would have to fight. In May and June the Union and Confederate armies clashed in three major battles. This was exactly what Grant wanted.

The fighting began on May 5 with the two-day **Battle of the Wilderness.** This battle occurred on virtually the same ground as the Battle of Chancellorsville the year before. The two armies met in a dense forest. The fighting was so heavy that the woods caught fire, causing many of the wounded to be burned to death. Unable to see in the smoke-filled forest, units got lost and fired on friendly soldiers, mistaking them for the enemy. One of these casualties was General Longstreet, Lee's second-in-command. He was accidentally shot and wounded by his own soldiers only three miles from where Stonewall Jackson had been shot the year before.

Grant took massive losses at the Battle of the Wilderness. However, instead of retreating as previous Union commanders had done after suffering heavy casualties, he moved his army around the Confederates and again headed south. Despite the high number of casualties, Union soldiers were proud that under Grant's leadership they would not retreat so easily.

Spotsylvania and Cold Harbor Two days later, on May 8, the Confederates caught up to the Union army near the little town of Spotsylvania Court House. The series of clashes that followed over nearly two weeks is called the **Battle of Spotsylvania.** The heaviest fighting took place on May 12. In some parts of the battlefield, the Union dead were piled four deep. When Northerners began to protest the huge loss of life, a determined Grant notified Lincoln, "I propose to fight it out on this line [course of action] if it takes all summer." Then he moved the Union army farther south.

In early June the armies clashed yet again at the **Battle of Cold Harbor,** just eight miles from Richmond. In a dawn attack on June 3, Grant launched two direct charges on the Confederates, who were behind strong fortifications. Some 7,000 Union soldiers fell—many in the first hour.

The Siege of Petersburg Unable to reach Richmond or defeat Lee's army, Grant moved his army around the capital and attacked Petersburg, a railroad center south of the city. He knew that if he could cut off shipments of food to Richmond, the city would have to surrender. However, the attack failed. In less than two months, Grant's army had suffered some 65,000 casualties. This toll

Focus on TECHNOLOGY

Civil War Submarine In 1864, the South had a secret weapon. Nothing like it had ever been seen before. It was the world's first successful military submarine, and the first such vessel to sink a ship in battle—something that would not happen again until World War I. Made from an old steam engine boiler, and cranked by hand, the Confederate *Hunley* was just 40 feet long. Once the craft submerged, the only light came from a candle. The flame would go out after about 25 minutes from lack of oxygen—a sign that the crew had better surface soon.

In February 1864, near Charleston, South Carolina, the *Hunley* rammed its torpedo into the *Housatonic,* and sank the Union ship. Then, mysteriously, the *Hunley* also sank. Now, in one of the largest recovery projects of its kind, the sub is being recovered and restored, and its crew of nine given heroes' burials.

READING CHECK
What happened at Spotsylvania and Cold Harbor?

LESSON PLAN

Focus Explain that Lee finally surrendered at Appomattox Court House, Virginia, in April 1865. Ask students to consider the costs of the Civil War. What were its major results?

Instruct Have students trace Sherman's route through Georgia. Ask how Sherman's march and Grant's dogged pursuit of Lee show the commitment of both generals to the idea of total war. Discuss how Lincoln's reelection led to the passage of the Thirteenth Amendment.

Assess/Reteach Ask students to identify the significance of the following in relation to the end of the Civil War and the redefinition of the nation: Gettysburg Address, Thirteenth Amendment, Appomattox Court.

ACTIVITY
Connecting with Culture

Ask students to prepare an oral reading of one of the following: the Gettysburg Address, selections from Stephen Vincent Benet's "John Brown's Body," or Walt Whitman's poem mourning the death of Lincoln, "O Captain! My Captain!" **(Verbal/Linguistic)**

READING CHECK
Union casualties were extremely heavy at Spotsylvania and Cold Harbor in May and June of 1864. At Cold Harbor, Grant ordered Union troops to make frontal assaults against extremely strong Confederate defenses.

CUSTOMIZE FOR ...
Gifted and Talented

Railroads played a central role in widening the economic gap between the North and the South. Later, they also played a leading part in the war that erupted between the two regions. Ask students to research the development of railroads in the United States and to draw a map showing the routes of the major railroads in both the North and the South in the 1850s.

ACTIVITY

Connecting with History and Conflict

Remind students that war is really about individual people, and that relationships between individuals often affect the lives of thousands. Sherman and Grant had a relationship built on loyalty. Despite what other Union commanders thought, Grant stood by Sherman. Divide students into groups. Have them research the lives of both men. Then have each group prepare and present a short skit demonstrating the personalities and philosophies of both men as Sherman convinces Grant to permit a daring move to "make Georgia howl." **(Verbal/Linguistic)**

BACKGROUND

Cryptology in the Civil War

Nearly as old as writing itself, secret codes have been used in times of war for thousands of years. During the Civil War, both the Union and Confederate armies relied on codes for their military communication. The code used by the Confederacy was easily broken by Union cryptanalysts. But the Union's code defied the Confederate's code-breakers. The coded Union messages were sometimes published in Confederate newspapers, with pleas to readers for deciphering help.

MAP SKILLS Grant's stubbornness and Sherman's campaign of total war brought the Civil War to a bloody close. **Movement** *Compare the size and movement of the Union and Confederate forces in the final months of the war. Why do you think Sherman met with little resistance?*

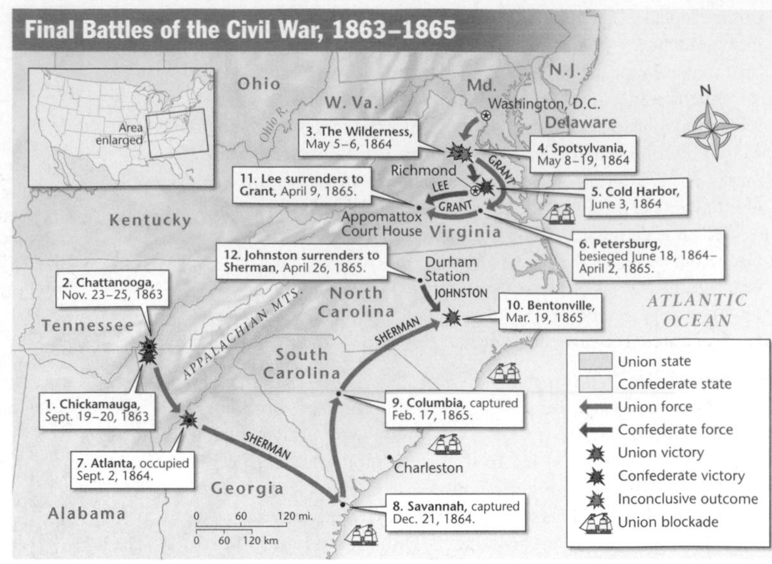

had a chilling effect on the surviving Union troops. At Cold Harbor, many soldiers pinned their names and addresses on their uniforms so their bodies could be identified.

Grant then turned to the tactic he had successfully used at Vicksburg. On June 18, 1864, he began the siege of Petersburg. Lee responded by building defenses. While he had lost many fewer men than Grant, it was becoming difficult for Lee to replace all of his casualties. He was willing to stay put and wait for the Northern election in November.

In the Shenandoah Grant recognized the importance of the Shenandoah Valley, both strategically and as a source of Southern supplies. In the summer of 1864, he decided to shut down that supply source once and for all. He told General Phil Sheridan, "Do all the damage to railroads and crops you can. . . . If the war is to last another year, we want the Shenandoah Valley to remain a barren waste." Sheridan carried out these orders to the letter. In the fall of 1864 he wrote Grant: "The people here are getting sick of the war." Grant answered: "Keep on, and your good work will cause the fall of Richmond."

In July 1864, one house that became a victim of Grant's policy belonged to Henrietta E. Lee. Her husband—the grandson of Revolutionary patriot and "rebel" Richard Henry Lee and a relative of Confederate General Robert E. Lee—was not at home. Henrietta Lee could not defend her home with weapons; all she had were words. She wrote the Union General a letter that began this way:

> *"General Hunter:*
>
> *Yesterday your underling, Captain Martindale, of the First New York Cavalry, executed your infamous order and burned my house. . . . the dwelling and every outbuilding, seven in number, with their contents, being burned. I, therefore, a helpless woman whom you have cruelly wronged, address you, a Major-General of the United States Army, and demand why this was done? What was my offence? My*

CAPTION ANSWERS

Map Skills Union manpower has become a vital factor. With his hands full facing Grant in Virginia, Lee could not reinforce Johnston and Hood against Sherman in Georgia.

RESOURCE DIRECTORY

Other Print Resources

Historical Outline Map Book *Union Advances,* p. 52

Technology

Color Transparencies *Fine Art,* E9

RESOURCE PRO® Primary Source Activity *A Teenager's Account of War,* found on Resource Pro, uses excerpts from Emma LeDonte's diary to show how young Southerners viewed and experienced the war.

husband was absent—an exile. He has never been a politician or in any way engaged in the struggle now going on . . . The house was built by my father, a Revolutionary soldier, who served the whole seven years for your independence. There I was born; there the sacred dead repose. . . ."

—Henrietta Lee, July 20, 1864

Little did Henrietta Lee know that this was just the beginning of the devastation of the South.

Sherman in Georgia

As Grant's army advanced against Lee, Sherman began to move south from Chattanooga, Tennessee, to threaten the city of Atlanta. Sherman's strategy was identical to Grant's in Virginia. He would force the main Confederate army in the West to attempt to stop his advance. If the Southern general took the bait, Sherman would destroy the enemy with his huge 98,000-man force. If the Confederates refused to fight, he would seize Atlanta, an important rail and industrial center.

The Capture of Atlanta Sherman's opponent in Georgia was General Joseph Johnston, the Confederate commander who had been wounded at the Battle of Seven Pines in Virginia in 1862. Johnston's tactics were similar to Lee's. He would engage the Union force to block its progress. At the same time, he would not allow Sherman to deal him a crushing defeat. In this way, he hoped to delay Sherman from reaching Atlanta before the presidential elections could take place in the North.

Despite Johnston's best efforts, by mid-July 1864 the Union army was just a few miles from Atlanta. Wanting more aggressive action, Confederate president Jefferson Davis replaced Johnston with General James Hood.

The new commander gave Davis—and Sherman—exactly what they wanted. In late July, Hood engaged the Union force in a series of battles. With each clash the Southern army lost thousands of soldiers. Finally, with the Confederate forces reduced from some 62,000 to less than 45,000, General Hood retreated to Atlanta's strong defenses. Like Grant at Petersburg, Sherman laid siege to the city. Throughout the month of August, Sherman's forces bombarded Atlanta. In early September the Confederate army pulled out and left the city to the Union general's mercy.

Sherman Marches to the Sea "War is cruelty," Sherman once wrote. "There is no use trying to reform it. The crueler it is, the sooner it will be over." It was from this viewpoint that the tough Ohio soldier conducted his military campaigns. Although a number of Union commanders considered Sherman to be mentally unstable, Grant stood by him. As a result, Sherman was fiercely loyal to his commander.

Now, Sherman convinced Grant to permit a daring move. Vowing to "make Georgia howl," in November 1864, Sherman led some 62,000 Union troops on a march to the sea to capture Savannah, Georgia. Before abandoning Atlanta, however, he ordered the city evacuated and then burned. After leaving Atlanta in ruins, Sherman's soldiers cut a

READING CHECK
What was Grant's policy toward the Shenandoah Valley, and how was the policy carried out?

VIEWING HISTORY *General Sherman's March to the Sea* shows the destruction caused by the Union advance. **Drawing Inferences** *What kinds of destruction are the Union troops causing here? What are the strategic purposes of this destruction?*

CUSTOMIZE FOR ...

Less Proficient Writers

Ask students to skim the section, list the main headings and subheadings, and write a sentence or phrase under each one that predicts the content it covers. Students should then test their predictions against the actual text when they have finished reading the section.

ACTIVITY

Connecting with Culture

Many popular songs were written during the Civil War years. Some songs, such as "While We Were Marching Through Georgia," "When Johnny Comes Marching Home Again," "The Battle Hymn of the Republic," and "Dixie," are still widely sung today.

Encourage interested students to research Civil War songs, and have them present a cabaret, which could be arranged in the chronological order in which the songs were written. Students could create a simple narrative structure describing the state of the war when various songs were written. **(Bodily/Kinesthetic; Musical/Rhythmic)**

BACKGROUND

Connections to Today

The New Market Battlefield Historical Park, now maintained by Richmond's Virginia Military Institute (VMI), commemorates one of the lesser battles of the Civil War. In May 1864 about 250 VMI cadets—average age 17—stopped 6,000 Union troops from entering the Shenandoah Valley. Needing the cadets to fill out his outnumbered army, Confederate General John C. Breckinridge is reported to have said: "Put the boys in, and may God forgive me for the order." Before the Union forces were forced into retreat, they had killed or wounded about one in four of the cadets.

READING CHECK

He wanted to deny the Confederates the Shenandoah Valley as either an avenue for moving troops into northern territory or as a food supply region. Grant ordered General Philip Sheridan to lay waste to the entire area in the summer of 1864. The Shenandoah Valley was thoroughly ravaged by Sheridan's Union troops.

CAPTION ANSWERS

Viewing History Union troops are destroying communication (telegraph) and transportation (railroad track and bridge) systems of the South, and burning what may be storehouses. They may also be welcoming escaped slaves.

BACKGROUND
Leadership and Timing

For many years, Lincoln had publicly opposed slavery. Yet as President, he did not automatically move to free all slaves. His priority in the first years of the Civil War was to preserve the Union at all costs. Many abolitionists criticized him for not freeing slaves as quickly as he could.

But Lincoln steadfastly refused to be hurried. He relied on his instincts and his own sense of timing. Lincoln first used his war powers as President to free slaves with the Emancipation Proclamation in 1863. As the tide of war turned toward the Union in 1864, Lincoln took the next step, insisting that his party adopt a platform calling for an amendment to the Constitution to abolish slavery in the United States forever. His successful reelection in 1864 gave him confidence that the majority of United States voters agreed with his approach, and, ultimately, Lincoln had the satisfaction of achieving both abolition and reunification.

BACKGROUND
Connections to Today

On March 4, 1865, with the end of the Civil War in sight, President Lincoln gave his Second Inaugural Address. In what was to become one of his most famous speeches, Lincoln spoke of the need "to bind up the nation's wounds" after nearly four years of bitter fighting. More than 135 years later, President George W. Bush spoke of the nation coming together once again to heal its wounds, this time in the aftermath of the September 11, 2001 terrorist attacks on New York City and Washington, D.C. Expressing the nation's sorrow as well as its resolve, Bush vowed that "whether we bring our enemies to justice or bring justice to our enemies, justice will be done."

nearly 300-mile-long path of destruction across Georgia. The Union troops destroyed bridges, factories, and railroad lines. They seized and slaughtered livestock. Grain that had recently been harvested for the Confederate troops went to Union soldiers instead.

As the Northerners approached Savannah, the small Confederate force there fled. On December 21, the Union army entered the city without a fight. "I beg to present you, as a Christmas gift, the city of Savannah," read General Sherman's message to Lincoln. For the President, it was the second piece of good news since the November election.

VIEWING HISTORY This campaign poster shows Lincoln running on the Union Party ticket. **Drawing Conclusions** *Do you think calling themselves the Union Party was a good strategy for the Republicans in 1864? Explain your answer.*

The Election of 1864

"I am going to be beaten," Lincoln said of his reelection chances in 1864, "and unless some great change takes place, badly beaten." Lincoln not only had to face a Democratic candidate, he also faced a brief challenge for the nomination of his own party. This challenge came from the Radical Republicans, those who were committed to emancipation and to "punishing" the South for the war. They were so angered when Lincoln pocket-vetoed the Wade-Davis Bill (which required stringent requirements for Southern states re-entering the Union), that they supported John C. Frémont for the nomination. Frémont eventually withdrew.

In an attempt to broaden Lincoln's appeal, the Republicans temporarily changed their name to the Union Party. They also dropped Vice President Hannibal Hamlin from the ticket and nominated Andrew Johnson of Tennessee to run with the President. Johnson was a Democrat and a pro-Union Southerner.

The Democrats nominated General George McClellan as their candidate. McClellan was only too happy to oppose Lincoln, who had twice fired him. The general was still loved by his soldiers, and Lincoln feared that McClellan would find wide support among the troops. McClellan promised that if elected, he would negotiate an end to the war.

Sherman's capture of Atlanta, however, changed the political climate in the North. Sensing that victory was near, Northerners became less willing to support a negotiated settlement. In November, with the help of ballots cast by Union soldiers, Lincoln won an easy victory, garnering 212 out of a possible 233 electoral votes.

A New Birth of Freedom

By reelecting Lincoln, voters showed not only their approval of his war policy, but also their increasing acceptance of his stand against slavery. Three months later, in February 1865, Congress joined Lincoln in that stand and passed the **Thirteenth Amendment** to the Constitution. It was ratified by the states and became law on December 18, 1865. In a few words, the amendment ended slavery in the United States forever:

> "*Neither slavery nor involuntary servitude, except as a punishment for crime whereof the party shall have been duly convicted, shall exist within the United States, or any place subject to their jurisdiction.*"
>
> —Thirteenth Amendment to the Constitution

In his Second Inaugural Address, in March 1865, Lincoln noted how slavery had divided the nation, but he also laid the groundwork for the effort to "bind up the nation's wounds."

CAPTION ANSWERS

Viewing History Answers will vary, but students should note that the Union Party name was an effort to make that party appealing to all voters who wanted to preserve the Union, regardless of previous party affiliation.

RESOURCE DIRECTORY

Teaching Resources

Learning with Documents booklet (Visual Learning Activity) *Defending Atlanta,* p. 50

Technology

Exploring Primary Sources in U.S. History CD-ROM *Second Inaugural Address, Abraham Lincoln*

“. . . It may seem strange that any men should dare ask a just God's assistance in wringing their bread from the sweat of other men's faces; but let us judge not that we be not judged.”

—Lincoln's Second Inaugural, March 1865

As President Lincoln prepared to begin his second term, it was clear to most Northerners that the war was nearly over. Lincoln said, “Fondly do we hope, fervently do we pray, that this mighty scourge of war may speedily pass away.”

The End of the War

As Grant strangled Richmond and Sherman prepared to move north from Savannah to join him, gloom deepened in the South. President Davis claimed that he had never really counted on McClellan's election, or on a negotiated peace. “The deep waters are closing over us,” Mary Chesnut observed in her diary.

Sherman Moves North In February 1865, General Sherman's troops left Savannah and headed for South Carolina. Since it had been the first state to secede from the Union, many Northerners regarded South Carolina as the heart of the rebellion. “Here is where the treason began and, by God, here is where it shall end,” wrote one Union soldier as the army marched northward.

Unlike Virginia and many other Confederate states, the Carolinas had seen relatively little fighting. Sherman had two goals as he moved toward Grant's position at Petersburg: to destroy the South's remaining resources and to crush Southerners' remaining will to fight. In South Carolina he did both. The Confederate army could do little but retreat in front of Sherman's advancing force. South Carolina was treated even more harshly than Georgia. In Georgia, for example, Union troops had burned very few of the houses that were in their path. In South Carolina, few houses were spared.

On February 17, the Union forces entered the state capital, Columbia. That night a fire burned nearly half of the city to the ground. Although no one could prove who started the fire, South Carolinians blamed Sherman's troops for the destruction. When the Union army moved into North Carolina, all demolition of civilian property ceased.

Surrender at Appomattox By April 1865, daily desertions had shrunk the Confederate army defending Richmond to fewer than 35,000 starving men. Realizing that he could no longer protect the city, on April 2 Lee tried to slip around Grant's army. He planned to unite his troops with those of General Johnston, who was retreating before Sherman's force in North Carolina. Lee hoped that together they would be able to continue the war.

Units of General Grant's army tracked the Confederates as they moved west. Each time Lee tried to turn his soldiers south, Grant's troops cut them off. On April 9, Lee's army arrived at the small Virginia town of Appomattox

Arlington National Cemetery

Arlington National Cemetery is located in Arlington, Virginia, across the Potomac River from Washington, D.C. This parcel of land once belonged to George Custis, who was the adopted son of George Washington. After Custis's daughter Mary inherited the property, she married a young army officer named Robert E. Lee, and they lived in the mansion Custis had built. During the Civil War, the Union army seized the property and used the mansion as a headquarters. The land became a military cemetery in 1864. In an 1882 Supreme Court case, Lee's descendants finally succeeded in having the U.S. government declared a trespasser on their property. The next year, Congress appropriated $150,000 to buy the property from the Lee family. Today, Arlington is the final resting place for many of the nation's military dead, and the mansion serves as a memorial to Robert E. Lee.

? Given the circumstances of the Civil War, do you think the Union was justified in seizing this property? Explain.

ACTIVITY
Connecting with Geography and History

As Union soldiers marched through South Carolina in 1865, they were conscious of that state's role in the beginning of the conflict. How much had changed in the four years since the shots were fired on Fort Sumter!

Divide students into groups, and assign one Southern state to each group. Have each group create a time line of its particular state's history during the Civil War years. Students may choose to use artwork, photographs, or facsimiles of historical documents to illustrate their time lines. **(Visual/Spatial)**

BACKGROUND
Recent Scholarship

In December 1862 President Lincoln said, “Fellow-citizens, *we* cannot escape history. The fiery trial through which we pass will light us down, in honor or dishonor, to the latest generation. . . . In *giving* freedom to the *slave,* we assure freedom to the free. . . . We shall nobly save, or meanly lose, the last best hope of Earth.” This statement has inspired a book of essays by leading scholars of Lincoln and the Civil War. Edited by James M. McPherson, a Pulitzer prize–winning history professor at Princeton University, *We Cannot Escape History: Lincoln and the Last Best Hope of Earth* contains a group of essays examining Lincoln's views on American History and considering his legacy.

TEST PREPARATION

Have students read the passage on this page from Lincoln's Second Inaugural Address, and then complete the sentence below.

Based on the passage, it is clear that—

(A) Lincoln believed the war had a greater purpose than either side knew.
B Lincoln thought Northerners were more religious than Southerners.
C Lincoln thought the North was winning because people there prayed more often.
D the North and the South had nothing in common.

CAPTION ANSWERS

Fast Forward to Today Sample answer: Given that the Civil War was raging, the Union had every right to seize and protect any land that Lee owned in Washington.

ACTIVITY

Connecting with History and Conflict

How did the generosity of Grant's terms of surrender parallel his stated desire to support restoration of peaceful relations between North and South? Have students list the ways Grant, by word and deed, took a leadership role in restoring the unity of the nation. Ask students to write a brief essay describing situations in their own lives when they have been part of a dispute's settlement. Can they compare ways in which they achieved reconciliation with the approach used by Grant? **(Verbal/Linguistic)**

INTERPRETING GRAPHS After four years and more than 10,500 battles, the Civil War claimed a staggering number of casualties. **Drawing Conclusions** *How does the total number of Civil War dead compare to those killed in other U.S. wars? Why do you think this is so? How does the information in the pie chart help to explain the outcome of the war?*

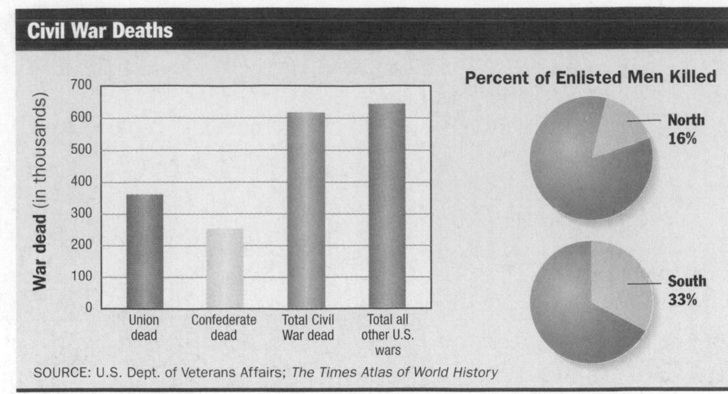

Court House. There, the Confederates were surrounded by a much larger Union force. Some of Lee's officers suggested that the army could scatter and continue to fight as **guerrillas**—soldiers who use surprise raids and hit-and-run tactics. Lee rejected this idea, fearing that it would bring more devastation to Virginia. Reluctantly he admitted, "There is nothing left for me to do but go and see General Grant, and I would rather die a thousand deaths." He knew the war was over.

That afternoon Lee and Grant met in a private home in the town. The house belonged to Wilmer McLean. He had not lived there long. In 1861, McLean had been living in Manassas, and the opening shots of the First Battle of Bull Run had landed in his front yard. To ensure the safety of his family, he had moved them away from the war—or so he thought—to the town of Appomattox Court House. Now the war was ending in his parlor.

When they met in McLean's house, General Lee was in his dress uniform, a sword at his side, and Grant was wearing his usual private's uniform, which was splattered with mud. They briefly chatted about the weather and their service in the Mexican War. Then Lee asked Grant about the terms of the surrender. These were generous. Southern soldiers could take their horses and mules and go home. They would not be punished as traitors so long as they obeyed the laws where they lived. Grant also offered to feed the starving Confederate army. After the two men signed the surrender papers, they talked for a few more minutes. Then Lee mounted his horse and rode away.

As news of the surrender spread through the Union army, soldiers began firing artillery salutes. Grant ordered the celebration stopped. He did not want rejoicing at the Southerners' misfortune because, as he pointed out, "the rebels are our countrymen again."

In the South, the news also met with mixed feelings. Nancy De Saussure recalled how she felt: "Joy and sorrow strove with each other. Joy in the hope of having my husband . . . return to me, but oh, such sorrow over our defeat!"

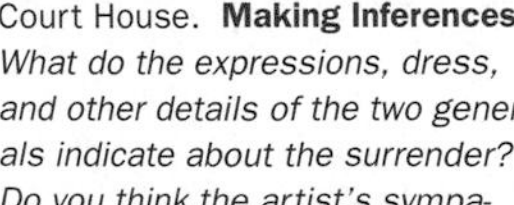

VIEWING HISTORY Lee surrenders to Grant at Appomattox Court House. **Making Inferences** *What do the expressions, dress, and other details of the two generals indicate about the surrender? Do you think the artist's sympathies were with the North or the South? Explain.*

Lincoln Is Assassinated

A few weeks after Lee's surrender, General Johnston surrendered to Sherman in North Carolina. Throughout May, other Confederate forces large and small also gave up.

CAPTION ANSWERS

Interpreting Graphs It almost equals those in all other U.S. wars because both sides were American and the obsolete tactics combined with new technology caused huge casualties. The pie charts show that the South lost a much larger percentage of its forces, and thus was short of manpower by the end of the war.

Viewing History General Lee looks dignified, elegant, and sadly heroic; his sword gives him the look of authority. Grant looks smaller and slightly deferential; he is positioned farther back in the painting. Both men look cordial and respectful of the other. Answers will vary about the artist's sympathies.

RESOURCE DIRECTORY

Teaching Resources

Units 1/2 booklet
- Section 4 Quiz, p. 42
- Chapter 4 Test, pp. 43, 46

Guide to the Essentials
- Section 4 Summary, p. 21
- Chapter 4 Test, p. 22

Other Print Resources

Chapter Tests with ExamView® Test Bank CD-ROM, Ch. 4

Technology

ExamView® Test Bank CD-ROM, Ch. 4
Social Studies Skills Tutor CD-ROM

Tragically, Abraham Lincoln did not live to see the official end of the war. Throughout the winter of 1864–1865, a group of Southern conspirators in Washington, D.C., had worked on a plan to aid the Confederacy. Led by John Wilkes Booth, a Maryland actor with strong Southern sympathies, the group plotted to kidnap Lincoln and exchange him for Confederate prisoners of war. After several unsuccessful attempts, Booth revised his plan. He assigned members of his group to kill top Union officials, including General Grant and Vice President Johnson. Booth himself would murder the President.

VIEWING HISTORY Lincoln's body was displayed in several major cities, including New York as shown here, on its way from Washington, D.C., to its resting place in Springfield, Illinois. **Drawing Conclusions** *Why do you think Lincoln was given such an elaborate funeral?*

On April 14, 1865, Booth slipped into the back of the President's unguarded box at Ford's Theater in Washington, D.C. Inside, the President and Mrs. Lincoln were watching a play. Booth pulled out a pistol and shot Lincoln in the head. Leaping over the railing, he fell to the stage, breaking his leg in the process. Booth then limped off the stage and escaped out a back alley. The army tracked Booth to his hiding place in a tobacco barn in Virginia. When he refused to surrender, they set the barn on fire. In the confusion that followed, Booth was shot to death, either by a soldier or by himself.

Mortally wounded, the unconscious President was carried to a boardinghouse across the street from the theater. While doctors and family stood by helplessly, Lincoln lingered through the night. He died early the next morning without regaining consciousness.

In the North, citizens mourned for the loss of the President who had led them through the war. Lincoln's funeral train took 14 days to travel from the nation's capital to his hometown of Springfield, Illinois. As the procession passed through towns and cities, millions of people lined the tracks to show their respect.

Both the North and the South had suffered great losses during the war, but both also gained by it. They gained an undivided nation, a democracy that would continue to seek the equality Lincoln had promised for it. They also gained new fellow citizens—the African Americans who had broken the bonds of slavery and claimed their right to be free and equal, every one.

Section 4 Assessment

READING COMPREHENSION

1. What did the **Battle of the Wilderness** reveal about Grant's strategy?
2. What happened at the **Battle of Spotsylvania** and the **Battle of Cold Harbor?**
3. What had the South hoped for in the election of 1864? Why did the election turn out differently?
4. What did the **Thirteenth Amendment** accomplish?
5. Who was John Wilkes Booth?

CRITICAL THINKING AND WRITING

6. **Analyzing Information** General Sherman said this about war: "The crueler it is, the sooner it will be over." Do you agree or disagree? Use examples from 1864 and 1865 to support your opinion.
7. **Writing an Editorial** Review the terms of surrender. Were they fair or too generous? Write the opening paragraph of an editorial stating your opinion.

Take It to the NET

Activity: Preparing an Oral Report Read about the events leading up to Lee's surrender to Grant. Report to your class on what you think is most interesting and important about the occasion. Use the links provided in the *America: Pathways to the Present* area of the following Web site for help in completing this activity.
www.phschool.com

Section 4 Assessment

Reading Comprehension

1. Under Grant's leadership, troops would not retreat quickly.
2. At Spotsylvania, despite huge losses, Grant persevered; at Cold Harbor, 7,000 Union troops fell in less than one hour.
3. For Lincoln's defeat, and McClellan's victory, as the latter had promised to negotiate to end the war. Sherman's capture of Atlanta changed the political climate in the North, leaving Northerners less willing to support negotiation.
4. The Thirteenth Amendment ended slavery in the United States forever.
5. He was a Southern conspirator who assassinated President Lincoln.

Critical Thinking and Writing

6. Students should assess military tactics and determine to what extent Union tactics such as Sheridan's Shenandoah campaign and Sherman's march to the sea contributed to ending the war.
7. Those who feel the terms were fair might claim it was necessary to offer easy terms because the former enemies were once again parts of one nation. Students who feel the terms were too generous might suggest that secession could be seen as treason and should be punished.

Take It to the NET

Students should demonstrate an understanding of the events that led to the end of the Civil War, including the Battle of Appomattox.

CAPTION ANSWERS

Viewing History Sample answers: He was respected for leading the Union to victory; an elaborate funeral was a display of Union solidarity and sorrow over Lincoln's death.

Reviewing Key Terms

Students should refer to the definitions of key terms in the chapter to write sentences that show an understanding of the Civil War era.

Reviewing Main Ideas

11. North: more railroad track; more factories for production of goods needed; a well-balanced economy; more money; functioning government; small army and navy; two-thirds of the nation's population lived there. South: home of most of the nation's military colleges; army did not need to initiate military action to win the war; fighting to preserve their way of life and self-government.

12. Union forces took control of the Cumberland and Tennessee rivers and seized parts of Mississippi, Tennessee, and Louisiana.

13. Union troops under Irvin McDowell were repulsed at Manassas in 1861; under McClellan were repulsed by Lee in 1862; under Burnside were beaten at Fredericksburg in 1862; under Hooker were beaten at Chancellorsville in 1863.

14. In May 1861 the Confederate government sent representatives to France and Great Britain. Though the South did not gain recognition, Great Britain did allow its ports to be used to build Confederate privateers.

15. He used the army to shut down opposition newspapers and denied others the use of the mails; used martial law to keep Kentucky in the Union camp. Kentucky citizens lost some of their constitutional rights.

16. While it did not bring an immediate end to slavery, it promised freedom when the North won the war. It caused many African American men to enlist in the military. It influenced both Great Britain and France in deciding not to intervene in the war.

17. There was some industrial growth. Women joined the Southern workforce in large numbers. The disruption of Southern farming, combined with the labor shortage and profiteering, caused shortages of food and other goods, as well as great inflation.

Chapter 4 Review and Assessment

creating a CHAPTER SUMMARY

Copy the time line (right) on a piece of paper and complete it by adding the important military and political events of the Civil War. Include a brief explanation of why each event was important. You may need to continue on several sheets of paper.

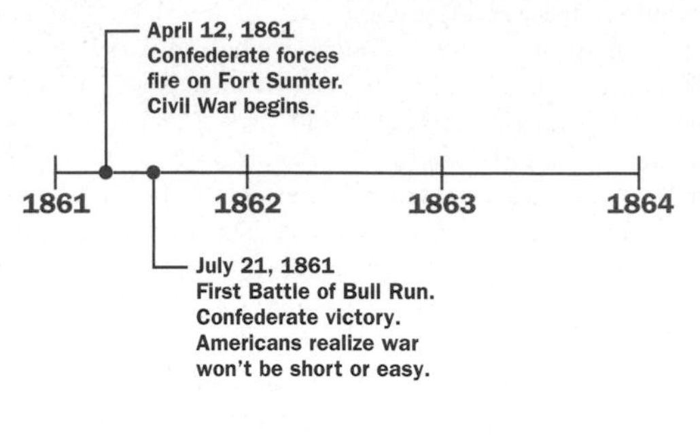
April 12, 1861
Confederate forces fire on Fort Sumter. Civil War begins.
1861
1862
1863
1864
July 21, 1861
First Battle of Bull Run. Confederate victory. Americans realize war won't be short or easy.

For additional review and enrichment activities, see the interactive version of *America: Pathways to the Present*, available on the Web and on CD-ROM.

★ Reviewing Key Terms

For each of the terms below, write a sentence explaining how it relates to the Civil War.

1. First Battle of Bull Run
2. war of attrition
3. Battle of Antietam
4. Copperhead
5. martial law
6. writ of *habeas corpus*
7. contraband
8. Pickett's Charge
9. siege
10. Thirteenth Amendment

★ Reviewing Main Ideas

11. List three strengths of the North and three strengths of the South. (Section 1)
12. What gains did Union forces make in the western part of the Confederacy in the first two years of the war? (Section 1)
13. Summarize Union efforts to capture Richmond in 1861–1863. (Section 1)
14. How and why did the South seek help from Europe? (Section 2)
15. Briefly describe three emergency measures Lincoln took during the war. (Section 2)
16. How did the Emancipation Proclamation affect the war? (Section 2)
17. How was the South's economy affected by the war? (Section 2)
18. What was the significance of the Battle of Gettysburg? (Section 3)
19. Why did Vicksburg surrender, and what was the importance of this Union victory? (Section 3)
20. What were the immediate and the long-term effects of Sherman's march to the sea? (Section 4)
21. What events led to Lee's surrender? (Section 4)

★ Critical Thinking

22. **Making Comparisons** Compare the Union and Confederate military strategies.
23. **Predicting Consequences** How might the war have been different if Lincoln had appointed Grant to lead the Union forces in July 1861? Explain your answer.
24. **Testing Conclusions** Lincoln came to believe that the Union could not survive if slavery were preserved. Give evidence to support this conclusion.
25. **Synthesizing Information** Why did the Civil War cost so many more American lives than wars before or since?

Creating a Chapter Summary

Year	Events
1861	• April 12 Confederate forces fire on Fort Sumter. Civil War begins. • July 21 First Battle of Bull Run, Confederate victory
1862	• March 9 Battle between the *Merrimack* and the *Monitor* • April 6–7 Battle of Shiloh • September 17 Battle of Antietam • December 13 Battle of Fredericksburg
1863	• January Emancipation Proclamation takes effect. • May 1–4 Battle of Chancellorsville • July 1–3 Battle of Gettysburg • July 4 Vicksburg surrenders. • November 19 Lincoln presents Gettysburg Address.
1864	• May 5–6 Battle of the Wilderness • June 3 Battle of Cold Harbor • September 2 Sherman occupies Atlanta. • December 21 Sherman captures Savannah. • April 9 Lee surrenders to Grant at Appomattox. • April 14 President Lincoln assassinated.

★ Skills Assessment

Analyzing Political Cartoons ▶

26. In this cartoon, England and France look on as a pair of combatants fight. Identify the two fighters.
27. In addition to the figure on the left, what other threat does the figure on the right face? Explain how you know.
28. What is being trampled? What does it stand for?
29. What do you think the political leanings of the cartoonist are? Explain your answer.

Interpreting Data

Turn to the "Civil War Deaths" graphs on page 192.

30. Which statement best describes the number of Civil War dead?
    A More Confederate soldiers died than Union soldiers.
    B More soldiers died in the Civil War than in all other U.S. wars combined.
    C More Union soldiers died than Confederate soldiers.
    D Twice as many Union soldiers died than Confederate soldiers.
31. Which statement best describes the percent, or fraction, of the total number of enlisted men killed?
    F Half of the soldiers who fought in the Civil War were killed.
    G A higher percentage of Confederate soldiers were killed than Union soldiers.
    H One third of all Union soldiers were killed.
    J More than a quarter of all Union soldiers were killed.

Applying the Chapter Skill: *Summarizing from Multiple Sources*

32. Reread two descriptions of battle by young boys who served in the Civil War: the quotation from Elisha Stockwell at the beginning of Section 2 and the one from the drummer boy at the beginning of Section 3. Create a summary of the two sources that expresses how it felt to be in a Civil War battle.

ACTIVITIES

Writing to LEARN

Writing to Persuade
In your view, would Lincoln have won the election of 1864 if the South had continued to triumph on the battlefield? Write an essay explaining your opinion. Include at least two reasons for your opinion, and support your reasons with specific details.

Primary Source CD-ROM

Working With Primary Sources Find additional information on the Civil War on the *Exploring Primary Sources in U.S. History CD-ROM* and use the selection(s) provided to complete the Chapter 4 primary source activity located in the *America: Pathways to the Present* area of the following Web site.
www.phschool.com

Take It to the NET

Chapter Self-Test As a review activity, take the Chapter 4 Self-Test in the *America: Pathways to the Present* area at the Web site listed below. The questions are designed to test your understanding of the chapter content.
www.phschool.com

ANSWERS TO ACTIVITIES

Writing to LEARN

Sample answer: Lincoln would have won the election because people did not want a negotiated settlement that might allow slavery to continue, which was part of McClellan's platform.

Primary Source CD-ROM

Direct students to the additional primary sources that can be found on the *Exploring Primary Sources in U.S. History CD-ROM.*

Take It to the NET

Additional support materials and activities for Chapter 4 of *America: Pathways to the Present* can be found in the Social Studies area at the Prentice Hall School Web site. **www.phschool.com**

18. After numerous defeats, Lee was forced to retreat, though both sides suffered huge losses. Lee never returned to Northern soil.
19. The siege depleted Confederate troops' rations, forcing them to surrender. The victory gave the Union control of the Mississippi River.
20. It brought widespread destruction to the South and created a long-lasting resentment of Southerners for Northerners.
21. Sheridan and Grant cut off Lee's supplies, forcing him to abandon Petersburg and Richmond. Then, hemmed in by Union forces, Lee surrendered at Appomattox Court House.

CRITICAL THINKING

22. The Union implemented the Anaconda Plan. Sherman and Grant were also able to win victories deep in southern territory. The Confederacy fought a primarily defensive war, hoping to wear down the Union's appetite for battle. But General Lee did march his troops into northern territory on two occasions.
23. Students may include a discussion of Grant's strong commanding skills, which may suggest that under his leadership the war might have been shorter, and more brutal.
24. Northerners were no longer content to let the slave system stand. Lincoln knew that slavery in the South would be an enduring source of friction even if the South could be brought back into the Union.
25. Advances in technology—both military and medical; the fact that both armies comprised Americans.

SKILLS ASSESSMENT

26. The seceding states, or the Confederacy, and the Union.
27. Copperheads, or anti-war Democrats, symbolized by the snake wrapped around the figure's leg.
28. The American flag: the United States and its ideals.
29. The cartoonist expresses the sentiments of a Union Democrat who supports the war. The Union figure is treated sympathetically, wearing white clothing and fighting two adversaries simultaneously—the Confederacy and the Copperheads.
30. C
31. F
32. Elisha Stockwell wants to go home, while the drummer boy wants to do his duty, regardless of the danger.

Federalism and States' Rights

Focus Remind students that the government of the United States is based on federalism, in which the national government shares power with the states. This system sometimes creates conflicts between the national government and the states. The Supreme Court has the authority to resolve such disputes.

Instruct As students read about each period in American history, tell them to think about the problems inherent in the country's system of government. Ask them why the balance of power at any given time tips toward either the federal government or the states.

Extend Encourage students to explore one of the periods described here. Tell them to find out whether the government in power at the time used its power wisely or overstepped its bounds. Ask them to consider whether it was inevitable that the federal government or the states had greater power at that time.

American Pathways
GOVERNMENT

Federalism and States' Rights

The Framers of the Constitution based the American system of government on federalism, which is the sharing of power between the national, or federal, government and state governments. This system set up a struggle for power between the two levels of government. The Supreme Court has served as the referee in this ongoing contest, which reached its climax in the Civil War.

1 The Growth of Nationalism

1787–1828 The Constitution created a federal system of government that strengthened what had been a weak national government. In the early 1800s, a sense of nationalism, along with westward expansion, prompted Congress and the Supreme Court to become more involved in issues affecting the states.

2 Sectionalism and Civil War

1828–1865 Nationalism turned into sectionalism as the federal government's policies in support of business and trade benefited the industrial North more than the agricultural South. Southern states, demanding their states' rights, denounced tariffs imposed by the federal government as well as calls for the abolition of slavery. The inability to resolve sectional conflicts, especially the slavery issue, ignited the Civil War.

Industry in Whitneyville, Connecticut (above left), and growing cotton along the Mississippi River (below left)

3 Reconstruction

1865–1877 The federal government's power over the states peaked during Reconstruction, when Congress put the Southern states under military rule and set the conditions for their reentry into the Union.

Federal troops in Atlanta, Georgia (right)

RESOURCE DIRECTORY

Teaching Resources

Units 1/2 booklet
- American Pathways Activity, pp. 104–105

American Pathways Thematic Posters

Technology

Companion Web site, www.phschool.com

Progressive Reforms

1890–1920 Cities and states often led the way in promoting Progressive reforms, which the federal government in some cases then applied to the entire nation. During this period, Congress took numerous actions to ensure the health and welfare of citizens and to prevent big businesses from limiting competition.

Two women protesting child labor (right)

From New Deal to Great Society

1932–1970 During the Great Depression, President Franklin Roosevelt's New Deal introduced many programs to assist the needy and regulate the economy. The federal government's involvement in areas formerly controlled by the states expanded.

The Civil Rights Movement

1954–1971 The Supreme Court, and later Congress, supported African Americans' efforts to secure their civil rights, despite firm resistance from state governments in the South.

Thurgood Marshall (left, center) outside the Supreme Court in Washington, D.C.

The Reagan Revolution

1980–Present President Ronald Reagan sought to limit the size—and the power—of the federal government while giving more responsibility to the states. He focused especially on cutting taxes, reducing government regulations, and reforming social welfare programs. Reagan's view of government has influenced politics to the present day.

Continuity and Change

1. Why did Southern states dislike the tariffs that Congress imposed?
2. Has power been evenly balanced between the federal government and the state governments? Explain your answer.

Take It to the NET: Creating a Study Guide
Print and complete the study guide for this topic found in the *America: Pathways to the Present* area of the following Web site. **www.phschool.com**

American Pathways

Take It to the NET

Students can print the American Pathways thematic study guide for this topic at the Prentice Hall School Web site, or you can provide students with copies of the study guide, which is found in the Units 1/2 booklet, the American Pathways Activity, pages 104–105. Students should use their texts to fill in a one-sentence description for each event on the study guide. When completed for each of the American Pathways topics, the thematic study guides will aid students in preparing for an end-of-course exam.

Answers

1. The tariffs were a heavy tax on imports designed to discourage foreign imports and encourage American manufacturing. The tariff greatly benefited the industrial North, but forced southerners to pay higher prices for manufactured goods. Also, southerners believed in states' rights and wanted to limit the power of the federal government.
2. Possible answer: The balance has shifted over time, reflecting the different views on the issue held by elected federal leaders. During Reconstruction, the federal government assumed its greatest control over the states. During the New Deal, the role of the federal government was greatly expanded into areas formerly controlled by the states. Since Ronald Reagan's presidency in the 1980s, most federal leaders have favored expanded powers for state governments and a reduction in the size of the federal government.

Chapter 5 Planning Guide

Resource Manager

	CORE INSTRUCTION	READING/SKILLS
Chapter-Level Resources **TEKS** 24(B), 24(C), 25(A), 25(B), 25(D)	Teaching Resources • Pacing Charts booklet • Block Scheduling booklet **Resource Pro® CD-ROM,** Ch. 5 **Prentice Hall Presentation Pro CD-ROM,** Ch. 5 **www.phschool.com** • eTeach	**Guided Reading Audiotapes (English/Spanish)** **Student Edition on Audio CD,** Ch. 5 **Social Studies Skills Tutor CD-ROM** **Color Transparencies,** B5, B6
1 Presidential Reconstruction 1. Learn about conditions in the South following the Civil War. 2. Analyze Lincoln's and Johnson's Reconstruction plans for similarities. 3. Find out how newly freed slaves began to rebuild their lives. **TEKS** 24(G), 25(C)	Teaching Resources **Units 1/2 booklet** • Section 1 Quiz, p. 50 **Learning Styles Lesson Plans booklet,** p. 26	**Guided Reading and Review booklet,** p. 50 **Guide to the Essentials,** p. 23 **Learning with Documents booklet,** p. 51 **Section Reading Support Transparencies**
2 Congressional Reconstruction 1. Discover how black codes and the Fourteenth Amendment were related. 2. Analyze the differences between Congress's Reconstruction plan and Andrew Johnson's. 3. Learn the significance of the Fifteenth Amendment. 4. Find out who supported the Republican governments of the South. **TEKS** 7(A), 7(C), 8(B), 19(B), 24(D), 24(G)	Teaching Resources **Units 1/2 booklet** • Section 2 Quiz, p. 51	**Guided Reading and Review booklet,** p. 51 **Guide to the Essentials,** p. 24 **Learning with Documents booklet,** p. 82 **Section Reading Support Transparencies**
3 Birth of the "New South" 1. Find out how farming in the South changed after the Civil War. 2. Explore how the growth of cities and industry began to change the South's economy after the war. 3. Learn how money designated for Reconstruction projects was used. **TEKS** 7(A), 8(B), 20(A), 24(H)	Teaching Resources **Units 1/2 booklet** • Section 3 Quiz, p. 52 **Learning Styles Lesson Plans booklet,** p. 27	**Guided Reading and Review booklet,** p. 52 **Guide to the Essentials,** p. 25 **Learning with Documents booklet,** p. 17 **Skills for Life booklet,** p. 7 **Section Reading Support Transparencies**
4 The End of Reconstruction 1. Learn about tactics used by the Ku Klux Klan to spread terror throughout the South. 2. Find out why Reconstruction ended. 3. Review the major successes and failures of Reconstruction. **TEKS** 7(A), 7(C), 8(B), 24(A)	Teaching Resources **Units 1/2 booklet** • Section 4 Quiz, p. 53	**Guided Reading and Review booklet,** p. 53 **Guide to the Essentials,** p. 26 **Section Reading Support Transparencies**

Enrichment/Pre-AP

Prentice Hall United States History Video Collection™
www.phschool.com
- Section Activities, Virtual Field Trip, Chapter Activities, Current Events Online

Biography, Literature, and Comparing Primary Sources booklet, pp. 17, 54–56
Great Debates booklet, p. 6
Historical Outline Map Book, p. 53
Sounds of an Era Audio CD

Biography, Literature, and Comparing Primary Sources booklet, pp. 119–120
American History Block Scheduling Support
Sounds of an Era Audio CD

Nystrom *Atlas of Our Country,* pp. 28–29

American History Block Scheduling Support
Historical Outline Map Book, p. 54
American Pathways Thematic Posters

Assessment

Core Assessment
ExamView® Test Bank, Ch. 5
ExamView® Test Bank CD-ROM, Ch. 5

Standardized Test Preparation
Diagnose and Prescribe
Diagnostic Tests for High School Social Studies Skills

Review and Reteach
Review Book for U.S. History

Practice and Assess
Test-taking Strategies With Transparencies
Test-taking Strategies Posters
Test Prep Book for U.S. History
Alternative Assessment Handbook
Document-Based Assessment

Teaching Resources
Units 1/2 booklet
- Section Quizzes, pp. 50–53
- Chapter Tests, pp. 54, 57

www.phschool.com Ch. 5 Self-Test

AmericanHeritage® Resources

From the Archives of American Heritage®, pp. 208, 219, 220
 **My Brush with History™ Videotapes**
www.americanheritage.com

iTEXT

Don't miss the exclusive interactive version of this textbook on the Web and on CD-ROM.

Chapter 5

Reconstruction

(1865–1877)

Introducing the Chapter

Though the outcome of the Civil War cemented the Union, the years that followed plunged the nation into dramatic social and economic changes. While African Americans obtained their liberty and southern society was transformed, Reconstruction involved a redefinition of social, economic, and political relationships between the North and the South as well as between the races.

Time Line Activity

To provide students with practice in using the time line, ask questions such as these:

1. What important events occurred in 1865? *(The Civil War ended, plans to pardon the South and restore the Union were made, and the Thirteenth Amendment ended slavery.)*
2. What did the Fourteenth Amendment do? *(It granted citizenship to all African Americans.)*
3. Where were slave markets abolished in 1873? *(Zanzibar)*

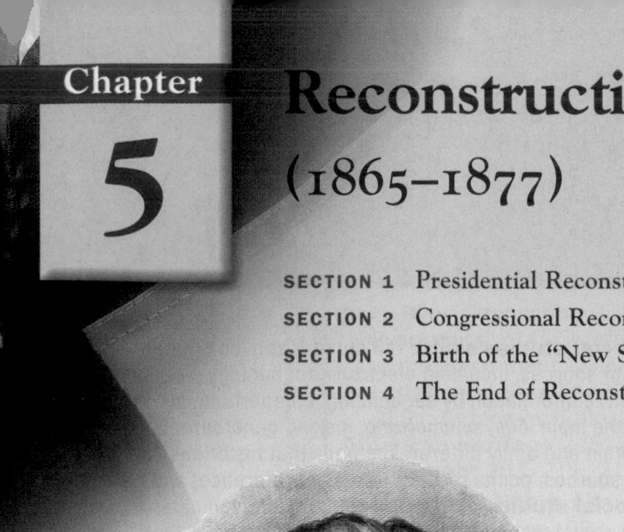

Chapter 5

Reconstruction (1865–1877)

Andrew Johnson

Following the Civil War, the South faced the challenge of rebuilding.

American Events

1865 The Civil War ends, and Presidents Lincoln and Johnson put forth plans to pardon the South and restore the Union. The Thirteenth Amendment ends slavery.

1866 The Ku Klux Klan forms, using terror to maintain white supremacy in the South.

1867 Angered by the southern states' attempts to limit rights of African Americans, Congress takes over Reconstruction and places the South under military rule.

1868 The Fourteenth Amendment grants blacks citizenship.

1870 The Fifteenth Amendment gives blacks the right to vote, and Republicans, including hundreds of freedmen, are elected to public office in the South.

Presidential Terms: Abraham Lincoln 1861–1865; Andrew Johnson 1865–1869; Ulysses S. Grant 1869–1877

1863 · 1866 · 1869

World Events

1864 Archduke Maximilian of Austria is made emperor of Mexico.

1867 Russia sells Alaska to the United States.

1869 The French-built Suez Canal opens in Egypt.

eTeach

Be sure to check out this month's online discussion with a Master Teacher. Go to **www.phschool.com**.

Resource Directory

Teaching Resources

Pacing Charts booklet

Block Scheduling booklet, p. 15

Units 1/2 booklet

- Chapter Summary, p. 49

Technology

Guided Reading Audiotapes (English/Spanish), Ch. 5

Student Edition on Audio CD, Ch. 5

Sounds of an Era Audio CD *Senator Robert Toombs on Secession,* 1960s recording (time: 30 seconds); *Former Slave Fountain Hughes,* 1941 recording (time: 20 seconds)

Prentice Hall United States History Video Collection™ Volume 10, *Reconstruction and Segregation (1865–1910)*

Prentice Hall Presentation Pro CD-ROM, Ch. 5

Resource Pro® CD-ROM

Social Studies Skills Tutor CD-ROM

Companion Web site, www.phschool.com

Reuniting a War-Torn Nation

Confederate states

Other states and territories

(1868) Date of readmission to the Union

Map shows 1863 borders.

1872
By 1872, all southern states have established public schools based in part on the success of the Freedmen's Bureau schools.

1877
Reconstruction ends when President Hayes withdraws federal troops from the South and Democrats regain control of southern politics.

Rutherford B. Hayes 1877–1881

1872 · **1875** · **1878**

1871
Britain legalizes labor unions.

1873
Slave markets are abolished in Zanzibar.

Reuniting a War-Torn Nation

Activating Prior Knowledge What was the first state to be readmitted to the Union? *(Tennessee was readmitted in 1866.)*

Previewing According to Johnson's Presidential Reconstruction plan, states were required to void secession, abolish slavery, and repudiate the confederate debt to be readmitted to the Union. Looking at the map, which states were last to meet these requirements? *(Texas, Mississippi, Georgia, and Virginia)*

BACKGROUND
About the Pictures

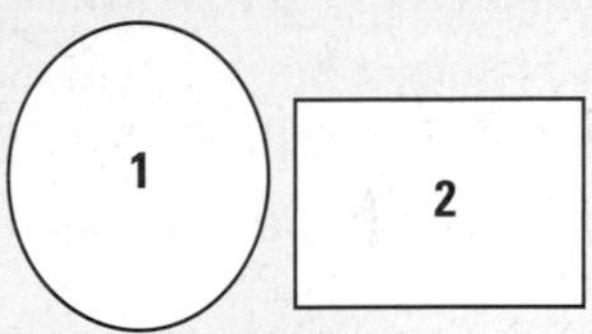

1. Contemporary engraving of Andrew Johnson, the seventeenth President of the United States.
2. The South was the main battleground of the Civil War, with hardly a farm or a family remaining unscarred by the time it was over.

BIBLIOGRAPHY

For the Teacher

Du Bois, W.E.B. ***Black Reconstruction.*** University of Notre Dame Press, 2001. (Classic account by the famous African American scholar.)

Foner, Eric. ***A Short History of Reconstruction.*** HarperCollins, 1990. (Abridgment of a definitive historical study of the era.)

Franklin, John Hope. ***Reconstruction After the Civil War.*** University of Chicago Press, 1995. (Sympathetic treatment of congressional efforts to reconstruct the old Confederacy.)

For the Student

Lester, Julius. ***This Strange New Feeling.*** Scholastic, 1997. (Three short stories about slavery and freedom, based on true accounts.)

Smith, John David. ***Black Voices from Reconstruction, 1865–1877.*** University Press of Florida, 1997. (Uses primary source material to detail the hopes, dreams, and disappointments of black people during the period after slavery.)

Don't miss the exclusive interactive version of this textbook on the Web and on CD-ROM.

Section 1 Presidential Reconstruction

SECTION OBJECTIVES

1. Learn about conditions in the South following the Civil War.
2. Analyze Lincoln's and Johnson's Reconstruction plans for similarities.
3. Find out how newly freed slaves began to rebuild their lives.

BELLRINGER

Warm-Up Activity Ask students to discuss the meaning of *reconstruct.* Ask them to think about how the concept relates to the period after the Civil War.

Activating Prior Knowledge Conduct a classroom discussion in which students speculate on the role Abraham Lincoln would have played in the Reconstruction had he not been assassinated. What do students think he would have emphasized more strongly: restoration of the Union or helping newly freed slaves achieve equality?

READING STRATEGY

As students read the section, have them apply absolute and relative chronology through the sequencing of significant individuals, events, and time periods in the years following the Civil War.

Section 1 Presidential Reconstruction

READING FOCUS

- What condition was the South in following the Civil War?
- How were Lincoln's and Johnson's Reconstruction plans similar?
- How did the newly freed slaves begin to rebuild their lives?

MAIN IDEA

Lincoln's and Johnson's Reconstruction plans focused on pardoning the Confederate states and restoring the Union quickly.

KEY TERMS

Reconstruction
pardon
Radical Republicans
pocket veto
Freedmen's Bureau

TAKING NOTES

Copy the diagram below. As you read, fill in the two circles with information about the two Presidents' Reconstruction plans. Place items that are similar in both plans in the area where the two circles overlap.

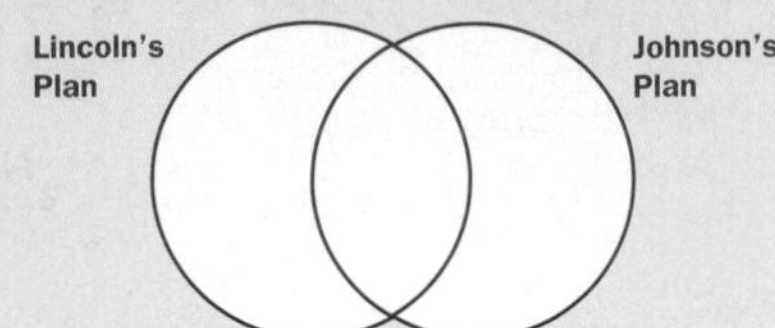

Setting the Scene The Civil War was over, and throughout the summer and fall of 1865, the soldiers who had made up the great armies of the Union and the Confederacy headed home. One was former Confederate soldier Val C. Giles, of Texas:

> "*I reached home in Govalle, outside of Austin . . . after an absence of four years and five months. Father and mother were not expecting me and were not at home, but my dog, Brave, was on guard. . . . It was not a 'deep-mouth welcome' that greeted me as I drew near, but a gruff emphatic warning to keep out. 'Brave, old boy,' I said, 'don't you know me?' He cocked up one ear and looked at me sideways. It finally dawned on him who I was, and he . . . circled wildly all around me, expressing in his dumb way his delight at my return. . . .*"
>
> —Val C. Giles

VIEWING HISTORY Many families eagerly awaited the return of loved ones at the end of the war. **Making Inferences** *What evidence is there in this photograph that this soldier's return home is an important event?*

Often the Confederate soldiers' homecomings contained as much sorrow as delight. Their cause had been defeated and their homes, in many cases, completely destroyed. Charleston, for example, was described by a journalist as a "city of ruins, of desolation, of vacant houses, of widowed women, of rotting wharves, of deserted warehouses, of weed-wild gardens, of miles of grass-grown streets, of acres of pitiful . . . barrenness."

Between 1865 and 1877, the federal government carried out a program to repair the damage to the South and restore the southern states to the Union. This program, known as **Reconstruction,** was hugely controversial at the time, and historians continue to debate its successes and failures to this day.

The War's Aftermath

At the start of Reconstruction, it was clear that the nation—especially the South—had been changed forever by the war. The changes reached into families and farms.

CAPTION ANSWERS

Viewing History Answers will vary. Students should note that both of the soldier's parents and one sibling have come out to greet him and appear to have dressed in fine clothes for the occasion. One of the neighboring families has also come out to greet the returning soldier.

RESOURCE DIRECTORY

Teaching Resources
Learning Styles Lesson Plans booklet, p. 26
Guided Reading and Review booklet, p. 50

Other Print Resources
Historical Outline Map Book *Reconstruction,* p. 53

Technology
Section Reading Support Transparencies
Guided Reading Audiotapes (English/Spanish), Ch. 5
Student Edition on Audio CD, Ch. 5
Sounds of an Era Audio CD *"When Johnny Comes Marching Home Again"* (time: 40 seconds)
Prentice Hall Presentation Pro CD-ROM, Ch. 5
Companion Web site, www.phschool.com

The Physical Toll War had destroyed two thirds of the South's shipping industry and about 9,000 miles of railroads. It had devoured farmland, farm buildings, and farm machinery; work animals and one third of all livestock; bridges, canals, and levees; and thousands of miles of roads. Factories, ports, and cities lay smoldering. The value of southern farm property had plunged by about 70 percent.

The Human Toll The Civil War destroyed a generation of young, healthy men—fathers, brothers, and husbands. The North lost 364,000 soldiers, including more than 38,000 African Americans. The South lost 260,000 soldiers, one fifth of its adult white men. One out of three southern men were killed or wounded. Many of the survivors were permanently scarred in mind or body. Fighting also resulted in countless civilian deaths. Children were made orphans; brides became widows.

VIEWING HISTORY This photograph of grave diggers by Alexander Gardner reminds viewers in grisly detail of the horrible human cost of the Civil War.

Southerners' Hardships The postwar South was made up of three major groups of people. Each group faced its own hardships and fears.

Black southerners Some 4 million freed people were starting their new lives in a poor region with slow economic activity. As slaves, they had received food and shelter, however inadequate. Now, after a lifetime of forced labor, many found themselves homeless, jobless, and hungry. Some freed slaves did choose to continue working on the plantations of their former masters. Others sought new jobs in the cities and in the West.

Plantation owners Planters lost slave labor worth about $3 billion. In addition, the Captured and Abandoned Property Act of 1863 allowed the federal government to seize $100 million in southern plantations and cotton. With worthless Confederate money, some farmers couldn't afford to hire workers. Others had to sell their property to cover debts.

Poor white southerners Many white laborers could not find work because of the new job competition from freedmen. Poor white families began migrating to frontier lands such as Mississippi and Texas to find new opportunities.

Punishment or Pardon? The fall of the Confederacy and the end of slavery raised difficult questions. How and when should southern states be allowed to resume their role in the Union? Should the South be punished for its actions, or be forgiven and allowed to recover quickly? Now that black southerners were free, would the races have equal rights? If so, how might those rights be protected? Did the Civil War itself point out a need for a stronger federal government? In Washington the debate over these questions launched new battles so fierce that some historians call Reconstruction an extension of the Civil War.

At stake were basic issues concerning the nation's political system. Yet it was not even clear which branch of government had the authority to decide these matters. On these key questions, the Constitution was silent. The Framers had made no provisions for solving the problems raised by the Civil War.

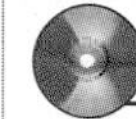

Sounds of an Era

Listen to "When Johnny Comes Marching Home Again" and other sounds from the Reconstruction period.

LESSON PLAN

Focus Explain that when the Civil War ended, the federal government struggled with the issue of how to put the nation back together. Discuss with students whether they think the South should have been treated harshly or dealt with leniently. What should the federal government have done to help newly freed slaves rebuild their lives?

Instruct Discuss the extent of the damage in the South caused by the Civil War and the suffering that resulted from it. Ask students why a harsh Reconstruction plan might be likely to increase the South's bitterness toward the federal government. Have student pairs summarize and compare Lincoln's and Johnson's Reconstruction plans. What were the elements of each? How did they differ?

Assess/Reteach Ask students to brainstorm, in order of urgency, a list of priorities that the United States faced as the country worked to reunite the North and the South.

ACTIVITY

Connecting with History and Conflict

Suggest that students analyze the statement in the text that Reconstruction was "an extension of the Civil War." Discuss how the issues involved in punishing or pardoning the South could continue to divide the North and South. Why would the reunion of the North and South after the war be especially difficult to accomplish? **(Verbal/Linguistic)**

CUSTOMIZE FOR ...

Less Proficient Writers

Have students list the three major groups of people in the postwar South. Then, have students make a bulleted list under each heading of the problems each group faced. Students don't have to write in complete sentences, but their lists should include all essential information.

Section 2
Congressional Reconstruction

Section Objectives

1. Discover how black codes and the Fourteenth Amendment were related.
2. Analyze the differences between Congress's Reconstruction plan and Andrew Johnson's.
3. Learn the significance of the Fifteenth Amendment.
4. Find out who supported the Republican governments of the South.

Bellringer

Warm-Up Activity Ask students to think about times in their lives when they experienced change. How did they and others react to the change? Did they want to go back to the way it had been before the change?

Activating Prior Knowledge Freed African American slaves and defeated Confederates alike experienced a great deal of upheaval during the Reconstruction years. Ask students to list some feelings, both positive and negative, that members of each group might have felt at that time.

Reading Strategy

In the late 1800s, southern states were putting ex-Confederates back in power and trying to keep freedmen in slave-like conditions. Ask students to analyze the social issue of treatment of minorities by listing some possible solutions to this problem. As they read, have them take specific notes on how Congress actually responded.

Section 2
Congressional Reconstruction

READING FOCUS

- How were black codes and the Fourteenth Amendment related?
- How did Congress's Reconstruction plan differ from Johnson's plan?
- What was the significance of the Fifteenth Amendment?
- Who supported the Republican governments of the South?

KEY TERMS

black codes
Fourteenth Amendment
civil rights
impeach
Fifteenth Amendment
carpetbagger
scalawag

MAIN IDEA

As southern states moved to limit freedmen's rights, Congress took over Reconstruction and passed new laws to protect African Americans' freedom.

TAKING NOTES

Create a cause-and-effect diagram like the one below. As you read, fill in the chart with the causes and effects discussed in the section.

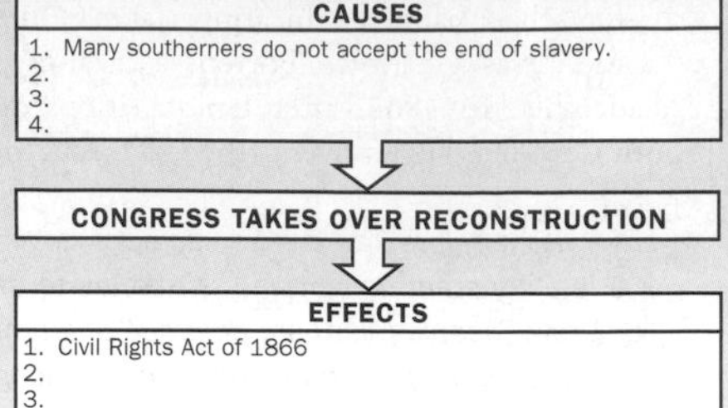

CAUSES
1. Many southerners do not accept the end of slavery.
2.
3.
4.
CONGRESS TAKES OVER RECONSTRUCTION
EFFECTS
1. Civil Rights Act of 1866
2.
3.

Setting the Scene For many African Americans, the initial surge of joy at gaining freedom quickly faded as they realized how many obstacles stood between them and true equality. Defeat in war had not changed the fact that white people still dominated southern society. As one white Georgian noted:

> "*[The freedman] has no land; he can make no crops. . . . He can scarcely get work anywhere but in the rice-fields and cotton plantations. . . . What sort of freedom is that?*"

Under Johnson's plan for Reconstruction, former Confederates were pardoned, state governments were restored, and the white leaders of those governments acted quickly to pass laws that severely restricted African Americans' newfound freedoms. These laws were known collectively as black codes.

VIEWING HISTORY According to Florida's black codes, a freedman without visible means of support could be fined. If the fine was not paid, the freedman's services could be auctioned off, as shown here. **Drawing Conclusions** *How does this photograph support the claim that black codes established virtual slavery?*

Black Codes

One by one, southern states met Johnson's Reconstruction demands and were restored to the Union. The first order of business in these new, white-run governments was to enact **black codes,** laws that restricted freedmen's rights. The black codes established virtual slavery with provisions such as these:

Curfews Generally, black people could not gather after sunset.

Vagrancy laws Freedmen convicted of vagrancy—that is, not working—could be fined, whipped, or sold for a year's labor.

Labor contracts Freedmen had to sign agreements in January for a year of work. Those who quit in the middle of a contract often lost all the wages they had earned.

Land restrictions Freed people could rent land or homes only in rural areas. This restriction forced them to live on plantations.

Caption Answers

Viewing History The African American men are being forced to allow their labor to be auctioned off by the white men on the porch, similar to the manner in which slaves had been auctioned off.

RESOURCE DIRECTORY

Teaching Resources
Guided Reading and Review booklet, p. 51

Technology
Section Reading Support Transparencies
Guided Reading Audiotapes (English/Spanish), Ch. 5
Student Edition on Audio CD, Ch. 5
Prentice Hall Presentation Pro CD-ROM, Ch. 5
Companion Web site, www.phschool.com

The Fourteenth Amendment

Southern defiance of Reconstruction enraged northern Republicans in Congress who blamed President Johnson for southern Democrats' return to power. Determined to bypass Johnson and put an end to his Reconstruction plan, Congress used one of its greatest tools: the power to amend the Constitution.

In early 1866, Congress passed a Civil Rights Act that outlawed the black codes. Johnson vetoed the measure. As President, Johnson was head of the Republican Party. Yet instead of leading congressional Republicans, he often found himself at odds with them. As an unelected former Democrat, Johnson had no real mandate to govern. (A mandate is voter approval of a politician's policies that is implied when he or she wins an election.) Lack of a mandate greatly limited Johnson's ability to influence Congress.

Congress overrode the President's veto. Then it took further action. Concerned that courts might strike down the Civil Rights Act, Congress decided to build equal rights into the Constitution. In June 1866, Congress passed the **Fourteenth Amendment,** which was ratified by the states in 1868. The amendment was a turning point, and its effects have echoed throughout American history. The amendment states:

KEY DOCUMENTS

> *"All persons born or naturalized in the United States . . . are citizens of the United States and of the State wherein they reside. No State shall make or enforce any law which shall abridge the privileges or immunities of citizens of the United States; nor shall any State deprive any person of life, liberty, or property, without due process of law; nor deny to any person within its jurisdiction the equal protection of the laws. . . ."*
>
> —Fourteenth Amendment, Section 1

Focus on GOVERNMENT

Civil Rights *The rights to which every citizen is entitled.*

The Historical Context The first Civil Rights Act, in 1866, guaranteed citizenship to African Americans. The second, in 1875, guaranteed them equal rights in public places. More fundamentally, in 1868, the Fourteenth Amendment made protection of civil rights part of the Constitution.

The Concept Today Violations of African Americans' civil rights continued and even increased following Reconstruction. Nearly a century later, the civil rights movement of the 1950s and 1960s fought to erase laws that discriminated against African Americans. Today it is illegal to discriminate on the basis of race.

Radical Reconstruction

The congressional Republicans who drafted the Fourteenth Amendment consisted of two major groups. One group was the Radical Republicans. Radicals were small in number but increasingly influential. Most Republicans, however, saw themselves as moderates. In politics, a moderate is someone who supports the mainstream views of the party, not the more extreme positions.

Moderates and Radicals both opposed Johnson's Reconstruction policies, opposed the spread of black codes, and favored the expansion of the Republican Party in the South. But moderates were less enthusiastic over the Radicals' goal of granting African Americans their **civil rights,** citizens' personal liberties guaranteed by law, such as voting rights and equal treatment. (See Focus on Government.) Racial inequality was still common in the North, and moderates did not want to impose stricter laws on the South than those in the North.

READING CHECK How did moderate Republicans in Congress differ from the Radical Republicans?

The North Grows Impatient This reluctance to grant civil rights began to dissolve in early 1866, as word spread of new violence against African Americans. In April, the famous Civil War nurse Clara Barton gave graphic testimony in Congress about injured black victims she had treated. During the next three months, white rioters went on rampages against African Americans in Memphis, Tennessee; New Orleans, Louisiana; and New York City. White police sometimes joined in the stabbings, shootings, and hangings that killed hundreds.

LESSON PLAN

Focus Explain that once southern state governments were reestablished under Johnson's plan, they began to undermine the plan. Ask students what southern states did to undermine Reconstruction. How did Congress respond?

Instruct Discuss how Republicans were able to bring radical political and social changes to the South. Ask students why Congress wanted to take over Reconstruction. How did the dissatisfaction of Congress with Johnson eventually lead to his impeachment? What was Congress hoping to accomplish by passing the Fourteenth and Fifteenth Amendments? What impact did the Fifteenth Amendment have on Reconstruction legislatures?

Assess/Reteach What was the intention of Congress in passing the Fourteenth Amendment? How did most members of Congress in the years just after the Civil War probably feel about black codes?

ACTIVITY: Connecting with Government

The phrases "due process" and "equal protection of the laws" in the Fourteenth Amendment are the foundations upon which many civil rights cases are argued today. Have students trace the historical development of the civil rights movement in the nineteenth century by supposing they are going to defend someone who has been discriminated against in employment, housing, education, or health care. Have them draw up the case to present to a court based on the Fourteenth Amendment. They should outline the case, explain the evidence, and lay out arguments based on due process and equal protection clauses. Students may then write up their cases or present them orally to the class. **(Logical/Mathematical; Verbal/Linguistic)**

READING CHECK
Moderate Republicans did not want full civil rights for African Americans, and felt threatened by the desire of Radical Republicans for a level of racial equality exceeding that found in northern states.

CUSTOMIZE FOR ...

ESL

Ask a volunteer to read aloud the excerpt from the Fourteenth Amendment on this page. Then have students take turns summarizing each sentence in the passage in their own words.

TEST PREPARATION

Have students read the excerpt from the Fourteenth Amendment on this page and then complete the sentence below.

The word *abridge* in the passage means—

A enforce.
(B) take away.
C connect.
D grant.

Activity

Connecting with Government

Create groups of four to six students. Group members should take on different roles, as representatives of the federal government, such as the President and senators, or representatives from various states. Each group should focus on one aspect of Reconstruction: political structure; social structure; or economic structure. After a group discussion, have each group state its perception of the reasoning that would have shaped plans for Reconstruction in the area on which the groups focus. **(Verbal/Linguistic)**

From the Archives of

American Heritage®

About the Presidents

Andrew Johnson (1865–1869) was impeached after two days of one-sided debate. The charges against the President were politically motivated. As his Secretary of the Navy wrote, "Those who may vote to convict . . . would as readily vote to impeach the President had he been accused of stepping on a dog's tail." The Senate had responsibility for conducting the trial. Members of Johnson's Cabinet were not allowed to testify on his behalf, and Radicals pressured undeclared Republican senators to convict Johnson. Among them, Senator Grimes buckled under the pressure and had a stroke. The Radicals even postponed the final vote to exert more pressure. In the end, however, seven Republican senators gave up their legislative careers to vote for Johnson's acquittal. Source: David Jacobs, "Andrew Johnson," *The American Heritage® Pictorial History of the Presidents of the United States,* vol. 1, 1968.

MAP SKILLS President Lincoln had hoped to restore southern state governments to "successful operation, with order prevailing and the Union reestablished," by December 1865. Under Radical Republican rule, however, this did not happen for more than a decade. Because of its adherence to Congressional demands, Tennessee was the only southern state not placed under northern military rule. **Place** *(a) Which state was the first to rejoin the Union? (b) How do you think southerners reacted to military rule by northern generals?*

Radical Rule of the South

Military District and Commander
- General Phillip Sheridan
- General Edward Ord
- General John Pope
- General Daniel Sickles
- General John Schofield
- (1868) Date of readmission to Union

Despite public outrage against the brutality, Johnson continued to oppose equal rights for African Americans. In the 1866 congressional elections, he gave speeches urging states not to ratify the Fourteenth Amendment. Angry northern voters responded by sweeping Radical Republicans into Congress. Now, Radicals could put their own Reconstruction plans into action.

Strict Laws Imposed Calling for "reform, not revenge," Radicals in Congress passed the Reconstruction Act of 1867. Historians note that this was indeed a "radical" act in American history. These are its key provisions:

1. It put the South under military rule, dividing it into five districts, each governed by a northern general. (See the map on this page.)
2. It ordered southern states to hold new elections for delegates to create new state constitutions.
3. It required states to allow all qualified male voters, including African Americans, to vote in the elections.
4. It temporarily barred those who had supported the Confederacy from voting.
5. It required southern states to guarantee equal rights to all citizens.
6. It required the states to ratify the Fourteenth Amendment.

Senator Charles Sumner of Massachusetts (top) and Thaddeus Stevens, a Congressman from Pennsylvania, were both leading spokesmen for the Radical Republicans in their fight to win civil rights for African Americans.

Congress and the President The stage was now set for a showdown that pitted President Johnson against two powerful Radical Republicans in Congress. Massachusetts Senator Charles Sumner, a founder of the Republican Party, was a passionate abolitionist who sought voting rights for black Americans. In the House, Johnson faced Thaddeus Stevens, a Pennsylvania congressman with a stern face and a personality to match. Stevens led the charge that threatened to bring down Johnson's presidency.

At face value, the contest was a test of wills between the President and his congressional adversaries. Yet it was also a power struggle between the legislative and executive branches of government, a test of the system of checks and balances established by the Constitution.

A Power Struggle The crisis began in early 1868, when Johnson tried to fire Secretary of War Edwin Stanton, a Lincoln appointee. Johnson wanted Stanton removed because, under the new Reconstruction Act, Stanton, a friend of the Radicals, would preside over military rule of the South.

The firing of Stanton directly challenged the Tenure of Office Act just passed by Congress in 1867. The act placed limits on the President's power to hire and fire government officials. Under the Constitution, the President must seek Senate approval for candidates to fill certain jobs, such as Cabinet posts.

Caption Answers

Map Skills Tennessee. Southerners generally disliked being governed by northerners. Southerners led a different lifestyle than northerners, and there was likely resentment at being governed by a recent enemy.

RESOURCE DIRECTORY

Other Print Resources

American History Block Scheduling Support *The Realities of Reconstruction,* found in the Expansion, Reconstruction, Immigration folder, includes interdisciplinary lesson suggestions and activities for Geography and History, Primary Sources, Biography, and Literature.

Technology

Color Transparencies *Political Cartoons,* B6

Sounds of an Era Audio CD *Campaign Song for Ulysses S. Grant* (time: one minute, 30 seconds)

RESOURCE PRO® **Primary Source Activity** *The Trial of President Johnson,* found on Resource Pro, describes the impeachment trial of President Johnson in the words of his bodyguard.

The Tenure of Office Act demanded that the Senate approve the firing of those officials as well, thereby limiting the President's power to create an administration to his own liking. The act also took away the President's constitutional powers as commander in chief of the armed forces.

Johnson Is Impeached Led by the fiery Stevens, the House found that Johnson's firing of Stanton was unconstitutional. On February 24, 1868, House members voted 126 to 47 to **impeach** him—to charge him with wrongdoing in office. The House drafted 11 articles of impeachment, including violation of the Tenure of Office Act and bringing "into disgrace, ridicule, hatred, contempt, and reproach the Congress of the United States." Johnson became the first President in United States history to be impeached.

As called for by the Constitution, the Senate tried President Andrew Johnson for "high crimes and misdemeanors." Chief Justice Salmon P. Chase presided over the proceedings. If two thirds of the senators were to vote for conviction, Johnson would become the only President ever removed from office. The historic vote took place on May 16, 1868. When all the "ayes" and "nays" were counted, Johnson had escaped by the closest of margins: one vote. The crisis set the precedent that only the most serious crimes, and not merely a partisan dispute with Congress, could remove a President from office.

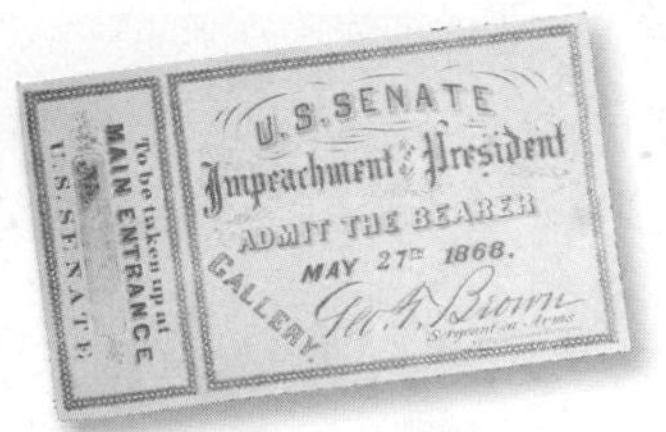

President Johnson was the first President to be impeached by the House of Representatives. The Senate found Johnson innocent, and he was not removed from office.

Grant Is Elected President Johnson, as the saying goes, "won the battle but lost the war." He served the remaining months of his term, but with no mandate and no real power. Rejected by the party that had never really embraced him, Johnson went back to Tennessee and regained his Senate seat—as a Democrat.

In the 1868 election, Republicans chose a trusted candidate who was one of their own: the victorious Civil War general, Ulysses S. Grant. In a close race, Grant beat Democrat Horatio Seymour, former governor of New York. Now, Congress and the President were allies, not enemies.

The Fifteenth Amendment

Across the South, meanwhile, freedmen were beginning to demand the rights of citizenship: to vote, to hold public office, to serve on juries, and to testify in court. In a letter to the Tennessee constitutional convention, Nashville freedmen eloquently presented the case for black voting rights:

> *"If [freedmen] are good law-abiding citizens, praying for its [the nation's] prosperity, rejoicing in its progress, paying its taxes, fighting its battles, making its farms, mines, work-shops and commerce more productive, why deny them the right to have a voice in the election of its rulers?"*
>
> —The "black citizens of Nashville," January 9, 1865

The letter received no known response. Yet African Americans, and their supporters in Congress, pressed on.

COMPARING PRIMARY SOURCES
Voting Rights for African Americans

The question of whether to extend voting rights to African Americans was hotly debated in the 1860s.

Analyzing Viewpoints Compare the main arguments made by the two writers.

In Favor of Voting Rights

"If impartial suffrage is excluded in rebel States, then every one of them is sure to send a solid rebel representative delegation to Congress, and cast a solid rebel electoral vote. They . . . would always elect the President and control Congress. . . . I am for negro suffrage in every rebel state. If it be just, it should not be denied; if it be necessary, it should be adopted; if it is a punishment to traitors, they deserve it."

—*Speech by Thaddeus Stevens, Radical Republican, January 3, 1867*

Opposed to Voting Rights

"Most of the whites are disenfranchised [not legally able to vote] and ineligible for office, whilst the Negroes are [granted] the right of voting. The political power is therefore thrown into the hands of a mass of human beings who, having just emerged from a state of servitude [slavery], are ignorant of the forms of government and totally unfit to exercise this, the highest privilege of a free people."

—*Henry William Ravenel, South Carolina planter, journal entry for February 24, 1867*

ACTIVITY
Connecting with Government

Divide students into groups representing Radical Republicans, Democrats, and moderate Republicans. Have students debate the issue of Johnson's impeachment, defending or opposing the action. They should look at the issues involved and also consider the motivations behind the impeachment. Encourage students to evaluate whether Johnson's actions constituted "high crimes and misdemeanors." Student groups may present their arguments to the class as a whole. **(Verbal/Linguistic)**

BACKGROUND
A Diverse Nation

Edmund G. Ross was a Radical Republican senator from Kansas who voted the party line for the radical Reconstruction measures. When it came to the trial of President Andrew Johnson in the Senate, however, he was uncertain. He insisted that Johnson be treated fairly, especially concerning the evidence presented at the trial. Radical Republicans pressured him, but he remained firm in his principles of fairness.

When the vote came in the Senate, six Republicans had defied their party, voting for acquittal and tying the vote. Ross's vote was crucial. He later described his feelings: "I almost literally looked down into my own grave. Friends, position, fortune, everything that makes life desirable to an ambitious man, were about to be swept away by the breath of my mouth, perhaps forever." When Ross voted "not guilty," he was denounced as a traitor and vilified by his colleagues. Ross served out his term, becoming more moderate and more independent of the Radical Republicans. But he was not reelected, and eventually he joined the Democratic Party.

TEST PREPARATION

Have students read the quote on this page and then answer the question below.

Why did the writer feel that freedmen should have the right to vote?

A Lincoln supported the idea.
B The freedmen had been slaves.
(C) Freedmen were contributing to the country.
D Freedmen supported radical Reconstruction.

ACTIVITY
Connecting with Citizenship

The Fourteenth Amendment gave freedmen citizenship. The Fifteenth Amendment gave them the right to vote. Trace the historical development of the civil rights movement in the nineteenth century by recalling with students the main points of the Fourteenth Amendment and having them compare these with the main points of the Fifteenth Amendment. Why do students think the Fourteenth Amendment did not include the right to vote? Why was it important to give African Americans voting rights? You might point out that the Fifteenth Amendment specifies people cannot be denied the right to vote based on race, color, or status as former slaves. What major sector of the population is not specified and is left out? **(Verbal/Linguistic)**

BACKGROUND
A Diverse Nation

To honor the passage of the Fifteenth Amendment, Baltimore, Maryland, held a parade and celebration on May 19, 1870. The crowd that gathered was large—at least 20,000 people. On this historic occasion, many heard a speech by Frederick Douglass, the great African American leader. According to a newspaper account that appeared the next day in the Baltimore *American,* Douglass began his speech by telling the crowd that he had often appeared before the people as a slave, sometimes as a fugitive slave, but always on behalf of the slave. "But today," said the newspaper article, "he was permitted to appear before them as an American citizen. How great the change!" Douglass went on to say: "The Fifteenth Amendment means that hereafter the black man is to have no excuse for ignorance, poverty, or destitution. Our excuse for such in the past is swept from us by the Fifteenth Amendment. We are to stand up and be responsible for our own existence, we must be independent men and citizens."

READING CHECK

The Fifteenth Amendment allowed hundreds of African Americans in southern states to become state senators and representatives in the 1870 elections.

American BIOGRAPHY

Blanche K. Bruce 1841–1898

A boy born into slavery in 1841 could expect little more than a life of servitude. Blanche K. Bruce was more fortunate than some. Growing up in Virginia and Missouri, he shared a tutor with his master's son. Later he attended Oberlin College in Ohio, until his money ran out. Bruce then moved to Mississippi and began recruiting Republicans from among freedmen on the plantations. In 1871 he ran for sheriff of Bolivar County, Mississippi. Bruce won the sheriff's post, and later held other government jobs as well. As a public servant, he worked to ease racial and political tensions, earning respect from Radical and moderate Republicans—even white planters. In 1874 Bruce won election to the United States Senate.

In February 1869, at the peak of Radical power, Congress passed the **Fifteenth Amendment** to the Constitution. It stated that no citizen may be denied the right to vote "by the United States or by any State on account of race, color, or previous condition of servitude." Ratified in March 1870, the Fifteenth Amendment was one of the enduring legacies of Reconstruction.

The Supreme Court added its weight to the federal Reconstruction effort in 1869. In *Texas* v. *White,* the Court ruled that it was illegal for any state to secede from the Union. The case also upheld Congress's right to restructure southern governments. The ruling added new support for federal power over states' rights.

The First Votes Even before the Fifteenth Amendment was ratified, the military had begun to register freedmen under the Reconstruction Act of 1867. Nearly 735,000 African Americans joined the voting rolls and their electoral power transformed politics in the South.

In 1867 and 1868, voters in southern states chose delegates to draft new state constitutions. Nearly 80 percent of the newly registered African American voters went to the polls, while most registered white voters did not participate. As a result, one quarter of the more than 1,000 delegates elected to the ten state conventions were black. In two states where African Americans outnumbered whites, Louisiana and South Carolina, voters chose majority-black delegations.

These integrated conventions wrote radical new constitutions for their states. Provisions in the new constitutions guaranteed the civil rights of all residents, opened political office to individuals without regard to wealth, and set up a system of public schools and orphanages. Ten Reconstruction state governments quickly adopted the new constitutions.

READING CHECK

How did the Fifteenth Amendment influence the composition of southern state legislatures?

Electing Black Leaders In 1870, with federal troops stationed across the South and with the Fifteenth Amendment in place, southern black men proudly voted in legislative elections for the first time. Most voted Republican, while many angry white voters again stayed home.

The results were dramatic. Before the election, African American voters made up a majority in five states—Alabama, Florida, Louisiana, Mississippi, and South Carolina—and a substantial minority in the other states undergoing Reconstruction. The unique circumstances of the election swept Republicans, including hundreds of freedmen, into public office in the South.

More than 600 African Americans were elected to state legislatures. However, African Americans remained the minority in nearly every state house in the South. The sole exception was South Carolina, where black legislators controlled the lower house and even, for a short time, the state senate. Individual black leaders could rise to positions of power in state government through alliances with white Republicans.

Louisiana gained a black governor, P.B.S. Pinchback, who had settled in that state after fighting for the Union during the Civil War. During Reconstruction, Pinchback had served as a state senator and eventually became lieutenant governor and then governor in 1872.

Integrating the Capitol The extension of the vote to freedmen led to the election of the first African Americans to the House of Representatives. Despite resistance from other representatives, their number gradually rose to eight by 1875.

RESOURCE DIRECTORY

Teaching Resources

Units 1/2 booklet
- Section 2 Quiz, p. 51

Guide to the Essentials
- Section 2 Summary, p. 24

Learning with Documents booklet (Key Documents) *Speeches by Blanche K. Bruce and Frederick Douglass,* p. 82

Biography, Literature, and Comparing Primary Sources booklet (Comparing Primary Sources) *On Voting Rights for African Americans,* pp. 119–120

In 1870, Hiram Revels of Mississippi became the first African American elected to the Senate. Four years later, Mississippi's state legislature sent to the Senate a former slave, Blanche K. Bruce. (See American Biography.) Louisiana chose P.B.S. Pinchback to represent it in the Senate, but other senators voted not to seat him in 1876. By that time, the climate in Washington, D.C., and the southern states had begun to shift against African American legislators.

A northerner's carpetbag

The Republican South

During Radical Reconstruction, the Republican Party was a mixture of people who had little in common but a desire to prosper in the postwar South. This bloc of voters included freedmen and two other groups.

Carpetbaggers Northern Republicans who moved to the postwar South became known as **carpetbaggers.** Southerners gave them this insulting nickname, which referred to a type of cheap suitcase made from carpet scraps. The name implied that these northerners had stuffed some clothes into a carpetbag and rushed in to profit from southern misery.

Carpetbaggers were often depicted as greedy men seeking to grab power or make a fast buck. Certainly the trainloads of northerners who disembarked in southern cities included some profiteers and swindlers. Yet historians point out that most carpetbaggers were honest, educated men. They included former union soldiers, black northerners, Freedmen's Bureau officials, businessmen, clergy, and political leaders.

Scalawags In the postwar South, to be white and a southerner and a Republican was to be seen as a traitor. Southerners had an unflattering name for white southern Republicans as well: **scalawag,** originally a Scottish word meaning "scrawny cattle." Some scalawags were former Whigs who had opposed secession. Some were small farmers who resented the planter class. Still others were former planters. Many scalawags, but not all, were poor.

Many southern whites, resenting the power of freedmen, carpetbaggers, and scalawags, criticized the Reconstruction governments as corrupt and incompetent. In reality, Reconstruction legislatures included honest men and dishonest men, qualified politicians and incompetent ones, literate men and a few illiterate ones. Today, most historians agree that these officials were no worse and no better than officials in other regions of the country at that time.

Section 2 Assessment

READING COMPREHENSION

1. Why were northern Republicans in Congress enraged by the **black codes** and the reports of violence against African Americans?
2. How did the moderate and Radical Republicans in Congress disagree over African American **civil rights?**
3. Who were the **carpetbaggers** and the **scalawags?**

CRITICAL THINKING AND WRITING

4. **Drawing Conclusions** How was the impeachment of Andrew Johnson a test of the Constitution's system of checks and balances?
5. **Comparing Points of View** Describe the gains made by African Americans under Radical Reconstruction governments in the South. How did white Democrats perceive Radical rule?

Take It to the NET

Activity: Drawing a Political Cartoon Learn more about southerners' perceptions of carpetbaggers, and then draw your own cartoon of a carpetbagger. Use the links provided in the *America: Pathways to the Present* area of the following Web site for help in completing this activity.
www.phschool.com

Section 2 Assessment

Reading Comprehension

1. Black codes created virtual slavery, rather than freedom and equality. The hypocrisy of these codes exemplified southern defiance of Reconstruction, as did incidents of violence in which African Americans were killed or wounded.
2. Moderates were less eager to support the Radicals' goal of granting civil rights to African Americans. Racial inequality in the North was still common, and moderates did not want to impose stricter laws on the South than those in the North.
3. Carpetbaggers were northern Republicans who moved to the postwar South. The nickname implied that these northerners had rushed in to profit from southern misery. Scalawags were white southern Republicans who, at the time, were viewed as traitors.

Critical Thinking and Writing

4. Congress used its constitutionally granted power to impeach a President who had been accused of acting unconstitutionally.
5. Answers may include the following: end of black codes; granting of civil rights, such as voting and equal treatment; ratification of the Fourteenth Amendment; election to public office. Southern white Democrats despised the Reconstruction governments. They felt that carpetbaggers and scalawags were the corrupt representatives of those governments, and that freedmen had been given too much power and protection.

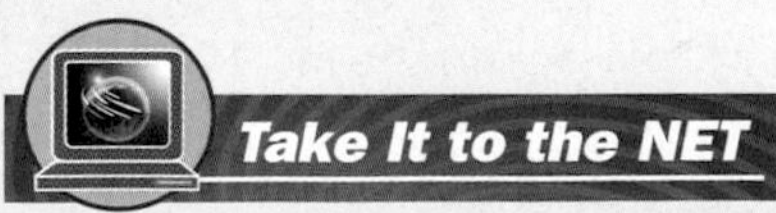
Take It to the NET

Illustrations should show the carpetbaggers' exploitation of the defeated South.

Section 3
Birth of the "New South"

Section Objectives

1. Find out how farming in the South changed after the Civil War.
2. Explore how the growth of cities and industry began to change the South's economy after the war.
3. Learn how money designated for Reconstruction projects was used.

Bellringer

Warm-Up Activity Ask students to think about the term *economic reorganization.* What do they suppose it means? Ask students if they know of any countries that have undergone economic reorganization in the last decade.

Activating Prior Knowledge Ask students to consider the types of people who might be drawn to help rebuild the South. Would it be likely that their interests would be mainly for the good of society, for their own personal gain, or both?

Reading Strategy

Have students read the Main Idea on this page. Ask them to rewrite it as a question. As they read, have them take notes that help answer that question and that help them support a point of view on one of the social studies issues or events described in the section.

Section 3

Birth of the "New South"

READING FOCUS

- How did farming in the South change after the Civil War?
- How did the growth of cities and industry begin to change the South's economy after the war?
- How was the money designated for Reconstruction projects used?

MAIN IDEA

The end of slavery brought about new patterns of agriculture in the South, while expansion of cities and industry led to limited economic growth.

KEY TERMS

sharecropping
tenant farming
infrastructure

TAKING NOTES

Copy the chart below. As you read, fill in details about economic changes that occurred in the South during Reconstruction.

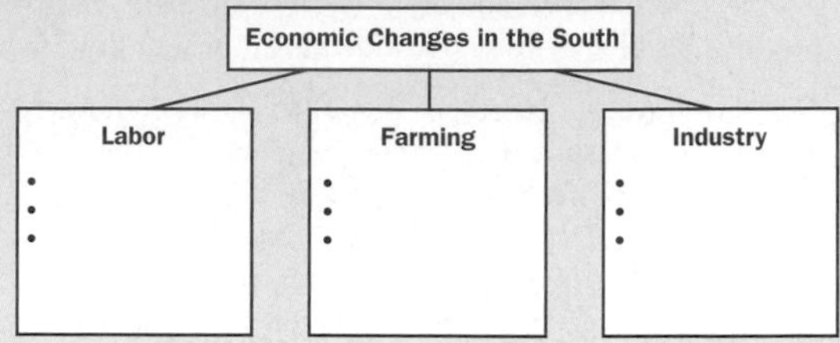

Setting the Scene Writing to a South Carolina newspaper late in 1865, a black soldier in the United States Army stated:

> "*We have been faithful in the field . . . and think that we ought to be considered as men, and allowed a fair chance in the race of life. It has been said that a black man can not make his own living, but give us opportunities and we will show the whites that we will not come to them for any thing.*"
>
> —Black Union soldier

This demand for a "fair chance in the race of life" was echoed by freedmen across the South. For most of them, the key to that fair chance was land. "Give us our own land and we can take care of ourselves," said one freedman, "but without land, our old masters can hire us or starve us as they please."

As you read in Section 1, proposals to distribute formerly white-owned land to freedmen received little political support. Few freedmen had the money to buy their own land, and even those who did often found that whites refused to sell or rent land to them. As a result, most freedmen had little choice but to work the land of others. They soon discovered, in one freedman's words, that "No man can work another man's land [without getting] poorer and poorer every year."

One black family in Alabama learned this lesson the hard way. The Holtzclaw family worked on the cotton farm of a white planter. Every year at harvest time they received part of the cotton crop as payment for their work. Most years, however, the Holtzclaws' share of the harvest didn't earn them enough money to feed themselves. Some years the planter gave them nothing at all. To earn more money, Mrs. Holtzclaw worked as a cook, while Mr. Holtzclaw hauled logs at a sawmill for 60 cents a day. Their children waded knee-deep in swamps gathering anything edible. This was not the freedom they had hoped for.

VIEWING FINE ART Despite emancipation, the cotton still needed to be picked. This painting by Winslow Homer (1876) shows young women in the fields, probably working just as their mothers had before the war, except for some small wages. **Making Comparisons** *Compare the details in this painting to the photograph on the next page.*

Caption Answers

Viewing Fine Art Similarities: the great size of the cotton fields is clear. The facial expressions are also very similar between the two illustrations. Differences: in the photo, the whole family is present in the field; the painting only shows two women. The dirt and dust that can be seen on each family member's clothing in the photo conveys the difficulty of the work.

Resource Directory

Teaching Resources
Learning Styles Lesson Plans booklet, p. 27
Guided Reading and Review booklet, p. 52

Technology
Section Reading Support Transparencies
Guided Reading Audiotapes (English/Spanish), Ch. 5
Student Edition on Audio CD, Ch. 5
Prentice Hall Presentation Pro CD-ROM, Ch. 5
Companion Web site, www.phschool.com

Changes in Farming

The Holtzclaws were part of an economic reorganization in the "New South" of the 1870s. It was triggered by the ratification of the Thirteenth Amendment in 1865, which ended slavery and shook the economic foundations of the South.

The loss of slave labor raised grave questions for southern agriculture. Would cotton still be king? If so, who would work the plantations? Would freed people flee the South or stay? How would black emancipation affect the poor white laborers of the South? No one really knew.

Wanted: Workers Although the Civil War left southern plantations in tatters, the destruction was not permanent. Many planters had managed to hang on to their land, and others regained theirs after paying off their debt. Planters complained, however, that they couldn't find people willing to work for them. Nobody liked picking cotton in the blazing sun. It seemed too much like slavery. Workers often disappeared to look for better, higher-paying jobs. For instance, railroad workers in Virginia in the late 1860s earned $1.75 to $2 a day. Plantation wages came to 50 cents a day at best. Women in the fields earned as little as 6 cents a day. In simple terms, planters had land but no laborers, while freedmen had their own labor but no land. Out of these needs came new patterns of farming in the South.

Sharecropping The most common new farming arrangement was known as **sharecropping.** A sharecropping family, such as the Holtzclaws, farmed some portion of a planter's land. As payment, the family was promised a share of the crop at harvest time, generally one third or one half of the yield. The planter usually provided housing for the family.

Sharecroppers worked under close supervision and under the threat of harsh punishment. They could be fined for missing a single workday. After the harvest, some dishonest planters simply evicted the sharecroppers without pay. Others charged the families for housing and other expenses, so that the sharecroppers often wound up in debt at the end of the year. Since they could not leave before paying the debt, these sharecroppers were trapped on the plantation.

INTERPRETING DIAGRAMS
Whether white or black, most southern farmers remained poor in the years following the Civil War—as did this Florida family (below right), thought to be sharecroppers or tenant farmers. The chart (below left) shows the cycle of debt that poor families faced. **Drawing Conclusions** *How did farmers get caught in a cycle of debt?*

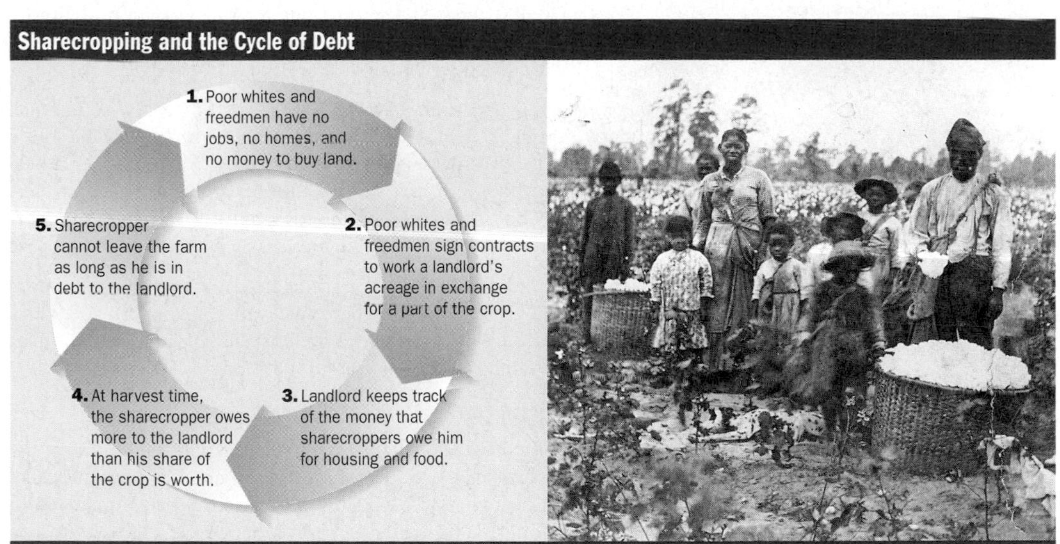

Sharecropping and the Cycle of Debt
1. Poor whites and freedmen have no jobs, no homes, and no money to buy land.
2. Poor whites and freedmen sign contracts to work a landlord's acreage in exchange for a part of the crop.
3. Landlord keeps track of the money that sharecroppers owe him for housing and food.
4. At harvest time, the sharecropper owes more to the landlord than his share of the crop is worth.
5. Sharecropper cannot leave the farm as long as he is in debt to the landlord.

LESSON PLAN

Focus Explain that the passage of the Thirteenth Amendment in 1865 and Reconstruction brought great economic changes to the South. Ask students what these changes were.

Instruct Discuss economic reorganization in the South. How did the end of slavery bring about new patterns of farming? Ask students why state governments poured money into creating infrastructure. What were the good and bad effects of this kind of business development? Why didn't the South become as industrialized as the North?

Assess/Reteach What do students think were the biggest challenges faced by the United States as a whole, and by southern states in particular, as the country tried to reunite and recover from the Civil War?

BACKGROUND
Recent Scholarship

In her book *The Dispossessed: America's Underclasses from the Civil War to the Present,* historian Jacqueline Jones writes that the sharecropping system had a "superficial simplicity" behind which "lay an intense power struggle between planter and field hand, a struggle that went to the heart of power relations in the rural South." One aspect of that struggle was the practice of fining sharecroppers up to a dollar a day for "time lost" if they refused to devote all their time to field work, as they had been forced to do when they were enslaved.

CUSTOMIZE FOR ...
Less Proficient Writers

Have students do library research to find out, by approximate percentages, how many freed African American slaves became sharecroppers or tenant farmers, moved to cities, or found other types of work. Have students display the information they discover in a pie chart.

CAPTION ANSWERS

Interpreting Diagrams Sharecroppers always had debts that exceeded what they earned in a given season. Therefore, sharecroppers remained in debt even after the harvest each year.

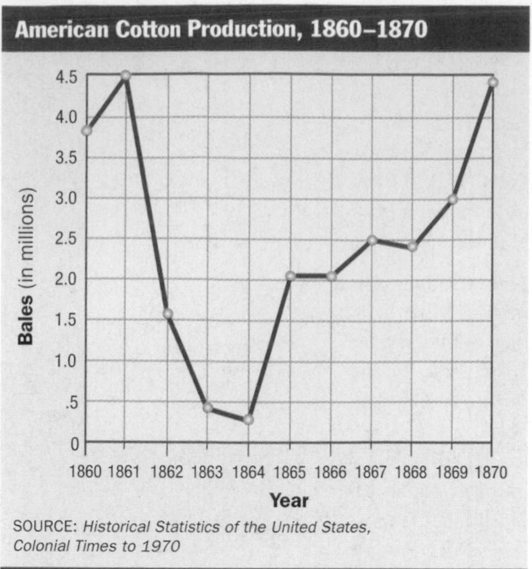

SOURCE: *Historical Statistics of the United States, Colonial Times to 1970*

INTERPRETING GRAPHS
Cotton production was the South's main economic activity until 1930. **Making Inferences** *What accounts for the drop in production in the middle of this graph?*

Tenant Farming If a sharecropper saved enough money, he might try **tenant farming.** Like sharecroppers, tenant farmers did not own the land they farmed. Unlike sharecroppers, however, tenant farmers paid to rent the land, just as you might rent an apartment today. Tenants chose which crops to plant and when and how much to work. As a result, the tenant farmers had a higher social status than sharecroppers.

The Holtzclaws managed to move from sharecropping to tenant farming. They rented 40 acres of land. They bought a mule, a horse, and a team of oxen. William Holtzclaw was a child at the time. "We were so happy at the prospects of owning a wagon and a pair of mules, and having only our father for boss, that we shouted and leaped for joy," he later recalled.

Effects on the South Changes in farming during Reconstruction affected the long-term health of the South's economy in several important ways:

Changes in the labor force Before the Civil War, 90 percent of the South's cotton was harvested by slaves. By 1875, white laborers, mostly tenant farmers, picked 40 percent of the crop.

Emphasis on cash crops Sharecropping and tenant farming encouraged planters to grow cash crops, such as cotton, tobacco, and sugar cane, rather than food crops. The South's postwar cotton production soon surpassed prewar levels. As a result of the focus on cash crops, the South had to import much of its food.

Cycle of debt By the end of Reconstruction, rural poverty was deeply rooted in the South, among blacks and whites alike. Both groups remained in a cycle of debt, in which this year's profits went to pay last year's bills. The Southern Homestead Act of 1866 attempted to break that cycle by offering low-cost land to southerners, black or white, who would farm it. By 1874, black farmers in Georgia owned 350,000 acres. Still, most landless farmers could not afford to participate in the land-buying program. In the cotton states, only about one black family in 20 owned land after a decade of Reconstruction.

READING CHECK
In what ways did the end of slavery change agriculture in the South?

Rise of merchants Tenant farming created a new class of wealthy southerners: the merchants. Throughout the South, stores sprang up around plantations to sell supplies on credit. "We have stores at almost every crossroad," a journalist observed. By 1880, the South had more than 8,000 rural stores. Some merchants were honest; others were not. Landlords frequently ran their own stores and forced their tenants to buy there at high prices.

After four years of tenant farming, the Holtzclaws watched as creditors carted away everything they owned. "They came and took our corn and, finally, the vegetables from our little garden, as well as the chickens and the pig," Holtzclaw said. The family had no choice but to return to sharecropping.

Cities and Industry

Southerners who visited the North after the Civil War were astounded at how industrialized the North had become. The need for large-scale production of war supplies had turned small factories into big industries that dominated the North's economy. Industrialization had produced a new class of wage earners.

Activity Connecting with Economics

Select students to take the roles of the following: sharecropper, tenant farmer, merchant. Have them tell one another about their situations and compare their lives. How are they similar? How are they different? Each group might also discuss how they would like to improve their situations. You might also suggest that groups present their situations, and then have them take questions from the class. **(Verbal/Linguistic)**

Background Recent Scholarship

The story of Reconstruction for African Americans is a story of 4 million people who experienced freedom only to find that freedom had its limitations. Nonetheless, they persevered. Generally, their stories are similar. Those who left rural life and farming traveled to southern urban centers, such as Atlanta, Georgia. In *To 'Joy My Freedom: Southern Black Women's Lives and Labors After the Civil War,* Tera W. Hunter details the individual stories of newly free African American women who moved to Atlanta. Atlanta was a key city in the South after the Civil War because it became the symbol in the New South of urbanization and industrial growth. And black women are key to understanding the African American community because their lives, work, and sacrifices informed the activities of the men, children, and other women in their communities.

READING CHECK
Sharecropping and tenant farming by emancipated African Americans and poor whites allowed destitute planters to get their land worked. Cash crops became the focus. Some former slaves found higher-paying non-agricultural jobs.

Caption Answers

Interpreting Graphs The Civil War.

RESOURCE DIRECTORY

Teaching Resources
Learning with Documents booklet (Primary Source Activity) *A Bleak Future for Freedmen,* p. 17

Other Print Resources
Nystrom *Atlas of Our Country* *Settling the West,* pp. 28–29

It had ignited city growth and generated wealth. Could all this happen in the South?

Some southern leaders saw a unique opportunity for their region. They urged the South to build a new, industrialized economy. One of the pro-business voices was that of Henry Grady, editor of the *Atlanta Constitution*. He called for a "New South" of growing cities and thriving industries.

The Growth of Cities Atlanta, the city so punished by Sherman's army, took Grady's advice. Only months after the war, the city was on its way to becoming a major metropolis of the South, as one observer noted:

> "*A new city is springing up with marvelous rapidity. The narrow and irregular and numerous streets are alive from morning till night . . . with a never-ending throng of . . . eager and excited and enterprising men, all bent on building and trading and swift fortune-making.*"
>
> —Visitor to Atlanta, 1865

San Antonio, Texas, prospered following the Civil War as a mercantile and cattle center. This 1872 photo shows a view of the east side of Main Plaza.

A major focus of Reconstruction, and one of its greatest successes, was the rebuilding and extension of southern railroads. By 1872, southern railroads were totally rebuilt and about 3,300 miles of new track laid, a 40 percent increase. Railroads turned southern villages into towns, and towns into cities where businesses and trade could flourish. Commerce and population rose not only in Atlanta, but also in Richmond, Nashville, Memphis, Louisville, Little Rock, Montgomery, and Charlotte. On the western frontier, the Texas towns of Dallas, Houston, and Fort Worth were on the rise.

Limits of Industrial Growth Despite these changes, Reconstruction did not transform the South into an industrialized, urban region like the North. Most southern factories did not make finished goods such as furniture. They handled only the early, less profitable stages of manufacturing, such as producing lumber or pig iron. These items were shipped north to be made into finished products and then sold.

Most of the South's postwar industrial growth came from cotton mills. New factories began to spin and weave cotton into undyed fabric. The value of cotton mill production in South Carolina rose from about $713,000 in 1860 to nearly $3 million by 1880. However, the big profits went to northern companies that dyed the fabric and sold the finished product.

Funding Reconstruction

The Republicans who led Congress agreed with southern legislatures on the importance of promoting business. The strong conviction that the growth of business would bring better times for everyone was called the "gospel of prosperity." It guided the Reconstruction efforts of Congress and the Reconstruction legislatures throughout the 1870s.

Raising Money In a sense, the postwar South was one giant business opportunity. The region's **infrastructure,** the public property and services that a society uses, had to be almost completely rebuilt. That included roads, bridges, canals, railroads, and telegraph lines. In addition to the rebuilding effort, some states used Reconstruction funds

Focus on CITIZENSHIP

Achievements of Black Legislators Thomas E. Miller defended the work of the South Carolina legislature in which he served: "We had built school houses, established charitable institutions . . . rebuilt bridges and reestablished ferries. In short, we had reconstructed the State and placed it upon the road to prosperity." The lithograph above shows seven African Americans who were elected to the United States Congress.

ACTIVITY
Connecting with Geography

Suggest that students choose a southern city mentioned in the text and research what it was like in the New South and what it is like today. Have them create a chart showing similarities and differences between the city in the past and present. Students might also prepare a written report summarizing changes and reasons for the changes. **(Visual/Spatial)**

BACKGROUND
Biography

Though he grew up on a slave-holding plantation, and his father died from a Yankee bullet, Henry W. Grady (1850–1889) used his platform as the editor of the Atlanta *Constitution* to present the idea of the New South, in which the past was put to rest. He gave his most famous speech, "The New South," before the New England Society of New York on December 22, 1886. In a speech frequently interrupted by applause, Grady said, "The New South is enamored of her new work. Her soul is stirred with the breath of a new life. The light of a grander day is falling fair on her face. She is thrilling with the consciousness of growing power and prosperity. As she stands upright, full-statured and equal among the people of the earth, breathing the keen air and looking out upon the expanding horizon, she understands that her emancipation came because in the inscrutable wisdom of God her honest purpose was crossed and her brave armies were beaten."

ACTIVITY
Connecting with History and Conflict

Ask students to suppose they are living in the year 1865, first as a poor African American sharecropper and then as a white southern planter whose plantation lies in ruins. Students should write two brief essays in which the characters tell how they hope their life will be ten years in the future. **(Verbal/Linguistic)**

TEST PREPARATION

Have students read the paragraph on the previous page that begins "Emphasis on cash crops" and then answer the question below.

Which of the following describes the South's economy after the Civil War?

A Most former slaves became land owners.
(B) There was greater reliance on cash crops than on food crops.
C There was decreased dependency on imports.
D All of the above.

Section 3 Assessment

Reading Comprehension

1. The work too closely resembled slavery; workers often left to look for better jobs and more money.
2. Tenant farmers rented land from a planter, chose which crops to plant, and decided how much to work, whereas sharecroppers farmed a portion of a planter's land in exchange for a share of the crop at harvest, and, oftentimes, housing.
3. As railroads were rebuilt in the South, and new track vastly extended, towns and villages were transformed into cities, trade and businesses flourished, allowing an increase in commerce and population.
4. Southern factories often did not make finished goods, but rather focused on the early stages of manufacturing. Profits from the cotton industry shifted to northern companies. Cotton from southern mills went north to facilities that dyed the fabric and sold the finished product.
5. Congress, private investors, and the levying of heavy taxes on individuals.

Critical Thinking and Writing

6. To increase and ensure profits; the subsequent need to import food into southern states would create further expense for those living in poverty.
7. Answers will vary. Students may want to mention that southern cities like Atlanta were devastated by the war.

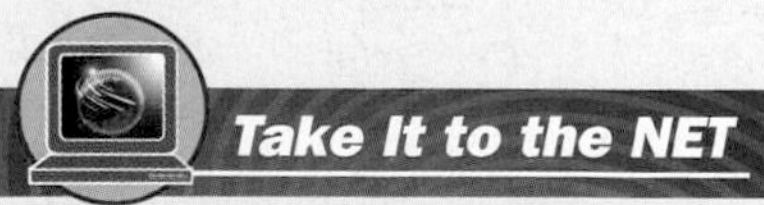

Invite students to take a Virtual Field Trip at **www.phschool.com**

INTERPRETING POLITICAL CARTOONS This cartoon, which appeared in *Harper's Weekly* in 1876, poked fun at President Grant's promise to "get to the bottom" of the corruption in government. **Making Inferences** *What does the cartoon imply about Grant's ability to investigate and put an end to corruption?*

to expand services to their citizens. For instance, following the North's example, all southern states created public school systems by 1872.

Reconstruction legislatures poured money into infrastructure. Some of the money came from Congress and from private investors. The rest, however, was raised by levying heavy taxes on individuals, many of whom were still deeply in debt from the war. White southerners, both wealthy and poor, resented this added financial burden. Spending by Reconstruction legislatures added another $130 million to southern debt. What further angered southerners was evidence that much of this big spending for infrastructure was being lost to corruption.

Corruption Today, corruption in government and business is vigorously uncovered and prosecuted. That was not the case a century ago. During Reconstruction, enormous sums of money changed hands rapidly in the form of fraudulent loans and grants. Participants in such schemes included blacks and whites, Republicans and Democrats, southerners and northern carpetbaggers. "You are mistaken if you suppose that all the evils . . . result from the carpetbaggers and negroes," a Louisiana man wrote to a northern fellow Democrat. Democrats and Republicans cooperated "whenever anything is proposed which promises to pay," he observed. The South Carolina legislature even gave $1,000 to the Speaker of the House to cover his loss on a horse race!

Scandal and corruption also reached to the White House. Early in Grant's second term, a scandal emerged involving the Credit Mobilier Company. Credit Mobilier had been set up by the owners of the Union Pacific Railroad to build their portion of the transcontinental railroad westward from Omaha. The Union Pacific gave the Credit Mobilier enormous sums of federal money. While some of this money paid for work, much of it went into the pockets of the Union Pacific officers and politicians who were bribed into ignoring the fraud.

Section 3 Assessment

READING COMPREHENSION

1. Why did planters have trouble finding people to work for them?
2. How did **sharecropping** and **tenant farming** differ?
3. How did railroads contribute to the growth of cities?
4. Why was southern industrial growth limited?
5. What were the sources of funding for Reconstruction programs?

CRITICAL THINKING AND WRITING

6. **Predicting Consequences** Why did sharecropping and tenant farming encourage planters to grow cash crops rather than food crops? What impact might this have had on people living in poverty?
7. **Creating an Outline** Create an outline for an essay in which you explain why the physical reconstruction of the South was necessary.

Take It to the NET

Activity: Virtual Field Trip Visit the Levi Jordan Plantation in Brazoria County, Texas, and learn how freed African Americans working on this plantation adapted to life as tenant farmers and sharecroppers after the Civil War. Use the links provided in the *America: Pathways to the Present* area of the following Web site for help in completing this activity.
www.phschool.com

Caption Answers

Interpreting Political Cartoons President Grant is "in over his head," meaning he is unaware of the scope and magnitude of the corruption problem he has promised to address. From the number of papers and notes coming from the barrel, the cartoonist is suggesting that the corruption comes from all parts of the government.

RESOURCE DIRECTORY

Teaching Resources

Units 1/2 booklet
- Section 3 Quiz, p. 52

Guide to the Essentials
- Section 3 Summary, p. 25

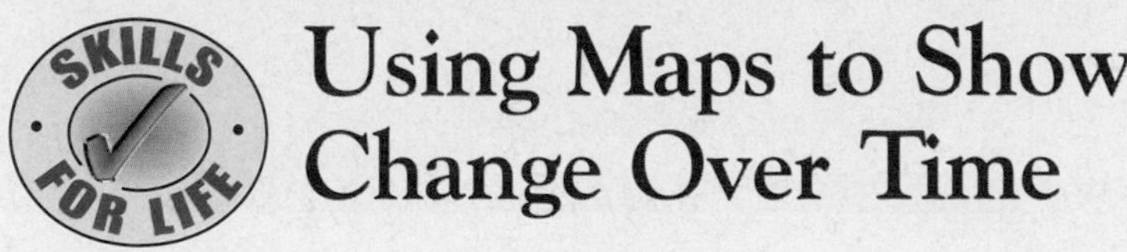

Using Maps to Show Change Over Time

Historians compare maps to help them identify changes over time. One far-reaching change that took place after the Civil War was the breakup of Southern plantations. The maps below show 2,000 acres of land before and after the Civil War.

The Barrow Plantation, Oglethorpe County, Georgia

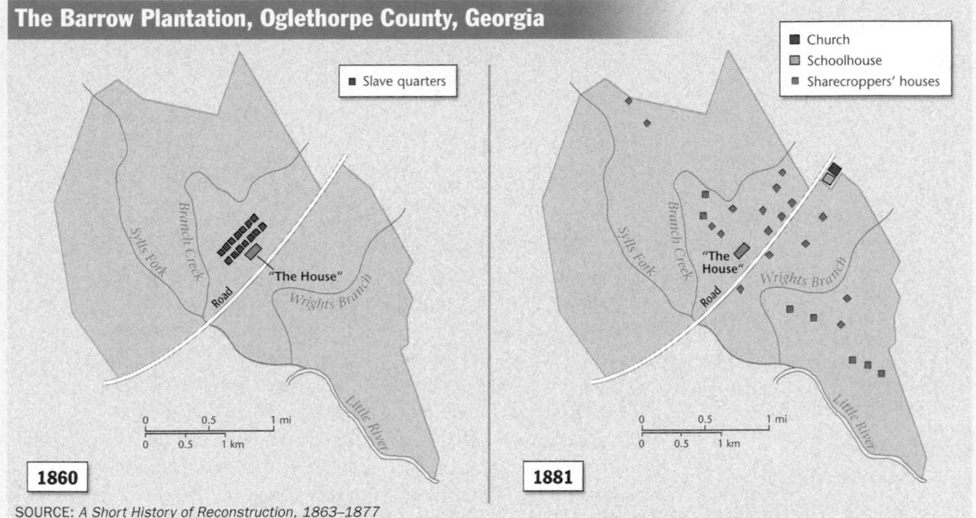

SOURCE: *A Short History of Reconstruction, 1863–1877*

LEARN THE SKILL

Use the following steps to analyze maps for evidence of change over time:

1. **Identify the location and time periods of the maps.** Most maps are labeled with the location and subject. If a date is not included, historians can often determine the date based on the style and content of the map.
2. **Identify the subject of the maps.** Maps can include information about geographic features as well as man-made features, such as buildings and roads.
3. **Analyze the map key and scale.** The key identifies what different symbols and colors represent on the map. The scale helps you determine the actual distance between features shown on the map.
4. **Analyze the data on the maps.** Compare the data to draw conclusions about change over the time period the maps indicate. Also use what you already know about events in the time period.

PRACTICE THE SKILL

Answer the following questions:

1. **(a)** What specific area of land do both maps show? **(b)** What dates are given on the maps? How long a time period is represented? **(c)** Is there anything unusual about the style of the maps? Explain.
2. **(a)** What geographic features are shown on both maps? **(b)** What man-made features are shown on each map? Are they the same on both maps?
3. **(a)** According to the key, what do the red squares on the 1860 map represent? **(b)** According to the key, what do the blue squares on the 1881 map represent? **(c)** How did the mapmaker show the difference between a church and a schoolhouse on the 1881 map? **(d)** What do you think the label "The House" means on each map? **(e)** On the 1881 map, approximately how far is "The House" from any other dwelling?
4. **(a)** How has the location of dwellings on the plantation changed during this time period? **(b)** What type of dwelling has disappeared? **(c)** What type of dwelling has been added? **(d)** What other new buildings have been added? **(e)** Summarize the changes to this plantation over time. What historical events helped produce these changes?

APPLY THE SKILL

See the Chapter Review and Assessment for another opportunity to apply this skill.

RESOURCE DIRECTORY

Teaching Resources

Skills for Life booklet, p. 14

Technology

Social Studies Skills Tutor CD-ROM

Interactive Practice in

- Geographic Literacy
- Critical Thinking and Reading
- Visual Analysis
- Communications

Using Maps to Show Change Over Time

Focus Students compare two historical maps to identify changes in the cultural landscape over time.

Instruct Explain that historical maps provide information about the cultural, or human-made, traits of a place. Ask students to use visual evidence from the maps, along with information they already have about the time periods, to suggest at least one cultural change that may have taken place. Then ask students what a map of this same area might be likely to show today.

Extend See the Skills for Life activity in the Resource Directory below.

ANSWERS

Practice the Skill

1. **(a)** The Barrow Plantation in Oglethorpe County, Georgia. **(b)** 1860 and 1881. 21 years. **(c)** The maps label "The House" on the map but use a key for other buildings. "The House" is not identified.
2. **(a)** Rivers and creeks. **(b)** 1860 map: Road, "The House," slave quarters; 1881 map: Road, "The House," church, schoolhouse, sharecroppers' houses. No.
3. **(a)** Slave quarters. **(b)** Sharecroppers' houses. **(c)** By color. **(d)** "The House" is the Barrow Plantation's main house, where the plantation owners lived. **(e)** Less than 1/8 mile (1/4 kilometer).
4. **(a)** In 1860 they were concentrated in a single area; by 1881 they had spread out across the entire plantation. **(b)** Slave quarters. **(c)** Sharecroppers' houses. **(d)** A church and a school. **(e)** The Civil War emancipated slaves, eliminating the need for slave quarters. By 1881 many former slaves had become sharecroppers and worked scattered plots of land.

Section 4

The End of Reconstruction

READING FOCUS

- What tactics did the Ku Klux Klan use to spread terror throughout the South?
- Why did Reconstruction end?
- What were the major successes and failures of Reconstruction?

MAIN IDEA

In the 1870s, white Democrats regained power in the South, and public interest in Reconstruction declined.

KEY TERMS

Enforcement Act of 1870
solid South
Compromise of 1877

TAKING NOTES

Copy the web diagram below. As you read, fill in supporting details for each heading.

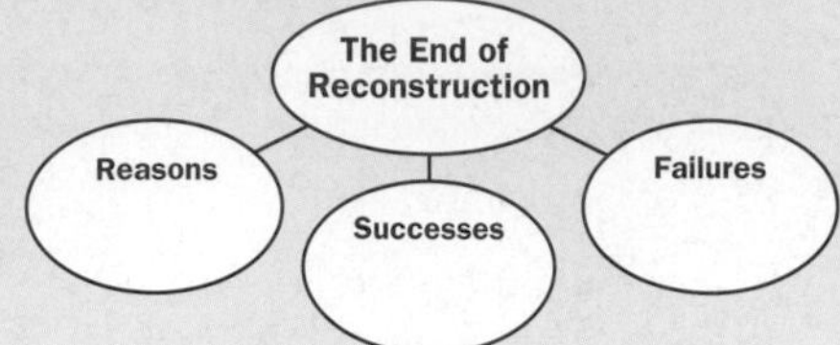

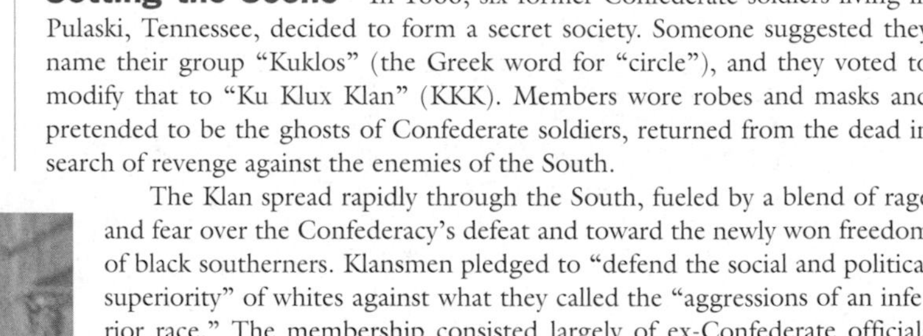

Members of the Ku Klux Klan (pictured below) left miniature coffins like this, containing written death threats, at the doors of many freedmen and their white supporters.

Setting the Scene In 1866, six former Confederate soldiers living in Pulaski, Tennessee, decided to form a secret society. Someone suggested they name their group "Kuklos" (the Greek word for "circle"), and they voted to modify that to "Ku Klux Klan" (KKK). Members wore robes and masks and pretended to be the ghosts of Confederate soldiers, returned from the dead in search of revenge against the enemies of the South.

The Klan spread rapidly through the South, fueled by a blend of rage and fear over the Confederacy's defeat and toward the newly won freedom of black southerners. Klansmen pledged to "defend the social and political superiority" of whites against what they called the "aggressions of an inferior race." The membership consisted largely of ex-Confederate officials and plantation owners who had been excluded from politics. The group also attracted merchants, lawyers, and other professionals. While the Klan was supposed to be a secret society, most members' identities were well known in their communities.

In 1867, at a convention in Nashville, Tennessee, the Klan chose its first overall leader, or "grand wizard," Nathan Bedford Forrest. Before the war, Forrest had grown wealthy as a cotton planter and slave trader. During the war, he had become known as one of the Confederacy's most brilliant generals. He also had ordered the massacre of more than 300 black men, women, and children when his troops captured Fort Pillow, Tennessee, in 1864.

As Reconstruction proceeded, Klan violence intensified. Arkansas Klansmen killed more than 300 Republicans, including a United States congressman, in 1868 alone. That year Klansmen murdered 1,000 people in Louisiana. Fully half of the adult white male population of New Orleans belonged to the KKK.

Spreading Terror

During Radical Reconstruction, the Klan sought to eliminate the Republican Party in the South by intimidating Republican voters, both white and black. The Klan's long-term goal was to keep African Americans in the role of submissive laborers.

Section 4

The End of Reconstruction

SECTION OBJECTIVES

1. Learn about tactics used by the Ku Klux Klan to spread terror throughout the South.
2. Find out why Reconstruction ended.
3. Review the major successes and failures of Reconstruction.

BELLRINGER

Warm-Up Activity Ask students if they know of any hate groups that are active today. What do they think motivates these groups?

Activating Prior Knowledge Ask students to state a reason why the Ku Klux Klan was formed and what the group intended to accomplish.

READING STRATEGY

Ask students to create a cause-and-effect chart or a graphic organizer entitled "Why Reconstruction Ended." The organizer should have at its center: "The End of Reconstruction," with various causes and effects shown coming outward from that starting point. As they read, have them add information to their chart.

ACTIVITY

Connecting with Government

The Enforcement Act of 1870 was one of many laws passed to protect civil rights. Have student groups trace the historical development of the civil rights movement in the late 1800s. Have student groups research similar acts (such as the Enforcement Acts of February 28, 1871, and April 20, 1871, the Civil Rights Acts of 1875, 1957, 1960, 1964, 1968, and 1991, and the Voting Rights Act of 1965). Have groups report on the intent and the rights protected by each of these laws. Then, hold a classroom discussion on why so many laws needed to be enacted. **(Verbal/Linguistic)**

RESOURCE DIRECTORY

Teaching Resources

Guided Reading and Review booklet, p. 53

Other Print Resources

American History Block Scheduling Support *The Reformers: A Struggle for Women's Rights,* found in the Prosperity, Depression, and War folder, includes interdisciplinary lesson suggestions and activities for Geography and History, Primary Sources, Biography, and Literature.

Technology

Section Reading Support Transparencies

Guided Reading Audiotapes (English/Spanish), Ch. 5

Student Edition on Audio CD, Ch. 5

Prentice Hall Presentation Pro CD-ROM, Ch. 5

RESOURCE PRO® **Visual Learning Activity** *America's Birthday Party,* found on Resource Pro, shows a list published in 1876 in the children's magazine *St. Nicholas,* citing major events in the first hundred years of the American republic.

Companion Web site, www.phschool.com

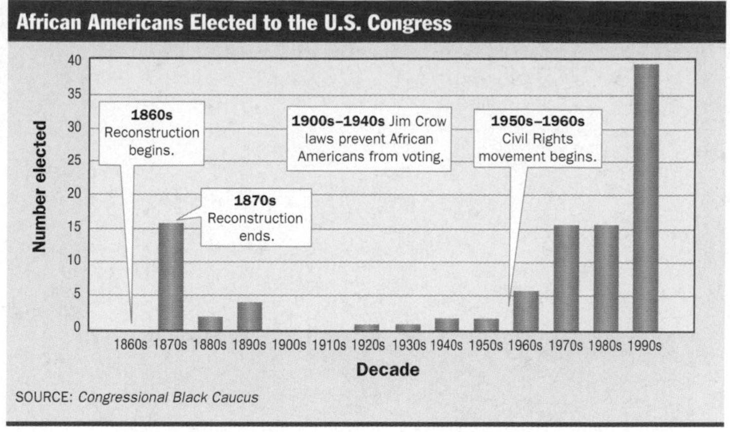

INTERPRETING GRAPHS
In many ways, Reconstruction was an unfinished revolution for African Americans. Corruption, violence, the return of Democratic rule in the South, and a faltering economy all contributed to a reversal of the civil and political gains made by African Americans during Reconstruction. **Analyzing Information** *How long did it take for African Americans to regain the same level of representation in the United States Congress they had held during Reconstruction?*

The Klan's terror tactics varied from place to place. Often, horsemen in long robes and hoods appeared suddenly at night, carrying guns and whips. They encircled the homes of their victims, and planted huge burning crosses in their yards. People were dragged from their homes and harassed, tortured, kidnapped, or murdered.

Anyone who didn't share the Klan's goals and hatreds could be a victim: carpetbaggers, scalawags, freedmen who had become prosperous—even those who had merely learned to read. With chilling frequency, black women went to claim the dead bodies of their husbands and sons.

The Federal Response The violence kindled northern outrage. At President Grant's request, Congress passed a series of anti-Klan laws in 1870 and 1871. The **Enforcement Act of 1870** banned the use of terror, force, or bribery to prevent people from voting because of their race. Other laws banned the KKK entirely and strengthened military protection of voters and voting places.

Using troops, cavalry, and the power of the courts, the government arrested and tried thousands of Klansmen. Within a year the KKK was virtually wiped out. Still, the thinly spread federal army could not be everywhere at once. As federal troops gradually withdrew from the South, black suffrage all but ended.

Reconstruction Ends

President Grant, who won reelection in 1872, continued to pursue the goals of Reconstruction, sometimes with energy. However, the widespread corruption in his administration reminded voters of all that was wrong with Reconstruction.

A Dying Issue By the mid-1870s, voters had grown weary of Republicans and their decade-long concern with Reconstruction. There were four main factors contributing to the end of Reconstruction:

Corruption Reconstruction legislatures, as well as Grant's administration, came to symbolize corruption, greed, and poor government.

The economy Reconstruction legislatures taxed and spent heavily, putting southern states deeper into debt. In addition, a nationwide economic

Focus on WORLD EVENTS

Alaska, the Midway Islands, and Mexico For the most part, Americans focused on rebuilding the nation during Reconstruction. Secretary of State William H. Seward, however, took a number of actions to expand the country's resources and trade. In 1866, Seward convinced the Senate to ratify his purchase of Alaska from Russia for $7.2 million. His opponents referred to Seward's purchase of Alaska's "walrus-covered icebergs" as "Seward's Folly." In an effort to expand trade with China, in 1867 Seward also annexed the Midway Islands, where coal-powered naval steamships could stop for refueling and repair on their voyages across the Pacific. Closer to home, Seward sent 50,000 American troops, who were already in Texas at the end of the Civil War, to Mexico to force the French to withdraw their troops from the country.

LESSON PLAN

Focus While southerners were fighting Reconstruction, the public began to lose interest in the program. Ask why public support for Reconstruction waned.

Instruct Discuss the southern backlash against Reconstruction. Ask students why they think it took a violent turn. Why was an organization like the Ku Klux Klan so effective even though the law was on the side of African Americans?

Analyze with students the Republicans' retreat from Reconstruction. Why did they abandon their dream of social justice and equality for all? Ask students if they think Reconstruction was a success or a failure, and why.

Assess/Reteach The Radical Republicans' dream of social equality and justice was abandoned in 1877. Ask student groups to write a slogan for a modern bumper sticker reflecting the feelings of betrayal African Americans might have felt at this time.

From the Archives of
AmericanHeritage®

Ku Klux Klan

In May 1867 the ex-Confederate general and guerrilla leader Nathan Bedford Forrest took his place as the first Grand Wizard in the recently formed Ku Klux Klan in Pulaski, Tennessee. As the 1868 elections approached, violence against former slaves hoping to vote became general throughout Tennessee. By the next spring, Grand Wizard Forrest oversaw an empire with toeholds in fourteen southern states. The Klan led riots against black suffragists in Mississippi, burned schools and whipped or lynched northern schoolteachers, and intimidated former slaves. Testifying before Congress in 1871, Forrest explained, "this organization was got up to protect the weak, with no political intention at all. . . ." Source: Nathan Ward, "The Time Machine," *American Heritage®* magazine, May/June 1992.

CAPTION ANSWERS

Interpreting Graphs 100 years.

ACTIVITY
Connecting with Today

The outcome of the 1877 election was the result of a compromise between Democrats and Republicans. Democrats conceded victory to Hayes over Tilden in exchange for certain promises to roll back the effects of Reconstruction.

In recent years, the results of another presidential election were hotly contested: the 2000 race between George W. Bush and Albert Gore. Have students research both postelection controversies and create a compare-and-contrast chart. Topics on the chart could include: percentage of popular vote received by both candidates; number of electoral votes under dispute; states with contested electoral votes; and how each contested election was resolved. **(Logical/Mathematical)**

From the Archives of
AmericanHeritage®

About the Presidents

Ulysses Simpson Grant (1869–1877) had trouble distinguishing between talent and friendship. Appointees and associates were implicated in one scam after another. Gold speculators wined and dined the President and then tried to use their influence to corner the gold market. The notorious "Whisky Ring," a network of IRS officers and whiskey distillers, reduced taxes on whiskey and pocketed the unreported revenue. The Treasury Department was also tied to this scandal. Grant himself was criticized for accepting costly gifts and favors. Source: Wilson Sullivan, "Ulysses S. Grant," *The American Heritage® Pictorial History of the Presidents of the United States,* vol. 1, 1968.

READING CHECK

The heavy taxes and corrupt public officials involved in Reconstruction were unpopular. The violence of the Ku Klux Klan was unsettling. President Rutherford B. Hayes ended the military occupation of southern states in the compromise settlement of the disputed presidential election of 1876.

CAPTION ANSWERS

Map Skills Louisiana, Florida, South Carolina, and Oregon.

MAP SKILLS In the tarnished election of 1876, the electoral votes in three states under federal control were disputed, but went to Hayes when he promised to end Reconstruction. **Location** *In which states were election results disputed?*

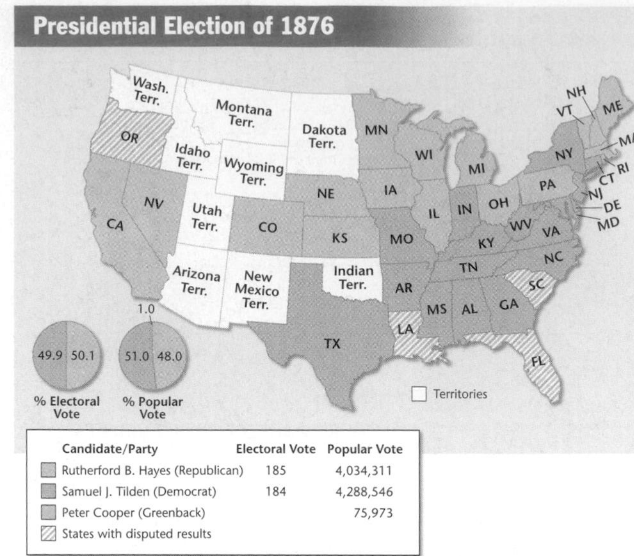

Candidate/Party	Electoral Vote	Popular Vote
Rutherford B. Hayes (Republican)	185	4,034,311
Samuel J. Tilden (Democrat)	184	4,288,546
Peter Cooper (Greenback)		75,973
States with disputed results		

downturn in 1873 diverted public attention from the movement for equal rights. In fact, northern voters had never fully supported the Radical Republicans' goal of racial equality.

Violence As federal troops withdrew from the South, some white Democrats were freer to use violence and intimidation to prevent freedmen from voting. This allowed white southerners to regain control of state governments.

The Democrats return to power The era of Republican control of the South was coming to a close. In 1872, the last ex-Confederates had been pardoned. They combined with other white southerners to form a new bloc of Democratic voters known as the **solid South.** Democrats of the solid South blocked many federal Reconstruction policies and reversed many reforms of the Reconstruction legislatures.

Supreme Court Limits Scope of Amendments The Supreme Court also played a role in bringing about the end of Reconstruction. In a series of cases, including the *Slaughterhouse Cases* in 1873, *United States* v. *Reese* in 1876, and *United States* v. *Cruikshank* in 1876, the Supreme Court narrowly interpreted the Fourteenth and Fifteenth amendments and placed the control of Americans' basic civil rights in the hands of the states. In short, the Court's decisions in these cases limited the federal government's ability to protect the civil and voting rights of African Americans.

READING CHECK What factors contributed to the end of Reconstruction?

The Compromise of 1877 Reconstruction politics took a final, sour turn in the presidential election of 1876. In that election, Republican Rutherford B. Hayes lost the popular vote to Democrat Samuel Tilden, who had the support of the solid South. The electoral vote, however, was disputed. The map above shows the results.

Hayes claimed victory based partly on wins in Florida, Louisiana, and South Carolina. Those states were still under Republican and federal control. Democrats submitted another set of tallies showing Tilden as the winner in those

RESOURCE DIRECTORY

Teaching Resources

Units 1/2 booklet
- Section 4 Quiz, p. 53
- Chapter 5 Test, pp. 54, 57

Guide to the Essentials
- Section 4 Summary, p. 26
- Chapter 5 Test, p. 27

Other Print Resources

Chapter Tests with ExamView® Test Bank CD-ROM, Ch. 5

Historical Outline Map Book *Election of 1876,* p. 54

Technology

Color Transparencies *Political Cartoons,* B5

ExamView® Test Bank CD-ROM, Ch. 5

Social Studies Skills Tutor CD-ROM

Successes and Failures of Reconstruction	
Successes	**Failures**
Union is restored.	Many white southerners remain bitter toward the federal government and the Republican Party.
The South's economy grows and new wealth is created in the North.	The South is slow to industrialize.
Fourteenth and Fifteenth amendments guarantee African Americans the rights of citizenship, equal protection under the law, and suffrage.	After federal troops are withdrawn, southern state governments and terrorist organizations effectively deny African Americans the right to vote.
Freedmen's Bureau and other organizations help many black families obtain housing, jobs, and schooling.	Many black and white southerners remain caught in a cycle of poverty.
Southern states adopt a system of mandatory education.	Racist attitudes toward African Americans continue, in both the South and the North.

INTERPRETING TABLES
Until recently, many historians believed that Reconstruction was a dismal failure. Today most historians argue that the truth is more complex. The cartoon below shows President Hayes "plowing under" Reconstruction programs. **Drawing Conclusions** *Do you think Reconstruction was more of a success or a failure? Why?*

states, and thus in the presidential race. (The eligibility of one Republican elector from Oregon was also called into question.) Congress set up a special commission to resolve the election crisis. Not surprisingly, the commission, which included more Republicans than Democrats, named Hayes the victor. However, Democrats had enough strength in Congress to reject the commission's decision.

Finally the two parties made a deal. In what became known as the **Compromise of 1877,** the Democrats agreed to give Hayes the victory in the presidential election he had not clearly won. In return, the new President agreed to remove the remaining federal troops from southern states. He also agreed to support appropriations for rebuilding levees along the Mississippi River, and to give huge subsidies to southern railroads. The compromise opened the way for Democrats to regain control of southern politics and marked the end of Reconstruction.

Section 4 Assessment

READING COMPREHENSION

1. Why did Congress pass the **Enforcement Act of 1870?**
2. What four factors contributed to the end of Reconstruction?
3. What was the **solid South?**
4. What was the **Compromise of 1877?** Why do you think the two parties made this compromise?

CRITICAL THINKING AND WRITING

5. **Drawing Conclusions** Do you agree with historian Samuel Eliot Morison, who said that "the North may have won the war, but the white South won the peace"?
6. **Writing an Opinion** What was the most significant success of Reconstruction? What was the most significant failure? Write an outline for an essay in which you state your opinions.

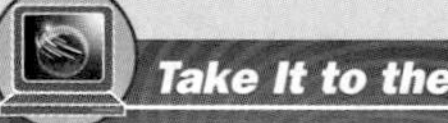

Take It to the NET

Activity: Writing a News Article
Prepare a newspaper article about the election of 1876. Use the links provided in the *America: Pathways to the Present* area of the following Web site for help in completing this activity.
www.phschool.com

Section 4 Assessment

Reading Comprehension

1. It banned the use of terror, force, or bribery as methods of preventing people from voting on the basis of race.
2. Corruption, the economy, violence, and the Democratic return to power in the South.
3. A new bloc of Democratic voters who blocked many federal Reconstruction policies and reversed many reforms of the Reconstruction legislatures.
4. The disputed results of the election of 1876 led to the Compromise of 1877 in which Democrats agreed to give Hayes the victory in the presidential election. In return, Hayes agreed to remove the remaining federal troops from southern states, and to give huge subsidies to southern railroads. Tilden and the Democrats made this compromise to open the way for Democrats to regain control of southern politics and end Reconstruction.

Critical Thinking and Writing

5. Students who agree might point to the long interval between the end of the war and the attainment of true civil rights by African Americans in the South.
6. Successes: rebuilt Union, stimulated economy; amendments passed; education in South; jobs and housing for freedmen; failures: corruption, poverty, and debt remained; freedmen prevented from voting; concerns of farmers and women not met.

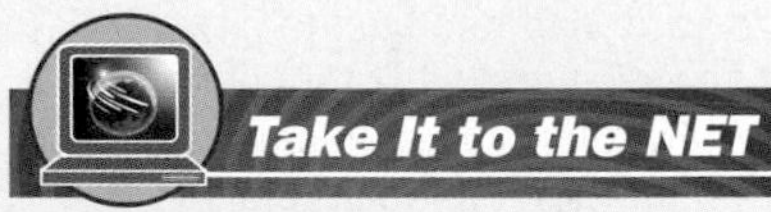

Take It to the NET

Students should demonstrate knowledge of the controversial circumstances surrounding the 1876 election.

CUSTOMIZE FOR ...

Less Proficient Readers

Ulysses S. Grant was a very popular leader in wartime, but an unpopular President. Have students make two lists about Grant. In one, have them list actions by Grant that made him popular. In the other, have them list actions taken by Grant that made him unpopular.

TEST PREPARATION

Have students read the section on the previous page called "The Democrats return to power," and then answer the question below.

What is the meaning of the phrase "solid South"?

A It refers to a group of southern states that supported Reconstruction.
(B) It refers to a bloc of voters that opposed Reconstruction.
C It refers to a group of southern states that resisted rejoining the Union.
D This phrase refers to the heavy, claylike soil of many southern states.

CAPTION ANSWERS

Interpreting Tables Answers will vary. Successes: the election of many African Americans to public office; African Americans were given rights they had never held under slavery. Failures: many white people ignored the rights newly granted to African Americans; many southern localities established "black codes," which returned African Americans to a position of near-slavery.

Chapter 5

Reviewing Key Terms

Students should refer to the definitions of key terms in the chapter to write sentences that show an understanding of the Reconstruction era.

Reviewing Main Ideas

11. Reconstituting southern state governments, cycle of debt, and loss of labor on plantations.

12. Lincoln's plan was tougher on the South. He supported a 10 percent allegiance requirement.

13. They attempted to create a new social order in the South and gain equal rights as citizens.

14. Congress blamed Johnson for southern Democrats' return to power and the southern defiance of Reconstruction. Johnson violated the Tenure of Office Act.

15. Through Reconstruction efforts, a Supreme Court decision that upheld the right of Congress to restructure southern governments, and through the Republican votes of freedmen who were benefiting from the Fifteenth Amendment.

16. They guaranteed the civil rights of all residents, opened political office to individuals without regard to wealth, and set up a system of public schools and orphanages.

17. The South became more industrialized and had to adjust to a new labor system. Still, it remained largely a farming economy.

18. It ended with the Compromise of 1877, which created an understanding between Democrats and Republicans. Hayes removed federal troops from southern states and opened the way for Democrats to regain control of southern politics.

Critical Thinking

19. (a) Reconstruction efforts helped to provide aid but sharecropping resulted in greater debt for farmers; (b) Former Confederates may have reluctantly accepted Reconstruction or turned to activities such as Klan membership; (c) Carpetbaggers benefited from southern poverty; (d) Much was accomplished despite the corruption and the blockage of policies by southern states.

Chapter 5 Review and Assessment

creating a CHAPTER SUMMARY

Copy the chart (right) on a piece of paper, and then complete it by adding information about key legislation passed during Reconstruction. Some entries have been completed for you as examples.

For additional review and enrichment activities, see the interactive version of *America: Pathways to the Present*, available on the Web and on CD-ROM.

Major Reconstruction Legislation		
Date	**Legislation**	**Description**
1865	13th Amendment	Abolished slavery
1865, 1866	Freedmen's Bureau	Provided services for war refugees and newly freed people
1867	Reconstruction Acts	
1868	14th Amendment	
1870	15th Amendment	
1875	Civil Rights Act	

★ Reviewing Key Terms

For each of the terms below, write a sentence explaining how it relates to the post-Civil War period.

1. Reconstruction
2. pardon
3. black codes
4. impeach
5. carpetbagger
6. scalawag
7. sharecropping
8. tenant farming
9. infrastructure
10. solid South

★ Reviewing Main Ideas

11. Name the three major problems the South faced at the end of the Civil War. (Section 1)
12. How did Lincoln's plan for Reconstruction compare to Johnson's plan? (Section 1)
13. How did African Americans try to improve their lives after emancipation? (Section 1)
14. Why did Johnson and Congress clash over Reconstruction? (Section 2)
15. How did Republicans gain control of southern governments? (Section 2)
16. In what ways were the new state constitutions radical? (Section 2)
17. In what ways did the economy of the South change after the Civil War, and in what ways did it remain unchanged? (Section 3)
18. Why did Reconstruction end? (Section 4)

★ Critical Thinking

19. **Comparing Points of View** Evaluate Reconstruction from the point of view of (a) a black sharecropper, (b) an ex-Confederate, (c) a carpetbagger, (d) a Radical Republican.
20. **Identifying Assumptions** Congress accused President Johnson of abusing his presidential powers, and Johnson thought that Congress overstepped its authority in carrying out Radical Reconstruction. What differing assumptions led to these conclusions?
21. **Recognizing Ideologies** Why were the strong policies of Radical Reconstruction largely ineffective in changing the attitudes of white southerners toward African Americans?
22. **Identifying Central Issues** Refer to the political cartoon depicting corruption during Grant's presidency in Section 3. Conduct research to learn more about one of the scandals pictured in the cartoon, such as the Whiskey Fraud, Secretary of War W. W. Belknap's impeachment, or the Back Pay Grab. Write a summary of the scandal and explain its impact on Reconstruction.

Creating a Chapter Summary

Major Reconstruction Legislation		
Date	**Legislation**	**Description**
1865	13th Amendment	Abolished slavery
1865, 1866	Freedman's Bureau	Provided services for war refugees and newly freed people
1867	Reconstruction Acts	Put the South under military rule, ordered these states to hold new elections, required states to allow all qualified males to vote, temporarily barred Confederacy supporters from voting, required southern states to guarantee equal rights to all citizens, required states to ratify the 14th Amendment
1868	14th Amendment	Established right of citizenship for all people born in the United States
1870	15th Amendment	Stated that no citizen would be denied the right to vote because of race, color, or previous condition of servitude
1875	Civil Rights Act	Stated that African Americans shall have unrestricted access to public places

★ Skills Assessment

Analyzing Political Cartoons ▶

23. This cartoon depicts President Grant riding in a carpetbag. (a) What does Grant represent? (b) What do the soldiers represent? (c) What does the woman represent?
24. State the central message of this cartoon.

Analyzing Primary Sources

Read this excerpt, and then answer the questions that follow.

> *"If [freedmen] are good law-abiding citizens, praying for its [the nation's] prosperity, rejoicing in its progress, paying its taxes, fighting its battles, making its farms, mines, work-shops and commerce more productive, why deny them the right to have a voice in the election of its rulers?"*
>
> —the "black citizens of Nashville," January 9, 1865

25. Which statement best represents the meaning of the quotation?
    - **A** Freedmen are responsible citizens.
    - **B** Freedmen deserve the right to vote because they earn money for the country.
    - **C** Freedmen deserve the right to vote because they are fulfilling the responsibilities of citizenship.
    - **D** Freedmen deserve to rule themselves.
26. What is the most likely reason the writers never received a response?
    - **F** White Tennesseans did not want freedmen to vote.
    - **G** White Tennesseans did not want freedman to become citizens.
    - **H** White Tennesseans thought freedmen should have economic rights, not political rights.
    - **J** White Tennesseans had already guaranteed freedmen the right to vote.

Applying the Chapter Skill: *Comparing Maps Over Time*

27. Refer to the maps on page 217. If the years of the maps were not labeled, would you be able to tell which map showed the plantation in 1860, and which showed the land in 1881? Explain your answer.

ACTIVITIES

Writing to LEARN

Writing an Opinion
Should Congress have accepted Johnson's Reconstruction plan, which allowed white Democrats and ex-Confederates to rejoin the political system (through voting and office holding)? Should Congress have worked with white southerners to uphold civil rights for African Americans? What were the consequences of not allowing the defeated Democrats to participate in the political process?

Primary Source CD-ROM

Working With Primary Sources Find additional information related to Reconstruction on the *Exploring Primary Sources in the U.S. History CD-ROM* and use the selection(s) provided to complete the Chapter 5 primary source activity located in the *America: Pathways to the Present* area of the following Web site.
www.phschool.com

Take It to the NET

Chapter Self-Test As a review activity, take the Chapter 5 Self-Test in the *America: Pathways to the Present* area at the Web site listed below. The questions are designed to test your understanding of the chapter content.
www.phschool.com

20. Both sides assumed that the other was overstepping boundaries and should have its power limited.
21. White southerners believed African Americans were inferior and that the government was treating them better than whites, themselves, were being treated. Plantation owners resented the changes because they lost their workforce.
22. Answers will vary, but should include a detailed summary, supported by facts, of one of the following scandals: Whiskey Fraud had whiskey distillers avoiding high taxes by bribing government officials; W. W. Belknap was Grant's Secretary of War who resigned to avoid impeachment for supposedly receiving bribes; Salary Grab, when the entire Republican Party was implicated for retroactively raising pay for congressmen and the President.

SKILLS ASSESSMENT

23. (a) Republican government. (b) Bayonet rule. (c) Southern Democrats.
24. Grant is oppressing the South, aided by martial rule.
25. C
26. G
27. On the earlier map, the slave quarters are all central to the main house. The later map shows the sharecroppers' houses spread out, demonstrating more independence and autonomy. The later map also has a church and a schoolhouse, buildings that would not have been available for slaves.

ANSWERS TO ACTIVITIES

Writing to LEARN

Sample answer: Congress opposed Johnson's Reconstruction policies, and with them the imposition of black codes. Had there been some room for compromise, some of the chaotic developments that characterized the era of Reconstruction might have been avoided, along with the growth and spread of the Ku Klux Klan.

Primary Source CD-ROM

Direct students to the additional primary sources that can be found on the *Exploring Primary Sources in U.S. History CD-ROM.*

Take It to the NET

Additional support materials and activities for Chapter 5 of *America: Pathways to the Present* can be found in the Social Studies area at the Prentice Hall School Web site. **www.phschool.com**

Chapter 6 Planning Guide

Resource Manager

	Core Instruction	Reading/Skills
Chapter-Level Resources **TEKS** 2(B), 24(A), 24(B)	Teaching Resources • Pacing Charts booklet • Block Scheduling booklet **Resource Pro® CD-ROM,** Ch. 6 **Prentice Hall Presentation Pro CD-ROM,** Ch. 6 **www.phschool.com** • eTeach	**Guided Reading Audiotapes (English/Spanish)** **Student Edition on Audio CD,** Ch. 6 **Social Studies Skills Tutor CD-ROM** **Color Transparencies,** B7, D6, F5, H9, H10, H11
1 A Technological Revolution 1. Learn how daily lives changed in the decades following the Civil War. 2. Find out how advances in electric power and communication affected people and businesses in this era. 3. Discover the effects the development of railroads had on industrial growth. 4. Think about the impact of the Bessemer process on American culture. **TEKS** 8(A), 22(A), 22(C), 23(A), 25(D)	Teaching Resources **Units 1/2 booklet** • Section 1 Quiz, p. 61 **Learning Styles Lesson Plans booklet,** p. 28	**Guided Reading and Review booklet,** p. 54 **Guide to the Essentials,** p. 28 **Skills for Life booklet,** p. 8 **Section Reading Support Transparencies**
2 The Growth of Big Business 1. Read to find out why American industrialists of the late 1800s were called both "robber barons" and "captains of industry." 2. Discover how social Darwinism affected Americans' views on big business. 3. Analyze the ways in which big businesses differed from smaller businesses. 4. Learn how industrialists gained a competitive edge over their rivals. **TEKS** 12(C), 19(B), 24(G)	Teaching Resources **Units 1/2 booklet** • Section 2 Quiz, p. 62 **Learning Styles Lesson Plans booklet,** p. 18	**Guided Reading and Review booklet,** p. 55 **Guide to the Essentials,** p. 29 **Learning with Documents booklet,** p. 18 **Section Reading Support Transparencies**
3 Industrialization and Workers 1. Find out about factors that led to a growing American work force betweeen 1860 and 1900. 2. Learn what factory work at the turn of the century was like. 3. Discover why it was sometimes necessary for entire families to work. **TEKS** 2(C), 8(B), 10(B), 22(C), 23(A), 24(H)	Teaching Resources **Units 1/2 booklet** • Section 3 Quiz, p. 63 **Learning Styles Lesson Plans booklet,** p. 29	**Guided Reading and Review booklet,** p. 56 **Guide to the Essentials,** p. 30 **Learning with Documents booklet,** p. 52 **Section Reading Support Transparencies**
4 The Great Strikes 1. Discover the impact of industrialism on the gulf between rich and poor. 2. Find out the goals of the early labor unions in the United States. 3. Learn why Eugene V. Debs formed the American Railway Union. 4. Study the causes and outcomes of the major strikes in the late 1800s. **TEKS** 2(C), 22(C)	Teaching Resources **Units 1/2 booklet** • Section 4 Quiz, p. 64	**Guided Reading and Review booklet,** p. 57 **Guide to the Essentials,** p. 31 **Section Reading Support Transparencies**

Enrichment/Pre-AP

Prentice Hall United States History Video Collection™
www.phschool.com
- Section Activities, Virtual Field Trip, Chapter Activities, Current Events Online

Great Debates booklet, p. 30
American History Block Scheduling Support
Nystrom *Atlas of Our Country,* pp. 28–29
Historical Outline Map Book, p. 82
Sounds of an Era Audio CD
Exploring Primary Sources in U.S. History CD-ROM

Great Debates booklet, p. 8
Sounds of an Era Audio CD
Exploring Primary Sources in U.S. History CD-ROM

Biography, Literature, and Comparing Primary Sources booklet, p. 57
American History Block Scheduling Support
Nystrom *Atlas of Our Country,* pp. 24–25, 30–31
Exploring Primary Sources in U.S. History CD-ROM

Biography, Literature, and Comparing Primary Sources booklet, pp. 18, 121
Sounds of an Era Audio CD
American Pathways Thematic Posters

Assessment

Core Assessment

ExamView® Test Bank, Ch. 6
ExamView® Test Bank CD-ROM, Ch. 6

Standardized Test Preparation

Diagnose and Prescribe

Diagnostic Tests for High School Social Studies Skills

Review and Reteach

Review Book for U.S. History

Practice and Assess

Test-taking Strategies With Transparencies
Test-taking Strategies Posters
Test Prep Book for U.S. History
Alternative Assessment Handbook
Document-Based Assessment

Teaching Resources

Units 1/2 booklet
- Section Quizzes, pp. 61–64
- Chapter Tests, pp. 65, 68

www.phschool.com Ch. 6 Self-Test

AmericanHeritage Resources

From the Archives of American Heritage®, pp. 244, 250
AmericanHeritage® My Brush with History™ Videotapes
www.americanheritage.com

Don't miss the exclusive interactive version of this textbook on the Web and on CD-ROM.

Chapter 6 Planning Guide

In Your Classroom

Customize for Individual Needs

Gifted and Talented

Teacher's Edition
- Customize for Gifted and Talented, pp. 241, 251

Teaching Resources
- Biography, Literature, and Comparing Primary Sources booklet, pp. 18, 57, 121

Technology
- Exploring Primary Sources in U.S. History CD-ROM *The Tall Office Building Artistically Considered, Louis H. Sullivan; Wealth, Andrew Carnegie; Spindle Top Gusher*

ESL

Teacher's Edition
- Customize for ESL, pp. 227, 239

Teaching Resources
- Guided Reading and Review booklet, pp. 54–57
- Guide to the Essentials (English/Spanish), Chapter 6

Technology
- Student Edition on Audio CD, Chapter 6
- Guided Reading Audiotapes (English/Spanish), Chapter 6
- Section Reading Support Transparencies

Less Proficient Readers

Teacher's Edition
- Customize for Less Proficient Readers, pp. 231, 249

Teaching Resources
- Guided Reading and Review booklet, pp. 54–57
- Guide to the Essentials (English/Spanish), Chapter 6

Technology
- Student Edition on Audio CD, Chapter 6
- Guided Reading Audiotapes (English/Spanish), Chapter 6
- Section Reading Support Transparencies

Less Proficient Writers

Teacher's Edition
- Customize for Less Proficient Writers, p. 245

Teaching Resources
- Guided Reading and Review booklet, pp. 54–57
- Guide to the Essentials (English/Spanish), Chapter 6

Technology
- Student Edition on Audio CD, Chapter 6
- Guided Reading Audiotapes (English/Spanish), Chapter 6
- Section Reading Support Transparencies

Teacher's Edition Index

Chapter 6 – Pacing Suggestions

For 90-minute Blocks

- Teach sections 1 and 2 using Transparencies B7, D6, F5, H10, and H11, and the Recent Scholarship note on page 239 for class discussions.

Running Out of Time?

If you are running short on time to cover this chapter, consider the following options:

- Use Prentice Hall Presentation Pro CD-ROM to create an outline for this chapter.
- Use the Section Summaries for Chapter 6, from **Guide to the Essentials (English/Spanish).**

TEKS Correlation

Chapter-Level	TEKS
	(2) History. The student understands the political, economic, and social changes in the United States from 1877 to 1898. The student is expected to: **(B)** analyze economic issues such as industrialization, the growth of railroads, the growth of labor unions, farm issues, and the rise of big business. **(24) Social studies skills.** The student applies critical-thinking skills to organize and use information acquired from a variety of sources, including electronic technology. The student is expected to: **(A)** locate and use primary and secondary sources such as computer software, databases, media and news services, biographies, interviews, and artifacts to acquire information about the United States. **(B)** analyze information by sequencing, categorizing, identifying cause-and-effect relationships, comparing, contrasting, finding the main idea, summarizing, making generalizations and predictions, and drawing inferences and conclusions.
1 A Technological Revolution	**(8) Geography.** The student uses geographic tools to collect, analyze, and interpret data. The student is expected to: **(A)** create thematic maps, graphs, charts, models, and databases representing various aspects of the United States. **(22) Science, technology, and society.** The student understands the impact of science and technology on the economic development of the United States. The student is expected to: **(A)** explain the effects of scientific discoveries and technological innovations such as electric power, the telegraph and telephone, petroleum-based products, medical vaccinations, and computers on the development of the United States. **(C)** analyze the impact of technological innovations on the nature of work, the American labor movement, and business. **(23) Science, technology, and society.** The student understands the influence of scientific discoveries and technological innovations on daily life in the United States. The student is expected to: **(A)** analyze how scientific discoveries and technological innovations, including those in transportation and communication, have changed the standard of living in the United States. **(25) Social studies skills.** The student communicates in written, oral, and visual forms. The student is expected to: **(D)** create written, oral, and visual presentations of social studies information.
2 The Growth of Big Business	**(12) Economics.** The student understands domestic and foreign issues related to U.S. economic growth from the 1870s to 1920. The student is expected to: **(C)** describe the impact of the Sherman Antitrust Act on businesses. **(19) Citizenship.** The student understands the importance of effective leadership in a democratic society. The student is expected to: **(B)** evaluate the contributions of significant political and social leaders in the United States such as Andrew Carnegie, Shirley Chisholm, and Franklin D. Roosevelt. **(24) Social studies skills.** The student applies critical-thinking skills to organize and use information acquired from a variety of sources, including electronic technology. The student is expected to: **(G)** support a point of view on a social studies issue or event.
3 Industrialization and Workers	**(2) History.** The student understands the political, economic, and social changes in the United States from 1877 to 1898. The student is expected to: **(C)** analyze social issues such as the treatment of minorities, child labor, growth of cities, and problems of immigrants. **(8) Geography.** The student uses geographic tools to collect, analyze, and interpret data. The student is expected to: **(B)** pose and answer questions about geographic distributions and patterns shown on maps, graphs, charts, models, and databases. **(10) Geography.** The student understands the effects of migration and immigration on American society. The student is expected to: **(B)** analyze the effects of changing demographic patterns resulting from immigration to the United States. **(22) Science, technology, and society.** The student understands the impact of science and technology on the economic development of the United States. The student is expected to: **(C)** analyze the impact of technological innovations on the nature of work, the American labor movement, and business. **(23) Science, technology, and society.** The student understands the influence of scientific discoveries and technological innovations on daily life in the United States. The student is expected to: **(A)** analyze how scientific discoveries and technological innovations, including those in transportation and communication, have changed the standard of living in the United States. **(24) Social studies skills.** The student applies critical-thinking skills to organize and use information acquired from a variety of sources, including electronic technology. The student is expected to: **(H)** use appropriate mathematical skills to interpret social studies information such as maps and graphs.
4 The Great Strikes	**(2) History.** The student understands the political, economic, and social changes in the United States from 1877 to 1898. The student is expected to: **(C)** analyze social issues such as the treatment of minorities, child labor, growth of cities, and problems of immigrants. **(22) Science, technology, and society.** The student understands the impact of science and technology on the economic development of the United States. The student is expected to: **(C)** analyze the impact of technological innovations on the nature of work, the American labor movement, and business.

Chapter 6

The Expansion of American Industry (1850–1900)

Introducing the Chapter

Beginning before the Civil War, rapid industrial progress transformed the United States, but relations between those who managed the industries and those who labored in them were filled with tensions. Conditions for workers grew worse.

Time Line Activity

To provide students with practice in using the time line, ask questions such as these:

1. What railroad was the first to connect the east and west coasts of the United States? *(The transcontinental railroad)*
2. What issues were the cause of the Great Railroad Strike? *(Dangerous working conditions and pay cuts)*
3. What railroad was completed that links eastern and western Canada? *(The Canadian Pacific Railway)*

Chapter 6

The Expansion of American Industry (1850–1900)

The steel-framed Syndicate Building in New York City.

American Events

1856 The Bessemer process is patented, paving the way for the mass production of steel and a new industrial age in America.

1859 Edwin L. Drake strikes oil in Titusville, Pennsylvania, marking the first successful oil well and the beginning of the commercial use of oil.

1869 Workers finish construction on the transcontinental railroad, the first railroad to connect the east and west coasts.

Presidential Terms: Franklin Pierce 1853–1857; James Buchanan 1857–1861; Abraham Lincoln 1861–1865; Andrew Johnson 1865–1869; Ulysses S. Grant 1869–1877

1850 • 1860 • 1870

World Events

1859 Charles Darwin publishes *On the Origin of Species.*

1861 Louis Pasteur introduces pasteurization.

1869 The Suez Canal is completed.

eTeach

Be sure to check out this month's online discussion with a Master Teacher. Go to **www.phschool.com**.

RESOURCE DIRECTORY

Teaching Resources

Pacing Charts booklet
Block Scheduling booklet, p. 19
Units 1/2 booklet
- Chapter Summary, p. 60

Technology

Guided Reading Audiotapes (English/Spanish), Ch. 6
Student Edition on Audio CD, Ch. 6
Sounds of an Era Audio CD *"Dallas Railway,"* 1930s recording (time: 30 seconds)
Prentice Hall United States History Video Collection™ Volume 11, *Industrialization and Urbanization*
Prentice Hall Presentation Pro CD-ROM, Ch. 6
Resource Pro® CD-ROM
Social Studies Skills Tutor CD-ROM
Companion Web site, www.phschool.com

Time Zones and the Growth of the Railroads, 1890

Pacific Time
Mountain Time
Central Time
Eastern Time

Railroads Built by 1870

Labor union poster of the United Mine Workers of America.

1876 — Korea becomes an independent nation.

1877 — Dangerous working conditions and wage cuts spark violent protests by railway workers in the Great Railroad Strike.

1882 — Samuel Dodd and John Rockefeller form the Standard Oil Trust, which would soon dominate the nation's oil industry.

1885 — The Canadian Pacific Railway opens, linking eastern and western Canada.

1889 — The Eiffel Tower is completed.

1890 — Congress passes the Sherman Antitrust Act.

1894 — The Pullman Strike leads President Cleveland to use federal force against striking workers.

Rutherford B. Hayes 1877–1881	James Garfield 1881 C. Arthur 1881–1885	Grover Cleveland 1885–1889	Benjamin Harrison 1889–1893	Grover Cleveland 1893–1897	William McKinley 1897–1901

1880 · 1890 · 1900

Time Zones and the Growth of the Railroads, 1890

Activating Prior Knowledge Which time zones had the greatest number of railroad lines in 1890? *(The Central and Eastern time zones)*

Previewing In which time zones did the number of railroad lines grow the most from 1870 to 1890? *(The Pacific and Mountain time zones)*

BACKGROUND
About the Pictures

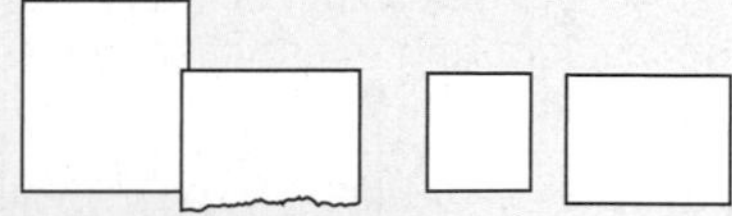

1. The Syndicate Building, also known as the Park Row Building, was constructed in lower Manhattan from 1896 to 1899 and stands 30 stories tall.
2. Constructing the transcontinental railroad required thousands of laborers such as these to perform dangerous, backbreaking work.
3. The United Mine Workers of America was founded in Columbus, Ohio, in 1890 when the Knights of Labor Trade Assembly No. 135 and the National Progressive Union of Miners and Mine Laborers joined together.

BIBLIOGRAPHY

For the Teacher

Boorstin, Daniel J. ***The Americans: The Democratic Experience.*** Random House, 1985. (A description of post–Civil War America, this book won the Pulitzer Prize when first published in 1973.)

Josephson, Matthew. ***The Robber Barons.*** Harvest Books, 1962. (This book was written in the 1930s at the height of the Depression, but it is still considered an important look at the rise of the titans of nineteenth-century American industry.)

For the Student

Riis, Jacob. ***How the Other Half Lives.*** Bedford/St. Martin's, 1996. (The wretchedness of urban slums in 1890 as described by a young New York reporter.)

Weisberger, Bernard. ***Captains of Industry.*** American Heritage Publishing, 1996. (A fast-moving, well-illustrated description of industrial leaders.)

Don't miss the exclusive interactive version of this textbook on the Web and on CD-ROM.

Section 1
A Technological Revolution

Section Objectives

1. Learn how daily lives changed in the decades following the Civil War.
2. Find out how advances in electric power and communication affected people and businesses in this era.
3. Discover the effects the development of railroads had on industrial growth.
4. Think about the impact of the Bessemer process on American culture.

Bellringer

Warm-Up Activity Write the following list of inventions on the chalkboard: typewriter, phonograph, telegraph, telephone. Ask students to decide which they consider the most important.

Activating Prior Knowledge Ask students to imagine how many times during the day they use a telephone. Have them list the number and types of calls they make on a given day. If they lived before the telephone was invented, how do they imagine they would have communicated the same types of information? How would their lives be different without telephones?

Reading Strategy

Tell students that they will be reading about daily life in the United States between 1865 and 1900. As they read, have them list the ways in which the United States changed during those 35 years to help them analyze economic issues such as the growth of railroads.

Section 1
A Technological Revolution

READING FOCUS

- Why did people's daily lives change in the decades following the Civil War?
- How did advances in electric power and communication affect life for people and businesses?
- What effects did the development of railroads have on industrial growth?
- What was the impact of the Bessemer process on American culture?

MAIN IDEA

In the years after the Civil War, new technology revolutionized American life.

KEY TERMS

patent
productivity
transcontinental railroad
Bessemer process
mass production

TAKING NOTES

As you read, complete this table listing some of the major technological innovations of the decades following the Civil War and their impact on American life.

A Technological Revolution		
Technology	**Examples**	**Impact on Daily Life and Business**
Electric power	Refrigerator	Reduced food spoilage

Setting the Scene Samuel Morse had worked for years on improving the telegraph and finally began to run out of money. Nearly broke, he anxiously awaited a bill to pass through Congress, which would provide him with funds to complete his work. The bill narrowly passed, to the surprise of many. Morse was greatly relieved. The next year he reached the climax of his success.

> *"And now at last the supreme moment had arrived. The line from Washington to Baltimore was completed, and on the 24th day of May, 1844, the company invited by the inventor . . . assembled to witness his triumph. True to his promise to Miss Annie Ellsworth, he had asked her to indite the first public message which should be flashed over the completed line, and she . . . chose the now historic words . . . 'What hath God wrought!' . . . Calmly he seated himself at the instrument and ticked off the inspired words in the dots and dashes of the Morse alphabet . . . the electromagnetic telegraph was no longer the wild dream of a visionary, but an accomplished fact."*
>
> —Samuel F.B. Morse

Below, Samuel Morse sends the first successful telegraph message, using Morse code, from the Supreme Court in Washington, D.C. Morse Code (inset) is still used today in amateur radio.

Little did Americans know as they entered the second half of the nineteenth century what other "wild dreams" would become reality. Samuel Morse's first successful telegraph message sent in 1844 marked the beginning of a second industrial revolution. The United States was on the verge of a major transformation. In the years after the Civil War, the United States developed into an industrial powerhouse. Inventors and scientists, backed by business leaders, created an explosion of inventions and improvements. Their efforts brought about a technological revolution that energized American industry and forever changed people's daily lives.

Activity
Connecting with Science and Technology

Share this quotation from the philosopher Alfred North Whitehead with students: "The greatest invention of the nineteenth century was the invention of the method of invention." Ask students to write paragraphs explaining what Whitehead meant, speculating on what "the method of invention" might be. **(Verbal/Linguistic)**

Resource Directory

Teaching Resources

Learning Styles Lesson Plans booklet, p. 28
Guided Reading and Review booklet, p. 54

Technology

Section Reading Support Transparencies
Guided Reading Audiotapes (English/Spanish), Ch. 6
Student Edition on Audio CD, Ch. 6
Prentice Hall United States History Video Collection™ Volume 11, *Industrialization and Urbanization*
Prentice Hall Presentation Pro CD-ROM, Ch. 6
Companion Web site, www.phschool.com

Changes in Daily Life

Most Americans today can flip a switch for light, turn a faucet for water, and talk to a friend a thousand miles away just by pressing a few buttons. It is hard for us to imagine life without these conveniences. In 1865, however, daily life was vastly different.

Daily Life in 1865 Indoor electric lighting did not exist in 1865. Instead, the rising and setting of the sun dictated the rhythm of a day's work. After dark, people lit candles or oil lamps if they could afford them. If they could not, they simply went to sleep, to rise at the first light of dawn.

Think about summers without the benefits of refrigeration! Ice was available in 1865, but only at great cost. People sawed blocks of ice out of frozen ponds during the winter, packed them in sawdust, and stored them in icehouses for later use.

By modern standards, long-distance communication was agonizingly slow. In 1860, most mail from the East Coast took ten days to reach the Midwest and three weeks to get to the West. An immigrant living on the frontier would have to wait several months for news from relatives in Europe.

Investing in Technology By 1900, this picture of daily life had changed dramatically for millions of Americans. The post–Civil War years saw tremendous growth in new ideas and inventions. Between 1790 and 1860, the Patent and Trademark Office of the federal government issued just 36,000 **patents**—licenses that give an inventor the exclusive right to make, use, or sell an invention for a set period of time. In contrast, 500,000 patents were issued between 1860 and 1890 for inventions such as the typewriter, telephone, and phonograph.

European and American business leaders began to invest heavily in these new inventions. The combination of financial backing and American ingenuity helped create new industries and expand old ones. By 1900, Americans' standard of living was among the highest in the world. This achievement was a result of the nation's growing industrial **productivity**—the amount of goods and services created in a given period of time.

Focus on ECONOMICS

Buying Stock The surge in inventions and patents could not have been possible without the money to finance them. How did inventors and entrepreneurs get the money they needed to develop their products and start their businesses? This country's free enterprise system provided the economic framework that could support these projects. The hopes of gaining substantial profits made business leaders more willing to take financial risks. They began to invest heavily in new inventions and businesses that they thought would be successful.

One way they did this was to buy stock in a company. A stock is a share representing a portion of ownership in a corporation. If a company sells 1,000 shares of stock, and an investor buys 100 of them, he or she owns 10 percent of the company. By purchasing a company's stock, an investor buys the right to receive a fraction of the company's profits.

New Forms of Energy

The blossoming of American inventive genius in the late 1800s had a profound effect on millions of people's lives. For example, scientists began developing new uses for petroleum, including fuels that would help power new machines. Electricity proved to be another productive energy source. It led to many important advances in the nation's industrial development and changed people's eating, working, and even sleeping habits.

Drake Strikes Oil In 1858, the Pennsylvania Rock Oil Company sent Edwin L. Drake to Titusville, Pennsylvania to drill for oil. The idea to drill for oil was new and many were skeptical of the project. Previously, oil had been obtained by either melting the fat from a whale or by digging large pits and waiting for oil to seep above ground—both of which were time-consuming and expensive. If the new method worked, it would be cheaper and more efficient.

READING CHECK
What were the benefits of Drake's new method of oil extraction?

LESSON PLAN

Focus Explain that the transformation of the United States in the late nineteenth century was due in large part to inventions that changed the way Americans lived and worked. Ask about the impact of the electric light.

Instruct Explain that conditions were ideal for a great surge in technology. Business leaders had capital to invest, and human and natural resources were abundant. Discuss how one invention often leads to others. Have students explain the effects of the technological innovations of electric power, the telegraph and telephone, and petroleum-based products on the development of the United States. Ask students to analyze the impact of technological innovations on the nature of work, the American labor movement, and business.

Assess/Reteach Ask students to list some of the ways in which new technology revolutionized American life in the years following the Civil War.

BACKGROUND
Connections to Today

Titusville, Pennsylvania, earned its place in history as the site of the world's first successful oil well, and, later, the site of the country's first oil refinery. But its oil-glory days are long past: Titusville's last refinery closed a half century ago. Today, Titusville is a sleepy little lumber and steel town of about 6,500 people. Still, civic pride in the town's oil heritage remains. Town slogans include "Where history meets technology" and "The birthplace of oil—in the valley that changed the world!" Titusville is home to the Drake Well Museum, where visitors tour replicas of Drake's oil derrick and engine house. From May through October, reproductions of the oil pioneer's steam engine and boiler operate, giving visitors a first-hand view of how oil was pumped from the nearly 70-foot-deep well. About 50,000 people visit the museum each year.

CUSTOMIZE FOR ...
ESL

Have students find or draw images of a refrigerator, an electric light, and an oil well. Have them label each image and add a sentence explaining the function of each.

READING CHECK
Drake's method was more efficient and less expensive.

Activity
Connecting with Science and Technology

Have small groups of students make presentations to the class that explain the differences between alternating current (AC) and direct current (DC). Their presentation should then describe the great "AC versus DC debate" of the 1880s and 1890s, in which Westinghouse eventually prevailed. **(Verbal/Linguistic)**

Background
Art History

The earliest existing photographs date from the 1820s. Technological advances in the mid-1800s allowed photographers to produce pictures on paper rather than glass. In the 1880s, George Eastman developed a hand-held camera that could be used by professionals and amateurs alike.

After spending nearly a year raising money and building the equipment needed for the project, Drake finally set up an oil well and began drilling using a steam-powered engine. In 1859, just as nervous investors had decided to call off the project, Drake struck oil. Oil quickly became a major industry.

As new uses for oil began to appear, the oil business grew rapidly. Titusville soon became one of several boom towns in northwestern Pennsylvania. Oil refineries, which transformed crude oil into kerosene, sprang up around the country. A byproduct of this process, gasoline, would eventually make oil even more valuable. Until the invention of the automobile in the late 1880s, however, gasoline was seen as a waste product and simply thrown away.

Edison, a Master of Invention Thomas A. Edison helped make another new source of energy, electric power, widely available. Born in 1847, Edison grew up tinkering with electricity. While working for a New York company, he improved the stock tickers that sent stock and gold prices to other offices. When his boss awarded him a $40,000 bonus, the 23-year-old Edison left his job and set himself up as an inventor.

In 1876, Edison moved into his "invention factory" in Menlo Park, New Jersey. The young genius, who had never received any formal science training, claimed that he could turn out "a minor invention every ten days and a big thing every six months or so."

Edison then began experimenting with electric lighting. His goal was to develop affordable, in-home lighting to replace oil lamps and gaslights. Starting around 1879, Edison and his fellow inventors tried different ways to produce light within a sealed glass bulb. They needed to find a material that would glow without quickly burning up when heated with an electric current.

The team experimented with various threadlike filaments with little success. In 1880, they finally found a workable filament made of bamboo fiber. This filament glowed, Edison said, with "the most beautiful light ever seen."

Edison's favorite invention, the phonograph, shown above, recorded sounds on metal foil wrapped around a rotating cylinder. The first words Edison recorded and then replayed on his phonograph were "Mary had a little lamb." This wondrous machine, introduced in 1877, gained Edison the nickname the "Wizard of Menlo Park."

Until the early 1880s, people who wanted electricity had to produce it with their own generator. Hoping to provide affordable lighting to many customers, Edison developed the idea of a central power station. In 1882, to attract investors, Edison built a power plant that lit dozens of buildings in New York City. Investors were impressed, and Edison's idea spread. By 1890, power stations across the country provided electricity for lamps, fans, printing presses, and many other newly invented appliances.

Electricity Is Improved Other inventors later improved upon Edison's work. Lewis Latimer, the son of an escaped slave, patented an improved method for producing the filament in light bulbs. He worked in Edison's laboratories, where he helped develop new advances in electricity. Latimer later wrote a landmark book about electric lighting.

Another major advance for electric lighting came from inventor George Westinghouse. In 1885, Westinghouse began to experiment with a form of electricity called alternating current. Edison had used direct current, which was expensive to produce and could only travel a mile or two. Alternating current could be generated more cheaply and travel longer distances.

RESOURCE DIRECTORY
Technology

Color Transparencies *The Way It Works,* H11

Sounds of an Era Audio CD *Thomas Edison on the Electric Age,* 1908 recording (time: one minute)

Westinghouse also used a device called a transformer to boost power levels at a station so that electricity could be sent over long distances. Another transformer at a distant substation could reduce power levels as needed. These aspects of Westinghouse's system made home use of electricity practical.

By the early 1890s, investors had used Edison's and Westinghouse's ideas and inventions to create two companies, General Electric and Westinghouse Electric. These companies' products encouraged the spread of the use of electricity. By 1898, nearly 3,000 power stations were lighting some 2 million light bulbs across the land.

Electricity's Impact on Business and Daily Life Electricity helped to improve the productivity of the business world and transform the nature of the workplace. Electric power was cheaper and more efficient than some previously existing power sources. For example, the electric sewing machine, first made in 1889, led to the rapid growth of the ready-made clothing industry. Before the electric sewing machine, workers had to physically push on a foot pedal to generate power. With electricity, a worker could produce more clothing in less time. As a result, the costs of producing each item of clothing decreased.

Rapidly growing industries, such as the ready-made clothing industry, opened up thousands of jobs for Americans looking for employment. Many of the country's new immigrants, especially women and children, found work making clothing in factories powered by electricity.

Household use of electric current revolutionized many aspects of daily life. To take but one example, electricity made the refrigerator possible. This invention reduced food spoilage and relieved the need to preserve foods by time-consuming means, such as smoking or salting.

Yet all Americans did not receive the benefits of electricity equally. Rural areas, especially, went without electricity for many decades. Even where electric power was available, many people could not afford the home appliances or other conveniences that ran on electricity.

Advances in Communications

In the late 1800s, thousands of people left their homes in Europe and the eastern United States to seek a new life in the West. One of the greatest hardships for these immigrants was leaving their loved ones behind. Would they ever hear from family and friends again? By 1900, thanks to many advances in communications, such fears of isolation had diminished.

The Telegraph The idea of sending messages over wires had occurred to inventors in the early 1700s. Several inventors actually set up working telegraph systems well before an American, Samuel F. B. Morse, took out a patent on telegraphy.

Morse may not have invented the telegraph, but he perfected it. He devised a code of short and long electrical impulses to represent the letters of the alphabet. Using this system, later called Morse code, he sent his first message in 1844. His success signaled the start of a communications revolution.

VIEWING HISTORY Here, visitors marvel at the electricity building, on display at the 1893 World's Columbian Exposition in Chicago. The building boasted more than 18,000 electric light bulbs and hosted other exhibits that showed the practical and entertainment value of electricity. **Drawing Conclusions** *Why do you think expositions such as this one were important? Who attended them?*

ACTIVITY
Connecting with Culture

Instruct students to keep an "electricity use log" for a 48-hour period. Students should note every time they use electricity, both directly (e.g., turning on a light) and indirectly (e.g., eating cafeteria food that has been cooked with electric power). After they have completed their logs, students should organize log entries into categories. (Categories might include illumination, food preservation, entertainment, and so on.) For each category, students should write a brief paragraph describing how that aspect of American culture would be different without electricity. **(Visual/Spatial)**

BACKGROUND
Connections to Today

Distress messages sent using Morse code have saved countless ships and thousands of lives. For a century, the Morse signal "SOS" (dit dit dit, dah dah dah, dit dit dit) has been universally recognized as a call for help. This may all soon be changing, however. The development of new, more advanced communications technologies has brought telegraphy and Morse code to the verge of obsolescence. Amateur radio operators are no longer required to learn Morse code to earn a license. And, in 1999, international regulations changed so that ships at sea were no longer required to carry equipment that enabled them to send an SOS using Morse code.

TEST PREPARATION

Have students read the passages under "Edison, a Master of Invention" on the previous page and then complete the sentence below.

The main idea of this section is that—

Ⓐ Edison's inventions led to the availability of cheap power, revolutionizing American life.
B Edison was a genius who received no formal education.
C later inventors improved on Edison's work.
D Edison invented the light bulb and the phonograph.

CAPTION ANSWERS

Viewing History It was important to celebrate the growing success of American technology in order to both encourage the continued development of new products and boost national morale. Most likely to attend these events were those who had more leisure time and education, those who had money to invest in technology, or those in the scientific community who wished to see where technology was heading.

ACTIVITY
Student Portfolio

You may wish to have students add the following to their portfolios: Many popular American folk songs concern the building of the railroads. Ask students to research the history of railroad songs and to prepare a written report or an oral presentation using an audiotape of the songs they researched. Suggest that students begin their research with books of American folk songs, such as Carl Sandburg's *The American Songbag.* **(Musical/Rhythmic)**

BACKGROUND
A Diverse Nation

Not everyone greeted the improvements in railroad transportation and travel with enthusiasm. *The Boston Courier* printed the following assertion as part of an editorial in 1827: "The project of a railroad from Boston to Albany is impracticable, as every one knows who knows the simplest rule of arithmetic, and the expense would be little less than the market value of the whole of Massachusetts; and which, if practicable, every person of common sense knows would be as useless as a railroad from Boston to the moon."

After the Civil War, several telegraph companies joined together to form the Western Union Telegraph Company. In 1870, Western Union had more than 100,000 miles of wire, over which some 9 million telegraph messages were transmitted. By 1900, the company owned more than 900,000 miles of wire and was sending roughly 63 million telegraph messages a year.

The Telephone In 1871, Alexander Graham Bell of Scotland immigrated to Boston, Massachusetts, to teach people with hearing difficulties. After experimenting for several years with an electric current to transmit sounds, Bell patented the "talking telegraph" on March 7, 1876. He had just turned 29. In 1885, Bell and a group of partners set up the American Telephone and Telegraph Company to build long-distance telephone lines.

The earliest local phone lines could connect only two places, such as a home and a business. Soon central switchboards with operators could link an entire city. The first commercial telephone exchange began serving 21 customers on January 28, 1878, in New Haven, Connecticut. The next year President Rutherford B. Hayes had a telephone installed at the White House. By 1900, 1.5 million telephones were in use.

Railroads Create a National Network

In 1850, steam-powered ships still provided much of the nation's transportation. Over the following decades, however, improvements in train and track design, plus the construction of new rail lines, gave railroads a big boost.

Before the Civil War, most of the nation's railroad tracks were in short lines that connected neighboring cities, mainly in the East. Since there was no standard track width, or gauge, each train could only travel on certain tracks. As a result, goods and passengers often had to be moved to different trains, which caused costly delays. To make matters worse, train travel was dangerous. No system of standard signals existed, and train brakes were unreliable.

The Transcontinental Railroad The rail business expanded greatly after the Civil War. The key event was the completion of the **transcontinental railroad,** a railway extending from coast to coast. When the project began in 1862, rail lines already reached from the East Coast to the Mississippi River. Now new rails were laid between Omaha, Nebraska, and Sacramento, California.

Because private investors did not see any likelihood of profit in building railroads beyond the line of settlement, the federal government stepped in to fund the completion of the transcontinental railroad. Members of Congress believed that the completion of a coast-to-coast railway would strengthen the country's economic infrastructure. Thus the federal government awarded huge loans and land grants to two private companies. The Central Pacific Railroad began laying track eastward out of Sacramento. The Union Pacific Railroad began work toward the west in Omaha.

Historians disagree as to whether it was a good idea for the government to provide funds for this project. Many believe that the government gave a much needed boost to

The World Wide Web

The growth and influence of the Internet in the second half of the 1990s was a turning point in the nation's economy, similar in scope to the vast economic changes brought about by the telegraph and railroads in the late 1800s. Estimates show that from 1996 to 2001, the number of people using the Internet worldwide skyrocketed from 45 million to over 400 million. Also during that time, the amount of revenue generated by the Internet jumped from $2.9 billion to over $700 billion.

Just as in the late 1800s, the world of business and daily life at the end of the twentieth century changed drastically with the advent of new technologies resulting from the Internet. The Internet became the next step in a process that began with the telegraph and the railroads to connect people and ideas in faster, more efficient ways. Moving beyond telegraph wires and railroad tracks, the United States, and indeed the world, is now connected through an infinite and invisible World Wide Web.

? What other recent technological innovations have changed the world of communications? What do you think will be the next step in this process? Explain.

CAPTION ANSWERS

Fast Forward to Today Possible answer: Faxes, cell phones, pagers, camcorders, digital cameras, high-speed passenger trains. Such innovations will continue to speed up the pace of everyday life. People are likely to become less reliant on traditional hard-wired telephones as they turn more and more to e-mail and cell phones.

RESOURCE DIRECTORY

Teaching Resources

Great Debates booklet (Decision-Making Activities) *Using Chinese Laborers to Build the Transcontinental Railroad,* p. 30

Other Print Resources

American History Block Scheduling Support *Linking the Nation: The Railroads,* found in the Expansion, Reconstruction, and Immigration folder, includes interdisciplinary lesson suggestions and activities for Geography and History, Primary Sources, Biography, and Literature.

Nystrom ***Atlas of Our Country*** *Settling the West,* pp. 28–29

Historical Outline Map Book *Political United States,* p. 82

Technology

Color Transparencies *The Way it Works,* H9

RESOURCE PRO® **Primary Source Activity** *Working on the Railroad,* found on Resource Pro, introduces students to a folk song by Thomas Casey about the hard life of an 1880s worker.

VIEWING HISTORY Workers from the Union and Central Pacific Railroads met at Promontory Summit, Utah, in 1869. The driving of the golden spike (inset) marked the completion of the transcontinental railroad. **Synthesizing Information** *Some have called this the greatest historical event in transportation in this country. Why was it such a joyous and momentous occasion?*

the railroad industry when the private sector was hesitant to invest. However, others argue that the government should not have gotten involved. One reason is that railroads built with federal aid did not operate as efficiently and profitably as those built by the private sector. For example, James J. Hill's Great Northern Railroad in the 1880s and 1890s had both lower rates and higher profits than the railroads built with federal aid.

Most of the workers on the transcontinental railroad were immigrants. Irish workers on the Union Pacific line used pickaxes to dig and level rail beds across the Great Plains at the rate of up to 6 miles a day. Chinese workers brought to the United States by the Central Pacific chiseled, plowed, and dynamited their way through the Sierra Nevada. Workers took pride in their labor. One work crew set a record for putting down track—an amazing ten miles in one day.

Finally, after seven years of grueling physical labor, the two crews approached each other in what is now Utah. On May 10, 1869, at a place called Promontory Summit, Central Pacific president Leland Stanford raised his hammer to drive the final golden spike into position. A telegraph operator beside the track tapped out a message to crowds throughout the country: "Almost ready now. Hats off. Prayer is being offered. . . . Done!" The nation had its first transcontinental railroad.

Railroad Developments By 1870, railroads could carry goods and passengers from coast to coast, but they still had problems. Trains were often noisy, dirty, and uncomfortable for travelers. The huge engines, spewing smoke and cinders as they thundered through the countryside, sometimes aroused fear and distrust.

In spite of the problems, train travel continued to expand and improve. The various new technologies emerging at this time all aided in the development of the national railroad system. Steel rails replaced iron rails, and track gauges and signals became standardized. Railroad companies also took steps to improve safety. In 1869, George Westinghouse developed more effective air

READING CHECK
What types of problems did railroads have in the late 1800s?

ACTIVITY
Connecting with Geography

Have students work in groups to create an illustrated and annotated map of the first transcontinental railroad. Their map should be illustrated with the major geographical barriers the builders faced, and annotated with notes that explain how each obstacle was overcome. **(Visual/Spatial)**

BACKGROUND
Biography

African American engineer Elijah McCoy (1843–1929) was born in Canada to escaped slaves. He studied in Edinburgh, Scotland, before settling in the United States. In 1872, while working for the Michigan Central Railroad, McCoy invented the lubricating cup—a device that continuously oiled the moving parts of factory machinery. Over the years he invented and sold nearly 60 kinds of devices and machine parts. It is sometimes said that the expression "the real McCoy," meaning the genuine article, came about because people insisted that the machinery they bought be equipped with McCoy's invention.

READING CHECK
The trains sometimes aroused fear because of their enormity, and passengers found the trains to be loud, unclean, and uncomfortable.

CUSTOMIZE FOR ...
Less Proficient Readers

Ask students to construct a cause-and-effect chart showing the effects of the growth of railroads, improved communications, and the availability of electric power.

CAPTION ANSWERS

Viewing History Joyous for workers because they spent seven years working on it; joyous for railroad owners because their profits and businesses would expand; momentous in history because it revolutionized transportation, businesses, and daily life.

ACTIVITY
Connecting with Economics

Remind students of the economic concept of the "factors of production"—the four factors that must be in place for economic production to occur (land, labor, capital, and management). Then have students review the five ways that railroads helped revolutionize business and industry. Have students identify how each factor of production played a role in the changes the railroads brought to business and industry. Students should present their analysis in the form of a chart. **(Logical/ Mathematical)**

BACKGROUND
Geography in History

During the United States' first century (and for centuries before), people relied on "solar time" to set their clocks. As its name implies, solar time is determined by the sun. Under solar time, noon is when the sun is highest in the sky. Typically, a small town would set its town clock at noon, and the other clocks in town would be set according to the town clock. But because the earth rotates east to west, solar noon is at different times in different locations. Even towns just a few miles to the east or west experience solar noon at a different time. Therefore, their clocks were never the same. (On average, solar time changed about five minutes for every 60 miles traveled east or west.) This never proved a problem until high-speed railroad travel and complex railroad schedules came along. The solution was "standard time," implemented through time zones. Because the railroad industry established standard time, it was for years known as "railroad time."

VIEWING HISTORY Citadel rock looms over the construction of the Union Pacific Railroad through Wyoming Territory in 1868. **Identifying Central Issues** *In what ways did the nation's growing transportation system help promote industrial growth?*

brakes. In 1887, Granville Woods patented a telegraph system for communicating with moving trains, thus reducing the risk of collision.

The growth of railroads also led to the development of many towns throughout the western part of the United States. Railroad owners, looking to expand their businesses and increase profits, began building towns near their railroads on land granted to them by the government.

Railroads and Time Zones Scheduling proved to be another problem for railroads. Throughout much of the 1800s, most towns set their clocks independently, according to solar time. But when trains started regular passenger service, time differences from town to town created confusion. So, in 1883, the railroads adopted a national system of time zones to improve scheduling. As a result, clocks in broad regions of the country showed the same time, a system we still use today.

Rail improvements such as this made life easier not only for passengers but also for businesses that shipped goods. By the end of the century, some 190,000 miles of rails linked businesses and their customers. Shipping costs dropped enormously. In 1865, shipping a barrel of flour from Chicago to New York cost $3.45. In 1895, it cost just 68 cents.

Railroads and Industry Although the development of canals, turnpikes, and steam-powered ships in the first half of the century had improved transportation, the transport of goods over long distances was still costly and inefficient. Railroads played a key role in revolutionizing business and industry in the United States in several ways.

A faster and more practical means of transporting goods Railroads were not as severely limited by geographic and natural factors, such as poor weather conditions. They could travel at higher speeds, and transport larger items in much greater quantities.

Lower costs of production Railroads were a cheaper way to transport goods. As shipping costs dropped, more goods could be sent at lower prices. As a result, businesses were able to receive the raw materials and resources needed to produce their products at much lower costs and in much less time.

Creation of national markets Higher speeds and lower costs now allowed a business to market and sell its finished products to locations nationwide, rather than

CAPTION ANSWERS

Viewing History Made shipping faster and cheaper, leading to lower costs of production; opened up national markets for selling and obtaining resources; stimulated the growth of other industries; provided a new model for the management of large businesses.

RESOURCE DIRECTORY
Technology

RESOURCE PRO® **Biography** *Washington A. Roebling,* found on Resource Pro, profiles the engineer who supervised the building of the Brooklyn Bridge.

just in a local region. Also, the resources needed to produce these goods could be obtained from anywhere in the country. These advances in commerce helped to link distant regions of the United States, furthering the national network of business, transportation, and communication.

A model for big business Because of the complexity and size of the railroad companies, with railroads came new administrative techniques for handling large numbers of workers and large quantities of materials and money. New methods of management also arose. The professional manager and the specialized department grew out of the railroad business.

Stimulation of other industries The growth of the railroad industry encouraged innovation in other industries. The replacement of iron rails with steel rails, for example, promoted the growth of the steel industry.

The Bessemer Process

Through the mid-1800s, the nation depended on iron for railroad rails and the frames of large buildings. But in the 1850s, Henry Bessemer in England and William Kelly in Kentucky independently developed a new process for making steel. In 1856, Bessemer received the first patent for the **Bessemer process.** Steel had long been produced by melting iron, adding carbon, and removing impurities. The Bessemer process made it much easier and cheaper to remove the impurities.

Locomotives, such as this Erie Locomotive from 1903, were an impressive sight to many Americans at the turn of the century.

233

ACTIVITY

Connecting with Science and Technology

Have students conduct research to identify the major steps in both the Bessemer process of producing steel and in the traditional method of producing steel. Have students create illustrated flowcharts that depict each process, and compare and contrast them. **(Visual/Spatial)**

BACKGROUND

Biography

John Roebling, the engineer who began to build the Brooklyn Bridge, died six months after construction began, in 1869, of injuries resulting from a construction accident. His son Colonel Washington Roebling took over, but he contracted the "bends," or caisson disease, in 1872 and was confined to his bed. His wife, Emily, acted as his messenger through the final phases of construction, which ended in 1883.

TEST PREPARATION

Have students read the section "Railroads and Industry" on these pages and then answer the question below.

Which of the following was NOT true of railroads in the 1800s?

- **A** They could transport larger quantities than ships.
- **B** They helped create nationwide markets.
- **Ⓒ** They made shipping by water obsolete.
- **D** They promoted the growth of other industries.

ACTIVITY
Connecting with Economics

Present the following facts to students: the Brooklyn Bridge cost $18 million to build. On the day it opened, 150,300 pedestrians crossed the bridge. Each paid a penny ($.01) for the privilege. Also on the first day, 1,800 vehicles crossed the bridge. Vehicles had to pay a nickel ($.05) to cross. Have students calculate the revenue earned on the Brooklyn Bridge's first day of operation. Then have them determine the percentage of the construction cost this amount represents. **(Logical/ Mathematical)**

BACKGROUND
Geography in History

The distance people could travel to work, as well as natural boundaries such as rivers and seashores, determined early city boundaries. In the late 1800s, bridges and streetcar lines eliminated these barriers and opened up an era of urban expansion in the east. Between 1855 and 1873, Boston absorbed several towns to the west and south and expanded north across its harbor. Fifteen years after the Brooklyn Bridge opened, New York City annexed the independent cities of Brooklyn and Queens.

READING CHECK
It allowed impurities to be removed cheaply and easily, enabling steel to be produced in mass quantities.

READING CHECK
How did the Bessemer process make steel more affordable?

Steel is lighter, stronger, and more flexible than iron. The Bessemer process made possible the **mass production,** or production in great amounts, of steel. As a result, a new age of building began. A majestic symbol of this new age that endures is the Brooklyn Bridge.

The Brooklyn Bridge After the Civil War, New York City grew in size as well as population. Many people who worked on the island of Manhattan lived in nearby Brooklyn. The only way to travel between Brooklyn and Manhattan was by ferry across the East River. In winter, ice or winds often shut down the ferry service. Could a bridge high enough to clear river traffic be built across such a large distance? Engineer John A. Roebling, a German immigrant, thought it could.

Roebling designed a suspension bridge with thick steel cables suspended from high towers to hold up the main span. That span, arching 1,595 feet above the

The Chicago Reliance Building

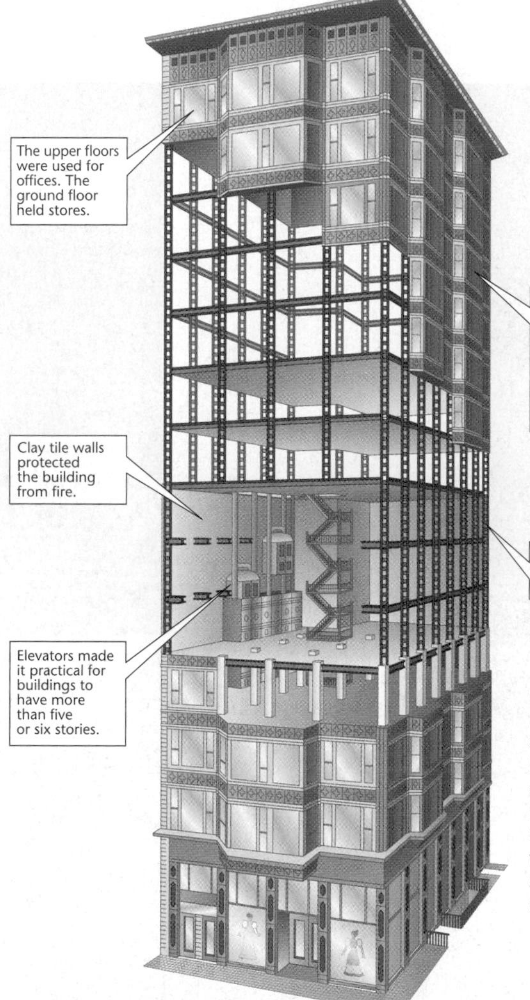
The upper floors were used for offices. The ground floor held stores.
Bay windows let in light and air. This was important at a time when few buildings had electric lights and no one had even dreamed of air conditioning.
Clay tile walls protected the building from fire.
The steel frame carried the weight of the building.
Elevators made it practical for buildings to have more than five or six stories.

VIEWING HISTORY The Bessemer process paved the way for the use of steel in building construction. Before steel, frameworks consisted of heavy iron. Steel acted as a much lighter framework and allowed the construction of taller buildings. The Reliance Building in Chicago, shown here, was built 16 stories high in the 1890s. At the time, 16 stories was enough to make a building a "skyscraper." **Analyzing Information** *How did various technologies combine to make skyscrapers possible?*

CAPTION ANSWERS

Viewing History The Bessemer process made possible the mass production of steel, which made steel cheap and easy to use for the construction of new buildings and bridges. Electricity aided the development of elevators.

RESOURCE DIRECTORY

Teaching Resources
Units 1/2 booklet
- Section 1 Quiz, p. 61

Guide to the Essentials
- Section 1 Summary, p. 28

Technology
Color Transparencies *The Way It Works,* H10; *American Photo,* F5
Exploring Primary Sources in U.S. History CD-ROM *The Tall Office Building Artistically Considered, Louis H. Sullivan*

river, would be the longest in the world. Roebling died shortly after construction of the Brooklyn Bridge began in 1869, so his son Washington took over the project. Washington was disabled in 1872 by a severe attack of decompression sickness ("the bends") while inspecting a foundation deep under the river. Other disasters followed, from explosions and fires, to dishonest dealings by a steel-cable contractor.

A Symbol of American Success Despite these problems, the Brooklyn Bridge was completed and opened with a ceremony on May 24, 1883. In the keynote address, congressman and future New York City mayor Abram Hewitt remarked on this great triumph:

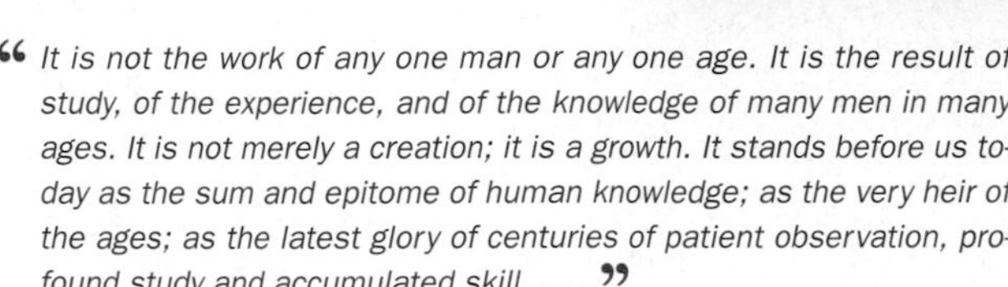

> "*It is not the work of any one man or any one age. It is the result of study, of the experience, and of the knowledge of many men in many ages. It is not merely a creation; it is a growth. It stands before us today as the sum and epitome of human knowledge; as the very heir of the ages; as the latest glory of centuries of patient observation, profound study and accumulated skill. . . .*"
>
> —Abram Stevens Hewitt

VIEWING HISTORY This 1883 lithograph by Currier and Ives reveals the atmosphere of triumph and celebration that accompanied the opening of the Brooklyn Bridge. **Demonstrating Reasoned Judgment** *How do you think images such as this influenced people's perceptions of the changes taking place in society?*

At nightfall, crowds gasped as electric light bulbs, which had been strung along the bridge, lit up the darkness and shimmered on the river below. The city celebrated with a magnificent fireworks display. Indeed, the entire United States celebrated, its inventive genius and hard work plainly visible for all the world to see.

Section 1 Assessment

READING COMPREHENSION

1. Why did the nation's industrial **productivity** rise in the late 1800s?
2. Why did the oil business change after Drake found oil in Pennsylvania?
3. How did inventions such as the light bulb and the telegraph change daily life in the late 1800s?
4. What were the advantages of building the **transcontinental railroad?**
5. What innovations did the **Bessemer process** encourage?

CRITICAL THINKING AND WRITING

6. **Determining Relevance** How did the system of patents encourage innovation and investment?
7. **Making Comparisons** Think of a modern convenience that you rely on. What benefits does this item bring to your life? Are there any drawbacks associated with this item?
8. **Writing a List** Create a list that compares the changes in business and daily life resulting from the telegraph and the railroad in the late 1800s with the changes resulting from the Internet in the late 1900s.

Take It to the NET

Virtual Field Trip Visit the Central Pacific Railroad Photographic History Museum to learn more about the completion of the transcontinental railroad and life surrounding the railroads in the middle of the nineteenth century. Use the links provided in the *America: Pathways to the Present* area of the following Web site for help in completing this activity.
www.phschool.com

Section 1 Assessment

Reading Comprehension

1. Due to new technology, the great increase in inventions, and the investments to fund them.
2. Using Drake's type of well made it much less expensive and easier to obtain large amounts of oil. The new process allowed an increase in demand to be satisfied.
3. They extended the usable hours of the day, allowed for efficient long-distance communication, and made possible the creation of entirely new industries.
4. Answers may include: reduce cost and increase efficiency of transportation; facilitate commerce; create national markets; stimulate other industries, like the steel industry.
5. Mass production of steel; large suspension bridges; steel frame construction in buildings.

Critical Thinking and Writing

6. By giving inventors and investors ownership of their ideas and creations, and the resulting profits.
7. Sample answers: personal computers or contact lenses.
8. Sample answers: A nationwide rail system made for a reduction in shipping prices. The Internet allows one to obtain news updates at any time throughout the day.

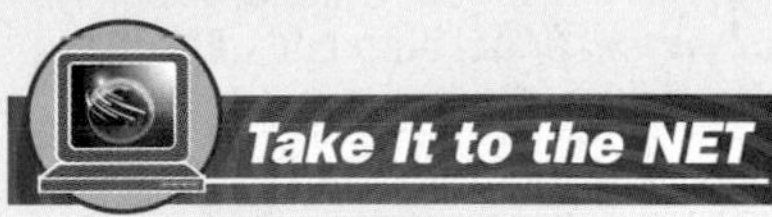

Invite students to take a Virtual Field Trip at **www.phschool.com**

Caption Answers

Viewing History They glorified and celebrated the new technologies and achievements of the time. The celebratory atmosphere depicted the public's view of American technological/business success and suggested that the United States was on the brink of something greater.

Using Cross-Sectional Maps

Focus Students compare the data provided in a cross-sectional map with that in a physical-political map.

Instruct To be sure students understand the information presented in the cross-sectional map, ask them to identify the locations on the map at elevations of 1,000 feet and 7,000 feet. Have them indicate the elevation at Bitter Creek. Ask students to think about some other useful subjects for cross-sectional maps. *(The ocean floor, rivers, and other waterways)*

Extend See the Skills for Life activity in the Resource Directory below.

ANSWERS

Practice the Skill

1. **(a)** The Rocky Mountains, Salt Lake Valley, Humboldt Valley, and the Sierra Nevada are on both maps. The Wyoming Basin and Independence Range appear only on the physical-political map. **(b)** No. The cross-sectional maps do not show the land area that lies north or south of the railroads. **(c)** No. The physical-political map shows some land to the east of Omaha, while the cross-sectional map ends at Omaha.
2. **(a)** Union Pacific: the highest elevation was about 7,500 feet above sea level, the lowest about 1,000 feet. Central Pacific: the highest elevation was just over 7,000 feet above sea level, the lowest about 300 feet. **(b)** The sharpest changes occurred heading east from Sacramento. **(c)** The most gradual changes occurred heading west from Omaha. **(d)** The Central Pacific Railroad: 700 miles; the Union Pacific Railroad: 1,100 miles.
3. **(a)** The Central Pacific Railroad was shorter but had more extreme changes in elevation. **(b)** Those working east from Sacramento, because of the Sierra Nevada mountains. **(c)** Union Pacific Railroad workers, because their route was longer and included more terrain at high elevation.

Using Cross-Sectional Maps

It is sometimes helpful to use more than one type of map to understand a particular piece of land. Physical-political maps show the land as if viewed from above, revealing distances across the surface. Cross-sectional maps show how the land would look if viewed from the side; they indicate the heights of mountains and valleys. The cross-sectional map below shows the changes in elevation along the route of the first transcontinental railroad. These changes posed a great challenge to workers building the railroad between 1862 and 1869.

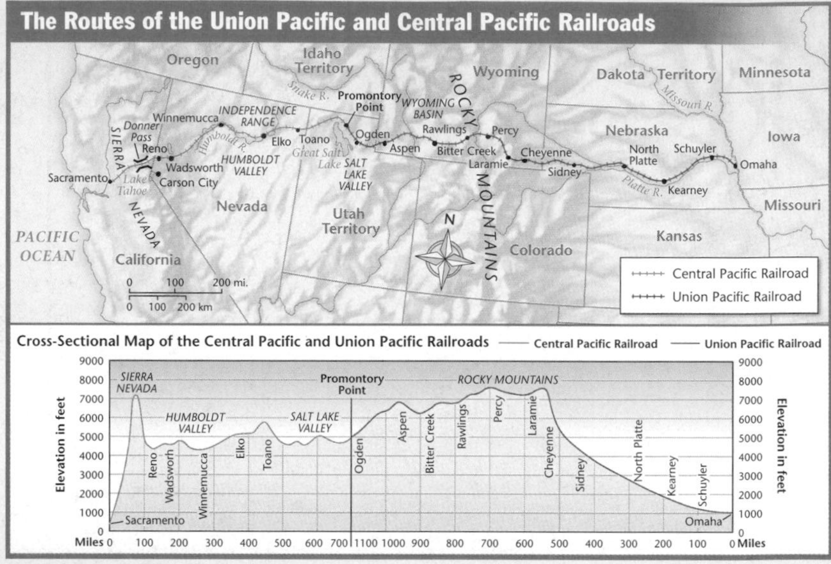

LEARN THE SKILL

Use the following steps to analyze a cross-sectional map:

1. **Study the region shown on both maps.** Compare the area covered and the elements shown on each map. Find several points that appear on both maps, and notice how they are depicted on each map.
2. **Analyze the information shown on the cross-sectional map.** Notice how changes in elevation are shown on the map (in this case, as the rising and falling of the green and red lines). Study the scale on the map, and notice both the distance covered across land and the elevation.
3. **Draw conclusions about the places or events depicted on the maps.** Use what you learn from both maps to better understand the landforms and the human activity in that area.

PRACTICE THE SKILL

Answer the following questions:

1. **(a)** Which landforms on the physical-political map correspond to those on the cross-sectional map? Which landforms appear on only one map? **(b)** Does the cross-sectional map show the same land area a the physical-political map? Explain. **(c)** Does the cro sectional map cover the same east-west distance as the physical-political map? Explain.
2. **(a)** What were the highest and lowest elevations of e railroad route? **(b)** Which 100-mile section on each ro had the sharpest changes? **(c)** Which 100-mile sectic on each route had the most gradual changes? **(d)** Ho long was each route?
3. **(a)** How do the length and elevation changes of the t routes compare? **(b)** Which railroad workers faced the greatest challenge at the start of the project: those w ing east from Sacramento, or those working west fror Omaha? Explain. **(c)** Which workers faced the greate overall challenge? Explain.

APPLY THE SKILL

See the Chapter Review and Assessment for another op tunity to apply this skill.

RESOURCE DIRECTORY

Teaching Resources
Skills for Life booklet, p. 15

Technology
Social Studies Skills Tutor CD-ROM
Interactive Practice in
- Geographic Literacy
- Critical Thinking and Reading
- Visual Analysis
- Communications

Section 2

The Growth of Big Business

READING FOCUS

- Why were American industrialists of the late 1800s called both "robber barons" and "captains of industry"?
- How did social Darwinism affect Americans' views on big business?
- In what ways did big businesses differ from smaller businesses?
- How did industrialists gain a competitive edge over their rivals?

KEY TERMS

social Darwinism
oligopoly
monopoly
cartel
vertical consolidation
economies of scale
horizontal consolidation
trust
Sherman Antitrust Act

TAKING NOTES

Copy the web diagram below. As you read, fill in examples relating to the growth of big business in the late 1800s.

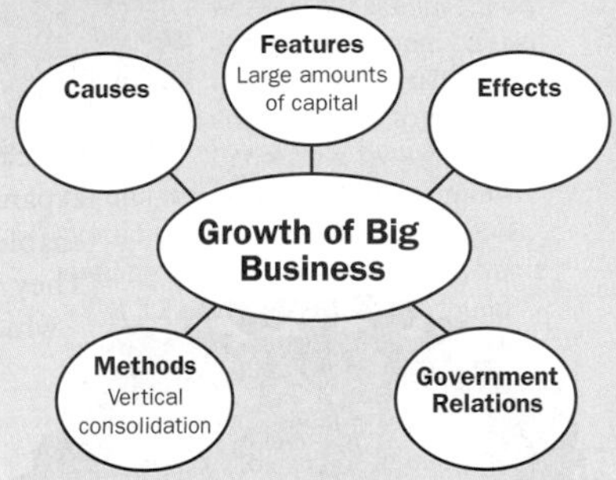

MAIN IDEA

Big business created wealth for its owners and for the nation, but it also prompted controversy and concern over its methods.

Setting the Scene

> "*A very important incident in my life occurred when one day in a train, a nice, farmer-looking gentleman approached me. . . . He pulled from a small green bag the model of the first sleeping car. This man was Mr. Woodruff, the inventor. Its value struck me like a flash. . . . [He] offered me an interest in the venture, which I promptly accepted. . . . I had not the money, and I did not see any way of getting it. But I finally decided to visit the local banker and ask him for a loan. . . . I really made my first considerable sum from this investment in the Woodruff Sleeping Car Company.*"
>
> —Andrew Carnegie

One of the most successful of all business leaders and industrialists in the late 1800s was Andrew Carnegie. He came from humble beginnings, but quickly understood and embraced the concept that "money could make money." He just needed a way to find it. Carnegie had an eye for recognizing a good investment. Making wise and sometimes risky investments would soon make him one of the richest and most successful businessmen in the world.

The period of invention after the Civil War set the stage for great industrial growth. Still, more than technology would be needed to transform the United States. It would take shrewd businesspeople and many investors willing to gamble on new products. Without huge amounts of capital, businesses could not build factories or market their inventions. To succeed, business leaders often combined funds and resources to create large companies. Thus was born the age of big business.

Wall Street in New York City was a prominent financial center in the late 1800s.

237

Section 2
The Growth of Big Business

Section Objectives

1. Read to find out why American industrialists of the late 1800s were called both "robber barons" and "captains of industry."
2. Discover how social Darwinism affected Americans' views on big business.
3. Analyze the ways in which big businesses differed from smaller businesses.
4. Learn how industrialists gained a competitive edge over their rivals.

Bellringer

Warm-Up Activity Have students describe a "mom and pop" business. Then have them write a definition of "big business" and explain how the two differ.

Activating Prior Knowledge Ask students to list reasons why this period in history saw the birth and rapid growth of many different types of big businesses.

Reading Strategy

Have students read the paragraphs under the heading "Robber Barons or Captains of Industry?" on the next page. Have them look for evidence to support each of these views of industrialists to help them understand and analyze the issue of industrialization and the rise of big business and the impact of the Sherman Antitrust Act on business.

RESOURCE DIRECTORY

Teaching Resources

Guided Reading and Review booklet, p. 55

Technology

Section Reading Support Transparencies
Guided Reading Audiotapes (English/Spanish), Ch. 6
Student Edition on Audio CD, Ch. 6
Prentice Hall Presentation Pro CD-ROM, Ch. 6
Companion Web site, www.phschool.com

resources. As a result, big businesses developed new systems of formal, written rules and created specialized departments.

Gaining a Competitive Edge

In their efforts to compete and earn higher profits, industrialists used many methods, fair or unfair, to gain a competitive edge over their rivals. They attempted to pay as little as they could for raw materials, labor, and shipping, hoping to maintain the most efficient businesses in their industry.

New Market Structures The lure of gaining enormous profits from new booming industries attracted many investors and entrepreneurs. However, the start-up costs of creating certain types of businesses were high and, as a result, only a few companies could compete in those industries. A market structure such as this, which is dominated by only a few large, profitable firms, is called an **oligopoly.** Many industries today are oligopolies, such as those that produce breakfast cereals, cars, and household appliances.

Some companies set out to gain a **monopoly,** or complete control of a product or service. To do this, a business bought out its competitors or drove them out of business. Once consumers had no other place to turn for a given product or service, the sole remaining company would be free to raise its prices.

Toward the end of the 1800s, federal and state governments passed laws to prevent certain monopolistic practices. Those laws did not prevent or destroy all monopolies, however. One reason was that political leaders refused to attack the powerful business leaders.

THE PROTECTORS OF OUR INDUSTRIES

INTERPRETING POLITICAL CARTOONS Some Americans were offended by the argument that business leaders protected jobs. **Drawing Conclusions** *What does this cartoon suggest about the relationship of workers to business leaders?*

Forming monopolies was not the only way to control an industry. Sometimes industrialists prospered by taking steps to limit competition with other firms. One way was to form a **cartel**—a loose association of businesses that make the same product. Members of the cartels agreed to limit the supply of their product and thus keep prices high.

Neither the monopolies nor the cartels were foolproof. Monopolies faced the threat of government action, and cartels tended to fall apart during hard economic times. To achieve a more reliable arrangement, industrialists came up with new strategies that would help them dominate their markets.

Carnegie Steel By the time he was 30, in 1865, Andrew Carnegie was making $50,000 a year, and he wanted to invest his wealth. The development of the Bessemer process persuaded Carnegie that steel would soon replace iron in many industries. During the early 1870s, near Pittsburgh, he founded the first steel plants to use the Bessemer process. These holdings would eventually grow into the Carnegie Steel Company, which he established in 1889.

Carnegie's business prospered. The company's wealth enabled him to make it even stronger. He soon had enough money to buy the companies that performed all the phases of steel production, from the mines that produced iron ore to the furnaces and mills that made pig iron and steel. He even bought the

ACTIVITY
Connecting with Economics

Have students reread the "Fast Forward to Today" feature on page 230, which draws parallels between the impact of technology on the United States economy in the late 1800s and in the late 1900s. Extend the parallel by asking students whether the growth of monopolies and trusts in the earlier period has any parallels today. Have them conduct research to determine how the antitrust and anti-monopoly legislation that grew out of the late 1800s has been applied to Microsoft, a leading business of the late 1900s. Students should share what they learn with the class. **(Verbal/Linguistic)**

BACKGROUND
A Diverse Nation

Many workers came from China to California during the Gold Rush of the mid-1800s. Chinese workers caught the attention of railroad owners, who recruited them when they found it difficult to attract other workers to the hard labor and low wages that were offered. Of the 12,000 men who worked to build the Central Pacific Railroad, 10,000 were Chinese. They were paid about $26 a month—less than the other workers—out of which they paid Central Pacific for their food and lodging. All other workers were paid $35 a month and given free food and lodging.

CAPTION ANSWERS

Interpreting Political Cartoons It depicts workers struggling to support the business leaders who mistakenly believe that they are protecting workers. In addition, the business leaders have literally grown fat upon the labor of the workers.

RESOURCE DIRECTORY

Technology

Color Transparencies *Cause-and-Effect Charts,* D6

RESOURCE PRO® **Visual Learning Activity** *Home of the Trusts,* found on Resource Pro, uses an antitrust cartoon by Thomas Nast to help students analyze political imagery.

Exploring Primary Sources in U.S. History CD-ROM *Spindle Top Gusher*

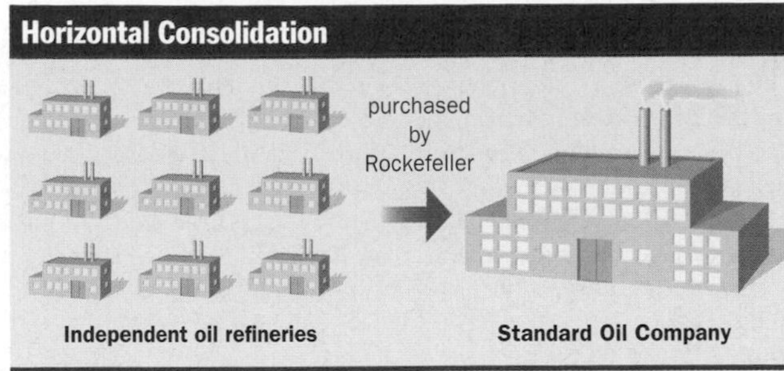

Vertical Consolidation

Coke fields — purchased by Carnegie
Iron ore deposits — purchased by Carnegie
Steel mills — purchased by Carnegie
Ships — purchased by Carnegie
Railroads — purchased by Carnegie

Carnegie Steel Company

Owns all phases of production

shipping and rail lines necessary to transport his products to market. Gaining control of the many different businesses that make up all phases of a product's development is known as **vertical consolidation.** (See diagram at right.)

This method of industrial control allowed Carnegie Steel to maintain very low production costs. This enabled Carnegie to cut his prices. He could charge less because of a phenomenon known as **economies of scale.** That is, as production increases, the cost of each item produced is lower. As Carnegie Steel expanded, its cost per item went down. Smaller companies were then at a disadvantage. Since they did not have the wealth to purchase all the phases of production, they were unable to cut their prices.

The Standard Oil Trust Oil was another industry that was about to become huge. In 1859, when Edwin L. Drake discovered oil in Titusville, Pennsylvania, many new opportunities for oil arose. The new ease of attaining oil and oil's growing usefulness excited many wealthy businessmen, including John D. Rockefeller. He had become rich from a grain and meat partnership during the Civil War, and he saw the oil business as a way to become even richer. In 1863, Rockefeller built an oil refinery near Cleveland, Ohio. The refinery expanded rapidly. In 1870, Rockefeller and several associates formed the Standard Oil Company of Ohio.

The large size of Standard Oil helped Rockefeller cut some of his production costs. For example, Standard Oil did not need to use all of the railroad services that other companies used, such as insurance and storage. Therefore, Rockefeller was able to negotiate with railroad companies to obtain refunds on part of the cost of transporting his oil. As a result of these refunds, he could set Standard Oil's prices lower than those of his competitors. As Rockefeller's company sold more oil, he was able to undersell his competitors by charging even less.

Rockefeller knew that he could expand his business further. He figured that if he could own his competitors' oil refineries, he would be able to create a giant oil company that had even lower production costs. This is another method of industrial control, called **horizontal consolidation,** which involves the bringing together of many firms in the same business. (See diagram above.)

Rockefeller soon had enough money to buy out his competitors, but the law stood in his way. State laws prohibited one company from owning the stock of another. If Rockefeller were to "buy out" his competitors, he would in effect be owning their stock. State governments feared that this practice would reduce competition and restrain, or hold back, free trade.

INTERPRETING DIAGRAMS Some companies grew more powerful through horizontal consolidation, in which companies simply bought competitors in their field (above left). Other companies grew more powerful through vertical consolidation, in which they controlled all the phases of production (above right). **Analyzing Information** *What problems might a business face when trying to compete with a company that has a vertical monopoly? With a company that has a horizontal monopoly?*

ACTIVITY
Connecting with Citizenship

Challenge students to identify what motivated John D. Rockefeller to accumulate such a mind-boggling amount of wealth. Record responses on the chalkboard. Then have students consider the reason Ida M. Tarbell gave: "Why this relentless, cruel, insistent accumulation of money when you are already buried in it? There seems to be only one explanation, that Mr. Rockefeller is the victim of a money-passion which blinds him to every other consideration in life, which is stronger than his sense of justice, his humanity, his affections, his joy in life, which is the one tyrannous, insatiable force of his being." **(Verbal/Linguistic)**

BACKGROUND
Connections to Today

The boom of mergers that took place in the late 1800s was echoed by a massive wave of mergers underway since the 1980s, when the Reagan administration set out to reverse antitrust laws that had been in place since the early 1900s. The Reagan administration's policies resulted in the takeover of about 28 percent of the 500 largest American corporations during the past twenty years. The merging of Time Warner and America Online, completed in 2001, is one example of the many companies affected.

CUSTOMIZE FOR ...
Gifted and Talented

To illustrate the delicate balance between economic development and fair treatment of workers, ask students to think about how industrialists like Andrew Carnegie and labor leaders like Samuel Gompers might have expressed their ideas through mass media today. Have students create "infomercials" for either industrialists or laborers. Suggest that students brainstorm a list of features that they would want to highlight in their "infomercials."

CAPTION ANSWERS

Interpreting Diagrams Vertical: Inability to compete on consumer price due to the fact that production costs will be affected by outside suppliers. Horizontal: The massive share of the market controlled in this way would make it very difficult for a competitor to break in. A large horizontal trust would always win a price war with any competitor because a large trust could better afford to withstand a short-term loss of revenue while under-selling any potential rival.

Section 2 Assessment

Reading Comprehension

1. Social Darwinism encouraged laissez faire policies because of the belief that society should not interfere with people's successes.
2. Answers may include: large amounts of capital, diversification to encompass the total production of a product, revised role of ownership, and new management methods.
3. Mainly by getting rid of competitors, thus forcing consumers to pay artificially high prices.
4. Public concerns over large trusts led Congress to attempt to stop trusts from limiting industrial competition and from restraining interstate commerce.

Critical Thinking and Writing

5. Both had enough wealth to invest in industries on the brink of expansion. Both gained industry-wide control by lowering production costs and realizing economies of scale. Rockefeller formed a trust; Carnegie did not.
6. Answers may include: industrialists increased the availability of goods, provided jobs, and endowed cultural institutions. However, many were ruthless and corrupt, stopping at nothing to gain control over the competition.

Encourage students to learn more about the personal histories and professional accomplishments of both Carnegie and Rockefeller.

Focus on ECONOMICS

The Panic of 1893 In 1893, a period of business expansion suddenly ended, sending a severe shock to the economy. During the "Panic of 1893," hundreds of banks closed, and more than 15,000 businesses failed, sinking the economy into a four-year depression. The resulting unemployment caused widespread misery, especially among workers and their families.

How does such a panic happen? At some point, businesses may begin churning out more goods than consumers want or can afford. Then they have to lower prices in order to sell their products. To cover their losses, they often cut wages and lay off workers. In turn, investors begin to fear that key businesses, heavily in debt, might not be able to repay their loans. Investors rush to sell stock, stock prices fall, and companies go bankrupt.

Samuel Dodd, Rockefeller's lawyer, had an idea to get around this ban. In 1882, the owners of Standard Oil and the companies allied with it agreed to combine their operations. They would turn over their assets to a board of nine trustees. In return, they were promised a share of the profits of the new organization. The board of trustees, which Rockefeller controlled, managed the companies as a single unit called a **trust.**

In time, 40 companies joined the trust. Because the companies did not officially merge, they did not violate any laws. Rockefeller's trust, a new kind of monopoly, controlled a high percentage of the nation's oil-refining capacity.

The Government Response Many Americans were skeptical and wary of trusts and other large business organizations. Americans who feared that trusts were limiting industrial competition began to demand government action to break up these industrial giants.

Despite questions about their practices, the large industrialists found sympathy and support from many government officials and leaders. The government was hesitant to interfere with the actions of big business. After all, these firms contributed mightily to the country's rising level of wealth. By the turn of the century, such mammoth companies as American Telephone and Telegraph, Swift and Armour, General Electric, Westinghouse, and Dupont were some of America's greatest success stories.

Congress did pass a law, however, in 1890, in an attempt to limit the amount of control a business could have over an industry. The **Sherman Antitrust Act** outlawed any combination of companies that restrained interstate trade or commerce.

The act, however, proved ineffective against trusts for nearly 15 years. Its vague wording essentially meant that the courts had to determine what the law said. As a result, the courts, which were largely pro-business in their views, enforced the law infrequently. The law actually *aided* giant corporations when it was applied successfully against labor unions. Federal officials argued that labor unions restrained trade because workers were combining to gain an advantage.

Section 2 Assessment

READING COMPREHENSION

1. How did the theory of **social Darwinism** affect the government's relationship to big business?
2. What were some features of the new big businesses?
3. How did methods such as **vertical** and **horizontal consolidation,** and factors such as **economies of scale** help companies dominate their markets?
4. Why did the **Sherman Antitrust Act** seek to stop big business from forming **trusts?**

CRITICAL THINKING AND WRITING

5. **Making Comparisons** Andrew Carnegie and John D. Rockefeller were both giant industrialists. Compare and contrast the ways they entered into, controlled, and dominated their respective industries.
6. **Writing to Persuade** Create an outline for a persuasive essay in which you explain why you view the nation's early industrialists as either "robber barons" or "captains of industry."

Biography To learn more about Andrew Carnegie or John D. Rockefeller, visit the links provided in the *America: Pathways to the Present* area of the following Web site. **www.phschool.com**

RESOURCE DIRECTORY

Teaching Resources
Units 1/2 booklet
• Section 2 Quiz, p. 62
Guide to the Essentials
• Section 2 Summary, p. 29

Technology
Color Transparency *Political Cartoons,* B7

Section 3 Industrialization and Workers

READING FOCUS

- What factors led to a growing American work force between 1860 and 1900?
- What was factory work like at the turn of the century?
- Why was it necessary for entire families to work?

KEY TERMS

piecework
sweatshop
division of labor

TAKING NOTES

As you read, complete the following chart to show some of the positive and negative effects of industrialization on workers.

Effects of Industrialization		
Event/Aspect	**Positive Effects**	**Negative Effects**
Growing work force	Opens up many new jobs for immigrants and ex-farmers	Supply of workers drives wages down; whole families forced to work

MAIN IDEA

Industry relied on its laborers, who worked in low-paying, unskilled jobs and often in unsafe factories.

Setting the Scene The abundant natural resources, inventive minds, and risk-taking entrepreneurs of the United States all contributed to the nation's industrial expansion. This expansion would not have been possible, however, without the millions of laborers who allowed the companies to succeed.

Sadie Frowne immigrated to the United States from Poland in 1899 when she was 13 years old. Her family, like so many others, hoped that America would provide greater opportunities for making money and living comfortably. Sadie began working in New York City, where she made skirts by machine.

> "*I was new at the work and the foreman scolded me a great deal. . . . I did not know at first that you must not look around and talk, and I made many mistakes with my sewing, so that I was often called a 'stupid animal.' . . . The machines go like mad all day, because the faster you work, the more money you get. Sometimes in my haste I get my finger caught and the needle goes right through it. It goes so quick, tho[ugh], that it does not hurt much. . . . We all have accidents like that. . . .*"
>
> —Garment worker Sadie Frowne

VIEWING HISTORY Industrialization led to a growing work force and new work environment. **Identifying Central Issues** *How did industrial workers respond to their working conditions?*

The Growing Work Force

Around 14 million people immigrated to the United States between 1860 and 1900. Most came in the hope of finding work in the country's booming industrial centers. During the Civil War, when labor was scarce, the federal government encouraged immigration by passing the Contract Labor Act in 1864. This law allowed employers to enter into contracts with immigrants. Employers would pay the cost of their passage in return for immigrants' agreeing to work for a certain amount of time, up to a year. Employers soon began actively recruiting foreign laborers.

In another dramatic population shift, some 8 or 9 million Americans moved to cities during the late 1800s. Most of them fled poor economic conditions on the nation's farms. A long drought beginning in 1887, combined with

Section 3 Industrialization and Workers

Section Objectives

1. Find out about factors that led to a growing American work force between 1860 and 1900.
2. Learn what factory work at the turn of the century was like.
3. Discover why it was sometimes necessary for entire families to work.

Bellringer

Warm-Up Activity Have students write down the words and phrases that they associate with the idea of work. Ask them to circle all the positive words and phrases on their list.

Activating Prior Knowledge Ask students what they know about child labor in the United States in the late 1800s. Are children permitted to work in this country today? Do other countries in the world permit child labor?

Reading Strategy

Before students read this section, ask them to look at the section's pictures and main headings. Have them write a prediction of what life was like for factory workers in late nineteenth-century America. As they read, have students compare their predictions with the information presented in the text to help analyze the social issue of immigrants and child labor.

Resource Directory

Teaching Resources

Learning Styles Lesson Plans booklet, p. 29
Guided Reading and Review booklet, p. 56

Other Print Resources

Nystrom *Atlas of Our Country* *The Second Wave of Immigration,* pp. 24–25; *The Third Wave of Immigration,* pp. 30–31

Technology

Section Reading Support Transparencies
Guided Reading Audiotapes (English/Spanish), Ch. 6
Student Edition on Audio CD, Ch. 6
Prentice Hall United States History Video Collection™ Volume 12, *Immigration and Cultural Change*
Prentice Hall Presentation Pro CD-ROM, Ch. 6
Companion Web site, www.phschool.com

Caption Answers

Viewing History Workers often became frustrated by dangerous conditions, strict work environments, and the repetitive nature of their work. Such sentiments eventually led large numbers of workers to join unions. Nevertheless, many others, including children, accepted harsh working conditions as a part of life and struggled on as best they could.

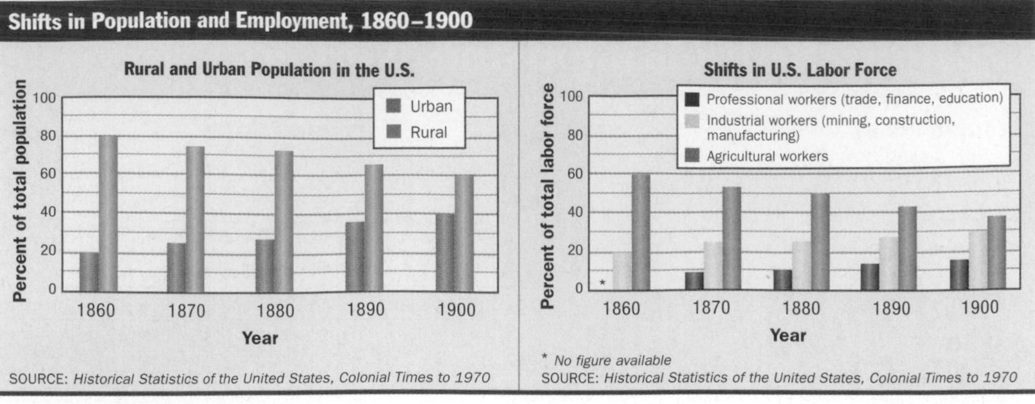

INTERPRETING GRAPHS Industrial growth in the mid- to late 1800s led to shifts in population and the work force. **Drawing Conclusions** *What do you think accounted for the rise in the percentage of professional workers?*

low prices and more competition from foreign wheat producers, left many farm families penniless. Plentiful work in the factories lured the former farmers, as did many of the new attractions of city life.

Factory Work

By 1860, most states had established a ten-hour workday, yet they rarely enforced it. Thus, most laborers worked twelve hours, six days a week—and even more when they had to meet production goals. An 1868 federal law granted government employees an eight-hour day, but this did not affect private industry.

In many industries, employers paid workers not by the time worked but by what they produced. Workers received a fixed amount for each finished piece they produced—for example, a few cents for a garment or a number of cigars. This system of **piecework** meant that those who worked the fastest and produced the most pieces earned the most money. Most piecework was performed in what came to be known as a **sweatshop**—a shop where employees worked long hours at low wages and under poor working conditions.

Increasing Efficiency In 1881, Frederick Winslow Taylor set out to improve worker efficiency in the steel plant where he was chief engineer. He began to study the workers, trying to see how much time they took to do various jobs. Then he broke down each task into a number of steps and determined how long each step should take. In the same way he also studied each motion needed in a task. The goal of Taylor's time and motion studies was to increase worker productivity and thereby increase profits.

Taylor used his studies as the foundation of an entire system for the scientific management of workers. In 1911, he described this system in his book, *The Principles of Scientific Management*:

> "*The work of every workman is fully planned out by the management at least one day in advance, and each man receives in most cases complete written instructions, describing in detail the task which he is to accomplish, as well as the means to be used in doing the work . . . and the exact time allowed for doing it.*"
>
> —Frederick Winslow Taylor

Focus on TECHNOLOGY

Technology and the Arts The emergence of clanging, greasy machines at the end of the nineteenth century entirely changed the American landscape. Many Americans, including writers and artists, were delighted with the new machines and the human progress they represented. Nathaniel Hawthorne described trip hammers as "very pleasant objects to look at, working so massively as they do, and yet so accurately, chewing up, as it were, the hot iron, and fashioning it into shape, with a sort of mighty and gigantic gentleness in their mode of action."

Lesson Plan

Focus Explain that in addition to technology and financial backing, an influx of new workers was needed. Ask students how this demand for labor affected life for many Americans.

Instruct Discuss with students why millions of workers came to work in industries. Help students compare a worker in a new pre–Civil War blacksmithy to a worker in a Carnegie steel plant. How did industrialization change employers, workers, and products?

Assess/Reteach Have students list industrialization's positive and negative aspects, such as the ability to immigrate and conditions for immigrants.

From the Archives of American Heritage®

Newsies

Horatio Alger's tales of a pious, lucky newsboy named Ragged Dick, published in 1867, created such a following that he went on to write 119 other stories about boys who overcome the odds to make it big. The books proved favorites for decades, selling more than seventeen million copies. Alger kept in touch with the subjects of his stories by frequenting the Newsboy's Lodging House on the top floor of the New York *Sun* Building, where some seventy-five boys between the ages of five and fifteen boarded and attended chapel for six cents a night. Eventually Alger set up a writing room and bed for himself there. His stories of "Mark the Match Boy" and many others came out of his consultations with New York urchins and toughs named Jack the Oyster, Pickle Nose, Cranky Jim, and Soggy Pants. But Alger had his critics. "The notion that yokels always succeed in the cities is a great delusion," wrote H. L. Mencken. Source: Nathan Ward, "The Time Machine," *American Heritage®* magazine, May/June 1993.

Caption Answers

Interpreting Graphs With the growth of business and cities, industry became more sophisticated and needed administrators, managers, accountants, sales people, etc.

Resource Directory

Teaching Resources

Learning with Documents booklet (Visual Learning Activity) *The Noble Face of Labor,* p. 52

Biography, Literature, and Comparing Primary Sources booklet (Literature) *The Stories of Horatio Alger,* p. 57

Other Print Resources

American History Block Scheduling Support *On the Job: Industrialism in America,* found in the Expansion, Reconstruction, and Immigration folder, includes interdisciplinary lesson suggestions and activities for Geography and History, Primary Sources, Biography, and Literature.

Some employers had their own, unscientific methods of improving efficiency. They simply increased the speed of factory machines or gave each employee more work. Increases in productivity, however, did not always translate into higher pay for workers. On the contrary, greater factory efficiency often led to layoffs because businesses no longer needed as many workers. In addition, many workers felt that these methods gave owners too much control over their work. As a result, most workers came to resent them.

READING CHECK
What was the goal of Taylor's studies?

The Division of Labor Athough its goal was to increase worker productivity, the methods used in scientific management brought about a change in the relationship between the worker and the product he or she created. Artisans traditionally made a product from start to finish. Doing so required them to perform a variety of tasks. In contrast, factory workers usually performed only one small task, over and over, and rarely even saw the finished product. This **division of labor** into separate tasks proved to be efficient, but it took much of the joy out of the work.

The relationship between workers and owners also changed. In smaller businesses, owners and workers had day-to-day interactions with each other. Because of the large size of new big businesses, owners seldom even visited the factory floor where workers toiled. In the worst cases, the workers, called "hands" or "operatives," were viewed as interchangeable parts in a vast and impersonal machine. One factory manager in 1883 declared, "I regard my people as I regard my machinery. So long as they can do my work for what I choose to pay them, I keep them, getting out of them all I can."

VIEWING FINE ART John Ferguson Weir's painting *Gun Foundry* presents a vivid image of the nation's industrial might. **Drawing Inferences** *What does the painting suggest about the conditions faced by workers?*

The Work Environment Unlike farmers, who had more flexibility in the pace they worked, factory workers were ruled by the clock, which told them when to start, take any breaks, and stop work. In addition, discipline within the factory was strict. To make a profit, factory managers needed to run an efficient operation. Thus they might fine or fire workers for a range of offenses, such as being late, talking, or refusing to do a task.

Workplaces were not always safe. The noise of the machines was deafening. Lighting and ventilation were poor. Fatigue, faulty equipment, and careless training resulted in frequent fires and accidents. Despite the harsh conditions, employers suffered no shortage of labor. Factory work offered higher pay and more opportunities than most people could hope to find elsewhere.

Laboring in factories or mines and performing dangerous work was unhealthy for all workers. But it especially threatened growing children. Many children became stunted in both body and mind. In 1892, social reformer Jacob Riis explained the impact of factory work on children in a book titled *Children of the Poor.* Riis wrote that people who spent their whole childhood on the factory floor grew "to manhood and womanhood . . . with the years that should have prepared them for life's work gone in hopeless and profitless drudgery." Thanks to Riis and others, the practice of child labor came under broad attack in the 1890s and early 1900s, prompting states to begin curbing this practice through legislation.

ACTIVITY
Connecting with History and Conflict

Direct students' attention to the quotation from the factory manager at the end of "The Division of Labor." Have students generate a rebuttal to this statement, following its construction, from the point of view of a factory worker. Students' statements should begin "I regard my managers as. . . ." **(Verbal/Linguistic)**

BACKGROUND
Biography

Frederick Taylor is often thought of as an apologist for management, but he went to great pains to argue that "scientific management" would actually benefit workers and, moreover, even lead to the end of labor conflicts. He wrote that "The majority of [employees and employers] believe that the fundamental interests of employees and employers are necessarily antagonistic. Scientific management, on the contrary, has for its very foundation the firm conviction that the true interests of the two are one and the same; that prosperity for the employer cannot exist through a long term of years unless it is accompanied by prosperity for the employee and vice versa; and that it is possible to give the workman what he most wants—high wages—and the employer what he wants—a low labor cost—for his manufactures."

READING CHECK
To increase the output of each worker, thus making the business more profitable.

CUSTOMIZE FOR ...
Less Proficient Writers

Have students create a "handbill" that states the rules of employment in a factory of this era. They can base the employment rules on the information included in the paragraph on this page headed "The Work Environment."

TEST PREPARATION

Have students reread the quotation from Frederick Winslow Taylor on the previous page and then answer the question below.

What was one of the results of using Taylor's theories of management?

A Factory workers took more pride in their work.
B Factory owners lost money.
C Owners visited factories more often.
(D) More factory workers were laid off.

CAPTION ANSWERS

Viewing Fine Art Conditions were dangerous and emphasized production over worker safety.

Section 3 Assessment

Reading Comprehension

1. Two population shifts occurred; farm to city and immigrants arriving in the U.S. Both groups sought work in the factories.
2. Piecework rewarded workers for products completed, not time worked. This led to inequity as not all workers could complete the same amount of product.
3. While increasing efficiency, the division of labor and Taylor's studies had a dehumanizing effect. Workers were treated like pieces of machinery whose performance could be precisely calculated.
4. Their income was often vital for family survival; no laws existed to prohibit child labor at this time. Families had no insurance for illness or unemployment.

Critical Thinking and Writing

5. Workers on farms may have had more of a connection to the work they were doing. Farm work was dictated more by nature than by technology—farmers could not work at night or in severe weather.
6. Outlines will vary. Possible answers include: lengthy work day, unpleasant working conditions, low pay.

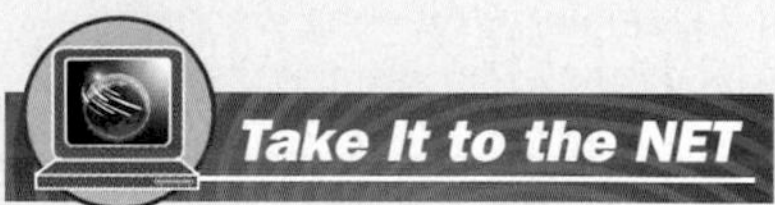

Invite students to take a Virtual Field Trip at **www.phschool.com**

VIEWING HISTORY Many children worked in hazardous conditions. The boys above worked in coal mines. The grime that covers their faces also clogged their lungs, leading to disease. The girl in the photo on the right operated heavy machinery in a textile mill. **Drawing Conclusions** *How do you think Americans at the time reacted to photos such as these?*

Working Families

In the 1880s, children made up more than 5 percent of the industrial labor force. By the end of the 1800s, nearly one in five children between the ages of 10 and 16 was employed. For many households, children's wages meant the difference between going hungry or having food on the table.

As a result, children often left school at the age of 12 or 13 to work. Girls sometimes took factory jobs so that their brothers could stay in school. If a mother could not make money working at home, she might take a factory job, leaving her children with relatives or neighbors. If an adult became ill, died, or could not find or keep a job, children as young as 6 or 7 had to bring in cash.

In the 1800s, families in need relied on private charities. These charities could not afford to help everyone, however. They had limited resources, so only the neediest received the food, clothing, and shelter that charities had to offer. Except in rare cases, government did not provide public assistance. Unemployment insurance, for example, did not exist, so workers received no payments as a result of layoffs or factory closings. The popular theory of social Darwinism held that poverty resulted from personal weakness. Many thought that offering relief to the unemployed would encourage idleness.

Section 3 Assessment

READING COMPREHENSION

1. Why did the American work force grow in the late 1800s?
2. How did **piecework** change the nature of factory work?
3. What were the effects of Taylor's scientific management studies and the **division of labor** on workers?
4. Why did children work?

CRITICAL THINKING AND WRITING

5. **Identifying Alternatives** Although it differed from factory work, work on family farms was also difficult and dangerous. Explain what you think were the key differences between the two types of work.
6. **Writing to Describe** Prepare an outline for an essay describing the daily life of a typical factory worker.

Virtual Field Trip Visit the Smithsonian Institute to learn more about sweatshops and labor conditions in the late 1800s and find out what they are like today. Use the links provided in the *America: Pathways to the Present* area of the following Web site for help in completing this activity.
www.phschool.com

Caption Answers

Viewing History Most probably began to sympathize with the children and advocate an end to child labor.

RESOURCE DIRECTORY

Teaching Resources

Units 1/2 booklet
- Section 3 Quiz, p. 63

Guide to the Essentials
- Section 3 Summary, p. 30

Section 4

The Great Strikes

READING FOCUS

- What impact did industrialization have on the gulf between rich and poor?
- What were the goals of the early labor unions in the United States?
- Why did Eugene V. Debs organize the American Railway Union?
- What were the causes and outcomes of the major strikes in the late 1800s?

MAIN IDEA

In the late 1800s, workers organized labor unions to improve their wages and working conditions.

KEY TERMS

socialism
craft union
collective bargaining
industrial union
scab
anarchist
Haymarket Riot
Homestead Strike
Pullman Strike

TAKING NOTES

As you read, complete the chart below, filling in the successes and failures of the labor unions.

Labor Unions	
Successes	**Failures**
The Knights of Labor protect railroad wages from being cut in 1885 through the use of the strike.	The Great Railroad Strike of 1877 turns violent, giving the public and the government a bad taste for unions.

Setting the Scene

> "What shall the workers do? Sit idly by and see the vast resources of nature and the human mind be utilized and monopolized for the benefit of the comparative few? No. The laborers must learn to think and act, and soon, too, that only by the power of organization, and common concert of action, can . . . their rights to life . . . be recognized, and liberty and rights secured."
>
> —Samuel Gompers

Industrialization had lowered the prices of consumer goods, but in the late 1800s most factory workers did not earn enough to buy them. The successful entrepreneurs of the era had worked hard. Many, like Carnegie, had used their wealth to provide money for good works. Still, in hard times only the poor went hungry. Increasingly, working men and women took their complaints directly and forcefully to their employers.

VIEWING HISTORY Many wealthy industrialists enjoyed great personal wealth and luxurious comforts (left). In stark contrast, many workers lived in crowded boarding houses (right). **Identifying Central Issues** *How did many workers respond to the contrast between the rich and poor?*

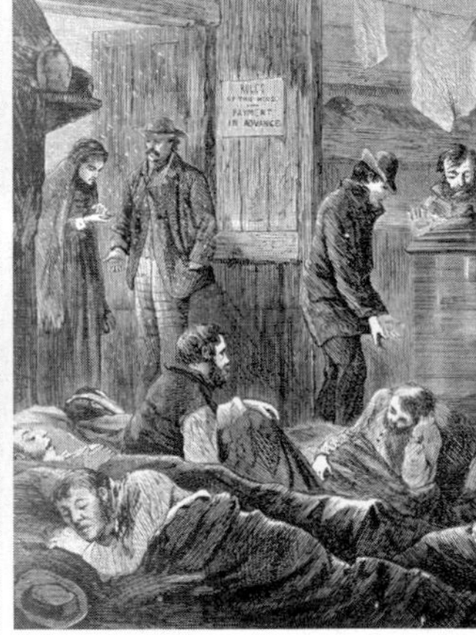

Gulf Between Rich and Poor

In 1890, the richest 9 percent of Americans held nearly 75 percent of the national wealth. In the best of times, the average worker could earn only a few hundred dollars a year. Many workers resented the extravagant lifestyles of many factory owners. Poor families had little hope of relief when hard times hit. Some suffered in silence, trusting that tomorrow would be better. Others became politically active in an effort to improve their lives. A few of these individuals were drawn to the idea of **socialism,** which was then gaining popularity in Europe.

Socialism is an economic and political philosophy that favors public instead of private control

Section 4

The Great Strikes

Section Objectives

1. Discover the impact of industrialism on the gulf between rich and poor.
2. Find out the goals of the early labor unions in the United States.
3. Learn why Eugene V. Debs formed the American Railway Union.
4. Study the causes and outcomes of the major strikes in the late 1800s.

Bellringer

Warm-Up Activity Have student pairs choose several possible courses of action in the following situation: Restaurant workers are told that unless they agree to work four additional evening hours each week for no extra pay, they will be fired. As students read, have them circle any option that uses collective bargaining.

Activating Prior Knowledge Have students list reasons why labor unions came into being during the late 1800s to help them analyze the growth of labor unions.

Reading Strategy

As students read, have them list each new development in the labor movement during these years. Then have them indicate on their lists whether each development came about due primarily to political ("p") or economic ("e") factors. As a group, review the lists and discuss students' responses. Ask students to analyze the treatment of minorities in work settings using their lists.

Caption Answers

Viewing History Many turned to labor unions and some turned to socialism to seek justice.

RESOURCE DIRECTORY

Teaching Resources

Guided Reading and Review booklet, p. 57

Technology

Section Reading Support Transparencies
Guided Reading Audiotapes (English/Spanish), Ch. 6
Student Edition on Audio CD, Ch. 6
Sounds of an Era Audio CD *"The Electric Light Quadrille,"* 1889 recording (time: one minute, 30 seconds)

RESOURCE PRO® **Literature Activity** *Sister Carrie,* found on Resource Pro, introduces students to factory life in the late 1800s with an excerpt from Theodore Dreiser's novel.
Prentice Hall Presentation Pro CD-ROM, Ch. 6
Companion Web site, www.phschool.com

Lesson Plan

Focus Explain to students that industrialization caused great inequalities in wealth in the late nineteenth century. Big business owners grew wealthy while workers toiled for low wages. Ask students how workers tried to improve their wages and working conditions.

Instruct Discuss why workers resented the wealth of business owners. Ask how socialism, anarchism, and labor unions were different approaches to solving the problems of workers. Ask how socialism and anarchism promised to improve workers' lives but ran counter to some American ideals. What did labor unions do to address workers' problems? Ask students to describe public reaction to the strikes. What pattern of events did the Pullman Strike set in motion?

Assess/Reteach Have students list the types of grievances experienced by workers that led to the development of labor unions.

Background

Interdisciplinary

Though the cost of manufactured consumer goods dropped because of industrialization, working-class women had difficulty affording them. Women's wages and job opportunities were far below those of men. African American women were even worse off, being excluded from most factory positions until World War I. Consider the average earnings of a working woman and the price of consumer goods: factories paid the average woman worker $5 a week, department stores paid $2 a week plus 5 percent commission, and families paid domestic servants $3 a week plus board. A ready-made blouse cost $1, a skirt $2, and a pair of shoes $1.50. Carfare for sales clerks was a nickel each way, and a dormitory bed cost $2.50 a week.

of property and income. Socialists believe that society at large, not just private individuals, should take charge of a nation's wealth. That wealth, they say, should be distributed equally to everyone.

Socialism began in the 1830s as an idealistic movement. Early Socialists believed that people should cooperate, not compete, in producing goods. Socialism then grew more radical, reflecting the ideas of a German philosopher named Karl Marx. In 1848, Marx, along with Friedrich Engels, wrote a famous pamphlet called the *Communist Manifesto.* In it they denounced the capitalist economic system and predicted that workers would one day overturn it.

Most Americans opposed socialism. The wealthy saw it as a threat to their fortunes. Politicians saw it as a threat to public order. Americans in general, including most workers, saw it as a threat to the deeply rooted American ideals of private property, free enterprise, and individual liberty.

The Rise of Labor Unions

A small percentage of American workers did become Socialists and called for an end to free enterprise. Far more workers, however, chose to work within the system by uniting to form labor unions.

Early Labor Unions The early years of industrialization had spawned a few labor unions, organized among workers in certain trades, such as construction and textile manufacturing. The first national labor organization was the National Trades Union, which was open to workers from all crafts. It survived only a few years before being destroyed by the panic and depression of 1837.

Strong local unions resurfaced after the Civil War. They began by providing help for their members in bad times, but soon became the means for expressing workers' demands to employers. These demands included shorter workdays, higher wages, and better working conditions.

National unions also began to reappear at this time. In Baltimore in 1866, labor activists formed the National Labor Union, representing some 60,000 members. In 1872, this union nominated a candidate for President. It failed, however, to survive a depression that began the following year. Indeed, unions in general suffered a steep decline in membership as a result of the poor economy.

Meeting posters and labor union badges such as these appeared around the country as labor unions grew more popular.

The Knights of Labor Another national union, the Noble and Holy Order of the Knights of Labor, formed in Philadelphia in 1869. The Knights hoped to organize all working men and women, skilled and unskilled, into a single union. Membership included farmers and factory workers as well as shopkeepers and office workers. The union recruited African Americans, 60,000 of whom joined. After 1881, the union also recruited women members.

Under the leadership of former machinist Terence Powderly, the Knights pursued broad social reforms. These included equal pay for equal work, the eight-hour workday, and an end to child labor. They did not emphasize higher wages as their primary goal.

The leaders of the Knights preferred not to use the strike as a tool. Most members, however, differed with their leadership on this issue. In fact, it was a strike that helped the Knights achieve their greatest strength. In 1885, when

RESOURCE DIRECTORY

Technology

Sounds of an Era Audio CD *"The Commonwealth of Toil,"* 1940s recording (time: 45 seconds)

unions linked to the Knights forced railroad owner Jay Gould to give up a wage cut, membership quickly soared to 700,000. Yet a series of failed strikes followed, some of them violent. Membership dropped off, and public support for the Knights waned. By the 1890s, the Knights had largely disappeared as a national force.

The American Federation of Labor A third national union, the American Federation of Labor (AFL) formed in 1886 under the leadership of Samuel Gompers, a London-born cigar maker. Unlike the Knights of Labor, the AFL was a **craft union.** Rather than organizing all workers, the AFL sought to organize only skilled workers in a network of smaller unions, each devoted to a specific craft.

Between 1886 and 1892, the AFL gained some 250,000 members. Yet they still represented only a tiny portion of the nation's total labor force. Few African Americans joined. In theory the AFL was open to African Americans, but local unions often found ways to exclude them from membership. Women, too, were not welcome in the AFL. Gompers opposed the membership of women because he believed that their presence in the work force would drive wages down.

Gompers and the AFL focused mainly on issues of workers' wages, hours, and working conditions. This so-called bread-and-butter unionism set the AFL apart from the Knights of Labor. The Knights had sought to help their members through political activity and education. The AFL relied on economic pressure, such as strikes and boycotts, against employers. By using these tactics, the AFL tried to force employers to participate in **collective bargaining,** a process in which workers negotiate as a group with employers. Workers acting as a group had more power than a single worker acting alone. To strengthen its collective bargaining power, the AFL pressed for a "closed shop," a workplace in which only union members would be hired.

The Wobblies The AFL's policies did not suit all workers. In 1905, in Chicago, 43 groups opposed to the AFL founded the Industrial Workers of the World (IWW), or Wobblies. The IWW, which focused on unskilled workers, was a radical union that included many Socialists among its leadership. A number of IWW strikes were violent on both sides. During World War I, many IWW leaders were convicted of promoting strikes in war-related industries.

Reaction of Employers By and large, employers disliked and feared unions. They preferred to deal with employees as individuals. In addition, they feared that if they had to pay higher wages and meet the other demands of unions, their costs would go up and they would be less competitive in the marketplace. As a result, employers took measures to stop unions, such as

1. forbidding union meetings;
2. firing union organizers;
3. forcing new employees to sign "yellow dog" contracts, in which workers promised never to join a union or participate in a strike;
4. refusing to bargain collectively when strikes did occur;
5. refusing to recognize unions as their workers' legitimate representatives.

In 1902, George F. Baer, the president of a mining company, reflected the opinions of many business leaders when he wrote: "The rights and interests of the laboring man will be protected and cared for—not by the labor agitators, but by the Christian men to whom God . . . has given control of the property interests of the country. . . . "

Focus on CULTURE

Labor Day The Knights of Labor sponsored the first Labor Day on September 5, 1882, as a tribute to the American worker. As the labor force grew, so did support for making this day an official national holiday. In 1887, five states passed laws giving Labor Day legal status. Finally, in 1894, days after President Cleveland sent troops to suppress the Pullman Strike, Congress passed the bill making Labor Day a national holiday. The "workingman's holiday," celebrated the first Monday of every September, has now also come to be associated with the end of summer vacations, a return to school, and one last long weekend for family barbecues and outdoor picnics before the autumn months arrive.

Sounds of an Era

Listen to the IWW song "The Commonwealth of Toil" and other sounds from the period of industrial expansion.

ACTIVITY
Connecting with Culture

Direct students' attention to the quotation from George F. Baer at the bottom of this page. In a class discussion, have students compare and contrast Baer's contention that "God has given control of the property interests of the country" to business owners of high moral principles with the central idea of social Darwinism, that the most "fit" would succeed and become rich. Ask: how are these two arguments similar and different? **(Verbal/Linguistic)**

BACKGROUND
Connections to Today

In the late 1800s workers injured on the job had no recourse. Yet as the country became more industrialized, worksite accidents became inevitable. Maryland passed the first state compensation law in 1902, but the Supreme Court declared that law, and all compensation laws of that era, unconstitutional. The first state compensation law to be held constitutional, that of Wisconsin, was enacted in 1911. By the end of that year ten states had passed workers' compensation laws. Today, all states have programs, financed by employers, to provide injured workers with both medical and financial benefits.

CUSTOMIZE FOR ...
Less Proficient Readers

Have students create a chart that indicates some of the differences in the approaches of the American Federation of Labor and the Knights of Labor. Topics that might be included in the chart: Inclusion of Women; Inclusion of African Americans; Attitude Towards Strikes; Inclusion of Unskilled Labor.

TEST PREPARATION

Have students read this statement, then complete the sentence below. "We know to our regret that too often are wives, sisters, and children brought into the factories and workshops only to reduce the wages and displace the labor of men—the heads of families." —Samuel Gompers

Gompers dislikes women in the workplace because—

A they should be taking care of their homes.
(B) they lower wages for the male employees.
C they make more money than men.
D he thinks they are not as capable.

Railroad Workers Organize

The first major incident of nationwide labor unrest in the United States occurred in the railroad industry. The violent strike of 1877 touched off a wave of strikes and bitter confrontations between labor, management, and the government in the decades to follow. It also led to reform and reorganization within the labor movement itself.

READING CHECK What prompted the railroad strike of 1877?

The Great Railroad Strike of 1877 The strike began in July 1877, when the Baltimore and Ohio Railroad announced a wage cut of 10 percent in the midst of a depression. This was the second wage cut in eight months. Railroads elsewhere imposed similar cuts, along with orders to run "double headers," trains with two engines and twice as many cars as usual. The unusually long trains increased the risk of accidents and the chance of worker layoffs.

Railway workers reacted with violence. Workers in Martinsburg, West Virginia, were the first to declare a strike. Strikers and sympathizers there were strong enough to turn back the local militia. Rioting spread rapidly to Pittsburgh, Chicago, St. Louis, and other cities. The governors in some of these states requested assistance from the federal government. President Rutherford B. Hayes responded by sending in federal troops to put down the strikes.

A week later in Pittsburgh, soldiers fired on rioters, killing and wounding many. A crowd of 20,000 angry men and women reacted to the shootings by setting fire to railroad company property, causing more than $5 million in damage. President Hayes again sent in federal troops. From the 1877 strike on, employers relied on federal and state troops to repress labor unrest. A new and violent era in labor relations had begun.

Debs and the American Railway Union At the time of the 1877 strike, railroad workers mainly organized into various "brotherhoods," which were basically craft unions. Eugene V. Debs had taken a leadership role in the Brotherhood of Locomotive Firemen. He spoke out against the 1877 strike. The mission of the brotherhood, according to Debs, was "not to antagonize capital." Although he was initially opposed to strikes because of their confrontational nature, Debs gained sympathy for the strike as he became more involved in the labor movement.

COMPARING PRIMARY SOURCES

Labor Unions

In 1883, the Senate Committee on Education and Labor held a series of hearings concerning the relationship between workers and management. The committee heard these opposing views about the need for labor unions.

Analyzing Viewpoints Compare the main arguments made by the two speakers.

Testimony of a Labor Leader

"The laws written [by Congress] and now in operation to protect the property of the capitalist and the moneyed class generally are almost innumerable, yet nothing has been done to protect the property of the workingmen, the only property that they possess, their working power, their savings bank, their school, and trades union."

—Samuel Gompers, labor leader

Testimony of a Factory Manager

"I think that . . . in a free country like this . . . it is perfectly safe for at least the lifetime of this generation to leave the question of how a man shall work, and how long he shall work, and what wages he shall get to himself."

—Thomas L. Livermore, manager of a manufacturing company

ACTIVITY

Connecting with History and Conflict

To enable all students to understand the different perspectives of the parties involved in labor disputes of the late nineteenth century, assign them the following roles: Pinkerton, scab, anarchist, laborer, immigrant, business owner, union leader. Based on their reading, students should write a description of their roles and what they hope to achieve in an industrial dispute. **(Verbal/Linguistic)**

BACKGROUND

Biography

Many people remember President Hayes as the man who sent American troops to attack American workers. In reality, though, Hayes was something of a humanitarian. As President, he championed meritocracy within the civil service system. In retirement, he focused his energies on social causes, among them reforming prisons to make them less cruel, and advancing education for African Americans in the South.

From the Archives of AmericanHeritage®

About the Presidents

Rutherford B. Hayes (1877–1881) seemed old-fashioned: he always wore a silk hat, frock coat, and black shoes. But in some ways, he was ahead of his time. He ended Reconstruction and turned away from the politics of the past. Declaring that the old spoils system should be abolished, he pleaded for a merit system instead. Though Congress didn't pass civil service reform under Hayes, reform would be the wave of the future. What's more, Hayes traveled more than any of his predecessors. He became the first President to see the West Coast. Source: Donald Young, "Rutherford B. Hayes," *The American Heritage® Pictorial History of the Presidents of the United States,* vol. 2, 1968.

READING CHECK

A steep cut in wages during a depression, combined with unsafe working conditions and an increased likelihood of layoffs.

RESOURCE DIRECTORY

Teaching Resources

Biography, Literature, and Comparing Primary Sources booklet (Comparing Primary Sources) *On Labor Unions,* p. 121

Biography, Literature, and Comparing Primary Sources booklet (Biography) *Mary Kenney O'Sullivan,* p. 18

Debs, however, never thought violence had a place in strikes. He believed that the violence of the 1877 strike had resulted in part from the disorganization and corruption that existed within the brotherhoods. As a solution to this problem, and in an attempt to avoid future violent strikes, Debs proposed a new **industrial union** for all railway workers. Industrial unions organized workers from all crafts in a given industry. The American Railway Union (A.R.U.), formed in 1893, would replace the existing craft brotherhoods and unite all railroad workers, skilled and unskilled. Its primary purpose would be to protect the wages and rights of all the employees.

VIEWING HISTORY Eugene V. Debs was arrested following the Pullman Strike in 1894. While in jail, Debs gained an interest in socialism. He would later combine his energetic style and his belief in socialism to conduct several unsuccessful presidential campaigns as leader of the Socialist Party. **Drawing Inferences** *What factors, including his core beliefs, ultimately led Debs to become a Socialist?*

> *"If fair wages [were] the return for efficient service, [then] harmonious relations may be established and maintained . . . and the necessity for strike and lockout, boycott and blacklist, alike disastrous to employer and employee, and a perpetual menace to the welfare of the public, will forever disappear."*
>
> —Eugene V. Debs

Strikes Rock the Nation

From 1881 to 1900, the United States faced one industrial crisis after another. Some 24,000 strikes erupted in the nation's factories, mines, mills, and rail yards during those two decades alone. Three events were particularly violent: the Haymarket Riot and the Homestead and Pullman strikes.

Haymarket, 1886 On May 1, 1886, groups of workers mounted a national demonstration for an eight-hour workday. "Eight hours for work, eight hours for rest, eight hours for what we will," ran the cry. Strikes then erupted in a number of cities.

On May 3, at Chicago's McCormick reaper factory, police broke up a fight between strikers and **scabs.** (A scab is a negative term for a worker called in by an employer to replace striking laborers. Using scabs allows a company to continue operating and to avoid having to bargain with the union.) The police action caused several casualties among the workers.

Union leaders called for a protest rally on the evening of May 4 in Chicago's Haymarket Square. A group of **anarchists,** radicals who oppose all government, joined the strikers. Anarchists addressed workers with fiery speeches, such as this one by newspaper editor August Spies:

> *"You have endured the pangs of want and hunger; your children you have sacrificed to the factory-lords. In short, you have been miserable and obedient slaves all these years. Why? To satisfy the insatiable greed, to fill the coffers of your lazy thieving master!"*
>
> —August Spies

At the May 4 event, someone threw a bomb into a police formation, killing one officer. In the riot that followed, gunfire between police and protesters killed dozens on both sides. Investigators never found the bomb thrower, yet eight anarchists were tried for conspiracy to commit murder. Four were

READING CHECK
What led to the riot in Haymarket?

ACTIVITY
Connecting with History and Conflict

During the last 20 years of the nineteenth century, there were about 24,000 strikes in the United States. To give students a sense of just how widespread and persistent the labor disputes of the period were, have them calculate, on average, how many strikes were occurring on any given day during the 1880s and 1890s. **(Logical/Mathematical)**

BACKGROUND
Connections to Today

Soon after the Haymarket Square riot, a monument was erected to honor the police, dedicated by Chicago "to her defenders in the riot of May 4, 1886." Another monument was also erected—to honor the workers. It quotes August Spies' last words before he was hanged: "The day will come when our silence will be more powerful than the voices you are throttling today." Over the years, both monuments have been vandalized repeatedly, and both have been the scenes of various protests. In some ways, then, the conflict at Haymarket Square is still ongoing.

CUSTOMIZE FOR ...
Gifted and Talented

Have students research August Spies, one of the anarchists convicted of inciting the Haymarket Riot. Then, have students write a diary entry from the point of view of Spies. Include his account of the riot, his arrest, and his feelings about the trial and his pending execution.

CAPTION ANSWERS

Viewing History He believed in the value of industrial unions, which united workers of all skill levels in a given industry. Debs also seems to have felt that relations between workers and management needed to become less confrontational, with more planning and cooperation between the two sides.

ACTIVITY
Connecting with Culture

Have students create charts that summarize the Haymarket, Homestead, and Pullman strikes. Their charts should consist of three columns, each headed by a name of one of the strikes, and five rows, respectively titled *Who, What, Where, When, Why,* and *How.* The bodies of the charts should answer appropriate questions about each strike. **(Visual/Spatial)**

BACKGROUND
Biography

"The Pinkertons" was the name commonly used to identify members of the Pinkerton National Detective Agency. Allan Pinkerton, who had emigrated from Scotland, established the agency in 1850. Pinkerton was originally a cooper (barrel maker), and it was while working in 1843 near Chicago that he accidentally discovered—and later captured—a gang of counterfeiters. He was rewarded with an appointment as deputy sheriff. He resigned from official police work to establish his detective agency. For 30 years, Pinkerton and his agency enjoyed a series of great successes, from capturing train robbers to stopping an assassination attempt against President-elect Abraham Lincoln. After the Civil War, the Pinkertons became famous to some—and infamous to others—as strikebreakers. Pinkerton reflected on his colorful life in a memoir, *Thirty Years a Detective.*

VIEWING HISTORY The violence of the Haymarket Riot, depicted here, troubled many Americans. **Recognizing Cause and Effect** *What were the effects of the incident at Haymarket on the union cause?*

hanged. Another committed suicide in jail. Governor John P. Altgeld of Illinois decided later that the convictions resulted from public outrage rather than evidence. He pardoned the remaining three anarchists.

To many unionists, the anarchists who took part in the **Haymarket Riot** would be heroes forever. To employers, however, they remained vicious criminals determined to undermine law and order. Much of the American public came to associate unions in general with violence and radical ideas.

Homestead, 1892 In the summer of 1892, while Andrew Carnegie was in Europe, his partner Henry Frick tried to cut workers' wages at Carnegie Steel. The union at the Carnegie plant in Homestead, Pennsylvania, called a strike.

Frick had a plan for defeating the union. On July 1, he called in the Pinkertons, a private police force known for their ability to break strikes. Under cover of darkness on July 5, some 300 Pinkertons moved up the Monongahela River on barges. In a shootout with strikers on shore, several people died and many were wounded.

At first Americans generally sympathized with the striking workers. Then, on July 23, anarchist Alexander Berkman tried and failed to assassinate Frick. Although Berkman was not connected with the strike, the public associated his act with the rising tide of labor violence.

The union admitted defeat and called off the **Homestead Strike** on November 20. Homestead reopened under militia protection. "I will never recognize the union, never, never!" Frick declared. Carnegie believed in unions and accepted their right to strike, as long as no violence took place. However, Carnegie Steel (and its successor, U.S. Steel) remained nonunionized until the late 1930s.

Pullman, 1894 Like the strike of 1877, the last of the great strikes involved the railroad industry. Inventor George Pullman had developed a luxury sleeping car that was slightly larger than existing railroad cars. Known as Pullman cars, they were so successful that Pullman needed a steady source of labor to meet growing demands. He believed he could attract a solid, dedicated labor force by constructing a town made just for workers.

Built in 1880, twelve miles south of Chicago's business district, the town of Pullman provided its workers with everything they could possibly need: parks, a miniature lake, schools, a theater, a church, and paved sidewalks lined with shade trees. Pullman also maintained remarkable health and sanitation conditions, athletic programs, and a military band.

READING CHECK
What were the benefits and drawbacks of Pullman's town?

However, Pullman held his town to high standards, which workers sometimes viewed as unfriendly. Many workers felt that Pullman exercised too much control over their lives. Pullman's ban on alcohol in the town, for example, angered many residents. While these factors did not directly cause a strike, they provided a tense backdrop for the events about to occur. Conditions in the town took a turn for the worse after the Panic of 1893. Pullman laid off workers and cut wages by 25 percent. Meanwhile, he kept rent and food prices in his town at the same levels.

In May 1894, a delegation of workers went to him to protest. In response, Pullman fired three of the workers, which led the local union to go on strike.

CAPTION ANSWERS

Viewing History It hurt the union cause because the public came to associate unions with violence and radicalism.

RESOURCE DIRECTORY

Teaching Resources
Units 1/2 booklet
- Section 4 Quiz, p. 64
- Chapter 6 Test, pp. 65, 68

Guide to the Essentials
- Section 4 Summary, p. 31
- Chapter 6 Test, p. 32

Other Print Resources
Chapter Tests with ExamView® Test Bank CD-ROM, Ch. 6

Technology
ExamView® Test Bank CD-ROM, Ch. 6
Social Studies Skills Tutor CD-ROM

Pullman refused to bargain and instead shut down the plant. Badly needing help, the workers turned to the newly formed American Railway Union and Eugene V. Debs for support.

One month earlier, the A.R.U. had achieved success when they supported striking workers on James J. Hill's Great Northern Railroad. Following that victory, membership in the union rose to over 150,000 members, 3,000 percent more than the previous year. The A.R.U.'s triumph led many railway workers to feel optimistic about their cause.

Although Debs was hesitant to join this strike, the delegates of the A.R.U. voted to support the strike and called for a boycott of Pullman cars throughout the country. Widespread local strikes followed. By June 1894, some 260,000 railway workers had joined in the **Pullman Strike.** Debs instructed strikers not to interfere with the nation's mail, but the strike got out of hand. It completely disrupted western railroad traffic, including delivery of the mail.

VIEWING HISTORY Angry railroad strikers look on as federal troops ride in to restore order. **Synthesizing Information** *Why did the government intervene in the Pullman Strike? Why did the government side against labor unions?*

Railroad owners, organized as the General Managers Association, turned to the federal government for help. By arguing that the mail had to get through and citing the Sherman Antitrust Act, Attorney General Richard Olney won a court order forbidding all union activity that halted railroad traffic. The American Railway Union, he argued, had formed an illegal trust and was restraining free trade. Two days later, on July 4, President Grover Cleveland sent in 2,500 federal troops to ensure that strikers obeyed the court order. A week later the strike was over.

The Pullman strike and its outcome set an important pattern. In the years ahead, factory owners appealed frequently for court orders against unions. The federal government regularly approved these appeals, denying unions recognition as legally protected organizations. This official government opposition helped limit union gains for more than 30 years.

Section 4 Assessment

READING COMPREHENSION

1. Why did **socialism** appeal to some Americans in the late 1800s?
2. How did early labor unions in the United States differ in their organization and in the methods they used to achieve their goals?
3. Why did the railroad strike in 1877 prompt Eugene V. Debs to create an **industrial union?**
4. How successful were labor unions at the end of the century?

CRITICAL THINKING AND WRITING

5. **Making Comparisons** Compare socialism and the labor movement as two different responses to the growing gulf between the rich and the poor. How did their goals differ?
6. **Writing a Letter** Write a letter to President Hayes regarding the strike in Martinsburg, West Virginia, in 1877. Try to persuade the President either to send troops in to stop the strike or to refuse to intervene.

Take It to the NET

Activity: Creating a Fact Sheet Prepare a fact sheet outlining a specific aspect of labor unions, for example, the role of labor unions in our society, or the experience of a labor union member in the late 1800s. Use the links provided in the *America: Pathways to the Present* area of the following Web site for help in completing this activity.
www.phschool.com

Section 4 Assessment

Reading Comprehension

1. The gap between rich and poor was vast. Socialism seemed to offer a political and economic philosophy which favored the public at large, rather than a few wealthy individuals.
2. Organization: inclusion of skilled or unskilled workers; by trade, or including all trades. Methods: collective bargaining, strikes, boycotts.
3. He disliked the violence of the strike. He felt that separate railway unions were too fractured, and that one union for the entire railroad industry would be efficient and effective.
4. Labor unions had only limited success at that time. They brought many of labor's pressing issues to light, but often met with violence and government opposition during strikes.

Critical Thinking and Writing

5. Socialists hoped to see all Americans share equally in the nation's wealth. The labor movement worked mostly within the free enterprise system, attempting to attain fair treatment for workers and owners.
6. Letters requesting federal troops might stress that the strikers had defied the state militia. Letters opposing intervention might say that the use of federal troops would only increase the violence.

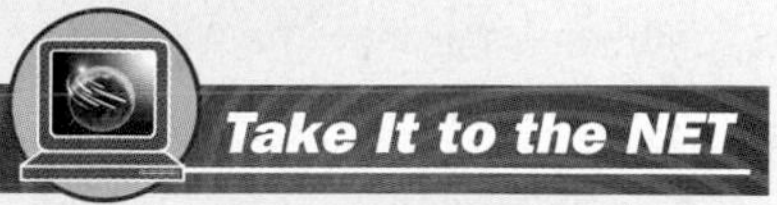

Take It to the NET

Answers will vary. Students might note the solidarity of the unions, the level of support they received, and the success or failure rate they had in achieving their goals.

Caption Answers

Viewing History The government was sympathetic to big business at the time. The government also felt that rail transport was a vital industry that must not be interrupted, particularly since railroads carried the nation's mail.

Chapter 6

Reviewing Key Terms

Students should refer to the definitions of key terms in the chapter to write sentences that show an understanding of the era of American industrial expansion.

Reviewing Main Ideas

15. Railroad expansion created great demand for steel rails; manufacturers could use railroads to sell their products nationwide; towns benefited from being located along rail lines.
16. Free enterprise was invaluable to the stimulation of big business because the lure of profits and success encouraged investment and innovation.
17. Horizontal consolidation, vertical consolidation, formation of trusts, underselling competitors.
18. It made the United States wealthy, opened up thousands of jobs, and created many new products at low costs. However, the safety and well-being of labor was not a priority.
19. They often resented these attempts for increased efficiency, as it gave employers too much control over their work and made the work less interesting.
20. Many young children left school and worked at hard labor in unhealthy conditions in order to help support their families.
21. They disallowed union meetings; fired union organizers; forced new employees to sign yellow dog contracts; refused to bargain collectively or recognize unions as workers' legitimate representatives.
22. Causes: the confining structure of Pullman's town, layoffs, and wage cuts. Effects: the federal government sent troops to restore order and end the strike. Union gains were minimal for years to come.

Critical Thinking

23. Answers will vary. Students might mention the impact of computers or other new electronic inventions.

Chapter 6 Review and Assessment

creating a CHAPTER SUMMARY

Copy this chart (right) on a piece of paper and complete it by adding information about how each of these important figures contributed to the period of industrial expansion in the United States.

Person	Impact
Thomas Edison	Helped bring electric power to businesses and homes. This new form of energy stimulated the growth of big business.
Henry Bessemer	
Andrew Carnegie	
John D. Rockefeller	
Frederick Winslow Taylor	
Samuel Gompers	
Eugene V. Debs	
George Pullman	

iTEXT 

For additional review and enrichment activities, see the interactive version of *America: Pathways to the Present*, available on the Web and on CD-ROM.

★ Reviewing Key Terms

For each of the terms below, write a sentence explaining how it relates to the period of industrial expansion in the United States.

1. transcontinental railroad
2. Bessemer process
3. mass production
4. social Darwinism
5. monopoly
6. vertical consolidation
7. economies of scale
8. trust
9. Sherman Antitrust Act
10. piecework
11. division of labor
12. socialism
13. collective bargaining
14. scab

★ Reviewing Main Ideas

15. How did new railroads and improvements in railway technology help spur economic growth? (Section 1)
16. Evaluate the impact of the free enterprise system in stimulating the age of big business. (Sections 1 and 2)
17. Name four methods that industrialists may have used to dominate their industry. (Section 2)
18. What were some positive and negative effects of rapid industrial growth? (Section 2)
19. How did workers react to attempts by employers to increase factory efficiency? (Section 3)
20. What problems did children face in industrialized America? (Section 3)
21. What steps did employers take to fight labor unions? (Section 4)
22. Analyze the causes and effects of the Pullman Strike. (Section 4)

★ Critical Thinking

23. **Making Comparisons** How have recent inventions such as the personal computer and the cell phone changed your daily life?
24. **Demonstrating Reasoned Judgment** Choose two visuals from the chapter and explain how they reflect the impact of industrialism on American society.
25. **Drawing Conclusions** Why do you think the federal government was friendly to the industrialists even when much of the public did not support them?
26. **Recognizing Ideologies** How did the emergence of beliefs in social Darwinism and/or socialism reflect the new challenges facing American society in the late 1800s?
27. **Expressing Problems Clearly** What challenges did labor unions have to overcome in order to achieve their main goals?

Creating a Chapter Summary

Person	Impact
Thomas Edison	Helped bring electric power to businesses and homes, stimulating the growth of big business
Henry Bessemer	Developed less expensive process for manufacturing steel
Andrew Carnegie	One of the most successful business leaders and industrialists of the late 1800s; first fortune in railroads, second in steel
John D. Rockefeller	Founded Standard Oil Company; great American philanthropist
Frederick Winslow Taylor	An "efficiency expert," invented the process of time and motion studies
Samuel Gompers	Founded American Federation of Labor
Eugene V. Debs	Established the American Railway Union to clean up corruption in unions and to eradicate violence in strikes
George Pullman	Pullman gave his workers good places to live, but he tried to control their lives. This led to the Pullman Strike of 1894, involving 120,000 railway workers.

★ Skills Assessment

Analyzing Political Cartoons ▶

28. In the background of this cartoon, a concerned citizen tries to alert Uncle Sam to the dangerous scene in the foreground. (a) What is the snake a symbol of? (b) How do you know? (c) Who is the woman? (d) How do you know?
29. What is the snake doing?
30. What is the cartoon's overall message?

Interpreting Data

Turn to the population and labor graphs in Section 3.

31. Which statement best summarizes the information shown in both graphs?
    - **A** The rural population decreased between 1860 and 1900.
    - **B** The number of industrial workers and city dwellers rose between 1860 and 1900.
    - **C** The percentage of professional workers decreased as people began moving away from farms.
    - **D** As people moved to the cities, a higher percentage of the population became industrial or professional workers.
32. What was the main reason for shifts in population and employment in the late 1800s?
    - **F** increasing immigration and decreasing farm prices
    - **G** the lure of new attractions in the nation's growing cities
    - **H** the growth of railroads and expansion of American industry
    - **J** high wages and incentives offered by factory owners

Applying the Chapter Skill: *Using Cross-Sectional Maps*

33. Use map resources to plot a route across the Appalachian Mountains from Raleigh, North Carolina, to Columbus, Ohio. Then draw a cross-sectional map of your route.

ACTIVITIES

Writing to LEARN

Writing to Describe
The Bessemer process helped create what has been termed the "age of steel" in the United States. Is the United States still in the age of steel? If not, how might you describe the present era? Write an essay expressing your view. Include specific examples.

Primary Source CD-ROM

Working With Primary Sources Find additional information on the period of industrial expansion on the *Exploring Primary Sources in U.S. History CD-ROM* and use the selection(s) provided to complete the Chapter 6 primary source activity located in the *America: Pathways to the Present* area of the following Web site.
www.phschool.com

Take It to the NET

Chapter Self-Test As a review activity, take the Chapter 6 Self-Test in the *America: Pathways to the Present* area at the Web site listed below. The questions are designed to test your understanding of the chapter content.
www.phschool.com

24. Answers might focus on the disparity in wealth represented in the illustration at the beginning of Section 4, or the heroism of railroad track gangs depicted in the photograph in Section 1.
25. Because of their contributions to the rising wealth of the country and the political power wielded by many of the industrialists.
26. Social Darwinism reflected free enterprise and laissez faire. Socialism emphasized the problems of wealth and the desire for its equal distribution to all, preserving the greater good rather than individual success.
27. They had to overcome their differences in order to remain united; deal with hostile employers who attempted to stop all union activity; and face disapproval by the federal government.

SKILLS ASSESSMENT

28. (a) Monopolies. (b) It is labeled, "Monopoly." (c) Liberty. (d) Lady Liberty is a common political symbol.
29. The snake has control of the Capitol and is attacking liberty.
30. That monopolies control the government and threaten freedom.
31. D
32. F
33. Answers will vary, but students should try to map out a direct route.

ANSWERS TO ACTIVITIES

Writing to LEARN

Answers will vary. Students should consider that while infrastructure development (requiring steel) is still important, in many ways the emphasis in this country has shifted to the gathering and dissemination of information.

Primary Source CD-ROM

Direct students to the additional primary sources that can be found on the *Exploring Primary Sources in U.S. History CD-ROM.*

Take It to the NET

Additional support materials and activities for Chapter 6 of *America: Pathways to the Present* can be found in the Social Studies area at the Prentice Hall School Web site. **www.phschool.com**

Chapter 7 Planning Guide

Resource Manager

	Core Instruction	Reading/Skills
Chapter-Level Resources **TEKS** 24(A), 24(B), 25(A), 25(B), 25(D)	Teaching Resources • Pacing Charts booklet • Block Scheduling booklet **Resource Pro® CD-ROM,** Ch. 7 **Prentice Hall Presentation Pro CD-ROM,** Ch. 7 **www.phschool.com** • eTeach	**Guided Reading Audiotapes (English/Spanish)** **Student Edition on Audio CD,** Ch. 7 **Social Studies Skills Tutor CD-ROM** **Color Transparencies,** A25, A26, A60, B8, E10, E11, E12, E13, H12, H13, H14
1 Moving West 1. Learn about the kinds of conditions that lured people to migrate to the West. 2. Find out where western settlers came from. 3. Describe how the American frontier shifted westward. **TEKS** 10(A), 10(B), 12(A)	Teaching Resources **Units 1/2 booklet** • Section 1 Quiz, p. 72	**Guided Reading and Review booklet,** p. 58 **Guide to the Essentials,** p. 33 **Learning with Documents booklet,** p. 19 **Section Reading Support Transparencies**
2 Conflict with Native Americans 1. Study the factors that caused changes in the life of the Plains Indians. 2. Find out how government policies and battlefield challenges affected the Indian Wars. 3. Learn about changes that occurred in federal Indian policies by 1900. **TEKS** 2(A), 12(A), 21(A), 21(C)	Teaching Resources **Units 1/2 booklet** • Section 2 Quiz, p. 73 **Learning Styles Lesson Plans booklet,** p. 30	**Guided Reading and Review booklet,** p. 59 **Guide to the Essentials,** p. 34 **Learning with Documents booklet,** p. 53 **Section Reading Support Transparencies**
3 Mining, Ranching and Farming 1. Learn how mining spread in the West. 2. Find out what caused the western cattle boom. 3. See what life was like for a cowboy on the Chisholm Trail. 4. Discover how settlers overcame barriers in farming the plains. **TEKS** 8(A), 20(E), 22(A), 22(B), 22(C)	Teaching Resources **Units 1/2 booklet** • Section 3 Quiz, p. 74	**Guided Reading and Review booklet,** p. 60 **Guide to the Essentials,** p. 35 **Section Reading Support Transparencies**
4 Populism 1. See why farmers complained about federal post–Civil War economic policies. 2. Find out how the government responded to organized protests by farmers. 3. Discover the Populists' key goals. 4. Understand the main point of William Jennings Bryan's Cross of Gold speech. 5. Learn about the legacy of Populism. **TEKS** 4(C), 5(B), 24(B), 24(C)	Teaching Resources **Units 1/2 booklet** • Section 4 Quiz, p. 75 **Learning Styles Lesson Plans booklet,** p. 31	**Guided Reading and Review booklet,** p. 61 **Guide to the Essentials,** p. 36 **Learning with Documents booklet,** p. 83 **Skills for Life booklet,** p. 16 **Section Reading Support Transparencies**

Enrichment/Pre-AP

Prentice Hall United States History Video Collection™
www.phschool.com
- Section Activities, Virtual Field Trip, Chapter Activities, Current Events Online

Nystrom *Atlas of Our Country,* pp. 28–29
Sounds of an Era Audio CD

Biography, Literature, and Comparing Primary Sources booklet, p. 125
Nystrom *Atlas of Our Country,* pp. 32–33
Historical Outline Map Book, p. 55
Sounds of an Era Audio CD
Exploring Primary Sources in U.S. HIstory CD-ROM

Biography, Literature, and Comparing Primary Sources booklet, p. 19, 58
American History Block Scheduling Support
Historical Outline Map Book, p. 56
Sounds of an Era Audio CD
Exploring Primary Sources in U.S. History CD-ROM

Great Debates booklet, p. 10
American History Block Scheduling Support
Sounds of an Era Audio CD
American Pathways Thematic Posters

Assessment

Core Assessment

ExamView® Test Bank, Ch. 7
ExamView® Test Bank CD-ROM, Ch. 7

Standardized Test Preparation

Diagnose and Prescribe

Diagnostic Tests for High School Social Studies Skills

Review and Reteach

Review Book for U.S. History

Practice and Assess

Test-taking Strategies With Transparencies
Test-taking Strategies Posters
Test Prep Book for U.S. History
Alternative Assessment Handbook
Document-Based Assessment

Teaching Resources

Units 1/2 booklet
- Section Quizzes, pp. 72–75
- Chapter Tests, pp. 76, 79

www.phschool.com Ch. 7 Self-Test

AmericanHeritage Resources

From the Archives of American Heritage®, pp. 271, 273, 275, 281
AmericanHeritage® My Brush with History™ Videotapes
www.americanheritage.com

Don't miss the exclusive interactive version of this textbook on the Web and on CD-ROM.

Chapter 7 Planning Guide
In Your Classroom

Customize for Individual Needs

Gifted and Talented

Teacher's Edition
- Customize for Gifted and Talented, p. 259

Teaching Resources
- Biography, Literature, and Comparing Primary Sources booklet, pp. 19, 58, 125

Technology
- Exploring Primary Sources in U.S. History CD-ROM *Geronimo: His Own Story, S. M. Barrett, ed.; The Old Chisholm Trail, Cowboy Song; Peary Reaches the North Pole, Robert E. Peary*

ESL

Teacher's Edition
- Customize for ESL, p. 269

Teaching Resources
- Guided Reading and Review booklet, pp. 58–61
- Guide to the Essentials (English/Spanish), Chapter 7

Technology
- Student Edition on Audio CD, Chapter 7
- Guided Reading Audiotapes (English/Spanish), Chapter 7
- Section Reading Support Transparencies

Less Proficient Readers

Teacher's Edition
- Customize for Less Proficient Readers, pp. 265, 281

Teaching Resources
- Guided Reading and Review booklet, pp. 58–61
- Guide to the Essentials (English/Spanish), Chapter 7

Technology
- Student Edition on Audio CD, Chapter 7
- Guided Reading Audiotapes (English/Spanish), Chapter 7
- Section Reading Support Transparencies

Less Proficient Writers

Teacher's Edition
- Customize for Less Proficient Writers, p. 275

Teaching Resources
- Guided Reading and Review booklet, pp. 58–61
- Guide to the Essentials (English/Spanish), Chapter 7

Technology
- Student Edition on Audio CD, Chapter 7
- Guided Reading Audiotapes (English/Spanish), Chapter 7
- Section Reading Support Transparencies

Teacher's Edition Index

Chapter 7 – Pacing Suggestions

For 90-minute Blocks

- Teach sections 1–4 using Transparencies A25, A26, A60, B8, E10, E11, E12, E13, H12, H13, and H14, and the Recent Scholarship note on page 273 for class discussions.

Running Out of Time?

If you are running short on time to cover this chapter, consider the following options:

- Use the Prentice Hall Presentation Pro CD-ROM to create an outline for this chapter.
- Use the Section Summaries for Chapter 7, from **Guide to the Essentials (English/Spanish).**

TEKS Correlation

Chapter-Level	TEKS
	(24) Social studies skills. The student applies critical-thinking skills to organize and use information acquired from a variety of sources, including electronic technology. The student is expected to: **(A)** locate and use primary and secondary sources such as computer software, databases, media and news services, biographies, interviews, and artifacts to acquire information about the United States. **(B)** analyze information by sequencing, categorizing, identifying cause-and-effect relationships, comparing, contrasting, finding the main idea, summarizing, making generalizations and predictions, and drawing inferences and conclusions. **(25) Social studies skills.** The student communicates in written, oral, and visual forms. The student is expected to: **(A)** use social studies terminology correctly. **(B)** use standard grammar, spelling, sentence structure, and punctuation. **(D)** create written, oral, and visual presentations of social studies information.
1 Moving West	**(10) Geography.** The student understands the effects of migration and immigration on American society. The student is expected to: **(A)** analyze the effects of changing demographic patterns resulting from migration within the United States. **(B)** analyze the effects of changing demographic patterns resulting from immigation to the United States. **(12) Economics.** The student understands domestic and foreign issues related to U.S. economic growth from the 1870s to 1920. The student is expected to: **(A)** analyze the relationship between private property rights and the settlement of the Great Plains.
2 Conflicts with Native Americans	**(2) History.** The student understands the political, economic, and social changes in the United States from 1877 to 1898. The student is expected to: **(A)** analyze political issues such as Indian policies, the growth of political machines, and civil service reform. **(12) Economics.** The student understands domestic and foreign issues related to U.S. economic growth from the 1870s to 1920. The student is expected to: **(A)** analyze the relationship between private property rights and the settlement of the Great Plains. **(21) Culture.** The student understands how people from various groups, including racial, ethnic, and religious groups, adapt to life in the United States and contribute to our national identity. The student is expected to: **(C)** analyze how the contributions of people of various racial, ethnic, and religious groups have helped to shape the national identity.
3 Mining, Ranching and Farming	**(8) Geography.** The student uses geographic tools to collect, analyze, and interpret data. The student is expected to: **(A)** create thematic maps, graphs, charts, models, and databases representing various aspects of the United States. **(20) Culture.** The student understands the relationship between the arts and the times during which they were created. The student is expected to: **(E)** identify the impact of popular American culture on the rest of the world. **(22) Science, technology, and society.** The student understands the impact of science and technology on the economic development of the United States. The student is expected to: **(A)** explain the effects of scientific discoveries and technological innovations such as electric power, the telegraph and telephone, petroleum-based products, medical vaccinations, and computers on the development of the United States. **(B)** explain how scientific discoveries and technological innovations such as those in agriculture, the military, and medicine resulted from specific needs. **(C)** analyze the impact of technological innovations on the nature of work, the American labor movement, and business.
4 Populism	**(4) History.** The student understands the effects of reform and third party movements on American society. The student is expected to: **(C)** evaluate the impact of third parties and their candidates such as Eugene Debs, H. Ross Perot, and George Wallace. **(5) History.** The student understands significant individuals, events, and issues of the 1920s. The student is expected to: **(B)** analyze the impact of significant individuals such as Clarence Darrow, William Jennings Bryan, Henry Ford, and Charles A. Lindbergh. **(24) Social studies skills.** The student applies critical-thinking skills to organize and use information acquired from a variety of sources, including electronic technology. The student is expected to: **(B)** analyze information by sequencing, categorizing, identifying cause-and-effect relationships, comparing, contrasting, finding the main idea, summarizing, making generalizations and predictions, and drawing inferences and conclusions. **(C)** explain and apply different methods that historians use to interpret the past, including the use of primary and secondary sources, points of view, frames of reference, and historical context.

Chapter 7

Looking to the West

(1860–1900)

Introducing the Chapter

After the Civil War, Americans moved west of the Mississippi River, taking over the land for farms, ranches, and mines, forcing out the original users, the Native Americans. The taming of the West became one of the great American myths.

Time Line Activity

To provide students with practice in using the time line, ask questions such as these:

1. What began the push of Indians off their traditional lands in the 1860s and 1870s? *(Federal land grants starting in 1862 spurred settlement of the West.)*
2. Which country began to move Indians onto reservations in 1871? *(Canada)*
3. What were two key battles between U.S. forces and Native Americans? *(The Battle of Little Bighorn in 1876 and the Wounded Knee Massacre in 1890)*

Chapter 7

Looking to the West (1860–1900)

Grand Canyon of the Yellowstone, by Thomas Moran, 1872

Longhorn steer

A Ute settlement in the Great Basin region

American Events

- **1862** Federal land grants ignite western settlement.
- **1867** Founding of Abilene, Kansas, spurs era of Texas cattle drives.
- **1872** Yellowstone National Park is created.
- **1876** Custer and his men are killed at Battle of Little Bighorn.

Presidential Terms: A. Lincoln 1861–1865 | A. Johnson 1865–1869 | U. S. Grant 1869–1877 | R. Hayes 1877–1881

1860 | 1870

World Events

- **1867** Swedish scientist Alfred Nobel invents dynamite.
- **1871** Canada begins forcing Indians onto reservations.

eTeach

Be sure to check out this month's online discussion with a Master Teacher. Go to **www.phschool.com**.

RESOURCE DIRECTORY

Teaching Resources

Pacing Charts booklet
Block Scheduling booklet, p. 20
Units 1/2 booklet
- Chapter Summary, p. 71

Technology

Guided Reading Audiotapes (English/Spanish), Ch. 7
Student Edition on Audio CD, Ch. 7
Sounds of an Era Audio CD *"The Cowboy's Life Is a Very Dreary Life,"* 1942 recording (time: 30 seconds)
Prentice Hall United States History Video Collection™ Volume 11, *Industrialization and Urbanization*
Prentice Hall Presentation Pro CD-ROM, Ch. 7
Resource Pro® CD-ROM
Social Studies Skills Tutor CD-ROM
Companion Web site, www.phschool.com

Statehood in the West

CANADA

Washington 1889

Oregon 1859

Montana 1889

North Dakota 1889

Minnesota

South Dakota 1889

Idaho 1890

Wyoming 1890

Nevada 1864

Utah 1896

Nebraska 1867

Iowa

Colorado 1876

Kansas 1861

California 1850

Missouri

Oklahoma 1907

Arizona 1912

New Mexico 1912

Arkansas

PACIFIC OCEAN

Texas 1845

MEXICO

Louisiana

1890 Date of statehood

State flag today

1882	Britain takes sole control of Egypt.
1885	Canada's transcontinental railroad completed despite uprising by Plains Indians.
1887	The Dawes Act allots land to individual Indians.
1889	"Boomers" race to stake claims as tracts of Indian Territory open in Oklahoma.
1890	Wounded Knee Massacre marks the end of the Indian wars. The Sherman Silver Purchase Act aims to boost silver currency.
1895	Russia's last czar, Nicholas II, begins his reign.
1896	Democratic presidential candidate William Jennings Bryan gives pro-silver "Cross of Gold" speech.
1900	Australian nationhood is approved by Britain.

J. Garfield 1881 · C. Arthur 1881–1885 · G. Cleveland 1885–1889 · B. Harrison 1889–1893 · G. Cleveland 1893–1897 · W. McKinley 1897–1901

1880 · 1890 · 1900

Statehood in the West

Activating Prior Knowledge Why do you think the dates of statehood are so close for many of the states shown? *(The western areas were settled rapidly in a wave of pioneers.)*

Previewing Many of the states shown have very regular shapes, unlike the shapes of states on the East Coast. What might be one reason? *(Possible answers: State boundaries were sometimes determined by natural borders, such as mountains. There were fewer of these natural borders in some of the country's midwestern plains areas, so the borders that were created had a very regular look.)*

BACKGROUND
About the Pictures

1. The teepee was an ideal shelter for the Utes because it was easy to disassemble and transport as they moved from place to place in pursuit of game animals and better land.
2. Longhorn cattle, originally bred in Texas, were a tough and hardy breed ideally suited for grazing on the sparse western plains. Soldiers returning from the Civil War found millions of Longhorns wandering wild in Texas.
3. American artist Thomas Moran painted the *Grand Canyon of Yellowstone* while on an expedition to document the natural wonders of the area. This painting was one of the major influences in convincing the government to set aside the area as the first national park.

BIBLIOGRAPHY

For the Teacher

Moynihan, Ruth B., Susan Armitage, and Christine Fischer Dichamp, eds. ***So Much to Be Done: Women Settlers on the Mining and Ranching Frontier.*** University of Nebraska Press, 1990. (Nineteen narratives by women from diverse environments and backgrounds in the nineteenth-century West.)

Unruh, John D., Jr., ***The Overland Emigrants and the Trans-Mississippi West, 1840–60.*** University of Illinois Press, 1993. (Reissue of a prizewinning account of the opening of the Oregon Trail.)

For the Student

Time-Life Books editors. ***Time-Life Books: The Old West.*** Prentice Hall, 1990. (A richly illustrated companion volume to a ten-hour miniseries, ***Faces and Voices of the Wild West.***)

"The Donner Party," KCTS Video, 90 minutes. (Part of the PBS series, ***The American Experience;*** an ill-fated journey west.)

Dakota Wars and Reservation Life. University of Nebraska. Film. (Depicts the lives of Native Americans of the Plains and their wars, including Custer's last stand.)

TEXT

Don't miss the exclusive interactive version of this textbook on the Web and on CD-ROM.

Section 1

Moving West

Section Objectives

1. Learn about the kinds of conditions that lured people to migrate to the West.
2. Find out where western settlers came from.
3. Describe how the American frontier shifted westward.

Bellringer

Warm-Up Activity Ask students what they would do if they were moving to another part of the country. What difficulties would they face in leaving their old home and in settling into a new one? Why might they want to move?

Activating Prior Knowledge Ask students if they are aware of people in their families who immigrated to this country. From what country did they come? Why did they immigrate?

Reading Strategy

As students read the section, have them list possible solutions to the following problems: how to obtain land, how to locate water, how to work prairie sod.

Activity

Connecting with Geography

Divide the class into groups to role-play homesteaders bound for Tucson, Boise, Jackson, Helena, or Cheyenne. Have each group research the climate and features of their destination. Have them analyze the effects of changing demographic patterns resulting from migration within the United States as each group reports on homesteading prospects. **(Logical/Mathematical)**

Caption Answers

Viewing History The plains were like nothing Easterners had seen before. But the plain, with no shelter and needing hard work to farm, was a huge challenge.

Section 1

Moving West

READING FOCUS

- What conditions lured people to migrate to the West?
- Where did the western settlers come from?
- How did the American frontier shift westward?

KEY TERMS

push-pull factors
Pacific Railway Acts
Morrill Land-Grant Act
land speculator
Homestead Act
Exoduster

TAKING NOTES

Copy the diagram below. As you read, fill in factors relating to settlement of the West.

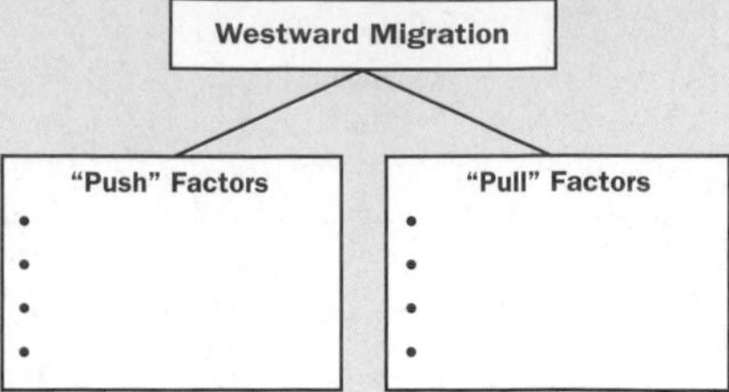

MAIN IDEA

With the help of the federal government, Americans and immigrants settled the region west of the Mississippi in a major migration during the second half of the 1800s.

VIEWING HISTORY Buffalo dot the landscape today in South Dakota's Badlands National Park. Majestic prairie scenes like this greeted early settlers. **Expressing Problems Clearly** *To many newcomers, the first sight of the Great Plains was both dazzling and daunting. Explain this statement.*

Setting the Scene At minus 50 degrees, a Montana winter night could turn a fatted steer into a furry icicle. In the Southwest, heat topping 110 degrees left the bleached bones of prospectors strewn across the desert. Describing the harsh winters of the open plains, one newspaper editor called western Kansas "a prairie where the cows give blue milk and the wind whips the long-tailed pigs to death."

After the Civil War, pioneers settled from the Mississippi River to the partly populated California coast. Newcomers from Vermont, or Kentucky, or Germany wrote home with fantastic tales of these strange lands:

> *"The wind was too fierce. . . . It actually blows the feathers off the chickens' backs. . . . I can't put up many pictures and things for everytime the door opens they all blow off the wall. . . . [W]e noticed how terrible loud everyone talks out here and now we find ourselves just shouting away at the top of our voices. . . . [U]nless you yell you can't be heard at all."*
>
> —South Dakota settler Mary Clark

Truly, you have to wonder: What moved people like Mary Clark to journey to this land of known and unknown dangers?

The Lure of the West

The settlers of the American West had many reasons for giving up their old, sometimes comfortable, lives for a new start in the wilderness. The West seized the American imagination. It kindled people's sense of adventure, their entrepreneurial spirit, and their appetite for profit and conquest.

When scholars study the reasons for major migrations, they look at what they call **push-pull factors**—events and conditions that either force (push) people to move elsewhere or strongly attract (pull) them to do so.

Push Factors Various conditions urged settlers westward. The Civil War had displaced thousands of farmers, former slaves, and other workers. Eastern

Resource Directory

Teaching Resources
Guided Reading and Review booklet, p. 58

Other Print Resources
Nystrom *Atlas of Our Country* *Settling the West,* pp. 28–29

Technology
Section Reading Support Transparencies
Guided Reading Audiotapes (English/Spanish), Ch. 7
Student Edition on Audio CD, Ch. 7
Color Transparencies *Fine Art,* E11, E12; *The Way It Works,* H13
Sounds of an Era Audio CD *Cowboy Dan Deering* (time: 40 seconds)
RESOURCE PRO® **Critical Thinking Activity** *Formulating Questions,* found on Resource Pro, extends students' application of this skill by having them compose questions on immigration from Europe to the United States.
Prentice Hall Presentation Pro CD-ROM, Ch. 7
Companion Web site, www.phschool.com

farmland was increasingly costly, certainly for many African Americans or for impoverished immigrants. Failed entrepreneurs sought a second chance in a new location. Ethnic and religious repression caused both Americans (such as the Mormons) and Europeans to seek freedom in the West. The open spaces also sheltered outlaws on the run.

Yet the West was more than just a refuge for discouraged people and shady characters. The region offered temptations and adventures that lured—pulled—settlers westward.

Pull Factor: Government Incentives Before the Civil War, the North and South had fought bitterly over whether the new territories of the West would allow or prohibit slavery. After the war, with those issues behind it, the federal government opened the way to western migration by giving away public lands—or selling them at rock-bottom prices.

Under the **Pacific Railway Acts** of 1862 and 1864, the government gave large land grants to the Union Pacific and Central Pacific railroads. The original act granted 10 square miles of public land on each side of the track for every mile of track laid. From 1850 to 1871, the railroads received more than 175 million acres of public land—an area more than one tenth the size of the whole United States and larger than the state of Texas.

Railroad expansion provided new avenues of migration into the American interior. The railroads sold portions of their land to arriving settlers at a handsome profit. Lands closest to the tracks drew the highest prices, because farmers and ranchers wanted to locate near railway stations.

To further encourage western settlement, Congress passed the **Morrill Land-Grant Act** of 1862. It gave state governments millions of acres of western lands, which the states could then sell to raise money for the creation of "land grant" colleges specializing in agriculture and mechanical arts. The states sold their land grants to bankers and **land speculators,** people who bought up large areas of land in the hope of selling it later for a profit.

The government program that really set the wagons rolling west was the **Homestead Act,** signed by President Lincoln in 1862. Under the act, for a small fee settlers could have 160 acres of land—a quarter-mile square—if they met certain conditions: They were at least 21 years old or the heads of families. They were American citizens or immigrants filing for citizenship. They built a house of a certain minimum size (usually 12 feet by 14 feet) on their claims and lived in it at least six months a year. Finally, they had to farm the land for five years in a row before claiming ownership.

The act created more than 372,000 farms. By 1900, settlers had filed 600,000 claims for more than 80 million acres under the Homestead Act.

Pull Factor: Private Property A key incentive to western settlement was the availability of legally enforceable, transferable property rights. The Homestead Act and state and local laws helped to limit settlers' risks and avoid a total free-for-all. Miners, cattle ranchers, and farmers all received certain rights to land and possessions. Land parcels were measured, registered, and deeded. Cattle branding established ownership. Enforcement of water rights provided stable water sources for crops and for human and animal consumption.

In time, established American economic concepts of private property, private enterprise, and a free market extended across the continent. One editor, hoping to raise the standards of a rather lawless town, reminded his readers that

Lesson Plan

Focus Tell students that after the Civil War, large numbers of Americans and Europeans continued moving into "the West," the area between the settled West Coast and the Mississippi River. Ask students what these people hoped to find.

Instruct Discuss the conditions that inspired people to head west. Explain that many Civil War veterans from New England sought larger, more fertile fields. Many African Americans wanted to leave the restrictive South and obtain land of their own. Ask students why the government gave land to homesteaders. How did railroads profit from the land the federal government granted to them? Who were the most successful homesteaders? What special challenges did frontier life present for African Americans? For women?

Assess/Reteach The second half of the nineteenth century was marked by a major migration of settlers from the eastern portion of the United States to the western portion. Can students list some areas to which these new settlers journeyed?

Background
Geography in History

African Americans who left the South for a better life in the West were met with both acceptance and rejection in their new homes. When a group of Exodusters arrived in Kansas in 1879, the governor vowed to help them. A Freedman's Relief Association provided food and medical supplies, and many white people offered jobs and homes. Within a few years, African Americans had bought more than twenty thousand acres of land and created the towns of Dunlap, Singleton, and Nicodemus. While life in the West was generally better than it had been in the South, African Americans still faced discrimination. In Denver the locals would not rent to or hire African Americans, and in communities such as Lincoln, Nebraska, African American migrants were expelled.

Customize For ...
Gifted and Talented

Explain that pressure for a homestead law began long before 1862. Ask students to discuss why Northerners opposed such a law until the Civil War. What factors might have made life easier for African Americans in the West?

Test Preparation

Have students reread the section on this page titled "Pull Factor: Government Incentives" and then answer the question below.

Which of these activities would a land speculator be likely to undertake?

A Creating a large agricultural college.

B Overseeing the donation of public lands for the creation of railroads.

C Inducing settlers to establish homestead farms.

(D) Buying up large areas of land very cheaply in the hope of selling it later for a profit.

Reading Comprehension

1. The Homestead Act offered land for a nominal fee, encouraging people to move to the West to begin farming. Settlers were attracted by the prospect of legal ownership of property.
2. The Pacific Railway Acts granted an enormous amount of territory to railroads. People followed the railroads west, either to lay track or to purchase some railroad land.
3. (a) Answers may include: white Easterners, African Americans, Germans, Irish, Italians, European Jews, Chinese, Mexicans.
(b) Different religions, languages, and traditions. For example, Germans and Scandinavians brought the Lutheran religion, which stressed hard work and education.

Critical Thinking and Writing

4. Answers will vary, but may include: The West had a spirit of equality; there were fewer class divisions; the hard work of any group of people was highly valued.
5. Answers may include references to the richness of the soil, the beauty of the prairie, and the joy of farming one's own land.

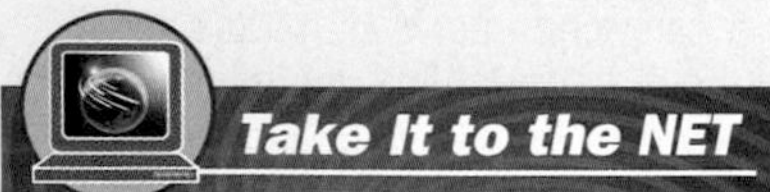

Flyers should highlight the advantages of moving to one of these new settlements. They should advertise plenty of land, inexpensive prices, favorable climate, and other selling points.

VIEWING HISTORY Settlers registered their claims at this land office in Round Pond, Oklahoma Territory. **Determining Relevance** *How did the surveying and registration of land claims encourage settlement and free enterprise in the West?*

"people who have money to invest go where they are protected by law."

Settlers From Far and Wide

New groups of settlers soon joined the mainly white easterners who first cut trails into the western wilderness. Cheap land and new jobs attracted people of other countries and ethnic groups. In growing towns and cities throughout the region, settlers spoke a rich mixture of languages and practiced a variety of customs.

German immigrants arrived in the last half of the 1800s, mainly seeking land to farm. They built orderly, tight-knit settlements from Texas to the upper Missouri River. They brought the Lutheran religion, with its strict ethics, and their traditional emphasis on hard work and education. Lutherans from Scandinavia settled the northern plains from Iowa to Minnesota to the Dakotas, many pursuing dairy farming.

Irish, Italians, European Jews, and Chinese tended to settle in concentrated communities, initially in West Coast cities. Eventually they gravitated to growing cities in the American interior, taking jobs in mining, railroad construction, and other trades. Ranching, mining, farm labor, and jobs in boom towns drew Americans and foreigners alike. Mexicans and Mexican Americans contributed to the growth of ranching.

After the Civil War, thousands of African Americans rode or even walked westward, often fleeing the violence and exploitation that followed Reconstruction. In 1879, Benjamin "Pap" Singleton led groups of southern blacks on a mass "Exodus," a trek inspired by the biblical account of the Israelites' flight from Egypt to a prophesied homeland. Hence, the settlers called themselves **Exodusters.** Some 50,000 or more Exodusters migrated west.

The Shifting Frontier

The "frontier" was not a line that moved westward in a unified motion. Various regions were settled at different times. Yet by 1890, settlements dotted the prairie every 10 miles or so. Towns gave rise to cities at a stunning pace. But one reality remained: The West was already occupied—by Native Americans.

Section 1 Assessment

READING COMPREHENSION

1. Why was the **Homestead Act** such a significant factor in the westward migration?
2. How did the **Pacific Railway Acts** influence Western settlement?
3. (a) What main groups of Americans and immigrants settled the West?
(b) Describe the contrasting cultural influences they brought to the region.

CRITICAL THINKING AND WRITING

4. **Drawing Inferences** Why do you think some African Americans faced less discrimination in the West than they had experienced in the East?
5. **Writing to Inform** You were an unemployed eastern factory worker with a family who moved to Kansas. Write a letter to a friend back East, describing this new place and explaining why you made this risky move.

Activity: Creating a Flyer
Research Exoduster towns such as Nicodemus, Kansas. Create a flyer to attract migrants to such a town. Use the links provided in the *America: Pathways to the Present* area of the following Web site for help in completing this activity.
www.phschool.com

Caption Answers

Viewing History They helped to secure land rights and ownership, without which people might have been reluctant to endure the risks and hardships of settlement in the West.

RESOURCE DIRECTORY

Teaching Resources
Units 1/2 booklet
- Section 1 Quiz, p. 72

Guide to the Essentials
- Section 1 Summary, p. 33

Learning with Documents booklet (Primary Source Activity) *African American Settlers*, p. 19

Section 2

Conflict With Native Americans

Section 2 Conflict With Native Americans

READING FOCUS

- What caused changes in the life of the Plains Indians?
- How did government policies and battlefield challenges affect the Indian wars?
- What changes occurred in federal Indian policies by 1900?

MAIN IDEA

American expansion into the West led to the virtual elimination of Native Americans.

KEY TERMS

Great Plains
nomad
reservation
Battle of Little Bighorn
Ghost Dance
Massacre at Wounded Knee
assimilation
Dawes Act
boomers
sooners

TAKING NOTES

As you read, complete this chart, listing federal Indian policies in the West and their outcomes.

Federal Indian Policies	Results
Treaties	Often violated by U.S.

SECTION OBJECTIVES

1. Study the factors that caused changes in the life of the Plains Indians.
2. Find out how government policies and battlefield challenges affected the Indian wars.
3. Learn about changes that occurred in federal Indian policies by 1900.

BELLRINGER

Warm-Up Activity Discuss with students the tremendous gulf of understanding implied between the Easterners' perception of the "Indian problem," versus the Native Americans' perception that what was at stake was their own existence as a civilization.

Activating Prior Knowledge Ask students to describe what they know already about the impact of western settlement on Native American people. Direct the class to list the areas of conflict that were most likely to arise between natives and new settlers.

READING STRATEGY

Have students use the headings and subheadings to create an outline of the section. Then, as they read, have them fill in supporting details and analyze how the contributions of Native Americans have helped to shape the national identity.

Setting the Scene Easterners called it "the Indian problem." What could and should be done with western Indians so that their lands could be used productively, as they saw it, for mining, ranching, and farming?

To Native Americans, the "problem" was a life-or-death battle. In the second half of the 1800s, they resisted an all-out assault on their warriors, their women and children, their homelands, their sources of food and shelter, and their ways of life. It was a race against time. They faced their fate in varying ways—with bloodthirsty anger, solemn faith, and cautious compromise. At last, when their time ran out, they faced resignation, fatigue, and heartbreak.

The Life of the Plains Indians

Long before eastern settlers arrived, changes had affected the lives of Native Americans on the **Great Plains,** the vast grassland between the Mississippi River and the Rocky Mountains. The changes blended with and altered traditions that had existed for generations.

Well into the 1800s, millions of buffalo ranged the Great Plains. These huge beasts provided life-sustaining supplies to the Plains Indians: meat, hides for making shelters and clothing, and a wealth of other uses. The opening of relations with French and American fur traders in the 1700s allowed the Plains Indians to exchange hides for guns, making buffalo hunting easier.

By the mid-1700s, horses' hooves thundered across the plains. The Spanish had brought horses to Mexico in the 1500s, and Native Americans obtained them through trading and raids. The impact of the horse on Native American culture was profound.

While many Indian nations continued to live mainly as farmers, hunters, and gatherers, others became **nomads.** These are people who travel from place to place, usually following available food sources, instead of living in one location. With horses, nomadic peoples were better able to carry their possessions as they followed the vast buffalo herds across the plains.

VIEWING FINE ART Artist George Catlin lived with the Plains Indians for years, producing more than 500 sketches and paintings of Native American life, including this work, *Buffalo Chase—Single Death.* **Analyzing Visual Information** *How does Catlin depict the equipment, skills, and character needed to hunt the buffalo?*

RESOURCE DIRECTORY

Teaching Resources

Learning Styles Lesson Plans booklet, p. 30
Guided Reading and Review booklet, p. 59
Learning with Documents booklet (Visual Learning Activity) *Western Expansion into Native American Land,* p. 53
Biography, Literature, and Comparing Primary Sources booklet (Comparing Primary Sources) *On Cultural Ties,* p. 125

Other Print Resources

Historical Outline Map Book *Indian Lands After 1850,* p. 55

Technology

Section Reading Support Transparencies
Guided Reading Audiotapes (English/Spanish), Ch. 7
Student Edition on Audio CD, Ch. 7
Prentice Hall Presentation Pro CD-ROM, Ch. 7
Companion Web site, www.phschool.com

CAPTION ANSWERS

Viewing Fine Art The hunter is depicted on a speeding horse with only a bow and arrow. He and the horse must move in closely to the thundering buffalo in order to hit it, a maneuver that appears to require courage, horsemanship, good timing, and good aim.

Lesson Plan

Focus Explain that as settlers from the U.S. and Europe poured into the West, they took up land that had been home to Native Americans for many generations. Ask students how Native Americans of the West were affected.

Instruct Discuss how cultural beliefs can lead to misunderstandings and even war. In what ways did Native American groups and settlers hold conflicting beliefs about land use and government? What role did their differences play in the Indian Wars of the late 1800s? How did attempts to "civilize" Native Americans contribute to their ruin?

Ask students to consider the results of dividing up Native American land. What was the effect of the homesteading rush in 1889?

Assess/Reteach Can students list alternative approaches to settlement of the West that might have avoided the terrible consequences to Native American peoples?

Background
A Diverse Nation

Some native peoples were outraged by the encroachment of the transcontinental railroad. On August 7, 1867, about 40 Cheyenne, led by Chief Pawnee Killer, derailed a train near Plum Creek in central Nebraska. At a Peace Commission conference in September 1867, General William Sherman told several chiefs, "We will build iron roads, and you cannot stop the locomotive any more than you can stop the sun or the moon, and you must submit, and do the best you can."

READING CHECK

Plains Indians began to obtain firearms and horses in the 1700s. Horses were used in Indian wars against rival Indian nations. These battles were quite fierce. Some Indians took to their horses and became nomads.

READING CHECK

What changes occurred in the culture of Plains Indians before the arrival of settlers?

The arrival of the horse also brought upheaval. Warfare among Indian nations, to gain possessions or for conquest, rose to a new intensity when waged on horseback. Success in war brought wealth and prestige. The rise of warrior societies led to a decline in village life, as nomadic Native Americans raided more settled groups.

Indian Wars and Government Policy

Before the Civil War, Native Americans west of the Mississippi continued to inhabit their traditional homelands. An uneasy peace prevailed, punctured by occasional hostilities as workers laid railroad track deeper into Indian lands and as the California gold rush of 1848 drew wagon trains across the plains. By the 1860s, however, Americans had discovered that the interior concealed a treasure chest of resources. The battle for the West was on.

Causes of Clashes Settlers' views of land and resource use contrasted sharply with Native American traditions. Many settlers felt justified in taking Indian land because, in their view, they would make it more productive. To Native Americans, the settlers were simply invaders. Increasing intrusions, especially into sacred lands, angered even chiefs who had welcomed the newcomers.

Making Treaties Initially, the government tried to restrict the movements of nomadic Native Americans by negotiating treaties. Some treaties arranged for the federal purchase of Indian land, often for little in return. Other treaties restricted Native Americans to **reservations,** federal lands set aside for them.

The treaties produced misunderstandings and outright fraud. The government continued its longtime practice of designating as "tribes" groups that often had no single leadership or even related clans or traditions. Federal agents selected "chiefs" to sign treaties, but the signers often did not represent the majority of their people. Honest government agents negotiated some pacts in good faith; others had no intention of honoring the treaties. Some sought bribes or dealt violently with tribes until they signed. Indian signers often did not know that they were restricted to the reservations, and that they might be in danger if they left.

The federal Bureau of Indian Affairs (BIA), a part of the Interior Department, was supposed to manage the delivery of critical supplies to the reservations. But widespread corruption within the BIA and among its agents resulted in supplies being mishandled or stolen.

The government made some attempts to protect the reservations, but their poorly manned outposts were no match for waves of land-hungry settlers. Unscrupulous settlers stole land, killed buffalo, diverted water supplies, and attacked Indian camps. After a treaty violation in 1873, Kicking Bird, a Kiowa, declared: "I have taken the white man by the hand, thinking him to be a friend, but he is not a friend; government has deceived us. . . ."

Native Americans reacted in frustration and anger. Groups who disagreed with the treaties refused to obey. Acts of violence on both sides set off cycles of revenge that occurred with increasing brutality.

Focus on GOVERNMENT

Acquiring Indian Lands From the 1860s to 1900, presidential administrations gained Native American lands however they could: through treaties, land purchases, forced relocation of Indians to reservations, wars—or simply looking the other way and letting settlers solve the problem. In 1875, after failed attempts to purchase the mineral-rich but sacred Black Hills of the Sioux, President Ulysses S. Grant gave General William T. Sherman the go-ahead for mining the treaty-protected territory. Sherman wrote that if the miners were to pour in, "I understand that the president and the Interior Department will wink at it." Word got out, and soon the hills were crawling with prospectors.

Battlefield Challenges

Federal lawmakers came to view the treaties as useless. In 1871, the government declared that it would make no more treaties and recognize no chiefs.

RESOURCE DIRECTORY

Other Print Resources

Nystrom *Atlas of Our Country* *Later Expansion of the United States,* pp. 32–33

Technology

Color Transparencies *Fine Art,* E10

Inconclusive Battles In 1865, one general urged the government to "finish this Indian war this season, so that it will stay finished." Yet the tragic conflicts would drag on for nearly three more decades.

Both sides lacked a coherent strategy along with the resources to achieve one. They reacted to each others' attacks in a long, exhausting dance of death. The Indians were outgunned, and suffered far more casualties. Yet in the end, they succumbed less to war than to disease and to lack of food and shelter.

The United States Army, spread across the South to monitor Reconstruction, had slim resources to send to the West. With infantry, cavalry, and artillery units spread thinly across the vast region, the Army could not build coordinated battle fronts. Battle lines constantly shifted as settlers moved into new areas. Most confrontations were small hit-and-run raids with few decisive outcomes. Still, experienced army generals managed to lead successful campaigns in some regions.

Indian warriors fought mostly on their own turf, employing tactics they had used against their traditional enemies for generations. Profit-seeking whites sold guns to the warriors. Native American groups made some alliances in attempts to defeat the intruders, but their efforts usually failed. Moreover, the army often pitted Indian groups against one another.

The Soldier's Life on the Frontier Who would volunteer for this army? Living conditions: $13 a month; a leftover Civil War uniform; rotten food. Duties: build forts; drive settlers from reservations; escort the mail; stop gunfights; prevent liquor smuggling and stagecoach robberies; protect miners, railroad crews, and visiting politicians; and—occasionally—fight Indians. Hazards: smallpox, cholera, and flu; accidents; endless marching; and death in battle. In fact, thousands of recruits—former Civil War soldiers, freed slaves, jobless men—did join the frontier army. Unlike the typical Indian warrior, the average soldier on the plains rarely saw battle. Up to a third of the men deserted.

American BIOGRAPHY

Chief Joseph 1840–1904

Born in 1840, *Hin-mah-too-yah-lat-kekt*, or "Thunder Rolling Down the Mountain," was better known by the name he got from his father, Joseph, a converted Christian. As his father lay dying in 1871, he made Joseph promise never to sell their scenic, fruitful homeland in the Northwest. The promise proved impossible to keep.

Forced to flee in 1877, the Nez Percé fought skillfully, but their chief found no joy in it. In his surrender speech, Joseph reportedly declared, "Hear me, my chiefs! I am tired. My heart is sick and sad. From where the sun now stands I will fight no more forever."

Chief Joseph's band was exiled to Indian Territory (Oklahoma), where all six of Joseph's children died. In 1885, the chief was returned to the modern-day state of Washington, but not to his father's land. He died in 1904 "of a broken heart," his doctor said.

Key Battles

Native Americans and the army met in battles throughout the interior West. In major engagements, the army usually prevailed.

The Sand Creek Massacre, 1864 The southern Cheyenne occupied the central plains, including parts of Colorado Territory. After some gruesome Cheyenne raids on wagon trains and settlements east of Denver, Colorado's governor took advantage of a peace campaign led by Cheyenne chief Black Kettle. Promised protection, Black Kettle and other chiefs followed orders to camp at Sand Creek.

Colonel John Chivington, who had so far failed to score a big military victory against the Cheyenne, now saw his chance. On November 29, 1864, his force of 700 men descended upon the encamped Cheyenne and Arapaho. While Black Kettle frantically tried to mount an American flag and a white flag of surrender, Chivington's men slaughtered between 150 and 500 people—largely women and children. The next year, many southern Cheyenne agreed to move to reservations.

> "*Nothing lives long.*
> *Only the earth and the mountains.*"
>
> —death song sung by a Cheyenne killed at Sand Creek, 1864

This 1864 poster promises cavalry recruits "all horses and other plunder taken from the Indians."

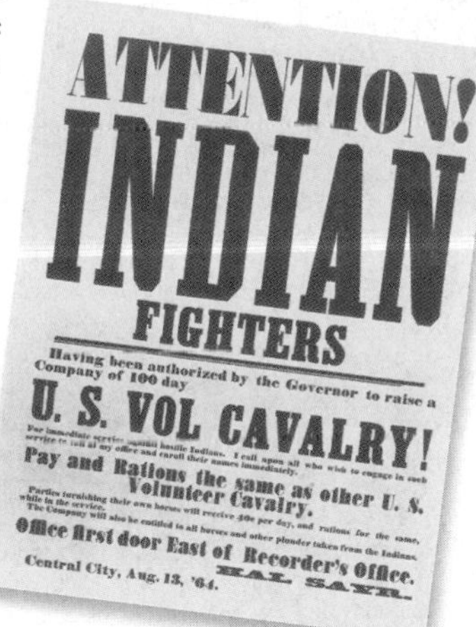

ATTENTION!
INDIAN
FIGHTERS
Having been authorized by the Governor to raise a Company of 100 day
U. S. VOL CAVALRY!
Pay and Rations the same as other U. S. Volunteer Cavalry.
Office first door East of Recorder's Office.
Central City, Aug. 13, '64.

ACTIVITY
Connecting with History and Conflict

Tell students that they are going to try to negotiate an agreement between the Native American tribes and the United States government. Divide the class into two groups. One group will represent the native peoples, while the other group advocates on behalf of the government. Have each group prepare their case by drawing up a list of grievances, as well as a proposal that states their needs. Have both groups consider the causes and effects of actions taken by Native Americans to expand economic opportunities and political rights in the United States. When the two groups come together, they should try to find a way to work out their differences. **(Verbal/Linguistic)**

BACKGROUND
A Diverse Nation

In studying native cultures historians face a major obstacle—a lack of documents written by Native Americans. Historians must rely on records left by white people. At best these documents reflect what the white people thought the native people wanted to say. There is, however, a rich oral tradition that provides insight into Native American history. Elders shared their stories with their descendants, and in so doing preserved important events, concepts, and beliefs. This oral tradition serves as a fertile source of understanding of the Native American experience.

ACTIVITY
Connecting with History and Conflict

Ask students to research and write a brief biography of one of the following Native American leaders of the West: Red Cloud, Sitting Bull, Black Kettle, Crazy Horse, Cochise, or Geronimo. **(Verbal/Linguistic)**

TEST PREPARATION

Have students read the section on this page with the heading "Inconclusive Battles" and then answer the question below.

Which of the following factors contributed to the decades-long duration of the battles between the United States Army and Native Americans?

A Lack of a coherent strategy by either side.

B The army's depleted resources due to the Civil War.

C Whites who sold guns to the Native American side for their own profit.

Ⓓ All of the above.

ACTIVITY
Connecting with Government

"There is no selfishness [among them], which is at the bottom of civilization."

—Henry Dawes, United States

" . . . you are taking my land from me; you are killing off our game, so it is hard for us to live. Now you tell us to work for a living . . . We do not interfere with you, and again you say, why do you not become civilized? We do not want your civilization! We would live as our fathers did, and their fathers before them."

—Crazy Horse, Oglala

Tell students to choose one of the quotations and write an essay reflecting on its meaning. Encourage students to consider the root of the conflict between Native Americans and the United States government. **(Verbal/Linguistic)**

BACKGROUND
Buffalo Soldiers

Certain African American regiments of the United States Cavalry, assigned to serve in the western United States in the years following the Civil War, were known as "buffalo soldiers." It is thought that the regiments received the name from the Native Americans whom they were sent to fight. Though the buffalo soldiers were African Americans, their officers were white. Though these soldiers were poorly equipped, they had a challenging assignment: to maintain order among the Native Americans, and also to control bandits, outlaws, and various lawbreakers hidden throughout the vast territories. Over the course of 30 years, buffalo soldiers participated in nearly 200 skirmishes of various sizes. The buffalo soldiers are remembered today as brave, disciplined, and courageous. Many buffalo soldiers received medals, including the Medal of Honor, the army's highest award.

CAPTION ANSWERS

Map Skills (a) They were pushed westward, away from areas with growing white settlement. (b) The Great Plains.

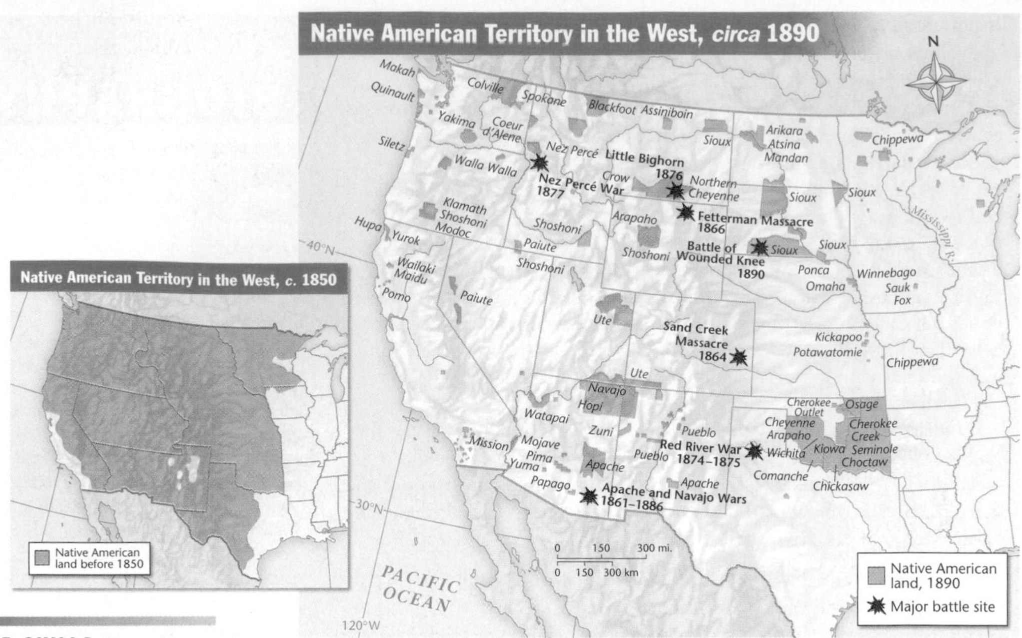

MAP SKILLS The main map at right shows Indian lands in 1890, compared with the land they roamed in 1850, shown in the inset map above. **Regions** *In what directions were Native Americans pushed as they lost territory?*

Sounds of an Era

Listen to *Black Elk Speaks*, an eyewitness account of the Battle of Little Bighorn, and other sounds from the era of the western settlement.

The Battle of Little Bighorn, 1876 The Sioux of the northern plains—Dakota, Wyoming, and Montana territories—powerfully resisted white expansion. In 1865, the government enraged the Sioux by deciding to build a road, the Bozeman Trail, through prime Sioux hunting grounds in the Bighorn Mountains.

Sioux chief Red Cloud launched a two-year war to block the project. In 1866, Sioux warriors slaughtered more than 80 soldiers under Captain W. J. Fetterman near Fort Phil Kearny. The war ended in the Fort Laramie Treaty of 1868, under which the United States abandoned the Bozeman Trail and created a large Sioux reservation in what is half of South Dakota today.

Sioux land protected by the treaty included the Black Hills—tall, dramatic, pine-covered mountains in South Dakota and Wyoming territories, held sacred by many Sioux. But in 1874, the government sent Lieutenant Colonel George A. Custer to investigate rumors of gold in the Black Hills. He reported that the hills cradled gold "from the grass roots down." This news was the starting gun in a mining race that overran the region.

The government offered to buy the Black Hills, and Red Cloud entered negotiations. But two Sioux chiefs, Sitting Bull and Crazy Horse, who had never signed the Fort Laramie Treaty, left the reservation. Hostilities resumed.

RESOURCE DIRECTORY

Technology

Color Transparencies *Historical Maps,* A25

Sounds of an Era Audio CD *"It Is a Good Day to Die,"* Sioux war song (time: 30 seconds)

RESOURCE PRO® Primary Source Activity *Talks with Otoe Chiefs,* found on Resource Pro, illustrates the United States government's treatment of Native Americans with a transcript of a meeting between Otoe chiefs and the United States Commissioner of Indian Affairs.

In June 1876, Custer was sent to round up the Indians. He moved his cavalry toward the Little Bighorn River in what is now Montana. There he met the full fury of the Sioux: nearly 2,000 warriors, the largest Indian force ever gathered on the plains. Custer, expecting a smaller enemy, had split his forces. The Sioux fell on their prey, wiping out Custer and his more than 200 soldiers within an hour.

The **Battle of Little Bighorn,** or "Custer's Last Stand," stunned Americans. The army flooded the area with troops and swiftly forced most of the Sioux back to their reservations. Crazy Horse was killed after surrendering in 1877. Sitting Bull and some remaining Sioux escaped to Canada, but starvation forced them to surrender and return to a reservation four years later.

The Battle of Wounded Knee, 1890 Under stress for a half-century, Native Americans saw the rise of religious prophets predicting danger or prosperity. A prophet of the plains, Wovoka, promised a return to traditional life if people performed purification ceremonies. These included the **Ghost Dance,** a ritual in which people joined hands and whirled in a circle.

The Ghost Dance caught on among the Teton Sioux, who, still struggling to adjust to reservation life, practiced it with great urgency, encouraged by Sitting Bull. In 1890, word spread that the Indians were becoming restless. The government agent at the Pine Ridge Reservation in South Dakota wired the army: "Indians are dancing in the snow and are wild and crazy. . . . We need protection and we need it now." The army dispatched the Seventh Cavalry, Custer's old unit, to the scene.

Hoping to calm the crisis, Indian police officers tried to arrest Sitting Bull. When he hesitated, the officers shot and killed him. His grieving followers, some 120 men and 230 women and children, surrendered and were rounded up at a creek called Wounded Knee. As they were being disarmed, someone fired a shot. Soldiers opened fire, killing more than 200 Sioux. The **Massacre at Wounded Knee** was the last major episode of violence in the Indian wars.

BIOGRAPHY

George Armstrong Custer
1839–1876

He had the stuff of a legendary hero: charming, fearless, and memorable in his long, golden curls and flamboyant uniform. He was also vain, heedless of authority, and foolhardy—qualities that would prove fatal.

Custer seemed to be born for war. Daring in battle, he achieved great distinction in the Civil War. At the war's end, he was sent to fight Indians, a job he relished. To the Sioux, he was the "chief of thieves" for entering their sacred Black Hills and spreading word of their gold wealth.

Court-martialed twice for various offenses, Custer at last found fame and adoration in his final impulsive act: rushing to his death in 1876 at the Battle of Little Bighorn. At "Custer's Last Stand," he became the heroic victim of legend and song.

New Policies Toward Native Americans

"I am the last Indian," Sitting Bull is reported to have said. Indeed, he was among the last to have lived the life of a free Native American, roaming with the buffalo herds across unobstructed plains, practicing traditional customs.

Critics of Federal Indian Policies While many white Americans called for the destruction of Native Americans, others, horrified by the government's policies, formed a growing peace movement. It found inspiration in Helen Hunt Jackson's 1881 publication *A Century of Dishonor.* Protesting what she

Apache chief Geronimo leads a band of renegades. Apache resistance ended with his surrender in 1886, the year of this photograph.

BACKGROUND
A Diverse Nation

The town of Wounded Knee has become a continuing symbol of Native American suffering. In March 1973 more than 200 members of the American Indian Movement (AIM) seized the trading post at Wounded Knee in an attempt to draw national attention to their platform. AIM leaders wanted reforms in the tribal government and demanded Senate hearings on United States treaties with Native American nations. In response federal law officers surrounded the area. "You have here," said one government official, "an arguable case of treason." The AIM occupation ended in surrender to the federal authorities, but it mobilized other Native American groups and focused attention on recovering the titles to their tribal territories.

ACTIVITY
Connecting with Culture

Tell students to research the Sioux. Have them investigate how the Sioux lived in the nineteenth century and how their culture has survived in the twenty-first century. How has their way of life changed over the years? Where do the Sioux live? What is their approximate population? After students complete their research, have them deliver an oral presentation on their findings. **(Verbal/Linguistic)**

BACKGROUND
Art History

In addition to relying on the buffalo for basic needs, the Native Americans of the Plains created beautiful things from the skins of buffalo and deer. Women's dresses, children's clothes, men's ceremonial shirts, shields, and robes were all made from the hides of the animals that roamed the plains. Each tribe had its own unique patterns and ways of applying decorations such as porcupine quills, beads, and feathers of the eagle, hawk, and crow. In *Buckskin & Buffalo,* author Colin F. Taylor examines the details and symbols that turned everyday objects into works of art.

CUSTOMIZE FOR ...
Less Proficient Readers

Ask students to rewrite the following incorrect statements:

- In the massacres at Sand Creek and Wounded Knee, Native Americans killed large numbers of United States cavalry.
- Most Native Americans were eager to become farmers like the white settlers.

Activity

Connecting with Economics

As students review the chart of Key Events in the Indian Wars, have them discuss the role that economics played in these battles. Encourage students to consider why the United States government felt compelled to acquire territories where native groups had lived. What were the forces that drove white people to conquer the land? Why was the drive to "strike it rich" such a powerful force in this chapter of history? Have students analyze the relationship between private property rights and the settlement of the Great Plains. How did the clash of values play out in the conflicts between Native Americans and whites? **(Verbal/Linguistic)**

Background

Connections to Today

Despite pressure from white Americans to assimilate, Native American tribes have managed to maintain their cultural identity. There are now more than 300 federally recognized tribes. Many of these tribes have prospered since the federal courts ruled that tribes could operate casinos on reservations if that type of gambling is legal in the states in which the reservations are located. As a result of the Indian Gaming Regulatory Act of 1988, many tribes have a chance to become self-sufficient. With economic success comes political clout as local officials seek out tribal leaders for their support.

Key Events in the Indian Wars, 1861–1890

Wars / Battles	Native American Nations / Homelands	Key Players	Description / Outcome
Apache and Navajo Wars 1861–1886	Apache in Arizona, New Mexico, and Colorado territories; Navajo in New Mexico, Colorado territories	• Geronimo • Col. Christopher "Kit" Carson	Carson kills or relocates many Apache to reservations in 1862. Clashes drag on until Geronimo's surrender in 1886. Navajo told to surrender in 1863, but before they can, Carson attacks, killing hundreds, destroying homelands. Navajos moved to New Mexico reservation in 1865.
Sand Creek Massacre 1864	Southern Cheyenne, Arapaho, in central plains	• Black Kettle • Col. John Chivington	Cheyenne massacres prompt Chivington to kill up to 500 surrendered Cheyenne and Arapaho led by Black Kettle.
Red River War 1874–1875	Comanche and southern branches of Cheyenne, Kiowa, and Arapaho, in southern plains	• Comanche war parties • Gen. William T. Sherman • Lt. Gen. Philip H. Sheridan	Southern plains Indians relocated to Oklahoma Indian Territory under 1867 Treaty of Medicine Lodge. After buffalo hunters destroy the Indians' food supply, Comanche warriors race to buffalo grazing areas in Texas panhandle to kill hunters. Sherman and Sheridan defeat warriors and open panhandle to cattle ranching.
Battle of Little Bighorn 1876	Northern plains Sioux in Dakota, Wyoming, and Montana territories	• Sitting Bull • Crazy Horse • Red Cloud • Lt. Col. George A. Custer	U.S. tries to buy gold-rich Black Hills from Sioux. Talks fail. Custer's 7th Cavalry is sent to round up Sioux, but meets huge enemy force. Custer and some 200 men perish in "Custer's Last Stand."
Nez Percé War 1877	Largest branch of Nez Percé, in Wallowa Valley of Idaho and Washington territories and Oregon	• Chief Joseph • Gen. Oliver O. Howard • Col. Nelson Miles	Howard orders Nez Percé to Idaho reservation; violence erupts. Joseph leads some 700 men, women, and children on 1,400-mile flight. His 200 warriors hold off Miles's 2,000 soldiers until halted 40 miles short of Canada. Sent to Indian Territory, many die of disease. In 1885, survivors moved to reservation in Washington Territory.
Battle of Wounded Knee 1890	Sioux at Pine Ridge Reservation, South Dakota	• Sitting Bull • U.S. 7th Cavalry	Ghost Dance raises fears of Sioux uprising; Sitting Bull killed in attempted arrest. His followers surrender and camp at Wounded Knee. Shots are fired; some 200 Sioux die.

INTERPRETING CHARTS This chart provides a brief summary of some of the key battles that were fought in various areas of the western interior. **Making Comparisons** *(a) What factors did many of these clashes have in common? (b) In what ways did they differ?*

saw as the government's broken promises and treaties, Jackson wrote, "It makes little difference . . . where one opens the record of the history of the Indians; every page and every year has its dark stain."

Attempts to Change Native American Culture As sincere as the reformers may have been, most believed that Native Americans still needed to be "civilized." That is, they should be made to give up their traditions, become Christians, learn English, adopt white dress and customs, and support themselves by farming and trades. Tribal elders were ordered to give up their religious beliefs and rituals. Christian missionaries ran schools on the reservations.

In 1879, Army Captain Richard H. Pratt opened the United States Indian Training and Industrial School in Carlisle, Pennsylvania. Children as young as 5 years old were taken from the reservations by coaxing, trickery, or force, and sent to Carlisle and other such schools to be educated "as Americans." The children were to be integrated into white society. This policy is called **assimilation,** the process by which one society becomes a part of another, more dominant society by adopting its culture.

In 1887, a federal law dismantled the Native American concept of shared land in favor of the principle of private property highly valued by Americans. The **Dawes Act** divided reservation land into individual plots. Each Native American family headed by a man received a plot, usually 160 acres. These landholders were granted U.S. citizenship and were subject to local, state, and federal laws. Many Indian sympathizers believed that the land allocations would make families self-supporting and create pride of ownership.

But the idea of taking up farming offended the beliefs of many Native Americans. Smohalla, a religious teacher from the Northwest, retorted: "You

Caption Answers

Interpreting Charts (a) These battles often resulted from attempts by U.S. forces to confine Native Americans to reservations. The fighting often occurred on the Great Plains. (b) Sometimes the army triggered the violence, and sometimes Native Americans did.

RESOURCE DIRECTORY

Technology

Color Transparencies *Historical Maps,* A60

Sounds of an Era Audio CD *John G. Neihardt* (time: 35 seconds)

Exploring Primary Resources in U.S. History CD-ROM *Geronimo: His Own Story, S. M. Barrett, ed.*

ask me to cut grass and make hay and sell it, and be rich like white men! But how dare I cut off my mother's hair?"

In reality, much reservation land was not suitable for farming. Many Native Americans had no interest or experience in agriculture. Some sold their land to speculators or were swindled out of it. Between 1887 and 1932, some two thirds of the 138 million acres of Indian land wound up in the hands of whites.

The Opening of Indian Territory For the some 55 Indian nations that had been forced into Indian Territory, worse trouble loomed. The territory contained the largest unsettled farmland in the United States—about 2 million unassigned acres. During the 1880s, as squatters overran the land, Congress agreed to buy out Indian claims to the region.

On the morning of April 22, 1889, tens of thousands of homesteaders lined up at the territory's borders. At the stroke of noon, bugles blew, pistols fired, and the eager hordes surged forward, racing to stake a claim.

> "*[W]ith a shout and a yell the swift riders shot out, then followed the light buggies or wagons and last the lumbering prairie schooner and freighters' wagons, with here and there even a man on a bicycle and many too on foot—above all a great cloud of dust hovering like smoke over a battlefield.*"
>
> —newspaper reporter, 1889

By sundown, these settlers, called **boomers,** had staked claims on almost 2 million acres. Many boomers discovered that some of the best lands had been grabbed by **sooners,** people who had sneaked past the government officials earlier to mark their claims. Under continued pressure from settlers, Congress created Oklahoma Territory in 1890. In the following years, the remainder of Indian Territory was opened to settlement.

It took a half-century, more than a thousand battles, and the deaths of about 950 United States soldiers to conquer the Native Americans. The clashes also took the lives of countless Indians used by the army as scouts and fighters; of settlers killed in Indian attacks; and of millions of Native American men, women, and children who died in battles or on squalid reservations.

VIEWING HISTORY Officials at the Carlisle, Pennsylvania, Indian school took before-and-after photographs of their students. **Analyzing Visual Information** *List details that show the changes undergone by these boys.*

Section 2 Assessment

READING COMPREHENSION

1. Describe early changes in the lifestyle of the Plains Indians.
2. Why were Indian treaties often unsuccessful?
3. How did the **Ghost Dance** lead to a tragic conflict?
4. Describe two major federal **assimilation** policies.

CRITICAL THINKING AND WRITING

5. **Identifying Assumptions** What assumptions about Native Americans did sympathetic easterners make when proposing improvements on the reservations?
6. **Writing a News Story** As an eastern reporter traveling with an army unit, report on one of the battles discussed in this section.

Take It to the NET

Activity: Creating a Presentation
Prepare a presentation on attempts to assimilate Indian students. Use the links provided in the *America: Pathways to the Present* area of the following Web site for help in completing this activity.
www.phschool.com

RESOURCE DIRECTORY

Teaching Resources

Units 1/2 booklet
- Section 2 Quiz, p. 73

Guide to the Essentials
- Section 2 Summary, p. 34

Section 2 Assessment

Reading Comprehension

1. Some early changes were caused by guns and horses, which facilitated buffalo hunting; the horses also supported the nomadic lifestyle and helped to confer status and wealth upon warriors.
2. Treaties were often fraught with misunderstandings and fraud. The government frequently designated "tribes" and "chiefs" to suit its own needs. Treaty violations resulted in violence on both sides.
3. A ritual dance was misinterpreted as an act of aggression and led to the Massacre at Wounded Knee. Chief Sitting Bull was killed. Further violence erupted as his followers were being disarmed. More than 200 Sioux were killed.
4. Reeducation forced elders to give up their traditions and beliefs; schools for Native American children instilled only "white" cultural ideas. The Dawes Act divided shared reservation land into separate plots.

Critical Thinking and Writing

5. Answers will vary, but may include that eastern "reformers" assumed that Native American ways of life, religion, education, and work were inferior to the ways of whites.
6. Answers may include that the Native Americans were usually heavily outgunned but not always outnumbered, or that the Native Americans were good fighters and worthy adversaries.

Student presentations should reflect the aspects of assimilation described in the chapter, focusing on the attempts by whites to do away with Native American culture.

Caption Answers

Viewing History Answers include: Their traditional garments were replaced with military-style uniforms; their long hair was cut; the traditional head scarf worn by the boy on the left was replaced with a cap.

Section 3 Mining, Ranching and Farming

Section Objectives

1. Learn how mining spread in the West.
2. Find out what caused the western cattle boom.
3. See what life was like for a cowboy on the Chisholm Trail.
4. Discover how settlers overcame barriers in farming the plains.

Bellringer

Warm-Up Activity Write the words *modernization* and *mechanization* on the chalkboard. Ask students to think about the positive and negative effects of these processes.

Activating Prior Knowledge How long do students think it took for word to spread throughout the country of gold's discovery in California in 1849? What are some ways students think this information might have traveled? How long would it take the information to travel around the country today?

Reading Strategy

As students read, have them notice the ways in which the farming, mining and ranching industries changed in the second half of the nineteenth century. Have students explain how scientific discoveries and technological innovations in agriculture resulted from specific needs.

Section 3 Mining, Ranching and Farming

READING FOCUS

- How did mining spread in the West?
- What caused the western cattle boom?
- What was life like for a cowboy on the Chisholm Trail?
- How did settlers overcome barriers in farming the plains?

MAIN IDEA

Mining, ranching, and farming developed from individual and family enterprises into major industries, transforming the West.

KEY TERMS

placer mining
long drive
homesteader
soddie
dry farming
bonanza farm
Turner thesis
stereotype

TAKING NOTES

As you read, complete this diagram to show the effects of settlement by various groups.

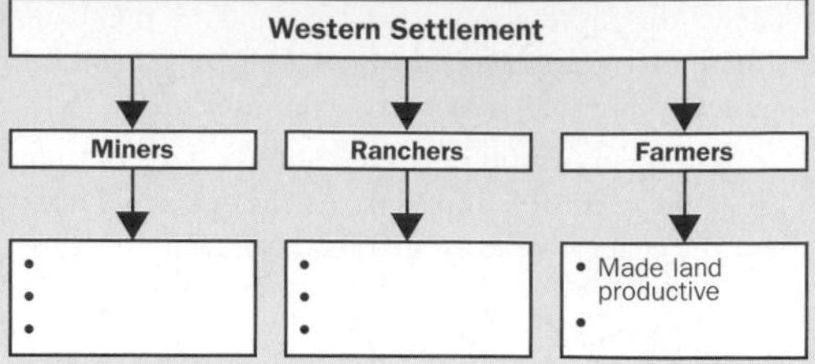

Setting the Scene Along with the armies of Custer and Sherman came virtual armies of miners, ranchers, and farmers that descended on the American West from the end of the Civil War to the end of the nineteenth century. Once unleashed, this force would remake the West. One railroad worker saw the transformation coming:

> "*The time is coming, and fast, too, when, in the sense it is now understood, THERE WILL BE NO WEST.*"
>
> —from the diary of a Union Pacific engineer

VIEWING HISTORY With the arrival of large mining operations, mining sites became sprawling industrial towns, like Virginia City, Nevada, shown here. **Analyzing Visual Information** *Describe the character and appearance of this mining site, using details from the photograph.*

He was right. By the late 1800s, the West of the Native Americans, of unplowed prairie, of thundering buffalo, had vanished. A new breed of Westerners had come here, they believed, on a mission: to unlock the potential of this land and make it fruitful.

The Spread of Western Mining

After the stunning discovery of gold at Sutter's Mill, California, in 1848, a surge of fortune-hunters, from single men to whole families, set their sights on the West Coast. Little did they know that on the way to California, their wagon wheels rolled over mountains even more rich in precious minerals.

Mining Moves Inland In 1859, rumors of gold "everywhere you stick your shovel" at Pikes Peak, Colorado, brought on a stampede of wagons painted with the slogan "Pikes Peak or Bust!" The rumors turned out to be exaggerated. But later that year, one of the biggest strikes ever, Nevada's Comstock Lode, sent prospectors converging on the ore-laden western mountain ranges. Over the next 30 years, the Comstock Lode would yield $400 million in gold and silver.

Almost simultaneously, a gold strike west of the little town of Denver, in what was then Kansas Territory, threw open the gates to the American interior.

Caption Answers

Viewing History The site is full of activity. Factories and homes for the workers are spread across the city. The mound in the center appears to be refuse produced by mining. Tracks indicate the presence of railroads for hauling the ore. The overall appearance is dirty and unappealing.

RESOURCE DIRECTORY

Teaching Resources

Guided Reading and Review booklet, p. 60
Literature, Biography, and Comparing Primary Sources booklet (Literature) *The Californian's Tale,* p. 58

Other Print Resources

Historical Outline Map Book *Opening the West,* p. 56

Technology

Section Reading Support Transparencies
Guided Reading Audiotapes (English/Spanish), Ch. 7
Student Edition on Audio CD, Ch. 7
Prentice Hall Presentation Pro CD-ROM, Ch. 7
Companion Web site, www.phschool.com

By 1861, the swarm of settlers caused the federal government to carve out Colorado Territory from western Kansas. The Homestake mine, opened in 1877 in the Black Hills of Dakota, was possibly the richest single mine ever uncovered in the world, producing a billion dollars' worth of ore.

One miner, William Parsons, perceived the national significance of the gold rush: "The Atlantic and Pacific coasts, instead of being, as they are now, divided countries, will become parts of a compact whole, joined and cemented together by bonds of mutual interest."

Early Mining, and Mining Towns At first, miners searched for metal in surface soil or in streambeds. The simplest tool was a shallow pan in which the miner scooped dirt and water, and then swished it around. Lighter particles washed over the edge while the gold stayed in the bottom of the pan. A technique called **placer mining** used this method on a larger scale. Miners shoveled loose dirt into boxes and then ran water over the dirt to separate it from gold or silver particles. (The word *placer,* of Spanish origin, rhymes with *passer.*)

These methods could be used by individuals, small groups of men, or even families. They came at the first whisper of a new strike, and tent communities popped up almost overnight. Larger strikes led to settled towns, even cities. Merchants, farmers, and other entrepreneurs came to supply miners' needs.

The easily gathered precious metal was skimmed off quickly. By the late 1850s and early 1860s, most of the precious metals that remained in the West lay locked in quartz and deeply buried. At that point, many prospectors straggled home, leaving mining settlements deserted ghost towns.

The large, deep veins of ore attracted the money and sophisticated technologies of large corporations. Using large work crews, they diverted streams and dug into the exposed beds. Workers tunneled into mountains and plunged into rickety mine shafts that sometimes became their graves. Huge drills replaced pickaxes. Hydraulic pumps pounded mountainsides with water. With the arrival of dynamite in the 1870s, miners blasted ore out of hillsides. Like other industries, mining had become the realm of big business.

The Cattle Boom

Mexicans taught Americans cattle ranching in the early 1800s. The Americans adopted Mexican ranching equipment and dress. They also learned from Mexican cattlemen the advantages of raising the hardy Texas longhorn cattle that thrived on the dry, grassy plains.

Demand Spurs Growth Several changes launched the West's legendary cattle industry. During the Civil War, many Texans left their ranches to serve in the Confederate army. They returned home to find up to 5 million cattle roaming wild in the grasslands, making available ample supplies of beef.

Prior to the war, pork had been Americans' meat of choice. But when cookbooks began snubbing pork as "difficult to digest" and "unwholesome," the nation went on a beef binge. Cattle that had sold for only $3 to $6 a head in Texas at the war's end now brought $40 a head in Illinois and $80 in New York. Soon, however, consumers began to complain about the tough beef from the Texas

Major Mining Strikes in the West, 1849–1880*

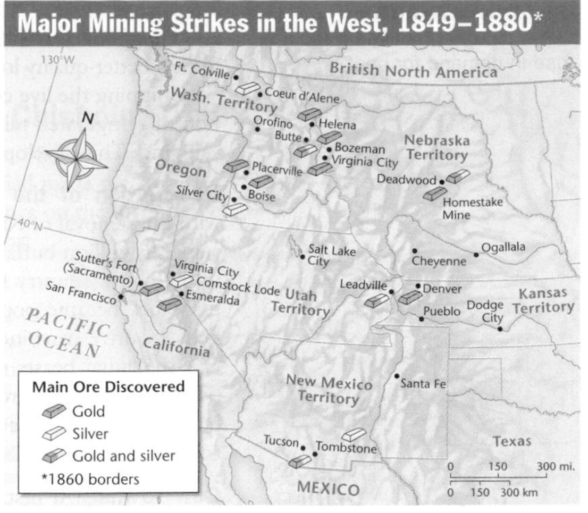

MAP SKILLS Mining spread throughout the interior West in the 1860s after a gold strike outside of Denver. **Place** *From the map, what can you tell about the characteristics of places where key mining strikes occurred?*

Lesson Plan

Focus Point out that opportunities for farming and ranching and the discovery of gold and silver attracted both individual settlers and big businesses. Ask students why big businesses were important in the development of the West.

Instruct Discuss how technology transformed the West. Ask students what new technology helped Great Plains farmers. Were there any negative aspects of mechanized farming? How did technology change the mining industry? Discuss how only a big business could afford to excavate ore.

Ask students what role railroads played in helping the ranching frontier to flourish. What caused the frontier's decline?

Assess/Reteach Ask students to list ten impacts of the discovery of gold in California. Have them organize the list in order of lasting importance.

Background

Pioneer Women

More than 800 diaries were written by women traveling west between 1840 and 1870. The writings offer a glimpse into the pioneer woman's life and challenges. About one in five women was pregnant or gave birth during the journey, although cultural taboos prevented women from writing about childbirth, even in diaries. A comprehensive collection of pioneer women's diaries is found in Johanna L. Stratton's *Pioneer Women, Voices from the Kansas Frontier.*

Activity

Connecting with Science and Technology

Have students learn more about methods used to extract precious metals from the earth. Tell students to make a chart or illustration showing how these methods worked. Have students analyze the impact of these technological innovations on the nature of mine work. **(Visual/Spatial)**

Customize For ...

ESL

Write the sentence under Main Idea on the chalkboard. Read it aloud slowly. Then have volunteers reread the sentence phrase by phrase and explain what each phrase means. Finally, have students look at the photographs in the section and talk about what they show.

Caption Answers

Map Skills Most appear to have occurred in mountainous areas (or at least in foothills) rather than in the plains.

Section 3 Assessment

Reading Comprehension

1. Large drills, hydraulic pumps, and dynamite replaced placer mining.
2. Texans returned to their ranches after the Civil War to find a cattle population boom. Increased demand for beef, refrigerated railroad cars, and the extension of rail lines into the West caused cattle ranching to become successful.
3. Cow towns were specifically developed along railroad lines to receive cattle on their way to market. These towns would often thrive until they became surrounded by farms.
4. Answers may include: building homes without wood, floods, prairie fires, dust storms, drought, insects that ravaged the crops, disease-carrying mosquitoes, financial worries.
5. The West was romanticized as a place full of outlaws, Indian fighters, cowboys, and happily prosperous farmers. Another stereotype is that issues of right and wrong were clearly defined in the West.

Critical Thinking and Writing

6. Drills, hydraulic pumps, and dynamite favored large mining corporations. Refrigerated railroad cars and open land with water resulted in vast cattle-ranching operations. Machines like automatic grain drills and techniques like dry farming and crop rotation created bonanza farms.
7. Answers might try to debunk some of the myths by explaining the difficulties and hardships involved in homesteading.

Take It to the NET

Invite students to take a Virtual Field Trip at **www.phschool.com**

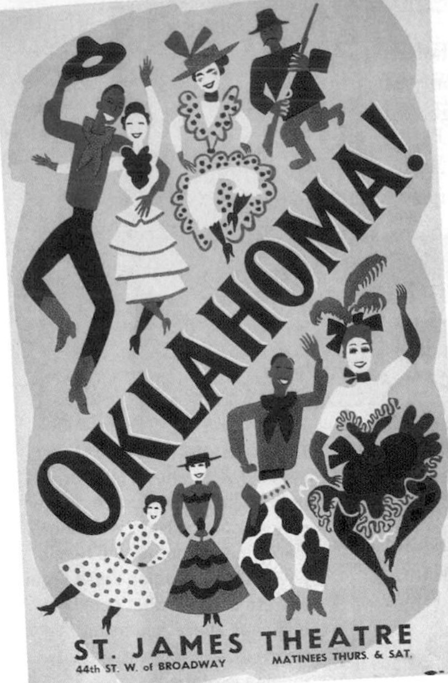

The 1943 Rodgers and Hammerstein musical "Oklahoma" is a love story that takes place during the settlement of Oklahoma Territory, where "the corn is as high as an elephant's eye." One song declares that "the farmer and the cowman should be friends," a reference to the frequent land feuds between the two groups.

outlaw, a miner, a gang leader, or a cowboy—anyone who dealt out righteous justice against evil.

Edward Wheeler's novel *Deadwood Dick, The Prince of the Road: or, the Black Rider of the Black Hills* was based on a real person. But the real Deadwood Dick was no outlaw. He was an African American named Nat Love. Entering a rodeo contest in a Dakota Territory mining town named Deadwood, Love won several roping and shooting contests. In his autobiography, Love wrote, "Right there the assembled crowd named me 'Deadwood Dick' and proclaimed me champion roper of the Western cattle country."

In 1883, William F. ("Buffalo Bill") Cody created his fantastically popular Wild West shows, contributing further to frontier myths. These events drew thousands of spectators to steer-roping contests, rodeos, and battle enactments between "good" cavalry regiments and "bad" Native Americans. One season featured the real-life Sitting Bull.

Most stories from the West supported stereotypes about men. The West was the place where a young man could find freedom and opportunity. He could lead a virtuous life and resist the forces of civilization that had made easterners soft. Many writers praised the West for having toughened the bodies and souls of young men. In his histories of the West, future President Theodore Roosevelt urged American men to experience the "strenuous life" of the West before they became too weak from the comforts of modern civilization.

Some male themes also appealed to women. In 1912, Juliette Low founded the American Girl Scouts in part because she feared that civilization had made girls too soft. Praising women homesteaders for their strength and intelligence, she made the scouting techniques of tracking, woodcraft, and wilderness survival the core of her program.

The Wild West remains fixed in popular culture, from the Dallas lawyer in a cowboy hat to western movies. Cowboy songs—"Home on the Range" and "Don't Fence Me In"—celebrate images of wide-open spaces and freedom from civilization. While myths of the Old West are more dramatic than the reality, the era produced many of the nation's most cherished images of itself.

Section 3 Assessment

READING COMPREHENSION

1. What technologies gradually replaced **placer mining?**
2. Why did cattle ranching become so successful after the Civil War?
3. Describe the rise of cow towns.
4. What hardships did **homesteaders** face?
5. What kinds of **stereotypes** were created about the Old West?

CRITICAL THINKING AND WRITING

6. **Analyzing Information** Describe the impact of new technologies and other factors on small entrepreneurs in mining, ranching, and farming.
7. **Writing to Narrate** Create a historical fiction narrative describing the experience of a homesteading family on the Great Plains.

Take It to the NET

Virtual Field Trip Travel the Chisholm Trail. Read about the challenges of getting Texas cattle herds to market. See how the trail's history is being preserved. Use the links provided in the *America: Pathways to the Present* area of the following Web site for help in completing this activity.
www.phschool.com

RESOURCE DIRECTORY

Teaching Resources
Units 1/2 booklet
- Section 3 Quiz, p. 74

Guide to the Essentials
- Section 3 Summary, p. 35

Section

4 Populism

READING FOCUS

- Why did farmers complain about federal post–Civil War economic policies?
- How did the government respond to organized protests by farmers?
- What were the Populists' key goals?
- What was the main point of William Jennings Bryan's Cross of Gold speech?
- What was the legacy of Populism?

MAIN IDEA

Economic crises led to organized protests by farmers seeking government relief. Economic reform became an election issue and led to the rise of Populism.

KEY TERMS

money supply
deflation
monetary policy
bimetallic standard
free silver
Bland-Allison Act
Sherman Silver Purchase Act
the Grange
Interstate Commerce Act
Populist
Cross of Gold speech

TAKING NOTES

Copy the web diagram below. As you read, fill in the blank circles to show the effects of economic instability from 1870 to 1900. Add more circles if needed.

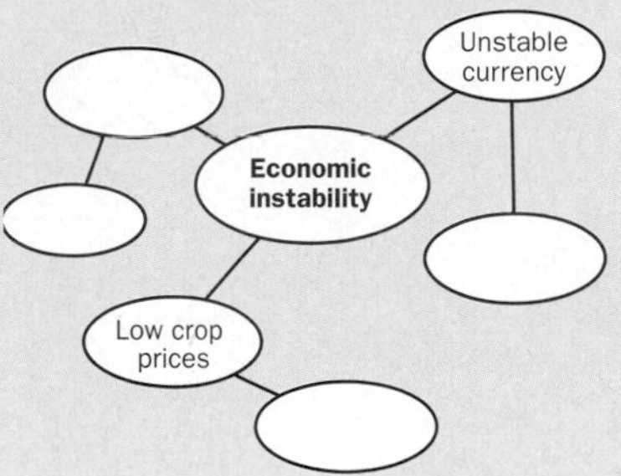

Setting the Scene American farmers have always struggled against two forces: nature and the economy. In the late 1800s, economic perils were as devastating to farmers as locusts or boll weevils. Ever since the end of the Civil War, farm production had risen. So too had debt, as farmers borrowed heavily to purchase the expensive new equipment that made possible such increased productivity.

Indebted farmers found themselves in an increasingly dangerous, even hopeless, position, as competition from abroad increased and crop prices went into a prolonged decline. Tenant farming increased as homesteaders lost their farms when they couldn't make their loan payments. The crisis struck farmers throughout the West and the South, both whites and blacks.

In 1890, a Congregational minister described the plight of the farmer:

> "*The farmers . . . are the bone and sinew of the nation; they produce the largest share of its wealth; but they are getting, they say, the smallest share for themselves. The American farmer is steadily losing ground. His burdens are heavier every year and his gains are more meager.*"
>
> —Washington Gladden

Wheat Prices 1866–1890

Price per bushel: $2.25, $2.00, $1.75, $1.50, $1.25, $1.00, 75¢, 50¢, 25¢, 0

Year: 1866, 1872, 1878, 1884, 1890

SOURCE: *Historical Statistics of the United States, Colonial Times to 1970*

INTERPRETING CHARTS
Farmers often suffered from unpredictable crop prices. **Drawing Conclusions** (a) What might have caused the sharpest price drop? (b) What happened to prices during the Panic of 1873?

The Farmers' Complaint

The American economy rested on shaky ground in the post–Civil War era. Twice, in 1873 and 1893, the collapse of a financially ailing railroad led to a cascading national panic. Banks failed. Businesses—which, like farmers, had also

Section 4

Populism

Section Objectives

1. See why farmers complained about federal post–Civil War economic policies.
2. Find out how the government responded to organized protests by farmers.
3. Discover the Populists' key goals.
4. Understand the main point of William Jennings Bryan's Cross of Gold speech.
5. Learn about the legacy of Populism.

Bellringer

Warm-Up Activity Ask students why merchants and service industries accept paper money or coins in return for goods and services. What gives these items value?

Activating Prior Knowledge In the years following the Civil War the government took steps to ensure the strength of the country's economy. What types of steps does the government take today?

Reading Strategy

Imagine you are a farmer in the late 1800s. List some of the problems you face and identify some of the organizations that promise to help you.

Activity

Connecting with Economics

Ask students to research the ways in which the federal government controls the money supply. Have them locate magazine and newspaper articles that focus on the Federal Reserve Bank's influence in recent times. Tell students to write a short report describing the influence of the Federal Reserve Bank on the economy. **(Logical/Mathematical)**

Caption Answers

Interpreting Charts Sample answer: (a) A sharp drop in demand after the war. (b) Wheat prices dropped sharply.

RESOURCE DIRECTORY

Teaching Resources

Learning Styles Lesson Plans booklet, p. 31
Guided Reading and Review booklet, p. 61

Technology

Section Reading Support Transparencies
Guided Reading Audiotapes (English/Spanish), Ch. 7
Student Edition on Audio CD, Ch. 7
Prentice Hall Presentation Pro CD-ROM, Ch.7
Companion Web site, www.phschool.com

Lesson Plan

Focus Explain that as farmers' incomes declined, they began to join together, many by supporting the Populist Party. Ask students what the farmers' complaints were. What reforms did the Populist Party promise to help them institute?

Instruct Discuss why Americans in the late 1800s were divided over the issue of tariffs. Ask how industrialists profited from tariffs and why farmers ultimately protested against them.

Assess/Reteach As the country expanded, many different groups raised their voices to seek the government's support. One such group was the Populists. Have students list the aims of the Populists. Are there groups today whose interests and main opinions resemble those of the Populists?

Background
Global Connections

As the world has become more complex, and countries more economically dependent on one another, international efforts to balance trade have grown in importance. In 1947, 23 countries signed on to GATT, the General Agreement on Tariffs and Trade. This set of trade agreements, designed to eliminate quotas and reduce tariff duties, played a key role in increasing world trade in the second half of the twentieth century. By 1995, when GATT was replaced by the World Trade Organization (WTO), 125 countries had become signatories to its agreements. GATT's most significant policy was to promote trade without discrimination, which required every member nation to open its markets equally to every other. Under GATT when a nation and its largest trading partners agreed to a tariff reduction, the cut applied to all other GATT members.

READING CHECK
The economic strength of the nation fluctuated wildly after the Civil War. Farm earnings plummeted during hard times while farm loans were being called.

READING CHECK
Why did farmers begin to ask for government help in solving their problems?

over-borrowed—went under. Unemployment soared. During both panics, farmers suffered the double disasters of falling crop prices and loans called in by banks desperate for cash.

Historically, the federal government rarely had intervened to stabilize the nation's economy, nor would most people have expected it to. But in their distress, farmers increasingly began to view government help as a right. In small but rapidly growing numbers, they voiced their demands.

Farmers and Tariffs One federal policy of concern to farmers was tariffs. Tariffs on imported goods discourage people from buying imports by making them more expensive. Thus, tariffs encourage the sale of goods produced at home.

Americans in the late 1800s were divided on the benefit of tariffs. Businesses claimed that tariffs protected American factory jobs—and their own profits. But because tariffs reduced foreign competition, they also encouraged American firms to raise their prices, which harmed workers and consumers in general.

Tariffs helped farmers by protecting them against competition from farm imports. But tariffs hurt farmers in two ways. First, they raised the prices of manufactured goods, such as farm machinery. Second, they kept foreigners from earning the U.S. currency they needed to buy American crops. Thus, tariffs indirectly reduced the world market for American farm products.

Whenever the government raised tariffs to benefit industry, farmers protested. They viewed tariff increases as proof that the government favored eastern manufacturers over western farmers.

The Money Issue Tariffs were not farmers' only concern in the late 1800s. For many, the key issue was the silver supply. The value of money is linked to the **money supply,** the amount of money in the national economy. If the government increases the money supply, the value of every dollar drops. This drop in value shows up as inflation, a widespread rise in prices on goods of all kinds.

People who borrow money benefit from inflation because the money they eventually pay back is worth less than the money they borrowed. Inflation also helps sellers, such as farmers, because it raises the prices of the goods they sell.

In contrast, if the government reduces the money supply, the value of each dollar becomes greater. This causes **deflation,** or a drop in the prices on goods. People who lend money are helped by deflation because the money they receive in payment of a loan is worth more than the money they lent out.

In the years following the Civil War, the nation's money supply shrank as the federal government took out of circulation the paper money issued during the war. As a result, the nation experienced a prolonged period of deflation.

Monetary policy, the federal government's plan for the makeup and quantity of the nation's money supply, thus emerged as a major political issue. Supporters of inflation pushed for an increase in the money supply. Supporters of deflation wanted a "tight money" policy of less currency in circulation.

Gold Bugs In 1873—the year of the worst economic panic in U.S. history to that point—supporters of tight money won a victory. Until that time, United States currency had been on a **bimetallic standard.** That is, currency consisted of gold or silver coins or United States treasury notes that could be traded in for gold or silver. In 1873, in order to prevent inflation and stabilize the economy, Congress put the nation's currency on a gold standard. This move reduced the amount of money

Focus on Economics

Monetary Policy *The federal government's plan for the size of the nation's money supply.*

The Historical Context Farmers in the late 1800s called for an increase in the money supply, which would cause higher prices and thus raise their incomes. Their opponents called for a continued "tight money" policy, in which the money supply is kept low.

The Concept Today The Federal Reserve System, established in 1913, controls the nation's money supply today. Led by its chairman, the "Fed" seeks to promote steady economic growth without causing high inflation.

RESOURCE DIRECTORY
Teaching Resources
Great Debates booklet (Great Debates) *How Should People Treat the Land?* p. 10

in circulation because the money supply was limited by the amount of gold held by the government. Conservative "gold bugs" were pleased. Many of them were big lenders, and they liked the idea of being repaid in currency backed by the gold standard.

Silverites The move to a gold standard enraged "silverites," mostly silver-mining interests and western farmers. They claimed that ending silver as a monetary standard would depress farm prices. Silverites called for **free silver,** the unlimited coining of silver dollars to increase the money supply.

The **Bland-Allison Act** of 1878, was, for the silverites, a step in the right direction. This act required the federal government to purchase and coin more silver, increasing the money supply and causing inflation. Passed by Congress, the Bland-Allison Act was vetoed by President Rutherford B. Hayes because he opposed the inflation it would create. Congress overrode Hayes's veto. Yet the act had only a limited effect, because the Treasury Department refused to buy more than the minimum amount of silver required under the act. The Treasury also refused to circulate the silver dollars that the law required it to mint.

In 1890, Congress passed the **Sherman Silver Purchase Act.** While not authorizing the free and unlimited coinage of silver that the silverites wanted, it increased the amount of silver the government was required to purchase every month. The law required the Treasury to buy the silver with notes that could be redeemed for either silver or gold. That plan backfired, as people turned in their silver Treasury notes for gold dollars, thus depleting the government's gold reserves. To protect the gold supply, President Grover Cleveland oversaw the repeal of the Silver Purchase Act in 1893.

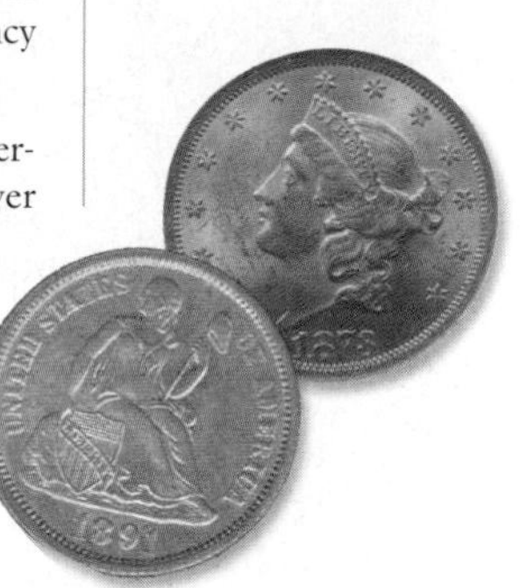

Gold vs. silver: an 1891 silver dime and an 1873 $20 gold coin

COMPARING PRIMARY SOURCES

Gold Bugs *vs.* Silverites

In this famous exchange, one "silverite" proposes the return to a bimetallic standard along with the unlimited coining of silver, while his opponent, a "gold bug," criticizes the proposal.

Analyzing Viewpoints Compare the main arguments made by the two scholars.

In Favor of Free Silver

"Our forefathers showed much wisdom in selecting silver, of the two metals, out of which to make the unit [of currency]. . . . [T]hey were led to adopt silver because it was the most reliable. It was the most favored as money by the people. It was scattered among all the people. . . . Gold was considered the money of the rich. . . . [With the coining of silver,] you increase the value of all property by adding to the number of monetary units in the land. You make it possible for the debtor to pay his debts; business to start anew, and revivify all the industries of the country. . . . The money lenders in the United States, who own substantially all our money, have a selfish interest in maintaining the gold standard."

—*pamphlet by Professor W. H. "Coin" Harvey, of Coin's Financial School, 1894*

Opposed to Free Silver

"Do you suppose that the farmers of this country really believe that with each ton of silver taken out of the mines by the silver law-makers in the Senate that there are created bushels of wheat[?] . . . Free coinage of silver then is absolutely certain to drive all our gold out of circulation. . . . [Hence] there will be no increase in the quantity of money. . . . The only way it would act would be by increasing the price of everything. . . . A dozen eggs, now selling at 15 cents, would sell for about 30 cents. . . . As [it] would inevitably result in a rise of prices it would immediately result in the fall of wages. . . . Are we willing to sacrifice the interests of the laboring classes to the demands of certain owners of silver mines . . . ?"

—*University of Chicago economist James Laurence Laughlin, in a public debate with "Coin" Harvey, 1895*

ACTIVITY Connecting with Economics

Have students debate the money issue. One team argues in favor of free silver, while the other team advocates on behalf of the gold standard. Have students prepare for the debate by listing various points that strengthen their position and weaken the opposition's. After the debate discuss which side was more persuasive. **(Verbal/Linguistic)**

BACKGROUND Global Connections

For many centuries, silver has been a major part of the monetary systems of most cultures. Because of its softness and malleability, silver is used for nearly all metalworking techniques, including casting, embossing, engraving, inlaying, and enameling. In ancient Rome silver was used to make plates, household utensils, and ornamental pieces; and during the Middle Ages, Europeans preferred silver to gold for metal artwork. Silverwork was especially popular among Renaissance artisans.

ACTIVITY

Connecting with Citizenship

To help students understand the role of organizations such as the Grange, divide them into at least two groups. Tell members of one group to role-play reporters from an eastern newspaper in 1870. Tell the other members to role-play Grange members. Pair reporters and Grangers and have them conduct interviews. **(Verbal/Linguistic)**

BACKGROUND

Connections to Today

At the height of its success, in the mid-1870s, the Grange had a national membership of nearly 800,000. These days, the Grange consists of more than 3,000 local Granges in more than 30 states. The local Granges hold frequent meetings, where members discuss issues of community concern. The National Grange has its own office building in Washington, D.C., a couple of blocks from the White House. The Grange has always been involved in legislative action. Its primary concerns include rural quality of life issues, farm programs, rural economic development, environmental issues, and taxation.

VIEWING HISTORY A teacher who farmed, studied law, and raised a family, Mary Elizabeth Lease (above) became a leading speaker and educator for Farmers' Alliance groups. The illustration below is from a book of Farmer's Alliance songs. **Drawing Inferences** *Why do you think education and a spirit of unity were key goals of these groups?*

Organizing Farmer Protests

Because farmers lived far from one another and usually relied on their own efforts, they tended not to organize protests against policies they opposed. In the late 1800s, however, farmers took advantage of improvements in communication and transportation to form several powerful protest groups.

The Grange In 1866, the Department of Agriculture sent Oliver H. Kelley on an inspection tour of southern farms. Disturbed by the farmers' isolation, the following year he founded the Patrons of Husbandry, or **the Grange.**

The Grange soon began helping farmers form cooperatives, through which they bought goods in large quantities at lower prices. The Grange also pressured state legislators to regulate businesses on which farmers depended, such as the operators of grain elevators that stored farmers' crops and the railroads that shipped goods to market.

Farmers' Alliances Although the Grange was popular (and still exists today), eventually farmers formed other political groups. In the 1880s, many farmers joined a network of Farmers' Alliances that were formed around the nation. The alliances launched harsh attacks on monopolies, such as those that controlled the railroads.

The Farmers' Alliance in the South, formed in Texas in the mid-1870s, grew especially powerful. It called for actions that many of the nation's farmers could support: federal regulation of the railroads, more money in circulation, creation of state departments of agriculture, antitrust laws, and farm credit.

Farmers' Alliances held special importance for women, who served as officers and won support for women's political rights. One of the most popular speakers was Kansas lawyer Mary Elizabeth Lease, who reportedly urged farmers to raise "less corn and more Hell!" African Americans worked through a separate but parallel "Colored Farmers' Alliance." Formed in 1886 in Lovelady, Texas, the group had a quarter of a million members by 1891.

A series of natural disasters gave special urgency to Farmers' Alliance programs. The Mississippi River flooded in 1882. In 1886 and 1887, Texas suffered a 21-month drought. Terrible blizzards, which killed thousands of cattle, struck the West in 1887. Increasingly, farmers wanted to know why the federal government was unwilling to respond to these disasters.

Government Responses Political power and influence were splintered during this period. Farmers often differed on how much federal help was needed, if any. On the other hand, business interests were not always strong enough to prevent legislation they disliked from becoming law. As one historian put it, "Big business was powerful; it was by no means all-powerful."

Meanwhile, fragmented political parties had difficulty rallying support for controversial proposals among their members in various regions of the country as well as among different economic and ethnic groups. In every election from 1880 to

CAPTION ANSWERS

Viewing History Sample answer: Education about issues important to farmers was helpful because information traveled slowly among the scattered farms. Unity among farmers created political power, provided support, and eased the isolation of farm families.

RESOURCE DIRECTORY

Other Print Resources

American History Block Scheduling Support *Farmers Unite: The Populist Party,* found in the Expansion, Reconstruction, and Immigration folder, includes interdisciplinary lesson suggestions and activities for Geography and History, Primary Sources, Biography, and Literature.

Technology

RESOURCE PRO® **Biography** *Mary Elizabeth Lease,* found on Resource Pro, profiles the crusader for the Farmers' Alliances and the Populist party.

RESOURCE PRO® **Visual Learning Activity** *The Farmer's Complaint,* found on Resource Pro, uses an 1875 poster to illustrate the plight of the American farmer.

1892, no candidate won a majority of the popular vote. Only rarely did the President's party command a majority in Congress. Presidents thus lacked the power to take bold action. In addition, some Presidents were influenced by promises of support from powerful business interests.

In 1887, Congress passed the Texas seed bill, which provided seed grain to drought victims. But President Cleveland, a Democrat, vetoed the bill, expressing the commonly held view that "though the people support the government, the government should not support the people."

On the issue of railroad regulation, some consensus emerged. Even some railroad owners backed moderate regulations, fearing more drastic measures. In 1887, Cleveland signed the **Interstate Commerce Act.** It regulated the prices that railroads charged to move freight between states, requiring the rates to be set in proportion to the distance traveled. The law also made it illegal to give special rates to some customers. While the act did not control the monopolistic railroad practices that angered farmers, it established the principle that Congress could regulate the railroads, a significant expansion of federal authority. The act also set up the Interstate Commerce Commission (ICC) to enforce the laws.

In 1890, President Benjamin Harrison approved the Sherman Antitrust Act. This act was meant to curb the power of trusts and monopolies. But during its first decade, enforcement was lax.

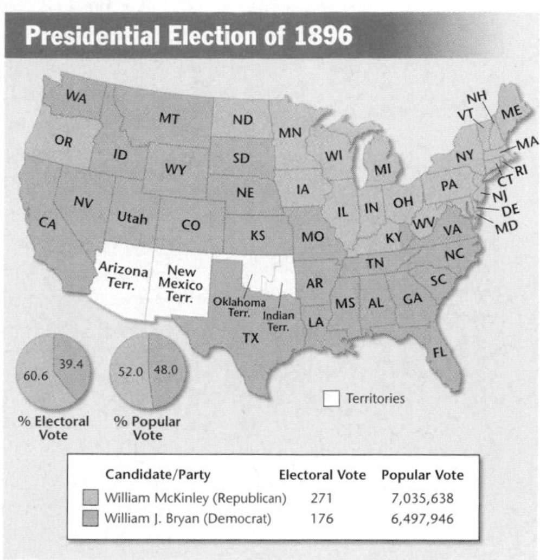

Candidate/Party	Electoral Vote	Popular Vote
William McKinley (Republican)	271	7,035,638
William J. Bryan (Democrat)	176	6,497,946

MAP SKILLS William Jennings Bryan was the candidate of the Democrats and the Populists in 1896. As the map shows, he won most of the western and southern states and nearly half the popular vote, yet he lost the election.
Analyzing Visual Information *Explain the reasons for Bryan's defeat.*

The Populists

In 1890, the various small political parties associated with the Farmers' Alliances began to enjoy success at the ballot box, especially in the South. In 1891, the Alliances founded the People's Party, a new national party that demanded radical changes in federal economic and social policies. The **Populists,** as followers of the new party were known, built their platform around the following issues:

1. An increased circulation of money.
2. The unlimited minting of silver.
3. A progressive income tax, in which the percentage of taxes owed increases with a rise in income. This tax would place a greater financial burden on wealthy industrialists and a lesser one on farmers.
4. Government ownership of communications and transportation systems.

Seeking the support of urban industrial workers, the Populists endorsed an eight-hour work day. For the same reason, they opposed the use of Pinkertons, the private police force that had been involved in the bloody Homestead Strike of 1892, as strikebreakers. Breaking through deeply rooted racial prejudice, Populists sought a united front of African American and white farmers. The poor of both races had a common cause, they argued. "You are kept apart that you may be separately fleeced of your earnings," said one party leader. The party drew some black sharecroppers and tenant farmers away from the Republican Party.

During the 1892 campaign, populism generated great excitement among its followers. But the party's presidential candidate, Iowan James B. Weaver, won barely a million votes. Cleveland returned to the presidency.

ACTIVITY
Connecting with Government

Tell students to research recent presidencies to find out whether the administration in power corresponded with a party majority in Congress. Have students look into the benefits a President has when his party has a majority in Congress. Tell students also to find out how a President's efforts can be stymied when the opposition party is in the majority. As students discuss recent presidencies, have them cite specific examples of both situations. **(Verbal/Linguistic)**

From the Archives of
AmericanHeritage®
About the Presidents

William McKinley (1897–1901) enjoyed a big advantage over William Jennings Bryan in his first election, which was a well-financed campaign. Businessman Marcus A. Hanna raised millions of dollars on McKinley's behalf. McKinley's campaign chest paid for pamphlets, posters, and buttons, as well as train fare for those wishing to visit McKinley in his home town of Canton, Ohio. On one day alone McKinley spoke to some 30,000 visitors. By contrast, Bryan's campaign had little money. Although Bryan crossed the country with his "silverite" message, warning that wealthy eastern financial interests should not be allowed to "crucify" ordinary working Americans "upon a cross of gold," McKinley beat Bryan with a comfortable electoral margin. Source: Donald Young, "William McKinley," *The American Heritage® Pictorial History of the Presidents of the United States,* vol. 2, 1968.

CUSTOMIZE FOR ...
Less Proficient Readers

Ask students to make a chart with two headings: *The Farmers* and *The Populists.* On one side students should list the complaints of farmers in 1896 about the money supply, the transportation system, and the disparity between the incomes of the rich and the poor. On the other side, they should list the promises of the Populist Party that addressed those complaints.

TEST PREPARATION

Have students reread the quote from President Cleveland on this page. Then have them answer the question below.

Which sentence below most closely paraphrases the quote from President Cleveland?

A The government is responsible for providing goods and services to citizens.
B The government and the people do not have a connection.
(C) The government should not be responsible for providing its people a living or food.
D The government exists for the people's good.

CAPTION ANSWERS

Map Skills Bryan failed to capture many of the most populous urbanized states in the East and Midwest, which had more electoral votes. Elections are determined by the electoral count, not by the popular vote.

VIEWING HISTORY This cartoon shows William Jennings Bryan holding a crown of thorns and a cross of gold, biblical images that he used in his famous speech. **Analyzing Visual Information** *Does this cartoon present Bryan in a positive or a negative light?*

Bryan's "Cross of Gold"

Populists renewed their vigor in the 1896 presidential campaign. In an election that focused mainly on currency issues, the Republicans ran moderate Ohio governor William McKinley on a gold-standard platform. William Jennings Bryan, a former silverite congressman from Nebraska and a powerful speaker, captured the Democratic nomination with an emotional plea for free silver.

Bryan addressed the 1896 Democratic Convention in Chicago on July 8, at the close of the debate over the party platform. Using images from the Bible, he stood with head bowed and arms outstretched and cried out at the climax of his speech, "You shall not press down upon the brow of labor this crown of thorns. You shall not crucify mankind upon a cross of gold!" So stunning was Bryan's speech that both the Democrats and the Populists nominated him for President. The **Cross of Gold speech** is one of the most famous in American history.

The 1896 campaign was one of marked contrasts. Bryan created a whirlwind of activity, traveling all over the country and making speeches at every stop. McKinley ran a more traditional campaign. He remained in his hometown of Canton, Ohio, greeting visitors and making a few speeches from his front porch.

Despite his best efforts, Bryan lost the election. He carried the Democratic West and South but none of the urban and industrial midwestern and northern states. In these states, factory workers feared that free silver might cause inflation, which would eat away the buying power of their wages. Thus, despite populism's broad appeal, it could not bridge the gap between America's cities and farms. Nor could populism slow America's transition from an agricultural nation to an industrial nation.

Populism's Legacy

By 1897, McKinley's administration had raised the tariff to new heights. In 1900, after gold discoveries in South Africa, the Canadian Yukon, and Alaska had increased the world's gold supply by more than $100 million, Congress returned the nation to a gold standard. To the surprise of many farmers, crop prices began a slow rise. The silver movement died, as did populism.

The goals of populism, however, lived on. In the decades ahead, other reformers, known as Progressives, applied populist ideas to urban and industrial problems. In so doing, they launched a new, historic era of reforms.

Section 4 Assessment

READING COMPREHENSION

1. What changes in economic policy did many farmers seek?
2. Explain the difference between a gold standard, a **bimetallic standard,** and **free silver.**
3. What did the government do to address farmers' complaints?
4. To whom did Bryan's **Cross of Gold speech** appeal, and why?

CRITICAL THINKING AND WRITING

5. **Drawing Conclusions** Few strong third parties such as the Populists have arisen in the nation's history. What caused the Populist Party to enjoy relative success in its time?
6. **Writing an Outline** Set up an outline for an analysis of the gold-versus-silver debate. Include facts on the currency plans put forward and who favored and opposed them.

Take It to the NET

Activity: Creating a Fact Sheet
Write a fact sheet comparing the Grange's early activities with its modern-day ones. Browse the Web site of the National Grange by using the link provided at the *America: Pathways to the Present* area of the following Web site for help in completing this activity.
www.phschool.com

Section 4 Assessment

Reading Comprehension

1. Increase in money supply, free silver, higher tariffs, regulation of rates charged by railroads and grain elevators.
2. Gold standard: limited the money supply to match the gold held by the government. Bimetallic standard: gold or silver coins or treasury notes that could be traded for gold or silver. Free silver: unlimited coining of silver dollars to increase the money supply.
3. The Bland-Allison Act put more silver into circulation and was inflationary. The Sherman Silver Purchase Act increased the government's silver supply but caused a depletion of its gold reserves. The Interstate Commerce Act made interstate rail shipping prices equitable.
4. It appealed to many Democrats, especially in the West and South, as well as many Populists, farmers, and other silverites. They applauded its support of free silver and the preservation of farming.

Critical Thinking and Writing

5. Political parties were fractured, leaving an opening for a new party. Populism appealed to diverse groups, including rural voters. Populism also drew on existing organizations like the Grange and the Farmers' Alliance.
6. Answers will vary, but might focus on inflation and deflation, or on the transformation of the United States from an agricultural into an industrial nation.

Take It to the NET

Fact sheets should compare the Grange's early activities, such as helping farmers form unions, with its modern-day activities of providing support to families involved in agriculture, as well as its involvement in broader environmental and conservation issues.

Caption Answers

Viewing History The cartoon portrays him in a negative light, suggesting that he is using the symbols of Christianity—the cross, the crown of thorns, and the Bible—to further his political career.

RESOURCE DIRECTORY

Teaching Resources

Units 1/2 booklet
- Section 4 Quiz, p. 75
- Chapter 7 Test, pp. 76, 79

Guide to the Essentials
- Section 4 Summary, p. 36
- Chapter 7 Test, p. 37

Learning with Documents booklet (Key Documents) *William Jennings Bryan, Cross of Gold Speech,* p. 83

Other Print Resources

Chapter Tests with ExamView® Test Bank CD-ROM, Ch. 7

Technology

Color Transparencies *Political Cartoons,* B8
Sounds of an Era Audio CD *"Cross of Gold"* (time: 40 seconds)
ExamView® Test Bank CD-ROM, Ch. 7
Social Studies Skills Tutor CD-ROM

Expressing Problems Clearly

Expressing a problem clearly is the first step toward understanding and solving it. Problems often arise out of situations that have many elements; this makes them complex or puzzling. Other problems are difficult because there are clearly several possible solutions; this makes these problems open to debate. The ability to express a problem clearly means being able to describe a complex situation or body of information so that possible solutions can be evaluated, and the problem can be solved.

In 1877, the United States was in the midst of a depression. On July 14, the Baltimore and Ohio Railroad announced a 10 percent wage cut. The passage below is from an editorial, "The Railroad Strike," which appeared in a business journal.

LEARN THE SKILL

Use the following steps to express problems clearly:

1. **Analyze the information.** Identify the difficulties faced by the persons or groups involved. Consider what led to the problem, including the historical context. Be aware of the point of view of those who are describing the problem.
2. **Identify the basic concepts involved.** Problems usually arise out of a specific set of circumstances. However, they often revolve around a general principle, such as fairness. To identify this concept, try to express the problem in terms of what each side wants for itself.
3. **Identify the function of the supporting details.** Note details that are not basic to the problem. Eliminating them from consideration can help you see the problem more clearly.
4. **Express the problem as simply and completely as possible.** Once you have identified the main area of dispute and have stripped away irrelevant details, you are ready to express the problem clearly.

PRACTICE THE SKILL

Answer the following questions:

1. **(a)** What difficulty were the railroad companies facing? What actions did they take? **(b)** What difficulty were the workers facing? What action did they take? **(c)** Who else may have been affected by the problem? Why? **(d)** How does the historical context affect this situation? **(e)** What is the point of view of the writer of this editorial?
2. **(a)** Explain what each party wants for itself. **(b)** Do you think the writer is interested in fairness, or unfairly favors one side? Explain.
3. **(a)** Is the detail that the Baltimore & Ohio Company is paying 10 percent to its stockholders important to understanding the problem? Explain. **(b)** Are there any details in this excerpt that are irrelevant to the problem? Explain.
4. **(a)** Describe the problem caused by the railroad strike. **(b)** Evaluate the editorial's proposed solution. **(c)** What other solutions might be possible?

"The present strike among the employees of most of our principal railroad lines, is an illustration of errors in judgment . . . committed by the employers as well as by the employees of the railroad companies. None can deny, as a fundamental principle, the absolute necessity of . . . 'making both ends meet.' This principle is as applicable to every line of business, whether small or large, as to every family, whether poor or rich. Now, the railroad companies, in order to make ends meet, had the choice of three different means: 1st, to pay less dividends to the stockholders, in case dividends are paid; 2d, to raise the rates of freight; 3d, to reduce expenses. . . .

Of these three ways to make ends meet, the railroad companies, or rather those who are supposed to have sound judgment enough to be entrusted with their management . . . chose the latter means; and this was unjust to the employees and unfortunate for the stockholders, and especially unfortunate for the community at large, which is highly interested in reliable railroad transportation. . . .

It should not be lost sight of that the railroad on which the strike began (the Baltimore & Ohio) has been paying, and has thus far continued to pay, 10 per cent dividends to its stockholders. We ask if it would not be more just all around to pay only 8 or 9, or even 6 or 7 per cent dividend, and thus, instead of reducing the already too scanty wages of their employees, enable the railroad company to increase their pay. They forget that the interest on the capital invested must be earned by the men they employ, without whom they could not earn anything. . . ."

—*The Manufacturer and Builder*, August 1877

APPLY THE SKILL

See the Chapter Review and Assessment for another opportunity to apply this skill.

RESOURCE DIRECTORY

Teaching Resources

Skills for Life booklet, p. 16

Technology

Social Studies Skills Tutor CD-ROM

Interactive Practice in
- Geographic Literacy
- Critical Thinking and Reading
- Visual Analysis
- Communications

Expressing Problems Clearly

Focus Students clearly express the dispute between railroad companies and their workers.

Instruct Have students write the following headings on a piece of paper: *Employees* and *Employers.* As they read the passage, have them list aspects of it that apply to each side in the dispute. Have them use this chart to organize information for the "Learn the Skill" activities. For more practice, have students bring in and analyze editorials from current newspapers.

Extend See the Skills for Life activity in the Resource Directory below.

ANSWERS

Practice the Skill

1. **(a)** They were having trouble making ends meet. Railroad management reduced expenses. **(b)** Their pay was reduced. They went out on strike. **(c)** People who use the railroad, because they rely on it to be dependable. **(d)** The nationwide depression contributed to the railroad's financial problems. **(e)** That it would be better to reduce the dividends than to cut workers' salaries.
2. **(a)** The railroad wants to remain profitable; the workers want to continue to earn the same amount of money. **(b)** More sympathetic to the workers, though he suggests a compromise, asking the railroads to consider lower dividends. He suggests this will benefit workers, patrons, and, ultimately, the railroad.
3. **(a)** Yes. This is a figure that the editorial writer thinks could be lowered to solve the problem. **(b)** Every family must make ends meet. The problem does not deal with family finances.
4. **(a)** Service to patrons is disrupted, workers earn no wages, and the railroad loses money. **(b)** The solution seems fair, but it might be difficult to get the stockholders to accept it. **(c)** Some possibilities include raising rates of freight, improving operating efficiency, combining routes, or closing underused stations.

Chapter 7

Reviewing Key Terms

Students should refer to the definitions of key terms in the chapter to write sentences that show an understanding of the era of westward expansion.

Reviewing Main Ideas

11. Pacific Railway Acts opened the West. Morrill Land Grant Act allowed states to sell western lands. Homestead Act sold land cheaply, luring settlers. Congress in the 1880s began to open Native American lands to white settlers.
12. Treaties lacked clarity and often were administered fraudulently. White settlers complicated the situation. Western army units were undermanned.
13. Capital, sophisticated equipment, and large firms were necessary to extract deep gold and silver deposits. Ranching grew after 1865 due to large herds of cattle, disappearance of buffalo, and expulsion of Native Americans from open lands. New devices and techniques made large farms possible.
14. They brought diversity of religion, education, and work ethics.
15. Gold standard: conservatives, lenders. Free silver: silver miners, western farmers.
16. Populism had wide appeal, other parties fractured. Goals: increase circulation; free silver; government ownership of some vital industries; eight-hour workday; progressive income tax.
17. Issue: currency. Players: Republican William McKinley on a gold-standard platform; Democrat William Jennings Bryan, a silverite. Outcome: McKinley wins election; Bryan strong in West and South.
18. Answers may refer to: stereotypes, characters in dime novels, Wild West shows.

Critical Thinking

19. Settlers wanted to farm the land. Native Americans co-existed with the land. Settlers tried to force their priorities on Native Americans, often leading to conflict.

Chapter 7

Review and Assessment

creating a CHAPTER SUMMARY

Copy this chart (right) on a piece of paper and complete it by adding information about major influences on western development. Some entries have been completed for you as examples.

For additional review and enrichment activities, see the interactive version of *America: Pathways to the Present*, available on the Web and on CD-ROM.

Forces That Shaped the West

Cause(s)	Event	Effect(s)
Gold and silver strikes in California and the western interior	Mining rushes	
	Ranching	
	Homesteading	Immigrants populate the West.
	Indian wars	
	Populism	

★ Reviewing Key Terms

For each of the terms below, write a sentence explaining how it relates to the period of frontier development in the West.

1. Pacific Railway Acts
2. Exoduster
3. reservation
4. Battle of Little Bighorn
5. long drive
6. soddie
7. bonanza farm
8. free silver
9. the Grange
10. Interstate Commerce Act

★ Reviewing Main Ideas

11. Describe four ways that the federal government encouraged the settlement of the West. (Section 1)
12. Why did it take decades for the government to bring the Indian wars to an end? (Section 2)
13. How did large mining, ranching, and farming industries evolve in the West? (Section 3)
14. How did the arrival of American and immigrant settlers change the culture of the West? (Section 3)
15. Which groups supported the gold standard, and which favored free silver? (Section 4)
16. Why did Populism take hold in the late 1800s, and what were its main goals? (Section 4)
17. Identify the key issues, the key players, and the outcome of the 1896 presidential election. (Section 4)
18. Describe the origins of some of the frontier myths around the turn of the century. (Section 4)

★ Critical Thinking

19. **Recognizing Ideologies** Analyze the beliefs of settlers and Native Americans that brought them into conflict.
20. **Drawing Conclusions** Evaluate the impact of the federal government's policy of assimilation of Native Americans in the late 1800s.
21. **Synthesizing Information** Explain the roles played by the following people in the development of the West: (a) Lieutenant Colonel George Armstrong Custer; (b) Chief Joseph of the Nez Percé; (c) Native American sympathist writer Helen Hunt Jackson; (d) cattle baron Charles Goodnight.
22. **Testing Conclusions** Give evidence to support these statements: (a) Private property rights encouraged the settlement of the West. (b) Homesteaders caused the spread of traditional values such as democracy and a strong work ethic.
23. **Recognizing Cause and Effect** Analyze the effects of the federal government's monetary policies, such as tariffs and the gold standard, on the following groups: (a) farmers; (b) businesses and banks.

Creating a Chapter Summary

Forces That Shaped the West

Cause(s)	Event	Effect(s)
Gold and silver strikes in California and the western interior	Mining rushes	Fortune hunters on their way to California find rich mineral strikes in other areas, too.
Increased supply *and* demand for beef after Civil War	Ranching	A cattle boom
Government incentives	Homesteading	Immigrants populate the West.
Usurpation of Native American land and resources by settlers	Indian wars	Annihilation of majority of Indian population
Farmers heavily in debt, facing stiff foreign competition and collapsing prices	Populism	Though eventually defeated, the movement gave voice to many for the first time and later gave rise to other movements.

★ Skills Assessment

Analyzing Political Cartoons ▶

24. This hot-air balloon holds aloft several Populist figures. (a) How do you know these men are Populists? (b) What is the balloon made of, and what do its components suggest?
25. What is the message of the words on the basket, "Platform of Lunacy"?
26. Analyze the elements of this cartoon and state the cartoonist's main message.

A PARTY OF PATCHES.
Grand Balloon Ascension—Cincinnati, May 20th, 1891.

Analyzing Primary Sources

Reread the two quotations in Comparing Primary Sources in Section 4, and then answer the questions that follow.

27. What is Professor Harvey's main reason for supporting free silver?
    - **A** Gold was considered the money of the rich.
    - **B** The Founding Fathers selected silver as the preferred coinage, and the people preferred it.
    - **C** Silver is a more reliable type of currency than gold.
    - **D** Coining silver would put more money in circulation, enabling debtors to clear their debts.
28. According to Laughlin, who would be harmed by the coinage of free silver?
    - **F** miners, farmers, and consumers
    - **G** consumers and silver lawmakers
    - **H** laborers, farmers, and consumers
    - **J** mine owners and pro-silver Senators

Applying the Chapter Skill: *Expressing Problems Clearly*

Review the skill on page 283. Then refer to Section 2 to write a paragraph that addresses these questions:

29. What was the central conflict between Native American groups and the United States, and how did their goals differ?
30. (a) What attempts were made to resolve the conflict, and what circumstances usually caused the efforts to fail? (b) What other solutions to the conflict could have been pursued?

ACTIVITIES

Writing to LEARN

Writing to Narrate
From what you have read in this chapter about the settlement of the West, create your own mythical frontier story. Choose for your hero a man or a woman who is one of these characters: a homesteader, a Native American, a cattle rancher, an army officer, or a miner. Use realistic details to demonstrate your understanding of life during that time. Also draw on what you have read about popular western stereotypes to make your hero larger than life.

Primary Source CD-ROM

Working With Primary Sources Find additional information on settlers in the West on the *Exploring Primary Sources in U.S. History CD-ROM* and use the selection(s) provided to complete the Chapter 7 primary source activity located in the *America: Pathways to the Present* area of the following Web site.
www.phschool.com

Take It to the NET

Chapter Self-Test As a review activity, take the Chapter 7 Self-Test in the *America: Pathways to the Present* area at the Web site listed below. The questions are designed to test your understanding of the chapter content.
www.phschool.com

20. Possible answers: the heavy-handed and arrogant nature of government assimilation efforts limited their effectiveness; cultural differences made assimilation impossible.
21. (a) Army moves vigorously against Sioux after Custer and troops were killed; (b) Chief Joseph and his people symbolize pain and upheaval experienced by Native Americans who were moved to reservations; (c) Jackson's writings publicize plight of Native Americans; (d) Charles Goodnight helped create booming cattle business in Texas.
22. (a) Private property rights allowed people to safely buy and settle western property; (b) Traditional values did move west with immigrant homesteaders, particularly German and Scandinavian Lutherans.
23. (a) Farmers: high tariffs bad, expenses rise, foreign markets close; gold standard bad, reduces farm income, tightens credit. (b) Business and banks: high tariffs good, industrial prices rise; gold standard good, makes lending profitable.

SKILLS ASSESSMENT

24. (a) "The People's Party" was the Populist Party. (b) A frail patchwork of Populist groups and causes, suggesting instability and division.
25. That Populists support crazy ideas.
26. Populists are full of hot air, expounding a patchwork of unrelated, unrealistic ideas.
27. C
28. H
29. The U.S. government wanted to mine, ranch, and farm Native American land.
30. (a) The government negotiated treaties but offered little in return for the purchase of the land or restricted the Native Americans. The government often did not honor the treaties or protect the reservations, and Native American groups who disagreed with the treaties refused to obey them. (b) Answers will vary.

ANSWERS TO ACTIVITIES

Writing to LEARN

Stories will vary but should include specific details from the chapter.

Primary Source CD-ROM

Direct students to the additional primary sources that can be found on the *Exploring Primary Sources in U.S. History CD-ROM.*

Take It to the NET

Additional support materials and activities for Chapter 7 of *America: Pathways to the Present* can be found in the Social Studies area at the Prentice Hall School Web site. **www.phschool.com**

Settling the Great Plains

Focus Explain that the two main groups that arrived on the Great Plains and drove off the Native Americans were ranchers and farmers. Ranchers and farmers had different needs and fought for control of the grasslands until the farmers finally won out.

Instruct Divide the class into two groups: farmers and ranchers. Ask the farmers to suppose that they are new settlers on an unplowed homestead on the Great Plains. Ask them to list their minimum needs (tools, seeds, etc.) for creating a successful farm on the plains. Ask the ranchers to suppose that they are starting a ranch in northern Texas after the Civil War. What are their minimum needs for creating a successful ranch? After students have completed their lists, determine which needs bring the two groups into conflict.

Discuss with students how the coming of railroads affected this process. What was the impact of railroads on farmers? How did the railroads impact ranchers?

Extend Ask students to find out about the other group that entered into the conflict over the use of the Great Plains: the sheepherders. Why did ranchers oppose the sheepherders?

Settling the Great Plains

Native Americans once hunted buffalo on the Great Plains and farmed its river valleys. By the 1860s, especially in Texas, cattle ranchers had taken over the open ranges of the Plains. That all changed with the expansion of railroads and the invention of barbed wire.

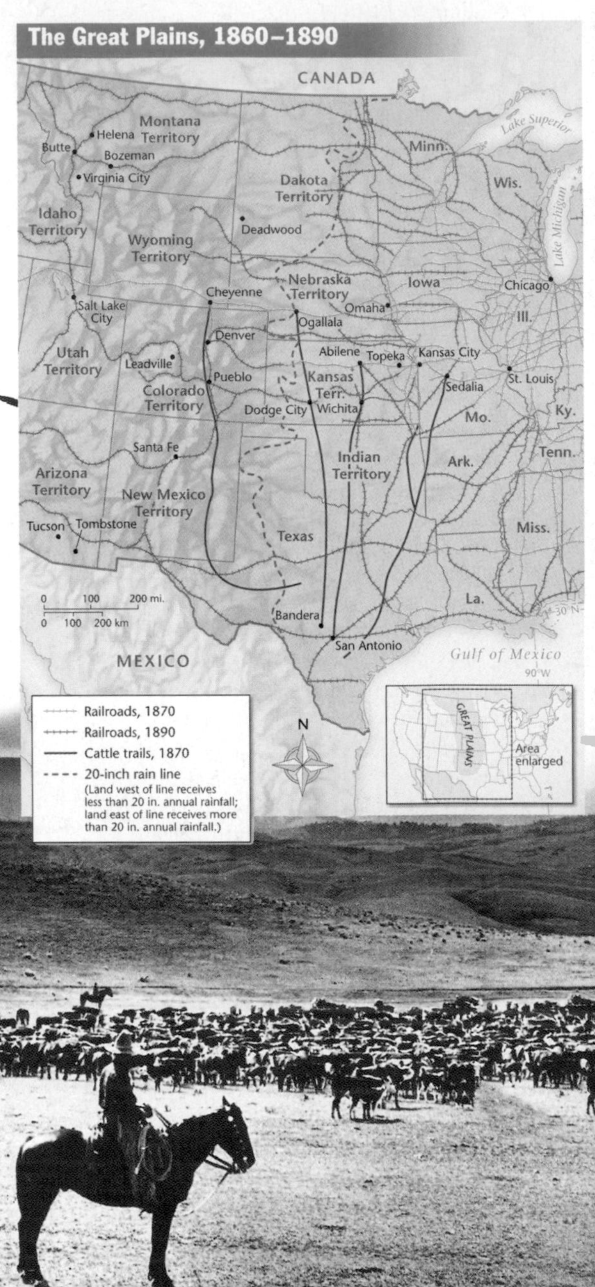

Transformation of the Plains

In 1870, no railroads crossed the Texas plains. Ranchers drove their cattle over long trails to railroad towns in Kansas and Colorado. This was the heyday of the open range. As railroads expanded, though, farmers settled in areas of higher rainfall and put up barbed-wire fences to keep cattle off their land. Ranchers sometimes responded violently, but the government stood by the farmers. By 1890, railroads crisscrossed the Plains, and ranchers were forced to retreat to their own fenced ranges.

Geographic Connection

Why might farmers prefer areas with more rain?

Answers

1. Basically, because plants need water in order to grow. More specifically, many crops have a minimum requirement for water that can be supplied most economically (without relying on irrigation) if rainfall is adequate. Also, crop yields tend to be higher when rainfall is greater.

RESOURCE DIRECTORY

Teaching Resources
Geography and History booklet, pp. 10–11

Other Print Resources
Nystrom *Atlas of Our Country* *Settling the West,* pp. 28–29

Technology
Prentice Hall United States History Video Collection™ Volume 11, *Industrialization and Urbanization*

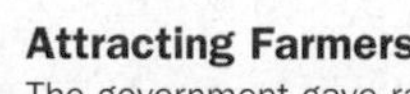

Attracting Farmers

The government gave railroads generous land grants for building lines across unsettled country on the Great Plains and in other parts of the country. Railroads such as the Hannibal and St. Joseph could cover expenses—and win future customers—by recruiting farmers to purchase and settle their land, as advertised in glowing posters like the one shown here.

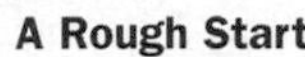

A Rough Start

The first settlers on the Plains lacked wood for building houses and had to build "soddies," or houses made of sod, which consists of dirt and grass. They also had to contend with hostile, gun-slinging cattlemen, whose herds trampled their crops until the farmers could build barbed-wire fences.

The Nation's Breadbasket

Early explorers had called the treeless Great Plains the "Great American Desert," fit only for buffalo and cattle herds. However, farmers proved them wrong and made the region one of the world's most productive grain belts. This poster contrasts the reputation of Kansas as "drouthy" (or drought-prone) with images of abundant rainfall and crops.

Geographic Connection
How did the physical and human geography of the Great Plains allow farmers to displace ranchers?

287

Answers

2. The availability of adequate rainfall allowed farmers to settle large areas of the Plains. The construction of railroads gave farmers access to the market and gave the railroads an incentive to attract farmers to settle the land. Government control over western land distribution allowed the government to protect farmers' land.

Chapter 8 Planning Guide
Resource Manager

	CORE INSTRUCTION	READING/SKILLS
Chapter-Level Resources **TEKS** 1(A), 24(B), 25(A)	Teaching Resources • Pacing Charts booklet • Block Scheduling booklet **Resource Pro® CD-ROM,** Ch. 8 **Prentice Hall Presentation Pro CD-ROM,** Ch. 8 **www.phschool.com** • eTeach	**Guided Reading Audiotapes (English/Spanish)** **Student Edition on Audio CD,** Ch. 8 **Social Studies Skills Tutor CD-ROM** **Color Transparencies,** A58, E14, G9, G10
1 Politics in the Gilded Age 1. Find out how business influenced politics during the Gilded Age. 2. Learn the ways in which government reformed the spoils system and regulated railroads. 3. Discover the effect the transition from depression to prosperity had on politics in the 1890s. **TEKS** 2(A), 12(B), 23(A)	Teaching Resources **Units 1/2 booklet** • Section 1 Quiz, p. 83 **Learning Styles Lesson Plans booklet,** p. 32	**Guided Reading and Review booklet,** p. 62 **Guide to the Essentials,** p. 38 **Section Reading Support Transparencies**
2 People on the Move 1. Share the experiences of immigrants in the late 1800s and early 1900s. 2. Analyze the different challenges faced by immigrants from Europe, Asia, and Mexico. **TEKS** 2(C), 5(A), 10(B), 11(A)	Teaching Resources **Units 1/2 booklet** • Section 2 Quiz, p. 84 **Learning Styles Lesson Plans booklet,** p. 33	**Guided Reading and Review booklet,** p. 63 **Guide to the Essentials,** p. 39 **Learning with Documents booklet,** p. 54 **Section Reading Support Transparencies**
3 The Challenge of the Cities 1. Find out why cities expanded in the late 1800s and early 1900s. 2. Review new developments that helped cities grow. 3. Learn how living conditions in cities changed. 4. State the results of city growth. **TEKS** 2(A), 2(C), 10(A), 11(A)	Teaching Resources **Units 1/2 booklet** • Section 3 Quiz, p. 85	**Guided Reading and Review booklet,** p. 64 **Guide to the Essentials,** p. 40 **Learning with Documents booklet,** p. 20 **Skills for Life booklet,** p. 10 **Section Reading Support Transparencies**
4 Ideas for Reform 1. Study the ways in which different movements helped the needy. 2. Learn how and where sociology developed. 3. Examine efforts to control immigration and personal behavior in the late 1800s. **TEKS** 2(C), 10(B), 21(D)	Teaching Resources **Units 1/2 booklet** • Section 4 Quiz, p. 86	**Guided Reading and Review booklet,** p. 65 **Guide to the Essentials,** p. 41 **Section Reading Support Transparencies**

Enrichment/Pre-AP

Prentice Hall United States History Video Collection™
www.phschool.com
- Section Activities, Virtual Field Trip, Chapter Activities, Current Events Online

American History Block Scheduling Support
Sounds of an Era Audio CD

Biography, Literature, and Comparing Primary Sources booklet, pp. 61, 125
American History Block Scheduling Support
Nystrom *Atlas of Our Country,* pp. 30–31
Sounds of an Era Audio CD
Exploring Primary Sources in U.S. History CD-ROM

Biography, Literature, and Comparing Primary Sources booklet, p. 20
American History Block Scheduling Support
Sounds of an Era Audio CD

American History Block Scheduling Support
Nystrom *Atlas of Our Country,* pp. 30–31
Exploring Primary Sources in U.S. History CD-ROM
American Pathways Thematic Posters

Assessment

Core Assessment
ExamView® Test Bank, Ch. 8
ExamView® Test Bank CD-ROM, Ch. 8

Standardized Test Preparation
Diagnose and Prescribe
Diagnostic Tests for High School Social Studies Skills

Review and Reteach
Review Book for U.S. History

Practice and Assess
Test-taking Strategies With Transparencies
Test-taking Strategies Posters
Test Prep Book for U.S. History
Alternative Assessment Handbook
Document-Based Assessment

Teaching Resources
Units 1/2 booklet
- Section Quizzes, pp. 83–86
- Chapter Tests, pp. 87, 90

www.phschool.com Ch. 8 Self-Test

AmericanHeritage Resources

From the Archives of American Heritage®, pp. 293, 294, 305
AmericanHeritage® My Brush with History™ Videotapes
www.americanheritage.com

Don't miss the exclusive interactive version of this textbook on the Web and on CD-ROM.

Chapter 8 Planning Guide
In Your Classroom

Customize for Individual Needs

Gifted and Talented

Teacher's Edition
- Customize for Gifted and Talented, pp. 293, 315

Teaching Resources
- Biography, Literature, and Comparing Primary Sources booklet, pp. 20, 61, 125

Technology
- Exploring Primary Sources in U.S. History CD-ROM *The New Colossus, Emma Lazarus; Poems by Chinese Immigrants at Angel Island; Twenty Years at Hull House, Jane Addams*

ESL

Teacher's Edition
- Customize for ESL, p. 299

Teaching Resources
- Guided Reading and Review booklet, pp. 62–65
- Guide to the Essentials (English/Spanish), Chapter 8

Technology
- Student Edition on Audio CD, Chapter 8
- Guided Reading Audiotapes (English/Spanish), Chapter 8
- Section Reading Support Transparencies

Less Proficient Readers

Teacher's Edition
- Customize for Less Proficient Readers, pp. 295, 303

Teaching Resources
- Guided Reading and Review booklet, pp. 62–65
- Guide to the Essentials (English/Spanish), Chapter 8

Technology
- Student Edition on Audio CD, Chapter 8
- Guided Reading Audiotapes (English/Spanish), Chapter 8
- Section Reading Support Transparencies

Less Proficient Writers

Teacher's Edition
- Customize for Less Proficient Writers, p. 307

Teaching Resources
- Guided Reading and Review booklet, pp. 62–65
- Guide to the Essentials (English/Spanish), Chapter 8

Technology
- Student Edition on Audio CD, Chapter 8
- Guided Reading Audiotapes (English/Spanish), Chapter 8
- Section Reading Support Transparencies

Teacher's Edition Index

Chapter 8 – Pacing Suggestions

For 90-minute Blocks

- Teach sections 2 and 3 using Transparencies A58, E14, G9, and G10, and the Recent Scholarship notes on pages 291, 295, 300, and 314 for class discussions.

Running Out of Time?

If you are running short on time to cover this chapter, consider the following options:

- Use Prentice Hall Presentation Pro CD-ROM to create an outline for this chapter.
- Use the Section Summaries for Chapter 8, from **Guide to the Essentials (English/Spanish).**

TEKS Correlation

Chapter-Level	TEKS
	(1) History. The student understands traditional historical points of reference from 1877 to the present. The student is expected to: **(A)** identify the major eras in U.S. history from 1877 to the present and describe their defining characteristics. **(24) Social studies skills.** The student applies critical-thinking skills to organize and use information acquired from a variety of sources, including electronic technology. The student is expected to: **(B)** analyze information by sequencing, categorizing, identifying cause-and-effect relationships, comparing, contrasting, finding the main idea, summarizing, making generalizations and predictions, and drawing inferences and conclusions. **(25) Social studies skills.** The student communicates in written, oral, and visual forms. The student is expected to: **(A)** use social studies terminology correctly.
1 Politics in the Gilded Age	**(2) History.** The student understands the political, economic, and social changes in the United States from 1877 to 1898. The student is expected to: **(A)** analyze political issues such as Indian policies, the growth of political machines, and civil service reform. **(12) Economics.** The student understands domestic and foreign issues related to U.S. economic growth from the 1870s to 1920. The student is expected to: **(B)** compare the purpose of the Interstate Commerce Commission with its performance over time. **(23) Science, technology, and society.** The student understands the influence of scientific discoveries and tech-noloigcal innovations on daily life in the United States. The student is expected to: **(A)** analyze how scientific discoveries and technological innovations, including those in transportation and communica-tion, have changed the standard of living in the United States.
2 People on the Move	**(2) History.** The student understands the political, economic, and social changes in the United States from 1877 to 1898. The student is expected to: **(C)** analyze social issues such as the treatment of minorities, child labor, growth of cities and problems of immigration. **(5) History.** The student understands significant individuals, events, and issues of the 1920s. The student is expected to: **(A)** analyze causes and effects of significant issues such as immigration, the Red Scare, Prohibition, and the changing role of women. **(10) Geography.** The student understands the effects of migration and immigration on American society. The student is expected to: **(B)** analyze the effects of changing demographic patterns resulting from immigration to the United States. **(11) Geography.** The student understands the relationship between population growth and modernization on the physical environment. The student is expected to: **(A)** identify the effects of population growth and distribution and predict future effects on the physical environment.
3 The Challenge of the Cities	**(2) History.** The student understands the political, economic, and social changes in the United States from 1877 to 1898. The student is expected to: **(A)** analyze political issues such as Indian policies, the growth of political machines, and civil service reform. **(C)** analyze social issues such as the treatment of minorities, child labor, growth of cities and problems of immigration. **(10) Geography.** The student understands the effects of migration and immigration on American society. The student is expected to: **(A)** analyze the effects of changing demographic patterns resulting from migration within the United States. **(11) Geography.** The student understands the relationship between population growth and modernization on the physical environment. The student is expected to: **(A)** identify the effects of population growth and distribution and predict future effects on the physical environment.
4 Ideas for Reform	**(2) History.** The student understands the political, economic, and social changes in the United States from 1877 to 1898. The student is expected to: **(C)** analyze social issues such as the treatment of minorities, child labor, growth of cities, and problems of immigrants. **(10) Geography.** The student understands the effects of migration and immigration on American society. The student is expected to: **(B)** analyze the effects of changing demographic patterns resulting from immigration to the United States. **(21) Culture.** The student understands how people from various groups, including racial, ethnic, and religious groups, adapt to life in the United States and contribute to our national identity. The student is expected to: **(D)** identify the political, social, and economic contributions of women to American society.

Chapter 8
Politics, Immigration, and Urban Life
(1870–1915)

Introducing the Chapter
The years from 1870 to 1915 saw a continuation of the social, economic, and political divisions that had characterized the nation even before the Civil War. This was not a "nation united" as much as it was a collection of political factions and machines, ghettos, neighborhoods, ethnic enclaves, and extremes of rich and poor all competing to realize their version of the "American Dream."

Time Line Activity
To provide students with practice in using the time line, ask questions such as these:

1. What did the events of 1873 and 1883 say about public attitudes about corruption? *(The arrest and imprisonment of Boss Tweed and changes in federal hiring practices showed a growing intolerance of corruption.)*
2. Where did new immigration centers open in 1892 and 1910 and why were the centers in these areas? *(In 1892 New York was a popular destination for European immigrants, while in 1910 San Francisco attracted heavier Asian immigration.)*
3. What was one of the defining events in Woodrow Wilson's presidency? *(The beginning of World War I in 1914)*

Chapter 8 Politics, Immigration, and Urban Life
(1870–1915)

RESTRICT ALL IMMIGRATION!
PROTECT YOURSELF AND YOUR CHILDREN AGAINST Ruinous Labor and Business Competition THROUGH UNRESTRICTED IMMIGRATION.

Boss Tweed cartoon

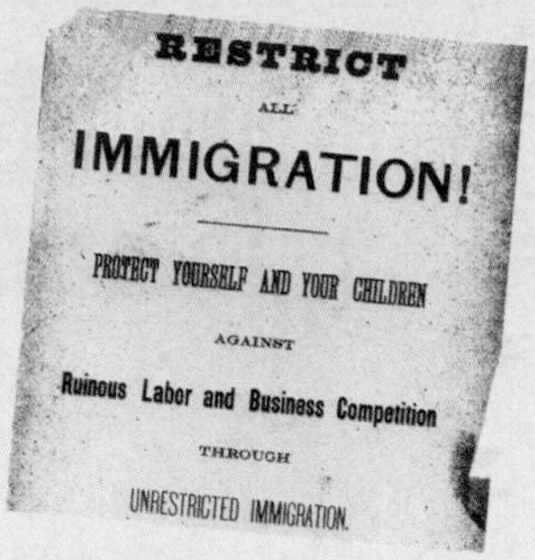

American Events

- **1873** New York City's Boss Tweed is sent to prison for corruption in city government.
- **1882** The Chinese Exclusion Act closes the door to new immigration from China.
- **1883** In response to scandals, the Pendleton Civil Service Act changes how the federal government hires and promotes workers.
- **1886** The United States officially accepts the Statue of Liberty as a gift from France.

Presidential Terms: U.S. Grant 1869–1877; R. Hayes 1877–1881; J. Garfield 1881; C. Arthur 1881–1885; G. Cleveland 1885–1889; B. Harrison 1889–1893

1870 · 1880 · 1890

World Events

- **1884** European powers meet at Berlin to divide up Africa.
- **1887** Sherlock Holmes debuts in *A Study in Scarlet*.

288 Chapter 8 • *Politics, Immigration, and Urban Life*

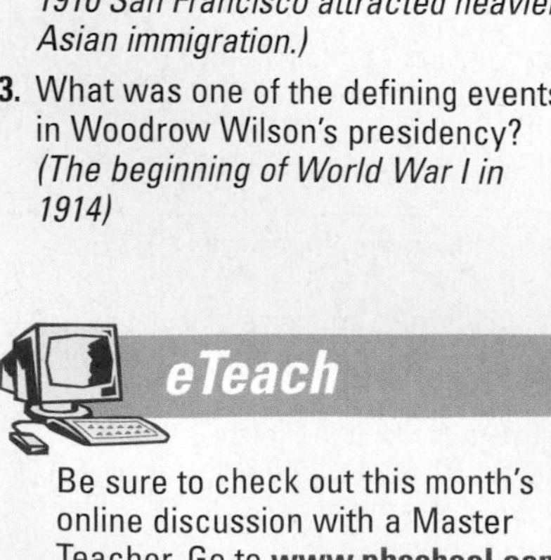

eTeach
Be sure to check out this month's online discussion with a Master Teacher. Go to **www.phschool.com**.

Resource Directory
Teaching Resources
Pacing Charts booklet
Block Scheduling booklet, p. 20
Units 1/2 booklet
- Chapter Summary, p. 82

Technology
Guided Reading Audiotapes (English/Spanish), Ch. 8
Student Edition on Audio CD, Ch. 8
Sounds of an Era Audio CD *"The Sidewalks of New York,"* 1895 recording (time: 30 seconds)
Prentice Hall United States History Video Collection™ Volume 12, *Immigration and Cultural Change*
Prentice Hall Presentation Pro CD-ROM, Ch. 8
Resource Pro® CD-ROM
Social Studies Skills Tutor CD-ROM
Companion Web site, www.phschool.com

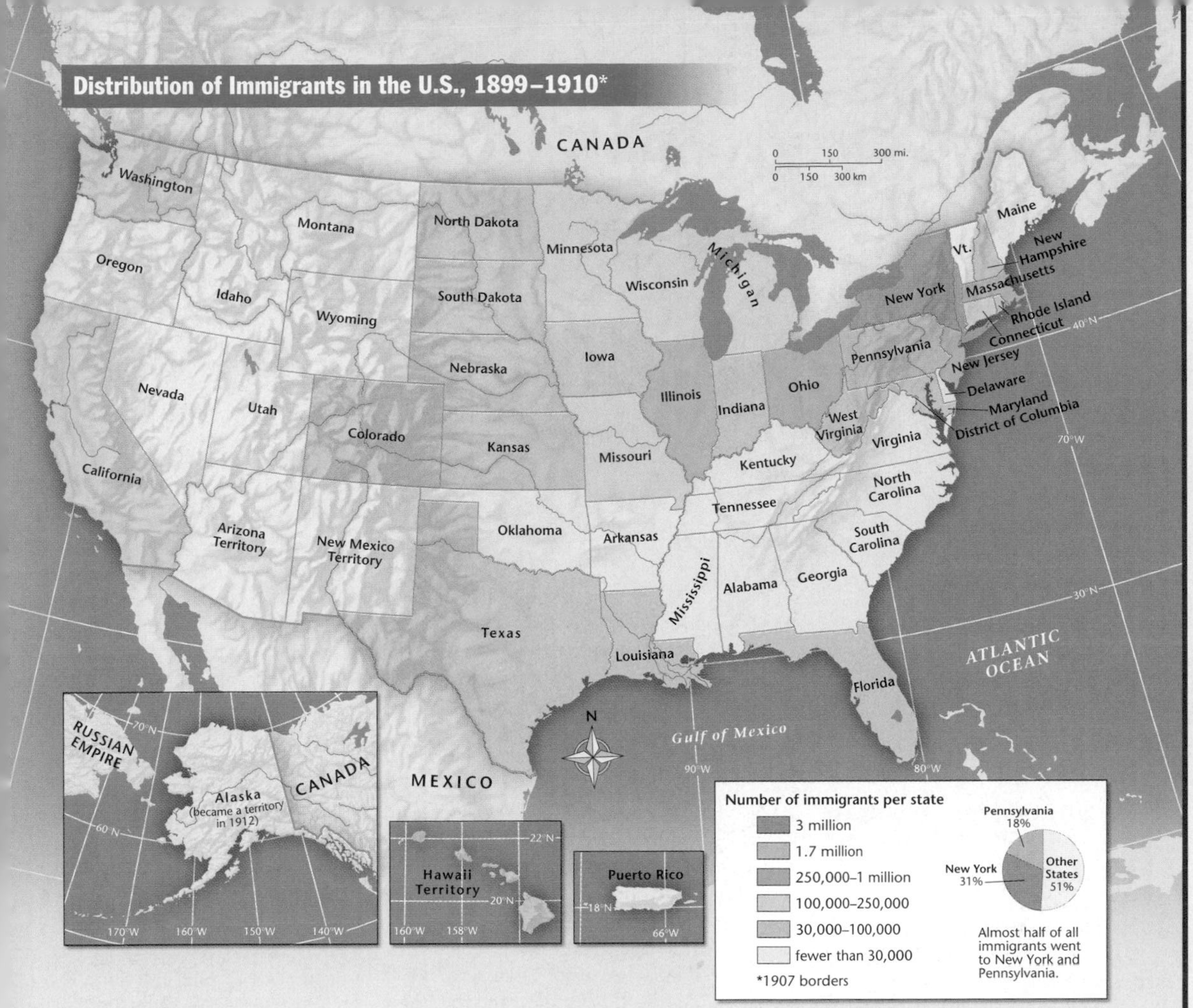

Distribution of Immigrants in the U.S., 1899–1910*

Number of immigrants per state
- 3 million
- 1.7 million
- 250,000–1 million
- 100,000–250,000
- 30,000–100,000
- fewer than 30,000

*1907 borders

Pennsylvania 18%
New York 31%
Other States 51%

Almost half of all immigrants went to New York and Pennsylvania.

1892 A new reception center for immigrants opens at Ellis Island.

1907 Immigration to the United States reaches an all-time high.

1910 The federal government begins processing immigrants at Angel Island in San Francisco Bay.

G. Cleveland 1893–1897 | W. McKinley 1897–1901 | T. Roosevelt 1901–1909 | W.H. Taft 1909–1913 | W. Wilson 1913–1921

1900 — 1910

1900 Boxer Rebellion occurs in China.

1905 Albert Einstein publishes the *Special Theory of Relativity.*

1912 The Titanic sinks.

1914 World War I begins in Europe.

Distribution of Immigrants in the U.S., 1899–1910

Activating Prior Knowledge Have students study the map on this page and then answer the following question, based on their prior knowledge: The east-west population distribution of immigrants to the United States at the end of the 1800s mirrors what earlier population movement? *(The western migration of settlers in the early 1800s)*

Previewing Ask students to study the map on this page and ask the following question: Based on the population distribution of immigrants shown on the map, which of the following three regions do you think contributed the most immigrants to the United States in the years 1899–1910: China, Mexico, or Europe? Why? *(Europe; because the state that gained the largest immigrant population is New York, gateway for European immigration to the U.S.)*

BACKGROUND
About the Pictures

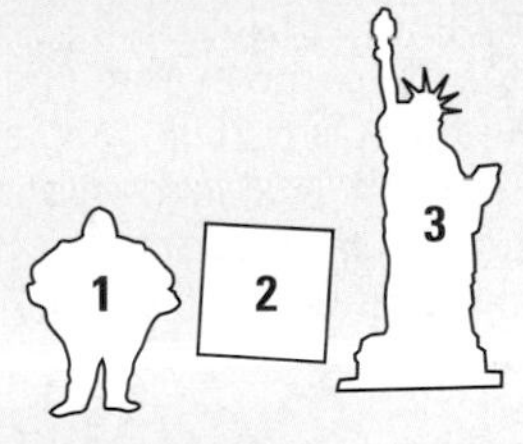

1. Published in 1871 by Thomas Nast, this political cartoon suggests William Marcy "Boss" Tweed is concerned only with money. Tweed, head of New York City's Democratic party during the 1870s, amassed millions of dollars in illegal funds. He was arrested and jailed in 1873.
2. During the 1880s cities like New York City saw a huge influx of immigrants. This created serious overcrowding, leading many Americans to oppose unrestricted immigration.
3. The Statue of Liberty, a gift from France, was erected in New York harbor in 1886. The statue has come to symbolize the values of the United States.

Don't miss the exclusive interactive version of this textbook on the Web and on CD-ROM.

BIBLIOGRAPHY

For the Teacher

Miller, Kerby A. ***Emigrants and Exile: Ireland and the Irish Exodus to North America.*** Oxford University Press, 1988. (The first "transatlantic" history of the Irish, the book offers a full account of the diverse waves of Irish emigration to North America.)

Schlereth, Thomas J. ***Victorian America: Transformations in Everyday Life, 1876–1915 (The Everyday Life in America Series, Vol. 4).*** Harperperennial Library, 1992. (A portrait of the daily life of Americans during the Victorian era.)

Takaki, Ronald. ***Strangers from a Different Shore: A History of Asian Americans.*** Little, Brown, 1989. (A comprehensive account of the Asian American immigrant experience.)

For the Student

Addams, Jane. ***Twenty Years at Hull House.*** Signet, 1999. (The autobiography of a pioneer of the settlement house movement, first published in 1910.)

Immigration: Growth of a Nation. Random House Media, 1985. Sound filmstrip. (A two-part feature in color.)

Section 1 Politics in the Gilded Age

Section Objectives

1. Find out how business influenced politics during the Gilded Age.
2. Learn the ways in which government reformed the spoils system and regulated railroads.
3. Discover the effect the transition from depression to prosperity had on politics in the 1890s.

Bellringer

Warm-Up Activity Ask students to list ideas they associate with the word *reformer.* In what areas of life are reformers trying to make changes today? What factors work against them?

Activating Prior Knowledge Certain private individuals made vast fortunes in the railroad industry in this era. Ask students to list some of the impacts of the expansion of the railroads on the life of the average person in the United States to help them analyze how technological innovations such as those in transportation have changed the standard of living in the United States.

Reading Strategy

Have students write the following headings from the section on a sheet of paper, leaving room under each: *The Business of Politics; Reforming the Spoils System; Regulating Railroads; Depression to Prosperity.* As they read, have them list important details under each of these headings.

Section 1 Politics in the Gilded Age

READING FOCUS

- How did business influence politics during the Gilded Age?
- In what ways did government reform the spoils system and regulate railroads?
- What effect did the transition from depression to prosperity have on politics in the 1890s?

MAIN IDEA

From 1877 to 1900, national politics was dominated by issues of corruption and reform.

KEY TERMS

Gilded Age
laissez-faire
subsidy
blue law
civil service
Pendleton Civil Service Act
rebate
Munn v. *Illinois*

TAKING NOTES

Copy the diagram below. As you read, fill in the two circles with events and issues of the Gilded Age that you can categorize as related to business or politics. Place events and issues that involved both politics and business in the area where the two circles overlap.

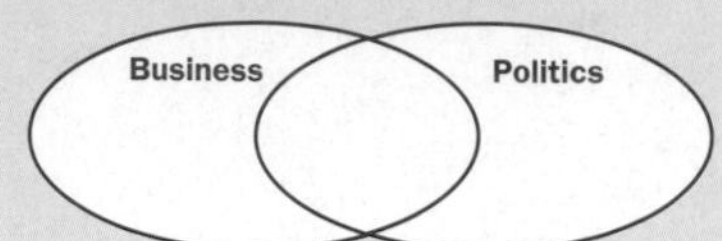

Setting the Scene Jay Gould never formally learned how to run a railroad, but he understood the stock market. By 1871, he had become the most powerful railroad man in New York. A decade later he controlled the largest rail network in the nation.

Gould began buying and selling shares of small railways in 1859 and rose to the position of Director of New York's Erie Railroad Company. In 1867, Cornelius Vanderbilt moved to buy stock in the Erie to combine it with his own New York Central Railroad. Gould, seeking to keep control out of Vanderbilt's hands, swiftly issued 50,000 new shares. Knowing the stock issue was illegal, Gould bribed members of the New York State Legislature to legalize his stock sale and to forbid the combination of the New York Central and Erie railroads. Vanderbilt had been stopped.

Now securely in control, Gould directed the Erie to pay his own private construction companies to lay track. No work was done. Gould pocketed the money, and the Erie's share price fell sharply. When several British shareholders tried to stop him, Gould refused to recognize their voting rights. A judge ruled against the shareholders when they sued.

Gould lived in a time when corruption was common among judges, politicians, and presidential advisors. Some corrupt individuals were caught and punished. Jay Gould, on the other hand, died a very wealthy man. His story illustrates the remarkable flavor of politics and business in the **Gilded Age**—a term coined by Mark Twain to describe the post-Reconstruction era. Gilded means "covered with a thin layer of gold," and "Gilded Age" suggests that a thin but glittering layer of prosperity covered the poverty and corruption of much of society. This was a golden period for America's industrialists. Their wealth helped hide the problems faced by immigrants, laborers, and farmers. It also helped cover up the widespread abuse of power in business and government.

INTERPRETING POLITICAL CARTOONS Jay Gould's wealth and social connections gave him tremendous power in the financial world, as this cartoon shows. **Making Inferences** *How did the cartoonist feel about Gould's power? Explain your answer.*

JAY GOULD'S NEW YORK BOWLING ALLEY

Caption Answers

Interpreting Political Cartoons The cartoonist takes a very negative view of Gould. The cartoon demonstrates the viewpoint that Gould has far too much power, and that he abuses this power.

RESOURCE DIRECTORY

Teaching Resources
Learning Styles Lesson Plans booklet, p. 32
Guided Reading and Review booklet, p. 62

Technology
Section Reading Support Transparencies
Guided Reading Audiotapes (English/Spanish), Ch. 8
Student Edition on Audio CD, Ch. 8
Prentice Hall Presentation Pro CD-ROM, Ch. 8
Companion Web site, www.phschool.com

The Business of Politics

The United States faced great challenges in Gould's day as it emerged from Reconstruction. Industrial expansion raised the output of the nation's factories and farms. Some Americans, such as speculators in land and stocks, quickly rose "from rags to riches." At the same time, depressions, low wages, and rising farm debt contributed to discontent among working people.

Laissez-faire Policies In the late 1800s, businesses operated largely without government regulation. This hands-off approach to economic matters, known by the French phrase ***laissez-faire,*** holds that government should play a very limited role in business. Supporters of this strategy maintain that if government does not interfere, the strongest businesses will succeed and bring wealth to the nation as a whole.

The term *laissez-faire* translates roughly as "allow to be" in French. Although the term probably originated with French economists in the mid-1700s, the theory of *laissez-faire* economics was primarily developed by Adam Smith in his 1776 book, *The Wealth of Nations.* A university professor in Scotland, Smith argued that government should promote free trade and allow a free marketplace for labor and goods.

In the late 1800s, most Americans accepted *laissez-faire* economics in theory. In practice, however, many supported government involvement when it benefited them. For example, American businesses favored high tariffs on imported goods to encourage people to buy American goods instead. American businesses also accepted government land grants and subsidies. A **subsidy** is a payment made by the government to encourage the development of certain key industries, such as railroads.

In this political cartoon, monopolies and trusts are depicted as controlling the government.

To ensure government aid, business giants during the Gilded Age supported friendly politicians with gifts of money. Some of these contributions were legal and some were illegal. Between 1875 and 1885, the Central Pacific Railroad reportedly budgeted $500,000 each year for bribes. Central Pacific co-founder Collis P. Huntington explained, "If you have to pay money to have the right thing done, it is only just and fair to do it."

Credit Mobilier Scandal Washington's generous financial support for railroad-building after the Civil War invited corruption. A notorious scandal developed when Congress awarded the Union Pacific Railroad Company loans and western land to complete the first transcontinental railroad. Like Jay Gould and the Erie Railroad, the owners of the Union Pacific hired an outside company—Credit Mobilier—to build the actual tracks that Union Pacific trains would ride upon. Credit Mobilier charged Union Pacific far beyond the value of the work done, and money flowed from the federal government through the Union Pacific railroad to the shareholders of Credit Mobilier.

Credit Mobilier's managers needed Congress to continue funding the Union Pacific. They gave cheap shares of valuable Credit Mobilier stock to those who agreed to support more funding. Congress did not investigate Credit Mobilier until 1872—three years after the Union Pacific had completed the transcontinental railroad. It was discovered that Credit Mobilier gave stock to representatives of both parties, including a future President, a future Vice President, several cousins of President Grant, and as many as thirty other officials. Unfortunately, Credit Mobilier was only one of many scandals that marked Grant's eight years as President.

READING CHECK
How did the government help private businesses in the Gilded Age?

Lesson Plan

Focus National politics during the Gilded Age was uninspired at best. Ask how business affected politics during the Gilded Age. Why were reformers unable to end corruption in politics and business?

Instruct Review with students the reasons some Americans demanded reform. Discuss the positions of the two major political parties. Which party was favored by wealthy Americans? Which party opposed blue laws? How did the cycle of depression of the early 1890s hurt Democrats and help Republicans? Ask students to list the efforts of Presidents Hayes and Arthur to end the spoils system and analyze civil service reform.

Assess/Reteach There was a great deal of corruption and scandal during this period of time. Ask students to discuss why they think neither state nor federal governments seemed able to control this widespread problem.

Background
Recent Scholarship

In *Nothing Like It in the World* author Stephen E. Ambrose provides an account of the construction of the transcontinental railroad. Ambrose documents the amazing brainpower and manpower that made the project a success. He compares the two railroad companies—the Union Pacific and the Central Pacific—to Civil War armies. At the peak of the project, both companies employed as many as 15,000 workers. Men toiled in all kinds of weather to lay tracks stretching from Omaha, Nebraska, to Sacramento, California. Ambrose shows that the Central Pacific workers—mostly Chinese—and the Union Pacific workers—mostly Irish—came together to create one of the last big projects done mostly by hand.

READING CHECK
Business regulation was lacking due to laissez faire policies. Also, government officials accepted bribes from business in return for subsidies, land grants, and other favorable action.

ACTIVITY
Connecting with Government

Tell students to find out the philosophical and political differences between the Democrats and the Republicans today. One way would be to obtain copies of the party platforms from the last presidential election. Another way would be to read recent newspaper articles detailing the way Democrats and Republicans have voted on important issues. Have students share their findings with the class. **(Verbal/ Linguistic)**

BACKGROUND
The Rotation System

Corrupt party officials used the so-called rotation system to reward lower-level party members. This is how the system worked: workers would stay at a position for a brief period—a month, a few weeks, or even a few days—and then be dropped from that position and go into the rotation to wait for another job. This form of corruption allowed powerful politicians to offer at least partial employment to a great many Loyalists—far more than were actually needed for the requirements of each position. This practice was common around the country at many federal offices—but not in Washington, where observers would have scrutinized it more closely. At the Port of New York, for example, the customs collector removed about one employee every three days.

The Spoils System Bribery was one consequence of the reliance of American politics on the spoils system. Under this system, elected officials appointed friends and supporters to government jobs, regardless of their qualifications. By the Gilded Age, government swarmed with unqualified, dishonest employees.

The spoils system appealed to many politicians because it ensured them a loyal group of supporters in future elections. Both Democrats and Republicans handed out jobs to pay off the people who had helped them get elected. But the system led to corruption when dishonest appointees used their jobs for personal profit.

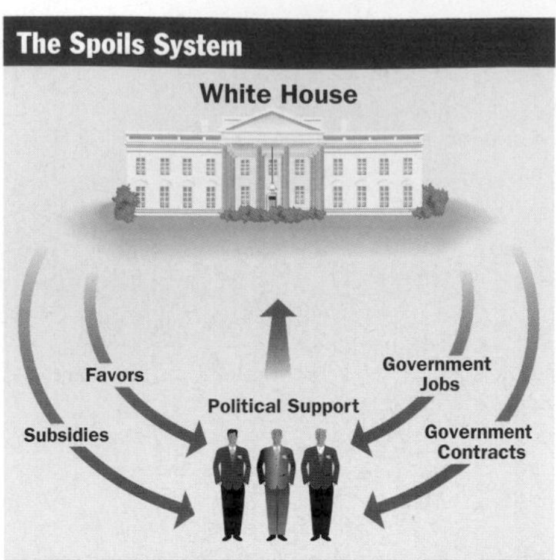

INTERPRETING DIAGRAMS Under the spoils system, individuals offered candidates their votes and support. If the candidate won office, he rewarded his supporters with jobs in his administration. More broadly, the spoils system also gave supporters access to money and political favors. **Determining Relevance** *Why did the spoils system weaken the effectiveness of government?*

Opposing Political Parties During the Gilded Age, the Democratic and Republican parties had roughly the same number of supporters. They differed greatly, however, in who those supporters were and in the positions that the parties took on major issues.

Republicans appealed to industrialists, bankers, and eastern farmers. The party was strongest in the North and the upper Midwest and was weak to nonexistent in the South. In general, Republicans favored a tight money supply backed by gold, high tariffs to protect American business, generous pensions for Union soldiers, government aid to the railroads, strict limits on immigration, and enforcement of **blue laws,** regulations that prohibited certain private activities that some people considered immoral.

As a rule, the Democratic Party attracted those in American society who were less privileged, or at least felt that way. These groups included northern urban immigrants, laborers, southern planters, and western farmers. Claiming to represent the interests of ordinary people, Democrats favored an increased money supply backed by silver, lower tariffs on imported goods, higher farm prices, less government aid to big business, and fewer blue laws.

Reforming the Spoils System

Since the two parties had roughly equal strength, presidential candidates needed the votes of almost all members of their party in order to win an election. To avoid offending party members, candidates generally avoided taking well-defined stands on controversial issues. Most states had very strong ties to one party or the other, so candidates often came from the few states that could swing either Democratic or Republican. Seven of the eight presidents who followed Andrew Johnson came from Ohio or New York.

Republicans whipped up support by "waving the bloody shirt." This meant recalling the bloodshed of the Civil War, a conflict they blamed on the Democrats. This tactic helped Republicans hold on to the presidency for much of the post-Reconstruction era.

Presidents of this period did make some efforts to exercise leadership. Indeed, the Gilded Age witnessed some important reforms in such areas as the spoils system and the railroads.

Hayes Fights the Spoils System After his election in 1877, Rutherford B. Hayes surprised many supporters by refusing to use the patronage system. Instead he appointed qualified political independents to Cabinet posts and fired employees who were not needed. By these actions Hayes began to reform the **civil service,** or the government's nonelected workers.

CAPTION ANSWERS

Interpreting Diagrams Politicians gave government jobs to their friends and supporters, who may have been unqualified, dishonest, or both.

RESOURCE DIRECTORY
Technology

RESOURCE PRO® **Critical Thinking Activity** *Distinguishing False from Accurate Images: Honest Graft,* found on Resource Pro, helps students apply this skill by examining a politician's attempted justification of "honest graft."

Hayes undertook these reforms without congressional backing, even from members of his own Republican Party. He further angered his party on July 11, 1878, when he removed fellow Republican Chester A. Arthur from an important patronage position in New York. Then, with the help of congressional Democrats, he replaced Arthur with one of his own appointments. These moves especially upset Senator Roscoe Conkling, a supporter of patronage in New York State.

Hayes had announced at the beginning of his presidency that he would not seek a second term. After his bold attack on the spoils system, he probably could not have won his party's nomination in any case. That attack strengthened the government but also helped weaken the Republicans.

A GREAT NATION IN GRIEF

PRESIDENT GARFIELD SHOT BY AN ASSASSIN

THOUGH SERIOUSLY WOUNDED HE STILL SURVIVES

THE WOULD-BE MURDERER LODGED IN PRISON.

President Garfield's assassination made the nation aware of the need for reform of the spoils system.

Garfield's Term Cut Short As the 1880 presidential election approached, the Republican Party was split into three factions. The Stalwarts, followers of Senator Conkling, defended the spoils system. The Half-Breeds, who followed Senator James G. Blaine of Maine, hoped to reform the spoils system while remaining loyal to the party. Independents opposed the spoils system altogether.

James A. Garfield, an Ohio congressman and ally of the Half-Breeds, won the party's presidential nomination. To balance the ticket, the Republicans chose as their vice-presidential candidate Chester A. Arthur, a New York Stalwart.

Garfield won a narrow victory over the Democratic candidate, General Winfield S. Hancock. However, his term was cut short. On July 2, 1881, a mentally unstable lawyer named Charles Guiteau shot Garfield as the President walked through a Washington, D.C., railroad station. When he fired his fatal shot, Guiteau cried out, "I am a Stalwart and Arthur is President now!" Garfield died three months later.

The public later learned that Guiteau, a loyal Republican, had expected a job from Garfield. When Garfield passed him over, Guiteau became so enraged that he decided to murder the President. The murder caused a public outcry against the spoils system.

Arthur Reforms the Civil Service Upon Garfield's death, Vice President Chester Arthur became President. Arthur had fought for (and benefited from) patronage in New York. Once in office, however, he urged Congress to support reform of the spoils system. With Garfield's assassination fresh in the nation's mind, President Arthur was able to obtain congressional support for this reform. As a result, the **Pendleton Civil Service Act** became law in 1883.

The act created a Civil Service Commission, which classified government jobs and tested applicants' fitness for them. It also stated that federal employees could not be required to contribute to campaign funds and could not be fired for political reasons.

INTERPRETING GRAPHS
Arthur's reforms protected thousands of jobs from political concerns. **Synthesizing Information** *Why did the rapid growth of the government work force encourage the spoils system?*

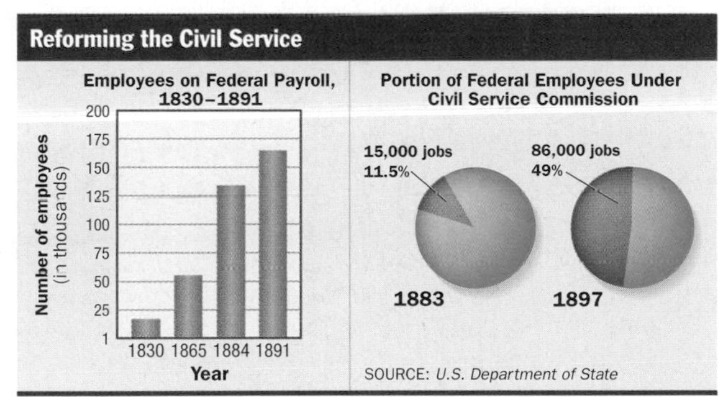

ACTIVITY
Student Portfolio

You may wish to have students add the following to their portfolios: Have students research the lives of the very wealthy during the Gilded Age. Students may select one person and present their findings in a report or skit that shows some of the details of the person's daily activities. **(Verbal/Linguistic; Bodily/Kinesthetic)**

From the Archives of
AmericanHeritage®

About the Presidents

James Abram Garfield (1881) had just appointed a new Postmaster General when *The New York Times* brought the "Star Route Frauds" to light. The *Times'* investigation revealed that thousands of dollars were being spent for deliveries to places that received mail no more than three times a year. With Garfield's approval, the Postmaster General began a thorough public investigation. In the scandal that unfolded, several high-ranking Republicans were implicated. Nevertheless, Garfield called on the Postmaster General to continue releasing his report. As it turned out, the scandal outlived Garfield. In time, it helped lead to civil service reform. Source: David Jacobs, "James Abram Garfield," *The American Heritage® Pictorial History of the Presidents of the United States,* vol. 2, 1968.

CUSTOMIZE FOR ...
Gifted and Talented

Ask students to write a paragraph explaining why Garfield's assassination by Charles Guiteau helped speed the end of the spoils system.

CAPTION ANSWERS

Interpreting Graphs An expanding government created more job openings for political appointees and was also difficult to police for corruption.

BACKGROUND
Connections to Today

In the twentieth century, the growing popularity of air travel resulted in a major decline in railroad use. In 1950 there were about 9,000 passenger trains in service, but by 1970 there were only about 450 trains still in operation. That year Congress created Amtrak, a federally supported corporation that operates almost all intercity passenger trains in the country. In recent years, decreased federal funding of Amtrak has caused controversy. Public concern over traffic and air congestion has caused many people to call for increased governmental support of rail travel.

From the Archives of
AmericanHeritage®

About the Presidents

When Chester Alan Arthur (1881–1885) took over as President, many Americans were worried. For good reason: he was seen as a tool of New York political boss Roscoe Conkling. He'd also been a firm supporter of the spoils system. But Arthur filled his new role with honesty and ability. He supported and signed into law the Pendleton Bill, which created the Civil Service Commission. He became a popular Chief Executive, but could not pacify feuding factions in his party. He never got a chance to run for a presidential term in his own right. Source: Michael Harwood, "Chester Alan Arthur," *The American Heritage® Pictorial History of the Presidents of the United States,* vol. 2, 1968.

Democrats Take Power In 1884, the Republicans nominated James G. Blaine, a former Secretary of State and senator from Maine, for President. The Democrats chose Grover Cleveland, former mayor of Buffalo and governor of New York.

Serious issues confronted the nation that year, such as high tariffs, unfair business practices, and unregulated railroads. Yet the campaign focused mostly on scandals. Had James G. Blaine received railroad stock options in return for favorable votes while he was in Congress? No one could prove that he had. Had Cleveland fathered a child out of wedlock while a bachelor in Buffalo? Cleveland admitted the rumor was true. Republicans jeered, "Ma, Ma, where's my Pa?" Democrats responded, "Going to the White House, ha, ha, ha!"

Cleveland became the first Democrat to capture the presidency since 1856. He owed at least some of his success to Republican independents who decided that Blaine was too corrupt to support. An unsympathetic newspaper editor called these Cleveland voters "Little Mugwumps." (*Mugwump* was an Algonquin word meaning "important chief.") The editor was suggesting that the independents were little men who wanted to be big chiefs.

Cleveland favored tight money policies, so most business interests backed him. Yet not all his policies were probusiness. He opposed high tariffs and took back from the railroads and other interests some 80 million acres of federal land that had been granted to them. In addition, Cleveland supported more government regulation of the powerful railroad companies.

Fast Forward to Today

Confederate Battle Flags

Memories of the Civil War still divided Americans after Reconstruction. In 1887, President Cleveland proposed returning captured Confederate battle flags held by the federal government to southern states. Cleveland was the first Democrat and nonveteran President elected since the Civil War, and his request unleashed a firestorm of anger from the 400,000 veterans of the Grand Army of the Republic. Governor Foraker of Ohio said, "The patriotic people of this state are shocked and indignant beyond anything I can express." Shaken by the reaction, Cleveland retreated from his proposal.

Today President Theodore Roosevelt returned the battle flags held by the federal government in 1905, but individual states and societies still hold other battle flags today. In 2000, the Virginia Senate urged the Minnesota Historical Society to return the battered flag of the 28th Virginia Infantry. The Minnesota 1st Volunteer had captured the flag at the Battle of Gettysburg after suffering terrible losses. "Absolutely not," replied Minnesota Gov. Jesse Ventura. "We took it. That makes it our heritage."

? Why were many northerners upset by Cleveland's proposal to return the flags?

Regulating Railroads

Railroad regulation had begun in 1869, when Massachusetts investigated claims that railroad companies were overcharging customers. By 1880, about 14 states had railroad commissions that looked into complaints about railroad practices. One of those practices was charging more for a short haul than for a long haul over the same track. Another practice was to offer **rebates,** or partial refunds, to favored customers. Others included keeping rates secret and charging different rates to different people for the same service.

Some of these practices can be justified by the economics of operating a railroad. For example, a short haul is more costly per mile than a long haul because the cost of loading and unloading the cargo is equal in both cases. Rebates were one legal way that railroads competed for customers. In any event, farmers and businesses opposed them because they favored some customers and kept others from predicting their costs.

In 1877 the Supreme Court, in ***Munn* v. *Illinois,*** allowed states to regulate certain businesses within their borders, including railroads. But railroad traffic often crossed state boundaries. Lawyers for the railroads argued that under the Constitution only the federal government could regulate interstate commerce. In 1886, in the *Wabash* case, the Supreme Court agreed. Interstate railroad traffic thus remained unregulated.

CAPTION ANSWERS

Fast Forward to Today At that time many of the veterans of the Union army were still alive. They would certainly have looked with great disfavor upon any proposal to return Confederate flags that they and their comrades had captured during hard-fought battles.

RESOURCE DIRECTORY

Other Print Resources

American History Block Scheduling Support *Linking the Nation: The Railroads,* found in the Expansion, Reconstruction, Immigration folder, includes interdisciplinary lesson suggestions and activities for Geography and History, Primary Sources, Biography, and Literature.

Pressure mounted on Congress to curb these abuses. As you read in the last chapter, in 1887 Congress responded by passing the Interstate Commerce Act. The act required that rates be set in proportion to the distance traveled and that rates be made public. It also outlawed the practice of giving special rates to powerful customers. Finally, it set up the nation's first federal regulatory board, the Interstate Commerce Commission (ICC), to enforce the act.

The Interstate Commerce Act did not give the ICC the power to set railroad rates. Also, to enforce its rulings, the ICC had to take the railroads to court, where it usually lost. Of the 16 cases involving the ICC that came before the Supreme Court between 1887 and 1905, the Court ruled against the ICC 15 times.

Focus on ECONOMICS

Regulation *Government can regulate an industry by deciding what services companies can offer and how much they may charge customers.*

The Historical Context Congress passed the Interstate Commerce Act to regulate the railroad industry. In later years, the federal government also regulated the air travel and trucking industries.

The Concept Today Under President Carter and President Reagan, the federal government stepped back and ended some regulations on air travel, trucking, and railroads. This process is known as deregulation. In 1995, Congress passed a bill to abolish the Interstate Commerce Commission the following year.

Depression to Prosperity

Boosted by vigorous industrial growth, American business generally grew during the late 1880s and into the 1890s. But in 1893 a depression struck, and prosperity did not return until around 1900. These ups and downs made the economy the hottest political issue of this period.

Focus on Tariffs Cleveland lost the 1888 presidential election to Republican Benjamin Harrison. The campaign had focused on tariffs. Cleveland favored a minor reduction in tariffs, while Harrison wanted an increase. Harrison's position won him plenty of business support and, ultimately, the presidency.

Among President Harrison's achievements was the signing of the Sherman Antitrust Act in 1890, described earlier. Like the Interstate Commerce Act, however, this seemingly bold action failed to curb the power of the largest corporations until well after the turn of the century.

Meanwhile, Harrison made good his campaign promise to business by approving a huge tariff increase in 1890. He also supported legislation on behalf of special business interests. Although he was thought to be conservative with public funds, Harrison dipped deep into the Treasury to award huge new pensions to dependents of Civil War soldiers.

These actions would later damage the economy, and they did not help Harrison in the election of 1892. Many new immigrants had swelled the ranks of the Democratic Party. Campaigning again for lower tariffs, Grover Cleveland was returned to the presidency.

Cleveland's Second Term Cleveland's second term started badly. Thanks in part to the drained treasury, a panic hit the country in 1893. This began a long depression, during which millions of workers lost their jobs or had their wages slashed. Despite the suffering, the government offered no help.

In 1894, Jacob S. Coxey, a wealthy Ohio quarry owner, demanded that government create jobs for the unemployed. Coxey called on unemployed workers to march on the nation's capital. "We will send a petition to Washington with boots on," he declared.

Many small "armies" started out on the protest march, but only Coxey's army reached Washington. Police arrested him and a few others for illegally carrying banners on the Capitol grounds and for trampling the grass. A song sung by

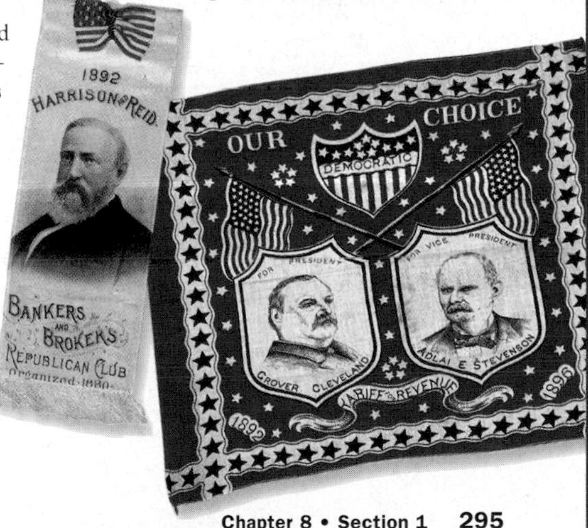

These campaign ribbons illustrate how presidential candidates attracted support from different groups of people.

ACTIVITY
Connecting with Government

In this activity, which may take place over more than one class session, students prepare a portion of an evening news broadcast dealing with one political event described in the section. The students' goal is to identify and present key issues related to a political event.

Have students work in small groups to create a segment for the evening news. Assign each group one of the following events: Hayes begins civil service reform; Garfield is assassinated; Arthur ends the spoils system; Cleveland wins the presidential election of 1884; Coxey's army marches on Washington. Each group should have anchor people, newsroom staff, and reporters on location. **(Visual/Spatial; Verbal/Linguistic)**

BACKGROUND
Recent Scholarship

Some historians consider Grover Cleveland to have been one of our most honest and moral presidents. In *Grover Cleveland: A Study in Character*, Alyn Brodsky writes: "Here, indeed, was that rarest of political animals: one who believed his ultimate allegiance was to the nation, not to the party." Brodsky compares Cleveland with Harry S. Truman, saying, "Like Truman, Cleveland was compassionate, courageous, scrupulous, ever prepared to follow his conscience and moral responsibility no matter the impediments that so often cluttered his path."

CUSTOMIZE FOR ...
Less Proficient Readers

Ask students to correct any of the following statements that are incorrect:

- Government regulations such as those established under the Interstate Commerce Act stopped unfair business practices.
- During the Gilded Age, the positions of the Republicans and Democrats were more or less interchangeable.
- President Arthur's assassination led to the end of the spoils system.

TEST PREPARATION

Have students reread the material under the heading "Regulating Railroads" on the previous page, and then complete the sentence below.

According to the text, railroads offered rebates to certain customers. Rebates are—

A higher prices, or surcharges.
(B) partial refunds.
C very comfortable seats.
D faster trains.

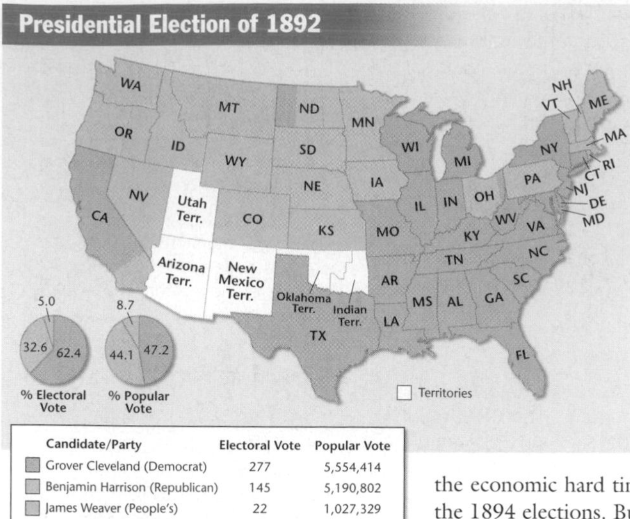

Candidate/Party	Electoral Vote	Popular Vote
Grover Cleveland (Democrat)	277	5,554,414
Benjamin Harrison (Republican)	145	5,190,802
James Weaver (People's)	22	1,027,329

MAP SKILLS Grover Cleveland returned to the White House after the 1892 election with the support of Southern Democrats and immigrants. **Place** *Compare this map to the map on page 289. How did the states that later attracted many immigrants vote in 1892?*

Coxey's supporters mocked the government for worrying more about its lawns than its citizens.

In his second term Cleveland managed to anger not only the unemployed but almost everyone else. In 1893, he upset farmers by repealing the Sherman Silver Purchase Act, which had become law just three years before. He enraged unions when he sent federal troops to Chicago during the Pullman strike of 1894.

By the time of his party's convention in 1896, Cleveland had turned many fellow Democrats against him. Hence, the President failed to win his party's nomination.

McKinley Wins in 1896 The Populists had emerged as a political power during the economic hard times of the early 1890s and had made gains in the 1894 elections. But in 1896, William Jennings Bryan, the presidential candidate of the Populists and Democrats, lost to the Republican candidate, William McKinley. McKinley was supported by urban workers and the middle class.

President McKinley oversaw a new tariff bill and a stronger gold standard. These actions brought Republicans an even more decisive victory against Bryan in 1900. McKinley won 292 electoral votes while Bryan only won 155. As the economy began to climb out of the 1890s depression, Republicans claimed credit with their slogan "A Full Dinner Pail."

McKinley did not live long enough to enjoy the effects of the returning prosperity. On September 6, 1901, McKinley went on a tour of the Pan-American Exposition in Buffalo, New York. Leon Czolgosz, a mentally ill man who called himself an anarchist, shot the President as he greeted the public there. McKinley died days later.

Section 1 Assessment

READING COMPREHENSION

1. Is the term **Gilded Age** a positive or negative description of this period? Explain.
2. What is the purpose of a **subsidy?**
3. How did the **Pendleton Civil Service Act** address the problems of the spoils system?
4. How did the Interstate Commerce Act affect railroads?

CRITICAL THINKING AND WRITING

5. **Recognizing Cause and Effect** Businesses sought political influence by making large contributions to politicians. How do you think these politicians voted on tariff legislation? Why?
6. **Creating an Outline** Create an outline for an essay in which you explain how economic issues affected the outcome of presidential elections during the Gilded Age.

Activity: Finding a Job Research a job from the variety of employment options offered by the federal government and civil service. Create a résumé that you could submit for the job you researched. Use the links provided in the *America: Pathways to the Present* area at the following Web site for help in completing this activity.
www.phschool.com

Section 1 Assessment

Reading Comprehension

1. Negative. It suggests that the positive and prosperous aspects of society were a thin, golden layer masking numerous problems, such as poverty and corruption.
2. To promote the expansion of industries deemed essential by the government.
3. It created a Civil Service Commission that classified government jobs, tested applicants, and stipulated that federal employees could not be required to contribute to campaign funds. In addition, federal workers could no longer be fired for political reasons.
4. It forced railroads to set rates according to distance and to make rates public and universal for all customers.

Critical Thinking and Writing

5. Sample answer: They voted for increased tariff regulation because it would help the businesspeople who had made contributions.
6. Outlines will vary but should be supported with facts from the text, and may include tariffs, government spending, and the gold standard.

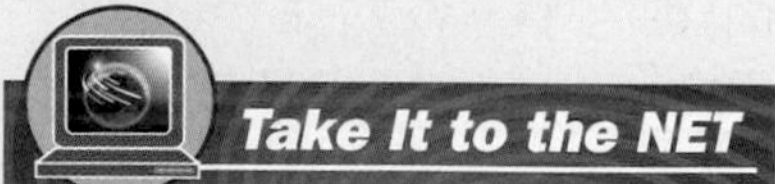

Resumes will vary but should be supported with research and should reference appropriate skills for the desired position.

Caption Answers

Map Skills Many of the states destined for an influx of immigrants voted for Harrison in 1892. However, Cleveland benefited by winning large future immigrant haven states such as New York and Texas.

RESOURCE DIRECTORY

Teaching Resources

Units 1/2 booklet
- Section 1 Quiz, p. 83

Guide to the Essentials
- Section 1 Summary, p. 38

Technology

Sounds of an Era Audio CD *William McKinley* (time: one minute)

Section 2 People on the Move

READING FOCUS

- What were the experiences of immigrants in the late 1800s and early 1900s?
- What different challenges did immigrants from Europe, Asia, and Mexico face?

MAIN IDEA

Millions of immigrants, representing many different cultures, arrived in the United States during the late 1800s and early 1900s.

KEY TERMS

pogrom
steerage
quarantine
ghetto
restrictive covenant
Chinese Exclusion Act
Gentlemen's Agreement
alien

TAKING NOTES

As you read, complete this chart listing the reasons why immigrants came to America and their experiences in their new land.

Place of Origin	Reasons for Immigration	Experiences in the United States
Europe	To escape religious persecution	Settled in cities in the East and the Midwest
Asia		
Mexico		

Setting the Scene

Peter Mossini was born in 1898 into a poor family in Sicily. He shared a small two-bedroom house with his parents and seven brothers and sisters. Peter's parents could not afford to send him to school, so at age ten he went to work in a factory. He earned about ten cents a day for eleven or twelve hours of work.

When Peter was still an infant, his father left home to find work in the coal mines of Pennsylvania. Peter's family survived on the money his father sent back in addition to the children's wages from the factory. Peter's father returned to Sicily in 1913, and the family once again struggled to get by. Following World War I, Peter saw no future for himself in his hometown of Santa Teresa di Riva:

> “*During the First World War, I was in the army, and I held to my idea about coming to America. Then, in 1919, my sister Josephine came [to America]. I was very close to her . . . She came by herself and she got married. She was doing very well over here. And I wanted to build a new life, better myself. Eventually, all my brothers and sisters came to the United States.*”
>
> —Peter Mossini

At age 22, Peter boarded a ship, the *Pesaro*, bound for America. Three months later he joined his sister in Portage, Pennsylvania.

It was sometimes said that America's streets were paved with gold. This myth held a grain of truth for the millions of immigrants who left a life of poverty behind. Like Peter, they came to America because it offered, if not instant wealth, then at least the chance to improve their lives. Some immigrants did get rich through hard work and determination. Many more managed to carve out a decent life for themselves and their families. For these immigrants, the chance to come to the United States was indeed a golden opportunity.

A family of immigrants arrives at Ellis Island in 1905.

Section 2 People on the Move

Section Objectives

1. Share the experiences of immigrants in the late 1800s and early 1900s.
2. Analyze the different challenges faced by immigrants from Europe, Asia, and Mexico.

Bellringer

Warm-Up Activity Ask students what immigrants entering the United States in 1900 might have thought as they saw the Statue of Liberty. Ask them to explain why the Statue of Liberty remains a potent symbol today, despite the fact that few immigrants now arrive by sailing into New York harbor.

Activating Prior Knowledge How do students think the experiences of new Americans around 1900 would compare to experiences of immigrants arriving in this country today?

Reading Strategy

Have students write down several questions they might ask about the experiences of immigrants around 1900. As they read the chapter, have them note the answers to their questions to help them analyze social issues such as the problems of immigrants.

Activity

Connecting with Geography

Have students trace the journey of an immigrant from a city in southern Italy, Russia, Japan, or China at the end of the nineteenth century. Using a world map, students should calculate the distance from the immigrant's former home to Boston, New York, or San Francisco. Students should map out two possible routes and state which route was probably more popular, and why. **(Visual/Spatial; Logical/Mathematical)**

Resource Directory

Teaching Resources

Learning Styles Lesson Plans booklet, p. 33
Guided Reading and Review booklet, p. 63
Learning with Documents booklet (Visual Learning Activity) *Passage to America,* p. 54

Other Print Resources

Nystrom *Atlas of Our Country* *The Third Wave of Immigration,* pp. 30–31

Technology

Section Reading Support Transparencies
Guided Reading Audiotapes (English/Spanish), Ch. 8
Student Edition on Audio CD, Ch. 8
Prentice Hall Presentation Pro CD-ROM, Ch. 8
Companion Web site, www.phschool.com

Lesson Plan

Focus Explain that the Gilded Age was marked by the arrival of new immigrants to the United States. Ask students what immigrants' lives were like.

Instruct Ask what drew immigrants to the United States. Have them compare the experiences of Europeans, Asians, and Mexicans. What special problems did Asian immigrants encounter? Ask students to analyze the role of fear and racism in discrimination against Asians. How did Americans respond to Asian customs, their willingness to work for low wages, and their success in California agriculture?

Assess/Reteach Ask students to write a first-person essay describing the experience, as they imagine it, of immigrating to a new country. Have them imagine that as new immigrants, they do not speak the language in the new country, and they find the customs and regulations completely unfamiliar. In the essay, have them reflect on the circumstances that may have caused them to immigrate to a new country.

Background
Global Connections

The emergence of the steamship resulted from fierce competition among several countries. The United Kingdom, Germany, the Netherlands, and the United States engaged in a development race that lasted from the late 1850s until the 1860s. Although the public was initially wary of traveling aboard steamships, eventually people accepted the greater speed of the steamship as a big advantage over its predecessor, the more sluggish sailing ship. In 1856 more than 95 percent of all immigrants journeyed to America on sailing ships. By 1873 only 3.2 percent came on sailing ships; the rest arrived on steamships.

VIEWING HISTORY While crossing the Atlantic, some passengers escaped crowded conditions in steerage by sleeping on deck in the open air. **Making Inferences** *Why did shipowners provide such poor conditions for immigrants in steerage?*

The Immigrant Experience

In the late 1800s, people in many parts of the world were on the move from farms to cities and from one country to another. Immigrants from around the globe were fleeing crop failures, shortages of land and jobs, rising taxes, and famine. Some were also escaping religious or political persecution.

Immigrants' Hopes and Dreams The United States received a huge portion of this global migration. In 1860, the resident population of the United States was 31.5 million people. Between 1865 and 1920, close to 30 million additional people entered the country.

Some of these newcomers dreamed of getting rich, or at least of securing free government land through the Homestead Act. Others yearned for personal freedoms. In America, they had heard, everyone could go to school, young men were not forced to serve long years in the army, and citizens could freely take part in a democratic government. Conditions in two countries, Italy and Russia, illustrate how economic problems and political persecution encouraged millions to immigrate to the United States.

"There [were] two classes of people in Sicily," Peter Mossini said, "the rich and the very poor." A few people owned most of the land and the poor lived as sharecroppers. In the late 1800s, the economy of southern Italy slipped into decline. The land was very poor, but the government of Italy demanded more and more money in taxes. Thousands of farmers lost their livelihood when a parasite killed many of the region's grapevines. Many tenant farmers found they simply could not afford to stay in their homes and still take care of their families. Skilled workers, too, could not find jobs. The United States offered a solution.

In Russia, Jews faced hostility from their Christian neighbors and the government. In the 1880s, a wave of **pogroms,** or violent massacres of Jews, swept across the country. The czar responded to the pogroms by sharply limiting where Jews could live and how they could earn a living. America offered freedom of religion and the opportunity to build a new life.

In the late 1800s, millions of immigrants brought their belongings and their dreams to the United States in a single steamer trunk.

Crossing the Ocean In the late 1800s, steam-powered ships could cross the Atlantic Ocean in two to three weeks. By 1900, on more powerful steamships, the crossing took just one week. Even this brief journey, however, could be difficult, especially for those who could not afford cabins. Most immigrants traveled in **steerage,** a large open area beneath the ship's deck. Steerage offered limited toilet facilities, no privacy, and poor food, but tickets were relatively cheap.

Crossing the vast Pacific Ocean took much longer, but the arrangements were similar. Passengers traveled in steerage, with few comforts. A person's country of origin, however, could make a difference in the conditions aboard a ship. Immigrants from Japan, whose power in the world was growing, often received better treatment than those from China, which at that time was a weak country.

Caption Answers

Viewing History Steerage passengers paid much less than other passengers. Also, there was no shortage of immigrants wishing to cross to America. For these reasons, ship owners had no incentive to improve conditions.

Resource Directory

Teaching Resources

Biography, Literature, and Comparing Primary Sources booklet (Literature) *The Statue of Liberty,* p. 61

Other Print Resources

American History Block Scheduling Support *Ellis Island: Gateway to America,* found in the Expansion, Reconstruction, Immigration folder, includes interdisciplinary lesson suggestions and activities for Geography and History, Primary Sources, Biography, and Literature.

Technology

Color Transparencies *American Diversity,* G10

Exploring Primary Sources in U.S. History CD-ROM *The New Colossus, Emma Lazarus*

Arriving in America Information about the number and origins of the nation's immigrants is not precise. Officials often misidentified the origins of immigrants. About one third of them were "birds of passage." These were usually young, single men who worked for a number of months or years and then returned home.

Historians estimate that about 10 million immigrants arrived between 1865 and 1890. Most came from northwestern and central European countries: about 2.8 million from Germany, another 1.8 million from Great Britain, and nearly 1.4 million from Ireland.

In the 1890s, the pattern of immigration shifted dramatically. Most new immigrants came from the countries of central, southern, and eastern Europe and the Middle East. Between 1890 and 1920 about 10 million Italians, Greeks, Slavs, Jews, and Armenians arrived. Around 3.8 million immigrants came from Italy alone. Another 3 million, primarily Jews, came from Russia.

Until the 1880s, decisions about whom to allow into the country were left to the states. In 1882, the federal government began excluding certain categories of immigrants. In 1891, the Office of the Superintendent of Immigration was formed to determine who was fit to settle in America and who was not.

Immigrants entered the United States through several port cities. European newcomers might come through Boston, Philadelphia, or Baltimore. Asians might enter through San Francisco or Seattle. Yet more than 70 percent of all immigrants came through New York City, which was called the "Golden Door."

Focus on CITIZENSHIP

Naturalization The process of becoming a United States citizen is called naturalization. A male immigrant seeking citizenship needed to meet several requirements, including "good moral character," "attachment to the Constitution," and (after 1906) proficiency in the English language. Only "free white persons" and people of African descent could apply.

A woman won citizenship by marrying a citizen or accompanying a husband through his naturalization. Her name did not appear on the naturalization certificate, but she could prove her citizenship with her husband's papers and their marriage certificate. Single women and widows could apply as individuals. Since female citizens did not enjoy the same rights as male citizens, many chose not to spend the money to become a citizen.

Immigrants From Europe

Throughout most of the 1800s, immigrants arriving in New York entered at the Castle Garden depot, near the southern tip of Manhattan. In 1892, the federal government opened a huge reception center for steerage passengers on Ellis Island in New York harbor, near where the Statue of Liberty had been erected in 1886. The statue, a gift from France, celebrated "Liberty Enlightening the World." It became a symbol of the United States as a place of refuge and hope.

Physical Exams In 1892, the federal government required all new immigrants to undergo a physical examination. Those who were found to have a contagious disease such as tuberculosis faced **quarantine,** a time of isolation to prevent the spread of a disease. They could even be deported. People with trachoma, an eye disease common among immigrants, were automatically sent back to their country.

Fiorello La Guardia, who later became mayor of New York City, worked as an interpreter at Ellis Island. "It was harrowing to see families separated," he remembered in the book *The Making of an Insurgent:*

INTERPRETING GRAPHS
Beginning in the 1890s, large numbers of immigrants arrived from eastern and southern Europe. **Analyzing Information** *Which region provided the greatest number of immigrants in 1910?*

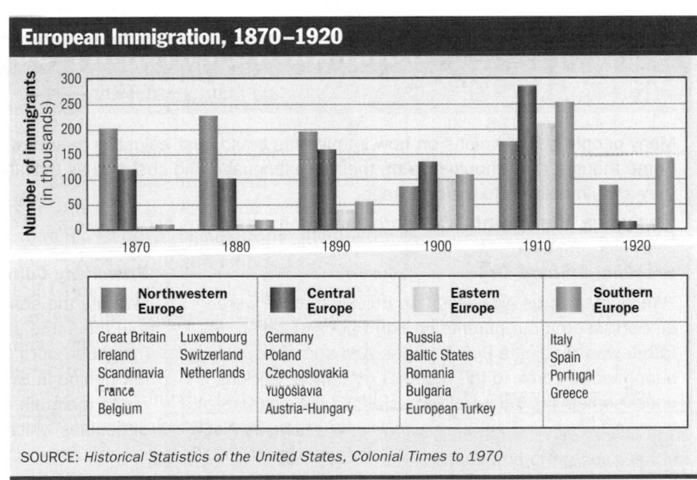

SOURCE: *Historical Statistics of the United States, Colonial Times to 1970*

ACTIVITY
Connecting with Citizenship

In 1892 the Office of the Superintendent of Immigration was established to determine who was "fit" for immigration into the United States. Divide students into an even number of groups and ask each group to design a test for immigration fitness. Suggest the following tests: physical fitness, intelligence, finances, and knowledge of United States history. Have groups administer their tests to each other. Discuss with students their feelings about being tested in this way. **(Bodily/Kinesthetic; Verbal/Linguistic)**

BACKGROUND
Global Connections

Between 1847 and 1860, a million people from Ireland arrived in the United States through the port of New York City alone. That was nearly half of all Europeans who landed in New York in those years. The Irish came in large part because blight had destroyed their country's entire potato crop, which was the mainstay of their diet. Famine conditions were aggravated by the inadequate response of the British government. Eventually over one million people died in Ireland from starvation and disease during the potato famine. America seemed a far cry from the disaster. One new arrival wrote, "Every day [in America] is like Christmas Day."

CUSTOMIZE FOR ...
ESL

Write the words *immigrant* and *immigration* on the chalkboard. Ask volunteers to define the words. Then have students look through the section text for dates, numbers, and the names of countries that are related to immigration and write them on the chalkboard.

CAPTION ANSWERS

Interpreting Graphs Central Europe.

Section 3
The Challenge of the Cities

Section Objectives

1. Find out why cities expanded in the late 1800s and early 1900s.
2. Review new developments that helped cities grow.
3. Learn how living conditions in cities changed.
4. State the results of city growth.

Bellringer

Warm-Up Activity Ask students to think about the expression "bright lights, big city." Then have them list the advantages and disadvantages of city life.

Activating Prior Knowledge Ask students if they know much about the history of immigration and settlement in their area. Can they identify some of the predominant ethnic groups in the community? Do they know at what point in time these ethnic groups settled in the area?

Reading Strategy

As students read, ask them to find evidence to support the following statement: "The arrival of large numbers of newcomers, from both within and outside the nation, radically changed the face of the nation's cities."

Activity
Connecting with Culture

Tell students to imagine that they are living around the year 1900. Their family has decided to abandon the family farm and move to a fast-growing city. Have students write a diary entry that describes how it feels to move from the country to a city. Encourage students to tell how everyday life in the city differs from life on a farm. **(Verbal/Linguistic)**

Section 3
The Challenge of the Cities

READING FOCUS

- Why did cities expand in the late 1800s and early 1900s?
- What new developments helped cities grow?
- How did living conditions in cities change?
- What were the results of city growth?

MAIN IDEA

Millions of people moved into the cities, creating new growth and new challenges.

KEY TERMS

suburb
tenement
dumbbell tenement
political machine
graft

TAKING NOTES

Copy the flowchart below. As you read, complete the following chart to show some of the effects of rapid population growth in the cities.

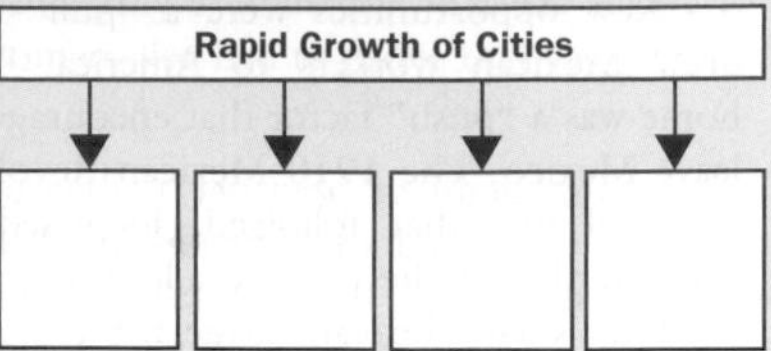

Setting the Scene New York's first European settlers lived at the southern tip of Manhattan Island. To the north, along the East River, colonial families like the Rutgers and Delanceys established estates in the countryside. As the city grew, wealthy sea captains and merchants built large houses there to be near the docks. Later, the city government planned a grid of roads in the fields. Developers divided the land for rows of narrow single-family homes to house the large middle-class families of the early 1800s.

These residents moved uptown as Irish and German immigrants began to arrive in the 1840s. Builders tore down single-family row houses to make room for five- and six-story apartment buildings that fit several families on each floor. An influx of Italian and Jewish immigrants in the 1890s again changed the character of the Lower East Side, as the area came to be known. The streets teemed during the day with merchants, shoppers, and children.

Most immigrants in New York City lived in cramped, overcrowded apartments. This family posed in a space that served as both a kitchen and a bedroom.

A Council of Hygiene and Public Health studied how these immigrants lived. To their shock, they found the old Delancey and Rutgers farms housed an amazing 240,000 people per square mile. The Council wrote:

> "*It is only because this rate of packing is somewhat diminished by intervening warehouses, factories, private dwellings, and other classes of buildings that the entire [apartment] population is not devastated by the domestic pestilences and infectious epidemics that arise from overcrowding and uncleanness. . . . Such concentration and packing of a population has probably never been equaled in any city as may be found in particular localities in New York.*"
>
> —Council of Hygiene and Public Health

Resource Directory

Teaching Resources
Guided Reading and Review booklet, p. 64
Learning with Documents booklet (Primary Source Activity) *New York Gangs,* p. 20

Technology
Section Reading Support Transparencies
Guided Reading Audiotapes (English/Spanish), Ch. 8
Student Edition on Audio CD, Ch. 8
Color Transparencies *Historical Maps,* A58
Sounds of an Era Audio CD *"The Bowery,"* 1893 recording (time: 45 seconds)
Prentice Hall Presentation Pro CD-ROM, Ch. 8
Companion Web site, www.phschool.com

Expanding Cities

But New York was not alone. Philadelphia, Chicago, St. Louis, New Orleans, and many other cities were bursting at the seams with newcomers. While millions of immigrants from around the world were settling in the cities of the United States, growing numbers of native-born Americans were moving there, too. Between 1880 and 1920, 11 million Americans left behind the economic hardship of their farms and headed for the opportunities of the cities. This migration within the country, combined with the new immigration, brought explosive growth to the nation's urban centers.

Women and men alike took part in the migration from rural to urban America. As factories produced more of the goods that farm women had once made, the need for women's labor on farms declined. In addition, as new machines replaced manual labor on many farms, the need for male farmhands shrank. The result was a striking shift in the nation's population. Between 1880 and 1910, the percentage of the nation's population living on farms fell from 72 to 54 percent.

Many African Americans took part in this internal migration. In 1870, fewer than a half million of the nation's 5 million African Americans lived outside the South. But after Reconstruction ended in 1877, segregation and acts of racial violence against African Americans increased. By 1890, partly as a result of these pressures, another 150,000 black southerners had left the South, and many rural African Americans had moved into nearby cities. Then, in the 1910s, the boll weevil destroyed cotton crops and floods ruined Alabama and Mississippi farmlands. These disasters drove several hundred thousand more African Americans out of the South, mostly to northern cities.

VIEWING FINE ART These two drawings give a bird's-eye view of Chicago in 1871 and many years later in 1916. **Making Comparisons** *What happened to the farmland at the city's edge between 1871 and 1916? What changes do you observe in the buildings in the city center?*

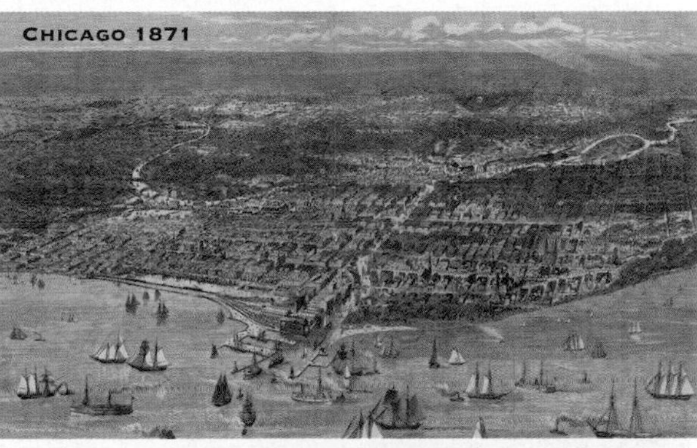

How Cities Grew

The arrival of large numbers of newcomers, from both within and outside the nation, radically changed the face of the nation's cities. Between 1865 and 1900 many features of modern city life, both good and bad, first appeared—from subways and skyscrapers to smog and slums.

Before the Civil War, cities were small in area, rarely extending more than three or four miles across. Most people lived near their workplace and walked wherever they had to go. The introduction of public, horse-drawn carriages that traveled on rails began to change this pattern. Appearing in many cities in the 1850s, they allowed people who could afford the fares to move outside the cities. Those people made their homes in the **suburbs**, or residential communities surrounding the cities.

Later in the 1800s, motorized methods of transportation made commuting much easier and advanced suburban growth. The first elevated trains, opened in 1868 in New York,

LESSON PLAN

Focus Tell students that people flocked to the nation's cities during the Gilded Age. Ask how this changed the cities.

Instruct To help students analyze the factors contributing to migration within the U.S., ask students about the Industrial Revolution's role in migration from rural areas to cities.

Assess/Reteach Have students research the population of New York City in 1860 and in 1900.

From the Archives of
American Heritage®

Two Fires

On the evening of October 7, 1871, Chicago firemen encountered the latest and biggest in a series of fires the city had seen during an unusually dry summer and fall. The next evening, around a quarter of nine, a fresh load of hay caught on fire in Catherine and Patrick O'Leary's barn at the corner of DeKoven and Jefferson streets. A tale sprang up almost instantly that one of their milk cows had kicked over a lantern, but there is no evidence for this; other possible explanations include arson, spontaneous combustion, and a discarded cigar or cigarette. Whatever the cause, high winds swiftly spread the flames, and the fire department, weary from the previous night's marathon effort, was slow to respond. The first company to reach the site attacked the wrong end of the fire, while the second one found its steam pumper broken and without fuel. By the time the whole department could be mobilized, the blaze was out of control. A couple of hours later a gasworks exploded, intensifying the conflagration, and then at 7:00 A.M. hydrants ran dry when the city waterworks caught fire. From then on, all anyone could do was pray for rain. Source: Frederic D. Schwarz, "The Time Machine," *American Heritage®* magazine, October 1996.

CAPTION ANSWERS

Viewing Fine Art The open land near Chicago filled with streets and buildings as the city grew. Newer, taller buildings were built in the city center.

ACTIVITY
Connecting with Geography

Specialized areas such as business districts, retail districts, and industrial districts emerged as a result of city expansion. Have students analyze the social issue of the growth of cities by assuming the role of city planner for a city of their choice. Ask them to choose one of the specialized areas mentioned and create a drawing of it, trying to arrange the district in the best interests of the city. **(Visual/Spatial)**

BACKGROUND
A Diverse Nation

Racial prejudice drove many Chinese out of small towns and forced them to work for other Chinese in service jobs in laundries and restaurants. By the turn of the century there were large Chinese communities in San Francisco and New York City. Chinese neighborhoods, called Chinatowns, were tight enclaves built around small businesses such as cigar manufacturing, groceries, barbershops, and restaurants. Scholar Ronald Takaki described the Chinatowns in American cities as "cultural islands, cut off from the mainland of American society, perceived by whites as strange places to visit as tourists."

Focus on GEOGRAPHY

Streetcar Suburbs The spread of streetcar lines created a new type of town: the streetcar suburb. Streetcars doubled or tripled the distance people could live from the central city while still traveling there to work each day. In many places, the same company that operated the streetcar line built middle-class homes and apartments in leafy suburbs to create demand for their services. Streetcar suburbs included West Philadelphia; East Cleveland; Piedmont Park near Charlotte, North Carolina; Roxbury and Dorchester near Boston; and Harlem, north of downtown New York. Many of these first suburbs later merged with their parent cities.

allowed commuters to bypass the congested streets. Cable cars, introduced in San Francisco in 1873, allowed quick access to the city's steep hills. Electric trolleys, first used in Richmond, Virginia, in 1888, replaced horse-drawn cars and reached even farther into the suburbs. Subway trains first appeared in Boston in 1897. Finally, the automobile, invented in the 1890s and mass-produced beginning in the 1910s, guaranteed that expansion into the suburbs would continue.

Cities grew upward as well as outward. Before the Civil War, buildings stood no more than five stories high. Yet as urban space became scarce, buildings were made taller and taller. To build these mammoth structures, engineers needed the strength of Bessemer steel girders.

To reach the upper floors, people relied on the speed and efficiency of elevators. In 1852 Elisha Graves Otis, an American, invented a safety device that made passenger elevators possible. The first one went into operation five years later. The first skyscraper, Chicago's Home Insurance Company Building, appeared in 1885. Ten stories tall, it was built with a framework of iron and steel and had four passenger elevators. Architect Louis Sullivan completed the ten-story Wainwright building in St. Louis in 1891. The Wainwright building consisted of a steel skeleton sheathed in red sandstone, granite, brick, and a form of baked red clay called terra cotta.

As cities expanded, specialized areas emerged within them. Banks, financial offices, law firms, and government offices were located in one central area. Retail shops and department stores were located in another central neighborhood. Industrial, wholesale, and warehouse districts formed a ring around the center of the city.

Urban Living Conditions

Some urban workers moved into housing built especially for them by mill and factory owners. The rest found apartments wherever they could. Many middle-class residents who moved to the suburbs left empty buildings behind. Owners converted these buildings into multifamily units for workers and their families.

Speculators also built many **tenements,** low-cost apartment buildings designed to house as many families as the owner could pack in. A group of dirty, run-down tenements could transform an area into a slum.

Conditions in the Slums Before long, because of poverty, overcrowding, and neglect, the old residential neighborhoods of cities gradually declined. Trees and grass disappeared. Hundreds of people were crammed into spaces meant for a few families. Soot from coal-fired steam engines and boilers made the air seem dark and foul even in daylight. Open sewers attracted rats and other disease-spreading vermin.

In 1905, journalist Eleanor McMain quoted a university student who described a block of tenements in the Italian district of New Orleans as "death traps, closely built, jammed together, with no side openings. Twenty-five per cent of the yard space is damp and gloomy. . . . Where the houses are three or more rooms in depth, the middle ones are dark, without outside ventilator. . . . There is no fire protection whatever."

Fire was a constant danger in cities. With tenement buildings so closely packed together, even a small fire could quickly consume a neighborhood. Once a fire started, it leaped easily from roof to roof. As a result, most large cities had major fires during this period. Chicago experienced one of the

Growing cities drew people from rural areas. This woman found work as a porter in a subway.

RESOURCE DIRECTORY
Other Print Resources

American History Block Scheduling Support *Ellis Island: Gateway to America,* found in the Expansion, Reconstruction, and Immigration folder, includes interdisciplinary lesson suggestions and activities for Geography and History, Primary Sources, Biography, and Literature.

Technology

Color Transparencies *Fine Art,* E14

most devastating: the Great Chicago Fire of 1871. Nobody knows for sure what started it, but before it was over, 18,000 buildings had burned, leaving some 250 people dead and 100,000 homeless. Property damage estimates reached $200 million, the equivalent of $2 billion today. A similar fire in Boston caused the equivalent of nearly $1 billion in damage.

Contagious diseases, including cholera, malaria, tuberculosis, diphtheria, and typhoid, thrived in crowded tenement conditions. Epidemics, such as the yellow fever that swept through Memphis, Tennessee, in the late 1870s and through New Orleans in the early 1900s, took thousands of lives. Children were especially vulnerable to disease. In one district of tenements in New York City, six out of ten babies died before their first birthday.

Diseases spread rapidly, especially during the summer months when apartments heated up like ovens. A heat wave lasting from August 5 to 13, 1896, took the lives of over 400 New Yorkers. The Chicago Health Department found that at least 80 percent of summer deaths among children under two were caused by preventable diseases. Chicago and New York City established fresh-air havens on their waterfronts for sick children to escape the deadly conditions of the slums.

Light, Air, and Water Scientists believed that lack of good ventilation helped disease spread. They pushed for reforms to improve air flow and natural light in tenements. One wrote:

> *"Simple ordinary outdoor air is a most valuable health resource . . . a balcony on a city street is a thousand times better than a room in a house closed for fear of drafts, curtained for fear of fading the furniture, and lighted by a lamp."*
>
> —Ellen Swallow Richards

In 1879, a change in New York laws required an outside window in every room. To accommodate windows in rows of buildings, an architect designed the **dumbbell tenement,** named for its dumbbell shape. Each building narrowed in the middle, and gaps on either side formed air shafts to bring light and air to inside rooms.

While an improvement, the gloomy air shaft was certainly not an open balcony. The tenement-dweller looked across the closed space to a brick wall and a neighbor's window only a few feet away. Rotting garbage collected at the bottom of the shaft. Little sunlight or fresh air reached apartments this way.

Scientists also linked diseases like cholera and typhoid to contaminated drinking water, which tenement residents drew from a common pipe or pump in the yard. Authorities feared that polluted city water drawn from local springs and rivers could cause epidemics. Boston, Cincinnati, and New York built reservoirs or waterworks to collect clean water far from the city and filter out impurities. City water companies later introduced chlorination and filtration. A 1901 New York City law required that hallway bathrooms replace

INTERPRETING DIAGRAMS
Architects designed the dumbbell tenement to fit as many people as possible into a city block while providing all rooms with light and air. **Drawing Conclusions** *How successful was the dumbbell tenement at meeting these two goals?*

The Dumbbell Tenement

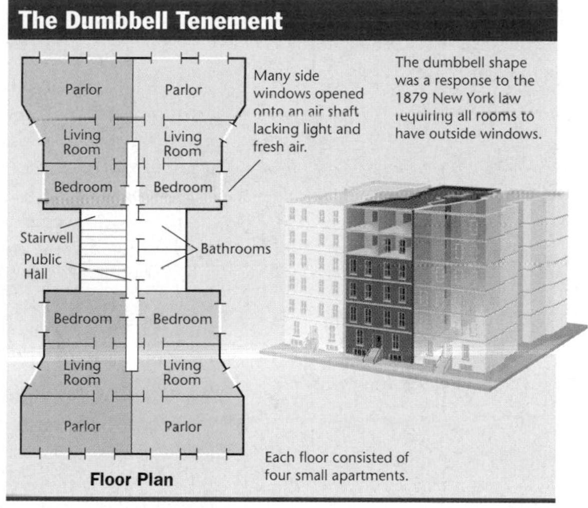

Parlor
Parlor
Living Room
Living Room
Bedroom
Bedroom
Stairwell
Public Hall
Bathrooms
Bedroom
Bedroom
Living Room
Living Room
Parlor
Parlor
Floor Plan
Many side windows opened onto an air shaft lacking light and fresh air.
The dumbbell shape was a response to the 1879 New York law requiring all rooms to have outside windows.
Each floor consisted of four small apartments.

Activity: Connecting with Science and Technology

Tell students to research some of the medical discoveries that have made many of the common nineteenth-century diseases obsolete or rare. Of the contagious diseases—yellow fever, cholera, malaria, tuberculosis, diphtheria, and typhoid—that claimed many lives, which ones are still a threat? Which of these diseases do we no longer see? How have we eradicated them? **(Verbal/Linguistic)**

Background: Geography in History

Thanks to the foresight of Andrew Jackson Downing, America's first major landscape architect, residents of crowded New York City enjoy the trees and wide-open spaces of Central Park. In 1848, after living through numerous riots and epidemics, Downing suggested creating a vast "lung" for the city. In 1858 a competition was held for the design of the park. The winners of the contest were Calvert Vaux and Frederick Law Olmsted. The result—Central Park—has been used as a model for public parks all over the world.

Customize for ... Less Proficient Writers

This section refers to the first development of urban parklands as "lungs of the cities." Ask students to think about nearby parklands, and to write a brief essay or poem about what that open space means to them.

Caption Answers

Interpreting Diagrams Dumbbell tenements did allow a great many people to be crammed into each city block. However, they were largely unsuccessful in providing adequate ventilation and sunlight.

ACTIVITY
Student Portfolio

You may wish to have students add the following to their portfolios: Frederick Law Olmsted is considered by many to be America's greatest landscape architect. He designed New York City's Central Park, Boston's city park system, and about 38 other major parks. Have students find out more about Olmsted's life and present a report about one of his major projects. **(Visual/Spatial)**

BACKGROUND
Biography

David Sarnoff (1891–1971) arrived in New York City from Russia in 1900 and exceeded the immigrant promise of America beyond his wildest dreams. Self-educated in Morse code, he got a job as a radio operator. By 1930 he was president of the Radio Corporation of America (RCA). By 1932 Sarnoff had added the National Broadcasting Corporation (NBC) to the ranks of RCA-owned companies. During World War II Sarnoff served as General Eisenhower's communications consultant. After the war he aggressively promoted the new color television industry for NBC.

READING CHECK

Urban growth caused city governments to become larger and more powerful. Revenue from increased taxes financed better fire fighting, drinking water, public transportation, and other city services.

backyard outhouses. Landlords installed small bathtubs and sinks with running water in most apartments.

How the Other Half Lives The American public learned about the horrors of tenement life in 1890 when a reporter named Jacob Riis published *How the Other Half Lives.* Hoping to generate public support for reform of the tenement "system," Riis painted a bleak picture of New York's future:

> *"Today three-fourths of [New York's] people live in the tenements. . . . We know now that there is no way out; that the 'system' that was the evil offspring of public neglect and private greed has come to stay, a storm-centre forever of our civilization. Nothing is left but to make the best of a bad bargain."*
>
> —Jacob Riis, *How the Other Half Lives*, 1890

American BIOGRAPHY

Jacob Riis
1849–1914

Some reformers worked to improve the lives of the urban poor. One was Jacob Riis. A native of Denmark, Riis had boarded a steamship bound for America in 1870 at the age of 21 and settled in New York City. There he personally experienced the dreadful conditions in which many new Americans lived.

Riis held various jobs before he landed a position as a police reporter in 1873. Riis honed his writing skills while covering New York's Lower East Side, a tenement slum bursting with immigrant families. He worked for the *New York Tribune* from 1877 to 1888 and the *New York Evening Sun* from 1888 to 1899. While working at the *Sun*, Riis wrote *How the Other Half Lives.*

In order to document his reporting, Riis mastered the new technology of flash photography. Drawings based on these photographs appeared in his book, and he showed the actual photographs of overcrowded rooms and run-down buildings in his lectures on the plight of immigrants. As a result of Riis's work, New York State passed the nation's first meaningful laws to improve tenements.

The Results of City Growth

Some city residents could avoid urban problems simply by leaving the cities. The middle and upper classes began moving to the suburbs in the late 1800s. As a result, the gap between the well-to-do and the poor widened.

A few cities preserved neighborhoods of mansions and luxury townhouses near the city center for the wealthiest residents. These areas included Beacon Hill in Boston, the Gold Coast in Chicago, and Nob Hill in San Francisco. Often, people living in these neighborhoods also owned country estates and were quite isolated from the nearby poverty.

Political Divisions Rapidly growing cities proved difficult to govern. Urban growth put pressure on city officials to improve police and fire protection, transportation systems, sewage disposal, electrical and water service, and health care. To deliver these services, cities raised taxes and set up offices to deal with people's needs.

Increased revenue and responsibilities gave city governments more power. Competition among groups for control of city government grew more intense. Some groups represented those members of the middle and upper classes who still lived in the cities. Other groups represented new immigrants, migrants from the countryside, and workers—people that now made up the majority of the population in most cities.

READING CHECK
Why did urban growth change the role of city government?

The Rise of Political Bosses The **political machine** was born out of these clashing interests. A political machine was an unofficial city organization designed to keep a particular party or group in power and usually headed by a single powerful "boss." Sometimes the boss held public office. More often, he handpicked others to run for office and then helped them win.

Political machines worked through the exchange of favors. Machines used an army of ward leaders, each of whom managed a city district, to hand out city jobs and contracts to residents of their ward and do other favors for them. In return, those residents were expected to give their votes to the machine's

RESOURCE DIRECTORY

Teaching Resources

Units 1/2 booklet
- Section 3 Quiz, p. 85

Guide to the Essentials
- Section 3 Summary, p. 40

Biography, Literature, and Comparing Primary Sources booklet (Biography) *Thomas Nast,* p. 20

candidates on election day. Similarly, individuals or companies wanting a favor from the city could get it by first paying some money to the machine. **Graft,** or the use of one's job to gain profit, was a major source of income for the machines.

Many people blamed the success of political machines on the large number of urban immigrants. They charged that corrupt politicians easily took advantage of immigrants who were poorly educated and unfamiliar with democracy. Immigrants tended to support political machines because they helped poor people at a time when neither government nor private industry would.

Cincinnati's George B. Cox, a former saloon owner, was an unusual example of a fairly honest political boss. A Republican, in 1879 he won election to the city council. In true machine fashion he used this post to guarantee election victories and business contracts for the party faithful. But he also worked with local reformers to improve the quality of the police force and city services.

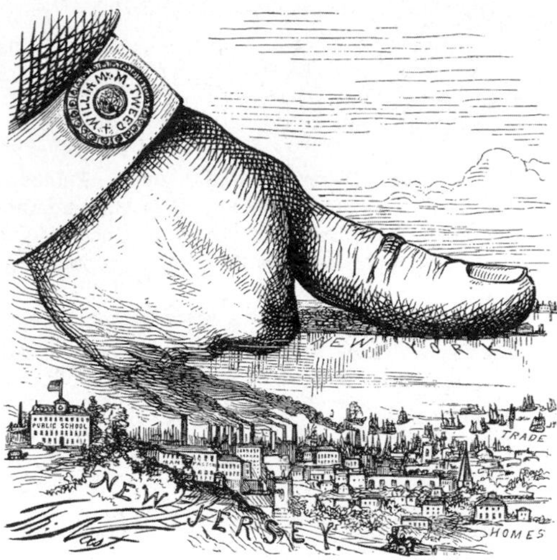

UNDER THE THUMB.

INTERPRETING POLITICAL CARTOONS This cartoon by Thomas Nast illustrates Boss Tweed's total control over New York City. **Recognizing Point of View** *Why did some people believe Boss Tweed's leadership helped New York City?*

Perhaps the most notorious boss was William Marcy Tweed. "Boss" Tweed controlled Tammany Hall, the political club that ran New York City's Democratic Party. Once Tweed and his pals gained access to the city treasury in 1870, they used various illegal methods to plunder it. Tweed and his friends padded bills for construction projects and supply contracts with fake expenses and kept the extra money for themselves. Through countless such instances of fraud and graft, the Tweed ring amassed many millions of dollars.

The brilliant political cartoons of German immigrant Thomas Nast helped bring Tweed down by exposing his methods to the public. Nast's cartoons depicted Tweed as a thief and a dictator who manipulated New York City politics for his own benefit. Convicted of crimes in 1873, Tweed eventually died in jail. Under new leaders, however, Tammany Hall dominated New York politics for another half century.

Section 3 Assessment

READING COMPREHENSION

1. Describe the living conditions in a **tenement** apartment.
2. What were three technological developments that enabled cities to house more people?
3. What contributed to the rise of **political machines?**
4. Why did some people criticize **graft?**

CRITICAL THINKING AND WRITING

5. **Drawing Inferences** Who benefited most from Boss Tweed's control of New York City? What does this tell you about the effects of political machines?
6. **Writing an Outline** Create an outline of the challenges city dwellers faced in the 1880s and 1890s.

Take It to the NET

Activity: Virtual Field Trip Visit the Lower East Side Tenement Museum in New York and learn how immigrants from Germany, Italy, and Russia lived from the 1850s to the 1930s. Use the links provided in the *America: Pathways to the Present* area of the following Web site for help in completing this activity.
www.phschool.com

Section 3 Assessment

Reading Comprehension

1. Overcrowded, unsanitary, disease-ridden, and run-down; but low-cost.
2. Answers should describe advancements in transportation and construction methods, and may include the invention of the elevator, the subway, and the cable car.
3. As city governments grew in size, wealth, and power, they became prizes to control. The machine enabled a local faction of one party to maintain control.
4. Graft is distasteful because it involves using one's position of power to exploit others.

Critical Thinking and Writing

5. Himself and his cohorts in Tammany Hall, revealing political machines as largely self-serving and detrimental to the population at large.
6. Answers will vary but may include: overcrowding, disease, danger of fires, contaminated water, lack of indoor plumbing.

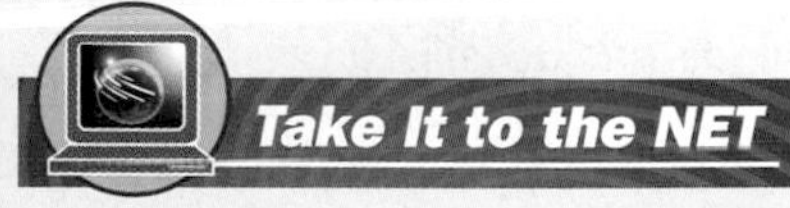

Invite students to take a Virtual Field Trip at **www.phschool.com**

TEST PREPARATION

Have students read the passage by Jacob Riis on the previous page and then complete the sentence below.

Based on the passage, you can tell that—

A Riis felt optimistic about the future of the tenements.
B Riis blamed only tenement owners for the plight of the poor.
C half of New York's population lived in tenements.
(D) Riis thought the tenement system was entrenched in city life and would be difficult to overcome.

Caption Answers

Interpreting Political Cartoons Some people believed that Boss Tweed's machine supplied needed city services for immigrants and the poor.

Analyzing Tables and Statistics

Focus Students learn to analyze statistics to see what they show, what they distort, and what they hide.

Instruct Begin the activity by asking students to review the data in the table. To give them warm-up practice in working with the statistics provided, ask them to identify peak years of immigration for these various population groups: Eastern Europeans, Southern Europeans, Central Europeans. Before they begin the Learn the Skill activity, ask the class to brainstorm various types of analyses they can do, using the statistics.

Extend See the Skills for Life activity in the Resource Directory below.

ANSWERS

Practice the Skill

1. **(a)** Estimated Number of Immigrants to the United States, by Region, 1871–1920. **(b)** Northwestern Europe, Central Europe, Eastern Europe, Southern Europe, Asia, the Americas, Africa, and Oceania. **(c)** *Historical Statistics of the United States, Colonial Times to 1970.* **(d)** Government data is considered reliable.
2. **(a)** 65,727. **(b)** Central Europe provided the largest number of immigrants. Africa provided the smallest number of immigrants.
3. **(a)** Central Europe. **(b)** 1891–1900.
4. When the U.S. unemployment rate was high, the immigration rate was relatively low. When unemployment was low, the immigration rate increased dramatically. A low unemployment rate may have signaled the availability of jobs in the United States and attracted immigrants.
5. **(a)** Answers will vary. **(b)** Answers will vary.

Analyzing Tables and Statistics

Statistical tables present large amounts of numerical data concisely and clearly. The patterns suggested by statistics must be carefully analyzed, however, and their sources evaluated for reliability. Once you have analyzed the data, you can draw conclusions about historical periods or trends.

Estimated Number of Immigrants to the United States, by Region, 1871–1920

Years	Northwestern Europe	Central Europe	Eastern Europe	Southern Europe	Asia[1]	The Americas[2]	Africa	Oceania
1871–1875	858,325	549,610	15,580	37,070	65,727	193,345	205	6,312
1876–1880	493,866	254,511	24,052	39,248	58,096	210,690	153	4,602
1881–1885	1,121,477	1,128,528	63,443	120,297	60,432	403,977	331	4,406
1886–1890	1,131,844	729,967	157,749	211,399	7,948	22,990	526	8,168
1891–1895	745,433	762,216	251,405	314,625	19,255	14,734	163	2,215
1896–1900	392,907	432,363	270,421	389,608	51,981	24,238	187	1,750
1901–1905	761,517	1,121,234	711,546	1,061,406	115,941	63,774	1,829	6,134
1906–1910	807,020	1,365,530	1,058,024	1,260,424	127,626	298,114	5,539	6,890
1911–1915	652,189	1,027,138	978,931	1,137,539	123,719	528,098	5,847	6,126
1916–1920	201,304	23,276	33,547	322,640	68,840	615,573	2,596	7,301

[1]No record of immigration from Korea prior to 1948. [2]No record of immigration from Mexico for 1886 to 1893.
SOURCE: *Historical Statistics of the United States, Colonial Times to 1970*

LEARN THE SKILL

Use the following steps to analyze tables and statistics:

1. **Determine what type of information is presented and decide whether the source is reliable.** The title of the table and the labels for the rows and columns tell you what information is presented. The source is most often found below the table. Government publications are usually reliable sources.
2. **Read the information in the table.** Note how the statistics are organized. This table provides the total number of immigrants who came from each region for a given five-year period.
3. **Find relationships among the statistics.** In this case, you can compare the number of immigrants who came to the United States from different regions or trace changes in the pattern of immigration from one region over time.
4. **Use the data to draw conclusions.** You can also use what you know from other sources. Compare patterns in the two sets of data.
5. **Share your data and conclusions.** Present and support your conclusions in a report, or create graphs or charts that help explain your data.

PRACTICE THE SKILL

Answer the following questions:

1. **(a)** What is the title of the table? **(b)** What geographical areas are covered? **(c)** What is the source of the statistics? **(d)** Are the data reliable?
2. **(a)** Between 1871 and 1875, how many immigrants came to the United States from Asia? **(b)** Between 1881 and 1885, which region provided the largest number of immigrants? The smallest number of immigrants?
3. **(a)** Between 1871 and 1920, which region provided the largest total number of immigrants? **(b)** During which decade did the Americas show the sharpest drop in the number of immigrants?
4. Between 1891 and 1900, the unemployment rate in the United States averaged 10.5 percent. Between 1901 and 1910, it averaged 4.5 percent. What conclusions can you draw about the relationship between the unemployment rate and the immigration rate for these time periods?
5. **(a)** Write a paragraph summarizing the conclusions you reached in Question 4. Support your conclusions with data from the table. **(b)** Create a line graph showing the pattern of immigration from one region from 1871–1920.

APPLY THE SKILL

See the Chapter Review and Assessment for another opportunity to apply this skill.

RESOURCE DIRECTORY

Teaching Resources
Skills for Life booklet, p. 17

Technology
Social Studies Skills Tutor CD-ROM
Interactive Practice in
- Geographic Literacy
- Critical Thinking and Reading
- Visual Analysis
- Communications

Section 4

Ideas for Reform

READING FOCUS

- How did different movements help the needy?
- How and where did sociology develop?
- What efforts were made to control immigration and personal behavior in the late 1800s?

MAIN IDEA

A variety of groups worked to improve social, economic, and political conditions in the cities.

KEY TERMS

social gospel movement
settlement house
sociology
nativism
temperance movement
prohibition
vice

TAKING NOTES

Copy the web diagram below. As you read, fill in each blank circle with important movements that focused on immigration, morality, or both.

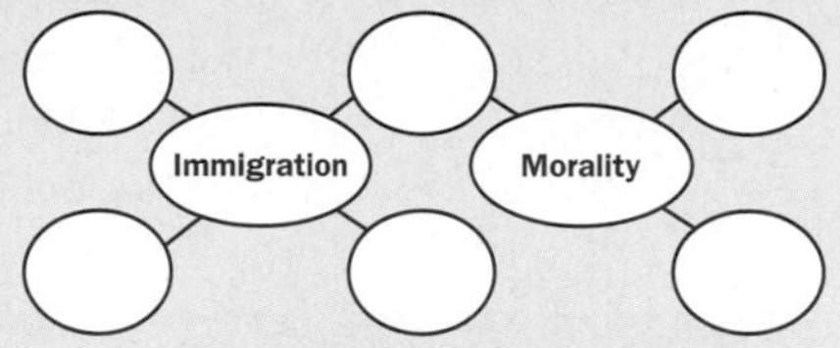

Setting the Scene

During the Gilded Age, saloons, places where men could meet to drink and gamble, could be found in nearly every city and town. Frances Willard paid her first visit to one at the age of 35. Unlike the customers, she arrived with a prayer group. Willard later wrote:

> *"The tall, stately lady who led us placed her Bible on the bar and read a psalm . . . and then one of the older women whispered to me softly that the leader wished to know if I would pray. It was strange, perhaps, but I felt not the least reluctance, and kneeling on the sawdust floor, with a group of earnest hearts around me, and behind them . . . a crowd of unwashed, unkempt, hard-looking drinking men, I was conscious that perhaps never in my life, save beside my sister Mary's dying bed, had I prayed as truly as I did then."*
>
> —Frances Willard

Temperance advocates pray outside a saloon.

Frances Willard described the experience as her "baptism" in the "Crusade." One week later she became president of the Chicago chapter of the Woman's Christian Temperance Union, an anti-alcohol group. Frances Willard was a reformer. Like many Americans of her time, she observed a problem in society and chose to confront it, motivated by her faith and her concern for the well-being of others. However, not everyone agreed with her wish to ban alcohol. Like many other crusaders, Frances Willard found that her personal goals could lead to conflict.

Helping the Needy

Many middle-class people were genuinely shocked by poor living and working conditions in the slums. One group of reformers, moved by social conscience or religious idealism, worked to improve society by helping the needy. They argued that prosperous Americans should fight poverty and improve unwholesome social conditions in cities.

Section 4

Ideas for Reform

SECTION OBJECTIVES

1. Study the ways in which different movements helped the needy.
2. Learn how and where sociology developed.
3. Examine efforts to control immigration and personal behavior in the late 1800s.

BELLRINGER

Warm-Up Activity Ask students to list what they consider the most effective ways to help needy people. Ask them to consider the pros and cons of each.

Activating Prior Knowledge Ask students to list some efforts in the local community to help people in need. Can students also name global organizations designed to help people? Have students list in order the types of help they consider most important to needy people.

READING STRATEGY

Have students write down these headings: *Controlling Immigrants* and *Helping the Needy.* As they read, have students list under the correct heading strategies used to reform cities.

ACTIVITY

Connecting with Citizenship

Have students investigate ways in which religious and civic groups promote social welfare in today's culture. What kinds of charitable efforts are made by churches, synagogues, and other organized religious or civic groups? How successful are these campaigns? Can students list such activities that take place in their community? Have students participated in any efforts to help those less fortunate than themselves? If so, what have they done? **(Verbal/Linguistic)**

RESOURCE DIRECTORY

Teaching Resources

Guided Reading and Review booklet, p. 65

Other Print Resources

Nystrom *Atlas of Our Country* *The Third Wave of Immigration,* pp. 30–31

Technology

Section Reading Support Transparencies
Guided Reading Audiotapes (English/Spanish), Ch. 8
Student Edition on Audio CD, Ch. 8
Prentice Hall Presentation Pro CD-ROM, Ch. 8
Companion Web site, www.phschool.com

Lesson Plan

Focus Point out that the rapid growth of the nation's cities led to many urban problems. Reformers worked to improve social, economic, and political conditions in the cities. How successful were they?

Instruct Discuss the events and trends that made some Americans wary of immigration. Examples include the assassination of President McKinley, corruption in city governments, and poor conditions in slums. How did members of groups like the nativists and the temperance movement try to control immigration and personal behavior?

Have students compare reformers who tried to outlaw certain behaviors with those who developed a "helping" approach. Which group more successfully achieved its goals?

Assess/Reteach Throughout the history of the United States, immigrants have had a hard time being accepted in their new country. Have students research other periods when immigration was a contentious political issue.

Background

Biography

Jane Addams wrote a memoir, *Twenty Years at Hull House,* in which she details her efforts to create the now-famous community center. In the introduction to a recent reprinting of Addams's memoir, author Ruth Sidel notes that Addams was influenced by the thinking of two men: Abraham Lincoln and her own father. Her father, a Quaker and state legislator, helped Addams develop her social conscience, reminding her every day of those less fortunate than she. Addams graduated from Rockford College and went on to study medicine. She was forced to halt her studies because of a medical condition. While visiting London in 1883, Addams saw the Toynbee Hall settlement house, which became her inspiration for Hull House.

The Charity Organization Movement In 1882, Josephine Shaw Lowell founded the New York Charity Organization Society (COS). The COS tried to make charity a scientific enterprise. Members kept detailed files on those who received help. In this way, COS leaders could more easily determine how to serve their clients. Yet keeping detailed files also allowed COS leaders to distinguish between the poor whom they considered worthy of help and those whom they deemed unworthy. This attitude sometimes led to unkind treatment of the needy.

Many COS members wanted immigrants to adopt American, middle-class standards of child-raising, cooking, and cleaning. They did not care how strange these customs seemed to people with different cultural backgrounds. This disturbed some immigrants, but others were grateful for the assistance.

The Social Gospel Movement In the 1880s and 1890s, urban churches began to provide social services for the poor who now surrounded them. They also tried to aim some reform campaigns in new directions. Instead of blaming immigrants for drinking, gambling, and other behaviors, the churches sought to treat the problems that drove people into such activities.

Soon a social reform movement developed within religious institutions. It was called the **social gospel movement** and it sought to apply the gospel (teachings) of Jesus directly to society. The movement focused on the gospel ideals of charity and justice, especially by seeking labor reforms. In 1908, followers of such views formed the Federal Council of the Churches of Christ. This organization supported providing improved living conditions and a larger share in the national wealth for all workers. Other religious organizations, including some Jewish synagogues, adapted the social gospel ideal for themselves.

VIEWING HISTORY Some reformers focused their efforts on helping immigrants adjust to life in the United States. This immigrant is learning English. **Analyzing Information** *What else is she learning?*

The Settlement Movement Thousands of young, educated women and men put the social gospel into practice in an innovative reform program called the settlement movement. These young reformers settled into a house in the midst of a poor neighborhood. From this **settlement house,** a kind of community center, they eventually offered social services.

The settlement movement had begun in Britain. Its founders believed that simply giving money to the poor never really helped them. In order to find out what would be most helpful, the young settlers had to live in poor neighborhoods. There they could witness the effects of poverty firsthand.

In 1889, inspired by the British settlement movement, Jane Addams and Ellen Gates Starr bought the run-down Charles Hull mansion in Chicago. They repaired it and opened its doors to their immigrant neighbors. At first, Starr and Addams simply wanted to get to know their neighbors, offering help when needed. Soon they began anticipating and responding to the needs of the community as a whole.

Over the decades that followed, Addams and Starr turned Hull House into a center of community activity. At Hull House, neighbors could attend cultural events, take classes, or display exhibits of crafts from their home countries. The

Resource Directory

Other Print Resources

American History Block Scheduling Support *Ellis Island: Gateway to America,* found in the Expansion, Reconstruction, Immigration folder, includes interdisciplinary lesson suggestions and activities for Geography and History, Primary Sources, Biography, and Literature.

Technology

RESOURCE PRO® **Biography** *Lillian Wald,* found on Resource Pro, profiles the public-health nurse, activist, fund-raiser, and champion of child welfare and women's rights.

RESOURCE PRO® **Primary Source Activity** *Hull House,* found on Resource Pro, uses excerpts from the writings of founder Jane Addams to encourage students' investigations of social service organizations.

Exploring Primary Sources in U.S. History CD-ROM *Twenty Years at Hull House, Jane Addams*

Caption Answers

Viewing History She is learning how to cook an American breakfast like an American woman.

VIEWING HISTORY Reformers offered help to newcomers by watching over their children while they worked. **Synthesizing Information** *What other services did settlement houses offer?*

settlement set up child-care centers, playgrounds, clubs, and summer camps for boys and girls; offices to help people find jobs and deal with legal problems; and health-care clinics. It also launched investigations of city economic, political, and social conditions. These actions laid the foundation for many later reforms.

Settlement houses like Hull House sprang up across the country. The Henry Street Settlement, founded by Lillian Wald on New York's Lower East Side, was originally a nurses' settlement to offer home health care to the poor. Its programs soon expanded to resemble many of those at Hull House. Missionaries, too, founded settlement houses, in part to gain converts but also to apply the social gospel in practical ways.

By 1910 there were more than 400 settlement houses. Most were supported by donations and staffed by volunteers or people willing to work for low wages and free room and board. Hundreds of college graduates, especially women excluded from other professions, became settlement workers. Except for leaders, such as Addams and Wald, most workers spent only a few years in these jobs. Many moved on to professional careers in social work, education, or government.

Few ever forgot their settlement experience. "I don't know that my attitude changed," wrote one former settlement worker, "but my point of view certainly did, or perhaps it would be more true to say that now I have several points of view." By helping its workers see social issues in new ways, the settlement houses energized the reform movement while improving the lives of the urban poor.

READING CHECK
What were the effects of the settlement movement?

The Development of Sociology

While settlement workers observed first-hand the problems of the slums, scholars in America and Europe were developing a scientific way of looking at how people lived. Philosopher Auguste Comte coined the term **sociology** to describe the study of how people interact with one another in a society. Sociology is a social science. Like a biologist studying animals, a sociologist collects data on societies, and measures the data against theories of human behavior.

ACTIVITY
Connecting with Citizenship

Have students analyze the effects of changing demographic patterns resulting from immigration to the United States by inviting small groups of students to plan a community center similar to Hull House. Tell students that they must take into account some of the current social problems facing our culture. Suggest that students list some of the services they would provide and some of the specialists who would work at the center. Students should also identify the neighborhood in which they would locate their community center, remembering to consider factors such as proximity to public transportation. **(Verbal/Linguistic)**

BACKGROUND
Connections to Today

During the 1990s the population of Asian immigrants in the United States nearly doubled, to at least 10.2 million people, according to the 2000 census. Chinese make up the largest Asian group in the United States, totaling 2.4 million people. The number of Asian Indians in the United States also nearly doubled. The 2000 census also shows an 83 percent increase in the Vietnamese population. Japanese, whose numbers fell by 6 percent, were the only Asian group whose population decreased in the United States during the 1990s.

READING CHECK
Settlement houses provided immediate assistance to urban poor in such forms as child care, health care, and legal assistance. They also contributed to long-term reforms in city government services for the poor.

CAPTION ANSWERS

Viewing History Health-care clinics, schooling, cultural events, legal aid, and help finding employment.

TEST PREPARATION

Have students reread the quotation on this page and answer the question below.

Based on that statement, what can be concluded about this person's settlement house experience?

A The worker did not learn much about the people who came to the settlement house.

(B) The worker learned a lot by working in the settlement house.

C The worker disliked the people who came to the settlement house.

D The worker did not learn about others' points of view in the settlement house.

ACTIVITY
Connecting with Culture

Instruct students to research ways in which the sentiments of the nativists may have influenced immigration policies in the United States and how those policies have evolved. Students should include the Comprehensive Immigration Law (1924) and the Immigration Bill (1965) in their research. Have students write a short essay on their findings. **(Verbal/Linguistic)**

BACKGROUND
Recent Scholarship

Were settlement movement founders altruists who respected the cultural pluralism of immigrant communities? Or were they "social controllers" trying to check the chaos of a rapidly urbanizing society and bent on Americanization? Focusing solely on the nationally important settlement houses can be misleading, suggests Ruth Crocker in *Social Work and Social Order: The Settlement Movement in Two Industrial Cities, 1889–1930.* Crocker looks at "second-tier" settlements, notably those founded by religious groups in Indiana. By highlighting the evangelical side of the movement and the support it received from the business community, she reveals a tendency toward social control that historians often do not discuss.

READING CHECK

Nativists felt threatened by urban immigrants who had attained political and financial power. They blamed immigrants for the problems, such as crime and poverty found in cities in the late 1800s.

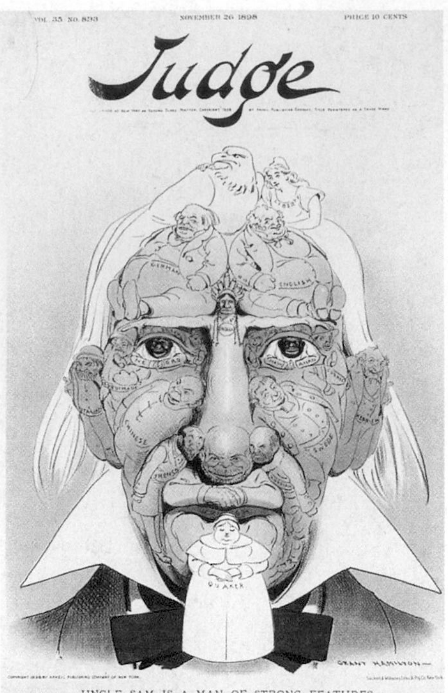

Judge
UNCLE SAM IS A MAN OF STRONG FEATURES.

INTERPRETING POLITICAL CARTOONS The caption on this magazine cover reads, "Uncle Sam is a man of strong features." **Recognizing Point of View** *What does this cartoon suggest about the artist's view of immigration?*

Sociology provided a scientific counterpart to the settlement houses' practical experience.

Sociologists studied cultures around the world to learn what institutions and practices define a society. The institutions in an American community might include houses of worship, local governments, schools, libraries, and museums. Practices might include the way that children relate to their parents or a community teaches students. In the late nineteenth century, many sociologists studied the effects of industrialization and urbanization on established communities. America's rapidly changing population provided them with many examples.

Controlling Immigration and Behavior

Many Americans linked the problems of the cities to the new immigrants. By controlling immigrants, they hoped to restore what they believed had been a past of purity and virtue. Groups were formed to pursue this goal. Some sought to keep immigrants out of the United States, while others wanted to change their behavior.

Nativism In the 1850s, the Know-Nothing Party had gained many followers by vowing to restrict immigration. Thirty years later this policy of **nativism,** or favoring native-born Americans over immigrants, reappeared. The rise of immigrants to positions of power in the cities helped provoke this new wave of antiforeign bias. Passage of the Chinese Exclusion Act in 1882 showed how politically effective the new nativists were.

Nativists did not oppose only Asian immigration. The American Protective Association, a nativist group founded in 1887, targeted immigrants in general as well as the Catholic Church. It called for the teaching of only American culture and the English language in schools and demanded tighter rules on citizenship and employment of aliens. Members of this secret society took an oath to hire and vote for Protestants alone.

Nativists won a victory in 1885, when Congress repealed the Contract Labor Act. Passed in 1864, the law had allowed employers to recruit foreign laborers. Even after the law's repeal, however, employers often illegally brought in foreign workers to replace striking employees. Such actions only heightened nativist feelings among workers.

There were nativists among the wealthy as well. The Immigration Restriction League was organized in 1894 by some Harvard College graduates. The League hoped to exclude immigrants considered unfit by requiring them to pass literacy tests. Its main targets were immigrants from southern and eastern Europe, whose cultures differed greatly from those of League members.

READING CHECK Why did nativists oppose immigration?

Prohibition Like nativism, another movement begun before the Civil War saw a revival later in the 1800s: the **temperance movement,** an organized campaign to eliminate alcohol consumption. Three groups dominated the new temperance movement: the Prohibition party, founded in 1869, the Woman's Christian Temperance Union, founded in 1874, and the Anti-Saloon League, founded in 1893. These groups opposed drinking on the grounds that it led to personal tragedies. They supported **prohibition,** a ban on the manufacture and sale of alcoholic beverages. One activist, Carry Nation, won fame by smashing illegal saloons with a hatchet in her home state of Kansas.

CAPTION ANSWERS

Interpreting Political Cartoons The cartoonist believed that immigration built the United States and continued to make it stronger.

RESOURCE DIRECTORY

Teaching Resources

Units 1/2 booklet
- Section 4 Quiz, p. 86
- Chapter 8 Test, pp. 87, 90

Guide to the Essentials
- Section 4 Summary, p. 41
- Chapter 8 Test, p. 42

Other Print Resources

Chapter Tests with ExamView® Test Bank CD-ROM, Ch. 8

Technology

ExamView® Test Bank CD-ROM, Ch. 8
Social Studies Skills Tutor CD-ROM

Prohibition groups also opposed drinking because of what they saw as the links among saloons, immigrants, and political bosses. Immigrant men often used saloons as social clubs, where they could relax and also find information about jobs. Prohibitionists believed that saloons undermined public morals. Some prohibitionists even claimed that saloons formed the center of a movement to take over the United States. "Foreign control or conquest is rapidly making us un-Christian, with immorality throned in power," one prohibitionist wrote in 1908.

At first, progress was slow. Early prohibitionists measured their success by towns and counties that agreed to ban alcohol. By 1890, only three states had gone completely "dry" and embraced prohibition: Maine, Kansas, and North Dakota.

Purity Crusaders As cities grew, drugs, gambling, prostitution, and other forms of vice became big business. **Vice** (immoral or corrupt behavior) was not unique to the cities. But large urban populations made vice highly visible and very profitable. Then as now, many residents fought to rid their communities of unwholesome and illegal activities.

"Purity crusaders" led the way. In 1873, Anthony Comstock founded the New York Society for the Suppression of Vice. The following year he won passage of a law that prohibited sending obscene materials through the United States mail. Material deemed obscene included descriptions of methods to prevent unwanted pregnancy. For decades the Comstock Law, as it came to be known, slowed the distribution of information about birth control.

Other purity crusaders attacked urban political machines, saying that machine-controlled police forces profited from vice. Police were known to demand payment from gamblers in return for ignoring illegal activities. On occasion, purity crusaders joined forces with other reformers to run for public office. By campaigning on an anti-vice platform, some succeeded in throwing machine candidates out of office. Usually the political machines regained power in later elections by mocking the self-righteous tone of many purists and by arguing that morality was a personal issue.

Focus on DAILY LIFE

Mrs. Winslow's Soothing Syrup
The WCTU found a target in the heavily advertised patent medicines that parents bought to cure illness and quiet crying babies. Mrs. Winslow's Soothing Syrup sold very well; it put children to sleep with a mix of alcohol and morphine, a narcotic made from opium. Other childhood remedies based on morphine included Dr. Fahrney's Teething Syrup, Dr. Seth Arnold's Cough Killer, and Carney Common Sense Cure. Although popular, these so-called medicines were addictive and harmful to children's health. The federal government outlawed Mrs. Winslow's Soothing Syrup in 1906.

Section 4 Assessment

READING COMPREHENSION

1. What was the purpose of the New York Charity Organization Society?
2. What is the purpose of **sociology?**
3. What was the goal of **nativist** movements?
4. How did **temperance** groups and purity crusaders differ from charity, **social gospel,** and **settlement** movements?

CRITICAL THINKING AND WRITING

5. **Identifying Assumptions** How might the anti-immigrant arguments of wealthy nativists have differed from those of less-affluent nativists?
6. **Drawing Inferences** What were two possible reasons for people to oppose purity crusaders?
7. **Journal Writing** Write three brief fictional journal entries from the point of view of a settlement house worker.

Take It to the NET

Activity: Creating a Poster
Research Hull House and create a poster designed to inform neighbors about the services offered at that settlement house. Use the links provided in the *America: Pathways to the Present* area of the following Web site for help in completing this activity.
www.phschool.com

Section 4 Assessment

Reading Comprehension

1. To take a scientific approach to providing charity. Also, to encourage immigrants to behave like middle-class Americans.
2. To examine, scientifically, how people live and interact with one another in a society.
3. To favor native-born Americans over immigrants.
4. Temperance groups and purity crusaders focused on banning alcohol and vice. The other groups focused on improving society by providing help to the needy.

Critical Thinking and Writing

5. Sample: Less wealthy nativists might have argued to restrict immigration so they would not have to compete for jobs. Wealthy nativists opposed immigrant cultures.
6. Answers will vary, but may include: morality is a personal issue; vice was big business; protection of First Amendment rights.
7. Answers will vary, but may include being shocked at the depth of poverty, or finding the work to be fulfilling.

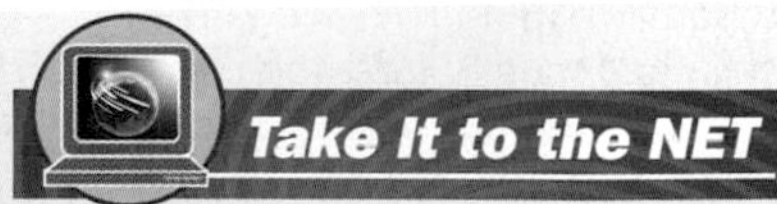

Take It to the NET

Posters will vary but should demonstrate knowledge of the services offered to immigrants and the poor at Hull House.

CUSTOMIZE FOR ...

Gifted and Talented

Ask students to identify the style of reform favored by Jacob Riis, based on this quotation from his article "The Battle with the Slum": "Government by the people must ever rest upon the people's ability to govern themselves, upon their intelligence and public spirit. The slum stands for ignorance, want, unfitness, for mob-rule. . . . Put it this way: you cannot let men live like pigs when you need their votes as freemen."

Chapter 8

Reviewing Key Terms

Students should refer to the definitions of key terms in the chapter to write sentences that show an understanding of politics, immigration, and urban life in the Gilded Age.

Reviewing Main Ideas

15. Business interests tried to influence politicians to vote in their favor by giving gifts and money.
16. The hiring of unqualified and often dishonest government employees. Corruption in government became an accepted practice.
17. Immigrants fled poor farming, working, and living conditions in their home countries.
18. More new immigrants during this period come from southern and eastern Europe.
19. Middle-class residents moved to the suburbs. Urban landowners built cheap tenements that became neglected, overcrowded, unsanitary, and unsafe.
20. Advantages: They helped poor immigrants when no help was given by government or private industry. Disadvantages: They illegally skimmed money from the city's income and hurt businesses.
21. By offering social services in community centers, such as classes, childcare, and health care. They also launched investigations of city economic, political, and social conditions, laying the foundation for later reforms.
22. They influenced the passage of the Chinese Exclusion Act and the repeal of the Contract Labor Act. They also founded the Immigration Restriction League.

Chapter 8 Review and Assessment

creating a CHAPTER SUMMARY

Copy this chart (right) on a piece of paper and complete it by adding important events and issues that fit each heading. Some entries have been completed for you as examples.

Politics, Immigration, and Urban Life in the Gilded Age	
Immigration and Nativism	• More immigrants arrive from eastern and southern Europe. • Mexican immigrants settle in the Southwest. • Asian immigrants face challenges in the West. •
Presidential Politics	
Urban Growth	
Political Machines	
Social Reform	

iTEXT

For additional review and enrichment activities, see the interactive version of *America: Pathways to the Present*, available on the Web and on CD-ROM.

★ Reviewing Key Terms

For each of the terms below, write a sentence explaining how it relates to the Gilded Age.

1. Gilded Age
2. *laissez-faire*
3. blue law
4. civil service
5. steerage
6. ghetto
7. Chinese Exclusion Act
8. suburb
9. tenement
10. political machine
11. graft
12. settlement house
13. nativism
14. prohibition

★ Reviewing Main Ideas

15. How did business influence politicians during the Gilded Age? (Section 1)
16. What problems did the spoils system create? (Section 1)
17. Why did so many people want to come to the United States between 1870 and 1915? (Section 2)
18. Starting in the 1890s, where did large numbers of immigrants come from? (Section 2)
19. How did slums develop in cities? (Section 3)
20. What were the advantages and disadvantages of political machines for urban residents? (Section 3)
21. How did the settlement movement seek to help the needy? (Section 4)
22. What actions did nativists take to restrict immigration? (Section 4)

★ Critical Thinking

23. **Drawing Inferences** What character trait did President Rutherford B. Hayes exhibit by his actions regarding the spoils system? Explain.
24. **Drawing Conclusions** What conclusion(s) can you draw from the fact that Tammany Hall dominated New York City for more than 50 years?
25. **Predicting Consequences** What might have been the effect if the United States had adopted all the ideas of the nativists?
26. **Making Comparisons** How and why did the experiences of Chinese immigrants differ from the experiences of immigrants from Italy and Russia?
27. **Recognizing Bias** Read the following quote about a charity reformer's visit to an immigrant home: "[they] upset the usual routine of their lives, opening windows, undressing children, giving orders not to eat this and that, not to wrap babies in swaddling clothes." (a) What does this quote reveal about the author's opinions? (b) How might a charity reformer describe the visit?

Creating a Chapter Summary

Politics, Immigration, and Urban Life in the Gilded Age	
Immigration and Nativism	• More immigrants arrive from eastern and southern Europe. • Mexican immigrants settle in the Southwest. • Asian immigrants face challenges in the West.
Presidential Politics	• Corruption common at high levels in government • Laissez faire attitude by government toward business • Credit Mobilier scandal in Grant's administration • Hayes reformed spoils system • Garfield shot and later died • Arthur ended spoils system.
Urban Growth	• Populations of cities swelled in years 1871–1900. • Slums and ghettos developed. • Suburbs developed. • Transportation caused cities to grow.
Political Machines	• Bosses arose to control problems in cities. • Graft a source of income for political machines
Social Reform	• Social service organizations sprang up to try to help immigrants and so improve city life. • Many people wrote about the problems of the cities and tried to suggest solutions.

★ Skills Assessment

Analyzing Political Cartoons ▶

28. This scene shows a strength contest once popular at fairs. The goal was to test one's strength in an attempt to ring the bell at the top of the column. Examine the scene. Who are the contestants?
29. Examine the game. (a) What are the contestants hitting? (b) What is the bell? (c) What is the mallet?
30. Read the caption. Describe the cartoonist's message in a brief paragraph.

Interpreting Data

Turn to the graph titled "European Immigration, 1870–1920" in Section 2.

31. In which of the following years did immigrants from central Europe outnumber immigrants from every other region?
    - **A** 1870
    - **B** 1880 and 1890
    - **C** 1900 and 1910
    - **D** 1920
32. Which sentence best describes immigration from eastern Europe from 1870 to 1920?
    - **F** Immigration increased steadily and then fell to near zero.
    - **G** The number of immigrants declined steadily.
    - **H** The number of immigrants increased steadily every decade.
    - **J** The number of immigrants stayed constant.

Applying the Chapter Skill: *Analyzing Tables and Skills*

33. Look back at the table on the Skills for Life page. World War I was fought from 1914 to 1918. How does the table reflect the influence of the war on immigration to the United States?

ACTIVITIES

Writing to LEARN

Writing to Compare and Contrast Today, the Democratic and Republican parties both try to appeal to the large American middle class. Write an essay comparing and contrasting the major parties of today with those in the Gilded Age. Be sure to address this question: Did all levels of society have a political voice in both eras?

Primary Source CD-ROM

Working With Primary Sources Find additional information on immigration and urban life on the *Exploring Primary Sources in the U.S. History CD-ROM* and use the selection(s) provided to complete the Chapter 8 primary source activity located in the *America: Pathways to the Present* area of the following Web site.
www.phschool.com

Take It to the NET

Chapter Self-Test As a review activity, take the Chapter 8 Self-Test in the *America: Pathways to the Present* area of the Web site listed below. The questions are designed to test your understanding of the chapter content.
www.phschool.com

CRITICAL THINKING

23. Sample answer: Integrity, because he refused to use the patronage system even though he angered his fellow Republicans and thus ensured that he could not win reelection.
24. That political machines, although corrupt, were entrenched in city politics and economics and were successful enough that there was no organized public outcry against them.
25. Sample answer: Immigration from some countries would have declined greatly; society would be less multicultural and less tolerant.
26. European immigrants generally fared better. For instance, Russian Jews found religious freedom in America. The Chinese had to contend with labor contracts and the Exclusion Act.
27. (a) The author feels charity reformers are arrogant. (b) A charity reformer might insist that immigrant behavior must be changed to American standards.

SKILLS ASSESSMENT

28. Trusts.
29. (a) Consumers. (b) Profits. (c) A tariff.
30. Powerful trusts are being assisted by tariffs. These trusts are abusing consumers in order to reap high profits.
31. C
32. F
33. Immigration from all parts of Europe decreased markedly.

ANSWERS TO ACTIVITIES

Writing to LEARN

Sample answer: Many segments of society in the Gilded Age had much less of a political voice than they do today. Women in the Gilded Age still could not vote; African Americans still faced various forms of social, political, and economic discrimination; and many immigrant groups were discriminated against and not considered citizens.

Primary Source CD-ROM

Direct students to the additional primary sources that can be found on the *Exploring Primary Sources in U.S. History CD-ROM.*

Take It to the NET

Additional support materials and activities for Chapter 8 of *America: Pathways to the Present* can be found in the Social Studies area at the Prentice Hall School Web site. **www.phschool.com**

Chapter 9 Planning Guide
Resource Manager

	Core Instruction	Reading/Skills
Chapter-Level Resources **TEKS** 24(B)	Teaching Resources • Pacing Charts booklet • Block Scheduling booklet **Resource Pro® CD-ROM,** Ch. 9 **Prentice Hall Presentation Pro CD-ROM,** Ch. 9 **www.phschool.com** • eTeach	**Guided Reading Audiotapes (English/Spanish)** **Student Edition on Audio CD,** Ch. 9 **Social Studies Skills Tutor CD-ROM** **Color Transparency,** E15
1 The Expansion of Education 1. Learn how and why public schools expanded during the late 1800s. 2. Find out how opportunities for higher education increased after the Civil War. 3. Discover the views of Booker T. Washington and W.E.B. Du Bois regarding African American education. **TEKS** 2(C), 8(A), 21(B), 24(D), 24(G), 25(D)	Teaching Resources **Units 1/2 booklet** • Section 1 Quiz, p. 94 **Learning Styles Lesson Plans booklet,** p. 21	**Guided Reading and Review booklet,** p. 66 **Guide to the Essentials,** p. 43 **Learning with Documents booklet,** pp. 84, 85 **Skills for Life booklet,** p. 16 **Section Reading Support Transparencies**
2 New Forms of Entertainment 1. Discover the new kinds of performances and recreation that Americans enjoyed at the turn of the century. 2. Find out what people were reading for education and entertainment. 3. Learn how American music was changing. **TEKS** 2(C), 24(A)	Teaching Resources **Units 1/2 booklet** • Section 2 Quiz, p. 95 **Learning Styles Lesson Plans booklet,** p. 34	**Guided Reading and Review booklet,** p. 67 **Guide to the Essentials,** p. 44 **Section Reading Support Transparencies**
3 The World of Jim Crow 1. Probe the kinds of discrimination encountered by African Americans after Reconstruction. 2. Find out how African Americans resisted this discrimination. **TEKS** 1(B), 2(C), 21(A), 24(A)	Teaching Resources **Units 1/2 booklet** • Section 3 Quiz, p. 96	**Guided Reading and Review booklet,** p. 68 **Guide to the Essentials,** p. 45 **Section Reading Support Transparencies**
4 The Changing Role of Women 1. Examine the issues in the debate over women's equality. 2. Discover how women's work in the home changed at the turn of the century. 3. Learn how stores and catalogs served women's new role as consumers. 4. Find out about the kinds of work that women did outside the home. **TEKS** 5(A), 18(B), 24(A), 25(D)	Teaching Resources **Units 1/2 booklet** • Section 4 Quiz, p. 97 **Learning Styles Lesson Plans booklet,** p. 35	**Guided Reading and Review booklet,** p. 69 **Guide to the Essentials,** p. 46 **Learning with Documents booklet,** p. 55 **Section Reading Support Transparencies**

Enrichment/Pre-AP

Prentice Hall United States History Video Collection™
www.phschool.com
- Section Activities, Virtual Field Trip, Chapter Activities, Current Events Online

Sounds of an Era Audio CD

Biography, Literature, and Comparing Primary Sources booklet, p. 62
Sounds of an Era Audio CD

Great Debates booklet, pp. 32–35
American History Block Scheduling Support
Nystrom *Atlas of Our Country*, pp. 30–31

Biography, Literature, and Comparing Primary Sources booklet, p. 127
Great Debates booklet, p. 34
American Pathways Thematic Posters

Assessment

Core Assessment
ExamView® Test Bank, Ch. 9
ExamView® Test Bank CD-ROM, Ch. 9

Standardized Test Preparation
Diagnose and Prescribe
Diagnostic Tests for High School Social Studies Skills

Review and Reteach
Review Book for U.S. History

Practice and Assess
Test-taking Strategies With Transparencies
Test-taking Strategies Posters
Test Prep Book for U.S. History
Alternative Assessment Handbook
Document-Based Assessment

Teaching Resources
Units 1/2 booklet
- Section Quizzes, pp. 94–97
- Chapter Test, p. 98

www.phschool.com Ch. 9 Self-Test

AmericanHeritage Resources

From the Archives of American Heritage®, p. 338
AmericanHeritage® My Brush with History™ Videotapes
www.americanheritage.com

Don't miss the exclusive interactive version of this textbook on the Web and on CD-ROM.

Chapter 9 Planning Guide
In Your Classroom

Customize for Individual Needs

Gifted and Talented

Teacher's Edition
- Customize for Gifted and Talented, pp. 331, 335

Teaching Resources
- Biography, Literature, and Comparing Primary Sources booklet, pp. 21, 62, 127

ESL

Teacher's Edition
- Customize for ESL, p. 321

Teaching Resources
- Guided Reading and Review booklet, pp. 66–69
- Guide to the Essentials (English/Spanish), Chapter 9

Technology
- Student Edition on Audio CD, Chapter 9
- Guided Reading Audiotapes (English/Spanish), Chapter 9
- Section Reading Support Transparencies

Less Proficient Readers

Teacher's Edition
- Customize for Less Proficient Readers, p. 325

Teaching Resources
- Guided Reading and Review booklet, pp. 66–69
- Guide to the Essentials (English/Spanish), Chapter 9

Technology
- Student Edition on Audio CD, Chapter 9
- Guided Reading Audiotapes (English/Spanish), Chapter 9
- Section Reading Support Transparencies

Less Proficient Writers

Teacher's Edition
- Customize for Less Proficient Writers, p. 329

Teaching Resources
- Guided Reading and Review booklet, pp. 66–69
- Guide to the Essentials (English/Spanish), Chapter 9

Technology
- Student Edition on Audio CD, Chapter 9
- Guided Reading Audiotapes (English/Spanish), Chapter 9
- Section Reading Support Transparencies

Teacher's Edition Index

Chapter 9 – Pacing Suggestions

For 90-minute Blocks

- Teach section 4 using Transparency E15, and the Recent Scholarship notes on pages 324 and 339 for class discussions.

Running Out of Time?

If you are running short on time to cover this chapter, consider the following options:

- Use the Prentice Hall Presentation Pro CD-ROM to create an outline for this chapter.
- Use the Section Summaries for Chapter 9, from **Guide to the Essentials (English/Spanish).**

TEKS Correlation

Chapter-Level	TEKS
	(24) Social studies skills. The student applies critical-thinking skills to organize and use information acquired from a variety of sources, including electronic technology. The student is expected to: **(B)** analyze information by sequencing, categorizing, identifying cause-and-effect relationships, comparing, contrasting, finding the main idea, summarizing, making generalizations and predictions, and drawing inferences and conclusions.
1 The Expansion of Education	**(2) History.** The student understands the political, economic, and social changes in the United States from 1877 to 1898. The student is expected to: **(C)** analyze social issues such as the treatment of minorities, child labor, growth of cities, and problems of immigrants. **(8) Geography.** The student uses geographic tools to collect, analyze, and interpret data. The student is expected to: **(A)** create thematic maps, graphs, charts, models, and databases representing various aspects of the United States. **(21) Culture.** The student understands how people from various groups, including racial, ethnic, and religious groups, adapt to life in the United States and contribute to our national identity. The student is expected to: **(B)** explain efforts of the Americanization movement to assimilate immigrants into American culture. **(24) Social studies skills.** The student applies critical-thinking skills to organize and use information acquired from a variety of sources, including electronic technology. The student is expected to: **(D)** use the process of historical inquiry to research, interpret, and use multiple sources of evidence. **(G)** support a point of view on a social studies issue or event. **(25) Social studies skills.** The student communicates in written, oral, and visual forms. The student is expected to: **(D)** create written, oral, and visual presentations of social studies information.
2 New Forms of Entertainment	**(2) History.** The student understands the political, economic, and social changes in the United States from 1877 to 1898. The student is expected to: **(C)** analyze social issues such as the treatment of minorities, child labor, growth of cities, and problems of immigration. **(24) Social studies skills.** The student applies critical-thinking skills to organize and use information acquired from a variety of sources, including electronic technology. The student is expected to: **(A)** locate and use primary and secondary sources such as computer software, databases, media and news services, biographies, interviews, and artifacts to acquire information about the United States.
3 The World of Jim Crow	**(1) History.** The student understands traditional historical points of reference in U.S. history from 1877 to the present. The student is expected to: **(B)** apply absolute and relative chronology through the sequencing of significant individuals, events, and time periods. **(2) History.** The student understands the political, economic, and social changes in the United States from 1877 to 1898. The student is expected to: **(C)** analyze social issues such as the treatment of minorities, child labor, growth of cities, and problems of immigrants. **(21) Culture.** The student understands how people from various groups, including racial, ethnic, and religious groups, adapt to life in the United States and contribute to our national identity. The student is expected to: **(A)** explain actions taken by people from racial, ethnic, and religious groups to expand economic opportunities and political rights in American society **(24) Social studies skills.** The student applies critical-thinking skills to organize and use information acquired from a variety of sources, including electronic technology. The student is expected to: **(A)** locate and use primary and secondary sources such as computer software, databases, media and news services, biographies, interviews, and artifacts to acquire information about the United States.
4 The Changing Role of Women	**(5) History.** The student understands significant individuals, events, and issues of the 1920s. The student is expected to: **(A)** analyze causes and effects of significant issues such as immigration, the Red Scare, Prohibition, and the changing role of women. **(18) Citizenship.** The student understands efforts to expand the democratic process. The student is expected to: **(B)** evaluate various means of achieving equality of political rights, including the 19th, 24th, and 26th amendments. **(24) Social studies skills.** The student applies critical-thinking skills to organize and use information acquired from a variety of sources, including electronic technology. The student is expected to: **(A)** locate and use primary and secondary sources such as computer software, databases, media and news services, biographies, interviews, and artifacts to acquire information about the United States. **(25) Social studies skills.** The student communicates in written, oral, and visual forms. The student is expected to: **(D)** create written, oral, and visual presentations of social studies information.

Chapter 9

Life at the Turn of the Twentieth Century

(1870–1915)

Introducing the Chapter

The growth of industry and urban areas in the late 1800s brought many cultural and social transformations to the United States. At the time, many Americans feared change and clung to old ideas about social roles, particularly those that affected women and African Americans.

Time Line Activity

To provide students with practice in using the time line, ask questions such as these:

1. What country granted voting rights to women in 1893? *(New Zealand)*
2. How did the outcome of *Plessy* v. *Ferguson* affect the cause of civil rights in the United States? *(The Supreme Court ruled in favor of separate but equal facilities for African Americans and whites, effectively making segregation legal.)*
3. What organization was formed in 1909 to advance the cause of African Americans? *(The NAACP)*

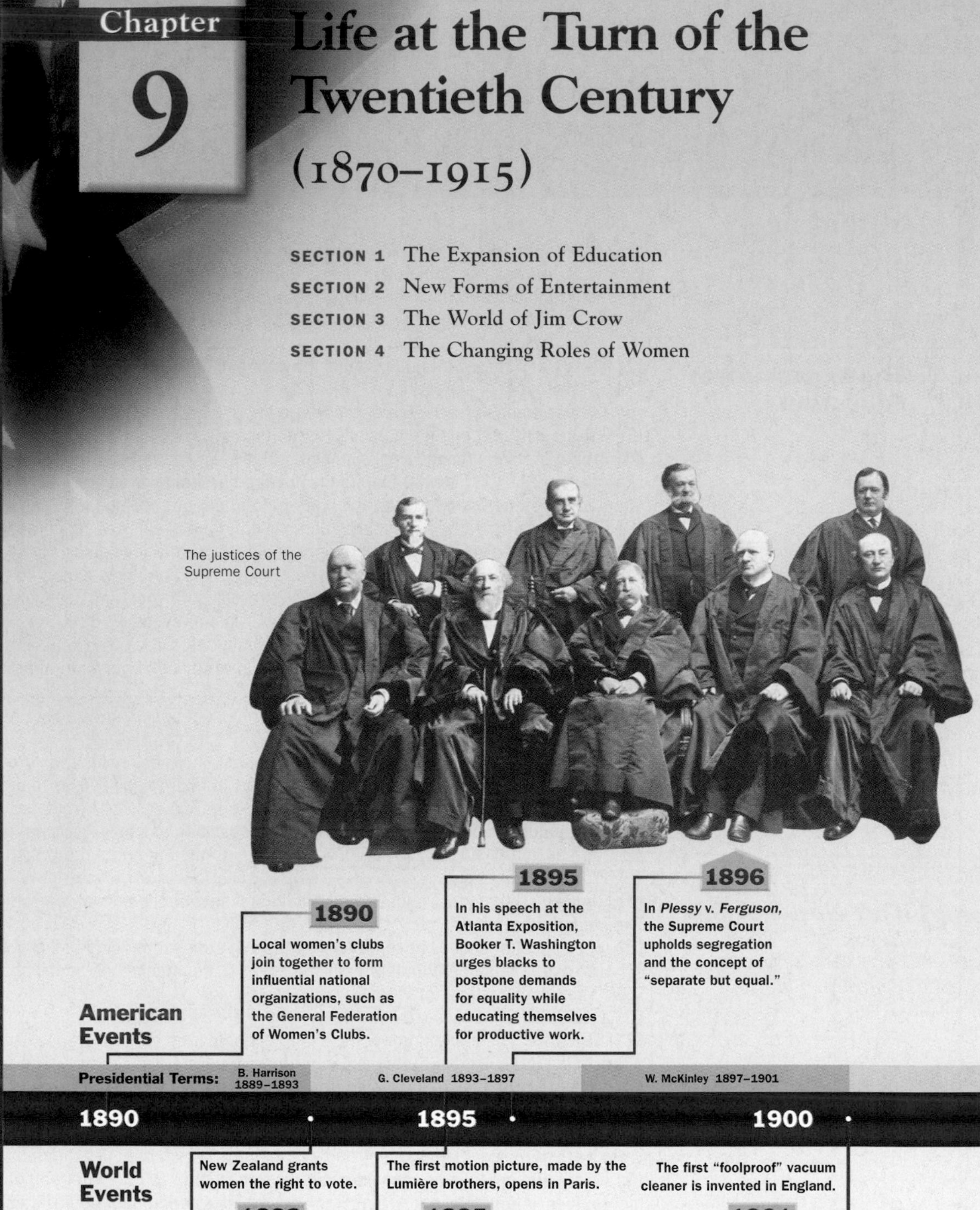

Chapter 9

Life at the Turn of the Twentieth Century (1870–1915)

The justices of the Supreme Court

American Events

1890 Local women's clubs join together to form influential national organizations, such as the General Federation of Women's Clubs.

1895 In his speech at the Atlanta Exposition, Booker T. Washington urges blacks to postpone demands for equality while educating themselves for productive work.

1896 In *Plessy* v. *Ferguson*, the Supreme Court upholds segregation and the concept of "separate but equal."

Presidential Terms: B. Harrison 1889–1893 | G. Cleveland 1893–1897 | W. McKinley 1897–1901

1890 | 1895 | 1900

World Events

1893 New Zealand grants women the right to vote.

1895 The first motion picture, made by the Lumière brothers, opens in Paris.

1901 The first "foolproof" vacuum cleaner is invented in England.

eTeach

Be sure to check out this month's online discussion with a Master Teacher. Go to **www.phschool.com**.

RESOURCE DIRECTORY

Teaching Resources

Pacing Charts booklet
Block Scheduling booklet, p. 21
Units 1/2 booklet
- Chapter Summary, pp. 93, 96

Technology

Guided Reading Audiotapes (English/Spanish), Ch. 9
Student Edition on Audio CD, Ch. 9
Sounds of an Era Audio CD *"Blue Back Speller,"* vowel exercise (time: 30 seconds)
Prentice Hall United States History Video Collection™ Volume 11, *Immigration and Cultural Change*
Prentice Hall Presentation Pro CD-ROM, Ch. 9
Resource Pro® CD-ROM
Social Studies Skills Tutor CD-ROM
Companion Web site, www.phschool.com

Daily Expenditure per Pupil in Public Schools, 1909–1910

In dollars:
- 24 and above
- 19–23
- 14–18
- 0–13

Newspapers and magazines offer information and entertainment.

1903 The huge success of the movie *The Great Train Robbery* signals the beginning of the silent movie era.

1905 W.E.B. Du Bois helps found the Niagara Movement, which promotes full civil liberties for African Americans.

1909 The National Association for the Advancement of Colored People is founded to fight for civil rights.

T. Roosevelt 1901–1909 | W. Taft 1909–1913 | W. Wilson 1913–1921

1905 | 1910 | 1915

1902 Italian tenor Enrico Caruso makes his first recording.

1914 Marcus Garvey founds the Universal Negro Improvement Association in Jamaica.

Daily Expenditure per Pupil in Public Schools, 1909–1910

Activating Prior Knowledge Which states had a daily expenditure of between 19 and 23 dollars per pupil? *(Oregon, Utah, Minnesota, Illinois, Indiana, Ohio, New York, and New Jersey)*

Previewing By looking at the map, why do you think the western states were able to spend so much more money per student than states like New York and Maryland? *(There were probably fewer students in western schools, so there was more money to spend per student.)*

Background
About the Pictures

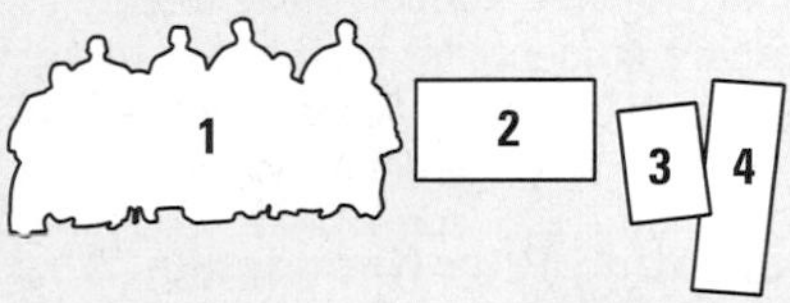

1. The judges of the Supreme Court who ruled on the *Plessy* v. *Ferguson* case in 1896.
2. Poster from *The Great Train Robbery,* one of the first movies to attract a vast, nationwide audience.
3. & 4. Newspapers such as the *Chicago Daily News* offered readers both information and entertainment. Magazines also expanded in this era, assisted by lowered postal rates.

Bibliography

For the Teacher

Abrahams, Roger D. ***Singing the Master: The Emergence of African Culture in the Plantation South.*** Penguin USA, 1993. (Uses primary sources to trace the impact of plantation traditions and songs on African American performance styles in the nineteenth and twentieth centuries.)

Lewis, David Levering. ***W.E.B. Du Bois: Biography of a Race, 1868–1919.*** Henry Holt, 1994. (The first 51 years of the life of the brilliant African American leader.)

For the Student

Blacks and the Constitution. PBS Video, 1987.

Ward, Geoffrey C. ***Baseball: An Illustrated History.*** Alfred A. Knopf, 1996. (Based on the acclaimed PBS series, this book recounts the history of baseball from its earliest days.)

Washington, Booker T. ***Up from Slavery.*** Oxford University Press, 2000. (Classic autobiography of the famous civil rights leader.)

Don't miss the exclusive interactive version of this textbook on the Web and on CD-ROM.

Section 1
The Expansion of Education

SECTION OBJECTIVES

1. Learn how and why public schools expanded during the late 1800s.
2. Find out how opportunities for higher education increased after the Civil War.
3. Discover the views of Booker T. Washington and W.E.B. Du Bois regarding African American education.

BELLRINGER

Warm-Up Activity Ask students if they think changes need to be made in American education in order to better prepare students for their future roles. Ask them to explain what they think these changes should be.

Activating Prior Knowledge What are some ways in which your students' educational experience would be different if they had attended a nineteenth-century-style one-room schoolhouse rather than a modern high school? Have them list some of the differences.

READING STRATEGY

As students read this section, have them make a list of examples of how educational opportunities expanded between 1870 and 1910. How did industrialization, the growth of railroads, the growth of labor unions, farm issues, and the rise of big business affect education?

Section 1
The Expansion of Education

READING FOCUS

- How and why did public schools expand during the late 1800s?
- How did opportunities for higher education increase after the Civil War?
- What were the views of Booker T. Washington and W.E.B. Du Bois regarding African American education?

MAIN IDEA

Education was a lofty goal that was out of reach of most nineteenth-century Americans. However, as the new century began, more and more Americans took advantage of educational opportunities.

KEY TERMS

literacy
assimilation
philanthropist
Niagara Movement

TAKING NOTES

Copy the diagram below. As you read, fill in the causes and effects of the expanding opportunities for education in America. You may add circles as needed.

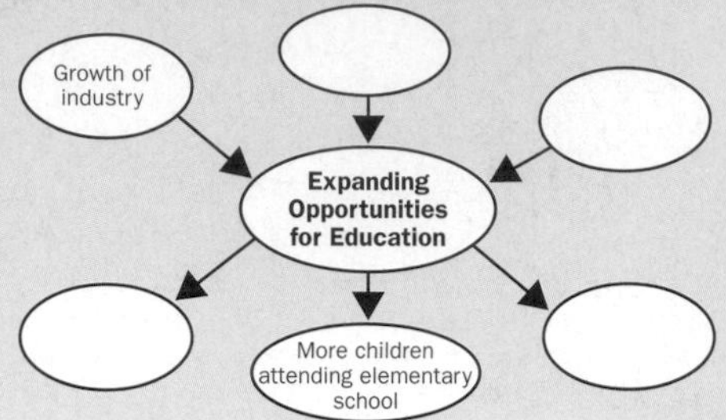

Setting the Scene From sparsely populated prairie towns to crowded city neighborhoods, schools were becoming more common and more important to Americans at the end of the nineteenth century. In frontier areas, families banded together to hire teachers for their one-room schoolhouses. City schools were larger and more crowded, and often served many immigrants. Mary Antin, whose father sent for his family from Russia after he had established himself in Boston, describes the importance of free schools to her family:

> "*Education was free. That subject my father had written about repeatedly, as comprising his chief hope for us children, the essence of American opportunity, the treasure that no thief could touch, not even misfortune or poverty. . . . A little girl from across the alley came and offered to conduct us to school. . . . No application made, no question asked, no examinations, no fees. The doors stood open for every one of us. The smallest child could show us the way.*"
>
> —Mary Antin

A teacher (far left) and her students stand in front of their sod school in Thomas County, Kansas, around 1880. The adult man is probably an immigrant who wants to learn English.

The Growth of Public Schools

Americans had long understood that a democratic society functioned best when its citizens could read and write. By the late 1800s, however, an education had become more than just a worthy goal. For a growing number of Americans, it was a necessary first step toward economic and social success. In recognition of this fact and in response to public demand, educational opportunities expanded.

By the time of the Civil War, more than half of the nation's white children were attending the nation's free public schools. Because most children had to help their families earn a living, however, many left school at an early age. A high school diploma was still the exception. In 1870, only 2 percent

RESOURCE DIRECTORY

Teaching Resources
Guided Reading and Review booklet, p. 66

Technology
Section Reading Support Transparencies
Guided Reading Audiotapes (English/Spanish), Ch. 9
Student Edition on Audio CD, Ch. 9

RESOURCE PRO® **Literature Activity** *The Promised Land,* found on Resource Pro, uses an excerpt from the autobiography of Mary Antin, a Jewish immigrant from Russia living in Boston, to show the importance of education to immigrant families.
Prentice Hall Presentation Pro CD-ROM, Ch. 9
Companion Web site, www.phschool.com

of all 17-year-olds graduated from high school. An even lower percentage of students went on to college.

The vast majority of American children attended school for only a few years and learned only to "read, and write, and 'cipher [do basic arithmetic]." What's more, in farm communities, older children often attended school only from November to April so that they could help in the fields. As industries grew after the Civil War, parents came to realize that their children needed more than basic skills to advance in life. They began pressuring local governments to increase school funding and to lengthen the school year. At the same time, reformers pressured state governments to limit child labor.

By 1900, 31 states had laws requiring children between the ages of 8 and 14 to attend school. Although unevenly enforced, these laws had a powerful effect. By 1910, nearly 72 percent of American children attended school, with more than a million students in high school.

School Days Early in the 1900s, about half of the nation's children attended one-room schools. There, children aged 6 to 14 were taught by a single teacher; often the older students helped the younger ones with their lessons. In the classic *Little House* novels based on her own life, Laura Ingalls Wilder describes these schools. *These Happy Golden Years* tells how Laura becomes a teacher when she is only 15 years old. She boards with a rural family, teaches in a drafty shanty, and has only five students—three of whom are older than she is!

Students in both rural and city schools learned many of their lessons by rote. They read aloud from texts such as the *McGuffey Readers*, and recited passages and facts from memory. As they got older, they studied geography, history, and grammar in addition to the "three Rs." Teachers often kept discipline with the threat of physical punishment. Erwin House was a student in 1876: "To a nervous child the discipline was indeed terrible. The long birch switches hanging on hooks against the wall haunted me day and night, from the time I entered school."

Other students loved school. Tony Longo, son of an Italian immigrant, went to a city school:

> "*I liked school. . . . The teacher told us stories about General Grant and Abraham Lincoln and other great Americans. She also taught us how to read and write in English. . . . For the Centennial celebration we had a pageant at school. I wore a white wig and played the role of George Washington. My father was very proud.*"
>
> —Tony Longo

Immigrants and Education Like the parents of Tony Longo and Mary Antin, many immigrants placed a high value on American public education. It was a way for their children to become successful Americans.

One of the most important functions of the public schools was to teach literacy skills. **Literacy** is the ability to read and write. For many immigrants, learning to read and write English was an important step in their quest to succeed in the United States. And it was not only children who went to school. Adults attended school at night to learn English and civics, which they needed to qualify for citizenship.

Public schools also played a role in assimilating immigrants. **Assimilation** is the process by which people of one culture become part of another culture.

Focus on DAILY LIFE

The *McGuffey Readers* At the end of the nineteenth century, all across America, schoolchildren could be heard reciting from their *McGuffey Eclectic Readers*. This series of textbooks was by far the most popular in the nation. The first *Reader* was published in 1830, and by 1922, about 122 million texts had been sold. Graded from first to sixth, *McGuffey Readers* included excerpts from great books. For rural families who lived far from libraries, the *Readers* might be their only exposure to good literature, such as works by Wordsworth and Shakespeare. *McGuffey Readers* also contained tales designed to teach moral lessons and good citizenship. Children often memorized verses like these:

> *"'Tis a lesson you should heed,*
> *Try, try again;*
> *If at first you don't succeed,*
> *Try, try again. . . ."*

READING CHECK
What were schools like in the early 1900s?

LESSON PLAN

Focus Explain that as the United States became more industrialized and urbanized after the Civil War, education became more important.

Instruct Discuss the expansion of education after the Civil War. What was the result of compulsory school laws? How did education encourage immigrants to assimilate? Who benefited from increased opportunities for higher education?

Ask students to analyze the impact of educational expansion on African Americans, on women, and on American society as a whole. How did Booker T. Washington's and W.E.B. Du Bois's approaches toward education for African Americans differ?

Assess/Reteach Have students discuss the types of changes that would result in a society in which education gradually, but steadily, became available to a wider variety of people.

READING CHECK
Many schools had only one room and one teacher with older students helping the younger ones. There were a growing number of city schools that were larger, however. Discipline was often imposed with physical force, and attendance was mandatory in most states for school-age children.

CUSTOMIZE FOR ...
ESL
Write the words *public education, literacy,* and *assimilation* on the chalkboard. Have volunteers define the words. Make sure that all students understand what they mean. Then lead a discussion about the importance of public education for literacy and the importance of literacy for assimilation. Encourage students to speak from their own experience.

Analyzing Political Cartoons for Point of View

Focus Students learn to analyze a political cartoon as historical evidence of ideas and attitudes about a past event.

Instruct Explain to students that one way of gaining insight into the views of a society of a bygone era is by studying political cartoons created in that era. Political cartoons, though prone to bias, often offer an inside perspective on past events not available from reading secondary sources. Post examples of present-day political cartoons, and ask students to analyze them using the techniques described in the activity.

Extend See the Skills for Life activity in the Resource Directory below.

ANSWERS

Practice the Skill

1. **(a)** She is a teacher. **(b)** He represents most men, who are happy to see a woman teaching school. **(c)** She is petitioning for suffrage, or the right to vote. **(d)** The man is opposed to her petition.
2. **(a)** Yes. **(b)** No. **(c)** Possible answer: In the first panel, the woman is teaching a classroom of children, which the man approves of. In the second panel, the woman is petitioning for the right to vote, but the man rejects her ideas.
3. **(a)** Women's right to vote. **(b)** The cartoonist implies that the man is hypocritical to be praising the woman for holding a job and guiding the development of the next generation (including boys), but to be angry with her for demanding the right to vote. **(c)** The man in the cartoon has the more typical viewpoint. **(d)** The cartoonist appears to support the woman's demand for suffrage. It is likely that the cartoon was not that effective at the time, as most people in society shared the man's point of view.

Analyzing Political Cartoons for Point of View

Political cartoons can tell you a great deal about the past. Political cartoonists try to influence public opinion about issues by exaggerating or highlighting certain details about the facts. A cartoon can often make a point more strongly than words alone. When you look at a political cartoon from the past, however, it is important to remember that there were different points of view when the event took place. To analyze the cartoon, be sure to consider the cartoonist's frame of reference—the place, time, and circumstances when the cartoon was created.

"The woman question" provided a wealth of material for cartoonists at the turn of the last century. The cartoon below was published early in the 1900s.

LEARN THE SKILL

Use the following steps to analyze a political cartoon for point of view:

1. **Identify the symbols used in the cartoon.** Cartoons often use visual images that stand for some other idea or event. For example, a heart is a commonly used symbol for love. A dove is a symbol for peace.
2. **Analyze the meaning of the symbols and words.** Use what you already know about the historical period and the cartoon itself to decide what the symbols refer to and how they are used as shorthand to represent actions or ideas. Summarize what is happening in the cartoon in your own words.
3. **Interpret the cartoon.** Determine what the cartoonist is saying about the political issue. Consider the cartoonist's frame of reference, and compare the cartoonist's representation with other opinions of the time and with the facts. Finally, draw conclusions about the cartoonist's point of view.

PRACTICE THE SKILL

Answer the following questions:

1. **(a)** In the left panel, what job is the woman doing? **(b)** What does the man represent, and what is his reaction to what the woman is doing? **(c)** In the right panel, what is the woman doing? **(d)** What is the man's reaction?
2. **(a)** In the early 1900s, would women have been likely to do the job shown in the left panel? **(b)** Would women have been likely to do what is shown in the right panel? **(c)** Summarize the action in the two panels; be sure to include the man's reaction.
3. **(a)** What political issue is the cartoon about? **(b)** What point is the cartoonist making by showing the man's two reactions side by side? **(c)** Which point of view—the man's or the cartoonist's—is more typical of the early 1900s? Explain. **(d)** What action is the cartoonist advocating? Do you think the cartoon was effective at the time? Explain.

APPLY THE SKILL

See the Chapter Review and Assessment for another opportunity to apply this skill.

RESOURCE DIRECTORY

Teaching Resources

Skills for Life booklet, p. 18

Technology

Social Studies Skills Tutor CD-ROM

Interactive Practice in
- Geographic Literacy
- Critical Thinking and Reading
- Visual Analysis
- Communications

Section 2

New Forms of Entertainment

READING FOCUS

- What new kinds of performances and recreation did Americans enjoy at the turn of the century?
- What were people reading for information and entertainment?
- How was American music changing?

MAIN IDEA

Americans flocked to new forms of entertainment, sports, and music during the period from the late 1880s to 1915.

KEY TERMS

vaudeville
yellow journalism
ragtime

TAKING NOTES

Copy the chart below. As you read, add types of entertainment to the first column, and details to the other two columns.

Type of Entertainment	How It Developed	Why People Enjoyed It
• Vaudeville	• Grew out of minstrel shows	• Inexpensive
•	•	• Lots of variety
•	•	•

Setting the Scene You can probably hum the following song, even though it was written in 1908. It has been baseball's "anthem" since that time, and is still sung at the seventh-inning stretch in ballparks today. But "Take Me Out to the Ballgame" also captures the spirit of the turn of the twentieth century in America.

> *"Take me out to the ball game*
> *Take me out with the crowd*
> *Buy me some peanuts and Cracker Jack*
> *I don't care if I never get back . . ."*
>
> —Jack Norworth

Many of the changes occurring in America at that time are reflected in this verse: more leisure time for working people, more money to spend on entertainment, the craze for sports, the introduction of snack foods, and a spirit of fun. The United States was becoming a more urban nation, and city dwellers began looking for entertainment in their own neighborhoods, as well as for recreation away from the dirty, crowded streets where they lived and worked. These factors would fuel a whole new commercial recreation industry designed to supply inexpensive entertainment for all Americans.

By 1898, baseball had become the American pastime. From 1891 to 1899, there was one professional league, with teams from Boston to St. Louis. The ball and glove shown above commemorate an 1899 college game.

Performances and Recreation

Many kinds of performances attracted audiences at this time. They ranged from live theater to a new medium: the moving picture show, or the "movies."

Vaudeville and Minstrel Shows The most popular kind of live theatrical performance was **vaudeville,** a type of inexpensive variety show that first appeared in the 1870s. Vaudeville performances consisted of comic sketches based on ethnic or racial humor; song-and-dance routines; magic acts; and performances by ventriloquists, jugglers, and animals. In 1899, the actor Edwin Milton Royle wrote, "The vaudeville theatre is an American invention. There is nothing like it anywhere else in the world." Although early vaudeville was

Section 2

New Forms of Entertainment

Section Objectives

1. Discover the new kinds of performances and recreation that Americans enjoyed at the turn of the century.
2. Find out what people were reading for education and entertainment.
3. Learn how American music was changing.

Bellringer

Warm-Up Activity Ask students how they like to entertain themselves during their free time. Ask them if they spend money on entertainment.

Activating Prior Knowledge Ask students what they know about the history of such popular American pastimes as baseball, basketball, visiting amusement parks, and going to movies. Do they know how long such amusements have been popular?

Reading Strategy

As students read the section, have them take notes to help analyze the relationship between culture and economy in the late nineteenth century. What impact did leisure activities have on the U.S. economy?

RESOURCE DIRECTORY

Teaching Resources

Learning Styles Lesson Plans booklet, p. 34
Guided Reading and Review booklet, p. 67
Biography, Literature, and Comparing Primary Sources booklet (Biography) *George M. Cohan,* p. 21

Technology

Section Reading Support Transparencies
Guided Reading Audiotapes (English/Spanish), Ch. 9
Student Edition on Audio CD, Ch. 9
Sounds of an Era Audio CD *"Mr. Moonman, Turn Out Your Light"* (time: 45 seconds)
RESOURCE PRO® **Critical Thinking Activity** *Recognizing Cause and Effect: America's Game,* found on Resource Pro, focuses on the development of American baseball to help students apply the skill.
Prentice Hall Presentation Pro CD-ROM, Ch. 9
Companion Web site, www.phschool.com

Lesson Plan

Focus Explain that urbanization and industrialization brought in their wake a new commercial entertainment industry. Ask students what the new forms of amusement were in the late 1800s. Did men and women prefer different forms of entertainment?

Instruct Discuss the kinds of popular amusements that emerged in the late 1800s. Ask what part sports played in mass entertainment. What was the influence of African American art on popular entertainment?

Assess/Reteach Have students list the forms of entertainment that were popular in the United States in the years between 1880 and 1915. Which of those amusements are still popular today?

Activity: Connecting with Culture

Many well-known American entertainers got their start in vaudeville. Have students research the early careers of W. C. Fields, Charlie Chaplin, Will Rogers, Lillian Russell, or another star who began in vaudeville for a description of the performer's act. Have students identify the impact of these popular performers on Americans and on the rest of the world. Then have students write and perform a skit based on their chosen performer's act. **(Verbal/Linguistic; Kinesthetic; Musical/Rhythmic)**

geared to male spectators, the shows soon sought a wider audience and presented themselves as family entertainment.

One of the sources of vaudeville was the minstrel show. A popular form of entertainment from the 1840s, minstrel shows began to die out as vaudeville gained popularity. Minstrel shows featured white actors in "blackface" (exaggerated make-up caricaturing African Americans). The shows perpetuated racial stereotypes with exaggerated imitations of African American music, dance, and humor. Nevertheless, black performers—also wearing blackface—sometimes performed in minstrel shows, as these were often the only stage jobs they could get. Once they were able to, many African American performers switched to vaudeville.

Focus on Technology

Snapshots Although professional photographers had been taking portraits for decades, it was not until the 1880s that ordinary people could become their own family photographers—and the snapshot was born. In 1888, George Eastman marketed a handheld camera that he had developed. The Kodak was so easy to use that its motto was, "You press the button—We do the rest." "The rest" included developing the film when the camera was sent to the company, and then returning the camera reloaded and ready to take more pictures. However, at $25 the Kodak was expensive. In 1900, Eastman came out with a new and even simpler camera called the Brownie (below right). It was marketed to children and cost only one dollar. Families all over America began snapping pictures of each other, and the family snapshot album became a staple of American culture.

Movies As the twentieth century began, vaudeville started getting competition from the movies. *The Great Train Robbery*, released in 1903, was a huge success and clearly demonstrated that profits could be made from movies. By 1908, the nation had 8,000 nickelodeons—theaters set up in converted stores or warehouses that charged a nickel admission. They showed short slapstick comedies and other films to as many as 200,000 people a day.

Improving technology and the increasing popularity of films led to longer, better movies and to bigger, more elaborate movie houses. Full-length dramas featured new stars such as Mary Pickford and Douglas Fairbanks. Charlie Chaplin began appearing in comedies. Early movies were silent and often accompanied by a live piano player. Soon audiences flocked to new movie palaces with names like The Empress and The Riviera, which often had full orchestras to accompany their films.

The Circus While circuses have a long history, it was the introduction of the circus train in 1872 that made the annual visit of the circus an anticipated event all over America. First, "advance men" arrived in a town to promote the performances. They often recruited young boys to hand out printed advertisements. Several days later, the circus train pulled in, and the big top went up. This was a show in itself, and hundreds of people often gathered to watch. Then the circus parade kicked off, and all the circus acts and performers marched through town to great fanfare. After the parade and advertising created great anticipation, the paid performances were held. At the turn of the century, there was hardly a town or a city in America where a youngster did not dream of running away to join the circus.

Amusement Parks The technology of the trolley—and the trolley lines themselves—led to the development of amusement parks. A similar technology helped to create their main attractions: mechanical rides like the steeplechase, the Ferris wheel, and the roller coaster.

As trolley lines were extended from the central cities out to less populated areas, "trolley parks" began to spring up at the end of the lines. Although many people still worked ten hours a day, a half-holiday on Saturday was becoming more common. Transportation companies encouraged ridership on weekends, and the inexpensive excursion from the city to an amusement park was just what the public wanted. These parks often featured music, games of skill, vaudeville productions, bathing beaches, and exciting rides. The business of the amusement park, according to the manager of Coney Island's Luna Park, was "the business of amusing the million."

Sports Another way "the million" were amused was by watching or participating in sports. While many enjoyed the spectator sports of boxing and horse racing, baseball was by far the most popular.

By 1860, groups such as firefighters, police officers, and teachers had formed baseball clubs in many American cities. When it became clear that there were large audiences for these games, entrepreneurs enclosed fields and charged admission. Teams formed leagues and began to play championship games. In 1869, the first true professional team, the Cincinnati Red Stockings, was formed. By the 1870s, the sport's best players were being paid. What Americans loved most about baseball was the speed, daring, and split-second timing of the game. Mark Twain called baseball "the very symbol, the outward and visible expression of the drive and push and rush and struggle of the raging, tearing, booming nineteenth century."

Two other games captured the interest of Americans during the late 1800s. Football emerged as a popular American sport when Walter Camp began adapting the European game of rugby during the 1880s. Basketball, the only major sport of exclusively American origin, was invented in 1891 by a physical education teacher, Dr. James Naismith of Springfield, Massachusetts, to keep athletes fit during winter.

VIEWING HISTORY Coney Island, the most spectacular of the turn-of-the-century amusement parks, was really three parks along the beach in Brooklyn, New York. By 1900, it had tens of thousands of visitors every day. **Drawing Conclusions** *How does this 1904 guidebook help explain Coney Island's appeal?*

Women also participated enthusiastically in many sports. When a bicycling fad swept the nation in the late 1800s, women joined in. Whether women were riding "bicycles built for two" or the new safety bicycles deemed suitable for female riders, the sport required practical clothing. Women athletes abandoned corsets, which wrapped tightly around their torsos and restricted their breathing. Women's involvement in sports also led to the popularity and acceptance of shirtwaists (ready-made blouses) that were tucked into shorter or split skirts.

Female college students also began playing basketball. However, recreation specialists thought that stiff competition and hard physical exertion were unhealthy for women, so they devised less demanding "women's rules." Ice-skating had long been a favorite recreation for women. Now they also played tennis, learned gymnastics, and swam, although society's strict dress codes required women to wear black cotton stockings under short dresses or bloomers.

What People Were Reading

The increase in education that you read about in the last section meant that reading for entertainment became a popular pastime for many Americans. Writers and publishers were quick to take advantage of this new, larger audience.

Newspapers For generations, newspapers had been a vital source of information for city dwellers. In the late 1800s, they became a popular form of entertainment as well. Taking advantage of new typesetting machinery that allowed printers to set whole lines of type quickly, publishers created larger and more interesting publications. They introduced new features, such as comics, sports sections, Sunday editions, women's pages, stories "hot off the wires," and graphic pictures.

Between 1870 and 1900, newspaper circulation soared from 2.6 to 15.1 million copies a day. Because of heated competition, publishers urged their reporters to discover lurid details of murders, vice, and scandal—anything to sell more papers. Such sensational news coverage came to be called **yellow journalism,** a reference to the yellow ink used in a popular comic strip of the era.

Hungarian-born Joseph Pulitzer, who owned the *St. Louis Post-Dispatch* and the *New York World*, said his purpose was to "expose all fraud and sham,

ACTIVITY
Student Portfolio

You may wish to have students add the following to their portfolios: Tell students that many middle- and upper-class Americans lived by Victorian morals that dictated proper behavior. These people had long been offended by popular amusements. Have students research Victorianism and write an essay contrasting the kinds of behavior embraced by forms of entertainment such as dancing, vaudeville, and sports with the code of behavior dictated by Victorianism. **(Verbal/Linguistic)**

BACKGROUND
Connections to Culture

For many years, Abner J. Doubleday, a West Point cadet, has been credited with organizing the first game of baseball in Cooperstown, New York, in 1839. Recently, however, two newspaper references were found indicating a version of baseball was played in New York City as early as 1823. The articles, both dated April 25, 1823, describe a game called "base ball," played regularly in Manhattan. In one, the author wrote of witnessing "a company of active young men playing the manly and athletic game of 'base ball.'" The spectator noted approvingly, "it is innocent amusement, and healthy exercise, attended with but little expense, and has no demoralizing tendency."

CUSTOMIZE FOR ...
Less Proficient Writers

Have students research the professional baseball teams that existed at the turn of the century. Have them design a pennant, with a logo, for one of the teams.

TEST PREPARATION

Have students read the quote by Edwin Milton Royle on page 327 and then complete the sentence below.

According to Royle, the most important contributing factors to the uniqueness of vaudeville were—

- **(A)** the variety of performers and types of acts presented.
- **B** the cities and states where vaudeville performances took place.
- **C** presenting African American minstrel performers and ventriloquists.
- **D** combining animal acts and juggling acts.

CAPTION ANSWERS

Viewing History Its cover points out that Coney Island had a wide variety of activities and entertainments for men, women, and children.

ACTIVITY
Connecting with Culture

Tell students to research the origin of a professional sports team in your area. Have students find out when the team was formed, where the team plays, how much money players earn, and how much community support the team receives. Then have students present an oral report on their findings. If possible, students should supply visuals, such as photographs and newspaper accounts. **(Verbal/Linguistic)**

BACKGROUND
Biography

The game of basketball was invented in 1891 by Canadian American James A. Naismith (1861–1939). As head of the physical education department at Springfield College in Massachusetts, Naismith was asked to devise a safe, indoor game for play during the cold winter months. Blending aspects of soccer, field hockey, football, and other sports, and removing (in theory) physical contact, Naismith invented a basketball game for nine players on each side. He coached the game at the University of Kansas, Lawrence, until 1908.

READING CHECK

They introduced spirituals to white audiences and earned enough money to save Fisk University.

Focus on ECONOMICS

The Newsboys' Strike "Extra! Extra!" and "Hot off the presses!" These were the cries of "newsies," the children who sold newspapers at the turn of the century. Aged 8 to 15, newsies were independent business persons. They bought their papers from the publishers and sold them at a small profit, but they could not get refunds on unsold papers. Marketing their papers aggressively, newsies vied with each other for the best street corners.

In 1899, New York newspaper sales were slowing. Hearst and Pulitzer feared that raising prices would cause them to lose customers—so they raised the cost to the newsies instead, cutting into their profits. Newsboys insisted that the *Journal* and the *World* roll back the increase. When the publishers refused, the newsboys boycotted their papers. Circulation went way down. After two weeks, the newsboys won a partial victory: the increase remained but unsold papers would now be refunded.

fight all public evils and abuses." Californian William Randolph Hearst used his father's gold-mining millions to put out the even more sensational *New York Journal.* While popular with many readers, yellow journalism troubled some observers. Critics charged that the "yellow press" intruded into private lives, invented facts, and sensationalized ordinary events by exaggerating them.

Magazines In 1879, Congress passed a law lowering the postal rates for periodicals. One result was the increased circulation and popularity of magazines, such as *McClure's, Cosmopolitan,* and *Munsey's.* Magazines appeared weekly or monthly and contained helpful articles, advertising, and fiction.

Many of the popular magazines of this era featured stories appealing to the average American's desire and determination to succeed. In many of Horatio Alger's stories, for example, the main character embodies the American dream of rising from "rags to riches" through cheerfulness, honesty, and hard work. Stories of this kind reminded the working poor of the seemingly boundless opportunities available to them in the nation's industrial cities.

Popular Fiction Rags-to-riches stories as well as adventure yarns also appeared as "dime novels," inexpensive books with a wide readership. More educated readers turned instead to serious novels by such writers as Henry James and Edith Wharton and to the social protest novels of Upton Sinclair and other reformers. Even the humorist Mark Twain satirized the attitudes and practices of the time in his popular novels, such as the classic *The Adventures of Huckleberry Finn* (1884).

Huck Finn was also an example of local color, a type of writing that describes the people and places of particular regions of the United States in accurate detail. In an author's note at the beginning of *Huck Finn,* Twain explains that seven different dialects used in the book have been written "pain-stakingly, and with the trustworthy guidance and support of personal familiarity with these several forms of speech." Local color writers satisfied their audience's hunger for information about distant parts of the country. For example, Sarah Orne Jewett depicted the people of Maine and many of New England's disappearing traditions, Bret Harte captured the excitement of the California Gold Rush, and Willa Cather described life on the Great Plains.

Musical Diversions

Music was an important part of life in the late 1800s. People went to concerts, operettas, and dances, or gathered around the piano at home. But this era also saw important changes that would influence American music forever.

The Negro Spiritual One series of concerts in 1871 helped make American music more inclusive by introducing African American religious folk songs called spirituals to white audiences. These concerts also helped save a struggling black university from financial ruin. When Fisk University found itself deeply in debt in 1871, the school's music teacher organized a highly successful fundraising concert tour featuring nine gifted students. The Fisk Jubilee Singers, all of whom had been slaves or were the children of former slaves, toured the United States, England, and Europe—and eventually raised $150,000 to secure their school's future.

READING CHECK
What were the accomplishments of the Fisk Jubilee Singers?

In the process of making the Negro spiritual acceptable to white audiences, the Jubilee Singers and similar groups transformed the musical form. It acquired

RESOURCE DIRECTORY

Teaching Resources

Units 1/2 booklet
- Section 2 Quiz, p. 95

Guide to the Essentials
- Section 2 Summary, p. 44

Biography, Literature, and Comparing Primary Sources booklet (Literature) *Around the World in 72 Days,* p. 62

Technology

Sounds of an Era Audio CD *"Maple Leaf Rag,"* 1916 recording (time: one minute); *"Florida Rag,"* 1907 recording (time: one minute)

characteristics of the European musical tradition with which whites were familiar. This new spiritual became identified as an American art form, as opposed to a purely African American one.

VIEWING HISTORY This painting of the Jubilee Singers by a British artist is on view at Fisk University. **Making Inferences** *Why do you think the group chose to be painted in formal clothing and posed against a classical backdrop?*

Ragtime and Jazz **Ragtime** originated among black musicians in the South and Midwest in the 1880s. This infectious music featured melodies with shifting accents over a steady, marching-band beat. In 1899, composer and piano player Scott Joplin wrote "Maple Leaf Rag," which was recorded in 1903. It became a huge hit, and ragtime became a rage all across the country.

Jazz grew out of the vibrant musical culture of New Orleans, a city with a heritage that included African, Spanish, French, and Latin American influences. The city also had a popular marching-band tradition. After the Civil War, African American bands experimented with new styles, such as "raggy" rhythms and a style based on the call-and-response patterns of some church services. These bands also played jazzed-up versions of familiar melodies, such as hymns or the mournful "blues" songs of Southern slaves and sharecroppers. New Orleans jazz styles slowly worked their way northward through towns along the Mississippi River. By 1915, thanks in part to the success of the phonograph, jazz and the dances associated with it were becoming a national passion.

Music at Home While African American influences were beginning to enrich American music, two new ways of enjoying music at home appeared on the scene. Both allowed people access to music without having to produce it themselves. In the player piano, a paper roll was "played" by wooden "fingers" to reproduce the music recorded on the roll. Foot pedals activated the machine, requiring no skill on the part of the human player. The phonograph was invented in 1877 by Thomas Edison, and was selling at a rate of more than 500,000 per year by 1914.

These two technological advances allowed new musical styles to spread quickly, thus creating nationwide hits and stars. And the popularity of the phonograph signaled the birth of the music business that is so important to America's culture and economy today.

Section 2 Assessment

READING COMPREHENSION

1. What was **vaudeville,** and why did it become popular?
2. How did movies change during this period?
3. What was the most popular spectator sport at this time?
4. What was **yellow journalism?**
5. Describe **ragtime** music.

CRITICAL THINKING AND WRITING

6. **Drawing Inferences** What role do you think compulsory education played in creating a larger market for newspapers and magazines?
7. **Writing to Explain** Briefly explain how the growth of cities led to the growth of entertainment and recreation.

Take It to the NET

Activity: Drawing a Cartoon
Read more about baseball or basketball in the late 1800s, and draw a cartoon about the sport. Use the links provided in the *America: Pathways to the Present* area of the following Web site for help in completing this activity.
www.phschool.com

Section 2 Assessment

Reading Comprehension

1. Vaudeville was a type of live variety show with comedy, magicians, song-and-dance routines, ventriloquists, jugglers, and animals. It appealed to an increasingly urban nation, where city dwellers sought affordable, local, mass entertainment.
2. Improving technology allowed longer, better movies to be made. Movies were often accompanied by small orchestras rather than by a single piano.
3. Baseball.
4. Sensational news coverage focusing on lurid details of murders, vice, and scandal.
5. Ragtime mixed shifting melodies with marching-band beats.

Critical Thinking and Writing

6. Sample answer: Increased literacy expanded the demand for magazines and newspapers.
7. Answers might point out that urban workers were gaining more leisure time and that the entertainment industry grew to cater to city customers who had more money to spend.

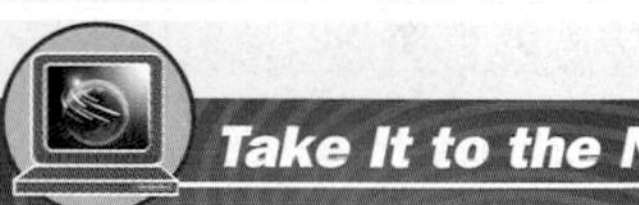

Cartoons will vary, but might show the uniforms and equipment used at the time.

CUSTOMIZE FOR ...

Gifted and Talented

Have students select a jazz or blues player from the early 1900s, such as Blind Lemon Johnson, Huddie "Leadbelly" Ledbetter, or Jelly Roll Morton, and research that artist's contribution to the beginnings of jazz. Students should report their findings to the class.

Caption Answers

Viewing History Answers will vary, but students may note that it was probably important to the group to be taken seriously and to have their music taken as seriously as was classical music from the European tradition.

Section 3
The World of Jim Crow

Section Objectives

1. Probe the kinds of discrimination encountered by African Americans after Reconstruction.
2. Find out how African Americans resisted this discrimination.

Bellringer

Warm-Up Activity Ask students to define the words *discriminate* and *discrimination.* Ask how a discriminating person is different from a discriminatory one.

Activating Prior Knowledge After the Civil War, the Reconstruction years saw many laws passed to begin to grant African Americans their civil rights. But there was a political backlash in the last part of the nineteenth century that lasted well into the twentieth century. Have students list the areas in which African Americans have had a long struggle for equality. Ask them how various laws have either helped or hindered that cause.

Reading Strategy

As students read this section, have them make a list of the methods white society used to prevent African Americans from achieving equality.

Section 3 The World of Jim Crow

READING FOCUS

- How were African Americans discriminated against after Reconstruction?
- How did African Americans resist this discrimination?

MAIN IDEA

African Americans found their hopes of equality dashed after Reconstruction by white attitudes, customs, and the law. Yet many blacks not only resisted discrimination but achieved success in spite of it.

KEY TERMS

poll tax
grandfather clause
segregation
Jim Crow
Plessy v. *Ferguson*
lynching
National Association for the Advancement of Colored People (NAACP)

TAKING NOTES

Copy the web diagram below. As you read, fill in the circles with examples of discrimination against African Americans and with examples of how blacks resisted discrimination.

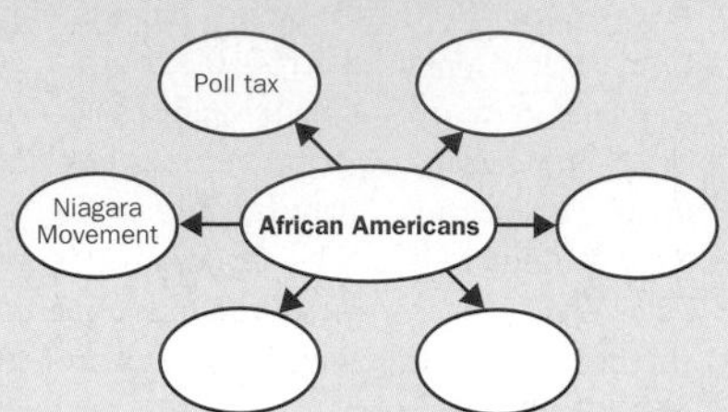

Setting the Scene Within a few years after the end of Reconstruction in the 1870s, African Americans began to see many of their newly won freedoms disappear. In the South, black Americans were prevented from voting and were subjected to repressive laws and intimidating violence. It did not take young African Americans long to recognize their inferior status in Southern society. Albon Holsey, who was a teenager in the first decade of the twentieth century, later recalled:

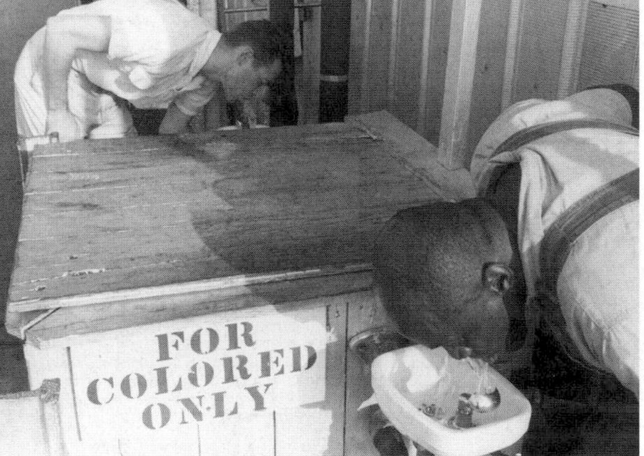

> *"At fifteen, I was fully conscious of the racial difference. . . . I knew then that I could never aspire to be President of the United States, nor Governor of my State, nor mayor of my city; I knew that the front door of white homes in my town were not for me to enter except as a servant; I knew that I could only sit in the peanut gallery at our theatre, and could only ride on the back seat of the electric car and in the Jim Crow car on the train. I had bumped into the color line. . . ."*
>
> —Albon Holsey

VIEWING HISTORY By the turn of the century, segregation was integral to life in the South. African American (then called *colored*) and white citizens had separate facilities, ranging from drinking fountains to public schools. **Making Inferences** *What effect do you think this separation had on both blacks and whites?*

Discrimination was also widespread in the North, but it was in the South that the color line was clearly drawn in all aspects of daily life. Nevertheless, in spite of the many obstacles placed in their path, African Americans at this time began to work together to fight discrimination and to become successful in spite of it.

Post-Reconstruction Discrimination

Booker T. Washington's belief that white Americans would be willing to accept hard-working African Americans as equal citizens was proving too optimistic.

Caption Answers

Viewing History Separating the races led to misunderstanding, distrust, and hostility. The inferiority of facilities for African Americans led whites to feel superior to African Americans, and left many African Americans feeling either inferior or angry and fearful.

RESOURCE DIRECTORY

Teaching Resources
Guided Reading and Review booklet, p. 68
Great Debates booklet (Great Debates) *Can Separate Be Equal?* pp. 32–35

Other Print Resources
Nystrom *Atlas of Our Country* *The Third Wave of Immigration,* pp. 30–31

Technology
Section Reading Support Transparencies
Guided Reading Audiotapes (English/Spanish), Ch. 9
Student Edition on Audio CD, Ch. 9
RESOURCE PRO® **Primary Source Activity** *Lynchings and Mob Law,* found on Resource Pro, provides students with a contemporary account of an Illinois lynching, written by Ida B. Wells.
Prentice Hall United States History Video Collection™ Volume 10, *Reconstruction and Segregation*
Prentice Hall Presentation Pro CD-ROM, Ch. 9
Companion Web site, www.phschool.com

Voting Restrictions for African Americans in the South, 1889–1908

Voting Restrictions	States										
	AL	AR	FL	GA	LA	MS	NC	SC	TN	TX	VA
Grandfather Clause	✓			✓	✓		✓				
Property Test	✓			✓	✓		✓				✓
Literacy Test	✓			✓	✓	✓	✓	✓			✓
Poll Tax	✓	✓	✓		✓	✓	✓	✓	✓	✓	✓

SOURCE: *The American Record: Images of the Nation's Past*

INTERPRETING CHARTS This chart shows how southern states tried to prevent African Americans from voting. **Analyzing Information** *Which kind of restriction was used by the most states? Which states had the widest variety of voting restrictions?*

Some southern whites, who in the past had used slavery to repress African Americans, now turned to other methods of oppression.

Voting Restrictions In many southern communities, whites were concerned that if African Americans were allowed to exercise their right to vote, they would gain too much political power. As a result, during the 1890s southern states began using several tactics to deny the vote to blacks. Some states required voters to own property or to pay a **poll tax,** a special fee that must be paid before a person was permitted to vote. Both of these requirements were beyond the financial reach of most African Americans. Voters also had to pass literacy tests. These tests were supposed to demonstrate that a voter could read, write, and meet minimum standards of knowledge. But, like the property requirement and the poll tax, literacy tests were really designed to keep African Americans from voting. In fact, blacks were often given much more difficult tests than whites.

To ensure that the literacy tests did not keep too many poor whites from voting, some states passed special laws with **grandfather clauses.** These laws exempted men from certain voting restrictions if they had already voted, or if they had ancestors (grandfathers) who had voted prior to blacks being granted suffrage. African Americans, of course, did not meet these qualifications and thus were required to take the literacy tests. All of these laws kept African Americans from voting while not singling out the group by name, which would have been unconstitutional.

Segregation During this period many states also instituted a system of legal **segregation.** This system ensured that African Americans were treated as second-class citizens. Segregation means separation of people by race. When this separation is the result of custom, it is called *de facto* segregation (meaning the condition exists in fact, but not in law). In the South, segregation was required by statutes called **Jim Crow** laws. The name came from a minstrel show routine called "Jump Jim Crow," in which a white entertainer in blackface and baggy clothes grinned broadly as he performed unflattering caricatures of African American song and dance.

Although segregation laws are usually associated with the South, they first appeared in the 1830s, when Massachusetts allowed railroad companies to separate black and white passengers. It was in the South,

INTERPRETING POLITICAL CARTOONS Literacy tests were designed to keep African Americans from voting. **Drawing Inferences** *According to this cartoon, what unexpected results did these tests sometimes have?*

"BY TH' WAY, WHAT'S THAT BIG WORD?"

LESSON PLAN

Focus Tell students that although African Americans were free, white society found many ways to suppress them. Despite this, many reached high levels of achievement after Reconstruction. Ask in what ways white society denied African Americans their freedom.

Instruct Review discrimination after Reconstruction. Which tactics did whites use to legally prohibit African Americans from doing certain things, inhibiting them from exercising their full rights? Have students analyze the African American response to discrimination. How did "community" help them overcome discrimination?

Assess/Reteach Have students research ways in which late-nineteenth-century African Americans helped their people make progress in spite of society's obstacles.

ACTIVITY
Connecting with Government

Tell students to learn about the voting patterns of African Americans in the most recent presidential election. Have students look into whether certain issues drew voters to a particular candidate or party, and if so, what those issues were. **(Logical/Mathematical)**

CAPTION ANSWERS

Interpreting Charts All but one of these states used the poll tax. Alabama, Louisiana, and North Carolina had the widest variety of restrictions.

Interpreting Political Cartoons They exposed the fact that there were many illiterate whites who would themselves have failed literacy tests if they had had to take the same difficult tests that African Americans were forced to take.

Section 3 Assessment

Reading Comprehension

1. African Americans often could not afford to pay the poll tax and were given more complex literacy tests than were whites. Grandfather clauses allowed illiterate white men to vote while excluding all African Americans.
2. Statutes that required segregation.
3. The murdering of an African American by white mob action without a lawful trial was used to intimidate other African Americans. Victims were sometimes mutilated or shot before being hanged.
4. The NAACP was formed in 1909 to abolish segregation and discrimination, to oppose racism, and to gain civil rights for African Americans.

Critical Thinking and Writing

5. The separate facilities set aside for African Americans that *Plessy* v. *Ferguson* declared legal were never, in fact, as comfortable or convenient as facilities for whites. African Americans were thus left with unequal treatment.
6. Answers might claim that preventing African Americans from voting was a violation of the Fifteenth Amendment.

Answers will vary, but should include key events, including the founding of the NAACP, important legal victories, protests, and recent social and political actions.

In this photograph, taken at Tuskegee Institute around 1900, Booker T. Washington (front, center) poses with some distinguished guests, including Charles W. Eliot, President of Harvard University (front, far left) and Andrew Carnegie (to the right of Washington).

Overcoming Obstacles In the early 1900s, African American mutual aid and benefit societies multiplied, and social workers and church groups founded settlement houses in black neighborhoods. The Young Men's and Young Women's Christian Associations developed separate recreational and guidance programs for African American youth. The National Urban League, founded in 1911, improved job opportunities and housing for blacks.

Also during this period, African American intellectuals began to publish literature, history, and groundbreaking sociological studies. George Washington Carver became known for his scientific and agricultural research at Tuskegee Institute. In 1897, Alexander Crummell founded the American Negro Academy, which promoted scholarly publications about African American culture and history. Academy members included Du Bois, the poet Paul Dunbar, and educator Anna Julia Cooper.

Black-owned businesses began appearing everywhere. To help these businesses, Booker T. Washington founded the National Negro Business League in 1900. By 1907, it had 320 branches.

In 1912, Madam C. J. Walker spoke at the annual meeting of the Negro Business League. By any standards, she was a successful business person. Walker came from a family of ex-slaves and sharecroppers and had worked as a servant and as a laundress. "I got myself a start by giving myself a start," Walker would later say. She did so by developing her own preparations for styling the hair of African American women. Walker moved to Denver, Colorado, in 1905, and set up a prosperous mail-order business for her hair products. She also established a chain of beauty parlors and training schools. By 1916 her company had 20,000 employees.

With her business a success, Walker moved to New York City. Her home became a gathering place for African American leaders. Walker supported black welfare, education, and civil rights with large contributions. She also made many speeches for the anti-lynching drives of the NAACP and for African American women's organizations. "The girls and women of our race must not be afraid to take hold of business endeavor," she said in her 1913 speech to the Negro Business League. "I want to say to every Negro woman present, don't sit down and wait for the opportunities to come. . . . Get up and make them!"

Section 3 Assessment

READING COMPREHENSION

1. How did the **poll tax**, literacy tests, and **grandfather clauses** limit African American suffrage?
2. What were **Jim Crow** laws?
3. How was **lynching** used to intimidate African Americans?
4. When and why was the **National Association for the Advancement of Colored People** formed?

CRITICAL THINKING AND WRITING

5. **Expressing Problems Clearly** How did *Plessy* v. *Ferguson* contribute to the denial of equal rights for African Americans?
6. **Writing an Editorial** Write an editorial criticizing the denial of suffrage to African Americans that might have appeared at the turn of the century.

Activity: Creating a Time Line
Read more about the NAACP from its founding until today, and create a time line of the major events in the NAACP's history. Use the links provided in the *America: Pathways to the Present* area of the following Web site for help in completing this activity.
www.phschool.com

RESOURCE DIRECTORY

Teaching Resources
Units 1/2 booklet
- Section 3 Quiz, p. 96

Guide to the Essentials
- Section 3 Summary, p. 45

Section 4

The Changing Roles of Women

READING FOCUS

- What were the issues in the debate over women's equality?
- How did women's work in the home change at the turn of the century?
- How did stores and catalogs serve women's new role as consumers?
- What kind of work did women do outside the home?

KEY TERMS

department store
rural free delivery (RFD)
mail-order catalog

TAKING NOTES

As you read, use a chart like the one below to keep track of the changes in women's activities during this period.

In the Home	Outside the Home
Cleaning/traditional	
Buying processed foods/new	

MAIN IDEA

Changes in women's lives, including new jobs, new educational opportunities, and new roles in the home and in the marketplace, fueled a debate over the proper role of women in society.

Setting the Scene "Women hain't no business a votin'," pronounced Josiah Allen, a fictional creation of the popular turn-of-the-century humorist Marietta Holley. "They had better let the laws alone, and tend to their housework. The law loves wimmin and protects 'em." His wife, Samantha, replied, "If the law loves wimmin so well, why don't he give her as much wages as men get for doin' the same work?" Most Americans around 1900 would have known exactly what Samantha and Josiah were arguing about. They would have called it *the woman question,* a wide-ranging debate about the roles of women in society. This debate grew out of several major developments of the era.

The Debate Over Women's Equality

For women like Samantha Allen, the woman question boiled down to a few key demands: Women should be able to vote. They should be able to control their own property and income, and they should have access to higher education and professional jobs. Women's rights advocates were countered by those who insisted that giving women economic and political power would upset the social order. Some argued that allowing women more public roles would destroy their femininity.

Sometimes the debate about the role of women occurred within one individual. Frederic Howe was a writer and reformer who believed in women's equality. When Howe married a woman who was a Unitarian minister, however, he found that he didn't want her to work anymore.

> *"I wanted my old-fashioned picture of a wife rather than [an] equal partner. Men and women fell in love, they married, had children; the wife cooked the meals, kept the house clean, entertained friends . . . cared for the family when sick, got the children ready for school and church, arranged the men's clothes . . . made cakes and pies for the church sociables. . . . She was careful of her conduct, and only had an opinion of her own in a whisper."*
>
> —Frederic Howe

These ladies are enjoying the annual horse show at the Islip Polo Club in 1915. They are also enjoying looser-fitting, more comfortable clothing than had been the style in the 1800s.

Section 4

The Changing Role of Women

SECTION OBJECTIVES

1. Examine the issues in the debate over women's equality.
2. Discover how women's work in the home changed at the turn of the century.
3. Learn how stores and catalogs served women's new role as consumers.
4. Find out about the kinds of work that women did outside the home.

BELLRINGER

Warm-Up Activity Ask students if they think women have full equality with men in American society today. Encourage them to explain their answers.

Activating Prior Knowledge Ask students to state their impression of the rights women had at the turn of the century. What were the short and long-term goals of those who struggled to increase opportunities for women? How did those rights compare to rights still sought today?

READING STRATEGY

As students read this section, have them look for evidence to support the following statement: "Although much had changed in women's lives by the turn of the century, much had stayed the same." Have students reflect on this statement as they identify the political, social, and economic contributions of women to American society at this time.

ACTIVITY

Connecting with Culture

For many women in the late 1800s, club membership provided the means for involvement in public life for the first time. Have groups choose a focus for a club and develop an agenda of activities around that focus. Have a recorder from each group report to the class, and discuss common activities. **(Verbal/Linguistic)**

RESOURCE DIRECTORY

Teaching Resources

Learning Styles Lesson Plans booklet, p. 35
Guided Reading and Review booklet, p. 69
Learning with Documents booklet (Visual Learning Activity) *The New Woman and the New Man,* p. 55

Technology

Section Reading Support Transparencies
Guided Reading Audiotapes (English/Spanish), Ch. 9
Student Edition on Audio CD, Ch. 9
Prentice Hall Presentation Pro CD-ROM, Ch. 9
Companion Web site, www.phschool.com

ACTIVITY
Connecting with Science and Technology

Have students research the typewriter or the telephone. Tell them to find out who invented the item and when. Also have students investigate the ways in which the typewriter or telephone changed people's lives. Encourage students to examine whether there was resistance to the invention and, if so, why. Then have students present an oral report on their findings. **(Verbal/Linguistic)**

BACKGROUND
A Diverse Nation

In the late nineteenth and early twentieth centuries, opportunities opened for white women to perform industrial jobs. In 1870, 18 percent of all women workers were employed in factories. By 1920, the number had risen to 24 percent. Unfortunately, most of these women worked in semiskilled or unskilled positions. Despite the fact that they worked long hours in unsanitary and often unsafe conditions, most of these women had little chance for career advancement. Many women worked in shoe factories, which paid better than textile factories. However, female shoemakers earned just 60 percent of what their male counterparts earned. In the early days of telephones, boys were employed as telephone operators because they had to run between switchboard connections. But when technology improved and concerns arose about the boys' rudeness, women began to replace them, and telephone operator positions came to be filled largely by underpaid women. Employers took advantage of women since they knew women couldn't earn more elsewhere.

READING CHECK
Attending lectures, lobbying for progressive social causes, socializing with other women, engaging in educational activities, and discussing the important topics of the day.

CAPTION ANSWERS

Viewing History It was not a job with high status, and it did not place women in competition with men.

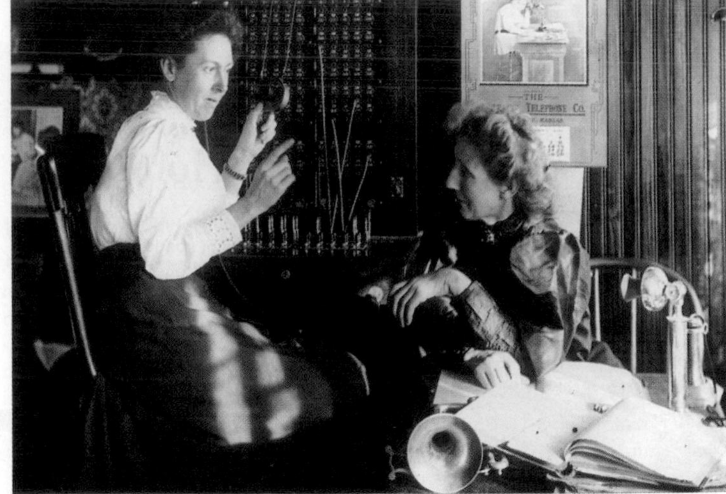

VIEWING HISTORY These telephone operators are on the cutting edge of a new technology and a new industry. **Drawing Conclusions** *Why do you think this job was deemed acceptable for women at the turn of the century?*

Most single female workers were between the ages of 16 and 24. Employers assumed that they would leave when they got married and rarely gave them supervisory jobs or advanced training. They also paid women an average of $3 to $5—about 30 to 60 percent—a week less than men. Self-supporting women were discouraged from entering fields that put them in competition with men. Many educated young women who wanted or needed to work became nurses or teachers. Then new technology opened up two other areas for female workers where they would not be competing with men. The typewriter appeared on the scene in the 1870s, and by 1900 more than one third of American clerical workers were women—usually typists supervised by men. The spread of telephone networks also provided jobs for women, who took telephone orders for department stores and worked as operators.

Much of American society believed that women did not have the mental capacity for professional training. In 1873, retired Harvard Medical School professor Edward H. Clarke warned that young women could not engage in studying and learning while retaining "uninjured health and a future secure from [sickness], hysteria, and other derangements of the nervous system." Three years before Clarke made this warning, the United States had 525 physicians, 67 ministers, and 5 lawyers who were women. Still, women professionals found most of their opportunities in women's colleges and in hospitals.

Volunteering for a Larger Role in Society Women in both the North and the South had performed important voluntary service during the Civil War. Afterward, their interest in voluntary work exploded. They formed hundreds of clubs and associations to facilitate their activities. At first, women joined these organizations primarily for intellectual and social reasons. They studied subjects of common interest, gave talks, or heard lectures by distinguished guests. Some groups, such as the New England Woman's Club, promoted specific causes such as temperance and girls' education. Others worked to establish new libraries and playgrounds. African American club women in Atlanta participated in a national adult education program. The Chicago Woman's Club read Karl Marx's writings and other theoretical works.

READING CHECK
What kinds of activities were popular in women's clubs?

Whatever their focus, these clubs gave their members invaluable experience in speaking, writing, and finance. They helped women increase

RESOURCE DIRECTORY

Teaching Resources
Units 1/2 booklet
- Section 4 Quiz, p. 97
- Chapter 9 Test, pp. 98, 101

Guide to the Essentials
- Section 4 Summary, p. 46
- Chapter 9 Test, p. 47

Other Print Resources
Chapter Tests with ExamView® Test Bank CD-ROM, Ch. 9

Technology
Color Transparencies *Fine Art,* E15
ExamView® Test Bank CD-ROM, Ch. 9
Social Studies Skills Tutor CD-ROM

their self-confidence and take their first steps toward public life. To increase their influence, women's groups combined into national associations. The Association for the Advancement of Women was formed in 1873, followed by the General Federation of Women's Clubs in 1890. These groups took on increasingly ambitious projects, including suffrage and the reform of political abuses. In doing so, they joined with other groups founded to pursue specific reforms, such as the Woman's Christian Temperance Union, established in 1874, and the National American Woman Suffrage Association, formed in 1890. This last group would carry the cause of women's suffrage to victory some 30 years later.

New Women, New Ideas By the early 1900s, the woman question had grown to include a number of issues besides economic and political rights. One was the question of lifestyle: How should women dress and behave? As more women entered the work force or went to college, they took this matter into their own hands. Because they valued convenience, they began to wear shorter hairstyles, raise their hemlines, and wear skirts and blouses that were more suited to their new activities.

Courting and marriage customs also changed. For example, instead of being limited to entertaining a man at home under the watchful eyes of their parents, many young women now went out on dates without supervision. "New women," as they were sometimes called, still hoped to marry. Yet they seemed to have higher expectations of fulfillment in marriage than earlier generations of women did. As a result, the divorce rate rose from one in twelve in 1900 to one in nine by 1916. Many "new women" who married began to push for the legalized spread of information about birth control, a campaign led by New York nurse Margaret Sanger. Such developments were shocking to more traditional Americans.

What was the consensus among women on the woman question? Although the majority wanted "their rights," most women still saw domestic fulfillment as their chief goal. The right to vote was another matter. The issue of the vote prompted huge numbers of women to support the suffrage movement in some way. Soon the vote would be the one issue on which women from many walks of life would unite.

Focus on CULTURE

The Gibson Girl Who was the most popular young woman in 1890s America? Definitely the Gibson Girl. In reality, she was the pen-and-ink creation of illustrator Charles Gibson, whose sketches in *Life* and other magazines helped set the fashion of the time. The Gibson Girl was modern but respectable, and changes in her appearance and activities mirrored the changing roles of women. She often wore the proper business attire of a shirtwaist and skirt; she participated in sports; and eventually she even appeared as a college graduate in cap and gown.

Section  Assessment

READING COMPREHENSION

1. Name three traditional household tasks that women no longer had to do at home after 1900.
2. How did the new system of **rural free delivery** lead to the popularity of **mail-order catalogs?**
3. (a) What kinds of jobs were acceptable for women in 1900? (b) What made these jobs acceptable?
4. How did volunteer work prepare women to be influential in public life?

CRITICAL THINKING AND WRITING

5. **Recognizing Cause and Effect** Use a flowchart to show which changes in society at large led to changes in the roles of women in this era.
6. **Writing a Letter** Parents of young women often objected to their daughters going to work outside the home. Write a letter from a young woman of 1900 in which she tries to convince her parents that she should get a clerical job.

Take It to the NET

Activity: Creating an Advertisement Read about the history of Sears, Roebuck and Company. Draw a poster that might have been used in 1900 to advertise the young company to potential shoppers. Use the links provided in the *America: Pathways to the Present* area of the following Web site for help in completing this activity.
www.phschool.com

Section 4 Assessment

Reading Comprehension

1. Baking bread, sewing clothing, butchering.
2. Rural free delivery made department store goods accessible to farming families in rural areas of the Midwest through mail-order catalogs.
3. (a) Teaching, nursing, clerical work, telephone operators, domestic work. (b) These jobs were low-paying, did not lead to promotion, and did not put women in competition with men.
4. Volunteer work gave women experience in speaking, writing, and finance, giving them the skills and confidence to pursue political and social change.

Critical Thinking and Writing

5. Flowcharts will vary, but changes might include: increase in educational opportunities, new technology in the workplace, less time needed for housework.
6. Possible answer: Perhaps the woman has a college education. She might then argue that she has an obligation to put her education to use.

Posters will vary, but should advertise practical, high-quality, reliable products aimed at the average person.

Reviewing Key Terms

Students should refer to the definitions of key terms in the chapter to write sentences that show an understanding of daily life between 1870 and 1915.

Reviewing Main Ideas

11. Legislation in many states began to limit child labor and require children to attend school; newly arrived immigrants were eager to send their children to public schools.
12. Washington urged African Americans to strengthen their vocational job skills. Du Bois called for full civil liberties for African Americans, urging them to use education to become leaders in professional fields.
13. Amusement parks and vaudeville appealed to city dwellers who now had the time and the money to seek entertainment near their homes. The technology of the trolley aided both the development and the accessibility of amusement parks.
14. Bicycling, basketball, ice skating, tennis, gymnastics, swimming. Women's participation in sports led to new clothing styles and the development of "women's rules" in competitive sports.
15. Ragtime evolved in the South and Midwest by combining shifting melodies with marching-band beats. Jazz originated in New Orleans and synthesized a variety of musical styles, including traditional hymns and the newer ragtime rhythms.
16. Requirements to own property and pay poll taxes in order to vote; court decisions overturning the Civil Rights Act and *Plessy* v. *Ferguson;* Jim Crow laws, which required discrimination.
17. The NAACP worked through the courts system to gain civil rights for African Americans.
18. People were able to shop more conveniently at chain stores with low prices, at department stores, and through mail-order catalogs.
19. Work at home became less demanding, increased opportunities for education existed, volunteer experience gave women skills and confidence.

Chapter 9 Review and Assessment

creating a CHAPTER SUMMARY

Copy this chart (right) and complete it by adding important information about changes in education, entertainment, the situation for African Americans, and the roles of women in the period from 1870 to 1915.

For additional review and enrichment activities, see the interactive version of *America: Pathways to the Present*, available on the Web and on CD-ROM.

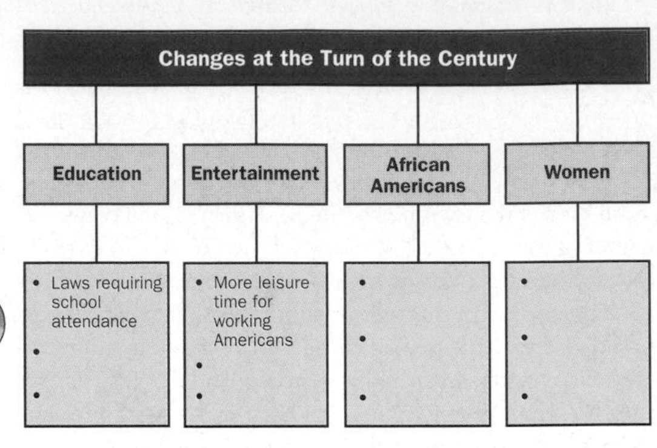

★Reviewing Key Terms

For each of the terms below, write a sentence explaining how it relates to daily life at the turn of the century.

1. literacy
2. assimilation
3. Niagara Movement
4. yellow journalism
5. ragtime
6. poll tax
7. grandfather clause
8. Jim Crow
9. *Plessy* v. *Ferguson*
10. rural free delivery

★ Reviewing Main Ideas

11. Why did public schools gain more students in the late 1800s? (Section 1)
12. Compare the ideas of Booker T. Washington and W.E.B. Du Bois. (Section 1)
13. Why were vaudeville and amusement parks popular during this time? (Section 2)
14. Which sports did women participate in, and what effects did their participation have? (Section 2)
15. Where and how did ragtime and jazz originate? (Section 2)
16. Describe three ways African Americans were discriminated against after Reconstruction. (Section 3)
17. How did the NAACP help African Americans during the early 1900s? (Section 3)
18. How did new sources of manufactured goods change how people shopped? (Section 4)
19. Why were more women entering the work force in the early 1900s? (Section 4)

★ Critical Thinking

20. **Analyzing Information** Use the following data to make a bar graph showing the increase in students earning bachelor's degrees from 1890 to 1920.

    1890: males—12,857; females—2,682
    1900: males—22,173; females—5,237
    1910: males—28,762; females—8,437
    1920: males—31,980; females—16,642

    During which decade did women make the most significant gains compared to men? Why?
21. **Testing Conclusions** Cite evidence to support this statement: The turn of the century saw the birth of the American mass entertainment industry.
22. **Identifying Central Issues** Why do you think southern whites were so determined to use custom and law to keep blacks separate from whites?
23. **Recognizing Bias** (a) What views of men and women are reflected in the quotation by Frederic Howe on page 337? (b) How did women challenge these views?

Creating a Chapter Summary

Changes at the Turn of the Century

Education	Entertainment	African Americans	Women
• Laws requiring school attendance	• More leisure time for working Americans	• Increased discrimination after end of Reconstruction	• Invention of the washing machine frees home-makers
• Expansion of higher education	• People began attending movies	• Segregation is legal	• Availability of ready-made food
• Increased opportunities for coeducation	• Popularity of attending sporting events	• Growth of civil rights organizations	• More women in the work-force

A GOVERNMENT OF THE PEOPLE
BY THE PEOPLE FOR THE PEOPLE
UNENFRANCHISED
ARE NOT THE WOMEN HALF THE NATION?

★ Skills Assessment

Analyzing Political Cartoons ▶

24. Read the words at the top of the cartoon. To what government do they refer? Describe how that kind of government should treat its citizens.
25. Identify the figures. (a) What does each figure represent? (b) How do you know?
26. Analyze the woman on the right. (a) Why is she shackled? (b) Why is she appealing to the man on the left? (c) Why does the cartoonist show the woman in the middle supporting the woman on the right?
27. Read the words at the bottom of the cartoon. What is the message of the cartoon?

Interpreting Data

Turn to the graph on illiteracy in the United States in Section 1.

28. In which year were illiteracy rates the highest?
    A 1870
    B 1880
    C 1890
    D 1920
29. Which of the following statements best summarizes the information in the graph?
    F Few people were able to read and write in the late 1800s.
    G About 10 percent of the United States population was illiterate in 1900.
    H During the period from 1870 to 1920, illiteracy rates dropped in the United States.
    J Literacy was an important requirement for citizenship in the United States.

Applying the Chapter Skill: *Analyzing Political Cartoons for Point of View*

30. Look back at the cartoon on page 333. Use the steps presented on the Skills for Life page in this chapter to analyze the cartoon. (a) What was the cartoonist's frame of reference? Explain. (b) Do you think his point of view is the same as that of the two men in the cartoon? Explain. (c) What is the point of view of the cartoonist? What action might he advocate?

ACTIVITIES

Writing to LEARN

Writing an Outline
Many kinds of social and cultural changes occurred in America at the turn of the century. Make five of these changes the main headings of an outline. Under each heading, write who welcomed each change and why, and also who resisted the change (if anyone) and why. Finally, write a short paragraph summarizing how these changes affected American society at the beginning of the twentieth century.

Primary Source CD-ROM

Working With Primary Sources Find additional information on life at the turn of the twentieth century on the *Exploring Primary Sources in U.S. History CD ROM* and use the selection(s) provided to complete the Chapter 9 primary source activity located in the *America: Pathways to the Present* area of the following Web site.
www.phschool.com

Take It to the NET

Chapter Self-Test As a review activity, take the Chapter 9 Self-Test in the *America: Pathways to the Present* area at the Web site listed below. The questions are designed to test your understanding of the chapter content.
www.phschool.com

CRITICAL THINKING

20. Students should create a bar graph. The 1920s, because more schools for women had been developed and coeducational opportunities had increased.
21. America become more urban, leisure time increased, technology advanced, and people had more money. These factors helped create a mass entertainment industry featuring such activities as movies, vaudeville, and spectator sports.
22. To prevent African Americans from gaining power and prestige in society.
23. Women as exclusively domestic and submissive, men as dominant breadwinners. Women challenged this viewpoint by gaining education, seeking employment, volunteering, and becoming active in political life.

SKILLS ASSESSMENT

24. The United States government. With equality.
25. (a) Kneeling figure: American women; standing woman: justice; the man: the government. (b) The seated woman's banner reads "unenfranchised," indicating the lack of female suffrage in America; the standing woman's headband reads "Justice"; the man is dressed as "Uncle Sam."
26. (a) Because her rights are limited. (b) She appeals to the government to grant women liberty and justice. c) To show that justice for women is a natural right.
27. That equality is the natural right of all Americans, not just male Americans.
28. A
29. H
30. (a) African Americans were prevented from voting and were subject to repressive laws and violence. (b) No, the cartoonist is making fun of them. (c) The cartoonist is against the literacy tests and favors equality.

ANSWERS TO ACTIVITIES

Writing to LEARN

Answers will vary, but should focus on facts from the chapter, particularly that while education expanded and new forms of entertainment emerged, many people in society resisted change, especially in the status of African Americans and women.

Primary Source CD-ROM

Direct students to the additional primary sources that can be found on the *Exploring Primary Sources in U.S. History CD-ROM.*

Take It to the NET

Additional support materials and activities for Chapter 9 of *America: Pathways to the Present* can be found in the Social Studies area at the Prentice Hall School Web site. **www.phschool.com**

Living Under Jim Crow

Focus Have students find the meaning of each of these words in a dictionary before they begin to read: *vehement, rookery, hovel, locality, consternation, glimpse.* Ask them to think, as they read, about how segregation shaped the attitudes of blacks and whites toward one another. Explain the allusion to Spanish-American heroes. *(In 1898 the United States declared war on Spain. African American troops served with distinction in the Spanish-American War, which the United States won resoundingly in just three months.)*

Instruct Ask students to think about a typical day in their family's life. Discuss with students how the presence of Jim Crow would affect such a day. Elicit specific examples.

To ensure that students grasp the writer's subtle points, call on volunteers to explain sentences such as the following:

- "There is no wonder that we die; the wonder is that we persist in living."
- "We had ruined his neighborhood of poor people; poor as we, poorer in manners at least."

Analyzing the Document Use this additional question to generate class discussion:

Critical Thinking: Demonstrating Reasoned Judgment Give evidence to support the speaker's statement: "I have seen very small white children hang their black dolls. It is not the child's fault, he is simply an apt pupil." *(Adult whites hanged African Americans under Jim Crow.)*

AmericanHeritage®

MY BRUSH WITH **HISTORY™**

ANONYMOUS

Living Under Jim Crow

The editors of *American Heritage* magazine have selected this account, published in 1902 and written by an unnamed African American woman living in the South. In it she described the world of Jim Crow—the daily frustrations and humiliations that African Americans had to endure as they struggled to build successful lives.

I AM A COLORED WOMAN, wife and mother. I have lived all my life in the South, and have often thought what a peculiar fact it is that the more ignorant the Southern whites are of us the more vehement they are in their denunciation of us. They boast that they have little intercourse with us, never see us in our homes, churches or places of amusement, but still they know us thoroughly.

They also admit that they know us in no capacity except as servants, yet they say we are at our best in that single capacity. What philosophers they are! The Southerners say we Negroes are a happy, laughing set of people, with no thought of tomorrow. How mistaken they are! The educated, thinking Negro is just the opposite. There is a feeling of unrest, insecurity, almost panic among the best class of Negroes in the South. In our homes, in our churches, wherever two or three are gathered together, there is a discussion of what is best to do. Must we remain in the South or go elsewhere? Where can we go to feel that security which other people feel? Is it best to go in great numbers or only in several families? These and many other things are discussed over and over. . . .

Even well-educated African Americans were often restricted to low-paying jobs.

I know of houses occupied by poor Negroes in which a respectable farmer would not keep his cattle. It is impossible for them to rent elsewhere. All Southern real estate agents have "white property" and "colored property." In one of the largest Southern cities there is a colored minister, a graduate of Harvard, whose wife is an educated, Christian woman, who lived for weeks in a tumble-down rookery because he could neither rent nor buy in a respectable locality.

Many colored women who wash, iron, scrub, cook or sew all the week to help pay the rent for these miserable hovels and help fill the many small mouths, would deny themselves some of the necessaries of life if they could take their little children and teething babies on the cars to the parks of a Sunday afternoon and sit under trees, enjoy the cool breezes and breathe God's pure air for only two or three hours; but this is denied them. Some of the parks have

344

RESOURCE DIRECTORY

Technology

AmericanHeritage® My Brush with History™ Videotapes *Living Under Jim Crow*

TEST PREPARATION

Have students use the excerpt on these pages to answer the following question.

Which of her neighbors' slights gave the speaker the most pain?

A The neighbors' allowing their children to hang their black dolls.

B The neighbors' failing to call on the speaker after her child died.

C The neighbors' expressing surprise that the speaker's children are clean and well cared for.

(D) The neighbors' unfriendliness and lack of even slight attention.

signs, "No Negroes allowed on these grounds except as servants." Pitiful, pitiful customs and laws that make war on women and babes! There is no wonder that we die; the wonder is that we persist in living.

A Neighborhood of Poor People

Fourteen years ago I had just married. My husband had saved sufficient money to buy a small home. On account of our limited means we went to the suburbs, on unpaved streets, to look for a home, only asking for a high, healthy locality. Some real estate agents were "sorry, but had nothing to suit," some had "just the thing," but we discovered on investigation that they had "just the thing" for an unhealthy pigsty. Others had no "colored property." One agent said that he had what we wanted, but we should have to go to see the lot after dark, or walk by and give the place a casual look; for, he said, "all the white people in the neighborhood would be down on me." Finally, we bought this lot. When the house was being built we went to see it. Consternation reigned. We had ruined his neighborhood of poor people; poor as we, poorer in manners at least. The people who lived next door received the sympathy of their friends. When we walked on the street (there were no sidewalks) we were embarrassed by the stare of many unfriendly eyes.

Two years passed before a single woman spoke to me, and only then because I helped one of them when a little sudden trouble came to her. Such was the reception, I a happy young woman, just married, received from people among whom I wanted to make a home. Fourteen years have now passed, four children have been born to us, and one has died in this same home, among these same neighbors. Although the neighbors speak to us . . . , not one woman has ever been inside of my house, not even at the times when a woman would doubly appreciate the slightest attention of a neighbor. . . .

White agents and other chance visitors who come into our homes ask questions that we must not dare ask their wives. They express surprise that our children have clean faces and that their hair is combed. . . .

We were delighted to know that some of our Spanish-American heroes were coming where

Jim Crow laws continued into the second half of the twentieth century, as this woman discovered in a Dallas, Texas, bus station in 1961.

we could get a glimpse of them. Had not black men helped in a small way to give them their honors? In the cities of the South, where these heroes went, the white school children were assembled, flags waved, flowers strewn, speeches made, and "My Country, 'tis of Thee, Sweet Land of Liberty," was sung. Our children who need to be taught so much, were not assembled, their hands waved no flags, they threw no flowers, heard no thrilling speech, sang no song of their country. And this is the South's idea of justice. Is it surprising that feeling grows more bitter, when the white mother teaches her boy to hate my boy, not because he is mean, but because his skin is dark? I have seen very small white children hang their black dolls. It is not the child's fault, he is simply an apt pupil. . . .

Source: Anonymous, *Independent* magazine, 1902.

Understanding Primary Sources

1. At what time of day did this woman and her husband have to go to look at a new house they were thinking of buying?
2. When she refers to her neighbors as "poor people," what does she mean?

American Heritage® MY BRUSH WITH **HISTORY**™  **Videotapes**

For more information about segregation and Jim Crow laws, view "Living Under Jim Crow."

345

CUSTOMIZE FOR ...

Gifted and Talented

Discuss the speaker's tone in the first two paragraphs. *(Sarcastic)* Have students read aloud examples that illustrate this tone.

Ask students to think of a time that they used sarcasm, humor, or "put-downs" to deal with a painful situation. Have them write a description of the situation and the strategy that they used to protect themselves.

CUSTOMIZE FOR ...

ESL

Students may need help with the following words and phrases:
denunciation harsh criticism
capacity role
on account of because of
assembled gathered together

CUSTOMIZE FOR ...

Less Proficient Readers

Discuss the differences between the lives of white and black children under Jim Crow. (Refer students particularly to the last paragraph in the selection.) Then discuss the challenges that confronted African American parents raising children under Jim Crow. The discussion might include areas such as schools and teachers, safety precautions, and places to play.

CUSTOMIZE FOR ...

Less Proficient Writers

In this passage, the writer lists many injustices experienced by her and her family. Ask students to select one of these injustices and state their own opinion about it in two or three sentences.

Answers

1. After dark.
2. "Poorer in manners," she calls them. They greet her with unfriendly eyes and do not speak to her.

Use this sample exam to help your students prepare for standardized tests.

Tips for Test Taking

You might want to remind your students of the following:

1. Read the directions carefully.
2. Read each question carefully.
3. For multiple choice questions, try to answer the question before you look at the choices. Read all the choices. Then, eliminate those that are absolutely incorrect.
4. For short answer questions, be sure to answer the question completely if there is more than one part.
5. Answer the easy questions first. Then, go back to the ones that will take more time.
6. Pace yourself. Be sure to set aside enough time for the writing questions.

TEST PREPARATION

Write your answers on a separate sheet of paper.

1. Which one of the following was a purpose of the Union naval blockade of the South during the Civil War?

   A To encourage Southerners to move to the North
   B To stop travel to the Confederate capital city
   C To prevent cotton from being sold in Europe
   D To limit the food exports of the South

2. The purpose of the Gettysburg Address was to

   A rally tired Confederate soldiers.
   B remind the nation about the reasons for fighting the Civil War.
   C help Union generals locate a house full of stored weapons.
   D outline Lincoln's reelection platform.

3. After the Civil War, the Radical Republicans believed

   A in completely restructuring society to guarantee equality to blacks.
   B that the North should rebuild the South.
   C that Southern military leaders could serve in the Congress.
   D that violence was the best way to settle social problems in the South.

4. Which one of the following groups provided food, clothing, and education to blacks in the South after the Civil War?

   A Progressives
   B Radical Republicans
   C Tweed Machine
   D Freedmen's Bureau

5. The sharecropping system in the South resulted in

   A higher wages in Southern industries.
   B annual debts for many farm families.
   C the government's giving each black family 40 acres of land.
   D the end of large-scale cotton production.

6. Which one of the following nineteenth-century business leaders is correctly paired with his area of industry?

   A John D. Rockefeller and oil
   B Andrew Carnegie and railroads
   C Edwin Drake and steel
   D Thomas A. Edison and the telephone

7. The Sherman Antitrust Act initially was unsuccessful because

   A it was not passed into law by Congress.
   B it was enforced infrequently by the courts.
   C President Harrison refused to support it.
   D Rockefeller turned his employees against it.

346

Diagnose and Prescribe
- Profile student skills with Diagnostic Tests A&B.
- Address student needs with program materials correlated to test questions.

Review and Reteach
- Provide cumulative content review with the Review Book.

Practice and Assess
- Build test-taking skills with Test-taking Strategies With Transparencies.

Use the chart and your knowledge of social studies to answer the following question.

Which Early Labor Union?
• Represented skilled workers • Consisted of a network of smaller "craft" unions • Focused on wages, hours, and working conditions • Excluded women and African Americans • Used strikes, boycotts, and collective bargaining • Wanted "closed shops"

8. The chart describes which one of the following early labor unions?

A National Labor Union

B Knights of Labor

C American Federation of Labor

D Industrial Workers of the World

9. What was the long-term result of the Pullman Strike of 1894?

A The federal government sided with business against labor unions.

B The Knights of Labor membership grew after they won the strike.

C Nonviolent methods helped the unions win the strike.

D Unskilled workers formed their own labor unions.

10. The Pendelton Civil Service Act

A limited government assistance to businesses.

B provided special jobs for Civil War veterans.

C opened up government jobs to African Americans.

D helped to end the spoils system.

Use the chart and your knowledge of social studies to answer the following question.

Immigration From Italy	
Year	**Number of Immigrants**
1900	100,135
1901	135,996
1902	178,375
1903	230,622
1904	193,296
1905	221,479
SOURCE: *Historical Statistics of the United States, Colonial Times to 1970*	

11. Which one of the following factors contributed to the rise in U.S. immigration from Italy around the turn of the century?

A Pogroms

B Steerage and quarantines

C High taxes and crop failures

D Revolution and civil war

12. Jane Addams operated Hull House as a center to

A assist the urban poor.

B fight immigration from Asia.

C aid men who fought in the Civil War.

D support Populist Party candidates.

Writing Practice

13. Describe how the Compromise of 1877 brought an end to Reconstruction.

14. Explain the methods businesses used to limit the power of unions.

15. What actions did the federal government take to encourage people to move to the West following the Civil War?

1. C
2. B
3. A
4. D
5. B
6. A
7. B
8. C
9. A
10. D
11. C
12. A
13. Answers should mention the disputed election victory of Rutherford B. Hayes. In exchange for the presidency, Hayes offered to remove the remaining federal troops from southern states.
14. Answers should include forbidding union meetings, firing union organizers, forcing new employees to sign contracts promising not to join unions, refusing to bargain with unions, and refusing to recognize unions as representatives of workers.
15. Answers should mention the Pacific Railway Acts, which expanded railway transportation; the Morrill Land-Grant Act, which gave states land to sell; and the Homestead Act, which gave settlers small parcels of western land if they agreed to settle and farm them.

Unit 3

Introducing the Unit

The United States on the Brink of Change (1890–1920) This unit presents the United States as it first begins to look outward and form its role as an important leader among nations of the world. Global situations and conflicts began to engage the United States as the nineteenth century came to a close. Meanwhile, at home, there were conflicts between different factions of society: between the rich and the poor, the working class and business owners, new immigrants and older settlers, former slaves and American society at large. As Americans dealt with their problems at home, tension between the great powers continued in Europe, resulting finally in the Great War (World War I), which compelled the United States to join in a worldwide conflict for the first time.

Using Historical Evidence

Direct students' attention to the painting on these pages. It depicts the U.S. fleet's return to New York harbor after a victory in the Spanish-American War. This war took place as imperialism spread worldwide. Under imperialism, stronger, richer nations took control of smaller, poorer nations. America's role as an imperialist nation is a sign of how much the new country had grown in power and strength.

Discuss this change with students. What were some positive aspects of this type of strength and power? What were some pitfalls? How did this imperialist posture affect America as the era of global conflict got under way?

eTeach

Be sure to check out this month's online discussion with a Master Teacher. Go to **www.phschool.com**.

Unit 3

The United States on the Brink of Change (1890–1920)

"Whether they will or no, Americans must begin to look outward."

Alfred T. Mahan
The Interest of America in Sea Power, 1897

This 1898 painting by Fred Pansing shows part of the U.S. fleet entering New York harbor following the Spanish-American War. ▶

RESOURCE DIRECTORY

Teaching Resources

Units 3/4 booklet
- American Pathways Activity, pp. 37–38
- History's Lasting Impact, pp. 39–40

Geography and History booklet, pp. 12–13

Other Print Resources

Prentice Hall Assessment System
- Document-Based Assessment

TECHNOLOGY CENTER

Take It to the NET

Prentice Hall School Web site offers student-appropriate Internet activities and links that extend core content. Visit us at the Social Studies area. **www.phschool.com**

AmericanHeritage®

My Brush with History™ Video Program This new video series lets your students learn history from the people who lived it.

RESOURCE PRO®

Teaching Resources on CD-ROM offer lesson-planning flexibility, test-generation capability, and resource manageability.

- **Presentation Pro CD-ROM** Provides you with multimedia lecture notes for each chapter.
- **Social Studies Skills Tutor CD-ROM** Provides interactive practice in Geographic Literacy, Critical Thinking and Reading, Visual Analysis, and Communications.
- **Interactive Constitution CD-ROM** Exploring active citizenship and civic responsibilities, this CD-ROM shows students how the Constitution affects their lives today.
- **Exploring Primary Sources in U.S. History CD-ROM** This interactive exploration of primary sources allows students to analyze and to evaluate writing and images from American history.
- **Guided Reading Audiotapes**
- **Student Edition on Audio CD**
- **Sounds of an Era Audio CD** Bring the sounds of American history to life in the classroom with music, speeches, poetry, interviews, and news reports.

Don't miss the exclusive interactive version of this textbook on the Web and on CD-ROM.

RESOURCE DIRECTORY

Technology

Color Transparencies *Historical Maps,* A27, A28, A29, A30, A31, A33, A34; *Political Cartoons,* B9, B10, B11; *Time Lines,* C5, C6; *Cause-and-Effect Charts,* D7, D8; *Fine Art,* E16; *American Photo,* F6; *American Diversity,* G11; *The Way It Works,* H15, H16

Section Reading Support Transparencies

Prentice Hall United States History Video Collection™ Volume 14, *The Progressive Movement;* Volume 15, *The United States and the World;* Volume 16, *The Great War*

Companion Web site, www.phschool.com

Chapter 10 Planning Guide
In Your Classroom

Customize for Individual Needs

Gifted and Talented

Teacher's Edition
- Customize for Gifted and Talented, p. 371

Teaching Resources
- Biography, Literature, and Comparing Primary Sources booklet, pp. 22, 63, 129

Technology
- Exploring Primary Sources in U.S. History CD-ROM *Roosevelt Corollary*

ESL

Teacher's Edition
- Customize for ESL, p. 353

Teaching Resources
- Guided Reading and Review booklet, pp. 70–73
- Guide to the Essentials (English/Spanish), Chapter 10

Technology
- Student Edition on Audio CD, Chapter 10
- Guided Reading Audiotapes (English/Spanish), Chapter 10
- Section Reading Support Transparencies

Less Proficient Readers

Teacher's Edition
- Customize for Less Proficient Readers, p. 359

Teaching Resources
- Guided Reading and Review booklet, pp. 70–73
- Guide to the Essentials (English/Spanish), Chapter 10

Technology
- Student Edition on Audio CD, Chapter 10
- Guided Reading Audiotapes (English/Spanish), Chapter 10
- Section Reading Support Transparencies

Less Proficient Writers

Teacher's Edition
- Customize for Less Proficient Writers, p. 375

Teaching Resources
- Guided Reading and Review booklet, pp. 70–73
- Guide to the Essentials (English/Spanish), Chapter 10

Technology
- Student Edition on Audio CD, Chapter 10
- Guided Reading Audiotapes (English/Spanish), Chapter 10
- Section Reading Support Transparencies

Teacher's Edition Index

Chapter 10 – Pacing Suggestions

For 90-minute Blocks

- Teach sections 1–4 using Transparencies A27, A28, A29, A30, B9, B10, C5, D7, and G11, and the Recent Scholarship note on page 369 for class discussions.

Running Out of Time?

If you are running short on time to cover this chapter, consider the following options:

- Use Prentice Hall Presentation Pro CD-ROM to create an outline for this chapter.
- Use the Section Summaries for Chapter 10, from **Guide to the Essentials (English/Spanish).**

TEKS Correlation

Chapter-Level	TEKS
	(24) Social studies skills. The student applies critical-thinking skills to organize and use information acquired from a variety of sources, including electronic technology. The student is expected to: **(A)** locate and use primary and secondary sources such as computer software, databases, media and news services, biographies, interviews, and artifacts to acquire information about the United States.
1 The Pressure to Expand	**(3) History.** The student understands the emergence of the United States as a world power between 1898 and 1920. The student is expected to: **(A)** explain why significant events and individuals, including the Spanish-American war, U.S. expansionism, Henry Cabot Lodge, Alfred Thayer Mahan, and Theodore Roosevelt, moved the United States into the position of a world power. **(9) Geography.** The student understands the impact of geographic factors on major events. The student is expected to: **(B)** identify and explain reasons for changes in political boundaries such as those resulting from statehood and international conflicts. **(24) Social studies skills.** The student applies critical-thinking skills to organize and use information acquired from a variety of sources, including electronic technology. The student is expected to: **(B)** analyze information by sequencing, categorizing, identifying cause-and-effect relationships, comparing, contrasting, finding the main idea, summarizing, making generalizations and predictions, and drawing inferences and conclusions.
2 The Spanish-American War	**(1) History.** The student understands traditional historical points of reference in U.S. history from 1877 to the present. The student is expected to: **(C)** explain the significance of the following dates: 1898, 1914–1918, 1929, 1941–1945, and 1957. **(3) History.** The student understands the emergence of the United States as a world power between 1898 and 1920. The student is expected to: **(A)** explain why significant events and individuals, including the Spanish-American war, U.S. expansionism, Henry Cabot Lodge, Alfred Thayer Mahan, and Theodore Roosevelt, moved the United States into the position of a world power. **(8) Geography.** The student uses geographic tools to collect, analyze, and interpret data. The student is expected to: **(B)** pose and answer questions about geographic distributions and patterns shown on maps, graphs, charts, models, and databases. **(12) Economics.** The student understands domestic and foreign issues related to U.S. economic growth from the 1879s to 1920. The student is expected to: **(D)** analyze the effects of economic policies including the Open Door Policy and Dollar Diplomacy on U.S. Diplomacy. **(E)** describe the economic effects of international military conflicts, including the Spanish-American War and World War I, on the United States. **(23) Science, technology, and society.** The student understands the influence of scientific discoveries and technological innovations on daily life in the United States. The student is expected to: **(B)** explain how technological innovations in areas such as space exploration have led to other innovations that affect daily life and standard of living. **(25) Social studies skills.** The student communicates in written, oral, and visual forms. The student is expected to: **(D)** create written, oral, and visual presentations of social studies information.
3 A New Foreign Policy	**(1) History.** The student understands traditional historical points of reference in U.S. history from 1877 to the present. The student is expected to: **(B)** apply absolute and relative chronology through the sequencing of significant individuals, events, and time periods. **(3) History.** The student understands the emergence of the United States as a world power between 1898 and 1920. The student is expected to: **(A)** explain why significant events and individuals, including the Spanish-American War, U.S. expansionism, Henry Cabot Lodge, Alfred Thayer Mahan, and Theodore Roosevelt, moved the United States into the position of a world power. **(9) Geography.** The student understands the impact of geographic factors on major events. The student is expected to: **(A)** analyze the effects of physical and human geographic factors on major events including the building of the Panama Canal. **(12) Economics.** The student understands domestic and foreign issues related to U.S. economic growth from the 1879s to 1920. The student is expected to: **(D)** analyze the effects of economic policies including the Open Door Policy and Dollar Diplomacy on U.S. Diplomacy.
4 Debating America's New Role	**(24) Social studies skills.** The student applies critical-thinking skills to organize and use information acquired from a variety of sources, including electronic technology. The student is expected to: **(G)** support a point of view on a social studies issue or event. **(25) Social studies skills.** The student communicates in written, oral, and visual forms. The student is expected to: **(C)** transfer information from one medium to another, including written to visual and statistical to written or visual, using computer software as appropriate.

Chapter 10

Becoming a World Power

(1890–1915)

Introducing the Chapter

By the 1890s, business and political leaders with dreams of empire were expanding into new markets and seizing control of territory abroad. Imperialism on the part of a country founded on freedom from colonialism troubled many United States citizens. The responsibilities of world power brought the government's conflicting domestic and international agendas to the forefront.

Time Line Activity

To provide students with practice in using the time line, ask questions such as these:

1. Who was President at the time the United States overthrew Hawaii's Queen Liliuokalani? *(Grover Cleveland)*
2. What act led the United States to declare war on Spain? *(The explosion of the U.S.S.* Maine *in 1898)*
3. What later action resulted from Austria's annexation of Bosnia and Herzegovina? *(The outbreak of World War I)*

Chapter 10 Becoming a World Power (1890–1915)

$50,000 REWARD.—WHO DESTROYED THE MAINE?—$50,000 REWARD.
NEW YORK JOURNAL AND ADVERTISER
DESTRUCTION OF THE WAR SHIP MAINE WAS THE WORK OF AN ENEMY

American Events

1890 Alfred T. Mahan's *The Influence of Sea Power Upon History, 1660–1783* urges the United States to build a powerful navy to protect markets abroad.

1893 American business groups, with the help of United States Marines, overthrow Hawaii's Queen Liliuokalani and set up a provisional government.

1898 The U.S.S. *Maine* explodes off the coast of Havana, Cuba, killing more than 250 American sailors. An outraged American public convinces Congress to declare war on Spain.

Presidential Terms: Grover Cleveland 1893–1897; William McKinley 1897–1901

1890 • 1894 • 1898 •

World Events

1895 Cuba rebels against Spanish rule.

1900 The Boxer Rebellion erupts in China.

eTeach

Be sure to check out this month's online discussion with a Master Teacher. Go to **www.phschool.com**.

RESOURCE DIRECTORY

Teaching Resources

Pacing Charts booklet
Block Scheduling booklet, p. 21
Units 3/4 booklet
- Chapter Summary, p. 3

Technology

Guided Reading Audiotapes (English/Spanish), Ch. 10
Student Edition on Audio CD, Ch. 10
Sounds of an Era Audio CD *"The Washington Post March,"* 1897 recording
Prentice Hall United States History Video Collection™ Volume 15, *The United States and the World*
Prentice Hall Presentation Pro CD-ROM, Ch. 10
Resource Pro® CD-ROM
Social Studies Skills Tutor CD-ROM
Companion Web site, www.phschool.com

World Imperialism, *circa* 1900

ARCTIC OCEAN
ATLANTIC OCEAN
PACIFIC OCEAN
INDIAN OCEAN
PACIFIC OCEAN
Equator

1 UNITED STATES — American possessions	4 CHINA — Chinese possessions	7 FRANCE — French possessions	10 JAPAN — Japanese possessions	13 RUSSIAN EMPIRE — Russian possessions
2 BELGIUM — Belgian possessions	5 DENMARK — Danish possessions	8 GERMANY — German possessions	11 OTTOMAN EMPIRE — Ottoman possessions	14 SPAIN — Spanish possessions
3 UNITED KINGDOM — British possessions	6 NETHERLANDS — Dutch possessions	9 ITALY — Italian possessions	12 PORTUGAL — Portuguese possessions	Independent country

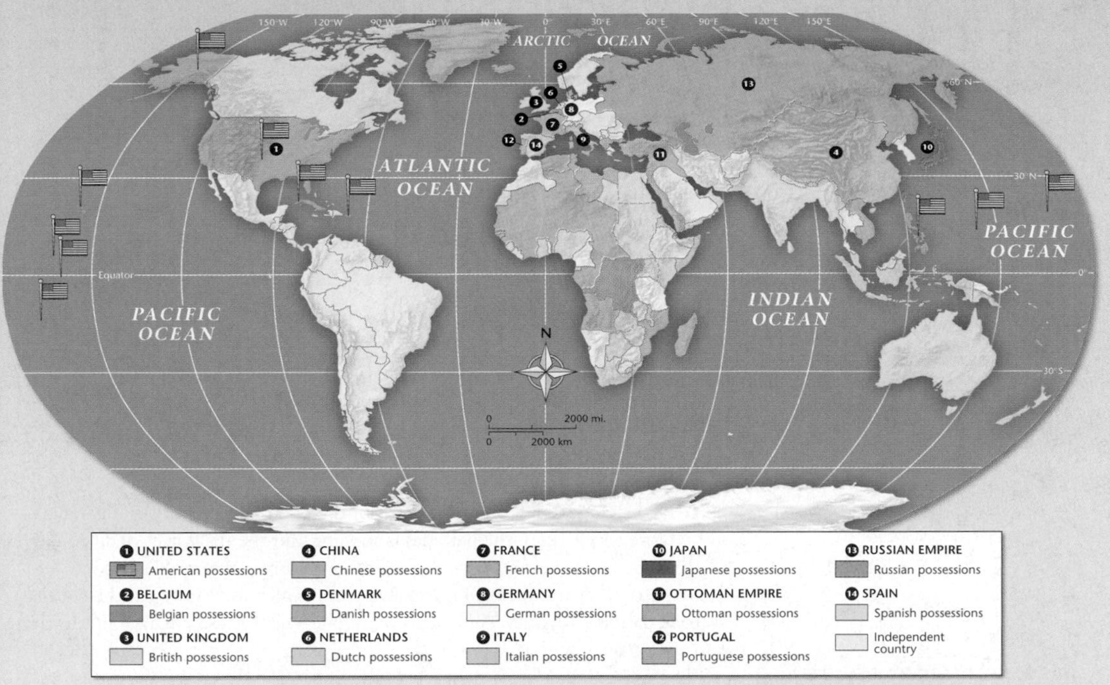

1903 Panama gives the United States control over the Panama Canal Zone for $10 million.

1904 President Roosevelt issues the Roosevelt Corollary to the Monroe Doctrine.

1907 The Great White Fleet tours the world as a display of the impressive naval power of the United States.

1914 President Wilson sends troops to Mexico to assist Mexican revolutionaries.

Theodore Roosevelt 1901–1909 | William Howard Taft 1909–1913 | Woodrow Wilson 1913–1921

1902 · 1906 · 1910 · 1914

1905 Japan defeats Russia in the Russo-Japanese War.

1908 Austria annexes Bosnia and Herzegovina.

1912 The First Balkan War begins.

1914 World War I begins.

World Imperialism, circa 1900

Activating Prior Knowledge Looking at the map, explain the saying current at this time that "the sun never sets on the British Empire." *(Great Britain had acquired so much territory that it was always daytime in some place under Britain's control.)*

Previewing Why do you think the United States bought Alaska and annexed islands in the Pacific? *(The United States was trying to intimidate the British in Canada by placing American territory on two sides of Canada. The annexed islands were to be used as refueling and repair stations for the rebuilt U.S. Navy.)*

BACKGROUND
About the Pictures

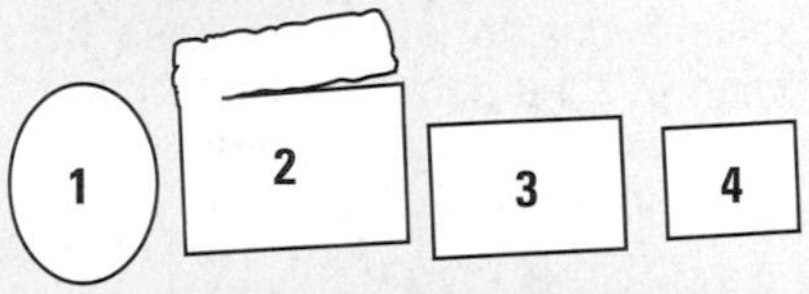

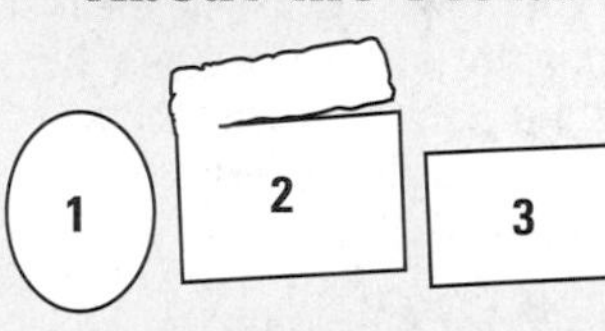

1. Until the 1893 overthrow of Queen Liliuokalani, Hawaii had been the only state in the United States to have a monarchical government.
2. The exact cause of the February 1898 explosion of the U.S.S. *Maine* was never discovered, but the speculation was sabotage by the Spanish.
3. British artist Edward Moran painted *Return of the Conquerors* in 1899. Moran moved to America in 1844, and by the time of his death in 1901 he was widely regarded as one of the foremost American painters of maritime subjects.
4. From 1911 until 1917, the United States was involved in the Mexican civil war. In 1916 General Pershing was dispatched to Mexico to apprehend the Mexican revolutionary leader Pancho Villa, who had been raiding American towns across the border. Pershing failed, however, and Pancho Villa escaped.

Don't miss the exclusive interactive version of this textbook on the Web and on CD-ROM.

BIBLIOGRAPHY

For the Teacher

McCullough, David. ***The Path Between the Seas: The Creation of the Panama Canal, 1870–1914.*** Simon & Schuster, 1977. (Lively and full account contains excerpts from original sources and reads as an epic adventure.)

Traxel, David. ***1898: The Birth of the American Century.*** Vintage, 1999. (A historian pinpoints 1898 as the year America entered the world stage.)

For the Student

O'Toole, G.J.A. ***The Spanish War: An American Epic—1898.*** Norton, 1986. (An anecdotal discussion of the explosion of the *Maine* with recent evidence and an analysis of the McKinley administration's role in the expansion of the conflict.)

Friar, William. ***Portrait of the Panama Canal: From Construction to the 21st Century.*** Graphic Arts Center Publishing Company, 1999. (A lively collection of historic and contemporary photos.)

Section 1 The Pressure to Expand

Section Objectives

1. Find out about the factors that led to the growth of imperialism around the world.
2. Learn about the ways in which the United States began to expand its interests abroad in the 1800s.
3. See the arguments made in favor of United States expansion in the 1890s.

Bellringer

Warm-Up Activity Write the following on the chalkboard: "The sun never sets on the British Empire." Ask students what they think the saying means. Explain that in the late 1800s, when this saying was popular, the United States was beginning to build its own empire. Ask what an empire is.

Activating Prior Knowledge Ask students, "Which of the current United States became part of this country's territory in the 1890s?" *(Hawaii)*

Reading Strategy

Before they read, ask students to write a question about each heading in the section. As they read, have them note answers to their questions.

Section 1

The Pressure to Expand

READING FOCUS

- What factors led to the growth of imperialism around the world?
- In what ways did the United States begin to expand its interests abroad in the late 1800s?
- What arguments were made in favor of United States expansion in the 1890s?

MAIN IDEA

In the late 1800s, as European nations took over vast areas in Africa and Asia, American leaders looked to extend American influence abroad.

KEY TERMS

imperialism
nationalism
annex
banana republic

TAKING NOTES

As you read, complete the diagram below to show some of the causes that led the United States to adopt a policy of political and economic expansion overseas.

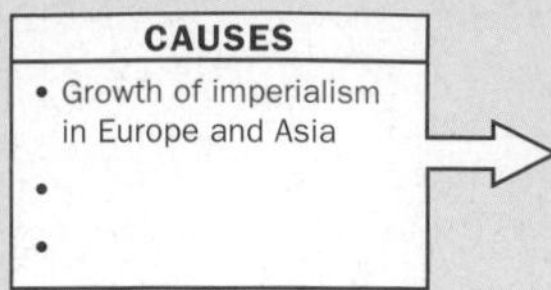

Setting the Scene

By the dawn of the twentieth century, industrialization had forever changed the national landscape and the daily lives of all Americans. The rise of cities, the beginnings of mass culture, westward expansion, and new coast-to-coast networks of travel and communications all strengthened the country's national identity. Americans wondered what these changes meant for the future of the country.

The development of the United States into an industrial powerhouse not only revolutionized the lives of all Americans, it also forced them to strengthen their ties to other nations more than ever before. Many Americans began to believe that the country had to protect its economic, political, and social interests internationally. A surge in European conquests for new lands and resources reinforced this new way of thinking about America's role in the world. Some Americans, such as Senator Henry Cabot Lodge, believed that the time was right for the United States to expand its interests abroad.

> *"Small States are of the past and have no future. The modern movement is all toward the concentration of people and territory into great nations and large dominions. The great nations are rapidly absorbing for their future expansion and their present defence all the waste places of the earth. . . . As one of the great nations of the world, the United States must not fall out of the line of march."*
>
> —Senator Henry Cabot Lodge, speech to Congress, 1895

VIEWING HISTORY This 1902 photograph shows a man in a car overlooking the Grand Canyon. **Determining Relevance** *What does this photograph suggest about the new pressures facing the United States?*

Growth of Imperialism

As the map on the previous page shows, Europe had reached new heights in its quest for territories to rule. The late 1800s marked the peak of European **imperialism,** with much of Africa and Asia under foreign domination. Under imperialism, stronger nations attempt to create

Caption Answers

Viewing History The United States, now industrialized, faces its past (the frontier) and must look to the future (a new frontier). Industrialized man appears confident about future expansion, yet somewhat nostalgic for the past.

RESOURCE DIRECTORY

Teaching Resources
Guided Reading and Review booklet, p. 70

Other Print Resources
Nystrom *Atlas of Our Country* *Later Expansion of the United States,* pp. 32–33

Technology
Section Reading Support Transparencies
Guided Reading Audiotapes (English/Spanish), Ch. 10
Student Edition on Audio CD, Ch. 10
Color Transparencies *Time Lines,* C5
Prentice Hall Presentation Pro CD-ROM, Ch. 10
Companion Web site, www.phschool.com

empires by dominating weaker nations—economically, politically, culturally, or militarily.

Why Imperialism Grew Several factors accounted for the burst of imperialistic activity in the late 1800s.

Economic factors The growth of industry in Europe created an increased need for natural resources, such as rubber and petroleum, which came from undeveloped areas of the world. Manufacturing nations also required new markets in which to sell their manufactured goods.

Nationalistic factors Competition among European nations for large empires was the result of a rise in **nationalism,** or devotion to one's nation. Nationalism usually suggests that a nation's people believe themselves, their ideals, and their goals to be superior to those of other nations. In the late 1800s, nationalist feelings grew stronger in many countries, causing several European nations to take strong actions to protect their interests. For example, when France acquired colonies in West Africa in the late 1800s, rival nations Great Britain and Germany seized lands nearby to stop French expansion.

Military factors Advances in military technology produced European armies and navies that were far superior to those in Africa and Asia. Also, Europe's growing navies required bases around the world for taking on fuel and supplies.

Humanitarian factors Humanitarian and religious goals spurred on imperialists. Colonial officials, doctors, and missionaries believed they had a duty to spread the blessings of Western civilization, including its law, medicine, and Christian religion.

Europe Leads the Way Improved transportation and communication made it easier for Great Britain, France, and Russia, all with long imperialist traditions, to extend their grip over far-flung lands. Great Britain, in particular, acquired so much new territory around the globe that people began to say "the sun never sets on the British Empire." Competition for new territory grew even more intense when Germany, unified in 1871, seized colonies in Africa and Asia.

By 1890, the United States was eager to join the competition for new territories. Supporters of expansion denied that the United States sought to **annex** foreign lands. (To annex is to join a new territory to an existing country.) Yet annexation did take place.

Expanding U.S. Interests

In his Farewell Address in 1796, President George Washington had advised Americans to "steer clear of permanent alliances" with other countries. For the next century, Americans generally followed Washington's advice. The nation's rapid economic growth along with the settlement of the West left the United States with little interest in foreign affairs.

As early as the 1820s, the Monroe Doctrine had been the main principle of foreign policy in the United States. Taking Washington's advice, under this doctrine, the United States had declared itself neutral in European wars and

Focus on WORLD EVENTS

The Sino-Japanese War After the Meiji Restoration in 1868, Japan entered a period of reform and modernization in which it grew to be an imperial power. (See the map, below left.) The Japanese began using Western military techniques, developed an advanced industrial economy, and even Westernized their political system. As Japan expanded economically, socially, and militarily, it experienced a rise in nationalism. In August 1894, conflict between China and Japan over Korea erupted into the Sino-Japanese War. Japan's more modern military easily defeated China's massive forces. As a result, China ceded Taiwan and other lands to Japan, signaling the status of Japan as a major world power.

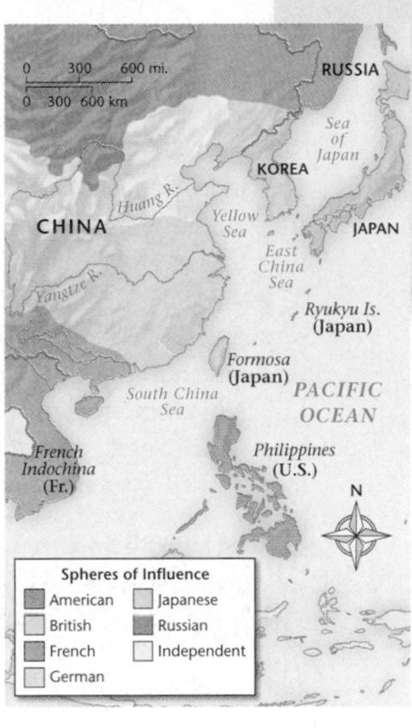

LESSON PLAN

Focus Explain that in the late 1800s, the United States needed new markets for its goods. Ask students how that need led to political entanglements abroad.

Instruct Discuss the worldwide growth of imperialism in the late 1800s. Ask students why stronger nations wanted to dominate weaker ones. What role did economics play in American expansion? Why did business leaders put so much pressure on the American government to find new markets for their goods? What other reasons were used to justify United States expansion?

Assess/Reteach What was the response of the United States government as European nations gained sovereignty over vast areas in Asia and Africa?

ACTIVITY

Connecting with Government

Have students discuss Henry Cabot Lodge's statement on the previous page. Ask them to consider the following questions: What are the "small states" of the past? Which "great nations" and "large dominions" is Lodge referring to? What does Lodge mean by "all the waste places of the earth"? Have students explain how sentiments such as these helped move the United States into the position of a world power. **(Verbal/Linguistic)**

CUSTOMIZE FOR ...

ESL

Write the words *imperialism, nationalism,* and *annex* on the chalkboard. Have volunteers define the words using a map of the world or a globe as a graphic aid.

ACTIVITY
Connecting with Culture

Discuss how nationalism affects a country's identity. Suggest that students think about how nationalism discourages friendly relations with other countries and fosters an insular feeling within a country. Encourage students to consider how cultivating a sense of superiority affects national pride. Have students identify and explain reasons for changes in political boundaries, such as those resulting from statehood and international conflicts. How do such events affect the nationalistic attitude of a country? You might challenge students to name countries that have suffered as a result of adopting a nationalist attitude. **(Verbal/Linguistic)**

BACKGROUND
Art History

Europeans who visited Japan in the 1850s and 1860s often returned with Japanese art. Wall scrolls were marked by clear, well-defined lines, a spare layout, and flat, bold colors. Impressionist painters, including Monet, Degas, and Toulouse-Lautrec, collected Japanese art and applied these techniques to their own work. An 1868 show of Japanese decorative arts made Japanese interior design popular in France.

READING CHECK

An expanded form of the Monroe Doctrine was used to justify American acquisition of territories from Mexico, the annexation of Texas and Midway, the purchase of Alaska, and highly favorable trade terms with Hawaii.

READING CHECK
What was the role of the Monroe Doctrine in shaping U.S. foreign policy?

warned other nations not to interfere in the Western Hemisphere. There were instances, however, when Americans "looked outward." Over time the Monroe Doctrine would be broadened to support American imperialism.

From the 1830s to 1850s, belief in the idea of Manifest Destiny helped the United States to justify its policies toward Mexico. The annexation of Texas and the acquisition of California and other southwestern lands were early steps toward claiming an American empire.

After the Civil War, American secretaries of state continued to apply the principles of the Monroe Doctrine. In 1866, for example, Secretary of State William H. Seward sent 50,000 troops to the Mexican border after France placed an emperor on the Mexican throne. In the face of this army, the French abandoned their colonial venture in Mexico. Then, in 1867, Seward bought Alaska from Russia. In addition to gaining more territory, Seward hoped that the presence of the United States on two sides of Canada would force the British out of that region. Most Americans ridiculed the undertaking. Seward, they said, was buying "walrus-covered icebergs" in a "barren, worthless, God-forsaken region." Seward, however, waged a successful campaign to educate the nation about Alaska's rich resources. In the end, the Senate ratified the purchase, and the United States took possession of what was then called "Seward's Folly."

Americans also showed their interest in the Pacific. In 1853, an American fleet led by Commodore Matthew C. Perry sailed into Tokyo Bay and convinced Japan to open trade relations with the United States. By the 1860s, the United States and several European countries had signed a series of treaties that allowed for expanded trade with China.

Now the U.S. government wanted control of some Pacific islands to use as refueling and repair stations for its naval vessels. To this end, Seward championed the annexation of the uninhabited Midway Islands in 1867. Eight years later the U.S. government signed a treaty with Hawaii. This agreement allowed Hawaiians to sell sugar in the United States duty-free, as long as they did not sell or lease territory to any foreign power.

COMPARING HISTORIANS' VIEWPOINTS
The Motivation Behind American Imperialism

Historians offer many different explanations for why the United States sought to expand its influence abroad.

Analyzing Viewpoints What factors do these historians describe as contributing to American expansionism?

Expansion to Solve Domestic Problems

"Spurred by a fantastic industrial revolution, which produced ever larger quantities of surplus goods, depressions, and violence, and warned by a growing radical literature that the system was not functioning properly, the United States prepared to solve its dilemmas with foreign expansion. Displaying a notable lack of absent-mindedness, Americans set out to solve their problems by creating an empire whose dynamic and characteristics marked a new departure in their history."

—*Walter LaFeber,* The New Empire: An Interpretation of American Expansion 1860–1898

Expansion to Restore a Sense of Security

"In a period of drastic social change, old maxims lost their sway over people who had good reason to take them for granted no longer; calm and thoughtful Americans, as well as frightened and anxious ones, felt compelled by events to reexamine the precepts of U.S. foreign policy. . . . Perhaps the United States could reaffirm its soundness by thrashing some country in a war or, more subtly, by demonstrating its ability to govern 'inferior' peoples in a colonial empire. Once indifferent to events outside their boundaries, Americans now searched abroad for means to internal salvation."

—*Robert L. Beisner,* From the Old Diplomacy to the New, 1865–1900

RESOURCE DIRECTORY

Other Print Resources

Historical Outline Map Book *The United States in the Caribbean, 1898–1917,* p. 58; *Central America and the Caribbean,* p. 81

Technology

Color Transparencies *Political Cartoons,* B9

RESOURCE PRO® **Visual Learning Activity** *Expansionism,* found on Resource Pro, uses a political cartoon from the British magazine *Puck* to present a critical view of United States territorial expansion.

Also of great concern to the United States were the Caribbean islands and Latin America. In 1870, President Ulysses S. Grant announced that in the future the Monroe Doctrine would protect all territories in these two regions from "transfer to a European power." Not long after, the United States was playing an active role in several diplomatic and military conflicts in Latin America.

Arguments for U.S. Expansion

By the 1890s, Americans were debating what foreign policy would best serve the United States. Some argued that the country should continue to avoid foreign entanglements. Others offered a variety of reasons for increased American involvement in international affairs.

Promoting Economic Growth A chief argument in favor of expansion was economic. By the late 1800s, the industrialists, inventors, and workers of the United States had built a powerful industrial economy. Americans alone, however, could not consume everything their nation produced. The overproduction of food and goods led to financial panics and frequent economic depressions. Protesting their plight, workers and farmers helped to convince business and political leaders that the United States must secure new markets abroad.

Many business leaders agreed that the economic problems of the nation could be solved only by expanding its markets. For this reason, they threw their support behind expansionist policies. Some American businesses already dominated international markets. Firms such as Rockefeller's Standard Oil and American Telephone and Telegraph had all become international businesses.

Other American business leaders had gone a step further and invested directly in the economies of other countries. In some cases their investments gave them political influence in those countries. In Central America, for example, an American named Minor C. Keith provided financial services to the Costa Rican government. In return, he won long-term leases for lands and railroad lines. By 1913, Keith's United Fruit Company not only exported 50 million bunches of bananas a year to the United States, it also dominated the governments and economies of Costa Rica, Guatemala, and Honduras. As a result, some people began calling the Central American nations **banana republics.**

Protecting American Security Lobbyists who favored a strong United States Navy formed a second force pushing for expansion. By the 1880s, U.S. warships left over from the Civil War were rusting and rotting. Naval officers joined with business interests to convince Congress to build modern steam-powered, steel-hulled ships to protect overseas trade.

The most influential of these officers was Captain (later Admiral) Alfred T. Mahan. In his 1890 book, *The Influence of Sea Power Upon History, 1660–1783,* Mahan argued that the nation's economic future hinged on gaining new markets abroad. In his view, the United States needed a powerful navy to protect these markets from foreign rivals.

Influenced by supporters of an expanded navy, Congress established a Naval Advisory Board in 1881. The board pushed to increase the navy's budget. Two years later, Congress authorized the building of three cruisers and two battleships, including the U.S.S. *Maine.* Finally, the Naval Act of 1890 called for the construction of more battleships, gunboats, torpedo boats, and

Value of United States Exports, 1870–1920

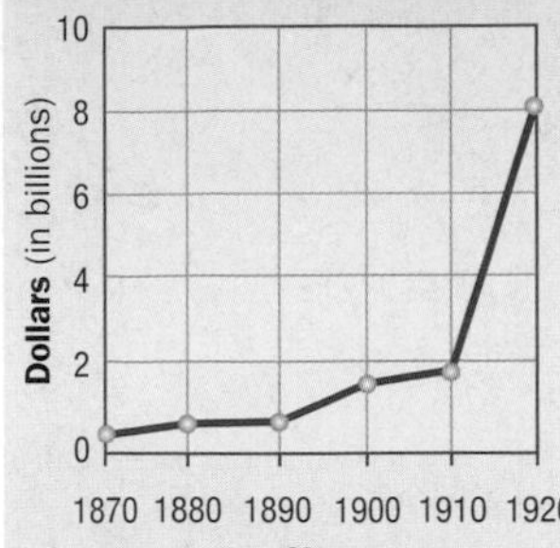

SOURCE: *Historical Statistics of the United States, Colonial Times to 1970*

INTERPRETING GRAPHS

Businesses eagerly sought new markets abroad in the late 1800s and early 1900s. **Analyzing Information** *By how much did U.S. exports increase between 1870 and 1920?*

ACTIVITY

Connecting with Economics

In the late 1800s, overproduction of goods in the United States created a need for American businesses to find foreign markets. Today the United States continues this search, just as other countries seek a place in the American market to sell their goods. To help students understand imports, exports, and the marketplace, have them list the names of the countries where their clothing and accessories were manufactured. Conduct a survey to determine which country has the largest share of the classroom market. Then ask students to discuss the dynamic relationship between U.S. international trade policies and the U.S. free enterprise system. **(Logical/Mathematical)**

BACKGROUND

Biography

John D. Rockefeller used his flair for numbers and details to build the Standard Oil Company, one of the country's earliest corporate successes. When he was just twenty years old, Rockefeller and a friend started a commodity brokerage. After the Civil War broke out, lubricating oil was needed to keep the Union trains rolling. Rockefeller perceived the need for petroleum products, and in 1863, he began a company that refined and sold oil. Prior to 1859, petroleum had not been commercially produced. During the next decade, annual production of petroleum reached nearly ten million barrels. It was used as an industrial lubricant, solvent, and fuel. Rockefeller's success resulted from his foresight, his ability to drive a hard bargain, and his efficiency. In his later years, Rockefeller devoted himself to philanthropy, providing funds to found the University of Chicago and to create several major philanthropic institutions.

TEST PREPARATION

Have students reread the section under the heading "Arguments for U.S. Expansion" on these pages and then complete the sentence below.

The main reason the U.S. practiced imperialism was—

A There was not enough room in the established U.S. territories for all the American people.

(B) The U.S. sought expanded markets for export of its manufactured goods.

C The U.S. wanted to increase its military security.

D The U.S. sought more places to dig for gold.

CAPTION ANSWERS

Interpreting Graphs By approximately 7.5 billion dollars.

cruisers. By 1900, the United States had one of the most powerful navies in the world. The expanded fleet suggested that the United States was willing and able to confront an enemy on the open sea.

Preserving American Spirit A third force for expansion consisted of people who feared that the United States was losing its vitality. Among them were Massachusetts Senator Henry Cabot Lodge, historian Frederick Jackson Turner, and a young politician from New York named Theodore Roosevelt. Worried that the closing of the frontier would sap the nation's energy, they argued that a quest for an empire might restore the country's pioneer spirit.

These and other leaders of the day drew on the doctrine of social Darwinism to justify the takeover of new territories, just as they had done earlier to defend the conquest of Native Americans. In the opinion of respected leaders such as Congregationalist minister Josiah Strong and Indiana senator Albert J. Beveridge, the civilizations produced by Anglo-Saxon and Teutonic (Germanic) peoples were superior to the societies they conquered. Social Darwinists believed that expansionism was not only this nation's destiny but also a noble pursuit, for it introduced Christianity and modern civilization to other "heathen" peoples around the world. This was an age when many intellectuals believed that certain racial and national groups were superior to others.

INTERPRETING POLITICAL CARTOONS As this 1901 political cartoon suggests, the United States relied on the principles of the Monroe Doctrine to block European involvement in Latin America. **Drawing Inferences** *What is the cartoonist suggesting about the role of the United States in world affairs?*

Americans Lean Toward Expansion Gradually public opinion warmed to the idea of expansionism. Although most Americans had accepted the conquest of Native Americans as right and inevitable, they did not see themselves as potential rulers of oppressed foreign peoples. Moreover, they did want new markets abroad and favorable trade relations. What they soon discovered was that political and military entanglements tended to follow. The United States would find itself in difficult, bloody, and painful foreign conflicts.

Section 1 Assessment

READING COMPREHENSION

1. Why did **imperialism** grow in Europe at the end of the 1800s?
2. How did the United States apply the Monroe Doctrine to its foreign policy throughout the 1800s?
3. Why did U.S. policymakers feel the need to secure new markets abroad?
4. Why did some believe that U.S. expansion was needed to preserve the "American spirit"?

CRITICAL THINKING AND WRITING

5. **Recognizing Cause and Effect** What effect did the growth of European imperialism have on United States attitudes toward foreign policy and expansion?
6. **Writing a List** Beginning with the Louisiana Purchase, write a chronological list tracing specific examples of American expansionism before 1880.

Take It to the NET

Activity: Writing a Letter If you were alive in 1867, would you have supported or opposed Seward's purchase of Alaska? Write a letter to the editor explaining your position. Use the links provided in the *America: Pathways to the Present* area of the following Web site for help in completing this activity.
www.phschool.com

Section 1 Assessment

Reading Comprehension

1. Industrial growth; nationalism; advances in military technology; humanitarian and religious goals.
2. To keep the Western Hemisphere free from intervention by European powers; to justify Manifest Destiny as well as the acquisition of overseas territories, such as Midway.
3. Foreign markets were seen as necessary to sell the nation's surplus products. American industrial and agricultural goods could not be consumed fast enough domestically to prevent recurring cycles of panic and depression.
4. They worried that the closing of the frontier would deplete the nation's energy; a quest for an empire might restore America's pioneer spirit. There was a belief that Americans could civilize and Christianize other peoples.

Critical Thinking and Writing

5. It created a sense of urgency for Americans. Many believed that the United States would need to acquire overseas territories in order to continue on the path toward becoming a great nation.
6. Answers should include territory acquired during westward expansion, as well as Alaska and Midway.

Take It to the NET

Answers will vary. For: the need for more land and new trading markets, Alaska's natural resources, and the potential to force the British out of Canada. Against: the cost involved, and the isolationist views of many Americans who did not want to be involved in European affairs.

Caption Answers

Interpreting Political Cartoons The United States is represented by the largest rooster and is in charge of the chicken coop (the Western Hemisphere). The U.S. protects its own interests and weaker nations by blocking strong European powers.

RESOURCE DIRECTORY

Teaching Resources
Units 3/4 booklet
- Section 1 Quiz, p. 4

Guide to the Essentials
- Section 1 Summary, p. 48

Technology
Color Transparencies *American Diversity,* G11

Section 2 The Spanish-American War

READING FOCUS

- How did the activities of the United States in Latin America set the stage for war with Spain?
- What were the events leading up to and following the Spanish-American War?
- What challenges did the United States face after the war?
- Why did the United States seek to gain influence in the Pacific?

MAIN IDEA

A swift victory in the Spanish-American War confirmed the status of the United States as a world power, but it left some people arguing over how to govern newly acquired territories.

KEY TERMS

arbitration
jingoism
Platt Amendment
sphere of influence
Open Door Policy

TAKING NOTES

As you read, complete this chart listing the effects of United States foreign policies on other nations after the Spanish-American War.

Effects of United States Foreign Policy	
Nation	**Policy and Effects**
Philippines	Annexed by U.S. after Spanish-American War. U.S. soldiers remain there. Fighting between U.S. and Philippines occurs. U.S. occupation continues until 1946.
Cuba	
Puerto Rico	
Hawaii	
China	

Setting the Scene The United States was poised on the edge of becoming a world power. All that was needed was something to push the country in that direction. The cautious McKinley administration resisted the growing demands of those in Congress and throughout the country who hungered for expansion. The time was not yet right. As they waited for action, Americans woke up to this newspaper headline in October 1897:

> "*EVANGELINA CISNEROS RESCUED BY THE JOURNAL: AN AMERICAN NEWSPAPER ACCOMPLISHES AT A SINGLE STROKE WHAT THE RED TAPE OF DIPLOMACY FAILED UTTERLY TO BRING ABOUT IN MANY MONTHS.*"
>
> —Headline in the *New York Journal,* October 10, 1897

Many would have been shocked to read in big, bold letters that a newspaper had acted outside the law to protect liberty and justice abroad. In this instance, the *Journal* staged the rescue of someone they described as a beautiful, young Cuban girl being held prisoner by the Spanish. Vivid headlines such as this attracted readers craving controversy and excitement. The sensational stories that followed increased newspaper circulations and resulted in huge profits for newspaper publishers.

Another year would pass before the United States fought a war that would forever change its role in world affairs. The newspapers did not cause the war, but they did help to reinforce and magnify a new set of assumptions among the American people regarding their place in the world. Americans began to feel that their nation was growing bigger and stronger. They were ready and willing to take action outside U.S. borders. In the process of expanding and becoming a world power, however, the United States increasingly found itself in conflict with other nations.

VIEWING HISTORY This illustration by Thure de Thulstrup depicts Cuban rebels charging into battle with the Spanish. **Analyzing Visual Information** *What do the details in the illustration tell you about the artist's view of the Cuban rebellion?*

Section 2 The Spanish-American War

Section Objectives

1. Read about United States activities in Latin America that set the stage for war with Spain.
2. Find out about events leading up to and following the Spanish-American War.
3. Discover challenges faced by the United States after the war.
4. Learn why the United States sought to gain influence in the Pacific.

Bellringer

Warm-Up Activity Write the word *sensationalism* on the chalkboard and ask students to define it and explain how it can trigger public reactions. Discuss news that might be called sensational.

Activating Prior Knowledge Can students name the country that had sovereignty over Cuba in the nineteenth century? *(Spain)*

Reading Strategy

As students read, have them jot down the key events that led to the Spanish-American War in 1898. Then have them review their list to make sure it is in chronological order. Ask students to briefly summarize the economic effects of the Spanish-American War on the United States. Have them state the importance of the year 1898 in American history.

Caption Answers

Viewing History The viewer is riding with the Cuban rebels and feels a sense of purpose and triumph. The machetes held high indicate charging forward and success. The artist most likely supports the rebellion.

RESOURCE DIRECTORY

Teaching Resources
Learning Styles Lesson Plans booklet, p. 36
Guided Reading and Review booklet, p. 71

Technology
Section Reading Support Transparencies
Guided Reading Audiotapes (English/Spanish), Ch. 10
Student Edition on Audio CD, Ch. 10
Color Transparencies *Historical Maps,* A27
Prentice Hall Presentation Pro CD-ROM, Ch. 10
Companion Web site, www.phschool.com

Lesson Plan

Focus An aggressive foreign policy brought the United States into conflict with other nations.

Ask what problems the United States faced as a new world power.

Instruct Discuss how United States intervention in Latin America and the Pacific resulted in conflict. Ask how conflict in the Caribbean developed into war with Spain. What were the major causes of the Spanish-American War? What lands did the United States gain?

Discuss how national pride and an aggressive foreign policy could be seen at work in events in Chile, Cuba, the Philippines, and Hawaii in the late 1800s. In what areas in the Pacific did the United States pursue an expansionist policy?

Assess/Reteach Ask students how the United States' position among nations changed as a result of the Spanish-American War.

READING CHECK

The United States forced Great Britain to accept the Cleveland administration's plan for resolving a dispute over South American territory. Thus, the United States proved itself to be the dominant power in the Western Hemisphere.

Setting the Stage for War

American expansionists paid close attention to the political and economic actions of countries in the Western Hemisphere. In the 1890s, several incidents took place that allowed the United States to strengthen its role in Latin American affairs.

Displays of United States Power In 1891, an angry Chilean mob attacked a group of American sailors on shore leave in Valparaíso. They killed two Americans and injured seventeen others. The U.S. government reacted strongly, forcing Chile to pay $75,000 to the families of the sailors who were killed or injured. Two years later, when a rebellion threatened the friendly republican government of Brazil, President Cleveland ordered naval units to Rio de Janeiro to protect United States shipping interests. This show of force broke the back of the rebellion.

READING CHECK How did the 1895 dispute between the United States and Great Britain reaffirm the validity of the Monroe Doctrine?

In the third and most important incident of the era, the United States confronted the nation then considered the most powerful in the world, Great Britain. Since the 1840s, Britain and Venezuela had disputed ownership of a piece of territory located at the border between Venezuela and British Guiana. In the 1880s, the dispute intensified when rumors surfaced of mineral wealth in this border area. President Cleveland's Secretary of State, Richard Olney, demanded in July 1895 that Britain acknowledge the Monroe Doctrine and submit the boundary dispute to **arbitration.** (Arbitration is the settlement of a dispute by a person or panel chosen to listen to both sides and come to a decision.) The British government replied that the doctrine had no standing in international law.

Eventually Britain backed down and agreed to arbitration. Concerned about the rising power of Germany in Africa, the British government realized that it needed to stay on friendly terms with the increasingly powerful United States.

Focus on WORLD EVENTS

José Martí Fights for Cuban Independence José Martí (1853–1895) dedicated his life to achieving Cuban independence. A patriot and a revolutionary, Martí had dreamed of *Cuba Libre* (a free Cuba) since the age of 15. A gifted writer, he wrote poems as a teenager and soon founded his own newspaper, *La patria libre (The Free Fatherland).*

Because of his revolutionary activity, Martí was forced to leave Cuba in 1871. He was deported to Spain, where he received a master's degree and a law degree. Martí finally settled in New York City in 1881, where he led the Cuban Revolutionary Party. In 1895, Martí left New York to stage attacks in Cuba with other revolutionaries. Later that year, he was killed in battle, just a few years before *Cuba Libre* became a reality.

The Cuban Rebellion By the mid-1890s, the United States had not only reaffirmed the Monroe Doctrine, it had also forced the world's most powerful nation to bow to its will. Events in Cuba soon paved the way for a far more spectacular display of American power.

An island nation off the coast of Florida, Cuba first rebelled against Spain in 1868. After ten years of fighting the rebels, Spain finally put in place a few meager reforms to appease the Cuban people. In 1895, after the island's economy had collapsed, Cubans rebelled again. This time Spain sent 150,000 troops and its best general, Valeriano Weyler, to put down the rebellion. In a desperate attempt to prevent civilians from aiding the rebels, Weyler instituted a policy of "reconcentration." He forced hundreds of thousands of Cubans into guarded camps. The prisoners, including women, children, and the elderly, lived in miserable conditions with little food or sanitation. Over two years, disease and starvation killed an estimated 200,000 Cubans.

Cuban exiles living in the United States, led by the journalist José Martí, urged the United States to intervene. Both Presidents Cleveland and McKinley refused. They were unwilling to spend the money that intervention would require and feared the United States would be saddled with colonial responsibilities it could not handle. Frustrated, Cuban guerrillas turned to the one tactic they knew would attract the U.S. government's attention: the destruction of American sugar plantations and mills in Cuba. As a result, business owners increased their pressure on the government to act.

RESOURCE DIRECTORY

Other Print Resources

American History Block Scheduling Support *The Spanish-American War: Door to Imperialism,* found in the Prosperity, Depression, and War folder, includes interdisciplinary lesson suggestions and activities for Geography and History, Primary Sources, Biography, and Literature.

Historical Outline Map Book *The Spanish-American War,* p. 57

Technology

Color Transparencies *Historical Maps,* A30

RESOURCE PRO® **Literature Activity** *The Open Boat,* found on Resource Pro, describes the harrowing experience of Stephen Crane, who survived the sinking of a munitions supply steamer returning from Cuba in 1897.

RESOURCE PRO® **Critical Thinking Activity** *Drawing Conclusions: The Explosion of the Maine,* found on Resource Pro, presents contemporary reports about the mysterious explosion of the *Maine* to help students apply this skill.

Yellow Journalism Demands for United States intervention in Cuba also came in large part from American newspapers. In the 1890s, a fierce competition for readers broke out between two New York City newspapers, the *New York World* and the *New York Morning Journal.* Both newspapers reported exaggerated and sometimes false stories about the events in Cuba in order to increase circulation. The battle pitted the *World's* established publisher, Joseph Pulitzer, against a newcomer to the city, the *Journal's* William Randolph Hearst.

Hearst bought the *Journal* when it was struggling in 1895. By luring experienced journalists from other papers, including the *World,* he managed to turn it into a success. Hearst used a variety of other techniques to increase the *Journal's* circulation, including printing sensational crime stories, using illustrations and vivid headlines to draw in the reader, and lowering the price to one penny.

Both Hearst and Pulitzer took advantage of the horrifying stories coming from Cuba about the "Butcher" Weyler and his barbed-wire concentration camps. Their sensational headlines and stories, known as yellow journalism, whipped up American public opinion in favor of the rebels. The intense burst of national pride and the desire for an aggressive foreign policy that followed came to be known as **jingoism.** The name came from a line in a British song of the 1870s: "We don't want to fight, yet by Jingo! if we do, We've got the ships, we've got the men, and got the money too."

The Spanish-American War

The stories printed in newspapers such as the *Journal* strengthened American sympathy for the Cuban rebels. Slowly the demand for U.S. intervention began to build.

Steps to War Early in 1898, riots erupted in Havana, the capital of Cuba. In response, President McKinley moved the battleship U.S.S. *Maine* into the city's harbor to protect American citizens and property. Several events followed that pushed the United States to war.

The de Lôme letter A few weeks later, in early February 1898, United States newspapers published a letter stolen from the Spanish ambassador to Washington, Dupuy de Lôme. The de Lôme letter, which described McKinley as "weak and a bidder for the admiration of the crowd," caused an outcry in the United States. The letter raised a commotion not just because it ridiculed McKinley, but mostly because of the sensationalism surrounding it. Because de Lôme was a Spaniard, the press now had a golden opportunity to intensify anti-Spanish sentiments.

The explosion of the U.S.S. Maine Then, on February 15, an explosion sank the *Maine,* killing more than 250 American sailors. The blast probably had been caused by a fire that set off ammunition, but the American public put the blame on Spain. (The exact cause of the explosion has never been determined.) The papers jumped on the chance to arouse more bitter feelings toward Spain. The *New York Morning Journal* asked, "How long shall the United States sit idle and indifferent within sound and hearing of rapine and murder? How long?" The Spanish were willing to enter into arbitration talks to determine more decisively if they were responsible, but that did not matter. An enraged American public called for war. Still, McKinley hesitated.

American BIOGRAPHY

William Randolph Hearst
1863–1951

William Randolph Hearst's first venture into newspaper publishing came in 1887, when he took control of the *San Francisco Examiner,* a faltering paper owned by his father. Hearst used a combination of investigative reporting and sensationalistic stories to increase circulation.

After achieving success with the *New York Morning Journal* several years later, Hearst went on to serve briefly in the United States House of Representatives. He continued to expand his publishing empire, acquiring newspapers in cities throughout the country. By 1935, he owned 28 major newspapers, 18 magazines, and several radio stations and news services. Although the era of rabid yellow journalism declined following the turn of the century, the innovations of Hearst and his competitors continue to influence journalism today.

INTERPRETING TABLES

Sales of Hearst's *New York Morning Journal* soared in 1898. **Synthesizing Information** *What factors led to the increased demand for papers such as the* Journal?

Morning Journal Sales

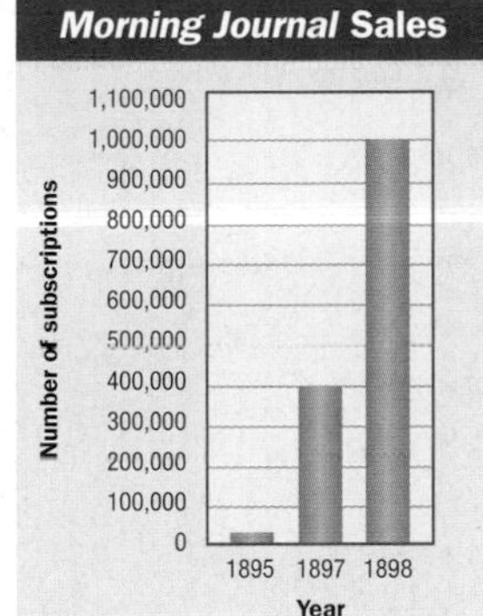

ACTIVITY
Connecting with Science and Technology

Tell students that developments in printing technology during the 1890s brought about intense competition among newspapers in major cities. As newspapers vied for increased readership, they took journalistic liberties in reporting the news. Have students discuss why they think publishers felt it was acceptable to embellish the truth in order to gain readers. Tell students to think about how journalistic ethics have changed over time, and why. **(Verbal/Linguistic)**

From the Archives of
AmericanHeritage®

Sousa's Greatest

On May 14, 1897, John Philip Sousa premiered his most inspired and glorious march, "The Stars and Stripes Forever." The march, which he had composed in his head as he strolled the deck of the steamship *Teutonic* while crossing from Liverpool to New York the previous November, brought down the house. A joyous audience made the Sousa Band repeat it twice more. Critics in the next day's papers were just as ecstatic. One called the piece "stirring enough to rouse the American eagle from his crag and set him to shriek exultantly while he hurls his arrows at the aurora borealis." The march's "jingoistic" character, as many critics called it, reflected the times—war with Spain was brewing. Although Sousa was already known as the March King, it took "The Stars and Stripes Forever" to make him immortal. Until his death in 1932, no audience would let him leave the podium without conducting it at least once. Source: Frederic D. Schwarz, "The Time Machine," *American Heritage®* magazine, May 1997.

CUSTOMIZE FOR ...
Less Proficient Readers

Have students write at least one cause for each of these effects: the Cuban rebellion, the sinking of the U.S.S. *Maine,* and greater circulation of the *New York World* newspaper.

CAPTION ANSWERS

Interpreting Tables Americans hungry for intervention/imperialism; the Spanish-American War; competition between papers led to lower prices and more sensational stories.

ACTIVITY
Connecting with Government

Encourage students to discuss Theodore Roosevelt's decision to cable naval commanders to prepare for military action against Spain. Was his action an example of extreme courage or cowardice? Remind students that Roosevelt took action when his boss was out of the office. Tell students to consider the ramifications of Roosevelt's action as they discuss whether they think it was right or wrong. **(Verbal/Linguistic)**

BACKGROUND
Biography

Puerto Rican nationalist Luis Muñoz Rivera (1859–1916) was elected head of a new liberal government in Puerto Rico only months before the United States invasion. In 1910, after sadly accepting the continuing U.S. presence, which he called "unworthy of the United States . . . and of the Puerto Ricans who have to endure it," Muñoz moved to Washington, D.C., as the island's representative in Congress. He died before the passage of the Jones Act of 1917, which granted United States citizenship to all Puerto Ricans.

BACKGROUND
Geography in History

In the era of coal-powered steamships, small Pacific islands acquired a strategic value far out of proportion to their size. Unlike wind-powered clipper ships, steamships needed to refuel often. Coal was bulky, and a ship could not carry enough to cross the Pacific. The U.S. and European navies acquired a series of harbors called "coaling stations" where a friendly government could assure a reliable supply of coal. The U.S. occupied Samoa's Pago Pago Harbor in 1878 and Hawaii's Pearl Harbor in 1887, many years before either nation was annexed.

CAPTION ANSWERS

Map Skills San Juan Hill; Santiago Harbor; Manila Bay.

Preparing in the Philippines On the other side of the world, the people of another of Spain's last remaining possessions, the Philippine Islands, also were rebelling. In the view of Theodore Roosevelt, then Assistant Secretary of the Navy, the Philippines could become a key base from which the United States might protect its Asian trade. On February 25, while his boss, the Secretary of the Navy, was out of the office, Roosevelt cabled naval commanders in the Pacific to prepare for military action against Spain. When President McKinley discovered what Roosevelt had done, he ordered most of the cables withdrawn, but he made an exception in the case of the cable directed to Admiral George Dewey. Dewey was told to attack the Spanish fleet in the Philippines if war broke out with Spain.

McKinley's war message Late in March, in a final attempt at a peaceful solution, McKinley sent a list of demands to Spain. These included compensation for the *Maine,* an end to the reconcentration camps, a truce in Cuba, and Cuban independence. Eager to find a peaceful settlement to the crisis, Spain accepted all but the last. McKinley decided he could not resist the growing cries for war. On April 11, he sent a war message to Congress. A few days later, rallying to the cry of "Remember the *Maine*!" Congress recognized Cuban independence and authorized force against Spain.

"A Splendid Little War" The war's first action took place not in Cuba but in the Philippines, as shown on the map on this page. On May 1, 1898, Admiral Dewey launched a surprise attack on Spanish ships anchored in Manila Bay, destroying Spain's entire Pacific fleet in just seven hours. In Cuba, meanwhile, United States warships quickly bottled up Spain's Atlantic fleet in the harbor at Santiago.

American army troops gathered in Tampa, Florida, to prepare for an invasion of Cuba. The group that received the most publicity was the First Volunteer Cavalry, known as the Rough Riders. Its leader, Theodore Roosevelt, had resigned his position as Assistant Secretary of the Navy and recruited a diverse group of volunteers that included cowboys, miners, policemen, and college athletes. On July 1, 1898, Roosevelt led the Rough Riders in a charge up San Juan Hill. This charge became the most famous incident of the war.

The Spanish fleet made a desperate attempt to escape Santiago harbor on July 3. In the ensuing battle, the United States Navy sank every Spanish ship,

MAP SKILLS Although the Spanish-American War was fought in two locations on opposite sides of the world, the United States defeated Spain in just nine weeks. **Location** *At what specific sites were the major battles of the war fought?*

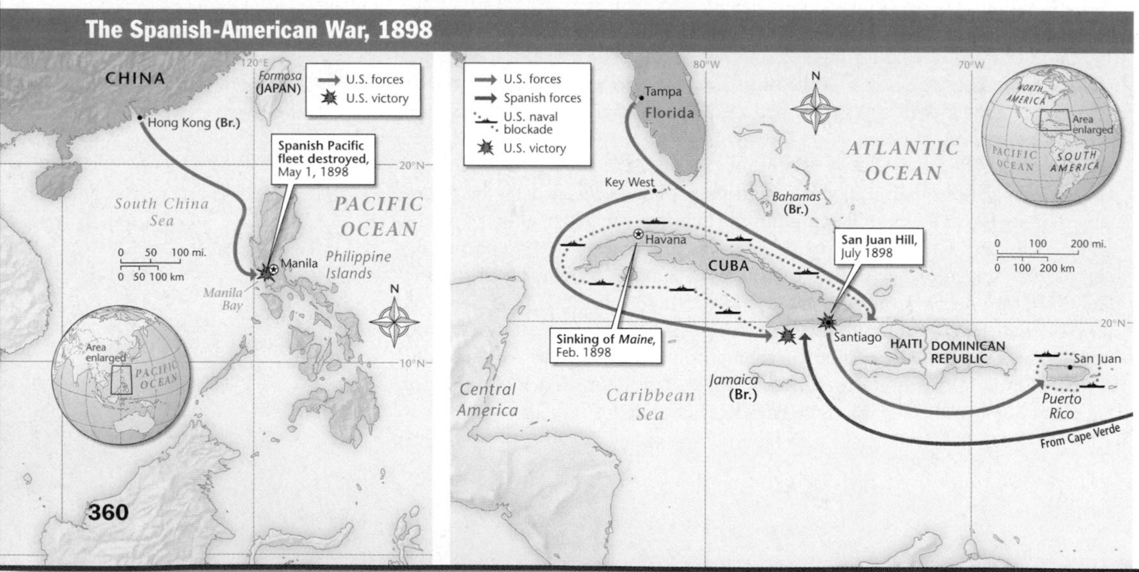

RESOURCE DIRECTORY

Teaching Resources
Learning with Documents booklet (Visual Learning Activity) *Wartime Propaganda,* p. 56

Technology
Color Transparencies *Fine Art,* E16
Sounds of an Era Audio CD *"Roosevelt's Charge"* and *"Teddy Roosevelt's Bugler"* (time: one minute, 30 seconds)
RESOURCE PRO® **Primary Source Activity** *Teddy Roosevelt: Letters Home,* found on Resource Pro, describes in detail the hardships and harsh conditions facing the Rough Riders.

setting off wild Independence Day celebrations back in the United States.

It had all seemed quite simple. Although 2,500 Americans had died in the short war, fewer than 400 died in battle. The remainder died from food poisoning, yellow fever, malaria, and inadequate medical care. Future Secretary of State John Hay captured the public mood when he wrote his friend Teddy Roosevelt that it had been "a splendid little war."

INTERPRETING POLITICAL CARTOONS European powers and Uncle Sam look on as the United States Navy defeats the Spanish. **Drawing Inferences** *Why do you think most of the European powers look upset by this turn of events?*

The Treaty of Paris The United States signed the Treaty of Paris with Spain in December 1898. In the treaty, the Spanish government recognized Cuba's independence. In return for a payment of $20 million, Spain also gave up the Philippines, Puerto Rico, and the Pacific island of Guam to the United States. These became "unincorporated" territories of the United States, which meant that these lands were not intended for eventual statehood.

The Senate ratified the treaty in February 1899, but not without great debate. A majority of senators supported the annexation of these territories, but many senators still remained passionately against such policies. Although the outnumbered anti-imperialists held their ground, the treaty narrowly passed by only one vote more than the two-thirds majority needed.

New Challenges After the War

With many in the United States divided over the issue of imperialism, developing a policy for dealing with the new territories proved to be difficult. How could the United States become a colonial power without violating the nation's most basic principle—that all people have the right to liberty?

Dilemma in the Philippines President McKinley was forced to justify this seeming departure from American ideals with his policy toward the Philippines.

> "*We could not leave them to themselves—they were unfit for self-government, and they would soon have anarchy and misrule worse than Spain's was. . . . There was nothing left for us to do but to take them all, and to educate the Filipinos, and uplift and civilize and Christianize them. . . .*"
>
> —President McKinley

Despite the fact that most Filipinos were already Christian, McKinley pressed on with his arguments for annexation. He made what was perhaps a more convincing argument when he warned that if the United States did not act first, European powers might try to seize the islands and new conflicts could result.

READING CHECK
Why did President McKinley want to annex the Philippines?

Filipino rebels had fought alongside American troops in the war against Spain with the expectation that victory would bring independence. But when rebel leader Emilio Aguinaldo issued a proclamation in January 1899 declaring the Philippines a republic, the United States ignored him. Mounting tensions between the rebel forces and American soldiers finally erupted into war in February. In the bitter three-year war that followed, more than 4,000 Americans were killed and nearly 3,000 more wounded. Fighting without restraint—and sometimes with great brutality—American forces killed some 16,000 Filipino

ACTIVITY
Connecting with History and Conflict

Have students stage a mock debate between 1900 campaign candidates William McKinley and William Jennings Bryan. Ask students to reflect on the importance of each figure and to consider how Bryan might have attacked McKinley's policies and how McKinley might have responded. **(Verbal/ Linguistic)**

BACKGROUND
A Diverse Nation

Despite the mounting tensions between blacks and whites in 1898, they fought side by side in the Spanish-American War. President McKinley appointed 100 black army officers to lead black troops. Four regiments of black buffalo soldiers headed for Cuba on the same ships as white troops, but the black soldiers were segregated and forced to remain below decks. African Americans were acutely aware of the irony that they were fighting against black Cubans for a country in which Jim Crow laws and policies forced southern blacks to take a back seat to whites.

READING CHECK
McKinley feared that a European power would seize the Philippines if the United States did not. McKinley also wanted the Philippines as a naval base for the protection of American shipping in Asian waters.

TEST PREPARATION

Have students read the passages on the previous page under the subheading "A Splendid Little War" and then answer the question below.

Based on facts from the text, why did John Hay describe the Spanish-American War as "a splendid little war"?

A He found the action stimulating.
B He thought the war was confined to a small geographic area.
(C) The war was relatively short, with few Americans dying in battle.
D He liked the way the battle coincided with Independence Day.

CAPTION ANSWERS

Interpreting Political Cartoons
Possibly because there is now another power in their presence, meaning more imperialist competition. They might also see growing U.S. power as a threat to European security.

rebels and as many as 200,000 Filipino civilians. Occasional fighting continued for years. The Philippines did not gain complete independence until 1946.

READING CHECK What was the purpose of the Teller Amendment?

The Fate of Cuba Supporters of Cuban independence had attached an amendment, called the Teller Amendment, to Congress's 1898 war resolution against Spain. The document promised that the United States would not annex Cuba. Yet American involvement in Cuba did not end with the victory over Spain in 1898. In order to protect American business interests in the chaotic environment that followed the war, President McKinley installed a military government in Cuba led by General Leonard Wood. The military government would remain in place for three years. This government organized a school system and restored economic stability. It also established a commission led by Major Walter Reed of the Army Medical Corps that discovered a cure for the deadly disease yellow fever.

Many Cubans felt that the United States had betrayed its goal of securing independence for Cuba. To some, it seemed that the United States had simply replaced Spain as Cuba's sovereign nation. In 1900, the U.S. military government authorized the Cubans to begin to draft a constitution. The new constitution was modeled on the United States Constitution and did not allow for continued American involvement in Cuba. The U.S. government, however, only agreed to remove its troops if the Cubans included provisions outlined in a document called the **Platt Amendment.** The Platt Amendment stipulated that the Cuban government could not enter any foreign agreements, must allow the United States to establish naval bases as needed on the island, and must give the United States the right to intervene whenever necessary. Cuba, which wanted an end to U.S. occupation, reluctantly agreed to the amendment. The

U.S. Foreign Intervention

Victory in the Spanish-American War touched off a new era in the United States. Its role in world affairs forever changed, the United States became involved in many foreign conflicts over the next century.

1898 The United States enters the Spanish-American War.

1917 After a time of neutrality, the United States enters World War I on the side of the Allies.

1941 After Japan bombs Pearl Harbor, the United States enters World War II.

1950 Following North Korea's invasion of South Korea, President Truman calls on American troops to defend South Korea.

1964 Congress passes the Gulf of Tonkin Resolution, authorizing the use of American military force in the war in Vietnam.

1991 The United States and its allies free Kuwait from Iraqi occupation in the Gulf War.

1999 After NATO launches airstrikes against Serbia, the United States commits troops to a NATO peacekeeping force in Kosovo.

? Since the Spanish-American War, the United States has become involved in many foreign conflicts. What foreign conflicts does the United States play a part in today? What is its role in these conflicts?

ACTIVITY
Connecting with History and Conflict

Have students write a short essay on U.S. intervention in foreign affairs. Suggest that students reflect on events at the end of the nineteenth century as they formulate their opinions on U.S. foreign intervention. Have students consider some of the following questions as they prepare their essay: Why and when should our government become involved in the affairs of another country? What specific situations warrant U.S. intervention? When should the U.S. stay out of another country's affairs? **(Verbal/Linguistic)**

BACKGROUND
Biography

Walter Reed (1851–1902) was a U.S. Army doctor who proved that yellow fever was transmitted by mosquitoes. Yellow fever is an infectious tropical and subtropical disease that affects humans, monkeys, and some other small mammals. Yellow fever was first recorded in the sixteenth century in South America. For the next 300 years, it was one of the greatest plagues in history. During the nineteenth century, many people believed that yellow fever was spread by *fomites*—bedding and clothing that had been used by a yellow-fever victim. Reed went to Cuba in 1899 after an outbreak of yellow fever in the U.S. garrison in Havana. After Reed's discovery, yellow fever was practically eliminated from Havana. The last outbreak of yellow fever in the U.S. took place in 1905 in New Orleans and other southern ports.

READING CHECK

Anti-imperialists in Congress had formulated the Teller Amendment to ensure that Cuba became independent after the war. The Teller Amendment forbade the United States from annexing Cuba.

CAPTION ANSWERS

Fast Forward to Today Balkans as peacekeeper; South Korea as peacekeeper; Iraq—enforcing the no-fly zones.

RESOURCE DIRECTORY

Teaching Resources

Biography, Literature, and Comparing Primary Sources booklet (Biography) *Walter Reed,* p. 22

Great Debates booklet (Great Debates) *Should the United States Have Colonies?* p. 14

Technology

Color Transparencies *Historical Maps,* A28; *Cause-and-Effect Charts,* D7

United States intervened militarily in Cuban affairs only twice while the Platt Amendment remained in force until 1934.

The United States and Puerto Rico Unlike Cuba, Puerto Rico did not become independent. The United States maintained a military government in the territory until 1900. The military aided in the development of infrastructure and education, and also acted as a police force. With the passage of the Foraker Act in 1900, the United States removed its military control and established a civil government, still under U.S. control. Gradually, the United States ceded more freedom and control to the Puerto Rican people.

In an attempt to stem a growing independence movement, the United States government granted Puerto Ricans American citizenship with the passage of the Jones Act in 1917. However, because the Constitution did not apply to United States territories, this citizenship was based only on the act of Congress. In addition, although Puerto Ricans could now elect their local legislatures, the United States retained the power to appoint key officials, such as the governor.

United States Acquisitions and Annexations, 1857–1904

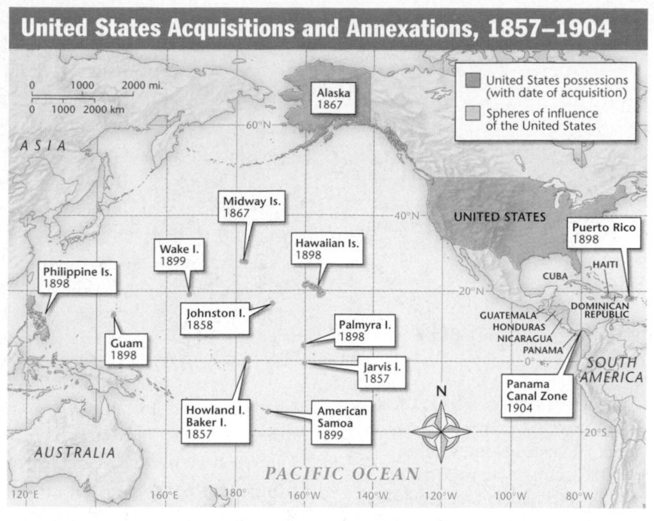

MAP SKILLS Between 1857 and 1904, the United States acquired many new territorial possessions around the globe. **Regions** *Why were so many of these new possessions located in the Pacific Ocean?*

Other Gains in the Pacific

The United States government intervened in other parts of the Pacific at the same time that events played out in the Spanish-American War. This intervention eventually brought about changes in the relationships of the United States with Hawaii, Samoa, and China.

Annexation of Hawaii Hawaii had become increasingly important to U.S. business interests in the late 1800s. In 1887, Hawaii and the United States renewed a trade treaty that allowed Hawaiian sugar to be sold duty-free in the United States. Hawaii also leased Pearl Harbor to the United States as a fueling and repair station for naval vessels. That same year, white Hawaiian-born planters forced the Hawaiian king, Kalakaua, to accept a new constitution that, in effect, gave them control of the government.

When the king died in 1891, his sister Liliuokalani came to the throne. A strong nationalist, Queen Liliuokalani opposed U.S. control of the islands and sought to reduce the power of foreign merchants. In 1893, with the help of the United States Marines, pineapple planter Sanford B. Dole removed Queen Liliuokalani from power. He proclaimed Hawaii a republic and requested that it be annexed by the United States.

When William McKinley was elected President, he supported the annexation. "We need Hawaii just as much and a good deal more than we did California. It is Manifest Destiny," McKinley said in early 1898. After briefly considering whether the Hawaiian people wished to be annexed, Congress was swayed by arguments that the United States needed naval stations in Hawaii in order to protect its world trade. In 1898, Congress approved the annexation of Hawaii.

ACTIVITY
Student Portfolio

You may wish to have students add the following to their portfolios: Explain that the United States government has considered petitions to repay Hawaiians for the seizure of their islands. Ask students to further research and report, either in writing or orally, on the history of Hawaii before and after its annexation. Encourage them to include ethnic composition, type of government, and lasting impact of United States plantations on the islands. Have them reflect on the effects of population growth and distribution that resulted from the annexation of Hawaii. **(Verbal/Linguistic)**

BACKGROUND
Connections to Today

Native Hawaiians waited 100 years for the United States government to acknowledge its part in the overthrow of the Hawaiian monarchy in 1893. On November 16, 1993, Congress admitted United States complicity in the 1893 overthrow of the Hawaiian monarchy and called for "reconciliation between the United States and the native Hawaiian people." Three weeks earlier, by a vote of 65 to 34, the Senate had backed the resolution that offered a formal apology to native Hawaiians.

CAPTION ANSWERS

Map Skills They provided stepping stones to Asian markets and stations for repairing and refueling vessels.

INTERPRETING POLITICAL CARTOONS Competition for trade in China led to Secretary Hay's Open Door Policy. This cartoon depicts Uncle Sam as holding the "key" to China's "open door." **Drawing Inferences** *Is the cartoonist being sympathetic toward, or critical of, Hay's Open Door Policy?*

Samoa The Polynesian islands of Samoa represented another possible stepping stone to the growing trade with Asia. Back in 1878, the United States had negotiated a treaty with Samoa offering protection in return for a lease on Samoa's fine harbor at Pago Pago. When Britain and Germany began competing for control of these islands in the 1880s, tension between these European powers and the United States almost led to war. Eventually the three nations arranged a three-way protectorate of Samoa in 1889. The withdrawal of Great Britain from Samoa in 1899 left Germany and the United States to divide up the islands. A year after the annexation of Hawaii, the United States had acquired the harbor at Pago Pago as well.

An Open Door to China China's huge population and its vast markets became increasingly important to American trade by the late 1800s. But the United States was not the only nation interested in China. Countries such as Russia, Germany, Britain, France, and Japan were seeking **spheres of influence,** or areas of economic and political control, in China. In 1899, John Hay, President McKinley's Secretary of State, wrote notes to the major European powers trying to persuade them to keep an "open door" to China. He wanted to ensure through his **Open Door Policy** that the United States would have equal access to China's millions of consumers. Hay's suggestions met with a cool response from the other countries.

Meanwhile, many Chinese resented foreign influence of any kind. A secret society called the Righteous and Harmonious Fists (the Western press called them "Boxers") started a rebellion in the spring of 1900 that led to the massacre of 300 foreigners and Christian Chinese. Although the European powers eventually defeated the Boxers, Secretary Hay feared that these imperialist nations would use the rebellion as an excuse to seize more Chinese territory. Thus, he issued a second series of Open Door notes. These notes reaffirmed the principle of open trade in China and made an even stronger statement about the intention of the United States to preserve it.

Section 2 Assessment

READING COMPREHENSION

1. How did yellow journalism and **jingoism** influence Americans' views of the Cuban rebellion?
2. What did John Hay mean when he called America's war with Spain a "splendid little war"?
3. How did U.S. policies, such as the **Platt Amendment,** secure control over its newly acquired territories?
4. What methods did the United States use to gain land and influence in the Pacific region?

CRITICAL THINKING AND WRITING

5. **Making Comparisons** In what ways was the Spanish-American War similar to the war between the United States and Mexico in 1846?
6. **Writing a News Story** Using information from this section, write a brief newspaper story with a sensational headline in the same style that was used in William Randolph Hearst's newspapers around the turn of the century.

Take It to the NET

Activity: Writing a Letter
Research the history of the American annexation of Hawaii in 1898 and the apology offered by our government in 1993. Consider whether you think the apology was sufficient. Write a letter to your representative in Congress expressing your views on the subject. Use the links provided in the *America: Pathways to the Present* area of the following Web site for help in completing this activity.
www.phschool.com

Section 2 Assessment

Reading Comprehension

1. Strengthened American sympathy for the Cuban rebels; nationalism and a demand for U.S. intervention began to build.
2. The war was short and victorious. American deaths in battle were relatively few.
3. The Platt Amendment made Cuba into an American satellite. The Treaty of Paris made the Philippines, Guam, and Puerto Rico American possessions outright. American forces fought a brutal campaign against Filipino rebels.
4. The United States proclaimed an Open Door trade policy in regard to China. The United States acquired partial control over Samoa by treaty and by declaring protectorate status. Hawaii was annexed to the United States in 1898.

Critical Thinking and Writing

5. In both wars the U.S. swiftly defeated weak and disorganized enemies and acquired important new territories from the defeated nations in the ensuing peace treaties.
6. Essays will vary, but should reflect the style presented in the section.

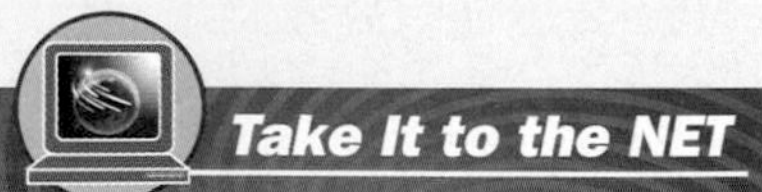

Take It to the NET

Answers will vary. Students may note that Hawaii was not annexed peacefully, but by subterfuge and force; the U.S. economic interests in Hawaii; the tone of the apology.

Caption Answers

Interpreting Political Cartoons Both. On the one hand, the cartoonist believes that "American diplomacy" is the key to China's open door. On the other hand, the cartoonist seems concerned about the U.S. having too large a role in the process.

RESOURCE DIRECTORY

Teaching Resources
Units 3/4 booklet
- Section 2 Quiz, p. 5

Guide to the Essentials
- Section 2 Summary, p. 49

Using a Time Zone Map

A system of worldwide standard time was devised in 1884. It divides the world into 24 time zones based on meridians of longitude. The time is the same throughout each zone. The Prime Meridian of 0°, which passes through Greenwich, England, is the starting point for calculating the time in each zone. The meridian of 180° longitude, halfway around the world, is the International Date Line. The calendar date to the east of this line is one day later than the date to the west.

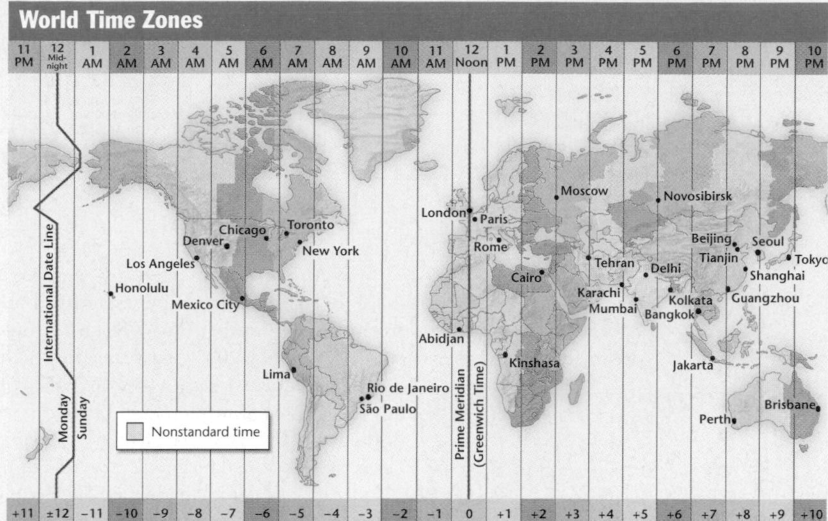

LEARN THE SKILL

Use the following steps to read a time zone map:

1. **Study the information on the map.** Locate the Prime Meridian and the International Date Line. Study any keys, labels, and color-coding. On this map, the 24 time zones are shown by colored bands. The numbers at the bottom of the map indicate the number of hours each time zone differs from time at the Prime Meridian (Greenwich time). For example, +3 means that local time is three hours later than Greenwich time. The numbers at the top of the map provide examples of how this system works if it is 12:00 noon in Greenwich.
2. **Determine where the time zones and date change.** Notice how closely the time zones correspond to the meridians of longitude and where they vary from these lines. Compare time zones in different areas.
3. **Compare the time in your zone with other zones around the world.** Find your time zone on the map. Determine how it differs from Greenwich time.

PRACTICE THE SKILL

Answer the following questions:

1. **(a)** How does the map indicate which line is the Prime Meridian? **(b)** What time is it at the International Date Line when it is noon in Greenwich? **(c)** How many different time zones does South America have?
2. **(a)** If it is 12:00 noon, Greenwich time, what time is it in Moscow, Russia? In Denver, United States of America? **(b)** If it is 2 P.M. in Abidjan, Cote d'Ivoire, what time is it in the zone labeled +7? In the zone labeled –4? **(c)** Why do you think some of the time zones follow geographical features and political boundaries rather than the meridians of longitude?
3. **(a)** If it is 12:00 noon in Greenwich, what time is it in your time zone? **(b)** If it is 1 A.M. in your time zone, what time is it in Karachi, Pakistan? In Guangzhou, China? **(c)** If it is 12:00 noon in São Paulo, Brazil, what time is it where you live? **(d)** If it is 9 P.M. on Wednesday where you live, what are the day and time in Brisbane, Australia?

APPLY THE SKILL

See the Chapter Review and Assessment for another opportunity to apply this skill.

Using a Time Zone Map

Focus Students will use a time zone map to calculate times in various locations in the world.

Instruct Ask students if they have seen pictures of Earth from space. Do they show a clear dividing line between day and night? Explain that as areas of Earth pass out of darkness and into sunlight, people experience sunrise. We say that sunrise occurs at a specific time in a certain area, but sunrise occurs continuously as Earth turns. Ask why people on Earth need agreed-upon times and time zones.

Extend See the Skills for Life Activity in the Resource Directory below.

Answers

Practice the Skill

1. **(a)** It is a clearly labeled, bright red line. **(b)** Midnight. **(c)** Three.
2. **(a)** Moscow: 2:00 P.M.; Denver: 5:00 A.M. **(b)** 9:00 P.M.; 10:00 A.M. **(c)** For convenience so that people doing business with one another are in the same time zone.
3. **(a)** Answers will vary. **(b)** Answers will vary. **(c)** Answers will vary. **(d)** Answers will vary.

RESOURCE DIRECTORY

Teaching Resources

Skills for Life booklet, p. 19

Technology

Social Studies Skills Tutor CD-ROM

Interactive Practice in

- Geographic Literacy
- Critical Thinking and Reading
- Visual Analysis
- Communications

Section 3
A New Foreign Policy

Section Objectives

1. Find out why the United States wanted to build the Panama Canal.
2. Learn about the goals of Roosevelt's "big stick" diplomacy.
3. Discover some ways in which the foreign policies of Presidents Taft and Wilson differed from those of President Roosevelt.

Bellringer

Warm-Up Activity Display a world map. Ask students how much time they think it took a ship to travel from New York to San Francisco before and after the building of the Panama Canal. Ask for an estimate of the distance between the two cities.

Activating Prior Knowledge Do students know the status of the Panama Canal today? *(By treaty, control of the Canal Zone territory was given over to the government of Panama on December 31, 1999.)*

Reading Strategy

As students read the section, have them note the effects of physical and human geographic factors on such events as the building of the Panama Canal and the establishment of the National Park Service. What are some ways in which the existence of the canal has changed the world? How has the establishment of the National Park Service impacted American life?

Section 3

A New Foreign Policy

READING FOCUS

- Why did the United States want to build the Panama Canal?
- What were the goals of Theodore Roosevelt's "big stick" diplomacy?
- In what ways did the foreign policies of Presidents Taft and Wilson differ from those of President Roosevelt?

MAIN IDEA

President Theodore Roosevelt conducted a vigorous foreign policy that suited the new status of the United States as a world power. Presidents Taft and Wilson took a different approach to influencing other nations.

KEY TERMS

concession
Roosevelt Corollary
dollar diplomacy

TAKING NOTES

Copy the flowchart below. As you read, fill in the boxes with some of the major effects of the new United States foreign policy.

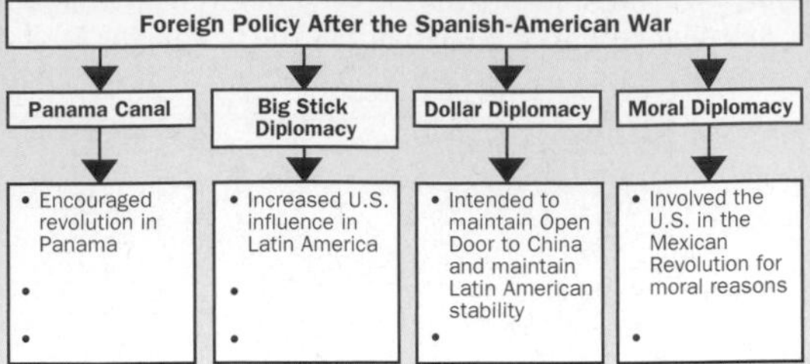

Foreign Policy After the Spanish-American War
Panama Canal
Big Stick Diplomacy
Dollar Diplomacy
Moral Diplomacy
• Encouraged revolution in Panama
•
•
• Increased U.S. influence in Latin America
•
•
• Intended to maintain Open Door to China and maintain Latin American stability
•
• Involved the U.S. in the Mexican Revolution for moral reasons
•

Setting the Scene By 1900, the United States had emerged as a genuine world power. It controlled several overseas territories and had a large and vigorous economy. These circumstances contributed to William McKinley's decisive victory in the presidential election of 1900. One year later McKinley was dead, cut down by an assassin's bullet. Theodore Roosevelt, McKinley's Vice President, was now President. The new President developed a foreign policy to support the nation's new role in the world. Under his leadership, the United States continued to intervene in the affairs of countries that were of economic and strategic interest to the nation.

Because of the uneven elevation in the canal zone, engineers had to design a series of locks to raise and lower the ships so that they could pass through the canal.

The Panama Canal

The Spanish-American War brought home to Americans the need for a shorter route between the Pacific and Atlantic oceans. A canal built across Central America would link the two oceans, making global shipping much faster and cheaper. It would also allow the United States Navy to move quickly from one ocean to the other in time of war.

Building the Canal The Isthmus of Panama was an ideal location for such a route. At that time, Panama was a province of the South American nation of Colombia. In 1879, a French company headed by Ferdinand de Lesseps had bought a 25-year **concession** from Colombia to build a canal across Panama. (A concession is a grant for a piece of land in exchange for a promise to use the land for a specific purpose.) Defeated by yellow fever and severe mismanagement, the company abandoned the project ten years later. It offered its remaining rights to the United States for $100 million. When the price fell to $40 million, Congress

Activity

Connecting with Geography

Tell students to use either a globe or a map of the world to chart routes from the Atlantic Ocean to the Pacific, without going through the Panama Canal. How many routes are possible between London and Los Angeles? How many routes are possible between Tokyo and New York? How does the Panama Canal shorten each route? **(Visual/Spatial; Logical/Mathematical)**

Resource Directory

Teaching Resources
Guided Reading and Review booklet, p. 72

Other Print Resources
Nystrom *Atlas of Our Country* *Later Expansion of the United States,* pp. 32–33
Historical Outline Map Book *The Panama Canal,* p. 59

Technology
Section Reading Support Transparencies
Guided Reading Audiotapes (English/Spanish), Ch. 10
Student Edition on Audio CD, Ch. 10
Color Transparencies *Historical Maps,* A29
Prentice Hall Presentation Pro CD-ROM, Ch. 10
Companion Web site, www.phschool.com

passed the Spooner Act in 1902 that authorized the purchase of the French assets. The act required that the United States work out a treaty with Colombia for a lease on the land.

Treaty negotiations went nowhere. Colombia was waiting for the French concession to expire in 1904 so that it could offer the isthmus at a higher price. Roosevelt was enraged by this attempt of Colombian "bandits" to "rob" the United States. Secretary of State John Hay sent a message to the American minister in Colombia in June 1903 essentially threatening Colombia if it did not reconsider.

> *"If Colombia should now reject the treaty or unduly delay its ratification, the friendly understanding between the two countries would be so seriously compromised that action might be taken by the Congress next winter which every friend of Colombia would regret."*
>
> —Secretary of State John Hay

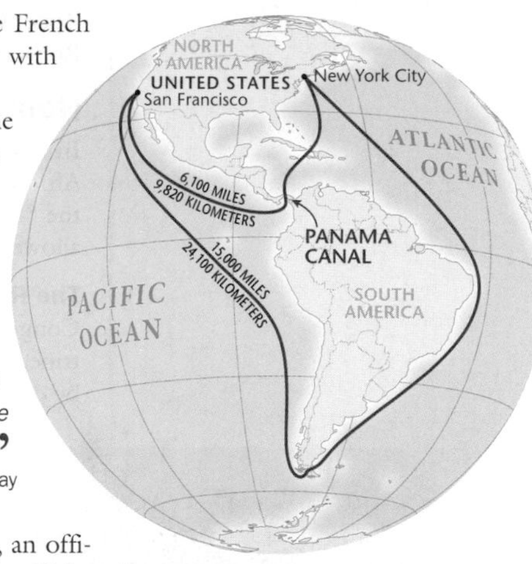

MAP SKILLS Compare the sea route from New York City to San Francisco (above) with and without the canal. **Movement** *By how many miles did the Panama Canal reduce the journey?*

Meanwhile, Roosevelt secretly made it clear to Philippe Bunau-Varilla, an official with the French company, that the United States would not interfere if the company organized a Panamanian revolution against Colombia.

The revolt took place in November 1903 with U.S. warships waiting offshore to provide support for the rebels. The United States immediately recognized an independent Panama and became its protector. In return, Panama signed the Hay-Bunau-Varilla Treaty in November 1903. The treaty gave the United States a permanent grant of a 10-mile-wide strip of land for a Canal Zone over which the United States would have complete sovereignty. In return, the Panamanians received a payment of $10 million.

Construction of the canal began in 1904. To complete this mammoth task, workers were brought in from several countries. Many of them had no construction experience whatsoever. After receiving proper training, the workers surpassed all expectations. They finished the canal in 1914, six months ahead of schedule and $23 million under budget.

Reaction to the Canal Roosevelt's opponents did not appreciate the methods he had used to secure the Canal Zone. A newspaper published by William Hearst commented, "Besides being a rough-riding assault upon another republic over the shattered wreckage of international law . . . , it is a quite unexampled instance of foul play in American politics."

Most Americans, however, convinced that the canal was vital to national security and prosperity, approved of President Roosevelt's actions in Panama. Two years after leaving office, Roosevelt gave a speech at the University of California at Berkeley in which he justified his methods:

> *"If I had followed traditional, conservative methods I would have submitted a dignified State paper of probably 200 pages to Congress and the debates on it would have been going on yet; but I took the Canal Zone and let Congress debate; and while the debate goes on the canal does also."*
>
> —Theodore Roosevelt, 1911

Workers on the Panama Canal wore identification badges like the ones shown here.

Despite the success of the Panama Canal as a link between the Atlantic and Pacific, its acquisition left a legacy of ill will among Latin Americans toward the United States. In recognition of the illegal means used to acquire the Canal

Lesson Plan

Focus The foreign policies of Presidents Roosevelt and Taft were crafted to suit America's new role as a world power. Ask how their approaches differed.

Instruct Point out that the United States did not settle in the territories it acquired in the late 1800s and early 1900s as the British did in parts of the British Empire. Ask: Why did Roosevelt and Taft pursue policies that involved American control of other countries? Why did the United States want to build the Panama Canal? How did Roosevelt get Colombia to agree? How did the tactics he used in Latin American countries differ from those he used in Asia?

Assess/Reteach President Roosevelt relied on the power of his personality to further his goals for American foreign policy. Though many Americans were opposed to his approach, he made a great deal of progress in a short amount of time. Can students state their own opinions of his methods? Do Presidents use the "personality" approach today?

Caption Answers

Map Skills By about 8,900 miles.

BACKGROUND
Biography

William Howard Taft (1857–1930) began and ended his career as a judge. Early on, Taft served as a superior court judge in Ohio. From 1892 until 1900, he was a judge of the U.S. Sixth Circuit Court of Appeals. In March of 1900, Taft resigned his judgeship when President McKinley appointed him chairman of the Second Philippine Commission. Taft particularly enjoyed his post in the Philippines and twice refused to leave when offered an appointment on the Supreme Court. After his defeat by Woodrow Wilson in the presidential election of 1912, Taft became a law professor at Yale. In 1921 President Harding appointed Taft Chief Justice of the United States Supreme Court. Taft served as chief justice until 1930, when he resigned because of poor health.

From the Archives of
AmericanHeritage®

About the Presidents

William Howard Taft (1909–1913) hoped to establish a system for working out disagreements between nations. Under Taft, treaties were drafted with Great Britain and France in 1911. These treaties included provisions for negotiating issues that might lead to war, but the Senate made important changes. One of Taft's main opponents in this disagreement was Theodore Roosevelt. Just back from an African safari, Roosevelt was ready to jump into politics again. In the end, Taft refused to sign the new Senate version. Source: Michael Harwood, "William Howard Taft," *The American Heritage® Pictorial History of the Presidents of the United States,* vol. 2, 1968.

CAPTION ANSWERS

Map Skills Military seizures and occupations.

Foreign Policy After Roosevelt

Under the presidency of Theodore Roosevelt, the United States assumed a forceful new role in foreign affairs. Roosevelt's successors were thrown into a complex mix of political alliances and world events that would require careful and creative policymaking. William Howard Taft and Woodrow Wilson continued the Roosevelt legacy, but each brought with them their own unique methods of diplomacy.

MAP SKILLS This map shows how frequently the United States intervened in the affairs of Latin American countries in the early 1900s. **Place** *What form did most of these interventions take?*

United States Interventions, 1898–1934

U.S. expeditionary force, 1916–1917
U.S. occupation, 1898–1902, 1906–1909, 1912, 1917–1922
U.S. seizure, 1914
U.S. occupation, 1915–1934
U.S. possession, 1898
Purchased from Denmark, 1917
U.S. leased naval base, 1903
United Fruit Co. organized for banana trade, 1899
U.S. occupation, 1924–1925
U.S. occupation, 1909–1910, 1912–1925, 1926–1933. Canal proposed, 1916
U.S. leased Corn Is., 1914
U.S. occupation, 1916–1924
U.S. acquired Canal Zone, 1904. Canal completed, 1914

Taft and Dollar Diplomacy William Howard Taft, elected to the presidency in 1908, was not as aggressive as Roosevelt in pursuing foreign policy aims. A distinguished lawyer from Ohio, Taft had served as Roosevelt's Secretary of War and had headed the commission that governed the Philippines.

Taft's main foreign policy goals were to maintain the open door to Asia and preserve stability in Latin America. As for the rest, he preferred "substituting dollars for bullets." By this he meant maintaining orderly societies abroad through increased American investment in foreign economies. Although some of Taft's contemporaries mocked his approach, calling it **dollar diplomacy,** Taft himself later used this term with pride.

Dollar diplomacy did not succeed as well as Taft had hoped. Although it increased the level of United States financial involvement abroad, the results were not always profitable. For example, when Taft's Secretary of State, Philander Knox, persuaded bankers from the United States to invest in railroad projects in China and Manchuria, Russia and Japan united in an effort to block the influence of the Americans. In addition, many U.S. investments in China were lost when the country's government collapsed in revolution in 1911.

Sounds of an Era

Listen to a campaign speech by William Howard Taft in 1908 and other sounds from the age of imperialism.

Dollar diplomacy also created enemies in Latin America, especially in the Caribbean and Central America, where local revolutionary movements opposed American influence. Although the United States reached new heights as an international power under Roosevelt and Taft, anti-colonialism abroad and anti-imperialism at home provided a growing check to further expansion.

Wilson and the Mexican Revolution American intervention in Mexico under President Woodrow Wilson led to even more anti-American feeling in Latin America. In 1911, a revolution forced Mexico's longtime dictator, Porfirio Diaz, to resign. The new president, Francisco Madero, promised democratic reforms but could not unite his deeply divided and impoverished country. In 1913, General Victoriano Huerta overthrew him and had him killed.

The United States was unsure how to respond to Huerta's illegal action. Americans had invested over $1 billion in Mexican oil, mines, land, and railways. When Huerta promised to protect foreign investments, most European countries recognized him. American investors urged President Wilson to do the same, but he refused. To him, Huerta was a "butcher" ruling without the consent of the

RESOURCE DIRECTORY

Teaching Resources

Units 3/4 booklet
- Section 3 Quiz, p. 6

Guide to the Essentials
- Section 3 Summary, p. 50

Learning with Documents booklet (Key Documents) *Theodore Roosevelt, the Strenuous Life,* p. 85

Biography, Literature, and Comparing Primary Sources booklet (Literature) *You're All Right, Teddy,* p. 63

Other Print Resources

American History Block Scheduling Support *The Spanish-American War: Door to Imperialism* and *Through Mud and Disease: Building the Panama Canal,* found in the Prosperity, Depression, and War folder, includes interdisciplinary lesson suggestions and activities for Geography and History, Primary Sources, Biography, and Literature.

Technology

Sounds of an Era Audio CD *William Howard Taft,* 1908 recording (time: one minute)

people. With this refusal, Wilson was announcing the end of Taft's "dollar diplomacy." From now on, the United States would apply moral and legalistic standards to foreign policy decisions.

Wilson's policy led him into a complex and bloody confrontation with Mexico. First, he interfered in Mexican politics. Another Mexican leader, Venustiano Carranza, began making military progress against Huerta. Wilson demanded that a truce be declared and that Mexico hold democratic elections in which Huerta could not run. When Huerta refused, Wilson decided to support Carranza and blocked all munitions from reaching Huerta's forces.

In April 1914, the brief arrest of American sailors in Tampico gave Wilson an excuse to act militarily. He sent the American navy to occupy Veracruz, Mexico's port on the Gulf of Mexico. Over a hundred Mexicans died resisting the occupation, and Mexico's political factions united against the United States. Deprived by the occupation of customs revenue and munitions, on July 15 Huerta resigned in favor of Carranza.

Wilson withdrew the navy, but was soon drawn into Mexican affairs again by the actions of peasant rebel leader Francisco "Pancho" Villa. Villa had once supported Carranza but now opposed him and gathered his armed forces in his strongholds in northern Mexico. The threat of civil war in Mexico again worried President Wilson, who encouraged Carranza and Villa to meet and negotiate. When neither of the two leaders would agree to such a meeting, Wilson felt he had to choose between them. He chose Carranza as the more stable of the two.

Wilson's decision to support Carranza infuriated Pancho Villa, who then began to pursue a more radical path in Mexico. Villa began terrorizing Americans in Mexico and raiding border towns in the United States. On March 9, 1916, his men crossed the U.S. border into Columbus, New Mexico, and burned the town, killing more than 15 people.

Wilson's "moral diplomacy" had not worked well. Carranza's government eventually adopted a constitution that curbed foreign ownership of Mexico's resources. Many American and Mexican lives had been lost, and American financial interests had lost ground. Wilson's interference in Mexican affairs soured relations between the two countries for years to come.

Focus on WORLD EVENTS

In Pursuit of Pancho Villa Besides wanting to take revenge on Wilson, Villa's other likely motive for terrorizing Americans along the border was to weaken Mexican support for the Carranza government. Villa knew that Wilson would respond to the terrorism with force. Any attempt by Wilson to interfere with Mexican affairs would make Carranza look weak.

Villa was right. Wilson sent General John J. "Black Jack" Pershing at the head of more than 5,000 American troops into Mexico to pursue Villa. Carranza authorized Wilson to do this, only to regret his decision later on. His strongest supporters were nationalists who saw American intervention as a violation of Mexican sovereignty. Threatened with a loss of power, Carranza demanded that the American troops leave, but was refused. Bloody clashes took place between Mexican and American troops. Pershing's pursuit of Villa failed. In 1917, with the United States on the brink of war in Europe, Wilson withdrew his troops.

Section 3 Assessment

READING COMPREHENSION

1. How did the United States secure the rights to build the Panama Canal?
2. (a) Why did Roosevelt issue the **Roosevelt Corollary?** (b) How did people in Latin America and the United States react to Roosevelt's declaration?
3. Why did Taft's **dollar diplomacy** and Wilson's actions in Mexico anger many Latin Americans?

CRITICAL THINKING AND WRITING

4. **Making Comparisons** How were Teddy Roosevelt and Andrew Jackson similar in the way in which they used the power of the presidency to achieve policy goals?
5. **Writing an Opinion** In two or three paragraphs, explain why you think that the United States adopted a new foreign policy in the 1900s and whether or not you think this policy was justified.

Take It to the NET

Activity: Creating a Time Line Read more about President Taft (1909–1913), and create a time line of his career. What do you consider his most important achievement? What did Taft consider his most important achievement? Use the links provided in the *America: Pathways to the Present* area of the following Web site for help in completing this activity.
www.phschool.com

Section 3 Assessment

Reading Comprehension

1. It secretly encouraged a revolution in Panama and sent military forces to protect it. It received a 10-mile-wide strip of land across the isthmus in return.
2. (a) It would allow U.S. intervention if Latin American countries took actions harmful to the U.S. or if their governments collapsed, inviting intervention from stronger nations. (b) Latin Americans were angered. The U.S. Congress was displeased, as these measures strengthened Roosevelt's powers while weakening those of Congress.
3. In Latin America, increased American investment in the economy angered local revolutionaries that opposed American influence. Wilson's moral stance during his direct intervention in Mexican affairs dictated how the civil war would go, angering many Mexicans.

Critical Thinking and Writing

4. Both were active Presidents who used high-handed tactics in pursuit of their policy goals. For example, Jackson refused to enforce the Supreme Court's decision stating that the removal of the Cherokee people was illegal. Roosevelt stage-managed the Panamanian revolution.
5. Essays will vary but should be supported with facts from the section.

Answers will vary. Students should include Taft's accomplishments both as a judge and as President. Taft considered his Supreme Court work to be his most important.

CUSTOMIZE FOR ...

Gifted and Talented

Next to Washington, Jefferson, and Lincoln, the fourth stone face on the slopes of Mount Rushmore is that of Theodore Roosevelt. Have students write one or two paragraphs explaining why some people might have wanted Roosevelt to be on this monument, while others felt that he did not belong.

Section 4 Debating America's New Role

Section Objectives

1. Examine the main arguments raised by the anti-imperialists.
2. See why imperialism appealed to many Americans.
3. Find out how American imperialism was viewed from abroad.

Bellringer

Warm-Up Activity Write the following sentence on the chalkboard: "Americans are always searching for a new frontier." Ask students what this might mean for other nations.

Activating Prior Knowledge Ask students to describe some situations that demonstrate the ways in which the debate concerning United States involvement in international affairs continues to this day.

Reading Strategy

Have students skim the section and use the headings and subheadings to create an outline. Then, as they read the section, have them fill in supporting details.

Section 4 Debating America's New Role

READING FOCUS

- What were the main arguments raised by the anti-imperialists?
- Why did imperialism appeal to many Americans?
- How was American imperialism viewed from abroad?

MAIN IDEA

After the Spanish-American War, the debate intensified over whether the United States should build an empire.

KEY TERMS

racism
compulsory
Great White Fleet

TAKING NOTES

As you read, complete this chart listing all of the arguments for and against imperialism.

Pro-Imperialism	Anti-Imperialism
• Offers new "frontier" for the American imagination and spirit	• Rejects the foundation of American ideals and democracy
•	•
•	•

Setting the Scene Before the Spanish-American War, U.S. citizens were already debating the consequences of an expanded role in world affairs. Walter Gresham, President Cleveland's Secretary of State in 1894, cautioned against "the evils of interference in affairs that do not specially concern us." Until the annexation of the Philippines in 1898, however, most citizens supported overseas involvement. The U.S. occupation of the Philippines quickly raised the voices of those wary of imperialism.

> *"Much as we abhor the 'criminal aggression' in the Philippines, greatly as we regret that the blood of the Filipinos is on American hands, we more deeply resent the betrayal of American institutions at home. The real firing line is not in the suburbs of Manila. The foe is of our own household. The attempt of 1861 was to divide the country. That of 1899 is to destroy its fundamental principles and noblest ideals."*
>
> —From the platform of the Anti-Imperialist League

INTERPRETING POLITICAL CARTOONS This cartoon depicts the imperialist powers about to carve up a slain China. **Analyzing Visual Information** *What is the cartoonist's attitude toward imperialism?*

The Anti-Imperialists

In November 1898, opponents of U.S. policy in the Philippines established the Anti-Imperialist League. Most of its organizers were well-to-do professionals. They included editor E. L. Godkin, Democratic politician William Jennings Bryan, settlement house leader Jane Addams, and novelist Mark Twain.

Moral and Political Arguments To support their position, the anti-imperialists used a variety of arguments. The strongest of these were moral and political in nature. Expansionist behavior, the anti-imperialists asserted, was a rejection of the nation's foundation of "liberty for all." As one prominent Republican and former senator from Missouri explained in 1899:

Caption Answers

Interpreting Political Cartoons The other powers appear ready to fight over their "share" of China as the United States looks on. The cartoonist seems to believe that imperialism perpetuates greed and violence.

RESOURCE DIRECTORY

Teaching Resources
Learning Styles Lesson Plans booklet, p. 37
Guided Reading and Review booklet, p. 73

Technology
Section Reading Support Transparencies
Guided Reading Audiotapes (English/Spanish), Ch. 10
Student Edition on Audio CD, Ch. 10
Prentice Hall Presentation Pro CD-ROM, Ch. 10
Companion Web site, www.phschool.com

“We regret that it has become necessary in the land of Washington and Lincoln to reaffirm that all men, of whatever race or color, are entitled to life, liberty, and the pursuit of happiness.”

—Carl Schurz

Other anti-imperialists promoted the idea that “the Constitution must follow the flag,” by which they meant that the American flag and laws went together. They argued that people in territories controlled by the United States should be entitled to the same guarantees in the Constitution as U.S. citizens. For example, labor leader Samuel Gompers objected to taking over countries in which U.S. labor laws did not apply. He pointed out that in Hawaii, half of the population consisted of “contract laborers, practically slaves,” who did not benefit from the laws that protected American workers.

In response to such an argument, expansionists claimed that the people of the Caribbean and the Pacific were not ready for democracy and that the United States was preparing them for liberty. Major General Douglas MacArthur, military governor of the Philippines in 1900, said, “We are planting in those islands . . . the best traditions, the best characteristics of Americanism.” Anti-imperialists, however, did not believe that any group of people should be forced to wait to enjoy liberty.

Finally, anti-imperialists noted that imperialism threatened the nation’s democratic foundations. The large standing armies that were employed to bring other nations under American control could be used just as easily to crush dissent at home.

Racial Arguments Other anti-imperialists saw racism at work in imperialism. **Racism** is a belief that differences in character or intelligence are due to one’s race. Many Americans of this period believed that people of Anglo-Saxon heritage were superior to other races. Many of the public officials who developed the country’s policies shared these sentiments.

African Americans were at first torn about imperialistic issues. As U.S. citizens, they wanted to support their country. But they recognized the racism that underlay imperialism. A leader of the A.M.E. Zion Church had this to say in 1899:

“Had the Filipinos been white and fought as bravely as they have, the war would have been ended and their independence granted a long time ago.”

—Bishop Alexander Walters

Although most southern Democrats also opposed imperialism, they did so for different reasons. Many southern politicians feared the effects of having to absorb more people of different races into the United States. Consequently, southern Democrats led the movement in the Senate against ratifying the treaty with Spain after the Spanish-American War. A number of anti-imperialists outside the South also feared that imperialist policies would encourage people

COMPARING PRIMARY SOURCES
Imperialism

The Spanish-American War heightened the debate between imperialist and anti-imperialist factions at home.

Analyzing Viewpoints Which of the viewpoints do you think most Americans supported?

Anti-Imperialist	*Pro-Imperialist*
“We assume that what we like and practice, and what we think better, must come as a welcome blessing to Spanish-Americans and Filipinos. This is grossly and obviously untrue. They hate our ways. They are hostile to our ideas. Our religion, language, institutions, and manners offend them.” —*William G. Sumner, Yale University professor, in an 1898 speech*	“Think of the tens of thousands of Americans who will invade mine and field and forest in the Philippines when a liberal government, protected and controlled by this republic, if not the government of the republic itself, shall establish order and equity there!” —*Albert J. Beveridge, leading imperialist and later United States senator, in an 1898 speech*

READING CHECK
Why did some anti-imperialists believe that “the Constitution must follow the flag”?

LESSON PLAN

Focus After the Spanish-American War, anti-imperialists launched heated debates over United States foreign policy. Ask what arguments these anti-imperialists used to support their case. How persuasive were they?

Instruct Discuss the arguments for and against imperialism. Why did professionals, southern Democrats, labor leaders, and African Americans oppose imperialism? Who supported imperialism? What role did the “frontier mentality” play? Discuss with students the way racism entered into the arguments of both imperialists and anti-imperialists.

Ask students how imperialism created a love-hate relationship between the United States and some countries.

Assess/Reteach Ask students to imagine what the United States would be like if all the areas involved in this country’s imperialist efforts were states today. What regions would that involve? How would the inclusion of these territories as states change the United States?

ACTIVITY
Connecting with History and Conflict

Tell students to imagine that they are one of the well-known anti-imperialists mentioned in the text—E. L. Godkin, William Jennings Bryan, Jane Addams, or Mark Twain. Then have students write a statement explaining their opposition to the government’s expansionist policies. Ask volunteers to read their statements aloud to the class. **(Verbal/Linguistic)**

READING CHECK
They believed that the United States should not acquire new territory unless the local inhabitants were immediately given all the rights and liberties enjoyed by American citizens.

TEST PREPARATION

Have students reread the following quote from this page: “The Constitution must follow the flag,” then have them answer the question below.

Which statement best paraphrases the quote?

A Wherever the American flag appears, people must obey the rules of the U.S.

B The U.S. flag is more important than the Constitution.

C Americans favor imperialism.

(D) The people in any place that the U.S. governs are entitled to the same rights as U.S. citizens.

Activity

Connecting with Government

Ask students to create a newspaper advertisement that attempts to persuade Americans to support the anti-imperialists' arguments. Students should focus on these issues for their ad: anti-imperialist arguments, effective ways to counter the appeal of imperialism, and the effect of imperialism on the image of the United States in Latin America and the Pacific. **(Visual/Spatial)**

Background

A Diverse Nation

The Filipino people were not blind to the irony of facing African American soldiers serving in the war against the Philippines (1898–1902). Joining the military was a way for African Americans to prove their patriotism, but as one African American soldier wrote from the Philippines, "I was struck by a question a little Filipino boy asked me, which ran this way: 'Why does the American Negro come . . . to fight us? . . . Why don't you fight those people in America who burn Negroes?'"

READING CHECK

The frontier spirit lived on after the domestic frontier was closed. Many Americans saw imperialist expansion as the next frontier to be conquered.

VIEWING FINE ART Edward Moran captured the triumph of the United States Navy in his 1899 painting *Return of the Conquerors.* **Identifying Central Issues** *How does this painting both reinforce and reflect imperialism's appeal to many Americans?*

of different racial backgrounds to move to the United States.

Economic Arguments Finally, anti-imperialists raised economic objections to expansionist policies. In their view, the time was not right for the United States to expand. First, expansion involved too many costs. Maintaining the necessary armed forces required more taxation, debt, and possibly even **compulsory,** or required, military service.

Samuel Gompers raised another concern. He argued that laborers coming to the United States from annexed territories would compete with American workers for jobs. Since these immigrants would work for lower wages, their presence would drive all wages down. The nation's industrialists raised yet another concern. They pointed out that goods produced cheaply in annexed countries could be imported to the United States without customs duties. This competition would hurt many American industries.

Imperialism's Appeal

Despite the strength of these arguments, imperialism maintained a powerful hold on the American imagination. Some people looked to a new frontier abroad to keep Americans from losing their competitive edge. The America of explorers and pioneers, who bravely chartered unknown territories and overcame great obstacles, was fast disappearing into the shadows of memory. In 1890, the director of the census had declared the frontier "closed." Imperialism offered a new kind of frontier for American expansion. Some proponents of expansionism believed that imperialism was a celebration of American tradition and creative spirit. In this editorial, Walter Hines Page dismissed the anti-imperialist notion that imperialism was a betrayal of American ideals:

READING CHECK
How did the "closing" frontier make imperialism more appealing to some Americans?

> “*It is temperament that tells, and not schemes of national policy, whether laid down in Farewell Addresses or in Utopian books. No national character was ever shaped by formula or by philosophy; for greater forces than these lie behind it,—the forces of inheritance and of events. Are we, by virtue of our surroundings and institutions, become a different people from our ancestors, or are we yet the same race of Anglo-Saxons, whose restless energy in colonization, in conquest, in trade, in 'the spread of civilization,' has carried their speech into every part of the world, and planted their habits everywhere?*”
>
> —Walter Hines Page, editor of the *Atlantic Monthly,* 1898

The growth and popularity of youth scouting programs during this period shows that many Americans shared a "frontier mentality." Sir Robert Baden-Powell, an army officer of the British Empire, had used scouting techniques (tracking, woodcraft, and wilderness survival) to great success in a battle in South Africa. A few years after he returned to Britain as a war hero, Baden-Powell founded the Boy Scout movement. Scouting appeared in the United States in 1910 and soon became immensely popular. Two years later, Juliette

Caption Answers

Viewing Fine Art The ships imply power and seem to "own" the waters. Americans may feel secure and proud when seeing images such as this.

RESOURCE DIRECTORY

Teaching Resources

Units 3/4 booklet
- Section 4 Quiz, p. 7
- Chapter 10 Test, pp. 8, 11

Guide to the Essentials
- Section 4 Summary, p. 51
- Chapter 10 Test, p. 52

Biography, Literature, and Comparing Primary Sources booklet (Comparing Primary Sources) *On the Race for Empire,* p. 129

Other Print Resources

Chapter Tests with ExamView® Test Bank CD-ROM, Ch. 10

Technology

Color Transparencies *Political Cartoons,* B10

RESOURCE PRO® **Biography** *Juliette Gordon Low,* found on Resource Pro, profiles the woman who founded the Girl Scouts in 1912.

ExamView® Test Bank CD-ROM, Ch. 10

Social Studies Skills Tutor CD-ROM

Low, a close friend and admirer of Baden-Powell, founded the American Girl Scouts. Low hoped to use the program both to build moral character in girls and to teach them skills that would make them "hardy" and "handy."

Many people were swayed by the practical advantages of imperialism. They agreed with the economic arguments that emphasized the need to gain access to foreign markets. Others embraced the strategic military reasons for expansion.

In December 1907, Roosevelt sent part of the United States Navy on a cruise around the world. The trip was designed to demonstrate the nation's impressive naval power to other nations. The **Great White Fleet,** as the gleaming white ships were called, made a big impression everywhere it sailed. For American citizens, the fleet clearly showed the benefits of having a powerful navy.

Imperialism Viewed From Abroad

Having begun a pattern of international involvement, the United States discovered that these actions frequently took on a life of their own. In the Caribbean and Central America, for example, the United States often had to defend governments that were unpopular with local inhabitants. In Latin America, the cry "Yankee, Go Home!" began to be heard. Even before the Panama Canal was completed in 1914, Panamanians began to complain that they suffered from discrimination.

On the other hand, because the United States was quickly becoming so powerful, other countries—even those fearful about maintaining their independence—began to turn to the United States for help. Both welcomed and rejected, the United States would spend the rest of the century trying to decide the best way to reconcile its growing power and national interests with its relationships with other nations.

Focus on CULTURE

The Media and Imperialism In addition to the pro-imperialist yellow journalism of the time, much of the popular media glorified the accomplishments of imperialist frontier heroes. Theodore Roosevelt's book on his heroic charge, *The Rough Riders,* drew much praise. However, satirist Finley Peter Dunne's character, "Mr. Dooley," suggested the book should be called *Alone in Cuba* to emphasize Roosevelt's boastfulness. Another book of this era, *Conquest of the Tropics* (1914), describes the history of the United Fruit Company, portraying railroad entrepreneur Minor Keith as one of "the hardy American type which listens and responds eagerly to the call of the wild."

Section 4 Assessment

READING COMPREHENSION

1. Why did some people believe that **racism** was at work in imperialism?
2. What were three economic arguments raised by the anti-imperialists?
3. How did imperialism's appeal go beyond what many saw as its practical advantages?
4. What was significant about the tour of the **Great White Fleet?**

CRITICAL THINKING AND WRITING

5. **Identifying Assumptions** How did expansionists and anti-imperialists view imperialism in relation to the original principles of American democracy? What different assumptions did people on the two sides make about the roots and goals of the United States?
6. **Writing an Opinion** Based on the arguments they made against imperialism, what role do you think the anti-imperialists believed the United States should play in world affairs?

Take It to the NET

Activity: Creating a Poster
Research the itinerary, composition, and purpose of the Great White Fleet. Create a tour poster advertising "appearances" along the route. Keep in mind the political purpose of the tour. Use the links provided in the *America: Pathways to the Present* area of the following Web site for help in completing this activity.
www.phschool.com

Section 4 Assessment

Reading Comprehension

1. Through the desire to bring American values to other countries, imperialism perpetuated the belief that Anglo-Saxons were superior, and other races were inferior and in need of "Americanization."
2. Expansion was too costly; laborers coming to the U.S. from annexed territories would compete with American workers for jobs; cheap, duty-free goods imported from overseas possessions would hurt American industries.
3. Imperialism was seen by some Americans as a way to reinvigorate the American frontier spirit. It would also give American missionaries the opportunity to spread Christianity.
4. It reinforced imperialism's appeal to Americans as it demonstrated the nation's impressive naval power to the world.

Critical Thinking and Writing

5. Anti-imperialists: expansion rejected the "liberty for all" aspect of American life. People in overseas U.S. territories should have full constitutional rights. Expansionists: Imperialism was a rebirth of the American frontier spirit and would spread civilization to other lands.
6. Defender of democratic ideals and institutions around the world to which all peoples deserved access.

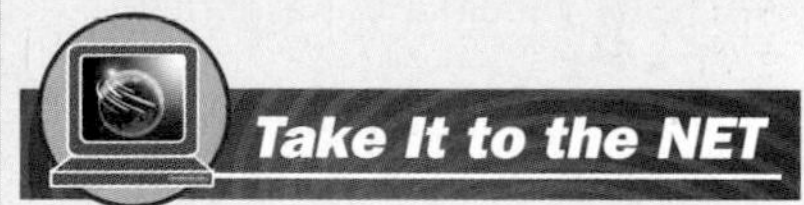

Student posters should advertise where the fleet was going, how many vessels there were, and why it was on tour.

CUSTOMIZE FOR ...
Less Proficient Writers
Ask students to imagine that they are a resident of one of the countries that the United States sought to rule. Can they write a list of words to describe how they would feel about this action?

Chapter 10

Reviewing Key Terms

Students should refer to the definitions of key terms in the chapter to write sentences that show an understanding of the causes of American imperialism and how it affected countries around the world.

Reviewing Main Ideas

14. New developments in communication and transportation fueled intensified competition among nations with long traditions of imperialism, now joined by the newly unified Germany.
15. Mahan: The economic future of the U.S. depended on new markets abroad and a navy to protect them. Lodge: worried about the effects of a disappearing frontier. Beveridge: expansionism was necessary because it introduced the ideas and customs of "superior" races to "primitive" societies.
16. Yellow journalism played on human rights abuses in Cuba and fanned public outrage over the destruction of American property. The public blamed the Spanish for the explosion aboard the *Maine.*
17. The Open Door Policy, initiated by John Hay, called for open trade in China. It was important for Americans because European nations and Japan were establishing spheres of influence in China, threatening to shut out American commerce.
18. It caused U.S. military intervention to become standard policy in Latin America.
19. Taft: maintain the open door to Asia; preserve stability in Latin America; Dollar Diplomacy. Wilson: willing to use military force in pursuit of his policy of "moral diplomacy," or promoting democracy around the world.
20. Anti-imperialists believed that imperialism betrayed the ideal of liberty for all people.

Chapter 10 Review and Assessment

creating a CHAPTER SUMMARY

Copy this cause-and-effect diagram (right) on a separate sheet of paper to show some of the causes and effects of American expansion during the late 1800s and early 1900s. Provide at least four causes and four effects.

CAUSES
- Pressure to find new markets abroad
-
-
-

AMERICAN EXPANSIONISM

EFFECTS
- Purchase of Alaska from Russia
-
-
-

iTEXT

For additional review and enrichment activities, see the interactive version of *America: Pathways to the Present*, available on the Web and on CD-ROM.

★ Reviewing Key Terms

For each of the terms below, write a sentence explaining how it relates to the era of imperialism in the United States.

1. imperialism
2. nationalism
3. annex
4. banana republic
5. arbitration
6. jingoism
7. Platt Amendment
8. sphere of influence
9. concession
10. dollar diplomacy
11. racism
12. compulsory
13. Great White Fleet

★ Reviewing Main Ideas

14. Why were the major European powers scrambling to seize new territory in the late 1800s? (Section 1)
15. Briefly explain the arguments of Alfred T. Mahan, Henry Cabot Lodge, and Albert J. Beveridge regarding expansionism. (Section 1)
16. Why did the American public favor war with Spain in 1898? (Section 2)
17. What was the Open Door Policy, and why was it important to the United States? (Section 2)
18. How did the Roosevelt Corollary affect United States policy in Latin America? (Section 3)
19. Describe the foreign policy goals of Taft and Wilson. (Section 3)
20. Explain why anti-imperialists believed that imperialism betrayed basic American principles. (Section 4)

★ Critical Thinking

21. **Synthesizing Information** In what sense were the expansionist policies of the United States in the late 1800s a continuation of the concept of Manifest Destiny?
22. **Identifying Central Issues** How did the popular theory of social Darwinism make it easier for some Americans to embrace imperialist policies in the late 1800s?
23. **Drawing Conclusions** During the late 1800s, the press fanned the flames of the Spanish-American War by publishing sensational stories about Spanish cruelties in Cuba. On what current issues has the press played a major role in influencing public opinion?
24. **Distinguishing Fact From Opinion** President McKinley's Secretary of State, John Hay, referred to the Spanish-American War as "a splendid little war." Can you think of any Americans, in addition to anti-imperialists, who might disagree with Hay's opinion?

Creating a Chapter Summary

American Expansionism

Causes	Effects
Pressure to find new markets abroad	Purchase of Alaska from Russia
Desire to protect American security	Spanish-American War
Desire to preserve American spirit of vitality	Annexation of Hawaii and Puerto Rico
Need for outposts for shipping traffic and steamship refueling	Construction of the Panama Canal

★ Skills Assessment

Analyzing Political Cartoons ▶

25. The caption to this 1904 political cartoon was "HIS 128th BIRTHDAY. 'Gee but this is an awful stretch!'" (a) Whose birthday is it? (b) How do you know? (c) What does the "awful stretch" refer to? (d) How do you know?
26. What is the cartoonist's view of United States imperialism?

Analyzing Primary Sources

Read this excerpt, and then answer the questions that follow.

> *"I hope that we can persuade our people on the one hand to act in a spirit of generous justice and genuine courtesy toward Japan, and on the other hand to keep the navy respectable in numbers and more than respectable in the efficiency of its units. If we act thus we need not fear the Japanese. But if . . . we show ourselves 'opulent, aggressive, and unarmed,' the Japanese may sometime work us an injury."*
>
> –President Theodore Roosevelt

27. This statement best reflects Roosevelt's support for
   - **A** the Monroe Doctrine.
   - **B** "Speak softly and carry a big stick."
   - **C** the Open Door Policy.
   - **D** the Roosevelt Corollary.
28. What is the most likely reason for Roosevelt's concern over Japan?
   - **F** He knew their military could easily defeat the military of the United States.
   - **G** The Japanese threatened to intervene if Western nations pursued trade with China.
   - **H** Laws were being proposed in the United States that discriminated against Japanese immigrants.
   - **J** The United States was interested in acquiring Japanese land.

Applying the Chapter Skill: *Using a Time Zone Map*

29. Review the time zone map on page 365. Name two cities on the map that are in the same time zone as New York City.

ACTIVITIES

Writing to LEARN

Writing a Persuasive Essay
The United States still intervenes in foreign countries when its interests are threatened. Write a letter to the editor of a newspaper in which you argue either for or against an interventionist foreign policy. Research recent examples of United States intervention in foreign countries and use them to support your arguments.

Primary Source CD-ROM

Working With Primary Sources Find additional information on American imperialism on the *Exploring Primary Sources in the U.S. History CD-ROM* and use the selection(s) provided to complete the Chapter 10 primary source activity located in the *America: Pathways to the Present* area of the following Web site: **www.phschool.com**

Take It to the NET

Chapter Self-Test As a review activity, take the Chapter 10 Self-Test in the *America: Pathways to the Present* area at the Web site listed below. The questions are designed to test your understanding of the chapter content. **www.phschool.com**

CRITICAL THINKING

21. Expansionism built on the belief that the U.S. was destined to expand across North America. The closing of the frontier led to the belief that the U.S. should acquire overseas territory.
22. Social Darwinism promoted the racist idea that Europeans and Americans were superior to other cultures and peoples. Social Darwinists applauded imperialism as a way to bring civilization to "inferior" countries.
23. Answers will vary. Students might cite press coverage of any issue currently in the news. Students may point out that the degree of sensationalism usually depends on the source that is covering the story.
24. The families of people who were injured or killed in the war would probably disagree with Hay, as would anyone who suffered as a result of the war.

SKILLS ASSESSMENT

25. (a) The birthday of the United States. (b) The eagle with the banner is a common symbol of the nation. (c) U.S. imperialism. (d) The eagle's wings stretch from Puerto Rico and Panama to the Philippines—places of strong U.S. involvement.
26. Sample response: The cartoonist may be suggesting that the United States is not justified in its involvements far from home.
27. B
28. H
29. Toronto and Lima.

ANSWERS TO ACTIVITIES

Writing to LEARN

Students' letters should take into account the imperialist and anti-imperialist arguments advanced in the chapter.

Primary Source CD-ROM

Direct students to the additional primary sources that can be found on the *Exploring Primary Sources in U.S. History CD-ROM.*

Take It to the NET

Additional support materials and activities for Chapter 10 of *America: Pathways to the Present* can be found in the Social Studies area at the Prentice Hall School Web site. **www.phschool.com**

BUILDING THE PANAMA CANAL

Focus Point out that the building of the Panama Canal is all the more remarkable when one realizes that it was undertaken with the earliest types of earth-moving equipment and without surveillance, computerized geological models, or even thorough knowledge of Panama's rugged jungle environment.

Instruct Explain that the Panama Canal was the largest engineering accomplishment of its day. The main challenges of the project fell into the categories of location, human-environmental interaction, and the movement of people and goods—three key factors in the study of geography.

Before they read, have students make a chart using these three factors as headings. Ask them to speculate about what specific challenges engineers might have faced in building the canal and to write down their ideas under the appropriate heading.

Extend After they read, have students add to their chart by filling in factual information under each of the three headings and comparing it with their original, speculative answers.

Geography & History

Building the Panama Canal

Constructing the Panama Canal was one of the greatest engineering feats of all time. Panama's physical and human geography presented several obstacles to the canal's planners and builders, but they overcame each challenge. When the canal was completed in 1914, it linked the Atlantic and Pacific Oceans, as well as the East and West Coasts of the United States.

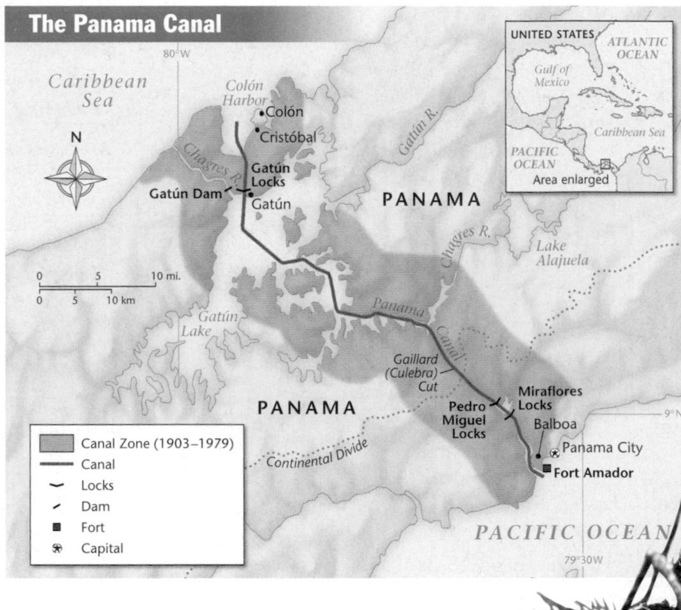

Flooding a River Valley

The greatest challenge was how to move ships across the Continental Divide, with an elevation of 312 feet above sea level. Digging a canal at sea level across the entire isthmus would have been much too expensive and time-consuming. However, the proposed route of the canal partly followed the course of the wild Chagres River, which had a record of violent floods. Engineers solved these problems by damming the Chagres River to create Gatún Lake, 85 feet above sea level. A series of locks would raise ships from the Atlantic Ocean to the lake. Ships could then travel across most of the isthmus at the level of the lake.

Cutting Across the Continental Divide

Workers would cut a deep gorge, later known as the Gaillard Cut (or Culebra Cut), to allow ships to cross the continental divide at the level of Gatún Lake before descending through another set of locks to the Pacific.

Geographical Connection **The inset map shows that the Atlantic Ocean lies east of the Pacific Ocean. According to the main map, in what direction do ships passing from the Pacific to the Atlantic actually travel through the Panama Canal?**

ANSWERS

1. They actually travel northwest. This is because of the peculiar orientation of the Isthmus of Panama.

RESOURCE DIRECTORY

Teaching Resources
Geography and History booklet, pp. 12–13

Other Print Resources
Nystrom *Atlas of Our Country* *Later Expansion of the United States,* pp. 32–33

Technology
Prentice Hall United States History Video Collection™ Volume 15, *U.S. and the World*

Solving Problems of Movement

One of the greatest challenges for planners was assembling a labor force to build the canal, because Panama did not have enough workers for the project. As a solution, workers were brought in from overseas, mainly from the United States and the West Indies. Another challenge was removing rock and soil from the canal bed and bringing in machinery and supplies for the workers. The engineers' solution was an extensive rail system.

How Locks Work

The canal's massive locks are an engineering marvel. The locks' lower gates serve as temporary dams to hold water so that ships can float in at the level of the canal above the locks. Then, the upper gates close, the lower gates open, and water flows out of the lock chamber. This lets ships float down to the next-lowest level. When the lower gates close and the gates at the upper end open, water floods in and raises ships. This drawing shows a lock chamber and gates under construction.

Eradicating Disease

Two deadly mosquito-borne diseases—malaria and yellow fever—threatened the canal's work force, but army physician William Gorgas devised an effective mosquito eradication program that saved thousands of lives.

Geographic Connection

What kinds of obstacles did the human and physical geography of Panama pose for the builders of the Panama Canal? How did they overcome those obstacles?

379

ANSWERS

2. Obstacles posed by the physical geography: The elevation of the Continental Divide, which required that ships be raised or that a deep gap be cut in the earth across the divide. Solution: A combination of both options—construction of locks to raise ships and the Gaillard Cut across the divide; the need to remove large amounts of earth and rock. Solution: Construction of a rail system; flooding along the Chagres River. Solution: Construction of a dam and the creation of Gátun Lake; the presence of disease-bearing mosquitoes. Solution: A mosquito eradication program.

   Obstacle posed by the human geography: The lack of an adequate labor force in Panama. Solution: Recruitment and transport of workers from other countries.

Chapter 11 Planning Guide
Resource Manager

	Core Instruction	Reading/Skills
Chapter-Level Resources **TEKS** 4(B)	Teaching Resources • Pacing Charts booklet • Block Scheduling booklet **Resource Pro® CD-ROM,** Ch. 11 **Prentice Hall Presentation Pro CD-ROM** **www.phschool.com** • eTeach	**Guided Reading Audiotapes (English/Spanish)** **Student Edition on Audio CD,** Ch. 11 **Social Studies Skills Tutor CD-ROM** **Color Transparencies,** B11, F6
1 The Origins of Progressivism 1. Learn the key goals of Progressives. 2. Find out how the ideas of progressive writers helped inspire new reform movements. 3. Discover which reform organizations and which women reformers took up progressive causes. 4. Understand why progressive reforms met with resistance. **TEKS** 1(A), 2(B), 4(A), 20(A), 24(C)	Teaching Resources **Units 3/4 booklet** • Section 1 Quiz, p. 15 **Learning Styles Lesson Plans booklet,** p. 38	**Guided Reading and Review booklet,** p. 74 **Guide to the Essentials,** p. 53 **Skills for Life booklet,** p. 388 **Section Reading Support Transparencies**
2 Progressive Legislation 1. Read about how Progressives wished to expand the role of government. 2. Discover the municipal and state reforms achieved by Progressives. 3. Learn what federal reforms Theodore Roosevelt championed as President. **TEKS** 4(A), 12(B), 12(C)	Teaching Resources **Units 3/4 booklet** • Section 2 Quiz, p. 16	**Guided Reading and Review booklet,** p. 75 **Guide to the Essentials,** p. 54 **Learning with Documents booklet,** p. 57 **Section Reading Support Transparencies**
3 Progressivism Under Taft and Wilson 1. Study the political conflicts that marked the presidency of William Howard Taft. 2. Find out who contended in the Election of 1912 and learn the outcome of that election. 3. Learn about the major policies that President Woodrow Wilson put into place. 4. Discover the limitations placed on the achievements of progressivism. **TEKS** 4(C), 8(B)	Teaching Resources **Units 3/4 booklet** • Section 3 Quiz, p. 17	**Guided Reading and Review booklet,** p. 77 **Guide to the Essentials,** p. 55 **Section Reading Support Transparencies**
4 Suffrage at Last 1. Learn the ways in which Susan B. Anthony and Elizabeth Cady Stanton formed a "bridge" to the twentieth-century suffrage effort. 2. Discover two main strategies pursued by suffrage leaders. 3. Read about the status of the suffrage movement by the turn of the century. 4. Find out why a new generation of leaders was needed in the suffrage effort. 5. Study the factors that led to a final victory for suffrage. **TEKS** 4(B), 5(A), 8(B), 17(B), 18(A), 18(B), 21(D)	Teaching Resources **Units 3/4 booklet** • Section 4 Quiz, p. 18 **Learning Styles Lesson Plans booklet,** pp. 38–39	**Guided Reading and Review booklet,** p. 77 **Guide to the Essentials,** p. 56 **Section Reading Support Transparencies**

Enrichment/Pre-AP

Prentice Hall United States History Video Collection™
www.phschool.com
- Section Activities, Virtual Field Trip, Chapter Activities, Current Events Online

Biography, Literature, and Comparing Primary Sources booklet, pp. 23, 64
American History Block Scheduling Support
Sounds of an Era Audio CD
Exploring Primary Sources in U.S. History CD-ROM

Great Debates booklet, p. 57
Nystrom *Atlas of Our Country,* pp. 30–31

Sounds of an Era Audio CD

Biography, Literature, and Comparing Primary Sources booklet, p. 131
Sounds of an Era Audio CD
Exploring Primary Sources in U.S. History CD-ROM

Assessment

Core Assessment
ExamView® Test Bank, Ch. 11
ExamView® Test Bank CD-ROM, Ch. 11

Standardized Test Preparation
Diagnose and Prescribe
Diagnostic Tests for High School Social Studies Skills

Review and Reteach
Review Book for U.S. History

Practice and Assess
Test-taking Strategies With Transparencies
Test-taking Strategies Poster
Test Prep for U.S. History
Alternative Assessment Handbook
Document-Based Assessment

Teaching Resources
Units 3/4 booklet
- Section Quizzes, pp. 387, 395, 402, 407
- Chapter Tests, pp. 408–409

www.phschool.com Ch. 11 Self-Test

AmericanHeritage® Resources

From the Archives of American Heritage®, pp. 394, 399
AmericanHeritage® My Brush with History™ Videotapes
www.americanheritage.com

Don't miss the exclusive interactive version of this textbook on the Web and on CD-ROM.

Chapter 11 Planning Guide

In Your Classroom

Customize for Individual Needs

Gifted and Talented

Teacher's Edition
- Customize for Gifted and Talented, pp. 393, 407

Teaching Resources
- Biography, Literature, and Comparing Primary Sources booklet, pp. 23, 64, 131

Technology
- Exploring Primary Sources in U.S. History CD-ROM *The Jungle, Upton Sinclair; Are Not the Women Half the Nation?*

ESL

Teacher's Edition
- Customize for ESL, p. 383

Teaching Resources
- Guided Reading and Review booklet, pp. 74–77
- Guide to the Essentials (English/Spanish), Chapter 11

Technology
- Student Edition on Audio CD, Chapter 11
- Guided Reading Audiotapes (English/Spanish), Chapter 11
- Section Reading Support Transparencies

Less Proficient Readers

Teacher's Edition
- Customize for Less Proficient Readers, p. 399

Teaching Resources
- Guided Reading and Review booklet, pp. 74–77
- Guide to the Essentials (English/Spanish), Chapter 11

Technology
- Student Edition on Audio CD, Chapter 11
- Guided Reading Audiotapes (English/Spanish), Chapter 11
- Section Reading Support Transparencies

Less Proficient Writers

Teacher's Edition
- Customize for Less Proficient Writers, p. 405

Teaching Resources
- Guided Reading and Review booklet, pp. 74–77
- Guide to the Essentials (English/Spanish), Chapter 11

Technology
- Student Edition on Audio CD, Chapter 11
- Guided Reading Audiotapes (English/Spanish), Chapter 11
- Section Reading Support Transparencies

Teacher's Edition Index

Chapter 11 – Pacing Suggestions

For 90-minute Blocks

- Teach sections 3 and 4 using Transparencies B11 and F6, and the Recent Scholarship note on pages 391 and 405 for class discussions.

Running Out of Time?

If you are running short on time to cover this chapter, consider the following options:

- Use the Prentice Hall Presentation Pro CD-ROM to create an outline for this chapter.
- Use the Section Summaries for Chapter 11, from **Guide to the Essentials (English/Spanish).**

TEKS Correlation

Chapter-Level	TEKS
	(4) History. The student understands the effects of reform and third party movements on American society. The student is expected to: **(B)** evaluate the impact of reform leaders such as Susan B. Anthony, W.E.B. DuBois, and Robert LaFollette on American society.
1 The Origins of Progressivism	**(1) History.** The student understands traditional historical points of reference in U.S. history from 1877 to the present. The student is expected to: **(A)** identify the major eras in U.S. history from 1877 to the present and describe their defining characteristics. **(2) History.** The student understands the political, economic, and social changes in the United States from 1877 to 1898. The student is expected to: **(B)** analyze economic issues such as industrialization, the growth of railroads, the growth of labor unions, farm issues, and the rise of big business. **(4) History.** The student understands the effects of reform and third party movements on American society. The student is expected to: **(A)** evaluate the impact of Progressive Era reforms including initiative, referendum, recall, and the passage of the 16th and 17th amendments. **(20) Culture.** The student understands the relationship between the arts and the times during which they were created. The student is expected to: **(A)** describe how the characteristics and issues of various eras in U.S. history have been reflected in works of art, music, and literature such as the paintings of Georgia O'Keeffe, rock and roll, and John Steinbeck's *The Grapes of Wrath.* **(24) Social studies skills.** The student applies critical-thinking skills to organize and use information acquired from a variety of sources including electronic technology. The student is expected to: **(C)** explain and apply different methods that historians use to interpret the past, including the use of primary and secondary sources, points of view, frames of reference, and historical context.
2 Progressive Legislation	**(4) History.** The student understands the effects of reform and third party movements on American society. The student is expected to: **(A)** evaluate the impact of Progressive Era reforms including initiative, referendum, recall, and the passage of the 16th and 17th amendments. **(12) Economics.** The student understands domestic and foreign issues related to U.S. economic growth from the 1870s to 1920. The student is expected to: **(B)** compare the purpose of the Interstate Commerce Commission with its performance over time. **(C)** describe the impact of the Sherman Antitrust Act on businesses.
3 Progressivism Under Taft and Wilson	**(4) History.** The student understands the effects of reform and third party movements on American society. The student is expected to: **(C)** evaluate the impact of third parties and their candidates such as Eugene Debs, H. Ross Perot, and George Wallace. **(8) Geography.** The student uses geographic tools to collect, analyze, and interpret data. The student is expected to: **(B)** pose and answer questions about geographic distributions and patterns shown on maps, graphs, charts, models, and databases.
4 Suffrage at Last	**(4) History.** The student understands the effects of reform and third party movements on American society. The student is expected to: **(B)** evaluate the impact of reform leaders such as Susan B. Anthony, W.E.B. DuBois, and Robert LaFollette on American society. **(5) History.** The student understands significant individuals, events, and issues of the 1920s. The student is expected to: **(A)** analyze causes and effects of significant issues such as immigration, the Red Scare, Prohibition, and the changing role of women. **(8) Geography.** The student uses geographic tools to collect, analyze, and interpret data. The student is expected to: **(B)** pose and answer questions about geographic distributions and patterns shown on maps, graphs, charts, models, and databases. **(17) Government.** The student understands the impact of constitutional issues on American society in the 20th century. The student is expected to: **(B)** analyze reasons for the adoption of 20th-century constitutional amendments. **(18) Citizenship.** The student understands efforts to expand the democratic process. The student is expected to: **(A)** identify and analyze methods of expanding the right to participate in the democratic process, including lobbying, protesting, court decisions, and amendments to the U.S. Constitution. **(B)** evaluate various means of achieving equality of political rights, including the 19th, 24th, and 26th amendments. **(21) Culture.** The student understands how people from various groups, including racial, ethnic, and religious groups, adapt to life in the United States and contribute to our national identity. The student is expected to: **(D)** identify the political, social, and economic contributions of women to American society.

Chapter 11

The Progressive Reform Era

(1890–1920)

Introducing the Chapter

At the turn of the century, many Americans hoped to change American society for the better. These reform-minded citizens, who were called Progressives, worked for many different causes at the national, state, and local levels. Many of their reforms had lasting effects on American society.

Time Line Activity

To provide students with practice in using the time line, ask questions such as these:

1. What was the aim of the Boxer Rebellion? *(To drive foreigners out of China)*
2. Which happened first: Theodore Roosevelt's third Presidential campaign, or the passage of the Clayton Antitrust Act? *(Roosevelt's third presidential campaign in 1912)*
3. What was Upton Sinclair's intention in publishing *The Jungle*? *(To expose the horrors of the meat-packing industry)*

Chapter 11

The Progressive Reform Era

(1890–1920)

Elephants carry a suffrage "plank" in a New York rally.

American Events

- **1890** The National American Woman Suffrage Association is founded.
- **1899** National Consumers' League is founded.
- **1900** Hurricane devastates Galveston, Texas; recovery produces new model for city government.

Presidential Terms: B. Harrison 1889–1893 | Grover Cleveland 1893–1897 | William McKinley 1897–1901 | Theodore Roosevelt 1901–1909

1890 · 1900

World Events

- **1900** The Boxer Rebellion fails to drive foreigners out of China.
- **1905** Albert Einstein puts forth his special theory of relativity.

eTeach

Be sure to check out this month's online discussion with a Master Teacher. Go to **www.phschool.com**.

RESOURCE DIRECTORY

Teaching Resources

Pacing Charts booklet
Block Scheduling booklet, p. 22
Units 3/4 booklet
- Chapter Summary, p. 14

Technology

Guided Reading Audiotapes (English/Spanish), Ch. 11
Student Edition on Audio CD, Ch. 11
Prentice Hall United States History Video Collection™ Volume 14, *The Progressive Movement*
Prentice Hall Presentation Pro CD-ROM, Ch. 11
Resource Pro® CD-ROM
Social Studies Skills Tutor CD-ROM
Companion Web site, www.phschool.com

Theodore Roosevelt's Conservation Legacy

Present-day national parks that originated prior to Roosevelt's administration
Present-day national monuments that originated prior to Roosevelt's administration
Present-day national parks that originated during Roosevelt's administration
Present-day national monuments that originated during Roosevelt's administration
Present-day national forests that originated during Roosevelt's administration

This first-edition copy of *The Jungle* was given by Sinclair to author Mark Twain.

1906 Upton Sinclair's *The Jungle* exposes unsanitary conditions in the meatpacking industry.

1912 Roosevelt runs for President under the new Progressive ("Bull Moose") Party and splits the GOP vote, giving the election to Wilson.

1914 The Clayton Antitrust Act gives the federal government broad anti-monopoly power.

1920 The Nineteenth Amendment is ratified.

William H. Taft 1909–1913 | Woodrow Wilson 1913–1921

1910 | 1920

1909 American Robert Peary reaches the North Pole.

1910 The Mexican Revolution begins.

1914 World War I begins in Europe.

1917 The Russian Revolution begins.

1919 The Treaty of Versailles is signed.

Theodore Roosevelt's Conservation Legacy

Activating Prior Knowledge What was the majority of the land set aside by Theodore Roosevelt intended for? *(National forests)*

Previewing Theodore Roosevelt viewed the presidency as a "bully pulpit" that he could use to rally Americans to support his causes. How does his conservation legacy illustrate this notion? *(He saw the enjoyment and appreciation of nature as an important part of American life. By setting aside so much land, he encouraged all Americans to utilize the land.)*

BACKGROUND
About the Pictures

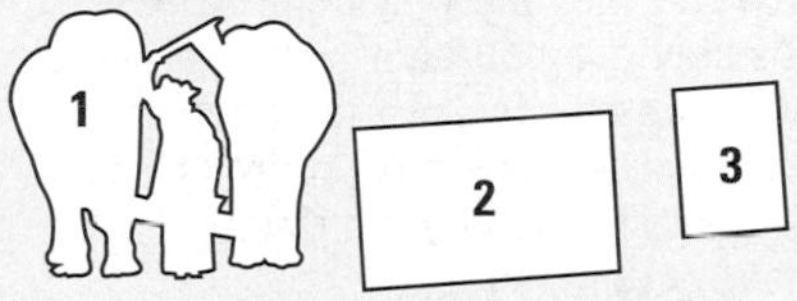

1. Elephants, the symbol of the Republican Party since the 1840s, are shown using their force and strength to represent the determination of women to gain the right to vote on a national basis.
2. The unnamed hurricane that hit Galveston, Texas, in 1900 stands as the deadliest natural disaster in United States history.
3. Upton Sinclair and other writers, dubbed "muckrakers" by President Theodore Roosevelt, used their journalistic skills to stimulate reforms.

BIBLIOGRAPHY

For the Teacher

Cott, Nancy F., editor. ***Root of Bitterness: Documents of the Social History of American Women.*** New York: Oxford, 1996. (Examines the range and depth of women's experience through historical sources such as diaries, letters, and petitions.)

Norris, Frank. ***The Octopus.*** Penguin, 1994. (Originally published in 1901, this is a classic turn-of-the-century epic of California wheat farmers struggling against the forces of greedy railroad interests.)

For the Student

Life History of the United States. Vols. 8–10. *The Progressive Era.* (Richly illustrated series by editors of *Life* magazine.)

The Progressives. McGraw Hill Films. (A brief history of the period.)

Don't miss the exclusive interactive version of this textbook on the Web and on CD-ROM.

Section 1 The Origins of Progressivism

Section Objectives

1. Learn the key goals of Progressives.
2. Find out how the ideas of progressive writers helped inspire new reform movements.
3. Discover which reform organizations and which women reformers took up progressive causes.
4. Understand why progressive reforms met with resistance.

Bellringer

Warm-Up Activity Ask students what cues they look for to determine whether they are making progress, possibly in a course or with a project. How does a society or a nation measure its progress? In what areas would students like to see the United States make progress today?

Activating Prior Knowledge Can students list the types of advancements in industry and technology that might have stimulated the Progressives to seek reforms? What political factors in this era might have stimulated reform?

Reading Strategy

As students read the section, have them create a list of the reforms the Progressives worked to bring about.

Ask them to evaluate the impact of Progressive Era reforms.

Activity

Student Portfolio

You may wish to have students add the following to their portfolios: Ask students to research and write a report on the reforms suggested and implemented by progressive educator John Dewey. Have students identify progressive elements in their own education, such as "hands-on" math and science activities, and include this information in their reports. Have students evaluate the impact of Dewey's reforms on American society. **(Verbal/Linguistic)**

Section 1

The Origins of Progressivism

READING FOCUS

- What were the key goals of Progressives?
- How did the ideas of progressive writers help to inspire new reform movements?
- What reform organizations and what women reformers took up Progressive causes?
- Why did Progressive reforms meet with resistance?

MAIN IDEA

At the end of the 1800s, problems resulting from rapid industrialization, immigration, and urban growth spurred the creation of many reform movements during what is known as the Progressive Era.

KEY TERMS

Progressive Era
muckraker
injunction

TAKING NOTES

Copy the chart below. As you read, fill in factors relating to the Progressive Era.

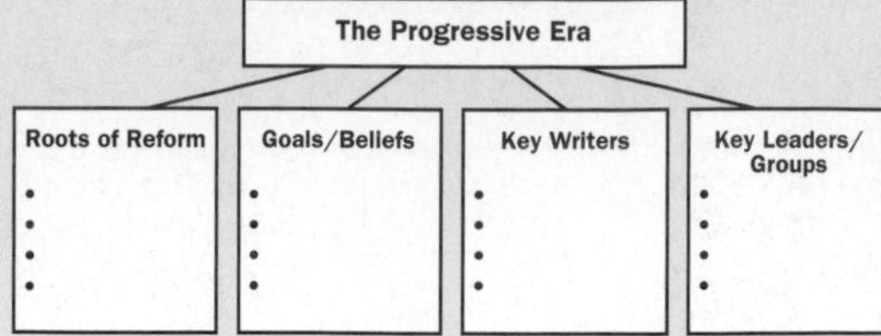

Setting the Scene In 1906, Upton Sinclair turned the nation's stomachs. That year, the writer and journalist published *The Jungle,* a novel based on his investigations of the turn-of-the-century meatpacking industry. Besides depicting the violent accidents, horrible illnesses, and painful deaths that came to packinghouse workers themselves, Sinclair sickened the public with descriptions of how meat—and what was *called* meat—was processed on the way to their dinner tables.

Workers at a Chicago stockyard package boiled hams on dingy tables. Sinclair and others pressed for tough sanitary standards in meatpacking plants.

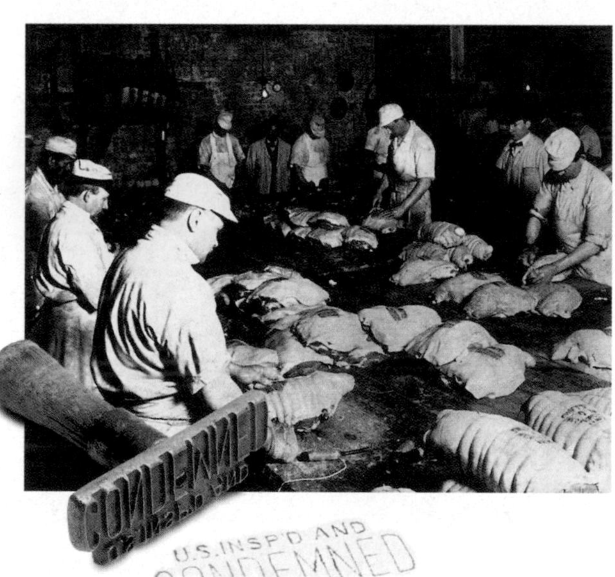

The main character in *The Jungle* is a naive, hard-working new immigrant from Lithuania who gratefully takes a job at a meatpacking house. Gradually, Sinclair's readers learn, as the worker does, the ugly secrets of what goes on inside the plant.

> *"It seemed they must have agencies all over the country, to hunt out old and crippled and diseased cattle to be canned. There were cattle which had been fed on 'whisky-malt,' the refuse [garbage] of the breweries, and had become what the men called 'steerly'—which means covered with boils. . . . It was stuff such as this that made the 'embalmed beef' that had killed several times as many United States soldiers as all the bullets of the Spaniards [in the Spanish-American War]."*
>
> —Upton Sinclair, *The Jungle*, 1906

Resource Directory

Teaching Resources

Learning Styles Lesson Plans booklet, p. 38
Guided Reading and Review booklet, p. 74
Biography, Literature, and Comparing Primary Sources booklet (Literature) *Horrors of the Meat-Packing Industry,* p. 64

Other Print Resources

American History Block Scheduling Support *The Reformers: A Struggle for Women's Rights,* found in the Prosperity, Depression, and War folder, includes interdisciplinary lesson suggestions and activities for Geography and History, Primary Sources, Biography, and Literature.

Technology

Section Reading Support Transparencies
Guided Reading Audiotapes (English/Spanish), Ch. 11
Student Edition on Audio CD, Ch. 11
Sounds of an Era Audio CD *Upton Sinclair Interview* (time: two minutes)
Exploring Primary Sources in U.S. History CD-ROM *The Jungle, Upton Sinclair*
Prentice Hall Presentation Pro CD-ROM, Ch. 11
Companion Web site, www.phschool.com

The Progressive Era

Revelations like these sent shock waves across a country that prided itself in being a modern land of progress and prosperity. Sinclair and others like him became leading figures in an era of reform movements that spread throughout American society at the turn of the twentieth century.

The Roots of Twentieth-Century Reform Many of these new reform movements were an outgrowth of earlier reform groups, such as the Populists. But while populism thrived mainly among western and southern farmers, many of the new reform movements arose in the cities of the Northeast, Midwest, and West Coast. They had their roots in movements such as nativism, prohibition, purity crusades, electoral reform, charity reform, social gospel philosophy, and the settlement houses.

The new reformers were reacting to the effects of rapid industrialization, immigration, and urbanization in the United States during the last decades of the 1800s. These changes contributed to the growth of the nation's cities and population.

Industrialization had brought a national prosperity that had come at a cost to some members of society. Industrial workers, like the farmers of the post–Civil War decades, suffered from low incomes and cycles of unemployment. Working conditions for men, women, and children in the factories were deplorable. Political corruption plagued governments at all levels.

Many Progressives maintained that private efforts to address the needs of workers, such as initiatives made by charities, were inadequate. What action, then, was needed? An active political debate produced a variety of attempts to bring about progress in society. Hence, historians refer to the period from about 1890 to 1920 as the **Progressive Era.**

The Progressives: Their Goals and Beliefs Progressivism was not a single unified movement. People who called themselves Progressives did not all share the same views. For the most part, their goals fell into four categories: social, moral, economic, and political. Some of these goals overlapped; some in fact conflicted.

Progressives included Republicans, Democrats, and members of other political parties. Yet in general, most reformers were people of average wealth who held in common at least four basic beliefs:

1. Government should be more accountable to its citizens.
2. Government should curb the power and influence of wealthy interests.
3. Government should be given expanded powers so that it could become more active in improving the lives of its citizens.
4. Governments should become more efficient and less corrupt so that they could competently handle an expanded role.

Reform in Modern Times

Urban changes and industrialization led to a period of social reforms in the 1960s and 1970s, as they had at the start of the century. Following World War II, many Americans moved from cities to new suburbs. City tax revenues declined. Economic and physical decay, inner-city poverty, and racial tensions set in. Wartime growth of heavy industry had produced workplace and environmental hazards, which were exposed by citizen activists.

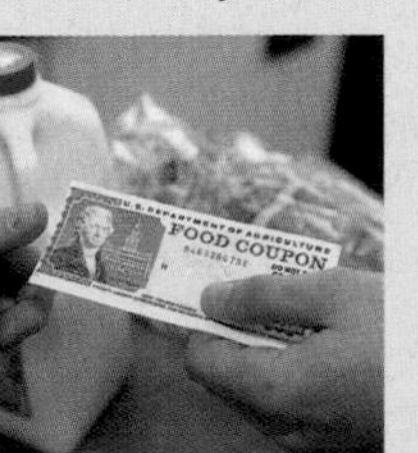

Responding to these needs, in 1964 President Lyndon B. Johnson launched his Great Society program. It established a permanent Food Stamp program; Medicare and Medicaid; and federal programs for education, immigration, literacy, jobs, and urban renewal.

Johnson's successor, Richard M. Nixon, sought to trim social programs, yet he promoted other reforms. In 1970, Nixon created the Environmental Protection Agency (EPA) to oversee the cleanup of pollution in the air, water, and soil. That same year the Occupational Safety and Health Administration (OSHA) was created to monitor workplace safety.

? What beliefs did Johnson and Nixon share with the Progressives regarding the functions of government? Explain.

Lesson Plan

Focus In the 1880s and 1890s, many concerned citizens worked to reform American society. Their efforts became known as progressivism. How did progressivism affect American life?

Instruct Discuss the theme of reform. In what ways does progressivism resemble populism? What reform ideas were new? Ask students to compare the ideas of Henry George and Edward Bellamy. What actions did each think the government should take to transform society?

Discuss the various progressive movements. How did journalists work to bring about reform? What kinds of reforms did women and labor unions hope to effect?

Assess/Reteach Ask students to suggest the types of Americans who would be drawn to support the various progressive movements. Which of the movements established at the turn of the twentieth century would be likely to find supporters today?

Background
Global Connections

In 1905, as progressivism caught fire in the United States, Einstein's theory of relativity—the idea that space and time are connected and that nothing is absolute, that even the passage of time is not uniform but varies in relation to an object's velocity—set the stage for a major rethinking of scientific truth. Publication of the more sweeping theory of general relativity in 1916 brought with it a questioning of the status quo and justified, some felt, revolutionary calls for change.

Customize for ...
ESL

Write the words *progress* and *progressive* on the chalkboard. Explain to students that progress is the root word of progressive. Have a volunteer look up *progress* in a dictionary and read the definition aloud. Have another student look up the word *progressive* and read its definition. Tell students that historians refer to the period between 1890 and 1920 as the Progressive Era. Ask them why.

Caption Answers

Fast Forward to Today Sample answer: They shared the belief that the federal government had a responsibility to provide certain services that affected Americans' health and well-being.

BACKGROUND
Connections to Today

Since *The Jungle* spurred reform in 1906, the federal government has worked to ensure the safety of the nation's food supply. Yet despite new technologies to protect food and oversight of the food industry by the Food and Drug Administration, about 5,000 deaths and about 76 million illnesses are caused by food poisoning each year. Experts say people are eating more raw and precooked foods, thus increasing the chances of infection from bacteria or viruses. Also, the variety of foods available from all over the globe has increased much faster than the FDA's ability to inspect them. Still, the American food supply remains the safest in the world.

ACTIVITY
Connecting with Citizenship

Tell students that in 1799 Thomas Jefferson wrote: "Our citizens may be deceived for awhile, and have been deceived; but as long as the presses can be protected, we may trust to them for light." Discuss the quotation's meaning as a class. Then ask: Would Thomas Jefferson have approved of the muckrakers? Have students write brief essays in response. **(Verbal/Linguistic)**

READING CHECK
Progressives pressed for efficient, honest, accountable government. They wanted government to be strong enough to protect the public from abuse at the hands of capitalists and bankers.

Igniting Reform: Writers and Their New Ideas

From the 1880s into the new century, lively debates emerged about how to reform society. The ideas of journalists and other writers had enormous influence on public opinion.

READING CHECK
In your own words, summarize the main beliefs of Progressives.

Two Early Reformers In 1879, reformer Henry George wrote *Progress and Poverty,* an effort to explain why poverty continued to plague such an advanced civilization. George, a journalist and self-taught economist, concluded that poverty arose because some people bought and held on to land until its price went up. This practice, known as speculation, prevented others from using the land productively.

To solve this problem, George proposed that the government charge landowners a single tax on the value of the land itself. In the past, landowners had been taxed on improvements to the land, such as houses and cultivation. A single tax would make speculation in land less attractive by increasing the cost of holding land without using it. George's ideas had a powerful effect. "Single tax" clubs sprang up everywhere.

In 1888, newspaper editor Edward Bellamy published *Looking Backward.* In this novel, a Boston man undergoes hypnosis in 1887 and wakes up in the year 2000. Upon waking, the man finds the United States transformed. In place of harsh working conditions, poverty, and political corruption, he finds a utopian country where the government has taken over the largest companies. The government has also reorganized the companies with the goal of meeting human needs rather than making profits. Bellamy wrote:

> "*In a word, the people of the United States concluded to assume the conduct of their own business, just as . . . years before they had assumed the conduct of their own government.*"
>
> —Edward Bellamy, *Looking Backward,* 1888

Bellamy's novel was a phenomenal bestseller. In response, more than 150 "Nationalist" clubs formed to promote his ideas. Bellamy's views also influenced the Populist Party platform in 1892.

INTERPRETING POLITICAL CARTOONS Theodore Roosevelt himself was willing to wield the muckrake to attack social problems. Here, he tries to clean up the meatpacking industry. **Determining Relevance** *(a) What does the rake represent, and how would the President use it to solve the problem? (b) What is the significance of the U.S. Capitol in the background?*

A DISGUSTING JOB BUT IT MUST BE DONE.

The Muckrakers Many reformers at the turn of the century worked to bring about change in a systematic manner. Relying heavily on scientific data and expert testimony, they first investigated issues of concern, such as conditions in slums and sweatshops. They then publicized the results of their investigations, so that the public would pressure legislators to pass and enforce new laws. Women's clubs and charitable groups provided leadership in pressuring officials to implement reforms.

Journalists such as Upton Sinclair played a key role in alerting the public to wrongdoing in politics and business. Theodore Roosevelt called such writers **muckrakers.** A *muckrake* is a rake or pitchfork used to clean manure and hay out of stables. Roosevelt took the term *muckraker* from John Bunyan's 1678 book *Pilgrim's Progress,* in which one of the characters was too busy raking filth on Earth to lift his eyes to heaven.

While Roosevelt approved of the legitimate exposure of wrongdoing, he condemned those who "earn their

CAPTION ANSWERS

Interpreting Political Cartoons (a) The rake represents federal regulations and standards intended to clean up the meatpacking industry and make meat products safe for consumers. (b) The Capitol refers to the pressure Roosevelt put on Congress to pass laws regulating the industry.

RESOURCE DIRECTORY
Teaching Resources
Biography, Literature, and Comparing Primary Sources booklet (Biography) *Ida Tarbell,* p. 23

VIEWING HISTORY New York City garment workers march on a picket line, holding protest signs in English and Hebrew (left); the National Women's Trade Union League (below) was founded in 1903 after the American Federation of Labor (AFL) continued to ban women from its ranks. **Recognizing Bias** *What barriers to fair treatment might both of these groups, male and female, have encountered on the job? Explain.*

livelihood by telling . . . scandalous falsehoods about honest men." Yet when Roosevelt read Upton Sinclair's *The Jungle,* he wrote the young novelist that "the specific evils you point out shall, if their existence be proved, and if I have power, be eradicated."

Despite the exaggerations of some authors, the muckrakers included many respected writers who identified and exposed serious abuses. Journalist Lincoln Steffens uncovered political corruption in St. Louis and other cities. In the 1904 book *The History of the Standard Oil Company,* Ida Tarbell, an investigative journalist, editor, teacher, and lecturer, revealed the abuses committed by the Standard Oil Trust.

Progressive Reform Organizations

Americans read the muckrakers' novels and newspaper accounts with enthusiasm. Whether angered or sickened by what they read, many Americans were inspired to take action by joining reform groups.

READING CHECK What factors prompted Americans to join reform organizations?

The Labor Movement The union movement grew in the 1890s, but only slowly. Employers discouraged union membership, preferring to deal with individual workers. If unions succeeded in forming, business leaders could often count on courts to issue **injunctions,** court orders that prohibit a certain activity. Courts often issued injunctions preventing workers from going on strike. Unions, however, continued to fight for better working conditions through collective rather than individual bargaining.

Socialists The Progressive Era saw a rise in the popularity of socialism, an economic and political philosophy favoring public or government control of property and income. Many American Socialists of this era wanted to end the capitalist system, distribute wealth more equally, and have government ownership of American industries. Writers Edward Bellamy and Upton Sinclair, among others, promoted Socialist ideas. Bellamy's *Looking Backward,* in particular, appealed to a wide spectrum of Americans, from military men to progressive women. Socialism also attracted some union members who hoped for fundamental change in the way the economy was organized.

Most Socialists hoped to accomplish their goals through the ballot box, not through revolution. In 1901 they formed the Socialist Party of America. By

Activity
Connecting with Culture

The labor movement of this period produced its own literature of protest and work songs. Ask students to locate the lyrics and music, or recordings, of some of the songs popular with workers of the time. (A good source is *Songs of Work and Protest* by Edith Fowke and Joe Glazer, New York: Dover Publications, 1973.) Possible songs include "Hallelujah, I'm a Bum," "The Preacher and the Slave," "Hold the Fort," "Bread and Roses," and "Solidarity Forever." Ask students to describe how the characteristics and issues of the Progressive Era were reflected in this music. Invite interested students to work together to perform the songs for the class. **(Musical/Rhythmic)**

Background
Interdisciplinary

Progressive ideas were slow to gain acceptance in the world of literature. Theodore Dreiser's first novel, *Sister Carrie* (1900), with its gritty depictions of urban life and a heroine who goes unpunished for her sins, was apparently too shocking for its time. The book failed miserably at first, selling fewer than 700 copies. It was rediscovered in later years and today is regarded as an important book for those who want to gain insight into issues and attitudes of the Progressive Era.

READING CHECK
Industrialization and urbanization had changed society in many ways. The writings of muckrakers and other reformers exposed serious problems that needed to be corrected.

TEST PREPARATION

Have students read the paragraph on this page called "The Labor Movement" and then complete the sentence below.

The main reason the union movement grew slowly in the 1890s is that—

- **A** not many immigrants were working in companies with unions.
- **B** most workers were opposed to unions.
- **Ⓒ** most employers discouraged union membership.
- **D** it was illegal to create new unions at this time.

Caption Answers

Viewing History Women, along with certain ethnic groups such as the Jewish men seen in the photograph, were often kept in low-level, low-paying jobs. Women and Jewish men often were paid less than non-Jewish men who did exactly the same work.

VIEWING HISTORY The International Ladies Garment Workers Union was formed in 1900. Activists such as those shown above fought hard to organize the garment industry. **Recognizing Cause and Effect** *Why do you think women activists targeted the garment industry, in particular, for reforms?*

1912 the party had won more than 1,000 city government offices.

Unlike the Socialists and some more radical reformers, most Progressives did not support sweeping economic and political changes. They did not want to lose the high standard of living and personal liberties that democracy and a free enterprise system had given them. Instead, Progressives wanted to free the existing government of corruption and refocus its energies toward guarding the welfare of workers and the poor.

Women's Groups Rising to new levels of civic activism, women played a pivotal role in the reform movements of the Progressive Era. Influential women's organizations formed around nearly every major reform issue.

One leading women's group was the National Consumers' League (NCL), organized in 1899 to unite local consumers' leagues. Through these groups, women investigated the conditions under which goods were made and sold. They also encouraged consumers to purchase goods only at shops that did not employ children or require overtime. Leagues insisted that factories obey state factory inspection laws and pay a minimum wage.

Although they shared many goals, Progressive women did not all agree on methods for reforming society. For example, from her perspective in an impoverished urban neighborhood, social worker Jane Addams made an argument that not all reformers shared. She maintained that women in cities needed government help in order to care for their families:

> "*Women who live in the country sweep their own dooryards and may either feed the refuse [scraps] of the table to a flock of chickens or allow it innocently to decay in the open air and sunshine. In a crowded city quarter, however, if the street is not cleaned by the city authorities no amount of private sweeping will keep the tenement free from grime; if the garbage is not properly collected and destroyed a tenement house mother may see her children sicken and die of diseases.*"
>
> —Jane Addams, *Ladies' Home Journal* article, 1910

READING CHECK
What types of groups became involved in Progressive reforms?

Whatever their interests, many women agreed that they needed the right to vote. The cause of women's suffrage was important to many Progressives.

Two Women Reformers

Because so many urban women and children worked in factories, women's organizations took a special interest in workplace reforms. Among the numerous women who rose to national prominence in labor movements were Florence Kelley and Mary Harris "Mother" Jones.

Florence Kelley A leader in the work for labor reform, Florence Kelley joined Jane Addams's Hull House in Chicago in 1891. When federal officials asked Addams to investigate local labor conditions, she recommended Kelley for the job. Largely through Kelley's efforts, in 1893 Illinois passed a law prohibiting child labor, limiting working hours for women, and regulating

ACTIVITY
Connecting with History and Conflict

While they did not have voting power, women often created ways to push progressive reform when legislators were slow to cooperate. Businesses that supported progressive social reform, for example, were put on a list of places where women should do their shopping. In order to be named to this "White List," businesses needed to meet certain criteria in harmony with reform. Divide students into groups to create at least five criteria suitable for a White List of today. Then have the groups compare their lists and justify their choices. **(Logical/Mathematical)**

BACKGROUND
Art History

The spirit of iconoclasm that marked the Progressive Era produced an important new movement in art known as the Ashcan school. Emerging in the early 1900s, it was led by a diverse group of painters known as "the Eight." These artists, among them Robert Henri, John Sloan, and Arthur B. Davies, rejected the conventional portraits and landscapes that had been the staple of nineteenth-century art. Instead, they depicted urban scenes, showing city life in all its shabby vitality. While the style of the art was conservative, the gritty realism of its content was entirely new.

READING CHECK
Women's groups, labor unions, and Socialists.

CAPTION ANSWERS

Viewing History Workplace conditions in the garment industry were some of the worst. That industry also employed large numbers of women and children.

RESOURCE DIRECTORY

Teaching Resources

Units 3/4 booklet
- Section 1 Quiz, p. 15

Guide to the Essentials
- Section 1 Summary, p. 53

sweatshop conditions. The governor put Kelley in charge of enforcing the law. She became so frustrated by the district attorney's refusal to prosecute cases that she earned a law degree in order to take legal action herself.

Kelley later served as general secretary of the National Consumers' League. Under her leadership, the NCL spearheaded national movements to outlaw child labor and protect workers, especially women. When criticized, Kelley would ask why "seals, bears, reindeer, fish, wild game in the national parks, buffalo" and numerous other creatures were worthy of government protection, "but not the children of our race and their mothers."

Mother Jones Irish immigrant Mary Harris Jones came to the reform movement late in her life, inspired by personal convictions and tragedies. Her husband, an iron worker, and her four children died in a yellow fever epidemic in Tennessee in 1867. She rebuilt her life, establishing a successful dressmaking business. Then, in 1871, she lost everything in the Great Chicago Fire.

From her laborer husband, Jones had learned of the difficult working conditions in factories. Now she also discovered what it meant to be poor and alone. She appealed to the Knights of Labor for assistance, and became interested in its efforts to improve workplace conditions. In the labor movement, "Mother Jones," as she came to be called, found her life's work. Across the country, she organized unions for workers, both men and women. A tireless worker, Jones became best known for organizing unions in the mines of West Virginia and Colorado. These mines had some of the worst working conditions. Company resistance to unions often turned violent. Well into her eighties, Jones gave fiery speeches at rallies, uttering her famous call, "Join the union, boys!"

Jones became a national speaker on behalf of both unions and child labor laws. In 1905, she helped found the International Workers of the World (IWW).

Florence Kelley (top) and Mary Harris "Mother" Jones (below) were two of the nation's most active women reformers.

Progressive Reforms Meet With Resistance

Progressives sought increased government involvement in people's lives—in housing, health care, and even in the content of the movies. This aspect of progressivism provoked resistance, often among the very people Progressives hoped to help. For example, Progressives saw child labor laws as critical to social progress. Yet, poor families who could not survive without the wages of their working children opposed the laws. Such disputes added to the perception that Progressives were insensitive to the poor.

Section 1 Assessment

READING COMPREHENSION

1. What were some of the historical roots of the **Progressive Era?**
2. How did Henry George and Edward Bellamy influence the rise of progressivism?
3. How did **injunctions** affect the growth of labor unions?
4. Identify some Progressive women's groups and their causes.

CRITICAL THINKING AND WRITING

5. **Recognizing Ideologies** What beliefs did most Progressives share?
6. **Writing to Persuade** Write a letter to the editor of a 1905 newspaper arguing why the paper should publish articles by muckrakers.

Take It to the NET

Activity: Writing a Summary
Choose a reform issue or organization from the Progressive Era and write a summary on how it survives today. Use the links provided in the *America: Pathways to the Present* area of the following Web site for help in completing this activity.
www.phschool.com

Section 1 Assessment

Reading Comprehension

1. Answers may include: nativism; prohibition; purity crusades; charity reform; social gospel philosophy; settlement houses.
2. Henry George: Combat poverty by charging a single tax to landowners based on the value of the land itself, discouraging speculation and decreasing poverty. Edward Bellamy: Government should take over the largest companies and reorganize them to focus more on human needs than on profits. Led to the development of "Nationalist" clubs; influenced the Populist Party platform.
3. They made it more difficult to go on strike. However, unions continued to fight through collective bargaining.
4. Answers may include: International Ladies Garment Workers Union to organize the garment industry; National Women's Trade Union League fought for labor laws; National Consumers' League fought to outlaw child labor and protect workers.

Critical Thinking and Writing

5. In general, Progressives wanted to rid the government of corruption and expand its role to regulate economic activity and enhance human welfare.
6. Answers will vary, but might state that while muckraking articles tend to be somewhat one-sided, they also point out some of the worst abuses in an industrializing society.

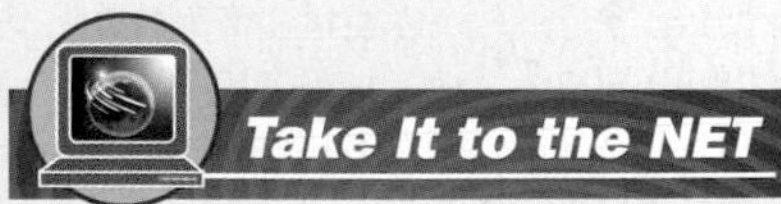

Sample answer: The Food and Drug Administration was founded during the Progressive Era and initially had limited powers. Through public support and legal initiatives, the FDA became the official regulating group for all food and drugs. It continues to oversee food and drug testing and regulations today.

Drawing and Testing Conclusions

Focus Students learn to analyze data to support a conclusion, and also how to test statements or opinions against facts to check a conclusion's validity.

Instruct Discuss with students the steps necessary to draw a conclusion and test its validity. Ask students to brainstorm ways to gather the necessary information to reach a conclusion. How can they check the validity of information they've gathered? How will they know when they have enough data? What steps should they take to sort through the information that is gathered so they may focus just on those pieces that are necessary to use in forming a conclusion? To validate the approach suggested in the book, ask students to describe other situations in which they would follow the same steps to draw and test conclusions.

Extend See the Skills for Life activity in the Resource Directory below.

ANSWERS

Practice the Skill

1. **(a)** The "Work Force and Labor Union Membership" chart.
   (b) Conclusion 2: Data is from "Average Union and Nonunion Hours and Earnings in Manufacturing Industries" chart. Conclusion 3: Data is from "Work Force and Labor Union Membership" chart. Conclusion 4: There is not sufficient data in the charts to test this conclusion. **(c)** The data support conclusions 1 and 2. They contradict conclusion 3, and are insufficient to evaluate conclusion 4.
2. **(a)** Conclusion 1 deals with a trend. **(b)** No.
3. **(a)** Percentage of total workforce in unions increased by 8.9% in the years between 1900 and 1920. **(b)** The data contradict conclusion 3. **(c)** No data is given that indicates the earnings that were last due to work stoppages. Therefore, Conclusion 4 is not valid.

Drawing and Testing Conclusions

Drawing conclusions involves using available and reliable information to find an answer or to form an opinion. Testing conclusions means checking statements or opinions against data known to be valid. If the data support the conclusion, then you have reason to believe the conclusion is sound.

Read the conclusions below. Note that the first one has been left for you to complete. Then examine the data in the tables.

Conclusions:

1. The 20-year period between 1900 and 1920 saw a steady and significant _______ in union membership.
2. By 1920, union workers earned more money than nonunion workers while working fewer hours.
3. In terms of a percent of the work force, more workers were union members in 1910 than in 1920.
4. The reason the vast majority of workers did not join labor unions in the early 1900s was that work stoppages led to pay stoppages and decreased earnings.

Work Force and Labor Union Membership

Year	Total Workers	Total Union Membership	Percentage of Work Force in Unions
1900	29,073,000	868,000	3.0
1910	37,371,000	2,140,000	5.7
1920	42,434,000	5,048,000	11.9

Union Membership by Industry

Year	Building	Textiles	Public Service
1900	153,000	8,000	15,000
1910	459,000	21,000	58,000
1920	888,000	149,000	161,000

Average Union and Nonunion Hours and Earnings in Manufacturing Industries

	Union		Nonunion	
Year	Weekly Hours	Hourly Earnings	Weekly Hours	Hourly Earnings
1900	53.0	$0.341	62.1	$0.152
1910	50.1	$0.403	59.8	$0.188
1920	45.7	$0.884	53.5	$0.561

SOURCE: *Historical Statistics of the United States, Colonial Times to 1970*

LEARN THE SKILL

Use the following steps to draw conclusions and to test their validity:

1. **Identify the type of data that is necessary to draw conclusions about your topic or to verify existing conclusions.** Consider the issue about which you want to draw a conclusion, or study existing conclusions you wish to verify. If supporting data are provided, decide if they are useful for the conclusions.
2. **Decide on the criteria by which the conclusions could be made or tested.** Conclusions based on trends require data that cover a period of time. Other more specific conclusions may need exact data.
3. **Draw conclusions by analyzing the data, or test the conclusions by comparing them with the data.** Decide whether there are sufficient data to draw a sound conclusion, and be sure you interpret the data correctly. To test conclusions, decide whether the data support or contradict the conclusions and whether additional information is needed to determine the validity of some conclusions.

PRACTICE THE SKILL

Answer the following questions:

1. **(a)** Consider the data needed to complete Conclusion 1. Which chart supplies these data? **(b)** Upon what data is each of the other conclusions based? **(c)** Are these data useful for either supporting or contradicting these conclusions?
2. **(a)** Does Conclusion 1 deal with a trend or with a specific point in time? **(b)** Would data covering a period of time be needed to support Conclusion 2?
3. **(a)** Use the data to complete Conclusion 1. **(b)** Do the data support or contradict Conclusion 3? **(c)** Do the data give you reason to agree with Conclusion 4? Explain.

APPLY THE SKILL

See the Chapter Review and Assessment for another opportunity to apply this skill.

RESOURCE DIRECTORY

Teaching Resources
Skills for Life booklet, p. 20

Technology
Social Studies Skills Tutor CD-ROM
Interactive Practice in
- Geographic Literacy
- Critical Thinking and Reading
- Visual Analysis
- Communications

Section 2 Progressive Legislation

READING FOCUS

- How did Progressives wish to expand the role of government?
- What municipal and state reforms did Progressives achieve?
- What federal reforms did Theodore Roosevelt champion as President?

MAIN IDEA

Because of public demand, local, state, and federal officials enacted major Progressive reforms in the early 1900s.

KEY TERMS

social welfare program
municipal
home rule
direct primary
initiative
referendum
recall
holding company

TAKING NOTES

In the left-hand column of the chart below, list Progressive reforms. As you read, place checkmarks to indicate what level(s) of government initiated each type of reform.

Progressive Reform	Municipal	State	Federal
Fight government corruption	√	√	√
Home rule	√		

Setting the Scene On March 25, 1911, about 500 workers, mostly Italian and Jewish girls, were on the job at the Triangle Shirtwaist Company. The company, which occupied the upper floors of a 10-story building in New York City, made tailored women's blouses. In the supposedly fireproof building, a small fire broke out. Feeding on fabric and rubbish, it swelled into an inferno.

Some workers fled to safety through the one open stairway to the roof. Surging to the other exits, employees found doors locked from the outside. Others piled onto the single, rusted fire escape; it collapsed, plunging them to their deaths. Ladders on the fire trucks were not long enough to reach the upper floors, so desperate women, their dresses aflame, leaped into the firemen's nets below. The nets tore open, killing many who fell to the pavement. Those trapped above perished in smoke and flames, some still hunched over their sewing machines. A total of 146 workers died.

In the aftermath, 29-year-old labor leader Rose Schneiderman addressed a public meeting held to discuss the causes of the fire. A Jewish immigrant from Poland, Schneiderman would become one of the nation's best-known women labor leaders. She attacked government resistance to reform:

> "*Every week I must learn of the untimely death of one of my sister workers. . . . But every time the workers come out in the only way they know to protest against conditions which are unbearable, the strong hand of the law is allowed to press down heavily upon us.*"
>
> —Rose Schneiderman, public address, 1911

Schneiderman helped stir powerful public support for reforms. Public and private groups called on the city to appoint fire inspectors, to make fire drills compulsory, to unlock and fireproof exits, and to require automatic sprinklers in buildings more than seven stories high. New York's Tammany government bowed to the pressure and adopted new workplace protections.

Firefighters wage a losing battle against the deadly blaze in the upper floors of the 10-story, 135-foot Asch Building housing the Triangle Shirtwaist Company.

Section 2 Progressive Legislation

SECTION OBJECTIVES

1. Read about how Progressives wished to expand the role of government.
2. Discover the municipal and state reforms achieved by Progressives.
3. Learn what federal reforms Theodore Roosevelt championed as President.

BELLRINGER

Warm-Up Activity Ask students to consider this statement by former Speaker of the House Thomas P. "Tip" O'Neill, Jr.: "All politics is local [politics]." Do students agree or disagree?

Activating Prior Knowledge After a period of rapid change, it is often necessary to slow down for a bit and regroup to assess the larger impacts of the changes that have taken place. In some ways, the era of progressive legislation marked such a point in United States history. Can students pinpoint a time in their own lives during which they experienced rapid change, followed by a period of reassessment?

READING STRATEGY

As students read the chapter, have them create a cause-and-effect chart. Under the heading "cause," have them list events that served as stimuli to reforms. Under the heading "effect," have them list legislation that resulted.

RESOURCE DIRECTORY

Teaching Resources

Guided Reading and Review booklet, p. 75

Other Print Resources

Nystrom *Atlas of Our Country* *The Third Wave of Immigration,* pp. 30–31

Technology

Section Reading Support Transparencies
Guided Reading Audiotapes (English/Spanish), Ch. 11
Student Edition on Audio CD, Ch. 11
Prentice Hall Presentation Pro CD-ROM, Ch. 11
Companion Web site, www.phschool.com

Lesson Plan

Focus Progressives succeeded in passing many reform bills in local, state, and federal legislatures. What were these laws, and what did they accomplish?

Instruct Discuss the alliance between machine politicians and reformers. What were they able to accomplish together? Why were they able to make more improvements by working together?

Ask what state and federal reforms were passed to protect workers. What was done to improve social conditions in the cities? Ask why it was important for city dwellers that utilities be regulated.

Discuss how state legislatures empowered voters. In what ways did voters gain more influence in government during the Progressive Era?

Assess/Reteach Ask students to list some ways in which demands from the public stirred the movement toward reform. Were there some types of reform that people in general wanted to see, but that government failed to provide?

Activity
Connecting with Economics

Discussing social welfare programs raises the question of how such programs should be financed. Progressives opposed the tariff as being unfair to poor people. They supported a progressive income tax to distribute the burden of taxation more fairly. Stage a classroom debate over the relative merits and fairness of the tariff versus the progressive income tax. To further the discussion, have students study the relative merits of three different types of tax codes—proportional, progressive, and regressive—and have them write brief descriptions of the positive and negative aspects of each. **(Logical/Mathematical)**

READING CHECK
Curbing the power of state governments and political bosses through home rule and civil service reform, respectively; ensuring the equitable delivery of services, such as public utilities and welfare programs.

Focus on GOVERNMENT

Good Government Clubs Determined to clean up corruption and make governments operate with business efficiency, a Good Government movement arose in the 1880s. Good Government clubs throughout the country promoted Progressive reforms and attracted new recruits, creating fertile ground for the future Progressive Party. In 1894, the clubs held a national conference in Philadelphia, with future President and Progressive Party candidate Theodore Roosevelt as the key speaker. The conference led to the founding of the National Municipal League. Municipal leagues thrive in many cities today.

An Expanded Role for Government

Rose Schneiderman was one of many Progressive leaders who sought more government regulation to protect workers' rights and business competition. But most Progressives opposed government control of businesses, except for companies that supplied essential services such as water and electricity.

Progressives also believed that government ought to increase its responsibility for the welfare, or well-being, of people. They sought more **social welfare programs,** which help ensure a minimum standard of living. Progressives pressed for social welfare programs such as unemployment benefits, accident and health insurance, and a social security system for the disabled and the elderly. Progressives envisioned a government that relied on experts and scientists to plan efficient programs managed by professionals, not politicians.

Municipal Reforms

Many of the earliest Progressive reforms were made at the city, or **municipal,** level. Those seeking reform of municipal governments came from within and outside of those governments. Cities were home to most of the settlement workers, club members, and professionals who pressed for changes. Some municipal reformers worked for **home rule,** a system that gives cities a limited degree of self-rule. Home rule allowed cities to escape domination by state governments controlled by political machines or by business or rural interests.

Municipal reformers sometimes seemed naive in their belief that they could abolish corruption. Some reformers also held negative views of immigrants, who they felt were responsible for many city problems. Still, the ideas of municipal activists formed an important part of the era's spirit of reform.

READING CHECK
Describe some of the goals of municipal reformers.

Attacking the Bosses Municipal reformers opposed the influence of political bosses. They argued that only a civil service system based on merit instead of favors would keep political appointees out of important jobs, such as those enforcing labor and public safety laws.

For the most part, political machines and bosses survived such attacks. In 1896, for example, Columbia University president Seth Low ran for mayor of New York City, supported by municipal reformers. To help in his campaign

against Tammany Hall's ward bosses, settlement houses sent children out to post handbills in their neighborhoods. Low lost that election but won in 1901. Still, the Tammany Hall machine returned to power in the next election.

In some cities, however, voter support for reforms prompted machine politicians to work with reformers. Together they improved city services, established public health programs and workplace reforms, and enforced tenement codes.

New Forms of Municipal Government Like the Triangle Shirtwaist fire, other catastrophes served to bring about reforms. On September 8, 1900, a powerful hurricane in the Gulf of Mexico slammed into the city of Galveston, Texas. The storm left more than 6,000 people dead when its 120-mile-per-hour winds and surging waves pounded the unprotected city for 18 hours. To manage the huge relief and rebuilding effort needed, the city created an emergency commission of five administrators to replace the mayor and aldermen. The commission handled the rebuilding with such efficiency that Galveston permanently instituted the commission form of government. Other cities rapidly adopted the Galveston model, adapting it to their needs.

In March 1913, Ohio's Great Miami River Basin flooded the city of Dayton, killing 360 people and causing damage of more than $100 million. In the aftermath, Dayton became the first large city to adopt a council-manager government. Typically, this system includes an elected city council, which sets laws and appoints a professional city manager to run city services.

Cities Take Over Utilities Reformers made efforts to regulate or dislodge the monopolies that provided city utilities such as water, gas, and electricity. Reform mayors Hazen S. Pingree of Detroit (1889–1897), Samuel M. Jones of Toledo (1897–1904), and Tom Johnson of Cleveland (1901–1909) worked within existing government structures to pioneer city control or ownership of utilities. By 1915, nearly two out of three cities had some city-owned utilities.

Providing Welfare Services Some reform mayors led movements for city-supported welfare services. Pingree provided public baths, parks, and a work-relief program for Detroit. Jones opened playgrounds, free kindergartens, and lodging houses for the homeless in Toledo. In his view, all people would become good citizens if social conditions were good.

VIEWING HISTORY The coastal city of Galveston, Texas, lacked a retaining wall to protect it from the powerful hurricanes that blow ashore from the Gulf of Mexico. In 1900, after a huge storm left wind and flood devastation, the city needed a new type of government to manage the relief and rebuilding effort. **Drawing Inferences** *What features or qualities would a municipal government need to handle a reconstruction job of the magnitude seen here?*

ACTIVITY
Connecting with Geography

Have students locate Galveston, Texas, and Dayton, Ohio, on a map. Discuss why each city is vulnerable to flooding. Then have students pinpoint other cities that they think would be vulnerable to flooding and tell why. **(Visual/Spatial)**

BACKGROUND
Recent Scholarship

At midnight on New Year's Eve, 1897, the nation's first- and fourth-largest cities—New York City and Brooklyn—officially merged to become (with Queens, Staten Island, and the Bronx) the megalopolis known as Greater New York. In *Gotham*, historians Edwin G. Burrows and Mike Wallace detail the history of the city's consolidation. Calling it "a municipal counterpart of the giant corporations busily being born," the authors portray municipal expansion and annexation as urban imperialism, not unlike that of "nationalist jingoes, railroad magnates, and corporate financiers."

BACKGROUND
A Diverse Nation

The nation's big cities were bursting with immigrants during the Progressive Era. According to the 1910 census, 13,515,886 immigrants entered the United States during the previous decade. Of those, approximately 3 million were eastern European, 2.3 million were German, and 1.3 million were Irish. The nation's largest city that year was New York, with a population of 4,766,883. Fully 40 percent of New Yorkers (about 2 million) were foreign born, providing a seemingly inexhaustible supply of labor for the city's factories and sweatshops.

TEST PREPARATION

Have students read the material on this page under the heading "New Forms of Municipal Government" and answer the question below.

Which of the following cities established a commission form of government following a natural disaster?

Ⓐ Galveston, Texas
B Detroit, Michigan
C New York City
D Dayton, Ohio

CAPTION ANSWERS

Viewing History Answers should include: Strong, honest leadership with clear-cut lines of responsibility; proper oversight to prevent the misuse or waste of cleanup funds; the ability to raise money to fund the rebuilding.

ACTIVITY
Connecting with Government

After discussing how progressive reforms at the state level gave more power to citizens, ask students: What law would you like to see passed if you had the power? Then have them work individually or in groups to write their own ballot initiatives or referenda. Have students explain how participation in the democratic process reflects our national identity. Afterward, discuss and vote on students' initiatives as a class.

ACTIVITY
Connecting with Science and Technology

In 1913 the new technology of moving pictures was used to improve the efficiency of factory workers. In a time-and-motion study at a factory in Providence, Rhode Island, a motion picture camera operator filmed a worker assembling a braiding machine. Based on the film, "waste motions" were eliminated. Afterward the worker assembled the machine in less than a quarter of the time previously needed.

Have students with access to video cameras use them to conduct their own time-and-motion studies. They should study a daily activity, such as making lunch, to see how quickly and efficiently it can be done. As they work, have them analyze the impact of technological innovations, such as the motion picture, on the nature of work. Have groups share their results with the class. **(Visual/Spatial; Bodily/Kinesthetic)**

State Reforms

Some governors and state legislators also promoted progressive reforms. Like the reform mayors, Progressives at the state level first worked to oust party bosses and give more power to citizens. Then they passed laws to increase the role of government in business regulation and social welfare.

More Power to Voters During the Progressive Era, voters gained more direct influence in lawmaking and in choosing candidates. (See diagram below.) Throughout the country, party leaders traditionally had handpicked candidates for public office. In Wisconsin, reform governor Robert M. La Follette instituted a **direct primary,** an election in which citizens vote to select nominees for upcoming elections. By 1916, all but three states had direct primaries. Many states also instituted the **initiative,** a process in which citizens can put a proposed new law directly on the ballot in the next election by collecting voters' signatures on a petition. Another lawmaking reform was the **referendum,** a process that allows citizens to approve or reject a law passed by the legislature. The **recall** procedure permits voters to remove public officials from office before the next election.

In 1904, Oregon began allowing voters, rather than the state legislature, to choose their United States senators. In 1913, the Seventeenth Amendment, allowing the direct election of senators, was ratified by the states.

Progressive Political Reforms

Before		Reforms	After
	Party leaders choose candidates for state and local offices.	**Direct Primaries** Voters select their party's candidates.	Power moves to voters.
	State legislatures choose U.S. senators.	**17th Amendment** U.S. senators are elected by popular vote.	
	Only members of the state legislature can introduce bills.	**Initiative** Voters can put bills before the legislature.	
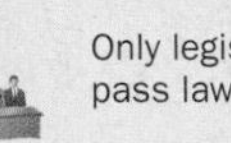	Only legislators pass laws.	**Referendum** Voters can vote on bills directly.	
	Only courts or the legislature can remove corrupt officials.	**Recall** Voters can remove elected officials from office.	

INTERPRETING DIAGRAMS This diagram shows the effects of some of the major reforms achieved by Progressives at all levels of government. **Synthesizing Information** *What type of reform do all these measures address, and why were such changes so important to Progressives?*

Reforms in the Workplace Motivated in part by the Triangle Shirtwaist fire, state reformers worked to curb workplace hazards. Some states established labor departments to provide information and dispute-resolution services to employers and employees. Other states developed workers' accident insurance and compensation systems. However, government efforts to control working conditions met legal opposition. Business owners contended that the government could not interfere with their constitutional right to make contracts with their employees. They also maintained that government workplace regulations violated their private property rights by attempting to dictate how they used their property.

The courts generally upheld these views. Reformers argued that the Constitution reserves police powers to the states, and the states could use these powers to intervene in the workplace to protect workers.

In principle, the courts acknowledged the reformers' reasoning. But in the case of *Lochner* v. *New York* (1905), the Supreme Court struck down a law setting maximum hours for bakers. The Court said that since the law had not been shown to protect public health, the law constituted an improper use of the state's police power and "an illegal interference with the rights of individuals . . . to make contracts."

The justices left open the possibility that if such a law *could* be shown to protect workers' health, it would be permissible. Reformers used this strategy in

CAPTION ANSWERS

Interpreting Diagrams The measures address voting reform, without which, the Progressives believed, citizens could not participate fully in the process of cleaning up government and making it more efficient and responsive.

Muller v. *Oregon*. In this 1908 case, the Court upheld an Oregon law that limited hours for female laundry workers to 10 hours a day. Reform lawyer Louis D. Brandeis represented the interests of the laundry workers. Using scientific evidence gathered by activists in the National Consumers' League, he argued that women's long work hours in laundries harmed their health.

Labor reformers succeeded on other fronts as well. By 1907, nearly two thirds of the states had abolished child labor, often defined as employment of children under the age of 14. Minimum wage laws for women and children also made headway, with Florence Kelley leading a national campaign. After Massachusetts adopted a minimum wage in 1912, eight other states followed.

Wisconsin's Reform Governor One of the most determined Progressives in U.S. politics was Robert M. La Follette of Wisconsin. "Fighting Bob" earned his nickname through efforts to clean up government and produce social welfare reforms. In three terms as a Progressive Republican governor (1901–1906), La Follette ousted party bosses and brought about structural changes such as a direct primary and civil service reform.

La Follette introduced a new way of running state government. He called on academic experts to help draft reform legislation. To get it passed, he had the voting roll call read publicly in the districts of legislators who opposed reform. He drew on academics and citizen committees to run regulatory agencies. The "Wisconsin Idea" of a public–academic alliance to improve government became known nationwide.

> *"If it can be shown that Wisconsin is a happier and better state to live in, that its institutions are more democratic, that the opportunities of all its people are more equal, that social justice more nearly prevails, that human life is safer and sweeter—then I shall rest content in the feeling that the Progressive movement has been successful. . . . [T]here is no reason now why the movement should not expand until it covers the entire nation."*
>
> —Robert M. La Follette, from his autobiography, *A Personal Narrative of Political Experiences*, 1913

La Follette took his ideas to the U.S. Senate, where he served from 1906 until his death in 1925. Famous for his independence from business interests, he successfully promoted Progressive legislation on the federal level. As the Progressive Party's candidate for President in 1924, La Follette lost, but received one sixth of the vote.

La Follette on the Firing Line
ROBERT MARION LA FOLLETTE

Progressive reform politician Robert M. La Follette earned the nickname "Fighting Bob."

Federal Reforms

A number of important Progressive reforms were made at the federal level. Beginning with President Theodore Roosevelt in 1901, the White House became a powerful voice for change. In a major expansion of federal authority, Roosevelt used his presidential powers vigorously in domestic matters, just as he did overseas. He viewed the presidency as a "bully pulpit"—an ideal platform from which to guide or rally the American public to support moral, worthy causes. In the process he created the modern presidency, in which the chief executive is a strong political force.

TR's "Square Deal" TR got a chance to flex his political muscle in May 1902, when the United Mine Workers called a strike to protest

ACTIVITY
Connecting with Government

Have students review the quote on this page by Robert La Follette. His goals as a Progressive reformer are clearly stated. Did the movement succeed in achieving the aims he described? Have groups of students research and then list the pros and cons of several of La Follette's reforms, such as the direct primary, civil service reforms, and incorporation of academics and citizen committees to run regulatory agencies. **(Verbal/Linguistic)**

BACKGROUND
Biography

One of the most effective reform governors in the nation was the plain-spoken governor of California, Hiram Johnson (1866–1945). The son of a Republican politician, Johnson ran for governor vowing to "kick the Southern Pacific out of politics." The Southern Pacific Railroad was not only the state's most powerful corporation, it was his own father's close political ally. But Johnson was, in his own words, a "natural rebel." He fought against "rotten big business and crooked politics," enacting so many progressive reforms that one journalist called his tenure a "political revolution."

CUSTOMIZE FOR ...
Gifted and Talented

Tell students that most Progressives were financially comfortable. Ask how much self-interest was involved in the Progressives' desire to maintain order and stability and the nation's high standard of living. Does self-interest on the part of reformers affect the value of their reforms?

ACTIVITY

Connecting with Economics

To gain insight into the complexity of resolving a nationwide strike, have students divide into groups representing different sides in the 1902 coal miners strike. The goal of the activity will be to have groups representing the union's or government's perspective gain greater insight into the issues and controversies of the strike and then share their discoveries with their classmates. **(Verbal/Linguistic)**

From the Archives of

AmericanHeritage®

About the Presidents

Theodore Roosevelt (1901–1909) accomplished several "firsts" as President. He was the first Vice President to become President and then be elected in his own right. He was the first Republican President from the East. He set up the first White House press room. Roosevelt was the first President to invite an African American—Booker T. Washington—to dinner at the White House. He was the first to leave U.S. soil while in office, on a visit to the Panama Canal in 1908. What's more, Roosevelt was the first President to fly in an airplane. The purchase of a Wright brothers' airplane during his presidency led to the U.S. Army Air Force. Source: Wilson Sullivan, "Theodore Roosevelt," *The American Heritage® Pictorial History of the Presidents of the United States,* vol. 2, 1968.

READING CHECK

By getting involved in labor disputes, breaking up harmful trusts, and successfully pushing Congress to regulate railroads and the food-processing industry.

CAPTION ANSWERS

Interpreting Charts Legislation such as the Hepburn Act and the Meat Inspection Act exemplify progressive reforms that allowed the federal government to intervene forcefully in the sphere of private business in order to protect the well-being of consumers.

Progressive Era Legislation

Legislation	Purpose
Sherman Antitrust Act, 1890	Outlawed monopolies and practices that restrained trade, such as price fixing.
National Reclamation Act, 1902	Created to plan and develop irrigation projects.
United States Forest Service, 1905	Created to manage the nation's water and timber resources.
Hepburn Act, 1906	Authorized the Interstate Commerce Commission to regulate railroad rates.
Pure Food and Drug Act, 1906	Banned interstate shipping of impure food and deliberate mislabeling of food and drugs.
Meat Inspection Act, 1906	Required federal inspection of meat processing to ensure sanitary conditions.
Department of Labor, 1913	Cabinet department created to promote the welfare and employment of working people.
16th Amendment, 1913	Gave Congress the power to levy an income tax.
17th Amendment, 1913	Provided for the direct election of senators.
Federal Reserve Act, 1913	Created Federal Reserve System of government banks to supervise private banks and provide a flexible money supply.
National Park Service, 1916	Created to administer the nation's parks.
18th Amendment, 1919	Prohibited the manufacture and sale of liquor. (Repealed in 1933.)
19th Amendment, 1920	Granted women full suffrage.
Women's Bureau, 1920	Created within the Department of Labor to improve the status of working women.

INTERPRETING CHARTS
Progressive reform touched many aspects of American life, including business, natural resources, labor, voting, and consumer protection. **Analyzing Information** *How did Progressive reforms result in a major expansion of federal power?*

their low wages. As winter approached and mine owners continued to refuse to talk to the union, TR decided to intervene. Lacking coal, the nation would be without a major source of heating fuel.

Roosevelt insisted that both sides submit to arbitration, a settlement in which an impartial third party decides on a legally binding solution. To pressure mine owners, TR threatened to use the army to seize and operate the mines. In 1903, arbitrators granted the miners a 10 percent raise and reduced their workday from 10 hours to 9. The arbitrators did not officially recognize the union, however. When Roosevelt called this a "square deal" for both sides in the coal strike, the phrase became a slogan of his presidency.

Antitrust Activism Although the Sherman Antitrust Act in 1890 was in place as a check on big business, it had never been vigorously enforced. Reversing this trend, Roosevelt's Attorney General used the act to sue the Northern Securities Company. Northern Securities was a **holding company,** a firm that buys up stocks and bonds of smaller companies. In doing so, it can create a monopoly. Northern Securities had brought about a modest decline in railroad rates by forming such a monopoly. But in 1904 the government convinced the Supreme Court that the company was in violation of the Sherman Act. The Court dissolved the company.

The Roosevelt administration filed 42 antitrust actions. The beef trust, Standard Oil, and the American Tobacco Company were either broken up or forced to reorganize. Like most Progressives, TR was not antibusiness. He did not wish to destroy trusts that did not harm the public. But he believed that government should regulate them.

Railroad Regulation An unelected President facing congressional opposition, Roosevelt proceeded with caution in his first term. He used his executive powers to achieve change, creating a political platform and a record on which to run in 1904. His comfortable victory over his Democratic opponent, Alton B. Parker, gave Roosevelt a mandate for his pursuit of reforms. He soon used his position to achieve a long-sought Progressive goal: regulation of the railroads.

After a battle with Congress, Roosevelt won passage of the 1906 Hepburn Act. The act moved the Interstate Commerce Commission (ICC) out of its largely weak advisory role and gave it strong enforcement powers that were essentially both legislative and judicial. The act authorized the ICC to set and limit railroad rates. Thus, the ICC became the first true federal regulatory agency.

READING CHECK
How did Roosevelt expand presidential authority?

Protecting Public Health Although Roosevelt denounced the muckrakers at first, public horror over numerous exposés of the food and drug industries persuaded him to respond. The result was the Pure Food and Drug Act and the Meat Inspection Act. The 1906 laws required accurate labeling of ingredients, strict sanitary conditions, and a rating system for meats.

RESOURCE DIRECTORY

Teaching Resources

Units 3/4 booklet
- Section 2 Quiz, p. 16

Guide to the Essentials
- Section 2 Summary, p. 54

Learning with Documents booklet (Primary Source Activity) *The Shame of the People,* p. 57

Great Debates booklet (Great Debates) *Marching for Child Labor Laws,* pp. 36–37

Technology

RESOURCE PRO® **Primary Source Activity** *Giving the Child a Chance,* found on Resource Pro, illustrates attempts made to stimulate interest in the crusade for children's rights, using an article published in *Harper's Weekly.*

A New Labor Department In response to pressure from labor and women's groups, in 1912 the government established a Children's Bureau. A Cabinet-level Department of Labor was added in 1913, and a Women's Bureau in 1920. The two new bureaus, both part of the Department of Labor, supported laws to benefit women and children. Julia Lathrop and Mary Anderson, the heads of these bureaus, became the first women in such federal posts.

Protecting the Environment TR also urged Congress to take further steps to protect the nation's natural resources. At the urging of explorers and nature writers such as John Wesley Powell and John Muir, Congress had established Yellowstone in Wyoming as the nation's first national park in 1872. Yosemite National Park in California had been created in 1890. Presidents Harrison and Cleveland had preserved some 35 million acres of forest land.

In 1905, Roosevelt named Gifford Pinchot, a forester, to head a new United States Forest Service. Pinchot sought to develop a policy for land and water use based on scientific data. At his recommendation, TR set aside more than 200 million acres for national forests, mineral reserves, and water projects. The National Reclamation Act, passed in 1902, used money from the sale of public lands to build irrigation systems in arid states.

Roosevelt and conservationist John Muir pose against the magnificent landscape of California's Yosemite National Park in this 1906 photograph.

New Constitutional Amendments During the Progressive Era, constitutional restraints on federal power gradually diminished. The Sixteenth Amendment, ratified in 1913, authorized Congress to collect federal income taxes. Previously, the government had relied on income from tariffs. Progressives had argued that tariffs pushed up the prices of goods for the working poor. The Sixteenth Amendment enabled the government to get more revenues from people with higher incomes. The Seventeenth Amendment (allowing direct election of senators) also was ratified in 1913. The Eighteenth Amendment, ratified in 1919, banned the production, sale, or import of alcoholic beverages. Not all Progressives favored Prohibition, but many thought it would protect society from the poverty and violence associated with drinking.

Section 2 Assessment

READING COMPREHENSION

1. Summarize the Progressives' views on regulating business.
2. Give examples of government reforms and **social welfare programs** at the municipal and state levels during the Progressive Era.
3. Describe the effect of each of these reforms: (a) **home rule;** (b) **direct primary;** (c) **initiative.**
4. What reforms did TR achieve under his square deal?

CRITICAL THINKING AND WRITING

5. **Synthesizing Information** Choose two constitutional amendments passed during the Progressive Era and explain how they expanded the role of government in citizens' lives.
6. **Writing a Conclusion** From what you know about TR's personality, beliefs, and leadership style, draw conclusions about how these characteristics affected his pursuit of Progressive reforms.

Take It to the NET

Activity: Virtual Field Trip To learn more about the Triangle Shirtwaist Factory fire, visit the links provided in the *America: Pathways to the Present* area of the following Web site.
www.phschool.com

Section 2 Assessment

Reading Comprehension

1. Progressives sought government regulation to protect workers' rights and business competition. They opposed government control, except in the cases of companies that supplied services like water and electricity.
2. Possible answers: Municipal: public baths in Detroit, free kindergartens in Toledo. State: workers' accident insurance, child labor legislation.
3. (a) Home rule: frees cities from domination by state governments; (b) direct primary: voters, not party leaders, choose candidates; (c) initiative: voters introduce a bill, then vote on it at the next election.
4. Antitrust activism; railroad regulation; transforming ICC into first regulatory agency; Pure Food and Drug Act, Meat Inspection Act; protecting the environment.

Critical Thinking and Writing

5. Answers may include: Sixteenth Amendment: introduced a graduated income tax. Eighteenth Amendment: prohibited alcohol manufacture, sale, and consumption.
6. Answers will vary, but might mention that TR's dynamic personality and energetic leadership style was well suited to the Progressive Era. He was not afraid to take on the railroads and large trusts.

Invite students to take a Virtual Field Trip at **www.phschool.com**

Section 3 Progressivism Under Taft and Wilson

Section Objectives

1. Study the political conflicts that marked the presidency of William Howard Taft.
2. Find out who contended in the election of 1912 and learn the outcome of that election.
3. Learn about the major policies that President Woodrow Wilson put into place.
4. Discover the limitations placed on the achievements of progressivism.

Bellringer

Warm-Up Activity Have students consider an election for class president with four students running for office. If half the class agreed to vote for one nominee and half the class voted for several, who would win? Explain how the election of 1912 was determined in a similar fashion.

Activating Prior Knowledge The elections of 1992 and 2000, like the election of 1912, each involved challenges by a third-party candidate. In students' opinions, what might the outcome of these elections have been without these third-party challenges?

Reading Strategy

As students read this section, have them each create a time line of reforms made during the Taft and Wilson presidencies.

Section 3 Progressivism Under Taft and Wilson

READING FOCUS

- What political conflicts marked the presidency of William Howard Taft?
- Who were the contenders in the Election of 1912, and what was the outcome?
- What major policies did President Woodrow Wilson help put in place?
- In what ways were the achievements of progressivism limited?

KEY TERMS

conservationist
New Nationalism
Bull Moose Party
Clayton Antitrust Act
Federal Trade Commission (FTC)
Federal Reserve System

TAKING NOTES

Copy the Venn diagram below. As you read, fill in the two circles with facts about the policies of Presidents Taft and Wilson. Where the circles overlap, fill in policies endorsed by both Presidents.

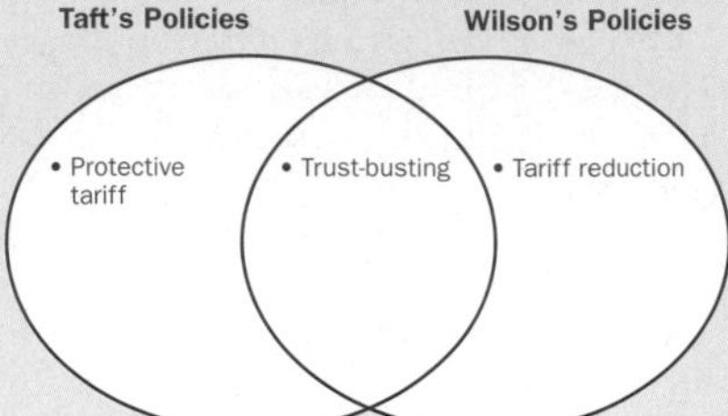

MAIN IDEA

Despite his solid record of reforms, President Taft alienated many Progressives. They broke away and formed their own party with Roosevelt as their candidate. Democrat Woodrow Wilson beat both men in 1912 and continued progressive reforms.

VIEWING HISTORY President Taft accomplished as much as or more than TR in some areas of progressive reform, yet he took several steps for which Progressives never forgave him. **Identifying Central Issues** *What factors made Taft's job so difficult?*

Setting the Scene The day after his election in 1904, Theodore Roosevelt announced he would not seek another term as President. One evening, as the 1908 campaign approached, Roosevelt was entertaining the Secretary of War, William Howard Taft, and his wife, Helen, at the White House. Suddenly the mischievous TR pretended to fall into a fortune teller's trance. "I see a man standing before me weighing about 350 pounds." (Taft was a portly man, more than 6 feet tall.)

"There is something hanging over his head. I cannot make out what it is; it is hanging by a slender thread. At one time it looks like the Presidency—then again it looks like the Chief Justiceship."

"Make it the Presidency!" exclaimed Mrs. Taft.

"Make it the Chief Justiceship!" cried Mr. Taft.

Helen Taft, a key political advisor to her husband, had her way. TR persuaded the reluctant Taft to run for the job, and made him his handpicked nominee on the Republican ticket in 1908.

Perhaps Taft should have listened instead to his mother: "I do not want my son to be President. His is a judicial mind and he loves the law." Taft would, in time, become the nation's highest judge, a job he dearly loved. But not until he served a fairly miserable four years as President.

Taft's Presidency

With TR's backing, Taft easily won the 1908 election over Democrat William Jennings Bryan, who tried for a third and last time to win the office. Taft pledged to carry on TR's progressive program. But from the beginning, Taft found his predecessor's shoes difficult to fill. He had neither Roosevelt's energy nor strength of personality to battle the powerful Republican congressmen who opposed progressive reforms. He created disappointment from the start by not appointing any Progressives to his Cabinet. Although in many ways he would fulfill his pledge to continue Roosevelt's reforms, in the

Caption Answers

Viewing History Taft had neither Roosevelt's sheer energy nor his ability to line up congressional support for his reforms. He also did not place Progressives in his Cabinet, and he disappointed Progressives on a few key issues, such as tariff reduction.

RESOURCE DIRECTORY

Teaching Resources
Guided Reading and Review booklet, p. 76

Technology
Section Reading Support Transparencies
Guided Reading Audiotapes (English/Spanish), Ch. 11
Student Edition on Audio CD, Ch. 11
Prentice Hall Presentation Pro CD-ROM, Ch. 11
Companion Web site, www.phschool.com

end he alienated Progressives and caused a crisis in the Republican Party.

INTERPRETING POLITICAL CARTOONS Taft's presidency quickly became entangled in controversy and conflict. **Drawing Inferences** *What details illustrate Taft's troubles? What does the cartoon suggest about TR's reaction to Taft's predicament?*

Conflict Over Tariffs In 1908, Taft had run on a Republican platform of lower tariffs, a Progressive goal that Roosevelt had not addressed. Taft promptly called a special session of Congress in 1909 to pass tariff reductions. The effort backfired on him. The House passed some reductions, while more traditional Republicans in the Senate added some highly protective tariff increases. The compromise measure, which Taft signed enthusiastically, was the Payne-Aldrich Tariff. Although not as protective as the McKinley Tariff Act of 1890, Payne-Aldrich was a protective measure. Progressives were furious with Taft.

The Ballinger-Pinchot Affair Progressives felt betrayed by Taft on another issue: the management of public lands. Taft's choice for Secretary of the Interior, Richard A. Ballinger, angered **conservationists,** people who favor the protection of natural resources. Ballinger opposed conservation policies on federal lands in the West, siding with business interests that sought unrestricted development.

Ballinger's views put him in conflict with Gifford Pinchot, head of the U.S. Forest Service. Pinchot favored scientific management of wilderness lands to allow both preservation and development. He had crafted many of TR's conservation policies. Pinchot's relationship with Taft, however, was strained.

In 1909, it became known that Ballinger had allowed a private group of businesspeople to obtain several million acres of Alaskan public lands containing rich coal deposits. Pinchot charged that Ballinger had improperly shown special preference to the purchasing group. When Pinchot protested to a congressional committee and aired suggestions of corruption on Ballinger's part, Taft fired Pinchot. Ballinger, although never found guilty of wrongdoing, eventually resigned. Pinchot remained a public hero, while Taft's popularity continued to slump.

Turmoil in the Republican Party

Angry Republican Progressives in the House now teamed up with Democrats to attack opponents of reform in the Republican Party. This so-called "old guard" of traditional Republicans controlled the House Rules Committee, which decides whether and how bills will be referred for action by the House. Through the Rules Committee, the old guard had been able to block much reform legislation.

To break this stranglehold, the progressive faction sought to curtail the powers of the old guard member and House Speaker, Joseph G. Cannon. In 1910, the House passed a resolution allowing the full membership, instead of the Speaker, to appoint the Rules Committee. The Speaker was barred from serving on the committee. The Republican Party was now bitterly split.

The Midterm Elections of 1910 Following Taft's election in 1908, Roosevelt had set off on a long safari to East Africa. He returned to the United States to a wildly cheering crowd in New York and a storm of protest against Taft. At first, Roosevelt refrained from criticizing his old

Focus on GEOGRAPHY

Environmental Management The nation's forests should be managed for "the greatest good of the greatest number in the long run." This summarizes the philosophy of conservationist Gifford Pinchot, head of the U.S. Forest Service from 1898 to 1909. After studying forestry in France, the young Pinchot returned home to find that "the nation was obsessed by a flurry of development." At that point he devoted his life to making forestry and conservation recognized professions and to promoting the scientific study and management of American forests.

LESSON PLAN

Focus In 1912 many groups associated with the progressive movement established a political party. Ask students why. Although the progressive candidate did not win the election, the new President, Woodrow Wilson, continued to institute progressive reforms.

Instruct Explain that while Roosevelt said, "I believe in a strong executive. I believe in power," Taft felt that the President should use restraint. Discuss Taft's unwillingness or inability to influence Congress. In what ways did Taft disappoint Roosevelt and his followers? How did Wilson increase the powers of the federal government?

Assess/Reteach Taft became President reluctantly, after much persuasion by Theodore Roosevelt. Do students think he should have walked away from the chance to run for President and followed his own instinct to become a judge instead? How did the decision to go along with Roosevelt's wishes affect Taft in the long run?

ACTIVITY

Connecting with Government

Ask each student to write two statements about each of the four candidates in the presidential election of 1912, following this format: "This candidate ________." Then invite pairs of students to exchange papers and identify the candidates described in each statement. **(Verbal/Linguistic)**

TEST PREPARATION

Have students read the section on this page titled "Conflict Over Tariffs" and then complete the sentence below.

The Payne-Aldrich Tariff that Taft signed—

- **Ⓐ** made Progressives furious.
- **B** was more protective than the McKinley Tariff Act of 1890.
- **C** showed that Taft was not able to compromise on tariffs.
- **D** made Taft very popular with the Progressives.

CAPTION ANSWERS

Interpreting Political Cartoons
The kittens and the puppy playing with the strands of yarn in which Taft has become entangled signify that the affairs of government have spiraled out of Taft's control. The caption suggests that Taft has been negligent. Meanwhile, TR looks on with amusement at Taft's inability to gain control of the situation.

Activity

Connecting with Geography

Have students imagine they are presidential campaign managers for either Roosevelt, Taft, or Wilson in 1912 and must plan a national campaign for their candidate. Students should consider the following: Where will the candidate go? How will he travel? Who will his audiences be? How will you publicize his candidacy? Students may want to work in teams, with each member responsible for different aspects of the finished product, e.g., creating a map, drawing up an itinerary, or outlining a speech. **(Visual/Spatial; Logical/Mathematical; Verbal/Linguistic)**

Background

TR and Women's Suffrage

"Rough Rider," "Bull Moose," safari hunter, and imperialist, Theodore Roosevelt was also an early proponent of voting rights for women. In his senior year at Harvard University, young Roosevelt wrote a paper in which he asserted that women should have equal rights with men. He even suggested they not change their last names when they married. As New York City police commissioner, he placed women in executive and other positions in his department. When the time was ripe for a constitutional amendment on women's suffrage, Roosevelt took the lead, while his progressive rivals, Taft and Wilson, lagged behind.

friend, but before long he plunged into the battle between Taft and the Progressives. Roosevelt campaigned for Progressive candidates for the 1910 midterm elections. He called for business regulation, welfare laws, workplace protection for women and children, income and inheritance taxes, and voting reform. TR called his plan the **New Nationalism.**

The congressional elections brought down the old guard. Democrats gained control the House and Senate, with Progressive Democrats and Republicans firmly in place in both houses.

The Republicans had their elephant mascot, the Democrats had their donkey, and the Progressives added a Bull Moose (above) to the zoo of political symbols. The "Bull Moose" himself, TR, escaped assassination, possibly thanks to the speech and eyeglass case (below) tucked inside his coat.

The Election of 1912

In early 1912, Roosevelt challenged Taft for the Republican presidential nomination. In the GOP primaries, voters preferred Roosevelt. But Taft, who controlled the Republican convention in Chicago, won the nomination handily.

Charging Taft's group with fraud, the Progressive Republicans marched out. Now Progressives vowed to form their own party. In August the Progressive Party held its convention. Spontaneous and intense, it had the feel of a religious revival. Gone were the party bosses. More women and young people attended. State delegations prayed together for their candidates: Roosevelt and his running mate, California Governor Hiram Johnson, a Progressive crusader.

When TR was asked about his physical readiness for a campaign, he said, "I feel fit as a bull moose!" The **Bull Moose Party** became the nickname of the Progressive Party—and the moose a symbol to challenge the Republican elephant and the Democratic donkey.

The Bull Moose Party The Bull Moose platform included tariff reduction, women's suffrage, more regulation of business, a child labor ban, an eight-hour workday, a federal workers' compensation system, and the direct election of senators. Many women joined the Progressive Party and campaigned for candidates. In states where women could vote, women ran for state and local offices.

Roosevelt ran a vigorous campaign. On October 14, at a speech in Milwaukee, TR was shot by a would-be assassin. With a bullet lodged in his lung, Roosevelt spoke for another hour and a half before seeking medical aid.

"Friends," TR addressed the crowd, "I shall ask you to be as quiet as possible. I don't know whether you fully understand that I have just been shot; but it takes more than that to kill a Bull Moose." He showed the crowd his bloodstained shirt, then continued his speech. It was classic TR.

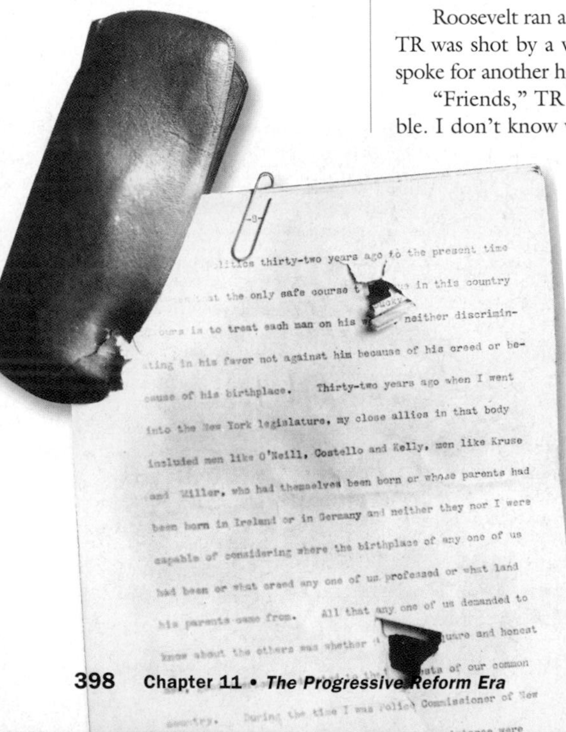

-8-

thirty-two years ago to the present time ... the only safe course ... in this country ... is to treat each man on his ... neither discriminating in his favor not against him because of his creed or because of his birthplace. Thirty-two years ago when I went into the New York legislature, my close allies in that body included men like O'Neill, Costello and Kelly, men like Kruse and Miller, who had themselves been born or whose parents had been born in Ireland or in Germany and neither they nor I were capable of considering where the birthplace of any one of us had been or what creed any one of us professed or what land his parents came from. All that any one of us demanded to know about the others was whether ... square and honest ... of our common country. During the time I was Police Commissioner of New

Taft's Record Taft's frequent complaints about his job ("politics makes me sick") are so often quoted that they threaten to overshadow his presidential legacy. Yet Taft did achieve a notable record on progressive causes. He reserved more public lands and brought more antitrust suits in four years than TR had in seven. He supported the Children's Bureau, the Sixteenth and Seventeenth amendments, and the Mann-Elkins Act of 1910. This act gave the Interstate Commerce Commission the power to regulate telephone and telegraph rates. Yet Taft remained at odds with Republican Progressives.

Wilson's New Freedom To head the Democratic ticket, the party chose New Jersey Governor Woodrow Wilson. Like Roosevelt, Wilson ran on a reform platform.

RESOURCE DIRECTORY

Technology

Color Transparencies *American Photo*, F6

Sounds of an Era Audio CD *Teddy Roosevelt,* 1912 recording (time: one minute, 45 seconds); *Woodrow Wilson,* 1912 recording (time: 50 seconds)

RESOURCE PRO® **Critical Thinking Activity** *Distinguishing False from Accurate Images,* found on Resource Pro, encourages students to apply this skill by analyzing a political cartoon.

Unlike Roosevelt, he criticized both big business and big government. As part of his "New Freedom" policy, he promised to enforce antitrust laws without threatening economic competition. His position was pure progressivism:

> *"A trust is an arrangement to get rid of competition. . . . I am for big business, and I am against the trusts. Any man who can survive by his brains, any man who can put the others out of the business by making the thing cheaper to the consumer at the same time that he is increasing its intrinsic value and quality, I take off my hat to, and I say: 'You are the man who can build up the United States. . . .'"*
>
> —Woodrow Wilson, campaign speech, 1912

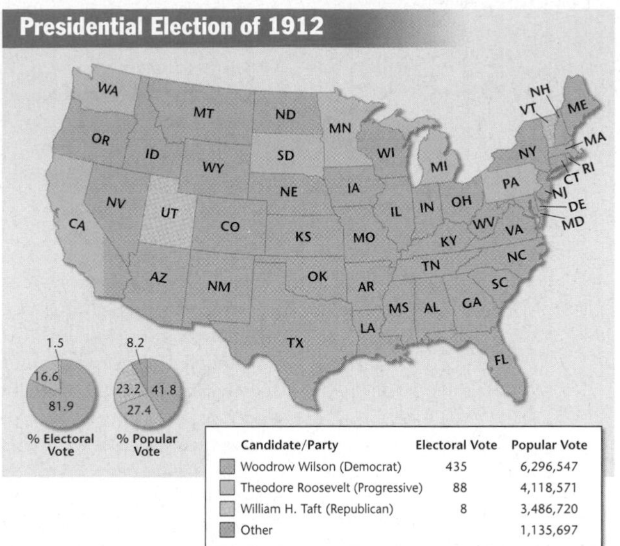

Candidate/Party	Electoral Vote	Popular Vote
Woodrow Wilson (Democrat)	435	6,296,547
Theodore Roosevelt (Progressive)	88	4,118,571
William H. Taft (Republican)	8	3,486,720
Other		1,135,697

MAP SKILLS In the 1912 presidential election, progressive ideas influenced the party platforms of the three major contenders. **Predicting Consequences** *What would have happened if Roosevelt had not run and Taft had received Roosevelt's votes?*

A Four-Way Election Four main candidates sought the presidency in 1912. Taft, despite his distaste for the job, fought to keep it for the Republicans. Roosevelt, eager to get his job back, represented his Bull Moose Progressives. Wilson headed the Democratic ticket. Labor leader Eugene V. Debs made the third of his eventual five presidential runs for the Socialists.

With the Republican vote split between Taft and Roosevelt, Wilson emerged the victor. He gained only about 42 percent of the popular vote, but he won the electoral vote by a landslide: 435 votes to TR's 88 and Taft's mere 8. (See election map, above.) The Democrats also took control of both houses of Congress.

Taft left office with few regrets. "I'm glad to be going," he told his successor. "This is the lonesomest place in the world."

Wilson's Policies as President

As president of Princeton University (1902–1910) and then as the governor of New Jersey (1911–1913), Wilson had acquired a reputation as a dedicated reformer. A former professor of political science, Wilson believed that one of his main duties as President was to offer major legislation to Congress, promote it publicly, and help guide it to passage. In that role he worked the Congress vigorously, keeping it in session for a full year and a half for the first time ever.

Tariffs and Taxes Wilson's first major victory was tariff reduction, a long-unfulfilled goal of Progressives. The Underwood Tariff Act of 1913 reduced average tariff rates from 40 percent to 25 percent. To make up for that loss of government revenue, in October 1913 Wilson signed into law a federal income tax, made legal with ratification of the Sixteenth Amendment earlier in the year.

Attacking the Trusts Despite the Sherman Act and the trustbusting under Roosevelt and Taft, a congressional committee concluded that a relatively small group of powerful men still controlled much of the nation's wealth, businesses, and credit. Wilson believed strongly that monopolies and trusts led

Sounds of an Era

Listen to speeches from 1912 by Roosevelt and Wilson, and other sounds from the Progressive Era.

BACKGROUND
Art History

The year after his defeat in the presidential election, Theodore Roosevelt was back in the public eye as art critic. In 1913 he attended the International Exhibition of Modern Art in New York City. Organized by the avant-garde artists known as "the Eight," the show introduced French cubist and post-impressionist painting to America. Roosevelt's review of the show was mixed. Referring to cubists and futurists as the "lunatic fringe," he compared a painting entitled "A Naked Man Going Downstairs" to the Navajo rug in his bathroom. "From the standpoint of decorative value, of sincerity, and of artistic merit," he wrote, "the Navajo rug is infinitely ahead of the picture."

From the Archives of
AmericanHeritage®

About the Presidents

Woodrow Wilson (1913–1921) met with Louis D. Brandeis in August 1912. It may have been the most important event of his campaign. Brandeis helped to convert Wilson to a progressive agenda. During his campaign, Wilson articulated the New Freedom, as preached to him by Brandeis. After Wilson's inauguration, progressivism took the form of far-reaching reforms. Lowering the tariff was one top priority. To emphasize its importance, the new President called a special session of Congress. The result was a tariff reform bill. As it turned out, however, a law attached to that bill had a more far-reaching effect: establishing the U.S. income tax. Source: Joseph L. Gardner, "Woodrow Wilson," *The American Heritage® Pictorial History of the Presidents of the United States,* vol. 2, 1968.

CUSTOMIZE FOR ...
Less Proficient Readers

Ask students to list the names of the presidential candidates in 1912—Debs, Taft, Roosevelt, and Wilson—at the top of a piece of paper. Then have them make notes under each name as they read, identifying each candidate, his political party in 1912, and his claim to be called a Progressive, even if he was not a member of the progressive party.

CAPTION ANSWERS

Map Skills Taft would have won the popular vote with 7,605,291 votes to Wilson's 6,296,547. But Taft still would have lost the election with a total of only 96 electoral votes to Wilson's 435.

ACTIVITY
Connecting with Economics

Reinforce students' understanding of Federal Reserve notes by inviting them to examine $1, $5, $10, and $20 bills. They should note the legend "Federal Reserve Note" at the top. Notes issued prior to 1996 bear a regional seal to the left of the portrait, indicating the name of the issuing Federal Reserve Bank. The letter designates the district in which the bank is located. After 1996 a universal seal is used and a letter and number identify the issuing bank. Have students compare the cities on the notes with the map of Federal Reserve districts in the book. **(Visual/Spatial)**

BACKGROUND
Interdisciplinary

While the rights of working men and women were debated in government, a rising young poet named Carl Sandburg was celebrating their lives in verse. In 1916 his first book, *Chicago Poems*, was published to widespread praise. Sandburg, a Socialist and the son of a laborer, was deeply sympathetic to the working class, as evidenced in such poems as "The Shovel Man," "Ice Handler," "Working Girls," and "Masses." The title poem, "Chicago," in its personification of the "City of the Big Shoulders," vividly captures the spirit of the rapidly growing industrial city.

to economic instability and the restriction of free enterprise. He did not want to create more government to monitor the trusts. He sought to get rid of trusts altogether.

With Wilson's guidance, in 1914 Congress passed the **Clayton Antitrust Act** to strengthen the Sherman Antitrust Act of 1890. Instead of simply making trusts illegal, as the Sherman Act had done, the Clayton Act spelled out specific activities that big businesses could not do. Companies could not prevent their buyers from purchasing goods from competitors. Some types of holding companies used to create monopolies were banned. Price cutting in local markets to squeeze out competitors was forbidden, as were some rebates.

Prior to the Clayton Act, courts often treated labor unions as monopolies. Clayton stated that unions could not be regarded as "illegal combinations [monopolies] in restraint of trade under the antitrust laws" because "the labor of a human being is not a commodity or article of commerce." The act therefore legalized unions as well as their key weapons: strikes, peaceful picketing, and boycotts. Courts were prevented from issuing injunctions against unions unless their activities led to "irreparable injury to property."

To enforce the Clayton Act and set up fair-trade laws, in 1914 Wilson and the Congress created the **Federal Trade Commission (FTC).** The FTC was given the power to order firms to "cease and desist" the practice of business tactics found to be unfair. Still, later court rulings weakened the Clayton Act.

The Federal Reserve System Congress did not give the FTC authority over banks. Wilson sought a total overhaul of the American banking system to promote competition in the industry and to ease the frequent panics that destabilized the U.S. economy. Bankers, however, had their own ideas about how to reform the system, and many viewed Wilson's plans as radical.

After a long, heated debate, Congress passed the Federal Reserve Act of 1913. The act created the **Federal Reserve System.** It divided the country into 12 districts, each with a Federal Reserve bank owned by its member

MAP SKILLS Initially, the 12 regional banks in the Federal Reserve System acted independently, sometimes in conflict. Changes to the system over the years have improved coordination among the regional banks while still allowing them to represent the interests of their member banks. **Analyzing Visual Information** *Which regions' banks might represent a large proportion of (a) farm interests; (b) urban interests; (c) manufacturing interests?*

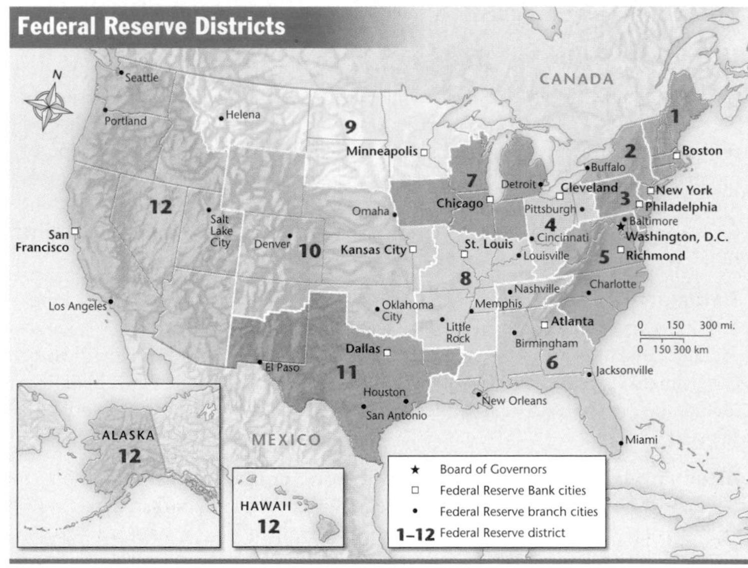

CAPTION ANSWERS

Map Skills Accept reasonable answers. (a) Areas with strong farming interests include 6–12. (b) Urban interests are strong in 1–5, 7, and 12. (c) Manufacturing dominates in 1–5 and in parts of 6, 7, 11, and 12.

RESOURCE DIRECTORY
Technology

RESOURCE PRO® **Biography** *Louis D. Brandeis,* found on Resource Pro, profiles the progressive Supreme Court justice.

banks. The system was supervised by a Federal Reserve Board appointed by the President.

The Federal Reserve banks were the central banks for their regions—the "bankers' banks." Every national bank was required to become a member of the Federal Reserve bank in its district and to deposit some of its capital and cash reserves in that bank. Member banks could borrow from the Federal Reserve to meet short-term demands. This helped to prevent bank failures that occurred when large numbers of depositors withdrew funds during an economic panic.

The system also created a new national currency known as Federal Reserve notes. The Federal Reserve could now expand or contract the amount of currency in circulation according to economic needs.

Another Wilson financial reform was the establishment of the Federal Farm Loan Board in 1916. This board and a system of Farm Loan Banks made loans available to farmers. Farmers could borrow money for five to forty years at rates lower than those offered by commercial banks.

Brandeis to the Supreme Court In 1916, with the presidential election approaching, Wilson took a number of steps aimed partly at attracting progressive voters. Early that year, Wilson nominated progressive lawyer Louis D. Brandeis to the Supreme Court. Brandeis was known for his brilliance and for fighting many public causes. He was known as "the people's lawyer."

Wilson's nomination of Brandeis to the Supreme Court drew a storm of protest. Opponents, including former President Taft, accused Brandeis of being too radical. Anti-Semitism also played a part in the opposition; Brandeis was the first Jewish Supreme Court nominee. Nevertheless, he was confirmed by the Senate and served on the Court with distinction until 1939. The appointment of Brandeis marked the peak of federal progressive reforms.

Also in the months preceding the 1916 election, Wilson oversaw federal legislation limiting the use of child labor in industry. Most states already had such laws. Yet the federal provision was struck down by the Supreme Court two years later. A federal ban on child labor would take another two decades.

Wilson Wins a Second Term By 1916, the historic progressive drive was winding down. TR did not want to run again. Instead, Roosevelt and the Bull Moose Party endorsed Wilson's Republican opponent, Charles Evans Hughes, a former governor of New York and Supreme Court justice. Wilson ran on the slogan that he had kept the country out of World War I, which had erupted in Europe two years before. He barely defeated Hughes, with 277 electoral votes to 254.

The Limits of Progressivism

By the mid-1910s, Progressives had made broad changes in society, government, and business. They had redefined and enlarged the role of government. Yet their influence was limited to certain sectors of society. Focused mainly on municipal problems, Progressives did little to aid tenant and migrant farmers

VIEWING HISTORY In 1916, Wilson had the election momentum of an incumbent, suggested in the campaign button above. The campaign truck at top publicized Wilson's record during his first term as President. **Analyzing Information** *Which of the slogans shown on this truck probably contributed most to Wilson's reelection?*

READING CHECK
List some progressive reforms achieved by Wilson.

ACTIVITY
Connecting with History and Conflict

Have students do research to find out more about Louis D. Brandeis and the controversy surrounding his Supreme Court nomination. Students should then use their findings to write their own newspaper editorials addressing the controversy and taking a position either for or against Brandeis's nomination. **(Verbal/Linguistic)**

BACKGROUND
Global Connections

Between 1910 and 1916, Mexico underwent a series of revolutions, prompting American business interests there to ask for U.S. military intervention to protect their property. President Wilson declined, adopting a policy of "watchful waiting" in hopes that a constitutional government would be elected. In 1916, however, attacks on Americans by guerrilla leader Pancho Villa provoked Wilson to send troops into Mexico, bringing the two nations briefly to the brink of war. Later that year, the establishment of a constitutional Mexican government, coupled with the increasing likelihood of United States involvement in World War I, caused Wilson to withdraw American troops.

READING CHECK
Reducing tariffs; appointing Louis D. Brandeis to the Supreme Court; sponsoring the Federal Farm Loan Board, the Federal Trade Commission, the Clayton Antitrust Act, and the Federal Reserve System.

TEST PREPARATION

Have students read the passages under "Brandeis to the Supreme Court" and then complete the sentence below.

Brandeis was most likely nicknamed "the people's lawyer" because—

A he was the first Jewish Supreme Court nominee.

B he was a brilliant lawyer.

(C) he pushed for progressive reform.

D he was nominated by Wilson, who was popular with the people.

CAPTION ANSWERS

Viewing History "Who keeps us out of war?" "Peace with honor." "Preparedness."

Section 3 Assessment

Reading Comprehension

1. (a) Reserved public lands; antitrust suits; supported the Children's Bureau; supported the Sixteenth and Seventeenth Amendments and the Mann-Elkins Act. (b) By appointing Richard A. Ballinger, then firing Pinchot; Ballinger resigns; continued decline in Taft's popularity.
2. Split Republican vote, allowing Democratic candidate, Wilson, to win.
3. Reducing tariffs; eliminating trusts; overhaul of the American banking system; attempted to impose federal limits on child labor.
4. (a) Legalized unions and strikes, limited the issuing of injunctions against unions. (b) Worked to eliminate unfair business tactics. (c) Established national banking system; created new form of currency; stabilized banking as a whole.

Critical Thinking and Writing

5. Payne-Aldrich: the Senate insisted on protective measures. Underwood: congressional acquiescence secured for significant cuts. Payne-Aldrich: Progressives furious with Taft. Underwood: major victory for Wilson.
6. Answers will vary, but should include references to: curbing the power of trusts; regulating business; creating Federal Reserve System, Federal Trade Commission, and Federal Farm Loan Board.

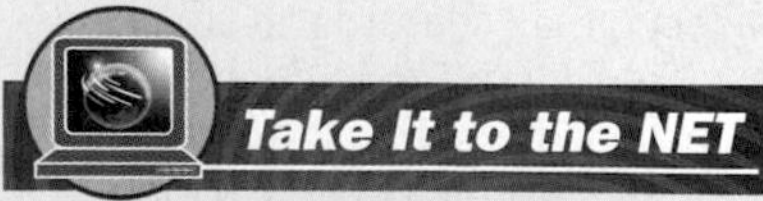

Take It to the NET

Answers will vary. Students should note the background, political position, and influence of the Progressive. They should also note to what extent the reformer's goals were achieved, and whether they were satisfied with their work.

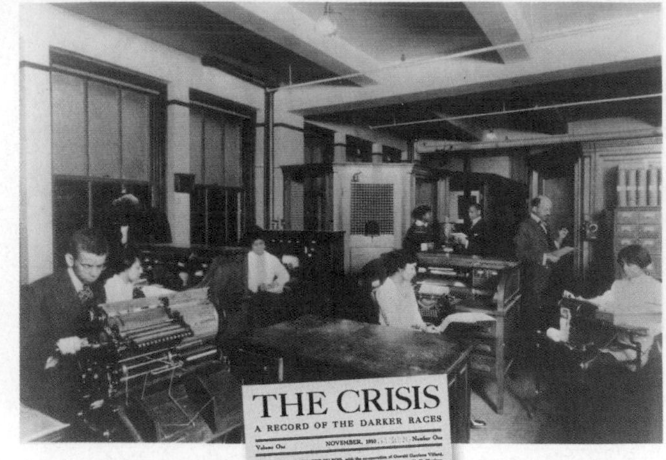

The journal of the NAACP is shown at right. Above is a photo of the offices of the NAACP, with W.E.B. Du Bois standing to the right at the back.

and nonunionized workers. Some Progressives supported immigration limits and literacy tests.

Social Justice and Progressivism The progressive Presidents took little action to pursue social justice reforms. Wilson allowed his Cabinet officers to extend the Jim Crow practice, begun under Taft, of separating the races in federal offices. Wilson also initially opposed a constitutional amendment on women's suffrage because his party platform had not endorsed it.

Many African Americans felt ignored by Progressives. Only a tiny group of Progressives, those who helped found the National Association for the Advancement of Colored People (NAACP) in 1909, concerned themselves with the worsening race relations and continued lynchings of the era. Although Roosevelt invited Booker T. Washington to the White House in 1901, he did little else to support African American rights. At the 1912 Progressive Party convention, Roosevelt declined to seat black delegates from the South for fear of alienating white southern supporters. In addition, some white southern Progressives who favored the women's vote did so because they realized that women's suffrage could double the white vote, putting African Americans further behind.

The End of Progressivism As more and more nations became involved in World War I, Americans worried about how long they could remain uninvolved. Soon, calls to prepare for war drowned out calls for reform in America. By the end of 1916, the reform spirit had nearly sputtered out. But one reform movement grew bolder: the drive for women's suffrage.

Section 3 Assessment

READING COMPREHENSION

1. (a) What progressive reforms did Taft achieve? (b) How did he offend **conservationists,** and what was the result?
2. What effect did the Bull Moose Party have on the election of 1912?
3. What reforms did Wilson seek?
4. What reforms resulted from the establishment of (a) the **Clayton Antitrust Act;** (b) **the Federal Trade Commission;** (c) the **Federal Reserve System?**

CRITICAL THINKING AND WRITING

5. **Making Comparisons** Compare and contrast the Payne-Aldrich Tariff and the Underwood Tariff Act. Describe the political battles and the outcomes of each.
6. **Writing an Introduction** Write a one-paragraph introduction to an essay on how reforms under President Wilson changed the size, scope, and role of the federal government.

Take It to the NET

Activity: Writing a Biography
Write a brief biography of a Progressive mentioned in this section. Discuss your subject's success or failure in achieving Progressive goals. Use the links provided in the *America: Pathways to the Present* area of the following Web site for help in completing this activity.
www.phschool.com

RESOURCE DIRECTORY

Teaching Resources
Units 3/4 booklet
- Section 3 Quiz, p. 17

Guide to the Essentials
- Section 3 Summary, p. 55

Section 4 Suffrage at Last

READING FOCUS

- In what ways were Susan B. Anthony and Elizabeth Cady Stanton a "bridge" to the twentieth-century suffrage effort?
- What two main strategies did suffrage leaders pursue?
- What was the status of the suffrage movement by the turn of the century?
- Why was a new generation of national leaders needed in the suffrage effort?
- What factors led to a final victory for suffrage?

KEY TERMS

civil disobedience
National American Woman Suffrage Association (NAWSA)
Congressional Union (CU)

TAKING NOTES

As you read, complete this chart, adding causes that led to the passage of women's suffrage.

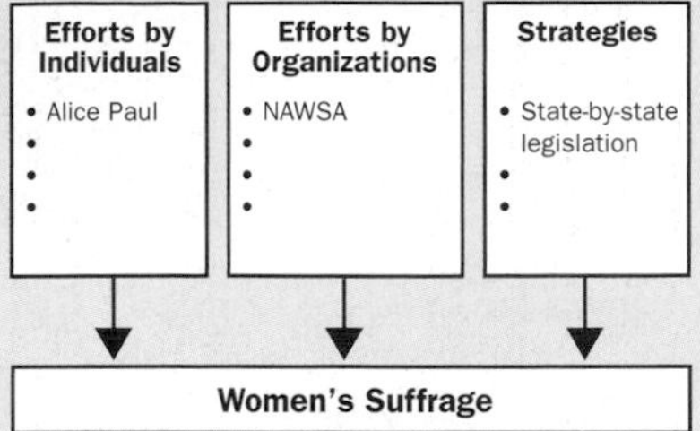

MAIN IDEA

Demonstrating their skills as organizers and activists, women won the right to vote with the ratification of the Nineteenth Amendment in 1920.

Setting the Scene For roughly 70 years, women's organizations actively campaigned for the right to vote. As the movement grew, so did resistance to it. Opponents included men and women from all age groups and income levels. Many viewed the idea of women's suffrage as unnecessary, at best. At worst, they saw it as a threat to the stability of American society and government.

In speeches and articles, anti-suffragists voiced the genuine fears of many Americans: Would women become "too masculine," as critics suggested? Would they be easily manipulated by politicians? Would politics distract them from their duties in the home?

One of the most persuasive arguments against suffrage was that women simply did not want to vote—a fact that was confirmed by some opinion polls in some areas. Yet note the language this popular magazine used to make generalizations about all women:

> "This is the negative reason why woman does not wish the ballot: she does not wish to engage in that conflict of wills which is the essence of politics; she does not wish to assume the responsibility for protecting person and property which is the essence of government. The affirmative reason is that she has other, and in some sense, more important work to do."
>
> —Lyman Abbott, "Why Women Do Not Wish the Suffrage," *The Atlantic Monthly*, September 1903

INTERPRETING CARTOONS As the women's suffrage movement gained strength, criticisms grew louder. **Drawing Inferences** *Give at least one possible explanation for the word* delusion *in the title of this cartoon.*

Anthony and Stanton: Preparing the Way

From the beginning, suffragists heard such arguments, and more. In their long struggle, they faced confrontations, ridicule, threats, and even violence.

Section 4 Suffrage at Last

Section Objectives

1. Learn the ways in which Susan B. Anthony and Elizabeth Cady Stanton formed a "bridge" to the twentieth-century suffrage effort.
2. Discover two main strategies pursued by suffrage leaders.
3. Read about the status of the suffrage movement by the turn of the century.
4. Find out why a new generation of leaders was needed in the suffrage effort.
5. Study the factors that led to a final victory for suffrage.

Bellringer

Warm-Up Activity Ask students if they intend to vote when they turn 18. How would they feel if a constitutional amendment raised the voting age to 25?

Activating Prior Knowledge Can students determine why some people would deny others the right to vote? Are they aware that voting rights are not universal in all nations?

Reading Strategy

As students read, have them construct a time line of events that led to the enactment of the Nineteenth Amendment. Time lines should start in 1848 and end in 1920.

Caption Answers

Interpreting Cartoons Possible answers: the delusion that women would get the right to vote; that women wanted the right to vote; that women were capable of making good voting choices.

RESOURCE DIRECTORY

Teaching Resources
Learning Styles Lesson Plans booklet, pp. 38–39
Guided Reading and Review booklet, p. 77

Technology
Section Reading Support Transparencies
Guided Reading Audiotapes (English/Spanish), Ch. 11
Color Transparencies *Political Cartoons,* B11
Student Edition on Audio CD, Ch. 11
Prentice Hall Presentation Pro CD-ROM, Ch. 11
Companion Web site, www.phschool.com

Lesson Plan

Focus Women won the right to vote in 1920 after a long, bitter fight. Ask students how the suffrage campaign achieved success.

Instruct Read students the following comment from a 1974 interview with the suffragist Alice Paul, then 89 years old: "I always feel . . . the movement is a sort of mosaic. Each of us puts in one little stone, and then you get a great mosaic at the end." (Quoted in Garraty, John A., ed. *Historical Viewpoints,* Vol. II. Harper & Row, 1983, p. 195.) Ask students what role civil disobedience played in Susan B. Anthony's efforts to gain suffrage. Have students compare the tactics of Catt and the NAWSA with those of Paul and the CU. How did the actions of both help the suffragists gain victory?

Assess/Reteach Gaining the right to vote was a long, arduous process for the women of the United States. Without dedication and persistence, this right might never have been won. As a class, discuss the ways in which the eventual passage of the Nineteenth Amendment opened the way toward ensuring equal rights for all Americans.

Activity

Connecting with Citizenship

Susan B. Anthony was one of many American activists who have used civil disobedience to protest an unfair law. Have students research other examples of civil disobedience in U.S. history, then use their findings to create original skits or role-plays. **(Bodily/Kinesthetic)**

READING CHECK
By personally lobbying Congress; cofounding the American Equal Rights Association; engaging in civil disobedience; and leading the National American Woman Suffrage Association.

American Biography

Susan B. Anthony 1820–1906

Like her father, a Quaker abolitionist, Susan B. Anthony was a crusader. She founded her own temperance group. She campaigned hard to get schools to open their doors to women and former slaves. As an abolitionist, Anthony faced armed mobs and threats. She fought for equal pay and an eight-hour workday for women.

Anthony ran a tireless campaign for women's voting rights as head of the National Woman Suffrage Association. For nearly 40 years, Anthony appeared before every Congress to demand a suffrage amendment. Anthony co-founded the National American Woman Suffrage Association, which she led for eight years, retiring in 1900. Devoting her life to her many causes, Anthony never married.

"Failure is impossible," Anthony declared before her death in 1906. Fourteen years later, her words came true with the ratification of the Nineteenth Amendment.

American women activists first formally demanded the right to vote in 1848 at the Seneca Falls Convention in New York. The meeting made famous the names of Lucretia Mott and Elizabeth Cady Stanton. A few years later, a young woman joined their cause: Susan B. Anthony. She, along with Stanton, would become the nation's most celebrated champions of women's suffrage.

Together, Anthony, a tireless strategist and organizer, and Stanton, a skilled speaker and writer, would take the women's suffrage movement into the twentieth century. In 1866, they founded the American Equal Rights Association and soon began publication of a newspaper, *The Revolution.* On its banner was emblazoned ". . . men, their rights and nothing more; women, their rights and nothing less."

The movement later split into two groups. Stanton and Anthony continued, as the National Woman Suffrage Association, to fight for a constitutional amendment for suffrage. Meanwhile, the newly formed American Woman Suffrage Association worked on the state level to win voting rights. When Wyoming entered the union in 1890, it became the first state to grant women full suffrage.

In 1872, Anthony led a group of women to the polls in Rochester, New York, where she insisted on voting. Anthony was arrested for this act of **civil disobedience.** Civil disobedience is a nonviolent refusal to obey a law in an effort to change it. While she awaited her trial, Anthony set out on a highly publicized lecture tour. During one of these lectures she asserted:

> *"The preamble of the Federal Constitution says: 'We, the people of the United States. . . . ' It was we, the people; not we, the white male citizens; nor yet we, the male citizens; but we, the whole people, who formed the Union. And we formed it, not to give the blessings of liberty, but to secure them; not to the half of ourselves and the half of our posterity, but to the whole people—women as well as men."*
>
> —Susan B. Anthony

Anthony was convicted at her trial and fined $100. She refused to pay the fine but was set free anyway. Legal maneuvering by the judge and her court-appointed lawyer prevented her from appealing the conviction and further pursuing her case.

READING CHECK
How did Susan B. Anthony contribute to the suffrage movement?

Suffragist Strategies

Suffragists continued to follow two paths toward their goal. One path was to press for a constitutional amendment giving women the vote. The most commonly used method of amending the Constitution required two thirds of each house of Congress to pass a measure. The measure then had to be ratified by three fourths of the state legislatures.

The other path pursued by suffragists was to get individual states to let women vote. At first this approach was more successful, especially in the western states. There, survival on the frontier required the combined efforts of men and women and encouraged a greater sense of equality between them.

Pushing for a federal amendment proved to be the more difficult approach. The first amendment introduced in Congress in 1868 stalled. In 1878, suffragists introduced a new amendment that adopted the wording of

Resource Directory

Teaching Resources

Biography, Literature, and Comparing Primary Sources booklet (Comparing Primary Sources) *On the Nineteenth Amendment,* p. 131

Technology

Exploring Primary Sources in U.S. History CD-ROM *Are Not the Women Half the Nation?*

RESOURCE PRO® **Literature Activity** *The "New" Woman,* found on Resource Pro, provides insight into the oppression of women at the turn of the century, with excerpts from Kate Chopin's novel, *The Awakening.*

RESOURCE PRO® **Visual Learning Activity** *When Women Have Rights,* found on Resource Pro, uses a 1913 cartoon to illustrate a popular antisuffrage argument.

Susan B. Anthony: "The right of citizens of the United States to vote shall not be denied or abridged by the United States or by any state on account of sex."

With this language, the proposed amendment received its first committee hearing. Elizabeth Cady Stanton described the chair of the committee, Senator Bainbridge Wadleigh of New Hampshire, as a picture of "inattention and contempt." "He stretched, yawned, gazed at the ceiling, cut his nails, sharpened his pencil, changing his occupation and position every two minutes."

Stalled again, the bill was not debated until 1887. It was then defeated in the Senate by a vote of 16 for, 34 against, and 26 absent. Supporters reintroduced the "Anthony Amendment," as the bill came to be called, every year until 1896. Then it disappeared, and did not resurface again until 1913.

Focus on CITIZENSHIP

Women in Law Practice Suffrage workers confronted strongly held attitudes about women and their proper social roles. When lawyer Myra Bradwell of Chicago was denied a state license to practice law in 1869, she took her case to the Supreme Court. In *Bradwell* v. *Illinois* (1873), the Court upheld the denial, reaffirming the "wide difference in the respective spheres and destinies of man and woman." Although Illinois had given Bradwell her license by 1890, most Americans believed that woman's proper sphere remained the home, not the workplace.

Suffrage at the Turn of the Century

In 1890, veteran leaders of the suffrage movement, including Anthony, Stanton, and Lucy Stone, were joined by younger leaders in forming the **National American Woman Suffrage Association (NAWSA).** Anthony served as president of NAWSA from 1892 until 1900.

By the time of NAWSA's founding, women had won many rights. For example, married women could now buy, sell, and will property. By 1900, growing numbers of women were demanding the vote. Some were participating in voluntary organizations that investigated social conditions. These women were publicizing their findings, suggesting reforms, lobbying officials, and monitoring enforcement of new laws. Working women were becoming more active in unions, picketing, and getting arrested. To many of these women, being denied the right to vote seemed ridiculous.

Yet from the late 1890s to 1910, the suffrage movement was in "the doldrums," as one historian put it. Years of legal efforts to win suffrage had failed. The rise of progressivism brought new political support, but it was not enough to turn the tide. The beloved leaders of the suffrage movement, Stanton and

COMPARING PRIMARY SOURCES

Voting Rights for Women

In the early 1900s, the longtime debate over women's suffrage entered a heated, final stage prior to the passage of the Nineteenth Amendment.

Analyzing Viewpoints Summarize the arguments made in the two quotations below.

In Favor of Women's Suffrage

"The great doctrine of the American Republic that 'all governments derive their just powers from the consent of the governed' justifies the plea of one-half of the people, the women, to exercise the suffrage. The doctrine of the American Revolutionary War that taxation without representation is unendurable justifies women in exercising the suffrage."

—*Robert L. Owen, senator from Oklahoma, 1910*

Opposed to Women's Suffrage

"In political warfare, it is perfectly fitting that actual strife and battle should be apportioned [given out] to man, and that the influence of woman, radiating from the homes of our land, should inspire to lofty aims and purposes those who struggle for the right. I am thoroughly convinced that woman can in no better way than this usefully serve the cause of political betterment."

—*Grover Cleveland,* Ladies' Home Journal, *October 1905*

ACTIVITY Student Portfolio

You may wish to have students add the following to their portfolios: Ask students to use an almanac to find the percentage of eligible women voting in each of the presidential elections since 1920 and to compare it with the percentage of eligible males voting. Students can show the statistics in a series of simple bar graphs or a table. **(Logical/Mathematical)**

BACKGROUND Recent Scholarship

African American women and men supported the movement for women's suffrage from the beginning. However, the movement, which was led by white women, included instances of racism and divisiveness, as Rosalyn Terborg-Penn's *African American Women in the Struggle for the Vote, 1850–1920* makes clear. In fact, some southern women suffrage leaders sought to both enfranchise the "best white women in the South" and disenfranchise American black women, thus preserving the inequalities of race and class.

BACKGROUND Biography

Born into slavery, Ida Bell Wells-Barnett (1862–1931) founded what was probably the first African American women's suffrage group, Chicago's Alpha Suffrage Club. As a journalist she was a strident crusader against the lynching of African Americans in the South, and in 1909 she helped organize the National Association for the Advancement of Colored People (NAACP). Her memoirs, *Crusade for Justice,* were published posthumously in 1970.

CUSTOMIZE FOR ...

Less Proficient Writers

Have students review the quote on this page from Susan B. Anthony. Then have them paraphrase the quote using their own words.

TEST PREPARATION

Have students read the quotation by Elizabeth Cady Stanton on this page and then complete the sentence below.

Based on Stanton's description of New Hampshire senator Bainbridge Wadleigh's behavior as he listened to a hearing about the Nineteenth Amendment, you can infer that Senator Wadleigh—

A avidly supported the proposed amendment.
B wanted to know more about Elizabeth Cady Stanton.
C did not like being a senator.
(D) did not support the proposed amendment.

ACTIVITY
Connecting with Culture

How did women's clothing styles reflect the shift in women's attitudes and roles in the early twentieth century? Have students do research and create a poster or bulletin board display illustrating various styles of women's clothing between 1890 and 1920. Illustrations can be original or taken from period publications. The display might be combined with a time line of the period showing important cultural and political milestones for women. **(Visual/Spatial)**

BACKGROUND
Global Connections

By 1915, as the American women's suffrage movement worked furiously toward its goal, only four nations had granted women the right to vote in national elections: New Zealand (1893), Australia (1902), Finland (1906), and Norway (1913). During and after World War I, more than two dozen nations granted women the vote, including Canada (1918), Germany, Austria, Poland, and Czechoslovakia (1919). In 1920 Hungary gave women the vote.

World War II led to even wider enfranchisement, with over 100 nations granting full voting rights to women by 1970. Today in some conservative Arab and Muslim countries, women are still denied the right to vote.

VIEWING HISTORY At the 1913 suffrage rally hundreds of participants were taunted and injured by opponents, yet the event was considered a success. **Drawing Conclusions** *What reasons might suffragists have had for viewing the rally as a victory?*

Anthony, died in 1902 and 1906, respectively—without seeing the realization of their life's work. It was time for a new generation to create momentum and take the cause of suffrage to victory.

A New Generation

One new leader who emerged to re-energize the movement was Carrie Chapman Catt, a former high school principal and superintendent of schools in Mason City, Iowa. A talented speaker and organizer, she headed NAWSA from 1900 to 1904, and then again after 1915. As head of NAWSA, Catt insisted on precinct-by-precinct political work with close coordination among districts.

Alice Paul also rose as a leader in the women's suffrage movement. She had learned tactics from the aggressive English suffrage movement while she was a student in England. In January 1913, she and a friend, Lucy Burns, took over the NAWSA committee that was working on congressional passage of the federal suffrage amendment.

Two months later, the two women had organized a parade of 5,000 women in Washington, D.C. The parade took place on the day before Woodrow Wilson's inauguration. It drew so much attention that few supporters greeted Wilson when he arrived at the train station. After the success of the rally, Paul transformed her committee into a new organization, the **Congressional Union (CU).**

A Split in the Movement Following Paul's action, a split occurred within the suffrage movement. Paul's CU called for an aggressive, militant campaign for the constitutional amendment. She planned to bypass existing state suffrage organizations and set up new ones in each state.

The leadership of NAWSA opposed Paul's plan, believing it would alienate moderate supporters. In February 1914, they expelled the Congressional Union from the organization. The CU went on to stage militant protests. They demonstrated in front of the White House. They set aflame a life-size dummy of Wilson, who was still refusing to back the suffrage amendment. They burned copies of his speeches. Exasperated authorities arrested CU members and sent them to prison, where they went on hunger strikes to protest horrible prison conditions.

This suffrage poster urges parents to consider the future of their daughters.

Meanwhile, NAWSA continued to back the state suffrage campaigns. The group focused its efforts on winning the vote in four eastern states: New York, Pennsylvania, Massachusetts, and New Jersey. In 1915, the suffrage campaigns failed in all four states. At that point, Carrie Chapman Catt was reinstated as NAWSA president and given free rein to bring about victory. Out of this challenge came her "Winning Plan."

This plan consisted of developing a large group of full-time leaders to work in "red-hot" campaigns for six years. In addition, NAWSA decided to focus on getting Congress to re-introduce the federal suffrage amendment.

By 1917, NAWSA had grown into the largest volunteer organization in the country, with 2 million members. In the fall of that year, it won an important victory when New York State voted for women's suffrage. New York, with its

CAPTION ANSWERS

Viewing History The event attracted much attention, in part because of the way the protesters were treated. Also, it upstaged the arrival of Wilson for his inauguration the next day.

RESOURCE DIRECTORY

Teaching Resources
Units 3/4 booklet
- Section 4 Quiz, p. 18
- Chapter 11 Test, pp. 19, 22

Guide to the Essentials
- Section 4 Summary, p. 56
- Chapter 11 Test, p. 57

Other Print Resources
Chapter Tests with ExamView® Test Bank CD-ROM, Ch. 11

Technology
Sounds of an Era Audio CD *Carrie Chapman Cott* (time: 30 seconds)
ExamView® Test Bank CD-ROM, Ch. 11
Social Studies Skills Tutor CD-ROM

large number of electoral votes in presidential elections, would now be courted by candidates seeking the support of the state's women voters.

Impact of World War I The United States entered World War I in April 1917. Women across the country hastened to do their patriotic duty by volunteering for ambulance corps and for medical work and by taking on jobs left by men. Arguments of separate spheres for women and men were forgotten during wartime.

In addition, Congress adopted the Eighteenth Amendment, prohibiting the sale of liquor. As a result of this action, liquor interests no longer had reason to fight suffrage.

Passage of Women's Suffrage

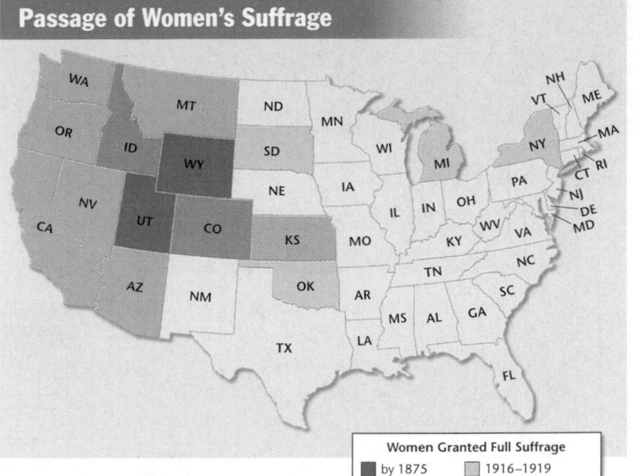

Women Granted Full Suffrage
- by 1875
- 1876–1900
- 1901–1915
- 1916–1919
- by the 19th Amendment, 1920

Map shows present-day borders.

MAP SKILLS Women's suffrage was already in place in many states by the time the Nineteenth Amendment was ratified. **Analyzing Visual Information** *What pattern do you see in the locations of states that did and did not pass suffrage at the state level?*

Victory for Suffrage

In 1918, Congress formally proposed the suffrage amendment. Its members finally succumbed to the political forces of states that had passed suffrage and to the unrelenting work of NAWSA. They also had been keenly embarrassed and disturbed by the treatment that the women of Alice Paul's Congressional Union had received in filthy jails, where some hunger strikers were force-fed. After the amendment was proposed in Congress, the ratification battle began. It would end in August, 1920, when Tennessee became the 36th state necessary to ratify the suffrage amendment.

As suffragist Carrie Chapman Catt commented when the exhausting battle of many decades was finally over, "It is doubtful that any man . . . ever realized what the suffrage struggle came to mean to women. . . . It leaves its mark on one, such a struggle." The Nineteenth Amendment marked the last major reform of the Progressive Era.

Section 4 Assessment

READING COMPREHENSION

1. Describe how Anthony and Stanton worked together to lead the suffrage movement.
2. Why was the suffrage movement in need of new leadership after the turn of the century?
3. How did the **National American Woman Suffrage Association** and the **Congressional Union** differ in their tactics?
4. (a) How did passage of the Nineteenth Amendment come about? (b) Why did the battle take so long?

CRITICAL THINKING AND WRITING

5. **Drawing Inferences** How do you think the state-by-state efforts of suffragists affected the effort to win a constitutional amendment on suffrage?
6. **Writing an Opinion** Identify the goals, strategies, and tactics of two of the suffrage leaders described in this section. Which leader or group do you think was most effective? Why? Write a brief paragraph expressing your opinion.

Take It to the NET

Activity: Writing an Essay Study the suffrage movement online. Write an essay comparing the suffrage movement to other struggles for liberty. Use the links provided in the *America: Pathways to the Present* area of the following Web site for help in completing this activity.
www.phschool.com

Section 4 Assessment

Reading Comprehension

1. Founded the American Equal Rights Association; published *The Revolution;* worked for a voting rights constitutional amendment; formed National American Woman Suffrage Association.
2. Suffrage efforts were failing; deaths of Stanton and Anthony.
3. CU: aggressive, militant tactics, wanted new state suffrage organizations. NAWSA opposed CU, fearing CU would alienate moderate supporters; NAWSA worked with old state organizations toward a federal suffrage amendment.
4. (a) Women in voluntary organizations and unions began to demand the right to vote. They pressed for a constitutional amendment and for individual states to allow women to vote. Ratification came in 1920. (b) Widely held attitudes about role of women; loss of momentum in suffrage movement; amendment bill stalled in Congress.

Critical Thinking and Writing

5. Successes in individual states contributed support for federal amendment allowing female suffrage.
6. Answers will vary but should be supported with facts from the section.

Take It to the NET

Answers will vary. Students might compare the opposition to, the tactics of, and the level of violence of the suffrage movement to other struggles for liberty, as well as the successfulness of each movement.

CUSTOMIZE FOR ...

Gifted and Talented

Ask students to list arguments used against women's suffrage. Then ask them to refute each of the arguments.

Caption Answers

Map Skills The states that adopted suffrage soonest were mostly in the West. The Northeast, Midwest, and South were slower to accept women as voters.

Reviewing Key Terms

Students should refer to the definitions of key terms in the chapter to write sentences that show an understanding of the Progressive Reform Era.

Reviewing Main Ideas

11. People: George, Bellamy, Kelley, Jones. Muckrakers such as Sinclair, Tarbell, Steffens. Ideas: honest government, government involvement in social welfare, giving more power to voters.
12. Progressives studied social problems using scientific methods. They publicized their results to pressure lawmakers. Muckrakers used investigative journalism to publicize progressive causes.
13. State reformers wanted to give more power to voters, for example, through direct primaries. They also championed labor and factory legislation. Urban reformers attacked political machines, took over utilities, and expanded welfare services.
14. Theodore Roosevelt sponsored antitrust initiatives; conserved natural resources; regulated railroads; and spearheaded reform of the meatpacking industry. Constitutional amendments expanded the power of the federal government.
15. He had not been elected, and he faced congressional opposition.
16. Taft achieved many progressive goals, such as increased prosecution of antitrust cases. He lost progressive support, however, because of events such as the Ballinger-Pinchot affair and his failure to lower the tariff.
17. His progressive beliefs and a split Republican vote.
18. Preparations for war began to occupy the nation.
19. To win suffrage in individual states and to pass a constitutional amendment allowing female suffrage.
20. Answers will vary but should be supported with facts from the section.

Critical Thinking

21. Possible answers: Henry George and the "single tax"; Upton Sinclair's expose of problems in the

Chapter 11 Review and Assessment

creating a CHAPTER SUMMARY

Copy the chart (right) on a piece of paper and complete it by adding information about the Progressive Era. Some entries have been completed for you as examples. Add as many entries as you can.

Progressive Era Reforms		
Municipal Level	**State Level**	**Federal Level**
Regulating utilities		Pure Food and Drug Act

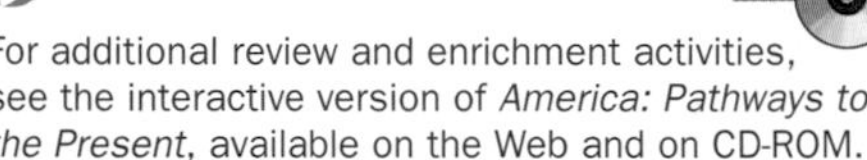

For additional review and enrichment activities, see the interactive version of *America: Pathways to the Present*, available on the Web and on CD-ROM.

★ Reviewing Key Terms

For each of the terms below, write a sentence explaining how it relates to the Progressive reforms.

1. Progressive Era
2. muckraker
3. injunction
4. municipal
5. holding company
6. conservationist
7. New Nationalism
8. Bull Moose Party
9. Federal Reserve System
10. civil disobedience

★ Reviewing Main Ideas

11. What people and ideas contributed to the rise of progressivism? (Section 1)
12. What were the typical methods of Progressive reformers? (Section 1)
13. Summarize progressive reforms at the municipal and state levels. (Section 2)
14. Describe progressive reforms at the national level. (Section 2)
15. Why did TR have to proceed with caution on pushing for reforms in his first term? (Section 2)
16. What were the main successes and failures of Taft's presidency? (Section 3)
17. What factors contributed to the election of Wilson in 1912? (Section 3)
18. Why did progressivism decline? (Section 3)
19. What two main approaches did women's organizations take to win suffrage? (Section 4)
20. Choose two leaders of the suffrage movement and describe their contributions to the cause. (Section 4)

★ Critical Thinking

21. **Drawing Conclusions** In what ways did reform movements benefit from the contributions of both men and women? Give examples.
22. **Drawing Inferences** Why do you think reformers at the municipal and state levels began by passing voting reforms and tackling corruption?
23. **Synthesizing Information** How did Roosevelt use the "bully pulpit," and how did his style shape the modern presidency?
24. **Making Comparisons** How did TR, Taft, and Wilson compare in their approaches to reform?
25. **Identifying Central Issues** What was the Clayton Antitrust Act, and why was it important to progressive reformers and labor leaders?
26. **Recognizing Cause and Effect** What kinds of reforms contributed to an increase in the size and role of government?
27. **Analyzing Information** What shift in public attitudes was necessary for social welfare programs to gain support and passage?

Creating a Chapter Summary

Progressive Era Reforms		
Municipal Level	**State Level**	**Federal Level**
Regulating utilities	Voting reforms, i.e., direct primary, initiative, referendum, recall	Pure Food and Drug Act
Workplace protections	Workplace protections	Sherman Antitrust Act
Home rule	Abolition of child labor	Constitutional amendments 16, 17, 18 and 19
Providing welfare services	Minimum wage laws	Establishment of Department of Labor, U.S. Forest Service, National Park Service, Women's and Children's Boards

meatpacking industry; Florence Kelley and Mother Jones working for labor reform.

22. Reformers needed to attack political machines in order to make governments honest and more accountable to voters before progressive reform legislation could be passed.

23. Roosevelt used his authority as President to push for reform. He believed in and exerted the power of the presidency.

24. TR: used personal skills to push aggressively for certain reforms. Taft: lacked TR's ability to push for reform legislation, compromised more, yet still made significant achievements. Wilson: believed it was the President's duty to submit bills to Congress. Thus, he pushed for progressive reform.

25. The Clayton Antitrust Act strengthened the Sherman Antitrust Act by specifying actions businesses could not do and by supporting unions. It showed that government was committed to regulating business and protecting workers.

26. New federal regulatory agencies such as the Federal Trade Commission and the Federal Reserve System increased the federal budget and the federal work force. Measures such as prohibition and federal income tax increased the role of government in citizens' lives.

27. Americans became accustomed to an increasing government role in their lives.

★ Skills Assessment

Analyzing Political Cartoons ▶

28. Examine this 1904 cartoon at right. (a) What does the octopus represent? (b) What does the octopus hold in its tentacles? (c) What is it reaching for?

29. Why is the octopus pictured on a globe?

30. (a) What overall point is the cartoonist trying to make? (b) Why was an octopus such a good choice for making this point?

Analyzing Primary Sources

Read the quotation from Jane Addams on page 386, and answer the questions that follow.

31. In comparing the lives of rural and urban women, Addams' main purpose was to point out

- **A** the problems that united women throughout the country.
- **B** their differing lifestyles and roles in American society.
- **C** the ways in which urban living presented new problems for women.
- **D** the reasons that rural children were healthier.

32. In this quotation, Addams made the argument for

- **F** better health services for children.
- **G** more and better government services in cities, to help families survive.
- **H** the need for garbage collection in rural areas, to prevent the spread of disease.
- **J** programs to get women and children out of tenement houses.

Applying the Chapter Skill: *Testing Conclusions*

33. Based on the results of the election of 1912, is it reasonable to conclude that most Americans favored some amount of progressive reform? Explain.

ACTIVITIES

Writing to LEARN

Writing a News Story
Write a brief newspaper or broadcast story on the 1900 Galveston hurricane. Identify the basic facts of the event, as well as immediate and long-term effects of the tragedy. Include fictional quotations from city government officials, reformers, and survivors of the devastation.

Primary Source CD-ROM

Working With Primary Sources Find additional information on the Progressive era on the *Exploring Primary Sources in U.S. History CD-ROM* and use the selection(s) provided to complete the Chapter 11 primary source activity located in the *America: Pathways to the Present* area of the following Web site.
www.phschool.com

Take It to the NET

Chapter Self-Test As a review activity, take the Chapter 11 Self-Test in the *America: Pathways to the Present* area at the Web site listed below. The questions are designed to test your understanding of the chapter content.
www.phschool.com

Skills Assessment

28. (a) Standard Oil Company.
(b) Government and industry.
(c) The White House.

29. To imply that Standard Oil was trying to control the entire world.

30. (a) That Standard Oil had a stranglehold on government and industry.
(b) It demonstrates the powerful, far-reaching control of the Standard Oil Company.

31. C

32. G

33. Yes. Roosevelt and Wilson, who both supported progressivism, between them gained almost 70 percent of the popular vote.

ANSWERS TO ACTIVITIES

Writing to LEARN

Answers will vary but should focus on the area hit, the amount of destruction, deaths, and how the rebuilding efforts led to a commission form of government.

Primary Source CD-ROM

Direct students to the additional primary sources that can be found on the *Exploring Primary Sources in U.S. History CD-ROM.*

Take It to the NET

Additional support materials and activities for Chapter 11 of *America: Pathways to the Present* can be found in the Social Studies area at the Prentice Hall School Web site. **www.phschool.com**

Fighting for Freedom and Democracy

Focus Remind students that Americans have gone to war numerous times to protect the country's freedom and democracy. In recent history, the United States has rallied troops to face down threats from Germans, Japanese, Russians, and, most recently, terrorists in Afghanistan.

Instruct Have students carefully read the description of each conflict in which the United States has been engaged. Tell students to discuss the differences between internal conflicts, which take place among groups living in the United States, and external conflicts, which occur outside United States borders. How does each kind of conflict affect the economy, government, and morale of the United States?

Extend Encourage students to focus on one of the time periods described in "Fighting for Freedom and Democracy." Tell students to write a report on the conflict. Why did Americans become involved? How did the role of the United States affect its citizens? How did the involvement of the United States affect the resolution of the conflict?

American Pathways
HISTORY

Fighting for Freedom and Democracy

Throughout the nation's history, Americans have stepped forward to risk their lives to protect freedom and democracy. More than 40 million Americans have fought in the nation's wars both at home and abroad, and more than one million have given their lives to preserve their country's cherished ideals.

1 From Colonies to Nation

1565–1783 As Europeans established a presence in North America, conflicts occurred among the competing nations as well as with Native Americans. Ultimately, the colonists' struggle to gain independence from Britain resulted in the creation of a new country built on the foundations of freedom, equality, and self-government.

Emanuel Gottlieb Leutze's *George Washington Crossing the Delaware* (left)

2 The New Nation Asserts Its Authority

1812–1848 In the first half of the nineteenth century, the United States asserted its sovereignty during the War of 1812 and the Mexican-American War, as well as with the proclamation of the Monroe Doctrine.

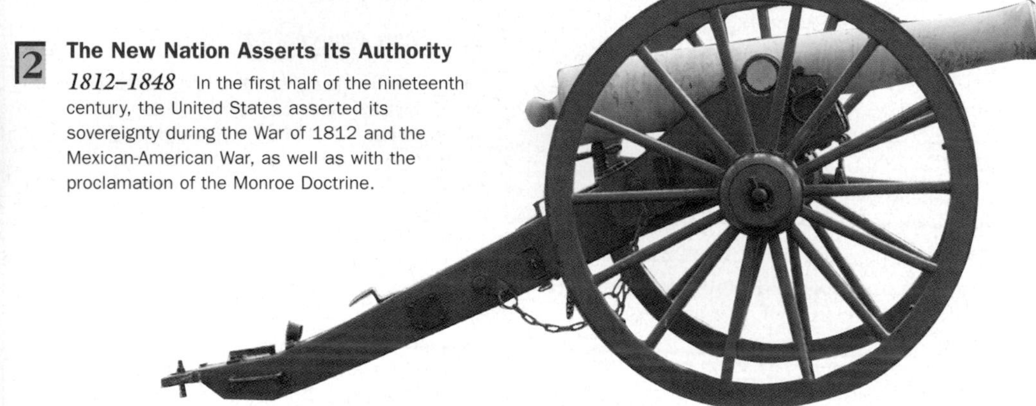

3 Civil War and Reunion

1861–1890 From 1861 to 1865, the Civil War split the nation in two as armies from the North and the South battled over the issues of states' rights and slavery. Although the Union was restored, conflicts developed over the status of freed African Americans during the Reconstruction period. In the West, Native Americans continued to resist the expansion of the United States.

A cannon used in the Battle of Gettysburg (above)

410

RESOURCE DIRECTORY

Teaching Resources

Units 3/4 booklet

- American Pathways Activity, pp. 37–38

American Pathways Thematic Posters

Technology

Companion Web site, www.phschool.com

Becoming a World Power and World War I

1890–1918 As a result of the industrial boom at the turn of the century, the United States expanded its foreign trade. When German submarines attacked neutral American merchant ships, the United States entered World War I and helped the French and English defeat the Germans. In the words of President Wilson, Americans fought "to make the world safe for democracy."

Allied troops fighting in the trenches during World War I (left)

Isolationism

1920–1940 The horrors of World War I convinced many Americans that the country should end foreign entanglements and curtail military expenditures.

World War II and the Cold War

1941–1991 Tensions between the United States and the Soviet Union developed at the end of World War II and lasted for 50 years until the collapse of the Soviet Union in 1991. Throughout that time, the goal of U.S. foreign policy was to prevent the spread of communism.

American troops landing in Normandy, France, on D-Day, June 6, 1944 (above)

Regional Conflicts and Terrorism

1991–Present In the post–Cold War period, the United States played a role in resolving many regional ethnic conflicts. The nation also struggled to preserve its freedoms in the face of terrorism.

Firemen raise an American flag amid the rubble of the World Trade Center following the terrorist attacks on New York and Washington, D.C., on September 11, 2001 (above).

Continuity and Change

1. What factors contributed to the country's relative isolationism between the two World Wars?
2. Explain how the Cold War began and ended.

Take It to the NET: Creating a Study Guide Print and complete the study guide for this topic found in the *America: Pathways to the Present* area of the following Web site. **www.phschool.com**

Take It to the NET

Students can print the American Pathways thematic study guide for this topic at the Prentice Hall School Web site, or you can provide students with copies of the study guide, which is found in the Units 3/4 booklet, the American Pathways Activity, pages 37–38. Students should use their texts to fill in a one-sentence description for each event on the study guide. When completed for each of the American Pathways topics, the thematic study guides will aid students in preparing for an end-of-course exam.

Answers

1. The savagery of World War I made Americans wary of involvement in foreign affairs. The stock market crash of 1929 and subsequent Depression limited American resources and kept American military budgets low.
2. The Cold War arose out of tensions between the United States and the Soviet Union at the end of World War II and from the deeply held philosophical differences between Soviet-backed communism and U.S.–supported capitalism. The Cold War ended following Soviet leader Mikhail Gorbachev's glasnost ("political openness") policies in the late 1980s, the subsequent collapse of Eastern European Communist governments, the destruction of the Berlin Wall, Strategic Arms Reduction agreements, and the dissolution of the Soviet Union at the beginning of 1992.

Chapter 12 Planning Guide

Resource Manager

	Core Instruction	Reading/Skills
Chapter-Level Resources TEKS 24(B)	Teaching Resources • Pacing Charts booklet • Block Scheduling booklet **Resource Pro® CD-ROM,** Ch. 12 **Prentice Hall Presentation Pro CD-ROM,** Ch. 12 **www.phschool.com** • eTeach	**Guided Reading Audiotapes (English/Spanish)** **Student Edition on Audio CD,** Ch. 12 **Social Studies Skills Tutor CD-ROM** **Color Transparencies,** A32, A33, A34, D8, H15, H16
1 The Road to War 1. Identify the main causes of World War I. 2. Understand how the conflict expanded to draw in much of Europe. 3. Analyze how the United States responded to the war in Europe. **TEKS** 1(C)	Teaching Resources **Units 3/4 booklet** • Section 1 Quiz, p. 26 **Learning Styles Lesson Plans booklet,** p. 40	**Guided Reading and Review booklet,** p. 78 **Guide to the Essentials,** p. 58 **Learning with Documents booklet,** p. 24 **Skills for Life booklet,** p. 21 **Section Reading Support Transparencies**
2 The United States Declares War 1. Discover how Germany's use of submarines affected the war. 2. Find out the steps the United States took toward war in early 1917. **TEKS** 3(B), 24(A), 26(A)	Teaching Resources **Units 3/4 booklet** • Section 2 Quiz, p. 27	**Guided Reading and Review booklet,** p. 79 **Guide to the Essentials,** p. 59 **Section Reading Support Transparencies**
3 Americans on the European Front 1. Analyze the preparations of the United States for World War I. 2. Study the ways in which the American troops helped turn the tide of the war. 3. Learn about conditions in Europe and the United States at the end of the war. **TEKS** 3(C), 8(B), 24(A)	Teaching Resources **Units 3/4 booklet** • Section 3 Quiz, p. 28	**Guided Reading and Review booklet,** p. 80 **Guide to the Essentials,** p. 60 **Section Reading Support Transparencies**
4 Americans on the Home Front 1. Learn about the steps the government took to finance the war and manage the economy. 2. Describe how the government enforced loyalty to the war effort. 3. Find out how the war changed the lives of Americans on the home front. **TEKS** 12(E), 15(B), 24(A), 24(F)	Teaching Resources **Units 3/4 booklet** • Section 4 Quiz, p. 29	**Guided Reading and Review booklet,** p. 81 **Guide to the Essentials,** p. 61 **Learning with Documents booklet,** p. 58 **Section Reading Support Transparencies**
5 Global Peacemaker 1. Discover the expectations that Wilson and the Allies brought to the Paris peace conference. 2. Learn about the important provisions of the peace treaty. 3. Find out how the federal government and ordinary Americans reacted to the end of the war. **TEKS** 3(D), 9(B), 24(A), 24(H)	Teaching Resources **Units 3/4 booklet** • Section 5 Quiz, p. 30 **Learning Styles Lesson Plans booklet,** p. 41	**Guided Reading and Review booklet,** p. 82 **Guide to the Essentials,** p. 62 **Learning with Documents booklet,** p. 86 **Section Reading Support Transparencies**

Enrichment/Pre-AP

Prentice Hall United States History Video Collection™
www.phschool.com
- Section Activities, Virtual Field Trip, Chapter Activities, Current Events Online

Biography, Literature, and Comparing Primary Sources booklet, p. 66
American History Block Scheduling Support
Historical Outline Map Book, p. 60
Sounds of an Era Audio CD

Biography, Literature, and Comparing Primary Sources booklet, p. 24
Sounds of an Era Audio CD
Exploring Primary Sources in U.S. History CD-ROM

Historical Outline Map Book, p. 61
Sounds of an Era Audio CD
Exploring Primary Sources in U.S. History CD-ROM

American History Block Scheduling Support
Nystrom *Atlas of Our Country,* pp. 30–31
Sounds of an Era Audio CD

Biography, Literature, and Comparing Primary Sources booklet, p. 133
Historical Outline Map Book, p. 62
Exploring Primary Sources in U.S. History CD-ROM
American Pathways Thematic Posters

Assessment

Prentice Hall Assessment System

Core Assessment
ExamView® Test Bank, Ch. 12
ExamView® Test Bank CD-ROM, Ch. 12

Standardized Test Preparation
Diagnose and Prescribe
Diagnostic Tests for High School Social Studies Skills

Review and Reteach
Review Book for U.S. History

Practice and Assess
Test-taking Strategies With Transparencies
Test-taking Strategies Posters
Test Prep Book for U.S. History
Alternative Assessment Handbook
Document-Based Assessment

Teaching Resources
Units 3/4 booklet
- Section Quizzes, pp. 26–30
- Chapter Tests, pp. 31–34

www.phschool.com Ch. 12 Self-Test

AmericanHeritage® Resources

From the Archives of American Heritage®, pp. 434, 439
AmericanHeritage® My Brush with History™ Videotapes
www.americanheritage.com

Don't miss the exclusive interactive version of this textbook on the Web and on CD-ROM.

Chapter 12 Planning Guide
In Your Classroom

Customize for Individual Needs

Gifted and Talented

Teacher's Edition
- Customize for Gifted and Talented, pp. 429, 433

Teaching Resources
- Biography, Literature, and Comparing Primary Sources booklet, pp. 24, 66, 133

Technology
- Exploring Primary Sources in U.S. History CD-ROM *Zimmermann Telegram; Diary of a World War I Ambulance Driver, William Stevenson; The Fourteen Points*

ESL

Teacher's Edition
- Customize for ESL, p. 415

Teaching Resources
- Guided Reading and Review booklet, pp. 78–82
- Guide to the Essentials (English/Spanish), Chapter 12

Technology
- Student Edition on Audio CD, Chapter 12
- Guided Reading Audiotapes (English/Spanish), Chapter 12
- Section Reading Support Transparencies

Less Proficient Readers

Teacher's Edition
- Customize for Less Proficient Readers, p. 423

Teaching Resources
- Guided Reading and Review booklet, pp. 78–82
- Guide to the Essentials (English/Spanish), Chapter 12

Technology
- Student Edition on Audio CD, Chapter 12
- Guided Reading Audiotapes (English/Spanish), Chapter 12
- Section Reading Support Transparencies

Less Proficient Writers

Teacher's Edition
- Customize for Less Proficient Writers, p. 441

Teaching Resources
- Guided Reading and Review booklet, pp. 78–82
- Guide to the Essentials (English/Spanish), Chapter 12

Technology
- Student Edition on Audio CD, Chapter 12
- Guided Reading Audiotapes (English/Spanish), Chapter 12
- Section Reading Support Transparencies

Teacher's Edition Index

Chapter 12 – Pacing Suggestions

For 90-minute Blocks

- Teach sections 1 and 3 using Transparencies A31, A32, A33, A34, C6, D8, H15, and H16, and the Recent Scholarship note on page 435 for class discussions.

Running Out of Time?

If you are running short on time to cover this chapter, consider the following options:

- Use the Prentice Hall Presentation Pro CD-ROM to create an outline for this chapter.
- Use the Section Summaries for Chapter 12, from **Guide to the Essentials (English/Spanish)**.

TEKS CORRELATION

Chapter-Level	TEKS
	(24) Social studies skills. The student applies critical-thinking skills to organize and use information acquired from a variety of sources, including electronic technology. The student is expected to: **(B)** analyze information by sequencing, categorizing, identifying cause-and-effect relationships, comparing, contrasting, finding the main idea, summarizing, making generalizations and predictions, and drawing inferences and conclusions.
1 The Road to War	**(1) History.** The student understands traditional historical points of reference in U.S. history from 1877 to the present. The student is expected to: **(C)** explain the significance of the following dates: 1898, 1914–1918, 1929, 1941–1945, and 1957.
2 The United States Declares War	**(3) History.** The student understands the emergence of the United States as a world power between 1898 and 1920. The student is expected to: **(B)** identify the reasons for U.S. involvement in World War I, including unrestricted submarine warfare. **(24) Social studies skills.** The student applies critical-thinking skills to organize and use information acquired from a variety of sources, including electronic technology. The student is expected to: **(A)** locate and use primary and secondary sources such as computer software, databases, media and news services, biographies, interviews, and artifacts to acquire information about the United States. **(26) Social studies skills.** The student uses problem-solving and decision-making skills, working independently and with others, in a variety of settings. The student is expected to: **(A)** use a problem-solving process to identify a problem, gather information, list and consider options, consider advantages and disadvantages, choose and implement a solution, and evaluate the effectiveness of the solution.
3 Americans on the European Front	**(3) History.** The student understands the emergence of the United States as a world power between 1898 and 1920. The student is expected to: **(C)** analyze significant events such as the battle of Argonne Forest and the impact of significant individuals, including John J. Pershing, during World War I. **(8) Geography.** The student uses geographic tools to collect, analyze, and interpret data. The student is expected to: **(B)** pose and answer questions about geographic distributions and patterns shown on maps, graphs, charts, models, and databases. **(24) Social studies skills.** The student applies critical-thinking skills to organize and use information acquired from a variety of sources, including electronic technology. The student is expected to: **(A)** locate and use primary and secondary sources such as computer software, databases, media and news services, biographies, interviews, and artifacts to acquire information about the United States.
4 Americans on the Home Front	**(12) Economics.** The student understands domestic and foreign issues related to U.S. economic growth from the 1870s to 1920. The student is expected to: **(E)** describe the economic effects of international military conflicts, including the Spanish-American War and World War I, on the United States. **(15) Government.** The student understands changes in the role of government over time. The student is expected to: **(B)** explain the impact of significant international events such as World War I and World War II on changes in the role of the federal government. **(24) Social studies skills.** The student applies critical-thinking skills to organize and use information acquired from a variety of sources, including electronic technology. The student is expected to: **(A)** locate and use primary and secondary sources such as computer software, databases, media and news services, biographies, interviews, and artifacts to acquire information about the United States. **(F)** identify bias in written, oral, and visual material.
5 Global Peacemaker	**(3) History.** The student understands the emergence of the United States as a world power between 1898 and 1920. The student is expected to: **(D)** analyze major issues raised by U.S. involvement in World War I, Wilson's Fourteen Points, and the Treaty of Versailles. **(9) Geography.** The student understands the impact of geographic factors on major events. The student is expected to: **(B)** identify and explain reasons for changes in political boundaries such as those resulting from statehood and international conflicts. **(24) Social studies skills.** The student applies critical-thinking skills to organize and use information acquired from a variety of sources, including electronic technology. The student is expected to: **(A)** locate and use primary and secondary sources such as computer software, databases, media and news services, biographies, interviews, and artifacts to acquire information. **(H)** use appropriate mathematical skills to interpret social studies information such as maps and graphs.

Chapter 12

The World War I Era

(1914–1920)

Introducing the Chapter

In the second decade of the twentieth century, a terrible war began in Europe, with the death toll eventually totaling an estimated 8 million combatants—and many more civilians. At first the United States vowed to maintain its neutrality. However, the nation finally declared war in order to support its allies and defend its commercial interests.

Time Line Activity

To provide students with practice in using the time line, ask questions such as these:

1. What impact did the assassination of Archduke Francis Ferdinand have on the United States? *(His 1914 assassination caused many people to call for the United States to enter the war, but President Wilson declared that the country would stay neutral.)*
2. Explain the significance of the following dates: 1914–1918. *(World War I was fought between 1914 and 1918.)*
3. Did the sinking of the *Lusitania* cause the United States to enter World War I? *(Not directly, but it did cause more Americans to be in favor of the entry of the United States into the war.)*

Chapter 12

The World War I Era

(1914–1920)

Assassination of Archduke Francis Ferdinand

"All the News That's Fit to Print." The New York Times. EXTRA 5:30 A.M.

LUSITANIA SUNK BY A SUBMARINE, PROBABLY 1,260 DEAD; TWICE TORPEDOED OFF IRISH COAST; SINKS IN 15 MINUTES; CAPT. TURNER SAVED, FROHMAN AND VANDERBILT MISSING; WASHINGTON BELIEVES THAT A GRAVE CRISIS IS AT HAND

American Events

1914 President Wilson announces American neutrality in the war.

1915 The sinking of the *Lusitania* angers Americans.

1916 With the Sussex pledge, Germany promises the United States that U-boats will warn ships before attacking.

Presidential Terms: Woodrow Wilson 1913–1921

1912 — 1914 — 1916

World Events

1914 Assassination of Archduke Francis Ferdinand triggers World War I.

1915 Poison gas is first used against the Allies.

1916 Millions of British, French, and German soldiers die in failed offensives at Verdun and the Somme River.

eTeach

Be sure to check out this month's online discussion with a Master Teacher. Go to **www.phschool.com.**

Resource Directory

Teaching Resources

Pacing Charts booklet

Block Scheduling booklet, p. 22

Units 3/4 booklet

- Chapter Summary, p. 25

Technology

Guided Reading Audiotapes (English/Spanish), Ch. 12

Student Edition on Audio CD, Ch. 12

Color Transparencies *Historical Maps,* A31; *Time Lines,* C6

Sounds of an Era Audio CD *"It's a Long Way to Tipperary,"* 1917 recording

Prentice Hall United States History Video Collection™ Volume 16, *The Great War*

Prentice Hall Presentation Pro CD-ROM, Ch. 12

Resource Pro® CD-ROM

Social Studies Skills Tutor CD-ROM

Companion Web site, www.phschool.com

The World at War, 1914–1918

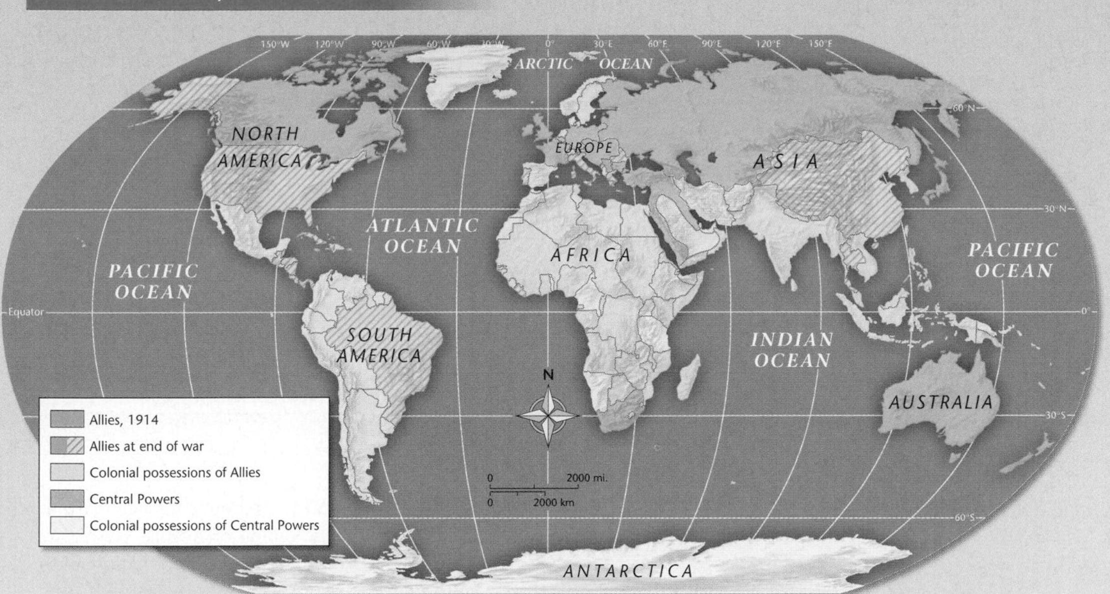

Allied soldiers on the Western Front

Department of Labor poster

1917
Germany ends Sussex pledge and resumes undeclared submarine warfare. Wilson declares war and sends the first units of the AEF to France under General Pershing.

1918
American troops fight at Belleau Wood, Château-Thierry, and the Argonne Forest.

1919
United States Senate rejects the Treaty of Versailles and membership in the League of Nations as American soldiers return from Europe.

Warren G. Harding 1921–1923

1918 **1920** **1922**

Revolutions in Russia overthrow the czar and bring the Bolsheviks to power.
1917

Central Powers agree to a truce with the Allies.
1918

Germany signs the Treaty of Versailles.
1919

The World at War, 1914–1918

Activating Prior Knowledge What country in South America had joined forces with the European Allies by the end of World War I? *(Brazil)*

Previewing Ask students to study the map and explain how the Great War eventually became known as World War I. *(Because most of the countries in the world had allegiance to one side or the other in the war)*

BACKGROUND
About the Pictures

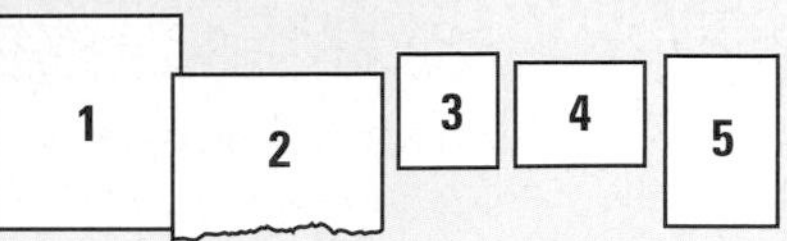

1. Archduke Francis Ferdinand and his wife, Sophia, were assassinated on June 28, 1914. Carried out by a Serbian named Gavrilo Princip, the assassination was one of the events that led to World War I.
2. The front page of *The New York Times* on May 7, 1915, the day following the sinking of the cruise ship *Lusitania,* which went down with many Americans on board.
3. General John J. Pershing (center) inspects British troops in Brest, France, during World War I.
4. Allied soldiers begin the dangerous task of going "over the top"—leaving the protection of the trenches and crossing "No Man's Land," an action often performed under heavy artillery and machine gun fire.
5. Poster used by the Department of Labor encouraging veterans of World War I to return to the workforce after their welcome home.

BIBLIOGRAPHY

For the Teacher

Horne, Alistaire. ***The Price of Glory.*** Penguin, 1994. (In-depth account of the grueling ten-month Battle of Verdun.)

Tuchman, Barbara W. ***The Guns of August.*** Macmillan, 1962. (Chronicle of the events that resulted in World War I.)

Winter, Denis. ***Soldiers of the Great War.*** Penguin, 1985. (Distillation of soldiers' personal experiences during World War I.)

For the Student

Remarque, Erich Maria. ***All Quiet on the Western Front.*** Ballantine, 1996. (Classic novel of the war from the German viewpoint; first published in 1929.)

Lawrence, T. E. ***The Seven Pillars of Wisdom.*** Anchor, 1991. (The author is the real Lawrence of Arabia, who helped unify various Arab factions against a common Turkish invader during World War I.)

Time-Life Books editors. ***Time-Life Books: This Fabulous Century, Vol. 2. 1910–1920.*** Time-Life, 1969. (Richly illustrated, comprehensive study of the era.)

Don't miss the exclusive interactive version of this textbook on the Web and on CD-ROM.

Section 1

The Road to War

Section Objectives

1. Identify the main causes of World War I.
2. Understand how the conflict expanded to draw in much of Europe.
3. Analyze how the United States responded to the war in Europe.

Bellringer

Warm-Up Activity Ask students to define the word *neutral.* Ask them to think of situations in which they remained neutral and others in which they took a stand. What conditions affected their choices?

Activating Prior Knowledge What impact might the presence of many first-generation European immigrants have had on the position of the United States toward entering the war?

Reading Strategy

As World War I began and then expanded throughout much of Europe, the United States remained neutral. Ask students to rewrite the statement above as a question. As they read the section, have them write down the answers to their question.

Activity

Student Portfolio

You may wish to have students add the following to their portfolios. Britain's Queen Victoria, who reigned from 1837 to 1901, has been called "Europe's grandmother" because so many monarchs were descended from her five children. Ask students to make a family tree tracing Victoria's descendents up to 1920. Have them highlight the names of the cousins who reigned during World War I. **(Logical/Mathematical)**

Caption Answers

Viewing History Nationalism.

Section 1

The Road to War

READING FOCUS

- What were the main causes of World War I?
- How did the conflict expand to draw in much of Europe?
- In what ways did the United States respond to the war in Europe?

MAIN IDEA

As World War I began and then spread to much of Europe, the United States tried to remain neutral as long as possible.

KEY TERMS

militarism
mobilization
Central Powers
Allies
stalemate
autocrat
propaganda

TAKING NOTES

As you read, complete the following cause-and-effect diagram that shows why World War I began.

CAUSES
• Assassination of Archduke Francis Ferdinand in Sarajevo • Competition for colonies in Africa, Asia, and the Pacific • •

↓

WORLD WAR I

Setting the Scene On June 28, 1914, Archduke Francis Ferdinand and his wife made a state visit to Sarajevo, the capital of Bosnia. Bosnia was a new province within the Austro-Hungarian Empire, and Francis Ferdinand was heir to the empire's throne. Although many Bosnians were upset with Austro-Hungarian rule, Francis Ferdinand decided to disregard growing tensions and visit his government's soldiers in Sarajevo.

The morning of his visit, a bomb thrown by a terrorist bounced off the archduke's car and exploded, injuring two officers in another car. Unfazed, Francis Ferdinand attended a state ceremony and then rode to the hospital to see the wounded officers. Gavrilo Princip, a second terrorist, just 19 years old, happened to spot the car as it slowly moved down a narrow street. One of Princip's friends saw what happened next:

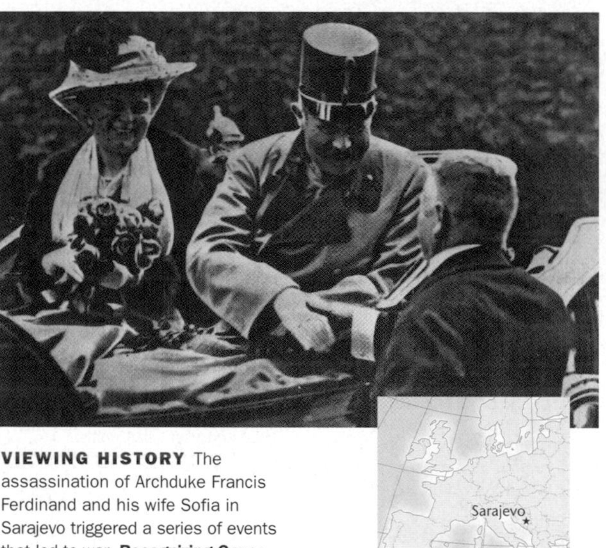

VIEWING HISTORY The assassination of Archduke Francis Ferdinand and his wife Sofia in Sarajevo triggered a series of events that led to war. **Recognizing Cause and Effect** *Which of the four causes of World War I contributed most directly to the murder in Sarajevo?*

> *"As the car came abreast he stepped forward from the curb, drew his automatic pistol from his coat and fired two shots. The first struck the wife of the Archduke, the Archduchess Sofia, in the abdomen. . . . She died instantly. The second bullet struck the Archduke close to the heart. He uttered only one word; 'Sofia'—a call to his stricken wife. Then his head fell back and he collapsed. He died almost instantly."*
>
> —Borijove Jevtic

Princip, a Bosnian nationalist, believed that Austria-Hungary had no right to rule Bosnia. Little did he know that his act of terrorism in Sarajevo would have grave consequences.

Resource Directory

Teaching Resources

Learning Styles Lesson Plans booklet, p. 40
Guided Reading and Review booklet, p. 78

Technology

Section Reading Support Transparencies
Guided Reading Audiotapes (English/Spanish), Ch. 12
Student Edition on Audio CD, Ch. 12
Color Transparencies *Historical Maps,* A32
Sounds of an Era Audio CD *"Castle Walk,"* 1914 recording by Europe's Society Orchestra (time: 45 seconds)
Prentice Hall Presentation Pro CD-ROM, Ch. 12
Companion Web site, www.phschool.com

Causes of World War I

The assassination of Archduke Francis Ferdinand ignited what was then called the Great War, later known as World War I. However, the main causes of the war existed well before 1914. Those causes included imperialism, militarism, nationalism, and a tangled system of alliances.

Imperialism A great scramble for colonies took place in the late 1800s. European powers rushed to claim the remaining uncolonized areas of the world, particularly in Africa, Asia, and the Pacific. Japan joined the roster of colonial powers when it won the Sino-Japanese War in 1895 and moved to acquire Korea, Taiwan, and territory on China's mainland.

By 1910, the most desirable colonies had been taken. Competition for the lands that remained led to conflict among the powers of Europe. Germany's leaders envied Britain and France—two countries that had begun colonizing early and controlled large, resource-rich empires. Leaders in Germany and other countries recognized that they could only expand in Africa by taking land away from other colonizers.

READING CHECK How did competition for colonies help lead to war?

Militarism By the early 1900s in Europe, diplomacy had taken a back seat to **militarism.** This policy involved aggressively building up a nation's armed forces in preparation for war and giving the military more authority over the government and foreign policy. The great powers of Europe—Austria-Hungary, France, Germany, Great Britain, and Russia—all spent large sums of money on new weapons and warships for expanding their armed forces. Their endless planning for war made war much more likely.

Nationalism Two kinds of nationalism contributed to World War I. The first was the tendency for countries such as the great powers to act in their own

The War in Europe, 1914–1918

Allies, 1918
Central Powers
Neutral nations
Russian territory ceded by Treaty of Brest-Litovsk
Farthest advance by Central Powers
Major battle

MAP SKILLS Before the war, Europe was a land of empires and alliances. When Austria-Hungary declared war on Serbia, much of the continent was drawn into the conflict. **Location** *Based on this map, which side, if any, had a geographical advantage in the war? Explain.*

Lesson Plan

Focus Explain that when war first broke out in Europe, most Americans wished to remain neutral. However, as the war continued, the United States moved to more active involvement. Ask what prompted this change.

Instruct Remind students that World War I did not erupt overnight. Ask about long-standing causes and discuss the reasons why each European nation became involved. Why did the system of secret European alliances fail to maintain peace? Discuss being both neutral and prepared. Did arms and troops buildup ensure United States entry into the war? Why or why not?

Assess/Reteach Ask students to consider the underlying causes of World War I: imperialism, militarism, and nationalism. In what ways did these trends lead to war? How did conflicts in central Europe (especially in Bosnia) cause the scope of the war to grow? Ask them to consider how new weapons changed the way soldiers fought.

READING CHECK

Competition for colonies led to frequent disputes between the Great Powers in the 1895–1914 period.

Customize for ...

ESL

Have students read the material under the heading "Causes of World War I." Then have them use the map on this page titled "The War in Europe, 1914–1918" to explain the causes of the war in their own words.

Test Preparation

Have students reread the section "Causes of World War I" on this page and then answer the question below.

Which of the below is an example of nationalism?

A The desire of a powerful nation to expand by seizing control of a smaller nation.

B The growth of a nation's military power in the interest of waging war.

(C) The longing of an ethnic minority for independence.

D The decision by a government to remain neutral in wartime.

Caption Answers

Map Skills The Allies, because the Central Powers were nearly surrounded by enemy nations.

ACTIVITY
Connecting with Government

Have students divide into groups of four to six. Each group will become the expert on one European nation. Each group is to prepare a "briefing book" for President Wilson—a document describing one of the major nations of Europe in June 1914. The document should include sections on the head of state and form of government; geographical features; economy, including major products and trade partners; military leaders; and ethnic and religious composition of the population. Each student should assume responsibility for one section of the document for the group's nation. **(Verbal/Linguistic)**

BACKGROUND
Getting to Stalemate

Before reaching stalemate, both sides suffered tremendous losses. In just the first five months of the war, approximately one million French soldiers were seriously injured or killed. The Germans also experienced huge losses in what was considered the world's worst bloodbath. Although the Germans had built up a formidable military, they had failed to anticipate the combined strength of their enemies. The result was a stalemate and a new form of battle known as *trench warfare.*

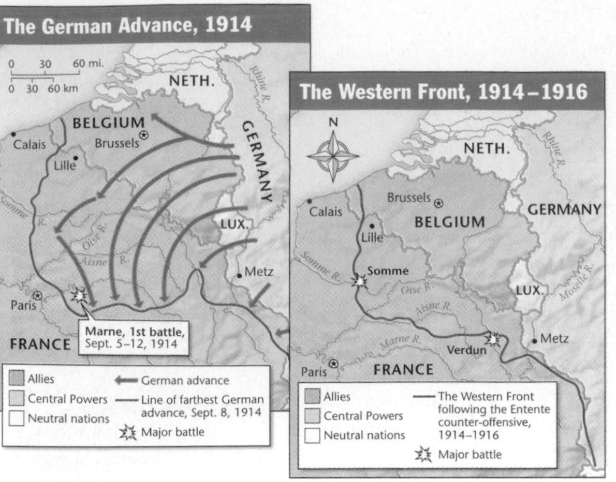

MAP SKILLS German troops advanced deep into French territory before British and French armies stopped them at the Battle of the Marne. **Movement** *Why did the battle lines change little after 1914?*

national interest. When such action went against the national interest of another nation, warfare could result.

One source of trouble was the German region of Alsace-Lorraine, a strip of land along Germany's border with France. The French people considered the return of Alsace-Lorraine, which had been conquered by Germany in 1871, a matter of national pride. German leaders valued the region's strong defenses and historic ties to Germany. These conflicting goals soured relations between France and Germany.

The second kind of nationalism occurred in countries with diverse ethnic populations, particularly those in central and eastern Europe. In Austria-Hungary, Hungarians and German-speaking Austrians governed millions of Czechs, Slovaks, Poles, and others who sought self-government. The empire also included Italians, Romanians, and Serbs who wished to join their compatriots in neighboring lands. Poles in Russia, Germany, and Austria-Hungary wanted to reunite and build an independent Poland. The longing of an ethnic minority for independence often led to violence.

As the most powerful Slavic country, Russia protected Slavs in Serbia and those under Austro-Hungarian rule. Russia's strong ties to the Serbs would play an important role in expanding the conflict beyond Serbia in 1914.

Alliances A complicated system of alliances developed among the nations of Europe during the late nineteenth century. Designed to bolster each nation's security, the alliances bound the great powers to come to each other's aid in the event of attack. Germany and Austria-Hungary were linked by treaty, as were Russia and France. Great Britain and France shared a looser alliance called the Entente Cordiale, or simply Entente. In 1914, this fragile balance of power, which had kept the peace for decades, led its creators into war.

As the need for soldiers increased, the British government used powerful national symbols to draw young people into Britain's all-volunteer army.

The Conflict Expands

At the time of the assassination of Francis Ferdinand, Bosnia was the focal point of a nationalist dispute between Austria-Hungary, which had recently annexed Bosnia, and its neighbor Serbia, which shared a language and common history with Bosnia. Convinced that Serbia was behind the assassination, Austria-Hungary used the event as an excuse to crush its small enemy. On July 28, 1914, Austria-Hungary declared war on Serbia.

This declaration of war set off a chain reaction that rapidly worked its way through Europe's complex web of alliances. On July 29, Russia, as Serbia's protector, began **mobilization**—the readying of troops for war. Germany, Austria-Hungary's chief ally, demanded that Russia stop mobilizing. Russia refused. At that point, Russia's ally, France, began to ready its troops, as did Germany.

On August 1, Germany declared war on Russia. Germany's military leaders had long prepared for this day. Their country lay between France to the west and Russia to the east. To avoid fighting both the French and Russian armies at the same time, Germany had developed a first-strike strategy. Known as the Schlieffen Plan, it called for a quick sweep through France to knock the French out of the war. Then, the German army would turn east and defeat Russia.

CAPTION ANSWERS

Map Skills Due to trenches.

RESOURCE DIRECTORY

Teaching Resources

Learning with Documents booklet (Primary Source Activity) *Thoughts on the War,* p. 24

Biography, Literature, and Comparing Primary Sources booklet (Literature) *A War Song,* p. 66

Other Print Resources

American History Block Scheduling Support *Liberty Bread and War Bonds: Supporting Our Soldiers in World War I,* found in the Prosperity, Depression, and War folder, includes interdisciplinary lesson suggestions and activities for Geography and History, Primary Sources, Biography, and Literature.

Historical Outline Map Book *Europe in World War I,* p. 60

Technology

Color Transparencies *Historical Maps,* A33, A34

Germany put the plan into action. To reach France as quickly as possible, the German army had to pass through Belgium, a country whose neutrality was protected by an international treaty. Germany had hoped that Britain would stay out of the war, but the invasion of Belgium brought Britain into the conflict on August 4.

One week after the war started, all the great powers of Europe had been drawn into it. The conflict divided them into two sides. Germany and Austria-Hungary made up the **Central Powers.** Russia, France, Serbia, and Great Britain were called the **Allies.**

Stalemate Each side felt confident of swift victory. A few months, experts said, and the war would be over. The experts were wrong.

Using the Schlieffen Plan, the German army quickly swept through Belgium and northern France. By September, they had advanced to within 30 miles of Paris. There, at the river Marne, a combined French and British force stopped their progress. Both sides then dug in and fortified their lines. Relatively equal in size and strength, the two sides reached a bloody **stalemate,** a situation in which neither side is able to gain the advantage.

Holed up in lines of muddy, rat-infested trenches, the two sides faced each other across an empty "no man's land." For months, each side tried to reach the other's lines to push back the enemy. But neither side was able to gain more than a few miles, and then only at an appalling human cost.

In the east, the poorly-armed Russian army invaded Germany and Austria-Hungary. Under the Schlieffen Plan, Germany expected to give some ground in the east to the Russian army while the bulk of the German army dealt a knockout blow to France. After capturing Paris, German troops would travel east to defeat the Russian army. However, Russia's early victories frightened Germany into sending soldiers to the Eastern Front ahead of schedule. There, German forces pushed the invading Russian armies back. However, the early transfer of troops away from France may have prevented a German victory in the west.

At the end of 1914, the Ottoman Empire, centered in what is now Turkey, entered the war on the side of the Central Powers. In the spring of 1915, Italy joined the Allies. Bulgaria joined the Central Powers that October, and Romania joined the Allies the following year. Each side hoped that a new ally would attack the enemy in a weak spot and break the stalemate. Instead, fronts in northern Italy and at Gallipoli, southwest of the Ottoman capital of Constantinople, brought the familiar pattern of trench warfare and costly, unsuccessful attacks.

Modern Warfare In 1914, the youth of Europe had marched off to fight, eager for a chance to be heroic. In earlier wars, a strong, swift offense led by troops on horseback often had been enough to secure victory in battle. The soldiers of World War I, however, came up against new killing machines of amazing efficiency. Defensive forces could use modern firepower, such as machine guns and rapid-fire

Focus on TECHNOLOGY

Gas Masks The German army first released chlorine gas into the Allied trenches in April 1915. The gas attacked the lungs and the eyes, causing panic, pain, and even death in enemy trenches. At first, soldiers covered their mouths with wet gauze for protection. Later, they received gas masks that allowed the wearer to breathe in and draw air through a canister that filtered out poisons. Putting on the clumsy, heavy gas mask became an essential part of a soldier's drill. Unfortunately, these masks could not protect against the more dangerous mustard gas used later in the war.

VIEWING HISTORY Trenches ranged from crudely dug foxholes (below) to a series of elaborate trenches stretching for miles. The German soldier at left wears a gas mask and holds a grenade. **Drawing Conclusions** *Why do you think the armies resorted to poison gas to attack fortifications like this?*

Activity
Connecting with Science and Technology

Ask students to research some of the new forms of weaponry used during World War I—such as machine guns, hand grenades, artillery shells, and torpedoes. Tell them to explore the role of science and industry in the development of these new weapons. Then have students give an oral report explaining their findings. **(Verbal/ Linguistic)**

Background
Interdisciplinary

One of the inventions that revolutionized twentieth-century warfare was the tank. By mounting the body of an armored car onto a tractor, the British improvised the first armored, tracked vehicle in July 1915. The prototype tank, called "Little Willie," was quickly succeeded by "Big Willie." The new weapon proved itself at the Battle of Cambria in late 1917, where more than 400 British tanks breached German lines. But the tanks were too slow to exploit the victory, necessitating the development of faster armored vehicles.

Caption Answers

Viewing History Poison gas could precede soldiers into areas like trenches, thereby attacking the enemy before the soldier arrived.

ACTIVITY
Connecting with Economics

Have students research the kind of trade that the United States was engaged in at the start of the war. What were our major imports and exports at the time? What were our most important markets? Ask students to consider why President Wilson acted to protect American commercial interests. Suggest to students that they think about how economic concerns affected political decisions. **(Logical/Mathematical)**

BACKGROUND
Art History

American painter John Singer Sargent (1856–1925) is best known for his portraits of famous and wealthy patrons. However, during World War I, Sargent was hired to create a large-scale war painting for the British government. From July through October 1918, Sargent lived at the Western Front. One day, Sargent witnessed the aftermath of a mustard gas attack by the Germans. Out of this experience, he produced *Gassed,* a moving painting that depicts a field full of gassed and blindfolded Allied soldiers.

Focus on CULTURE

The War Poets The horrors of modern warfare had a major impact on British culture. Wilfred Owen was one of several soldiers in their late teens and twenties whose poems expressed anger at older leaders who sent them to fight and die under ghastly circumstances. Owen's poem, "Dulce et Decorum Est," contrasts school lessons that "it is fitting and sweet to die for one's country" with harsh images of death in a gas attack. Another poem, "The Parable of the Old Man and the Young," compares the war to a biblical story in which Abraham is asked to sacrifice his son, Isaac, but is told not to kill him at the last minute. Owen's poem has a different ending:

> *"But the old man would not so, but slew his son,*
>
> *And half the seed of Europe, one by one."*

artillery, to stop advancing soldiers. Ripped apart by machine guns, hand grenades, or artillery shells, and choked by poison gases, soldiers found that heroism came at a terrible price.

If soldiers charging across no man's land toward the enemy survived the artillery shells that rained down upon them, the enemy's machine guns, firing 450 rounds a minute, mowed them down. The generals, unaccustomed to the new weaponry, assumed that superiority in troop numbers would bring them victory. They repeatedly ordered soldiers to go "over the top" of the trenches to attack the enemy. That strategy, however, produced only a mounting pile of dead infantry. In the Battle of the Somme in 1916, for example, the British suffered some 20,000 deaths in a single day of combat.

Morale sank. Desperate, the armies began using any tactic available. Erasing the distinction between soldier and civilian, they burned fields, killed livestock, and poisoned wells. They tunneled under the no man's land to plant bombs below enemy trenches. German submarines torpedoed any ship they believed to be carrying arms to the Allies. A British naval blockade slowly starved the German people. None of these tactics brought a quick end to the conflict.

The American Response

Newspapers in the United States had recorded the march toward war in bold headlines. "Austria Declares War, Rushes Vast Army into Serbia; Russia Masses 80,000 Men on Border." Americans read the news with mounting alarm. How could all of these great countries of beauty and culture be at war with one another?

Some Americans felt personally involved. More than a third of the nation's 92 million people were immigrants or the children of immigrants. About a quarter of these were German American, and another eighth were Irish American. Both of these groups felt hostility toward Great Britain because of past conflicts and the current war. For that reason, they favored the Central Powers over the Allies.

Most Americans, however, opposed the Central Powers. Millions of Americans traced their roots to Britain, and others identified with British history, literature, and culture. Recent immigrants from Italy and parts of Austria-Hungary hoped that a defeat of the Central Powers would lead to independence for or expansion of their homelands.

Another source of mistrust was Kaiser Wilhelm II of Germany. The Kaiser, or emperor, was an **autocrat**—a ruler with unlimited power. His rule offended supporters of democracy. Americans also saw the Germans as a people of frightening militarism and cold-blooded efficiency. Reporters who had rushed to Europe to witness the German advance fueled this view. Richard Harding Davis described the August 1914 invasion as "not men marching, but a force of nature like a tidal wave, an avalanche, or a river flooding its banks." Americans read that the Germans killed civilians and destroyed libraries, cathedrals, and even entire towns in Belgium and France.

While civilians suffered severely under German occupation, some of the worst stories of German crimes were not true. British newspapers published false **propaganda,** or information intended to sway public opinion, that spread throughout the United States. These stories turned American public opinion against Germany.

RESOURCE DIRECTORY

Teaching Resources

Units 3/4 booklet
- Section 1 Quiz, p. 26

Guide to the Essentials
- Section 1 Summary, p. 58

Technology

Sounds of an Era Audio CD *Herbert Hoover on the Battle of the Somme,* 1928 recording (time: 40 seconds)

American Neutrality Trade strongly influenced the American position on the war. Between 1897 and 1914, American commercial investments overseas had increased five-fold, from $700 million to $3.5 billion. German submarines and a British naval blockade of the North Sea placed those investments at risk. To protect the investments, on August 4, 1914, President Wilson officially proclaimed the United States a neutral country. The American government protested the actions of both sides and tried to act as peacemaker.

The Preparedness Movement American business leaders welcomed the proclamation of neutrality. Still, those who had strong commercial ties to Great Britain urged that the United States get ready for war. Their watchword was "preparedness." They wanted their country to be in a position to aid Great Britain if necessary. In December 1914, preparedness supporters organized a National Security League to "promote patriotic education and national sentiment and service among people of the United States."

By the late summer of 1915, the movement's leaders had persuaded the government to set up camps to train American men for combat. By the summer of 1916, Wilson had worked out an agreement with Congress for large increases in the armed forces.

VIEWING HISTORY This "peace ship" traveled to Europe in 1915 with hopes of ending the war. Jane Addams, second from the left in the front row, joined the delegation. **Recognizing Ideologies** *How did the peace movement differ from the preparedness movement?*

The Peace Movement When World War I broke out, a peace movement also swung into gear. Its members consisted primarily of former Populists, Midwest progressives, and social reformers. Women were particularly active. On August 29, 1914, suffragists, dressed in black and carrying a banner of a dove, marched down New York City's Fifth Avenue. In November 1915, a group of social reformers founded the American Union Against Militarism.

Congress also included some peace advocates. They insisted on paying for preparedness through a tax on the makers of arms and through higher income taxes. Claude Kitchin, a member of Congress from North Carolina, predicted that when people discovered "that the income tax will have to pay for the increase in the army and navy, . . . preparedness will not be so popular." Congress increased taxes, but the preparedness movement remained strong.

Section 1 Assessment

READING COMPREHENSION

1. How did nationalism contribute to the start of World War I?
2. Which countries were known as the **Allies?** Which countries were known as the **Central Powers?**
3. What were two causes of the **stalemate** in the West?
4. What was the main reason that the United States stayed neutral at the start of World War I?

CRITICAL THINKING AND WRITING

5. **Checking Consistency** The alliance system in Europe was designed to maintain peace. Yet it seemed to make the conflict worse once the fighting began. Explain the apparent inconsistency.
6. **Writing to Persuade** Write an essay in which you express your support for the preparedness movement. Persuade your readers that the United States had no choice but to be ready to go to war.

Take It to the NET

Activity: Interpreting a Poem
Read a poem about World War I and write a short essay about the meaning of the poem. Discuss how the writer felt about the war. What symbols does the writer use? Use the links provided in the *America: Pathways to the Present* area of the following Web site for help in completing this activity.
www.phschool.com

Section 1 Assessment

Reading Comprehension

1. The tendency for countries such as the Great Powers to act in their own national interest, which sometimes went against the national interest of another nation; in countries with diverse ethnic populations, the longing of an ethnic minority for independence often led to violence.
2. Allies: Russia, France, Serbia, Great Britain. Central Powers: Germany, Austria-Hungary, Turkey.
3. Answers should include two of the following: similar size and strength of opposing armies; neither side had an ally to break the stalemate and attack; early transfer of troops away from France.
4. President Wilson wanted to protect American commercial investments overseas.

Critical Thinking and Writing

5. Sample answer: Alliances tend to widen the conflict by involving nations that have no concern with the issues that caused the war.
6. Essays should use facts from the section to persuade readers of their point. Answers may describe American support for neutrality, the National Security League, and the need to protect commercial ties to Great Britain.

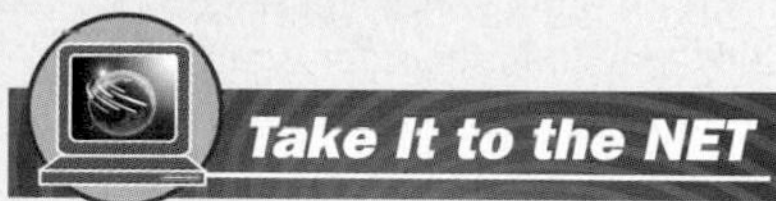

Take It to the NET

Essays will vary, but might address the horrors of war or the soldier's desire to return home to loved ones.

Identifying and Analyzing Alternatives

Focus Students will identify and analyze alternative solutions to a problem.

Instruct As a class, work through the question in steps 1–3. You might want to divide students into small groups for consideration of step 4. Ask each group to submit a sentence stating the goal of the United States regarding the war in Europe and at least three steps likely to achieve that goal. Have each group tell which of these steps the nation actually took.

Extend See the Skills for Life activity in the Resource Directory below.

ANSWERS

Practice the Skill

1. **(a)** World War I and the United States response to it. **(b)** Answers will vary but should reflect an understanding of chapter material.
2. **(a)** Neutrality. **(b)** Intervening to protect small, democratic nations against German aggression.
3. Possible answers: **(a)** It is difficult to expect people not to judge or feel strong sympathy when small, democratic nations suffer aggression. **(b)** It may lead to wider war or unnecessary bloodshed. American interests may be injured. **(c)** No. **(d)** No. It is presumed that this standard is clearly understood by all. **(e)** No, because the standard for action is not clear.
4. **(a)** Answers will vary. **(b)** Make sure students explain their answers and demonstrate an understanding of the problem. **(c)** Answers will vary.

Identifying and Analyzing Alternatives

Identifying alternatives means finding one or more possible ways to achieve a goal or to solve a problem. You have read about the conflict in the United States over how to respond to the war escalating in Europe. President Woodrow Wilson favored one response. Former President Theodore Roosevelt favored another.

LEARN THE SKILL

Use the following steps to identify and analyze alternatives:

1. **Identify the nature of the problem under discussion.** Before you can identify alternative solutions to a problem, you must understand what the problem is.
2. **Note the solutions proposed.** Write down the main points of each proposed solution.
3. **Evaluate the potential effectiveness of each solution.** Consider the strengths and weaknesses of each proposal.
4. **Consider other alternatives.** Recall the nature of the problem under discussion. Then, using the insights you gained by following the preceding steps, think of other possible solutions.

A

"My thought is of America. . . .[T]his great country of ours . . . should show herself in this time of peculiar trial a nation fit beyond others to exhibit the fine poise of undisturbed judgment, the dignity of self-control, the efficiency of dispassionate [unemotional] action; a nation that neither sits in judgment upon others nor is disturbed in her own counsels and which keeps herself fit and free to do what is honest and disinterested and truly serviceable for the peace of the world."

—Woodrow Wilson, *Appeal for Neutrality*
August 18, 1914

PRACTICE THE SKILL

Answer the following questions:

1. **(a)** What is the issue that both passages address? **(b)** What do you already know about this issue from your reading?
2. **(a)** What does Passage A suggest is the proper response of the United States to the war in Europe? **(b)** What does Passage B suggest is the proper response?
3. **(a)** What difficulties do you see in Wilson's suggestion that the United States not judge the actions of other nations? **(b)** What might happen if the United States acts in a "disinterested" way, as Wilson suggests? **(c)** Is Roosevelt clear about what he means when he refers to a nation that "does ill"? **(d)** Does Roosevelt explain how nations should be judged "highly civilized" or "well-behaved"? **(e)** Is his solution practical?
4. **(a)** What do you think should have been the goal of the United States in responding to the war in Europe? **(b)** What steps were most likely to achieve that goal? **(c)** Write a brief paragraph outlining your alternative solution.

B

"Our true course should be to judge each nation on its conduct, unhesitatingly to antagonize every nation that does ill [at the point] it does ill, and equally without hesitation to act. . . .

One of the greatest of international duties ought to be the protection of small, highly civilized, well-behaved and self-respecting states from oppression and conquest by their powerful military neighbors. . . .

I feel in the strongest way that we should have interfered, at least to the extent of the most emphatic diplomatic protest and at the very outset—and then by whatever further action was necessary—[when Germany invaded Belgium]."

—Theodore Roosevelt
America and the World War, 1915

APPLY THE SKILL

See the Chapter Review and Assessment for another opportunity to apply this skill.

420 Chapter 12 • *The World War I Era*

RESOURCE DIRECTORY

Teaching Resources
Skills for Life booklet, p. 21

Technology
Social Studies Skills Tutor CD-ROM
Interactive Practice in
- Geographic Literacy
- Critical Thinking and Reading
- Visual Analysis
- Communications

Section
2 The United States Declares War

READING FOCUS

- How did Germany's use of submarines affect the war?
- What moves did the United States take toward war in early 1917?

MAIN IDEA

German submarine warfare helped push the United States into World War I.

KEY TERMS

U-boat
Sussex pledge
Zimmermann note
Russian Revolution

TAKING NOTES

Copy this flowchart. As you read, fill in the boxes with some of the major events that caused the United States to declare war on Germany. The first box has been completed to help you get started.

German U-boats begin sinking Allied ships, killing 1,200 aboard the *Lusitania* in 1915.
↓
[ ]
↓
Wilson asks Congress to declare war on Germany.

Setting the Scene The fighting in Europe continued with no end in sight. In October 1916, *The New York Times* explained why American voters wanted a leader who would keep the United States out of war:

> "*The voters . . . have seen lives lost, property ruined, privations suffered, on a greater scale than the world had ever known, and they have seen existence become harder, not only for the men who are fighting, but for all the inhabitants of the stricken countries. They have seen nation after nation drawn in, until the roll of the original combatants has been doubled.*"

Many Americans hoped that the United States would not be the next country to be drawn in. Nevertheless, friction between the United States and Germany increased from 1914 to 1917. The preparedness movement continued to gain support in the United States, and the pressure to join in the war intensified. Ultimately, actions by the Central Powers pushed Congress and the President into entering the war on the side of the Allies.

German Submarine Warfare

One action that provoked angry calls for war in the United States was the German use of submarine warfare. This tactic was effective militarily, but it cost the Germans dearly in terms of American public opinion.

The German **U-boat,** short for *Unterseeboot*, or submarine, was a terrifying new weapon that changed the rules of naval warfare. Germany deployed them to prevent munitions and food from reaching Britain's ports. At first, U-boats rose to the surface to allow the crew of merchant ships to abandon ship before their ship was attacked. After Britain armed merchant ships to fire on exposed U-boats, Germany abandoned the old rules and permitted U-boats to remain hidden and fire on merchant ships without warning.

The U-boat enabled Germany to break a stalemate at sea. In the years leading up to the war, Britain and Germany competed to build the largest, strongest

This German poster urged U-boats on their mission. The translation is "U-boats: Go out!"

Section 2
The United States Declares War

SECTION OBJECTIVES

1. Discover how Germany's use of submarines affected the war.
2. Find out the steps the United States took toward war in early 1917.

BELLRINGER

Warm-Up Activity Ask students what makes a country one of the great nations of the world. What domestic conditions and foreign alliances characterize a great nation? What countries are great nations today? Why?

Activating Prior Knowledge Did everyone in the United States agree that going to war was the best approach? In what ways did President Wilson take a political risk by keeping the United States out of the war in its early years?

READING STRATEGY

Ask students to imagine that they are members of Congress in 1917, and they helped decide that the United States would go to war against Germany and the other Central Powers. As they read the section, have them identify the reasons for U.S. involvement in World War I, including unrestricted submarine warfare.

ACTIVITY
Connecting with History and Conflict

Have students discuss the impact of Germany's aggressive use of U-boats. In small groups, have them examine the issue and suggest that they consider why the submarine attacks proved to be the turning point in American sentiment toward the war. **(Logical/Mathematical)**

RESOURCE DIRECTORY

Teaching Resources
Guided Reading and Review booklet, p. 79

Technology
Section Reading Support Transparencies
Guided Reading Audiotapes (English/Spanish), Ch. 12
Student Edition on Audio CD, Ch. 12
Sounds of an Era Audio CD *"I Didn't Raise My Boy to be a Soldier,"* 1916 recording (time: one minute)
Prentice Hall Presentation Pro CD-ROM, Ch. 12
Companion Web site, www.phschool.com

Section 2 Assessment

Reading Comprehension

1. Answers should include: ships had no warning or defense against U-boats; submarines attacked American and other neutral ships; the German government broke its promises about restricting its submarines.
2. (a) It created a temporary peace. (b) By resuming unrestricted submarine warfare, Germany hoped to defeat Britain and win the war in France before American entry into the war could make a difference.
3. Though Wilson did not take it seriously, the Zimmermann note enraged Americans because it was an attempt to secretly draw Mexico into the war and ultimately reward it with U.S. territory.

Critical Thinking and Writing

4. Sample answer: The United States would have had to keep its commercial vessels out of waters patrolled by U-boats. This would have been politically unpopular and economically damaging.
5. Answers may vary, but should chronicle Germany's use of the submarine, the sinking of unarmed ships, and the dissolving of the Sussex pledge.

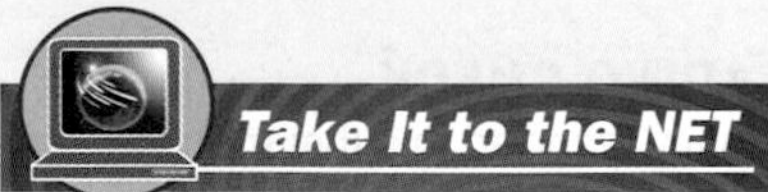

Take It to the NET

Posters will vary, but should convey the importance of the specific job, the idea that women in the workforce were vital to the country's success, and a sense of patriotism.

Focus on CITIZENSHIP

The Price of Pacifism One of the fifty votes against the House war resolution came from Montana's Representative Jeannette Rankin, the first woman elected to Congress. Elected only a few months earlier, she said, "I want to stand by my country, but I cannot vote for war." Rankin faced a strong backlash over her vote. The Republican Party refused to nominate her for the Senate in 1918. She ran as an independent candidate but lost.

Rankin returned to Congress in 1941. When Japan bombed Pearl Harbor that December and the President asked Congress for a declaration of war, Rankin voted no once again.

Neither Wilson nor Mexico took the **Zimmermann note** seriously. Already divided by civil war, Mexico could not have launched a successful invasion of the United States. The telegram's release, however, scored another public relations victory for Great Britain. The United States edged closer to war.

Revolution in Russia By early 1917, Russia already had suffered enormous casualties in the war: more than 1.5 million killed, roughly 2.5 million taken prisoner, and millions more wounded. Austro-Hungarian and German forces had advanced deep into Russian territory. Poorly fed and miserably equipped, the Russians fell back farther and farther into their country's interior.

Then, in March 1917, Czar Nicholas II, Russia's autocratic leader, was forced to give up the throne. The Russian monarchy was replaced with a republican government. This **Russian Revolution** cheered the prowar faction in the United States. Concern over being allied with the autocratic government of the czar had slowed the nation's move toward entry into the war. The fall of the czar removed a last stumbling block to joining the Allies.

The War Resolution Between March 16 and March 18, Germany sank the United States ships *City of Memphis, Illinois,* and *Vigilancia.* Wilson's patience had run out. On March 20, the President's Cabinet voted unanimously for war. Casting the issue in idealistic terms, Wilson told Congress on April 2 that "the world must be made safe for democracy." He stated:

> "*It is a fearful thing to lead this great peaceful people into war, the most terrible and disastrous of all wars, civilization itself seeming to be in the balance. But the right is more precious than peace.*"
>
> —Woodrow Wilson

Members of Congress, ambassadors, and Supreme Court justices stood up and cheered the President's call to war. A war resolution passed 82 to 6 in the Senate and 373 to 50 in the House. On April 6, 1917, the President signed it.

Section 2 Assessment

READING COMPREHENSION

1. Why did Germany's use of **U-boats** lead to conflict with the United States?
2. (a) How did the **Sussex pledge** affect relations between the United States and Germany? (b) Why did Germany end the pledge?
3. Why did the **Zimmermann note** enrage Americans?

CRITICAL THINKING AND WRITING

4. **Identifying Alternatives** Consider the causes that brought the United States into World War I. (a) What would the United States have had to do to avoid the conflict altogether? (b) Why did the United States not take such steps?
5. **Writing to Inform** Write a paragraph explaining why President Wilson asked Congress to arm American merchant ships.

Take It to the NET

Activity: Creating a Poster
Research some of the women's organizations that contributed to the war effort in Europe. Create a recruitment poster encouraging women to join one of these organizations. Use the links provided in the *America: Pathways to the Present* area of the following Web site for help in completing this activity.
www.phschool.com

RESOURCE DIRECTORY

Teaching Resources
Units 3/4 booklet
- Section 2 Quiz, p. 27

Guide to the Essentials
- Section 2 Summary, p. 59

Biography, Literature, and Comparing Primary Sources booklet (Biography) *Jeannette Rankin,* p. 24

Americans on the European Front

READING FOCUS

- How did the United States prepare to fight in World War I?
- In what ways did American troops help turn the tide of war?
- What were conditions like in Europe and in the United States at the end of the war?

MAIN IDEA

American troops helped the Allies defeat the Central Powers in World War I.

KEY TERMS

Selective Service Act
American Expeditionary Force (AEF)
convoy
zeppelin
armistice
genocide

TAKING NOTES

Copy this flowchart. As you read, fill in the boxes with significant events, beginning with the declaration of war by the United States and ending with the Allied victory. The first box has been completed to help you get started.

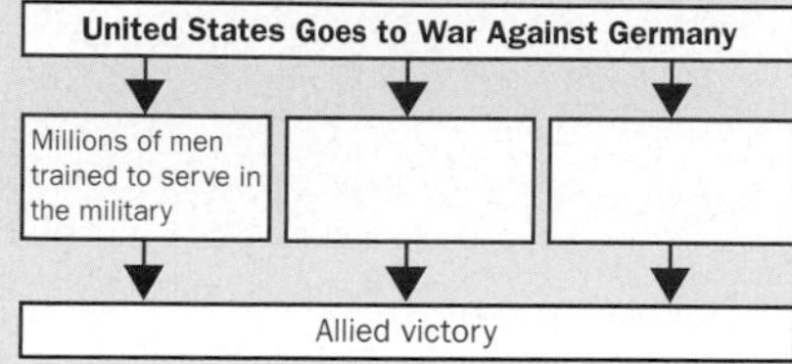
United States Goes to War Against Germany
Millions of men trained to serve in the military
Allied victory

Setting the Scene Woodrow Wilson brought the United States into war with the support of Congress and most of the country. But in April 1917, despite the success of the preparedness movement, the United States was far from ready to send an army to the European front. With a little more than 100,000 men in uniform, the United States army was outranked in size by the armies of 16 other countries. The country's 15,500 marines were far from Europe, patrolling several Central American countries and American possessions in the Pacific. The National Guard, 132,000 strong, needed training. The United States was simply not ready for war.

The Allies desperately needed replacement troops. In June, President Wilson agreed to send a small force to Europe under the command of General John J. Pershing. A veteran of the Spanish-American War, the general had also taught for a time at West Point. Pershing would need all his experience and skills to lead the American forces against a determined German army.

Preparing for War

Instead of a full-sized army, a cautious Congress sent the Allies naval support, supplies, arms, and $3 billion in loans. The token force of 14,500 men led by General Pershing served mainly to boost Allied morale. After landing in France, Pershing realized that he needed more troops. He recommended that the army number 1 million men by 1918 and 3 million the following year.

Draftees and Volunteers Congress passed a **Selective Service Act** in May 1917, authorizing a draft of young men for military service. During the Civil War, the draft had sparked riots. Now, however, the general feeling that this was the "war to end all wars" led to wide acceptance of the draft. By November 1918, more than 24 million men had registered for the draft. From those, a lottery picked 3 million draftees to serve in the war. Volunteers and National Guardsmen made up the remainder of what was called the **American Expeditionary Force (AEF).**

I WANT YOU
FOR U.S. ARMY
NEAREST RECRUITING STATION

VIEWING HISTORY James Montgomery Flagg's poster called on Americans to join the military. **Drawing Inferences** *Why do you think this poster was effective?*

Section 3
Americans on the European Front

Section Objectives

1. Analyze the preparations of the United States for World War I.
2. Study the ways in which the American troops helped turn the tide of the war.
3. Learn about conditions in Europe and the United States at the end of the war.

Bellringer

Warm-Up Activity Are allies automatically equals? Can allies exist without a common enemy? Ask students what kinds of relationships allies share.

Activating Prior Knowledge Have students list five ways in which the entry of the United States into the war would change the Allies' situation. Then have them list five ways in which the entry of the United States into the war would change the Central Powers' situation.

Reading Strategy

Ask students to create a list of this section's boldfaced headings and subheadings. Under each one, have them write a one-sentence prediction of what the content will be. Then have them check their predictions against the actual text.

Caption Answers

Viewing History It inspired patriotism while at the same time bringing the war to a personal level, making a direct appeal to the viewer.

Resource Directory

Teaching Resources
Guided Reading and Review booklet, p. 80

Technology
Section Reading Support Transparencies
Guided Reading Audiotapes (English/Spanish), Ch. 12
Student Edition on Audio CD, Ch. 12
Color Transparencies *Cause-and-Effect Charts,* D8
RESOURCE PRO® **Primary Source Activity** *Women on the War Front,* found on Resource Pro, uses an excerpt from *Two Colored Women with the American Expeditionary Forces* to show how African American women contributed to the war effort.
Prentice Hall Presentation Pro CD-ROM, Ch. 12
Companion Web site, www.phschool.com

Lesson Plan

Focus Point out that the United States quickly became fully involved in the war. Ask what roles Americans played abroad. How did American efforts affect the war?

Instruct Discuss why President Wilson preferred to send money and supplies to the Allies rather than troops. Ask students what the difficulties are in organizing an army in a short amount of time. Have them list the steps required to create an army large enough to fight a war on the scale of World War I.

Ask students to locate on a map the major battles of the war involving Americans and to describe their outcomes.

Ask what events turned the tide of the war. What role did American troops play in ending the war? Ask students why they think the Allies insisted on total surrender.

Assess/Reteach Have students list the European countries involved in World War I. Ask students to create lists of descriptive phrases to describe each country's likely response to the entry of the United States into the war.

Activity

Connecting with Citizenship

Tell students to form two groups—one made up of American soldiers just arriving in France and the other made up of British and French soldiers who have been stationed at the Western Front. Have students conduct a role-playing exercise in which the Allied soldiers orient the Americans. Tell members of the American Expeditionary Force to ask questions about what has been going on and what they can expect to do and see. **(Bodily/Kinesthetic)**

VIEWING HISTORY New soldiers learn how to attack with bayonets at a training camp in the United States. **Recognizing Cause and Effect** *Why was training important to the war effort?*

Among the Americans who served their country were thousands of women. Some 11,000 women volunteered to serve in uniform as nurses, drivers, and clerks. Another 14,000 women served abroad, as civilians working for the government or for private agencies.

Training for War The military's next challenge was to transform draftees into soldiers who were armed and ready to fight. In September, draftees began to arrive at new and expanded training camps around the country. At these camps, they learned how to use a bayonet and a rifle, dig a trench, put on a gas mask, and throw a grenade. American and British lecturers told them about German crimes in Belgium and the strategies of trench warfare.

The military planned to give new soldiers several months of training in the United States and France before shipping them off to battle. In reality, soldiers did not always receive that much training. The task of building an army of millions and transporting it to France in time to be of help meant that training would sometimes be cut short.

The Convoy System In addition to building a fighting force, the War Department had to worry about transporting its troops overseas safely. In April 1917 alone, German U-boats had sunk more than 400 Allied and neutral ships.

Starting in May 1917, all merchant and troop ships traveled in a **convoy.** A convoy consisted of a group of unarmed ships surrounded by a ring of destroyers, torpedo boats, and other armed naval vessels equipped with hydrophones to track and destroy submarines. Between April and December 1917, merchant marine losses dropped by half.

The convoy system was remarkably successful in carrying American troops to Europe. Despite several scares, U-boats did not sink a single United States troopship traveling to Europe. A relatively small number of Americans lost their lives on the return trip.

Focus on CITIZENSHIP

Conscientious Objectors Some men refused to fight when they were drafted. Most of these men belonged to religious groups that opposed war, such as the Quakers. They were known as "conscientious objectors" because they objected to fighting as a matter of conscience. Most conscientious objectors were allowed to serve in a noncombatant (nonfighting) position. Sometimes they were resented by other soldiers. General Leonard Wood called conscientious objectors "enemies of the Republic, fakers and active agents of the enemy."

American Soldiers in Europe From the time the AEF arrived in France in June 1917, Pershing kept American troops independent of the Allied armies. In Pershing's view, the Allies had become too accustomed to defensive action. He wanted to save his men's strength for offensive moves.

American troops surprised the British and French soldiers on the front lines with their strength, good health, and energy. They resembled the European soldiers who had gone to war in 1914, not the exhausted forces that survived after several years of fighting. By 1918, European armies could only recruit new soldiers among much older men, boys turning 18, and wounded soldiers returning from the hospital.

Members of the American Expeditionary Force were called doughboys, although no one is sure why. The nickname had been in use for years, but it stuck with World War I soldiers. The name could have come from the white adobe dust that stuck to the boots of soldiers during the Mexican War. On the other hand, Civil War soldiers might have picked up the nickname from their uniform buttons, which looked like flour dumplings, or from the white flour they used to keep their belts white.

Resource Directory

Technology

Sounds of an Era Audio CD *General Pershing,* 1917 recording (time: 30 seconds)

RESOURCE PRO® **Biography** *Henry Johnson,* found on Resource Pro, profiles the most famous African American soldier of World War I.

Caption Answers

Viewing History Most soldiers were new to the armed forces and needed to learn how to dig trenches and fight with bayonets and modern weapons.

The more than 300,000 African Americans who volunteered or were drafted served in segregated units. Most black soldiers never saw combat, though many fought with distinction and nearly 4,000 died or were wounded. The marines refused to accept African Americans altogether, and the navy used them for menial tasks only. The army, too, used African Americans mostly for manual labor.

These assignments distressed many African Americans. The 369th Infantry Regiment, which came to be known as the Harlem Hell Fighters, was especially eager to fight. Its members persuaded their white officers to loan the regiment to the French, who integrated the regiment into the French army. Because of their distinguished service, the entire regiment received France's highest combat medal, the Croix de Guerre.

The Western Front, 1917–1918

GREAT BRITAIN
London
Thames R.
English Channel
Calais
Lille
Paris
NETH.
Brussels
Cologne
BELGIUM
GERMANY
LUX.
Metz
Strasbourg
FRANCE
Meuse R.
Rhine R.
Moselle R.
Aisne R.
Oise R.
Seine R.
Marne R.
0 30 60 mi.
0 30 60 km
Ypres, 3rd battle, July 31–Nov. 10, 1917
Cantigny, May 28, 1918
Belleau Wood, June 6–July 1, 1918
Château-Thierry, June 4, 1918
Marne, 2nd battle, July 18–Aug. 6, 1918
St. Mihiel, Sept. 12–16, 1918
Meuse-Argonne offensive, Sept. 26–Nov. 11, 1918
Allies
Central Powers
Neutral nations
Limit of final German advance, 1918
American Expeditionary Force attacks
Armistice Line, Nov. 11, 1918
Major battle
Area enlarged

Turning the Tide of War

As American involvement in the war expanded, events in Russia shook the alliance. In November 1917, followers of Vladimir Lenin, called Bolsheviks, violently overthrew Russia's republican government. Until that spring, Lenin had been living in Switzerland. He had promised to make peace with Germany if he successfully won control of his native land, and for that reason Germany helped arrange his return to Russia.

Lenin signed a truce with Germany in December and a final peace treaty on March 3, 1918. Germany won vast territories in western Russia that included much of the country's industry and richest farmland. More important, Russia's exit from the war freed the Germans from the two-front war they had been forced to fight. Germany sent hundreds of thousands of troops west for one final offensive before American troops could reinforce the British and French armies in large numbers.

German forces attacked British lines on March 21, 1918. For the first time since 1914, they successfully broke through the trenches and advanced deep into Allied territory. Their aim was to split British troops in northern France from French armies to the east, and eventually to capture Paris. From March through May 1918, German forces turned all their energies toward pounding the French and British lines. By the end of May, they were only about 50 miles from Paris.

Americans Save Paris American forces came to the rescue. General Pershing dispatched troops to the front to turn back the German offensive. American troops attacked and recaptured the village of Cantigny on May 28. One week later, soldiers from the Marine Corps and the army stopped German attacks at Belleau Wood and Château-Thierry, east of Paris. Marching out from Paris, the men received this word from their leader, Brigadier General James G. Harbord: "We dig no trenches to fall back on. The Marines will hold where they stand." At the battle of Château-Thierry, they did just that.

MAP SKILLS After the final German offensive faltered, American troops helped the British and French push the Germans back across land Germany had held since the start of the war. General Pershing (above, center) directed American forces in Europe. **Place** *In what region of France did American troops have the greatest impact?*

ACTIVITY
Connecting with History and Conflict

Ask students to research the impact of John J. Pershing during World War I. Have students analyze his actions and their importance to the war effort, including his determination not to mix American troops with those of other countries. **(Verbal/Linguistic)**

BACKGROUND
A Diverse Nation

African Americans entered the war only after passage of the Selective Service Act, which allowed *all* able-bodied American men between the ages of 21 and 31 to enlist. The Harlem Hell Fighters got their name from the French and Germans, who were impressed with the persistence of the 369th Infantry. On September 29, 1918, this unit engaged in heavy combat, capturing the town of Sechault, along with prisoners, cannons, and machine guns. Then the 369th Infantry led a dawn assault on the enemy, overpowering the Germans.

TEST PREPARATION

Have students read the first two paragraphs under the heading "Turning the Tide of War" and then answer the question below.

How did Lenin's victory in the Russian Revolution affect the course of World War I?

A There was no effect.
(B) Germany and Russia signed a truce.
C France and Russia signed a truce.
D Lenin's victory caused the United States to enter the war.

CAPTION ANSWERS

Map Skills American troops had the greatest impact on France east of Paris.

ACTIVITY
Connecting with Geography

To analyze significant events such as the battle of Argonne Forest, have students make a detailed map of France showing the locations mentioned in the text—the Marne river, Paris, Amiens, St. Mihiel, the Argonne Forest, and the region of the Meuse river. Tell students to identify where and when the battles took place. **(Visual/Spatial)**

BACKGROUND
Geography in History

The Meuse-Argonne Offensive was a very difficult campaign. There were numerous obstacles. The land to the north of Verdun was in disarray as a result of previous battles. It was difficult for tanks to get through the Argonne Forest, which was located in a mass of rivers and ridges. In addition to the physical obstacles, the American soldiers were inexperienced. Fortunately, the British had secured a huge supply of high-explosive shells, as well as a copy of the Germans' battle plans.

READING CHECK

American soldiers drove the Germans out of their heavily defended position at St. Mihiel in September 1918. Later that month, more than one million men of the American Expeditionary Force participated in a major Allied offensive in the Meuse-Argonne region of northern France. This attack routed the Germans and forced the German army into headlong retreat.

Trench Warfare on the Western Front
Underground "dugout" shelters allowed soldiers to take cover during enemy bombardment.
Artillery bombardments turned the "no man's land" into rough terrain that slowed advancing infantry.
Periscopes allowed soldiers to observe the enemy without making themselves vulnerable to gunfire.
Sandbags protected soldiers from enemy bullets.
A "fire step" boosted troops above sandbags to shoot at the enemy.

INTERPRETING DIAGRAMS
Protected by rows of barbed wire, sandbags, and armed soldiers, trenches were very difficult to capture. Neither side could advance on the Western Front without losing thousands of men in the attack.
Drawing Inferences *How did tanks overcome the obstacles of barbed wire, sandbags, and enemy guns?*

At a loss of over half of their troops, they helped the French save Paris, blunted the edge of the German advance, and began to turn the tide of the war.

In mid-July, the Germans launched a massive attack on French positions on the river Marne. The French were joined by 28,000 American troops in a counter-attack that forced the Germans back across the river and into retreat. The Second Battle of the Marne ended any German hopes for victory.

Allied Counterattack After turning back the Germans outside Paris, the Allies took heart. About 250,000 new American soldiers were arriving in France each month, and thousands more were ready to leave training camps in France for the front line.

Using a new weapon, the tank, which could cross trenches and roll through barbed wire, the Allies began to break the German lines. On August 8, at the battle of Amiens, the Allied armies stopped the German advance in the north and recaptured Germany's gains from earlier in the year. General von Ludendorff, sensing the end was near, called it the "black day of the German army." He advised Kaiser Wilhelm to seek a peace settlement. The Allies, however, insisted on total surrender before peace talks.

In September, some 500,000 American troops, assisted by 100,000 French soldiers, began to hit the final German strongholds. In the battle of St. Mihiel, the first major military effort entirely in American hands, General Pershing and his troops ousted the Germans from a long-held position. The final Allied assault, the Meuse-Argonne Offensive, began on September 26, 1918. Over a million AEF troops began the drive to expel the Germans from France and to cut their supply lines. Soon after, the German army was in full retreat from the Argonne Forest and the region of the Meuse river.

READING CHECK
How did American soldiers contribute to the Allied counterattack?

War in the Air The Americans entered the war with only 55 planes, all too primitive to use in war. The United States quickly manufactured hundreds of planes to match the technology used by the Allies. Very different from modern aircraft, World War I planes were built from wooden frames covered with cloth. The pilot, and sometimes a copilot, sat in an open-air cockpit.

CAPTION ANSWERS

Interpreting Diagrams Tanks were able to roll right over these obstacles with their heavy, durable treads.

RESOURCE DIRECTORY

Other Print Resources
Historical Outline Map Book *The Western Front, 1914–1918,* p. 61

Technology
Color Transparencies *The Way It Works,* H15, H16

RESOURCE PRO® **Literature Activity**
A Poet Describes War, found on Resource Pro, uses e. e. cummings's short poem, "look at this," to express the tragedy of war.

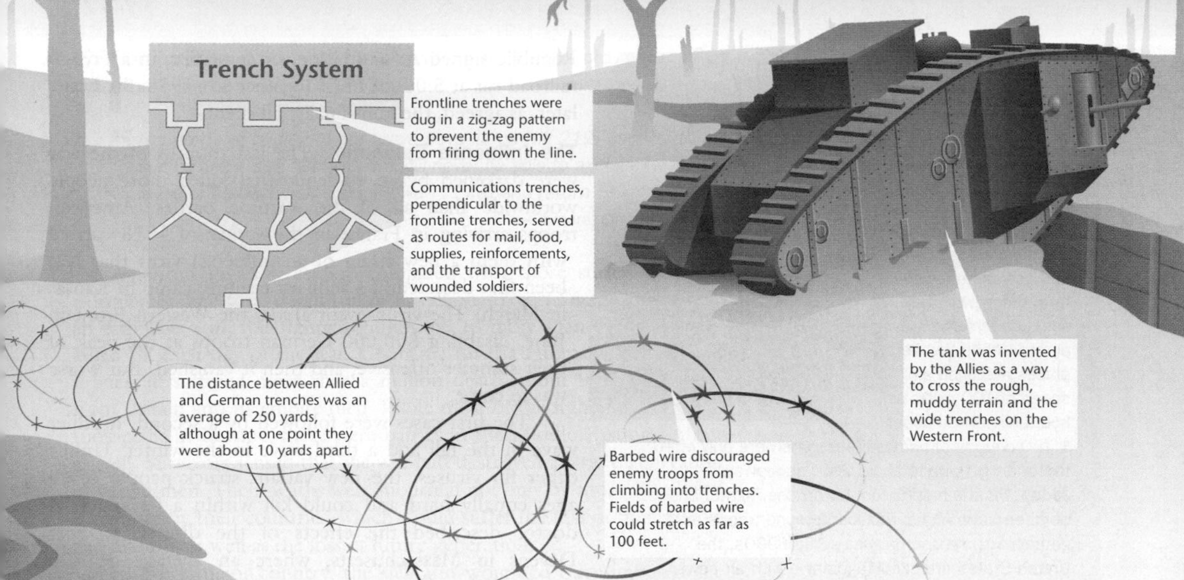

Trench System
Frontline trenches were dug in a zig-zag pattern to prevent the enemy from firing down the line.
Communications trenches, perpendicular to the frontline trenches, served as routes for mail, food, supplies, reinforcements, and the transport of wounded soldiers.
The distance between Allied and German trenches was an average of 250 yards, although at one point they were about 10 yards apart.
Barbed wire discouraged enemy troops from climbing into trenches. Fields of barbed wire could stretch as far as 100 feet.
The tank was invented by the Allies as a way to cross the rough, muddy terrain and the wide trenches on the Western Front.

Aircraft were first used to scout enemy positions, but soon flyers engaged each other in dogfights with pistols and later with machine guns. Each side had its "aces," such as the American Captain Eddie Rickenbacker, who downed 26 enemy fighters. Pilots also shot down hot-air balloons that were used for observation, and fired on individual soldiers on the ground. German **zeppelins,** or floating airships, and German bombers launched more than 100 raids on London, killing almost 1,500 civilians.

The airplane took on a new role in the 1918 offensive. American Colonel Billy Mitchell organized a fleet of more than 1,400 planes to drop bombs on enemy positions and on the railroads that carried supplies to the front. Bombing was not very effective at destroying targets, but frequent bombing raids frightened and confused enemy soldiers. Bombing raids would become a devastating weapon in the future.

Ending the War

The Allies pressed on against their enemy. The Central Powers collapsed, one by one, in the face of Allied attacks and domestic revolutions. Two of Germany's allies, Bulgaria and the Ottoman Empire, made a separate peace with the Allies in autumn. Austria-Hungary splintered in October as Poles, Hungarians, Czechs, and Slovaks declared their independence from the emperor.

The German commanders begged for peace, still hoping to dictate some terms before the fighting crossed onto German soil. The Allies refused. In the last week of October, the German naval command ordered the fleet to leave port and confront the British Navy for one final battle. Sailors in the German port of Kiel recognized that defeat was only a matter of time and further fighting would cause needless loss of life, so they mutinied on October 29. The revolt quickly spread to other ships and ports as well as to factories and industrial cities, pressuring the generals to bring the war to an end. By November 10, the Kaiser had fled to Holland. A civilian representative of the new German

James Cochran was an American soldier from Philadelphia who died in the war at the age of 19. His family honored his memory with a locket containing a photograph and a lock of his hair.

ACTIVITY
Connecting with History and Conflict

Tell students to make a list of the various countries that belonged to the Central Powers during the war. Then have them make a chart showing the actions that each country took following the collapse of the Central Powers. **(Visual/Spatial)**

BACKGROUND
A Stab in the Back

World War I came to an end with the signing of the Armistice document on November 11, 1918. The German delegation was led by a civilian politician, Matthias Erzberger. German generals, such as Erich Ludendorff, refused to concede that their situation was hopeless at the time of the Armistice's signing. He implied that victory was denied the military due to evil unnamed civilian forces. He compared himself to the hero Siegfried of ancient German tales, saying that like Siegfried, he had been "stabbed in the back." His belief that the German army was undefeated in the field, reiterated throughout the 1920s, contributed to the instability of the Weimar Republic government that ruled Germany after World War I.

CUSTOMIZE FOR ...
Gifted and Talented Students

Ask students to analyze the impact of new weapon technologies on the progress of World War I. Then have them list ways in which a war fought from the air was different from a land-based war.

Section 4
Americans on the Home Front

Section Objectives

1. Learn about the steps the government took to finance the war and manage the economy.
2. Describe how the government enforced loyalty to the war effort.
3. Find out how the war changed the lives of Americans on the home front.

Bellringer

Warm-Up Activity Ask students what the term *home front* implies about the nature of American life during the war. Why could life not continue normally while the nation was involved in a war overseas?

Activating Prior Knowledge World War I brought many women into the paid labor force for the first time. How might this change have affected American families? Ask students to name some other periods of time during the twentieth century when women entered the paid labor force in large numbers.

Reading Strategy

Tell students that as they read, they should look for evidence to support the following statement, which appears on this page: "Waging war required many sacrifices at home." On a sheet of paper, have students describe the economic effects of World War I on the United States.

Section 4

Americans on the Home Front

READING FOCUS

- What steps did the government take to finance the war and manage the economy?
- How did the government enforce loyalty to the war effort?
- How did the war change the lives of Americans on the home front?

MAIN IDEA

Americans and their government took extraordinary steps at home to support the war effort.

KEY TERMS

Liberty Bond
price controls
rationing
daylight saving time
sedition
vigilante

TAKING NOTES

As you read, prepare an outline of this section. Use Roman numerals to indicate the major headings of this section, capital letters for the subheadings, and numbers for the supporting details. The sample below will help you get started.

I. Financing the War
II. Managing the Economy
  A. New agencies are founded to organize the economy.
    1. War Industries Board oversees production.
    2. ____________
    3. ____________
  B. ____________

Setting the Scene

> "*I hate war, because war is murder, desolation and destruction. If one-tenth of what has been spent on preparedness for war had been spent on the prevention of war the world would always have been at peace.*"
>
> —Henry Ford

Henry Ford's words appeared in the *Detroit Free Press* on August 12, 1915, when the United States still practiced neutrality. Ford vowed that he would burn down his factories before allowing them to make goods for the war in Europe.

Two years later, the United States was at war, and Ford had orders to build 16,000 tanks and 20,000 tractors for the United States government. A new Ford factory that would build anti-submarine ships was rising in Dearborn, Michigan, with the help of $10 million in federal aid. Henry Ford and his workers, along with the rest of the nation, had joined the war effort.

Waging war required many sacrifices at home. Despite the efforts of the preparedness movement, the American economy was not ready to meet the demands of modern warfare. War required huge amounts of money and personnel. As President Wilson explained, now "there are no armies . . . ; there are entire nations armed."

VIEWING HISTORY The United States government used posters to whip up sentiment against the "Huns"—the Germans—and to sell bonds to fund the war effort. **Recognizing Bias** *How does this poster depict German soldiers?*

Financing the War

The government launched a vigorous campaign to raise money from the American people. It borrowed money by selling **Liberty Bonds,** special war bonds to support the Allied cause. Like all bonds, they could later be redeemed for the original value of the bonds plus interest. By selling war bonds to enthusiastic Americans, Secretary of the Treasury William Gibbs McAdoo raised more than $20 billion. These funds allowed the United States to pay about one quarter of its war costs and still loan more than $10 billion to the Allies during and just after the war.

Caption Answers

Viewing History They are not depicted as human, but rather as savage and bloodthirsty.

Resource Directory

Teaching Resources
Guided Reading and Review booklet, p. 81

Technology
Section Reading Support Transparencies
Guided Reading Audiotapes (English/Spanish), Ch. 12
Student Edition on Audio CD, Ch. 12
Sounds of an Era Audio CD *"Over There,"* 1917 recording (time: 40 seconds)

RESOURCE PRO® **Literature Activity** *Selling the War,* found on Resource Pro, uses an excerpt from the propaganda folder *Why America Fights Germany* to show how the government galvanized popular sentiment against Germany.
Prentice Hall Presentation Pro CD-ROM, Ch. 12
Companion Web site, www.phschool.com

Responding to the slogan "Every Scout to Save a Soldier," Boy Scouts and Girl Scouts set up booths on street corners and sold bonds. The government hired popular commercial artists to draw colorful posters and recruited famous screen actors to lead public rallies to buy bonds. An army of 75,000 "four-minute men" gave brief (four-minute) speeches before movies, plays, and school or union meetings to persuade audiences to buy bonds.

Buying war bonds was one of several ways that civilians could support Americans at the front and demonstrate their patriotism. Patriotism is the love of one's country and the willingness to fight to defend its ideals and institutions.

Sounds of an Era

Listen to "Over There" and other sounds from the World War I era.

Managing the Economy

The government also called on industry to switch from producing commercial goods to war goods. In 1918, Wilson won authority to set up a huge bureaucracy to manage this process. Business leaders flocked to Washington to take up posts in thousands of new agencies. Because they gave their service for a token salary, they were called "dollar-a-year" men and women.

New Agencies A War Industries Board, headed by financier Bernard Baruch, oversaw the nation's war-related production. The board had far-reaching powers. It doled out raw materials, told manufacturers what and how much to produce, and even fixed prices.

A War Trade Board licensed foreign trade and punished firms suspected of dealing with the enemy. A National War Labor Board, set up in April 1918 under former President Taft, worked to settle any labor disputes that might disrupt the war effort. Labor leader Samuel Gompers promised to limit labor problems in war-production industries. A separate War Labor Policies Board, headed by Harvard law professor Felix Frankfurter, set standards for wages, hours, and working conditions in the war industries. Labor unions won limited rights to organize and bargain collectively.

Regulating Food and Fuel Consumption In August 1917, Congress passed the Lever Food and Fuel Control Act. This act gave the President the power to manage the production and distribution of foods and fuels vital to the war effort.

Using the slogan "Food will win the war," the government began to manage how much food people bought. Under the leadership of engineer and future President Herbert Hoover, the Food Administration worked to increase farm output and reduce waste. Hoover had the power to impose **price controls,**

VIEWING HISTORY At this shipyard, women workers replaced men who left to join the military. **Synthesizing Information** *Based on this photograph, describe some of the changes that wartime brought to the workplace.*

Lesson Plan

Focus Point out that World War I brought many changes at home, including unprecedented government control of the economy and of news and information. How did the war lead to the suppression of civil liberties?

Instruct Discuss the extent of the sacrifices that were required of Americans at home. Have students list changes in American life caused by the war and then categorize the changes.

Ask how the War Industries Board controlled industry. Have students compare the operations of a small manufacturing company before and during the war. Ask in what ways the War Labor Policies Board controlled workers. Why did business and labor cooperate with these boards? Would business and labor have cooperated with them in peacetime?

Assess/Reteach Ask students to imagine what it would be like to live in the United States during wartime. Have them discuss the ways in which their own daily lives would be affected. What industries would be affected today by wartime, and in what ways? How do they think a war would affect the economy?

Activity

Connecting with Citizenship

As head of the United States Food Administration during World War I, Herbert Hoover relied on slogans to help remind people to conserve food so there would be enough to feed the army. The slogan "Meatless, Wheatless, and Sweetless" was used, as were many different posters. The posters carried slogans such as "Food is Ammunition—Don't waste it."

Have students research these posters, and then ask them to make up their own posters and slogans to encourage food conservation. **(Visual/Spatial)**

Customize For ...

Gifted and Talented Students

Tell students that in 1929, Herbert Hoover said, "Absolute freedom of the press to discuss public questions is a foundation stone of American liberty." Have students write a few paragraphs explaining how Woodrow Wilson would have responded if Hoover had made that statement in 1917. They should also indicate if they agree with Hoover or with Wilson, and why.

Test Preparation

Have students read the passage under "New Agencies" on this page and then answer the question below.

How did labor leader Samuel Gompers affect the United States war effort?

- **A** Gompers had no effect on the war effort.
- **B** Gompers slowed the war effort.
- **Ⓒ** Gompers encouraged union members to support the war effort.
- **D** Gompers supported Germany in opposition to the U.S.

Caption Answers

Viewing History Possible answers include: women worked in jobs traditionally held by men; African Americans were hired by companies that previously discriminated against them.

Section 4 Assessment

Reading Comprehension

1. Price controls and rationing gave the President the ability to control the production and distribution of foods and fuels vital to the war effort.
2. Answers may include: Liberty Bonds, rationing, price controls, daylight savings time.
3. The government censored the press and banned certain films, thereby challenging any media influences that threatened the war effort.

Critical Thinking and Writing

4. (a) To raise money for the war costs. (b) By purchasing Liberty Bonds, civilians had a way of demonstrating their patriotism and supporting America's war efforts.
5. Answers will vary, but should include a discussion of being identified with the enemy, loyalty, and fear of espionage.

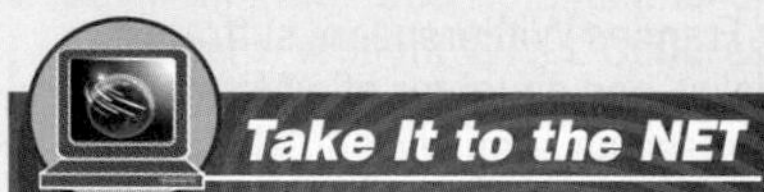

Graphs should be clearly constructed and should accurately present the historical data provided.

With the help of workers in the Woman's Land Army, farmers were able to harvest crops despite a labor shortage.

Changing People's Lives

American patriotism and war fever made military styles and activities more acceptable at home. Children joined scouting programs with military-style uniforms, marching, and patriotic exercises. Military drill became part of many school programs. By the summer of 1918, all able-bodied males in colleges and universities had become army privates, subject to military discipline.

Social Mobility for Minorities and Women After the war, Americans would turn away from military trends and other war-related activities. But other social changes that occurred during the war would have more lasting effects. The war virtually stopped the flow of immigrants from Europe, and the armed forces had taken many young men out of the labor pool. Businesses, especially war-related industries, suddenly needed workers. These wartime conditions drew some people into higher paying jobs. Factory owners and managers that had discriminated against African Americans and Mexican Americans now actively recruited them.

The African Americans who had left the South to work in northern factories added to a steady stream of migrants that had already started in the late 1800s. The stream turned into a flood during the war, when some 500,000 African Americans joined what came to be called the Great Migration.

The diminished work force also created new opportunities for women. Some women found jobs on farms, thanks to organizations such as the Woman's Land Army. Others moved into jobs as telegraph messengers, elevator operators, letter carriers, and similar jobs that were previously open only to men. A few earned management positions.

As a result of the war, about 400,000 women joined the industrial work force for the first time. In 1917, a speaker for the Women's Trade Union League proclaimed, "At last, after centuries of disabilities and discrimination, women are coming into the labor and festival of life on equal terms with men." Such pronouncements, while premature, celebrated what seemed to be a major social change.

Section 4 Assessment

READING COMPREHENSION

1. What was the role of **price controls** and **rationing** on the home front in World War I?
2. What were three ways that the government intervened in the economy to help the war effort?
3. How did the government deal with newspapers, magazines, and movies during the war?

CRITICAL THINKING AND WRITING

4. **Drawing Inferences** (a) What was the primary purpose of selling Liberty Bonds? (b) What else did the government's efforts to sell bonds accomplish?
5. **Writing an Opinion** Write a short speech discussing anti-German sentiment. Why do you think people reacted the way they did to the use of German words in the United States?

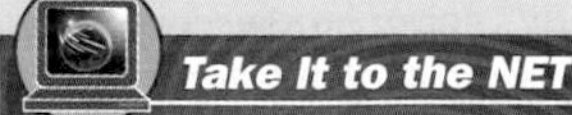

Activity: Creating a Graph Interpret historical data to create a bar graph of the financial costs of World War I. Use the links provided in the *America: Pathways to the Present* area of the following Web site for help in completing this activity.
www.phschool.com

RESOURCE DIRECTORY

Teaching Resources

Units 3/4 booklet
- Section 4 Quiz, p. 29

Guide to the Essentials
- Section 4 Summary, p. 61

Learning with Documents booklet (Visual Learning Activity) *Women's Roles in World War I*, p. 58

Section 5

Global Peacemaker

READING FOCUS

- What expectations did Wilson and the Allies bring to the Paris Peace Conference?
- What were the important provisions of the peace treaty?
- How did the federal government and ordinary Americans react to the end of war?

KEY TERMS

Fourteen Points
self-determination
spoils
League of Nations
reparations
Versailles Treaty

TAKING NOTES

Copy this incomplete Venn diagram. As you read, write the key peace proposals offered by President Wilson and the Allied leaders in the appropriate sections. If both sides supported a proposal, include it in the space where the circles overlap.

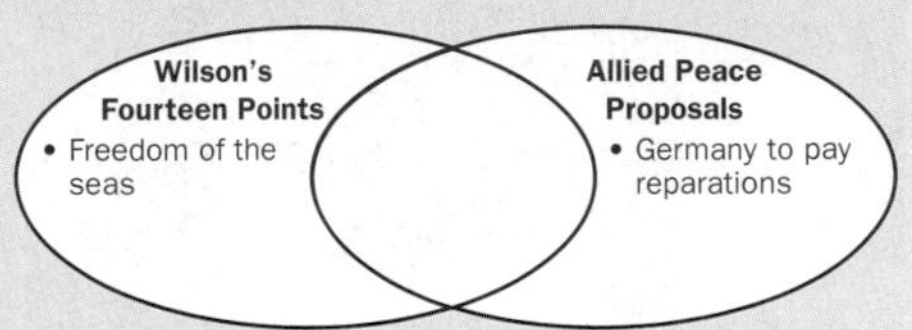

MAIN IDEA

When the fighting ended in Europe, President Wilson pressed for a treaty that would bring peace to the postwar world.

Setting the Scene On January 8, 1918, President Wilson stood before the Congress of the United States. The war had not ended, yet Wilson talked about peace. He hoped that the world could "be made safe for every peace-loving nation which, like our own, wishes to live its own life, determine its own institutions, be assured of justice and fair dealing by the other peoples of the world as against force and selfish aggression."

Wilson's program for reaching these goals came to be called the **Fourteen Points,** for the number of provisions it contained. Wilson's first point called for an end to entangling alliances, a key cause of the war. He wrote:

> *"Open covenants of peace, openly arrived at, after which there shall be no private international understandings of any kind but diplomacy shall proceed always frankly and in the public view."*
>
> —Woodrow Wilson

The remaining provisions of the Fourteen Points dealt with a variety of issues related to keeping the peace after the war. They included the removal of trade barriers among nations and the reduction of military forces. Wilson also called for the right of Austria-Hungary's ethnic groups to **self-determination,** or the power to make decisions about one's own future.

Wilson hoped that these points would form the basis of peace negotiations. Germany assumed that they would. At first, the Allies appeared to cooperate. But it soon became clear that Wilson's colleagues did not share his idealism. The Allies discarded Wilson's proposals one by one as they met to map out a future for Europe.

VIEWING HISTORY Crowds greet returning soldiers at a victory parade in New York City. **Drawing Inferences** *How did American attitudes toward Europe change in 1919 and 1920?*

The Paris Peace Conference

In January 1919, an international peace conference convened in Paris. Wilson decided to head the United States delegation. Although the Republican-controlled Senate would have the final word on the treaty,

Section 5

Global Peacemaker

Section Objectives

1. Discover the expectations that Wilson and the Allies brought to the Paris peace conference.
2. Learn about the important provisions of the peace treaty.
3. Find out how the federal government and ordinary Americans reacted to the end of the war.

Bellringer

Warm-Up Activity Ask students to explain the expression "At what cost peace?" How could this expression be applied to other wars the United States has fought?

Activating Prior Knowledge How did actions taken by President Wilson before and during the war affect his ability to negotiate a peace settlement? Would he be likely to have the support of the United States Congress?

Reading Strategy

As students read, have them analyze major issues raised by U.S. involvement in World War I, such as the changing role of the U.S. in world affairs and changes the war brought to the American home front.

Activity: Connecting with Government

When Wilson presented the Versailles Treaty to Congress with the provision to establish the League of Nations, he asked: "Dare we reject it and break the heart of the world?" Discuss Wilson's statement with students. Have them write essays in which they analyze major issues raised by the Treaty of Versailles. **(Verbal/Linguistic)**

Caption Answers

Viewing History Many people wanted the United States to withdraw from European affairs and focus on issues at home.

Resource Directory

Teaching Resources

Guided Reading and Review booklet, p. 82
Learning Styles Lesson Plans booklet, p. 41
Learning with Documents booklet (Key Documents) *Woodrow Wilson, The Fourteen Points,* p. 86

Technology

Section Reading Support Transparencies
Guided Reading Audiotapes (English/Spanish), Ch. 12
Student Edition on Audio CD, Ch. 12
Exploring Primary Sources in U.S. History CD-ROM *The Fourteen Points*
Prentice Hall Presentation Pro CD-ROM, Ch. 12
Companion Web site, www.phschool.com

ACTIVITY
Connecting with Culture

Ask students to read the text. Then divide the class into small groups. Have the groups discuss ideas for a mural on the risks and dangers of modern warfare. They could consider the following questions:

- What statements would you like to make?
- What images come to mind when you think of these dangers?
- How might you turn the images into a mural?

Have the groups share their ideas. Then take a class vote on the best ones. The class could then organize and carry out one or more of the best mural ideas. **(Visual/Spatial)**

BACKGROUND
Interdisciplinary

Many African American artists who sought increased opportunities to express themselves after World War I found an audience through publication in a magazine called *The Crisis: A Record of the Darker Races.* The magazine was first established in 1910 by the newly formed organization National Association for the Advancement of Colored People (NAACP), and edited by W.E.B. DuBois.

By the end of World War I, *The Crisis* had a monthly circulation of 100,000. When Jesse Redmon Fauset became the magazine's literary editor in 1919, she published the work of many young African American novelists and poets, such as Arna Bontemps, Langston Hughes, and Countee Cullen. *The Crisis* helped establish a literary movement in the 1920s called the Harlem Renaissance.

Europe After World War I

New nation

Allied-occupied zone

MAP SKILLS Britain, France, and the United States redrew the map of Europe at the Paris Peace Conference. **Regions** *Which three participants in the war lost the most territory in central and eastern Europe?*

humiliate Germany. In 1871, the new German Empire had been founded in the same hall at Versailles.

Reactions at Home

On July 8, treaty in hand, Wilson returned home to great acclaim. But many legislators had doubts about the results of the peace conference. Some senators opposed the treaty because it committed the United States to the League of Nations. These senators were called the "irreconcilables," because they could not be reconciled to, or made to accept, the treaty. Irreconcilables argued that joining the League would threaten American independence.

Senator Henry Cabot Lodge, chair of the Foreign Relations Committee, led another group called the "reservationists." This group accepted the League of Nations but wanted to impose reservations, or restrictions, on American participation. In particular, they wanted a guarantee that the Monroe Doctrine would remain in force. Wilson's point that compliance with the League's decisions was "binding in conscience only, not in law," failed to persuade them.

Wilson Tours the Country Determined to win grass-roots support for the League, Wilson took to the road in September. In 23 days, he delivered three dozen speeches across the country. After this tremendous effort, he suffered a stroke that paralyzed one side of his body. He would remain an invalid, isolated from his Cabinet and visitors, for the rest of his term.

During his illness, Wilson grew increasingly inflexible. Congress would have to accept the treaty and the League as he envisioned it, or not at all. In November 1919, the Senate voted on the treaty with Lodge's reservations included. The Senate rejected the treaty by a vote of 39 for, 55 against. When the treaty came up without the reservations, it failed again, 38 to 53. In the face of popular dismay at this outcome, the Senate reconsidered the treaty in March 1920, but once again the treaty was rejected.

A Formal End to Hostilities On May 20, 1920, Congress voted to disregard the Treaty of Versailles and declare the war officially over. Steadfast to his principles, Wilson vetoed the resolution. Finally, on July 2, 1921, another joint resolution to end the war passed. By that time, a Republican President, Warren G. Harding, was in office, and he signed it. Congress ratified separate peace treaties with Germany, Austria, and Hungary that October.

Difficult Postwar Adjustments The war spurred the United States economy, giving a big boost to American businesses. The United States was now the world's largest creditor nation. In 1922, a Senate debt commission calculated that European countries owed $11.5 billion to the United States.

The decline of the European powers thrust the United States into a position of unexpected strength. Britain, once the banker to the world

Focus on GEOGRAPHY

Multinational States Two countries created at the Paris Peace Conference were designed as multinational states. These were Czechoslovakia, a country dominated by Czechs and Slovaks, and Yugoslavia, or the Kingdom of the South Slavs, which included Serbs, Croats, Slovenes, and others. Czechoslovakia flourished as a democracy between the two world wars, but Yugoslavia stayed intact only under the strong hand of kings and dictators. Czechoslovakia split peacefully in 1993. Yugoslavia broke up violently into several countries in the 1990s, and many borders are still unsettled.

CAPTION ANSWERS

Map Skills Germany, Austria-Hungary, and Russia.

RESOURCE DIRECTORY

Teaching Resources

Units 3/4 booklet
- Section 5 Quiz, p. 30
- Chapter 12 Test, pp. 31, 34

Guide to the Essentials
- Section 5 Summary, p. 62
- Chapter 12 Test, p. 63

Other Print Resources

Chapter Tests with ExamView® Test Bank CD-ROM, Ch. 12

Historical Outline Map Book *Europe After World War I,* p. 62

Technology

RESOURCE PRO® **Primary Source Activity** *Mrs. Wilson's Role,* found on Resource Pro, illustrates how First Lady Edith Wilson became the "voice" of the President after he suffered a stroke.

ExamView® Test Bank CD-ROM, Ch. 12

Social Studies Skills Tutor CD-ROM

and center of the greatest colonial empire, had spent much of its great wealth on the war. Britain's economy never adjusted to peacetime, and the nation's power declined in comparison to that of the United States. The German invasion had devastated France, and Germany was weakened by the Treaty of Versailles. Yet even though the United States enjoyed unparalleled power, it chose to turn away from international affairs and focus on its concerns at home.

The return to peace had caused problems for the country at large. By April 1919, about 4,000 servicemen a day were being mustered out of the armed forces. But nobody had devised a plan to help returning troops merge back into society. The federal agencies that controlled the economy during the war had abruptly canceled war contracts. As a result, jobs proved scarce. The women who had taken men's places in factories and offices also faced readjustment. To free up jobs for returning soldiers, many women left their jobs voluntarily or were fired.

Like white troops, black soldiers came home to a hero's welcome. When they went to find jobs, however, their reception was different. Their contributions to the war had not earned black soldiers more respect from others. African Americans still faced discrimination in housing and employment, and lynchings and race riots continued.

Postwar Gloom Many artists and intellectuals in the United States entered the postwar years with a sense of gloom or disillusionment. They expressed their feelings in books and other artistic works. Social reformers had been encouraged by the government-business collaboration during the war. For most of them, the end of the war also ended an era of optimism. Alice Lord O'Brian, a military post exchange director from Buffalo who was twice decorated by the French, expressed the views of many who took part in the war. In a letter home she stated:

> "*We all started out with high ideals. . . . [A]fter being right up here almost at the front line . . . I cannot understand what it is all about or what has been accomplished by all this waste of youth.*"
>
> —Alice Lord O'Brian

Focus on GOVERNMENT

Checks and Balances *This is the system, established by the Constitution, that enables each of the three branches of the federal government to check the other branches.*

The Historical Context After President Wilson signed the Versailles Treaty, the treaty went to the Senate. There, a two-thirds vote in favor of the treaty was needed for the treaty to become official in the United States. The Senate, however, failed to approve the treaty.

The Concept Today Many people complain today that the branches of government should work together more and check each other less. Yet the system of checks and balances helps keep government responsible to the voters.

Section 5 Assessment

READING COMPREHENSION

1. Describe three of Woodrow Wilson's **Fourteen Points.**
2. How did the Allies both encourage and discourage **self-determination** in Europe?
3. Why did France and Britain demand **reparations** from Germany?
4. How did the United States eventually make peace with Germany?

CRITICAL THINKING AND WRITING

5. **Synthesizing Information** Why do you think many Americans opposed the Versailles Treaty?
6. **Drawing Inferences** Why did the Fourteen Points fail as a basis of peace negotiations?
7. **Writing a List** Compile a list of ten descriptive phrases that characterize the United States and Europe after the war.

Take It to the NET

Activity: Historical Recreations
Choose one of the Big Four leaders. Research your representative and recreate a meeting of the conference in your class. Use the links provided in the *America: Pathways to the Present* area of the following Web site for help in completing this activity.
www.phschool.com

Section 5 Assessment

Reading Comprehension

1. Answers should include three of the following: an end to entangling alliances; removal of trade barriers among nations; reduction of military forces; the right of Austria-Hungary's ethnic groups to self-determination.
2. Encouraged by giving independence to some countries; discouraged by disregarding the wishes of other countries. Allies were inconsistent in their application of self-determination.
3. To punish Germany for its role in the war.
4. The U.S. Senate approved a separate peace treaty with Germany in October 1921. Prior to that, President Warren G. Harding had signed a Congressional resolution declaring an end to the conflict without regard to the Treaty of Versailles in the summer of 1921.

Critical Thinking and Writing

5. It committed the United States to the League of Nations, which caused concern about American independence and whether or not the Monroe Doctrine would remain in effect.
6. Sample answer: The Fourteen Points did not serve the ends of the other Allies; especially France and Britain; they wanted to cripple Germany by taking its territory and demanding reparations.
7. Answers will vary but should be supported by facts from the section. Sample answer: postwar gloom.

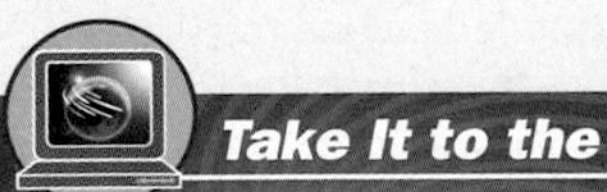

Answers will vary, but should focus on the disagreement between the Allies over postwar conduct.

CUSTOMIZE FOR ...

Less Proficient Writers

Ask students to list a set of three or four reasons either for or against the United States' participation in the League of Nations. Additionally, they could illustrate one of their reasons as a political cartoon.

TEST PREPARATION

Have students read the section on the previous page under "Reactions at Home" and then answer the question below.

What United States political figure, active in 1921, supported the position of the "irreconcilables"?

A Woodrow Wilson
B Henry Cabot Lodge
(C) Warren G. Harding
D none of the above

Chapter 12

Reviewing Key Terms

Students should refer to the definitions of key terms in the chapter to write sentences that show an understanding of the World War I era.

Reviewing Main Ideas

15. Imperialism, militarism, nationalism, and alliances were the deeper causes. The triggering cause was the assassination of Archduke Francis Ferdinand.
16. Answers should include the objectives of the Schlieffen Plan and the fact that it failed, the failure of the Russian invasion of Germany, the beginning of trench warfare, and the fact that modern weapons gave the overwhelming advantage to defending forces.
17. Most Americans favored the Allies. President Wilson decided on a position of neutrality. Both the preparedness movement, which urged the United States to get ready for war, and the peace movement began promoting their views.
18. The triggering cause was the continued sinking of neutral ships, which harmed American commercial interests. Other causes included the Zimmermann note, the Russian Revolution, and an anti-German bias among Americans.
19. Machine guns, hand grenades, long-range artillery, poison gases, tanks, the convoy system, and the use of airplanes as fighters and bombers.
20. They stopped the German advance on Paris and then led a counterattack that helped end the war.
21. To be sure that the United States would produce enough for the war effort, the government established new federal agencies to oversee industry and labor, as well as food consumption.
22. The government censored printed material and films to promote the Allied cause to the American people and to ensure that spies did not gain access to damaging material. The Espionage and Sedition Acts blunted criticism of the government.
23. There was widespread popular support for the treaty, but many senators opposed membership in the League.

Chapter 12 Review and Assessment

creating a CHAPTER SUMMARY

Copy this chart (right) on a piece of paper and complete it by adding important events that occurred in each year. Some entries have been completed for you as examples.

Year	Events
1914	• Gavrilo Princip assassinates Archduke Francis Ferdinand. • War breaks out between the Central Powers and the Allies. •
1915	
1916	
1917	
1918	
1919	
1920	

iTEXT

For additional review and enrichment activities, see the interactive version of *America: Pathways to the Present*, available on the Web and on CD-ROM.

★ Reviewing Key Terms

For each of the terms below, write a sentence explaining how it relates to World War I.

1. militarism
2. Central Powers
3. Allies
4. stalemate
5. U-boat
6. Zimmermann note
7. American Expeditionary Force (AEF)
8. convoy
9. armistice
10. Liberty Bond
11. sedition
12. Fourteen Points
13. League of Nations
14. Versailles Treaty

★ Reviewing Main Ideas

15. What were the main causes of World War I? (Section 1)
16. Describe the first three months of the war in Europe in your own words. (Section 1)
17. What were the reactions in the United States to the outbreak of the war in Europe? (Section 2)
18. Why did the United States declare war on Germany? (Section 2)
19. Name some of the military innovations introduced during World War I. (Section 3)
20. How did American troops help turn the tide of the war on the battlefield? (Section 3)
21. Why and how did the government try to control the economy at home? (Section 4)
22. Why and how did the government influence what people said about the war? (Section 4)
23. What was the American reaction to the Versailles Treaty and to the League of Nations? (Section 5)

★ Critical Thinking

24. **Predicting Consequences** What might have happened on the European front if General Pershing had decided to combine the American troops with other Allied armies instead of keeping them independent?
25. **Drawing Inferences** Do you think that women played a key role in World War I? Why or why not?
26. **Testing Conclusions** Many young people in Europe and the United States felt that they bore the heaviest costs of the war. Cite evidence showing whether they were correct.
27. **Supporting a Position** Do you think the Sedition Act was a good way to deal with critics during wartime? Explain.
28. **Identifying Central Issues** It is often said that Woodrow Wilson won World War I, but then "lost the peace." Explain your understanding of this statement.

Creating a Chapter Summary

Year	Events
1914	• Gavrilo Princip assassinates Archduke Francis Ferdinand. • War breaks out between the Central Powers and the Allies. • United States declares its neutrality.
1915	• British ship *Lusitania* is sunk by Germans. • Poison gas used on Western Front in an attempt to break stalemate.
1916	• Germany signs the Sussex pledge. • Huge offensives at Verdun and the Somme River; many German, French, and British casualties.
1917	• Russian revolution. • Germany ends Sussex pledge. • United States enters war.
1918	• American troops finally end stalemate, pushing back the Western Front. • Influenza epidemic spreads throughout the world. • Central Powers agree to a cease-fire.
1919	• United States Senate rejects Versailles Treaty and refuses to join League of Nations. • Germany signs the Treaty of Versailles.
1920	• Congress votes to disregard the Treaty of Versailles and declares the war officially over.

THE CHILD WHO WANTED TO PLAY BY HIMSELF.
President Wilson: "Now come along and enjoy yourself with the other nice children. I promised that you'd be the life and soul of the party."

★ Skills Assessment

Analyzing Political Cartoons ▶

29. Analyze the images in this 1919 cartoon. (a) Who is the man? (b) What does the little boy represent? (c) How can you tell?
30. Who does the man in the cartoon want the "child" to play with?
31. Why does the "child" want to play alone?
32. Explain the meaning of the cartoon.

Interpreting Data

Turn to the table of casualties in Section 5.

33. Which two countries suffered the greatest number of soldiers killed?
    A Russia and France
    B Germany and Austria-Hungary
    C Russia and Austria-Hungary
    D Germany and Russia
34. What can you conclude about casualties in "Other" Allied countries from this table?
    F These countries suffered as many casualties as the British Empire and France.
    G Their casualties were comparable to the total casualties in Bulgaria.
    H Unlike soldiers from France or Russia, soldiers in Romania, Serbia, and other small Allied countries were more likely to be killed in battle than wounded.
    J "Other" Allies suffered fewer casualties because they entered the war in 1916 or later.

Applying the Chapter Skill: *Identifying Alternatives*

35. The United States chose to go to war with Germany in 1917 largely because of continued German submarine attacks on neutral shipping. Identify alternative solutions to this problem of U-boat attacks. Discuss your alternative in a written proposal to President Wilson.

ACTIVITIES

Writing to LEARN

Writing to Compare
Compare the peacemaking ability of the United States today with its peacemaking ability after the war. What characteristics does it take for a country to serve as a peacemaker? Does the United States have these characteristics today? Did it have them in Wilson's time?

Primary Source CD-ROM

Working With Primary Sources Find additional information on World War I on the *Exploring Primary Sources in U.S. History CD-ROM* and use the selection(s) provided to complete the Chapter 12 primary source activity located in the *America: Pathways to the Present* area of the following Web site.
www.phschool.com

Take It to the NET

Chapter Self-Test As a review activity, take the Chapter 12 Self-Test in the *America: Pathways to the Present* area at the Web site listed below. The questions are designed to test your understanding of the chapter content.
www.phschool.com

ANSWERS TO ACTIVITIES

Writing to LEARN

Essays might focus on characteristics such as power and influence, and on the role of military might and democratic values.

Primary Source CD-ROM

Direct students to the additional primary sources that can be found on the *Exploring Primary Sources in U.S. History CD-ROM.*

Take It to the NET

Additional support materials and activities for Chapter 12 of *America: Pathways to the Present* can be found in the Social Studies area at the Prentice Hall School Web site. **www.phschool.com**

CRITICAL THINKING

24. The American troops might have adopted the Europeans' defensive posture and not have taken the offensive against the Germans outside Paris; Paris might have fallen; the war might have been lost.
25. Yes; they moved into important jobs, helped Food Administration programs succeed, served in the American Expeditionary Force at home and at the front.
26. Historians agree that the young men of all the major European combatant nations were, as a generational group, largely wiped out by the war (American casualties were lower). Young soldiers could sense that their leaders had failed to adapt their battle plans to the realities of the enormous firepower of twentieth century weapons.
27. Possible answer: the Sedition Act was a bad idea because, in disregarding the First Amendment, it undermined the goals President Wilson claimed the United States was fighting for.
28. Sample answer: Wilson had directed the victorious U.S. war effort, yet was unable to influence the Allies in the peace settlement.

SKILLS ASSESSMENT

29. (a) President Wilson. (b) The U.S. (c) "U.S.A." is printed on his hat.
30. He wants him to play with the other children in the "Temple of Peace." In other words, Wilson wants the U.S. to join the League of Nations.
31. Congress was reluctant to involve the nation in alliances that could pull it into international disputes.
32. Wilson looks foolish to the world because he can't get the U.S. to agree to an organization he proposed.
33. D
34. H
35. Answers might include suggesting to Wilson that he prohibit American ships from entering the war zone, or that he prohibit Americans from traveling to or from Great Britain.

A Flyer on the Edge

Focus Have students find the meaning of each of these words in a dictionary before they begin to read: *flinching, burlesque, strafing, airdrome, grotesque, contemptible, cur.* Ask them to consider, as they read, the long-term emotional effects of the war on those who fought it.

Instruct Ask students to review the passage from the viewpoint of a World War I historian. What information about World War I can you gain from the pilot's diary? What information can you discern from it about the emotions and morale of fighting men? What other types of sources would you need to consult to become an expert on World War I?

Analyzing the Document Use this additional question to generate class discussion:

Critical Thinking: Testing Conclusions Do you think that the pilot is correct when he writes that, after a war has ended, defeated enemies become objects of charity, while politicians look for another war? Give examples to support your answer. *(Answers will vary. Some students may argue that the pilot is correct; for example, the United States gave aid to Germany after World War II and then went to war against North Korea. Other students may answer that compassion dictates that a vanquished population receive aid and that subsequent wars are unavoidable.)*

AmericanHeritage®

MY BRUSH WITH **HISTORY**™

by ANONYMOUS

A Flyer on the Edge

The dangers of war took a heavy toll on the men who served in uniform, not only the soldiers in the trenches but also those who fought in the skies overhead. The passage below, selected by the editors of *American Heritage* magazine, is from the diary of an unknown pilot in World War I. As you read the following excerpt, think about how the psychological stresses of modern warfare affected those who fought to defend freedom.

WE'VE LOST A LOT OF GOOD MEN. It's only a question of time until we all get it. I'm all shot to pieces. I only hope I can stick it. I don't want to quit. My nerves are all gone and I can't stop. I've lived beyond my time already.

It's not the fear of death that's done it. I'm still not afraid to die. It's this eternal flinching from it that's doing it and has made a coward out of me. Few men live to know what real fear is. It's something that grows on you, day by day, that eats into your constitution and undermines your sanity. I have never been serious about anything in my life and now I know that I'll never be otherwise again. But my seriousness will be a burlesque for no one will recognize it.

Here I am, twenty-four years old, I look forty and I feel ninety. I've lost all interest in life beyond the next patrol. No one Hun will ever get me and I'll never fall into a trap, but sooner or later I'll be forced to fight against odds that are too long or perhaps a stray shot from the ground will be lucky and I will have gone in vain. Or my motor will cut out when we are trench strafing or a wing will pull off in a dive. Oh, for a parachute! The Huns are using them now. I haven't a chance, I know, and it's this eternal waiting around that's killing me. I've even lost my taste for liquor. It doesn't seem to do me any good now. I guess I'm stale. Last week I actually got frightened in the air and lost my head. Then I found ten Huns and took them all on and I got one of them down out of control. I got my nerve back by that time and came back home and slept like a baby for the first time in two months. What a blessing sleep is! I know now why men go out and take such long chances

Airplanes, originally used for reconnaissance, fought in aerial "dogfights" toward the end of the war.

444

RESOURCE DIRECTORY

Technology

AmericanHeritage® My Brush with History™ Videotapes *A Flyer on the Edge*

TEST PREPARATION

Have students use the excerpt on these pages to answer the following question.

Based on the passage, you can tell that—

Ⓐ the pilot's mental and emotional health is very frail.

B the pilot is mourning the loss of things that he may never experience, such as getting married and having children.

C the pilot is angry with himself for not using his family connections to stay out of the war.

D the pilot has post-traumatic stress syndrome.

and pull off such wild stunts. No discipline in the world could make them do what they do of their own accord. I know now what a brave man is. I know now how men laugh at death and welcome it. I know now why Ball went over and sat above a Hun airdrome and dared them to come up and fight with him. It takes a brave man to even experience real fear. A coward couldn't last long enough at the job to get to that stage. What price salvation now?

More than 8 million soldiers died in World War I, making it the costliest war in history to that time.

THOUGHTS ABOUT WAR

War is a horrible thing, a grotesque comedy. And it is so useless. This war won't prove anything. All we'll do when we win is to substitute one sort of Dictator for another. In the meantime we have destroyed our best resources. Human life, the most precious thing in the world, has become the cheapest. After we've won this war by drowning the Hun in our own blood, in five years' time the sentimental fools at home will be taking up a collection for these same Huns that are killing us now and our fool politicians will be cooking up another good war. Why shouldn't they? They have to keep the public stirred up to keep their jobs and they don't have to fight and they can get soft berths for their sons and their friends' sons. To me the most contemptible cur in the world is the man who lets political influence be used to keep him away from the front. For he lets another man die in his place.

The worst thing about this war is that it takes the best. If it lasts long enough the world will be populated by cowards and weaklings and their children. And the whole thing is so useless, so unnecessary, so terrible! . . .

The devastation of the country is too horrible to describe. It looks from the air as if the gods had made a gigantic steam roller, forty miles wide and run it from the coast to Switzerland, leaving its spike holes behind as it went. . . .

I've lost over a hundred friends, so they tell me—I've seen only seven or eight killed—but to me they aren't dead yet. They are just around the corner, I think, and I'm still expecting to run into them any time. I dream about them at night when I do sleep a little and sometimes I dream that some one is killed who really isn't. Then I don't know who is and who isn't. I saw a man in Boulogne the other day that I had dreamed I saw killed and I thought I was seeing a ghost. I can't realize that any of them are gone. Surely human life is not a candle to be snuffed out. . . .

Source: Anonymous, *War Birds: Diary of an Unknown Aviator,* Doran, 1926.

Understanding Primary Sources

1. **(a)** What is the writer's attitude toward war? **(b)** How does he feel about politicians and their role in war? **(c)** Why does the writer feel this way?
2. **(a)** In the author's opinion, what are his chances of surviving the war? **(b)** From what you've learned about World War I, is this a reasonable position?

American Heritage® MY BRUSH WITH **HISTORY**™ **Videotapes**

For more information about the experience of World War I, view "A Flyer on the Edge."

445

CUSTOMIZE FOR ...
ESL

Students may need help with the following words and phrases:
Huns a derogatory term for Germans
dictator a ruthless ruler who wields near-total power
wild stunts reckless feats

CUSTOMIZE FOR ...
Less Proficient Readers

Divide students into small groups and have each group discuss one of the following statements from the diary:
- "Here I am, twenty-four years old, I look forty and I feel ninety."
- "I haven't a chance, I know, and it's this eternal waiting around that's killing me."
- "To me the most contemptible cur in the world is the man who lets political influence be used to keep him away from the front. For he lets another man die in his place."

After groups have concluded their discussion, have them explain to the class what the pilot's statements mean.

CUSTOMIZE FOR ...
Less Proficient Writers

The writer uses many powerful negative phrases in this passage to express his fear and anxiety. Have students imagine that they are a pilot who is still optimistic, who is not worn down from fright and fatigue. Ask them to write a few sentences that express such a pilot's feelings as he or she prepares to take a flight.

CUSTOMIZE FOR ...
Gifted and Talented

Have students write an essay on what real fear is, based on the pilot's diary. Encourage students not merely to recapitulate the pilot's description (in the second paragraph) of what fear does, but to describe what provokes "real fear." Ask them to use the pilot's wartime experiences as examples. You might also suggest that students explain the pilot's assertion, "It takes a brave man to even experience real fear."

ANSWERS

1. **(a)** He thinks it's horrible, a "grotesque comedy." **(b)** He feels that politicians are fools, and cowards for protecting their sons from war and sending others to die in their places. He is risking his life while the politicians are safe at home.
2. **(a)** He thinks it's "only a question of time" until he dies. **(b)** Answers will vary.

TEST PREPARATION

Use this sample exam to help your students prepare for standardized tests.

Tips for Test Taking

You might want to remind your students of the following:

1. Read the directions carefully.
2. Read each question carefully.
3. For multiple choice questions, try to answer the question before you look at the choices. Read all the choices. Then, eliminate those that are absolutely incorrect.
4. For short answer questions, be sure to answer the question completely if there is more than one part.
5. Answer the easy questions first. Then, go back to the ones that will take more time.
6. Pace yourself. Be sure to set aside enough time for the writing questions.

TEST PREPARATION

Write your answers on a separate sheet of paper.

Use the information in the map to answer the following question.

United States Overseas Possessions, 1900

PACIFIC OCEAN; Philippines; Guam; Puerto Rico; 0–2000 mi.; 0–2000 km; N, S, E, W

1. How did the United States gain the territories labeled on the map?

   A Through the Monroe Doctrine
   B By treaty after World War II
   C Through a ruling of the United Nations
   D By winning the Spanish-American War

2. Who argued that naval power was crucial to the success of United States involvement overseas?

   A Samuel Gompers
   B William Randolph Hearst
   C Alfred T. Mahan
   D William Howard Taft

3. Which one of these was the main argument for those who supported United States imperialism?

   A Colonies would give the United States a place to sell products.
   B Colonies would provide students for United States colleges and universities.
   C The Constitution must go wherever the flag goes.
   D The United States needed naval bases in China and Japan.

Use the chart and your knowledge of social studies to answer the following question.

?????
• Settled the United Mine Workers' strike • Passed the Hepburn Act, giving the ICC the power to limit railroad rates • Created the Department of Labor • Was a leader in the conservation of natural resources • Changed the Monroe Doctrine • Won the Nobel peace prize for ending the Russo-Japanese War

4. Which one of these is a correct title for the information in the chart?

   A Progressive reforms of Woodrow Wilson
   B Accomplishments of Theodore Roosevelt
   C Accomplishments of Admiral Alfred T. Mahan
   D Actions of Roosevelt canceled by Taft

5. What did the Muckrakers do in the Progressive Era?

   A They helped sell war bonds during World War I.
   B They were the leaders in the Red Scare.
   C They exposed problems present in American society.
   D They did not want the United States to have colonies.

Diagnose and Prescribe
- Profile student skills with Diagnostic Tests A&B.
- Address student needs with program materials correlated to test questions.

Review and Reteach
- Provide cumulative content review with the Review Book.

Practice and Assess
- Build test-taking skills with Test-taking Strategies With Transparencies.

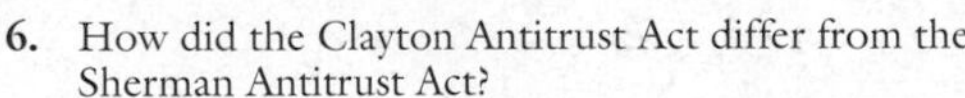

6. How did the Clayton Antitrust Act differ from the Sherman Antitrust Act?

   A The Sherman Antitrust Act divided the nation into 12 banking districts.

   B The Clayton Antitrust Act applied equally to businesses and unions.

   C The Sherman Antitrust Act applied only to railroads and transportation.

   D The Clayton Antitrust Act listed specific actions businesses could not do.

Use the information in the chart to answer the following question.

1912 Election Results			
Candidate	**Party**	**Popular Vote**	**Percentage**
Woodrow Wilson	Democrat	6,293,152	41.8%
Theodore Roosevelt	Progressive	4,119,207	27.4
William Howard Taft*	Republican	3,486,333	23.2
Eugene V. Debs	Socialist	900,369	6.0

*Incumbent

SOURCE: *New York Times Almanac 2001*

7. Which one of the following conclusions is correct?

   A Most of the Republican votes came from the Western states.

   B The American people voted for change in 1912.

   C The Democrats spent more money than the Republicans.

   D Taft would have won if Debs had not been in the race.

8. Susan B. Anthony and Carrie Chapman Catt were two of the leaders in the fight for the

   A rejection of prohibition.

   B approval of the Treaty of Versailles.

   C right of women to vote.

   D passage of the Clayton Antitrust Act.

9. Which one of the following contributed to the decision of the United States to enter World War I?

   A Germany's unrestricted submarine warfare

   B Mobilization of their armies by the Central Powers

   C The failure of the convoy system

   D The success of the czar in ending the Russian Revolution

10. Who was the commander of the American Expeditionary Force (AEF) in World War I?

    A Louis D. Brandeis

    B Arthur Zimmermann

    C John J. Pershing

    D David Lloyd George

11. Which of the following best describes Woodrow Wilson's Fourteen Points?

    A A statement of the goals for peace put forth by the United States following World War I

    B The American fighting plan for World War I

    C A list of Progressive Era reforms

    D The constitutional amendments planned by Progressives

Writing Practice

12. What actions did the Progressives take to change the United States government?

13. Describe the major reasons for the entry of the United States into World War I.

14. What steps did the government take to manage the economy during World War I?

TEST PREPARATION

1. D
2. C
3. A
4. B
5. C
6. D
7. B
8. C
9. A
10. C
11. A
12. Answers might mention reform-oriented writers and muckrakers; labor unions and women's groups; social welfare programs; implementation of workplace safety, minimum wage, and child labor reforms; new antitrust legislation; establishment of the Federal Trade Commission and the Federal Reserve System; and others.
13. Answers might mention the German use of the submarine, especially against neutral ships and passenger liners; and British control of U.S.–German communications and encouragement of anti-German sentiment among the American public.
14. Answers might mention the establishment of government agencies to oversee war-related production and labor, rationing, and the regulation of food and fuel consumption, and the enforcement of daylight saving time.

Unit 4

Introducing the Unit

Boom Times to Hard Times (1920–1938) The decades between World War I and World War II saw dramatic changes in society and the economy. The 1920s were an era of social experimentation, flourishing of the arts, and rapid economic growth. They were also a decade of political corruption and financial collapse, resulting in a worldwide economic Depression. Though challenged by this economic crisis, Americans pulled together and were able to help one another through the hard times, spurred on by massive governmental programs designed to restore the country's infrastructure while keeping its citizens busily engaged.

Using Historical Evidence

In the 1920s, New York City's Times Square first came into prominence as a crossroads of culture. As the painting on these pages shows, it was a lively scene, even in the dark of night. Crowds thronged there to enjoy the theater, the cinema, and simply the activity.

As students study the painting, discuss ways in which it depicts the liveliness of the Roaring Twenties. It was painted in 1925—at the height of an era of prosperity and optimism. How do students think the painting might be different if it had been painted six years later—during the heart of the Depression? Would the lively crowds be there? How many of the theater marquees would be brightly lit? How would people be dressed?

Unit 4

Boom Times to Hard Times (1920–1938)

"We are moving forward to a greater freedom, to greater security for the average man than he has ever known before in the history of America."

Franklin D. Roosevelt
Fireside chat, September 1934

Howard Thain's painting, *The Great White Way, Times Square, 1925*, captures the upbeat mood of the 1920s. ▶

RESOURCE DIRECTORY

Teaching Resources
Units 3/4 booklet
- American Pathways Activity, pp. 82–83
- History's Lasting Impact, pp. 84–85

Geography and History booklet, pp. 14–15

Other Print Resources
Prentice Hall Assessment System
- Document-Based Assessment

eTeach

Be sure to check out this month's online discussion with a Master Teacher. Go to **www.phschool.com**.

Chapter 13 Postwar Social Change, 1920–1929
Chapter 14 Politics and Prosperity, 1920–1929
Chapter 15 Crash and Depression, 1929–1933
Chapter 16 The New Deal, 1933–1941

449

TECHNOLOGY CENTER

Take It to the NET

Prentice Hall School Web site offers student-appropriate Internet activities and links that extend core content. Visit us at the Social Studies area. **www.phschool.com**

AmericanHeritage®

My Brush with History™ Video Program This new video series lets your students learn history from the people who lived it.

RESOURCE PRO®

Teaching Resources on CD-ROM offer lesson-planning flexibility, test-generation capability, and resource manageability.

- **Presentation Pro CD-ROM** Provides you with multimedia lecture notes for each chapter.
- **Social Studies Skills Tutor CD-ROM** Provides interactive practice in Geographic Literacy, Critical Thinking and Reading, Visual Analysis, and Communications.
- **Interactive Constitution CD-ROM** Exploring active citizenship and civic responsibilities, this CD-ROM shows students how the Constitution affects their lives today.
- **Exploring Primary Sources in U.S. History CD-ROM** This interactive exploration of primary sources allows students to analyze and to evaluate writing and images from American history.
- **Guided Reading Audiotapes**
- **Student Edition on Audio CD**
- **Sounds of an Era Audio CD** Bring the sounds of American history to life in the classroom with music, speeches, poetry, interviews, and news reports.

Don't miss the exclusive interactive version of this textbook on the Web and on CD-ROM.

RESOURCE DIRECTORY

Technology

Color Transparencies *Historical Maps,* A35; *Political Cartoons,* B12, B13; *Cause-and-Effect Charts,* D9; *Fine Art,* E17; *American Photo,* F7; *American Diversity,* G9, G12; *The Way It Works,* H17
Section Reading Support Transparencies
Prentice Hall United States History Video Collection™ Volume 17, *The Roaring Twenties;* Volume 18, *The Great Depression and the New Deal*
Companion Web site, www.phschool.com

Chapter 13 Planning Guide
Resource Manager

	Core Instruction	Reading/Skills
Chapter-Level Resources **TEKS** 24(B), 25(A), 25(D)	Teaching Resources • Pacing Charts booklet • Block Scheduling booklet **Resource Pro® CD-ROM,** Ch. 13 **Prentice Hall Presentation Pro CD-ROM,** Ch. 13 **www.phschool.com** • eTeach	**Guided Reading Audiotapes (English/Spanish)** **Student Edition on Audio CD,** Ch. 13 **Social Studies Skills Tutor CD-ROM** **Color Transparencies,** E17, G19
1 Society in the 1920s 1. Learn how women's roles changed in the 1920s. 2. Find out how the nation's cities and suburbs were affected by Americans on the move from rural areas. 3. Read about America's heroes of the 1920s, and come to see the reasons for their popularity. **TEKS** 5(A), 5(B), 8(B), 10(A), 10(B), 11(A), 21(D)	Teaching Resources **Units 3/4 booklet** • Section 1 Quiz, p. 42	**Guided Reading and Review booklet,** p. 83 **Guide to the Essentials,** p. 64 **Learning with Documents booklet,** p. 25 **Section Reading Support Transparencies**
2 Mass Media and the Jazz Age 1. See how the mass media helped create common cultural experiences. 2. Realize why the decade of the 1920s was called the Jazz Age, and learn how the jazz spirit affected the arts. 3. Discover how the writers of the Lost Generation responded to popular culture. 4. Find out about some of the subjects explored by the writers of the Harlem Renaissance. **TEKS** 1(A), 20(A), 20(B), 20(C), 20(E)	Teaching Resources **Units 3/4 booklet** • Section 2 Quiz, p. 43 **Learning Styles Lesson Plans booklet,** p. 42	**Guided Reading and Review booklet,** p. 84 **Guide to the Essentials,** p. 65 **Learning with Documents booklet,** p. 59 **Skills for Life booklet,** p. 15 **Section Reading Support Transparencies**
3 Cultural Conflicts 1. Learn about the effects of Prohibition on society. 2. Discover the issues of religion that were at the core of the Scopes trial. 3. Find out how racial tensions changed after World War I. **TEKS** 5(B), 7(A)	Teaching Resources **Units 3/4 booklet** • Section 3 Quiz, p. 44 **Learning Styles Lesson Plans booklet,** p. 43	**Guided Reading and Review booklet,** p. 85 **Guide to the Essentials,** p. 66 **Learning with Documents booklet, p. 59** **Section Reading Support Transparencies**

Enrichment/Pre-AP

Prentice Hall United States History Video Collection™
www.phschool.com
- Section Activities, Virtual Field Trip, Chapter Activities, Current Events Online

Biography, Literature, and Comparing Primary Sources booklet, p. 25
Great Debates booklet, p. 38
Sounds of an Era Audio CD
Exploring Primary Sources in U.S. History CD-ROM

Biography, Literature, and Comparing Primary Sources booklet, p. 67
American History Block Scheduling Support
Sounds of an Era Audio CD
Exploring Primary Sources in U.S. History CD-ROM

Biography, Literature, and Comparing Primary Sources booklet, p. 135
Sounds of an Era Audio CD
American Pathways Thematic Posters

Assessment

Core Assessment
ExamView® Test Bank, Ch. 13
ExamView® Test Bank CD-ROM, Ch. 13

Standardized Test Preparation
Diagnose and Prescribe
Diagnostic Tests for High School Social Studies Skills

Review and Reteach
Review Book for U.S. History

Practice and Assess
Test-taking Strategies With Transparencies
Test-taking Strategies Posters
Test Prep Book for U.S. History
Alternative Assessment Handbook
Document-Based Assessment

Teaching Resources
Units 3/4 booklet
- Section Quizzes, pp. 42–44
- Chapter Tests, pp. 45, 48

www.phschool.com Ch. 13 Self-Test

AmericanHeritage Resources

From the Archives of American Heritage®, pp. 454, 469
AmericanHeritage® My Brush with History™ Videotapes
www.americanheritage.com

Don't miss the exclusive interactive version of this textbook on the Web and on CD-ROM.

Chapter 13 Planning Guide

In Your Classroom

Customize for Individual Needs

Gifted and Talented

Teacher's Edition
- Customize for Gifted and Talented, pp. 461, 469

Teaching Resources
- Biography, Literature, and Comparing Primary Sources booklet, pp. 25, 67, 135

Technology
- Exploring Primary Sources in U.S. History CD-ROM *A Flapper's Appeal to Parents, Ellen Welles Page; Charles Lindbergh's Transatlantic Flight, The Japan Times; The Report of the Committee on Recent Economic Changes; As I Grew Older, Langston Hughes*

ESL

Teacher's Edition
- Customize for ESL, pp. 463, 469

Teaching Resources
- Guided Reading and Review booklet, pp. 83–85
- Guide to the Essentials (English/Spanish), Chapter 13

Technology
- Student Edition on Audio CD, Chapter 13
- Guided Reading Audiotapes (English/Spanish), Chapter 13
- Section Reading Support Transparencies

Less Proficient Readers

Teacher's Edition
- Customize for Less Proficient Readers, p. 471

Teaching Resources
- Guided Reading and Review booklet, pp. 83–85
- Guide to the Essentials (English/Spanish), Chapter 13

Technology
- Student Edition on Audio CD, Chapter 13
- Guided Reading Audiotapes (English/Spanish), Chapter 13
- Section Reading Support Transparencies

Less Proficient Writers

Teacher's Edition
- Customize for Less Proficient Writers, p. 455

Teaching Resources
- Guided Reading and Review booklet, pp. 83–85
- Guide to the Essentials (English/Spanish), Chapter 13

Technology
- Student Edition on Audio CD, Chapter 13
- Guided Reading Audiotapes (English/Spanish), Chapter 13
- Section Reading Support Transparencies

Teacher's Edition Index

Chapter 13 – Pacing Suggestions

For 90-minute Blocks

- Teach section 1 using Transparencies E17 and G19, and the Recent Scholarship note on page 461 for class discussions.

Running Out of Time?

If you are running short on time to cover this chapter, consider the following options:

- Use the Prentice Hall Presentation Pro CD-ROM to create an outline for this chapter.
- Use the Section Summaries for Chapter 13, from **Guide to the Essentials (English/Spanish).**

TEKS Correlation

Chapter-Level	TEKS
	(24) Social studies skills. The student applies critical-thinking skills to organize and use information acquired from a variety of sources, including electronic technology. The student is expected to: **(B)** analyze information by sequencing, categorizing, identifying cause-and-effect relationships, comparing, contrasting, finding the main idea, summarizing, making generalizations and predictions, and drawing inferences and conclusions. **(25) Social studies skills.** The student communicates in written, oral, and visual forms. The student is expected to: **(A)** use social studies terminology correctly. **(D)** create written, oral, and visual presentations of social studies information.
1 Society in the 1920s	**(5) History.** The student understands significant individuals, events, and issues of the 1920s. The student is expected to: **(A)** analyze causes and effects of significant issues such as immigration, the Red Scare, Prohibition, and the changing role of women. **(B)** analyze the impact of significant individuals such as Clarence Darrow, William Jennings Bryan, Henry Ford, and Charles A. Lindbergh. **(8) Geography.** The student uses geographic tools to collect, analyze, and interpret data. The student is expected to: **(B)** pose and answer questions about geographic distributions and patterns shown on maps, graphs, charts, models, and databases. **(10) Geography.** The student understands the effects of migration and immigration on American society. The student is expected to: **(A)** analyze the effects of changing demographic patterns resulting from migration within the United States. **(B)** analyze the effects of changing demographic patterns resulting from immigration to the United States. **(11) Geography.** The student understands the relationship between population growth and modernization on the physical environment. The student is expected to: **(A)** identify the effects of population growth and distribution and predict future effects on the physical environment. **(21) Culture.** The student understands how people from various groups, including racial, ethnic, and religious groups, adapt to life in the United States and contribute to our national identity. The student is expected to: **(D)** identify the political, social, and economic contributions of women to American society.
2 Mass Media and the Jazz Age	**(1) History.** The student understands traditional historical points of reference in U.S. history from 1877 to the present. The student is expected to: **(A)** identify the major eras in U.S. history from 1877 to the present and describe their defining characteristics. **(20) Culture.** The student understands the relationship between the arts and the times during which they were created. The student is expected to: **(A)** describe how the characteristics and issues of various eras in U.S. history have been reflected in works of art, music, and literature such as the paintings of Georgia O'Keeffe, rock and roll, and John Steinbeck's *The Grapes of Wrath.* **(B)** describe the impact of significant examples of cultural movements in art, music, and literature on American society, including the Harlem Renaissance. **(C)** identify examples of American art, music, and literature that transcend American culture and convey universal themes. **(E)** identify the impact of popular American culture on the rest of the world.
3 Cultural Conflicts	**(5) History.** The student understands significant individuals, events, and issues of the 1920s. The student is expected to: **(B)** analyze the impact of significant individuals such as Clarence Darrow, William Jennings Bryan, Henry Ford, and Charles A. Lindbergh. **(7) History.** The student understands the impact of the American civil rights movement. The student is expected to: **(A)** trace the historical development of the civil rights movement in the 18th, 19th, and 20th centuries, including the 13th, 14th, 15th amendments.

Chapter 13

Postwar Social Change

(1920–1929)

Introducing the Chapter

American society changed in many ways following World War I, as the Jazz Age introduced a variety of new styles, tastes, and manners. Conflict arose between Americans ready to adopt these new manners and new ways and Americans who tried to resist the forces of change.

Time Line Activity

To provide students with practice in using the time line, ask questions such as these:

1. What spurred the nationwide popularity of jazz? *(Broadcasting live jazz performances by radio)*
2. What famous discovery of this era changed the way we look at the ancient past? *(The discovery of King Tutankhamen's tomb in Egypt)*
3. What achievement combined bravery and technology to enthrall the world? *(Charles Lindbergh's successful transatlantic solo flight in 1927)*

Chapter 13 Postwar Social Change (1920–1929)

Newspaper headline shows unrest in Chicago.

The Chicago Daily Tribune. FINAL EDITION

TROOPS ACT; HALT RIOTING

Campaign for Prohibition succeeds.

The Shadow of Danger

If you believe that the traffic in Alcohol does more harm than good—help stop it!

Strengthen America Campaign

Heavyweight champion Jack Dempsey, sports hero of the 1920s.

American Events

1919 Race riots erupt in Chicago and other cities. Marcus Garvey launches the first of his Black Star Line ships for the Universal Negro Improvement Association.

1920 The Eighteenth Amendment institutes Prohibition. The Nineteenth Amendment gives women the right to vote.

1923 Louis Armstrong makes his first jazz recording. Duke Ellington begins playing in Harlem's jazz clubs. Jazz is made more popular by a growing radio audience.

1924 Women governors are elected in Wyoming and Texas.

Presidential Terms: Woodrow Wilson 1913–1921; Warren G. Harding 1921–1923; Calvin Coolidge 1923–1929

1918 • 1920 • 1922 • 1924

World Events

1920 Dutch painter Piet Mondrian publishes his ideas on "neoplastic" style.

1922 King Tutankhamen's tomb is discovered in Egypt.

1924 First Winter Olympic games are held in Chamonix, France.

eTeach

Be sure to check out this month's online discussion with a Master Teacher. Go to **www.phschool.com**.

RESOURCE DIRECTORY

Teaching Resources

Pacing Charts booklet

Block Scheduling booklet, p. 23

Units 3/4 booklet

- Chapter Summary, p. 41

Technology

Guided Reading Audiotapes (English/Spanish), Ch. 13

Student Edition on Audio CD, Ch. 13

Sounds of an Era Audio CD *"Livery Stable Blues"* (time: 45 seconds)

Prentice Hall United States History Video Collection™ Volume 17, *The Roaring Twenties*

Prentice Hall Presentation Pro CD-ROM, Ch. 13

Resource Pro® CD-ROM

Social Studies Skills Tutor CD-ROM

Companion Web site, www.phschool.com

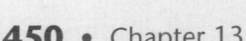

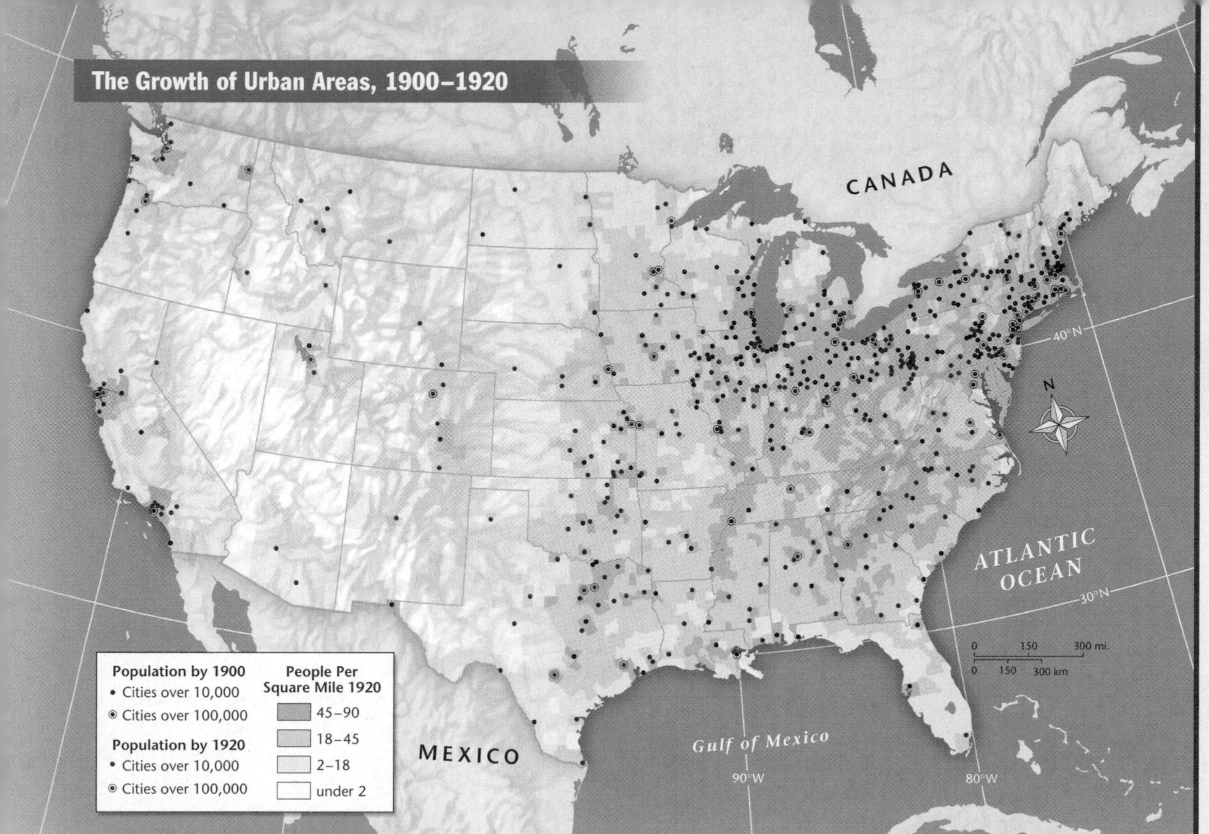

The Growth of Urban Areas, 1900–1920

CANADA

MEXICO

Gulf of Mexico

ATLANTIC OCEAN

Population by 1900
• Cities over 10,000
◉ Cities over 100,000

Population by 1920
• Cities over 10,000
◉ Cities over 100,000

People Per Square Mile 1920
45–90
18–45
2–18
under 2

Sixth Avenue Elevated at Third Street, 1928, by John Sloan.

Actress Lillian Gish, star of silent films and "talkies."

1925 The Scopes trial stirs a national debate on evolution.

1926 Gertrude Ederle becomes the first woman to swim across the English Channel.

1927 Aviator Charles Lindbergh completes the first nonstop transatlantic solo flight.

Herbert Hoover 1929–1933

1926 · 1928 · 1930

1925 Japan enacts universal male suffrage.

1928 *The Threepenny Opera* by Bertolt Brecht and Kurt Weill debuts in Berlin.

1929 The term *apartheid* is introduced in South Africa.

The Growth of Urban Areas, 1900–1920

Activating Prior Knowledge Where were more people per square mile concentrated—in the eastern or western part of the United States? *(Eastern)*

Previewing Between 1900 and 1920, there were changes regarding the places many people chose to live. Looking at the map, find one such change that took place. *(More people chose to live in large cities in 1920 than in 1900.)*

BACKGROUND
About the Pictures

1. The Chicago Race Riots of 1919 shocked the nation and after five days of rioting left 38 people dead and hundreds more injured.
2. During the 1920s, anti-alcohol groups attempted to sway the public toward supporting Prohibition because the enforcement of Prohibition laws was proving to be nearly impossible without public support.
3. The heavyweight boxing match between American Jack Dempsey and Frenchman Georges Carpentier was the first boxing match broadcast over the radio. Grossing over one million dollars in ticket sales, the fight lasted only 11 minutes as Dempsey completely overpowered Carpentier.
4. New York's trolley system was extensive, providing transportation to most parts of the city. New York was also one of the first cities to run its trolleys through underground tunnels, or subways.
5. One of the most prolific and popular actresses of the twentieth century, Lillian Gish had a career that spanned 75 years, beginning with her first film in 1912 and ending with her last in 1987.

BIBLIOGRAPHY

For the Teacher

Delany, Sarah Louise and Elizabeth. ***Having Our Say: The Delany Sisters' First 100 Years.*** Dell, 1996. (Two noted African American centenarians share their memories, in memorable fashion.)

Lemann, Nicholas. ***The Promised Land, The Great Black Migration and How It Changed America.*** Vintage, 1992. (Scholarly examination of the tremendous impact of this mass movement on both cities and rural areas.)

For the Student

Editors of Time-Life Books. ***The Jazz Age: The 20s (Our American Century).*** Time-Life, 1998. (Colorful, lively account of an interesting era.)

Willis-Thomas, Deborah, et al. ***Van Der Zee.*** Harry N. Abrams, 1998. (Harlem in its heyday as seen by its most famous photographer.)

Don't miss the exclusive interactive version of this textbook on the Web and on CD-ROM.

Section 1

Society in the 1920s

Section Objectives

1. Learn how women's roles changed in the 1920s.
2. Find out how the nation's cities and suburbs were affected by Americans on the move from rural areas.
3. Read about America's heroes of the 1920s, and come to see the reasons for their popularity.

Bellringer

Warm-Up Activity Ask students if they have ever moved and, if so, for what reasons. Which state or region of the country do they think currently provides the best opportunity for good jobs and advancement?

Activating Prior Knowledge Have students research the populations of several major American cities based on data from the 1920 census and the 1930 census. Which cities experienced the greatest growth in population?

Reading Strategy

Have students copy the headings in this section. As they read, they should write down at least two key points under each heading.

Section 1

Society in the 1920s

READING FOCUS

- How were women's roles changing during the 1920s?
- How were the nation's cities and suburbs affected by Americans on the move from rural areas?
- Who were some American heroes of the 1920s? What made them popular with the American public?

KEY TERMS

flapper
demographics
barrio

TAKING NOTES

Copy the chart below. As you read, fill in details relating to various social changes of the 1920s.

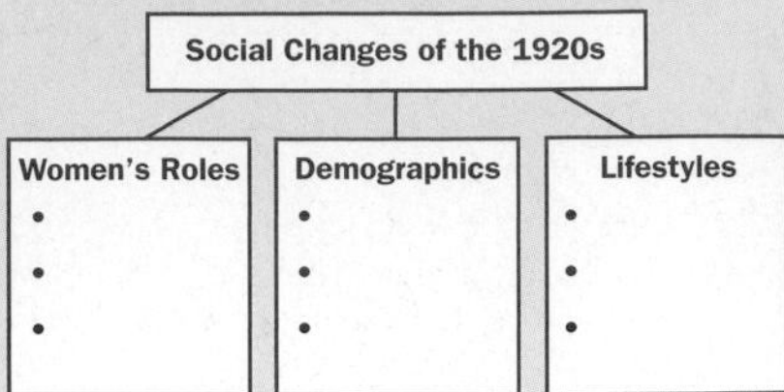

MAIN IDEA

The 1920s were a time of rapid social change, in which many young people, particularly young women, adopted new lifestyles and attitudes. As its rural population decreased, the United States became an urban nation, and traditional values were increasingly challenged.

VIEWING HISTORY Flappers defined a new style of dress. **Drawing Inferences** *How does this young woman's attitude reflect the mood of the 1920s?*

Setting the Scene The decade of the 1920s stands out as a time of rapid change in American society. Much of the change had its roots in the previous century. In the late 1800s, industrialization and immigration began transforming the United States into an urban nation. Farm families streamed into the cities. Along with masses of immigrants, the new arrivals helped form a more complex urban culture.

The Great War accelerated those changes. Millions of young people had marched off to war full of enthusiasm. Many returned bearing the scars of that war: shell shock, permanent injury, and the effects of poison gas. Many also came back disillusioned, a condition they shared with others who had stayed home during the war. Together, they questioned the ideas and attitudes that had led to the war. Their challenge of traditional values helped ignite a revolution in manners and morals.

The **flapper** symbolized this revolution. The term described a new type of young woman: rebellious, energetic, fun-loving, and bold. One author depicted the flapper this way:

> *"Breezy, slangy, and informal in manner; slim and boyish in form; covered in silk and fur that clung to her as close as onion skin; with carmined [vivid red] cheeks and lips, plucked eyebrows and close-fitting helmet of hair; gay, plucky and confident."*
>
> —Preston Slosson, *The Great Crusade and After,* 1930

Many older Americans held more traditional views of how young women were supposed to behave in public. They disapproved not only of the flappers' display of free manners but also of the behavior of the young men who flocked around them.

Of course, not all young women became flappers, and not everyone questioned traditional values. Still, those who did had a lasting effect on society. They helped create what we think of today as modern America.

Caption Answers

Viewing History The flapper wears a carefree smile and kicks up her leg, as though dancing the Charleston. Her knee-length skirt, short hair, and cloche hat are some of the new fashions appearing in the 1920s.

RESOURCE DIRECTORY

Teaching Resources

Guided Reading and Review booklet, p. 83
Learning with Documents booklet (Primary Source Activity) *The Younger Generation,* p. 25

Technology

Section Reading Support Transparencies
Guided Reading Audiotapes (English/Spanish), Ch. 13
Student Edition on Audio CD, Ch. 13
Sounds of an Era Audio CD *"Have You Seen Rosie's Sister?"* 1925 recording (time: one minute)
Exploring Primary Sources in U.S. History CD-ROM *A Flapper's Appeal to Parents, Ellen Welles Page*
Prentice Hall Presentation Pro CD-ROM, Ch. 13
Companion Web site, www.phschool.com

Women's Changing Roles

Women stood at the center of much of the social change in the 1920s. Both single and married women had been in the work force for a long time. During the war, their numbers rose and they moved into better, higher-paying jobs. After the Nineteenth Amendment was adopted in 1920, all American women could vote. These experiences made them eager for still greater equality with men. Without intending to, the rebellious flapper brought all women closer to that goal.

The Flapper Image The flapper represented only a small number of American women, yet her image had a wide impact on fashion and on behavior. Stylish young women began wearing dresses shorter than their mothers did, to the dismay of some guardians of decency. The fashion page of the *New York Times* declared in July 1920 that "the American woman . . . has lifted her skirts far beyond any modest limitation." At that time, hemlines had risen to just nine inches above the ground. By 1927, they would rise to knee-length or even higher. Between 1913 and 1928, the average amount of fabric used to make a woman's outfit shrank from 19.5 yards to just 7 yards.

Women also broke with the past in other ways. While most of their mothers had grown their hair long and then pinned it up, young women bobbed, or cut short, their hair. Instead of wide-brimmed hats, they wore the close-fitting "cloche," whose bell shape accentuated the new hairstyles. They also began wearing heavy makeup, a practice formerly associated only with actresses or prostitutes.

Women's manners changed as well. Before the 1920s, "proper" women rarely drank anything much stronger than wine, much less smoked, in public. By the end of the decade, many women were doing both, in part to defy Prohibition, but also to express their new freedom. Between 1918 and 1928, the number of cigarettes produced in the United States more than doubled. Though men were smoking more (many switching from cigars and pipes to cigarettes), the new woman smoker accounted for a large part of the increase. All these changes shocked American society and enraged many parents.

Women Working and Voting Although many women bobbed their hair and wore shorter skirts, most did not embrace a flapper lifestyle. Some women adopted the new fashions simply because they were more convenient.

Convenience was an issue for young working women, as they had less time to spend maintaining elaborate wardrobes or hairstyles. During the 1920s, about 15 percent of wage-earning women became professionals and about 20 percent held clerical positions. Generally, these were single white women, although the percentage of married women working increased from 23 percent of the total female work force in 1920 to 29 percent in 1930.

Businesses remained prejudiced against women seeking professional posts. Many hospitals refused to hire female doctors, and many legal firms rejected female lawyers or offered them secretarial jobs. Employers seldom trained women for jobs beyond the entry level or paid them on as high a scale as men. Few women advanced to leadership positions. Employers expected women to quit if they married and became pregnant.

Fast Forward to Today

Women in the Workplace

Over time, the nature of women's work has changed to accommodate the needs of the labor market and changes in attitudes about women working outside the home. In a rural setting, women looking for outside work have typically found their choices more limited than in a city. As more and more people moved from rural areas in the 1920s, growing urban economies made room for women to enter the paid work force. The 1920s saw many women securing clerical jobs, work once reserved for men. From the 1920s to today, work available to women in the United States has expanded from jobs women have traditionally held, such as teaching and nursing, to include a range of options never before available.

As shown by the chart below, the percentage of women in the labor force has risen from the 1920s to the 1990s.

? What types of jobs are limited to rural areas or to cities today?

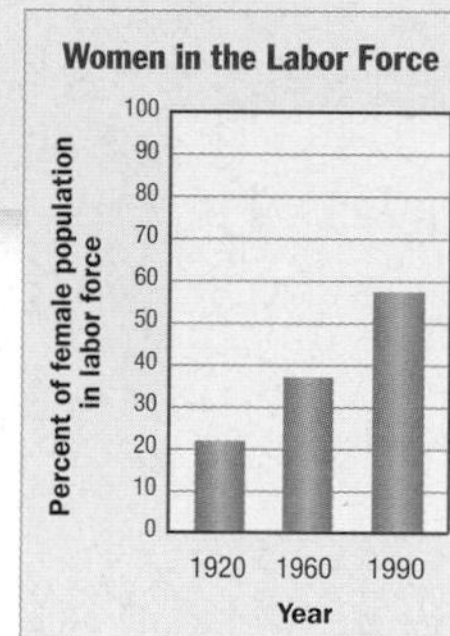

Lesson Plan

Focus The 1920s was a time of rapid social change. Ask students what new social and demographic trends appeared. How did they affect the country?

Instruct Discuss the changing role of women in society and the impact of suffrage on the country. How did the newly gained right to vote affect the number of women holding elective office?

Have students identify the reasons people began to move. Why did many African Americans migrate from the South to the North? Why did migrants come to the United States from Mexico and Canada? Why were Americans able to leave the cities and move to the suburbs?

Ask students why Americans needed heroes in the 1920s. Who were they and what qualities did they possess?

Assess/Reteach Ask students to contemplate the impact on a society of a vast migration from rural areas into cities. How would this movement impact education, housing, employment, culture, and society in general? What would be some positive results of this movement? What would be some negative results?

Caption Answers

Fast Forward to Today Clerical, financial, industrial, and medical jobs are found in cities today. Rural areas today have many small businesses, as well as agriculture-related jobs.

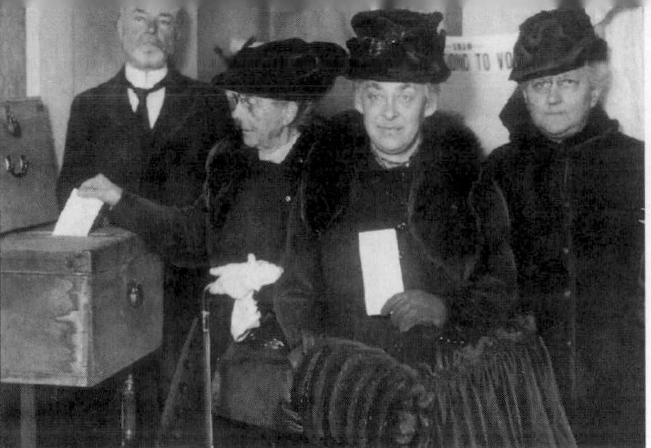

VIEWING HISTORY In 1920, women in New York City vote after the adoption of the Nineteenth Amendment. **Drawing Conclusions** *Why do you think more women did not turn out to vote in the early 1920s?*

Like the situation of women at work, women's status in politics changed little. As of 1920, women could vote in all elections. At first, some politicians feared that women might vote as a bloc, or special-interest group. That did not happen. Most women voted along the same lines as men. Moreover, relatively few women voted at all, especially in the early years after gaining national suffrage. Only about 35 percent of women voters went to the polls in 1920. In 1923, a survey asked women in Chicago why they did not vote in the mayoral election. Most notably, about a third said that they lacked interest. Another eleven percent said that they did not think women should vote at all.

Early on, women did not exercise their right to vote for a number of reasons. Women who lived in rural areas or had children to look after had to make special arrangements to get to the polls. Sometimes women's families discouraged them from voting. Other women were not comfortable with the idea of voting. In short, women had yet to make voting a habit, and it would take time for the habit to develop.

As the decade wore on, more women voted, but their choices did not change politics greatly. In national elections, women voted in patterns similar to men's. In local elections, however, women's votes often differed from men's, perhaps because women were more familiar with the candidates and issues.

After the Nineteenth Amendment was adopted, the alliance that worked for suffrage split, weakening its ability to push bills through Congress. Progressive reformers did lobby successfully for the Sheppard-Towner Act of 1921, the first major federal welfare measure concerned with women's and children's health. A constitutional amendment calling for an end to child labor failed, however. So did the Equal Rights Amendment (ERA), introduced in Congress for the first time in 1923. The original wording of the ERA stated that "Men and women shall have equal rights throughout the United States and every place subject to its jurisdiction." Some reformers opposed the ERA because it would make the laws requiring special working conditions for women unconstitutional.

Despite their disagreements, women worked together to win political office. Jeannette Rankin of Montana won election to the U.S. House of Representatives in 1916, becoming the first woman to serve in either house of Congress. Miriam A. Ferguson from Texas and Nellie Tayloe Ross of Wyoming, both wives of former governors, were elected governors themselves in 1924. By 1928, there were 145 women in 38 state legislatures. Thus, although women did not increase their political power as quickly as suffragists had hoped, they did lay a foundation for future participation in government on a larger scale.

READING CHECK
How did women influence politics in the 1920s?

Americans on the Move

In addition to social changes, many changes in **demographics** occurred in the 1920s. Demographics are the statistics that describe a population, such as data on race or income. The major demographic change of the 1920s was a movement away from the countryside. The 1920 census showed that for the first time in the nation's history, more Americans lived in urban areas than in rural areas.

Rural-Urban Split The 1920s magnified the gap between rural and urban society. One aspect of that gap was economic. Farmers had done well for the first two decades of the century. After the war, however, market prices dropped while the costs of operation rose. By the early 1920s, many farmers were economically stressed.

From the Archives of
American Heritage®

Women Who Smoke

Having recently secured the right to vote, America's women rose up in early 1922 to defend an even more fundamental liberty: the right to smoke. In February newspapers reported the shocking news that smoking was common among female students at Northwestern University, the University of Chicago, Columbia University's Teacher's College, and other institutions of higher learning. Barnard College even allowed unrestricted use of the "devil's weed." Barnard's permissive attitude was not universal throughout New York City, however. On March 27, with no warning, police began to enforce an ordinance that banned smoking by females in restaurants, hotels, and other public gathering places. Women were outraged. The bill's sponsor defended it saying that ". . . [Y]oung fellows go into restaurants to find women folk sucking cigarettes. What happens? The young fellows . . . vampired by these smoking women, desert their homes, their wives and children, rob their employers and even commit murder so that they can get money to lavish on these smoking women." Source: Frederic D. Schwarz, "The Time Machine," *American Heritage®* magazine, February 1997.

READING CHECK

In a very limited manner. Many women failed to vote. Women who did vote had little effect on national politics, but did impact local campaigns. By the end of the decade, many women had been elected to state legislatures, and two female state governors had been elected.

CAPTION ANSWERS

Viewing History Disinterest; difficulty finding child care; family members may have discouraged it.

RESOURCE DIRECTORY

Teaching Resources

Biography, Literature, and Comparing Primary Sources booklet (Biography) *Lillian Moller Gilbreth,* p. 25

Great Debates booklet (Decision-Making Activities) *Lobbying for Indian Immigration,* p. 38

Technology

Color Transparencies *Fine Art,* E17; *American Diversity,* G19

RESOURCE PRO® **Primary Source Activity** *Growing Up Black,* found on Resource Pro, provides an excerpt from Daisy Bates's autobiography describing the effects of segregation on her and her African American and white neighbors in the 1920s South.

Meanwhile, the industrial and commercial economy began to boom. This prosperity bypassed much of rural America. Many farmers reluctantly left the land and headed to cities. During the decade, some 6 million people moved from rural to urban areas.

This migration, combined with urban prosperity, had important effects on society. Attendance at public high schools rose from 2.2 million in 1920 to 4.4 million by 1930. Some of this rise came from an increase in urban population and greater prosperity, but an important part of it resulted from a change in the labor pool. On farms, most older children played vital roles as laborers, so they often had to drop out of school to help their parents. In cities, children needed more education to compete in urban-based industry.

Rural and urban America also split over cultural issues. You read earlier about the change in manners and morals. This general shift away from traditional values took place mainly in the cities. Most rural populations wanted to preserve traditional values, not defy them. They frowned on the flappers and other aspects of society that they deemed immoral or dangerous.

African Americans in the North As you have read, the passage of Jim Crow laws, as well as new job opportunities in the North, produced the Great Migration of blacks from the South to northern cities. This migration continued from the late 1800s through World War I. The boom in northern industries further encouraged this demographic shift.

Throughout the early 1900s, jobs for African Americans in the South had been scarce and low-paying. Many factories refused to hire blacks for anything other than menial jobs. As industries expanded during the 1920s, many jobs opened up for African Americans in the North. In 1860, 93 percent of all African Americans lived in the South. By 1910, this figure had dropped to 89 percent. By 1930, it had fallen far more, to 80 percent.

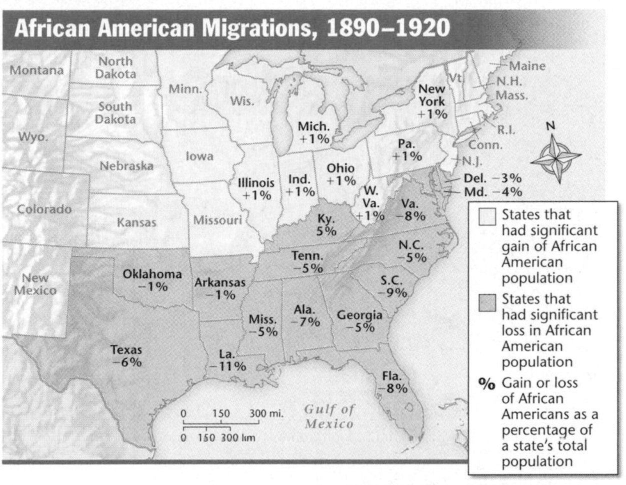

MAP SKILLS The migration of African Americans from the South to the North helped alter the populations of both regions. **Movement** *Which states lost the largest percentages of their black populations?*

Yet the North was no promised land. African American factory workers often faced anger and hatred from whites, who believed that migrants would work for lower wages and take their jobs. African American women generally worked for very low wages as household help for whites.

Other Migration After World War I, masses of refugees applied for entry into the United States. During the 1920s, Congress acted to limit immigration, especially from southern and eastern Europe and also from China and Japan. Since the limits did not apply to nations in the Americas, employers turned to immigrants from Mexico and Canada to fill low-paying jobs.

In the West, Mexicans supplied most of this labor, migrating to work on the farms of California and the ranches of Texas. In the Northeast, Canadians from the French-speaking province of Quebec traveled south to work in the paper mills, potato fields, and forests of New England and New York.

Migrants also took jobs in the cities. Los Angeles, for example, became a magnet for Mexicans and developed a distinct **barrio,** or Spanish-speaking neighborhood. New York also attracted a Spanish-speaking population—Puerto Ricans migrating in the hope of a better life in the United States.

ACTIVITY
Connecting with Geography

Have half of your students conduct research to find out the percentage of Americans who were living in rural areas and the percentage of Americans who were living in urban areas in 1920. Have the second half find the same data for the year 1930. Then have students cooperate to create a line graph that shows the changes during the 1920s. Ask them how the graph emphasizes the demographic changes of 1920s America. **(Visual/Spatial)**

BACKGROUND
Connections to Today

Most African Americans who migrated to the North during the late nineteenth and early twentieth centuries settled in urban areas. Urban areas were the seats of the economic opportunities the migrants sought. Upon arrival, a combination of poverty on the part of the new migrants and racism on the part of property owners ensured that African Americans were forced to settle in less desirable parts of towns. This settlement pattern is still in evidence today: many northern cities still have segregated neighborhoods, and many primarily African American areas are the same ones that were created during the early twentieth-century migrations from the South.

CUSTOMIZE FOR ...
Less Proficient Writers

Have students create two lists with the headings: *Jobs in the Country* and *Jobs in the City.* Have them list some of the jobs they could imagine someone a little older than themselves holding in the country and in the city in the 1920s. Have them put a star next to each job that would require a high school education or more.

TEST PREPARATION

Have students review the material on the previous page about migration of Mexicans to United States cities and then complete the sentence below.

According to the text, the word *barrio* means—

A region.
Ⓑ neighborhood.
C country.
D state.

CAPTION ANSWERS

Map Skills Louisiana lost 11 percent of its African American population. South Carolina lost 9 percent.

ACTIVITY
Connecting with Geography

Have small groups of students conduct research on the demographic history of their own city (or nearest large city) during the 1920s. Students should consider library and Internet research, as well as contacting a local historical society to answer such questions as: Did suburbs develop in the 1920s? Does evidence of the demographic changes of the 1920s still exist today? Have students present their findings in the form of a report. Their report should evaluate whether changes in the 1920s in their city were typical of changes occurring in other American cities at the time. **(Verbal/Linguistic)**

BACKGROUND
An American Hero

"Lindbergh . . . has qualities of heart and head that all of us would like to possess," said *The New York Times.* On his flight across the Atlantic, Lindbergh seemed to carry the hopes and dreams of a nation struggling to come to grips with itself following World War I. It is estimated that 25,000 tons of newsprint alone were used to record his flight and 5,000 poems were written to commemorate it.

Growth of the Suburbs As a result of the migrations of the 1920s, American suburbs grew. Suburban growth had begun to accelerate in the late nineteenth century. Cities built transportation systems that used electric trolleys—cars that ran on rails laid in the streets, and were powered by overhead wires. Trolleys allowed people to get from their suburban homes to jobs and stores in the city cheaply.

During the 1920s, buses replaced trolleys in many areas. Buses did not need rails and overhead wires, and thus were less expensive and easier to route. By the mid-1920s, about 70,000 buses were operating throughout the United States. At the same time, the automobile became more affordable to middle-class families and offered even greater flexibility in travel.

New York City provides a good example of the demographic changes that occurred during the 1920s. The number of residents decreased in Manhattan, the heart of the city, while the suburb of Queens saw its population double.

American Heroes

The changing morals of the 1920s made many Americans hungry for the values of an earlier time. Many in the nation became fascinated with heroes. Some were admired for their bravery and modesty, others for the way they showed Americans how to meet new challenges, with spirit and vitality. Among the decade's heroes, none became more famous than Charles Lindbergh.

"Lucky Lindy" The sky was drizzling rain at Roosevelt Field on Long Island, New York, on the morning of May 20, 1927. A 25-year-old Minnesotan, Charles Lindbergh, climbed into the cockpit of his plane, the *Spirit of St. Louis,* and revved the engine. He had not slept much, but he did not dare wait any longer. Two other teams were waiting on the airfield, hoping to be the first to fly nonstop from

MAP SKILLS Charles Lindbergh's transatlantic flight helped foster the development of commercial aviation. Lindbergh is shown below with his *Spirit of St. Louis.* **Location** *What body of water did Lindbergh cross from New York to Paris?*

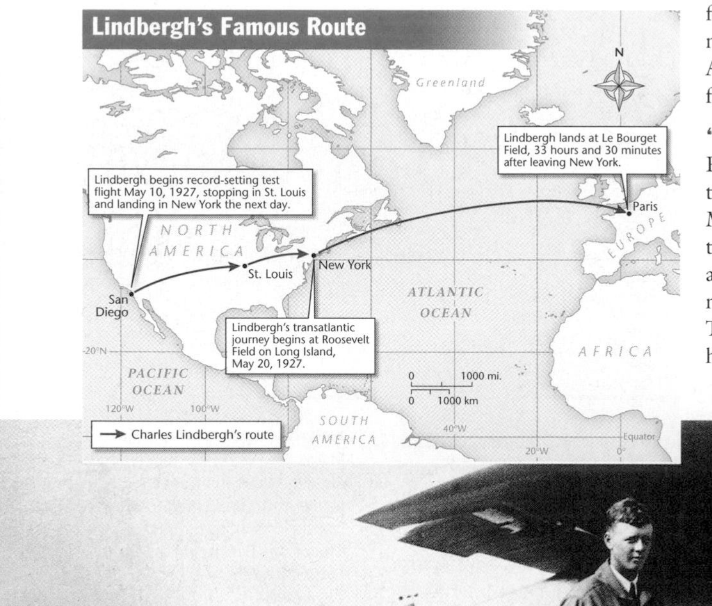

456

CAPTION ANSWERS

Map Skills The Atlantic Ocean.

RESOURCE DIRECTORY

Technology

Sounds of an Era Audio CD *Charles Lindbergh,* 1927 recording (time: 40 seconds)

Exploring Primary Sources in U.S. History CD-ROM *Charles Lindbergh's Transatlantic Flight, The Japan Times*

The Last Flight of Amelia Earhart

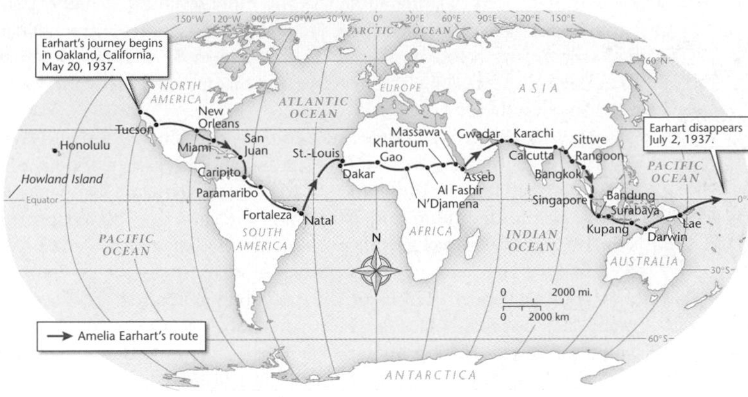

MAP SKILLS The map shows the route aviator Amelia Earhart and navigator Fred Noonan took in their attempt to fly around the world. **Regions** *What continents did Earhart and Noonan fly over on their journey?*

New York to Paris. The prize was $25,000, and Lindbergh was determined to capture it.

In those days, flying was an infant science. Orville and Wilbur Wright had achieved the first powered, sustained, and controlled airplane flight only two decades earlier, in 1903. Radio and navigation equipment were primitive at best, and Lindbergh had no autopilot to switch on if he grew tired. Flying solo, he would have to stay awake and alert for the entire flight.

The minute Lindbergh's plane was aloft, the news flashed by telegraph and telephone to news desks around the nation. Americans everywhere took notice and began to wait eagerly for the latest word. The newspapers fed this hunger, printing some 27,000 columns of information about Lindbergh in the first few days after his departure.

After a brutal flight over the Atlantic Ocean, battling icy weather and fighting off sleep, "Lucky Lindy" landed safely in an airfield outside Paris, 33½ hours after he had left New York. America went wild with jubilation. Lindbergh was brought home on a navy cruiser, given the Congressional Medal of Honor, and celebrated with parades throughout the nation.

Yet despite this frenzy of hero-worship, Lindbergh remained modest and calm. He refused offers of millions of dollars in publicity fees. To millions of Americans, Lindbergh was proof that the solid moral values of the old days lived on in the heartland of America. The public's fascination with Lindbergh may have played a role in a great tragedy for him, however, when one night his firstborn son was kidnapped from his crib. The child was later found murdered. Ironically, the murder case brought Lindbergh and his family more media attention than ever before.

Amelia Earhart Lindbergh's feat inspired later flyers, including Amelia Earhart. In 1928, Earhart became the first woman to fly across the Atlantic, although she was only a passenger. In 1932, she made the trip on her own, becoming the first woman to fly solo across the Atlantic. Later Earhart set another record, as the first person to fly solo from Hawaii to California, a challenge that had resulted in the deaths of many aviators before her. In 1937, Earhart and her navigator, Fred Noonan, tried to fly around the world. After completing two thirds of the trip, they disappeared mysteriously while crossing the Pacific Ocean.

Amelia Earhart helped open the field of aviation to more women.

ACTIVITY
Connecting with Geography

Have students study the map of Amelia Earhart's last flight. Then have them conduct research in order to create similar annotated maps of Charles Lindbergh's famous 1927 solo flight from New York to Paris. **(Visual/ Spatial)**

BACKGROUND
Biography

Charles Lindbergh's contributions to aviation went far beyond his historic transatlantic flight. Lindbergh and his wife, Anne Morrow Lindbergh (who often served as his copilot and navigator), flew and pioneered many new international air routes for Transcontinental Air Transport and Pan American World Airways. During World War I, Lindbergh served as an aviation consultant to Ford Motor Company and the United Aircraft Corporation. During World War II, he became a civilian test pilot, working to maximize the effectiveness of American fighter planes. He also flew combat missions: 50 in all. After the war, Lindbergh accompanied an American military mission to Germany to analyze aviation developments there. He also continued his work as a consultant, serving, among others, the Department of Defense. Few other individuals have played such a fundamental role in the development of aviation.

CAPTION ANSWERS

Map Skills North America, South America, Africa, Asia, and Australia.

Section 1 Assessment

Reading Comprehension

1. The bold and rebellious spirit of the flapper inspired women of the 1920s to pursue equality and to challenge their roles in society.
2. Low market prices and higher operational costs caused many farmers to move to cities, which were experiencing an economic boom. Job opportunities in expanding industries drew African Americans north. Mexicans and Canadians arrived to fill low-paying positions as immigration from Europe and Asia became restricted. Expanded transportation systems spurred the growth of suburbs.
3. Many Mexicans seeking work moved to Los Angeles, where they lived in a common neighborhood in which Spanish was the primary language.

Critical Thinking and Writing

4. Sample answer: Young people today question traditional values; challenge traditional roles; and favor fashions, manners, and morals that might shock the older generation.
5. Answers will vary, but might point out that voter turnout among women in the early 1920s was surprisingly low.

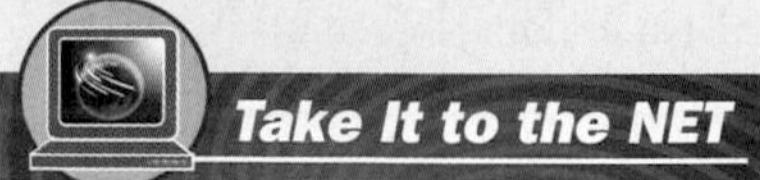

Students should note the achievements of and important facts about both aviators: Lindbergh's solo, nonstop, transatlantic flight, the kidnapping of his baby, and his involvement in politics; Earhart becoming the first woman to fly solo across the Atlantic Ocean, creating opportunities for American women in aviation, and her mysterious disappearance.

Caption Answers

Viewing History The spectators are wearing coats. Thus, the air and the water are probably cold. The grease is probably to keep Ederle warm and to help her swim faster. It is a highly publicized swim since there are spectators and someone helping her to prepare.

Sports Heroes Though spectator sports had long been popular with the American public, they became big business in the 1920s. The new, heavy commercialization of sports led to larger audiences and more revenues. A highly publicized fight between boxers Jack Dempsey and Georges Carpentier in 1921 broke the record for ticket sales, taking in $1 million. Dempsey won the fight to become the heavyweight champion of the world and a new American hero.

Another hero, Jim Thorpe, starred as a professional football player in the 1920s. By then he was in the late stages of his career, and his role was to attract fans to the games. Earlier, he had won Olympic gold medals in the decathlon and pentathlon and had also played professional baseball. Thorpe, a Native American, was elected the first president of what later became the National Football League.

Of all the sports heroes of the era, none generated more excitement than baseball's George Herman "Babe" Ruth, known as "the Sultan of Swat." During his career with the Boston Red Sox and then with the New York Yankees, Ruth hit 714 home runs, a record that was unbroken for nearly 40 years. In 1927, the champion enthralled Americans by setting the legendary record of 60 home runs in a 154-game season.

VIEWING HISTORY At Cape Gris Nez, France, Gertrude Ederle is greased up in preparation for her swim across the English Channel. **Analyzing Visual Information** *What does the photograph show about the difficulties of a Channel swim and what the feat might mean to the public?*

Women who excelled in sports included Hazel Wightman and Helen Wills, Olympic and Wimbledon tennis stars, and Gertrude Ederle, who smashed record after record in women's freestyle swimming. Ederle won one gold and two bronze medals in the 1924 Olympic Games. Newspapers hailed her as the "bob-haired, nineteen-year-old daughter of the Jazz Age." Her coach explained that her feat was a product of modern times. Thirty years previously, he said, "corsets and other ridiculously unnecessary clothing" would have hampered her physical conditioning. In 1926, Ederle became the first woman to swim the English Channel, having made an unsuccessful attempt the year before. She covered some 35 miles, taking into account crosscurrents and rough water. Her time beat the men's record by nearly two hours.

Besides being eager spectators, more Americans participated in amateur sports during the 1920s. With wide-ranging transportation, such as buses and automobiles, plus more leisure time, people took up golf, tennis, swimming, and many other types of recreation.

Section 1 Assessment

READING COMPREHENSION

1. How did the **flapper** symbolize change for women in the 1920s?
2. What conditions brought about the **demographic** shifts of the 1920s?
3. How did a **barrio** develop in Los Angeles during the 1920s?

CRITICAL THINKING AND WRITING

4. **Making Comparisons** How is today's youth culture similar to the youth culture of the 1920s?
5. **Writing a News Brief** Write a short news article and headline reporting on women voting in 1920 after the adoption of the Nineteenth Amendment.

Take It to the NET

Activity: Writing a Biography
Research the lives of Charles Lindbergh and Amelia Earhart. Use the links provided in the *America: Pathways to the Present* area of the following Web site for help in completing this activity.
www.phschool.com

RESOURCE DIRECTORY

Teaching Resources
Units 3/4 booklet
- Section 1 Quiz, p. 42

Guide to the Essentials
- Section 1 Summary, p. 64

Technology
Exploring Primary Sources in U.S. History CD-ROM *The Report of the Committee on Recent Economic Changes*

Section 2 Mass Media and the Jazz Age

READING FOCUS

- How did the mass media help create common cultural experiences?
- Why are the 1920s called the Jazz Age, and how did the jazz spirit affect the arts?
- How did the writers of the Lost Generation respond to the popular culture?
- What subjects did the Harlem Renaissance writers explore?

KEY TERMS

mass media
Jazz Age
Lost Generation
Harlem Renaissance

TAKING NOTES

Copy the web diagram below. As you read, fill in the blank circles with details on how the mass media affected American life.

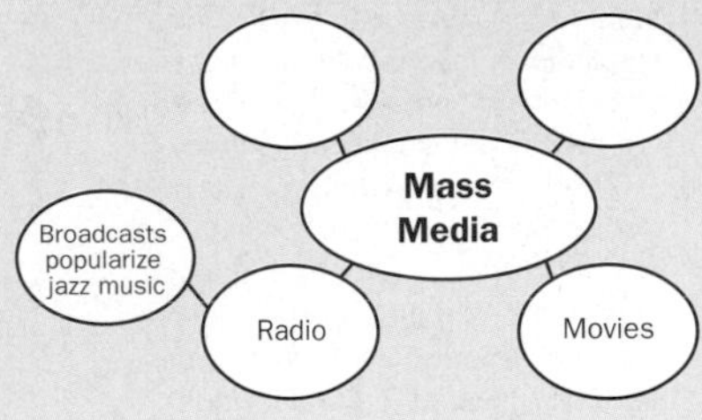

MAIN IDEA

In the 1920s, the mass media provided information and entertainment as never before. The decade was an especially creative period for music, art, and literature.

Setting the Scene Before 1900, few people outside Los Angeles had even heard of a dusty little subdivision northwest of the city. Its founder, a religious man, hoped that it would remain a quiet town, where citizens valued proper behavior. In the early 1900s, however, filmmakers began moving there. They were attracted by the large work force in nearby Los Angeles; by the variety of landscapes, from desert to snowy mountains; and by the warm climate and the sun they needed to light their films.

These pioneer filmmakers faced many difficulties. Director Cecil B. DeMille set up his first studio in a rented barn, which he shared with horses and a carriage. DeMille later wrote, "I expected to be working like a horse: what did it matter being housed like one?"

In the early 1920s, DeMille became known for his stylish comedies that dealt with the changing romance customs of the time, and for his epics, which were designed to appeal to mass audiences. The barn he rented grew into a huge movie complex and the small suburb it was located in—Hollywood—soon became the center of the entertainment film industry. The town's main avenue displayed a strip of expensive shops and bars. Stars drove the streets in luxurious cars, trailed by reporters. In turn, what grew out of Hollywood in the 1920s—its culture of movies, movie stars, and entertainment reporters—helped create the beginnings of a common national culture.

VIEWING HISTORY Hollywood's Mulholland Drive is shown in this 1924 photo. The now-famous sign in the hills was erected to promote a real-estate development. **Analyzing Visual Information** *What details in the photograph show Hollywood's past and future?*

The Mass Media

Hollywood's new fame reflected a major trend of the 1920s. Before that time, the United States had been largely a collection of regional cultures. Interests, tastes, and attitudes varied widely from one region to another. Most Americans simply did not know much about the rest of the country, talk with people in other regions, or even read the same news as other Americans.

Section 2 Mass Media and the Jazz Age

Section Objectives

1. See how the mass media helped create common cultural experiences.
2. Realize why the decade of the 1920s was called the Jazz Age, and learn how the jazz spirit affected the arts.
3. Discover how the writers of the Lost Generation responded to popular culture.
4. Find out about some of the subjects explored by the writers of the Harlem Renaissance.

Bellringer

Warm-Up Activity Ask students what new source of information became popular in the 1990s. *(The Internet)* How has it affected communication? In what other ways has it affected life in the United States?

Activating Prior Knowledge Many artists, writers, and performers of this era are still known today. Ask students if they can identify individuals such as Duke Ellington, Louis Armstrong, Ernest Hemingway, Greta Garbo, and Charlie Chaplin.

Reading Strategy

As students read, have them write down facts that will help them define what the Jazz Age was. Then have them use their notes to write a one-sentence definition.

Caption Answers

Viewing History The road looks new and barren. Thus, Hollywood in the 1920s had not yet been built up very much. The future is indicated by the sign which, in shortened form, would signify that the word "Hollywood" had become synonymous with "movies."

RESOURCE DIRECTORY

Teaching Resources
Learning Styles Lesson Plans booklet, p. 42
Guided Reading and Review booklet, p. 84

Technology
Section Reading Support Transparencies
Guided Reading Audiotapes (English/Spanish), Ch. 13
Student Edition on Audio CD, Ch. 13
Prentice Hall Presentation Pro CD-ROM, Ch. 13
Companion Web site, www.phschool.com

LESSON PLAN

Focus In the 1920s developments in communication, entertainment, and the arts contributed to the growth of a distinctly American culture. Ask students what these developments were. How did they affect life in the United States?

Instruct Discuss the role of the mass media. How did newspapers and radio help to create a national culture?

Ask students how radio helped make jazz a part of American culture. Who were some of the most well-known jazz musicians during the 1920s?

Discuss the role of other art forms and artists in the 1920s. How did writers of the Lost Generation express their discontent with American culture? What was the contribution of the Harlem Renaissance to American literature?

Assess/Reteach Ask students to discuss some of the reasons why the decade of the 1920s saw such an outpouring of creativity in all areas of the arts.

BACKGROUND
Interdisciplinary

The stunning growth of the popularity of films during the 1920s was accompanied by the growth of their influence on American culture. For the first time, movies set trends. In 1929 a study revealed that chorus girls and flappers, as portrayed on the big screen, had become the standards by which women judged their appearance and behavior. "These modern pictures," a sixteen-year-girl of the time said, "give me a feeling to imitate their ways."

Focus on TECHNOLOGY

Adding Sound to Movies The system used to record and play sound in *The Jazz Singer* (below) was known as Vitaphone, which used a 16-inch rotating wax disk to record the movie's singing and speech. The sound was then synchronized with the film and amplified by loudspeakers in the theater. The Vitaphone system offered the best sound quality of its time.

Another method of making sound movies involved recording sound directly onto film. Although the early use of this method produced poor sound quality and distortion, by the 1930s it became the preferred technology for making "talkies."

The 1920s changed all that. Films, nationwide news gathering, and the new industry of radio broadcasting produced the beginnings of a national culture. As you have read, early in the decade few American women dressed in the flapper style or smoked and drank in public. Such customs became common cultural experiences because of the growth of the mass media. The **mass media** are print and broadcast methods of communicating information to large numbers of people.

Movies From their beginnings in the 1890s, motion pictures had been a wildly popular mass medium, and through the 1920s, audiences grew. Between 1910 and 1930, the number of theaters rose from about 5,000 to about 22,500. By 1929, when the total population was less than 125 million, the nation's theaters sold roughly 80 million tickets each week. Moviemaking had become the fourth largest business in the country.

This growth occurred throughout the silent film era. In 1927, the success of the first sound film, *The Jazz Singer,* changed the course of the movie industry. Starring vaudeville performer Al Jolson, the movie included speech, singing, music, and sound effects. Audiences loved it. As more theaters played "talkies," the industry's boom continued.

Some actors never made the shift from silent films to sound films. Foreign actors, for example, often faced the choice of learning English or giving up their movie careers. Other actors moved more smoothly to talkies. Greta Garbo, a glamorous star of the silent screen, retained her popularity in speaking roles despite a heavy Swedish accent. Silent screen actress Lillian Gish won renown for playing the part of the delicate heroine. She readily transferred her expressive gestures and heart-rending glances to speaking roles. Charlie Chaplin extended the silent era. Dressed in his famous tattered suit, derby hat, and cane, Chaplin had delighted American audiences since 1914 with his silent comedy. In the era of sound, Chaplin added music to his films and successfully continued his soundless portrayal of the "little tramp."

Newspapers and Magazines Americans followed the off-screen lives of their favorite stars in two other mass media—newspapers and magazines. During the 1920s, newspapers increased both in size and in circulation, or readership. In 1900, a hefty edition of the *New York Times* totaled only 14 pages. By the mid-1920s, however, newspapers even in mid-sized American cities often totaled more than 50 pages a day, and Sunday editions were enormous. In fact, the use of newsprint roughly doubled in the United States between 1914 and 1927.

Even as newspapers grew and gained more readers, the number of independently owned newspapers fell. Many disappeared as a result of mergers. A newspaper chain, owned by a single individual or company, often bought up two of a city's established papers and merged them. Thus they created one newspaper with potentially twice the circulation. The larger the circulation, the more money that advertisers would pay to market their products in the paper and the greater the profits for the publisher. Between 1923 and 1927, the number of chains doubled, and the total number of newspapers they owned rose by 50 percent.

Profits, not quality, drove most of these newspaper chains. To attract readers, especially in the cities, many chains published tabloids. A tabloid is a compact newspaper that relies on large headlines, few words, and many pictures to tell a

RESOURCE DIRECTORY

Technology

Sounds of an Era Audio CD *"Society Blues,"* 1921 recording (time: 30 seconds)

RESOURCE PRO® **Critical Thinking Activity** *Testing Conclusions: The Jazz Age,* found on Resource Pro, provides a partial glossary of terms and expressions to help students test their conclusions about the values of the era.

story. Tabloids of the 1920s replaced serious news with entertainment that focused on fashion, sports, and sensational stories about crimes and scandals. This content sold papers, as publisher William Randolph Hearst knew well. Hearst once said that he wanted his New York tabloid the *Daily Mirror* to be "90 percent entertainment, 10 percent information—and the information without boring you."

During the 1920s, sales of magazines rose, too. By 1929, Americans were buying more than 200 million copies of such popular magazines as the *Saturday Evening Post, Reader's Digest, Ladies' Home Journal,* and *Time.* These magazines provided a variety of information in a form that most people could easily digest. Advertisers, eager to reach so many potential customers, often ran full-page ads promoting their products.

With the rise of newspapers and magazines as mass media, Americans began to share the same information, read about the same events, and encounter the same ideas and fashions. Thus newspapers and magazines helped create a common popular culture.

Radio As a mass medium, radio barely existed until the 1920s. Before that time, relatively few Americans had radio sets, and those they had were all homemade. They used their radios to communicate with each other one-on-one. In 1920, Frank Conrad, an engineer with the Westinghouse Electric Company, set up a radio transmitter in his garage in Pittsburgh. As an experiment, he began sending recorded music and baseball scores over the radio. The response was so great that Westinghouse began broadcasting programs on a regular basis. Soon the nation had its first commercial radio station, Pittsburgh's KDKA.

At first, the only advertising on KDKA was the occasional mention of its sponsor, Westinghouse. Yet even that was enough to increase the sales of Westinghouse products, mainly home appliances. In the coming years, radio would become a profitable medium for advertisers.

Radio enjoyed tremendous growth. By 1922, more than 500 stations were on the air, and Americans eagerly bought radios to listen to them. To reach more people, networks such as the National Broadcasting Company (NBC) linked many individual stations together. Each station in the network played the same programming. Soon much of the country was listening to the same jokes, commercials, music, sports events, religious services, and news. Other companies imitated NBC, building networks of their own.

The Jazz Age

Both the growing radio audience and the great African American migration to the cities helped make a music called jazz widely popular in the 1920s. This music features improvisation, a process by which musicians make up music as they are playing it rather than relying completely on printed scores. It also has a type of off-beat rhythm called syncopation.

Jazz Arrives Jazz grew out of the African American music of the South, especially ragtime and blues. By the early 1900s, bands in New Orleans were

Growth of the Mass Media in the 1920s

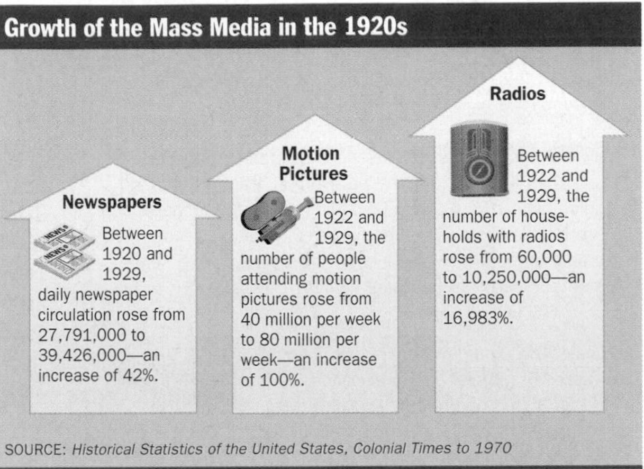

Newspapers
Between 1920 and 1929, daily newspaper circulation rose from 27,791,000 to 39,426,000—an increase of 42%.
Motion Pictures
Between 1922 and 1929, the number of people attending motion pictures rose from 40 million per week to 80 million per week—an increase of 100%.
Radios
Between 1922 and 1929, the number of households with radios rose from 60,000 to 10,250,000—an increase of 16,983%.

SOURCE: *Historical Statistics of the United States, Colonial Times to 1970*

INTERPRETING DIAGRAMS
The decade of the 1920s saw an explosion in forms of mass communication. **Making Comparisons** *Which form of mass communication grew the most during this decade?*

READING CHECK
What social changes were brought about by the mass media?

ACTIVITY
Connecting with Culture

Play a recording of one of the jazz greats, such as Duke Ellington or Louis Armstrong. Have students listen to the music and then discuss how it expresses the mood of the 1920s. **(Musical/Rhythmic)**

BACKGROUND
Recent Scholarship

In the 1920s African Americans made history through music, literature, and social movements. One of the many notable African Americans living during this time was Carter G. Woodson, generally known as the "Father of Black History," who was one of the first to point out that African Americans had a rich history worthy of significant study. Jacqueline Goggin, in *Carter G. Woodson: A Life in Black History,* explains how Woodson's work, capitalizing on the tide of the Harlem Renaissance, prompted Americans to celebrate Negro History Week in the second week of February, a week framed by the birthdays of Abraham Lincoln and Frederick Douglass. From 1926 until 1976, Americans recognized Negro History Week. In 1976 the entire month of February was designated as Black History Month.

READING CHECK
The United States began to have a national culture. Americans were listening to the same radio programs, reading about the same events in newspapers, and seeing the same movies. Newspaper chains began to replace independent newspapers.

CUSTOMIZE FOR ...
Gifted and Talented
Have students research the roots of jazz. Then have them write a paragraph or two explaining how jazz is a uniquely American art form.

TEST PREPARATION
Have students read the material on these pages about the growth of popularity of magazines, and then answer the following question.

What is an important reason why advertisers began to run full-page ads in magazines in the 1920s?

A This practice suddenly became legal.
B Television wasn't invented yet.
C It was illegal to show advertisements in movie theaters.
(D) Magazines suddenly became very popular, with large numbers of readers who would see the advertisements.

CAPTION ANSWERS
Interpreting Diagrams Radio.

ACTIVITY

Connecting with Culture

Provide Paul Whiteman's recording of "Rhapsody in Blue" to the class. Direct them to listen to the recording with the aim of interpreting the music in light of George Gershwin's description of it. Then have students discuss what makes it, in Gershwin's words, "a sort of musical kaleidoscope of America." **(Musical/Rhythmic)**

BACKGROUND

Biography

James van der Zee (1886–1983) turned his pride in his Harlem neighbors and his skill as a photographer into a priceless archive of images. The son of Ulysses S. Grant's maid and butler, van der Zee first thought of a career as a musician. But it was with his camera, in the elaborately decorated studio area of his "Guarantee Photo" shop, that he made his reputation. Acknowledged to be the first great African American photographer, van der Zee made more than 75,000 photo portraits during his career, photographing people both ordinary and famous.

The heyday of van der Zee's career corresponded with the years of the Harlem Renaissance. By the 1940s more individuals owned cameras themselves, and people did not often go to a studio to have portraits made. Van der Zee continued to work during these years, largely in obscurity. Then in 1968 his work was rediscovered and became a major portion of an exhibit, "Harlem On My Mind," at New York's Metropolitan Museum of Art.

American BIOGRAPHIES

Duke Ellington (1899–1974)

Edward Kennedy Ellington was born in Washington, D.C. At 17, "Duke," as Ellington was called, played in Washington's clubs at night and painted signs during the day. In 1923, Ellington and several other musicians moved to New York City and formed a band. This band, under various names and in one form or another, continued to play with Ellington until his death at age 75.

Although Ellington was an excellent pianist, his greatest talents were as a band leader, an arranger, and a composer. He wrote at least a thousand pieces in his long career, including music for concerts, Broadway shows, films, and operas. Among his most memorable tunes are "Mood Indigo," "Solitude," "In a Sentimental Mood," "Blue Harlem," and "Bojangles."

Louis Armstrong (1901–1971)

Louis Armstrong, nicknamed "Satchmo," was born and grew up in New Orleans, where he learned to sing and play the trumpet. In 1922, Armstrong was invited to play the trumpet in Chicago, and in 1923, he made his first recordings with King Oliver's Creole Jazz Band. Armstrong's showmanship and virtuosity soon became evident, especially when he performed his improvised extended solos. Because of Armstrong, long solos became key elements of jazz ensemble performances.

Armstrong also improvised with his voice, replacing words with nonsense syllables in a style known as "scat" singing. His first scat recording, "Heebie Jeebies," encouraged many jazz vocalists to sing scat. His Hot Five and Hot Seven ensemble recordings are among his most notable early recordings.

playing the new mix of styles. Although jazz recordings were available in the 1910s, many radio listeners began hearing the new sound for the first time in the 1920s. Soon jazz became a nationwide craze. Younger people in particular loved to dance to the new music. By 1929, a survey of stations showed that two thirds of all radio air time was devoted to jazz.

Some Americans were horrified by jazz. Its syncopated rhythms and improvisations were too suggestive of the free manners and morals of the age. Eventually, however, Americans from many walks of life embraced the music. The great symphony conductor Leopold Stokowski declared that jazz was "an expression of the times, of the breathless, energetic, superactive times in which we are living." The 1920s came to be called the **Jazz Age.**

Jazz Clubs and Dance Halls One of the most popular places to listen to jazz was Harlem, a district on the northern end of the island of Manhattan. By one count, Harlem had some 500 jazz clubs. A dozen of them, including the Cotton Club, Connie's Inn, and the Saratoga Club, catered to the rich and famous. At clubs such as these, musicians, most of whom were black, performed for audiences that were primarily white.

Nearly all the great jazz musicians played in the Harlem clubs at one time or another. Jelly Roll Morton, a jazz pianist from New Orleans, arranged his band's music in a way that encouraged group improvisation. This gave his band a smooth, modern sound. Benny Goodman, known as the "King of Swing," began playing jazz professionally as a teenager in the early 1920s. His "big band" helped make jazz popular with white audiences. Goodman's 1936 quartet, which included African American musicians Lionel Hampton and Teddy Wilson, was the first popular racially mixed jazz group. Two musicians, in particular, made important contributions to jazz beginning in the 1920s: Louis Armstrong, who wowed audiences with his brilliantly improvised trumpet solos, and Duke Ellington, an arranger, composer, and bandleader, whose works are played widely to this day.

When flappers danced to jazz on the radio or to a live jazz band, most likely they did the Charleston. This dance took over the dance halls and ballrooms in the 1920s and became a national fad. The Charleston embodied the Jazz Age. It was wild and reckless, full of kicks and twists and pivots. Unlike traditional ballroom dancing, the Charleston could be danced with a partner, in a group, or all alone.

Sounds of an Era

Listen to a 1927 recording of "East St. Louis Toodle-oo" by Duke Ellington.

The Jazz Spirit The jazz spirit ran through all the arts of the 1920s. People spoke of "jazz poetry" and "jazz painting." However, jazz most strongly influenced other forms of music. Composers in the Jazz Age, such as George Gershwin, mixed jazz elements into more familiar-sounding music. Gershwin, the son of

RESOURCE DIRECTORY

Teaching Resources

Biography, Literature, and Comparing Primary Sources booklet (Literature) *The Weary Blues,* p. 67

Other Print Resources

American History Block Scheduling Support *The Harlem Renaissance During the Jazz Age,* found in the Prosperity, Depression, and War folder, includes interdisciplinary lesson suggestions and activities for Geography and History, Primary Sources, Biography, and Literature.

Technology

Sounds of an Era Audio CD *"Rhapsody in Blue"* (time: one minute, 30 seconds); *"West End Blues"* (time: 45 seconds); *"East St. Louis Toodle-oo,"* 1927 recording (time: one minute, 15 seconds)

RESOURCE PRO® **Literature Activity** *Tales of the Jazz Age,* found on Resource Pro, highlights the shallow, carefree rebellion of the flapper culture.

Russian immigrants, won overnight success in 1924 with his *Rhapsody in Blue.* First played by bandleader Paul Whiteman's orchestra, this piece throbbed with jazz rhythms. Not quite jazz and not quite symphony, it was, instead, a magical blend of the two. The basic form of this rhapsody came to Gershwin in a sudden rush of insight while riding a train. He said that he heard the music in the rhythmic noise of the train:

> "*I heard it as a sort of musical kaleidoscope of America—of our vast melting pot, of our unduplicated national pep, of our blues, our metropolitan madness.*"
>
> —George Gershwin, 1924

Painting Like jazz musicians, American painters of the 1920s did not shy away from taking the pulse of American life. Painters such as Edward Hopper and Rockwell Kent showed the nation's rougher side, from cities to coal mines, from the streets to the barrooms.

By contrast, a young artist named Georgia O'Keeffe painted natural objects such as flowers, animal bones, and landscapes. However simple her images, they always suggest something greater than themselves. A range of hills, for example, seems almost to shudder with life. O'Keeffe continued to paint until her death in 1986 at the age of nearly 100.

VIEWING HISTORY Edward Hopper painted this scene, titled *Automat,* in 1927. The Automat was a popular restaurant chain in which one could purchase a snack or meal from a vending machine and then eat at a table. **Drawing Inferences** *What does the painting suggest about Hopper's view of the culture of the times?*

Literature Several modern writers began fruitful careers during the 1920s. Novelist Sinclair Lewis attacked American society with savage irony. His targets included the prosperous conformist (*Babbit,* 1922), the medical business (*Arrowsmith,* 1925), and dishonest ministers (*Elmer Gantry,* 1927). In *Main Street* Lewis, showing no mercy, depicts small-town Americans as a

> "*savorless people, gulping tasteless food, and sitting afterward, coatless and thoughtless, in rocking-chairs prickly with inane decorations, listening to mechanical music, saying mechanical things about the excellence of Ford automobiles, and viewing themselves as the greatest race in the world.*"
>
> —Sinclair Lewis, *Main Street* (1920)

Lewis refused a Pulitzer Prize in 1926, but in 1930 he became the first American to receive the Nobel prize for literature.

Another writer destined for the Nobel prize was playwright Eugene O'Neill. In a career stretching from the 1920s into the 1950s, he wove dark, poetic tragedies out of the material of everyday American life. Until his time, most American theaters had shown only European plays or light comedies. The power of O'Neill's work proved to the public that the American stage could achieve a greatness rivaling that of Europe.

The Lost Generation American society in the 1920s troubled one group of important writers. This group rejected the quest for material possessions that

ACTIVITY Student Portfolio

You may wish to have students add the following to their portfolios: Ask students to research the life and writings of F. Scott Fitzgerald in order to determine whether he invented the concept of the "flapper." Have them write a brief essay defending their point of view. **(Verbal/Linguistic)**

BACKGROUND Art History

Edward Hopper's (1882–1967) paintings reflected the character of the people and the land realistically and objectively. Hopper saw America as a lonely place, often silhouetted in harsh shades of light, as depicted in his paintings "Early Sunday Morning" (1930) or "Room in Brooklyn" (1932). In the midst of the depression, Hopper's works achieved national recognition when New York's Museum of Modern Art mounted a one-man retrospective show in 1933.

CUSTOMIZE FOR ...

ESL

Have students research music, art, fiction, or poetry of the era, and present to the class their favorite example of an artistic expression from the Jazz Age.

CAPTION ANSWERS

Viewing History Sample answer: It shows a view of a lonely, isolated, impersonal world.

ACTIVITY
Connecting with Culture

Have students choose one of the expatriate writers of the Lost Generation listed on this page and read one or more of his or her shorter works (poem, short story, or essay). Students should search for evidence of the writer's dissatisfaction with American culture at the time. Have the students present brief readings of the work to the class, along with an interpretation of its cultural critique. **(Verbal/Linguistic)**

BACKGROUND
A Diverse Nation

The Harlem Renaissance inspired many artists to create masterpieces of language and tone. Claude McKay's "The Tropics in New York," Jean Toomer's "Cane," and Georgia Douglas Johnson's "Common Dust" are among the many works that express the feelings of both urban and rural African Americans. Langston Hughes's poem "I, Too" epitomizes the sense of possibility and the deep frustrations that African Americans felt at the time. Carl Van Doren, the editor of *Century* magazine and a Pulitzer Prize winner for biography, observed: "What American literature decidedly needs at this moment is color, music, gusto, the free expression of gay or desperate moods. If the Negroes are not in a position to contribute to these items, I don't know what Americans are."

Artists of the Jazz Age (left to right): Writer F. Scott Fitzgerald and his wife, Zelda Sayre Fitzgerald, a writer and painter; poet Edna St. Vincent Millay; and writer and anthropologist Zora Neale Hurston.

seemed to occupy so many Americans. Its members also scorned American popular culture as artless and uninspired. Postwar society so repelled them that they left the United States for Europe. These expatriates, or people who live outside their homeland, found Europe more intellectually stimulating.

The most prominent of these writers settled in Paris. They included Sherwood Anderson, Archibald MacLeish, Hart Crane, E. E. Cummings, John Dos Passos, Ernest Hemingway, and F. Scott Fitzgerald. Another notable American writer, Gertrude Stein, had been living in Paris for some time and had come into contact with many of the expatriates. Stein remarked to Hemingway that he and the other expatriate writers were all a **Lost Generation,** a group of people disconnected from their country and its values. Hemingway introduced Stein's term to the reading public when he used it in his 1926 novel *The Sun Also Rises.*

F. Scott Fitzgerald was both part of the Lost Generation and part of the Jazz Age. Some people believe Fitzgerald helped create the flapper culture with his novel *This Side of Paradise,* published in 1920. His 1925 masterpiece *The Great Gatsby* focused on the wealthy, sophisticated Americans of the Jazz Age whom he found to be self-centered and shallow.

After Hemingway made the term *Lost Generation* famous, it was taken up by the flappers. They liked to imagine themselves as rebels against the culture of their time, living a fast and dangerous life. The words of a popular poet of the day, Edna St. Vincent Millay, captured the flapper's attitude toward life:

> "*My candle burns at both ends;*
> *It will not last the night;*
> *But ah, my foes, and oh, my friends—*
> *It gives a lovely light!*"
>
> —Edna St. Vincent Millay, "First Fig," 1920

Focus on CULTURE

Twenties Slang Every generation coins its own terms and phrases. The youth culture of the 1920s was no different. In addition to "flappers" and "speakeasies," the decade spoke its share of slang, some of which is still in use today.

baloney *Nonsense; untrue*
bee's knees *The best; cutest*
copacetic *Excellent, used as an exclamation*
gold digger *A woman in search of a wealthy man*
goofy *Silly, clumsy, stupid*
hard-boiled *Unfeeling or tough*
jazz baby *Another word for* flapper
peppy *Energetic*
ritzy *High class*
swell *Terrific*

The Harlem Renaissance

For African Americans, New York City's Harlem was becoming the cultural center of the United States. The number of African Americans living in Harlem grew from 50,000 in 1914 to about 200,000 in 1930. Not just a national center for jazz, Harlem also became the home of an African American literary awakening of the 1920s known as the **Harlem Renaissance.**

James Weldon Johnson emerged as a leading writer of the Harlem group. Johnson lived in two worlds, the political and the literary. As executive secretary of the National Association for the Advancement of

RESOURCE DIRECTORY

Teaching Resources
Units 3/4 booklet
- Section 2 Quiz, p. 43

Guide to the Essentials
- Section 2 Summary, p. 65

Technology
Sounds of an Era Audio CD *"I, Too, Am America"* (time: 35 seconds)
Exploring Primary Sources in U.S. History CD-ROM *As I Grew Older, Langston Hughes*

Colored People (NAACP), he led the group during an active period in its history. At the same time, he pursued a writing career that inspired younger members of the Harlem group. His most famous work, *God's Trombones* (1927), is a collection of sermons in rhythmic verse modeled after the style of traditional black preaching.

Other writers followed Johnson's lead. Alain Locke's 1925 book *The New Negro* celebrated the blossoming of African American culture. Locke noted that both African and American heritages could be enriching, not conflicting. Zora Neale Hurston came to New York in 1925, became an anthropologist, and gained fame as a writer with her poignant novel *Their Eyes Were Watching God* (1937). Dorothy West, another accomplished writer, tackled the dual themes of being black and being a woman.

The leading poets of the Harlem Renaissance were Claude McKay and Countee Cullen. McKay produced a large body of work, including *Harlem Shadows* (1922), and was a voice of protest against the sufferings of African Americans in white society. The gifted Cullen is best known for his 1925 collection of poems called *Color*. He also brought to light the talents of fellow writers in *Caroling Dusk: An Anthology of Verse by Negro Poets* (1927).

The Harlem writer perhaps most studied today is Langston Hughes, a poet, short story writer, journalist, and playwright whose career stretched into the 1960s. Hughes spoke with a clear, strong voice about the joys and difficulties of being human, being American, and being black:

> "*I, too, sing America.*
> *I am the darker*
> *brother.*
> *They send me to eat*
> *in the kitchen*
> *When company comes,*
> *But I laugh,*
> *And eat well,*
> *And grow strong. . . .*
> *Tomorrow,*
> *I'll be at the table*
> *When company*
> *comes.*
> *Nobody'll dare*
> *Say to me,*
> *'Eat in the*
> *kitchen,'*
> *Then.*
> *Besides,*
> *They'll see how*
> *beautiful I am*
> *And be*
> *ashamed—*
>
> *I, too, am*
> *America.*"
>
> —Langston Hughes, "I, Too," 1926

Harlem Renaissance poet and writer Langston Hughes

Section 2 Assessment

READING COMPREHENSION

1. What social changes were brought about by the **mass media?**
2. Who were some of the major figures of the **Jazz Age?**
3. Why is the term **Lost Generation** used to describe some writers of the 1920s?
4. How might the jazz spirit have influenced the poetry that came out of the **Harlem Renaissance?**

CRITICAL THINKING AND WRITING

5. **Making Comparisons** What do the novels of Sinclair Lewis and F. Scott Fitzgerald say about Americans in the 1920s?
6. **Writing an Opinion** What do you think about the balance of entertainment and information in today's news media?

Take It to the NET

Activity: Drawing a Cartoon
Learn more about popular entertainment in the 1920s, and then draw a cartoon about the music, movies, sports, or arts of the Jazz Age. Use the links provided in the *America: Pathways to the Present* area of the following Web site for help in completing this activity.
www.phschool.com

Section 2 Assessment

Reading Comprehension

1. Encouraged a national popular culture to develop: affected fashion, consumerism, and what music became popular (jazz).
2. Sample answer: Louis Armstrong, Duke Ellington, Langston Hughes, George Gershwin, Edna St. Vincent Millay.
3. Gertrude Stein first used the term to describe American writers who felt disconnected from their country and its values. The country lost these writers; they, in turn, lost their country.
4. Possible answer: the jazz spirit contributed rhythm and subject matter to poetry.

Critical Thinking and Writing

5. Beneath a transparent sophistication, Americans were represented as shallow, uncouth, and self-centered.
6. Answers will vary but might compare the present news media with the mass media represented within the section.

Take It to the NET

Cartoons will vary. Students should demonstrate an understanding of the trends in 1920s music, movies, sports, and arts, including the increasing influence of African Americans on popular entertainment.

Supporting a Position

Focus Students learn the steps necessary to build a convincing argument in support of a position.

Instruct As a group, brainstorm a topic to complete step 1. Try to choose a topic about which students have differing positions. Divide the class into smaller groups, based on their position on the topic. Have each group come up with three reasons to support its position, and ask each group to also find evidence to support its position. List the reasons for supporting each position on the board. Were the arguments made by any group sufficient to change the position of a member of another group? Ask students to analyze what made the argument persuasive.

Extend See the Skills for Life activity in the Resource Directory below.

ANSWERS

Practice the Skill

1. **(a)** He does not think talkies will replace live theater. **(b)** The first sentence of the second paragraph. **(c)** Possible answer: Talkies will never replace live theater for two reasons: they are not as thrilling as live performances and they are not economically viable.
2. **(a)** Live theater is more thrilling than a film could ever be; talkies are not profitable; talkies cannot take advantage of the lucrative foreign market in non–English-speaking countries. **(b)** He is dismissive. **(c)** Strengthens, because he describes Hollywood's certainty of its ultimate success as "optimistic," which could be translated as "unrealistic."
3. **(a)** He gives no evidence for his first reason; he cites a director of talkies; no talkie has yet paid for itself; talkies can't make money in small towns or non-English markets. **(b)** The second and third points could be verified; the first point is opinion.
4. **(a)** Answers will vary, but should include Fisher's three main points. **(b)** Answers will vary.

Supporting a Position

When you take a position on an issue, you have a better chance of winning others to your side if you can back up your argument with solid reasons and evidence.

The movie industry introduced the first "talkie"—a movie with sound—in 1927. At that time, many people predicted that these films would replace traditional stage productions. (In recent years, some people have made a similar prediction with regard to computers replacing books, newspapers, and magazines.) In 1929, Irving Norton Fisher discussed this issue in a letter to his father. Fisher would later become a drama critic and author. In his letter, he takes a position on talkies.

Nov. 14, 1929.

Dear Father:—

Yours of the 10th just here. For which many thanks, as I know how pressed for time you must be. It's incredible that the stock market can go any lower, and yet each new day seems to be worse than the day before. . . .

I'm free to confess I don't entirely agree with all you say about "talkies" replacing the theatre. Any more than I believe that artificial flowers can ever replace those produced by nature. There is no mechanical way of thrilling the human mind as the actual presence of an actor or singer thrills it. And from what Sidney Howard said after directing three "talkies" in Hollywood himself, the whole thing is still in the balance. No talkie has yet paid for itself.—They are so much more expensive than other films, and the whole foreign market (formerly so lucrative) is automatically cut out, except for English-speaking countries. Formerly, movies didn't begin to make money until the returns began accumulating from the small towns in U.S. (which are still unequipped for "talkies") and from foreign countries. Of course Hollywood is optimistic, who wouldn't be if his livelyhood [sic] *depended on it, but it is by no means an assured thing! . . .*

—Your very loving son,
Irving N. Fisher

LEARN THE SKILL

Use the following steps to support a position:

1. **State your position clearly in a sentence.** To take a position on any issue, you must be clear as to what that position is. Writing it out in a sentence forces you to organize your thoughts.
2. **Identify at least three reasons for your position.** To be convincing, you must do more than say what you believe; you must say why you believe it. Think of reasons for your side—or against the opposing position. Pointing out the weakness of an opposing idea can be very effective. Also consider your audience. Think of what reasons will be most effective with those you are trying to persuade.
3. **Support each reason with evidence.** To build a solid case for your position, use facts to support each reason.
4. **Add a conclusion.** This is your chance to sum up and drive your point home.

PRACTICE THE SKILL

Answer the following questions:

1. **(a)** What position does Irving Norton Fisher take on the issue of talkies replacing live theater? **(b)** What part of his letter states this position? **(c)** Restate Fisher's position in your own words, as if you were using it to begin an essay or a speech.
2. **(a)** What reasons does Fisher give for his position? **(b)** How does Fisher treat the opposing position? **(c)** Does this strengthen or weaken his argument? Explain your reasoning.
3. **(a)** What evidence does Fisher give for each of his reasons? **(b)** Is the evidence factual, or just opinion masquerading as fact?
4. **(a)** Fisher's argument is part of an informal letter and does not have a conclusion. Write a conclusion for his argument. **(b)** Write a short paragraph that takes one of these positions: the position of Fisher's father (that talkies would become popular and replace live theater); or the position that, in the future, computers will (or will not) replace books, newspapers, and magazines.

APPLY THE SKILL

See the Chapter Review and Assessment for another opportunity to apply this skill.

RESOURCE DIRECTORY

Teaching Resources
Skills for Life booklet, p. 22

Technology
Social Studies Skills Tutor CD-ROM
Interactive Practice in
- Geographic Literacy
- Critical Thinking and Reading
- Visual Analysis
- Communications

Section

3 Cultural Conflicts

READING FOCUS

- What were the effects of Prohibition on society?
- What issues of religion were at the core of the Scopes trial?
- How did racial tensions change after World War I?

MAIN IDEA

Rapid social change after World War I caused conflicts among people with differing beliefs and values.

KEY TERMS

bootleggers
speakeasies
fundamentalism
Scopes trial

TAKING NOTES

Create a chart like the one below. As you read, fill the chart with some of the effects of Prohibition.

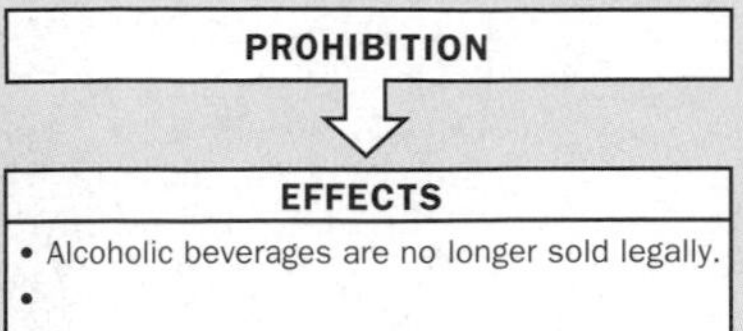

PROHIBITION
EFFECTS
• Alcoholic beverages are no longer sold legally.
•
•

Setting the Scene

Prohibition of all alcoholic beverages became the law of the land when the Eighteenth Amendment to the Constitution took effect on January 16, 1920. Yet for many people, life went on as before. Even President Harding did not heed the law, as the daughter of former President Theodore Roosevelt witnessed:

> "*Though violation of the Eighteenth Amendment was a matter of course in Washington, it was rather shocking to see the way Harding disregarded the Constitution he was sworn to uphold. . . . there were always, at least before the unofficial dinners, cocktails in the upstairs hall outside the President's room. . . . One evening . . . a friend of the Hardings asked me if I would like to go up to the study. . . . No rumor could have exceeded the reality; . . . trays with bottles containing every imaginable brand of whiskey stood about. . . .*"
>
> —Alice Roosevelt Longworth, *Crowded Hours*, 1933

Prohibition forced many beer companies to find new beverages to brew, as these labels show.

Prohibition

The main goals of Prohibition seemed worthy: (1) Eliminate drunkenness and the resulting abuse of family members and others. (2) Get rid of saloons, where prostitution, gambling, and other forms of vice thrived. (3) Prevent absenteeism and on-the-job accidents stemming from drunkenness. Congress passed the Volstead Act in 1919 to provide a system for enforcing the Eighteenth Amendment, but it was widely ignored—especially in the large cities along the coasts and in the upper Midwest. A 1924 report showed Kansans obeying the law at a rate of about 95 percent and New Yorkers at a rate of only about 5 percent. Thus Prohibition sharpened the contrast between urban and rural moral values during the 1920s.

Bootlegging Liquor, beer, and wine could no longer be manufactured, sold, or transported in the United States. Americans who chose to defy the Volstead Act needed to find a private source of alcoholic beverages. For this they turned to a new type of criminal: the bootlegger.

Section 3

Cultural Conflicts

Section Objectives

1. Learn about the effects of Prohibition on society.
2. Discover the issues of religion that were at the core of the Scopes trial.
3. Find out how racial tensions changed after World War I.

Bellringer

Warm-Up Activity Ask students to consider what might happen if the making, selling, importing, and exporting of soft drinks were made illegal. Do they think all Americans would stop drinking soda? What unwanted effects might such a law have?

Activating Prior Knowledge What moods and changes in society might have brought about Prohibition? Do students think the majority of American citizens were in favor of Prohibition or opposed to it?

Reading Strategy

As students read, have them list the types of conflicts that divided Americans during the 1920s. Ask them to note ways these problems could have been eased.

Activity

Connecting with Geography

Tell students that in 1925 the first issue of *The New Yorker* magazine appeared with a famous editorial statement vowing that the slick, expensive magazine of fiction, essays, cartoons, and reviews was not designed for "the old lady from Dubuque." Ask students to write a brief essay about the divisions in American society pointed out by that statement. **(Verbal/Linguistic)**

Resource Directory

Teaching Resources

Learning Styles Lesson Plans booklet, p. 43
Guided Reading and Review booklet, p. 85

Technology

Section Reading Support Transparencies
Guided Reading Audiotapes (English/Spanish), Ch. 13
Student Edition on Audio CD, Ch. 13
Prentice Hall Presentation Pro CD-ROM, Ch. 13
Companion Web site, www.phschool.com

Lesson Plan

Focus Explain that rapid changes in American life after World War I led to differences in values among Americans. Ask students what major conflicts arose.

Instruct Discuss the institution of Prohibition and its failure. How did Prohibition contribute to the expansion of organized crime? Ask students to explain why some Americans argued that even though alcohol was bad, it should be legal.

Ask students how the Scopes trial pointed out divisions in American society. Why was the trial of lasting importance?

Discuss racial tensions in the 1920s. Why did violence by whites against blacks increase in the North? Why did membership in the Klan grow? How did African Americans react to the violence?

Assess/Reteach Many complex and divisive issues faced the United States after World War I. Have students list some of society's major conflicts at this time. Then, have them state which of those conflicts have been resolved by now, and which still cause problems.

VIEWING HISTORY The government struggled to stop the illegal flow of liquor during Prohibition. Federal agents are shown destroying cases of beer during a raid in Philadelphia. **Analyzing Information** *What were the biggest problems in enforcing Prohibition?*

In the old days, **bootleggers** merely had been drinkers who hid flasks of liquor in the leg of their boots. Now the term was used to describe suppliers of illegal alcohol. Some bootleggers operated stills—devices used to produce alcohol from corn, grain, potatoes, or other fruit and vegetable sources. Others smuggled liquor overland from Canada or by ship from the Caribbean. A smuggler's ship might anchor far off the coast, where its illegal cargo would be loaded onto speedboats fast enough to outrace Coast Guard cutters. The boats would then head to secluded harbors where trucks were waiting to carry the liquor to warehouses. From there, it would be transported to retail outlets. Those outlets included restaurants, nightclubs, and speakeasies.

Speakeasies were bars that operated illegally. These bars flourished in the cities. One observer estimated that there were 700 speakeasies and 4,000 bootleggers in Washington, D.C., a city with only 300 licensed saloons before Prohibition. The whole state of Massachusetts had 1,000 saloons before Prohibition, while during it Boston alone had 4,000 speakeasies and 15,000 bootleggers. A customer could not just stroll into a speakeasy. A heavy gate usually blocked the entrance, and the customer had to show a membership card or be recognized by a guard. A

COMPARING PRIMARY SOURCES

The Eighteenth Amendment

Violations of Prohibition led Congress to hear testimony on whether the Eighteenth Amendment should be repealed.

Analyzing Viewpoints Compare the main arguments made by the two speakers.

In Favor of Repeal

"I will concede that the saloon was odious [offensive], but now we have delicatessen stores, pool rooms, drug stores, millinery shops, private parlors, and 57 other varieties of speakeasies selling liquor and flourishing."

—*Representative Fiorello La Guardia of New York, 1926*

Against Repeal

"Instead of lowering our standards, we urge that the law be strengthened. . . .The closing of the open saloon . . . has resulted in better national health; children are born under better conditions, homes are better, and the mother is delivered from the fear of a drunken husband."

—*Ella A. Boole, president of the National Woman's Christian Temperance Union, 1926*

Caption Answers

Viewing History Bootleggers and owners of speakeasies were clever in eluding the police. Many people disregarded Prohibition laws. There was not enough money to enforce Prohibition properly. Organized crime was hard to fight.

RESOURCE DIRECTORY

Teaching Resources

Biography, Literature, and Comparing Primary Sources booklet (Comparing Primary Sources) *On the Eighteenth Amendment,* p. 135

number of speakeasies rejected the standard gate for a more creative entrance, as a French diplomat observed in New York City:

> "*Some speakeasies are disguised behind florists' shops, or behind undertakers' coffins. I know one, right in Broadway, which is entered through an imitation telephone-box; it has excellent beer. . . .*"
>
> —Paul Morand, 1929

Organized Crime Supplying illegal liquor was a complex operation, involving manufacture, transportation, storage, and sales. This complexity, and bootlegging's huge potential for profit, helped lead to the development of organized crime.

At first, local gangsters operated independently, competing to supply liquor. Then some of them found that by joining forces they could create an organization large and efficient enough to handle the entire bootlegging operation. When these organizations tried to expand their territory, they clashed with other gangs. As rival groups fought for control with machine guns and sawed-off shotguns, gang wars and murder became commonplace. The streets of American cities became a battleground.

Successful bootlegging organizations often moved into other illegal activities, including gambling, prostitution, and a highly profitable business called racketeering. In one kind of "racket," gangsters bribed police or other government officials to ignore their illegal operations. In another, gangsters forced local businesses to pay a fee for "protection." Those who refused to pay might be gunned down or have their businesses blown to bits. In one period of a little more than a year, racketeers set off 157 bombs in Chicago. Terrified citizens went along with the gangsters' demands. The supporters of Prohibition had never dreamed that their ideals would bear such evil fruit.

Al Capone The most notorious of the gangster organizations operated in Chicago. There, bootlegging had added immense wealth to an already successful gambling, prostitution, and racketeering business that reached into nearly every neighborhood, police station, and government office.

In 1925, a young gangster murdered his way to the top of Chicago's organized crime network. He was Al Capone, nicknamed "Scarface." Capone was a ruthless criminal with a talent for avoiding jail. With so much money at his disposal ($60 million a year from bootlegging alone), Capone easily bought the cooperation of police and city officials. Politicians, even judges, took orders from him.

The government fought back with improved law enforcement. The Federal Bureau of Investigation (FBI), headed by J. Edgar Hoover, became a dedicated, independent force against organized crime during the 1920s. Still, Capone managed for years to slip out of any charges brought against him. Finally, in 1931, a federal court convicted him of income-tax evasion and sent him to prison. Bootlegging remained a problem, however, until Prohibition ended in 1933.

VIEWING HISTORY Chicago gangster Al Capone (left) confers with his lawyer in this 1929 photo. **Synthesizing Information** *Why was it so difficult for the government to bring Capone to justice?*

Issues of Religion

Prohibition highlighted the differences between urban and rural areas of the country. Another issue that tended to split Americans along urban and rural lines was the teaching of evolution. Many Americans felt that the theory of evolution conflicted with their

Activity: Connecting with Culture

Share this quotation from a noted historian with students: "As an attempt to restore morality, Prohibition probably produced the opposite effect. The willingness to break the law contributed to a wider decline in moral standards." Conduct a whole-class debate on the historian's position. Ask: Did Prohibition result in an improvement or decline in morality in America? **(Verbal/Linguistic)**

From the Archives of American Heritage®

Sister Aimee

On January 1, 1923, in Los Angeles, Aimee Semple McPherson opened the 5,300-seat Angelus Temple, home base for her Church of the Four Square Gospel. Sister Aimee, as she was known, had a riveting stage presence, her charisma was overwhelming, and she knew how to draw a crowd. Aimee preached almost every day and on Sunday, three times. As colored lights played over her pure white gown, she spoke of love and redemption instead of sin and damnation. Vaudevillian musical acts and elaborately staged allegorical scenes rounded out her services. One observer saw the proceedings as "a sensuous debauch served up in the name of religion"; another called them "supernatural whoopee." Within five years the church had 30,000 members. In a short time, however, scandals and lawsuits had turned off the lights on Aimee's career. Source: Frederic D. Schwarz, "The Time Machine," *American Heritage®* magazine, December 1997.

Customize for ... ESL

Have students reread the section "Organized Crime" on this page. Then have them define the terms "bootlegging," "racket," "protection," and "gangster" as they apply to organized crime.

Caption Answers

Viewing History Though Capone was known as a ruthless criminal, the government was only able to convict him of tax evasion. Capone had enough money and power to avoid prosecution by bribing police and city officials.

Activity
Connecting with Culture

Have students cooperate in conducting research and creating a Venn diagram that compares and contrasts the lives and careers of Billy Sunday and Aimee Semple McPherson. The students' diagram should include such things as biographical backgrounds, numbers of followers, promotional techniques, use of media, and so on. Have the students share the diagram with the class, highlighting remarkable similarities and differences between the two evangelists. **(Visual/Spatial)**

Background
Biography

John T. Scopes, whose name lives in history as the moniker of the famous trial, led a life otherwise free from conflict and the media spotlight. After the trial, he refused his old teaching position (which was offered to him) and instead accepted a scholarship funded by scientists and journalists to attend the prestigious University of Chicago. He studied geology for two years, and then went to work for Gulf Oil Corporation, which sent him to Venezuela in 1925. He returned to the United States in 1929. Scopes later worked as a geologist for the United Gas Corporation. From 1940 to 1963, when he retired, he worked at the company's headquarters in Louisiana. Scopes died in 1970.

Fundamentalist preacher Billy Sunday drew large crowds at religious revivals.

religious beliefs. The teaching of this theory in some public schools during the 1920s touched off a debate that continues today.

Fundamentalism Before the teaching of evolution became an issue, many Americans already felt uneasy with certain changes in society. During the early part of the century, challenges to traditional beliefs came from several directions:

1. Science and technology were taking a larger role in everyday life.
2. War and the widespread problems of modern society were causing more people to question whether God took an active role in human affairs or if God even existed.
3. Some scholars were saying that the Bible was a document written by humans and that it contained contradictions and historical inaccuracies.

In response to these challenges, between 1910 and 1915, religious traditionalists published a series of 12 pamphlets called *The Fundamentals.* They stated a set of beliefs that have since come to be called **fundamentalism.** In addition to supporting traditional Christian ideas about Jesus, fundamentalists argued that God inspired the Bible, so it cannot contain contradictions or errors. They declared that the Bible is literally true and that every story in it actually took place as described.

Fundamentalism gained tremendous attention in the 1920s. The most famous fundamentalist preacher of the time was Billy Sunday, a former professional baseball player. Sunday's sermons on the evils of alcohol made him an influential figure in the Prohibition movement. His series of more than 300 religious revival meetings attracted an estimated total attendance of 100 million. Another popular preacher, Aimee Semple McPherson, was a master of theatrical presentation. Her followers gave $1.5 million to build her the massive Angelus Temple in Los Angeles, where she preached to huge crowds. "Sister Aimee," as she was called, owned her own radio station, which allowed her to broadcast her revival meetings. By doing so, she used radio in an innovative way: to broaden the reach of her ministry.

Evolution and the Scopes Trial The theory of evolution deeply disturbed fundamentalists. This theory states that human beings and all other living species developed over time from simpler life forms.

Fundamentalists denounced the evolution theory, saying that it contradicts the history of creation as stated in the Bible. They worked for the passage of laws to prevent public schools from teaching evolution. When Tennessee passed such a ban in 1925, a science teacher named John T. Scopes agreed to challenge it as unconstitutional, thus denying him personal and religious freedom. He defied the law and was arrested for teaching evolution. Thus began the case popularly known as the **Scopes trial.**

VIEWING HISTORY William Jennings Bryan (right) and Clarence Darrow (left) faced off on the issue of evolution in Dayton, Tennessee, in 1925. **Drawing Inferences** *What constitutional issue was at the heart of the matter?*

The case became a battle between two of the country's greatest lawyers. William Jennings Bryan, an outspoken fundamentalist, volunteered to help prosecute Scopes. Clarence Darrow, a passionate supporter of free speech, volunteered to help defend him. Both men were known for their debating skills. Bryan had run for President three times. Darrow had won fame for defending political and labor activists such as Eugene V. Debs.

The trial took place in the small town of Dayton, Tennessee, in the withering heat of July 1925. In this new era of mass media, journalists swarmed around the courthouse, telegraphing some 2 million words of

Caption Answers

Viewing History Freedom of speech.

Resource Directory

Technology

Sounds of an Era Audio CD *Billy Sunday,* 1923 recording (time: one minute)

Resource Pro® Visual Learning Activity *The Ku Klux Klan,* found on Resource Pro, uses a 1923 drawing from *Life* magazine to enhance students' understanding of how artists use symbols to convey political viewpoints.

reporting to their papers over the ten days of the trial. This was the first trial ever broadcast over American radio.

On the surface, the case was a simple one. The judge ruled that the jury should determine only whether Scopes had taught evolution, which he readily admitted he had. The jury took just a few minutes to find Scopes guilty, and the judge fined him $100. However, more complex issues were at stake, including the clash between the country's modern beliefs and its traditional values.

The dramatic climax of the case came when Darrow put Bryan himself on the stand to testify as an expert on the Bible. Darrow set about testing the logic of Bryan's faith by citing passages from the Bible and forcing him to try to explain them. In the process, Darrow ridiculed fundamentalist beliefs. Under Darrow's intense, often brutal, questioning, Bryan admitted that even he did not interpret all of the Bible literally. He kept fighting back, however, at one point saying, "I am simply trying to protect the word of God."

This grueling battle exhausted Bryan, who died just a few days after the trial ended. Fundamentalists saw Bryan as a martyr for their cause. Modernists saw Darrow as a defender of science and reason. Although fundamentalists considered the trial a setback, their movement remained active. In later decades, it would grow in membership and strength.

Racial Tensions

Americans clashed over race in the 1920s. African Americans took part in the Great Migration to the North in the early 1900s for two main reasons. They wanted to take advantage of greater job opportunities in the North, and they wanted to escape the increasing violence against African Americans in the South. Many of them, however, found both racial prejudice and violence in the North.

Violence Against African Americans During the summer of 1919, mob violence between white and black Americans erupted in about 25 cities. That summer became known as the "Red Summer" for all the blood that was spilled. Omaha, Tulsa, and Washington, D.C., all suffered periods of racial turmoil. The worst of these race riots, however, occurred in Chicago.

The African American population of Chicago had doubled since 1910. This increase led to overcrowded neighborhoods and heightened tensions between blacks and whites. An incident at a beach on Lake Michigan touched off the violence. On one especially hot July day, stone-throwing had erupted between whites and blacks on a beach typically used only by whites. Meanwhile, a 17-year-old black boy, swimming just offshore with his friends, accidentally floated into the "whites only" area. A white man, who had been throwing rocks at the swimmers for some time, struck the boy, and he drowned. Furious blacks accused the whites of killing him, and more fights broke out. The riot spread through the city. For several days, chaos reigned in parts of Chicago. By the end, some 23 African Americans and 15 whites were dead, another 537 people were wounded, and the destruction caused by rioting had left hundreds homeless.

The Chicago Daily Tribune. FINAL EDITION

TROOPS ACT; HALT RIOTING

CAR MEN VOTE TOMORROW ON LOWDEN PLAN

5 REGIMENTS BEGIN PATROL OF RIOT AREAS

Zone Quiet as a Church, Says Dickson

SNIPERS FIRE UPON SOLDIERS; CALM SETS IN

TURKS, TARTARS, PERIL ARMENIA

BRUNDAGE, HOYNE TO PUNISH MOBS

U.S. WILL RETAIL $125,500,000 OF FOOD TO PUBLIC

Race riots broke out in several cities in the summer of 1919.

Focus on GOVERNMENT

How Laws Are Challenged When the state of Tennessee passed a law banning the teaching of evolution in 1925, John T. Scopes disagreed with the law and took action to challenge it. In the American system of checks and balances, individuals, organizations, and state and local governments can challenge the meaning of a law, and even its constitutionality, by going to court.

Interest groups often assist individuals in preparing their case if the case can be used to "test" the legitimacy of a law that the group opposes. For example, Scopes was assisted in his case by the American Civil Liberties Union (ACLU). They resolved to take the Scopes case through the court system all the way to the United States Supreme Court. By doing so, they hoped that the court would find the law, and other similar laws, to be unconstitutional.

Because Scopes' $100 fine was later thrown out by the Tennessee Supreme Court, however, the case never had the opportunity to reach the Supreme Court.

ACTIVITY
Connecting with History and Conflict

Have students locate the transcript from the Scopes trial, especially the sections in which Clarence Darrow examines William Jennings Bryan. Have them review the transcript to determine which people spoke during this part of the trial (Darrow, Bryan, attorneys, the judge, etc.) and assign students to play each role. Then have students present a readers' theater or sketch reenacting the climax of one of the most famous trials in history. **(Bodily/Kinesthetic)**

BACKGROUND
A Tragic Outrage

The boy whose death precipitated the 1919 Chicago riots was named Eugene Williams. The Cook County Coroner, in investigating the boy's death, created a chilling portrait of racist mob mentality and a teenager's terrifying last minutes: "We find that the deceased, Eugene Williams, a peaceable citizen, in bathing suit, had entered the water at said beach, the exact time unknown, and was in the water clinging to a railroad tie, that numerous stones were thrown by the white men in his direction, preventing him, for fear of bodily injury, from landing, deceased being compelled to remain out in the deep water of the lake until he released his hold on the railroad tie and drowned. . . . We recommend that the parties who threw stones at the deceased and all rioters who participated in the affray above described be apprehended and prosecuted."

CUSTOMIZE FOR ...
Less Proficient Readers

Ask students to explain the following: why Prohibition divided Americans, why the Scopes trial generated heated debate among Americans, and why the Ku Klux Klan experienced a revival in the 1920s.

TEST PREPARATION

Have students review the information about the Scopes trial and then complete the sentence below.

The Scopes Trial received nationwide attention—

A because two well-known lawyers were arguing the case.

B because its subject matter reflected the divided emotions of the country.

C because it was the first trial ever broadcast nationally, on the radio.

(D) for all the reasons stated above.

ACTIVITY

Connecting with History and Conflict

Have students research and report on lynchings in their state or a selected state during the 1920s. How many lynchings took place? What events led to particular lynchings? What were the results of these acts of cruelty? Have students present their findings in oral presentations and/or written reports. **(Verbal/Linguistic)**

BACKGROUND

A Diverse Nation

Ku Klux Klan activity dropped sharply in the late 1920s, owing in large part to the scandal in Indiana. Yet the Klan was to enjoy a final spurt of popularity at the end of the decade. In 1928, Alfred E. Smith became the Democratic presidential nominee. Smith's candidacy disturbed the Klan, and Klansmen used it as a way to rally sympathy and recruit new members. What was it about Smith's candidacy that created so much excitement? Smith was a Roman Catholic—the first to run for President—and the Klan viewed Catholicism as a threat to the United States.

READING CHECK

Several northern cities experienced race riots in 1919. The revived Ku Klux Klan engaged in violent attacks against African Americans and other groups in many states. Southern states continued to deny suffrage to African Americans.

Some whites also directed racial violence against specific individuals. During the 1920s, the lynchings of the Jim Crow era continued. Many of these new crimes were the work of an old enemy of racial harmony, the Ku Klux Klan.

This 1920s poster illustrates the Ku Klux Klan's views on immigration.

Revival of the Klan During Reconstruction, President Grant's campaign against the Ku Klux Klan had largely eliminated it. However, in 1915 a former Methodist circuit preacher from Atlanta, Colonel William J. Simmons, revived the organization. The Klan used modern fundraising and publicity methods to increase its influence and size. By 1922, Klan membership had grown to about 100,000. Two years later, it had ballooned to 4 million. The new Klan was no longer just a southern organization. In fact, the state with the greatest number of Klansmen was Indiana. The Klan's focus shifted, too. The organization vowed to defend their own white-Protestant culture against any group, not just blacks, that seemed to them un-American:

> "*Klansmen are to be examples of pure patriotism. They are to organize the patriotic sentiment of native-born white, Protestant Americans for the defense of distinctively American institutions. Klansmen are dedicated to the principle that America shall be made American through the promulgation [circulation] of American doctrines, the dissemination [spread] of American ideals, the creation of wholesome American sentiment, the preservation of American institutions.*"
>
> —Klansman's Manual, 1925

During the early 1920s, Klan members carried out many crimes against African Americans, Catholics, Jews, immigrants, and others. They rode by night, beating, whipping, even killing their victims, terrorizing blacks and whites alike. Then, in 1925, the head of the Klan in Indiana was sentenced to life imprisonment for assaulting a girl who later poisoned herself. The nation was finally shocked into action, and police began to step up enforcement. By 1927, Klan activity had diminished once again.

Fighting Discrimination Increasing violence against African Americans rallied the efforts of the NAACP. During the 1920s, the NAACP worked in vain to pass federal anti-lynching laws. A proposed law passed the House of Representatives in 1922 but died in the Senate. Law enforcement improved at the state level, and the number of lynchings gradually decreased. Ten lynchings were reported in 1929.

During the 1920s, the NAACP also worked to protect the voting rights of African Americans, but again it had only limited success. For example, the Supreme Court struck down as unconstitutional a Texas law prohibiting blacks from voting in the Democratic primary. Yet the Texas legislature got around the law by giving political parties the right to decide who could vote in primary elections. African Americans in the South still could not exercise their full political rights.

READING CHECK

Where and how did racial issues surface in the 1920s?

The Garvey Movement Some African Americans, frustrated by continued violence and discrimination, dreamed of a new homeland where they could live in peace. An African American named Marcus Garvey worked to make that dream a reality. Garvey had come to New York City from his native Jamaica in 1916 to establish a new headquarters for his Universal Negro Improvement Association (UNIA).

Through the UNIA, Garvey sought to build up African Americans' self-respect and economic power. African Americans were encouraged to buy shares

RESOURCE DIRECTORY

Teaching Resources

Units 3/4 booklet
- Section 3 Quiz, p. 44
- Chapter 13 Test, pp. 45, 48

Guide to the Essentials
- Section 3 Summary, p. 66
- Chapter 13 Test, p. 67

Other Print Resources

Chapter Tests with ExamView® Test Bank CD ROM, Ch. 13

Technology

ExamView® Test Bank CD-ROM, Ch. 13
Social Studies Skills Tutor CD-ROM

in Garvey's Negro Factories Corporation, a set of small black-owned businesses. He also urged African Americans to return to "Motherland Africa" to create a self-governing nation. Garvey's message of racial pride and independence attracted a large number of followers to his black nationalist movement. Garvey held regular UNIA meetings in Harlem, and his followers could be seen in military-style uniforms reflecting their status, whether as members of the marching band, the Black Cross Nurses, or the African Legion. Several respected African American leaders, such as W.E.B. Du Bois, criticized the movement, however. They objected to Garvey's call for separation of the races, as well as his careless business practices.

Garvey gathered $10 million for a steamship company, the Black Star Line, that would carry his followers back to the motherland. Corruption and mismanagement plagued the shipping line, however, and in 1925, Garvey was jailed on mail fraud charges relating to the sale of stock in the steamship company. From prison the same year, he wrote in an essay: "Why should we be discouraged because somebody laughs at us today? Who [is] to tell what tomorrow will bring forth? . . . We see and have changes every day, so pray, work, be steadfast and be not dismayed."

Garvey's sentence was later commuted, and he was deported to Jamaica in 1927. Without his leadership, the UNIA in America collapsed. Still, Garvey's ideas remained an inspiration to later "black pride" movements.

VIEWING HISTORY This ship belonged to Marcus Garvey's Black Star Line steamship company, founded in 1919. It was one of many enterprises Garvey (left) hoped would strengthen the African American community. **Drawing Conclusions** *Was Marcus Garvey a successful leader?*

Section 3 Assessment

READING COMPREHENSION

1. What were the goals of Prohibition?
2. How did organized crime profit from **bootleggers** and **speakeasies** during Prohibition?
3. How were religious issues and **fundamentalism** at odds with the teaching of evolution?
4. Which positions did William Jennings Bryan and Clarence Darrow each represent in the **Scopes trial?**
5. Why were many African Americans drawn to Marcus Garvey's message and movement?

CRITICAL THINKING AND WRITING

6. **Predicting Consequences** How might life in the 1920s have been different without Prohibition?
7. **Synthesizing Information** Consider the racial tensions that existed in the 1920s and those that exist today. Why are racial issues difficult to resolve?
8. **Writing a Conclusion** Write a short essay that supports the following conclusion: Differences between traditional and modern beliefs were responsible for the cultural conflicts of the 1920s.

Take It to the NET

Activity: Creating a Poster
Research arguments for and against Prohibition, and then create a poster that either promotes Prohibition or calls for its repeal. Use the links provided in the *America: Pathways to the Present* area of the following Web site for help in completing this activity.
www.phschool.com

CUSTOMIZE FOR ...

Gifted and Talented

Have students research Marcus Garvey and the Universal Negro Improvement Association (UNIA), then have them write a paragraph from the point of view of one of Garvey's followers that explains why they joined the UNIA.

Section 3 Assessment

Reading Comprehension

1. Eliminate drunkenness and the abuses it caused; eliminate saloons, where vice thrived; prevent job absenteeism and accidents stemming from drunkenness.
2. Organized crime had the resources necessary to handle all aspects of the illegal liquor trade. In return, each gang made money from each speakeasy and bootlegger operating within its territory.
3. Fundamentalists believe the Bible is true in a literal sense. The theory of evolution contradicts the history of creation as stated in the Bible.
4. Bryan: fundamentalist; prosecution. Darrow: supporter of free speech; defense.
5. His movement seemed to offer an escape from continued violence and discrimination. Garvey urged his followers to take pride in being African American and to strive for economic advancement.

Critical Thinking and Writing

6. Sample answer: Organized crime may not have developed at all, or at least not to the extent that it did.
7. Answers will vary, but might include references to the long history of racial tension in the United States.
8. Essays will vary, but might focus on the Scopes trial, or the fact that Prohibition was more effective in rural areas than it was in large cities.

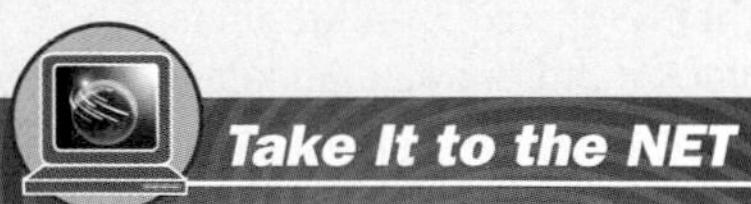

Take It to the NET

Answers will vary. For: the elimination of family or workplace problems caused by drunkenness; the elimination of crime associated with alcohol. Against: the interference with individuals' rights; the economic loss involved.

Caption Answers

Viewing History Sample answer: Garvey was successful as a symbol of both African American pride and the hope of economic advancement. He performed poorly, however, in the day-to-day management of his various business enterprises. Consequently, his empire collapsed.

Chapter 13

Reviewing Key Terms

Students should refer to the definitions of key terms in the chapter to write sentences that show an understanding of the social changes of the 1920s.

Reviewing Main Ideas

11. Women started smoking, wearing makeup, and drinking. Women began moving into office jobs, but were still denied equal pay and leadership positions. Some began to seek political offices.
12. A great number of people moved to cities; African Americans moved north; immigrants from Mexico and Canada entered the country; American suburbs greatly expanded.
13. Sample answer: Charles Lindbergh for his bravery and ability to meet a new challenge; Gertrude Ederle, as a sports hero, for her swim across the English Channel.
14. Development of national popular culture, expansion of movie industry, expansion of size and circulation of newspapers and magazines, development of radio.
15. Growing radio audiences helped to popularize jazz.
16. A group of expatriate American writers in the 1920s. They were troubled by what they saw as a greedy, materialistic world that lacked moral values.
17. Their work explored traditional black culture, being female, being Americans, the experiences of African Americans in society, and being human.
18. Differences between urban and rural moral values: speakeasies flourished in cities. Large numbers of formerly law-abiding citizens were willing to break the law by drinking.
19. The division between fundamentalist, traditional values and modern scientific belief.
20. Mob violence between African Americans and whites, lynchings, and the revival of the Ku Klux Klan.

Chapter 13 Review and Assessment

creating a CHAPTER SUMMARY

Copy this chart (right) on a piece of paper and complete it by adding information about the effects of important social changes and conflicts that occurred in the 1920s. Some entries have been completed for you as examples.

Conflict and Change in the 1920s	
Change/Conflict	**Impact on Society**
Women win the right to vote.	Their vote influences local politics.
Prohibition takes effect.	
Farm prices drop.	

For additional review and enrichment activities, see the interactive version of *America: Pathways to the Present*, available on the Web and on CD-ROM.

★ Reviewing Key Terms

For each of the terms below, write a sentence explaining how it relates to the 1920s.

1. flapper
2. demographics
3. barrio
4. mass media
5. Jazz Age
6. Lost Generation
7. bootleggers
8. speakeasies
9. fundamentalism
10. Scopes trial

★ Reviewing Main Ideas

11. How did women's roles change during the 1920s? (Section 1)
12. What types of demographic change occurred during the 1920s? (Section 1)
13. Name two American heroes from the 1920s and tell why they were popular at that time. (Section 1)
14. What types of changes occurred with the rise of mass media in the 1920s? (Section 2)
15. Explain the significance of radio broadcasting in the Jazz Age. (Section 2)
16. What was the Lost Generation? What trends in society did they find troubling? (Section 2)
17. How were the experiences of African Americans reflected by the writers of the Harlem Renaissance? (Section 2)
18. What cultural conflicts did Prohibition highlight? (Section 3)
19. What divisions in American society did the Scopes trial reflect? (Section 3)
20. Describe the racial conflicts experienced in the 1920s. (Section 3)

★ Critical Thinking

21. Drawing Conclusions Why did women fail to have an immediate impact on national elections after the passage of the Nineteenth Amendment?
22. Drawing Inferences Evaluate the possible impact of racial tensions of the 1920s on the growth of the Universal Negro Improvement Association (UNIA).
23. Comparing Points of View Evaluate Prohibition from the point of view of (a) a law officer, (b) the owner of a legal bar, (c) a bootlegger, (d) a member of the National Woman's Christian Temperance Union.
24. Demonstrating Reasoned Judgment Explain the meaning of this statement: "For many African Americans, migration to the North was a mixed success."

Creating a Chapter Summary

Conflict and Change in the 1920s	
Change/Conflict	**Impact on Society**
Women win the right to vote.	Their vote influences local politics.
Prohibition takes effect.	Organized crime grows.
Farm prices drop; urban economy grows.	Migration from rural to urban areas
Mass media develops, including radio.	Heightened awareness of national issues and figures; instant transmission of news
Scopes teaches theory of evolution.	"Showdown" between supporters of theory of evolution versus fundamentalists
Racial tensions increase after WWI.	Urban riots

★ Skills Assessment

Analyzing Political Cartoons ▶

25. Herbert Hoover famously referred to Prohibition as a "noble experiment." Who does the nurse to the right of Hoover represent? Why would the cartoonist choose this particular nurse to assist in the "experiment"?
26. Why are the doctor and his syringe made to seem frightening?
27. What is the cartoonist's message?

Analyzing Primary Sources

Reread the poem below, "First Fig" by Edna St. Vincent Millay, from Section 2:

(1) "My candle burns at both ends;
(2) It will not last the night;
(3) But ah, my foes, and oh, my friends—
(4) It gives a lovely light!"

28. Which of the following best expresses the speaker's meaning in lines one and two?
    - **A** She feels bright.
    - **B** She lives in a dark world.
    - **C** She stays up all night.
    - **D** The pace of her life is dangerously fast.
29. Which of the following best expresses the meaning of lines three and four?
    - **F** Her lifestyle is exciting while it lasts.
    - **G** She feels bright and lovely.
    - **H** Her friends and foes approve of her lifestyle.
    - **J** Her life is quiet.

Applying the Chapter Skill: *Supporting a Position*

30. Review the steps involved in supporting a position outlined on page 466. Then reread the Comparing Primary Sources quotes on page 468. What reasons does each speaker give as evidence to support his or her position on the Eighteenth Amendment?

"YES, IT'S A NOBLE EXPERIMENT."

ACTIVITIES

Writing to LEARN

Writing to Describe
Consider that radio broadcasts were a new experience for Americans in the 1920s. Imagine turning on a radio and hearing jazz for the first time. Describe what the experience might have been like for a teenager, for the teenager's parents, and for the grandparents.

Primary Source CD-ROM

Working With Primary Sources Find additional information on the 1920s on the *Exploring Primary Sources in U.S. History CD-ROM* and use the selection(s) provided to complete the Chapter 13 primary source activity located in the *America: Pathways to the Present* area of the following Web site.
www.phschool.com

Take It to the NET

Chapter Self-Test As a review activity, take the Chapter 13 Self-Test in the *America: Pathways to the Present* area at the Web site listed below. The questions are designed to test your understanding of the chapter content.
www.phschool.com

CRITICAL THINKING

21. Relatively few women voted, and those who did voted largely along the same lines as men.
22. A postwar recession increased competition between blacks and whites for the same jobs.
23. (a) Difficult to enforce, and not enough resources to properly enforce it. (b) Bars could not legally sell alcohol and faced a loss of livelihood. (c) Lucrative. (d) In favor of Prohibition as a social reform.
24. Although they came in search of a better life, African Americans still met with racism in the North. For instance, African American women often had to work as household help for whites at low wages that kept them trapped in poverty.

SKILLS ASSESSMENT

25. Virtue. She looks tough, as if Prohibition was an effort to force Americans to live virtuous lives.
26. Possible answer: To suggest that the "cure" (Prohibition) was worse than the "disease" (drinking alcoholic beverages).
27. It is a bad idea to forcibly inflict the preferences of a minority (temperance advocates) onto the nation as a whole.
28. D
29. F
30. For repealing: Prohibition has led to alcohol being sold successfully, and in great quantities, from many new sources other than saloons. Against repealing: Prohibition has increased the general health of the nation, leading to better conditions for children and families, and has lessened instances of domestic abuse.

ANSWERS TO ACTIVITIES

Writing to LEARN

Sample answer: Teenagers would have enjoyed the exciting new sound of jazz—a sound that they had probably never heard before. They would have loved to dance to it. Parents may have resisted jazz at first but could have grown to like it as it influenced other forms of familiar music. Grandparents probably did not approve of the suggestive music that reflected the morals of the time.

Primary Source CD-ROM

Direct students to the additional primary sources that can be found on the *Exploring Primary Sources in U.S. History CD-ROM.*

Take It to the NET

Additional support materials and activities for Chapter 13 of *America: Pathways to the Present* can be found in the Social Studies area at the Prentice Hall School Web site. **www.phschool.com**

The Arts in America

Focus Tell students that to gain insight into a particular period in American history, one needs only to look at America's creative side. The arts are a mirror of the national mood, reflecting joys and fears, the need to escape pain, and the need to comfort one another.

Instruct As students read the text and study the photographs, tell them to consider how the arts of each period tell something about what was happening at the time. Discuss with students how the mood of the country is expressed through literature, film, music, and the visual arts.

Extend Encourage students to examine one specific time period, looking at how the arts reflect that era. Tell students that they may focus on one art form, such as music, film, literature, or the visual arts, such as painting and sculpture.

American Pathways
CULTURE

The Arts in America

Throughout the nation's history, the arts have reflected the era in which they were created. Newspapers and magazines have brought the latest information into American homes. Books, movies, and music often have focused on issues of national concern.

1 Early American Arts and Crafts

1732–1776 The colonial period abounded with artisans such as Paul Revere, news printers such as Benjamin Franklin, and writers such as Franklin, Thomas Paine, and Thomas Jefferson.

A bowl made by Paul Revere (right)

2 A New Nation

1783–1860 A spirit of improvement swept the new nation, leading to increased interest in education and the arts. Transcendental writers Ralph Waldo Emerson and Henry David Thoreau celebrated both the individual and the natural world, and female intellectuals like Margaret Fuller sought to raise awareness of women's new roles in society.

Henry David Thoreau (far left) and Ralph Waldo Emerson (left)

THE GREAT TRAIN ROBBERY
SENSATIONAL AND STARTLING "HOLD UP" OF THE "GOLD EXPRESS" BY FAMOUS WESTERN OUTLAWS

3 Civil War to World War I

1861–1918 Following the Civil War, Americans embraced new forms of popular entertainment, including vaudeville, minstrel shows, ragtime music, jazz, and motion pictures.

A poster for the 1903 film *The Great Train Robbery* (right)

RESOURCE DIRECTORY

Teaching Resources

Units 3/4 booklet
- American Pathways Activity, pp. 82–83

American Pathways Thematic Posters

Technology

Companion Web site, www.phschool.com

American Pathways

4 The Jazz Age

1920–1929 The popularity of jazz soared during the Roaring Twenties, and its spirit ran through many of the other arts of the time.

Louis Armstrong's Hot Five jazz band (below) and record labels from the 1920s (right)

5 The Great Depression and World War II

1929–1945 During this period, serious works of art dealt with the despair of the Depression and the war, while entertainment largely sought to offer a means of escape from these harsh realities.

American author John Steinbeck (above)

6 Postwar Turmoil and Change

1945–Present After World War II, Americans experienced a time of rapid cultural and social change. Writers and other artists explored subjects such as youthful rebellion, civil rights, environmental issues, and the Vietnam War.

American artist Georgia O'Keeffe (above)

Continuity and Change

1. What work of art created in colonial times helped bring about the American Revolution? Explain.
2. How did Ernest Hemingway and F. Scott Fitzgerald view the era in which they lived?

Take It to the NET: Creating a Study Guide Print and complete the study guide for this topic found in the *America: Pathways to the Present* area of the following Web site. **www.phschool.com**

477

Take It to the NET

Students can print the American Pathways thematic study guide for this topic at the Prentice Hall School Web site, or you can provide students with copies of the study guide, which is found in the Units 3/4 booklet, the American Pathways Activity, pages 82–83. Students should use their texts to fill in a one-sentence description for each event on the study guide. When completed for each of the American Pathways topics, the thematic study guides will aid students in preparing for an end-of-course exam.

Answers

1. Possible answers: *Common Sense* and the Declaration of Independence both called on Americans to throw off British tyranny.
2. Possible answer: As part of the "lost generation," they rejected American popular culture and the postwar society's quest for material possessions.

Chapter 14 Planning Guide
Resource Manager

	Core Instruction	Reading/Skills
Chapter-Level Resources	Teaching Resources • Pacing Charts booklet • Block Scheduling booklet **Resource Pro® CD-ROM,** Ch. 14 **Prentice Hall Presentation Pro CD-ROM,** Ch. 14 **www.phschool.com** • eTeach	**Guided Reading Audiotapes (English/Spanish)** **Student Edition on Audio CD,** Ch. 14 **Social Studies Skills Tutor CD-ROM** **Color Transparencies,** G12, H17
1 A Republican Decade 1. Learn about events that fueled the Red Scare of the early 1920s. 2. Find out about conflicts that led to the major labor strikes of 1919. 3. See how Republican leadership during the Harding and Coolidge presidencies shaped the 1920s. 4. Discover the issues that shaped the presidential election of 1928. **TEKS** 5(A), 15(C), 20(A)	Teaching Resources **Units 3/4 booklet** • Section 1 Quiz, p. 52 **Learning Styles Lesson Plans booklet,** p. 44	**Guided Reading and Review booklet,** p. 86 **Guide to the Essentials,** p. 68 **Skills for Life booklet,** p. 23 **Section Reading Support Transparencies**
2 A Business Boom 1. Understand the role businesses and consumers play in a consumer economy. 2. Find out how Henry Ford and the automobile were important to the 1920s. 3. Discover the ways in which industrial growth affected the economy of the 1920s. 4. See how the economic boom bypassed some people and benefited others. **TEKS** 5(B), 10(A), 22(C), 23(A), 23(B), 25(C)	Teaching Resources **Units 3/4 booklet** • Section 2 Quiz, p. 53 **Learning Styles Lesson Plans booklet,** p. 45	**Guided Reading and Review booklet,** p. 87 **Guide to the Essentials,** p. 69 **Section Reading Support Transparencies**
3 The Economy in the Late 1920s 1. See why the economy in the late 1920s appeared healthy to most Americans. 2. Observe the danger signs that were present in the economy of the late 1920s. **TEKS** 13(A), 13(B), 25(C), 25(D)	Teaching Resources **Units 3/4 booklet** • Section 3 Quiz, p. 54	**Guided Reading and Review booklet,** p. 88 **Guide to the Essentials,** p. 70 **Section Reading Support Transparencies**

Enrichment/Pre-AP

Prentice Hall United States History Video Collection™
www.phschool.com
- Section Activities, Virtual Field Trip, Chapter Activities, Current Events Online

Biography, Literature, and Comparing Primary Sources booklet, p. 26
American History Block Scheduling Support
Sounds of an Era Audio CD

Biography, Literature, and Comparing Primary Sources booklet, pp. 68–69, 137–138
Nystrom *Atlas of Our Country,* pp. 30–32
Sounds of an Era Audio CD

American Pathways Thematic Posters

Assessment

Core Assessment

ExamView® Test Bank, Ch. 14
ExamView® Test Bank CD-ROM, Ch. 14

Standardized Test Preparation

Diagnose and Prescribe

Diagnostic Tests for High School Social Studies Skills

Review and Reteach

Review Book for U.S. History

Practice and Assess

Test-taking Strategies With Transparencies
Test-taking Strategies Posters
Test Prep Book for U.S. History
Alternative Assessment Handbook
Document-Based Assessment

Teaching Resources
Units 3/4 booklet
- Section Quizzes, pp. 52–54
- Chapter Test, p. 55

www.phschool.com Ch. 14 Self-Test

AmericanHeritage Resources

From the Archives of American Heritage®, pp. 486, 488
AmericanHeritage® My Brush with History™ Videotapes
www.americanheritage.com

Don't miss the exclusive interactive version of this textbook on the Web and on CD-ROM.

Chapter 14 Planning Guide
In Your Classroom

Customize for Individual Needs

Gifted and Talented

Teacher's Edition
- Customize for Gifted and Talented, pp. 481, 493

Teaching Resources
- Biography, Literature, and Comparing Primary Sources booklet, pp. 26, 68–69, 137–138

ESL

Teacher's Edition
- Customize for ESL, p. 495

Teaching Resources
- Guided Reading and Review booklet, pp. 86–88
- Guide to the Essentials (English/Spanish), Chapter 14

Technology
- Student Edition on Audio CD, Chapter 14
- Guided Reading Audiotapes (English/Spanish), Chapter 14
- Section Reading Support Transparencies

Less Proficient Readers

Teacher's Edition
- Customize for Less Proficient Readers, p. 483

Teaching Resources
- Guided Reading and Review booklet, pp. 86–88
- Guide to the Essentials (English/Spanish), Chapter 14

Technology
- Student Edition on Audio CD, Chapter 14
- Guided Reading Audiotapes (English/Spanish), Chapter 14
- Section Reading Support Transparencies

Less Proficient Writers

Teacher's Edition
- Customize for Less Proficient Writers, pp. 487, 501

Teaching Resources
- Guided Reading and Review booklet, pp. 86–88
- Guide to the Essentials (English/Spanish), Chapter 14

Technology
- Student Edition on Audio CD, Chapter 14
- Guided Reading Audiotapes (English/Spanish), Chapter 14
- Section Reading Support Transparencies

Teacher's Edition Index

Chapter 14 – Pacing Suggestions

For 90-minute Blocks

- Teach sections 1 and 2 using Transparencies G12 and H17, and the Recent Scholarship note on page 487 for class discussions.

Running Out of Time?

If you are running short on time to cover this chapter, consider the following options:

- Use the Prentice Hall Presentation Pro CD-ROM to create an outline for this chapter.
- Use the Section Summaries for Chapter 14, from **Guide to the Essentials (English/Spanish).**

TEKS Correlation

Chapter-Level	TEKS
1 A Republican Decade	**(5) History.** The student understands significant individuals, events, and issues of the 1920s. The student is expected to: **(A)** analyze causes and effects of significant issues such as immigration, the Red Scare, Prohibition, and the changing role of women. **(15) Government.** The student understands changes in the role of government over time. The student is expected to: **(C)** evaluate the effects of political incidents such as Teapot Dome and Watergate on the views of U.S. citizens concerning the role of the federal government. **(20) Culture.** The student understands the relationship between the arts and the times during which they were created. The student is expected to: **(A)** describe how the characteristics and issues of various eras in U.S. history have been reflected in works of art, music, and literature such as the paintings of Georgia O'Keeffe, rock and roll, and John Steinbeck's *The Grapes of Wrath.*
2 A Business Boom	**(5) History.** The student understands significant individuals, events, and issues of the 1920s. The student is expected to: **(B)** analyze the impact of significant individuals such as Clarence Darrow, William Jennings Bryan, Henry Ford, and Charles A. Lindbergh. **(10) Geography.** The student understands the effects of migration and immigration on American society. The student is expected to: **(A)** analyze the effects of changing demographic patterns resulting from migration within the United States. **(22) Science, technology, and society.** The student understands the impact of science and technology on the economic development of the United States. The student is expected to: **(C)** analyze the impact of technological innovations on the nature of work, the American labor movement, and business. **(23) Science, technology, and society.** The student understands the influence of scientific discoveries and technological innovations on daily life in the United States. The student is expected to: **(A)** analyze how scientific discoveries and technological innovations, including those in transportation and communication, have changed the standard of living in the United States. **(B)** explain how technological innovations in areas such as space exploration have led to other innovations that affect daily life and the standard of living. **(25) Social studies skills.** The student communicates in written, oral, and visual forms. The student is expected to: **(C)** transfer information from one medium to another, including written to visual and statistical to written or visual, using computer software as appropriate.
3 The Economy in the Late 1920s	**(13) Economics.** The student understands significant economic developments between World War I and World War II. The student is expected to: **(A)** analyze causes of economic growth and prosperity in the 1920s. **(B)** analyze the causes of the Great Depression, including the decline in worldwide trade, the stock market crash, and bank failures. **(25) Social studies skills.** The student communicates in written, oral, and visual forms. The student is expected to: **(C)** transfer information from one medium to another, including written to visual and statistical to written or visual, using computer software as appropriate. **(D)** create written, oral, and visual presentations of social studies information.

Chapter 14

Politics and Prosperity (1920–1929)

Introducing the Chapter

Coming out of World War I, Americans were focused on returning to normal and improving the nation's economy. Through three one-term presidencies, the country saw an economic boom, labor troubles, and the seeds of an economic disaster that loomed as the decade ended.

Time Line Activity

To provide students with practice in using the time line, ask questions such as these:

1. What impact did the Russian Revolution have on the public's perception of Communists in the United States? *(Communists were viewed as "subversives" whose movements and actions were held under suspicion.)*
2. What incident revealed the Harding administration's corruption? *(The Teapot Dome scandal of 1923)*
3. What medical breakthrough occurred during this decade? *(The 1928 discovery of penicillin by Scottish scientist Alexander Fleming)*

Chapter 14

Politics and Prosperity (1920–1929)

Coolidge backers sang this song to show their support.

THE OFFICIAL
CAMPAIGN SONG OF THE HOME TOWN COOLIDGE CLUB OF PLYMOUTH, VERMONT
KEEP COOL AND KEEP COOLIDGE
MUSIC BY BRUCE HARPER WORDS BY IDA CHEEVER GOODWIN
BAND, ORCHESTRA, MALE QUARTET & MIXED QUARTET, ARRANGEMENTS MAY BE OBTAINED FROM THE PUBLISHERS
PUBLISHED BY HOME TOWN COOLIDGE CLUB, PLYMOUTH, VERMONT

American Events

1919 During a Red Scare, the Palmer raids target suspected Communists and other "subversives." Labor strikes are widespread.

1920 Sacco and Vanzetti are arrested and later tried and convicted for murder. They are executed in 1927.

1923 Senate hearings on Teapot Dome reveal corruption in the Harding administration.

Presidential Terms: Woodrow Wilson 1913–1921 | Warren G. Harding 1921–1923 | Calvin Coolidge 1923–1929

1918 • 1920 • 1922 • 1924

World Events

1920 The Russian Civil War ends.

1921 The Chinese Communist Party is founded.

1923 In Germany, Hitler's Beer Hall Putsch fails.

1924 Soviet leader Vladimir Ilyich Lenin dies.

eTeach

Be sure to check out this month's online discussion with a Master Teacher. Go to **www.phschool.com**.

Resource Directory

Teaching Resources
- **Pacing Charts booklet**
- **Block Scheduling booklet,** p. 23
- **Units 3/4 booklet**
  - Chapter Summary, p. 51

Technology
- **Guided Reading Audiotapes (English/Spanish),** Ch. 14
- **Student Edition on Audio CD,** Ch. 14
- **Prentice Hall United States History Video Collection™** Volume 17, *The Roaring Twenties*
- **Prentice Hall Presentation Pro CD-ROM,** Ch. 14
- **Resource Pro® CD-ROM**
- **Social Studies Skills Tutor CD-ROM**
- **Companion Web site, www.phschool.com**

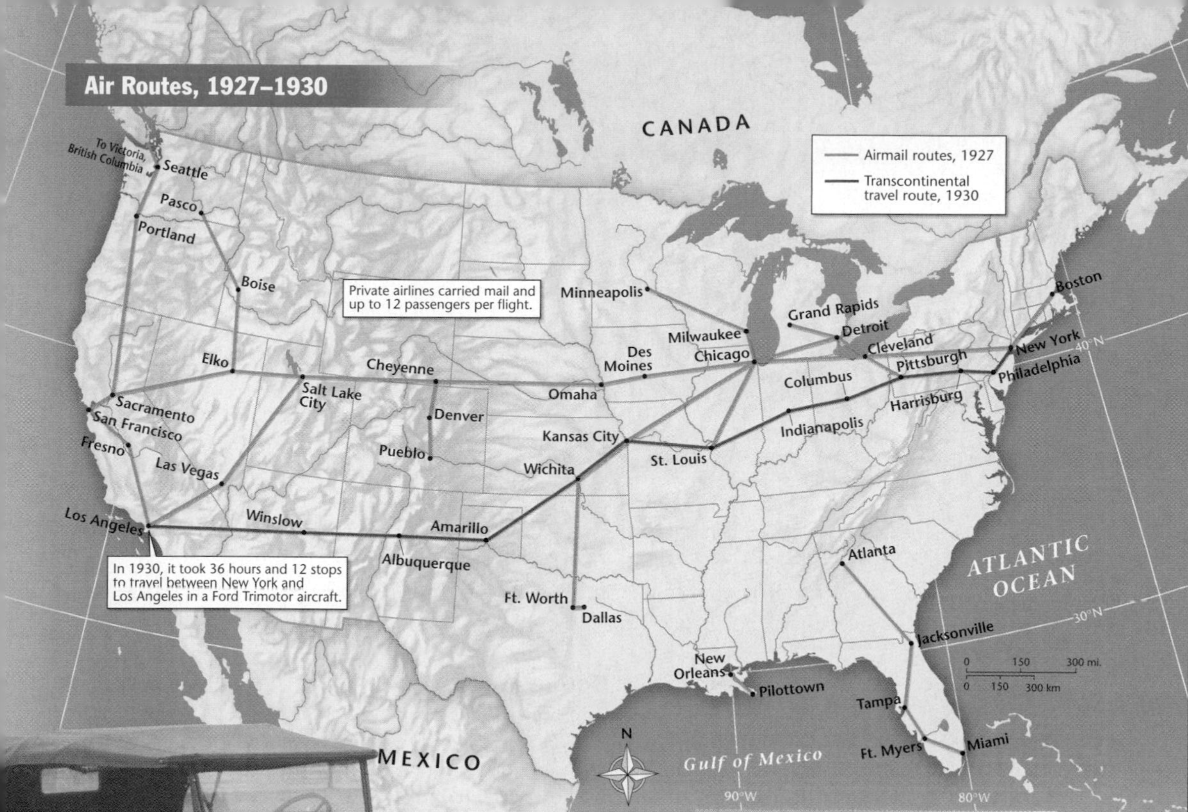

Air Routes, 1927–1930

Airmail routes, 1927
Transcontinental travel route, 1930

Private airlines carried mail and up to 12 passengers per flight.

In 1930, it took 36 hours and 12 stops to travel between New York and Los Angeles in a Ford Trimotor aircraft.

A 1929 Model A Ford Phaeton

Hard times forced many farmers to auction their land, equipment, animals, and homes.

1927 Ford's Model A automobile replaces the Model T.

1928 Nations signing the Kellogg-Briand Pact vow to resolve disputes peacefully.

1929 Home building falls by 25 percent. Two hundred companies own nearly half of all industry. Stock values reach $87 billion in October.

Herbert Hoover 1929–1933

1926 · 1928 · 1930

1928 Penicillin is discovered by Scottish scientist Alexander Fleming.

1929 The National Revolutionary Party is established in Mexico.

Air Routes, 1927–1930

Activating Prior Knowledge Did airlines of this time serve people in all parts of the country? *(No. Mail and passenger routes were limited.)*

Previewing How do you think the achievements of Charles Lindbergh and Amelia Earhart affected the airlines? *(Their exploits helped popularize the industry.)*

BACKGROUND
About the Pictures

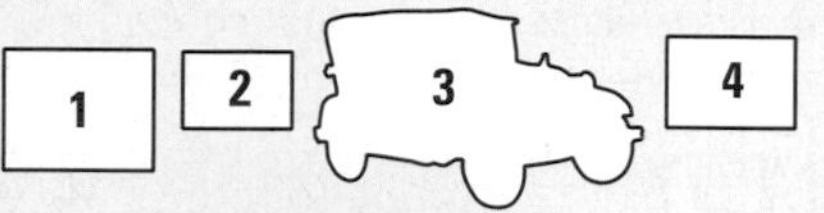

1. The trial and execution of Nicola Sacco and Bartolomeo Vanzetti caused great controversy not only in the United States but also internationally. In France a mob of people protesting the case besieged the American embassy, requiring French police and soldiers to defend the building.
2. During the 1920s most presidential campaign paraphernalia consisted of printed material, such as this song book endorsing Calvin Coolidge.
3. Originally introduced in 1927, the Ford Model A was a drastic improvement over the earlier Model T. The Model A had hydraulic brakes, a three-speed transmission complete with clutch, and safety glass for the front windshield.
4. Farmers unable to pay their bills would be forced to auction off their farm equipment and possessions at extremely low prices, reducing many of them to poverty.

BIBLIOGRAPHY

For the Teacher

Coolidge, Calvin (author), and Peter Hannaford (editor). ***The Quotable Calvin Coolidge: Sensible Words for a New Century.*** New York: Images from the Past, 2001. (Fascinating collection of Coolidge quotations, with an insightful introduction.)

Sacco, Nicola, and Bartolomeo Vanzetti (authors), and Marian Denman Frankfurter (editor), ***The Letters of Sacco and Vanzetti.*** New York: Penguin, 1997. (This collection of letters from the condemned prisoners, originally published in 1928, was reissued to coincide with the seventieth anniversary of their execution.)

For the Student

Gourley, Catherine. ***Wheels of Time: A Biography of Henry Ford.*** Brookfield, Connecticut: Millbrook Press, 1997. (Written in association with the Henry Ford Museum, this book contains many archival photographs.)

Monroe, Judy. ***The Sacco and Vanzetti Controversial Murder Trial: A Headline Court Case.*** New York: Enslow Publishers, 2000. (Did Sacco and Vanzetti get a fair trial? This book will stimulate classroom debate.)

Don't miss the exclusive interactive version of this textbook on the Web and on CD-ROM.

Section 1 A Republican Decade

Section Objectives

1. Learn about events that fueled the red scare of the early 1920s.
2. Find out about conflicts that led to the major labor strikes of 1919.
3. See how Republican leadership during the Harding and Coolidge presidencies shaped the 1920s.
4. Discover the issues that shaped the presidential election of 1928.

Bellringer

Warm-Up Activity Write on the chalkboard: "The business of the American people is business." Ask students what they think the quote means and why it might have appealed to Americans after World War I.

Activating Prior Knowledge Can students state their impressions of the American economy as World War I ended? What type of direction do students think most people wanted from the government at this time?

Reading Strategy

Have students copy the headings in this section. As they read, have them write down at least two key points under each heading. Have them focus particularly on the causes and effects of significant issues such as the red scare.

Section 1 A Republican Decade

READING FOCUS

- What events fueled the Red Scare of the early 1920s?
- What conflicts led to the major labor strikes of 1919?
- How did Republican leadership during the Harding and Coolidge presidencies shape the 1920s?
- What issues influenced the presidential election of 1928?

MAIN IDEA

Republican administrations of the 1920s pursued pro-business economic policies and an isolationist foreign policy.

KEY TERMS

communism
Red Scare
isolationism
disarmament
quota
Teapot Dome scandal
Kellogg-Briand Pact

TAKING NOTES

Copy the cause-and-effect diagram below. As you read, fill in the causes leading to the red scare and the effects the scare had on domestic issues.

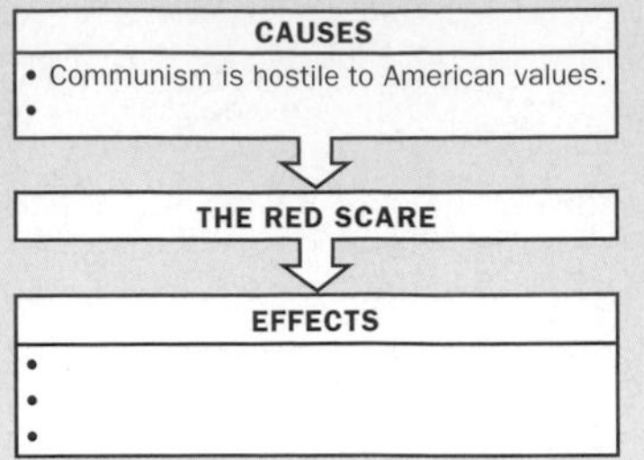

CAUSES
• Communism is hostile to American values.
THE RED SCARE
EFFECTS

VIEWING HISTORY President Warren G. Harding had promised a return to "normalcy." **Drawing Inferences** *What sort of leadership were Americans seeking in the early 1920s?*

Setting the Scene In 1920, the memory of World War I remained fresh. The Senate still refused to accept the Versailles Treaty, and debates on America's participation in the League of Nations continued. At the same time, a harsh economic downturn had begun, bringing an end to a brief postwar boom. Emerging from the shadow of the war and putting the economy back on track became significant issues in the 1920 presidential race.

The eventual winner, Republican Warren G. Harding, had the style of a leader. With his deep voice and dignified manner of speaking, he impressed people as honest and kind. But Harding doubted his own ability to serve as President, as did many of his critics. One Democrat called Harding's speeches "an army of pompous phrases moving across the landscape in search of an idea."

Nonetheless, one of his campaign speeches struck a chord with Americans. In it, Harding spelled out what the nation required in order to shake off the gloom of war:

> *"America's present need is not heroics, but healing; not nostrums [fake cures] but normalcy; not revolution, but restoration; not agitation, but adjustment; not surgery, but serenity; not the dramatic, but the dispassionate; not experiment, but equipoise [stability]; not submergence in internationality, but sustainment in triumphant nationality."*
>
> —Warren G. Harding, Boston, May 14, 1920

Harding's call for a return to "normalcy" became a hallmark of his campaign speeches. Voters got the message. In a nation weary of war abroad and sacrifice at home, the mere promise of "normalcy" gave Harding a landslide victory over Democrat James Cox and his running mate, Franklin D. Roosevelt.

Caption Answers

Viewing History Americans wanted strong, reassuring leaders who promised stability and prosperity.

Resource Directory

Teaching Resources

Learning Styles Lesson Plans booklet, p. 44
Guided Reading and Review booklet, p. 86
Learning with Documents booklet (Primary Source Activity) *Industrializing the USSR,* p. 26
Biography, Literature, and Comparing Primary Sources booklet (Biography) *Walter Lippmann,* p. 26

Technology

Section Reading Support Transparencies
Guided Reading Audiotapes (English/Spanish), Ch. 14
Student Edition on Audio CD, Ch. 14
Prentice Hall Presentation Pro CD-ROM, Ch. 14
Companion Web site, www.phschool.com

The Red Scare

"Normalcy" appealed to Americans in 1920 because events within the country and abroad seemed anything but normal. Upheaval in faraway Russia and a series of strikes and bombings at home convinced many people that political violence posed a real threat to the United States.

The Russian Revolution As you read in an earlier chapter, Russia's absolute ruler, Czar Nicholas II, lost his hold on power in March 1917. The czar's popularity had been declining as a result of several tragically poor decisions, including leading his country into World War I. The war brought devastating casualties and severe food shortages. With riots in the streets and the army too weak to protect him, Nicholas was forced to abdicate. A new government formed, led by Alexander Kerensky. Kerensky pledged to remain in the European war, a decision that hurt him politically. Weary of war and political turmoil, Russia's workers and peasants fell under the sway of more radical ideas.

Promising "peace, land, and bread," revolutionary leader Vladimir I. Lenin undermined Kerensky's power. Although in the minority, Lenin and his followers took the name Bolsheviks, Russian for "majority," and adopted the red flag as their party's emblem. With such slogans as "End the war! All land to the peasants!" the Bolsheviks overthrew Kerensky's government on November 6, 1917. They then made peace with Germany and put all privately owned farms, industries, land, and transportation under government ownership.

Civil war broke out almost immediately. Lenin's Red Army, often simply called the Reds, met resistance from several armies, known collectively as the Whites. The Whites included former landowners, government officials, Russian army leaders and others. Britain, France, Japan, and the United States, whose investments in Russia had been seized by Bolsheviks, backed the Whites.

After more than two and a half years, the Reds triumphed in 1920. Two years later, their new nation became known as the Union of Soviet Socialist Republics (USSR), or the Soviet Union.

Lenin made communism the official ideology of Russia and, later, the Soviet Union. This ideology was openly hostile to American beliefs and values, such as capitalism, private ownership of land and business, and First Amendment freedoms. For Lenin and his followers, **communism** meant the following:

1. The government owned all land and property.
2. A single political party controlled the government.
3. The needs of the country always took priority over the rights of individuals.

If isolated, a Communist country could be open to attack. For communism to survive, Lenin believed that it would have to be spread throughout the world.

To a working class long oppressed by czarist rule, communism's appeal lay in the promise of a classless society, its wealth shared according to need. In practice communism evolved into something far different, especially when shaped by Joseph Stalin, who led the Soviet Union after Lenin's death in 1924. Instead of "peace, land, and bread," Stalin used terror to force the peasantry onto collectivized farms. The result was great famine.

American Fears Russia's intention to spread communism to other countries alarmed many Americans. They distrusted Europeans already, blaming them for starting World War I. Some Americans grew concerned that among the masses of

Focus on GOVERNMENT

The Origins of Communism The communal sharing of wealth is an old concept, one often embraced by religious groups. The Shakers, who settled in New York in the mid-eighteenth century, worked together and shared wealth and property, as did the later Amana colonies of Iowa. Eventually, the huge disparities of wealth created by industrialization transformed communism into a general social ideal.

Followers of this ideal soon split into factions. Both Socialists and Communists believed that wealth should be shared according to need but differed on how to achieve this goal. Some socialists put their hopes in democratic processes and labor unions, others in terrorism. Communists adopted Lenin's idea of the "dictatorship of proletariat," which referred to a period when workers would rule through a single authoritarian party. The party would regulate all activities until it had achieved a classless society and a world union of socialist republics. At left, Lenin addresses a crowd.

LESSON PLAN

Focus As the country entered the post–World War I era, the mood was one of discontent and fear. Americans turned to the Republican Party for security. Ask students what policies the Republicans followed in the 1920s to encourage economic and social stability.

Instruct Discuss why Americans were feeling insecure and frightened about the future after World War I. Why did the Russian Revolution and postwar economic adjustments make people feel uneasy? Why did labor disputes increase?

Ask students to describe the economic and foreign policies of Harding and Coolidge. How were laws restricting immigration an attempt to restore normalcy?

Assess/Reteach Do students feel that the government's pro-business stance in the 1920s was compatible or incompatible with the prevailing isolationist mood? Discuss.

CUSTOMIZE FOR ...

Gifted and Talented

Have students compare and contrast the main tenets of a Communist versus a capitalist regime. Ask them to address such aspects as landownership, political parties, and individual rights.

ACTIVITY
Connecting with Economics

To help students understand the red scare, propose that communism will replace the capitalist system. Divide students into groups and assign to each one of the following roles: factory worker, factory owner, investor, government official, consumer. From the perspective determined by each of their roles, have students decide if the new system would improve or worsen their lives. How might the wish for "normalcy" have intensified these views? **(Verbal/Linguistic)**

BACKGROUND
Connections to Today

During the Red Scare, when then–U.S. Attorney General A. Mitchell Palmer relentlessly pursued "subversives," thousands of people—mainly immigrants—were arrested and held without trial. In the immediate aftermath of the September 11, 2001, terrorist attacks in New York City, Washington, D.C., and Pennsylvania, the United States government showed that it had learned from history's lessons. Congress quickly passed House Concurrent Resolution 227, declaring "that in the quest to identify, bring to justice and punish the perpetrators and sponsors of the terrorist attacks. . . the civil rights and civil liberties of all Americans, including Arab Americans, American Muslims, and Americans from South Asia, should be protected. . . ."

READING CHECK

Abroad: The Bolshevik seizure of power in Russia; Communist agitation in Germany; a Communist regime in Hungary. In U.S.: red scare; strikes; bomb explosions; mistrust of recent immigrants.

INTERPRETING POLITICAL CARTOONS Anarchists on American soil were a matter of concern at the time of this 1919 illustration. **Analyzing Visual Information** *How does the artist use symbolism to convey a message?*

European immigrants entering the United States were Communists and other radicals. American worries about foreigners from Europe reached new heights.

In early 1919, Russian-backed Communists tried to overthrow the new German government, and Communists came to power in Hungary. Similar chaos threatened to seep into the United States, or so many people thought. In February, shipyard workers went on strike in Seattle, and the mayor proclaimed them "revolutionists." In April, a number of bombs were sent through the mail, addressed mainly to government officials—including Seattle's mayor. One of the bombs reached its destination and exploded, severely injuring a Georgia senator's housekeeper. Newspapers whipped up the public's anxiety with sensational stories about these events. Soon the United States was in the grip of a **Red Scare,** an intense fear of communism and other politically radical ideas. Americans called for known Communists to be jailed or driven out of the country.

READING CHECK
What events abroad and in the United States caused concern among war-weary Americans?

Schenck* v. *U.S. To some people, a 1919 Supreme Court decision seemed to justify jailing Communists. During World War I, a war opponent named Charles Schenck had mailed letters to men who were drafted, urging them not to report for duty. He was convicted of breaking the Espionage Act, a wartime law aimed at spies and people who opposed the war. Schenck appealed the case, claiming that he was only exercising his right to speak freely.

In the Court's written opinion, Justice Oliver Wendell Holmes, Jr., said that the government is justified in silencing free speech when there is a "clear and present danger" to the nation. He compared what Schenck had done to shouting "Fire!" in a crowded theater. Such an action could cause a dangerous panic. Some have argued that in equating what was reasonable with what was constitutional, Holmes expanded the powers of the Supreme Court beyond the original intent of the Constitution.

Gitlow* v. *New York The Supreme Court's decision in another radical speech case in this period had later significance. The state of New York had convicted Bernard Gitlow, a Socialist, of "criminal anarchy" for publishing calls in 1919 to overthrow the government by force. Gitlow appealed on the basis that New York had violated his constitutional guarantees of freedom of speech and of the press.

In the past, the Supreme Court had argued that the Bill of Rights protected individuals only against actions of the federal, not the state, governments. In this case, the Court upheld Gitlow's conviction, saying that he had indeed urged people to violent revolution. At the same time, it affirmed that the Fourteenth Amendment protected civil rights against restriction by state governments. Since *Gitlow,* the Court has used the Fourteenth Amendment to make other provisions of the Bill of Rights apply to state actions.

The Palmer Raids In June 1919, bombs exploded in several cities. One explosion severely damaged the home of A. Mitchell Palmer, the Attorney General of the United States. Although Palmer escaped injury, the bombings convinced him that radicals were conspiring to overthrow the government. He began a campaign to identify and root out groups whose activities posed a "clear and present danger" to the country.

Later that year the Justice Department, headed by Palmer, set up a special force to conduct raids and arrest suspected "subversives" (people trying to subvert, or overthrow, the government). Targets included Communists, Socialists,

CAPTION ANSWERS

Interpreting Political Cartoons The American flag, a symbol of freedom and democracy, is used to show how the United States can be destroyed by the "flames" of anarchy.

and anarchists, or people who oppose all government. Palmer approached the task zealously. On the night of December 31, 1919, he stated: "Any movement, however cloaked or dissembled, designed to undermine the government, will be met with unflinching, persistent, aggressive warfare."

On January 2, 1920, federal agents in 33 cities arrested thousands of suspected radicals, and without evidence, charged them with anarchy. Most of the suspects had been born overseas. Many were completely innocent. Still, more than 500 of them were later deported, or sent back to their homeland.

At first, Palmer received strong support for his actions. The army's chief of staff urged that those deported be sent away on "ships of stone with sails of lead." Popular preacher Billy Sunday suggested that a firing squad would save money on ships.

The Red Scare created such a frenzy that in April 1920, the New York State Assembly voted to expel five recently elected Socialist members. Many people protested that the assembly was violating the public's right to choose its own representatives, but the Socialists never took office.

Americans expected the worst on May 1, 1920, an annual Socialist holiday honoring workers and labor organizations. On that day, according to Palmer, the nation would experience a general labor strike and widespread bombings. Newspapers predicted a major crisis. When May 1 came and went quietly, the press turned on Palmer, and Americans lost faith in him.

Sacco and Vanzetti The Red Scare played a part in one of the most controversial events in United States history. The story began on April 15, 1920, when gunmen robbed and killed the guard and paymaster of a shoe factory in South Braintree, Massachusetts. A few weeks later, police arrested two Italian immigrants in connection with the crime.

One, Nicola Sacco, was a shoemaker, and the other, Bartolomeo Vanzetti, was a fish peddler. Both of them were also anarchists. Police found guns on both men when they were arrested; Sacco's gun was the same model used in the crime. Yet many Americans suspected that the two men were arrested mainly because they were immigrants with radical beliefs. The case drew international attention and controversy.

After a trial that many observers called unfair, a jury found Sacco and Vanzetti guilty. Their lawyers appealed the case to higher courts again and again for years, but the convictions were upheld. The two men were sentenced to death in April 1927, and despite mass protests, they died in the electric chair four months later.

Labor Strikes

A wave of strikes helped fuel the Red Scare in 1919. Strikers included telephone operators in New England, machinists in Ohio, and construction workers in Texas. The number of strikes per month climbed from around 175 in March of that year to around 370 in August. Many Americans believed that Communist "agitators" were behind this labor unrest. Most of the strikes, however, had a simpler cause. In

COMPARING HISTORIANS' VIEWPOINTS

The Sacco and Vanzetti Verdict

Over the years, historians have examined and reexamined evidence and transcripts from the Sacco and Vanzetti trial. Opinions regarding their guilt or innocence, and the fairness of the trial, have changed over time.

Analyzing Viewpoints Compare the main arguments made by the writers.

Vanzetti Was Innocent

"Even if one accepts the possibility that someone other than Sacco fired the [murder weapon], Sacco knew who that someone was.

Vanzetti's innocence is, at least for me, confirmed by . . . contradictions to the court testimony. . . . Yet it would have been like Vanzetti to go to the chair rather than betray a friend."

—*Francis Russell,* Tragedy in Dedham: The Story of the Sacco-Vanzetti Case

Opposed to the Verdict

"Any attempt to establish the guilt or innocence of Sacco and Vanzetti must be based upon an analysis of the evidence. . . . The revelations of the state police files, the grand jury proceeding, and the prosecution notebooks show that virtually every piece of evidence against the two men ultimately rested upon falsehoods and fabrications."

—*William Young and David E. Kaiser,* Postmortem: New Evidence in the Case of Sacco and Vanzetti

CUSTOMIZE FOR ...

Less Proficient Readers

Have students create a who, what, when, where, why, and how list of the events that led to the arrest, conviction, and execution of Sacco and Vanzetti. They should take into account Justice Felix Frankfurter's observation: "Outside the courtroom the Red hysteria was rampant; it was allowed to dominate within."

ACTIVITY

Connecting with History and Conflict

Upon learning that he had been sentenced to death, Bartolomeo Vanzetti addressed the judge. In part, he said, " . . . my conviction is that I have suffered for things that I am guilty of. I am suffering because I am a radical and indeed I am a radical; I have suffered because I was an Italian, and indeed I am an Italian . . . but I am so convinced to be right that if you could execute me two times, and if I could be reborn two other times, I would live again to do what I have done already." Hold a classroom discussion in which students analyze Vanzetti's statement. Do they think Vanzetti is admitting he is guilty of the crime of which he has been convicted? Or do they think he means that he is "guilty" merely of being an Italian and a radical? After the discussion, have students write a paragraph expressing their interpretation of Vanzetti's statement. **(Verbal/Linguistic)**

BACKGROUND

The Never-Ending Wrong

The writer Katherine Anne Porter believed fervently in the innocence of Sacco and Vanzetti, and she was part of a group protesting their innocence. Porter became disillusioned not only with the trial, but also with her fellow protesters. Fifty years after the 1927 execution of Sacco and Vanzetti, Porter wrote,". . . [t]here are many trials such as these in which the victim was already condemned to death before the trial took place. . . . These are trials in which the judge, the counsel, the jury, and the witnesses are the criminals, not the accused."

But what stung Porter most 50 years later was that the protest leaders themselves had wanted to see Sacco and Vanzetti executed because of their propaganda value as martyrs. Wrote Porter, "I remarked to our Communist leader that even then, at that late time, I still hoped the lives of Sacco and Vanzetti might be saved and that they would be granted another trial. 'Saved?' she said. 'Who wants them saved? What earthly good would they do us alive?'"

Activity

Connecting with Citizenship

Have students review this quote by Calvin Coolidge: "There is no right to strike against the public safety by anybody, anywhere, anytime." What is their opinion of the quote? Have them play the role of a newspaper editorial writer who is writing a brief essay to comment on the Boston police strike, either for or against. Have students write their editorial specifically in response to Coolidge's statement. **(Verbal/Linguistic)**

Background

Biography

Emma Goldman (1869–1940), a native of Lithuania, immigrated to the United States from Russia in 1885. "Red Emma," as she became known, was an active member of anarchist and socialist groups both before and after her arrival in this country and was a popular lecturer on the topics of anarchism and social problems. She also lectured about many European dramatists, including Henrik Ibsen, August Strindberg, George Bernard Shaw, and others.

Early in her career, Goldman advocated violence as an acceptable way to solve problems in a society. Over time, she rejected that approach. Even so, these early views, as well as her outspoken protests against the United States' entry into World War I, marked her as a dangerous subversive, and she was among those deported during the Palmer raids of 1919.

early 1919, prices of food, clothing, housing, and other necessities soared. By 1920, inflation brought the cost of living to twice that of prewar levels. Most workers went on strike because the standard of living they had achieved during World War I had declined.

The Boston Police Strike Boston police officers had not received a pay increase since the start of the war. In September 1919, they took steps to organize a union, even though department rules banned labor unions. After the Boston police commissioner fired 19 officers for union activity, the whole force voted to strike.

Rioting broke out in Boston within hours after the police walked off the job, and it lasted through the night. In the morning, the mayor sent out a volunteer police force to restore order. Later in the day, Massachusetts governor Calvin Coolidge called out the state guard, but by then, calm had largely returned to Boston. "There is no right to strike against the public safety by anybody, anywhere, anytime," Coolidge stated. The future President gained national attention for his firm response to the strike.

Steel and Coal Strikes Later in September, steelworkers launched a strike against the United States Steel Corporation. At the time, steelworkers put in 12-hour shifts, and their work week averaged more than 65 hours. Backed by the American Federation of Labor (AFL), the workers asked for an 8-hour day and a 48-hour week. Some 350,000 workers walked off the job.

The strike nearly shut down a huge steel mill in Gary, Indiana, and it affected plants in several other cities as well. Claiming that the strike was the work of Communists, U.S. Steel set out to stop it. The company hired a private police force, which killed 18 strikers and beat hundreds more.

The company also brought in thousands of African American workers from the South to break the strike. The state and federal governments supported management by supplying troops to control the strikers and protect the strikebreakers. After ten weeks, the AFL called off the strike when workers, realizing that they could not win, started heading back to work.

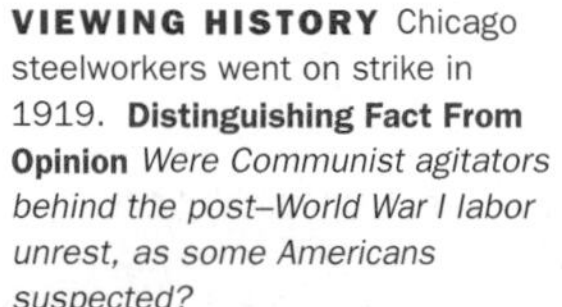

VIEWING HISTORY Chicago steelworkers went on strike in 1919. **Distinguishing Fact From Opinion** *Were Communist agitators behind the post–World War I labor unrest, as some Americans suspected?*

Caption Answers

Viewing History No. The main cause of labor unrest had to do with the fact that wages were too low to keep up with the rising cost of living.

RESOURCE DIRECTORY

Technology

Sounds of an Era Audio CD *Warren Harding*

Soft-coal miners also went on strike in that troubled fall of 1919, demanding higher wages. Their union, the United Mine Workers of America (UMW), had made a no-strike agreement during the war that they claimed had ended with the armistice. The Wilson administration argued that the agreement was still in effect. When the miners struck in November, Attorney General Palmer persuaded a court to order the strikers back to work. Regardless, the miners continued their walkout until early December, when a coal shortage developed. To end the strike, a government-established coal commission granted the miners a 14 percent pay raise.

Strikes Decline Most Americans opposed strikes. They saw them as anti-American and likely to result in violence. They also distrusted labor unions and the immigrant workers they represented, assuming they were influenced by radical ideas. Actually, the largest labor union by far in the United States, the AFL, did not fit this description at all. At its convention in 1919, the AFL went out of its way to declare its opposition to labor radicalism and to communism. Nevertheless, the union stuck by its main goals—to fight for higher wages, shorter hours, and the right to organize workers.

Membership in labor unions peaked at 5 million workers during the Red Scare of 1919–1920. Then it dropped sharply to a level that stayed fairly steady throughout the 1920s. When union growth leveled, the number of strikes declined. These changes to organized labor had a range of causes. Public opposition hurt unions, as did the lack of support from the government. President Wilson called the Boston police strike a "crime against civilization" and warned that striking for higher wages only drove up prices. Other causes were economic. The economic downturn that began in 1920 severely reduced the number of employed workers. The following economic boom brought higher wages, which undercut both the workers' desire to seek union representation and their need to strike.

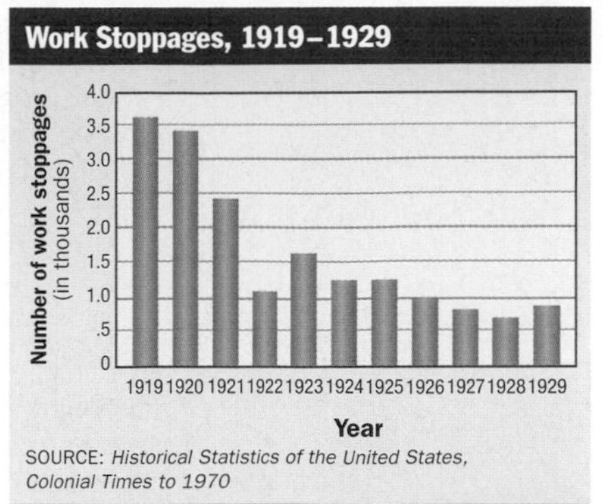

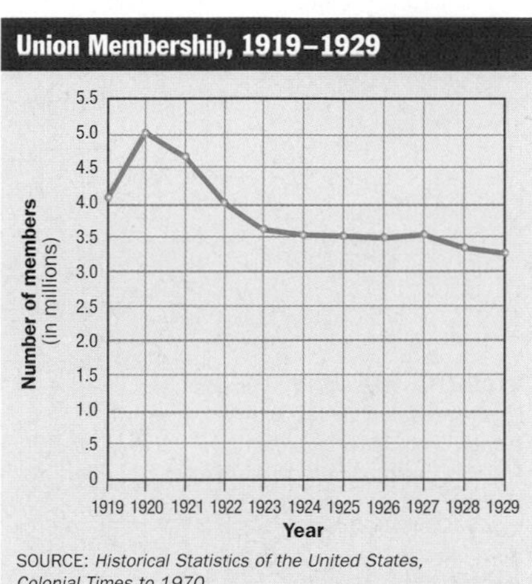

INTERPRETING GRAPHS
The post–World War I years were stormy ones for labor and business, until a booming economy caused wages to rise. **Making Comparisons** *How do union membership and the number of work stoppages reflect changes in labor?*

Republican Leadership

The Red Scare had important political consequences. Americans felt that the Republican Party was more likely to restore stability than the Democratic Party. Starting with the 1920 election, Republicans solidified their power and dominated all three branches of government for the rest of the decade. Republican Presidents Warren G. Harding, Calvin Coolidge, and Herbert Hoover served from 1921 to 1933. Republicans held the majority in Congress during this period. In addition, Supreme Court decisions of the era reflected the influence of its new chief justice, former President William Howard Taft, appointed by Harding in 1921.

Republican leaders agreed on basic policies and goals. Generally, they favored business and sought social stability. Many of these leaders were, in fact, businessmen who believed that social stability promoted economic growth.

The Harding Presidency

President Harding took office as the Red Scare and the labor strikes were beginning to subside. In that respect, the country did seem to be getting back to "normalcy."

Sounds of an Era

Listen to President Harding's speech "Return to Normalcy" and other sounds from the 1920s.

ACTIVITY
Connecting with Citizenship

Harding's election was the first ever broadcast by radio, on station KDKA in Pittsburgh. Have students research this election, and then have a group of interested students create a radio play in which they simulate a portion of the broadcast election results.
(Verbal/Linguistic)

BACKGROUND
A Diverse Nation

Many advances in aviation technology occurred during the 1920s, allowing the business of carrying passengers by air to expand. New navigational instruments were available by the end of the decade which allowed aircraft to be flown safely in conditions of poor visibility, such as bad weather or darkness. There were also powerful and reliable new aircraft engines of an improved air-cooled radial design (such as the engine which powered Charles Lindbergh's *Spirit of St. Louis* on his transatlantic flight). These and other advances allowed commercial air travel to begin to be seen as a realistic alternative for the traveling public.

TEST PREPARATION

Have students read the paragraphs under "The Boston Police Strike" on the previous page and then complete the sentence below.

Based on the passage, you can infer that—

- **(A)** Coolidge believed this strike should be stopped, as it presented a danger to the general public.
- **B** Coolidge did not support strikes under any circumstances.
- **C** Coolidge favored expanding the role of government to stop all strikes.
- **D** Coolidge sympathized with the police officers.

CAPTION ANSWERS

Interpreting Graphs As union membership leveled off throughout the 1920s, work stoppages fell to a much lower level than had been the case in 1919–1920.

ACTIVITY

Connecting with Government

President Harding was famous for his long-winded, convoluted oratorical style, which he called "bloviating"—a made-up word that is a conjunction of "blowhard" and "oration." Here is an example of a portion of one of Harding's "bloviations," taken from his Presidential Inaugural Address: "We have mistaken unpreparedness to embrace it to be a challenge of the reality, and due concern for making all citizens fit for participation will give added strength of citizenship and magnify our achievement."

Have students study this long-winded sentence fragment, and then have them read current news accounts to find modern-day examples of "bloviation." **(Verbal/Linguistic)**

From the Archives of

American Heritage®

About the Presidents

Warren G. Harding (1921–1923) was worrying about his chances of re-election to the Senate when a group of powerful Republicans asked him how he'd like to be President. He had the qualities they were looking for in a candidate: pro-business, conservative, and isolationist. But above all, they knew they could control Warren Harding. After giving him their party's nomination, the powerbrokers kept Harding from campaigning. They were afraid he'd say too much. When he won the election, they demanded paybacks. Harding knew his friends were not the most talented men in government, but he gave them jobs anyway. Later he admitted, "I am not worried about my enemies. It is my friends that are keeping me awake nights." Source: David Jacobs, "Warren G. Harding," *The American Heritage® Pictorial History of the Presidents of the United States,* vol. 2, 1968.

Caption Answers

Viewing History Possible answer: Ford, Firestone, and (to a lesser extent) Edison represent big business. Harding shared their interest in encouraging the growth of business. He also most likely shared their antipathy to labor unions.

Harding made some wise Cabinet appointments. An able administrator, Herbert Hoover reorganized the office of Secretary of Commerce. Charles Evans Hughes, a former Supreme Court justice, worked for world peace as Secretary of State. One of the nation's most powerful businessmen, Andrew Mellon, became Treasury Secretary. Serving under Harding and his two Republican successors, Mellon shaped the economic policies of the 1920s.

Harding showed poor judgment in many of his other appointments, however. He gave important jobs to friends and acquaintances, many of whom were inexperienced, incompetent, or dishonest. These choices eventually overwhelmed his presidency and his life.

Foreign Policy After the war, many Americans wished to avoid political or economic alliances with foreign countries, a policy called **isolationism.** Harding's opposition to American membership in the League of Nations reflected those wishes, and he made no attempt to join. Yet the President wanted to establish international peace and stability. To reach this goal, he worked with other nations, while carefully avoiding "entangling alliances" that might threaten the independence of the United States.

One road to peace and stability involved finding ways to prevent war. Harding called for **disarmament,** a program in which the nations of the world would voluntarily give up their weapons. He convened the Washington Conference in 1921 to discuss this plan. At the conference, several major military powers signed a treaty limiting the size of their navies.

The United States, now a major economic power, continued to engage in trade throughout the world. Harding promoted the expansion of trade, saying that American business must "go on to the peaceful commercial conquest of the world." He also acted to protect business at home. In 1922, Congress, with Harding's support, passed the Fordney-McCumber Tariff, which raised import taxes to historically high levels. The tariff especially discouraged imports that competed with goods made by new American industries, such as china, toys, and chemicals.

The new tariff angered the European nations who faced demands from the United States to pay their American war debts. To raise the money necessary to pay off those debts, Europeans needed to sell goods to the United States. Yet the tariff acted as a barrier to their exports. Great Britain and France argued forcefully for the cancellation of their debts. To resolve the issue, Congress agreed in 1922 to scale back those debts to a level that better suited each country's ability to pay.

VIEWING HISTORY President Harding (seated center) with (seated from left) Henry Ford, Thomas Edison, tire manufacturer Harvey Firestone, and William Anderson, Methodist Bishop of Cincinnati. **Drawing Inferences** *What goals and ideals might Harding and his companions in this photo have had in common?*

The United States hoped to apply the same approach to another sensitive international issue, German war reparations. In the early 1920s, inflation left Germany's economy in ruins. The German government simply could not afford the huge bill for war costs that the Allies demanded in the Versailles Treaty. Along with the British, the United States pushed for a plan to help the German economy recover enough to pay its debts. A special commission developed the Dawes Plan, which the Allies and Germany signed in 1924. The plan set a payment schedule, reorganized the German national bank, and approved a loan to Germany.

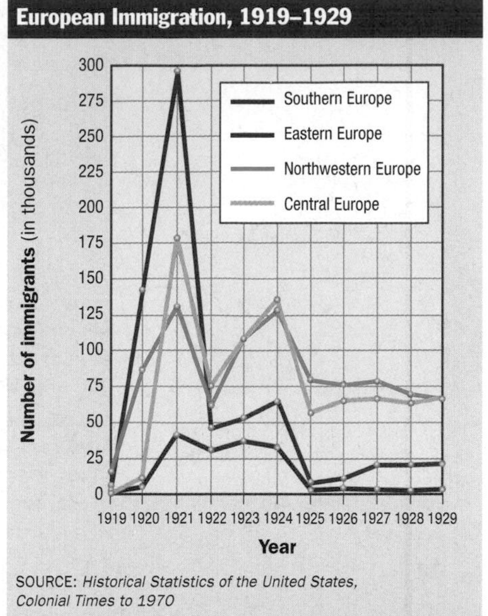

SOURCE: *Historical Statistics of the United States, Colonial Times to 1970*

INTERPRETING GRAPHS
The graph shows European immigration to the United States before and after immigration legislation was passed. **Analyzing Information** *Describe the effect of Harding's immigration policies on the number of immigrants from eastern and southern Europe as shown by the graph.*

Domestic Issues As Americans became more isolationist, they also became more nativist. Nativism is a movement favoring native-born Americans over immigrants. It had first appeared in the 1800s, but after World War I it flared up again, for several reasons:

Patriotism Many Americans believed that foreigners could never be fully loyal to the United States.

Religion Nativists, who were mostly Protestants, had long mistrusted immigrants who were Catholics, Orthodox Christians, or Jews.

Urban conditions Americans often blamed the problems in cities, such as slums and corruption, on the immigrants who lived in them.

Jobs Workers feared that immigrants would take their jobs away from them.

Red Scare Some immigrants came from the most unstable parts of Europe, where World War I had started. Nativists believed that these immigrants might hold or adopt radical political ideas, and spread them to the United States.

Nativists reacted to the sharp postwar rise in immigration with calls for government action. In 1921, at Harding's request, Congress passed a law restricting immigration. Although only a temporary measure, the law included an important feature whose impact would long be felt: a **quota,** or numerical limit, imposed on immigrants representing certain ethnic groups or nations. According to the law, a group's numerical limit equaled 3 percent of that group's total United States population as of the 1910 census.

A permanent measure, the National Origins Act, passed in 1924. This law reduced the quota to 2 percent and based it on the census of 1890. In 1890, the population of immigrants from Italy, Poland, Russia, and other southern and eastern European countries was low. As a result, the law severely limited continued immigration from those countries. The law went further, prohibiting the entry of "aliens ineligible to citizenship," a category that referred specifically to the Japanese. (The Chinese Exclusion Act had already shut down immigration from China.)

Recall that social stability became a basic goal of Republicans in the 1920s. President Harding believed that restrictions on immigration helped the cause of social stability. He also believed that restrictions on the civil rights of American citizens hurt that cause. In 1921, in front of a segregated audience in Birmingham, Alabama, Harding made a surprisingly bold speech on equality:

> *"I want to see the time come when black men will regard themselves as full participants in the benefits and duties of American citizenship; . . . We cannot go on . . . with one great section of our population . . . set off from real contribution to solving national issues, because of division on race lines."*
>
> —Warren G. Harding, October 26, 1921

ACTIVITY
Connecting with Citizenship

As he left office in 1969, Charles de Gaulle, then president of France, commented: "Patriotism is when love of your own people comes first; nationalism, when hate for people other than your own comes first." Hold a classroom discussion about this statement, and then ask students to write brief essays in response to it. Have students include their own definitions of patriotism and nationalism in the essays and give examples of each, either contemporary or historical. **(Verbal/Linguistic)**

BACKGROUND
Recent Scholarship

One outgrowth of virulent nativist sentiment was legislation such as the Chinese Exclusion Act of 1882. This act, which remained in force in the U.S. until 1943, arose from anti-Chinese demonstrations in San Francisco in the 1870s and 1880s. It was intended to protect American jobs and wages from what was seen as an uncontrollable influx of immigrants from China.

Claiming America: Constructing Chinese American Identities During the Exclusion Era is a collection of essays about the formation of an ethnic identity during the time that immigration from China was barred and the rights of Chinese living in America were severely restricted. The book presents accounts of Chinese immigrants as well as essays that describe the struggle of members of the next generation to define their identity as Chinese Americans and to achieve the kinds of opportunities afforded other immigrant populations.

CUSTOMIZE FOR ...
Less Proficient Writers

Have students reread the section "The Coolidge Presidency." Then have students list specific actions or decisions by Coolidge that supported his opinion that "the chief business of the American People is business."

CAPTION ANSWERS

Interpreting Graphs Immigration legislation was passed in 1921 and in 1924. These acts caused a sharp drop in the number of immigrants from both southern and eastern Europe, but especially from southern Europe.

Activity

Connecting with Government

The Teapot Dome affair was but one of many corruption scandals to blemish the American presidency over the centuries. Divide the class into small groups. Ask each group to research and offer an oral report on a corruption scandal that erupted during a presidency, such as the "Whiskey Ring" scandal during U. S. Grant's presidency or the Iran-Contra affair that occurred during Ronald Reagan's presidency. What has been the effect of such political incidents on the views of U.S. citizens concerning the role of the federal government? **(Verbal/Linguistic)**

From the Archives of

AmericanHeritage®

About the Presidents

Calvin Coolidge (1923–1929) believed in laissez faire in domestic matters, whereas in foreign affairs he was an active diplomat. When an earthquake devastated Japan, he sent the Pacific fleet to help. His excellent international appointments improved U.S. relations abroad. Coolidge himself set a precedent by addressing the Sixth InterAmerican Conference in Havana, Cuba. The United States took part in several conferences sponsored by the League of Nations as well. But the isolationist tendencies of the 1920s prevented U.S. entry into the Permanent Court of International Justice, which Coolidge favored. Isolationism also led to the Immigration Act of 1924. This act included a provision, which Coolidge opposed, banning Japanese immigration. Twenty years later, this ban would help lead to war in the Pacific. Source: Michael Harwood, "Calvin Coolidge," *The American Heritage® Pictorial History of the Presidents of the United States,* vol. 2, 1968.

The Democrats in 1924 tried to use public anger over the Teapot Dome affair to defeat the Republicans, as this campaign artifact shows.

African American onlookers cheered the President's words, but the white members of the audience responded with shocked silence. Later, Harding introduced federal anti-lynching legislation, but his proposal died in the Senate.

The Teapot Dome Scandal At the start of 1923, the economy was growing steadily. A period of prosperity had begun, and Harding enjoyed strong popularity. Then, major corruption scandals in Harding's administration came to light. There was no evidence that the President was involved in the scandals. In fact, Harding became terribly disturbed when he heard of the scandals, and the strain may have contributed to his death, possibly from heart problems, on August 2, 1923.

By 1924, the extent of the corruption in Harding's administration was widely known. One official had stolen government funds. Others had taken bribes in return for help in getting contracts approved or laws passed. Several other officials were also accused of wrong-doing, and two committed suicide.

The worst Harding scandal came to be known as the **Teapot Dome scandal.** In 1921 and 1922, Harding's Secretary of the Interior, Albert B. Fall, secretly gave oil-drilling rights on government oil fields in Elk Hills, California, and Teapot Dome, Wyoming, to two private oil companies. In return, Fall received more than $300,000 in illegal payments and gifts disguised as loans.

The Coolidge Presidency

Vice President Calvin Coolidge was visiting his parents in Vermont on August 3, 1923, when word arrived of Harding's death. At 2:30 A.M., by the light of a kerosene lamp, Coolidge's father, a justice of the peace, administered to him the oath of office of President of the United States.

Coolidge was still widely respected for his actions as governor of Massachusetts. He had played no part in the Harding scandals. In fact, one Democrat said that Coolidge's "great task was to restore the dignity and prestige of the presidency when it had reached the lowest ebb in our history." After finishing Harding's term, Coolidge ran in the 1924 election, defeating Democrat John W. Davis and Progressive Robert M. La Follette with the slogan "Keep cool with Coolidge." Coolidge had a reputation as a skilled public speaker, but in private he was a man of few words. Someone said of him that "he could be silent in five languages."

Laissez Faire In one sentence, Coolidge summed up a major theme of the Republican decade: "The chief business of the American people is business." The best that the government could do, he believed, was to leave business alone and allow it to grow. This laissez-faire business policy helped fuel the tremendous economic boom of the 1920s.

For the most part, Congress supported a laissez-faire approach to business. It lowered income and inheritance tax rates and approved higher tariffs that benefited domestic manufacturing. Coolidge was so insistent on a minimal role for government that when Herbert Hoover, his Secretary of Commerce, urged him to regulate the buying of stocks on easy credit, he refused. When Mississippi River flood victims appealed to him for help, he said that government had no duty to protect citizens "against the hazards of the elements."

Coolidge's effort to have government do less drew criticism from those who saw it as a failure to take action. In 1926, the noted newspaper columnist Walter Lippmann said: "Mr. Coolidge's genius for inactivity is developed to a very high point. It is a grim, determined, alert inactivity, which keeps Mr. Coolidge occupied constantly."

RESOURCE DIRECTORY

Teaching Resources

Units 3/4 booklet

- Section 1 Quiz, p. 52

Guide to the Essentials

- Section 1 Summary, p. 68

Technology

Sounds of an Era Audio CD *Calvin Coolidge,* 1924 recording (time: one minute, 15 seconds)

Kellogg-Briand Pact Coolidge continued Harding's approach to international issues. He wanted peace and stability without getting the United States too deeply involved with other nations. Coolidge, however, left most foreign-policy decisions up to his Secretary of State, Frank B. Kellogg.

In 1927, Kellogg received an unusual suggestion from French Foreign Minister Aristide Briand. Briand thought that their two countries should formally agree not to declare war on each other. An isolationist at heart, Kellogg feared that such a treaty might entangle the United States with France. When other nations agreed to participate, however, Kellogg helped Briand iron out the details. Under the **Kellogg-Briand Pact,** 15 nations pledged not to use the threat of war in their dealings with one another. More than 60 nations eventually joined the pact. Outlawing war seemed to be a good idea, but the pact was unrealistic and unworkable because it had no provisions for enforcement. By 1941, many of the nations that had signed the pact would be at war.

INTERPRETING POLITICAL CARTOONS Calvin Coolidge, shown here with a saxophone, was known for his support of big business. **Analyzing Information** *What does this cartoon say about Coolidge and big business? Write a caption for the cartoon.*

The Election of 1928

As Coolidge neared the end of his first full term, he was asked about his political plans. "I do not choose to run for President in 1928" was his brief and famous reply. In his place, Republicans nominated Herbert Hoover. During and after World War I, Hoover had won respect for programs he ran in Europe to ease hunger. He had held Cabinet posts under Harding and Coolidge.

Hoover's main opponent was Alfred E. Smith of New York, a popular Democratic governor. Prohibition emerged as a major issue of the presidential campaign, as did religion. Smith was the first Roman Catholic to be nominated for President, and he opposed Prohibition. Hoover, a Protestant, vigorously supported Prohibition, which he called a "noble experiment." The contest reflected the basic urban-rural split in the country, as Smith drew most of his votes from the large cities, while Hoover did best in small towns. Drawn especially by the Prohibition debate, women voted in fairly large numbers for the first time and made a strong impact on both parties. Hoover captured about 21 million popular votes to 15 million for Smith, and he won in the electoral college by a huge margin. Americans expected that what they called the "Coolidge prosperity" would continue under Hoover.

Section 1 Assessment

READING COMPREHENSION

1. Why did **communism** seem to pose a threat to capitalist nations?
2. How did the **Red Scare** contribute to America's policy of **isolationism** in the 1920s?
3. What was the **Teapot Dome scandal?**
4. What was the **Kellogg-Briand Pact** and how did it reflect Republican foreign policy in the 1920s?

CRITICAL THINKING AND WRITING

5. **Identifying Central Issues** What led Americans to suspect that Communists were the source of labor unrest in the 1920s?
6. **Write a Letter to the Editor** Suppose you observed the trial of Sacco and Vanzetti. Write a letter telling whether or not you think the defendants received a fair trial.

Take It to the NET

Activity: Writing a Biography
Write a brief biography of one of the three Republican Presidents of the 1920s. Include stands on important issues and highlights from the presidency. Use the links provided in the *America: Pathways to the Present* area of the following Web site for help in completing this activity.
www.phschool.com

Section 1 Assessment

Reading Comprehension

1. Communist system: government owns all land and property; one-party government, needs of the nation supersede individual rights. Communism antithetical to capitalist philosophies of free enterprise and private sector ownership of industrial facilities.
2. Many of the suspected radicals swept up in the Palmer raids were immigrants. This contributed to the desire of Americans to adopt an isolationist stance.
3. Corruption in the Harding administration.
4. The Kellogg-Briand Pact was an agreement declaring warfare to be illegal. The United States, France, and some 60 other nations were signatories. This pact reflected the Republican desire to avoid foreign wars.

Critical Thinking and Writing

5. With the red scare as a backdrop, the number of strikes per month more than doubled in mid-1919. Blaming Communists was related to the prevalent belief that labor unions contained large numbers of immigrant radicals.
6. Letters will vary, but should be supported with facts from the section.

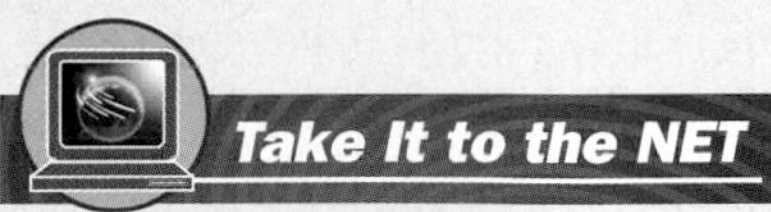

Take It to the NET

Answers will vary. Students should demonstrate knowledge of the major policies and accomplishments of Presidents Warren Harding, Calvin Coolidge, or Herbert Hoover.

Caption Answers

Interpreting Political Cartoons Big business likes what Coolidge has to say. Possible caption: "Dancing to Coolidge's tune."

Evaluating Advertisements

Focus Students learn to analyze an advertisement as a historical document to gain insight into ideas, attitudes, and values of an era.

Instruct As you and your students analyze the historical ad shown in the book, focus particularly on the ad's message and its possible historical interpretations. Ask students to discuss their impressions of the effectiveness of the ad. Particularly, do they think it is likely that the lady would reject the man for "slovenliness" for the reason stated in the ad? Ask students to think of, or bring in, examples of modern-day advertisements that use the type of persuasion shown in this ad.

Extend See the Skills for Life Activity in the Resource Directory below.

ANSWERS

Practice the Skill

1. **(a)** Garters to hold up men's socks. **(b)** The ad shows two available garter styles; gives price range; states that no metal can touch the wearer. **(c)** The "problem" the ad promises to solve is the rejection of the man's proposal because he appears slovenly to the woman due to his sagging socks and exposed calves. **(d)** Men: the need to present a neat appearance and to be successful; the concern about being rejected by women. Women: the concern about having husbands who will not be embarrassments in social situations.
2. **(a)** Answers will vary but should be based on facts about the 1920s. **(b)** That men will be more desirable to women if they use Paris Garters.
3. **(a)** Being neat, well-dressed, successful, and attractive to the opposite sex; caring about others' opinions. **(b)** The dress of the people in the ad, the furnishings of the room, the art-deco style border around the ad. **(c)** Answers will vary but should be well supported. Sample answer: Ads create a desire for products and manipulate people into buying them.

Evaluating Advertisements

Advertisements offer more than evidence of the consumer goods and services produced in a historical period. They often hold clues to widely held ideas, attitudes, and values. However, when using advertisements as historical evidence, keep in mind that their stated or unstated messages may reflect what the advertisers want readers to believe, value, or desire—rather than the reality for most people of the time.

By the 1920s, "situational" ads depicted not only products and what they did, but also the ways these products might enhance the lives of typical consumers. One such ad from the 1920s is shown below.

LEARN THE SKILL

Use the following steps to evaluate historical advertisements:

1. **Identify the subject of the advertisement.** What product or service does the advertisement promote?
2. **Analyze the advertisement's reliability as historical evidence.** Consider both the product itself and the way it is advertised.
3. **Study the advertisement to learn more about the historical period.** Consider the product and its purpose, the situation depicted in the advertisement, the text, and the visuals.

PRACTICE THE SKILL

Answer the following questions:

1. **(a)** What product or service does this advertisement promote? **(b)** What facts about the product does it provide? **(c)** What is the situation of the ad—in other words, what "problem" will this product solve for the people depicted in the ad? **(d)** What strategy does this advertisement use to appeal particularly to men? How does the ad try to appeal to women?
2. **(a)** Do you think the people depicted in the advertisement represent typical consumers of the 1920s? Explain. **(b)** In this ad, what is the unstated message that the advertiser is using to persuade people to buy the product?
3. **(a)** What social or cultural values are promoted in the advertisement? **(b)** What clues to the time period are given in the photograph? **(c)** In general, do you think advertisements reflect consumers' desires for products or create the desire for such products? Explain your reasoning.

APPLY THE SKILL

See the Chapter Review and Assessment for another opportunity to apply this skill.

RESOURCE DIRECTORY

Teaching Resources
Skills for Life booklet, p. 23

Technology
Social Studies Skills Tutor CD-ROM
Interactive Practice in
- Geographic Literacy
- Critical Thinking and Reading
- Visual Analysis
- Communications

Section 2

A Business Boom

READING FOCUS

- What role do businesses and consumers play in a consumer economy?
- How were Henry Ford and the automobile important to the 1920s?
- In what ways did industrial growth affect the economy of the 1920s?
- Why did the economic boom bypass some people and benefit others?

KEY TERMS

consumer economy
installment plan
Gross National Product (GNP)
assembly line

TAKING NOTES

Copy this flowchart. As you read, fill in the boxes with some of the factors that caused a business boom in the 1920s.

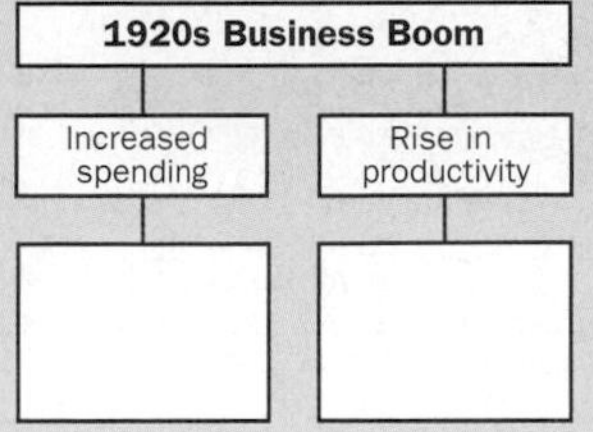

MAIN IDEA

During the 1920s, new products and Americans' power to purchase them grew rapidly, producing a decade of enormous business growth.

Setting the Scene Until the 1920s, shopping centers did not exist. Food was not "fast." Billboards did not line the nation's highways, because there were no highways, few cars, and relatively few advertisements.

The decade of the 1920s gave birth to much of the popular culture we know in modern America. The nation's first shopping center opened in Kansas City, giving consumers a more convenient way to shop. The first fast-food chain, A&W Root Beer, began selling burgers and soft drinks.

A popular roadside advertising campaign for shaving cream found its start in the mid-1920s. Signs that were evenly spaced apart compelled motorists to read each successive message: "Your shaving brush . . . has had its day . . . so why not . . . shave the modern way." Advertising became big business in the 1920s, with companies spending $3.2 billion on ads in 1927.

VIEWING HISTORY The nation's first modern shopping center, the Country Club Plaza, opened in Kansas City, Missouri, in 1922. **Making Comparisons** *How does it compare to the shopping malls of today?*

A Consumer Economy

After a period of uncertainty following World War I, the United States economy made a rapid adjustment. By 1920, incomes had resumed the upward trend begun during the war. Between 1914 and 1926, average wages rose more than 28 percent. The number of millionaires in the United States more than doubled in the same period.

Much of this growth resulted from a new focus on the consumer. In fact, the 1920s saw the development of a **consumer economy,** one that depends on a large amount of spending by consumers—individuals who use, or consume, products. Increased spending leads to larger profits for businesses, which in turn pushes up wages and encourages even more spending.

Traditionally, Americans valued thrift. They bought mainly what they needed, and much less of what they merely wanted, or what was nonessential. Several factors helped spark more buying in this decade, including higher wages, clever advertising, new products, lower costs, and the widespread availability of credit.

Section 2

A Business Boom

Section Objectives

1. Understand the role businesses and consumers play in a consumer economy.
2. Find out how Henry Ford and the automobile were important to the 1920s.
3. Discover the ways in which industrial growth affected the economy of the 1920s.
4. See how the economic boom bypassed some people and benefited others.

Bellringer

Warm-Up Activity Ask students what items are commonly bought on credit. Ask how American life would be different if credit disappeared.

Activating Prior Knowledge What, in students' opinions, constitutes a consumer society? Have the class list some aspects of a consumer society. Then have them list some positive and negative aspects of such a society.

Reading Strategy

Have students reread the Main Idea on this page. Then have them rewrite it as a question. As they read, have them take notes about events that help answer the question.

Caption Answers

Viewing History The first shopping mall was large, but not nearly as large as many malls are today.

RESOURCE DIRECTORY

Teaching Resources
Learning Styles Lesson Plans booklet, p. 45
Guided Reading and Review booklet, p. 87

Other Print Resources
Nystrom *Atlas of Our Country* *The Third Wave of Immigration,* pp. 30–32

Technology
Section Reading Support Transparencies
Guided Reading Audiotapes (English/Spanish), Ch. 14
Student Edition on Audio CD, Ch. 14
Prentice Hall Presentation Pro CD-ROM, Ch. 14
Companion Web site, www.phschool.com

Lesson Plan

Focus In the 1920s, the nation experienced an economic change that resulted in phenomenal business growth. Ask students what this change was. How did it affect American life?

Instruct Discuss the development of the consumer economy in the 1920s. Ask students to explain the link between buying on credit and the business boom. Why did the sale of consumer items skyrocket? How did the system of paying in installments contribute to the development of new products? What effect did it have on the material quality of American life?

Ask students how the consumer economy encouraged innovation. Why was it in Henry Ford's interest to be able to produce more cars in less time? What process did he adapt in order to do this?

Assess/Reteach Ask students to list a series of developments in manufacturing that might have given rise to the consumer society of the 1920s. In what ways did this first consumer era in American society mirror the current day? How is the current consumer society different?

Background
Global Connections

After the devastation of the war in Europe and the deaths of more than 100,000 Americans of the 2 million who had been shipped "over there," Americans wanted to withdraw from world affairs and focus on improving their lives at home. Material dreams, not the idealistic dreams that sent Americans to fight in Europe, were the important ones. Calvin Coolidge defined business as "one of the great contributing forces to the moral and spiritual advancement of the race."

Catalogs brimming with exciting new goods tempted consumers to buy on credit.

Buying on Credit Until the 1920s, middle-class Americans generally paid cash for everything. Borrowing money for any purchase but a house or land was considered unthrifty, even immoral. During the 1920s, new kinds of consumer goods, such as automobiles and refrigerators, became widely available. Americans wanted these modern conveniences, but they cost a great deal. Unless manufacturers sold more of these goods, they would go out of business. To increase their profits, manufacturers developed and financed buying on the **installment plan.** On an installment plan, the customer makes partial payments (installments) at set intervals over a period of time until the total debt is paid. Installment plans fueled the growth of consumer spending.

Clever advertising made this form of buying acceptable to the American people. People who otherwise would not spend beyond their means were encouraged to buy all kinds of items, even though interest charges ranged from 11 to 40 percent. By 1929, Americans were using the installment plan to buy 60 percent of all cars sold; 70 percent of all furniture; 80 percent of all vacuum cleaners, radios, and refrigerators; and 90 percent of all washing machines.

Electric Power Refrigerators, washing machines, and other power-hungry appliances created a surge in the demand for electricity. Between 1913 and 1927, the number of electric power customers more than quadrupled. The number of people who had electric lights jumped from 16 percent to 63 percent in about the same time. Part of this increase came from the expanding housing industry. New homes, wired for electricity, could now be filled with electric appliances.

Although cities gained electric power rapidly, the countryside did not. By 1925, for example, power plants supplied only 4 percent of American farms with electricity. Running power lines to scattered farming communities simply cost too much. Instead, some farmers created their own source of electricity by building wind-powered generators.

Spending on Goods and Services, 1928

Item	Percent of Budget Spent
Food	27%
Clothing	13%
Shelter	12%
Fuel and light	4%
Furniture and furnishings	2%
Health and education	3%
Automobile	5%
Sundries:	
Tobacco, candy, soft drinks, gum	5%
Recreation (theater, ball games)	3%
Miscellaneous (trolley, stationery)	4%
Savings and insurance	12%
Taxes	10%
Total	**100%**

SOURCE: *Setting a Course: American Women in the 1920s*

INTERPRETING TABLES A study of family spending habits during the late 1920s reveals lifestyle choices as well as economic realities. **Drawing Conclusions** *What does the sundries category say about life in the 1920s?*

The growth of General Electric Company illustrates how the increasing use of electricity went hand in hand with the jump in consumer sales. General Electric was formed in 1892 to take over Thomas Edison's electric light business. During the 1920s, the company grew dramatically by selling a variety of household electric appliances. It also sold electric motors and other products for industry. Between 1919 and 1929, the value of electrical products of this kind more than doubled, from nearly $1 billion to $2.3 billion. General Electric rode this wave of consumer buying to become one of the world's largest companies.

Advertising General Electric's product line included electric toasters, ovens, sewing machines, coffee pots, irons, and vacuum cleaners. Other companies offered similar appliances, as well as a vast array of other goods, from telephones to cosmetics. To rise above the competition, manufacturers needed an edge: mass-media advertising.

By the 1920s, marketers had developed a new approach to advertising. In the past, advertisements had provided fairly basic information about a product. A magazine ad for clothing, for example, might have noted its quality of fabric, smart design, and affordable price. Advertising in the 1920s, especially in mass magazines, spoke less about the product and more about how the product could enhance the consumer's image. "A woman is only as old as her complexion," stated one cosmetics ad from 1923. For postal service, consumers were advised, "Air mail is socially correct." Ads like these appealed to

Caption Answers

Interpreting Tables That life was somewhat more simple in the 1920s than it is today.

Resource Directory

Teaching Resources

Learning with Documents booklet (Visual Learning Activity) *Advertising Techniques of the 1920s,* p. 60

Biography, Literature, and Comparing Primary Sources booklet (Literature) *Superpower,* pp. 68–69

Technology

Sounds of an Era Audio CD *Will Rogers,* 1925 recording (time: one minute, 40 seconds)

such emotions as insecurity and fear. Other ads used celebrities to associate an image with their products. This kind of ad might show a movie star using a product and claiming to adore it. The ad implied that anyone who used the product could be as stylish as a movie star.

The new advertising had its critics. Some saw it as a waste of time and money. Others condemned its use of psychology to persuade people to buy products. Advertising also had its defenders. One professional "ad man" claimed that advertising for modern products served a vital educational purpose:

> "*The vacuum cleaner was introduced by educational advertising. The advertising was done partly by manufacturers anxious to sell vacuum cleaners, and partly by electric-light companies anxious to sell current. . . . But the result has been a public benefit, an increasing willingness to spend money to lighten the human burden, to cut down the waste of human energy spent in the operation of living.*"
>
> —Earnest Elmo Calkins, *Business the Civilizer,* 1928

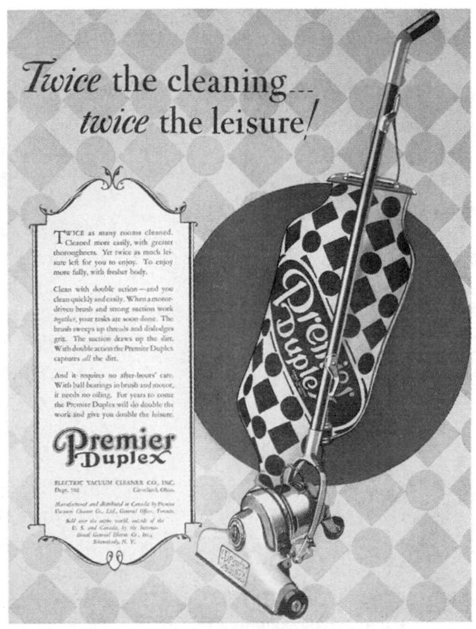

Twice the cleaning...
twice the leisure!
Premier Duplex

Electrical appliances such as the vacuum cleaner changed the nature of housework.

Rise in Productivity Electric power, persuasive advertising, and the installment plan all helped consumers go on a buying spree in the 1920s. Without an increased volume of goods to buy, however, the consumer economy could not have developed as rapidly as it did. In order to meet consumer demand, productivity needed to increase. Productivity is a worker's level of output, whether in goods or in services, over a given period. One measure of productivity is the **Gross National Product (GNP),** which is the total value of goods and services a country produces annually. From 1921 to 1929, the GNP grew at an average rate of 6 percent per year. The preceding decade had seen a growth rate of less than 1 percent.

Productivity rose in part because the nation developed new resources, new management methods, and new technologies. Major oil fields had been discovered in Texas, Oklahoma, and California around the turn of the century. These discoveries provided the resources to power industrial growth. You have read about Frederick Winslow Taylor's time-and-motion studies in the late 1800s, designed to increase worker efficiency. By the 1920s, industrial managers as well as labor leaders had come to accept Taylor's management principles. Application of those principles helped workers produce more goods. The increasing use of new machines and other kinds of technology also significantly increased workers' output. In addition, technology proved useful in solving production problems, such as how to make more automobiles in less time.

READING CHECK
What factors allowed for a rise in productivity in the 1920s?

Ford and the Automobile

The first automobile appeared in Germany in the 1880s. In 1892, Charles and Frank Duryea of Springfield, Massachusetts, developed a marketable car, and several other American inventors soon followed their lead. Over the next 28 years, about 8 million cars rolled out of factories and onto America's roads. Yet in the ten years after that period, during the 1920s, the number of registered cars rose by more than 15 million. Much of this rapid growth in production resulted from the efforts of the inventive businessman Henry Ford.

ACTIVITY
Connecting with Science and Technology

Have students select a common household item whose parts they are familiar with and draw a design for an assembly line to produce it. As they design the assembly line, have them analyze the impact of this type of technological innovation on the nature of work, the American labor movement, and businesses. **(Visual/Spatial; Logical/Mathematical)**

BACKGROUND
Geography in History

American roads could scarcely keep up with Ford's assembly line. Most were intended for horses and cattle, and none were planned with a national network in mind. In 1919, Lt. Col. Dwight D. Eisenhower left Washington, D.C., with a party of 60 military trucks to test the feasibility of a coast-to-coast trip. Two months and over eight repaired bridges later, he arrived in San Francisco, convinced of the need for government action. A concerned General Pershing proposed an 8,000-mile interstate highway system to the President and Congress in 1922, but little progress was made until Eisenhower became President in the 1950s.

READING CHECK
Rapidly growing GNP; new advertising techniques; electric power for homes and industries; a plentiful supply of oil; efficient manufacturing techniques; and easy credit terms for installment purchasing.

CUSTOMIZE FOR ...
Gifted and Talented

Have students construct their own advertisement for a current product. Ask them to explain how their ad appeals to some human emotion or desire and to discuss whether their claim about the product is realistic.

Activity
Student Portfolio

You may wish to have students add the following to their portfolios: Ask students to research the beginning of the national highway system and the construction of U.S. Highway 66 and write a report. Ask them to include a map of the highway with their report. Have students analyze how the development of this highway reflected changing demographic patterns resulting from migration within the United States. **(Visual/Spatial)**

Background
The Model T

There is some debate about whether Henry Ford was oblivious to consumer tastes regarding color. Ford biographer Robert Lacey says in *Ford: The Men and the Machine* that the only reason Ford's Model T was offered to customers in "any color so long as it's black" was because an engineer in the Ford plant discovered that black dried faster than any other color. Tin Lizzies originally came in green with a red stripe.

Ford and the "Model T" In the late 1880s, Ford worked as an engineer with a lighting company. In his spare time he began inventing a "horseless carriage." In 1896, Ford perfected his first version of a lightweight, gas-powered car he called the "quadricycle." By 1903, he had started his own automobile company. Five years later, Ford sold 30,000 of an improved vehicle that he called the Model T.

Ford's Assembly Line Ford wanted to "democratize the automobile," producing even more cars and selling them at prices ordinary people could afford. This goal set him apart from all other car makers and made him one of the most influential people of the century.

To achieve his goal, he adapted the **assembly line** for his factories. An assembly line is a manufacturing process in which each worker does one specialized task in the construction of the final product. In the past, an individual worker might build an entire product from start to finish. Since that type of manufacturing process required each worker to master hundreds of tasks, it was too inefficient for the mass production of something as complex as an automobile. On an assembly line, one worker might install windshields on all the cars. Another might mount the tires or weld a certain part in place or apply the paint.

Ford did not invent the assembly line, but he made it more efficient. His specially designed assembly line moved while each worker stayed in place, instead of moving from vehicle to vehicle. Critics of Ford's system claimed that the assembly line, with its endless repetition of tasks, strained workers both physically and mentally. Ford admitted that he would be bored working on an assembly line but insisted that his employees enjoyed it. At Ford's Highland Park, Michigan, factory, the assembly line turned out a Model T every 24 seconds. Between 1908 and 1927, Ford built half of the automobiles produced in the entire world, more than 15 million cars.

By making large numbers of identical automobiles in an identical way, Ford could take advantage of economies of scale, a concept you have read about in an earlier chapter. The more automobiles he made, the less each one cost. In 1914,

INTERPRETING DIAGRAMS The layout of the main buildings at Ford's River Rouge facility was designed to maximize efficiency. Locate the power house in the late 1920s photo by its eight smoke stacks. **Analyzing Information** *Trace the work process from delivery of raw materials to finished automobile. What steps must be taken along the way?*

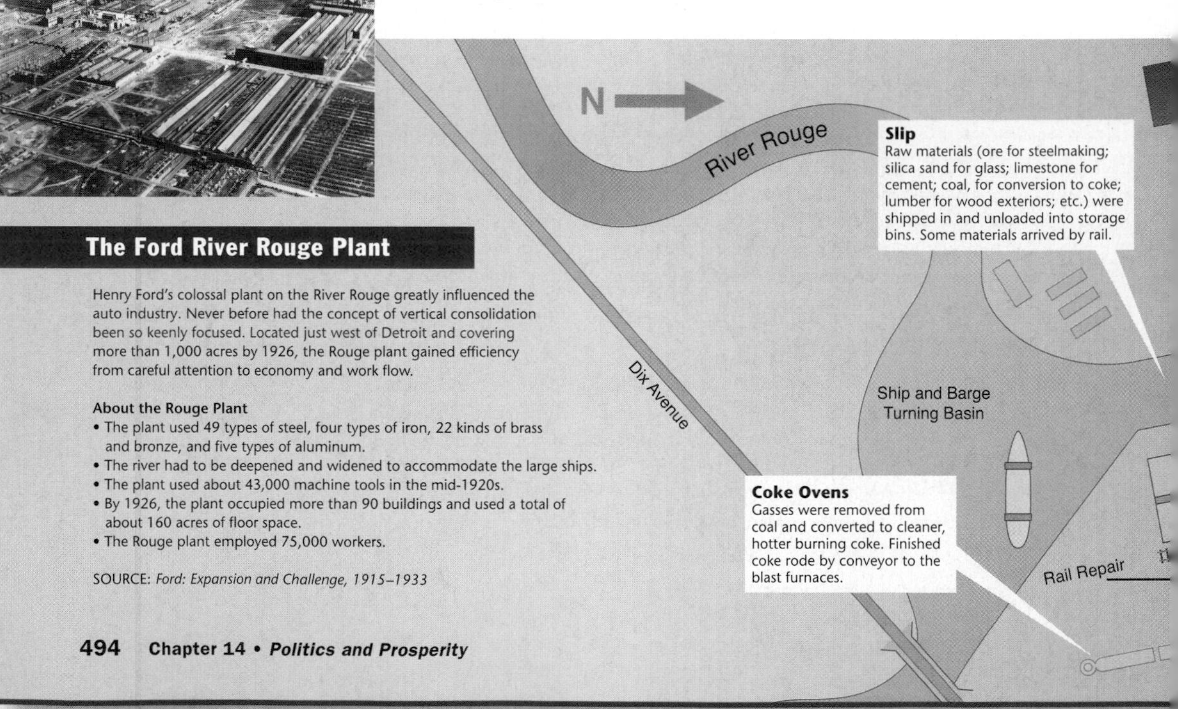
N
River Rouge
Dix Avenue
Slip
Raw materials (ore for steelmaking; silica sand for glass; limestone for cement; coal, for conversion to coke; lumber for wood exteriors; etc.) were shipped in and unloaded into storage bins. Some materials arrived by rail.
Ship and Barge Turning Basin
Coke Ovens
Gasses were removed from coal and converted to cleaner, hotter burning coke. Finished coke rode by conveyor to the blast furnaces.
Rail Repair

The Ford River Rouge Plant

Henry Ford's colossal plant on the River Rouge greatly influenced the auto industry. Never before had the concept of vertical consolidation been so keenly focused. Located just west of Detroit and covering more than 1,000 acres by 1926, the Rouge plant gained efficiency from careful attention to economy and work flow.

About the Rouge Plant
- The plant used 49 types of steel, four types of iron, 22 kinds of brass and bronze, and five types of aluminum.
- The river had to be deepened and widened to accommodate the large ships.
- The plant used about 43,000 machine tools in the mid-1920s.
- By 1926, the plant occupied more than 90 buildings and used a total of about 160 acres of floor space.
- The Rouge plant employed 75,000 workers.

SOURCE: *Ford: Expansion and Challenge, 1915–1933*

Caption Answers

Interpreting Diagrams Work flow: Raw materials are delivered over water into the slip (or by rail) and are deposited into bins. The "High Line" transports materials from bins for processing: ore goes to blast furnaces, then (as metals) to foundry. Open hearth rolling mill makes steel. Engines, steel, windshields, etc. proceed to "B Building" for assembly. Coke ovens provide fuel for the plant. The power house produces electricity.

RESOURCE DIRECTORY
Technology
Color Transparencies *The Way It Works,* H17

the first year Ford's assembly line was in full swing, his company sold Model T's at $490 each. This price was almost half of what a car had cost in 1910. The following year he dropped the price to $390.

The Model T was a utilitarian, or practical, vehicle. It was available in a limited range of styles, but built with essentially the same engine and other basic parts. While early Model T's came in a variety of colors, Ford eventually switched to cheaper and more durable black paint. Ford's competitors, however, realized that the American public wanted different colors and styles of cars. When General Motors introduced its low-priced Chevrolet in several colors, Ford lost many customers. Not until 1925 did he introduce a choice of colors for his "improved" Model T. The last Model T was produced in 1927, making way for the Model A.

Ford's success came partly from vertical consolidation, which, as you have read, means controlling the businesses that make up phases of a product's development. From Ford's huge new plant built on the River Rouge, he was able to take a load of raw ore on any morning and roll it off the line as a car the next day. Much of the ore came from Ford's own iron mines and was forged in his own blast furnaces and steel mills, which were fired by coal from his 16 coal mines. Wood used in the car came from his 700,000 acres of forests, and glass for windshields from his own glassworks. He hauled materials over his own railroad and on his own fleet of ships. Company workshops made nearly all the tools used in his factories. Furthermore, he built this entire empire with profits from the Model T.

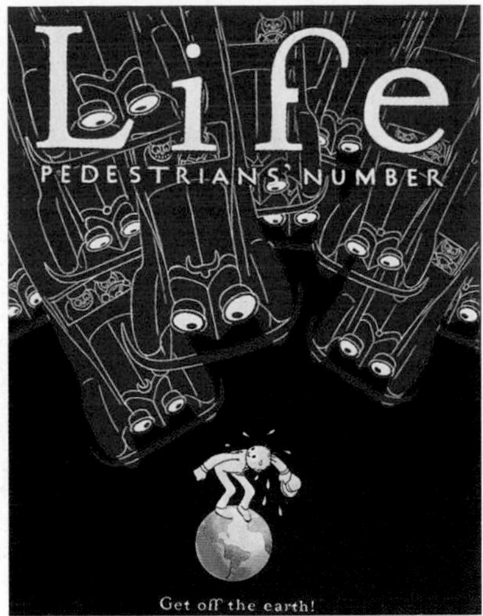

ANALYZING VISUAL INFORMATION Automobiles are the subject of this 1925 *Life* magazine cover. **Making Comparisons** *What do the illustration and its caption, "Get off our earth," say about the impact of the automobile on society in the 1920s?*

A Complex Businessman Like the empire he ran, Henry Ford was complex. He had both admirable qualities and personal failings. For example, he won praise in 1914 for introducing a $5-a-day pay rate for many of his workers. At the time, other factories paid only about half that amount. Yet he was not always so generous. He ran his company harshly and used violence to fight unions. During World War I, Ford devised an Americanization program for his

Open Hearth and Rolling Mill
Steel was made and processed here.

Bins
Machines unloaded the railcars and ships, dumping tons of raw materials at a time into concrete bins.

B Building
Ford workers made WWI Eagle boats, car bodies, and Fordson tractors. Production stopped in 1927 for installation of the Model A assembly line.

Glass Plant

Paper Mill

Kilns

A Building

High Line
The beginning of the intra-factory rail system. It transported raw materials from the bins for processing.

Fabricating Shop

Blast Furnaces
Processed ores, melting them down into iron and other metals for use in the foundry.

Motor Assembly

Pig Iron Building

Power House
Requiring eight smoke stacks, the power house produced enough light and current for both the Rouge and Highland plants.

Foundry
Molten metals were poured into molds to create castings for engine blocks and other parts. Parts moved on for assembly.

Miller Road

ACTIVITY
Connecting with Science and Technology

Have groups of students conduct time-and-motion studies of various simple activities such as creating a paper airplane, alphabetizing a group of books, or collating stacks of paper. Instruct the groups to collaborate to devise the simplest, most efficient method of accomplishing the assigned task, with the goal of using the least number of motions in the shortest amount of time. Have each group create a chart describing its recommended method. **(Bodily/Kinesthetic)**

BACKGROUND
Biography

Frank B. Gilbreth (1868–1924) and Lillian E. Gilbreth (1878–1972) were a husband-and-wife team whose breakthrough time-and-motion studies, conducted during the first years of the twentieth century, helped usher in the era of mass production. They wrote a series of influential books. Frank Gilbreth was the first "efficiency expert" to use motion pictures to study surgical operations. He also lectured widely. The Gilbreths carried their notions home, adapting many of their methods from industry to bring efficiency to the raising of their 12 children. Two of their children, Frank B. Gilbreth, Jr., and Ernestine Gilbreth Carey, recorded the results in two funny and popular books, *Cheaper by the Dozen* (1949) and *Belles on Their Toes* (1950).

CUSTOMIZE FOR ...
ESL

Write the phrase *assembly line* on the chalkboard. Ask students to look closely at the illustration of an assembly line on this page. Have volunteers read the captions aloud and describe the steps involved in assembling Model Ts.

TEST PREPARATION

Have students read the paragraph that begins "Ford's success came partly from vertical consolidation . . .", then answer the question below.

How did Ford acquire the raw materials (such as coal) needed to operate the River Rouge plant?

A The Standard Oil Trust provided all of Ford's raw materials at a special discount.

B Ford worked with independent contractors.

C Rival automobile manufacturers sold raw materials to Ford.

(D) Ford owned coal mines, forests, iron mines, and rail and shipping resources.

CAPTION ANSWERS

Analyzing Visual Information The man standing on the globe is threatened by the cars surrounding him. It seems to say that there are so many cars that they are taking over the planet.

ACTIVITY
Connecting with Economics

Have students research the growth in auto ownership during the 1920s. If they can, have them find out what percentage of these cars were manufactured by the Ford Motor Company. Have them use transfer information from one medium to another to present the first set of findings as a graph, and the second set of findings as a pie chart. **(Logical/Mathematical)**

BACKGROUND
Interdisciplinary

Though some people heralded the rise in productivity brought about by mass production, others found the development profoundly dehumanizing. One artist who applied his satirical genius to this situation was the actor and filmmaker Charlie Chaplin. The 1936 film *Modern Times* portrayed Chaplin's popular Little Tramp character as a victim of modern factory efficiency.

The most hilarious scenes in the film depict the Tramp as a hapless assembly-line worker who suffers the indignity of being fed by a remorseless "lunch-machine" and is whirled away on the cogs of a monstrous piece of equipment.

BIOGRAPHY

Henry Ford
1863–1947

Henry Ford was born on a Michigan farm during the Civil War, the son of Irish immigrants. Although Ford is best known as an industrialist, not all his energies were devoted to the Ford Motor Company. His pursuits were diverse, at the very least.

In 1915, he sailed a rented ocean liner across the Atlantic in a hopeless effort to talk Europe out of fighting World War I. He purchased the *Dearborn Independent* in 1918, but then used his newspaper to run a series of articles that blamed Jews for the world's problems. In 1927, however, after being sued for slander, he apologized for these attacks and sold the paper.

As a nod to his early years on the farm, he recreated a rural American town, Greenfield Village, as well as a museum of American artifacts that can still be visited today.

foreign-born workers. In return for higher pay, workers had to enroll in English and civics classes and let investigators inspect their homes. The company held elaborate graduation ceremonies in which workers shed their previous ethnic identities and became "Americans." When postwar inflation made the pay incentive less attractive, the program declined. Although he showed genius in giving millions of Americans a car they could afford, he stubbornly refused to keep up with their changing tastes. By 1936, the Ford Motor Company had slipped to third place in the automobile industry.

Industrial Growth

Through Ford's genius, automobile making became the nation's biggest single manufacturing industry in the 1920s. By the late twenties, automakers used 15 percent of America's steel, 80 percent of its rubber, half of its glass, 65 percent of its leather upholstery, and 7 billion gallons of its gasoline every year. Naturally, the industries that provided those materials, such as steelmaking and oil refining, also grew.

Thousands of new businesses arose to serve automobile travel, including garages, car dealerships, motels ("motor hotels"), campgrounds, gas stations, and restaurants. Thanks to the automobile, suburbs expanded, in turn boosting the housing industry. Truck lines began hauling the nation's freight, and motorized buses traveled new routes through both city and countryside. By 1929, about 3.7 million people owed their jobs directly or indirectly to the automobile industry. In that year, the nation spent nearly $2 billion to build and maintain its roads and bridges.

Businesses unrelated to the automobile industry also boomed. As you have read, movie making, radio broadcasting, and publishing all flourished. One industry that greatly expanded during the late 1920s was aviation. This industry had begun to develop during the war, with the production of military aircraft. The first domestic airlines, however, had limited success. They flew small planes, mainly over local routes, and many of them stayed in business only a short time. The public's fascination with Charles Lindbergh and Amelia Earhart helped boost the industry's fortunes. Aircraft companies began designing larger, faster planes. By late in the decade, air transport of mail and other goods, as well as passengers, had improved.

Electric power fueled homes, businesses, and a consumer economy. Workers stand on an electric power generator in 1924.

Under Republican laissez-faire policies, which limited government regulation of business, the value of the nation's businesses soared. Between 1919 and 1929, the 200 top American companies nearly doubled their total worth, which rose from $43 billion to $81 billion. Government and industry seemed eager to prove that the chief business of the American people truly was business.

Even with limited regulation and a business boom, the power of monopolies declined. Rapid business expansion opened up new opportunities for smaller companies. These competitors rushed in to challenge the giant steel and oil monopolies. For example, when banker J. P. Morgan created the U.S. Steel Corporation in 1901, it controlled about 60 percent of the steel business. By 1930, it had grown enormously. Yet its competitors also had grown, and in that year, U.S. Steel controlled only about 39 percent of the steel business. Likewise, the companies that had once made

RESOURCE DIRECTORY

Teaching Resources

Units 3/4 booklet
- Section 2 Quiz, p. 53

Guide to the Essentials
- Section 2 Summary, p. 69

Biography, Literature, and Comparing Primary Sources booklet (Comparing Primary Sources)
On the McNary-Haugen Bill (1927), pp. 137–138

up the Standard Oil Trust grew with the demand for oil products during the 1920s. Even so, by 1930 they controlled only about half of the nation's oil business.

Purchasing expensive tractors and other equipment helped put many farmers into debt in the 1920s.

Bypassed by the Boom

While most Americans enjoyed a better standard of living, others struggled to survive. Unskilled laborers, including many African American migrants, remained poor. Their wages and working conditions did not improve, nor did those for workers in several major industries, including agriculture.

For some sectors of the farm economy, the 1920s brought not prosperity but devastation. Farm prices had stayed high during the war and just afterward, as American farmers supplied food to the United States and to war-torn Europe. After the war, however, the recovering European farm industry and cheaper food imports helped to push American products out of the European market. The huge wartime demand shrank, and American farm prices, especially for wheat and hogs, plummeted.

During more prosperous times, many farmers had borrowed money to buy new tractors and other machinery. Their new equipment allowed them to expand their operations, so they bought more land as well. In the late 1920s, when most Americans spent freely on consumer goods, these farmers could not even pay back their loans. Many of them abandoned agriculture. Others hung on to the only way of life they had ever known, going even further into debt every day.

The same dwindling demand for goods hurt producers of cotton textiles and bituminous (soft) coal. These industries had expanded to meet wartime needs, but after the war they failed to uncover new markets for their products. The resulting low profits kept wage rates down. Railroads suffered, too, not just from shrinking demand but also from mismanagement, competition from trucking firms, and labor unions that fought against wage cuts and layoffs.

Section 2 Assessment

READING COMPREHENSION

1. What conditions made a **consumer economy** possible in the 1920s?
2. What is an **installment plan?**
3. How did the **Gross National Product** change during the 1920s?
4. How did Henry Ford change his **assembly line** to increase efficiency?

CRITICAL THINKING AND WRITING

5. **Making Comparisons** How did postwar economic conditions favor automobile workers and yet undermine the farming industry?
6. **Writing a List** List all the factors that led to increased consumer spending in the 1920s.

Take It to the NET

Activity: Writing a Summary
Research several inventions from the 1920s and write a summary of how they affected consumer goods or business in general. Use the links provided in the *America: Pathways to the Present* area of the following Web site for help in completing this activity.
www.phschool.com

Section 2 Assessment

Reading Comprehension

1. Increased wages and incomes; technologically advanced new consumer products; lower costs; clever advertising; widespread availability of credit.
2. A payment plan in which the customer makes partial payments at set intervals over a period of time until the total debt is paid.
3. It grew markedly, at an average rate of 6 percent per year.
4. His assembly line moved, while the workers stayed in place.

Critical Thinking and Writing

5. Automobile workers benefited from new businesses that fostered auto travel. However, the postwar recovery of European agriculture and cheaper food imports helped to reduce European demand for American farm products. Prices plummeted as the wartime demand shrank.
6. Higher wages; higher incomes; clever advertising; new products; lower costs; availability of credit.

Take It to the NET

Answers will vary. Examples may include inventions or scientific developments such as the television, the discovery of penicillin, and the liquid-fueled rocket.

Section 3
The Economy in the Late 1920s

Section Objectives

1. See why the economy in the late 1920s appeared healthy to most Americans.
2. Observe the danger signs that were present in the economy of the late 1920s.

Bellringer

Warm-Up Activity Discuss with students the many elements that combine to influence the economy for a country as diverse and globally interconnected as the United States. Talk about ways in which an economic situation in this country could have worldwide implications.

Activating Prior Knowledge Ask students to talk about what they know about the current state of the United States economy. Can they state some descriptive terms that they may have heard or read about in the news? How does today's economy compare with the economy of the late 1920s?

Reading Strategy

Have students write down three questions they might ask to help them better understand the economy of the 1920s. As they do so, have them analyze the causes of economic growth and prosperity in the 1920s.

Section 3
The Economy in the Late 1920s

READING FOCUS

- Why did the economy of the late 1920s appear healthy to most Americans?
- What danger signs were present in the economy of late 1920s?

MAIN IDEA

During the 1920s, rising wealth and a booming stock market gave Americans a false sense of faith in the economy. In fact, there were signs that the economy was in trouble.

KEY TERMS

welfare capitalism
speculation
buying on margin

TAKING NOTES

Copy the web diagram below. As you read, add reasons showing that Americans in the 1920s had confidence in the nation's economy.

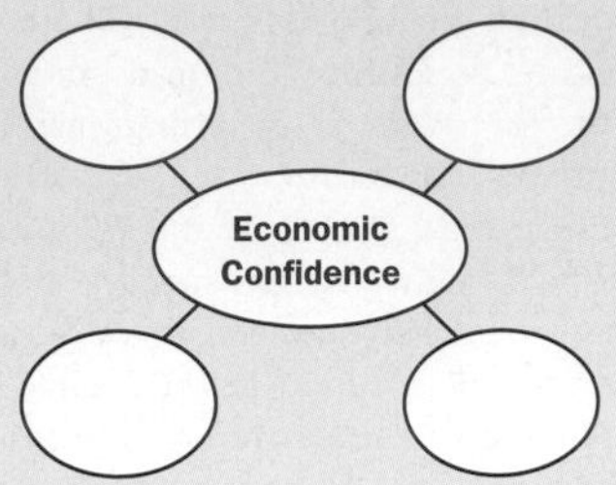

Many Americans expected Herbert Hoover to oversee continued prosperity.

Setting the Scene The mood of most Americans in the late 1920s was optimistic, and with good reason. Medical advances had greatly reduced deaths from whooping cough, diphtheria, and other serious diseases. Since 1900 the number of infant deaths had declined, and life expectancy had increased by more than 10 years, to an average of 59 years for men and 63 years for women.

The brightest hopes seemed to come from the economy. During a campaign speech in 1928, Herbert Hoover reflected on Republican economic policies. Hoover sought to keep the government out of business in order to preserve "the American system of rugged individualism," and to continue prosperity:

> "*[T]he greatness of America has grown out of a political and social system and a method of control of economic forces distinctly its own—our American system—which has carried this great experiment in human welfare further than ever before in all history. We are nearer today to the ideal of the abolition of poverty and fear from the lives of men and women than ever before in any land.*"
>
> —Herbert Hoover, New York City, October 1928

Economy Appears Healthy

As you have read, Hoover easily won the 1928 election, benefiting from years of prosperity under previous Republican presidents. Americans widely admired this self-made millionaire for the way he had organized food relief in Europe during and after World War I. He had also worked effectively as Secretary of Commerce under Presidents Harding and Coolidge. People expected that the good times would get even better under Hoover.

"Wonderful Prosperity" As Hoover took office, the American economy seemed to be in fine shape. In 1925, the market value of all stocks was $27 billion. Over the next few years, stocks soared. In 1928 alone, stock values rose by more than $11 billion. Because the stock market was widely regarded as the nation's economic weathervane, the *New York Times* could describe the

RESOURCE DIRECTORY

Teaching Resources
Guided Reading and Review booklet, p. 88

Technology
Section Reading Support Transparencies
Guided Reading Audiotapes (English/Spanish), Ch. 14
Student Edition on Audio CD, Ch. 14
Prentice Hall Presentation Pro CD-ROM, Ch. 14
Companion Web site, www.phschool.com

year as one "of unprecedented advance, of wonderful prosperity." By early October 1929, stock values hit $87 billion.

Many working people had prospered in the post-World War I period. Since 1914, the value of workers' wages had risen more than 40 percent. Although certain industries were troubled and some workers lost jobs in the shift to new technologies, unemployment averaged below 4 percent. Even such critics of capitalism as journalist Lincoln Steffens made optimistic predictions: "Big business in America," Steffens said in 1928, "is producing what the Socialists held up as their goal: food, shelter and clothing for all. You will see it during the Hoover administration."

"Everybody Ought to Be Rich" People had unusually high confidence in the business world during the 1920s. For some, business success became almost a religion. One of the decade's best-selling books was *The Man Nobody Knows* (1925). Written by Bruce Barton, an advertising executive, it told the biblical story of Jesus' life in business terms. Barton portrayed Jesus as a managerial genius who "picked up twelve men [a reference to Jesus' 12 apostles, or followers] from the bottom ranks of business and forged them into an organization that conquered the world."

Similarly, Americans trusted the advice of corporate leaders such as John J. Raskob. In a 1929 article titled "Everybody Ought to Be Rich," Raskob stated that savings of only $15 a week over 20 years could bring a $400-a-month income from investments. "I am firm in my belief," Raskob said, "that anyone not only can be rich, but ought to be rich." Statements such as this encouraged Americans to make investments that in an earlier era would have seemed far too risky.

Market Speculation

Stock market speculation was almost a sport in the 1920s: The cartoon at left shows stockbrokers fishing for new clients from the top of the New York Stock Exchange. Though market investment is now more regulated than it was in the 1920s, Americans continue to speculate on stocks, both by buying on margin and by practicing other forms of high-risk trading.

One trading method involves what are known as call options. An investor may buy the right to purchase a certain stock before an expiration date, but at a price set near its current value (the "strike price"). Profit is made this way: If the stock goes up in price, the investor then "calls" in that option. In other words, he or she exercises the right to buy the stock at the lower rate set earlier. The investor then turns around and sells the same stock at its currently higher market price, or the option itself may be sold.

Some brokers have used the Internet to lure option speculators into making unwise investments. While the stock market has more government oversight than it did in the 1920s, buyers must still make their decisions carefully.

How could investors lose money by buying call options? Explain.

Welfare Capitalism Following the violent labor strikes of 1919, the postwar economy stabilized. Many larger companies launched strategies to meet some of their workers' demands. By doing so, they believed they could avoid union intervention, prevent strikes, and keep productivity high. This new approach to labor relations became known as **welfare capitalism.** Employers raised wages and provided such benefits as paid vacations, health plans, recreation programs, and English classes for recent immigrants, all in the interest of strengthening company loyalty and morale. Employers also set up "company unions," which they controlled, as channels for workers to express their concerns. As a result of welfare capitalism, organized labor lost members during the 1920s.

Economic Danger Signs

A climbing stock market, consumer confidence, and labor stability all pointed the way to a bright future. Yet despite the apparent prosperity, all was not well. Only later did many people recognize the warning signs of an unsound economy.

Uneven Prosperity Despite the stock market success stories, it was mainly the rich who got richer. Huge corporations rather than small businesses

Lesson Plan

Focus The United States was a confident, burgeoning place in the late 1920s. By all indications, the American economy was robust and the pace of innovation in fields such as manufacturing and medicine was rapid. Ask students to describe the reasons for late-1920s optimism.

Instruct Discuss the danger signs that lurked in the shadows of the apparently healthy economic indicators. Encourage students to analyze situations such as uneven prosperity, a growth in personal debt, a roller-coaster stock market, and surplus manufacturing capability. How do students think such warning signs should have been managed? To what extent would students say many of those situations grew out of natural human optimism and enthusiasm for an economy that nobody thought would ever stop growing?

Assess/Reteach Have students discuss how it would be possible for an economy to seem healthy to its core when it was in fact teetering on collapse.

Activity

Connecting with Science and Technology

As students read in the section "Setting the Scene," the late 1920s was a time when many dangerous diseases were conquered. Have students research the progress made in curing whooping cough and diphtheria, or in diminishing the rate of infant mortality in this era. Have students create visual presentations that summarize the progress made in these efforts. **(Visual/Spatial)**

Test Preparation

Have students review the material on this page under the heading "Welfare Capitalism" and then complete the sentence below.

Welfare capitalism is—

A giving money to people on welfare to make personal investments.

(B) the employers' practice of providing a living wage and benefits to employees.

C employee benefits made possible because of union negotiations.

D a tax paid by employed people to help support unemployed people.

Caption Answers

Fast Forward to Today Investors could lose money if the daily price of the stock declines steadily from the "strike price" after the call option has been purchased.

ACTIVITY
Connecting with Economics

An "installment" purchase is one in which a consumer buys an expensive item, such as a car or furniture, by making many small payments over a long time. In the years between 1920 and 1929, the number of installment purchases quintupled, reaching $6 billion per year. Have students research the growth of installment purchases during this decade and create a graph or table that demonstrates this growth. **(Logical/Mathematical)**

BACKGROUND
Geography in History

Hoover Dam, on the Nevada-Arizona border, controls the flow of the Colorado River. It has had more than one name. The project was begun while Herbert Hoover was Secretary of Commerce in the Harding administration, and he is generally credited with helping solve a series of problems that made the dam possible. When the dam was dedicated in 1936, it was named after him.

However, after Hoover left office, the dam became known as the Boulder Canyon Dam or the Boulder Dam. This change may have occurred because the new administration of Franklin D. Roosevelt did not want to promote such an impressive reminder of its immediate predecessor. Nonetheless, in 1947, the name Hoover Dam was officially restored to the project, and it retains that name to this day.

READING CHECK

Wealth was very unevenly distributed. Many families were on the brink of poverty. Large corporations dominated the industrial scene. Individual wealth was concentrated amongst a very small segment of the population.

CAPTION ANSWERS

Interpreting Diagrams Sixty-five percent of families earned below $2,000 a year.

READING CHECK
Describe the distribution of wealth in the United States in the 1920s. How were families affected?

dominated industry. In 1929, some 200 large companies controlled 49 percent of American industry.

Similarly, a small proportion of families held most of the nation's personal wealth. In 1929, the richest Americans—24,000 families, or just 0.1 percent of the population—had incomes of more than $100,000. They also held 34 percent of the country's total savings.

By contrast, 71 percent of individuals and families earned less than $2,500 a year, an amount some budget experts at the time considered the minimum standard of living. Nearly 80 percent of all families had no savings. Many people earned so little that almost every family member, children included, had to work just to get by.

Government tax policy contributed to this imbalance. Andrew Mellon, Secretary of the Treasury and one of the richest people in the nation, successfully pushed Congress to reduce taxes. Mellon's tax plan, however, gave the largest tax cuts to the wealthiest Americans. He believed that continued high taxation of the wealthy, imposed during the war, would hinder business expansion.

Personal Debt Many Americans became accustomed to credit spending during the 1920s. However, the resulting increase in personal debt signaled trouble. As you have read, assembly-line production made consumer items more affordable and available. People bought radios, vacuum cleaners, refrigerators, and other exciting new products, whether or not they had the money to pay for them. They believed that they could count on future income to cover their debts. Traditionally, Americans had feared debt and postponed buying goods until they had the cash to pay for them. Now, however, talk of unending prosperity eased worries about going into debt. Installment plans, boasting of "easy terms," made even luxury items seem affordable.

Personal Debt and Income Distribution in the 1920s

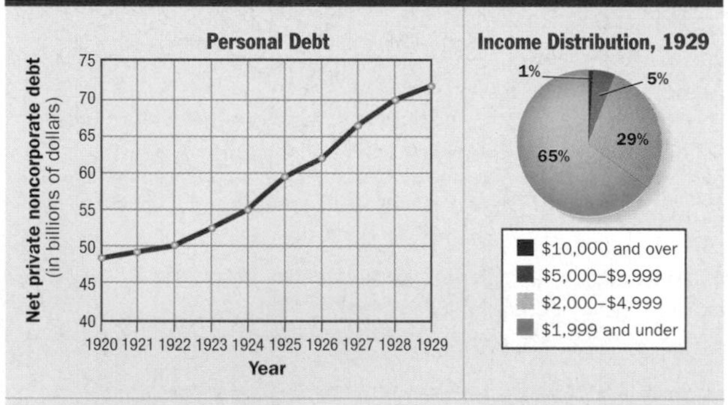

Personal Debt

Net private noncorporate debt (in billions of dollars)

75, 70, 65, 60, 55, 50, 45, 40

1920 1921 1922 1923 1924 1925 1926 1927 1928 1929

Year

Income Distribution, 1929

1%, 5%, 29%, 65%

$10,000 and over
$5,000–$9,999
$2,000–$4,999
$1,999 and under

SOURCE: *Historical Statistics of the United States, Colonial Times to 1970*

INTERPRETING DIAGRAMS
The circle graph (right) shows how unevenly the country's wealth was distributed in the 1920s. The line graph (left) shows the rise in personal debt. **Analyzing Information** *What percentage of American families earned less than $2,000 a year in 1929?*

Playing the Stock Market Fed by the optimism of the age, a "get-rich-quick" attitude prevailed during the 1920s. The dizzying climb of stock prices encouraged widespread **speculation,** the practice of making high-risk investments in hopes of getting a huge return.

Before World War I, only the wealthy played the stock market. Now the press reported stories of how ordinary people were making fortunes. Many small investors entered the market, often spending their life savings. To attract these less wealthy investors, stockbrokers encouraged a practice called **buying on margin.** This option allowed investors to purchase a stock for only a fraction of its price (10 to 50 percent) and borrow the rest. The brokers charged high interest rates and could demand payment of the loan at any time. If the stock price went up, however, borrowers could sell the stock at a price high enough to pay off both the loan and the interest charges and still make money.

Too Many Goods, Too Little Demand Rising productivity had brought prosperity, but eventually it created a problem. By the late 1920s, the country's warehouses were overstocked; they held more goods than consumers would

RESOURCE DIRECTORY

Teaching Resources

Units 3/4 booklet
- Section 3 Quiz, p. 54
- Chapter 14 Test, pp. 55, 58

Guide to the Essentials
- Section 3 Summary, p. 70
- Chapter 14 Test, p. 71

Other Print Resources

Chapter Tests with ExamView® Test Bank CD-ROM, Ch. 14

Technology

ExamView® Test Bank CD-ROM, Ch. 14
Social Studies Skills Tutor CD-ROM

buy. Wages had risen, but people still could not afford to buy goods as fast as the assembly lines turned them out.

Although the stock market kept rising, overproduction caused some industries to slow in the late 1920s. The automobile industry, which had helped create American prosperity, slumped after 1925. Industries that depended on it, including steel, rubber, and glass, also declined. Housing construction, which also caused a "ripple effect" on the economy, fell by 25 percent between 1928 and 1929.

Trouble for Farmers and Workers As you have read, falling farm prices left many farmers unable to repay their debts for land and machinery. These farmers often lost their farms. Some rural banks gave farmers extra time to meet their obligations, but those banks struggled when loans were not repaid. About 6,000 rural banks failed during the 1920s.

Congress responded to the farm problem with the McNary-Haugen farm relief bill. This measure was designed to increase the prices farmers received for their crops. Congress passed the bill twice, in 1927 and 1928, but each time President Coolidge vetoed it, believing that it was not the government's job to provide such assistance. Farmers continued to suffer.

Life remained exceedingly hard for many factory workers as well. While companies grew wealthy, most laborers still worked long hours for low wages. Conditions were especially bad in distressed industries, such as coal mining and textiles. In the rayon mills of Elizabethton, Tennessee, for instance, women worked 56-hour weeks, earning 16 to 18 cents an hour—about $10 a week.

To some observers, these factors—uneven wealth, rising debt, stock speculation, overproduction, and the hardships of farmers and workers—clearly signaled trouble in the economy. In 1928, Belle Moskowitz, who had managed Al Smith's losing presidential campaign that year, predicted that "growing unemployment, business depression, or some false step" would soon trigger a reaction against Republican policies.

VIEWING HISTORY Auctioneers grew increasingly busy through the late 1920s, as distressed farmers defaulted on loans for expensive equipment and other items. **Identifying Alternatives** *What economic choices did farmers face after they repaid their loans?*

Section 3 Assessment

READING COMPREHENSION

1. What reasons did corporations have for practicing **welfare capitalism** in the 1920s?
2. Why was **speculation** in the stock market so popular in the 1920s?
3. How does a stockbroker profit from an investor **buying on margin?**

CRITICAL THINKING AND WRITING

4. **Recognizing Cause and Effect** How does a widespread increase in personal debt affect a nation's economy?
5. **Writing to Persuade** Write an essay from the perspective of someone living in the 1920s and feeling optimistic about his or her finances. Persuade your readers that the economy is sound, despite all the existing danger signs.

Take It to the NET

Activity: Creating a Diagram
Research more on how the economy of the 1920s functioned. Create a chart or diagram showing what factors affected the economy and how the economy affected people's lives. Use the links provided in the *America: Pathways to the Present* area of the following Web site for help in completing this activity.
www.phschool.com

Section 3 Assessment

Reading Comprehension

1. They hoped to meet workers' demands while avoiding union intervention, preventing strikes, and keeping productivity high.
2. The optimism of the age, the prevalence of a "get-rich-quick" mentality, and the rise in stock values.
3. The brokers charge high interest rates and could demand payment of the loan at any time.

Critical Thinking and Writing

4. If future earning potential is curtailed by an economic downturn, people become unable to pay back their loans. This, in turn, devastates the finances of lenders.
5. Essays will vary, but should persuade the reader and be supported with facts from the section.

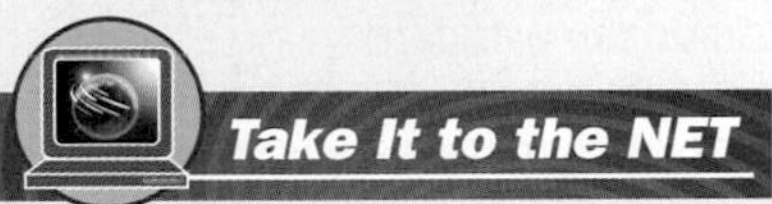

Take It to the NET

Sample answer: Mass production made goods easier to manufacture in large quantities; more production often led to higher wages and lower unemployment; higher wages led to more consumer spending; and the presence of mass-marketed goods made consumer spending easy to accomplish.

CUSTOMIZE FOR ...

Less Proficient Writers

Have students place the following events in the correct chronological order:

- Herbert Hoover is elected.
- The general public begins participation in the stock market.
- The value of the stock market increases by $11 billion in one year.
- Personal debt of Americans exceeds $70 billion.

CAPTION ANSWERS

Viewing History They could continue to farm, and probably incur more debt doing so. They could try to work in another industry, but that might involve moving to a city. Such a change would be difficult for those who had never done any other work besides farming.

Chapter 14

Reviewing Key Terms

Students should refer to the definitions of key terms in the chapter to write sentences that show an understanding of the era of politics and prosperity.

Reviewing Main Ideas

11. Labor strikes and terrorist acts. The government responded with the Palmer raids.
12. Though Schenck contended that he was only exercising free speech, the Supreme Court declared that Schenck's actions created a "clear and present danger" to the nation.
13. It raised import taxes, with special protection for new American industrial products, furthering a break from foreign countries. It also impeded European repayment of American war debt.
14. Harding appointed dishonest and incompetent friends and acquaintances to high office. This resulted in widespread corruption, such as the Teapot Dome Scandal. Coolidge was respected for his actions as governor of Massachusetts; he had no part in the Harding scandals; he was a skilled public speaker.
15. Advertising no longer sold only products; it also sought to make new consumer goods seem glamorous. Fewer hard facts about the products were presented. Instead, advertising focused on such things as how the product would make one more stylish.
16. An increase in productivity due to the development of new resources, new management methods, and new technologies.
17. Ford produced cars that working people could afford. Auto-making became the nation's biggest single manufacturing industry. Scores of related new businesses arose.
18. Republican laissez-faire policies caused rapid business expansion, opening up new opportunities for competitors to the giant monopolies. The automobile, steel, oil and electrical industries boomed as did the publishing, motion picture, and machine-making industries.
19. It furthered the imbalance, giving the largest tax cuts to the wealthiest Americans.

Chapter 14 Review and Assessment

creating a CHAPTER SUMMARY

Copy this chart (right) on a piece of paper and complete it by showing how Republican leadership affected American life and the economy in the 1920s.

Administrations	Policies, Legislation, and Major Events
Wilson	Labor strikes, Palmer raids
Harding	"Normalcy"
Coolidge	
Hoover	

For additional review and enrichment activities, see the interactive version of *America: Pathways to the Present*, available on the Web and on CD-ROM.

★ Reviewing Key Terms

For each of the terms below, write a sentence explaining how it relates to the post-World War I period.

1. communism
2. disarmament
3. quota
4. Teapot Dome scandal
5. Kellogg-Briand Pact
6. installment plan
7. assembly line
8. welfare capitalism
9. speculation
10. buying on margin

★ Reviewing Main Ideas

11. What events of 1919 caused the Red Scare? How did the government respond? (Section 1)
12. Explain why the Supreme Court decision in *Schenck* v. *U.S.* seemed to justify jailing Communists. (Section 1)
13. Describe how the Fordney-McCumber Tariff of 1922 reflects a policy of isolationism. (Section 1)
14. What events brought disgrace upon the Harding presidency? How did Coolidge restore respect to the office? (Section 1)
15. How did the advertising industry help to develop a consumer economy? (Section 2)
16. What helped the growth of the Gross National Product (GNP) during the 1920s? (Section 2)
17. Describe Henry Ford's impact on American business and society. (Section 2)
18. How did a decade of Republican government affect the economy? (Section 3)
19. Evaluate the impact of the government's tax policy on income distribution in 1929. (Section 3)
20. What issues faced farm and factory workers in the late 1920s? (Section 3)

★ Critical Thinking

21. **Comparing Points of View** Evaluate welfare capitalism from the point of view of (a) a factory worker, (b) a labor union leader, and (c) a factory owner.
22. **Expressing Problems Clearly** Explain the American public's opposition to the wave of labor strikes that occurred from 1919 to 1920.
23. **Recognizing Bias** How did the bombing of A. Mitchell Palmer's home in 1919 affect Palmer's actions as Attorney General of the United States?
24. **Determining Relevance** How might changing social customs and attitudes have affected the spending habits of Americans during the 1920s?
25. **Recognizing Ideologies** Identify the domestic issues that led to passage of immigration legislation in the 1920s. Why were immigration quotas favored? What was the impact of the legislation?

Creating a Chapter Summary

Administrations	Policies, Legislation, and Major Events
Wilson	Labor strikes, Palmer raids
Harding	"Normalcy"
Coolidge	Laissez-faire business policy, Kellogg-Briand Pact
Hoover	Rising productivity, rising personal debt, stock market boom, stock market crash

★ Skills Assessment

Analyzing Political Cartoons ▶

26. This cartoon appeared in 1924. (a) Who was President in 1924? (b) What were the major news items regarding the presidential administration in 1924?
27. Describe the scene in the cartoon. What is it satirizing?
28. Why are Cabinet members advertised as being for sale?

Analyzing Primary Sources

Reread President Harding's quote from the first page of Section 1, and then answer the questions that follow.

29. Which statement best represents the meaning of the quotation?
    - **A** Americans need to commit to radical reforms.
    - **B** The nation's problems can be solved with international assistance.
    - **C** The nation should look calmly inward and proceed with caution.
    - **D** The nation's heroes will lead the country to triumph.
30. Harding's message was effective because
    - **F** the heroic actions taken in World War I were no longer admired.
    - **G** Americans were seeking the stability and normalcy Harding promised.
    - **H** voters were looking for Harding to deliver dramatic solutions to their problems.
    - **J** sustaining international ties was important to the American public.
31. **Applying the Chapter Skill: Analyzing Advertising** Turn to the vacuum cleaner ad in Section 2. What does the ad say about life in the 1920s? What does the ad promise that the vacuum cleaner will do for the consumer?

ACTIVITIES

Writing to LEARN

Writing an Opinion
Consider the beliefs and fears that helped fuel the Red Scare in the 1920s. What events led up to the Red Scare? How did fears of Communism develop, and were those fears justified? Explain your reasoning.

Primary Source CD-ROM

Working With Primary Sources Find additional information about the 1920s on the *Exploring Primary Sources in U.S. History CD-ROM* and use the selection(s) provided to complete the Chapter 14 primary source activity located in the *America: Pathways to the Present* area of the following Web site.
www.phschool.com

Take It to the NET

Chapter Self-Test As a review activity, take the Chapter 14 Self-Test in the *America: Pathways to the Present* area at the Web site listed below. The questions are designed to test your understanding of the chapter content.
www.phschool.com

ANSWERS TO ACTIVITIES

Writing to LEARN

Sample response: The belief that communism would spread to America and the fear of violence. It was understandable to a certain extent since Lenin vowed to stir up revolutions in other countries, but the widespread paranoia that took place in America resulted in raids and arrests of innocent people.

Primary Source CD-ROM

Direct students to the additional primary sources that can be found on the *Exploring Primary Sources in U.S. History CD-ROM.*

Take It to the NET

Additional support materials and activities for Chapter 14 of *America: Pathways to the Present* can be found in the Social Studies area at the Prentice Hall School Web site. **www.phschool.com**

20. Falling farm prices left farmers unable to repay their debts, facing the loss of their farms. Factory workers faced long hours for low wages and in poor conditions.

CRITICAL THINKING

21. (a) Support, due to increased wages and benefits. (b) Oppose, as it would mean a decrease in union membership. (c) Mixed, had to offer employees more money and benefits, but avoided strikes and could thereby maintain increased productivity.
22. They believed Communists and other radicals were behind the labor unrest. This activity was thought to be un-American.
23. It caused him to believe that radicals were conspiring to overthrow the government, leading him to create a campaign to identify and eliminate groups like Communists, Socialists, and anarchists.
24. New advertising techniques made it seem acceptable to purchase on credit. Advertising also sold "image" as well as products. Such changes in the 1920s encouraged people to purchase what they wanted, not just items they needed.
25. Americans associated immigrants with Communism and radical politics. Laborers feared immigrant competition for jobs. Nativism was on the rise in the U.S. Quotas were favored because they sharply restricted immigration from eastern and southern Europe as well as Japan.

SKILLS ASSESSMENT

26. (a) Calvin Coolidge. (b) Financial scandals, such as the Teapot Dome scandal, that had characterized the previous Harding administration.
27. The scene shows the Capitol, White House, Washington Monument, the armed forces, and members of Harding's administration for sale. It is satirizing the scandals in Harding's administration.
28. In the Teapot Dome affair, a Cabinet secretary (Albert Fall) gave away oil rights on government land in exchange for money.
29. C
30. G
31. The advertisement exemplifies the excitement over new consumer goods. It promises that cleaning can be done more thoroughly in much less time with the vacuum cleaner, thus increasing one's leisure time.

Taking to the Highway

Focus Explain that when automobiles were first invented, they were purchased more by sports enthusiasts or hobbyists than as a practical means of transportation. Early automobiles had no roofs and traveled slowly on dirt roadways built for horses and buggies. The first cars were owned by very few individuals and were relatively expensive.

Instruct Ask students to list the types of changes that would be necessary in order for American society to increase its reliance on cars for transportation. Have them consider the design of early cars, including the fact that they did not have roofs, as well as the fact that they were relatively expensive to purchase. How did design modifications and the introduction of mass production influence the popularity of automobiles?

Discuss with students the 1921 establishment of the federal highway system. Have them consider how this uniform system of connected roads would have influenced the increased use of cars. Ask students to list the ways in which the increased use of cars across the United States affected the development of the country.

Extend Ask students to compare and contrast the development of the national railway system with the development of the interstate highway system. In what ways are the two systems similar? How are they different? How did the rise of auto travel ultimately affect the railroads?

Geography & History

Taking to the Highway

Car ownership expanded rapidly during the 1910s and the 1920s. By 1927, some 54 percent of American families owned a car. The growing popularity of car travel and the usefulness of trucks during World War I led to calls for federally funded highways. In 1926, the first nationwide system of numbered highways was introduced, as shown on this map.

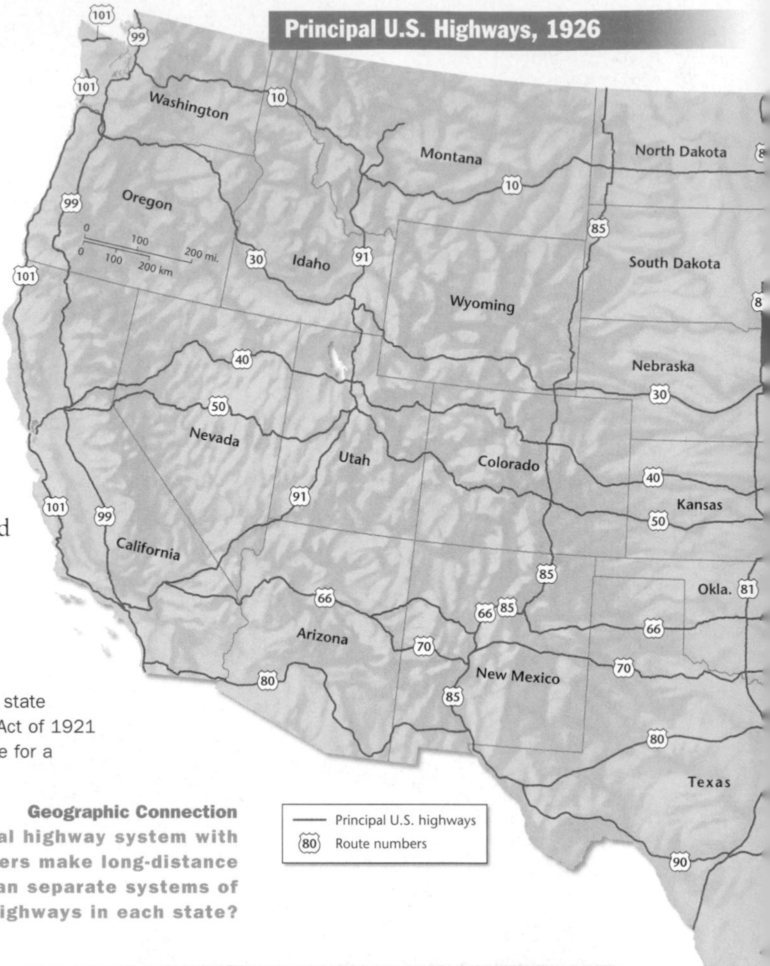

Principal U.S. Highways, 1926

— Principal U.S. highways
(80) Route numbers

Aid for Highways
The first paved highways were built with state and local funding. The Federal Highway Act of 1921 provided federal funding for the first time for a national system of paved highways.

Geographic Connection
How would a federal highway system with uniform route numbers make long-distance travel easier than separate systems of numbered highways in each state?

The Difficulties of Early Car Travel
When cars were first introduced in the 1890s and early 1900s, they had to travel on poorly maintained dirt roads that often turned to mud when it rained.

Answers

1. Travelers would be able to follow the same route number as they passed from one state to another.

RESOURCE DIRECTORY

Teaching Resources
Geography and History booklet, pp. 14–15

Other Print Resources
Nystrom *Atlas of Our Country* *United States Political Map,* pp. 38–39

Technology
Prentice Hall United States History Video Collection™ Volume 17, *The Roaring Twenties*

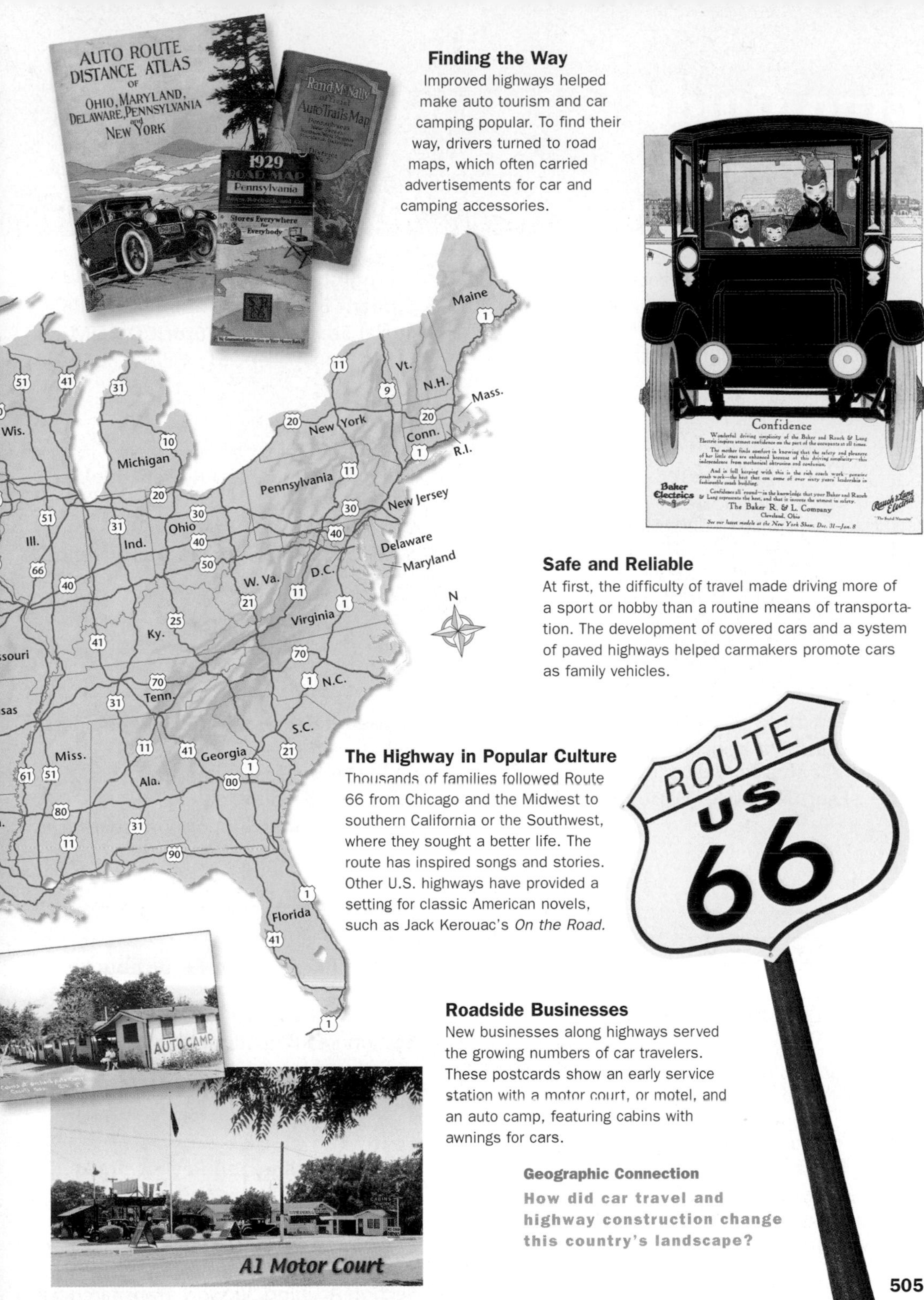

Finding the Way
Improved highways helped make auto tourism and car camping popular. To find their way, drivers turned to road maps, which often carried advertisements for car and camping accessories.

Safe and Reliable
At first, the difficulty of travel made driving more of a sport or hobby than a routine means of transportation. The development of covered cars and a system of paved highways helped carmakers promote cars as family vehicles.

The Highway in Popular Culture
Thousands of families followed Route 66 from Chicago and the Midwest to southern California or the Southwest, where they sought a better life. The route has inspired songs and stories. Other U.S. highways have provided a setting for classic American novels, such as Jack Kerouac's *On the Road.*

Roadside Businesses
New businesses along highways served the growing numbers of car travelers. These postcards show an early service station with a motor court, or motel, and an auto camp, featuring cabins with awnings for cars.

Geographic Connection
How did car travel and highway construction change this country's landscape?

505

Answers

2. It created a network of paved highways and a landscape of roadside businesses along them. It promoted the development of camping facilities, resorts, and tourist attractions.

Chapter 15 Planning Guide
Resource Manager

	CORE INSTRUCTION	READING/SKILLS
Chapter-Level Resources 1(A), 25(A), 25(B), 25(D)	Teaching Resources • Pacing Charts booklet • Block Scheduling booklet **Resource Pro® CD-ROM,** Ch. 15 **Prentice Hall Presentation Pro CD-ROM,** Ch. 15 **www.phschool.com** • eTeach	**Guided Reading Audiotapes (English/Spanish)** **Student Edition on Audio CD,** Ch. 15 **Social Studies Skills Tutor CD-ROM** **Color Transparencies,** A35, B12, F7
1 The Stock Market Crash 1. Learn about events that led to the stock market's Great Crash in 1929. 2. See how the Great Crash produced a ripple effect throughout the nation's economy. 3. Become familiar with the main causes of the Great Depression. 1(B), 13(B), 13(C)	Teaching Resources **Units 3/4 booklet** • Section 1 Quiz, p. 62	**Guided Reading and Review booklet,** p. 89 **Guide to the Essentials,** p. 72 **Section Reading Support Transparencies**
2 Social Effects of the Depression 1. Understand how poverty spread during the Great Depression. 2. Find out about social problems that were caused by poverty in the 1930s. 3. Discover how some people struggled to survive hard times. 9(A), 13(C), 21(D), 24(A)	Teaching Resources **Units 3/4 booklet** • Section 2 Quiz, p. 63 **Learning Styles Lesson Plans booklet,** p. 46	**Guided Reading and Review booklet,** p. 90 **Guide to the Essentials,** p. 73 **Skills for Life booklet,** p. 17 **Section Reading Support Transparencies**
3 Surviving the Great Depression 1. Read about ways Americans pulled together to survive the Great Depression. 2. See the signs of change Americans began to notice in the early 1930s. 13(C), 17(B)	Teaching Resources **Units 3/4 booklet** • Section 3 Quiz, p. 64	**Guided Reading and Review booklet,** p. 91 **Guide to the Essentials,** p. 74 **Section Reading Support Transparencies**
4 The Election of 1932 1. Find out how President Hoover responded to the Great Depression. 2. Learn what Roosevelt meant when he offered Americans a "new deal." 3. Realize why the election of 1932 was a significant turning point in American politics. 20(A)	Teaching Resources **Units 3/4 booklet** • Section 4 Quiz, p. 65 **Learning Styles Lesson Plans booklet,** p. 47	**Guided Reading and Review booklet,** p. 92 **Guide to the Essentials,** p. 75 **Learning with Documents booklet,** p. 87 **Section Reading Support Transparencies**

Enrichment/Pre-AP

Prentice Hall United States History Video Collection™
www.phschool.com
- Section Activities, Virtual Field Trip, Chapter Activities, Current Events Online

Biography, Literature, and Comparing Primary Sources booklet, p. 70
American History Block Scheduling Support

American History Block Scheduling Support
Sounds of an Era Audio CD
Exploring Primary Sources in U.S. History CD-ROM

Biography, Literature, and Comparing Primary Sources booklet, p. 27
Exploring Primary Sources in U.S. History CD-ROM

Biography, Literature, and Comparing Primary Sources booklet, p. 139
Sounds of an Era Audio CD
American Pathways Thematic Posters

Assessment

Core Assessment
ExamView® Test Bank, Ch. 15
ExamView® Test Bank CD-ROM, Ch. 15

Standardized Test Preparation
Diagnose and Prescribe
Diagnostic Tests for High School Social Studies Skills

Review and Reteach
Review Book for U.S. History

Practice and Assess
Test-taking Strategies With Transparencies
Test-taking Strategies Posters
Test Prep Book for U.S. History
Alternative Assessment Handbook
Document-Based Assessment

Teaching Resources
Units 3/4 booklet
- Section Quizzes, pp. 62–65
- Chapter Tests, pp. 66, 69

www.phschool.com Ch. 15 Self-Test

AmericanHeritage® Resources

From the Archives of American Heritage®, p. 526
AmericanHeritage® My Brush with History™ Videotapes
www.americanheritage.com

Don't miss the exclusive interactive version of this textbook on the Web and on CD-ROM.

Chapter 15 Planning Guide
In Your Classroom

Customize for Individual Needs

Gifted and Talented

Teacher's Edition
- Customize for Gifted and Talented, p. 527

Teaching Resources
- Biography, Literature, and Comparing Primary Sources booklet, pp. 27, 70, 139

Technology
- Exploring Primary Sources in U.S. History CD-ROM *The Grapes of Wrath, John Steinbeck; Depression Photograph, Dorothea Lange; This Land Is Your Land, Woody Guthrie*

ESL

Teacher's Edition
- Customize for ESL, p. 517

Teaching Resources
- Guided Reading and Review booklet, pp. 89–92
- Guide to the Essentials (English/Spanish), Chapter 15

Technology
- Student Edition on Audio CD, Chapter 15
- Guided Reading Audiotapes (English/Spanish), Chapter 15
- Section Reading Support Transparencies

Less Proficient Readers

Teacher's Edition
- Customize for Less Proficient Readers, p. 509

Teaching Resources
- Guided Reading and Review booklet, pp. 89–92
- Guide to the Essentials (English/Spanish), Chapter 15

Technology
- Student Edition on Audio CD, Chapter 15
- Guided Reading Audiotapes (English/Spanish), Chapter 15
- Section Reading Support Transparencies

Less Proficient Writers

Teacher's Edition
- Customize for Less Proficient Writers, p. 523

Teaching Resources
- Guided Reading and Review booklet, pp. 89–92
- Guide to the Essentials (English/Spanish), Chapter 15

Technology
- Student Edition on Audio CD, Chapter 15
- Guided Reading Audiotapes (English/Spanish), Chapter 15
- Section Reading Support Transparencies

Teacher's Edition Index

Chapter 15 – Pacing Suggestions

For 90-minute Blocks

- Teach sections 1, 2, and 4 using Transparencies A35, B12, and F7, and the Recent Scholarship note on page 515 for class discussions.

Running Out of Time?

If you are running short on time to cover this chapter, consider the following options:

- Use Prentice Hall Presentation Pro CD-ROM to create an outline for this chapter.
- Use the Section Summaries for Chapter 15, from **Guide to the Essentials (English/Spanish).**

TEKS Correlation

Chapter-Level	**TEKS** **(1) History.** The student understands traditional historical points of reference in U.S. history from 1877 to the present. The student is expected to: **(A)** identify the major eras in U.S. history from 1877 to the present and describe their defining characteristics. **(25) Social studies skills.** The student communicates in written, oral, and visual forms. The student is expected to: **(A)** use social studies terminology correctly. **(B)** use standard grammar, spelling, sentence structure, and punctuation. **(D)** create written, oral, and visual presentations of social studies information.
1 The Stock Market Crash	**(1) History.** The student understands traditional historical points of reference in U.S. history from 1877 to the present. The student is expected to: **(B)** apply absolute and relative chronology through the sequencing of significant individuals, events, and time periods. **(13) Economics.** The student understands significant economic developments between World War I and World War II. The student is expected to: **(B)** analyze the causes of the Great Depression, including the decline in worldwide trade, the stock market crash, and bank failures. **(C)** analyze the effects of the Great Depression on the U.S. economy and government.
2 Social Effects of the Depression	**(9) Geography.** The student understands the impact of geographic factors on major events. The student is expected to: **(A)** analyze the effects of physical and human geographic factors on major events including the building of the Panama Canal. **(13) Economics.** The student understands significant economic developments between World War I and World War II. The student is expected to: **(C)** analyze the effects of the Great Depression on the U.S. economy and government. **(21) Culture.** The student understands how people from various groups, including racial, ethnic, and religious groups, adapt to life in the United States and contribute to our national identity. The student is expected to: **(D)** identify the political, social, and economic contributions of women to American society. **(24) Social studies skills.** The student applies critical-thinking skills to organize and use information acquired from a variety of sources including electronic technology. The student is expected to: **(A)** locate and use primary and secondary sources such as computer software, databases, media and news services, biographies, interviews, and artifacts to acquire information about the United States.
3 Surviving the Great Depression	**(13) Economics.** The student understands significant economic developments between World War I and World War II. The student is expected to: **(C)** analyze the effects of the Great Depression on the U.S. economy and government. **(17) Government.** The student understands the impact of constitutional issues on American society in the 20th century. The student is expected to: **(B)** analyze reasons for the adoption of 20th-century constitutional amendments.
4 The Election of 1932	**(20) Culture.** The student understands the relationship between the arts and the times during which they were created. The student is expected to: **(A)** describe how the characteristics and issues of various eras in U.S. history have been reflected in works of art, music, and literature such as the paintings of Georgia O'Keeffe, rock and roll, and John Steinbeck's *The Grapes of Wrath.*

Chapter 15

Crash and Depression

(1929–1933)

Introducing the Chapter

When the economy of the high-flying 1920s crashed in 1929, the bleak years of the Great Depression began. Behind the headlines and photos of stock-buying-and-selling frenzy and destitution grew a debate that cut to the very political, social, and economic fiber of the country and changed forever how Americans look at government.

Time Line Activity

To provide students with practice in using the time line, ask questions such as these:

1. What single event led to the Great Depression? *(The Great Crash of October 29, 1929)*
2. What famous building was completed at the height of the Depression? *(The Empire State Building)*
3. What were conditions like in the Soviet Union in 1932? *(There was widespread famine.)*

Chapter 15

Crash and Depression

(1929–1933)

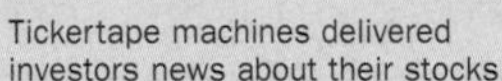

Tickertape machines delivered investors news about their stocks.

American Events

1929 Oct. 29: Stock prices tumble in what is known as the Great Crash. Investors lose millions of dollars, and the economy sinks into a devastating depression.

1930 Congress passes the Hawley-Smoot tariff, the highest import tax in American history, in an effort to protect domestic industries. World trade suffers as a result.

1931 The Empire State Building, the world's tallest, opens in New York City.

Presidential Terms: Herbert Hoover 1929–1933

1929 — 1930 — 1931

World Events

1929 The term *apartheid* is introduced in South Africa.

1930 Five nations meet at the London Naval Conference.

1931 Japanese troops occupy Manchuria.

eTeach

Be sure to check out this month's online discussion with a Master Teacher. Go to **www.phschool.com**.

Resource Directory

Teaching Resources

Pacing Charts booklet

Block Scheduling booklet, p. 24

Units 3/4 booklet

- Chapter Summary, p. 61

Technology

Guided Reading Audiotapes (English/Spanish), Ch. 15

Student Edition on Audio CD, Ch. 15

Sounds of an Era Audio CD *"Brother Can You Spare a Dime?"* 1932 recording

Prentice Hall United States History Video Collection™ Volume 18, *The Great Depression and the New Deal*

Prentice Hall Presentation Pro CD-ROM, Ch. 15

Resource Pro® CD-ROM

Social Studies Skills Tutor CD-ROM

Companion Web site, www.phschool.com

The Dust Bowl, 1933–1940

CANADA

MEXICO

PACIFIC OCEAN

ATLANTIC OCEAN

Gulf of Mexico

Washington, Oregon, California, Nevada, Idaho, Montana, Wyoming, Utah, Arizona, Colorado, New Mexico, North Dakota, South Dakota, Nebraska, Kansas, Oklahoma, Texas, Minnesota, Iowa, Missouri, Arkansas, Louisiana, Wisconsin, Illinois, Michigan, Indiana, Ohio, Kentucky, Tennessee, Mississippi, Alabama, Georgia, Florida, South Carolina, North Carolina, Virginia, West Virginia, Pennsylvania, New York, Maryland, Delaware, New Jersey, District of Columbia, Conn., R.I., Massachusetts, Vt., N.H., Maine

- Severe wind erosion
- Slight wind erosion
- Dust Bowl

0 150 300 mi.
0 150 300 km

Franklin D. Roosevelt at his inauguration in 1933.

1932 President Hoover authorizes troops to remove Bonus Army protesters after Congress refuses to give them an advance on a pension bonus.

1932 The American people, hopeful about Franklin Delano Roosevelt's "New Deal," overwhelmingly elect him to be the nation's 32nd President.

1933 Congress passes the Twenty-first Amendment, which repeals Prohibition.

Franklin D. Roosevelt 1933–1945

1932 **1933**

1932 Famine strikes the Soviet Union.

1933 Hitler and the Nazis take over Germany.

The Dust Bowl, 1933–1940

Activating Prior Knowledge What region of the United States was most heavily affected by the drought that caused the Dust Bowl? *(The Midwest)*

Previewing What role did climatic conditions play in creating the Dust Bowl? *(Overcultivated areas with severe wind erosion and a lack of rainfall experienced the worst effects.)*

BACKGROUND
About the Pictures

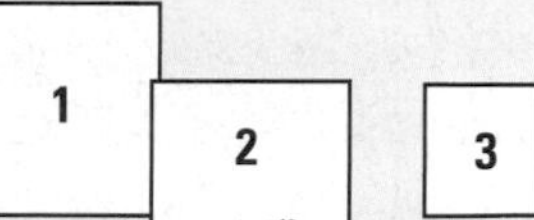

1. The stock ticker machine was a small telegraph receiver connected to the New York Stock Exchange. It would print out the stock trade information on long, thin rolls of paper known as ticker tape. The phrase "ticker-tape parade" originated when brokerage offices on Wall Street threw their used ticker-tape rolls out of the windows during parades.
2. At the time it was completed, the Empire State Building in New York City was the tallest in the world. All 100 stories were completed in just over 400 days, an average of 4½ stories built each week. Over 7 million hours of work were required to complete the building.
3. Franklin Delano Roosevelt's inauguration was on March 4, 1933.

BIBLIOGRAPHY

For the Teacher

Brendon, Piers. ***The Dark Valley: A Panorama of the 1930s.*** Knopf, 2000. (A vivid portrait of conditions around the world during the 1930s.)

Watkins, T. H. ***The Great Depression: America in the 1930s.*** Little, Brown, 1995. (Companion volume to the PBS video.)

For the Student

The Great Depression. 420 minutes. PBS Video, 1993. (Seven one-hour segments produced by the Public Broadcasting Service.)

The Grapes of Wrath. 129 minutes. Zenger. Black-and-white film. (Dramatization of John Steinbeck's novel about the Depression.)

Don't miss the exclusive interactive version of this textbook on the Web and on CD-ROM.

Section 1
The Stock Market Crash

Section Objectives

1. Learn about events that led to the stock market's Great Crash in 1929.
2. See how the Great Crash produced a ripple effect throughout the nation's economy.
3. Become familiar with the main causes of the Great Depression.

Bellringer

Warm-Up Activity Ask students to take the perspective of a bank customer who wants to withdraw savings and is told by the teller that there is no money. What might be the cause of such a situation? What options would the customer have?

Activating Prior Knowledge Ask students if they have ever heard a description of conditions during the Great Depression. What are their impressions of that time?

Reading Strategy

Have students copy the time line on the previous pages. Then, as they read, have them add more information to the time line. Have them apply absolute and relative chronology through the sequencing of significant individuals, events, and time periods as they analyze how one event led to the next. Have them analyze the causes of the Great Depression, including the decline in worldwide trade, the stock market crash, and bank failures.

Section 1

The Stock Market Crash

READING FOCUS

- What events led to the stock market's Great Crash in 1929?
- Why did the Great Crash produce a ripple effect throughout the nation's economy?
- What were the main causes of the Great Depression?

KEY TERMS

Dow Jones Industrial Average
Black Tuesday
Great Crash
business cycle
Great Depression

TAKING NOTES

As you read, complete the following diagram to show some of the causes and effects of the Stock Market's Great Crash in 1929.

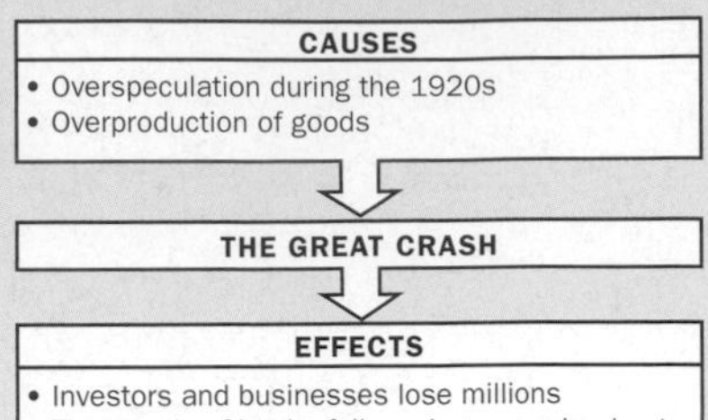

CAUSES
• Overspeculation during the 1920s
• Overproduction of goods
THE GREAT CRASH
EFFECTS
• Investors and businesses lose millions
• Thousands of banks fail, savings are wiped out

MAIN IDEA

In October 1929, panic selling caused the United States stock market to crash. The crash led to a worldwide economic crisis called the Great Depression.

Setting the Scene On October 29, 1929, fear gripped the floors of the New York Stock Exchange as investors watched millions of dollars slip away. The "wonderful prosperity" of the 1920s had come to an abrupt end. Writers Gordon Thomas and Max Morgan-Witts captured the scene:

> *"A messenger struggling through the crowd suddenly found himself yanked by his hair off his feet. The man who held him kept screaming he had been ruined. He would not let the boy go. The terrified youth at last broke free, leaving the man holding tufts of his hair. Crying in pain, the messenger fled the Exchange. His hair never regrew.*
>
> *Behind, he left a scene of increasing pandemonium. As huge blocks of shares continued to be dumped, . . . 1,000 brokers and a support army of 2,000 page boys, clerks, telephonists . . . and official recorders could sense this was going to be the 'day of the millionaire's slaughter.'*
>
> *William Crawford, swept along helplessly by the great tide of people, would always remember how 'they roared like a lot of lions and tigers. They hollered and screamed, they clawed at one another's collars. It was like a bunch of crazy men.'"*
>
> —Gordon Thomas and Max Morgan-Witts from *The Day the Bubble Burst*

VIEWING HISTORY As stock market prices fell, the ticker tape could not report market activity fast enough. Nervous investors crowded into Wall Street hoping to hear the latest news. **Identifying Central Issues** *Why did investors panic in October 1929?*

The Market Crashes

Before the panic on that fateful October day, most people saw no reason to worry. In early 1928, the **Dow Jones Industrial Average,** an average of stock prices of major industries, had climbed to 191. By Hoover's Inauguration

Caption Answers

Viewing History As stock prices dropped sharply, investors began to lose millions of dollars. Many tried to sell their stocks as soon as they could to avoid losing their entire investments. They believed they faced financial ruin.

RESOURCE DIRECTORY

Teaching Resources

Guided Reading and Review booklet, p. 89
Biography, Literature, and Comparing Primary Sources booklet (Literature) *The Stock Market Crash,* p. 70

Other Print Resources

American History Block Scheduling Support *The Great Depression: A Struggle to Survive,* found in the Prosperity, Depression, and War folder, includes interdisciplinary lesson suggestions and activities for Geography and History, Primary Sources, Biography, and Literature.

Technology

Section Reading Support Transparencies
Guided Reading Audiotapes (English/Spanish), Ch. 15
Student Edition on Audio CD, Ch. 15
RESOURCE PRO® **Biography** *Woody Guthrie,* found on Resource Pro, profiles the folk songwriter and singer who chronicled the woes of ordinary Americans during the Depression.
Prentice Hall Presentation Pro CD-ROM, Ch. 15
Companion Web site, www.phschool.com

Day, March 4, 1929, it had risen another 122 points. By September 3, the Dow Jones average reached an all-time high of 381.

The rising stock market dominated the news. Keeping track of prices became almost as popular as counting Babe Ruth's home runs. Eager, nervous investors filled brokerage houses to catch the latest news coming in on the ticker tape. Prices for many stocks soared far above their real value in terms of the company's earnings and assets.

Black Thursday After the peak in September, stock prices fell slowly. Some brokers began to call in loans, but others continued to lend even more. One bank official assured the nervous public: "Although in some cases speculation has gone too far, . . . the markets generally are now in a healthy condition."

When the stock market closed on Wednesday, October 23, the Dow Jones average had dropped 21 points in an hour. The next day, Thursday, October 24, worried investors began to sell, and stock prices fell. Investors who had bought General Electric stock at $400 a share sold it for $283 a share.

Again, business and political leaders told the country not to worry. Another banking executive said that only a nation as rich as the United States could "withstand the shock of a $3 billion paper loss on the Stock Exchange in a single day without serious effects to the average citizen." President Hoover maintained that the nation's business "is on a sound and prosperous basis."

Black Tuesday To stop the panic, a group of bankers pooled their money to buy stock. This action stabilized prices, but only for a few days. By Monday, prices were falling again. Investors all over the country raced to get their money out of the stock market. On October 29, **Black Tuesday,** a record 16.4 million shares were sold, compared with the average 4 million to 8 million shares a day earlier in the year.

This collapse of the stock market is known as the **Great Crash.** Despite efforts to halt it, the Crash continued beyond Black Tuesday. By November 13, the Dow Jones average had fallen from its September high of 381 to 198.7. Overall losses totaled $30 billion. The Great Crash was part of the nation's **business cycle,** a span in which the economy grows, then contracts.

Focus on ECONOMICS

Business Cycle *The periodic growth and contraction of a nation's economy.*

The Historical Context The Crash of 1929 brought an abrupt end to the economic expansion of the 1920s and ushered in a prolonged period of economic contraction known as the Great Depression. During the Depression, political leaders debated whether to stimulate the economy through higher government spending or to rely on the natural operation of the free market to restore economic expansion and prosperity.

The Concept Today The American economy continues to alternate between periods of higher growth and slower growth, or contraction. Both the federal government, through its taxing and spending fiscal policies, and the Federal Reserve, through its monetary policies that regulate the nation's supply of money, seek to prevent shocks that would bring about severe downturns in the economy.

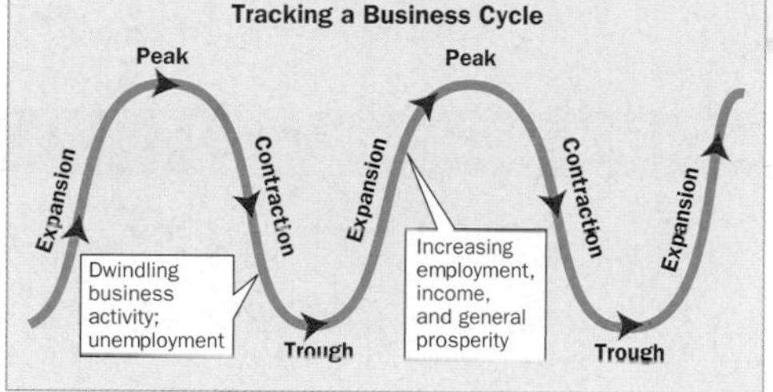

The Ripple Effect of the Crash

Initially the effects of the Crash were felt only by those who were heavily invested in the stock market. By 1929, that number was about 4 million people out of a population of 120 million. Some investors lost everything. One wealthy Bostonian who lost heavily in the market wrote in his diary, "The profit in my little book melted yesterday to seven thousand. It is probably nil [nothing] today. . . . My dreams of a million—where are they?"

Within a short time, however, the effects of the Great Crash began to ripple throughout the nation's economy. Soon millions of people who had never owned a share of stock were affected. The following list explains how the effects of the Crash spread to all Americans.

READING CHECK
Who felt the effects of the Great Crash?

LESSON PLAN

Focus Explain that the stock market crash in October 1929 brought on a depression more severe than any the nation had ever experienced. Ask what events led to the crash.

Instruct Have students think about conditions on the day after the crash. Explain that it took time for the effects of the crash to reach businesses and services, and few Americans understood at first how the event would affect them. Ask how a general economic failure might affect various employers.

Assess/Reteach Can students state the cause-and-effect relationship between the stock market crash and the onset of the Great Depression? In their statement, they should describe the impact of these events both nationally and internationally.

ACTIVITY
Connecting with Economics

Suggest that students learn how to read the stock market reports in the daily newspaper. Ask them to pick one or two stocks that are traded on the New York Stock Exchange and chart the progress of their stocks for at least one week. Students might also be interested in writing to the corporations for annual reports. Addresses can be found in a business directory such as the one published by Standard & Poor's. **(Logical/Mathematical)**

READING CHECK
The Great Crash affected American society as a whole.

CUSTOMIZE FOR ...
Less Proficient Readers
Have students make two columns on a piece of paper. Tell them to list the positive signs of the 1920s economy in the right-hand column and the negative signs in the left-hand column as they read. Then ask them to write one or two sentences explaining the seriousness of the negative indications.

ACTIVITY
Connecting with Economics

Invite students to imagine that they are living in the early 1930s. To help them analyze the effects of the Great Depression on the U.S. economy and government, organize them into small groups to discuss how their lives would be affected if the banks in their region closed. After discussions have proceeded for a few minutes, point out that there were no credit cards in the 1930s. Advise them to consider this fact as they continue their discussions. (Groups will have to confront such issues as how to negotiate paychecks to raise funds for everyday expenses and how to pay for needs in such an environment.) Have a spokesperson from each group report its conclusions to the class. **(Verbal/Linguistic)**

BACKGROUND
Economics

Most bank runs lasted just a day or two, and sometimes only hours. So bankers tried to combat them by slowing down the rate of withdrawals while reassuring customers that the bank would not fail. One Arkansas bank resisted a run by paying only in silver coins and making customers provide their own bags. Forced to carry away heavy bags of savings, some customers changed their minds and left their money in the bank. In 1932, banks in Urbana, Illinois, prevented a run in nearby Champaign from spreading to Urbana by closing for five days. Meanwhile, teams of volunteers pressured depositors into signing no-withdrawal pledges. When the strategy worked, the concept of a "bank holiday" spread. The following year, a national bank holiday was the first action ordered by new President Franklin D. Roosevelt.

Risky loans hurt banks Banks earn their profits on the interest they earn from lending out their deposits. Throughout the 1920s, banks loaned huge sums of money to many high-risk businesses. When stock prices fell, these businesses were unable to repay their loans.

Consumer borrowing Banks also make money on loans they lend to consumers. Consumers had borrowed heavily from banks throughout the 1920s to purchase consumer goods. When banks called in their loans, customers did not have cash to pay them.

Bank runs The Great Crash resulted in widespread bank runs. Fearful that banks would run out of money, people rushed to make withdrawals from their accounts. To pay back these deposits, banks had to recall loans from borrowers. However, many businesses and consumers hurt by falling stock prices could not repay their loans. Even if loans were repaid, banks could not get the money fast enough to pay all the depositors demanding their money.

Bank failures The combination of unpaid loans and bank runs meant that many banks across the country failed. Thousands of banks closed their doors when they could not return their depositors' money. In just a few years, more than 5,500 banks failed.

Savings wiped out Bank failures wiped out what little savings people had. By 1933, the money from 9 million savings accounts had vanished.

Cuts in production Businesses now could not borrow money to use to produce more goods. In addition, businesses lacked any incentive to spend money producing goods. Few people had money to buy them.

Rise in unemployment As businesses cut back on production, they laid off workers. Unemployment grew.

INTERPRETING DIAGRAMS
After the Great Crash, each sector of the economy experienced a damaging cycle of events. Each cycle also directly influenced the others. **Expressing Problems Clearly** *How did the events following the Great Crash interact and affect one another?*

Effects of the Great Crash, 1929

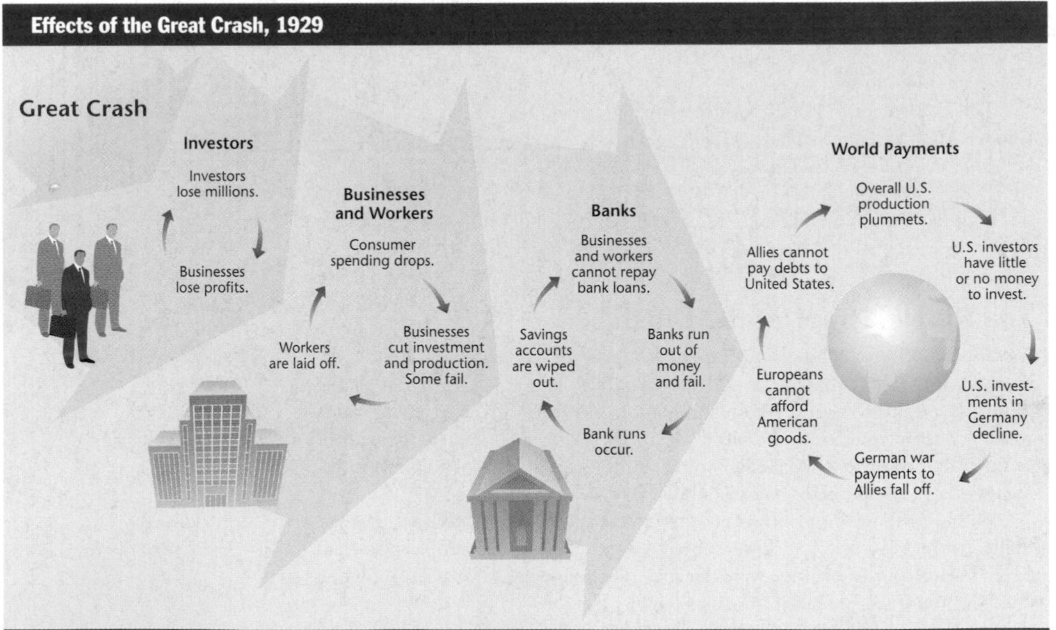

RESOURCE DIRECTORY
Technology
Color Transparencies *American Photo,* F7
RESOURCE PRO® **Critical Thinking Activity** *Identifying Central Issues: Signs of Trouble,* found on Resource Pro, helps students apply the skill by analyzing a graph of income distribution in the United States in 1929.

CAPTION ANSWERS

Interpreting Diagrams Sample answer: Businesses and consumer spending suffer when investors lose money. Layoffs occur. Loans go unpaid. Banks fail. Tariffs prevent Europeans from purchasing U.S. goods. Reparations payments and declining U.S. overseas investments severely harm European economies.

Further cuts in production As unemployment grew and incomes shrank, consumers spent less and less money and businesses produced still fewer goods. The overall output of goods in the economy dropped.

Economic Contraction The results of the Great Crash described above are all symptoms of an economy beginning to contract. A contraction is an economic decline marked by a falling output of goods and services. A particularly long and severe contraction is known as a depression. The contraction that began with the Great Crash triggered the most severe economic downturn in the nation's history—the **Great Depression.** The Great Depression lasted from 1929 until the United States entered World War II in 1941.

Impact on Workers and Farmers With no money and little incentive to produce more goods, factories throughout the country began to close. Thousands of workers lost their jobs or endured pay cuts. In August 1931, Henry Ford shut down his Detroit automobile factories, putting at least 75,000 people out of work.

Soon after local factories closed, small local businesses began to suffer as well. Restaurants and other small businesses closed because customers could no longer afford to go to them. Formerly wealthy families dismissed household workers. Farm prices, already low, fell even more, bringing disaster to many families. In 1929, a bushel of wheat had sold for $1.18; in 1932 it brought a mere 49 cents. Cotton dropped from 19 to 6.5 cents a pound.

By 1932, more than 12 million people were unemployed, which accounted for about a quarter of the labor force. (See the graph to the right.) Others worked only part-time or had their wages cut. The Gross National Product (GNP)—the total value of goods and services a country produces annually—dove from $103 billion in 1929 to just $56 billion in 1933.

Impact on the World By the 1930s, international banking, manufacturing, and trade had made nations around the world interdependent. For example, Latin America depended on U.S. markets for its goods. Europeans depended on the United States for investments and loans. When the world's leading economy fell, the global economic system began to crumble or contract in much the same way the U.S. economy had.

After World War I, the United States had insisted that France and Britain, its wartime allies, repay their war debts. At the same time, Congress kept import taxes high, making it hard for European nations to sell goods in the United States. With economies weakened by the war and little chance of selling goods in the United States, the Allies had to rely on Germany's reparations payments for income.

As long as American companies invested in Germany, reparations payments continued. But with the Depression, investments fell off. German banks failed, Germany suspended reparations, and the Allies, in turn, stopped paying their debts. Industrial production fell by 40 percent in Germany, 14 percent in Britain, and 29 percent in France. Europeans could no longer afford to buy American-made goods. Thus the American stock market crash started a downward cycle in the global economy.

Economic Impact of the Great Depression

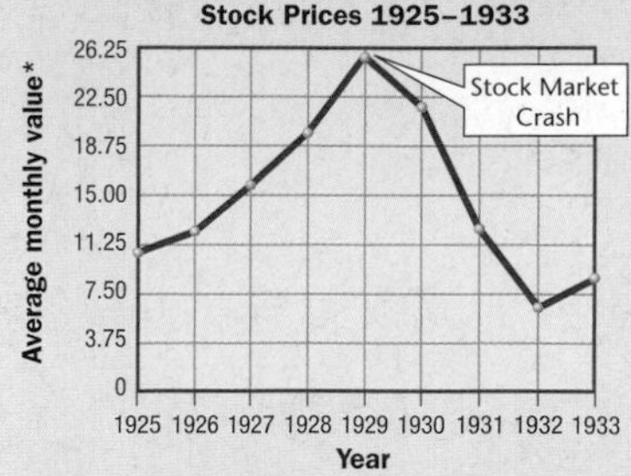

*Based on Standard and Poor's index of common stocks

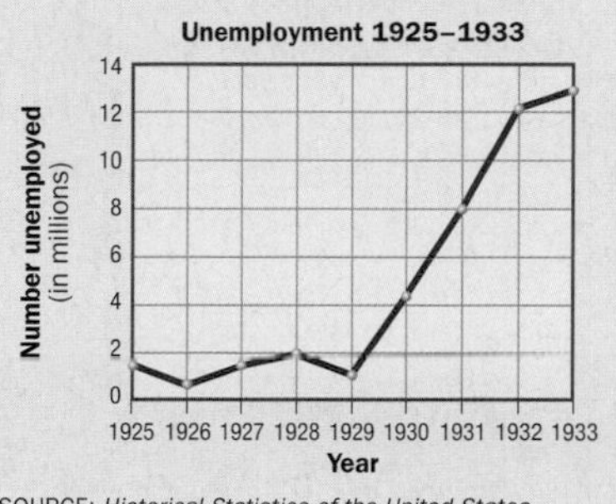

SOURCE: *Historical Statistics of the United States, Colonial Times to 1970*

INTERPRETING GRAPHS
The stock market crash caused a series of economic disasters.
Analyzing Information *Roughly how many people became unemployed between 1929 and 1933?*

ACTIVITY
Connecting with Economics

Ask students to suppose it is 1931. Half the class will write editorials explaining why this is a good time to invest in the stock market. The other half will write editorials about why *not* to buy stocks. Tell each student to exchange his or her editorial with a classmate who has taken the other position. Then have students write letters to the editor, responding to the arguments in the editorial they have received. **(Verbal/ Linguistic)**

BACKGROUND
Global Connections

The contraction in the global economy that accompanied the Depression actually benefited some of the world's developing nations. India's loss of foreign markets for its cotton, for example, encouraged the growth of its own textile industry. The collapse of Brazil's coffee market provided a powerful stimulus to industrial development in that country. No longer able to afford imported goods, Brazilians began to manufacture their own. By 1939, Brazilian factories were making more than 90 percent of the clothing, furniture, and other items Brazilians used in everyday life. Mexico's industrial sector experienced a similarly tremendous growth during the 1930s, largely because the cost of foreign manufactures was prohibitive to Depression-era Mexicans.

TEST PREPARATION

Have students review the material beneath the heading "Impact on Workers and Farmers" and then answer the question below.

Which of the following Depression-era events might have caused small businesses to fail?

- **A** Factory closures.
- **B** Bank failures.
- **C** Unemployment.
- **(D)** All of the above.

CAPTION ANSWERS

Interpreting Graphs Approximately 11 million.

INTERPRETING POLITICAL CARTOONS This cartoon was published three weeks before the Great Crash, at the beginning of a "bear market." A bear market exists when the stock market falls for a period of time. **Analyzing Visual Information** *What effect did the cartoonist predict the bear market would have on Wall Street?*

Underlying Causes of the Depression

The stock market crash of 1929 did not cause the Great Depression. Rather, both the Great Crash and the Depression were the result of deep underlying problems with the country's economy.

An Unstable Economy Overall, the seemingly prosperous economy of the 1920s lacked a firm base. National wealth was unevenly distributed, with most money in the hands of a few families who tended to save or invest rather than buy goods. Industry produced more goods than most consumers wanted or could afford. Farmers and many workers had not shared in the economic boom. The uneven prosperity of the 1920s made rapid recovery from an economic downturn impossible.

Overspeculation During the 1920s, speculators bought stocks with borrowed money and then pledged those stocks as *collateral* to buy more stocks. Collateral is an item of value that a borrower agrees to forfeit to the lender if the borrower cannot repay the loan. Brokers' loans went from under $5 billion in mid-1928 to $850 billion in September 1929. The stock market boom was based on borrowed money and optimism instead of real value.

Government Policies Mistakes in monetary policy were also to blame. During the 1920s, the Federal Reserve system, which regulates the amount of money in circulation, cut interest rates to spur economic growth. Then in 1929, worried about overspeculation, the Federal Reserve limited the money supply to discourage lending. As a result, there was too little money in circulation to help the economy recover after the Great Crash.

Section 1 Assessment

READING COMPREHENSION

1. What is the **Dow Jones Industrial Average?**
2. What happened on **Black Tuesday?**
3. Which part of the **business cycle** did the **Great Depression** represent?
4. What could cause a country's Gross National Product to decrease?
5. How did the unstable economy in the 1920s contribute to the Great Depression?

CRITICAL THINKING AND WRITING

6. **Recognizing Cause and Effect** How did the Great Depression have such a huge impact on the economies of other countries?
7. **Making Comparisons** Many people today use credit cards and charge accounts to buy on credit. Is this practice as dangerous now as it was in 1929? Why or why not?
8. **Writing to Inform** It is the day after Black Tuesday. Write a brief newspaper report describing the scene at local banks.

Take It to the NET

Activity: Writing a Diary Entry
Research the events of October 1929 leading up to the Great Crash. Then write a diary entry from the perspective of a stockbroker in New York noting your experiences. How are you affected by the crash? What is your reaction? Use the links provided in the *America: Pathways to the Present* area of the following Web site for help in completing this activity.
www.phschool.com

Section 1 Assessment

Reading Comprehension

1. The average of stock prices of major industries.
2. A record 16.4 million shares of stock were sold off on Wall Street, causing the stock market to crash.
3. A trough.
4. Widespread unemployment resulting from a lack of demand for products and the inability of businesses to obtain loans with which to finance their manufacturing operations.
5. The unbalanced economy had no stable base to fall back upon. Production far outstripped demand; wealth was unevenly distributed; the boom in stock market prices was based mainly on borrowed money, not real value.

Critical Thinking and Writing

6. Interdependence of the world's economies; high U.S. tariffs; the breakdown of reparations payments; declining European demand for American goods.
7. Answers will vary, but should display an understanding of how the credit situation and the distribution of wealth in the 1920s differed from today.
8. Answers should reflect the shock and sense of panic that swept the nation at that time.

Take It to the NET

Students should research the weaknesses of the stock market. They may also note a sense of optimism before the Great Depression set in, noting that during the Great Crash it appeared as if only the very wealthy would be hit hardest.

Caption Answers

Interpreting Political Cartoons The cartoonist predicts prolonged hard times ahead. The investor clings to the bear's tail in a desperate attempt to slow down a bear market gaining speed. The twisted buildings suggest a Wall Street losing its sense of order and stability.

RESOURCE DIRECTORY

Teaching Resources
Units 3/4 booklet
- Section 1 Quiz, p. 62

Guide to the Essentials
- Section 1 Summary, p. 72

Section 2 Social Effects of the Depression

READING FOCUS

- How did poverty spread during the Great Depression?
- What social problems were caused by poverty in the 1930s?
- How did some people struggle to survive hard times?

MAIN IDEA

By the early 1930s, wage cuts and growing unemployment had brought widespread suffering across the United States.

KEY TERMS

Hooverville
Dust Bowl

TAKING NOTES

As you read, complete this chart by listing examples of how the Great Depression affected different parts of American society.

Effects of the Great Depression	
Social Groups	**Effects**
City laborers	Many lost their jobs, became homeless, lived in poverty, some resorted to living in "Hoovervilles"
Farmers	
Women	
Children	
Men	
Racial minorities	

Setting the Scene Many Americans thought the Depression would not last. They were soon proved wrong. Hard times continued and eventually spread to all levels of society. Those who never imagined they would one day have to ask friends, neighbors, or even the government for money found themselves with no other option. In this account from 1934, a "middle-class" college graduate details the awkwardness and pain associated with what she described as "becoming one of them," or joining the ranks of the poor:

> *"Two years ago I was living in comfort and apparent security. My husband had a good position in a well-known orchestra and I was teaching a large and promising class of piano pupils. When the orchestra was disbanded we started on a rapid down-hill path. My husband was unable to secure another position. My class gradually dwindled away. We were forced to live on our savings.*
>
> *In the early summer of 1933 I was eight months pregnant and we had just spent our last twelve dollars on one month's rent for an apartment. . . . [which] lacked the most elementary comforts such as steam heat, bathtubs, sunlight, and running hot water. They usually are infested with mice and bedbugs. Ours was. . . .*
>
> *What then, did we do for food when our last money was spent on rent? So strong was the influence of our training that my husband kept looking feverishly for work when there was no work, and blaming himself because he was unable to find it. . . . An application to the Emergency Home Relief Bureau was the last act of our desperation."*
>
> —From Ann Rivington [pseudonym], "We Live on Relief," *Scribner's Magazine*, April 1934

Poverty Spreads

Imagine that the bank where you have a savings account suddenly closes. Your money is gone. Or your parents lose their jobs and cannot pay the rent or mortgage. One day you come home to find your furniture and all of your belongings on the sidewalk—you have been evicted.

WORK-IS-WHAT-I
WANT-AND-NOT-CHARITY
WHO-WILL-HELP-ME-
GET-A-JOB-7 YEARS-
IN-DETROIT. NO MONEY
SENT AWAY. FURNISH-
BEST-OF-REFERENCES
PHONE

VIEWING HISTORY The number of people without jobs rose dramatically after the Crash. **Drawing Inferences** *What can you tell from this man's sign about the social view of charity in the 1930s?*

Section 2 Social Effects of the Depression

SECTION OBJECTIVES

1. Understand how poverty spread during the Great Depression.
2. Find out about social problems that were caused by poverty in the 1930s.
3. Discover how some people struggled to survive hard times.

BELLRINGER

Warm-Up Activity Ask students to discuss how they would cut back on their expenses if their cash funds were limited. Have students describe how they might feel if this happened.

Activating Prior Knowledge Do students know anyone who was directly affected by the Depression? Ask students to interview that person about his or her memories. Can the interview subject state how living through the Depression affected him or her in later life?

READING STRATEGY

Before students read, have them list the section headings and one sentence telling what they think each section might be about. Then, as they read, have them review the sentences they wrote and modify them if necessary.

RESOURCE DIRECTORY

Teaching Resources
Learning Styles Lesson Plans booklet, p. 46
Guided Reading and Review booklet, p. 90

Technology
Section Reading Support Transparencies
Guided Reading Audiotapes (English/Spanish), Ch. 15
Student Edition on Audio CD, Ch. 15
Prentice Hall Presentation Pro CD-ROM, Ch. 15
Companion Web site, www.phschool.com

CAPTION ANSWERS

Viewing History Many people did not look favorably upon charity. Most unemployed people wanted to work for food or money and not receive handouts or direct aid. To accept charity without working may have been shameful or damaging to one's pride.

Lesson Plan

Focus Explain that the effects of the stock market crash filtered through all levels of society. Ask how the Great Depression changed American life.

Instruct Explain that the crash most severely affected those with the least money. Have them describe how the Depression affected each of the following groups: farm families, men, women, African Americans, Hispanics, and Asians. Compare rural poverty to urban poverty and ask students if they think they could have survived the Depression more easily in the country or in a city. Discuss the human toll of the Depression. How did poverty affect people's health?

Assess/Reteach Ask students to research the types of social services that were available to assist poor people in the 1930s. What types of organizations could people turn to for help? Prior to the election of 1932, what role did the federal government play in assisting those in need?

Activity
Connecting with Culture

Ask students to write a description of what they consider the worst economic, military, or political crisis that the United States has experienced in their own lifetime. Then ask them to explain to the class how the incident they chose compares in terms of severity to the situation described in the Ann Rivington quote on the previous page. **(Verbal/Linguistic)**

VIEWING HISTORY Makeshift huts served as homes for the homeless and unemployed in this New York City Hooverville. **Making Comparisons** *Do "Hoovervilles" exist today? Under what conditions do the homeless now live?*

People at all levels of society faced these situations during the Great Depression. Professionals and white-collar workers, who had felt more secure in their jobs than laborers, suddenly were laid off with no prospects of finding another position. Those whose savings disappeared could not understand why banks no longer had the money they had deposited for safekeeping.

"Hoovervilles" The hardest hit were those at the bottom of the economic ladder. Some unemployed laborers, unable to pay their rent, moved in with relatives. Others drifted around the country. In 1931, census takers estimated the homeless population in New York City alone at 15,000.

Homeless people sometimes built shanty towns, with shacks of tar paper, cardboard, or scrap material. These shelters of the homeless came to be called **Hoovervilles,** mocking the President, whom people blamed for not resolving the crisis.

A woman living in Oklahoma visited one Hooverville: "Here were all these people living in old, rusted-out car bodies," she noted. "There were people living in shacks made of orange crates. One family with a whole lot of kids were living in a piano box."

Many homeless and jobless people, rather than staying in one place, became drifters, hitchhiking from one "hobo jungle" to another. Thousands rode the rails—or jumped on trains illegally to travel across the country. They slept in boxcars or open freight cars. By 1933, an estimated one million people were on the move, risking jail, injury, or death.

Farm Distress Farm families suffered as low crop prices cut their income. When they could not pay their mortgages, they lost their farms to the banks, which sold them at auction. In the South, landowners expelled tenant farmers and sharecroppers. In protest against low prices, farmers dumped thousands of gallons of milk and destroyed crops. These desperate actions shocked a hungry nation.

The Dust Bowl For thousands of farm families in the Midwest, the harsh conditions of the Depression were made even more extreme by another major crisis of the decade. The origin of this one was not economic, but environmental. Between 1931 and 1940, so much soil blew out of the central and southern Great Plains that the region became known as the **Dust Bowl.**

Focus on GEOGRAPHY

Weather in the Dust Bowl The Great Plains is called "America's breadbasket." Deep, fertile soils, a long growing season, and flat land make it ideal for farming. But the region has always experienced severe weather. Hot and humid tropical air masses come from the Gulf of Mexico. Cold polar air masses rush southward from above the Arctic Circle. When these air masses collide, powerful storms with fierce updrafts are created. The complex root systems of the grasslands had protected the soil from weather. As you have read, however, when farmers plowed the land, this natural protection was lost.

Caption Answers

Viewing History Many homeless people still live on the streets today. However, in modern times, there are more shelters and relief programs for the homeless than there were during the 1930s.

RESOURCE DIRECTORY

Other Print Resources

American History Block Scheduling Support *Nature's Fury: The Dust Bowl,* found in the Prosperity, Depression, and War folder, includes interdisciplinary lesson suggestions and activities for Geography and History, Primary Sources, Biography, and Literature.

Technology

Color Transparencies *Historical Maps,* A35

Sounds of an Era Audio CD *"The Grapes of Wrath"* (time: 40 seconds)

RESOURCE PRO® **Literature** *The Psychological Effects of the Depression,* found on Resource Pro, expresses the economic and psychological damage of the Depression through an excerpt from the book *Studs Lonigan.*

Exploring Primary Sources in U.S. History CD-ROM *The Grapes of Wrath, John Steinbeck*

The Dust Bowl was created, in part, by dust storms that began in the early 1930s. Farmers said the storms were the result of a severe drought. While drought was a major factor in creating the Dust Bowl, it was not the only factor. Farming practices also contributed.

As long as there was a thick layer of prairie grasses to protect topsoil, severe weather could not harm the land. When farmers plowed the land, however, they stripped the soil of its natural protection. Winds picked up the dark, nutrient-rich topsoil and carried it eastward, sometimes for hundreds of miles, leaving behind barren, shifting dunes of grit and sand. The map below shows the extent of soil erosion across the plains.

The most severe storms of the dry years were called "black blizzards." Time after time, dirt was swept up and dropped by the ton over states and cities far to the east. The dirt darkened the sky in New York City and Washington, D.C. It stained the snows of New England red and dropped on ships hundreds of miles off the Atlantic Coast. The drought and winds persisted for more than seven years, bringing ruin to the farmers.

The combination of terrible weather and low prices for farm products caused about 60 percent of Dust Bowl families to lose their farms. More than 440,000 people left Oklahoma during the 1930s. Nearly 300,000 people left Kansas. Thousands of families in Oklahoma, Texas, Kansas, and other southwestern Plains states migrated to California. Many found work on California's farms as laborers. About 100,000 of the Dust Bowl migrants headed to cities such as Los Angeles, San Francisco, and San Diego. Relief did not come to the Dust Bowl region until the early 1940s, when the rains finally arrived and World War II drove farm prices up.

Sounds of an Era

Listen to a reading from John Steinbeck's *The Grapes of Wrath* and other sounds from the Great Depression.

MAP SKILLS Drought combined with over-farming to reduce the Great Plains to dust. **Regions** *How did farmers destroy the region's natural protection against severe weather?*

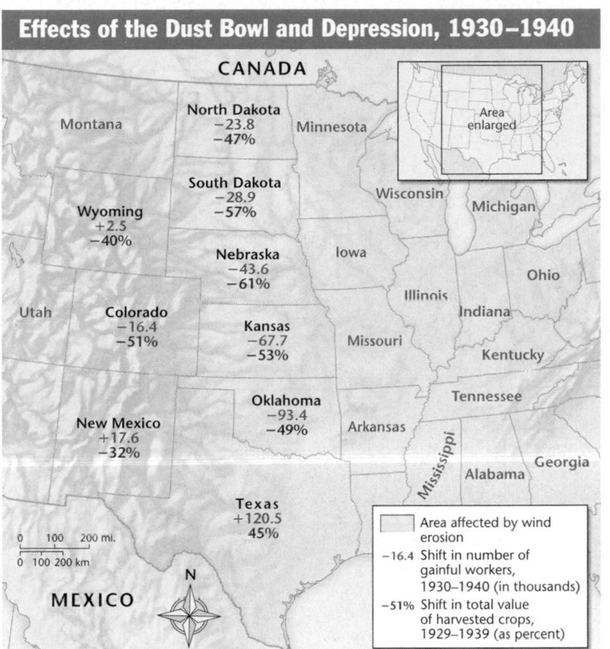

Poverty Strains Society

As the Depression wore on, it took a serious physical and psychological toll on the entire nation. Unemployment and fear of losing a job caused great anxiety. People became depressed; many considered suicide, and some did take their own lives.

Impact on Health "No one has starved," President Hoover declared, but some did, and thousands more went hungry. Impoverished people who could not afford food or shelter got sick more easily. Children suffered most from the long-term effects of poor diet and inadequate medical care.

"All last winter we never had a fire except about once a day when Mother used to cook some mush or something," one homeless boy recalled. "When the kids were cold they went to bed. I quit high school, of course."

In the country, people grew food. In cities, they sold apples and pencils, begged for money to buy food, and fought over the contents of restaurant garbage cans. Families who had land planted "relief gardens" to feed themselves or so they could barter food for other items. One historian recalled:

ACTIVITY
Connecting with Geography

Point out that the Dust Bowl was the result of decades of natural and human conditions and developments. Then organize the class into five groups. Have each locate and use primary and secondary sources such as computer software, databases, media and news services, biographies, interviews, and artifacts to investigate one of the following areas of Great Plains history: (1) its physical geography and natural environment; (2) native inhabitants and their lifestyles; (3) the role of technology in frontier agriculture; (4) climate, conditions, and population trends in the late 1800s; and (5) soil conservation methods in use today. Have each group select a spokesperson to present its findings to the class. **(Verbal/Linguistic)**

BACKGROUND
Recent Scholarship

In *Bad Land: An American Romance,* Jonathan Raban observes that most people date the "downfall" of the midwestern homesteaders to the "Dirty Thirties." Raban's reading of 800 family memoirs collected in Montana, however, leads him to conclude that the exodus from midwestern farmlands began much earlier. In fact, Raban found that more people left their farms between 1917 and 1928 than between 1929 and 1940. The dry spell actually began with a rainless spring in 1917 and culminated in the terrible winter of 1919. The roots of the already-overgrazed grasses died. Ruined farmers went on to other jobs in nearby towns. Those who had held on through the first dry spell went west when the second one occurred.

CAPTION ANSWERS

Map Skills Farmers destroyed the sod by cultivating the land too extensively. This exhausted the soil and broke up the prairie grass that had held topsoil in place, thus allowing the topsoil to erode.

ACTIVITY
Connecting with Culture

Organize students into groups to create collages that compare and contrast life during the Depression with life today. Have each group search current newspapers and magazines, as well as books about modern times and the Depression, for photos that show similarities or differences in the experiences of farmers, workers, homeless people, women, and others now and then. Remind students to photocopy the images they select so as not to damage the source materials. Groups should then arrange, label, and mount their images on a piece of posterboard to complete their collage. **(Visual/Spatial)**

BACKGROUND
Preserving the Past

Jobless men in worn-out clothes, hungry babies, and desperate mothers—Dorothea Lange's photos stirred public attention in the 1930s and created a powerful historical record of the decade's suffering. "She told me . . . that she was thirty-two," Lange recalled of the migrant mother. "She said that they had been living on frozen vegetables and the birds that the children killed. She had just sold the tires from her car to buy food. There she sat in that lean-to tent with her children huddled around her, and seemed to know that my pictures might help her." Indeed, images such as this helped lead to the creation of government camps for migrant workers. Lange's photographs also inspired John Steinbeck's important Depression-era novel *The Grapes of Wrath*.

READING CHECK

Widespread malnutrition led to reduced resistance to diseases such as tuberculosis. The increase of such diseases, poor diet, and lack of medical care seriously weakened millions of Americans, especially children.

CAPTION ANSWERS

Viewing Fine Art They aroused public attention and helped to create political support for aid to unemployed and homeless people.

READING CHECK
How did the Great Depression impact people's health?

> *"In Detroit nearly one out of every seven persons was on relief [government aid]. Children scavenged through the streets like animals for scraps of food, and stayed away from school. . . . Among high school students in the inner city the incidence of tuberculosis tripled. Each day four thousand children stood in bread lines. With their sunken, lifeless eyes, sallow cheeks, and distended bellies, some resembled the starving children in Europe during the war."*
>
> —Robert Conot

Stresses on Families Living conditions declined as families moved in together, crowding into small houses or apartments. The divorce rate dropped because people could not afford separate households. People gave up even small pleasures like an ice cream cone or a movie ticket.

Men who had lost jobs or investments often felt like failures because they could no longer provide for their families. If their wives or children were working, men thought their own status had fallen. Many were embarrassed to be seen at home during normal work hours. They were ashamed to ask friends for help.

Women faced other problems. Those who had depended on a husband's paycheck worried about feeding their hungry children. Working women were accused of taking jobs away from men. Even in the better times of the 1920s, Henry Ford had fired married women. "We do not employ married women whose husbands have jobs," he explained. During the Depression, this practice became common. In 1931, the American Federation of Labor endorsed it. Most school districts would not hire married women as teachers, and many fired those who got married.

Many women continued to find work, however, because poor-paying jobs such as domestic service, typing, and nursing were considered "women's work." The greatest job losses

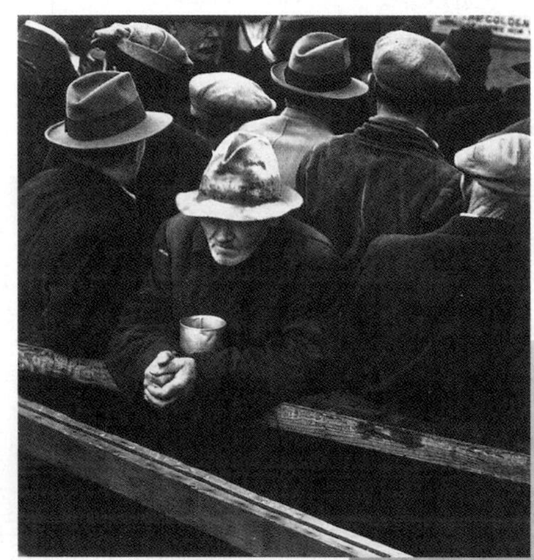

VIEWING FINE ART Dorothea Lange's most famous photographs, the "Migrant Mother" series (1936, right), have become a symbol of the Depression. The face of the undernourished mother displays a numbness to her destitute surroundings, yet a certain determination to pull through it all. Above is another of Lange's most famous photographs, "White Angel Breadline." **Determining Relevance** *What effect did Lange's photographs have on the general public?*

RESOURCE DIRECTORY

Technology

Exploring Primary Sources in U.S. History CD-ROM *Depression Photograph, Dorothea Lange*

of the Depression were in industry and other areas that seldom hired women.

Discrimination Increases Hard economic times put groups of Americans in competition with one another for a shrinking number of jobs. This produced a general rise in suspicions and hostilities against minorities. African Americans, Hispanics, and in the West, Asian Americans all suffered as white laborers began to demand the low-paying jobs typically filled by these minorities. Hispanics and Asian Americans lost not only their jobs but also their country. Thousands were deported—even those born in the United States.

Black unemployment soared—about 56 percent of black Americans were out of work in 1932. Some white citizens declared openly that blacks had no right to jobs if whites were out of work. Gordon Parks, a photographer who rode the rails to Harlem, later wrote:

> *"To most blacks who had flocked in from all over the land, the struggle to survive was savage. Poverty coiled around them and me with merciless fingers."*
>
> —Photographer Gordon Parks

Because government relief programs often discriminated against African Americans, black churches and organizations like the National Urban League gave private help. The followers of a Harlem evangelist known as Father Divine opened soup kitchens that fed thousands every day. Discrimination was even worse in the South, where African Americans were denied civil rights such as access to education, voting, and health care. Lynchings increased.

The justice system often ignored the rights of minority Americans. In March 1931, near Scottsboro, Alabama, nine black youths who had been riding the rails were arrested and accused of raping two white women on a train. Without being given the chance to hire a defense lawyer, eight of the nine were quickly convicted by an all-white jury and sentenced to die.

The case of the "Scottsboro boys" was taken up, and sometimes exploited, by northern groups, most notably the Communist Party. The party helped supply legal defense and organized demonstrations, which, after many years, helped overturn the convictions, but four of the "boys" spent many years in jail.

American BIOGRAPHY

Dorothea Lange
1895–1965

"The camera is an instrument that teaches people how to see without a camera," said photographer Dorothea Lange. Born in New Jersey in 1895, Lange decided at a young age to be a photographer. In 1919, Lange opened a portrait studio in San Francisco where she photographed wealthy clients. Beyond the windows of her studio, she could see the spreading effects of the Depression. She thought about the vast difference "between what I was working on in the printing frames [in the studio] and what was going on in the street."

Lange's first exhibition, in 1934, landed her an assignment to photograph the hundreds of migrant workers streaming into California from the Dust Bowl. Lange's photographs showed the world the desperation and bravery of families displaced by the Depression.

Lange continued to document the suffering and mistreatment of other Americans until her death in 1965. But she will be forever linked in people's minds to the 1930s and the human courage that she made a part of the nation's permanent record.

Stories of Survival

A generation of Americans would live to tell their grandchildren how they survived the Depression. Wilson Ledford first felt the effects of the Depression in March 1930 when he was 15, living in Chattanooga, Tennessee, with his mother and younger sister. Wilson had worked part time and after school in a grocery store since he was 11. By 1930, his family could no longer afford Chattanooga. They moved back to Cleveland, Tennessee, a nearby small town. They survived on the rent Wilson's mother received on a house and 15 acres of land, which she still owned. The property brought in $6 a month in rent—except when the tenants were out of work. After taxes and insurance, the family had about a dollar a week to live on. Wilson "swapped work with neighbors." He looked after the family horse and cow, chopped wood for the fireplace, tended the garden that provided family food, and raised corn to feed the animals:

ACTIVITY
Connecting with Citizenship

Ask students to write letters to the editor as 1930s citizens, expressing their opinions about the employment policies applied to women or minorities. Select a representative sample of letters and read them to the class. Ask students why these practices existed during the Depression and how employment practices today have—or have not—changed since that time. Have students identify the political, social, and economic contributions of women and minorities to American society. **(Verbal/Linguistic)**

BACKGROUND
A Diverse Nation

The Scottsboro case became the cause célèbre for civil rights in the 1930s and resulted in two important legal precedents. The U.S. Supreme Court in 1932, in *Powell* v. *Alabama,* ordered a new trial on the grounds that the defendants had not received adequate counsel. In 1933, the defendants were tried and convicted a second time. But the next year, in *Norris* v. *Alabama,* the Court reversed this second set of convictions because African Americans were excluded from serving on juries in Alabama. Tried yet a third time, five of the defendants were found guilty and sentenced to long prison terms. The last of the Scottsboro defendants was paroled in 1950.

CUSTOMIZE FOR ...
ESL

Have students imagine that they are one of the Depression-era children described on this page. Then have them make a list of the hardships they would experience in their daily lives. Can they list some solutions to these difficult problems?

TEST PREPARATION

Have students read the quotation by the homeless boy under "Impact on Health" on the previous page and then complete the sentence below.

Based on the passage, you can infer that the reason the writer quit high school was—

- **A** he was too cold to go to school.
- **(B)** his first priority was getting enough to eat and staying warm.
- **C** he was not interested in studying.
- **D** he had to help his mother make dinner.

VIEWING HISTORY Many Americans reluctantly waited in "souplines" such as this when they did not have enough money to buy food. **Drawing Inferences** *What do you think was the hardest part of such an experience? What made it easier?*

> *"We had to raise most of what we ate since money was so scarce. . . . Sometimes I plowed for other people when I could get the work. . . . I got 15 cents an hour for plowing, and I furnished the horse and plow."*
>
> —Wilson Ledford

Nothing was wasted. Wilson's mother kept chickens and traded eggs at the store for things they could not grow or raise. Overalls cost 98 cents; shoes were $2. She bought a pig for $3 and raised it for meat, and she made jelly from wild blackberries. Despite the family's own poverty, she gave extra milk and butter to "some poor people, a woman with three small children who lived in a one-room shack with a dirt floor."

Wilson never got to high school, "as survival was more important." The Ledfords had no radio, but Wilson made his own entertainment. Wilson and some other boys cleaned the rocks off a field, graded it, and made a baseball diamond. Baseballs were precious. "You could buy a pretty good baseball for a quarter and a real good one for 50 cents. . . . If we lost a ball during the game, everyone had to go hunt for it."

In the summer of 1932, when he was 17, Wilson got a job in Chattanooga delivering ice. He worked there again the next summer: "I worked twelve hours a day, six days a week, and made $3.00 a week." When the icehouse closed in the fall, Wilson hitchhiked throughout the Southeast looking for work, but never had any success. "I pumped up so many tires for people I rode with, I had blisters all in my hands. Finally I got back home."

Later Wilson bought a truck to haul coal, cotton, and oranges, then worked nights in a woolen mill while carrying ice during the day. Finally, "I got a call from Chickamauga Dam and I went to work there. That was a good job working on the dam. I made 60 cents an hour. Times were better by then, but did not start booming until World War II started."

Section 2 Assessment

READING COMPREHENSION

1. Who lived in **Hoovervilles?**
2. What factors led to the creation of the **Dust Bowl** in the 1930s?
3. What were some causes and effects of increased discrimination during the Great Depression?
4. What can you learn about the Depression from Wilson Ledford's experiences?

CRITICAL THINKING AND WRITING

5. **Identifying Central Issues** Explain the effect the Depression had on the psychology of many Americans. Why do you think the Depression changed people's goals and expectations?
6. **Writing an Interview** In an effort to learn firsthand what it was like to live during the Great Depression, write ten questions that you might ask someone who lived through it.

Activity: Writing a Newspaper Article Write a newspaper article describing the conditions faced by those living in the Dust Bowl during the Great Depression. Be sure to include a lot of details for the readers back home. Use the links provided in the *America: Pathways to the Present* area of the following Web site for help in completing this activity.
www.phschool.com

Section 2 Assessment

Reading Comprehension

1. Unemployed laborers and their families.
2. Exposure of topsoil due to overintensive agriculture, drought, and wind erosion.
3. Causes: Competition for scarce, low-paying jobs, and a legal system that continued to disregard civil rights for nonwhites. Effects: Deportations, lynchings, high African American unemployment.
4. His experiences demonstrate the hardships of finding work, which was often only temporary or was located far from home. Yet, he and his family made the best of the situation in order to survive.

Critical Thinking and Writing

5. Answers will vary, but students might note the feelings of hopelessness and the loss of pride many Americans felt. Well-educated people could not find jobs. Many people had to rely on friends, family, or the government for help. The goals and expectations of most people were only to survive, not to prosper.
6. Questions will vary but should be supported with facts from the section.

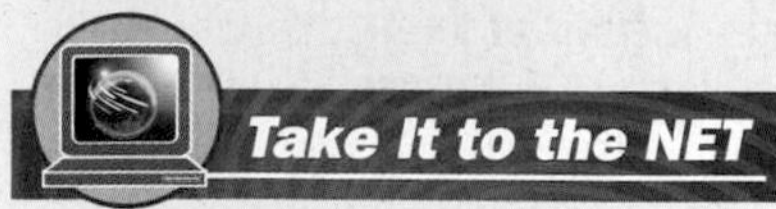

Articles should describe weather and environmental conditions faced by farmers in the Dust Bowl. Students should note both the great size of the storms and the damage they caused.

Caption Answers

Viewing History The hardest part was probably the pride that many Americans had to swallow when they accepted relief such as this. The experience was made easier because people knew that many others were forced to accept public assistance as well.

RESOURCE DIRECTORY

Teaching Resources
Units 3/4 booklet
- Section 2 Quiz, p. 63

Guide to the Essentials
- Section 2 Summary, p. 73

Drawing Inferences

Drawing inferences is a way of interpreting what you read. When you draw inferences about a person's character, you add what you know to what an author tells you, including facts about the person's words and actions, and ideas that are implied but not directly stated in the text.

Gordon Parks eventually became a successful photographer and writer. But when the Great Depression hit, he was only a teenager, on his own and desperately in need of a job and a place to live. When he tried to get a room in a cheap hotel, he was refused because he was black (Passage A). Later, Parks determined to become a photographer (Passage B).

LEARN THE SKILL

Use the following steps to draw inferences:

1. **Identify stated facts.** Identify what the person actually said and did. Determine what information is directly stated.
2. **Identify unstated ideas.** Distinguish between what is implied by the facts and what is suggested by the perspective of the author.
3. **Add what you know.** Use information you know about the historical period and about human nature to help you understand the person's actions.
4. **Draw inferences about the person's character.** Keep the point of view of the author in mind, and be wary of authors who may have a bias.

PRACTICE THE SKILL

Answer the following questions:

1. Summarize the facts in each passage.
2. **(a)** What does Passage A suggest about Parks's reaction to racism? Explain. **(b)** Where does Parks suggest what he wants you to think? **(c)** What do you think the author of Passage B wants you to feel about Parks? Explain.
3. **(a)** How does your knowledge of the Depression help you understand what Parks does in Passage A? **(b)** How does your understanding of human nature help you evaluate Parks's decision to tell the truth in Passage B? Explain.
4. **(a)** From the passages, what inferences can you draw about Parks as a teenager? As an adult? **(b)** How do the two passages help you understand Gordon Parks?

APPLY THE SKILL

See the Chapter Review and Assessment for another opportunity to apply this skill.

A

"Mike tells me you're looking for a room and work. That so?" [the manager] asked, squinting down . . . at me.

"That's right."

"You look like a clean-cut colored boy."

"I'm a boy. I don't know what my color's got to do with it."

"Don't go gittin' your dander up. I think I got a proposition for you." I waited. "How'd you like to have a room and a job both?"

"Where?"

"Right here. I'm needin' a boy to clean this place. You'll git a room in the back and a half a buck a day. . . ."

"I'd like to know why I can't just pay and sleep here?"

"Look, I ain't no expert on race problems," the . . . man said impatiently. "I'm just givin' you a proposition. Whyn't you try it and see how things work out?"

"Give me twenty-five cents more a day and some food."

"Hell, fellow, you'll be makin' a buck a day with all that. That's big dough round these parts."

"Sorry," I said, turning as if I were going.

"Just a second." I had bluffed him into a decision. "Okay. . . ."

—Gordon Parks, *Voices in the Mirror: An Autobiography*

B

"Early in 1938, Parks walked through the door of an upscale women's clothing store in St. Paul and asked if they might need any fashions photographed. The manager wasn't interested, but the fellow's wife convinced him to give Parks a chance. Parks borrowed a Speed Graphic camera on credit, and spent a day photographing models. But when he developed the film, he was devastated to find that he had double-exposed all but one shot. [His wife] suggested he take a chance and blow up the one good picture. When the store manager saw it, he was thrilled. Where were the rest? Parks told the truth. He was allowed to reshoot. Soon his pictures filled the windows of Frank Murphy's store. That was the beginning. . . ."

—Dick Russell, *Black Genius and the American Experience*

SKILLS FOR LIFE

Drawing Inferences

Focus Students will learn how to use historical material to draw inferences about a person's character.

Instruct Discuss with students what life was like for a young African American artist such as Gordon Parks in the first part of the last century. What opportunities might come his way? What obstacles would he have to overcome? Have students read passage A. Ask them to describe how Parks must have felt as he had to assert himself to get what he needed. What do his actions indicate about his character? Have students read passage B. Ask students to describe ways in which his behavior in this passage is consistent with his behavior in passage A.

Extend See the Skills for Life activity in the Resource Directory below.

ANSWERS

Practice the Skill

1. Sample answers: A: Parks is looking for a job and a place to live; he resents being referred to as "colored"; he rejects the first offer by the hotel manager. B: Parks was first rejected for a photographer's job at a clothing store; the manager's wife intervened; only one photograph came out; when asked, Parks told the truth; he was allowed to shoot more photos and was hired; it was the start of his career.
2. **(a)** It angered him, but he dealt with the situation calmly. **(b)** At the end of the passage. **(c)** To respect his determination, honesty, and talent.
3. **(a)** He was desperate for a job, food, and a place to live. He took a big chance, as jobs were scarce. **(b)** That telling the truth is the right thing to do even when it isn't easy.
4. **(a)** As a teenager, he was proud and determined with a bit of a temper, and good at manipulating people. As an adult, he was still determined but showed integrity and no temper. **(b)** They show his development from a headstrong, rather desperate boy to a mature, honest man.

RESOURCE DIRECTORY

Teaching Resources

Skills for Life booklet, p. 24

Technology

Social Studies Skills Tutor CD-ROM

Interactive Practice in
- Geographic Literacy
- Critical Thinking and Reading
- Visual Analysis
- Communications

Section 3
Surviving the Great Depression

Section Objectives

1. Read about ways Americans pulled together to survive the Great Depression.
2. See the signs of change Americans began to notice in the early 1930s.

Bellringer

Warm-Up Activity Ask students to recall a time in their lives when friends, neighbors, or strangers worked together to solve a problem or helped one another through an unpleasant situation.

Activating Prior Knowledge Have students find out about the history of the Depression in your local area. What government programs were put in place to help out-of-work citizens? Are there examples of Depression-era government-funded buildings, bridges, or highways that students can find?

Reading Strategy

As students read the section, have them make a list of the strategies that helped Americans survive the Depression years.

Section 3

Surviving the Great Depression

READING FOCUS

- In what ways did Americans pull together to survive the Great Depression?
- What signs of change did Americans begin to notice in the early 1930s?

MAIN IDEA

Americans survived the Great Depression with determination and even humor. They helped one another, looked for solutions, and waited for the hard times to pass.

KEY TERMS

penny auction
Twenty-first Amendment

TAKING NOTES

As you read, prepare an outline of this section. Use Roman numerals to indicate the major headings of this section, capital letters for the subheadings, and numbers for the supporting details.

I. Americans Pull Together
 A. Farmers Stick Together
  1. Worked together to minimize impact of Great Depression
  2. ______
  3. ______
 B. Young People Ride the Rails
  1. Young people left home to seek a better life.
  2. ______
  3. ______

Setting the Scene No one who lived through the Great Depression ever forgot it. Long after the economy rebounded, many from the "Depression generation," even those who recovered enough to live a very comfortable life, would continue to pinch pennies as if financial ruin were just around the corner. Many Americans avoided buying on credit, instead saving for years to pay cash for needed items. Others even stuffed money under their mattresses rather than trust their life savings to banks.

Americans Pull Together

Not all the memories of the Depression were bad or despairing, as one reporter noted:

> "*The great majority of Americans may be depressed. They may not be well pleased with the way business and government have been carried on, and they may not be at all sure that they know exactly how to remedy the trouble. They may be feeling dispirited. But there is one thing they are not, and that is—beaten.*"
>
> —Journalist Gerald W. Johnson, 1932

VIEWING HISTORY Traveling hobos gave each other helpful information about certain areas with symbols such as these. They were usually written on sidewalks, fences, or buildings using chalk or coal. **Drawing Inferences** *How did such a symbol system help hobos and the homeless? Why do you think they wanted to help each other?*

Hobo Symbols

Symbol	Meaning	Symbol	Meaning
	Kind-hearted woman lives here		Bad-tempered owner
	Food for work		Unsafe place
	Good place for a handout		Good water
	Can sleep in barn		Doctor won't charge

Throughout the country people pulled together to help one another. Tenant groups formed to protest rent increases and evictions. Neighbors, in difficult circumstances themselves, helped those they saw as worse off than themselves. One woman remembered:

> "*There were many beggars, who would come to your back door, and they would say they were hungry. I wouldn't give them money because I didn't have it. But I did take them in and put them in my kitchen and give them something to eat.*"
>
> —Depression survivor Kitty McCulloch

Caption Answers

Viewing History These symbols pointed fellow hobos toward welcoming places and away from dangerous ones. The system was mutually beneficial. It was in each person's best interest to keep the system alive. By sticking together, these people could survive the Depression.

Resource Directory

Teaching Resources

Guided Reading and Review booklet, p. 91
Biography, Literature, and Comparing Primary Sources booklet (Biography) *Babe Didrickson Zaharias,* p. 27

Technology

Section Reading Support Transparencies
Guided Reading Audiotapes (English/Spanish), Ch. 15
Student Edition on Audio CD, Ch. 15
Sounds of an Era Audio CD *Kitty McCulloch* (time: 20 seconds)

RESOURCE PRO® **Primary Source Activity** *The Forgotten Man,* found on Resource Pro, uses two letters written to President Hoover during the Depression to show the way many American workers viewed their President and the economic breakdown of the country.
Exploring Primary Sources in U.S. History CD-ROM *This Land Is Your Land, Woody Guthrie*
Prentice Hall Presentation Pro CD-ROM, Ch. 15
Companion Web Site, www.phschool.com

McCulloch also gave one beggar a pinstripe suit belonging to her husband, who, she explained, already had three others.

Farmers Stick Together Farmers also worked together to minimize the impact of the Depression. When a farmer was unable to pay the mortgage on his farm, the bank would foreclose on the property and then sell it at an auction. In some farm communities, local farmers met secretly and agreed to keep bids low during the auction. In what were known as **penny auctions,** farmers would bid mere pennies on land and machines auctioned by the banks in order to help their struggling neighbors. Buyers then returned the farms and machinery to their original owners. As one farmer recalled about his farming community:

> "*The aim of our organization was pure survival. All the farmer asked was more time to see him through the depression years. If they won, they had saved (temporarily at least) their home and means of livelihood, and the means of paying their just debts. If they lost, they would be no worse off. They knew they had nothing to lose, so they decided to fight. . . .*"
>
> —Harry Haugland

In the first two months of 1933, more than 70 foreclosure sales on farms were blocked by penny auctions. The success of penny auctions as well as the threat of violence at some farm auctions led some states to pass laws suspending foreclosures on farms. For example, in February 1933, the Iowa state legislature passed a "foreclosure moratorium law," which gave farmers more time to pay back their mortgages.

Young People Ride the Rails At the height of the Great Depression, many young people left their homes, either out of necessity or the desire to seek a better life. In the mid-1930s roughly 250,000 teenagers were living on the road, illegally riding the rails of freight trains. Some rode the rails to find work; others hungered for adventure. Clarence Lee, who left home when he was 16, recalled:

> "*I wanted to stay home and fight poverty with my family. But my father told me I had to leave. . . . But I didn't have it in my mind to leave until he told me, 'Go fend for yourself. I cannot afford to have you around any longer.'*"
>
> —Clarence Lee

Jim Mitchell also left home at 16. He was not forced to leave, but he could not deal with the pressures of home life after his father lost his job and was unable to support the family. "The quickest and easiest way to get out," he recalled, "was go jump a train and go somewhere."

Young people riding the rails faced danger every day. They were vulnerable to train-related injuries, the possibility of being arrested by police, or even the threat of being shot at by angry farmers. These hobos, as they are sometimes called, witnessed the Depression in all parts of the country firsthand. Many who rode the rails described their experiences as some of the loneliest times of their

Focus on CULTURE

Monopoly With everyday life so difficult during the Depression, people needed a way to get their minds off their troubles. In response to this need, Charles B. Darrow, an unemployed man living in Germantown, Pennsylvania, created a compelling board game. Called Monopoly®, the game allowed people to live the fantasy of acquiring land, houses, and hotels that they could rent or sell to fellow players. Darrow brought Monopoly to executives at Parker Brothers, a leading board game company, to see if they would produce it. The company rejected Darrow's game, saying that it had 52 design errors. Determined to make the game a success, Darrow worked on correcting the flaws and produced Monopoly on his own. Darrow sold so many sets so quickly that Parker Brothers reconsidered its decision and agreed to produce it. The game was introduced in 1935 and was a bestseller in its first year. Since then, an estimated 500 million people have played Monopoly.

READING CHECK
Why did so many young people ride the rails in the 1930s?

LESSON PLAN

Focus Explain that Americans who lived through the Great Depression never forgot the pain of that time, and their feelings about banks, business, government, and money changed forever. Ask what characteristics helped Americans to survive those troubled times.

Instruct Discuss how living through the Great Depression brought out courage, kindness, charity, and humor in many Americans. Ask students why crises bring out these characteristics. You might want to have students share their recollections from the Warm-Up Activity. Discuss the signs of changing times that gave Americans hope. Ask students to explain the impact of the repeal of Prohibition.

Assess/Reteach Ask students to discuss some favorite pastimes of the Depression, such as going to movies and playing board games, like Monopoly. How do they think such diversions helped people cope with their situations?

BACKGROUND
Homelessness

Evictions were commonplace during the 1930s. Those already marginalized before the Depression, including many African Americans, suffered especially heavily. Writer Langston Hughes observed, "[T]he Depression had brought everyone down a peg or two. And the Negroes had but a few pegs to fall."

TEST PREPARATION

Have students review the quote by Clarence Lee on this page and then complete the sentence below.

Clarence Lee's attitude toward leaving his family during the Depression could best be described as—

A indifferent.
(B) reluctant.
C hostile.
D eager.

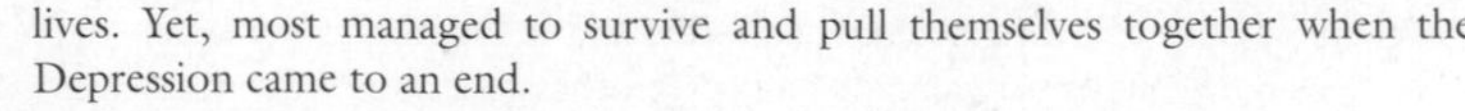

lives. Yet, most managed to survive and pull themselves together when the Depression came to an end.

Activity
Connecting with Culture

The Empire State Building was designed in the Art Deco style. Ask students to bring to class copies of photographs of the Empire State Building, or another building built in the same time period that illustrates the Art Deco style, and to describe its prominent features. **(Verbal/Linguistic; Visual/Spatial)**

Background
Biography

Although Will Rogers (1879–1935) lived most of his life as an entertainer in New York and California, he never forgot his Cherokee roots. His father had wanted him to remain on the family's ranch in Indian Territory (now Oklahoma), but Rogers was more interested in trick roping than in roping cattle. However, audiences proved more responsive to the humorous political and social observations he made while performing his rope tricks, and this commentary soon became the focus of his act. In the 1920s he expanded his stage monologue into printed form in a nationally syndicated newspaper column. The radio program he launched in 1930 gave him his greatest influence on public opinion. Rogers rarely commented on Indian issues, but became the broader voice of all peoples who felt dispossessed and powerless in American society.

READING CHECK
There was very little clamor for political upheaval. Some Americans did support the Communist and Socialist political parties in the hope of distributing wealth more evenly. The idea of social justice gained many followers.

READING CHECK
What political solutions did some Americans seek in the 1930s?

Seeking Political Solutions As bad as conditions were, few Americans called for radical political change. In Europe, economic problems brought riots and political upheaval, but in the United States most citizens trusted the democratic process to handle their problems. As one writer wryly observed:

> "*Ten million unemployed continue law-abiding. No riots, no trouble, no multi-millionaires cooked and served with cranberry sauce, alas.*"
>
> —William Saroyan, 1936

For some Americans, however, radical and reform movements offered new solutions to the country's problems, by promising a fairer distribution of wealth. The Communist Party had about 14,000 members, mainly intellectuals and labor organizers. In the 1932 election, the Communist candidate polled just over 100,000 votes. Socialists, who called for gradual social and economic changes rather than revolution, did better. Their presidential candidate, Norman Thomas, won 881,951 votes in 1932, about 2.2 percent of the total vote.

Voting figures and party membership do not reflect the notable interest in radical and reform movements in the 1930s. Those who were part of those movements remember the decade as a high point of cooperation among different groups of Americans—students, workers, writers, artists, and professionals of all races. They worked together for social justice in cases such as that of the Scottsboro boys.

INTERPRETING POLITICAL CARTOONS Showing the darker side of Depression humor, an end-of-the-year cartoon in *Life* magazine summed up the hopes and disasters of 1929. **Drawing Conclusions** *Why did Americans use humor to fight their despair?*

Depression Humor For the most part, Americans gritted their teeth and waited out the hard times. Jokes and cartoons helped people through their troubles. The term "Hooverville" was at first a joke. People who slept on park benches huddled under "Hoover blankets"—old newspapers. Empty pockets turned inside out were "Hoover flags." When Babe Ruth was criticized for requesting a salary of $80,000, higher than Hoover's, he joked, "I had a better year than he did."

People fought despair by laughing at it. In 1929, humorist Will Rogers quipped, "When Wall Street took that tail spin, you had to stand in line to get a window to jump out of." A cartoon that showed two men jumping out of a window arm-in-arm was captioned "The speculators who had a joint account."

Signs of Change

Looking back, we know that the Great Depression began to ease when the United States entered into World War II in 1941. Americans suffering through the Depression, of course, had no idea when the hard times would end. They looked for signs of change, and even in the early 1930s there were some.

Prohibition Is Repealed In February 1933, just 15 years after it passed the Eighteenth Amendment banning the sale of alcoholic beverages, Congress passed the **Twenty-first Amendment,** repealing Prohibition. The amendment was ratified by the end of the year.

Some people, including President Hoover, regretted the repeal, but most welcomed it as an end to a failed social experiment and as a curb on gangsters who profited from bootlegging. Control of alcohol returned to the states, eight of which chose to continue the ban on liquor sales.

Caption Answers

Interpreting Political Cartoons Sample answer: To forget their worries and to share their misery.

RESOURCE DIRECTORY
Teaching Resources
Units 3/4 booklet
- Section 3 Quiz, p. 64

Guide to the Essentials
- Section 3 Summary, p. 74

The Empire State Building For many, a dramatic symbol of hope was the new Empire State Building, begun in 1930. John J. Raskob, the developer of the gleaming new skyscraper, won the race to build the world's tallest building. Some 2,500 to 4,000 people worked on its construction on any given day. The cost of the construction was about $41 million (including land). Because of the Depression, projected building costs were cut in half.

The 102-story Empire State Building soared 1,250 feet into the sky and was topped with a mooring mast for blimps. The building's 67 elevators, traveling 1,000 feet per minute, brought visitors to its observation deck. The building officially opened on May 1, 1931, when President Hoover pressed a button in Washington, D.C. that turned on the building lights, illuminating the New York City skyline. On the first Sunday after it opened, more than 4,000 people paid a dollar each to make the trip to the top.

The End of an Era By the mid-1930s, it was clear that an era was ending. One by one, symbols of the 1920s faded away. In 1931, organized crime gangster Al Capone was at last brought down, convicted of tax evasion and sent to prison. The frugal former President Calvin Coolidge, who presided over the freewheeling prosperity of the 1920s, died in January 1933. Baseball legend Babe Ruth retired in 1935. The Depression-era labor policies of automaker Henry Ford, once admired for his efficiency, made him labor's prime enemy.

In 1932, the nation was horrified when the infant son of aviation hero Charles Lindbergh and Anne Morrow Lindbergh was kidnapped and murdered. Somehow this tragedy seemed to echo the nation's distressed condition and its fall from the heights of its energy and heroism in the 1920s.

VIEWING HISTORY Workers like the man shown above looked out over New York City as they labored to complete the Empire State Building. **Determining Relevance** *How was the Empire State Building a symbol of hope?*

Section 3 Assessment

READING COMPREHENSION

1. What were **penny auctions** and how did they help farmers overcome some of the hardships of the Great Depression?
2. Why was there an interest among some Americans in radical and reform movements? How did American involvement in these movements differ from the political movements occurring in some parts of Europe at the same time?
3. Why was the **Twenty-first Amendment** passed? Why do you think it was passed during the Great Depression?

CRITICAL THINKING AND WRITING

4. **Making Comparisons** Cite three events in American history that reflect the same qualities of cooperation and endurance exhibited by Americans during the Depression.
5. **Writing an Opinion** In a time of crisis, the building of an expensive skyscraper such as the Empire State Building might have been seen as wasteful. Instead, many Americans found it inspiring. What might account for this view of the project?

Take It to the NET

Activity: Virtual Field Trip Take a tour showing the construction of the Empire State Building. What kinds of conditions did the workers encounter? Write a poem or an essay based on the images you see. Use the links provided in the *America: Pathways to the Present* area of the following Web site for help in completing this activity.
www.phschool.com

Section 3 Assessment

Reading Comprehension

1. A penny auction occurred when a bank foreclosed on a farm and put it up for auction. Neighbors of the foreclosed farmer would buy his property for only pennies, then return it to him in order to help him out.
2. Many Americans became interested in radical social movements because they felt the current government had failed them. Unlike the situation in many European countries, American involvement in these movements was nonviolent and did not seriously challenge the government.
3. It passed because many people wanted to lift the ban on the sale and consumption of alcohol. It was passed during the Depression to help people socialize during tough times and to lessen the activity of gangsters and bootleggers.

Critical Thinking and Writing

4. Answers will vary but might include the American Revolution, the war efforts for both World War I and II, the civil rights movement, and the women's movement.
5. Sample answer: The skyscraper was a symbol of American pride in spite of the Depression, and the project provided jobs for many people.

Invite students to take a Virtual Field Trip at **www.phschool.com**

CUSTOMIZE FOR ...

Less Proficient Writers

Have students make an advertisement or poster designed to encourage Depression-era Americans to help one another through the hard times.

CAPTION ANSWERS

Viewing History The tallest building in the world symbolized progress and success in a time when people were losing hope.

Section 4
The Election of 1932

Section Objectives

1. Find out how President Hoover responded to the Great Depression.
2. Learn what Roosevelt meant when he offered Americans a "new deal."
3. Realize why the election of 1932 was a significant turning point in American politics.

Bellringer

Warm-Up Activity Ask students to consider why elections are important and to provide specific examples of how elections are an avenue of change.

Activating Prior Knowledge Ask students if they have ever heard the "theme song" of the Democratic Party, "Happy Days Are Here Again." This song was written in 1929 and became associated with FDR. Have students research the lyrics to the song and see how they relate to the conditions at the time FDR took office.

Reading Strategy

Have students skim the section, reading headings and the first sentence of each paragraph. Then have them list the main headings on a sheet of paper. Under each heading, have them write a sentence or phrase predicting the content of that part of the section. When students have finished reading, have them compare their predictions with the actual content.

Section 4 The Election of 1932

READING FOCUS

- How did President Hoover respond to the Great Depression?
- What did Roosevelt mean when he offered Americans a "new deal"?
- Why was the election of 1932 a significant turning point for American politics?

MAIN IDEA

As the Depression worsened, people blamed Hoover and the Republicans for their misery. The 1932 presidential election brought a sweeping victory for Democrat Franklin D. Roosevelt and profound changes in the role of government.

KEY TERMS

Hawley-Smoot tariff
Reconstruction Finance Corporation (RFC)
Bonus Army

TAKING NOTES

As you read, complete this chart listing some ideas of the presidential candidates in 1932.

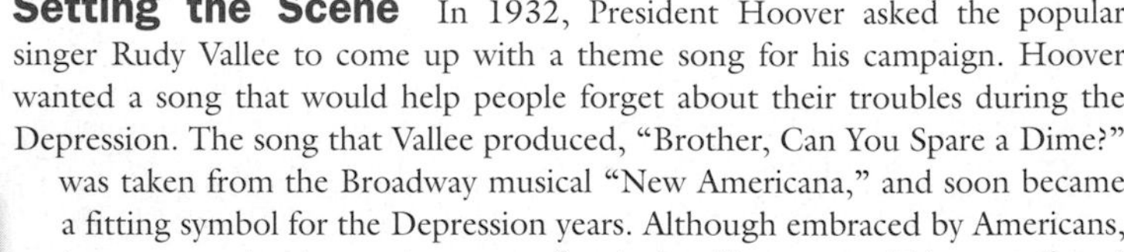

Candidate	Ideas on Government
Herbert Hoover	• Believed in minimal government action • Strict view of government (less government is better) •
Franklin Delano Roosevelt	• Willing to experiment with government roles • Supported broadening the role of government •

Setting the Scene In 1932, President Hoover asked the popular singer Rudy Vallee to come up with a theme song for his campaign. Hoover wanted a song that would help people forget about their troubles during the Depression. The song that Vallee produced, "Brother, Can You Spare a Dime?" was taken from the Broadway musical "New Americana," and soon became a fitting symbol for the Depression years. Although embraced by Americans, it was not quite the rousing song of optimism Hoover would have preferred as a campaign song.

> "*Once I built a railroad*
> *I made it run*
> *Made it race against time.*
> *Once I built a railroad*
> *Now it's done*
> *Brother, can you spare a dime?*"

In contrast, the Democratic candidate for President in 1932, Franklin Delano Roosevelt, built his campaign around a much different tune:

> "*Happy days are here again,*
> *The skies above are clear again*
> *Let us sing a song of cheer again—*
> *Happy days are here again.*"

VIEWING HISTORY This *New Yorker* cover drawing of FDR's inauguration in 1933 shows Roosevelt, the new President, in contrast with Hoover. **Recognizing Bias** *Do you think this drawing is being critical of Hoover or of the American public's perception of the two candidates?*

As the election approached, Hoover, known as the "great engineer" for his exceptional engineering career, tried desperately to "engineer" the United States out of the Depression. His strict adherence to his political beliefs, however, would put severe limits on what he was able to accomplish.

Hoover's Limited Strategy

For a few months after the stock market crash, President Hoover, along with business leaders, insisted that the key to recovery was confidence. Hoover

Caption Answers

Viewing History Based on election results, it probably shows how many Americans saw the two candidates, but at the same time it is making a caricature of them both. Roosevelt's big smile may be interpreted as being somewhat fake. Hoover appears to be excessively grim and pessimistic.

RESOURCE DIRECTORY

Teaching Resources

Learning Styles Lesson Plans booklet, p. 47
Guided Reading and Review booklet, p. 92
Biography, Literature, and Comparing Primary Sources booklet (Comparing Primary Sources) *On Ending the Depression,* p. 139

Technology

Section Reading Support Transparencies
Guided Reading Audiotapes (English/Spanish), Ch. 15
Student Edition on Audio CD, Ch. 15
RESOURCE PRO® **Visual Learning Activity** *Veterans March on Washington,* found on Resource Pro, uses a political cartoon to help students understand veterans' issues.
Prentice Hall Presentation Pro CD-ROM, Ch. 15
Companion Web site, www.phschool.com

blamed the Great Depression on "world-wide economic conditions beyond our control"—not on problems in the United States economy. Taking Hoover's advice, business and government leaders tried to maintain public confidence in the economy. Even as factories closed, Hoover administration officials insisted that conditions would improve soon.

Voluntary Action Fails Hoover believed that voluntary controls by businesses in the United States were the best way to end the economic crisis. He quickly organized a White House conference of business leaders and got their promise to maintain wage rates. At first, many firms did keep wages up. By the end of 1931, however, companies were quietly cutting workers' pay.

Hoover held rigidly to his principle of voluntary action. A shy man, he was successful in business but inexperienced in politics. As a result, he showed less flexibility when it came to political compromise. Often unwilling to budge from his views, Hoover was ultimately unable to make his plan attractive to the American people. After a year of misery, the public began to blame him and the Republicans for the crisis.

The Government Acts Despite his staunch beliefs and continual reassurances to the public, Hoover knew that he had to do something to alleviate the suffering of so many Americans. Even before the Depression began, Congress, with the support of Hoover, passed the Agricultural Marketing Act in June 1929. The act provided a form of relief for farmers by creating a Federal Farm Board, which was designed to stabilize the prices of farm crops. The program proved to be a failure, however, losing over $150 million and sending farm prices on another downward spiral.

VIEWING HISTORY Boulder Dam, seen here under construction, was built with massive steel bar columns, and used as much steel as the Empire State Building. **Synthesizing Information** *What did Hoover hope to accomplish by spending money to build Boulder Dam?*

As a result of the worsening Depression, the Republicans took a beating in the 1930 midterm elections. After the election, Republicans no longer controlled the House, and their majority in the Senate was reduced to just one seat. As the hardships continued and criticisms increased, Hoover took an even more active approach. To create jobs, the government spent more on new public buildings, roads, parks, and dams. Construction on Boulder Dam (later renamed Hoover Dam) began in 1930. A President's Emergency Committee on Employment advised the President to create local relief programs.

In an attempt to protect domestic industries from foreign imports, in 1930 Congress passed the **Hawley-Smoot tariff,** the highest import tax in history. The tariff backfired. European countries raised their own tariffs, bringing a sudden slowdown in international trade. Hoover suspended the Allies' payments of their war debts, but Europe's economies grew weaker.

In early 1932, Hoover set up the **Reconstruction Finance Corporation (RFC),** which gave government credit to a number of institutions, such as large industries, railroads, and insurance companies. The act also lent money to banks so that they could extend loans. Also that year, Congress passed the

Lesson Plan

Focus The 1932 presidential election presented an opportunity for change. What was the outcome of this election? How did the new administration change the direction of American government?

Instruct Explain that Hoover believed a positive outlook and voluntary contributions by business leaders would end the economic crisis. His administration did, however, take more direct action than had former governments. Ask students to state the results of the Hawley-Smoot tariff and the Reconstruction Finance Corporation.

Discuss what Roosevelt meant when he offered Americans a "new deal." What programs was he referring to? Ask why the 1932 election signaled a shift in the relationship between the people and the government.

Assess/Reteach To what degree do students think Hoover was responsible for the onset of the Great Depression? Have them review actions he took (or did not take) and analyze them.

Activity
Connecting with Culture

Have students create poems or song lyrics, of the same length and meter as those in Setting the Scene, to reflect either the despair of the Depression or hope for a better future. Call on students to read their compositions to the class. Have them describe how the characteristics and issues of the Depression era are reflected in their compositions. **(Musical/Rhythmic)**

Test Preparation

Have students review the material on this page under the heading "The Government Acts" and then answer the question below.

What was the purpose of the Agricultural Marketing Act of 1929?

A To raise the prices of farm crops.
(B) To stabilize the prices of farm crops.
C To supervise farm foreclosures.
D To turn farms over to the government.

Caption Answers

Viewing History He hoped that building projects such as the Boulder Dam would help to create jobs and increase productivity.

Home Loan Bank Act, which, by discounting mortgage rates, helped homeowners save their homes and farmers keep their farms. The RFC reflected the theory that prosperity at the top would help the economy as a whole. To many people, however, it seemed that the government was helping bankers and big business leaders while ordinary people went hungry. Despite the RFC, banks continued to fail.

READING CHECK
What did Hoover think of direct federal relief?

Hoover's Unpopularity Grows Despite his support of these programs, Hoover insisted that state and local governments should handle relief. Hoover argued that direct federal relief would destroy people's self-respect and create a large bureaucracy. His refusal to provide direct aid brought bitter public reaction and negative publicity. Although his World War I relief work had earned him the title "Great Humanitarian," Hoover's attitude toward Depression relief made him seem cold and hard-hearted.

Many people blamed Hoover, not always fairly, for their problems. While people went hungry, newspapers showed a photograph of him feeding his dog on the White House lawn. People booed when he said such things as "Our people have been protected from hunger and cold."

Private charities and local officials could not meet the demands for relief as Hoover wanted. Finally, in 1932, Hoover broke with tradition and let the RFC lend the states money for unemployment relief. But it was too little and too late.

As the Depression deepened, some economists backed the ideas of British economist John Maynard Keynes. Keynes argued that massive government spending could help a collapsing economy and encourage more private spending and production of goods and services. This economic theory was not yet widely accepted, however.

Veterans March on Washington A low point for Hoover came in the summer of 1932, when 20,000 jobless World War I veterans and their families encamped in Washington, D.C. The **Bonus Army,** as they called themselves,

Philosophy of Government

FDR's New Deal represented the birth of a new philosophy of the government's role in American life. Since the days of FDR, Americans have had differing opinions on what the size and role of the government should be.

1933 Roosevelt's New Deal greatly expands the role of government for social and welfare programs.

1964 In the tradition of FDR, President Johnson promises a "Great Society," which would provide legislation to combat poverty and offer health care.

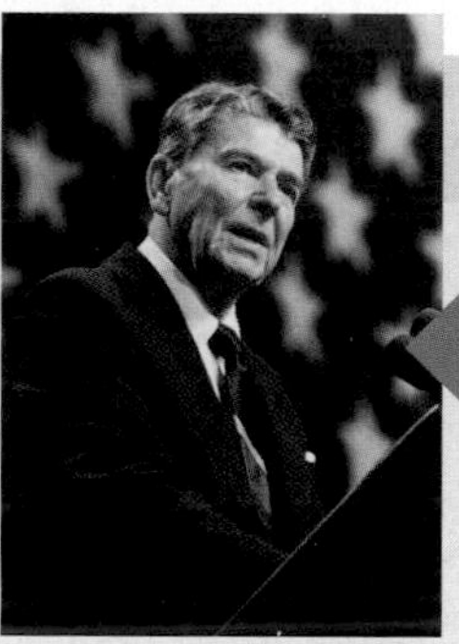

1981 Conservatives, who believe in a minimal role for the government, score a victory when President Reagan begins to cut social welfare spending.

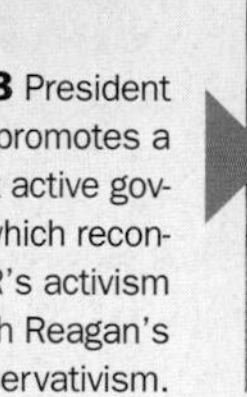

1993 President Clinton promotes a smaller, but active government, which reconciles FDR's activism with Reagan's conservativism.

? **What are possible consequences of both a large government role in social welfare and a limited government role?**

ACTIVITY
Connecting with Government

Have students create political cartoons that reflect public opinion in the 1930s about Hoover's actions or attitudes in dealing with the Depression. Suggest that cartoons focus on a specific subject or policy area, such as unemployment, relief aid, or Hoover's handling of the Bonus Army. Display selected cartoons and ask the class to interpret their meaning. **(Visual/Spatial)**

From the Archives of
American Heritage®

About the Presidents

Herbert Hoover (1929–1933) believed deeply in hard work and self-reliance. He was determined to keep a balanced budget. For Hoover, giant public works projects to aid recovery were out of the question. So was direct federal aid to individuals. He believed that the Constitution would not permit direct aid, and that a "handout" would only worsen the panic. Instead he called on private industry and volunteers to assume more responsibility. "Prosperity cannot be restored by raids upon the public treasure," he said. Source: Saul Braun, "Herbert Hoover," *The American Heritage® Pictorial History of the Presidents of the United States,* vol. 2, 1968.

READING CHECK
Hoover favored state and local relief efforts, as opposed to direct federal relief. He feared that federal relief would needlessly expand the size of the federal government and would create a culture of dependence.

Caption Answers

Fast Forward to Today Possible answer: Government involvement in social welfare can provide a lifeline to those in need, but requires tax increases. A limited role keeps government small, but may leave many needy people adrift.

RESOURCE DIRECTORY

Technology
Color Transparencies *Political Cartoons,* B12
Sounds of an Era Audio CD *Breakup of the Bonus Army,* 1932 recording (time: 30 seconds)

VIEWING HISTORY MacArthur's troops set fire to the Bonus Army camps after driving out the protesters. **Determining Relevance** *Why do you think the government's response to the Bonus Army hurt Hoover at election time?*

wanted immediate payment of a pension bonus that had been promised for 1945. The House of Representatives agreed, but the Senate said no. Most of the Bonus Army then went home, but a few thousand stayed, living in shacks.

Although the bonus marchers were generally peaceful, a few violent incidents prompted Hoover to call in the army. General Douglas MacArthur decided to use force to drive the marchers out of Washington. Armed with bricks and stones, the Bonus Army veterans faced their own country's guns, tanks, and tear gas. Many people were injured. Hoover was horrified, but he took responsibility for MacArthur's actions. In the next election, the lingering image of this ugly scene would help defeat him.

A "New Deal" for America

"I pledge myself to a new deal for the American people," announced presidential candidate Franklin Delano Roosevelt as he accepted the Democratic Party's nomination at its Chicago convention in July 1932. Delegates cheered, and an organ thundered out the song "Happy Days Are Here Again." The Republicans, in June, had again named Hoover as their candidate. As the presidential campaign took shape, the differences between the two candidates became very clear.

In Franklin and Eleanor Roosevelt, the Democrats had a remarkable political couple ready to bring them to victory. Franklin, nicknamed "FDR" by the press, was born in 1882. He graduated from Harvard University and took a job in a law firm, although his main interest was politics. He was elected twice to the New York State Senate before becoming Assistant Secretary of the Navy under President Wilson.

In 1920, FDR ran for Vice President but lost. The following summer, he came down with polio and never walked without help again. He spent much of the 1920s recovering at Warm Springs, Georgia, but with his wife's help kept up his political interests.

Eleanor Roosevelt, a niece of Theodore Roosevelt, was born in 1884 into a wealthy family. She married her distant cousin Franklin in 1905. During the 1920s, in New York State, Eleanor worked for several causes, including public housing legislation, state government reform, birth control, and better conditions for working women. By 1928,

Focus on GOVERNMENT

The Twentieth Amendment On March 2, 1932, Congress proposed the Twentieth Amendment to the Constitution. Called the "Lame Duck Amendment," its purpose was to shorten the period between election day in November and the time when congressional representatives and the President take office. Prior to this amendment, elected officials took office on March 4. During this post-election period of over four months, those who had lost the election were "lame ducks," and would spend this time without having much influence or effectiveness. The amendment changed the inauguration date to January 20, cutting the lame duck period in half. By October 15, 1933, every state had ratified the amendment. The first presidential term to be affected would be FDR's second term, which began on January 20, 1937.

ACTIVITY
Student Portfolio

You may wish to have students add the following to their portfolios: Challenge students to design campaign literature for Franklin D. Roosevelt's 1932 election campaign. The format for the brochures should be a tri-folded piece of standard-size 8-1/2-by-11-inch paper. Each brochure should contain illustrations, slogans, and information about the issues and candidate, laid out in a logical and visually engaging manner that will attract voters to support Roosevelt. **(Visual/Spatial)**

BACKGROUND
A Diverse Nation

Hardships for rural African Americans mounted during the Depression, often spurred by policies of the New Deal that were of benefit to the nation as a whole. Historian Jacqueline Jones writes in her book *The Dispossessed* that NRA (National Recovery Act) minimum-wage legislation spurred mechanization of the tobacco industry and put many African Americans out of work. The crop-reduction programs of the AAA (Agricultural Adjustment Administration) severely cut demand for farm labor and provided ready cash for planters to invest in labor-saving machinery. The long-term effects of major development programs such as the TVA (Tennessee Valley Authority) are well known, but the fate of more than 840 Santee-Cooper (South Carolina) families living along the flood plain of a proposed dam is all but forgotten.

CUSTOMIZE FOR ...
Gifted and Talented

Ask students to decide which of the following Presidents would have agreed with FDR and which would have supported Hoover on the issue of controls on business growth and power: Washington, McKinley, Theodore Roosevelt, Coolidge, Wilson. Ask students to explain their decisions based on evidence from the words and actions of the former Presidents.

CAPTION ANSWERS

Viewing History Sample answer: It was Hoover's decision to use the army. Therefore, he probably felt it necessary to "take the heat."

ACTIVITY
Connecting with Citizenship

Analyze with students the problems of image in a presidential campaign. Ask in what ways image is unavoidable. In what ways can image mask the truth? Did Hoover's image mask his real strengths? What was FDR's image? What about his image appealed to many Americans? **(Verbal/Linguistic)**

BACKGROUND
Connections to Today

In one respect, the 1932 election was the first modern presidential campaign. The Democratic National Committee had hired Charles Michelson as the first publicity specialist in American politics in 1928. Armed with a large budget, he developed a well-planned and coordinated media campaign. Michelson wrote the speeches for prominent Democrats and got anti-Hoover stories placed in newspapers and on radio. These tactics reflected Michelson's decision to make Hoover himself, and not the Depression, the issue in the campaign. The nation's widespread suffering facilitated this strategy. In such circumstances, the shy Hoover was no match for a public relations genius like Michelson.

READING CHECK

Democrats, Republicans, immigrants, laborers, and urban workers.

when FDR was persuaded to run for governor of New York, Eleanor was an experienced political worker and social reformer.

After FDR's success as governor of New York (1929–1932), his supporters believed him ready to try for the presidency. With his broad smile and genial manner, he represented a spirit of optimism that the country badly needed.

Unlike Hoover, FDR was ready to experiment with governmental roles. Though from a wealthy background, he had genuine compassion for ordinary people, in part because of his disability. He was also moved by the great gap between the nation's wealthy and the poor.

As governor of New York, Roosevelt had worked vigorously for Depression relief. In 1931, he set up an unemployment commission and a relief administration, the first state agencies to aid the poor in the Depression era. When, as a presidential candidate, FDR promised the country a "new deal," he had similar programs in mind.

COMPARING PRIMARY SOURCES

Fighting the Depression

Sharp philosophical differences characterized the presidential campaign of 1932.

Analyzing Viewpoints Compare the statements made by the two candidates.

Against Drastic Measures

"We are told by the opposition that we must have a change, that we must have a new deal. It is not the change . . . to which I object but the proposal to alter the whole foundations of our national life which have been built through generations of testing and struggle."

—*Herbert Hoover, speech at Madison Square Garden, October 31, 1932*

For Drastic Measures

"I have recounted to you in other speeches, and it is a matter of general information, that for at least two years after the Crash, the only efforts made by the [Hoover administration] to cope with the distress of unemployment were to deny its existence."

—*Franklin D. Roosevelt, campaign address, October 13, 1932*

The Election of 1932

Hoover, the incumbent candidate for President, summed up the choice that voters had in 1932:

> *"This campaign is more than a contest between two men. . . . It is a contest between two philosophies of government."*
>
> —President Herbert Hoover, October 1932

This statement also accurately describes the long-term impact of the 1932 presidential election. It was a historic battle between those who believed that the federal government could not and should not try to fix people's problems, and those who felt that large-scale problems such as the Depression required the government's help. The election would have an enormous effect on public policy for decades to come.

Still arguing for voluntary aid to relieve the Depression, Hoover attacked the Democratic platform. If its ideas were adopted, he said, "this will not be the America which we have known in the past." He sternly resisted the idea of giving the national government more power.

Roosevelt, by contrast, called for "a reappraisal of values" and controls on business:

> *"I feel that we are coming to a view through the drift of our legislation and our public thinking in the past quarter century that private economic power is . . . a public trust as well."*
>
> —Franklin Delano Roosevelt, 1932

While statements like this showed FDR's new approach, many Americans did not support Roosevelt because of his ideas as much as they opposed Hoover because he had been too passive. Even longtime Republicans deserted him. A reserved man by nature, Hoover became grim and isolated. He gave few campaign speeches. Crowds jeered his motorcade.

READING CHECK

From what groups did FDR receive support in the 1932 election?

FDR won the presidency by a huge margin of 7 million popular votes. Much of his support came from groups that had begun to turn to the

RESOURCE DIRECTORY

Teaching Resources

Units 3/4 booklet
- Section 4 Quiz, p. 65
- Chapter 15 Test, pp. 66, 69

Guide to the Essentials
- Section 4 Summary, p. 75
- Chapter 15 Test, p. 76

Learning with Documents booklets (Key Documents) *Franklin D. Roosevelt, First Inaugural Address,* p. 87

Other Print Resources

Chapter Tests with ExamView® Test Bank CD-ROM, Ch. 15

Technology

ExamView® Test Bank CD-ROM, Ch. 15
Social Studies Skills Tutor CD-ROM

Democrats in 1928: urban workers, coal miners, and immigrants of Catholic and Jewish descent.

On a rainy day in 1933, FDR stood before a Depression-weary crowd and took the oath of office of President of the United States. As reporter Thomas Stokes observed, a stirring of hope moved through the crowd when Roosevelt said, "This nation asks for action and action now."

Phrases like this foreshadowed a sweeping change in the style of presidential leadership and government response to its citizens' needs. Ultimately, such changes altered the way many Americans viewed their government and its responsibilities.

In the depths of the Great Depression, many Americans had to give up cherished traditional beliefs in "making it on their own." They turned to the government as their only hope. Thus, as you will read in the next chapter, the Roosevelt years saw the beginning of many programs that changed the role of government in American society.

The words of FDR's Inaugural Address gave much of the country renewed hope for the future:

> *"So first of all let me assert my firm belief that the only thing we have to fear is fear itself."*
>
> —President Franklin Delano Roosevelt, First Inaugural Address, 1933

Having overcome fear in his own life many times, Roosevelt spoke with conviction and confidence, reassuring a frightened nation.

Presidential Election of 1932

% Electoral Vote: 88.9, 11.1

% Popular Vote: 57.4, 39.7, 2.9

Candidate/Party	Electoral Vote	Popular Vote
Franklin D. Roosevelt (Democrat)	472	22,821,857
Herbert Hoover (Republican)	59	15,761,841
Other		1,160,615

MAP SKILLS Franklin D. Roosevelt and the Democratic Party won the popular vote in 1932 as well as a huge margin of electoral votes. **Location** *Which states' electoral votes did Hoover win?*

Section  Assessment

READING COMPREHENSION

1. How did President Hoover hope to end the Depression and its hardships?
2. What was the intent of the **Hawley-Smoot tariff** and the **Reconstruction Finance Corporation?**
3. How did the **Bonus Army** conflict contribute to Hoover's downfall?
4. Describe Franklin Delano Roosevelt's appeal to the American voter in 1932.

CRITICAL THINKING AND WRITING

5. **Distinguishing Fact From Opinion** Do you think the criticisms of Hoover were justified, or might the Depression have brought failure for any President? Explain.
6. **Writing a News Story** Take the position of a reporter covering FDR's inaugural speech. Write a brief newspaper report describing what the President said and how Americans responded to the speech.

Take It to the NET

Activity: Analyzing Primary Sources Read several of FDR's campaign speeches. What issues did he focus on? Referring to the map of the election of 1932 above or online, did FDR win the states in which he made campaign stops? Use the links provided in the *America: Pathways to the Present* area of the following Web site for help in completing this activity. **www.phschool.com**

Section 4 Assessment

Reading Comprehension

1. Hoover believed that the economy would correct itself if Americans remained confident. He relied on voluntary actions from businessmen to maintain this confidence. He finally, and reluctantly, agreed to allow some direct federal assistance to be used for relief efforts.
2. Hawley-Smoot tariff: to protect American products from cheaper foreign imports, keeping money in the United States economy. RFC: to stabilize large banks and corporations with government aid.
3. It made Hoover appear unconcerned with the problems of the average American, who made up the largest part of the voting public.
4. He intended to bring in a new philosophy of government, one that would expand the government to provide more for the common people.

Critical Thinking and Writing

5. Possible answer: no single person's policies and personality could have compensated for the deep flaws in the economy. On the other hand, Hoover appeared cold and hard-hearted, unwilling to provide enough government money either for relief or to stimulate economic recovery.
6. Answers will vary, but might mention that FDR seemed to symbolize hope and action.

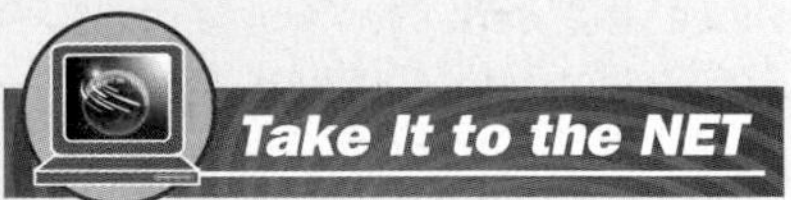

Students should note FDR's concern for the economic situation in the United States, which was suffering from the Great Depression.

Caption Answers

Map Skills Maine, New Hampshire, Vermont, Connecticut, Pennsylvania, and Delaware.

Chapter 15

Chapter 15 Review and Assessment

creating a CHAPTER SUMMARY

Copy this cause-and-effect diagram (right) on a piece of paper and complete it by filling in the major causes and effects of the Great Depression.

iTEXT

For additional review and enrichment activities, see the interactive version of *America: Pathways to the Present*, available on the Web and on CD-ROM.

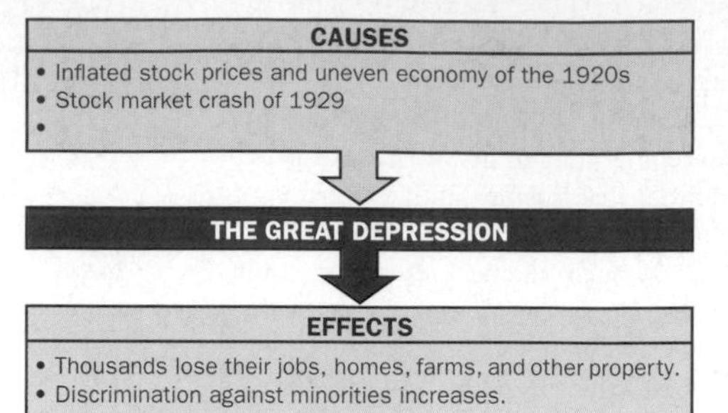
CAUSES
• Inflated stock prices and uneven economy of the 1920s
• Stock market crash of 1929
•
THE GREAT DEPRESSION
EFFECTS
• Thousands lose their jobs, homes, farms, and other property.
• Discrimination against minorities increases.
•

★ Reviewing Key Terms

For each of the terms below, write a sentence explaining how it relates to the Great Depression.

1. Dow Jones Industrial Average
2. Black Tuesday
3. Great Crash
4. business cycle
5. Great Depression
6. Hooverville
7. Dust Bowl
8. penny auction
9. Twenty-first Amendment
10. Hawley-Smoot tariff
11. Reconstruction Finance Corporation (RFC)
12. Bonus Army

★ Reviewing Main Ideas

13. How did overspeculation in the stock market endanger the economy? (Section 1)
14. Why did the Great Depression in the United States affect countries worldwide? (Section 1)
15. How did the Depression affect those at the bottom of the economic scale? (Section 2)
16. Why were farm families hit particularly hard by the Depression? (Section 2)
17. Give specific examples of Americans helping one another to survive the Depression. (Section 3)
18. In what ways did the end of Prohibition mark the end of an era? (Section 3)
19. Why was President Hoover criticized for his handling of the Great Depression? (Section 4)
20. Compare and contrast Hoover's strategy for ending the Great Depression with Roosevelt's. (Section 4)

★ Critical Thinking

21. **Determining Relevance** During the Depression, some economists turned to the ideas of British economist John Maynard Keynes, who argued that massive government spending could help a collapsing economy. Do you agree with Keynes's approach? To what extent are Keynes's views still at work in the American economy today?
22. **Drawing Conclusions** The Great Depression led to hardships for almost everyone, from the very wealthy to the very poor. Do you think this had an impact on traditional American assumptions regarding the work ethic and the theory of social Darwinism?
23. **Demonstrating Reasoned Judgment** Think about some of the examples of Depression humor in this chapter, such as the cartoon in Section 3, and the use of President Hoover's name to describe certain symbols of the Depression. (a) What is the tone of this "humor"? (b) Would you describe it as funny? (c) Think about examples of humor in today's culture. What differences and similarities can you find between now and then?
24. **Recognizing Ideologies** How did the political ideologies of Hoover and Roosevelt affect their decision making?

Reviewing Key Terms

Have students refer to the definitions of key terms in the chapter to write sentences that show an understanding of the causes and effects of both the stock market crash and the Great Depression.

Reviewing Main Ideas

13. Speculation resulted in enormous blocks of stocks being purchased with borrowed money. Thus, the rise in stock prices during the 1920s had no solid foundation.
14. The Great Depression affected other countries by slowing or halting World War I reparation payments and international trade. The world's economies had also become heavily interdependent in many ways during the 1920s.
15. Those at the bottom of the economic scale were hit hardest by the Depression. Many people were left homeless and jobless.
16. Farmers could not meet their payments on loans for land and machinery; natural disasters such as the Dust Bowl ruined farms; prices for farm products fell sharply.
17. Sample answers: soup kitchens were set up; people agreed to keep bids low on foreclosed farm property; some poor people gave food to those who were even worse off.
18. The repeal of Prohibition symbolized a nationwide desire to ease the psychological rigors of the Depression. Repeal also greatly weakened the organized crime networks that had plagued the 1920s.
19. Americans thought that under Hoover's leadership, the government was not doing enough to relieve their problems. What assistance he did offer was too little and too late.
20. Hoover planned to end the Depression through voluntary actions from businessmen and restoring consumer confidence; FDR planned to end the Depression through government intervention, increasing the role government played in helping citizens.

Creating a Chapter Summary

Causes
- Inflated stock prices and uneven economy of the 1920s
- Stock market crash of 1929
- Congress passes the Hawley-Smoot tariff.

Effects
- Thousands lose their jobs, homes, farms, and other property.
- Discrimination against minorities increases.
- Loan failures, bank runs, bank failures, cuts in production, rise in unemployment
- "Hoovervilles"
- Farm distress
- Election of FDR with his promise of a "new deal"

★ Skills Assessment

Analyzing Political Cartoons ▶

25. This political cartoon appeared in 1931. Who is the figure at the center of the cartoon?
26. What is the crowd doing?
27. Do you think the cartoonist is criticizing Hoover or those who are blaming him? Explain.

Interpreting Data

Turn to the series of three graphs in Section 1.

28. About how many banks suspended their business in 1933?
    A about 2,000
    B about 2,300
    C about 1,500
    D about 4,000
29. Which of the following statements best summarizes the data on the unemployment graph?
    F The numbers of unemployed people peaked in 1929.
    G Unemployment was low in 1925.
    H Unemployment increased dramatically between 1929 and 1933.
    J Unemployment decreased after 1933.
30. Which of the following can you NOT tell from these graphs?
    A the percentage of Americans unemployed in 1930
    B the average monthly value of stock prices in 1932
    C the change in stock prices from 1927 to 1932
    D the total number of bank suspensions from 1925 to 1933

Applying the Chapter Skill: *Drawing Inferences*

31. Review the steps needed to draw inferences in the Skills for Life feature on page 519. Then, reread the American Biography on Dorothea Lange on page 517 and study her photographs. Taking into account what you know about the Depression, what inferences can you draw about Lange's attitude toward the Depression? Why do you think she depicts it the way she does?

ACTIVITIES

Writing to LEARN

Writing a Letter
It is 1932. You want to preserve this period in history in a letter that your grandchildren can read in the 2000s. List the main events leading up to the Depression. Include details of daily life in difficult economic times, as well as the upcoming presidential election. Note how your life has been permanently changed by the Depression. Then write a draft of your letter in which you explain your experiences and those of the people around you. Make sure you use enough detail to bring your experiences to life.

Primary Source CD-ROM

Working With Primary Sources Find additional information on the Great Depression on the *Exploring Primary Sources in U.S. History CD-ROM* and use the selection(s) provided to complete the Chapter 15 primary source activity located in the *America: Pathways to the Present* area of the following Web site.
www.phschool.com

Take It to the NET

Chapter Self-Test As a review activity, take the Chapter 15 Self-Test in the *America: Pathways to the Present* area at the Web site listed below. The questions are designed to test your understanding of the chapter content.
www.phschool.com

CRITICAL THINKING

21. Answers will vary, but students should demonstrate a knowledge of Keynesian theory and the ability to give examples from today's economy.
22. Sample answer: Yes, because even those individuals who worked hard were not able to make ends meet. The government had to intervene in people's lives in order to help them to survive.
23. (a) It is dark and sarcastic. (b) In a way. This type of humor gave people a way to laugh in spite of their misery and despair. (c) Answers will vary but should be supported by examples from today.
24. Hoover believed that government should be as unobtrusive as possible. He was hesitant to use the government to provide direct relief, even during the Depression. Roosevelt believed in social welfare programs and was willing to expand the role of government in order to help people.

SKILLS ASSESSMENT

25. President Hoover.
26. Blaming their problems on Hoover.
27. The cartoonist is criticizing both sides. The cartoon seems to be mocking the fact that Hoover is blamed for everyone's troubles, but it also shows Hoover as ineffective.
28. D
29. H
30. A
31. Students should infer that Lange felt that the Great Depression was a tragedy for America, but one that America would survive. Her depictions of Depression-era Americans are meant to show both the crisis they were facing and their perseverance.

ANSWERS TO ACTIVITIES

Writing to LEARN

Answers will vary, but should be supported with facts or quotations from the chapter.

Primary Source CD-ROM

Direct students to the additional primary sources that can be found on the *Exploring Primary Sources in U.S. History CD-ROM.*

Take It to the NET

Additional support materials and activities for Chapter 15 of *America: Pathways to the Present* can be found in the Social Studies area at the Prentice Hall School Web site. **www.phschool.com**

AFTERNOON IN THE BALLPARK

Focus Have students find the meaning of each of these words in a dictionary before they begin to read: *revered, buoyant, bunting, luster, jaunty.* Ask them to think about the selection's two themes as they read: the historic opening game of the 1932 World Series and the emergence of FDR as the front runner on the presidential "playing field."

Instruct Ask students to describe what they already know about the social, political, and economic climate of the country in 1932. Write key ideas on the chalkboard. Then ask them to explain the significance to the writer of the "bright autumn afternoon" of October 1, 1932. Ask a volunteer to read aloud the last two paragraphs of the selection. Discuss the significance to the writer of seeing then-Governor Roosevelt.

Ask students to consider today's baseball heroes and their feats (for example, Mark McGwire and Sammy Sosa's 1998 shattering of Roger Maris's single-season home run record). How might they respond to seeing a famous baseball player or other sports star today?

Analyzing the Document Use this additional question to generate class discussion:

Critical Thinking: Predicting Consequences Based on the passage, which candidate do you think the people of Chicago supported in the election of 1932? *(Franklin D. Roosevelt. Fleming remarks that Hoover was booed in Chicago. Americans blamed Hoover and the Republicans for the Depression.)*

AmericanHeritage®

MY BRUSH WITH **HISTORY**™

by TOM FLEMING

Afternoon in the Ballpark

Both the boom times of the 1920s and the hard times of the 1930s produced numerous heroes and celebrities. Thanks to advances such as radio, these national heroes were familiar to Americans all across the country. Seeing one in person was a memorable experience. In the passage below, Tom Fleming recalls the day he saw three: the President, the man who would become the next President, and the greatest baseball player of his era.

LIKE EVERY AMERICAN BOY in the twenties and thirties, I revered Babe Ruth as the greatest name in baseball. What made him come alive for me was a genuine American League baseball that my father brought home after one of his trips to New York. Ruth had fouled it off, and Dad had jumped up and caught it one-handed. "Just for you," he said. That was at Yankee Stadium, the "House that Ruth built."

Babe Ruth in action, 1929

Of course, I wanted to see Babe Ruth play too, but this wasn't easy. Dad and I were Cub fans. Ruth was an American Leaguer with the Yankees, so when they came to Chicago, they played the White Sox in Comiskey Park on the South Side.

In the fall of 1932 it became clear that Babe would be coming to Wrigley Field (the Cubs and Yankees had reached the World Series). It was beyond expectation that I would actually get to see those games; I hoped that perhaps I could sneak into the coach's office in the high school locker room and catch a few plays on his radio before the bell rang for afternoon classes.

One evening in September Dad came home in an unusually buoyant mood. I was doing a jigsaw puzzle at the family game table in the den. I watched him take off his suit coat and drape it deliberately over the back of his desk chair. As he unbuttoned his vest, he leaned forward and took a small envelope from his inside coat pocket.

Inside the envelope was a pair of tickets to the October 1 home opener of the World Series—the Cubs and the Yankees at Wrigley Field.

"Now you can see Babe Ruth," he said.

Our beloved Wrigley Field had been transformed for the Series, with red, white, and blue bunting draped everywhere. Temporary stands had been set up in the outfield to accommodate the huge crowd. Our seats were only six rows back from the playing field on the left-field side, between the end of the Cubs' dugout and third base.

"There's your man," Dad said, pointing to left field as we settled in. Sure enough, there he

532

RESOURCE DIRECTORY

Technology

AmericanHeritage® My Brush with History™ Videotapes *Afternoon in the Ballpark*

TEST PREPARATION

Have students use the excerpt on these pages to answer the following question.

What is the main idea of the excerpt?

A Roosevelt was a popular governor.

B Fleming's father applauded Hoover while other spectators booed.

C Many people lost their jobs during the Depression.

(D) Seeing Roosevelt made Fleming realize that he was part of the larger world of politics.

was warming up with his teammates—the Bambino, the Sultan of Swat, the Colossus of Clout—Babe Ruth, all six feet two inches and 215 pounds of him.

When the players left the field, the announcer introduced President Hoover, who was in the stands for the big game. The applause was scattered, and I was shocked to hear boos. (As a Boy Scout I thought you didn't do such a thing to a President.) When Governor Franklin D. Roosevelt was introduced, there was much more applause and fewer boos. Both men were on the campaign trail for the presidential election coming up that November. If I had been politically conscious, I would have known right then that Mr. Hoover was in trouble, for it seemed most fans felt Hoover wasn't having nearly as good a year as Ruth.

Charlie Root took the mound for the Cubs. He was in trouble from the first pitch. With the first two Yankees on base on a walk and a throwing error by the shortstop Billy Jurges, Ruth lumbered up to the plate. He promptly did what he was famous for—lofted one of his patented homers out to the center field seats.

The Cubs lifted our hearts with some good hitting, especially from Kiki Cuyler, but they never seemed to get real control of the game. The score was 4 to 4 when Ruth stepped into the box at the top of the fifth inning.

RUTH CALLS HIS SHOT How lucky we were to be on the third-base side. As a left-handed batter, Ruth faced us, and we could see his every move and gesture. Root was very careful. After each strike the Babe raised his right arm, showing one finger for a strike, then two, to keep the stands posted on the duel between him and the pitcher. The crowd reacted wildly. When the count stood at 2 and 2, Ruth stepped back a bit and then pointed grandly to the outfield, making a big arc with his right hand.

Dad poked me in the ribs.

"Look at him point, son! Look at him point! He's calling a home run!"

The very air seemed to vibrate. I held my breath, digging my fingernails into my palms.

Ruth stepped back into the batter's box, ready for Root's next pitch. It came in knee-high, and the Babe connected solidly with his great swing. The crowd let out a volcanic, spontaneous gasp of awe. Everybody knew it was gone, gone, gone as it soared high and out over the center-field score board for one of the longest homers ever hit out of Wrigley Field.

The Babe started his trip around the bases. When he rounded second and came toward us, we saw a triumphant smile on his face. Past third, he leaned over and pointed into the Cub dugout. I can only guess what he said to the Cub bench jockeys, although I probably wouldn't have known all the words then.

Root and Hartnett, the Cub battery, later denied that Ruth had called his shot or pointed. I guess that as great competitors they didn't want to give Ruth any more luster than he already had. Dad and I knew that Babe Ruth had pointed though. The Yankees went on to win, 7 to 5, and four of their runs were provided by Babe Ruth. That was the Sultan of Swat at his greatest.

As we were leaving the ballpark, a loud siren wailed just below us, and we rushed over to the ramp railing to see what was going on. Below was the big white touring car of the city greeter, and beside him on the back seat was Governor Roosevelt—gray felt hat and cigarette holder at the jaunty angle cartoonists loved to draw. For a brief moment my eyes locked with his as he looked up at the people lining the railing.

At that moment I realized I was seeing a new star about to enter a more serious arena. That day was a capsule of life. I passed from my boyhood interests to those of the greater game of politics on that bright autumn afternoon of October 1, 1932.

Source: *American Heritage* magazine, November 1990.

Understanding Primary Sources

1. What was the public's reaction when President Herbert Hoover was introduced?
2. Why was this reaction particularly significant in 1932?

American Heritage® MY BRUSH WITH **HISTORY**™

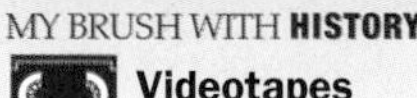

Videotapes

For more information about life during the Great Depression and the 1932 election, view "Afternoon in the Ballpark."

533

CUSTOMIZE FOR ...
ESL

Students may need help with the following words and phrases:
genuine real, authentic
fouled it off hit a foul ball
jigsaw puzzle a picture cut into pieces, which players fit together
accommodate make room for

CUSTOMIZE FOR ...
Less Proficient Readers

To ensure that all students understand the game of baseball, first divide students into small groups. Then have students in each group act as either readers or baseball players. Readers should take turns reading aloud passages that contain references to the game, while baseball players take turns explaining what the references mean. (For example, a reader reads aloud, "Charlie Root took the mound for the Cubs," and a baseball player explains that "the mound" is the pitcher's mound, so the sentence means that Root is pitching.)

CUSTOMIZE FOR ...
Less Proficient Writers

In the passage, the boy closely observes every move that Babe Ruth makes. Have students list each of the Babe's actions while he is at bat, writing one sentence to describe each action.

CUSTOMIZE FOR ...
Gifted and Talented

After students read the selection, have them write a continuation of Fleming's memoir. Tell students to begin with Fleming's concluding sentence, "I passed from my boyhood interests to those of the greater game of politics on that bright autumn afternoon of October 1, 1932." Students' continuations might include the presidential election of 1932 and the New Deal, as regarded by the young Fleming.

ANSWERS

1. He received only scattered applause and some boos.
2. It was a presidential election year in the midst of the Great Depression.

Chapter 16 Planning Guide
Resource Manager

	Core Instruction	Reading/Skills
Chapter-Level Resources **TEKS** 13(D), 24(A), 24(B), 25(D)	Teaching Resources • Pacing Charts booklet • Block Scheduling booklet **Resource Pro® CD-ROM,** Ch. 16 **Prentice Hall Presentation Pro CD-ROM,** Ch. 16 **www.phschool.com** • eTeach	**Guided Reading Audiotapes (English/Spanish)** **Student Edition on Audio CD,** Ch. 16 **Social Studies Skills Tutor CD-ROM** **Color Transparencies,** B13, D9
1 Forging a New Deal **1.** Explore Franklin and Eleanor Roosevelt's roles in restoring the nation's hope. **2.** Learn about the major New Deal programs that were created in the first hundred days, and find out about some of FDR's key players in these programs. **3.** Discover what caused the New Deal to falter. **4.** Review the key goals and accomplishments of the Second New Deal. **5.** Interpret the significance of the outcome of the 1936 election. **TEKS** 11(B), 13(E), 19(B), 21(A), 21(D), 24(C)	Teaching Resources **Units 3/4 booklet** • Section 1 Quiz, p. 73 **Learning Styles Lesson Plans booklet,** p. 48	**Guided Reading and Review booklet,** p. 93 **Guide to the Essentials,** p. 77 **Learning with Documents booklet,** pp. 28, 62 **Section Reading Support Transparencies**
2 The New Deal's Critics **1.** Learn about some of the New Deal's short-comings and limitations. **2.** Discover the chief complaints of FDR's critics inside and outside of politics. **3.** See how the court-packing fiasco harmed FDR's reputation. **TEKS** 16(B), 24(C)	Teaching Resources **Units 3/4 booklet** • Section 2 Quiz, p. 74 **Learning Styles Lesson Plans booklet,** p. 49	**Guided Reading and Review booklet,** p. 94 **Guide to the Essentials,** p. 78 **Skills for Life booklet,** p. 25 **Section Reading Support Transparencies**
3 Last Days of the New Deal **1.** Learn about factors that led to the recession of 1937 and about the Roosevelt administration's response to this situation. **2.** Find out about triumphs and setbacks experienced by unions during the New Deal era. **3.** Discover some effects of the New Deal on American culture. **4.** See what lasting effects can be attributed to the New Deal. **TEKS** 8(A), 13(E), 15(A), 20(A), 22(A), 24(G)	Teaching Resources **Units 3/4 booklet** • Section 3 Quiz, p. 75	**Guided Reading and Review booklet,** p. 95 **Guide to the Essentials,** p. 79 **Section Reading Support Transparencies**

Enrichment/Pre-AP

Prentice Hall United States History Video Collection™
www.phschool.com
- Section Activities, Virtual Field Trip, Chapter Activities, Current Events Online

Great Debates booklet, pp. 16, 18
American History Block Scheduling Support
Nystrom *Atlas of Our Country*, pp. 34–35
Sounds of an Era Audio CD
Exploring Primary Sources in U.S. History CD-ROM

Biography, Literature, and Comparing Primary Sources booklet, pp. 71, 141–142
Sounds of an Era Audio CD

Biography, Literature, and Comparing Primary Sources booklet, p. 28
Sounds of an Era Audio CD
American Pathways Thematic Posters

Assessment

Core Assessment
ExamView® Test Bank, Ch. 16
ExamView® Test Bank CD-ROM, Ch. 16

Standardized Test Preparation
Diagnose and Prescribe
Diagnostic Tests for High School Social Studies Skills

Review and Reteach
Review Book for U.S. History

Practice and Assess
Test-taking Strategies With Transparencies
Test-taking Strategies Posters
Test Prep Book for U.S. History
Alternative Assessment Handbook
Document-Based Assessment

Teaching Resources
Units 3/4 booklet
- Section Quizzes, pp. 73–75
- Chapter Tests, pp. 76, 79

www.phschool.com Ch. 16 Self-Test

AmericanHeritage Resources

From the Archives of American Heritage®, p. 538
AmericanHeritage® My Brush with History™ Videotapes
www.americanheritage.com

Don't miss the exclusive interactive version of this textbook on the Web and on CD-ROM.

Chapter 16 Planning Guide

In Your Classroom

Customize for Individual Needs

Gifted and Talented

Teacher's Edition
- Customize for Gifted and Talented, pp. 539, 555

Teaching Resources
- Biography, Literature, and Comparing Primary Sources booklet, pp. 28, 71, 141–142

Technology
- Exploring Primary Sources in U.S. History CD-ROM *First Inaugural Address, Franklin D. Roosevelt*

ESL

Teacher's Edition
- Customize for ESL, pp. 541, 549

Teaching Resources
- Guided Reading and Review booklet, pp. 93–95
- Guide to the Essentials (English/Spanish), Chapter 16

Technology
- Student Edition on Audio CD, Chapter 16
- Guided Reading Audiotapes (English/Spanish), Chapter 16
- Section Reading Support Transparencies

Less Proficient Readers

Teacher's Edition
- Customize for Less Proficient Readers, p. 547

Teaching Resources
- Guided Reading and Review booklet, pp. 93–95
- Guide to the Essentials (English/Spanish), Chapter 16

Technology
- Student Edition on Audio CD, Chapter 16
- Guided Reading Audiotapes (English/Spanish), Chapter 16
- Section Reading Support Transparencies

Less Proficient Writers

Teacher's Edition
- Customize for Less Proficient Writers, p. 537

Teaching Resources
- Guided Reading and Review booklet, pp. 93–95
- Guide to the Essentials (English/Spanish), Chapter 16

Technology
- Student Edition on Audio CD, Chapter 16
- Guided Reading Audiotapes (English/Spanish), Chapter 16
- Section Reading Support Transparencies

Teacher's Edition Index

Chapter 16 – Pacing Suggestions

For 90-minute Blocks

- Teach sections 1 and 2 using Transparencies B13 and D9, and the Recent Scholarship notes on pages 539, 547, and 550 for class discussions.

Running Out of Time?

If you are running short on time to cover this chapter, consider the following options:

- Use the Prentice Hall Presentation Pro CD-ROM to create an outline for this chapter.
- Use the Section Summaries for Chapter 16, from **Guide to the Essentials (English/Spanish).**

TEKS Correlation

Chapter-Level	TEKS
	(13) Economics. The student understands significant economic developments between World War I and World War II. The student is expected to: **(D)** evaluate the effectiveness of New Deal measures in ending the Great Depression. **(24) Social studies skills.** The student applies critical-thinking skills to organize and use information acquired from a variety of sources, including electronic technology. The student is expected to: **(A)** locate and use primary and secondary sources such as computer software, databases, media and news services, biographies, interviews, and artifacts to acquire information about the United States. **(B)** analyze information by sequencing, categorizing, identifying cause-and-effect relationships, comparing, contrasting, finding the main idea, summarizing, making generalizations and predictions, and drawing inferences and conclusions. **(25) Social studies skills.** The student communicates in written, oral, and visual forms. The student is expected to: **(D)** create written, oral, and visual presentations of social studies information.
1 Forging a New Deal	**(11) Geography.** The student understands the relationship between population growth and modernization on the physical environment. The student is expected to: **(B)** trace the development of the conservation of natural resources, including the establishment of the National Park System and efforts of private nonprofit organizations. **(13) Economics.** The student understands significant economic developments between World War I and World War II. The student is expected to: **(E)** analyze how various New Deal agencies and programs such as the Federal Deposit Insurance Corporation, the Securities and Exchange Commission, and Social Security continue to affect the lives of U.S. citizens. **(19) Citizenship.** The student understands the importance of effective leadership in a democratic society. The student is expected to: **(B)** evaluate the contributions of significant political and social leaders in the United States such as Andrew Carnegie, Shirley Chisholm, and Franklin D. Roosevelt. **(21) Culture.** The student understands how people from various groups, including racial, ethnic, and religious groups, adapt to life in the United States and contribute to our national identity. The student is expected to: **(A)** explain actions taken by people from racial, ethnic, and religious groups to expand economic opportunities and political rights in American society. **(D)** identify the political, social, and economic contributions of women to American society. **(24) Social studies skills.** The student applies critical-thinking skills to organize and use information acquired from a variety of sources, including electronic technology. The student is expected to: **(C)** explain and apply different methods that historians use to interpret the past, including the use of primary and secondary sources, points of view, frames of reference, and historical context.
2 The New Deal's Critics	**(16) Government.** The student understands the changing relationship among the three branches of the federal government. The student is expected to: **(B)** evaluate the impact of events, including Franklin Roosevelt's attempt to increase the number of U.S. Supreme Court justices, on the relationship among the legislative, executive, and judicial branches of government. **(24) Social studies skills.** The student applies critical-thinking skills to organize and use information acquired from a variety of sources, including electronic technology. The student is expected to: **(C)** explain and apply different methods that historians use to interpret the past, including the use of primary and secondary sources, points of view, frames of reference, and historical context.
3 Last Days of the New Deal	**(8) Geography.** The student uses geographic tools to collect, analyze, and interpret data. The student is expected to: **(A)** create thematic maps, graphs, charts, models, and databases representing various aspects of the United States. **(13) Economics.** The student understands significant economic developments between World War I and World War II. The student is expected to: **(E)** analyze how various New Deal agencies and programs such as the Federal Deposit Insurance Corporation, the Securities and Exchange Commission, and Social Security continue to affect the lives of U.S. citizens. **(15) Government.** The student understands changes in the role of government over time. The student is expected to: **(A)** evaluate the impact of New Deal legislation on the historical roles of state and federal governments. **(20) Culture.** The student understands the relationship between the arts and the times during which they were created. The student is expected to: **(A)** describe how the characteristics and issues of various eras in U.S. history have been reflected in works of art, music, and literature such as the paintings of Georgia O'Keeffe, rock and roll, and John Steinbeck's *The Grapes of Wrath.* **(22) Science, technology, and society.** The student understands the impact of science and technology on the economic development of the United States. The student is expected to: **(A)** explain the effects of scientific discoveries and technological innovations such as electric power, the telegraph and telephone, petroleum-based products, medical vaccinations, and computers on the development of the United States. **(24) Social studies skills.** The student applies critical-thinking skills to organize and use information acquired from a variety of sources, including electronic technology. The student is expected to: **(G)** support a point of view on a social studies issue or event.

Chapter 16

The New Deal

(1933–1941)

Introducing the Chapter

President Roosevelt's New Deal—the name given to the vast collection of programs and policies formulated to combat the Depression—proved to be only partially successful at ending the nation's misery. But though critics were quick to point to the New Deal's many failures, it was hard to argue against its resounding success in bringing hope to a weary nation. Moreover, the New Deal influenced the social, political, and cultural life and attitudes of Americans in ways that are still apparent today.

Time Line Activity

To provide students with practice in using the time line, ask questions such as these:

1. Who was a popular opponent of FDR and the New Deal? *(Father Coughlin, whose radio show attracted up to 10 million listeners)*
2. What important project was completed in 1937? *(The Golden Gate Bridge in San Francisco)*
3. Name an event that took place in 1938 and foreshadowed World War II. *(Germany invaded and annexed Austria.)*

Chapter 16

The New Deal

(1933–1941)

SECTION 1 Forging a New Deal
SECTION 2 The New Deal's Critics
SECTION 3 Last Days of the New Deal

Campaigning in 1932, Roosevelt greets a miner in Elm Grove, West Virginia.

Union poster from an oil painting by Ben Shahn, late 1930s

American Events

1933 FDR's New Deal is launched, creating new legislation and several major federal agencies.

1934 The American Liberty League is founded. Father Coughlin attracts millions of listeners to his radio show.

1935 As the Depression continues, FDR launches the Second New Deal. The Social Security system is created.

1936 Workers stage a sit-down strike at automobile plants in Michigan.

Presidential Terms: Franklin D. Roosevelt 1933–1945

1932 • **1934** • **1936**

World Events

1933 Germany opens the first concentration camps.

1934 Communists begin the 6,000-mile "Long March" across China.

1936 The Spanish Civil War begins.

eTeach

Be sure to check out this month's online discussion with a Master Teacher. Go to **www.phschool.com**.

RESOURCE DIRECTORY

Teaching Resources

Pacing Charts booklet
Block Scheduling booklet, p. 24
Units 3/4 booklet
- Chapter Summary, p. 72

Technology

Guided Reading Audiotapes (English/Spanish), Ch. 16
Student Edition on Audio CD, Ch. 16
Sounds of an Era Audio CD *Will Rogers April 30, 1933 recording* (time: one minute, 30 seconds)
Prentice Hall United States Video Collection™ Volume 18, *The Great Depression and the New Deal*
Prentice Hall Presentation Pro CD-ROM, Ch. 16
Resource Pro® CD-ROM
Social Studies Skills Tutor CD-ROM
Companion Web site, www.phschool.com

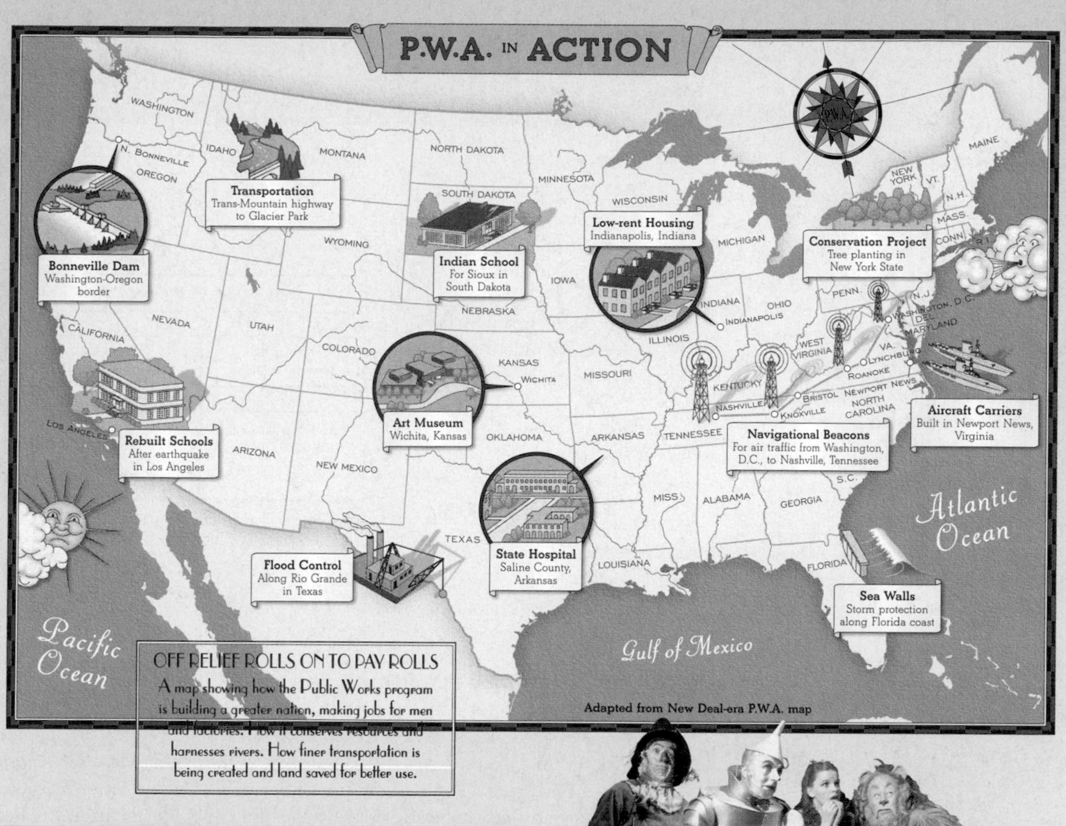

The Wizard of Oz (1939) delighted Depression-era audiences.

1937
San Francisco's Golden Gate Bridge is completed. FDR attempts to "pack" the Supreme Court. The U.S. economy collapses into recession again.

1941
James Agee's *Let Us Now Praise Famous Men* is published.

1938 — **1940** — **1942**

1937
The Sino-Japanese War breaks out.

1938
Germany invades and annexes Austria.

1941
The United States enters World War II.

P.W.A. in Action

Activating Prior Knowledge What is an example of a public works program that improved ground transportation? *(The Trans-Mountain highway to Glacier Park.)*

Previewing How did the public works programs help boost Americans' morale? *(The programs provided jobs and improved the country by providing housing, improving transportation, harnessing energy, and building schools and museums.)*

BACKGROUND
About the Pictures

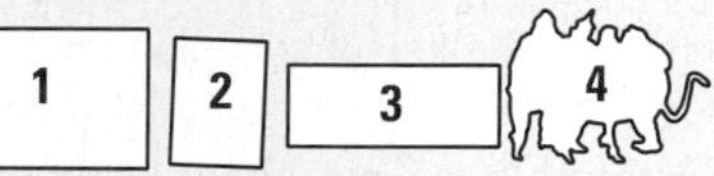

1. When accepting the Democratic Party's nomination in 1932, Roosevelt said, "I pledge you, I pledge myself, to a new deal for the American people."
2. Shahn was a painter and graphic artist who used his artwork to champion important social and political causes.
3. Constructed under the supervision of Joseph B. Strauss, this enormous suspension bridge is 4,200 feet wide at its main span and has "earthquake-proof" foundations.
4. Written by L. Frank Baum, the book *Wonderful Wizard of Oz* was first made into a musical stage performance in 1901 and later became the cinematic adventure beloved by children of all generations.

BIBLIOGRAPHY

For the Teacher

Allan, Frederick Lewis. ***Since Yesterday: The 1930s in America, September 3, 1929–September 3, 1939.*** HarperCollins, 1986. (A close-up view of the era by a respected magazine editor.)

Steinbeck, John. ***The Harvest Gypsies: On the Road to* The Grapes of Wrath.** Heyday Books, 1996. (A collection of newspaper articles written by Steinbeck in 1936, based on interviews with workers in federal migrant labor camps.)

For the Student

Leuchtenberg, William E. ***Franklin D. Roosevelt and the New Deal, 1932–1940.*** HarperCollins, 1963. (An introduction to the New Deal.)

Warren, Robert Penn. ***All the King's Men.*** Harvest Books, 1996. (A fictionalized account of the life of Huey Long.)

Don't miss the exclusive interactive version of this textbook on the Web and on CD-ROM.

Section 1
Forging a New Deal

Section Objectives

1. Explore Franklin and Eleanor Roosevelt's roles in restoring the nation's hope.
2. Learn about the major New Deal programs that were created in the first hundred days, and find out about some of FDR's key players in these programs.
3. Discover what caused the New Deal to falter.
4. Review the key goals and accomplishments of the second New Deal.
5. Interpret the significance of the outcome of the 1936 election.

Bellringer

Warm-Up Activity Have students imagine a situation in which all members of their household were out of work, had no hope of finding a job, and had no government benefits. Ask them how they would want their government leaders to respond.

Activating Prior Knowledge Ask students to list some current government programs that are designed to help families that are out of work.

Reading Strategy

Have students write two column headings on a sheet of paper: *New Deal* and *Second New Deal.* As they read, have them list details from the section in the appropriate column, note the significance of each detail, and evaluate the effectiveness of New Deal measures in ending the Depression.

Section 1 Forging a New Deal

READING FOCUS

- How did Franklin and Eleanor Roosevelt work to restore the nation's hope?
- What major New Deal programs were created in the first hundred days, and who were some of FDR's key players in these programs?
- What caused the New Deal to falter?
- What were the key goals and accomplishments of the Second New Deal?
- What did the outcome of the 1936 election indicate?

MAIN IDEA

President Roosevelt sought to end the Great Depression through the federal programs of the New Deal.

KEY TERMS

New Deal
hundred days
public works program
Civilian Conservation Corps (CCC)
Agricultural Adjustment Administration (AAA)
Tennessee Valley Authority (TVA)
Second New Deal
Wagner Act
closed shop
Social Security system

TAKING NOTES

As you read, fill in the chart below with key goals of the first and second phases of the New Deal.

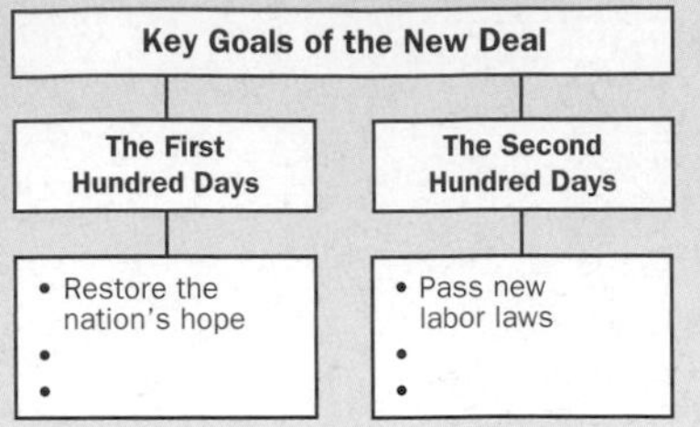

Setting the Scene

A desperate nation anticipating Franklin Delano Roosevelt's "new deal" for America had to wait an agonizingly long time for it to begin. Presidential elections took place in November, but the inauguration of the victor did not occur until the following March 4—a full four-month wait. The lengthy time interval had made sense in earlier days, when vote counting took longer and the President-elect often needed more time to travel to the capital.

By 1933, however, improvements in communication and transportation had eliminated the need for such a long wait, and the disadvantages of the delay were abundantly clear. Hoover remained in office as a "lame duck"—a leader whose authority is weakened because he or she is about to leave office. Meanwhile, the Depression deepened.

The situation prompted Congress to pass the Twentieth Amendment—nicknamed the "lame-duck amendment"—which changed the date of the inaugural to January 20. Ratified in early 1933, the amendment did not take effect until the next election. Roosevelt, therefore, became the last President to be inaugurated in March. While the nation waited, FDR prepared for what would be the biggest change in the federal government since its inception.

VIEWING HISTORY Whenever a presidential administration changes hands from one political party to another, many members of the old administration lose their government jobs. **Drawing Inferences** *(a) Who are the elephants in this cartoon, and what are they doing? (b) What point is the cartoonist trying to make?*

Restoring the Nation's Hope

As he prepared plans for rescuing the economy, FDR, along with the new First Lady, Eleanor, went about restoring Americans' sense of hope. Building public confidence in the future was essential to calming panic and creating support for the President's plans.

A test of the new administration's approach to crises came shortly after he took office. World War I veterans staged a second Bonus March on Washington. This time, the White House provided campsites for the veterans. Even more astounding, Eleanor Roosevelt paid them a visit.

Caption Answers

Viewing History (a) Republican public officeholders put out of work when Roosevelt, a Democrat, took office. They are looking for work. (b) The cartoonist is pointing out the irony that the failure of Hoover, a Republican, to ease severe unemployment at the start of the Great Depression caused him and those in his administration to lose their own jobs.

Resource Directory

Teaching Resources
Learning Styles Lesson Plans booklet, p. 48
Guided Reading and Review booklet, p. 93

Other Print Resources
Nystrom *Atlas of Our Country* *People on the Move,* pp. 34–35

Technology
Section Reading Support Transparencies
Guided Reading Audiotapes (English/Spanish), Ch. 16
Student Edition on Audio CD, Ch. 16
Sounds of an Era Audio CD *President Roosevelt's First Inauguration Speech, 1933 recording* (time: 50 seconds); *President Roosevelt's First "Fireside Chat," March 12, 1933* (time: 45 seconds)
Exploring Primary Sources in U.S. History CD-ROM *First Inaugural Address, Franklin D. Roosevelt*
Prentice Hall Presentation Pro CD-ROM, Ch. 16
Companion Web site, www.phschool.com

When she walked up to a group of marchers, "They looked at me curiously and one of them asked my name and what I wanted," she recalled later. By the time she left, the veterans were waving and calling out, "Good-bye and good luck to you!" The First Lady told reporters afterward how polite the marchers had been. By this act, she demonstrated compassion and soothed popular fears about renewed radical agitation.

FDR, in his First Inaugural Address, March 4, 1933, told Americans, "The only thing we have to fear is fear itself." The first Sunday after taking office, Roosevelt spoke to the nation over the radio in the first of what became regular "fireside chats." His easy manner and confidence helped renew people's hopes for the future.

In campaigning for the White House, FDR had promised "bold, persistent experimentation." No one knew exactly what that meant—only that someone was going to do something. As reporter Arthur Krock noted, Washington "welcomes the 'New Deal,' even though it is not sure what the New Deal is going to be."

Even Roosevelt himself had no sure plan for government under his leadership. Nevertheless, the new President's optimism and willingness to experiment won him the support of the American people. He had promised "a new deal for the American people," and he kept his word. The term **New Deal** came to refer to the relief, recovery, and reform programs of FDR's administration that were aimed at combating the Great Depression.

Sounds of an Era

Listen to excerpts from FDR's First Inaugural Address, one of his fireside chats, and other sounds from the New Deal era.

The First Hundred Days

From his inauguration in March through June 1933, a period known as the **hundred days,** Roosevelt pushed program after program through Congress to provide relief, create jobs, and stimulate economic recovery. He based some of these programs on the work of federal agencies that had controlled the economy during World War I and on agencies set up by states to ease the Depression. Former Progressives figured prominently, inspiring New Deal legislation or administering programs.

Stabilizing Financial Institutions FDR's first step was to restore public confidence in the nation's banks. On March 5, 1933, he ordered all banks to close for the next four days. He then pushed Congress to pass the Emergency Banking Act, which was approved on March 9. The act authorized the government to inspect the financial health of all banks.

Many Americans had been terrified by the prospect of losing all their savings in a bank failure. By his actions, FDR hoped to assure the American people that their banks would not fail. Indeed, government inspectors found that most banks were healthy, and two thirds had reopened by March 15.

After the brief "bank holiday," Americans regained confidence in the banking system. They began to put more money back into their accounts than they took out. These deposits allowed banks to make loans that would help stimulate the economy. Congress increased public confidence further by passing the Glass-Steagall Banking Act of 1933. It established a Federal Deposit Insurance Corporation (FDIC) to insure bank deposits.

VIEWING HISTORY A Detroit, Michigan, bank opens under a new charter following the "bank holiday" ordered by FDR. **Drawing Inferences** *(a) Why do you think the bank is so crowded? (b) How would you react to the bank closings if you were a bank customer in March 1933?*

Lesson Plan

Focus Explain that FDR fulfilled his promise to take action to combat the Depression. Though the New Deal suffered setbacks, FDR's attitude and programs uplifted the nation.

Instruct Explain that the Depression had deeply demoralized the nation by the time FDR became President. Ask students to name the programs FDR created. What were the problems with this New Deal? How did the Second New Deal address the shortcomings of the first one?

Discuss FDR's choice of advisers and policymakers. How did FDR's political appointments reflect his commitment to change? Ask how Eleanor Roosevelt redefined the role of First Lady.

Assess/Reteach Ask students to discuss the underlying assumption of the New Deal: that government can and should help restore economic stability through creation of jobs and funding of economic initiatives. Do students agree or disagree with that basic premise?

Activity

Connecting with Government

Ask students to discuss ways in which the government can build and maintain public confidence. Encourage students to consider why it is important for the government to win the public's trust and what happens when the government loses the public's trust. Have students list some current government programs that create positive feelings among the public. Make sure students understand the changes in the role of government over time. **(Verbal/Linguistic)**

Customize for ...

Less Proficient Writers

To construct an outline of the section, have students first list each boldfaced title in the section and then write a sentence or phrase about each title.

Caption Answers

Viewing History (a) Many of the people in the photograph probably showed up simply to reassure themselves that the bank was indeed open again and functioning properly. Some customers undoubtedly came in order to withdraw their savings. However, there were probably some in the photograph who actually deposited money that day. (b) Answers might mention that such an occurrence would be very frightening to experience. A bank closing might make one reluctant to ever put any more money into a bank.

ACTIVITY

Connecting with Government

During the first 100 days of FDR's administration, many federal programs passed through Congress to provide relief, create jobs, and stimulate the economy. Stage a classroom discussion in which students evaluate the effectiveness of New Deal measures in ending the Great Depression. To help students understand these New Deal programs, have them create public works programs within their school. Divide students into small groups to develop a public works project. Each group should identify the goal of the project, the people who would qualify to work on it, and the way in which it would affect the school community. **(Logical/Mathematical)**

From the Archives of

American Heritage®

About the Presidents

Franklin Delano Roosevelt (1933–1945) used two forms of public communication that contributed to his administration's success. First, he met with the press about twice a week. These free-and-easy, back-and-forth sessions put his achievements and plans in the headlines. Even more important were his radio "fireside chats." On these occasions, Roosevelt talked about his programs and purposes to the nation. His soothing voice inspired confidence. Source: Wilson Sullivan, "Franklin Delano Roosevelt," *The American Heritage® Pictorial History of the Presidents of the United States,* vol. 2, 1968.

Congress also moved to correct problems that had led to the stock market crash. The Federal Securities Act, passed in May 1933, required companies to provide information about their finances if they offered stock for sale. The next year Congress set up the Securities and Exchange Commission (SEC) to regulate the stock market. Congress also gave the Federal Reserve Board power to regulate the purchase of stock on margin.

In July 1933, Roosevelt took a further step to stimulate the economy. He decreased the value of U.S. currency by taking it off the gold standard. He hoped that this action would raise the prices of farm products and other goods. He also hoped that a devalued American currency would stimulate export trade. FDR's move pleased many in Congress, who thought it would make paying off New Deal debts easier. Others, including his budget director, Lewis Douglas, thought it was "the end of Western civilization."

Providing Relief and Creating Jobs FDR's next step was to help overburdened local relief agencies. He persuaded Congress in May to establish a Federal Emergency Relief Administration (FERA), which sent funds to these agencies. Harry Hopkins, a former settlement worker and a longtime Roosevelt friend and advisor, directed this agency. Hopkins professed a strong belief in helping people find work:

> "*Give a man a dole [handout], and you save his body and destroy his spirit. Give him a job and pay him an assured wage and you save both the body and the spirit.*"
>
> —FERA administrator Harry Hopkins

To help people who were out of work, the FERA also put federal money into **public works programs,** government-funded projects to build public facilities. One of these programs, set up in November 1933, was the Civil Works Administration (CWA). The CWA put the unemployed to work building or improving roads, parks, airports, and other facilities. The agency was a tremendous morale booster to its 4 million employees. As a former insurance salesman

VIEWING HISTORY This worker for the Civilian Conservation Corps (right) is planting seedlings in Montana. The poster below proclaims the benefits of CCC labor. **Drawing Conclusions** *If you had been a young person during the Depression, what effect might these images have had on you? Why?*

CAPTION ANSWERS

Viewing History These images would undoubtedly have inspired hope for Depression-era youths who would be given the opportunity to earn wages for performing interesting, useful, and healthy outdoor work. These workers would also receive free lodging and meals—in and of themselves powerful inducements for a generation of young people who often found it difficult to get enough to eat.

RESOURCE DIRECTORY

Teaching Resources

Learning with Documents booklet (Primary Source Activity) *A Fireside Chat: The NIRA,* p. 28

Great Debates booklet (Great Debates) *Who Is Responsible for the Elderly and Unemployed?* p. 18

NOTABLE PRESIDENTS
Franklin Delano Roosevelt

32nd President
1933–1945

"The only thing we have to fear is fear itself."
—First Inaugural Address, 1933

Courage in times of crisis was perhaps Franklin Delano Roosevelt's greatest strength. His first crisis was personal rather than political. In 1921, Roosevelt was stricken with polio, which paralyzed his legs and threatened to destroy what had been a promising political career. (Roosevelt had been the Democratic vice-presidential candidate the year before.)

Roosevelt returned to politics in 1928, running for governor of New York. Despite having to be helped or carried onto podiums to speak, Roosevelt campaigned energetically and won the election. Four years later he ran for President. In a campaign dominated by the gloom of the Great Depression, FDR's confidence helped bring him victory.

As President, Roosevelt fought the Depression through what he called "bold, persistent experimentation." "It is common sense to take a method and try it," he explained. "If it fails, admit it frankly and try another. But above all, try something." This commitment to action gave Americans much-needed hope.

Roosevelt showed a similar commitment as commander in chief during World War II. After the attack on Pearl Harbor in 1941, Roosevelt rallied a shocked nation and oversaw the creation of the greatest military force ever seen up to that time. Elected President for a record fourth time in 1944, Roosevelt died in April 1945, just months before the victorious end of the war.

Connecting to Today

Should government programs to help the elderly and the poor be temporary responses to crises such as the Great Depression, or should such programs be permanent? Defend your position.

Take It to the NET **Biography** To read more about Franklin Delano Roosevelt, visit the links provided in the *America: Pathways to the Present* area at the following Web site. **www.phschool.com**

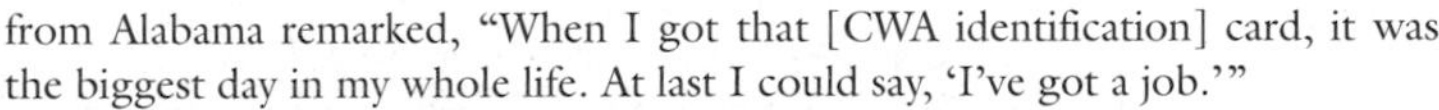

from Alabama remarked, "When I got that [CWA identification] card, it was the biggest day in my whole life. At last I could say, 'I've got a job.'"

The **Civilian Conservation Corps (CCC)** became FDR's favorite program. Established in March 1933, the CCC put more than 2.5 million young, unmarried men to work maintaining forests, beaches, and parks. CCC workers earned only $30 a month, but they lived in camps free of charge and received food, medical care, and job training. Eleanor Roosevelt persuaded the CCC to fund similar programs for young women.

Public works programs also helped Native Americans. John Collier, FDR's commissioner of Indian Affairs, used New Deal funds and Native American workers to build schools, hospitals, and irrigation systems. The Indian Reorganization Act of 1934 ended the sale of tribal lands begun under the Dawes Act (1887) and restored some lands to Indian owners.

Regulating the Economy The sharp decline of industrial prices in the early 1930s had caused many business failures and much unemployment. The National Industrial Recovery Act (NIRA) of June 1933 sought to bolster those prices. The NIRA established the National Recovery Administration (NRA), which set out to balance the unstable economy through extensive planning.

This planning took the form of industry-wide codes to spell out fair business practices. The federal codes regulated wages, restraining wage competition. They controlled working conditions, production, and prices, and set a minimum wage. They gave organized labor collective bargaining rights, which allowed workers to negotiate as a group with employers. NRA officials wrote some of the codes, and they negotiated the details of some codes with the affected businesses. Many codes, however, were drawn up by the largest companies in an

VIEWING HISTORY The National Recovery Administration (NRA) attempted to stabilize the economy by regulating business practices.

ACTIVITY
Student Portfolio

You may wish to have students add the following to their portfolios: Ask students to research a particular New Deal public works program, such as the Civil Works Administration (CWA), the Civilian Conservation Corps (CCC), or the Public Works Administration (PWA). Students should focus on the attitudes and experiences of the individuals whose lives were affected by these programs. Some New Deal agencies and programs continue to affect the lives of U.S. citizens today. Students can present their findings in a written or oral report. **(Verbal/Linguistic)**

BACKGROUND
Recent Scholarship

FDR's struggle with polio was carefully concealed from the public. Although the public knew that he could not walk without assistance, they never fully understood the extent of his condition. In *FDR's Splendid Deception,* Hugh Gregory Gallagher explores how the press and the Secret Service protected FDR, and why. Gallagher maintains that FDR's illness was a critical factor in shaping his political ambitions and achievements. Gallagher writes that despite FDR's ongoing attempts to minimize the extent of his impairment, he raised money for research, education, and care for polio victims.

BACKGROUND
Reforming Society

With FDR's enactment of the New Deal, a horde of young, idealistic lawyers came to Washington eager to reform American society. These students and protégés of Harvard University's Felix Frankfurter—who were accordingly nicknamed "hot dogs"—incurred the disapproval of conservatives. One bureaucratic spokesperson complained of the "plague of young lawyers settled upon Washington."

CUSTOMIZE FOR ...
Gifted and Talented

As they read, have students analyze the difficulties of forging government programs that provide equal benefits for and satisfaction to all citizens. Have students discuss what limits the democratic process places on the ability of a government to implement broad new programs.

ACTIVITY

Connecting with Economics

Have students find out about local or regional projects, such as bridges or buildings, that were carried out by the Public Works Administration (PWA) or the Works Progress Administration (WPA). Suggest that students contact your local or state public works department for information. If possible, encourage students to bring in photos and other pertinent information about these projects. Have students share their findings, including how many people worked on the project, how long it took them to complete it, and how much they were paid. **(Verbal/Linguistic)**

BACKGROUND

A Diverse Nation

In the late 1920s, farming was still a way of life for many Americans. In 1929 two-fifths of the country's citizens lived in rural places. (The U.S. Census defined *rural* as any place with fewer than 2,500 inhabitants.) One-quarter of the country's jobs were related to agriculture. When a worldwide agricultural depression began in 1926, many Americans were affected, especially those in the cotton belt—the area going west from South Carolina to Texas—and those in the wheat belt—the area running south from Minnesota and North Dakota to Kansas and Oklahoma. When the financial crisis struck at the end of the decade, farmers were ill prepared to cope.

Focus on GEOGRAPHY

Florida's Overseas Highway: A New Deal Project Like a string of pearls, the Florida Keys dangle from the tip of Florida out into the Gulf of Mexico. In the early 1900s, the Florida East Coast Railroad connected the mainland to the popular island of Key West. But in 1935, the strongest hurricane ever recorded in the Western Hemisphere smacked into the Keys with winds of up to 250 miles an hour, destroying the railroad. The Public Works Administration stepped in with a $3.6 million loan that largely financed the construction of a highway over the old railroad bed. Officially opened on July 4, 1938, the 110-mile-long Overseas Highway is the longest overwater road in the world. Part of U.S. Highway 1, it links the Keys with 42 bridges. FDR celebrated this engineering feat by driving the route from Miami to Key West in 1939.

industry. This practice pleased businesses but drew criticism from people concerned that industry influence would bias the codes against workers.

For a brief time, the codes stopped the tailspin of industrial prices. But by the fall of 1933, when higher wages went into effect, prices rose, too. Consumers stopped buying. The cycle of rising production and falling consumption returned, and many more businesses failed, causing more unemployment. Businesses complained that the codes were too complicated and the NRA's control was too rigid.

To this day, one of the most visible parts of the NIRA's efforts is the work carried out by its Public Works Administration (PWA). Directed by Secretary of the Interior Harold Ickes, the PWA launched projects ranging from the Grand Coulee Dam on the Columbia River in Washington State, to New York City's Triborough Bridge, to the causeway that connects Key West to the Florida mainland.

Assisting Homeowners and Farmers The Depression caused many middle-income homeowners to fall behind in paying their mortgages. The Home Owners' Loan Corporation (HOLC) refinanced mortgages—that is, changed the terms of the mortgages—to make the payments more manageable. Between June 1933 and June 1936, the HOLC made about 1 million low-interest loans. Even with these low-interest-rate loans, however, many owners lost their homes because they could not pay their mortgages.

The National Housing Act of 1934 established the Federal Housing Administration (FHA), a government-owned corporation. The FHA, which exists today, was created to improve housing standards and conditions, to insure mortgages, and to stabilize the mortgage market.

Many farmers were losing their homes and their land because of the low prices they received for their products. The **Agricultural Adjustment Administration (AAA),** set up in May 1933, tried to raise farm prices through subsidies, or government financial assistance. The AAA used proceeds from a new tax to pay farmers *not* to raise certain crops and livestock. Lower production, it was hoped, would cause prices to rise.

Under this program, some farmers plowed under crops that were already growing. Many Americans could not understand how the federal government could encourage the destruction of food while so many people were hungry.

The TVA One public works project proved especially popular. The **Tennessee Valley Authority (TVA),** created in May 1933, helped farmers and created jobs in one of the country's least developed regions. By reactivating a hydroelectric power facility started during World War I, the TVA provided cheap electric power (in cooperation with the Rural Electrification Administration), flood control, and recreational opportunities to the entire Tennessee River valley, as shown on the map on the next page.

Key Players in the New Deal

Roosevelt surrounded himself with eager and hard-working advisors. Some became members of the Cabinet or, like Harry Hopkins, headed one of the new agencies. Columbia University Professors Raymond Moley, Adolf A. Berle, and Rexford G. Tugwell became the three key members of FDR's so-called "brain trust," an informal group of intellectuals who helped draft policies.

RESOURCE DIRECTORY

Teaching Resources

Great Debates booklet (Great Debates) *Should the Federal Government Interfere in Local Matters?,* p. 16

Other Print Resources

American History Block Scheduling Support *Alphabet Soup: New Deal Legislation,* found in the Prosperity, Depression, and War folder, includes interdisciplinary lesson suggestions and activities for Geography and History, Primary Sources, Biography, and Literature.

Historical Outline Map Book *Tennessee Valley Authority,* p. 63

Technology

Color Transparencies *Cause-and-Effect Charts,* D9

RESOURCE PRO® **Primary Source Activity** *Providing Emergency Relief,* found on Resource Pro, uses excerpts from Frances Perkins's *The Roosevelt I Knew* to demonstrate her impressions of the New Deal President.

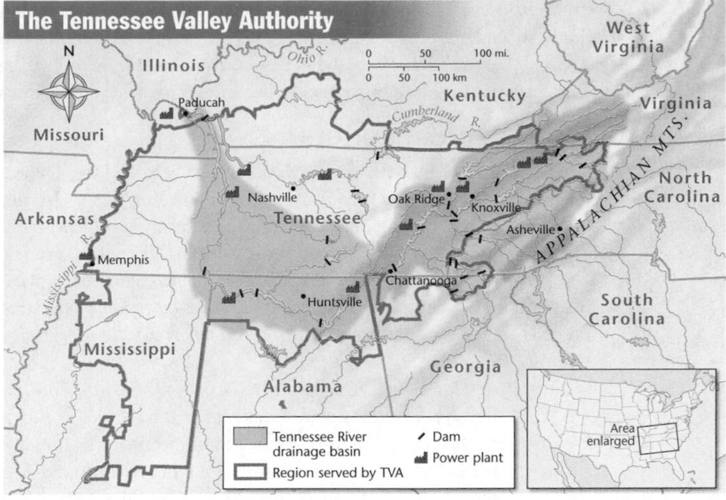

MAP SKILLS The massive TVA project combined the activities of many government agencies to control flooding of the Tennessee River, provide hydroelectric power and irrigation for farms, improve navigation, and provide recreation. The photograph below shows the interior of a dam in Norris, Tennessee. **Regions** *(a) Which states benefited from the TVA? (b) What formed the boundary of TVA activity in the East?*

Groundbreaking Appointments Roosevelt was the first President ever to appoint a woman to a Cabinet post. Frances Perkins, a former Progressive who had headed the New York State Industrial Commission, became Secretary of Labor. She held this job until 1945. Perkins successfully pressed for laws that would help both wage earners and the unemployed. Perkins was one of more than two dozen women who held key New Deal positions.

FDR's administration also broke new ground by hiring African Americans in more than a hundred policymaking posts. One of Roosevelt's key appointees, Mary McLeod Bethune, held the highest position of any African American woman in the New Deal. Bethune was a former elementary school teacher, a college president, and the founder of the National Council of Negro Women. She entered government service with a reputation as one of the country's most influential spokespersons for African American concerns.

Appointed director of the Division of Negro Affairs of the National Youth Administration (NYA) in 1936, Bethune advised FDR on programs that aided African Americans. In the process, she increased her level of influence. She forged a united stand among black officeholders by organizing a Federal Council on Negro Affairs. This unofficial group, known as the "black Cabinet," met weekly to hammer out priorities and increase African American support for the New Deal.

READING CHECK
What historic appointments did FDR make to his administration?

Eleanor Roosevelt Among FDR's most important colleagues was his wife, Eleanor. She threw herself into supporting the New Deal and traveled widely for her husband, whose disability made traveling difficult. She reported to him on conditions in the country and on the effects of his programs. At times, the First Lady took stands that embarrassed her husband. For example, in 1938, she attended a Birmingham, Alabama, meeting of the Southern Conference for Human Welfare, an interracial group. She knew she was expected to obey local Jim Crow laws that required blacks and whites to sit on opposite sides of the auditorium. In protest, she sat in the center of the aisle, between the divided races. Her act received wide publicity, and no one missed its symbolism.

ACTIVITY
Connecting with Government

Have students conduct research to learn about women who have held Cabinet-level positions. What were their backgrounds? What did they accomplish as Cabinet members? Were they considered successful? Have students identify the political contributions of women in American society. **(Verbal/Linguistic)**

BACKGROUND
Biography

Frances Perkins (1882–1965) pushed for a minimum wage, a maximum work week, unemployment compensation for disabled workers, and a limit on the hiring of children under age 16. Perkins said of the New Deal: "Its value was psychological. It made people feel better, and in that terrible period of depression they needed to feel better." Among her most notable achievements was the establishment of the Department of Labor and the Bureau of Labor Statistics.

READING CHECK
FDR was the first President to appoint a woman (Frances Perkins) to a Cabinet post. He hired African Americans in more than 100 policymaking posts, including at least one African American woman, Mary McLeod Bethune.

CAPTION ANSWERS

Map Skills (a) Virginia, North Carolina, Georgia, Alabama, Mississippi, Tennessee, and Kentucky. (b) The Appalachian Mountains.

CUSTOMIZE FOR ...
ESL

Write the following words on the chalkboard: *What, Who, Where, When, Why.* Ask volunteers to make up a question about the New Deal using each of these words. For example: *What was the New Deal?* Write the questions on the chalkboard. Then help students formulate answers to these questions.

ACTIVITY
Connecting with Citizenship

Tell students to explore the interests and accomplishments of a recent First Lady. As students do their research, have them consider the following questions: What kinds of issues did she address and how? How did the public receive her efforts? How assertive can a First Lady be in pursuing her own national agenda? Invite students to share their findings in an oral report. **(Verbal/Linguistic)**

BACKGROUND
The First Lady

Eleanor Roosevelt was personally responsible for persuading Harry Hopkins to create a women's division within the Federal Emergency Relief Administration (FERA). And in late 1933, Mrs. Roosevelt sponsored a White House Conference on the Emergency Needs of Women. By spring 1934, more than 300,000 women—more than 50 percent of those who qualified for relief—were employed on various public works projects. At the same time, these women were usually paid less than men.

American BIOGRAPHY

Eleanor Roosevelt 1884–1962

Anna Eleanor Roosevelt, a niece of Theodore Roosevelt, was born in New York City on October 11, 1884. A member of a wealthy family, Eleanor attended private schools. In 1905, she married her distant cousin Franklin, and they had six children.

During World War I, Eleanor Roosevelt joined the war effort as a volunteer for the Red Cross. After the war, she became involved in social and political reforms. In 1922, she joined the Women's Trade Union League and became a leader in the New York State Democratic Party.

Eleanor Roosevelt reshaped the role of First Lady. Besides traveling widely to observe the effects of the New Deal on Americans, she held her own press conferences at the White House, which were for women correspondents only. She lectured widely, and in 1935, she started a newspaper column called "My Day." She used the column to drum up support for the New Deal.

Within a year after Franklin's death in 1945, Eleanor gained further admiration as a delegate to the United Nations. In that role, she led the campaign to approve a Declaration of Human Rights. She worked vigorously for human rights causes until her death in 1962.

Eleanor Roosevelt's activities troubled some Americans. In their view, a First Lady should act only as a gracious hostess at state dinners. Gradually, however, the public got used to her unconventional style, and many came to admire her for her political skills, her humanity, and her idealism.

The New Deal Falters

The zeal and energy with which New Dealers attacked the Depression pleased many observers, at least at first. But when the new programs failed to bring about significant economic improvement, criticism began to mount. Many worried that New Deal agencies were giving increasing power to the federal government. Former President Hoover warned against "a state-controlled or state-directed social or economic system. . . . That is not liberalism; it is tyranny," he said.

The Supreme Court also attacked FDR's programs. In 1935, the Court declared the NIRA unconstitutional because it gave the President lawmaking powers and regulated local, rather than interstate, commerce. The following year, the Court also struck down the tax that funded AAA subsidies to farmers. Two of the most important elements of the New Deal had crumbled. It was time to reassess.

A Second New Deal

Most of the public remained behind Roosevelt. The midterm elections of 1934 showed overwhelming nationwide support for FDR's administration. In 1935, the President launched a new, even bolder burst of activity. Many historians call this period and the legislation it produced the **Second New Deal,** or the Second Hundred Days. In part, it was FDR's response to critics who said he was not doing enough for ordinary Americans. The Second New Deal included more social welfare benefits, stricter controls over business, stronger support for unions, and higher taxes on the rich.

New and Expanded Agencies New agencies attacked joblessness even more aggressively than before. The Works Progress Administration (WPA), an agency set up in 1935 and lasting eight years, provided work for more than 8 million citizens. The WPA built or improved tens of thousands of playgrounds, schools, hospitals, and airfields, and it supported the creative work of many artists and writers. The National Youth Administration, established in June 1935 within the WPA, provided education, jobs, recreation, and counseling for young men and women ages 16 through 25.

The Second New Deal responded to the worsening plight of agricultural workers. The original AAA had ignored many of the farm workers who did not own land. In the Southwest, for example, Mexican American farm workers struggled to survive. Many of these migrant workers were forced to return to Mexico. Others tried to form unions, causing fierce resistance from farming associations. In the South, when landlords accepted the AAA subsidies and took land out of production, many tenants and sharecroppers were left without land to farm.

In May 1935, Rexford Tugwell, an economist in FDR's Department of Agriculture, set up the Resettlement Administration. The agency loaned money to owners of small farms and helped resettle tenants and sharecroppers on productive land. In 1937, the Farm Security Administration (FSA) replaced

RESOURCE DIRECTORY

Teaching Resources

Learning with Documents booklet (Visual Learning Activity) *Promoting the WPA,* p. 62

Technology

Sounds of an Era Audio CD *Dorothy Thompson on Eleanor Roosevelt,* 1936 recording

Tugwell's agency. It loaned more than $1 billion to farmers and set up camps for migrant workers.

Rural Electrification The New Deal also brought electricity to the American countryside. By the 1930s, nearly 90 percent of Americans in urban areas had electricity, compared to only about 10 percent in rural areas. The free market did not encourage private companies to provide power because of the high cost of running power lines to remote areas.

Roosevelt believed that the government had an obligation to provide this essential service where private enterprise would not. In 1935, Congress created the Rural Electrification Administration (REA), which offered loans to electric companies and farm cooperatives for building power plants and extending power lines, as well as to farmers and other rural residents to wire their homes and barns.

Within four years, about 25 percent of rural households had electricity. In time, the REA brought power to 98 percent of U.S. farms. Demand for electric appliances grew, benefiting manufacturing companies and local merchants.

New Labor Legislation Labor unions had liked the NIRA provision known as 7a, which granted them the right to organize and bargain collectively. When the NIRA was declared unconstitutional, workers began to demand new legislation to protect their rights.

In July 1935, Congress responded. It passed the National Labor Relations Act, called the **Wagner Act** after its leading advocate, New York Senator Robert Wagner. The Wagner Act legalized such union practices as collective bargaining and **closed shops,** which are workplaces open only to union members. It also outlawed spying on union activities and blacklisting, a practice in which employers agreed not to hire union leaders. The act set up the National Labor Relations Board (NLRB) to enforce its provisions. The

READING CHECK
Why did Roosevelt see a need to launch a second New Deal?

INTERPRETING CHARTS
The New Deal created an alphabet soup of new federal agencies, greatly expanding the bureaucracy and authority of the government. **Synthesizing Information** *Write a statement explaining the major goals of these agencies.*

Major New Deal Agencies

Agency	Purpose
Federal Emergency Relief Act (FERA), 1933	Provided funds to state relief agencies.
Civil Works Administration (CWA), 1933	Provided federal jobs in building and improving roads and public facilities.
Tennessee Valley Authority (TVA), 1933	Provided hydroelectric power, flood control, and recreational opportunities to the Tennessee River Valley and surrounding areas.
Home Owners Loan Corporation (HOLC), 1933	Provided low-cost mortgage refinancing to homeowners facing foreclosure.
Civilian Conservation Corps (CCC), 1933	Provided jobs to young, unmarried men (and, later, women) to work on conservation and resource development projects.
Public Works Administration (PWA), 1933	Sponsored massive public works projects such as dams and hydroelectric plants.
National Recovery Administration (NRA), 1933	Worked with industries to establish codes outlining fair business and labor practices.
Federal Deposit Insurance Corporation (FDIC), 1933	Insured bank deposits up to $5,000.
Agricultural Adjustment Administration (AAA), 1933	Attempted to raise farm prices by paying farmers to lower farm output.
Federal Housing Administration (FHA), 1934	Improved housing standards and conditions and provided home financing.
Securities and Exchange Commission (SEC), 1934	Regulated the stock market and protected investors from dishonest trading practices.
Works Progress Administration (WPA), 1935	Gave the unemployed work in building construction and arts programs.
National Labor Relations Board (NLRB), 1935	Enforced provisions of the Wagner Act, which included the right to collective bargaining and other union rights.
National Youth Administration (NYA), 1935	Provided education, jobs, recreation, and counseling for youth ages 16 to 25.
Rural Electrification Administration (REA), 1935	Provided loans for building power plants, extending power lines to rural areas, and wiring homes.
Social Security Administration (SSA), 1935	Provided old-age pensions, disability payments, and unemployment benefits.

ACTIVITY
Connecting with Economics

Tell students to learn about migrant farm workers in the West and Southwest. Encourage students to find answers to some of the following questions. Which countries do migrant workers come from? How do they get here? Do they belong to unions? Do the unions provide ample protection? Who was César Chávez and what did he accomplish? Who are some of the contemporary leaders of the farm workers' movement? Have students explain actions taken by migrant farm workers to expand their economic opportunities and political rights in American society.
(Verbal/Linguistic)

BACKGROUND
FDR

By passing legislation that redistributed corporate wealth and empowered unions, FDR made enemies among the country's business leaders. In his acceptance speech for the Democratic nomination in June 1936, FDR addressed a crowd in Philadelphia. He compared the patriots' efforts in 1776 to free themselves from "royalists who held special privileges from the crown" to his own fight against the new "economic royalists . . . who sought to regiment the people, their labor, and their property." Although FDR's policies were unpopular with business leaders, they made him a hero among the working class.

READING CHECK
It was an effort to assist agricultural workers and to silence critics who claimed that FDR was giving more aid to businesses and wealthy people than to the average citizen.

TEST PREPARATION

Ask students to study the chart "Major New Deal Agencies" on this page and then answer the question below.

Which of the following agencies provided benefits when a worker was unemployed?

A Home Owners Loan Corporation.
B Public Works Administration.
(C) Social Security Administration.
D Rural Electrification Administration.

CAPTION ANSWERS

Interpreting Charts Sample answer: The major New Deal agencies aimed to promote economic recovery, stabilize the nation's financial system, improve the nation's infrastructure, and improve the quality of life for all Americans.

Section 1 Assessment

Reading Comprehension

1. His easy, confident manner; his direct communication to the American people in "Fireside Chats" helped create hope; he renewed confidence in economic institutions through such actions as the Bank Holiday of 1933; the Glass-Steagall Banking Act of 1933; the creation of the SEC.
2. They employed a great number of people to build and maintain public facilities such as roads and public beaches. This activity rejuvenated people through employment. The nation itself benefited through the work that was being accomplished.
3. It helped farmers and created jobs in one of the country's least developed regions. The TVA provided cheap electric power, flood control, and recreational opportunities.
4. It legalized important union practices such as collective bargaining and closed shops, while outlawing both spying on union activities and blacklisting. The National Labor Relations Board was established to enforce the provisions of the Wagner Act.

Critical Thinking and Writing

5. The first New Deal was energetic, but it failed to create economic recovery by itself. Two of its lynchpin programs, the NILB and the AAA, were declared unconstitutional by the Supreme Court. The Second New Deal instituted bolder programs than the first, reaching out to more Americans and increasing FDR's popularity.
6. Answers will vary but should be supported with facts from the section.

The Social Security system marked a major expansion of the federal government's role as a caretaker of its citizens.

Supreme Court upheld the constitutionality of the Wagner Act in *NLRB* v. *Jones and Laughlin* (1939). The landmark case established the federal government's ability to regulate interstate commerce. In 1938, the Fair Labor Standards Act banned child labor and established a minimum wage for all workers covered under the act.

Social Security In 1935, Congress also passed the Social Security Act. The act established a **Social Security system** to provide financial security, in the form of regular payments, to people who could not support themselves. This system offered three types of insurance:

Old-age pensions and survivors' benefits Workers and their employers paid equally into a national insurance fund. Retired workers or their surviving spouses were eligible to start receiving Social Security payments at age 65. The act did not cover farm and domestic workers until it was amended in 1954.

Unemployment insurance Employers with more than eight employees funded this provision by paying a tax. The government distributed the money to workers who lost their jobs. States administered their own programs, with federal guidance and financial support.

Aid for dependent children, the blind, and the disabled The federal government gave grants to states to help support needy individuals in these categories.

The 1936 Election

No one expected the Republican presidential candidate of 1936, Kansas governor Alfred M. Landon, to beat the popular incumbent President. But few could have predicted the extent of FDR's landslide. Roosevelt carried every state except Maine and Vermont, winning 523–8 in the electoral college.

FDR's landslide victory showed that most Americans supported the New Deal. Yet the New Deal still had many critics with their own sizable followings.

Section 1 Assessment

READING COMPREHENSION

1. What steps did FDR take to restore the nation's hope and boost public confidence in economic institutions?
2. What role did **public works programs** play in Roosevelt's plans for economic recovery?
3. What benefits did the **Tennessee Valley Authority** bring about?
4. How was the **Wagner Act** a triumph for organized labor?

CRITICAL THINKING AND WRITING

5. **Making Comparisons** Compare the success of the early New Deal programs with those of the Second New Deal. Explain why the early programs faltered, and how the Second New Deal gave FDR a boost in the 1936 election.
6. **Writing a Conclusion** Write a statement that analyzes the types of programs created under the New Deal and then draws conclusions about FDR's view of the role of government. Give evidence to support your conclusions.

Take It to the NET

Activity: Yesterday and Today A New Deal program that survives today is the Tennessee Valley Authority (TVA). Research the TVA's beginnings and find out how it has changed to meet present-day needs. Summarize your findings in a brief report. Use the links provided in the *America: Pathways to the Present* area of the following Web site for help in completing this activity.
www.phschool.com

Take It to the NET

Answers will vary, but should demonstrate a knowledge of the origins of the TVA and an understanding of how it has changed to remain a part of present-day society.

RESOURCE DIRECTORY

Teaching Resources

Units 3/4 booklet
- Section 1 Quiz, p. 73

Guide to the Essentials
- Section 1 Summary, p. 77

Technology

RESOURCE PRO® **Critical Thinking Activity** *Recognizing Ideologies: The Role of Government,* found on Resource Pro, helps students understand the ideology behind the Social Security Act of 1935.

Section 2

The New Deal's Critics

READING FOCUS

- What were some of the shortcomings and limits of the New Deal?
- What were the chief complaints of FDR's critics inside and outside of politics?
- How did the court-packing fiasco harm FDR's reputation?

MAIN IDEA

A variety of critics pointed out the shortcomings of the New Deal as well as its potential for restricting individual freedom.

KEY TERMS

American Liberty League
demagogue
nationalization
deficit spending

TAKING NOTES

Copy the chart below. As you read, fill in criticisms of the New Deal.

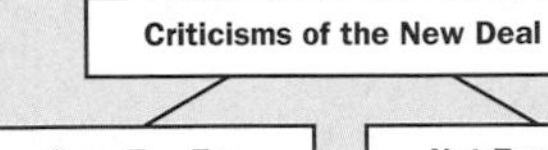

Setting the Scene

To the poor and the jobless who benefited from New Deal programs, Franklin Delano Roosevelt was a true hero. One mill worker expressed the thoughts of many citizens:

> "*Roosevelt is the only President we ever had that thought the Constitution belonged to the pore [poor] man too. . . . Yessir, it took Roosevelt to read in the Constitution and find out them folks way back yonder that made it was talkin' about the pore man right along with the rich one.*"
>
> —Testimony by mill worker George Dobbin in 1939, collected in *These Are Our Lives,* Federal Writers Project of the Works Progress Administration (1939)

Letters thanking the President poured into the White House. One letter read, "There ain't no other nation in the world that would have sense enough to think of WPA and all the other *A*'s."

Yet the New Deal inspired its share of critics, and the criticism would swell as the Depression dragged on. One critic wrote, "If you could get around the country as I have and seen the distress forced upon the American people, you would throw your darn NRA and AAA, and every other . . . *A* into the sea."

The Limitations of the New Deal

For all its successes, the New Deal fell short of many people's expectations. The Fair Labor Standards Act, for example, covered fewer than one quarter of all gainfully employed workers. It set the minimum wage at 25 cents an hour, which was well below what most covered workers already made. New Deal agencies also were generally less helpful to women and minority groups than they were to white men.

Women Many aspects of New Deal legislation put women at a disadvantage. The NRA codes, for example, permitted lower wages for women's work in almost a quarter of all cases. In relief and job programs, men and boys received strong preference. In accordance with the social customs of the time, jobs went to male "heads of families," unless the men were unable to work.

"COME ALONG. WE'RE GOING TO THE TRANS-LUX TO HISS ROOSEVELT."

INTERPRETING POLITICAL CARTOONS In this cartoon, rich people are going to a fancy hotel to "hiss"—that is, protest—FDR. **Analyzing Visual Information** *How does the cartoonist depict wealth? Why did some rich people oppose Roosevelt's policies?*

Section 2

The New Deal's Critics

SECTION OBJECTIVES

1. Learn about some of the New Deal's shortcomings and limitations.
2. Discover the chief complaints of FDR's critics inside and outside of politics.
3. See how the court-packing fiasco harmed FDR's reputation.

BELLRINGER

Warm-Up Activity Write the following statement on the chalkboard: "I feel that our President is doing an outstanding job, and I agree with his policies." Do students agree? Ask them to consider the reasons people criticize their leaders.

Activating Prior Knowledge Have students speculate on some possible objections to the New Deal. List these on the chalkboard. What groups might feel that the New Deal did not represent their best interests?

READING STRATEGY

Have students scan the section and note the main headings. Have them turn each main heading into a question. As they read, have them answer the questions they have created.

CAPTION ANSWERS

Interpreting Political Cartoons Wealthy people are portrayed in the cartoon as being selfish and elitist. The New Deal antagonized some wealthy people who opposed the "Wealth Tax Act," the requirement to pay Social Security taxes, and the general principle of government intervention in the economy.

RESOURCE DIRECTORY

Teaching Resources

Learning Styles Lesson Plans booklet, p. 49
Guided Reading and Review booklet, p. 94
Biography, Literature, and Comparing Primary Sources booklet (Literature) *In Search of Work: African Americans*, p. 71

Technology

Section Reading Support Transparencies
Guided Reading Audiotapes (English/Spanish), Ch. 16
Student Edition on Audio CD, Ch. 16
Prentice Hall Presentation Pro CD-ROM, Ch. 16
Companion Web site, www.phschool.com

Lesson Plan

Focus Explain that the many far-reaching programs of the New Deal did not provide benefits to all people. Ask students why President Roosevelt and the New Deal sparked criticism.

Instruct Ask how the New Deal failed to address the problems of many women and African Americans. Ask students to describe the opposition from the right and the left, respectively. Discuss the role of anti–New Dealers such as Huey Long and Father Coughlin, and ask students to consider why such demagogues often find eager audiences.

Explore the court-packing scheme. Ask students how that episode provoked widespread public disapproval of Roosevelt and damaged his standing in Congress.

Assess/Reteach Have students discuss the ways that the New Deal and its supporters and detractors demonstrated the effectiveness of America's system of checks and balances in government.

No New Deal provision protected domestic service, the largest female occupation. In 1942, an African American domestic worker in St. Louis pleaded with the President to ask employers, the "rich people," to "give us some hours to rest in and some Sundays off and pay us more wages." Working 14-hour days, she earned only $6.50 per week. A brutally honest official wrote back to her:

> *"State and Federal labor laws, which offer protection to workers in so many occupations, have so far not set up standards for working conditions in domestic situations. There is nothing that can be done . . . to help you and others in this kind of employment."*
>
> —Roosevelt administration official

African Americans Federal relief programs in the South, including public works projects, reinforced racial segregation. As a rule, African Americans were not offered jobs at a professional level. They were kept out of skilled jobs on dam and electric power projects, and they received lower pay than whites for the same work. Because the Social Security Act excluded both farmers and domestic workers, it failed to cover nearly two thirds of working African Americans. One black American expressed deep disappointment with FDR's policies:

> *"All the prosperity he had brought to the country has been legislated and is not real. Nothing he has ever started has been finished. My common way of expressing it is that we are in the middle of the ocean like a ship without an anchor. No good times can come to the country as long as there is so much discrimination practiced. . . . I don't see much chance for our people to get anywhere when the color line instead of ability determines the opportunities to get ahead economically."*
>
> —Testimony by Sam T. Mayhew in 1939, collected in *Such As Us* (1978)

WORLD'S HIGHEST STANDARD OF LIVING
There's no way like the American Way

VIEWING HISTORY This photograph, taken at a relief center in Louisville, Kentucky, highlights the struggle of African Americans to overcome the effects of both the Depression and prejudice. **Analyzing Visual Information** *What contrast was the photographer trying to point out in this picture?*

Yet the New Deal did nothing to end discriminatory practices in the North. In many black neighborhoods, for example, white-owned businesses continued to employ only whites. In the absence of help from the federal government, African Americans took matters into their own hands. Protesters picketed and boycotted such businesses with the slogan "Don't shop where you can't work."

The early Depression had seen an alarming rise in the number of lynchings. The federal government again offered no relief. A bill to make lynching a federal crime was abandoned by Congress in 1938. NAACP leader Walter White recalled in 1948 that FDR had given this explanation for his refusal to support these measures:

> *"Southerners, by reason of seniority rule in Congress, are chairmen or occupy strategic places on most of the Senate and House committees. If I come out for the anti-lynching bill now, they will block every bill I ask Congress to pass to keep America from collapsing. I just can't take that risk."*
>
> —President Franklin Roosevelt

Caption Answers

Viewing History All of the people on the billboard, which touts the nation's high standard of living, are white. All the people in the relief line are African Americans. The photographer might have been commenting on discrimination in New Deal relief programs.

RESOURCE DIRECTORY

Technology

Sounds of an Era Audio CD *Marian Anderson*

Although African Americans in the North had not supported FDR in 1932, by 1936 many had joined his camp. Often the last hired and first fired, they had experienced the highest unemployment rates of any group during the Depression. For this reason, those who did gain employment appreciated many of the New Deal programs.

Other aspects of Roosevelt's record also had some appeal to many African Americans. He appointed more African Americans to policymaking posts than any President before him. The Roosevelts also seemed genuinely concerned about the fate of African Americans. These factors help to explain FDR's wide support among black voters.

Political Critics

Under the desperate conditions of the Great Depression, reactions to the New Deal ran strong. People with widely differing political views criticized the New Deal, both for what it did and for what it did not do.

New Deal Does Too Much A number of Republicans, in Congress and elsewhere, opposed Roosevelt. They knew something had to be done about the Depression, but they believed that the New Deal went too far.

These critics included many wealthy people who regarded FDR as their enemy. Early in the New Deal, they had disapproved of certain programs, such as the TVA and rural electrification, that they considered to be socialistic. The Second New Deal gave them even more to hate, as FDR pushed through a series of higher taxes aimed at the rich. One of these was the Revenue Act of 1935, also known as the Wealth Tax Act. This act raised the tax rate on individual incomes over $50,000 as well as on the income and profits of corporations.

The Social Security Act also aroused political opposition. Some of FDR's enemies claimed that it penalized successful, hardworking people by forcing them to pay into the system. Others saw the assignment of Social Security numbers as the first step toward a militaristic, regimented society. They predicted that soon people would have to wear metal dog tags engraved with their Social Security numbers.

A group called the **American Liberty League,** founded in 1934, spearheaded much of the opposition to the New Deal. It was led by former Democratic presidential candidate Alfred E. Smith, the National Association of Manufacturers, and leading business figures.

The league charged the New Deal with limiting individual freedom in an unconstitutional, "un-American" manner. To them, programs such as compulsory unemployment insurance smacked of "Bolshevism," a reference to the political philosophy of the founders of the Soviet Union.

New Deal Does Not Do Enough Many Progressives and Socialists also attacked the New Deal. But these critics charged that FDR's programs did not provide enough help.

Muckraking novelist Upton Sinclair believed that the nation's entire economic system needed to be reformed in order to cure what he believed to be a "permanent crisis." A Socialist, he sought solutions that went far beyond New Deal–style reforms. In 1934, Sinclair ran for governor of California on the Democratic ticket. His platform, "End Poverty in California" (EPIC), called for a new economic system in which the state would take over factories and farms.

Focus on CULTURE

Marian Anderson and the DAR One of the greatest concert singers of her time, Marian Anderson first achieved widespread fame in Europe. At the time, opportunities for African Americans in the United States were limited. In 1935, however, Anderson successfully debuted in New York City. The following year, at the Roosevelts' invitation, she became the first African American to perform at the White House. In 1939, Anderson attempted to rent Constitution Hall in Washington, D.C., to stage a concert. The owners of the hall, the prestigious Daughters of the American Revolution (DAR), denied Anderson's request. In protest, Eleanor Roosevelt and other important members resigned from the group and then arranged for Anderson to perform on the steps of the Lincoln Memorial. An audience of some 75,000, including both blacks and whites, attended the concert on Easter, April 9, 1939.

Anderson's moving performance included a patriotic rendering of "America."

READING CHECK
What were the main criticisms of the New Deal?

ACTIVITY
Connecting with History and Conflict

Stage a classroom debate about the merits of the New Deal. Tell one team to take the stance that the New Deal went too far, and have the other team argue that the New Deal was necessary to revive the economy. Suggest that all debate participants become familiar with the New Deal programs so that they can argue their positions convincingly. **(Verbal/Linguistic)**

BACKGROUND
Recent Scholarship

Most historians see a modernized "New South" emerging only after it received massive federal assistance during the New Deal. But Roger Biles, writing in the *Journal of Southern History* ("The Persistence of the Past: Memphis in the Great Depression"), shows that while Memphis accepted such aid, it held on to its old values and customs. The city's political elite at first supported FDR, but by the Second New Deal had begun to attack New Dealers as too liberal. Characterizing federal authorities as "professional agitators and adventurers" pressuring the South toward a "centralization of government," they became leaders in the later backlash against the welfare state.

READING CHECK
Upton Sinclair and Midwestern Progressives criticized the New Deal for not doing enough. Wealthy Americans felt that with legislation such as Social Security and the "Wealth Tax," FDR's program had gone too far. Many people deplored the court-packing scheme.

CUSTOMIZE FOR ...
Less Proficient Readers

Ask students to construct two two-column charts, which they will complete as they read. The first chart will be used to identify conservative critics of the New Deal in one column and the reasons behind their criticisms in the other; the second chart will be used to identify liberals who criticized the New Deal and their reasons for doing so.

TEST PREPARATION

Have students read the quotation by Roosevelt on the previous page and then complete the sentence below.

From the passage, you can infer that—

- **A** Southerners did not have considerable power in Congress.
- **B** FDR opposed the anti-lynching bill.
- **(C)** Southerners in Congress did not support the anti-lynching bill.
- **D** FDR was not interested in helping African Americans.

ACTIVITY
Connecting with Government

Ask students to create a political advertisement for a candidate opposed to President Roosevelt. The ad may identify particular or general criticisms. It may also identify specific actions the opponent hopes to take if elected. **(Visual/Kinesthetic)**

BACKGROUND
A Diverse Nation

Many African Americans felt left out by the New Deal and turned to the Communist Party. Hosea Hudson, for example, an African American farmer from rural Georgia, joined the party. Angered by the 1931 case of the Scottsboro Boys, Hudson organized unemployed African Americans in Birmingham, Alabama, to meet weekly and discuss social issues. The Communist Party's legal arm, the International Labor Defense (ILD), defended the Scottsboro Boys.

READING CHECK
Huey Long's Share-the-Wealth idea put pressure on FDR to tax wealthy Americans. The criticisms from demagogues like Long and Father Coughlin had little direct impact on the course of the New Deal. However, their large followings represented something of a threat to FDR should New Deal policies fail to show results.

INTERPRETING POLITICAL CARTOONS In this cartoon, Uncle Sam is being restrained by New Deal agencies and policies. **Drawing Inferences** *What point is the cartoonist trying to make? Does the cartoon favor or criticize the New Deal? Support your answers with details from the drawing.*

EPIC clubs formed throughout the state, and Sinclair won the primary. Terrified opponents then used shady tactics to discredit him. They produced fake newsreels showing people who spoke with a Russian accent endorsing Sinclair. Associated unfairly with communism, Sinclair lost the election.

The New Deal had only limited success in eliminating poverty. This fact contributed to a revival of progressivism in Minnesota and Wisconsin. Running for the United States Senate, Wisconsin Progressive Robert La Follette, Jr., argued that "devices which seek to preserve the unequal distribution of wealth . . . will retard or prevent recovery." His brother Philip also took a radical stand, calling for a redistribution of income. Philip's ideas persuaded the state Socialist Party to join the Progressives after he won the Wisconsin governorship in 1934.

Other Critics

READING CHECK
What influence did demagogues have during the Depression?

Some New Deal critics were **demagogues,** leaders who manipulate people with half-truths, deceptive promises, and scare tactics. Two such demagogues attracted strong followings during the Depression.

Father Coughlin One such demagogue was Father Charles E. Coughlin (CAWG-lin), a dynamic speaker who used the radio to broadcast his message. Throughout the 1930s, the so-called Radio Priest held listeners spellbound from his studio in Detroit. In 1934, Father Coughlin's weekly broadcasts reached an audience estimated at more than 10 million people.

Coughlin achieved popularity even though he sometimes contradicted himself. One time he advocated the **nationalization,** or government takeover and ownership, of banks and the redistribution of their wealth. Another time he defended the sanctity of private property, including banks. At first he supported FDR and the New Deal. Later he denounced them, through his radio show and through the organization he formed in 1934 called the National Union for

CAPTION ANSWERS

Interpreting Political Cartoons The cartoon suggests that New Deal programs, represented by restraints on Uncle Sam, interfere with American freedoms and the free market. It is critical of the New Deal.

RESOURCE DIRECTORY

Teaching Resources
Biography, Literature, and Comparing Primary Sources booklet (Comparing Primary Sources) *On the New Deal,* pp. 141–142

Technology
Color Transparencies *Political Cartoons,* B13
Sounds of an Era Audio CD *"Share the Wealth," Huey Long* (time: 20 seconds)

Social Justice. Coughlin's attacks on FDR grew increasingly reckless. In 1936, he called him "Franklin 'Double-crossing' Roosevelt" and described him as a "great betrayer and liar."

By the end of the 1930s, Coughlin was issuing openly anti-Jewish statements. He also began showering praise on Adolf Hitler and Benito Mussolini, two menacing leaders who were rising to power in Europe. Coughlin's actions alarmed many Americans, and he lost some of his support. In 1942, Roman Catholic officials ordered him to stop broadcasting his show.

At top, Father Coughlin addresses some 6,000 members of his National Union for Social Justice in Detroit, 1936. Above, Louisiana's Huey Long gestures in the flamboyant style for which he was famous.

Huey Long A powerful figure in Louisiana politics, Huey Long was a different type of demagogue. Long was a country lawyer who had grown up in poverty. He won the governorship of Louisiana in 1928 and became a United States senator in 1932. Unlike many other southern Democrats, Long never used racial attacks to build a base of power. Instead, he worked to help the underprivileged by improving education, medical care, and public services. He also built an extraordinarily powerful and ruthless political machine in his home state.

Originally a supporter of FDR, Long broke with him early in the New Deal. "Unless we provide for redistribution of wealth in this country, the country is doomed," he said. While in the Senate, Long developed a program called Share-Our-Wealth. It would limit individual income to $1 million and inheritance to $5 million. The government would take the rest in steep progressive income taxes. Thus the plan would confiscate large fortunes. It would then redistribute that wealth by giving every family a minimum $5,000 "household estate" and a minimum annual income of $2,500. Long also sought other improvements for Americans: shorter working hours, more veterans' benefits, payments for education, and pensions for the elderly.

COMPARING HISTORIANS' VIEWPOINTS

Roosevelt and the New Deal

Historians disagree on the effectiveness of the New Deal in combating the Depression and improving the lives of Americans.

Analyzing Viewpoints Compare the viewpoints of these two historians.

Criticism of the New Deal

"[New Deal measures] have not been administered with any special care to preserve the best features of private industry and encourage it to bring about recovery. The relief measures have been inefficient and expensive. They have resulted in a tremendous burden of taxation. . . . There has been no effort to preserve conditions under which a man, striving for a private job and doing his job well, shall be encouraged and preferred to the man on WPA. . . . More men have gone out of business in the last five years than have gone into business because of the complete uncertainty whether they can survive a constant Government interference."

—*Robert A. Taft, "A Conservative Critique: The New Deal and the Republican Program"*

Praises for the New Deal

"What then did the New Deal do? . . . [It] expanded the authority of the presidency, recruited university-trained administrators, won control of the money supply, established central banking, imposed regulations on Wall Street, . . . rescued debt-ridden farmers and homeowners, . . . fostered unionization of the factories, drastically reduced child labor, . . . established minimal working standards, enabled thousands of tenants to buy their own farms, built camps for migrants, introduced the Welfare State with old-age pensions, unemployment insurance, . . . subsidized painters and novelists, composers and ballet dancers, . . . [and] gave women greater recognition. . . ."

—*William E. Leuchtenburg,* The FDR Years: On Roosevelt and His Legacy

ACTIVITY
Connecting with History and Conflict

Ask students to do enough additional research to enable them to write a short essay comparing the career and tactics of Father Coughlin with those of William Joyce, another controversial radio broadcaster who was active during World War II. Joyce, known by the nickname "Lord Haw-Haw," was a Nazi sympathizer who had lived in England before the war. Joyce used his fluent command of the English language to make wartime pro-German radio broadcasts from Germany, which were heard in Great Britain. Lord Haw-Haw was considered a war criminal in Great Britain, where he was executed in 1946. Ask students to explore in their essays the similarities between the views of Father Coughlin and those of William Joyce. Students may also wish to give their opinion as to whether or not such people should have been allowed to make radio broadcasts at all. **(Verbal/ Linguistic)**

BACKGROUND
Biography

Huey Long (1893–1935) was a powerful and controlling figure who dominated Louisiana politics in the late 1920s and early 1930s. After a term as governor, he left to serve in the U.S. Senate, but just before leaving office he fired the current lieutenant governor and replaced him with two successors who obeyed Long from Washington. Long eventually took personal control of all educational, police, and fire fighter appointments, gaining control of an unprecedented amount of the state's bureaucracy. Long was at the height of his power when he was assassinated by Carl Austin Weiss. If Long had lived, he had the potential to significantly influence the presidential election of 1936.

CUSTOMIZE FOR ...
ESL

List the following words on the chalkboard: *demagogue, nationalization,* and *private property.* Have students first define each word and then use the information in the section to write a paragraph that includes all three words.

ACTIVITY
Connecting with Economics

Tell students to do some research to learn about the current state of the federal budget. Does the federal government have a deficit? What is the federal debt? Encourage students to read about the reasons for the current conditions. Have students explain their findings in an oral report. **(Verbal/Linguistic)**

BACKGROUND
Recent Scholarship

In writing *Recollections of the New Deal: When the People Mattered,* Thomas Eliot relied on his old letters to his mother and a friend to present a look back at his role in the New Deal. Eliot arrived in Washington at the age of 26, one year out of Harvard Law School, took a job in the Labor Department, and went on to write the Social Security Act. Eliot, who was in his eighties when he wrote the book, said, "The present configuration of our governmental process is largely an outgrowth of the New Deal or an adverse reaction to it. And every economic recession makes one realize that if that recession deepens, the 'crisis management' of the thirties will be only too relevant."

Focus on ECONOMICS

Deficit and Debt The terms *federal deficit* and *federal debt* (or *national debt*) are often confused. A federal deficit occurs when the government spends more money in its annual budget than it receives in revenues during that year. To cover a deficit, the government borrows money by issuing bonds, which are essentially IOUs to those who buy the bonds. The federal debt is the money the government owes to its bondholders. The government could have a great deal of federal debt, but not be practicing deficit spending. That is, it could be spending no more than it earns each year, yet it still could be paying off old debt, much like individuals who owe money on their credit cards. The chart below, for example, shows the deficit rising and falling during the Depression, as federal revenues and spending varied. The debt chart at the bottom, however, shows steady increases in government borrowing for New Deal programs.

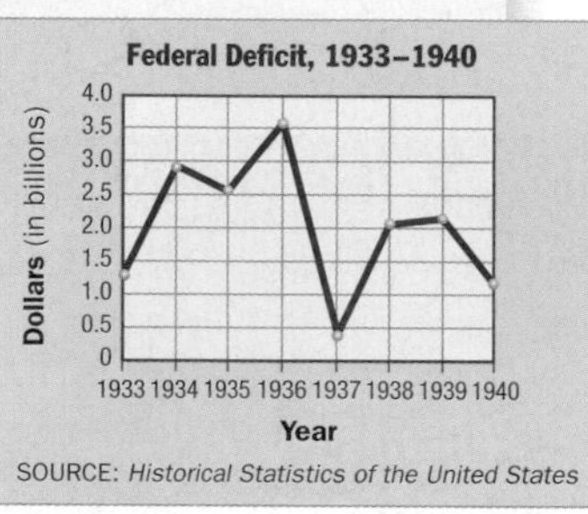

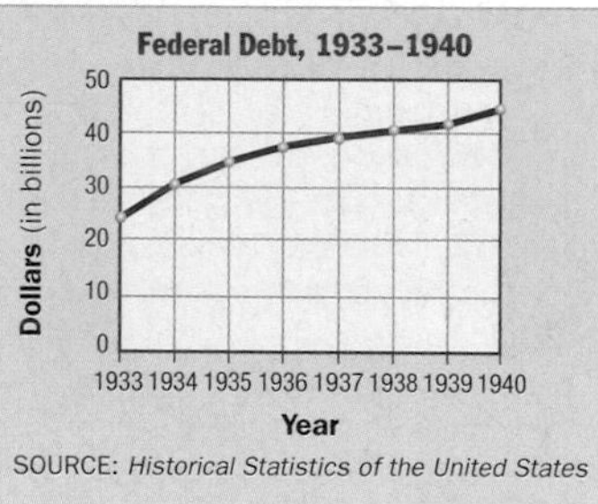

Long's program for helping all Americans achieve wealth attracted many followers. His success helped push FDR to propose new taxes on wealthy Americans in the Second New Deal. Meanwhile, Long himself began to eye the presidency. But in September 1935, the son-in-law of one of Long's political enemies shot and killed him.

Long and Coughlin never seriously threatened FDR or the New Deal. But their influence warned Roosevelt that if he failed to solve the nation's problems, he risked losing mass support.

Modern-Day Critics

Although many of the people who directly benefited from the New Deal are now gone, their children and grandchildren still pass down individual stories of hope and help that came to their families through programs like the WPA. To many Americans, FDR's bold actions place him among the nation's greatest Presidents. Yet some modern-day critics question whether the New Deal achieved the greatest good for the greatest number of Americans.

Some historians and economists have examined this question in recent years and found the New Deal lacking. They say that New Deal programs actually hindered economic progress and threatened America's core beliefs in free enterprise. Further, they charge that the programs created a bloated and dangerously powerful federal bureaucracy and encouraged inefficient use of resources.

For example, critics maintain that New Deal employment programs created "make work" jobs instead of allowing the free market to determine what jobs, and how many, were needed. These job programs were financed by heavy tax increases, which took money out of the economy and gave people less money to spend on products that would boost production and create jobs.

Modern critics also attack the policy of paying farmers not to plant. They contend that market demand should have been allowed to determine the supply and price of farm products. In a time of hunger, the program wasted precious resources, they note—from dumped milk to burned wheat. The program encouraged some farmers to plant crops on poor land just so that they could later take the land out of production and get paid for doing so. This caused marginal soil to erode further and become depleted. Farm production quotas penalized efficient and less-efficient farmers equally, while the free market would have weeded out inefficiency and rewarded productivity.

Finally, the New Deal receives criticism from people who oppose **deficit spending**—paying out more money from the annual federal budget than the government receives in revenues. Deficit spending to fund New Deal programs required the government to borrow money. Government borrowing produced what economists call the "crowding-out effect"—making less money available for private borrowing by businesses and consumers.

At the heart of the question is a difference in ideologies. Some people believe that the New Deal violated the free-market system that Americans have traditionally cherished. Others believe that providing direct relief to many of the nation's suffering citizens was worth the compromise. These debates continue today.

RESOURCE DIRECTORY

Teaching Resources

Units 3/4 booklet
- Section 2 Quiz, p. 74

Guide to the Essentials
- Section 2 Summary, p. 78

Technology

RESOURCE PRO® **Visual Learning Activity**
FDR Tries to Pack the Court, found on Resource Pro, features a political cartoon that illustrates a common response to FDR's attempt to add more justices to the Supreme Court.

The Court-Packing Fiasco

INTERPRETING POLITICAL CARTOONS FDR's request to Congress to allow him to appoint more Supreme Court justices (friendly to his New Deal programs) caused an uproar that damaged the President politically. **Analyzing Visual Information** *In this cartoon, what do you think the donkey represents, and what is the cartoonist trying to portray?*

Roosevelt received criticism not only for his programs, but also for his actions. No act aroused more opposition than his attempt to "pack" the Supreme Court.

Throughout the early New Deal, the Supreme Court had caused FDR his greatest frustration. The Court had invalidated the NIRA, the AAA, and many state laws from the Progressive Era. In February 1937, FDR proposed a major court-reform bill.

The Constitution had not specified the number of Supreme Court justices. Congress had last changed the number in 1869. By Roosevelt's time, the number nine had become well established. Arguing that he merely wanted to lighten the burden of the aging justices, FDR asked Congress to allow him to appoint as many as six additional justices, one for each justice over 70 years old. Roosevelt's real intention was to "pack" the Court with judges supportive of the New Deal.

Negative reaction came swiftly from all sides. Critics blasted the President for trying to inject politics into the judiciary. They warned Congress not to let him undermine the constitutional principle of separation of powers. With several dictators ruling in Europe, the world seemed already to be tilting toward tyranny. If Congress let FDR reshape the Supreme Court, critics worried, the United States might head down the same slope.

Strong opposition forced FDR to withdraw his reform bill. He also suffered political damage. Many Republicans and Southern Democrats united against further New Deal legislation. This alliance remained a force for years to come.

In the end, FDR still wound up with a Court that tended to side with him. Some older justices retired, allowing the President to appoint justices who favored the New Deal. Even earlier, however, the Court, acting on lawsuits filed by New Deal adversaries, had begun to uphold measures from the Second New Deal, including the Wagner Act. The Court may have been reacting to public opinion, or it may have decided that those measures were better thought out and more skillfully drafted than earlier ones.

Section 2 Assessment

READING COMPREHENSION

1. What effects did the New Deal have on women and minorities?
2. Why did the **American Liberty League** view the New Deal as unconstitutional and un-American?
3. Why did Upton Sinclair and Robert La Follette believe that the New Deal did not go far enough?
4. Describe FDR's "court-packing" maneuver and its outcome.

CRITICAL THINKING AND WRITING

5. **Making Comparisons** Compare and contrast the criticisms of two New Deal–era demagogues, Father Coughlin and Huey Long.
6. **Writing an Opinion** Review the arguments made by modern-day supporters and critics of the New Deal, and reread Comparing Historians' Viewpoints. Write a statement explaining which arguments you agree with, and why.

Take It to the NET

Activity: Analyzing Primary Sources Read or listen to the "fireside chat" in which FDR explains his controversial court-packing plan to the nation. What is his argument? Do you agree or disagree with it? Explain. Use the links provided in the *America: Pathways to the Present* area of the following Web site for help in completing this activity.
www.phschool.com

Section 2 Assessment

Reading Comprehension

1. It allowed lower wages for their work and favored white males in job programs. Federal relief programs in the South enforced racial segregation. The Social Security Act excluded farmers and domestic workers, the primary areas in which African Americans and women worked.
2. It felt the New Deal limited individual freedom too radically and that its compulsory programs resembled Bolshevik philosophies.
3. Sinclair believed that the nation's entire economic system needed to be reformed along Socialist lines. La Follette believed that wealth needed to be evenly distributed.
4. After the court struck down some early New Deal programs, FDR pressed for legislation to increase the number of Supreme Court justices, hoping to appoint justices friendly to the New Deal. The resulting negative reaction caused political damage to FDR and increased opposition to New Deal legislation.

Critical Thinking and Writing

5. Coughlin and Long shared strident and combative methods to present their views, but only Coughlin used racial attacks. Also, Coughlin retracted his early support for wealth redistribution, while Long never lost faith in his Share-the-Wealth philosophy.
6. Answers will vary, but should be persuasive and supported by facts from the section.

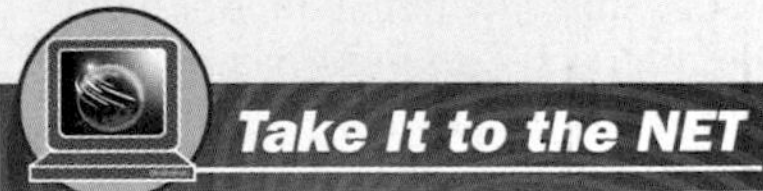

Take It to the NET

Answers will vary but should include an examination of FDR's desire to gain support for the New Deal by adding justices to the Supreme Court bench who would approve of his programs.

Caption Answers

Viewing History The donkey represents Democrats, most likely in the Democrat-controlled Congress. They, like many other critics, balked at FDR's request to add Justices to the Supreme Court.

Distinguishing Fact From Opinion

Focus Analyze a speaker's use of facts and opinions in a political speech.

Instruct Divide students into small groups to examine the speech and identify the various facts and opinions used by the speaker. Ask each group to report its findings. If groups draw different conclusions about which statements are facts and which are opinions, have the whole class discuss the examples. Then ask students whether or not they think the speaker in this case has made an effective argument. What facts might he have used to strengthen his points?

Extend See the Skills for Life activity in the Resource Directory below.

ANSWERS

Practice the Skill

1. **(a)** The decisions of the Supreme Court are matters of public record and can thus be easily verified. **(b)** Possible answers: the statements about the growth of the national debt, billions spent by government, higher taxes, the percent of income paid in taxes, and the growth in the number of public officials. They could be verified in government publications.
2. **(a)** It is an appeal to emotion and does not define "foundations of freedom." **(b)** Possible answers: "must" has invaded independence of Congress; Congress has abandoned its responsibility; torrent of waste; freedom has changed to slavery to the government; and New Deal developments have polluted the foundation of liberty. They are opinions because they cannot be proven or verified, and they contain sweeping generalizations and emotion-packed words.
3. **(a)** He states that they were overthrown by the Supreme Court, the guardian of constitutional rights. **(b)** No, he gives no specific examples—he just makes a sweeping accusation. **(c)** Answers will vary, but should note the unsupported statements listed in question 2.

Distinguishing Fact From Opinion

A fact is something that can be proved to be true by checking an encyclopedia or other trusted source. An opinion is a judgment that reflects beliefs or feelings. Historical materials such as speeches, letters, and diaries often contain both facts and opinions. The ability to distinguish between facts and opinions will help you determine the soundness of a writer's ideas and reach your own conclusions about historical events.

In the excerpt below from a speech given at the 1936 Republican National Convention, Herbert Hoover criticizes the New Deal.

LEARN THE SKILL

Use the following steps to distinguish between fact and opinion in historical materials:

1. **Determine which statements are facts.** Remember that facts can be verified in other sources.
2. **Determine which statements are opinions.** Sometimes authors signal opinions with phrases such as "I believe" or "I think," but often they do not. Other clues that indicate opinions are emotion-packed words and sweeping generalizations. (A sweeping generalization is a broad statement about a group of people, things, or events, such as, "Politicians are corrupt.")
3. **Evaluate opinions as you read.** Generally, an opinion is more reliable when the author gives facts to support it.

PRACTICE THE SKILL

Answer the following questions:

1. **(a)** For what reason is Hoover's first statement, about the Supreme Court, easily recognizable as a fact? **(b)** Find two other statements of fact in the excerpt. How might you prove each one is a statement of fact?
2. **(a)** What indicates that the final sentence of the first paragraph is an opinion rather than a fact? **(b)** Find two other statements of opinion in the excerpt. What indicates that they are opinions?
3. **(a)** How does Hoover support his opinion that many New Deal acts "were a violation of the rights of men and of self-government"? **(b)** Does he present any facts to support his statement that the Congress has "abandoned its responsibility"? **(c)** In your opinion, how good a job has Hoover done in supporting his opinions? Explain your answer.

APPLY THE SKILL

See the Chapter Review and Assessment for another opportunity to apply this skill.

"The Supreme Court has reversed some ten or twelve of the New Deal major enactments. Many of these acts were a violation of the rights of men and of self-government. Despite the sworn duty of the Executive and Congress to defend these rights, they have sought to take them into their own hands. That is an attack on the foundations of freedom.

More than this, the independence of the Congress, the Supreme Court, and the Executive are pillars at the door of liberty. For three years the word 'must' has invaded the independence of Congress. And the Congress has abandoned its responsibility to check even the expenditures [spending] of money. . . .

We have seen these gigantic expenditures and this torrent of waste pile up a national debt which two generations cannot repay. . . .

Billions have been spent to prime the economic pump. . . . We have seen the frantic attempts to find new taxes on the rich. Yet three-quarters of the bill will be sent to the average man and the poor. He and his wife and his grandchildren will be giving a quarter of all their working days to pay taxes. Freedom to work for himself is changed into a slavery of work for the follies of government. . . .

We have seen the building up of a horde of political officials. We have seen the pressures upon the helpless and destitute to trade political support for relief. Both are a pollution of the very foundations of liberty."

—Herbert Hoover, *American Ideals Versus the New Deal*

RESOURCE DIRECTORY

Teaching Resources
Skills for Life booklet, p. 25

Technology
Social Studies Skills Tutor CD-ROM
Interactive Practice in
- Geographic Literacy
- Critical Thinking and Reading
- Visual Analysis
- Communications

Section 3

Last Days of the New Deal

READING FOCUS

- What factors led to the recession of 1937, and how did the Roosevelt administration respond?
- What triumphs and setbacks did unions experience during the New Deal era?
- What effects did the New Deal have on American culture?
- What lasting effects can be attributed to the New Deal?

KEY TERMS

recession
national debt
revenue
coalition
sit-down strike

TAKING NOTES

Copy the chart below on a piece of paper. As you read, fill in the blanks by listing various effects of the New Deal.

Effects of the New Deal			
Economic	Political	Social	Cultural

MAIN IDEA

Ultimately, the New Deal did not end the Depression. Yet it had lasting effects on many aspects of American life.

Setting the Scene In 1936, writer James Agee and photographer Walker Evans made a six-week journey among the nation's poorest citizens, the tenant farmers of Alabama. Evans's photographs and Agee's descriptions were later published as *Let Us Now Praise Famous Men,* a book that left powerful images of the Great Depression in the nation's consciousness. The book bore witness to the survival of human dignity in the midst of deepest poverty. Here Agee, who shared meager lodgings with families, describes one farmer's revolving door of debt and despair:

> *"Years ago the Ricketts were, relatively speaking, almost prosperous. Besides their cotton farming they had ten cows and sold the milk, and they lived near a good stream and had all the fish they wanted. Ricketts went $400 into debt on a fine young pair of mules. One of the mules died before it had made the first crop; the other died the year after; against his fear . . . Ricketts went into debt for other, inferior mules; his cows went one by one . . . ; he got congestive chills; his wife got pellagra [a disease caused by dietary deficiencies]; a number of his children died; . . . for ten consecutive years now . . . they have not cleared or had any hope of clearing a cent at the end of the year. . . .*
>
> *WPA work is available to very few tenants: they are, technically, employed, and thus have no right to it: and if by chance they manage to get it, landlords are more likely than not to intervene. They feel it spoils a tenant to be paid wages, even for a little while."*
>
> —James Agee, *Let Us Now Praise Famous Men,* 1941

VIEWING HISTORY Walker Evans's photographs captured both the plight and the dignity of the impoverished farm families he visited. **Analyzing Visual Images** *What impressions come to mind when you study this picture? Explain.*

Section 3
Last Days of the New Deal

Section Objectives

1. Learn about factors that led to the recession of 1937 and about the Roosevelt administration's response to this situation.
2. Find out about triumphs and setbacks experienced by unions during the New Deal era.
3. Discover some effects of the New Deal on American culture.
4. See what lasting effects can be attributed to the New Deal.

Bellringer

Warm-Up Activity Write the term *federal government* on the chalkboard. Ask students to brainstorm a list of words they associate with the term. Explain that many modern attitudes and beliefs concerning the government stem from the New Deal era.

Activating Prior Knowledge Ask students to discuss whether government alone has the power to reverse an economic crisis. What other factors must come into play for a steady recovery to occur?

Reading Strategy

Before students read the section, have them make a table. Across the top, have them list these categories: *economics, culture, citizenship,* and *society.* Then, as they read the section, have students list the works of art, literature, or music in a column at the side of the table, and then indicate which aspects of New Deal society they reflect. Have students describe how characteristics and issues of the New Deal era are reflected in these works.

RESOURCE DIRECTORY

Teaching Resources

Guided Reading and Review booklet, p. 95

Technology

Section Reading Support Transparencies
Guided Reading Audiotapes (English/Spanish), Ch. 16
Student Edition on Audio CD, Ch. 16
Prentice Hall Presentation Pro CD-ROM, Ch. 16
Companion Web site, www.phschool.com

Caption Answers

Viewing History Sample answers: The family's shack and their tattered, dirty clothing suggest extreme poverty. The individuals and their facial expressions suggest resignation, malnutrition, weariness, dignity amid misfortune, and family togetherness.

Lesson Plan

Focus Point out that the New Deal did not succeed in ending the Depression but that it did have a great impact on the nation's political, social, and cultural life. Ask students to list ways that this impact is felt today.

Instruct Ask students what the recession of 1937 revealed about the New Deal and the economy. Discuss the changes that the New Deal introduced to the nation. Ask students to describe changes affecting labor unions. Ask them to consider the role of government in helping to make union gains possible.

Discuss government support for the arts as an important part of the New Deal. Ask students to discuss the benefits and drawbacks of government funding of the arts.

Assess/Reteach Ask students to discuss the ways in which government-funded art programs of the New Deal era helped creative people make a record of the time in which they lived. If students were recipients of similar types of grants today, which aspects of society would they choose to depict, and how?

Background
Art History

Mexican-born muralist Diego Rivera (1886–1957) was commissioned to work on several building lobbies during the Depression, including that of the Detroit Institute of the Arts. Rivera's bright, expansive murals integrated elements of Mexican folk art and modern industrial themes.

Unemployment, 1933–1940

Number unemployed (in millions)

0 2 4 6 8 10 12 14

1933 1934 1935 1936 1937 1938 1939 1940

Year

SOURCE: *Historical Statistics of the United States, Colonial Times to 1970*

INTERPRETING GRAPHS Combating unemployment was one of Roosevelt's greatest challenges during the Depression. **Analyzing Visual Information** *(a) From your reading of Section 2, explain why unemployment rose during 1937. (b) By about how much did unemployment decline over the course of the New Deal?*

The Recession of 1937

The New Deal was no miracle cure for the Great Depression. While massive government spending led to some temporary economic improvement, in August 1937, the economy collapsed again. Industrial production fell, as did employment levels. The nation entered a **recession,** a period of slow business activity.

The new Social Security tax was partly to blame for this recession. The tax came directly out of workers' paychecks, through payroll deductions. With less money in their pockets, Americans bought fewer goods.

Americans also had less money because FDR had cut way back on expensive programs such as the WPA. The President had become distressed at the rising **national debt,** or the total amount of money the federal government borrows and has to pay back. (See Focus on Economics, page 550.) The government borrows when its **revenue,** or income, does not keep up with its expenses. To fund the New Deal, the government had to borrow massive amounts of money. As a result, the national debt rose from $21 billion in 1933 to $43 billion by 1940.

After 1937, Harry Hopkins and other advisors persuaded FDR to expand the WPA and other programs that had been cut back. The increased spending provided some economic relief. Still, hard times lasted until well into the 1940s.

Unions Triumph

The New Deal changed the way many Americans thought about labor unions. New federal protections for unions under the 1935 Wagner Act made union membership more attractive to workers. Membership rose from about 3 million in 1933 to 10.5 million by 1941, a figure representing 11.3 percent of the nonagricultural work force. By 1945, some 36 percent were unionized, the all-time high for unions in the United States.

A New Labor Organization Activism by powerful union leaders helped increase membership. The cautious and craft-based American Federation of Labor (AFL) had done little to attract unskilled industrial workers during the half-century of its existence. In 1935, United Mine Workers President John L. Lewis joined with representatives of seven other AFL unions to try to change this situation. They created a Committee for Industrial Organization (CIO) within the AFL.

Although the AFL did not support its efforts, the CIO sought to organize the nation's unskilled workers in mass-production industries. It sent organizers into steel mills, auto plants, and southern textile mills and encouraged all workers to join. In response, the AFL suspended CIO unions in 1936.

Two years later, the CIO had 4 million members. In November 1938, this **coalition,** or alliance of groups with similar goals, changed its name to the Congress of Industrial Organizations. John L. Lewis became its first president. The aim of this coalition of industrial unions was to challenge conditions in industry. Their main tool was the strike.

CIO chief John L. Lewis addresses 10,000 textile workers in Massachusetts in 1937.

Caption Answers

Interpreting Graphs (a) New Deal jobs programs provided initial relief, but only for certain segments of society. Critics charged that government spending on jobs programs and public works projects wasted resources, interfered with free market economics, and needlessly expanded the government bureaucracy. Also, the WPA and certain other jobs programs had their funding reduced in 1937. (b) By approximately four million workers.

Resource Directory

Teaching Resources

Biography, Literature, and Comparing Primary Sources booklet (Biography) *Emma Tenayuca,* p. 28

Technology

RESOURCE PRO® **Literature Activity** *In Search of Work: Migrant Farmers,* found on Resource Pro, uses an excerpt from John Steinbeck's *The Grapes of Wrath* to illustrate the plight of tenant farmers during the Depression.

VIEWING HISTORY
Automobile workers stage a successful sit-down strike during the winter of 1936–1937 at the Fisher Body Plant No. 1, in Flint, Michigan. Here, workers guard a window during the strike. **Drawing Inferences** *Make a list of the possible challenges these men faced during this long sit-down strike.*

An Era of Strikes The Wagner Act legalized collective bargaining and required companies to bargain in good faith with certified union representatives. But the act did not force companies to accept unions' demands. Although the Wagner Act was designed to bring about industrial peace, in the short term it led to a wave of dramatic strikes.

Many of these work stoppages took the form of sit-down strikes. A weapon often used by the Congress of Industrial Organizations, the **sit-down strike** is a strike in which laborers stop working but refuse to leave the building. Supporters outside the workplace set up picket lines. Together, the strikers and the picket lines prevent the company from bringing in scabs, or non-union substitute workers. In areas where local authorities were New Deal Democrats, the workers' actions sometimes went unchallenged, making the sit-down strike an effective tool.

The first sit-down strikes took place in early 1936 at three huge rubber-tire plants in Akron, Ohio. The success of the sit-downs led to similar strikes later in the year at several General Motors (GM) auto plants. The most famous began on December 31, 1936. In this strike, laborers associated with the United Auto Workers (UAW) occupied GM's main plants in Flint, Michigan, and refused to leave.

GM executives turned off the heat and blocked entry to the plants so that the workers could not receive food. They also called in the police against the picketers outside. Violence erupted. The wife of a striker grabbed a bullhorn and urged other wives to join the picketers.

Women—both workers' wives and female employees—later organized food deliveries to supply the strikers. They set up a speakers' bureau to present the union's position to the public, and formed a Women's Emergency Brigade to take up picket duty. Governor Frank Murphy of Michigan and President Roosevelt refused to use the militia against the strike. By early February General Motors had given in.

Not all labor strikes were as successful. Henry Ford continued to resist unionism. In 1937, at a Ford Motor Company plant near Detroit, his men beat UAW officials when the unionists tried to distribute leaflets. Walter Reuther, a future UAW president, later testified about the incident:

READING CHECK
What made sit-down strikes effective to some extent?

ACTIVITY
Connecting with History and Conflict

Engage students in a discussion about labor disputes. Talk about why some companies, such as General Motors, have experienced many strikes in recent years. Discuss why the federal government sometimes intervenes and whether its actions are effective. It might help to bring in news articles about recent strikes to give students a clearer idea of some of the issues. **(Verbal/Linguistic)**

ACTIVITY
Connecting with Culture

This activity may take place over several class periods. Working in groups of four or six, students should create a newspaper special edition that highlights the major people and events of the New Deal. The newspaper could include such features as news stories about New Deal programs or developments, profiles of key figures, political cartoons about people or events, and editorials. The newspaper could also evaluate the impact of New Deal legislation on the historical roles of state and federal governments. Based on their abilities and interests, students may take on various roles, such as cartoonist, editorial writer, reporter, or layout and production designer. **(Verbal/Linguistic; Visual/Spatial)**

READING CHECK
They prevented the company from bringing in substitute workers.

CUSTOMIZE FOR ...
Gifted and Talented
Ask students to analyze the difficulties of forging government programs that provide equal benefit and satisfaction to all citizens. Have students discuss what limits the democratic process places on the ability of a government to implement broad new programs, such as universal health care.

CAPTION ANSWERS

Viewing History Sample answer: Workers may have battled cold, since it was winter and the company might have turned off the heat; hunger, if friends and family were unable to get enough food to them; anxiety in wondering whether or not the strike would lead to violent confrontation; and boredom.

ACTIVITY
Connecting with Culture

Tell students to bring in books, such as *The Good Earth, The Grapes of Wrath, Their Eyes Were Watching God,* and *Let Us Now Praise Famous Men,* that were written during the 1930s and early 1940s. Encourage students to read one of these books and write a summary telling what the book is about and how it describes the characteristics and issues of the era of the Great Depression. **(Verbal/Linguistic)**

BACKGROUND
Interdisciplinary

Technological developments changed the culture of the New Deal period. Specifically, the integration of sound with moving pictures revitalized the motion picture industry. Adding sound was first accomplished by using a sound-on-film synchronization system, Phonofilm, patented by Lee DeForest in 1919. By 1933, when techniques had been developed to eliminate camera noise from recordings, improve microphones (so that actors could move while they spoke), and edit a soundtrack, all of the major studios had converted to sound, increasing their profits by 600 percent.

> *"They picked me up about eight different times and threw me down on my back on the concrete. While I was on the ground they kicked me in the face, head, and other parts of my body. . . . I never raised a hand."*
> —Walter Reuther

Companies and the police were not the only instigators of violence. Mobs of striking unionists sometimes attacked strikebreakers trying to enter or leave a plant, or they destroyed company property. Unions generally opposed such actions, instead encouraging passive resistance. Still, strikers often fought back with bottles, bricks, stones, and bats.

Like Ford, the Republic Steel Company refused to sign with steelworkers' unions until war loomed in 1941. At one strike against Republic Steel on May 30, 1937, Chicago police killed several picketers and injured dozens. This Memorial Day tragedy was a sign that labor, despite its triumphs, still faced many challenges. Another sign came in the form of a Supreme Court ruling. In 1939, the Court outlawed the sit-down strike as being too potent a weapon and an obstacle to negotiation.

The New Deal's Effects on Culture

Artists created enduring cultural legacies for the nation during the Great Depression. They were aided by federal funds allocated by Congress to support the popular and fine arts and to provide jobs.

Literature Several works of literature destined to become classics emerged during this period. One example is Pearl Buck's novel *The Good Earth* (1931), a saga of peasant struggle in China. In 1937, folklorist Zora Neale Hurston published *Their Eyes Were Watching God,* a novel about a strong-willed African American woman and the Florida town in which she lives. John Steinbeck wrote *The Grapes of Wrath* (1939), a powerful tale about Dust Bowl victims who travel to California in search of a better life. Funding from *Fortune* magazine allowed James Agee and Walker Evans to live for weeks with Alabama sharecroppers. The result of their experiences was the nonfiction masterpiece *Let Us Now Praise Famous Men* (1941).

Focus on CULTURE

The Grapes of Wrath The 1939 novel by John Steinbeck epitomizes the despair of downtrodden farmers during the Depression. The story pits powerful banks and corporate farming interests against powerless farmers. This bitter critique is told through the experiences of the Joad family, "Okies" forced to travel to California in an endless search for migrant labor. The family finds human kindness in the midst of misfortune, cruelty, hunger, and hopelessness. Steinbeck's intimate, searing portrayals shocked the nation and aroused sympathy for migrant workers.

Radio and Movies The new medium of radio became a major source of entertainment for American families. Comedy shows of the 1930s produced stars such as Jack Benny, Fred Allen, George Burns, and Gracie Allen. The first daytime dramas, called soap operas because soap companies often sponsored them, emerged in this period. These 15-minute stories, designed to provoke strong emotional responses, were meant to appeal to women who remained at home during the day. Symphonic music and opera also flourished on the radio.

By 1933, the movies had recovered from the initial setback caused by the early Depression. Americans needed an escape from hard times, and the movies provided that escape. For a quarter, customers could see a double feature (introduced in 1931) or take the whole family to a drive-in theater (introduced in 1933). Federal agencies used motion pictures to publicize their work. The Farm Security Administration, for example, produced documentaries of American agricultural life.

Some Hollywood studios concentrated on optimistic films about common people who triumphed over evil, such as Warner Brothers' *Mr. Smith Goes to Washington* (1939). Comedies were

RESOURCE DIRECTORY
Technology

Sounds of an Era Audio CD *"King Porter Stomp," Benny Goodman* (time: one minute); *"The People, Yes," Carl Sandburg* (time: 50 seconds)

RESOURCE PRO® **Biography** *Jacob Lawrence,* found on Resource Pro, profiles one of the finest artists of the WPA Federal Arts Project, long considered the foremost African American painter of his time.

Social Security

1935 "Young people have come to wonder what would be their lot when they came to old age," says FDR, signing into law the Social Security Act. It provides retirement pensions financed by a tax on employers and employees. Initally, retirees received a one-time payment, averaging $58.08.

1939 Act is amended to include benefits for spouses, minor children, and survivors, paid in monthly checks.

1950 Act is amended to increase the number of workers covered in the program from about 50 percent to nearly all workers; cost-of-living increases are enacted.

1956 Act is amended to cover disabled Americans.

1965 Creation of Medicare gives Social Security recipients health insurance.

2000 Social Security Trustees report that payment of full benefits can be guaranteed only through 2037. With the huge "baby boom" generation nearing retirement, concern about funding for the system prompts intense debate on proposals to reform Social Security.

? **Why do you think the federal government kept enlarging the Social Security system and extending its benefits?**

very popular, too. In this era, the zany Marx Brothers produced such comic classics as *Monkey Business* (1931) and *Duck Soup* (1933), both of which had first premiered as stage shows.

The greatest box-office hits were movies that distracted Americans from the gloom of the Depression. *The Wizard of Oz,* released in 1939, allowed viewers to escape to a whole different world. Moviegoers flocked to musicals that featured large orchestras and lavishly choreographed dance numbers. No one understood the needs of Depression-era audiences better than Walt Disney, whose Mickey Mouse cartoons delighted moviegoers everywhere. Disney also released the classic cartoon *Snow White and the Seven Dwarfs* (1938) during this period.

The WPA and the Arts FDR believed that the arts were not luxuries that people should have to give up in hard times. For this reason, he earmarked WPA funds to support unemployed artists, musicians, historians, theater people, and writers. The Federal Writers' Project, established in 1935, assisted more than 6,000 writers, including Richard Wright, Saul Bellow, Margaret Walker, and Ralph Ellison. Historians with the project surveyed the nation's local government records, wrote state guidebooks, and collected life stories from about 2,000 former slaves.

Other government projects supported music and the visual arts The Federal Music Project started community symphonies and organized free music lessons. It also sent music specialists to lumber camps and small towns to collect and preserve a fast-disappearing folk music heritage.

The Federal Art Project, begun in 1935, put thousands of artists to work. They painted some 2,000 murals, mainly in public buildings. They also produced about 100,000 other paintings, 17,000 sculptures, and many other works of art.

ACTIVITY
Connecting with Culture

Tell students to write a short essay about the value of entertainment during the Depression. Suggest that students consider why comedies, such as those by the Marx Brothers, and fantasies, such as *The Wizard of Oz,* were popular. Have them explain the effect of scientific discoveries and technical innovations, such as talking films, on the development of the United States. Encourage students to think about the growing influence of popular culture at this time. **(Verbal/Linguistic)**

BACKGROUND
A Diverse Nation

In the 1930s, blacks continued to experience greater unemployment than whites. However, many African Americans benefited from the WPA. By 1939, nearly one-third of all African American families were being paid by the WPA. Thanks to WPA funding, community theaters and arts centers sprang up in African American neighborhoods.

In 1937 more than 4,000 people a month attended lectures and other events at the Harlem Community Art Center. In the late 1930s, many southern blacks registered to vote, spurred on largely by their participation in the WPA.

TEST PREPARATION

Have students read the quotation by Walter Reuther on the previous page and then complete the sentence below.

You can tell from the passage that—

A Reuther's resistance encouraged more violence against him.

(B) Reuther was determined to remain passive even when being beaten.

C Ford's men did not seriously intend to harm Reuther.

D Reuther was determined to resist the men by any means necessary.

CAPTION ANSWERS

Fast Forward to Today The Social Security system has grown in part because the nation's population has continued to grow. Also, the postwar economic boom made more federal money available for social programs, especially during the time in which Johnson's Great Society initiatives were enacted.

ACTIVITY
Connecting with Government

Have students work in small groups to make a visual presentation that analyzes the effects of the Great Depression on the U.S. economy and government. Students might choose to make a simple chart, or they might create a collage or poster. Encourage students to take a creative approach but to be sure to include specific examples from this era of history. **(Visual/Spatial)**

BACKGROUND
Geography in History

The Great Depression had a catastrophic impact on the United States. It was equally damaging to the economies of other nations, whose fortunes were becoming ever more tightly interconnected. Japan's burden of a rapidly growing population and a lack of territorial resources was exacerbated by the economic depression. In response, militarist Japanese leaders promoted aggressive expansion into areas rich in natural resources, such as the northern Chinese province of Manchuria. The stage was thus being set for World War II, President Roosevelt's greatest challenge.

READING CHECK

FDR believed that the arts were necessities, not luxuries. Art and theater could create awareness of social problems, while employing many and fostering hope.

VIEWING FINE ART New Deal support for the arts led to many lasting works, including this mural painted by Thomas Hart Benton in 1930 for the New School of Social Research in New York City. **Analyzing Visual Information** *How does this mural celebrate the values and spirit of the era? Support your answer with specifics from the painting.*

The Federal Theatre Project, directed by Vassar College Professor Hallie Flanagan, was the most controversial project. Flanagan used drama to create awareness of social problems. Her project launched the careers of many actors, playwrights, and directors who later became famous, including Burt Lancaster, Arthur Miller, John Houseman, and Orson Welles.

READING CHECK

Why did the federal government fund new arts programs during the Depression?

Accusing the Federal Theatre Project of being a propaganda machine for international communism, the House Un-American Activities Committee (HUAC) investigated the project in 1938 and 1939. In July 1939, Congress eliminated the project's funding.

Lasting New Deal Achievements

The New Deal attacked the Great Depression with a barrage of programs that affected nearly every American. The New Deal did not end the nation's suffering, but it led to some profound changes in American life. Voters began to expect a President to formulate programs and solve problems. People accepted more government intervention in their lives, and they grew accustomed to a much larger government. Laborers demanded more changes in the workplace.

The New Deal did not vanish completely when the Depression ended. Its accomplishments continued in many forms. This legacy ranges from physical monuments that dot the American landscape to towering political and social achievements that still influence American life.

Public Works and Federal Agencies Many New Deal bridges, dams, tunnels, public buildings, and hospitals exist to this day. These durable public works are visual reminders of this extraordinary period of government intervention in the economy.

Some of the federal agencies from the New Deal era have also endured. The Tennessee Valley Authority remains a model of government planning. The Federal Deposit Insurance Corporation still guarantees bank deposits. The Securities and Exchange Commission continues to monitor the workings of the stock exchanges.

CAPTION ANSWERS

Viewing Fine Art The mural celebrates hard work and economic activity. Muscular men are shown doing heavy physical labor; other details depict construction, factory work, and shipping.

RESOURCE DIRECTORY

Teaching Resources

Units 3/4 booklet
- Section 3 Quiz, p. 75
- Chapter 16 Test, pp. 76, 79

Guide to the Essentials
- Section 3 Summary, p. 79
- Chapter 16 Test, p. 80

Other Print Resources

Chapter Tests with ExamView® Test Bank CD-ROM, Ch. 16

Technology

ExamView® Test Bank CD-ROM, Ch. 16
Social Studies Skills Tutor CD-ROM

And in rural America, farmers still plant according to federal crop allotment policies adopted after the Supreme Court struck down AAA crop-reduction plans.

Social Security Despite its enduring support throughout American society, the Social Security system has had many critics. At first, Social Security came under attack because its payments were very low.

For a long time the system discriminated against women. It assumed, for example, that the male-headed household was typical. A mother could lose benefits for her children if a man, whether providing support for her or not, lived in her house. Women who went to work when their children started school rarely stayed in the work force long enough or earned high enough wages to receive the maximum benefits from the system. In addition, when a male recipient died, his benefits ended, leaving his family without an income.

In 1939, Congress and the Social Security Administration developed a series of amendments to the system attempted to address some of the weaknesses in the system. The amendments raised benefit amounts and provided monthly benefit checks instead of one-time payments. They also provided benefits for recipients' dependents and survivors. Later amendments included farm workers and others previously excluded from coverage, and added disability coverage.

A Legacy of Hope Of all of its achievements, perhaps the New Deal's greatest was to restore a sense of hope. People poured out their troubles to the President and First Lady. Eleanor and Franklin Roosevelt received thousands of letters daily during the late Depression era. Every letter contained a story of continued personal suffering. In their distress, people looked to their government for support. Indeed, government programs did mean the difference between survival and starvation for millions of Americans.

Nevertheless, economic recovery in the United States would not come until well into the 1940s, and it did not come through more New Deal programs. The return of a robust economy was set in motion on the battlefields of Europe in the late 1930s, where another test of American character was brewing: a second world war.

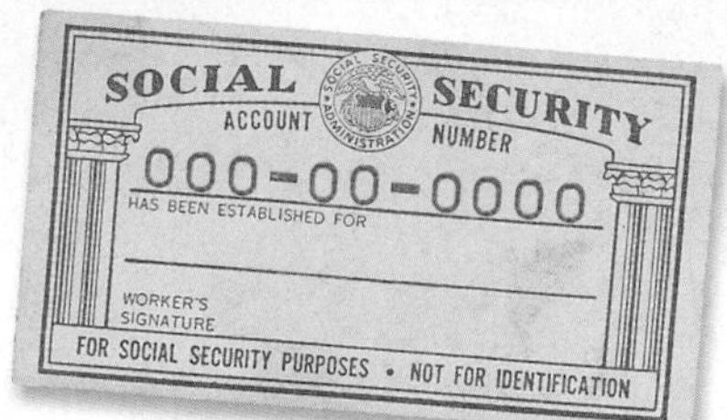

Sample Social Security card, with zeroes representing an individual's Social Security number

Section 3 Assessment

READING COMPREHENSION

1. Why did the United States slide back into a **recession** in 1937?
2. Why did FDR become concerned about the **national debt?**
3. (a) What gains and setbacks did unions experience during the New Deal era? (b) What impact did the Congress of Industrial Organizations (CIO) have on union strategies?
4. What did critics dislike about the Social Security system?

CRITICAL THINKING AND WRITING

5. **Testing Conclusions** FDR's advisors concluded that certain actions were needed to combat the recession of 1937. What actions did they recommend, and what were the consequences?
6. **Writing an Opinion** Write an essay that examines the legacy of the New Deal. In your opinion, what positive or negative effects did it have on the country? Should the federal government have become involved in creating jobs in theater and the other arts?

Take It to the NET

Activity: Interdisciplinary Connections Examine examples of federally funded arts projects during the New Deal. State your opinion on whether federal sponsorship of the arts was valuable and appropriate. Explain your reasoning. Use the links provided in the *America: Pathways to the Present* area of the following Web site for help in completing this activity.
www.phschool.com

Section 3 Assessment

Reading Comprehension

1. Social Security taxes meant that workers had less money to spend and bought fewer goods; consumers also had less money because programs such as the WPA had been reduced in size.
2. New Deal programs had required borrowing massive amounts of money, causing the national debt to rise dramatically.
3. (a) Wagner Act protections and activism by union leaders allowed unions to grow dramatically. Strikes were used as a tool, sometimes successfully, but sometimes leading to violent opposition. Eventually the sit-down type of strike was outlawed by the Supreme Court. (b) The CIO helped to unite and organize the nation's unskilled workers in mass-production industries, using the strike as the main tool in the quest for better wages and working conditions.
4. The payments were low, and women were discriminated against.

Critical Thinking and Writing

5. They advised restoring the programs that had been reduced in scope; they were proven right, as economic conditions slowly improved.
6. Essays will vary, but should address both the overall impact of the New Deal and the question of whether or not federal funding for the arts was justified.

Take It to the NET

Opinions will vary and may include a discussion of how the New Deal arts projects provided work for a great number of jobless artists who could convey themes of the time through their work. Art could provide enjoyment for the public during a time of tremendous trial and change. At the same time, such programs were opposed by some politicians who claimed that government funds were being used to create Communist propaganda.

Reviewing Key Terms

Students should refer to the definitions of key terms in the chapter to write sentences that show an understanding of the New Deal era.

Reviewing Main Ideas

11. The Bank Holiday served to enable the nation's banks to pause and reassess. It also coincided with the beginning of a federal inspection of all banks. These actions helped alleviate Americans' fears that banks were too unstable to be entrusted with personal savings.
12. By bolstering industrial prices; by instituting industry-wide codes to regulate industrial procedures and thus balance the unstable economy. The PWA offshoot of the NIRA undertook several highly successful public works construction projects.
13. The landslide reelection of FDR indicated that the American public heartily approved of the New Deal.
14. Its programs fell short of covering many segments of society, including women and minorities.
15. Their main criticism was that New Deal policies limited individual freedom and were therefore unconstitutional. They maintained that the New Deal philosophy was similar to Bolshevism.
16. The Court had struck down two major New Deal programs, the NIRA and the AAA. FDR wanted to pack the Supreme Court with justices who favored the New Deal.
17. Social Security taxes meant that workers had less money to spend and thus bought fewer goods; consumer spending had also been hurt because programs such as the WPA had had their budgets trimmed; national debt rose because of New Deal spending.
18. Because the New Deal legalized unions, relations between workers and employers were permanently changed, and unions became more powerful.
19. Federal funds were allocated by Congress to employ writers, painters, theater actors, and other artists to provide jobs for these people and to allow the public to benefit from their creative work.

Chapter 16 Review and Assessment

creating a CHAPTER SUMMARY

Copy this web diagram (right) on a piece of paper and complete it by adding information about New Deal programs and laws. Add as many circles as you need. Some entries have been completed for you as examples.

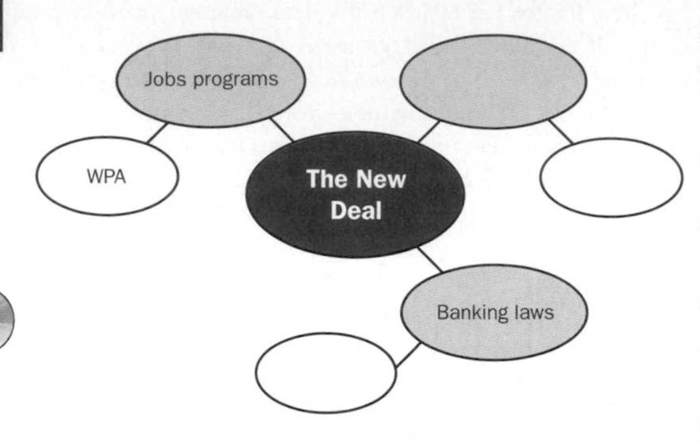

iTEXT

For additional review and enrichment activities, see the interactive version of *America: Pathways to the Present*, available on the Web and on CD-ROM.

★ Reviewing Key Terms

For each of the terms below, write a sentence explaining how it relates to the New Deal era.

1. New Deal
2. hundred days
3. Tennessee Valley Authority (TVA)
4. Second New Deal
5. Wagner Act
6. Social Security system
7. demagogue
8. nationalization
9. national debt
10. sit-down strike

★ Reviewing Main Ideas

11. Why did FDR begin the New Deal by closing the nation's banks? (Section 1)
12. How did the National Industrial Recovery Act aim to help businesses? (Section 1)
13. What did the 1936 election reveal about voters' attitudes toward the New Deal? (Section 1)
14. What were some of the limitations of the New Deal? (Section 2)
15. What was the main criticism of the New Deal by the American Liberty League? (Section 2)
16. Why did President Roosevelt attempt to "pack" the Supreme Court? (Section 2)
17. What factors led to the recession of 1937? (Section 3)
18. What permanent changes took place for labor unions as a result of the New Deal? (Section 3)
19. How did the New Deal support the popular and fine arts in America? (Section 3)

★ Critical Thinking

20. **Identifying Central Issues** Do you think that the New Deal was a success or a failure? Explain, citing information from the chapter.
21. **Comparing Points of View** (a) How did Eleanor Roosevelt view her role as First Lady? (b) How did her critics view that role? (c) How and why did these view point differ?
22. **Demonstrating Reasoned Judgment** (a) Why did the Supreme Court strike down the National Industrial Recovery Act? (b) Do you agree with the court's decision? Why or why not?
23. **Identifying Alternatives** Choose a present-day social or economic problem and state whether a New Deal type of approach would help to solve it. Explain your reasoning.
24. **Recognizing Ideologies** Compare the viewpoints of supporters and critics of the New Deal. Describe the beliefs and values that influenced the opinions of each side.

Creating a Chapter Summary

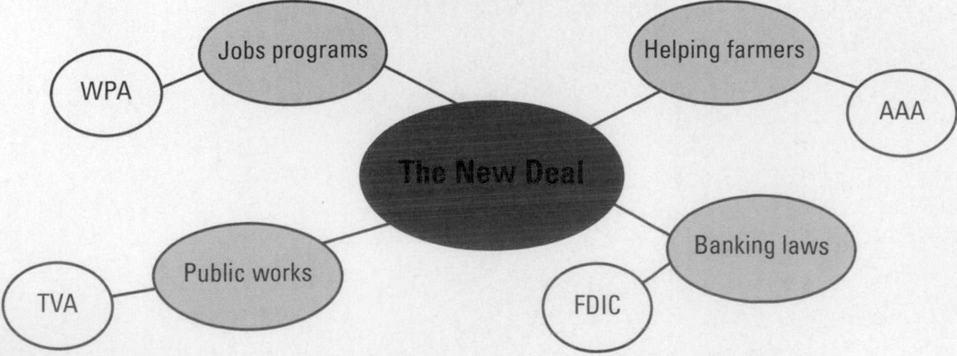

★ Skills Assessment

Analyzing Political Cartoons ▶

25. In this New Deal–era cartoon, (a) Who is the magician? (b) What does the rabbit represent?
26. (a) What does the caption "Old Reliable" mean? (b) Summarize the cartoon's message.

Analyzing Primary Sources

Turn to the quotation from Sam T. Mayhew in Section 2. Then answer the questions that follow.

27. What statement *best* summarizes Mayhew's opinion of the New Deal?
    - **A** Roosevelt's policies were harmful to all Americans because they were never put into action.
    - **B** Roosevelt should have provided more leadership during the Depression instead of letting the country drift.
    - **C** The New Deal failed to bring prosperity to all of America because its benefits were given out by race, not ability.
    - **D** Discrimination on the basis of color caused the Great Depression to worsen in the United States.
28. What does Mayhew mean when he says, "All the prosperity he had brought to the country has been legislated and is not real"?
    - **F** Laws to relieve the Depression were passed but not carried out.
    - **G** Congress passed laws to create new opportunities for Americans, but those opportunities did not become a reality for African Americans.
    - **H** Politicians misled Americans into believing that the New Deal had brought prosperity.
    - **J** Roosevelt himself did not bring any real prosperity to the country; Congress did, through the legislation it passed.

Applying the Chapter Skill: *Distinguishing Fact From Opinion*

29. Suppose you could use these three sources for a report on the 1936 election: (a) a speech by Alfred M. Landon, (b) a political encyclopedia, (c) Franklin Roosevelt's diary for 1936. Which source would you turn to for verifiable facts about the election? Why? Which sources would you turn to for opinions? Why?

THIS IS ONE RABBIT THAT NEVER FAILED ME!
SPENDING
OLD RELIABLE!

ACTIVITIES

Writing to LEARN

Writing an Interview
By the late 1930s, the TVA was well established. Write an interview that might have taken place between a reporter and a farmer, a homeowner, a banker, or some other person living in the region affected by the TVA. Begin the interview by reviewing the purpose of the TVA project.

Primary Source CD-ROM

Creating a Multimedia Presentation Find additional information on the New Deal on the *Exploring Primary Sources in U.S. History CD-ROM* and use the selection(s) provided to complete the Chapter 16 primary source activity located in the *America: Pathways to the Present* area of the following Web site.
www.phschool.com

Take It to the NET

Chapter Self-Test As a review activity, take the Chapter 16 Self-Test in the *America: Pathways to the Present* area at the Web site listed below. The questions are designed to test your understanding of the chapter content.
www.phschool.com

ANSWERS TO ACTIVITIES

Writing to LEARN

Answers will vary but should show an understanding of the TVA project.

Primary Source CD-ROM

Direct students to the additional primary sources that can be found on the *Exploring Primary Sources in U.S. History CD-ROM.*

Take It to the NET

Additional support materials and activities for Chapter 16 of *America: Pathways to the Present* can be found in the Social Studies area at the Prentice Hall School Web site. **www.phschool.com**

CRITICAL THINKING

20. Answers will vary but should be supported with specific facts from the chapter.
21. Answers will vary but should show an understanding that Eleanor Roosevelt performed many active roles in promoting government programs and in alleviating suffering.
22. (a) It gave the President legislative powers and regulated local, not interstate, commerce. (b) Opinions will vary, but should reflect an understanding of the separation of powers and Congress's power to regulate interstate commerce.
23. Essays will vary, but should be supported with specific examples and address themes and topics introduced in the chapter.
24. Supporters: the government has a responsibility to provide aid to its citizens in times of crisis, justifying huge New Deal spending. Though the New deal did not end the Depression, it provided relief and hope for many people. Opponents: were angered by government interference in a free enterprise economy. They felt that free market policies would have been more effective than the New Deal at ameliorating the Depression. Opponents also felt that the New Deal imposed an inordinately large tax burden upon the wealthy. Some critics opposed the crop subsidies paid to farmers, the creation of a huge bureaucracy, and massive spending.

SKILLS ASSESSMENT

25. (a) FDR. (b) New Deal spending.
26. (a) That FDR can be relied on to think he has solved Depression-era problems. (b) FDR's answer to the ills of the Depression is always more government spending.
27. C
28. G
29. For reliable facts about the election, you would choose the encyclopedia as a source because it presents facts that have been checked and confirmed. For opinions, you would choose the Landon and Roosevelt sources because they are first-person accounts and reflect the participants' personal beliefs and feelings, unconfirmed by other sources.

Use this sample exam to help your students prepare for standardized tests.

TIPS FOR TEST TAKING

You might want to remind your students of the following:

1. Read the directions carefully.
2. Read each question carefully.
3. For multiple choice questions, try to answer the question before you look at the choices. Read all the choices. Then, eliminate those that are absolutely incorrect.
4. For short answer questions, be sure to answer the question completely if there is more than one part.
5. Answer the easy questions first. Then, go back to the ones that will take more time.
6. Pace yourself. Be sure to set aside enough time for the writing questions.

TEST PREPARATION

Write your answers on a separate sheet of paper.

1. Charles Lindbergh was admired by many Americans in the 1920s after he
   - **A** made many popular silent films.
   - **B** set records in Major League baseball.
   - **C** flew alone across the Atlantic Ocean.
   - **D** became a commercial radio announcer.

2. Which one of the following best describes the Harlem Renaissance?
   - **A** A system of registering African Americans to vote
   - **B** A very popular nightclub in New York City
   - **C** A program to end Jim Crow laws in the southern states
   - **D** An African American literary and artistic movement

3. Support for African American businesses and a back-to-Africa movement were part of whose program?
   - **A** Marcus Garvey
   - **B** W.E.B. Du Bois
   - **C** James Weldon Johnson
   - **D** Jim Thorpe

4. Which one of the following best describes the Red Scare of the 1920s?
   - **A** A part of the Ku Klux Klan program
   - **B** A type of popular music, especially among teenagers
   - **C** A period of fear of communism and radical ideas
   - **D** A plan to limit immigration from eastern Europe

Use the information in the graph to answer the following question.

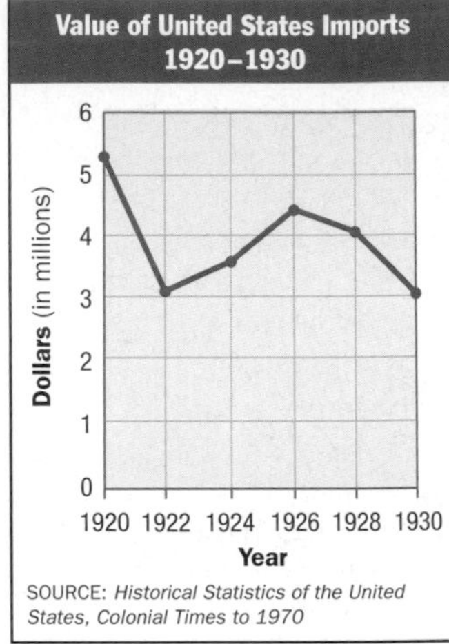

5. Which one of the following statements best explains the information in the graph?
   - **A** United States tariffs reduced imports into the country during the 1920s.
   - **B** No one had money in the 1920s to buy imports.
   - **C** World War I effectively ended all international trade.
   - **D** New immigrants bought many things from their former countries.

6. The assembly line was first used in manufacturing by
   - **A** J. P. Morgan.
   - **B** Walter Chrysler.
   - **C** A. Mitchell Palmer.
   - **D** Henry Ford.

562

Diagnose and Prescribe
- Profile student skills with Diagnostic Tests A&B.
- Address student needs with program materials correlated to test questions.

Review and Reteach
- Provide cumulative content review with the Review Book.

Practice and Assess
- Build test-taking skills with Test-taking Strategies With Transparencies.

Use the information in the chart to answer the following question.

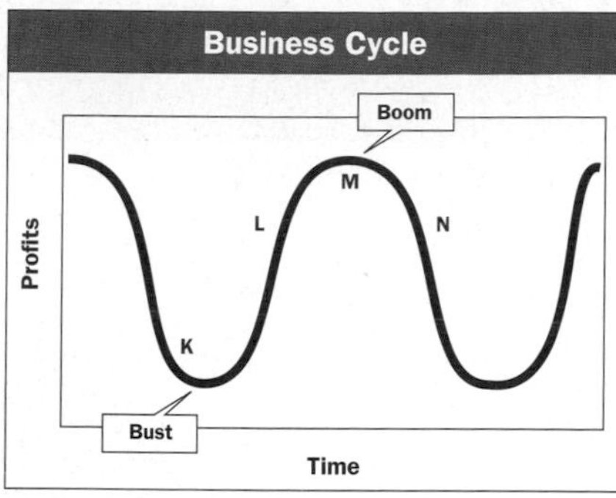

7. At what point in the business cycle was the U.S. economy just before the Great Crash occurred?
   - **A** K
   - **B** L
   - **C** M
   - **D** N

8. Which one of the following was an action taken by President Hoover to fight the Depression?
   - **A** Giving assistance directly to individuals
   - **B** Closing down all the nation's banks
   - **C** Establishing the Social Security Act
   - **D** Providing jobs through public works programs

9. Which one of the following was one of the first actions taken by Franklin D. Roosevelt when he became President?
   - **A** Ending prohibition in the country
   - **B** Creating the Reconstruction Finance Corporation
   - **C** Closing down all the nation's banks
   - **D** Establishing the 12 Federal Reserve Banks

10. The New Deal–era law that gives money to people who are retired or without work is the
    - **A** Wagner Act.
    - **B** National Youth Administration.
    - **C** Social Security Act.
    - **D** National Industrial Recovery Act.

11. Putting young men to work restoring and maintaining forests, beaches, and parks was the purpose of Roosevelt's
    - **A** Civilian Conservation Corps.
    - **B** American Federation of Labor.
    - **C** Tennessee Valley Authority.
    - **D** Federal Emergency Relief Administration.

12. Which one of the following effectively ended the Depression and restored the U.S. economy?
    - **A** The Public Works Administration
    - **B** The Security and Exchange Commission
    - **C** World War II
    - **D** The Bonus Army march on Washington

Writing Practice

13. Describe the changing role of women in the 1920s.
14. What were the three major causes of the Depression?
15. Describe the actions taken during the New Deal to change the financial system of the United States.

1. C
2. D
3. A
4. C
5. A
6. D
7. C
8. D
9. C
10. C
11. A
12. C
13. Answers might mention that women worked outside the home more often, adopted more casual social manners, and in a few instances were elected to public office.
14. Answers should explain the unstable economy, overspeculation, and mistakes in government economic policies.
15. Answers might include the Glass-Steagall Banking Act, the establishment of the Securities and Exchange Commission, the Social Security Act, and the refinancing of home mortgages.

Unit 5

Introducing the Unit

Hot and Cold War (1931–1960)

World War II was a devastating worldwide experience. Americans fought to defend democracy against German and Japanese forces. Americans at home endured shortages and hardships in a spirit of cooperation and patriotism. After the war ended there were new problems to confront. The shaky alliance between the United States and the Soviet Union, established for the sake of convenience during the war, fell into a state of undeclared belligerence called the Cold War. As that hostility intensified, and as the United States sought to contain the expansion of communism around the world, some Americans were accused of disloyalty and even treason.

Using Historical Evidence

Direct students' attention to the photograph on these pages. Reflect with them on the fact that the soldiers landing on the shores of Normandy are heading into a terrifying battle situation. Note that the soldiers in the photograph look eager. Note particularly the body position of the man in the foreground on this page. He seems to be leaning forward, almost as though he were eager to meet the enemy. Note also the expressions of others as they leap off the end of the landing craft.

Discuss with students the soldiers' attitude and spirit. What do students think lay behind that? What do students think it would have been like to be one of these soldiers?

Unit 5

Hot and Cold War (1931–1960)

"It is not enough to fight. It is the spirit which we bring to the fight that decides the issue. It is morale that wins the victory."

George C. Marshall
Military Review, October 1948

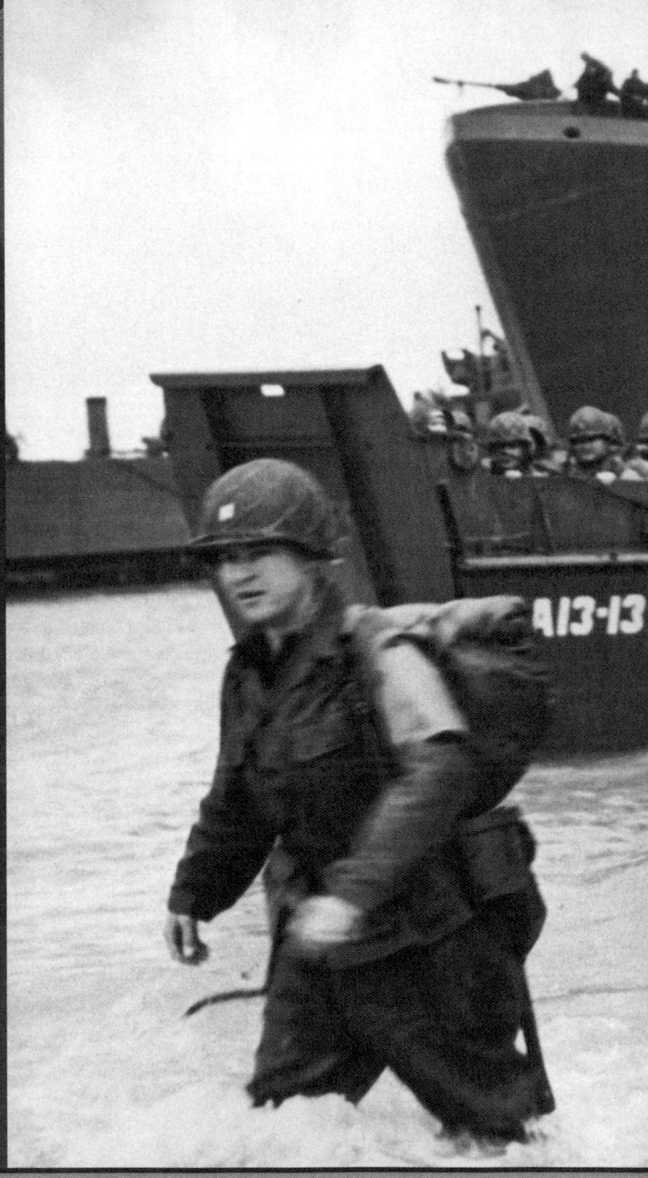

U.S. soldiers disembark from Coast Guard landing craft on the shores of Normandy after the main D-Day invasion. ▶

564

RESOURCE DIRECTORY

Teaching Resources

Units 5/6/7 booklet
- American Pathways Activity, pp. 47–48
- History's Lasting Impact, pp. 49–50

Geography and History booklet, pp. 16–17

Other Print Resources

Prentice Hall Assessment System
- Document-Based Assessment

eTeach

Be sure to check out this month's online discussion with a Master Teacher. Go to **www.phschool.com**.

Chapter 17 World War II: The Road to War, 1931–1941
Chapter 18 World War II: Americans at War, 1941–1945
Chapter 19 The Cold War, 1945–1960
Chapter 20 The Postwar Years at Home, 1945–1960

565

TECHNOLOGY CENTER

Take It to the NET

Prentice Hall School Web site offers student-appropriate Internet activities and links that extend core content. Visit us at the Social Studies area. **www.phschool.com**

AmericanHeritage®

My Brush with History™ Video Program This new video series lets your students learn history from the people who lived it.

RESOURCE PRO®

Teaching Resources on CD-ROM offer lesson-planning flexibility, test-generation capability, and resource manageability.

- **Presentation Pro CD-ROM** Provides you with multimedia lecture notes for each chapter.
- **Social Studies Skills Tutor CD-ROM** Provides interactive practice in Geographic Literacy, Critical Thinking and Reading, Visual Analysis, and Communications.
- **Interactive Constitution CD-ROM** Exploring active citizenship and civic responsibilities, this CD-ROM shows students how the Constitution affects their lives today.
- **Exploring Primary Sources in U.S. History CD-ROM** This interactive exploration of primary sources allows students to analyze and to evaluate writing and images from American history.
- **Guided Reading Audiotapes**
- **Student Edition on Audio CD**
- **Sounds of an Era Audio CD** Bring the sounds of American history to life in the classroom with music, speeches, poetry, interviews, and news reports.

iTEXT

Don't miss the exclusive interactive version of this textbook on the Web and on CD-ROM.

RESOURCE DIRECTORY

Technology

Color Transparencies *Historical Maps,* A36, A37, A38, A39, A40, A41, A42, A43, A44, A45, A46, A47; *Political Cartoons,* B14, B15; *Time Lines,* C7; *Cause-and-Effect Charts,* D10; *Fine Art,* E18; *American Photo,* F8; *The Way it Works,* H18

Section Reading Support Transparencies

Prentice Hall United States History Video Collection™ Volume 19, *World War II;* Volume 20, *Post-War USA*

Companion Web site, www.phschool.com

Chapter 17 Planning Guide

Resource Manager

	Core Instruction	Reading/Skills
Chapter-Level Resources **TEKS** 8(B), 24(B), 25(A), 25(B)	Teaching Resources • Pacing Charts booklet • Block Scheduling booklet **Resource Pro® CD-ROM,** Ch. 17 **Prentice Hall Presentation Pro CD-ROM,** Ch. 17 **www.phschool.com** • eTeach	**Guided Reading Audiotapes (English/Spanish)** **Student Edition on Audio CD,** Ch. 17 **Social Studies Skills Tutor CD-ROM** **Color Transparencies,** A36, A37, A38, A39, A40
1 The Rise of Dictators 1. Find out how the government and the economy of the Soviet Union changed under Stalin. 2. Discover the origins and goals of Italy's fascist government. 3. See how Hitler rose to power in Germany and Europe in the 1930s. 4. Learn about the causes and results of the Spanish Civil War. **TEKS** 1(B), 6(A)	Teaching Resources **Units 5/6/7 booklet** • Section 1 Quiz, p. 4 **Learning Styles Lesson Plans booklet,** p. 50	**Guided Reading and Review booklet,** p. 96 **Guide to the Essentials,** p. 81 **Section Reading Support Transparencies**
2 Europe Goes to War 1. Understand how the German invasion of Poland led to war with Britain and France. 2. See what wartime victories and setbacks Germany experienced in Western Europe. 3. Find out why the Battle of Britain was an important victory for Britain. **TEKS** 1(B), 25(C)	Teaching Resources **Units 5/6/7 booklet** • Section 2 Quiz, p. 5 **Learning Styles Lesson Plans booklet,** p. 51	**Guided Reading and Review booklet,** p. 97 **Guide to the Essentials,** p. 82 **Learning with Documents booklet,** p. 63 **Skills for Life booklet,** p. 26 **Section Reading Support Transparencies**
3 Japan Builds an Empire 1. Discover the causes and effects of Japan's growing military power. 2. See why the Manchurian Incident was a turning point for Japan's civil government. 3. Find out about the initial outcome of Japan's war against China. 4. Learn why Japan looked beyond China for future expansion. **TEKS** 1(B), 26(B)	Teaching Resources **Units 5/6/7 booklet** • Section 3 Quiz, p. 6	**Guided Reading and Review booklet,** p. 98 **Guide to the Essentials,** p. 83 **Section Reading Support Transparencies**
4 From Isolationism to War 1. Find out why the United States chose neutrality in the 1930s. 2. See how American involvement in the European conflict grew from 1939 to 1941. 3. Discover why Japan's attack on Pearl Harbor led the United States to declare war. **TEKS** 6(A), 8(A)	Teaching Resources **Units 5/6/7 booklet** • Section 4 Quiz, p. 7	**Guided Reading and Review booklet,** p. 99 **Guide to the Essentials,** p. 84 **Learning with Documents booklet,** p. 88 **Section Reading Support Transparencies**

Enrichment/Pre-AP

Prentice Hall United States History Video Collection™
www.phschool.com
- Section Activities, Virtual Field Trip, Chapter Activities, Current Events Online

---

Biography, Literature, and Comparing Primary Sources booklet, p. 29
Historical Outline Map Book, p. 64
Exploring Primary Sources in U.S. History CD-ROM

Biography, Literature, and Comparing Primary Sources booklet, pp. 72, 143
Historical Outline Map Book, p. 65
Sounds of an Era Audio CD

Historical Outline Map Book, p. 66

Great Debates booklet, p. 20
Sounds of an Era Audio CD
Exploring Primary Sources in U.S. History CD-ROM
American Pathways Thematic Posters

Assessment

Core Assessment
ExamView® Test Bank, Ch. 17
ExamView® Test Bank CD-ROM, Ch. 17

Standardized Test Preparation
Diagnose and Prescribe
Diagnostic Tests for High School Social Studies Skills

Review and Reteach
Review Book for U.S. History

Practice and Assess
Test-taking Strategies With Transparencies
Test-taking Strategies Posters
Test Prep Book for U.S. History
Alternative Assessment Handbook
Document-Based Assessment

Teaching Resources
Units 5/6/7 booklet
- Section Quizzes, pp. 4–7
- Chapter Tests, pp. 8, 11

www.phschool.com Ch. 17 Self-Test

AmericanHeritage Resources

From the Archives of American Heritage®
AmericanHeritage® My Brush with History™ Videotapes
www.americanheritage.com

Don't miss the exclusive interactive version of this textbook on the Web and on CD-ROM.

Chapter 17 Planning Guide

In Your Classroom

Customize for Individual Needs

Gifted and Talented

Teacher's Edition
- Customize for Gifted and Talented, p. 569

Teaching Resources
- Biography, Literature, and Comparing Primary Sources booklet, pp. 29, 72, 143

Technology
- Exploring Primary Sources in U.S. History CD-ROM *Berlin Diary, William Shirer; Lend Lease; Pearl Harbor, Daniel K. Inouye*

ESL

Teacher's Edition
- Customize for ESL, p. 577

Teaching Resources
- Guided Reading and Review booklet, pp. 96–99
- Guide to the Essentials (English/Spanish), Chapter 17

Technology
- Student Edition on Audio CD, Chapter 17
- Guided Reading Audiotapes (English/Spanish), Chapter 17
- Section Reading Support Transparencies

Less Proficient Readers

Teacher's Edition
- Customize for Less Proficient Readers, p. 583

Teaching Resources
- Guided Reading and Review booklet, pp. 96–99
- Guide to the Essentials (English/Spanish), Chapter 17

Technology
- Student Edition on Audio CD, Chapter 17
- Guided Reading Audiotapes (English/Spanish), Chapter 17
- Section Reading Support Transparencies

Less Proficient Writers

Teacher's Edition
- Customize for Less Proficient Writers, p. 587

Teaching Resources
- Guided Reading and Review booklet, pp. 96–99
- Guide to the Essentials (English/Spanish), Chapter 17

Technology
- Student Edition on Audio CD, Chapter 17
- Guided Reading Audiotapes (English/Spanish), Chapter 17
- Section Reading Support Transparencies

Teacher's Edition Index

Chapter 17 – Pacing Suggestions

For 90-minute Blocks

- Teach sections 1, 2, 3, and 4 using Transparencies A36, A37, A38, A39, and A40, and the Recent Scholarship note on page 577 for class discussions.

Running Out of Time?

If you are running short on time to cover this chapter, consider the following options:

- Use the Prentice Hall Presentation Pro CD-ROM to create an outline for this chapter.
- Use the Section Summaries for Chapter 17, from **Guide to the Essentials (English/Spanish).**

TEKS Correlation

Chapter-Level	TEKS
	(8) Geography. The student uses geographic tools to collect, analyze, and interpret data. The student is expected to: **(B)** pose and answer questions about geographic distributions and patterns shown on maps, graphs, charts, models, and databases. **(24) Social studies skills.** The student applies critical-thinking skills to organize and use information acquired from a variety of sources, including electronic technology. The student is expected to: **(B)** analyze information by sequencing, categorizing, identifying cause-and-effect relationships, comparing, contrasting, finding the main idea, summarizing, making generalizations and predictions, and drawing inferences and conclusions. **(25) Social studies skills.** The student communicates in written, oral, and visual forms. The student is expected to: **(A)** use social studies terminology correctly. **(B)** use standard grammar, spelling, sentence structure, and punctuation.
1 The Rise of Dictators	**(1) History.** The student understands traditional historical points of reference in U.S. history from 1877 to the present. The student is expected to: **(B)** apply absolute and relative chronology through the sequencing of significant individuals, events, and time periods. **(6) History.** The student understands the impact of significant national and international decisions and conflicts from World War II and the Cold War to the present on the United States. The student is expected to: **(A)** identify reasons for U.S. involvement in World War II, including the growth of dictatorships and the attack on Pearl Harbor.
2 Europe Goes to War	**(1) History.** The student understands traditional historical points of reference in U.S. history from 1877 to the present. The student is expected to: **(B)** apply absolute and relative chronology through the sequencing of significant individuals, events, and time periods. **(25) Social studies skills.** The student communicates in written, oral, and visual forms. The student is expected to: **(C)** transfer information from one medium to another, including written to visual and statistical to written or visual, using computer software as appropriate.
3 Japan Builds an Empire	**(1) History.** The student understands traditional historical points of reference in U.S. history from 1877 to the present. The student is expected to: **(B)** apply absolute and relative chronology through the sequencing of significant individuals, events, and time periods. **(26) Social studies skills.** The student uses problem-solving and decision-making skills, working independently and with others, in a variety of settings. The student is expected to: **(B)** use a decision-making process to identify a situation that requires a decision, gather information, identify options, predict consequences, and take action to implement a decision.
4 From Isolationism to War	**(6) History.** The student understands the impact of significant national and international decisions and conflicts from World War II and the Cold War to the present on the United States. The student is expected to: **(A)** identify reasons for U.S. involvement in World War II, including the growth of dictatorships and the attack on Pearl Harbor. **(8) Geography.** The student uses geographic tools to collect, analyze, and interpret data. The student is expected to: **(A)** create thematic maps, graphs, charts, models, and databases representing various aspects of the United States.

Chapter 17

World War II: The Road to War

(1931–1941)

Introducing the Chapter

Economic conditions in Europe and Russia following the end of World War I and the Russian Revolution were devastating. Conditions were ripe for the rise to power of new leaders, totalitarian in approach, who promised to relieve countries of poverty and chaos. Joseph Stalin in Russia, Adolf Hitler in Germany, and (to a lesser extent) Benito Mussolini in Italy each took actions, ostensibly to revitalize their countries, which would result in further devastation and vast destruction.

The prevailing mood in the United States during the 1930s was isolationist as Americans coped with the economic crisis of the depression. But when Japanese forces struck Pearl Harbor on December 7, 1941, the United States could remain neutral no longer.

Time Line Activity

To provide students with practice in using the time line, ask questions such as these:

1. What action taken by Japan in 1931 would have far-reaching global consequences? *(The Japanese army invaded Manchuria.)*
2. What 1938 meeting between two leaders failed to forestall World War II? *(The meeting between Neville Chamberlain and Adolf Hitler)*
3. What 1939 action began World War II? *(The invasion of Poland by Germany)*

eTeach

Be sure to check out this month's online discussion with a Master Teacher. Go to **www.phschool.com**.

Chapter 17 World War II: The Road to War (1931–1941)

This German election poster translates to "Our Last Hope: Hitler."

Adolf Hitler

American Events

1934 The United States cuts tariffs on foreign goods to benefit trade and international relations.

1935 Congress passes the first Neutrality Act banning the sale of arms to countries at war.

Presidential Terms: Herbert Hoover 1929–1933; Franklin D. Roosevelt 1933–1945

1931 — 1933 — 1935

World Events

1931 Japanese army overruns Manchuria.

1933 Adolf Hitler is named Chancellor of Germany.

1934 Joseph Stalin begins the Great Purge of Soviet citizens.

RESOURCE DIRECTORY

Teaching Resources

Pacing Charts booklet
Block Scheduling booklet, p. 25
Units 5/6/7 booklet
- Chapter Summary, p. 3

Technology

Guided Reading Audiotapes (English/Spanish), Ch. 17
Student Edition on Audio CD, Ch. 17
Prentice Hall United States History Video Collection™ Volume 19, *World War II*
Prentice Hall Presentation Pro CD-ROM, Ch. 17
Resource Pro® CD-ROM
Social Studies Skills Tutor CD-ROM
Companion Web site, www.phschool.com

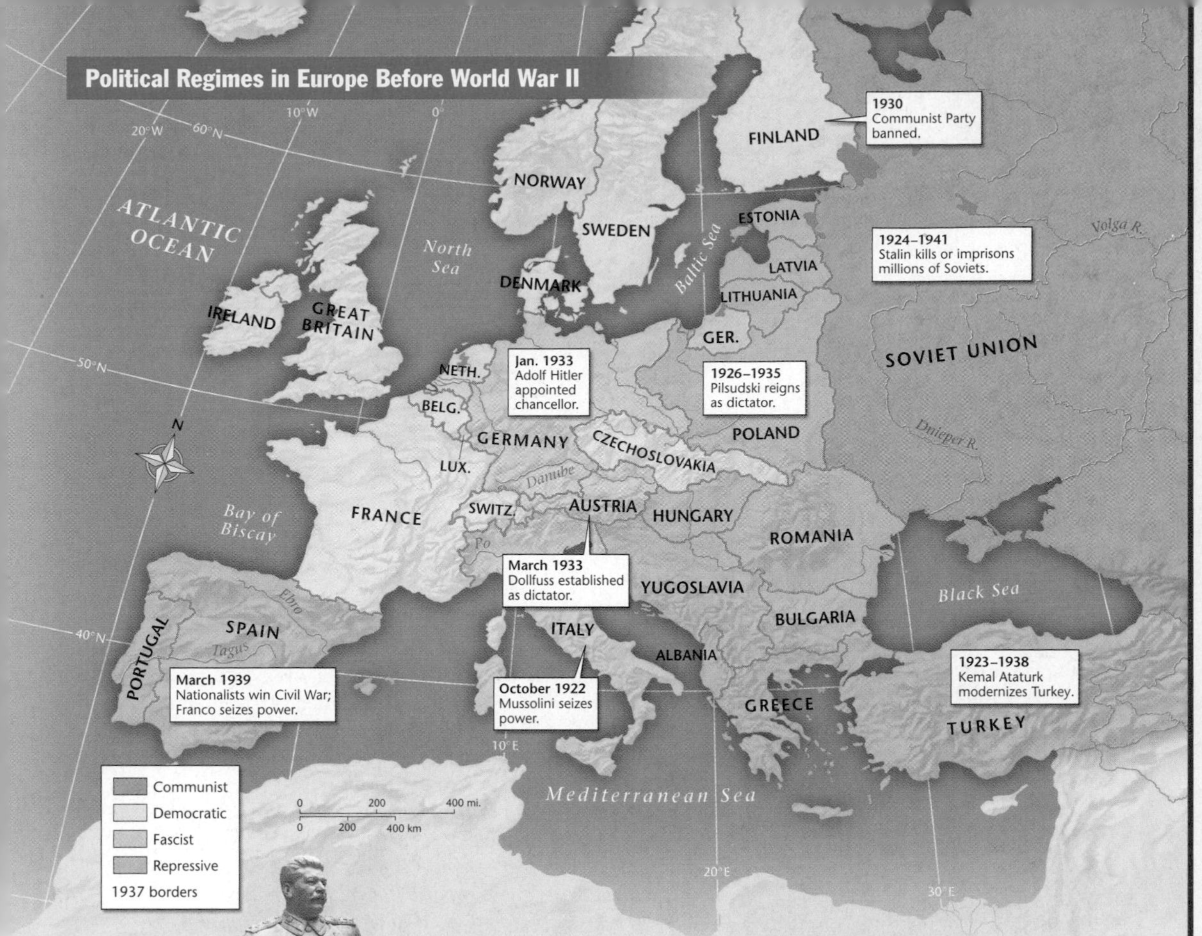

Political Regimes in Europe Before World War II

1930 Communist Party banned.

1924–1941 Stalin kills or imprisons millions of Soviets.

Jan. 1933 Adolf Hitler appointed chancellor.

1926–1935 Pilsudski reigns as dictator.

March 1933 Dollfuss established as dictator.

March 1939 Nationalists win Civil War; Franco seizes power.

October 1922 Mussolini seizes power.

1923–1938 Kemal Ataturk modernizes Turkey.

FINLAND, NORWAY, SWEDEN, ESTONIA, LATVIA, LITHUANIA, DENMARK, IRELAND, GREAT BRITAIN, NETH., BELG., GER., GERMANY, LUX., CZECHOSLOVAKIA, POLAND, SOVIET UNION, FRANCE, SWITZ., AUSTRIA, HUNGARY, ROMANIA, YUGOSLAVIA, BULGARIA, ITALY, ALBANIA, GREECE, TURKEY, SPAIN, PORTUGAL

ATLANTIC OCEAN, North Sea, Baltic Sea, Bay of Biscay, Mediterranean Sea, Black Sea, Volga R., Dnieper R., Danube, Po, Ebro, Tagus

	Communist
	Democratic
	Fascist
	Repressive
1937 borders	

0 200 400 mi.
0 200 400 km

Joseph Stalin

1939 Congress repeals the arms embargo.

1940 Roosevelt sends 50 destroyers to Britain in exchange for military bases in the Western Hemisphere.

1941 Roosevelt proposes lend-lease program to aid the Allies. Japan bombs Pearl Harbor and brings the United States into the war.

1937 · 1939 · 1941

1936 Italy conquers Ethiopia.

1937 Marco Polo Bridge incident leads Japan to invade China.

1938 Chamberlain and Hitler meet at the Munich Conference.

1939 Invasion of Poland begins World War II.

1940 Germany defeats France and attacks Britain by air.

Political Regimes in Europe Before World War II

Activating Prior Knowledge What was the political system of the Allied countries? *(Democratic)*

Previewing Czechoslovakia was one of the first countries to become dominated by Germany. Looking at the map, give two reasons for this. *(Czechoslovakia was the lone democratic country surrounded by more repressive political regimes, and a section of Czechoslovakia was bordered by Germany on three sides.)*

BACKGROUND
About the Pictures

1. One of Hitler's campaign strategies was using propaganda like this poster to manipulate the voters he was trying to reach.
2. On August 2, 1934, Hitler assumed both the role of Führer (German for *the leader*) and Chancellor of Germany.
3. Through statues like this, Stalin became widely recognizable and inspired a cult-like fanaticism among his people.

BIBLIOGRAPHY

For the Teacher

Kershaw, Ian. ***Hitler, 1936–1945: Nemesis.*** W. W. Norton, 2000. (A chilling, definitive biography.)

Prange, Gordon William. ***At Dawn We Slept: The Untold Story of Pearl Harbor.*** Penguin, 2001. (Exhaustively researched, detailed account of the attack on Pearl Harbor.)

Radzinsky, Edvard. ***Stalin: The First In-Depth Biography Based on Explosive New Documents from Russia's Secret Archives.*** Anchor, 1997. (From behind the iron curtain comes one of the first biographies written with access to previously secret information.)

For the Student

Raymer, Edward C. ***Descent Into Darkness: Pearl Harbor, 1941: A Navy Diver's Memoir.*** Presidio Press, 1996. (Find out what it was like to dive at Pearl Harbor following the attack, trying to salvage ships and search for remains.)

Rooney, Andy. ***My War.*** Public Affairs, 2000. (A first-hand account of the war experiences of a 19-year-old.)

Don't miss the exclusive interactive version of this textbook on the Web and on CD-ROM.

Section 1
The Rise of Dictators

Section Objectives

1. Find out how the government and the economy of the Soviet Union changed under Stalin.
2. Discover the origins and goals of Italy's fascist government.
3. See how Hitler rose to power in Germany and Europe in the 1930s.
4. Learn about the causes and results of the Spanish Civil War.

Bellringer

Warm-Up Activity The world of the 1930s was a tremendously unstable place, due to economic crisis and a slow recovery from the devastation of World War I. Several leaders catapulted to power on this shaky foundation, including Joseph Stalin, Adolf Hitler, and Benito Mussolini. Ask students to reflect on the global conditions that created opportunities for those leaders.

Activating Prior Knowledge What do students know about conditions in Europe and Russia in the 1930s? Ask students to recall what they learned about the terms of the Versailles Treaty, in relation to Germany. In what ways might France's fury with Germany, and its desire for punishment and revenge, now give rise to a bitter harvest?

Reading Strategy

As students read the section, have them make notes on conditions that led to a growth of dictatorships in the 1930s.

Section 1 The Rise of Dictators

READING FOCUS

- How did Stalin change the government and the economy of the Soviet Union?
- What were the origins and goals of Italy's fascist government?
- How did Hitler rise to power in Germany and Europe in the 1930s?
- What were the causes and results of the Spanish Civil War?

MAIN IDEA

Dictators in the Soviet Union, Italy, Germany, and Spain formed brutal, repressive governments in the 1920s and 1930s. They were motivated by their political beliefs and a desire for power.

KEY TERMS

totalitarian
fascism
purge
Nazism
Axis Powers
appeasement

TAKING NOTES

As you read, complete this chart listing the actions of dictators in the Soviet Union, Italy, and Germany in the 1930s.

Country	Actions Taken
Soviet Union	• Combined farms into collectives • Sent millions to labor camps in Siberia •
Germany	
Italy	

Adolf Hitler presided over massive party rallies, including this one at Nuremberg.

Setting the Scene In September 1936, German dictator Adolf Hitler called hundreds of thousands of his followers to a week-long rally in the German city of Nuremberg. Included with political meetings and parades was a nighttime ceremony: the Oath under the Cathedral of Light. A Nazi Party booklet described the beginning of the ceremony.

> *"180,000 people look to the heavens. 150 blue spotlights surge upward hundreds of meters, forming overhead the most powerful cathedral that mortals have ever seen.*
>
> *There, at the entrance, we see [Hitler]. He too stands for several moments looking upward, then turns and walks, followed by his aides, past the long, long columns, 20 deep, of the fighters for his idea. An ocean of Heil-shouts and jubilation surrounds him."*
>
> *—The Party Rally of Honor*

Amid waving red banners and circling searchlights, Hitler led the audience of 180,000 in a "holy oath" to Germany.

Grand spectacles like the Nuremberg Party Rally were essential to Hitler's **totalitarian** rule. A totalitarian government exerts total control over a nation. It dominates every aspect of life, using terror to suppress individual rights and silence all forms of opposition. The pride and unity of the Nuremberg rally hid the fact that people who disagreed with Hitler were silenced, beaten, or killed. Hitler's power rested on the destruction of the individual.

Hitler and Italy's Benito Mussolini governed by a philosophy called **fascism.** Fascism emphasizes the importance of the nation or an ethnic group and the supreme authority of the leader. In the Soviet Union, Joseph Stalin based his totalitarian government on a vicious form of communism. Like fascism, communism relies upon a strong, dictatorial government that does not respect individual rights and freedoms. Historically, however, Communists and Fascists have been natural enemies.

RESOURCE DIRECTORY

Teaching Resources
Learning Styles Lesson Plans booklet, p. 50
Guided Reading and Review booklet, p. 96

Technology
Section Reading Support Transparencies
Guided Reading Audiotapes (English/Spanish), Ch. 17
Student Edition on Audio CD, Ch. 17
Prentice Hall Presentation Pro CD-ROM, Ch. 17
Companion Web site, www.phschool.com

Stalin's Soviet Union

While Lenin led the Soviet Union, the worldwide Communist revolution he sought never materialized. Even in his own country, economic failure threatened Communist control of the government. Lenin eased up on the drive to convert all property to public ownership. His New Economic Policy (NEP) allowed some private business to continue. Stalin took over after Lenin's death in 1924. Stalin decided to abandon the NEP and take "one great leap forward" to communism. He launched the first of a series of five-year plans to modernize agriculture and build new industries from the ground up.

Stalin's Economic Plans To modernize agriculture, Stalin encouraged Soviet farmers to combine their small family farms into huge collective farms owned and run by the state. Facing widespread resistance, Stalin began forcing peasants off their land in the late 1920s.

The state takeover of farming was completed within a few years, but with terrible consequences. In the Ukraine and other agricultural regions, Stalin punished resistant farmers by confiscating much or all of the food they produced. Millions of people died from starvation, and millions more fled to the cities. Stalin also sent approximately 5 million peasants to labor camps in Siberia and northern Russia. In addition to the human cost, the collectivization campaign caused agricultural production to fall dramatically. Food shortages forced Stalin to introduce rationing throughout the country.

Stalin pursued rapid industrialization with more success. He assigned millions of laborers from rural areas to build and run new industrial centers where iron, steel, oil, and coal were produced. Because Stalin poured money and labor into these basic industries rather than housing, clothing, and consumer goods, the Soviet people endured severe shortages of essential products, and their standard of living fell sharply. Still, by 1940 Stalin had achieved his goal of turning the Soviet Union into a modern industrial power.

Stalin's Reign of Terror During the economic upheaval, Stalin completed his political domination of the Soviet Union through a series of **purges.** In political terms, a purge is the process of removing enemies and undesirable

Labor Camps in the Western Soviet Union, *circa* 1936

MAP SKILLS Stalin presided over a vast expansion of the Soviet Union's system of labor camps. **Place** *What hardships did prisoners experience in the northernmost camps?*

Lesson Plan

Focus Fascist dictators seized control in several nations scarred by World War I. Ask how these leaders were able to rise to power and what types of actions people took during the 1930s to attempt to repel the dictators' advances.

Instruct Point out that Hitler and Mussolini promised to restore economic prosperity to the countries they led. Ask students to describe how they used expansion as a way to bolster national pride. How did activities in Spain mirror what was going on in Germany and Italy?

Assess/Reteach Ask students to list motivations on the part of leaders in Germany, Italy, and Spain in the 1930s. Then have them list motivations of those citizens who supported these leaders.

Activity

Connecting with Culture

Organize students into groups to discuss the psychology behind Hitler's popularity in Germany. To help them relate this phenomenon to their everyday experience, suggest that they explore why individuals often go along with the actions of the "crowd," even when they are not comfortable doing so. Tell groups to identify other factors in Germany that contributed to this mass psychology of support for Hitler. Ask them to decide if, given a similar set of circumstances, a leader like Hitler could hold such appeal in some nation today. Have a spokesperson from each group report its conclusions to the class. **(Logical/Mathematical)**

Customize For ...

Gifted and Talented

Ask students to write an essay in which they describe how Stalin's actions in Russia began in support of the principles of the Russian Revolution, but soon went in a direction that was different in many respects. Ask them to focus on the following elements: economics, industrialization, political control, treatment of dissidents.

Caption Answers

Map Skills Extreme cold added to difficult working and living conditions.

ACTIVITY
Connecting with Citizenship

Ask students to write letters to the editor, in the role of Italians of the 1920s or 1930s, explaining why they support (or do not support) Mussolini as the leader of Italy. Ask several students from each side of the issue to read their letters to the class. **(Verbal/Linguistic)**

BACKGROUND
Daily Life

As he made war in Africa, Mussolini preserved the appearance of Italy's economic "miracle" by keeping the nation on a peacetime footing. As a result, when restrictions finally came, they were very harsh. In 1939 sugar and soap were rationed throughout Italy, followed by fats in 1940 and other foodstuffs in 1941. Most civilians were limited to less than 1,000 calories a day, although a well-organized black market in food flourished. Italians were permitted one new pair of shoes or a few articles of clothing per year, but not both. Newspapers were limited to four pages, later reduced to two. By the end of 1941, all civilian gasoline-powered vehicles had been forbidden on the nation's streets and highways. Only a few cars and buses continued to run, powered by methane from Italy's Po Valley.

READING CHECK

Stalin removed his enemies from government through purges. He had his enemies arrested, often on false charges. Stalin used show trials to find these individuals guilty, after which they were executed, deported, or imprisoned.

CAPTION ANSWERS

Viewing History Mussolini's head is pictured prominently over a map of Italy's conquest, giving him credit for the victory. His image is surrounded by a light glow.

READING CHECK
How did Stalin establish total control of the Soviet Union?

individuals from power. Stalin "purified" the Communist Party by getting rid of his opponents and anyone else he believed to be a threat to his power or to his ideas. The Great Purge began in 1934 with a series of "show trials," in which the only possible verdict was "guilty." Stalin's reign of terror did not stop there, however. He and his followers purged local party offices, collective farms, the secret police, and the army of anyone whom he considered a threat.

By 1939, his agents had arrested more than 7 million people from all levels of society. A million were executed, and millions more ended up in forced labor camps. Nearly all of the people were innocent victims of Stalin's paranoia. But the purges successfully eliminated all threats to Stalin's power, real or imagined.

Fascism in Italy

As in the Soviet Union, Italy's totalitarian government arose from the failures of World War I. Benito Mussolini had fought and been wounded in the war. He believed strongly that the Versailles Treaty should have granted Italy more territory. A talented speaker, Mussolini began to attract followers, including other dissatisfied war veterans, opponents of the monarchy, Socialists, and anarchists. In 1919, Mussolini and his supporters formed the revolutionary Fascist Party.

Calling himself *Il Duce* ("the leader"), Mussolini organized Fascist groups throughout Italy. He relied on gangs of Fascist thugs, called Blackshirts because of the way they dressed, to terrorize and bring under control those who opposed him. By 1922, Mussolini had become such a powerful figure that when he threatened to march on Rome, the king panicked and appointed him prime minister.

Strikes and riots had plagued Italy since World War I. Mussolini and the Fascists vowed to end Italy's economic problems. In the name of efficiency and order, they suspended elections, outlawed all other political parties, and established a dictatorship.

Italy's ailing economy improved under *Il Duce*'s firm command. Other European nations noted his success with the Italian economy and applauded him as a miracle worker. They would soon choke on their words of praise, however, for Mussolini had dreams of forging a new Roman Empire. A Fascist slogan summed up Mussolini's expansionist goals: "The Country Is Nothing Without Conquest."

In October 1935, Mussolini put those words into practice by invading the independent African kingdom of Ethiopia. The Ethiopians resisted fiercely, but the large Italian army, using warplanes and poison gas, overpowered the Ethiopian forces. By May 1936, Ethiopia's emperor had fled to England and the capital, Addis Ababa, was in Italian hands.

VIEWING HISTORY This poster announced, "Italy finally has its empire," after the conquest of Ethiopia. The letters *A.O.* are the Italian abbreviation for East Africa—the site of Mussolini's empire. **Drawing Inferences** *How does this poster glorify Mussolini?*

Hitler's Rise to Power

While Mussolini was gaining control in Italy, a discontented Austrian painter was rising to prominence in Germany. Like Mussolini, Adolf Hitler had been wounded while serving in World War I. He, too, felt enraged by the terms of the peace settlement, which stripped Germany of land and colonies and imposed a huge burden of debt to pay for the damage done to France, Belgium, and Britain. He especially hated the war-guilt clause—the section of the Versailles Treaty that forced Germany to accept the blame for starting the war.

The Nazi Party In 1919, Hitler joined a small political group that became the National Socialist German Workers' Party, or Nazi Party. The philosophy and policies of this party came to be called **Nazism.** Nazism was a form of fascism shaped by Hitler's fanatical ideas about German nationalism and racial superiority.

Hitler's powerful public-speaking abilities quickly made him a leader of his party. The Nazis held mass meetings at which Hitler spoke passionately against Germany's national humiliation. One such meeting in 1921 drew more than 8,000 people. Nazi posters helped to boost attendance:

> "*White collar and manual workers of our people, you alone have to suffer the consequences of this unheard-of treaty. Come and protest against Germany being burdened with the war guilt. Protest against the peace treaty of Versailles which has been forced upon us. . . .*"
>
> —Nazi poster, Munich, Germany, March 1921

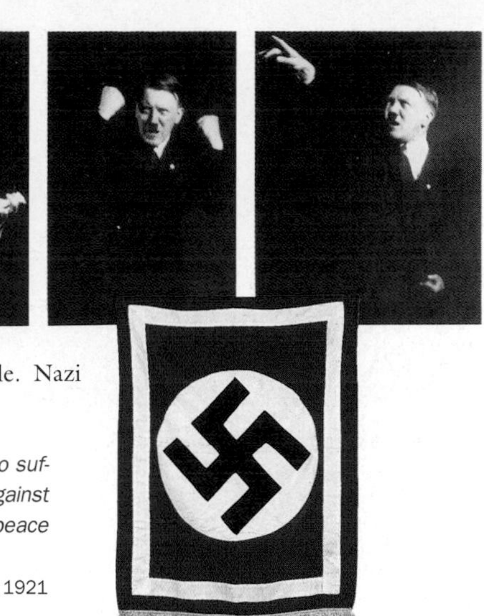

Adolf Hitler spoke with a charismatic passion that helped him expand the reach of the Nazi Party. The party's symbol, the swastika, is shown here.

In November 1923, with some 3,000 followers, Hitler tried to overthrow the German government. Authorities easily crushed the uprising. Although a German court sentenced Hitler to five years in prison, he spent only nine months in confinement.

While in prison, Hitler began writing an autobiography, *Mein Kampf* ("My Struggle"). In it Hitler outlined the Nazi philosophy, his views of Germany's problems, and his plans for the nation. According to *Mein Kampf,* Germany had been weakened by certain groups that lived within its borders. In particular, Hitler bitterly criticized the nation's Jewish population, which he blamed for Germany's defeat in World War I.

In *Mein Kampf,* Hitler proposed, in defiance of the Versailles Treaty, strengthening Germany's military and expanding its borders to include Germans living in other countries. He also called for purifying the so-called "Aryan race" (blond, blue-eyed Germans) by removing from Germany those groups he considered undesirable. In time, removal came to mean the mass murder of millions of Jews and other peoples.

After Germany's economy recovered from an inflationary crisis in the mid-1920s, the Great Depression hit in the early 1930s. The German people, facing more poverty, looked to their political leaders for help. In response, Hitler and the Nazis promised to stabilize the country, rebuild the economy, and restore the empire that had been lost.

Hitler Becomes Chancellor Hitler's promises gradually won him a large following. In the 1930 elections, the Nazi Party became the largest group in the *Reichstag* (the lower house of the German parliament). In 1932, Hitler placed second to Paul von Hindenburg, a general in World War I, in the presidential election. In January 1933, the elderly President Hindenburg made Hitler chancellor, or head of the German government.

Hitler soon moved to suspend freedom of speech and freedom of the press. Thousands of Nazi thugs, called storm troopers or Brownshirts, waged a violent campaign that silenced those opposed to Hitler's policies. In the March elections, the Nazis gained enough seats to

Focus on CULTURE

The Berlin Olympics Hitler used the 1936 Olympic Games, hosted by Berlin, to spotlight his theory of the racial superiority of "Aryan" Germans. To link the Nazi regime with the heritage of ancient Greece, Hitler introduced the custom of carrying a torch from the birthplace of the Olympics to the modern games.

Hitler hoped that German athletes would sweep the competition and awe the world. Instead, an African American runner, Jesse Owens, won four gold medals, as well as the support of the crowd.

ACTIVITY
Connecting with Government

Have half the class create flow charts showing the process by which Mussolini came to power in Italy. Have the other half chart Hitler's rise in Germany. Then pair students from each half to compare their flow charts and find similarities and differences in how these two leaders gained control of their nations. Call on pairs to report their findings to the class. **(Visual/Spatial)**

BACKGROUND
Global Connections

The swastika, a hooked cross with arms facing in a clockwise-rotating direction, is an ancient symbol with cultural significance in many parts of the world. Its name derives from the Sanskrit word *svastika,* which means "conducive to well-being." The swastika denoted good fortune and appeared on ancient Mesopotamian coins, as well as in early Christian and Byzantine art. It was also present in Mayan and other pre-Columbian cultures in the Americas. In India, Hindus continue to use the swastika today to mark doorways and the opening pages of account books. To Buddhists it symbolizes the footprints of the Buddha, and Tibetan Buddhists use it as a clothing decoration. In 1910 German poet Guido von List, mistakenly believing the swastika to be Teutonic in origin, suggested it as an anti-Semitic symbol. The Nazi party adopted it in 1919.

VIEWING HISTORY Germany's democratically elected assembly, the *Reichstag*, gave Hitler dictatorial powers in March 1933. **Drawing Conclusions** *What does this photograph indicate about the* Reichstag*'s independence from Hitler?*

dominate the *Reichstag*. Less than three weeks later, the *Reichstag* building burned down in a suspicious fire. Hitler blamed the Communists and used the disaster to convince the parliament to pass an Enabling Bill which gave him dictatorial powers. When Hindenburg died in August 1934, Hitler became both chancellor and president. He gave himself the title *Der Führer* ("the leader").

Germany Rearms Determined to put Germans to work while restoring Germany's military might, the Nazis secretly began spending money on rearming and expanding the armed forces in violation of the Versailles Treaty. They also hired unemployed workers to build massive public buildings and a network of highways known as the *autobahn*. Unemployment fell to near zero, industry prospered, and, by 1936, the Depression had ended in Germany. In addition, the Nazis were now in a position to put Hitler's expansion plans into action.

Like Mussolini, Hitler saw expansion as a way to bolster national pride. He also longed to see Germany return to a dominant position in the world. To do this, he believed, Germans needed more territory, or what he called *lebensraum* ("living space"), to the east. Hitler's main goal, therefore, became the conquest of eastern Europe and the Soviet Union. First, he needed to assert German military power within Germany's own borders.

On March 7, 1936, German troops entered the Rhineland, a region in western Germany. The Versailles Treaty had expressly banned German military forces from this region, which Germany had used as a base for the 1914 attack on France and Belgium. Since the Allies had taken no action in 1935 when Hitler revealed Germany's illegal rearmament, he had reason to believe that the Allies would not enforce the treaty.

MAP SKILLS Germany annexed Austria and dismembered Czechoslovakia without triggering a war. **Place** *What advantage did Germany gain by stationing troops in the Rhineland?*

ACTIVITY
Connecting with History and Conflict

Organize students into small groups. Ask them to speculate how history would have been affected if Britain and France had resisted Germany's militarization of the Rhineland in 1936. Have a spokesperson from each group summarize its discussion for the class. Then springboard from the groups' conclusions to a general class discussion of the value of appeasement as an instrument of foreign policy. **(Logical/Mathematical)**

BACKGROUND
Biography

Jesse Owens (1913–1980), the tenth child of African American sharecroppers in the South, gave an outstanding performance at the 1936 Olympic Games in Berlin, Germany. The Nazi dictator Adolf Hitler expected the Games to showcase German athletes' superiority since he believed that the Nazis were destined to rule "non-Aryan," or inferior, peoples. Before the eyes of the world, Owens proved Hitler wrong by winning four gold medals in track and field events. After the Games, Owens said, "[I] learned that the false leaders and sick movements of this earth must be stopped in the beginning, for they turn humanity against itself."

CAPTION ANSWERS

Viewing History The swastikas on the banners and the eagle sculpture illustrate the Nazi Party's total control of the Reichstag.

Map Skills With troops in the Rhineland, Hitler could threaten Belgium and France with invasion more easily. This event also convinced Hitler that Britain and France would acquiesce to additional German territorial demands.

RESOURCE DIRECTORY

Other Print Resources

Historical Outline Map Book *Aggression in Europe*, p. 64

Technology

Exploring Primary Sources in U.S. History CD-ROM *Berlin Diary, William Shirer*

Still, Hitler took an enormous gamble in remilitarizing the Rhineland. The German army was not ready for war. However, neither Britain nor France chose to react to this blatant violation of the Versailles Treaty. The British and French had not forgotten the awful costs of World War I, and their leaders were reluctant to challenge Hitler.

Also in 1936, Hitler signed an alliance with the Italian dictator, Mussolini. Their agreement created what Mussolini called an "axis" between Rome and Berlin, the capitals of the two nations. Germany and Italy, joined later by Japan, became known as the **Axis Powers.**

Germany Expands Two years later, the German Army was much stronger. Hitler began to press his homeland of Austria for *Anschluss,* or political union with Germany. In March 1938, after Austria's chancellor refused to surrender his country to Germany, Hitler ordered German troops into the country. Most Austrians warmly welcomed the Nazis, who were often presented with flowers by cheering crowds. When Britain and France protested the German actions, Hitler replied that the affair concerned only the German people.

VIEWING HISTORY Upon his return to London from Munich in September 1938, Neville Chamberlain showed crowds the agreement that promised "peace in our time." **Drawing Conclusions** *Why did Chamberlain sign the Munich Agreement?*

Several months later, Hitler demanded the Sudetenland, an industrial region of western Czechoslovakia with a heavily German population and many fortifications crucial to Czechoslovakia's defense. Neville Chamberlain, the British prime minister, met with Hitler twice to try to resolve the issue. Chamberlain pursued a policy of **appeasement,** or giving in to a competitor's demands in order to keep the peace. Hitler kept increasing his demands, so Chamberlain and the French president, Édouard Daladier, met with Hitler and Mussolini in Munich, Germany, in September 1938.

Because Britain and France were unprepared for a conflict, they agreed to sacrifice the Sudetenland, in the hopes that Hitler's appetite for territory would be satisfied. Although France was bound by treaty to defend Czechoslovakia, Daladier and Chamberlain agreed to let Hitler annex the Sudetenland on his own terms. No one consulted Czechoslovakia's leaders. British crowds cheered Chamberlain upon his return home for achieving what he called "peace for our time."

The Spanish Civil War

While Britain and France struggled to maintain peace with Germany, civil war was raging in Spain. Spain's democratic government held what would be the country's last free elections under the old republic in February 1936.

Numerous political parties vied for power, including small Fascist and Communist organizations. In this atmosphere, labor strikes, assassinations, and street battles became commonplace.

A group backed by liberal parties won, and five months later the military began a rebellion against the newly elected government, whose supporters were called the Republicans. General Francisco Franco led the rebels, who became known as the Nationalists. By October, the Nationalists had formed their own government, a military dictatorship under the rule of Franco.

The uprising turned into a fierce civil war between the Nationalists and the Republicans. Both sides turned to foreign powers for help. Germany and Italy provided planes, tanks, and soldiers to the Nationalists. Their aid attracted international attention in 1937 when Hitler's Condor Legion

German bombers left the Spanish city of Guernica in ruins.

ACTIVITY
Connecting with Culture

Invite students to imagine that they are Sudetenlanders on October 5, 1938, as German troops march into their town. Have them write diary entries to record their feelings on that day about Czechoslovakia, Germany, Hitler, and appeasement. Remind students that not all the region's residents were ethnic Germans, and that not all favored annexation by Germany. Call on volunteers to share their diary entries with the class. **(Verbal/Linguistic)**

BACKGROUND
Biography

Britain's King Edward VIII, who abdicated the throne in 1936 to marry divorcée Wallis Warfield Simpson, played an awkward role in British-German relations of the late 1930s. Honored by Nazi officials, Edward, now the Duke of Windsor, met with Adolf Hitler, to the consternation of many Britons. He was estranged from the royal family, even after the onset of World War II, when he accepted a position as a liaison officer with the French. After the conquest of France by Germany, he was approached with a Nazi plan to reinstate him as King of England. He rejected this plan and sat out the war in Bermuda.

TEST PREPARATION

Have students review the section "Germany Expands," and then answer the question below.

What is meant by a "policy of appeasement"?

A Fighting an enemy by all means.
B Finding ways to please an ally.
Ⓒ Giving in to the demands of an enemy in an effort to maintain peace.
D Attacking an enemy to achieve peace.

CAPTION ANSWERS

Viewing History He believed that giving in to Hitler's demands would prevent war.

Section 1 Assessment

Reading Comprehension

1. (a) In an attempt to modernize agriculture and other industries, he created a system of collective farming and poured money into other basic industries, turning the Soviet Union into a modern industrial power.
   (b) Stalin confiscated land of resistant farmers and sent peasants to distant labor camps, causing food shortages and the need for rationing.
2. At the onset of the Great Depression, Hitler and the Nazis promised to stabilize the country, rebuild the economy, and restore the empire that had been lost. Through these promises, he gained the support of many Germans.
3. Still feeling the aftermath of World War I, neither country was prepared for war; they desired peace.
4. Both Spanish Nationalists and Republicans sought help from foreign powers. Germany and Italy provided support to the Nationalists; the Soviet Union supported the Republicans; Britain, France, and the United States did not intervene, but people came from many countries, including the U.S., to aid the Republicans.

Critical Thinking and Writing

5. (a) Totalitarian leaders felt free to act against other nations, or against domestic opponents. (b) Democratic nations were reluctant to use force.
6. Sample answer: 1933–Hitler became chancellor; 1935–Hitler admitted that Germany was rearming; 1936–German troops entered the Rhineland, Hitler signed an alliance with Mussolini, 1938–Britain and France sacrifice the Sudentenland, Hitler takes over Austria.

Take It to the NET

Editorials should mention concern about German aggression and note that most Americans felt that European conflicts did not concern the United States.

Caption Answers

Viewing Fine Art Answers will vary, but may mention that the painting includes more elements of human suffering than does the photograph.

VIEWING FINE ART Spanish artist Pablo Picasso painted *Guernica* to convey the horrors of the Spanish Civil War to a world audience. **Making Comparisons** *Which do you think illustrates the raid more effectively,* Guernica *or the photograph on the previous page? Explain.*

bombed the northern Spanish town of Guernica into ruins. Attacking on a market day, German pilots incinerated the town center and fired on civilians from the air. One person, watching the attack from nearby hills, described it as "a preview of the end of the world." In fact, the attack was a preview of the destruction that would strike hundreds of cities in Britain, Germany, Poland, and other countries a few years later.

The Soviet Union sent arms and supplies to the Republicans. Although Britain, France, and the United States did not intervene, some 40,000 foreigners volunteered to fight for the Republicans as part of the International Brigades. Mostly young and many of them Communist, the soldiers of the International Brigades came from about 50 countries, including the United States.

In March 1939, the Nationalist army finally took the Spanish capital of Madrid and ended the civil war. Franco kept firm control of the government after the war and ruled Spain until his death in 1975.

Section 1 Assessment

READING COMPREHENSION

1. (a) How did Stalin change the Soviet economy? (b) How did he change the lives of the Soviet people?
2. Why did many Germans support Hitler and **Nazism** in the early 1930s?
3. Why did Britain and France pursue a policy of **appeasement** with Hitler?
4. How did the Spanish Civil War highlight divisions in Europe?

CRITICAL THINKING AND WRITING

5. **Making Comparisons** (a) How did leaders of totalitarian states feel about using force against people and nations they considered their enemies? (b) How did that compare with how leaders of democratic countries such as Britain and France felt about using force against other nations?
6. **Creating a Time Line** Create a time line of important events in Germany in the 1930s.

Take It to the NET

Activity: Writing an Editorial
Take notes on the reaction to German aggression in Europe, particularly following the Munich Conference. Write an editorial for an American newspaper reacting to the events you've studied. Use the links provided in the *America: Pathways to the Present* area of the following Web site for help in completing this activity.
www.phschool.com

RESOURCE DIRECTORY

Teaching Resources
Units 5/6/7 booklet
- Section 1 Quiz, p. 4

Guide to the Essentials
- Section 1 Summary, p. 81

Biography, Literature, and Comparing Primary Sources booklet (Biography) *Winston Churchill,* p. 29

Technology
Color Transparencies *Historical Maps,* A36, A37

Section 2

Europe Goes to War

READING FOCUS

- How did the German invasion of Poland lead to war with Britain and France?
- What wartime victories and setbacks did Germany experience in western Europe?
- Why was the Battle of Britain an important victory for Britain?

KEY TERMS

blitzkrieg
collaboration
Resistance
Allies

TAKING NOTES

As you read, prepare an outline of this section. Use Roman numerals to indicate the major headings of the section, capital letters for the subheadings, and numbers for the supporting details.

I. Invasion of Poland
A. Hitler invades Czechoslovakia.
B. Stalin and Hitler agree to divide Eastern Europe between them.
C. German *blitzkrieg* attack overwhelms Poland in three weeks.
II. War in the West

MAIN IDEA

After war began in September 1939, Germany easily conquered Poland, France, and several smaller countries, but Britain successfully defended itself against German air attacks.

Setting the Scene Neville Chamberlain's triumphant return from the Munich Conference in 1938 did not cheer everyone. Winston Churchill, a member of the British Parliament, believed that sacrificing part of Czechoslovakia to preserve peace was a fatal mistake. He made a dire prediction about this choice: "Britain and France had to choose between war and dishonor," Churchill said. "They chose dishonor. They will have war."

Churchill thought that Hitler had no intention of stopping his military machine and that Chamberlain's peace agreement would give Britain only a few more months of peace. He and other members of Parliament urged Chamberlain to reconsider Britain's policy toward Germany. Alfred Duff Cooper, the head of the British navy, chose to resign rather than accept that policy. In his resignation speech to Parliament, he insisted that Hitler had to be confronted with British might, not appeased:

> "*That is the deep difference between the Prime Minister and myself throughout these days. The Prime Minister has believed in addressing Herr Hitler through the language of sweet reasonableness. I have believed that he was more open to the language of the mailed [armored] fist.*"
>
> —Alfred Duff Cooper, First Lord of the Admiralty, 1938

Winston Churchill succeeded Neville Chamberlain as prime minister in May 1940.

Hitler had promised that the Sudetenland was all he wanted. But in March 1939, only six months after annexing the Sudetenland, Hitler occupied the western half of Czechoslovakia and divided the rest of the country among his allies. Most Czechs were hostile to Hitler and bitterly opposed to the German occupation. The following month, Italian forces invaded and occupied Albania, a nation on the Balkan Peninsula north of Greece. Although no shots had been fired, peace in Central Europe was rapidly breaking down.

Section 2
Europe Goes to War

Section Objectives

1. Understand how the German invasion of Poland led to war with Britain and France.
2. See what wartime victories and setbacks Germany experienced in western Europe.
3. Find out why the Battle of Britain was an important victory for Britain.

Bellringer

Warm-Up Activity Germany's initial forays in World War II were vastly successful, largely thanks to the form of attack they pioneered, called *blitzkrieg* ("lightning war"), which combined air and land attacks plus the element of surprise. This approach resulted in rapid victories in Poland, the Netherlands, Luxembourg, Belgium, and France. What types of tactical advantages did these early victories give Germany?

Activating Prior Knowledge In war, opposing sides often benefit from new techniques and approaches. *Blitzkrieg* was the new technique applied by the Germans in World War II. What are some techniques students recall from their reading that were pioneered in the Civil War and World War I?

Reading Strategy

Ask students to rewrite the Main Idea of this section as a question. As they read the section, have them write down answers to their question.

RESOURCE DIRECTORY

Teaching Resources
Learning Styles Lesson Plans booklet, p. 51
Guided Reading and Review booklet, p. 97
Biography, Literature, and Comparing Primary Sources booklet (Comparing Primary Sources) *On Arming Europe,* p. 143

Technology
Section Reading Support Transparencies
Guided Reading Audiotapes (English/Spanish), Ch. 17
Student Edition on Audio CD, Ch. 17
Sounds of an Era Audio CD *Winston Churchill,* 1940 recording (time: 15 seconds)
Prentice Hall Presentation Pro CD-ROM, Ch. 17
Companion Web site, www.phschool.com

Lesson Plan

Focus Germany's momentum afforded the country an early advantage. Yet forces in Britain were determined to beat back the enemy. What advantages did Britain have over Germany as the Battle of Britain was waged?

Instruct Discuss with students how Hitler combined military and strategic advances to gain momentum at the beginning of the war. In what ways did he catch others in Europe by surprise? Was his early onslaught inevitable, or could it have been prevented? In retrospect, how did Chamberlain's policy of appeasement wind up affording Hitler an advantage?

Assess/Reteach Have students create a time line of major events in the first years of World War II. Have them suggest an answer to this question: By the end of 1941, which country held the advantage?

Activity

Connecting with Citizenship

Have students create political cartoons about appeasement and the results of the Munich Conference. Tell them that their cartoons can either support or oppose Chamberlain's action at Munich, but should express a point of view from 1938—in other words, without taking into account what students know about subsequent events. Select cartoons for interpretation by the class. **(Visual/Spatial)**

READING CHECK

Britain and France had promised to help Poland in the case of a German attack. However, the invasion of Poland was so rapid that Poland was devoured by Germany and Russia before Britain and France could offer the Poles any substantive assistance.

Caption Answers

Interpreting Political Cartoons It implies that the terms of the pact will not last long.

Invasion of Poland

The March invasion of Czechoslovakia ended Chamberlain's hope of working peacefully with Hitler. Britain and France abandoned their policy of appeasement and prepared for war. After Hitler took Czechoslovakia, British and French leaders warned him that any further German expansion would risk war. On March 31, 1939, they formally pledged their support to Poland, agreeing to come to its aid if Germany invaded. By now, however, Hitler did not believe their warning.

Hitler did have one major concern. As in 1914, Germany could ill afford to fight a war on two fronts at the same time. Hitler wanted to deal with Britain and France, his foes to the west, without having to fear an attack from the east.

Hitler's Pact With Stalin Nazi Germany and the Soviet Union had been sworn enemies, but Hitler and Stalin recognized that they had much to gain by working together. Stalin refused to believe that Hitler's long-term plans included conquering the Soviet Union. In August, he and Hitler signed a ten-year Nonaggression Pact, which eliminated the danger of a Soviet invasion from the east.

A secret document attached to the pact divided up the independent states of eastern Europe between Germany and the Soviet Union. One week later, on September 1, 1939, Hitler invaded Poland. On September 3, Britain and France declared war on Germany.

WONDER HOW LONG THE HONEYMOON WILL LAST?

INTERPRETING POLITICAL CARTOONS The unlikely alliance between Nazi Germany and the Communist Soviet Union stunned western observers. **Drawing Inferences** *What does the caption imply about the Nonaggression Pact?*

Lightning War Britain, France, and Poland together made an impressive alliance, at least on paper. They had more soldiers and more infantry divisions than Germany. Each German division, however, had superior firepower—more machine guns, artillery, and other weapons. Germany also boasted six panzer, or armored, divisions organized around more than 2,000 tanks.

In addition, the Germans practiced a new form of attack that they unveiled in the invasion of Poland. Called ***blitzkrieg*** ("lightning war"), this new military tactic included a fast, concentrated air and land attack that took the enemy's army by surprise. The German *stuka,* a divebombing warplane, began the *blitzkrieg* by shattering defenses and terrorizing civilians. Then the tanks and mobile artillery of the panzer divisions punched through enemy lines, encircling and capturing opposing troops. Finally, the infantry moved in to defeat the enemy and occupy the country.

Using the *blitzkrieg* tactic, German troops overran Poland in less than a month. Britain and France watched helplessly from hundreds of miles away, unable to aid Poland in time. Meanwhile, in mid-September, Soviet forces joined the German attack. Under the secret terms of his Nonaggression Pact with Hitler, Stalin seized eastern Poland for the Soviet Union.

War in the West

After Poland fell, the war entered a quiet period. The British and French held back their troops, fearing tremendous losses. The American press dubbed this lack of combat the "phony war." The Germans labeled the lull in fighting the *sitzkrieg* ("sit-down war"). For the next several months, German troops sat and waited while French forces held their defenses.

READING CHECK
How did Britain and France react to the fall of Poland?

The key to these defenses was the Maginot Line, a massive string of fortifications along France's border with Germany. A triumph of modern technology, the Maginot Line provided housing for troops, recreational areas, and even air

RESOURCE DIRECTORY

Other Print Resources

Historical Outline Map Book *World War II in Europe and North Africa,* p. 65

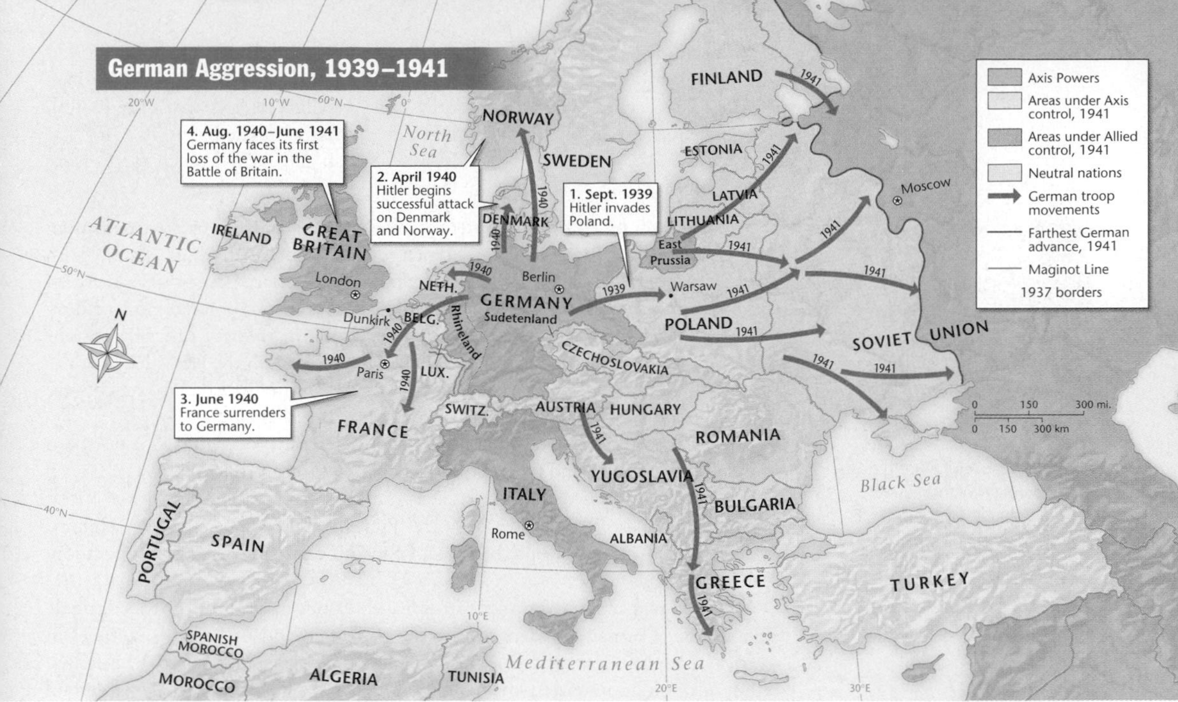

conditioning. Underground rail lines connected its main sections. Thick concrete walls and extra-heavy artillery stood ready to fend off any invading army. The Maginot Line had two major problems, however. It protected only the part of the French border that faced Germany, leaving France open to an attack through Belgium. In addition, all of its heavy guns pointed east, toward Germany. If the Germans got around the line, those guns would be useless.

Germany Attacks On April 9, 1940, the phony war came to an end as Hitler began a successful attack on Denmark and Norway. Then, on May 10, German troops launched a *blitzkrieg* on the Netherlands, Belgium, and Luxembourg. Although British and French troops rushed to Belgium to defend their neighbor, they were too late. The German army overran Luxembourg in a day, the Netherlands in five days, and Belgium in less than three weeks. Meanwhile, in mid-May, German motorized divisions in Belgium invaded northern France, skirting the end of the Maginot Line. They raced from there all the way to the English Channel, splitting the main French armies to the south from the British and French troops in northern France and Belgium.

Dunkirk The German drive west divided British and French troops into two pockets, one in the north and one in the south. In the face of Germany's advance, French and British forces in the north retreated to the coastal city of Dunkirk. There, over a nine-day period in late May and early June, one of the greatest rescues in the history of warfare took place. While some troops fought to slow the advancing Germans, others hastily

MAP SKILLS Germany overran northern and western Europe in 1940, conquered Yugoslavia and Greece in the spring of 1941, and invaded the Soviet Union in June 1941. **Location** *How does this map illustrate the dire situation of the Allies in 1941?*

This 1940 British painting depicts the difficult circumstances surrounding the retreat from Dunkirk.

ACTIVITY
Connecting with Geography

Pair students to take the role of generals in the German military writing memos to Hitler. Each pair's memo should explain why German control of Austria, Czechoslovakia, Poland, Belgium, Denmark, or France is important to Hitler's goal of conquering all of Europe. Call on at least one pair for each country to read its memo to the class. **(Verbal/Linguistic)**

BACKGROUND
Recent Scholarship

World War II was the greatest military conflict ever known. In *A World at Arms: A Global History of World War II,* Gerhard L. Weinberg argues that this struggle was qualitatively different from World War I. While the first major war of the twentieth century brought unprecedented casualties and unveiled horrific new weapons, World War II was a struggle for the total reordering of the globe. It resulted in an Allied victory at last, but only after mobilizing huge numbers of soldiers and civilians and concluding in a series of titanic battles around the world.

CUSTOMIZE FOR ...
ESL

Photocopy a map of Europe, and ask students to use a pencil to shade in the countries conquered by Hitler by 1941.

TEST PREPARATION

Have students read the material on these pages under the heading "War in the West." Then ask them to complete the sentence below.

One main weakness of the Maginot Line was that—

A it did not have enough heavy artillery.
B it faced Belgium, rather than Germany.
C it was too far away from Germany.
(D) it only protected the part of the French border that faced Germany.

CAPTION ANSWERS

Map Skills By 1941 the Axis controlled most of continental Europe, and the invasion of the Soviet Union had nearly reached the capital, Moscow.

ACTIVITY
Connecting with History and Conflict

Have students work alone or in pairs to write a poem or rap that expresses the experiences or feelings of persons who lived through the Battle of Britain. Suggest that their compositions might be from the perspective of an attacking *Luftwaffe* pilot, an RAF defender, or a British soldier or civilian on the ground during an attack. Invite students to present their work to the class. **(Musical/Rhythmic)**

BACKGROUND
Technology

Britain's defense against German air raids was greatly aided by a new technology called radar, an acronym for Radio Detection and Ranging. World War I had demonstrated the military threat posed by aircraft. So in the 1930s, scientists in Europe, Russia, Japan, and the United States developed devices for finding distant objects from their reflection of high frequency sound waves the radars sent out. By 1939 the British had 18 radar stations operating as an early-warning air defense system. These stations could detect planes up to 185 miles away. This gave RAF fighters vital time during the Battle of Britain to get into the air before the attackers arrived. Radar also controlled the searchlights used with anti-aircraft guns, making ground-based fire more accurate during night-time raids, when airborne defenses were less effective.

Adolf Hitler posed before the Eiffel Tower during a victory tour of German-occupied Paris.

assembled a makeshift fleet consisting mainly of tugboats, yachts, and other small private craft. Braving merciless attacks by the *Luftwaffe* (the German air force), about 900 vessels carried some 340,000 soldiers across the English Channel to Great Britain. Although Dunkirk marked a retreat for the British, the remarkable boatlift saved British and some French forces from almost certain capture by the Germans.

The Fall of France Hitler's armies turned and swept south through France. On June 10, the French government abandoned Paris. With France's defeat only a matter of time, Italy declared war on France and Britain on the same day. On June 14, German troops entered Paris, and on June 22 France and its more than 1.5 million soldiers officially surrendered. Adolf Hitler himself traveled to France to join the armistice negotiations and to make a brief victory tour of Paris. The British and French were stunned by the speed of Germany's conquest of France.

According to the surrender terms, Germany occupied the northern three fifths of France and the entire Atlantic Coast southward to Spain. The French government supervised the unoccupied south from the vacation resort of Vichy, and this zone became known as Vichy France. Under General Henri-Philippe Pétain, Vichy France adopted a policy of **collaboration,** or close cooperation, with Germany.

Free France, a government-in-exile in London, continued the struggle against the German invaders from bases in Britain and in France's colonies in Africa. Led by General Charles de Gaulle, the Free French also backed the underground **Resistance** movement in France. The Resistance consisted of groups of French citizens whose activities ranged from distributing anti-German leaflets to sabotaging German operations in France.

Until the summer of 1940, Hitler had experienced nothing but success. German armies had conquered most of Western Europe. He seemed to be on the verge of destroying the **Allies,** the group of countries who opposed the Axis Powers. Eventually, the United States and the Soviet Union would join the Allies, but at that time Great Britain stood alone.

VIEWING HISTORY London's St. Paul's Cathedral survived the Battle of Britain while surrounding buildings were reduced to rubble. The cathedral became a powerful symbol of Britain's spirit of defiance. **Drawing Conclusions** *How did this spirit help defeat the* Luftwaffe*?*

The Battle of Britain

As France fell, Hitler amassed troops on the French coast. His next invasion target, Great Britain, lay just 20 miles away, across the English Channel. Winston Churchill, now Britain's prime minister, pledged that the British would defend their island at all costs:

> *"We shall fight on the beaches, we shall fight on the landing grounds, we shall fight in the fields and in the streets, we shall fight in the hills; we shall never surrender."*
>
> —Winston Churchill

Relentless Attack Britain's large and well-equipped navy stood between Hitler and England. To neutralize the British navy, Germany would have to control the air. Hitler turned to the *Luftwaffe* to destroy Britain's air defenses. In August 1940, he launched the greatest air assault the world had yet seen. This intense attack, called the Battle of Britain, would continue well into September. Day after day, as many as 1,000 planes rained bombs on Britain.

The 1923 Hague Draft Rules of Air Warfare prohibited attacks on civilians. At first, the Germans only targeted British ports, airfields, and radar installations. Later they attacked aircraft factories and oil storage tanks. In late August, a

CAPTION ANSWERS

Viewing History British civilians endured the bombs long enough for British pilots to defeat the *Luftwaffe*. The British refused to surrender.

RESOURCE DIRECTORY

Teaching Resources

Learning with Documents booklet (Visual Learning Activity) *Germans March at the Arc de Triomphe*, p. 63

Biography, Literature, and Comparing Primary Sources booklet (Literature) *This Was His Hour*, p. 72

Technology

Color Transparencies *Historical Maps,* A38

group of German bombers strayed off course and dropped their bombs on London. Two nights later, perhaps in retaliation, British planes bombed Berlin. A new, more deadly type of air war was about to begin.

In early September, Hitler ordered massive bombing raids on London and other cities to try to break the British people's will to resist. These attacks included firebombs, which carried a mix of chemicals that burned at a temperature high enough to set buildings on fire. The bombing of London, called the Blitz, would continue off and on until May 1941. The bombing of population centers, by both sides, would continue throughout the war.

Courageous Defense Britain's Royal Air Force (RAF), although greatly outnumbered, stoutly defended its homeland. In a typical raid, slow-moving German bombers, accompanied by speedy fighter planes, would cross the English Channel at a height of about 15,000 feet. RAF pilots in British Spitfires and Hurricanes dodged the German fighter planes while trying to shoot down the bombers. They inflicted heavy damage on the attackers, sometimes flying six or seven missions a day. Hundreds of RAF pilots died defending Britain, but German losses were higher. "Never in the field of human conflict was so much owed by so many to so few," said Churchill, praising the courageous resistance of the RAF.

The British people showed equal bravery. In December 1940, German bombing of London started some 1,500 fires, setting the center of the historic city ablaze. Despite massive losses, the British people kept their will to fight. By the end of 1941, when the German air raids ended, some 20,000 Londoners had been killed and more than 70,000 injured.

Besides courageous pilots and citizens, Britain had another advantage. By February 1940, scientists in Britain had cracked the code that Germany used for top-secret communications. By deciphering coded messages, the British military could get a general idea of Hitler's battle plans. They knew, for example, that Hitler would not invade Britain until the *Luftwaffe* established air superiority—which it never did.

Focus on DAILY LIFE

London in the Blitz Some Londoners sought nighttime shelter from the Blitz in the stations of London's Underground subway system. The authorities tried to discourage the practice for safety reasons, but they were overwhelmed by the number of people who hurried underground in advance of air raids. Eventually, London Transport allowed civilians to spend the night on the tracks and platforms and even provided special trains to supply them with coffee and snacks.

Section 2 Assessment

READING COMPREHENSION

1. How did relations between Britain and Germany change between the Munich Conference and the invasion of Poland?
2. What were three reasons why Germany was able to defeat Poland in less than a month?
3. What was the French policy of **collaboration** with Germany?
4. Why were aircraft crucial to Germany's planned invasion of Britain?

CRITICAL THINKING AND WRITING

5. **Identifying Alternatives** (a) Why did Britain and France choose not to attack Germany in 1939 and 1940? (b) What were the possible disadvantages of attacking Germany?
6. **Demonstrating Reasoned Judgment** Do you think bombing cities is a fair act of war? Explain your answer.
7. **Creating a Time Line** Construct a time line of important events in Europe in 1939 and 1940.

Take It to the NET

Virtual Field Trip The Maginot Line was designed to shield France from German aggression following World War I. Take a virtual tour of these historic fortifications and write a summary of what you learn on the journey. Use the links provided in the *America: Pathways to the Present* area of the following Web site for help in completing this activity.
www.phschool.com

Section 2 Assessment

Reading Comprehension

1. The invasion of Czechoslovakia ended Chamberlain's hope of working peaceably with Hitler. Britain abandoned its policy of appeasement and prepared for war.
2. Answers may include: use of *blitzkrieg* for the first time; more advanced military than Poland; France and Britain were unable to aid Poland in time; Soviet Union came to Germany's aid, and under the secret terms of the Nonaggression Pact, seized eastern Poland.
3. Answers will vary. Students may note that the policy of collaboration allowed southern France to remain temporarily free of German occupying troops.
4. To neutralize Britain's navy so that German troops could invade with some hope of success.

Critical Thinking and Writing

5. (a) They felt safe behind the Maginot Line. Also, Britain and France lacked enthusiasm for the war. (b) The risks consisted of defeat and high casualties.
6. Answers will vary, but should pertain to issues and events described in the section.
7. Time lines will vary and may include: Hitler's takeover of Czechoslovakia; invasion of Poland; Hitler's attacks against Denmark and Norway; the fall of France; Battle of Britain.

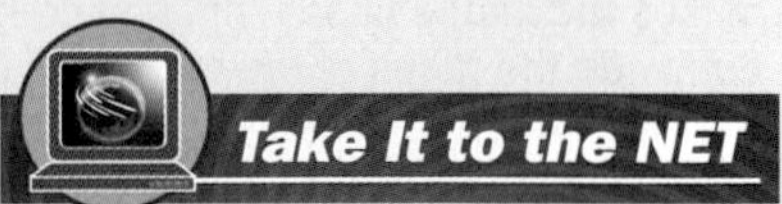

Invite students to take a Virtual Field Trip at **www.phschool.com**

RESOURCE DIRECTORY

Teaching Resources
Units 5/6/7 booklet
- Section 2 Quiz, p. 5

Guide to the Essentials
- Section 2 Summary, p. 82

Technology
Sounds of an Era Audio CD *Edward R. Murrow on the London Blitz,* 1940 recording (time: one minute)

Examining Photographs

Focus Analyze a photograph as historical evidence, taking into account the point of view of the photographer.

Instruct If possible, display collections of World War II photographs. Ask students to note the subjects, background, quality of light, and mood. Encourage them to try to determine the photographer's style or point of view. Discuss the importance of being able to analyze a photographer's point of view.

Extend See the Skills for Life activity in the Resource Directory below.

ANSWERS

Practice the Skill

1. **(a)** A group of soldiers watching other soldiers wading to their ship. **(b)** It tells when and where the photo was taken and explains why the soldiers are wading to the ship. **(c)** The soldiers are in very deep water and are struggling to reach the ship.
2. **(a)** Yes, the situation was desperate, and soldiers were willing to wade to the ships. **(b)** Answers will vary. Sample answer: a feeling of aloneness, of grim determination. **(c)** Answers will vary. Sample answers: there is open water on both sides of the wading men, making them look lost. The tilted angle makes the image unsettling, and you don't see the faces of the men on the ship. **(d)** Sample answers: the photographer may have chosen the angle of the photograph and to stand behind the men on the ship. **(e)** Answers will vary. Sample answer: the photographer might have taken a picture of one of the men being pulled into the ship, happy at being rescued, or a man on the ship shouting encouragement. A change in the camera angle would have made the image less unsettling.
3. **(a)** Answers will vary. **(b)** Answers will vary. Sample answer: photographs can convey the feeling and immediacy of an event in ways that aren't always possible in writing.

Examining Photographs

Photographs are a form of visual evidence that can provide valuable information about an event or a historical period. Photographers, however, like other observers of events, have their own points of view. By their choice of subject, lighting, and camera angle, photographers can influence what is seen and how it is perceived. They may also distort the appearance of objects in their photographs to create an illusion or to convey a particular mood. For these reasons, you should always analyze photographs carefully.

LEARN THE SKILL

Use the following steps to examine photographs:

1. **Study the photograph to identify the subject.** Look at the photograph as a whole; then study the details. If a title and a caption are provided, refer to them for more information.
2. **Analyze the reliability of the photograph as a source of information.** Note how the photograph conveys information and how it creates a mood or an emotion. Think about other ways the event or scene might have been photographed.
3. **Study the photograph to learn more about the historical period.** Think about how the photograph fits with what you already know. Consider what the photograph adds to your understanding of the historical period.

PRACTICE THE SKILL

Answer the following questions:

1. **(a)** What do you see in the picture? **(b)** How does the caption help you understand the photograph? **(c)** What visual details of the men in the water help you understand what happened at Dunkirk?
2. **(a)** Do you think the photograph depicts the situation accurately? Explain. **(b)** What mood or emotion do you think the photographer wanted viewers to feel? **(c)** What aspects of the photograph help to create this feeling? **(d)** What choices might the photographer have made before taking this picture? **(e)** What other choices (of subject or camera angle, for example) might the photographer have made to give a different impression of Dunkirk? Explain.
3. **(a)** Briefly summarize what you already know about the evacuation at Dunkirk. Does this photograph in any way contradict what you already know, or does it add to your understanding? Explain. **(b)** What can photographs like this contribute to your knowledge of an event that written sources cannot?

APPLY THE SKILL

See the Chapter Review and Assessment for another opportunity to apply this skill.

▲ Soldiers of the British Expeditionary Force wade to the safety of one of 900 vessels that evacuated Allied troops trapped on the beaches of Dunkirk, France, May 1940.

RESOURCE DIRECTORY

Teaching Resources
Skills for Life booklet, p. 26

Technology
Social Studies Skills Tutor CD-ROM
Interactive Practice in
- Geographic Literacy
- Critical Thinking and Reading
- Visual Analysis
- Communications

Section 3

Japan Builds an Empire

READING FOCUS

- What were the causes and effects of Japan's growing military power?
- Why was the Manchurian Incident a turning point for Japan's civilian government?
- What was the initial outcome of Japan's war against China?
- Why did Japan look beyond China for future expansion?

KEY TERMS

Manchurian Incident
puppet state
Burma Road
Greater East Asia Co-Prosperity Sphere

TAKING NOTES

Copy this flowchart. As you read this section, fill in the boxes with some of the major events that led to Japan's invasion of China in 1937.

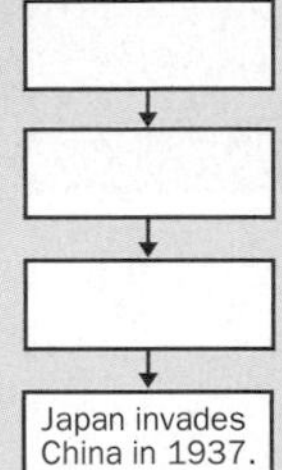

Japan invades China in 1937.

MAIN IDEA

The Japanese military expanded Japan's power into China and southeast Asia and came to dominate Japan's government.

Setting the Scene

Japan emerged from isolation in the mid-1800s. The United States forced Japan to open its markets to foreigners when Matthew Perry sailed into Tokyo Bay in 1853. That event pushed Japan to strengthen its military and modernize its economy in order to defend itself. Japan also developed a constitutional government, although the emperor remained a respected figure and the divine leader of the nation.

By engaging in wars against China (1894–1895) and Russia (1904–1905), Japan expanded its sphere of influence in East Asia. It took control of Korea and gained considerable influence over the northern Chinese province of Manchuria, where it stationed soldiers. By the eve of World War I, Japan had developed into the strongest nation in East Asia and one of the most powerful nations in the world.

VIEWING HISTORY The rising sun was the symbol of Imperial Japan. **Synthesizing Information** *Why was this an appropriate symbol for Japan in the early 1900s?*

Growing Military Power

During World War I, Japan joined the Allies. Although Japan played just a minor military role, it conquered several German possessions in the Pacific and won access to markets abandoned by the Europeans. As a result, Japan's economy prospered.

After the war, Japan enacted political reforms that resulted in a two-party parliamentary system and a sharp increase in the number of people allowed to vote. Japan also slowed its territorial expansion. It helped found the League of Nations and signed international agreements designed to keep the peace. By signing the 1928 Kellogg-Briand Pact, Japan condemned war and pledged to solve all disagreements peacefully. Japan would soon show how little influence such international peace agreements really had.

Democracy in Crisis In the early 1920s, a series of recessions rocked Japan's economy. As in Germany, conditions grew worse after 1930 because of the Great Depression. Japan's industries depended on selling their goods to foreign countries, but many of the nation's trading partners put high tariffs on Japanese goods to protect their own businesses. The resulting industrial decline led to

Section 3

Japan Builds an Empire

SECTION OBJECTIVES

1. Discover the causes and effects of Japan's growing military power.
2. See why the Manchurian Incident was a turning point for Japan's civil government.
3. Find out about the initial outcome of Japan's war against China.
4. Learn why Japan looked beyond China for future expansion.

BELLRINGER

Warm-Up Activity Though Japan sided with the Allies in World War I, during the 1920s and 1930s a series of economic and political crises changed the balance of power in Japan. Eventually, a more militaristic regime took control and launched an invasion of China. This action was a turning point in Japan's relationships with the rest of the world.

Activating Prior Knowledge Ask students to state what they know about Japan's role in world affairs prior to World War I. Were the Japanese primarily nationalist or internationalist in outlook at that time?

READING STRATEGY

Have students write down the main headings of this section. As they read, have them take notes about the contents under each heading. Then, have students write a brief sentence to summarize material under each of the headings.

CAPTION ANSWERS

Viewing History Japan was extending its military and economic reach across Asia and the Pacific.

RESOURCE DIRECTORY

Teaching Resources
Guided Reading and Review booklet, p. 98

Technology
Section Reading Support Transparencies
Guided Reading Audiotapes (English/Spanish), Ch. 17
Student Edition on Audio CD, Ch. 17
Prentice Hall Presentation Pro CD-ROM, Ch. 17
Companion Web site, www.phschool.com

Lesson Plan

Focus Japan was a very isolated nation in the 1930s, by choice. As militaristic Japanese leaders sought to increase Japanese territory, there was a very strong, negative global response. What was the response of the Japanese military leaders to this attempt to thwart Japanese nationalistic intentions?

Instruct Though Japan was never actually ruled by the military, this aspect of the government came to hold more and more control over decisions that were made. Ask students to discuss the impact of the increased efforts by Japan to dominate China. The response of the United States was to attempt to "quarantine" Japan. But there could be no further response from the United States because of a series of "neutrality acts." Ask students to speculate about what might have happened if these neutrality acts had not been in place.

Assess/Reteach What risk did the United States and other nations run by condemning Japanese actions in China? Could this risk have been avoided?

Activity

Connecting with History and Conflict

Invite students to create time lines comparing events related to Japan's rise in Asia with those associated with Germany's rise in Europe. Suggest to students that they plot German events on one side of their time line and Japanese events on the other. Then have students use information from their time lines to write a paragraph summarizing how the paths Germany and Japan followed were similar and how they differed. **(Visual/Spatial)**

Japanese troops in Manchuria

massive layoffs, strikes, and widespread political discontent. Many Japanese blamed the new multiparty system of government. Politicians, they believed, had taken too long to deal with the mounting economic problems. While economic conditions were worsening, some politicians had enriched themselves by taking bribes from the huge family-owned companies that dominated the economy.

The Japanese military, too, expressed dissatisfaction with democracy. At the Washington Conference in 1922, the Japanese government had accepted limits on the size of its navy. Later it had cut the strength of the army and prevented the military from challenging the Chinese troops in Manchuria.

Rise of Nationalism Several radical nationalist groups formed in response to the government's perceived weaknesses. They demanded a return to traditional ways and an end to multiparty rule, powerful businesses, and other Western-style institutions. Radicals assassinated several business and political leaders. By committing terrorism, they hoped to force the military to take over the government. Some members of the military, especially younger officers, supported the radicals.

The Manchurian Incident

Japan, located on a chain of volcanic islands, experienced a population explosion in the 1900s. By 1930, the population neared 65 million, and it was growing by about one million people per year. Japan lacked the land needed to feed its rising population and the raw materials and markets needed to power the Japanese economy. Many Japanese saw the acquisition of Manchuria as a solution to these problems, both for its coal and iron ore and for its immense areas of undeveloped land.

In September 1931, a Japanese army stationed in Manchuria took matters into its own hands. Claiming that Chinese soldiers had tried to blow up a railway line, they captured several cities in southern Manchuria. Chinese troops withdrew from the area. Japan's civilian government tried but failed to prevent the army from taking further action. By February 1932, the army had seized all of Manchuria. World leaders and most Japanese expressed shock at what came to be called the **Manchurian Incident.**

In response, Japan announced that Manchuria was now the independent state of Manchukuo, under Japanese protection. Japan installed a new head of state—P'u-I, China's last emperor from a Manchurian dynasty—with Japanese advisors to run the government. In fact, Manchukuo was a **puppet state,** or a supposedly independent country under the control of a powerful neighbor. Japan sent more than a million farmers, entrepreneurs, and soldiers with the goal of securing Manchuria as a Japanese colony.

The United States and Britain protested that Japan had broken the Kellogg-Briand Pact, but they did not act to halt Japan's aggression. The League of Nations ordered Japan to end its occupation of Manchuria. Japan refused and withdrew from the League instead.

The Manchurian Incident greatly increased the army's power over the government, but some radicals in the military wanted complete control. In 1932, naval officers helped assassinate the prime minister. Other military leaders did not support the assassins, but they used this opportunity to end the multiparty government, putting the parliamentary system itself in danger. In 1936, an uprising by junior military officers resulted in the murder of several high government officials. The uprising failed, but it gave the military even greater power. Civilian politicians began to

General Joseph Stilwell
1883–1946

One high-ranking American soldier witnessed Japan's aggression in China from a local perspective. A West Point graduate, Joe Stilwell served in the Philippines and France before returning to the United States where he learned Chinese. From 1926 to 1929 and 1932 to 1946, Stilwell lived in China, where he represented the United States Army and developed close ties to Jiang Jieshi. Stilwell rose from Jiang's chief of staff to commander of U.S. forces in China, Burma, and India. During World War II, he played an important role in defending South Asia from Japan and in keeping China's links to the West open.

Resource Directory

Other Print Resources

Historical Outline Map Book *World War II in the Pacific,* p. 66

Technology

Color Transparencies *Historical Maps,* A39

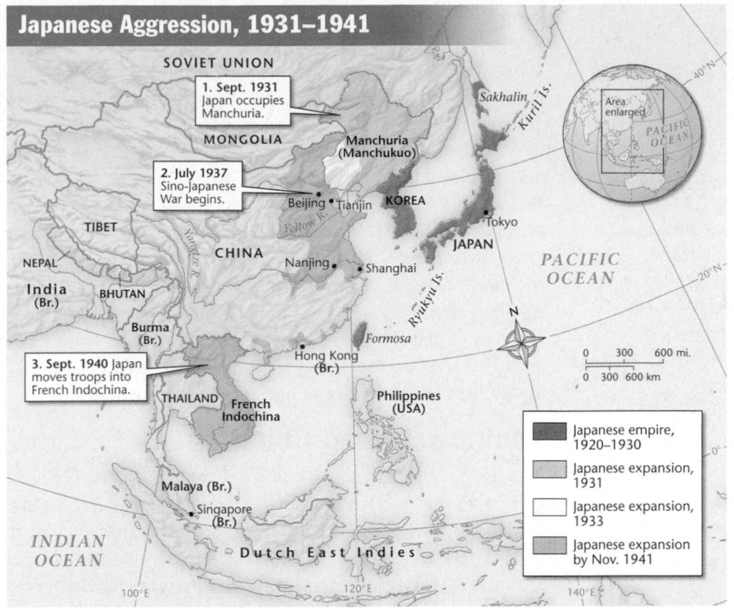

MAP SKILLS Japan's gradual expansion in Asia led to an outright war with China in 1937. **Location** *List three countries or colonial possessions that appeared to be likely targets of Japanese aggression in November 1941. Explain your reasoning.*

fear for their lives so much that they dared not criticize the military. The new prime minister said:

> *"The military are like an untamed horse left to run wild. If you try head-on to stop it, you'll get kicked to death. The only hope is to jump on from the side and try to get it under control while still allowing it to have its head to a certain extent."*
>
> —Hirota Koki

Japan's military leaders never actually seized control of the government. However, they took a much stronger hand in governing the nation, especially in the area of foreign policy. They began to develop Manchuria as a base for even further Japanese expansion in Asia.

War Against China

In July 1937, Japan resumed its invasion of China. The Japanese army turned a minor clash at the Marco Polo Bridge outside Beijing into a full-scale war. By the end of the month, Japanese forces occupied the major cities of Beijing and Tianjin and threatened the rest of northern China. The Chinese Nationalist army, led by General Jiang Jieshi (jyawng jeh SHEE), fiercely resisted the invasion. In battle after battle, however, Japan's superior weapons overcame China's huge manpower advantage. Japanese warplanes ruthlessly bombed Chinese cities. During the "Rape of Nanjing," Japanese soldiers brutalized or killed at least 100,000 civilians, including women and children, in the former capital of China.

READING CHECK How successful was Japan's 1937 invasion of China?

The United States and other nations condemned Japan's actions. President Roosevelt spoke out against international aggression, saying that "the epidemic of world lawlessness is spreading" and calling for a "quarantine" to protect peaceful nations. Meanwhile, Congress passed a series of Neutrality Acts that prevented the United States from becoming involved in foreign conflicts. The

ACTIVITY
Connecting with History and Conflict

Select students to represent Japan and China in presenting their case in the Manchurian Incident to the rest of the class. Then have the class, acting as the League of Nations, debate and evaluate actions it might take in response to the crisis. After a time, announce that Japan has withdrawn from the League. Have the class discuss how this development affects their ability to resolve the Manchuria issue. **(Logical/Mathematical)**

BACKGROUND
Global Connections

Korea became a Japanese protectorate in 1905 against the wishes of the Korean people, and then became part of the Japanese Empire in 1910 when its king was forced to abdicate. During World War II the Japanese converted Korea into what one historian has called "a slave labor camp under armed guard." Millions of Koreans were required to work, in Korea and elsewhere, to support the Japanese war effort. Korean men were drafted into Japan's army, and tens of thousands of Korean women were forced to serve as prostitutes for Japanese troops. Many Koreans were sent to work in Japan, making up nearly one-third of that nation's labor force by 1945. Some 25 percent of the casualties from the atomic bomb that U.S. forces dropped on Hiroshima in August 1945 were Koreans.

READING CHECK

It was initially successful, as the superior weapons and tactics of the Japanese consistently beat the Chinese. However, the Chinese received aid from the Soviet Union, the United States, and Great Britain. The Chinese Communists led a guerrilla campaign against the Japanese, whose offensive lost momentum. The conflict settled down to a stalemate.

CUSTOMIZE FOR ...
Less Proficient Readers

Ask students to describe what is meant by a "Puppet State." Have them define this type of government, using their own terms.

TEST PREPARATION

Ask students to review the quote by Hirota Koki on this page, and then complete the sentence below.

According to the quotation on this page, Hirota Koki would probably favor—

- **A** stopping them head on.
- **B** tricking the military leaders into thinking he is cooperating with them.
- Ⓒ controlling the military by giving them some of what they want.
- **D** avoiding the military, letting them go their own way.

CAPTION ANSWERS

Map Skills Possible answers include: the Dutch East Indies, because Japan needed oil and rubber; Thailand, Malaya, and Burma, because Japan had recently moved troops into nearby French Indochina; and the Philippines, because its American military bases lay near territory Japan's leaders wished to control, such as the Dutch East Indies.

Section 3 Assessment

Reading Comprehension

1. (a) A Japanese army stationed in Manchuria. (b) The Manchurian incident was launched by the Japanese Army on its own, not by the civilian government; whereas Germany's attack on Poland was launched by Hitler.
2. Though Japanese troops controlled the cities, Mao Zedong's Chinese guerrillas dominated the countryside, causing a stalemate.
3. (a) To liberate Asia from European colonizers. (b) Japan needed the region's natural resources to carry on its war against China.

Critical Thinking and Writing

4. Answers will vary somewhat, but should show an understanding of how the effects of a population boom in Japan led the Japanese to look overseas for resources and for land upon which to expand.
5. Paragraphs will vary, but should reflect an understanding of the growing power that the military began to wield in Japan's government during the 1930s, and the waning influence of Japanese civilian government officials at that time.

Entries should note that after the initial shock of the attack, most sailors tried to man battle stations and carry out their duties. The severity of the attacks should be conveyed through the amount of damage done and the number of casualties.

Fast Forward to Today

An American Partner in the Pacific

Since the 1930s and 1940s, when they competed for control of the Pacific, Japan and the United States have become important allies and trading partners. The two countries share concerns about aggressive moves by North Korea and China.

Japan had renounced war and had limited the use of its much-reduced military to defense purposes after World War II. In 1998, the Japanese government announced that Japan would offer noncombat support to American troops in "areas surrounding Japan." This bill upset many Japanese who were unwilling to send any troops overseas, even in noncombat roles, to avoid association with Japan's wartime past.

? Why did the United States and Japan come into conflict in the 1930s and 1940s?

Soviet Union also voiced its concern and backed up its words with arms, military advisors, and warplanes for China. Later, Britain sent a steady stream of supplies to the Chinese over the **Burma Road,** a 700-mile-long highway linking Burma (present-day Myanmar) to China.

The war brought two longtime enemies together. Jiang and Chinese Communist leader Mao Zedong, who were locked in a bitter struggle for power, put aside their differences to fight the Japanese. When direct resistance failed, Jiang withdrew his armies to the mountains of remote Sichuan province in the south. Mao split his army into small groups of soldiers who organized bands of Chinese guerrilla fighters to harass the Japanese. While Japanese troops controlled the cities, these guerrillas dominated the countryside. By 1939, the war in China had reached a stalemate.

Looking Beyond China

Meanwhile, the start of the war in Europe distracted European powers from the defense of their colonies in East Asia. Japanese leaders took this opportunity to expand their influence in the region to its south. In 1940, Japan's prime minister announced a **Greater East Asia Co-Prosperity Sphere** to be led by the Japanese, extending from Manchuria in the north to the Dutch East Indies in the south. Japan declared it would liberate Asia from European colonizers. In reality, Japan needed the region's natural resources, especially oil and rubber, to carry on its war against China. In this way, Japan's co-prosperity sphere resembled Hitler's invasion of other countries for *lebensraum* ("living space").

In September 1940, Japan allied itself with Germany and Italy through the Tripartite Pact. That same month, Japan moved troops into the northern part of French Indochina, with the reluctant permission of the Vichy government of France. With the Netherlands in German hands, Japan also set its sights on the oil-rich Dutch East Indies. Then, in April 1941, the Japanese signed a neutrality pact with the Soviet Union. The stage was now set for Japan to challenge the Europeans and Americans for supremacy in Asia.

Section 3 Assessment

READING COMPREHENSION

1. (a) Who among the Japanese was responsible for the conquest of Manchuria? (b) How was this invasion different from Germany's invasion of Poland?
2. Why was Japan unable to win the war in China?
3. (a) According to Japan, what was the purpose of the **Greater East Asia Co-Prosperity Sphere?** (b) What was Japan's real goal?

CRITICAL THINKING AND WRITING

4. **Drawing Conclusions** What do Japan's actions indicate about the way economic problems affect foreign policy? Cite evidence from your reading.
5. **Writing an Opinion** Read the quote from Hirota Koki. Write a paragraph defending or criticizing Hirota's response to the military's actions.

Take It to the NET

Activity: Writing a Newspaper Article The massacre at Nanjing was a terrible episode of World War II. Using eyewitness accounts and other primary sources, write a newspaper article on this topic. Use the links provided in the *America: Pathways to the Present* area of the following Web site for help in completing this activity.
www.phschool.com

Caption Answers

Fast Forward to Today America protested Japan's aggression against China in the 1930s. The United States government feared for the security of the Philippines, which was an American possession at that time. FDR cut off American oil exports to Japan in 1941 in response to the Japanese occupation of French Indochina. Amidst worsening U.S.–Japanese relations, Japan attacked the U.S. Pacific Fleet at Pearl Harbor, killing more than 2,000 Americans.

RESOURCE DIRECTORY

Teaching Resources

Units 5/6/7 booklet
- Section 3 Quiz, p. 6

Guide to the Essentials
- Section 3 Summary, p. 83

Section 4

From Isolationism to War

READING FOCUS

- Why did the United States choose neutrality in the 1930s?
- How did American involvement in the European conflict grow from 1939 to 1941?
- Why did Japan's attack on Pearl Harbor lead the United States to declare war?

KEY TERMS

Neutrality Acts
cash and carry
America First Committee
Lend-Lease Act

TAKING NOTES

As you read, complete this chart by listing reasons why people supported or opposed the involvement of the United States in the war.

Supported Involvement in the War	Opposed Involvement in the War
• Britain was defending American ideals of freedom and democracy. • The Axis Powers would eventually declare war on the United States. •	

MAIN IDEA

United States foreign policy changed slowly from neutrality to strong support for the Allies. Japan's surprise attack on Pearl Harbor immediately brought the United States into the war with the full support of the people.

Setting the Scene During the 1930s, the United States largely turned away from international affairs. Instead, the government focused its energies on solving the domestic problems brought about by the Great Depression. Even as Italy, Germany, and Japan threatened to shatter world peace, the United States clung to its policy of isolationism. The horrors of World War I still haunted many Americans who refused to be dragged into another foreign conflict. President Franklin Roosevelt assured Americans that he felt the same way:

> "*I have seen war. I have seen war on land and sea. I have seen blood running from the wounded. I have seen men coughing out their gassed lungs. I have seen the dead in the mud. I have seen cities destroyed. I have seen two hundred limping, exhausted men come out of line—the survivors of a regiment of one thousand that went forward forty-eight hours before. I have seen children starving. I have seen the agony of mothers and wives. I hate war.*"
>
> —Franklin D. Roosevelt, address at Chautauqua, New York, August 1936

VIEWING HISTORY Franklin Roosevelt used "fireside chats" to speak directly to Americans during the Depression and later as the United States drew closer to war.

Few people in the United States agreed with the actions or the ideas of the Fascists, the Nazis, or the Japanese radicals. Most Americans sympathized with the victims of aggression. Still, nothing short of a direct attack on the United States would propel Americans into another war.

The United States Chooses Neutrality

American isolationism increased in the early 1930s, although President Roosevelt, elected in 1932, favored more international involvement. The demands of carrying out the New Deal kept Roosevelt focused on domestic issues, however. He was more concerned with lifting the United States out of the Depression than with addressing foreign concerns.

Section 4
From Isolationism to War

SECTION OBJECTIVES

1. Find out why the United States chose neutrality in the 1930s.
2. See how American involvement in the European conflict grew from 1939 to 1941.
3. Discover why Japan's attack on Pearl Harbor led the United States to declare war.

BELLRINGER

Warm-Up Activity Ask students to choose a place in the world where there is currently armed conflict and to describe the involvement of the United States in that area, if any. Ask them to consider under what conditions the United States should intervene in a conflict between other nations.

Activating Prior Knowledge Ask students if they recall the word "isolationism" from the class study of World War I. Can they define it? What situations in the United States might cause the country to adopt an isolationist attitude in the years leading up to World War II?

READING STRATEGY

Have students create a concept map by drawing five large circles on a piece of paper and labeling each circle with a heading from the section. Have them add supporting information in smaller circles and draw lines connecting them to the large circles.

RESOURCE DIRECTORY

Teaching Resources
Guided Reading and Review booklet, p. 99

Technology
Section Reading Support Transparencies
Guided Reading Audiotapes (English/Spanish), Ch. 17
Student Edition on Audio CD, Ch. 17
Prentice Hall Presentation Pro CD-ROM, Ch. 17
Companion Web site, www.phschool.com

Lesson Plan

Focus Fascist dictators seized control in several nations scarred by World War I, while military leaders in Japan pursued a policy of expansion. Ask how the United States responded to the growing worldwide conflict, and what finally propelled the United States into the war.

Instruct Discuss why the United States was reluctant to enter the war. What were the events that overcame this reluctance?

Assess/Reteach Ask students how events at Pearl Harbor created the necessary momentum to propel the United States into the war in Europe.

Background

American Isolationism

American isolationism in the late 1930s had significant support. The America First Committee was not only vocal but also influential in gathering support from a cross-section of Americans against intervening in the war in Europe. Among the public figures who supported the America First Committee were former President Herbert Hoover; labor leader John L. Lewis; historian Charles Beard; architect Frank Lloyd Wright; chairman of Sears, Roebuck Robert Wood; and possibly the most famous American of his generation, Charles Lindbergh.

These Spring Days It's Hard to Keep Your Mind on Your Work!

INTERPRETING POLITICAL CARTOONS Domestic issues kept Congress and the President from focusing on the increasingly tense situation in Europe. **Predicting Consequences** *What did this cartoonist believe would happen if the United States did not act against Hitler and Mussolini?*

In 1930, Congress had passed the Hawley-Smoot tariff to protect American industries from foreign competitors. In response, other nations raised their tariff walls against American goods. Although they were reduced in 1934, these trade barriers prolonged the Depression and isolated the United States.

Congress again prevented international involvement by passing a series of **Neutrality Acts.** The first of these, in 1935, banned the United States from providing weapons to nations at war. The second, in 1936, banned loans to such nations. The third, in 1937, permitted trade with fighting nations in nonmilitary goods as long as those nations paid cash and transported the cargo themselves. This policy became known as **cash and carry.**

The Neutrality Acts prevented the United States from selling arms even to nations that were trying to defend themselves from aggression. By doing this, as FDR pointed out later, the Neutrality Acts encouraged aggression. By the end of 1938, Italy had conquered Ethiopia, Japan had invaded China, and Germany had taken Austria and the Sudetenland. The United States watched warily from a distance, protected by the Atlantic and Pacific oceans.

American Involvement Grows

As the decade wore on, the American economy recovered somewhat. Unemployment and business failures no longer required the nation's full attention. At the same time, Germany and Japan stepped up their aggression against neighboring countries. This combination of events softened Americans' isolationist views.

American opinion shifted even further against the Axis Powers in September 1939, when Germany invaded Poland. At that time, almost no one believed that America should enter the war against Germany. But many people felt that the United States shared Britain's interests, and given the constraints of neutrality, President Roosevelt began to look for ways to send more aid to the Allies.

Comparing Primary Sources

Assistance for Britain

After France fell and Britain stood alone against Germany, Americans debated whether to assist Britain and what form that assistance should take.

Analyzing Viewpoints Compare the statements of the two speakers.

Opposed to Aid

"When England asks us to enter this war, she is considering her own future, and that of her Empire. In making our reply, I believe we should consider the future of the United States and that of the Western Hemisphere. . . . I ask you to look at the map of Europe today and see if you can suggest any way in which we could win this war if we entered it. . . . If we concentrate on our own and build the strength that this nation should maintain, no foreign army will ever attempt to land on American shores."

—Charles Lindbergh, Address to the America First Committee, April 23, 1941

In Favor of Aid

"The Nazi masters of Germany have made it clear that they intend . . . to enslave the whole of Europe, and then to use the resources of Europe to dominate the rest of the world. . . . the Axis not merely admits but proclaims that there can be no ultimate peace between their philosophy of government and our philosophy of government. . . . [Britain is] putting up a fight which will live forever in the story of human gallantry."

—Franklin D. Roosevelt, Arsenal of Democracy speech, December 29, 1940

Caption Answers

Interpreting Political Cartoons The United States would not be safe from the effects of violence, as symbolized by the powder keg.

Resource Directory

Teaching Resources

Learning with Documents booklet (Primary Source Activity) *Einstein's Letter to FDR,* p. 29

Great Debates booklet (Great Debates) *How Much Should the United States Be Involved in World Affairs?* p. 20

Technology

Exploring Primary Sources in U.S. History CD-ROM *Lend Lease*

Debating the American Role Three weeks after the invasion of Poland, Roosevelt asked Congress to revise the Neutrality Acts to make them more flexible. Congress did so by repealing the arms embargo and providing Britain and France with the weapons they needed. A later amendment allowed American merchant ships to transport these purchases to Britain. The neutrality legislation was effectively dead.

In June 1940, France fell to the Germans, and Hitler prepared to invade Britain. France's rapid collapse shocked Americans, who had expected the Allies to defend themselves effectively against Germany. Now Britain stood alone against Hitler, and many Americans supported "all aid short of war" for Britain. Roosevelt successfully pressed Congress for more aid. On September 2, the United States agreed to send 50 old destroyers to Britain in return for permission to build bases on British territory in the Western Hemisphere. Some Americans saw this exchange as a dangerous step toward direct American military involvement. Two days after the trade, a group of isolationists formed the **America First Committee** to block further aid to Britain. At its height, this group attracted more than 800,000 members, including Charles Lindbergh.

During the presidential campaign of 1940, both Roosevelt and his Republican opponent, Wendell Willkie, supported giving aid to the Allies. They disagreed, however, on how much aid should be given and on what the aid should be. As election day approached, Willkie sharpened his attack, saying that if FDR won, he would plunge the nation into war. To counter this charge, FDR assured all parents: "Your boys are not going to be sent into any foreign wars." In reality, both men knew that war would be hard to avoid.

Lend-Lease In November 1940, Roosevelt won reelection to a third term as President. His easy victory encouraged him to push for greater American involvement in the Allied cause. To continue battling Germany, Britain needed American equipment. Britain, however, faced a financial crisis. Prime Minister Churchill, in a letter to FDR, confessed that his country was nearly bankrupt. "The moment approaches," he wrote in December, "when we shall no longer be able to pay cash for shipping and other supplies."

In December 1940, Roosevelt introduced a bold new plan to keep supplies flowing to Britain. He proposed providing war supplies to Britain without any payment in return. Roosevelt explained his policy to the American people by

READING CHECK
Why did Roosevelt press Congress for aid to Britain?

VIEWING HISTORY Members of the "Mothers' Crusade" knelt and prayed outside the Capitol to stop Congress from passing the Lend-Lease Act, Bill 1776. **Drawing Inferences** *How did these protesters hope to sway votes?*

ACTIVITY
Connecting with Government

Have students substantiate or refute these two explanations offered by historians as the reasons for American involvement in World War II: (a) Roosevelt saw the war as a way to end the economic depression in the United States. (b) Roosevelt knew that involvement in the war would guarantee the United States a key role in the postwar peace process. **(Logical/Mathematical; Verbal/Linguistic)**

BACKGROUND
Geography in History

The Axis occupation of Europe and North Africa made getting Lend-Lease supplies to the Soviets difficult and dangerous. Goods had to be transported north on the Arctic Ocean to the Barents Sea port of Murmansk, or south around Africa to present-day Iran and then by rail to the USSR. The long southern route maximized exposure to German submarines. (The southern route became much shorter and somewhat safer after the Mediterranean was reopened to Allied shipping in late 1943 in the wake of the defeat of Italy.) The northern route was hazardous because of the extreme weather. Arctic ice sometimes forced ships close to the coast of German-held Norway, where they came within range of air attack. Some Lend-Lease planes headed for Russia were flown across the Bering Strait from Alaska. Others flew in stages from the United States to Brazil, across the Atlantic to West Africa, across Africa to British-held Egypt, and finally north to the Soviet Union.

READING CHECK
With France and Poland already under Nazi control, Britain was the last remaining European power opposing the Nazis (until Hitler invaded the Soviet Union). In that situation, President Roosevelt's lobbying of Congress on behalf of aiding Britain was in keeping with the sentiments of many Americans.

CUSTOMIZE FOR ...
Less Proficient Writers
Have students read the quote on this page in which FDR justifies the Lend-Lease Act. Then ask them to rewrite his quote in their own words, to offer a similarly logical justification of the program.

TEST PREPARATION
Have students read the section "Lend-Lease" on this page and then answer the question below.

What did Roosevelt mean when he said that when your neighbor's house is on fire you lend, not sell, him a hose?

A America should charge Britain lower rates for supplies.
(B) America should send Britain what it needs in an emergency without payment.
C America should stay out of foreign problems.
D It was time for America to join the fight on Britain's side.

CAPTION ANSWERS

Viewing History The protestors used their roles as mothers to attack the aid bill as a threat to their sons' lives. By praying, they hoped to appeal to the lawmakers' religious beliefs by equating religion with pacifism.

the use of a simple comparison: If your neighbor's house is on fire, you don't sell him a hose. You lend it to him and take it back after the fire is out.

The America First Committee campaigned strongly against this new type of aid. Nevertheless, Congress passed the **Lend-Lease Act** in March 1941, authorizing the President to aid any nation whose defense he believed was vital to American security. FDR immediately began sending aid to Britain. After Germany attacked the Soviet Union, the United States extended lend-lease aid to the Soviets as well. By the end of the war, the United States had loaned or given away more than $49 billion worth of aid to some 40 nations.

Japan Attacks Pearl Harbor

Although Roosevelt focused his attention on Europe, he was aware of Japan's aggressive moves in the Pacific. In July 1940, Roosevelt began limiting what Japan could buy from the United States. In September, he ended sales of scrap iron and steel. He hoped to use the threat of further trade restrictions to stop Japan's expansion. A year later, however, Japanese forces took complete control of French Indochina. In response, Roosevelt froze Japanese financial assets in the United States. Then he cut off all oil shipments. As you have read, Japan desperately needed raw materials, and this embargo encouraged Japan to look to the lightly defended Dutch East Indies for new supplies of oil. For the next few months, leaders in the United States and Japan sought ways to avoid war with each other.

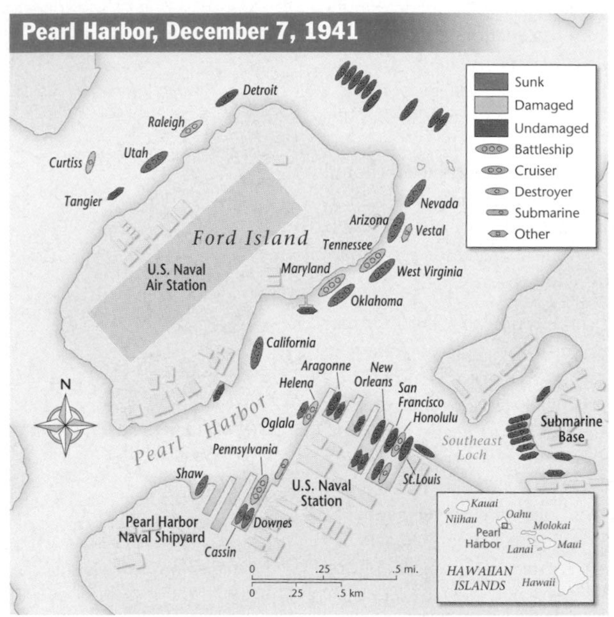

MAP SKILLS The Japanese attack on Pearl Harbor was surprising and swift. **Location** *Where did the Japanese inflict the most damage?*

Final Weeks of Peace While Japanese and American diplomats negotiated, a militant army officer took power in Japan. General Tojo Hideki, who supported war against the United States, became prime minister in October 1941. Yet Roosevelt still hoped for peace, and he continued negotiations.

More than a year earlier, American technicians had cracked a top-secret Japanese code. Knowing this code allowed them to read intercepted diplomatic messages. By November 27, based on decoded messages, American military leaders knew that Japanese aircraft carriers were on the move in the Pacific. They expected an attack, but they did not know where.

Indeed, a Japanese fleet of 6 aircraft carriers and more than 20 other ships was already on the move. Its target was Pearl Harbor, the naval base on the Hawaiian island of Oahu that served as the home of the U.S. Pacific Fleet. Japan's leaders had gambled that they could cripple the American fleet and then achieve their goals in Asia before the United States could rebuild its navy and challenge Japan.

The Attack Shortly after 7:00 on the morning of December 7, an American army radar operator on Oahu noticed a large blip on his radar screen. He called his headquarters to report that planes were headed toward the island. The only officer on duty that Sunday morning believed that the planes were American. "Don't worry about it," the officer told the radar operator, and he hung up the

BACKGROUND
Connections to Today

Few events in U.S. history have forever changed the very course of the country itself. Pearl Harbor was one of those events. The same can be said of September 11, 2001. Addressing Congress nine days after the terrorist attacks on the World Trade Center and the Pentagon, President George W. Bush said, "Americans have known wars—but for the past 136 years, they have been wars on foreign soil, except for one Sunday in 1941 . . . . Americans have known surprise attacks—but never before on thousands of civilians. All of this was brought upon us in a single day—and night fell on a different world, a world where freedom itself is under attack."

BACKGROUND
Global Connections

The idea of a surprise attack on Pearl Harbor came from Admiral Osoroku Yamamoto, the commander-in-chief of the Japanese navy. It appears to have been inspired by a fictional book he read and by an actual historic air attack. In the 1925 book *The Great Pacific War,* British author Hector Bywater presented a fictional account of a war between the United States and Japan that began with the destruction of the U.S. fleet. The actual air attack was a British strike in November 1940 on the Italian fleet at its base at Taranto, in southern Italy. Launched from an aircraft carrier 180 miles out to sea, the raid took the Italians completely by surprise. Three battleships and a cruiser were hit; three of the battleships were heavily damaged. That same month Yamamoto began planning a similar attack on Pearl Harbor.

CAPTION ANSWERS

Map Skills East of Ford Island where most of the battleships lay.

RESOURCE DIRECTORY

Teaching Resources

Learning with Documents booklet (Key Documents) *Franklin D. Roosevelt, Message Asking for War Against Japan,* p. 88

Technology

Color Transparencies *Historical Maps,* A40

Exploring Primary Sources in U.S. History CD-ROM *Pearl Harbor, Daniel K. Inouye*

phone. Less than an hour later, more than 180 Japanese warplanes streaked overhead. Half of the Pacific Fleet lay at anchor in Pearl Harbor, crowded into an area less than three miles square.

Japanese planes bombed and strafed (attacked with machine-gun fire) the fleet and the airfields nearby. By 9:45, the attack was over. In less than two hours, some 2,400 Americans had been killed and nearly 1,200 wounded. Nearly 200 American warplanes had been damaged or destroyed; 18 warships had been sunk or heavily damaged, including 8 of the fleet's 9 battleships. Japan had lost just 29 planes.

Wearing a black armband to mourn those killed at Pearl Harbor, Roosevelt signed a declaration of war against Japan on December 8, 1941.

United States Declares War

The attack on Pearl Harbor stunned the American people. Calling December 7, 1941, "a date which will live in infamy," Roosevelt the next day asked Congress to declare war on Japan:

> "*Hostilities exist. There is no blinking at the fact that our people, our territory, and our interests are in grave danger. With confidence in our armed forces—with the unbound determination of our people—we will gain the inevitable triumph—so help us God.*"
>
> —Franklin D. Roosevelt, December 8, 1941

Within hours after Roosevelt finished speaking, Congress passed a war resolution. Only one of its members, pacifist Jeannette Rankin of Montana, voted against declaring war. Even the America First Committee called on its members to back the war effort.

On December 11, Germany and Italy declared war on the United States. For the second time in the century, Americans had been drawn into a world war. Once more, their contributions would make the difference between victory and defeat for the Allies.

Sounds of an Era

Listen to Roosevelt's speech and other sounds from World War II.

Section 4 Assessment

READING COMPREHENSION

1. (a) What was required by the **Neutrality Acts?** (b) Did they succeed in keeping the United States neutral? Why or why not?
2. Why did Roosevelt ask Congress to pass the **Lend-Lease Act?**
3. In your own words, describe relations between Japan and the United States before the attack on Pearl Harbor.

CRITICAL THINKING AND WRITING

4. **Recognizing Cause and Effect** (a) How much did President Roosevelt consider American public opinion when deciding how to respond to the conflict in Europe? (b) Why did he need to consider public opinion at all?
5. **Writing a News Story** Write a short newspaper article on the fall of France from an American point of view. Explain the consequences for the United States.

Take It to the NET

Activity: Writing a Diary Entry
Read eyewitness accounts of the Pearl Harbor bombing online. Next, write a personal diary entry as if you were present for this historic event. Use the links provided in the *America: Pathways to the Present* area of the following Web site for help in completing this activity.
www.phschool.com

Section 4 Assessment

Reading Comprehension

1. (a) The Neutrality Acts required: banning the United States from providing weapons and loans to nations at war; nations at war to pay cash for all nonmilitary goods and be responsible for transporting the goods from the United States—cash and carry. (b) Yes, for a limited time, until the revisions which created a more flexible Neutrality Act of 1939. Events such as the German invasion of Poland convinced the American public of the need for America to provide weapons to nations fighting the Axis powers.
2. Because the nations which needed American military equipment were running out of money with which to pay for it. Lend-Lease allowed nations such as Great Britain to pursue their war efforts with the idea that they would pay back their debts to the United States at a later date.
3. Answers will vary. Students might state that relations were cool; the United States was unhappy with Japan's expansionist policies.

Critical Thinking and Writing

4. (a) He wanted to right the American economy before becoming involved in foreign affairs, and he moved slowly in regard to the war in Europe because he felt he needed the support of the American people before taking action. (b) Because no American President can succeed in anything without popular support. Also, FDR hoped to win the 1940 Presidential election and to get legislation he favored (such as scrapping the neutrality laws) passed.
5. Articles will vary but should be supported with facts from the section.

Take It to the NET

Student articles should note the brutality of the Nanjing Massacre. Students should note that all of the casualties were either surrendered soldiers or civilians.

RESOURCE DIRECTORY

Teaching Resources

Units 5/6/7 booklet
- Section 4 Quiz, p. 7
- Chapter 17 Test, pp. 8, 11

Guide to the Essentials
- Section 4 Summary, p. 84
- Chapter 17 Test, p. 85

Other Print Resources

Chapter Tests with ExamView® Test Bank CD-ROM, Ch. 17

Technology

Sounds of an Era Audio CD *Broadcast from KGU, Honolulu,* December 7, 1941, recording (time: 15 seconds); *Broadcast from Washington,* December 7, 1941, recording (time: 15 seconds); *Roosevelt's Declaration of War,* 1941 recording (time: one minute); *"We Hold These Truths,"* December 15, 1941, recording (time: one minute, 30 seconds)
ExamView® Test Bank CD-ROM, Ch. 17
Social Studies Skills Tutor CD-ROM

Chapter 17 Review and Assessment

creating a CHAPTER SUMMARY

Copy this diagram (right) on a piece of paper and complete it by adding important events and issues that fit each heading.

Time Period	Important Events
The Rise of Dictators	• Stalin takes control of the Soviet Union and nationalizes most of the economy. • Millions die during Stalin's collectivization campaign and Communist purges. • Mussolini overthrows the Italian government shortly after World War I.
Europe Goes to War	
Japan Builds an Empire	
From Isolationism to War	

For additional review and enrichment activities, see the interactive version of *America: Pathways to the Present*, available on the Web and on CD-ROM.

★ Reviewing Key Terms

For each of the terms below, write a sentence explaining how it relates to the years leading up to the entry of the United States into war.

1. totalitarian
2. fascism
3. Nazism
4. Axis Powers
5. appeasement
6. *blitzkrieg*
7. collaboration
8. Allies
9. Manchurian Incident
10. puppet state
11. Neutrality Acts
12. cash and carry
13. America First Committee
14. Lend-Lease Act

★ Reviewing Main Ideas

15. (a) How did Hitler come to power in Germany? (b) How did Mussolini come to power in Italy? (Section 1)
16. List three ways that individuals in the Soviet Union suffered under Stalin. (Section 1)
17. What role did aircraft play in the German attacks on Poland? (Section 2)
18. (a) How did the Blitz affect life in Britain? (b) Did it succeed in discouraging Britain from resisting? Why or why not? (Section 2)
19. Describe the relationship between the military and the civilian government in Japan in the 1930s. (Section 3)
20. What problems did Japan face in China in 1939 and 1940? (Section 3)
21. What steps did Roosevelt take to help Britain up until the attack on Pearl Harbor? (Section 4)
22. Describe the events leading up to and following the attack on Pearl Harbor. (Section 4)

★ Critical Thinking

23. **Predicting Consequences** If Britain and France had not adopted a policy of appeasement, would Adolf Hitler have been as successful as he was in overrunning Europe?
24. **Making Comparisons** (a) What characteristics did fascism under Mussolini and Hitler have in common with communism under Stalin? (b) What are two important differences between fascism and communism?
25. **Synthesizing Information** In what ways did the Spanish Civil War foreshadow the events that occurred in 1939 and later, throughout Europe?
26. **Recognizing Ideologies** How was the idea of the Greater East Asia Co-Prosperity Sphere designed to appeal to Asians? (b) Why do you think Japan failed to win lasting support from most non-Japanese within this region?
27. **Identifying Central Issues** Why didn't Roosevelt declare war on Germany in 1939?

Reviewing Key Terms

Students should refer to the definitions of key terms in the chapter to write sentences that show an understanding of the decade of tension and conflict leading up to World War II.

Reviewing Main Ideas

15. (a) Germany was suffering economically at the time, and Hitler attracted Germans with promises of stabilizing the economy and restoring Germany to a strong international position. The growing strength of the Nazi party forced President Hindenburg to appoint Hitler Chancellor in January 1933. (b) Mussolini believed strongly that the Versailles Treaty should have granted Italy more territory, and he would later seek it himself. His talent as a public speaker attracted followers and led to the founding of the Italian Fascist party. Through terror and threats, his power grew.
16. Sample answer: peasants were forced off their lands in favor of large, collective farms; food shortages and rationing occurred; purges exiled and executed large numbers of people.
17. Aircraft, which play a central role in *blitzkrieg*, allowed fast, concentrated, surprise attacks, contributing significantly to a quick victory in Poland.
18. (a) The Blitz was destructive, and many sought shelter in subway stations at night. (b) No, they kept their will to fight. In 1940 they cracked Germany's code for top-secret communications. The superb performance of the Royal Air Force in the Battle of Britain inspired the nation.
19. The military gradually took power away from the civilian government.
20. In China, the war had reached a stalemate. At home, the lack of raw materials was hurting the Japanese economy, particularly after July 1940, when the United States began to curtail exports to Japan.
21. The Neutrality Act of 1939 allowed Britain to buy goods on a cash-and-carry basis; a later amendment allowed American merchant ships to transport these purchases to Britain; the United States sent 50 destroyers to Britain in return for permission to build bases on British territory in the Western Hemisphere; the Lend-Lease

Creating a Chapter Summary

Time Period	Important Events
The Rise of Dictators	• Stalin takes control of the Soviet Union and nationalizes most of the economy. • Millions die during Stalin's collectivization campaign and Communist purges. • Mussolini overthrows the Italian government shortly after World War I.
Europe Goes to War	• Hitler makes a pact with Stalin. • Germany invades Poland. • Germany conquers Denmark, Norway, Luxembourg, and the Netherlands. • Germany invades and conquers France. • Germany loses the Battle of Britain.
Japan Builds an Empire	• Rise of militaristic nationalism in Japan • Japan invades Manchuria. • Japan continues its invasion of China.
From Isolationism to War	• United States remains neutral in early years of the war. • Interest grows in America to become involved on European front. • America First Committee opposes war. • FDR establishes Lend-Lease program to aid allies. • Japan attacks Pearl Harbor. • U.S. enters the war.

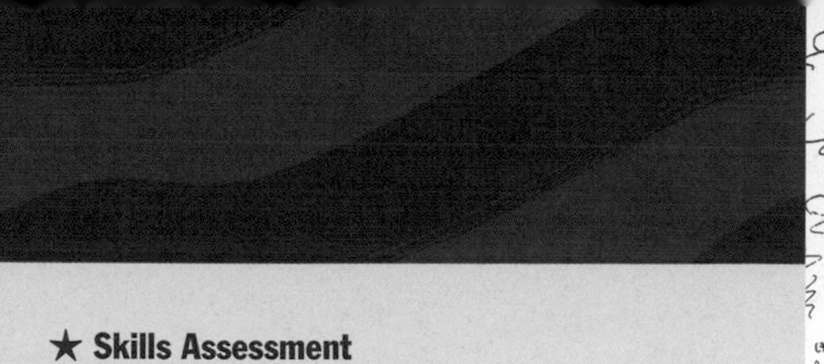

"Sometimes I wonder -- would we speed things up if we used turtles instead of snails?"
"ALL OUT" AID TO BRITAIN

act allowed for the flow of supplies to Britain without pay.

22. Japan's actions in China and Indochina led the U.S. to freeze Japanese assets in the United States and stop exporting raw materials to Japan. Japanese and American diplomats negotiated to avoid war, while General Tojo Hideki came to power in Japan. Tojo's regime planned and carried out the Japanese attack on Pearl Harbor. After the attack the United States declared war on Japan. Subsequently, Germany and Italy declared war on the United States.

★ Skills Assessment

Analyzing Political Cartoons ▶

28. Analyze the images in this May 4, 1941, cartoon. (a) What does the tank represent? (b) Whom do the men represent?

29. Why is it significant that the tank is riding on the backs of snails?

30. What point is the cartoonist making by having the men ask this question?

Analyzing Primary Sources

Read the excerpt from Roosevelt's speech asking Congress to declare war on Japan. Then answer the questions below.

31. How would you describe the tone of Roosevelt's speech?

- **A** serious but optimistic
- **B** joyful
- **C** pessimistic
- **D** angry

32. What is the most likely reason that Roosevelt began this speech with the words, "hostilities exist"?

- **F** to inform members of Congress that Japan has bombed Pearl Harbor.
- **G** to inform the Japanese that the United States is hostile to the Axis Powers.
- **H** to give Japan an opportunity to make peace with the United States.
- **J** to convince members of Congress that their only option is to declare war.

Applying the Chapter Skill: *Examining Photographs*

33. Study the photograph of St. Paul's Cathedral in London on p. 578. (a) What do you think was the purpose of this photo? (b) How did the photographer add drama to a picture of St. Paul's among damaged buildings? (c) Do you think this photo reflects the experiences of ordinary Londoners during the Blitz? Explain your answer.

ACTIVITIES

Writing to LEARN

Writing an Opinion
If a foreign power threatens a neighbor of the United States, and American intervention can stop the aggression, should the United States intervene? Does the United States have a responsibility to act? How should the President and Congress determine when to act and when to avoid a conflict? Write an essay to explain your answer.

Primary Source CD-ROM

Working With Primary Sources Find additional information on World War II on the *Exploring Primary Sources in U.S. History CD-ROM* and use the selection(s) provided to complete the Chapter 17 primary source activity located in the *America: Pathways to the Present* area of the following Web site.
www.phschool.com

Take It to the NET

Chapter Self-Test As a review activity, take the Chapter 17 Self-Test in the *America: Pathways to the Present* area at the Web site listed below. The questions are designed to test your understanding of the chapter content.
www.phschool.com

CRITICAL THINKING

23. Sample answer: Probably not; Hitler might not have been able to fight Czechoslovakia in the east and Britain and France in the west at the same time.

24. (a) Single-party control of the government; lack of individual rights. (b) Communist governments have complete ownership of land and property, and call for worldwide revolution. Fascist regimes allow private business ownership and do not favor worldwide revolution.

25. Other countries were drawn into a civil war within Spain. Similarly, the German attack on Poland eventually plunged virtually all of Europe into war.

26. (a) As a way to liberate Asia from European colonizers. (b) Their method of colonization was similar to that of European powers, and thus met with objection.

27. American Presidents cannot declare war. Only Congress can declare war. Americans were unwilling to fight then, and had no commitments in Europe at the time.

SKILLS ASSESSMENT

28. (a) Aid to Britain. (b) Americans policy makers and weapons manufacturers supplying aid to Britain.

29. The flow of aid was slow in starting.

30. America was not doing enough to send aid, though it claimed to be.

31. A

32. J

33. (a) To show the cathedral, which survived the bombing, as an example of Britain's refusal to surrender. (b) By capturing one of the buildings in the foreground as the upper stories fell to the ground. (c) Yes, because many areas of London were damaged during the blitz, but like the cathedral, British people refused to give in despite the bombing.

ANSWERS TO ACTIVITIES

Writing to LEARN

Pro-intervention: Students may cite the dangers to American interests abroad and the suffering of innocent people living under tyranny. Anti-intervention: Students may note the possibility of American casualties and the idea that America should not intervene in the business of other nations.

Primary Source CD-ROM

Direct students to the additional primary sources that can be found on the *Exploring Primary Sources in U.S. History CD-ROM.*

Take It to the NET

Additional support materials and activities for Chapter 17 of *America: Pathways to the Present* can be found in the Social Studies area at the Prentice Hall School Web site. **www.phschool.com**

Chapter 18 Planning Guide
Resource Manager

	Core Instruction	Reading/Skills
Chapter-Level Resources **TEKS** 6(B), 24(A)	Teaching Resources • Pacing Charts booklet • Block Scheduling booklet **Resource Pro® CD-ROM,** Ch. 18 **Prentice Hall Presentation Pro CD-ROM,** Ch. 18 **www.phschool.com** • eTeach	**Guided Reading Audiotapes (English/Spanish)** **Student Edition on Audio CD,** Ch. 18 **Social Studies Skills Tutor CD-ROM** **Color Transparencies,** A41, A42, A43, A44, E18, F8, H18
1 Mobilization 1. Find out how Roosevelt mobilized the armed forces. 2. Learn about ways in which the government prepared the economy for war. 3. See how the war affected daily life on the home front. **TEKS** 1(C), 7(A), 12(E), 15(B)	Teaching Resources **Units 5/6/7 booklet** • Section 1 Quiz, p. 15 **Learning Styles Lesson Plans booklet,** p. 52	**Guided Reading and Review booklet,** p. 100 **Guide to the Essentials,** p. 86 **Section Reading Support Transparencies**
2 Retaking Europe See Teacher's Edition p. 600 for Section Objectives 1–5. **TEKS** 6(C), 8(B), 19(B)	Teaching Resources **Units 5/6/7 booklet** • Section 2 Quiz, p. 16	**Guided Reading and Review booklet,** p. 101 **Guide to the Essentials,** p. 87 **Section Reading Support Transparencies**
3 The Holocaust 1. Find out about some ways in which Germany persecuted Jews in the 1930s. 2. See how Germany's policies toward Jews developed from murder into genocide. **TEKS** 1(B), 8(B)	Teaching Resources **Units 5/6/7 booklet** • Section 3 Quiz, p. 17	**Guided Reading and Review booklet,** p. 102 **Guide to the Essentials,** p. 88 **Section Reading Support Transparencies**
4 The War in the Pacific 1. Learn about advances Japan made in Asia and the Pacific in late 1941 and 1942. 2. See which Allied victories turned the tide of war in the Pacific. 3. Read about the strategy of the United States in the struggle to reconquer the Pacific Islands. 4. Discover why the battles of Iwo Jima and Okinawa were important. 5. Understand how the Manhattan Project brought the war to an end. **TEKS** 6(A), 8(A)	Teaching Resources **Units 5/6/7 booklet** • Section 4 Quiz, p. 18	**Guided Reading and Review booklet,** p. 103 **Guide to the Essentials,** p. 89 **Learning with Documents booklet,** p. 30 **Skills for Life booklet,** p. 27 **Section Reading Support Transparencies**
5 The War's Social Impact 1. Learn how African Americans, Mexican Americans, and Native Americans experienced the war at home. 2. Find out about difficulties Japanese Americans faced. 3. See how the war changed conditions for working women. **TEKS** 7(A), 14(A), 21(A)	Teaching Resources **Units 5/6/7 booklet** • Section 5 Quiz, p. 19 **Learning Styles Lesson Plans booklet,** p. 53	**Guided Reading and Review booklet,** p. 104 **Guide to the Essentials,** p. 90 **Learning with Documents booklet,** p. 64 **Section Reading Support Transparencies**

Enrichment/Pre-AP

Prentice Hall United States History Video Collection™
www.phschool.com
- Section Activities, Virtual Field Trip, Chapter Activities, Current Events Online

Historical Outline Map Book, pp. 65, 67
Sounds of an Era Audio CD
Exploring Primary Sources in U.S. History CD-ROM

Sounds of an Era Audio CD
Exploring Primary Sources in U.S. History CD-ROM

Biography, Literature, and Comparing Primary Sources booklet, p. 74
Historical Outline Map Book, p. 66
Sounds of an Era Audio CD
Exploring Primary Sources in U.S. History CD-ROM

Biography, Literature, and Comparing Primary Sources booklet, pp. 30, 145
American History Block Scheduling Support
Nystrom *Atlas of Our Country*, pp. 32–33, 34–35
Sounds of an Era Audio CD
Exploring Primary Sources in U.S. History CD-ROM
American Pathways Thematic Posters

Assessment

Core Assessment
ExamView® Test Bank, Ch. 18
ExamView® Test Bank CD-ROM, Ch. 18

Standardized Test Preparation
Diagnose and Prescribe
Diagnostic Tests for High School Social Studies Skills

Review and Reteach
Review Book for U.S. History

Practice and Assess
Test-taking Strategies With Transparencies
Test-taking Strategies Posters
Test Prep Book for U.S. History
Alternative Assessment Handbook
Document-Based Assessment

Teaching Resources
Units 5/6/7 booklet
- Section Quizzes, pp. 15–19
- Chapter Tests, pp. 20, 23

www.phschool.com Ch. 18 Self-Test

AmericanHeritage Resources

From the Archives of American Heritage®, pp. 596, 616
AmericanHeritage® My Brush with History™ Videotapes
www.americanheritage.com

Don't miss the exclusive interactive version of this textbook on the Web and on CD-ROM.

Chapter 18 Planning Guide

In Your Classroom

Customize for Individual Needs

Gifted and Talented

Teacher's Edition
- Customize for Gifted and Talented, pp. 595, 601, 617, 621, 627

Teaching Resources
- Biography, Literature, and Comparing Primary Sources booklet, pp. 30, 74, 145

Technology
- Exploring Primary Sources in U.S. History CD-ROM *What Should You Bring Overseas? Bill Steele; "Gee, Mom, I Want to Go Home," Army Song; Night, Elie Wiesel; Japanese Internment Photograph; Rosie the Riveter Poster*

ESL

Teacher's Edition
- Customize for ESL, p. 611

Teaching Resources
- Guided Reading and Review booklet, pp. 100–104
- Guide to the Essentials (English/Spanish), Chapter 18

Technology
- Student Edition on Audio CD, Chapter 18
- Guided Reading Audiotapes (English/Spanish), Chapter 18
- Section Reading Support Transparencies

Less Proficient Readers

Teacher's Edition
- Customize for Less Proficient Readers, pp. 603, 605, 613

Teaching Resources
- Guided Reading and Review booklet, pp. 100–104
- Guide to the Essentials (English/Spanish), Chapter 18

Technology
- Student Edition on Audio CD, Chapter 18
- Guided Reading Audiotapes (English/Spanish), Chapter 18
- Section Reading Support Transparencies

Less Proficient Writers

Teacher's Edition
- Customize for Less Proficient Writers, p. 625

Teaching Resources
- Guided Reading and Review booklet, pp. 100–104
- Guide to the Essentials (English/Spanish), Chapter 18

Technology
- Student Edition on Audio CD, Chapter 18
- Guided Reading Audiotapes (English/Spanish), Chapter 18
- Section Reading Support Transparencies

Teacher's Edition Index

Chapter 18 – Pacing Suggestions

For 90-minute Blocks

- Teach sections 1, 2, 3, 4, and 5 using Transparencies A41, A42, A43, A44, E18, F8, and H18, and the Recent Scholarship notes on pages 612, 617, and 627 for class discussions.

Running Out of Time?

If you are running short on time to cover this chapter, consider the following options:

- Use the Prentice Hall Presentation Pro CD-ROM to create an outline for this chapter.
- Use the Section Summaries for Chapter 18, from **Guide to the Essentials (English/Spanish).**

TEKS Correlation

Chapter-Level	TEKS
	(6) History. The student understands the impact of significant national and international decisions and conflicts from World War II and the Cold War to the present on the United States. The student is expected to: **(B)** analyze major issues and events of World War II such as fighting the war on multiple fronts, the interment of Japanese-Americans, the Holocaust, the battle of Midway, the invasion of Normandy, and the development of and Harry Truman's decision to use the atomic bomb. **(24) Social studies skills.** The student applies critical-thinking skills to organize and use information acquired from a variety of sources including electronic technology. The student is expected to: **(A)** locate and use primary and secondary sources such as computer software, databases, media and news services, biographies, interviews, and artifacts to acquire information about the United States.
1 Mobilization	**(1) History.** The student understands traditional historical points of reference in U.S. history from 1877 to the present. The student is expected to: **(C)** explain the significance of the following dates: 1898, 1914–1918, 1929, 1941–1945, and 1957. **(7) History.** The student understands the impact of the American civil rights movement. The student is expected to: **(A)** trace the historical development of the civil rights movement in the 18th, 19th, and 20th centuries, including the 13th, 14th, and 15th amendments. **(12) Economics.** The student understands domestic and foreign issues related to U.S. economic growth from the 1870s to 1920. The student is expected to: **(E)** describe the economic effects of international military conflicts, including the Spanish-American War and World War I, on the United States. **(15) Government.** The student understands changes in the role of government over time. The student is expected to: **(B)** explain the impact of significant international events such as World War I and World War II on changes in the role of the federal government.
2 Retaking Europe	**(6) History.** The student understands the impact of significant national and international decisions and conflicts from World War II and the Cold War to the present on the United States. The student is expected to: **(C)** explain the roles played by significant military leaders during World War II, including Omar Bradley, Dwight Eisenhower, Douglas MacArthur, George Marshall, and George Patton. **(8) Geography.** The student uses geographic tools to collect, analyze, and interpret data. The student is expected to: **(B)** pose and answer questions about geographic distributions and patterns shown on maps, graphs, charts, models, and databases. **(19) Citizenship.** The student understands the importance of effective leadership in a democratic society. The student is expected to: **(B)** evaluate the contributions of significant political and social leaders in the United States such as Andrew Carnegie, Shirley Chisholm, and Franklin D. Roosevelt.
3 The Holocaust	**(1) History.** The student understands traditional historical points of reference in U.S. history from 1877 to the present. The student is expected to: **(B)** apply absolute and relative chronology through the sequencing of significant individuals, events, and time periods. **(8) Geography.** The student uses geographic tools to collect, analyze, and interpret data. The student is expected to: **(B)** pose and answer questions about geographic distributions and patterns shown on maps, graphs, charts, models, and databases.
4 The War in the Pacific	**(6) History.** The student understands the impact of significant national and international decisions and conflicts from World War II and the Cold War to the present on the United States. The student is expected to: **(A)** identify reasons for U.S. involvement in World War II, including the growth of dictatorships and the attack on Pearl Harbor. **(8) Geography.** The student uses geographic tools to collect, analyze, and interpret data. The student is expected to: **(A)** create thematic maps, graphs, charts, models, and databases representing various aspects of the United States.
5 The War's Social Impact	**(7) History.** The student understands the impact of the American civil rights movement. The student is expected to: **(A)** trace the historical development of the civil rights movement in the 18th, 19th, and 20th centuries, including the 13th, 14th, and 15th amendments. **(14) Economics.** The student understands the economic effects of World War II, the Cold War, and increased worldwide competition on contemporary society. The student is expected to: **(A)** describe the economic effects of World War II on the home front, including rationing, female employment, and the end of the Great Depression. **(21) Culture.** The student understands how people from various groups, including racial, ethnic, and religious groups, adapt to life in the United States and contribute to our national identity. The student is expected to: **(A)** explain actions taken by people from racial, ethnic, and religious groups to expand economic opportunities and political rights in American society.

Chapter 18

World War II: Americans at War

(1941–1945)

INTRODUCING THE CHAPTER

"The peace, freedom, and security of 90 percent of the world is being jeopardized by the remaining 10 percent . . ." said President Roosevelt about the war raging in Europe. Many Americans, opposed to intervention, were convinced only after the attack on Pearl Harbor that the United States should be involved in the war. With the American entry into World War II, there was no longer any question about the role of the United States in world affairs.

TIME LINE ACTIVITY

To provide students with practice in using the time line, ask questions such as these:

1. In what year did the United States declare war on Japan, Germany, and Italy? *(1941)*
2. Which two countries were engaged in the Battle of Midway, and which country was victorious? *(The United States and Japan; the United States)*
3. In what year did the Japanese begin *kamikaze* attacks? *(1944)*

Chapter 18

World War II: Americans at War

(1941–1945)

Ration cards and points

American troops in the South Pacific

American Events

1941 A. Philip Randolph threatens to march on Washington to end discrimination in war industries. The United States declares war on Japan, Germany, and Italy.

1942 Japan conquers the Philippines. The United States defeats the Japanese navy at the Battle of Midway. Japanese Americans are interned in camps.

Presidential Terms: Franklin D. Roosevelt 1933–1945

1940 — **1941** — **1942**

World Events

1941 Hitler invades the Soviet Union. Hong Kong falls to Japan.

1942 Allied troops land in North Africa. The Battle of Stalingrad begins.

eTeach

Be sure to check out this month's online discussion with a Master Teacher. Go to **www.phschool.com**.

RESOURCE DIRECTORY

Teaching Resources

Pacing Charts booklet
Block Scheduling booklet, p. 25
Units 5/6/7 booklet
- Chapter Summary, p. 14

Technology

Guided Reading Audiotapes (English/Spanish), Ch. 18
Student Edition on Audio CD, Ch. 18
Prentice Hall United States History Video Collection™ Volume 19, *World War II*
Prentice Hall Presentation Pro CD-ROM, Ch. 18
Resource Pro® CD-ROM
Social Studies Skills Tutor CD-ROM
Companion Web site, www.phschool.com

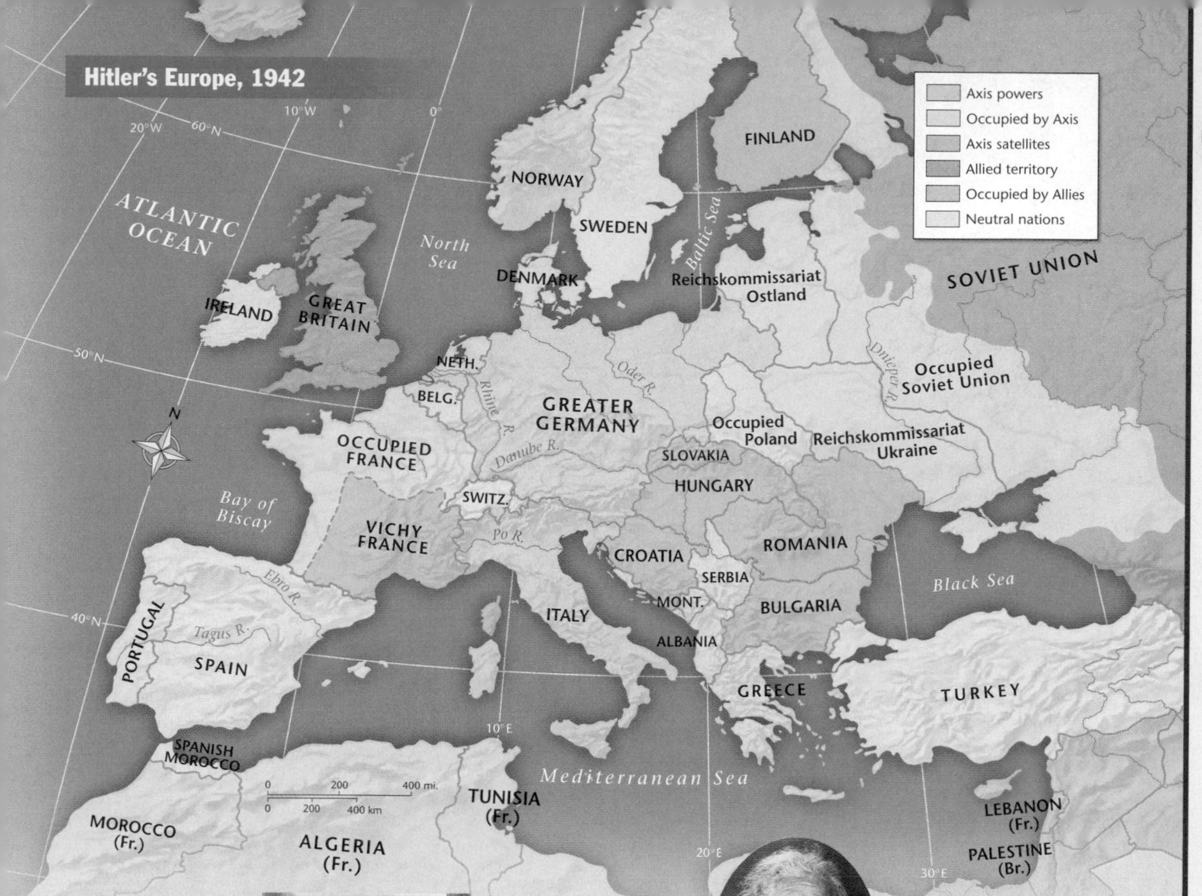

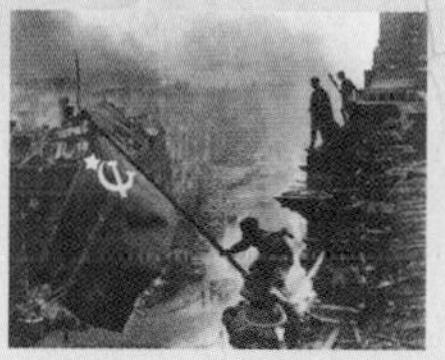

Hitler's Europe, 1942

Axis powers
Occupied by Axis
Axis satellites
Allied territory
Occupied by Allies
Neutral nations

ATLANTIC OCEAN
North Sea
IRELAND
GREAT BRITAIN
NORWAY
SWEDEN
FINLAND
DENMARK
Baltic Sea
Reichskommissariat Ostland
SOVIET UNION
Occupied Soviet Union
NETH.
BELG.
GREATER GERMANY
Occupied Poland
Reichskommissariat Ukraine
OCCUPIED FRANCE
VICHY FRANCE
SWITZ.
SLOVAKIA
HUNGARY
ROMANIA
CROATIA
SERBIA
MONT.
ALBANIA
BULGARIA
ITALY
GREECE
TURKEY
Black Sea
Bay of Biscay
PORTUGAL
SPAIN
SPANISH MOROCCO
MOROCCO (Fr.)
ALGERIA (Fr.)
TUNISIA (Fr.)
Mediterranean Sea
LEBANON (Fr.)
PALESTINE (Br.)

A Soviet soldier raises his country's flag over the ruined *Reichstag* in Berlin.

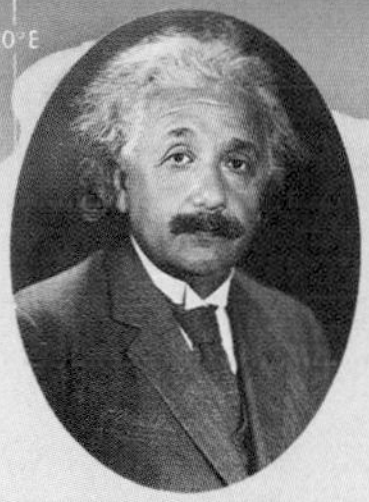

A letter written by Albert Einstein led to the development of the atomic bomb.

1943 Americans help defeat Axis armies in North Africa and invade Italy. Troops in the Pacific take Guadalcanal and begin island-hopping campaign.

1944 American and British troops lead the D-Day invasion of France.

1945 Harry S Truman becomes President after Roosevelt's death. American troops liberate Western Germany. The United States drops atomic bombs on Hiroshima and Nagasaki.

Harry S Truman 1945–1953

1943 | 1944 | 1945

1943 Jews in Warsaw ghetto rebel. Germany invades Italy after Mussolini is overthrown.

1944 Japan begins *kamikaze* attacks. De Gaulle leads Allies into Paris.

1945 Hitler commits suicide. Germany and Japan surrender.

Hitler's Europe, 1942

Activating Prior Knowledge According to this map, how many countries were Allied territory? *(Two: Great Britain and the Soviet Union)*

Previewing Considering the location of the Allied territories, what advantage did the Allies have? *(They were positioned on either side of the Axis powers, satellites, and territories, so they could attack on both fronts.)*

BACKGROUND
About the Pictures

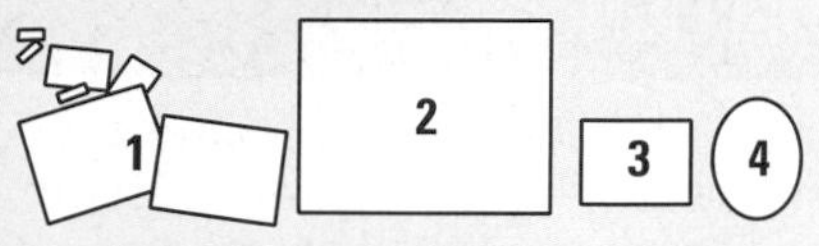

1. Ration cards were distributed to help limit quantities and to conserve resources during wartime.
2. The everyday hardships and difficult conditions the soldiers faced together during war helped them create strong bonds of friendship among themselves.
3. After breaking their pact with the Soviet Union and launching a large-scale attack, Germany was finally defeated.
4. Despite the fact that Einstein's name became closely associated with atomic weaponry, he was a pacifist, wishing to prevent any further use of atomic bombs.

BIBLIOGRAPHY

For the Teacher

Brokaw, Tom. ***The Greatest Generation.*** Random House, 2001. (The veteran television announcer has assembled a moving collection of first-hand reminiscences based on hundreds of letters and interviews with people who lived through World War II.)

Prange, Gordon William. ***At Dawn We Slept: The Untold Story of Pearl Harbor.*** Penguin, 2001. (This minutely researched book provides a definitive account of the attack on Pearl Harbor, from both the Japanese and United States perspectives.)

Roeder, George. ***The Censored War: American Visual Experience During World War II.*** Yale University Press, 1993. (A collection of wartime photographs, many used for propaganda, and many from the National Archives.)

For the Student

Hersey, John. ***Hiroshima.*** Vintage, 1989. (Harrowing account of the bombing.)

Selden, Kyoko, and Mark Selden, eds. ***The Atomic Bomb: Voices from Hiroshima and Nagasaki.*** Sharpe, 1989. (Accounts of the bombing by survivors.)

iTEXT

Don't miss the exclusive interactive version of this textbook on the Web and on CD-ROM.

Section 1

Mobilization

Section Objectives

1. Find out how Roosevelt mobilized the armed forces.
2. Learn about ways in which the government prepared the economy for war.
3. See how the war affected daily life on the home front.

Bellringer

Warm-Up Activity Ask students to suppose they were President Roosevelt on December 8, 1941. What are the three most important things that must be done to prepare the country for war?

Activating Prior Knowledge Ask students to list some facts they know about the United States' involvement in World War II. In particular, do they know in what year the U.S. entered the war? In what year did the war end?

Reading Strategy

Have students write the heading "Economic Effects of World War II" on a piece of paper. As they read the chapter, have them list effects that are described. These should include rationing, female employment, and the end of the Great Depression.

Background

Geography in History

The United States' "Good Neighbor Policy" paid dividends during the war. The Latin American nations provided vital war materials—rubber, quinine, tin—along with naval and air bases. Brazil sent troops to Europe, and Mexico had an air squadron in the Pacific. The Mexican and Cuban navies patrolled the Caribbean for German submarines. In return, the U. S. provided military equipment and loans to these nations.

Section 1 Mobilization

READING FOCUS

- How did Roosevelt mobilize the armed forces?
- In what ways did the government prepare the economy for war?
- How did the war affect daily life on the home front?

MAIN IDEA

The United States quickly mobilized millions of Americans to fight the Axis powers. The government organized the economy to supply the military.

KEY TERMS

Selective Training and Service Act
GI
Office of War Mobilization
Liberty ship
victory garden

TAKING NOTES

As you read, complete the following flowchart to show some of the effects that America's entry into war had on the economy of the United States.

United States Enters the War → Industries adapt to produce war goods. | [blank] | [blank] | [blank]

Millions of Americans traded their civilian clothes for military fatigues (above) as the United States prepared to fight the Axis.

Setting the Scene Well before the Japanese attack on Pearl Harbor, officials in the United States had begun to prepare for war. President Roosevelt made his concerns and worries clear to the American people in a radio address in December 1940. He stated that the Axis nations, especially Germany, posed a direct threat to the security of the United States. He appealed to American business owners and workers to support Britain's defensive efforts or face the ultimate task of defending their own land against the "brute force" of the Axis.

> *"We must be the great arsenal of democracy. For us this is an emergency as serious as war itself. We must apply ourselves to our task with the same resolution, the same sense of urgency, the same spirit of patriotism and sacrifice as we would show were we at war."*
>
> —Franklin D. Roosevelt, fireside chat, December 29, 1940

FDR understood that the outcome of the war in Europe ultimately depended on his country's ability to produce planes, tanks, guns, uniforms, and other war materials for the Allies.

Mobilizing the Armed Forces

FDR realized that a crucial step that he had to take was to strengthen the armed forces if the United States were to enter the war on the side of the Allies. In September 1940, Congress authorized the first peacetime draft in the nation's history. The **Selective Training and Service Act** required all males aged 21 to 36 to register for military service. A limited number of men was selected from this pool to serve a year in the army. The United States also boosted its defense spending from $2 billion at the start of the year to more than $10 billion in September.

As the United States prepared for the possibility of war, thousands of American men received official notices to enter the army. In what came to be known as the "Four Freedoms speech," FDR shared his vision of what these troops would be fighting for:

Resource Directory

Teaching Resources
Learning Styles Lesson Plans booklet, p. 52
Guided Reading and Review booklet, p. 100

Technology
Section Reading Support Transparencies
Guided Reading Audiotapes (English/Spanish), Ch. 18
Student Edition on Audio CD, Ch. 18
Color Transparencies *Time Lines,* C7

RESOURCE PRO® Primary Source Activity *Experiences of an African American Soldier,* found on Resource Pro, uses narrative by World War II veteran Timuel Black to show some of the hardships and injustices African American soldiers faced.
Exploring Primary Sources in U.S. History CD-ROM *What Should You Bring Overseas? Bill Steele*
Prentice Hall Presentation Pro CD-ROM, Ch. 18
Companion Web site, www.phschool.com

> “We look forward to a world founded upon four essential freedoms. The first is freedom of speech and expression. . . . The second is freedom of every person to worship God in his own way. . . . The third is freedom from want [need]. . . . The fourth is freedom from fear.”
>
> —Franklin D. Roosevelt, State of the Union Message, January 6, 1941

Artist Norman Rockwell illustrated these four freedoms in a series of paintings that the government distributed in poster form during the war. After the attack on Pearl Harbor, feelings of patriotism swept over the United States. Tens of thousands of men volunteered to serve in the military.

OURS...to fight for
FREEDOM FROM WANT

Norman Rockwell's *Freedom From Want* was widely reproduced during the war.

The GI War World War II greatly changed the lives of the men and women who were uprooted from home and sent far away to fight for their country. More than 16 million Americans served as soldiers, sailors, and aviators in the war. They called themselves **GIs,** an abbreviation of "Government Issue."

During the war, American GIs slogged through swamps, crossed hot deserts and turbulent seas, and flew through skies pounded by enemy guns. Soldiers on the front lines often found their experience in the war was a daily struggle just to stay alive. Between battles, the typical GI dreamed of home and a cherished way of life. When asked what he was fighting for, a young marine replied, "What I'd give for a piece of blueberry pie." American soldiers knew that they were fighting to preserve the freedoms that they held dear.

Diversity in the Armed Forces Americans from all ethnic and racial backgrounds fought during World War II. More than 300,000 Mexican Americans served their country, primarily in the army.

Some 25,000 Native Americans also served in the military. A group of Navajos developed a secret code, based on their language, that the enemy could not break. The marines recruited more than 400 Navajos to serve as radio operators. These "code talkers," as they became known, provided an important secure communications link in several key battles of the war.

Nearly a million African Americans joined the military. At first, officials limited most black troops to supporting roles. By late 1942, however, faced with mounting casualties, military authorities reluctantly gave African Americans the opportunity to fight. African Americans fought in separate units. One such group, called the Tuskegee Airmen, became the first African American flying unit in the United States military. In late 1944, heavy casualties forced the army to accept African Americans into some white combat units.

Women in the Military Not all who served in the military were men. By the war's end, roughly 350,000 American women had volunteered for military service. Faced with a personnel shortage, officials agreed to use women in almost all areas except combat. Many worked as clerks, typists, airfield control tower operators, mechanics, photographers, and drivers. Others ferried planes around the country and towed practice targets for antiaircraft gunners.

INTERPRETING POLITICAL CARTOONS Bill Mauldin created the characters of GIs Willie and Joe for the Army newspaper, *Stars and Stripes.* **Distinguishing False From Accurate Images** *What does this cartoon say about the GIs who fought in World War II?*

"Me future is settled, Willie. I'm gonna be a perfessor on types o' European soil."

Preparing the Economy for War

The United States entered the war at a time when the production levels of the other Allies had dropped sharply. Bombing campaigns and German advances had affected production in Britain and the Soviet Union, and Japan's conquests in the Pacific threatened to cut off

Lesson Plan

Focus Explain that as factories shifted into wartime production, new opportunities arose for workers and businesses. Ask students how these opportunities changed American life.

Instruct Discuss why it was crucial for American industries to begin making war supplies rather than consumer goods. What happened in Europe and in the Pacific to make it necessary for the United States to become the "arsenal of democracy"? Have students restate this slogan in their own words: "Production lines are battle lines."

Assess/Reteach Ask what types of steps the United States took to mobilize its troops. Can students list some major impacts this type of nationwide action would have had on American society?

Caption Answers

Interpreting Political Cartoons Possible answer: GIs were ordinary people. They made jokes about some of the hardships of army life.

Customize For ...

Gifted and Talented

Ask students to write a short paper on what facts of the African American experience in World War II they think were the most important in beginning the movement for equality. Discuss the importance of leadership and experience in a large institution such as the military and the significance of the contrast between the nation's stated goals and its discriminatory actions.

ACTIVITY
Connecting with Economics

Ask students to research some of the new products developed by the petrochemical industry during the war, such as artificial rubber, nylon, and plastics. Tell them to find out why these new products were needed. Have students share what they learned with the class. **(Verbal/Linguistic)**

BACKGROUND
Economics in History

The term from economics often applied to such outstanding production accomplishments as those of the Liberty ships is *production miracle.* Miracle, indeed: at times, the Kaiser shipyards could produce a huge ship in not forty days, but *four.*

From the Archives of
American Heritage®

Husbands Off to War

So many married men had joined the armed forces in the first year of American involvement in World War II that a new book appeared to help their wives cope. In *So Your Husband's Gone to War,* published by Doubleday, former advertising writer Ethel Gorman covered everything from preparing for furloughs and coping with a smaller apartment to giving parties for women and restraining the office "wolf" who proves too helpful. Source: Nathan Ward, "The Time Machine," *American Heritage®* magazine, December 1992.

supplies of such vital raw materials as rubber, oil, and tin. President Roosevelt pushed industries to move quickly into the production of war equipment.

War Production FDR knew that the federal government would have to coordinate the production of American businesses to meet Allied demand. The government had already assumed tremendous power over the economy during the New Deal. Now the Supreme Court, filled with Roosevelt appointees, tended to support FDR's attempts to boost the government's power even further.

In January 1942, the government set up the War Production Board (WPB) to direct the conversion of peacetime industries to industries that produced war goods. It quickly halted the production of hundreds of civilian consumer goods, from cars to lawn mowers to bird cages, and encouraged companies to make goods for the war. The armed forces decided which companies would receive contracts to manufacture military hardware, but the WPB set priorities and allocated raw materials.

As the war went on, the government established dozens of additional agencies to deal with war production, labor questions, and scarce resources. In May 1943, the President appointed James F. Byrnes, a longtime member of Congress and a close presidential advisor, to head the **Office of War Mobilization.** The office would serve as a superagency in the centralization of resources. Working from a makeshift office in the White House, Byrnes had such broad authority that he was often called the "assistant president." Some people said that Byrnes ran the country while FDR ran the war.

As production of consumer goods stopped, factories converted to war production. The Ford Motor Company built a huge new factory to make B-24 Liberator bombers using the same assembly-line techniques used to manufacture cars. Henry J. Kaiser introduced mass production techniques into shipbuilding and cut the time needed to build one type of ship from 200 days to 40 days. The vessels that made Kaiser famous were called **Liberty ships.** They were large, sturdy merchant ships that carried supplies or troops.

To motivate businesses and guarantee profits, the government established the "cost-plus" system for military contracts. The military paid development and production costs and added a percentage of costs as profit for the manufacturer. Pride and patriotism also motivated business executives. As in World War I, thousands went to Washington, D.C., to work in the new federal agencies that coordinated war production. They received a token "dollar-a-year" salary from the government while still remaining on their own companies' payrolls.

VIEWING HISTORY Henry J. Kaiser's Liberty ship *Robert E. Peary* (above) was built in a matter of days. A button (right) shows the spirit of workers building airplanes for the war effort. **Drawing Conclusions** *Why was military production so important to winning the war?*

Each year of the war, the United States raised its production goals for military materials, and each year it met these goals. In 1944, American production levels doubled those of all the Axis nations put together. By the middle of 1945, the nation had produced approximately 300,000 airplanes; 80,000 landing craft; 100,000 tanks and armored cars; 5,600 merchant ships (including about 2,600 Liberty ships); 6 million rifles, carbines, and machine guns; and 41 billion rounds of ammunition.

The Wartime Work Force War production benefited workers, too, ending the massive unemployment of the 1930s. As the graphs on the next page show, unemployment virtually vanished during the war. Not only did people find

CAPTION ANSWERS

Viewing History Possible answer: Because winning the war would require the United States to produce enough military equipment to supply not only its own vast forces, but also to make good the shortfalls of supply being experienced by Britain, the Soviet Union, and other Allied nations.

RESOURCE DIRECTORY

Technology
Color Transparencies *American Photo,* F8

jobs, they also earned more money for their work. Average weekly wages in manufacturing, adjusted for inflation, rose by more than 50 percent between 1940 and 1945. Under pressure to produce high-quality goods in a hurry, the American labor force delivered. A journalist wrote of a war production factory: "Not a day passes but you'll hear somebody say to a worker who seems to be slowing down, 'There's a war on, you know!'"

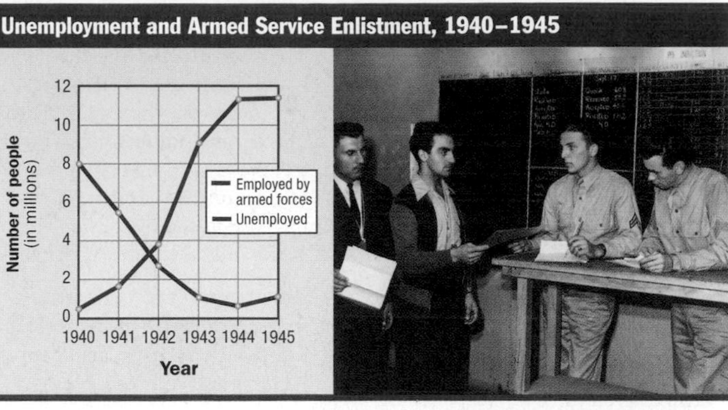

INTERPRETING CHARTS Ten years of high unemployment came to an end as workers joined the military or found jobs in defense industries. **Analyzing Information** *In what year did the number of people in the armed forces increase by 5 million?*

With more people working, union membership rose. From 1940 to 1941, the number of workers belonging to unions increased by 1.5 million. Union membership continued to rise sharply once the United States entered the war, increasing from 10.5 million in 1941 to 14.8 million in 1945.

Two weeks after the attack on Pearl Harbor, labor and business representatives agreed to refrain from strikes and "lockouts." A lockout is a tactic in which an employer keeps employees out of the workplace to avoid meeting their demands. As the cost of living rose during the war, however, unions found the no-strike agreement hard to honor. The number of strikes rose sharply in 1943 and continued to rise in the last two years of the war.

The most serious strikes occurred in the coal industry. John L. Lewis, head of the United Mine Workers union, called strikes on four occasions in 1943. Lewis and the miners had watched industry profits and the cost of living soar while their wages stayed the same. Secretary of the Interior Harold L. Ickes finally negotiated an agreement with Lewis. Meanwhile, Congress passed the Smith-Connally Act in June 1943, limiting future strike activity.

Financing the War The United States government vowed to spend whatever was necessary to sustain the war effort. Federal spending increased from \$8.9 billion a year in 1939 to \$95.2 billion in 1945. The Gross National Product (GNP) more than doubled. Overall, between 1941 and 1945, the federal government spent about \$321 billion—ten times as much as it had spent in World War I.

Higher taxes paid for about 41 percent of the cost of the war. The government borrowed the rest of the money from banks, private investors, and the public. The Treasury Department launched bond drives to encourage Americans to buy war bonds to help finance the war. Total war bond sales brought in about \$186 billion.

READING CHECK How did the government pay for the war effort?

During the Depression, British economist John Maynard Keynes had argued in favor of deficit spending to get the economy moving. While spending did increase during the 1930s, the government failed to generate large deficits until World War II. The country could not afford to pay all the costs of war, so deficits provided a way to postpone some payments until after the war. High levels of deficit spending helped the United States field a well-equipped army and navy, bring prosperity to workers, and pull the United States out of the Depression. It also boosted the national debt from \$43 billion in 1940 to \$259 billion in 1945.

ACTIVITY
Connecting with Culture

Direct students' attention to the last sentence in the first paragraph on this page ("There's a war on, you know!"). Explain that several such common expressions and words came out of the World War II era. Have students identify at least three others and research their etymology. **(Verbal/Linguistic)**

BACKGROUND
Global Connections

The Great Depression ended with the start of World War II. The war fueled economic growth in the United States as well as in the other countries involved in the war. By 1943 there was virtually no unemployment in the United States. In Great Britain the labor force grew by 2.9 million. Germany and Japan both entered the war hoping that their economies would also get a much-needed boost. In Japan 3.2 million people became employed during the war years.

READING CHECK
The government paid for the war effort through higher taxes; borrowing from banks, private investors, and the public; and the sale of war bonds.

TEST PREPARATION

Have students read the section "The Wartime Work Force" on these pages and then answer the question below.

By approximately how much did union membership increase in the United States between 1941 and 1945?

A 10.5 million
(B) 4.3 million
C 14.8 million
D 3.4 million

CAPTION ANSWERS

Interpreting Charts 1943.

Focus on DAILY LIFE

Black Markets Despite rationing and shortages, people could buy rare goods if they were willing to pay a high price. Nylon stockings could be found for $5 a pair in most cities, if not in the stores. Gas stations, shoe stores, and groceries sold rationed goods to trusted customers "off-ration," or without ration coupons, at a higher price. These deals were known as the black market. They hurt the war effort by taking resources away from war production and upsetting Americans who played by the rules and stuck to their rations. Because it depended on thousands of personal relationships and small trades, the black market was impossible to defeat.

Daily Life on the Home Front

The war affected the daily lives of most Americans. Nearly everyone had a relative or a friend in the military, and people closely followed war news on the radio. During the war, nearly 30 million people moved, including soldiers, families of soldiers, and civilians relocating to take jobs in military production. The end of the Depression helped lift Americans' spirits. One measure of people's optimism was an increase in the birthrate. The population grew by 7.5 million between 1940 and 1945, nearly double the rate of growth for the 1930s.

Shortages and Controls Wartime jobs gave many people their first extra cash since the Depression. Still, shortages and rationing limited the goods that people could buy. Familiar consumer items were simply unavailable "for the duration." Metal to make zippers or typewriters went instead into guns, and rubber went to make tires for army trucks instead of for bicycles. Nylon stockings, introduced in 1939, vanished from shops because the nylon was needed for parachutes.

The supply of food also fell short of demand. The government needed great amounts of food for the military. In addition, the closing of shipping lanes and enemy occupation of foreign countries cut off some of America's supplies of sugar, tropical fruits, and coffee.

Worried that shortages would cause price increases, the government used tough measures to head off inflation. In April 1941, the Office of Price Administration (OPA) was established by an executive order. The OPA's job was to control inflation by limiting prices and rents. Such controls sometimes backfired, however. For example, companies would cut back on the production of goods whose prices did not allow for a substantial profit. Such cutbacks could cause the very shortages they were supposed to prevent. Also, people found ways of getting around the limits. Still, the OPA accomplished its main task, keeping inflation under control. The cost of living rose, but not nearly as much as it had in World War I.

The OPA also oversaw rationing during the war. The goal of rationing was a fair distribution of scarce items. Beginning in 1943, the OPA assigned point values to items such as sugar, coffee, meat, butter, canned fruit, and shoes. It issued ration books of coupons worth a certain number of points for categories of food or clothing. Once consumers had used up their points, they could not buy any more of those items until they received new ration books or traded coupons with neighbors. Gasoline for cars was strictly rationed, too, on the basis of need. Signs asked, "Is this trip necessary?" Customers found some shortages and ration rules confusing, but any complaint could be answered with the question, "Don't you know there's a war on?"

VIEWING HISTORY Shoppers needed ration points (right) as well as cash to buy rationed goods. **Drawing Inferences** *Why did Americans support rationing?*

Popular Culture With so many goods unavailable, Americans looked for other ways to spend their money. Civilians bought and read more books and magazines. They purchased recordings of popular songs, such as "White Christmas" by Irving Berlin, a sentimental favorite of both soldiers and civilians. They flocked to baseball games, even though most of their favorite players had gone off to war. Millions of Americans—about 60 percent of the population—also went to the movies every week.

ACTIVITY
Connecting with Culture

Ask students to interview older relatives or other appropriate adults about their experience and memories of the home front during World War II, and to share what they learn with the class. **(Verbal/Linguistic)**

BACKGROUND
Art History

Popular movies of the era include some of the best ever made, like *Citizen Kane* (1941), *The Maltese Falcon* (1941), and *Yankee Doodle Dandy* (1942). Not surprisingly, many of them, like *Casablanca* (1942), were war films. Many film stars of the era volunteered for the armed services, sold war bonds, or made movies to train servicemen.

CAPTION ANSWERS

Viewing History Americans recognized that rationing was essential to the war effort.

RESOURCE DIRECTORY

Teaching Resources
Units 5/6/7 booklet
- Section 1 Quiz, p. 15

Guide to the Essentials
- Section 1 Summary, p. 86

Technology
Color Transparencies *Fine Art,* E18

Enlisting Public Support The government understood the need to maintain morale. It encouraged citizens to participate in the war effort while persuading them to accept rationing and conserve precious resources. Roosevelt established the Office of War Information in June 1942 to work with magazine publishers, advertising agencies, and radio stations. It hired writers and artists to create posters and ads that stirred Americans' patriotic feelings.

One popular idea was the **victory garden,** a home vegetable garden planted to add to the home food supply and replace farm produce sent to feed the soldiers. Soon people in cities and suburbs were planting tomatoes, peas, and radishes in backyards, empty parking lots, and playgrounds. By 1943, victory gardens produced about one third of the country's fresh vegetables.

Victory gardens gave people a chance to help the war effort and to add fresh vegetables to their food rations.

The war became a part of everyday life in many ways. People drew their shades for nighttime "blackouts," which tested their readiness for possible bombing raids. Men too old for the army joined the Civilian Defense effort, wearing their CD armbands as they tested air raid sirens. Women knit scarves and socks or rolled bandages for the Red Cross.

The government encouraged efforts to recycle scrap metal, paper, and other materials for war production. In one drive, people collected tin cans, pots and pans, razor blades, old shovels, and even old lipstick tubes. The collection drives kept adults and children actively involved in the war effort. "Play your part." "Conserve and collect." "Use it up, wear it out, make it do or do without." These slogans echoed throughout the United States and reminded people on the home front of their important contributions to the war effort.

Section 1 Assessment

READING COMPREHENSION

1. Describe three ways that individual Americans contributed to the war effort.
2. How did the government pay for the war effort?
3. What was the purpose of the **Office of War Mobilization?**
4. What effect did shortages have on the economy?

CRITICAL THINKING AND WRITING

5. **Making Comparisons** (a) How were African Americans in the military treated differently from white soldiers? (b) How were women in the military treated differently from men? (c) Why do you think the military insisted on these differences at the start of the war?
6. **Writing to Describe** Write a paragraph detailing daily life from the point of view of an American in the early 1940s. Include the effects of the mobilization for war.

Take It to the NET

Activity: Analyzing Primary Sources Select a primary source from the American home front during World War II (for example, a letter, a poster, or an oral history). Describe the source you selected in a brief report. What did the source reveal about the home front? Use the links provided in the *America: Pathways to the Present* area at the following Web site for help in completing this activity.
www.phschool.com

Section 1 Assessment

Reading Comprehension

1. Sample answers: Volunteering for military service; planting victory gardens; joining the Civilian Defense effort.
2. Through higher taxes, borrowing money, sale of war bonds, and deficit spending.
3. It served as an agency specializing in the centralization of resources.
4. They limited the goods people could buy; rationing occurred; supply of consumer goods fell short of demand.

Critical Thinking and Writing

5. (a) At first, African American troops were limited to supporting roles, and even when given the opportunity to fight, they were generally assigned to separate units. (b) Women were used in many different roles, but were excluded from combat. (c) These differences reflected existing roles in society at that time.
6. Paragraphs will vary, but should be descriptive and use supporting facts from the section.

Take It to the NET

Reports will vary, but should demonstrate insight into the wartime mood and conditions on the home front.

Section 2
Retaking Europe

SECTION OBJECTIVES

1. See where Americans joined the struggle against the Axis.
2. Find out how the war in the Soviet Union changed from 1941 to 1943.
3. Learn about the role air power played in the war in Europe.
4. Read about why the invasion of Western Europe succeeded.
5. Discover some events that marked the end of the war in Europe.

BELLRINGER

Warm-Up Activity Ask students if they have ever used the term *D-Day.* If so, what did they mean by it?

Activating Prior Knowledge Do students know individuals who fought in World War II? Where and when did these people fight? As students read this section, have them note any engagements in World War II in which people they know might have been involved.

READING STRATEGY

As students read this section, have them analyze the major issues and events of World War II, such as fighting the war on multiple fronts, the battle of Midway, and the invasion of Normandy.

ACTIVITY
Connecting with Citizenship

Have students generate lists of the principles or ideals of the United States (e.g., popular sovereignty, limited government, freedom, equality, etc.) and then compare and contrast these ideals with the principles of the Atlantic Charter. Ask: Did the principles of the Atlantic Charter fully and faithfully reflect American principles? Have students present their answers in the form of paragraphs. **(Verbal/Linguistic)**

Section

2 Retaking Europe

READING FOCUS

- Where did Americans join the struggle against the Axis?
- How did the war in the Soviet Union change from 1941 to 1943?
- What role did air power play in the war in Europe?
- Why did the invasion of Western Europe succeed?
- What events marked the end of the war in Europe?

KEY TERMS

Atlantic Charter
carpet bombing
D-Day
Battle of the Bulge

TAKING NOTES

As you read, complete the following chart by listing wartime events in different regions of Europe and North Africa.

Region	Events
Western Europe	• Allied navies battle Germany for control of the Atlantic Ocean. •
Eastern Europe	
North Africa and Italy	

MAIN IDEA

To secure victory in Europe, the Allies waged war in the Atlantic Ocean, North Africa, the Soviet Union, and Western Europe between 1941 and 1945.

Setting the Scene In August 1941, unknown to the rest of the world, two warships quietly lay at anchor off the coast of Newfoundland. Aboard were Prime Minister Winston Churchill and President Franklin D. Roosevelt. Both men believed that the United States would soon join Great Britain militarily as an ally in war. The two leaders met in secret to discuss the war's aims and to agree on a set of principles to guide them in the years ahead. After several days of talks, they issued a joint declaration of those principles, which included the following:

Churchill and Roosevelt met secretly to negotiate the Atlantic Charter while the United States was still neutral.

> *"First, their countries seek no aggrandizement [enlargement], territorial or other.*
>
> *Second, they desire to see no territorial changes that do not accord with the freely expressed wishes of the peoples concerned.*
>
> *Third, they respect the right of all peoples to choose the form of government under which they will live; . . .*
>
> *Sixth, after the final destruction of the Nazi tyranny, they hope to see established a peace which will afford to all nations the means of dwelling in safety within their own boundaries, . . .*
>
> *Eighth, they believe that all of the nations of the world . . . must come to the abandonment of the use of force. . . ."*
>
> —Franklin D. Roosevelt and Winston S. Churchill, August 14, 1941

The declaration of principles became known as the **Atlantic Charter.** After the war, this charter would form the basis for the United Nations.

RESOURCE DIRECTORY

Teaching Resources
Guided Reading and Review booklet, p. 101

Other Print Resources
Historical Outline Map Book *World War II in Europe and North Africa,* p. 65

Technology
Section Reading Support Transparencies
Guided Reading Audiotapes (English/Spanish), Ch. 18
Student Edition on Audio CD, Ch. 18
Color Transparencies *The Way It Works,* H18; *Historical Maps,* A41
Prentice Hall Presentation Pro CD-ROM, Ch. 18
Companion Web site, www.phschool.com

Americans Join the Struggle

The United States entered the war in December 1941, at a critical time for the Allies. London and other major British cities had suffered heavy damage during the Battle of Britain. The Germans' *blitzkrieg* had extended Nazi control across most of Europe. In North Africa, a mixed German and Italian army was bearing down on British forces. Many people feared that Germany could not be stopped.

The Battle of the Atlantic At sea, Britain and the United States desperately struggled to control the Atlantic trade routes vital to British survival. Britain relied on shipments of food and supplies from the United States and from its territories overseas. As allied merchant ships crossed the Atlantic, German U-boats, or submarines, sailed out from ports in France to attack them. To protect themselves better, Allied ships formed convoys led by American and British warships. The Germans countered with groups of as many as 20 U-boats, called wolf packs, that carried out coordinated nighttime attacks on the convoys.

After the United States entered the war, U-boats began attacking merchant ships within sight of the American coast. Although Allied warships used underwater sound equipment called sonar to locate and attack U-boats, the wolf packs experienced great success. In the Atlantic, they sank nearly 175 ships in June 1942 alone. Allied convoys later developed better defensive strategies, including the use of long-range sub-hunting aircraft, and the U-boat success rate plummeted.

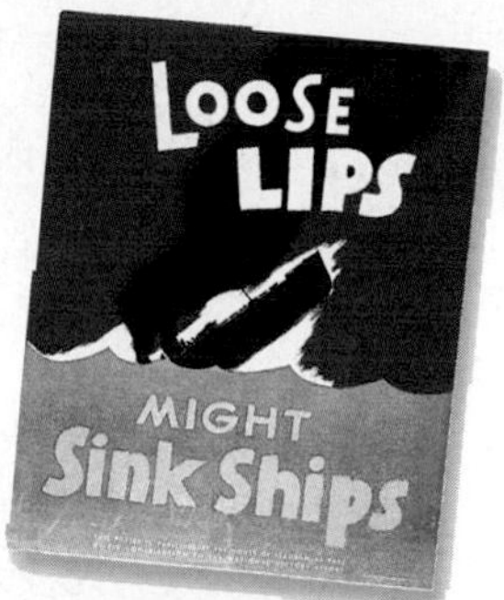
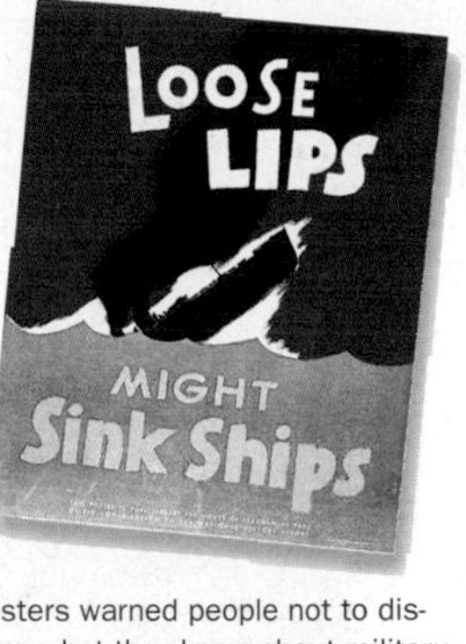

Posters warned people not to discuss what they knew about military movements for fear of espionage.

MAP SKILLS After stopping the German offensive, the Allies were able to reconquer Europe from the south, east, and west. **Place** *Which regions saw fighting in 1943?*

Allied Advances in Europe and North Africa, 1942–1945

601

LESSON PLAN

Focus The Allies were on the defensive when the United States entered the war. Ask students to consider how the Allies planned to win victory in Europe.

Instruct Discuss the factors that mobilized diverse groups of Americans to enter the armed forces. Ask students to explain how Roosevelt's vision of freedom might have been a unifying force. Have students identify the reasons for U.S. involvement in World War II, including the attack on Pearl Harbor. Ask how discrimination and segregation affected some groups in the military. How did the armed forces benefit from diversity?

Ask why the Soviet Union continually pressured the Allies to open a front in Western Europe. Why did Churchill insist on attacking Germany through North Africa and Italy? How were D-Day and the Battle of the Bulge significant?

Assess/Reteach Have students view a world map and identify areas of the world that were involved in World War II. Were there any areas that were not affected?

CAPTION ANSWERS

Map Skills The Soviet Union, North Africa, Sicily, and Italy.

CUSTOMIZE FOR ...

Gifted and Talented

Ask students to write a short paper on one or more aspects of the harsh and gritty Battle of the Atlantic. Suggest to the students such things as the difficulty for submarine crews of living in a confined space on lengthy war patrols; the horrors of being on board a surface ship that has been torpedoed by a U-boat; and the difficulties for Allied pilots of flying long patrols in search of U-boats.

ACTIVITY
Connecting with History and Conflict

Explain that the age of the typical soldier in World War II ranged from late teens to early twenties. Ask students to assume the role of a citizen in this age group during World War II. Have them write a letter to President Roosevelt explaining their views on either of the following topics: the role of women in the military or segregation in the armed forces. Letters should respectfully suggest to Roosevelt a change the students feel is acceptable. Ask why they think the government did not change its policies at the time. **(Verbal/Linguistic)**

BACKGROUND
Biography

Erwin Rommel (1891–1944) first joined the German army in 1910. During World War I his courage, leadership, and rapport with his men were recognized early. Though offered many promotions, he chose to remain on the front lines. With the outbreak of World War II, Rommel was on the front lines again, first in France and then in Libya and North Africa. He became known as "The Desert Fox" because of his fearless surprise attacks. As the fighting in Africa progressed, Rommel became increasingly disenchanted with his Italian allies and the German command itself. Undersupplied by his government and overwhelmed by the opposition, Rommel was forced to concede defeat. He was sent to France, where he realized that the beaches of Normandy were a logical place for an Allied invasion. He tried to communicate this warning to his superiors, but he was ignored.

By autumn of 1943, Rommel became convinced that the war was unwinnable, and he became involved with an unsuccessful attempt to remove Hitler from power. Not wanting to turn the popular Rommel into a martyr, Hitler sent two generals to Rommel with poison and the suggestion that taking the poison would spare his reputation. Rommel complied, and he died on October 14, 1944.

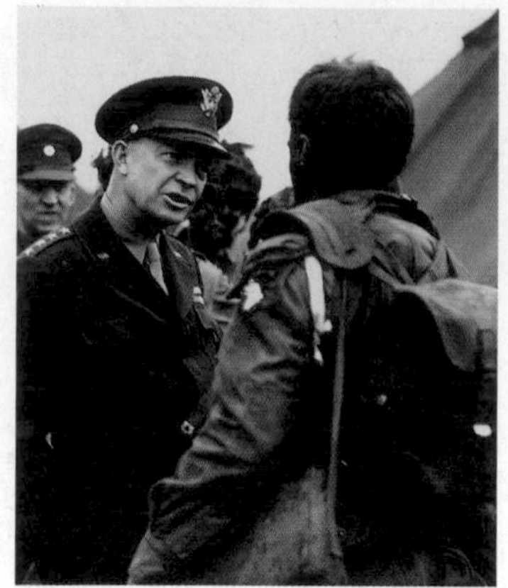

General Dwight D. Eisenhower (left) was named commander of U.S. troops in Europe in June 1942.

The North Africa Campaign Starting in August 1940, a British army had successfully battled Italian troops in the Egyptian and Libyan deserts of North Africa. Then, in February 1941, Hitler sent General Erwin Rommel and a German division to reinforce the Italians. Rommel, who earned the nickname "Desert Fox" for his shrewd tactics, won several battles. The Germans pushed deep into British-controlled Egypt and threatened the Middle East. Rommel's offensive failed, however, in November 1942, when the British under General Bernard Montgomery won a decisive victory at El Alamein. The German army retreated west.

A few days later, Allied troops landed in the French territories of Morocco and Algeria on the northwest coast of North Africa. This largely American force, under the command of American General Dwight D. Eisenhower, quickly pushed eastward. Meanwhile, British troops chased Rommel westward from Egypt. In response, Hitler sent some 20,000 combat troops across the Mediterranean Sea from Italy to reinforce Rommel's army in Tunisia. There, in February 1943, the inexperienced Americans suffered a major defeat of the war while trying to defend the Kasserine Pass. They learned from their defeat, however, and by early May 1943, the Allied armies had the Axis forces in North Africa trapped. Despite Hitler's instructions to fight to the death, about 240,000 Germans and Italians surrendered.

Churchill and Roosevelt met again in January 1943 at Casablanca, Morocco. At this Casablanca Conference, they mapped out their strategy for the rest of the war. They decided to maintain the approach of dealing with Europe first. They would continue to concentrate Allied resources on Europe before trying to win the war in the Pacific. Churchill and Roosevelt also agreed to accept nothing less than the unconditional surrender of Italy, Germany, and Japan.

The Invasion of Italy Control of North Africa freed the Allies to make the next move toward retaking Europe. They decided to target Italy, which lay to the north, across the Mediterranean. In July 1943, the U.S. Seventh Army, under General George S. Patton, invaded the large island of Sicily with British forces.

VIEWING HISTORY The ancient monastery at Monte Cassino was destroyed in the battle to break through German defenses in Italy. **Expressing Problems Clearly** *Describe the obstacles Allied troops faced in Italy.*

RESOURCE DIRECTORY
Technology

RESOURCE PRO® Biography *Jacqueline Cochran,* found on Resource Pro, profiles a veteran of the World War II Women's Air Force Service Pilots.

RESOURCE PRO® Critical Thinking Activity *Predicting Consequences: After the Army—What?* found on Resource Pro, helps students apply this skill by having them explore possible postwar lifestyle changes for returning servicemen and women.

RESOURCE PRO® Visual Learning Activity *The North African Front,* found on Resource Pro, uses information from the chapter and a photograph of American soldiers in Tunisia to challenge students' perception of detail.

Exploring Primary Sources in U.S. History CD-ROM *"Gee, Mom, I Want to Go Home," army song*

CAPTION ANSWERS

Viewing History Mountainous terrain, destroyed bridges, blocked roads, and elaborate German Army defenses.

With the Italian mainland in jeopardy, Italians lost faith in Mussolini's leadership. An official Fascist council voted to remove him from office, and King Victor Emmanuel III had him arrested. The Fascist Party was promptly disbanded, but the Germans freed Mussolini and evacuated him to northern Italy.

In September 1943, as Allied troops threatened to overrun the south and take Rome, Italy's new government surrendered. On October 13, the government declared war on Germany. The German army in Italy, however, continued to resist, blocking roads and destroying bridges as it retreated northward through the mountainous Italian peninsula. The Germans set up Mussolini as the puppet ruler of a fascist Italian state in northern Italy.

By November, the Allied advance had stalled in the face of a stiffened German defense. The town of Cassino, the key to the German defensive line, stood between the Allies and Rome. In January 1944, the Allies made a surprise move. They landed an American army unit behind German lines on the beach at Anzio, just 35 miles south of Rome. However, the American commander took too long to organize his forces. A German force blocked off the beach in time to trap the Allied troops. For the next four months, the Germans fiercely attacked the trapped soldiers. Before the Americans finally broke through German defenses in May 1944, tens of thousands of American soldiers had been killed or wounded.

Meanwhile, the Allies attacked Cassino and succeeded in breaking through the German line. Joining with the forces from Anzio, the Allied army quickly captured Rome. They faced more months of heavy fighting, however, before the Germans in northern Italy finally surrendered in April 1945. That same month, Mussolini was shot and killed by Italians as he tried to flee across the northern Italian border.

Focus on WORLD EVENTS

The Siege of Leningrad At the northern reaches of the Eastern Front, Hitler's armies began a nearly three-year siege of Leningrad in September 1941. Despite German artillery attacks, the Soviets sustained a heroic effort to transport food and supplies to the city's three million inhabitants across the frozen surface of Lake Ladoga, Leningrad's only link to the Soviet Union. About 660,000 residents died of starvation and disease before the Germans retreated in January 1944. Leningrad was awarded the Order of Lenin and the title "Hero City of the Soviet Union" in gratitude for its stand against Hitler.

War in the Soviet Union

As the Allies battled their way across North Africa and into Italy, an epic struggle unfolded in eastern Europe. In *Mein Kampf,* Hitler had called for the conquest of the Soviet Union, to give the German people "living space." Hitler believed that Germany had to be self-sufficient, which meant that it needed its own sources of oil and food. By 1941, Hitler had taken control of huge oilfields in Romania. Now he planned to seize the farmlands of the Ukraine. After losing the Battle of Britain, Hitler decided to turn his war machine to the east. He broke his pact with Stalin and launched an attack against the Soviet Union.

The Germans Advance, 1941–1942 The attack began in the early morning hours of June 22, 1941. Nearly 3.6 million German and other Axis troops poured across the length of the Soviet border, from Finland in the north to Romania in the south. Nearly 3 million Red Army soldiers, poorly trained and badly equipped, mobilized to oppose the *blitzkrieg.*

The intensity and the brutality of the German attack took the Soviet defenders by surprise. The *Luftwaffe* quickly gained control of the air, and German ground troops drove deep into Soviet territory. Germany captured hundreds of thousands of Soviet soldiers who were trapped by the German army's quick advances. Soviet citizens who suffered badly under Stalin, including Ukrainians and Lithuanians, welcomed the Germans as liberators. Their enthusiasm ended quickly as German troops introduced forced labor and began executing civilians.

READING CHECK
How successful was the invasion of the Soviet Union in its first few months?

ACTIVITY
Connecting with Geography

Ask students to work in groups to make a detailed map of the theater of war in either Europe or North Africa, including battle lines and the dates of important events. **(Visual/Spatial)**

BACKGROUND
Military Technology

One of the obstacles facing the landing at Anzio was a shortage of LSTs. LST stood for "Landing Ship Tank." Many different types of landing craft were used by the Allies to land troops on beaches. Of these, the LST was the largest and arguably the most important. They were so crucial to the war effort that Winston Churchill once remarked, "Sometimes I think the whole war depends on some damned thing called an LST." In some ways, he was right: it was a critical piece of equipment. (Naval personnel, who knew the LSTs were prime targets for enemy attack, sometimes said that LST stood for "Large Slow Target.")

READING CHECK
It was widely successful in the first few months. The German air forces gained near total control of the air, and German ground troops took hundreds of thousands of Russian prisoners and penetrated deep into Russian territory.

CUSTOMIZE FOR ...
Less Proficient Readers
Have students work together to make a time line of the major battles and events in the European and North African theaters of war. The time line should begin in 1941 and end in 1945.

Activity
Student Portfolio

You may wish to have students add the following to their portfolios: Ask students to prepare a detailed report about one battle of World War II or about one military leader, such as Omar Bradley, Dwight Eisenhower, or Douglas MacArthur. Suggest that students locate old issues of *Yank* magazine in the library and read eyewitness accounts written by soldiers who actually participated in the battles as background for their reports. **(Verbal/Linguistic)**

Background
Interdisciplinary

It is instructive to compare Soviet and American casualties from World War II. About 27 million Soviets died as a result of the war. The comparable figure for Americans is about 40,000 lives lost. As one historian put it, "More Russian soldiers died in the one great battle for Stalingrad than Americans did in *all* the battles in the *entire* war." The Battle of Stalingrad stands as the deadliest battle in human history. Before the battle, about 500,000 people lived in Stalingrad. At the end of the battle, only about 1,500 of them were still alive. All told, this single battle claimed more than one million lives—a mind-boggling death toll. Soviet resentment of a perceived lack of American appreciation of such facts as these helped fuel the Cold War.

The *Reichstag*

In the final days of World War II, a Soviet soldier celebrated the final conquest of Berlin by raising a Soviet flag over the ruined *Reichstag* building. His act was only one of many turning points in German history that occurred at the *Reichstag* (left).

On February 27, 1933, four weeks after Hitler became chancellor, the main chamber of the *Reichstag* burned in a suspicious fire attributed to the Communists. Hitler used the fire as a pretext to win dictatorial powers and end the legislature's independence. The *Reichstag* building housed Nazi exhibitions in the late 1930s and suffered from Allied bombing during World War II.

After 1945, the heavily damaged *Reichstag* was located within West Berlin, but the new east-west boundary divided it from nearby buildings. The West German government, uncomfortable with Berlin's isolated location and its Nazi associations, chose the university town of Bonn as its capital instead. Partially restored as a museum, the *Reichstag* occasionally served as a backdrop for speeches and concerts protesting Communist acts in the east.

Today When Germany reunited in 1990, Chancellor Helmut Kohl opted to move the national capital back to unified Berlin. Germany chose to replace part of the old building so as to create a new *Reichstag* unburdened by its past history. To replace the destroyed roof, British architect Norman Foster designed a futuristic glass dome that reflected light into the building and opened the parliamentary chamber up to the outside. Visitors may climb to the very top of the dome for views of Berlin. In 1999, 60 years after World War II began, the German Parliament returned to the *Reichstag* building.

How did the history of the *Reichstag* building parallel the history of democracy in Germany?

Ten days after the invasion began, Stalin broadcast a message to his people: "In case of a forced retreat of the Red Army," he said, "all rolling stock [trains] must be evacuated; to the enemy must not be left a single engine, a single railway car, not a single pound of grain or gallon of fuel." Now, as the army began to retreat, it carried out this policy, destroying everything that might be useful to the enemy. In the meantime, Stalin asked Roosevelt for help through the Lend-Lease program. American aid began to flow and lasted until the end of the war.

By that autumn, German armies had advanced several hundred miles into the Soviet Union. German troops threatened the capital, Moscow, and nearly surrounded the historic city of Leningrad, now known as St. Petersburg. Stalin desperately urged his allies to launch an attack on Western Europe. This action would take pressure off the Soviet Union's Red Army by forcing Hitler to fight on two fronts at once. Churchill did not feel ready to commit to a risky invasion. Later, at Casablanca, he would persuade Roosevelt instead to invade Italy, which he called the "soft underbelly" of Europe. The Soviet people would have to confront the bulk of the German army on their own.

The Battle of Stalingrad The cold Russian winter stopped Germany's advance in October, and the Soviets regained some of their lost territory. The next summer brought a new German offensive aimed at oil fields to the southeast. The Red Army decided to make its stand at Stalingrad, a major rail and industrial center on the Volga River. In mid-September 1942, the Germans began a campaign of firebombing and shelling that lasted more than two months. Soviet fighters took up positions in the charred rubble that remained of Stalingrad. There they engaged the advancing German troops in bitter house-to-house combat, but lost most of the city.

In mid-November, taking advantage of harsh winter weather, Soviet forces launched a fierce counterattack. As Hitler had ruled out a retreat, the German army was soon surrounded in the ruined city with few supplies and no hope of escape. In late January, the Red Army launched a final assault on the freezing enemy. A German soldier later described the experience:

> *"Completely cut off, the men in field grey just slouched on, invariably filthy and invariably louse-ridden, their weary shoulders sagging, from one defence position to another. The icy winds of those great white wastes which stretched for ever beyond us to the east lashed a million crystals of razor-like snow into their unshaven faces, skin now loose-stretched over bone, so utter was the exhaustion, so utter the starvation."*
>
> —A German infantryman at Stalingrad, December 1942

Caption Answers

Fast Forward to Today The 1933 Reichstag fire and its aftermath served as a reminder that democracy in Germany had come to a grinding halt. The 1999 reopening of the renovated Reichstag building symbolized that democracy had returned to all of Germany.

RESOURCE DIRECTORY
Technology

RESOURCE PRO® Literature Activity *Dispatches from the Battle Front,* found on Resource Pro, features war correspondent Ernie Pyle's descriptions of the front lines of the European theater and the lives of the U.S. servicemen who fought there.

On January 31, 1943, more than 90,000 surviving Germans surrendered. In all, Germany lost some 330,000 troops at Stalingrad. Soviet losses are unknown, but estimates range as high as 1,100,000.

The Battle of Stalingrad proved to be the turning point of the war in the east. Germany's seemingly unstoppable offensive was over. After their victory, Soviet forces began a long struggle to regain the territory lost to the Germans. As the Red Army slowly forced the German invaders back, Stalin continued to push for the long-promised Soviet invasion of Western Europe.

American BIOGRAPHY

George Marshall
1880–1959

A graduate of Virginia Military Institute, George Marshall had served in France during World War I, where he aided in planning major Allied victories. He became Army Chief of Staff in 1939 and used his position to urge President Roosevelt to strengthen the army in preparation for war. As the highest-ranking general in the United States during the war, he was among the first leaders to recommend an early invasion of Western Europe. After the war, he left his post as Army Chief of Staff to become Secretary of State under President Truman. His work to rebuild Europe with American aid gained him the Nobel peace prize in 1953.

The Allied Air War

To be successful, a major invasion of Western Europe by land forces needed the support of air power. By 1943, Allied pilots had gained plenty of battle experience. Aside from fighting off German attacks, Britain's Royal Air Force (RAF) had carried out long-range bombing of Germany, as well as Germany's oil facilities in Romania.

As you read earlier, German warplanes started to target cities during the Battle of Britain and British warplanes followed suit. After abandoning attempts to pinpoint targets, the RAF developed a technique called **carpet bombing,** in which planes scattered large numbers of bombs over a wide area. German cities suffered heavy damage as a result.

Allied bombing of Germany intensified after the United States entered the war. In a typical American raid, hundreds of B-17 Flying Fortresses took off from Britain, escorted by fighters. They rained bombs on German aircraft factories, railway lines, ball-bearing plants, bridges, and cities. With these massive raids, the Allies aimed to destroy Germany's ability to fight the war.

In the spring of 1943, the Allies stepped up their bombing campaign yet again in preparation for an eventual Allied invasion. Like British civilians during the Blitz, Germans came to spend nights in underground air raid shelters while enemy planes flew above. On the night of July 28, 1943, firebombing turned Hamburg into one huge blaze. A survivor recalled that "a storm started, a shrill howling in the street. It grew into a hurricane so that we had to abandon all hope of fighting the fire." The Hamburg fire department coined the term "firestorm" to describe this combination of flames driven by fierce heat-generated winds. More than 40,000 civilians died in four attacks on Hamburg.

By 1944, British and American commanders were conducting coordinated air raids—American planes bombing by day and RAF planes bombing by night. At its height, some 3,000 planes took part in this campaign.

The Invasion of Western Europe

Stalin was not the only leader calling for an invasion of Western Europe. George Marshall, the top American general and FDR's Chief of Staff, voiced the same opinion. At every Allied strategy conference after the United States entered the war, he pushed for an attack on the German forces occupying France. In late 1943, the British finally agreed to go along with Marshall's proposal. The invasion, code-named Operation Overlord, would be launched from Great Britain. Marshall chose General Eisenhower to be the supreme commander of the invasion forces.

The Allies began a massive military buildup in southern England. Polish, Dutch, Belgian, and French troops joined the American, British, and Canadian forces already in place. In response, the Germans strengthened their defenses

ACTIVITY

Connecting with History and Conflict

Have student groups research the use of carpet bombing versus targeted bombing in different conflicts, such as the Vietnam War and the Gulf War. Have students list the strengths and weaknesses and parameters for the use of each method. **(Verbal/Linguistic)**

BACKGROUND

Connections to History and Conflict

In contrast to the Royal Air Force's "carpet bombing," the American bomber command focused on its opposite: "precision bombing." In precision bombing, bombers attacked specific targets, such as factories or road junctions. The Americans felt they could achieve such precision because of a device called the Norden bombsight. Named for its inventor, Carl Norden, the bombsight was basically an early analog computer consisting of gyroscopes, mirrors, and a telescope. By sighting through it, bombardiers could calculate the exact moment to release their bomb loads. Theoretically, the bombsight was so accurate that a bombardier could hit a 100-foot circle from an altitude of four miles. In practice, it was less accurate, but still fairly effective. Airmen often claimed it could "put a bomb in a pickle barrel." The bombsight was a closely guarded military secret, and bombardiers had to swear to guard its secret with their lives.

CUSTOMIZE FOR ...

Less Proficient Readers

Have students read the section on the Battle of Stalingrad. Ask them to write a paragraph briefly explaining what they feel to be the most important reason for the massive German defeat at Stalingrad.

ACTIVITY
Connecting with Today

Divide the class into small groups. Assign each group the task of creating an illustrated travel brochure for a trip to the Normandy beaches today. The students' brochure should identify the ruins, monuments, and other attractions that modern visitors to the site of the historic invasion can view. **(Visual/Spatial)**

BACKGROUND
Etymology

Today, the term *D-Day* is used almost exclusively to refer to June 6, 1944, when the great Allied invasion of Europe began. Originally, however, D-Day referred to the day on which any military operation or offensive was set to commence. The time of the day that operations began was called "H-Hour." These terms were used most often in the case of amphibious operations—i.e., landings from the sea, such as the island campaigns in the Pacific. The etymology of the two terms follows the same pattern: the "D" in D-Day is simply an abbreviation for "day"; the "H" in H-Hour is an abbreviation for "hour."

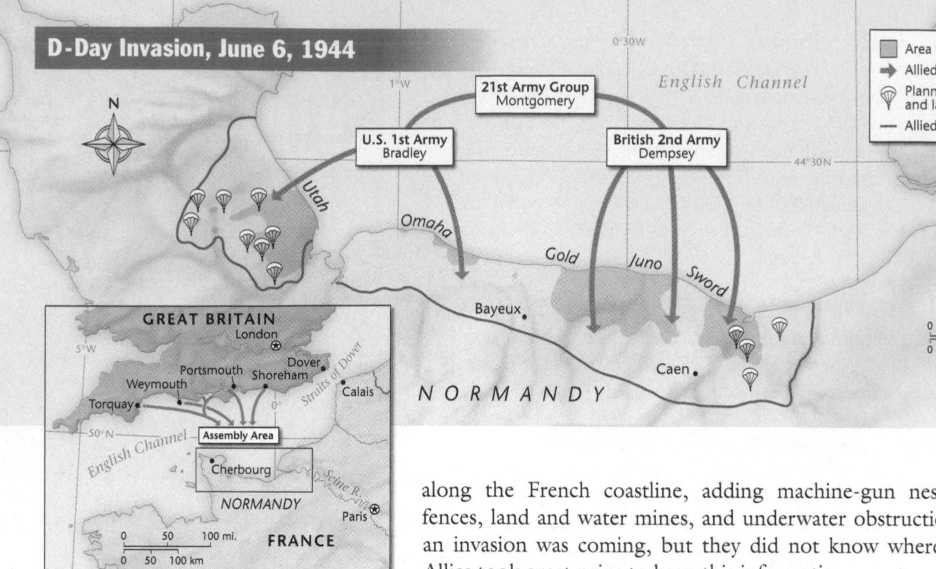

MAP SKILLS Allied troops began the liberation of Western Europe on the beaches of Normandy on June 6, 1944. **Movement** *Cite evidence to show that the Allies carefully planned most aspects of the invasion.*

along the French coastline, adding machine-gun nests, barbed-wire fences, land and water mines, and underwater obstructions. They knew an invasion was coming, but they did not know where or when. The Allies took great pains to keep this information secret.

D-Day Shortly after midnight on June 6, 1944, some 4,600 invasion craft and warships slipped out of their harbors in southern England. As the ships crossed the English Channel, about 1,000 RAF bombers pounded German defenses at Normandy. Meanwhile, some 23,000 airborne British and American soldiers, in a daring nighttime maneuver, parachuted behind enemy lines.

At dawn on **D-Day,** the day the invasion of Western Europe began, Allied warships in the channel began a massive shelling of the coast. Some 1,000 American planes continued the RAF's air bombardment. Then, around 150,000 Allied troops and their equipment began to come ashore along 60 miles of the Normandy coast in the largest landing by sea in history.

Despite the advice of his generals to launch a quick counterattack, Hitler hesitated. Thanks to a complex Allied deception, he feared a second, larger invasion at the narrowest part of the English Channel near Calais. Nevertheless, the limited German force at Normandy resisted fiercely. At Omaha Beach, the code name for one landing site, the Allies suffered some 2,000 casualties. One Allied soldier later explained his experience of landing at Omaha Beach:

> "*It seemed like the whole world exploded. There was gunfire from battleships, destroyers, and cruisers. The bombers were still hitting the beaches. . . . As we went in, we could see small craft from the 116th Infantry that had gone in ahead, sunk. There were bodies bobbing in the water, even out three or four miles.*"
>
> —Lieutenant Robert Edlin

In spite of the heavy casualties of D-Day, within a week a half million men had come ashore. By late July, the Allied force in France numbered some 2 million troops.

Liberating France Air power helped the Allies establish a beachhead at Normandy and also held off German reinforcements by blowing up bridges throughout the region. Allied troops engaged in intense fighting on the ground. In early August, General Patton used a *blitzkrieg* to open a hole in the German

Sounds of an Era

Listen to a live description of the D-Day invasion and other sounds from World War II.

CAPTION ANSWERS

Map Skills The Allies divided the attacking forces into five groups with assigned landing points and defined goals to meet in the first day. Allied forces entered the English Channel from different ports and met at a gathering point in the Channel before attacking.

RESOURCE DIRECTORY

Other Print Resources

Historical Outline Map Book *Germany Divided,* p. 67

Technology

Color Transparencies *Historical Maps,* A42

Sounds of an Era Audio CD *D-Day Invasion,* 1944 recording (time: 40 seconds)

lines and burst out of Normandy. Armored units of his U.S. Third Army drove deep into enemy territory and then encircled and destroyed the opposing forces. After breaking German defenses, Patton led his army on a successful sweep across northern France.

In Paris, an uprising started by the French Resistance freed the city from German control. On August 25, 1944, a French division of the U.S. First Army officially liberated Paris. That same day, General Charles de Gaulle arrived in the city, prepared to take charge of the French government.

British and Canadian forces freed Brussels and Antwerp in Belgium a few days later. In mid-September, a combined Allied force attacked the Germans occupying the Netherlands. At about the same time, American soldiers crossed the western border of Germany.

The Battle of the Bulge The Nazis fought desperately to defend their conquests. To the north, the Allied attack on the Netherlands faltered at the Rhine River. Meanwhile, Hitler reinforced the army with thousands of additional draftees, some as young as 15. Then, in mid-December 1944, Germany launched a counterattack in Belgium and Luxembourg. The German attack smashed into the U.S. First Army and pushed it back, forming a bulge in the Allied line. The resulting clash came to be known as the **Battle of the Bulge.**

Many small units, cut off from the rest of the American army, fought gallantly against overwhelming odds. From his headquarters near Paris, Eisenhower ordered more troops to the scene. General Patton rapidly moved his U.S. Third Army north to help stop the German advance. In just a few weeks, the First and Third armies, under the overall direction of General Omar N. Bradley, knocked the Germans back and restarted the Allied drive into Germany.

The Battle of the Bulge was the largest battle in Western Europe during World War II, and the largest battle ever fought by the United States Army. It involved some 600,000 GIs, of whom about 80,000 were killed, wounded, or captured. German losses totaled about 100,000. After this battle, most Nazi leaders recognized that the war was lost.

The War in Europe Ends

In March 1945, as Allied bombers continued to strike German cities, American ground forces under General Bradley crossed the Rhine River and moved toward Berlin from the west. Meanwhile, Soviet troops pushed into Germany from the east.

Soviet Forces Advance The struggle between German and Soviet forces from 1941 to 1945 dwarfed the fighting in France. At any given time, more than 9 million soldiers were fighting on the eastern front. The costs of this struggle were horrific. Some 11 million Soviet and 3 million German soldiers died, accounting for more than two thirds of the soldiers killed in all of World War II. Current estimates place the total of Soviet civilian and military deaths at about 18 million.

After the hardships their nation had endured, Soviet leaders considered the capture of Berlin, Germany's capital, a matter of honor. In late April 1945, Soviet troops fought their way into Berlin. As they had in Stalingrad, they fought German soldiers for each ruined house and street in the destroyed city.

Allied soldiers parachute into France during the D-Day invasion.

ACTIVITY Connecting with Geography

Have a small group of students create a map similar to the one on the previous page that depicts the Battle of the Bulge. The map should clearly show the basic disposition and movement of Allied and German forces, and depict the "bulge" in the Allied line. **(Visual/Spatial)**

ACTIVITY Connecting with Culture

Have students create a bulletin-board display that celebrates V-E Day. The display should include newspaper headlines, photographs of celebrations, first-person accounts, and other memorabilia of the historic day. **(Visual/Spatial)**

TEST PREPARATION

Have students read the section "D-Day" on the previous page and then answer the question below.

Of all the brave acts surrounding the D-Day invasion, what was arguably the most risky?

- **(A)** Parachuting behind enemy lines at night.
- **B** Operating one of the small landing craft used to transfer soldiers from troopships to the beach.
- **C** Bombing German defenses on the French coast.
- **D** Serving on a warship protecting the invasion fleet.

Section 2 Assessment

Reading Comprehension

1. It contained terms agreed to by Great Britain and the U.S. to govern war behavior and define their aims.
2. (a) The intensity of the attack took the Soviets by surprise. (b) During the retreat, the Soviets destroyed any items that could be of use to the Germans; the cold, harsh weather; the vast size of the Soviet Union.
3. (a) To drop many bombs over a wide area, causing heavy damage. (b) Carpet bombing, along with more precise American bombing, enabled the Allies to strike all over Germany with lower risk for Allied casualties.
4. It represented the opening of the Allied invasion of Western Europe.

Critical Thinking and Writing

5. The Soviet Union bore the heaviest cost of fighting Germany.
6. Battle of Stalingrad: Turning point of war in the east; German surrender and loss showed that Germany's seemingly unstoppable offensive was over. Battle of the Bulge: Battle resulted in great German losses, after which most Nazi leaders recognized that the war was lost.
7. Entries may include: February 1941: Hitler sends General Rommel to reinforce Italian troops in North Africa; November 1942: British victory at El Alamein, and U.S. and British forces land in northwest Africa; July 1943: U.S. and British forces invade Sicily; Winter 1942–1943: Battle of Stalingrad; June 1944: D-Day; August 1944: Paris liberated; December 1944: Battle of the Bulge; May 1945: Germany surrenders.

Take It to the NET

Invite students to take a Virtual Field Trip at **www.phschool.com**

CAPTION ANSWERS

Viewing History Soviet troops invaded Germany from the east and conquered Berlin with heavy losses in the final weeks of the war in Europe.

VIEWING HISTORY A United States soldier (left) and a Soviet soldier (right) share a moment of camaraderie after meeting at the Elbe River in April 1945. **Recognizing Cause and Effect** *How did Soviet assaults in 1945 help end the war?*

While some Soviet troops attacked Berlin, other elements of the Red Army continued to drive west. On April 25, at the Elbe River, they connected with American troops pushing east.

Germany Surrenders As the Soviet army surrounded Berlin, Hitler refused to take his generals' advice to flee the city. Instead, he chose to commit suicide in his underground bunker in Berlin on April 30, 1945. A few days later, on May 8, 1945, Germany's remaining troops surrendered.

When the fighting in Europe came to an end, American soldiers rejoiced, and civilians on the home front celebrated V-E Day (Victory in Europe Day). They knew, however, that the war would not be over until the Allies had defeated Japan.

The Yalta Conference In February 1945, months before the fall of Berlin, Roosevelt, Churchill, and Stalin met at Yalta, a city in the Soviet Union near the Black Sea. Building on discussions at Teheran, in Iran, at the end of 1943, they gathered to plan the final defeat of Germany and to decide the shape of the postwar world. The leaders agreed to split Germany into four zones, each under the control of one of the major Allies, including France. They planned a similar division of the city of Berlin, which would lie deep inside the Soviet zone. Stalin promised to allow elections in the nations of Eastern Europe that his army had liberated from the Germans. He also promised to enter the war against Japan within three months of Germany's surrender.

Stalin did not fulfill his promises at Yalta. He refused, for example, to honor his pledge of free elections in Eastern Europe. Critics of Yalta accused Roosevelt and Churchill of not doing enough to prevent Soviet domination of half of Europe. The issue of Eastern Europe would be at the heart of the conflict that later arose between the Soviet Union and the Western Allies.

Section 2 Assessment

READING COMPREHENSION

1. Why was the **Atlantic Charter** significant?
2. (a) Why did the German invasion of the Soviet Union succeed at first? (b) What factors helped the Soviet army defeat the Germans?
3. (a) What was the goal of **carpet bombing**? (b) What advantage did carpet bombing have over a conventional attack on Germany?
4. Explain the significance of the D-Day invasion.

CRITICAL THINKING AND WRITING

5. **Identifying Alternatives** How did the Allied decision to delay an invasion of Western Europe and fight instead in North Africa and Italy affect the Soviet Union?
6. **Making Comparisons** Explain why Stalingrad and the Battle of the Bulge marked two different turning points for Germany during the war.
7. **Writing a Time Line** Create a time line that lists important events in the war in Europe and in North Africa between 1941 and 1945.

Take It to the NET

Activity: Virtual Field Trip D-Day is one of the most memorable events of World War II. Take a virtual field trip examining different aspects of the Normandy invasion. Then, write a summary of your field trip. Use the links provided in the *America: Pathways to the Present* area of the following Web site for help in completing this activity.
www.phschool.com

RESOURCE DIRECTORY

Teaching Resources

Units 5/6/7 booklet
- Section 2 Quiz, p. 16

Guide to the Essentials
- Section 2 Summary, p. 87

Section 3

The Holocaust

READING FOCUS

- In what ways did Germany persecute Jews in the 1930s?
- How did Germany's policies toward Jews develop from murder into genocide?

MAIN IDEA

During World War II, the Nazis carried out a brutal plan that resulted in the deaths of 6 million Jews and millions of other victims.

KEY TERMS

anti-Semitism
Holocaust
concentration camp
Kristallnacht
Warsaw ghetto
Wannsee Conference
death camp
War Refugee Board (WRB)
Nuremberg Trials

TAKING NOTES

Copy the web diagram below and fill in the circles with examples of German persecution of Jews.

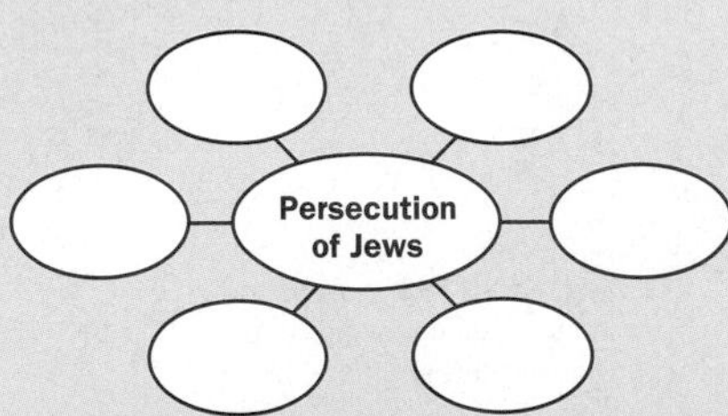

Setting the Scene Jews in Europe faced persecution for their religious beliefs for centuries. In the mid-1800s, a new form of anti-Jewish prejudice arose based on racial theories. Some thinkers claimed that Germanic peoples whom they called "Aryans" were superior to Middle Eastern peoples called Semites. Semitic peoples included Arabs and Jews, but the term often applied only to Jews.

Although most scholars rejected those theories, others used them to justify the continued persecution of "non-Aryans." By the 1880s, Europeans used the term **anti-Semitism** to describe discrimination or hostility, often violent, directed at Jews. Despite the rise of anti-Semitism, most European countries repealed old anti-Jewish laws between the mid-1800s and World War I.

The suffering caused by World War I and the hardships of the Great Depression led many to look to these old theories to restore national pride and a sense of purpose. In *Mein Kampf,* Adolf Hitler revived the idea of Aryan superiority and expressed an especially hateful view of Jews. In particular, he despised the mixing of the two "races":

> "*Let the desolation which Jewish hybridization daily visits on our nation be clearly seen, this blood-poisoning that can be removed from our body national only after centuries or nevermore; let it be pondered, further, how racial decay drags down, indeed often annuls, the final Aryan values of our German nation. . . .*"
>
> —Adolf Hitler, from *Mein Kampf,* 1925

Building upon historic anti-Semitism, the Nazis planned to exclude Jews from all areas of German life. A sign turns away shoppers from a Jewish-owned store during the April 1, 1933, boycott.

Persecution in Germany

When Hitler became Germany's leader in 1933, he made anti-Semitism the official policy of the nation. No other persecution of Jews in modern history equals the extent and brutality of the **Holocaust,** Nazi Germany's systematic murder of European Jews. In all, some six million Jews, about two thirds of Europe's

Section 3

The Holocaust

SECTION OBJECTIVES

1. Find out about some ways in which Germany persecuted Jews in the 1930s.
2. See how Germany's policies toward Jews developed from murder into genocide.

BELLRINGER

Warm-Up Activity Ask students to define the word *genocide.* Ask students if they are aware of any racial, ethnic, or cultural groups in the past or in the present against which genocide has been committed.

Activating Prior Knowledge Ask students to search for the dictionary definition of *holocaust.* Can they state a list of synonyms for that word? Have a discussion about the power of certain words in our language, such as *holocaust,* to call up a host of emotions. What are some emotions that are stirred amongst students by the word *holocaust?*

READING STRATEGY

As students read the section, have them create a time line of the events related to the Holocaust. For each event, have students write a sentence that analyzes the event's historic importance.

ACTIVITY

Connecting with History and Conflict

Assign segments of *Mein Kampf* as outside reading to students. Have students summarize and analyze their excerpts in written or oral reports. **(Verbal/Linguistic)**

RESOURCE DIRECTORY

Teaching Resources

Guided Reading and Review booklet, p. 102

Technology

Section Reading Support Transparencies
Guided Reading Audiotapes (English/Spanish), Ch. 18
Student Edition on Audio CD, Ch. 18
Prentice Hall Presentation Pro CD-ROM, Ch. 18
Companion Web site, www.phschool.com

Lesson Plan

Focus During World War II, the Nazis undertook the annihilation of Jews, Romany, people with physical and mental disabilities, and others whom they considered to be inferior. Ask students how the Nazis tried to accomplish this task.

Instruct Ask students why Germany might have wanted a scapegoat during the 1930s. How did anti-Semitism become official government policy? In what ways did the Nazis use this policy to persecute Jews during the 1930s?

Assess/Reteach Ask students to contemplate the enormity of the Nazis' plan, "The Final Solution," to systematically annihilate many millions of people. Hold a classroom discussion that analyzes both the stark cruelty of the "Solution" and the horrific brutality experienced as it was carried out.

READING CHECK
It was meant to exclude German Jews from all aspects of political, economic, and social life.

Jewish population, would lose their lives. Some 5 to 6 million other people would also die in Nazi captivity.

READING CHECK
What was the goal of Nazi persecution of Jews in the mid-1930s?

Nazi Policies Early Nazi persecution aimed to exclude Germany's Jews from all aspects of the country's political, social, and economic life. On April 1, 1933, the Nazis ordered a one-day boycott of businesses owned by Jews. In 1935, the Nuremberg laws stripped Jews of their German citizenship, and outlawed marriage between Jews and non-Jews. Nazi-controlled newspapers and radio constantly attacked and caricatured Jews as enemies of Germany.

In 1938, the Nazis enacted new policies to make life even more difficult for the Jewish people. Most Jews had already lost their jobs. The Nazis now forced Jews to surrender their own businesses to Aryans for a fraction of their value. Jewish doctors and lawyers were forbidden to serve non-Jews, and Jewish students were expelled from public schools.

A Jew was defined as any person who had three or four Jewish grandparents, regardless of his or her current religion, as well as any person who had two Jewish grandparents and practiced the Jewish religion. At the request of Switzerland, the destination of many refugees, the Nazis marked Jews' identity cards with a red letter "J." The Nazis also gave Jews new middle names—"Sarah" for women and "Israel" for men—which appeared on all documents. Eventually, Jews in Germany and German-occupied countries were forced to sew yellow stars marked "Jew" on their clothing. These practices exposed Jews to public attacks and police harassment.

VIEWING HISTORY At bottom, a Jewish shopkeeper sweeps up shop windows left shattered by *Kristallnacht.* Below, the "J" stamp on this girl's identification paper identifies her as Jewish. **Synthesizing Information** *In what other ways did the Nazis organize the persecution of the Jews?*

Hitler's Police When Hitler first came to power, the Gestapo, Germany's new secret state police, was formed to identify and pursue enemies of the Nazi regime. Hitler also formed the SS, or *Schutzstaffel,* an elite guard that developed into the private army of the Nazi party. By 1939, the Gestapo had become part of the SS.

The duties of the SS included guarding the **concentration camps,** or places where political prisoners are confined, usually under harsh conditions. In addition to Communists, the Nazi camps soon held many other classes of people whom they considered "undesirable"—mainly Jews, but also homosexuals, Jehovah's Witnesses, Gypsies, and the homeless.

Kristallnacht Despite the ever-increasing restrictions on their lives, many Jews believed they could endure persecution until Hitler lost power. Older people believed staying in Germany was safer than starting a new life with no money in a foreign country. Their illusions were destroyed on the night of November 9, 1938, when Nazi thugs throughout Germany and Austria looted and destroyed Jewish stores, houses, and synagogues.

This incident became known as ***Kristallnacht,*** or "Night of the Broken Glass," a reference to the broken windows of the Jewish shops. Nearly every synagogue was destroyed. The Nazis arrested thousands of Jews that night and shipped them off to concentration camps. These actions were followed by an enormous fine to make Jews pay for the damage of *Kristallnacht.* After that night, Germany's remaining Jews sought any means possible to leave the country.

Refugees Seek an Escape From 1933 through 1937, about 130,000 Jews, or one in four, fled Germany with Nazi encouragement. At first, most refugees moved to neighboring European nations. As the numbers grew, however, Jews began to seek protection in the United States, Latin America,

Caption Answers

Viewing History They set up concentration camps and death camps, and organized mobile killing units.

RESOURCE DIRECTORY

Technology

Color Transparencies *Historical Maps,* A43

Exploring Primary Sources in U.S. History CD-ROM *Night, Elie Wiesel*

and British-ruled Palestine. Few countries, however, welcomed Jewish refugees as long as the Depression prevented their own citizens from finding work.

Responding to criticism, President Roosevelt called for an international conference to discuss the growing numbers of Jewish refugees. The Evian Conference, held in France in July 1938, failed to deal with the situation. With the exception of the Dominican Republic, each of the 32 nations represented, including the United States, refused to open its doors to more immigrants.

From Murder to Genocide

As German armies overran most of Europe, more and more Jews, including many who had fled Germany, came under their control. In 1939, for example, the invasion of Poland brought some 2 million additional Jews under German control. Nazi plans for dealing with these Jews included the establishment of ghettos, areas in which members of a minority group are concentrated. In Warsaw, the Nazis rounded up more than 400,000 Jews, about 30 percent of the Polish capital's population, and confined them in an area that was less than 3 percent of the entire city. They sealed off the **Warsaw ghetto** with a wall topped with barbed wire and guarded by Germans. Jews received little food, and hunger, overcrowding, and a lack of sanitation brought on disease. Each month, thousands of Jews died in the ghetto. The Nazis, however, sought more efficient ways of killing Jews.

The *Einsatzgruppen* During the invasion of the Soviet Union, Hitler ordered *Einsatzgruppen,* or mobile killing squads, to shoot Communist political leaders as well as all Jews in German-occupied territory. Typically, they rounded up their victims, drove them to gullies or freshly dug pits, and shot them. In a ravine called Babi Yar outside Kiev, the Nazis killed more than 33,000 Jews in two days.

Although Hitler considered mass murder by firing squad acceptable in a war zone, he found the method unsuitable for the conquered nations of western and central Europe. In January 1942, Nazi officials met at the **Wannsee Conference** outside Berlin to agree on a new approach. They developed a plan to achieve what one Nazi leader called the "final solution to the Jewish question." Ultimately, the plan would lead to the construction of special camps in Poland where **genocide,** or the deliberate destruction of an entire ethnic or cultural group, was to be carried out against Europe's Jewish population.

The Death Camps The Nazis chose poison gas as the most effective way to kill people. A pesticide called Zyklon B proved to be the most efficient killer. In January 1942, the Nazis opened a specially designed gas chamber disguised as a shower room at the Auschwitz camp in western Poland. The Nazis outfitted six such camps in Poland. Unlike concentration camps, which functioned as prisons and centers of forced labor, these **death camps** existed primarily for mass murder.

Jews in Poland, the Netherlands, Germany, and other lands were crowded into train cars built for cattle and transported to these extermination centers. Most of them were told they were going to "the East" to work. At four of the six death camps, nearly all were murdered soon after they arrived. On arrival at the two largest camps, Auschwitz and Majdanek, prisoners were organized into a line and quickly inspected. The elderly, women with children, and those who looked too weak to work were herded into gas chambers and killed. Jewish

VIEWING HISTORY The Nazis forced Jews to wear armbands or bright yellow stars marked "Jew" in Germany (top), in occupied lands, including France (center), and in the Netherlands (bottom). Jews caught without a star were deported or killed. **Predicting Consequences** *Why did the stars make life more difficult for Jews?*

Focus on WORLD EVENTS

Rescue in Denmark One country managed to save almost its entire Jewish community from destruction during the war. In October 1943, Danish fishermen secretly ferried nearly all of Denmark's 8,000 Jews across the water to neutral Sweden. A German official had alerted the Danish resistance that the Jews were about to be deported. Denmark's success was as rare as it was remarkable. Rescue was much more difficult in countries where the Jewish population was much greater than in Denmark, where the non-Jewish population was unwilling to help, or where there was no safe haven nearby.

ACTIVITY
Connecting with History and Conflict

Direct students to research the origin and use of the term *genocide.* Students should provide a complete etymological history, noting its Greek roots and the term's creation in relationship to the Holocaust. **(Verbal/Linguistic)**

BACKGROUND
Jewish Refugees

On May 13, 1939, the Hamburg-American liner *St. Louis* left Germany bound for Cuba, carrying 930 Jewish refugees, 734 of whom were bearing United States immigration papers. When the *St. Louis* docked in Havana on May 27, however, the refugees were told that Cuban authorities would not allow them ashore. United States officials refused to waive quota restrictions then in effect, and the doomed vessel sailed back to Europe. Frantic workers from Jewish relief agencies finally persuaded four European countries to take in the refugees—but only those who settled in Britain remained free of Nazi persecution.

CUSTOMIZE FOR ...
ESL

Write the word *holocaust* on the chalkboard. Have a volunteer look up its meanings in the dictionary and read them. Ask students to make a collage of holocaust pictures that conveys the significance of the Jewish Holocaust.

TEST PREPARATION

Have students read the section "The *Einsatzgruppen*" on this page and then answer the question below.

What is the nearest translation of the German term *"Einsatzgruppen"*?

A Broken glass.
B Sitting in judgment.
C Enemy troops.
(D) Mobile killing squads.

CAPTION ANSWERS

Viewing History The bright yellow star singled out Jews for public assaults and official persecution.

ACTIVITY
Connecting with History and Conflict

Every year about half a million people from all over the world visit—or make a pilgrimage to—what remains of Auschwitz. A sign at the entrance of the infamous death camp says: "You are entering a place of exceptional horror and tragedy. Please show your respect for those who suffered and died here by behaving in a manner suitable to the dignity of their memory." Most visitors do not need this reminder. In addition, tour guides, museums, and various permanent and changing exhibits help keep the memories of the victims of Auschwitz alive. Have students contemplate what it might be like to visit Auschwitz by writing a "diary entry" of a trip there as a modern-day traveler. **(Verbal/Linguistic)**

BACKGROUND
Recent Scholarship

Although the Holocaust is one of the central events of the twentieth century, there is growing disagreement about how it should be studied. Reflecting the opinion of many current scholars, Steven T. Katz of Boston University says that in the Holocaust "the distinctive features of modernity," including nationalism, bureaucracy, and the rise of the secular state, "come together in a unique way." Thus, the Holocaust can and should be studied in its unique aspects. But Ruth R. Wisse, professor of Yiddish and comparative literature at Harvard, argues that the Holocaust is too often studied apart from the context of the long history of persecution of the Jewish people.

prisoners carried the dead to the crematoria, or huge ovens where the bodies were burned.

Those who were selected for work endured almost unbearable conditions. The life expectancy of a Jewish prisoner at Auschwitz was a few months. Men and women alike had their heads shaved and a registration number tattooed on their arms. They were given one set of clothes and slept in crowded, unheated barracks on hard wooden pallets. Their daily food was usually a cup of imitation coffee, a small piece of bread, and thin, foul-tasting soup made with rotten vegetables. Diseases swept through the camps and claimed many who were weakened by harsh labor and starvation. Others died from torture or from cruel medical experiments. At periodic "selections," German overseers sent weak prisoners to the gas chambers.

Estimated Jewish Losses in the Holocaust

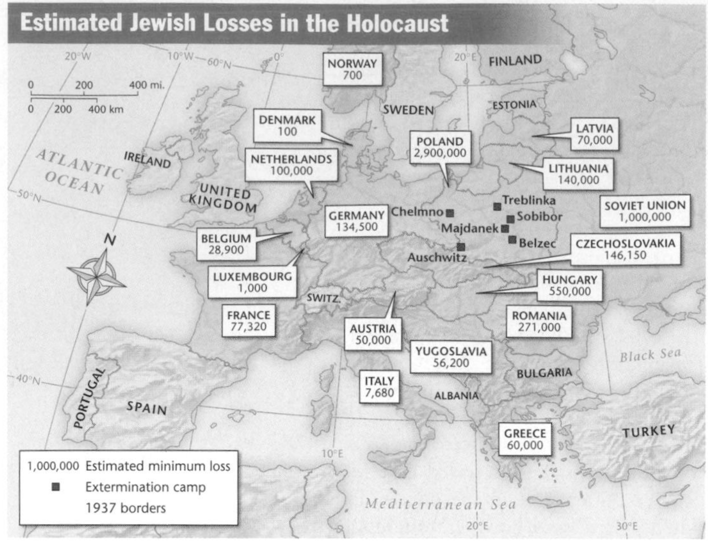

MAP SKILLS The horror of the Holocaust touched many nations in Europe. **Place** *Which country do you think was most altered by the Holocaust?*

The number of people killed in the labor and death camps is staggering. At Auschwitz, the main Nazi killing center, 12,000 victims could be gassed and cremated in a single day. There the Nazis killed as many as 1.5 million people, some 90 percent of them Jews.

Fighting Back Some Jews resisted the Nazis. In Poland, France, and elsewhere, Jews joined underground resistance groups. Jews in several ghettos and camps took part in violent uprisings. In August 1943, rioting Jews damaged the Treblinka death camp so badly that it had to be closed. However, uprisings often came too late to save many people, and they were quickly crushed by the Germans.

Escape was the most common form of resistance. Most attempts failed, and most of those who escaped were later caught, but a few people managed to bring word of the death camps to the outside world. After several prisoners escaped from Treblinka, word got back to the Warsaw ghetto about the fate of nearly 300,000 Jews from Warsaw who had been sent there in 1942. As a result, in April 1943, the approximately 50,000 Jews still in the Warsaw ghetto rose up against a final deportation to Treblinka. For some 27 days, Jews armed with little more than pistols and homemade bombs held out against more than 2,000 Germans with tanks and artillery. Although the Germans defeated the rebellion, Warsaw's Jews had brought the deportation drive to a standstill, if only for a time.

Jews in the Lodz ghetto in Poland board a train for deportation to the Chelmno death camp. The Germans seized the Jews' belongings and did not tell the deportees where they were going.

Rescue and Liberation The United States government knew about the mass murder of Jews by the Nazis as early as November 1942. The press showed little interest in reporting the story. Congress did not raise immigration quotas, and even the existing quotas for Jews went unfilled.

Finally, in January 1944, over the objection of the State Department, Roosevelt created the **War Refugee Board (WRB)** to try to help people threatened by the Nazis. Despite

CAPTION ANSWERS

Map Skills Poland.

RESOURCE DIRECTORY

Teaching Resources
Units 5/6/7 booklet
- Section 3 Quiz, p. 17

Guide to the Essentials
- Section 3 Summary, p. 88

Technology
Sounds of an Era Audio CD *Edward R. Murrow* (time: one minute, 30 seconds)

its late start, the WRB's programs helped save some 200,000 lives. With WRB funding, for example, Swedish diplomat Raoul Wallenberg rescued thousands of Hungarian Jews by issuing them special Swedish passports. A WRB effort to bring Jews to the United States met with less success. Some 1,000 refugees were rescued and brought to an army camp in Oswego, New York, but Roosevelt would not expand the program.

As Allied armies advanced in late 1944, the Nazis abandoned the camps outside Germany and moved their prisoners to camps on German soil. On the eve of liberation, thousands of Jews died on death marches from camp to camp as their German guards moved them ahead of advancing armies. In 1945, American troops were able to witness the horrors of the Holocaust for the first time. A young soldier described the conditions he discovered as he entered the barracks at Buchenwald:

VIEWING HISTORY The faces of these newly liberated prisoners reflect the starvation and horrors they experienced in a concentration camp in Ebensee, Austria. **Recognizing Cause and Effect** *How did the liberation of the camps lead to the Nuremberg trials?*

> “*The odor was so bad I backed up, but I looked at a bottom bunk and there I saw one man. He was too weak to get up; he could just barely turn his head. . . . He looked like a skeleton; and his eyes were deep set. He didn't utter a sound; he just looked at me with those eyes, and they still haunt me today.*”
>
> —Leon Bass, American soldier

Horrified by the death camps and by Germany's conduct during the war, the Allies placed a number of former Nazi leaders on trial. They charged them with crimes against peace, crimes against humanity, and war crimes. An International Military Tribunal composed of members selected by the United States, Great Britain, the Soviet Union, and France conducted the **Nuremberg Trials** in November 1945. Of the 24 Nazi defendants, 12 received the death sentence. More significant than the number of convictions, the trials established the important principle that individuals must be responsible for their own actions. The tribunal firmly rejected the Nazis' argument that they were only “following orders.”

Section 3 Assessment

READING COMPREHENSION

1. Why was ***Kristallnacht*** a critical event for Jews living under Nazi control?
2. (a) What was the purpose of a **concentration camp?** (b) What was the purpose of a **death camp?**
3. How did the United States respond to news of the **Holocaust** during the war?

CRITICAL THINKING AND WRITING

4. **Identifying Central Issues** How did the Nazis implement their plans for genocide?
5. **Writing to Inform** Write a short paragraph from the point of view of a Jewish teenager living in the Warsaw Ghetto in 1942.

Take It to the NET

Activity: Virtual Field Trip Visit the United States Holocaust Memorial Museum online. Select one of the several online exhibits available and write an essay describing the exhibit's effectiveness. Use the links provided in the *America Pathways to the Present* area of the following Web site for help in completing this activity.
www.phschool.com

CUSTOMIZE FOR ...

Less Proficient Readers

Have students read the section “From Murder to Genocide,” and examine the map on the previous page. Ask them to make a list of the names of the six death camps. Have the students indicate which two death camps were also work camps by underlining the names of those camps.

Section 3 Assessment

Reading Comprehension

1. Many Jews living under Nazi rule thought they could endure persecution until Hitler lost power. The devastation of *Kristallnacht* forced them to realize that outlasting Hitler would not be possible and that they should try to leave Germany by any means possible.
2. (a) To confine Jews, political prisoners, and others, and act as a forced labor camp. (b) The mass murder of (primarily) Jews.
3. At first the United States was unresponsive, showing little interest in reporting the stories, not raising immigration quotas, and not filling the existing quota for Jews. Later, Roosevelt, over the objection of the State Department, created the War Refugee Board to try to help people threatened by the Nazis.

Critical Thinking and Writing

4. During the invasion of Russia, German *Einsatzgruppen* (mobile killing units) carried out mass shootings of Russian Jews. At the Wannsee Conference in January 1942, the Nazis decided to set up death camps to systematically murder Jews using poison gas.
5. Paragraphs will vary, but should reflect an understanding of ghettoization as it is described in the chapter.

Invite students to take a Virtual Field Trip at **www.phschool.com**

Caption Answers

Viewing History The Allies called for Nazi leaders to be put on trial due in large part to the horrors revealed when the camps were liberated.

Section 4 The War in the Pacific

Section Objectives

1. Learn about advances Japan made in Asia and the Pacific in late 1941 and 1942.
2. See which Allied victories turned the tide of war in the Pacific.
3. Read about the strategy of the United States in the struggle to reconquer the Pacific Islands.
4. Discover why the battles of Iwo Jima and Okinawa were important.
5. Understand how the Manhattan Project brought the war to an end.

Bellringer

Warm-Up Activity Ask students to write one sentence describing what they think is the most important way the use of nuclear weapons has changed the world.

Activating Prior Knowledge Can students recall and list some significant events that led up to the war between Japan and the United States? What was the single most significant event?

Reading Strategy

Have students sketch a map that shows the areas where fighting took place in the Pacific Ocean. As they read the section, have them mark the major battle sites on their map. Also have them note who won each battle.

Section 4

The War in the Pacific

READING FOCUS

- What advances did Japan make in Asia and the Pacific in late 1941 and 1942?
- Which Allied victories turned the tide of war in the Pacific?
- What was the strategy of the United States in the struggle to reconquer the Pacific islands?
- Why were the battles of Iwo Jima and Okinawa important?
- How did the Manhattan Project bring the war to an end?

KEY TERMS

Bataan Death March
Geneva Convention
Battle of the Coral Sea
Battle of Midway
Battle of Guadalcanal
island-hopping
Battle of Leyte Gulf
kamikaze
Battle of Iwo Jima
Battle of Okinawa
Manhattan Project

TAKING NOTES

As you read, prepare an outline of this section. The sample below will help you get started.

I. Japan attacks American and British bases across the Western Pacific.
A. American troops at Bataan and Corregidor surrender.
B. POWs are forced on Bataan Death March.
C. Allies defend India and extend aid to China.
D. Battle of the Coral Sea ends threat to Australia.
II. ______________________

MAIN IDEA

Fierce fighting and heavy casualties characterized the war in the Pacific Ocean as the Allied forces struggled to turn back Japanese advances.

VIEWING HISTORY A Japanese soldier patrols the ruins of Bataan in the Philippines. **Drawing Inferences** *Why was the United States unable to defend the Philippines successfully?*

Setting the Scene The bombing of Pearl Harbor was only the first of several sudden attacks across the Pacific. Japanese forces attacked American bases on Wake Island on December 8 and on Guam on December 10. Just hours after striking Pearl Harbor, Japanese warplanes bombed Clark Field, the main American air base in the Philippines. Although news of Pearl Harbor had reached Douglas MacArthur, the commanding general, the Americans at Clark Field failed to prepare for an attack. The Japanese destroyed about half of MacArthur's airplanes, which were lined up in rows on the ground.

Within days, a large Japanese force landed on the main Philippine island of Luzon. MacArthur withdrew most of his troops southward to the Bataan Peninsula. There he set up defenses, hoping the navy would be able to evacuate his army to safety.

American and Filipino troops held out on the Bataan Peninsula under Japanese fire for several months as hopes of rescue dimmed. Realizing that the situation was hopeless, President Roosevelt ordered MacArthur to escape to Australia. In March 1942, the general reluctantly boarded a torpedo boat and set off through Japanese-controlled waters to the safety of the southern Philippines. There, he boarded an airplane for Australia. Upon his arrival, MacArthur made a promise to the people of the Philippines and to his army: "I shall return."

The Japanese Advance, 1941–1942

The Japanese struck Pearl Harbor and Clark Field to try to gain military control of the Western Pacific. By shattering American forces everywhere in the region, they hoped that the United States would withdraw, leaving them easy access to the natural resources of Southeast Asia. Oil from the Dutch East Indies and rubber from British Malaya would give Japan the economic independence it

Caption Answers

Viewing History American troops were surprised by the Japanese, and the Philippines were too distant from the United States to reinforce with new American troops in time to make a difference.

Resource Directory

Teaching Resources
Guided Reading and Review booklet, p. 103

Other Print Resources
Historical Outline Map Book *World War II in the Pacific,* p. 66

Technology
Section Reading Support Transparencies
Guided Reading Audiotapes (English/Spanish), Ch. 18
Student Edition on Audio CD, Ch. 18
Color Transparencies *Historical Maps,* A44
Exploring Primary Sources in U.S. History CD-ROM *Japanese Internment Photograph*
Prentice Hall Presentation Pro CD-ROM, Ch. 18
Companion Web site, www.phschool.com

needed. With this goal in mind, the Japanese attacked a number of other Allied colonies in December 1941. By early March 1942, they had overrun the British strongholds of Hong Kong and Singapore, seized the Dutch East Indies and Malaya, and invaded Burma. Japan's southern offensive swept aside British, American, and Dutch naval power in Southeast Asia and brought a wide band of colonies into the Japanese empire. Japan then turned its attention to securing the Philippines.

American and Filipino prisoners captured by the Japanese in the Philippines

The Philippines Fall Facing starvation and renewed Japanese attacks, most of Bataan's defenders surrendered in early April 1942. About 2,000 soldiers and nurses escaped to the fortified island of Corregidor, just off the tip of the peninsula, to join the fort's defenders. American troops on Corregidor survived another month of continual Japanese bombardment by living in the rock tunnels of the fortress. Finally, running low on ammunition and food, more than 11,000 Americans and Filipinos surrendered to invading Japanese forces on May 6.

With the fall of the Bataan Peninsula in early April and Corregidor in May, the Japanese captured about 76,000 Filipinos and Americans as prisoners of war. Already weakened by disease and lack of food, these prisoners faced a grueling test in the tropical heat. Their Japanese captors split them into groups of 500 to 1,000 and force-marched them some 60 miles to a railroad junction. There, the prisoners were boarded on a train that took them to within eight miles of an army camp and then walked the rest of the way.

During the march, many prisoners were treated brutally. They were denied water and rest and many were beaten and tortured. At least 10,000 prisoners died during the 6- to 12-day journey. Many were executed by the guards when they grew too weak to keep up. Their ordeal became known as the **Bataan Death March.** Those who survived were sent to primitive prison camps, where an additional 15,000 or more died.

The brutality of Japanese soldiers in Bataan defied accepted international standards of conduct toward prisoners of war. Those standards had been spelled out in 1929 in the third **Geneva Convention.** "Prisoners of war," the convention stated, "shall at all times be humanely treated and protected, particularly against acts of violence. . . ."

Defending China and Burma China joined the Allies on December 9, 1941, by officially declaring war on Germany, Italy, and its longtime foe, Japan. The United States had already sent military advisors and Lend-Lease arms and equipment to China. They hoped to strengthen China and thus divert Japan from the drive to conquer Southeast Asia.

Shortly after the war began, China's Nationalist leader Jiang Jieshi asked an American general, Joseph Stilwell, to serve as his chief of staff. Stilwell led the Chinese armies defending Burma, an important link between the Allies and Jiang's base in southwestern China. Despite the support of volunteer American aviators called the "Flying Tigers," China's ragtag forces fared poorly against the well-trained Japanese. They lost control of China's lifeline, the Burma Road, and retreated back into China. British and Indian troops in Burma fled west into India, which now also faced the threat of Japanese invasion.

Focus on GOVERNMENT

War Crimes in the Pacific Word of the Bataan Death March did not reach the American public until a few years later when three soldiers escaped from their prison camp. As at Nuremberg, Japanese leaders accused of crimes against humanity faced a trial after the war. A United States military commission tried and convicted the general blamed for organizing the march. He was one of seven Japanese executed for war crimes.

Lesson Plan

Focus As Allied forces struggled to defeat the Axis Powers in Europe, they were also fighting fiercely against the Japanese in the Pacific.

Instruct Explain that initially the Japanese had the upper hand in the Pacific. Ask students why they think this was so. What military successes did Japan have between 1941 and 1942?

Discuss the strategies used by the Allies in the Pacific from 1943 to 1945. Why was it important that the Allies get control of the islands? Why did so many casualties result? Ask students to explain the significance of the Battle of Okinawa.

Discuss the history of the atomic bomb and have students explain the Manhattan Project. Ask them if they think Truman would have dropped the atomic bomb if he had known the bomb's delayed effects. Ask students to compare the use of the atomic bomb with the Allied conventional bombing raids against German cities discussed in Section 2.

Assess/Reteach Ask students to consider Truman's position as he contemplated the use of the atomic bomb. American casualties in the Pacific were heavy and mounting. The bombing of Germany with conventional bombs had been an accepted practice in the war in Europe. He saw in the use of the atomic bomb a quick and certain way to bring the war to a close. In students' opinions, did this justify the use of the atomic bomb?

Activity

Connecting with Government

Douglas MacArthur's statement, "I shall return," is among the most famous utterances to come out of World War II. Have students include it in a booklet they make that records the most famous quotations of the war era. Quotations should be selected for their historical importance and their fame. Students should write an annotation for each quotation that identifies its author and explains its context. **(Verbal/Linguistic)**

Test Preparation

Have the students read the section dealing with the American defeat in the Philippines, and then answer the following question.

On what date did the last American troops in the Philippines surrender to the Japanese?

A December 7, 1941
(B) May 6, 1942
C December 10, 1941
D August 5, 1943

ACTIVITY

Connecting with Geography

Ask students to find out about and visit World War II memorials in your community. Students also might interview a veteran of the war (possibly through contacting the local VFW post), and ask questions about his or her branch of service, locations of service, assignments, rank, and conditions experienced. Have them report to the class what they have learned. **(Verbal/Linguistic)**

From the Archives of

AmericanHeritage®

Thirty Seconds over Tokyo

Four months after Pearl Harbor it turned out that Japan could be surprised, too. On April 18, 1942, the world-renowned aviator Lt. Col. James H. Doolittle commanded a daring raid by sixteen B-25 bombers on Japan. Doolittle's bombers took off from the carrier *Hornet* while it was deep in Japanese-controlled waters but still 800 miles from Japan itself. There was no thought of returning to the carrier. The planes would drop their bombs, then fly on another 1,000 miles to land in China. True to plan, the pilots bombed military and industrial targets in Tokyo, Yokohama, and other cities. One bomber went down inside the Soviet border, where its surveying crew was detained; three of eight Americans captured in Japanese territory were executed. The raid had caused little damage, but it offered a gleam of triumph in a theater where the Allies had thus far known little but disaster. Its leader was made a brigadier general the very next day. Source: Nathan Ward, "The Time Machine," *American Heritage®* magazine, April 1992.

MAP SKILLS United States forces advanced from island to island across the Pacific toward Japan. **Location** *Why was the Battle of the Coral Sea important to the Allied cause?*

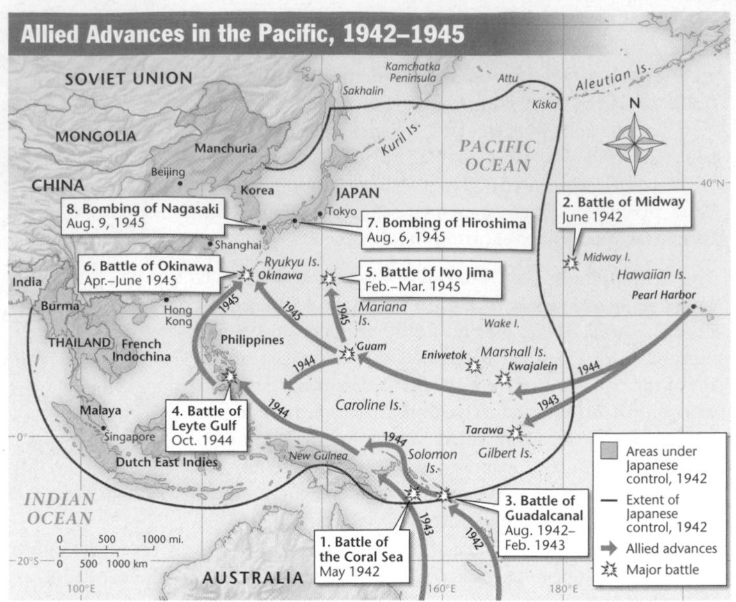

The War at Sea At Pearl Harbor, Japan had not achieved one of its main goals: to destroy the three aircraft carriers that formed the heart of the Pacific Fleet. Two of the carriers, the *Lexington* and the *Enterprise,* had been away at sea during the attack, accompanied by the fleet's heavy cruisers. The third, the *Saratoga,* was undergoing repairs in California. These carriers would prove to be important American weapons in the war at sea.

Since World War I, the design of carriers and the aircraft that relied on them had improved tremendously. Carriers had become floating airfields, greatly extending the area in which warplanes could fly. These planes now included dive bombers and torpedo bombers capable of destroying enemy ships. Japan had used aircraft carriers as a base for the attack on Pearl Harbor.

In April 1942, a group of American B-25 medium bombers took off from the aircraft carrier *Hornet* on their own secret mission. Led by Lieutenant Colonel James Doolittle, the planes flew 650 miles to Japan to carry out a daring American counterattack. Doolittle's squadron dropped bombs on Tokyo and other cities before crash landing in China. Most of the pilots survived. The Doolittle raid caused little physical damage, but it shocked Japan's leadership and boosted Allied morale at a crucial time.

Japanese forces continued to advance across the Pacific, and the battered American navy fought desperately to stop them. The fall of the Dutch East Indies opened the way to Australia. In May 1942, a largely American naval group engaged a superior Japanese fleet in the Coral Sea, northeast of Australia. In the **Battle of the Coral Sea,** aircraft launched from aircraft carriers bombed and strafed enemy ships more than 70 miles away. The five-day battle cost both sides more than half their planes. The Japanese destroyed the *Lexington* and badly damaged the *Yorktown,* another carrier. One Japanese carrier sank, another lost most of its planes, and a third was put out of action. The battle was a draw, but it prevented the Japanese from invading Australia.

RESOURCE DIRECTORY

Teaching Resources

Learning with Documents booklet (Primary Source Activity) *Guadalcanal,* p. 30

Caption Answers

Map Skills Although inconclusive, the Battle of the Coral Sea caused Japanese losses that were severe enough to remove the immediate threat to Australia by preventing a Japanese landing in southern New Guinea.

The Battle of the Coral Sea also opened a new chapter in naval warfare. It was the first naval combat carried out entirely by aircraft. The enemy ships never came within sight of one another. From now on, aircraft and aircraft carriers would play the central role in naval battles.

Allied Victories Turn the Tide

In the summer of 1942, while the Soviet Union resisted German attacks and the Allies prepared to invade North Africa, two critical battles took place in the Pacific. The fight for Midway Island, near Hawaii, and for Guadalcanal, near the Coral Sea, changed the course of the war in the Pacific.

The Battle of Midway Japanese Admiral Yamamoto Isoroku, architect of the Pearl Harbor attack, hoped to destroy what remained of the United States Pacific Fleet by luring it into battle near Midway Island, some 1,100 miles northwest of Hawaii. Yamamoto committed a large part of Japan's navy to his planned invasion of Midway. He believed, correctly, that American Admiral Chester Nimitz would use all his resources to protect the island so vital to the defense of Hawaii.

The **Battle of Midway** opened on June 4, 1942, with a wave of Japanese bomber attacks on the island and a simultaneous, unsuccessful American strike on the Japanese fleet. As in the Battle of the Coral Sea, the Battle of Midway was fought entirely from the air. At first, American planes based on Midway's airfields tried to fend off the Japanese carrier-based bombers. Then the American carriers intervened. Their warplanes surprised Japan's carriers at a vulnerable time as the Japanese were refueling planes and loading them with bombs. Aboard the targeted Japanese ships, fuel hoses caught fire and bombs stacked on the decks exploded. The Americans swiftly sank three of the four heavy Japanese carriers and finished off the fourth, the *Hiryu*, the next day. Before the *Hiryu*'s destruction, planes from that carrier had managed to disable the *Yorktown*, which was later sunk by a Japanese submarine. The other two American carriers, the *Enterprise* and the *Hornet*, emerged undamaged.

Japanese planes attack an American aircraft carrier during the Battle of Midway. The black clouds of smoke come from antiaircraft fire.

The sinking of four Japanese carriers, combined with the loss of some 250 planes and most of Japan's skilled naval pilots, was a devastating blow to the Japanese navy. The American victory owed much to Commander Joseph Rochefort, who broke the Japanese code JN-25 in time to learn crucial information before the attack began. After the Battle of Midway, Japan was unable to launch any more offensive operations in the Pacific.

The Battle of Guadalcanal The victory at Midway allowed the Allies to take the offensive in the Pacific. Their first goal was to capture Guadalcanal in the Solomon Islands, where the Japanese were building an airfield to threaten nearby Allied bases and lines of communication with Australia.

When more than 11,000 marines landed on the island in August 1942, the 2,200 Japanese who were defending the island fled into the jungle. The **Battle of Guadalcanal** provided the marines with their first taste of jungle warfare. They slogged through swamps, crossed rivers, and hacked through tangles of vines in search of the enemy. The marines made easy targets for Japanese snipers hidden in the thick underbrush or in the tops of palm trees.

ACTIVITY
Connecting with Government

Divide the class into small groups and assign each group a battle from World War II. Have each group create a table for the assigned battle that summarizes its basic characteristics (the date of battle, its location, the composition of the fighting forces, the major weapons used, the results of the battle, and so on). Assemble the tables into a class reference booklet. **(Logical/Mathematical)**

BACKGROUND
Recent Scholarship

In 1998 the National Geographic Society launched its Midway Expedition, a search for the carriers—Japanese and American—that were sunk during the Battle of Midway. In May the expedition located and filmed the wreck of the *Yorktown,* lying more than three miles beneath the waters of the Pacific Ocean. Members of the expedition, led by famed discoverer of the *Titanic,* Bob Ballard, were ecstatic. So too were veterans of the famous ship. The discovery of the *Yorktown* was international news, and millions of people saw film and photographs of her—upright and stately—where she had come to rest during what was arguably the most important battle of the Pacific War.

BACKGROUND
Code-Breaker

An American World War II cryptologist, Lt. Cmdr. Joseph Rochefort, is credited with breaking the Japanese naval code JN-25. Using code messages he intercepted, Rochefort discovered that the Japanese intended to attack Midway Island in June 1942. He was able to pass this information on to the headquarters of the United States Pacific Fleet. This preparation enabled the Americans to prevail at Midway, which ultimately ensured Japan's defeat.

CUSTOMIZE FOR ...
Gifted and Talented

Ask students to write a short paper in which they reflect upon why the American victory at Midway was so critical to the Allied war effort. Suggest to the students such aspects as that Midway marked an irrevocable halt to Japan's expansion in the central Pacific; that the battle was a major turning point in the war; and that Midway remains one of the most important naval battles in history.

ACTIVITY
Connecting with Technology

Have students research the B-29 bomber, one of the most impressive and decisive weapons of World War II. Students may present the results of their research on a poster, a bulletin board, or even a Web site. **(Logical/Mathematical)**

BACKGROUND
Connections to History and Conflict

The famous—or infamous—Japanese *kamikaze* planes were not the only suicidal weapons the Japanese used in the war in the Pacific. Several Japanese submarines were equipped with *kaitens,* or human-piloted torpedoes. The 48-foot-long weapons had a range of 27 miles, and kaiten pilots tried to drive their explosive vessels against the hulls of enemy ships. Most kaiten pilots missed their intended targets, but lost their lives nevertheless: a kaiten that ran out of fuel simply sank, until the pressure of the deep water crushed it and its pilot.

READING CHECK

They were effective because they inflicted massive amounts of damage.

Estimated World War II Deaths

Country	Military Deaths	Civilian Deaths	Total Deaths
Axis			
Germany	3,250,000	2,350,000	5,600,000
Italy	226,900	60,000	286,900
Japan	1,740,000	393,400	2,133,400
Allies			
France	122,000	470,000	592,000
Great Britain	305,800	60,600	366,400
United States	405,400	—	405,400
Soviet Union	11,000,000	6,700,000	17,700,000
China	1,400,000	8,000,000	9,400,000

SOURCE: *World War II: A Statistical Survey*

INTERPRETING TABLES
Accurate death tolls are hard to determine, but scholars do not dispute the horrific human cost of the war. **Analyzing Information** *Which nation suffered the greatest human loss?*

Both sides landed thousands of reinforcements in five months of fighting. After several fierce naval battles, the American navy took control of the waters around the island in November, limiting Japanese troop landings. Japan's outnumbered forces finally slipped off the island in February 1943. The Allies had conquered their first piece of Japanese-held territory. Now they made plans for rolling back Japan's other conquests.

Struggle for the Islands

From Guadalcanal, American forces began **island-hopping,** a military strategy of selectively attacking specific enemy-held islands and bypassing others. By capturing only a few crucial islands, the United States effectively cut off the bypassed islands from supplies and reinforcements and rendered those islands useless to the Japanese. This strategy also allowed the Americans to move more quickly toward their ultimate goal—Japan itself.

Island-Hopping in the Pacific In 1943 and 1944, the Allies pushed north from Australia and west across the Central Pacific. Forces under General MacArthur and Admiral William Halsey leapfrogged through the Solomon Islands while Admiral Nimitz led a similar island-hopping campaign in the Gilbert Islands. After seizing the island of Tarawa, Nimitz used it to launch bombing raids on Japanese bases in the Marshall Islands. By February 1944, these attacks had crippled Japanese air power, allowing Nimitz's forces to seize Kwajalein and Eniwetok at the northwest end of the island group.

From the Marshalls, Nimitz captured parts of the Mariana Islands in June. For the first time, Japan was within reach of long-range American bombers. By the end of 1944, B-29 Superfortresses were dropping tons of explosives on Japanese cities.

The Philippines Campaign As American forces pushed toward Japan in the summer of 1944, military planners decided to bypass the Philippine Islands. MacArthur vigorously opposed this strategy, claiming that the United States had an obligation to free the Filipino people. The general's arguments persuaded Roosevelt, who reversed the decision.

In mid-October, some 160,000 American troops invaded the Philippine island of Leyte. After the beach was secure, General MacArthur dramatically waded ashore from a landing craft. News cameras recorded the historic event as MacArthur proclaimed, "People of the Philippines, I have returned."

While American troops fought their way inland, the greatest naval battle in world history developed off the coast. More than 280 warships took part in the three-day **Battle of Leyte Gulf.** The Japanese high command directed nearly every warship still afloat to attack the United States Navy. This was the first battle in which Japanese ***kamikazes,*** or suicide planes, were used. *Kamikaze* pilots loaded their aircraft with bombs and then deliberately crashed them into enemy ships to inflict maximum damage. Despite this tactic, the American force virtually destroyed the Japanese navy and emerged victorious.

READING CHECK
Why were *kamikaze* attacks effective?

Japanese land forces in the Philippines continued to resist, however. American troops needed two months to liberate Leyte. Some 80,000 Japanese defenders were killed and fewer than 1,000 Japanese surrendered. The battle for the Philippines' capital city of Manila, on the island of Luzon, was equally hard fought. Fighting left most of Manila in ruins and some 100,000 Filipino civilians dead. Not until June 1945 did the Allies control the Philippines.

CAPTION ANSWERS

Interpreting Tables The Soviet Union.

Iwo Jima and Okinawa

The fighting grew deadlier as American troops moved closer to Japan. One of the bloodiest battles of the war took place on the tiny volcanic island of Iwo Jima, less than 700 miles from Japan. The island's steep, rocky slopes were honeycombed with caves and tunnels. The natural terrain protected more than 600 Japanese guns, many encased in concrete bunkers. In November 1944, American bombers, based in the recently conquered Marianas, began to pound Iwo Jima from the air. For 74 days, American planes and warships poured nearly 7,000 tons of bombs and more than 20,000 shells onto Iwo Jima's defenders.

In mid-February 1945, marines stormed the beaches. They encountered furious resistance from the Japanese. After three days of combat, the marines had advanced only about 700 yards inland. Eventually nearly 110,000 American troops took part in the campaign. Although opposed by fewer than 25,000 Japanese, the marines needed almost a month to secure the island. The enemy fought almost to the last defender. Only 216 Japanese were taken prisoner.

In the **Battle of Iwo Jima,** American forces suffered an estimated 25,000 casualties. The United States awarded 27 Medals of Honor for actions on Iwo Jima, more than in any other single operation of the war. Admiral Nimitz described the island as a place in which "uncommon valor was a common virtue." A photo of servicemen raising the United States flag on Mt. Surabachi came to symbolize the struggles and sacrifices of American troops during World War II.

The **Battle of Okinawa,** fought from April to June 1945, was equally bloody. The small island of Okinawa, little more than 350 miles from Japan itself, was historically Japanese soil. It was the last obstacle to an Allied invasion of the Japanese home islands. With this in mind, many of the island's nearly 100,000 defenders had pledged to fight to the death.

The Allies gathered some 1,300 warships and more than 180,000 combat troops to drive the enemy from Okinawa in an effort second only to the Normandy invasion in size. Japanese pilots flew nearly 2,000 *kamikaze* attacks against this fleet. As American soldiers stormed ashore, defenders made equally desperate *banzai* charges—attacks in which the soldiers tried to kill as many of the enemy as possible until they themselves were killed.

On February 19, 1945—the first day of the invasion—Marines fought to win a foothold on Iwo Jima under intense Japanese fire.

ACTIVITY
Connecting with Geography

Divide the class into small groups. To give the class an idea of the inverse relationship between the size of Iwo Jima and the carnage that took place there, have each group superimpose an outline of Iwo Jima on a map of your community or nearest large city drawn to the same scale, and write a brief comparison. **(Visual/Spatial)**

BACKGROUND
Art History

Photography played a vital role in bringing the war to the American people at home. One acclaimed photograph, which became emblematic of the American effort in World War II, was Joe Rosenthal's study of six victorious marines hoisting the American flag on the isle of Iwo Jima. Rosenthal said of the shot: "I want[ed] to get at least one picture of an American flag on top of this hill." One writer later suggested that more people learned about the fight for Iwo Jima because of Rosenthal's photograph than because of any books or articles they have read on the subject.

TEST PREPARATION

Have students read the description of Japanese *kamikaze* pilots on the previous page and then complete the sentence below.

From the name these pilots were given, you can tell that—

- **A** the Japanese liked calamities.
- **B** the Japanese thought the Americans were like the Mongols.
- **C** the Japanese thought Japan could be saved only by a natural disaster.
- **(D)** the Japanese thought they had a divine mission to defend their islands.

ACTIVITY
Connecting with Government

Have students argue in favor of one of the following positions: naval blockade; A-bomb demonstration; the invasion of Japan; immediate use of the atomic bomb; relaxation of position on unconditional surrender. Students might research the opinions of a top policy-maker—such as Henry L. Stimson, Ralph A. Bard, or James Franck—regarding the use of the atomic bomb. **(Verbal/Linguistic; Logical/ Mathematical)**

BACKGROUND
Connections to Today

In November 2001 President George W. Bush issued a presidential order that had not been given since World War II: to allow military tribunals to try accused terrorists connected to the September 11, 2001, terrorist attacks on the United States. Military tribunals permit prosecutors to withhold sensitive information about national security that they would otherwise have to disclose in a criminal trial. Tribunals allow military officers to serve as both judge and jury, and instead of a unanimous verdict, the votes of two thirds of the panel would be needed to convict a defendant. Although the order gives Defense Secretary Donald Rumsfeld the power to detain anyone, it requires that the suspect be "treated humanely, without any adverse distinction based on race, color, [or] religion."

Kamikaze attacks took a toll on the United States Navy in the final year of the war.

One soldier described the long, hard-fought campaign to take Okinawa:

> *"Our attack pattern was: barrage a hill with bombs and shells, move up the foot soldiers, hold it against counterattacks, fight down the reverse slope, then start on the next one. We would attack during the day, dig in for the night—not for sleep, but for safety. A hole was never deep enough when the Japanese started their barrage. And then, at night, they would come, a screaming* banzai *or a single shadow."*
>
> —An American GI at Okinawa

In June, when the Japanese resistance finally ended after almost three months, only 7,200 defenders remained to surrender. For American forces, the nearly 50,000 casualties made the Battle of Okinawa the costliest engagement of the Pacific war. At long last, however, the Allies had a clear path to Japan.

The Manhattan Project

The next challenge for American soldiers was to prepare themselves for the invasion of Japan. After the grueling battles at Iwo Jima and Okinawa, they knew how costly such an invasion would be. Unknown to them, however, work was nearly complete on a bomb that would make the invasion unnecessary.

In August 1939, Roosevelt had received a letter from Albert Einstein, a brilliant Jewish physicist who had fled from Europe. In his letter, Einstein suggested that an incredibly powerful new type of bomb could be built by the Germans. Determined to build the bomb before Germany did, Roosevelt organized the top secret **Manhattan Project** to develop an atomic bomb.

Scientists had already succeeded in splitting the nucleus of the uranium atom. To make an atomic bomb, however, they had to discover how to create a chain reaction. In such a reaction, particles released from the splitting of one atom would cause another atom to break apart, and so on. In theory, the energy released by the splitting of so many atoms would produce a massive explosion. In 1942, Enrico Fermi produced the first controlled chain reaction in a laboratory at the University of Chicago. Scientists worked to design a bomb that could store the raw materials and trigger a much more powerful chain reaction on demand.

On July 16, 1945, Manhattan Project scientists field-tested the world's first atomic bomb in the desert of New Mexico. With a blinding flash of light, the explosion blew a huge crater in the earth and shattered windows some 125 miles away. As he watched, J. Robert Oppenheimer, who had supervised the building of the bomb, remembered the words of the *Bhagavad Gita*, the Hindu holy book: "Now I am become Death, the destroyer of worlds."

VIEWING HISTORY A single atomic bomb leveled the city of Hiroshima. **Making Comparisons** *How was the atomic bomb different from other war technology?*

The Decision to Drop the Bomb Once the bomb was ready, the question became whether or not to use it against Japan. There were a number of alternative possibilities for ending the war:

1. a massive invasion of Japan, expected to cost millions of Allied casualties
2. a naval blockade to starve Japan, along with continued conventional bombing
3. a demonstration of the new weapon on a deserted island to pressure Japan to surrender

CAPTION ANSWERS

Viewing History It was the most powerful weapon ever created and had the potential to destroy hundreds of thousands of lives with a single bomb.

RESOURCE DIRECTORY

Teaching Resources

Units 5/6/7 booklet
- Section 4 Quiz, p. 18

Guide to the Essentials
- Section 4 Summary, p. 89

Biography, Literature, and Comparing Primary Sources booklet (Literature) *Hiroshima,* p. 74

Technology

Sounds of an Era Audio CD *Roosevelt's Funeral,* April 1945 recording (time: 45 seconds); *President Truman,* 1945 recording (time: 50 seconds)

4. a softening of Allied demands for an unconditional surrender

An advisory group of scientists, military leaders, and government officials, called the Interim Committee, met in the spring of 1945 to debate these ideas. It could not recommend any of the alternatives. Heavy American casualties at Iwo Jima and Okinawa were a factor in the committee's support for using the bomb.

The final decision, however, rested with President Harry S Truman, who had taken office barely three months earlier, after Roosevelt's sudden death in April 1945. Truman had no difficulty making up his mind. He considered the bomb to be a military weapon and had no doubt that it should be used. Truman never regretted his decision. "You should do your weeping at Pearl Harbor," he said to his critics in 1963.

Japanese officials signed documents of surrender aboard the USS *Missouri.*

Japan Surrenders On August 6, 1945, an American plane, the *Enola Gay,* dropped a single atomic bomb on Hiroshima, a city in southern Japan and the site of a large army base. A blast of intense heat annihilated the city's center and its residents in an instant. Many buildings that survived the initial blast were destroyed by fires spread by powerful winds. Perhaps 80,000 died and at least as many were injured by fire, radiation sickness, and the force of the explosion. At least 90 percent of the city's buildings were damaged or totally destroyed. A Hiroshima resident described the scene after the bombing:

> "*Wherever you went, you didn't bother to take the roads. Everything was flat, nothing was standing, no gates, pillars, walls, or fences. You walked in a straight line to where you wanted to go. Practically everywhere you came across small bones that had been left behind.*"
>
> —Hiroshima survivor

Three days later, a second bomb was dropped on Nagasaki. On August 14, the government of Japan accepted the American terms for surrender. The next day, Americans celebrated V-J Day (Victory in Japan Day). The formal surrender agreement was signed on September 2, 1945, aboard the USS *Missouri* in Tokyo Bay. The long and destructive war had finally come to an end.

Section 4 Assessment

READING COMPREHENSION

1. What was Japan's military strategy immediately after the attack on Pearl Harbor?
2. How did the **Battle of Midway** and the **Battle of Guadalcanal** change the course of the war in the Pacific?
3. How did the **Battle of Okinawa** influence the decision to use the atomic bomb against Japan?

CRITICAL THINKING AND WRITING

4. **Making Comparisons** (a) In what ways did naval power play a different role in the Pacific war than it did in the war in Europe? (b) Why were aircraft carriers crucial to the Japanese and American war efforts?
5. **Writing to Explain** Write a brief essay that explains why the Japanese were able to advance so easily in 1941 and early 1942.

Take It to the NET

Activity: Writing a Magazine Article Select a battle, issue, or military unit from the War in the Pacific. Research your subject online, and then write a magazine article on that theme. Be sure to incorporate primary sources. Use the links provided in the *America: Pathways to the Present* area of the following Web site for help in completing this activity.
www.phschool.com

CUSTOMIZE FOR ...

Gifted and Talented

Ask students to write an essay stating their view as to whether or not the use of atomic weapons by the United States to end the war was justified. To do this, the students should compare the bombing of Hiroshima and Nagasaki to the highly destructive conventional bombing raids carried out by the Americans and the British against German cities.

Section 4 Assessment

Reading Comprehension

1. To continue attacking in several different areas of the Pacific, before the United States would have time to respond. In this way, the Japanese hoped to gain unrestricted access to territory in Southeast Asia.
2. The losses sustained by Japan during the Battle of Midway prevented the Japanese from launching any further offensive operations in the Pacific. In the Battle of Guadalcanal, the Americans conquered their first piece of Japanese-held territory.
3. The vast number of casualties at Okinawa led to the decision to use the atomic bomb, rather than sustain the heavy losses that would undoubtedly be incurred if Japan itself were invaded.

Critical Thinking and Writing

4. (a) Europe: Allied naval power used primarily to defeat the German U-boats; Pacific: Naval battles there were the most significant of the war. Establishing naval supremacy in the Pacific was essential to the success of the American island-hopping strategy. (b) Carrier-based aircraft could attack the opposing fleet from a great distance without the need for a land base. Aircraft carriers themselves were (and are) highly mobile. Thus, air strikes could be carried out anywhere in the Pacific.
5. Answers will vary, but should reflect an understanding of the following elements: surprise attacks; time America needed to respond; Britain, Netherlands preoccupied with war in Europe.

Take It to the NET

Articles will vary but should thoroughly represent the chosen topic, and be supported with various primary sources.

Making Decisions

Focus Students will gain insight into the process of decision-making by reading about the process of deciding to drop the atomic bomb on Japan.

Instruct Review with students the historical context of this document. America was at the end of a war that had been very costly in terms of lives and resources. President Truman had at his disposal a new kind of weapon that would bring the war to a rapid end. Should he use it? It was a heart-wrenching decision, because dropping the bomb would cause many innocent people to be injured or killed. Have students review his options. How many of them would have made the same decision?

Extend See the Skills for Life activity in the Resource Directory below.

ANSWERS

Practice the Skill

1. **(a)** Whether to use the atomic bomb or not. To end the war in Japan. **(b)** Yes. Truman had to find a way to end the war.
2. **(a)** Truman knew that Japan still had 5,000 attack planes, 17 garrisons on Kyushu, and more than 2 million soldiers. **(b)** The United States would probably lose between a quarter of a million and a half million men.
3. (1) Attacking the island of Kyushu, then Honshu; (2) blockading Japan and using conventional weaponry; (3) dropping the bomb in an area with a very small population; (4) dropping the atomic bomb on military-manufacturing areas.
4. **(a)** 1 and 2 would lead to great loss of American life but no definite end of the war, and 3 would not be shocking enough to force surrender. **(b)** Pros: 1 and 2 didn't have the bomb's horrific results; 3 had fewer Japanese civilian casualties. Cons: In 1 and 2 the war would go on longer, with many casualties on both sides. In 3 the Japanese would not surrender.
5. **(a)** To drop the bomb on military-manufacturing areas. **(b)** He felt this would bring the war to a faster end with fewest American casualties.

Making Decisions

Some decisions are more difficult to make than others. A good way to learn decision-making skills is to look at the choices others have made and how they made them.

One of the most famous—and most analyzed—decisions in history was President Harry S Truman's decision to drop the atomic bomb on Japan during World War II. The decision was made after Germany had surrendered. Truman feared that defeating Japan might be more difficult because "the Japanese were self-proclaimed fanatic warriors who made it all too clear that they preferred death to defeat in battle." He describes his decision at right.

LEARN THE SKILL

Use the following steps to make decisions:

1. **Identify the problem and express it clearly.** First determine *whether* a decision is needed; then clarify *what* needs to be decided. What is the issue you want to resolve or the goal you want to achieve?
2. **Gather information.** Find out facts about the issue. Be sure that your sources are reliable.
3. **Identify options.** Be sure to consider all the ways an issue might be handled. Stating the options clearly will help you decide.
4. **Predict consequences.** Identify the pros and cons of each choice.
5. **Make a decision.** Evaluate your options; choose the one with the most acceptable consequences.

PRACTICE THE SKILL

Answer the following questions:

1. **(a)** What issue did President Truman need to resolve? What was his goal? **(b)** Was a decision necessary? Explain your answer.
2. **(a)** What information was Truman given about Japan's military strength? **(b)** What information was he given on the projected casualties should the United States invade Japan?
3. What options did Truman identify?
4. **(a)** What did Truman think would be the consequences of each of these options? **(b)** What pros and cons did he consider?
5. **(a)** What did President Truman decide? **(b)** What was his reasoning?

APPLY THE SKILL

See the Chapter Review and Assessment for another opportunity to apply this skill.

"[O]n June 18, I met with the Joint Chiefs of Staff to discuss what I hoped would be our final push against the Japanese. We still hadn't decided whether or not to use the atomic bomb, and the chiefs of staff suggested that we plan an attack on Kyushu, the Japanese island on their extreme west, around the beginning of November, and follow up with an attack on the more important island of Honshu. But the statistics that the generals gave me were as frightening as the news of the big bomb. The chiefs of staff estimated that the Japanese still had five thousand attack planes, seventeen garrisons on the island of Kyushu alone, and a total of more than two million men on all of the islands of Japan. General Marshall then estimated that, since the Japanese would unquestionably fight even more fiercely than ever on their own homeland, we would probably lose a quarter of a million men and possibly as many as a half million in taking the two islands. I could not bear this thought, and it led to the decision to use the atomic bomb.

We talked first about blockading Japan and trying to blast them into surrender with conventional weaponry; but Marshall and others made it clear that this would never work, pointing out that we'd hit Germany in this way and they hadn't surrendered until we got troops into Germany itself. Another general also pointed out that Germany's munitions industries were more or less centralized and that our constant bombings of these facilities never made them quit, and Japan's industries were much more spread apart and harder to hit. Then, when we finally talked about the atomic bomb, on July 21, coming to the awful conclusion that it would probably be the only way the Japanese might be made to surrender quickly, we talked first about hitting some isolated area, some low-population area where there would not be too many casualties but where the Japanese could see the power of the new weapon. Reluctantly, we decided against that as well, feeling that that just wouldn't be enough to convince the fanatic Japanese. And we finally selected four possible target areas, all heavy military-manufacturing areas: Hiroshima, Kokura, Nagasaki, and Niigata."

—*Where the Buck Stops: The Personal and Private Writings of Harry S Truman*, Margaret Truman (ed.)

RESOURCE DIRECTORY

Teaching Resources
Skills for Life booklet, p. 27

Technology
Social Studies Skills Tutor CD-ROM
Interactive Practice in
- Geographic Literacy
- Critical Thinking and Reading
- Visual Analysis
- Communications

Section

5 The Social Impact of the War

READING FOCUS

- How did African Americans, Mexican Americans, and Native Americans experience the war at home?
- What difficulties did Japanese Americans face?
- In what ways did the war change conditions for working women?

MAIN IDEA

While the war brought new opportunities for women and some racial and ethnic minorities, Japanese Americans were the victims of widespread intolerance.

KEY TERMS

Congress of Racial Equality (CORE)
bracero
barrio
interned
Nisei

TAKING NOTES

As you read, complete this chart listing the experiences of women and minorities during the war.

Women	• Women fill jobs at factories and shipyards. •
African Americans	
Mexican Americans	
Japanese Americans	

Setting the Scene To win the war, the United States needed to draw upon all its resources, including its people. For several groups in American society, this need opened up opportunities that had not existed before the war. Taking advantage of those opportunities proved difficult, however, especially for racial and ethnic minorities. Prejudice still blocked many people from advancing freely.

Early in the war, most defense industries refused to accept African Americans. A. Philip Randolph, a powerful union leader, thought that mass protest might force the government to end this discrimination. He called for a march on Washington, D.C., under the slogan "We loyal Negro American citizens demand the right to work and fight for our country." Critics, including President Roosevelt, feared that a protest march by African Americans might hurt national unity and lead to violence. Randolph replied:

> "*We seek the right to play our part in advancing the cause of national defense and national unity. But certainly there can be no national unity where one tenth of the population are denied their basic rights as American citizens. . . . One thing is certain and that is if Negroes are going to get anything out of this national defense, which will cost the nation 30 or 40 billions of dollars that we Negroes must help pay in taxes as property owners and workers and consumers, we must fight for it and fight for it with gloves off.*"
>
> —A. Philip Randolph, press release, January 15, 1941

Segregation in the military mirrored conditions at home. Members of an African American field artillery unit (above) fire shells in Germany.

African Americans

African Americans had struggled for decades to end discrimination. Yet the Jim Crow system still endured in the South, and African Americans in the North faced unofficial discrimination in employment, education, and housing.

Economic Discrimination In 1941, industries searched for millions of new workers to meet the demands of the Lend-Lease program. Still, one out of five potential African American workers remained jobless. Government

Section 5

The War's Social Impact

SECTION OBJECTIVES

1. Learn how African Americans, Mexican Americans, and Native Americans experienced the war at home.
2. Find out about difficulties Japanese Americans faced.
3. See how the war changed conditions for working women.

BELLRINGER

Warm-Up Activity Write the words *injustice* and *inequality* on the chalkboard. Have students describe an incident that they associate with these words.

Activating Prior Knowledge Ask students what they know about the involvement of minorities, particularly African Americans, Native Americans, Hispanics, and Japanese Americans, in World War II.

READING STRATEGY

As students read the section, have them list and then analyze how the contributions of people of various racial, ethnic, and religious groups helped shape the national identity during World War II.

RESOURCE DIRECTORY

Teaching Resources

Learning Styles Lesson Plans booklet, p. 53
Guided Reading and Review booklet, p. 104

Technology

Section Reading Support Transparencies
Guided Reading Audiotapes (English/Spanish), Ch. 18
Student Edition on Audio CD, Ch. 18
Prentice Hall Presentation Pro CD-ROM, Ch. 18
Companion Web site, www.phschool.com

LESSON PLAN

Focus Point out that women and Americans of different ethnic groups were recruited to support the war effort. Ask what impact the war had on these Americans.

Instruct Although the war provided opportunities for African Americans, it did not end discrimination. Have students list examples of continued discrimination and describe efforts to promote racial equality.

Ask students what new job opportunities opened for Mexican Americans and Native Americans. How did both groups face cultural challenges as their interaction with the dominant society increased? Discuss why Japanese Americans were treated so harshly during the war. What civil rights were violated by their internment?

Assess/Reteach While World War II hastened the demand for and the rate of social change on the home front, it also caused many Americans to experience new kinds of discrimination. Have students list each ethnic group that experienced discrimination in the United States during World War II.

BACKGROUND Biography

Adam Clayton Powell, Jr. (1908–1972), charismatic minister from Harlem, used the pulpit and his oratorical skills to mobilize frustrated African Americans into positive political action. He echoed the sentiments of many fellow African Americans of his time when he said: "If the Negro is good enough to drive tanks on the battlefronts of Europe and Asia, he's good enough to work on the assembly lines of America." In 1944 Powell became one of only two African Americans in Congress and gained admiration for his "Powell Amendments"—attachments to bills that called for the cut-off of federal funds to any organization that practiced racial discrimination.

BIOGRAPHY

A. Philip Randolph 1889–1979

While working his way through college in New York and later as a ship's waiter, A. Philip Randolph began work as a union organizer. Starting in 1925, Randolph gradually won recognition for the Brotherhood of Sleeping Car Porters, a railway union composed largely of African Americans. The union won higher wages and cuts in working hours and travel requirements in 1937.

After World War II, Randolph continued as a labor leader, and became a vice president of the combined AFL and CIO labor union in 1955. When the civil rights movement got under way, the march that Randolph had wanted to hold years before finally took place. In August 1963, he directed the March on Washington, D.C., and stood beside Martin Luther King, Jr., as King gave his famous "I Have a Dream" speech.

agencies set up to help the unemployed during the Depression honored employers' requests for "whites only." Randolph hoped that his March on Washington would persuade the President to end this discrimination. He told Roosevelt to expect thousands of marchers in the capital on July 4. Roosevelt tried to talk Randolph out of the march, but Randolph refused.

Finally, on June 25, 1941, the President signed Executive Order 8802, opening jobs and job training programs in defense plants to all Americans "without discrimination because of race, creed, color, or national origin." The order also created the Fair Employment Practices Committee (FEPC) to hear complaints about job discrimination in defense industries and government. The committee had no real power, and many defense employers ignored its recommendations. Still, it was a beginning. For the first time in American history, the government acted against discrimination in employment. Randolph called off his march.

As a result, African Americans shared in some of the wartime prosperity. During the 1940s, more than 2 million African Americans migrated from the South to cities in the North. They found new job opportunities but also encountered new problems. Segregation forced most African Americans to live in poor housing in overcrowded urban ghettos. A 1941 survey showed that 50 percent of all African American homes were substandard, compared to only 14 percent of white homes.

To make matters worse, white workers and homeowners often feared and resented the newcomers. Resentments escalated into violence in some cities. In June 1943, a race riot in Detroit killed 34 people and caused millions of dollars worth of damage. Later that summer, a riot also broke out in New York City.

Soldiers and Segregation African American and white soldiers risked their lives equally in the war. Yet the American military strictly segregated white and African American troops. When they came home on leave, African Americans in army uniform still faced prejudice. Alexander J. Allen, who worked for the Baltimore Urban League during the war, remarked, "It made a mockery of wartime goals to fight overseas against fascism only to come back to the same kind of discrimination and racism here in this country." In Kansas, for instance, the owner of a lunch counter refused to serve a group of African American GIs. One GI recalled:

> *"'You know we don't serve coloreds here,' the man repeated. . . .We ignored him, and just stood there inside the door, staring at what we had come to see—the German prisoners of war who were having lunch at the counter. . . . We continued to stare. This was really happening. It was no jive talk. The people of Salina would serve these enemy soldiers and turn away black American GIs."*
>
> —Lloyd Brown

Divided Opinions In a 1942 poll, six out of ten whites believed that black Americans were satisfied with existing conditions and needed no new opportunities. Government attitudes mirrored this lack of concern. Roosevelt declined to disrupt the war effort to promote social equality. "I don't think, quite frankly," he said in late 1943, "that we can bring about the millennium [a period of human perfection] at this time."

RESOURCE DIRECTORY

Other Print Resources

Nystrom *Atlas of Our Country* *Later Expansion of the United States,* pp. 32–33; *People on the Move,* pp. 34–35

These attitudes forced African Americans to work for change on their own. The *Pittsburgh Courier,* an African American newspaper, launched a "Double V" campaign. The first *V* stood for victory against the Axis powers, the second for victory in winning equality at home.

Another step was the founding of the **Congress of Racial Equality (CORE)** in Chicago in 1942. CORE believed in using nonviolent techniques to end racism. In May 1943, it organized its first sit-in at a restaurant called the Jack Spratt Coffee House. Groups of CORE members, including at least one African American, filled the restaurant's counter and booths. They refused to leave until everyone was served. The sit-in technique ended Jack Spratt's discriminatory policies and quickly spread to CORE groups in other cities. These efforts paved the way for the civil rights movement that would begin in the next decade.

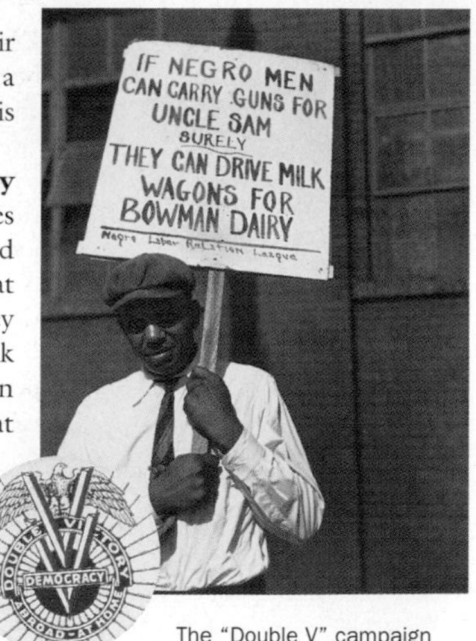

The "Double V" campaign urged victory over enemies overseas and over racial discrimination at home. This man (above) protested outside a Chicago milk company in 1941.

Mexican Americans

Like African Americans, both Mexican American citizens and Mexicans working in the United States faced discrimination during the war. Mexican Americans joined the armed forces, and the wartime economy brought new job opportunities in defense industries. By 1944, about 17,000 Mexican American citizens and Mexicans working in the United States held jobs in the Los Angeles shipyards, where none had worked three years before. Mexican Americans also found jobs in shipyards and aircraft factories in California and in Washington, Texas, and New Mexico. Some headed for other war production centers such as Detroit, Chicago, Kansas City, and New York.

The *Bracero* Program In agriculture, a shortage of farm laborers led the United States to seek help from Mexico. In 1942, an agreement between the two nations provided for transportation, food, shelter, and medical care for thousands of ***braceros,*** Mexican farm laborers brought to work in the United States. Between 1942 and 1947, more than 200,000 *braceros* worked on American farms and, occasionally, in other industries. The program brought a rise in the Latino population of Los Angeles and other cities in southern California. Many lived in Spanish-speaking neighborhoods called ***barrios.*** Crowded conditions and discrimination often created tensions, however.

COMPARING PRIMARY SOURCES
Integration of the Armed Forces

Discussion about desegregating the armed forces during World War II aroused strong feelings on both sides.
Analyzing Viewpoints What arguments does each side use to support its viewpoint?

In Favor of Integration

"Though I have found no Negroes who want to see the United Nations lose this war, I have found many who, before the war ends, want to see the stuffing knocked out of white supremacy. . . . If freedom and equality are not vouchsafed [granted] the peoples of color, the war for democracy will not be won. . . We demand the abolition of segregation and discrimination in. . . [all] branches of national defense."

—*A. Philip Randolph, African American labor and civil rights leader, November 1942*

Opposed to Integration

"In this hour of national crisis, it is much more important that we have the full-hearted co-operation of the thirty million white southern Americans than that we satisfy the National Association for the Advancement of Colored People. . . .If they be forced to serve with Negroes, they will cease to volunteer; and when drafted, they will not serve with that enthusiasm and high morale that has always characterized the soldiers and sailors of the United States."

—*W. R. Poage, Texas state representative, 1941*

ACTIVITY
Student Portfolio

Have students write journal entries in which they answer and explain their answers to this question: Were the *braceros* exploited by the United States, or were they given opportunities? **(Verbal/Linguistic)**

BACKGROUND
Connections to Today

The men of the 99th Pursuit Squadron, formed in 1942, were the first African Americans to fly in the Army Air Forces. They were known as the "Black Eagles" because of their success in escorting all-white bomber crews over Europe. The 99th was commanded by Benjamin O. Davis, Jr., the son of the man who became the first African American general. This squadron later became part of the 332nd Fighter Group. In 1991 Davis wrote about the exploits of the Black Eagles in his autobiography. By the early 1990s more than 5,500 African American officers made up 5.6 percent of the officers in the United States Air Force.

CUSTOMIZE FOR ...
Less Proficient Writers

Have students list the headings in this section. Then ask them to select one heading and summarize its contents in a brief paragraph.

TEST PREPARATION

Have students read the quote by Lloyd Brown on the previous page, and then complete the sentence below.

The main reason the writer is disturbed by what he sees is that—

Ⓐ the restaurant refused black soldiers but would serve enemy prisoners.
B he hates German soldiers.
C he is angry because the man isn't giving him the proper respect as a soldier.
D he is disturbed that the Germans aren't in jail.

Zoot Suit Riots In the 1940s, some young Mexican Americans in Los Angeles began to wear an outfit known as the "zoot suit," featuring a long draped jacket and baggy pants with tight cuffs. "Zoot-suiters" often wore a slicked-back "ducktail" haircut. This look offended many people, especially sailors who came to Los Angeles on leave from nearby military bases. Groups of sailors roamed the streets in search of zoot-suiters, whom they beat up and humiliated for looking "un-American." One Spanish newspaper, *La Opinión,* urged Mexican American youths not to respond with more violence, but some took revenge on the sailors when they could.

Early in June 1943, the street fighting grew into full-scale riots. Local newspapers usually blamed Mexican Americans for the violence. Police often arrested the victims rather than the sailors who had begun the attacks. Army and navy officials finally intervened by restricting GIs' off-duty access to Los Angeles.

Native Americans

The war also changed the lives of Native Americans. In addition to the 25,000 Native Americans who joined in the armed forces, many others migrated to urban centers to work in defense plants. Roughly 23,000 Native Americans worked in war industries around the country.

Life in the military or in the cities was a new experience for many Native Americans who had lived only on reservations. They had to adapt quickly to white culture. At the end of the war, those who had moved away often did not return to reservation life. For some, the cultural transition brought a sense of having lost their roots.

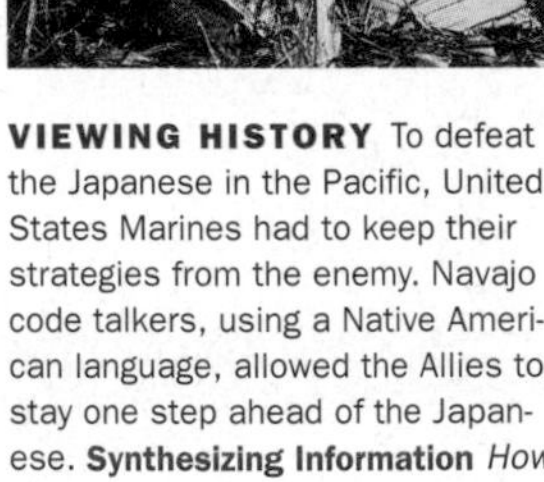

VIEWING HISTORY To defeat the Japanese in the Pacific, United States Marines had to keep their strategies from the enemy. Navajo code talkers, using a Native American language, allowed the Allies to stay one step ahead of the Japanese. **Synthesizing Information** *How else did the armed forces benefit from diversity?*

Japanese Americans

Japanese Americans suffered official discrimination during the war. In late 1941, they were a tiny minority in the United States, numbering only 127,000 (about 0.1 percent of the entire population). Most lived on the West Coast, where racial prejudice against them had always been strong. About two thirds of Japanese Americans had been born in the United States. Although they were native-born citizens, they still often met hostility from their white neighbors.

Hostility grew into hatred and hysteria after Japan attacked Pearl Harbor. Rumors flew about sabotage on the West Coast. The press increased people's fears with inaccurate reports carrying headlines such as "Jap Boat Flashes Message Ashore" and "Japanese Here Sent Vital Data to Tokyo." Such reports left Americans feeling that Japanese spies were everywhere.

Japanese Internment As a result of these prejudices and fears, the government decided to remove all "aliens" from the West Coast. On February 19, 1942, President Roosevelt signed Executive Order 9066. It authorized the Secretary of War to establish military zones on the West Coast and remove "any or all persons" from such zones. Officials told foreign-born Italians and Germans to move away from the coast, but within a few months they canceled those orders. The government set up the War Relocation Authority to move out everyone of Japanese ancestry—about 110,000 people, both citizens and noncitizens. They would be **interned,** or confined, in camps in remote areas far from the coast.

Relocation took place so fast that Japanese Americans had little time to secure their property before they left. Many lost their businesses, farms, homes, and other valuable assets. Henry Murakami, a resident of California,

ACTIVITY
Connecting with History and Conflict

Ask students to suppose that they are writing for a magazine distributed to the armed services during World War II. Ask them to write an editorial about the Zoot Suit riots, expressing an opinion about the actions of sailors before and during the riots. **(Verbal/Linguistic)**

BACKGROUND
Geography in History

Japanese Americans provided most of California's fresh produce in 1940, although they constituted less than 1% of the state's population. The internment of Japanese American farmers and grocers after Pearl Harbor threw parts of California's agricultural sector into chaos. While the government scrambled to feed its troops and encouraged Americans to start victory gardens, California had lost its primary providers of fruits and vegetables.

BACKGROUND
Connections to Today

Fearing that Japanese Americans might act as spies and help Japan invade the United States, the U. S. government moved Japanese American families to relocation camps during World War II. Some 60 years later, the United States offered a very different response to Muslim and Arab Americans following the terrorist attacks of September 11, 2001. President George W. Bush said, "We are in a fight for our principles, and our first responsibility is to live by them. No one should be singled out for unfair treatment or unkind words because of their ethnic background or religious faith."

CAPTION ANSWERS

Viewing History A Japanese American army unit was the most decorated in American history; African Americans, Mexican Americans, and women signed up to serve in significant numbers.

RESOURCE DIRECTORY

Teaching Resources

Biography, Literature, and Comparing Primary Sources booklet (Biography) *Navajo Code Talkers,* p. 30

Biography, Literature, and Comparing Primary Sources booklet (Comparing Primary Sources) *On Japanese American Internment,* p. 145

Other Print Resources

American History Block Scheduling Support *The Internment of Japanese Americans During World War II,* found in the Prosperity, Depression, and War folder, includes interdisciplinary lesson suggestions and activities for Geography and History, Primary Sources, Biography, and Literature.

remembers losing the $55,000 worth of fishing nets that had been his livelihood:

> *"When we were sent to Fort Lincoln [in Bismarck, North Dakota] I asked the FBI men about my nets. They said, 'Don't worry. Everything is going to be taken care of.' But I never saw the nets again, nor my brand-new 1941 Plymouth, nor our furniture. It all just disappeared. I lost everything."*
>
> —Henry Murakami

VIEWING HISTORY Five months after the attack on Pearl Harbor, the Mochida family waits for a bus to take them from Hayward, California, to a camp. **Recognizing Bias** *Why did the United States intern Japanese Americans like the Mochidas?*

Japanese Americans had no idea where they were going when they boarded buses and trains for the camps. Monica Sone, who lived in Seattle, imagined her camp would be "out somewhere deep in a snow-bound forest, an American Siberia. I saw myself plunging chest deep in the snow, hunting for small game to keep us alive." She and her family packed their winter clothes, only to end up in Camp Minidoka, on the sun-baked prairie of central Idaho, where the normal July temperature is about 90 degrees Fahrenheit.

All the camps were located in desolate areas. Families lived in wooden barracks covered with tar paper, in rooms equipped only with cots, blankets, and a light bulb. People had to share toilet, bathing, and dining facilities. Barbed wire surrounded the camps, and armed guards patrolled the grounds. Although the government referred to these as relocation camps, one journalist pointed out that they seemed "uncomfortably close to concentration camps."

Legal Challenges A few Japanese Americans challenged the internment policy in the courts. Four cases eventually reached the Supreme Court, which ruled that the wartime relocation was constitutional. In one case, California resident Fred Toyosaburo Korematsu, a defense-plant worker, was arrested for refusing to report to a relocation center. Korematsu appealed, saying that his civil rights had been violated.

The Supreme Court, in *Korematsu* v. *United States* (1944), ruled that the relocation policy was not based on race. The majority opinion said that "the military urgency of the situation demanded that all citizens of Japanese ancestry be segregated from the West Coast temporarily." The dissenting opinion, however, labeled the policy "an obvious racial discrimination."

Early in 1945, the government allowed Japanese Americans to leave the camps. Some returned home and resumed their lives, but others found that they had lost nearly everything. As time passed, many Americans came to believe that the internment had been a great injustice. In 1988, Congress passed a law awarding each surviving Japanese American internee a tax-free payment of $20,000. More than 40 years after the event, the United States government also officially apologized.

Japanese Americans in the Military During the war, the military refused to accept Japanese Americans into the armed forces until early 1943. Despite the government's harsh treatment of Japanese civilians, thousands volunteered and eventually more than 17,000 fought in the United States armed services. Most were **Nisei**, or citizens born in the United States to Japanese immigrant parents, and some volunteered while in internment camps. Many all-Nisei units won recognition for their courage in Europe. In fact, the soldiers of the

READING CHECK
What was the record of Japanese American soldiers in World War II?

ACTIVITY
Connecting with Government

Focus students' attention on the two opposing views expressed by the Supreme Court in the landmark case, *Korematsu* v. *United States.* Assign teams to uphold each of the opinions in a whole-class debate. Have students debate this resolution: "That the relocation of Japanese Americans was made necessary by wartime." **(Verbal/Linguistic)**

BACKGROUND
Recent Scholarship

The decision to relocate Japanese Americans to internment camps has been debated for more than 50 years. In his book *All the Laws but One: Civil Liberties in Wartime,* Chief Justice of the United States Supreme Court William H. Rehnquist writes that the legacy of that complex decision is "... that the courts will pay more careful attention to the basis for the government's claims of necessity as a reason for curtailing civil liberty. The laws will thus not be silent in time of war, even though they will speak with a different voice."

READING CHECK
They had an outstanding record in World War II, receiving medals and recognition for their bravery in combat. The all-Japanese 442nd Regimental Combat Team won more medals for bravery than any other regiment in United States history.

CUSTOMIZE FOR ...
Gifted and Talented
Ask students to write a short paper in which they consider why the U.S. Supreme Court upheld the constitutionality of internment camps for Japanese Americans in the 1944 *Korematsu* case. Students should consider the following questions: Was the Court's decision based purely on racism? Was it evidence of the High Court's unwillingness to rule against the federal government in a time of war? Did the justices really feel that Japanese Americans represented a genuine risk in terms of sabotage and espionage, or were there other reasons?

CAPTION ANSWERS

Viewing History After Pearl Harbor, many people thought that West Coast Japanese Americans were potential spies or saboteurs. There had been considerable ill will between Caucasians and Japanese Americans even before the war.

ACTIVITY
Connecting with Culture

Have students provide dramatic readings from sections of the book *The Good War* by Studs Terkel, an oral history of World War II that includes many descriptions of life in the United States at the time. Focus students' attention on the role of women. **(Verbal/Linguistic)**

BACKGROUND
Connections to Today

In June 2000 President Bill Clinton presented the Medal of Honor, the nation's highest military award, to 22 Nisei veterans of World War II (15 of these were awarded posthumously). All but two of the recipients were members of the 442nd Regimental Combat Team. Many of the recipients volunteered for service right out of internment camps. At the ceremony, President Clinton said that these soldiers "did not give up on their country when too many of their countrymen gave up on them." He added, "They risked their lives above and beyond the call of duty, and in doing so, they did more than defend America. In the face of painful prejudice, they helped to define America at its best."

all-Japanese 442nd Regimental Combat Team won more medals for bravery than any other unit in United States history.

Working Women

Women of all ages and ethnic and economic backgrounds went to work in the wartime economy. Many of them joined the work force out of a sense of patriotism. They wanted to support their husbands, boyfriends, sons, and brothers who had marched off to war. Others realized that the war gave them an opportunity to work at jobs that would otherwise be closed to them.

New Kinds of Jobs Before the war, most women who worked for wages were single and young. They worked mainly as secretaries, sales clerks, household servants, and in other low-paying jobs traditionally held by women. Except for teaching and nursing, few women entered professional careers. Women with factory jobs usually worked in industries that produced clothing, textiles, and shoes, while men dominated the higher-paying machinery, steel, and automobile industries. Almost everywhere, women earned less than men.

The motto of the women's Auxiliary Reserve Pool (top) during World War II was "Prepared and Faithful." The worker (bottom) is assembling an aircraft.

Like World War I, World War II brought women into different parts of the work force. As men were drafted into the armed forces, many factory jobs fell vacant. These higher-paying positions lured many women away from traditional women's jobs. They moved eagerly into manufacturing, particularly in the defense industries. Many women who had never worked outside the home also took jobs in the aircraft factories, shipyards, and other industrial sites that directly supported the war effort. The number of working women rose by almost one third, from 14.6 million in 1941 to about 19.4 million in 1944. Women at one point made up about 35 percent of the total civilian labor force.

A popular song in 1942 told the story of a fictional young woman called Rosie the Riveter. Rosie was a home front hero. She worked in a defense plant, driving rivets into the metal plates of aircraft, while her boyfriend Charlie served in the marines. The government used images of Rosie in posters and recruitment films of the 1940s to attract new women workers. In time, Rosie the Riveter became the popular name for all women who worked in war-production jobs, including riveters, steelworkers, and welders.

Benefits and Problems of Employment On the whole, women enjoyed working in war-related industries. Employment outside the home made a big difference in their lives, giving them self-confidence as well as economic independence. For example, Josephine McKee, a Seattle mother of nine who worked at the Boeing Aircraft Company, used her earnings to pay off debts from the Depression. Other women found the work more interesting and challenging than what they had done before. Evelyn Knight left a job as a cook to work in a navy yard. She explained, "After all, I've got to keep body and soul together, and I'd rather earn a living this way than to cook over a hot stove." Many women took jobs for patriotic reasons. One rubber plant worker declared, "Every time I test a batch of rubber, I know it's going to help bring my three sons home quicker."

Sounds of an Era

Listen to "Rosie the Riveter" and other sounds from World War II.

African American women had long worked in greater proportion than white women. Generally, though, only cooking, cleaning, child care, and other domestic jobs were open to them. When they applied for defense jobs, African American women often faced prejudice based on both their gender and race. Some women fought back. Through lawsuits and other forms of protest,

RESOURCE DIRECTORY

Teaching Resources
Units 5/6/7 booklet
- Section 5 Quiz, p. 19
- Chapter 18 Test, pp. 20, 23

Guide to the Essentials
- Section 5 Summary, p. 90
- Chapter 18 Test, p. 91

Learning with Documents booklet (Visual Learning Activity) *Campaigns on the Home Front,* p. 64

Other Print Resources
Chapter Tests with ExamView® Test Bank CD-ROM, Ch. 18

Technology
Sounds of an Era Audio CD *Mary Anderson, Director of the Women's Bureau,* 1942 recording (time: 30 seconds); *"Rosie the Riveter"* (time: one minute, 30 seconds)
Exploring Primary Sources in U.S. History CD-ROM *Rosie the Riveter Poster*
ExamView® Test Bank CD-ROM, Ch. 18
Social Studies Skills Tutor CD-ROM

African American women improved their chances in the work force. From 1940 to 1944, the percentage of African American women in industrial jobs increased from 6.8 percent to 18 percent. The number working in domestic service dropped from 59.9 percent to 44.6 percent.

In spite of the benefits of working, women faced a number of problems both inside and outside the workplace. They often encountered hostile reactions from other workers, particularly in jobs previously filled only by men. They also earned much less pay than men doing the same jobs. The National War Labor Board declared in the fall of 1942 that women who performed "work of the same quality and quantity" as men should receive equal pay. Employers widely ignored this policy.

What's Become of Rosie the Riveter?

VIEWING HISTORY Government campaigns aimed at women changed their message once the war was over. Posters such as this one tried to persuade women to give up their factory jobs and return to full-time homemaking. **Drawing Inferences** *Why were women being urged out of the work force?*

Working women had to figure out what to do with their children while they were on the job. More than half a million women with children under the age of 10 worked during the war, and day-care centers were scarce. They were forced to rely on family members and friends to care for their children. Furthermore, a typical woman's workday did not end after eight hours at the plant. Most working women also shouldered the burden of cooking, cleaning, and otherwise maintaining the household.

After the War The government drive to bring women to defense plants assumed that when the war was over, women would leave their jobs and return home. War work was just "for the duration." While many women wanted to continue working at the war's end, the pressures to return home were intense. Returning servicemen expected to get their jobs back.

As the economy returned to peacetime, twice as many women as men lost factory jobs. Some women were content to leave once the wartime sense of urgency ended. Others, however, had discovered new satisfactions in the workplace that made them want to keep on working. Some women also continued to work part time to bring in additional income.

Section 5 Assessment

READING COMPREHENSION

1. (a) What was the goal of A. Philip Randolph's march? (b) What was the significance of **CORE?**
2. How did Mexican Americans contribute to the war effort through the ***bracero*** program and in other ways?
3. (a) What challenges did women confront when taking jobs outside the home? (b) What were some benefits of wartime jobs for women?

CRITICAL THINKING AND WRITING

4. **Recognizing Bias** Although women workers were recruited during the war, they were pressured to leave their jobs and return to domestic work once it ended. What underlying beliefs does this series of events suggest?
5. **Writing an Opinion** Write a short paragraph explaining why you think the government acted more harshly against Japanese Americans than against people of Italian and German ancestry.

Take It to the NET

Activity: Writing an Encyclopedia Entry Investigate key roles women played during World War II. Take detailed notes. Then using your findings, write an encyclopedia entry for "Women's Roles During World War II." Use the links provided in the *America: Pathways to the Present* area of the following Web site for help in completing this activity.
www.phschool.com

Section 5 Assessment

Reading Comprehension

1. (a) For African Americans to gain the right to work and fight for their country. (b) Through its nonviolent search for equality, CORE paved the way for the civil rights movement.
2. They joined the armed forces, worked in defense industries, and *braceros* worked primarily on farms, but also in other industries.
3. (a) They often encountered hostile reactions from male workers; they earned much less than men doing the same jobs; they had to arrange child care while at work; and they had to maintain their household responsibilities in addition to their work outside the home. (b) Promoted self-confidence and economic independence; it was interesting and challenging and gave them opportunities to work in fields that were not previously open to women.

Critical Thinking and Writing

4. That women's place was still in the home, and that their work for the war effort was only temporary. Men returning from the war needed their jobs back, and women were expected to relinquish those jobs and resume their roles at home.
5. Paragraphs will vary, but should discuss the feelings of many Americans after the attack on Pearl Harbor—the growing prejudices and fears that Japanese Americans would sabotage facilities on the West Coast. That the war brought long-simmering animosity toward Japanese Americans into the open should also be mentioned. Bias against Japanese in the United States was stronger than bias against European immigrants at that time.

Take It to the NET

Entries will vary, but should reflect an understanding of the key activities of American women in the war.

Caption Answers

Viewing History To accommodate the employment needs of men returning from the war.

Chapter 18 Review and Assessment

creating a CHAPTER SUMMARY

Copy this chart (right) on a piece of paper and complete it by adding important events and issues that fit each heading. Some entries have been completed for you as examples.

Time Period	Important Events
The Home Front	• The armed forces draft millions of men to fight. • The economy converts to meet the needs of war. • Food and consumer goods are rationed. •
War in Europe (1941–1945)	
War in Asia and the Pacific (1941–1945)	
The Holocaust	

iTEXT

For additional review and enrichment activities, see the interactive version of *America: Pathways to the Present*, available on the Web and on CD-ROM.

★ Reviewing Key Terms

For each of the terms below, write a sentence explaining how it relates to the role of the United States in World War II.

1. Selective Training and Service Act
2. Office of War Mobilization
3. victory garden
4. Atlantic Charter
5. carpet bombing
6. D-Day
7. Holocaust
8. concentration camp
9. death camp
10. Bataan Death March
11. Battle of Midway
12. *kamikaze*
13. Manhattan Project
14. *bracero*
15. Nisei

★ Reviewing Main Ideas

16. How did World War II end the Depression? (Section 1)
17. What changes did American businesses make at the start of the war? (Section 1)
18. Where did the United States battle Germany and Italy in 1942 and 1943? (Section 2)
19. What was the D-Day operation? (Section 2)
20. Why did many Jews remain in Germany after 1933? (Section 3)
21. What was Hitler's "final solution"? (Section 3)
22. (a) What were the benefits of "island-hopping"? (b) List three islands or island groups in the order that they were captured by the United States. (Section 4)
23. Why did Truman decide to use the atomic bomb against Japan? (Section 4)
24. What strategies did African Americans use to gain equal rights during World War II? (Section 5)
25. What changes took place in the kinds of jobs women held before and during World War II? (Section 5)

★ Critical Thinking

26. **Recognizing Cause and Effect** Why were there shortages of sugar, coffee, and gasoline during World War II?
27. **Testing Conclusions** Some historians claim that Germany made a fatal mistake by declaring war on the United States in December 1941. Cite evidence to defend or disprove this claim.
28. **Identifying Assumptions** Why did military planners believe that an attack on Japan would be much more costly and dangerous than the D-Day invasion and eventual defeat of Germany?
29. **Predicting Consequences** How might the changes that the war brought for African Americans have affected the later civil rights movement?

REVIEWING KEY TERMS

Students should refer to the definitions of key terms in the chapter to write sentences that show an understanding of the World War II era.

REVIEWING MAIN IDEAS

16. The economy was boosted by the massive production of goods to supply the Allied forces.
17. They stopped producing consumer goods, converting to weapons and other wartime production. American businesses also built new factories and developed new mass production techniques.
18. In the Atlantic, North Africa, Sicily, and Italy; and by bombing German cities from the air.
19. The invasion of Western Europe begun by Allied forces at Normandy on June 6, 1944. D-Day was the largest landing by sea in history.
20. They believed that they could endure persecution, which would be easier than starting a new life in a foreign country, until Hitler lost power.
21. To annihilate all Jews and others considered "undesirable" by the Nazis. The killing was done by mobile killing squads in Russia and in six death camps in Poland.
22. (a) By selectively attacking specific enemy-held islands and bypassing others, the United States effectively cut off the bypassed islands from supplies and reinforcements, rendering them useless to Japan, and allowing Americans to move more quickly toward their ultimate goal—Japan. (b) Possible answer: Guadalcanal, Tarawa, Kwajalein, Iwo Jima, Okinawa.
23. To prevent the further loss of American troops and to end the war.
24. They launched the "Double V" campaign to win equality at home, founded CORE, and used activism to try to end discrimination.
25. Before the war women worked mainly as secretaries, sales clerks, household servants, and with the exception of teaching and nursing, seldom entered professional careers. In wartime, women worked in higher-paying positions in manufacturing and the defense industry.

CREATING A CHAPTER SUMMARY

Time Period	Important Events
The Home Front	• The armed forces draft millions of men to fight. • The economy converts to meet the needs of war. • Food and consumer goods are rationed. • The national debt rises to finance the wartime economy.
War in Europe (1941–1945)	• The Germans invade the Soviet Union. • Americans join the war in 1941. • The North African campaign is conducted. • The Allied air war intensifies. • Western Europe is invaded on D-Day. • The Allies invade Germany.
War in Asia and the Pacific (1941–1945)	• Japanese attack Pearl Harbor in 1941. • Japan attacks the Philippines and British and Dutch possessions in the Far East. • U.S. aircraft bomb Tokyo and Yokohama. • The Americans defeat the Japanese at Midway and Guadalcanal. • American victories in the Solomon, Gilbert, and Marshall islands, the Philippines, and at Iwo Jima and Okinawa • The U.S. drops atomic bombs on Hiroshima and Nagasaki. • World War II ends.
The Holocaust	• Germany builds concentrations camps. • *Kristallnacht* takes place in Germany. • Jews seek to escape Germany. • Jews, Romany, and other ethnic minorities are captured and transferred to concentration camps. • German mobile killing squads and death camps begin the mass murder of Jews. • The death camps and the concentration camps are liberated in 1945 after six million Jews had been murdered by the Nazis.

★ Skills Assessment

Analyzing Political Cartoons ▶

30. What does the woman in the cartoon symbolize?
31. What is the significance of her having her own "man-size" pay?
32. What point does the man's speech make?
33. Examine both figures. What message is conveyed by the woman's huge size and by the man's clothing?

Analyzing Primary Sources

Turn to the quotation in Section 4 about fighting in Okinawa.

34. Which phrase best describes the American campaign on Okinawa?
    - **A** long and hard-fought
    - **B** easy
    - **C** completely safe
    - **D** over in one day
35. According to the description of the fighting, you can infer that the terrain on Okinawa was
    - **F** flat and sandy.
    - **G** heavily wooded.
    - **H** rocky.
    - **J** hilly.
36. **Writing** Write a brief paragraph describing how you think the GIs felt during the long nights on Okinawa.

Applying the Chapter Skill: *Making Decisions*

37. Turn to Section 4 and to page 622, and read again about the decision to drop the atomic bomb. (a) What were the potential consequences of a naval blockade to starve Japan? (b) Why do you think Truman and the Interim Committee rejected this option?

ACTIVITIES

Writing to LEARN

Writing a Persuasive Essay
The horrible slaughter of six million Jews during the Holocaust is an example of genocide. Research and write an essay on a more recent case where one group tried to carry out a campaign of genocide against another ethnic group. In your essay, include the global community's reaction to the killings.

Primary Source CD-ROM

Working With Primary Sources Find additional information on World War II on the *Exploring Primary Sources in U.S. History CD-ROM* and use the selection(s) provided to complete the Chapter 18 primary source activity located in the *America: Pathways to the Present* area of the following Web site.
www.phschool.com

Take It to the NET

Chapter Self-Test As a review activity, take the Chapter 18 Self-Test in the *America: Pathways to the Present* area at the Web site listed below. The questions are designed to test your understanding of the chapter content.
www.phschool.com

ANSWERS TO ACTIVITIES

Writing to LEARN

Essays will vary but could focus on campaigns of genocide that include Cambodia, Laos, Haiti, Kosovo, or Rwanda.

Primary Source CD-ROM

Direct students to the additional primary sources that can be found on the *Exploring Primary Sources in U.S. History CD-ROM.*

Take It to the NET

Additional support materials and activities for Chapter 18 of *America: Pathways to the Present* can be found in the Social Studies area at the Prentice Hall School Web site. **www.phschool.com**

Critical Thinking

26. The closing of shipping lanes and enemy occupation of foreign countries limited the supply of sugar and coffee to the United States during World War II. Gasoline was rationed because it was needed for the war effort.

27. Answers will vary but should be supported with facts from the chapter.

28. The Japanese were reluctant to surrender and fought to the last defender. The D-Day landings took place in an occupied country, rather than in Germany proper. Also, British and American D-Day planners knew that the vast majority of German troops were pinned down on the Eastern Front fighting the Russians.

29. For the first time in American history, the government acted (with Executive Order 8802) against discrimination in employment. Also, the founding of CORE and the creation of the sit-in technique paved the way for the civil rights movement that would later follow.

Skills Assessment

30. Women who entered the labor force in support of the war effort.

31. It means that women enjoyed working in traditionally male jobs and making good wages while doing so.

32. Women were expected to give up their new jobs once men returned home from the war.

33. Women empowered by gainful employment are threatening to men. Such women might become the dominant partner in a marriage, and might force their husbands to wear aprons.

34. A

35. J

36. Paragraphs will vary, but should be descriptive and should mention that nights on Okinawa were very frightening and dangerous.

37. (a) No definite end to the war, humanitarian disaster in Japan.
(b) Primarily because it would delay the ending of the war and could only be successful if the blockade were accompanied by an Allied ground invasion of Japan's home islands.

LOCKING HORNS WITH THE BULL

Focus Have students find the meaning of each of these words in a dictionary before they begin to read: *transmission, meteorologist, keen, court-martial, insubordination.* Ask them to think, as they read, about the responsibilities that Roddewig had despite his young age.

Instruct Explain that the work of radio operators was critical during World War II. After World War I, the U.S. Navy led the world in radio innovation. (Unlike the telegraph and telephone, radio was developed mainly for military use.) The interception of radio transmissions became routine during World War II. When decoded, such transmissions significantly influenced the movements of all naval forces. Discuss Roddewig's responsibilities as a radio operator during the war.

Analyzing the Document Use this additional question to generate class discussion:

Critical Thinking: Identifying Assumptions Why did Roddewig think that his naval career was sure to end in disgrace? *(Because he, a lowly third-class radioman, had told a four-star admiral to "shut up.")*

AmericanHeritage®

MY BRUSH WITH **HISTORY**™

by ROBERT RODDEWIG

Locking Horns With the Bull

United States Navy radiomen at work during World War II

In the passage below, Robert Roddewig, a sailor on the battleship USS *Missouri* in the final months of World War II, describes a nerve-wracking experience in the waters near Japan. As you read, think about the responsibilities that Roddewig had despite his young age.

Admiral William F. "Bull" Halsey

THE YEAR WAS 1945. As an eighteen-year-old eligible for the draft, I had enlisted in the Navy before graduation from high school in Davenport, Iowa. After boot camp and radio school, at Farragut, Idaho, I was assigned to the staff of Adm. William F. "Bull" Halsey aboard the *Missouri*, an *Iowa*-class battleship.

I felt honored to pull duty as a staff member with a four-star admiral. Halsey usually selected the *New Jersey*, another *Iowa*-class ship, but the *Jersey* had steamed stateside for some badly needed maintenance and repair. The *Missouri* got the call.

There were seven radio transmitting-and-receiving stations aboard the *Missouri*, and I usually spent my four hours handling routine communications among ships of the fleet. I had been onboard several weeks and had not even seen the admiral. Then I was transferred to the radio station just behind the ship's bridge. I would be copying coded messages from several military shore stations. When decoded, these transmissions would help our meteorologists map weather conditions over possible Japanese bombing targets. I quickly came to realize the importance of my work. The safety of our carrier pilots might well depend upon the accuracy and thoroughness of the radiomen on duty behind the bridge.

To obtain weather information I usually copied station NPG Honolulu or an Army station from Andrews Air Force Base on Guam. These were clear stations with little interference of any kind. But station KCT from Vladivostok, U.S.S.R., was different.

If our planes were to raid the Japanese islands of Hokkaido or Honshu, we needed the weather report from KCT. The Japanese, knowing this, constantly jammed the KCT frequency with music, loud laughter, foreign languages—anything and everything to drown out the signal. It required keen concentration to find our signal and stay on it while totally ignoring all the "trash."

RESOURCE DIRECTORY

Technology

AmericanHeritage® **My Brush with History**™ **Videotapes** *Locking Horns with the Bull*

TEST PREPARATION

Have students use the excerpt above to answer the following question.

From what you read, which statement best describes Admiral Halsey?

Ⓐ He understood the importance of the contributions of all his staff members.

B He hated war.

C His nickname came from the way he bullied his staff.

D He had little interest in the task that Roddewig was carrying out.

Interference From a Loud Voice
One evening I was copying KCT with the usual Japanese garbage jamming my frequency. I had my eyes closed, and I was concentrating totally on that faint but distinctive signal: Dit dah dit. I automatically hit the R key on the typewriter (or mill, as the Navy called it). Dah dit dit dit, B. Dit dit dit, S.

Then a loud voice behind me asked, "Are they jamming our station?"

"Yes, sir," I replied, my concentration broken. I hit the space bar of the mill several times to indicate missed letters. I found the signal once again.

"Are you able to copy it?" The voice again. I hit the space bar several more times before finding my signal once more. "Will you be able to get enough for us?" And the space-bar routine again. But this time I blurted out, "Shut up!"

When the transmission was complete, I pulled the message from my machine. Wondering if the blank spaces would ruin our mapmaking effort, I turned in my seat—and looked up at four stars on each lapel of a brown shirt. I had just met Admiral Halsey.

Oh my . . . , I thought. I was an insignificant radioman, third class, and I had told an admiral to shut up.

At nineteen years my life would end. I would be fortunate to get a court-martial for insubordination along with a dishonorable discharge from the Navy.

"Sir, are you the one I told to 'shut up'?"

This tough-looking admiral was standing there with arms folded and legs apart in a mild inverted Y, brown naval field cap pulled to his brow, jaw jutting menacingly with lips pressed firmly together. I could see now why they called him Bull Halsey.

"Yes, lad," he blared.

"I apologize, sir. I did not know it was you. I have no excuse, sir."

The admiral broke his stance and began to pace the floor. "Lad," he bellowed, "when I come into this radio shack and speak to you while you are on that radio, you do not tell me to shut up! Do you understand?"

His voice boomed like the nine 16-inch guns attached to the ship's three main turrets.

Launched in 1944, the battleship USS Missouri *was nearly 900 feet long and had a crew of 1,900.*

"Yes, sir, I understand." I was frozen at attention and, I am certain, tears were welling in my eyes.

Then, stopping in front of me and looking me straight in the eye, he went on in a very calm and friendly voice. "If I or anyone else ever bothers you while you are on that radio, you do not tell them to shut up. What you tell them is to get the . . . out of here and that's an order. Do you understand, lad?"

I could only look at him and stammer, "Yes, sir."

We saluted. Admiral Halsey went on his way. I never met him again.

Source: *American Heritage* magazine, September 1997.

Understanding Primary Sources

1. How did Admiral Halsey respond when an underling told him to "shut up" under these circumstances?
2. What does this response imply about Halsey's character and leadership ability?

American Heritage® MY BRUSH WITH HISTORY™

 **Videotapes**

For more information about World War II in the Pacific, view "Locking Horns With the Bull."

633

CUSTOMIZE FOR ...
ESL
Students may need help with the following words and phrases:
draft the choosing of a person or persons for required military service
pull duty to perform an assignment
four-star admiral an admiral whose high rank is indicated by four stars on his or her uniform
jamming making a radio broadcast impossible to understand by broadcasting on the same call frequency

CUSTOMIZE FOR ...
Less Proficient Readers
Group students in pairs and ask them to dramatize the story. First have students copy the dialogue between Admiral Halsey and the sailor. Have one student in each pair take the part of the admiral and the other the part of the sailor. Tell "admirals" to stand in back of "sailors," who are seated at a desk. After all the pairs have practiced the dramatizations, call on several pairs of volunteers to perform for the class.

CUSTOMIZE FOR ...
Less Proficient Writers
Have students do research to find out more about the life of Admiral Halsey. Ask them to find out these facts: What year was he born? When did he die? What were his years of military service? List at least three of his major achievements as an admiral. Why was he known as "Bull"?

CUSTOMIZE FOR ...
Gifted and Talented
Have students revise the story by assuming the role of Admiral Halsey and writing a diary entry that describes his encounter with the radioman. Encourage students to complete the following sentences and incorporate them into their diary entries:
- I interrupted the radioman because . . .
- When the radioman told me to shut up, I felt . . .
- After the radioman apologized, I decided to . . .

Answers
1. Halsey initially upbraided the radioman but then acknowledged the importance of his job and put him at ease.
2. Answers will vary; Halsey's actions show that he was confident enough to relax military protocol slightly under difficult circumstances while maintaining control and giving support.

Chapter 19 Planning Guide
Resource Manager

	CORE INSTRUCTION	READING/SKILLS
Chapter-Level Resources **TEKS** 24(A)	Teaching Resources • Pacing Charts booklet • Block Scheduling booklet **Resource Pro® CD-ROM,** Ch. 19 **Prentice Hall Presentation Pro CD-ROM,** Ch. 19 **www.phschool.com** • eTeach	**Guided Reading Audiotapes (English/Spanish)** **Student Edition on Audio CD,** Ch. 19 **Social Studies Skills Tutor CD-ROM** **Color Transparencies,** A45, A46, A47, B14, D10
1 Origins of the Cold War 1. Learn why 1945 was a critical year in United States foreign relations. 2. Discover some of the postwar goals of the United States and the Soviet Union. 3. Find out how the iron curtain tightenend the Soviet hold over Eastern Europe. 4. See how the Truman Doctrine complemented the policy of containment. **TEKS** 1(B), 6(D), 15(B), 24(B), 24(C), 24(G), 26(A)	Teaching Resources **Units 5/6/7 booklet** • Section 1 Quiz, p. 27	**Guided Reading and Review booklet,** p. 105 **Guide to the Essentials,** p. 92 **Learning with Documents booklet,** pp. 31, 68 **Skills for Life booklet,** p. 28 **Section Reading Support Transparencies**
2 The Cold War Heats Up 1. Find out how the Marshall Plan, the Berlin airlift, and NATO helped to achieve American goals in postwar Europe. 2. Realize how Communist advances affected American foreign policy. 3. See how the Cold War affected American life at home. **TEKS** 6(D), 14(C), 24(H)	Teaching Resources **Units 5/6/7 booklet** • Section 2 Quiz, p. 28 **Learning Styles Lesson Plans booklet,** p. 54	**Guided Reading and Review booklet,** p. 106 **Guide to the Essentials,** p. 93 **Section Reading Support Transparencies**
3 The Korean War 1. Observe the ways Communist expansion in Asia set the stage for the Korean War. 2. Learn who fought in the Korean War and about the war's three stages. 3. Discover the different effects of the Korean War. **TEKS** 1(B), 6(E), 6(H), 9(B), 14(C), 25(D)	Teaching Resources **Units 5/6/7 booklet** • Section 3 Quiz, p. 29	**Guided Reading and Review booklet,** p. 107 **Guide to the Essentials,** p. 94 **Learning with Documents booklet,** p. 89 **Section Reading Support Transparencies**
4 The Continuing Cold War 1. Discover some characteristics of the McCarthy era. 2. See how the Cold War was waged in Southeast Asia, the Middle East, and Latin America during the 1950s. 3. Understand how the arms race developed. **TEKS** 6(D), 6(F), 24	Teaching Resources **Units 5/6/7 booklet** • Section 4 Quiz, p. 30 **Learning Styles Lesson Plans booklet,** p. 55	**Guided Reading and Review booklet,** p. 108 **Guide to the Essentials,** p. 95 **Section Reading Support Transparencies**

Enrichment/Pre-AP

Prentice Hall United States History Video Collection™
www.phschool.com
- Section Activities, Virtual Field Trip, Chapter Activities, Current Events Online

Biography, Literature, and Comparing Primary Sources booklet, p. 31
Historical Outline Map Book, pp. 68, 77
Sounds of an Era Audio CD

Biography, Literature, and Comparing Primary Sources booklet, pp. 147–148
American History Block Scheduling Support
Sounds of an Era Audio CD

American History Block Scheduling Support
Historical Outline Map Book, p. 69
Sounds of an Era Audio CD

Biography, Literature, and Comparing Primary Sources booklet, p. 75
Historical Outline Map Book, p. 78
Sounds of an Era Audio CD
American Pathways Thematic Posters

Assessment

Core Assessment
ExamView® Test Bank, Ch. 19
ExamView® Test Bank CD-ROM, Ch. 19

Standardized Test Preparation
Diagnose and Prescribe
Diagnostic Tests for High School Social Studies Skills

Review and Reteach
Review Book for U.S. History

Practice and Assess
Test-taking Strategies With Transparencies
Test-taking Strategies Posters
Test Prep Book for U.S. History
Alternative Assessment Handbook
Document-Based Assessment

Teaching Resources
Units 5/6/7 booklet
- Section Quizzes, pp. 27–30
- Chapter Tests, pp. 31, 34

www.phschool.com Ch. 19 Self-Test

AmericanHeritage Resources

From the Archives of American Heritage®, p. 639
AmericanHeritage® My Brush with History™ Videotapes
www.americanheritage.com

Don't miss the exclusive interactive version of this textbook on the Web and on CD-ROM.

Chapter 19 Planning Guide

In Your Classroom

Customize for Individual Needs

Gifted and Talented

Teacher's Edition
- Customize for Gifted and Talented, pp. 637, 653

Teaching Resources
- Biography, Literature, and Comparing Primary Sources booklet, pp. 31, 75, 147–148

ESL

Teacher's Edition
- Customize for ESL, p. 661

Teaching Resources
- Guided Reading and Review booklet, pp. 105–108
- Guide to the Essentials (English/Spanish), Chapter 19

Technology
- Student Edition on Audio CD, Chapter 19
- Guided Reading Audiotapes (English/Spanish), Chapter 19
- Section Reading Support Transparencies

Less Proficient Readers

Teacher's Edition
- Customize for Less Proficient Readers, pp. 641, 645

Teaching Resources
- Guided Reading and Review booklet, pp. 105–108
- Guide to the Essentials (English/Spanish), Chapter 19

Technology
- Student Edition on Audio CD, Chapter 19
- Guided Reading Audiotapes (English/Spanish), Chapter 19
- Section Reading Support Transparencies

Less Proficient Writers

Teacher's Edition
- Customize for Less Proficient Writers, p. 647

Teaching Resources
- Guided Reading and Review booklet, pp. 105–108
- Guide to the Essentials (English/Spanish), Chapter 19

Technology
- Student Edition on Audio CD, Chapter 19
- Guided Reading Audiotapes (English/Spanish), Chapter 19
- Section Reading Support Transparencies

Teacher's Edition Index

Chapter 19 – Pacing Suggestions

For 90-minute Blocks

- Teach sections 2, 3, and 4 using A45, A46, A47, B14, and D10, and the Recent Scholarship notes on pages 647 and 649 for class discussions.

Running Out of Time?

If you are running short on time to cover this chapter, consider the following options:

- Use the Prentice Hall Presentation Pro CD-ROM to create an outline for this chapter.
- Use the Section Summaries for Chapter 19, from **Guide to the Essentials (English/Spanish).**

TEKS Correlation

Chapter-Level	TEKS
	(24) Social studies skills. The student applies critical-thinking skills to organize and use information acquired from a variety of sources, including electronic technology. The student is expected to: **(A)** locate and use primary and secondary sources such as computer software, databases, media and news services, biographies, interviews, and artifacts to acquire information about the United States.
1 Origins of the Cold War	**(1) History.** The student understands traditional historical points of reference in U.S. history from 1877 to the present. The student is expected to: **(B)** apply absolute and relative chronology through the sequencing of significant individuals, events, and time periods. **(6) History.** The student understands the impact of significant national and international decisions and conflicts from World War II and the Cold War to the present on the United States. The student is expected to: **(D)** describe U.S. responses to Soviet aggression after World War II, including the Truman Doctrine, the Marshall Plan, the North Atlantic Treaty Organization, and the Berlin airlift. **(15) Government.** The student understands changes in the role of government over time. The student is expected to: **(B)** explain the impact of significant international events such as World War I and World War II on changes in the role of the federal government. **(24) Social studies skills.** The student applies critical-thinking skills to organize and use information acquired from a variety of sources, including electronic technology. The student is expected to: **(B)** analyze information by sequencing, categorizing, identifying cause-and-effect relationships, comparing, contrasting, finding the main idea, summarizing, making generalizations and predictions, and drawing inferences and conclusions. **(C)** explain and apply different methods that historians use to interpret the past, including the use of primary and secondary sources, points of view, frames of reference, and historical context. **(G)** support a point of view on a social studies issue or event. **(26) Social studies skills.** The student uses problem-solving and decision-making skills, working independently and with others, in a variety of settings. The student is expected to: **(A)** use a problem-solving process to identify a problem, gather information, list and consider options, consider advantages and disadvantages, choose and implement a solution, and evaluate the effectiveness of the solution.
2 The Cold War Heats Up	**(6) History.** The student understands the impact of significant national and international decisions and conflicts from World War II and the Cold War to the present on the United States. The student is expected to: **(D)** describe U.S. responses to Soviet aggression after World War II, including the Truman Doctrine, the Marshall Plan, the North Atlantic Treaty Organization, and the Berlin airlift. **(14) Economics.** The student understands the economic effects of World War II, the Cold War, and increased worldwide competition on contemporary society. The student is expected to: **(C)** describe the impact of the Cold War on the business cycle and defense spending. **(24) Social studies skills.** The student applies critical-thinking skills to organize and use information acquired from a variety of sources, including electronic technology. The student is expected to: **(H)** use appropriate mathematical skills to interpret social studies information such as maps and graphs.
3 The Korean War	**(1) History.** The student understands traditional historical points of reference in U.S. history from 1877 to the present. The student is expected to: **(B)** apply absolute and relative chronology through the sequencing of significant individuals, events, and time periods. **(6) History.** The student understands the impact of significant national and international decisions and conflicts from World War II and the Cold War to the present on the United States. The student is expected to: **(E)** analyze the conflicts in Korea and Vietnam and describe their domestic and international effects. **(H)** identify the origins of major domestic and foreign policy issues currently facing the United States. **(9) Geography.** The student understands the impact of geographic factors on major events. The student is expected to: **(B)** identify and explain reasons for changes in political boundaries such as those resulting from statehood and international conflicts. **(14) Economics.** The student understands the economic effects of World War II, the Cold War, and increased worldwide competition on contemporary society. The student is expected to: **(C)** describe the impact of the Cold War on the business cycle and defense spending. **(25) Social studies skills.** The student communicates in written, oral, and visual forms. The student is expected to: **(D)** create written, oral, and visual presentations of social studies information.
4 The Continuing Cold War	**(6) History.** The student understands the impact of significant national and international decisions and conflicts from World War II and the Cold War to the present on the United States. The student is expected to: **(D)** describe U.S. responses to Soviet aggression after World War II, including the Truman Doctrine, the Marshall Plan, the North Atlantic Treaty Organization, and the Berlin airlift. **(F)** describe the impact of the GI Bill, the election of 1948, McCarthyism, and Sputnik I. **(24) Social studies skills.** The student applies critical-thinking skills to organize and use information acquired from a variety of sources, including electronic technology.

Chapter 19

The Cold War

(1945–1960)

Introducing the Chapter

American foreign policy after World War II remained consistent with the nation's wartime activities: force would be used to oppose authoritarian regimes that the United States considered a threat to the free world. At home the federal government would use strong, and sometimes questionable, measures to counter what it perceived to be threats to the nation's internal security.

Time Line Activity

To provide students with practice in using the time line, ask questions such as these:

1. Why did Churchill, Truman, and Stalin meet in Potsdam? *(To plan the postwar world)*
2. What was the stated purpose of the Eisenhower Doctrine? *(To defend Middle East countries against Communist aggression)*
3. What two events in 1949 would have been very threatening to those who opposed the worldwide expansion of communism? *(The Communist victory in China and the successful Soviet test of an atomic bomb)*

Chapter 19 The Cold War (1945–1960)

SECTION 1 Origins of the Cold War
SECTION 2 The Cold War Heats Up
SECTION 3 The Korean War
SECTION 4 The Continuing Cold War

Churchill, Truman, and Stalin (left to right) at the Potsdam Conference

American Events

1945 The United States, Britain, and the Soviet Union meet at Yalta, and later at Potsdam, to plan the postwar world. The United Nations is founded.

1947 The Truman Doctrine promises support to nations resisting Communist aggression.

1948 The Marshall Plan provides U.S. aid to Europe. The Berlin airlift brings supplies to West Berlin.

1949 NATO is formed to defend Europe against the Communists.

1950 The Korean War begins. Senator Joseph McCarthy launches his anti-Communist campaign.

Presidential Terms: F.D. Roosevelt 1933–1945; Harry S Truman 1945–1953

1944 • 1946 • 1948 • 1950

World Events

1946 Soviet leader Joseph Stalin predicts the worldwide triumph of communism.

1949 Communists win control of China. The Soviets test an atomic bomb.

eTeach

Be sure to check out this month's online discussion with a Master Teacher. Go to **www.phschool.com**.

RESOURCE DIRECTORY

Teaching Resources

Pacing Charts booklet
Block Scheduling booklet, p. 26
Units 5/6/7 booklet
- Chapter Summary, p. 26

Technology

Guided Reading Audiotapes (English/Spanish), Ch. 19
Student Edition on Audio CD, Ch. 19
Prentice Hall United States History Video Collection™ Volume 20, *Post-War USA*
Prentice Hall Presentation Pro CD-ROM, Ch. 19
Resource Pro® CD-ROM
Social Studies Skills Tutor CD-ROM
Companion Web site, www.phschool.com

NATO and the Warsaw Pact, 1955

NATO members
Warsaw Pact members

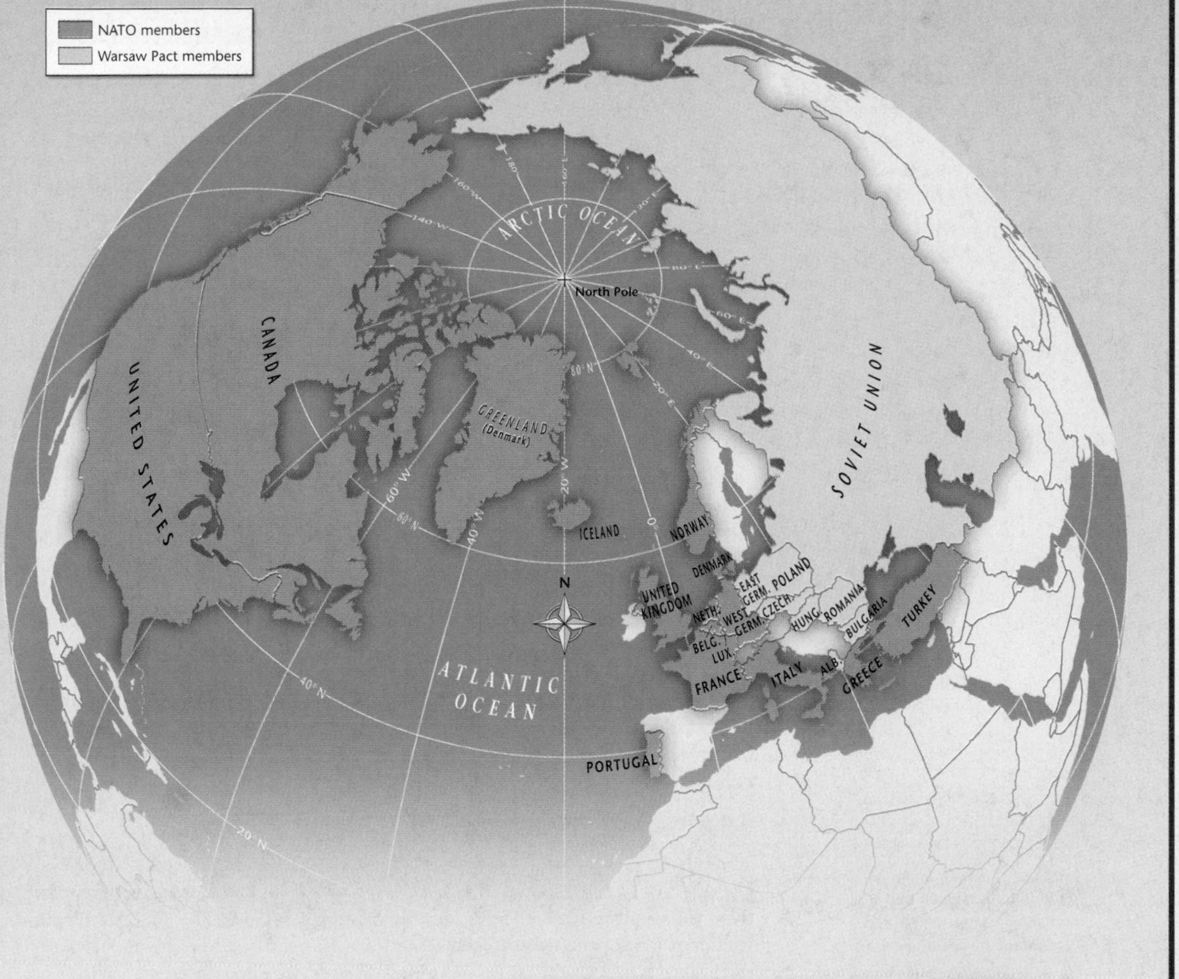

1953 The Rosenbergs are executed for spying for the Soviets.

1953 The Soviets test a hydrogen bomb.

1954 Senator Joseph McCarthy is formally censured by the Senate.

1955 The Warsaw Pact is formed.

1957 The President proclaims the Eisenhower Doctrine, promising to use force to defend Middle Eastern countries against Communist aggression.

1957 The Soviet Union launches the *Sputnik* satellite.

Dwight D. Eisenhower 1953–1961

1952 · 1954 · 1956 · 1958

NATO and the Warsaw Pact, 1955

Activating Prior Knowledge Ask students to explain where the term "iron curtain" comes from. *(It is the imaginary line drawn between NATO and the Warsaw Pact members.)*

Previewing Why was the formation of NATO necessary? *(To create an alliance that would counterbalance the threat of communism)*

BACKGROUND About the Pictures

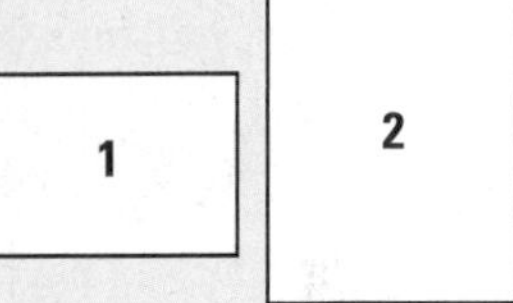

1. Though the three men met as allies, the ties that bound them were very weak. Each was heavily focused on his own motives and interests.
2. Through the Marshall Plan, over $13 billion worth of aid was distributed to European nations over the course of four years.

BIBLIOGRAPHY

For the Teacher

Kennan, George F. ***Memoirs: 1925–1950.*** Knopf, 1983. (A personal view of the era by the definitive statesman of the policy of "containment.")

McCullough, David. ***Truman.*** Touchstone, 1993. (A comprehensive biography of the Cold War President.)

For the Student

Orwell, George. ***Nineteen Eighty-Four.*** New American Library Classics, 1990. (A haunting, futuristic indictment of the totalitarian state.)

Solzhenitsyn, Aleksandr I. ***One Day in the Life of Ivan Denisovich.*** Signet Classic, 1998. (A famous Russian dissident's moving account of life in a Soviet prison camp.)

Don't miss the exclusive interactive version of this textbook on the Web and on CD-ROM.

Section 1 Origins of the Cold War

Section Objectives

1. Learn why 1945 was a critical year in United States foreign relations.
2. Discover some of the postwar goals of the United States and the Soviet Union.
3. Find out how the iron curtain tightened the Soviet hold over Eastern Europe.
4. See how the Truman Doctrine complemented the policy of containment.

Bellringer

Warm-Up Activity Write the following questions on the chalkboard and ask students to write an answer: What do you think a "cold war" is? Why was this war considered "cold" and not "hot"? What made it a war?

Activating Prior Knowledge Ask students to describe the relationship between the United States and the Soviet Union at the end of World War II. What were their areas of agreement? What were some areas of conflict?

Reading Strategy

As students read, have them make a list of events that led to the development of the Cold War. Have students list the date of each event. Then, have students arrange the dates in chronological order.

Activity
Student Portfolio

You may wish to have students add the following to their portfolios: Have student write an essay in response to this question: Had the United States and the Soviet Union been able to avoid the deep split that made them enemies and to instead remain allies, what benefits might have resulted? In the essay, have students describe U.S. responses to Soviet aggression after World War II, including the Truman Doctrine, the Marshall Plan, the North Atlantic Treaty Organization, and the Berlin airlift.

Section 1

Origins of the Cold War

READING FOCUS

- Why was 1945 a critical year in United States foreign relations?
- What were the postwar goals of the United States and the Soviet Union?
- How did the iron curtain tighten the Soviet Union's hold over Eastern Europe?
- How did the Truman Doctrine complement the policy of containment?

KEY TERMS

satellite nation
iron curtain
Cold War
containment
Truman Doctrine

TAKING NOTES

As you read, complete this chart to show how the Soviets tightened their hold on Eastern Europe and how the United States responded to the increasing Soviet threat. Add as many rows as you need.

Soviet Actions	U.S. Actions
Stalin refuses to allow free elections in Poland.	Truman criticizes Soviets for not allowing Polish elections.

MAIN IDEA

At the end of World War II, conflicting goals for the future of Europe led to growing hostility between the United States and the Soviet Union.

Setting the Scene "I know you will not mind my being brutally frank when I tell you that I can personally handle Stalin," President Roosevelt told Winston Churchill during World War II. "He thinks he likes me better, and I hope he will continue to." By 1944, Roosevelt was so sure of Stalin's cooperation that he began calling the Soviet dictator "Uncle Joe."

A Roosevelt advisor later wrote that the President did not have "any real comprehension of the great gulf that separated [their] thinking." Nor did he understand just what a wily and difficult adversary Stalin would turn out to be. Churchill, however, clearly understood the situation. "Germany is finished," he declared. "The real problem is Russia. I can't get the Americans to see it."

1945—A Critical Year

The wartime cooperation between the United States and the Soviet Union was a temporary arrangement. There had been a history of bad feelings between the two nations ever since the Russian Revolution of 1917. During that revolt, President Wilson had dispatched American troops to Russia to support anti-Communist resistance. The United States had not even recognized the legal existence of the Soviet government until 1933. These actions caused considerable resentment in the Soviet Union.

Churchill, Roosevelt, and Stalin (left to right) met at Yalta to discuss postwar Europe.

As wartime allies, the Soviets disagreed bitterly with their American and British partners over battle tactics and postwar plans. The United States was angered by the nonaggression pact that Stalin had signed with Hitler (which Hitler had broken), and Stalin was angry that the Allies had not invaded Europe sooner, to take the pressure off the Russian front. As the end of the war approached, relations between the Communist Soviet Union and the two Western democracies grew increasingly tense.

Resource Directory

Teaching Resources
Guided Reading and Review booklet, p. 105
Learning with Documents booklet (Primary Source Activity) *Uncle Joe,* p. 31

Other Print Resources
Historical Outline Map Book *Europe After World War II,* p. 68

Technology
Section Reading Support Transparencies
Guided Reading Audiotapes (English/Spanish), Ch. 19
Student Edition on Audio CD, Ch. 19
Prentice Hall Presentation Pro CD-ROM, Ch. 19
Companion Web site, www.phschool.com

Differences at Yalta In February 1945, Roosevelt met with Stalin and Churchill at Yalta to work out the future of Germany and Poland. They agreed on the division of Germany into American, British, French, and Soviet occupation zones. (Later, the American, British, and French zones were combined to create West Germany. The Soviet zone became East Germany.) Roosevelt and Churchill rejected Stalin's demand that Germany pay the Soviet Union $20 billion in war damages.

At the meeting, Roosevelt pressed Stalin to declare war on Japan. The atomic bomb had not yet been tested, and the President wanted Soviet help if an invasion of Japan became necessary. Stalin promised to enter the war against Japan soon after Germany surrendered, in exchange for Soviet control over two Japanese islands.

Poland proved the most difficult issue at Yalta. The Red Army had occupied that country and supported the Communist-dominated government. Stalin opposed the return of Poland's prewar government, then in exile in London. Historically, Poland provided an invasion route into Russia, as Hitler had just demonstrated. The Polish government, Stalin insisted, must be sympathetic to Soviet security needs. The Yalta meeting stalled until Stalin agreed on elections to let Poles choose their government, using the Communist-dominated regime as a framework. However, disputes about Poland were not over; they would continue to strain American-Soviet relations for years to come.

The United Nations One item on which the leaders at Yalta all agreed was the creation of the United Nations (UN), a new international peacekeeping organization. The League of Nations, founded after World War I, had failed largely because the United States refused to join. This time, policymakers got congressional support for the UN.

In April 1945, delegates from 50 nations met in San Francisco to adopt a charter, or statement of principles, for the UN. The charter stated that members would try to settle their differences peacefully and would promote justice and cooperation in solving international problems. In addition, they would try to stop wars from starting and "take effective collective measures" to end those that did break out.

All member nations belonged to the UN's General Assembly. Representatives of 11 countries sat on a Security Council. The United States, the Soviet Union, Great Britain, France, and China had permanent seats on the Security Council and a veto over proposed policies.

VIEWING HISTORY President Truman called the United Nations "a victory against war itself." In this photograph, Truman and representatives from other member nations look on as Secretary of State Edward Stettinius signs the UN charter in June 1945. **Drawing Conclusions** *Why do you think Congress agreed to United States membership in the UN even though it had not supported the League of Nations?*

Truman Takes Command Roosevelt never lived to see his dream of the United Nations fulfilled. On April 12, 1945, just two weeks before the UN's first meeting, the President died while vacationing at Warm Springs, Georgia. Although he was in poor health and noticeably tired, his unexpected death shocked the nation. No one was more surprised than Vice President Harry S Truman, who suddenly found himself President.

Few Vice Presidents have been less prepared to become President. Although he had spent ten years in Congress, Truman had been Vice President for only a few months. Roosevelt had never involved him in major foreign policy

Lesson Plan

Focus Having defeated a common enemy in World War II, the United States and the Soviet Union then became enemies themselves. Ask students what both sides sought to gain after World War II.

Instruct Discuss how the United States and the Soviet Union became bitter rivals after World War II. Was the Cold War the result of a mistake, or were there powerful forces at work that made the conflict inevitable? Point out the differing views of Joseph Stalin held by Roosevelt and Churchill, and discuss what effect the personalities of Western leaders might have had on Soviet policy.

Assess/Reteach Can students think of any way that the hostility between the United States and the Soviet Union could have been avoided? Are there any safeguards in place today that would prevent a cold war from erupting again?

Customize for ...

Gifted and Talented

Have students enact a meeting of the United Nations General Assembly. Ask them to choose a current or historical world event to discuss and conduct research to prepare them for the meeting. Students can assume the roles of the secretary-general and delegates from member nations. Students should debate the situation and vote on a proposed solution.

Caption Answers

Viewing History Sample Answer: The lack of American participation in the League of Nations led to that organization's downfall, and thus to global war. American participation in the UN was thought of as a way to prevent another global war.

ACTIVITY
Connecting with History and Conflict

Your students may take several periods to complete the following activity: Their task is to reenact a meeting between President Truman and Soviet Foreign Minister Molotov. Divide the class into several groups of four to six students each. Each group should assign two students to role-play the officials and two students to act as coaches. Each team should develop a list of overall goals and specific demands for the meeting. Students should consider the desires, fears, and political systems of their respective countries.

The goal of the activity is to help students understand the political perspective of each official and his respective nation. **(Verbal/Linguistic)**

READING CHECK

Postwar plans for Poland and Germany continued to create divisions between the views of Attlee and Truman on the one hand, and Stalin on the other. Truman informed Stalin, in general terms only, of U.S. possession of an atomic bomb.

discussions. Truman at first seemed willing to compromise with the Soviets. But before long his attitude hardened.

The Potsdam Conference Truman's first meeting with Stalin occurred in July 1945 in the Berlin suburb of Potsdam. During the conference, Churchill was replaced by Clement Attlee, who had just won the British election. Thus, new representatives from Britain and the United States now faced off against Stalin. They continued to debate the issues that had divided them at Yalta, including the future of Germany and of Poland. Stalin renewed his demand for war payments from Germany, and Truman insisted on the promised Polish elections.

At Potsdam, Truman got word that the atom bomb had been tested in New Mexico. Hoping to intimidate Stalin, Truman told him that the United States had a new weapon of extraordinary force. Stalin, who already knew of the bomb from Soviet spies, simply nodded and said that he hoped it would be put to good use. Stalin's casual manner hid his concern over America's new strategic advantage.

READING CHECK

Summarize what happened at the Potsdam Conference.

Conflicting Postwar Goals

Shortly after Truman took office, he scolded the Soviet Foreign Minister, Vyacheslav Molotov, for the Soviet Union's failure to allow Polish elections. Molotov was offended by Truman's bluntness. "I have never been talked to like that in my life," Molotov protested. "Carry out your agreements and you won't get talked to like that," Truman snapped.

The American View Tensions over Poland illustrated the differing views of the world held by American and Soviet leaders. Americans had fought to bring democracy and economic opportunity to the conquered nations of Europe and

NOTABLE PRESIDENTS
Harry S Truman

"We must build a new world, a far better world—one in which the eternal dignity of man is respected."

—Radio address to the UN conference, 1945

Harry S Truman has been called the ultimate common man—but he was a common man who became President. Truman tried careers as a bank clerk, a farmer, and a haberdasher, but he was more successful as a military officer during World War I. He entered politics in Missouri in 1922. In spite of his connection to corrupt Democratic Party boss Thomas Prendergast, Truman earned a reputation for personal integrity and skillful management, both as a judge and as a United States senator.

When Vice President Truman was catapulted into the presidency by FDR's death in 1945, he expressed shock and asked reporters to pray for him. He also put a sign on his desk that said, "The buck stops here," and took responsibility for dropping the atomic bombs on Japan that ended World War II, the Truman Doctrine, the Berlin airlift, sending troops to Korea, integrating the military, and initiating other civil rights reforms. His election to a second term surprised the pundits of his day, and the reforms of his Fair Deal were eventually supported by both parties. Today, Truman is regarded as a common man who faced uncommon challenges with considerable success.

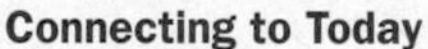
33rd President 1945–1953

Connecting to Today

Truman's reputation for personal integrity no doubt contributed to his reelection in 1948. How did the issue of personal integrity influence the election of 2000, between George W. Bush and Al Gore?

Take It to the NET **Biography** To read more about Harry S Truman, visit the links provided in the *America: Pathways to the Present* area of the following Web site. **www.phschool.com**

RESOURCE DIRECTORY

Teaching Resources

Learning with Documents booklet (Visual Learning Activity) *What They Fear Most,* p. 68

Other Print Resources

Historical Outline Map Book *Europe,* p. 77

Asia. The United States hoped to see these goals achieved in the postwar world. An economically strong and politically open world would also serve American interests by providing markets for its products.

The Soviet View After losing more than 20 million people during the war and suffering widespread destruction, the Soviet Union was determined to rebuild in ways that would protect its own interests. One way was to establish **satellite nations,** countries subject to Soviet domination, on the western borders of the Soviet Union. These governments would be sympathetic to Communist goals.

The Soviet Union also looked forward to the spread of communism throughout the world. According to Communist doctrine, revolution to overthrow the capitalist system was inevitable, and the role of Communist governments was to support and speed up these revolutionary processes in other countries. Stalin thus refused to cooperate with new agencies such as the World Bank and the International Monetary Fund, intended to help build strong capitalist economies. Instead, Stalin installed or supported totalitarian Communist governments in Eastern Europe.

Soviets Tighten Their Hold

The Soviet Union quickly gained political control over nations that the Red Army had freed from the Nazis. The promised elections in Poland did not take place for nearly two years. By that time, Poland's Soviet-installed government had virtually eliminated all political opposition. The Soviets sponsored similar takeovers in other nations of Eastern Europe.

Albania and Bulgaria In Albania, Communist guerrilla forces had driven out the Germans by 1944. When elections were held the following year, all anti-Communist leaders had been silenced. Soviet troops rolled into Bulgaria in 1944, and the Communists secured their hold on the country by 1948.

Czechoslovakia The Czechs desperately tried to hold on to their democratic multiparty political system. The Communist candidate won 40 percent of the vote in free elections in 1946, but Communist repression in neighboring nations hurt the popularity of the Czech Communists. They plotted to take power, therefore, by replacing all non-Communist police officers with party members. Sure of support from the Soviet Union, they also staged rallies, strikes, and a violent uprising. By 1948, Czechoslovakia was a Soviet satellite nation.

Hungary and Romania After Communist candidates lost elections in Hungary in late 1945, Soviet troops remained there and demanded Communist control of the police. The arrest of anti-Communist leaders allowed the Communists to

COMPARING HISTORIANS' VIEWPOINTS

The Origins of the Cold War

Early in the Cold War, the United States and the Soviet Union blamed each other for increased tensions. Historians continue to analyze the outbreak of the Cold War.

Analyzing Viewpoints Would Gaddis agree that "Soviet policies were reasonably cautious and conservative"?

American Policy Led to the Cold War

"By overextending policy and power and refusing to accept Soviet interests, American policy-makers contributed to the Cold War. . . . There is evidence that Soviet policies were reasonably cautious and conservative, and that there was at least a basis for accommodation. But . . . [a]s American demands for democratic governments in Eastern Europe became more vigorous, as the new administration delayed in providing economic assistance to Russia and in seeking international control of atomic energy, policy-makers met with increasing Soviet suspicion and antagonism. Concluding that Soviet-American cooperation was impossible, they came to believe that the Soviet state could be halted only by force or the threat of force."

—Barton Bernstein, "American Foreign Policy and the Origins of the Cold War," 1989

Stalin's Actions Led to the Cold War

"Would there have been a Cold War without Stalin? Perhaps. Nobody in history is indispensable. But Stalin had certain characteristics that set him off from others in authority. . . . He alone pursued personal security by depriving everyone else of it: no Western leader relied on terror to the extent that he did. He alone transformed his country into an extension of himself: no Western leader could have succeeded at such a feat, and none attempted it. He alone saw war and revolution as acceptable means with which to pursue ultimate ends: no Western leader associated violence with progress to the extent that he did. Did Stalin therefore seek a Cold War? The question is a little like asking: 'Does a fish seek water?'"

—John Lewis Gaddis, We Now Know: Rethinking Cold War History, *1997*

ACTIVITY
Connecting with Government

Fearing the threat of communism, the United States government established a containment policy to provide financial and military support to countries potentially subject to Communist influence. To help students understand this policy, have them describe an example of a current threat their parents fear might influence them (the students). Ask them to list three ways their parents could try to "contain" this threatening influence. Then, as a group, make a list of parental containment policies and compare them with the postwar containment policies of the United States government. **(Verbal/Linguistic)**

From the Archives of **AmericanHeritage®**

Naming the New War

On April 16, 1947, Bernard Baruch gave a name to something that had been developing for several years but was still inchoate in the public mind: the Cold War. In a speech before the legislature of his native South Carolina, on the occasion of the unveiling of his portrait, the venerable financier, humanitarian, and presidential adviser said: "Let us not be deceived—we are today in the midst of a Cold War. Our enemies are to be found abroad and at home. Let us never forget this: Our unrest is the heart of their success." The phrase was not original with Baruch. In his autobiography he attributed it to his longtime friend the journalist Herbert Bayard Swope. As early as October 1945 George Orwell had used the same words to refer to a hostile peace, and the following March the London Observer employed them to describe Soviet policy toward Britain. Neither one drew much attention, so commentators made do with references to "current world events" or "Russia's actions in Europe" until Baruch crystallized the situation in a compact, convenient form. Source: Frederic D. Schwarz, "The Time Machine," *American Heritage®* magazine, April 1997.

Activity
Connecting with Culture

Have students locate and use primary source materials from the Cold War era. They could do library research to find newspaper and magazine articles from 1946. Students might focus on how journalists reported on the speeches made by Stalin and Churchill. Or they might search for editorials and cartoons that reflect the political and emotional climate at the time. Have students present an oral report on their findings. **(Verbal/Linguistic)**

Background
Geography in History

Despite its geographical proximity to the Soviet Union, Finland remained neutral during the Cold War. Finland is one of the world's most geographically remote countries. Approximately one-third of the country lies north of the Arctic Circle. Because of its location, Finland experiences harsh weather conditions. The mean annual temperature in Helsinki, the capital, is 5.3 degrees Celsius, or 42 degrees Fahrenheit. More than 5 million people live in Finland. Three-quarters of the country's surface area is covered with forests. The country is also known for its many lakes and islands. During the 1940s, Finland surrendered about one-tenth of its land to the Soviet Union.

VIEWING HISTORY Not only did Stalin dominate the Soviet Union and its satellites, he was also a commanding figure on the world stage. **Synthesizing Information** *Why do you think the Allies found Stalin such a difficult adversary?*

win new elections held in 1947. The Red Army also stayed in Romania, and in 1945 the Soviets forced the Romanian king to name a Communist as prime minister. Less than two years later, the prime minister forced the king to step down.

East Germany While the Western Allies wanted a strong, rebuilt Germany at the center of Europe, Stalin was determined that the Germans would never threaten his nation again. He established national control of all East German resources and installed a brutal totalitarian government there. In 1949, under the Communist government, the country became known as the German Democratic Republic.

Finland and Yugoslavia In spite of the Soviet successes occurring all around them, two countries did manage to maintain a degree of independence from the Soviet Union. Finland signed a treaty of cooperation with the Soviets in 1948. The treaty required Finland to remain neutral in foreign affairs but allowed it to manage its own domestic affairs. In Yugoslavia, Communists gained control in 1945 under the leadership of Josip Broz, better known as Tito. A fiercely independent dictator, Tito refused to take orders from Stalin, who unsuccessfully tried to topple him in 1948. For the next three decades, Tito would pursue his own brand of communism relatively free from Soviet interference.

The Iron Curtain

In a February 1946 speech, Stalin predicted the ultimate triumph of communism over capitalism. Yet he knew that it would be years before the Soviets were strong enough militarily to directly confront the United States. In the meantime, Stalin called on Communists to spread their system by other means. He established Cominform, an agency intended to coordinate the activities of Communist parties around the world.

A month after Stalin's speech, Winston Churchill responded. Although recently defeated for reelection as prime minister, Churchill remained a powerful voice of opposition to the Soviet Union. Speaking in Fulton, Missouri, he condemned the division of Europe that Stalin had already accomplished:

Winston Churchill coined the phrase "iron curtain."

KEY DOCUMENTS

> *"From Stettin in the Baltic to Trieste in the Adriatic, an iron curtain has descended across the Continent. Behind that line lie all the capitals of . . . Central and Eastern Europe. . . . The Communist parties, which were very small in all these Eastern States of Europe, have been raised to pre-eminence and power far beyond their numbers and are seeking everywhere to obtain totalitarian control. . . . This is certainly not the Liberated Europe we fought to build up. Nor is it one which contains the essentials of permanent peace."*
>
> —"Iron Curtain" speech, Winston Churchill, March 5, 1946

Churchill also called on Americans to help keep Stalin from enclosing any more nations behind the **iron curtain** of Communist domination and oppression.

These two speeches of 1946—by Stalin and by Churchill—set the tone for the **Cold War,** the competition that developed between the United States and the Soviet Union for power and influence in the world. For nearly 50 years, until the collapse of the Soviet Union in 1991, the Cold War was characterized by political and economic conflict and military tensions. The rivalry stopped just short of a

Caption Answers

Viewing History Answers will vary, but students may note that Stalin was ruthless and secretive and not above lying to allies and adversaries alike.

RESOURCE DIRECTORY

Teaching Resources

Biography, Literature, and Comparing Primary Sources booklet (Biography) *George F. Kennan,* p. 31

Technology

Sounds of an Era Audio CD *"Iron Curtain Speech," Winston Churchill* (time: 50 seconds)

MAP SKILLS The division between Soviet-controlled nations and non-Communist countries is easily seen on this map. **Location** *How does the map illustrate the Soviet Union's policy of protecting itself from its non-Communist rivals in Europe?*

"hot" war—a direct military engagement—between the two competing nations. However, United States military forces did engage in combat in other nations as part of the American effort to defeat Soviet-supported uprisings and invasions wherever they occurred.

INTERPRETING POLITICAL CARTOONS In this cartoon, United States Secretary of State James Byrnes is portrayed as a determined suitor. **Drawing Inferences** *(a) Whom is Byrnes courting? (b) How does the cartoonist rate his chances of success? (c) Explain how the cartoon conveys this opinion.*

Containment

In a long telegram to the State Department in early 1946, George Kennan, a top American diplomat stationed in Moscow, analyzed Soviet behavior and policy. Later, in an anonymous journal article, Kennan warned that the Soviets had "no real faith in the possibility of a permanently happy coexistence of the Socialist and capitalist worlds" and that they also believed in the inevitable triumph of communism. Therefore, Kennan concluded that the Soviet Union "cannot be easily defeated or discouraged by a single victory on the part of its opponents . . . but only by intelligent long-range policies." According to Kennan, the "United States policy toward the Soviet Union must be that of a long-term, patient but firm and vigilant containment of Russian expansive tendencies."

The American policy of **containment** emerged from Kennan's analysis. This policy recognized the possibility that Eastern Europe was already lost to communism. It called for the United States to resist Soviet attempts to form Communist governments elsewhere in the world.

Critics saw containment as too moderate an approach to Soviet-American relations. They called for action to push the Communists out of Eastern Europe, Russia, and anywhere else they had taken power. Kennan, however, argued that the Soviet system "bears within it the seeds of its own decay" and would eventually crumble. Thus, although containment remained controversial, it became the cornerstone of America's Cold War foreign policy.

The Truman Doctrine

President Truman soon had an opportunity to apply the policy of containment. Since 1945, the Soviet Union had been making threats against Turkey.

ACTIVITY
Connecting with Geography

Tell students to imagine that they are growing up in Vienna, Austria, during the Cold War. Have them think about what it might have been like to live in a city that is situated just west of the iron curtain. Suggest that students consider the kinds of tensions the Viennese might have experienced, whether there was trade across the iron curtain, and whether there was curiosity about life on the other side. Encourage students to write a journal entry from the point of view of a Viennese teenager in the late 1940s. Remind students that a Viennese teenager would also have vivid memories of World War II. **(Verbal/Linguistic)**

BACKGROUND
Interdisciplinary

The Cold War proved to be a great boon to science and technology. Byproducts of this era of research included smoke detectors, hang gliders, the Minuteman ICBM, and the first microwave oven. Percy Spencer, a war hero and scientist at Raytheon, developed the microwave oven in 1946. While experimenting with a magnetron—the part of a radar set that produces microwave energy—he felt a chocolate bar in his pocket begin to melt. Spencer then placed popcorn kernels and raw eggs in front of the magnetron. The microwave energy caused the temperature of each to increase so quickly that they exploded. Spencer and other Raytheon scientists then created an oven that could harness microwave energy to cook food. Unfortunately, at 750 pounds, the oven was hardly ready for consumer use. It wasn't until 1955 that the microwave oven was small enough to fit into a home kitchen.

CUSTOMIZE FOR ...
Less Proficient Readers

Ask students to explain what the iron curtain was. Have them list facts about life on both sides of the iron curtain.

TEST PREPARATION

Have students read the quotation by Winston Churchill on the previous page and then complete the sentence below.

The main significance of the iron curtain that Churchill describes is that—

A it stretches from Stettin in the Baltic to Trieste in the Adriatic.
B it divides Central and Eastern Europe.
Ⓒ it was instituted by the Soviet Union and threatens peace and democracy.
D it is part of postwar liberated Europe.

CAPTION ANSWERS

Map Skills The map shows that Soviet leaders wanted to create a buffer zone of satellite nations between Russia's western border and the nations of western Europe.

Interpreting Political Cartoons The nations of Eastern Europe. The cartoonist seems to believe the effort is futile: the iron curtain dwarfs Byrnes and his bouquet of roses while Stalin looks over the top and smiles. The cartoonist makes the wall/obstacle high and strong.

Section 1 Assessment

Reading Comprehension

1. Satellites were countries subject to Soviet domination. Stalin wanted satellites in order to speed up communism's spread and to protect the Soviet western border in case of another war.
2. It seemed that there was an impermeable barrier between the capitalist West and the Communist East.
3. A cold war has no direct military fighting between the main antagonists. It is instead a stealthy contest to gain influence in world affairs. A "hot" war is a direct military engagement.
4. The policy of containment set out the United States aim to stop the spread of communism, and the Truman Doctrine gave justification for American efforts to intervene against communism on behalf of oppressed nations.

Critical Thinking and Writing

5. Sample answer: The two speeches outlined the opposing positions in the Cold War.
6. Letters will vary but should be supported with facts from the section.

Students may summarize the Yalta or Potsdam conferences, which focused mainly on the future of Germany and Poland.

VIEWING HISTORY President Truman was named Man of the Year by *Time* in 1949. Behind him on the *Time* cover is the Doomsday Clock, showing how close the world was to nuclear destruction. **Drawing Inferences** *What reason for honoring Truman does the* Time *cover suggest?*

Stalin wanted control of the Dardanelles, a narrow strait in Turkey that would give Soviet ports on the Black Sea access to the Mediterranean. In addition, a civil war had broken out in nearby Greece in the closing days of World War II. There, Communists fought to overthrow the government that had returned to power after the Axis invaders had withdrawn.

Still suffering from the economic devastation of the war, Great Britain announced in February 1947 that it could no longer afford to provide aid to Greece and Turkey. The British suggested that the United States take over responsibility for defending the region. Undersecretary of State Dean Acheson reported that at that moment Great Britain "handed the job of world leadership, with all its burdens and all its glory, to the United States."

State Department officials developed a plan to provide American aid to Greece and Turkey. To head off congressional opposition, Acheson warned of grave dangers if the United States failed to act. "Only two great powers remain in the world," he observed, "the United States and the Soviet Union."

In March 1947, in a speech before a joint session of Congress, Truman called on the United States to take a leadership role in the world. In a statement of principles known as the **Truman Doctrine,** he established another major policy that would guide American actions in the Cold War.

KEY DOCUMENTS

> "*Nearly every nation must choose between alternative ways of life. The choice is too often not a free one. One way of life is based upon the will of the majority. . . . The second way of life is based upon the will of a minority forcibly imposed upon the majority. . . . I believe that it must be the policy of the United States to support free peoples who are resisting attempted subjugation [conquest] by armed minorities or by outside pressures. I believe that we must assist free peoples to work out their own destinies in their own way.*"
>
> —Truman Doctrine, March 12, 1947

Responding to Truman's appeal, Congress approved $400 million in aid for Greece and Turkey. In addition, the United States soon established military bases in both countries. During the next four decades, the Truman Doctrine and the policy of containment would lead the United States into controversial involvements in both "hot" and "cold" conflicts around the world.

Section 1 Assessment

READING COMPREHENSION

1. What is a **satellite nation?** Why did Stalin want these satellites?
2. Why was the term **iron curtain** a good description of the Soviet presence in Eastern Europe?
3. What is the difference between the **Cold War** and a "hot" war?
4. How do the policy of **containment** and the **Truman Doctrine** complement one another?

CRITICAL THINKING AND WRITING

5. **Drawing Conclusions** What effect do you think the Stalin and Churchill speeches of 1946 had on American public opinion? Explain your answer.
6. **Writing a Letter to the Editor** In 1947, some Americans thought that containment was a wise policy and others felt that it was too moderate. Support one of these positions in a 1947 letter to the editor.

Take It to the NET

Activity: Writing a News Article Select an important international conference of the Cold War period, and write an article summarizing what was accomplished at the conference. Use the links provided in the *America: Pathways to the Present* area of the following Web site for help in completing this activity.
www.phschool.com

Caption Answers

Viewing History The use of the Doomsday Clock suggests that Truman is keeping the world at peace (but just barely).

RESOURCE DIRECTORY

Teaching Resources
Units 5/6/7 booklet
- Section 1 Quiz, p. 27

Guide to the Essentials
- Section 1 Summary, p. 92

Recognizing Cause and Effect

History is more than a list of events; it is a study of relationships among events. Recognizing cause and effect means examining how one event or action brings about another—which, in turn, may bring about still more events. Each one becomes a link in a growing chain of events. The statements below deal with the events and attitudes leading to the Cold War.

LEARN THE SKILL

Use the following steps to recognize cause and effect:

1. **Identify the two parts of a cause-effect relationship.** A cause is an event, action, or idea that brings about an effect. As you read, look for key words that signal a cause-effect relationship. Words and phrases such as *because, due to,* and *on account of* signal causes. Words and phrases such as *so, thus, therefore,* and *as a result* signal effects.
2. **Remember that events can have more than one cause and more than one effect.** Several causes can combine to lead to one event. So, too, can a single cause have more than one effect.
3. **Understand that an event can be both a cause and an effect.** A cause can lead to an effect, which in turn can be the cause of another event—forming a chain of related events. You can illustrate the chain by making a cause-effect diagram like this one:

A

Because President Roosevelt believed that postwar cooperation with the Soviet Union was necessary, he viewed Stalin as a partner—if not an ally—in formulating a peace.

B

Unlike Roosevelt, President Truman was persuaded by advisors that the Soviet Union would become a "world bully" after the war. As a result, he adopted a "get tough" policy whose aim was to block any possibility of Soviet expansion.

C

The Soviets, for their part, believed that the United States was intent on global domination and meant to encircle the Soviet Union with anti-Communist states.

D

Due to mounting distrust between the United States and the Soviet Union, each power came to view the postwar peace negotiations as an opportunity to test the other's global objectives. Thus, negotiating the status of Poland became the first such test. Other tests included the plans for former German satellite states and the policies for the occupation of Germany. Each power regarded its own positions in these negotiations as essentially defensive, but each viewed the other's stances as aggressive and expansionist. Together these tests and stances produced the Cold War, an armed and dangerous truce that lasted for 45 years.

PRACTICE THE SKILL

Answer the following questions:

1. **(a)** Read statements A through C. Which statements contain both a cause and an effect? **(b)** Which is the cause and which is the effect in each statement? **(c)** Which words, if any, signal the cause-effect relationship?
2. **(a)** In Statement D, find an example of a cause that has more than one effect. **(b)** Give an example of an effect that has more than one cause in Statement D.
3. **(a)** What is the chain of related events in Statement D? Explain it in one or two sentences. **(b)** Draw a diagram showing the chain of related events.

APPLY THE SKILL

See the Chapter Review and Assessment for another opportunity to apply this skill.

Recognizing Cause and Effect

Focus Students distinguish between causes and effects and recognize multiple causes and effects.

Instruct Present this quotation from Harry Truman: "There is nothing new in the world except the history you do not know." Why, then, is it important to study the causes and effects of historical events?

Ask students to cite causes of the Cold War. Discuss events in the world today that are similar to those that caused the Cold War.

Extend See the Skills for Life activity in the Resource Directory below.

ANSWERS

Practice the Skill

1. **(a)** A and B. **(b)** A: Cause—Roosevelt believed that postwar cooperation with the Soviet Union was necessary; Effect—He viewed Stalin as a partner in formulating peace. B: Cause—Truman was persuaded that the Soviet Union would become a "world bully"; Effect—he adopted a tough policy to block Soviet expansion. **(c)** *Because* signals cause. *As a result* signals effect.
2. **(a)** Cause: mounting distrust between the U.S. and the Soviet Union. Effects: negotiations on Poland, the former German satellite states, and the occupation of Germany used as ways to test the other nation's global objectives. **(b)** Effect: the Cold War. Causes: mounting distrust; negotiations viewed as tests; defensive positions seen as aggressive stances.
3. **(a)** Mistrust of one another, led the United States and the Soviet Union to test each other's objectives in postwar peace negotiations over the future of Poland, the former German satellite states, and the occupation of Germany. These tests and the distrust they caused led to the Cold War. **(b)** Diagrams should include events described in **3 (a)**.

RESOURCE DIRECTORY

Teaching Resources

Skills for Life booklet, p. 28

Technology

Social Studies Skills Tutor CD-ROM

Interactive Practice in

- Geographic Literacy
- Critical Thinking and Reading
- Visual Analysis
- Communications

Section 2
The Cold War Heats Up

SECTION OBJECTIVES

1. Find out how the Marshall Plan, the Berlin Airlift, and NATO helped to achieve American goals in postwar Europe.
2. Realize how Communist advances affected American foreign policy.
3. See how the Cold War affected American life at home.

BELLRINGER

Warm-Up Activity Write on the chalkboard, "The buck stops here." Ask students if they know what this famous quotation means. Tell them that President Truman kept it on his desk, and ask how it reflected his political style.

Activating Prior Knowledge Ask students to recall the conditions under which Harry Truman assumed office in 1945. What do they think were some of the biggest challenges he confronted? How do they think he responded to those challenges?

READING STRATEGY

As students read, have them list major challenges the United States faced in its efforts to oppose communism. Then have them describe the solutions carried out. Encourage students to describe the impact of the Cold War on the business cycle and defense spending.

ACTIVITY
Connecting with Government

Ask students to identify the major United States foreign policy efforts discussed in this section. Then have them analyze those actions and decide whether each was aimed more at confrontation or at peacemaking. Students should support their analysis with specific facts from the text. **(Logical/Mathematical)**

Section 2
The Cold War Heats Up

READING FOCUS

- How did the Marshall Plan, the Berlin airlift, and NATO help to achieve American goals in postwar Europe?
- How did Communist advances affect American foreign policy?
- How did the Cold War affect American life at home?

MAIN IDEA

As the Cold War intensified, American foreign policy focused on rebuilding and unifying Western Europe. At home, Americans began to suspect Communist infiltration of their own society and government.

KEY TERMS

Marshall Plan
Berlin airlift
North Atlantic Treaty Organization (NATO)
collective security
Warsaw Pact
House Un-American Activities Committee (HUAC)
Hollywood Ten
blacklist
McCarran-Walter Act

TAKING NOTES

Copy the chart below. As you read, fill in details illustrating the effects of the Cold War on American foreign policy and on life at home.

The U.S. Responds to the Cold War		
In Europe	Regarding Nuclear Weapons	At Home

Setting the Scene The end of World War II caused a profound change in the way world leaders and ordinary citizens thought about war. The devastation caused by the atomic bombs dropped on Japan and the efforts of the Soviet Union to acquire similar weapons instilled fear in both East and West. In his last State of the Union address, President Truman declared:

> "*[W]e have entered the atomic age and war has undergone a technological change which makes it a very different thing from what it used to be. War today between the Soviet empire and the free nations might dig the grave not only of our Stalinist opponents, but of our own society, our world as well as theirs. . . . Such a war is not a possible policy for rational men.*"
>
> —President Harry S Truman

Anxiety about a "hot" and catastrophic nuclear war became a backdrop to the Cold War policies of both the United States and the Soviet Union.

A 1946 American atomic bomb test creates the signature mushroom cloud over the Pacific Ocean.

The Marshall Plan

In addition to worrying about the new threat of nuclear war, American policymakers were determined not to repeat the mistakes of the post–World War I era. This time the United States would help restore the war-torn nations so that they might create stable democracies and achieve economic recovery. World War II had devastated Europe to a degree never seen before. About 21 million people had been made homeless. In Poland, some 20 percent of the population had died. Nearly 1 of every 5 houses in France and Belgium had been damaged or destroyed. Across

RESOURCE DIRECTORY

Teaching Resources
Learning Styles Lesson Plans booklet, p. 54
Guided Reading and Review booklet, p. 106

Technology
Section Reading Support Transparencies
Guided Reading Audiotapes (English/Spanish), Ch. 19
Student Edition on Audio CD, Ch. 19
Sounds of an Era Audio CD *George Marshall, June 5, 1947* (time: one minute); *President Truman, 1948* (time: 30 seconds)
Prentice Hall Presentation Pro CD-ROM, Ch. 19
Companion Web site, www.phschool.com

Europe, industries and transportation were in ruins. Agriculture suffered from the loss of livestock and equipment. In France alone, damage equaled three times the nation's annual income.

These conditions led to two fundamental shifts in American foreign policy that were designed to strengthen European democracies and their economies. The first was the Truman Doctrine. The other was the **Marshall Plan,** which called for the nations of Europe to draw up a program for economic recovery from the war. The United States would then support the program with financial aid.

The plan was unveiled by Secretary of State George C. Marshall in 1947. The Marshall Plan was a response to American concerns that Communist parties were growing stronger across Europe, and that the Soviet Union might intervene to support more of these Communist movements. The plan also reflected the belief that United States aid for European economic recovery would create strong democracies and open new markets for American goods.

Marshall described his plan in a speech at Harvard University in June 1947:

KEY DOCUMENTS

> *"It is logical that the United States should do whatever it is able to assist in the return of normal economic health in the world, without which there can be no political stability and no assured peace. Our policy is directed not against any country or doctrine but against hunger, poverty, desperation, and chaos. Its purpose should be the revival of a working economy in the world so as to permit the emergence of political and social conditions in which free institutions can exist."*
>
> —Marshall Plan speech, George C. Marshall, June 5, 1947

Shipments Financed by the Marshall Plan, 1948–1951

Shipment	Total Value (in millions of dollars)
Food, feed, fertilizer	3,209.5
Fuel	1,552.4
Cotton	1,397.8
Other raw materials	2,327.6
Machinery and vehicles	1,428.1
Other	88.9
Total	**10,004.3**

SOURCE: *Statistical Abstract of the United States*

ANALYZING TABLES The photo shows a parade in Athens, Greece, following the unloading of sacks of flour delivered by the Marshall Plan. The table identifies the kinds of goods the Marshall Plan provided.
Drawing Conclusions *What made up the largest percentage of goods delivered? Why do you think this was so?*

The Soviet Union was invited to participate in the Marshall Plan, but it refused the help and pressured its satellite nations to do so too. Soviet Foreign Minister Vyacheslav Molotov called the Marshall Plan a vicious American scheme for using dollars to "buy its way" into European affairs. In fact, Soviet leaders did not want outside scrutiny of their country's economy.

In 1948, Congress approved the Marshall Plan, which was formally known as the European Recovery Program. Seventeen Western European nations joined the plan: Austria, Belgium, Denmark, France, Greece, Iceland, Ireland, Italy, Luxembourg, the Netherlands, Norway, Portugal, Sweden, Switzerland, Turkey, the United Kingdom, and West Germany. Over the next four years, the United States allocated some $13 billion in grants and loans to Western Europe. The region's economies were quickly restored, and the United States gained strong trading partners in the region.

The Berlin Airlift

One of the nations that benefited from the Marshall Plan was West Germany. By 1948, American, British, and French leaders had become convinced that Stalin was not going to allow the reunification of Germany. Therefore the

LESSON PLAN

Focus Fearing the further spread of communism, the United States developed a new foreign policy called containment. Ask students how this policy was enacted.

Instruct Explain that the events in Berlin, Germany, from 1948 to 1949 highlighted Cold War tensions. Discuss why the blockade of one city caused so much anxiety to people around the world. What might the Soviets have hoped to gain by such a move? Why is the incident a good example of the Cold War and of the policy of containment?

Assess/Reteach Can students list some areas of American society in which Communist infiltration was suspected? What might have been the impact on American society if these various areas were, in fact, infiltrated, as suspected?

CUSTOMIZE FOR ...

Less Proficient Readers

Have students reread the section "The Marshall Plan." Then have students list what the U.S. would do under the plan, its results, and how the U.S. benefited from implementing the plan.

CAPTION ANSWERS

Analyzing Tables Food, feed, fertilizer. These goods are the most important for immediate human survival and for the ability to produce food in the future.

ACTIVITY
Connecting with Economics

Tell students to calculate how much of the $13 billion in grants and loans went to each of the 17 Western European nations that participated in the Marshall Plan. Tell students to use primary and secondary sources to research the population of each country in 1948. Then tell students to estimate which countries received more aid and which got less, depending on their population. **(Logical/Mathematical)**

BACKGROUND
The Berlin Airlift

The Berlin airlift remains one of the most dramatic and unforgettable events of the Cold War between the Soviet bloc and the Western allies. During the months of February, March, and April more tonnage traveled to West Berlin via airlift than had previously been arriving by truck, rail, and barge combined. To underscore the success of the operation, a 24-hour "Easter Parade" was staged, ending at noon on Easter Sunday, April 16, 1949. During the "parade," an amazing 1,398 flights were made, delivering almost 13,000 tons of coal to West Berlin.

Western Allies prepared to merge their three occupation zones to create a new nation, the Federal Republic of Germany, or West Germany. The western part of Berlin, which lay in the Soviet zone, would become part of West Germany. The Soviets responded in 1949 by forming a Communist state, the German Democratic Republic, or East Germany.

Capitalist West Berlin and Communist East Berlin became visible symbols of the developing Cold War struggle between the Soviet Union and the Western powers. Hundreds of thousands of Eastern Europeans left their homes in Communist-dominated nations, fled to East Berlin, and then crossed into West Berlin. From there they booked passage to freedom in the United States, Canada, or Western Europe.

Stalin decided to close this escape route by forcing the Western powers to abandon West Berlin. He found his excuse in June 1948, when a new German currency was introduced in West Germany, including West Berlin. Stalin considered the new currency and the new nation it represented to be a threat. The city of West Berlin—located within East Germany—was a symbol of that threat. The Soviets used the dispute over the new currency as an excuse to block Allied access to West Berlin. All shipments to the city through East Germany were banned. The blockade threatened to create severe shortages of food and other supplies needed by the 2.5 million people in West Berlin.

Truman did not want to risk starting a war by using military force to open the transportation routes. Nor did he want to give up West Berlin to the Soviets. Instead, Truman decided on an airlift, moving supplies into West Berlin by plane. During the next 15 months, British and American military aircraft made

MAP SKILLS The map shows the location of West Berlin within East Germany. In the photo below, German children wave to an American airplane during the Berlin airlift. **Location** *How did Berlin's location make it difficult to supply?*

646

CAPTION ANSWERS

Map Skills It was isolated within Communist East Germany (and lies inland, not on the coast). Therefore, supplies being moved overland to West Berlin from western Europe had to pass through Soviet-controlled territory.

RESOURCE DIRECTORY

Teaching Resources

Biography, Literature, and Comparing Primary Sources booklet (Comparing Primary Sources) *On Joining NATO,* pp. 147–148

Other Print Resources

American History Block Scheduling Support *The Berlin Wall: Past and Present,* found in The Nation After World War II folder, includes interdisciplinary lesson suggestions and activities for Geography and History, Primary Sources, Biography, and Literature.

Technology

Color Transparencies *Historical Maps,* A45

more than 200,000 flights to deliver food, fuel, and other supplies. At the height of the **Berlin airlift,** nearly 13,000 tons of goods arrived in West Berlin daily.

The Soviets finally gave up the blockade in May 1949, and the airlift ended the following September. By that time, the Marshall Plan had helped achieve economic stability in the capitalist nations of Western Europe, including West Germany. Berlin, however, remained a focal point of East-West conflict.

NATO

In the early postwar period, the international community looked to the United Nations to protect nations from invasion or destabilization by foreign governments, and to maintain world peace. However, the Soviet Union's frequent use of its veto power in the Security Council prevented the UN from effectively dealing with a number of postwar problems. Thus it became clear that Western Europe would have to look beyond the UN for protection from Soviet aggression. In 1946, the Canadian foreign minister, Louis St. Laurent, proposed creating an "association of democratic peace-loving states" to defend Western Europe against attack by the Soviet Union.

American officials expressed great interest in St. Laurent's idea. Truman was determined to prevent the United States from returning to pre–World War II isolationism. The Truman Doctrine and the Marshall Plan soon demonstrated his commitment to making America a leader in postwar world affairs. Yet Truman did not want the United States to be the only nation in the Western Hemisphere pledged to defend Western Europe from the Communists. For this reason, a Canadian role in any proposed organization became vital to American support.

Not all Americans agreed that such an organization was a good idea. Ohio Senator Robert Taft thought that the pact was "not a peace program; it is a war program." He continued, "We are undertaking to arm half the world against the other half. We are inevitably starting an armament race." On the other hand, Senator Tom Connally favored joining such an association:

> "*From now on, no one will misread our motives or underestimate our determination to stand in defense of our freedom. . . . The greatest obstacle that stands in the way of complete recovery [from World War II] is the pervading and paralyzing sense of insecurity. The treaty is a powerful antidote to this poison. . . . With this protection afforded by the Atlantic Pact, Western Europe can breathe easier again.*"
>
> —Texas Senator Tom Connally, 1949

In April 1949, Canada and the United States joined Belgium, Britain, Denmark, France, Iceland, Italy, Luxembourg, the Netherlands, Norway, and Portugal to form the **North Atlantic Treaty Organization (NATO).** Member nations agreed that "an armed attack against one or more of them . . . shall be considered an attack against them all." This principle of mutual military assistance is called **collective security.** Having dropped its opposition to military treaties with Europe for the first time since the Monroe Doctrine, the United States now became actively involved in European affairs. In 1955,

Focus on WORLD EVENTS

Operation Little Vittles The Berlin airlift was called "Operation Vittles," (*vittles* is slang for food) by American servicemen. It provided the necessities of life to Berliners. But one USAF pilot, Lieutenant Gail Halvorsen, felt that the children needed more than necessities, and he began dropping candy to the children of Berlin. Halvorsen rigged up tiny parachutes made of handkerchiefs and fabric scraps. As he flew over groups of children who had gathered to watch the planes, he wiggled the wings of his aircraft to signal that the parachuted candy was about to be dropped. German children began calling him "Uncle Wiggly Wings." Soon other pilots joined this Operation Little Vittles, and donations of handkerchiefs as well as thousands of pounds of candy began arriving at American air bases. Eventually, Operation Little Vittles dropped more than 250,000 miniature parachutes and some 23 tons of candy.

ACTIVITY
Connecting with Citizenship

Engage students in a discussion about the concept that led to the formation of NATO. Ask students to consider the advantages and disadvantages to citizens whose nations joined NATO. Do those citizens gain a greater sense of security? Or do they acquire a false sense of security? How does the expectation of an attack affect member nations? Is there a need for NATO in the post–Cold War era? **(Verbal/Linguistic)**

BACKGROUND
Recent Scholarship

The Cold War dominated post–World War II American life. An excellent, balanced account of this situation can be found in *We Now Know: Rethinking Cold War History,* by John Lewis Gaddis. In this work, Gaddis covers such interesting topics as the manner in which the Russian and American spheres of influence that formed in Europe after World War II were indelibly stamped with the domestic characteristics found within the respective structures of the two superpowers themselves. Written after the Cold War had ended, this work represents refreshingly recent scholarship on the subject.

CUSTOMIZE FOR ...
Less Proficient Writers

Have students list the Americans' reasons for and against joining NATO. Do students agree or disagree with the idea of "collective security"?

ACTIVITY
Connecting with Government

Have students trace the steps that the United States took to counter communism from 1945 to 1949. Then have them discuss as a group how the nation's foreign policy began to shift after Truman's announcement in 1949 that the Soviet Union had developed nuclear weapons technology. **(Logical/Mathematical)**

BACKGROUND
Civil Defense

Successful Soviet development of a nuclear bomb created widespread fear of a "sneak" attack by the Soviets. The Civil Defense Administration (CDA) was set up to oversee warning, evacuation, and communications systems. Thousands of Americans built backyard bomb shelters, while schoolchildren learned to "duck and cover." In 1955 the CDA staged the first nationwide nuclear air raid drill, dubbed "Operation Alert '55," in which 60 cities underwent mock hydrogen bomb attacks and were evacuated.

READING CHECK

The strength of the Chinese Communists grew during World War II. In the renewal of the civil war that followed the end of World War II, the Communists quickly gained the upper hand. The United States began to cut back on its aid to the Nationalist Chinese, whose cause now seemed hopeless. The Communists gained control of all of mainland China in 1949, causing the Nationalists to flee to Taiwan.

Early Cold War Crises, 1944–1949

Year	Crisis	Significance
1944–1949	Poland, Albania, Bulgaria, Czechoslovakia, Hungary, Romania, and East Germany become Soviet satellite nations.	Communist power grows with the Soviet Union's domination of Eastern Europe.
1948–1949	The Soviet Union blockades West Berlin. Truman initiates Berlin airlift to supply the city with food, fuel, and other necessities.	Tensions increase between the United States and the Soviet Union, with Berlin a focal point of East-West conflict.
1949	The Soviet Union develops nuclear weapons technology. China falls to Communist dictator Mao Zedong.	The United States no longer has the upper hand in weapons technology. Communism spreads to the most populous nation in Asia.

INTERPRETING CHARTS
A series of crises stepped up demands on the American government to deal effectively with the spread of communism. **Making Comparisons** *(a) How are the two entries in the last row different from those that came before? (b) How did they affect American public opinion?*

the Soviet Union responded to the formation of NATO by creating the **Warsaw Pact,** a military alliance with its satellite nations in Eastern Europe.

Communist Advances

In 1949, two events heightened American concerns about the Cold War. The first was President Truman's terrifying announcement that the Soviet Union had successfully tested an atomic bomb. Then, just a few weeks later, Communist forces took control of China.

The Soviet Atomic Threat "We have evidence that within recent weeks an atomic explosion occurred in the USSR," Truman told reporters in September 1949. The news jolted Americans. New York, Los Angeles, and other American cities were now in danger of suffering the horrible fate of Hiroshima and Nagasaki.

Truman's response to the Soviet atomic threat was to forge ahead with a new weapon to maintain America's nuclear superiority. In early 1950, he gave approval for the development of a hydrogen, or thermonuclear, bomb that would be many times more destructive than the atomic bomb. The first successful thermonuclear test occurred in 1952, reestablishing the United States as the world's leading nuclear power.

At about the same time, Truman organized the Federal Civil Defense Administration. The new agency flooded the nation with posters and other information about how to survive a nuclear attack. These materials included plans for building bomb shelters and instructions for holding air raid drills in schools. Privately, however, experts ridiculed these programs as almost totally ineffective. Not until the late 1950s did civil defense become a more important federal government priority.

China Falls to the Communists The Communist takeover of China also came as a shock to many Americans. However, in actuality the struggle between China's Nationalists and Communists had been going on since the 1920s. (See Section 3.) During World War II, the Communist leader Mao Zedong and the Nationalist leader Jiang Jieshi (also known as Chiang Kai-shek) grudgingly cooperated to resist the invading Japanese. But the war also enabled Mao to strengthen his forces and to launch popular political, social, and economic reforms in the regions of China that he controlled.

READING CHECK
Describe how China fell to the Communists.

As World War II drew to a close, the fighting between the Communists and government forces resumed. The Truman administration at first provided economic and military assistance to Jiang. Despite this aid, by 1947 Mao's forces had occupied much of China's countryside and had begun to take control of the northern cities. When Jiang asked for more American help, Truman and his advisors concluded that Mao's takeover of China probably could not be prevented. While continuing to give some aid to Jiang, the United States decided to focus instead on saving Western Europe from Soviet domination.

In early 1949, China's capital of Peking (now Beijing) fell to the Communists. A few months later, Mao proclaimed the creation of a Communist state, the People's Republic of China. The defeated Jiang and his followers withdrew to the island of Taiwan, off the Chinese mainland. There they continued as the Republic of China, claiming to be the legitimate government of the entire

CAPTION ANSWERS

Interpreting Charts (a) These entries reflect the fact that communism had spread from Europe to Asia by 1949. (b) This made communism seem like a worldwide threat to Americans, who were shocked and frightened by this development. Anti-Communist feeling increased in the United States. In addition, many Americans questioned the ability and loyalty of their own government officials.

RESOURCE DIRECTORY

Technology

Color Transparencies *Historical Maps,* A46

RESOURCE PRO® Critical Thinking Activity *Identifying Central Issues: Cold War Policy,* found on Resource Pro, uses a speech by Christian A. Herter, Undersecretary of State in 1957, to help students apply this skill.

Chinese nation. With American support, the Republic of China also held on to China's seats in the UN's General Assembly and Security Council.

Many Americans viewed the "loss of China" as a stain on the record of the Truman administration. Members of Congress and others who held this view called for greater efforts to protect the rest of Asia from communism. Some Americans also began to suspect the loyalties of those involved in making military and foreign policy.

The Cold War at Home

Throughout the Great Depression, tens of thousands of Americans had joined the Communist Party, which was a legal organization. Many were desperate people who had developed serious doubts about the American capitalist system, partly because of the economic collapse of the 1930s. Others were intellectuals who were attracted to Communist ideals. After World War II, however, improved economic times, as well as the increasing distrust of Stalin, caused many people to become disillusioned with communism. Most American Communists quit the party, although some remained members, whether active or not. Now, as a new red scare began to grip America, their pasts came back to haunt them.

During the presidencies of Truman and his successor, Dwight D. Eisenhower, concern about the growth of world communism raised fears of a conspiracy to overthrow the government, particularly when a number of Communist spies were caught and put on trial. These fears launched an anti-Communist crusade that violated the civil liberties of many Americans. Anyone who had ever had Communist party ties and many who had never even been Communists were swept up in the wave of persecutions.

The Loyalty Program As the Truman administration pursued its containment policy abroad, government officials launched programs to root out any element of communism that might have infiltrated the United States. Exposure of a number of wartime spy rings in 1946 increased the anxiety of many Americans. (In recent years, new evidence of Soviet infiltration has come to light. It is known, for instance, that Soviet spies gathered information on the United States nuclear program that helped the Soviet Union advance its own atomic development.)

When Republicans made big gains in the 1946 congressional elections, Truman worried that his rivals would take political advantage of the loyalty issue. To head off this possibility, he began his own investigation, establishing a federal employee loyalty program in 1947. Under this program, all new employees hired by the federal government were to be investigated. In addition, the FBI checked its files for evidence of current government employees who might be engaged in suspicious activities. Those accused of disloyalty were brought before a Loyalty Review Board.

While civil rights were supposed to be safeguarded, in fact those accused of disloyalty to their country often had little chance to defend themselves. Rather than being considered innocent until proven guilty, they found that the accusation alone made it difficult to clear their names. The Truman program examined several million government employees, yet only a few hundred were actually removed from their jobs. Nonetheless, the loyalty program added to a climate of suspicion taking hold in the nation.

Focus on CULTURE

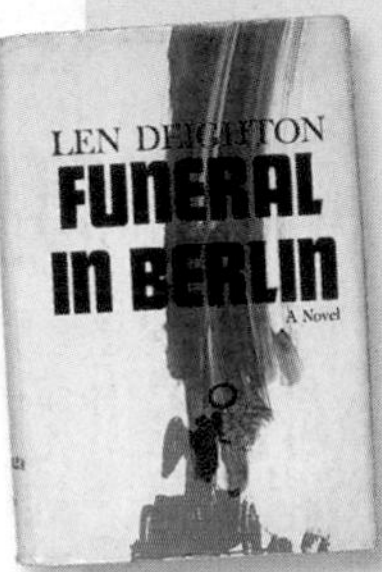

The Rise of the Spy Novel The Cold War produced real spies, as well as the fear of spies where none existed. But perhaps the most famous Cold War spies were the fictional espionage agents in spy novels. James Bond, for example, is a post-war British Secret Service agent whose exploits continue in countless movies. The author of the Bond novels, Ian Fleming, had served in British naval intelligence during the war. John Le Carré, who was in the British Foreign Service in West Germany, created another famous British intelligence agent, George Smiley, who battles the Soviet master spy Karla in a series of novels. In Le Carré's classic *The Spy Who Came in From the Cold,* agents and double agents struggle to cross (and get doublecrossed!) at the Berlin Wall. Len Deighton's *Funeral in Berlin* also features a dangerous passage between East and West in the divided city of Berlin, where heroes and villains, secrets and spies, often slipped through the iron curtain on their shadowy missions.

ACTIVITY
Connecting with Culture

To help students understand the "red scare," have them research communism to gain a better grasp of its ideals. Tell students to find out why thousands of Americans had been drawn to the Communist Party during the 1920s and the Depression. What did it offer that our capitalist system didn't? Engage students in a discussion about communism and its appeal at the time. **(Verbal/Linguistic)**

BACKGROUND
Recent Scholarship

In 1943 the U.S. Army built a secret laboratory at Los Alamos, New Mexico. Sitting high atop a mesa, the laboratory was far removed from the people whom it was designed to protect. Two years later the lab had created two atomic bombs, both of which were used to end World War II. In 1993, 50 years after the lab had opened, the workers at Los Alamos faced another daunting task: providing advice on how to disassemble portions of the deadly nuclear arsenal. In *The Good Servant: Making Peace with the Bomb at Los Alamos*, Janet Bailey examines how the scientists at Los Alamos coped with the dramatic change brought about by the end of the Cold War.

TEST PREPARATION

Have students review the section entitled "The Cold War at Home," and then have them answer the question below.

In 1947, how did Truman demonstrate his concern about Communist infiltration?

A He put suspected Communists on trial.

(B) He required government employees to have background checks before they started their jobs.

C He campaigned in favor of officials who were committed to rooting out Communists.

D He took no action.

Activity
Connecting with Culture

In the late 1940s and early 1950s, the film and television industries were often a target of investigation by the House Un-American Activities Committee (HUAC). Have students work in small groups to list three activities by the film and television industry today that might be considered un-American, and three activities that would be considered "good" for Americans. **(Logical/Mathematical)**

Background
Biography

Dalton Trumbo (1905–1976) was arguably the most talented member of the Hollywood Ten. As a result of his refusal to testify before the House Un-American Activities Committee, he spent 11 months in prison in 1950 and was blacklisted. After his blacklisting, he continued to write, but under pseudonyms. Trumbo won an Oscar in 1956 for the script for *The Brave One,* written under the name Robert Rich. By 1960 Trumbo was writing under his own name again, creating the scripts for the epics *Exodus* and *Spartacus.* He was also the author of the searing antiwar novel *Johnny Got His Gun.*

HUAC As the Loyalty Review Board carried out its work, Congress pursued its own loyalty programs. The **House Un-American Activities Committee,** known as **HUAC,** had been established in 1938 to investigate disloyalty on the eve of World War II. Now it began a postwar probe of Communist infiltration of government agencies and, more spectacularly, a probe of the Hollywood movie industry.

Claiming that movies had tremendous power to influence the public, in 1947 HUAC charged that numerous Hollywood figures had Communist leanings that affected their filmmaking. In fact, some Hollywood personalities were or had been members of the Communist Party. Others in the industry had openly supported various causes and movements with philosophical similarities to communism (which, of course, did not make them Communists or disloyal in any way). With government encouragement, Hollywood had also produced some movies favorable to the Soviet Union and its people. These films had been made during the war, when the United States and the Soviet Union had been allies.

Many movie stars protested HUAC's attitude and procedures. Actor Frederic March asked Americans to consider where it all could lead: "Who's next? . . . Is it you, who will have to look around nervously before you can say what's on your mind? . . . This reaches into every American city and town."

The Hollywood Ten In September and October of 1947, HUAC called a number of Hollywood writers, directors, actors, and producers to testify. They were a distinguished group, responsible for some of Hollywood's best films of the previous decade. Facing the committee, celebrities who were accused of having radical political associations had little chance to defend themselves. The committee chairman, Republican Representative J. Parnell Thomas of New Jersey, first called witnesses who were allowed to make accusations based on rumors and other flimsy evidence. Then the accused were called.

Over and over the committee asked, "Are you now or have you ever been a member of the Communist Party?" When some of those called before HUAC attempted to make statements, they were denied permission. Invoking their Constitutional rights, ten of the accused declined to answer the committee's questions. The **Hollywood Ten** were cited for contempt of Congress and served jail terms ranging from six months to a year.

The HUAC investigations had a powerful impact on filmmaking. Nervous motion picture executives denounced the Hollywood Ten for having done a disservice to their industry. The studios compiled a **blacklist,** a list circulated among employers, containing the names of persons who should not be hired. Many other entertainment figures were added to the Hollywood blacklist simply because they seemed subversive or because they opposed *the idea* of a blacklist. The list included actors, screenwriters, directors, and broadcasters.

In the past, Hollywood had been willing to make movies on controversial subjects such as racism and anti-Semitism. Now studios resisted all films dealing with social problems and concentrated on pure entertainment.

The McCarran-Walter Act While HUAC carried out its work in the House, Democrat Pat McCarran led a Senate hunt for Communists in the movie industry, labor unions, the State Department, and the UN. Senator McCarran became convinced that most disloyal Americans were immigrants from Communist-dominated parts of the world.

VIEWING HISTORY Actor Humphrey Bogart protested HUAC's actions against other actors, and then ended up having to clear his own name. *Red Channels* was an index of blacklisted actors published in 1950. **Drawing Inferences** *How do these two items demonstrate the climate of suspicion at that time?*

Caption Answers

Viewing History The poster shows that people, especially prominent people in the arts, felt they had to prove their loyalty to the United States by denouncing communism. The blacklist shows that there were many people whose loyalty was suspect and that retaliation against them caused them to lose their livelihoods.

Resource Directory

Teaching Resources
Units 5/6/7 booklet
- Section 2 Quiz, p. 28

Guide to the Essentials
- Section 2 Summary, p. 93

Technology
Sounds of an Era Audio CD *House Un-American Activities Committee Testimony,* 1948 recording (time: 40 seconds)

Resource Pro® Primary Source Activity *The Rise of Joseph McCarthy,* found on Resource Pro, provides students with an insider's description of how the stage was set for the McCarthy hearings with a chapter from Senator Charles E. Potter's book *Days of Shame.*

At his urging, Congress passed the **McCarran-Walter Act** in 1952. This law reaffirmed the quota system for each country that had been established in 1924. It discriminated against potential immigrants from Asia and from Southern and Central Europe. President Truman vetoed McCarran's bill, calling it "one of the most un-American acts I have ever witnessed in my public career." Congress, however, passed the bill over the President's veto.

Spy Cases Inflame the Nation Two famous spy cases helped fuel the suspicion that a conspiracy within the United States was helping foreign Communists gain military and political successes overseas. In 1948, HUAC investigated Alger Hiss, who had been a high-ranking State Department official before he left government service. Whittaker Chambers, a former Communist who had become a successful *Time* magazine editor, accused Hiss of having been a Communist in the 1930s. Hiss denied the charge and sued Chambers for slander. Chambers then declared that Hiss had been a Soviet spy.

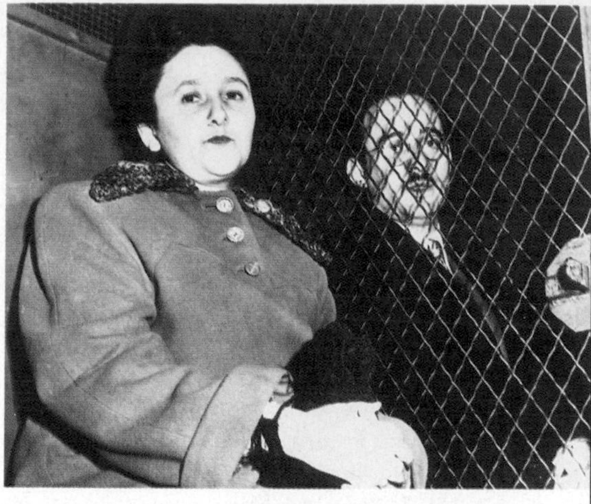

VIEWING HISTORY Ethel and Julius Rosenberg were the first U.S. civilians to be executed for espionage. **Drawing Conclusions** *How did spy cases affect Americans' perception of a Communist threat to society?*

Too much time had passed for the spying charge to be pressed. After two trials, Hiss was convicted of perjury for lying in the slander case. In 1950, he went to prison for four years. Not all Americans were convinced that he was guilty, and the case was debated for years. For most people, however, the case seemed to prove that there was a real Communist threat in the United States.

Several months after Hiss's conviction, Julius and Ethel Rosenberg, a married couple who were members of the Communist Party, were accused of passing atomic secrets to the Soviets during World War II. After a highly controversial trial, the Rosenbergs were convicted of espionage and executed in 1953. The case was another event that inflamed anti-Communist passions and focused attention on a possible internal threat to the nation's security.

Like the Hiss case, the Rosenbergs' convictions were debated for years afterward. Careful work by historians in once-classified American records and in secret Soviet records opened at the end of the Cold War indicate that both Alger Hiss and Julius Rosenberg were guilty. While Ethel Rosenberg may have had some knowledge of her husband's activities, it now appears that she was not guilty of espionage.

Section 2 Assessment

READING COMPREHENSION

1. What was the **Marshall Plan,** and why was it instituted?
2. What was the importance of the **Berlin airlift?**
3. How did **NATO** demonstrate the principle of **collective security?**
4. What did the **HUAC** hearings and the **McCarran-Walter Act** show about American attitudes?

CRITICAL THINKING AND WRITING

5. **Identifying Central Issues** What dangers to a free society are posed by the kind of tactics used by HUAC and by the creation of blacklists?
6. **Writing a Conclusion** How well did the United States respond to Cold War threats? Support your conclusion with three examples.

Take It to the NET

Activity: Writing an Editorial
Read more about the Marshall Plan. Then write a newspaper editorial supporting or criticizing the plan. Use the links provided in the *America: Pathways to the Present* area of the following Web site for help in completing this activity.
www.phschool.com

Section 2 Assessment

Reading Comprehension

1. A program for the economic recovery of postwar Europe. American policymakers hoped it would keep Communist governments from gaining more power, and strengthen European economies as well as foreign trade.
2. The Berlin Airlift allowed West Berlin to remain free from Communist domination and allowed President Truman to avoid using military force to end an early Cold War standoff.
3. Every nation that joined NATO had to agree that a military attack on any member nation would be viewed as an attack upon the alliance as a whole, and that all NATO member nations would defend the nation that had been attacked.
4. They demonstrated the paranoia and distrust on the part of Americans toward communism.

Critical Thinking and Writing

5. HUAC used mainly rumors and false accusations to gather information, leading to innocent people being accused and imprisoned; the movie industry suffered greatly, as no one wanted to make films that might appear controversial; Americans in general were fearful of speaking their minds, thinking anyone could be a government informer.
6. Answers will vary but should be supported with facts from the section.

Sample answer: It was important to fight communism and to boost U.S. exports.

Caption Answers

Viewing History The spy cases made Americans more convinced of the existence of a Communist conspiracy within the nation.

Section 3

The Korean War

Section Objectives

1. Observe the ways Communist expansion in Asia set the stage for the Korean War.
2. Learn who fought in the Korean War, and about the war's three stages.
3. Discover the different effects of the Korean War.

Bellringer

Warm-Up Activity Set up a row of dominoes in the front of the classroom. Knock over the first domino so that it causes the whole line to fall. Ask students to explain what this "domino effect" has to do with containing communism in the 1950s and with the outbreak of war in Korea.

Activating Prior Knowledge Ask the class to list what they know about Korea and about its history during the second half of the last century. What is the political situation like in Korea today?

Reading Strategy

Have students copy the headings in this section on a sheet of paper. As they read, have them add two or three key facts under each heading to create an outline that helps them analyze the conflict in Korea and its domestic and international effects.

Section 3

The Korean War

READING FOCUS

- How did Communist expansion in Asia set the stage for the Korean War?
- Who fought in the Korean War, and what were the three stages of the war?
- What were the effects of the Korean War?

MAIN IDEA

To repel a North Korean invasion of South Korea, American and other UN troops fought against Communist forces for three years. The result was a return to prewar Korean borders.

KEY TERMS

38th parallel
Korean War
military-industrial complex

TAKING NOTES

Copy the diagram below. As you read, fill in the causes and effects of the Korean War.

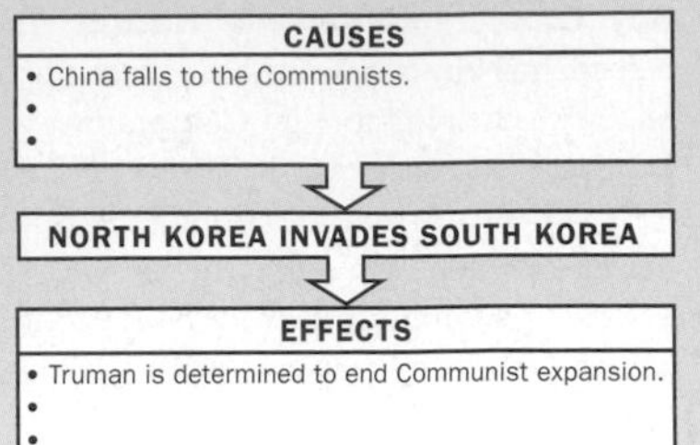

CAUSES
• China falls to the Communists.
•
•
NORTH KOREA INVADES SOUTH KOREA
EFFECTS
• Truman is determined to end Communist expansion.
•
•

Setting the Scene The Korean War is sometimes called America's forgotten war, but the soldiers who fought in Korea never forgot it. In June of 1950, American troops struggled to push back the Communists, who had made huge advances. One American marine recalled the fierce fighting:

> *"To push the North Koreans back across the river we had to kick them off a series of ridges. . . . It was straight uphill. No cover. There were machine guns, mortars, grenades going off. The volume of fire was terrific. They were pouring everything they had into us. Guys were cursing and yelling and dropping all around me. . . ."*
>
> —Arnold Winter

Later in 1950, both sides dug in to hold their positions. Infantryman Tom Clawson said later, "I didn't realize it at the time, but when I got to Korea the war of movement had just ended. What they called the sitting war had taken its place." He described what "the sitting war" was like:

American soldiers dig in during the Korean War.

> *"You spent hours every day improving your position, working on the foxholes and trenches and bunkers. But I never liked to get too fancy, because sooner or later we'd be shifted to a different position. . . . Most times [after going on patrol] you'd return to the place you started from, but the day would always come when you wouldn't. You'd come back and move directly to a new position. But all the positions were always somewhere on the same ridgeline."*
>
> —Tom Clawson

Although it lacked the glory of World War II and the turmoil of the Vietnam War, the Korean conflict had important effects on the United States.

RESOURCE DIRECTORY

Teaching Resources
Guided Reading and Review booklet, p. 107

Other Print Resources
Historical Outline Map Book *The Korean War,* p. 69

Technology
Section Reading Support Transparencies
Guided Reading Audiotapes (English/Spanish), Ch. 19
Student Edition on Audio CD, Ch. 19
Prentice Hall Presentation Pro CD-ROM, Ch. 19
Companion Web site, www.phschool.com

Communist Expansion in Asia

While the attention of most Americans was focused on the Communist threat in Europe, events were unfolding in Asia that would cause the Cold War to flare up into a "hot" military confrontation. The roots of this armed conflict were found in the Chinese Civil War and in Japanese aggression in both China and Korea before and during World War II.

The Chinese Civil War As you recall, before World War I, foreign powers exerted considerable influence in China and even held some Chinese territory. One of these powers was Japan. Another was Germany. After Germany was defeated in World War I, the Allies gave Japan control over former German possessions, thus increasing Japanese power in China. In 1919, Chinese protesters began calling for a stronger, more independent China. Some demanded democracy and nationalism. Others, impressed by the results of the Russian Revolution of 1917, thought that communism was the way to build a strong nation.

In the mid-1920s, the Nationalist Party led by Jiang Jieshi gained strength in northern China and captured Beijing. Meanwhile, the Communists had made gains around Shanghai. In 1927, Jiang sent troops to attack the Communists and their supporters. The result was a massacre that would lead to civil war.

The Communists were led by Mao Zedong. He gained support for the Communist cause in southeastern China by redistributing land to the peasants and offering them schooling and health care. Determined to consolidate his power, Jiang continued to pursue the Communists. In 1934, Mao and his followers began retreating before Jiang's forces. After the Long March, Mao began rebuilding his forces in the north of China.

As you read in Section 2, the Nationalists and the Communists had cooperated to resist invading Japanese forces, but after World War II the Chinese Civil War became more intense. The Nationalists lost support because of their harsh treatment of the population, high taxes, and corruption. Mao's land reforms and his promise of equality, as well as his military victories, led the Communists to power in 1949. The Nationalists fled to Taiwan, where they still claimed to be the legitimate government of China.

Dividing Korea In addition to seeking territory and influence in China before World War I, Japan had also annexed the Korean peninsula. Japanese rule of Korea was harsh, and Koreans hoped that their nation would be restored after the Japanese were finally defeated in World War II. However, the war ended before careful plans for Korean independence could be worked out. In 1945, the Allies agreed on a temporary solution. Soviet soldiers accepted the surrender of Japanese troops north of the **38th parallel,** the latitude line running across Korea at approximately the midpoint of the peninsula; American forces did the same south of the parallel. While the dividing line was never intended to be permanent, Korea was divided—temporarily—into a Soviet-occupied northern zone and an American-occupied southern zone. Soon a pro-American government formed in South Korea and a Communist regime was established in North Korea. Occupying forces withdrew from both zones in 1948 and 1949.

Focus on WORLD EVENTS

The Long March In the fall of 1934, some 85,000 Communist troops found themselves surrounded by Nationalist forces in southeastern China. They broke through the Nationalist lines and began a 6,000-mile, year-long trek to Northwest China, near the Soviet border. Constantly under both air and ground attack by the Nationalists, they crossed 24 rivers and 18 mountain ranges. In the first three months, the Communists lost more than half their army, and only about 8,000 survivors finally reached their destination. During the Long March, Mao Zedong's leadership made him the undisputed head of the Chinese Communist Party. In spite of their often desperate circumstances, the Communist troops treated the peasants with respect, paid for goods they needed, and did not damage crops. This behavior—and the heroic ordeal of the Long March itself—inspired many young Chinese to join the Communist cause.

READING CHECK
How did Korea become a divided nation?

LESSON PLAN

Focus The momentum of the Cold War carried the United States into troubled political waters. The Korean War was a costly, difficult conflict, fought primarily to help suppress the spread of communism in Asia.

Instruct Explain that in its efforts to fight Communist aggression, the United States engaged in its own aggressive policies, both at home and abroad. Discuss whether those actions were justified in order to oppose communism. Encourage students to support their opinions with facts and reasoning.

Assess/Reteach Looking back from today, what do students think about efforts such as the Korean War? Does the end—the suppression of communism—justify the means—a costly, bloody war?

BACKGROUND
Geography in History

A few months before North Korea launched the Korean War, Secretary of State Dean Acheson gave a speech on American postwar military commitments at Washington, D.C.'s National Press Club. In the case of Soviet attack, Acheson said, the United States would only defend countries within its Pacific defense perimeter. Because China had recently fallen to the Communists, Acheson drew this line off the coast of Asia. The islands of Japan, the Philippines, and Okinawa fell under American protection, but South Korea did not. Although American historians have found no proof, many suspect that Acheson's speech encouraged Communist leaders to invade South Korea.

READING CHECK
Japan had occupied Korea prior to World War I. After Japan's defeat in World War II, Korea was temporarily occupied by Russian troops in the north and American troops in the south. The departure of all occupation troops in the late 1940s left a Communist government north of the 38th parallel and a Western-oriented non-Communist government in the south.

CUSTOMIZE FOR ...
Gifted and Talented

Have students research the route of the Long March. Then have them make a map detailing the route, noting dates and events along an accompanying time line.

Activity
Connecting with Government

Tell students to find out about the current status of relations between the U.S. and Korea. Are U.S. troops stationed on the Korean peninsula? If so, how many and what is their purpose? What do the South Korean people think of the American troops? What do the North Koreans think about the troops? Tell students to write a short report describing what they have learned about the situation in Korea. **(Verbal/Linguistic)**

Background
Connections to Today

In September 1999 a report revealed that American soldiers had killed as many as 300 South Korean refugees in July 1950. Soon after the report was released, an investigative panel was set up to look into the matter. The panel spent 18 months gathering evidence, visiting the site, and reviewing aerial photographs, testimony, and other relevant documents. Bernard E. Trainor, a retired Marine lieutenant general who led a platoon in the Korean War, was on the panel. In an article he wrote for the *Washington Post*, Trainor said, "It was not the deliberate murder of innocents, but an act of desperation by frightened, green troops who acted out of self-preservation." He was referring to the chaotic situation in South Korea during the opening phase of the war. In January 2001 President Clinton released a statement taking responsibility for the deaths at No Gun Ri. South Korean president Kim accepted Clinton's deepest regrets on behalf of our country.

The Korean Conflict

Koreans on both sides of the dividing line wanted to unify their nation. In June 1950, the **Korean War** broke out when North Korean troops streamed across the 38th parallel, determined to reunite Korea by force. The invasion took the United States by surprise. It also alarmed Americans, who were sure—wrongly, it turned out—that the action had been orchestrated by the Soviet Union. The fall of China to the Communists had been a shock to the United States; now it seemed as though communism was on the advance again. Faced with what he viewed as a clear case of aggression, President Truman was determined to respond. He recalled earlier instances "when the strong had attacked the weak." Each time that the democracies failed to act, Truman remembered, it had encouraged the aggressors. "If this [invasion of South Korea] was allowed to go unchallenged, it would mean a third world war, just as similar incidents brought on the second world war," Truman said.

The UN Police Action After the defeat of the Chinese Nationalists in 1949, the United States had blocked Communist China's admission to the United Nations. The Soviet delegation had walked out in protest, and thus could not exercise its veto when President Truman brought the issue of North Korean aggression to the UN. The United States gained unanimous approval for resolutions that branded North Korea an aggressor and that called on member states to help defend South Korea and restore peace.

President Truman wasted no time. He commanded the American Seventh Fleet to protect Taiwan, and he ordered American air and naval support for the South Koreans. Later he sent ground troops as well. Although Truman did not go to Congress for a declaration of war as required by the Constitution, both Democrats and Republicans praised him for his strong action. Members of the House stood and cheered when they heard of it.

The UN set up the United Nations Command and asked the United States to choose the commander of the UN forces. Eventually, 16 member nations contributed troops or arms, but Americans made up roughly 80 percent of the troops that served in the UN police action in Korea.

MAP SKILLS These maps show the back-and-forth nature of the fighting in the Korean War. **Movement** *Examine the maps and the movements of UN troops. Why do you think China entered the war when it did?*

The Korean War, 1950–1953

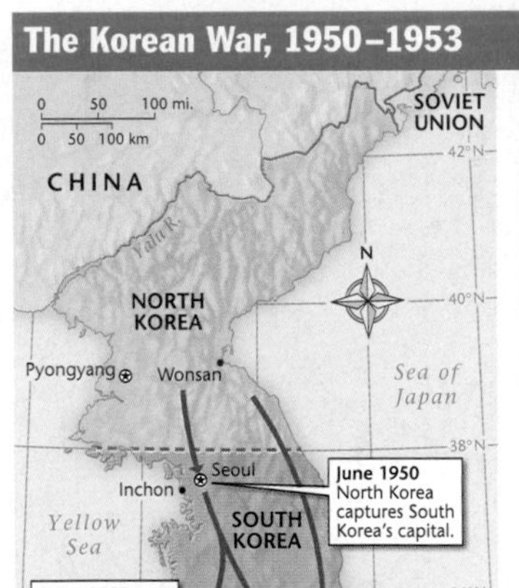

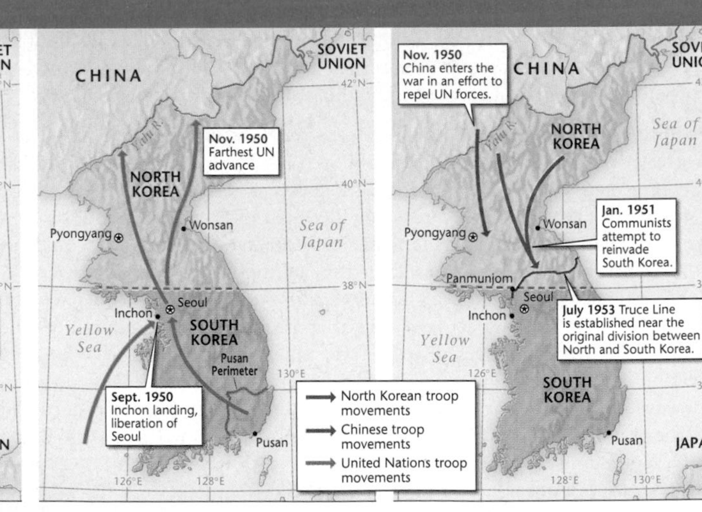

Caption Answers

Map Skills To stop the northward progression of UN troops.

Resource Directory

Other Print Resources

American History Block Scheduling Support *Korea: The Unknown War,* found in The Nation After World War II folder, includes interdisciplinary lesson suggestions and activities for Geography and History, Primary Sources, Biography, and Literature.

Technology

Color Transparencies *Historical Maps,* A47

Sounds of an Era Audio CD *General Douglas MacArthur, April 19, 1951* (time: 45 seconds)

RESOURCE PRO® **Biography** *Marguerite Higgins,* found on Resource Pro, profiles a female journalist who overcame discrimination to become a war correspondent in Korea.

Waging the War A hero of two world wars and a strong anti-Communist, General Douglas MacArthur was Truman's choice to lead the UN forces in Korea. MacArthur was based in Japan, where he headed the postwar occupation. He was responsible for establishing Western democracy there and for creating Japan's new democratic constitution. He had been less successful in implementing democracy in South Korea, where he also commanded American occupation forces. There, MacArthur had supported Korean president Syngman Rhee, despite Rhee's brutal elimination of his opponents.

Despite a difficult personality, MacArthur was an excellent military strategist, and he developed a bold plan to drive the invaders from South Korea. With Soviet tanks and air power, the North Koreans had swept through South Korea in just weeks. Only a small part of the country, near the port city of Pusan, remained unconquered.

MacArthur suspected that the North Koreans' rapid advance had left their supply lines stretched thin. He decided to strike at this weakness. After first sending forces to defend Pusan, in September 1950 he landed troops at Inchon in northwestern South Korea, and attacked enemy supply lines from behind.

MacArthur's strategy worked. Caught between UN forces in the north and in the south, and with their supplies cut off, the invaders fled back across the 38th parallel. UN troops pursued them northward. American and South Korean leaders began to boast of reuniting Korea under South Korean control. Such talk alarmed the Chinese Communists, who had been in power less than a year and who did not want a pro-Western nation next door.

As UN troops approached North Korea's border with China, the Chinese warned them not to advance any farther. MacArthur ignored the warning. On November 24, 1950, the general announced his "Home by Christmas" offensive, designed to drive the enemy across the North Korean border at the Yalu River into China and end the war. However, Chinese troops poured across the Yalu to take the offensive. The Chinese and the North Koreans pushed the UN forces back into South Korea. A stalemate developed.

MacArthur favored breaking the stalemate by opening a second front. He wanted the Chinese opposition forces of Jiang Jieshi on the island of Taiwan to return to the mainland to attack the Chinese Communists. Truman opposed this strategy, fearing it could lead to a widespread war in Asia. Unable to sway Truman, MacArthur sent a letter to House Minority Leader Joseph Martin in March 1951, attacking the President's policies. Martin made the letter public. On April 11, Truman fired MacArthur for insubordination.

MacArthur returned home to a hero's welcome. In an address to a joint session of Congress on April 19, he made an emotional farewell:

> "*Since I took the oath at West Point, the hopes and dreams [of youth] have all vanished. But I still remember the refrain of one of the most popular barracks ballads of that day, which proclaimed most proudly that old soldiers never die, they just fade away. And like the old soldier of that ballad, I now close my military career and just fade away, an old soldier who tried to do his duty as God gave him the light to see that duty. Good-bye.*"
>
> —General Douglas MacArthur, 1951

American BIOGRAPHY

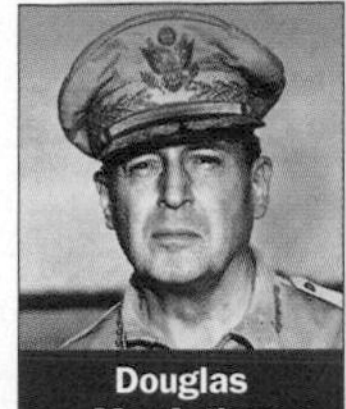
Douglas MacArthur
1880–1964

The son of an army officer, Douglas MacArthur graduated from West Point at the top of his class. Cited for bravery in World War I, he became a general by the time he was 38, and Army Chief of Staff in 1930.

During World War II, MacArthur commanded American forces in Asia. He organized the defense of the Philippines and the island-hopping campaign against the Japanese in the Pacific. After commanding American Occupation forces in both Japan and South Korea, MacArthur led the UN forces in the Korean War. His dispute with President Truman led the President to fire him for insubordination.

Although a hero to those he commanded and to much of the American public, MacArthur was disliked by many political leaders, who viewed him as overly ambitious. MacArthur, in turn, had little respect for either Roosevelt or Truman; he thought both were soft on communism. His attitude made MacArthur an anti-Communist hero. Yet his characteristic contempt for anyone with authority over him led him to take actions that undermined his otherwise brilliant career.

Sounds of an Era

Listen to MacArthur's speech to Congress and other sounds from the Cold War period.

ACTIVITY
Connecting with History and Conflict

Have students work in small groups to analyze the conflict between President Truman and General MacArthur. Have them list two or three beliefs held by each. What goals did they have in common? Why did they come into conflict? Whose views do students favor more? **(Verbal/Linguistic)**

BACKGROUND
MacArthur's Dismissal

Although President Truman had no qualms about his decision to dismiss General MacArthur, his decision prompted a huge outcry from the public, as well as from members of the Republican Party. In the first two days after the firing, the White House received 250,000 telegrams protesting the decision. During a private meeting of Republican members of Congress, one senator proposed that Congress impeach Truman. After MacArthur delivered his famous farewell speech, members of Congress rushed to touch the fired general. Meanwhile, back at the White House, President Truman and his aides watched in disbelief. Despite the outpouring of support for MacArthur, Truman knew he had made the right decision.

TEST PREPARATION

Have students review the text in the section "Waging the War," and then ask them to complete the sentence below.

The main reason Truman fired MacArthur was that—

A they did not agree on the best way to fight the Korean War.
B Truman did not like MacArthur.
Ⓒ MacArthur was insubordinate to his commander in chief.
D MacArthur did not like Truman.

Section 3 Assessment

Reading Comprehension

1. It is the latitude line that divides Korea in half. After World War II, Communists controlled the northern half, while the south was supported by the United States.
2. (a) It began when North Korean troops crossed the 38th parallel in an attempt to reunite North and South Korea by force. (b) The North Koreans were aided by the Chinese; the South Koreans had the aid of the United States, along with some other UN member countries.
3. For insubordination after MacArthur wrote a letter to a U.S. Congressman blasting Truman's policies.
4. Answers can include: the frustration caused in the United States, ambiguities of the war, a huge increase in defense spending, and the beginning of the military-industrial complex.

Critical Thinking and Writing

5. Success: the Communist forces were successfully evicted from South Korea. Failure: North Korea remained under Communist control, and many American lives were sacrificed for little apparent gain.
6. Time lines will vary but should be supported with facts from the section.

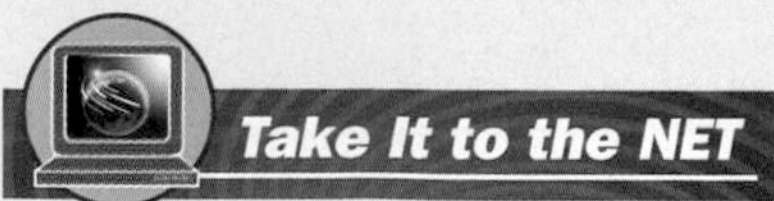

Collages should accurately reflect the nature of the Korean War.

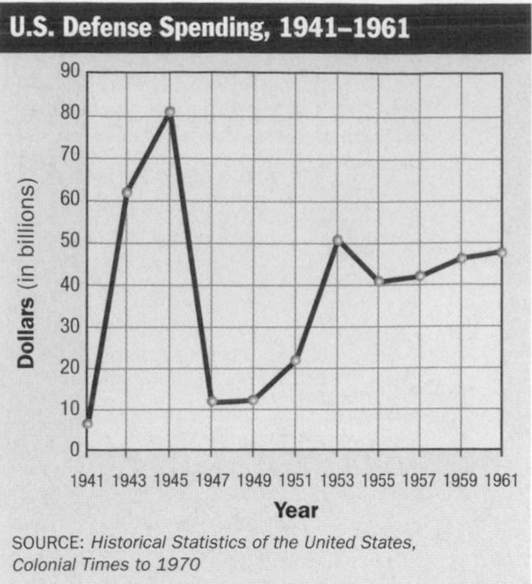

INTERPRETING GRAPHS The competition for world leadership led to an arms race between the United States and the Soviet Union. **Recognizing Cause and Effect** *What was the cause of the sharpest rise in American defense spending in the post–World War II era? Why do you think spending did not drop off abruptly again, the way it did after World War II?*

Once tempers cooled, MacArthur did, in fact, fade from view, and Truman was able to keep the war limited. However, the struggle dragged on for over two more years, into the presidency of Dwight D. Eisenhower. When peace talks stalled, Eisenhower's threat to use atomic weapons got the talks going again. Finally, a truce was signed in 1953, leaving Korea divided at almost exactly the same place as before the war, near the 38th parallel.

The Effects of the Korean War

The Korean War caused enormous frustration in the United States. Americans wondered why roughly 34,000 of their soldiers had been killed and 103,000 wounded for such limited results. They questioned whether their government was serious about stopping communism. On the other hand, Communist forces had been pushed back beyond the 38th parallel. What's more, this containment had occurred without nuclear war. It seemed that Americans would have to get used to more limited wars and more limited victories.

Americans would have to get used to other changes as well. One change was in the military itself. Although President Truman had ordered the integration of the armed forces in 1948, the Korean War was the first war in which white Americans and African Americans served in the same units.

The Korean War also led to a huge increase in military spending. The military had taken less than a third of the federal budget in 1950; a decade later, military spending made up about half of federal expenditures. At the same time, the United States came to accept the demands of permanent mobilization. Over a million American soldiers were stationed around the world. At home, the military establishment became more powerful as it developed links to the corporate and scientific communities. These ties created a powerful **military-industrial complex** that employed 3.5 million Americans by 1960.

The Korean War also helped to shape future U.S. policy in Asia. Hoping that Japan could help to maintain the balance of power in the Pacific, the United States signed a peace treaty with that nation in September 1951. In addition, the Korean War further poisoned relations with Communist China, leading to a diplomatic standoff that would last more than 20 years.

Section 3 Assessment

READING COMPREHENSION

1. What was the importance of the **38th parallel?**
2. (a) How did the **Korean War** begin? (b) Who fought on each side?
3. Why did President Truman fire General MacArthur?
4. Name two effects of the war.

CRITICAL THINKING AND WRITING

5. **Drawing Conclusions** Considering containment and the Truman Doctrine, do you think the Korean War was a success or a failure? Why?
6. **Creating a Time Line** Make a time line of the important events of the Korean War.

Take It to the NET

Activity: Creating a Collage
Make a collage about one aspect of the Korean War. Download or copy maps, photos, newspaper headlines, and quotes from soldiers. Use the links provided in the *America: Pathways to the Present* area of the following Web site for help in completing this activity.
www.phschool.com

Caption Answers

Interpreting Graphs The Korean War. Americans felt that the enemy had not been totally defeated in the sense that the Nazis and the Japanese had been defeated in World War II. Americans felt that the Communist threat continued, and that the U.S. must remain ready for another war.

RESOURCE DIRECTORY

Teaching Resources

Units 5/6/7 booklet
- Section 3 Quiz, p. 29

Guide to the Essentials
- Section 3 Summary, p. 94

Learning with Documents booklet (Key Documents) *General Douglas MacArthur, Address to Congress,* p. 89

Technology

RESOURCE PRO® **Visual Learning Activity** *Civilian Control of the Military,* found on Resource Pro, uses a cartoon to present one view of Truman's controversial firing of General MacArthur during the Korean War.

Section 4

The Continuing Cold War

READING FOCUS

- What were the characteristics of the McCarthy era?
- How was the Cold War waged in Southeast Asia, the Middle East, and Latin America during the 1950s?
- How did the arms race develop?

KEY TERMS

McCarthyism
arms race
deterrence
brinkmanship
ICBM
Sputnik
U-2 incident

TAKING NOTES

As you read, prepare an outline of the first section. Follow the model below.

The McCarthy Era

I. McCarthy's Rise to Power
A. McCarthy needed a popular issue for the 1952 election.
1. ________
2. ________
B. ________

MAIN IDEA

During the 1950s, the Cold War spread around the world. At home, McCarthyism caused fear and distrust.

Setting the Scene Communist aggression in Korea was already heightening Americans' fear of communism when Wisconsin Senator Joseph McCarthy held up a piece of paper and declared, "I have here in my hand a list of 205 [people] who were known to the secretary of state as being members of the Communist Party and who, nevertheless, are still working and shaping policy at the State Department." In the Cold War atmosphere of 1950, McCarthy's charges quickly gained so much support that only the most courageous spoke out against him. One such person was Edward R. Murrow, who concluded his TV show on McCarthy by saying that "[t]his is no time for men who oppose Senator McCarthy to keep silent." He explained:

> "*[T]he line between investigating and persecuting is a very fine one and the junior Senator from Wisconsin has stepped over it repeatedly. . . . We must not confuse dissent with disloyalty. We must remember always that accusation is not proof. . . . We can deny our heritage and our history, but we cannot escape responsibility for the result. . . .*"
>
> —Edward R. Murrow

The McCarthy Era

In 1950, it seemed to many Americans that the events in Asia supported McCarthy's sensational charges. However, the famous list of 205 known State Department Communists turned out to be the names of people who were still employed by the government, even though they had been accused of disloyalty under Truman's loyalty program. When pressed for details, the senator reduced the number from 205 to 57. Nevertheless, McCarthy's accusations sparked an anti-Communist hysteria and national search for subversives that caused suspicion and fear across the nation.

McCarthy's Rise to Power Joseph McCarthy's first term in the Senate had been undistinguished and he needed an issue to arouse public support. He found that issue in the menace of communism. Piling baseless accusations on top of unprovable charges, McCarthy took his crusade to the floor of the Senate and engaged in the smear tactics that came to be called **McCarthyism.** Not only was McCarthy reelected, but he became

ANALYZING POLITICAL CARTOONS The caption of this cartoon cites Senator McCarthy's famous claim to have proof of subversion "in his hand." **Drawing Conclusions** *(a) According to the cartoon, what does McCarthy really have, instead of proof? (b) What is the message of the cartoon?*

"I Have Here In My Hand—"

Section 4 The Continuing Cold War

Section Objectives

1. Discover some characteristics of the McCarthy era.
2. See how the Cold War was waged in Southeast Asia, the Middle East, and Latin America during the 1950s.
3. Understand how the arms race developed.

Bellringer

Warm-Up Activity Discuss with students the concepts of loyalty and patriotism. Do they think that it is possible to be a "true American" while supporting an ideology or belief such as communism?

Activating Prior Knowledge Ask students if they are familiar with the concept of "blacklisting" as practiced during the McCarthy era.

Reading Strategy

As students read, have them list some of the ways in which the United States government sought to suppress and contain the spread of communism in the 1950s.

Caption Answers

Analyzing Political Cartoons (a) Bogus evidence that "stinks." (b) McCarthy is a liar and not to be believed.

RESOURCE DIRECTORY

Teaching Resources
Learning Styles Lesson Plans booklet, p. 55
Guided Reading and Review booklet, p. 108

Technology
Section Reading Support Transparencies
Guided Reading Audiotapes (English/Spanish), Ch. 19
Student Edition on Audio CD, Ch. 19
Prentice Hall Presentation Pro CD-ROM, Ch. 19
Companion Web site, www.phschool.com

Lesson Plan

Focus The Cold War era created many tense and difficult political situations for the United States. The new availability of the atomic bomb complicated the situation enormously. Discuss whether there was any precedent in United States history for the ideological warfare of the 1950s.

Instruct Discuss the ways in which America's military strategy changed from the end of World War II to the 1950s, as the enemy shifted from Hitler's German army to forces in Stalin's Russia. Discuss with students the ways in which the beginnings of the nuclear weapons race complicated matters still further.

Assess/Reteach Ask students to state ways in which the tension between the United States and the Soviet Union spilled over into U.S. domestic affairs, such as the Senate hearings conducted by Joseph McCarthy.

Activity

Connecting with Culture

Have students research the media's coverage of the McCarthy era. Have them look for news stories and editorials from the early 1950s. Tell students to photocopy several articles and bring them to class. Engage students in a discussion of the way in which the news media handled the story. What did the news coverage reveal about a newspaper or magazine and its particular slant? Why was this story difficult to cover? What were the complexities of the story? **(Verbal/Linguistic)**

VIEWING HISTORY Army counsel Joseph Welch listens as Senator Joseph McCarthy discusses Communist infiltration into the army. **Analyzing Visual Information** *(a) What emotion do you think Welch is experiencing? Why do you think he feels that way? (b) What was the result of the Army-McCarthy hearings?*

chairman of an investigations subcommittee. Merely being accused by McCarthy caused people to lose their jobs and reputations.

McCarthy soon took on larger targets. He attacked former Secretary of State George Marshall, a national hero and a man of unquestioned integrity. McCarthy claimed that Marshall was involved in "a conspiracy so immense and an infamy so black as to dwarf any previous venture in the history of man," because of his inability to stop the Communist triumph in China.

Even other senators came to fear McCarthy. They worried that opposition to his tactics would brand them as Communist sympathizers. But there were a few exceptions. As early as June 1950, Republican Senator Margaret Chase Smith of Maine presented a Declaration of Conscience to the Senate. She denounced McCarthy for having "debased" the Senate "to the level of a forum of hate and character assassination sheltered by the shield of congressional immunity. . . ."

Focus on CITIZENSHIP

Declaration of Conscience

Margaret Chase Smith's declaration to the Senate made it clear that Senator McCarthy, far from protecting American values as he claimed, was really putting American principles in danger:

"Those of us who shout the loudest about Americanism in making character assassinations are all too frequently those who, by our own words and acts, ignore some of the basic principles of Americanism—

The right to criticize;
The right to hold unpopular beliefs;
The right to protest;
The right of independent thought.

The exercise of these rights should not cost one single American citizen his right to a livelihood nor should he be in danger of losing his reputation nor should he be in danger . . . merely because he happens to know someone who holds unpopular beliefs."

McCarthy's Fall In early 1954, when one of his assistants was drafted, McCarthy charged that even the army was full of Communists. Army officials, in turn, charged McCarthy with seeking special treatment for his aide. As charges and countercharges flew back and forth, the senator's subcommittee voted to investigate the claims.

The Army-McCarthy hearings began in late April 1954. Democrats asked that the hearings be televised, hoping that the public would see McCarthy for what he was. Ever eager for publicity, the senator agreed. For weeks, Americans were riveted to their television sets. Most were horrified by McCarthy's bullying tactics and baseless allegations.

By the time the hearings ended in mid-June, the senator had lost even his strongest supporters. The Senate formally condemned him for his reckless actions. Unrepentant, McCarthy charged his accusers with being tools of the Communists, but he no longer had credibility. Although McCarthy remained in the Senate, his power was gone.

Eventually this second red scare, much like the one that followed World War I, subsided. But the nation was damaged by the era's suppression of free speech and open, honest debate.

The Cold War in the 1950s

American Cold War policy entered a new phase when Republican Dwight D. Eisenhower became President in 1953. Eisenhower's Secretary

Caption Answers

Viewing History (a) Answers may vary from despair to disgust. Welch knows that McCarthy is both a liar and a dangerous person. (b) They brought about McCarthy's downfall because they showed him as a bully whose accusations were baseless and unfair.

Resource Directory

Other Print Resources

Historical Outline Map Book *The Middle East,* p. 78

Technology

Color Transparencies *Political Cartoons,* B14

Sounds of an Era Audio CD *Army-McCarthy Hearings,* 1954 recording (time: 40 seconds)

RESOURCE PRO® **Literature Activity** *The Hunt for Witches and Communists,* found on Resource Pro, focuses on *The Crucible,* Arthur Miller's play about the Salem witch trials of 1692, which he wrote in response to the McCarthy hearings.

of State, John Foster Dulles, was a harsh anti-Communist who considered winning the Cold War to be a moral crusade. Dulles believed that Truman's containment policy was too cautious. Instead, he called for a policy to roll back communism where it had already taken hold.

As a military leader, Eisenhower recognized the risks of confronting the Soviets. He acted as a brake on Dulles's more extreme views. In Eisenhower's judgment, the United States could not intervene in the affairs of the Soviet Union's Eastern European satellites. So when East Germans revolted in 1953, and Poles and Hungarians in 1956, the United States kept its distance as Soviet troops crushed the uprisings. Eisenhower felt that any other response risked war with the Soviet Union. He wanted to avoid that at all costs. Thus containment remained an important part of American foreign policy in the 1950s.

Southeast Asia In July 1953, Eisenhower fulfilled a campaign promise to bring the Korean War to an end. The sudden death of Stalin in March and the rapid rise of more moderate Soviet leaders contributed to the resolution of this conflict. Meanwhile, the United States began providing substantial military aid to support France, which was trying to retain control of its colony, Vietnam. When an international conference divided Vietnam, like Korea, into a Communist north and an anti-Communist south, the United States provided aid to South Vietnam, but—for the time being—resisted greater involvement. (See Chapter 24.)

The Middle East The Cold War was also played out in the historic tensions of the Middle East. In the 1930s and 1940s, the Holocaust had forced many Jews to seek safety in Palestine, the Biblical home of the Jewish people, now controlled by the British. Calls for a Jewish state intensified. In 1947, the British turned the question over to the UN, which created two states in the area, one Jewish and one Arab. In May 1948, the Jews in Palestine proclaimed the new nation of Israel. Israel's Arab neighbors, who also viewed Palestine as their ancient homeland, attacked the Jewish state in 1948. Israel repelled the Arab assault, and the UN mediated new borders. As Arab hostility to the idea of a Jewish state continued, the United States supported Israel, while the Soviet Union generally backed Arab interests.

Meanwhile, the United States also worked to prevent oil-rich Arab nations from falling under the influence of the Soviet Union. In 1952, a nationalist leader gained control in Iran. Fearful that he would be neutral—or worse, sympathetic to Communism—the United States backed groups that overthrew the nationalist government and restored the pro-American Shah of Iran to power.

Next came the Suez crisis of 1956. When Egypt's ruler, Gamal Abdel Nasser, sought Soviet support, the United States and Great Britain cut off their aid to Egypt. Nasser responded by seizing the British-owned Suez Canal. This canal was a vital waterway that passed through Egypt and allowed Middle East oil to reach Europe via the Mediterranean. In late 1956, British and French forces attacked Egypt to regain control of the canal, despite prior assurances they would not rely on force. Reacting to Soviet threats of "dangerous consequences," a furious Eisenhower persuaded his NATO allies to withdraw from Egypt, which retained control of the canal.

To combat further Soviet influence in the Middle East, the President announced the Eisenhower Doctrine in

MAP SKILLS Following the 1948 war, Israel controlled most of what had been Palestine, but Egypt barred Israel and all nations trading with Israel from using the Suez Canal. **Location** *(a) Why do you think the Suez Canal was important to Israel and to its trading partners? (b) What do you think Egypt's purpose was in denying access to Israel?*

ACTIVITY
Connecting with Citizenship

Many people knew that Senator McCarthy's claims were exaggerated at best. Why, then, was he able to gain so much power and ruin the lives of so many people? Have students discuss the question as a group and then write a brief answer on their own. **(Verbal/Linguistic)**

BACKGROUND
Interdisciplinary

The quasi-religious fervor of Senator McCarthy's anti-Communist crusade was mirrored in *The Crucible,* Arthur Miller's allegorical dramatization of the Salem witch trials. Miller, who later became the target of an HUAC hearing, created in his play a parable of American society under McCarthyism. It was poorly received when it opened on Broadway in 1953, but it went on to become Miller's most frequently produced play.

TEST PREPARATION

Have students read the section "The Cold War in the 1950s" and then answer the question below.

Which of the following actions would John Foster Dulles probably have supported?

A A softening of relations with the Soviet Union.
B Continuing Truman's policy of containment without alteration.
C Avoiding involvement in Vietnam.
(D) Removing Communist regimes already in power.

CAPTION ANSWERS

Map Skills The canal runs through Egyptian territory, linking the Red Sea to the Mediterranean. It is vitally important for trade, especially for tankers carrying oil to Europe from the Persian Gulf region. Barring Israel (and ships docking there) from the canal would seriously disrupt and weaken the Israeli economy.

ACTIVITY

Connecting with Government

Have students evaluate the following questions with regard to the CIA: Could there be any situation in which it would be right for the CIA to topple governments and assassinate leaders? Was there justification for such actions in Guatemala and Cuba? How far should the United States go to protect American companies in foreign lands? **(Logical/ Mathematical)**

BACKGROUND

Biography

The bloody fighting between Arabs and Jews that erupted after Israel's declaration of independence in 1948 ended with a truce in 1949. The chief mediator of that truce was UN diplomat Ralph J. Bunche (1904–1971). Formerly a U.S. State Department official, Bunche joined the United Nations at its inception and later oversaw UN peacekeeping operations in the Suez, the Congo, and Cyprus. For his mediation of the Arab-Israeli war, Bunche became the first African American to be awarded the Nobel peace prize.

From *Sputnik* to Space Station

When the Soviets launched *Sputnik* in 1957, they also launched the space race. NASA was established in 1958 to oversee an American space program that could compete with the Soviets. However, in 1961, the Soviets scored another win: the first man in space. Competition continued through the 1960s, but the Americans raised the stakes by landing on the moon in 1969.

The two nations also continued to launch orbiting satellites. In 1973, the American *Skylab* became the first successful space station, but the Soviet *Mir*, launched in 1986, was the most successful, remaining in orbit until 2001. *Mir*, which means "peace" in Russian, also changed the nature of space exploration: it became a cooperative venture. Crews from many nations visited *Mir*, including the United States beginning in 1995. And in 1998, when the United States and Russia began assembling the International Space Station, to which many nations will eventually contribute, a new era of cooperation had truly begun.

? Which kind of "space race" do you think would lead to more progress: competition or cooperation? Explain your reasoning.

January 1957. This policy stated that the United States would use force "to safeguard the independence of any country or group of countries in the Middle East requesting aid against [Communist-inspired] aggression." Eisenhower used his doctrine in 1958 to justify landing troops in Lebanon to put down a revolt against its pro-American government.

Latin America The United States also acted to support pro-American governments and to suppress Communist influences in Latin America, especially where American companies had large investments. Since the mid-1920s, the United States had exercised control over the economies of some ten Latin American nations. In Central America, United States troops had invaded Nicaragua and Honduras to prop up leaders who supported American interests. In 1947, the United States signed the Rio Pact, a regional defense alliance with 18 other nations in the Western Hemisphere. The next year, the United States led the way in forming the Organization of American States (OAS) to increase cooperation among the nations of the hemisphere.

In 1954, the CIA helped overthrow the government of Guatemala on the grounds that its leaders were sympathetic to radical causes. The CIA takeover restored the property of an American corporation, the United Fruit Company, which had been seized by the Guatemalan government. Such actions fueled a Soviet perception that America was escalating the Cold War.

The Arms Race

Throughout the 1950s, the United States and the Soviet Union waged an increasingly intense struggle for world leadership. Nowhere was this competition more dangerous than in the **arms race,** the struggle to gain weapons superiority.

The Growth of Nuclear Arsenals In August 1953, less than a year after the United States exploded its first thermonuclear device, the Soviet Union successfully tested its own hydrogen bomb. As part of the policy of deterrence begun by President Truman, Eisenhower stepped up American weapons development. **Deterrence** is the policy of making the military power of the United States and its allies so strong that no enemy would dare attack for fear of retaliation. Between 1954 and 1958, the United States conducted 19 hydrogen bomb tests in the Pacific. One of these explosions, in March 1954, was over 750 times more powerful than the atomic bomb that had been dropped on Nagasaki in World War II. Japanese fishermen some 90 miles from the blast suffered severe radiation burns. The test was a chilling warning that nuclear war could threaten the entire world with radioactive contamination.

Brinkmanship American policymakers used the fear of nuclear war to achieve their Cold War objectives. In 1956, Secretary of State John Dulles made it clear that the United States was prepared to risk war to protect its national interests. Dulles explained the policy of **brinkmanship** this way: "The ability to get to the verge without getting into the war is the necessary art. If you cannot master it, you inevitably get into war. If you try to run away from it, if you are scared to

CAPTION ANSWERS

Fast Forward to Today Possible answer: Competition and cooperation can both result in progress in terms of exploring space. Competition worked best during the Cold War. Cooperation works well in the post–Cold War era.

RESOURCE DIRECTORY

Teaching Resources

Units 5/6/7 booklet
- Section 4 Quiz, p. 30
- Chapter 19 Test, pp. 31, 34

Guide to the Essentials
- Section 4 Summary, p. 95
- Chapter 19 Test, p. 96

Biography, Literature, and Comparing Primary Sources booklet (Literature) *The Ugly American*, p. 75

Other Print Resources

Chapter Tests with ExamView® Test Bank CD-ROM, Ch. 19

Technology

Color Transparencies *Cause-and-Effect Charts,* D10

Sounds of an Era Audio CD *President Eisenhower's Farewell Address,* 1961 recording (time: 40 seconds)

ExamView® Test Bank CD-ROM, Ch. 19

Social Studies Skills Tutor CD-ROM

go to the brink, you are lost." Many Americans agreed with the reaction of Illinois senator Adlai Stevenson: "I am shocked that the Secretary of State is willing to play Russian roulette with the life of our nation." Still, the Eisenhower administration relied on the policy of brinkmanship.

Cold War in the Skies To carry hydrogen bombs to their targets, American military planners relied mainly on airplanes. Unable to match this strength, the Soviets focused on long-range rockets known as intercontinental ballistic missiles, or **ICBMs.** Americans also worked to develop ICBMs. However, in part because of its dependence on conventional air power, the United States lagged behind the Soviet Union in missile development.

The size of this technology gap became apparent in 1957, when the Soviets used one of their rockets to launch ***Sputnik,*** the first artificial satellite to orbit Earth. The realization that the rocket used to launch *Sputnik* could carry a hydrogen bomb to American shores added to American shock and fear.

This 1959 *Newsweek* illustration shows Soviet leader Khruschev (left) and President Eisenhower (right) using missiles to maintain a balance of power.

In May 1960, the Soviet military again demonstrated its arms capabilities by using a guided missile to shoot down an American U-2 spy plane over Soviet territory. Because these spy planes flew more than 15 miles high, American officials had assumed that they were invulnerable to attack. The **U-2 incident** shattered this confidence, and made Americans willing to expend considerable resources to catch up to—and surpass—the Soviet Union.

One legacy of the Cold War was the creation of what Eisenhower called a "permanent armaments industry of vast proportions." As he left office, he warned that the existence of this military-industrial complex, employing millions of Americans and having a financial stake in war-making, could become a threat to peace:

> *"Our arms must be mighty, ready for instant action. . . . We recognize the imperative need for this development. Yet we must not fail to comprehend its grave implications. . . . [In] government, we must guard against the acquisition of unwarranted [unnecessary] influence, whether sought or unsought, by the military-industrial complex. The potential for the disastrous rise of misplaced power exists and will persist."*
>
> —Dwight D. Eisenhower, Farewell Address, 1961

Section 4 Assessment

READING COMPREHENSION

1. What was **McCarthyism?**
2. What was the **arms race?**
3. How did the policy of **deterrence** influence U.S. actions during the Cold War?
4. How did ***Sputnik*** and the **U-2 incident** affect American public opinion and policy?

CRITICAL THINKING AND WRITING

5. **Identifying Alternatives** When could President Eisenhower have chosen an alternative to containment and the arms race? How might history have been different if he had done so?
6. **Writing a Letter** Write a letter urging a senator of 1952 to oppose Senator McCarthy.

Activity: Writing a Diary Entry
Learn more about *Sputnik* and how Americans reacted to it. Write a diary entry as if you were an American of 1957 who has just heard about the launch of the Soviet satellite. Use the links provided in the *America: Pathways to the Present* area of the following Web site for help in completing this activity.
www.phschool.com

Section 4 Assessment

Reading Comprehension

1. Using baseless rumors and unfounded accusations to destroy someone's reputation and career, a tactic perfected by Senator Joseph McCarthy.
2. The struggle between the United States and the Soviet Union to achieve weapons superiority, particularly in the area of nuclear weapons.
3. It allowed Secretary of State John Foster Dulles to use brinkmanship as a strategy. Dulles's actions put the United States in diplomatic positions where threatening to apply military force presented the danger of starting a war.
4. Americans were shocked and frightened that the Soviet Union was technologically ahead of the United States in the arms race and in space travel. This caused U.S. public opinion and policy to favor a large military buildup to surpass the Soviet Union.

Critical Thinking and Writing

5. Sample answer: President Eisenhower could have intervened when Soviet troops crushed an East German uprising in 1953. This would have caused the United States and the Soviet Union to get into a "hot" war with one another.
6. Answers will vary but should be supported with facts from the section.

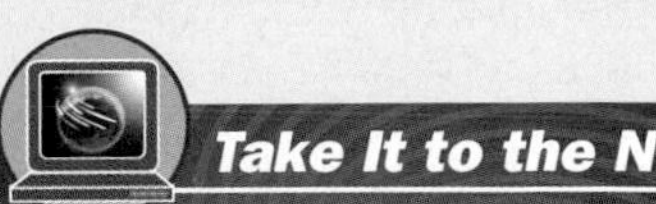

Sample response: Americans were afraid of the dangers posed by Soviet missile development.

CUSTOMIZE FOR ...

ESL

Ask students to write the column headings "Problem" and "Solution" on a piece of paper. In the first column have them list the problems the United States faced in Asia, the Middle East, and Latin America, and in the second column have them write the solutions the United States attempted to carry out.

Chapter 19

Reviewing Key Terms

Students should refer to the definitions of key terms in the chapter to write sentences that show an understanding of the Cold War.

Reviewing Main Ideas

11. Yalta: Germany be divided into zones, Poland hold elections, and the United Nations be formed. Potsdam: Truman and Stalin tried to resolve outstanding issues from Yalta, and Truman alluded to the atomic bomb to intimidate Stalin.
12. U.S.: to bring economic prosperity back to Europe and install democratic governments in recovering nations. Soviet Union: to dominate the satellite nations on its western border and spread communism.
13. Through containment, the U.S. hoped to prevent additional domination by the Soviet Union or internal Communist governments. The Truman Doctrine made it U.S. policy to intervene on behalf of nations in danger of having elected governments overthrown by Communist forces.
14. It helped European nations rebuild economies and gave the U.S. new allies and trading partners.
15. (a) A U.S.–Soviet war could result in the destruction of both nations. (b) By authorizing work on the hydrogen bomb.
16. To provide collective security against Soviet aggression.
17. The Soviet test of an atomic bomb and the establishment of a Communist government in mainland China.
18. (a) The administration began to investigate the background of prospective federal government employees. Congress investigated communism in Hollywood and passed the McCarran-Walter Act, restricting immigration from Communist-leaning regions. (b) They created paranoia and mistrust.
19. China's Nationalist government lost popular support due to corruption and harsh policies, while the Communists won the people's loyalty with reforms.
20. One: Communist invasion of South Korea. Two: United Nations' forces drive North Koreans across the 38th parallel. Three: Stalemate as the

Chapter 19 Review and Assessment

creating a CHAPTER SUMMARY

Copy the diagram (right) onto a piece of paper. Complete it by filling in the the most important causes and effects of the Cold War.

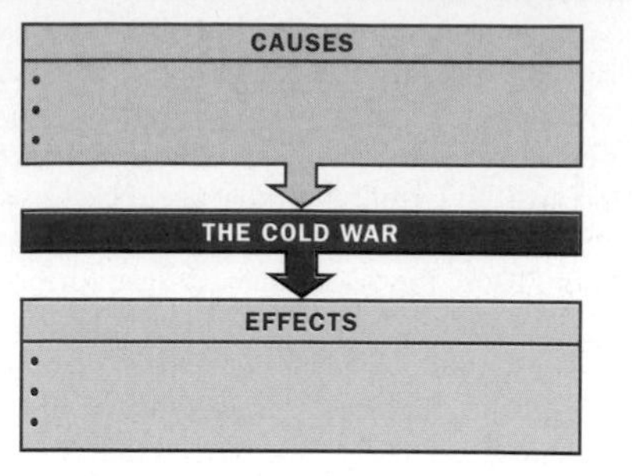

For additional review and enrichment activities, see the interactive version of *America: Pathways to the Present*, available on the Web and on CD-ROM.

★ Reviewing Key Terms

For each of the terms below, write a sentence explaining how it relates to the Cold War.

1. satellite nation
2. iron curtain
3. containment
4. Marshall Plan
5. Warsaw Pact
6. HUAC
7. blacklist
8. 38th parallel
9. brinkmanship
10. U-2 incident

★ Reviewing Main Ideas

11. What decisions were reached at Yalta and Potsdam? (Section 1)
12. Summarize the postwar goals of the United States and the Soviet Union. (Section 1)
13. How did the United States hope to use the policy of containment and the Truman Doctrine to respond to the Soviet creation of an iron curtain? (Section 1)
14. What did the Marshall Plan accomplish in Europe? (Section 2)
15. (a) What was the Soviet atomic threat? (b) How did President Truman respond to it? (Section 2)
16. What was the purpose of NATO? (Section 2)
17. What Communist advances worried Americans in 1949? (Section 2)
18. (a) Describe the efforts by the Truman administration and Congress to stop Communist influence in the United States. (b) How did this anti-Communist effort affect the nation? (Section 2)
19. How did the Communists gain control of China? (Section 3)
20. Describe the three phases of the Korean War. (Section 3)
21. Describe the rise and fall of Senator Joseph McCarthy. (Section 4)
22. How did the Cold War play out in Southeast Asia, the Middle East, and Latin America? (Section 4)
23. Describe the arms race of the 1950s. (Section 4)

★ Critical Thinking

24. **Recognizing Ideologies** Explain how the differing ideologies of the Soviets and the United States were reflected in their Cold War policies.
25. **Predicting Consequences** (a) What principles of American foreign policy did the Berlin airlift put into action? (b) What do you think might have happened if the United States and Britain had not tried the airlift or if the airlift had failed?
26. **Identifying Central Issues** Why do you think that Americans were so willing to believe that Communists had infiltrated the movie industry and the American government?
27. **Expressing Problems Clearly** General MacArthur wanted to pursue the Korean War more aggressively, but President Truman was more cautious. Explain the pros and cons of each position.

Creating a Chapter Summary

The Cold War

Causes	Effects
• U.S. and Soviet Union have had a bad relationship since the Russian Revolution of 1917. • U.S. is angered by Stalin's nonaggression pact with Hitler. • Stalin is angry that U.S. did not invade Europe sooner. • U.S. rejects Soviet Union's demand for war reparations. • Soviets expand sphere of influence. • Stalin predicts triumph of communism over capitalism and urges expansion of communism. • Soviets gain nuclear capability. • China becomes Communist.	• Winston Churchill describes the "iron curtain." • Truman adopts policy of containment (the Truman Doctrine). • NATO is established. • Truman establishes a Loyalty Program for government employees. • McCarthy uses the issue of communism to become a powerful senator. • Korean War is fought. • Eisenhower tries to defeat communism in Southeast Asia, the Middle East, and Latin America. • Beginning of U.S. involvement in Vietnam; beginning of U.S.–Soviet arms buildup • Beginning of U.S.–Soviet space race

★ Skills Assessment

Analyzing Political Cartoons ▶

28. Examine the images in this 1949 cartoon. (a) What is the flame that the man is about to douse? (b) What does the flame represent?
29. (a) What does the man represent? (b) How can you tell?
30. What is the cartoonist's message?

Analyzing Primary Sources

Turn to the excerpt from the Truman Doctrine at the end of Section 1.

31. What was the main purpose of Truman's speech?
    - **A** to frighten the Soviet government
    - **B** to make clear how the United States would respond to Communist aggression
    - **C** to win congressional approval of his containment policy
    - **D** to expand the Cold War
32. What group or groups did Truman promise to help?
    - **F** subjugated minorities
    - **G** armed resistance movements
    - **H** majorities whose freedom was threatened
    - **J** all of the above
33. According to Truman, what two groups might try to subjugate free peoples?
    - **A** free peoples and armed minorities
    - **B** subjugated minorities and outside forces
    - **C** the majority and outsiders
    - **D** outside forces and armed minorities

Applying the Chapter Skill: *Recognizing Cause and Effect*

34. Look back at the Skills for Life page, and review the steps for recognizing cause and effect. Then create a cause-and-effect chain to explain what led to the Marshall Plan and what impact it had.

ACTIVITIES

Writing to LEARN

Writing to Persuade
Review the policy of brinkmanship as stated by John Foster Dulles in Section 4 as well as Adlai Stevenson's objection to that policy. Take a position for or against brinkmanship, and write an editorial that might have appeared in 1956. Create a well-reasoned argument, and support it with specific details.

Primary Source CD-ROM

Working With Primary Sources Find additional information on the Cold War on the *Exploring Primary Sources in U.S. History CD-ROM* and use the selection(s) provided to complete the Chapter 19 primary source activity located in the *America: Pathways to the Present* area of the following Web site.
www.phschool.com

Take It to the NET

Chapter Self-Test As a review activity, take the Chapter 19 Self-Test in the *America: Pathways to the Present* area at the Web site listed below. The questions are designed to test your understanding of the chapter content.
www.phschool.com

ANSWERS TO ACTIVITIES

Writing to LEARN

Sample responses may include: In certain situations, the threat of massive retaliation is worth the price of peace; it is a dangerous policy that could easily lead to all-out war and destruction.

Primary Source CD-ROM

Direct students to the additional primary sources that can be found on the *Exploring Primary Sources in U.S. History CD-ROM.*

Take It to the NET

Additional support materials and activities for Chapter 19 of *America: Pathways to the Present* can be found in the Social Studies area at the Prentice Hall School Web site. **www.phschool.com**

Chinese Communists enter the fighting, resulting in stalemate.

21. McCarthy gained popularity by crusading against communism, and he lost power when he accused the army of housing Communists.
22. Southeast Asia: The U.S. attempted to prevent a Vietnamese Communist government from coming to power in the 1950s. Middle East: The Soviets supported Arab nations; the U.S. supported Israel. Latin America: The U.S. helped bring down a Communist-leaning government in Guatemala.
23. A competition for weapons superiority between the U.S. and the Soviet Union. Both nations tried to build enough nuclear weapons to frighten other nations (but mainly each other).

CRITICAL THINKING

24. The Soviet Union worked to rebuild itself and protect its borders. The U.S. helped rebuild European countries that opposed communism.
25. (a) The Truman Doctrine and the policy of containment. (b) West Berlin could have fallen under Soviet domination.
26. Students may note that both the government and the movie industry had significant influence over Americans' everyday lives. Perhaps this made both seem susceptible to infiltration.
27. MacArthur's position might have ended all Communist domination in China and Korea, but it also could have led to larger war. Truman's position was safer for the U.S., but would not end Communist influence in Asia.

SKILLS ASSESSMENT

28. (a) The torch held by the Statue of Liberty. (b) Liberty.
29. (a) Cold War hysteria; exaggerated fear of communism. (b) The cartoon's date, and the "hysteria" label.
30. Cold War hysteria is threatening American civil liberties.
31. C
32. H
33. D
34. European countries suffer huge losses in World War II; Soviet Union attempts to dominate nearby nations; U.S. uses Marshall Plan to intervene on behalf of non-Communist European countries; the economies of these countries begin to recover; U.S. gains influence and trading partners.

American Innovations in Technology

Focus Tell students that American innovation and invention have fueled our growth and made us a powerful player in the global economy. From the start, American inventions have made us a desirable trading partner. Today our economy reaps many benefits from the technological advances that come from our innovations.

Instruct Tell students to read all of the text carefully. Then ask them to think about how scientific and technological innovations have benefited American citizens. Have them consider how our technical know-how has made us a key player in the world. Why do other countries admire our scientific and technological prowess?

Extend Tell students to research one of the inventions mentioned. Suggest that students learn about the inventor and his or her invention. Tell them to explore the effects of the invention on American culture. Encourage interested students to examine an important invention that wasn't mentioned on these pages but that played a large role in American history.

American Pathways

SCIENCE & TECHNOLOGY

American Innovations in Technology

Technological innovation has always spurred the nation's economic growth. From the Industrial Revolution to the Information Age, American inventiveness has resulted in new and improved products for consumers and increased profits for businesses.

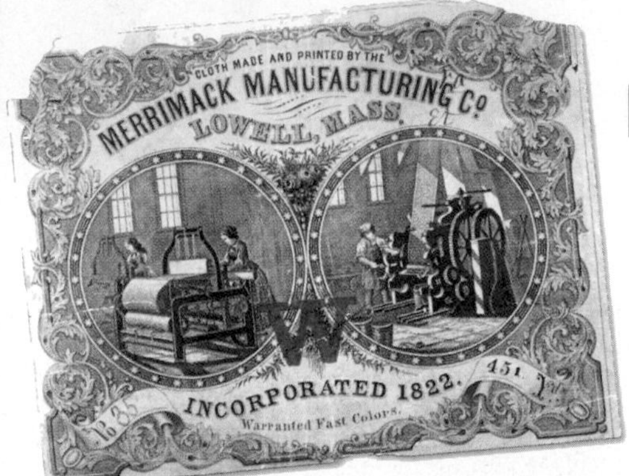

1 A Young and Growing Economy

1790–1850 As the nation expanded westward, a number of innovations such as the cotton gin, the mechanical reaper, and centralized textile factories improved agriculture and encouraged trade.

A textile mill label from Lowell, Massachusetts (left)

2 Industrial Expansion

1850–1890 New inventions such as the telephone and the light bulb, as well as other technological advances such as the first electric power stations, played an important role in the massive industrial expansion that occurred after the Civil War.

Corliss steam engine at the 1876 Centennial Exhibition (left) and the receiving device for Alexander Graham Bell's first telephone call (above)

664

RESOURCE DIRECTORY

Teaching Resources

Units 5/6/7 booklet

- American Pathways Activity, pp. 47–48

American Pathways Thematic Posters

Technology

Companion Web site, www.phschool.com

3 **Becoming a Superpower**

1900–1945 The Allies won two world wars in part because of American technological skills, including the ability to apply assembly-line and other mass-production techniques to the manufacture of war materials.

Boeing B-17 bomber production during the 1940s (above)

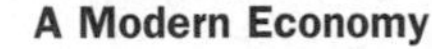

4 **A Modern Economy**

1945–Present The modern American economy has benefited from a steady stream of innovations, especially in the fields of biotechnology, electronics, plastics, aerospace, and computer science.

High-tech devices (above) and an implantable replacement heart (left)

Continuity and Change

1. How did the Erie Canal encourage the growth of agriculture in the West?
2. How did the assembly line improve productivity in the automobile industry?

Take It to the NET: Creating a Study Guide
Print and complete the study guide for this topic found in the *America: Pathways to the Present* area of the following Web site. **www.phschool.com**

Students can print the American Pathways thematic study guide for this topic at the Prentice Hall School Web site, or you can provide students with copies of the study guide, which is found in the Units 5/6/7 booklet, the American Pathways Activity, pages 47–48. Students should use their texts to fill in a one-sentence description for each event on the study guide. When completed for each of the American Pathways topics, the thematic study guides will aid students in preparing for an end-of-course exam.

Answers

1. By improving east-west transportation, the Erie Canal helped populate the West and provided farmers there with a faster route to east coast markets.
2. Workers stayed in one place while the assembly line moved the vehicles to them. Also, workers specialized in just one part of the assembly. These factors enabled the assembly line to greatly speed the production of vehicles.

Chapter 20 Planning Guide
Resource Manager

	Core Instruction	Reading/Skills
Chapter-Level Resources **TEKS** 24(B)	Teaching Resources • Pacing Charts booklet • Block Scheduling booklet **Resource Pro® CD-ROM,** Ch. 20 **Prentice Hall Presentation Pro CD-ROM,** Ch. 20 **www.phschool.com** • eTeach	**Guided Reading Audiotapes (English/Spanish)** **Student Edition on Audio CD,** Ch. 20 **Social Studies Skills Tutor CD-ROM** **Color Transparency,** B15
1 The Postwar Economy 1. Find out how businesses reorganized after World War II. 2. Learn how technology transformed life after World War II. 3. Discover ways in which the nation's workforce changed after World War II. 4. See how subways and highway systems grew after World War II. 5. Understand how postwar conditions affected consumer credit. **TEKS** 6(F), 8(A), 14(B), 22(A), 22(B), 22(C), 22(D), 23(A) 24(F), 24(H), 25(D)	Teaching Resources **Units 5/6/7 booklet** • Section 1 Quiz, p. 38 **Learning Styles Lesson Plans booklet,** p. 56	**Guided Reading and Review booklet,** p. 109 **Guide to the Essentials,** p. 97 **Learning with Documents booklet,** p. 66 **Section Reading Support Transparencies**
2 The Mood of the 1950s 1. Find out why comfort and security were so important to Americans in the 1950s. 2. Learn about the accepted roles of men and women during the 1950s. 3. See how some people challenged conformity in the 1950s. **TEKS** 20(A), 20(B), 24(A)	Teaching Resources **Units 5/6/7 booklet** • Section 2 Quiz, p. 39 **Learning Styles Lesson Plans booklet,** p. 57	**Guided Reading and Review booklet,** p. 110 **Guide to the Essentials,** p. 98 **Section Reading Support Transparencies**
3 Domestic Politics and Policy 1. Discover Truman's Domestic policies as outlined in the Fair Deal. 2. Learn how Truman won the election of 1948. 3. Understand the Republican approach to government during the Eisenhower presidency. **TEKS** 10(A), 17(B), 19(A), 19(C), 24(A), 24(D), 24(H)	Teaching Resources **Units 5/6/7 booklet** • Section 3 Quiz, p. 40	**Guided Reading and Review booklet,** p. 111 **Guide to the Essentials,** p. 99 **Learning with Documents booklet,** p. 32 **Skills for Life booklet,** p. 29 **Section Reading Support Transparencies**

Enrichment/Pre-AP

Prentice Hall United States History Video Collection™
www.phschool.com
- Section Activities, Virtual Field Trip, Chapter Activities, Current Events Online

Biography, Literature, and Comparing Primary Sources booklet, p. 20
American History Block Scheduling Support
Sounds of an Era Audio CD
Exploring Primary Sources in U.S. History CD-ROM

Biography, Literature, and Comparing Primary Sources booklet, pp. 149–150
Sounds of an Era Audio CD

Biography, Literature, and Comparing Primary Sources booklet, pp. 76–77
Sounds of an Era Audio CD
American Pathways Thematic Posters

Assessment

Core Assessment
ExamView® Test Bank, Ch. 20
ExamView® Test Bank CD-ROM, Ch. 20
Standardized Test Preparation

Diagnose and Prescribe
Diagnostic Tests for High School Social Studies Skills

Review and Reteach
Review Book for U.S. History

Practice and Assess
Test-taking Strategies With Transparencies
Test-taking Strategies Posters
Test Prep Book for U.S. History
Alternative Assessment Handbook
Document-Based Assessment

Teaching Resources
Units 5/6/7 booklet
- Section Quizzes, pp. 38–40
- Chapter Tests, pp. 41, 44

www.phschool.com Ch. 20 Self-Test

AmericanHeritage® Resources

From the Archives of American Heritage®, pp. 682, 683, 684
AmericanHeritage® My Brush with History™ Videotapes
www.americanheritage.com

Don't miss the exclusive interactive version of this textbook on the Web and on CD-ROM.

Chapter 20 Planning Guide

In Your Classroom

Customize for Individual Needs

Gifted and Talented

Teacher's Edition
- Customize for Gifted and Talented, p. 677

Teaching Resources
- Biography, Literature, and Comparing Primary Sources booklet, pp. 20, 76–77, 149–150

Technology
- Exploring Primary Sources in U.S. History CD-ROM *Dr. Salk and His Vaccine*

ESL

Teacher's Edition
- Customize for ESL, p. 669

Teaching Resources
- Guided Reading and Review booklet, pp. 109–111
- Guide to the Essentials (English/Spanish), Chapter 20

Technology
- Student Edition on Audio CD, Chapter 20
- Guided Reading Audiotapes (English/Spanish), Chapter 20
- Section Reading Support Transparencies

Less Proficient Readers

Teacher's Edition
- Customize for Less Proficient Readers, p. 673

Teaching Resources
- Guided Reading and Review booklet, pp. 109–111
- Guide to the Essentials (English/Spanish), Chapter 20

Technology
- Student Edition on Audio CD, Chapter 20
- Guided Reading Audiotapes (English/Spanish), Chapter 20
- Section Reading Support Transparencies

Less Proficient Writers

Teacher's Edition
- Customize for Less Proficient Writers, p. 683

Teaching Resources
- Guided Reading and Review booklet, pp. 109–111
- Guide to the Essentials (English/Spanish), Chapter 20

Technology
- Student Edition on Audio CD, Chapter 20
- Guided Reading Audiotapes (English/Spanish), Chapter 20
- Section Reading Support Transparencies

Teacher's Edition Index

Chapter 20 – Pacing Suggestions

For 90-minute Blocks

- Teach sections 1 and 3 using Transparency B15, and the Recent Scholarship note on page 685 for class discussions.

Running Out of Time?

If you are running short on time to cover this chapter, consider the following options:

- Use the Prentice Hall Presentation Pro CD-ROM to create an outline for this chapter.
- Use the Section Summaries for Chapter 20, from **Guide to the Essentials (English/Spanish).**

TEKS Correlation

Chapter-Level	TEKS
	(24) Social studies skills. The student applies critical-thinking skills to organize and use information acquired from a variety of sources including electronic technology. The student is expected to: **(B)** analyze information by sequencing, categorizing, identifying cause-and-effect relationships, comparing, contrasting, finding the main idea, summarizing, making generalizations and predictions, and drawing inferences and conclusions.
1 The Postwar Economy	**(6) History.** The student understands the impact of significant national and international decisions and conflicts from World War II and the Cold War to the present on the United States. The student is expected to: **(F)** describe the impact of the GI Bill, the election of 1948, McCarthyism, and Sputnik I. **(8) Geography.** The student uses geographic tools to collect, analyze, and interpret data. The student is expected to: **(A)** create thematic maps, graphs, charts, models, and databases representing various aspects of the United States. **(14) Economics.** The student understands the economic effects of World War II, the Cold War, and increased worldwide competition on contemporary society. The student is expected to: **(B)** identify the causes and effects of prosperity in the 1950s. **(22) Science, technology, and society.** The student understands the impact of science and technology on the economic development of the United States. The student is expected to: **(A)** explain the effects of scientific discoveries and technological innovations such as electric power, the telegraph and telephone, petroleum-based products, medical vaccinations, and computers on the development of the United States. **(B)** explain how scientific discoveries and technological innovations such as those in agriculture, the military, and medicine resulted from specific needs. **(C)** analyze the impact of technological innovations on the nature of work, the American labor movement, and business. **(D)** use the process of historical inquiry to research, interpret, and use multiple sources of evidence. **(23) Science, technology, and society.** The student understands the influence of scientific discoveries and technological innovations on daily life in the United States. The student is expected to: **(A)** analyze how scientific discoveries and technological innovations, including those in transportation and communication, have changed the standard of living in the United States. **(24) Social studies skills.** The student applies critical-thinking skills to organize and use information acquired from a variety of sources including electronic technology. The student is expected to: **(F)** identify bias in written, oral, and visual material. **(H)** use appropriate mathematical skills to interpret social studies information such as maps and graphs. **(25) Social studies skills.** The student communicates in written, oral, and visual forms. The student is expected to: **(D)** create written, oral, and visual presentations of social studies information.
2 The Mood of the 1950s	**(20) Culture.** The student understands the relationship between the arts and the times during which they were created. The student is expected to: **(A)** describe how the characteristics and issues of various eras in U.S. history have been reflected in works of art, music, and literature such as the paintings of Georgia O'Keeffe, rock and roll, and John Steinbeck's *The Grapes of Wrath.* **(B)** describe the impact of significant examples of cultural movements in art, music, and literature on American society, including the Harlem Renaissance. **(24) Social studies skills.** The student applies critical-thinking skills to organize and use information acquired from a variety of sources including electronic technology. The student is expected to: **(A)** locate and use primary and secondary sources such as computer software, databases, media and news services, biographies, interviews, and artifacts to acquire information about the United States.
3 Domestic Politics and Policy	**(10) Geography.** The student understands the effects of migration and immigration on American society. The student is expected to: **(A)** analyze the effects of changing demographic patterns resulting from migration within the United States. **(17) Government.** The student understands the impact of constitutional issues on American society in the 20th century. The student is expected to: **(B)** analyze reasons for the adoption of 20th-century constitutional amendments. **(19) Citizenship.** The student understands the importance of effective leadership in a democratic society. The student is expected to: **(A)** describe the qualities of effective leadership. **(C)** identify the contributions of Texans who have been President of the United States. **(24) Social studies skills.** The student applies critical-thinking skills to organize and use information acquired from a variety of sources including electronic technology. The student is expected to: **(A)** locate and use primary and secondary sources such as computer software, databases, media and news services, biographies, interviews, and artifacts to acquire information about the United States. **(D)** use the process of historical inquiry to research, interpret, and use multiple sources of evidence. **(H)** use appropriate mathematical skills to interpret social studies information such as maps and graphs.

Chapter 20

The Postwar Years at Home

(1945–1960)

INTRODUCING THE CHAPTER

As the United States emerged from World War II, the American Dream of having a secure job and owning a house came within reach for many Americans. Fueled by the postwar baby boom, the economy rocketed forward in the late 1940s and 1950s.

TIME LINE ACTIVITY

To provide students with practice in using the time line, ask questions such as these:

1. What event took place in 1947 that would have a huge impact on later technological development? *(The transistor was invented.)*
2. What 1951 event would eventually lead to a cultural revolution? *(Alan Freed played the first rock-and-roll music on a Cleveland radio station.)*
3. What 1957 event would lead to a space race between the United States and the Soviet Union? *(The Soviet Union launched* Sputnik.*)*

Chapter 20

The Postwar Years at Home (1945–1960)

Plastic flamingos were popular lawn ornaments in the 1950s.

A Levittown suburb

This sign sat on President Truman's desk.

American Events

- **1944** Congress passes the GI Bill of Rights.
- **1946** Dr. Spock publishes *The Common Sense Book of Baby and Child Care.*
- **1947** Congress passes the Taft-Hartley Act. The first transistor is invented, spurring growth in computers and electronics.

Presidential Terms: Franklin D. Roosevelt 1933–1945; Harry S Truman 1945–1953

1940 · 1945 · 1950

World Events

- **1947** Thor Heyerdahl and his crew sail the raft *Kon-Tiki* from Peru to Polynesia.
- **1949** English novelist George Orwell's *Nineteen Eighty-Four* is published.

eTeach

Be sure to check out this month's online discussion with a Master Teacher. Go to **www.phschool.com**.

RESOURCE DIRECTORY

Teaching Resources

Pacing Charts booklet
Block Scheduling booklet, p. 26
Units 5/6/7 booklet
- Chapter Summary, p. 37

Technology

Guided Reading Audiotapes (English/Spanish), Ch. 20
Student Edition on Audio CD, Ch. 20
Prentice Hall United States History Video Collection™ Volume 20, *Postwar USA*
Prentice Hall Presentation Pro CD-ROM, Ch. 20
Resource Pro® CD-ROM
Social Studies Skills Tutor CD-ROM
Companion Web site, www.phschool.com

Regional Migration, 1940–1960

Net regional migration by race, 1940–1960

—— Limit of population zone

Black migration White migration

2,000 / 1,000 / 0

Approximate number of migrants (in thousands)

The Growth of Suburban St. Louis, Missouri 1950–1960

Increases in percentages: 100 / 70 / 50 / 20 / Decrease / No basis for comparison

City of St. Louis

Singer, songwriter, and guitarist Chuck Berry greatly influenced rock-and-roll.

1951 Disc jockey and music promoter Alan Freed begins hosting a radio show, featuring music that comes to be known as "rock-and-roll."

1953 The double-helix model for DNA is formulated in London.

1954 Successful tests are conducted on a polio vaccine.

1955

1956 The Federal-Aid Highway Act funds an interstate highway system.

1957 The Soviet Union launches *Sputnik.*

1958 Congress passes the National Defense Education Act and establishes the National Aeronautics and Space Administration.

1959 The Soviet Union launches three lunar probes.

1960

Dwight D. Eisenhower 1953–1961

Regional Migration, 1940–1960

Activating Prior Knowledge Most of the migrating African Americans moved in what general direction? *(Northward)*

Previewing What does the map of suburban St. Louis show about regional migration? *(People were leaving the city for the suburbs.)*

Background

About the Pictures

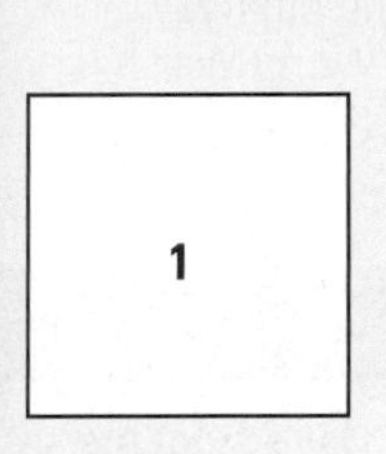

1. Designed and built by Levitt and Sons, Inc. in the 1950s, Levittown was a planned suburban development in Pennsylvania that was then reproduced in communities across the United States.
2. Flamingos, along with dogs, ducks, and frogs, began appearing on lawns in two-dimensional forms in 1946. In 1957 a man named Don Featherstone sculpted the first three-dimensional plastic flamingo, soon to be found on suburban lawns everywhere.
3. This phrase is a reply to the act of "passing the buck," or transferring responsibility from one person to the next and avoiding blame. Truman wanted to make clear that he would take all responsibility for the actions of his administration.
4. Berry's music drew from a broad range of influences, including rhythm and blues, country-western, gospel, and music from the Caribbean to create his brand of rock-and-roll.

Bibliography

For the Teacher

Halberstam, David. ***The Fifties.*** Fawcett, 1994. (A comprehensive look at the social, political, economic, and cultural history of the 1950s.)

Marling, Karal Ann. ***As Seen on TV: The Visual Culture of Everyday Life in the 1950s.*** Harvard University Press, 1996. (Combines social commentary with a vivid recapturing of the dawn of the television era.)

For the Student

Drake, Albert. ***Fifties Flashback: A Nostalgic Trip!*** California Bill's Automotive, 2000. (A car buff offers nostalgic memories of the way things were in the 1950s.)

Stolley, Richard B. ***The American Dream: The 50s.*** Time-Life Books, 2000. (Richly illustrated and comprehensive study of the 1950s.)

Don't miss the exclusive interactive version of this textbook on the Web and on CD-ROM.

Section 1
The Postwar Economy

Section Objectives

1. Find out how businesses reorganized after World War II.
2. Learn how technology transformed life after World War II.
3. Discover ways in which the nation's workforce changed after World War II.
4. See how suburbs and highway systems grew after World War II.
5. Understand how postwar conditions affected consumer credit.

Bellringer

Warm-Up Activity Have students think of an invention that would be totally new to a person from the 1950s who was suddenly transported to the present.

Activating Prior Knowledge Television was a new phenomenon in the 1950s. Can students list some ways they think the introduction of television into homes changed families' lives?

Reading Strategy

Have students make a chart with two headings, one reading *Causes of Prosperity,* the other reading *Effects of Prosperity.* As they read the section, have them identify the causes and effects of prosperity in the 1950s.

Section 1

The Postwar Economy

READING FOCUS

- How did businesses reorganize after World War II?
- How did technology transform life after World War II?
- In what ways did the nation's work force change following World War II?
- Why did suburbs and highway systems grow after World War II?
- How did postwar conditions affect consumer credit?

MAIN IDEA

The "American Dream," characterized by a home in the suburbs and a car in the garage, became reality for many people in the postwar years.

KEY TERMS

per capita income
conglomerate
franchise
transistor
baby boom
GI Bill of Rights

TAKING NOTES

Copy the outline below. As you read, fill in information about the postwar economy. Use Roman numerals to indicate the major headings, capital letters for the subheadings, and numbers for the supporting details.

1950s Economic Expansion
I. Businesses Reorganize
A. Corporate expansion accompanies growth.
1. ______
2. ______
B. ______

VIEWING HISTORY A wounded World War II soldier returns to his family in New York. **Drawing Conclusions** *What were some expectations of former servicemen and their families after the war?*

Setting the Scene When American soldiers returned from the battlefields, they wanted to put the horrors of the war behind them and enjoy the comforts of home. During the war, many items were rationed or not produced at all. Many people had simply put their money into savings. Now most Americans were eager to acquire everything the war—and before that, the Depression—had denied them.

The marriage rate increased dramatically after the war, and the population boomed. Fueled by a growing economy, suburbs sprang up with look-alike houses in answer to a postwar housing shortage. One writer observed:

> *"Socially, these communities have neither history, tradition, nor established structure. . . . Everybody lives in a 'good neighborhood'; there is, to use that classic American euphemism, no 'wrong side of the tracks.'"*
>
> —Harry Henderson, "The Mass-Produced Suburbs," *Harper's,* 1953

Suburban families enjoyed incomes that were considerably higher than those in rural communities. They spent large sums of money on recreation. By the end of the 1950s, about 75 percent of families owned a car, and even more owned a TV set. America's consumer economy was thriving.

Businesses Reorganize

During the postwar years, the United States embarked on one of its greatest periods of economic expansion. The gross national product (GNP) more than doubled, jumping from $212 billion in 1945 to $504 billion in 1960. **Per capita income,** the average annual income per person, increased from $1,223 to $2,219 during the same period.

Caption Answers

Viewing History After the war, servicemen and their families wanted to be able to buy items that they couldn't afford during the Depression, or that were rationed during the war.

RESOURCE DIRECTORY

Teaching Resources
Learning Styles Lesson Plans booklet, p. 56
Guided Reading and Review booklet, p. 109

Technology
Section Reading Support Transparencies
Guided Reading Audiotapes (English/Spanish), Ch. 20
Student Edition on Audio CD, Ch. 20
Prentice Hall Presentation Pro CD-ROM, Ch. 20
Companion Web site, www.phschool.com

Major corporate expansion accompanied economic growth. Industrialists fully intended to provide consumers the goods they desired, as they reconverted their businesses to civilian production at the end of the war. At the same time, American industry had benefited from technological advances made during the war. Research and development—funded by the government—helped create a variety of new products, such as radar and the computer, that could be used in the civilian economy.

READING CHECK
How did the war influence corporate expansion?

In the 1950s, a few large firms dominated many industries. General Motors, Ford, and Chrysler overshadowed all competitors in the automobile industry; General Electric and Westinghouse enjoyed similar positions in the electrical industry. The Great Depression, however, had made many giant corporations wary of investing all their resources in a single business. A **conglomerate,** a corporation made up of three or more unrelated businesses, was better able to defend against economic downturns. For this reason, some corporations chose to become conglomerates. In the event one industry or area of the economy failed, the conglomerate could rely on its earnings in another industry. International Telephone and Telegraph, for example, purchased Avis Rent-a-Car, Sheraton Hotels, Hartford Fire Insurance, and Continental Baking.

At the same time, another kind of expansion took place. In 1954, salesman Ray Kroc was amazed when two brothers who owned a restaurant in San Bernardino, California, gave him an order for their eighth Multimixer, a brand of milkshake machine. With eight machines, the restaurant could make 40 milkshakes at once. Because of the restaurant's fast, efficient service and its prime location along a busy highway, it was experiencing great success. Intrigued by the possibilities, Kroc purchased the two brothers' idea of assembly-line food production. He also acquired the restaurant's name: McDonald's. Kroc built a nationwide chain of fast-food restaurants by selling eager entrepreneurs the right to open a **franchise**—a business that contracts to offer certain goods and services from a larger parent company. Franchise agreements vary from one company to the next, but generally the contracts allow each owner to use the company's name, suppliers, products, and production methods. Each franchise, then, is operated as a small business whose owners profit from the parent company's guidance. Franchise owners assume less risk than small business owners, in that they sell a product that is well known—and presumably liked by the consumer. Many other restaurant franchises followed.

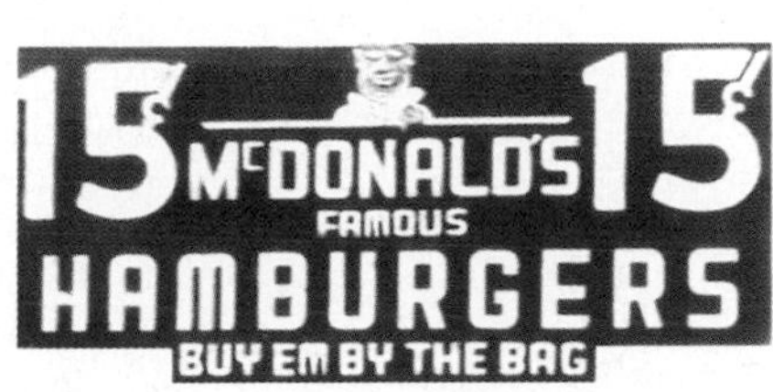

This sign at the original fast-food restaurant in San Bernardino, California, advertised the McDonald brothers' hamburgers.

The franchise system flourished in the 1950s. Other kinds of businesses, such as clothing stores and automobile muffler shops, also adopted the franchise method. Some small businesses suffered from the growth of the franchise system. As nationwide chains grew popular with consumers, independent businesses declined, unable to compete successfully.

Technology Transforms Life

Meanwhile, developments in technology spurred industrial growth. Rushing to keep up with demand, businesses produced hundreds of new products, such as dishwashers and gas-powered lawnmowers, aimed at saving the consumer time and money. Eager Americans filled their homes with the latest inventions.

Television Americans fell in love with television in the 1950s. The technology for television had been developed throughout the late 1920s and 1930s, but then stalled during the war. After World War II, television became enormously

Westerns featuring Hopalong Cassidy aired on TV during the 1950s.

LESSON PLAN

Focus The nation's economy boomed during the postwar years. Ask students how this boom changed American life.

Instruct Explain that after World War II, people wanted to enjoy the comforts that war had denied them. Ask students to explain why the economy expanded after World War II. What new ways of organizing businesses developed in response to the growing economy?

Ask students for examples of new technology after World War II that changed American culture and work. How did the widespread use of the automobile lead to the growth of consumer credit? Why does a credit-driven economy move faster than a cash-only economy? Have students describe the relationship between the growth of white-collar jobs, the creation of the suburbs, and the "car culture."

Assess/Reteach Ask students to explain how scientific discoveries and technological innovations that made their way into society in the 1950s arose from specific needs. What was the impact of those innovations on the nature of work and businesses?

ACTIVITY: Connecting with Culture

Have students write journal entries in which they address the idea of living in a new suburb that, as Harry Henderson wrote, has "neither history, nor tradition, nor established structure" but is a "'good neighborhood.'" What are the advantages and disadvantages of life in such a community? **(Verbal/Linguistic)**

READING CHECK
Industry benefited from government-funded technological advances made during the war to create new products for consumers in the postwar years.

CUSTOMIZE FOR ...
ESL

Model an outline of the section, using the major and minor subsection headings, on the chalkboard. Divide students into six groups and have each group read one subsection. Then have a volunteer from each group come up to the chalkboard and, with help, fill in the section of the outline assigned to his or her group. Students should copy the entire outline on a piece of paper.

ACTIVITY
Connecting with Culture

Today we take business franchises for granted, but after World War II the franchise was a new concept, designed to address the growing consumer demand in the United States. Divide students into small groups and have them list as many franchises as possible in five minutes. Discuss how the increasing number of franchises contributed to the growing economy after World War II. Then have the groups list two positive and two negative effects of franchises. **(Logical/Mathematical)**

BACKGROUND
Technology

Television's growth into a powerful force in public opinion was foreshadowed by the results of televising the 36-day hearing on Senator Joseph McCarthy's charges of subversion by U.S. Army officers and civilian officials in 1954. As a result of viewing McCarthy's brutal and overbearing manner at the hearing, his popularity waned, and public opinion began to turn against him.

popular. Although taped programs later became the norm, live broadcasts in the early days of television made the shows especially exciting to watch.

In 1955, the average American family watched television four to five hours a day. Children grew up on such programs as *Howdy Doody* and *The Mickey Mouse Club*. Teenagers danced to rock-and-roll music played on *American Bandstand*, a forerunner to today's MTV. Other viewers followed comedies, including *I Love Lucy* and *Father Knows Best*. A 1949 *McCall's* article described the importance of television at the time: "Many couples credit television, which simultaneously eased baby-sitting, entertainment, and financial problems, with having brought them closer. . . . Though often contemptuous of many programs, they speak of TV gratefully as 'something we can share.' . . ."

Three large networks controlled television programming. As had been the case with radio, they raised the money to broadcast their shows by selling advertising time. Television became a powerful new medium for advertisers, allowing them to reach millions of viewers. As a result, Americans watched their favorite shows interrupted by commercials, a practice that continues today.

The Computer Industry Another innovation appeared in the 1950s that would transform American life in the years to come. Wartime research led to the development of ever more powerful calculators and computers. During the 1950s, American businesses reached out to embrace the computer industry. Grace Hopper, a research fellow at Harvard University's computation laboratory, pioneered the creation of software that ran computers. She also introduced the term *debugging*—which was born when she removed a moth that had become caught in a relay switch and had caused a large computer to shut down. Today the term means "ridding a computer program of errors."

In 1947, scientists at Bell Telephone Laboratories invented the first **transistor,** a tiny circuit device that amplifies, controls, and generates electrical signals. The transistor could do the work of a much larger vacuum tube, but took up less

Fast Forward to Today

Television Viewing

After inventor Philo Taylor Farnsworth transmitted the first electronic television image in 1927, he hoped that television would become an important educational tool. Instead, he was dismayed at the programs he saw on television in the 1950s and 1960s, as well as the amount of time people spent watching TV. He refused to allow his children to watch television when they were growing up, telling them, "I don't want it in your intellectual diet."

Today many adults share Farnsworth's concerns about television content and viewing habits. Researchers have suggested links between TV viewing and lower reading scores for children, obesity, and violent behavior. The introduction of program rating systems and the v-chip, which allows parents to block out programs that have certain ratings, came about in response to such concerns.

The graph (left) and chart (above) indicate television's popularity with the American public over time.

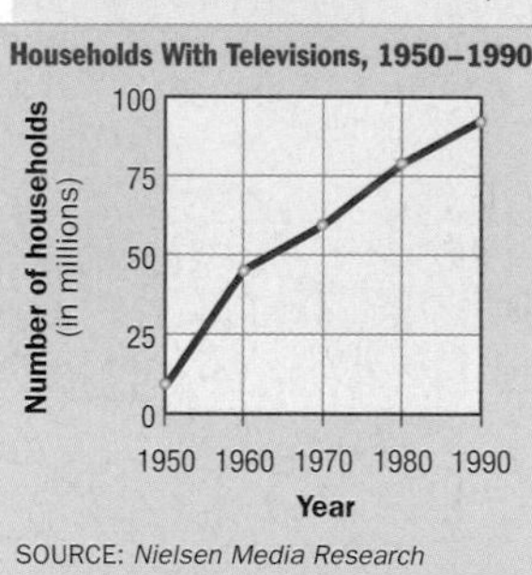

Average Household TV Viewing Hours, 1950–1990

Year	Average Daily Viewing per Household
1950	4 hours, 35 minutes
1960	5 hours, 6 minutes
1970	5 hours, 56 minutes
1980	6 hours, 36 minutes
1990	6 hours, 55 minutes

SOURCE: *Nielsen Media Research*

? Study the graph (left), "Households With Televisions, 1950–1990." Why would more people have acquired TV sets in the 1950s than in any of the other decades shown? Explain.

CAPTION ANSWERS

Fast Forward to Today Television first became widely available in the 1950s. Since it quickly became wildly popular, it seemed that everyone wanted to purchase a television set, hence the buying spree of the 1950s. The likely reason for slower sales of television sets in later decades is that almost 50 million households already possessed at least one television set by 1960.

RESOURCE DIRECTORY

Teaching Resources

Biography, Literature, and Comparing Primary Sources booklet (Biography) *Ray A. Kroc,* p. 20

Learning with Documents booklet (Visual Learning Activity) *The Miracle of Television,* p. 66

Other Print Resources

American History Block Scheduling Support *The Age of Affluence and "Trouble in the Fields": The Decline of the Family Farm,* found in the Nation After World War II folder, includes interdisciplinary lesson suggestions and activities for Geography and History, Primary Sources, Biography, and Literature.

Technology

Exploring Primary Sources in U.S. History CD-ROM *Dr. Salk and His Vaccine*

space and generated less heat. The transistor could be used in radios, computers, and other electronic devices, and greatly changed the electronics industry. Because of the transistor, giant machines that once filled whole rooms could now fit on a desk. Calculations that had taken hours could now be performed in fractions of a second. The Census Bureau purchased one of the first new computer systems to tally the 1950 census.

VIEWING HISTORY The vacuum tube (top left) was used in radios prior to the invention and development of the transistor (bottom left). The transistor radio (top) was among many new electronic products the invention made possible. **Making Comparisons** *Compare the size of the vacuum tube to that of the transistor. How did the size of the tube limit its uses?*

Nuclear Power An entirely new industry, the generation of electrical power through the use of atomic energy, resulted from the research that had produced the atomic bomb. Nuclear fission, which involves splitting uranium or plutonium atoms, could produce a huge explosion if the reaction occurred quickly. But fission, carefully controlled, could also produce heat to generate steam and drive electrical turbines. In 1954, the Navy produced the first nuclear-powered submarine, which had a small reactor in the hull. The submarine's technology provided a model for the first nuclear power plant on land, which opened in Shippingport, Pennsylvania, in 1957. The 1956 children's book *The Walt Disney Story of Our Friend the Atom,* by scientist Heinz Haber, explored the potential uses of atomic energy during peacetime. The accompanying Disney film, *Our Friend the Atom,* gave many children their first glimpse into what has since been referred to as the atomic age.

Advances in Medicine Americans also found hope in developments made in medicine. In 1954, Dr. Jonas Salk and Dr. Thomas Francis conducted a successful field test of a vaccine to prevent one of the most feared diseases—poliomyelitis. Before the vaccine, the disease, known commonly as polio, had killed or disabled more than 20,000 children in the United States every year. As you have read, Franklin D. Roosevelt suffered the effects of polio throughout much of his life. Just before the polio vaccine's success was to be reported, Salk wrote to FDR's widow Eleanor: "The scientific report, that may mark the beginning of the end of the scourge of polio, is to be made on the Tenth Anniversary of Mr. Roosevelt's untimely death. Wherever you may be, or whatever your thoughts, I would like you to know that a part of his great spirit will be within me, living as it was during his great life, while we all share the knowledge that may bring the fulfillment of the dream he had many years ago." Salk's injected vaccine, together with an oral version developed later by Dr. Albert Sabin, effectively eliminated the threat of polio.

Research in the development of drugs used to fight bacterial infections had been underway long before the start of World War II. By 1944, advances in the production of antibiotics such as penicillin were saving countless lives. During the 1950s, doctors discovered other antibiotics that were effective against penicillin-resistant bacteria.

Doctors who had served during the war saving the lives of wounded soldiers helped usher in a new era of surgical advances. Surgical techniques developed during the war allowed doctors to correct heart defects, and the specialty of heart surgery grew rapidly.

VIEWING HISTORY Jonas Salk is shown administering his new polio vaccine. **Drawing Inferences** *How did the availability of the vaccine change the lives of Americans?*

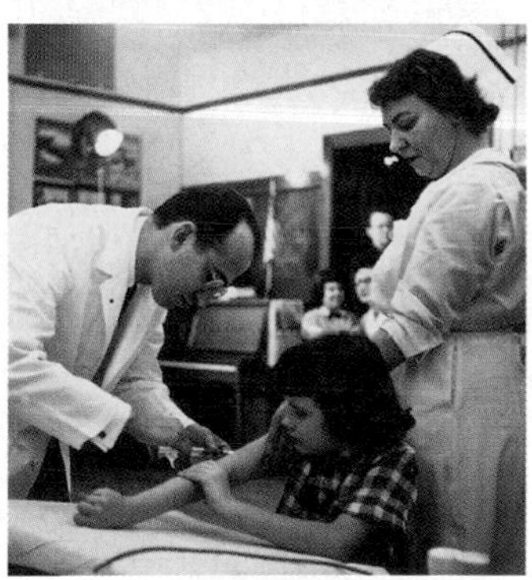

Changes in the Work Force

In earlier years, most Americans made a living as blue-collar workers, producing goods or performing services that depended on manual labor. After the war, however, new machines performed many of the jobs previously done by people. Some blue-collar workers found their way into white-collar jobs. Young people, particularly former servicemen with new college degrees,

ACTIVITY
Connecting with Science and Technology

The first nuclear-powered submarine was the USS *Nautilus.* Direct students to conduct research on this historic vessel and then create a multimedia presentation or a written report about the history and accomplishments of the *Nautilus.* **(Visual/Spatial)**

BACKGROUND
Interdisciplinary

The new nuclear technology had few detractors and fewer restrictions. From the 1940s to the early 1970s, the federal government exposed as many as 1,800 people to radiation in experiments that provided little or no medical benefit. In early 1994, Congressman Ed Markey (Democrat, Massachusetts) said that "the appalling truth is that in some cases American citizens were used as nuclear calibration instruments."

CAPTION ANSWERS

Viewing History The vacuum tube is much bigger than the transistor and could not be used in small electronic devices.

Viewing History Polio had been responsible for killing or disabling more than 20,000 children in the U.S. every year. Adults, including Franklin Roosevelt, also contracted the disease. After the vaccine was available, parents could feel more optimistic about their children's safety as well as their own.

ACTIVITY
Connecting with Culture

Draw students' attention to this comment by C. Wright Mills: "When white-collar people get jobs, they sell not only their time and energy but their personalities as well." Invite volunteers to explain what Mills meant by his remark. Then conduct a whole-class debate in response to the comment. Students could focus on such approaches as: 1) whether or not they agree with the statement, and 2) if students think his statement reflects a problem, what they think should be done to address the problem. Encourage students to make the connection between conformity at their school and conformity in the workplace. **(Verbal/Linguistic)**

BACKGROUND
Interdisciplinary

It is difficult to overstate the influence that the GI Bill of Rights had on the postwar housing boom in the United States. Between 1945 and 1965, about 20 percent—one in five—of all the single-family houses built in the country were financed, at least in part, by mortgages guaranteed by the GI Bill of Rights.

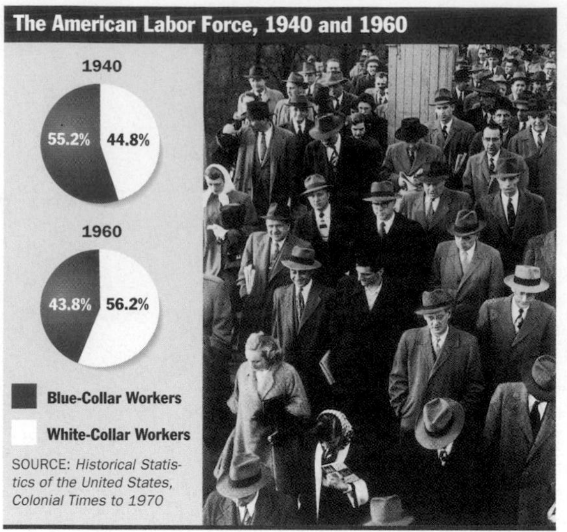

INTERPRETING GRAPHS
These Chicago-area commuters (above right) display some of the conformity that characterized the labor force in the 1950s. The graph above shows the American labor force in 1940 and 1960. **Making Comparisons** *How did the labor force change from 1940 to 1960? Be specific.*

also gravitated toward white-collar jobs as they entered the work force for the first time. Corporate expansion meant that more people were needed to keep growing organizations running. By 1956, a majority of American workers held white-collar jobs, managing offices, working in sales, and performing professional and clerical duties in which manual labor was not an essential element.

The growth of the service industry had a great effect on the lives of Americans. The new white-collar workers felt encouraged by the working conditions they found: the buildings were clean, the offices bright. Physically, the work was less exhausting than blue-collar labor, it was not as dangerous, and some workers had the opportunity to rise into executive positions. But office jobs had their drawbacks. Employment in large corporations was often impersonal. White-collar workers in large companies had less connection with the products and services that their companies provided. Employees sometimes felt pressure to dress, think, and act alike. Sociologist C. Wright Mills commented: "When white-collar people get jobs, they sell not only their time and energy but their personalities as well."

In the blue-collar sector, working conditions and wages improved during the 1940s and 1950s. During this period, workers in some unions won important gains, such as guaranteed cost-of-living increases, designed to adjust wages to keep up with the rate of inflation. By 1955, nearly 33 percent of the total labor force in the United States was unionized. In that year, the two largest unions, the American Federation of Labor (AFL) and the Congress of Industrial Organizations (CIO), merged. The new and more powerful organization, called the AFL-CIO, remains a major force today.

Suburbs and Highways

With so many people working and making a better living than ever before, the **baby boom** that had begun in the mid-1940s continued. The birthrate, which had fallen to 19 births per 1,000 people during the Depression, soared to more than 25 births per 1,000 in its peak year of 1957.

INTERPRETING GRAPHS
The graph shows the trend in the birthrate from 1930 to 1960. **Synthesizing Information** *Overall, which decade shows the lowest number of births, and which shows the highest number of births?*

Live Births, 1930–1960

Number of births (in millions): 0, 0.5, 1.0, 1.5, 2.0, 2.5, 3.0, 3.5, 4.0, 4.5

Year: 1930, 1935, 1940, 1945, 1950, 1955, 1960

Peak year, 1957. 4,308,000 births

SOURCE: *Historical Statistics of the United States, Colonial Times to 1970*

Moving to the Suburbs Seeking more room, growing families retreated from the noise and pollution of aging cities and bought new houses in suburbs that ringed the urban areas. World War II veterans expanded their economic opportunities with the help of the Servicemen's Readjustment Act of 1944, commonly known as the **GI Bill of Rights,** which gave them low-interest mortgages to purchase new homes and provided them with educational stipends to go to college or graduate school.

Developers like William J. Levitt began to cater to the demand for housing. Levitt built new communities in the suburbs, pioneering mass-production techniques in home building. He bought precut and preassembled materials, and built houses in just weeks

CAPTION ANSWERS

Interpreting Graphs In 1940 there were 10.4% more blue-collar workers than white-collar workers, but in 1960 there were 12.4% more white-collar workers than blue-collar workers.

Interpreting Graphs Births were lowest during the 1930s and highest during the 1950s.

RESOURCE DIRECTORY

Technology
Color Transparencies *Political Cartoons,* B15
Sounds of an Era Audio CD *"Route 66," Nat King Cole Trio* (time: one minute, 30 seconds)

instead of months. Proud of his creations, Levitt gave his name to the new towns. By the late 1940s, there was a Levittown on Long Island that included more than 17,000 homes. Another in Bucks County, Pennsylvania, had about 16,000 homes, and a third Levittown in Willingsboro, New Jersey, appeared in the late 1950s. Other developers adopted Levitt's techniques, and new communities sprang up all over the United States.

For the first time, many average Americans could afford to buy their own home. While most fully enjoyed life in their new houses, others complained that the developments all looked too much alike. Folk singer Malvina Reynolds expressed her distaste for the new communities with these words from "Little Boxes," a popular song of the era:

> *"Little boxes on the hillside*
> *Little boxes made of ticky-tacky*
> *Little boxes on the hillside*
> *Little boxes all the same.*
>
> *There's a green one and a pink one*
> *And a blue one and a yellow one*
> *And they're all made out of ticky-tacky*
> *And they all look just the same."*
>
> —Malvina Reynolds, "Little Boxes"

Levitt and other developers built not just houses, but entire communities.

Cars and Highways Suburban growth brought with it other changes. Following their customers, some stores began to move from cities to shopping centers located in the suburbs. Many Americans, living in suburbs built beyond the reach of public transportation, depended more and more on automobiles. Suburban resident Agnes Geraghty recalled, "When we came here [to the suburbs] our first goal was to buy a new car. I mean with all the traveling that we needed to do, our old car just didn't cut it. We soon realized that task was a little more complicated than we anticipated. A car was a real status symbol and hey, who didn't want to impress the neighbors?"

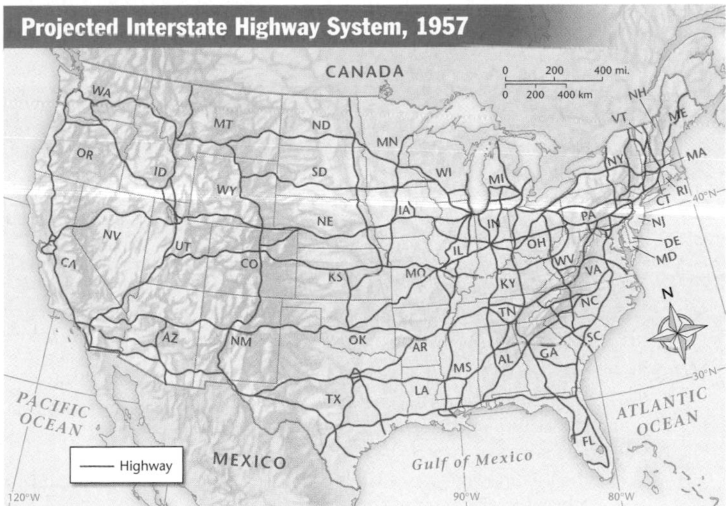

MAP SKILLS Increasingly dependent on the automobile, Americans needed new and better roads. **Place** *How did roads built under the Interstate Highway Act contribute to changes in American culture?*

ACTIVITY
Connecting with Geography

Assign students the task of obtaining a copy of a map of a Levittown, or provide one for them. Direct the students to compare and contrast that community's layout with the layout of an earlier American city and a contemporary American suburb. Have students point out similarities and differences in the communities' structures. Have them pose and answer questions about geographic distributions and patterns shown on their maps. Use the presentation as a springboard into a discussion about changes in the geography of population centers in the United States. **(Visual/Spatial)**

BACKGROUND
Connections to Today

While the houses of Levittown, New York, were commonly criticized as "little boxes" and as symbols of a cheapened mass culture, many commentators think they look better as time goes on. Historian Alexander O. Boulton, for instance, has pointed out that far from being "made of ticky-tacky," the Levittown houses were unusually well-designed and built. In addition, Levittown residents have modified their homes in so many ways through the years that those homes still in original condition are sought after as rarities. In Boulton's words, Levittown "now seems not the model of mass conformity, but a monument to American individualism."

TEST PREPARATION

Have students read the excerpt from the song "Little Boxes" on this page and then complete the sentence below.

The main reason the songwriter dislikes the new housing development is that—

A the houses resemble boxes.
(B) all the houses look the same.
C the houses are in poor taste.
D she dislikes pastel colors.

CUSTOMIZE FOR ...
Less Proficient Readers

Ask students to write one or two sentences showing how each of the following developments changed American life during the postwar period: corporate expansion, technological advances, changes in the workforce, changes in farm work and life, the move to the suburbs, and consumer credit.

CAPTION ANSWERS

Map Skills Roads are shorter and have more intersections on the East Coast. Roads in the West are spaced farther apart and intersect less often.

Section 1 Assessment

Reading Comprehension

1. Average annual income per person.
2. Conglomerates allowed more security for a company, through investing in multiple businesses rather than just one. Franchises allowed a larger parent company to expand to many locations, operated locally as small businesses, while still under the parent company's guidance.
3. To amplify, control, and generate electrical signals. Transistors greatly impacted the electronics industry because they took up much less physical space and made possible rapid improvements in early computers.
4. Couples with children increasingly left cities to raise their children in the suburbs. The GI Bill of Rights gave World War II veterans economic and educational opportunities that helped them gain better-paying jobs, enabling them to purchase homes in the suburbs.

Critical Thinking and Writing

5. Students should note that the author's bias is to assume that television viewers will consist almost entirely of married couples who have children.
6. Answers will vary, but should be descriptive, and supported with facts from the section.

Research should chronicle the phases of development and testing of the vaccine, including dates, milestones, and advancements in technology, from 1908 to 1961.

Focus on DAILY LIFE

1950s Car Culture In the 1950s, cars increasingly became part of many social and cultural events. Families took long vacations traveling by car with campers hitched to the rear and went on Sunday drives in their station wagons. Teenagers would cruise about town with no particular destination. Drivers sat in their parked cars at outdoor movie theaters and watched double features, with the sound coming through a speaker hooked onto the car door. At drive-in restaurants, waitresses delivered food right to the car, placing orders on trays that attached to the door.

You'll get BIG-CAR quality
at lowest cost

The car culture was fed by consumer demand for the latest "dream car" to come from the Detroit automakers. Such cars were large and stylish, with powerful engines, chrome accents, and long tail fins projecting off the rear fenders.

The ad above prompts consumers to "See the USA" by automobile.

To meet the demand, automakers started introducing new car designs every year. People eagerly awaited the unveiling of the latest models. During the 1950s, American automakers produced up to 8 million new cars each year. From 1948 to 1958, passenger car sales increased by more than 50 percent.

Growth in the car industry created a need for more and better roads. The 1956 Federal-Aid Highway Act—sometimes called the Interstate Highway Act—provided $25 billion to build an interstate highway system more than 40,000 miles long. The project provided a national web of new roads and theoretically allowed for the evacuation of major cities in the event of nuclear attack.

The car culture inspired the development of many new businesses including gas stations, repair shops, and parts stores. Americans, especially teenagers, flocked to drive-in movies and restaurants. Families, encouraged by car advertisements that urged them to "See the USA," headed off for vacations at national parks, seaside resorts, and amusement parks.

The Growth of Consumer Credit

Eager to cash in on the increasing number of cars on the road, gasoline companies began offering credit cards to loyal customers. These cards allowed people to charge gas purchases when they were traveling. Americans found the cards convenient and easy to use.

Lending agencies picked up the credit card idea and made borrowing easy. Just as installment plans of the 1920s encouraged consumers to purchase beyond their means, credit cards introduced in the 1950s encouraged similar spending. The Diner's Club credit card appeared in 1950, followed at the end of the decade by the American Express card, and then by the BankAmericard (later called Visa). Total consumer credit debt rose from more than $8 billion in 1946 to more than $56 billion in 1960.

Americans used their credit to purchase washing machines, vacuum cleaners, and television sets. The United States had become, in the words of economist John Kenneth Galbraith, "the affluent society."

Section 1 Assessment

READING COMPREHENSION

1. What is **per capita income?**
2. How did **conglomerates** and **franchises** evolve in the postwar economy?
3. What is the purpose of a **transistor** and how did it contribute to other developments?
4. How did the **baby boom** and the **GI Bill of Rights** affect suburban growth?

CRITICAL THINKING AND WRITING

5. **Recognizing Bias** Reread the excerpt from the article on television viewing that begins, "Many couples credit television. . . ." What is the author's bias in the article?
6. **Writing to Describe** Write a paragraph that shows in detail what it would be like to move from an apartment in the city to a house in a Levittown after World War II.

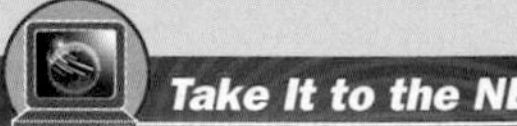

Activity: Creating a Fact Sheet
Research the history of polio up to the creation and testing of a vaccine in the 1950s. Use the links provided in the *America: Pathways to the Present* area of the following Web site for help in completing this activity.
www.phschool.com

RESOURCE DIRECTORY

Teaching Resources

Units 5/6/7 booklet
- Section 1 Quiz, p. 38

Guide to the Essentials
- Section 1 Summary, p. 97

Section 2

The Mood of the 1950s

READING FOCUS

- Why were comfort and security so important to Americans in the 1950s?
- What were the accepted roles of men and women during the 1950s?
- How did some people challenge conformity during the 1950s?

MAIN IDEA

After World War II, many Americans enjoyed economic prosperity. While some welcomed the conformity of the 1950s, others felt it was restrictive and rebelled against it.

KEY TERMS

rock-and-roll
beatnik

TAKING NOTES

Copy the chart below. As you read, fill in details that describe the mood of the 1950s.

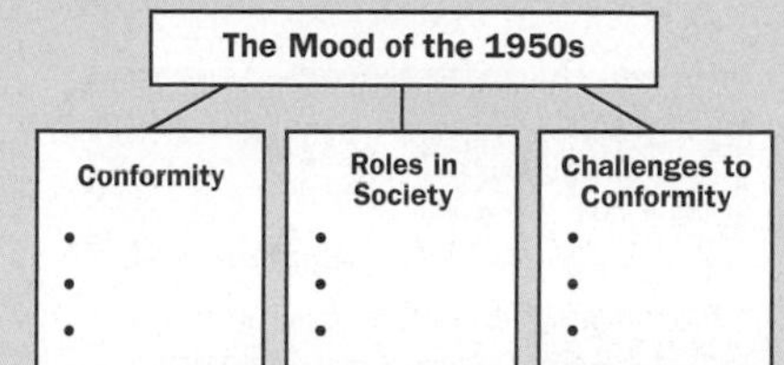

Setting the Scene Most Americans were comfortable during the 1950s. They valued security over adventure, reflecting the mood of a nation still recovering from years of economic depression and war. One historian who grew up in the 1950s wrote:

> “*The spreading of huge organizations, the rapidity of technological change, the rise of suburbia, the standardization of life posed new challenges, but for the most part people coped with them. That may not be very dramatic. But it is the truth about daily life as most people knew it and lived it. . . . Life in the 1950s . . . was a better life than they, or almost anyone else, had ever known.*”
>
> —Geoffrey Perrett, *A Dream of Greatness: The American People, 1945–1963*

Americans applauded the apparent harmony between individuals and groups in the United States that conformity seemed to encourage. Compromise, rather than conflict, was the way disagreements could be settled. People wanted to enjoy their newly won prosperity and provide even better opportunities for their children.

One of many 1950s fads: By wearing special glasses, audiences could see “3-D movies,” films that produced an effect of three dimensions.

Comfort and Security

In the past, sociologist David Riesman observed, Americans had valued individuality. Now most preferred conformity. Riesman cited *Tootle the Engine,* a children’s story in the popular Little Golden Book series. Tootle, a young train engine, found it was more fun to play in the fields than it was to stay on the tracks. His fellow citizens in “Engineville” worked hard to break him of the habit. Tootle finally absorbed the lesson of his peers: “Always stay on the track no matter what.” The story, Riesman believed, was a powerful parable for the young people of the 1950s.

Section 2
The Mood of the 1950s

SECTION OBJECTIVES

1. Find out why comfort and security were so important to Americans in the 1950s.
2. Learn about the accepted roles of men and women during the 1950s.
3. See how some people challenged conformity in the 1950s.

BELLRINGER

Warm-Up Activity Ask students to decide what they consider to be the “proper” roles for men and women in their society today. Do their views of gender-based roles differ from those of their parents or grandparents? If so, how?

Activating Prior Knowledge Have the class list some aspects of 1950s culture with which they are familiar, under such headings as *Art, Music, Television, Theater, Fashion,* etc.

READING STRATEGY

Have students write two headings on a piece of paper: *Conformity* and *Nonconformity.* As they read the section, have them note relevant information in the appropriate column. Then have them write a sentence explaining whether conformity or nonconformity was more prevalent in the 1950s than it is in American life today.

ACTIVITY

Connecting with Culture

This activity may take place over several class periods: Have groups of four to six students brainstorm topics concerning life in the 1950s, write questions for potential interviews, and select possible subjects to interview. Students may focus their interview questions on a specific population, for example, women. The goal of the project is to identify significant aspects of life in the 1950s and learn about them through first-person accounts. **(Verbal/Linguistic)**

RESOURCE DIRECTORY

Teaching Resources

Learning Styles Lesson Plans booklet, p. 57
Guided Reading and Review booklet, p. 110

Technology

Section Reading Support Transparencies
Guided Reading Audiotapes (English/Spanish), Ch. 20
Student Edition on Audio CD, Ch. 20
Prentice Hall Presentation Pro CD-ROM, Ch. 20
Companion Web site, www.phschool.com

Lesson Plan

Focus In the 1950s, many Americans enjoyed unprecedented prosperity and security. Ask students if this comfort was worth the price of conformity.

Instruct Ask students how people behave when they want to fit into a group. How did the Great Depression and World War II affect Americans' need for security? Discuss other factors, such as the fear of communism, that led to increased conformity. Remind students that not everyone wanted to conform. Ask how rock and roll challenged middle-class mores in the 1950s. What distinguished the beatniks?

Discuss men's and women's roles in the postwar era. Ask students to define those roles and to compare them with the roles of men and women today.

Assess/Reteach Ask students to discuss conformity in American life today. How does the proliferation of franchise clothing stores and restaurants contribute to that sense of conformity? What approaches would students who do not wish to conform take toward clothing and entertainment?

READING CHECK

Fearing communism and threats of nuclear war, many Americans sought comfort in their religion. Attendance in churches and at synagogues increased. Evangelists catered to the trend toward religion by delivering sermons over the radio or on television.

Youth Culture Some called the youth of the 1950s the "silent generation." The silent generation seemed to have little interest in the problems and crises of the larger world.

The strong economy of the 1950s allowed more young people to stay in school rather than having to leave early to find a job. Before World War I, most youths left school in their mid-teens to help support their families. In the 1920s, however, more and more children were able to complete secondary school. Because jobs were scarce during the Depression, many teenagers stayed in school. By the 1950s, most middle-class teenagers were expected to stay in school, holding only part-time jobs, if they worked at all. With more leisure time, some young people appeared to devote all their energies to organizing parties and pranks, joining fraternities and sororities, and generally pursuing entertainment and fun.

Some teenagers, most of them girls, baby-sat in their spare time. Young parents who moved to the suburbs were less able to turn to members of their extended family for help with child-care. By the 1950s, baby-sitting had for the first time become a job done not by relatives, but by the young daughters of friends and neighbors. By the end of the decade, half of all teenage girls were employed as part-time baby sitters.

Businesses seized the opportunity to sell products to the youth market. Advertisements and movies helped to build an image of what it meant to be a teenager in the 1950s. The girls were shown in bobby socks and poodle skirts, and the boys wore letter sweaters. These images created a greater sense of conformity in style. The media's ideal of the clean-cut teen could also be seen on such television shows as *Leave It to Beaver* and *Father Knows Best.* Magazines targeting youth, including *Seventeen, Datebook, Teen,* and *Cool,* offered plenty of advice to teenagers—not only on how to dress, but on how best to behave, especially when it came to dating.

Teenage girls collected items such as silver and linens in anticipation of marriage, which was often just after high school. The number of teenage brides rose in the 1950s, so that by 1954, close to half of all brides were in their teens, typically marrying grooms just slightly older.

American BIOGRAPHY

Billy Graham
b. 1918

Evangelist Billy Graham gained a wide following during the 1950s. Born in Charlotte, North Carolina, William Franklin Graham, Jr., was the son of a prosperous dairy farmer. In 1939, he was ordained as a Southern Baptist minister, and he went on to graduate from college in 1943.

Graham then joined an organization founded to minister to young soldiers during World War II. Following the war, he appeared at tent revivals and religious rallies in the United States and Europe.

Thousands of Americans flocked to hear Graham preach throughout the United States. His direct style of speaking made religion accessible, and he became known as fundamentalism's chief spokesperson. In addition to his televised crusades, Graham founded *Decision* magazine and wrote several books. Graham's prominence continued to grow, and in 1996, he was awarded the Congressional Gold Medal.

A Resurgence in Religion In the 1950s, Americans, who had drifted away from religion in earlier years, flocked back to their churches and synagogues. The renewed interest in religion was a response in part to the Cold War struggle against "godless communism." Some looked to religion to find hope in the face of the threat of nuclear war.

Evidence of the newfound commitment to religion was abundant. In 1954, Congress added the words "under God" to the Pledge of Allegiance, and the next year it required the phrase "In God We Trust" to appear on all American currency. Like other aspects of American life, religion became more commercial. Those in need could call Dial-a-Prayer, and new slogans that sounded a lot like advertising—"the family that prays together stays together," for example—became commonplace. Evangelists used radio and television to carry their messages to more people than ever before. By the end of the 1950s, about 95 percent of all Americans said they felt connected to some formal religious group.

READING CHECK

Why did some Americans return to religion in the 1950s?

Men's and Women's Roles

Americans in the post–World War II years were keenly aware of the roles that they were expected to play as men and women. These roles were defined by

RESOURCE DIRECTORY

Teaching Resources

Biography, Literature, and Comparing Primary Sources booklet (Comparing Primary Sources) *On Rock and Roll,* pp. 149–150

Technology

Sounds of an Era Audio CD The Feminine Mystique, *Betty Friedan*

RESOURCE PRO® **Critical Thinking Activity** *Determining Relevance: Wages, Hours, and Unions,* found on Resource Pro, uses graphs of American work statistics between 1900 and 1960 to help students apply this skill.

RESOURCE PRO® **Literature Activity** *Nonconformity in the 1950s,* found on Resource Pro, features a passage from the novel *On the Road* by Jack Kerouac, the author whose work and life are often considered synonymous with the "Beat Generation."

social and religious traditions that had broad appeal to Americans. Men were expected to go to school and then find jobs to support wives and children. Theirs was the public sphere, the world away from home, where they earned money and made important political, economic, and social decisions.

Women were expected to play a supporting role in their husbands' lives. They kept house, cooked meals, and raised children. Many parents turned to pediatrician Dr. Benjamin Spock for child-care advice. His book *The Common Sense Book of Baby and Child Care* (1946) had a major impact on child-rearing practices. Most middle-class women settled into the domestic role and took on the demands of raising children and maintaining their suburban homes. In 1956, *Life* magazine published "Busy Wife's Achievements." The article profiled a housewife who had married at the age of 16, had four children, and kept busy with the PTA, Campfire Girls, and charity causes. She served as "home manager, mother, hostess, and useful civic worker." Her family duties and community service were typical of many middle-class suburban women.

Challenges to Conformity

Social conformity made it easy to mask the differences among individuals and groups. Not all Americans fit the model of American middle-class life described above, however.

Women at Work Many women had enjoyed working outside the home during World War II and were reluctant to give up their good jobs. Some women, single and married, worked simply to make ends meet. Although the norm was for women to leave their jobs once they were married, not all women did. In 1950, about 24 percent of all married American women had jobs. By 1960, the figure had risen to 31 percent. Married women with jobs had first begun to outnumber unmarried women with jobs near the end of World War II; in the postwar years, the gap grew even larger.

Most of the women who worked outside the home held jobs as secretaries, teachers, nurses, and sales clerks. Besides the satisfaction of earning their own money, women wanted to be able to buy the items that were part of "the good life," such as cars and electric appliances.

In 1963, Betty Friedan published a critique of the 1950s ideal of womanhood. In *The Feminine Mystique,* Friedan lashed out at the culture that made it difficult for women to choose alternative roles. Millions of women, Friedan charged, were frustrated with their roles in the 1950s:

> "*It was unquestioned gospel [in the 1950s] that women could identify with nothing beyond the home—not politics, not art, not science, not events large or small, war or peace, in the United States or the world, unless it could be approached through female experience as a wife or mother or translated into domestic detail!*"
>
> —Betty Friedan, *The Feminine Mystique*

Youthful Rebellions Young people also challenged the norms of 1950s society. Some young people rejected the values of their parents and felt

Focus on DAILY LIFE

Tupperware Parties Tupperware, a line of flexible plastic containers designed by Earl Silas Tupper, became popular after World War II. Many women sold Tupperware from their homes in the 1950s, making the "Tupperware party" a fixture of the suburban social scene. Sales "hostesses" invited friends and acquaintances over for product demonstrations in an atmosphere designed to make the buyer feel relaxed and at home. At the party's end, the hostess took product orders, earning a commission from her sales. As buyers and sellers, some women found home-based sales to be less intimidating than the door-to-door sales that were also popular in the 1950s. In 1954, Tupperware vice president Brownie Wise, the pioneer of home parties, was the first woman to appear on the cover of *BusinessWeek.* Above is a 1946 ad for Tupperware.

INTERPRETING GRAPHS
The graph shows the numbers of single and married women in the labor force from 1900 to 1960.
Making Comparisons *Which years show more single women than married women in the work force?*

Female Labor Force, 1900–1960

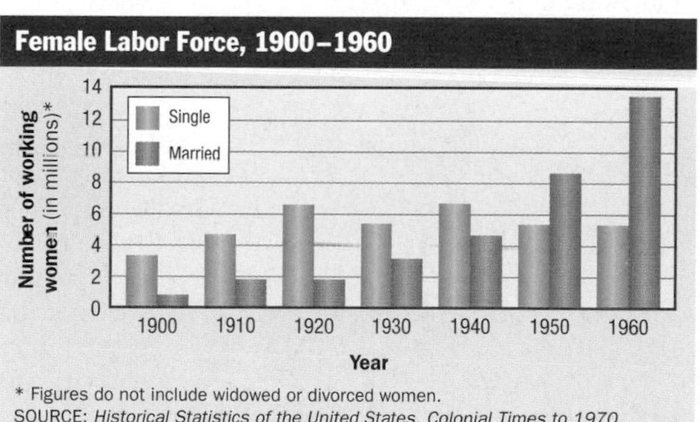

* Figures do not include widowed or divorced women.
SOURCE: *Historical Statistics of the United States, Colonial Times to 1970*

ACTIVITY
Connecting with Culture

Have students create an editorial cartoon about the 1950s, focusing on the need and desire to conform or on the challenges to conformity posed by beatniks. **(Visual/Spatial)**

BACKGROUND
Interdisciplinary

Betty Friedan found her inspiration through a college alumni project. In 1957 she began interviewing her former classmates for a report on their activities 15 years after graduating from Smith College. She found most of them dealing with, as she later wrote, "a strange stirring, a sense of dissatisfaction, a yearning . . ." and "the silent question—'Is this all?'" Friedan wanted to write a magazine article about this discontent, but all of the women's magazines she submitted it to rejected the story. So instead, Friedan wrote a book: *The Feminine Mystique.*

CUSTOMIZE FOR ...
Gifted and Talented

Ask students to consider this statement by writer Annie Dillard about her early life in *American Childhood:* "Every woman stayed alone in her house in those days, like a coin in a safe. Amy [Dillard's sister] and I lived alone with our mother most of the day." What is the mood of Dillard's statement? What image does she create of a woman's life in the 1950s?

CAPTION ANSWERS

Interpreting Graphs Single women in the workforce outnumbered married women in 1900, 1910, 1920, 1930, and 1940.

ACTIVITY
Connecting with Culture

Have the class read (or listen to) the lyrics of several popular songs from the 1950s. Challenge students to identify the theme of each song, the ideas each song expresses, and the tone or mood of each song. Then have the class compare and contrast these elements of 1950s rock-and-roll to the songs students listen to today. How are they alike and different? **(Musical/Rhythmic)**

BACKGROUND
Music History

"What was the first rock-and-roll record?" is a common question asked by music fans. In 1992 Jim Dawson and Steve Propes attempted to answer, or at least illuminate, that question in a book of the same name. While providing no definitive answer, they suggest 50 candidates for the title of "first rock-and-roll record." The nominees include Jazz at the Philharmonic, "Blues, Part 2" (1944); Helen Humes, "Be-Baba-Leba" (1945); Bill Monroe, "We're Gonna Rock, We're Gonna Roll" (1948); John Lee Hooker, "Boogie Chillen" (1948); Ruth Brown, "Teardrops from My Eyes" (1950); Hank Williams, "Kaw-Liga" (1953); Bill Haley and His Comets, "(We're Going to) Rock Around the Clock" (1954); and Elvis Presley, "Heartbreak Hotel" (1956).

COMPARING PRIMARY SOURCES
Rock-and-Roll Music

When the defiant beat of rock-and-roll burst onto the American scene in the mid-1950s, few people remained impartial about its sound or its impact.

Analyzing Viewpoints What does each viewpoint below say about the relationship between rock-and-roll music and juvenile delinquency?

In Favor of Rock-and-Roll

"If my kids are home at night listening to my radio program, and get interested enough to go out and buy records and have a collection to listen to and dance to, I think I'm fighting delinquency."

—Radio disc jockey Alan Freed, the *New York Times, January 12, 1958*

Opposed to Rock-and-Roll

"Rock 'n' roll . . . is sung, played and written for the most part by [mentally deficient] goons and by means of its almost imbecilic repetition and sly, lewd, in plain fact, dirty lyrics . . . it manages to be the [warlike] music of every sideburned delinquent on the face of the earth."

—Singer Frank Sinatra, the *New York Times, January 12, 1958*

Teenagers listened to the new rock-and-roll music on record players.

misunderstood and alone. A few films, such as *Rebel Without a Cause,* released in 1955, captured these feelings of alienation. The movie's young star, James Dean, became a teen idol and a film legend.

Holden Caulfield, the main character in J. D. Salinger's 1951 novel *The Catcher in the Rye,* is troubled by the "phonies" he sees at boarding school and in the world around him. Throughout the book, Holden struggles to preserve his own integrity despite the fierce pressure to conform. Many readers could relate to this experience.

Young people sought a style they could call their own. In 1951, disc jockey Alan Freed began hosting a radio show in Cleveland, Ohio, playing what was called black rhythm-and-blues music for a largely black audience. Though other white—and black—disc jockeys were playing rhythm-and-blues at the time, the music did not have a wide audience. Freed's charismatic on-air style quickly drew a broad audience of teenage listeners, both black and white. Freed's program, "Moondog Rock 'n' Roll Party" gave important exposure to the music, which grew out of rhythm-and-blues and came to be called **rock-and-roll.** Teenagers across the nation quickly became fans of the driving beat and simple melodies that characterized rock-and-roll. They rushed to buy records of their favorite performers: African American stars such as Chuck Berry, Little Richard, and Fats Domino; and white musicians including Bill Haley and the Comets, Jerry Lee Lewis, and Buddy Holly.

Elvis Presley was a star performer in the early days of rock-and-roll.

One of the best-known rock-and-roll singers was Elvis Presley. Presley's performances showcased his flamboyant style and good looks. He attracted hordes of screaming teenage girls everywhere he went. Presley released many records that became huge hits, including "Don't Be Cruel," "Hound Dog," and "Heartbreak Hotel." From the United States, rock music spread to Europe and Asia, becoming popular with listeners and influencing musicians. Early songs by The Beatles, a British group that first performed in 1957, were inspired by American rock-and-roll.

Many adults disliked the new music, fearing it would cause a rise in immorality. For some people, opposition to rock-and-roll had to

RESOURCE DIRECTORY

Teaching Resources

Units 5/6/7 booklet
- Section 2 Quiz, p. 39

Guide to the Essentials
- Section 2 Summary, p. 98

Technology

Sounds of an Era Audio CD *"Hand Clappin',"* *Red Prysock* (time: 45 seconds)

do with race. Rock-and-roll, in its appeal to both black and white teenagers, and in its black rhythm-and-blues origins, threatened many who were comfortable with racial segregation in the 1950s and who were uncomfortable with the idea of black and white teenagers attending the same concerts and dancing to the same music. Despite some efforts to ban rock concerts and keep records out of stores, rock-and-roll's popularity continued to soar.

Members of the "Beat Generation," called **beatniks,** launched a different kind of challenge. Beatniks, some of them writers, some artists, some simply participants in the movement, promoted spontaneity, or acting at a moment's notice without planning. They stressed spirituality and the need for release from the world of money and property. Beatniks challenged traditional patterns of respectability and shocked other Americans with their more open sexuality and their use of illegal drugs.

Author Jack Kerouac, whom many considered the leader of the beat generation, gathered with others in coffee houses in San Francisco, California, to share ideas and experiences. The unconventional Kerouac published his best-selling novel *On the Road* in 1957. He typed the first complete draft in less than a month, and on one continuous roll of paper. This was a reflection of his free-flowing, spontaneous writing method. The novel's "wild form," as Kerouac described it, was meant to reflect an open approach to life. One of Kerouac's friends, Allen Ginsberg, used the unstructured and chaotic style of the Beat Movement to write his influential epic poem "Howl," which begins, "I saw the best minds of my generation destroyed by madness . . ."

VIEWING HISTORY Jack Kerouac, author of *On the Road,* performs at a poetry reading in 1959. **Drawing Conclusions** *What was it about Kerouac and his work that appealed to people?*

Section 2 Assessment

READING COMPREHENSION

1. Why did some people call 1950s youth the "silent generation"?
2. Why did Americans renew their interest in religion during the 1950s?
3. How did **rock-and-roll** influence life in the 1950s?
4. How did **beatniks** challenge conformity?

CRITICAL THINKING AND WRITING

5. **Making Comparisons** Describe the roles of men and women in 1950s society.
6. **Writing an Interview** Ask a relative, a neighbor, or a friend who grew up in the 1950s about what life was like for young people at that time. Write your interview in question-and-answer format.

Take It to the NET

Activity: Writing a Report
Research the history of rock-and-roll and write a brief report on its social impact. Use the links provided in the *America: Pathways to the Present* area of the following Web site for help in completing this activity.
www.phschool.com

Section 2 Assessment

Reading Comprehension

1. They seemed to have little interest in the problems of the larger world; the stronger economy allowed the youth generation to stay in school, delaying their entry into the workforce and "real world" responsibilities.
2. In part as a response to the Cold War's "godless communism," Americans turned to religion to find hope in the face of the threat of nuclear war. As a result, religion grew more commercial, thereby attracting even more interest.
3. It gave young people a style of their own, causing adults to fear a rise in immorality and some to oppose this type of music on a racial basis, preferring segregation to watching young blacks and whites enjoy attending concerts together.
4. Stressing spirituality and the need for release from the material world, beatniks challenged traditional patterns of respectability.

Critical Thinking and Writing

5. Men assumed the public sphere. They worked outside the home and brought in money to support the family. Women primarily played a supporting role, working within the home, raising children, and managing the family, though some women did work outside the home.
6. Answers will vary, but questions included in the interview should reflect themes from the section.

Take It to the NET

Reports should focus on the social impact of rock-and-roll, including its effects on racial issues, youth culture, and the relationship between the generations. Students should demonstrate an understanding of the connection between social identity, age, class, and musical style that continues today.

Caption Answers

Viewing History Kerouac's fans found his spontaneity and his writing style to be refreshing.

Section 3
Domestic Politics and Policy

Section Objectives

1. Discover Truman's domestic policies as outlined in the Fair Deal.
2. Learn how Truman won the election of 1948.
3. Understand the Republican approach to government during the Eisenhower presidency.

Bellringer

Warm-Up Activity Ask students to think of someone in a leadership position whom they admire, for example, a teacher, coach, or member of the clergy. Ask students to describe that person's leadership style and explain why they think it's effective.

Activating Prior Knowledge Have students reflect on what they know about Eisenhower's popularity as a World War II general. How did that popularity influence his prospects as a candidate for President?

Reading Strategy

Have students put the names *Truman* and *Eisenhower* on top of a piece of paper. As they read the section, have them note and evaluate the contributions of these political leaders.

Section 3
Domestic Politics and Policy

READING FOCUS

- What were Truman's domestic policies as outlined in his Fair Deal?
- How did Truman win the election of 1948?
- What was the Republican approach to government during the Eisenhower presidency?

MAIN IDEA

Presidents Harry Truman and Dwight Eisenhower used two very different styles of leadership to meet the challenges they faced during the postwar period.

KEY TERMS

reconversion
Taft-Hartley Act
Modern Republicanism
National Aeronautics and Space Administration (NASA)
National Defense Education Act

TAKING NOTES

Copy the web diagram below. As you read, fill in each blank circle with details about Eisenhower's policies.

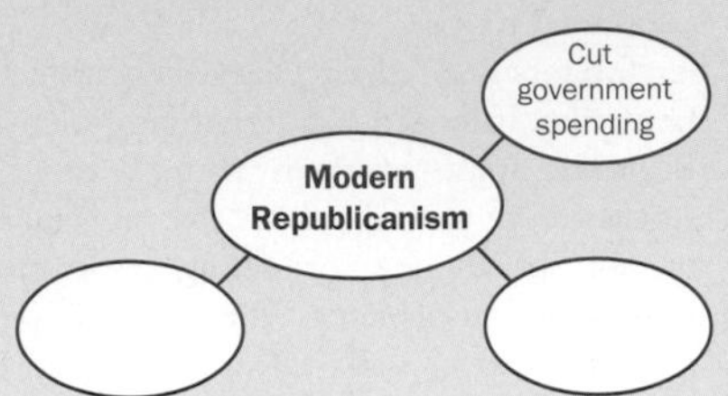

Setting the Scene The 1950s were conservative years— politically as well as culturally. The government felt public pressure to maintain the nation's newly won prosperity. Democrat Harry Truman first struggled with the problems of moving to a peacetime economy, and then fought for a reform program blocked repeatedly by Congress.

Republican Dwight Eisenhower took a more low-key approach to the presidency. One economic advisor, Gabriel Hauge, recalled that Eisenhower was "very decent, wholesome in his instincts, terribly free of the little meannesses that often plague great men's lives." His genial, reassuring manner made him one of the most popular Presidents in the years following World War II.

VIEWING HISTORY These former servicemen are picketing the entrance to a Pennsylvania coal mine in 1946 to demand jobs. **Analyzing Information** *One of the signs held in the photo reads "Fought for U.S.A., Now Discarded." What is the complaint this man is making?*

Truman's Domestic Policies

Harry Truman wanted to follow in Franklin Roosevelt's footsteps, but he often appeared ill-prepared for the presidency. He seemed to have a scattershot approach to governing, offering a new batch of proposals in every speech. People wondered where his focus lay.

The Peacetime Economy Truman's first priority was **reconversion**—the social and economic transition from wartime to peacetime. Soldiers wanted to return home, and politicians were flooded with messages that warned, "No boats, no votes." Truman responded quickly and got most soldiers home by 1946.

Lifting the economic controls that had kept wartime inflation in check proved a more difficult challenge. Most Americans had limited access to consumer goods during World War II. Now they wanted those goods, and they wanted them right away. In an effort to make the economy more responsive to consumer preferences, the government eased the controls in July 1946, and prices soared almost 25 percent. Since wages failed to keep up with prices, many people still could not enjoy the fruits of their years of sacrifice.

Caption Answers

Viewing History The man is saying that he and the other men with picket signs fought for their country in World War II. Without a job, he feels mistreated by the same country he fought for.

RESOURCE DIRECTORY

Teaching Resources
Guided Reading and Review booklet, p. 111

Technology
Section Reading Support Transparencies
Guided Reading Audiotapes (English/Spanish), Ch. 20
Student Edition on Audio CD, Ch. 20
Prentice Hall Presentation Pro CD-ROM, Ch. 20
Companion Web site, www.phschool.com

In some ways, the economic issues facing the United States at the end of World War II were similar to those at the end of World War I. Workers demanded wage increases that they had forgone for the sake of the war effort. In 1946, nearly 4.6 million workers went on strike, more than ever before in the United States. Strikes hit the automobile, steel, electrical, coal, and railroad industries, and affected nearly everyone in the country.

Although Truman agreed that workers deserved higher wages, he thought that their demands were inflationary. That is, he feared that such increases would push the prices of goods still higher. In his view, workers failed to understand that big wage increases might destroy the health of the economy.

VIEWING HISTORY Truman sits at his desk in the White House. **Analyzing Information** *Why would Truman place a sign reading "The buck stops here" on his desk?*

In the spring of 1946, a railroad strike caused a major disruption in the economy. In response, Truman asked Congress for the power to draft the striking workers into the army. He would then be able to order them as soldiers to stay on the job. Determining that Truman's request was an overreaction to the strike, the Senate refused to go along.

Truman's White House took other steps to limit the power of labor unions as well. When John L. Lewis and his United Mine Workers defied a court order against a strike, the Truman administration asked a judge to serve Lewis with a contempt of court citation. The court fined Lewis $10,000 and his union $3.5 million.

Congress went even further than Truman: In 1947, it passed the **Taft-Hartley Act.** This act allowed the President to declare an 80-day cooling-off period during which strikers had to return to work, in strikes in industries that affected the national interest. Reflecting the widespread anti-Communist feelings gripping the United States at the time, the measure also required union officials to sign oaths that they were not Communists. Furious union leaders complained bitterly about the measure, and Truman vetoed it. Congress, however, passed the act over Truman's veto.

Truman's Fair Deal Truman had supported Roosevelt's New Deal, and now, playing on the well-known name, he devised a program he called the Fair Deal. The Fair Deal extended the New Deal's goals.

Truman agreed with FDR that government needed to play an active role in securing economic justice for all American citizens. As the war ended, he introduced a 21-point program that included legislation designed to promote full employment, a higher minimum wage, greater unemployment compensation for workers without jobs, housing assistance, and a variety of other items. Over the next ten weeks, Truman added more proposals to the Fair Deal. By early 1946, he had asked for a national health insurance program and legislation to control atomic energy.

The leader of the United Mine Workers, John Lewis (left), opposed the Taft-Hartley Act cosponsored by Senator Robert Taft (right).

Truman ran into tremendous political opposition in Congress from a coalition of conservative Democrats and Republicans. Opponents rejected the majority of the Fair Deal initiatives. One measure that passed was the Employment Act of 1946, which created a Council of Economic Advisors to advise the President.

As the 1946 midterm elections approached, it seemed to many people that Truman was little more than a bungling bureaucrat. Among the remarks often heard about Truman were, "You just sort of forget about Harry until he makes another mistake," and "To err is Truman," adapted

LESSON PLAN

Focus Presidents Truman and Eisenhower presented Americans with different approaches to government and to the challenges facing the post-war nation. How did they disagree about the proper role of government and the way to solve the nation's social problems?

Instruct Discuss the tasks that needed to be accomplished to return the nation to stability after World War II. Ask students to assess how well Truman carried out each of these tasks and show how he was a New Dealer in his view of the appropriate role of government in American life. Ask how the Fair Deal extended Roosevelt's New Deal.

Assess/Reteach Ask students to summarize the differences in Truman and Eisenhower's governing styles. In what ways was each leader most effective?

ACTIVITY

Connecting with Economics

Have students conduct research to determine the total numbers of American servicemen and women who were overseas at the end of World War II. Have them also determine the total population of the United States at the time. Direct students to calculate the percentage of the country's population that was repatriated at the end of the war to analyze the effects of changing demographic patterns resulting from migration within the United States. Have students speculate on the effects such a percentage of returning people might have had on the American economy. **(Logical/Mathematical)**

TEST PREPARATION

Have students reread the section "Truman's Fair Deal" on this page and then have them answer the question below.

Which of the following statements is NOT correct?

A The Fair Deal extended FDR's New Deal.

(B) Truman was able to gain wide support for the Fair Deal from both parties.

C The aim of the Fair Deal was economic justice.

D The Fair Deal proposed an increase in the minimum wage.

CAPTION ANSWERS

Viewing History Truman means that as President, he is the man responsible for what happens in his administration, and that he is not afraid of making decisions.

BACKGROUND
Connections to Today

Since the full integration of the army in the Korean War, the armed forces have provided merit-based promotion in a too-often racist society. Thousands of people of color have achieved positions of authority and responsibility in the armed forces where such success might have been unattainable in civilian life during the latter half of the twentieth century. Today, the U.S. armed forces are widely recognized as, if not perfectly color-blind, more so, as a whole, than the society that they serve.

From the Archives of
AmericanHeritage®

About the Presidents

Harry S. Truman (1945–1953) called the Eightieth Congress back for a special session starting on July 26, 1948. This date, he said, was "Turnip Day" in his home state. He asked the legislature to halt rising prices and to meet the housing crisis. The Republican platform, he pointed out, called for such action. This proved to be a trap for Congress. If they passed the bills, they would strengthen the President. If not, they would remain the "do-nothing Eightieth Congress." They ignored Truman's challenge. After the July "turnip session," Truman made Congress a major election issue. His strategy worked, helping him achieve an upset victory over opponent Tom Dewey. Source: David Jacobs, "Harry S. Truman," *The American Heritage® Pictorial History of the Presidents of the United States,* vol. 2, 1968.

from a well-known saying. Truman's support in one poll dropped from 87 percent just after he assumed the presidency to 32 percent in November 1946. The results of the 1946 elections reflected many people's feelings that Truman was not an effective leader. Republicans won majorities of both houses of Congress.

The 80th Congress battered the President for the next two years. Under the leadership of the conservative Republican senator Robert A. Taft of Ohio, commonly known as "Mr. Republican," the Republican Party worked hard to reduce the size and the power of the federal government, to decrease taxes, and to block Truman's liberal goals. On civil rights initiatives, in particular, Truman found opposition throughout his presidency.

VIEWING HISTORY Harry Truman became the first President ever to campaign in Harlem, the heart of New York City's African American community. The campaign button (top) supports his civil rights stance. **Synthesizing Information** *How did Truman's support of civil rights cause a split in the Democratic Party?*

Truman on Civil Rights While holding in private many of the racial prejudices he had learned growing up, Truman recognized that as President he had to take action on civil rights. In a letter to a friend, he wrote, "I am not asking for social equality, because no such things exist, but I am asking for equality of opportunity for all human beings, and, as long as I stay here, I am going to continue that fight."

Truman had publicly supported civil rights for many years. In September 1946, he met with a group of African American leaders to discuss the steps that needed to be taken to achieve their goals. They asked Truman to support a federal anti-lynching law, abolish the poll tax as a voting requirement, and establish a permanent board to prevent discriminatory practices in hiring. Congress refused to address any of these concerns, so in December 1946, Truman appointed a biracial Committee on Civil Rights to look into race relations. This group produced a report demanding action on the concerns listed above. It also recommended that a permanent civil rights commission be established.

A majority of the members of Congress disagreed with the report, and as a result, Congress took no action. In July 1948, Truman banned discrimination in the hiring of federal employees. He also ordered an end to segregation and discrimination in the armed forces. Real change came slowly, however. Only with the onset of the Korean War in 1950 did the armed forces make significant progress in ending segregation.

The Election of 1948

Truman decided to seek another term as President in 1948. He had no reason to expect victory, however, because even in his own party, his support was disintegrating. The southern wing of the Democratic Party, protesting a moderate civil rights plank in the party platform, split off from the main party. These segregationists formed the States' Rights, or Dixiecrat Party and nominated Governor J. Strom Thurmond of South Carolina for President.

Meanwhile, the liberal wing of the Democratic Party deserted Truman to follow Henry Wallace, who headed the Progressive Party ticket. Wallace had been Franklin Roosevelt's second Vice President, and many Democrats believed that he was the right person to carry out the measures begun by Roosevelt. Most recently Wallace had served as Truman's Secretary of Commerce. Wallace had resigned, however, because he did not support Truman's Cold War policies.

CAPTION ANSWERS

Viewing History Segregationist southern Democrats formed a separate party, the States' Rights Party.

RESOURCE DIRECTORY

Teaching Resources

Biography, Literature, and Comparing Primary Sources booklet (Literature) *Conformity in the 1950s*, pp. 76–77

Technology

RESOURCE PRO® **Visual Learning Activity** *Auto Strike, 1950,* found on Resource Pro, illustrates the continuing rift between workers and management in a photograph of United Auto Workers members preparing for a strike.

RESOURCE PRO® **Primary Source Activity** *Harry Truman: Off the Record,* found on Resource Pro, uses excerpts from the private papers of the former President to provide students with an additional perspective on the issues of that era.

Running against Republican Thomas E. Dewey, governor of New York, Truman crisscrossed the country by train. He campaigned not so much against Dewey as against the Republican Congress, which the President repeatedly mocked as the "do-nothing" 80th Congress. Truman's campaign style was blunt and effective. In off-the-cuff speeches, he challenged all Americans: "If you send another Republican Congress to Washington, you're a bigger bunch of suckers than I think you are." "Give 'em hell, Harry," the people yelled as Truman got going. And he did.

Among other things, Truman vehemently attacked Congress's farm policy. In the past, a federal price-support program had permitted farmers to borrow money to store surplus crops until someone bought the produce. Recently, however, Congress had kept the Commodity Credit Corporation, responsible for buying the surplus, from buying or leasing storage bins. Unforeseen by legislators of either party, the 1948 harvest was especially good. With commercial storage space filled, farmers were forced to sell their surpluses on the open market at very low prices. Truman attacked Congress, saying it had "stuck a pitchfork in the farmers' backs."

On election day, although virtually all experts and polls had picked Dewey to win, Truman scored an astounding upset. Furthermore, Democrats won control of Congress. With this victory, Truman stepped out of FDR's shadow to claim the presidency in his own right.

Truman looked forward to a chance to push further for his legislative goals. Over the next four years, however, the Fair Deal scored only occasional successes. Instances of corruption among federal officials hurt Truman's image.

Longtime Democratic control over the White House frustrated many Republicans, who were opposed to any legacy of the New Deal. Debate over presidential term limits had flared up after Roosevelt won his unprecedented third and fourth terms. Up until that time, the two-term presidency had been upheld by custom—as set by George Washington—rather than by law. Republicans, together with southern Democrats, moved for the passage of a constitutional amendment limiting a President to two terms. The amendment won more than enough votes in both houses. Truman was silent on the matter, and Americans showed little concern for the issue. It was in the absence of public opposition, rather than with any overwhelming public support, that the Twenty-second Amendment was adopted in 1951. It states, in part:

KEY DOCUMENTS

> *"No person shall be elected to the office of the President more than twice, and no person who has held the office of President, or acted as President, for more than two years of a term to which some other person was elected President shall be elected to the office of the President more than once."*
>
> —The Twenty-second Amendment

The amendment's passage did little to keep politicians from debating the issue. Since then analysts have wondered if term limitations render a second-term President less effective than one empowered to seek reelection.

Focus on GOVERNMENT

Predicting the Election Truman's upset in the 1948 election caught many experts and pollsters off guard, but it was likely no surprise to the many people who voted for him. After that election, embarrassed newspapers and polling organizations wondered how their predictions could have been wrong. A post-election study revealed the polling had stopped too soon to take into account late gains made by Truman as his campaign picked up momentum: Polls taken after the election revealed that many Truman voters had made up their minds in the last two weeks before the election. Although the election was held in November, one of the major polling organizations based its predictions on surveys taken in mid-August. Another stopped polling in mid-October. Newspaper reporters compounded these errors in judgment by relying too heavily on poll results in making their own predictions.

The *Chicago Daily Tribune* was so certain of Truman's defeat that it printed this edition before all the votes were tallied.

ACTIVITY
Connecting with Government

Ask students to compare the personalities of Truman and Eisenhower. Ask how Eisenhower's personality helped him win the election of 1952. Encourage students to use what they know about the 1950s to explain how Eisenhower's style fit the mood of the country at the time. **(Logical/Mathematical)**

From the Archives of AmericanHeritage®

Truman on TV

On October 5, 1947, Harry S. Truman became the first President to address the nation on television from the White House. The subject of his speech was the need for Americans to conserve food in order to feed Europe. Truman declined the opportunity to hog the cameras. Instead, he appeared as the last of five speakers, coming on after rousing talks from the Secretaries of Agriculture, State, and Commerce and the Chairman of the Citizens Food Committee. With only a few hundred thousand television sets in the entire country, the vast majority of Americans listened to the program on radio. In 1951 Truman made another accommodation to technology that would have far-reaching results. He let reporters use recording machines to tape his remarks at press conferences, not for broadcast, but so they could check their notes. In 1955 his successor, Dwight D. Eisenhower, allowed his conferences to be filmed for broadcast, with the understanding that his press secretary could edit them first. From there, it was only a short step to live broadcasts, sound bites, one-liners, and all the fulsome vapidity that characterizes American politics in the information age. Source: Frederic D. Schwarz, "The Time Machine," *American Heritage®* magazine, October 1997.

CUSTOMIZE FOR ...
Less Proficient Writers

Have students read the quote by Harry Truman on the previous page. Then have them make two columns, one headed *Social Equality* and one headed *Equal Opportunity.* Have students list aspects of American life that represent Social Equality, versus those that represent Equal Opportunity. Then have students discuss the differences between those two terms.

Activity
Student Portfolio

You may wish to have students add the following to their portfolios: Intelligent and witty, Adlai M. Stevenson, governor of Illinois from 1949 to 1953, ran for President against Eisenhower in 1952 and 1956. Ask students to research Stevenson's life and career, focusing on his bids to occupy the Oval Office, and to write and perform a monologue to convey the information. **(Verbal/Linguistic; Bodily/Kinesthetic)**

Background
Biography

At the very end of the Checkers speech, after he invited people to contact the Eisenhower campaign, Nixon made a final promise and a final plea to the "folks" watching: "But let me say this last word. Regardless of what happens, I am going to continue this fight. I am going to campaign up and down America until we drive the crooks and Communists and those that defend them out of Washington, and remember, folks, Eisenhower is a great man. Folks, he is a great man, and a vote for Eisenhower is a vote for what is good for America."

From the Archives of
American Heritage®

About the Presidents

Dwight David Eisenhower (1953–1961) often spoke out against the idea of a welfare state—one that gives handouts to those in need. Nevertheless, New Deal policies were continued during his administration. The National Defense Education Act of 1958 made student loans available. The Department of Health, Education, and Welfare was created. Ten million more people joined the Social Security rolls while Eisenhower was President. Source: Charles L. Mee, Jr., "Dwight David Eisenhower," *The American Heritage® Pictorial History of the Presidents of the United States,* vol. 2, 1968.

The "I like Ike" message was seen in many places in 1952, even on cosmetics containers.

The amendment contained specific language that allowed Truman to be reelected. Nonetheless, he decided not to run again in 1952. Instead, the Democrats chose Adlai Stevenson, governor of Illinois, as their presidential candidate.

Eisenhower and the Republican Approach

Running against Stevenson for the Republicans was Dwight Eisenhower, former commander in chief of the Allied forces. As a public figure, Eisenhower's approach to politics differed from that of Harry Truman. Whereas Truman was a scrappy fighter, Ike—as the people affectionately called Dwight Eisenhower—had always been a talented diplomat. During World War II, Eisenhower forged agreements among Allied military commanders. His easygoing charm gave Americans a sense of security.

By 1952, Americans across the land were chanting, "I like Ike." The Republicans devised a "K_1C_2" formula for victory, which focused on three problems: Korea, communism, and corruption. Eisenhower promised to end the Korean War, and the Republican Party guaranteed a tough approach to the Communist challenge. Eisenhower's vice-presidential running mate, Californian Richard M. Nixon, hammered on the topic of corruption in government.

The Checkers Speech In spite of his overwhelming popularity, Eisenhower's candidacy hit a snag in September 1952. Newspapers accused Richard Nixon of having a special fund, set up by rich Republican supporters. "Secret Nixon Fund!" and "Secret Rich Man's Trust Fund Keeps Nixon in Style Beyond His Salary," screamed typical headlines. In fact, Nixon had done nothing wrong, but the accusation that he had received illegal gifts from political friends was hard to shake.

Nixon's broadcast of his "Checkers" speech on national television was well received by viewers.

Soon, cries arose for Eisenhower to dump Nixon from the ticket. Eisenhower decided to allow Nixon to save himself, if he could. In response to the allegation, Nixon delivered a televised speech, emotionally denying wrongful use of campaign funds. He also gave a detailed account of his personal finances. In response to the charge that he was living above his means, he described his wife, Pat, as wearing a "respectable Republican cloth coat."

The emotional climax of the speech came when Nixon admitted that he had, in fact, received one gift from a political supporter:

> "*It was a little cocker spaniel dog. . . . Black and white spotted. And our little girl—Tricia, the 6-year-old—named it Checkers. And you know the kids love that dog and I just want to say this right now, that regardless of what they say about it, we're going to keep it.*"
>
> —Richard Nixon, September 23, 1952

At the end of his speech, Nixon requested that the American people contact the Eisenhower campaign to register their opinions as to whether or not he should stay on the Republican ticket. People from all across the nation called, wired, and wrote to Eisenhower, demanding that Nixon continue as his running mate. Nixon had turned a political disaster into a public relations bonanza.

Support for Eisenhower continued to grow through the fall. Ike got 55 percent of the popular vote and swept into office with a Republican Congress.

Sounds of an Era

Listen to part of Richard Nixon's "Checkers" speech and other sounds from the postwar years.

Eisenhower as President Ike's natural inclination was to work behind the scenes. "I am not one of those desk-pounding types that likes to stick out his jaw and look like he is bossing the show," Eisenhower said. Critics misinterpreted his

RESOURCE DIRECTORY

Teaching Resources

Learning with Documents booklet (Primary Source Activity) *Enforcing* Brown *v.* Board of Education, p. 32

Technology

Sounds of an Era Audio CD *"The Checkers Speech," Richard Nixon* (time: one minute)

apparent lack of leadership, joking about an Eisenhower doll—you wound it up and it did nothing. Eisenhower defended his approach, declaring:

> "I'll tell you what leadership is. It's persuasion—and conciliation—and education—and patience. It's long, slow tough work. That's the only kind of leadership I know or believe in—or will practice."
>
> —Dwight Eisenhower

The American people approved of Ike's style. In 1956, Eisenhower once again faced Stevenson and easily won reelection. This time he garnered an even greater margin of victory, with almost 58 percent of the vote. The Democrats, however, having regained control of Congress in midterm elections, continued to lead both houses after the 1956 election.

Modern Republicanism In domestic matters, Eisenhower was determined to slow the growth of the federal government. He also wanted to limit the President's power and increase the authority of Congress and the courts. Eisenhower was not, however, interested in completely reversing the New Deal.

READING CHECK
What were Eisenhower's domestic priorities?

Ike's priorities included cutting spending, reducing taxes, and balancing the budget. He called this approach to government "dynamic conservatism" or **Modern Republicanism.** He intended to be "conservative when it comes to money, liberal when it comes to human beings."

In the tradition of past Republican Presidents such as Coolidge and Hoover, Eisenhower favored big business. His Cabinet was composed mostly of successful businessmen, plus one union leader. Critics charged that the Eisenhower Cabinet consisted of "eight millionaires and a plumber."

Modern Republicanism sought to encourage and support corporate America. Eisenhower's administration transferred control of about $40 billion worth of

NOTABLE PRESIDENTS
Dwight D. Eisenhower

34th President
1953–1961

"I am no politician as you well know."
—Eisenhower, as he prepared to assume the presidency

Born in Texas in 1890, Dwight Eisenhower grew up in Abilene, Kansas. After high school he attended the United States Military Academy at West Point. As supreme commander of the Allied Expeditionary Force during World War II, Eisenhower oversaw the D-Day landings in France and the final defeat of Germany. After the war, he served as Army Chief of Staff, president of Columbia University, and then head of NATO, the North Atlantic Treaty Organization. In 1952, he ran for President as a Republican and won a landslide victory in the general election.

Eisenhower was a strong defender of American interests abroad, yet he also feared that high military spending would harm the economy. Therefore, Eisenhower endorsed a military strategy of relying on nuclear weapons, rather than more costly conventional armies, in conflicts around the world.

At home, Eisenhower generally favored restraint in government actions and spending.

Eisenhower's critics sometimes complained about his low-key approach to the presidency and accused him of providing weak leadership. Yet he offered the nation stability and reassurance during a dangerous period of the Cold War.

Connecting to Today
How might experience as a military leader help a President? Can you think of any ways in which such experience might not be helpful? Explain.

Take It to the NET Biography To read more about Dwight Eisenhower, visit the links provided in the *America: Pathways to the Present* area at the following Web site. **www.phschool.com**

ACTIVITY
Connecting with Citizenship

Remind students of the existence and purpose of presidential libraries, and assign them the task of learning about the Eisenhower presidential library. Students should conduct research to learn about its official name and location, facilities, and attractions. **(Verbal/Linguistic)**

BACKGROUND
Recent Scholarship

The decade of the 1950s was peaceful and prosperous on the surface. Most Americans seemed comfortable with the conservative patterns of their lives. Beneath this calm exterior, however, lay the seeds of the turbulence that unfolded in the 1960s. In *The Fifties,* David Halberstam describes the Cold War and anti-Communist fervor that culminated in the war in Vietnam, assesses the growing impact of television on American life, and highlights the social and sexual tensions festering beneath the surface that helped create the lively and colorful counterculture of the 1960s.

READING CHECK
Eisenhower wanted to slow the growth of the federal government; to limit the President's power; and to increase the authority of Congress and the courts. He looked to cut spending, reduce taxes, and balance the budget. He did, however, support certain aspects of the New Deal.

TEST PREPARATION

Have students reread the quotation by Richard Nixon on the previous page and then complete the sentence below.

From this passage, you can infer that—

A Nixon feels guilty about accepting the gift.
B Nixon secretly blames his daughter for making him take the gift.
(C) Nixon knows that his emotional story will win public approval.
D Nixon doesn't understand why anyone would get angry over him accepting a dog as a pet for his children.

VIEWING HISTORY Scientists (left to right) William Pickering, James Van Allen, and Wernher von Braun raise a model of the first U.S. satellite, *Explorer-I*. The scientists participated in the satellite program. **Drawing Conclusions** *Why did the government find it important to establish a space program in the 1950s?*

offshore oil lands from the federal government to the states so that the states could lease oil rights to corporations. It worked to end government competition with big business.

Ike's attempt to balance the budget backfired. His cuts in government spending caused the economy to slump. When that happened, tax revenues dropped, and the deficit grew larger instead of smaller. Economic growth, which had averaged 4.3 percent between 1947 and 1952, fell to 2.5 percent between 1953 and 1960. The country suffered three economic recessions during Eisenhower's presidency, from 1953 to 1954, from 1957 to 1958, and again from 1960 to 1961.

Despite America's economic troubles, Eisenhower helped the country maintain a mood of stability. He also underscored the basic commitment the government had made during the New Deal: to ensure the economic security of all Americans. For example, in 1954 and 1956, Social Security was extended to make eligible 10 million additional workers. In 1955, the minimum wage was raised from 75 cents to $1 an hour.

Meeting the Technology Challenge When the Soviet Union launched *Sputnik* in 1957, as described in the previous chapter, many Americans grew concerned that the United States was losing its competitive edge. Others feared a nuclear attack would soon follow. In 1958, the United States government responded by creating the **National Aeronautics and Space Administration (NASA),** as an independent agency for space exploration.

The same year, Congress passed and President Eisenhower signed into law the **National Defense Education Act.** The measure was designed to improve science and mathematics instruction in the schools so that the United States could meet the scientific and technical challenge from the Soviet Union. The act provided millions of dollars in low-cost loans to college students and significant reductions in repayments if they ultimately became teachers. The federal government also granted millions to state schools for building science and foreign language facilities.

Section 3 Assessment

READING COMPREHENSION

1. What issues did Truman face during the period of **reconversion?**
2. What was the **Taft-Hartley Act?**
3. What was **Modern Republicanism?** Why did Eisenhower embrace it?
4. Why was the **National Aeronautics and Space Administration (NASA)** created?
5. What was the **National Defense Education Act?**

CRITICAL THINKING AND WRITING

6. **Making Comparisons** Compare what President Truman and President Eisenhower each saw as the federal government's role in domestic matters.
7. **Writing a Letter** Review the issues that led to the passage of the Twenty-second Amendment. Write a letter to your state senator registering your opinion as to whether the amendment should be repealed.

Take It to the NET

Activity: Writing a News Article Investigate the early years of America's space program. Write an article on some aspect of NASA's first operations. Use the links provided in the *America: Pathways to the Present* area of the following Web site for help in completing this activity.
www.phschool.com

Section 3 Assessment

Reading Comprehension

1. Answers may include: lifting economic controls while attempting to check inflation; workers demanding wage increases; 1946 railroad strike.
2. It allowed the President to declare an 80-day cooling-off period when strikes occurred in industries affecting national interests. During this time, strikers had to return to work while the government conducted an investigation. It also stipulated that union leaders had to declare under oath that they did not belong to the Communist party.
3. Policies of cutting spending, reducing taxes, and balancing the budget. He was determined to slow the growth of the government and support big business.
4. As a response to the concern that the U.S. was losing its technological edge to Russia and the fear that a nuclear attack was forthcoming.
5. A law designed to improve science and mathematics instruction in the schools so that the U.S. could meet the scientific and technical challenge from the Soviet Union.

Critical Thinking and Writing

6. Truman believed in an active, positive role for the federal government in social and economic matters; Eisenhower wanted to curb the role of the federal government in these areas.
7. Letters will vary, but should be supported with facts from the section.

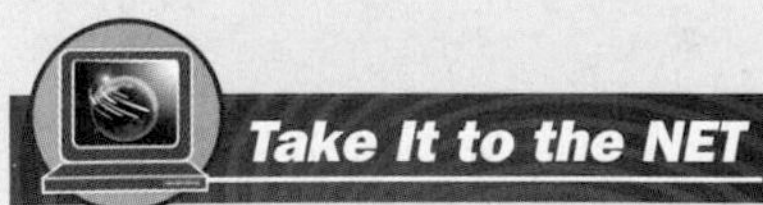

Take It to the NET

Students' answers will vary, but may include an exploration of the reasons for the founding of NASA in 1958 and descriptions of the growth and development of early operations.

Caption Answers

Viewing History As a world power, the United States wanted to compete with the Soviet Union on many levels. Soviet advances in space exploration, such as *Sputnik*, made NASA a priority.

RESOURCE DIRECTORY

Teaching Resources

Units 3/4 booklet
- Section 3 Quiz, p. 40
- Chapter 20 Test, pp. 41, 44

Guide to the Essentials
- Section 3 Summary, p. 99
- Chapter 20 Test, p. 100

Other Print Resources

Chapter Tests with ExamView® Test Bank CD-ROM, Ch. 20

Technology

ExamView® Test Bank CD-ROM, Ch. 20
Social Studies Skills Tutor CD-ROM

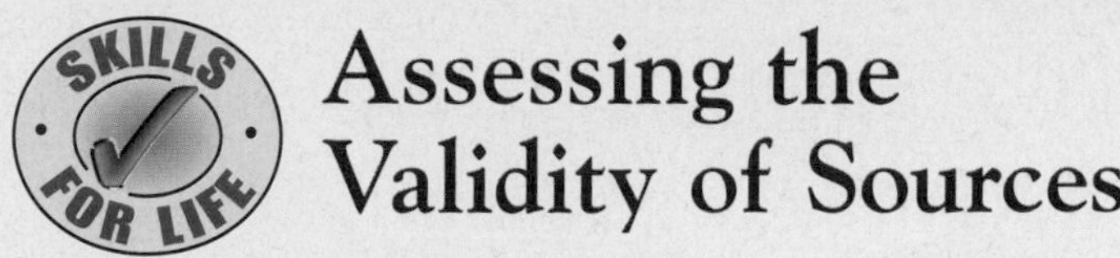

Assessing the Validity of Sources

Sometimes it seems that information is everywhere: in newspapers, magazines, and books; on television, radio, and the Internet. How can you tell which information is reliable? Your teacher or librarian can point you toward good sources, such as well-respected encyclopedias, publishers, and Web sites, but you can also make judgments about the validity of sources yourself. The sources at right discuss President Truman's veto of the 1947 Taft-Hartley Act.

LEARN THE SKILL

Use the following steps to assess the validity of sources:

1. **Determine what kind of information you need.** For current statistics, you need an up-to-date source. To learn about a historical event, you may want a primary source from the time. Remember, however, that causes and effects may have been unclear to the people writing when the event occurred.
2. **Ask yourself if the information is generally accurate.** Does it agree with sources you already know are reliable, such as a current encyclopedia?
3. **Check the qualifications of the author or publisher.** Is the author an expert on the subject? Is the magazine generally well respected? Is the Web site hosted by a reliable organization?
4. **Consider whether the author seems objective or biased.** An author who is trying to persuade might mention only certain facts, use "loaded" language, or state opinions as if they are proven facts.

PRACTICE THE SKILL

Answer the following questions:

1. **(a)** Do you need recent information to research this event? Explain. **(b)** What are the benefits of using a primary source such as A? **(c)** What might be one benefit of using a secondary source such as B?
2. **(a)** How might you check the information found in Source A for accuracy? **(b)** Source B includes extensive footnotes citing bibliographic sources. How does this information help you judge its reliability?
3. **(a)** What are the qualifications of the author of Source A for writing about this subject? **(b)** Do you have confidence in the author and publisher of Source B? Explain.
4. **(a)** Why is the author of Source A writing about this subject? Is he likely to be objective? Explain. **(b)** Does Source B seem to be objective or biased? Explain.

APPLY THE SKILL

See the Chapter Review and Assessment for another opportunity to apply this skill.

A

"My fellow countrymen:

At noon today I sent the Congress a message vetoing the Taft-Hartley labor bill. I vetoed this bill because I am convinced it is a bad bill. It is bad for labor, bad for management, bad for the country. . . .

This bill is deliberately designed to weaken labor unions. When the sponsors of the bill claim that by weakening unions, they are giving rights back to individual working men, they ignore the basic reason why unions are important in our democracy. Unions exist so that laboring men can bargain with their employers on a basis of equality. . . .

We have been told, by the supporters of the Taft-Hartley bill, that it would reduce industrial strife.

On the contrary, I am convinced that it would increase industrial strife. . . . because a number of its provisions deprive workers of legal protection of fundamental rights. They would then have no means of protecting those rights except by striking. . . ."

—Harry S Truman, radio address, June 20, 1947

B

"Several quite important political factors indicated that signing the measure would be [Truman's] wisest course. The . . . desire of the nation for remedial labor legislation, plus the large majorities given the bill by Congress, made it fairly obvious that a veto would be overridden. Thus Truman would be placed in the embarrassing position of having tried to withhold legislation that the people demanded. . . .

But . . . [s]igning the proposal would be inconsistent with . . . the requests made in [Truman's] State of the Union message. . . . Then there was the apparently honest conviction that the bill would actually increase industrial strife. Reports of various competent advisers . . . indicated that the legislation was fundamentally unworkable. . . . "

—R. Alton Lee, *Truman and Taft-Hartley: a question of mandate,* University of Kentucky Press, 1966

RESOURCE DIRECTORY

Teaching Resources

Skills for Life booklet, p. 29

Technology

Social Studies Skills Tutor CD-ROM

Interactive Practice in
- Geographic Literacy
- Critical Thinking and Reading
- Visual Analysis
- Communications

ASSESSING THE VALIDITY OF SOURCES

Focus Students learn to compare and contrast the validity of primary and secondary material in seeking to understand a historical situation.

Instruct After students have read passage A, ask them to discuss the ways in which President Truman attempted to justify his actions. Do his arguments make sense? Next, have students read passage B, in which they gain more background on the situation. Truman's decision was very costly politically. How do students view his decision now, with more information on the background of the situation? Have students explain the usefulness of analyzing both primary and secondary sources in attempting to reconstruct a historical event.

Extend See the Skills for Life activity in the Resource Directory below.

ANSWERS

PRACTICE THE SKILL

1. **(a)** No. Most facts about the event are already known. **(b)** It is possible to find out Truman's views on the situation and how he thought he could convince the nation. **(c)** It is possible to gain more perspective and to hear an unbiased view.
2. **(a)** Though it might be helpful to read the bill itself for more background, the statements made by Truman are statements of opinion, not fact. **(b)** Footnotes and extensive bibliographic citation help support the validity of the author's assertions.
3. **(a)** The author of source A is the man who made the actual decision—President Truman. **(b)** A university press is generally considered a reliable source because the material it publishes is usually reviewed by experts for accuracy.
4. **(a)** Because he is trying to defend an unpopular stance he has taken by vetoing a bill. He is unlikely to be objective, because he is involved in the decision. **(b)** Source B appears to be objective because he presents both sides of the argument.

Reviewing Key Terms

Students should refer to the definitions of key terms in the chapter to write sentences showing an understanding of domestic issues during the postwar era.

Reviewing Main Ideas

11. The conglomerate system led to the formation of giant corporations that owned businesses in many different areas of the economy. The franchise system meant that local businesses were sometimes pushed out of business by large chains.

12. New electronic components, such as transistors, aided in the development of new and improved products. Peaceful uses of atomic energy were also explored.

13. Suburbs developed because of urban decay, an increase in population, cheap and plentiful housing, improved roads, and availability of automobiles and fuel.

14. They seemed to have little interest in national and international issues; the stronger economy allowed the youth generation to stay in school; teenagers seemed to be mainly interested in enjoying themselves.

15. Men working as breadwinners, active in society and politics. Women at home in suburbia, tending to the house and children. Young people in school, pursuing fun in their free time. The media encouraged conformity in appearance and behavior, promoting, for example, the image of bobby socks and letter sweaters for teens.

16. They gave young people identities of their own as they rebelled against rigid societal roles and expectations.

17. The Fair Deal promoted full employment, a higher minimum wage, greater unemployment compensation, housing assistance, national health insurance, and atomic energy legislation. A coalition of conservative Democrats and Republicans in Congress opposed most of the Fair Deal initiatives.

18. He supported civil rights, appointing a biracial Committee on Civil Rights and banning discrimination in the hiring of federal employees and

Chapter 20 Review and Assessment

creating a CHAPTER SUMMARY

Copy this flowchart (right) on a piece of paper and complete it by adding information about life in the United States after World War II.

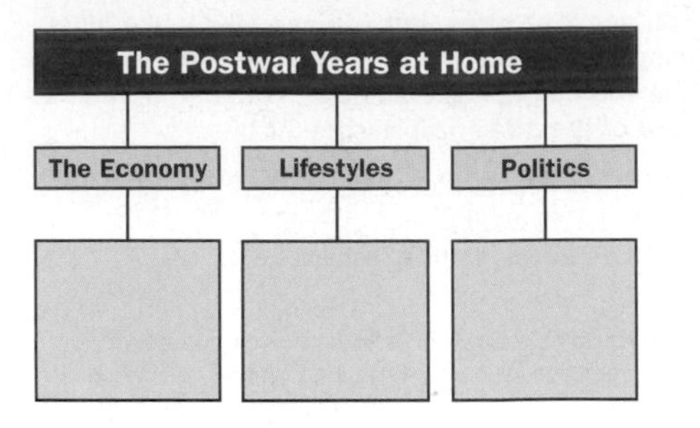

iTEXT

For additional review and enrichment activities, see the interactive version of *America: Pathways to the Present*, available on the Web and on CD-ROM.

★ Reviewing Key Terms

For each of the terms below, write a sentence explaining how it relates to the postwar years.

1. per capita income
2. conglomerate
3. franchise
4. transistor
5. GI Bill of Rights
6. reconversion
7. Taft-Hartley Act
8. modern republicanism
9. National Aeronautics and Space Administration (NASA)
10. National Defense Education Act

★ Reviewing Main Ideas

11. How did the conglomerate and the franchise system change the American economy after World War II? (Section 1)
12. What technological advances took place during the postwar years? (Section 1)
13. What factors contributed to the development of the suburbs from 1945 to 1960? (Section 1)
14. Explain why children of the baby boom were sometimes called the "silent generation." (Section 2)
15. What was the model middle-class lifestyle of the 1950s? Give examples showing how the media fostered expectations of "the good life." (Section 2)
16. Why did young people identify with rock-and-roll and the beat movement in the 1950s? (Section 2)
17. Describe Truman's Fair Deal program and the congressional response to it. (Section 3)
18. What was Truman's stand on civil rights issues? (Section 3)
19. What effect did Eisenhower's leadership style have on his presidency? (Section 3)

★ Critical Thinking

20. **Recognizing Cause and Effect** How did Americans' experiences throughout the Depression and World War II affect consumer spending during the 1950s?
21. **Demonstrating Reasoned Judgment** Which technological advance of the 1950s—atomic energy, computers, or television—do you think has had the most far-reaching impact on the way Americans live? Explain why you think so.
22. **Identifying Central Issues** What economic changes occurred in the United States from 1945 to 1960? Explain why the changes occurred.
23. **Making Comparisons** Analyze the conflicts between labor unions and the Truman administration just after World War II. How did the situation compare to labor disputes that followed World War I?
24. **Identifying Assumptions** Why was the outcome of the 1948 election a surprise to some people? What issues did Truman raise in his campaign that helped secure his victory?

Creating a Chapter Summary

The Postwar Years at Home

The Economy	Lifestyles	Politics
Businesses reorganize.	Alan Freed begins playing rock-and-roll in Cleveland.	Congress passes the GI Bill.
Efforts to reconvert the economy from wartime to peacetime	Americans begin to buy televisions.	Congress passes the Taft-Hartley Act.
The Fair Deal	Baby boom begins.	Very close election of 1948
	Housing boom in suburbs	White House is Republican for the first time in 20 years in 1953.
	Surge of auto use, highway construction	

★ Skills Assessment

Analyzing Political Cartoons ▶

25. A cartoonist drew this view of suburban life in 1952. (a) What is most striking about this community? (b) What do you know about such communities?
26. Read the caption. What is the cause of the woman's dilemma?
27. What is the cartoonist saying about life in a 1950s suburb?

Interpreting Data

Turn to the chart "Average Household TV Viewing Hours, 1950–1990" in Section 1.

28. During what year was TV viewing at its lowest point?
    A 1950
    B 1960
    C 1970
    D 1980
29. By how much time did average daily television viewing per household increase from 1950 to 1960?
    F 1 hour, 29 minutes
    G 31 minutes
    H 29 minutes
    J 45 minutes

Applying the Chapter Skill: *Assessing the Validity of Sources*

30. Using the library or the Internet, find five other sources of information on the Taft-Hartley Act. How does the validity of those five sources compare to that of the two sources used on the skill page at the end of this chapter?

"I'm Mrs. Edward M. Barnes. Where do I live?"

ACTIVITIES

Writing to LEARN

Journal Writing
What it would be like to return to life at home after serving in World War II? Finding a job, reconnecting with friends and family, and adjusting to postwar social and economic conditions were some of the issues that returning soldiers faced. Write a journal entry from a returning soldier's point of view that addresses some of these topics.

Primary Source CD-ROM

Working With Primary Sources Find additional information on the post–World War II years on the *Exploring Primary Sources in U.S. History CD-ROM* and use the selection(s) provided to complete the Chapter 20 primary source activity located in the *America: Pathways to the Present* area of the following Web site. **www.phschool.com**

Take It to the NET

Chapter Self-Test As a review activity, take the Chapter 20 Self-Test in the *America: Pathways to the Present* area at the Web site listed below. The questions are designed to test your understanding of the chapter content. **www.phschool.com**

ANSWERS TO ACTIVITIES

Writing to LEARN

Answers will vary, but should explore social, economic, and political themes discussed in the chapter.

Primary Source CD-ROM

Direct students to the additional primary sources that can be found on the *Exploring Primary Sources in U.S. History CD-ROM.*

Take It to the NET

Additional support materials and activities for Chapter 20 of *America: Pathways to the Present* can be found in the Social Studies area at the Prentice Hall School Web site. **www.phschool.com**

segregation and discrimination in the armed forces.

19. Eisenhower's behind-the-scenes leadership increased his popularity with the American people. The stability and reassurance he offered led to his reelection.

Critical Thinking

20. People were eager to buy everything that the war and the Depression had denied them.
21. Answers will vary. Students may point out that television has been blamed for such problems as violence and consumerism; computers have become elements of daily life, changing both work and recreation; and atomic energy has raised concerns about waste disposal, accidents, and terrorism.
22. Answers may vary, but should include: under President Truman, inflation set in as wartime economic controls were lifted and wages remained low. There was overall prosperity during Eishenhower's term, with three recessions caused by his efforts to reduce federal government size and balance the budget.
23. In both cases, workers demanded increases that they had forgone for the war effort; the number of strikes soared and affected many industries; in both time periods unemployment was a problem, and strong anti-Communist feelings dominated.
24. Truman's support, even from his own party, had fallen. Truman stressed that the Republican Congress did little to effect progress. He attacked its farm policy, giving him the farmers' support.

Skills Assessment

25. (a) Its uniformity. (b) Prefabricated communities were built of affordable, mass-produced houses in the postwar years by Levitt and other developers.
26. She cannot distinguish her home from the others.
27. It lacks individuality and originality.
28. A
29. G
30. Answers will vary, but students should check the qualifications of the author or publisher for the five sources. For example, they should note if a Web site is a personal home page or if it is hosted by a reliable organization, such as the government or a university.

The Rise of the Suburbs

Focus Explain that before the postwar building boom, only the wealthy could afford to live in the suburbs. After the war, prosperity and government programs to finance mortgages started a suburban building boom that changed the way many Americans lived.

Instruct Show students a detailed map of the nearest large city and its surrounding suburbs. Ask students to point out the core city, beltways, and "edge cities."

Ask students to list ways in which the development of suburban housing changed American life. Ask them to consider:

- The family: How did suburban housing encourage nuclear, as opposed to extended, families?
- The environment: What impact did the growth of suburbs have on wildlife, quality of air and water, and amount of farmland?
- Integration: Did the growth of suburbs encourage or discourage integration of housing and schools?

Extend Many observers thought that the shopping mall would become the "community center" of the suburbs, filling the roles of Main Street, the town common, the city square, and the neighborhood playground. Ask students how successful they think shopping malls have been in creating a sense of community. What activities other than shopping, such as eating meals, taking an exercise class, or going to a movie, are available in shopping malls?

Geography & History

The Rise of the Suburbs

In the decades after World War II, millions of Americans moved from older cities to new suburban developments. By the 1960s, a new landscape of single-family homes and shopping malls had spread across the land. This phenomenon was not new: Commuter suburbs on rail and streetcar lines had attracted affluent and middle-class home buyers since the 1800s. What was new was the massive scale of the movement, made possible by government subsidies and widespread car ownership.

The Government's Role

The Federal Housing Administration offered low-cost loans to homebuyers, and the GI Bill made these loans even cheaper for veterans. These loans promoted suburban development by favoring new single-family houses over existing multifamily housing in cities. Meanwhile, the Interstate Highway Act of 1956 provided government funding for superhighways that gave cars easy access to the suburbs.

Urban Decay

City residents moved to the suburbs to fulfill dreams of home ownership and to flee crime and congestion. Increasingly, city neighborhoods, such as this one in Washington, D.C., fell victim to decay and abandonment.

Geographic Connection

Why did people move from the inner cities to the suburbs?

Answers

1. City dwellers sought to pursue dreams of home ownership and to flee crime and congestion. Government programs (subsidized loans, highway construction) promoted suburban single-family development over multifamily urban housing.

RESOURCE DIRECTORY

Teaching Resources
Geography and History booklet, pp. 16–17

Other Print Resources
Nystrom *Atlas of Our Country* *Land Use, Population, and Ethnicity,* pp. 46–47

Technology
Prentice Hall United States History Video Collection™ Volume 20, *Post-War USA*

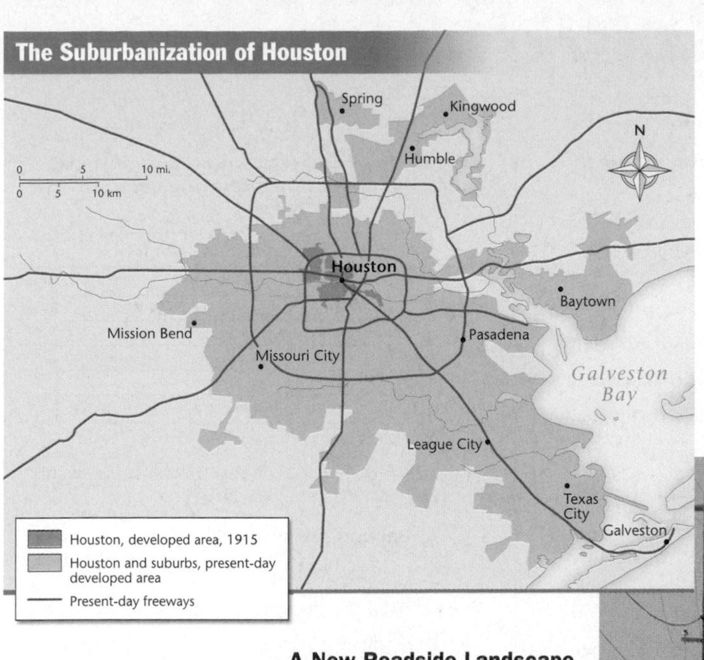

One City's Example

In 1915, before most people owned cars, Houston, Texas, was a compact city, and most people walked or took a streetcar to work. With the growth in car ownership and the construction of freeways and suburban developments, Houston has expanded to cover a much larger area, organized around car travel and major highways.

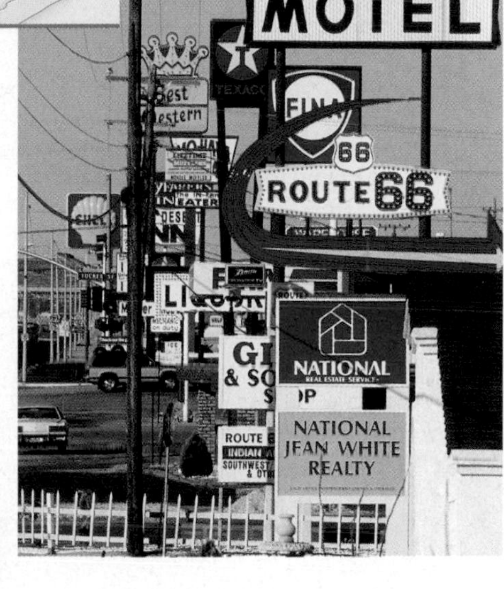

A New Roadside Landscape

Billboards and retail businesses sprang up along suburban highways to serve a growing population of drivers.

Geographic Connection

How did the geography of cities and suburbs change as a result of growth along suburban highways?

New Commercial Centers

At first, suburbs were mainly residential, and people traveled into the city to shop and work. Then open-air malls were built to serve suburban shoppers. By the 1960s, covered malls and office parks had begun to replace traditional downtown city districts as places to shop and work.

Geographic Connection

How do you think the growth of suburban malls and roadside businesses affected traditional downtown businesses?

Answers

2. Suburbs expanded, primarily along highways. Roadside businesses developed. The suburban landscape, which once focused on walking and public transportation lines, is now mainly organized around car travel and major highways.
3. Traditional downtown businesses lost customers to suburban malls and roadside businesses. Downtown districts lost some of their former commercial importance.

TEST PREPARATION

Use this sample exam to help your students prepare for standardized tests.

Tips for Test Taking

You might want to remind your students of the following:

1. Read the directions carefully.
2. Read each question carefully.
3. For multiple choice questions, try to answer the question before you look at the choices. Read all the choices. Then, eliminate those that are absolutely incorrect.
4. For short answer questions, be sure to answer the question completely if there is more than one part.
5. Answer the easy questions first. Then, go back to the ones that will take more time.
6. Pace yourself. Be sure to set aside enough time for the writing questions.

Write your answers on a separate sheet of paper.

1. Which one of the following is a correct statement about Stalin's "show trials" in the Soviet Union in the 1930s?

   A The rights of the accused were fully protected.

   B The juries always found Communists not guilty.

   C Guilt was determined before the trial began.

   D Few people were actually punished by the trials.

2. Why did British and French leaders follow a policy of appeasement when dealing with Germany?

   A They were not ready to fight a war with Hitler.

   B The two countries were following isolationist policies.

   C As Axis Powers, they could ignore the growing German strength.

   D Their main interests were in East Asia and not Western Europe.

> **"Never . . . was so much owed by so many to so few."**
>
> *—Winston Churchill*

3. British Prime Minister Winston Churchill was speaking about

   A American military forces who invaded France during D-Day.

   B British pilots who defeated the Germans in the Battle of Britain.

   C British troops who ended German expansion in North Africa.

   D Soviet soldiers who stopped the Germans in central Russia.

Use the chart and your knowledge of social studies to answer the following question.

The Road to World War II

Year	Event
1936	Germany occupies the Rhineland
1938	Austria taken over by Germany
1938	Germany divides up Czechoslovakia
1939	???
1940	Germany invades and conquers France

4. Which one of the following items replaces the question marks on the chart?

   A England begins bombing raids on Germany.

   B Italy and Germany invade Spain.

   C Germany declares war on the Soviet Union.

   D Germany invades and conquers Poland.

5. During World War II, why did the government ration sugar, butter, and other foods?

   A To stop the Germans from buying up foods and exporting them to Germany

   B To prevent deflation of the nation's money

   C To make sure items in short supply were available for all people

   D To keep the military from getting more food than it needed

6. Which battle in World War II ended Japan's ability to carry out offensive operations in the Pacific?

   A Midway

   B Coral Sea

   C Leyte Gulf

   D Okinawa

692

Diagnose and Prescribe
- Profile student skills with Diagnostic Tests A&B.
- Address student needs with program materials correlated to test questions.

Review and Reteach
- Provide cumulative content review with the Review Book.

Practice and Assess
- Build test-taking skills with Test-taking Strategies With Transparencies.

TEST PREPARATION

Use the information in the map to answer the following question.

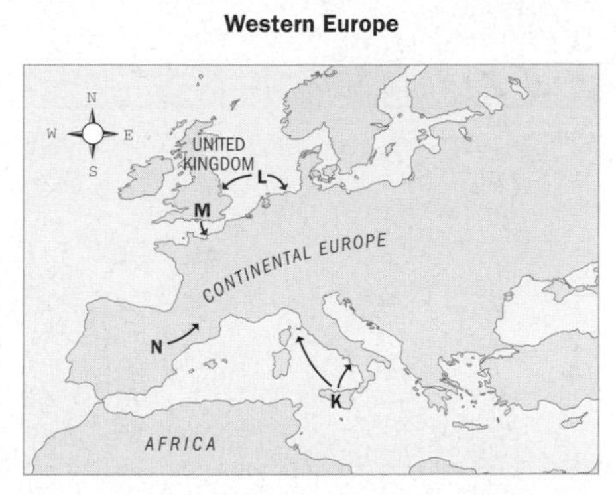

7. Which one of the arrows represents Operation Overlord on D-Day, June 6, 1944, when Western Europe was invaded by Allied forces?

   A K

   B L

   C M

   D N

> **"The President shall be Commander in Chief of the Army and Navy of the United States. . . ."**
>
> *—Article II, Section 2, United States Constitution*

8. This part of the United States Constitution provided the basis for President Harry S Truman to

   A open up trade with China.

   B make General Dwight Eisenhower the next President.

   C help rebuild the Soviet Union after World War II.

   D fire General Douglas MacArthur.

Use the information in the graph and your knowledge of social studies to answer the following question.

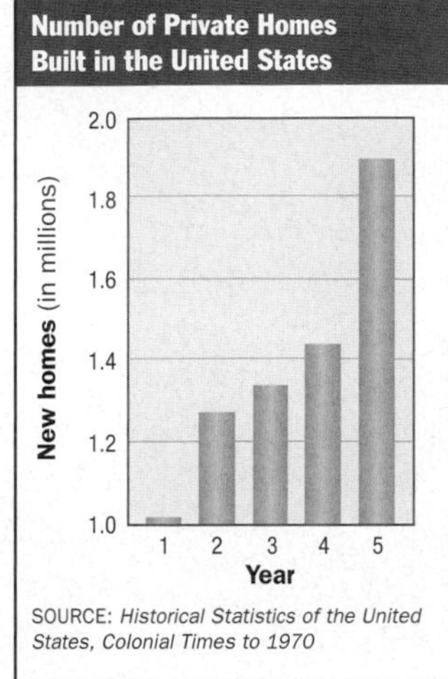

SOURCE: *Historical Statistics of the United States, Colonial Times to 1970*

9. The information on housing best describes which five-year period?

   A 1930–1935

   B 1936–1940

   C 1941–1945

   D 1946–1950

Writing Practice

10. What was the intended purpose of the U. S. Neutrality Acts passed during the 1930s? What was their actual effect? Explain why this happened.

11. What promises were made at the Yalta Conference and which of these were kept?

12. Describe three components of the Fair Deal as proposed by President Harry S Truman.

1. C
2. A
3. B
4. D
5. C
6. A
7. C
8. D
9. D
10. The purpose was to keep the U.S. out of future wars. In effect, the acts encouraged German aggression, because they made it difficult for the United States to help countries trying to defend themselves against German attacks.
11. Stalin promised to enter the war against Japan and to allow Poland to have free elections. He kept the first promise (just barely) and allowed Polish elections only after a long delay in which he eliminated political opposition to communism there.
12. Answers could discuss any three of the following: legislation to promote full employment; a higher minimum wage; increased unemployment compensation; housing assistance; a national health insurance program; or congressional action in regard to controlling atomic energy.

Unit 6

Introducing the Unit

A Period of Turmoil and Change (1950–1975) The third quarter of the twentieth century found many Americans restless for change. For African Americans, it was a time to demand equal opportunities in education, housing, and citizenship. Many American students supported these demands, and the movement for civil rights evolved into a protest movement that opposed the United States policies in Vietnam as well as in domestic activities. President Kennedy offered a steadying hand in the early days of civil rights protests; after Kennedy was assassinated in 1963, President Johnson had to deal with the unrest. He also inherited the deteriorating situation in Vietnam. Johnson's decision to escalate United States involvement in that war and the growing United States protest movement combined to cripple his presidency.

Using Historical Evidence

Direct students' attention to the photograph on these pages. Have students list the various factions they see represented in the photograph. Also note that there are protestors from many different parts of the country. Point out that many protestors are African American, but there are also members of other ethnic groups.

Talk with students about why Washington, D.C., became the focus of so many civil rights and antiwar protests. Who were the protestors trying to reach? Do students agree with the strategy of gathering large groups of protestors in the nation's capital?

eTeach

Be sure to check out this month's online discussion with a Master Teacher. Go to **www.phschool.com**.

Unit 6 A Period of Turmoil and Change (1950–1975)

"In a democratic society like ours, relief must come through an aroused popular conscience that sears the conscience of the people's representatives."

Felix Frankfurter, Supreme Court Justice
Baker v. Carr, 1962

Thousands showed their support for the civil rights movement at the March on Washington in 1963. ▶

694

RESOURCE DIRECTORY

Teaching Resources

Units 5/6/7 booklet
- American Pathways Activity, pp. 95–96
- History's Lasting Impact, pp. 97–98

Geography and History booklet, pp. 18–19

Other Print Resources

Prentice Hall Assessment System
- Document-Based Assessment

695

RESOURCE DIRECTORY

Technology

Color Transparencies *Historical Maps,* A48, A49, A50, A51; *Political Cartoons,* B16, B17; *Time Lines,* C8; *American Photo,* F9; *The Way It Works,* H19

Section Reading Support Transparencies

Prentice Hall United States History Video Collection™ Volume 20, *Post-War USA*

Companion Web site, www.phschool.com

TECHNOLOGY CENTER

Take It to the NET

Prentice Hall School Web site offers student-appropriate Internet activities and links that extend core content. Visit us at the Social Studies area. **www.phschool.com**

AmericanHeritage®

My Brush with History™ Video Program This new video series lets your students learn history from the people who lived it.

RESOURCE PRO®

Teaching Resources on CD-ROM offer lesson-planning flexibility, test-generation capability, and resource manageability.

- **Presentation Pro CD-ROM** Provides you with multimedia lecture notes for each chapter.
- **Social Studies Skills Tutor CD-ROM** Provides interactive practice in Geographic Literacy, Critical Thinking and Reading, Visual Analysis, and Communications.
- **Interactive Constitution CD-ROM** Exploring active citizenship and civic responsibilities, this CD-ROM shows students how the Constitution affects their lives today.
- **Exploring Primary Sources in U.S. History CD-ROM** This interactive exploration of primary sources allows students to analyze and to evaluate writing and images from American history.
- **Guided Reading Audiotapes**
- **Student Edition on Audio CD**
- **Sounds of an Era Audio CD** Bring the sounds of American history to life in the classroom with music, speeches, poetry, interviews, and news reports.

Don't miss the exclusive interactive version of this textbook on the Web and on CD-ROM.

Chapter 21 Planning Guide
Resource Manager

	Core Instruction	Reading/Skills
Chapter-Level Resources **TEKS** 7(A), 24(A), 24(B)	Teaching Resources • Pacing Charts booklet • Block Scheduling booklet **Resource Pro® CD-ROM,** Ch. 21 **Prentice Hall Presentation Pro CD-ROM,** Ch. 21 **www.phschool.com** • eTeach	**Guided Reading Audiotapes (English/Spanish)** **Student Edition on Audio CD,** Ch. 21 **Social Studies Skills Tutor CD-ROM** **Color Transparencies,** B16, F9
1 Demands for Civil Rights 1. Learn about events that led to a rise in African American influence in the twentieth century. 2. Find out how Americans responded to the *Brown* v. *Board of Education* decision. 3. Discover how the Montgomery bus boycott affected the civil rights movement. 4. See how other minorities began to demand civil rights in the 1960s. **TEKS** 8(B), 17(A), 26(A)	Teaching Resources **Units 5/6/7 booklet** • Section 1 Quiz, p. 52 **Learning Styles Lesson Plans booklet,** p. 58	**Guided Reading and Review booklet,** p. 112 **Guide to the Essentials,** p. 101 **Learning with Documents booklet,** pp. 33, 92 **Section Reading Support Transparencies**
2 Leaders and Strategies 1. Find out how early groups laid the foundation for the civil rights movement. 2. Understand the philosophy of nonviolence. 3. Realize how SNCC gave students a voice in the civil rights movement. **TEKS** 7(B), 20(A), 21(A)	Teaching Resources **Units 5/6/7 booklet** • Section 2 Quiz, p. 53	**Guided Reading and Review booklet,** p. 113 **Guide to the Essentials,** p. 102 **Learning with Documents booklet,** p. 67 **Section Reading Support Transparencies**
3 The Struggle Intensifies 1. Identify the goals of sit-ins and Freedom Rides. 2. Find out the reaction to James Meredith's integration at the University of Mississippi. 3. Understand how the Birmingham events affected attitudes toward the civil rights movement. **TEKS** 24(D), 24(H), 25(D)	Teaching Resources **Units 5/6/7 booklet** • Section 3 Quiz, p. 54 **Learning Styles Lesson Plans booklet,** p. 59	**Guided Reading and Review booklet,** p. 114 **Guide to the Essentials,** p. 103 **Learning with Documents booklet,** p. 33 **Skills for Life booklet,** p. 30 **Section Reading Support Transparencies**
4 The Political Response 1. Learn about Kennedy's approach to civil rights. 2. Find out why civil rights leaders proposed a march on Washington. 3. Learn the goals of the Civil Rights Act of 1964. **TEKS** 7(C), 7(D), 8(A), 18(A), 18(B), 19(C)	Teaching Resources **Units 5/6/7 booklet** • Section 4 Quiz, p. 55	**Guided Reading and Review booklet,** p. 115 **Guide to the Essentials,** p. 104 **Learning with Documents booklet,** p. 91 **Section Reading Support Transparencies**
5 The Movement Takes a New Turn 1. Learn about Malcolm X's approach to gaining civil rights. 2. Become familiar with the major goals of the black power movement. 3. See why violent riots erupted in many urban streets. 4. Find out how the tragic events of 1968 affected the nation. **TEKS** 1(B), 24(C)	Teaching Resources **Units 5/6/7 booklet** • Section 5 Quiz, p. 56	**Guided Reading and Review booklet,** p. 116 **Guide to the Essentials,** p. 105 **Section Reading Support Transparencies**

Enrichment/Pre-AP

Prentice Hall United States History Video Collection™
www.phschool.com
- Section Activities, Virtual Field Trip, Chapter Activities, Current Events Online

Biography, Literature, and Comparing Primary Sources booklet, p. 33
Great Debates booklet, p. 40
Sounds of an Era Audio CD
Exploring Primary Sources in U.S. History CD-ROM

Biography, Literature, and Comparing Primary Sources booklet, pp. 78–79, 151–152
American History Block Scheduling Support

Sounds of an Era Audio CD
Exploring Primary Sources in U.S. History CD-ROM

American History Block Scheduling Support
Sounds of an Era Audio CD
Exploring Primary Sources in U.S. History CD-ROM

Sounds of an Era Audio CD
American Pathways Thematic Posters

Assessment

Core Assessment
ExamView® Test Bank, Ch. 21
ExamView® Test Bank CD-ROM, Ch. 21

Standardized Test Preparation
Diagnose and Prescribe
Diagnostic Tests for High School Social Studies Skills

Review and Reteach
Review Book for U.S. History

Practice and Assess
Test-taking Strategies With Transparencies
Test-taking Strategies Posters
Test Prep Book for U.S. History
Alternative Assessment Handbook
Document-Based Assessment

Teaching Resources
Units 5/6/7 booklet
- Section Quizzes, pp. 52–56
- Chapter Tests, pp. 57, 60

www.phschool.com Ch. 21 Self-Test

AmericanHeritage® Resources

From the Archives of American Heritage®, pp. 701, 719, 726
AmericanHeritage® My Brush with History™ Videotapes
www.americanheritage.com

Don't miss the exclusive interactive version of this textbook on the Web and on CD-ROM.

Chapter 21 Planning Guide

In Your Classroom

Customize for Individual Needs

Gifted and Talented

Teacher's Edition
- Customize for Gifted and Talented, pp. 711, 713

Teaching Resources
- Biography, Literature, and Comparing Primary Sources booklet, pp. 33, 78–79, 151–152

Technology
- Exploring Primary Sources in U.S. History CD-ROM *Brown v. Board of Education; Letter from a Birmingham Jail, Martin Luther King, Jr.; I Have a Dream, Martin Luther King, Jr.; Reynolds v. Sims*

ESL

Teacher's Edition
- Customize for ESL, p. 719

Teaching Resources
- Guided Reading and Review booklet, pp. 112–116
- Guide to the Essentials (English/Spanish), Chapter 21

Technology
- Student Edition on Audio CD, Chapter 21
- Guided Reading Audiotapes (English/Spanish), Chapter 21
- Section Reading Support Transparencies

Less Proficient Readers

Teacher's Edition
- Customize for Less Proficient Readers, pp. 703, 705, 721

Teaching Resources
- Guided Reading and Review booklet, pp. 112–116
- Guide to the Essentials (English/Spanish), Chapter 21

Technology
- Student Edition on Audio CD, Chapter 21
- Guided Reading Audiotapes (English/Spanish), Chapter 21
- Section Reading Support Transparencies

Less Proficient Writers

Teacher's Edition
- Customize for Less Proficient Writers, p. 725

Teaching Resources
- Guided Reading and Review booklet, pp. 112–116
- Guide to the Essentials (English/Spanish), Chapter 21

Technology
- Student Edition on Audio CD, Chapter 21
- Guided Reading Audiotapes (English/Spanish), Chapter 21
- Section Reading Support Transparencies

Teacher's Edition Index

Chapter 21 – Pacing Suggestions

For 90-minute Blocks

- Teach section 3 using Transparencies B16 and F9, and the Recent Scholarship note on page 711 for class discussions.

Running Out of Time?

If you are running short on time to cover this chapter, consider the following options:

- Use the Prentice Hall Presentation Pro CD-ROM to create an outline for this chapter.
- Use the Section Summaries for Chapter 21, from **Guide to the Essentials (English/Spanish).**

TEKS Correlation

Chapter-Level	TEKS
	(7) History. The student understands the impact of the American civil rights movement. The student is expected to: **(A)** trace the historical development of the civil rights movement in the 18th, 19th, and 20th centuries, including the 13th, 14th, and 15th amendments. **(24) Social studies skills.** The student applies critical-thinking skills to organize and use information acquired from a variety of sources, including electronic technology. The student is expected to: **(A)** locate and use primary and secondary sources such as computer software, databases, media and news services, biographies, interviews, and artifacts to acquire information about the United States. **(B)** analyze information by sequencing, categorizing, identifying cause-and-effect relationships, comparing, contrasting, finding the main idea, summarizing, making generalizations and predictions, and drawing inferences and conclusions.
1 Demands for Civil Rights	**(8) Geography.** The student uses geographic tools to collect, analyze, and interpret data. The student is expected to: **(B)** pose and answer questions about geographic distributions and patterns shown on maps, graphs, charts, models, and databases. **(17) Government.** The student understands the impact of constitutional issues on American society in the 20th century. The student is expected to: **(A)** analyze the effects of 20th-century landmark U.S. Supreme Court decisions such as *Brown* v. *Board of Education, Regents of the University of California* v. *Bakke,* and *Reynolds* v. *Sims.* **(26) Social studies skills.** The student uses problem-solving and decision-making skills, working independently and with others, in a variety of settings. The student is expected to: **(A)** use a problem-solving process to identify a problem, gather information, list and consider options, consider advantages and disadvantages, choose and implement a solution, and evaluate the effectiveness of the solution.
2 Leaders and Strategies	**(7) History.** The student understands the impact of the American civil rights movement. The student is expected to: **(B)** identify significant leaders of the civil rights movement, including Martin Luther King, Jr. **(20) Culture.** The student understands the relationship between the arts and the times during which they were created. The student is expected to: **(A)** describe how the characteristics and issues of various eras in U.S. history have been reflected in works of art, music, and literature such as the paintings of Georgia O'Keeffe, rock and roll, and John Steinbeck's *The Grapes of Wrath.* **(21) Culture.** The student understands how people from various groups, including racial, ethnic, and religious groups, adapt to life in the United States and contribute to our national identity. The student is expected to: **(A)** explain actions taken by people from racial, ethnic, and religious groups to expand economic opportunities and political rights in American society.
3 The Struggle Intensifies	**(24) Social studies skills.** The student applies critical-thinking skills to organize and use information acquired from a variety of sources, including electronic technology. The student is expected to: **(D)** use the process of historical inquiry to research, interpret, and use multiple sources of evidence. **(H)** use appropriate mathematical skills to interpret social studies information such as maps and graphs. **(25) Social studies skills.** The student communicates in written, oral, and visual forms. The student is expected to: **(D)** create written, oral, and visual presentations of social studies information.
4 The Political Response	**(7) History.** The student understands the impact of the American civil rights movement. The student is expected to: **(C)** evaluate government efforts, including the Civil Rights Act of 1964, to achieve equality in the United States. **(D)** identify changes in the United States that have resulted from the civil rights movement such as increased participation of minorities in the political process. **(8) Geography.** The student uses geographic tools to collect, analyze, and interpret data. The student is expected to: **(A)** create thematic maps, graphs, charts, models, and databases representing various aspects of the United States. **(18) Citizenship.** The student understands efforts to expand the democratic process. The student is expected to: **(A)** identify and analyze methods of expanding the right to participate in the democratic process, including lobbying, protesting, court decisions, and amendments to the U.S. Constitution. **(B)** evaluate various means of achieving equality of political rights, including the 19th, 24th, and 26th amendments. **(19) Citizenship.** The student understands the importance of effective leadership in a democratic society. The student is expected to: **(C)** identify the contributions of Texans who have been President of the United States.
5 The Movement Takes a New Turn	**(1) History.** The student understands traditional historical points of reference in U.S. history from 1877 to the present. The student is expected to: **(B)** apply absolute and relative chronology through the sequencing of significant individuals, events, and time periods. **(24) Social studies skills.** The student applies critical-thinking skills to organize and use information acquired from a variety of sources, including electronic technology. The student is expected to: **(C)** explain and apply different methods that historians use to interpret the past, including the use of primary and secondary sources, points of view, frames of reference, and historical context.

Chapter 21

The Civil Rights Movement

(1950–1968)

Introducing the Chapter

The 1950s and 1960s were a time of great progress and great frustration for African Americans. Through nonviolent protests and an extremely focused civil rights struggle, African Americans ended institutional segregation and secured voting rights in the South. Lack of progress on economic issues, especially in urban areas, however, drove some to vent their anger through bitter violence.

Time Line Activity

To provide students with practice in using the time line, ask questions such as these:

1. What event took place in 1954 that would forever change the United States? *(The Supreme Court's historic* Brown v. Board of Education *of Topeka, Kansas, ending school segregation)*
2. What did President Eisenhower do in 1957 that supported the Supreme Court's 1954 decision? *(He sent troops to Little Rock, Arkansas, to assist the integration of a high school.)*
3. What important international leader was jailed in 1962? *(Nelson Mandela)*

Chapter 21

The Civil Rights Movement (1950–1968)

This protester picketed a restaurant in Georgia.

American Events

1954 In a unanimous decision, the Supreme Court rules that segregation in public schools is unconstitutional in *Brown* v. *Board of Education of Topeka, Kansas.*

1955 Thousands of African Americans participate in the Montgomery, Alabama, bus boycott to protest discrimination in public transportation.

1957 Eisenhower sends troops to Little Rock, Arkansas, to facilitate integration at Central High School.

Presidential Terms: Harry S Truman 1945–1953; Dwight D. Eisenhower 1953–1961

1950 — 1954 — 1958

World Events

1954 Vietnamese Communists defeat the French at Dien Bien Phu.

1956 Sudan becomes an independent nation.

eTeach

Be sure to check out this month's online discussion with a Master Teacher. Go to **www.phschool.com**.

Resource Directory

Teaching Resources

Pacing Charts booklet

Block Scheduling booklet, p. 27

Units 5/6/7 booklet

- Chapter Summary, p. 51

Technology

Guided Reading Audiotapes (English/Spanish), Ch. 21

Student Edition on Audio CD, Ch. 21

Prentice Hall United States History Video Collection™ Volume 20, *Post-War USA*

Prentice Hall Presentation Pro CD-ROM, Ch. 21

Resource Pro® CD-ROM

Social Studies Skills Tutor CD-ROM

Companion Web site, www.phschool.com

Civil Rights Events, 1945–1968

▲ Seven days of race-related riots occurred in the Watts area of Los Angeles, California, in 1965.

More than 200,000 black and white Americans peacefully marched on Washington, D.C., to further civil rights in 1963.

- ▲ Racial violence, 1945–1965
- ▲ Racial violence, 1966–1968
- ■ Peaceful demonstration, 1945–1965
- ■ Peaceful demonstration, 1966–1968

The Watts riot in the summer of 1965.

1961 Freedom Riders challenge segregation on interstate buses.

1964 Congress passes the Civil Rights Act of 1964.

1968 The assassinations of Martin Luther King, Jr., and Robert F. Kennedy mark a tragic point in the civil rights movement.

John F. Kennedy 1961–1963

Lyndon B. Johnson 1963–1969

1962 · 1966

1959 Fidel Castro rises to power in Cuba.

1962 Nelson Mandela is jailed in South Africa.

1966 The Chinese Cultural Revolution begins.

Civil Rights Events, 1945–1968

Activating Prior Knowledge In which state was there the greatest number of peaceful demonstrations? *(Alabama)*

Previewing Were there more incidents of racial violence and fewer peaceful demonstrations during the period from 1945 to 1965 or during the period from 1966 to 1968? *(There were more incidents of racial violence and fewer peaceful demonstrations from 1966 to 1968.)*

BACKGROUND
About the Pictures

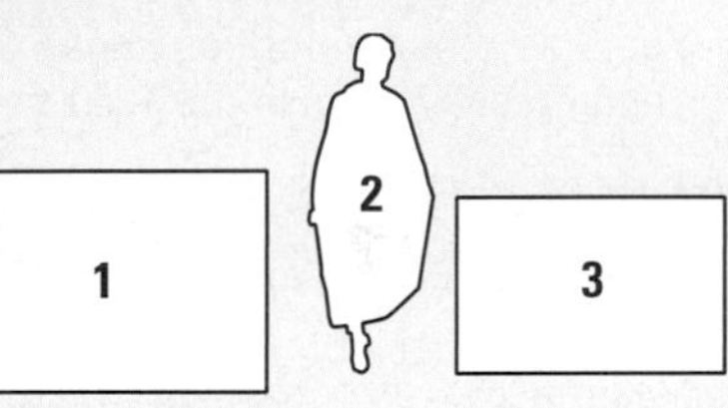

1. This protest began in response to the arrest of Rosa Parks, who had refused to remove herself from the "whites only" section of a bus.
2. After the success of the bus boycotting, which led to the desegregation of seating on buses, picketing and protests broke out all over for various American rights to be upheld.
3. Frustrated by social injustice, many African Americans burned stores and reeked havoc in this riot, which eventually ended in 34 deaths and over 1,000 injuries.

BIBLIOGRAPHY

For the Teacher

Branch, Taylor. ***Parting the Waters: America in the King Years, 1954–1963.*** Touchstone, 1989. (Chronicles the times from Eisenhower to Kennedy.)

Raines, Howell. ***My Soul Is Rested: Movement Days in the Deep South Remembered.*** Viking, 1983. (First-person accounts of participants in major civil rights events.)

For the Student

Ellison, Ralph. ***Invisible Man.*** Random House, Vintage, 1995. (Awarded the 1952 National Book Award for fiction, uses the experiences of an idealistic young African American to depict the alienation of American society.)

Eyes on the Prize. PBS Video. (Comprehensive six-part series on the history of the civil rights movement from 1954.)

iTEXT

Don't miss the exclusive interactive version of this textbook on the Web and on CD-ROM.

Section 1 Demands for Civil Rights

Section Objectives

1. Learn about events and cultural trends that led to a rise in African American influence in the twentieth century.
2. Find out how Americans responded to the Supreme Court's decision in *Brown* v. *Board of Education.*
3. Discover how the Montgomery bus boycott affected the civil rights movement.
4. See how other minorities began to demand civil rights in the 1960s.

Bellringer

Warm-Up Activity Ask students to consider the role of sports in American life. Ask if sports stars should be considered heroes. What qualities does a "hero" possess? Ask students who their heroes are. Why?

Activating Prior Knowledge Ask students if they are familiar with the term *boycott.* If they are, have them describe some situations where boycotts might be used to influence political decisions. What impressions do students have of the use of boycotts as a political tool?

Reading Strategy

This section describes some significant events in the historical development of the civil rights movement in the twentieth century. As students read the section, have them make a list of the important events described and write a one-sentence description of the importance of each of these events.

Caption Answers

Viewing History Robinson publicly broke a professional race barrier and was an inspirational role model.

Section 1

Demands for Civil Rights

READING FOCUS

- What events and cultural trends led to a rise in African American influence in the twentieth century?
- How did Americans respond to the Supreme Court's decision in *Brown* v. *Board of Education?*
- How did the Montgomery bus boycott affect the civil rights movement?
- How did other minorities begin to demand civil rights in the 1950s?

KEY TERMS

Brown v. *Board of Education of Topeka, Kansas*
Montgomery bus boycott
integration

TAKING NOTES

As you read, complete the following chart to show how each person affected the civil rights movement in its early years.

Person	Impact on Civil Rights
Branch Rickey	Hired Jackie Robinson, ending segregation in the Major Leagues
Thurgood Marshall	
Earl Warren	
Jo Ann Robinson	
Dwight Eisenhower	
Rosa Parks	
Orval Faubus	

MAIN IDEA

Following World War II, African Americans began to push harder in the civil rights movement and brought about significant results.

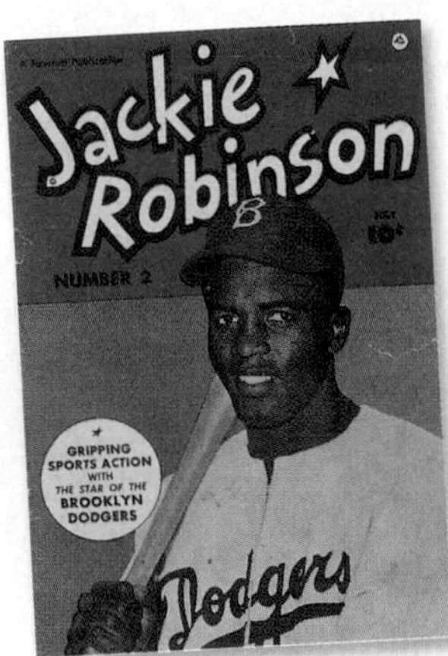

VIEWING HISTORY After his brilliant first season with the Brooklyn Dodgers, Jackie Robinson was featured on baseball cards like the one above, issued in 1951. **Determining Relevance** *How did Robinson's career serve the cause of civil rights?*

Setting the Scene In August 1945, Branch Rickey, the general manager of the Brooklyn Dodgers, called a young man named Jackie Robinson into his office. Rickey told Robinson of his plan to challenge the rule in Major League Baseball that required African Americans to play in a separate Negro League. Rickey wanted Robinson, a promising athlete in college and a World War II veteran, to be the first player to break the color barrier.

To test how Robinson would respond to the pressure he was likely to face, Rickey acted the part of those who might try to discourage him. He roared insults at Robinson and threatened him with violence. "Mr. Rickey," Robinson finally said, "do you want a ballplayer who's afraid to fight back?" Rickey answered, "I want a player with guts enough not to fight back."

In 1947, Robinson joined the Brooklyn Dodgers, becoming the first African American to play in the Major Leagues. Despite many instances of prejudice, Robinson behaved with dignity and had a sparkling first season. He was named Rookie of the Year in 1947. In 1949, he was voted the league's most valuable player. Just as important, Robinson fostered pride in African Americans around the country and paved the way for other African Americans to follow him into professional sports.

The Rise of African American Influence

Before and during World War II, African Americans were not treated as equals by a large portion of American society. After the war, however, the campaign for civil rights began to accelerate. Millions of people believed that the time had come to demand that the nation live up to its creed that all are equal before the law. Several factors contributed to this growing demand.

African American Migration After the Civil War, many African Americans migrated to large northern cities. Between 1910 and 1940, the black population of New York City leaped from 60,000 to 450,000. Other cities experienced a similar growth in black population. Out of these expanding black communities

RESOURCE DIRECTORY

Teaching Resources
Learning Styles Lesson Plans booklet, p. 58
Guided Reading and Review booklet, p. 112

Technology
Section Reading Support Transparencies
Guided Reading Audiotapes (English/Spanish), Ch. 21
Student Edition on Audio CD, Ch. 21
Sounds of an Era Audio CD, *Reaction to* Brown v. Board of Education, 1954 (time: about one minute)
Prentice Hall Presentation Pro CD-ROM, Ch. 21
Companion Web site, www.phschool.com

emerged a number of prominent African American citizens, including doctors and lawyers, who gained political influence. They were able to form alliances with political machines. In effect, they could offer their votes in return for social gains.

The New Deal During the Depression, Roosevelt and the Democrats began to court black votes and gain African Americans' support for New Deal policies. Under Roosevelt, the number of African Americans working for the federal government increased significantly.

READING CHECK How did World War II affect African Americans in the United States?

World War II Perhaps the greatest stimulus to the changing racial climate in the United States was World War II. During the war, increased demands for labor in northern cities led to a rise in the black population in the North. This increase in numbers gave African Americans considerable voting power in some northern cities.

Another impact of World War II was ideological. The war, fought largely over the racism and discrimination taking place in Europe, opened many people's eyes to the racism and discrimination taking place in the United States. This realization did not spread to everyone, nor did it have a sudden impact. Rather, these new ideas crept into the ideological climate of the country.

Rise of the NAACP Amidst these cultural changes, the NAACP—the National Association for the Advancement of Colored People—worked hard in the courts to challenge segregation laws throughout the country. For years the NAACP had tried to get the 1896 *Plessy* v. *Ferguson* decision overturned. That decision held that segregation of the races in public institutions and accommodations was constitutional as long as facilities were "separate but equal." In practice, equal facilities were rarely—if ever—the case.

One of the NAACP's greatest assets was its legal team. Leading the NAACP's Legal Defense Fund was Thurgood Marshall, who had joined the association in the 1930s. Known as "Mr. Civil Rights," Marshall fought many battles over segregation in the courts and achieved great gains. His success was bolstered by the support of an exceptional team of lawyers.

VIEWING HISTORY Thurgood Marshall talks to reporters in New York City in 1955, after the Supreme Court ordered the desegregation of public schools. Marshall later became the first African American Supreme Court Justice. **Analyzing Information** *How did Marshall's efforts lead to gains in civil rights and prepare him for the* Brown v. Board of Education *case?*

One lawyer in particular, Oliver Hill, from Virginia, won many civil rights suits that focused on issues of discrimination in education and wages. According to the *Washington Post,* Hill's team of lawyers had succeeded in winning more than $50 million in higher pay and better educational facilities for black students and teachers. Little by little, Marshall and Hill managed to chip away at the "separate but equal" clause of *Plessy* v. *Ferguson*. Finally, in 1951, they took on the greatest and most important fight of all.

Brown v. *Board of Education*

In 1951, Oliver Brown sued the Topeka, Kansas, Board of Education to allow his 8-year-old daughter Linda to attend a school that only white children were allowed to attend. She passed the school on her way to the bus that took her to a distant school for African Americans. After appeals, the case reached the Supreme Court. There, Thurgood Marshall argued on behalf of Brown and against segregation in America's schools.

On May 17, 1954, in ***Brown* v. *Board of Education of Topeka, Kansas,*** the Supreme Court issued its historic ruling.

Lesson Plan

Focus Point out to students that many alterations in social, economic, and demographic conditions coalesced in the 1950s to create a sense that gains in civil rights were possible.

Instruct Ask the students to voice their opinions as to what issues, in addition to the gains made by African Americans during World War II, made the 1950s seem like the right time to mount a serious challenge to the legality of *Plessy* v. *Ferguson.*

Assess/Reteach Discuss with students the role of the NAACP. Ask students to explain why the NAACP was well positioned in the 1950s to move ahead on civil rights issues.

Activity: Connecting with Citizenship

The civil rights movement included different groups with many priorities, all working toward the larger goal of social equality. To help students understand this concept, divide the class into three groups. Have groups form organizations with the common goal of social equality for all young adults. Have each group state its own aims, create an acronym for itself, and describe one way it will attempt to achieve its aims. Discuss how groups might support each other in their aims. **(Logical/Mathematical)**

READING CHECK

Due to the demands for labor in northern cities, the black population in the North grew, giving African Americans considerable voting power in some northern cities. The war heightened awareness of racial discrimination in the United States.

Caption Answers

Viewing History Marshall was a successful lawyer who possessed a superb understanding of desegregation cases. He had won many civil rights battles in court in the 1930s and 1940s. These successes paved the way for victory in *Brown* v. *Board of Education.*

Activity
Connecting with Government

Brown v. *Board of Education* and its implementation provide a good model for how our federal system works. As a class, evaluate the impact of events and the role played by the legislative, judicial, and executive branches of government, as well as federal and state governments, in *Brown* and its aftermath. After discussion, challenge students to create diagrams illustrating these interrelationships. Display the finished diagrams and talk about what they show. **(Verbal/Linguistic; Visual/Spatial)**

Background
Biography

The great-grandson of a freed slave, Thoroughgood (he later changed the name to Thurgood) Marshall (1908–1993) spent more than 20 years as the NAACP's chief legal counsel challenging institutional racism. In 1967 President Johnson appointed Marshall the Supreme Court's first African American associate justice. Marshall maintained a staunchly liberal presence on what soon became an increasingly conservative Court. He opposed the death penalty and favored affirmative action and other remedies for discrimination. By the time he retired in 1991, he had become, in the words of one Harvard Law School professor, "the great dissenter . . . part of the conscience of the Court."

READING CHECK
It was unconstitutional (because it forced African Americans to use dilapidated facilities) and could not be applied to public education.

READING CHECK
What did the Supreme Court say about the "separate but equal" clause?

> *"Does segregation of children in public schools solely on the basis of race . . . deprive the children of the minority group of equal educational opportunities? We believe that it does. . . . To separate them from others of similar age and qualifications solely because of their race generates a feeling of inferiority as to their status in the community that may affect their hearts and minds in a way unlikely to ever be undone. . . . We conclude that in the field of public education the doctrine of 'separate but equal' has no place. Separate educational facilities are inherently unequal."*
>
> —Chief Justice Earl Warren

In a unanimous decision, the Court declared that the "separate but equal" doctrine was unconstitutional and could not be applied to public education. A year later, the Court ruled that local school boards should move to desegregate "with all deliberate speed."

Reaction to *Brown* v. *Board of Education*

The public's reaction to the Supreme Court's ruling was mixed. African Americans rejoiced. Many white Americans, even if they did not agree, accepted the decision and hoped that desegregation could take place peacefully. President Eisenhower, who privately disagreed with the *Brown* ruling, said only that "the Supreme Court has spoken and I am sworn to uphold the constitutional processes in this country, and I am trying. I will obey." Not everyone, however, was willing to obey.

The ruling in *Brown* v. *Board of Education* caused many southern whites, especially in the Deep South, to react with fear and angry resistance. In Georgia, Governor Herman Talmadge made it clear that his state would "not tolerate the mixing of the races in the public schools or any other tax-supported institutions." The Ku Klux Klan also became more active, threatening those who advocated acceptance of the *Brown* decision. The congressional representatives of states in the Deep South joined together in March 1956 to protest the Supreme Court's order to desegregate public schools.

More than 90 members of Congress expressed their opposition to the Court's ruling in what was known as the "Southern Manifesto." The congressmen asserted

MAP SKILLS Many states were slow to integrate their public schools after the *Brown* decision. **Place** *Which states had the highest increase in the percentage of African Americans attending integrated schools?*

African Americans Attending Integrated Southern Schools

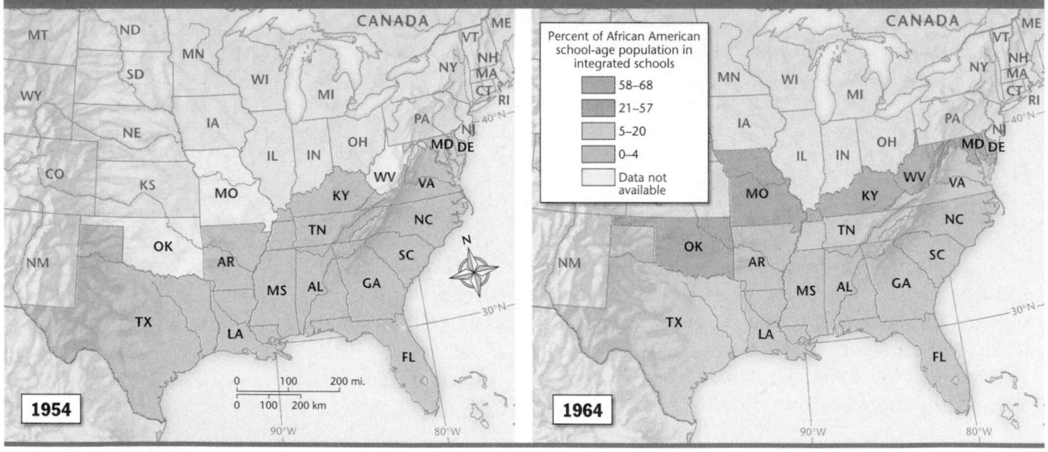

Percent of African American school-age population in integrated schools: 58–68; 21–57; 5–20; 0–4; Data not available

1954

1964

Caption Answers

Map Skills Texas, Tennessee, Virginia, Maryland, and Delaware.

RESOURCE DIRECTORY

Teaching Resources

Great Debates booklet (Great Debates) *Integrating the University of Georgia,* p. 40

Biography, Literature, and Comparing Primary Sources booklet (Biography) *Thurgood Marshall,* p. 33

Learning with Documents booklet (Primary Source Activity) *Enforcing* Brown *v.* Board of Education, p. 33

Learning with Documents booklet (Key Documents) Brown *v.* Board of Education, p. 92

Technology

RESOURCE PRO® **Biography** *Maria Latigo Hernandez and Pedro Hernandez,* found on Resource Pro, profiles two Mexican immigrants who sought relief in the United States from Mexico's famine and chaos in the early twentieth century.

Exploring Primary Sources in U.S. History CD-ROM Brown *v.* Board of Education that the Supreme Court had overstepped its bounds and had "no legal basis for such action." The decision, they claimed, violated states' rights and was an example of "judicial usurpation." Many believed that desegregation would lead to violence and chaos in several southern states. As a result, they refused to comply with the court's ruling:

> "*We pledge ourselves to use all lawful means to bring about a reversal of this decision, which is contrary to the Constitution, and to prevent the use of force in its implementation.*"
>
> —From the Congressional Record, 84th Congress, 2nd session

The Montgomery Bus Boycott

In 1955, the nation's attention shifted from the courts to the streets of Montgomery, Alabama. In December, Rosa Parks, a seamstress who had been the secretary of the Montgomery NAACP for 12 years, took a seat in the middle section of a bus, where both African Americans and whites usually were allowed to sit. African Americans, however, were expected to give up their seats for white passengers if no available seats remained. When a white man got on at the next stop and had no seat, the bus driver ordered Parks to give up hers. She refused. Even when threatened with arrest, she held her ground. At the next stop, police seized her and ordered her to stand trial for violating the segregation laws.

Rosa Parks's arrest in 1955 touched off the successful Montgomery bus boycott. Here, one year later, she smiles after the Supreme Court ruled bus segregation to be unconstitutional.

Civil rights leaders in Montgomery quickly met and, after Jo Ann Robinson of the Women's Political Council (WPC) suggested the idea, decided to organize the **Montgomery bus boycott.** The plan called for African Americans to refuse to use the entire bus system until the bus company agreed to change its segregation policy. Robinson and other members of the WPC wrote and distributed leaflets announcing the boycott. Martin Luther King, Jr., the 26-year-old minister of the Baptist church where the original boycott meeting took place, soon became the spokesperson for the protest movement. He proclaimed:

> "*There comes a time when people get tired . . . tired of being segregated and humiliated, tired of being kicked about by the brutal feet of oppression. We have no alternative but to protest.*"
>
> —Martin Luther King, Jr.

The morning of the first day of the boycott, King roamed the streets of Montgomery. He was anxious to see how many African Americans would participate, and recorded his observations:

> "*During the rush hours the sidewalks were crowded with laborers and domestic workers, many of them well past middle age, trudging patiently to their jobs and home again, sometimes as much as twelve miles. They knew why they walked, and the knowledge was evident in the way they carried themselves. And as I watched them I knew that there is nothing more majestic than the determined courage of individuals willing to suffer and sacrifice for their freedom and dignity.*"
>
> —Martin Luther King, Jr.

Over the next year, 50,000 African Americans in Montgomery walked, rode bicycles, or joined car pools to avoid the city buses. Despite losing money,

Activity: Connecting with Economics

Help students grasp the economic impact of the Montgomery bus boycott by having them calculate approximately how much money the boycott cost the bus company. Students should conduct research to find out the cost of a typical bus fare in Montgomery in 1955. Based on the statistic cited in the text (50,000 African Americans boycotted buses for one year), have students create formulas for assessing the financial impact of the boycott. Have students compare their results and how they arrived at them. Have students analyze this method of expanding the right to participate in the democratic process.
(Logical/Mathematical)

From the Archives of AmericanHeritage®

Racism on the Gridiron

On November 5, 1946, Penn State and the University of Miami canceled a football game scheduled for the end of the month over the presence of two black players on the Penn State team. The president of Miami had banned the pair on grounds of good fellowship, saying he hoped to avoid "unfortunate incidents" and "not catapult very important, not-well-understood interracial problems into a football game." The dean of athletics at Penn State insisted that the boys were regular members of the Penn State team and declined to place any conditions on their participation. Similar disagreements were cropping up elsewhere. Earlier in the season a pair of smaller colleges had worked out a solution to the American dilemma: Fresno State's black players sat out a game at Oklahoma City but would be allowed to play in a return match at Fresno. Source: Frederic D. Schwarz, "The Time Machine," *American Heritage®* magazine, November 1996.

TEST PREPARATION

Have students read the quote from the "Southern Manifesto" on this page and then complete the sentence below.

According to the southern members of Congress who opposed *Brown* v. *Board of Education,* the legal basis for the decision was—

- **(A)** in violation of states' rights.
- **B** strongly supported by precedent.
- **C** designed to favor northern states.
- **D** designed to favor southern states.

The Boycott

The boycott has often been an effective form of protest throughout United States history. When Britain passed the Stamp Act in 1765, the colonists responded by organizing a boycott of certain British goods. The boycott proved to be effective when the British merchants who had lost profits on their goods pressured Parliament into repealing the act.

The actual term "boycott" did not come into use until the 1880s in Ireland. A land agent there, Charles Boycott, had refused to comply with a new land reform law designed to lower rents. As a result, his tenants and employees turned against him. He soon found himself isolated and poor.

In modern times, boycotts are often initiated to protest the actions of corporations. Recently, a successful boycott was waged on the tuna industry. The nets used to catch tuna had killed many dolphins and raised environmental concerns. Now, almost all commercial tuna fishing is "dolphin-friendly." Other boycotts have centered around religious, political, and civil or human rights issues.

U.S. Department of Commerce
Dolphin Safe

? Why do you think boycotts are effective? What types of boycotts are the hardest for boycotters to endure? Explain.

the bus company refused to change its policies. Finally, in 1956, the Supreme Court ruled that bus segregation, like school segregation, was unconstitutional.

The Montgomery bus boycott encouraged a new generation of leaders in the African American community, most notably Martin Luther King, Jr. In addition, it gave minority groups hope that steps toward equality could be made through peaceful protest.

Resistance in Little Rock

In the fall of 1957, Arkansas Governor Orval Faubus declared that he could not keep order if he had to enforce **integration,** or the bringing together of different races. In blatant defiance of the Supreme Court's *Brown* decision, Governor Faubus posted Arkansas National Guard troops at Central High School in Little Rock, Arkansas, and instructed them to turn away the nine African American students who were supposed to attend the school that year. Outside the school, mobs of angry protesters gathered to prevent the entry of the black students. One of those students, 15-year-old Elizabeth Eckford, remembered that day:

VIEWING HISTORY African American students like Elizabeth Eckford (below, right) had to endure the insults of white students who disagreed with the the Court's *Brown* v. *Board* decision. **Recognizing Cause and Effect** *What finally caused President Eisenhower to support desegregation?*

> *"[The Arkansas national guardsmen] glared at me with a mean look and I was very frightened and didn't know what to do. I turned around and the crowd came toward me. They moved closer and closer. Somebody started yelling 'Lynch her! Lynch her!' I tried to see a friendly face somewhere in the mob—someone who maybe would help. I looked into the face of an old woman and it seemed a kind face, but when I looked at her again, she spat on me."*
>
> —Elizabeth Eckford

President Eisenhower could no longer avoid the issue of segregation. Faubus's actions were a direct challenge to the Constitution and to Eisenhower's authority as President. Eisenhower acted by placing the National Guard under federal command. He then sent soldiers to Arkansas to protect

ACTIVITY
Connecting with History and Conflict

Ask students to imagine they were principals or administrators of Little Rock's Central High School during desegregation from 1957 to 1958. How would they keep order and promote tolerance among their students? Have small student groups come up with concrete strategies and written guidelines for the school. Have each group present its strategy to the class. Afterward, discuss what various groups' strategies have in common and how well students think they might work. Have students analyze this situation in light of changes in the United States that have resulted from the civil rights movement. **(Logical/Mathematical)**

BACKGROUND
Biography

As Chief Justice of the United States Supreme Court from 1953 to 1969, Earl Warren (1891–1974) led the court in its historic rewriting of civil rights law and criminal procedures. Warren came to the court from California, where he had had a successful political career culminating in his election as governor in 1942. During his tenure on the bench, Warren presided over 75 rulings, many of which, as in *Brown* v. *Board of Education,* were to have far-reaching consequences. In the 1960s, conservative groups tried but failed to have him removed from the bench. Warren also served as chairman of the special committee that investigated the Kennedy assassination in 1963.

CAPTION ANSWERS

Fast Forward to Today Boycotts are effective because businesses have to choose between losing profits or changing their methods. The most effective boycotts are probably those in which the seller has only one type of product on the market. A corporation that has only one line of business has nothing to fall back on if consumers stop purchasing that one item.

Viewing History The defiance of Arkansas Governor Orval Faubus, who refused to obey the Supreme Court's orders. Eisenhower saw this as a threat to the Constitution and to his authority as President.

RESOURCE DIRECTORY

Teaching Resources

Units 5/6/7 booklet
- Section 1 Quiz, p. 52

Guide to the Essentials
- Section 1 Summary, p. 101

the nine students. In a speech to the nation on September 24, 1957, Eisenhower justified his actions:

> "*Our personal opinions about the decision have no bearing on the matter of enforcement; the responsibility and authority of the Supreme Court to interpret the Constitution are very clear. . . . Mob rule cannot be allowed to override the decisions of our courts. . . . In the present case the troops are there, pursuant to law, solely for the purpose of preventing interference with the orders of the Court.*"
>
> —President Eisenhower

Other Voices of Protest

African Americans were not the only minority group to demand equal rights after World War II. Mexican Americans, for example, also struggled to achieve equality. In one case, a funeral home in Texas refused to bury Felix Longoria, a World War II veteran who had died in the Philippines. Protests in the Mexican American community over the refusal finally led to the soldier's burial in Arlington National Cemetery in Washington, D.C. Groups like the Community Service Organization and the Asociación Nacional México-Americana found that peaceful protest could slowly bring about some of the results Mexican Americans desired.

Native Americans faced a unique situation. The federal government managed the reservations where most Native Americans lived in terrible poverty. In 1953, however, the government adopted a new approach, known as "termination," which sought to eliminate reservations altogether. The government's goal was to assimilate Native Americans into the mainstream of American life.

The policy of termination met with resistance, and in time the federal government discarded it. Yet the problems of the Native Americans remained: poverty, discrimination, and little real political representation. For Native Americans, the civil rights advances of the 1950s were mere tokens of the real gains that were needed.

Focus on CITIZENSHIP

Dr. Hector Garcia When Latino veterans returned to the United States from battle in World War II, they faced discrimination and prejudice at every turn. Latino veterans were often denied employment, housing, and military benefits afforded to white Americans. Many were still denied the right to vote and hold office.

Dr. Hector P. Garcia, who served as a combat surgeon during the war, decided that he had to act. In 1948, he organized a group that would protect the interests and rights of Latino veterans: the American G.I. Forum. Through the years, the G.I. Forum worked tirelessly to battle discrimination and improve conditions for Latinos in the United States. The Forum's activities included providing funds for higher education, raising money to help poor Latinos pay poll taxes so they could vote, and winning a Supreme Court case allowing Latinos to serve on juries. Today, the G.I. Forum continues to thrive as it works to promote and protect Latino rights.

Section 1 Assessment

READING COMPREHENSION

1. What was the principle behind the Supreme Court's ruling in ***Brown* v. *Board of Education?***
2. What were the goals of the Southern Manifesto?
3. How did President Eisenhower react to the incident over **integration** in Little Rock, Arkansas?
4. How did Mexican Americans and Native Americans assert their rights in the 1950s?

CRITICAL THINKING AND WRITING

5. **Making Comparisons** The Montgomery bus boycott proved to be an effective form of nonviolent protest against segregation. Can you find other examples of effective boycotts in American history?
6. **Writing a News Story** Take the position of a reporter stationed at Central High School in Little Rock, Arkansas, on the day when nine African American students are to be integrated into the school. Write a brief news story describing the scene.

Take It to the NET

Activity: Analyzing Primary Source Access the full *Brown* v. *Board of Education of Topeka, Kansas,* unanimous Supreme Court decision. Read the entire majority opinion. What arguments were used? How was the Constitution cited? Use the links provided in the *America: Pathways to the Present* area of the following Web site for help in completing this activity.
www.phschool.com

Section 1 Assessment

Reading Comprehension

1. That what the "separate but equal" doctrine really meant is that African Americans were forced to use public facilities that were vastly inferior to the facilities routinely made available to whites.
2. To oppose desegregation of schools, asserting that the Supreme Court had no legal basis for its decision, and that the decision violated states' rights.
3. He placed the Arkansas National Guard under federal command and sent additional soldiers from the regular army to Arkansas to protect the students. He was determined to uphold the rule of law and to prevent one state from flouting the Supreme Court and the Constitution.
4. Mexican Americans—through peaceful protest; Native Americans—through resistance to the termination policy.

Critical Thinking and Writing

5. Answers will vary but may include: the colonists' boycott of certain British goods after the passage of the Stamp Act in 1765; the more recent boycott of the tuna industry, which has helped raise environmental awareness and protect dolphins.
6. Answers will vary, but should be supported with facts from the section.

Take It to the NET

Answers will vary, but should explore arguments and constitutional references made in the *Brown* v. *Board of Education* case, such as: that segregated schools will always be of unequal quality, and that a segregated educational system violates the equal protection section of the Fourteenth Amendment.

CUSTOMIZE FOR ...

Less Proficient Readers

Have students select one of the events described in this section and list four reasons why the event is important to the history of civil rights in the United States.

Section 2
Leaders and Strategies

Section Objectives

1. Find out how early groups laid the foundation for the civil rights movement.
2. Understand the philosophy of nonviolence.
3. Realize how SNCC gave students a voice in the civil rights movement.

Bellringer

Warm-Up Activity Ask students to think of ways that people can protest without resorting to violence. What advantages do these tactics have?

Activating Prior Knowledge Are students familiar with nonviolent protest strategies? Ask if they can list some, such as sit-ins, boycotts, and peaceful demonstrations.

Reading Strategy

Have students analyze nonviolent protest as a means of achieving equality of political rights. As they read the section, they should list various strategies described, and then offer a one-sentence response stating which of the various approaches, in their opinion, is most effective.

Section 2

Leaders and Strategies

READING FOCUS

- How did early groups lay the groundwork for the civil rights movement?
- What was the philosophy of nonviolence?
- How did SNCC give students a voice in the civil rights movement?

MAIN IDEA

The civil rights movement of the 1960s consisted of many separate groups and leaders. While the methods used by these groups differed, they shared the same goal of securing equal rights for all Americans.

KEY TERMS

interracial
Congress of Racial Equality (CORE)
Southern Christian Leadership Conference (SCLC)
nonviolent protest
Student Nonviolent Coordinating Committee (SNCC)

TAKING NOTES

As you read, complete the chart below listing the prominent civil rights organizations in the early 1960s and their goals and characteristics.

Civil Rights Group	Features
NAACP	Focused on gaining legal equality. Appealed mainly to middle- and upper-class African Americans.
National Urban League	
CORE	
SCLC	
SNCC	

Setting the Scene

“*It really hit me when I was fifteen years old, when I heard about Martin Luther King, Jr., and the Montgomery bus boycott. Black people were walking the streets for more than a year rather than riding segregated buses. To me it was like a great sense of hope, a light. . . . That more than any other event was the turning point for me, I think. It gave me a way out.*

When I graduated from high school, I enrolled at the American Baptist Theological Seminary in Nashville. . . . While I was there I began attending these workshops, studying the philosophy and discipline of nonviolence: the life and times of Gandhi, the works of Henry Thoreau, and the philosophy of civil disobedience. And we began to think about how we could apply these lessons to the problem of segregation.”

—John Lewis

VIEWING HISTORY The NAACP was one of many civil rights groups committed to improving the status of African Americans. **Analyzing Visual Information** *(a) How are the images in this poster intended to rally support for the NAACP? (b) What does the poster tell you about the goals of this organization?*

In the 1960s, many young people, like John Lewis, became active in the struggle for civil rights. They knew that battling segregation and gaining civil rights would require organization and strong commitment.

Laying the Groundwork

The civil rights movement of the 1950s and 1960s was a grass-roots effort of ordinary citizens determined to end racial injustice in the United States. Although no central organization directed the movement, several major groups formed to share information and coordinate civil rights activities. Each of these groups had its own priorities, strategies, and ways of operating, but they all helped to focus the energies of thousands of Americans committed to securing civil rights for all citizens.

NAACP Behind the case of *Brown* v. *Board of Education* was the National Association for the Advancement of Colored People (NAACP),

Caption Answers

Viewing History (a) The images show positive interaction between African Americans and white Americans, either enjoying life together or working together to create “one” society. (b) The NAACP is portrayed as an organization working for an integrated society in which different racial groups can coexist happily for the benefit of all.

RESOURCE DIRECTORY

Teaching Resources
Guided Reading and Review booklet, p. 113

Technology
Section Reading Support Transparencies
Guided Reading Audiotapes (English/Spanish), Ch. 21
Student Edition on Audio CD, Ch. 21
Prentice Hall Presentation Pro CD-ROM, Ch. 21
Companion Web site, www.phschool.com

one of the oldest civil rights organizations in the United States. The group formed in 1909 as an **interracial** organization—one with both African Americans and white Americans as members.

W.E.B. Du Bois, a prominent African American scholar, was a founding member. Du Bois had been the first African American to receive a doctoral degree from Harvard University. He served as the NAACP's director of publicity and research and also edited the NAACP magazine, *Crisis*. Du Bois summarized the NAACP's goals this way:

> "*The main object of this association is to secure for colored people, and particularly for Americans of Negro descent, free and equal participation in the democracy of modern culture. This means the clearing away of obstructions to such participation . . . and it means also the making of a world democracy in which all men may participate.*"
>
> —W.E.B. Du Bois

From the start, the NAACP focused on challenging the laws that prevented African Americans from exercising their full rights as citizens. The NAACP worked to secure full legal equality for all Americans and to remove barriers that kept them from voting.

In the 1920s and 1930s, lynching was still a threat to African Americans, particularly in the South. Working to end such violence, the NAACP succeeded in getting two anti-lynching bills passed by the House of Representatives in the 1930s. Southern leaders in the Senate prevented the bills from becoming law, but the NAACP continued to keep the issue of lynching in the public eye.

The NAACP was more successful in its lawsuits that challenged segregation laws. In the 1920s and 1930s, it won a number of legal battles in the areas of housing and education.

The NAACP appealed mainly to educated, middle- and upper-class African Americans and some liberal white Americans. Critics charged that it was out of touch with the basic issues of economic survival faced by many poorer African Americans.

National Urban League One organization that took on economic issues was the National Urban League, founded in 1911. The League sought to assist people moving to major American cities. It helped African Americans moving out of the South find homes and jobs and ensured that they received fair treatment at work. League workers also looked for migrant families on ship docks and at train stations and found safe, clean apartments for them. They also insisted that factory owners and union leaders allow African American workers the opportunity to learn the skills that could lead to better jobs.

CORE Founded by pacifists in 1942, the **Congress of Racial Equality (CORE)** was dedicated to bringing about change through peaceful confrontation. It too was interracial, with both African American and white members. During World War II, CORE organized demonstrations against segregation in cities including Baltimore, Chicago, Denver, and Detroit.

In the years after World War II, CORE director James Farmer worked without pay in order to keep the organization alive. The growing interest in civil rights in the 1950s gave him a new base of support and allowed him to

Focus on CULTURE

"We Shall Overcome" The anthem of the civil rights movement, which brought together activists from all backgrounds, similarly arose through a combination of diverse efforts. "We Shall Overcome" has its roots in an African American spiritual from the days of slavery and from a gospel song called "I'll Overcome Someday," by Minister Charles Albert Tindley.

In 1945, tobacco strikers in South Carolina adopted the song, which had been passed by oral tradition down through the generations. The song later reached white folk singers Pete Seeger and Guy Carawan, who changed the lyrics and altered the melody. They renamed the song "We Shall Overcome," and began teaching it to young activists. The song spread quickly across the nation, unifying all those fighting for civil rights. The successful folk group Peter, Paul, and Mary made the song popular to audiences across the country.

"We Shall Overcome" soon became not only a symbol of the movement, but also a source of pride and determination. An SCLC leader remarked: "You really have to experience it to understand the kind of power it has for us. When you get through singing it, you could walk over a bed of hot coals, and you wouldn't even feel it!"

STUDENT NONVIOLENT COORDINATING COMMITTEE
WE SHALL OVERCOME

LESSON PLAN

Focus Explain that the civil rights movement was not a monolithic organization under the sway of a single leader. The groups were as diverse as the people in the movement. Ask students to note in what ways the movement was diverse and in what ways it was united.

Instruct Ask students to read the first quotation by Martin Luther King, Jr., under the subheading "A New Voice For Students." Then discuss these questions: Do you agree with King's view that the failure to fight oppression made African Americans guilty of cooperating with evil? What values and beliefs did King hold that caused him to view the struggle this way?

Assess/Reteach Ask students to analyze the significance of the inclusion of students into the civil rights movement.

ACTIVITY
Connecting with Culture

"We Shall Overcome" is one of many songs sung by 1960s civil rights marchers and their supporters. Have students locate the music and lyrics to other notable songs of the movement, such as "Oh Freedom," "Which Side Are You On?" "We Shall Not Be Moved," "Keep Your Eyes on the Prize," "Woke Up This Morning with My Mind Stayed on Freedom," "Ain't Gonna Let Nobody Turn Me Around," and "This Little Light of Mine." Students can perform the songs for the class, or have the class listen to recordings. Have them describe how characteristics and issues of the civil rights era are reflected in these songs. **(Musical/Rhythmic)**

CUSTOMIZE FOR ...
Less Proficient Readers

As they read the section, have students list the key organizations and people mentioned and describe the contributions of each to the civil rights movement.

ACTIVITY
Connecting with Government

At this time, Martin Luther King, Jr.'s, birthday—January 15—is celebrated as a national holiday. But the process of officially designating it as such was a long and difficult one. Have students research the governmental process by which King's birthday was made a holiday, as well as the controversy surrounding it. Ask students to share their findings with the class. **(Verbal/ Linguistic)**

BACKGROUND
A Diverse Nation

After the death of Martin Luther King, Jr., in 1968, his widow, Coretta Scott King (b. 1927), remained active in various civil rights issues. In the 1993 edition of her book, *My Life with Martin Luther King, Jr.,* she wrote: "One reason so many young people became involved in the Movement was television. The Movement began in Montgomery just when the electronic era was beginning. Students were educated about social issues through the nightly news."

American BIOGRAPHY

Martin Luther King, Jr.
1929–1968

Born in Atlanta, Georgia, in 1929, King grew up amid all the symbols of southern segregation—separate schools, stores, churches, and public places. Although he had white playmates as a child, those social ties ended when he reached school age. King's father, Martin Luther King, Sr., and his grandfather were both prominent and respected Baptist preachers. He was raised with a sense of personal pride and dignity that went beyond the limitations of segregation.

Even in high school, young Martin was an inspiring and eloquent public speaker. Graduating early from high school, he went to Morehouse College in Atlanta. He earned a divinity degree at Crozer Theological Seminary in Pennsylvania, and then a doctorate in theology at Boston University in 1955. There he met and married Coretta Scott.

King's opponents would attack him physically and verbally, and he would often go to jail for his beliefs. Death threats were frequent. As King had sometimes predicted, he did not live to see the success of the movement. He was assassinated in Memphis, Tennessee, in April 1968, at the age of 39. King's accused killer, a white southerner named James Earl Ray, was convicted in 1969 and sentenced to 99 years in prison.

turn CORE into a national organization, one that would play a major role in the confrontations that lay ahead.

The Philosophy of Nonviolence

Growing opposition to the gains made by African Americans through the *Brown* decision and the Montgomery bus boycott resulted in increasing violence and hostility toward African Americans. Even so, rising new leaders such as Martin Luther King, Jr., preached a philosophy of nonviolence. They asked anyone involved in the fight for civil rights not to retaliate with violence out of fear or hate.

The SCLC In 1957, Martin Luther King, Jr., and other African American clergymen began a new and significant civil rights organization, the **Southern Christian Leadership Conference (SCLC).** SCLC advocated the practice of **nonviolent protest,** a peaceful way of protesting against restrictive racial policies. Nonviolent protesters do not resist even when attacked by opponents. In its first official statement, SCLC set out this principle:

> “*To understand that nonviolence is not a symbol of weakness or cowardice, but as Jesus demonstrated, nonviolent resistance transforms weakness into strength and breeds courage in the face of danger.*”
>
> —SCLC statement

SCLC shifted the focus of the civil rights movement to the South. Earlier organizations had been dominated by northerners. Now southern African American church leaders moved into the forefront of the struggle for equal rights. Among them, Martin Luther King, Jr., became a national figure. (See the American Biography on this page.)

Dr. King Leads the Way When the Montgomery bus boycott began, Martin Luther King, Jr., was a young Baptist preacher. Within a few years he would become one of the most loved and admired—and also one of the most hated—people in the United States. King became not only a leader in the African American civil rights movement but also a symbol of nonviolent protest for the entire world.

As he became more and more involved in the civil rights movement, King was influenced by the beliefs of Mohandas K. Gandhi. Gandhi had been a leader in India's long struggle to gain independence from Great Britain, an effort that finally succeeded in 1947. Gandhi preached a philosophy of nonviolence as the only way to achieve victory against much stronger foes. Those who fight for justice must peacefully refuse to obey unjust laws, Gandhi taught. They must remain nonviolent, regardless of the violent reactions such peaceful resistance might provoke—a tactic that requires tremendous discipline and courage.

The philosophy of protest advocated by King had other sources as well. American author Henry David Thoreau had been an advocate of civil disobedience in the mid-1800s. Thoreau, who opposed the 1846 war with Mexico, refused to pay his taxes, and as a result, was jailed. He then wrote about this experience and the principles behind his actions in his famous essay "*Civil Disobedience.*"

As the Montgomery boycott ended and boycotters prepared to ride the newly-integrated buses, King began training volunteers for what they might expect in the months ahead. Films, songs, and skits showed Gandhi's activities

RESOURCE DIRECTORY

Teaching Resources

Biography, Literature, and Comparing Primary Sources booklet (Comparing Primary Sources) *On School Integration,* pp. 151–152

Biography, Literature, and Comparing Primary Sources booklet (Literature) *SNCC Workers,* pp. 78 79

Learning with Documents booklet (Visual Learning Activity) *Nonviolent Resistance,* p. 67

Other Print Resources

American History Block Scheduling Support *Martin Luther King, Jr.'s, Nonviolent Way to Civil Rights,* found in the Nation After World War II folder, includes interdisciplinary lesson suggestions and activities for Geography and History, Primary Sources, Biography, and Literature.

and demonstrated the success of passive resistance in India. Bus riders were advised to follow 17 rules for maintaining a nonviolent approach in case they encountered confrontations on the buses as they traveled through the South. These rules included the following:

> *"Pray for guidance and commit yourself to complete nonviolence in word and action as you enter the bus. . . . Be loving enough to absorb evil and understanding enough to turn an enemy into a friend. . . . If cursed, do not curse back. If pushed, do not push back. If struck, do not strike back, but evidence love and good will at all times. . . . If another person is being molested, do not arise to go to his defense, but pray for the oppressor and use moral and spiritual force to carry on the struggle for justice. . . ."*
>
> —Leaflet distributed throughout the city

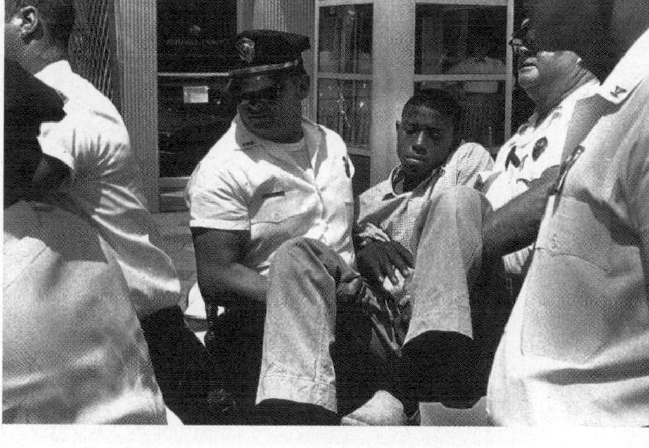

VIEWING HISTORY Police arrested SNCC member Eddie Brown at a 1962 protest rally in Albany, Georgia. **Analyzing Visual Information** *How do Brown's actions reflect the philosophy of nonviolent protest?*

As a result of his role in the Montgomery boycott, King gained national prominence. He went on to play a key role in almost every major civil rights event. His work earned him the Nobel peace prize in 1964.

A New Voice for Students

Nonviolent protest was a practical strategy in the civil rights struggle. It also represented a moral philosophy. "To accept passively an unjust system is to cooperate with that system; thereby the oppressed become as evil as the oppressor," King said. "Noncooperation with evil is as much a moral obligation as is cooperation with good."

The Formation of SNCC A new, student organization conceived by the SCLC took a somewhat different approach. The **Student Nonviolent Coordinating Committee,** usually known as **SNCC** (pronounced "snick"), began in 1960 at a meeting in Raleigh, North Carolina, for students active in the struggle. SCLC executive director Ella Baker thought that the NAACP and SCLC were not keeping up with the demands of young African Americans. She wanted to give them a way to play an even greater role in the civil rights movement.

READING CHECK
What led to the formation of SNCC?

Nearly 200 students showed up for the first SNCC meeting. Most came from southern communities, but some northerners attended as well. Baker delivered the opening address. "The younger generation is challenging you and me," she told the adults present. "They are asking us to forget our laziness and doubt and fear, and follow our dedication to the truth to the bitter end."

Martin Luther King, Jr., spoke next to the young audience, calling the civil rights movement "a revolt against the apathy and complacency of adults in the Negro community. . . ." At the end of the meeting, the participants organized a temporary coordinating committee.

A month later, student leaders met with Baker and other SCLC and CORE leaders and voted to maintain their independence from other civil rights groups. By the end of the year, the Student Nonviolent Coordinating Committee was a permanent and separate organization. It was interracial at first, though that changed in later years.

ACTIVITY
Connecting with History and Conflict

Have students reread the guidelines for nonviolent resistance used by civil rights activists. ("If cursed, do not curse back. If pushed, do not push back. If struck, do not strike back.") Have them study the photos on these pages. Then pose the question: Could you have done it? Would you have made a good SNCC volunteer? Why or why not? Have students write their answers and reasons in the form of a paragraph. Then have students meet in small groups, share their responses, and draw conclusions about what qualities are necessary to succeed at nonviolent resistance. Have students explain the nonviolent resistance movement in the context of actions taken by African Americans to expand economic opportunities and political rights in American society. **(Verbal/Linguistic)**

BACKGROUND
Biography

Baptist minister Jesse Jackson (b. 1941) was a close aide to Martin Luther King, Jr. Until 1971 Jackson headed Operation Breadbasket, a Southern Christian Leadership Conference program to expand educational and job opportunities for African Americans. He then founded People United to Save Humanity. In 1984 he unsuccessfully ran for the Democratic presidential nomination, but his candidacy spurred African American voter registration. "Hands that picked cotton in 1884," said Jackson, "will pick the President in 1984."

READING CHECK
It developed out of existing organizations to give a stronger voice to youth activists.

TEST PREPARATION

Have students read the material in the section "A New Voice For Students" and then answer the question below.

What did Martin Luther King, Jr., probably mean by the word "noncooperation"?

- **A** Working as a team with other people.
- **(B)** Refusing to cooperate with something a person believes is wrong.
- **C** Gathering with other people to form a company, or a corporation.
- **D** Supporting evil actions.

CAPTION ANSWERS

Viewing History Eddie Brown offers no resistance whatsoever, even while police officers are carrying him away.

Section 2 Assessment

Reading Comprehension

1. The National Urban League assisted poor African Americans economically by helping them move to cities, obtain employment there, and find a place to live. CORE leaders concentrated on bringing about change through peaceful confrontation. CORE organized demonstrations against segregation during World War II.
2. Nonviolence, civil disobedience.
3. It gave the movement a younger focus and energy. Its members were idealistic activists who pushed for social change and forced others to confront their demands.
4. He was soft-spoken, and seemed humble and accessible. He was a sincere speaker and a strong leader.

Critical Thinking and Writing

5. Strengths: Nonviolent protest preserves the moral integrity of the protesters because they refuse to use violence against their oppressors. In this way, they may also win the respect and support of other people. Weaknesses: Nonviolent protesters often encounter violent resistance but have no way to protect themselves.
6. Agendas will vary, but should be supported with facts from the section.

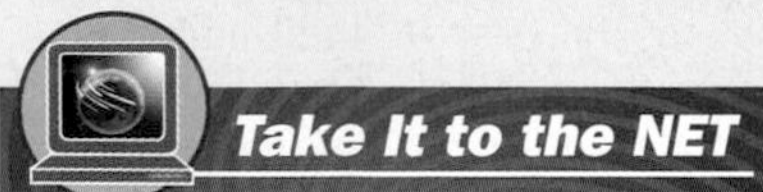

Students should create a chart comparing past goals and accomplishments of the organization they select with that group's present endeavors. Encourage students to highlight both similarities and differences.

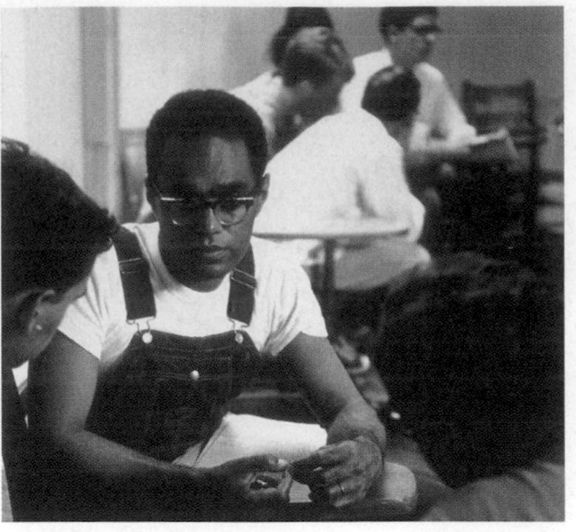

VIEWING HISTORY Robert Moses helped train SNCC volunteers in Ohio in 1964. **Drawing Conclusions** *Why was Bob Moses well suited to be a leader of SNCC?*

SNCC filled its own niche in the American civil rights movement. The focus of the civil rights movement shifted away from church leaders alone and gave young activists a chance to make decisions about priorities and tactics. SNCC also sought more immediate change, as opposed to the gradual change advocated by most of the older organizations.

Robert Moses One of SNCC's most influential leaders was Robert Moses, a Harvard graduate student and a mathematics teacher in Harlem. As the civil rights movement developed, he wanted to be involved. He first went to work for SNCC in Atlanta, and later headed for Mississippi to recruit black and white volunteers to help rural blacks register to vote.

While Martin Luther King, Jr., spoke with eloquence and passion, Moses was more soft-spoken. He took time to gather his thoughts, and then he spoke slowly. Todd Gitlin, a white student-activist leader, later noted that Moses was loved and trusted "precisely because he seemed humble, ordinary, accessible." Gitlin went on to describe Moses's style of oratory:

> *"He liked to make his points with his hand, starting with palm downturned, then opening his hand outward toward his audience, as if delivering the point for inspection, nothing up his sleeve. The words seemed to be extruded [thrust forth], with difficulty, out of his depths. What he said seemed earned. . . . To teach his unimportance, he was wont [accustomed] to crouch in the corner or speak from the back of the room, hoping to hear the popular voice reveal itself."*
>
> —Todd Gitlin

With fresh new ideas and strong leaders like Bob Moses, SNCC became a strong and vital organization for students wanting to take part in the civil rights movement. As the struggle intensified, SNCC became a powerful force, and many students found that they would risk almost anything for their beliefs.

Section 2 Assessment

READING COMPREHENSION

1. What functions did the National Urban League and **CORE** serve for African Americans?
2. What was Dr. King's approach to civil rights?
3. What role did **SNCC** play in the movement?
4. Why was Bob Moses an effective leader?

CRITICAL THINKING AND WRITING

5. **Determining Relevance** What do you think are some of the strengths and weaknesses of nonviolent protest as a means to bring about social change?
6. **Writing a List** As a student in the 1960s, you have been asked to help organize a local chapter of SNCC. Write an agenda for organizing such a group, listing strategies you would use to recruit members and to work for change.

Take It to the NET

Activity: Yesterday and Today Select one of the civil rights organizations discussed in this section and research its goals and strategies in the present day. Create a chart comparing this group's historic actions to its actions today. Use the links provided in the *America: Pathways to the Present* area of the following Web site for help in completing this activity.
www.phschool.com

Caption Answers

Viewing History The sincere, low-key style of Bob Moses was well suited to the SNCC because he was able to earn the trust of his audiences.

RESOURCE DIRECTORY

Teaching Resources
Units 5/6/7 booklet
- Section 2 Quiz, p. 53

Guide to the Essentials
- Section 2 Summary, p. 102

Section 3

The Struggle Intensifies

READING FOCUS

- What were the goals of sit-ins and Freedom Rides?
- What was the reaction to James Meredith's integration at the University of Mississippi?
- How did the events in Birmingham, Alabama, affect the nation's attitudes toward the civil rights movement?

KEY TERMS

sit-in
Freedom Ride

TAKING NOTES

Copy this flowchart. As you read, fill in the boxes with the tactics and outcomes of the civil rights protests mentioned in this section.

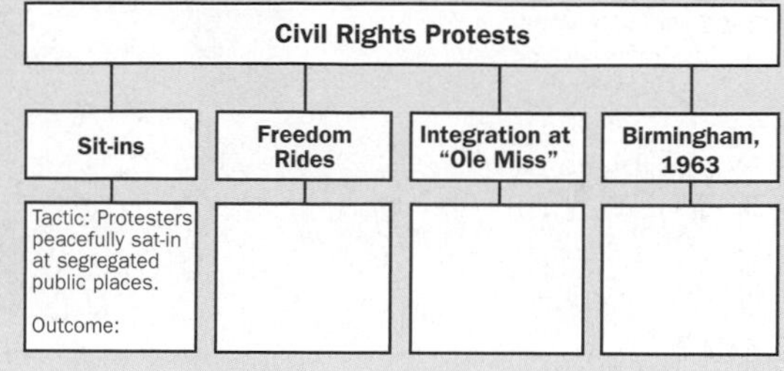

MAIN IDEA

The tactics of nonviolent protest, including sit-ins and boycotts, challenged segregation and brought change, but also generated violent confrontations.

Setting the Scene As a child in the rural Mississippi town of Centreville, Anne Moody grew up wondering what "the white folks' secret" was. "Their homes were large and beautiful with indoor toilets and every other convenience that I knew of at the time," she observed. "Every house I had ever lived in was a one- or two-room shack with an outdoor toilet." Moody was horrified when 14-year-old Emmett Till, visiting from Chicago, was killed in Mississippi supposedly because he had whistled at a white woman.

While in college, Moody became involved in the civil rights movement. She joined the NAACP and also worked with CORE and SNCC. She took part in the first sit-ins in Jackson, Mississippi, in 1963. Like so many other students in the 1960s, Moody was jailed for taking part in civil rights demonstrations.

Worse was the reaction from her family at home. Her mother, afraid for the lives of her relatives, begged Moody to end her involvement with the civil rights movement. The local sheriff had warned that Moody should never return to her hometown. Moody's brother had been beaten up and almost lynched by a group of white boys. Her sister angrily told her that her activism was threatening the life of every African American in Centreville.

Against all that resistance, Moody persevered. She participated in demonstrations, helped force the desegregation of local facilities, and remained determined to do everything she could to make the South a better place for African Americans. But it was never easy, and the gains came at tremendous personal cost. Like many other Americans committed to changing society through nonviolent means, Moody learned that challenging white supremacy often provoked an ugly and violent reaction.

Anne Moody joined a SNCC voter registration drive during her first year at Tougaloo College. She said of her fellow SNCC workers, "I had never known people so willing and determined to help others."

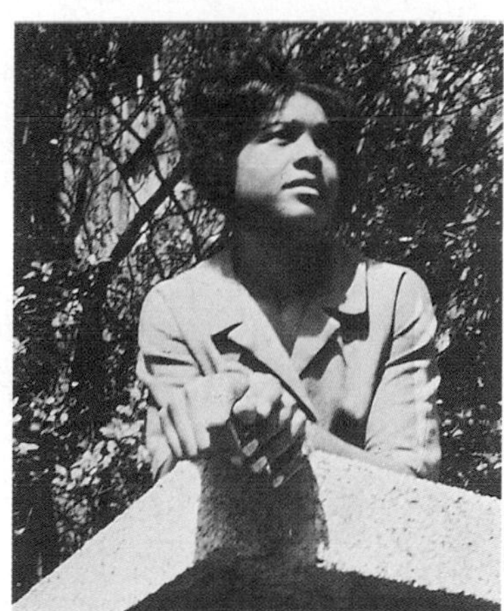

Sit-ins Challenge Segregation

As you read in an earlier chapter, the Congress of Racial Equality (CORE) created the **sit-in** in 1943 to desegregate the Jack Spratt Coffee House in Chicago. In this technique, a group of CORE members simply sat down at a segregated lunch counter or other public place. If they were refused service at first, they simply stayed where they were.

Section 3
The Struggle Intensifies

SECTION OBJECTIVES

1. Identify the goals of sit-ins and Freedom Rides.
2. Find out the reaction to James Meredith's integration at the University of Mississippi.
3. Understand how the events in Birmingham, Alabama, affected the nation's attitudes toward the civil rights movement.

BELLRINGER

Read aloud the quotation by John Lewis on the opposite page. Then ask students to weigh carefully this question: Could you have endured what the lunch-counter protesters did without either fleeing or defending yourself? Ask what motivated Lewis and the other protesters to suffer the abuse of the white segregationists.

READING STRATEGY

Remind students that civil rights workers faced violence, even death, from opponents of change. Have students list techniques they might use when confronted with this problem. Then have them read the section to find out what actually happened.

RESOURCE DIRECTORY

Teaching Resources
Learning Styles Lesson Plans booklet, p. 59
Guided Reading and Review booklet, p. 114

Technology
Section Reading Support Transparencies
Guided Reading Audiotapes (English/Spanish), Ch. 21
Student Edition on Audio CD, Ch. 21
Prentice Hall Presentation Pro CD-ROM, Ch. 21
Companion Web site, www.phschool.com

Lesson Plan

Focus Explain that as civil rights activists put the philosophy of nonviolence into action, protests began to sweep the South. Ask students to describe what happened as a result of these protests.

Instruct Discuss what issues made the civil rights movement so unstoppable. Ask students to consider the following factors in their examination of the movement: the people involved, the tactics, the moral philosophy of the movement, the reactions of whites, and television and newspaper images of the violence.

Assess/Reteach At the time of nonviolent protests, many people who sympathized with the aims of the civil rights movement nonetheless did not agree with the methods used. In students' opinions, did the end justify the means?

Activity
Connecting with Geography

Have students use a historical atlas of the United States to broaden their understanding of Anne Moody's background growing up in Centreville, Mississippi. Have them use the appropriate mathematical skills to interpret social studies information as they use an atlas to do the following: locate Centreville on a map, find out its population, calculate the town's distance from a major city, identify transportation routes by which a person could travel to Centreville, and describe the economy of the area in which the town is located. Then discuss the picture that emerges from this information. **(Visual/Spatial; Logical/Mathematical)**

READING CHECK
They were subjected to physical abuse and often served time in jail.

Caption Answers

Viewing History It forced business owners to decide between serving the protesters or risking a disruption of business.

VIEWING HISTORY Signs like the one below were clear indications of how institutionalized segregation was in the South. At right, John Salter, Jr., Joan Trumpauer, and Anne Moody (left to right) held a sit-in in at a Jackson, Mississippi, lunch counter in May 1963. A hostile crowd registered their response by mocking and pouring food on the three activists. **Synthesizing Information** *Why was the sit-in often a successful tactic?*

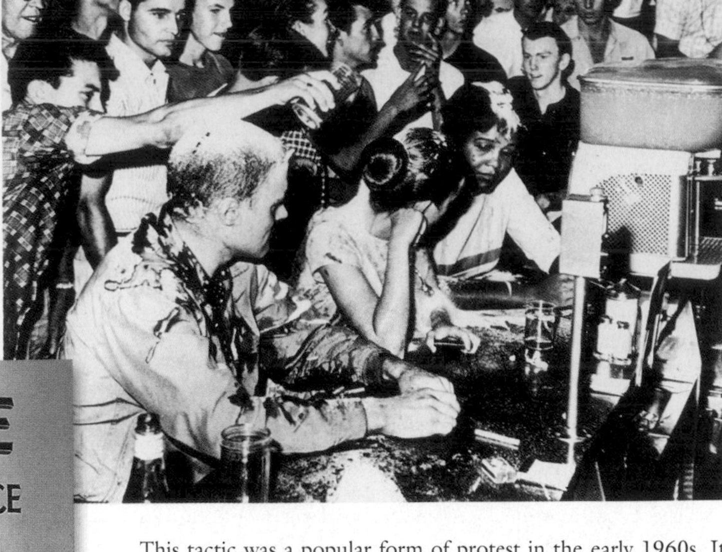

This tactic was a popular form of protest in the early 1960s. It often worked because it forced business owners to decide between serving the protesters or risking a disruption and loss of business. In some places, sit-ins brought strong reactions. John Lewis, a SNCC activist, participated in sit-ins in Nashville, Tennessee, in the 1960s. He remembered the experience:

> *"It was a Woolworth in the heart of the downtown area, and we occupied every seat at the lunch counter, every seat in the restaurant. . . . A group of young white men came in and they started pulling and beating primarily the young women. They put lighted cigarettes down their backs, in their hair, and they were really beating people. In a short time police officials came in and placed all of us under arrest, and not a single member of the white group, the people that were opposing our sit-in, was arrested."*
>
> —John Lewis

READING CHECK
What often happened to those who participated in sit-ins?

Soon, thousands of students were involved in the sit-in campaign, which gained the support of SCLC. Martin Luther King, Jr., told students that arrest was a "badge of honor." By the end of 1960, some 70,000 students had participated in sit-ins, and 3,600 had served time in jail. The protests began a process of change that could not be stopped.

The Freedom Rides

In *Boynton* v. *Virginia* (1960), the Supreme Court expanded its earlier ban on segregation on interstate buses. As a result, bus station waiting rooms and restaurants that served interstate travelers could not be segregated either.

In 1961, CORE, with aid from SNCC, organized and carried out the **Freedom Rides.** They were designed to test whether southern states would obey the Supreme Court ruling and allow African Americans to exercise the rights newly granted to them.

Violence Greets the Riders The first Freedom Ride departed Washington, D.C., on May 4, 1961. Thirteen freedom riders, both African Americans and

RESOURCE DIRECTORY

Teaching Resources
Learning with Documents booklet (Primary Source Activity) *Protecting the Freedom Riders,* p. 33

Technology
Color Transparencies *American Photo,* F9
Sounds of an Era Audio CD *A Sit-in in Nashville, Tennessee* (time: one minute, 30 seconds)
RESOURCE PRO® **Biography** *Sidney Poitier,* found on Resource Pro, profiles the actor whose movies in the 1950s and 1960s dramatically portrayed the evils of racism in United States society.

white Americans, boarded two interstate buses heading south. (See the map of the route below.) At first the group encountered only minor conflicts. In Atlanta the two buses split up and headed for the Deep South. There the trip turned dangerous.

In Anniston, Alabama, a heavily armed white mob met the first bus at the terminal. The bus attempted to leave. CORE director James Farmer described what happened next:

> “*Before the bus pulled out, however, members of the mob took their sharp instruments and slashed tires. The bus got to the outskirts of Anniston and the tires blew out and the bus ground to a halt. Members of the mob had boarded cars and followed the bus, and now with the disabled bus standing there, the members of the mob surrounded it, held the door closed, and a member of the mob threw a firebomb into the bus, breaking a window to do so. Incidentally, there were some local policemen mingling with the mob, fraternizing with them while this was going on.*”
>
> —James Farmer

The riders escaped before the bus burst into flames, but many were beaten by the mob as they stumbled out of the vehicle, choking on the smoke. They had anticipated trouble, since they meant to provoke a confrontation. The level of violence, however, took them by surprise.

As a result of the savage response, Farmer considered calling off the project. SNCC leaders, though, begged to go on. Farmer warned, “You know that may be suicide.” Student activist Diane Nash replied, “If we let them stop us

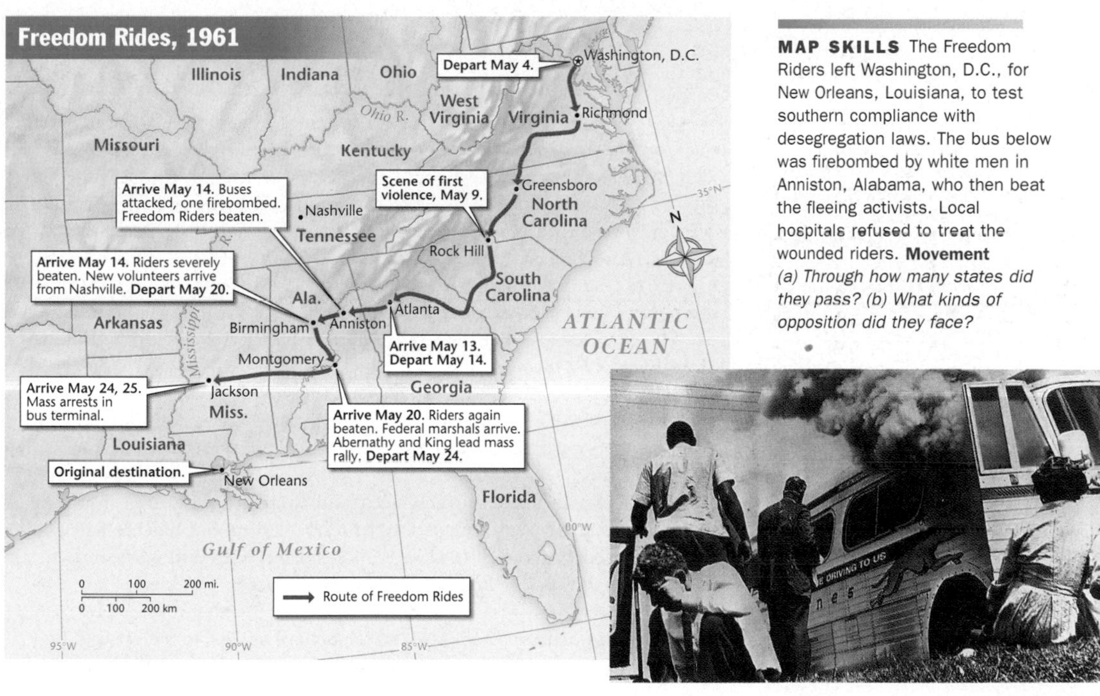

MAP SKILLS The Freedom Riders left Washington, D.C., for New Orleans, Louisiana, to test southern compliance with desegregation laws. The bus below was firebombed by white men in Anniston, Alabama, who then beat the fleeing activists. Local hospitals refused to treat the wounded riders. **Movement** *(a) Through how many states did they pass? (b) What kinds of opposition did they face?*

ACTIVITY
Connecting with Citizenship

Explain to students that at the time of the Freedom Rides, virtually no southern newspapers were covering the civil rights movement. Only the white-owned *Tennessean* in Nashville, which supported civil rights, did so. *The Atlanta Journal and Constitution* ran editorials but did not report stories. Have students write letters to the editor of a southern newspaper urging the paper to cover civil rights activity in the region and supporting their position with reasons and examples. Display finished letters and discuss which are most persuasive and why. **(Verbal/Linguistic)**

BACKGROUND
Recent Scholarship

Ordinary people doing extraordinary things helped the civil rights movement succeed in the United States. In *Voices of Freedom: An Oral History of the Civil Rights Movement from the 1950s through the 1980s,* Henry Hampton and Steve Fayer provide oral commentary by hundreds of Americans involved in the struggle. Based on interviews for the *Eyes on the Prize* television series, the book offers first-person accounts of such historic events as the sit-ins of 1960, the freedom rides of 1961, and the Birmingham protests of 1963.

CUSTOMIZE FOR ...
Gifted and Talented

Have students pick one event from the Freedom Rides map on this page. They should research the event and prepare a report, including primary sources from that time period.

CAPTION ANSWERS

Map Skills (a) Six states. (b) Beatings and a firebombing.

ACTIVITY
Student Portfolio

You may wish to have students add the following to their portfolios: Ask students to compare the civil rights movement in the United States with the African independence movements of the late 1950s and early 1960s. Encourage them to research the leaders, goals, and challenges of the movements, as well as any inspirational symbols, slogans, or songs. Ask them to conclude with a paragraph addressing this question: How did events in Africa challenge America's image as the protector of democracy? **(Verbal/ Linguistic)**

BACKGROUND
Interdisciplinary

Most Americans in the early 1960s were more focused on President Kennedy's New Frontier and its faith in a future based on science and technology than on civil rights activism. In January 1961, *Time* magazine chose 15 scientists as its "Men of the Year" with the following testimonial: "Statesmen and savants, builders and even priests are their servants. . . . Science is at the apogee of its power."

Major Civil Rights Protests, 1954–1965

Year	Event and Outcome
1954	***Brown* v. *Board of Education*** Supreme Court ruled against the "separate but equal" doctrine and ordered the desegregation of all public schools. Violent protests in southern states followed.
1955–1956	**Montgomery Bus Boycott** Bus company desegregated its buses. Martin Luther King, Jr., emerged as an important civil rights leader.
1960s	**Sit-ins** Peaceful actions sparked violent reactions and many protesters were jailed. The tactic gained momentum for the civil rights movement.
1961	**Freedom Rides** Attempts to desegregate interstate travel led to mob violence. The Interstate Commerce Commission banned segregation in interstate transportation.
1962	**James Meredith Enrolls at the University of Mississippi** The Supreme Court upheld Meredith's right to enter the all-white institution. Violence erupts on the campus.
1963	**Protest Marches and Boycotts in Birmingham, Alabama** Violence against peaceful demonstrators shocked the nation. Under pressure, Birmingham desegregated public facilities.
1963	**March on Washington** More than 200,000 people demonstrated in an impressive display of support for civil rights.
1965	**Selma March** State troopers attacked marchers. President Johnson used federal force to protect the route from Selma to Montgomery, and thousands joined the march, which was designed to call attention to the issue of voting rights.

INTERPRETING CHARTS
The visibility of early civil rights protests led to advances in civil rights on both the local and national level. **Making Comparisons** *What do most of these protests have in common? How do they differ?*

with violence, the movement is dead! . . . Your troops have been badly battered. Let us pick up the baton and run with it."

National Reactions Photographs of the smoldering bus in Anniston horrified the country. Burke Marshall, the Assistant Attorney General who headed the Justice Department's Civil Rights Division, was astonished "that people—presumably otherwise sane, sensible, rational—would have this kind of reaction simply to where people were sitting on a bus."

The violence intensified in Birmingham and Montgomery. Upon their arrival in Jackson, Mississippi, the riders met no mobs but were arrested immediately. New volunteers arrived to replace them and were also arrested. This first Freedom Ride died out in Jackson, but about 300 Freedom Riders continued the protest throughout that summer. Attorney General Robert Kennedy had at first been reluctant to lend federal support to the protest, but now he sent federal marshals to protect the Freedom Riders.

Kennedy then took further measures. He pressured the Interstate Commerce Commission to issue a ruling that prohibited segregation in all interstate transportation—trains, planes, and buses. The Justice Department sued local communities that did not comply.

Integration at "Ole Miss"

In 1961, James Meredith, an African American Air Force veteran, fought a personal battle for equal rights. Meredith was a student at Jackson State College, but he wanted to transfer to the all-white University of Mississippi, known as "Ole Miss." After being rejected, Meredith got legal help from the NAACP. It filed a lawsuit claiming that Meredith's application was turned down on racial grounds.

In the summer of 1962, the Supreme Court upheld Meredith's claim. Mississippi Governor Ross Barnett, however, declared that Meredith could not enroll, regardless of what the Court said. Barnett personally blocked the way to the admissions office.

The issue became a standoff between the governor and the Justice Department. President Kennedy sent federal marshals to accompany Meredith to the campus. Crowds of angry white protesters, who had gathered around campus, destroyed their vehicles. As violence erupted on campus, tear gas covered the grounds. Two bystanders were killed and hundreds of people hurt. Finally, President Kennedy sent army troops to restore order, but federal marshals continued to escort Meredith to class. A month later, Meredith wrote an article for the *Saturday Evening Post* describing his experiences:

> *" It hasn't been all bad. Many students have spoken to me very pleasantly. They have stopped banging doors and throwing bottles into my*

CAPTION ANSWERS

Interpreting Charts Possible answers: In common: The protesters were peaceful, but the response from whites was often violent. These protests posed a challenge to existing discriminatory laws and practices by urging desegregation. Differences: Some were marches, others were boycotts; some relied on courageous individuals, others involved large masses of people.

RESOURCE DIRECTORY

Technology

Color Transparencies *Political Cartoons,* B16

dormitory now. One fellow from my home town sat down at my table in the cafeteria. 'If you're here to get an education, I'm for you,' he said. 'If you're here to cause trouble, I'm against you.' That seemed fair enough to me."

—James Meredith, 1962

Clash in Birmingham

Elsewhere, civil rights leaders looked for chances to protest segregation nonviolently. The Reverend Fred Shuttlesworth, head of the Alabama Christian Movement for Human Rights, in Birmingham, invited Martin Luther King, Jr., and the SCLC to visit the city in April 1963. Birmingham's population was 40 percent African American, but King called it "the most segregated city in America." Victory there could be a model for resistance.

King and Shuttlesworth planned boycotts of downtown stores and attempts to integrate local churches. Business leaders, fearing disruptions and lost sales, tried to negotiate with Shuttlesworth to call off the plan, without success.

When reporters wanted to know how long King planned to stay, he drew on a biblical story and told them he would remain until "Pharaoh lets God's people go." Birmingham police commissioner Eugene "Bull" Connor, a determined segregationist, replied, "I got plenty of room in the jail."

From Birmingham Jail The campaign began nonviolently with protest marches and sit-ins. City officials declared that the marches violated a regulation prohibiting parades without a permit. They obtained a court injunction, which directed the protesters to cease demonstrations. King decided to disobey the court orders and set an example of civil disobedience. Connor then arrested King and other demonstrators. When a group of white clergy criticized the campaign as an ill-timed threat to law and order by an "outsider," King responded from his cell. In his "Letter from Birmingham Jail," he defended his tactics and his timing:

"*Frankly, I have yet to engage in a direct-action campaign that was 'well timed' in the view of those who have not suffered unduly from the disease of segregation. For years now I have heard the word 'Wait!' It*

VIEWING HISTORY President Kennedy supported the Supreme Court's decision to allow James Meredith to enroll at the University of Mississippi. **Synthesizing Information** *How did the various branches and levels of government interact over this issue?*

COMPARING PRIMARY SOURCES
Integrating Schools

In parts of the Deep South, the battle for equal rights continued to be fought at the nation's schoolhouse doors each September, long after the Supreme Court ordered schools to desegregate in 1954.

Analyzing Viewpoints How do these two speeches, made about a month apart, reflect the divisions in the country?

For School Integration

"Nearly nine years have elapsed since the Supreme Court ruled that state laws requiring or permitting segregated schools violate the Constitution. . . . Since that time it has become increasingly clear that neither violence nor legalistic measures will be tolerated as a means of thwarting court-ordered desegregation."

—President Kennedy, message to Congress February 28, 1963

Against School Integration

"I draw the line in the dust and toss the gauntlet before the feet of tyranny and I say segregation now, segregation tomorrow, segregation forever."

—Alabama Governor George Wallace, Inaugural Address, January 14, 1963

ACTIVITY
Connecting with Culture

This activity may take place over several class periods: Divide the class into groups of three. Have each student in the group make or find three images relating to the civil rights movement to include in a collage. The group should decide on a title for the artwork, perhaps borrowing a film or television series title (such as *Mississippi Burning* or *Eyes on the Prize*), using a line from a speech (such as "I have a dream"), or making up a title. One student from each group should present the finished collage to the class. **(Visual/Kinesthetic)**

BACKGROUND
Connections to Today

On September 15, 1963, a bomb exploded outside the Sixteenth Street Baptist Church in Birmingham, Alabama, killing four black girls. Although an FBI investigation concluded that four Ku Klux Klansmen were responsible, FBI director J. Edgar Hoover closed the case without filing any charges. In the 1970s Alabama's attorney general reopened the case and succeeded in convicting one suspect of murder. An FBI review of the case in the early 1990s led to the conviction of a second suspect in May 2001. Other cases from the civil rights era have also recently been reopened. In 1994 a jury convicted the assassin of civil rights leader Medgar Evers, who was killed in 1963.

CUSTOMIZE FOR ...
Gifted and Talented

After students have read the statement on the previous page by Assistant Attorney General Burke Marshall, ask them to analyze why whites reacted as they did to the Freedom Rides. What was at stake from the point of view of white segregationists? Why did African Americans riding a bus alongside whites seem so threatening to them?

TEST PREPARATION

Have students read the quotation by Martin Luther King, Jr., on these pages and then complete the statement below.

The reason King gives to defend the timing of his campaign note is that—

- **A** only segregationists can plan well timed campaigns.
- **B** African Americans only know how to wait.
- **Ⓒ** there is no such thing as perfect timing in a fight to overcome segregation.
- **D** direct-action campaigns cannot be well timed.

CAPTION ANSWERS

Viewing History The U.S. Supreme Court ruled that Meredith could enroll at the University of Mississippi. President Kennedy sent troops and federal marshals to uphold the Supreme Court's decision in the face of Mississippi Governor Barnett's defiance of the Court.

Section 3 Assessment

Reading Comprehension

1. Angry white mobs harassed, and sometimes physically attacked, the sit-in participants. Sit-ins generated tremendous publicity around the country, which aided the civil rights movement as a whole.
2. The nation was shocked by the violence; the federal government began to support the protesters.
3. In both cases the President supported the Supreme Court's decision to allow the students to be integrated. The government supported the students, intervening and sending escorts to accompany them to school in the face of resistance.
4. Martin Luther King, Jr., wanted to bring about the integration of public facilities and to end discrimination in hiring practices. He also wanted to use Birmingham as a model for the desegregation of other southern cities.

Critical Thinking and Writing

5. Answers will vary but may include: working through established political channels, voting for candidates who supported their cause, or initiating letter-writing campaigns.
6. Answers will vary. Encourage students to support their responses by considering their own views toward the strategy of nonviolence.

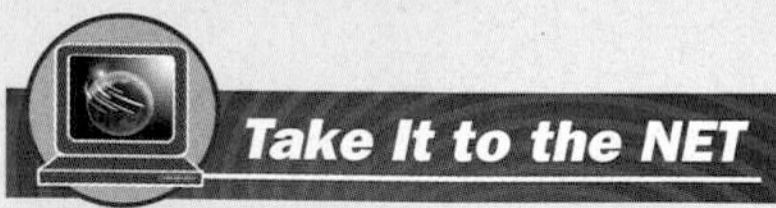

Invite students to take a Virtual Field Trip at **www.phschool.com**

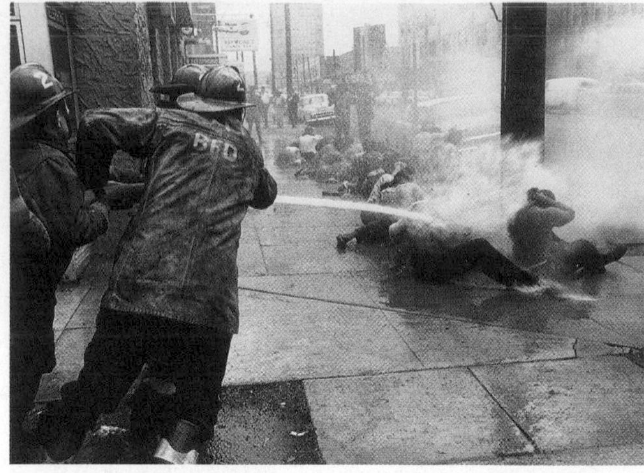

VIEWING HISTORY Police in Birmingham, Alabama, used high-powered hoses to break up civil rights marches in 1963. Television coverage of this brutal treatment of peaceful demonstrators prompted widespread sympathy for the movement. **Identifying Central Issues** *What was the outcome of the Birmingham crisis?*

rings in the ear of every Negro with piercing familiarity. This 'Wait!' has almost always meant 'Never.'"

—"Letter from Birmingham Jail," Martin Luther King, Jr., 1963

After more than a week, King was released on bail. Soon after, he made a difficult decision: to let young people join the campaign. Though dangerous, it would test the conscience of the Birmingham authorities and the nation.

As they marched with the adults, "Bull" Connor arrested more than 900 of the young people. Police used high-pressure fire hoses, which could tear the bark from trees, on the demonstrators. They also brought out trained police dogs that attacked marchers' arms and legs. When protesters fell to the ground, policemen beat them with clubs and took them off to jail.

The Nation Watches Television cameras brought the scenes of violence to people across the country. Even those unsympathetic to the civil rights movement were appalled. As reporter Eric Sevareid observed, "A newspaper or television picture of a snarling police dog set upon a human being is recorded in the permanent photo-electric file of every human brain."

In the end, the protesters won. A compromise arranged by Assistant Attorney General Burke Marshall led to desegregation of city facilities and fairer hiring practices. An interracial committee was set up to aid communication.

The success of the Birmingham marches was just one example that proved how effective nonviolent protest could be. Sometimes the technique did not work, or worked only slowly. Nevertheless, nonviolent protest as a means to social change had earned itself a place of honor in the history of civil rights in the United States.

Section 3 Assessment

READING COMPREHENSION

1. What reaction did **sit-ins** provoke?
2. How did the violent response to the **Freedom Rides** and the Birmingham marches aid the civil rights movement?
3. Compare the government's response to the controversy at "Ole Miss" with its response to the Little Rock controversy in 1957.
4. What was the aim of the Birmingham campaign?

CRITICAL THINKING AND WRITING

5. **Identifying Alternatives** If student protesters had not chosen nonviolent protest, what other peaceful options might they have used?
6. **Writing to Persuade** In May 1961, an article in the *New York Times* urged the Freedom Riders to call off their plans, saying, "Non-violence that deliberately provokes violence is a logical contradiction." Write two paragraphs explaining why you agree or disagree with this opinion.

Take It to the NET

Activity: Virtual Field Trip Visit the National Civil Rights Museum online and tour the exhibits it has provided. Select the exhibit in the museum that interests you the most and summarize what you see in that exhibit in a brief essay. Use the links provided in the *America: Pathways to the Present* area of the following Web site for help in completing this activity.
www.phschool.com

Caption Answers

Viewing History City facilities were desegregated, more equitable hiring practices were instituted, and an interracial committee was established to aid in communication.

RESOURCE DIRECTORY

Teaching Resources
Units 5/6/7 booklet
- Section 3 Quiz, p. 54

Guide to the Essentials
- Section 3 Summary, p. 103

Technology
Exploring Primary Sources in U.S. History CD-ROM *Letter from Birmingham Jail, Martin Luther King, Jr.*

Understanding Public Opinion Polls

Elected officials are always interested in public opinion—first, so they can support the policies their constituents favor; and second, so they can be reelected. Public opinion polls that use scientific polling techniques are a good way of finding out what the public thinks at a particular time and how these opinions change over time. Professional polling organizations follow a complex process to provide reliable public opinion data. In the 1960s, civil rights was a divisive issue. Samples of polling about civil rights conducted by the Gallup Organization appear at right.

LEARN THE SKILL

Use the following steps to understand opinion polls:

1. **Define the universe being polled.** In polling, a *universe* is the whole population that the poll aims to measure—for example, all adults in the country or all the members of a political party or region. After defining the universe, pollsters interview a randomly selected sample of people representing that universe. Unless noted, the universe is assumed to be all the adults in the nation or region being polled.
2. **Examine the questions.** Polling questions should be simply worded and objective, and should not lead toward a particular answer.
3. **Analyze the results.** If they include answers from subgroups of the universe, ask yourself why the pollster chose these groups. What are the differences between the groups? Use your knowledge of the historical period to determine what events might have affected results. Consider how the polling results might be used by a politician or other decision-maker.

PRACTICE THE SKILL

Answer the following questions:

1. **(a)** What is the universe of Poll C? **(b)** Of Poll D? **(c)** What subgroup is singled out in Poll A?
2. **(a)** How is the first question in Poll C different from the questions in the other polls? **(b)** Why do you think the pollster gives "No opinion" or "Don't know" as options? **(c)** Do you think the polls contain any leading questions? Explain.
3. **(a)** Why do you think Poll A breaks out only one region of the country? **(b)** Why do you think the pollster asks the same question in Polls B and D? **(c)** What kind of information can you learn from Poll C that you cannot learn from the others? **(d)** How might decision-makers or candidates use each of these polls?

A. Integration, June 23, 1961

The United States Supreme Court has ruled that racial segregation in the public schools is illegal. This means that all children, no matter what their race, must be allowed to go to the same schools. Do you approve or disapprove of this decision?

	South Only
Approve............62%	*Approve..........24%*
Disapprove.........33%	*Disapprove.....69%*
No opinion...........5%	*No opinion........7%*

B. Integration, Nov. 14, 1962

Do you think the Kennedy Administration is pushing racial integration too fast, or not fast enough?

Too fast.............42%	*About right......31%*
Not fast enough...12%	*No opinion.......15%*

C. Most Important Problem, Oct. 2, 1963

What do you think is the most important problem facing this country today?

Racial problems.............52%
International problems (Russia—threat of war)........25
Unemployment........5
Cost of living...........3
Other problems.....13
Don't know.............5
108%

Which political party do you think can do a better job of handling the problem you just mentioned—the Republican Party or the Democratic Party?

Democratic........30%
Republican........20
No opinion........50

(Note: table [at left] adds to more than 100% since some persons named more than one problem.)

D. Integration, Oct. 13, 1963

Do you think the Kennedy Administration is pushing integration too fast, or not fast enough?

Too fast..............50%	*About right......27%*
Not fast enough...11%	*No opinion.......12%*

APPLY THE SKILL

See the Chapter Review and Assessment for another opportunity to apply this skill.

Understanding Public Opinion Polls

Focus Students learn how to study historical polling data to gain insight into the opinions of the American people about a pressing or divisive issue.

Instruct Discuss with students why it is important in a democracy to monitor public opinion. Ask students to describe how shifts in public opinion could impact the results of elections. Do students think officials should modify their stances in response to opinions?

Extend See the Skills for Life activity in the Resource Directory below.

ANSWERS

Practice the Skill

1. **(a)** All adults in the nation. **(b)** All adults in the nation. **(c)** Adults in the South.
2. **(a)** It is the only question that allows individuals to suggest and rank national problems rather than having them react to a stated issue. **(b)** Some people may not have enough information to offer an opinion in answer to a given question. **(c)** The question in Polls B and D might be considered a leading question because of the word "pushing." While each question leaves out the possibility that people feel the Kennedy Administration is moving at the right speed, that is one of the answer options.
3. **(a)** That is the region of the country that is most concerned with the issues of integration and segregation. **(b)** The pollster wants to see how opinions have changed over time. **(c)** What other issues are on the minds of Americans and how important the issue of racial integration is to the population, compared with other issues. **(d)** These polls might be used to influence government policies and election platforms.

RESOURCE DIRECTORY

Teaching Resources
Skills for Life booklet, p. 30

Technology
Social Studies Skills Tutor CD-ROM
Interactive Practice in
- Geographic Literacy
- Critical Thinking and Reading
- Visual Analysis
- Communications

Section 4 The Political Response

Section Objectives

1. Learn about President Kennedy's approach to civil rights.
2. Find out why civil rights leaders proposed a march on Washington.
3. Learn the goals of the Civil Rights Act of 1964.
4. Discover how African Americans fought to gain voting rights.

Bellringer

Warm-Up Activity Ask students if they plan to vote when they reach voting age. Why or why not? How many students would vote if it meant facing possible harassment or violence? Explain that protection of voters' rights was an important aspect of the civil rights movement.

Activating Prior Knowledge Ask students to recall stories of elections where votes were in dispute. Focus particularly on the 2000 presidential election, when some voters in Florida claimed that their votes went uncounted, or were counted improperly. Ask students to talk about how they would feel if they were one of those voters.

Reading Strategy

As students read, have them analyze how effective the civil rights movement was by making a list of all the major cause-and-effect relationships they can find.

Section 4 The Political Response

READING FOCUS

- What was President Kennedy's approach to civil rights?
- Why did civil rights leaders propose a march on Washington?
- What were the goals of the Civil Rights Act of 1964?
- How did African Americans fight to gain voting rights?

MAIN IDEA

Continuous civil rights protests in the 1960s gradually made politicians respond to public opinion and move forward with strong civil rights legislation.

KEY TERMS

March on Washington
filibuster
cloture
Civil Rights Act of 1964
Voting Rights Act of 1965
Twenty-fourth Amendment

TAKING NOTES

As you read, complete this chart showing some of the provisions of major civil rights legislation passed in the 1960s.

Legislation	Provisions
Civil Rights Act of 1964	• Increased Justice Department authority to enforce school desegregation and ensure fair voting practices •
Voting Rights Act of 1965	
Twenty-fourth Amendment	

Setting the Scene

In October 1960, just weeks before the presidential election, John F. Kennedy had an opportunity to make a powerful gesture of goodwill toward African Americans. Martin Luther King, Jr., had been arrested in Georgia and sentenced to four months of hard labor. His family feared for his life in the prison camp. Kennedy called Coretta Scott King, Dr. King's wife, and offered his help. Then, Robert Kennedy, John's younger brother, persuaded the Georgia sentencing judge to release King on bail. Word of the Kennedys' actions spread quickly throughout the African American community, and many switched their votes from Nixon to Kennedy. These votes were crucial in Kennedy's slim margin of victory in the election.

President Kennedy confers with his brother, Attorney General Robert Kennedy, outside the White House in 1962. Both Kennedy brothers played key roles in the civil rights movement.

Kennedy on Civil Rights

As a senator from Massachusetts, John F. Kennedy had voted for civil rights measures but had never actively pushed the issue. During his presidential campaign, however, Kennedy had sought and won many African American votes with bold rhetoric. In 1960, he proclaimed, "If the President does not himself wage the struggle for equal rights—if he stands above the battle—then the battle will inevitably be lost."

Once in office, however, Kennedy moved slowly on issues such as fair housing. He did not want to anger southern Democratic senators whose votes he needed on other issues. Yet Kennedy did appoint a number of African Americans to prominent positions. For example, Thurgood Marshall joined the United States Circuit Court and later became the first African American Supreme Court Justice. At the same time, however, Kennedy also named a number of segregationists to federal courts.

As the civil rights movement gained momentum and violence began to spread, Kennedy could no longer avoid the issue. He was deeply disturbed by the scenes of violence in

RESOURCE DIRECTORY

Teaching Resources
Guided Reading and Review booklet, p. 115

Technology
Section Reading Support Transparencies
Guided Reading Audiotapes (English/Spanish), Ch. 21
Student Edition on Audio CD, Ch. 21
Prentice Hall Presentation Pro CD-ROM, Ch. 21
Companion Web site, www.phschool.com

the South that flooded the media. The race riots surrounding the Freedom Rides in 1961 embarrassed the President when he met with Soviet leader Nikita Khrushchev. Observers around the world watched the brutality in Birmingham early in 1963. Aware that he had to respond, Kennedy spoke to the American people on television:

> "*We preach freedom around the world, and we mean it, and we cherish our freedom, here at home, but are we to say to the world, and much more importantly, to each other that this is the land of the free except for the Negroes? . . . The time has come for this nation to fulfill its promise.*"
>
> —President John F. Kennedy, television address, June 1963

Hours after Kennedy's broadcast, civil rights leader Medgar Evers was gunned down outside his home. Evers had been an NAACP field secretary in Mississippi. He worked on recruiting NAACP members and organized various voter-registration drives throughout the state. Police charged a white supremacist, Byron de la Beckwith, with the murder. After two hung juries failed to convict him, Beckwith was set free in 1964. (Beckwith was convicted of murder in 1994 after the case was reopened.) The timing of the Evers murder made it clear that the government needed to take action.

Earlier in his term, Kennedy had proposed a modest civil rights bill. After the crisis in Birmingham, he introduced a far stronger one. The bill would prohibit segregation in public places, ban discrimination wherever federal funding was involved, and advance school desegregation. Powerful southern segregationists in Congress, however, kept the bill from coming up for a vote.

READING CHECK
Why did civil rights violence embarrass Kennedy when he met with world leaders?

The March on Washington

To focus national attention on Kennedy's bill, civil rights leaders proposed a march on Washington, D.C. Kennedy feared the march would alienate Congress and cause racial violence. Yet when he could not persuade organizers to call off the march, he gave it his support.

The **March on Washington** took place in August 1963. More than 200,000 people came from all over the country to call for "jobs and freedom," the official slogan of the march. Labor leader A. Philip Randolph directed the march. Participants included religious leaders and celebrities such as writer James Baldwin, entertainer Sammy Davis, Jr., and baseball player Jackie Robinson. Leading folk singers of the early 1960s, such as Joan Baez and Bob Dylan, were also there. Dylan's powerful protest song "Blowin' in the Wind" was performed at the march by the popular group Peter, Paul, and Mary:

> "*How many years can a mountain exist*
> *Before it's washed to the sea?*
> *Yes, 'n' how many years can some people exist*
> *Before they're allowed to be free.*
> *Yes, 'n' how many times can a man turn his head,*
> *Pretending he just doesn't see?*
> *The answer, my friend, is blowin' in the wind,*
> *The answer is blowin' in the wind.*"
>
> —Bob Dylan, ©1962

VIEWING HISTORY Bob Dylan raised social consciousness about civil rights issues with his songs. Here, he plays on the back porch of the SNCC office in Greenwood, Mississippi, in 1963. **Determining Relevance** *Why do you think music played an important role in the civil rights movement?*

LESSON PLAN

Focus Explain that few politicians of the early 1960s were willing to risk taking a strong stand for civil rights. Ask students to note what events or circumstances forced them to change their minds.

Instruct Tell students that John Kennedy was from Massachusetts and Lyndon Johnson was from Texas. Discuss Kennedy's and Johnson's reactions to the civil rights crisis. How might each man's origins have played a role in his handling of civil rights issues?

Assess/Reteach Presidents Kennedy and Johnson took different approaches to civil rights legislation. Kennedy had made promises to voters to advance the cause of civil rights. However, many in Congress were opposed to these measures. He needed to move cautiously in promoting civil rights legislation, or else risk losing these legislators' support for other measures. Lyndon Johnson's actions as President in regard to civil rights were far more vigorous. He pressed ahead wholeheartedly in backing civil rights legislation, and he deserves much of the credit for the passage of the Civil Rights Act of 1964 and the Voting Rights Act of 1965.

READING CHECK
It seemed hypocritical since Kennedy was attempting to promote democracy and freedom abroad.

TEST PREPARATION

Ask students to review the quotation by John F. Kennedy on this page and then complete the sentence below.

According to Kennedy, to preach freedom around the world and then deny it to African Americans in this country is an example of—

A disloyalty.
B dishonesty.
C revolution.
(D) hypocrisy.

CAPTION ANSWERS

Viewing History Political songs sent strong messages to much of the public; such songs bonded civil rights activists together, giving them a sense of pride in what they were doing.

ACTIVITY
Connecting with History and Conflict

What do Americans remember about the March on Washington and other signal events of the civil rights era? Have students work in pairs or small groups to conduct interviews of people who lived through that time. Students should prepare a list of questions beforehand; if they have access to video equipment, they can record the interviews and create a mini-documentary. Discuss the interviews as a class. Ask: What did people remember best? What shaped their impressions? **(Verbal/Linguistic; Visual/Spatial)**

ACTIVITY
Connecting with Science and Technology

Have students research how the advent of television changed the news media and affected events, including the early civil rights movement. Students can use their findings to make a time line of media and information technology from the 1940s to the present. **(Visual/Spatial)**

BACKGROUND
Connections to Today

In August 1993, 75,000 people—far fewer than the 250,000 who came in 1963—gathered in Washington, D.C., for the 30th anniversary of the March on Washington. The theme of the 1993 march, "Jobs, Justice and Peace," was chosen by African American leaders to focus on the gap between the promise of 1963 and the reality 30 years later. "When we were segregated, we said, if we could sit all over the bus, things would be all right," said one civil rights leader. "We have since discovered the bus has flat tires and burned-out pistons. We have got to rebuild the bus."

Martin Luther King, Jr. (above), delivers his famous "I Have a Dream" speech at the March on Washington (below) in 1963.

Sounds of an Era

Listen to Martin Luther King, Jr.'s "I Have a Dream" speech and other sounds from the civil rights movement.

The march was peaceful and orderly. After many songs and speeches, Martin Luther King, Jr., delivered what was to become his best-known address. With power and eloquence, he spoke to all Americans:

> *"I have a dream that one day this nation will rise up and live out the true meaning of its creed, 'We hold these truths to be self-evident, that all men are created equal.' I have a dream that one day on the red hills of Georgia, the sons of former slaves and the sons of former slave owners will be able to sit down together at the table of brotherhood. . . . I have a dream that my four little children will one day live in a nation where they will not be judged by the color of their skin, but by the content of their character. . . . When we allow freedom to ring, when we let it ring from every village and every hamlet, from every state and every city, we will be able to speed up that day when all of God's children, black men and white men, Jews and Gentiles, Protestants and Catholics, will be able to join hands and sing in the words of the old Negro spiritual: 'Free at last. Free at last. Thank God Almighty, we are free at last.'"*
>
> —"I Have a Dream" speech, Martin Luther King, Jr., August 28, 1963

King's words echoed around the country. President Kennedy, watching the speech on television, was impressed with King's skill. But still the civil rights bill remained stalled in Congress.

The Civil Rights Act of 1964

Three months after the March on Washington, President Kennedy was assassinated, and his civil rights bill was not much closer to passage. The new President, Lyndon Johnson, was finally able to move the legislation along.

Johnson's Role Lyndon Johnson, a former member of Congress from Texas, had voted against civil rights measures during the Truman administration. As Senate majority leader, however, he had worked successfully to get a civil rights bill passed in 1957. Upon becoming President, he was eager to use his

RESOURCE DIRECTORY

Teaching Resources

Learning with Documents booklet (Key Documents) *Martin Luther King, Jr., "I Have a Dream,"* p. 91

Other Print Resources

American History Block Scheduling Support *Presidential Power; Changes in the Twentieth Century,* found in The Nation After World War II folder, includes interdisciplinary lesson suggestions and activities for Geography and History, Primary Sources, Biography, and Literature.

Technology

Sounds of an Era Audio CD *"I Have a Dream," Martin Luther King, Jr.* (time: 30 seconds)

Exploring Primary Sources in U.S. History CD-ROM *I Have a Dream, Martin Luther King, Jr.*

political skills to build support for Kennedy's bill. In his first public address, he told Congress and the country that nothing "could more eloquently honor President Kennedy's memory than the earliest possible passage of the civil rights bill." Johnson promised African American leaders that he would push for the measure "with every energy [he] possessed," and he made good on that commitment.

Johnson let Congress know that he would accept no compromise on civil rights. After the House of Representatives passed the bill, civil rights opponents in the Senate started a lengthy **filibuster,** exercising their right of unlimited day-and-night debate. (A filibuster is a tactic in which senators prevent a vote on a measure by taking the floor and refusing to stop talking.) Johnson finally enlisted his former colleague, Republican minority leader Everett Dirksen, to support the rarely used procedure called **cloture**—a three-fifths vote to limit debate and call for a vote. In June 1964, the Senate voted for cloture, which successfully ended the filibuster. Soon after, the bill passed with support from both Democrats and Republicans.

The Provisions of the Act The **Civil Rights Act of 1964** had an impact on many areas, including voting, schools, and jobs. It gave the Justice Department the authority to act vigorously in school desegregation and voting rights cases. The law's major sections (called titles) included these provisions:

1. Title I banned the use of different voter registration standards for blacks and whites.
2. Title II prohibited discrimination in public accommodations, such as motels, restaurants, gas stations, theaters, and sports arenas.
3. Title VI allowed the withholding of federal funds from public or private programs that practice discrimination.
4. Title VII banned discrimination on the basis of race, sex, religion, or national origin by employers and unions, and also created the Equal Employment Opportunity Commission (EEOC) to investigate charges of job discrimination.

A Profile in Courage When Congress voted on the Civil Rights Act of 1964, southern Congressmen opposed to racial discrimination faced a difficult choice: They could vote for their beliefs, or risk losing reelection. Only one representative from a state in the Deep South, Charles Weltner of Georgia, voted for the bill.

In 1966, Weltner faced another moral dilemma. At that time, the Democratic Party required all its members to take an oath of support for all Democratic candidates. The oath meant that Weltner would have to support a vehement segregationist, Lester Maddox, for governor of Georgia. Weltner shocked the country when he decided to give up his seat in Congress rather than support Maddox. Weltner's action meant the end of his congressional career. Years later, in 1991, he received the prestigious "Profile in Courage" Award for his heroism.

BACKGROUND
Building a New South

Southerners were caught off guard when Representative Charles Weltner voted in favor of the Civil Rights Act of 1964, arguing, "We can offer resistance and defiance, with their harvest of strife and tumult. We can suffer continued demonstrations, with their wake of violence and disorder. Or, we can acknowledge this measure as the law of the land. We can accept the verdict of the Nation. . . . I would urge that we at home now move on to the unfinished task of building a new South. We must not remain forever bound to another lost cause."

From the Archives of
American Heritage®

About the Presidents

Lyndon Baines Johnson (1963–1969) served in Congress from 1937 to 1961, when he became JFK's Vice President. After Kennedy's assassination, President Johnson used his skills as a legislative leader to push his domestic programs through Congress. Under his influence, Congress passed a strong civil rights act, laws that provided federal aid to mass transportation and to education, and the anti-poverty bill. This all occurred within a nine-month period. At the time, one commentator said, "LBJ has been hurling himself about Washington like an elemental force." Source: Wilson Sullivan, "Lyndon Baines Johnson," *The American Heritage® Pictorial History of the Presidents of the United States,* vol. 2, 1968.

CUSTOMIZE FOR ...

ESL

Ask students to reread the passage from the speech by Martin Luther King, Jr., on this page. Have them rephrase the speech in their own words, then write a sentence summarizing King's main point. Explain why the speech is regarded as one of the most powerful in American history.

ACTIVITY
Connecting with Geography

Have students work individually or in pairs to research and create thematic maps of the civil rights movement. Encourage students to be creative in choosing map subjects. Maps might show, for example, where and when key events took place, routes of Freedom Rides and/or marches, the state-by-state progress of school desegregation, or the various places Martin Luther King lived and traveled. Display all finished maps in the classroom or compile into a class atlas of the civil rights movement. **(Visual/Spatial)**

BACKGROUND
Geography in History

In a 1965 article entitled "Next Stop: the North," Martin Luther King, Jr., declared his intention to begin focusing on the problems of urban blacks. "Our movement has been essentially regional, not national," he wrote. King pointed out that the movement had made great progress, but only in the South. "In the North," he wrote, "the Negro's repellent slum life was altered not for the better but for the worse." King was right in his assessment of the problem, but wrong when he predicted that despite their "cynicism" and "urban sophistication," northern blacks would embrace nonviolence.

Civil Rights Measures

Measure	Purpose
Truman's Executive Orders, 1948	• Required equality in the armed forces • Established the Committee on Equality of Treatment and Opportunity in the Armed Services • Banned discrimination in the hiring of federal employees
Civil Rights Act of 1957	• Established a federal Civil Rights Commission • Created a Civil Rights Division in the Department of Justice • Increased efforts to protect voting rights
Civil Rights Act of 1960	• Strengthened the 1957 act by giving courts more power to enforce fair voting practices • Prescribed criminal penalties for bombing and bomb threats
Kennedy's Executive Orders, 1962	• Increased enforcement of previous acts and the *Brown* v. *Board of Education* ruling • Prohibited racial and religious discrimination in housing built or purchased with federal aid
Twenty-fourth Amendment, 1964	• Eliminated the poll tax as a voting requirement
Civil Rights Act of 1964	• Banned discrimination in public accommodations • Authorized the attorney general to institute suits to desegregate schools • Outlawed discrimination in employment on the basis of race, sex, or religion • Furthered efforts at protecting voting rights
Voting Rights Act of 1965	• Eliminated literacy tests as a voting requirement • Gave federal officials the power to supervise voter registration
Open Housing Law, 1968	• Prohibited discrimination in the sale or rental of most housing

INTERPRETING CHARTS The federal government passed a significant number of civil rights measures following World War II. **Analyzing Information** *(a) Which civil rights issues did each of these measures address? (b) Which do you think were the most effective?*

Fighting for the Vote

Even with a strong new law, change came slowly. Civil rights leaders pushed harder for expanded rights, most notably voting rights.

Freedom Summer In 1964, leaders of the major civil rights groups organized a voter registration drive in Mississippi. About a thousand African American and white volunteers, mostly college students, joined in what came to be called Freedom Summer. Many white Mississippians were already angry about the new Civil Rights Act before the volunteers arrived. The Ku Klux Klan held rallies to intimidate the volunteers.

Soon, three young civil rights workers, James Chaney, Andrew Goodman, and Michael Schwerner, were reported missing. Later in the summer, FBI agents found their bodies buried in a new earthen dam a few miles from where their burned-out station wagon had been found. These three murders were only part of the turbulence reported that summer. Civil rights leaders also reported about 80 mob attacks. Volunteers were beaten up and a few wounded by gunfire. About a thousand were arrested. African American churches and homes were burned or firebombed.

The Democratic Convention Newly registered Mississippi voters, along with members of SNCC, organized the Mississippi Freedom Democratic Party (MFDP). The MFDP sent delegates to the Democratic national convention in the summer of 1964. The delegates argued that they, not politicians from the segregated party organization, were the rightful representatives.

One delegate was Fannie Lou Hamer, who had lost her job on a cotton plantation when she tried to register to vote. She told the convention about her experiences in one voter drive:

> "*I began to scream, and one white man got up and began to beat me on my head and tell me to 'hush.'. . . All of this is on account we want to register, to become first class citizens, and if the Freedom Democratic Party is not seated now, I question America.*"
>
> —Fannie Lou Hamer

President Johnson offered a compromise to the Freedom Party: he would choose two MFDP delegates to sit among Mississippi's 68 seats. Johnson also promised that the rules of the convention would be changed in 1968 to eliminate

CAPTION ANSWERS

Interpreting Charts (a) Truman: segregation, discrimination; 1957 Act: voting rights; 1960 Act: voting rights; Kennedy: segregation, discrimination, voting rights; Twenty-fourth Amendment: voting rights; 1964 Act: discrimination, segregation, voting rights; 1965 Act: voting rights; 1968 Housing Law: discrimination. Many of these measures also increased the federal government's power to punish civil rights breaches. (b) Answers will vary.

RESOURCE DIRECTORY

Teaching Resources
Units 5/6/7 booklet
- Section 4 Quiz, p. 55

Guide to the Essentials
- Section 4 Summary, p. 104

Technology

RESOURCE PRO® **Primary Source Activity** *Registering to Vote in Mississippi,* found on Resource Pro, uses the testimony of Fannie Lou Hamer to show why hundreds of civil rights workers volunteered to spend the summer of 1964 in Mississippi.

RESOURCE PRO® **Visual Learning Activity** *A White House Demonstration,* found on Resource Pro, uses a 1965 photo of a civil rights demonstration to enrich students' understanding of the pressure on Congress to pass the Voting Rights Act.

Exploring Primary Sources in U.S. History CD-ROM *Reynolds* v. *Sims*

discrimination. Leaders of the MFDP rejected Johnson's offer, believing that it fell short of the gains they were seeking.

The Selma March Many black southerners still had trouble obtaining their voting rights. In Selma, Alabama, police and sheriff's deputies arrested people just for standing in line to register to vote. To call attention to the voting rights issue, King and other leaders decided to organize a protest march. They would walk from Selma to the state capital, Montgomery, about 50 miles away.

As the marchers set out on a Sunday morning in March 1965, armed state troopers on horseback charged into the crowd with whips, clubs, and tear gas. TV pictures of the attack again shocked many viewers. In response, President Johnson put the Alabama National Guard under federal control. He sent members of the National Guard, along with federal marshals and army helicopters, to protect the march route. When the Selma marchers started out again, supporters from all over the country flocked to join them. By the time the march reached Montgomery, its ranks had swelled to about 25,000 people.

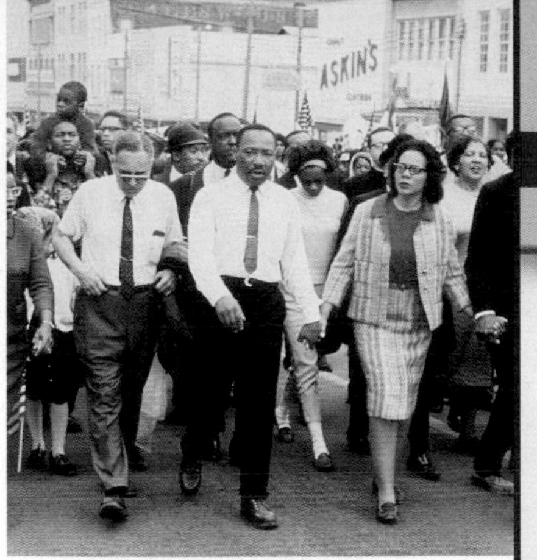

VIEWING HISTORY The Selma March, led here by Martin Luther King, Jr., and his wife, Coretta Scott King, impelled President Johnson to push for the Voting Rights Act of 1965. Between 1960 and 1970, about 2 million new African American voters registered to vote. **Recognizing Cause and Effect** *How did the Selma March focus attention on the issue of voting rights?*

The Voting Rights Act Reacting to Selma, Johnson went on national television, promising a strong new law to protect voting rights. Raising his arms, Johnson repeated, "And . . . we . . . shall . . . overcome!" That summer, despite another filibuster, Congress passed the **Voting Rights Act of 1965.**

Under the act, federal officials could register voters in places where local officials were blocking registration by African Americans. The act also effectively eliminated literacy tests and other barriers. In the year after the law passed, more than 400,000 African Americans registered to vote in the Deep South.

Legal Landmarks Together, the Civil Rights Act of 1964 and the Voting Rights Act of 1965 created an entirely new voting population in the South. This new block of voters meant that more black Americans would be elected to political office. Another legal landmark was the **Twenty-fourth Amendment** to the Constitution, ratified in 1964. This amendment outlawed the poll tax, which was still being used in several southern states to keep poor African Americans from voting.

For some African Americans, new laws were not nearly enough. Impatient with the slow pace of progress, they were ready to listen to more militant leaders.

Section 4 Assessment

READING COMPREHENSION

1. Why did President Kennedy hesitate at first to support civil rights wholeheartedly? How did his position change?
2. How did the **Civil Rights Act of 1964** overcome the **filibuster** some senators used to try to block it?
3. What events led to the passage of the **Voting Rights Act of 1965?**

CRITICAL THINKING AND WRITING

4. **Recognizing Cause and Effect** How did President Johnson's previous experience in Congress help achieve the passage of civil rights legislation?
5. **Writing a News Story** Write a short news story describing the scene at the March on Washington.

Take It to the NET

Activity: Analyzing Primary Sources Access the full text of Martin Luther King, Jr.'s "I Have a Dream" speech. Then write an analysis of the speech. To whom was the speech addressed? What terms did King use for persuasion? Use the links provided in the *America: Pathways to the Present* area of the following Web site for help in completing this activity.
www.phschool.com

Section 4 Assessment

Reading Comprehension

1. Having won the presidency by a very narrow margin, JFK was afraid of alienating white southerners in Congress, whose votes he needed to support other measures. He soon decided to back stronger civil rights legislation.
2. President Johnson urged the Senate to take a cloture vote to limit debate and call for a vote. This was done, and the bill passed with bipartisan support.
3. The violence that occurred during the 1965 Selma-to-Montgomery march.

Critical Thinking and Writing

4. Johnson used his skills as a political consensus builder and played on the nation's sorrow over Kennedy's death to ensure passage of the Civil Rights Act of 1964 and the Voting Rights Act of 1965.
5. Answers will vary, but should be descriptive and supported with facts from the section.

Take It to the NET

Responses will vary, but should note that the speech was addressed to all Americans. They should cite specific examples of King's persuasiveness, a result of the eloquence of his language.

CUSTOMIZE FOR ...

Less Proficient Readers

Have students list the four major sections of the Civil Rights Act of 1964 and explain each in their own words.

CAPTION ANSWERS

Viewing History The idea to march from Selma to Montgomery was daring and was certain to attract attention. Police brutality shown on television led many to sympathize with the marchers. It also caused President Johnson to act to protect the marchers, and later, to sign the 1965 Voting Rights Act.

Section 5
The Movement Takes a New Turn

Section Objectives

1. Learn about Malcolm X's approach to gaining civil rights.
2. Become familiar with the major goals of the black power movement.
3. See why violent riots erupted in many urban streets.
4. Find out how the tragic events of 1968 affected the nation.

Bellringer

Warm-Up Activity Ask students what kinds of activities go on in schools that are against the rules. Then explain the difference between the terms *de jure* and *de facto.*

Activating Prior Knowledge Why do students think that some parts of the civil rights movement became nonviolent? Why do students think that some parts of the civil rights movement became violent? Do they think the movement needs to exist today?

Reading Strategy

As students read this section, have them identify the significant leaders at this stage of the civil rights movement. Have students list ways in which these leaders' strategies differed from those who were most influential before.

Section 5

The Movement Takes a New Turn

READING FOCUS

- What was Malcom X's approach to gaining civil rights?
- What were the major goals of the black power movement?
- Why did violent riots erupt in many urban streets?
- How did the tragic events of 1968 affect the nation?

KEY TERMS

Nation of Islam
black nationalism
black power
de jure segregation
de facto segregation

TAKING NOTES

As you read, prepare an outline of this section. Use Roman numerals to indicate the major headings of this section, capital letters for subheadings, and numbers for the supporting details.

I. Malcolm X and Black Nationalism
A. Black Nationalism
B. Opposition to Integration
1. Malcolm X rejects ideas of integration and nonviolent protest.
2. ______
II. The Black Power Movement
A. ______

MAIN IDEA

Gains in civil rights came so slowly that some African Americans rejected nonviolence and called for more radical action. Increases in social unrest culminated in 1968 with the assassinations of Martin Luther King, Jr., and Robert F. Kennedy.

VIEWING HISTORY Author James Baldwin wrote movingly of the black experience. **Identifying Central Issues** *What did Baldwin foresee happening to African Americans in the 1960s?*

Setting the Scene James Baldwin's essays and novels included powerful descriptions of the African American experience that touched both black and white Americans deeply. As a strong voice for the civil rights movement, Baldwin wrote about the damaging effects of segregation in the United States. He recounted "the Negro's past, of . . . death and humiliation; fear by day and night; fear as deep as the marrow of the bone; doubt that he was worthy of life, since everyone around him denied it. . . ."

In 1963, in the bestseller *The Fire Next Time,* Baldwin told how generations of oppression and suffering had set African Americans apart but had also made them stronger. Now, he said, African Americans were tired of promises. Their anger was ready to erupt. As Baldwin put it, "The Negro himself no longer believes in the good faith of white Americans—if, indeed, he ever could have."

Over time, the passage of two civil rights acts would help African Americans to win court battles that would tear down segregation. But in the meantime, African Americans still faced economic and social discrimination. Many were angry at the slow pace of change. Growing anger led to a deep divide within the civil rights movement.

Malcolm X and Black Nationalism

Outside the mainstream civil rights movement, more radical and militant political leaders emerged. The most well known of these was Malcolm X, born Malcolm Little in Omaha, Nebraska, in 1925. His father, a Baptist minister who spread the "back-to-Africa" message of Marcus Garvey, died when Little was a child. Growing up in ghettos in Detroit, Boston, and New York, Little turned to crime. At age 20, he was arrested for burglary and served seven years in prison. While in jail he joined the **Nation of Islam,** a group often called the Black Muslims. Viewing white society as oppressive, it preached black separation and self-help.

Caption Answers

Viewing History He believed their anger was ready to erupt.

RESOURCE DIRECTORY

Teaching Resources
Guided Reading and Review booklet, p. 116

Technology
Section Reading Support Transparencies
Guided Reading Audiotapes (English/Spanish), Ch. 21
Student Edition on Audio CD, Ch. 21
RESOURCE PRO® **Literature Activity** *Sins of the Father,* found on Resource Pro, uses an essay from Eldridge Cleaver's *Soul on Ice* to show Cleaver's view that there could be mutual respect between the races if "white youth" could repudiate the evils of the past.
Prentice Hall Presentation Pro CD-ROM, Ch. 21
Companion Web site, www.phschool.com

Black Nationalism Elijah Muhammad, the leader of the Nation of Islam, taught that Allah (the Muslim name for God) would bring about a "Black Nation," a union among all nonwhite peoples. According to Elijah Muhammad, one of the keys to self-knowledge was knowing one's enemy. For him, the enemy of the Nation of Islam was white society.

Members of the Nation of Islam did not seek change through political means but waited for Allah to create the Black Nation. In the meantime, they tried to lead righteous lives and worked hard to become economically self-sufficient.

Released from prison in 1952, Malcolm Little changed his name to Malcolm X. (The name Little, he said, had come from slaveowners.) He spent the next 12 years as a minister of the Nation of Islam, winning followers with his fiery speeches. He spread the ideas of **black nationalism,** a belief in the separate identity and racial unity of the African American community.

Opposition to Integration Malcolm X disagreed with both the tactics and the goals of the early civil rights movement. He called the March on Washington the "Farce on Washington," and voiced his irritation at "all of this non-violent, begging-the-white-man kind of dying . . . all of this sitting-in, sliding-in, wading-in, eating-in, diving-in, and all the rest." Instead of preaching brotherly love, he rejected ideas of integration. Asking why anyone would want to join white society, he noted:

VIEWING HISTORY Malcolm X was a leading minister of the Nation of Islam until 1964. **Making Comparisons** *How did black nationalism differ from other kinds of civil rights activism?*

> "*No sane black man really wants integration! No sane white man really wants integration! No sane black man really believes that the white man ever will give the black man anything more than token integration. No! The Honorable Elijah Muhammad teaches that for the black man in America the only solution is complete separation from the white man. . . . The American black man should be focusing his effort toward building his own businesses, and decent homes for himself. As other ethnic groups have done, let the black people, wherever possible, however possible, patronize their own kind, hire their own kind, and start in those ways to build up the black race's ability to do for itself. That's the only way the American black man is ever going to get respect.*"
>
> —Malcolm X

Malcolm X and Elijah Muhammad came to disagree about many things, including political action. In 1964, Malcolm X left the Nation of Islam and formed his own religious organization, called Muslim Mosque, Inc. He then made a pilgrimage, or religious journey, to Mecca, the holy city of Islam, in Saudi Arabia.

Seeing millions of Muslims of all races worshipping together peacefully had a profound effect on Malcolm X. It changed his views about separatism and hatred of white people. When he returned, he was ready to work with other civil rights leaders and even with white Americans on some issues. It seemed as if Malcolm X might become one of the leaders in a unified civil rights movement. His change of heart, however, had earned him some enemies.

Malcolm X had only nine months to spread his new beliefs. In February 1965, he was shot to death at a rally in New York. Three members of the Nation of Islam were charged with the murder. Malcolm X's message of black nationalism lived on, however. He particularly influenced younger members of SNCC, the Student Nonviolent Coordinating Committee.

READING CHECK
How did Malcolm X's views change after his pilgrimage in 1964?

Lesson Plan

Focus Explain that nonviolent protests resulted in early gains, but that progress subsequently seemed to stall. Ask students how African Americans reacted to continuing discrimination.

Instruct Discuss the alternatives to nonviolent confrontation that evolved in the civil rights movement. How did the views of Malcolm X differ from those of Martin Luther King, Jr.?

Point out President Johnson's comment on the last page of the section. Then discuss the answers to his and the following questions: Why, after so much progress for civil rights, did anger and violence erupt? Why did African Americans become cynical about the goal of nonviolent integration pursued by Martin Luther King, Jr.?

Assess/Reteach Have students evaluate the progress made in civil rights since the 1960s. In what areas have gains in equality been made? In what areas does inequality still prevail?

Activity
Connecting with Culture

Have students research black nationalism in America, beginning with abolitionist David Walker, whose *Appeal to the Coloured Citizens of the World* (1829) articulated the fundamental beliefs of black nationalism for the first time. Allow individuals or small groups to focus on an aspect of the topic in depth: e.g., chronology of black nationalism, explanation of black nationalist thought, profiles of individual leaders, or readings from black nationalist texts. Have groups present their findings orally, in writing, or in a chart or diagram. **(Verbal/Linguistic; Visual/Spatial)**

READING CHECK
He changed his views about separatism and white people.

Caption Answers

Viewing History Leaders like Malcolm X hoped to see African Americans succeed economically and politically without joining white society. They were thus opposed to Dr. King's desire for an integrated society (although Malcolm X himself eventually softened on this issue).

Test Preparation

Have students read the quotation by Malcolm X on this page and then answer the question below.

What did Malcolm X advocate for blacks in society?

- **(A)** Total segregation.
- **B** Social segregation, but integration in business pursuits.
- **C** Integration with other ethnic groups but segregation from whites.
- **D** Total integration.

Activity

Connecting with History and Conflict

Stage a mock panel debate between supporters of nonviolent protest, such as Martin Luther King, Jr., and Black Power advocates, such as Malcolm X or Stokely Carmichael, in 1966. Panel members on both sides should become familiar with the moral, social, and political arguments of their positions and try to refute the arguments of the opposition. **(Verbal/Linguistic)**

Background

Interdisciplinary

The growth of the civil rights movement in the early to mid-1960s coincided with the emergence of "soul," a gospel-influenced form of rhythm and blues popularized by Aretha Franklin and Wilson Pickett, among others. Soul, according to rock-and-roll historian Robert Palmer, "came to represent a self-consciously 'black' idiom, proudly displaying its roots in gospel singing . . . ." With the growth of the Black Power movement, the assassination of Martin Luther King, Jr., and race riots in the inner cities, however, soul began to lose its appeal. By the end of the decade, soul had metamorphosed into the harder-edged funk, which in turn was influenced by the psychedelic counterculture.

The Black Power Movement

One SNCC leader who heard Malcolm's message was Stokely Carmichael. Born in Trinidad, in the West Indies, in 1941, Carmichael came to the United States at the age of 11 and was soon involved in protests. At Howard University in Washington, D.C., he and other students became actively involved in the Washington chapter of SNCC.

SNCC Shifts Gears As Carmichael rose to SNCC leadership, the group became more radical. After being beaten and jailed for his participation in demonstrations, he was tired of nonviolent protest. He called on SNCC workers to carry guns for self-defense. He wanted to make the group exclusively black, rejecting white activists.

The split in the civil rights movement became obvious in June 1966. At a protest march in Greenwood, Mississippi, while King's followers were singing "We Shall Overcome," Carmichael's supporters drowned them out with "We Shall Overrun." Then Carmichael, just out of jail, jumped into the back of an open truck to challenge the moderate leaders:

> *"This is the twenty-seventh time I have been arrested, and I ain't going to jail no more! . . . The only way we gonna stop them white men from whippin' us is to take over. We been saying freedom for six years—and we ain't got nothin'. What we gonna start saying now is 'black power!'"*
>
> —Stokely Carmichael, public address, June 1966

VIEWING HISTORY Members of the Black Panthers marched in New York City in 1968 to protest the trial of Huey P. Newton. Newton had been convicted of voluntary manslaughter in the death of a police officer. His conviction was later overturned. **Identifying Central Issues** *What efforts did the Black Panthers make to improve the quality of life in black communities?*

As he repeated "We . . . want . . . black . . . power!" the audience excitedly echoed the new slogan. Carmichael's idea of **black power** resonated with many African Americans. It was a call "to unite, to recognize their heritage, to build a sense of community . . . to begin to define their own goals, to lead their own organizations and support those organizations."

The Black Panthers In the fall of 1966, a new militant political party, the Black Panthers, was formed by activists Bobby Seale and Huey Newton. The Panthers wanted African Americans to lead their own communities. They demanded that the federal government rebuild the nation's ghettos to make up for years of neglect. The Panthers also wanted to combat what they saw as police brutality in the ghettos. Often, as a result of their monitoring the police, they became engaged in direct confrontation with white authorities. Newton repeated the words of Chinese Communist leader Mao Zedong: "Power flows from the barrel of a gun." Although they did organize some beneficial community programs, the Panthers more often found themselves in violent encounters with police.

Black power gave rise to the slogan "Black is beautiful," which fostered racial pride. It also led to a serious split in the civil rights movement. More radical groups like SNCC and the Black Panthers moved away from the NAACP and other more moderate organizations.

Caption Answers

Viewing History They tried to combat what they saw as police brutality and implored the federal government to rebuild and revitalize ghetto areas.

RESOURCE DIRECTORY

Technology

RESOURCE PRO® **Critical Thinking Activity** *Demonstrating Reasoned Judgment: How to Respond,* found on Resource Pro, presents passages from four of America's most powerful civil rights leaders to help students apply this skill.

Riots in the Streets

The early civil rights movement focused on battling ***de jure* segregation,** racial separation created by law. Changes in the law, however, did not address the more difficult issue of ***de facto* segregation,** the separation caused by social conditions such as poverty. *De facto* segregation was a fact of life in most American cities, not just in the South.

There were no "whites only" signs above water fountains in northern cities, yet discrimination continued in education, housing, and employment. African Americans were kept out of well-paying jobs, job-training programs, and suburban housing. Inner-city schools were rundown and poorly equipped.

Residents of ghetto neighborhoods viewed police officers as dangerous oppressors, not upholders of justice. James Baldwin remarked that a white police officer in one of these neighborhoods was "like an occupying soldier in a bitterly hostile country." Eventually, frustration and anger boiled over into riots and looting. In 1964, riots ravaged Rochester, New York; New York City; and several cities in New Jersey.

One of the most violent riots occurred in the Los Angeles neighborhood of Watts. On August 11, 1965, police in Watts pulled over a 21-year-old black man for drunk driving. At first the interaction was friendly among the police, the suspect, and a crowd of Watts residents that had gathered. When the suspect resisted arrest, however, one police officer panicked and began swinging his riot baton. The crowd was outraged, and the scene touched off six days of rioting.

Thousands of people filled the streets, burning cars and stores, stealing merchandise, and sniping at firefighters. When the national guard and local police finally gained control, 34 people were dead and more than a thousand had been injured. Violence spread to other cities in 1966 and 1967. Cries of "Burn, baby, burn" replaced the gentler slogans of the earlier civil rights movement.

A concerned federal government set up a special National Advisory Commission on Civil Disorders, headed by former Illinois Governor Otto Kerner, to investigate. In 1968, the Kerner Commission report declared flatly that the riots were an explosion of the anger that had been smoldering in the inner-city ghettos. It declared that "our nation is moving toward two societies, one black, one white—separate and unequal."

Focus on ECONOMICS

***De facto* Challenges** The fight against *de facto* segregation faced different challenges than the fight against *de jure* segregation. One problem was that the civil rights movement lost much of its political support as the Nixon administration assumed power in 1969. Another had to do with changes taking place within the African American community. Not all civil rights organizations joined in this fight. Some activists believed that the real struggle was against legal barriers and not against residential patterns. Because there was less solidarity among civil rights groups, protests lost much of their strength.

African American solidarity was also weakened as a result of the increasing number of black Americans who had "made it" by the early 1970s. Many began moving to suburbs, attending college, and obtaining better jobs. As a result, some African Americans became disconnected from the intense struggle with poverty in the city ghettos.

Overall, the statistics looked promising. The number of black Americans living in poverty decreased from more than 40 percent in 1959 to about 20 percent in 1968. Between 1960 and 1977, the number of African Americans enrolled in college increased by 500 percent. Yet, for those African Americans living in inner cities, conditions had not improved. For example, in 1970, 60 percent of African Americans living in cities had low-level service jobs, compared to 33 percent of white Americans also living in cities.

Tragedy Strikes in 1968

In the troubled decade of the 1960s, the most shattering year was 1968. A series of tragic events hit with such force that, month by month, the nation seemed to be coming apart. Against a backdrop of domestic violence, chaos, and confrontation, many Americans began to believe that the chance of achieving peaceful social change through political activism was hopeless.

For many Americans, the memory of President Kennedy's assassination in 1963 was still vivid and haunting five years later. They looked to other leaders to carry on the spirit and idealism of the Kennedy years. But in 1968, people's hopes were again shattered by the burst of bullets from assassins' guns.

Martin Luther King, Jr., Is Assassinated In 1968, Dr. King turned his attention to economic issues. Convinced that poverty bred violence, he broadened his approach to attack economic injustice. Calling his new crusade the

ACTIVITY
Connecting with Culture

Ask students to locate protest poems, prose, songs, and art from the 1960s and to include several in a notebook. Suggest that they begin by examining the writings of James Baldwin and Malcolm X. **(Verbal/Linguistic)**

BACKGROUND
Connections to Today

In 1992 race riots again paralyzed the city of Los Angeles. The cause was eerily similar to that of 1965: outrage over the mistreatment of a black citizen by white police officers. In April 1992 four white LAPD officers, who had been caught on videotape beating a black motorist, were found innocent of brutality by a jury. As news of the acquittal spread, riots and mayhem erupted around the city. Five days later, 58 people were dead and thousands more were injured. Since then, the LAPD has come under scrutiny for brutality, corruption, and fabricating testimony. As a result of the most recent investigation, dozens of convictions were overturned.

CUSTOMIZE FOR ...
Less Proficient Writers

Have students make a chart illustrating the key occurrences in the chain of events that led from nonviolent protests to the ghetto riots.

ACTIVITY
Student Portfolio

You may wish to have students add the following to their portfolios: Tell students that in 1958, Martin Luther King, Jr., wrote: "The problem of race is indeed America's greatest moral dilemma." Despite the progress of the civil rights movement, some would argue that race is still our greatest moral dilemma. Have students write a short essay addressing the question of whether, in their opinion, King's statement still holds true today. Have them view King's statement in the context of the civil rights movement. **(Verbal/Linguistic)**

From the Archives of
American Heritage®

Other Fires

Amid all the love-ins, acid tests, and dreamy good feeling, the summer of 1967 also saw some of the greatest internal violence since the Civil War as riots broke out in at least 70 American cities from Grand Rapids to Boston, Buffalo to Tampa. The riots shared a bleak uniformity—each with an inciting police incident, brutality either real or alleged, looting, and fire bombing. Source: Nathan Ward, "The Time Machine," *American Heritage®* magazine, July 1992.

READING CHECK

He favored assisting the poor and disadvantaged in the United States, rather than investing money in fighting an unpopular war abroad.

VIEWING HISTORY Assassinations in 1968 shocked the nation. Above, Martin Luther King, Jr., lies mortally wounded, while companions point frantically to the direction from which shots were fired. At right, busboy Jay Romero is the first to reach Robert Kennedy after he was shot in a hotel kitchen just after winning the California primary. **Identifying Central Issues** *What effect did these murders have?*

Poor People's Campaign, King began planning a Poor People's March on Washington. Traveling around the United States to mobilize support, he went to Memphis, Tennessee, in early April. There he offered his assistance to striking garbage workers who were seeking better working conditions.

King spoke eloquently, referring to threats made against his life:

> "*We've got some difficult days ahead. But it doesn't matter with me now, because I've been to the mountain top. And I don't mind. Like anybody, I would like to live a long life. . . . But I'm not concerned about that now. I just want to do God's will. And He's allowed me to go up to the mountain. And I've looked over. And I've seen the promised land.*"
>
> —Martin Luther King, Jr., April 3, 1968

The next day, as King stood on the balcony of his motel, a bullet fired from a high-powered rifle tore into him. An hour later, King was dead.

King's assassination sparked violent reactions across the nation. In an outburst of rage and frustration, some African Americans rioted, setting fires and looting stores in more than 120 cities. The riots, and the police response to them, left close to 50 people dead. President Johnson ordered flags on federal buildings to be flown at half mast to honor King, but it took more than 50,000 troops to quell the violence. For many Americans of all races, King's death eroded faith in the idea of nonviolent change.

Robert F. Kennedy Is Assassinated Senator Robert F. Kennedy, who had served his brother John as Attorney General, was another major crusader for civil rights. In 1968, he decided to enter the race for the Democratic presidential nomination. President Johnson had lost support from many Democrats because of America's involvement in the Vietnam War. After Senator Eugene McCarthy lost to Johnson in the New Hampshire primary by only six percentage points, Kennedy realized that Johnson was vulnerable. On March 16, Kennedy entered the campaign. His candidacy received a critical boost on March 31, when Johnson stunned the nation by announcing that he would not run for a second term as President.

In the years since his brother's death, Robert Kennedy had reached out to many Americans, including Chicanos in the California farm fields, Native Americans in the Southwest, African Americans in the Mississippi delta, and poor white families in New York tenements. Opposed to the Vietnam War, he condemned the killing of both Americans and Vietnamese. He criticized the Johnson administration for financing a war instead of funding the programs needed to help the poor and disadvantaged at home.

READING CHECK
Why had Robert Kennedy represented a source of hope for many Americans?

Kennedy spent the spring of 1968 battling McCarthy in the Democratic primary elections. On June 4, he won a key victory in California's primary. But just

CAPTION ANSWERS

Viewing History The murders dashed people's hopes for the civil rights movement and for strong leadership.

RESOURCE DIRECTORY

Teaching Resources

Units 5/6/7 booklet
- Section 5 Quiz, p. 56
- Chapter 21 Test, pp. 57, 60

Guide to the Essentials
- Section 5 Summary, p. 105
- Chapter 21 Test, p. 106

Other Print Resources

Chapter Tests with ExamView® Test Bank CD-ROM, Ch. 21

Technology

ExamView® Test Bank CD-ROM, Ch. 21
Social Studies Skills Tutor CD-ROM
Sounds of an Era Audio CD *Report of Robert Kennedy Assassination* (time: one minute)

after midnight, after giving his victory speech in a Los Angeles hotel, Robert Kennedy was shot by an assassin. He died the next day.

When the shooting was reported, several campaign workers who had watched the speech on TV were waiting for Kennedy in his hotel room. One of them, civil rights leader John Lewis, later said, "We all just fell to the floor and started crying. To me that was like the darkest, saddest moment." Kennedy's death ended many people's hopes for an inspirational leader who could heal the nation's wounds.

Legacy of the Movement

At times, both black and white Americans wondered whether real progress in civil rights was possible. Many young activists felt frustrated and discouraged when the movement failed to bring changes quickly. Lyndon Johnson was devastated by the violence that exploded near the end of his presidency. "How is it possible," he asked, "after all we've accomplished?" Still, the measures passed by his administration had brought tremendous change. Segregation was now illegal. Because of voter registration drives, thousands of African Americans could now vote. The power they wielded changed the nature of American political life.

Between 1970 and 1975, the number of African American elected officials rose by 88 percent. Black mayors were elected in Atlanta, Detroit, Los Angeles, and Newark, New Jersey. Others served in Congress and state legislatures. In 1966, Barbara Jordan became the first African American elected to the Texas state senate since Reconstruction. Six years later she was elected to the United States Congress. Jordan noted what made the movement necessary:

> "*The civil rights movement called America to look at itself in a giant mirror. . . . Do the black people who were born on this soil, who are American citizens, do they really feel that this is the land of opportunity, the land of the free? . . . America had to say no.*"
>
> —Texas Representative Barbara Jordan

American BIOGRAPHY

Shirley Chisholm 1924–

In 1968, Shirley Chisholm became the first black woman elected to Congress. Running from New York's twelfth district as a Democrat, Chisholm overcame social obstacles facing both women and African Americans.

Chisholm, born in Brooklyn, New York, in 1924, had long held a deep interest in social welfare, particularly the social welfare of children. In her early 30s, Chisholm was the director for a child-care center in New York. Her career in politics began in 1964 when she was elected to the New York state assembly. Four years later she gained national attention when she won a seat in the U.S. House of Representatives. She would win the next six elections, serving in the House until 1983.

Her early career in politics was marked by her outspoken criticism of the seniority system in Congress and U.S. involvement in the Vietnam War. Her major work involved sponsoring legislation that would help the urban poor and increase funding for child welfare programs.

Section 5 Assessment

READING COMPREHENSION

1. How did **black nationalism** reflect a change from the early days of the civil rights movement?
2. How did the Black Panthers reflect Stokely Carmichael's idea of **black power?**
3. What did the Kerner Commission conclude about the race riots occurring in American cities?
4. What impact did the 1968 assassinations have on the legacy of the civil rights movement?

CRITICAL THINKING AND WRITING

5. **Distinguishing Fact From Opinion** Malcom X once said that for African Americans "the only solution is complete separation from the white man." Do you believe this statement to be a fact or an opinon? Explain your answer.
6. **Writing to Persuade** Black nationalists believed that African Americans should establish separate communities. Write a brief paper defending or opposing this position.

Take It to the NET

Activity: Creating a Time Line
Do further research on the civil rights movement from 1965–1970. Create a poster-sized time line for these years, incorporating images and quotations you find in your research. Be sure to include events covered in this section. Use the links provided in the *America: Pathways to the Present* area of the following Web site for help in completing this activity.
www.phschool.com

Section 5 Assessment

Reading Comprehension

1. It rejected the idea of racial integration and suggested that blacks needed to develop a separate identity and racial unity.
2. By stressing that African Americans should build their own communities, just as Carmichael had wanted to make SNCC an all-black organization. Both Carmichael and the Black Panthers disdained nonviolence and became more radical.
3. That the riots were a result of pent-up anger, and that the nation was moving toward two separate and unequal societies of African Americans and whites.
4. They marked an end to the civil rights movement; Americans lost faith in nonviolent protest, in their leaders, and in affecting change through political action.

Critical Thinking and Writing

5. Possible answer: The statement is an opinion; it expresses Malcolm X's conclusion about the complex problem of race relations in the United States.
6. Answers will vary, but should build a case for the student's viewpoint and be supported with facts from the section.

Take It to the NET

Student time lines should indicate events in the civil rights movement from 1965 to 1970.

REVIEWING KEY TERMS

Students should refer to the definitions of key terms in the chapter to write sentences that show an understanding of the civil rights movement.

REVIEWING MAIN IDEAS

13. By declaring "separate but equal" unconstitutional, and finding support as well as violent opposition to this ruling, the nation faced dilemmas of integration and racial uprisings.
14. Sample answers: By law, blacks were permitted to attend the same school as whites; the Ku Klux Klan became more active; the Southern Manifesto was created.
15. Sample answer: The NAACP had many legal successes, including *Brown* v. *Board of Education.* CORE organized demonstrations against segregation and became a national organization by the 1950s.
16. King's approach of nonviolent protest was influenced by Mohandas Gandhi's ideas, espoused during India's struggle for independence from Britain.
17. Activists placed groups of African Americans and whites on Freedom Rides to the South. After the groups were attacked at bus terminals, the federal government forced local authorities to uphold desegregation policies for interstate bus travelers.
18. After Kennedy's assassination, Johnson lobbied Congress to pass the Civil Rights Act of 1964 and the Voting Rights Act of 1965.
19. Civil Rights Act: created consistent standards for voter registration; prohibited discrimination in public places; allowed withholding of federal funds from programs that practiced discrimination; outlawed discrimination in the workplace; created the EEOC. Voting Rights Act: allowed federal officials to register voters in places where local officials were blocking African American registration; eliminated literacy tests and other barriers to voting; allowed for federal supervision of voter registration.

Chapter 21 Review and Assessment

creating a CHAPTER SUMMARY

Copy this web diagram (right). Add more circles to each of the four categories of civil rights participants. Fill in the circles with details about each person you add.

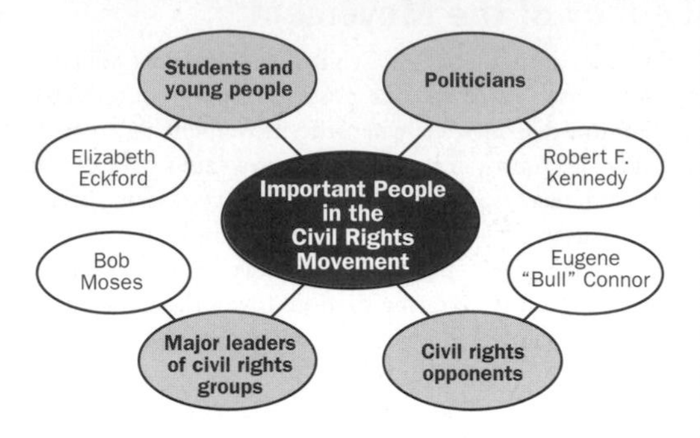

For additional review and enrichment activities, see the interactive version of *America: Pathways to the Present*, available on the Web and on CD-ROM.

★ Reviewing Key Terms

For each of the terms below, write a sentence explaining how it relates to the civil rights movement.

1. Montgomery bus boycott
2. integration
3. interracial
4. nonviolent protest
5. sit-in
6. Freedom Ride
7. filibuster
8. cloture
9. Twenty-fourth Amendment
10. black nationalism
11. black power
12. *de facto* segregation

★ Reviewing Main Ideas

13. How did the Supreme Court's decision in *Brown* v. *Board of Education* set the stage for a civil rights movement? (Section 1)
14. What were three effects of the *Brown* decision? (Section 1)
15. Name two groups that worked for African American rights *before* the 1960s. What did they accomplish? (Section 2)
16. What new approach did Martin Luther King, Jr., bring to the civil rights movement? What was the inspiration for his philosophy? (Section 2)
17. How did activists work to desegregate the interstate bus system? (Section 3)
18. What was President Johnson's role in passing civil rights legislation? (Section 4)
19. What did the Civil Rights Act of 1964 and the Voting Rights Act of 1965 accomplish? (Section 4)
20. What is the Nation of Islam? (Section 5)
21. What major changes occurred in the civil rights movement in the mid- to late 1960s? (Section 5)

★ Critical Thinking

22. **Identifying Assumptions** What assumptions did the federal government make when it created the termination policy to promote Native American assimilation into mainstream American culture?
23. **Formulating Questions** Make a list of five questions that you might ask a student activist from the 1960s to find out his or her reasons for taking part in the civil rights movement.
24. **Synthesizing Information** SNCC began as an alternative to existing civil rights groups. How did SNCC maintain itself as an alternative organization, and how did it change over time?
25. **Demonstrating Reasoned Judgment** Many people who lived through the 1960s would agree that the country lost its sense of hope after the deaths of Martin Luther King, Jr., and Robert F. Kennedy. Do you think that people in the United States today have regained a sense of hope?

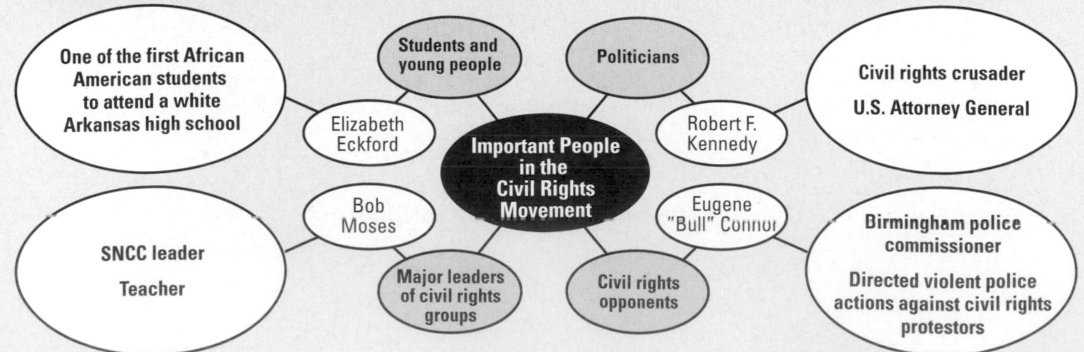

★ **Skills Assessment**

Analyzing Political Cartoons ▶

26. Examine both panels of the cartoon. What does the man represent?
27. (a) What does the first pit represent? (b) What does the second pit represent?
28. What is the man's overall goal, and what obstacles does he face?
29. What point is the cartoonist trying to make?

Analyzing Primary Sources

Read the excerpt from Martin Luther King, Jr.'s "I Have a Dream" speech in Section 4. Then answer the following questions.

30. Which of the following best *summarizes* King's dream?
   - **A** that Americans of all religions will be free at last
   - **B** that all Americans will achieve true equality and freedom
   - **C** that African Americans will form a brotherhood
   - **D** that children will not be judged by their color
31. King hopes that his dream will be fulfilled
   - **F** sometime in the future.
   - **G** in his children's lifetime.
   - **H** in the twentieth century.
   - **J** today.

Applying the Chapter Skill: *Using Autobiography and Biography*

32. Reread the excerpt on the Skills for Life page.
   (a) Why was Ralph Abernathy a reliable source for information about the civil rights movement?
   (b) How might Abernathy's association with Martin Luther King, Jr., have affected his point of view toward those events?

ACTIVITIES

Writing to LEARN

Writing to Inform
Reread the list of provisions of the 1964 Civil Rights Act in Section 4. Look through current newspapers and news magazines. Then write an essay describing how these laws and regulations still affect American life and politics today.

Primary Source CD-ROM

Working With Primary Sources Find additional information on the civil rights movement on the *Exploring Primary Sources in U.S. History CD-ROM* and use the selection(s) provided to complete the Chapter 21 primary source activity located in the *America: Pathways to the Present* area of the following Web site.
www.phschool.com

Take It to the NET

Chapter Self-Test As a review activity, take the Chapter 21 Self-Test in the *America: Pathways to the Present* area at the Web site listed below. The questions are designed to test your understanding of the chapter content.
www.phschool.com

ANSWERS TO ACTIVITIES

Writing to LEARN

Students' answers will vary, but should demonstrate the relevance of the Civil Rights Act in American life and politics today. For example, more recent cases of discrimination in the workplace sometimes appear in current newspaper accounts.

Primary Source CD-ROM

Direct students to the additional primary sources that can be found on the *Exploring Primary Sources in U.S. History CD-ROM.*

Take It to the NET

Additional support materials and activities for Chapter 21 of *America: Pathways to the Present* can be found in the Social Studies area at the Prentice Hall School Web site. **www.phschool.com**

20. An organization dedicated to black separation and self-help.
21. It changed from a mainstream, nonviolent movement to a collection of splinter groups advocating various degrees of militancy. It also became younger and less church-inflenced.

CRITICAL THINKING

22. The government assumed that Native Americans wanted to assimilate into mainstream American culture, and that the best way to improve their existing living conditions was for them to abandon their traditional ways of life and become "Americanized."
23. Sample questions: Why did you join the civil rights movement? Did your opinions of race relations change as a result of your participation? Do you agree that the use of nonviolent confrontation is the most effective way of achieving equality?
24. SNCC gave a voice to the youth generation. It maintained its individuality by deliberately choosing to remain autonomous, seeking immediate change, and through such activities as helping to organize the Mississippi Freedom Democratic Party. SNCC became less interracial and more radical over time.
25. Students' outlooks are likely to vary depending on individual situations, but they should reflect thoughtful consideration of today's major issues in relation to the issues that were current at the time of the 1968 assassinations.

SKILLS ASSESSMENT

26. African Americans.
27. (a) Racial inequality. (b) Economic inequality.
28. He is seeking equality in American society, but racism and lack of economic opportunity prevent him from achieving it.
29. Economic inequality is as effective as racism in preventing equality between blacks and whites.
30. B
31. G
32. (a) He was a firsthand observer, his tone is matter-of-fact, and he doesn't seem to exaggerate.
(b) He was a strong partisan of King's views and worked closely with him, meaning that his views would be favorable.

Encounters With Segregation

Focus Have students find the meaning of each of these words in a dictionary before they begin to read: *defunct, premise, freestanding, sparse, Jim Crow.* Ask them to consider, as they read, how a greater understanding of segregation might have changed white Americans' attitudes toward civil rights.

Instruct Have students role-play Bruce Killebrew and Joan W. Musbach talking to each other, as adults, about their childhood experiences of race. Have students work in pairs to outline conversations and choose roles. Tell them to construct conversations so that they give information in a manner that is consistent with both characters. Then have them perform their conversations for the class.

Analyzing the Document Use this additional question to generate class discussion:

Critical Thinking: Making Comparisons How were Bruce Killebrew's and Joan W. Musbach's experiences alike? How were they different? *(They were alike in that both students became aware of current issues dealing with race through personal experience. They were different in that Killebrew was inspired by integration, whereas Musbach was shocked and saddened by segregation.)*

AmericanHeritage®

MY BRUSH WITH **HISTORY**™

by BRUCE KILLEBREW and JOAN W. MUSBACH

COLORED WAITING ROOM

Encounters With Segregation

The two passages below describe how two white Americans became aware of the system of racial segregation that existed in many parts of the country. In the first account, Bruce Killebrew recalls the integration of his third-grade class. In the second account, Joan W. Musbach remembers the day that she, as a high school student, came face to face with her own ignorance about segregation.

A VIRGINIA CLASSROOM In 1954 my father was stationed at the Pentagon in Washington, D.C., and we lived on the now-defunct South Post of Fort Myer. My friends and I had a grand time romping through the nearby Civil War battlefields, taking turns being Yankee and Rebel. I couldn't decide whether to favor the Blue or the Gray. At the age of eight I'd really never thought about the issues that fueled the fighting.

Then, one day in the first week of September 1954, at the beginning of the year for our small military elementary school at Fort Myer, there were new faces in my class—and reporters from United Press and *Army Times* taking pictures. They were photographing the class while I led the Pledge of Allegiance for the first integrated class in the formerly Confederate state of Virginia. The two new students were black, and to me and the rest of my third-grade classmates they did not seem any different from the rest of us kids. But I was very proud to have been chosen to lead the Pledge of Allegiance on that day.

The event would help shape this nation's future, and my own. It brought

Bruce Killebrew (far left) leads the Pledge of Allegiance for one of the first integrated classes in Virginia.

RESOURCE DIRECTORY

Technology

AmericanHeritage® My Brush with History™ Videotapes *Encounters With Segregation*

TEST PREPARATION

Have students use the excerpt on these pages to answer the following question.

Why did newspaper reporters appear in Bruce Killebrew's class in the first week of school?

A Newspaper reporters in every town cover the beginning of the school year.

B Killebrew's school was particularly noteworthy because it was located on a military base.

C The reporters expected violence in the newly integrated school.

(D) Killebrew's was the first integrated class in Virginia.

home to me the idea that all men are created equal and have the right to equal opportunity. Much of my life as an individual and a social worker has been based on the premise I learned in that classroom in 1954.

A Midwestern Café On a crisp, cool, sunny Saturday in January, a Midwestern café—a free-standing building with one counter, stools in front, grill behind—became the site of the most memorable experience of my high school years.

It was 1960. I was a senior member of the debate team from John J. Ingels High School, in Atchison, Kansas. I was growing up within sixty miles of the origin of the 1954 Supreme Court case, *Brown* v. *Board of Education*, but, as of 1960, had never heard of Linda Brown or the case that bears her name. I was soon to discover that there was a great deal about which I was unaware.

We finished the Saturday-morning rounds and then went out for lunch before returning to the college to hear the semifinalists announced. We chose an appealing-looking cafeteria near the college. I was the only girl on the trip, and I was still just entering when Mr. Phipps and the boys turned around and came back out. I was busy talking and didn't ask why we had left. I assumed the cafeteria was too crowded. We got into Mr. Phipps's old car and drove a few blocks to a café. Business was sparse, and we spread out down the red-plastic-covered stools along the counter. John, my partner, was seated beside me. The waitress came down the counter distributing menus. John did not get one. We called this to her attention, and she quickly informed us that blacks were not served in there. I was shocked. I had never heard of such a thing. We all got up and went to the car, and Mr. Phipps went to a nearby hamburger stand and bought hamburgers and sodas for us all to eat in the car.

John wouldn't eat. He sat in the corner of the back seat, speechless. We didn't know what to say either. We just ate our hamburgers and went back to the college.

As I thought about the incident, I realized that John was the victim of our ignorance as well as of the prejudice of the management of the cafeteria and the café. He had probably never been exposed to such humiliation before, protected by parents or other adults who would have avoided such an incident. Strange as it may seem, a carful of high school students and their teacher were unaware of the segregation of public services just across the river from where they lived.

The look on John's face as we ate our hamburgers ensured that I would never forget that crisp January Saturday or the Kansas City café where I met Jim Crow.

The countless small conflicts of a segregated society flared up nationwide in diners and lunchrooms such as this one.

Source: *American Heritage* magazine, April 1991 and April 1994.

Understanding Primary Sources

1. What do Mr. Phipps and the boys do after they go into the first cafeteria near the college?
2. Why might they have done this?

American Heritage® MY BRUSH WITH **HISTORY**™ **Videotapes** — **For more information about the fight against segregation, view "Encounters With Segregation."**

731

CUSTOMIZE FOR ... ESL

Students may need help with the following words and phrases:

the Pentagon headquarters of the U.S. Department of Defense
integrated including persons of different races or ethnicities
social worker a person whose job involves finding and providing services for needy people
distributing handing out
segregation a system that reinforces prejudice by separating people of different races or ethnicities

CUSTOMIZE FOR ... Less Proficient Readers

After students read the selection, have them form small groups. Tell groups to reenact both stories. Circulate to check students' understanding of the main characters and issues. Then reconvene the class. Ask groups to tell how reenacting the stories changed or increased their understanding. Ask which roles were more or less comfortable to play and why.

CUSTOMIZE FOR ... Less Proficient Writers

Ask students to write a list of words that describe the emotions felt by Bruce Killebrew and Joan W. Musbach. Then ask them to write sentences using those words.

CUSTOMIZE FOR ... Gifted and Talented

Have students write a fictional account of how Joan Musbach's debate partner, John, came face to face with segregation. Accounts may treat the incident that Musbach describes or go further back in time to John's childhood. Call on volunteers to read their accounts aloud.

Answers

1. They turn around and come back out without eating.
2. They probably were refused service.

Expanding Civil Rights

Focus Remind students that the acquisition of civil rights has been a long and gradual process. At the time of the writing of the Constitution, only white males could vote. Over the course of the last 200 years, groups such as African Americans, Native Americans, and women have gained the right to vote. Laws have been passed banning discrimination against such groups.

Instruct Tell students to read the text carefully and look over the photographs. Ask students to think about why it has been necessary to pass laws to enforce civil rights. Ask students whether legislation is all that's needed to change people's attitudes. What else needs to happen to ensure "liberty and justice for all"?

Extend Encourage students to focus on one aspect of the struggle for civil rights. For example, students might choose to explore the suffrage movement or the civil rights era of the 1950s and 1960s. Tell students to research this era. Who were some of the prominent leaders? What were some of the biggest obstacles to obtaining civil rights?

American Pathways

CITIZENSHIP

Expanding Civil Rights

When the Constitution was written, only white male property owners had the right to vote. Over the past two centuries, though, the term "government by the people" has become more of a reality. Civil rights have been expanded for many groups, including Native Americans, African Americans, women, and young adults.

The Bill of Rights

1791 The first ten amendments to the United States Constitution were added in 1791. Known as the Bill of Rights, these amendments guaranteed freedom of belief and expression, freedom and security of the person, and fair and equal treatment before the law. Throughout American history, many people have worked to make these constitutional guarantees a reality for all Americans.

President Washington's cabinet (right)

Rights for African Americans

1868 and 1870 Two amendments ratified during the Reconstruction period sought to improve the civil rights of African Americans. The Fourteenth Amendment, ratified in 1868, granted citizenship to African Americans and declared that states could not "deprive any person of life, liberty, or property, without due process of law" or "deny to any person . . . the equal protection of the laws." The Fifteenth Amendment, ratified in 1870, was intended to protect any citizen from being denied the right to vote because of race or color. Still, for nearly another century, African Americans were systematically prevented from voting.

African American voters casting ballots in the 1876 election (left)

Suffrage for Women

1900–1920 Women made important civil rights gains with the ratification of the Nineteenth Amendment in 1920, which gave all American women the right to vote.

An American suffragette (left)

RESOURCE DIRECTORY

Teaching Resources

Units 5/6/7 booklet

- American Pathways Activity, pp. 95–96

American Pathways Thematic Posters

Technology

Companion Web site, www.phschool.com

Rights for Native Americans

1924 As European settlers migrated westward, they pushed many Indian groups off their lands. The result for many Native Americans was the loss of their sovereignty, culture, and territory. To help prevent further losses, Congress ratified the General Citizenship Act in 1924. It granted Native Americans the rights of citizenship, including the right to vote in federal elections.

The Civil Rights Era

1954–1968 In the period following World War II, thousands of ordinary Americans worked to end racial and ethnic injustice in the United States. The civil rights movement, especially, won significant victories in the battle to secure equal rights for all Americans, including African Americans, Latinos, Native Americans, and women.

Martin Luther King, Jr., and his wife, Coretta Scott King, lead a protest march from Selma to Montgomery, Alabama, in 1965 (above).

Suffrage for Young Adults

1971 Ratified in 1971, the Twenty-sixth Amendment set the minimum voting age at 18. Many of those who backed the amendment began to work for its passage during World War II. Its ratification was spurred by the Vietnam War.

An 18-year-old voter (left)

Rights for the Disabled

1990 The Americans with Disabilities Act guarantees disabled Americans equal opportunity in employment and public accommodations. The act has succeeded in breaking down many of the barriers that prevented the disabled from achieving equality.

Continuity and Change

1. How long did the system of Jim Crow, or legal segregation, last? What finally ended it?
2. What did minority groups do to try to gain their civil rights?

Take It to the NET: Creating a Study Guide Print and complete the study guide for this topic found in the *America: Pathways to the Present* area of the following Web site. **www.phschool.com**

733

Take It to the NET

Students can print the American Pathways thematic study guide for this topic at the Prentice Hall School Web site, or you can provide students with copies of the study guide, which is found in the Units 5/6/7 booklet, the American Pathways Activity, pages 95–96. Students should use their texts to fill in a one-sentence description for each event on the study guide. When completed for each of the American Pathways topics, the thematic study guides will aid students in preparing for an end-of-course exam.

Answers

1. Jim Crow lasted from about 1877 to 1954. It ended with the Supreme Court's decision in *Brown* v. *Board of Education of Topeka.*
2. Minority groups formed organizations, such as the NAACP and the American Indian Movement, to push the government to end discrimination.

Chapter 22 Planning Guide

Resource Manager

	Core Instruction	Reading/Skills
Chapter-Level Resources **TEKS** 24(A), 24(B), 24(D)	Teaching Resources • Pacing Charts booklet • Block Scheduling booklet **Resource Pro® CD-ROM,** Ch. 22 **Prentice Hall Presentation Pro CD-ROM,** Ch. 22 **www.phschool.com** • eTeach	**Guided Reading Audiotapes (English/Spanish)** **Student Edition on Audio CD,** Ch. 22 **Social Studies Skills Tutor CD-ROM** **Color Transparencies,** A48, A49, B17, H19
1 The New Frontier 1. Learn about factors that affected the election of 1960. 2. Find out about domestic programs pursued by President Kennedy. 3. Read about circumstances that surrounded Kennedy's assassination. **TEKS** 1(B), 8(B), 17(B), 18(B), 20(A), 25(D)	Teaching Resources **Units 5/6/7 booklet** • Section 1 Quiz, p. 64 **Learning Styles Lesson Plans booklet,** p. 60	**Guided Reading and Review booklet,** p. 117 **Guide to the Essentials,** p. 107 **Learning with Documents booklet,** p. 68 **Skills for Life booklet,** p. 31 **Section Reading Support Transparencies**
2 The Great Society 1. Discover Lyndon Johnson's path to the presidency. 2. Find out about some of the goals and programs of the Great Society. 3. Learn about some of the cases that made the Warren Court both important and controversial. **TEKS** 14(D), 18(A), 19(C), 25(D)	Teaching Resources **Units 5/6/7 booklet** • Section 2 Quiz, p. 65	**Guided Reading and Review booklet,** p. 118 **Guide to the Essentials,** p. 108 **Learning with Documents booklet,** pp. 34, 94 **Section Reading Support Transparencies**
3 Foreign Policy in the Early 1960s 1. Understand the goals and the outcome of the Bay of Pigs invasion. 2. Read to find out about events that led to the Berlin Crisis and the Cuban Missile Crisis. 3. Discover the goals of the Alliance for Progress and the Peace Corps. 4. Find out about Cold War conflicts in which Johnson became involved. **TEKS** 1(B), 6(D)	Teaching Resources **Units 5/6/7 booklet** • Section 3 Quiz, p. 66 **Learning Styles Lesson Plans booklet,** p. 61	**Guided Reading and Review booklet,** p. 119 **Guide to the Essentials,** p. 109 **Learning with Documents booklet,** p. 93 **Section Reading Support Transparencies**

Enrichment/Pre-AP

Prentice Hall United States History Video Collection™
www.phschool.com
- Section Activities, Virtual Field Trip, Chapter Activities, Current Events Online

Biography, Literature, and Comparing Primary Sources booklet, p. 80
Sounds of an Era Audio CD
Exploring Primary Sources in U.S. History CD-ROM

American History Block Scheduling Support
Sounds of an Era Audio CD

Biography, Literature, and Comparing Primary Sources booklet, pp. 34, 153
American History Block Scheduling Support
Sounds of an Era Audio CD
American Pathways Thematic Posters

Assessment

Core Assessment
ExamView® Test Bank, Ch. 22
ExamView® Test Bank CD-ROM, Ch. 22

Standardized Test Preparation
Diagnose and Prescribe
Diagnostic Tests for High School Social Studies Skills

Review and Reteach
Review Book for U.S. History

Practice and Assess
Test-taking Strategies With Transparencies
Test-taking Strategies Posters
Test Prep Book for U.S. History
Alternative Assessment Handbook
Document-Based Assessment

Teaching Resources
Units 5/6/7 booklet
- Section Quizzes, pp. 64–66
- Chapter Tests, pp. 67, 70

www.phschool.com Ch. 22 Self-Test

AmericanHeritage Resources

From the Archives of American Heritage®, pp. 740, 756
AmericanHeritage® My Brush with History™ Videotapes
www.americanheritage.com

Don't miss the exclusive interactive version of this textbook on the Web and on CD-ROM.

Chapter 22 Planning Guide
In Your Classroom

Customize for Individual Needs

Gifted and Talented

Teacher's Edition
- Customize for Gifted and Talented, pp. 753, 757

Teaching Resources
- Biography, Literature, and Comparing Primary Sources booklet, pp. 34, 80, 153

Technology
- Exploring Primary Sources in U.S. History CD-ROM *Colonel Glenn Rides into Space; On the Cuban Missile Crisis, John F. Kennedy and Nikita Khrushchev*

ESL

Teacher's Edition
- Customize for ESL, p. 737

Teaching Resources
- Guided Reading and Review booklet, pp. 117–119
- Guide to the Essentials (English/Spanish), Chapter 22

Technology
- Student Edition on Audio CD, Chapter 22
- Guided Reading Audiotapes (English/Spanish), Chapter 22
- Section Reading Support Transparencies

Less Proficient Readers

Teacher's Edition
- Customize for Less Proficient Readers, p. 755

Teaching Resources
- Guided Reading and Review booklet, pp. 117–119
- Guide to the Essentials (English/Spanish), Chapter 22

Technology
- Student Edition on Audio CD, Chapter 22
- Guided Reading Audiotapes (English/Spanish), Chapter 22
- Section Reading Support Transparencies

Less Proficient Writers

Teacher's Edition
- Customize for Less Proficient Writers, p. 749

Teaching Resources
- Guided Reading and Review booklet, pp. 117–119
- Guide to the Essentials (English/Spanish), Chapter 22

Technology
- Student Edition on Audio CD, Chapter 22
- Guided Reading Audiotapes (English/Spanish), Chapter 22
- Section Reading Support Transparencies

Teacher's Edition Index

Chapter 22 – Pacing Suggestions

For 90-minute Blocks

- Teach sections 2 and 3 using Transparencies A48, A49, B17, and H19, and the Recent Scholarship notes on pages 748, 754, and 757 for class discussions.

Running Out of Time?

If you are running short on time to cover this chapter, consider the following options:

- Use the Prentice Hall Presentation Pro CD-ROM to create an outline for this chapter.
- Use the Section Summaries for Chapter 22, from **Guide to the Essentials (English/Spanish).**

TEKS Correlation

Chapter-Level	TEKS
	(24) Social studies skills. The student applies critical-thinking skills to organize and use information acquired from a variety of sources, including electronic technology. The student is expected to: **(A)** locate and use primary and secondary sources such as computer software, databases, media and news services, biographies, interviews, and artifacts to acquire information about the United States. **(B)** analyze information by sequencing, categorizing, identifying cause-and-effect relationships, comparing, contrasting, finding the main idea, summarizing, making generalizations and predictions, and drawing inferences and conclusions. **(D)** use the process of historical inquiry to research, interpret, and use multiple sources of evidence.
1 The New Frontier	**(1) History.** The student understands traditional historical points of reference in U.S. history from 1877 to the present. The student is expected to: **(B)** apply absolute and relative chronology through the sequencing of significant individuals, events, and time periods. **(8) Geography.** The student uses geographic tools to collect, analyze, and interpret data. The student is expected to: **(B)** pose and answer questions about geographic distributions and patterns shown on maps, graphs, charts, models, and databases. **(17) Government.** The student understands the impact of constitutional issues on American society in the 20th century. The student is expected to: **(B)** analyze reasons for the adoption of 20th-century constitutional amendments. **(18) Citizenship.** The student understands efforts to expand the democratic process. The student is expected to: **(B)** evaluate various means of achieving equality of political rights, including the 19th, 24th, and 26th amendments. **(20) Culture.** The student understands the relationship between the arts and the times during which they were created. The student is expected to: **(A)** describe how the characteristics and issues of various eras in U.S. history have been reflected in works of art, music, and literature such as the paintings of Georgia O'Keeffe, rock and roll, and John Steinbeck's *The Grapes of Wrath.* **(25) Social studies skills.** The student communicates in written, oral, and visual forms. The student is expected to: **(D)** create written, oral, and visual presentations of social studies information.
2 The Great Society	**(14) Economics.** The student understands the economic effects of World War II, the Cold War, and increased worldwide competition on contemporary society. The student is expected to: **(D)** identify actions of government and the private sector to expand economic opportunities to all citizens. **(18) Citizenship.** The student understands efforts to expand the democratic process. The student is expected to: **(A)** identify and analyze methods of expanding the right to participate in the democratic process, including lobbying, protesting, court decisions, and amendments to the U.S. Constitution. **(19) Citizenship.** The student understands the importance of effective leadership in a democratic society. The student is expected to: **(C)** identify the contributions of Texans who have been President of the United States. **(25) Social studies skills.** The student communicates in written, oral, and visual forms. The student is expected to: **(D)** create written, oral, and visual presentations of social studies information.
3 Foreign Policy in the Early 1960s	**(1) History.** The student understands traditional historical points of reference in U.S. history from 1877 to the present. The student is expected to: **(B)** apply absolute and relative chronology through the sequencing of significant individuals, events, and time periods. **(6) History.** The student understands the impact of significant national and international decisions and conflicts from World War II and the Cold War to the present on the United States. The student is expected to: **(D)** describe U.S. responses to Soviet aggression after World War II, including the Truman Doctrine, the Marshall Plan, the North Atlantic Treaty Organization, and the Berlin airlift.

Chapter 22 The Kennedy and Johnson Years (1961–1969)

Introducing the Chapter

The contrast between the presidencies of John F. Kennedy and Lyndon Johnson is striking. While Kennedy articulated plans for domestic reform, few of his programs actually advanced through Congress, perhaps because of his preoccupation with foreign affairs. When Johnson took office after Kennedy's death, he used his legislative skills to push through Congress some of the most significant social programs in the nation's history.

Time Line Activity

To provide students with practice in using the time line, ask questions such as these:

1. In what year did the first U.S. astronaut go into space? *(1961)*
2. In what year did a country in Africa gain independence from France, and what was that country? *(1962; Algeria)*
3. What 1966 Supreme Court ruling gave rights to people accused of crimes? *(The Miranda ruling)*

Chapter 22 The Kennedy and Johnson Years (1961–1969)

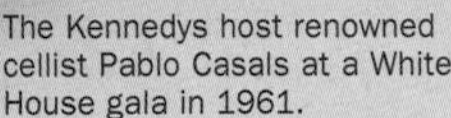

The Kennedys host renowned cellist Pablo Casals at a White House gala in 1961.

Lyndon Johnson rides his horse, Lady B, at his Texas ranch in 1963.

American Events

1960 Kennedy and Johnson win election by a razor-thin margin.

1961 Kennedy launches his New Frontier program. The first U.S. astronaut goes into space. The failed Bay of Pigs invasion is a U.S. foreign policy disaster.

1962 The Cuban Missile Crisis brings the superpowers to the brink of nuclear war.

1963 On November 22, Kennedy is assassinated in Dallas; Johnson becomes President.

1964 Johnson wins election. He launches a "war on poverty" with a series of programs known as the Great Society.

Presidential Terms: John F. Kennedy 1961–1963; Lyndon B. Johnson 1963–1969

1960 • 1962 • 1964

World Events

1961 In a showdown with Kennedy, Soviets build the Berlin Wall.

1962 Algeria wins independence from France, a colonial power in Africa.

1964 UN peacekeepers are sent to Cyprus amid Greek-Turk hostilities.

eTeach

Be sure to check out this month's online discussion with a Master Teacher. Go to **www.phschool.com**.

RESOURCE DIRECTORY

Teaching Resources
Pacing Charts booklet
Block Scheduling booklet, p. 27
Units 5/6/7 booklet
- Chapter Summary, p. 63

Technology
Guided Reading Audiotapes (English/Spanish), Ch. 22
Student Edition on Audio CD, Ch. 22
Sounds of an Era Audio CD *"The President Twist"* (time: 45 seconds)
Prentice Hall United States History Video Collection™ Volume 20, *Post-War USA*
Prentice Hall Presentation Pro CD-ROM, Ch. 22
Resource Pro® CD-ROM
Social Studies Skills Tutor CD-ROM
Companion Web site, www.phschool.com

Nuclear Threat From Cuba

CANADA
Seattle
2,843 miles
Chicago
New York
Washington, D.C.
ATLANTIC OCEAN
Denver
1,819 miles
1,333 miles
1,139 miles
1,317 miles
2,000 miles, 17 minutes
1,500 miles, 15 minutes
1,000 miles, 12 minutes
Los Angeles
2,299 miles
Atlanta
Houston
924 miles
761 miles
Miami
Gulf of Mexico
243 miles
1,103 miles
Havana
CUBA
MEXICO
Mexico City

Nuclear Threat From the U.S.S.R.

About 5,000 miles
UNITED STATES
SOVIET UNION

Teacher and students in the federal Head Start program begun under Johnson.

1965 Johnson sends the Marines to support a U.S.-backed government in the Dominican Republic. U.S. involvement in Vietnam deepens. Medicare and Medicaid programs are created.

1966 The Warren Court's landmark *Miranda* ruling gives rights to persons accused of crimes.

1968 Amid race riots and Vietnam War protests, Johnson's popularity plummets. He announces he will not run for reelection.

1966 — 1968

1965 Rhodesia declares independence from Britain.

1966 China's Cultural Revolution begins.

Nuclear Threat From Cuba

Activating Prior Knowledge Which is greater, the distance between Cuba to Washington, D.C., or the distance from Russia to the continental United States? By about how much? *(The distance from Russia to the United States is greater. The difference is about 4,000 miles.)*

Previewing Why would the United States object to Soviet missiles in Cuba? *(The proximity of Cuba to the United States meant that missiles from Cuba could arrive in the United States very quickly, giving the United States very little time to respond.)*

BACKGROUND

About the Pictures

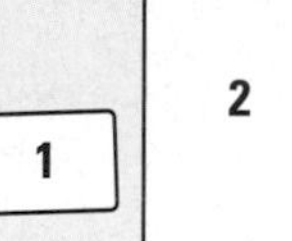

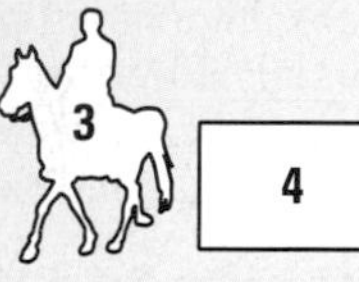

1. Kennedy's narrow win (only 118,550 out of 70 million votes) over the Republican candidate, Richard Nixon, spurred allegations of vote fraud in the state of Illinois.
2. The Kennedys become well known for their associations with people of glamour, style, and intellect.
3. Wishing to honor President Kennedy's memory, one of Johnson's highest priorities became signing the Civil Rights Act into law.
4. The Head Start program, created under the Economic Opportunity Act, provided needed social services, including preschool, for children in low-income families.

BIBLIOGRAPHY

For the Teacher

Bechschloss, Michael, editor. ***Taking Charge: The Johnson White House Tapes.*** Simon & Schuster, 1997. (Warts-and-all, behind-the-scenes glimpse of Johnson as President.)

Freedman, Lawrence. ***Kennedy's Wars: Berlin, Cuba, Laos, Vietnam.*** Oxford University Press, 2000. (Uses newly released material to insightfully analyze Kennedy's performance.)

Reeves, Richard. ***President Kennedy: Profile of Power.*** Touchstone, 1994. (Comprehensive account of Kennedy's 1960 presidential campaign.)

For the Student

Brown, Claude. ***Manchild in the Promised Land.*** Simon & Schuster, 1999. (Autobiography of an African American youth from poverty in Harlem to a law degree from Howard University.)

Kennedy, John F. ***Profiles in Courage.*** Harperperennial, 2000. (A first-rate book about political integrity.)

Kennedy, Robert F. ***Thirteen Days.*** Norton, 1999. (Gripping account of the Cuban missile crisis by the President's brother and closest adviser, who served as attorney general of the United States.)

Don't miss the exclusive interactive version of this textbook on the Web and on CD-ROM.

Section 1
The New Frontier

Section Objectives

1. Learn about factors that affected the election of 1960.
2. Find out about domestic programs pursued by President Kennedy.
3. Read about circumstances that surrounded Kennedy's assassination.

Bellringer

Warm-Up Activity Ask students to picture a political campaign for President waged without television appearances, interviews, or campaign commercials. How would voters learn about the candidates? What do voters learn about candidates from television?

Activating Prior Knowledge What do students know about the Kennedy presidency? Ask if students are familiar with the famous phrase from Kennedy's inauguration: "Ask not what your country can do for you; ask what you can do for your country." Ask students to explain why this statement had a tremendous impact on the American people.

Reading Strategy

As students read this section, have them make a list, in chronological order, of the programs that Kennedy proposed.

Section 1
The New Frontier

READING FOCUS

- What factors affected the election of 1960?
- What domestic programs did President Kennedy pursue?
- What circumstances surrounded Kennedy's assassination?

MAIN IDEA

Following a narrow election victory, President John F. Kennedy proposed a number of changes in domestic policy, many of which were defeated in Congress.

KEY TERMS

mandate
New Frontier
Warren Commission

TAKING NOTES

Copy the chart below. As you read, fill in details relating to Kennedy's New Frontier program.

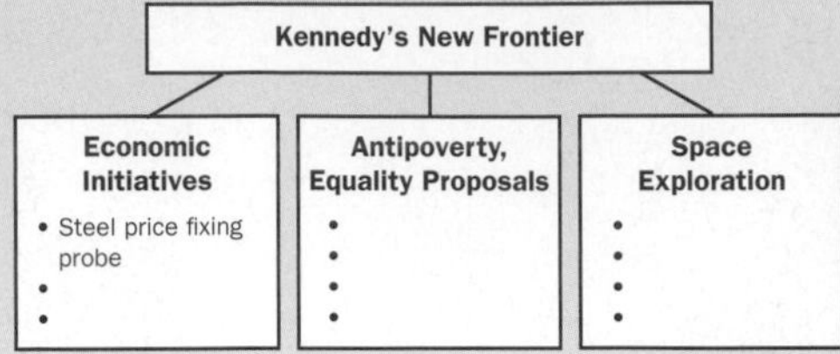

Setting the Scene On September 26, 1960, American politics changed forever. From a CBS television studio in Chicago, two presidential candidates—Republican Richard Nixon and Democrat John F. Kennedy—faced off in the first of four live, televised debates broadcast by all the networks. This debate focused on domestic issues.

Nixon was a tough, veteran campaigner who had gained plenty of political experience as a member of Congress and as Eisenhower's Vice President. Yet he was not in peak form. He had kept a grueling campaign schedule and had been sidelined in the hospital for two weeks with a serious knee injury. Nixon arrived at the studio 10 pounds underweight, having ignored advice to get a new shirt with a collar that fit. He refused makeup, except for a pasty beard stick called "Lazy Shave" to cover his perpetual "five o'clock shadow." According to biographer Stephen A. Ambrose, Nixon stood under the hot studio lights "half slouched, his 'Lazy Shave' powder faintly streaked with sweat, his eyes exaggerated hollows of blackness, his jaw, jowls, and face dropping with strain." Nixon had prepared his mind for the battle, but not his appearance.

Senator Kennedy, on the other hand, arrived in Chicago after a campaign swing through California that included plenty of rest and sunshine. Tanned, relaxed, and smiling, he breezed into the studio. The camera favored his young, handsome face, and Kennedy spoke directly to the camera, paying little attention to his opponent and addressing the viewing voters instead.

In a CBS studio in Chicago, a relaxed John Kennedy (seated) browses his notes as he prepares to meet Richard Nixon (at the podium) in the first of their four televised debates in the fall of 1960.

Who won the debate? Surveys showed that most of the 70 million TV viewers thought Kennedy won. Yet many radio listeners gave the victory to Nixon. Analysts still disagree over whether the debate was the turning point in the election.

The undisputed winner that night was television itself. The presidential debates of 1960 put TV in the national spotlight and made it the communications vehicle of choice for politicians.

RESOURCE DIRECTORY

Teaching Resources

Guided Reading and Review booklet, p. 117
Learning Styles Lesson Plans booklet, p. 60
Learning with Documents booklet (Visual Learning Activity) *Close Allies,* p. 68

Technology

Section Reading Support Transparencies
Guided Reading Audiotapes (English/Spanish), Ch. 22
Student Edition on Audio CD, Ch. 22
Sounds of an Era Audio CD *President John F. Kennedy's Inaugural Address,* 1961 recording (time: 40 seconds)
Prentice Hall Presentation Pro CD-ROM, Ch. 22
Companion Web site, www.phschool.com

The Election of 1960

Kennedy, a Massachusetts Democrat, had served in the United States House of Representatives and Senate for 14 years, following distinguished service in the United States Navy in World War II. Yet the senator faced serious obstacles in his quest for the presidency.

A New Type of Candidate John Kennedy was only 43 years old, and many questioned whether he had the experience needed for the nation's highest office. (While he was the youngest person ever to be *elected* President, Kennedy was not the youngest ever to serve. Theodore Roosevelt became President at age 42 when William McKinley was assassinated.) In addition, Kennedy was a Roman Catholic, and no Catholic had ever been elected President. Kennedy helped put an end to the religion issue when he won the primary of the largely Protestant state of West Virginia.

With that hurdle behind him, he campaigned hard, promising to spur the sluggish economy. During the last years of the Eisenhower administration, the Gross National Product (GNP) had grown very slowly, and the economy had suffered several recessions. During the campaign, Kennedy proclaimed that it was time to "get America moving again."

Senator John F. Kennedy, the 1960 Democratic presidential candidate, greets supporters during a campaign stop.

A Narrow Kennedy Victory Kennedy and his running mate, Lyndon Baines Johnson, won the election by an extraordinarily close margin. Although the electoral vote was 303 to 219 in Kennedy's favor, he won by fewer than 119,000 popular votes out of nearly 69 million cast. In Illinois and Texas, Nixon could have inched by Kennedy with just a few thousand more votes, and accusations were made that the Democrats had won these states through fraud.

As a result of this razor-thin victory, Kennedy entered office without a strong **mandate,** or public endorsement of his proposals. Without a mandate, Kennedy would have difficulty pushing his more controversial measures through Congress.

Sounds of an Era

Listen to John F. Kennedy's Inaugural Address and other sounds from the Kennedy-Johnson era.

Presidential Election of 1960

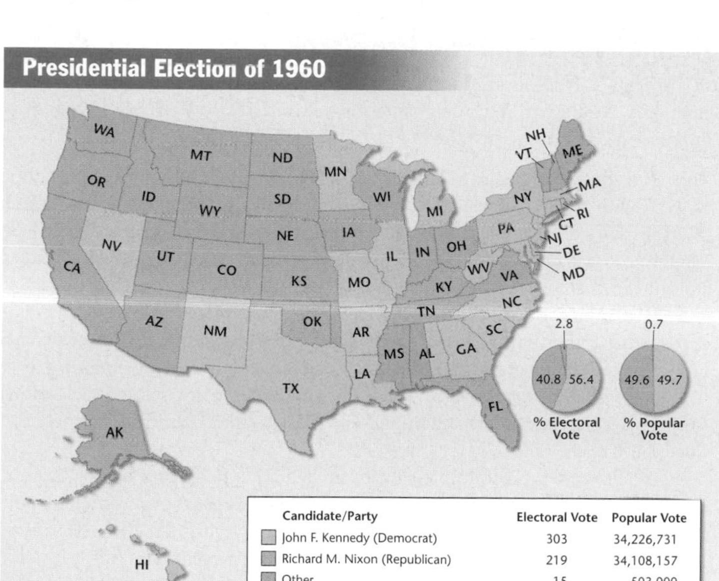

Candidate/Party	Electoral Vote	Popular Vote
John F. Kennedy (Democrat)	303	34,226,731
Richard M. Nixon (Republican)	219	34,108,157
Other	15	503,000

MAP SKILLS Kennedy and Nixon fought a head-to-head contest in the 1960 presidential election. **Regions** *(a) From what areas did each candidate draw the most votes? (b) Compare the popular vote and the electoral college vote, and explain the election outcome.*

Lesson Plan

Focus During the hard-fought election of 1960, John F. Kennedy promised new programs. Ask what those programs were. Why did so few of them make it through Congress?

Instruct Discuss the importance of a "mandate for change" for a reform-minded President. Why did Kennedy lack such a mandate? How did this lack hamper Kennedy? Ask students to describe Kennedy's New Frontier.

Discuss Kennedy's assassination. Ask students to describe the nation's response. What were the results of the Warren Commission's investigation into the assassination?

Assess/Reteach Ask students to speculate on what the United States would be like if Kennedy had not been assassinated, and had been able to serve two full terms. In what ways might this have affected the country?

Activity

Connecting with Government

Direct students to locate, or provide them with, a transcript of one of the historic Nixon-Kennedy debates. Have students identify a particularly interesting excerpt from the transcript to act out. Direct one student to assume the role of Nixon, a second student to assume the role of Kennedy, and a third student to assume the role of the moderator, Howard K. Smith. These students should then perform the debate excerpt for the class. Use the activity as a springboard into a discussion about the Nixon-Kennedy debates in particular, and the role of television in politics generally. **(Bodily/Kinesthetic)**

Customize for ...

ESL

Have volunteers read the following statements aloud:

- Kennedy defeated Nixon by a wide margin in 1960.
- Kennedy was able to move most of his New Frontier legislation through Congress.
- Kennedy was killed at the end of his fourth year as President.

Tell students these statements are incorrect, and ask them to correct them as they read. When students are finished, have volunteers read their corrected statements aloud.

Test Preparation

Have students reread the section "Setting the Scene" on the previous page and then answer the question below.

What is one plausible reason most television viewers felt that Kennedy had won the debate while most radio listeners felt that Nixon had won?

Ⓐ People listening to radio couldn't be influenced by Kennedy's and Nixon's appearance.
B Kennedy's arguments were more persuasive.
C Nixon appeared more trustworthy.
D Kennedy looked tired and pale.

Caption Answers

Map Skills (a) Kennedy: the South, much of the Northeast, and parts of the Midwest. Nixon: the West and parts of the Midwest, as well as Florida, Virginia, and Maine. (b) The popular vote was very close, but Kennedy won a substantial margin of the electoral votes, giving him the victory.

ACTIVITY
Student Portfolio

You may wish to have students add the following to their portfolios: Ask students to research and prepare either a written or oral report on the folk revival in popular music in the early 1960s (focusing on artists such as Bob Dylan and Joan Baez) and its relation to increasing demands for social reform in the nation. How does this music reflect the life and times in which it was created? **(Verbal/Linguistic)**

BACKGROUND
Connections to Earlier Events

Kennedy's phrase "Ask not what your country can do for you; ask what you can do for your country" is arguably his most famous utterance. Yet it is not entirely original. In 1884 Oliver Wendell Holmes wrote, "It is now the moment . . . to recall what our country has done for each of us, and to ask ourselves what we can do for our country in return." In 1904 LeBaron Russell Briggs wrote, "As has often been said, the youth who loves his Alma Mater will always ask, not 'What can she do for me?' but 'What can I do for her?'" And, in 1916, Warren Harding said, ". . . we must have a citizenship less concerned about what the government can do for it and more anxious about what it can do for the nation."

READING CHECK
Improving the economy, assisting the poor and disadvantaged, environmental issues, advancing the space program.

The President's children, Caroline Kennedy and John F. Kennedy, Jr., created an atmosphere of fun and family life in the Oval Office.

Kennedy nevertheless took office with vigor and confidence. In his Inaugural Address, he inspired a generation of young people by urging them to put patriotism before personal interests:

> *"My fellow Americans, ask not what your country can do for you; ask what you can do for your country."*
>
> —John F. Kennedy, Inaugural Address, 1961

Kennedy's Domestic Programs

In a speech early in his presidency, Kennedy said that the nation was poised at the edge of a **"New Frontier."** The name stuck. It referred to Kennedy's proposals to improve the economy, assist the poor, and speed up the space program.

The Economy Concerned about the continuing recession, Kennedy hoped to work with business leaders to promote economic growth. Often, however, he faced resistance from executives who were suspicious of his plans. Their worst fears were realized in the spring of 1962. When the U.S. Steel Company announced that it was raising the price of steel by $6 a ton, other firms did the same. Worried about inflation, Kennedy called the price increase unjustifiable and charged that it showed "utter contempt for the public interest." He ordered a federal investigation into the possibility of price fixing.

Under that pressure, U.S. Steel and the other companies backed down. Business leaders remained angry, and the stock market fell in its steepest drop since the Great Crash of 1929.

To help end the economic slump, in 1963 Kennedy proposed a large tax cut over three years. At first, the measure would reduce government income and create a budget deficit. Kennedy believed, however, that the extra cash in taxpayers' wallets would stimulate the economy and eventually bring in added tax revenues. However, as often happened, the President's proposal became stuck in Congress.

READING CHECK
What domestic issues did President Kennedy attempt to address?

RESOURCE DIRECTORY

Technology

RESOURCE PRO® **Biography** *Dr. Frances Kelsey,* found on Resource Pro, profiles the woman whose struggle to prevent FDA approval of thalidomide, a drug later linked to birth defects, won her the Distinguished Civilian Service Medal from President Kennedy.

Combating Poverty and Inequality Kennedy also was eager to take action against poverty and inequality. In his first two years in office, he hoped that he could help the poor simply by stimulating the economy. In 1962, though, author Michael Harrington described the lives of the poor in his powerful book, *The Other America*. Harrington's book revealed that while many Americans were enjoying the prosperity of the 1950s, a shocking one fifth of the population was living below the poverty line. Kennedy became convinced that the poor needed direct federal aid.

Kennedy's ambitious plans for federal education aid and medical care for the elderly both failed in Congress. Some measures did make it through Congress, however. Congress passed both an increase in the minimum wage and the Housing Act of 1961, which provided $4.9 billion for urban renewal. Congress also approved the Twenty-fourth Amendment, which outlawed the poll tax. In June 1963, Congress passed the Equal Pay Act. Added into the Fair Labor Standards Act of 1938, a New Deal program, the Equal Pay Act stated that all employees doing substantially the same work in the same workplace must be given equal pay.

Other Kennedy Initiatives In the face of congressional roadblocks, Kennedy, like many Presidents, sought to achieve his goals through executive orders. Among them were orders on providing equal opportunity in housing and establishing an expanded program of food distribution to needy families. Other orders established the President's Committee on Equal Employment, the President's Commission on the Status of Women, and the President's Council on Aging.

Other acts in Kennedy's shortened presidency—some carried out in collaboration with Congress—included the following:

1. an executive order providing improved surplus food to unemployed Americans;
2. the largest, fastest defense buildup in peacetime history, as Kennedy boosted missile programs;
3. an Area Redevelopment law to help communities plagued with long-term unemployment;
4. changes in Social Security extending benefits to 5 million people and allowing Americans to retire and collect benefits at age 62;
5. a law doubling federal resources to combat water pollution;
6. the creation of National Seashore Parks, a part of the National Park System;
7. the expansion and increase of the minimum wage;
8. the creation of the first federal program to address juvenile delinquency;
9. changes in the welfare system aimed at helping ailing families instead of encouraging dependency on government benefits;
10. the construction of the world's largest nuclear power plant, in Hanford, Washington;
11. tightening of food and drug laws to protect against untested drugs;
12. signing of a Trade Expansion Act to reduce American protectionism and encourage free trade;
13. signing of the Nuclear Test Ban Treaty, the first nuclear weapons agreement.

INTERPRETING GRAPHS
At bottom, Defense Department workers inspect the *Friendship 7* capsule after John Glenn's historic flight and splashdown. The chart below shows changes in NASA funding over two decades. **Analyzing Visual Information** *What accounts for the sudden surge in funding during the late 1950s?*

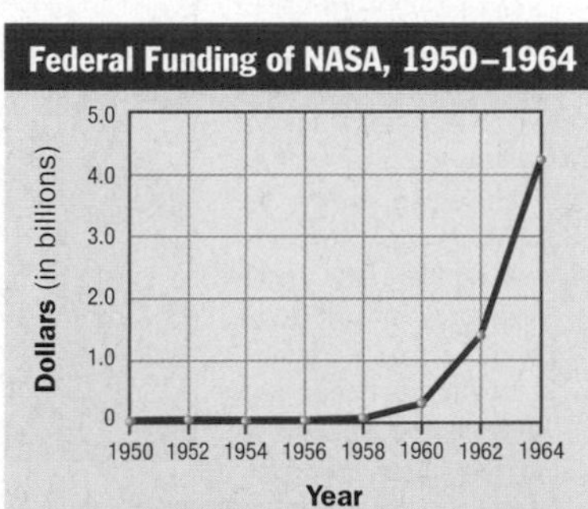

SOURCE: *Historical Statistics of the United States, Colonial Times to 1970*

739

ACTIVITY
Connecting with History and Conflict

Have pairs or small groups of students cooperate to compare Kennedy's domestic programs with those of the New Deal. Ask them to create a chart that presents the results of their comparison.

BACKGROUND
The Nuclear Test Ban Treaty

Signed during Kennedy's administration, the Nuclear Test Ban Treaty had its origins in concern about the dangers of radioactive fallout from nuclear weapons testing. Discussions had been underway since the mid-1950s, but the Cuban Missile Crisis of 1962 threw the problem into sharp focus. The world's three nuclear powers of the time, the Soviet Union, the United States, and Great Britain, agreed on the basic terms of a treaty with only ten days of discussion in the summer of 1963.

The treaty banned nuclear weapons testing in the atmosphere, in outer space, and underwater. Underground testing was still permitted, as was the maintenance of nuclear stockpiles and nuclear weapons buildup. Still, the treaty was regarded as an important first step. Within a few months, more than 100 other countries had signed the treaty.

TEST PREPARATION

Ask students to read the material in the section "The Space Program" on the next page and then answer the question below.

What 1961 event caused NASA to accelerate its space program and send a person into outer space?

A The Cuban Missile Crisis.
B The Cold War.
C A decision to send humans to the moon.
(D) The Soviet's successful launch of a peopled spacecraft.

CAPTION ANSWERS

Interpreting Graphs The launch of the Soviet satellite *Sputnik* in 1957 frightened and energized the United States into building a first-rate space program.

ACTIVITY

Connecting with Citizenship

This activity may continue over more than one class period: Divide the class into groups of four to six students. The goal of the project is to create an oral history of the Kennedy assassination. Ask students to interview people over the age of 45 about their memories of the event. Have them present the results of their interview in the form of a television news magazine segment. **(Verbal/Linguistic)**

From the Archives of

American Heritage®

Rush to Judgment

By 1967 theories about the assassination of President Kennedy were many. One magazine offered a review of 25 alternative theories grown up since the Warren Commission's report. They included the suggestion that original autopsy pictures had been destroyed to arguments over how many shots had been fired to the assertion that the killer's killer had been injected with cancer while in prison. But the most spectacular theory belonged to New Orleans district attorney Jim Garrison, who arrested respected New Orleans businessman Clay Shaw. According to Garrison, Shaw was part of a conspiracy funded by a rightist Cuban anti-Castro group that was angry with Kennedy for the failed Bay of Pigs invasion. After a trial filled with ever-widening charges and shadowy figures, Shaw was acquitted in 1969. Source: Nathan Ward, "The Time Machine," *American Heritage®* magazine, May/June 1992.

Focus on CULTURE

Camelot The name *Camelot* came to represent the energetic, idealistic image of the Kennedy White House. The Broadway musical *Camelot*, which opened in 1960, portrayed the legendary kingdom of the British King Arthur. Arthur dreamed of transforming medieval Britain from a country in which "might makes right," or the strong always get their way, into one in which power would be used to achieve what is right.

The Kennedys themselves embodied the royal, romantic spirit of Camelot. The President and First Lady made the White House a stage for high culture, inviting the best artists, musicians, and thinkers. Jacqueline Kennedy, an intelligent and beautiful woman, brought an atmosphere of style and grace to the White House. She personally supervised its renovation and redecoration, acquiring tasteful furnishings that reflected the Kennedys' interest in American cultural history.

The couple's young children, Caroline and John, Jr., added to the lively atmosphere. They played with their father in the Oval Office and in a swimming pool and treehouse on the White House lawn. The fact that the Kennedys had young children made it all the more tragic when Camelot came to a sudden end.

The Space Program Kennedy was also successful in his effort to breathe life into the space program. Following the Soviet Union's launch of the *Sputnik* satellite in 1957, government agencies and private industries had been working furiously with the National Aeronautics and Space Administration (NASA) to place a manned spacecraft in orbit around Earth. As part of the Mercury program, seven test pilots were chosen to train as astronauts in 1959. Government spending and the future of NASA became uncertain, however, when a task force appointed by Kennedy recommended that NASA concentrate on exploratory space missions without human crews.

All of that changed in April 1961. The Soviet Union announced that Yuri Gagarin had circled Earth on board the Soviet spacecraft *Vostok*, becoming the first human to travel in space. Gagarin's flight rekindled Americans' fears that their technology was falling behind that of the Soviet Union.

On May 5, 1961, the United States made its own first attempt to send a person into space. Astronaut Alan Shepard made a 15-minute flight that reached an altitude of 115 miles. Unlike Gagarin's flight, Shepard's flight did not orbit Earth. Nevertheless, its success convinced Kennedy to move forward. On May 25, Kennedy issued a bold challenge to the nation. He said the United States "should commit itself to achieving the goal, before this decade is out, of landing a man on the moon."

The nation accepted the challenge, and funding for NASA was increased. Less than a year later, on February 20, 1962, John Glenn successfully completed three orbits around Earth and landed in the Atlantic Ocean near the Bahamas. Later that year Kennedy outlined the reasons for American space exploration:

> "*We set sail on this new sea because there is new knowledge to be gained, and new rights to be won, and they must be won and used for the progress of all people. . . . [O]nly if the United States occupies a position of preeminence can we help decide whether this new ocean will be a sea of peace or a new, terrifying theater of war.*"
>
> —John F. Kennedy, speech at Rice University, Houston, Texas, 1962

Over the course of the decade, NASA flights brought the country closer and closer to its goal. Finally, on July 20, 1969, astronaut Neil Armstrong became the first person to walk on the moon. Unfortunately, Kennedy would not live to see the fulfillment of the goal he set in motion.

Kennedy Is Assassinated

On November 22, 1963, as Kennedy looked ahead to the reelection campaign the following year, he traveled to Texas to mobilize support. Texas Governor John Connally and his wife, Nelly, met the President and the First Lady, Jacqueline Kennedy, at the airport in Dallas. Together they rode through the streets of downtown Dallas in an open limousine, surrounded by Secret Service agents. Newspapers had published the parade route ahead of time, and it was jammed with thousands of supporters hoping for a glimpse of the President.

The motorcade slowed as it turned a corner in front of the Texas School Book Depository. Its employees had been sent to lunch so they could watch the event outside. Yet one man stayed behind. From a sixth-floor window, he aimed his rifle.

RESOURCE DIRECTORY

Teaching Resources

Units 5/6/7 booklet
- Section 1 Quiz, p. 64

Guide to the Essentials
- Section 1 Summary, p. 107

Biography, Literature, and Comparing Primary Sources booklet (Literature) *A Grieving Nation*, p. 80

Technology

Sounds of an Era Audio CD *Walter Cronkite on Kennedy's Death,* 1963 recording (time: 15 seconds); *A Dallas Reporter on Kennedy's Assassination* (time: one minute); *"A Taste of Honey"* (time: one minute)

Exploring Primary Sources in U.S. History CD-ROM *Colonel Glenn Rides into Space*

Suddenly shots rang out. Bullets struck both Connally and Kennedy. Connally would recover from his injuries. The President, slumped over in Jacqueline's lap, was mortally wounded.

The motorcade sped to nearby Parkland Memorial Hospital, where doctors made what they knew was a hopeless attempt to save the President. Kennedy was pronounced dead at 1:00 P.M. An aide delivered the news to a dazed Lyndon Johnson, addressing him as "Mr. President."

As the news spread by radio and TV bulletins, the country came to a halt in stunned disbelief. By the time Air Force One arrived in Washington, thousands of people had gathered in the streets. They stood in near silence, except for the sounds of weeping. America was shattered. Millions remained glued to their televisions for days as the impact of the tragedy sank in.

The prime suspect in Kennedy's murder was Lee Harvey Oswald, a former marine and supporter of Cuban leader Fidel Castro. He was apprehended within an hour of the President's death, but revealed little information to the police.

Two days after Kennedy's assassination, the TV cameras rolled as Oswald was being transferred from one jail to another. As the nation watched, a Dallas nightclub owner, Jack Ruby, stepped through the crowd of reporters and fatally shot Oswald.

On his third birthday, November 25, 1963, John F. Kennedy, Jr., salutes as his father's casket passes by in the funeral procession for President Kennedy. Other family members, from left, are JFK's brother Edward M. Kennedy; the late President's daughter, Caroline, almost age 6; his wife, Jacqueline Kennedy; and his brother Robert F. Kennedy.

On November 29, President Johnson appointed The President's Commission on the Assassination of President John F. Kennedy. It was better known as the **Warren Commission,** after its chairman, Supreme Court Chief Justice Earl Warren. After months of investigation, the Warren Commission determined that Oswald had acted alone in shooting the President. Neither Oswald, Jack Ruby, nor any other American or foreigner was involved in a conspiracy to commit the crime, the commission concluded.

Since then, the case has been explored in millions of pages of books, magazine and newspaper accounts, and formal and informal reports. It continues to be the topic of reenactments and television documentaries. Some investigations support the theory that Oswald was involved in a larger conspiracy, and that he was killed in order to protect others who had helped plan Kennedy's murder. The whole story probably will never be known.

Section 1 Assessment

READING COMPREHENSION

1. Explain the role of television in the 1960 presidential election, and describe the election outcome.
2. How did lack of a **mandate** affect Kennedy's administration?
3. Describe some of the successes and failures of Kennedy's **New Frontier.**
4. What were the conclusions of the **Warren Commission?**

CRITICAL THINKING AND WRITING

5. **Making Comparisons** Compare the advantages and disadvantages that Richard Nixon had going into the 1960 debates with John F. Kennedy.
6. **Writing a Conclusion** Why do you think the goal of a moon landing was so important to Kennedy? What effects do you think the successful NASA mission had on the country?

Take It to the NET

Activity: Virtual Field Trip Visit the John F. Kennedy Memorial and Library to learn more about JFK's life and work. Use the links provided in the *America: Pathways to the Present* area of the following Web site for help in completing this activity.
www.phschool.com

Section 1 Assessment

Reading Comprehension

1. It marked the beginning of television as a major influence on political campaigns. TV viewers thought Kennedy won the first debate; radio listeners felt the victory belonged to Nixon. Ultimately, Kennedy did win the election, but by a narrow margin.
2. Without a mandate, Kennedy had difficulty pushing his more controversial measures through Congress.
3. Successes: the space program, passage of the Twenty-fourth Amendment, Housing Act of 1961. Failures: the stock market decline, inability to push through education, medical care, or tax-cutting plans.
4. It determined that Oswald had acted alone in shooting the President and ruled out any conspiracy theories.

Critical Thinking and Writing

5. Disadvantages: Nixon felt and looked exhausted due to vigorous campaigning and his recent hospitalization for a knee injury. Nixon was not telegenic, which proved to be a disadvantage in televised debates. John F. Kennedy was well-rested and telegenic. Advantages: Nixon was mentally prepared. In addition, he had a great deal of campaign experience. As a Vice President and former Senator and Congressman, Nixon had considerable experience in high public office.
6. To remain technologically competitive with the Soviet Union, and to determine how space would be used in the times ahead. It renewed Americans' pioneer spirit and gave them a sense of security in this accomplishment.

Take It to the NET

Invite students to take a Virtual Field Trip at **www.phschool.com**

Exploring Oral History

Focus Students will analyze the content of oral history excerpts.

Instruct Ask student groups to consider the following: Twenty Americans have been selected to answer questions about the presidency of John Kennedy. Ask each group to write questions about the 20 citizens that might provide useful information when historians try to evaluate their testimony. (Questions might include age, level of political activity, level of education).

Extend See the Skills for Life activity in the Resource Directory below.

ANSWERS

Practice the Skill

1. **(a)** John Lewis, Atlanta city council member and civil rights leader. **(b)** In 1983, 20 years after the event. **(c)** He loved and admired President Kennedy because of his concern for civil rights. **(d)** No. Lewis's admiration has not lessened over time.
2. **(a)** Lewis heard the news of the assassination on the radio. But his organization had worked closely with Kennedy on racial issues, and Lewis felt he knew the President. **(b)** As a civil rights leader who saw Kennedy as supportive, Lewis probably viewed the event as especially tragic. **(c)** The civil rights legislation passed after Kennedy's death probably made Lewis view Kennedy as a man who played a pivotal role in progress. **(d)** That he favored government intervention on domestic issues such as civil rights, and that he believed government should be accessible to the people.
3. **(a)** That it gave people a feeling of hope about issues such as civil rights. **(b)** That although Kennedy's administration may not have made big changes in the laws, they did begin to change attitudes and made minorities feel hopeful and that they had a friend in the White House.

Exploring Oral History

Oral history is made up of people's verbal accounts and recollections of former times and events. Historians collect oral history through interviews, which may take place at the time of an event or at some later date, perhaps even decades later. These interviews are primary sources that record not only facts about the past, but also people's opinions, feelings, and impressions—all important for putting together a picture of the past.

The excerpt below is from an interview with John Lewis on the twentieth anniversary of President Kennedy's death. In 1963, Lewis was chairperson of the Student Nonviolent Coordinating Committee and one of the leaders of the civil rights March on Washington.

LEARN THE SKILL

Use the following steps to analyze an oral history:

1. **Identify the nature of the oral account.** Determine who was interviewed, that person's relationship to the event, and any factors that might have influenced the person's recollection of the event.
2. **Determine the reliability of the evidence.** Consider whether the person was in a position to observe events first-hand, or to judge events impartially. Also consider the length of time between the event and the interview.
3. **Study the evidence to learn more about the historical event.** Note any new facts you learn from the interview, as well as new insights into people's attitudes at the time of the event.

PRACTICE THE SKILL

Answer the following questions:

1. **(a)** Who was interviewed? **(b)** When did the interview take place? **(c)** What was Lewis's attitude toward Kennedy at the time of his death? Why? **(d)** Did that attitude change in any way over time?
2. **(a)** What was Lewis's relationship to the event he is describing? **(b)** How might Lewis's role in the civil rights movement have affected his interpretation of the event? **(c)** How might events after Kennedy's death have affected the account? **(d)** What do Lewis's views reveal about his political perspective?
3. **(a)** What impact does Lewis think Kennedy's presidency had on government policy and the nation? **(b)** What can you learn about Kennedy's presidency from Lewis's account?

An Interview with John Lewis: Remembering President Kennedy's Assassination

"I was living in Atlanta then, but I had gone back to Nashville for a trial. I was getting into a car to go to the Nashville airport when I heard it on the radio. And to me, it was the saddest moment in my life. I had grown up to love and to admire President Kennedy. I remember crying on the plane.

I saw him as a sort of guy that listened. Sincere. Caring. People argue and say that he didn't really do anything. But he did listen, and during that period from 1961 to 1963, I'll tell you, I think probably for the first time in modern American history, we felt, 'Well, we have a friend in the White House.' On some things we disagreed. We'd call them up and argue and debate with them on some issue, and we said a lot of different things, and sometimes it was harsh. But we saw the Kennedy administration during that period as a sympathetic referee in the whole struggle for civil rights.

His campaign had created a sense of hope, a sense of optimism for many of us. When someone asked him about the civil rights sit-ins that year, he said, 'By sitting down, these young people are standing up for the very best in American tradition.'"

—*Newsweek*, November 28, 1983

APPLY THE SKILL

See the Chapter Review and Assessment for another opportunity to apply this skill.

RESOURCE DIRECTORY

Teaching Resources
Skills for Life booklet, p. 31

Technology
Social Studies Skills Tutor CD-ROM
Interactive Practice in
- Geographic Literacy
- Critical Thinking and Reading
- Visual Analysis
- Communications

Section 2

The Great Society

READING FOCUS

- What was Lyndon Johnson's path to the presidency?
- What were some of the goals and programs of the Great Society?
- What were some of the cases that made the Warren Court both important and controversial?

MAIN IDEA

President Johnson's Great Society programs aimed to improve America's economy and provide substantial government aid to its citizens, especially the poor.

KEY TERMS

Great Society
Head Start
Volunteers in Service to America (VISTA)
Medicare
Medicaid
Immigration Act of 1965
Miranda rule
apportionment

TAKING NOTES

Copy the web diagram below. As you read, fill in details relating to President Johnson's Great Society programs.

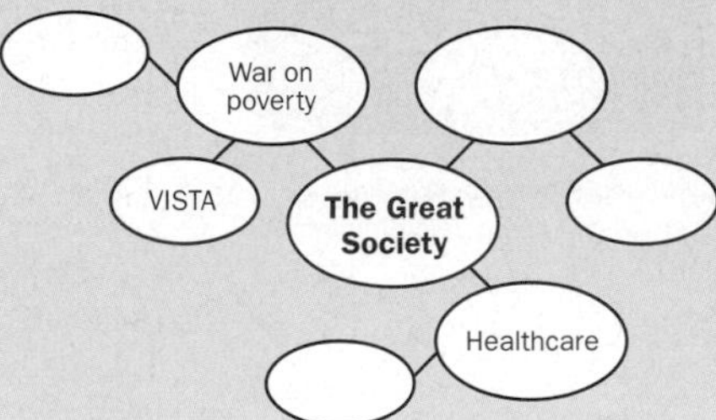

Setting the Scene At 2:35 P.M. on November 22, 1963, about 90 minutes after John F. Kennedy was pronounced dead, Lyndon Baines Johnson stood inside Air Force One on an airstrip at Dallas's Love Field. He was flanked by his wife, Lady Bird, and by Jacqueline Kennedy, who was bearing up with "amazing strength and calm," according to an account by the *Houston Chronicle*. According to the Constitution, LBJ had *immediately* become the thirty-sixth President from the moment of Kennedy's death. Johnson, however, insisted on taking the oath of office before leaving Dallas.

Federal District Judge Sarah T. Hughes was rushed to the airport to administer the oath. "The President and Mrs. Johnson were very serious and very calm," Judge Hughes told the *Chronicle* afterward. "He thanked us and told us he would rely on God's help."

Two minutes later, Air Force One took off for the capital, bearing Kennedy's body. Lady Bird Johnson, the new First Lady, began her White House diary that day.

"Friday, November 22, 1963 DALLAS

"It all began so beautifully. . . ."

A sad and solemn Lyndon Johnson is sworn in as President aboard Air Force One shortly after President Kennedy's assassination. On Johnson's right is his wife, Lady Bird, and on his left is Kennedy's grief-stricken widow, Jacqueline.

LBJ's Path to the White House

The grief of a nation, and the responsibility for healing it, hung heavily upon the new President. Johnson began the recovery process in a speech to Congress:

> *"All I have I would have given gladly not to be standing here today. . . . No words are sad enough to express our sense of loss. No words are strong enough to express our determination to continue the forward thrust of America that [Kennedy] began. . . . [T]he ideas and the ideals which he so nobly represented must and will be translated into effective action."*
>
> —Lyndon Johnson, address to a joint session of Congress, November 27, 1963

Section 2
The Great Society

SECTION OBJECTIVES

1. Discover Lyndon Johnson's path to the presidency.
2. Find out about some of the goals and programs of the Great Society.
3. Learn about some of the cases that made the Warren Court both important and controversial.

BELLRINGER

Warm-Up Activity Ask students what they think is great about American society. Was it as great in Johnson's time? What differences are evident?

Activating Prior Knowledge Ask students if they can name some Great Society initiatives that are still part of the federal government today. *(Head Start, Medicare and Medicaid, the Department of Housing and Urban Development)*

READING STRATEGY

As students read, ask them to create a chart describing the key elements of Johnson's Great Society program. Have them identify ways in which actions made by the government in introducing the Great Society program expanded economic opportunities for all citizens.

ACTIVITY

Connecting with Today

Have students ask appropriate older adults to share their recollections of the day Kennedy was assassinated and Lyndon Johnson became the thirty-sixth President of the United States. Have students share what they learn with the class. **(Verbal/Linguistic)**

RESOURCE DIRECTORY

Teaching Resources
Guided Reading and Review booklet, p. 118

Technology
Section Reading Support Transparencies
Guided Reading Audiotapes (English/Spanish), Ch. 22
Student Edition on Audio CD, Ch. 22
Sounds of an Era Audio CD *"The Times They Are A-Changing," Bob Dylan* (time: almost two minutes)
Prentice Hall Presentation Pro CD-ROM, Ch. 22
Companion Web site, www.phschool.com

Johnson's nose-to-nose form of persuasion could be intimidating.

Although he came to the Oval Office through tragedy, Johnson found himself in a job he had long sought. LBJ's road to the presidency was laid carefully and cunningly, through years of skillful political maneuvering and strong leadership.

Lyndon Johnson arrived in the United States House of Representatives in 1937 as a New Deal Democrat from Texas. In 1948, he won a seat in the Senate, but only by a tiny margin of 87 votes. He was jokingly dubbed "Landslide Lyndon"—a nickname that stuck for the rest of his career.

In the Senate, Johnson demonstrated both political talent and an unstoppable ambition. In 1953, he became the youngest Senator ever to be elected Minority Leader. When the Democrats won control of the Senate the following year, LBJ became Majority Leader. In this powerful post he became famous for his ability to use the political system to accomplish his goals. He controlled the legislative agenda and the votes to get bills passed by rewarding his friends and punishing his enemies. Johnson inspired fear and awe among his colleagues.

He was "not a likeable man," former Secretary of State Dean Acheson once told him. But Johnson was more concerned with accomplishment than popularity, and his single-minded intensity enabled him to get his way. Other senators marveled at the "Johnson treatment," in which he carefully researched a bill, and then approached in a hallway or office the legislator whose vote he needed. If he thought it was the best way to persuade the legislator, he would attack, "his face a scant millimeter from his target, his eyes widening and narrowing, his eyebrows rising and falling," according to columnists Rowland Evans, Jr.,

NOTABLE PRESIDENTS
Lyndon Baines Johnson

"In a land of great wealth, families must not live in hopeless poverty."

—Inaugural Address, January 20, 1965

Lyndon Johnson rose to the presidency under the worst of circumstances—the assassination of President John F. Kennedy—and governed during one of the nation's most divisive periods. President Johnson waged war on poverty in America. But another war, half a world away, drained funds from his ambitious domestic agenda.

Born to a financially struggling political family in Texas, Johnson became a school teacher during the 1920s, witnessing the harsh poverty of his students, mostly Mexican Americans. His concerns led him into politics. Johnson served for nearly 12 years in the House as a New Deal Democrat. In 1948, he won election to the Senate. Shrewd and determined, LBJ fought his way up to become, at age 46, the youngest-ever Senate Majority Leader.

In the 1960 Democratic primaries, Johnson had to settle for the No. 2 spot on Kennedy's ticket. As Vice President, Johnson was restless and powerless. But power came all too soon, when Kennedy's death launched him into the Oval Office.

36th President 1963–1969

LBJ moved quickly to pursue his Great Society programs, designed to lift Americans out of poverty and promote equal rights. But Johnson had inherited a problem: the escalating war against communism in Vietnam. The conflict was political and military quicksand.

In the 1968 primaries, facing low public support and a growing challenge from Robert F. Kennedy, a war-weary LBJ withdrew his candidacy. At the end of his term, he retired to his beloved Texas ranch with his wife, Claudia "Lady Bird" Johnson.

Connecting to Today

Have crises overseas had a strong effect on any recent presidencies? Why or why not?

Take It to the NET Biography To read more about Lyndon Johnson, visit the links provided in the *America: Pathways to the Present* area of the following Web site. **www.phschool.com**

LESSON PLAN

Focus After taking office following Kennedy's assassination, Lyndon Johnson moved many reform bills through Congress as part of his goal of achieving a "Great Society." Ask what Johnson's most important reform bills were. Why did some Americans criticize Johnson's program?

Instruct Discuss why LBJ was able to succeed where Kennedy had failed. Remind students that Congress, as well as LBJ, wanted to pass legislation proposed by the slain President as a memorial and as a way of reassuring the country. Ask to what extent LBJ's political experience helped him move legislation through Congress.

Ask students to describe the impact of Chief Justice Earl Warren on the Supreme Court. What were some landmark cases handed down by the Court under Warren?

Assess/Reteach When Johnson assumed the Presidency, the nation was in mourning. He demonstrated his leadership capabilities by moving ahead with an aggressive domestic program. Ask students to discuss the impact of Johnson's programs on American life, both in his time and today.

RESOURCE DIRECTORY

Teaching Resources

Learning with Documents booklet (Primary Source Activity) *President Johnson's Thanksgiving Address,* p. 34

Technology

Color Transparencies *Political Cartoon,* B17

Sounds of an Era Audio CD *"Great Society Speech,"* 1964 recording (time: 40 seconds)

and Robert Novak. Johnson might grab his victim by the lapels or by the shoulders, flattering, cajoling, and shouting in turn. Nearly without fail, he got the vote he wanted.

When Johnson's bid for the Democratic nomination failed in 1960, he accepted Kennedy's invitation to run for the vice presidency. Once elected, however, Johnson was frustrated with the job, which lacked any real power. He was also unhappy being away from Congress, where he had been so effective.

Yet Johnson was not powerless for long. While it had been a long journey to the vice presidency, it was a tragically short trip to the Oval Office in 1963.

Sounds of an Era

Listen to Lyndon Johnson's Great Society speech and other sounds from the Kennedy-Johnson era.

The Great Society

Johnson was aware that the American people needed some action that would help heal the wound caused by the loss of their President. To that end, he used all the talents he had developed as Senate Majority Leader to push through Congress an extraordinary program of reforms on domestic issues.

Johnson's agenda included Kennedy's civil rights and tax-cut bills. It also embraced laws to aid public education, provide medical care for the elderly, and eliminate poverty. By the spring of 1964, he had begun to use the phrase *Great Society* to describe his goals. In a speech that year he told students:

> *"Your imagination, your initiative, and your indignation will determine whether we build a society where progress is the servant of our needs, or a society where old values and new visions are buried under unbridled [unrestrained] growth. For in your time we have the opportunity to move not only toward the rich society and the powerful society, but upward toward the Great Society."*
>
> —Lyndon Johnson, speech at the University of Michigan, May 1964

Johnson's **Great Society** was a series of major legislative initiatives that continued into his second term. The Great Society programs included major poverty relief, education aid, healthcare, voting rights, conservation and beautification projects, urban renewal, and economic development in depressed areas.

The Election of 1964 Johnson's early successes paved the way for his landslide victory over Republican Barry Goldwater in the election of 1964. Goldwater, a senator from Arizona, held conservative views that seemed excessive to many Americans, as well as to many members of his own party.

For example, he opposed civil rights legislation, and he believed that military commanders should be allowed to use nuclear weapons as they saw fit on the battlefield. The Johnson campaign took advantage of voters' fears of nuclear war. It aired a controversial television commercial in which a little girl's innocent counting game turned into the countdown for a nuclear explosion.

Johnson received 61 percent of the popular vote and an overwhelming 486 to 52 tally in the electoral college. The Democrats won majorities in both houses of Congress: 295 Democrats to 140 Republicans in the House of Representatives and 68 to 32 in the Senate. "Landslide Lyndon" now had the mandate to move ahead even more aggressively.

Focus on GOVERNMENT

The "Daisy" Campaign Commercial

It aired only once, on September 7, 1964. Yet the Johnson campaign's chilling, black-and-white "daisy" commercial became one of the most famous in history. The camera zeroes in on a little girl holding a daisy. She counts the petals as she pulls them off: "One, two, three, four . . ." At "nine," a man's voice begins counting down to zero: ". . . three, two, one . . ." The image of the girl fades to the mushroom cloud of a nuclear blast.

The ad made no mention of Johnson's opponent, Barry Goldwater, but its message was clear: America in the hands of Goldwater risked nuclear war. Republicans cried foul. "This horror-type commercial is designed to arouse basic emotions and has no place in the campaign," the head of the Republican National Committee complained.

The protest backfired. Although the ad was pulled, the controversy caused TV news shows to play it over and over. The little girl with the daisy appeared on the cover of *Time* magazine.

ACTIVITY
Connecting with Citizenship

Share with students Johnson's description of the Great Society in the Background note below. Lead a class discussion in which students, using Johnson's description as a springboard, identify the qualities that any "great society" would have. Record and organize responses on the board. **(Verbal/Linguistic)**

BACKGROUND
Interdisciplinary

In the speech described on this page, Johnson went on to describe the "Great Society." He said the "Great Society rests on abundance and liberty for all. It demands an end to poverty and racial injustice. . . . The Great Society is a place where every child can find knowledge to enrich his mind and to enlarge his talents. It is a place where leisure is a welcome chance to build and reflect. . . . It is a place where man can renew contact with nature. . . . But most of all, the Great Society is not a safe harbor, a resting place, a final objective, a finished work. It is a challenge constantly renewed, beckoning us toward a destiny where the meaning of our lives matches the marvelous products of our labor. . . ."

TEST PREPARATION

Have students read Johnson's quotation on this page and then answer the question below.

What does Johnson mean when he speaks of the "rich" society, the "powerful" society, and the "Great" society?

A He envisions a society where no one will be either rich or poor.

(B) He sees a society that treats all its citizens with decency and respect.

C He does not think it matters if individual citizens are wealthy.

D He does not think it matters if the United States is powerful.

The Tax Cut Like Kennedy, Johnson believed that a budget deficit could be used to improve the economy. Not everyone agreed. To gain conservatives' support for Kennedy's tax-cut bill, which was likely to bring about a deficit, Johnson also agreed to cut government spending. With that agreement, the measure passed and worked just as planned. When the tax cut went into effect, the Gross National Product (GNP) rose by 7.1 percent in 1964, by 8.1 percent in 1965, and by 9.5 percent in 1966. The deficit, which many people feared would grow, actually shrank because the renewed prosperity generated new tax revenues. Unemployment fell, and inflation remained in check.

The War on Poverty Growing up in an impoverished area of rural Texas, Johnson had experienced the pain of poverty firsthand. He now pressed for the antipoverty program that Kennedy had begun to consider.

In his 1964 State of the Union message, Johnson vowed, "This administration today, here and now, declares unconditional war on poverty in America." The Economic Opportunity Act, passed in the summer of 1964, was created to combat several causes of poverty, including illiteracy, unemployment, and inadequate public services. The act provided nearly $950 million for 10 separate projects, including work training programs. The act also gave poor people a voice in defining housing, health, and education policies in their own neighborhoods.

Two of the best-known programs created under the act were Head Start and VISTA. **Head Start** is a preschool program for children from low-income families that also provides healthcare, nutrition services, and social services. **Volunteers in Service to America (VISTA)** sent volunteers to help people in poor communities. Under Presidents Bush and Clinton, VISTA was merged with other national service programs.

INTERPRETING GRAPHS
The cartoon above depicts Johnson playing Congress like a piano, with Great Society programs flowing forth like music. One of those programs, the Elementary and Secondary Education Act, was passed by Congress in 1965. **Analyzing Visual Information** *How does the graph illustrate the overall effect of this legislation?*

Aid to Education Johnson's education initiatives moved through Congress as well. The Elementary and Secondary Education Act of 1965 provided $1.3 billion in aid to states, based on the number of children in each state from low-income homes. The funds went to public and private schools, including parochial schools. Johnson signed the Education Act into law in the small Texas school he had attended as a child. The graph at left shows federal aid to schools from 1959 to 1972.

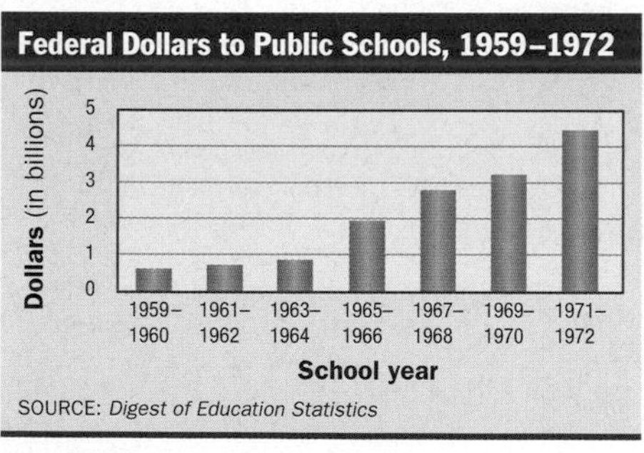

Medicare and Medicaid President Johnson also focused attention on the increasing cost of medical care. Harry Truman had proposed a medical assistance plan as part of his Fair Deal program, but it had never been passed into law. In 1965, Johnson used his leadership skills to push through Congress two new programs, Medicare and Medicaid.

Medicare provides hospital and low-cost medical insurance to most Americans age 65 and older. "No longer will older Americans be denied the healing miracle of modern medicine," Johnson declared. "No longer will illness crush and destroy the savings that they have so carefully put away." **Medicaid** provides low-cost health insurance coverage to poor Americans of any age who cannot afford their own private health insurance.

ACTIVITY
Connecting with Government

Have students select one of the agencies or programs established by one of the pieces of Great Society legislation and report on its fate today. Does it still exist? What activities does it engage in? Have students visit federal government Web sites to conduct their research and provide oral or written reports of what they learn. **(Verbal/Linguistic)**

BACKGROUND
A Diverse Nation

The war on poverty is continuing today. The focal point of poverty, however, is not predominantly among African Americans in the North and in urban areas, as popular perception might have it. The 2000 census data shows that poor whites (22 million) outnumber poor African Americans (14.9 million).

CAPTION ANSWERS

Interpreting Graphs It shows that the 1965 law significantly increased federal funding for public schools.

RESOURCE DIRECTORY
Technology

RESOURCE PRO® **Visual Learning Activity** *The Job Corps,* found on Resource Pro, uses a photograph from a Job Corps training course to illustrate how job training was considered a major weapon in Johnson's war on poverty.

RESOURCE PRO® **Critical Thinking Activity** *Recognizing Cause and Effect,* found on Resource Pro, helps students apply this skill with a graph showing trends in poverty and the economy from 1948 to 1987.

Great Society Legislation, 1964–1966	
Legislation	**Purpose**
Economic Opportunity Act, 1964	Created to combat causes of poverty such as illiteracy. Set up community action programs to give the poor a voice in defining local housing, health, and education policies.
Volunteers in Service to America (VISTA), 1964	Sent volunteers to help people in poor communities.
Medicare, 1965	Provided hospital and low-cost medical insurance for most Americans age 65 and older.
Medicaid, 1965	Provided low-cost health insurance for poor Americans of any age who could not afford their own private health insurance.
Elementary and Secondary Education Act of 1965	Provided education aid to states based on the number of children from low-income homes.
Immigration Act of 1965	Eliminated strict quotas for individual countries and replaced them with more flexible limits.
The Department of Housing and Urban Development (HUD), 1965	Established to oversee the nation's housing needs and to develop and rehabilitate urban communities. HUD also provided money for rent supplements and low-income housing.
The National Foundations of the Arts and Humanities, 1965	Offered grants to artists and scholars.
Water Quality Act, 1965; Clean Water Restoration Act, 1966	Brought about water and air quality standards and provided funding for environmental research.
The National Traffic and Motor Vehicle Safety Act, 1966	Established safety standards for all vehicles to protect consumers.

INTERPRETING CHARTS As this chart shows, Great Society legislation addressed a wide range of topics. **Synthesizing Information** *Which pieces of legislation attempted to combat poverty?*

These broad-based healthcare programs were the most important pieces of social welfare legislation since the passage of the Social Security Act in 1935. They demonstrated the government's commitment to provide help to needy Americans.

Immigration Reform The Great Society also revised the immigration policies that had been in place since the 1920s. Laws passed in 1921 and 1924 had set quotas, or numerical limits, for newcomers from each foreign nation. Low quotas—based on the 1890 census, before the arrival of new waves of immigrants—had been established for countries from southern and eastern Europe.

The **Immigration Act of 1965** replaced the varying quotas with a limit of 20,000 immigrants per year from any one country outside the Western Hemisphere. In addition, the act set overall limits of 170,000 immigrants from the Eastern Hemisphere and 120,000 from the Western Hemisphere. Family members of United States citizens were exempted from the quotas, as were political refugees. In the 1960s, some 350,000 immigrants entered the United States each year; in the 1970s, the number rose to more than 400,000 a year.

READING CHECK
Under President Johnson, how did the role of the federal government change?

The Warren Court

The Kennedy-Johnson years featured many of the landmark decisions of the famous, and controversial, Warren Court. As it had in earlier civil rights cases,

ACTIVITY

Connecting with Culture

Ask students to draw a political cartoon illustrating either a criticism of Johnson's Great Society legislation or a response to LBJ's critics. In the latter case, have students reflect on LBJ's contributions as President of the United States. **(Visual/Spatial)**

BACKGROUND

Biography

In 1965 lawyer Marian Wright Edelman (b. 1939) became the first African American woman admitted to the Mississippi bar. Edelman is the founder and president of the Children's Defense Fund, an advocacy group that promotes the health and welfare of children. Edelman summarizes the Fund's philosophy as follows: "Children cannot eat rhetoric and they cannot be sheltered by commissions. I don't want to see another commission that studies the needs of kids. We need to help them."

READING CHECK
It became more activist. The primary focus of Johnson's Great Society program was to vastly increase to government's role in tackling social problems.

CAPTION ANSWERS

Interpreting Charts The Economic Opportunity Act, VISTA, Medicare, Medicaid, Elementary and Secondary Education Act, and HUD.

ACTIVITY
Student Portfolio

You may wish to have students add the following to their portfolios: Three Supreme Court cases, *Gideon* v. *Wainright, Escobelo* v. *Illinois,* and *Miranda* v. *Arizona,* dealt with the rights of individuals accused of crimes. Have students analyze the effects of these landmark cases. Next, ask students to work in groups to write dialogue for a drama in which police officers, suspects, and lawyers discuss these cases and refer to instances in which individual rights may have been violated. **(Verbal/Linguistic)**

BACKGROUND
Recent Scholarship

Lyndon Johnson's presidency has faced substantial criticism from historians. In *Flawed Giant: Lyndon Johnson and His Times, 1961–1973,* Robert Dallek provides a more balanced account of LBJ's presidential years. Dallek argues that by pushing too hard for political victory, Johnson promised more than he could deliver. But Dallek also suggests that while some Great Society measures have fallen into disrepute, the overall initiative made a difference in people's lives.

The members of the Warren Court, shown here on Nov. 22, 1965 are: (standing, left to right) Byron White, William Brennan, Potter Stewart, Abe Fortas; (seated, left to right) Tom Clark, Hugo Black, Earl Warren, William Douglas, and John Marshall Harlan.

the Supreme Court under Chief Justice Earl Warren overturned many old laws and rulings and established new legal precedents.

Social Issues The Warren Court made the first attempt to define obscenity in the 1957 case *Roth* v. *United States,* ruling that obscene materials were "utterly without redeeming social importance." In an explosive 1962 case, the Court ruled that religious prayer in public schools was unconstitutional according to the First Amendment principle of separation of church and state *(Engel* v. *Vitale).* In 1965, the Court struck down a Connecticut law that prohibited the use of birth control *(Griswold* v. *Connecticut).*

VIEWING HISTORY The Warren Court issued rulings that angered many Americans, as this popular sign below shows. **Recognizing Ideologies** *What beliefs might have caused critics to oppose some of these rulings?*

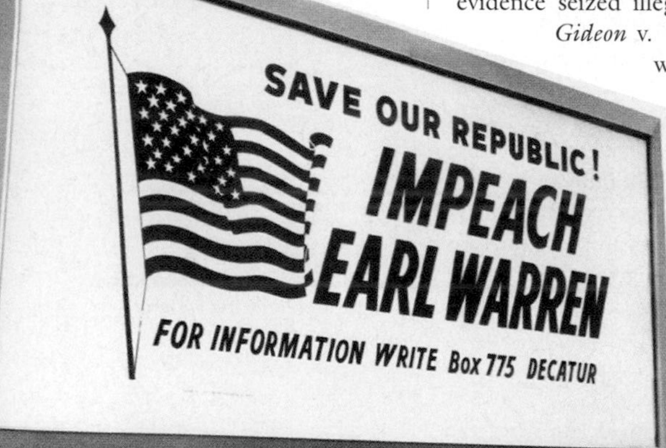
SAVE OUR REPUBLIC!
IMPEACH
EARL WARREN
FOR INFORMATION WRITE Box 775 DECATUR

Criminal Procedure The Warren Court was concerned with safeguarding the constitutional rights of the individual against the power of the government. In particular, the Court handed down several decisions protecting the rights of persons accused of crimes.

Mapp v. *Ohio* (1961) established the exclusionary rule, which states that evidence seized illegally cannot be used in a trial. The Court's decision in *Gideon* v. *Wainwright* (1963) stated that suspects in criminal cases who could not afford a lawyer had the right to free legal aid. In *Escobedo* v. *Illinois* (1964), the justices ruled that accused individuals had to be given access to an attorney while being questioned.

The Court's decision in *Miranda* v. *Arizona* (1966) stated that a suspect must be warned of his or her rights before being questioned. As a result of this **Miranda rule,** police must inform accused persons that they have the right to remain silent; that anything they say can be used against them in court; that they have a right to an attorney; and that if they cannot afford an attorney, one will be appointed for them.

"One Person, One Vote" The Warren Court also handed down a series of decisions on **apportionment,**

CAPTION ANSWERS

Viewing History Students' answers should note that most criticism of the Warren Court pertained to the fact that many people thought the Supreme Court under Earl Warren was too liberal.

RESOURCE DIRECTORY

Teaching Resources

Learning with Documents booklet (Key Documents) *Lyndon B. Johnson, The Great Society,* p. 94

Other Print Resources

American History Block Scheduling Support *Presidential Power: Changes in the Twentieth Century,* found in The Nation After World War II folder, includes interdisciplinary lesson suggestions and activities for Geography and History, Primary Sources, Biography, and Literature.

or the distribution of the seats in a legislature among electoral districts. Over the years, many Americans had moved from rural to urban areas, but most state governments had not reapportioned their electoral districts to reflect that fact. As a result, in many states, rural areas had more power in state legislatures—and urban areas had less power—than their populations should have given them.

The Warren Court's decision in the case of *Baker* v. *Carr* (1962) declared that state legislative districts had to be divided on the basis of "one person, one vote." In other words, each person's vote should carry the same weight, regardless of where in the state the person lived. This decision prevented the party in power from drawing district lines in unfair ways to give itself more potential votes. In *Reynolds* v. *Sims* (1964), the Supreme Court held that state legislative districts not based on the "one person, one vote" formula violated the equal protection clause of the Fourteenth Amendment.

Many of these decisions were, and remain, controversial. Some people argued that the justices had gone too far in their "loose construction" of the Constitution. A number of Warren Court rulings are under vigorous attack from conservatives today.

American Biography

Earl Warren
1891–1974

One of the most important chief justices in history, Earl Warren led a Supreme Court that brought sweeping changes to American law and society. His decisions delighted liberals but surprised and angered many in his own Republican Party.

Earl Warren earned his law degree at the University of California at Berkeley. From 1925 to 1953, he won various posts in California: Alameda County district attorney, state attorney general, and finally governor. Warren's only election defeat was as Thomas E. Dewey's vice presidential running mate in 1948. In 1953, President Eisenhower appointed him the fourteenth Chief Justice of the United States—a choice Ike would later regret. Warren served as Chief Justice until he retired in 1969.

Effects of the Great Society

At first, the Great Society seemed enormously successful. Opinion polls taken in 1964 showed Johnson to be more popular than Kennedy had been at a comparable point in his presidency.

In time, however, criticisms began to surface. New programs raised expectations that often could not be met. From 1965 through 1968, bloody race riots erupted in poor areas of major cities, giving urgency to Johnson's plans for Great Society programs. But military spending on Vietnam took ever-bigger bites out of the federal budget.

COMPARING HISTORIANS' VIEWPOINTS
The Great Society

Historians disagree about the effectiveness of President Johnson's Great Society programs.

Analyzing Viewpoints Compare the main arguments made by the two writers.

In Support of the Great Society

"In 1965 and early 1966 . . . the President and his economic advisors gratefully accepted the fiscal dividends provided by the booming economy as a means of bringing the Great Society closer to reality. Prosperity helped in two vital ways: by creating new jobs and by generating additional federal income that could be used to fund new social programs. Congress, which frequently approves new federal activities but then starves them to death by providing little or no money for their operation, funded the programs it authorized during 1965 and 1966 quite generously."

—*Jim F. Heath,*
The Decade of Disillusionment:
The Kennedy-Johnson Years

In Opposition to the Great Society

"In fact the war on poverty was destined to be one of the great failures of twentieth-century liberalism. Most of its programs could be grouped under two strategies. One of these emphasized opening new opportunities for poor people. . . . The other strategy, recognizing that mere opportunity would not be enough for many of the poor, provided subsidies to increase their consumption of food, shelter, and medical care. . . . Taken together, the programs spawned by these two strategies did little to diminish inequality and therefore, by definition, failed measurably to reduce poverty."

—*Allen J. Matusow,*
The Unraveling of America:
A History of Liberalism in the 1960s

Activity
Connecting with History and Conflict

Assign student pairs or small groups the task of creating a table that identifies and describes the landmark decisions of the Warren Court. The students should write a brief introduction to or caption for their table, which should at least include the names, parties to, dates, and impact of each of the decisions. **(Verbal/Linguistic)**

Background
Connections to Today

An enduring legacy of LBJ's aid to education is Head Start—a program begun in 1965 to prepare economically disadvantaged preschoolers for school. Now administered by the Department of Health and Human Services, Head Start works through local communities to provide nutritious lunches, medical and family services, and educational preparation. Head Start receives bipartisan support in Congress and serves more than 11 million children, mostly under the age of five.

CUSTOMIZE FOR ...
Less Proficient Writers

Have students reread the section "Criminal Procedure." Then, have students list the four cases mentioned in the section and write a brief description of each case in their own words.

Section 2 Assessment

Reading Comprehension

1. He became a member of the House in 1937, won a seat in the Senate in 1948, and became Senate Majority Leader in 1954. When his bid for the Democratic nomination in 1960 failed, he became Kennedy's vice presidential candidate. Kennedy's assassination made him President.
2. Goals: to provide government assistance to the poor, to improve the economy, the education system, and the environment. Programs: Head Start, VISTA, The Elementary and Secondary Education Act of 1965, Medicare, Medicaid.
3. It replaced the varying quotas, with a limit of 20,000 immigrants per year from any one country outside the Western Hemisphere. It also set overall limits of 170,000 immigrants for the Eastern Hemisphere and 120,000 from the Western Hemisphere. Family members of U.S. citizens and political refugees were exempted from the quotas.
4. By requiring police to inform suspects of their rights, it safeguarded the rights of the accused.

Critical Thinking and Writing

5. Answers will vary, but views should be supported with facts from the section.
6. Some students may say that the courts took actions that tackled social problems and benefited society, while others may believe that the court overstepped its bounds—for example, in protecting the rights of the accused rather than the rights of the victim.

Fact sheets should cite the accomplishments of either Jacqueline Kennedy or Lady Bird Johnson as First Ladies.

Caption Answers

Viewing History Sample answer: He hoped that early education would improve student performance in later years. A more educated workforce could result in a healthier economy, lower crime rates, and greater prosperity for Americans.

VIEWING HISTORY A teacher instructs young students in the Head Start program. **Predicting Consequences** *What long-term effects do you think the Johnson administration hoped to achieve through the Head Start program?*

Meanwhile, some Americans complained that too many of their tax dollars were being spent on poor people. For decades following the Great Society, a major political debate continued over the criticism that antipoverty programs encouraged poor people to become dependent on government aid and created successive generations of families on welfare instead of in jobs. Other critics argued that Great Society programs put too much authority into the hands of the federal government. They opposed the expansion of the federal bureaucracy that accompanied the new programs.

Nevertheless, the number of Americans living in poverty in the United States was cut in half during the 1960s and early 1970s. Michael Harrington, author of *The Other America,* argued that the federal government should have allocated even more public funds to fight poverty. He noted, "What was supposed to be a social war turned out to be a skirmish and, in any case, poverty won."

In the midst of praise and criticism, Johnson himself was proud of his Great Society programs. In his view, they were "major accomplishments without equal or close parallel in the present era."

Before his death, John Kennedy had focused more on foreign affairs than domestic. When Johnson took office, he threw his energies into problems at home. The next section describes Kennedy's actions on the world stage and, after JFK's death, the beginnings of the conflict in Southeast Asia that would eventually consume the resources that Johnson had hoped to spend on domestic programs. LBJ's inability to contain that conflict undermined and finally ended the Great Society.

Section 2 Assessment

READING COMPREHENSION

1. Briefly outline LBJ's rise to the presidency.
2. List the key goals of the **Great Society** and some of the programs created to meet those goals.
3. Describe the changes made by the **Immigration Act of 1965.**
4. How did the **Miranda rule** change law enforcement in the United States?

CRITICAL THINKING AND WRITING

5. **Demonstrating Reasoned Judgment** Do you think Johnson's Great Society programs were a success? What questions would you ask yourself in order to make this judgment?
6. **Writing an Opinion** What positive or negative effects do you think the Warren Court has had on society today? Use examples to support your opinion.

Take It to the NET

Activity: Creating a Fact Sheet
Read about the lives and activities of either Jacqueline Kennedy or Lady Bird Johnson. Create a fact sheet that describes the contributions of these First Ladies to their husbands' presidencies and to the nation. Use the links provided in the *America: Pathways to the Present* area of the following Web site for help in completing this activity.
www.phschool.com

RESOURCE DIRECTORY

Teaching Resources

Units 5/6/7 booklet
- Section 2 Quiz, p. 65

Guide to the Essentials
- Section 2 Summary, p. 108

Technology

RESOURCE PRO® **Literature Activity** *The Invisible Poor,* found on Resource Pro, features an excerpt from Michael Harrington's bestseller *The Other America,* which inspired Kennedy and shocked middle-class Americans into supporting actions against poverty.

Section 3

Foreign Policy in the Early 1960s

READING FOCUS

- What were the goals of the Bay of Pigs invasion, and what was the outcome?
- What events led to the Berlin crisis and to the Cuban Missile Crisis?
- What were the goals of the Alliance for Progress and the Peace Corps?
- Which Cold War conflicts did Johnson become involved in?

KEY TERMS

Bay of Pigs invasion
Berlin Wall
Cuban Missile Crisis
Limited Test Ban Treaty
Alliance for Progress
Peace Corps

TAKING NOTES

Copy the chart below. As you read, fill in facts about the outcomes of Cold War crises under Kennedy and Johnson.

Cold War Crises Under Kennedy and Johnson	Outcomes
Bay of Pigs	Failed invasion; United States humiliated

MAIN IDEA

The Cold War intensified as President Kennedy and President Johnson became involved in anti-Communist conflicts in Latin America, Europe, and Southeast Asia.

Setting the Scene Although they would have liked to dedicate more of America's resources to improving conditions at home, both Kennedy and Johnson found themselves in the front lines of the Cold War. It was a dangerous and expensive battle, but, as Kennedy argued, it was one worth fighting:

> "*Let every nation know, whether it wishes us well or ill, that we shall pay any price, bear any burden, meet any hardship, support any friend, oppose any foe to assure the survival and the success of liberty.*"
>
> —John F. Kennedy, Inaugural Address, 1961

As President at the height of the Cold War between the Soviet Union and the United States, Kennedy spoke boldly. In the crises he faced as President, though, Kennedy found that he had to act more cautiously to prevent a local conflict from sparking a global war.

The Bay of Pigs Invasion

Kennedy's first foreign crisis arose in Cuba, an island about 90 miles off the Florida coast. The United States had been concerned about Cuba ever since 1959, when Fidel Castro overthrew the U.S.-backed dictator Fulgencio Batista. Some Cubans had supported Castro because he promised to improve the lives of poor people. Castro claimed that the poor were being exploited by wealthy Cubans and by United States companies operating in Cuba.

Once in power, the Castro government seized large, privately owned plantations and property owned by foreign corporations, including some U.S. businesses. The United States broke diplomatic relations with Cuba and refused to accept Castro as the country's legitimate leader. When Castro developed ties to the Soviet Union, American officials began to fear that Cuba could become a model for revolutionary upheaval throughout Latin America.

A Plan to Overthrow Castro After Kennedy became President, he was informed about a plan that President Eisenhower had approved in 1960. Under

Cuba's Fidel Castro (left) poses with his ally and supporter, Soviet leader Nikita Khrushchev, at a United Nations meeting.

Section 3

Foreign Policy in the Early 1960s

SECTION OBJECTIVES

1. Understand the goals and the outcome of the Bay of Pigs invasion.
2. Read to find out about events that led to the Berlin Crisis and the Cuban Missile Crisis.
3. Discover the goals of the Alliance for Progress and the Peace Corps.
4. Find out about Cold War conflicts in which Johnson became involved.

BELLRINGER

Warm-Up Activity Ask students to think about the way the United States pursues relationships with other countries. Ask them to list what they think should be the goals of our foreign policy.

Activating Prior Knowledge Ask students to discuss ways in which United States foreign policy changed after World War II. In particular, how did the worsening relationship between the Soviet Union and the United States impact decisions that were made in Washington?

READING STRATEGY

Before students read this section, have them write one question for each of the main headings. As they read, have them look for answers to those questions. Have them reflect on the impact of significant international decisions that took place during this era.

ACTIVITY

Connecting with History and Conflict

Have student groups research and prepare a brief (one page or less) biography of Fidel Castro's early life (before the revolution in Cuba). Have student groups compare their biographies and together compile a list of facts about Castro. **(Verbal/Linguistic)**

RESOURCE DIRECTORY

Teaching Resources

Learning Styles Lesson Plans booklet, p. 61
Guided Reading and Review booklet, p. 119
Learning with Documents booklet (Key Documents) *John F. Kennedy, Inaugural Address,* p. 93

Technology

Section Reading Support Transparencies
Guided Reading Audiotapes (English/Spanish), Ch. 22
Student Edition on Audio CD, Ch. 22
Prentice Hall Presentation Pro CD-ROM, Ch. 22
Companion Web site, www.phschool.com

Lesson Plan

Focus The foreign policies of Presidents Kennedy and Johnson were grounded in the Cold War. Ask how Kennedy reacted to Communist challenges. How did Johnson continue many of Kennedy's foreign policies?

Instruct Discuss the Bay of Pigs fiasco. Why was the United States concerned about Castro? Why did Kennedy agree to support the invasion? Have students make a time line of the Cuban Missile Crisis events on the chalkboard. Ask them to identify the most critical time period of the crisis.

Ask students to explain the underlying political goal of the Alliance for Progress and the Peace Corps. How successful were these programs?

Assess/Reteach In what ways has the end of the Cold War modified the relationship between the United States and the former Soviet Union? Ask students to discuss the changes in attitudes that have resulted from this altered situation.

READING CHECK

Fidel Castro had seized U.S. property and was on good terms with the Soviet Union. The United States did not recognize Castro's government. Kennedy was motivated to act because he believed that the Cuban example might trigger revolutionary upheavals in other Latin American nations.

READING CHECK

Why did President Kennedy want to overthrow Fidel Castro?

this plan, the Central Intelligence Agency (CIA) was training a group of Cubans to invade Cuba and overthrow Castro. The training took place in Guatemala, a nearby Central American country. Kennedy and his advisors expected the Cuban people to help the invaders defeat Castro.

Resistance to the plan soon surfaced, however. When Democratic Senator J. William Fulbright, head of the Foreign Relations Committee, learned of the scheme, he called it an "endless can of worms." He warned the President:

> *"To give this activity even covert [secret] support is of a piece with the hypocrisy and cynicism for which the United States is constantly denouncing [condemning] the Soviet Union in the United Nations and elsewhere. This point will not be lost on the rest of the world—nor on our own consciences. . . . The Castro regime is a thorn in the flesh; but it is not a dagger in the heart."*
>
> —Senator J. William Fulbright, memorandum to Kennedy, March 29, 1961

Despite such reservations and those of some military leaders, Kennedy accepted the advice of the CIA and agreed to push ahead with the invasion plan.

A Military Catastrophe The **Bay of Pigs invasion,** shown on the map below, took place on April 17, 1961. It was a total disaster. An airstrike failed to destroy Cuba's air force, and Cuban troops were more than a match for the 1,500 U.S.-backed invaders. When Kennedy's advisors urged him to use American planes to provide air cover for the attackers, he refused. Rather than continue a hopeless effort, he chose simply to accept defeat.

The United States lost a great deal of prestige in the disastrous attack. To begin with, the invasion was clumsy and incompetent. Furthermore, America's support of an effort to overthrow another nation's government was exposed to the world. The United States faced anger from other countries in Latin America for violating agreements not to interfere in the Western Hemisphere. European

MAP SKILLS This map traces the ill-fated Bay of Pigs invasion authorized by President Kennedy in 1961. The photo below shows a Cuban beachfront resort littered with artillery shells following the invasion. **Regions** *(a) How many countries played a role in the incident in some form? (b) How do you think this complexity affected the outcome of the operation?*

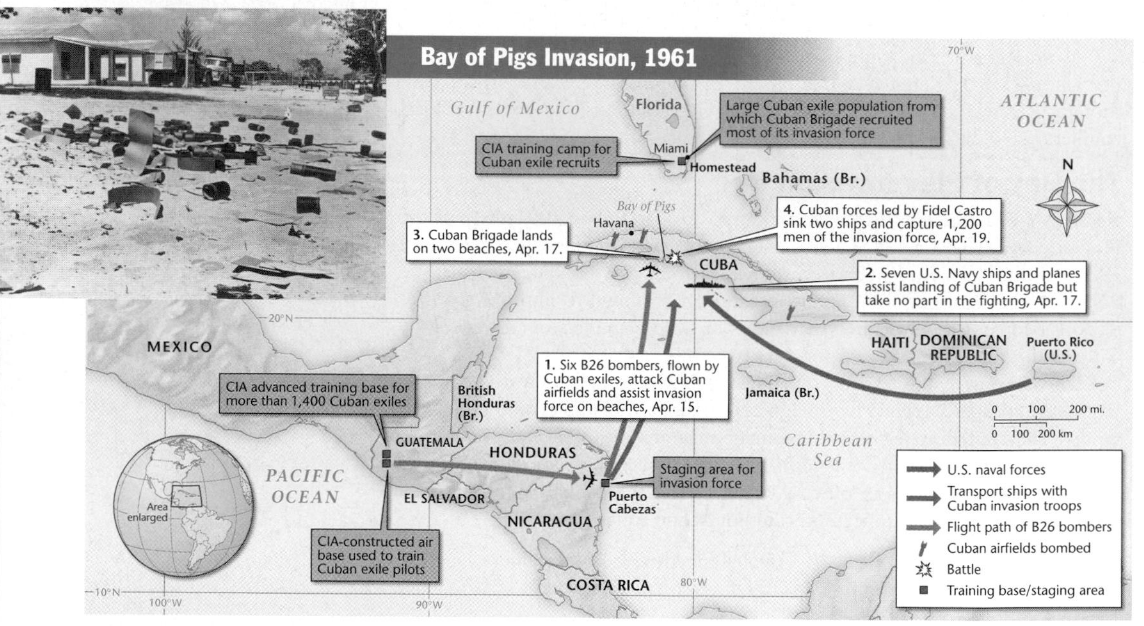

Caption Answers

Map Skills (a) Four (the United States, Cuba, Nicaragua, and Guatemala; the U.S. territory of Puerto Rico was involved as well). (b) Sample answer: It probably hampered the coordination of the operation, contributing to its failure.

RESOURCE DIRECTORY

Other Print Resources

American History Block Scheduling Support *The Berlin Wall: Past and Present,* found in The Nation After World War II folder, includes interdisciplinary lesson suggestions and activities for Geography and History, Primary Sources, Biography, and Literature.

Technology

Color Transparencies *Historical Maps,* A48

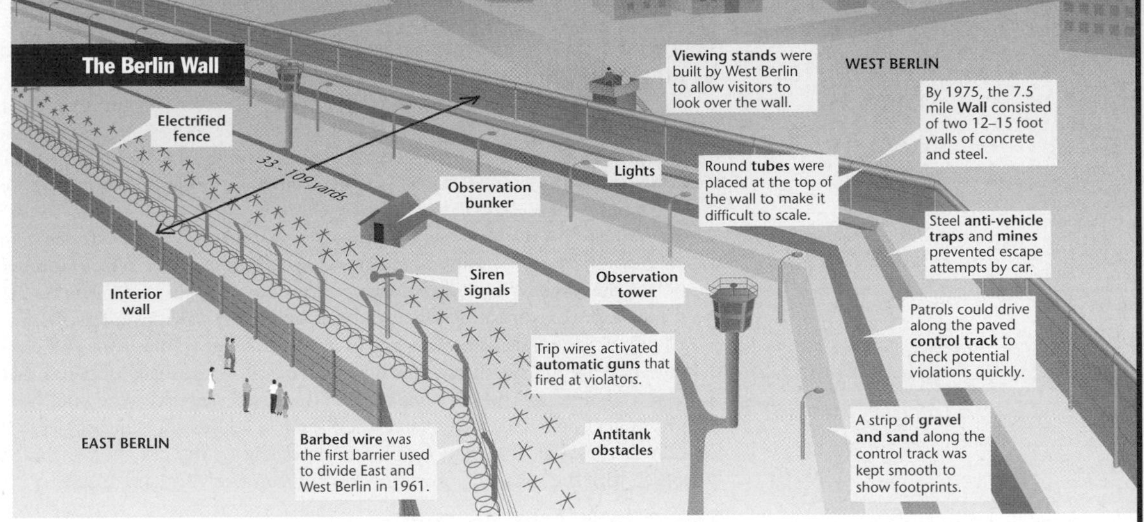
The Berlin Wall
Viewing stands were built by West Berlin to allow visitors to look over the wall.
WEST BERLIN
By 1975, the 7.5 mile Wall consisted of two 12–15 foot walls of concrete and steel.
Electrified fence
33 - 109 yards
Lights
Round tubes were placed at the top of the wall to make it difficult to scale.
Observation bunker
Steel anti-vehicle traps and mines prevented escape attempts by car.
Interior wall
Siren signals
Observation tower
Patrols could drive along the paved control track to check potential violations quickly.
Trip wires activated automatic guns that fired at violators.
A strip of gravel and sand along the control track was kept smooth to show footprints.
EAST BERLIN
Barbed wire was the first barrier used to divide East and West Berlin in 1961.
Antitank obstacles

leaders, who had high hopes for the new President, were concerned about the kind of leadership he would provide.

The Berlin Crisis

Upset by the failure at the Bay of Pigs, Kennedy was now even more determined to prove his toughness against communism. Later in 1961, he had another opportunity when a new crisis arose over a familiar issue: Berlin.

Rekindled Tensions Over Germany After World War II, the Allies had divided Germany into zones. The United States, Great Britain, the Soviet Union, and France each controlled one sector of the country. While the zones were meant to be temporary, the lines between them had hardened as Cold War tensions increased among the former Allies. In time, the western regions had been combined to form the nation of West Germany. The sector controlled by the Soviet Union became East Germany. The city of Berlin, although located completely inside East Germany, had also been divided among the World War II victors.

The Soviet attempt to cut off access to Berlin in 1948 had failed as a result of President Truman's successful Berlin airlift. Now the Soviets made another effort to resolve problems in Berlin on their own terms. They demanded a peace treaty that would make the division of the city permanent. Their goal was to cut off the large flow of East Germans escaping into West Germany, particularly through Berlin.

Kennedy feared that the Soviet effort in Germany was part of a larger plan to take over the rest of Europe. Adding to his fears, his first meeting with Soviet leader Nikita Khrushchev, in Vienna, Austria, in June 1961, went poorly. When Khrushchev made a public ultimatum regarding Germany, Kennedy felt bullied by the Soviet leader.

Kennedy Takes Action Upon returning home, Kennedy decided to show the Soviets that the United States would not be intimidated. He asked Congress for a huge increase of more than $3 billion for defense. He doubled the number of young men being drafted into the armed services and called up reserve forces for active duty. At the same time, he sought more than $200 million for a

INTERPRETING DIAGRAMS
Below, West Berliners peer through the newly built Berlin Wall into East Berlin near Checkpoint Charlie. Initially, tubes on the top of the wall were supposed to prevent escapees from getting a grip to pull themselves over. Later, as shown in the diagram of a typical checkpoint in the 1980s (top), a whole range of deadly deterrents were installed. **Analyzing Visual Information** *As depicted in the diagram, what other hazards were added to prevent escape?*

ACTIVITY
Connecting with Geography

Have students use a historical atlas or help small groups conduct Internet research to locate a map of Berlin, circa 1961. Have the students research and organize information on the city at that time, using the map as a visual aid. **(Verbal/Linguistic)**

BACKGROUND
Connections to Today

When the Berlin Wall that divided East and West Germany for 28 years was torn down on November 9, 1989, a witness said that spectators "seemed to be drawn by the sense that . . . the barrier of concrete and steel that had figured so prominently in the history of this city and the world might soon be relegated to history." The reunification of Germany one year later proved to be just part of the collapse of the iron curtain.

CUSTOMIZE FOR ...
Gifted and Talented

Have students analyze the impact of the construction of a physical barrier, such as the Berlin Wall, in your city or town. Ask them to consider the implications of such a construction from political, economic, social, and purely practical perspectives. Have them write a "newspaper editorial" that expresses an opinion about this action.

TEST PREPARATION

Have students read the quotation by Senator Fulbright on the previous page and then answer the question below.

What is the main reason that the senator opposed the plan to overthrow Castro?

A He had no objection to the Castro regime.
(B) He thought it was wrong for the United States to take the kind of actions it denounced other nations for taking.
C He wanted the plan to be carried out openly, not secretly.
D He thought the Soviet Union would retaliate.

CAPTION ANSWERS

Interpreting Diagrams Reinforced walls, barbed wire, sirens, electrified fencing, trip wires that activated automatic weapons, patrol vehicles, antivehicle traps and mines, bright lights, and a smooth sand-and-gravel strip that showed footprints.

ACTIVITY
Connecting with History and Conflict

Foreign policy during the Kennedy and Johnson administrations consisted of maintaining safety from nuclear threat by blocking the establishment of Communist governments in other—particularly neighboring—countries. To help students understand this concept, have them describe their neighborhoods. Then ask them to list characteristics of their neighborhoods that make them feel safe and those that make them feel threatened. **(Verbal/Linguistic)**

BACKGROUND
Recent Scholarship

Robert S. McNamara served as Secretary of Defense under Presidents Kennedy and Johnson. He was thus a key adviser to President Kennedy during the Cuban Missile Crisis. The book *Dereliction of Duty: Lyndon Johnson, Robert McNamara, the Joint Chiefs of Staff and the Lies That Led to Vietnam,* by historian and active-duty Army officer H. R. McMaster, is highly critical of Robert McNamara and makes important parallels between the Cuban Missile Crisis and the Vietnam conflict. McMaster contends that McNamara learned all the wrong lessons from the Cuban Missile Crisis. He points out that President Kennedy relied heavily upon advice from Robert McNamara and other civilian advisers among the National Security Council Staff during the Cuban Missile Crisis. The successful outcome of that crisis, writes McMaster, gave McNamara an exaggerated sense of the ability of civilians to devise military strategy. McMaster feels that as a consequence of this situation, McNamara would later use his authority as Secretary of Defense to repeatedly either overrule or ignore advice from the Joint Chiefs of Staff during the Vietnam War.

program to build fallout shelters across the country. He argued that the United States had to be prepared if the crisis led to nuclear war.

Kennedy appeared on television to tell the American people that West Berlin was "the great testing place of Western courage and will, a focal point where our solemn commitments . . . and Soviet ambitions now meet in basic confrontation." The United States, he said, would not be pushed around: "We do not want to fight—but we have fought before."

In August 1961, the Soviets responded by building a wall to separate Communist and non-Communist Berlin. The **Berlin Wall** became a somber symbol of the Cold War. Still, by stopping the flow of East Germans to the West, the Soviet Union had found a way to avoid a showdown over East Berlin.

Although the immediate crisis was over, the tensions of the Cold War continued. Speaking in Frankfurt, Germany, in June 1963, Kennedy declared that the United States "will risk its cities to defend yours because we need your freedom to protect ours." Two days later, the President addressed a cheering crowd near the Berlin Wall. To symbolize his commitment to the city, he concluded his speech with the rousing words, *"Ich bin ein Berliner,"* or "I am a Berliner."

The Cuban Missile Crisis

Kennedy also had a chance to restore American prestige in another crisis with Cuba. The Soviet Union, disturbed by the attempted Bay of Pigs invasion, had pledged to support Castro's government. On October 16, 1962, photographs taken from an American spy plane revealed that the Soviets were building missile bases on Cuban soil—only about 90 miles from the Florida coast. What followed was the **Cuban Missile Crisis,** a terrifying standoff between the United States and the Soviet Union that brought the superpowers to the brink of nuclear war.

Kennedy's Options The Soviet missiles in Cuba did not radically change the military balance between the United States and

MAP SKILLS U.S. spy plane photographs such as the one at right showed missile bases under construction in Cuba. The map shows the naval blockade of Cuba, put in place during tense diplomatic negotiations to avert a nuclear disaster. Khrushchev offered to withdraw the missiles from Cuba if Kennedy promised not to invade the island. **Location** *What details in the map help to explain (a) why the Soviet Union wanted a military presence in Cuba, and (b) why Kennedy was determined to prevent that from happening?*

Cuban Missile Crisis, 1962

1. **Oct. 16** CIA provides President Kennedy with evidence of Soviet missile bases under construction in Cuba.
2. **Oct. 22** President Kennedy announces a naval "quarantine" of Cuba.
3. **Oct. 24** Soviet ships reverse course upon learning of the blockade.
4. **Oct. 28** Premier Khrushchev offers to withdraw missiles from Cuba in exchange for removal of the quarantine and a U.S. pledge not to invade Cuba.
5. **Oct. 28** President Kennedy accepts the offer. Soviet missile bases are dismantled by mid-November.

Soviet missile base | U.S. naval quarantine | U.S. naval base

N; Florida; Miami; BAHAMAS; ATLANTIC OCEAN; Havana; CUBA; Guantanamo; HAITI; DOMINICAN REPUBLIC; JAMAICA; Caribbean Sea; 0 100 200 mi.; 0 100 200 km; 80°W; 70°W; 20°N

RESOURCE DIRECTORY

Teaching Resources

Biography, Literature, and Comparing Primary Sources booklet (Biography) *Robert F. Kennedy,* p. 34

Technology

Color Transparencies *Historical Maps,* A49

RESOURCE PRO® **Primary Source Activity** *Cuban Missile Crisis,* found on Resource Pro, uses excerpts from Ted Sorenson's *Kennedy* to explain the tension and danger of the crisis.

Exploring Primary Sources in U.S. History CD-ROM *On the Cuban Missile Crisis, John F. Kennedy and Nikita Khrushchev*

CAPTION ANSWERS

Map Skills (a) Because of Cuba's proximity to the United States. (b) The bases were being constructed in the northern half of Cuba, close to Florida, and the missiles could conceivably reach targets throughout the United States.

the Soviet Union. The Soviets could already inflict serious damage on the United States from bases within their own country. Yet installing missiles so close to the United States seemed to be an effort by the Soviets to intimidate the Americans. Kennedy was convinced that the missiles presented a direct challenge to which he must respond.

But how? The President quickly assembled his top advisors in a series of secret meetings. They outlined four possible responses:

1. Engage in further negotiations with Khrushchev. This option, although peaceful, would give the Soviets more time to finish building the missile bases. It also risked making Kennedy look hesitant and weak in the face of the bold Soviet move.
2. Invade Cuba. This would eliminate the missile threat and achieve the additional goal of ousting Fidel Castro. A Cuban invasion had failed before, though, and this plan risked all-out nuclear war with the Soviets.
3. Blockade Cuba. This action would prevent Soviet ships from making further missile deliveries. It would force Khrushchev either to back off or to take aggressive action against U.S. warships. However, no one knew how the Soviet leader might react to this step.
4. Bomb the missile sites. A series of airstrikes could quickly knock out the missiles. Yet would the Soviets launch a counterstrike, and where?

VIEWING HISTORY This famous photograph shows Kennedy in the Oval Office. The photo is often used to evoke the loneliness of the presidency. **Drawing Inferences** *From what you know about Kennedy's previous foreign policy experiences, what factors might have weighed heavily on him as he made his decision on the Cuban missiles?*

Attorney General Robert Kennedy argued against the airstrike option. It seemed, he said, too much like the Japanese attack on Pearl Harbor that had launched the United States into World War II. At one point former Secretary of State Dean Acheson joined the discussions and declared that the United States had to knock out the Soviet missiles. He was asked what would happen next. His response points out the very real danger of a local conflict escalating, or expanding, into a widespread war:

Acheson: I know the Soviet Union well. I know what they are required to do in the light of their history and their posture around the world. I think they will knock out our missiles in Turkey.

An advisor: Well, then what do we do?

Acheson: I believe under our NATO treaty . . . we would be required to respond by knocking out a missile base inside the Soviet Union.

Another advisor: Then what do they do?

Acheson: That's when we hope that cooler heads will prevail, and they'll stop and talk.

Kennedy Decides President Kennedy ordered United States forces on full alert. U.S. bombers were armed with nuclear missiles. The navy was ready to move, and army and marine units prepared to invade Cuba.

Kennedy listened to the different views of his advisors, grilling them with questions. Then, in solitude, he weighed the options, facing one of the most dangerous and agonizing decisions any President has had to make.

On Monday, October 22, Kennedy went on television and radio to confirm the press reports that had begun to circulate about Cuba. "[U]nmistakable evidence has established the fact that a series of offensive missile sites is now in

ACTIVITY

Connecting with History and Conflict

The threat of a nuclear holocaust was very real in the 1960s. Ask students to use the *Reader's Guide to Periodical Literature* or the Internet to locate and report on contemporary magazine articles about building, stocking, and living in fallout shelters. **(Verbal/Linguistic)**

BACKGROUND

Cuba and the United States

Since the Communist revolution in 1959, Cuban leader Fidel Castro has insisted that the small United States naval base in Guantanamo Bay on the eastern coast of Cuba is "a dagger plunged into Cuban soil." It has been there since 1903—five years after the end of the Spanish-American War—and some 70,000 United States military personnel and their families live and work at the base.

CUSTOMIZE FOR ...

Less Proficient Readers

Have students write two column headings on a piece of paper: *Kennedy's Trouble Spots* and *Johnson's Trouble Spots.* After they read the section, ask them to list each of the foreign affairs crises discussed in the section in the appropriate column and briefly describe the crisis and its resolution.

CAPTION ANSWERS

Viewing History Sample answer: He did not want to repeat the embarrassment of the failed Bay of Pigs invasion. He needed to take a firm stand against the Soviet Union for several reasons: to curb aggressive designs on the part of the Russians; to uphold the Monroe Doctrine; and to restore America's position of strength in foreign affairs.

ACTIVITY
Connecting with Today

Have students ask appropriate older adults to share their recollections of the Cuban Missile Crisis and the Cold War in general. Have students share what they learn with the class. **(Verbal/ Linguistic)**

From the Archives of
AmericanHeritage®

About the Presidents

John Fitzgerald Kennedy (1961–1963) won rave reviews for the first three months of his presidency. He announced the formation of the Peace Corps to send volunteer workers to developing countries. His administration continued Eisenhower's Food for Peace Program, helping to solve the problem of agricultural surplus while winning friends abroad. He also launched the Alliance for Progress for Latin-American economic cooperation and social development. Kennedy's live press conferences only added to his glamour. Some commentators suggested that Kennedy's first 100 days might surpass FDR's. Then came the Bay of Pigs. The disaster cost him prestige abroad and the support of liberals at home. Source: Joseph L. Gardner, "John Fitzgerald Kennedy," *The American Heritage® Pictorial History of the Presidents of the United States,* vol. 2, 1968.

1960s Bomb Shelter

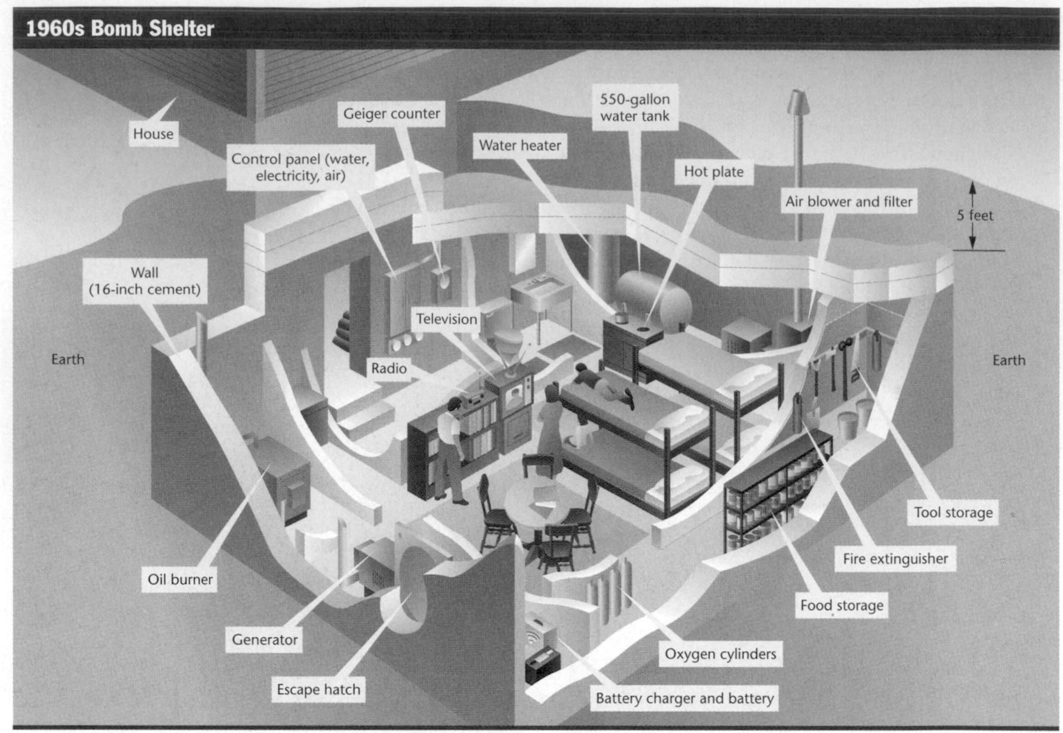

INTERPRETING DIAGRAMS Many Americans hoped they could survive a nuclear war in a basement shelter that would protect them from radioactive fallout, the deadly particles that rain down after an atomic blast. **Analyzing Visual Information** *Which features of this fallout shelter are intended to provide safety for the family, and which provide comfort and necessities for living?*

preparation on that imprisoned island," he said. The President then announced his decision: He had authorized a naval "quarantine" around Cuba. He was careful not to call the action a "blockade" because a blockade is an act of war. He demanded that Khrushchev "halt and eliminate this clandestine, reckless and provocative threat. . . ."

America did not desire confrontation, Kennedy said, but neither would it shrink from aggression. He told Americans:

> *"The path we have chosen for the present is full of hazards. . . . The cost of freedom is always high—and Americans have always paid it. And one path we shall never choose, and that is the path of surrender or submission."*
>
> —President Kennedy, television and radio address to the nation, October 22, 1962

The World Waits The two most powerful nations in the world stood teetering on the brink of disaster. "The immediate public reaction was a mixture of anger and fear—but no panic—as they rallied in support of the president," one reporter later recalled. Some people huddled in their bomb shelters, expecting the worst.

The naval quarantine went into effect on Wednesday, October 24. On October 25, a Soviet ship reached the quarantine line and was stopped by the navy. Because it was carrying only oil, it was allowed to proceed. Meanwhile, a dozen more Soviet cargo ships were steaming toward the blockade. Then, to

CAPTION ANSWERS

Analyzing Diagrams Accept reasonable answers. Safety: thick cement walls, Geiger counter, air filter, escape hatch, oxygen cylinders, fire extinguisher. Comfort and necessities: television, radio, oil burner, generator, battery charger, food storage, tool storage, hot plate, water tank and heater.

RESOURCE DIRECTORY

Teaching Resources

Biography, Literature, and Comparing Primary Sources booklet (Comparing Primary Sources) *On the Cold War,* p. 153

Technology

Color Transparencies *The Way It Works,* H19

everyone's great relief, the Soviet ships suddenly reversed direction. Khrushchev had called them back.

As a U.S. Navy patrol plane flies overhead, the American destroyer U.S.S. *Barry* pulls alongside the Soviet freighter *Anesov* during the American naval blockade of Cuba.

Disaster Avoided The crisis was not yet over, however. In Cuba, construction on the existing missile sites continued. On October 26, Khrushchev sent Kennedy a long letter in which he pledged to remove the missiles if Kennedy promised that the United States would end the quarantine and stay out of Cuba. A second letter delivered the next day demanded that the United States remove its missiles from Turkey in exchange for the withdrawal of Soviet missiles in Cuba. Kennedy publicly accepted the terms of the first note. He responded to the second note through secret negotiations and eventually met the demand.

With that, the crisis ended. As Secretary of State Dean Rusk observed to President Kennedy, "We have won a considerable victory. You and I are still alive."

The Cuban Missile Crisis brought the world closer than ever before to nuclear war. Such a war would have caused unimaginable death and destruction—far more, for example, than the atomic bombings of Japan in 1945, in part because more-powerful hydrogen bombs had replaced those early atomic weapons.

Kennedy emerged from the confrontation as a hero. He had stood up to the Soviets and shown that the United States would not be pushed around. His reputation, and that of the Democratic Party, improved just in time for the midterm congressional elections that were only weeks away.

The Aftereffects The Cuban Missile Crisis led to a number of efforts to reduce the risk of nuclear war. Once the confrontation was over, Kennedy and Khrushchev established a "hot line" between their two nations to allow the Soviet and American leaders to communicate quickly in the event of a future crisis. In addition, in the summer of 1963 the two countries (along with Great Britain) signed the first nuclear treaty since the development of the atomic bomb.

This agreement, the **Limited Test Ban Treaty**, banned nuclear testing above the ground. By doing so, it sought to eliminate the radioactive fallout that threatened to contaminate human, animal, and plant life.

The treaty still permitted underground nuclear testing, and the United States and the Soviet Union continued to build bigger and bigger bombs. Nonetheless, as Kennedy noted, the treaty marked "an important first step toward peace, a step toward reason, a step away from war."

The Alliance for Progress

The Soviet Union and the United States competed not only by building up their military forces, but also by seeking allies in the developing countries of Latin America, Asia, and Africa. Many of these countries were terribly poor. Communist revolutionary movements in some of these countries were gaining support by promising people a better future.

To counter these revolutionary movements, Kennedy tried to promote "peaceful revolution"—that is, to help build stable governments that met the needs of their citizens and also were allied with the democratic countries of the West. Two months after taking office, Kennedy called on all the people of the Western Hemisphere to join in a new **Alliance for Progress,** or *Alianza para Progreso.* The Alliance would be

Focus on WORLD EVENTS

Memoirs of the Crisis Many policymakers on both sides of the Cuban Missile Crisis composed memoirs of the event. In *Thirteen Days: A Memoir of the Cuban Missile Crisis*, Robert F. Kennedy recalled with awe what the American team had experienced:

> *"We saw as never before the meaning and responsibility in the power of the United States, . . . the responsibility we had to people around the globe who had never heard of us, who had never heard of our country or of the men sitting in that room determining their fate. . . ."*

Likewise, Russian leader Nikita Khrushchev set down his recollections in *Khrushchev Remembers:*

> *"I found myself in the difficult position of having to decide on a course of action which would answer the American threat but which would also avoid war. Any fool can start a war, and once he's done so, even the wisest of men are helpless to stop it—especially if it's a nuclear war."*

ACTIVITY
Connecting with Government

The Nuclear Test Ban Treaty was signed during Kennedy's administration in 1963. The treaty banned nuclear weapons testing in the atmosphere, in outer space, and underwater. Underground testing was still permitted, as was the maintenance of nuclear stockpiles and nuclear weapons buildup. Have students research the positions of Russia, the United States, and Great Britain on nuclear weapons testing today. **(Verbal/Linguistic)**

BACKGROUND
Recent Scholarship

In 1997 Harvard University professors Ernest R. May and Philip D. Zelikow published *The Kennedy Tapes,* an edited transcript of tapes made in the White House during the Cuban Missile Crisis. Only President Kennedy and possibly Robert Kennedy knew the tapes were being made. The book is riveting: readers learn that, despite being pressed by advisers to invade Cuba, President Kennedy maintained that "The question really is to what action we take which lessens the chances of a nuclear exchange." He referred to firing nuclear weapons as "a hell of an alternative." He was also concerned about the effects of a nuclear attack on the United States, asking at one point, "What is it we ought to do for the population in affected areas?" Above all else, the transcripts provide insight into the tense, minute-by-minute discussions that took place when the world almost went to nuclear war. The authors say, "these tapes record the decision-making of democracy."

CUSTOMIZE FOR ...
Gifted and Talented

Direct students to read *Thirteen Days: A Memoir of the Cuban Missile Crisis* or *The Kennedy Tapes,* or view a production of *The Missiles of October,* and write a review.

ACTIVITY

Connecting with Economics

During President Kennedy's administration, Social Security benefits were extended, and the age of eligibility for Social Security was lowered from 65 to 62. Have students research the current eligibility requirements for Social Security today, the current benefit rates, and the long-term prospects for this program. Have them present their findings in a chart, graph, or table. **(Logical/Mathematical)**

BACKGROUND

Connections to Geography

In speaking of the Alliance for Progress, Kennedy was always careful to include Spanish words and phrases to forge a closer bond with Latin American officials. Thus he spoke of *Alianza para Progreso* as "a vast cooperative effort, unparalleled in magnitude and nobility of purpose, to satisfy the basic needs of the American people for homes, work and land, health and schools—*techo, trabajo y tierra, salud y escuela.*" "Our motto," Kennedy said, "is what it has always been—progress yes, tyranny no—*progreso si, tirania no!*"

a vast cooperative effort to satisfy the basic needs of people in North, Central, and South America for homes, work, land, health, and schools.

The task was a huge undertaking. The administration pledged $20 billion over ten years to promote economic development and social reform and to prevent revolution. All citizens in the Western Hemisphere, Kennedy declared, had "a right to social justice," and that included "land for the landless, and education for those who are denied education."

Soon, however, Latin Americans began to question the benefits of the Alliance. Some viewed it simply as a tool of the United States to stop the spread of communism. Because of such doubts, the Alliance for Progress never lived up to Kennedy's expectations.

The Peace Corps

Kennedy's hope for a world in which nations worked together peacefully to solve problems was also reflected in his establishment of the **Peace Corps** in 1961. This program sent volunteers abroad as educators, health workers, and technicians to help developing nations around the world.

Paul Cowan was typical of many Peace Corps volunteers. After graduating from college in 1963, he worked in the civil rights movement, tutoring African American children in Maryland. In 1965, Cowan and his wife, Rachel, joined the Peace Corps and prepared to work in South America. After a training program at the University of New Mexico, they went to the city of Guayaquil in Ecuador to do community development work. Their job was to raise the standard of living in

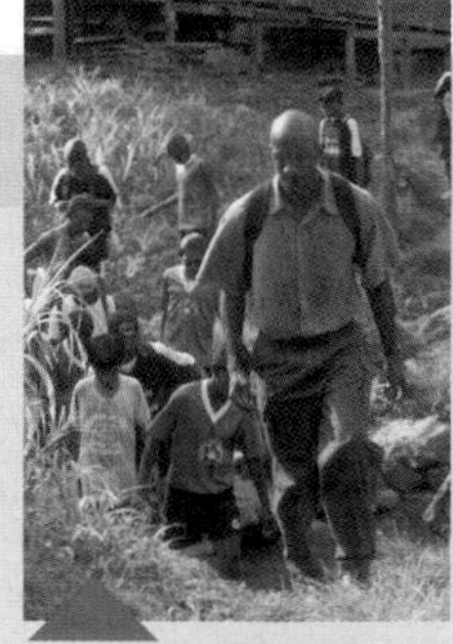

The Peace Corps

The idea for an overseas voluntary service organization began late at night on October 14, 1960. Kennedy, in an unscheduled speech to students at the University of Michigan, challenged them to devote two years of their lives helping people in developing countries. The idea took off. With the official creation of the Peace Corps a year later, the first volunteers accepted assignments in a handful of countries.

The mission of the Peace Corps, as set by Congress in 1961, was to meet the need for trained workers in participating countries and to promote mutual understanding between Americans and other peoples. "Life in the Peace Corps will not be easy," President Kennedy said in authorizing the organization. The more than 163,000 Peace Corps volunteers who served during the last four decades discovered the truth of Kennedy's statement. They have served in 135 countries, working side by side with local citizens—for low wages and only basic provisions—to improve impoverished areas of the world.

The mission and reach of the Peace Corps has expanded in recent years. In 1990, President George Bush celebrated the "talented Americans who are . . . to become the first Peace Corps volunteers to serve in Eastern Europe"—in Hungary and Poland. A special "Crisis Corps," created in 1995, provided workers who were trained to respond to humanitarian and natural disasters such as hurricanes. And in 2000, the Peace Corps announced that volunteers in Africa and in the Crisis Corps would be trained to provide education on HIV/AIDS. A "domestic Peace Corps," Americorps, founded in 1994, trains workers in local community service projects in the United States. Volunteers receive various benefits, including money for college, in return for their service.

 **What is the meaning of the Peace Corps slogan, "The toughest job you'll ever love"?**

CAPTION ANSWERS

Fast Forward to Today It means that service in the Peace Corps is demanding and difficult, but that it also offers a highly rewarding sense of accomplishment.

RESOURCE DIRECTORY

Teaching Resources
Units 5/6/7 booklet
- Section 3 Quiz, p. 66
- Chapter 22 Test, pp. 67, 70

Guide to the Essentials
- Section 3 Summary, p. 109
- Chapter 22 Test, p. 110

Other Print Resources
Chapter Tests with ExamView® Test Bank CD-ROM, Ch. 22

Technology
ExamView® Test Bank CD-ROM, Ch. 22
Social Studies Skills Tutor CD-ROM

poor areas and to work with local governments to provide services such as garbage removal and clean water.

Johnson's Foreign Policy

In 1963, Lyndon Johnson assumed the presidency upon Kennedy's death. His foreign policy, like Kennedy's, focused on containing communism around the world.

The Dominican Republic In 1965, Johnson received word that the military-backed government in the Dominican Republic, a Caribbean nation close to Cuba, had been attacked by rebels. Johnson feared that the disruption might endanger American citizens living there. Arguing (wrongly, it turned out) that Communist elements were causing the disruption, Johnson sent 22,000 marines to the Dominican Republic. Their presence tipped the balance away from the rebels. Within a few months a provisional government backed by the United States was put in place. Elections were held the following year.

Vietnam Johnson also became deeply involved in the ongoing conflict in Southeast Asia between Communist North Vietnam and non-Communist South Vietnam. Like Kennedy, Johnson was determined to prevent the spread of communism there. By 1963, about 16,000 American military advisors were in South Vietnam. The United States was also contributing economic aid to the South Vietnamese government.

In his 1964 campaign for President, Johnson opposed more direct United States involvement in the war. Yet, before long he faced the prospect of a Communist takeover of South Vietnam, which he could not tolerate. During 1965, American involvement in the conflict deepened as more and more troops and money were sent to prop up the South Vietnamese government.

COMPARING PRIMARY SOURCES
The Cold War

The United States and its allies continued to battle Communist expansion in the 1960s.

Analyzing Viewpoints What strategy did each of the speakers below want to pursue during the Cold War?

For Moderation in the Cold War

"The issues called the cold war . . . must be met with determination, confidence, and sophistication. . . . [C]hannels of communication should be kept open. . . . Our discussion, public or private, should be marked by civility; our manners should conform to our own dignity and power and to our good repute throughout the world."

—Secretary of State Dean Rusk, speech at the University of California, Berkeley, March 20, 1961

For Aggressiveness in the Cold War

"[I]t is really astounding that our government has never stated its purpose to be that of complete victory over the tyrannical forces of international communism. . . . And we need an official act, such as the resumption of nuclear testing, to show our own peoples and the other freedom-loving peoples of the world that we mean business."

—Arizona Senator Barry Goldwater, address to the United States Senate, July 14, 1961

Section 3 Assessment

READING COMPREHENSION

1. Describe the causes and effects of the **Bay of Pigs invasion.**
2. (a) Why did tensions reignite over the division of Germany? (b) Why was the **Berlin Wall** built?
3. What goals did the **Alliance for Progress** and the **Peace Corps** attempt to fulfill?
4. In what ways did Johnson continue Kennedy's approach to the Cold War?

CRITICAL THINKING AND WRITING

5. **Drawing Inferences** What can you infer about the Soviet Union's foreign policy goals from its actions in the Cold War crises of the 1960s?
6. **Journal Writing** Write a fictional entry from a personal journal of President Kennedy during the Cuban Missile Crisis. Include details that demonstrate your understanding of the difficulties Kennedy faced.

Take It to the NET

Activity: Creating a Brochure
Create a brochure about the Peace Corps. Include facts about why people volunteer, where they serve, and what kinds of work they do. Use the links provided in the *America: Pathways to the Present* area of the following Web site for help in completing this activity.
www.phschool.com

Section 3 Assessment

Reading Comprehension

1. Causes: Castro's seizure of American property and his friendship with Soviet leaders; to prevent other revolutionary upheavals throughout Latin America. Effects: The United States lost prestige; European leaders began to have doubts about Kennedy, other Latin American nations expressed anger.
2. (a) The Soviets demanded a peace treaty that would make the division of the city permanent. (b) To separate Communist and non-Communist Berlin and stop the flow of East Germans escaping into West Germany, particularly through Berlin.
3. Alliance for Progress: to create a vast cooperative effort to improve the lives of people in North, Central and South America, and to stop the threat of communism. Peace Corps: to send American volunteers to work in developing countries on programs, such as public health and sanitation, which would help the local inhabitants make better lives for themselves. Both initiatives were part of Kennedy's vision for cooperation among nations to solve problems.
4. Johnson's dispatch of United States marines to the Dominican Republic showed that he shared Kennedy's concern over the threat of communism in Latin America; Johnson also continued, and greatly expanded, Kennedy's policy of supporting South Vietnam.

Critical Thinking and Writing

5. Students might infer that the Soviet Union was determined to increase its political influence and spread communism to many different parts of the world; the Russians also worked to weaken United States influence globally.
6. Entries will vary but should reflect the issues, both humanitarian and political, that President Kennedy faced.

Brochures should highlight the purposes and practices of volunteerism in the Peace Corps.

Chapter 22

Reviewing Key Terms

Students should refer to the definitions of key terms in the chapter to write sentences that show an understanding of the respective administrations of John F. Kennedy and Lyndon Johnson.

Reviewing Main Ideas

11. According to television viewers, Kennedy was the victor, as he appeared far more composed than Nixon. Radio listeners, however, favored Nixon, as he was well-prepared to discuss the issues.
12. Kennedy wanted to cut taxes, offer health care and other benefits to the elderly, aid education, help poor Americans, protect the environment, and help troubled young people. Many of Kennedy's proposals died in Congressional committees. This was due in part to Kennedy's lack of a broad electoral mandate.
13. That Lee Harvey Oswald bore sole responsibility for killing President Kennedy.
14. The Civil Rights Act and the Voting Rights Act, tax relief, medical benefits for the elderly and the poor, educational assistance, programs to fight poverty, easing immigration restrictions, funding for cultural and consumer measures, environmental protection.
15. *Griswold* v. *Connecticut* (1965): the Court ruled that states could not prohibit birth control; *Baker* v. *Carr* (1962): held that state reapportionment had to be on the basis of "one person, one vote"; *Miranda* v. *Arizona* (1966): the Court ruled that police must make suspects aware of their rights before questioning begins.
16. Sample answer: It created new social programs and used government to attack social problems head-on, especially through the launching of the war on poverty. Gains were limited by the increase in military spending for the Vietnam War.
17. Kennedy appeared inexperienced in the eyes of European leaders; the Bay of Pigs was a blow to American prestige; Latin American leaders were angry at the U.S. attempt to overthrow a government in the Western Hemisphere.

Chapter 22 Review and Assessment

creating a CHAPTER SUMMARY

Copy this chart (right) on a piece of paper and complete it by adding information about key events and policies of the Kennedy and Johnson administrations. Some entries have been completed for you as examples.

Major Events/ Actions	Kennedy	Johnson
Domestic Policy	• 1960 debates • •	• Tax cut • •
Foreign Policy	• Bay of Pigs • • •	• Dominican Republic uprising • •

For additional review and enrichment activities, see the interactive version of *America: Pathways to the Present*, available on the Web and on CD-ROM.

★ Reviewing Key Terms

For each of the terms below, write a sentence explaining how it relates to the Kennedy-Johnson years.

1. mandate
2. New Frontier
3. Great Society
4. Medicare
5. Medicaid
6. Immigration Act of 1965
7. Miranda rule
8. apportionment
9. Limited Test Ban Treaty
10. Peace Corps

★ Reviewing Main Ideas

11. Describe the outcome of the first Nixon-Kennedy debate and the reasons for that outcome. (Section 1)
12. What domestic programs did Kennedy propose, and why were they largely unsuccessful? (Section 1)
13. What actions were taken to investigate Kennedy's assassination? (Section 1)
14. What domestic programs did Johnson propose? (Section 2)
15. Describe three landmark decisions handed down by the Supreme Court under Chief Justice Earl Warren. (Section 2)
16. Identify the major effects of the Great Society. (Section 2)
17. What consequences to President Kennedy and the United States resulted from the failed Bay of Pigs invasion? (Section 3)
18. Describe the Berlin crisis of 1961. (Section 3)
19. Why did Kennedy establish the Peace Corps? (Section 3)
20. What was Johnson's approach to foreign policy? (Section 3)

★ Critical Thinking

21. **Making Comparisons** What policies and programs would you recommend as part of an effort to eliminate poverty? How would they be similar to, or different from, the programs of Johnson's Great Society?
22. **Predicting Consequences** How did the beliefs of Presidents Kennedy and Johnson about the spread of communism influence their foreign policy decisions?
23. **Drawing Inferences** In what ways did the Warren Court help to uphold the principle that a person is "innocent until proven guilty"?
24. **Drawing Conclusions** Would you characterize Johnson as a weak or a powerful politician? Explain your reasoning.

Creating a Chapter Summary

Major Events/Actions	Kennedy	Johnson
Domestic Policy	• 1960 debates • The New Frontier • Space program	• Tax cut • The Great Society • War on poverty • Aid to education • Medicare and Medicaid
Foreign Policy	• Bay of Pigs • Berlin Crisis • Cuban Missile Crisis • Peace Corps • Alliance for Progress	• Dominican Republic uprising

★ Skills Assessment

Analyzing Political Cartoons ▶

25. This cartoon was printed in November 1962. (a) Who are the two men? (b) What are they trying to do?
26. What does the monster represent?
27. (a) What is the message of the cartoon? (b) What event do you think inspired the cartoon?

LET'S GET A LOCK FOR THIS THING.

Analyzing Primary Sources

Reread the two quotations in Comparing Primary Sources in Section 3 and then answer the questions that follow.

28. Which statement best describes Secretary of State Dean Rusk's view of the Cold War?
    - **A** The Cold War is not a serious threat to the United States and does not require a strong American response.
    - **B** The United States should be cautious in its discussions with the Soviet Union.
    - **C** The United States should be firm but honorable in its Cold War diplomacy.
    - **D** The United States must live up to its reputation as a superpower by being tough on communism.
29. Which statement best describes Senator Barry Goldwater's view of the Cold War?
    - **F** A strong statement of America's goal of eliminating communism should be backed up by military action.
    - **G** The United States should use nuclear weapons to protect people's freedom.
    - **H** The United States government has waged a tyrannical fight against communism.
    - **J** American businesses should help fight communism and protect freedom-loving peoples.

Applying the Chapter Skill: ***Exploring Oral History***

30. Interview one or two adults who remember Kennedy's assassination. Ask them if they can recall what they were doing when they heard the news. Have them describe their reaction to the tragedy as well as its impact on the nation.

ACTIVITIES

Writing to LEARN

Writing to Inform
What advantages and disadvantages did Kennedy and Johnson have as Presidents? Write a summary that includes factors such as their backgrounds, their leadership styles, their personality traits, public opinion of them, and the circumstances surrounding their presidencies. In what ways were the two men alike, and in what ways did they differ?

Primary Source CD-ROM

Working With Primary Sources Find additional information on the Kennedy and Johnson administrations on the *Exploring Primary Sources in U.S. History CD-ROM.* Use the selection(s) provided to complete the Chapter 22 primary source activity located in the *America: Pathways to the Present* area of the following Web site. **www.phschool.com**

Take It to the NET

Chapter Self-Test As a review activity, take the Chapter 22 Self-Test in the *America: Pathways to the Present* area at the Web site listed below. The questions are designed to test your understanding of the chapter content. **www.phschool.com**

18. Tensions mounted when the Russians pressed for a permanent division of Berlin to prevent East Germans from fleeing to the West. Kennedy's June 1961 meeting with Kruschev failed to resolve the issue; Kennedy took steps to strengthen U.S. military forces; the immediate crisis passed when the Russians built the Berlin Wall in August 1961 to prevent escapes, but Berlin continued to be a source of tension.
19. Because he felt that nations should work together to solve problems peacefully.
20. Like Kennedy, Johnson was determined to contain communism. This led Johnson to dramatically expand the American role in the war in Vietnam.

CRITICAL THINKING

21. Answers will vary, but should either support or refute Johnson's approach to the war on poverty.
22. Sample answer: It led them to attempt to counter communism everywhere. One result was foreign policy disasters such as the Bay of Pigs. Other aspects, such as Kennedy's strong stand in the Cuban Missile Crisis, were more successful. Actions by Kennedy and Johnson made it much more difficult for the U.S. government to consider withdrawing from South Vietnam.
23. In general, the Warren Court tended to uphold the rights of individuals against what the Court regarded as the arbitrary power of national, state, and local government. The *Miranda* case, in its protection of the rights of criminal suspects, is a perfect example of this philosophy.
24. Answers will vary, but should be supported with facts from the section, and reflect students' consideration of the issues.

SKILLS ASSESSMENT

25. John F. Kennedy and Nikita Kruschev.
26. The threat of nuclear war.
27. (a) That the superpowers need to do more to prevent the outbreak of nuclear war. (b) The Cuban Missile Crisis.
28. C
29. F
30. Answers will vary. Students' questions should pursue themes introduced in the chapter.

ANSWERS TO ACTIVITIES

Writing to LEARN

Answers will vary but should be supported with facts from the section.

Primary Source CD-ROM

Direct students to the additional primary sources that can be found on the *Exploring Primary Sources in U.S. History CD-ROM.*

Take It to the NET

Additional support materials and activities for Chapter 22 of *America: Pathways to the Present* can be found in the Social Studies area at the Prentice Hall School Web site. **www.phschool.com**

Chapter 23 Planning Guide
Resource Manager

	CORE INSTRUCTION	READING/SKILLS
Chapter-Level Resources **TEKS** 19(B), 24(A), 25(D)	Teaching Resources • Pacing Charts booklet • Block Scheduling booklet **Units 5/6/7 booklet** • Chapter Summary, p. 73 **Resource Pro® CD-ROM,** Ch. 23 **Prentice Hall Presentation Pro CD-ROM,** Ch. 23 **www.phschool.com** • eTeach	**Guided Reading Audiotapes (English/Spanish)** **Student Edition on Audio CD,** Ch. 23 **Social Studies Skills Tutor CD-ROM** **Color Transparencies,** E20, G12, H20
1 The Women's Movement 1. Discover the background of the women's movement. 2. Find out how women organized to gain support and to effect change. 3. Observe the impact of feminism. 4. Learn which groups opposed the women's movement and why. **TEKS** 7(D), 21(D), 24(F)	Teaching Resources **Units 5/6/7 booklet** • Section 1 Quiz, p. 74	**Guided Reading and Review booklet,** p. 120 **Guide to the Essentials,** p. 111 **Learning with Documents booklet,** p. 35 **Skills for Life booklet,** p. 25 **Section Reading Support Transparencies**
2 Ethnic Minorities Seek Equality 1. Learn how Latinos sought equality during the 1960s and the early 1970s. 2. Find out how Asian Americans fought discrimination during this period. 3. See the ways in which Native Americans confronted their unique problems. **TEKS** 7(D), 8(B), 21(A), 21(C)	Teaching Resources **Units 5/6/7 booklet** • Section 2 Quiz, p. 75	**Guided Reading and Review booklet,** p. 121 **Guide to the Essentials,** p. 112 **Section Reading Support Transparencies**
3 The Counterculture 1. Find out about social changes promoted by the counterculture. 2. Learn how the music world of the 1960s and 1970s contributed to the cultural changes of this era. **TEKS** 20(A), 20(B), 20(C), 20(E)	Teaching Resources **Units 5/6/7 booklet** • Section 3 Quiz, p. 76 **Learning Styles Lesson Plans booklet,** p. 62	**Guided Reading and Review booklet,** p. 122 **Guide to the Essentials,** p. 113 **Section Reading Support Transparencies**
4 The Environmental and Consumer Movements 1. Read about efforts begun in the 1960s to protect the environment. 2. Understand how the government tried to balance jobs and environmental protection. 3. Find out how the consumer movement began, and what it tried to accomplish. **TEKS** 11(B), 24(B)	Teaching Resources **Units 5/6/7 booklet** • Section 4 Quiz, p. 77 **Learning Styles Lesson Plans booklet,** p. 63	**Guided Reading and Review booklet,** p. 123 **Guide to the Essentials,** p. 114 **Learning with Documents booklet,** p. 69 **Section Reading Support Transparencies**

Enrichment/Pre-AP

Prentice Hall United States History Video Collection™
www.phschool.com
- Section Activities, Virtual Field Trip, Chapter Activities, Current Events Online

Biography, Literature, and Comparing Primary Sources booklet, pp. 155–156
Great Debates booklet, p. 22
American History Block Scheduling Support
Sounds of an Era Audio CD
Exploring Primary Sources in U.S. History CD-ROM

Biography, Literature, and Comparing Primary Sources booklet, pp. 35, 82
Great Debates booklet, p. 42
Nystrom *Atlas of Our Country,* pp. 32–33, 36–37
Sounds of an Era Audio CD

American History Block Scheduling Support
Sounds of an Era Audio CD
American Pathways Thematic Posters

Assessment

Core Assessment

ExamView® Test Bank, Ch. 23
ExamView® Test Bank CD-ROM, Ch. 23

Standardized Test Preparation

Diagnose and Prescribe
Diagnostic Tests for High School Social Studies Skills

Review and Reteach
Review Book for U.S. History

Practice and Assess
Test-taking Strategies With Transparencies
Test-taking Strategies Posters
Test Prep Book for U.S. History
Alternative Assessment Handbook
Document-Based Assessment

Teaching Resources
Units 5/6/7 booklet
- Section Quizzes, pp. 74–77
- Chapter Tests, pp. 78, 81

www.phschool.com Ch. 23 Self-Test

AmericanHeritage Resources

From the Archives of American Heritage®, p. 766
AmericanHeritage® My Brush with History™ Videotapes
www.americanheritage.com

Don't miss the exclusive interactive version of this textbook on the Web and on CD-ROM.

Chapter 23 Planning Guide

In Your Classroom

Customize for Individual Needs

Gifted and Talented

Teacher's Edition
- Customize for Gifted and Talented, p. 773

Teaching Resources
- Biography, Literature, and Comparing Primary Sources booklet, pp. 35, 82, 155–156

Technology
- Exploring Primary Sources in U.S. History CD-ROM *Debate on the Equal Rights Amendment, Representatives Emmanuel Celler and Edith Green*

ESL

Teacher's Edition
- Customize for ESL, p. 779

Teaching Resources
- Guided Reading and Review booklet, pp. 120–123
- Guide to the Essentials (English/Spanish), Chapter 23

Technology
- Student Edition on Audio CD, Chapter 23
- Guided Reading Audiotapes (English/Spanish), Chapter 23
- Section Reading Support Transparencies

Less Proficient Readers

Teacher's Edition
- Customize for Less Proficient Readers, pp. 765, 775

Teaching Resources
- Guided Reading and Review booklet, pp. 120–123
- Guide to the Essentials (English/Spanish), Chapter 23

Technology
- Student Edition on Audio CD, Chapter 23
- Guided Reading Audiotapes (English/Spanish), Chapter 23
- Section Reading Support Transparencies

Less Proficient Writers

Teacher's Edition
- Customize for Less Proficient Writers, p. 783

Teaching Resources
- Guided Reading and Review booklet, pp. 120–123
- Guide to the Essentials (English/Spanish), Chapter 23

Technology
- Student Edition on Audio CD, Chapter 23
- Guided Reading Audiotapes (English/Spanish), Chapter 23
- Section Reading Support Transparencies

Teacher's Edition Index

Chapter 23 – Pacing Suggestions

For 90-minute Blocks

- Teach section 2 using Transparencies E20, G12, and H20, and the Recent Scholarship note on page 773 for class discussions.

Running Out of Time?

If you are running short on time to cover this chapter, consider the following options:

- Use Prentice Hall Presentation Pro CD-ROM to create an outline for this chapter.
- Use the Section Summaries for Chapter 23, from **Guide to the Essentials (English/Spanish).**

TEKS Correlation

Chapter-Level	TEKS
	(19) Citizenship. The student understands the importance of effective leadership in a democratic society. The student is expected to: **(B)** evaluate the contributions of significant political and social leaders in the United States such as Andrew Carnegie, Shirley Chisholm, and Franklin D. Roosevelt. **(24) Social studies skills.** The student applies critical-thinking skills to organize and use information acquired from a variety of sources including electronic technology. The student is expected to: **(A)** locate and use primary and secondary sources such as computer software, databases, media and news services, biographies, interviews, and artifacts to acquire information about the United States. **(25) Social studies skills.** The student communicates in written, oral, and visual forms. The student is expected to: **(D)** create written, oral, and visual presentations of social studies information.
1 The Women's Movement	**(7) History.** The student understands the impact of the American civil rights movement. The student is expected to: **(D)** identify changes in the United States that have resulted from the civil rights movement such as increased participation of minorities in the political process. **(21) Culture.** The student understands how people from various groups, including racial, ethnic, and religious groups, adapt to life in the United States and contribute to our national identity. The student is expected to: **(D)** identify the political, social, and economic contributions of women to American society. **(24) Social studies skills.** The student applies critical-thinking skills to organize and use information acquired from a variety of sources including electronic technology. The student is expected to: **(F)** identify bias in written, oral, and visual material.
2 Ethnic Minorities Seek Equality	**(7) History.** The student understands the impact of the American civil rights movement. The student is expected to: **(D)** identify changes in the United States that have resulted from the civil rights movement such as increased participation of minorities in the political process. **(8) Geography.** The student uses geographic tools to collect, analyze, and interpret data. The student is expected to: **(B)** pose and answer questions about geographic distributions and patterns shown on maps, graphs, charts, models, and databases. **(21) Culture.** The student understands how people from various groups, including racial, ethnic, and religious groups, adapt to life in the United States and contribute to our national identity. The student is expected to: **(A)** explain actions taken by people from racial, ethnic, and religious groups to expand economic opportunities and political rights in American society. **(C)** analyze how the contributions of people of various racial, ethnic, and religious groups have helped to shape the national identity.
3 The Counterculture	**(20) Culture.** The student understands the relationship between the arts and the times during which they were created. The student is expected to: **(A)** describe how the characteristics and issues of various eras in U.S. history have been reflected in works of art, music, and literature such as the paintings of Georgia O'Keeffe, rock and roll, and John Steinbeck's *The Grapes of Wrath.* **(B)** describe the impact of significant examples of cultural movements in art, music, and literature on American society, including the Harlem Renaissance. **(C)** identify examples of American art, music, and literature that transcend American culture and convey universal themes. **(E)** identify the impact of popular American culture on the rest of the world.
4 The Environmental and Consumer Movements	**(11) Geography.** The student understands the relationship between population growth and modernization on the physical environment. The student is expected to: **(B)** trace the development of the conservation of natural resources, including the establishment of the National Park System and efforts of private nonprofit organizations. **(24) Social studies skills.** The student applies critical-thinking skills to organize and use information acquired from a variety of sources including electronic technology. The student is expected to: **(B)** analyze information by sequencing, categorizing, identifying cause-and-effect relationships, comparing, contrasting, finding the main idea, summarizing, making generalizations and predictions, and drawing inferences and conclusions.

Chapter 23

An Era of Activism

(1960–1975)

INTRODUCING THE CHAPTER

Inspired by the civil rights movement, women, Latinos, and Native Americans struggled to achieve equality in the 1960s and 1970s through protests. The movement for social change affected almost every aspect of American society from the environment to consumer awareness.

TIME LINE ACTIVITY

To provide students with practice in using the time line, ask questions such as these:

1. What was an important outcome of the publication of Rachel Carson's *Silent Spring? (Many people credit that book with launching the environmental movement.)*
2. Who was India's first woman prime minister? *(Indira Gandhi)*
3. What important environmental events took place in 1970? *(The first Earth Day was celebrated, the Environmental Protection Agency was established, and Congress passed the Clean Air Act.)*

Chapter 23 An Era of Activism (1960–1975)

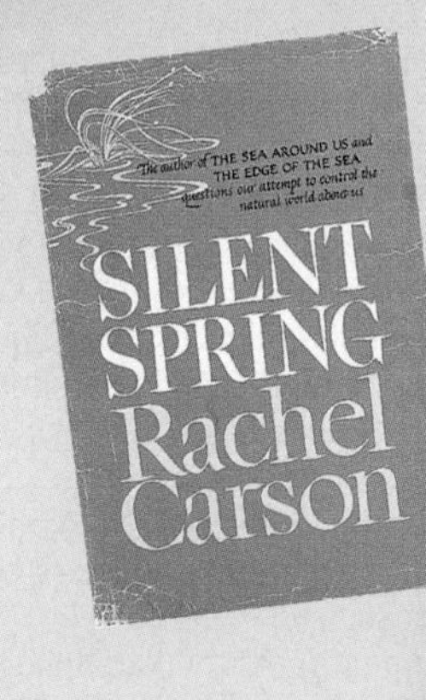

American Events

1962 Rachel Carson's book *Silent Spring* launches the environmental movement.

1963 *The Feminine Mystique* by Betty Friedan inspires the women's movement.

1965 Ralph Nader's *Unsafe at Any Speed* is published, initiating the consumer protection movement.

1966 The National Organization for Women is formed.

1967 César Chávez's United Farm Workers organize a nationwide boycott of grapes picked on nonunion farms.

Presidential Terms: D. Eisenhower 1953–1961 | John F. Kennedy 1961–1963 | Lyndon B. Johnson 1963–1969

1960 — 1965

World Events

1960 In Ceylon (now Sri Lanka), Sirimavo Bandaranaike is elected the world's first female prime minister.

1963 Soviet cosmonaut Valentina Tereshkova becomes the first woman in space.

1966 Indira Gandhi becomes prime minister of India.

eTeach

Be sure to check out this month's online discussion with a Master Teacher. Go to **www.phschool.com**.

RESOURCE DIRECTORY

Teaching Resources

Pacing Charts booklet
Block Scheduling booklet, p. 28
Units 5/6/7 booklet
- Chapter Summary, p. 73

Technology

Guided Reading Audiotapes (English/Spanish), Ch. 23
Student Edition on Audio CD, Ch. 23
Prentice Hall United States History Video Collection™ Volume 20, *Post-War USA*
Prentice Hall Presentation Pro CD-ROM, Ch. 23
Resource Pro® CD-ROM
Social Studies Skills Tutor CD-ROM
Companion Web site, www.phschool.com

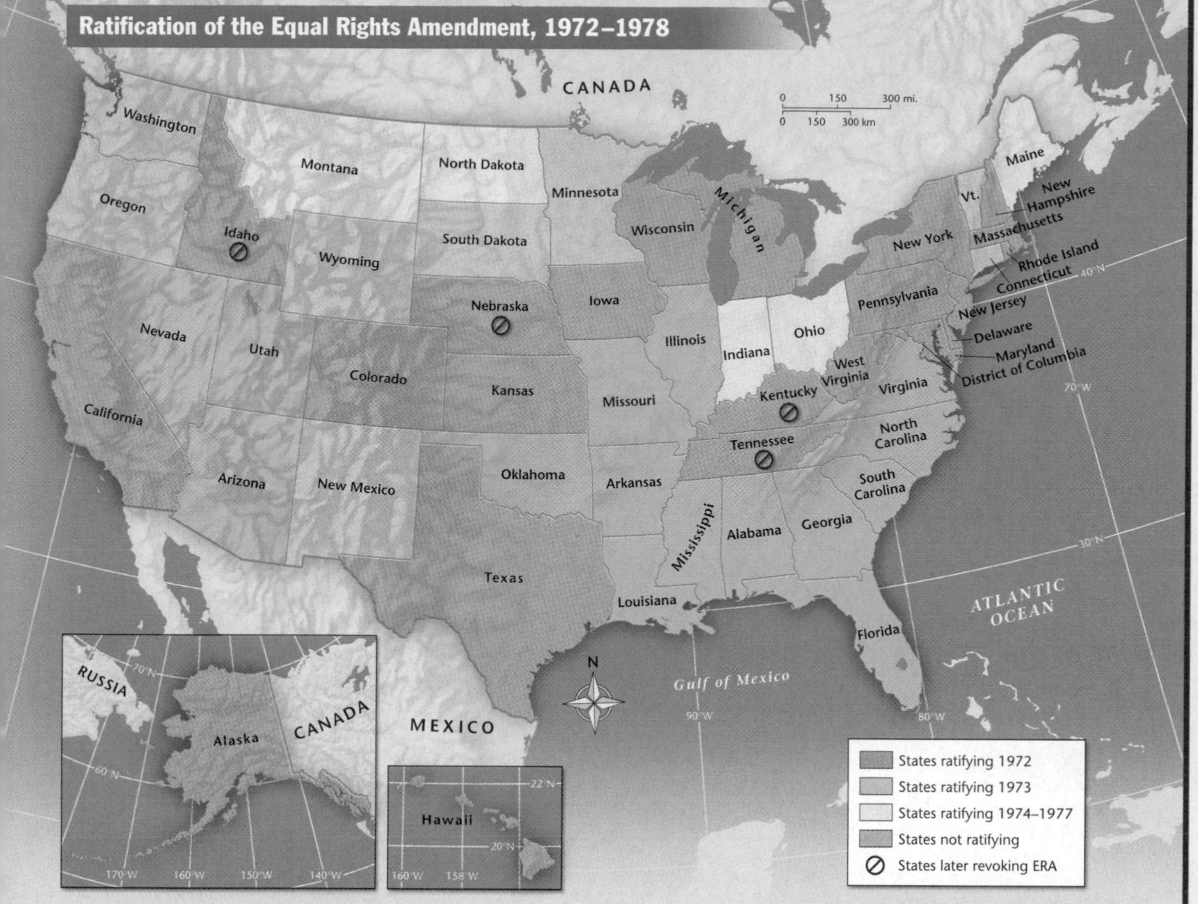

Ratification of the Equal Rights Amendment, 1972–1978

- States ratifying 1972
- States ratifying 1973
- States ratifying 1974–1977
- States not ratifying
- ⊘ States later revoking ERA

1969 The Woodstock festival celebrates rock music and the counterculture.

1970 The first Earth Day is celebrated, the Environmental Protection Agency is established, and Congress passes the Clean Air Act.

1973 The Supreme Court legalizes abortion in *Roe* v. *Wade*. Protesters from the American Indian Movement take over the reservation at Wounded Knee.

Richard M. Nixon 1969–1974 | Gerald R. Ford 1974–1977

1970 | 1975

1971 Greenpeace is founded in Vancouver, Canada.

1973 The Vietnam War ends with the signing of a formal peace agreement in Paris.

Ratification of the Equal Rights Amendment, 1972–1978

Activating Prior Knowledge Which states ratified the Equal Rights Amendment (ERA) between 1974 and 1977? *(Indiana, Ohio, Montana, Maine, and North Dakota)*

Previewing To become law, the ERA had to be ratified by 38 states within 10 years of its introduction in 1972. By looking at the map, calculate whether the ERA was passed into law by 1978. *(By 1978 there were not 38 states that had ratified the ERA, so it did not pass into law.)*

BACKGROUND About the Pictures

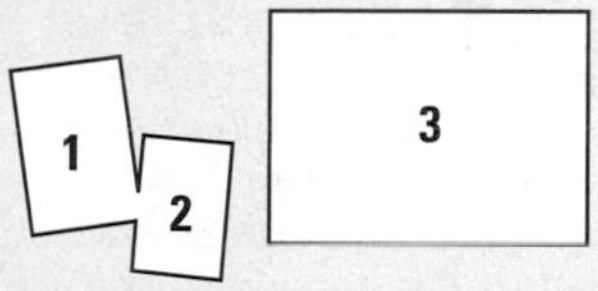

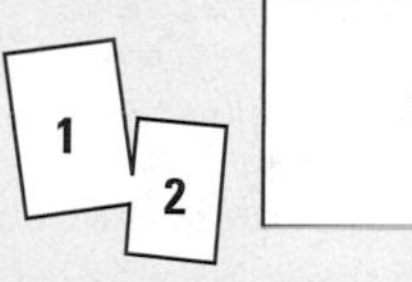

1. *Silent Spring* illustrated the harmful environmental effects of heavy chemical pesticide use and discouraged dependence on them in favor of a more varied approach to pest control.
2. Friedan's book shed light on women's feelings of frustration and inadequacy stemming from their reliance on their husbands for economic, emotional, and intellectual stability.
3. The boycott and strike lasted five years and, after many conflicts and court battles, ended in favor of the United Farm Workers.

BIBLIOGRAPHY

For the Teacher

Carson, Rachel. ***Silent Spring.*** Houghton Mifflin, 1994. (Classic, groundbreaking book on environmental awareness.)

Friedan, Betty. ***The Feminine Mystique.*** W. W. Norton, 2001. (A critique of postwar inequities and discrimination against women.)

For the Student

Momaday, N. Scott. ***House Made of Dawn.*** HarperCollins, 1999. (The Pulitzer Prize–winning novel of a young Native American caught between the white world and the ways of his people; written by an Oklahoma Kyowa.)

Unger, Irwin, and Unger, Debi (editors). ***The Times Were a Changin': The Sixties Reader.*** Three Rivers Press, 1998. (A collection of documents that brings central 1960s issues to life.)

Don't miss the exclusive interactive version of this textbook on the Web and on CD-ROM.

Section 1 The Women's Movement

Section Objectives

1. Discover the background of the women's movement.
2. Find out how women organized to gain support and to effect change.
3. Observe the impact of feminism.
4. Learn which groups opposed the women's movement and why.

Bellringer

Warm-Up Activity Write the terms *feminist* and *women's libber* on the chalkboard. Ask students to list five words that help describe each. Have them rank the words in order from most positive to most negative.

Activating Prior Knowledge Ask students to state their opinions as to the lasting impact of women's liberation activities of the 1960s and 1970s.

Reading Strategy

Ask students to write the following three columns on a piece of paper: *Social Conditions for Women in the 1950s, Steps Taken by Feminists to Change Conditions,* and *Opposition to the Feminist Movement.* As students read the section, have them note relevant information in the appropriate columns.

Activity

Connecting with Citizenship

Tell students to use names, acronyms, and other terms they encounter in this section to create a crossword puzzle on the women's rights movement. Suggest that they construct the filled-in puzzle first, then number the appropriate boxes and write the corresponding horizontal and vertical clues. (You may want to display a crossword puzzle from a newspaper or puzzle book as a model for students to follow.) Have students exchange an uncompleted version of their work and see if they can fill in one another's puzzles. **(Logical/Mathematical)**

Section 1 The Women's Movement

READING FOCUS

- What was the background of the women's movement?
- How did women organize to gain support and to effect change?
- What was the impact of feminism?
- Which groups opposed the women's movement and why?

MAIN IDEA

The women's movement, which was dedicated to ending discrimination based on gender, found inspiration in the civil rights movement and other activist causes.

KEY TERMS

feminism
National Organization for Women (NOW)
Roe v. *Wade*
Equal Rights Amendment (ERA)

TAKING NOTES

Copy the web diagram below. As you read, write the conditions that led to the women's movement in the bubbles on the left. Write the effects on the right.

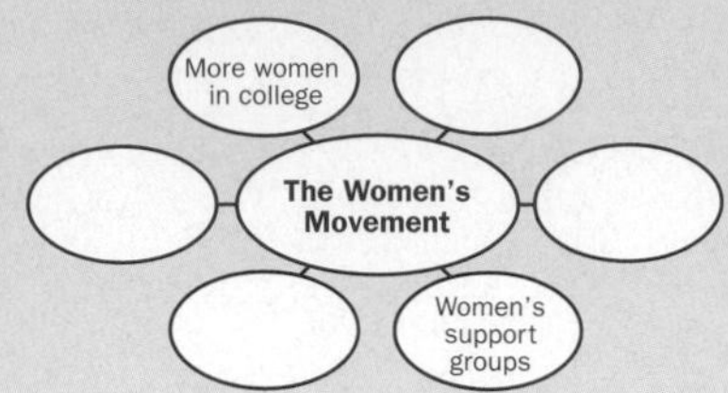

Setting the Scene Songwriter Bob Dylan's 1964 hit "The Times They Are A-Changin'" reflected the atmosphere of the sixties. The fifties had been primarily a time of unprecedented prosperity and security, but not all groups had participated equally. The sixties ushered in an era of activism, as these groups and their supporters seized the opportunity to make their voices heard. One demand for change came from women who did not want to be limited to the traditional roles of wife and mother. These women demanded the same opportunities as men. Pop singer Helen Reddy's 1971 song exemplified this new point of view:

> "*I am woman, hear me roar*
> *In numbers too big to ignore,*
> *And I know too much to go back*
> *and pretend. . . .*
> *Yes, I've paid the price*
> *But look how much I gained.*
> *If I have to, I can do anything.*
> *I am strong, I am invincible,*
> *I am woman.*"
>
> —Ray Burton and Helen Reddy

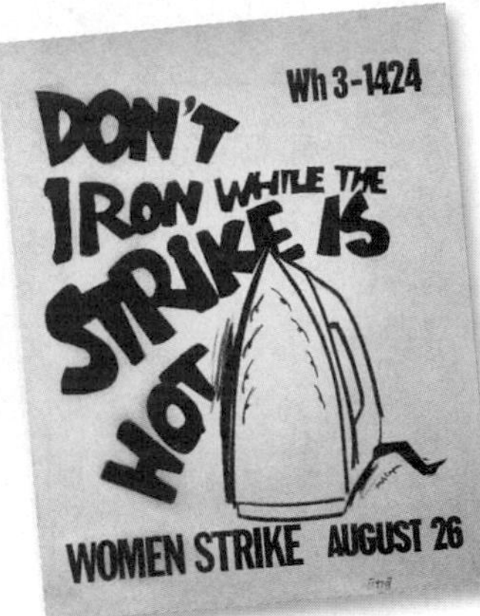

On August 26, 1970, the anniversary of the passage of the constitutional amendment granting women suffrage, thousands of women took the day off from jobs and household chores to observe Women's Equality Day.

These lyrics reflect the sense of self-confidence and strength that helped to create the new women's movement in the 1960s and continued to drive it forward into the 1970s.

Background of the Women's Movement

The crusade for women's rights was not new in 1960. In the late 1800s, particularly, women had worked for the right to vote and for equality in education and in jobs. The term **feminism,** which came to be associated with the 1960s, had first come into recorded use in 1895 to describe the theory of political, economic, and social equality of men and women. Feminists were those who believed in this equality or took action to bring it about.

Resource Directory

Teaching Resources
Guided Reading and Review booklet, p. 120

Technology
Section Reading Support Transparencies
Guided Reading Audiotapes (English/Spanish), Ch. 23
Student Edition on Audio CD, Ch. 23
Prentice Hall Presentation Pro CD-ROM
Companion Web site, www.phschool.com

While much progress had been made since the 1890s, the full equality sought by feminists had not been achieved. The women's movement of the 1960s sought to change aspects of American life that had been accepted for decades. The 1950s stereotype of women still placed them in the home, married and raising children. For many women, this stereotype did not reflect either reality or necessity. As had been the case in earlier decades, many women needed to work in order to support themselves or to help support their families. Furthermore, World War II had opened many new employment opportunities for women. During and after the war, more and more women entered the labor force. By the beginning of the 1960s, about 38 percent of all women held jobs. In addition, many women were educated, and looked forward to putting their education to use in professional careers.

The new women's movement chose symbols of power to represent its cause.

Education and Employment An increasing number of women began going to college after World War II. In 1950, only 25 percent of all Bachelor of Arts degrees were earned by women. Twenty years later, in 1970, the number was 43 percent. Better-educated women had high hopes for the future, but they were often discouraged by the discrimination they faced when they looked for jobs or tried to advance in their professions.

In many cases, employers were reluctant to invest in training women because they expected female employees to leave their jobs after a few years to start families. Other employers simply refused to hire qualified women because they believed that home and family should be a woman's only responsibility.

Women who did enter the work force often found themselves underemployed, performing jobs and earning salaries below their abilities. Working women earned less than working men doing similar or even identical jobs. In 1963, women, on average, were paid only 59 cents for each dollar that men earned. By 1973, this figure had dropped to 57 cents. This financial inequality created a growing sense of frustration among women and led to renewed demands for equal pay for equal work.

The Impact of the Civil Rights Movement While social, educational, and economic conditions set the scene for the women's movement, the civil rights movement provided a "how to" model for action. It also provided inspiration. Black and white women had joined in the struggle for civil rights and gained valuable skills from their work in the movement. At the same time, they had endured frustration over their second class status in civil rights organizations. As they worked to end racial discrimination, women were expected to make coffee and do clerical work while men made most of the policy decisions. Frustrated over their assigned roles, women began to apply the techniques that had been successful in the civil rights movement to a new movement that would address their own concerns.

The civil rights movement also provided women with legal tools to fight discrimination. One such tool was the 1964 Civil Rights Act. Originally, the section of the act called Title VII prohibited discrimination based on race, religion, or national origin. When Congress debated the bill, however, some opponents of civil rights added an amendment to outlaw discrimination on the basis of gender. This action was a strategy to make the entire bill look ridiculous, so that it would fail in the final vote. To the dismay of its opponents, both the amendment and the bill passed. The

INTERPRETING GRAPHS
Women's incomes continued to lag behind men's earnings, partly because many low-paying jobs were traditionally considered "women's work." **Making Comparisons** *How did the gap change between 1950 and 1975?*

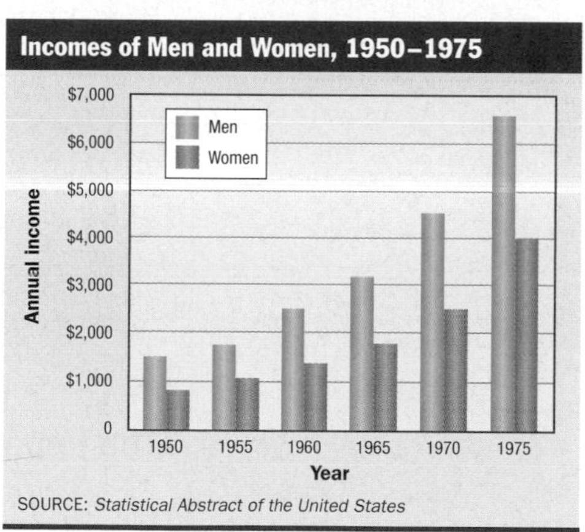

Lesson Plan

Focus Women were among the first groups to note the successes of the civil rights movement and to apply them to the inequalities of their own lives. Ask students how the women's movement affected American society.

Instruct Discuss the conditions in American society that feminists wanted to change. Ask students to list the ways in which employers discriminated—and in some cases continue to discriminate—against women.

Ask students to list the kinds of action taken by feminists to improve conditions for women. Which were most successful?

Assess/Reteach Ask students to consider the ways in which the Women's Liberation Movement improved women's lives. Are there also ways in which this movement created more challenges for women? Have students list some of those challenges.

Background

Workplace Opportunities

In the late 1960s and early 1970s, women created a vast network of health clinics, legal centers, newspapers, counseling centers, and professional caucuses for their needs. But since "men and institutions resisted radical challenges," according to one historian, women found it difficult to break through the "glass ceiling" in business. Women with college degrees were earning half as much as men with similar education, and one-third of all working women held clerical jobs. Even by the late 1970s, very few women were executives or upper-level managers.

Customize For ...

Less Proficient Readers

Ask students to correct the following incorrect statements.

- In the 1960s women were paid the same wages as men.
- The civil rights movement learned techniques and tactics from the women's movement.

Caption Answers

Interpreting Graphs In dollar amounts, the gap grew larger. In percentages, it grew smaller.

new Civil Rights Act now had a provision that gave women a legal framework to challenge discrimination.

Even with the added boost of the new legislation, progress took time. Women soon discovered that the Equal Employment Opportunity Commission (EEOC) set up by the bill did not take women's discrimination claims seriously. Nevertheless, Title VII would be tremendously important as the women's movement gained strength.

Women's Groups Organize

As the 1960s unfolded, women began to meet in groups to compare experiences. Women active in the civil rights movement met to look for ways in which they could play a larger role in that struggle. Soon they went beyond politics, exploring other aspects of their lives. The growing movement drew women who were active in other forms of protest and reform. They included student radicals, opponents of the Vietnam War and the draft, and workers for welfare rights and other social issues. Another important influence was Betty Friedan's 1963 book *The Feminine Mystique.* The dissatisfied housewives that Friedan described in her book began meeting, too, to discuss their lives and their roles in society.

Support Groups Meeting in kitchens and living rooms, women began gathering in consciousness-raising groups, which were dedicated to increasing their members' awareness of women's situation in society. One participant, Nancy Hawley, who was a community activist in Boston, Massachusetts, was troubled by patterns she saw at work. "Though many of us were working harder than the men," she noted, "we realized we were not listened to and often ignored." Growing numbers of women recognized the negative attitudes, or sexism, directed toward them. Many told of being ridiculed for attending women's groups. Such lack of support outside the group made their bond stronger within the group.

Organizing NOW In 1966, a group of 28 professional women, including Betty Friedan, established the **National Organization for Women (NOW).** These women were frustrated that existing women's groups were unwilling to pressure the Equal Employment Opportunity Commission to take women's grievances more seriously. The goal of NOW was "to take action to bring American women into full participation in the mainstream of American society now."

NOW sought fair pay and equal job opportunities. It attacked the "false image of women" in the media, such as advertising that used sexist slogans or photographs. NOW also called for more balance in marriages, with men and women sharing parenting and household responsibilities. A year after NOW was founded, it had 1,000 members. Only four years later, some 15,000 women had joined.

For some women, NOW seemed too extreme; for others, it was not extreme enough. Some saw NOW—and the women's movement in general—as mainly benefiting white, middle-class women. Nonetheless, NOW served as a rallying point to end sex discrimination and to promote equality for all women.

The Impact of Feminism

The women's movement came of age in the early 1970s. In August 1970, a New York City march celebrating the fiftieth anniversary of women's suffrage drew

Focus on CULTURE

The Feminine Mystique Betty Friedan's book *The Feminine Mystique* caused a sensation in the suburbs of America. It addressed the women who had everything that society said they should want: husbands who were good providers, healthy children, a house in the suburbs—often even the time and money to furnish and refurnish the comfortable homes they ran for their families. But many of these women were not happy, and when they said so, they were often called "neurotic" or not normal. Friedan called it "the problem that had no name"—the dissatisfaction of not being able to realize one's own full potential. Many women were dissatisfied with being regarded only as support services for their families, with constantly subordinating their own need for personal growth and fulfillment to the needs of their families, and with second-class citizenship in law and in the marketplace. Friedan gave these women the courage to ask, "Is this all?"—and her book helped women realize that it doesn't have to be.

ACTIVITY

Connecting with Citizenship

During the civil rights movement, women learned protest tactics that they then used to fight their own battle against discrimination. To help students understand how protest tactics allowed the civil rights movement to bring about changes in the United States, divide them into small groups to design a campaign for youth rights. Each group should create an identifying acronym, give one example of a discriminatory practice against youth, and describe a peaceful tactic that could be used to change this practice. **(Verbal/Linguistic)**

From the Archives of

AmericanHeritage®

ERA

On March 22, 1972, by a vote of 84 to 8, the Senate passed the Equal Rights Amendment, a goal of feminists for half a century. Since the House had given equally lopsided approval the previous fall, the amendment went to the states for ratification. Thirty-two minutes after the Senate vote, Hawaii became the first to ratify; New Hampshire and Nebraska followed the next day. Support for the idea of equality quickly swept the country, with both major parties endorsing the amendment. Within a year of the Senate vote, 30 of the required 38 states had passed the ERA. Boosters confidently predicted a quick completion of the process. Over the remainder of 1973, though, no more states added their names to the list. In 1974, even as polls showed three-quarters of Americans in favor, just three states gave their consent. One state ratified in 1975 and one in 1977, raising the total to 35, but that was all. The ERA's time limit expired in 1982, and since then, there has been no serious attempt to get it through Congress again. Source: Frederic D. Schwarz, "The Time Machine," *American Heritage®* magazine, February 1997.

RESOURCE DIRECTORY

Teaching Resources

Biography, Literature, and Comparing Primary Sources booklet (Comparing Primary Sources) *On Working Mothers,* pp. 155–156

Technology

Color Transparencies *Fine Art,* E20

tens of thousands of demonstrators supporting women's equality. More women began identifying themselves as feminists. Even those who did not join feminist groups could now find new kinds of information and opinions on women's issues. One new source was a book called *Our Bodies, Ourselves.* This handbook, published in 1970 by a women's health collective in Boston, encouraged women to understand their own health issues. It sold 200,000 copies in the first several years after its publication and three million by 1990.

In 1972, journalist Gloria Steinem and several other women founded *Ms.* magazine. Devoted to feminist issues, *Ms.* provided women with viewpoints that were decidedly different from those in *Good Housekeeping, Ladies' Home Journal,* and other women's magazines of the day. All 300,000 copies of the preview issue sold out in eight days. Only one year later, *Ms.* had nearly 200,000 subscribers. While not all readers considered themselves feminists, the magazine familiarized its audience with the arguments and issues of the women's movement.

READING CHECK
What were some of the effects of the women's movement?

A Shift in Attitudes Slowly the women's movement brought a shift in attitudes and in the law. For example, in 1972, Congress passed a prohibition against gender discrimination as part of the Higher Education Act. A survey of first-year college students revealed a significant change in career goals—and opportunities. In 1970, men interested in fields such as business, law, engineering, and medicine outnumbered women by eight to one. Five years later, the margin had dropped to three to one. More women entered law school and medical school. Women were finally admitted to military academies to be trained as officers.

In 1971, the National Women's Political Caucus was formed to expand women's participation in politics. By working from within the system, women were able to gain broader support for the goals of the women's movement. Women also became more influential in politics. New Yorker Shirley Chisholm, who was a founder of the National Women's Political Caucus, served in the House of Representatives from 1969 to 1983. In 1972, she ran for President, winning 152 delegates to the Democratic National Convention before she withdrew from the race. Chisholm's candidacy demonstrated that an African American woman

COMPARING PRIMARY SOURCES

Working Mothers

In the early years of the women's movement, experts disagreed over the issue of working mothers.

Analyzing Viewpoints What assumptions and biases about women and about children are revealed by each author? What reasonable argument does each author use?

In Favor of Working Mothers

"At the present time, one can say anything—good or bad—about children of employed mothers and support the statement by some research finding. But there is no definitive evidence that children are less happy, healthy, adjusted, because their mothers work. The studies that show working women to be happier, better, more mature mothers do not get much publicity."

—*Betty Friedan,* The Feminine Mystique, *1963*

Opposed to Working Mothers

"To work or not to work? Some mothers have to work to make a living. Usually their children turn out all right, because some reasonably good arrangement is made for their care. But others grow up neglected and maladjusted. . . . It doesn't make sense to let mothers go to work making dresses in a factory or tapping typewriters in an office, and have them pay other people to do a poorer job of bringing up their children."

—*Benjamin Spock, M.D.,* Baby and Childcare, *1957 first published in 1946*

ACTIVITY
Connecting with Culture

Challenge students to write short stories about a woman in the early 1960s who finds herself wanting or needing to enter the workplace and the obstacles she must confront in doing so. As they write their stories, have students consider and identify the political, social, and economic contributions of women to society. **(Verbal/Linguistic)**

BACKGROUND
Biography

In 1970 Betty Friedan (b. 1921) helped create the National Women's Political Caucus, and led a national Women's Strike for Equality. Friedan continually encouraged women "to march, to picket, and to speak up for equal rights." A frequent target of her attacks was the advertising industry, which she claimed promoted an image of women as the "weaker sex." In her 1981 book *The Second Stage*, Friedan assumed a more moderate stance, and criticized earlier feminists for trying to emulate the male realm rather than "affirm the differences between men and women."

READING CHECK
The formation of NOW and women's support groups; increasing numbers of women enrolled in law schools and medical schools in the 1970s. Gender discrimination in higher education is outlawed by Congress.

TEST PREPARATION

Have students read the section "The Impact of Feminism" on these pages and then answer the question below.

In what way did the 1972 Higher Education Act reflect the influence of the women's movement?

- Ⓐ The act included a prohibition against gender discrimination.
- **B** The act did not reflect the influence of the women's movement.
- **C** The act supported the continuation of gender discrimination.
- **D** The act explicitly supported equal rights for men and women.

ACTIVITY
Connecting with Government

Have students work in pairs to create a handbill, leaflet, or pamphlet that supports or opposes ratification of the ERA. Tell students that their literature should include illustration and information that would attract readers to its position. Display student work and have the class decide which piece is the most compelling for each side of the issue. **(Verbal/Linguistic; Visual/Spatial)**

BACKGROUND
Connections to Today

Some of the lasting effects of the social movements of the 1960s and 1970s were in the areas of environmental awareness and health education. When DDT manufacturers fought back against Rachel Carson, it was just one of many occasions in American history when businesses gave profits a higher priority than safety. Until well into the 1990s, tobacco companies refused to accept evidence showing that cigarette smoking can cause cancer. Sometimes companies cover up facts they have discovered; in the early 1990s Dow Corning was cited for ignoring evidence that their silicone breast implants might be harmful to women.

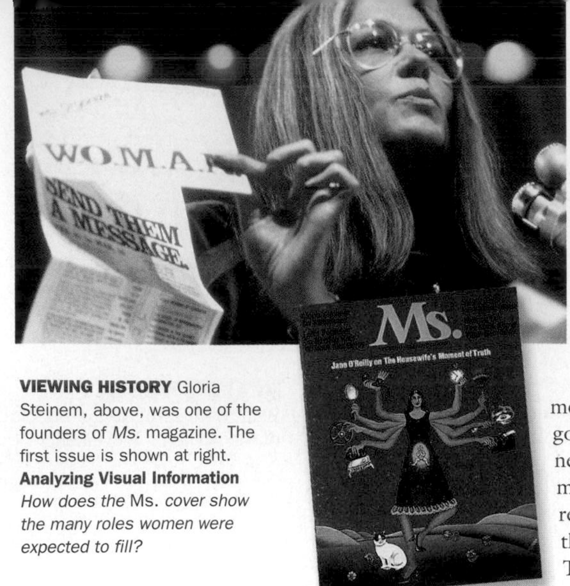

VIEWING HISTORY Gloria Steinem, above, was one of the founders of *Ms.* magazine. The first issue is shown at right. **Analyzing Visual Information** *How does the* Ms. *cover show the many roles women were expected to fill?*

could gain support for national office. And she paved the way for Geraldine Ferraro's selection as the Democratic Party's vice presidential candidate in 1984.

Many women did not actively participate in or support the women's movement. Still, most agreed with NOW's goal to provide women with better job opportunities. Many were also pleased that the women's movement brought a greater recognition of issues important to women. These issues included the need for child-care facilities, shelters for homeless women, more attention to women's health concerns, and increased awareness of sexual harassment.

Despite many shared concerns, the women's movement continued to be divided regarding some of its goals and strategies. Radical feminists emphasized the need to end male domination, sometimes even rejecting men, marriage, and childbearing. Other women rejected the strong opinions of the radicals, fearing they would cause a split in the women's movement. These women emphasized that they sought only equality with men, not rejection of them.

Roe* v. *Wade One issue that had the potential to divide the movement was abortion. NOW and other groups worked to reform the laws governing a woman's decision to choose an abortion instead of continuing an unwanted pregnancy. Many states outlawed or severely restricted access to abortion. Women who could afford to travel to another state or out of the country could usually find legal medical services, but poorer women often turned to abortion methods that were not only illegal but unsafe.

A landmark social and legal change came in 1973, when the Supreme Court legalized abortion in the controversial ***Roe* v. *Wade*** decision. The justices based their decision on the constitutional right to personal privacy, and struck down state regulation of abortion in the first three months of pregnancy. However, the ruling still allowed states to restrict abortions during the later stages of pregnancy. The case was, and remains, highly controversial, with radical thinkers on both sides of the argument.

The Equal Rights Amendment Many women also took part in the campaign for a change to the Constitution that would make discrimination based on a person's sex illegal. In 1972, Congress approved passage of the **Equal Rights Amendment (ERA)** to the Constitution:

"Equality of rights under the law shall not be denied or abridged by the United States or by any State on account of sex."

—Equal Rights Amendment, 1972

Many women demonstrated in favor of ratification of the ERA.

To become law, the amendment had to be ratified by 38 states. Thirty states did so quickly. When a few others also ratified it, approval seemed certain. By 1977, 35 states had ratified the amendment, but opposition forces were gaining strength. The effort to add the ERA to the Constitution limped along until the 1982 deadline for ratification and then died.

CAPTION ANSWERS

Viewing History It shows each hand of an eight-handed woman doing a different task. Tasks include traditional housework, work outside the home, and looking pretty (the mirror).

RESOURCE DIRECTORY

Teaching Resources

Units 5/6/7 booklet
- Section 1 Quiz, p. 74

Guide to the Essentials
- Section 1 Summary, p. 111

Learning with Documents booklet (Primary Source Activity) *The Equal Rights Amendment,* p. 35

Great Debates booklet (Great Debates) *What are Equal Rights?* p. 22

Technology

Sounds of an Era Audio CD *Bella Abzug on the ERA,* 1970 recording

Exploring Primary Sources in U.S. History CD-ROM *Debate on the Equal Rights Amendment, Representatives Emmanuel Celler and Edith Green*

Opposition to the Women's Movement

It was a woman, conservative political activist Phyllis Schlafly, who led a national campaign to block ratification of the ERA. She said this about the amendment:

> *"It won't do anything to help women, and it will take away from women the rights they already have, such as the right of a wife to be supported by her husband, the right of a woman to be exempted from military combat, and the right . . . to go to a single-sex college."*
>
> —Phyllis Schlafly

Women already had legal backing for their rights, Schlafly argued. ERA supporters contested Schlafly's charges about the supposed effects of the ERA, such as the establishment of coed bathrooms and the end of alimony. Nevertheless, arguments such as Schlafly's were instrumental in preventing the ERA from being ratified before the deadline.

Schlafly was not alone in her opposition to the ERA and to the women's movement in general. Many men were also hostile to the feminist movement, which was sometimes scornfully called "women's liberation" or "women's lib."

Nor were all women sympathetic to the goals of the women's movement. Some women responded by stressing their desire to remain at home and raise children. They were happy with women's traditional roles and resented being told that they should feel dissatisfied. These women felt that their roles as wives, and particularly as mothers, were being undervalued by the women's movement. The result, as these women saw it, was less rather than more respect for women and for the important task of raising the next generation.

Opposition came from other quarters as well. Some African American women felt that combating racial discrimination was more important than battling sex discrimination. In 1974, NOW's African American president, Aileen Hernandez, acknowledged that "Some black sisters are not sure that the feminist movement will meet their current needs." Many working-class women felt removed from the movement, too. They believed they were being encouraged to give up homemaking in order to take up undesirable paid labor.

Nevertheless, the women's movement continued to make gains, to change minds, and to expand opportunities for women. In so doing, it became one of several important strands of reform in the era of activism.

VIEWING HISTORY Phyllis Schlafly spoke out against the ERA. **Determining Relevance** *Do you think the fact that Schlafly was a woman made her a more effective or less effective advocate for her point of view? Explain your answer.*

Section 1 Assessment

READING COMPREHENSION

1. What is **feminism?**
2. (a) When was **NOW** formed? (b) What was its purpose?
3. Who was Shirley Chisholm?
4. Explain the ***Roe* v. *Wade*** decision.
5. (a) What was the **ERA?** (b) How many states eventually ratified it?

CRITICAL THINKING AND WRITING

6. **Identifying Assumptions** (a) What beliefs led many women to support the women's movement? (b) What beliefs led others to oppose it?
7. **Writing an Opinion** Would there have been a successful women's movement without the example of the civil rights movement? Support your opinion in a paragraph.

Take It to the NET

Activity: Making a Poster Learn more about the battle over ratification of the ERA. Make a poster either for or against ratification. Use the links provided in the *America: Pathways to the Present* area of the following Web site for help in completing this activity.
www.phschool.com

Section 1 Assessment

Reading Comprehension

1. Feminism is the belief in women's rights. In the 1890s feminism was defined as the theory of political, economic, and social equality for both men and women.
2. (a) 1966. (b) NOW was dedicated to gaining fair and equal pay and treatment for American women.
3. A founder of the National Women's Political Caucus, she served in the House of Representatives from 1969 to 1983 and ran for President in 1972.
4. It legalized abortion during the first three months of pregnancy, based on the constitutional right to personal privacy.
5. (a) The Equal Rights Amendment, approved by Congress in 1972, would have added a constitutional amendment banning discrimination based on sex. (b) 35.

Critical Thinking and Writing

6. (a) That women should fight discrimination just as African Americans had in the civil rights movement; that women (more and more of whom were well educated) were doing work equal to men but not being compensated equally. (b) Many men disliked feminism, and many women saw no need for an expanded role; African American women were more concerned with civil rights; many housewives thought feminism devalued the roles of wife and mother.
7. Answers will vary, but opinions should be supported with facts from the section.

Take It to the NET

Posters should strongly support or oppose ratification using relevant historical facts and images to persuade the viewer.

Caption Answers

Viewing History Answers will vary, but should be well reasoned and well supported.

Recognizing Bias

Focus Students will practice recognizing bias in two written selections.

Instruct After students have read the selections, have them analyze the following quotation using the feature skills.

"As radical feminists we recognize that we are engaged in a power struggle with men, and that the agent of our oppression is man insofar as he identifies with and carries out the supremacy privileges of the male role. For while we realize that the liberation of women will ultimately mean the liberation of men from their destructive role of oppressor, we have no illusion that men will welcome this liberation without a struggle."

Extend See the Skills for Life activity in the Resource Directory below.

ANSWERS

Practice the Skill

1. **(a)** A: ERA passage will give too much power to the federal government. B: ERA passage will end legal discrimination against women. **(b)** No, each one is one-sided.
2. **(a)** Stated: the opening statement notes the passage will be an "objection to ERA." **(b)** Unstated: the author does not state her position clearly.
3. **(a)** A: none. B: The 14th and 15th amendments information; the date and events when Susan B. Anthony voted; the number of "legal discriminations" against women on state books; the ERA language. **(b)** Yes. Possible answers: A: The ERA is a power grab by Washington. States rights pertaining to women will go to the national government. B: The ERA will give women 100 percent protection of the Constitution.
4. **(a)** A: Supreme Court actions over the last 25 years have been bad. The federal government has too much power and wants more. B: Discrimination against women is built into the government. Women deserve equality and can only get it through "their own" Amendment. **(b)** A, by saying that everyone who doesn't agree is a fool. **(c)** B has more material that can be verified.

Recognizing Bias

Recognizing bias means being aware of information and ideas that are one-sided or that present only a partial view of a subject. Bias may be stated or unstated. A writer may admit partisanship, or bias, and then support one side of an issue. Unstated bias—when a source presents only one side of an issue while suggesting that it presents the whole picture—is more difficult to detect. The ability to spot bias will help you analyze information and make sound judgments about the reliability of sources.

Bias is often attached to issues that have emotional impact—issues that also inspire strong expressions of different points of view. One such issue was the Equal Rights Amendment (ERA).

LEARN THE SKILL

Use the following steps to recognize bias:

1. **Decide whether or not the source presents only one side of an issue.** Writing from a single viewpoint signals imbalance—and bias.
2. **Look for unstated as well as stated bias.** Look for clear statements of a position that signal stated bias. Also look for indications that a source is presenting only one side of the issue while suggesting it covers all sides; that is unstated bias.
3. **Determine whether the presentation of the issue is supported by opinions or verifiable facts.** Sometimes what appear to be facts are actually opinions disguised as facts. Remember, you can check the accuracy of facts in other sources.
4. **Examine the source for hidden assumptions or generalizations that are not supported by facts.** Look for sweeping generalizations and for claims that opposing opinions are worthless.

PRACTICE THE SKILL

Answer the following questions:

1. **(a)** What is the overall message of each passage? **(b)** Does either passage present both sides of the issue? Explain.
2. **(a)** Is the bias in Passage A stated or unstated? Explain. **(b)** Is the bias in Passage B stated or unstated? Explain.
3. **(a)** Which details in the passages can be checked for accuracy? **(b)** Are any opinions presented as though they were facts? Give an example.
4. **(a)** What hidden assumptions or generalizations do you find in the passages? **(b)** Which passage ridicules the opposing point of view? How does it do so? **(c)** How much would you rely on each passage for information about the ERA? Explain your reasoning.

APPLY THE SKILL

See the Chapter Review and Assessment for another opportunity to apply this skill.

A.

"My primary objection to ERA is that it's a broad, general amendment which is open to interpretation. I think only an absolute fool would give an open amendment to the Supreme Court in light of what the Court has done in the last twenty-five years.

The ERA is a power grab by Washington. States' rights pertaining to women will go to the national government. We've already given up power to the feds in other Constitutional amendments. Why give up more power?"

—Opponent of ERA, in *The Politics of the Equal Rights Amendment*, 1979

B.

"The 14th and 15th amendments, written in 1868 and 1870, said: 'All persons born or naturalized in the U.S. are citizens and have the right to vote.'

Susan B. Anthony, considering herself to be a person, registered and voted in 1872. She was arrested, brought to trial, convicted of the crime of voting—because she was a woman, and the word persons mentioned in our Constitution did not mean women. . . . If she were alive today, Susan B. Anthony might vote, but she would still see 1000 legal discriminations against women upon various state statute books. . . .

The solution of the problem of giving women 100 per cent protection of the Constitution . . . is the adoption of the Equal Rights for Women Amendment which reads: Equality of rights under law shall not be denied or abridged by the United States or by any state on account of sex."

——Proponent of ERA, in *Delta Kappa Gamma Magazine*, Fall 1969

RESOURCE DIRECTORY

Teaching Resources
Skills for Life booklet, p. 32

Technology
Social Studies Skills Tutor CD-ROM
Interactive Practice in
- Geographic Literacy
- Critical Thinking and Reading
- Visual Analysis
- Communications

Section 2

Ethnic Minorities Seek Equality

READING FOCUS

- How did Latinos seek equality during the 1960s and early 1970s?
- How did Asian Americans fight discrimination during this period?
- In what ways did Native Americans confront their unique problems?

MAIN IDEA

Inspired by the civil rights movement, Latinos, Asian Americans, and Native Americans organized to seek equality and to improve their lives.

KEY TERMS

Latino
migrant farm worker
United Farm Workers (UFW)
Japanese American Citizens League (JACL)
American Indian Movement (AIM)
autonomy

TAKING NOTES

As you read, complete the chart below to describe each group's struggle for equality.

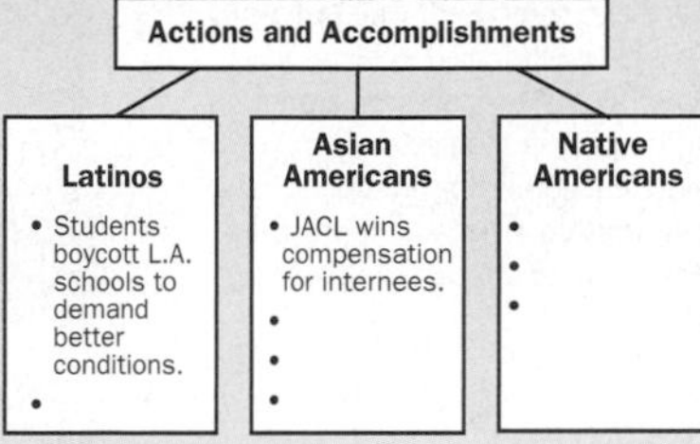

Actions and Accomplishments
Latinos
• Students boycott L.A. schools to demand better conditions.
•
Asian Americans
• JACL wins compensation for internees.
•
•
•
Native Americans
•
•
•

Setting the Scene

Inspired by the civil rights and women's movements, other ethnic and racial groups began to fight for equality during the 1960s and 1970s. In May 1970, journalist Rubén Salazar predicted the future of one of these new movements, the Chicano movement in Los Angeles, California. "We are going to overthrow some of our institutions," he said. "But in the way Americans have always done it: through the ballot, through public consensus. That's a revolution." Three months later, Salazar was killed in the rioting that broke out after police tried to stop a Chicano anti–Vietnam War demonstration.

After his death, Salazar became a martyr to the Chicano movement. His ideals and his death also point to the connection between the Chicano movement and other activist causes of the era, such as the antiwar and civil rights movements. In addition, Salazar's words show how these movements of the 1960s and 1970s fit into the long tradition of American reform—a tradition that is marked by change "through the ballot, through public consensus"—and occasionally marred by violence.

VIEWING HISTORY César Chávez leads a United Farm Workers Union march in 1965. **Checking Consistency** *Does this peaceful protest by Latino migrant workers correspond to the description of the "revolution" described by Rubén Salazar? Explain your answer.*

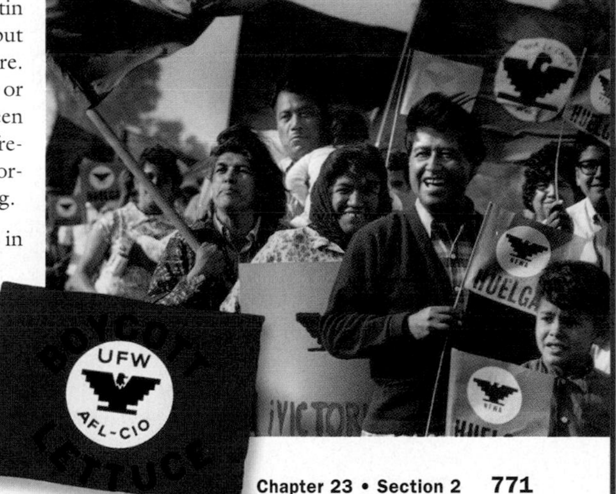

Latinos Fight for Change

People whose family origins are in Spanish-speaking Latin America, or **Latinos,** come from many different places, but they share the same language and some elements of culture. Whether their origins are in Puerto Rico, Cuba, Mexico, or other parts of the Americas, Latinos have often been regarded as outsiders by other Americans. They have frequently been denied equal opportunities in many important areas, including employment, education, and housing.

The Latino Population Spanish-speaking people lived in many parts of the present-day United States before English-speaking settlers arrived, and their numbers have grown steadily. In the late 1960s and early 1970s, for example, immigration from Central and South America increased, and between 1970 and 1980, census figures for people "of Spanish origin" rose from 9 million to 14.6 million. Specific groups

Section 2
Ethnic Minorities Seek Equality

Section Objectives

1. Learn how Latinos sought equality during the 1960s and early 1970s.
2. Find out how Asian Americans fought discrimination during this period.
3. See the ways in which Native Americans confronted their unique problems.

Bellringer

Warm-Up Activity Ask students to consider the dilemma faced by all ethnic Americans from the early days of mass immigration: whether to assimilate or to try to retain their native culture. Ask students to note what is gained and lost by assimilation.

Activating Prior Knowledge Ask students to consider the ways in which the civil rights movement, originally launched to improve the circumstances of African Americans, became a model for other minority groups. What techniques were adapted to support various struggles?

Reading Strategy

Have students skim the section and use the headings and subheadings to create an outline. Then, as they read, have them fill in appropriate details in the section outline.

Caption Answers

Viewing History Yes, in that it is a peaceful protest designed to change minds and laws.

RESOURCE DIRECTORY

Teaching Resources
Guided Reading and Review booklet, p. 121

Technology
Section Reading Support Transparencies
Guided Reading Audiotapes (English/Spanish), Ch. 23
Student Edition on Audio CD, Ch. 23
Prentice Hall Presentation Pro CD-ROM
Companion Web site, www.phschool.com

Lesson Plan

Focus Inspired by the civil rights movement, other ethnic minorities such as Latinos, Asian Americans, and Native Americans began to struggle for greater equality. Ask how their struggles differed.

Instruct Discuss how cultural differences among different groups of Latinos have led to many Latino movements rather than a single unified effort for equality in American society. Read this comment by Daniel Villanueva, a TV executive: "We need a Spanish Bobby Kennedy or Martin Luther King. Right now he's just not there." Discuss what a "Spanish Martin Luther King" might have been able to do that Cesar Chavez did not do.

Assess/Reteach Ask students to consider Latino, Asian American, and Native American groups' efforts to fight discrimination and secure equal rights. What were the primary concerns of each group? In what areas have the various groups succeeded in accomplishing their goals? In what areas does more work remain to be done?

Activity

Connecting with Citizenship

Have students work in groups to research and create time lines that compare major events in the civil rights movement for Asian Americans, Latinos, or Native Americans with major events in the African American civil rights movement. Be sure students focus on actions taken by people from these various ethnic groups to expand economic opportunities and political rights in American society. Display time lines for each movement and have students hypothesize how one movement might have influenced another. **(Visual/Spatial)**

Caption Answers

Viewing History Elements such as family values (the father and son); music (the blue note); the ancient and sophisticated cultures of Mexico (the Aztec eagle); the power of the UFW (its flag); Chicano political and labor power (the fist and the words).

VIEWING HISTORY Mexico's northern neighbors, California and Texas, traditionally received the majority of Mexican immigrants. This mural is located in Los Angeles. **Analyzing Visual Information** *What elements does the mural use to show Chicano cultural pride?*

tended to settle in certain areas. In the 1960s, Cubans, fleeing Fidel Castro's Communist rule, went first to Florida. Many of these refugees were educated professionals, and they became successful citizens of Miami and other American cities. The Puerto Ricans who moved to the Northeast, and the Mexicans who settled in the West and Southwest, usually had less education and found it harder to succeed in American society.

Mexican Americans, also known as Chicanos, have always made up the largest group of Latinos in the United States. In the 1960s, they began to organize against discrimination in education, employment, and the legal system, leading to *el Movimiento Chicano*—the Chicano movement.

Cultural Identity Chicano activists began encouraging Mexican Americans to take pride in their culture and its dual heritage from Spain and the ancient cultures of Mexico. Some of these activists also claimed that Anglos—white, English-speaking non-Latinos—had undermined Mexican Americans' control over their lives through economic pressure and through institutions such as the Roman Catholic Church, the media, and the schools.

This claim was supported by conditions in the Los Angeles barrios, or Latino neighborhoods. There, schools were crowded and run-down, with high dropout rates. In March 1968, 10,000 Mexican American students walked out of five such Los Angeles high schools to protest their unequal treatment. Latino students in other parts of California, and in the states of Colorado and Texas, followed their example. They demanded culturally sensitive courses, better facilities, and Latino teachers and counselors.

Organizing to Fight Discrimination The students were not the only protesters in the Latino community. Throughout the 1960s, organizers struggled to unite Latino farm workers. César Chávez became a hero to millions of Americans, both Latino and Anglo, in his effort to improve conditions for migrant workers. Moving from farm to farm, and often from state to state to provide the labor needed to plant, cultivate, and harvest crops, **migrant farm workers** were some of the most exploited workers in the country. They spent long hours doing backbreaking work for low pay, and their children had little opportunity for education.

Growing up among these farm workers, Chávez came to believe that unions offered them the best opportunity to gain bargaining power and

Focus on WORLD EVENTS

The Cuban Revolution In the 1950s, a young Cuban lawyer began organizing opposition to the corrupt regime of the Cuban dictator Fulgencio Batista. By 1959, Fidel Castro and his small band of guerrilla fighters had driven Batista from the country. When he took power, Castro promised an honest administration, full civil and political liberties, and moderate reforms. Instead, he imposed a one-party dictatorship, nationalized farms and industries, and suppressed all political dissent. Many Cubans—skilled workers, educated professionals, wealthy owners of businesses and farms, intellectuals and journalists—felt betrayed by Castro and chose to emigrate. Hundreds of thousands left Cuba, and many settled in the United States.

Resource Directory

Teaching Resources

Biography, Literature, and Comparing Primary Sources booklet (Biography) *Delores Huerta,* p. 35

Technology

Color Transparencies *American Diversity,* G12

Sounds of an Era Audio CD *César Chávez,* 1973 recording (time: 30 seconds)

RESOURCE PRO® **Literature Activity** *Perspectives of Women of Color,* found on Resource Pro, expresses the hopes of women of color with a poem by Puerto Rican–born poet Judith Ortiz Cofer.

to resist the economic power of their employers. In the 1960s, he and fellow-activist Dolores Huerta began to organize Mexican field hands into what became the **United Farm Workers (UFW).** They went from door to door and field to field. By 1965, the union had 1,700 members.

The UFW's first target was the grape growers of California. Chávez, like Martin Luther King, Jr., believed in nonviolent action. In 1967, when growers refused to grant more pay, better working conditions, and union recognition, Chávez organized a successful nationwide consumer boycott of grapes picked on nonunion farms. Later boycotts of lettuce and other crops also won consumer support across the country.

Chávez's efforts generated angry opposition and even brought him death threats. He responded this way:

> "*It's not me who counts, it's the Movement. And I think that in terms of stopping the Movement—this one or other movements by poor people around the country—the possibility is very remote. . . . The tide for change now has gone too far.*"
>
> —César Chávez

In 1975, California passed a law requiring collective bargaining between growers and union representatives. Workers finally had a legal basis to ask for better working conditions. By encouraging them to demand equality, the UFW had brought Latino migrant farm workers into the movement for civil rights.

While Chávez was organizing farm workers, other Chicanos took a different approach: they sought political power. In 1961, voters in San Antonio, Texas, elected Henry B. González to Congress. Another Texan, Elizo "Kika" de la Garza, went to the House of Representatives in 1964. Joseph Montoya of New Mexico was elected to the Senate in 1962. At the same time, new political groups formed to support Latino interests. In Texas, José Angel Gutiérrez spearheaded the formation of the political party *La Raza Unida* in 1970. This new party worked for better housing and jobs, and also backed Latino political candidates.

Yet a different approach was taken by Reies López Tijerina, who argued that the Anglo culture had stolen the Chicanos' land and heritage. To call attention to broken treaties, his *Alianza Federal de Mercedes* ("Federal Alliance of Land Grants") marched on the New Mexico state capital, Santa Fe, in 1966. At about the same time, the Mexican American Legal Defense and Educational Fund (MALDEF) began providing legal aid to help Mexican Americans defend their rights. It also encouraged Mexican American students to become lawyers.

BIOGRAPHY

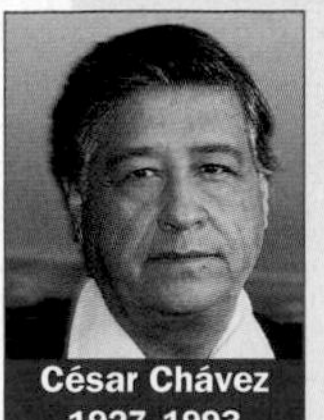
César Chávez
1927–1993

Before the Depression, César Chávez's father was a successful farmer and a local postmaster in Yuma, Arizona. In 1937, when César was 10, the family lost their farm because they could not afford the taxes. They became migrant workers in California. Because the family was always on the move, young César attended more than 30 different schools while working part time in the fields. Even so, the Chávez family fostered a powerful sense of independence. Chávez recalled, "I don't want to suggest we were that radical, but I know we were probably one of the strikingest families in California." After serving in the Navy, Chávez returned to California and worked as an organizer for the Community Services Organization before launching his own farm workers union.

Asian Americans Fight Discrimination

Ever since they first arrived in the United States, Americans of Chinese and Japanese ancestry have faced racial discrimination. Prejudice against Japanese Americans reached a peak during World War II, and the Communist takeover of China in 1949 caused negative feelings toward Chinese Americans. Still, the years after the war brought positive changes for Asian Americans.

Japanese Americans After the War As you have read, Japanese American citizens living along the West Coast were interned in camps during World War II. The government had feared that they were a risk to American security following Japan's attack on Pearl Harbor. Not only had they been unjustly detained and deprived of their rights as citizens, but they had also lost hundreds of millions of

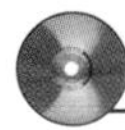

Sounds of an Era

Listen to a speech by César Chávez and other sounds from the activist movements of the 1960s and 1970s.

ACTIVITY
Connecting with Government

Ask students to research the Congressional Hispanic Caucus. Who are its members? What are its goals? How successful has the caucus been in reaching its goals? Have students present their information in a three-paragraph paper, with appropriate details covering each question above. **(Verbal/Linguistic)**

BACKGROUND
Recent Scholarship

The movement for Latino rights followed on the heels of the African American struggle for civil rights and the women's campaign for equality. Today, Latinos, like members of other groups, are trying to define their own role in American society. In *Mexican Americans: The Ambivalent Minority,* Peter Skerry argues that the Mexican American population faces different challenges from those faced by other groups. Focusing on San Antonio and Los Angeles and drawing on recent history, he suggests that assimilation will occur, but only within the context of radical changes in American institutions.

CUSTOMIZE FOR ...
Gifted and Talented

Ask students to analyze the success of the grape boycott and compare it with the Montgomery bus boycott. What made them different? Have students write a short essay in which they compare the work and tactics of César Chávez with those of Martin Luther King, Jr.

ACTIVITY
Connecting with Government

Divide the class into four groups. Have each student in Group One write a newspaper editorial supporting the compensation of Native Americans for the loss of their tribal lands. Tell students in Group Two to write editorials on why Native Americans should *not* be compensated. Have those in Groups Three and Four write similar editorials for each side on the compensation of Japanese Americans for their internment during World War II. You may then wish to have Groups One and Three and Groups Two and Four exchange editorials. Each student should write a letter to the editor opposing the position taken in the editorial he or she receives. **(Verbal/Linguistic)**

BACKGROUND
A Diverse Nation

Attempts to correct injustices against Native Americans often created other problems. When the Chippewa in Minnesota sued the government in 1975 to regain 100,000 acres that they claimed had been taken, in the words of one sympathetic historian, "through theft, trickery, ignorance, or for failing to pay taxes that were, in fact, illegal," the suit hurt white farmers who had bought the land in good faith. Because of the pending claims, banks wouldn't lend these farmers money to buy machinery, and no one would buy the land.

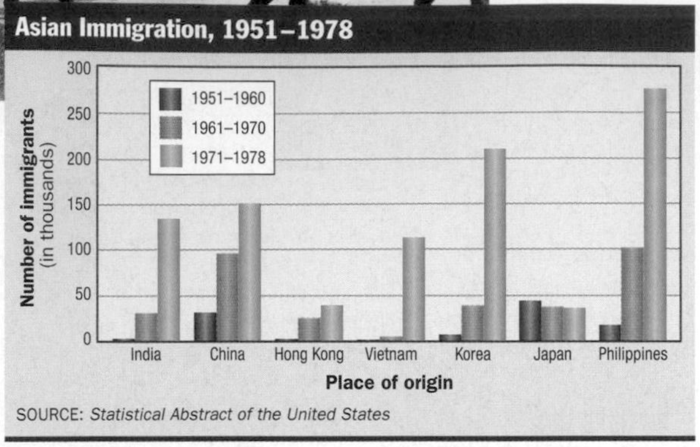

dollars in homes, farms, and businesses. After the war, many of those who had been interned sought compensation for these losses through the **Japanese American Citizens League (JACL).** In 1948, the JACL won passage of the Japanese American Claims Act. Under this act, Congress eventually paid relatively small amounts for property losses, with some claims not being settled until 1965. (It was not until 1988, however, that the United States apologized to Japanese American internees and paid them further monetary compensation.)

Economic and Political Advances Although Asian Americans as a group were well educated, in 1960 they earned less than white Americans. In California, for example, for each $51 a white man was paid, a Chinese man would earn $38 and a Japanese man, $43. College graduates faced prejudice when they tried to move into management positions. In the 1960s and 1970s, Asian Americans made economic gains faster than other minorities. Nonetheless, they still faced discrimination and relied on the example of the civil rights movement to push for change.

When Hawaii became a state in 1959, Asian Americans gained a voice in Congress. The new state sent Hiram Leong Fong, a Chinese American, to the Senate, and Daniel K. Inouye, a Japanese American, to the House of Representatives.

Asian Immigration, 1951–1978

SOURCE: *Statistical Abstract of the United States*

INTERPRETING GRAPHS The photo above shows the JACL participating in the 1963 Civil Rights March in Washington, D.C. Patterns of immigration from Asia changed dramatically from the 1950s to the 1970s. **Analyzing Information** *(a) Which two countries did the greatest number of Asian immigrants come from in the 1950s? In the 1970s? (b) What do you think might have accounted for this change?*

Native Americans Face Unique Problems

As the original inhabitants of North America, Native Americans have always occupied a unique social and legal position in the United States. Although the cultures and languages of Indian peoples varied, white society tended to view all Native Americans as one group. By 1871, the United States government no longer recognized Indian nations as independent powers. At the same time, it did not extend full citizenship to Native Americans, either. Instead, state and federal agencies limited self-government for Native Americans and often worked to destroy their traditional lifestyles. In 1924, the Snyder Act granted citizenship to all Native Americans born in the United States, but they continued to be recognized as citizens of their own nations or tribal groups as well. Even then, many states denied suffrage to Native Americans. It was not until 1948 that Arizona and New Mexico granted Indians the right to vote.

As a whole, Native Americans have routinely been denied equal opportunities. They have had higher rates of unemployment, alcoholism, and suicide, as well as a shorter life expectancy, than white Americans. Many communities have suffered from poverty and poor living conditions. Like other nonwhite groups, Native Americans have been the victims of centuries-old stereotypes reinforced by the images in movies and other media.

Native Americans also have had some grievances unique to their situation. The land now occupied by the United States was once theirs, and treaties made between Indian nations and the United States have repeatedly been broken by the American government.

Land Claims Traditional lands have a special role in most Native American cultures. "Everything is tied to our homeland," declared D'Arcy McNickle, a

CAPTION ANSWERS

Interpreting Graphs (a) 1950s: Japan and China. 1970s: the Philippines and Korea. (b) Answers will vary. They may include the fact that Japan's economy greatly improved over this period, so fewer Japanese may have felt the need to emigrate for economic reasons. At the same time, the Communists were tightening their hold over China and refusing to let Chinese people emigrate.

RESOURCE DIRECTORY

Teaching Resources

Great Debates booklet (Decision-Making Activities) *Native American Fishing Rights on Trial,* p. 42

Other Print Resources

Nystrom *Atlas of Our Country* *Later Expansion of the United States,* pp. 32–33; *The Fourth Wave of Immigration,* pp. 36–37

Technology

RESOURCE PRO® **Visual Learning Activity** *Changing Attitudes Toward Native Americans,* found on Resource Pro, portrays attempts made in the 1960s and 1970s to challenge stereotypes about Native Americans.

RESOURCE PRO® **Biography** *Vine Deloria Jr.,* found on Resource Pro, profiles the man who, through his books, emerged as the leading spokesman for Native American nationalism.

Native American anthropologist, in 1961. Yet, many years after pioneers first moved onto Native American territory, state and federal governments continued to take over traditional tribal lands. Protecting what was left became a major goal of Native American activists.

A government project in New York State triggered one early protest. According to a 1794 treaty, the Seneca Nation owned the land on its Allegany reservation. In 1956, when the federal government wanted to build a dam there, Congress held hearings that did not include the Seneca. Legal actions by the tribe and a 1961 appeal to President John Kennedy failed to halt the project. After the Kinzua Dam was completed, however, Congress agreed to pay $15 million in damages to the Seneca, but this award did not restore their hunting and fishing lands, homes, and sacred sites. In response, other Native American tribes, such as the Seminole, brought successful lawsuits for violations of treaty rights and failure to make promised payments.

The American Indian Movement In 1968, two Chippewa activists, Dennis Banks and George Mitchell, set out the goals of a new activist organization, the **American Indian Movement (AIM).** Banks called it "a new coalition that will fight for Indian treaty rights and better conditions and opportunities for our people." Following the example of militant black groups, AIM focused first on the special problems of Native Americans living in cities by setting up patrols and encouraging racial and cultural pride in young people. Eventually, AIM also fought for Native American legal rights, including **autonomy,** or self-government. It also sought control of natural resources on Native American lands, and the restoration of lands illegally taken from Indian nations. Many people, both white and Native American, criticized AIM's militant approach. Nevertheless, AIM continued to confront the government over Indian-rights issues.

VIEWING HISTORY AIM leader Dennis Banks leads a protest march in South Dakota. **Drawing Inferences** *Why do you think Banks chose to pose in front of Mount Rushmore?*

Confronting the Government Native American activists used standoffs with the federal government to call attention to issues that mainstream America had long ignored. In 1972, demonstrators protesting the violation of treaties between the United States and various Indian groups formed the Broken Treaties Caravan. They traveled to Washington, D.C., and occupied the Bureau of Indian Affairs' offices for six days. Other protests were even more dramatic.

In 1969, more than 75 Native American protesters landed on Alcatraz Island in San Francisco Bay. They claimed the 13-acre rock under the terms of the Fort Laramie Treaty of 1868, which allowed male Native Americans to file homestead claims on federal lands. Others joined the group, planning to turn the deserted island into an educational and cultural center. The occupation failed. Federal marshals eventually removed the last protesters after a year and a half. But the episode drew national attention to Native American grievances.

An even more dramatic confrontation came in 1973 at the Oglala Sioux village of Wounded Knee, South Dakota. In 1890, the army's Seventh Cavalry had massacred more than 200 Sioux men, women, and children there. The Pine Ridge reservation around the village was one of the country's poorest, with half of its families living on welfare. In February 1973, AIM took over the village and

READING CHECK
Describe two Native American protests.

ACTIVITY
Connecting with Culture

Cultural pride and education are very important tools for gaining self-determination. To help students understand the importance of cultural heritage and the ways in which it is taught, have them list as many aspects as possible of their own cultural heritage and recall briefly how they learned about them. **(Verbal/Linguistic)**

BACKGROUND
Biography

During the turbulent decade of the 1960s, Ben Nighthorse Campbell (b. 1933), a Northern Cheyenne, channeled an angry adolescence into the study of martial arts. It eventually earned him the captaincy of the 1964 United States Olympic Judo Team at the Tokyo games. In 1982, Campbell became the first Native American to serve in Congress since the 1930s. In 1992, he was elected to represent Colorado in the United States Senate.

READING CHECK
The Broken Treaties Caravan arrived in Washington, D.C., in 1972 and took over the offices of the Bureau of Indian Affairs. Violence erupted during the 1973 confrontation between American Indian Movement members and federal agents at Wounded Knee.

CUSTOMIZE FOR ...
Less Proficient Readers

Ask students to correct the following incorrect statements.

- Native Americans have rates of unemployment and alcoholism roughly equal to those of whites.
- The Seneca protest against the building of the Kinzua Dam succeeded in halting its construction.
- AIM's main goal was to secure more government handouts for Native Americans.

TEST PREPARATION

Have students reread the section "The American Indian Movement" on this page and then answer the question below.

One of the legal rights sought for Native Americans was *autonomy.* Which of the following is the best definition for autonomy?

A Independence.
B Freedom.
(C) Self-government.
D Legal authority.

CAPTION ANSWERS

Viewing History It is a famous symbol of national pride for white Americans and so would attract attention. Also, symbolically, Banks is bringing his grievances to the "attention" of the most honored of American leaders.

Section 2 Assessment

Reading Comprehension

1. Latinos are from Spanish-speaking Latin America, and Chicanos are Mexican Americans.
2. The UFW pressed for improved working conditions and higher wages for migrant farm workers. They orchestrated consumer boycotts to force recalcitrant farm owners to grant concessions to migrant laborers.
3. It organized Japanese Americans in an attempt to gain compensation for property losses sustained by Japanese Americans who were interned during World War II.
4. The American Indian Movement (AIM).

Critical Thinking and Writing

5. Native Americans used the aggressive tactics of militant black groups, such as taking over government buildings and creating standoffs with federal authorities. Native Americans wanted to protect what was left of Native American tribal lands and customs, and to gain autonomy. Latinos and Asian Americans, on the other hand, did not seek autonomy.
6. Answers will vary, but should be supported with facts from the section.

Encourage students to include both personal history and professional accomplishments in their biographical research.

VIEWING HISTORY Echoes of history surrounded the Sioux village of Wounded Knee during the AIM protest there. **Identifying Alternatives** *(a) Why did some people who sympathized with AIM's goals object to the organization's tactics? (b) What other tactics might AIM have used? Do you think they would have been as effective?*

refused to leave until the United States government agreed to investigate the treatment of Indians and the poor conditions on the reservation, and to review more than 300 treaties. Other Native American leaders supported the occupation. Onondaga Chief Oren Lyons, speaking for the Iroquois, said:

> *"We support the Oglala Sioux Nation or any Indian Nation that will fight for its sovereignty. . . . The issue here at Wounded Knee is the recognition of the treaties between the United States Government and the sovereign nations that were here before."*
>
> —Onondaga Chief Oren Lyons

Federal marshals and FBI agents put the village under siege, and agents arrested some 300 people, including news reporters and outside supporters. The standoff finally ended in May, when protesters agreed to surrender their weapons and to leave the reservation. In exchange, the government consented to reexamine Indian treaty rights. But during the siege, two AIM members had been killed and about a dozen people hurt, including two federal marshals.

Government Response Native American activism brought some positive government action. The Kennedy and Johnson administrations tried to bring jobs and income to some reservations by encouraging industries to locate there and by leasing reservation lands to energy and development corporations. But many Native Americans worried about the effects that these projects would have on the land, and later sought to renegotiate or cancel many of the leases.

A number of laws passed in the 1970s favored Native American rights. The Indian Education Act of 1972 gave parents and tribal councils more control over schools and school programs. The Indian Self-Determination and Education Assistance Act of 1975 upheld Native American autonomy and let local leaders administer federally supported social programs for housing and education. Native Americans also continued to win legal battles to regain land, mineral, and water rights.

Section 2 Assessment

READING COMPREHENSION

1. What are the family origins of **Latinos** and of Chicanos?
2. How did the **UFW** help **migrant farm workers?**
3. What was the purpose of the **Japanese American Citizens League?**
4. Which Native American group led the protest at Wounded Knee?

CRITICAL THINKING AND WRITING

5. **Making Comparisons** How and why was the Native Americans' struggle for equality different from that of Latinos and Asian Americans?
6. **Writing to Inform** Write a paragraph about one protest covered in this section. Include its purpose and its effect.

Take It to the NET

Activity: Writing a Biography Use both primary and secondary sources to write a biography of the United Farm Workers' founder César Chávez. Include quotes and important dates in his life. Use the links provided in the *America: Pathways to the Present* area of the following Web site for help in completing this activity. **www.phschool.com**

Caption Answers

Viewing History (a) The tactics were extreme and sometimes led to violence. (b) As an alternative, AIM might have kept their protests peaceful and thus might not have alienated potential supporters. Another alternative that might have worked better would have been to act within the political system by trying to win over influential politicians to AIM's positions.

RESOURCE DIRECTORY

Teaching Resources

Units 5/6/7 booklet
- Section 2 Quiz, p. 75

Guide to the Essentials
- Section 2 Summary, p. 112

Biography, Literature, and Comparing Primary Sources booklet (Literature) *Native American Voices,* p. 82

Technology

RESOURCE PRO® **Critical Thinking Activity** *Identifying Assumptions: The Beeah Tribe,* found on Resource Pro, allows students to identify assumptions by examining a satirical critique of the Bureau of Indian Affairs.

Section 3

The Counterculture

READING FOCUS

- What social changes were promoted by the counterculture?
- How did music both reflect and contribute to the cultural changes of this era?

MAIN IDEA

In the 1960s, a youth culture blossomed that promoted freedom and individuality. The counterculture's new attitudes toward personal relationships, drugs, and music shocked many Americans but ultimately changed American society.

KEY TERMS

counterculture
Woodstock festival

TAKING NOTES

Copy the web diagram below. As you read, fill in the characteristics of the counterculture and the changes they caused.

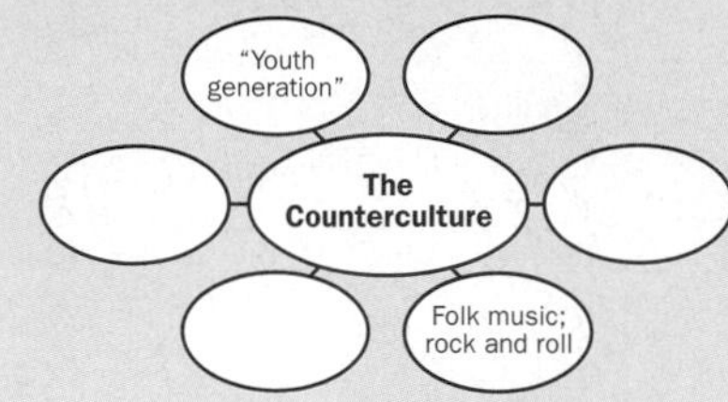

Setting the Scene

If the man in the gray flannel suit was the symbol of the 1950s, then the long-haired hippie dressed as outrageously as possible in bright colors, beads, and flowers was the symbol of the 1960s. The former looked adult and responsible, and was clearly dressed for nine-to-five success. He was the organization man, and conformed to the culture of his time. The latter, the hippie, rejected the gray flannel suit and the regimented life it represented. The hippie generation favored "flower power" over corporate and military power, and eventually influenced the dominant culture.

A Time of Change

In the 1960s, many young people adopted values that ran counter to, or against, the mainstream culture that they saw around them. Members of this **counterculture** valued youth, spontaneity, and individuality. Also called hippies, these young people promoted peace, love, and freedom. And they experimented with new styles of dress and music, freer attitudes toward sexual relationships, and the recreational use of drugs. The result was often a "generation gap," or a lack of understanding and communication between the older and younger generations.

The so-called youth generation had an enormous influence on American society. First of all, it was the largest generation in American history. The "baby boom" that followed World War II resulted in a huge student population in the 1960s. By sheer numbers, the baby boomers became a force for change. The music industry rushed to produce the music they liked; clothing designers copied the styles they

The hippie (seated below) is doing his best *not* to look like the man of the fifties (at left).

Section 3

The Counterculture

Section Objectives

1. Find out about social changes promoted by the counterculture.
2. Learn how the music world of the 1960s and 1970s contributed to the cultural changes of this era.

Bellringer

Warm-Up Activity Ask students to think about the meaning of the compound word counterculture. Ask them to consider how far the values, attitudes, and activities of young people in the 1960s ran "counter" to traditional American culture.

Activating Prior Knowledge Have students suggest words and phrases that describe, to them, the meaning and lasting impact of the 1960s counterculture movement.

Reading Strategy

As students read the section, have them note details that support the following sentence from this page: "In the 1960s, many young people adopted values that ran counter to, or against, the mainstream culture that they saw around them."

Activity

Connecting with History and Conflict

Invite students to imagine they are living in the 1960s. Then organize them into groups to create five-minute skits about the counterculture and the generation gap. Group members should take the roles of hippie youth, "responsible" adults, and their college-age children. The hippies and adults should defend their lifestyles and question the others' values, while the college students decide which way of life they will follow and why. Have each group perform its skit for the class. **(Bodily/Kinesthetic)**

RESOURCE DIRECTORY

Teaching Resources

Learning Styles Lesson Plans booklet, p. 62
Guided Reading and Review booklet, p. 122

Technology

Section Reading Support Transparencies
Guided Reading Audiotapes (English/Spanish), Ch. 23
Student Edition on Audio CD, Ch. 23
Prentice Hall Presentation Pro CD-ROM
Companion Web site, www.phschool.com

Lesson Plan

Focus Explain that in the 1960s, a youth culture rejected conventional norms and values. Ask what norms and values were embraced by the counterculture. How did the counterculture affect American life?

Instruct Discuss the aspects of American life that hippies rejected. What sort of life did hippies want to build for themselves? Discuss the reactions of other Americans to hippies and would-be hippies. Why did hippies attract so much attention? Why did some more conservative Americans feel threatened by the hippie lifestyle? Ask students which aspects of the counterculture some people considered dangerous.

Assess/Reteach Have students list the aspects of American society that were affected by the counterculture. Then have them analyze each aspect to see whether the impact of the counterculture endured beyond the era to this day.

introduced; universities changed college courses and rules to accommodate them. Politicians, too, found that they could not ignore the voice of the baby boom generation.

Sixties Style The look of the 1960s was distinctive, frivolous, and free. But it was also a signal of changing attitudes. The counterculture rejected restrictions and challenged authority. Many young women gave up the structured hairstyles of the 1950s and began wearing their hair long and free. They also chose freer fashions, such as loose-fitting dresses. Men, too, let their hair grow long and wore beards. Their clothing was as different from a gray flannel suit as they could make it—and that was the point. These styles announced a rejection of the corporate world and its uniform. Of course, hippie dress itself became a kind of uniform for the youth generation.

Many members of the counterculture identified with the poor and downtrodden around the world and at home. They fought for the civil rights of minority groups in the United States, and sided with those they believed were oppressed abroad. Hippies often adopted the dress of working people, including blue jeans, plain cotton shirts, peasant blouses, and other simple garments. They also sought out apparel of indigenous peoples, such as ponchos from South America, dashikis from Africa, jewelry made by Native Americans, and other handmade items.

The colorful look of the sixties was not confined to clothing. Hippies painted their cars—and their bodies. And this spirit of fun and irreverence also invaded the art world. The Pop Art of the 1960s, such as paintings by Andy Warhol and Roy Lichtenstein, featured realistic depictions of the artifacts of modern life. Scorned at the time, these satirical paintings of soup cans and comic books now hang in art museums. Another style, Op Art, captured the spirit of the sixties with its fluorescent colors and dizzying optical illusions. Many of the images were—or looked as though they were—created under the influence of psychedelic drugs. Op Art was especially popular for posters and album covers showcasing popular rock groups.

VIEWING HISTORY The Andy Warhol painting (above) and the Op Art poster (at right) show the irreverance of 1960s artists. **Making Comparisons** *What do the two art works have in common? How are they different?*

The Sexual Revolution Just as participants in the counterculture demanded more freedom to make personal choices in how they dressed, they also demanded more freedom to choose how they lived. Their new views of sexual conduct, which rejected many traditional restrictions on behavior, were labeled "the sexual revolution." Some of those who led this revolution argued that sex should be separated from its traditional ties to family life. Many of them also experimented with new living patterns. Some hippies rejected traditional relationships and lived together in communal groups, where they often shared property and chores. Others simply lived together as couples, without getting married.

The sexual revolution in the counterculture led to more open discussion of sexual subjects in the mainstream media. Newspapers, magazines, and books published articles that might not have been printed just a few years earlier. The 1962 book by Helen Gurley Brown, *Sex and the Single Girl*, became a bestseller. In 1966, William H. Masters and Virginia E. Johnson shocked many people

Caption Answers

Viewing History They are alike in that both rebel against mainstream formal artistic tradition and middle class culture. The Warhol pokes fun at American consumer conformist culture; the poster makes visual reference to psychedelic drugs. They differ in that Warhol's work represents a type of realism while the Op Art design represents a drug-induced hallucination.

Resource Directory

Technology

RESOURCE PRO® **Literature Activity** *The Flower Children,* found on Resource Pro, uses lyrics from the song "San Francisco (Be Sure to Wear Flowers in Your Hair)" to describe the group of young people who called themselves "flower children."

RESOURCE PRO® **Visual Learning Activity** *Reflections of the Counterculture,* found on Resource Pro, displays popular buttons that were worn in the 1960s to express views on contemporary issues.

when they published *Human Sexual Response,* a report on their scientific studies of sexuality.

The Drug Scene Some members of the 1960s counterculture also turned to psychedelic drugs. These powerful chemicals cause the brain to behave abnormally. Users of psychedelic drugs experience hallucinations and other altered perceptions of reality. The beatniks of the 1950s, who were an inspiration to the 1960s counterculture, had experimented with drugs, but the beatniks had been relatively few in number. In the 1960s, the use of drugs, especially marijuana, became much more widespread among the nation's youth.

One early proponent of psychedelic drug use was researcher Timothy Leary. Leary worked at Harvard University with Richard Alpert on the chemical compound lysergic acid diethylamide, commonly known as LSD. The two men were fired from their research posts in 1963 for involving undergraduates in experiments with the drug. Leary then began to preach that drugs could help free the mind. He advised listeners, "Tune in, turn on, drop out."

Leary's view presented just one side of the drug scene. On the other side lay serious danger. The possibility of death from an overdose or from an accident while under the influence of drugs was very real. Three leading musicians of the 1960s—Janis Joplin, Jim Morrison, and Jimi Hendrix—died of complications from drug overdoses. And they were not the only ones. Their deaths represented the tragic excesses to which some people were driven by their reliance on drugs to enhance or to escape from reality.

Focus on CULTURE

Hair Nothing seemed to provoke adult disapproval of the youth culture as much as their long hair. Young people themselves viewed growing their hair long as a sign of rebellion. African American youth also saw the longer, natural Afro style as a symbol of racial pride, and wore it instead of straightening their hair in imitation of conventional white hairstyles. Even the Broadway rock musical about the clash between the hippie generation and their elders was called *Hair.*

On the more serious side, many high schools banned "long, shaggy hair" and beards. Some students sued for their right to express themselves, and the responses of the courts were mixed. In 1967, a federal court upheld the expulsion of a boy for wearing long hair, and the Supreme Court refused to hear the case. But two years later, two other federal courts ruled in favor of long-haired teenagers.

The Music World

Music both reflected and contributed to the cultural changes of the 1960s. The rock and roll of the 1950s had begun a musical revolution, giving young people a music of their own that scandalized many adults. The early 1960s saw a new interest in folk music. Members of the counterculture turned to traditional songs that had been passed down from generation to generation of "folk," or ordinary people around the world. They also favored songs of protest against oppression; songs of laborers, such as sailors and railroadmen, and songs that originated under slavery.

The year 1964 marked a revolution in rock music that some called the British Invasion. It was the year that the Beatles first toured America. The "Fab Four" had already taken their native England by storm. They became a sensation in the United States as well, not only for their music but also for their irreverent sense of humor and their "mop top" long hair. The Beatles heavily influenced the music of the period, as did another British group, the Rolling Stones. Mick Jagger of the Stones was a dramatic and electrifying showman. Another exciting performer was Texan Janis Joplin, a hard-drinking singer whose powerful interpretations of classic blues songs catapulted her to superstardom.

Woodstock The diverse strands of the counterculture all came together at the Woodstock Music and Art Fair in August 1969. About 400,000 people gathered for several days in a large pasture in Bethel, New York, to listen to the major bands of the rock world. Despite brutal heat and rain, those who attended the **Woodstock festival** recalled the event with something of a sense of awe for the fellowship they experienced there. Police avoided confrontations with those

READING CHECK
Describe some influences on American music of the sixties.

ACTIVITY
Connecting with Culture

Have students work in groups of two or three to create the lyrics for a "folk song" protesting discrimination against women in the 1960s and 1970s, or the oppression of one of the groups discussed in Section 2 of this chapter. Suggest that groups put their lyrics to the melody of a song that they know. Then invite students to perform the compositions. Have them describe how the characteristics of the era are reflected in these works. **(Musical/Rhythmic)**

BACKGROUND
Biography

Joan Baez (b. 1941) is a folk singer and political activist who was a leader in the 1960s revival of folk songs, and who also performed at the Woodstock festival. Like many artists at that time, she was active in protest movements, often singing for free at benefit concerts and political rallies. In 1964 she refused to pay federal taxes that went toward war expenses, and was twice jailed.

READING CHECK
Folk music became popular in the early 1960s; the Beatles and the Rolling Stones exposed Americans to British pop music trends; blues music was given a new interpretation by Janis Joplin.

CUSTOMIZE FOR ...
ESL

Ask students to work in pairs or groups of three to develop a set of five questions about the section content. Each group should have a question beginning with *who, what, why, when,* and *how.* Have groups exchange question sheets and decide on consensus answers.

TEST PREPARATION

Have students reread the quote about Woodstock on the next page and then answer the question below.

Which of the following statements would Tom Law probably agree with concerning Woodstock?

A It was about more than music.
B The gathering was incredibly peaceful.
C The event was a phenomenon.
(D) All of the above.

Section 3 Assessment

Reading Comprehension

1. The group that rejected mainstream American culture, holding different values and experimenting with different lifestyles. It drew its adherents mainly from the vast population of college students resulting from the postwar baby boom.
2. Pop Art is the realistic depiction of items from everyday life in American culture. Op Art used fluorescent colors and strange imagery, reminiscent of psychedelic drugs, in its images.
3. Many young Americans rejected the idea of sex being tied to marriage and experimented with different lifestyles. The counterculture also encouraged experimentation with drugs, especially the psychedelic drugs that some believed would expand the user's imagination.
4. Woodstock had been peaceful.

Critical Thinking and Writing

5. (a) That it was repressed sexually and overly conservative in dress and politics; that middle-aged corporate types were insensitive to the needs of the poor; that mainstream traditional marriages suppressed individuality. (b) Answers will vary, but students should offer evidence to support their respective viewpoints.
6. Letters will vary but should be supported with facts from the section.

Posters should demonstrate knowledge of the performers' work and be visually attractive.

VIEWING HISTORY This group of hippies lived together in a commune and traveled around in their outrageously painted bus. **Drawing Inferences** *How are they showing their rejection of traditional social customs?*

attending by choosing not to enforce drug laws. The crowd remained under control. Tom Law was at Woodstock:

> *"The event was so much bigger than the music. It was a phenomenon. It was absolutely a phenomenon. And it was also the most peaceful, civilized gathering that was probably happening on the planet at the time."*
>
> —Tom Law

Other Americans, however, viewed both the festival and the mood it reflected with disgust. Even as some of the older generation began growing their hair longer and wearing "hipper" clothing, they were alarmed at the changes they saw around them. These changes also disturbed many in the younger generation. In particular, some in the mainstream culture deplored the drugs, sex, and nudity they saw at the Woodstock festival and around the country. To them, the counterculture represented a rejection of morals and honored values, and seemed a childish reaction to the problems of the era.

Altamont The fears of those who criticized Woodstock came true at another rock festival held at the Altamont Speedway in California in December 1969. There, 300,000 people gathered for a concert by the Rolling Stones. When promoters of the concert failed to provide adequate security, the Stones hired a band of Hell's Angels, an infamous and lawless motorcycle gang, to keep order. The cyclists ended up beating one man to death when he approached the stage with a gun. This ugly violence contradicted the values preached by the counterculture. It also signaled that the era of "peace and love" would not last forever.

Despite their celebration of simple lifestyles, most hippies were children of the comfortable middle class. American corporations marketed such items as bell-bottom blue jeans and stereo equipment to them, and they eagerly bought the products. When the counterculture fell apart, the hippies melted right back into the mainstream. By the 1980s, many baby boomers who had protested the values of 1950s and 1960s mainstream America would hold executive positions in the same corporations they had once denounced.

Section 3 Assessment

READING COMPREHENSION

1. What was the **counterculture?**
2. What are Pop Art and Op Art?
3. What new attitudes toward sexual activity and drugs were promoted by the counterculture?
4. How was the Altamont concert different from the **Woodstock festival?**

CRITICAL THINKING AND WRITING

5. **Identifying Assumptions** (a) What assumptions about mainstream culture were made by the counterculture? (b) Were they fair? Explain.
6. **Writing a Letter to the Editor** It is 1967, and you are the parent of a teenager. Write a letter to the editor either for or against a rule banning "hippie dress" at your child's school.

Activity: Creating an Ad Learn more about sixties folk music and create an ad for a concert featuring several folk performers. Use the links provided in the *America: Pathways to the Present* area of the following Web site for help in completing this activity.
www.phschool.com

Caption Answers

Viewing History By living communally, dressing in "hippie" styles, and riding on—as well as in—a bus painted in a wild color scheme.

RESOURCE DIRECTORY

Teaching Resources

Units 5/6/7 booklet
- Section 3 Quiz, p. 76

Guide to the Essentials
- Section 3 Summary, p. 113

Section 4 The Environmental and Consumer Movements

READING FOCUS

- What efforts were begun in the 1960s to protect the environment?
- How did the government try to balance jobs and environmental protection?
- How did the consumer movement begin, and what did it try to accomplish?

KEY TERMS

Nuclear Regulatory Commission (NRC)
Environmental Protection Agency (EPA)
Clean Air Act
Clean Water Act

TAKING NOTES

Copy the diagram below. As you read, fill in the two circles with the goals and accomplishments of each movement. Place items that apply to both where the circles overlap.

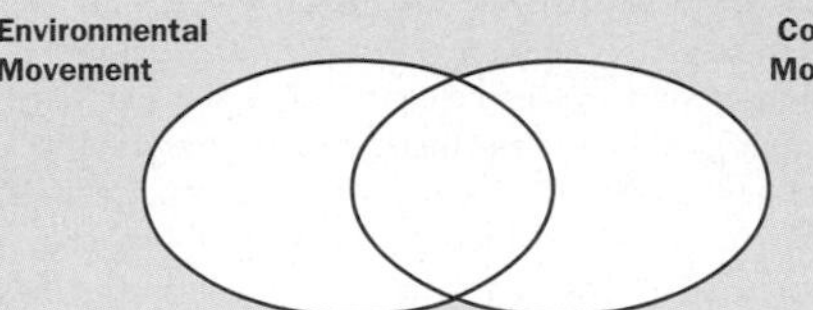

MAIN IDEA

Conditions that came to light in the 1960s as well as the activist mood of the period helped to create movements for preserving the environment and for ensuring the safety of consumer products.

Setting the Scene In 1958, a woman in Massachusetts wrote a letter to a friend—and set off a revolution. The letter writer was Olga Owens Huckins, and the friend was Rachel Carson. An airplane had sprayed Huckins's neighborhood with DDT to control mosquitoes, and the next day she had found dead birds in her yard. She asked Carson, a biologist, to look into the connection. The result was *Silent Spring*, the 1962 book that started the environmental movement.

Carson begins *Silent Spring* with "A Fable for Tomorrow." In the fable, she describes a lovely country town surrounded by farms and wilderness, by beauty and the sounds of wildlife. She continues:

> *"Then a strange blight crept over the area and everything began to change. Some evil spell had settled on the community: mysterious maladies swept the flocks of chickens; the cattle and sheep sickened and died. Everywhere was a shadow of death. The farmers spoke of much illness among their families. . . . There was a strange stillness. The birds, for example—where had they gone? . . . [T]here was now no sound; only silence lay over the fields and woods and marsh. . . . No witchcraft, no enemy action had silenced the rebirth of new life in this stricken world. The people had done it themselves."*
>
> —Rachel Carson in *Silent Spring*

Rachel Carson was already recognized as a distinguished naturalist when she wrote *Silent Spring*.

Protecting the Environment

Carson's fable links two protest movements of the 1960s and 1970s. Both the environmental movement and the consumer movement demanded honesty and accountability from industry and government. Consumer advocates insisted upon safety for customers and workers. Environmentalists went further: they called for actions that would preserve and restore the earth's environment and resources. According to environmental activists, the very products that people used in an effort to improve their world and their lives—to control mosquitoes, for example—were damaging not only the health of the environment but the health of the people as well.

Like the women's movement, the environmental movement of the 1960s had roots in the American past. In the late 1890s and early 1900s,

Section 4 The Environmental and Consumer Movements

Section Objectives

1. Read about efforts begun in the 1960s to protect the environment.
2. Understand how the government tried to balance jobs and environmental protection.
3. Find out how the consumer movement began, and what it tried to accomplish.

Bellringer

Warm-Up Activity Ask students to recall how many decisions they made on each day of the past week that affected the environment. Discuss how and why they made these decisions. How many of their decisions were good for the environment?

Activating Prior Knowledge Are students aware of the types of concerns that gave rise to the environmental movement of the late 1960s? Can they list some situations that have improved as a result of this movement?

Reading Strategy

The text states that "the environmental movement and the consumer movement demanded honesty and accountability from industry and government." As students read the section, have them look for evidence to support this statement.

Activity: Connecting with Government

Have students research the major pieces of environmental legislation that have been passed since 1970. Then, have them make a table that lists the legislation down one column and the categories *Restore Natural Resources, Eliminate Toxic Dumps, Cleaner Industries,* and *Eliminate Sources of Pollution.* Have students note which pieces of legislation impacted which areas of the environment. Which categories have been most affected by environmental legislation? **(Logical/Mathematical)**

RESOURCE DIRECTORY

Teaching Resources
Learning Styles Lesson Plans booklet, p. 63
Guided Reading and Review booklet, p. 123

Technology
Section Reading Support Transparencies
Guided Reading Audiotapes (English/Spanish), Ch. 23
Student Edition on Audio CD, Ch. 23
Prentice Hall Presentation Pro CD-ROM
Companion Web site, www.phschool.com

Lesson Plan

Focus Inspired by other protest movements, environmentalists and consumer advocates demanded action to preserve the environment and to protect the buyers and users of products in America. Ask students what triggered these movements. How successful were they?

Instruct Explain that many environmental problems grew out of the rapid development of technology, industry, and transportation after World War II. Have students list some voluntary measures that people undertake to preserve the environment. What role should the federal government play in regulating the environment? Should it determine how communities dispose of trash or how manufacturers package items?

Assess/Reteach Have students analyze the progress that has been made in cleaning up the environment over the past thirty years. What areas still need improvement?

Background

Then and Now

Despite the truth of Rachel Carson's assertions about the hazards of the chemical DDT, there is another side to DDT. Before its widespread agricultural use, DDT was used to kill malaria-carrying mosquitoes. DDT drastically lowered the spread of malaria, a disease that in India alone claimed about 800,000 lives every year. DDT, now banned, was once the means to the survival of millions.

READING CHECK
That chemical insecticides such as DDT were destroying the environment by killing animals and plants. She pointed out that these chemicals moved through nature's food chain to affect many different types of animal and plant species.

Caption Answers

Fast Forward to Today It suggests that if pollution is reduced and habitat is restored, animal species on the brink of extinction can be restored to healthy, self-sustaining population levels.

The Return of the Bald Eagle

In 1963, a year after *Silent Spring* was published, bald eagles were near extinction, with only 417 breeding pairs in the lower 48 states. They were declared an endangered species in 1967. In 1972, DDT was banned, and a year later the Endangered Species Act was passed. The eagles were put under the protection of this act in 1978. Efforts to save the bald eagle included bringing young eaglets from Canada and Alaska and then releasing them in the continental United States, and breeding eagles in captivity and then releasing their offspring into the wild. By 1999, the eagles had made a strong recovery; there were more than 5,000 breeding pairs, and the species was removed from the endangered list. Posing with an eagle named Challenger at an Independence Day ceremony, President Bill Clinton said, "It's hard to think of a better way to celebrate the birth of a nation than to celebrate the rebirth of our national symbol."

? What does the return of the bald eagle suggest about saving other endangered species? Explain your answer.

Progressives had worked to make public lands and parks available for the enjoyment of the population. New Deal programs of the 1930s included tree-planting projects in an effort to put people back to work—and to conserve forests and farmlands. The modern environmental movement, however, would not have started without Rachel Carson.

Rachel Carson Marine biologist Rachel Carson grew up wanting to become a writer. Her mother taught her to appreciate nature and encouraged Carson's growing interest in zoology. In the 1930s and 1940s, Carson combined her talents and began to write about scientific subjects for general audiences. In 1951, she published *The Sea Around Us,* which was an immediate bestseller and won the National Book Award. This book, and her next, *The Edge of the Sea,* made her famous as a naturalist. One of Carson's main themes was that human beings are part of nature, and that all parts of nature interact. She also believed that people carry a great responsibility for the health of nature because they have the power to change the environment. *Silent Spring,* her most influential book, warned against the abuse of that power.

In *Silent Spring,* Carson spoke out against the use of chemical pesticides, particularly DDT. She argued that DDT had increased agricultural productivity but killed various other plants and animals along with the insect pests that were its target. She stated:

> *"The most alarming of all man's assaults upon the environment is the contamination of air, earth, rivers, and sea with dangerous and even lethal materials. This pollution is for the most part irrecoverable. . . . In this now universal contamination of the environment, chemicals are the sinister and little-recognized partners of radiation in changing the very nature of the world."*
>
> —Rachel Carson in *Silent Spring*

As Carson explained, chemicals sprayed on crops enter into living organisms and move from one to another in a chain of poisoning and death. Specifically, in the 1960s, the lingering effects of DDT threatened to destroy many species of birds and fish, including the national symbol, the bald eagle.

Silent Spring caused a sensation. The chemical industry fought back vigorously, arguing that Carson confused the issues and left readers "unable to sort fact from fancy." The public, however, was not persuaded by this attack on Carson. So great was national concern that a special presidential advisory committee was appointed. It called for continued research and warned against the widespread use of pesticides. Eventually DDT was banned in the United States, and other chemicals came under stricter control. (For more on the impact of *Silent Spring,* see the "Geography and History" feature that follows this section.)

READING CHECK
What was Rachel Carson's main argument in *Silent Spring?*

It was not only DDT that worried people. They became more conscious of poisonous fumes in the air, oil spills on beaches, and toxic wastes buried in the ground. In the mid-1960s, President Lyndon Johnson addressed environmental concerns in his plans for the Great Society:

Resource Directory

Teaching Resources
Learning with Documents booklet (Visual Learning Activity) *Preserving the Environment,* p. 69

Technology
Color Transparencies *The Way It Works,* H20
Sounds of an Era Audio CD *Rachel Carson on* Silent Spring, 1963 recording (time: 50 seconds)

"The water we drink, the food we eat, the very air that we breathe, are threatened with pollution. Our parks are overcrowded, our seashores overburdened. Green fields and dense forests are disappearing."

—Lyndon Johnson

Johnson promised that environmental legislation would be part of his broader reform program.

Nuclear Power During the 1960s, concern about the overuse of nonrenewable resources, such as oil and gas, encouraged the development of nuclear power plants to generate electricity. Many people considered nuclear plants to be better than coal-burning plants because they caused less air pollution. Nuclear plants, however, discharged water used to cool the reactor into local waterways. This discharge raised water temperatures, killing fish and plant life. As time went on, objections to nuclear power plants began to develop.

These objections were also fueled by a growing concern about the possibility of nuclear plant accidents. The fear was that in the event of an accident, radioactivity would be released into the air, causing serious damage—or even death—to all plant and animal life in the surrounding area. The **Nuclear Regulatory Commission (NRC),** created in 1974, tried to address these fears as it oversaw the use of nuclear materials in civilian life. Its chief goal was to ensure that nuclear power plants and facilities were operated safely.

Public Response People from all walks of life were becoming alarmed by environmental problems. Biologist Barry Commoner, for example, warned about rapid increases in pollution in his 1971 book *The Closing Circle*. Meanwhile, the Sierra Club, an organization founded in 1892 to further nature conservation, became active in opposing power projects that the group thought would harm the environment. But it was an environmental catastrophe off the coast of California in 1969 that captured the public's attention. The result of an oil platform blowout, the Santa Barbara oil spill fouled beaches and killed thousands of birds and other wildlife. President Richard Nixon visited the site, and declared, "The Santa Barbara incident has frankly touched the conscience of the American people." And the American people were ready to respond.

Grassroots environmental movements began springing up around the country. Groups supporting conservation efforts and opposing such actions as the building of dams and nuclear plants gained attention. In 1969, Senator Gaylord Nelson of Wisconsin announced plans to hold a national day of discussion and teaching about the environment. The following year, on April 22, 1970, Americans celebrated the first Earth Day. Organizers stressed the important role that Americans could play in improving awareness of environmental issues and in bringing an end to environmental damage. Earth Day would become a yearly observance. Its aim was to heighten concern for the environment, to increase awareness about environmental issues, and to clean up pollution and litter.

VIEWING HISTORY Concern about Earth and its resources prompted Earth Day rallies, mass cleanup activities, and protests against nuclear power plants. **Expressing Problems Clearly** *(a) What is the sign carried by the protester really asking people to do? (b) According to environmental activists, why is this action necessary?*

ACTIVITY
Connecting with Citizenship

Have each student write a letter to the President of the United States explaining why he or she supports or opposes the opening of new nuclear power plants; the expansion of oil drilling offshore or in the Alaskan wilderness; or the growing of food crops that have been genetically altered to make them resistant to insects without the use of pesticides. In their letters, have students analyze the impact of these technological innovations and projects on the nature of work, the American labor movement, and businesses. Call on students to read their letters to the class. **(Verbal/Linguistic)**

BACKGROUND
Geography in History

Fishermen in the northeastern United States and Quebec were shocked when fish began disappearing from many local streams and lakes in the 1970s. The culprit was acid precipitation, rain and snow made as acidic as vinegar or lemon juice by pollutants from coal- and oil-burning power plants in the Ohio Valley. Ironically, the Clean Air Act had worsened the problem when it tried to disperse local pollution by ordering smokestacks to be built over 500 feet tall. Pollutants were not reduced, but blown far from the source by high-altitude westerly winds.

CUSTOMIZE FOR ...
Less Proficient Writers

Ask students to study the section photos and read the captions. Have them use the photos to write sentences that explain the section's main ideas.

TEST PREPARATION

Have students read the section "Rachel Carson" on these pages and then answer the question below.

What was the name of the program proposed by Lyndon Johnson to address what he felt were the American people's most important concerns?

A The New Deal
B A Challenge to Americans
C Let Freedom Ring
(D) The Great Society

CAPTION ANSWERS

Viewing History (a) The sign is really asking people to take care of their planet if they want to preserve it as a safe place to live. (b) This is essential because the Earth is being poisoned by pesticides and other pollutants and is in danger of being made uninhabitable by pollution and the potential for accidents at nuclear power plants.

ACTIVITY
Connecting with Geography

Ask each student to bring to class a picture that supports or shows the need for one of the environmental laws listed in the chart. Tell students that they may either look in newspapers and magazines for a picture or take their own photo of some local place that shows the need for or effects of one of these laws. Have students describe how their picture is related to the law they have chosen to illustrate. **(Visual/Spatial)**

BACKGROUND
Biography

The only child of immigrant parents, Ralph Nader studied the *Congressional Record* in his spare time and by age 14 had read the works of Progressive-era muckrakers Ida Tarbell, Lincoln Steffens, and Upton Sinclair. At Harvard Law School, Nader wrote an article on auto safety that appeared in *The Nation* magazine. When General Motors tried to discredit Nader after *Unsafe at Any Speed* was published, he sued the company. GM settled the case, and Nader used the settlement money to launch the modern consumer movement. In 1971 he founded Public Citizen, one of the largest consumer and public interest groups in America. Nader made an unsuccessful bid for the Presidency in 2000 as a candidate for the Green Party, an independent party that emphasizes social justice, nonviolence, and ecological responsibility.

READING CHECK

The Alaska Native Claims Settlement Act and later acts set aside large blocks of territory, ensuring that the Alaskan landscape would not be spoiled by development projects.

Major Environmental Landmarks, 1964–1976

Legislation	Description
Wilderness Act, 1964	Designated lands to be maintained and preserved for public enjoyment.
Rare and Endangered Species Act, 1966	Established protection for rare, endangered, and threatened plants and animals.
Environmental Protection Agency, 1970	Created as an independent federal agency to administer the laws that affect the environment.
Clean Air Act, 1970	Instituted a research and development program to prevent and control air pollution.
Clean Water Act, 1972	Established regulations for preventing urban and industrial water pollution.
Resource Conservation and Recovery Act, 1974	Established guidelines for storage and/or disposal of existing hazardous waste.
Safe Drinking Water Act, 1974	Established guidelines for safe drinking water.
Toxic Substance Control Act, 1976	Enacted to regulate the commercial manufacture, processing, and distribution of chemical substances.

INTERPRETING CHARTS The government responded to environmental activism by enacting laws and creating federal agencies. **Analyzing Information** *Which of these laws directly affect human health and safety?*

Government Actions The efforts of environmental activists and the concern of the public at large helped spur the federal government to create a new agency that would set and enforce national pollution-control standards. In 1970, President Nixon established the **Environmental Protection Agency (EPA)** by combining existing federal agencies concerned with air and water pollution.

One of the EPA's early responsibilities was to enforce the **Clean Air Act.** Passed by Congress in 1970 in response to public concerns about air pollution, the Clean Air Act was designed to control the pollution caused by industries and car emissions. The EPA forged an agreement with car manufacturers to install catalytic converters (devices that convert tailpipe pollutants into less dangerous substances) in cars to reduce harmful emissions.

In 1972, the EPA gained further responsibilities when Congress enacted the **Clean Water Act** to regulate the discharge of industrial and municipal wastewater. The act also provided for grants to build better sewage-treatment facilities. As the nation's watchdog against polluters, the EPA continues to monitor and reduce air and water pollution. It regulates the disposal of solid waste and the use of pesticides and toxic substances.

Balancing Jobs and the Environment

Efforts to clean up and preserve the environment did not come without a cost. Many industry leaders worried that the new regulations would be confusing to follow and overly costly to businesses. They raised concerns that the increased costs associated with cleaning up the air and water would result in the loss of jobs. Government and industry worked to balance the demands of economic development and environmental protection.

The development of oil fields in Alaska provides an example of how the government tried to achieve this balance. Construction began in 1974 on an 800-mile pipeline designed to carry oil across the frozen landscape to ice-free ports in the southern part of Alaska. This development of the oil industry created new jobs and expanded revenues for the state. At the same time, it brought increased concern over the welfare of the Alaskan wilderness and the rights of native Alaskans. The Alaska Native Claims Settlement Act of 1971 had set aside millions of acres of land for the state's native groups, to be used partly for conservation purposes. In 1978, and again in 1980, additional land was added to the state's protected conservation areas.

READING CHECK How did the government try to balance jobs and environmental protection in Alaska?

The Consumer Movement

Just as the birth of the environmental movement was credited to Rachel Carson, the consumer movement of the 1960s was also associated with one individual. Ralph Nader was this era's most important and visible champion of consumer rights. However, the consumer movement, too, had earlier roots. The Pure Food and Drug Act of 1906, for example, had been one early effort to maintain safety standards and protect the public. In the 1960s and early 1970s, though, the consumer movement grew far larger and stronger and had more far-reaching effects.

CAPTION ANSWERS

Interpreting Charts Clean Air Act, Clean Water Act, Resource Conservation and Recovery Act, Safe Drinking Water Act, Toxic Substance Control Act pertain to human health. The establishment of the Environmental Protection Agency is the most sweeping action of those listed.

RESOURCE DIRECTORY

Teaching Resources

Units 5/6/7 booklet
- Section 4 Quiz, p. 77
- Chapter 23 Test, pp. 78, 81

Guide to the Essentials
- Section 4 Summary, p. 114
- Chapter 23 Test, p. 115

Other Print Resources

Chapter Tests with ExamView® Test Bank CD-ROM, Ch. 23

American History Block Scheduling Support *Fueling the Nation: Energy and the Environment,* found in The Nation After World War II folder, includes interdisciplinary lesson suggestions and activities for Geography and History, Primary Sources, Biography, and Literature.

Technology

Sounds of an Era Audio CD *Ralph Nader to the National Press Club,* 1966 recording

RESOURCE PRO® Primary Source Activity *The Desecration of America,* found on Resource Pro, features excerpts from a 1961 *Atlantic Monthly* article by Vance Packard in which he examines the state of the countryside with dismay.

ExamView® Test Bank CD-ROM, Ch. 23

Social Studies Skills Tutor CD-Rom

Attorney Ralph Nader spearheaded the new consumer effort. Nader had been a serious activist all his life. While a student at Princeton University in the early 1950s, Nader protested the spraying of campus trees with DDT. His interest in automobile safety began while he was attending Harvard Law School. In 1964, Daniel Patrick Moynihan, then Assistant Secretary of Labor, hired Nader as a consultant on the issue of automobile safety regulations. The government report Nader wrote developed into a book, *Unsafe at Any Speed: The Designed-in Dangers of the American Automobile*, published the next year. It began:

> "*For over half a century the automobile has brought death, injury, and the most inestimable sorrow and deprivation to millions of people. . . . [T]his mass trauma began rising sharply four years ago reflecting new and unexpected ravages by the motor vehicle. A 1959 Department of Commerce report projected that 51,000 persons would be killed by automobiles in 1975. That figure will probably be reached in 1965, a decade ahead of schedule.*"
>
> —Ralph Nader in *Unsafe at Any Speed*

Like the muckrakers of the Progressive Era, Nader drew attention to the facts with passionate arguments. He called many cars "coffins on wheels," pointing to dangers such as a tendency of some models to flip over. The automobile industry, he charged, knew about these problems but continued to build over one million cars before confronting the safety problems.

Nader's book was a sensation. In 1966, he testified before Congress about automobile hazards. That year, Congress passed the National Traffic and Motor Vehicle Safety Act. The *Washington Post* noted, "Most of the credit for making possible this important legislation belongs to one man—Ralph Nader. . . . A one-man lobby for the public prevailed over the nation's most powerful industry."

Nader broadened his efforts and investigated the meatpacking business, helping to secure support for the Wholesome Meat Act of 1967. He next looked into problems in other industries. Scores of volunteers, called "Nader's Raiders," signed on to help. They turned out report after report on the safety of such products as baby food and insecticides, and they inspired consumer activism. As ordinary Americans began to stand up for their rights, consumer protection offices began to respond to their many complaints.

VIEWING HISTORY Ralph Nader was a "one-man lobby" for consumer safety. **Making Comparisons** *How were the tactics of Ralph Nader and his "raiders" different from those of other activists of the 1960s?*

Section 4 Assessment

READING COMPREHENSION

1. What is Earth Day?
2. When was the **Environmental Protection Agency** formed and what is its purpose?
3. Describe the **Clean Air Act** and the **Clean Water Act.**
4. Explain the importance of *Unsafe at Any Speed.*

CRITICAL THINKING AND WRITING

5. **Recognizing Cause and Effect** Explain how Rachel Carson's concern with DDT initiated the environmental movement.
6. **Writing an Opinion** Do you think the United States should rely more on nuclear power plants? Write a paragraph that supports your opinion.

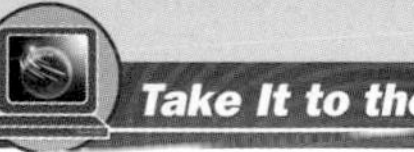

Take It to the NET

Activity: Preparing Testimony Research the EPA or the NRC. Write out testimony you might give in congressional hearings about funding the agency. Use the links provided in the *America: Pathways to the Present* area of the following Web site for help in completing this activity. **www.phschool.com**

Section 4 Assessment

Reading Comprehension

1. A yearly celebration begun in 1970 to increase public awareness of environmental issues and concerns.
2. The EPA was formed in 1970 to monitor pollution and enforce environmental regulations.
3. The Clean Air Act was designed to regulate air pollution from industries and cars, while the Clean Water Act regulates wastewater disposal and finances the construction of sewage treatment facilities.
4. Ralph Nader's book used colorful language and passionate arguments to raise public awareness of the dangers of automobiles. It demonstrated the impact one person could have on as powerful an entity as the auto industry.

Critical Thinking and Writing

5. Carson's concerns over DDT led her to write the book *Silent Spring*. The book's awakening of public concern over harmful pesticides led people to consider a host of other environmental concerns and to act on them.
6. Answers will vary but should be supported with facts from the section.

Take It to the NET

Students should incorporate their opinions with facts and data to create a persuasive testimony, and may choose to include an examination of other government-funded agencies.

Caption Answers

Viewing History Nader and his raiders worked within the system, lobbying Congress directly and turning out reports to influence public opinion and policy-makers. This approach was very different from, for example, the confrontational activities engaged in by AIM.

Chapter 23

Reviewing Key Terms

Students should refer to the definitions of key terms in the chapter to write sentences that show an understanding of the many different social movements that grew out of the civil rights movement of the 1960s.

Reviewing Main Ideas

11. Fair pay, equal job opportunities, overcoming sexism in the media, sharing domestic responsibilities with men.

12. The ERA was initially approved by Congress in 1972 and sent to the states for ratification. To become law, 38 states needed to ratify it. By 1977, 35 states had ratified the amendment. However, as opposition grew, the deadline for ratification passed without the required number of states on board.

13. Opposition from both men and women. Some women enjoyed being housewives and did not want to work outside of the home, while other women felt that the ERA would hurt the rights women already had.

14. He organized the UFW and led the movement. Chávez was successful in bringing about consumer boycotts of farm products produced by nonunion farms.

15. The JACL persuaded Congress to pass the Japanese American Claims Act in 1948, providing some reparation for treatment of Japanese Americans during World War II.

16. To obtain better treatment for Native Americans; to fight for the observance of treaties made by the U.S. government with Native American nations; and to gain autonomy.

17. The youth culture favored colorful and casual clothing, nontraditional views about sex and relationships, and a willingness to experiment with drugs.

18. The Rolling Stones were giving a concert. They hired a group of Hell's Angels for security. During the show the bikers killed a man who was carrying a gun.

…rson wrote the popular book *Silent* …, which examined the effect of … other pesticides on the …nt. The popularity of the

Chapter

23 Review and Assessment

creating a CHAPTER SUMMARY

Copy the chart (right) on a piece of paper. Use it to organize information about some of the groups that challenged the status quo in the 1960s and 1970s.

For additional review and enrichment activities, see the interactive version of *America: Pathways to the Present*, available on the Web and on CD-ROM.

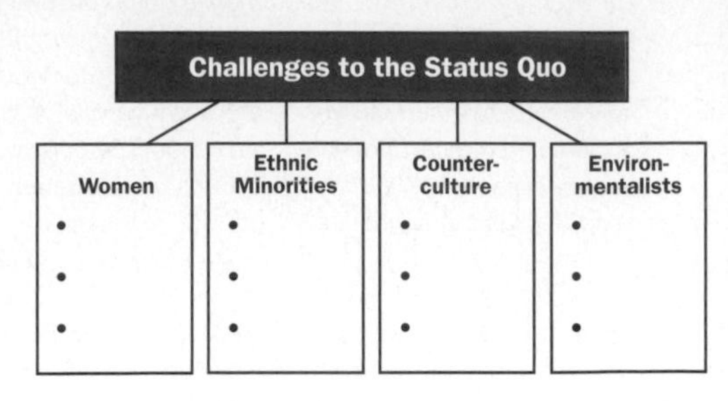

★ Reviewing Key Terms

For each of the terms below, write a sentence explaining how it relates to the activism of the 1960s and 1970s.

1. feminism
2. *Roe* v. *Wade*
3. Latino
4. migrant farm worker
5. United Farm Workers (UFW)
6. autonomy
7. counterculture
8. Woodstock festival
9. Nuclear Regulatory Commission (NRC)
10. Environmental Protection Agency (EPA)

★ Reviewing Main Ideas

11. What were the goals of NOW? (Section 1)
12. Describe the effort to ratify the ERA. (Section 1)
13. What opposition did the women's movement encounter? (Section 1)
14. What role did César Chávez play in the Chicano struggle for equal rights? (Section 2)
15. What did the JACL accomplish? (Section 2)
16. What were the goals of the American Indian Movement? (Section 2)
17. Describe three new attitudes of the youth culture of the 1960s and 1970s. (Section 3)
18. What happened at the Altamont festival? (Section 3)
19. Describe how Rachel Carson influenced the environmental movement. (Section 4)
20. What were two of the targets of Ralph Nader's consumer movement? (Section 4)

★ Critical Thinking

21. **Determining Relevance** (a) How did the civil rights movement affect groups as diverse as women, Native Americans, and environmentalists? (b) Do you think that these groups would have been as successful without the example of the civil rights activists? Explain your answer.
22. **Identifying Central Issues** (a) What underlying problem in American society did the women's movement, the Chicano movement, and the American Indian Movement try to address? (b) What kinds of changes were all three groups fighting for?
23. **Making Comparisons** What was the attitude of the counterculture toward "the establishment" (institutions such as government and big business) and how did they show it? Compare their attitudes and actions to those of the environmental and consumer movements.
24. **Demonstrating Reasoned Judgment** Balancing the demands of economic development and environmental protection often involves making tradeoffs. Choose a current environmental issue or use one that was discussed in the chapter, and write a paragraph suggesting how to balance those demands.

Creating a Chapter Summary

Challenges to the Status Quo

Women	Ethnic Minorities	Counterculture	Environmentalists
• After WW II, women were better educated, sought more opportunities • Civil rights movement gave women new tools to fight discrimination. • Gradual shift in attitudes and laws	• Heightened sense of cultural identity • Greater organization in fight against discrimination • Many different ethnic groups worked to secure their rights.	• Birth of "baby boom" generation after WW II • New styles of parenting, influenced by Dr. Spock and others • Identification by many members of the generation with certain lifestyles and trends in music and culture	• Landmark books *Silent Spring* and *Unsafe at Any Speed* • Earth Day protests attract many. • Beginning with The Great Society, government programs begin to favor restoration and protection of environment.

★ Skills Assessment

Analyzing Political Cartoons ▶

25. Examine the images in the cartoon. What do the ships represent?
26. Who are the people standing on the shore, and what do they represent?
27. Explain the humor in the dialogue, as well as the serious point it is making.

Analyzing Primary Sources

Dennis Banks restated the goals of the American Indian Movement in a speech marking the group's second anniversary. Read the following excerpt from his speech, and answer the questions that follow.

> "*The government and churches have demoralized, dehumanized, massacred, robbed, raped, promised, made treaty after treaty, and lied to us. . . . We must now destroy this political machine that man has built to prevent us from self-determination.*"
>
> —Dennis Banks

28. Which of the following was one of AIM's goals as expressed by Dennis Banks?
   - **A** to join the government
   - **B** to make no changes to Native American lifestyles
   - **C** to make radical changes in order to gain self-determination
   - **D** to enter into a new treaty with the government
29. How did Banks suggest that AIM achieve its goals?
   - **F** through peaceful demonstration
   - **G** by destroying the political machine built by the government and churches
   - **H** by joining churches
   - **J** by ignoring the problem

Applying the Chapter Skill: *Recognizing Bias*

30. Look back at the Skills for Life page. Then choose a quoted passage in this chapter, and use the steps for recognizing bias to evaluate that passage.

ACTIVITIES

Writing to LEARN

Writing an Explanation
During the 1960s and 1970s, César Chávez's United Farm Workers organized successful consumer boycotts of grapes, lettuce, and other produce. Explain how boycotts such as these achieve their goals. You may wish to do more reading about the UFW boycotts.

Primary Source CD-ROM

Working With Primary Sources Find additional information on the activism of the 1960s and 1970s on the *Exploring Primary Sources in U.S. History CD-ROM* and use the selection(s) provided to complete the Chapter 23 primary source activity located in the *America: Pathways to the Present* area of the following Web site.
www.phschool.com

Take It to the NET

Chapter Self-Test As a review activity, take the Chapter 23 Self-Test in the *America: Pathways to the Present* area at the Web site listed below. The questions are designed to test your understanding of the chapter content.
www.phschool.com

ANSWERS TO ACTIVITIES

Writing to LEARN

Sample answer: Boycotts have direct economic effects in that they draw upon consumers to stop buying certain products or using certain services.

Primary Source CD-ROM

Direct students to the additional primary sources that can be found on the *Exploring Primary Sources in U.S. History CD-ROM.*

Take It to the NET

Additional support materials and activities for Chapter 23 of *America: Pathways to the Present* can be found in the Social Studies area at the Prentice Hall School Web site. **www.phschool.com**

book helped start the environmental movement of the 1960s.

20. He targeted both the automobile and meatpacking industries.

CRITICAL THINKING

21. (a) It demonstrated nonviolent methods that would be used by later social movements. (b) Other groups probably would not have been as successful without the roadmap that the civil rights movement provided them.

22. (a) They addressed the unfair and unequal treatment received by a large group within American society. (b) To be treated the same as white males, with the same career opportunities, the same protections under law, and the same respect within society.

23. They viewed themselves collectively as the polar opposite of the traditional "establishment." They demonstrated their views by listening to rock music, spurning the traditional hair and clothing styles of their parents, and by other alternative actions—such as sometimes living in communes. The environmental and consumer movements were different in that they did not reject all of mainstream American culture but focused on one aspect of society or government and tried to effect change on that issue.

24. Answers will vary but should be supported with specific examples and should address themes introduced in the chapter.

SKILLS ASSESSMENT

25. The arrival of Europeans in the Americas.

26. They are Native Americans, representing the original inhabitants of the Americas.

27. The words are a play on the sentiment that one generation hands down all that it has achieved to the next generation. The cartoonist is saying that Native Americans quickly lost everything they had when the Europeans arrived.

28. C

29. G

30. Sample response: César Chávez assumes that the arguments of labor movements are correct by stating that the labor movements probably cannot be stopped from achieving their goals.

The Environmental Movement

Focus Tell students that when *Silent Spring* appeared in 1962, *ecology* was not a familiar word to most Americans. There was virtually no way for Americans to recycle glass, paper, metal, or plastic. The Environmental Protection Agency did not exist. Most Americans did not know about the ozone layer, and store clerks would have cast strange looks at a shopper who wanted to reuse grocery bags. The publication of *Silent Spring* marks the moment when the American public began to learn about the choices required to safeguard life on Earth.

Instruct Discuss with students the costs and benefits of environmental legislation. Bring up scenarios in which citizens might be angered by the costs and inconvenience of environmental regulations (i.e., consumers facing increasing water bills due to laws mandating cleaner drinking water, or land owners restricted from certain building practices in order to protect the environment). Do they think that environmental legislation is too costly or infringes on their right to live the way they want to? Can the students think of any examples in which environmental restrictions have improved quality of life? What benefits do they bring to society? Have students discuss if the benefits of environmental restrictions outweigh the costs.

Extend Ask students to monitor the local news for reports on environmental issues in your community. Have students outline the persons or groups involved, the environmental problems, and the potential costs to individuals. Students may present this information in a chart.

Geography & History

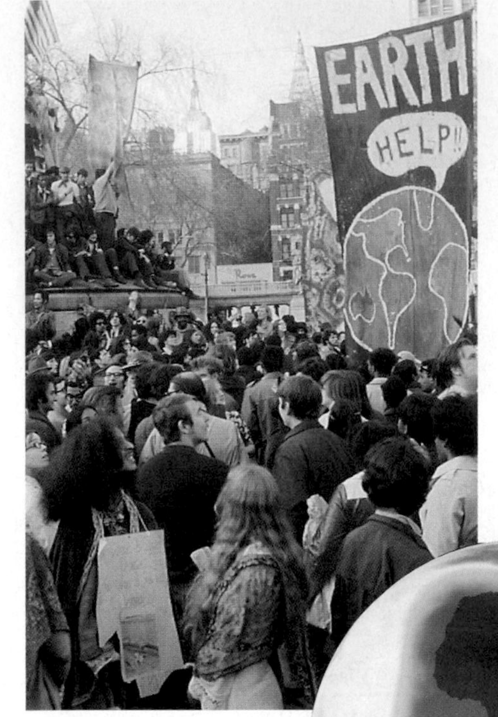

The Environmental Movement

The publication of Rachel Carson's book *Silent Spring* in 1962 helped spark an awareness of environmental problems during the 1960s. A growing environmental movement led to the first Earth Day in 1970—which featured demonstrations like the one shown here—to raise public awareness of environmental problems.

Environmental Legislation

Concerned citizens pressed the federal government to protect the environment. The 1963 Clean Air Act was followed by the tougher Clean Air Acts of 1970 and 1990, which required states to reduce high levels of pollution. In response to air quality concerns, carmakers and other industries acted to produce more fuel-efficient cars and to reduce harmful emissions. A 1980 law established a trust fund (known as the Superfund) to clean up hazardous waste sites.

Geographic Connection

In the image to the left, areas shaded in blue have below-normal ozone levels. Based on this image, what areas suffer from ozone loss?

Growing Concerns

While they continued to fight pollution in the 1980s and 1990s, scientists also addressed the thinning ozone layer and a growing "ozone hole" over Antarctica, shown in the remote sensing image on the right. Certain chemicals cause ozone in the atmosphere to break down, exposing Earth to higher levels of harmful ultraviolet radiation from the sun. An international accord in 1987 committed the world's nations to reducing gases that harm the ozone layer. Another concern was the accumulation of "greenhouse gases" released by industry and motor vehicles (right), which could raise temperatures globally.

RESOURCE DIRECTORY

Teaching Resources
Geography and History booklet, pp. 18–19

Other Print Resources
Nystrom *Atlas of Our Country* *Land Use, Population, and Ethnicity,* pp. 46–47

Technology
Prentice Hall United States History Video Collection™ Volume 20, *Post-War USA*

Protecting the Mojave

Environmental scientists have worked to protect open space and to preserve wildlife diversity and habitat. In 1994, Congress created the Mojave National Preserve, which protects part of the Mojave Desert from development.

One State's Example

This map of California shows just a few of that state's environmental achievements. The Sacramento and San Joaquin rivers feed canals and aqueducts that provide water to California's farms and cities as well as the Sacramento–San Joaquin Delta—a network of wetlands and inland waterways that flow into San Francisco Bay. Environmental organizations and the government have acted to ensure that enough fresh water flows into the delta and bay to protect fish and other species in danger of extinction. Meanwhile, air quality districts covering the state's largest cities have imposed strict air pollution standards.

Geographic Connection

Why might tougher air quality standards be needed in urban areas?

California Environmental Progress

Saving the California Condor

When California condors were almost extinct in the wild in the 1980s, scientists began a program to breed young condors in captivity at the Los Angeles Zoo and the San Diego Wild Animal Park. They have since released these birds in protected areas such as the Sespe Condor Sanctuary.

Geographic Connection

Why do environmentalists seek protection of nature preserves and wild areas?

Answers

1. Antarctica, portions of the Atlantic and Pacific oceans near Antarctica, and the southern tip of South America.
2. Urban areas have concentrations of the industrial activity and car traffic that cause air pollution.
3. To preserve wildlife diversity and habitat, and to protect endangered species from extinction.

Chapter 24 Planning Guide

Resource Manager

	CORE INSTRUCTION	READING/SKILLS
Chapter-Level Resources **TEKS** 6(E), 24(A), 24(B)	Teaching Resources • Pacing Charts booklet • Block Scheduling booklet **Resource Pro® CD-ROM,** Ch. 24 **Prentice Hall Presentation Pro CD-ROM,** Ch. 24 **www.phschool.com** • eTeach	**Guided Reading Audiotapes (English/Spanish)** **Student Edition on Audio CD,** Ch. 24 **Social Studies Skills Tutor CD-ROM** **Color Transparencies,** A50, A51, C8
1 The War Unfolds 1. Learn about the events that led to the war between North Vietnam and South Vietnam. 2. Become familiar with the Vietnam policies of President Kennedy and Robert McNamara. 3. See how President Johnson changed the course of the war. **TEKS** 8(A), 16(A)	Teaching Resources **Units 5/6/7 booklet** • Section 1 Quiz, p. 85 **Learning Styles Lesson Plans booklet,** p. 64	**Guided Reading and Review booklet,** p. 124 **Guide to the Essentials,** p. 116 **Skills for Life booklet,** p. 26 **Section Reading Support Transparencies**
2 Fighting the War 1. Learn how battlefield conditions in Vietnam affected American soldiers. 2. Be able to describe the course of the war between 1965 and 1968. 3. List reasons why the Tet Offensive was a turning point in the war. **TEKS** 8(B), 20(C), 22(B)	Teaching Resources **Units 5/6/7 booklet** • Section 2 Quiz, p. 86	**Guided Reading and Review booklet,** p. 125 **Guide to the Essentials,** p. 117 **Learning with Documents booklet,** p. 36 **Section Reading Support Transparencies**
3 Political Divisions 1. Find out about the role played by students in the protest movements of the 1960s. 2. Learn why President Johnson decided not to seek reelection. 3. Discover how the Vietnam War affected the election of 1968. **TEKS** 8(A), 8(B), 24(C), 24(F), 25(D)	Teaching Resources **Units 5/6/7 booklet** • Section 3 Quiz, p. 87 **Learning Styles Lesson Plans booklet,** p. 65	**Guided Reading and Review booklet,** p. 126 **Guide to the Essentials,** p. 118 **Learning with Documents booklet,** p. 24 **Section Reading Support Transparencies**
4 The End of the War 1. Learn how President Nixon's policies led to American withdrawal from Vietnam. 2. Discover why President Nixon campaigned promising to restore law and order. 3. See what happened in Vietnam after the withdrawal of American forces. 4. Determine the legacy of the Vietnam War. **TEKS** 1(B), 8(B), 24(C), 24(D), 24(F)	Teaching Resources **Units 5/6/7 booklet** • Section 4 Quiz, p. 88	**Guided Reading and Review booklet,** p. 127 **Guide to the Essentials,** p. 119 **Section Reading Support Transparencies**

Enrichment/Pre-AP

Prentice Hall United States History Video Collection™
www.phschool.com
- Section Activities, Virtual Field Trip, Chapter Activities, Current Events Online

---

American History Block Scheduling Support
Historical Outline Map Book, p. 70
Sounds of an Era Audio CD

Biography, Literature, and Comparing Primary Sources booklet, pp. 36, 83
Sounds of an Era Audio CD

Great Debates booklet, p. 24
American History Block Scheduling Support
Sounds of an Era Audio CD

Biography, Literature, and Comparing Primary Sources booklet, p. 157
Great Debates booklet, p. 44
Sounds of an Era Audio CD
Exploring Primary Sources in U.S. History CD-ROM
American Pathways Thematic Posters

Assessment

Core Assessment
ExamView® Test Bank, Ch. 24
ExamView® Test Bank CD-ROM, Ch. 24

Standardized Test Preparation
Diagnose and Prescribe
Diagnostic Tests for High School Social Studies Skills

Review and Reteach
Review Book for U.S. History

Practice and Assess
Test-taking Strategies With Transparencies
Test-taking Strategies Posters
Test Prep Book for U.S. History
Alternative Assessment Handbook
Document-Based Assessment

Teaching Resources
Units 5/6/7 booklet
- Section Quizzes, pp. 85–88
- Chapter Tests, pp. 89, 91

www.phschool.com Ch. 24 Self-Test

AmericanHeritage Resources

From the Archives of American Heritage®, p. 807
AmericanHeritage® My Brush with History™ Videotapes
www.americanheritage.com

Don't miss the exclusive interactive version of this textbook on the Web and on CD-ROM.

Chapter 24 Planning Guide
In Your Classroom

Customize for Individual Needs

Gifted and Talented

Teacher's Edition
- Customize for Gifted and Talented, pp. 795, 799

Teaching Resources
- Biography, Literature, and Comparing Primary Sources booklet, pp. 36, 83, 157

Technology
- Exploring Primary Sources in U.S. History CD-ROM *The Vietnam Veterans Memorial*

ESL

Teacher's Edition
- Customize for ESL, pp. 807, 813

Teaching Resources
- Guided Reading and Review booklet, pp. 124–127
- Guide to the Essentials (English/Spanish), Chapter 24

Technology
- Student Edition on Audio CD, Chapter 24
- Guided Reading Audiotapes (English/Spanish), Chapter 24
- Section Reading Support Transparencies

Less Proficient Readers

Teacher's Edition
- Customize for Less Proficient Readers, pp. 793, 803

Teaching Resources
- Guided Reading and Review booklet, pp. 124–127
- Guide to the Essentials (English/Spanish), Chapter 24

Technology
- Student Edition on Audio CD, Chapter 24
- Guided Reading Audiotapes (English/Spanish), Chapter 24
- Section Reading Support Transparencies

Less Proficient Writers

Teacher's Edition
- Customize for Less Proficient Writers, p. 815

Teaching Resources
- Guided Reading and Review booklet, pp. 124–127
- Guide to the Essentials (English/Spanish), Chapter 24

Technology
- Student Edition on Audio CD, Chapter 24
- Guided Reading Audiotapes (English/Spanish), Chapter 24
- Section Reading Support Transparencies

Teacher's Edition Index

Chapter 24 – Pacing Suggestions

For 90-minute Blocks

- Teach sections 1, 2, and 4 using Transparencies A50, A51, and C8, and the Recent Scholarship note on page 807 for class discussions.

Running Out of Time?

If you are running short on time to cover this chapter, consider the following options:

- Use Prentice Hall Presentation Pro CD-ROM to create an outline for this chapter.
- Use the Section Summaries for Chapter 24, from **Guide to the Essentials (English/Spanish)**.

TEKS Correlation

Chapter-Level	TEKS
	(6) History. The student understands the impact of significant national and international decisions and conflicts from World War II and the Cold War to the present on the United States. The student is expected to: **(E)** analyze the conflicts in Korea and Vietnam and describe their domestic and international effects. **(24) Social studies skills.** The student applies critical-thinking skills to organize and use information acquired from a variety of sources including electronic technology. The student is expected to: **(A)** locate and use primary and secondary sources such as computer software, databases, media and news services, biographies, interviews, and artifacts to acquire information about the United States. **(B)** analyze information by sequencing, categorizing, identifying cause-and-effect relationships, comparing, contrasting, finding the main idea, summarizing, making generalizations and predictions, and drawing inferences and conclusions.
1 The War Unfolds	**(8) Geography.** The student uses geographic tools to collect, analyze, and interpret data. The student is expected to: **(A)** create thematic maps, graphs, charts, models, and databases representing various aspects of the United States. **(16) Government.** The student understands the changing relationships among the three branches of the federal government. The student is expected to: **(A)** evaluate the impact of events, including the Gulf of Tonkin Resolution and the War Powers Act, on the relationship between the legislative and executive branches of government.
2 Fighting the War	**(8) Geography.** The student uses geographic tools to collect, analyze, and interpret data. The student is expected to: **(B)** pose and answer questions about geographic distributions and patterns shown on maps, graphs, charts, models, and databases. **(20) Culture.** The student understands the relationship between the arts and the times during which they were created. The student is expected to: **(C)** identify examples of American art, music, and literature that transcend American culture and convey universal themes. **(22) Science, technology, and society.** The student understands the impact of science and technology on the economic development of the United States. The student is expected to: **(B)** expain how scientific discoveries and technological innovations such as those in agriculture, the military, and medicine resulted from specific needs.
3 Political Divisions	**(8) Geography.** The student uses geographic tools to collect, analyze, and interpret data. The student is expected to: **(A)** create thematic maps, graphs, charts, models, and databases representing various aspects of the United States. **(B)** pose and answer questions about geographic distributions and patterns shown on maps, graphs, charts, models, and databases. **(24) Social studies skills.** The student applies critical-thinking skills to organize and use information acquired from a variety of sources including electronic technology. The student is expected to: **(C)** explain and apply different methods that historians use to interpret the past, including the use of primary and secondary sources, points of view, frames of reference, and historical context. **(F)** identify bias in written, oral, and visual material. **(25) Social studies skills.** The student communicates in written, oral, and visual forms. The student is expected to: **(D)** create written, oral, and visual presentations of social studies information.
4 The End of the War	**(1) History.** The student understands traditional historical points of reference in U.S. history from 1877 to the present. The student is expected to: **(B)** apply absolute and relative chronology through the sequencing of significant individuals, events, and time periods. **(8) Geography.** The student uses geographic tools to collect, analyze, and interpret data. The student is expected to: **(B)** pose and answer questions about geographic distributions and patterns shown on maps, graphs, charts, models, and databases. **(24) Social studies skills.** The student applies critical-thinking skills to organize and use information acquired from a variety of sources including electronic technology. The student is expected to: **(C)** explain and apply different methods that historians use to interpret the past, including the use of primary and secondary sources, points of view, frames of reference, and historical context. **(D)** use the process of historical inquiry to research, interpret, and use multiple sources of evidence. **(F)** identify bias in written, oral, and visual material.

Chapter 24

The Vietnam War

(1954–1975)

Introducing the Chapter

The 1960s and 1970s were decades of deep division and turmoil in the United States. Under Presidents Kennedy and Johnson, the country became increasingly involved in trying to stop a Communist takeover in Vietnam. As the war continued to cost more and more lives and money while achieving little apparent success, many Americans began to question their government's role there. At the same time, a youthful counterculture arose that was critical of the traditional values of many Americans.

Time Line Activity

To provide students with practice in using the time line, ask questions such as these:

1. Which President first applied the domino theory to the situation in Southeast Asia? *(President Eisenhower)*
2. What power did President Johnson gain by virtue of the Gulf of Tonkin Resolution? *(The authority to escalate the war in Vietnam)*
3. In what way was the passage of the Twenty-sixth Amendment related to the Vietnam War? *(It was argued that if 18-year-olds could be drafted to fight in the war, they should be able to vote.)*

Chapter 24 The Vietnam War (1954–1975)

President Kennedy (left) and Vice President Johnson at the 1961 inauguration.

American Events

1954 After the French defeat in Vietnam, the United States starts to support the newly established nation of South Vietnam with military advisors and aid.

1963 U.S. involvement in Vietnam increases. President Kennedy is assassinated.

1964 The Gulf of Tonkin Resolution gives President Johnson complete authority to escalate the war in Vietnam.

1968 A year of crises unfolds with the assassinations of Martin Luther King, Jr., and Robert Kennedy. Violence erupts at the Democratic National Convention in Chicago.

Presidential Terms: Dwight D. Eisenhower 1953–1961; John F. Kennedy 1961–1963; Lyndon B. Johnson 1963–1969

1954 · 1960 · 1966

World Events

1961 The Berlin Wall is built.

1967 The Six-Day War takes place in the Middle East.

1968 The Tet Offensive begins.

eTeach

Be sure to check out this month's online discussion with a Master Teacher. Go to **www.phschool.com**.

RESOURCE DIRECTORY

Teaching Resources

Pacing Charts booklet
Block Scheduling booklet, p. 29
Units 5/6/7 booklet
- Chapter Summary, p. 84

Technology

Guided Reading Audiotapes (English/Spanish), Ch. 24
Student Edition on Audio CD, Ch. 24
Prentice Hall United States History Video Collection™ Volume 20, *Post-War USA*
Prentice Hall Presentation Pro CD-ROM, Ch. 24
Resource Pro® CD-ROM
Social Studies Skills Tutor CD-ROM
Companion Web site, www.phschool.com

Major Players in the Vietnam Conflict

NORTH AMERICA
UNITED STATES
ARCTIC OCEAN
SOVIET UNION
FRANCE
EUROPE
ASIA
CHINA
ATLANTIC OCEAN
AFRICA
VIETNAM
PACIFIC OCEAN
PACIFIC OCEAN
SOUTH AMERICA
INDIAN OCEAN
AUSTRALIA
ANTARCTICA
Equator

Vietnam

CHINA
BURMA
LAOS
Gulf of Tonkin
17th Parallel
THAILAND
VIETNAM
CAMBODIA
Gulf of Thailand

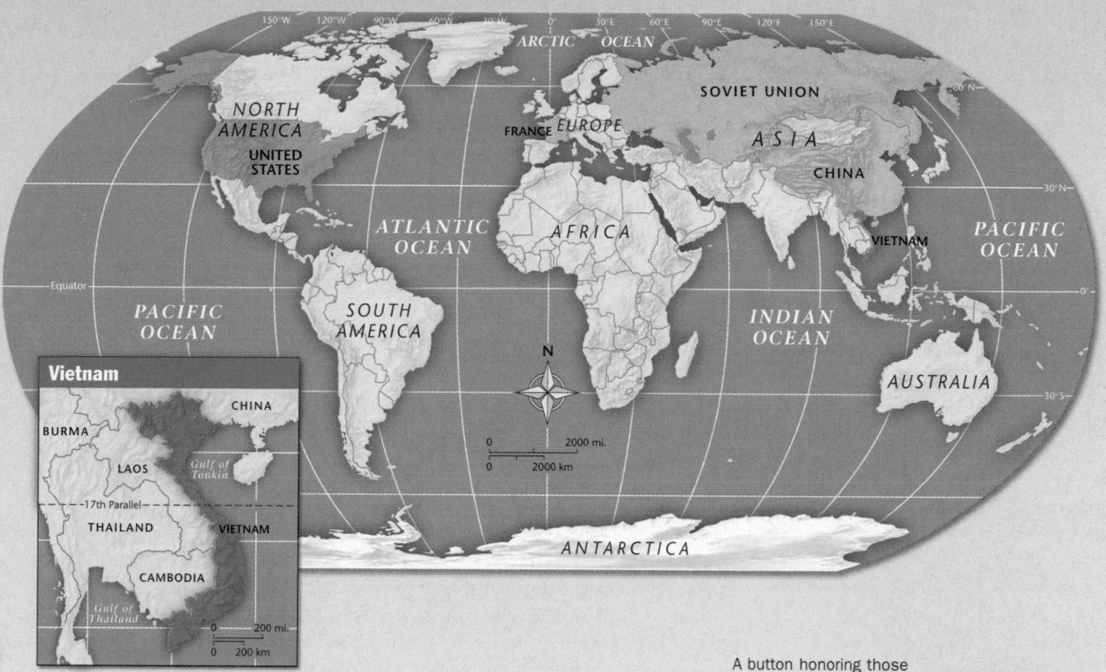

Antiwar protests sweep the nation.

A button honoring those missing in action in Vietnam.

MIA
MISSING OR PRISONER

1970 Four students protesting the Vietnam War are killed by National Guardsmen at Kent State. A similar incident at Jackson State results in two student deaths.

1971 The Twenty-sixth Amendment lowers the voting age to 18. Proponents argue that if 18-year-olds can fight in Vietnam, they should be able to vote.

1973 American troops withdraw from Vietnam, but returning veterans received a mixed welcome at home.

Richard M. Nixon 1969–1974 | Gerald R. Ford 1974–1977 | Jimmy Carter 1977–1981

1972 | 1978

1971 India and Pakistan go to war.

1973 The Vietnam War ends with the signing of a formal peace agreement in Paris.

1975 Communists take over South Vietnam, Cambodia, and Laos.

Major Players in the Vietnam Conflict

Activating Prior Knowledge Which countries were the major players in the Vietnam War? *(China, France, the Soviet Union, and the United States)*

Previewing What did the United States fear would happen if there was a Communist takeover of Vietnam? *(The U.S. feared that if Vietnam fell to the Communists, Laos, Cambodia, Burma, and Thailand would fall as well.)*

Background: About the Pictures

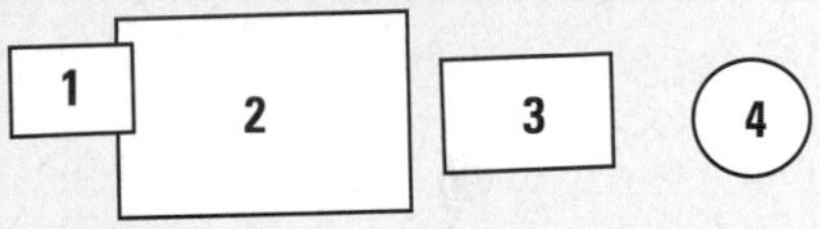

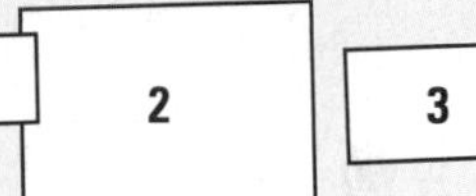

1. Inauguration day on January 20, 1961, was one of the coldest in United States history. The cold weather and snowfall the night before created one of the largest traffic jams ever as thousand of cars were left stranded by people trying to get to the ceremonies.
2. The terrain of Vietnam caused many problems for American soldiers as both their training and equipment proved unsuitable for the jungle climate.
3. Antiwar protests became common as more and more American soldiers were killed in Vietnam. Like the soldiers fighting, the majority of the antiwar protesters were young people.
4. Buttons such as this one were used to commemorate soldiers missing in action in Vietnam. Even today, many American soldiers remain unaccounted for.

Bibliography

For the Teacher

Fitzgerald, Frances. ***Fire in the Lake: The Vietnamese and the Americans in Vietnam.*** Random House, 1989 edition. (Considered the classic history of the war.)

Sheehan, Neil. ***A Bright Shining Lie: John Paul Vann and America in Vietnam.*** Random House, 1989. (The war seen through the story of one American officer.)

For the Student

Kovic, Ron. ***Born on the Fourth of July.*** Pocket Books, 1996. (A personal account by a disillusioned Vietnam veteran; later made into an Academy Award–winning film.)

O'Brien, Tim. ***The Things They Carried.*** Broadway Books, 1999. (A blending of fact and fiction on coming to terms with Vietnam.)

Vietnam: A Television History. PBS Video. (Award-winning 13-hour history of the War.)

Don't miss the exclusive interactive version of this textbook on the Web and on CD-ROM.

Section 1

The War Unfolds

SECTION OBJECTIVES

1. Learn about the events that led to the war between North Vietnam and South Vietnam.
2. Become familiar with the Vietnam policies of President Kennedy and Robert McNamara.
3. See how President Johnson changed the course of the war.

BELLRINGER

Warm-Up Activity Ask students to brainstorm words, phrases, and images that come to mind when they hear the word *Vietnam.*

Activating Prior Knowledge Some students may have family members or family friends who had a connection to the Vietnam War. Ask those students who are aware of such a connection to describe what it is.

READING STRATEGY

Ask students to write the following column headings: *Background of the War, Kennedy's Vietnam Policy, Johnson Commits to Containment.* As students read the section, have them take notes in each column and reflect on the domestic and international effects of the conflict.

ACTIVITY

Connecting with History and Conflict

Ask each student to create a chart to illustrate the buildup of American forces in Vietnam, starting with the 675 military advisers provided before 1960. Have students continue to add to the chart to reflect the progress of the war. As they create the chart, have them contemplate the challenges of changing relationships among nations that caused the United States to enter the Vietnam conflict. **(Visual/Spatial)**

Section 1

The War Unfolds

READING FOCUS

- What events led to the war between North Vietnam and South Vietnam?
- What were the Vietnam policies of President Kennedy and Robert McNamara?
- How did President Johnson change the course of the war?

MAIN IDEA

The United States entered the Vietnam War to defeat Communist forces threatening South Vietnam.

KEY TERMS

domino theory
Vietminh
Geneva Accords
Viet Cong
National Liberation Front
Gulf of Tonkin Resolution

TAKING NOTES

Copy the chart below. As you read, fill in some of the causes of the Vietnam War and its early effects on the United States.

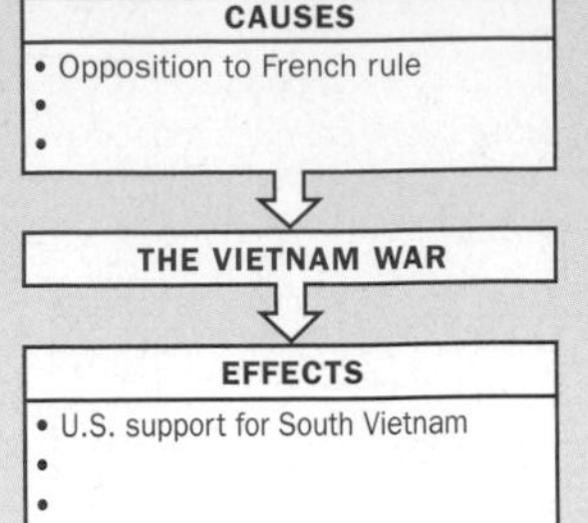

CAUSES
• Opposition to French rule
•
•
THE VIETNAM WAR
EFFECTS
• U.S. support for South Vietnam
•
•

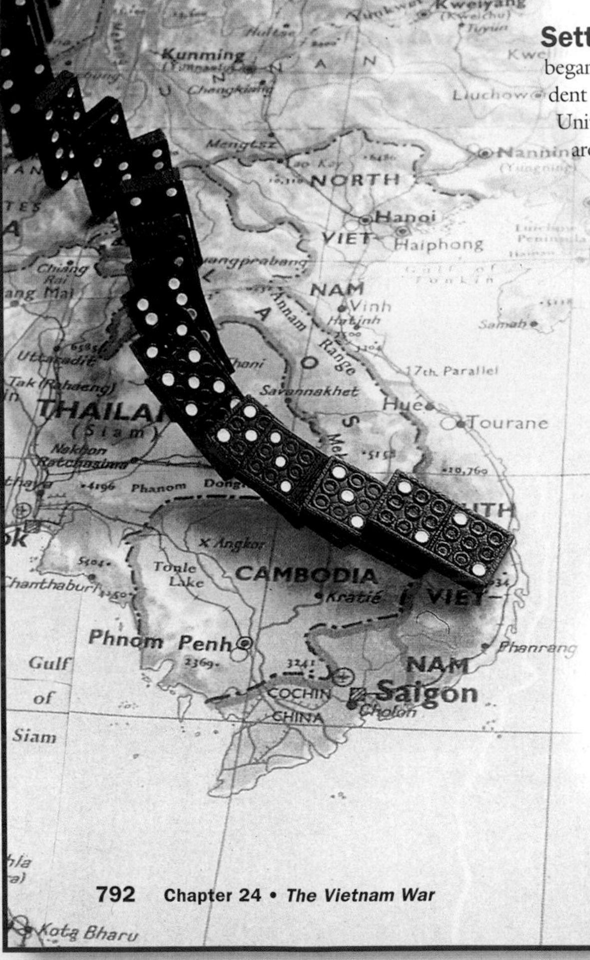

Setting the Scene American involvement in Vietnam began during the early years of the Cold War. It was based on President Harry S Truman's policy of containment which called for the United States to resist Soviet attempts to spread communism around the world. At a news conference in 1954, President Dwight D. Eisenhower described the principle that became associated with American involvement in Southeast Asia:

> "*You have a row of dominoes set up, you knock over the first one, and what will happen to the last one is the certainty that it will go over very quickly.*"
>
> —Dwight D. Eisenhower

The **domino theory,** described above, refers to the fear that if one Southeast Asian nation fell to the Communists, the others would also fall. A Communist takeover of Vietnam, because of its geographic location, posed a threat to Cambodia, Laos, Burma, and Thailand.

Background of the War

Vietnam had a history of nationalism that extended back nearly 2,000 years. The Vietnamese spent much of that time resisting attempts by neighboring China to swallow their small country. In the 1800s, France established itself as a new colonial power in Vietnam, and the French met similar resistance from the Vietnamese.

Ho Chi Minh, who sympathized with Communist ideas, fought for independence before, during, and after World War II. He was head of the League for the Independence of Vietnam, commonly called the **Vietminh.**

RESOURCE DIRECTORY

Teaching Resources
Learning Styles Lesson Plans booklet, p. 64
Guided Reading and Review booklet, p. 124

Other Print Resources
Historical Outline Map Book *War in Southeast Asia,* p. 70

Technology
Section Reading Support Transparencies
Guided Reading Audiotapes (English/Spanish), Ch. 24
Student Edition on Audio CD, Ch. 24
Color Transparencies *Time Lines,* C8
Prentice Hall Presentation Pro CD-ROM, Ch. 24
Companion Web site, www.phschool.com

Ho Chi Minh aroused his people's feelings of nationalism against French control. The French opposed the Vietminh by forming the Republic of Vietnam, headed by the emperor Bao Dai. War between these opposing forces continued until May 1954, when the Vietminh defeated the French after a long siege at a fortress in Dien Bien Phu.

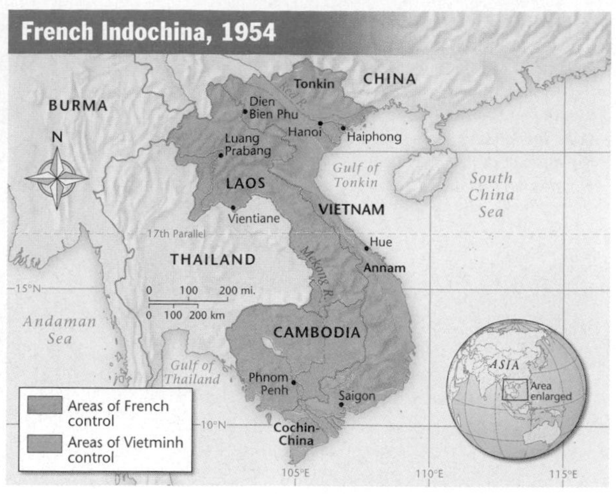

MAP SKILLS After World War II, France struggled to keep control of its colonies in Southeast Asia. The Vietminh was fighting for Vietnamese independence. **Regions** *In early 1954, where was the largest region of Vietminh (Ho Chi Minh's) control?*

A Divided Vietnam In April 1954, an international conference met in Geneva, Switzerland. After the French defeat in Vietnam, representatives of Ho Chi Minh, Bao Dai, Cambodia, Laos, France, the United States, the Soviet Union, China, and Britain arranged a peace settlement. As a result of the **Geneva Accords,** Vietnam was divided into two separate nations in July 1954. Although the border between the two nations was often referred to as the 17th parallel, the demarcation line set in Geneva was actually a few miles south of the parallel.

Ho Chi Minh became president of the new Communist-dominated North Vietnam, with its capital in Hanoi. Ngo Dinh Diem, a former Vietnamese official who had been living in exile in the United States, became president of anti-Communist South Vietnam, with its capital in Saigon. The Geneva agreements called for elections to be held in 1956 to unify the country. South Vietnam refused to support this part of the agreement, claiming that the Communists would not hold fair elections. As a result, Vietnam remained divided.

United States Involvement After World War II, President Truman had pledged American aid to any nation threatened by Communists. Beginning in 1950, the United States provided economic aid to the French effort in Vietnam as a way of gaining French support for the policy of containment in Europe. After the French defeat, the United States began to support anti-Communist South Vietnam.

President Eisenhower pledged his support to South Vietnam's Diem. In 1960, Eisenhower provided about 675 United States military advisors to assist in South Vietnam's struggle against the North. Thus the United States became involved in the Vietnam War.

Kennedy's Vietnam Policy

When President John F. Kennedy took office in 1961, he was determined to prevent the spread of communism at all costs. This meant strengthening

"Personally, I find it a rather unrewarding job."

INTERPRETING POLITICAL CARTOONS This cartoon uses an open sedan chair, similar to a kind of personal transportation popular in Southeast Asia, to make a political point. **Drawing Inferences** *(a) Who are the two men "carrying" President Diem of South Vietnam? (b) What has brought Diem's progress to a halt? (c) Why is the man in front complaining? (d) Explain the point the cartoonist is making.*

Lesson Plan

Focus Explain that in the 1960s, Presidents Kennedy and Johnson were determined to maintain South Vietnam under an anti-Communist government. Ask how the United States became involved in Vietnam. How did the American presence in Vietnam escalate?

Instruct Discuss Eisenhower's decision to support Diem and Kennedy's decision to increase United States support for the Diem regime. What other decisions might those Presidents have made? Ask students to list the most probable results of those other decisions. Could the nation accept those results today? Why would the results have been unacceptable in the late 1950s and early 1960s?

Assess/Reteach Ask students to state the original rationale for the involvement of the United States in the war in Vietnam. Can they describe ways in which this initial involvement could be linked to other world affairs, especially the Cold War?

Customize For ...

Less Proficient Readers

Have students reread the section "A Divided Vietnam." Then have students write down the following dates: April 1954, July 1954, and 1956. Have students list the event that took place during each of these dates, including what countries were involved.

Caption Answers

Map Skills The Tonkin region.

Interpreting Political Cartoons President Kennedy and a Vietnamese peasant. The peasant has sat down. He finds supporting Diem "unrewarding." The cartoonist is saying that the United States cannot "carry" the Diem government if the Vietnamese people do not support it.

ACTIVITY
Connecting with History and Conflict

Hold an informal, whole-class debate on the ethics of the Kennedy administration's encouragement of the coup in Vietnam. Ask: Are such actions inappropriate interference in another country, or are such actions justifiable methods of achieving larger goals? Poll the class before and after the debate to determine students' positions on the issue and whether, and why, the debate caused any of them to change their views. **(Verbal/Linguistic)**

BACKGROUND
Biography

Many people in the United States began calling U.S. activities in Vietnam "McNamara's war," owing to McNamara's unparalleled clout in shaping the country's Vietnam policies. Critics used the term derisively, but McNamara was quick to defend himself: "I don't object to its being called 'McNamara's war,'" he retorted. "I think it is a very important war and I am pleased to be identified with it and do whatever I can to win it."

VIEWING HISTORY Buddhist monks protested Ngo Dinh Diem's government by burning themselves to death on the streets of Saigon. **Identifying Central Issues** *How does this photograph symbolize the difficult problems Johnson inherited in Vietnam?*

and protecting the government that the United States had helped create in South Vietnam.

Kennedy sent Vice President Lyndon Johnson to Vietnam to assess the situation there. Diem told Johnson that South Vietnam would need even more aid if it was to survive. In response, Kennedy increased the number of American military advisors to Vietnam. By the end of 1963, that number had grown to more than 16,000.

Military aid by itself could not ensure success. Diem lacked support in his own country. He imprisoned people who criticized his government and filled many government positions with members of his own family. United States aid earmarked for economic reforms went instead to the military and into the pockets of corrupt officials.

Diem's Downfall Diem launched an unpopular program which relocated peasants from their ancestral lands to "strategic hamlets." These government-run farming communities were intended to isolate the peasants from Communist influences seeping into South Vietnam.

In addition, Diem was a Catholic in a largely Buddhist country. When Diem insisted that Buddhists obey Catholic religious laws, serious opposition developed. In June 1963, a Buddhist monk burned himself to death on the streets of Saigon. Photographs showing his silent, grisly protest appeared on the front pages of newspapers around the world. Other monks followed the example, but their martyrdom did not budge Diem.

Kennedy finally realized that the struggle against communism in Vietnam could not be won under Diem's rule. United States officials told South Vietnamese military leaders that the United States would not object to Diem's overthrow. With that encouragement, military leaders staged a coup in November 1963. They seized control of the government and assassinated Diem as he tried to flee.

McNamara's Role One of the American officials who helped create the Kennedy administration's Vietnam policy was Robert McNamara, President Kennedy's Secretary of Defense. A Republican with a strong business background, McNamara became one of Kennedy's closest

American BIOGRAPHY

Robert McNamara
b. 1916

Robert McNamara was born in San Francisco, California, and grew up across the bay in Oakland. He attended the University of California at Berkeley and went on to earn a graduate degree at Harvard Business School in 1939. McNamara served in the air force during World War II. After the war, he took a job at the Ford Motor Company. Through hard work and solid business decisions, McNamara moved quickly up the corporate ladder. He took over the presidency of Ford Motors in November 1960. This rising star caught the eye of President Kennedy, who offered him a position in his Cabinet just one month later.

CAPTION ANSWERS

Viewing History It shows the unpopularity of the United States–backed Diem among his own people.

RESOURCE DIRECTORY

Other Print Resources

American History Block Scheduling Support *Vietnam: The War at Home,* found in The Nation After World War II folder, includes interdisciplinary lesson suggestions and activities for Geography and History, Primary Sources, Biography, and Literature.

Technology

Sounds of an Era Audio CD *President John F. Kennedy,* 1961 recording (time: one minute)

advisors on Vietnam. Later he helped shape the policies that drew the United States deeper into the war.

As Secretary of Defense, McNamara applied his business knowledge, managing to cut costs while modernizing the armed forces. He turned the Pentagon's thinking away from reliance on the threat of nuclear bombs toward the development of a "flexible response" to military crises. He also began to focus his attention on how to handle the conflict in Vietnam.

Later, under Lyndon Johnson, McNamara pushed for direct American involvement in the war. In 1963, however, he still questioned whether a complete withdrawal was not the better alternative. Looking back on that period later, McNamara revealed his feelings:

> "*I believed that we had done all the training we could. Whether the South Vietnamese were qualified or not to turn back the North Vietnamese, I was certain that if they weren't, it wasn't for lack of our training. More training wouldn't strengthen them; therefore we should get out. The President (Kennedy) agreed.*"
>
> —Robert McNamara

As you will read later in this chapter, the United States did not withdraw. It continued to back South Vietnam and the military leaders who took over the government.

Johnson Commits to Containment

Three weeks after Diem's assassination, President Kennedy himself fell to an assassin's bullet in Dallas, Texas. Lyndon Johnson assumed the presidency and faced an escalating crisis in Vietnam. Johnson believed strongly in the need for containment:

> "*The Communists' desire to dominate the world is just like the lawyer's desire to be the ultimate judge on the Supreme Court. . . . You see, the Communists want to rule the world, and if we don't stand up to them, they will do it. And we'll be slaves. Now I'm not one of those folks seeing Communists under every bed. But I do know about the principles of power, and when one side is weak, the other steps in.*"
>
> —Lyndon Johnson

Communist Advances Diem's successors established a new military government in South Vietnam that proved to be both unsuccessful and unpopular. The ruling generals bickered among themselves and failed to direct the South Vietnamese army effectively. Communist guerrillas in the south, known as **Viet Cong,** and their political arm, called the **National Liberation Front,** gained control of more territory and earned the loyalty of an increasing number of the South Vietnamese people. Ho Chi Minh and the North Vietnamese aided the Viet Cong throughout the struggle.

Just after Johnson assumed office, he met with Henry Cabot Lodge, who was the United States ambassador to South Vietnam. Lodge told the new President that he faced some tough choices if he wanted to save Vietnam.

Focus on GOVERNMENT

The Powers of the President The United States Constitution divides military power between the executive and legislative branches. It makes the President commander in chief of the army and navy, but gives Congress the power to declare war and the power to raise an army and navy.

Throughout American history, Presidents have used their extensive authority as commander in chief to order military operations without a formal declaration of war. The Gulf of Tonkin Resolution, passed by Congress in 1964, was not a declaration of war, but it gave the President expanded powers to conduct the war in Vietnam.

The nation's anguish over the Vietnam War led Congress to pass the War Powers Act in 1973. The act places close limits on the President's war-making powers: If there is no declaration of war by Congress, it requires the President to

1. notify Congress within 48 hours of committing American troops to combat, and
2. end the combat within 60 days unless Congress authorizes a longer period.

In addition, the act gives Congress the power to end the combat at any time by passing a resolution to that effect.

READING CHECK
Describe the new military government in South Vietnam.

ACTIVITY
Connecting with Government

Refer students to the Constitution and have them identify and study the sections that specify the war-making powers of the President and the Congress. Then have students consider both the Gulf of Tonkin Resolution and the War Powers Act in light of constitutional provisions. Students should then write paragraphs arguing that either the Gulf of Tonkin Resolution or the War Powers Act is closer to the intentions of the Framers. **(Verbal/Linguistic)**

BACKGROUND
Interdisciplinary

The term "Viet Cong" comes from the Vietnamese term *Viet Nam Cong San,* which means "Vietnamese Communists." The term was first used by officials in Diem's regime—and perhaps originally by Diem himself—as a disparaging name for the Communists. The Communists themselves did not use or like the term. They called themselves such things as the People's Liberation Armed Forces or the National Front for the Liberation of Vietnam.

READING CHECK
Corrupt, incompetent, and unpopular.

CUSTOMIZE FOR ...
Gifted and Talented

Ask students to write one or two sentences describing the level of United States involvement in the Vietnam War under Presidents Eisenhower, Kennedy, and Johnson.

TEST PREPARATION

Have students read the quote on this page by Lyndon Johnson and then answer the question below.

Who is Johnson referring to when he talks about the "weak" side?

- **A** The Communists
- **(B)** Vietnam
- **C** The United States
- **D** China

Section 1 Assessment

Reading Comprehension

1. It demonstrated the fear on the part of the American government that if one Southeast Asian country fell to communism, others would follow; defying the U.S. policy of containment.
2. (a) The League for the Independence of Vietnam; (b) Communist guerrillas in the South; (c) the political wing of the Viet Cong.
3. Vietnam was divided into two separate nations. Unification and nationwide elections set for 1956 were prevented by South Vietnam.
4. Diem's policies of relocating peasants and persecuting Buddhists made him unpopular in his own country. Kennedy realized that the struggle against communism could not be won under Diem's rule.

Critical Thinking and Writing

5. Students should include the fact that the resolution gave the President almost complete control over U.S. actions in Vietnam. This usurped the constitutional right of Congress to declare war.
6. Essays will vary but should be supported with facts from the section.

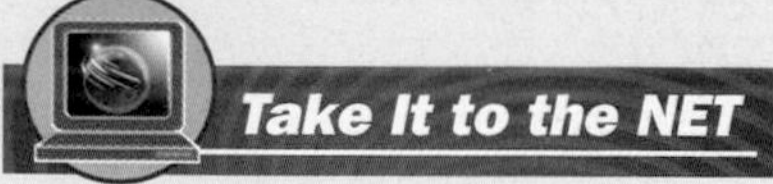

Answers will vary. Students should demonstrate knowledge of the early events of the Vietnam conflict.

GULF OF TONKIN RESOLUTION
Joint Resolution of Congress
H.J. RES 1145 • August 7, 1964
Public Law 88-408; 78 Stat. 384 • August 10, 1964

Resolved by the Senate and House of Representatives of the United States of America in Congress assembled,

That the Congress approves and supports the determination of the President, as Commander in Chief, to take all necessary measures to repel any armed attack against the forces of the United States and to prevent further aggression.

Section 2. The United States regards as vital to its national interest and to world peace the maintenance of international peace and security in southeast Asia. Consonant with the Constitution of the United States and the Charter of the United Nations and in accordance with its obligations under the Southeast Asia Collective Defense Treaty, the United States is, therefore, prepared, as the President determines, to take all necessary steps, including the use of armed force, to assist any member or protocol state of the Southeast Asia Collective Defense Treaty requesting assistance in defense of its freedom.

Section 3. This resolution shall expire when the President shall determine that the peace and security of the area is reasonably assured by international conditions created by action of the United Nations or otherwise, except that it may be terminated earlier by concurrent resolution of the Congress.

The Gulf of Tonkin Resolution tipped the balance of power between Congress (upper photo) and the White House (lower photo).

Johnson was determined to do whatever was needed to win the war. "I am not going to lose Vietnam," he said. Johnson recalled the Communist takeover of China in 1949. Referring to the fact that many Americans had blamed the "loss of China" on the Truman administration, Johnson went on: "I am not going to be the President who saw Southeast Asia go the way China went." Johnson did not want the Southeast Asian "dominoes" to be set in motion by the fall of Vietnam.

Expanding Presidential Power In August 1964, Johnson made a dramatic announcement: North Vietnamese torpedo boats had attacked United States destroyers in the international waters of the Gulf of Tonkin, 30 miles from North Vietnam. Those attacks would change the course of the war.

Details about the attacks were sketchy, and some people doubted that they had even taken place. In any case, Johnson used the Gulf of Tonkin incident to deepen American involvement in Vietnam. The President asked Congress for and obtained a resolution giving him authority to "take all necessary measures to repel any armed attack against the forces of the United States and to prevent further aggression."

Congress passed this **Gulf of Tonkin Resolution** on August 7 by a vote of 416 to 0 in the House of Representatives and 88 to 2 in the Senate. Johnson had been waiting for some time for an opportunity to propose the resolution, which, he noted, "covered everything." The President now had nearly complete control over what the United States did in Vietnam, even without an official declaration of war from Congress.

Section 1 Assessment

READING COMPREHENSION

1. How did the **domino theory** explain American involvement in Southeast Asia?
2. What were (a) the **Vietminh,** (b) the **Viet Cong,** and (c) the **National Liberation Front?**
3. What were the results of the **Geneva Accords?**
4. Why did American officials support the overthrow of Diem's government?

CRITICAL THINKING AND WRITING

5. **Drawing Conclusions** Write a paragraph explaining how the Gulf of Tonkin Resolution affected the balance of power between the President and Congress.
6. **Writing an Outline** Write an outline for an essay from the perspective of Robert McNamara in 1963 in which you present President Kennedy with two options—withdraw from Vietnam or fully support Diem.

Take It to the NET

Activity: Writing an Editorial Research events and media coverage from the early years of the Vietnam conflict. Then write an editorial as if it were 1965, and you do not know the eventual outcome of the war. Use the links provided in the *America: Pathways to the Present* area of the following Web site for help in completing this activity.
www.phschool.com

RESOURCE DIRECTORY
Teaching Resources
Units 5/6/7 booklet
- Section 1 Quiz, p. 85

Guide to the Essentials
- Section 1 Summary, p. 116

Sequencing

The order in which events occur is called sequence. When you are using several sources to gather information, each source may tell only part of the story. You will need to use sequencing to understand the order in which events took place. And when you are preparing your own report, presenting facts in sequence will help your audience understand your message.

These passages describe events in the 1950s and early 1960s that led to increased American involvement in Vietnam.

LEARN THE SKILL

Use the following steps to present information in sequence:

1. **Identify the order in which events happened.** Look for time-order words such as *later, earlier, now, then, finally, before,* and *after.* Also note any dates, including specific days, months, or parts of the year.
2. **Use visual aids to organize the information.** Make a list of events from all your sources, and the dates the events occurred. Then sort the events by date, and write them in a flowchart or a time line. Now you can add the events that don't have specific dates by inserting them according to clues given by time-order words.
3. **Explain how events are connected.** Present the information in your own words, using dates and time-order words to help your audience understand the sequence of events.

PRACTICE THE SKILL

Answer the following questions:

1. **(a)** Which years are identified in Source A, and what events occurred during those years? **(b)** Which years are identified in Source B, and what events occurred during those years? **(c)** Which time-order words in the sources help you understand the order of events?
2. **(a)** According to both sources, what events occurred in 1961? **(b)** What other event is described in both sources? **(c)** What information not given in Source A is provided by Source B?
3. Create a flowchart or a time line that shows all the events that are described in both sources. Include dates.

APPLY THE SKILL

See the Chapter Review and Assessment for another opportunity to apply this skill.

A

"When Kennedy took office in early 1961 he continued the policies of Truman and Eisenhower in Southeast Asia. . . .

One day in June 1963, a Buddhist monk sat down in the public square in Saigon and set himself afire. More Buddhist monks began committing suicide by fire to dramatize their opposition to the Diem regime. Diem's police raided the Buddhist pagodas and temples, wounded thirty monks, arrested 1,400 people, and closed down the pagodas. . . .

Earlier in 1963, Kennedy's Undersecretary of State, U. Alexis Johnson, was speaking before the Economic Club of Detroit: '. . . Why is [Southeast Asia] desirable, and why is it important? First, it provides a lush climate, fertile soil, rich natural resources, a relatively sparse population in most areas, and room to expand. . . .'

This is not the language that was used by President Kennedy in his explanations to the American public. He talked of Communism and freedom. In a news conference February 14, 1962 he said: 'Yes, as you know, the U.S. for more than a decade has been assisting the government, the people of Vietnam, to maintain their independence.'"

—Howard Zinn, *A People's History of the United States*

B

"In 1961, Diem asked for more U.S. assistance, saying, 'The level of their [the Communists] attacks is already such that our forces are stretched to their utmost.'

Kennedy was willing to help, but he was wary of sending in combat troops. Instead, he took measures to enhance the fighting ability of the [South Vietnamese]. . . .

In late August [1963], disapproval of Diem intensified when he declared martial law in South Vietnam and ordered a military crackdown on Communist activists. Once again his troops also targeted Buddhists. . . .

Though the raids momentarily halted the Buddhist uprisings, they infuriated many South Vietnamese and millions of Americans. Kennedy, in response to mounting public outrage over the crackdown, temporarily halted all economic and military aid to South Vietnam on October 2, 1963."

—John M. Dunn, *The Vietnam War: A History of U.S. Involvement*

SEQUENCING

Focus Students learn to construct a sequence of historical events by reviewing documents that describe different portions of the sequence.

Instruct As students sequence the statements in passage A, they may notice a discrepancy. The Undersecretary of State and the President appear to emphasize different approaches to selling the "benefits" of United States involvement in Vietnam. Kennedy speaks of fighting communism and helping the Vietnamese people stay free. The Undersecretary speaks about the benefits to America of exploiting the natural resources of Vietnam. Do students think that both points of view reflect American policies? What might be the importance of the fact that one statement was made a year later than the other? Why might it be significant that President Kennedy made his remarks at a press conference, while the Undersecretary spoke to a group of business leaders?

Extend See the Skills for Life activity in the Resource Directory below.

ANSWERS

PRACTICE THE SKILL

1. **(a)** Early 1961: Kennedy takes office; February 14, 1962: Kennedy talks about helping the people of Vietnam defend their freedom; 1963: Johnson speaks of the benefits of exploiting Vietnam's natural resources; June 1963: Buddhist monks self-immolate to protest the Diem regime and Diem cracks down. **(b)** 1961: Diem asks for more assistance; late August 1963: Diem declares martial law and a crackdown on Communists and Buddhists; October 2, 1963: Kennedy rescinds economic and military aid to South Vietnam. **(c)** A: early, earlier. B: late.
2. **(a)** Kennedy sends aid to South Vietnam. **(b)** Buddhist uprisings. **(c)** Diem's declaration of martial law; U.S. withdrawal of economic and military aid.
3. The flowchart or time line should include all the dates and events from **1. (a)** and **(b)**.

RESOURCE DIRECTORY

Teaching Resources
Skills for Life booklet, p. 33

Technology
Social Studies Skills Tutor CD-ROM
Interactive Practice in
- Geographic Literacy
- Critical Thinking and Reading
- Visual Analysis
- Communications

Section 2
Fighting the War

Section Objectives

1. Learn how battlefield conditions in Vietnam affected American soldiers.
2. Be able to describe the course of the war between 1965 and 1968.
3. List reasons why the Tet Offensive was a turning point in the war.

Bellringer

Warm-Up Activity Ask students to consider how they would define a "just" war. Is any war just? Does the way the war is waged, including the types of weapons and damage inflicted, determine whether or not it is just?

Activating Prior Knowledge Ask students if they are familiar with the phrases "My Lai massacre" and "the Tet Offensive." Can anyone describe what each of those phrases refers to?

Reading Strategy

Read the section that summarizes the effects of the war on American soldiers and Vietnamese civilians. As you read, list the different ways in which the soldiers and the civilians suffered.

Activity
Connecting with History and Conflict

Write the word *morale* on the board, and challenge students to define it in the context of soldiers at war. Ask students what factors might have increased the morale of American troops in Vietnam, and what factors might have decreased it. Record salient responses on the board in the form of a web graphic organizer. Then have students assess the importance of morale in Vietnam, and in any armed conflict. How important is morale to achieving victory? **(Verbal/Linguistic)**

Section 2 Fighting the War

READING FOCUS

- How did battlefield conditions in Vietnam affect American soldiers?
- How would you describe the course of the war between 1965 and 1968?
- Why was the Tet Offensive a turning point in the war?

MAIN IDEA

The violence and brutality of the Vietnam War affected civilians as well as soldiers.

KEY TERMS

land mine
saturation bombing
fragmentation bombs
Agent Orange
napalm
escalation
Ho Chi Minh Trail
hawks
doves
Tet Offensive

TAKING NOTES

As you read, prepare an outline of this section. Use Roman numerals for the major headings of the section, capital letters for the subheadings, and numbers for the supporting details. The sample below will help you get started.

I. Battlefield Conditions
- **A. One Soldier's Story**
  - **1.** ____________
  - **2.** ____________
- **B. The Ground War**
  - **1.** ____________
  - **2.** ____________

Setting the Scene Nearly 3 million Americans served in the Vietnam War. These soldiers found themselves thousands of miles from home, fighting under conditions that were far different from those they had seen in films. Marine Corps officer James Webb served as rifle platoon and company commander in the An Hoa Basin near Da Nang:

> *"We moved through the boiling heat with 60 pounds of weapons and gear, causing a typical Marine to drop 20 percent of his body weight while in the bush. When we stopped we dug chest-deep fighting holes and slit trenches for toilets. We slept on the ground under makeshift poncho [tents]. . . . Sleep itself was fitful, never more than an hour or two at a stretch for months at a time as we mixed daytime patrolling with night-time ambushes, listening posts, foxhole duty, and radio watches. Ringworm, hookworm, malaria, and dysentery were common, as was trench foot when the monsoons came."*
>
> —James Webb

American soldiers encountered unfamiliar terrain and conditions when they landed in Vietnam.

798 Chapter 24 • *The Vietnam War*

RESOURCE DIRECTORY

Teaching Resources

Guided Reading and Review booklet, p. 125
Biography, Literature, and Comparing Primary Sources booklet (Literature) *Experiences of a Young Soldier in Vietnam,* p. 83

Technology

Section Reading Support Transparencies
Guided Reading Audiotapes (English/Spanish), Ch. 24
Student Edition on Audio CD, Ch. 24
Prentice Hall Presentation Pro CD-ROM, Ch. 24
Companion Web site, www.phschool.com

Battlefield Conditions

When Americans first started arriving in Vietnam in large numbers, they encountered all the frustrations of guerrilla warfare. American forces had superior arms and supplies. The Viet Cong, however, had some advantages of their own. For one thing, they were familiar with the swamps and jungles of Vietnam. In addition, they could find protection across the border in Cambodia and Laos. Finally, the Viet Cong could often count on the support of the local population.

American soldiers found the war confusing and disturbing. They were trying to defend the freedom of the South Vietnamese, but the people seemed indifferent to the Americans' effort. The dishonest and inept government in Saigon may have caused that indifference. "We are the unwilling working for the unqualified to do the unnecessary for the ungrateful," Kit Bowen of the First Infantry Division wrote to his father in Oregon.

American troops never knew what to expect next, and they never could be sure who was a friend and who was an enemy. The Vietnamese woman selling soft drinks by the roadside might be a Viet Cong ally, counting government soldiers as they passed. A child peddling candy might be concealing a live grenade.

In the face of this uncertain situation, one GI wrote home:

> *"The VC [Viet Cong] are getting much stronger, so I think this war is going to get worse before it gets better. . . . I try and take great pride in my unit and the men I work with. A lot of the men have been in a lot of trouble and have no education or money. But I feel honored to have them call me a friend."*
>
> —Letter home from an American soldier

READING CHECK
What were battlefield conditions like for American soldiers?

One Soldier's Story Many American soldiers went to war enthusiastic about the job they were being asked to do for their country. Some, like Ron Kovic of Long Island, worried about the Communist threat. Kovic was afraid that Communists "were infiltrating our schools, trying to take over our classes and control our minds." After high school, he joined the marines to do his part to defend his country. He proudly served a tour in Vietnam and signed up for a second tour. This second tour of duty would take a terrible toll on Kovic's body and mind.

Ron Kovic confronted his fears by making an aggressive effort to be a good soldier. But the horrors of war came to haunt him after he accidentally killed a

Lesson Plan

Focus American soldiers were not prepared for the brutality of the fighting in Vietnam, and Americans at home were shocked by the violence they witnessed on their television screens. Ask why American forces had little success in Vietnam. How did the war affect Vietnamese civilians?

Instruct Ask students to explain how a guerrilla war differs from a conventional war. Discuss why the superior firepower of the American forces was not more successful against the Viet Cong. Ask students whether the Vietnam War meets the definition of "total war," one in which destruction of property and civilian life is carried out to persuade the enemy that continuing the conflict is not worth the cost.

Assess/Reteach Conditions in Vietnam were uncomfortable and often terrifying for American soldiers. Yet their equipment and technology were superior. The Viet Cong were skillful and wily adversaries, whose intimate knowledge of their surroundings far outweighed their lack of supplies and weapons. Have students compare and contrast the advantages and disadvantages of the two sides.

READING CHECK
Conditions were very difficult. American soldiers discovered that superior firepower had a sharply limited effect on an enemy that used guerrilla tactics and was often assisted by South Vietnamese civilians.

CUSTOMIZE FOR ...
Gifted and Talented

As students read this section, have them create two lists. In the first, they should name the strengths the United States brought to the war. In the second, they should list the factors that might have undercut those strengths in the actual war effort.

ACTIVITY
Student Portfolio

You may wish to have students add the following to their portfolios: Present the following quotation by an American army officer after the total destruction of the village of Ben Tre in January 1968: "It became necessary to destroy the town in order to save it." Then ask students to write a brief explanation of why those opposed to the war frequently quoted this statement. **(Verbal/Linguistic)**

BACKGROUND
Biography

By the early 1990s, Brigadier General Sherian Grace Cadoria, born in 1940 in Marksville, Louisiana, was the highest-ranking African American woman in the United States armed forces. She served in Vietnam from January 1967 to October 1969. She remembers her arrival: "I interviewed for a protocol job. When I got there, the colonel told me I couldn't do the job. He said, 'You can't travel, you can't carry luggage, it's too heavy. Women can't do this.' And I said, 'Nobody said I couldn't carry those hundred-pound bags of cotton when I was just a child.'"

American soldiers like this one endured extremely difficult battlefield conditions in Vietnam.

United States corporal. Later he shot at shadowy figures in a village hut, only to learn that his unit had killed and wounded innocent children.

The final blow for Ron Kovic came when a sniper's bullet entered his spine. As his spinal column was severed and he lost the feeling in his legs, all he could think of was "the worthlessness of dying right here in this place at this moment for nothing." Kovic survived the bullet wound but was paralyzed from the chest down. The injury caused him to feel, in his words, "like a big clumsy puppet with all his strings cut." Kovic later wrote about his experiences in the book *Born on the Fourth of July.*

The Ground War The Viet Cong lacked the sophisticated equipment of the United States troops, so they avoided head-on clashes. Instead they used guerrilla warfare tactics, working in small groups to launch sneak attacks and practice sabotage. They often frustrated American search parties by hiding themselves in elaborate underground tunnels. Some of these were equipped with running water and electricity. The largest contained hospitals, stores, and weapons storage facilities.

The various booby traps set by the guerrilla fighters posed constant hazards to the Americans. A soldier might step into a punji trap—a camouflaged pit filled with razor-sharp stakes that were sometimes poisoned. The pressure of a footstep could set off a **land mine**—an explosive device planted in the ground. Many soldiers were wounded or killed by grenades, which were triggered by concealed trip wires. GIs could go weeks without making contact with the enemy—in fact, most never did—but there was always the possibility of sudden danger.

The war was also devastating for Vietnamese civilians. Because American soldiers were never sure who might be sympathetic to the Viet Cong, civilians

INTERPRETING DIAGRAMS
Some components of the Viet Cong tunnel system are shown below. **Drawing Conclusions** *How did these tunnels help the Viet Cong hold out against superior firepower?*

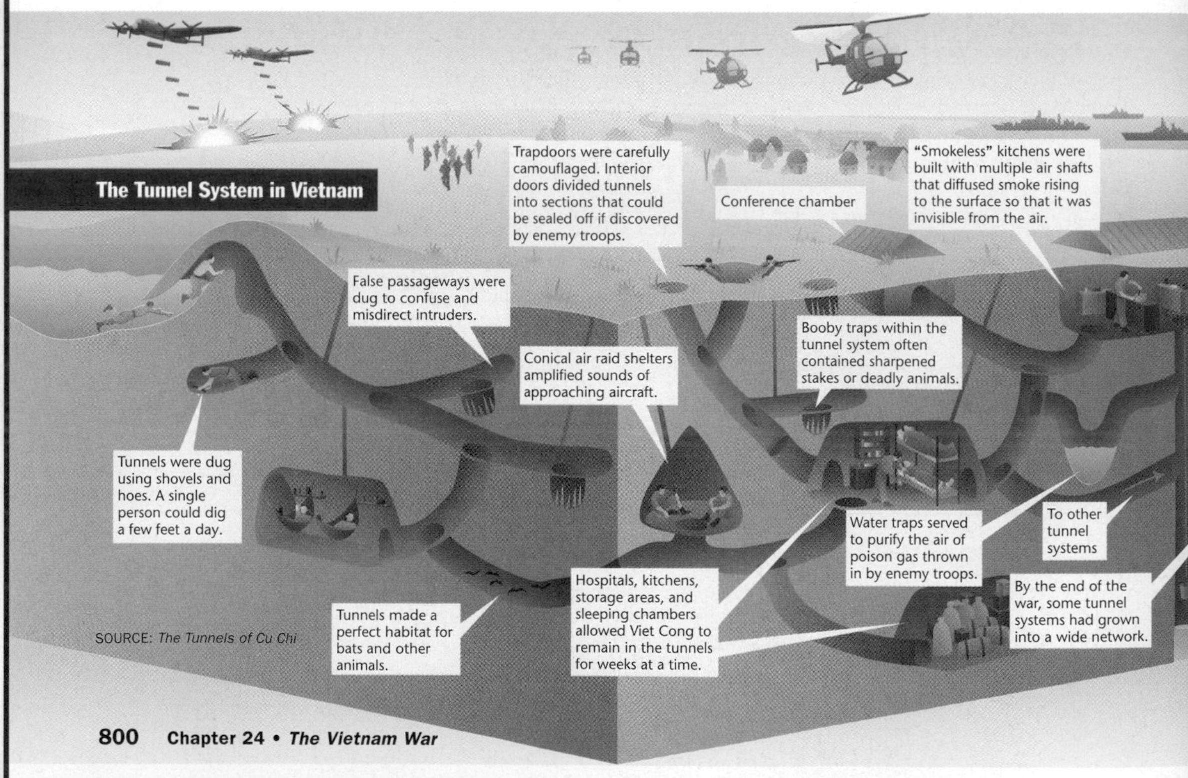

The Tunnel System in Vietnam
Trapdoors were carefully camouflaged. Interior doors divided tunnels into sections that could be sealed off if discovered by enemy troops.
Conference chamber
"Smokeless" kitchens were built with multiple air shafts that diffused smoke rising to the surface so that it was invisible from the air.
False passageways were dug to confuse and misdirect intruders.
Conical air raid shelters amplified sounds of approaching aircraft.
Booby traps within the tunnel system often contained sharpened stakes or deadly animals.
Tunnels were dug using shovels and hoes. A single person could dig a few feet a day.
Water traps served to purify the air of poison gas thrown in by enemy troops.
To other tunnel systems
Hospitals, kitchens, storage areas, and sleeping chambers allowed Viet Cong to remain in the tunnels for weeks at a time.
By the end of the war, some tunnel systems had grown into a wide network.
Tunnels made a perfect habitat for bats and other animals.
SOURCE: The Tunnels of Cu Chi

CAPTION ANSWERS

Viewing History Answers will vary but may include fear, confusion, and frustration.

RESOURCE DIRECTORY

Teaching Resources

Biography, Literature, and Comparing Primary Sources booklet (Biography) *John McCain III,* p. 36

Learning with Documents booklet (Primary Source Activity) *An Army Nurse Remembers,* p. 36

Technology

Color Transparencies *Historical Maps,* A50

suffered as much as soldiers. As the struggle intensified, the destruction worsened. The war affected everyone in Vietnam. Le Thanh, a North Vietnamese, recalled the horrors he had witnessed as a child in the 1960s:

> *"Nobody could get away from the war. It didn't matter if you were in the countryside or the city. While I was living in the country I saw terrible things. . . . I saw children who had been killed, pagodas and churches that had been destroyed, monks and priests dead in the ruins, schoolboys who were killed when schools were bombed."*
>
> —Le Thanh

VIEWING HISTORY In addition to killing and injuring many civilians, the war also forced many Vietnamese to flee their homes. **Recognizing Cause and Effect** *What impact do you think the war had on Vietnamese culture? Explain your answer.*

The Air War In April 1966, the Americans introduced the huge B-52 bomber into the war to smash roads and heavy bridges in North Vietnam. During air raids, these planes could drop thousands of tons of explosives over large areas. This **saturation bombing** tore North Vietnam apart.

Many of the bombs used in these raids threw pieces of their thick metal casings in all directions when they exploded. These **fragmentation bombs** were not confined to the north alone. They were also used in the south, where they killed and maimed countless civilians. Near the village of My Thuy Phuong, the war suddenly intruded on the life of a peasant who later described the frightening incident:

> *"One day I was walking back home from the ricefield, carrying tools on my shoulder. Then behind me I heard a large, loud noise. A very bad noise. I looked back and saw an American helicopter following me, shooting down the path toward me. I was very scared, so [I] jumped into the water by the side. Just one moment later, the bullets went right by. So scary."*
>
> —Vietnamese peasant

United States forces also used chemical weapons against the Vietnamese. Pilots dropped an herbicide known as **Agent Orange** on dense jungle landscapes. By killing the leaves and thick undergrowth, the herbicide exposed Viet Cong hiding places. Agent Orange also killed crops. Later it was discovered that Agent Orange caused health problems in livestock and in humans, including Vietnamese civilians and American soldiers.

Another destructive chemical used in Vietnam was called **napalm.** When dropped from airplanes, this jellylike substance splattered and burned uncontrollably. It also stuck to people's bodies and seared off their flesh.

The Course of the War, 1965–1968

After winning the election in 1964, President Johnson started a gradual military **escalation,** or expansion, of the war. Enemy gains in South Vietnam led Johnson to devote ever more American money and personnel to the conflict. Initially, United States soldiers had gone to Vietnam to advise the South Vietnamese. Now they took on the task of propping up the South Vietnamese government, which was led by military officer Nguyen Cao Ky.

Focus on CULTURE

The Ballad of the Green Berets
For several weeks in 1966, the number one song in the United States was "The Ballad of the Green Berets." This song, written by Staff Sergeant Barry Sadler, popularized American patriotism and honored the United States Army Special Forces, known as the Green Berets:

"Put silver wings on my son's chest
Make him one of America's best,
He'll be a man they'll test one day,
Have him win the Green Beret."
—Barry Sadler, medic in Vietnam War

ACTIVITY
Connecting with History and Conflict

Have students identify one of the many different weapons used by either side during the Vietnam War. The weapon may be a firearm, an aircraft, a ground vehicle, or any other piece of military hardware. Students should then compile and present brief reports on the weapon, identifying such things as its name, type, purpose, situations in which the weapon was used, the importance of the weapon to the war effort, and so on. Have students explain how scientific discoveries and technological innovations such as those in the military resulted from specific needs. **(Verbal/Linguistic)**

BACKGROUND
Interdisciplinary

As American herbicides destroyed crops in the South Vietnamese countryside, in the United States the Environmental Protection Agency (EPA) ordered a near-total ban on the pesticide dichlorodiphenyltrichloroethane (DDT). Although the use of DDT had resulted in dramatically increased crop yields, it was suspected to be a carcinogen and a possible cause of birth defects in humans and animals. DDT was banned in the United States and most other industrialized countries in the early 1970s.

TEST PREPARATION

Have students review the material under the heading "The Air War," and then answer the question below.

What is "saturation bombing"?

A Dropping bombs that contain water.
B Bombing dams to cause floods.
Ⓒ Blanketing a large area with thousands of tons of explosives.
D Sending out underwater bombs from submarines.

CAPTION ANSWERS

Viewing History Churches and schools were destroyed; the culture was disrupted.

ACTIVITY
Connecting with Citizenship

Have pairs of students cooperate to create a Venn diagram that compares and contrasts the "hawks" and "doves" of the Vietnam era. Cells in the diagram should include at least definitions of the terms, leading members of each school of thought, their basic positions, and any concerns or goals they had in common. **(Visual/Spatial)**

BACKGROUND
Biography

One of the leading doves was Senator Eugene McCarthy, Democrat from Wisconsin. He voiced the thoughts of many doves when he said, "The war in Vietnam . . . is central to all problems in America. A war of questionable legality and questionable constitutionality. A war which is diplomatically indefensible. . . . A war which cannot be defended in the context of the judgement of history. . . . A war which is not defensible even in military terms. . . . Finally, it is a war which is morally wrong."

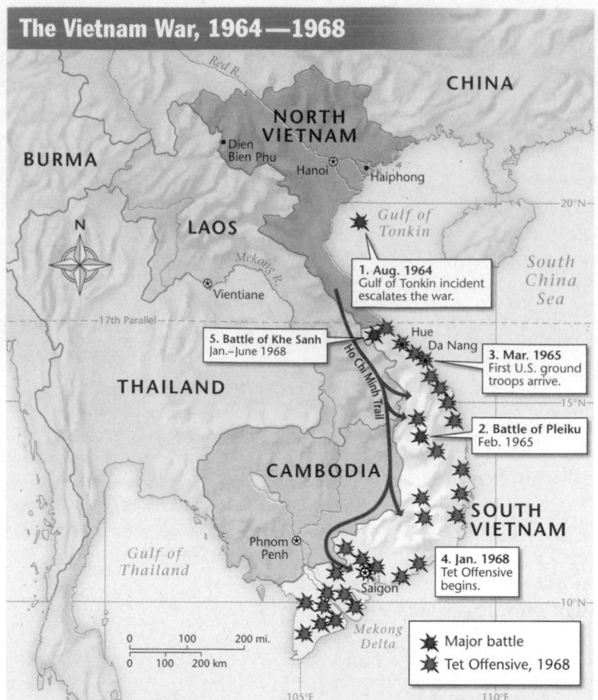

MAP SKILLS The Ho Chi Minh Trail, shown in the map above, was an important supply route for the Viet Cong and North Vietnamese troops. **Movement** (a) *Why do you think the Ho Chi Minh Trail was located exactly where it was?* (b) *How did it contribute to the Tet Offensive?*

Intensifying the War

By 1965, the Viet Cong were steadily expanding within South Vietnam. North Vietnamese troops and supplies poured into the south via the **Ho Chi Minh Trail,** a supply route that passed through Laos and Cambodia. In February, a Viet Cong attack at Pleiku within South Vietnam killed 8 Americans and wounded 126. President Johnson responded by authorizing the bombing of North Vietnam.

Two weeks after the Pleiku attack, General William Westmoreland, the commander of United States forces in Vietnam, requested more soldiers. He asked Johnson for two battalions of marines to protect the American airfield at Da Nang. Johnson heeded the request, beginning a rapid buildup of American combat troops. At the start of 1965, some 25,000 American soldiers were stationed in Vietnam. By the end of the year, the number had risen to 184,000.

Despite this large buildup of American troops, between 1965 and 1967 the war was at a stalemate. The American objective was not to conquer North Vietnam but rather to force the enemy to stop fighting. In 1965, President Johnson authorized Operation Rolling Thunder—the relentless bombing campaign that continued for almost three years. Although the bombing produced heavy damage, it failed to stop the Viet Cong. The enemy dug thousands of miles of tunnels through which troops and supplies moved south from North Vietnam.

United States forces launched search and destroy missions, but their victories failed to have a significant effect on the course of the war. Nothing seemed to diminish the enemy's willingness or ability to continue fighting. When the Viet Cong suffered heavy losses, North Vietnam sent new troops.

Hawks and Doves As the war unfolded, it came under increasing criticism at home from both **hawks**—those who supported the war—and **doves**—those who opposed the war. Senator J. William Fulbright, a Democrat and a leading dove, raised questions about the expansion of the war. As head of the Senate Foreign Relations Committee, Fulbright held televised hearings to examine U.S. policy in 1966.

At the hearings, Secretary of State Dean Rusk defended American involvement in Vietnam. George Kennan, who had helped draft U.S. foreign policy after World War II, opposed involvement in Vietnam. He argued that Vietnam was not strategically important to the United States and that Americans should not be called upon to solve the problems of that nation. Although both sides gave voice to their opinions, the war continued in Vietnam.

The Tet Offensive: A Turning Point

In 1967, Nguyen Van Thieu succeeded Ky as president of South Vietnam. Ky and Thieu were more effective leaders than Diem had been, but they remained

CAPTION ANSWERS

Map Skills (a) It allowed Viet Cong and North Vietnamese troops to travel in neighboring countries where they thought the United States would not attack them. (b) It allowed the North Vietnamese government to provide the Viet Cong with ammunition and other supplies for the Tet Offensive.

RESOURCE DIRECTORY

Technology

Sounds of an Era Audio CD *Walter Cronkite,* 1968 recording (time: one minute, 20 seconds)

authoritarian. Neither was able to put together an army that could successfully defend the country. The Americans brought with them advanced weaponry and new tactics that achieved some success. However, the American forces failed to drive out the Viet Cong, who were masters at jungle warfare. Month after month the fighting continued. United States planes bombed North Vietnam, and the flow of American soldiers into the south increased. Their number climbed to 385,000 by the end of 1966; to 485,000 by the end of 1967; and to 536,000 by the end of 1968. Despite the large United States presence in South Vietnam, the Communist forces intensified their efforts.

Those efforts reached a climax early in 1968, during Tet, the Vietnamese New Year. On January 30, the Viet Cong and North Vietnamese launched a major offensive. The **Tet Offensive,** shown on the map on the previous page, included surprise attacks on major cities and towns and American military bases throughout South Vietnam. In Saigon, the South Vietnamese capital, the Viet Cong attacked the American embassy and the presidential palace. Fierce fighting continued in Saigon for several weeks.

The War in Vietnam Escalates

Year	Event
1964	Gulf of Tonkin Resolution passes. Gradual military escalation begins.
1965	President Johnson responds to attacks against American troops by authorizing the bombing of North Vietnam and by rapidly increasing the number of American combat troops in South Vietnam.
1966–1967	The number of American soldiers in South Vietnam continues to increase.
1968	The Viet Cong and North Vietnamese launch the Tet Offensive.

INTERPRETING CHARTS
This chart shows several examples of the escalation of the Vietnam War beginning in 1964.
Determining Relevance *How did the Gulf of Tonkin Resolution contribute to this escalation?*

Communist Brutality During the Tet Offensive, Communists were uncommonly brutal, slaughtering anyone they labeled an enemy, including minor officials, teachers, and doctors. While the Communists had control of Hue, they ordered all civil servants, military personnel, and those who had worked for the Americans to report to special locations. Of those who obeyed, some 3,000 to 5,000 were killed. Their bodies were found in mass graves after American and South Vietnamese forces retook the city.

Massacre at My Lai Surrounded by brutality and under extreme distress, American soldiers also sometimes committed atrocities. Such brutality came into sharp focus at My Lai, a small village in South Vietnam. In response to word that My Lai was sheltering 250 members of the Viet Cong, a United States infantry company moved in to clear out the village in March 1968. Rather than enemy soldiers, the company found women, children, and old men. Lieutenant William L. Calley, Jr., was in charge. First he ordered, "Round everybody up." Then he gave the command for the prisoners to be killed. Private Paul Meadlo later described what happened to one group of Vietnamese:

> "*We huddled them up. We made them squat down. . . . I poured about four clips [about 68 shots] into the group. . . . Well, we kept right on firing. . . . I still dream about it. . . . Some nights, I can't even sleep. I just lay there thinking about it.*"
>
> —Private Paul Meadlo

Probably more than 400 Vietnamese died in the My Lai massacre. Even more would have perished without the heroic actions of a helicopter crew which stepped in to halt the slaughter. At great risk to himself and his crew, pilot Hugh Thompson landed the helicopter between the soldiers and the fleeing Vietnamese. He ordered his door gunner, 18-year-old Lawrence Colburn, to fire his machine gun at the American troops if they began shooting the villagers. Thompson got out, confronted the leader of the soldiers, and then arranged to evacuate the civilians. Thompson's crew chief, Glenn Andreotta, pulled a child from a ditch full of dead bodies.

Sounds of an Era

Listen to television journalist Walter Cronkite's editorial about the Tet Offensive and other sounds from the Vietnam era.

ACTIVITY
Connecting with History and Conflict

Tell students that in the wake of the My Lai massacre, Americans agonized over the question of who was responsible for the action. Were the men firing the weapons mainly at fault? Or was it the commanding officer at the scene? What responsibility did superior officers, who were not at My Lai, have for the massacre? Have students discuss these questions in small groups, then present their conclusions in a class discussion. **(Verbal/Linguistic)**

BACKGROUND
Connecting with Culture

The Tet Offensive was able to succeed as a widespread surprise attack largely because of cultural assumptions made by American military planners. They knew that Tet (Tet Nguyen Dan) is the most important holiday in Vietnamese culture. Tet celebrates the beginning of the new year on the Vietnamese lunar calendar and is observed with gifts, family visits, and religious services. Many Vietnamese believe that people's actions during Tet will determine their fortune throughout the following year. Because of Tet's importance, American planners assumed that the Communists would not launch an attack during the holiday. Indeed, many members of South Vietnam's army were on holiday leave, adding to the offensive's effectiveness. Additionally, President Johnson had called a halt to bombing during this time, as he had during other Tet holidays.

CUSTOMIZE FOR ...
Less Proficient Readers

Ask students to write two or three sentences about the hardships and dangers confronting American soldiers in Vietnam and two or three sentences about the hardships and dangers the war brought to Vietnamese civilians.

CAPTION ANSWERS

Interpreting Charts It allowed the President to take action—including escalating the war—without the approval of Congress.

Such breaches of the rules of military combat did not go unpunished. Pilot Thompson testified about Calley's conduct at My Lai. Although at first his testimony was covered up, eventually, in 1971, Lieutenant Calley began serving a sentence of life in prison with hard labor for his role in the massacre. Many Americans saw him as a scapegoat, however, and public outcry was such that President Nixon reduced his life sentence to 20 years. Calley was released on good behavior three years later. The heroics of the helicopter crew also did not go unnoticed. In 1998, the United States honored all three men with the Soldier's Medal, the highest award for bravery unrelated to fighting an enemy.

The Tet Offensive became a turning point in the war. Even though the Viet Cong were turned back with heavy losses, they had won a psychological victory. Secretary of State Dean Rusk commented on the American public's reaction to Tet:

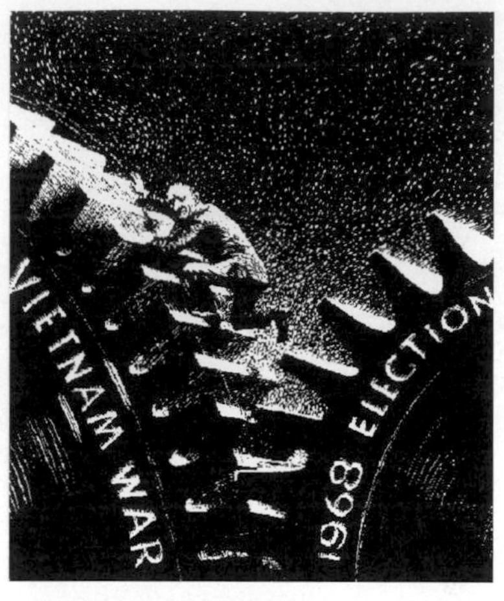

INTERPRETING POLITICAL CARTOONS This British cartoon appeared in 1967. **Drawing Inferences** *(a) What does the cartoonist think of President Johnson's chances for reelection? (b) How does the cartoon convey this opinion?*

> *"[E]ven though it was a considerable military set-back for the North Vietnamese and Vietcong out there on the ground, it was, in effect, a brilliant political victory for them here in the United States. I'm not sure I fully understand the reasons why that should have occurred, but it became very clear after the Tet offensive that many people at the grass roots, . . . finally came to the conclusion that if we could not tell them when this was going to end, and we couldn't in any good faith, that we might as well chuck it."*
>
> —Dean Rusk

The Tet Offensive demonstrated that the Viet Cong could launch a massive attack on targets throughout South Vietnam. Furthermore, as images of the fighting flooded American television, many people at home began to express reservations about American involvement in Vietnam. Many Americans were discouraged, believing that U.S. troops had not been allowed to win the war. In spite of the vocal antiwar protesters, a majority of Americans supported a policy tougher than the one pursued by the administration. President Johnson, caught in the middle, saw his popularity plunge.

Section 2 Assessment

READING COMPREHENSION

1. How did the use of **land mines** and **fragmentation bombs** make the war especially brutal for soldiers and civilians?
2. Why did the early military action result in a stalemate?
3. How were **Agent Orange** and **napalm** used during the war?
4. What was the **Ho Chi Minh Trail?**

CRITICAL THINKING AND WRITING

5. **Analyzing Information** Why was the Tet Offensive a turning point in the Vietnam War? Support your answer with examples.
6. **Writing a Letter to the Editor** Write a letter to the editor of a newspaper. The year is 1968. Write your letter from the point of view of a hawk in support of the war or a dove opposed to the war.

Take It to the NET

Activity: Creating a Diary Entry Investigate battlefield conditions during the Vietnam War. Use your research to write a diary entry from the viewpoint of an American soldier in Vietnam. Use the links provided in the *America: Pathways to the Present* area of the following Web site for help in completing this activity.
www.phschool.com

Section 2 Assessment

Reading Comprehension

1. Land mines planted in the ground were intended to stop advancing soldiers, but could be set off by the footstep of anyone, soldier or civilian. The casings of fragmentation bombs flew in all directions after exploding, killing many.
2. Despite a buildup in American troops, the relentlessness of the Viet Cong kept the war at a stalemate; the U.S. goal was not to conquer North Vietnam, but to force North Vietnam and the Viet Cong to stop fighting.
3. Agent Orange: herbicide that killed leaves and thick undergrowth, exposing Viet Cong positions. Napalm: flammable jelly that splattered and burned uncontrollably, sticking to bodies and burning people to death. Both substances were dropped from aircraft.
4. A supply route from North Vietnam, passing through Laos and Cambodia, which allowed supplies and troops from the North for the Viet Cong to be moved into South Vietnam.

Critical Thinking and Writing

5. Answers should expand on the theme that the Viet Cong won a psychological victory, even though the Americans won a military victory.
6. Letters will vary but should be supported with facts from the section.

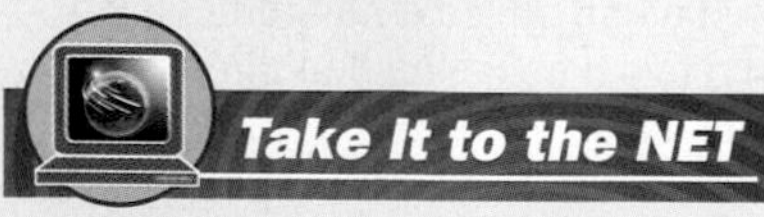

Take It to the NET

Answers will vary. Students should demonstrate knowledge of the difficult terrain and climate conditions in Vietnam and the chaotic nature of the fighting itself.

Caption Answers

Interpreting Political Cartoons The cartoonist does not think Johnson will be reelected. In the cartoon, Johnson is about to be ground up by the convergence of the Vietnam War and the upcoming election.

RESOURCE DIRECTORY

Teaching Resources

Units 5/6/7 booklet
- Section 2 Quiz, p. 86

Guide to the Essentials
- Section 2 Summary, p. 117

Section 3

Political Divisions

READING FOCUS

- What role did students play in the protest movements of the 1960s?
- Why did President Johnson decide not to seek reelection?
- How did the Vietnam War affect the election of 1968?

MAIN IDEA

The Vietnam War created deep divisions in the Democratic Party and in the nation as a whole.

KEY TERMS

generation gap
New Left
teach-in
conscientious objector
deferment
Middle America

TAKING NOTES

Copy the chart below. As you read, fill in each box with examples and events that reflected the growing divisions among the American people.

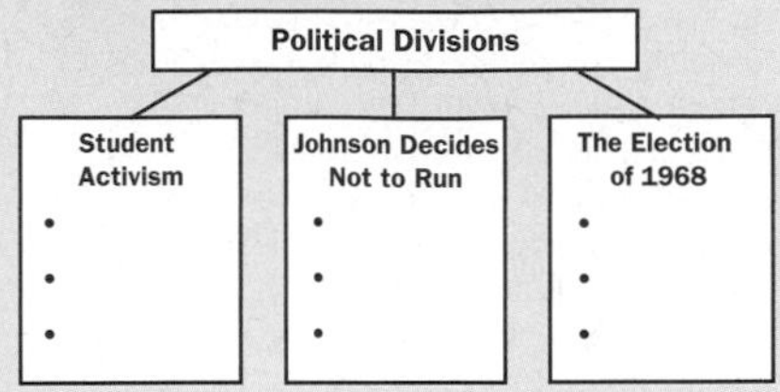

Setting the Scene As the war in Vietnam unfolded, many loyal and patriotic Americans favored increasing the war effort in order to bring about military victory. Others believed that the war was morally wrong and urged immediate withdrawal of U.S. troops. Opposing viewpoints created deep divisions within the United States:

> "*A feeling is widely and strongly held that . . . we are trying to impose some U.S. image on distant peoples we cannot understand, and that we are carrying the thing to absurd lengths. Related to this feeling is the increased polarization that is taking place in the United States, with seeds of the worst split in our people in more than a century.*"
>
> —John McNaughton, aide to Robert McNamara

Student Activism

In the early 1960s, members of the baby-boom generation began to graduate from high school. Postwar prosperity gave many of these students opportunities

Students were in the forefront of protests against the Vietnam War.

Section 3

Political Divisions

Section Objectives

1. Find out about the role played by students in the protest movements of the 1960s.
2. Learn why President Johnson decided not to seek reelection.
3. Discover how the Vietnam War affected the election of 1968.

Bellringer

Warm-Up Activity Ask students whether the decade in which they are living seems to have a particular theme or identity. Ask them to suggest adjectives that might describe its general tone and compare these adjectives to descriptions of the 1960s and early 1970s.

Activating Prior Knowledge What do students today know about the activities and lifestyles of students of the early 1960s and 1970s? What type of music was popular then? What type of clothing?

Reading Strategy

Have students write the main headings *Student Activism* and *Resistance to War* on a sheet of paper. As you read the section, write important details in the column under each heading.

Activity

Connecting with History and Conflict

Ask students to find illustrated books and magazines about the Vietnam War and to select one image that they think best represents the entire war. Students may present their chosen image to the class with a description and explanation of why they chose it. **(Visual/Spatial)**

RESOURCE DIRECTORY

Teaching Resources
Learning Styles Lesson Plans booklet, p. 65
Guided Reading and Review booklet, p. 125
Learning with Documents booklet (Key Documents) *The Port Huron Statement,* p. 95

Technology
Section Reading Support Transparencies
Guided Reading Audiotapes (English/Spanish), Ch. 24
Student Edition on Audio CD, Ch. 24
Prentice Hall Presentation Pro CD-ROM, Ch. 24
Companion Web site, www.phschool.com

Lesson Plan

Focus Explain that during the 1960s, college campuses erupted in student protests. The most dramatic, and perhaps the most effective, protests were against the war in Vietnam. Ask why college students became activists.

Instruct Note that the Port Huron Statement on this page begins with a generational identification: "We are people of this generation." Ask students why they think Hayden began the statement with those words. Discuss how the civil rights movement strengthened students' belief in their ability to bring about change. Ask why student activists, trained in the civil rights movement, worked to change their schools and to stop the Vietnam War. Also, ask why some SDS members transformed themselves into the weathermen, a group that engaged in violence and terrorism.

Assess/Reteach Ask students to discuss their opinion concerning a national army draft. Are they in favor of a draft or opposed to it? Under what circumstances do they think individuals should be exempted from the draft? Are they in favor of the types of deferments and exemptions that were available during the Vietnam War?

Background
Military Service

In percentage terms, there were very few conscientious objectors during the Vietnam era. By 1970, a total of about 22,000 men had been approved as conscientious objectors. This number represents about one tenth of one percent of the total number of men who had been registered for military service. Interestingly, a higher percentage of men were classified as conscientious objectors during World War II (about one third of one percent), which enjoyed much wider support. This highlights the fact that conscientious objectors, as a rule, choose this course of action because of their beliefs about war in general, and not based on a value judgment about any particular conflict.

Focus on Citizenship

Twenty-sixth Amendment Before 1971, nearly all states required voters to be at least 21 years old. (Georgia had allowed 18-year-olds to vote since 1943.) A movement to lower the voting age to 18 nationwide sparked controversy in the 1960s.

Opponents of the effort to lower the voting age pointed to radical student activists and asked, "Do you want people like that to take part in a national election?" Those who favored a lower voting age argued that if 18-year-olds were old enough to fight for their country in Vietnam, they were old enough to vote.

The Twenty-sixth Amendment, ratified in 1971, states: "The right of citizens of the United States, who are eighteen years of age or older, to vote shall not be abridged by any state on account of age."

unknown to previous generations. Instead of going directly into the working world after high school, many young men and women could afford to continue their education. College enrollments swelled with more students than ever before.

Change was in the air. It had been building for a while, even through the conformist years of the 1950s. The popular culture of that decade, including rock-and-roll music and rebellious youths on the movie screen, indicated that many young Americans were not satisfied with the values of their parents. The early 1960s saw a widening of this **generation gap.**

Students for a Democratic Society The civil rights movement, discussed in an earlier chapter, also became a steppingstone to other movements for change. Civil rights activists were among those who helped organize Students for a Democratic Society (SDS) in 1960. The organization's declaration of principles and goals, called the Port Huron Statement, appeared in 1962. Written largely by Tom Hayden, a student at the University of Michigan, the statement explained some of the feelings behind a student movement that was gaining strength in the United States:

> "*We are people of this generation, bred in at least modest comfort, housed now in universities, looking uncomfortably at the world we inherit. When we were kids the United States was the wealthiest and strongest country in the world. . . . As we grew, however, our comfort was penetrated by events too troubling to dismiss. . . . We would replace power rooted in possession, privilege, or circumstance by power and uniqueness rooted in love, reflectiveness, reason, and creativity. As a social system we seek the establishment of a democracy of individual participation.*"
>
> —Port Huron Statement

SDS was a tiny organization at the start. Still, it had a major influence on the development of a new political movement that came to be called the **New Left.** Members of the New Left believed that problems such as poverty and racism called for radical changes.

The Free Speech Movement Student activism led to confrontation at the University of California at Berkeley in September 1964. Students became angry when the university administration refused to allow them to distribute civil rights leaflets outside the main gate of the campus.

The students, who had fought for equal rights in the South, argued that their right to free speech was being challenged. They resisted the university's effort to restrict their political activity. When police came to arrest one of their leaders, students surrounded the police car and prevented it from moving. The free speech movement was underway.

The university administration tried to find a compromise, but then its governing board stepped in. The board had the final word over university policy. It decided to hold student leaders responsible for their actions and filed charges against some of them.

On December 2, 1964, thousands of irate students took over the university administration building. That night police moved in. They arrested more than 700 students. Other students, supported by some faculty members, went on strike. They stopped attending classes to show their support for the free speech demonstrators.

Berkeley remained the most radical campus, but student activism spread to other colleges and universities across the United States. In the spring of 1965, activists at several schools launched protests against regulations they thought curbed their freedom. Students at Michigan State University and elsewhere challenged social restrictions, such as the hours when women and men could visit each other's dormitories. Students also sought greater involvement in college policy-making. Others left their campuses to work in campaigns to improve conditions in the inner cities.

The Teach-in Movement Students were among the first to protest the Vietnam War. Some opposed what they regarded as American imperialism. Others viewed the conflict as a civil war that should be resolved by the Vietnamese alone.

As escalation began, antiwar activists used new methods to protest the war. The first **teach-in** took place at the University of Michigan in March 1965 when a group of faculty members decided to make a public statement against the war. Some 50 or 60 professors taught a special night session in which issues concerning the war could be aired.

To their surprise, several thousand people showed up and made the evening a monumental success. Soon other teach-ins followed at colleges around the country. Supporters as well as opponents of the war appeared at the early teach-ins, but soon antiwar voices dominated the sessions.

Draft Resistance A Selective Service Act allowing the government to draft men between the ages of 18 and 26 had been in place since 1951. Relatively few people refused to be drafted in the first half of the 1960s. Most who did were **conscientious objectors** who opposed fighting in the war on moral or religious grounds.

Draft Registration

Since the Civil War, the United States has used a draft in wartime to meet its military needs. During the Vietnam War, about 1.8 million men were drafted between 1964 and 1973. Because college students could receive draft deferments, a large proportion of draftees were young men from minority communities who were too poor to afford college. Reacting to complaints about the system, Congress eliminated the deferment in 1971.

Another effort to make the draft more evenhanded was the lottery system instituted in 1969. This random drawing determined how likely a young man was to be called for military service. Despite these changes, opposition to the draft continued. Some young men burned their draft cards in protest. Thousands even left the country to avoid the draft. In 1973, Congress ended the draft, and the United States converted to an all-volunteer military force.

Today male citizens ages 18 through 25 are required by law to register with the Selective Service System. In a national crisis, if the country needs more soldiers than an all-volunteer service can provide, the draft can be resumed.

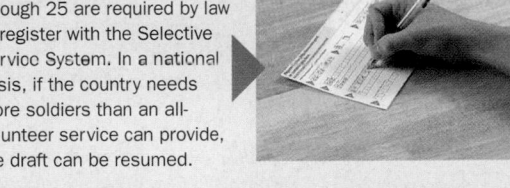

? Why do you think the government requires draft registration?

Activity: Connecting with Culture

Have selected students conduct Internet and other forms of research to identify the major religions in the United States whose pacifist creeds lead members to seek conscientious objector status. Students should learn something about each sect (central beliefs, total memberships, and so on) and share what they learn with the class. **(Verbal/Linguistic)**

From the Archives of American Heritage®

Dr. King Decries the War

April 1967 brought proclamations, draft-card burnings, and mass demonstrations against the United States' continuing grim entanglement in Vietnam. In New York City's Riverside Church on April 4, the Reverend Dr. Martin Luther King, Jr., encouraged conscientious objection to the draft on a nationwide scale, called the U.S. government the "greatest purveyor of violence in the world today," and offered a five-point plan for a peaceful American withdrawal. It was Dr. King's strongest statement yet on the war, in which "twice as many Negroes as whites" were serving (this view has been challenged in recent years). "If America's soul becomes totally poisoned," he warned, "part of the autopsy must read Vietnam."
Source: Nathan Ward, "The Time Machine." *American Heritage®* magazine, April 1992.

Customize for ...

ESL

Ask students to create a list of the goals of the free-speech, draft-resistance, and antiwar movements.

Caption Answers

Fast Forward to Today To enhance military preparedness.

ACTIVITY
Student Portfolio

Have students write journal entries in which they express their thoughts and feelings about the student protesters of the late 1960s. Journal entries might address such questions as: Are the protesters admirable figures? Were the protesters "anti-American"? Were their methods appropriate or inappropriate? **(Verbal/Linguistic)**

BACKGROUND
Global Connections

Immediately after the Tet Offensive, polls showed that most Americans had come to oppose America's involvement in Vietnam. Most historians view this as the turning point in the war. One wrote, "it hardly mattered whether [the North Vietnamese] won their battles . . . or lost . . . . The point was that by engaging the Americans in fierce combat—even accepting loss ratios of as much as ten-to-one [i.e., ten of their soldiers injured or killed for every one American soldier injured or killed], which was an inevitable consequence of the vastly superior American firepower—the North Vietnamese could exact the steady and large toll of American casualties that would destroy the American public's will to continue. It worked precisely as Hanoi had calculated . . . . After Tet, the Americans stopped looking for a fight and started looking for a way out . . . ."

In July 1965, President Johnson doubled the number of men who could be drafted into the armed forces. By the end of the year he had doubled the number again. These actions led to the rise of a draft-resistance movement that urged young men not to cooperate with their local draft boards.

As more and more young men were called into service and sent to fight in Vietnam, Americans began to question the morality and fairness of the draft. College students could receive a **deferment,** or official postponement of their call to serve. Usually this meant they would not have to go to war. Those who could not afford college did not have this avenue open to them. In 1966, the Selective Service System announced that college students who ranked low academically could be drafted.

In 1967, resistance to the military draft began to sweep the country. Many young men tried to avoid the draft by claiming that they had physical disabilities. Others applied for conscientious-objector status. Still others left the country. By the end of the war an estimated 100,000 draft resisters were believed to have gone to countries such as Canada.

VIEWING HISTORY New York City Transportation Union members demonstrate in favor of the Vietnam War in 1967. **Drawing Inferences** *Why do you think those in favor of the war felt it necessary to hold demonstrations like this one?*

Continued Protests In the first six months of 1968, more than 200 major demonstrations erupted at colleges and universities around the country. One of the most dramatic incidents took place in April of 1968 at Columbia University in New York City. Students there linked the issues of civil rights and the war. An SDS chapter sought to get the university to cut its ties with a research institute that did work for the military. At the same time, an African American student organization tried to halt construction of a gymnasium that would encroach upon a nearby minority neighborhood in Harlem.

Together these two groups took over the president's office. Finally the president of Columbia called the police, and hundreds of students were arrested. A student sympathy strike followed, and the university closed early that spring.

Johnson Decides Not to Run

Continuing protests and a growing list of American casualties had steadily increased public opposition to Johnson's handling of the war. By 1967, Secretary of Defense Robert McNamara had lost faith in the war effort. Privately, he urged the President to turn more of the fighting over to the South Vietnamese and to stop the bombing of North Vietnam. Johnson, fearful of risking defeat on the battlefield, ignored the proposal.

As a result of the Tet Offensive, polls showed for the first time that a majority of Americans opposed the war. Television news coverage of Tet increased the impact that the attack had on the public. Millions watched as news anchor Walter Cronkite, known for his objectivity and trustworthiness, said in February of 1968, "It now seems more certain than ever that the bloody experience in Vietnam is to end in stalemate." President Johnson

CAPTION ANSWERS

Viewing History To counteract the demonstrations by those against the war and the publicity they received. They wanted to show that many people disagreed with the vocal antiwar protesters.

RESOURCE DIRECTORY

Teaching Resources

Learning with Documents booklet (Visual Learning Activity) *Antiwar Demonstrations,* p. 24

Great Debates booklet (Great Debates) *Should the U.S. Have Stayed in Vietnam?* p. 24

Other Print Resources

American History Block Scheduling Support *Vietnam: The War at Home,* found in The Nation After World War II folder, includes interdisciplinary lesson suggestions and activities for Geography and History, Primary Sources, Biography, and Literature.

Technology

Sounds of an Era Audio CD *President Johnson,* 1968 recording (time: 30 seconds)

RESOURCE PRO® **Primary Source Activity** *LBJ Withdraws from the Race,* found on Resource Pro, uses a passage from Johnson's memoirs to describe the reasons behind his decision to withdraw from the 1968 presidential race.

heard Cronkite's assessment of the war and reacted with dismay. Reportedly he said, "If I've lost Cronkite, I've lost Middle America."

After the Tet Offensive, Johnson rarely left the White House for fear of being assaulted by angry crowds of protesters. He said he felt like "a jackrabbit in a hailstorm, hunkering up and taking it." In early 1968, Johnson watched the campaign of antiwar candidate Eugene McCarthy gain momentum. On March 12, McCarthy almost beat the President in the New Hampshire Democratic primary.

Four days later, another critic of the war, Robert Kennedy, joined the race for the Democratic nomination. Kennedy, the younger brother of President John Kennedy and a senator from New York, had been speaking out against the war in Congress. In March 1967, a year before he announced his candidacy, Kennedy had said this in a speech in the Senate:

> *"All we say and all we do must be informed by our awareness that this horror is partly our responsibility; not just a nation's responsibility but yours and mine. It is we who live in abundance and send our young men out to die. It is our chemicals that scorch the children and our bombs that level the villages. We are all participants. To know this and feel the burden of this responsibility is not to ignore important interests, not to forget that freedom and security must, at times, be paid for in blood. Still, even though we must know as a nation what it is necessary to do, we must also feel as men the anguish of what we are doing."*
>
> —Robert Kennedy

Now Kennedy was running against Johnson for the Democratic nomination for President.

On March 31, 1968, President Johnson declared dramatically in a nationally televised speech that he would not run for another term as President:

> *"I do not believe that I should devote an hour or a day of my time to any personal partisan causes or to any duties other than the awesome duties of this office—the presidency of your country. Accordingly, I shall not seek, and I will not accept, the nomination of my party for another term."*
>
> —Lyndon Johnson

The Election of 1968

Even before Johnson's announcement, the same issues that were dividing the American public had led to a split in the Democratic Party.

The Democratic Convention Delegates to the Democratic convention met in Chicago that summer to nominate candidates for President and Vice President. By the time the Democrats convened, their party was in shreds. Robert Kennedy had been assassinated in June, and party regulars thought McCarthy was too far out of the mainstream. Instead they supported Vice President Hubert Humphrey, longtime advocate of social justice and civil rights. Humphrey, however, was hurt by his defense of Johnson's policies on Vietnam. In the face of growing antiwar protest, he hardly seemed the one to bring the party together.

Focus on CULTURE

The Living Room War Television played a major role in influencing public opinion. Nightly news broadcasts brought the Vietnam War into the living rooms of more than 60 million American viewers. Scenes of dying soldiers and desperate civilians led many viewers to question American involvement in Vietnam.

VIEWING HISTORY Robert Kennedy announced his candidacy in March 1968. Here, he is campaigning in Nebraska. **Determining Relevance** *How much do you think Robert Kennedy's entrance into the race affected Johnson's decision not to seek reelection? Explain your answer.*

ACTIVITY
Connecting with Culture

Have interested students cooperate to make a collage that depicts "The United States in 1968." Images should be selected to convey the social and political turmoil of that watershed year. Students may compile their images using a computer if they wish. **(Visual/Spatial)**

BACKGROUND
Interdisciplinary

President Johnson's announcement that he would not seek a second term was shocking in and of itself. Yet his nationally televised speech included two other main points that were almost as stunning to the American people: Johnson, in the same speech, declared that he had ordered a significant cutback in the bombing of North Vietnam, and that he was requesting to open peace talks with North Vietnam's Communist government.

BACKGROUND
Global Connections

In 1969 the National Chicano Moratorium Committee staged its own antiwar demonstrations. These protesters argued that Vietnam was a racial war, with black and brown Americans being used against their brothers and sisters in developing nations. In the first six months of 1968, more than 200 major demonstrations erupted at colleges and universities around the country.

TEST PREPARATION

Ask students to read the quote from Lyndon Johnson on this page and then answer the question below.

What did President Johnson mean by the phrase "personal partisan causes"?

Ⓐ Pursuits that would benefit only himself.
B The beliefs of fellow Americans.
C Activities against the war in Vietnam.
D Activities in support of the war in Vietnam.

CAPTION ANSWERS

Viewing History Answers will vary. Students should note that Robert Kennedy was popular in his own right and might have gotten additional support from those who had supported his brother, President John F. Kennedy. He would have been a formidable opponent.

Activity
Connecting with Science and Technology

Remind students of the important impact that television had during this period in American history, conveying such things as President Johnson's speeches, footage of the Tet Offensive, and images of police handling protesters at the Democratic National Convention. Then have student pairs research, in both real and percentage terms, the growth of television viewership in the U.S. from 1960 to 1970. Students should create line graphs that show such data as the number of televisions in the U.S., the average number of televisions per household, and the average numbers of hours watched. Have students share their graphs with the class and use them in a class discussion on the role television played in 1960s America. **(Logical/Mathematical)**

Background
Recent Scholarship

The Vietnam War had a savage impact on American society, particularly on its soldiers. In *Working-Class War: American Combat Soldiers and Vietnam,* Christian G. Appy observes that African Americans and young men from small towns were overrepresented in the military, as were the working class. (This view of the exact racial composition of the U.S. Vietnam-era Army has been challenged and is still being debated.) Once in Vietnam, many soldiers found the purposes of the war unclear. They had been sent to fight communism, but soon that struggle lost meaning as they simply tried to stay alive.

READING CHECK

Complete chaos reigned. The Democratic Party was splintered. Antiwar demonstrators clashed with police in the streets of Chicago.

Caption Answers

Viewing History Viewers were horrified and disgusted by the violence, which they associated with the Democrats. It made the law-and-order promises of Richard Nixon all the more appealing.

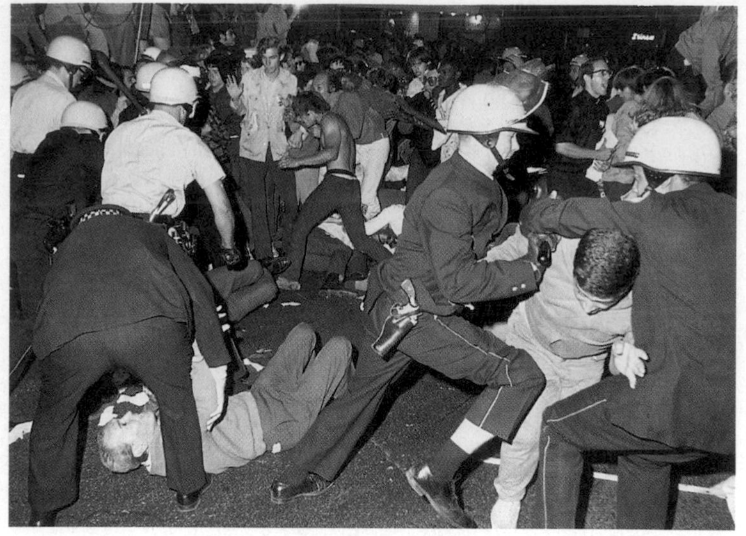

VIEWING HISTORY As the Democrats gathered in Chicago for their 1968 convention, antiwar protesters gathered too. Chicago police (under the direction of Democratic Mayor Richard Daley) and National Guardsmen used nightsticks, tear gas, and rifles against the demonstrators and others caught up in the protests. **Determining Relevance** *How do you think television broadcasts of scenes like the one at right affected the election? Explain.*

The climax came when the convention delegates voted down a peace resolution and seemed ready to nominate Humphrey for President. As thousands of protesters gathered for a rally near the convention hotel, the police moved in, using their nightsticks to club anyone on the street, including bystanders, hotel guests, and reporters. Historian Theodore H. White vividly recorded the scene that took place in Chicago during the Democratic convention in August 1968:

> "*Slam! Like a fist jolting, like a piston exploding from its chamber, comes a hurtling column of police . . . into the intersection, and all things happen too fast: first the charge as the police wedge cleaves through the mob; then screams, whistles, confusion. . . . And as the scene clears, there are little knots in the open clearing—police clubbing youngsters, police dragging youngsters, police rushing them by the elbows, their heels dragging, to patrol wagons. . . .*"
>
> —Theodore H. White

Much of the violence took place in front of television cameras, while crowds chanted "The whole world is watching." As the convention delegates voted, Senator Abraham Ribicoff of Connecticut denounced the "Gestapo tactics on the streets of Chicago," provoking an angry scene with Chicago mayor Daley. In the end, Humphrey was nominated, but the Democratic Party had been further torn apart.

READING CHECK

Describe what happened at the Democratic National Convention.

The Republicans and the Nation Choose Nixon The Republicans had already held their convention in early August. They had chosen Richard M. Nixon, who had narrowly lost the presidential election of 1960 to John Kennedy. During his campaign, Nixon backed law and order and boasted of a secret plan to end the war in Vietnam.

Nixon was determined to stay "above the fray" and act presidential during the campaign. Therefore he let his running mate, Governor Spiro Agnew of Maryland, make harsh accusations, such as calling Humphrey "squishy soft"

RESOURCE DIRECTORY

Teaching Resources

Units 5/6/7 booklet
- Section 3 Quiz, p. 87

Guide to the Essentials
- Section 3 Summary, p. 118

on communism. With a well-run and well-financed campaign, Nixon quickly took the lead in public-opinion polls.

Adding to the Democrats' problems was a third-party candidate for President. Alabama governor George C. Wallace, who had been a lifelong Democrat, had gained national fame for playing on racial tensions among southerners. In 1968, representing the American Independent Party, he appealed to blue-collar voters in the North who resented campus radicals and antiwar activists. Wallace won support by attacking those he called "left-wing theoreticians, briefcase-totin' bureaucrats, ivory-tower guideline writers, bearded anarchists, smart-aleck editorial writers, and pointy-headed professors."

Late in the campaign, Humphrey began to catch up to Nixon in the public-opinion polls. But even though President Johnson stopped the bombing of North Vietnam on October 31, it was too late. Many disillusioned Democrats stayed home on election day, voting for no one.

The election, held on November 5, was close. Nixon won 43.4 percent of the popular vote—less than one percentage point more than Humphrey's 42.7 percent. Even so, Nixon gained 302 electoral votes to 191 for Humphrey and 45 for Wallace. Although Democrats kept control of both houses of Congress, the Republicans had regained the White House.

The war significantly influenced the election of 1968. Nixon's win marked the start of a Republican hold on the presidency that would last, with one interruption, for more than 20 years. This political shift reflected how unsettling the 1960s had become for mainstream Americans, a group sometimes called **Middle America.** In an era of chaos and confrontation, Middle America turned to the Republican Party for stability.

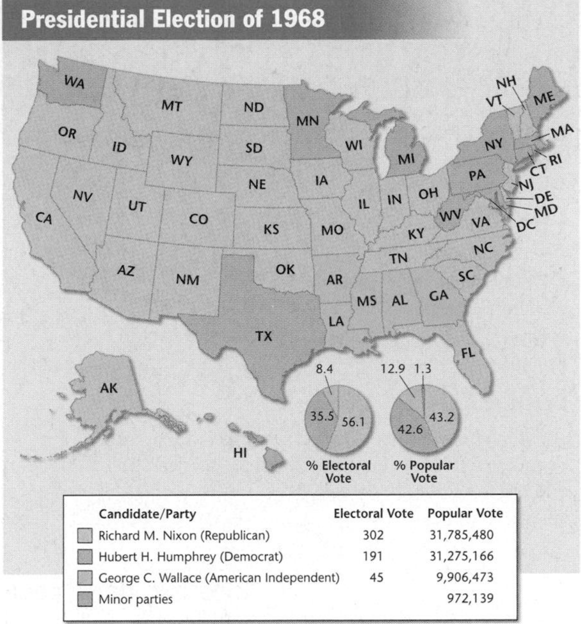

Candidate/Party	Electoral Vote	Popular Vote
Richard M. Nixon (Republican)	302	31,785,480
Hubert H. Humphrey (Democrat)	191	31,275,166
George C. Wallace (American Independent)	45	9,906,473
Minor parties		972,139

MAP SKILLS This map shows the results of the election of 1968. **Regions** *(a) Where did Humphrey draw most of his support? (b) Where was Wallace's support? (c) What do you think might have happened if Wallace had given up his candidacy and returned to the Democratic Party?*

Section 3 Assessment

READING COMPREHENSION

1. What was the **generation gap?**
2. Who participated in **teach-ins?**
3. What is a **conscientious objector?**
4. Why did some Americans oppose the practice of **deferment?**
5. Describe the group sometimes referred to as **Middle America.**

CRITICAL THINKING AND WRITING

6. **Making Comparisons** Write a brief summary comparing the different viewpoints that Americans held regarding the Vietnam War.
7. **Writing a List** List several reasons why students played a major role in the protest movements of the 1960s.

Take It to the NET

Activity: Analyzing Primary Sources Select a primary source associated with student activism. Prepare a brief analysis of this source, including point of view, bias, and audience. Use the links provided in the *America: Pathways to the Present* area of the following Web site for help in completing this activity.
www.phschool.com

Section 3 Assessment

Reading Comprehension

1. Many young Americans rejected the conservative values of their parents.
2. Professors and students; at first both supporters and opponents of the war attended, but soon antiwar voices prevailed.
3. People who opposed fighting in wars on moral and religious grounds.
4. They felt it was unfair to excuse college students from the draft, but not those who could not afford to go to college. The latter group included many members of minority groups. Thus, deferments were seen as discriminatory.
5. Mainstream Americans who turned to the Republican Party for stability during the 1960s.

Critical Thinking and Writing

6. Answers will vary but should be supported with facts from the section.
7. Lists will vary but may include: discontent with current society; the draft impacted them directly; and a desire to end the war.

Answers will vary. Students should prepare a clear, detailed analysis of the student activism primary source.

Caption Answers

Map Skills (a) The Northeast. (b) The South. (c) Answers will vary, but students should note that much of Wallace's support was from traditional Democrats and might have gone to Humphrey, thus making the election much closer.

Section 4
The End of the War

Section Objectives

1. Learn how President Nixon's policies led to American withdrawal from Vietnam.
2. Discover why President Nixon campaigned promising to restore law and order.
3. See what happened in Vietnam after the withdrawal of American forces.
4. Determine the legacy of the Vietnam War.

Bellringer

Warm-Up Activity Ask students whether it is possible for a United States President to continue a course of action strongly opposed by most of the American people. In what ways can the people make their opinions known to the President?

Activating Prior Knowledge Do your students think Lyndon Johnson would have been reelected if he had not withdrawn in 1968? Do they think Robert Kennedy would have become President if he had not been assassinated? How would either of these outcomes have affected the war in Vietnam?

Reading Strategy

Have students skim the section, reading headings and the first sentence of each paragraph. Then have them list the main headings on a sheet of paper. Under each heading, have them write a sentence or phrase predicting the content of that part of the section. When students have finished reading, have them compare their predictions with the actual content.

Section 4
The End of the War

READING FOCUS

- How did President Nixon's policies lead to American withdrawal from Vietnam?
- Why did President Nixon campaign promising to restore law and order?
- What happened in Vietnam after the withdrawal of American forces?
- What was the legacy of the Vietnam War?

KEY TERMS

Paris peace talks
Vietnamization
silent majority
POW
MIA

TAKING NOTES

As you read, complete a time line of events leading up to the end of war in Vietnam.

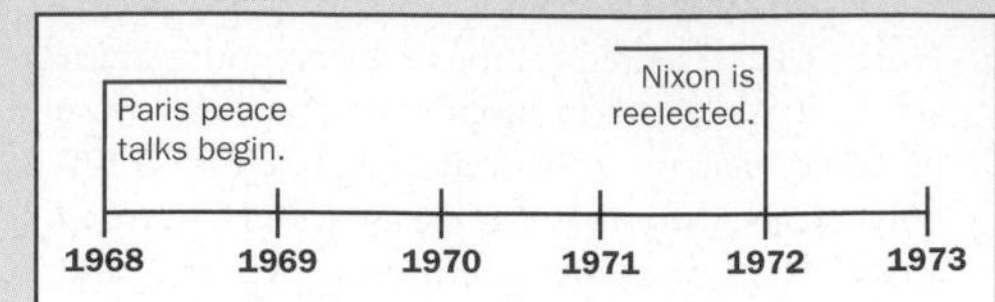

MAIN IDEA

The end of the Vietnam War involved slow-moving peace negotiations, the gradual withdrawal of American troops, and the fall of South Vietnam.

Setting the Scene A year after his election, President Nixon was still seeking—and receiving—the support of Middle America. But he was also well aware of increasing opposition to the Vietnam War. On November 3, 1969, Nixon gave a speech about Vietnam. Sometimes called the "silent majority speech" because of the President's appeal to those he felt quietly supported his policies, the address reviewed the history of America's participation in the Vietnam conflict. Nixon noted that under his administration, "United States casualties have declined" and that "we are finally bringing American men home." He also acknowedged, however, that the war was far from over, and posed the question, "[W]hat is the best way to end it?"

> *"My fellow Americans, I am sure you can recognize from what I have said that we really only have two choices open to us if we want to end this war.*
>
> *I can order an immediate, precipitate withdrawal of all Americans from Vietnam without regard to the effects of that action. Or we can persist in our search for a just peace through a negotiated settlement if possible, or through continued implementation of our plan for Vietnamization if necessary, a plan in which we will withdraw all of our forces from Vietnam on a schedule in accordance with our program, as the South Vietnamese become strong enough to defend their own freedom.*
>
> *I have chosen this second course. It is not the easy way. It is the right way. . . .*
>
> *And so tonight—to you, the great silent majority of my fellow Americans—I ask for your support."*
>
> —Richard Nixon

President Richard Nixon in the White House

Nixon's Vietnam Policy

As President Johnson's term drew to a close, he cut back on the bombing of North Vietnam and called for peace negotiations. The **Paris peace talks** began

RESOURCE DIRECTORY

Teaching Resources
Guided Reading and Review booklet, p. 127

Technology
Section Reading Support Transparencies
Guided Reading Audiotapes (English/Spanish), Ch. 24
Student Edition on Audio CD, Ch. 24
Color Transparencies *Historical Maps,* A51
Prentice Hall Presentation Pro CD-ROM, Ch. 24
Companion Web site, www.phschool.com

in May 1968, but failed to produce an agreement. Richard Nixon's claim that he had a secret plan to end the war in Vietnam helped him win the presidency in November.

Withdrawing Troops In June 1969, President Nixon announced a new policy known as **Vietnamization.** This involved removing American forces and replacing them with South Vietnamese soldiers. By 1972, American troop strength dropped to 24,000. As much as Nixon wanted to defuse antiwar sentiment at home, he was determined not to lose the war. Therefore, as he withdrew American troops, he ordered secret bombing raids on the major targets shown on the map at right.

The War Spreads to Cambodia President Nixon also widened the war beyond the borders of Vietnam. In April 1970, Nixon publicly announced that United States and South Vietnamese ground forces were moving into neighboring Cambodia. Their goal was to clear out Communist camps there, from which the enemy was mounting attacks on South Vietnam. The United States, he asserted, would not stand by like "a pitiful helpless giant" while the Viet Cong attacked from Cambodia:

> *"We take this action not for the purpose of expanding the war into Cambodia but for the purpose of ending the war in Vietnam and winning the just peace we all desire. We have made and we will continue to make every possible effort to end this war through negotiation at the conference table rather than through more fighting on the battlefield."*
>
> —Richard Nixon

Nixon knew that the invasion of Cambodia would not win the war, but he thought it would help at the bargaining table. He was willing to intensify the war in order to strengthen the American position at the peace talks. Nixon's actions, however, brought chaos and civil war in Cambodia and a fresh wave of protests at home.

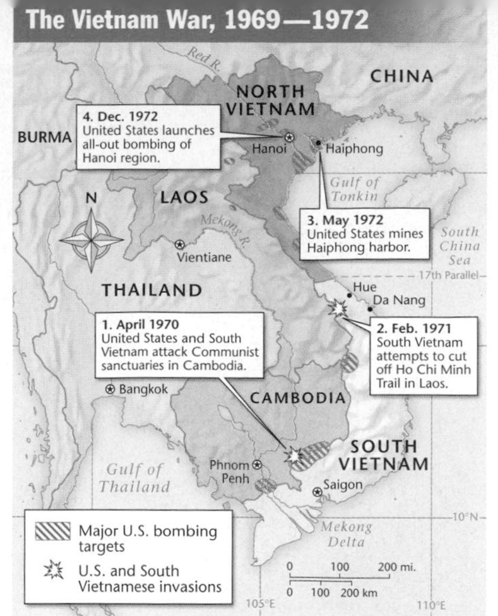

MAP SKILLS Although Nixon began withdrawing troops from Vietnam in 1968, he stepped up bombing raids. **Location** *According to this map, in what areas were United States bombing raids concentrated during the later years of the war?*

Nixon Calls for Law and Order

One of Nixon's campaign pledges had been to restore law and order in the country. This need seemed particularly apparent to Americans in October 1969 when one SDS faction turned to violence. This group called their organization the Weathermen, after a line in a Bob Dylan song—"You don't need a weatherman to know which way the wind blows." They were determined to bring about a revolution immediately. In October, the group converged on Chicago. Dressed in hard hats, boots, and work gloves, members of the Weathermen rampaged through the streets wielding pipes, clubs, rocks, and chains. They tangled with police (as they had planned), regrouped, and came back for still another confrontation. This kind of violence alarmed Americans and turned some against the antiwar movement.

The Silent Majority President Nixon recognized that student radicals, antiwar protesters, and the counterculture in general had never appealed to many Americans. Despite widespread discontent on college

Focus on GOVERNMENT

The Pentagon Papers In June 1971, *The New York Times* began publishing articles based on a classified government study of American involvement in the Vietnam War. The study, which came to be called the Pentagon Papers, revealed that government officials had lied to Congress and the American people about the war. Presidents had made secret policy decisions, such as giving military aid to France and waging an undercover war against North Vietnam in the early 1960s. Such revelations shocked the public and led to a growing distrust of government that would be reinforced by the events of the 1970s.

Lesson Plan

Focus Explain that antiwar protests grew in strength and frequency until President Nixon finally managed to bring the war to a close. Ask how opposition to the war affected the election of 1968. How did the war finally end?

Instruct Ask students to list the reasons for growing opposition to the war. Ask why Lyndon Johnson could not end the war. What steps finally led to the cease-fire and withdrawal of American forces? Why did Nixon's escalation of the bombing and the invasion of Cambodia cause such outrage? Tell students that Nixon's adviser Henry Kissinger hoped that "jugular diplomacy" would force the North Vietnamese into making some concessions at the negotiating table.

Assess/Reteach What do students think today of Nixon's desire to secure "peace with honor"? Ask them to share their opinions of his peace talks/bombing raids approach. Can students suggest other courses of action Nixon might have followed more successfully?

Activity
Student Portfolio

You may wish to have students add the following to their portfolios: Explain that once President Nixon had determined that the United States should no longer seek victory in Vietnam, he tried to find a way to gain "peace with honor." Ask students to write a brief description of how the Vietnamization policy seemed to placate both antiwar protesters and conservatives who did not think the United States should abandon Vietnam to its fate. **(Verbal/Linguistic)**

Customize For ...
ESL

Ask students to make time lines, beginning with 1960, identifying the major dates in the Vietnam War.

Caption Answers

Map Skills On the Vietnam-Cambodia border and in the Hanoi area.

ACTIVITY

Connecting with History and Conflict

Direct students to prepare a report on the contemporary media coverage given to the shootings at Kent State. Have them locate magazine and newspaper reports of the incident and analyze them. Students' analyses should consider such things as presentation, accuracy, and bias. Challenge students to explain how the reporting of Kent State did or did not reflect the spirit of the times. **(Verbal/Linguistic)**

BACKGROUND

Service Women

"I felt like Lady Macbeth. I couldn't get the blood of Vietnam off my hands," remembers Jean Fury, who served as a nurse in the war. "Part of me had held on, hoping that I'd be proven right, that all those sacrifices were worth something." On Veterans Day, 1993, Fury and the other 11,500 women who had served in Vietnam were honored with a permanent tribute in the form of a bronze statue of two servicewomen in action. "I didn't realize how much your sacrifice equaled and even exceeded that of the men," said General Colin Powell at the groundbreaking ceremony for the memorial in July 1993.

COMPARING PRIMARY SOURCES

The Tragedy of Kent State

In May 1970, the National Guard opened fire on a crowd of antiwar protesters at Kent State University in Ohio and killed four students. Reaction to the incident was strong but mixed.

Analyzing Viewpoints Compare the main arguments made by these two women.

In Support of the National Guard's Actions

"He told me they didn't fire those shots to scare the students off. He told me they fired those shots because they knew the students were coming after them, coming for their guns. People are calling my husband a murderer; my husband is not a murderer. He was afraid."

—Wife of a member of the National Guard, quoted in Newsweek *magazine, May 18, 1970*

Opposed to the National Guard's Actions

"Nixon acts as if the kids had it coming. But shooting into a crowd of students, that is violence. They say it could happen again if the Guard is threatened. They consider stones threat enough to kill children. I think the violence comes from the government."

—Mother of Jeffrey Glenn Miller, a student killed at Kent State, quoted in Life *magazine, May 15, 1970*

campuses, not all students agreed with the antiwar protesters. Some firmly supported American involvement in Vietnam. Others questioned the war but were troubled by the lawlessness and radicalism of many antiwar protests. These students did not receive the press coverage of their more outspoken classmates. But they did make their opinions known by writing letters to campus newspapers or by challenging the actions of antiwar groups in court.

Likewise, many adults held student protesters responsible for rising crime, growing drug use, and permissive attitudes toward sex. Some of these Americans expressed their patriotism by putting flag decals on their car windows or by attaching bumper stickers that read "My Country, Right or Wrong" and "Love It or Leave It." In the 1969 speech quoted at the beginning of this section, Nixon referred to this large group of Americans as the **silent majority.** To strengthen his position on law and order, Nixon aimed to discourage protest, especially against the war. In his "silent majority speech" he declared, "If a vocal minority, however fervent its cause, prevails over reason and the will of the majority, this nation has no future as a free society."

Kent State and Jackson State Tensions between antiwar activists and law-and-order supporters reached a peak in 1970. The U.S. invasion of Cambodia in 1970 fueled the protest movement on college campuses in the United States. At Kent State University in Ohio, students reacted angrily to the President's actions. They broke windows in the business district downtown. They also burned the army ROTC building, which had become a hated symbol of the war.

In response, the governor of Ohio ordered the National Guard to Kent State. Tension mounted. When students threw rocks at them, the guardsmen loaded their guns and donned gas masks. They hurled tear gas at the students, ordering them to disperse. Then the guardsmen retreated to another position. At the top of a hill, they suddenly turned and began firing on the students below.

Seconds later, four students lay dead, with nine others wounded. Two of the dead had been demonstrators 250 feet away from the guardsmen. The other two were bystanders, almost 400 feet away.

This famous photograph of the shooting of a student at Kent State University horrified the nation.

Similar violence flared at Jackson State, a nearly all-black college in Mississippi. A confrontation between students and police left two students dead and eleven wounded.

These attacks horrified Americans. In a sign of the deep divisions in the nation, 100,000 construction workers marched in an angry demonstration in New York City in support of the President.

American Withdrawal

The war dragged on, as did the Paris peace talks. In January 1972, while running for a second term as President, Nixon announced that North Vietnam had refused to accept a proposed settlement. At the end of March, the North Vietnamese began a major assault

RESOURCE DIRECTORY

Teaching Resources

Biography, Literature, and Comparing Primary Sources booklet (Comparing Primary Sources) *On the Tragedy of Kent State*, p. 157

Great Debates booklet (Decision-Making Activity) *Helping to Heal a War-Torn Nation*, p. 44

Technology

RESOURCE PRO® **Critical Thinking Activity** *Drawing Conclusions: Military Spending,* found on Resource Pro, charts the increase in military spending that many people thought was prolonging the Vietnam War.

VIEWING HISTORY The photo at left shows Vietnamese evacuees boarding an American helicopter near the American Embassy in Saigon in 1975. In the smaller photo, an American official punches a man trying to board the last plane out of Nha Trang; the plane was already overcrowded with fleeing refugees. **Drawing Inferences** *What do these photos suggest about the way the United States ended its involvement in Vietnam?*

on South Vietnam. This led Nixon to order the most intensive bombing campaign of the war. The United States bombed the North Vietnamese capital of Hanoi and mined North Vietnamese harbors.

Just days before the 1972 election, National Security Advisor Henry Kissinger announced, "Peace is at hand." As it turned out, the settlement was not actually final. After Nixon's reelection in November and another round of B-52 bombings of North Vietnam in December, peace finally arrived. In January 1973, the United States, South Vietnam, North Vietnam, and the Viet Cong signed a formal agreement in Paris. Among the provisions in the agreement were these:

1. The United States would withdraw all its forces from South Vietnam within 60 days.
2. All prisoners of war would be released.
3. All parties to the agreement would end military activities in Laos and Cambodia.
4. The 17th parallel would continue to divide North and South Vietnam until the country could be reunited.

READING CHECK
How did peace finally arrive?

Aftermath of the War in Asia

American involvement in the war came to an end in 1973, but the fighting between North and South Vietnam continued for another two years. Americans had believed that they could defend the world from communism anywhere, at any time. American technology and money, they assumed, could always bring victory. Vietnam proved that assumption to be false.

South Vietnam Falls After the withdrawal of American forces, South Vietnamese soldiers steadily lost ground to their North Vietnamese enemies. In the spring of 1975, the North Vietnamese launched a campaign of strikes against strategic cities throughout South Vietnam, the final objective being the seat of government in Saigon.

South Vietnamese forces crumpled in the face of this campaign. On April 29, 1975, with Communist forces surrounding Saigon, the United States carried out a dramatic last-minute evacuation. American helicopters airlifted more than 1,000 Americans and nearly 6,000 Vietnamese from the city to aircraft carriers waiting offshore. On April 30, North Vietnam completed its conquest of South Vietnam, and the Saigon government officially surrendered. After decades of fighting, Vietnam was a single nation under a Communist government.

ACTIVITY
Connecting with History and Conflict

Invite student groups to conduct research on various aspects of the Paris peace talks and provide a brief presentation to the rest of the class. Different presentations could include the settings of the talks, the major issues that were discussed, the attitudes of the participants, or the general mood or atmosphere that prevailed. **(Verbal/Linguistic)**

BACKGROUND
Connections to Today

One of the lasting images of the war in Vietnam for Americans is the scene of the final hours of the United States presence in Saigon (now Ho Chi Minh City). Helicopters that swooped down to the roof of the U.S. embassy were immediately filled with diplomatic and military personnel, then jammed to overflowing with frantic refugees before flying off to safety. For nearly 25 years afterward, the massive building was a reminder of the war, but no longer. The State Department decided in 1997 to demolish the old building and replace it with a sleek new consulate, designed to foster commercial ties. Many people in the city see the change as symbolic of a new era. As one Vietnamese said, "The relationship between the United States and Vietnam is different now. We are doing trade, not fighting a war."

READING CHECK
The Paris Peace Treaty was signed in January 1973 in the wake of a North Vietnamese offensive the previous spring and two final, massive American bombing campaigns.

CUSTOMIZE FOR ...
Less Proficient Writers

Ask students to restate, in their own words, the four conditions for American withdrawal from Vietnam agreed upon when the formal peace agreement was signed in Paris in January 1973.

CAPTION ANSWERS

Viewing History It looks like a hasty, desperate, disorganized retreat that left many would-be refugees behind.

ACTIVITY

Connecting with History and Conflict

Organize students into groups, and have each group create a project entitled "The Legacy of the Vietnam War." Student projects may honor veterans, express concerns, identify postwar policy implications, or convey anything else students feel is the true legacy of America's experience in Vietnam. Projects may take any suitable form, including reports, artwork, bulletin-board displays, songs, and so on. Have groups present their projects to the rest of the class. **(Verbal/Linguistic; Visual/Spatial)**

BACKGROUND

Connections to Today

Some analysts estimate that as many as one million South Vietnamese civilians were forced into "re-education" camps by the new Communist rulers of the country. That amounts to one out of every 20 people. Some were held in the camps for more than ten years. The camps varied widely in terms of how they treated prisoners, but some were horrid. One account tells of a cell built to hold 20 people housing 80, forcing prisoners to take turns breathing through the cell's single air hole. Countless prisoners were tortured, starved, forced into hard labor, and killed outright. Many South Vietnamese who avoided the camps were still forced to endure "re-education" on a smaller scale (say, for weeks at a local prison). That so many Vietnamese fled their home country by boat, risking drowning and pirate attacks, is testament to the brutality of the victorious Communist rule in the former South Vietnam.

Southeast Asia After the War One reason for American involvement in Vietnam was the belief in the domino theory. As you recall, this was the assumption that the entire region would collapse if the Communists won in Vietnam. With the North Vietnamese victory, two additional dominoes did topple—Laos and Cambodia. The rest of the region, however, did not fall.

The suffering of the Cambodian people was one of the most tragic effects of the war in Vietnam. In April 1975, Cambodia fell to the Khmer Rouge, a force of Communists led by the fanatical Pol Pot. In five years of fighting, Cambodia had already suffered as many as a half million civilian casualties, mostly by American bombs. Worse was to come. The Khmer Rouge in effect declared war on anyone "tainted" with Western ways, and they killed as many as 1.5 million Cambodians—a quarter of the population. Many were shot, while the rest died of starvation, from disease, from mistreatment in labor camps, or on forced marches.

Although not so extreme, Vietnam's new leaders also forced hundreds of thousands of South Vietnamese soldiers, civil servants, and other professionals into "re-education camps." Meanwhile, more than 1.5 million Vietnamese fled their country by boat, leaving behind all personal possessions in their determination to escape. In addition to these refugees, hundreds of thousands of Cambodians and Laotians also fled their homelands, many making their way to the United States.

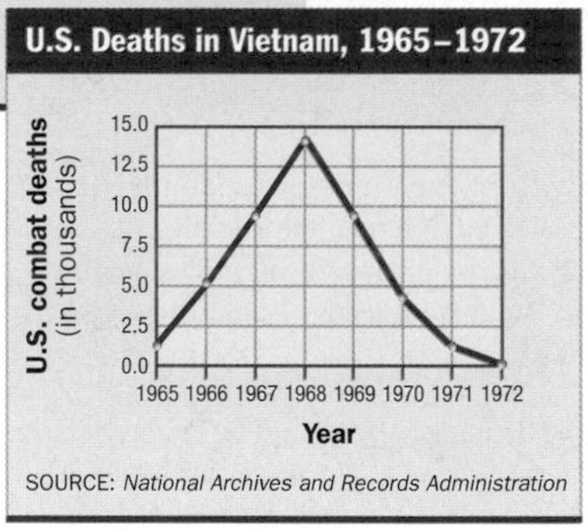

U.S. Forces in Vietnam, 1965 – 1972

Military forces (in thousands): 0–550; Year: 1965–1972

SOURCE: *National Archives and Records Administration*

U.S. Deaths in Vietnam, 1965–1972

U.S. combat deaths (in thousands): 0.0–15.0; Year: 1965–1972

SOURCE: *National Archives and Records Administration*

INTERPRETING GRAPHS United States involvement in Vietnam peaked in 1968. **Analyzing Information** *(a) How many United States soldiers were in Vietnam in 1968? (b) When did American casualties begin to decrease? (c) Judging from the two graphs, what is one reason for this decrease?*

The Legacy of the War

The Vietnam War resulted in more than 58,000 Americans dead and 300,000 wounded. In addition, more than 2,500 Americans were listed as **POWs** (prisoners of war) and **MIAs** (missing in action) at the end of the war. Many of them remain unaccounted for. After Vietnam, soldiers came home to a reception that was quite different than the ones their fathers and grandfathers had received following the World Wars. There were no welcoming ticker-tape parades. Many veterans complained that Americans did not appreciate the sacrifices they had made for their country.

Counting the Costs The Vietnam War was the longest and the least successful war in American history. The costs of the war were enormous. The United States spent at least $150 billion on the war. This expense resulted in growing inflation and economic instability.

The costs of the war were high for Vietnam as well. More bombs rained down on Vietnam than had fallen on all the Axis powers during World War II. The number of dead and wounded Vietnamese soldiers ran into the millions, with countless civilian casualties. The landscape itself would long bear the scars of war. In 1994, the United States announced an end to the long-standing American trade embargo against Vietnam. The next year the United States agreed to restore full diplomatic relations with its former enemy.

CAPTION ANSWERS

Interpreting Graphs Over 500,000. 1969. Casualties began to decrease when the United States began withdrawing troops.

RESOURCE DIRECTORY

Teaching Resources

Units 5/6/7 booklet
- Section 4 Quiz, p. 88
- Chapter 24 Test, p. 89, 92

Guide to the Essentials
- Section 4 Summary, p. 119
- Chapter 24 Test, p. 120

Other Print Resources

Chapter Tests with ExamView® Test Bank CD-ROM, Ch. 24

Technology

Sounds of an Era Audio CD *John Kerry's "Winter Soldier" speech,* 1971 recording (time: 50 seconds)

Exploring Primary Sources in U.S. History CD-ROM: *The Vietnam Veterans Memorial*

ExamView® Test Bank CD-ROM, Ch. 24

Social Studies Skills Tutor CD-ROM

The Vietnam Veterans Memorial Aside from the Civil War, the Vietnam War divided the nation more than any other conflict in American history. The issues were so difficult and emotional that for many years something was forgotten—that the Americans who died in Vietnam should be honored with a national monument.

In 1979, a group of veterans began making plans for a Vietnam Veterans Memorial. They wanted to recognize the courage of American GIs during the Vietnam ordeal and to help heal the wounds the war had caused. A Vietnam veteran named Jan Scruggs started a fund for the memorial. Eventually, he won support from Congress to build a monument in Washington, D.C., near the Lincoln Memorial. The question quickly arose: How could the memorial honor the people who gave their lives, while avoiding the hard political issues surrounding the war?

Scruggs's committee held a contest. Famous architects and artists submitted their ideas. Many were surprised when the winner was a 21-year-old college student named Maya Ying Lin. Her idea was to build a long wall of black granite, cut down into the ground. This wall would display the names of every American man and woman who died in the Vietnam War.

Lin had a reason for each element of the memorial. She chose black granite because it reflects light like a mirror, allowing visitors to see reflections of themselves and the nature around them. She put the memorial on a slope that led below ground level to create a quiet place where visitors could think about life and death and sorrow. She placed the names in the order people died, rather than in alphabetical order, so that the individual passing of each life would be emphasized. The memorial was to be long, but not tall, so that visitors could easily see and touch every name.

Lin's concept suited the needs of a nation that needed to heal. Her simple, abstract design would allow visitors to carry their own beliefs to the memorial, without creating images that might disturb or distract them. The Vietnam Veterans Memorial was completed in 1982, and ever since, people have added to it by leaving personal tokens at the wall in memory of their loved ones.

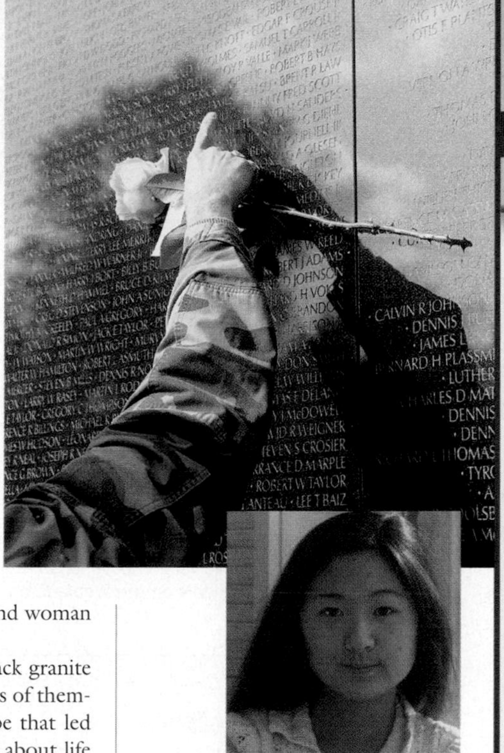

VIEWING HISTORY A Vietnam veteran holds a flower as he points to a name on the Memorial, which was designed by Maya Lin (lower photo). **Determining Relevance** *How do you think listing the names on the wall has contributed to the Memorial's popularity?*

Section 4 Assessment

READING COMPREHENSION

1. What terms were finally agreed to at the **Paris peace talks?**
2. What event led to American withdrawal from Vietnam?
3. Why was President Nixon's policy known as **Vietnamization?**
4. Who are **POWs** and **MIAs?**

CRITICAL THINKING AND WRITING

5. **Determining Relevance** How did violence at Kent State and Jackson State affect American public opinion? Explain your answer.
6. **Making a List** Do you think the United States made every effort to win the war in Vietnam? List reasons why or why not.

Take It to the NET

Activity: Creating a Time Line
Much has happened in Vietnam since the end of the war. Create a time line of important events in Vietnam from 1974 to the present. Use the links provided in the *America: Pathways to the Present* area of the following Web site for help in completing this activity.
www.phschool.com

Section 4 Assessment

Reading Comprehension

1. U.S. to withdraw all forces from South Vietnam within 60 days; all POWs to be released; all parties would end military activities in Laos and Cambodia; the 17th parallel would continue to divide North and South Vietnam until the country could be reunited.
2. The signing of the peace agreement in Paris in January 1973.
3. Because American troops were replaced with South Vietnamese soldiers.
4. POWs: prisoners of war; MIAs: missing in action.

Critical Thinking and Writing

5. This violence horrified Americans and displayed the sharp divisions the war had caused in American society.
6. Answers will vary, but might consider such topics as whether President Nixon had a realistic plan for ending the war, or the impact that antiwar demonstrators had on Nixon's actions.

Take It to the NET

Student time lines should indicate events in Vietnam from 1974 to the present. Examples may include: uniting of North and South Vietnam as Socialist Republic of Vietnam; admission to United Nations; overthrow of Pol Pot's government in Cambodia; reestablishing diplomatic relations with the United States.

TEST PREPARATION

Have students read the paragraph on the previous page titled "Southeast Asia After the War" and then answer the question below.

Who were the Khmer Rouge?

A A group of French student activists.
B A group of South Vietnamese who continued to fight after the U.S. left.
C A North Vietnamese religious group.
(D) A group of Communists in Cambodia.

Caption Answers

Viewing History Answers will vary. Many students may note that the list draws visitors because they can find and touch the names of their loved ones, and leave mementos in their honor.

Reviewing Key Terms

Students should refer to the definitions of key terms in the chapter to write sentences that show an understanding of the Vietnam War.

Reviewing Main Ideas

11. Johnson used the Gulf of Tonkin Resolution to justify devoting ever-increasing American resources to the war. In 1965, this included a massive influx of American troops and the beginning of Operation Rolling Thunder.
12. It gave the President almost complete control over U.S. actions in Vietnam, even without an official declaration of war from Congress.
13. The doubts of Americans at home increased since the Viet Cong had achieved a psychological victory even though they had suffered a devastating military defeat.
14. The guerrilla warfare in the jungle was confusing and frightening, and soldiers never knew who their friends or enemies were.
15. Guerrilla warfare tactics. Also, they were familiar with the swamps and jungles; they could find protection across the border in Cambodia and Laos; and they could often count on the support of the local population.
16. They participated in various activities, such as violent and nonviolent antiwar protests, teach-ins, draft resistance, and the free-speech movement.
17. Nixon gained support by claiming to have a secret plan to end the war; many Democrats abstained from voting because their party was split; Humphrey was hurt by his support of Johnson's policies.
18. To destroy Viet Cong and North Vietnamese bases there.
19. North Vietnam took over South Vietnam. Communist regimes also took over in Laos and Cambodia, but the rest of the region did not fall to communism.

Chapter 24 Review and Assessment

creating a CHAPTER SUMMARY

Copy this chart (right) on a piece of paper and complete it by adding information about U.S. involvement in Vietnam under each President from Truman through Nixon.

U.S. Involvement in Vietnam		
President	**Action (date)**	**Result**
Truman	Sent economic aid to French in Vietnam (1950)	U.S. began to fight the spread of communism.
Eisenhower	Provided military advisors to South Vietnam (1960)	U.S. became involved in the Vietnam War.
Kennedy	• Increased military aid • Supported overthrow of Diem (1963)	
Johnson		
Nixon		

iText

For additional review and enrichment activities, see the interactive version of *America: Pathways to the Present*, available on the Web and on CD-ROM.

★ Reviewing Key Terms

For each of the terms below, write a sentence explaining how it relates to the Vietnam War.

1. domino theory
2. Viet Cong
3. Gulf of Tonkin Resolution
4. land mine
5. Agent Orange
6. escalation
7. Ho Chi Minh Trail
8. conscientious objector
9. Middle America
10. Vietnamization

★ Reviewing Main Ideas

11. How did the Vietnam War escalate under President Johnson? (Section 1)
12. How did the Gulf of Tonkin Resolution expand presidential power? (Section 1)
13. Why was the Tet Offensive a turning point in the war? (Section 2)
14. Why was the war so hard on American soldiers fighting in Vietnam? (Section 2)
15. What advantages did the Viet Cong have in the war? (Section 2)
16. What methods did student activists use during the 1960s to oppose the war in Vietnam? (Section 3)
17. How did the war influence the election of 1968? (Section 3)
18. Why did Richard Nixon authorize the invasion of Cambodia in 1970? (Section 4)
19. What happened in Southeast Asia after American withdrawal from Vietnam? (Section 4)

★ Critical Thinking

20. **Comparing Points of View** Evaluate American involvement in Vietnam from the point of view of the following: a hawk, a dove, a conscientious objector, and a soldier.
21. **Drawing Conclusions** If you had been a student during the Vietnam War, do you think your views of the conflict would have changed or remained the same throughout the course of the war? What factors might have influenced your views?
22. **Checking Consistency** President Nixon promised to end the war in Vietnam. Yet he authorized the heaviest bombing raids of the war, and he expanded the war into Cambodia. Were these actions consistent with his promise? Explain.
23. **Drawing Inferences** Why do you think Vietnam veterans came home to a different reception than the ones veterans of the two World Wars received?
24. **Predicting Consequences** Since the end of the Vietnam War, government officials have advised caution in global affairs. How do you think Americans would react to United States involvement in "another Vietnam"? Explain your answer.

Creating a Chapter Summary

U.S. Involvement in Vietnam		
President	**Action (date)**	**Result**
Truman	Sent economic aid to French in Vietnam (1950)	U.S. began to fight the spread of communism.
Eisenhower	Provided military advisers to South Vietnam (1960)	U.S. became involved in the Vietnam War.
Kennedy	• Increased military aid (1961) • Supported overthrow of Diem (1963) • McNamara encouraged withdrawal (1963). • Kennedy assassinated (1963)	U.S. became more involved in Vietnam War.
Johnson	• Creates a policy of escalation (1965) • Congress passes Gulf of Tonkin Resolution (1964). • Tet Offensive (1968) • Massacre at My Lai (1968) • Johnson decides not to run for reelection (1968).	• War begins to escalate. • Johnson gains much broader powers. • Viet Cong gain advantage. • Americans become more vocal against the war.
Nixon	• Nixon promises he has "secret plan" to end the war (1968). • Nixon announces plan for "Vietnamization" (1969). • Nixon calls for law and order (1969). • Peace talks begin (1968). • Nixon launches saturation bombing and attacks on Cambodia (1969–1970). • Peace treaty is signed (1973).	• Student protests continue. • Student protesters are killed at Kent State and Jackson State.

★ **Skills Assessment**

Analyzing Political Cartoons ▶

25. Examine the images in the cartoon. (a) Who are the two men? (b) What is the occasion shown in the cartoon?
26. (a) What is the significance of the documents held by the man on the right? (b) What does the gravestone refer to?
27. What is the message of the cartoon?

Analyzing Primary Sources

Read this excerpt, and then answer the questions that follow.

> “*You have a row of dominoes set up, you knock over the first one, and what will happen to the last one is the certainty that it will go over very quickly.*”
>
> —Dwight D. Eisenhower

28. Which statement best represents the meaning of the quotation?
    - **A** Southeast Asian nations will support one another in the fight against communism.
    - **B** If one Southeast Asian nation falls to communism, others will also fall.
    - **C** The strongest Southeast Asian nation will remain standing after the others fall to communism.
    - **D** No one can predict what will happen if communism spreads in Southeast Asia.
29. Which of the following events supports the idea expressed in the quotation?
    - **F** American forces could not bring about victory in Vietnam.
    - **G** After decades of fighting, Vietnam became a single nation under a Communist government.
    - **H** Laos and Cambodia became Communist nations.
    - **J** The Vietnam War divided the American people.

Applying the Chapter Skill: *Sequencing*

30. Look back at the Skills for Life page. Write a paragraph telling, in sequence, the events described in the sources.

ACTIVITIES

Writing to LEARN

Writing a Conclusion
Why do you think that what began as a distant war in a small country that very few Americans had ever heard of ended up causing such a crisis in American society? In examining this question, consider the original causes of the war in Vietnam, the causes of American involvement and escalation, and the actions of both the U.S. government and ordinary citizens at home.

Primary Source CD-ROM

Working With Primary Sources Find additional information on the Vietnam War on the *Exploring Primary Sources in U.S. History CD-ROM* and use the selection(s) provided to complete the Chapter 24 primary source activity located in the *America: Pathways to the Present* area of the following Web site.
www.phschool.com

Take It to the NET

Chapter Self-Test As a review activity, take the Chapter 24 Self-Test in the *America: Pathways to the Present* area of the Web site listed below. The questions are designed to test your understanding of the chapter content.
www.phschool.com

ANSWERS TO ACTIVITIES

Writing to LEARN

Students might suggest the U.S. fear that communism was spreading; the real and alleged incidents Presidents cited to step up involvement; the war's violence and brutality affected civilians as well as soldiers.

Primary Source CD-ROM

Direct students to the additional primary sources that can be found on the *Exploring Primary Sources in U.S. History CD-ROM.*

Take It to the NET

Additional support materials and activities for Chapter 24 of *America: Pathways to the Present* can be found in the Social Studies area at the Prentice Hall School Web site. **www.phschool.com**

CRITICAL THINKING

20. Hawks: supported goals of war; Doves: felt we did not belong in Vietnam and wanted to pull out; Conscientious Objectors: objected to war on moral and religious levels; Soldiers: some wanted to serve their country, others were horrified by the war's conditions and wished to withdraw.
21. Students' answers should demonstrate an understanding that the views of many Americans changed from acceptance to strong disapproval. Factors that influenced this shift in opinion included student protests and television coverage of the brutality of war.
22. Mainly inconsistent: Though Nixon seemed to be pulling the U.S. out of the war with his policy of Vietnamization, his attack on Cambodia served to expand and complicate the war. Nixon's two massive bombing campaigns against North Vietnam in 1972 did, however, contribute to finally ending the war.
23. It was an unpopular war and veterans were not viewed as heroes and defenders of democracy as they had been in previous wars.
24. They would object to becoming involved in such a conflict, as this type of distant conflict against a guerrilla force which enjoys local support is difficult to pull out of, has a terrible cost in lives lost, and is probably doomed to failure.

SKILLS ASSESSMENT

25. (a) Richard Nixon and a man representing the American voter. (b) The 1972 presidential election.
26. (a) Nixon was elected President in 1968 by claiming that he had a secret plan to end the war in Vietnam. (b) The number of U.S. soldiers killed in Vietnam despite Nixon's secret plan to end the war.
27. That Nixon's 1968 campaign promise to end the war was completely bankrupt. Meanwhile, U.S. soldiers continue to die in Vietnam as Nixon runs for reelection.
28. B
29. H
30. Answers should include the order in which the events occurred and an explanation of how they are connected.

Use this sample exam to help your students prepare for standardized tests.

Tips for Test Taking

You might want to remind your students of the following:

1. Read the directions carefully.
2. Read each question carefully.
3. For multiple choice questions, try to answer the question before you look at the choices. Read all the choices. Then, eliminate those that are absolutely incorrect.
4. For short answer questions, be sure to answer the question completely if there is more than one part.
5. Answer the easy questions first. Then, go back to the ones that will take more time.
6. Pace yourself. Be sure to set aside enough time for the writing questions.

TEST PREPARATION

Write your answers on a separate sheet of paper.

1. The United States Supreme Court, in *Brown* v. *Board of Education* (1954), ended

A mandatory poll taxes and literacy tests.
B racial segregation in public schools.
C discrimination in employment and housing.
D separation of the races in buses and trains.

2. Which one of the following African Americans became known nationally as a result of the Montgomery, Alabama, bus boycott?

A Martin Luther King, Jr.
B James Meredith
C Malcolm X
D Barbara Jordan

3. Which one of the following issues was addressed by the Civil Rights Act of 1964?

A Racial discrimination in public colleges and universities
B Racial discrimination in voter registration standards
C Racial segregation in public schools
D Racial segregation in buses and taxis

4. Which decision of the United States Supreme Court requires police officials to inform suspects of their constitutional rights before questioning them?

A *Mapp* v. *Ohio* (1961)
B *Baker* v. *Carr* (1962)
C *Engel* v. *Vitale* (1962)
D *Miranda* v. *Arizona* (1966)

Use the table and your knowledge of social studies to answer the following question.

African American Elected Officials*	
Year	Number
1970	1,469
1980	4,890
1985	6,016
1990	7,335

*National, state, and local governments
SOURCE: *Statistical Abstract of the United States, 1995*

5. Which one of the following was the primary cause of the trend shown in the table?

A *Brown* v. *Board of Education*, 1954
B Southern Manifesto, 1956
C Civil Rights Act, 1964
D Voting Rights Act, 1965

6. Which one of the following events during the Cold War almost led to war between the United States and the Soviet Union?

A The Bay of Pigs invasion
B The Cuban Missile Crisis
C The Gulf of Tonkin incident
D The Tet Offensive

7. Which one of the following helped to further the women's movement of the 1960s and 1970s?

A The failed social welfare policies of President Lyndon Johnson
B The perceived threat to the suffrage movement
C The high rate of inflation throughout the 1960s
D The publication of *The Feminine Mystique* by Betty Friedan

820

Diagnose and Prescribe
- Profile student skills with Diagnostic Tests A&B.
- Address student needs with program materials correlated to test questions.

Review and Reteach
- Provide cumulative content review with the Review Book.

Practice and Assess
- Build test-taking skills with Test-taking Strategies With Transparencies.

Use the graph and your knowledge of social studies to answer the following question.

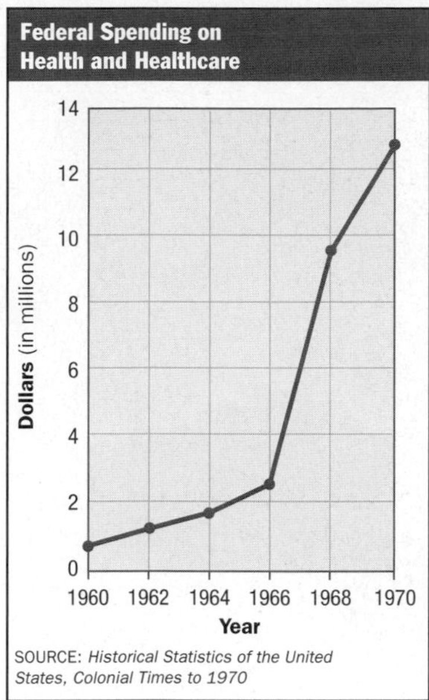

8. Which one of the following caused the trend shown in the line graph?

A Policies of the New Frontier

B Demands of the civil rights movement

C Programs of the Great Society

D The war in Vietnam

9. United States public opinion shifted against the Vietnam War following

A the battle of Dien Bien Phu.

B the assassination of President Ngo Dinh Diem.

C Operation Rolling Thunder.

D the Tet Offensive.

10. Which President established the Environmental Protection Agency (EPA), the federal agency designed to set and enforce national pollution-control standards?

A John Kennedy

B Lyndon Johnson

C Richard Nixon

D Jimmy Carter

11. Which one of the following was the legal basis for the involvement of the United States in Vietnam?

A A declaration of war by Congress

B The Geneva Accords

C The Gulf of Tonkin Resolution

D The Paris agreement

12. President Nixon's policy of Vietnamization was designed to

A replace Americans in Vietnam with South Vietnamese soldiers.

B bomb North Vietnam until it surrendered.

C stop the use of the Ho Chi Minh Trail.

D extend the fighting into Laos and Cambodia.

Writing Practice

13. Describe the major social programs of President Johnson's "Great Society."

14. Describe the role of César Chávez in the fight against discrimination.

15. How did Rachel Carson affect the movement for a cleaner environment?

1. B
2. A
3. B
4. D
5. D
6. B
7. D
8. C
9. D
10. C
11. C
12. A
13. Answers should mention the Economic Opportunity Act (including the Head Start and VISTA programs), the Elementary and Secondary Education Act of 1965, Medicare and Medicaid, and the Immigration Act of 1965.
14. Answers should mention that César Chávez organized migrant Latino farmworkers in an effort to provide better working conditions for them. He founded the United Farm Workers union and organized a successful national boycott of crops grown on nonunion farms.
15. Rachel Carson, a marine biologist and author, wrote *Silent Spring,* a book in which she explained the dangers of the use of chemical pesticides, particularly DDT. The book was a sensation and led to the eventual illegalization of DDT and control of other chemicals in the United States.

Unit 7

Unit 7

Continuity and Change (1969 to the Present)

INTRODUCING THE UNIT

Continuity and Change (1969 to the Present) The presidencies of Nixon, Ford, and Carter were marked, in succession, by tumult and recovery in government and by a deepening economic crisis. Seeking to re-ignite America's economy, citizens elected conservative Ronald Reagan by a landslide in 1981. He was followed by George H.W. Bush, who led Americans into war in the Persian Gulf in 1991. Bill Clinton presided over a dramatic phase of economic growth in the United States, but his tenure was marred by friction with Congress and scandal. The first President of the twenty-first century, George W. Bush, wants to minimize government's influence in everyday life and to limit United States involvement abroad.

USING HISTORICAL EVIDENCE

Direct students' attention to the picture on these pages. Discuss with students their memories of the transition from one century to another. How do they think the twenty-first century will differ from the twentieth? What types of improvements do they hope for in society and in technology?

Discuss the condition of the world as the twentieth century ended. What situations do students think were most important in the last years of the century? How do they imagine those situations will change, now and in the future?

"The challenge . . . is to make and keep our communities places where we can tolerate, even celebrate, our differences, while pulling together for the common good. 'Of many, one' is the main challenge, I believe; it is my hope for our country and the world."

Ruth Bader Ginsburg,
Supreme Court Justice, 1998

Americans across the nation celebrated the arrival of the new century with fireworks and festivities, like this celebration in San Francisco, California. ▶

RESOURCE DIRECTORY

Teaching Resources

Units 5/6/7 booklet
- American Pathways Activity, pp. 132–133
- History's Lasting Impact, pp. 134–135

Geography and History booklet, pp. 20–21

Other Print Resources

Prentice Hall Assessment System
- Document-Based Assessment

eTeach

Be sure to check out this month's online discussion with a Master Teacher. Go to **www.phschool.com**.

Chapter 25 Nixon, Ford, Carter, 1969–1981
Chapter 26 The Conservative Revolution, 1980–1992
Chapter 27 Entering a New Era, 1992 to the Present

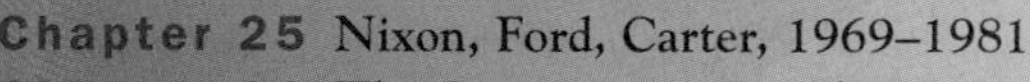

823

TECHNOLOGY CENTER

Prentice Hall School Web site offers student-appropriate Internet activities and links that extend core content. Visit us at the Social Studies area. **www.phschool.com**

AmericanHeritage®

My Brush with History™ Video Program This new video series lets your students learn history from the people who lived it.

RESOURCE PRO®

Teaching Resources on CD-ROM offer lesson-planning flexibility, test-generation capability, and resource manageability.

- **Presentation Pro CD-ROM** Provides you with multimedia lecture notes for each chapter.
- **Social Studies Skills Tutor CD-ROM** Provides interactive practice in Geographic Literacy, Critical Thinking and Reading, Visual Analysis, and Communications.
- **Interactive Constitution CD-ROM** Exploring active citizenship and civic responsibilities, this CD-ROM shows students how the Constitution affects their lives today.
- **Exploring Primary Sources in U.S. History CD-ROM** This interactive exploration of primary sources allows students to analyze and to evaluate writing and images from American history.
- **Guided Reading Audiotapes**
- **Student Edition on Audio CD**
- **Sounds of an Era Audio CD** Bring the sounds of American history to life in the classroom with music, speeches, poetry, interviews, and news reports.

Don't miss the exclusive interactive version of this textbook on the Web and on CD-ROM.

RESOURCE DIRECTORY

Technology

Color Transparencies *Historical Maps,* A52, A53, A54, A57, A59; *Political Cartoons,* B18, B19, B20; *Time Lines,* C9, C10; *Fine Art,* E19, E20; *American Photo,* F10; *American Diversity,* G13, G14, G15; *The Way It Works,* H20
Section Reading Support Transparencies
Prentice Hall United States History Video Collection™ Volume 20, *Post-War USA*
Companion Web site, www.phschool.com

Chapter 25 Planning Guide
Resource Manager

	CORE INSTRUCTION	READING/SKILLS
Chapter-Level Resources TEKS 24(A)	Teaching Resources • Pacing Charts booklet • Block Scheduling booklet **Resource Pro® CD-ROM,** Ch. 25 **Prentice Hall Presentation Pro CD-ROM,** Ch. 25 **www.phschool.com** • eTeach	**Guided Reading Audiotapes (English/Spanish)** **Student Edition on Audio CD,** Ch. 25 **Social Studies Skills Tutor CD-ROM** **Color Transparencies,** A57, B18, C9, H20
1 Nixon's Domestic Policy 1. Find out how Richard Nixon's personality affected his relationship with his staff. 2. See how Nixon's domestic policies differed from those of his predecessors. 3. Learn how Nixon applied his "southern strategy." 4. Describe the first moon landing. **TEKS** 8(A), 19(A), 24(B), 24(G)	Teaching Resources **Units 5/6/7 booklet** • Section 1 Quiz, p. 100	**Guided Reading and Review booklet,** p. 128 **Guide to the Essentials,** p. 121 **Section Reading Support Transparencies**
2 Nixon's Foreign Policy 1. Learn how Henry Kissinger relaxed tensions between the U.S. and the Communist powers. 2. Find out about Nixon's policy toward the People's Republic of China. 3. Discover how Nixon reached an agreement with the Soviet Union on limiting nuclear arms. **TEKS** 1(B), 24(B), 24(G), 26(A)	Teaching Resources **Units 5/6/7 booklet** • Section 2 Quiz, p. 101 **Learning Styles Lesson Plans booklet,** p. 66	**Guided Reading and Review booklet,** p. 129 **Guide to the Essentials,** p. 122 **Section Reading Support Transparencies**
3 The Watergate Scandal 1. See how the Nixon White House battled its political enemies. 2. Find out about Nixon's reelection campaign. 3. Learn about the Watergate break-in, and see how the story of the scandal unfolded. 4. Discover the events that led directly to Nixon's resignation. **TEKS** 15(C), 16(A), 16(B), 24(B), 24(G)	Teaching Resources **Units 5/6/7 booklet** • Section 3 Quiz, p. 102	**Guided Reading and Review booklet,** p. 130 **Guide to the Essentials,** p. 123 **Learning with Documents booklet,** p. 71 **Skills for Life booklet,** p. 34 **Section Reading Support Transparencies**
4 The Ford Administration 1. Find out how Gerald Ford became President. 2. See the types of economic problems the Ford administration faced. 3. Learn about the foreign policy actions Ford took. 4. See how Americans celebrated the nation's bicentennial. **TEKS** 1(B), 24(B)	Teaching Resources **Units 5/6/7 booklet** • Section 4 Quiz, p. 103	**Guided Reading and Review booklet,** p. 131 **Guide to the Essentials,** p. 124 **Learning with Documents booklet,** p. 37 **Section Reading Support Transparencies**
5 The Carter Administration 1. Discover some changes Jimmy Carter brought to the presidency. 2. Learn how Carter dealt with domestic issues. 3. Find out about Carter's foreign policies. 4. Discover some factors that influenced the outcome of the 1980 election. **TEKS** 17(A), 26(A)	Teaching Resources **Units 5/6/7 booklet** • Section 5 Quiz, p. 104 **Learning Styles Lesson Plans booklet,** p. 67	**Guided Reading and Review booklet,** p. 132 **Guide to the Essentials,** p. 125 **Learning with Documents booklet,** p. 96 **Section Reading Support Transparencies**

Enrichment/Pre-AP

Prentice Hall United States History Video Collection™
www.phschool.com
- Section Activities, Virtual Field Trip, Chapter Activities, Current Events Online

American History Block Scheduling Support

Sounds of an Era Audio CD

Biography, Literature, and Comparing Primary Sources booklet, pp. 85, 159
Sounds of an Era Audio CD
Exploring Primary Sources in U.S. History CD-ROM

American History Block Scheduling Support

Biography, Literature, and Comparing Primary Sources booklet, p. 37
Great Debates booklet, p. 26
Sounds of an Era Audio CD
American Pathways Thematic Posters

Assessment

Core Assessment
ExamView® Test Bank, Ch. 25
ExamView® Test Bank CD-ROM, Ch. 25

Standardized Test Preparation
Diagnose and Prescribe
Diagnostic Tests for High School Social Studies Skills

Review and Reteach
Review Book for U.S. History

Practice and Assess
Test-taking Strategies With Transparencies
Test-taking Strategies Posters
Test Prep Book for U.S. History
Alternative Assessment Handbook
Document-Based Assessment

Teaching Resources
Units 5/6/7 booklet
- Section Quizzes, pp. 100–104
- Chapter Tests, pp. 105, 108

www.phschool.com Ch. 25 Self-Test

AmericanHeritage Resources

From the Archives of American Heritage®, pp. 841, 848
AmericanHeritage® My Brush with History™ Videotapes
www.americanheritage.com

Don't miss the exclusive interactive version of this textbook on the Web and on CD-ROM.

Chapter 25 Planning Guide

In Your Classroom

Customize for Individual Needs

Gifted and Talented

Teacher's Edition
- Customize for Gifted and Talented, pp. 843, 855

Teaching Resources
- Biography, Literature, and Comparing Primary Sources booklet, pp. 37, 85, 159

Technology
- Exploring Primary Sources in U.S. History CD-ROM *Bugging at Watergate*

ESL

Teacher's Edition
- Customize for ESL, p. 827

Teaching Resources
- Guided Reading and Review booklet, pp. 128–132
- Guide to the Essentials (English/Spanish), Chapter 25

Technology
- Student Edition on Audio CD, Chapter 25
- Guided Reading Audiotapes (English/Spanish), Chapter 25
- Section Reading Support Transparencies

Less Proficient Readers

Teacher's Edition
- Customize for Less Proficient Readers, p. 847

Teaching Resources
- Guided Reading and Review booklet, pp. 128–132
- Guide to the Essentials (English/Spanish), Chapter 25

Technology
- Student Edition on Audio CD, Chapter 25
- Guided Reading Audiotapes (English/Spanish), Chapter 25
- Section Reading Support Transparencies

Less Proficient Writers

Teaching Resources
- Guided Reading and Review booklet, pp. 128–132
- Guide to the Essentials (English/Spanish), Chapter 25

Technology
- Student Edition on Audio CD, Chapter 25
- Guided Reading Audiotapes (English/Spanish), Chapter 25
- Section Reading Support Transparencies

Teacher's Edition Index

Chapter 25 – Pacing Suggestions

For 90-minute Blocks

- Teach sections 1, 2, 3, 4, and 5 using Transparencies A57, B18, C9, and H20, and the Recent Scholarship notes on pages 840 and 849 for class discussions.

Running Out of Time?

If you are running short on time to cover this chapter, consider the following options:

- Use the Prentice Hall Presentation Pro CD-ROM to create an outline for this chapter.
- Use the Section Summaries for Chapter 25, from **Guide to the Essentials (English/Spanish).**

TEKS CORRELATION

Chapter-Level	TEKS
	(24) Social studies skills. The student applies critical-thinking skills to organize and use information acquired from a variety of sources, including electronic technology. The student is expected to: **(A)** locate and use primary and secondary sources such as computer software, databases, media and news services, biographies, interviews, and artifacts to acquire information about the United States.
1 Nixon's Domestic Policy	**(8) Geography.** The student uses geographic tools to collect, analyze, and interpret data. The student is expected to: **(A)** create thematic maps, graphs, charts, models, and databases representing various aspects of the United States. **(19) Citizenship.** The student understands the importance of effective leadership in a democratic society. The student is expected to: **(A)** describe the qualities of effective leadership. **(24) Social studies skills.** The student applies critical-thinking skills to organize and use information acquired from a variety of sources, including electronic technology. The student is expected to: **(B)** analyze information by sequencing, categorizing, identifying cause-and-effect relationships, comparing, contrasting, finding the main idea, summarizing, making generalizations and predictions, and drawing inferences and conclusions. **(G)** support a point of view on a social studies issue or event.
2 Nixon's Foreign Policy	**(1) History.** The student understands traditional historical points of reference in U.S. history from 1877 to the present. The student is expected to: **(B)** apply absolute and relative chronology through the sequencing of significant individuals, events, and time periods. **(24) Social studies skills.** The student applies critical-thinking skills to organize and use information acquired from a variety of sources, including electronic technology. The student is expected to: **(B)** analyze information by sequencing, categorizing, identifying cause-and-effect relationships, comparing, contrasting, finding the main idea, summarizing, making generalizations and predictions, and drawing inferences and conclusions. **(G)** support a point of view on a social studies issue or event. **(26) Social studies skills.** The student uses problem-solving and decision-making skills, working independently and with others, in a variety of settings. The student is expected to: **(A)** use a problem-solving process to identify a problem, gather information, list and consider options, consider advantages and disadvantages, choose and implement a solution, and evaluate the effectiveness of the solution.
3 The Watergate Scandal	**(15) Government.** The student understands changes in the role of government over time. The student is expected to: **(C)** evaluate the effects of political incidents such as Teapot Dome and Watergate on the views of U.S. citizens concerning the role of the federal government. **(16) Government.** The student understands the changing relationships among the three branches of the federal government. The student is expected to: **(A)** evaluate the impact of events, including the Gulf of Tonkin Resolution and the War Powers Act, on the relationship between the legislative and executive branches of government. **(B)** evaluate the impact of events, including Franklin Roosevelt's attempt to increase the number of U.S. Supreme Court justices, on the relationships among the legislative, executive, and judicial branches of government. **(24) Social studies skills.** The student applies critical-thinking skills to organize and use information acquired from a variety of sources, including electronic technology. The student is expected to: **(B)** analyze information by sequencing, categorizing, identifying cause-and-effect relationships, comparing, contrasting, finding the main idea, summarizing, making generalizations and predictions, and drawing inferences and conclusions. **(G)** support a point of view on a social studies issue or event.
4 The Ford Administration	**(1) History.** The student understands traditional historical points of reference in U.S. history from 1877 to the present. The student is expected to: **(B)** apply absolute and relative chronology through the sequencing of significant individuals, events, and time periods. **(24) Social studies skills.** The student applies critical-thinking skills to organize and use information acquired from a variety of sources, including electronic technology. The student is expected to: **(B)** analyze information by sequencing, categorizing, identifying cause-and-effect relationships, comparing, contrasting, finding the main idea, summarizing, making generalizations and predictions, and drawing inferences and conclusions.
5 The Carter Administration	**(17) Government.** The student understands the impact of constitutional issues on American society in the 20th century. The student is expected to: **(A)** analyze the effects of 20th-century landmark U.S. Supreme Court decisions such as *Brown* v. *Board of Education, Regents of the University of California* v. *Bakke,* and *Reynolds* v. *Sims.* **(26) Social studies skills.** The student uses problem-solving and decision-making skills, working independently and with others, in a variety of settings. The student is expected to: **(A)** use a problem-solving process to identify a problem, gather information, list and consider options, consider advantages and disadvantages, choose and implement a solution, and evaluate the effectiveness of the solution.

Chapter 25

Nixon, Ford, Carter

(1969–1981)

Introducing the Chapter

The election of President Nixon in 1968 led to a 24-year period of almost uninterrupted Republican control of the White House. The new President's domestic and foreign policies marked a shift in national politics. But Nixon's leadership style led to scandal and his own eventual downfall. Gerald Ford tried to heal the nation after the scandal, but the country's trust in its highest office was severely shaken. It was no surprise, then, when a Washington outsider, Jimmy Carter, was elected to the White House in 1976.

Time Line Activity

To provide students with practice in using the time line, ask questions such as these:

1. What 1973 event in the Middle East would have severe economic implications in the United States? *(The embargo on oil shipments imposed by the Arab members of OPEC)*
2. What 1978 event has had lasting international repercussions, even though it did not fully resolve a conflict? *(The Camp David Accords)*
3. What action taken by the Soviet Union in 1979 resulted in a 1980 U.S. Olympic boycott? *(The Soviet Union invaded Afghanistan.)*

Chapter 25

Nixon, Ford, Carter (1969–1981)

An intercontinental ballistic missile (ICBM)

Apollo 11 astronaut Buzz Aldrin

American Events

1969 The United States achieves the first moon landing.

1972 Nixon travels to China and the Soviet Union to pursue détente. The United States and the Soviet Union sign the SALT I treaty.

1973 Senate investigation of the Watergate scandal reveals White House involvement.

1974 Nixon becomes the first U.S. President to resign. Ford becomes the first nonelected Vice President to assume office as President.

Presidential Terms: Richard M. Nixon 1969–1974

1968 • 1970 • 1972 • 1974

World Events

1971 China joins the United Nations.

1973 OPEC imposes an embargo on oil shipments.

eTeach

Be sure to check out this month's online discussion with a Master Teacher. Go to **www.phschool.com**.

RESOURCE DIRECTORY

Teaching Resources

Pacing Charts booklet
Block Scheduling booklet, p. 29
Units 5/6/7 booklet
- Chapter Summary, p. 99

Technology

Guided Reading Audiotapes (English/Spanish), Ch. 25
Student Edition on Audio CD, Ch. 25
Prentice Hall United States History Video Collection™ Volume 20, *Post-War USA*
Prentice Hall Presentation Pro CD-ROM, Ch. 25
Resource Pro® CD-ROM
Social Studies Skills Tutor CD-ROM
Companion Web site, www.phschool.com

OPEC Nations, 1975

*Organization of Petroleum Exporting Countries

A 1976 bicentennial quarter

Jimmy Carter's less aggressive leadership style challenged the idea of an "imperial presidency."

1975 Ford signs the Helsinki Accords on European security.

1976 The United States celebrates the bicentennial of the signing of the Declaration of Independence.

1978 President Carter negotiates the Camp David Accords to promote peace in the Middle East.

1980 The United States leads a boycott of the Moscow summer Olympics.

1981 American hostages held in Iran are returned to the United States.

Gerald R. Ford 1974–1977 | Jimmy Carter 1977–1981 | Ronald Reagan 1981–1989

1976 · 1978 · 1980 · 1982

1975 Cambodia captures the *Mayaguez*, an American merchant ship.

1979 The Soviet Union invades Afghanistan.

1980 A rescue attempt fails to free American hostages in Iran.

OPEC Nations, 1975

Activating Prior Knowledge Which countries were Arab members of the Organization of Petroleum Exporting Countries (OPEC)? *(Kuwait, Iran, Iraq, Qatar, United Arab Emirates, and Saudi Arabia)*

Previewing How did these countries react when the United States backed Israel in its war with the Arab nations of Egypt and Syria in 1973? *(They stopped shipping oil to the United States, and OPEC greatly increased its prices to other countries.)*

Background
About the Pictures

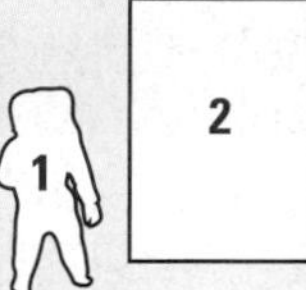

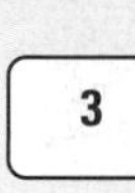

1. Buzz Aldrin was part of the *Apollo 11* crew, along with Neil Armstrong and Michael Collins. He was the second person to walk on the moon.
2. Some of the first U.S. ICBMs to go operational were the *Atlantis* and the *Titan I*, capable of travelling 7,500 miles and 6,300 miles, respectively.
3. After the Watergate scandal, Nixon resigned, saying he "no longer had a strong enough political base" to stay in office.
4. In 1976 thousands of communities across the United States held various festivals and celebrations in honor of the Declaration of Independence and the events that led to its creation.
5. Before leaving office, Carter was able to create an environmental "superfund" to go toward any disasters that might occur, and he set aside 100 million acres of Alaskan land for preservation.

Bibliography

For the Teacher

Lukas, J. Anthony. ***Common Ground: A Turbulent Decade in the Lives of Three American Families.*** Vintage, 1986. (A study of the impact of school busing on three economically diverse families.)

Wills, Garry. ***Nixon Agonistes: The Crisis of the Self-Made Man.*** Cherokee Publishing Company, 1990. (A critical and probing analysis of Richard Nixon and his most famous crisis.)

For the Student

The Right Stuff. Bantam, 1983. (Award-winning look at astronauts, based on Tom Wolfe's best-seller.)

All the President's Men. Warner Home Video, 1976. Video. (Fast-paced depiction of *Washington Post* reporters Bob Woodward and Carl Bernstein and the story they uncovered about the Watergate break-in.)

Don't miss the exclusive interactive version of this textbook on the Web and on CD-ROM.

Section 1 Nixon's Domestic Policy

Section Objectives

1. Find out how Richard Nixon's personality affected his relationship with his staff.
2. See how Nixon's domestic policies differed from those of his predecessors.
3. Learn how Nixon applied his "southern strategy" to the issue of civil rights and to the selection of Supreme Court justices.
4. Describe the first moon landing.

Bellringer

Warm-Up Activity Write the word *leadership* on the chalkboard. Ask students to list ideas they associate with this term. Explain that Nixon, upon taking office, exercised a new type of leadership.

Activating Prior Knowledge Ask students to state what they already know about Nixon's presidency. What were important national issues at the time of his election? What did his successful election indicate about the mood of the country?

Reading Strategy

Have students list the section headings, and as they read, have them add supporting information so that after reading the section, they can outline its main points.

Background

Connections to Today

When Richard Milhous Nixon died on April 22, 1994, at age eighty-one, biographer Garry Wills wrote of him: "In some areas of politics, he seemed to know almost everything about anything—except about himself. His strengths and weaknesses fed upon each other. He was a small bitter man and a very grand diplomat. Who can read that riddle? Some of us have spent much of our lives trying to read it, with little better success than his own."

Section 1 Nixon's Domestic Policy

READING FOCUS

- How did Richard Nixon's personality affect his relationship with his staff?
- How did Nixon's domestic policies differ from those of his predecessors?
- How did Nixon apply his "southern strategy" to the issue of civil rights and to his choice of Supreme Court justices?
- Describe the first manned moon landing.

KEY TERMS

deficit spending
Organization of Petroleum Exporting Countries (OPEC)
embargo
New Federalism

TAKING NOTES

Copy the chart below. As you read, fill in details about the Nixon administration. Add more boxes as needed.

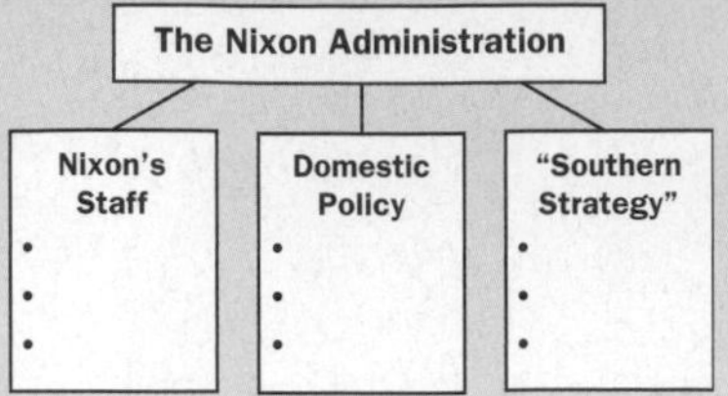

MAIN IDEA

President Richard Nixon relied on several close advisors to help him move the country in a new direction.

Although he was a private man, Nixon loved the applause of a crowd.

Setting the Scene Richard Nixon's victory in 1968 was, for him, particularly sweet. His earlier bid for the presidency, in 1960, had failed. Two years later he had lost another election, for governor of California. Deeply unhappy, Nixon had vowed to retire from politics. Instead, he came back from those bitter defeats to win the nation's highest office at a time when the country sorely needed strong leadership.

Nixon grew up in a low-income family in Whittier, California. He never got over his sense of being an outsider. In 1963, he described how that feeling drove him to achieve:

> " *What starts the process really are laughs and slights and snubs when you are a kid. Sometimes it's because you're poor or Irish or Jewish or Catholic or ugly or simply that you are skinny. But if you are reasonably intelligent and if your anger is deep enough and strong enough, you learn that you can change those attitudes by excellence, personal gut performance. . . .* "
>
> —Richard Nixon, 1963

Nixon in Person

Unlike most politicians, Richard Nixon was a reserved and remote man. Uncomfortable with people, he often seemed stiff and lacking in humor and charm. He overcame these drawbacks by using modern campaign techniques to get his message across.

Many Americans looked beyond Nixon's personality traits. They respected him for his experience and his service as Vice President under Eisenhower. Many others, though, neither trusted nor liked him.

According to Patrick Buchanan, then a Nixon speech writer, there was "a mean side to his nature." He was willing to say or do anything to defeat his

RESOURCE DIRECTORY

Teaching Resources
Guided Reading and Review booklet, p. 128

Technology
Section Reading Support Transparencies
Guided Reading Audiotapes (English/Spanish), Ch. 25
Student Edition on Audio CD, Ch. 25
RESOURCE PRO® Visual Learning Activity *The Imperial President,* found on Resource Pro, depicts what some people termed Nixon's "imperial presidency" in two humorous posters from the early 1970s.

Prentice Hall Presentation Pro CD-ROM, Ch. 25
Companion Web site, www.phschool.com

enemies. Those enemies included his political opponents, the government bureaucracy, the press corps, and leaders of the antiwar movement.

Nixon was fully prepared to confront these forces. He wrote, "I believe in the battle, whether it's the battle of the campaign or the battle of this office, which is a continuing battle. It's always there wherever you go."

Insulating himself from people and the press, Nixon had few close friends. He found support and security in his family: his wife Pat and their two daughters. He also established lasting associations with several activists in his political campaigns. Away from the White House, he stayed far from crowds by spending time at his estates in Florida and California.

Nixon believed the executive branch of government had to be strong to be successful. When he took office, he gathered a close circle of trusted advisors around him to pursue that goal.

Nixon's Staff

Cabinet members, representatives of the executive branch departments, have historically been a President's top advisors. Many have been independent-minded people. More than most other post–World War II Presidents, Nixon avoided his Cabinet and preferred to rely on his White House staff to develop his policies. Staff members were team players. They gave him unwavering loyalty.

Two key appointees had direct access to Nixon. They shielded him from the outside world and carried out his orders. One was H. R. Haldeman, an advertising executive who had campaigned tirelessly for Nixon. He became chief of staff. Haldeman once summarized how he served the President: "I get done what he wants done and I take the heat instead of him." The other key staffer was lawyer John Ehrlichman. Ehrlichman served as Nixon's personal lawyer and rose to the post of chief domestic advisor.

Haldeman and Ehrlichman framed issues and narrowed options for the President. They also stood between the President and anybody else who wanted to speak to him. Together they became known as the "Berlin Wall" for the way they protected Nixon's privacy.

A third trusted advisor was John Mitchell, a lawyer. Mitchell had worked with Nixon in New York and had managed his presidential campaign. Nixon asked him to be Attorney General just after the 1968 election. Mitchell had great influence with the President, often speaking with him several times a day.

Another of Nixon's closest advisors did not fit the mold of Haldeman, Ehrlichman, and Mitchell. Henry Kissinger, a Harvard government professor, had no previous ties to Nixon. Still, he acquired tremendous power in the Nixon White House. Nixon first appointed Kissinger to be his national security advisor, and then, in 1973, to be Secretary of State. Kissinger played a major role in shaping foreign policy, both as an advisor to the President and in behind-the-scenes diplomacy.

VIEWING HISTORY The Oval Office in the White House saw many meetings of Nixon and his inner circle of advisors. Left to right in this photo are Kissinger, Ehrlichman, the President, and Haldeman. **Synthesizing Information** *What role did Nixon's advisors play in his presidency?*

Domestic Policy

The Vietnam War and domestic policy had both been important in the 1968 political campaign. As you have read, restoring law and order was one element of Nixon's domestic policy. Other domestic issues also required attention, and on these, Nixon broke with many of the policies of Presidents Kennedy and Johnson.

Lesson Plan

Focus Explain that as President, Nixon displayed a penchant for secrecy that would develop into an obsession. Point out that this trait would have an important impact on Nixon's presidency.

Instruct Explain that domestically, Nixon hoped to steer the nation in a more conservative direction than had his Democratic predecessors. This proved difficult in the realm of economics, where inflation caused by war spending forced Nixon to act contrary to his stated goals. Explain that the oil crisis further aggravated the nation's economic problems. Discuss the nation's dependence on petroleum. Ask students what might happen if fuel prices rose suddenly today. Point out Nixon's greater success in instituting conservative policies in the area of social programs and law and order.

Assess/Reteach Ask students how Nixon's domestic advisers helped implement his plans. Can students describe how important it is for a President to select a cabinet that represents his views?

Customize for ...

ESL

Ask students to read the quotation by Richard Nixon on the previous page. Ask how Nixon's personal characteristics and the qualities he valued in his aides are reflected in this quote. In the discussion, have students choose specific words or phrases from the quotation that best reveal Nixon's sensibility.

Test Preparation

Have students read the quotation by Nixon in the second paragraph on this page and then complete the sentence below.

From the quote, you can infer that Nixon—

A believed the three branches of government should work together.

B was prepared to take a passive role in government.

C thought that he could trust most people in the government.

(D) was suspicious of people and took an aggressive stance as President.

Caption Answers

Viewing History They analyzed information for him, provided advice, carried out his orders, protected him from criticism, and guarded his privacy.

ACTIVITY
Connecting with Economics

Invite students to imagine they are members of the President's Council of Economic Advisors in 1973. Have them use information from the graph on this page to write a short report to the President summarizing economic trends since 1968 and suggesting actions the President might take to deal with any undesirable conditions that have developed. What actions might the government take to expand economic opportunities to all citizens? **(Logical/Mathematical; Verbal/Linguistic)**

BACKGROUND
Oil and the Economy

Few products had as great an influence on the American economy in the 1970s as oil—an influence that continues today. Crude oil is the main component of gasoline and other fuels that power automobiles, trucks, trains, planes, and ships. It is also used to generate heat and electricity for the nation's factories and their machines. Thus, oil prices influence not only what it costs to transport a product, but also the cost of manufacturing it. In addition, petrochemicals derived from petroleum are major components in products such as plastics, fertilizer, synthetic rubber and other fibers, paints, solvents, and many other cleaning agents. Rising oil prices increase the cost of these products as well as all other products that use or are made from them.

READING CHECK

The United States was already headed for an energy crisis due to the growing population, the low output of natural gas, the nation's decline in oil production, price controls on domestic oil, underutilization of coal as a fuel, and the nation's dependency upon imported oil.

CAPTION ANSWERS

Interpreting Graphs 1974. Increased energy needs, underutilization of coal and natural gas, decreased domestic production of oil, price controls on domestic oil mandated by Nixon, and especially the Arab Oil Embargo of 1973.

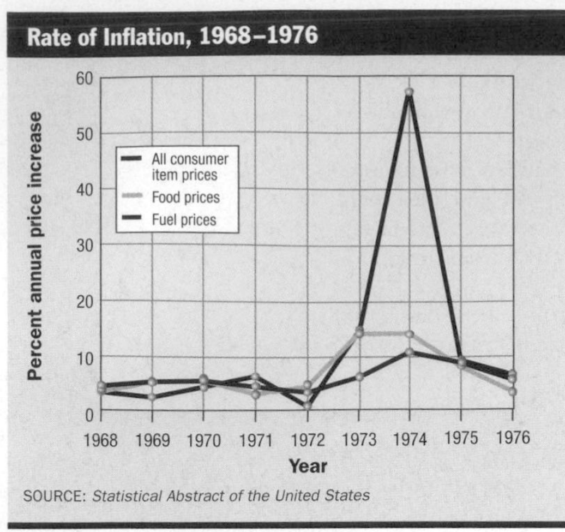

INTERPRETING GRAPHS
Rising oil prices in the 1970s had a strong impact on all parts of the American economy. **Analyzing Information** *When did fuel prices reach their peak? What caused fuel prices to rise so dramatically?*

Inflation The economy was shaky when Nixon took office. Largely because of rising spending for the Vietnam War, inflation had doubled between 1965 and 1968. In addition, the government was spending more than it was taking in from taxes, so the budget deficit was growing. Unemployment was also growing.

Nixon's first priority was to halt inflation. He wanted to bring federal spending under control, even if it led to further unemployment. He was determined, though, to avoid imposing government controls on wages and prices. He had seen such controls in action while working for the Office of Price Administration during World War II. "I will not take the nation down the road of wage and price controls, however politically expedient [helpful] they may seem," he said in 1970.

During Nixon's first few years in office, however, federal spending proved difficult to control. Unemployment and inflation both continued to rise. Although Republicans traditionally aimed for a balanced budget, Nixon began to consider **deficit spending,** or spending more money in a year than the government receives in revenues. In this way he hoped to stimulate the economy. Proposed by British economist John Maynard Keynes during the Great Depression, deficit spending had restored prosperity during World War II. "I am now a Keynesian in economics," Nixon announced in 1971, to many people's surprise.

Finally, in an attempt to slow the high rate of inflation, the President imposed a 90-day freeze on wages, prices, and rents in August 1971, and a 60-day general price freeze in June 1973. Pressure from business and labor, however, led him to lift these controls, and inflation again soared.

Oil Crisis In some ways, the United States had been heading toward an energy crisis long before Nixon took office. The nation's growing population and economy used more energy each year. Coal was plentiful, but environmental concerns discouraged its use. Federal regulations imposed in the mid-1950s kept the price of natural gas low, which meant producers had little incentive to raise their output. Furthermore, the nation's oil production began to decline in 1972. Americans depended on cheap, imported oil for about a third of their energy needs.

READING CHECK
What was the state of the nation's fuel supply before the oil embargo?

Nixon's oil price controls served to aggravate the energy problem. Refineries let supplies run so low during the price freezes that demand could not be met after the controls were lifted.

Unrest in the Middle East turned the energy problem into a crisis. In 1973, Israel and the Arab nations of Egypt and Syria went to war. The United States backed its ally Israel. In response, the Arab members of the **Organization of Petroleum Exporting Countries (OPEC)** imposed an **embargo,** or ban, on the shipping of oil to the United States. OPEC, a group of nations that cooperates to set oil prices and production levels, also quadrupled its prices. The cost of foreign oil skyrocketed.

Higher oil prices, in turn, worsened inflation. A loaf of bread that had cost 28 cents earlier in the 1970s now cost 89 cents. Americans had paid 25 cents a gallon for gas but now paid 65 cents. Consumers reacted to the higher prices by cutting back on spending. The result was a recession.

RESOURCE DIRECTORY

Teaching Resources
Great Debates booklet (Decision-Making Activity) *Redistributing Government Power,* p. 46

Other Print Resources
American History Block Scheduling Support *Presidential Power: Changes in the Twentieth Century,* found in The Nation After World War II folder, includes interdisciplinary lesson suggestions and activities for Geography and History, Primary Sources, Biography, and Literature.

Technology
Color Transparencies *Historical Maps,* A57
RESOURCE PRO® **Biography** *Maggie Kuhn,* found on Resource Pro, profiles the founder of the Gray Panthers, a protest movement that emerged in the early 1970s.

Social Programs President Nixon hoped to halt the growth of government spending by cutting back or shutting down some of the social programs that had mushroomed under Johnson's Great Society. Critics claimed that these programs were wasteful, encouraged "welfare cheaters," and discouraged people from seeking work.

Nixon had voiced similar complaints in his campaign, but he now faced a dilemma. On the one hand, he wanted to please conservative voters who demanded cutbacks. On the other hand, he hoped to appeal to traditionally Democratic blue-collar voters and others who favored social programs.

Nixon called for a new partnership between the federal government and the state governments known as the **New Federalism.** Under this policy, states would assume greater responsibility for the well-being of their own citizens. Congress passed a series of "revenue-sharing" bills that granted federal funds to state and local governments to use as they wished.

The "Southern Strategy"

Nixon believed he had little to gain by supporting advances in civil rights. Few African Americans had voted for him in the 1960 race against John Kennedy, and in 1968, he had won just 12 percent of the black vote. Besides, he reasoned, any attempt to appeal to black voters might cost him the support of many white southern voters.

Explaining his position, Nixon once observed that "there are those who want instant integration and those who want segregation forever. I believe that we need to have a middle course between those two extremes." In effect, this meant a slowdown in desegregation.

Nixon's aim was to find the proper "southern strategy" to win over white southern Democrats. Republican Senator Strom Thurmond of South Carolina, who had left the Democratic Party in 1948, became Nixon's strongest southern

Energy Shortages

Oil shortages caused enormous frustration in the United States during the 1970s. As shown in the photo left, lines at gas stations were long, often extending for blocks. Many people began to buy energy-efficient foreign cars instead of the "gas-guzzling" American models. Midwestern farmers had difficulty finding fuel to dry out their crops before they spoiled. Winter heating-oil shortages led to school closings in Colorado.

Electricity shortages can also cause hardships. When disruption is minor, an area may experience a brownout, a temporary reduction in electrical power. Blackouts, complete cuts to power, are more serious. Recently, electricity shortages forced "rolling blackouts" in California, shutting off power to selected areas at hours of peak usage. Homes and businesses without alternative energy sources, such as gas-powered generators or solar energy, could not operate computers or other electrical machines and appliances. Low supplies also meant higher prices, which demonstrators (above) in California protested by burning their electricity bills. In any state, energy shortages can have serious negative effects on the economy.

? How are oil shortages of the 1970s similar to more recent energy shortages?

ACTIVITY
Connecting with Citizenship

Organize students in pairs to develop a "southern strategy" for the Democratic Party to help presidential candidate George McGovern win the South in the 1972 election. Have them present their strategy in a memo to the Democratic National Committee. Then call on pairs to explain their strategy and the reasoning behind it to the class. **(Verbal/ Linguistic)**

BACKGROUND
Presidential Power

One way Nixon cut government programs he did not like was through impoundment, a practice whereby a President refuses to spend money allocated by Congress. The Constitution is silent on whether the President must spend all the funds Congress appropriates, and Presidents dating back to Jefferson had practiced impoundment. But Nixon's use was unprecedented in both its scope and intent. By 1973 he had impounded more than $20 billion, much of which Congress had earmarked for construction of low-rent housing, mass transit, food stamps, and medical research. In 1974 Congress retaliated by passing the Congressional Budget and Impoundment Control Act, which limited a President's ability to impound appropriated funds and established the budget process the federal government uses today.

CAPTION ANSWERS

Fast Forward to Today The United States is still heavily dependent upon oil for the nation's energy needs. Much of this oil is still obtained from overseas suppliers. Domestic production of oil in the United States continues to be inadequate for the nation's needs.

ACTIVITY
Connecting with Government

Have students write newspaper "help wanted" ads for a Supreme Court justice in the late 1960s or early 1970s. Tell them to consider what characteristics President Nixon would want in someone he would appoint to the Court as they list required qualifications for the position in their ads. **(Verbal/Linguistic)**

BACKGROUND
Geography in History

Despite the introduction of busing, the desegregation movement rapidly lost relevance for northern cities. Many middle-class white Americans abandoned city schools for suburban school districts and private schools in the 1960s and 1970s. This exodus, sometimes called "white flight," created de facto segregation in states like New Jersey and New York. A Harvard Graduate School of Education study noted in the late 1990s that the most drastic shift toward resegregation since 1954 took place between 1991 and 1994. By 1997 the 10 largest inner-city school districts in the United States had African American and Hispanic majorities.

VIEWING HISTORY In 1974, police escorts help Boston schools to comply with court-ordered busing. **Drawing Conclusions** *Why did Nixon oppose busing?*

supporter. To keep Thurmond and his colleagues happy, Nixon sought to cut funding for the enforcement of fair housing laws. He also made it easier to meet desegregation requirements.

The Justice Department, headed by John Mitchell, tried to prevent the extension of certain provisions of the Voting Rights Act of 1965 that were due to expire in 1970. This law had greatly increased the number of African Americans who could vote in the South. Congress went ahead with the extension, but through the efforts of his Attorney General, Nixon had made his point to white southern voters.

Another controversial racial issue was the use of busing to end school segregation. In several cities, federal courts ordered school systems to bus students to other schools in order to end the pattern of all-black or all-white schools. Particularly in northern cities, such as Detroit and Boston, some white students and their parents responded to busing with boycotts or violent protests.

In 1971, the Supreme Court issued guidelines for busing that went against Nixon's views. A federal judge in North Carolina had ruled that voluntary integration was not working. In *Swann* v. *Charlotte-Mecklenburg Board of Education,* the Court agreed, saying that busing was one possible option for ending school segregation.

Nixon, who had long opposed busing, then went on television to say he would ask Congress to halt it. He also allowed the Department of Health, Education, and Welfare to restore federal funding to school districts that were still segregated. Nixon's refusal to enforce the Court ruling did not halt busing in the country, but his opposition did limit it.

Focus on GOVERNMENT

The Imperial Presidency Nixon took a broad view of his powers as President of the United States and is counted among several Presidents, including Andrew Jackson and Theodore Roosevelt, who sought to expand the powers of the office. Nixon worked to extend executive privileges to include rights historically reserved for kings and emperors, such as the right to use public funds at his discretion and the right to shield himself from prosecution. Because of these efforts, Nixon contributed to what came to be called the "imperial presidency." The term is sometimes used by critics who think the powers of the presidency have become too strong.

Nixon's Supreme Court

During the election campaign, Nixon had criticized the Supreme Court for being too liberal and easy on criminals. In his first term, four of the nine justices either died, resigned, or retired. This gave him the extraordinary opportunity to name four new justices and thus reshape the Court. Nixon first named Warren Burger as Chief Justice, replacing Earl Warren. Burger, a moderate, was easily confirmed by the Senate in 1969.

CAPTION ANSWERS

Viewing History Nixon was opposed to "instant integration," and busing would fall under that heading. Nixon made little, if any, effort to win the votes of African Americans, who were never a part of his election strategy. Also, desegregation was not favored by the white southern Democrats Nixon *was* trying to win over.

RESOURCE DIRECTORY

Teaching Resources

Units 5/6/7 booklet
- Section 1 Quiz, p. 100

Guide to the Essentials
- Section 1 Summary, p. 121

Later nominations reflected Nixon's southern strategy and conservative views. The Senate rejected his first two nominees from the South, with opponents charging the men showed racial bias. Nixon successfully appointed Harry A. Blackmun (1970); Lewis F. Powell, Jr. (1972); and William H. Rehnquist (1972). All three were respected jurists who generally tilted the Court in a more conservative direction. As Justice Blackmun's tenure continued, however, he became increasingly liberal in his decisions.

The First Moon Landing

The Nixon years witnessed the fulfillment of President Kennedy's commitment in 1961 to achieve the goal, "before this decade is out, of landing a man on the moon." That man was *Apollo 11* astronaut Neil A. Armstrong.

On July 20, 1969, at 10:56 P.M. Eastern Daylight Time, Armstrong descended from the *Eagle* lunar landing craft and set foot on the moon's surface. Armstrong radioed back the famous message: "That's one small step for man, one giant leap for mankind."

VIEWING HISTORY Astronaut Buzz Aldrin takes a walk on the moon. **Drawing Inferences** *Why was the government so committed to the space program?*

Television viewers around the world witnessed this triumph of the *Apollo* program, carried out by the National Aeronautics and Space Administration (NASA). The *Apollo 11* crew included Edwin E. "Buzz" Aldrin, Jr., who landed with Armstrong in the *Eagle,* and Michael Collins, who remained in the *Apollo 11* command module circling the moon.

Aldrin joined Armstrong in the two-hour moon walk, during which they collected rock and soil samples and set up scientific instruments to monitor conditions on the moon. They also photographed the landing site, a dusty plain in an area called the Sea of Tranquillity.

The *Eagle* and its crew stayed on the moon for 21 hours and 36 minutes before lifting off to rejoin Collins for the return trip. After a safe splashdown, the astronauts were quarantined for 18 days to ensure that they had not picked up any unknown lunar microbes. They emerged to a hero's welcome.

Section 1 Assessment

READING COMPREHENSION

1. What is **deficit spending?** How did Nixon attempt to control inflation?
2. Why was the United States vulnerable to **OPEC?**
3. How did the 1973 oil **embargo** affect the United States?
4. What was the **New Federalism?**
5. Describe the busing issues and events of the 1970s.

CRITICAL THINKING AND WRITING

6. **Recognizing Bias** How was Nixon's image of himself as an outsider reflected in the way he ran the White House? Use specific examples in your explanation.
7. **Writing to Persuade** Write an outline for a persuasive essay either supporting or opposing Nixon's domestic policies.

Take It to the NET

Activity: Writing a Newspaper Article Research an area of President Nixon's domestic policy, and write a newspaper article on the topic you selected. Use the links provided in the *America: Pathways to the Present* area of the following Web site for help in completing this activity.
www.phschool.com

Section 1 Assessment

Reading Comprehension

1. Spending more money in a year than the government receives in revenues.
2. The United States depended on cheap, imported oil for about one-third of its energy needs.
3. Foreign oil prices skyrocketed; inflation worsened; and higher prices caused people to cut back on spending, which resulted in a recession.
4. A partnership between the federal government and the state governments granting the states greater responsibility for the well-being of their own citizens. This included the introduction of block grants of federal money to states. The individual states then decided how to spend their respective federal grants.
5. Federal courts in several cities ordered school systems to desegregate immediately by busing African American students to formerly all-white schools and vice versa. Boycotts and violent protests resulted in some (mostly northern) cities. The Supreme Court ruled in favor of busing, but Nixon impeded the process. He asked Congress, unsuccessfully, to halt busing, and he restored federal funding to segregated school districts.

Critical Thinking and Writing

6. Sample answer: His penchant for secrecy, and the fact that Nixon essentially ignored his Cabinet and relied instead on a very small circle of advisors.
7. Outlines will vary but should persuade the reader by using facts from the section.

Articles will vary, but should demonstrate an understanding of Nixon's domestic policies overall, with a focus on one particular issue.

Caption Answers

Viewing History Sample answer: To win the "space race" that had been going on for a decade between the United States and the Soviet Union.

Section 2
Nixon's Foreign Policy

Section Objectives

1. Learn about the role Henry Kissinger played in relaxing tensions between the United States and the major Communist powers.
2. Find out about Nixon's policy toward the People's Republic of China.
3. Discover how Nixon reached an agreement with the Soviet Union on limiting nuclear arms.

Bellringer

Warm-Up Activity Present students with the following situation: The United States is locked in a costly competition with powerful enemies for influence around the world, and no one is winning. How should the United States break the stalemate? Explain that Nixon faced a similar predicament during his presidency.

Activating Prior Knowledge Ask students to state what they know about relations between the United States and China in the years following World War II, leading up to the 1970s. Was there open dialogue and freedom of movement between the two countries at that time?

Reading Strategy

As students read the section, have them take notes on the following topics: (a) Henry Kissinger and American foreign policy; (b) United States relations with China; and (c) United States relations with the Soviet Union. Have students consider the challenges of changing relationships among nations.

Section 2

Nixon's Foreign Policy

READING FOCUS

- What role did Henry Kissinger play in relaxing tensions between the United States and the major Communist powers?
- What was Nixon's policy toward the People's Republic of China?
- How did Nixon reach an agreement with the Soviet Union on limiting nuclear arms?

MAIN IDEA

President Nixon's foreign policy led to more positive relationships with China and the Soviet Union.

KEY TERMS

realpolitik
détente
SALT I

TAKING NOTES

Copy the web diagram below. Include three or four blank circles. As you read, fill in each blank circle with important facts about U.S. relations with China and the Soviet Union during Nixon's presidency.

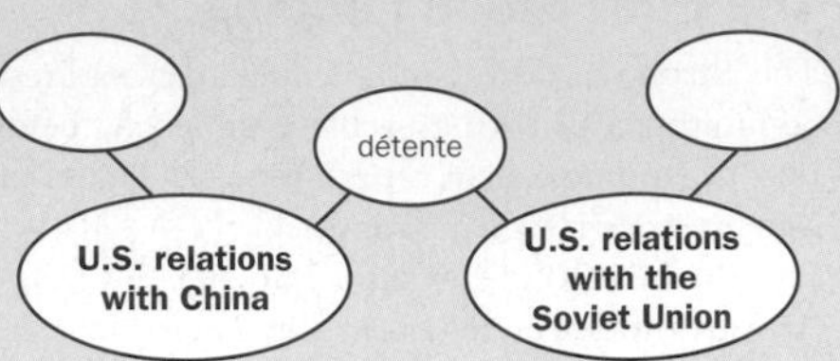

VIEWING HISTORY President Nixon owed the success of much of his foreign policy to his national security advisor, and later, Secretary of State, Henry Kissinger. **Demonstrating Reasoned Judgment** *Why did Nixon rely so heavily on Kissinger's advice?*

Setting the Scene As President, Richard Nixon's greatest achievements came in the field of foreign policy. "I've always thought this country could run itself domestically without a President," he observed. In his first Inaugural Address, Nixon set the stage for a new direction in foreign relations:

> *"After a period of confrontation, we are entering an era of negotiation. Let all nations know that during this administration our lines of communication will be open. We seek an open world. Open to ideas, open to the exchange of goods and people. A world in which no people, great or small, will live in angry isolation. We cannot expect to make everyone our friend, but we can try to make no one our enemy."*
>
> —Nixon's First Inaugural Address, January 20, 1969

Nixon's creative approach to foreign affairs helped ease Cold War tensions. Aided by the skillful diplomacy of Henry Kissinger, Nixon helped establish ties with China and crafted stronger relations with the Soviet Union.

Henry Kissinger

While Nixon had a keen understanding of foreign policy, he relied heavily on Henry Kissinger in charting his course. Kissinger quickly gained the President's confidence. By the time Nixon appointed Kissinger Secretary of State in 1973, he was a dominant figure in the administration.

Practical Politics Kissinger had written his doctoral dissertation on Klemens von Metternich, an Austrian statesman and diplomat in the nineteenth century who had helped maintain stability in Europe amid liberal change. Kissinger's studies in European history gave him an admiration for ***realpolitik,*** a German term meaning "practical politics." Nations that follow this policy make decisions based on maintaining their own strength rather than following moral principles. Kissinger would later apply this approach to his dealings with China and the Soviet Union.

RESOURCE DIRECTORY

Teaching Resources
Learning Styles Lesson Plans booklet, p. 66
Guided Reading and Review booklet, p. 129

Technology
Section Reading Support Transparencies
Guided Reading Audiotapes (English/Spanish), Ch. 25
Student Edition on Audio CD, Ch. 25
Color Transparencies *Time Lines,* C9
Prentice Hall Presentation Pro CD-ROM, Ch. 25
Companion Web site, www.phschool.com

Caption Answers

Viewing History Kissinger was a foreign affairs expert, and he knew how to persuade Nixon. The two men had much in common. For instance, both were by nature intensely suspicious. Nixon and Kissinger also both liked to operate under a cloak of secrecy.

Nixon liked to be flattered, and he liked people who could talk tough. Kissinger, who understood what Nixon wanted from an advisor, soon became the man Nixon talked to most. "Henry, of course, was not a personal friend," Nixon later said, but the two spoke five or six times a day, sometimes in person, sometimes by phone, and often for hours at a time.

Both men were suspicious and secretive. They tended not to seek consensus, or general agreement with others, but to keep information to themselves. "They tried not to let anyone else have a full picture, even if it meant deceiving them," noted Lawrence Eagleburger, a State Department official.

Kissinger's actual influence in shaping American foreign policy was broader than his official role as Secretary of State. He knew how to frame questions in ways the President wanted. He could condense complex foreign policy issues into briefing papers that gave Nixon clear options for making decisions. In his memoirs, Kissinger wrote:

> "Nixon could be very decisive. Almost invariably during his Presidency, his decisions were courageous and strong and often taken in loneliness against all expert advice. But wherever possible Nixon made these decisions in solitude on the basis of memoranda or with a few very intimate aides."
>
> —Henry Kissinger, *The White House Years*

Public Opinion Kissinger also understood the power of the press. He had a remarkable ability to use the media to shape public opinion. Journalists depended on him for stories, so they were afraid to anger him. "You know you are being played like a violin," a *Time* magazine reporter observed, "but it's still extremely seductive."

Kissinger's efforts in ending the Vietnam War and easing Cold War tensions made him a celebrity. He shared the 1973 Nobel peace prize with North Vietnam's Le Duc Tho (who refused it); he appeared on 21 *Time* magazine covers; and in a 1973 Gallup poll, he led the list of the most-admired Americans. Kissinger's efforts in the Nixon administration left a lasting mark on American foreign policy.

American BIOGRAPHY

Henry Kissinger
b. 1923

Like a number of other German Jews, 15-year-old Henry Kissinger and his family fled Nazi Germany in 1938 and settled in New York City. During the day, the young immigrant worked at a shaving brush company. At night he completed high school courses. Kissinger became a naturalized citizen in 1943, and served in the United States Army during World War II. Kissinger had attended City College of New York before the war and later transferred to Harvard. There he completed both undergraduate and graduate degrees. As a Harvard professor, Kissinger became a recognized expert on foreign relations. Nixon lured him away from Harvard in 1969 by offering him a job as his national security advisor.

After his years in Washington, D.C., Kissinger went on to become a foreign policy consultant and lecturer. He has written several books, including the first volume of his memoirs, *The White House Years* (1979).

Relaxing Tensions

Nixon and Kissinger's greatest accomplishment was in bringing about **détente,** or a relaxation in tensions, between the United States and the world's two Communist giants. China and the Soviet Union were sworn enemies of the United States. Nixon's willingness to conduct talks with them stunned many observers. In the 1950s, Nixon had been one of the most bitter and active anti-Communists in government. He had made his reputation by demanding that the United States stand firm against the Communist threat.

As President, however, Nixon dealt imaginatively with both China and the Soviet Union. Nixon distrusted government bureaucracy, so he kept much of his diplomacy secret. Bypassing Congress, and often bypassing his own advisors, he and Kissinger reversed the direction of postwar American foreign policy.

Nixon drew on Kissinger's understanding that foreign affairs were more complex than a simple standoff between the United States and communism.

READING CHECK
What were some obstacles to achieving détente?

LESSON PLAN

Focus Tell students that Nixon hoped to have an especially powerful impact as President in the field of foreign policy. Ask students to evaluate the success of Nixon's efforts.

Instruct Discuss the role of Henry Kissinger in shaping Nixon's foreign policy. What skills made Kissinger such a valued aide? What did he offer Nixon that other advisers could not? Tell students that relations with China improved during Nixon's presidency. Ask how Nixon's reputation as a strong anti-Communist enabled him to approach China.

Assess/Reteach Ask students to consider some of the long-term impacts of the reestablishment of diplomatic relations between the United States and China. Have students answer this question from political, economic, social, and cultural perspectives.

ACTIVITY
Connecting with History and Conflict

During the Nixon administration, United States relations with the Soviet Union and China changed dramatically as Nixon negotiated with these countries to resolve long-standing conflicts. Ask students to think of the different ways in which conflicts are resolved. Have them work in small groups to choose a conflict experienced by a member of the group. Then have groups list three ways in which the conflict might be resolved, and evaluate the benefits and drawbacks of each method. **(Verbal/Linguistic; Logical/Mathematical)**

READING CHECK
The fact that China and the Soviet Union were sworn enemies of the U.S.; Nixon having been a bitter and active anti-Communist in the 1950s; American relations with mainland China and the Soviet Union had been poor for the previous two decades.

TEST PREPARATION

Have students read the quotation by Henry Kissinger on this page and then complete the sentence below.

Kissinger means by the phrase "taken in loneliness" that—

A Nixon had no one to help him.
(B) Nixon's decisions went against the advice most people gave him.
C Nixon was a lonely man.
D Nixon insisted on making decisions with no outside help or advice.

ACTIVITY
Connecting with Citizenship

Have students create a campaign document that could be used to inform voters about key components of Nixon's foreign policy. Ask students to highlight people and strategies employed by Nixon during his administration. **(Visual/Spatial)**

BACKGROUND
Geography in History

The split between China and the Soviet Union began in 1956 after Soviet Premier Nikita Khrushchev denounced the policies of Josef Stalin and crushed a rebellion in Hungary. Chinese leaders worried because Stalin's economic and political policies were the model for Communist China's policies, and because in suppressing the Hungarian Revolution the Soviets seemed to be forcing their style of communism on other Communist nations. By 1960 continued Soviet criticism of China's policies, coupled with Khrushchev's withdrawal of Soviet aid, brought an open split, and both nations fortified their long common border. When border clashes occurred between Chinese and Soviet forces in the late 1960s, China's leaders felt the need to look to the West for protection from their former ally.

VIEWING HISTORY Chinese premier Zhou Enlai and President Richard Nixon congratulate each other on the new ties between their nations. **Determining Relevance** *Why was it important for the press to capture such moments?*

The Soviet Union and China, once allies, had become bitter enemies. This stunning development had the potential to reshape global politics. "The deepest international conflict in the world today," Kissinger noted, "is not between us and the Soviet Union but between the Soviet Union and Communist China."

A New Approach to China

The most surprising policy shift was toward China. In 1949, the Communists had taken power and established the People's Republic of China. Many Americans saw all Communists as part of a united plot to dominate the world. As a result, the United States did not formally recognize the new Chinese government. In effect, the United States officially pretended that it did not exist.

Even when the Chinese-Soviet alliance crumbled, the United States clung to its position. It insisted that the government of Jiang Jieshi, which was set up on the island of Taiwan when the Nationalists fled the Chinese mainland, was the rightful government of all China.

Opportunity for Change Quietly, Nixon began to prepare the way for a new policy of *realpolitik*. His first foreign policy report to Congress in 1970 began:

> “*The Chinese are a great and vital people who should not remain isolated from the international community. . . . United States policy is not likely soon to have much impact on China's behavior, let alone its ideological outlook. But it is certainly in our interest, and in the interest of peace and stability in Asia and the world, that we take what steps we can toward improved practical relations with Peking [Beijing].*”
>
> —Richard Nixon, report to Congress, 1970

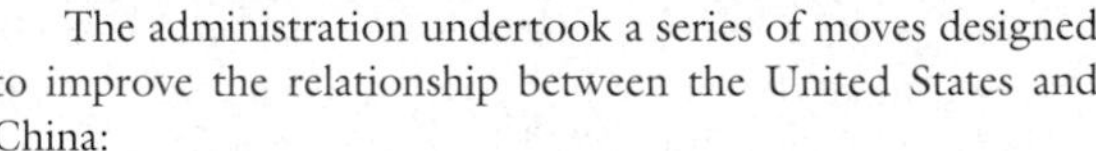

The President and First Lady Pat Nixon head a group touring the Great Wall of China.

The administration undertook a series of moves designed to improve the relationship between the United States and China:

1. In January and February 1970, American and Chinese ambassadors met in Warsaw, Poland.
2. In October 1970, in a first for an American President, Nixon referred to China by its official title, the People's Republic of China.
3. In March 1971, the United States government lifted restrictions on travel to China.
4. In April 1971, an American table-tennis team accepted a Chinese invitation to visit the mainland, beginning what was called "ping-pong diplomacy."
5. In June 1971, the United States ended its 21-year embargo on trade with the People's Republic of China.

In July 1971, after extensive secret diplomacy by Kissinger, Nixon made the dramatic announcement that he planned to visit China the following year. He would be the first United States President ever to travel to that country.

Nixon understood that the People's Republic was an established government that would not simply disappear. Other nations had recognized the government, and it was time for the United States to do the same. Similarly, other countries wanted to give China's seat in the United Nations to the People's Republic. The United States could no longer

CAPTION ANSWERS

Viewing History Sample answer: To show the world the new tone set by the trip and to bolster Nixon's support in the United States.

RESOURCE DIRECTORY

Technology

Sounds of an Era Audio CD *Nixon on the People's Republic of China,* July 15, 1971 (time: 55 seconds)

convince the world to oppose this change. In October 1971, Taiwan lost its seat in the United Nations to the People's Republic of China.

Benefiting From Friendship Nixon had other motives as well. He recognized that he could use Chinese friendship as a bargaining chip in his negotiations with the Soviet Union. (In other words, the Soviet Union might compromise with the United States in order to keep the United States and China from developing too close a relationship.) Press coverage of the trip would give Nixon a boost at home. Also, he believed that he could take this action without suffering political damage, because of his reputation as a strong anti-Communist.

Nixon traveled to China in February 1972. He met with Mao Zedong, the Chinese leader who had led the revolution in 1949. He spoke with Premier Zhou Enlai about international problems and ways of dealing with them. He and his wife Pat toured the Great Wall and other Chinese sights, all in front of television cameras that sent the historic pictures home.

When he returned to the United States, Nixon waited in his plane until prime time so that his return would be seen by as many television viewers as possible. Formal relations were not yet restored—that would take a few more years—but the basis for diplomatic ties had been established. While some members of Congress remained outspoken in their opposition to Communist China, most members—and most Americans—applauded Nixon for taking a more realistic approach to Asia.

NOTABLE PRESIDENTS

Richard M. Nixon

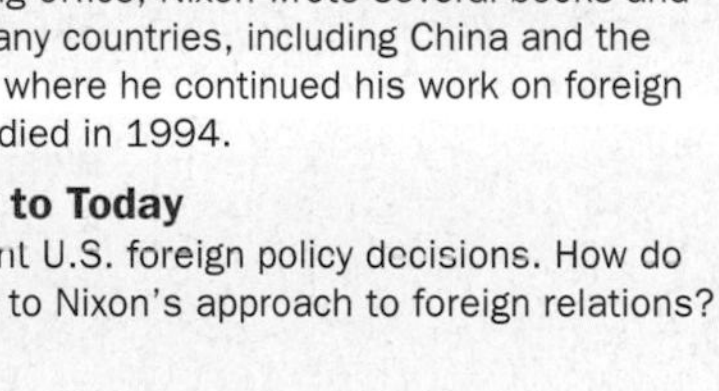

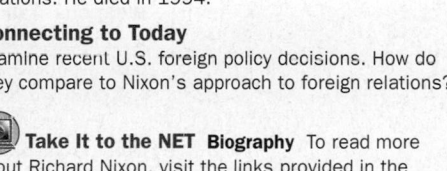

37th President 1969–1974

"In trusting too much in government, we have asked of it more than it can deliver."

—Second Inaugural Address, 1973

Born in Yorba Linda, California, in 1913, Richard Milhous Nixon spent his early years in southern California. He worked at his family's gas station and grocery store while attending Whittier College, and then moved to North Carolina, where he graduated from the Duke University School of Law.

Nixon returned to California to practice law. A few years later, in 1940, he married Patricia Ryan. Nixon served as a naval officer during World War II. When the war was over, Nixon began his political career, winning a seat as a Republican in the U.S. House of Representatives. During this time, Nixon gained national prominence for his lead role within the House Un-American Activities Committee (HUAC) in 1948. While serving on HUAC, Nixon showed himself to be an aggressive politician, while gaining many admirers, as well as critics, for his anti-Communist zeal.

After two terms in the House, Nixon was elected to the United States Senate, and then served as Vice President during the Eisenhower administration, from 1953 to 1961.

Many believe Nixon's greatest successes while President were in the field of foreign relations. However, his foreign policy achievements are often overshadowed by the Watergate scandal, and what many saw as Nixon's failure to preserve the trust of the American people. The scandal forced Nixon to resign from office in 1974, the only President in United States history to do so.

After leaving office, Nixon wrote several books and traveled to many countries, including China and the Soviet Union, where he continued his work on foreign relations. He died in 1994.

Connecting to Today

Examine recent U.S. foreign policy decisions. How do they compare to Nixon's approach to foreign relations?

Take It to the NET Biography To read more about Richard Nixon, visit the links provided in the *America: Pathways to the Present* area of the following Web site. **www.phschool.com**

ACTIVITY

Connecting with History and Conflict

The SALT I treaty negotiated between the Soviet Union and the United States marked a major step forward in relations between the two countries. Have students create an illustrated time line of the history of arms control negotiations between the Soviet Union (and the independent post-Soviet republics) and the United States. The time line should highlight the important successes and failures of these negotiations. **(Visual/Spatial)**

BACKGROUND

Connections to Today

Though Richard Nixon reestablished diplomatic relations with China, he remained watchful and somewhat wary of that vast country. At the time, he told his speechwriter William Safire, "We may have created a Frankenstein." In his last book, *Beyond Peace,* written shortly before his death, Nixon noted: "The giant is awake and is beginning to move the world." Nixon felt certain that economic freedom in China would ultimately lead to political freedom, ". . . but only," he wrote, "if economic freedom is not suppressed by frightened political dictators or sabotaged by shortsighted U.S. policies cutting back on trade with China because of its human rights abuses."

ACTIVITY
Connecting with History and Conflict

Organize students into groups to analyze SALT I and develop a theory to explain why it banned ABM systems in addition to limiting offensive missiles. Tell groups to also see if they can agree as a group whether or not SALT I would have reduced their fears of nuclear war had they been old enough to vote at the time the treaty was signed. Have representatives of each group explain its conclusions and reasoning to the class. **(Logical/Mathematical)**

BACKGROUND
Global Connections

In the 1970s the Soviet Union's rise as a nuclear superpower intensified the Cold War. In 1971, for the first time, the Soviet Union surpassed the United States in total number of land- and submarine-based nuclear missiles. A confident Foreign Minister Andrei Gromyko boasted that in world affairs, "No question of any significance . . . can now be decided without the Soviet Union or in opposition to it."

Nuclear Missiles Limited in SALT I, 1972

SLBM Submarine-Launched Ballistic Missile

Average range: 600–3,500 miles. These missiles, launched by submarines beneath the surface, are a type of IRBM (Intermediate-Range Ballistic Missile) with smaller warheads and a shorter range than ICBMs. The advantage of submarine-launched missiles is that they are difficult for the enemy to locate and destroy.

Poseidon C-3 Introduced in 1971, the Poseidon had a range of about 2,800 miles and could carry multiple warheads.

ICBM Intercontinental Ballistic Missile

Range: Up to 8,000 miles. These are missiles fired from underground silos. After an initial burst of power, they travel most of the distance to their target by momentum.

Minuteman III This missile was the most widely deployed ICBM around the time of the SALT talks. It was the first missile to carry Multiple Independent Re-entry Vehicles (MIRVs), meaning that a single Minuteman missile can send warheads to several targets.

ABM Anti-Ballistic Missile

In the late 1960s, both the United States and the Soviet Union deployed interceptor missile systems meant to destroy incoming ballistic missiles. The United States built these missiles mainly to protect ICBM launch sites. Safeguard, the ABM program created under Nixon, was shut down in 1975 because it was judged to be unreliable.

Spartan The Spartan missile had a range of 465 miles.

Sprint This smaller missile had a 25-mile range.

INTERPRETING DIAGRAMS The SALT I Treaty limited the stockpiling of missiles in various categories. **Synthesizing Information** *Which type of missile is used to ward off other missiles?*

Limiting Nuclear Arms

Several months after his 1972 China trip, Nixon visited the Soviet Union. He received as warm a welcome in Moscow as he had in Beijing. In a series of friendly meetings between Nixon and Premier Leonid I. Brezhnev, the two nations reached several decisions. They agreed to work together to explore space, eased longstanding trade limits, and completed negotiations on a weapons pact.

Balancing the Superpowers Nixon viewed arms control as a vital part of his foreign policy. Like many Americans, he was worried about the superpowers' growing stockpiles of nuclear weapons. The Limited Test Ban Treaty of 1963 had ended testing of new bombs in the atmosphere, but underground testing continued. The two superpowers were making bigger and more powerful bombs all the time. Some people feared that the world might be destroyed unless these weapons were brought under control.

Nixon was determined to address the nuclear threat and to deal creatively with the Soviet Union at the same time. He had taken office with the intention of building more nuclear weapons to keep ahead of the Soviet Union, but he came to believe that this kind of arms race made little sense. Each nation already had more than enough weapons to destroy its enemy many times over. The nuclear age demanded balance between the superpowers.

Weapons Talks To address the issue, the United States and the Soviet Union had begun the Strategic Arms Limitation Talks in 1969. In 1972, the talks produced a treaty that would limit offensive nuclear weapons. This treaty was ready for Nixon to sign during his visit to Moscow.

The first Strategic Arms Limitation Treaty, known as **SALT I,** included a five-year agreement that froze the number of intercontinental ballistic missiles (ICBMs) and submarine-launched ballistic missiles (SLBMs) at 1972 levels. The treaty also included an agreement restricting the development and deployment of antiballistic missile defense systems (ABMs), which were designed to shoot down attacking missiles.

CAPTION ANSWERS

Interpreting Diagrams Anti-Ballistic Missile (ABM).

RESOURCE DIRECTORY

Teaching Resources

Units 5/6/7 booklet
- Section 2 Quiz, p. 101

Guide to the Essentials
- Section 2 Summary, p. 122

While Congress approved SALT I and the treaty went into effect, some government officials were troubled by the agreement. They worried that the treaty's limitation on missiles might leave the United States unprepared to defend itself in an emergency. One solution was to improve conventional weapons, which were not limited by the treaty. Therefore, Secretary of Defense Melvin Laird made the Pentagon's approval contingent on a commitment to move ahead with plans to build a better bomber and a larger submarine. At the same time, both the United States and the Soviet Union began to develop a new technology that used multiple nuclear warheads on a single missile, and was correspondingly more destructive.

SALT I was a triumph for the Nixon administration and an important step forward. Yet it did not reduce the number of warheads the two nations possessed. Nor did it stop them from improving nuclear weapons in other ways. Still, it helped to ease what had been growing concerns about the arms race, and it demonstrated the willingness of the United States and the Soviet Union to work together toward a common goal. In showing that arms control agreements between the superpowers were possible, SALT I paved the way for more progress in the future.

About a year before the signing of SALT I, Nixon pointed out that the potential benefits of negotiating with the Soviet Union went beyond the issue of limiting nuclear arms:

> "*Perhaps for the first time, the evolving strategic balance allows a Soviet-American agreement which yields no unilateral [one-sided] advantages. The fact [that] we have begun to discuss strategic arms with the USSR is in itself important. Agreement in such a vital area could create a new commitment to stability, and influence attitudes toward other issues.*"
>
> —Richard Nixon

Focus on GOVERNMENT

Shuttle Diplomacy After the Arab-Israeli War in 1973, Kissinger undertook what came to be known as shuttle diplomacy, traveling back and forth between Middle Eastern capitals to arrange peace. In April 1974, he secured a cease-fire agreement between Israel and Syria, whose forces had been fighting on the Golan Heights. In June, President Nixon visited the Middle East to recognize the success of Kissinger's efforts to reduce tensions in the region. Others holding the office of Secretary of State since Kissinger have followed his lead, using shuttle diplomacy to further U.S. foreign policy goals.

Section 2 Assessment

READING COMPREHENSION

1. How did Kissinger use ***realpolitik*** to carry out Nixon's foreign policy?
2. What is the meaning of **détente?** Why was it difficult to achieve détente with Communist nations?
3. What did the term "ping-pong diplomacy" refer to in the Nixon administration? What steps were taken to improve the relationship between the United States and China?
4. What were Nixon's concerns about nuclear weapons?
5. What was **SALT I?**

CRITICAL THINKING AND WRITING

6. **Identifying Central Issues** What were Nixon's policies toward China and the Soviet Union? Why were they so surprising at the time?
7. **Drawing Conclusions** Why did Nixon and Kissinger believe it was important to relax the tensions between the United States and both China and the Soviet Union?
8. **Writing an Opinion** Considering the limitations of SALT I, do you think it was an important treaty? Make a list of reasons to support your opinion.

Take It to the NET

Activity: Writing an Editorial
Research an aspect of President Nixon's foreign policy that interests you. Write an editorial for your local newspaper reacting to the events or policies you have studied. Use the links provided in the *America: Pathways to the Present* area of the following Web site for help in completing this activity.
www.phschool.com

Section 2 Assessment

Reading Comprehension

1. He used the policy of making decisions based on maintaining the strength of one's nation rather than following moral principles in his dealings with China and the Soviet Union.
2. A relaxation in tensions. China and the Soviet Union were sworn enemies of the U.S.
3. The U.S. National Table Tennis team traveled to mainland China in order to play against the Chinese National team in April 1971. This was part of the Nixon era warming of relations between the two countries. This effort included other measures, such as the U.S. government lifting restrictions on travel to China.
4. He was worried about the superpowers' growing stockpiles of nuclear weapons, and he shared the concern of the American people that the growing arsenal posed a threat to the world if weapons went uncontrolled.
5. The Strategic Arms Limitation Treaty signed by the United States and the Soviet Union in 1972. This was the culmination of arms control talks that had begun in 1969 with the goal of limiting offensive nuclear weapons.

Critical Thinking and Writing

6. His policies involved working to improve American relations with both Communist China and the Soviet Union. This plan was surprising because in the past, Nixon had insisted on a firm stand against Communist countries.
7. Former allies, China and the Soviet Union had become enemies. This new relationship had the potential to reshape global politics.
8. Possible answer: It was the first step toward limiting arms on the part of the United States and the Soviet Union, and it opened the door to further discussions between the two superpowers.

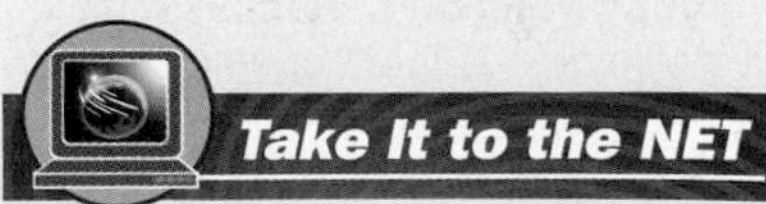

Editorials will vary, but should thoroughly examine one of Nixon's foreign policies, presenting facts as well as opinion.

Section 3 The Watergate Scandal

Section Objectives

1. See how the Nixon White House battled its political enemies.
2. Find out how the Committee to Reelect the President conducted itself during Nixon's reelection campaign.
3. Learn about the Watergate break-in, and see how the story of the scandal unfolded.
4. Discover the events that led directly to Nixon's resignation.

Bellringer

Warm-Up Activity Ask students how they would feel if they discovered that the President might have broken the law. Ask them to discuss the impact of such news and its effect on the perception of the symbolic role of the President.

Activating Prior Knowledge Can students list other Presidents who were subjected to Congressional investigations? What were the outcomes of those investigations?

Reading Strategy

As students read, have them take notes on the various events related to the Watergate scandal. Have them use the terms *Who, What, When, Where,* and *Why* to help them organize each piece of information.

Section 3 The Watergate Scandal

READING FOCUS

- How did the Nixon White House battle its political enemies?
- How did the Committee to Reelect the President conduct itself during Nixon's reelection campaign?
- What was the Watergate break-in, and how did the story of the scandal unfold?
- What events led directly to Nixon's resignation?

MAIN IDEA

The break-in at the Watergate apartment complex started a scandal that led to President Nixon's resignation.

KEY TERMS

wiretap
Watergate scandal
special prosecutor
impeach

TAKING NOTES

Copy the cause-and-effect diagram below. As you read, add information about the Watergate scandal and Nixon's resignation.

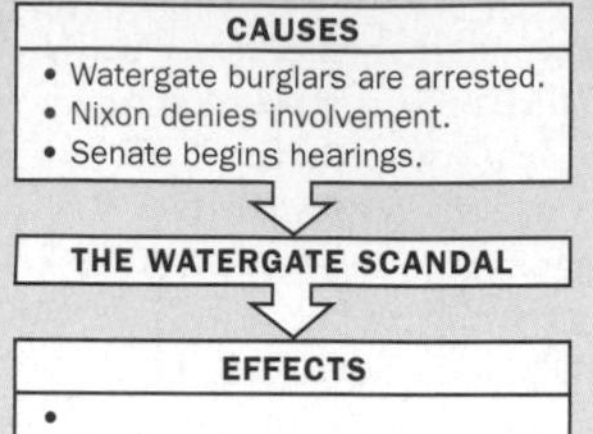

CAUSES
• Watergate burglars are arrested.
• Nixon denies involvement.
• Senate begins hearings.
THE WATERGATE SCANDAL
EFFECTS
•
•

Setting the Scene

President Nixon was determined to win an overwhelming victory in the 1972 election. With such a mandate, he would be in a strong position to move his programs through Congress. Fiercely loyal aides carried out schemes to help ensure that the President would win, some of them committing crimes in the process. When Nixon tried to hide their illegal actions, he involved himself in a scandal that ended his presidency and shook the foundations of American government.

In a detailed chronicle of the events surrounding the fall of Richard Nixon, author Theodore H. White observed:

> “*The true crime of Richard Nixon was simple: he destroyed the myth that binds America together, and for this he was driven from power.*
>
> *The myth he broke was critical—that somewhere in American life there is at least one man who stands for law, the President. . . . It was that faith that Richard Nixon broke, betraying those who voted for him even more than those who voted against him.*”
>
> —Theodore H. White, *Breach of Faith*

INTERPRETING POLITICAL CARTOONS This 1973 cartoon pokes fun at Nixon for compiling an "enemies list." **Drawing Inferences** *What message is conveyed by the two lists in the cartoon?*

ENEMY LIST
FRIENDLY LIST
SEC'Y OF LISTS
STAYSKAL 1973 CHICAGO TODAY
"YOU THOUGHT OF ANOTHER NAME? OH, GOOD, SIR... FOR WHICH LIST?"

Battling Political Enemies

The President's suspicious and secretive nature caused the White House to operate as if it were surrounded by political enemies. Nixon's staff tried to protect him at all costs from anything that might weaken his political position.

The Enemies List One result of this mind-set was what became known as the "enemies list." Special counsel Charles W. Colson helped develop a list of prominent people who were seen as unsympathetic to the administration. It included politicians such as Senator Edward Kennedy, reporters such as Daniel

Caption Answers

Interpreting Political Cartoons Sample answer: Nixon has more enemies than he has friends.

RESOURCE DIRECTORY

Teaching Resources

Guided Reading and Review booklet, p. 130

Technology

Section Reading Support Transparencies
Guided Reading Audiotapes (English/Spanish), Ch. 25
Student Edition on Audio CD, Ch. 25
Prentice Hall Presentation Pro CD-ROM, Ch. 25
Companion Web site, www.phschool.com

Schorr, and a number of outspoken performers such as comedian Dick Gregory and actors Jane Fonda and Steve McQueen. Aides then considered how to harass these White House "enemies." One idea, for example, was to arrange income tax investigations of people on the list.

Wiretaps In 1968, Nixon had campaigned as a man who believed in law and order. Sometimes, however, he was willing to take illegal actions. In 1969, someone in the National Security Council appeared to have leaked secret information to the *New York Times.* In response, Nixon ordered Henry Kissinger to install **wiretaps,** or listening devices, on the telephones of several members of his own staff. He also ordered wiretaps on some news reporters' phones. These wiretaps, installed for national security reasons, were legal at the time. Yet they would lead to other, illegal wiretaps, many of them for political purposes.

The Plumbers In the spring of 1971, Daniel Ellsberg, a former Defense Department official, handed the *New York Times* a huge, secret Pentagon study of the Vietnam War. In June 1971, as you have read, the *New York Times* began to publish this study, which became known as the Pentagon Papers. The documents showed that previous Presidents had deceived Congress and the American people about the real situation in Vietnam.

Nixon was furious that Ellsberg could get away with leaking secret government information. He was even more furious when leaks to the press continued. He and Kissinger were in the midst of secret discussions with China and the Soviet Union, and he did not want those talks to become public.

Nixon approved a plan to organize a special White House unit to stop government leaks. The group, nicknamed the Plumbers, included E. Howard Hunt, a spy novelist and former CIA agent, and G. Gordon Liddy, a former FBI agent. In September 1971, with approval from White House chief domestic advisor John Ehrlichman, the undercover unit broke into the office of Ellsberg's psychiatrist. The Plumbers hoped to find and disclose damaging information about Ellsberg's private life. Their goal was to punish Ellsburg for leaking the Pentagon Papers.

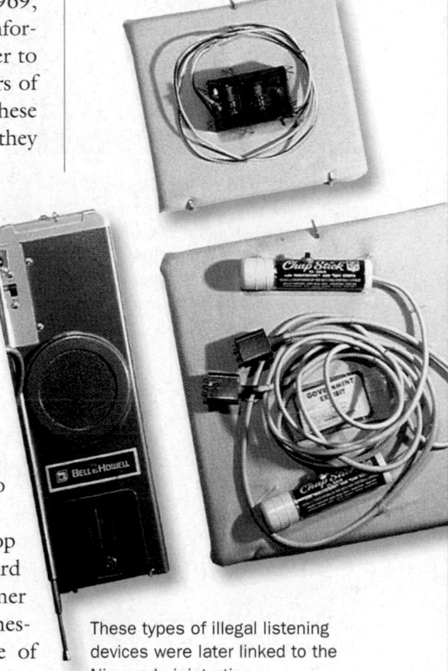

These types of illegal listening devices were later linked to the Nixon administration.

Nixon's Reelection Campaign

Determined to ensure Nixon's victory in 1972, the Committee to Reelect the President used similarly questionable tactics. Headed by John Mitchell, who resigned as Attorney General to assume command, the Committee launched a special fund-raising campaign. It wanted to collect as much money as possible before a new law made it necessary to report such contributions. The money would fund both routine campaign activities and unethical actions hidden from the public.

Though a few of the Committee's actions might have been considered annoying pranks, others were damaging. In 1972, people on the Committee payroll made up a letter attempting to discredit Edmund Muskie, a Democratic senator from Maine and a leading presidential contender. Then they leaked the letter to a conservative New Hampshire newspaper.

Charging Muskie with making insulting remarks about French Canadians living in the state, the letter was timed to arrive two weeks before the New Hampshire primary. The letter also claimed that Muskie's wife was an alcoholic. The normally composed Muskie broke down in tears in front of TV cameras, seriously hurting his candidacy.

READING CHECK
Why did the press leaks infuriate Nixon?

LESSON PLAN

Focus Tell students that Nixon's suspicious nature and his willingness to use his presidential power for partisan political ends set in motion a series of events that compromised the presidency itself. Ask students how the people of the United States reacted to presidential wrongdoing.

Instruct Discuss the atmosphere in the White House as described in this section. What does the existence of the "enemies list" reveal about Nixon's view of the world? Ask students to consider the fact that Nixon harassed those he perceived as hostile by arranging income tax investigations of them. Are such actions an abuse of power? Why or why not?

Assess/Reteach Ask students to list Nixon's attributes as President, both positive and negative. Do they think that, in the end, the value of his accomplishments outweighs the impact of his illegal actions?

ACTIVITY
Connecting with Government

Ask students to create a poem or a rap that expresses their evaluation of Richard Nixon as President. Remind students to consider Nixon's strengths and successes as well as his flaws and failures before forming an opinion about him. Invite students to present their creations to the class. **(Musical/Rhythmic)**

READING CHECK
Nixon was a deeply suspicious and insecure person. Also, leaks might disturb the secret talks he and Kissinger were having with China and the Soviet Union.

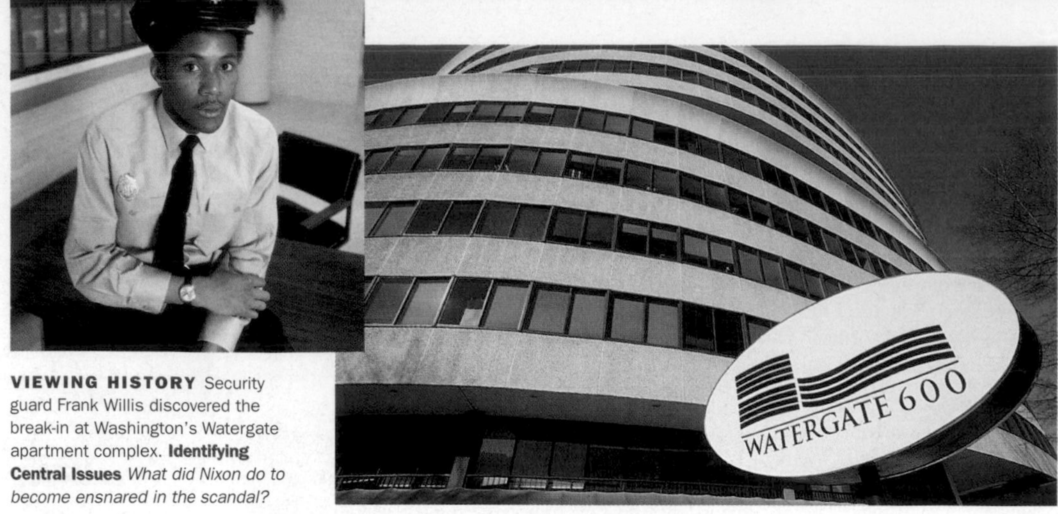

VIEWING HISTORY Security guard Frank Willis discovered the break-in at Washington's Watergate apartment complex. **Identifying Central Issues** *What did Nixon do to become ensnared in the scandal?*

Attempts such as this to sabotage Nixon's political opponents came to be known as "dirty tricks." They included sending hecklers to disrupt Democratic campaign meetings and assigning spies to join the campaigns of major candidates.

The Watergate Break-In

Within the Committee to Reelect the President, a group formed to gather intelligence. The group, which included "Plumbers" Liddy and Hunt, masterminded several outlandish plans.

One scheme called for wiretapping top Democrats to try to find damaging information about delegates at their convention. Twice, Committee leader John Mitchell refused to go along—not because the plan was illegal, but because it was too expensive. Finally, in March 1972, he approved a different idea. Liddy would oversee the wiretapping of phones at Democratic National Committee headquarters in the Watergate apartment complex in Washington, D.C.

The first break-in to install illegal listening devices failed. A second attempt early on the morning of June 17, 1972, ended with the arrest of the five men involved. One suspect was James McCord, a former CIA employee working as a security officer for the Committee to Reelect the President. The Watergate burglars carried money that could be linked to the Committee, thus tying the break-in directly to Nixon's reelection campaign.

When the FBI traced the money carried by the Watergate burglars to the reelection committee, Nixon contacted the CIA. He authorized that organization to try to persuade the FBI to stop its investigation on the grounds that the matter involved "national security."

This action would come back to haunt the President. Although he had not been involved in planning the break-in, Nixon was now part of the illegal coverup. The break-in and the coverup became known as the **Watergate scandal.**

In the months following the Watergate break-in, the incident barely reached the public's notice. Behind the scenes in the White House, some of the President's closest aides worked feverishly to keep the truth hidden.

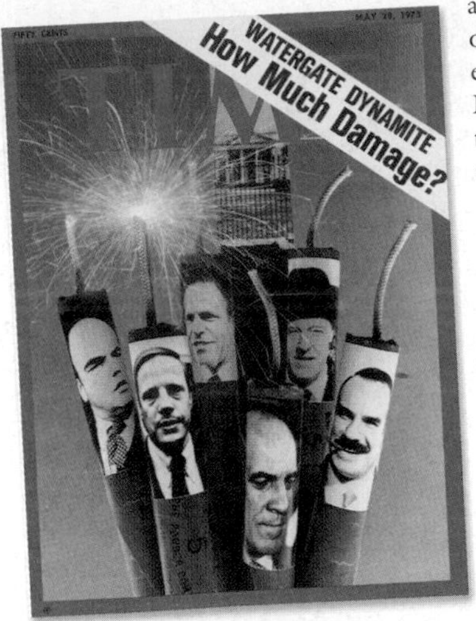

A May 1973 *Time* magazine cover shows some players in the Watergate scandal, from left, John Ehrlichman; John W. Dean III; H. R. Haldeman; James McCord, Jr.; E. Howard Hunt; and G. Gordon Liddy.

ACTIVITY
Connecting with History and Conflict

Point out to the class that some historians believe that Nixon could have minimized the Watergate scandal by admitting to his role in the affair before it became a major political crisis. Then pair students to develop two 60-second statements: one in which Nixon reveals his involvement to the American people and explains why he did it, and another in which Nixon tells his advisers why he will not—or cannot—admit to any wrongdoing. Call on pairs to present one or both of their statements to the class. **(Verbal/Linguistic; Bodily/Kinesthetic)**

BACKGROUND
Youth Vote in 1972

The 1972 Republican campaign received much support from young people, despite Nixon's and Agnew's criticisms of youth in general and the still-fresh memories of Kent State. Young Republicans, according to *Life* magazine in September 1972, comprised "the nation's largest bloc of first-time voters, 2.5 million of them, mostly 18 to 24 years old." By early fall in 1972, "Young Voters for the President" claimed 10,000 college volunteers on more than 90 campuses. On election day Nixon got 52 percent of the votes cast by those under 30.

BACKGROUND
Recent Scholarship

Richard Nixon's complicity in the Watergate affair led him to become the first President of the United States ever to resign from office. That step became necessary when tape recordings of presidential conversations demonstrated beyond the shadow of a doubt that he had been involved in a massive cover-up attempt. In *Abuse of Power: The New Nixon Tapes,* Stanley I. Kutler provides transcripts of recordings released only after a lengthy court case in which Nixon fought tenaciously to keep the tapes from being aired publicly.

CAPTION ANSWERS

Viewing History He ordered the CIA to attempt to halt the FBI Watergate investigation.

RESOURCE DIRECTORY

Teaching Resources

Learning with Documents booklet (Visual Learning Activity) *Wanted,* p. 71

In the summer of 1972, Nixon advisors H. R. Haldeman, John Ehrlichman, John Mitchell, and others launched a scheme to bribe the Watergate defendants. They distributed hundreds of thousands of dollars in illegal "hush money" to buy their silence. Also, to shield the President, Mitchell and other top officials coached the defendants about how to commit perjury by lying under oath in court.

Their efforts paid off in the November presidential election. Nixon trounced Senator George McGovern of South Dakota, a liberal Democrat, by 520 to 17 electoral votes and a sizable majority of the popular vote. Nixon had the mandate he wanted, though he did not get a Republican majority in either house of Congress.

The Scandal Unfolds

Despite Nixon's victory in the election, the Watergate story refused to go away. Newspapers such as the *Washington Post* continued to ask probing questions of administration officials. Nixon himself had proclaimed publicly that "no one in the White House staff, no one in this administration, presently employed, was involved in this very bizarre incident." Not everyone believed him.

The Watergate Trial The trial of the Watergate burglars began in January 1973 before Judge John J. Sirica. All the defendants either pleaded guilty or were found guilty. Meanwhile, the White House and the President himself were becoming more deeply involved. In March 1973, just before the judge handed down the sentences, Nixon personally approved the payment of "hush money" to defendant E. Howard Hunt.

At sentencing time, Judge Sirica was not convinced that the full story had yet been told. Criticizing the prosecution, he said:

> "I have not been satisfied, and I am still not satisfied that all the pertinent facts that might be available—I say might be available—have been produced before an American jury. . . . I would hope that the Senate committee is granted the power by Congress . . . to try to get to the bottom of what happened in this case."
>
> —Judge John J. Sirica

To prompt the burglars to talk, Sirica sentenced them to long prison terms, up to 40 years. Their sentences could be reduced, he suggested, if they cooperated with the upcoming Senate hearings on Watergate.

Watergate Chronology

1972

June: Five men linked to Nixon's reelection campaign are arrested for breaking into the Democratic National Committee headquarters.

1973

April: Nixon denies knowledge of the break-in.

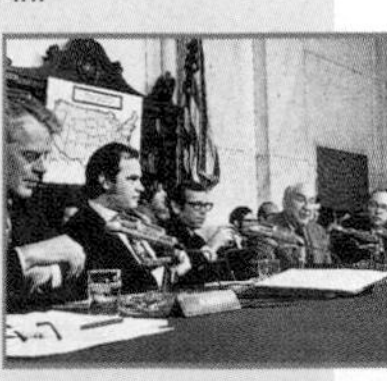

May: The Senate Select Committee on Presidential Campaign Activities begins hearings (right).

June: Former Nixon counsel John Dean tells the committee that Nixon authorized a coverup.

July: The committee discovers that Nixon had been secretly recording presidential conversations since 1971 and orders Nixon to release certain tapes. Nixon refuses.

August: Special Prosecutor Archibald Cox sues Nixon for the tapes.

October: Nixon offers summaries of the tapes, which Cox rejects. Nixon fires Cox, setting off a series of firings known as the "Saturday Night Massacre." The House takes steps to impeach Nixon. Nixon releases all but two of the requested tapes.

November: An 18½-minute gap is found on one of the tapes.

1974

January: Nixon claims "executive privilege."

April: Nixon is ordered to surrender more tapes and related documents. Nixon supplies 1,254 pages of edited transcripts. Special Prosecutor Leon Jaworski sues Nixon for the originals.

July: The Supreme Court orders Nixon to surrender the tapes and documents. The House Judiciary Committee recommends impeachment.

August: Nixon releases transcripts that prove he learned of the break-in as early as June 23, 1972, and ordered the coverup. Nixon resigns August 9. His resignation speech is televised (right).

INTERPRETING TIME LINES As the investigation unfolded, it became increasingly clear that Nixon had something to hide. **Analyzing Information** *How was the investigation an example of the federal system of checks and balances?*

ACTIVITY
Connecting with Government

This activity might take place over several class periods. Divide the class into groups of four. Have students explore the Constitution's guidelines for impeachment, as well as the charges and evidence against President Nixon. Then ask students to debate whether or not Nixon should have been impeached for his involvement in Watergate. **(Logical/Mathematical; Verbal/Linguistic)**

From the Archives of
AmericanHeritage®

About the Presidents

The presidency of Richard Nixon (1969–1974) defies simple assessments. While his presidency was scandal-ridden, and Nixon stands as the only President ever forced to resign from office, his historic legacy is complex. Nixon had acute political intelligence and a knack for innovative policy making. In domestic policy he oversaw the creation of the Occupational Safety and Health Administration and the Environmental Protection Agency. In foreign policy he pursued détente with the Soviet Union and opened relations with the People's Republic of China. In doing so, Nixon laid the foundation for stable relations between the United States and the world's dominant Communist powers. Source: Adapted from Henry F. Graff's *The Presidents,* Scribner's, 1984, by the editors of *American Heritage®* magazine.

CAPTION ANSWERS

Interpreting Time Lines Congress and the Supreme Court checked the abuses of the executive branch of the federal government.

ACTIVITY
Student Portfolio

You may wish to have students add the following activity to their portfolios: Suggest that students research and prepare a biographical file of the major figures in Watergate, their roles, and what happened to them in the aftermath of the scandal. The file could include figures in the Nixon administration, in the press, and in Congress. **(Verbal/Linguistic)**

BACKGROUND
Biography

Senator Samuel Ervin, Jr. (1896–1985), of North Carolina headed the seven-member Senate committee on Watergate. He won praise not only for his easy southern manner but also for his doggedness in pursuing evidence against Nixon and resisting the President's claims to "executive privilege." Ervin, who called the United States Constitution "the finest thing to come out of the mind of man," served in the United States Senate for more than 20 years until he retired in 1974. He wrote two books, *The Whole Truth: The Watergate Conspiracy* (1980) and *Humor of a Country Lawyer* (1983).

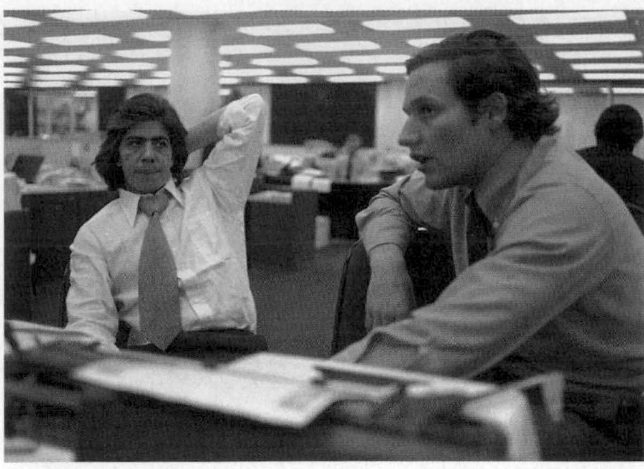

VIEWING HISTORY Reporters Carl Bernstein (left) and Bob Woodward of the *Washington Post* persisted in tracking down information to uncover the Watergate story. **Recognizing Cause and Effect** *How did their reporting affect the official investigation?*

Woodward and Bernstein Meanwhile, two *Washington Post* reporters were following a trail of leads. Bob Woodward and Carl Bernstein, both young and eager, sensed that the trail would lead to the White House.

Even before the election, Woodward and Bernstein had learned about the secret funds of the Committee to Reelect the President. They had written about the political spying and sabotage. As they began to realize who was involved, they called John Mitchell and asked him to verify their story. He denied it angrily.

The Senate Investigates In February 1973, a Senate Select Committee on Presidential Campaign Activities had begun to investigate the Watergate affair. James McCord, one of the convicted Watergate burglars, responded to his lengthy prison sentence by testifying before the committee in secret session. He gave members a vague sense of what had gone on, and he suggested that Nixon staffers were involved. The stories by Woodward and Bernstein helped the probe. In turn, leaks from the Senate committee aided these and other reporters.

As rumors of White House involvement grew, Nixon tried to protect himself. In April 1973, he forced Haldeman and Ehrlichman, his two closest aides, to resign. On national television he proclaimed that he would take final responsibility for the mistakes of others, for "there can be no whitewash at the White House."

The investigation ground on. In May 1973, the Senate committee, chaired by Senator Sam Ervin of North Carolina, began televised public hearings on Watergate. Millions of Americans watched, fascinated, as the story unfolded like a mystery thriller. John Dean, the President's personal legal counselor, sought to save himself by testifying that Nixon knew about the coverup. Other staffers described illegal activities at the White House.

COMPARING PRIMARY SOURCES
Should Nixon Be Impeached?

In July 1974, the House Judiciary Committee debated the possible impeachment of President Richard Nixon.
Analyzing Viewpoints Compare the main arguments made by the two speakers.

In Favor of Impeachment

"My faith in the Constitution is whole, it is complete, it is total, and I am not going to sit here and be an idle spectator to the diminution [lessening], the subversion [undermining], the destruction of the Constitution. . . . The Framers confided in the Congress the power if need be to remove . . . a President swollen with power and grown tyrannical."

—Texas Representative Barbara Jordan, Democrat

Opposed to Impeachment

"As the trust is placed in Congress to safeguard the liberties of the people through the . . . powers to remove a President, so must Congress's vigilance be fierce in seeing that the trust is not abused. . . . Not only do I not believe that any crimes by the President have been proved beyond a reasonable doubt, but I do not think the proof even approaches the lesser standards of proof which some of my colleagues . . . suggested we apply."

—Michigan Representative Edward Hutchinson, Republican

CAPTION ANSWERS

Viewing History It provided leads that kept the investigation going.

RESOURCE DIRECTORY

Teaching Resources

Biography, Literature, and Comparing Primary Sources booklet (Literature) *Unraveling the Story of Watergate*, p. 85

Biography, Literature, and Comparing Primary Sources booklet (Comparing Primary Sources) *On Nixon's Impeachment*, p. 159

Technology

Color Transparencies *Political Cartoons*, B18

Sounds of an Era Audio CD *Nixon's Watergate Speeches*

Exploring Primary Sources in U.S. History CD-ROM *Bugging at the Watergate*

The most dramatic moment came when Alexander Butterfield, a former presidential assistant, revealed the existence of a secret taping system in the President's office that recorded all meetings and telephone conversations. The system had been set up to provide a historical record of Nixon's presidency. Now those audiotapes could show whether or not Nixon had been involved in the coverup.

The "Saturday Night Massacre" In an effort to demonstrate honesty, Nixon agreed in May 1973 to the appointment of a special Watergate prosecutor. A **special prosecutor** works for the Justice Department but conducts an independent investigation of claims of wrongdoing by government officials. Archibald Cox, a Harvard law professor, took the post and immediately asked for the tapes. Nixon refused to release them. When Cox persisted, Nixon ordered him fired on Saturday, October 20, 1973. This action triggered a series of resignations and firings that became known as the "Saturday Night Massacre."

An Administration in Jeopardy By that time, Nixon was in serious trouble. His public approval rating plummeted. After Cox's firing, *Time* magazine declared, "The President Should Resign."

Leon Jaworski of Texas, Cox's replacement as special prosecutor, also asked for the tapes. Nixon then tried to demonstrate innocence by releasing edited transcripts of some of his White House conversations. He carefully cut out the most damaging evidence. Still, many people were angry and disillusioned when they read even the edited comments of some of the conversations in the Oval Office.

Meanwhile, a subplot had emerged in the troubled White House. Vice President Spiro Agnew stood accused of evading income taxes and taking bribes. Early in October 1973, just ten days before the "Saturday Night Massacre," he resigned in disgrace. To succeed Agnew, Nixon named Gerald R. Ford, the House Minority Leader. For nearly two months, until the Senate confirmed Ford, the nation had a President in big trouble—and no Vice President.

American BIOGRAPHY

Barbara Jordan
1936–1996

Born in Houston, Texas, Barbara Jordan grew up in a segregated society. She graduated from Texas Southern University, and then earned a law degree from Boston University.

Barbara Jordan's political career included many "firsts." In 1966, she became the first African American in the Texas state senate since Reconstruction. In 1972, Jordan became the first African American woman from Texas elected to the House of Representatives.

As a member of the House Judiciary Committee, Jordan took part in the Watergate hearings in July 1974. Her strong opinions were based on her belief that Nixon's actions threatened the Constitution.

Jordan was reelected to the House in 1974 and 1976. Retiring from politics in 1978, she taught political ethics at the Lyndon B. Johnson School of Public Affairs (University of Texas). Jordan was the keynote speaker at the Democratic conventions in 1976 and 1992.

Hearings Begin Nixon had to make another move. After the "Saturday Night Massacre," Congress had begun the process to help them determine if they should **impeach** the President—to charge him with misconduct while in office.

In July 1974, the House Judiciary Committee, which included 21 Democrats and 17 Republicans, began to hold hearings to determine if there were adequate grounds for impeachment. This debate, like the earlier hearings, was broadcast on national television. The country watched anxiously as even Republicans deserted the President. Representative M. Caldwell Butler of Virginia spoke for many of them when he said:

> "*For years we Republicans have campaigned against corruption and misconduct. . . . But Watergate is our shame. Those things have happened in our house and it is our responsibility to do what we can to clear it up. . . . In short, power appears to have corrupted. It is a sad chapter in American history, but I cannot condone what I have heard; I cannot excuse it; and I cannot and will not stand for it.*"
>
> —Representative M. Caldwell Butler, 1974

ACTIVITY
Connecting with History and Conflict

Invite students to research library and other resources for primary or secondary sources regarding one of the following topics: the Saturday Night Massacre, Nixon's release of the tapes following the Supreme Court's ruling, or Nixon's last day as President. Then have them use the information they gather to write a news story of the event that might have appeared in the newspaper the next day. **(Verbal/Linguistic)**

BACKGROUND
A Vice President Resigns

Calls for Nixon's resignation or impeachment after the Saturday Night Massacre were also linked to Spiro Agnew's resignation as Vice President. Agnew's verbal attacks on opponents of the Vietnam War and the network news media during Nixon's first term had made him a hero of political conservatives. But they also earned him the disdain of majority Democrats in the House and Senate. On the day he left office, Agnew pleaded *nolo contendere,* or "no contest," to tax evasion, for which he was fined $10,000 and placed on three years' unsupervised probation.

CUSTOMIZE FOR ...
Gifted and Talented

Have students research and report on the process of impeachment, including who is responsible for initiating the process.

TEST PREPARATION

Have students reread the section under the heading "The Saturday Night Massacre" and then answer the question below.

Who supervises the activities of a special prosecutor?

A The Supreme Court
B Congress
C The President
(D) The Justice Department

VIEWING HISTORY In this famous photograph, former President Richard Nixon offers the crowd his familiar salute as he leaves Washington, D.C., following his resignation. **Drawing Conclusions** *Why is the Watergate scandal an important part of American political history?*

By sizable tallies, the House Judiciary Committee voted to impeach the President on charges of obstruction of justice, abuse of power, and refusal to obey a congressional order to turn over his tapes. To remove him from office, a majority of the full House of Representatives would have to vote for impeachment, and the Senate would then have to hold a trial, with two thirds of the senators present voting to convict. The outcome seemed obvious.

Nixon Resigns

On August 5, after a brief delay, Nixon finally obeyed a Supreme Court ruling and released the tapes. They contained a disturbing gap of $18\frac{1}{2}$ minutes, during which the conversation had been mysteriously erased. Still, the tapes gave clear evidence of Nixon's involvement in the coverup.

Three days later, Nixon appeared on television and painfully announced that he would leave the office of President the next day. On August 9, 1974, Nixon resigned, the first President ever to do so. That same day, in a smooth constitutional transition, Vice President Gerald Ford was sworn in. "Our long national nightmare is over," he said.

The Watergate scandal still stands as a low point in American political history. Government officials abused the powers granted to them by the people. A President was forced to resign in disgrace. Many Americans lost a great deal of faith and trust in their government.

However, the scandal also proved the strength of the nation's constitutional system, especially its balance of powers. When members of the executive branch violated the law instead of enforcing it, the judicial and legislative branches of government stepped in and stopped them. As President Ford said upon taking office, "Our constitution works. Our great republic is a government of laws, not of men."

Section 3 Assessment

READING COMPREHENSION

1. Why did Nixon keep an "enemies list"? How was the list used?
2. Describe the use of **wiretaps** within the Nixon White House.
3. How did the public learn about Nixon's role in the **Watergate scandal?**
4. What role did the **special prosecutor** play in the Watergate investigation?
5. Describe what became known as the "Saturday Night Massacre."
6. What does it mean to **impeach?**

CRITICAL THINKING AND WRITING

7. **Posing Questions** Write three questions you would want to ask President Richard Nixon if you were a member of the House Judiciary Committee preparing for impeachment hearings.
8. **Writing an Opinion** Write an outline for an essay in which you evaluate Nixon's role in the Watergate scandal, and state your opinion as to whether or not he should have resigned.

Activity: Organizing a Debate
Investigate events leading up to the Watergate scandal. Participate in a classroom debate on whether to impeach President Nixon. Use the links provided in the *America: Pathways to the Present* area of the following Web site for help in completing this activity.
www.phschool.com

Section 3 Assessment

Reading Comprehension

1. His suspicious and secretive nature and his staff's attempt to protect him at all costs. To formulate plans to harass White House enemies through such methods as income tax investigations.
2. Nixon ordered Kissinger to install the wiretaps on the telephones of several members of President Nixon's staff and on some news reporters' phones to monitor the flow of information out of, and in regard to, the White House.
3. Through articles in the *Washington Post* investigated and written by Woodward and Bernstein, and through the Senate investigation that began in February 1973.
4. Archibald Cox asked for the tapes in his capacity as an independent investigator working on behalf of the Justice Department. Nixon refused and eventually ordered Cox to be fired, which triggered the "Saturday Night Massacre."
5. A series of resignations and firings.
6. To charge the President with misconduct while in office.

Critical Thinking and Writing

7. Answers will vary.
8. Outlines will vary but should be supported with facts from the section.

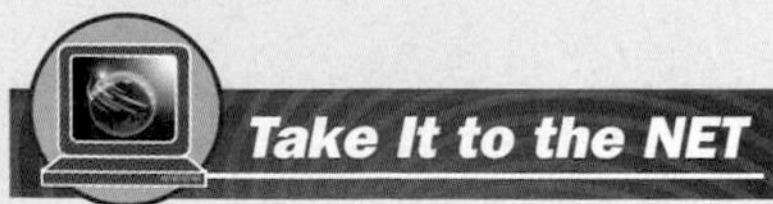

Students should consider the charges and evidence against President Nixon and explore the Constitution's guidelines for impeachment.

Caption Answers

Viewing History The contempt for law demonstrated by the Watergate conspirators; Nixon was the first President to resign; Americans became cynical in their views of government. One positive aspect is that the structure of government proved to be strong and resilient.

RESOURCE DIRECTORY

Teaching Resources
Units 5/6/7 booklet
- Section 3 Quiz, p. 102

Guide to the Essentials
- Section 3 Summary, p. 123

Creating a Multimedia Presentation

The Space Age helped launch new technologies as well as put men on the moon. Today, "reports" are no longer limited to handwritten or typewritten papers. With the help of computers, audio recorders, scanners, VCRs, and more, you can add graphics, photos, and maps; intersperse a written report with audio segments and video clips; and even make your own Web site with quizzes and links.

LEARN THE SKILL

Use the following steps to create a multimedia presentation:

1. **Define your topic.** Multimedia presentations are best suited to topics that have a variety of aspects or subtopics and that lend themselves to visual or audio segments. But your topic should not be so broad that you cannot cover it thoroughly.
2. **Make a "blueprint"—a written plan—for your project.** Find out what media are available to you. Brainstorm! List main subtopics, key sources of information, and the sequence and description of segments. If you are working with a team, assign roles to all team members.
3. **Develop your presentation.** Set deadlines for each main task. Do research, write scripts, and gather materials. Collecting more material than you need will give you flexibility in editing and assembling your work. As in a written report, make sure your ideas flow logically.
4. **Present your work.** The best presentations are interactive, so try to involve your audience in the presentation.

PRACTICE THE SKILL

Answer the following questions:

1. **(a)** Do you think the history of space flight would be too broad or too narrow a topic, or would it be manageable? Explain. **(b)** Evaluate the first moon landing as a topic. **(c)** What audio or video segments might you use for each of these topics?
2. **(a)** Suppose your topic is the first moon landing. What might your subtopics be? **(b)** Besides NASA's Web site (www.nasa.gov), what other sources might be helpful? (Don't forget "stills," such as magazine photographs, newspaper headlines, or diagrams. You might also do your own research by taping interviews with people who watched the moon landing on television as it happened.) **(c)** Create a blueprint for your presentation.
3. **(a)** How much time will you need to gather or create materials? **(b)** How much time will you need to write a script? **(c)** Create a schedule and assign tasks.
4. **(a)** Who is your audience? It might be your classmates, a community group, or younger students. **(b)** How will you involve your audience in the presentation?

APPLY THE SKILL

See the Chapter Review and Assessment for another opportunity to apply this skill.

Creating a Multimedia Presentation

Focus Students will learn how to gather together and organize material to create a multimedia presentation.

Instruct Talk with students about the types of topics that are appropriate for multimedia presentations. Topics should be focused and should suggest both visual and audio components. Ask students if they think a multimedia presentation has the potential to be more engaging than a written presentation. What elements do they think will help make a presentation interesting? Brainstorm with students to generate a list of subjects that would lead naturally to a multimedia treatment.

Extend See the Skills for Life activity in the Resource Directory below.

ANSWERS

Practice the Skill

1. **(a)** Too broad; it is more than fifty years long, and would require detailed explanation of many different events. **(b)** The first moon landing is a good topic: it can be described in relatively brief terms; there are many examples of photographs and audio clips that would make an effective presentation. **(c)** The history of space flight: stills and video of rocket launches and spaceship recoveries, audio tapes of astronauts in space, photos and video of returning astronauts, photos and videos of Earth and outer space as seen from spacecraft, and the *Challenger* disaster. The first moon landing: flight video and interviews with those astronauts.
2. **(a)** Possible answers: the astronauts, the flight, the moonwalk, the public reaction. **(b)** Possible answers: the National Air and Space Museum, which maintains an online gallery with many images of *Apollo* artifacts. **(c)** Answers will vary.
3. **(a)** Answers will vary, but should be realistic. **(b)** Answers will vary. **(c)** Answers will vary.
4. **(a)** Answers will vary. **(b)** Answers will vary.

RESOURCE DIRECTORY

Teaching Resources

Skills for Life booklet, p. 34

Technology

Social Studies Skills Tutor CD-ROM

Interactive Practice in
- Geographic Literacy
- Critical Thinking and Reading
- Visual Analysis
- Communications

Section 4 The Ford Administration

Section Objectives

1. Find out how Gerald Ford became President, and learn why he pardoned Richard Nixon.
2. See the types of economic problems the Ford administration faced.
3. Learn about the foreign policy actions Ford took.
4. See how Americans celebrated the nation's bicentennial.

Bellringer

Warm-Up Activity Ask students to think of a time when they excused or forgave a friend, classmate, or family member. What does offering a pardon imply about the guilt or innocence of the person pardoned?

Activating Prior Knowledge Based on what students know about Richard Nixon's involvement in the Watergate scandal, do they agree or disagree with Gerald Ford's decision to pardon him?

Reading Strategy

Have students skim the section and use the headings and subheadings to create an outline for the section. As they read, have them fill in appropriate supporting details under each heading.

Activity

Connecting with Government

Have students take the role of presidential advisers and write a memo to President Ford that recommends a course of action for Richard Nixon's pardon. Tell students that their memos should convince Ford why he should or should not pardon the former President and suggest when he should reveal this decision to Nixon and the American people. **(Verbal/Linguistic)**

Section 4 The Ford Administration

READING FOCUS

- How did Gerald Ford become President, and why did he pardon Richard Nixon?
- What economic problems did the Ford administration face?
- What actions in foreign policy did President Ford take during his term?
- How did Americans celebrate the nation's bicentennial?

KEY TERMS

stagflation
War Powers Act
Helsinki Accords
bicentennial

TAKING NOTES

As you read, prepare an outline of this section. Use Roman numerals to indicate the major headings, capital letters for the subheadings, and numbers for the supporting details.

The Ford Administration
I. Ford Becomes President
A. Background
1. Served in House of Representatives
2. ____________

MAIN IDEA

After becoming President, Gerald Ford worked to reunite the country while facing economic problems at home and challenges abroad.

Setting the Scene The new President, Gerald R. Ford, faced a difficult job. In his autobiography he recalled the situation he faced when he took office in August 1974:

> "*The years of suspicion and scandal that had culminated in Nixon's resignation had demoralized our people. They had lost faith in their elected leaders and in their institutions. I knew that unless I did something to restore their trust, I couldn't win their consent [approval] to do anything else. . . . The New Frontier and Great Society promises of the 1960s had been partly responsible for the national disillusionment. The country didn't need more promises. It yearned for performance instead.*"
>
> —Gerald R. Ford, *A Time to Heal*

President Gerald Ford is shown with his wife Betty Ford, the new First Lady, after taking the oath of office.

Ford had to help the United States emerge from its worst political scandal. At the same time, the economy was in trouble, and the divisions over the Vietnam War had hardly begun to heal.

Ford Becomes President

"Jerry" Ford was one of the most popular politicians in Washington when he was appointed Vice President in October 1973, following Spiro Agnew's resignation. A football star at the University of Michigan, Ford had played on the national championship teams of 1932 and 1933, and had been a college all-star. After earning a law degree and serving in the navy during World War II, he entered politics. In 1948, he won election to the House of Representatives, where he rose to become Minority Leader in 1965. He was an unassuming man who believed in hard work and self-reliance.

Ford described himself as "conservative in fiscal affairs, moderate in domestic affairs, internationalist in foreign affairs." Over the years, he had opposed much government spending—federal aid to education, the antipoverty program,

Resource Directory

Teaching Resources
Guided Reading and Review booklet, p. 131

Technology
Section Reading Support Transparencies
Guided Reading Audiotapes (English/Spanish), Ch. 25
Student Edition on Audio CD, Ch. 25
Prentice Hall Presentation Pro CD-ROM, Ch. 25
Companion Web site, www.phschool.com

and spending for mass transit. He had supported defense spending and measures for law and order.

Nixon saw Ford as a noncontroversial figure who might bolster his own support in Congress. When Ford was confirmed as Vice President, Congress and the public were interested mainly in his reputation for honesty, integrity, and stability. Some, however, questioned whether he was qualified to take over the presidency if that became necessary. Despite Ford's long experience in Congress, he had little experience as an administrator or in foreign affairs. Ford acknowledged his own limitations when he was sworn in, saying, "I am a Ford, not a Lincoln."

When Nixon resigned in August 1974, Ford became the first nonelected President. Other Vice Presidents who had moved into the White House had been elected to the vice presidency as part of the national ticket. To fill the vice-presidential vacancy, Ford named former New York Governor Nelson Rockefeller. This created the unique situation of having both a President and a Vice President who had been appointed, not elected.

VIEWING HISTORY Betty Ford described her husband as "an accidental Vice President, and an accidental President, and in both jobs he replaced disgraced leaders." **Predicting Consequences** *What political risks did President Ford take when he pardoned Richard Nixon?*

The Nixon Pardon

Ford became President at the end of a turbulent time in the country's history. The nation was disillusioned by Watergate. During the scandal, many Americans had wondered whether the Constitution would survive Nixon's actions. Few people looked forward to the prospect of an impeachment trial. It would have been only the second in United States history; the first was that of Andrew Johnson in 1868. When Ford assumed the presidency, the nation needed a leader who could take it beyond the ugliness of Watergate.

In response to this public mood, President Ford declared that it was a time for "communication, conciliation, compromise and cooperation." Americans were on his side. *Time* magazine noted "a mood of good feeling and even exhilaration in Washington that the city had not experienced for many years."

All too quickly, Ford lost some popular support. Barely a month after Nixon had resigned, Ford pardoned the former President for "all offenses" he might have committed, avoiding further prosecution. On national television, Ford explained that he had looked to God and his own conscience in deciding "the right thing" to do about Nixon and "his loyal wife and family":

> *"Theirs is an American tragedy in which we have all played a part. It could go on and on and on, or someone must write the end to it. I have concluded that only I can do that, and if I can I must. . . . My conscience tells me that only I, as President, have the constitutional power to firmly shut and seal this book. My conscience tells me that it is my duty not merely to proclaim domestic tranquility but to use every means that I have to ensure it."*
>
> —Gerald R. Ford, September 8, 1974

Ford expected criticism of the pardon, but he underestimated the widespread negative reaction. Many of Nixon's loyalists were facing prison for their role in Watergate. The former President, however, walked away without a penalty. Although some people supported Ford's action, his generous gesture

READING CHECK
Describe the public mood during the Watergate scandal. How did Ford respond to this mood?

LESSON PLAN

Focus Explain that when Vice President Ford stepped up to the presidency after Nixon resigned in 1974, Americans were cheered by his honesty. However, Ford's administration failed to provide strong leadership. Ask what problems it faced.

Instruct Review the constitutional requirements for the office of President and discuss Ford's qualifications. What about Ford made him suitable as Nixon's Vice President but less suitable as President? Discuss Ford's reasons for pardoning Nixon; then review the public's reaction to Ford's well-intentioned action.

Discuss the efforts of the Ford administration to control inflation and increase productivity. Ask students to consider the results of these efforts. Why did the WIN program fail?

Assess/Reteach In 2001 Gerald Ford was given the Profiles in Courage award by the John F. Kennedy Library. He was cited for his bravery in pardoning Nixon. Ask students to discuss Ford's receipt of this award. Do they agree that he was deserving of it? If so, in what ways could his action be seen as courageous?

READING CHECK
The public was disillusioned, losing faith in the constitutional system, and dreading an impeachment trial. President Ford tried to create a mood of good feeling and communication.

CUSTOMIZE FOR ...
Less Proficient Readers
Ask students to find evidence in the text to help them assess President Ford's effectiveness in healing the wounds of Watergate, restoring the health of the economy, and maintaining peace and good relationships with other nations. Have them work together to create a report card to record their assessments, including comments.

TEST PREPARATION
Have students read the quote by President Ford on this page and then complete the sentence below.

The word *tranquility* in the passage means—

Ⓐ calm.
B happiness.
C power.
D tragedy.

CAPTION ANSWERS

Viewing History He risked alienating those who thought Nixon should be punished for Watergate, like the conspirators who went to jail. This might affect his political future, including support for his policies while in office and any future run for office. The public might lose faith in Ford's judgement. Ford also risked that the Republicans would suffer in the 1974 midterm election.

Activity

Connecting with Economics

This activity might take place over more than one class period. Divide students into groups of four. Have each group create a program designed to increase public acceptance of Ford's WIN campaign. Then have students rate the potential effectiveness of the WIN campaign overall. **(Verbal/ Linguistic; Logical/Mathematical)**

From the Archives of

American Heritage®

About the Presidents

Gerald Ford (1974–1977) became the first President to reach the White House by way of the Twenty-Fifth Amendment and provided the nation with a "time to heal" after the Watergate scandal. Raised in a modest Midwestern home, he used his athletic ability to gain entrance into the University of Michigan, where he not only starred on the football team, but received good enough grades to enter Yale Law School. After earning his law degree, he joined the Navy in the dark days of 1942 and fought in the Pacific, serving until 1946. Upon entering politics, he rose quickly through Republican ranks. All these experiences shaped Ford, who would always be essentially conservative, optimistic, and loyal to the institutions under which he thrived. Source: Adapted from Henry F. Graff's *The Presidents,* Scribner's, 1984, by the editors of *American Heritage*® magazine.

Focus on GOVERNMENT

Granting Pardons The President's power to "grant reprieves and pardons for offenses against the United States, except in cases of impeachment," is provided by Article II, Section 2 of the Constitution. Most often, pardons are given to individuals who have been convicted in court. President Ford's pardon of Nixon was unusual in that it was awarded before a trial ever took place. Whoever is granted a pardon must, in turn, accept it in order for that pardon to be carried out. Though Nixon was never convicted of his alleged crimes, he was seen to have admitted guilt when he accepted his pardon.

backfired. Some people suggested that a bargain had been made when Nixon resigned. Many also criticized the new President's judgment. Ford was occasionally booed when he made public speeches, just as Johnson and Nixon had been for their stands on the Vietnam war. To counter the reactions, he went before a House committee in October to explain his reasons. The public, angry both at Watergate and the pardon, voted a number of Republicans out of office in the 1974 congressional elections.

Economic Problems

While focusing on the Watergate scandal, the nation had paid less attention to other issues. In the meantime, some conditions had grown worse. Now, facing a hostile Congress, the new administration found it hard to provide direction.

The Economy Stalls Months of preoccupation with Watergate had kept Nixon from dealing with the economy. By 1974, inflation was at about 11 percent, much higher than it had been in the past. Unemployment climbed from about 5 percent in January 1974 to just over 7 percent by the year's end. Home building, usually a sign of a healthy economy, slowed as interest rates rose. The fears of investors brought a drop in stock prices.

Usually, federal policymakers had to deal with either inflation (the result of a rapidly growing economy) or unemployment (the result of a slow economy). Most economists believed that each of those trends could balance out the other. For example, a moderate rise in inflation would help lower the rate of unemployment. Now, however, inflation and unemployment both rose, while the economy remained stalled and stagnant. Economists named this new situation **stagflation.**

By the time Ford assumed the presidency, the country was in a recession, a period in which the economy is shrinking. Not since Franklin Roosevelt took office during the Great Depression had a new President faced such harsh economic troubles.

Ford's approach—like Herbert Hoover's in the early 1930s—was to try to restore public confidence. Early in October 1974, he sent Congress an economic program called "WIN," or "Whip Inflation Now." The President asked Americans to wear red and white "WIN" buttons; to save money, not spend it; to conserve fuel; and to plant vegetable gardens to counter high grocery store prices. The WIN campaign

INTERPRETING GRAPHS Ford's administration saw the worst economic slump in the United States since the Great Depression. **Analyzing Information** *In what year were consumer prices highest in the 1970s? When did unemployment peak in this decade?*

"Stagflation," 1970–1979

SOURCE: *Statistical Abstract of the United States*

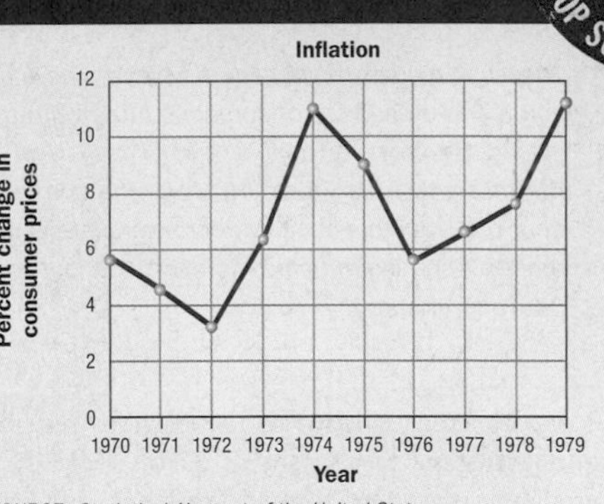

SOURCE: *Statistical Abstract of the United States*

Caption Answers

Interpreting Graphs 1979; 1975.

RESOURCE DIRECTORY

Other Print Resources

American History Block Scheduling Support *Presidential Power: Changes in the Twentieth Century,* found in The Nation After World War II folder, includes interdisciplinary lesson suggestions and activities for Geography and History, Primary Sources, Biography, and Literature.

depended on people voluntarily changing their everyday actions, but it had no real incentives. It soon faded away.

Eventually, Ford recognized the need for more direct action. The Federal Reserve tightened the money supply to control inflation, but the recession only worsened. Job layoffs were widespread. Unemployment soared to over 8 percent in 1975. Congress then backed an antirecession spending program. Despite his belief in less government spending, Ford backed an increase in unemployment benefits; he also supported a multibillion-dollar tax cut. While the economy did recover slightly, inflation and unemployment remained high.

Conflicts With Congress In spite of his long experience as a congressional leader, President Ford was often at odds with the Democratic-controlled Congress. He basically believed in limited government, while Congress wanted the government to take a more active role in the economy. Jerold F. terHorst, Ford's first press secretary, noted how Ford's own sense of decency came into conflict with his view of government:

> "*If he saw a schoolkid in front of the White House who needed clothing, he'd give him the shirt off his back, literally. Then he'd go right in the White House and veto a school-lunch bill.*"
>
> —Jerold F. terHorst

Ford vetoed bills to create a consumer protection agency and to fund programs for education, housing, and health care. Congress responded by creating its highest percentage of veto overrides since the presidency of Franklin Pierce in the 1850s.

Foreign Policy Actions

In foreign policy, Ford generally followed Nixon's approach and worked for détente. He kept Henry Kissinger on as Secretary of State. In 1974 and 1975, Ford made a series of trips abroad. He met with European leaders and was the first American President to visit Japan. Ford also visited China in order to continue improving the political and trade ties that Nixon had initiated. In Africa and elsewhere, the administration acted to develop relationships with countries that had recently gained independence after many years of colonial rule.

Southeast Asia In his policy toward Southeast Asia, Ford paid the price for Nixon's poor relationship with Congress. In 1973, Congress, angry at the growth of the "imperial presidency," had passed the **War Powers Act** over Nixon's veto. This law was designed to limit a President's ability to involve the United States in foreign conflicts without receiving a formal declaration of war from Congress. It stated that:

1. Within 48 hours of committing troops to overseas combat, the President must notify Congress of the reasons for this decision and the expected length of the mission.
2. The troops may not stay overseas for more than 60 days without congressional approval.
3. Congress can demand that the President bring the troops home.

In the spring of 1975, North Vietnam began a new offensive against the South. Ford asked for military aid to help South Vietnam meet the attack, but Congress rejected his request. Most Americans had no wish to become involved in Vietnam again, and Congress was willing to do anything—including using the War Powers Act if necessary—to make sure the United States stayed out of the war.

VIEWING HISTORY Continuing Nixon's policy of détente, President Ford (right) met with Soviet General Secretary Leonid Brezhnev (left) and other leaders at a 1975 summit in Finland. **Drawing Conclusions** *In what ways did Ford follow Nixon's policy of détente?*

ACTIVITY
Connecting with Culture

Ask students to research and report on the celebrations of the bicentennial that may have taken place in your community or one nearby. Reports should include descriptions of special projects and festivities. **(Verbal/Linguistic)**

BACKGROUND
Recent Scholarship

In the late 1960s and early 1970s the United States began to learn its limits in both foreign and domestic affairs. The Vietnam War taught America that it could not do everything it wanted to on the world stage. Nor could the President pursue an agenda at home without restraint. In *The Limits of Power: The Nixon and Ford Administrations,* John Robert Greene observes how the nation and the Republican Presidents in these years struggled to deal with these new limits and to come to terms with a new American attitude toward government.

CAPTION ANSWERS

Viewing History He kept Kissinger on as Secretary of State. He visited China, as had Nixon, and also met with Soviet leader Leonid Brezhnev.

Section 4 Assessment

Reading Comprehension

1. Inflation and unemployment were high as the economy continued to shrink.
2. It was designed to limit a President's ability to involve the United States in foreign conflicts without receiving a formal declaration of war from Congress.
3. The United States, Canada, the Soviet Union, and about 30 European countries pledged economic cooperation, respect for existing national boundaries, and promised to promote human rights.
4. The 200th anniversary of the signing of the Declaration of Independence.

Critical Thinking and Writing

5. Answers should reflect an understanding of Ford's wish to bring an end to Watergate and of the widespread, negative public reaction to his decision.
6. Articles will vary, but should be supported with facts from the section.

Take It to the NET

Time lines should chronicle the Ford presidency and may include some of the following events: Nixon's resignation, Ford's inauguration, the Nixon pardon, stagflation, "WIN," the War Powers Act, the Helsinki Accords.

Caption Answers

Viewing History Sample answer: Dignity, joy, pride, and strength.

VIEWING HISTORY Majestic tall ships sail past the Statue of Liberty in celebration of the bicentennial. **Drawing Inferences** *What images of the nation's past do these ships bring to mind?*

By late April, the South Vietnamese capital, Saigon, was about to fall. Ford agreed to an American airlift that helped evacuate thousands of Americans and Vietnamese.

Southeast Asia remained a foreign policy problem even after the fall of South Vietnam. In May 1975, soldiers from Communist Cambodia (which had fallen to the Khmer Rouge) captured the *Mayaguez,* an American merchant ship cruising in Cambodian waters. When protests by the United States went unanswered, Ford sent the marines to recapture the ship. The crew was retrieved, but at a high cost: 41 Americans were killed. Later investigations showed that the Cambodian government apparently had been preparing to return both ship and crew. For the administration, however, the incident was a chance to dispel the impression of American weakness in the region.

Europe and the Soviet Union On another foreign policy front, President Ford signed the **Helsinki Accords,** a series of agreements on European security made at a 1975 summit meeting in Finland. The United States, Canada, the Soviet Union, and about 30 European countries pledged to cooperate economically, respect existing national boundaries, and promote human rights. Ford also continued Strategic Arms Limitation Talks (SALT) with the Soviet Union, holding out hope for further limits on nuclear weapons.

The Nation's Birthday

Americans held a nationwide birthday party to mark July 4, 1976, the **bicentennial,** the 200th anniversary of the signing of the Declaration of Independence. Throughout the summer, people in small towns and big cities across the country celebrated with parades, concerts, air shows, political speeches, and fireworks. With so many Americans discouraged by Watergate, Vietnam, and the recession, the celebrations could not have been better timed.

On the Fourth of July, more than 200 sailing ships paraded into New York City's harbor while millions watched from many countries. Cities across the nation staged spectacular fireworks shows and long parades. Many observers saw in the bicentennial celebrations a revival of optimism after years of gloom.

Section 4 Assessment

READING COMPREHENSION

1. How did **stagflation** and recession harm the economy in the 1970s?
2. What was the purpose of the **War Powers Act?**
3. Who participated in the **Helsinki Accords,** and what were the agreements?
4. What did the **bicentennial** commemorate?

CRITICAL THINKING AND WRITING

5. **Predicting Consequences** What might have happened if Ford had not pardoned Nixon?
6. **Writing a News Story** Write the lead article for a local newspaper on July 4, 1976. Describe the significance of the nationwide celebrations on that day in the context of recent events.

Take It to the NET

Activity: Creating a Time Line
Investigate the key events of the Ford presidency, from his inauguration to his defeat in the 1976 election. Create a time line of Ford's term in office using pictures and quotations. Use the links provided in the *America: Pathways to the Present* area of the following Web site for help in completing this activity.
www.phschool.com

RESOURCE DIRECTORY

Teaching Resources
Units 5/6/7 booklet
- Section 4 Quiz, p. 103

Guide to the Essentials
- Section 4 Summary, p. 124

Learning with Documents booklet (Primary Source Activity) *1976: The Bicentennial Year,* p. 37

Section

5 The Carter Administration

READING FOCUS

- What changes did Jimmy Carter bring to the presidency?
- How did Carter deal with domestic issues?
- What ideals guided Carter's foreign policy?
- What factors influenced the outcome of the 1980 election?

KEY TERMS

incumbent
deregulation
amnesty
affirmative action
Camp David Accords
dissident

TAKING NOTES

Copy the chart below. As you read, fill in the major initiatives President Carter took and the results of each action.

The Carter Administration		
Policy	**Action**	**Result**
Economy	Cut government spending	Increased unemployment and business failures
Energy		
Civil Rights		
Foreign Relations		

MAIN IDEA

Jimmy Carter's human rights diplomacy brought notable accomplishments in foreign policy, but his inability to work effectively with Congress blocked the success of his domestic programs.

Setting the Scene The 1976 presidential campaign brought surprises for both political parties. Gerald Ford, who said at first that he would not be a candidate for President, later changed his mind. Even though Ford was the **incumbent**—the current office holder—he faced strong opposition from conservative fellow Republicans inside his own party. The Democrats nominated a candidate few Americans had even heard of at the start of the campaign: James Earl ("Jimmy") Carter, Jr., a former governor of Georgia. Carter went on to defeat Ford by a narrow margin.

In his Inaugural Address, President Carter outlined his beliefs:

> *"The American dream endures. We must once again have full faith in our country—and in one another. . . . Our commitment to human rights must be absolute, our laws fair, our natural beauty preserved; the powerful must not persecute the weak, and human dignity must be enhanced."*
>
> —Jimmy Carter, Inaugural Address, January 20, 1977

Carter's Presidency

Jimmy Carter, a southerner with no national political experience, was different from his recent predecessors in the White House. His family had lived for generations in the rural South. A 1946 graduate of the United States Naval Academy, Carter served as an engineering officer on nuclear submarines. When his father died, he took over management of the family's peanut farm and warehouse. He entered politics in 1962 and was elected governor of Georgia in 1970.

Carter was a born-again Baptist whose deeply felt religious faith was central to his view of the world. While holding his own strong religious beliefs, though, Carter respected those of others.

At first, people responded warmly to Carter's "down home" approach. They loved it when he and his wife Rosalynn dismissed their limousine after the inauguration and strolled

Abandoning the traditional limousine ride, President Jimmy Carter takes an inaugural stroll with his wife Rosalynn and daughter Amy.

Section 5

The Carter Administration

Section Objectives

1. Discover some changes Jimmy Carter brought to the presidency.
2. Learn how Carter dealt with domestic issues.
3. Find out about the ideals that guided Carter's foreign policy.
4. Discover some factors that influenced the outcome of the 1980 election.

Bellringer

Warm-Up Activity Ask students how they would rate the honesty of the current President and administration. Ask if they can envision any situation in which a President should be less than completely open and honest with the public.

Activating Prior Knowledge Jimmy Carter was celebrated for his honesty, his righteousness, and his moral certainty, qualities that have served him well in the years since his presidency. Can students name some of the types of activities in which Carter has been engaged since his presidency?

Reading Strategy

Have students write the words *Jimmy Carter* in the center of a web diagram. Then as they read the section, have them note major details about Carter in surrounding circles.

Activity

Connecting with Government

Ask students to create political cartoons that express an opinion on the election of Jimmy Carter as President. Suggest to students that their cartoons could focus on some aspect of Carter's personal background, his level of political experience, or his status as a Washington "outsider" in presenting a viewpoint on what his presidency might be like. **(Visual/Spatial)**

RESOURCE DIRECTORY

Teaching Resources
Learning Styles Lesson Plans booklet, p. 67
Guided Reading and Review booklet, p. 132

Technology
Section Reading Support Transparencies
Guided Reading Audiotapes (English/Spanish), Ch. 25
Student Edition on Audio CD, Ch. 25
Prentice Hall Presentation Pro CD-ROM, Ch. 25
Companion Web site, www.phschool.com

Lesson Plan

Focus Explain that in 1976, Jimmy Carter, former governor of Georgia, was elected President. Ask what promises Carter made to the American people.

Instruct Discuss how Ford's failure to convey a "presidential" image on television affected the election of 1976. Ask students which recent President they think has had the strongest "presidential" image, and whether that President was also a good leader.

Discuss how Carter's outsider status and his choice of other outsiders as his key advisers hampered his ability to work with Congress.

Assess/Reteach Ask students to analyze the degree to which Carter's essential human decency, as perceived by the electorate, influenced his election. Why was this quality so important to voters in the election of 1976?

READING CHECK

Sample answer: He had a "down-home" approach; he eliminated many of the ceremonial details of White House life; he appointed many more women and minorities to his staff than previous administrations had. He came to office as an untarnished "Washington outsider."

VIEWING HISTORY The Carters brought an informal style to the presidency. In spite of the President's low-key image, he was known among friends as a "super-achiever." **Identifying Central Issues** *Why do you think Carter's style appealed to many people?*

down Pennsylvania Avenue with their young daughter. He spoke to the nation on television wearing a cardigan sweater instead of a business suit. He eliminated many of the ceremonial details of White House life, such as trumpets to announce his entrance at official receptions. Some critics, however, began to complain about a lack of dignity and ceremony in the presidency.

The new President appointed many more women and minorities to his staff than previous administrations had done. Of about 1,200 full-time appointees, 12 percent were women, 12 percent were African American, and another 4 percent were Hispanic. In nominating federal judges, he chose four times as many women as had all previous Presidents combined.

Carter's lack of connections to Washington had helped him in the election campaign, since he had not been tarnished by failure or scandal. Once he became President, though, the "Washington outsider" role had disadvantages. The White House staff and other close advisors were also southerners, mostly Georgians. They had little sense of how crucial it was for the President to work with Congress. Carter himself was uneasy with Congress's demands and found it difficult to get legislation passed. He had no congressional experience and no former colleagues in Congress. He lacked Lyndon Johnson's ability to win over reluctant politicians.

READING CHECK
How did Carter attempt to become a different kind of President?

Carter's Domestic Policies

Jimmy Carter had little success in promoting his domestic programs. Looking back, he wrote, "I quickly learned that it is a lot easier to hold a meeting, reach a tentative agreement, or make a speech than to get a controversial program through Congress."

That was not the only problem. As the *New York Times* columnist Tom Wicker observed, Carter "never established a politically coherent administration." His strategies were not clearly defined. Public support faded as his programs floundered.

Economic Issues Carter inherited an unstable economy. Like his predecessors, he had trouble controlling inflation without hurting economic growth. To prevent another recession, Carter tried to stimulate the economy with government deficit spending. As deficits grew, the Federal Reserve Board increased the money supply. However, inflation then rose to about 10 percent.

In an attempt to stop inflation, slow the economy, and reduce the deficit, Carter then cut federal spending. The cuts fell mostly on social programs,

Caption Answers

Viewing History Sample answer: His down-to-earth style was a refreshing contrast to Nixon's imperial and dishonest administration.

RESOURCE DIRECTORY

Teaching Resources

Learning with Documents booklet (Key Documents) *Barbara Jordan, Keynote Address to the Democratic National Convention,* p. 96

Biography, Literature, and Comparing Primary Sources booklet (Biography) *Patricia Roberts Harris,* p. 37

Technology

RESOURCE PRO® **Primary Source Activity** *A Crisis of Confidence,* found on Resource Pro, presents an excerpt from a televised address in which President Carter talks about factors he sees "threatening to destroy the social and political fabric of America."

angering liberal Democrats. At the same time, the slowdown in the economy increased unemployment and the number of business failures. The situation became worse in 1980, when the new federal budget called for increased government spending. In reaction, bond prices fell and interest rates soared. Americans lost confidence in Carter and his economic advisors.

Deregulation Carter had more success in the area of **deregulation**—the reduction or removal of government controls in several industries. In the late 1800s and early 1900s, agencies such as the Interstate Commerce Commission had been established to regulate rates and business practices. Over time, government regulations had multiplied. Carter argued that they hurt competition and increased consumer costs.

To encourage greater energy production, Carter proposed removing controls on prices for oil and natural gas. He also took steps to deregulate the railroad, trucking, and airline industries. While consumer groups and many liberal Democrats opposed deregulation, it continued during the next two administrations, both of which were Republican.

Energy Issues In the late 1970s, more than 40 percent of the oil used in the United States came from other countries. OPEC, the Organization of Petroleum Exporting Countries, had been raising oil prices steadily since 1973. In April 1977, Carter presented his energy program to Congress and the public. He asked people to save fuel by driving less and using less heat and air conditioning in their homes and offices. He also created a new Cabinet department, the Department of Energy, to coordinate the federal programs promoting conservation and researching new energy sources. Carter called the need for energy conservation the "moral equivalent of war."

Representatives from states that produced oil and gas fiercely opposed Carter's energy plan. Many proposals were stalled in Congress for months. In 1978, though, the National Energy Act finally passed. It included these directives:

1. Tax sales of inefficient, "gas-guzzling," cars.
2. Convert new utilities to fuels other than oil or natural gas.
3. Deregulate prices for domestic oil and natural gas.
4. Provide tax credits or loans to homeowners for using solar energy and improving the insulation in their homes.
5. Fund research for alternative energy sources such as solar energy and synthetic fuels.

Nuclear power seemed to be a promising alternative energy source. Serious questions remained about its cost and safety, however. In March 1979, people's doubts appeared to be confirmed by an accident at the nuclear power plant at Three Mile Island, near Harrisburg, Pennsylvania. A partial meltdown of the reactor core occurred, releasing some radiation. About 140,000 people who lived near the plant fled their homes, terrified by the idea of a radioactive leak. The story made headlines around the world.

COMPARING PRIMARY SOURCES
On Nuclear Energy

The need to reduce the dependence on foreign oil prompted viewpoints strongly for and against nuclear power.

Analyzing Viewpoints What are the main concerns of each of the speakers below?

In Favor of Nuclear Energy

"When you debate the issue of nuclear energy, you are actually debating the issue of growth. Growth will be the key issue for the remainder of this century, and it is the resolution of that issue which will determine the lifestyles of most Americans for generations. . . . Economic growth has been inextricably linked to the growth of the supply of energy throughout history."

—*Senator James A. McClure (Idaho), addressing the National Conference on Energy Advocacy, February 2, 1979*

Opposed to Nuclear Energy

"If this country . . . continues to rely more and more on nuclear power a meltdown disaster is almost predictable. . . . For years now, the utilities and nuclear power industry have refused to listen to scientific logic and reasoning concerning the dangers of this technology. . . . Perhaps it is time for emotion and for passion and for commitment to stir our souls and our hearts and our minds once again into action."

—*Dr. Helen Caldicott, in* Nuclear Madness, What You Can Do!, *1980*

ACTIVITY
Connecting with Economics

Pair students to determine how each of the provisions of the National Energy Act of 1978 could be expected to contribute to energy conservation. Call on pairs to report their conclusions to the class. **(Logical/Mathematical)**

BACKGROUND
Connections to Today

The election of born-again Baptist Jimmy Carter encouraged evangelical Christians to again become involved with politics and government. This group was not very active in politics after losing the battle over teaching evolution in public schools in the 1920s. Until the 1970s they were less politically active than other Americans and less likely than other Christians to support their churches' involvement in political issues. However, Carter's campaign, which stressed the need for a return of morality to government, was one of the events that gave many evangelical Christians a new sense of entitlement and political legitimacy. They responded by becoming more involved in politics than most other Christians. From this transformation, the conservative political movement known today as the "religious right" was born.

ACTIVITY
Connecting with Citizenship

Invite students to imagine that they are living in the late 1970s. Have them write letters to the editor explaining why they support or oppose President Carter's pardon of Vietnam draft evaders or the Supreme Court's ruling in the *Bakke* decision. Select letters representing each side of each issue to share with the class. **(Verbal/Linguistic)**

BACKGROUND
Art History

In an amazing coincidence, just nine days before the partial meltdown at Three Mile Island, Columbia Pictures released a movie entitled *The China Syndrome,* a nuclear industry term for a theoretical scenario in which a reactor meltdown bores a hole in the earth all the way to China. The movie, starring Michael Douglas, Jane Fonda, and Jack Lemmon, is about a serious accident at a fictional nuclear power plant. Its story line magnified public concern over the TMI accident. Also unsettling was that the movie had been based on a real event in Alabama in 1975, when a failed system nearly caused a meltdown of a reactor's nuclear fuel and threatened a possible real "China syndrome."

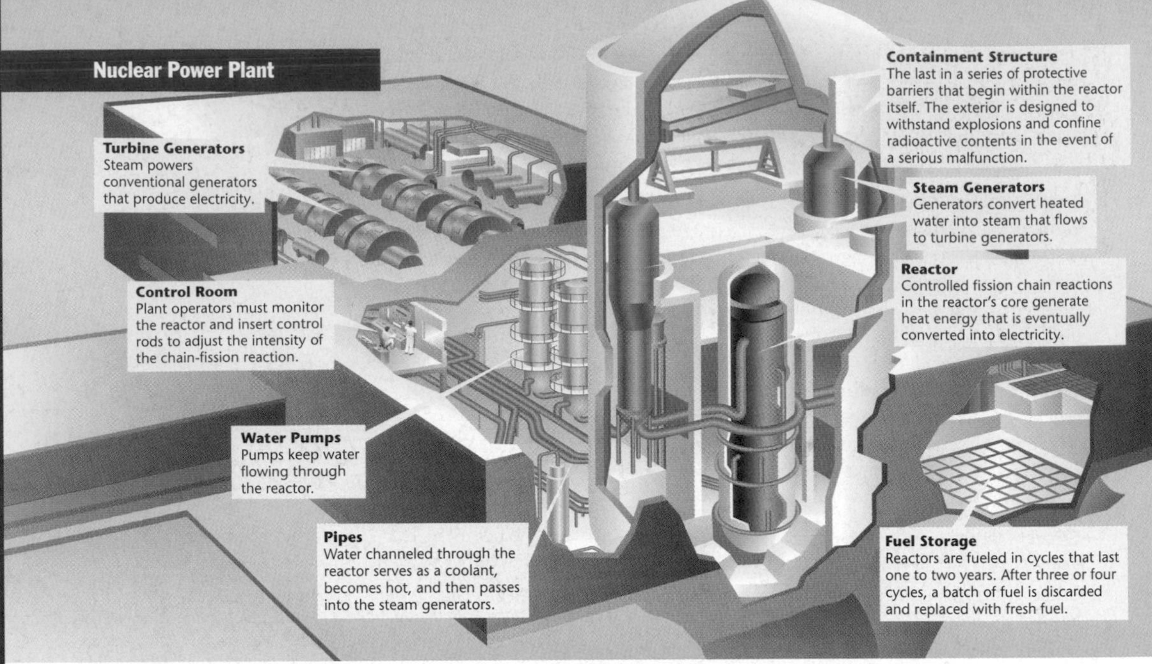

Nuclear Power Plant
Turbine Generators
Steam powers conventional generators that produce electricity.
Control Room
Plant operators must monitor the reactor and insert control rods to adjust the intensity of the chain-fission reaction.
Water Pumps
Pumps keep water flowing through the reactor.
Pipes
Water channeled through the reactor serves as a coolant, becomes hot, and then passes into the steam generators.
Containment Structure
The last in a series of protective barriers that begin within the reactor itself. The exterior is designed to withstand explosions and confine radioactive contents in the event of a serious malfunction.
Steam Generators
Generators convert heated water into steam that flows to turbine generators.
Reactor
Controlled fission chain reactions in the reactor's core generate heat energy that is eventually converted into electricity.
Fuel Storage
Reactors are fueled in cycles that last one to two years. After three or four cycles, a batch of fuel is discarded and replaced with fresh fuel.

INTERPRETING DIAGRAMS Inside a nuclear power plant, a series of steps lead to the production of electricity. **Synthesizing Information** *What element is used to cool the reactor?*

Carter named a commission to investigate the accident at Three Mile Island. The commission's report identified operator errors that had made the initial problem worse. In his response to the report, Carter noted "very serious shortcomings in the way that both the government and the utility industry regulate and manage nuclear power." He proposed reorganizing the Nuclear Regulatory Commission, the agency in charge of nuclear power. He also called on utility companies to improve standards.

Civil Rights Issues Carter's concern for moral values influenced his approach to domestic questions. Soon after taking office, he carried out his promise to grant **amnesty**—a general pardon—to those who had evaded the draft during the Vietnam War. Because that war still divided Americans, reactions were mixed.

As governor of Georgia, Carter had had a good civil rights record. As President, Carter tried to move beyond the civil rights battles of the 1950s and 1960s. Many of Carter's staff appointments, such as the United Nations ambassadorship for Andrew Young, won the approval of African Americans. On the other hand, many African Americans were disappointed by the President's weak support for social programs.

In 1978, the Supreme Court ruled on a civil rights case that would have important effects on **affirmative action** policies. First enacted during Lyndon Johnson's presidency, such policies aim to make up for past discrimination against women and members of minority groups by increasing their opportunities in areas such as employment and education. Allan Bakke, a white applicant, was refused admission to the medical school at the University of California (Davis) in 1973 and 1974. He sued the school, saying that its affirmative action policy amounted to "reverse discrimination." Specifically, Bakke charged that the policy of reserving 16 of 100 class spaces for minority group applicants violated both the Civil Rights Act of 1964 and the Constitution.

CAPTION ANSWERS

Interpreting Diagrams Water.

RESOURCE DIRECTORY

Teaching Resources

Great Debates booklet (Great Debates) *What Should Be the Rights of the Accused?* p. 26

Technology

Color Transparencies *The Way It Works,* H20

In a complex ruling in *Regents of the University of California* v. *Bakke,* the Court ordered that Bakke be admitted to the California medical school. It also upheld the school's right to consider race as one factor in admission decisions, but it did not allow the use of numerical quotas. While the Court decision supported the concept of affirmative action, the case signaled the start of a backlash against the policy.

Carter's Foreign Policy

Although Jimmy Carter had little diplomatic experience when he took office, his personal beliefs greatly influenced his decisions on foreign affairs. Support for human rights was the cornerstone of Carter's foreign policy.

Camp David Accords Carter's commitment to finding ethical solutions to complicated problems was most visible in the Middle East. In that unstable region, Israel and the Arab nations had fought several wars, most recently in 1967 and 1973. In 1977, though, Egypt's President Anwar el-Sadat made a historic visit to Israel to begin negotiations with Prime Minister Menachem Begin. The two men had such different personalities, however, that they had trouble compromising. Carter intervened, sending Secretary of State Cyrus Vance to invite them to Camp David, the presidential retreat in the Maryland hills.

At Camp David in September 1978, Carter assumed the role of peacemaker. He practiced highly effective personal diplomacy to bridge the gap between Sadat and Begin. They finally agreed on a framework for peace that became known as the **Camp David Accords.** Under the resulting peace treaty, Israel would withdraw from the Sinai peninsula, which it had occupied since 1967. Egypt, in return, became the first Arab country to recognize Israel's existence as a nation.

The Camp David Accords, of course, did not solve all the problems in the Middle East. Among the remaining problems were issues concerning the Palestinians. Many had fled their homes when Arab nations declared war on Israel immediately after that country was established in 1948. Still, as Secretary of State Vance noted:

VIEWING HISTORY President Carter congratulates Egypt's President Sadat (left) and Israel's Prime Minister Begin (right) on the signing of the Camp David Accords. **Drawing Conclusions** *What were the major achievements of the accords?*

> *"The Camp David Accords rank as one of the most important achievements of the Carter administration. First, they opened the way to peace between Egypt and Israel, which transformed the entire political, military, and strategic character of the Middle East dispute. Genuine peace between Egypt and Israel meant there would be no major Arab-Israeli war, whatever the positions of [other Arab groups]."*
>
> —Cyrus Vance, *Hard Choices*

Soviet-American Relations Several issues complicated the relationship between the United States and the Soviet Union. Détente was at a high point when Carter took office. However, Carter's stand on human rights angered Soviet leaders, undermining the efforts of the two nations to work together. The Soviets were especially annoyed when the President spoke in support of Soviet **dissidents**—writers and other activists who criticized the actions of their government. Soviet citizens were denied the right to speak freely or to criticize their political leaders. Carter believed that such rights were essential

ACTIVITY
Connecting with History and Conflict

To emphasize the importance of the Carter administration in bringing stability to the Middle East, divide students into groups of three to form peace negotiation teams. Each group should assign one student to play Anwar el-Sadat of Egypt, another to be Menachem Begin of Israel, and the third to play President Carter. Have each group then role-play the Camp David peace negotiations. **(Verbal/Linguistic)**

BACKGROUND
Biography

Few former Presidents have shown the dedication to serving humanity as that displayed by Jimmy Carter. After leaving office in 1981, he founded the Carter Presidential Center, an organization devoted to democracy and human rights. As a private citizen he also monitored elections and mediated disputes in Nicaragua, Panama, Ethiopia, and Haiti. In 1994 Carter helped to settle a nuclear-weapons dispute between the United States and North Korea, and his involvement in Bosnia helped bring the war there to an end in 1995. Carter's activities as a founder and volunteer carpenter with Habitat for Humanity, an organization that builds houses for low-income people, have also enhanced his reputation as an ex-President, which now far exceeds that of his White House years.

CUSTOMIZE FOR ...
Gifted and Talented

Have students analyze to what extent a President's personal beliefs should affect administration policy and presidential actions. Ask whether or not Carter's insertion of his own morality into his foreign policy was appropriate. Responses can take the form of a speech either defending or criticizing Carter's use of personal morality in formulating policy.

TEST PREPARATION

Have students read the quotation by Cyrus Vance on this page and then complete the sentence below.

From the passage, you can infer that Vance believed—

A that peace was instantly enacted with the signing of the Accords.

B that the Accords were a minor achievement for Carter.

(C) that Israel and Egypt were the key players in maintaining peace in the Middle East.

D that the Accords would have no real effect on the region.

CAPTION ANSWERS

Viewing History Peace was secured between Israel and Egypt. Israel withdrew from the Sinai peninsula, and Egypt extended formal diplomatic recognition to Israel.

ACTIVITY
Student Portfolio

You may wish to have students add the following to their portfolios: Ask students to respond to the following statement by President Carter: "The great democracies are not free because we are strong and prosperous. I believe we are strong and influential because we are free." Students should explain the relationship between freedom and strength. **(Verbal/Linguistic)**

BACKGROUND
Human Rights

A legacy of the Carter era is the link between human rights and diplomacy. As Winston Lord, Assistant Secretary of State for East Asian and Pacific Affairs (1993–1997), described the post–Cold War 1990s: "There are still security considerations, but increasingly the thrust of the debate in foreign policy today is economics versus human rights. . . . I find myself going from a meeting with Amnesty International or Asia Watch in the morning to one with the Chamber of Commerce in the afternoon."

Focus on WORLD EVENTS

The Panama Canal In the early 1900s, President Theodore Roosevelt had been proud of the way the United States had gained control of land for the Panama Canal. Many Latin Americans, though, resented the continuing United States presence in Panama.

In spite of bitter debate in Congress, in 1978 President Carter convinced the Senate to ratify two treaties dealing with the canal. One treaty was an agreement to return the canal to Panama by the year 2000. The other gave the United States the right to take military action to keep the canal open. The pacts protected American interests while improving relations with Latin America.

and was outspoken in defending them, even when such a defense caused international friction.

In spite of the discord, a second round of Strategic Arms Limitation Talks (SALT II) led Carter and Soviet leader Leonid Brezhnev to sign a new treaty in June 1979. More complicated than SALT I, this agreement limited the number of nuclear warheads and missiles held by each superpower.

Late in 1979, before the Senate could ratify SALT II, the Soviet Union invaded Afghanistan, a country on its southern border, to bolster a Soviet-supported government there. Carter telephoned Brezhnev and told him that the invasion was "a clear threat to the peace." He added, "Unless you draw back from your present course of action, this will inevitably jeopardize the course of United States–Soviet relations throughout the world." A United Nations resolution also called for Soviet withdrawal.

Carter halted American grain shipments to the Soviet Union and took other steps to show United States disapproval of Soviet aggression. Realizing that SALT II surely would be turned down, he removed the treaty from Senate consideration. (Although SALT II was never ratified, both countries followed the terms of the treaty based on its signing.) Carter also imposed a boycott on the 1980 summer Olympic Games to be held in Moscow. Eventually, some 60 other nations joined the Olympic boycott. Détente was effectively dead.

The Iran Hostage Crisis Iran, Afghanistan's neighbor to the west, was the scene of the worst foreign policy crisis of the Carter administration. For years the United States had supported the shah (or king) of Iran, Mohammad Reza Shah Pahlavi. The shah had taken many steps to modernize Iran. He was also a reliable supplier of oil and a pro-Western force in the region. For these reasons, Americans overlooked the corruption and harsh repression of the shah's government.

In January 1979, revolution broke out in Iran. It was led by Muslim fundamentalists, who wanted to bring back traditional ways, and by liberal critics of the shah, who wanted more political and economic reforms. As the revolution spread, the shah fled the country. He was replaced by an elderly Islamic leader, the Ayatollah Ruholla Khomeini, who had been in exile. Khomeini and his followers were aggressively anti-Western and planned to make Iran a strict Islamic state.

In October, out of concern for the shah's health, Carter let him enter the United States for medical treatment. Many Iranians were outraged. On November 4, 1979, angry followers of Khomeini seized the American embassy in Tehran and took Americans, mostly embassy workers, hostage.

VIEWING HISTORY Iranian protestors express anti-American sentiment in Tehran, where the American embassy was seized. **Identifying Central Issues** *What events led to the hostage crisis?*

For 444 days, revolutionaries imprisoned 52 hostages in different locations. The prisoners were blindfolded and moved from place to place. Some were tied up and beaten. Others spent time in solitary confinement and faced mock executions intended to terrorize them. One of the hostages, Kathryn Koob, described part of her experiences:

> "*[T]he sounds outside the embassy were nerve-wracking. . . . There seemed to be a continuous crowd of people shouting anti-American slogans, listening to the exhortations [cries] of the students and mullahs [clergymen] who were always on hand. In addition to the crowd noises, there were three or four loudspeakers blaring newscasts. . . . As I sat confined in my chair I thought . . . I just can't take this.*"
>
> —Kathryn Koob, *Guest of the Revolution*

CAPTION ANSWERS

Viewing History For years, the U.S. backed the shah of Iran, whose corrupt government was harshly repressive. After Iran's shah was replaced by the anti-Western Ayatollah Khomeini, Carter allowed the former shah to obtain medical treatment in the United States. Outraged Iranians seized the American embassy and took hostages.

RESOURCE DIRECTORY

Teaching Resources

Units 5/6/7 booklet
- Section 5 Quiz, p. 104
- Chapter 25 Test, pp. 105, 108

Guide to the Essentials
- Section 5 Summary, p. 125
- Chapter 25 Test, p. 126

Other Print Resources

Chapter Tests with ExamView® Test Bank CD-ROM, Ch. 25

Technology

Sounds of an Era Audio CD *Carter on Hostages in Iran* (time: 35 seconds)

RESOURCE PRO® **Biography** *Andrew Young,* found on Resource Pro, profiles the civil rights leader and President Carter's ambassador to the United Nations.

ExamView® Test Bank CD-ROM, Ch. 25

Social Studies Skills Tutor CD-ROM

Meanwhile, the American public became more impatient for the hostages' release. President Carter tried many approaches to secure the hostages' freedom. He broke diplomatic relations with Iran and froze all Iranian assets in the United States. Khomeini held out, insisting that the shah be sent back for trial. In April 1980, Carter authorized a risky commando rescue mission. It ended in disaster when several helicopters broke down in the desert, and eight American soldiers were killed. The government was humiliated, and Carter's popularity dropped further. Even after the shah died in July, the standoff continued. Carter's chances for reelection appeared dim.

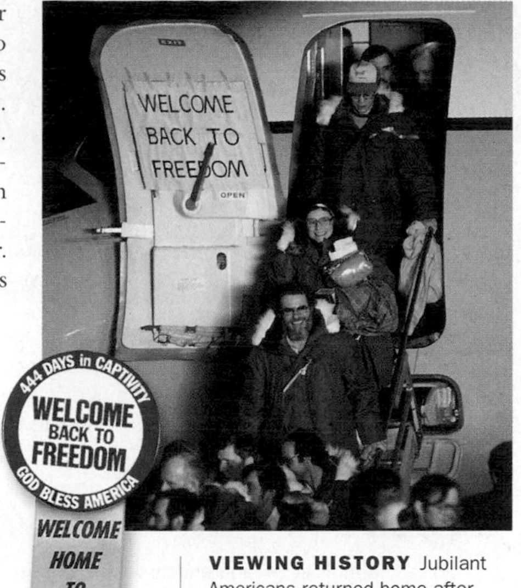

444 DAYS in CAPTIVITY
WELCOME BACK TO FREEDOM
GOD BLESS AMERICA
WELCOME HOME TO FREEDOM

VIEWING HISTORY Jubilant Americans returned home after being held hostage by Iranians. **Drawing Conclusions** *How did Carter's handling of the hostage crisis affect his career?*

The 1980 Election

Despite Carter's achievements in the Middle East and his commitment to serious goals, his administration had lost the confidence of many Americans. Rising inflation in early 1980 dropped his approval rating to 21 percent in public opinion polls. Unemployment was still over 7 percent. At times Carter himself seemed to have lost confidence. In two speeches in July, he spoke of a national "crisis of confidence" and a "national malaise."

In the Democratic primaries leading up to the 1980 elections, Massachusetts Senator Edward M. Kennedy won a large number of delegate votes. Kennedy withdrew just as the Democratic National Convention began, however, and Carter was nominated again. Nonetheless, many people were ready for the optimism of the Republican candidate, Ronald Reagan. A leading conservative, Reagan had failed to win his party's nomination in 1976. In 1980, however, Reagan won the nomination, and went on to win the election by a landslide.

After months of secret talks, the Iranians agreed to release the 52 hostages in early 1981. Not until the day Carter left office, however, were they allowed to come home. Newly elected President Reagan sent Carter, as a private citizen, to greet the hostages as they arrived at a U.S. military base in West Germany.

Section 5 Assessment

READING COMPREHENSION

1. What is an **incumbent?**
2. What issues concerning **deregulation, amnesty,** and **affirmative action** came up during Carter's presidency?
3. What were the **Camp David Accords?**
4. Why did the United States and the Soviet Union clash over Soviet **dissidents?**

CRITICAL THINKING AND WRITING

5. **Making Comparisons** List examples of the positive and negative results of Carter's approach to foreign policy.
6. **Writing a Letter to the Editor** Write a letter in which you support or oppose Carter's program to conserve energy.

Take It to the NET

Activity: Brainstorming
Research the Iran Hostage Crisis. With your class, explore alternative ways that could have been used to approach the crisis. Use the links provided in the *America: Pathways to the Present* area of the following Web site for help in completing this activity.
www.phschool.com

Section 5 Assessment

Reading Comprehension

1. The current office holder.
2. President Carter removed price controls on oil and natural gas in the hope of increasing energy production. He also began to deregulate the railroad, trucking and airline industries. He granted amnesty to those who had evaded the draft during the Vietnam War; the 1978 Supreme Court ruling in *Regents of the University of California* v. *Bakke* started a backlash against affirmative action.
3. A framework for peace between Egypt and Israel, which was brokered by President Carter.
4. Carter believed that it was wrong for Russian leaders to deny Soviet citizens the right to speak freely and to criticize their political leaders.

Critical Thinking and Writing

5. Positive: Camp David Accords initiated Middle East peace talks; the Panama Canal treaties showed U.S. willingness to deal fairly with other nations. Negative: Carter had very little success in dealing with the Soviet Union; his response to the Iran hostage crisis was clumsy and ineffective.
6. Letters will vary but should be supported with facts from the section.

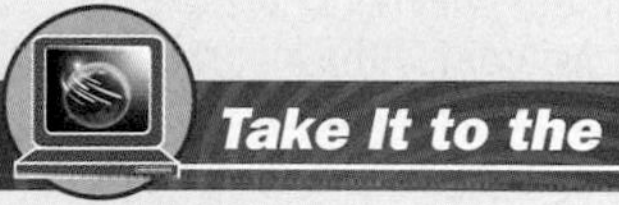

Students should evaluate the effectiveness of President Carter's decisions in regard to the hostage crisis and should also consider alternative courses of action.

Caption Answers

Viewing History It caused his popularity to plunge and damaged his chances for reelection.

Chapter 25 Review and Assessment

Reviewing Key Terms

Students should refer to the definitions of key terms in the chapter to write sentences that show an understanding of the respective administrations of Nixon, Ford, and Carter.

Reviewing Main Ideas

13. The bills would satisfy conservatives who wanted a smaller government. This technique also reassured those who favored social programs that they would continue with greater discretion to state governments.
14. Nixon made little attempt to appeal to African Americans or press for civil rights. He preferred to court the votes of southern white Democrats.
15. Kissinger practiced *realpolitik*, or acting in the nation's best interests rather than upon moral principles. Kissinger gained Nixon's trust in regard to foreign affairs and supported Nixon's use of secret negotiations.
16. Nixon was convinced that Communist China could no longer be ignored by the United States. He lifted travel restrictions for Americans who wished to visit China, arranged for the American Ambassador in Warsaw to meet with his Chinese counterpart, welcomed the initiation of "ping-pong diplomacy," and allowed trade to resume between the two nations. Nixon visited the People's Republic of China in 1972.
17. The committee adopted a no-holds-barred approach to winning, using "dirty tricks" against political opponents. These included a vicious criticism of Senator Edmund Muskie and his wife, and spies in an opponent's campaign staff.
18. Nixon attempted to indirectly pressure the FBI into dropping its Watergate investigation. He was also fully aware beforehand that one of the burglars had been paid to keep quiet.
19. He wanted to put an end to a very unpleasant episode and get on with the nation's real business. The public reaction was extremely negative. Many people felt that Nixon should share the fate of the Watergate conspirators who were going to jail.
20. Ford confronted the faltering economy by federal funding for unemployment compensation, the voluntary

creating a CHAPTER SUMMARY

Copy this chart (right) on a piece of paper and complete it by adding information about the issues and policies under each President's administration. Some entries have been completed for you as examples.

Presidents and Issues, 1969–1981				
President	**Economic Issues**	**Foreign Policy**	**Civil Rights**	**Energy Issues**
Nixon				Oil crisis
Ford	Stagflation			
Carter		Camp David Accords		

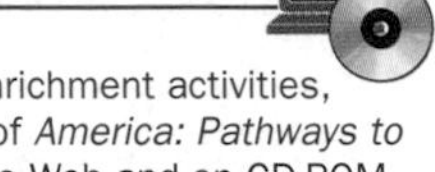

For additional review and enrichment activities, see the interactive version of *America: Pathways to the Present*, available on the Web and on CD-ROM.

★ Reviewing Key Terms

For each of the terms below, write a sentence explaining how it relates to the Nixon, Ford, or Carter administration.

1. deficit spending
2. embargo
3. *realpolitik*
4. détente
5. special prosecutor
6. impeach
7. Helsinki Accords
8. incumbent
9. deregulation
10. amnesty
11. affirmative action
12. Camp David Accords

★ Reviewing Main Ideas

13. How did the New Federalism fit into Nixon's approach to domestic policy? (Section 1)
14. What was Nixon's "southern strategy"? (Section 1)
15. How did Henry Kissinger affect American foreign policy under President Nixon? (Section 2)
16. How did the Nixon administration change United States policy toward China? (Section 2)
17. What measures did the Committee to Reelect the President take to win the 1972 election? (Section 3)
18. What illegal actions did Nixon take in attempting to cover up the Watergate break-in? (Section 3)
19. Why did Ford grant Nixon a pardon? (Section 4)
20. What programs did Ford propose to solve the nation's economic problems? (Section 4)
21. How did Carter's lack of Washington experience affect his administration? (Section 5)
22. Evaluate the impact of the Iran hostage crisis on the 1980 presidential election. (Section 5)

★ Critical Thinking

23. **Synthesizing Information** How did the Watergate scandal shape politics in the 1970s?
24. **Drawing Conclusions** In 1975, Congress refused President Ford's request to send military aid to South Vietnam. Which do you think played a larger role in Congress's decision—the War Powers Act or public opinion? Why?
25. **Checking Consistency** Although Americans complained about fuel shortages during the 1970s, many did not support Carter's energy program or try to conserve oil and gas. How do you explain this inconsistent behavior?
26. **Identifying Central Issues** How did the relationship between the United States and the Soviet Union evolve during the 1970s?
27. **Making Comparisons** In what ways was "Nixon the President" different from "Nixon the Congressman"? How can you account for this change?

Creating a Chapter Summary

Presidents and Issues, 1969–1981				
President	**Economic Issues**	**Foreign Policy**	**Civil Rights**	**Energy Issues**
Nixon	Deficit spending	Détente; reestablishment of diplomatic relations with China	Slowdown in desegregation	Oil crisis
Ford	Stagflation	Helsinki Accords	Congress overrides vetoes to establish Consumer Protection Agency and to fund programs for education, housing, and health care.	Encouraging people to conserve fuel
Carter	Deregulation	Camp David Accords	Amnesty; affirmative action	Safety of nuclear power; establishment of Department of Energy

★ Skills Assessment

Analyzing Political Cartoons ▶

28. This cartoon appeared during the Watergate scandal. What is Nixon doing?
29. What symbolism is used? What is the meaning behind the symbolism?
30. What is the cartoon's message? Write a caption that could be used with the cartoon.

Interpreting Data

Turn to the line graph on page 828 titled "Rate of Inflation, 1968–1976," in Section 1.

31. When did overall consumer prices reach their peak?
    A 1968
    B 1971
    C 1974
    D 1976
32. What is the best description of the rate of inflation during the period from 1968 to 1972?
    F stayed about the same
    G rose steadily
    H dropped steadily
    J rose and dropped wildly from year to year
33. Using this graph and the information in this chapter, examine the relationship between food and fuel prices. Write a paragraph that explains how food prices might be affected by changes in fuel prices.

Applying the Chapter Skill: *Creating a Multimedia Presentation*

34. Review the major topics discussed in this chapter. Develop a blueprint for a mulitmedia presentation on a topic you have not yet explored. Consider using information from previous chapters to provide a background for your topic.

ACTIVITIES

Writing to LEARN

Writing an Opinion
Partly due to the Watergate scandal, Congress and the press keep a watchful eye on top government officials. They probe any questionable activity — past or present, public or private. Is this level of watchfulness good or bad for the country? Support your opinion in an essay.

Primary Source CD-ROM

Working With Primary Sources Find additional information on the Nixon, Ford, and Carter administrations on the *Exploring Primary Sources in U.S. History CD-ROM* and use the selection(s) provided to complete the Chapter 25 primary source activity located in the *America: Pathways to the Present* area of the following Web site.
www.phschool.com

Take It to the NET

Chapter Self-Test As a review activity, take the Chapter 25 Self-Test in the *America: Pathways to the Present* area at the Web site listed below. The questions are designed to test your understanding of the chapter content.
www.phschool.com

ANSWERS TO ACTIVITIES

Writing to LEARN

Essays might consider the benefit or harm to the government of continuing investigations, the rights of high government officials, and whether such a mood of suspicion encourages or discourages people from entering politics.

Primary Source CD-ROM

Direct students to the additional primary sources that can be found on the *Exploring Primary Sources in U.S. History CD-ROM.*

Take It to the NET

Additional support materials and activities for Chapter 25 of *America: Pathways to the Present* can be found in the Social Studies area at the Prentice Hall School Web site. **www.phschool.com**

and unsuccessful "WIN" program, and proposing a large tax cut.

21. Carter's "outsider" status helped to get him elected. However, neither he nor his staff were ever able to master the art of working effectively with members of Congress.
22. Carter's inability to resolve the hostage crisis hurt him considerably in the 1980 election.

CRITICAL THINKING

23. Many Americans lost a great deal of faith in their government. However, the scandal also proved the strength of the constitutional system.
24. The Vietnam War had become highly unpopular in the United States by the early 1970s. Therefore, public opinion was probably the most important factor in the decision by Congress to deny further military aid to South Vietnam.
25. Possible answer: It is often very difficult to get people to make significant changes in the way they behave.
26. During Nixon's presidency, through détente and SALT I, relations improved. During Carter's presidency, relations soured due to strife over dissidents and the Soviet Union's invasion of Afghanistan. The latter interfered with the passing of SALT II, disrupted American grain shipments to Russia, and caused an American boycott of the Moscow Olympics.
27. The most evident change was in his attitudes toward communism. As a member of Congress, Nixon was staunchly anti-Communist. However, as President, he sought to improve relations with Communist countries. This change was due primarily to changing times and to the differences between the job of Congressman and that of being the President.

SKILLS ASSESSMENT

28. He is trapped in a web.
29. The symbolism of a spider's web. Spools of recording tape are also caught in the web, a reference to the White House tapes, central to the Watergate scandal. The symbolism is that Nixon and the tapes are inextricably linked in the scandal.
30. Nixon has trapped himself in a web of lies. Sample caption: "Caught in his own web."
31. C
32. F
33. Answers will vary, but blueprints should include subtopics, key sources of information, and the sequence and description of segments.

A Cold War Test

Focus Have students find the meaning of each of these words in a dictionary before they begin to read: *mecca, familiarity, anachronistic, vernacular, apocalyptic, admonishment, tranquility, indelibly.* Ask them to consider, as they read, the positive and negative effects of high defense spending on a nation's economy.

Instruct Ask students to review the selection and find evidence that Greenfield's direct exposure to the Cold War both scared and thrilled him. *(Greenfield indicates his discomfort at the thunderous noise that preceded the launching and describes his awe at the rocketing missile.)* How is Greenfield's ambivalence a metaphor for the feelings of the nation as a whole? *(Many Americans were impressed by U.S. power yet afraid that it could destroy the world.)*

Have students find examples in the selection of routine American and Soviet practices during the Cold War. *(Security checks, other preliminaries to boarding Navy ships)*

Analyzing the Document Use this additional question to generate class discussion:

Critical Thinking: Determining Relevance What purpose do specific details—such as the names of TV programs that Greenfield watched, types of clothing that he wore, and things that he did in his free time—serve in Greenfield's story? *(Such details strengthen the story by creating in the reader's mind images of "an average 12-year-old in 1974.")*

AmericanHeritage®

MY BRUSH WITH **HISTORY**™

by CRAIG B. GREENFIELD

A Cold War Test

A Poseidon missile is launched from a submarine.

The Cold War decades were a boom time for the American defense industry. The billions spent each year to develop and produce modern weapons not only helped protect the nation, but also boosted its economy. In the passage below, Craig B. Greenfield, whose father worked for a defense contractor, describes a visit to see his father's handiwork in action.

IT WAS **1974.** As your average twelve-year-old, my world was one of mischievous after-school activities, mixed with the usual sandlot sports, awkward encounters with girls, and homework. With the exception of the trendy peace-sign belt buckle and fingers-gesturing peace-sign T-shirt that I owned, I had only a faint familiarity with the politics of peace and war in faraway Vietnam. In fact, my only real exposure to those events came from those television voices that came between "Gilligan's Island" and "Adam 12," who spoke of the specter of nuclear holocaust that losing to communism in Asia might invite.

The nuclear-powered strategic missile submarine USS Lafayette underway

All that changed one winter with a brief but profound encounter with the inner workings and realities of the Cold War.

My family had taken a vacation that December. With my father employed as an electrical engineer by the Sperry Corporation, a leading Long Island defense contractor, and my mother keeping busy with her family at home, we set out for Fort Lauderdale to combine some sunshine with the duty of visiting all our recently retired relatives. A much-anticipated highlight of this trip for me was to be a visit to the newly opened Disney World. But compared with the show I was to see, that children's mecca turned out to be just a roadside attraction.

We were relaxing in the cool comfort of my uncle's condominium when my father proudly announced that he had arranged for a side trip to Cape Canaveral for what he called, in the acronymistic vernacular of the defense industry, a DASO, or "daytime at sea operation," wherein a Poseidon missile would be launched from an actual submarine. Although I viewed this devel-

RESOURCE DIRECTORY

Technology

AmericanHeritage® My Brush with History™ Videotapes *A Cold War Test*

TEST PREPARATION

Have students use the excerpt on these pages to answer the following question.

Which statement best describes the speaker's feelings about Cold War weapons development and production?

- Ⓐ He feels that U.S. military preparedness helped end the Cold War and is grateful.
- **B** He feels proud of his father's achievement.
- **C** He feels that high defense spending prevented the United States from adequately addressing problems such as poverty.
- **D** He feels that the nation should have done more to prepare militarily.

opment as one more dreaded lengthy car ride full of slap fighting with my brother, to my father, who had worked hard on developing submarine navigation systems, it was a rare and valuable chance to see his engineering achievement at work—a demonstration otherwise possible only in an apocalyptic armed launch situation.

With a quick good-bye we set off on our three-hour journey to Port Canaveral, neighboring the cape, where so many televised space shots originated, my father's excitement manifesting itself in driving at a clip that ultimately got him ticketed.

The Missile Launch We arrived at Cape Canaveral and were processed in true Cold War fashion: security clearance, identification cards, and a short, sharp admonishment to stay only in certain areas of the host Navy ship during our day at sea. Then we proceeded up the gangplank and onto the huge auxiliary ship *Compass Island* (EAG 153), which had seen action over the years as a part of the U.S. Military Sealift Command.

I spent the hours-long voyage out to sea exploring the ship and listening to a succession of lectures about this and that capability, guidance system, and the like on both the *Compass Island* and the day's feature attraction, the five-hundred-foot long Poseidon submarine USS *Lafayette* (SSBN 616), which rode regally beside us until it majestically submerged into the sparkling Atlantic water, trailed only by its perfect wake and the indiscreet presence of an antenna-laden Soviet "fishing trawler."

At dusk, with the Florida sun low on the horizon, everyone aboard became aware of the countdown that had actually been going on all day. With fifteen seconds left and our formidable companion well hidden under the sea, the boat buzzed with anticipation and excitement.

At about five seconds to launch, our immense host ship began to rock to and fro, despite the relative tranquillity of the Atlantic shortly before. At four seconds to launch the boat was heaving so violently that all of us had to brace ourselves. At three seconds to launch the rumbling became so loud that I imagined myself being in the center of a thunderclap. At two seconds to launch, with the blocks-long ship in its turbulent pitch and roll and the noise of eruption becoming ever louder, the inside missile hatch of the submarine blew open explosively far below. Finally, rising on a column of fire, the thirty-four-foot body of the C-3 Poseidon missile emerged from the boiling sea and, with a zig right and a zag left, rocketed skyward and headed toward its destination in the Indian Ocean, nearly three thousand miles away. As I gazed awestruck, my jaw opened wide, that image implanted itself indelibly in my memory.

Today, more than twenty years later, with the disintegration of Soviet communism receding into history, what occurred on that winter day at sea seems almost to have been staged for a movie rather than the profound and scary reality that it was.

However, that vivid childhood memory allows me as an adult to appreciate fully the magnitude of the resources involved in that endeavor called the Cold War. Having personally lived with the practical realities of the Cold War—and having been fed, clothed, and educated with the money that the employment of thousands like my father in the defense industry brought—I greet these new historical developments with both a sense of hope for a peaceful future and a sense of what brought them about.

Source: *American Heritage* magazine, July 1995.

Understanding Primary Sources

1. What was the Soviet "fishing trawler" carrying?
2. How would these items be used?

American Heritage® MY BRUSH WITH HISTORY™ 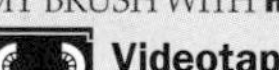 **Videotapes**

For more information about the Cold War, view "A Cold War Test."

CUSTOMIZE FOR ... ESL

Students may need help with the following words and phrases:

sandlot sports games such as baseball, kickball, softball, and soccer that children played on vacant lots
nuclear holocaust destruction of the world by a nuclear accident or by nuclear weapons
defense contractor firm that produces weapons and other supplies for the military
gangplank movable bridge used to board or leave a ship
a clip that ultimately got him ticketed a speed above the legal limit that resulted in a police officer issuing a ticket

CUSTOMIZE FOR ... Less Proficient Readers

Have students use their textbooks to make a time line of key events in the Cold War from 1947 to 1991. Completed time lines should include events such as the establishment of NATO (1949), the House Un-American Activities Committee hearings (late 1940s and early 1950s), the Cuban Missile Crisis (1962), and the escalation of the Vietnam War (1964).

CUSTOMIZE FOR ... Less Proficient Writers

Have students review the events on the ship that took place immediately before the missile was launched. Ask them to list the events in the following order: five seconds before launch; four seconds before launch; three seconds before launch; two seconds before launch; and at launch. Using their own words, have them summarize the events at those instants.

CUSTOMIZE FOR ... Gifted and Talented

How does hindsight affect our understanding of historical events? Have students analyze Greenfield's observation that his "vivid childhood memory allows [him] as an adult to appreciate fully the magnitude of the resources involved in that endeavor called the Cold War." How does Greenfield's upbringing influence his perceptions of the Cold War?

Answers

1. It was "antenna-laden."
2. Presumably, the antennas were radioing intelligence information to the Soviets.

Chapter 26 Planning Guide

Resource Manager

	Core Instruction	Reading/Skills
Chapter-Level Resources **TEKS** 25(A)	Teaching Resources • Pacing Charts booklet • Block Scheduling booklet **Resource Pro® CD-ROM,** Ch. 26 **Prentice Hall Presentation Pro CD-ROM,** Ch. 26 **www.phschool.com** • eTeach	**Guided Reading Audiotapes (English/Spanish)** **Student Edition on Audio CD,** Ch. 26 **Social Studies Skills Tutor CD-ROM** **Color Transparencies,** F10, G13, G14
1 Roots of the New Conservatism 1. Find out about the major events in Ronald Reagan's political career. 2. Learn how conservatism evolved in the years between the 1930s and the 1970s. 3. Discover why the 1980 election marked a turning point in United States history. **TEKS** 11(B), 18(C), 21(C)	Teaching Resources **Units 5/6/7 booklet** • Section 1 Quiz, p. 112 **Learning Styles Lesson Plans booklet,** p. 68	**Guided Reading and Review booklet,** p. 133 **Guide to the Essentials,** p. 127 **Learning with Documents booklet,** p. 98 **Skills for Life booklet,** p. 35 **Section Reading Support Transparencies**
2 The Reagan Revolution 1. Read to find out how President Reagan attempted to change the economy. 2. Find out how Reagan changed the federal government. 3. Reflect on major initiatives and key foreign policy crises of Reagan's first term. 4. Explore the ways in which the economy moved from recession to recovery in the early 1980s. **TEKS** 14(D), 15(D), 22(B)	Teaching Resources **Units 5/6/7 booklet** • Section 2 Quiz, p. 113	**Guided Reading and Review booklet,** p. 134 **Guide to the Essentials,** p. 128 **Learning with Documents booklet,** p. 97 **Section Reading Support Transparencies**
3 Reagan's Second Term 1. Observe the ways in which the United States experienced a renewal of patriotism in the 1980s. 2. Find out about some important social debates that continued through Reagan's term in office. 3. See how the economy evolved during the 1980s. 4. Discover how Reagan's hands-off style of governing led to problems. 5. Consider the legacy of Reagan's presidency. **TEKS** 15(C), 16(B)	Teaching Resources **Units 5/6/7 booklet** • Section 3 Quiz, p. 114	**Guided Reading and Review booklet,** p. 135 **Guide to the Essentials,** p. 129 **Learning with Documents booklet,** p. 72 **Section Reading Support Transparencies**
4 The George H. W. Bush Presidency 1. See what challenges George H. W. Bush faced during the 1988 presidential election. 2. Find out how the Cold War came to an end. 3. Learn about the ways in which the United States played a new international role after the Cold War. 4. Observe the effect domestic issues had on Bush's presidency. **TEKS** 6(G), 9(B), 18(C), 22(A)	Teaching Resources **Units 5/6/7 booklet** • Section 4 Quiz, p. 115 **Learning Styles Lesson Plans booklet,** p. 69	**Guided Reading and Review booklet,** p. 136 **Guide to the Essentials,** p. 130 **Section Reading Support Transparencies**

Enrichment/Pre-AP

Prentice Hall United States History Video Collection™
www.phschool.com
- Section Activities, Virtual Field Trip, Chapter Activities, Current Events Online

Sounds of an Era Audio CD

Great Debates booklet, p. 28
American History Block Scheduling Support
Exploring Primary Sources in U.S. History CD-ROM

Biography, Literature, and Comparing Primary Sources booklet, pp. 88, 161

Biography, Literature, and Comparing Primary Sources booklet, p. 38
American History Block Scheduling Support
Nystrom *Atlas of Our Country,* pp. 34–35
Sounds of an Era Audio CD
American Pathways Thematic Posters

Assessment

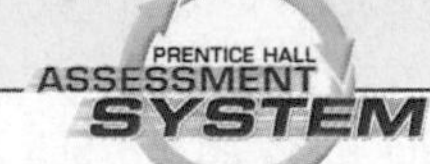

Core Assessment
ExamView® Test Bank, Ch. 26
ExamView® Test Bank CD-ROM, Ch. 26

Standardized Test Preparation
Diagnose and Prescribe
Diagnostic Tests for High School Social Studies Skills

Review and Reteach
Review Book for U.S. History

Practice and Assess
Test-taking Strategies With Transparencies
Test-taking Strategies Posters
Test Prep Book for U.S. History
Alternative Assessment Handbook
Document-Based Assessment

Teaching Resources
Units 5/6/7 booklet
- Section Quizzes, pp. 112–115
- Chapter Tests, pp. 116, 119

www.phschool.com Ch. 26 Self-Test

AmericanHeritage Resources

From the Archives of American Heritage®, pp. 878, 884
AmericanHeritage® My Brush with History™ Videotapes
www.americanheritage.com

Don't miss the exclusive interactive version of this textbook on the Web and on CD-ROM.

Chapter 26 Planning Guide
In Your Classroom

Customize for Individual Needs

Gifted and Talented

Teacher's Edition
- Customize for Gifted and Talented, pp. 865, 885

Teaching Resources
- Biography, Literature, and Comparing Primary Sources booklet, pp. 38, 88, 161

Technology
- Exploring Primary Sources in U.S. History CD-ROM *A Time for Choosing, Ronald Reagan*

ESL

Teacher's Edition
- Customize for ESL, p. 879

Teaching Resources
- Guided Reading and Review booklet, pp. 133–136
- Guide to the Essentials (English/Spanish), Chapter 26

Technology
- Student Edition on Audio CD, Chapter 26
- Guided Reading Audiotapes (English/Spanish), Chapter 26
- Section Reading Support Transparencies

Less Proficient Readers

Teacher's Edition
- Customize for Less Proficient Readers, p. 873

Teaching Resources
- Guided Reading and Review booklet, pp. 133–136
- Guide to the Essentials (English/Spanish), Chapter 26

Technology
- Student Edition on Audio CD, Chapter 26
- Guided Reading Audiotapes (English/Spanish), Chapter 26
- Section Reading Support Transparencies

Less Proficient Writers

Teacher's Edition
- Customize for Less Proficient Writers, pp. 877, 887

Teaching Resources
- Guided Reading and Review booklet, pp. 133–136
- Guide to the Essentials (English/Spanish), Chapter 26

Technology
- Student Edition on Audio CD, Chapter 26
- Guided Reading Audiotapes (English/Spanish), Chapter 26
- Section Reading Support Transparencies

Teacher's Edition Index

Chapter 26 – Pacing Suggestions

For 90-minute Blocks

- Teach section 1 using Transparencies F10, G13, and G14, and the Recent Scholarship note on page 872 for class discussions.

Running Out of Time?

If you are running short on time to cover this chapter, consider the following options:

- Use the Prentice Hall Presentation Pro CD-ROM to create an outline for this chapter.
- Use the Section Summaries for Chapter 26, from **Guide to the Essentials (English/Spanish).**

TEKS Correlation

Chapter-Level	TEKS **(25) Social studies skills.** The student communicates in written, oral, and visual forms. The student is expected to: **(A)** use social studies terminology correctly.
1 Roots of the New Conservatism	**(11) Geography.** The student understands the relationship between population growth and modernization on the physical environment. The student is expected to: **(B)** trace the development of the conservation of natural resources, including the establishment of the National Park System and efforts of private nonprofit organizations. **(18) Citizenship**. The student understands efforts to expand the democratic process. The student is expected to: **(C)** explain how participation in the democratic process reflects our national identity. **(21) Culture.** The student understands how people from various groups, including racial, ethnic, and religious groups, adapt to life in the United States and contribute to our national identity. The student is expected to: **(C)** analyze how the contributions of people of various racial, ethnic, and religious groups have helped to shape the national identity.
2 The Reagan Revolution	**(14) Economics.** The student understands the economic effects of World War II, the Cold War, and increased world-wide competition on contemporary society. The student is expected to: **(D)** identify actions of government and the private sector to expand economic opportunities to all citizens. **(15) Government.** The student understands changes in the role of government over time. The student is expected to: **(D)** predict the effects of selected contemporary legislation on the roles of state and federal governments. **(22) Science, technology, and society.** The student understands the impact of science and technology on the economic development of the United States. The student is expected to: **(B)** explain how scientific discoveries and technological innovations such as those in agriculture, the military, and medicine resulted from specific needs.
3 Reagan's Second Term	**(15) Government.** The student understands changes in the role of government over time. The student is expected to: **(C)** evaluate the effects of political incidents such as Teapot Dome and Watergate on the views of U.S. citizens concerning the role of the federal government. **(16) Government.** The student understands the changing relationships among the three branches of the federal government. The student is expected to: **(B)** evaluate the impact of events, including Franklin Roosevelt's attempt to increase the number of U.S. Supreme Court justices, on the relationships among the legislative, executive, and judicial branches of government.
4 The George H. W. Bush Administration	**(6) History.** The student understands the impact of significant national and international decisions and conflicts from World War II and the Cold War to the present on the United States. The student is expected to: **(G)** analyze reasons for the Western victory in the Cold War and the challenges of changing relationships among nations. **(9) Geography.** The student understands the impact of geographic factors on major events. The student is expected to: **(B)** identify and explain reasons for changes in political boundaries such as those resulting from statehood and international conflicts. **(18) Citizenship.** The student understands efforts to expand the democratic process. The student is expected to: **(C)** explain how participation in the democratic process reflects our national identity. **(22) Science, technology, and society.** The student understands the impact of science and technology on the economic development of the United States. The student is expected to: **(A)** explain the effects of scientific discoveries and technological innovations such as electric power, the telegraph and telephone, petroleum-based products, medical vaccinations, and computers on the development of the United States.

Chapter 26 The Conservative Revolution (1980–1992)

Introducing the Chapter

After the political, social, and cultural upheavals of the 1960s and 1970s, many Americans felt change had gone too far and wanted to return to smaller government and more conservative ideas. The policies of Ronald Reagan and his successor, George H.W. Bush, carried out the social and economic goals of "New Right" conservatives.

Time Line Activity

To provide students with practice in using the time line, ask questions such as these:

1. In what year did unemployment reach a 40-year high? *(1982)*
2. What definitive anti-apartheid action was made by the United States and Great Britain in 1986? *(Both governments banned most trade with South Africa, seeking a change in that country's laws.)*
3. What action did George H.W. Bush take in 1990 that went against one of his campaign pledges? *(He raised taxes.)*

Chapter 26 The Conservative Revolution (1980–1992)

Nancy Reagan and Ronald Reagan

Space Shuttle *Columbia*

American Events

1980 Conservatives sweep the 1980 federal elections. Ronald Reagan is elected President, and Republicans win control of the Senate.

1981 President Reagan cuts income tax rates and announces plans to curb government spending.

1982 Unemployment reaches a 40-year high of 10.8 percent during a sharp recession.

1984 Reagan wins a second term in office aided by an economic boom.

Presidential Terms: Jimmy Carter 1977–1981; Ronald Reagan 1981–1989

1980 · 1982 · 1984

World Events

1982 Argentina and Great Britain battle for control of the Falkland Islands.

1984 Indira Gandhi, prime minister of India, is assassinated.

eTeach

Be sure to check out this month's online discussion with a Master Teacher. Go to **www.phschool.com**.

Resource Directory

Teaching Resources

Pacing Charts booklet

Block Scheduling booklet, p. 28

Units 5/6/7 booklet

- Chapter Summary, p. 111

Technology

Guided Reading Audiotapes (English/Spanish), Ch. 26

Student Edition on Audio CD, Ch. 26

Sounds of an Era Audio CD *Barry Goldwater,* 1964 recording (time: 10 seconds); *Ronald Reagan,* 1981 recording (time: 20 seconds)

Prentice Hall United States History Video Collection™ Volume 20, *Post-War USA*

Prentice Hall Presentation Pro CD-ROM, Ch. 26

Resource Pro® CD-ROM

Social Studies Skills Tutor CD-ROM

Companion Web site, www.phschool.com

Cold War Events, 1980–1989

ARCTIC OCEAN
Fall of Berlin Wall, 1989
GERMANY
Collapse of Soviet Union, 1991
SOVIET UNION
Chernobyl Disaster, 1986
Tiananmen Square, 1989
CHINA
Los Angeles Olympic Games, 1984
UNITED STATES
Grenada Invasion, 1983
GRENADA
ATLANTIC OCEAN
Contra Rebellion, 1983–1990
NICARAGUA
Equator
PACIFIC OCEAN
INDIAN OCEAN
PACIFIC OCEAN
N
0 2000 mi.
0 2000 km

USA and allies
American military aid
Other Western military aid
Communist countries
Soviet military aid
Western and Soviet aid

1986 Americans learn that presidential aides illegally sold arms to Iran and sent money to support anti-Communist rebels in Nicaragua.

1990 President Bush agrees to raise taxes to fight budget deficits.

1991 American troops lead an international force to liberate Kuwait and defeat Iraq in Operation Desert Storm.

George H. W. Bush 1989–1993

1986 · 1988 · 1990 · 1992

1985 Britain and the United States ban most trade with South Africa over apartheid.

1987 Palestinians rebel against Israel.

1989 China crushes Beijing protests.

1990 Germany is reunified.

1991 Gorbachev resigns, and the Soviet Union dissolves into 15 republics.

Cold War Events, 1980–1989

Activating Prior Knowledge Which of the Cold War events displayed on this map took place in Communist countries? *(The collapse of the Soviet Union, the Chernobyl disaster, Tiananmen Square, and the fall of the Berlin Wall)*

Previewing Ask students what effect they think the Cold War events had on the 1984 Olympics. *(Because the Olympics were held in the United States, they were very pro-American, and some Communist countries boycotted the games.)*

BACKGROUND
About the Pictures

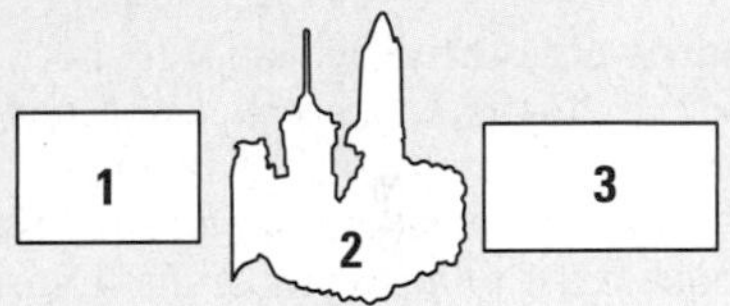

1. President Reagan's wife, Nancy, was his closest adviser and confidante.
2. The explosion of the *Challenger* space shuttle in 1987 was one of the greatest domestic tragedies that occurred during Reagan's presidency.
3. The stated goal of Operation Desert Storm was the liberation of oil-rich Kuwait from invading Iraqi forces.

BIBLIOGRAPHY

For the Teacher

Atkinson, Rick. ***Crusade: The Untold Story of the Persian Gulf War.*** Houghton Mifflin, 1993. (A *Washington Post* reporter looks at the war three years later.)

Hunter-Gault, Charlayne. ***In My Place.*** Vintage, 1993. (A successful journalist remembers her youth as one of the first two African American students at the University of Georgia.)

For the Student

Ashe, Arthur, and Arnold Rampersad. ***Days of Grace: A Memoir.*** Ballantine, 1994. (Reflections by the African American tennis champion and activist who died of AIDS.)

Erdrich, Louise. ***Love Medicine: New and Expanded Version.*** HarperCollins, 1993. (Updated version of the author's first novel of Native American life.)

Don't miss the exclusive interactive version of this textbook on the Web and on CD-ROM.

Section 1 Roots of the New Conservatism

Section Objectives

1. Find out about the major events in Ronald Reagan's political career.
2. Learn how conservatism evolved in the years between the 1930s and the 1970s.
3. Discover why the 1980 election marked a turning point in United States history.

Bellringer

Warm-Up Activity Ask students what the terms *conservative* and *conservatism* mean to them. Ask them to identify two contemporary issues that would fit their definitions of the terms.

Activating Prior Knowledge Ask students if they can answer the following question: What aspect of American society in 1980 most likely led to the election of Ronald Reagan? *(The condition of the United States economy)*

Reading Strategy

As students read the section, have them list significant events and individuals in the growth of the conservative movement. Then ask students to write a sentence that evaluates the impact of each event and individual on American society.

Activity

Connecting with Citizenship

Invite students to imagine that they are media consultants for presidential candidate Ronald Reagan in 1980. In this role, each student is to prepare a 15-second "sound bite" for the candidate to use in explaining to interviewers why Reagan switched political parties. Select students to deliver their sound bites to the class. **(Verbal/Linguistic)**

Section 1 Roots of the New Conservatism

READING FOCUS

- What were the major events in Ronald Reagan's political career?
- How did conservatism evolve in the years between the 1930s and the 1970s?
- Why did the 1980 election mark a turning point in United States history?

KEY TERMS

Reagan Democrat
New Right
televangelism

TAKING NOTES

Copy this flowchart. As you read, fill in the boxes with some of the major events in the history of the conservative movement. The first box has been completed to help you get started.

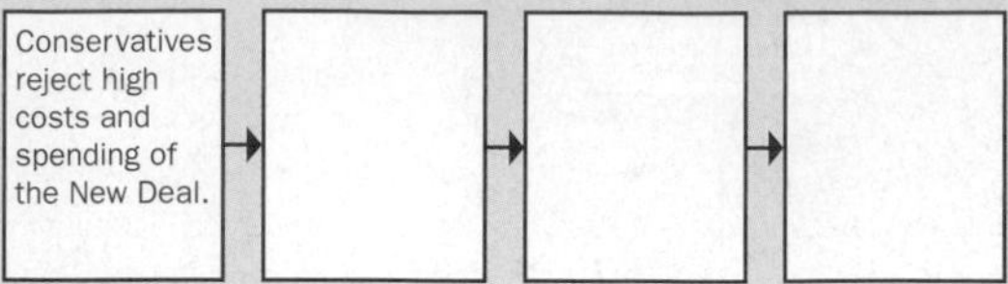
Conservatives reject high costs and spending of the New Deal.

MAIN IDEA

After decades of federal government expansion and social and cultural change, a conservative movement gained strength during the 1970s. In 1980, it brought Ronald Reagan to power.

Setting the Scene Two weeks after Ronald Reagan won the presidency in 1980, Richard Nixon wrote to the president-elect to recommend advisors for top positions:

> "*Washington needs new men and new ideas. By your appointments, you can give the country a sense of excitement, hope and drive to government which we have not seen since FDR.*"
>
> —Richard Nixon

With this 1980 campaign poster, Ronald Reagan appealed to voters' patriotism and their unhappiness with the direction of the country.

By most accounts, Reagan succeeded. Six years after the Watergate scandal drove Nixon from the White House, Reagan arrived in Washington at the head of a more conservative and powerful Republican Party. Reagan achieved many of his goals through the strength of his administration and the appeal of his warm personality and firm beliefs.

Although the 1980 election appeared to mark a sudden shift in American politics, the roots of change lay deep in the past. The new President voiced the growing frustrations of voters around the country who believed that government had grown too large and had lost touch with the needs of the people. Reagan's own political journey reflected the growing conservatism of millions of Americans.

Reagan's Political Career

Reagan was originally a Democrat who considered Franklin D. Roosevelt, architect of the New Deal, his political hero. When Reagan began his career as a movie actor in Hollywood, he became actively involved in the political affairs of the actors' union.

After World War II, Reagan found himself less comfortable with the Democratic Party, and he joined the Republican Party in the 1950s. He served as a spokesman for General Electric, making speeches that praised capitalism and attacked government regulation. He also spoke out strongly against

Resource Directory

Teaching Resources

Learning Styles Lesson Plans booklet, p. 68
Guided Reading and Review booklet, p. 133

Technology

Section Reading Support Transparencies
Guided Reading Audiotapes (English/Spanish), Ch. 26
Student Edition on Audio CD, Ch. 26
Color Transparencies *American Photo,* F10
Prentice Hall Presentation Pro CD-ROM, Ch. 26
Companion Web site, www.phschool.com

Communists in the United States. Ronald Reagan was now clearly in the conservative camp.

Reagan gained national attention in 1966, when he was elected governor of California. Likable, photogenic, and committed to conservative values, he gained support for cutbacks in social programs in his state. During his eight years as governor, Reagan eliminated California's budget deficit by modestly increasing taxes and reforming state spending. He called for similar reforms of social programs run by the federal government.

The Evolution of Conservatism

Reagan's political transition took place against the backdrop of a national debate over the proper size and scope of government. During the prosperous 1920s, conservative Republicans had won national elections by promising to keep taxes low and minimize spending. The Great Depression reshaped the debate with Franklin Roosevelt's introduction of New Deal programs that greatly enlarged the size and cost of the federal government.

New Deal Opponents New Deal agencies, which provided banking regulation, assistance to farmers, aid for the unemployed, and a great deal more, changed the role of the President and the federal government. Critics argued that in a capitalist country, government should not undertake these tasks. They said that the nation could not afford the high federal spending and substantial budget deficits that resulted.

Some of these critics joined to form the American Liberty League. Established in 1934, this organization included both industrialists and politicians. The Liberty League sought to teach respect for the rights of individuals and property and to underscore the importance of individual enterprise. All of these values, members claimed, were being undermined by FDR's large government programs.

In 1937, an attempt by Roosevelt to "pack" the Supreme Court by adding new justices caused a backlash. Conservatives in both major political parties formed a coalition that opposed further New Deal legislation. Nevertheless, Republicans struggled to overcome Roosevelt's enduring popularity as President. Led by Roosevelt and later by Harry S Truman, the Democrats kept control of the White House for twenty years.

From Eisenhower to Goldwater The election of Dwight D. Eisenhower as President in 1952 began eight years of Republican rule. Eisenhower called his approach to government "modern Republicanism." He accepted the basic outlines of the New Deal and never attempted to dismantle the federal bureaucracy. The federal bureaucracy even expanded, as it did in 1953 with the creation of a Department of Health, Education, and Welfare, headed by Oveta Culp Hobby.

In 1964, the Republican candidate for President, Senator Barry Goldwater of Arizona, ran on a staunchly conservative platform. Facing Democrat Lyndon B. Johnson, Goldwater opposed government activism, including social security, federal civil rights

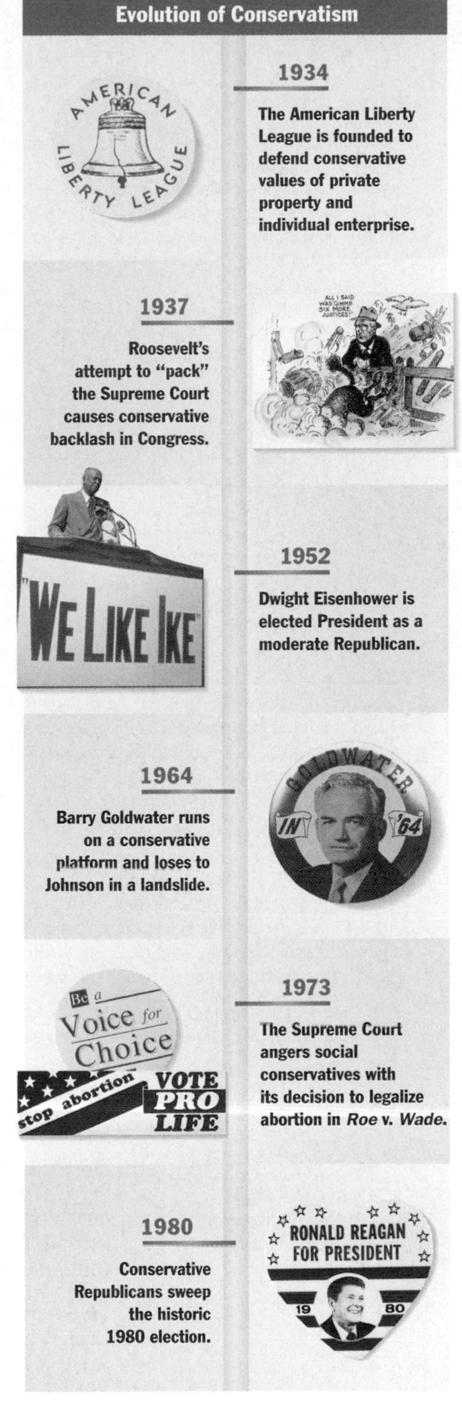

LESSON PLAN

Focus Explain that many Americans had long opposed the expansion of the federal government. This opposition came to a head in the 1980s with a well-organized conservative shift. Ask students what issues the New Right targeted.

Instruct Explain that the conservative movement of the 1980s was part of an ongoing opposition to government growth after the 1930s. Review the shift in the role of government brought by the New Deal.

Discuss the aims of the various government programs that had been instituted over the years. Did critics argue with those aims, with the methods, or with both? Have students discuss the social issues that helped bring the New Right together.

Assess/Reteach Ask students to compare and contrast views of Ronald Reagan and Jimmy Carter in the following areas: the role of government in funding social programs; the role of government in regulating industry; the role of the United States as a world leader.

ACTIVITY
Connecting with Government

Organize students into groups and ask each group to rank the following Presidents in order, from least to most conservative: Franklin D. Roosevelt, Dwight D. Eisenhower, Lyndon B. Johnson, Richard Nixon, Jimmy Carter, and Ronald Reagan. Have each group present its ranking to the class. Call on group members to justify differences between rankings. **(Logical/Mathematical)**

BACKGROUND
Biography

The title "Father of the New Right" may belong to late Senator Barry M. Goldwater (1909–1998) of Arizona. As a senator he became a critic of the Eisenhower administration and leader of conservative Republicans. Goldwater lost the presidential race in 1964 by 16 million votes, partly because his tough promilitary rhetoric frightened many people. So did his famous quote: "Extremism in the defense of liberty is no vice." He was reelected to the Senate in 1968 and served until his retirement in 1987.

CUSTOMIZE FOR ...
Gifted and Talented

Have students analyze the approaches to government growth taken by different Republican leaders: Eisenhower, Goldwater, Nixon, and Reagan. How did each leader's philosophy reflect the times? What factors made Reagan's viewpoint "an idea whose time had come"? Have students answer these questions in a brief essay.

Liberal Republicans

Historically, the Democratic Party and Republican Party have included coalitions of both liberals and conservatives. Liberal Republicans dominated their party's presidential nominations from the 1930s to the 1960s. However, Goldwater defeated a liberal Republican in the primaries to win the nomination with conservative support. At the 1964 convention, Goldwater denounced "moderation" in a fiery speech that inspired his followers but upset many liberals and moderates in the GOP.

Today Old coalitions have broken up, and the two major parties are clearly divided by philosophy on a national level. The conservative wing of the Republican Party, strengthened by conservative ex-Democrats, controls most leadership positions in the GOP. Some liberal Republicans and conservative Democrats still flourish at state and local levels, but they face difficulties running for Congress or the presidency. One of the few liberal Republicans in the Senate, James Jeffords of Vermont (above), broke his lifelong ties to his party in 2001 to become an Independent aligned with Democrats. He said,

> "Looking ahead, I can see more and more instances where I will disagree with [President George W. Bush] on very fundamental issues: the issues of choice [abortion rights], the direction of the judiciary, tax and spending decisions, missile defense, energy and the environment, and a host of other issues, large and small."

 **How did Goldwater's 1964 campaign lay the foundation for later Republican victories?**

laws and antipoverty programs. He also demanded a military buildup against a possible Soviet attack.

Many members of the Republican Party, particularly in the Northeast, felt Goldwater was too conservative to lead their party. Johnson portrayed Goldwater as a dangerous extremist and crushed him in the 1964 election. Goldwater only won his home state of Arizona and several southern states that were unhappy with federal desegregation initiatives. Some analysts concluded that Goldwater's conservatism would never gain wide support. His victory in the South, however, showed that southern conservatives might break their historic ties to the Democrats if a Republican candidate better represented their conservative views.

The Great Society Conservatives found themselves silenced for a time following Goldwater's decisive defeat in 1964. The Democratic landslide in the election gave liberals the political upper hand in the mid-1960s. Congress cooperated as President Johnson pushed ahead with his Great Society program, an extension of the New Deal, starting in 1965.

"Is a new world coming?" Johnson asked. "We welcome it, and we will bend it to the hopes of man."

The Great Society promised something for everyone. The Office of Economic Opportunity helped the poor and gave them a voice in handling their own affairs. Medicare provided medical care for the elderly, while Medicaid gave similar aid to the poor. The Great Society included the most far-reaching school support program in American history. In 1965, a new Department of Housing and Urban Development gave Cabinet-level visibility to the effort to revive the nation's cities and provide good housing for all Americans. However, the Great Society cost billions of dollars annually and raised expectations beyond what the government could meet.

Nixon and the Welfare State In 1968, Richard Nixon won the presidency, bringing Republicans back to power. Nixon wanted to trim social welfare programs, which he believed encouraged people not to work, and to bring the budget under control.

READING CHECK
How did conservatives feel about Johnson's Great Society?

Yet in fact, the federal government continued to grow during Nixon's presidency. The Occupational Safety and Health Act (OSHA) of 1970 provided for employee rights in the workplace and demanded that safety standards be maintained with federal enforcement regulation. Also in 1970, the Environmental Protection Agency (EPA) was created to oversee federal antipollution laws. Opponents of government growth criticized these efforts for interfering with private enterprise.

Social Issues Many conservatives were deeply troubled by rapid cultural changes of the period. Rock music was becoming increasingly shocking, its lyrics more openly sexual and drug-oriented. The use of illegal drugs became widespread, and a wave of radical and often violent student protests swept

ACTIVITY
Connecting with Government

Have students take on the role of a journalist covering a political campaign. Have each student prepare six questions to ask as he or she interviews one candidate from the New Right and one with liberal views. Some students can take the role of the candidates and answer the questions. Questions and answers should help explain how participation in the democratic process reflects our national identity. **(Verbal/Linguistic)**

BACKGROUND
Art History

The social changes and unrest of the 1960s were reflected in the movies of the period. "It would have been foolish to believe that movies, that most creative of art forms, could have remained unaffected by the change and torment in our society," remembers Jack Valenti, then president of the Motion Picture Association of America. "The result of all this was the emergence of a 'new kind' of American movie—frank and open and made by filmmakers subject to very few self-imposed restraints. . . . I knew that the mix of new social currents . . . and the possible intrusion of government into the movie arena demanded my immediate action." The result, in November 1968, was the introduction of the voluntary film rating system that, with a few modifications, is still in use today.

READING CHECK

They opposed it. Conservatives such as Barry Goldwater hoped to dismantle Social Security and block new civil rights legislation. Richard Nixon worried about the money spent on Johnson's welfare programs.

CAPTION ANSWERS

Fast Forward to Today Goldwater's campaign relied on the conservatives in the Republican Party. When he won the nomination, it demonstrated that conservatives could gain enough support without having to compromise with liberal Democrats.

RESOURCE DIRECTORY

Teaching Resources

Learning with Documents booklet (Primary Source Activity) *Speaking for the President,* p. 38

Technology

Color Transparencies *American Diversity,* G13, G14

college campuses. Reagan's strong opposition to riots at the University of California at Berkeley encouraged many voters to support him in his successful 1966 run for governor of California. One of his first acts as governor was to dismiss that university's president for being too soft on student protests.

The sexual revolution was another source of conservative concern. The use of the new birth control pill encouraged promiscuity, critics said. Also, after the 1973 Supreme Court ruling in *Roe* v. *Wade* legalized abortion, anti-abortion forces launched a campaign to overturn that decision. The movement for gay and lesbian rights further angered many conservative Americans.

The women's movement caused still another rift. As women worked for equal rights and began to gain new opportunities, some conservatives reacted vigorously. A woman's place was at home, they argued. Phyllis Schlafly, who campaigned against ratification of the Equal Rights Amendment, echoed the desire to retain women's traditional roles.

VIEWING HISTORY Richard Nixon, shown here at Grand Teton National Park, signed legislation to extend federal oversight of the environment. **Recognizing Ideologies** *Why were some conservatives unhappy with Richard Nixon's acts as President?*

Civil Rights Some government programs that were aimed at ending racial segregation and discrimination also disturbed conservatives. Most people supported the desegregation of public schools following *Brown* v. *Board of Education* in 1954. However, many questioned why their children had to be bused to distant schools each day for diversity's sake when neighborhood schools were much closer.

Another controversy involved affirmative action programs. These programs committed the government and private companies to give special consideration to groups discriminated against in the past, both women and members of minority groups. Some critics called affirmative action programs "reverse discrimination." This issue attracted some Democratic blue-collar workers to the Republican ranks, where they would help elect Ronald Reagan to the presidency. The **Reagan Democrats,** as they were known, would help Republicans win many victories in the 1980s.

Turning Point: The Election of 1980

In 1976, Ronald Reagan had challenged President Gerald Ford for the Republican nomination. He lost this contest by a narrow margin. In 1980, Reagan again sought the nomination. Republican moderates claimed that he, like Goldwater in 1964, was too conservative to defeat the Democratic President, Jimmy Carter. However, social changes were underway that would prove this prediction wrong.

The New Right Coalition By 1980, conservative groups had formed a powerful political coalition known as the **New Right.** A key concern of many conservatives in the New Right was the size of government and its role in the economy. They proposed cutting government-funded social programs.

Other groups in the New Right wanted to restore what they considered Christian values to society. Members of the Moral Majority, led by the Reverend Jerry Falwell of Virginia,

Focus on WORLD EVENTS

Margaret Thatcher Ronald Reagan found a strong ally in Margaret Thatcher, Britain's first woman prime minister. Thatcher governed from 1979 to 1990 and shared Reagan's support for free enterprise and his hostility toward communism. Like Reagan, Thatcher won office in difficult economic times by promising to cut taxes and reduce the size of government. Although her tough economic policies forced many inefficient factories and mines to close, she succeeded in curbing labor strife and in invigorating other sectors of the economy.

ACTIVITY

Connecting with Government

Ask students to do research to find the strategies, slogans, and advertisements used by the three candidates in their 1980 presidential campaigns. Have them demonstrate or read samples from each campaign in class. **(Verbal/Linguistic)**

BACKGROUND

Connections to Today

Despite the growth of conservatism, one of the greatest successes for women's rights came in the 1970s. This was the passage of Title IX of the Education Amendments of 1972 forbidding schools to practice gender discrimination in educational programs or activities. Girls' athletics have proved a major beneficiary of this law, which requires girls to have equal equipment, coaching, and opportunity to participate in interscholastic sports. As a result, the number of girls in high school interscholastic sports has grown from fewer than 300,000 in 1971 to more than 2.4 million today. Nowhere has the effect of Title IX been felt more than in soccer, considered a boys' sport in 1971. Because of this law, women players were able to lead the United States to its first Olympic medal in women's soccer in 1996 and a world championship in 1999.

TEST PREPARATION

Have students read the quote on the previous page by President Johnson and then answer the following question.

President Johnson said, "Is a new world coming? We welcome it, and we will bend it to the hopes of man." Which statement below best paraphrases President Johnson's statement?

- **(A)** Change lies ahead, and we will tame it to help society.
- **B** Change is bad and must be avoided.
- **C** Change is inevitable, but we can slow it.
- **D** Humankind has no control over the future.

CAPTION ANSWERS

Viewing History Nixon expanded the role of the federal government in regulating working conditions and protecting the environment; conservatives wanted to reduce the federal government's powers.

Section 1 Assessment

Reading Comprehension

1. They felt that it undermined the rights of individuals, property, and individual enterprise; and that the nation could not afford the high federal spending and resulting deficits.
2. Primarily because the government continued to grow larger under both Eisenhower and Nixon.
3. By offering the hope of ending forced busing and affirmative action.
4. Moral Majority televangelists and those who wanted to reduce both the size of the government and its social programs.

Critical Thinking and Writing

5. Reagan was very effective in televised debates and speeches due to his talent as a witty and optimistic public speaker. The New Right also used television to propagate conservative views that Reagan shared.
6. Answers will vary but should be supported with facts from the section.

President Reagan voiced the growing frustrations of voters who believed the government was too large. He proposed that decreasing the size of the bureaucracy and limiting government intervention in people's lives would solve the economic problems facing America.

VIEWING HISTORY Jerry Falwell and other televangelists helped change the way political candidates portrayed themselves and their opponents in the media. **Identifying Assumptions** *What were some of the issues addressed by the New Right?*

wanted to follow the dictates of the Bible and revive the traditional values they believed had strengthened the country in the past.

Falwell and other evangelists used the power of television to reach millions of people. In a format that became known as **televangelism,** they appealed to viewers to contribute money to their campaign. They delivered fervent sermons on specific political issues and used the money they raised to back conservative politicians.

A Reagan Landslide The growing strength of conservatives in the Republican Party gave Ronald Reagan the GOP presidential nomination in 1980. During the campaign, Reagan seized on growing discontent. His attacks on incumbent Jimmy Carter's handling of the economy were particularly effective. Criticizing Carter's economic record, he poked fun at the President's use of technical language:

> "*I'm talking in human terms and he is hiding behind a dictionary. If he wants a definition, I'll give him one. A recession is when your neighbor loses his job. A depression is when you lose yours. A recovery is when Jimmy Carter loses his.*"
>
> —Ronald Reagan, 1980

The continuing hostage crisis in Iran, as well as other issues, hurt Carter, and Reagan won in a landslide. He gained 51 percent of the popular vote to Carter's 41 percent. (Illinois Representative John Anderson, a Republican, ran as a moderate third-party candidate.) Carter carried but six states and the District of Columbia, including his home state of Georgia. Carter won only 49 electoral votes while Reagan picked up 489.

Swept along by Reagan's popularity, the Republicans gained control of the Senate for the first time since Eisenhower's first term. Several noted Democratic senators, including Frank Church of Idaho and Birch Bayh of Indiana, lost their seats to underdog Republican challengers. Conservatives now controlled the nation's agenda.

Section 1 Assessment

READING COMPREHENSION

1. Why did conservatives oppose Franklin Roosevelt's New Deal?
2. Why were some conservatives dissatisfied with Republican Presidents like Eisenhower and Nixon?
3. How did Reagan appeal to the voters who became known as **Reagan Democrats?**
4. What groups were part of the **New Right?**

CRITICAL THINKING AND WRITING

5. **Recognizing Cause and Effect** How did Reagan use modern technology and new political techniques to increase his popularity?
6. **Writing an Outline** Create an outline describing the goals of conservative politicians in 1980 and how they worked to accomplish these goals.

Take It to the NET

Activity: Analyzing Primary Sources Study Ronald Reagan's first inaugural address online. How does this address reflect the evolution of conservatism in America? Use the links provided in the *America: Pathways to the Present* area of the following Web site for help in completing this activity.
www.phschool.com

Caption Answers

Viewing History The size and role of government; following dictates of the Bible; reviving traditional values.

RESOURCE DIRECTORY

Teaching Resources
Units 5/6/7 booklet
- Section 1 Quiz, p. 112

Guide to the Essentials
- Section 1 Summary, p. 127

Technology
Sounds of an Era Audio CD *Ronald Reagan* (time: 5 seconds)

Analyzing Trends in Electoral College Maps

As you recall, votes in a presidential election are not cast directly for a presidential candidate but rather for presidential electors—the members of the electoral college. Each state has as many electoral votes as it has members of Congress: two for its two Senate seats, plus at least one more based on its representation in the House, which is in turn determined by the state's population. In all states but Maine and Nebraska, it's "winner take all": The candidate with the most popular votes gets *all* of a state's electoral votes. Therefore, it's not surprising that states and regions with the largest population—and most electoral votes—get the most attention from presidential candidates.

Electoral college maps show shifts in population—and political clout. Maps that also show election results reveal where the strength of a candidate or a party lies.

LEARN THE SKILL

Use the following steps to analyze trends shown in electoral college maps:

1. **Determine what information the maps provide.** In some electoral college maps, population size determines the size of each state on the map. Other maps just use the number of electoral votes. Still others show election results.
2. **Look for differences between the maps.** Note differences in population and electoral votes for particular states and for regions over time.
3. **Draw conclusions about population shifts and party strengths.** Relate what you know from other sources to what you see on the maps.

PRACTICE THE SKILL

Answer the following questions:

1. **(a)** What kind of information does Map A provide? How does the map present the information? **(b)** Does Map B provide more, less, or the same kind of information as Map A? Explain. **(c)** How is Map C different from Map A?
2. Between 1948 and 1980: **(a)** Which two states gained the most population? **(b)** Which two states lost the most population? **(c)** Which region(s) gained political clout?
3. **(a)** If you had been a candidate in 1948, where would you have concentrated your resources? **(b)** In 1980, what regions would you have concentrated on? **(c)** What conclusions can you draw about the changes in the political landscape between 1948 and 1980?

APPLY THE SKILL

See the Chapter Review and Assessment for another opportunity to apply this skill.

A. Electoral College Votes, Election of 1948

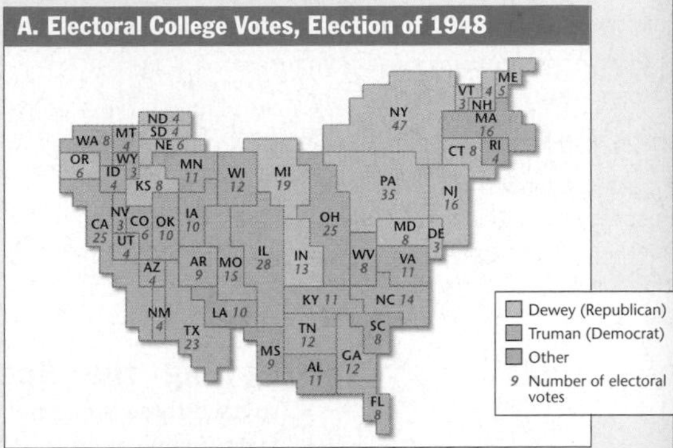

B. Electoral Votes of Each State, 1980

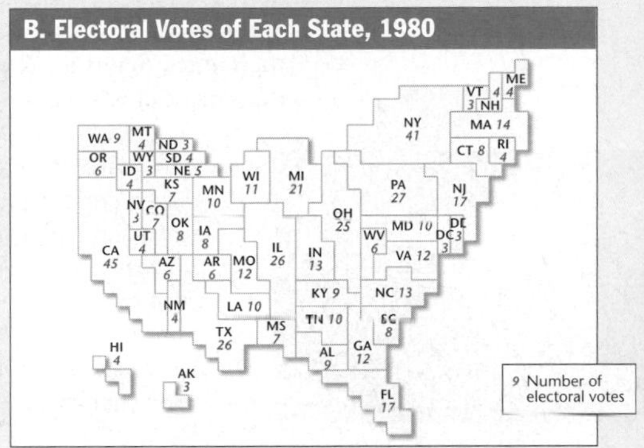

C. Electoral College Votes, Election of 1980

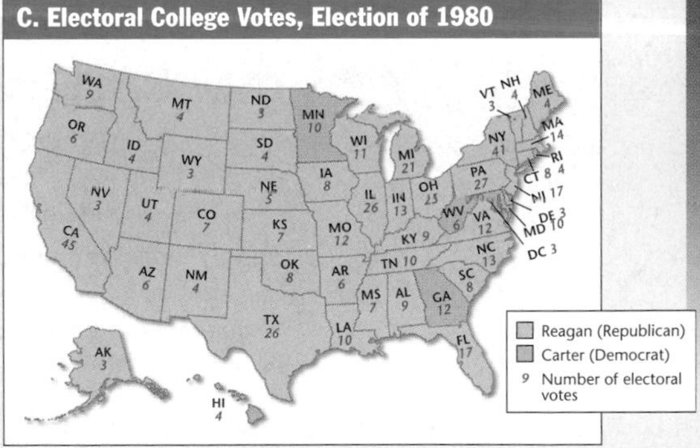

ANALYZING TRENDS IN ELECTORAL COLLEGE MAPS

Focus Students learn to analyze trends in population and regional political influence by comparing electoral college maps.

Instruct Discuss with students how the electoral college system may influence campaigns and issues. States that don't traditionally vote Democratic or Republican and/or that have many electoral votes receive the most attention from candidates. Issues that are important to these key "swing" states could dominate politics to the exclusion of other issues. Discuss recent election campaigns in view of the electoral votes in each state.

Extend See the Skills for Life activity in the Resource Directory below.

ANSWERS

PRACTICE THE SKILL

1. **(a)** Map A shows the number of electoral votes of each state, the relative population of each state, and which candidate won the electoral votes of each state in the election of 1948. The number of electoral votes is included in an outline of the state, sized to reflect its population compared to that of other states, and the states won by each candidate are color-coded. **(b)** Map B provides less information than Map A. It doesn't show the election results for a given year. **(c)** Map C shows the states with geographical boundaries and doesn't represent each state sized to reflect its population; it shows the results of a different election.
2. **(a)** California and Florida. **(b)** New York and Pennsylvania. **(c)** The South and the West.
3. **(a)** In the Northeast, particularly New York and Pennsylvania. **(b)** The West, the Southwest, and the Middle Atlantic States. **(c)** From 1948 to 1980, some of the political clout has shifted out of the Northeast into the West and the Southwest.

RESOURCE DIRECTORY

Teaching Resources
Skills for Life booklet, p. 35

Technology
Social Studies Skills Tutor CD-ROM
Interactive Practice in
- Geographic Literacy
- Critical Thinking and Reading
- Visual Analysis
- Communications

Section 2 The Reagan Revolution

SECTION OBJECTIVES

1. Read to find out how President Reagan attempted to change the economy.
2. Find out how Reagan changed the federal government.
3. Reflect on major initiatives and key foreign policy crises of Reagan's first term.
4. Explore the ways in which the economy moved from recession to recovery in the early 1980s.

BELLRINGER

Warm-Up Activity Ask students to suggest their own ideas for a fair method of taxing people to pay for government services. What kinds of income or purchases would they tax? How would they make sure the tax was fair?

Activating Prior Knowledge Did everyone in the United States agree with the principles of the Conservative Revolution? What percentage of voters favored Ronald Reagan in the 1980 election? Which leaders represented other viewpoints?

READING STRATEGY

Have students skim the section and write down main headings, then rewrite each heading as a question. As they read, have students answer their questions and reflect on actions of government and the private sector to expand economic opportunities to all citizens.

ACTIVITY

Connecting with Economics

Pair students and have each pair develop two diagrams: one illustrating how business growth is stimulated according to Keynesian theory and the other showing how supply-side economics creates business growth. Select pairs to explain and interpret their diagrams for the class. **(Visual/Spatial; Logical/Mathematical)**

Section 2

The Reagan Revolution

READING FOCUS

- How did President Reagan attempt to change the economy?
- In what ways did Reagan change the federal government?
- What were the major initiatives and key foreign policy crises of Reagan's first term?
- How did the economy move from recession to recovery in the early 1980s?

MAIN IDEA

Ronald Reagan worked to boost the nation's pride and prosperity by cutting taxes, shrinking the federal government, and increasing defense spending.

KEY TERMS

supply-side economics
New Federalism
Strategic Defense Initiative (SDI)

TAKING NOTES

As you read, prepare an outline of this section. Use Roman numerals to indicate the major headings of the section, capital letters for the subheadings, and numbers for the supporting details. The sample below will help you get started.

I. Changing the Economy
A. Supply-Side Economics
1. "Reaganomics" reverses earlier theories of high spending and debt.
2. ______
B. Cutting Taxes
1. ______
2. ______
II. Changing the Government

Setting the Scene During the 1980 campaign, Ronald Reagan stressed three broad policies that he would pursue if elected President: slashing taxes, eliminating unnecessary government programs, and bolstering the defense capability of the United States. His goals were to reshape the federal government and restore the country's strength and prosperity. As he addressed the United States for the first time as President, he reaffirmed his promises to the American people:

Ronald Reagan takes the oath of office with his wife, Nancy, at his side.

> "*In the days ahead I will propose removing the roadblocks that have slowed our economy and reduced productivity. Steps will be taken aimed at restoring the balance between various levels of government. Progress may be slow, measured in inches and feet, not miles, but we will progress. It is time to reawaken this industrial giant, to get government back within its means, and to lighten our punitive tax burden. And these will be our first priorities, and on these principles there will be no compromise.*"
>
> —Ronald Reagan, First Inaugural Address, 1981

In his first term, Reagan moved aggressively to put his principles into action.

Changing the Economy

President Reagan brought to Washington a plan for economic change that conservatives had long sought to implement. In simple terms, he wanted to put more money back into people's pockets, instead of into tax coffers.

Supply-Side Economics Reagan's main goal was to spur business growth. His economic program, dubbed "Reaganomics," rested on the theory of supply-side economics. This theory reversed earlier policies based on the ideas of English economist John Maynard Keynes.

RESOURCE DIRECTORY

Teaching Resources
Guided Reading and Review booklet, p. 134

Technology
Section Reading Support Transparencies
Guided Reading Audiotapes (English/Spanish), Ch. 26
Student Edition on Audio CD, Ch. 26
Exploring Primary Sources in U.S. History CD-ROM *A Time for Choosing, Ronald Reagan*
Prentice Hall Presentation Pro CD-ROM, Ch. 26
Companion Web site, www.phschool.com

In the 1920s and 1930s, Keynes had argued that the government could best improve the economy by increasing consumers' demand for goods. This meant giving people more money—either directly, through government payments and programs, or indirectly, by creating jobs. Once people had more money to spend, Keynes argued, they would purchase more goods and services, which would cause the economy to grow.

Keynesian theory had helped explain the Great Depression and the recovery that took place as the United States began a massive military spending program during World War II. In the postwar years, most economists accepted Keynesian arguments. Federal spending was seen as an essential tool for keeping the economy healthy.

In contrast to Keynesian theory, **supply-side economics** focused not on the demand for goods but on the supply of goods. It predicted that cutting taxes would put more money into the hands of businesses and investors—those who supplied the goods for consumers to buy.

The theory assumed that businesses would then hire more people and produce more goods and services, making the economy grow faster. The real key, therefore, was encouraging business leaders to invest in their companies. Their individual actions would create and promote greater national economic abundance. But without tax cuts, high taxes would discourage entrepreneurs from investing, and drain needed capital from the economy.

Cutting Taxes Reagan's first priority was a tax cut. In October 1981, a 5 percent cut went into effect, followed by 10 percent cuts in 1982 and 1983. In 1986, during Reagan's second term, Congress passed the most sweeping tax reform in history. The law closed loopholes that had allowed some people to avoid paying their fair share of taxes. It simplified the tax system by reducing the number of income brackets that determined how much tax a person paid. While all taxpayers benefited from these measures, wealthy Americans benefited most. The tax rate on the highest incomes dropped from 70 percent before Reagan took office to 50 percent in 1984, and to 28 percent after the 1986 tax reform.

Focus on ECONOMICS

Tax Reform Before the 1986 tax reform, taxpayers were able to exclude money spent on many different types of expenses from taxation, including money spent on child care, medical bills, and political contributions. Over time, these categories of expenses, known as deductibles, multiplied, making it easier for many people to find new and innovative ways to lower their taxes. By using their deductions creatively, taxpayers could effectively choose how much to pay in taxes. The elimination of so many loopholes in 1986 meant that the top tax rate could drop from 50 percent to 28 percent without a serious loss of revenue.

Changing the Government

As you read in the previous section, for generations, conservatives had criticized government growth. Now, however, they had a Chief Executive committed to limiting both the size and the role of the federal government.

Cutting Regulations Reagan embarked on a major program of deregulation. Like President Carter before him, Reagan wanted to eliminate government regulations that he believed stifled free market competition.

By the time of Reagan's presidency, regulation had been expanding for nearly a century. The Interstate Commerce Commission, established in 1887, was the first step. Government regulations grew during the Progressive Era of the early 1900s and in the New Deal years of the 1930s. Regulation was intended to protect

INTERPRETING GRAPHS
Reagan reduced the top income tax rate from 70 percent to 28 percent. **Analyzing Information** *What was the top income tax rate when Reagan ran for reelection in 1984?*

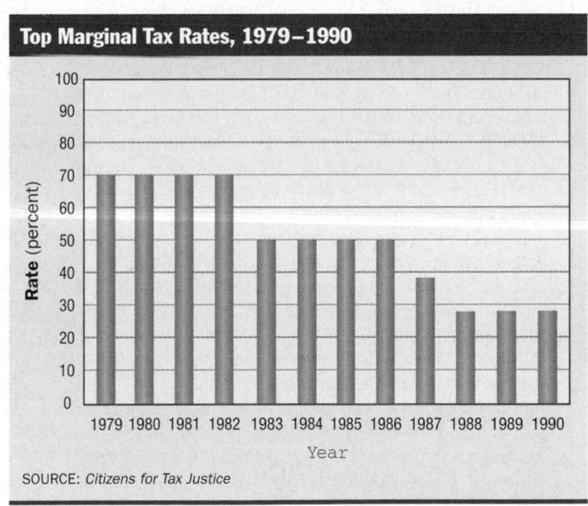

SOURCE: *Citizens for Tax Justice*

LESSON PLAN

Focus Explain that Reagan's actions and policies in his first term as President were intended to carry out the conservative ideas and principles on which he had campaigned. Ask students to name those principles.

Instruct Explain the two competing theories of economics that modern U.S. governments have followed: Keynesian and supply-side. Explore ways in which tax policies and other actions, such as deregulation, are outgrowths of the economic policy that an administration is following. Discuss how the military buildup, increased spending on weapons, and overseas military expeditions such as the invasion of Grenada fit in with Reagan's agenda.

Assess/Reteach Ask students to research the top five spending areas of the federal government, both today and in 1984. Has the percentage of government support for various programs gone up, gone down, or stayed the same? Are the five categories the same, or have they changed?

CAPTION ANSWERS

Interpreting Graphs 50 percent.

ACTIVITY
Connecting with History and Conflict

Have students choose one of the major topics or issues of Reagan's first term —for instance, supply-side economics, Grenada, or "Star Wars"—and draw a political cartoon that expresses an opinion or point of view about that issue. Display finished cartoons in class. **(Visual/Spatial)**

BACKGROUND
Recent Scholarship

Instrumental in challenging the assumptions that created the American welfare state, Ronald Reagan played a major role in the revival of conservatism in the 1980s. In *Exit with Honor: The Life and Presidency of Ronald Reagan,* William E. Pemberton describes the accomplishments of one of the most popular and publicly acclaimed Presidents of the twentieth century, while also pointing to Reagan's weaknesses as a manager in both foreign and domestic affairs.

companies from unfair competition, workers from unsafe working conditions, and consumers from ineffective or unsafe products.

Reagan continued and expanded the deregulation of the energy, transportation, and banking industries begun under the Carter administration. He cut the number and size of regulatory agencies like the Environmental Protection Agency, which had its budget, and therefore its functions, reduced. Reagan argued that regulations made life difficult for producers, which meant fewer jobs for workers and higher prices for consumers. The more that businesses spent to comply with government rules, he charged, the less they could spend on new factories and equipment.

READING CHECK
Why did Reagan roll back regulation of industries?

Reagan also challenged the powers of labor unions. In August 1981, the Professional Air Traffic Controllers Organization (PATCO) called a strike to win higher pay and improved working conditions. The move threatened to interrupt air travel across the country because air traffic controllers determine how and where the nation's commercial aircraft fly between airports. Reagan gave the 13,000 strikers two days to return to work, and when most chose to stay out on strike, he fired them. His decisive move caused short-term problems in the air traffic control system, but Reagan savored a victory that "convinced people who might have thought otherwise that I meant what I said."

Slowing Federal Growth Reagan also attempted to cut the size of the federal government. The President believed that any American could succeed through individual effort. This belief ran counter to the argument on which welfare was based: that government should help people who could not help themselves. Reagan charged that the government had become too intrusive in people's lives:

NOTABLE PRESIDENTS
Ronald Reagan

"I find no national malaise. I find nothing wrong with the American people."

—Ronald Reagan, 1980

Ronald Reagan was born in rural Tampico, Illinois, in 1911. The first in his family to go to college, Reagan became a radio sportscaster after graduating. His ability to spin dramatic stories from a few dry facts helped him become known in later years as the "Great Communicator." During a business trip to California in 1937, Reagan took a screen test at the Warner Brothers studio. He spent the next ten years building a film career.

In 1947, Reagan became president of the film actors' union, the Screen Actors' Guild. In the mid-1950s, he became the spokesman for General Electric. He spoke against communism and the "containment" policy.

In 1966, Reagan was elected governor of California. Likable and articulate, Reagan was a natural politician who appealed to any audience. In the presidential election of 1980, he asked the voters, "Are you better off today than you were four years ago?" The answer was apparent in his landslide victory over President Carter.

40th President 1981–1989

In 1984, Reagan was reelected, becoming the third Republican President to win reelection since the Depression. Americans remember Reagan for his presidential style—unassuming, personable, candid, and optimistic. A later President, Bill Clinton, summed it up: "[Reagan's] unwavering hopefulness reminded us that optimism is one of our most fundamental virtues."

Connecting to Today

Ronald Reagan reminded Americans how important the role of the President is in helping overcome national self-doubt. How has the self-confidence of the United States changed since 1980? Explain.

Take It to the NET Biography To read more about Ronald Reagan, visit the links provided in the *America: Pathways to the Present* area of the following Web site. **www.phschool.com**

RESOURCE DIRECTORY

Teaching Resources

Great Debates booklet (Great Debates) *How Should We Deal with Environmental Dangers?* p. 28

> “It is . . . my intention . . . to make [government] work—work with us, not over us; to stand by our side, not ride on our back. Government can and must provide opportunity, not smother it; foster productivity, not stifle it.”
>
> —Ronald Reagan, First Inaugural Address, 1981

Drawing support from opponents of the programs created by Lyndon Johnson's Great Society, Reagan attacked these issues head-on. The administration eliminated public service jobs that were part of an employment training program. It reduced unemployment compensation. It lowered welfare benefits and reduced spending on food stamps. It raised fees for Medicare patients. Despite cuts in these specific programs, total federal spending on social welfare rose between 1980 and 1982, although more slowly than it might have risen without cuts.

While he cut back the role of the federal government, Reagan sought to give more responsibility to state and local governments. Borrowing a term from the Nixon administration, he called his plan the **New Federalism.** Under this plan, the federal government would no longer tell states exactly how federal aid had to be used. Rather, it would let states create and pay for programs as they saw fit.

The New Federalism program never worked as planned. A recession early in Reagan's presidency left a number of cities and states nearly bankrupt. They now had more responsibility, but not enough money for the programs formerly funded directly by the federal government.

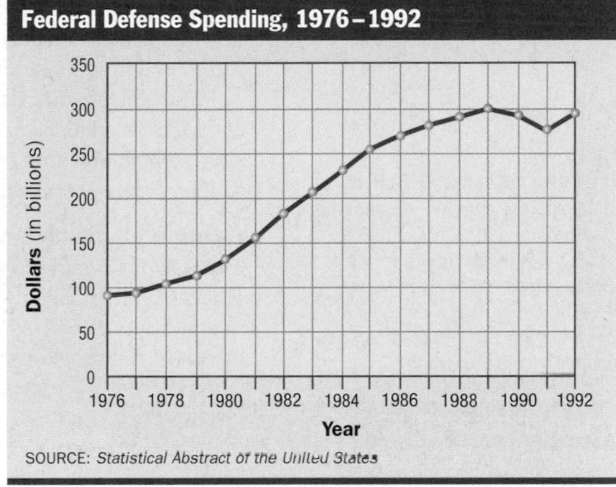

INTERPRETING GRAPHS
Notice the change in defense spending in the early 1980s. **Analyzing Information** *By how much did the defense budget increase during President Reagan's two terms in office?*

Reagan's Foreign Policy

While taking decisive measures to change the direction of domestic policy, Reagan was equally determined to defend American interests in the Cold War. He believed in a tough approach toward the Soviet Union, which he called an "evil empire." He favored large defense budgets to strengthen both conventional military forces and the nuclear arsenal.

Military Buildup The costs of the buildup were enormous. Over a five-year period, the United States spent an unprecedented $1.1 trillion on defense. These expenditures contributed to the growing budget deficits. Conservatives considered this the cost of fighting the Cold War.

Much of this money went into new weapons and new technology. The United States continued to develop new missiles, such as the intercontinental MX, as well as new bombers and submarines that could carry nuclear weapons. Reagan also explored ways to protect American territory against nuclear attack. In 1983, Reagan announced the **Strategic Defense Initiative (SDI),** popularly known as "Star Wars" after the 1977 film. SDI proposed the creation of a massive satellite shield in space to intercept and destroy incoming Soviet missiles.

Trouble Spots Abroad Relations with the Soviet Union remained frosty during Reagan's first term. The Soviets criticized the American defense buildup. They also complained when the United States stationed new intermediate-range nuclear missiles in Western Europe.

ACTIVITY
Connecting with Science and Technology

Have students use the text description as a guide to create drawings that depict how the planned "Star Wars" anti-missile defense system would have worked. Have students explain how the technological innovations featured in this system arose from specific perceived needs. Display selected drawings on classroom walls. **(Visual/Spatial)**

BACKGROUND
Global Connections

SDI greatly alarmed the Soviets because it threatened the belief, held by both nations throughout the Cold War, that neither could "nuke" the other without itself being destroyed by a retaliatory attack. The Soviets feared SDI would give the United States first-strike capability. When they could not dissuade President Reagan from the program, the Soviets went ahead with a similar project for the USSR. Research and development of these systems, designed to use lasers to shoot down missiles, was extraordinarily expensive. Scientists and military experts still dispute whether SDI would have worked. However, whether practical or not, its development further strained the weak Soviet economy.

CUSTOMIZE FOR ...
Less Proficient Readers

Ask students to make a cause-and-effect chart that shows, first, Reagan's policy priorities in his first term; second, the moves taken to implement them; and third, the results.

CAPTION ANSWERS

Interpreting Graphs It nearly doubled, from approximately $150 billion to $290 billion.

Activity
Connecting with Economics

Have one student group argue their position for the theory of supply-side economics in a debate; another student group should oppose the theory. Each group should use specific details and examples. The rest of the class should supply questions for each group to answer as part of the debate and discuss the argument made by each group. **(Verbal/Linguistic)**

Background
Geography in History

The outcome of the invasion of Grenada, the Western Hemisphere's smallest nation, was never in doubt. At 133 square miles in area, the island republic is less than one-tenth the size of Rhode Island, and Grenada's principal ally, Cuba, lay at the other end of the Caribbean. Grenada's neighbors supplied soldiers and police for the invasion. The United States landed 7,000 troops within one week, and Cuban and Marxist troops who survived the initial fighting retreated into the island's jungles. Resistance was so light that the United States began withdrawing its troops after less than a month.

Reagan salutes an honor guard of American soldiers with Secretary of Defense Caspar Weinberger (right).

The United States encountered difficulties in the Middle East as well. The country of Lebanon had become a battleground for a variety of armed political groups, some backed by neighboring countries. In 1982, Reagan sent several thousand marines to Beirut, the Lebanese capital, as part of a peacekeeping force. In October 1983, a terrorist truck loaded with explosives crashed through the gates of a marine barracks, killing 241 Americans.

The attack horrified the nation. Many Americans demanded an immediate withdrawal from Lebanon, and by the following February, all the troops had left.

The North African nation of Libya, under General Qaddafi, sponsored terrorist attacks on American and Israeli targets in Europe. Responding to one such incident, a bombing in West Berlin in which an American serviceman was killed, Reagan ordered air attacks on Libya on April 14, 1986.

INTERPRETING GRAPHS
Examine the graph below showing the federal deficit from 1980 to 1992. **Synthesizing Information** *What happened to the federal deficit during Reagan's years in office? How did Reagan's policies contribute to that trend?*

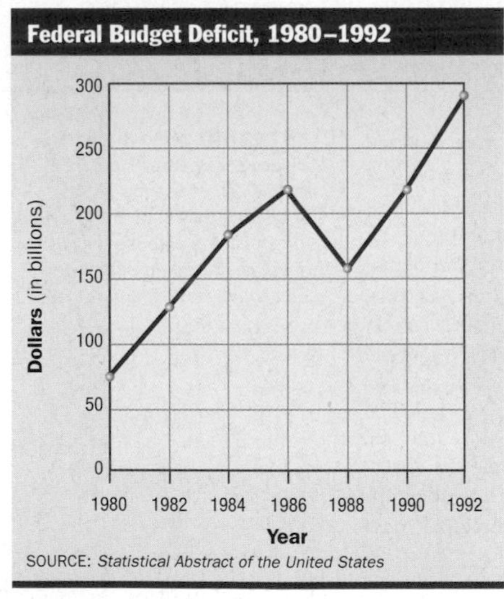

Fighting Communism in the Americas Reagan feared that Communist forces would gain power and threaten American interests in the Western Hemisphere. In El Salvador, the United States supported a repressive military regime in its efforts to resist guerrillas, some of whom were Marxists. Reagan increased military aid to El Salvador to the level of about $1 million a day. In Nicaragua, as you will read in the next section, the United States helped guerrillas who were fighting to overthrow that nation's leftist government.

Reagan claimed a victory over communism on the tiny Caribbean island of Grenada. He ordered United States military forces to Grenada in October 1983, after a military group staged a coup and installed a government sympathetic to Communist Cuba. The official aim of the invasion was to safeguard several hundred American medical students on the island. However, United States forces also overthrew the Grenadian government and remained in Grenada to oversee free elections.

Recession and Recovery

During Reagan's first two years in office, the United States experienced the worst economic downturn since the Great Depression. The Federal Reserve Bank raised interest rates to reduce inflation. However, high interest rates hurt businesses and discouraged Americans from borrowing to purchase goods or invest in new equipment. Foreign competition also cost thousands of American jobs. By 1982, unemployment had

Caption Answers

Interpreting Graphs It increased dramatically overall; Reagan's increase in defense spending and his tax cuts encouraged the trend.

RESOURCE DIRECTORY

Teaching Resources
Units 5/6/7 booklet
- Section 2 Quiz, p. 113

Guide to the Essentials
- Section 2 Summary, p. 128

Learning with Documents booklet (Key Documents) *Ronald Reagan, "These Are the Boys of Pointe du Hoc,"* p. 97

Other Print Resources
American History Block Scheduling Support *Presidential Power: Changes in the Twentieth Century,* found in The Nation After World War II folder, includes interdisciplinary lesson suggestions and activities for Geography and History, Primary Sources, Biography, and Literature.

Technology
RESOURCE PRO® **Visual Learning Activity** *Passing the Economic Buck,* found on Resource Pro, reveals two cartoonists' suggestions of why successive administrations were unable to control government waste and inefficiency.

reached a postwar high of 10.8 percent and several hundred businesses were going bankrupt each week.

The 1981–1982 recession did, however, pave the way for a healthier economy. The high interest rates cooled down inflation, and as Reagan's tax cuts took effect, consumer spending began to rise. By 1983, both inflation and unemployment had already dropped below 10 percent. Business leaders gained new confidence, and increased their investments. The stock market pushed upward. Republicans claimed that the recovery demonstrated the wisdom of supply-side economics.

An important prediction of the supply-side theorists had not come true, however. Cuts in tax rates were supposed to generate so much economic growth that the government's tax revenues would actually increase. As a result, the federal deficit, or the amount by which the government's spending exceeds its income in a given year, was supposed to decrease.

During the 1980 campaign, Reagan had vowed to balance the federal budget if elected. But, the combination of tax cuts and defense spending pushed the deficit up, not down. The deficit ballooned from nearly $80 billion in 1980 to a peak of $221 billion in 1986.

While the rising deficits did help the government cut back on domestic spending, they drove the nation as a whole deeper into debt. The national debt, the total amount of money owed by the government, rose from $909 billion in 1980 to $3.2 trillion in 1990. Future generations would have to bear the burden of interest payments on this monumental debt.

In spite of these challenges, many Americans supported President Reagan. They shared his values and principles. In 1981, the nation reacted with horror when Reagan was wounded in an assassination attempt. The courage and humor with which he faced the situation only reinforced Americans' respect for their President.

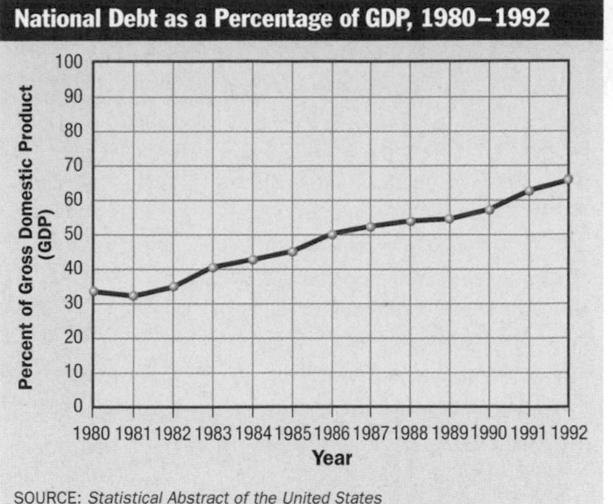

INTERPRETING GRAPHS As the federal government continued to spend more money than it received in taxes, the federal debt rose as a percentage of Gross Domestic Product (GDP). **Analyzing Information** *Review the definitions of national debt and Gross Domestic Product in the glossary and explain in your own words what it means if the national debt represents 60 percent of GDP.*

Section 2 Assessment

READING COMPREHENSION

1. How was **supply-side economics** expected to change the role of the federal government in the economy?
2. (a) What were Reagan's foreign policy goals? (b) How did the **Strategic Defense Initiative** support these goals?
3. Describe the course of the United States economy in the early 1980s.

CRITICAL THINKING AND WRITING

4. **Identifying Central Issues** What major shifts in philosophy and policies did Reagan bring to the federal government?
5. **Drawing Conclusions** What consequences could result from cutting regulations enforced by the federal government?
6. **Writing to Persuade** Write a short paragraph defending or opposing American intervention in Grenada in 1983.

Take It to the NET

Activity: Analyzing Primary Sources Select a speech from Ronald Reagan's first term as President. What does this speech reveal about President Reagan and his policies? Use the links provided in the *America: Pathways to the Present* area of the following Web site for help in completing this activity.
www.phschool.com

TEST PREPARATION

Have students reread the paragraphs under the subheading "Fighting Communism in the Americas" and then complete the sentence below.

A fact from this selection is that—

A Americans were unconcerned with the actions taking place in Lebanon.

(B) the United States supported a repressive military regime in El Salvador.

C Communist forces had power in Latin America and threatened American interests there.

D in Grenada, the United States intervened only to safeguard American medical students.

Section 2 Assessment

Reading Comprehension

1. Government would put more money in the hands of the businesses, rather than individuals, by cutting taxes, encouraging investment, and through deregulation.
2. (a) To inaugurate a major military buildup and to take a hard line against the Soviet Union. (b) It seemed to offer a sophisticated new defense against the Soviet Union's nuclear weapons.
3. A sharp recession followed by an economic recovery during which time both inflation and unemployment dropped.

Critical Thinking and Writing

4. An emphasis on limiting the size and role of the federal government domestically, and a foreign policy of strengthening the military.
5. Health and pollution problems could increase; consumers' rights and worker safety might be compromised.
6. Paragraphs will vary, but should persuade the reader with facts from the section.

Answers will vary but might focus on Reagan's foreign policy concerns and his goals of reducing government size and maintaining adequate levels of defense spending.

CAPTION ANSWERS

Interpreting Graphs Sample answer: The federal government had borrowed, and needed to repay, a sum of money equal to 60 percent of the total value of goods and services produced in the United States in a year.

Section 3
Reagan's Second Term

Section Objectives

1. Observe the ways in which the United States experienced a renewal of patriotism in the 1980s.
2. Find out about some important social debates that continued through Reagan's term in office.
3. See how the economy evolved during the 1980s.
4. Discover how Reagan's hands-off style of governing led to problems.
5. Consider the legacy of Reagan's presidency.

Bellringer

Warm-Up Activity Ask students to think about the American belief that all people are "created equal." In what ways is this belief reflected in social and economic policies?

Activating Prior Knowledge Ask students to state what patriotism means to them. Can they list some concrete symbols of patriotism or some specific acts that they would define as patriotic?

Reading Strategy

As students read the section, have them list the key events and crises described. Then, for each event, have them summarize the significance of its outcome.

Section 3

Reagan's Second Term

READING FOCUS

- In what ways did the United States experience a renewal of patriotism in the 1980s?
- What were some important social debates that continued through Reagan's term in office?
- How did the economy evolve during the 1980s?
- How did Reagan's hands-off style of governing lead to problems?
- What was the legacy of Reagan's presidency?

KEY TERMS

AIDS
Sandinista
Contra
Iran-Contra affair
INF Treaty
entitlement

MAIN IDEA

After a decisive reelection victory in 1984, Reagan continued his conservative policies on economic and social issues. In domestic and foreign affairs, the administration had key successes but also some serious missteps.

TAKING NOTES

As you read, complete the chart below to show some of the accomplishments and important events of Reagan's presidency.

Important Events
Reagan appointed conservatives to the Supreme Court.

Setting the Scene Campaigning for reelection in 1984, Ronald Reagan asked voters if they were better off than they had been four years before. As they roared their approval, he told them, "You ain't seen nothing yet." His campaign advertisements, such as one depicting "Morning in America," heralded a new day of optimism.

VIEWING HISTORY Geraldine Ferraro (right) made history when Walter Mondale (left) asked her to be the first woman to run for Vice President on a major-party ticket. **Drawing Conclusions** *Why did Reagan defeat Walter Mondale easily?*

Reagan faced Democrat Walter Mondale, former Vice President under Carter. Mondale's running mate was New York Representative Geraldine Ferraro, the first woman ever on a major party's presidential ticket.

The relative strength of the economy and Reagan's popularity gave the President a landslide victory over Mondale. Reagan took 59 percent of the popular vote and all the electoral votes except those of the District of Columbia and Mondale's home state of Minnesota. It was the second largest electoral-vote margin in history.

Patriotic Renewal

Reagan wanted to recreate the sense of community he had known in his youth and to help revive the virtues that had made America strong. The nation had endured turbulence in the years following the Vietnam War. The 1980s offered several occasions to celebrate patriotic renewal.

The 1984 Olympic Games were held in Los Angeles, the first time the Summer Games had come to the United States in half a century. The opening ceremonies, televised worldwide to hundreds of millions of viewers, were festive, patriotic affairs.

Some Communist countries, including the Soviet Union and East Germany, boycotted the games. The move was in retaliation to an American-led boycott of the 1980 Moscow games to protest the Soviet invasion of Afghanistan in 1979. As a result of the 1984 boycott, the United States won an unusually high number of medals.

Two years later, in 1986, the nation celebrated the centennial of the Statue of Liberty in New York harbor. This monument, a welcoming sight to many

Caption Answers

Viewing History The economy was booming, and many Americans were satisfied with Reagan's leadership.

Resource Directory

Teaching Resources

Guided Reading and Review booklet, p. 135
Biography, Literature, and Comparing Primary Sources booklet (Comparing Primary Sources) *On the Legacy of the Civil Rights Movement,* p. 161
Biography, Literature, and Comparing Primary Sources booklet (Literature) *Masters of the Universe,* p. 88

Technology

Section Reading Support Transparencies
Guided Reading Audiotapes (English/Spanish), Ch. 26
Student Edition on Audio CD, Ch. 26
Sounds of an Era Audio CD *Ronald Reagan,* 1984 campaign speech (time: 20 seconds)
Prentice Hall Presentation Pro CD-ROM, Ch. 26
Companion Web site, www.phschool.com

immigrants as they entered the United States, was a symbol of freedom around the world. But the copper lady in flowing robes had deteriorated over the course of a century. Now, after a massive campaign to refurbish the statue, the nation held a spectacular centennial celebration.

The following year, the United States celebrated the 200th anniversary of the Constitution, drafted in 1787. Government and private groups sponsored lectures, workshops, and meetings focusing on the features of the Constitution that had made the nation strong. This observance helped renew the public's appreciation of such enduring ideas as balanced government and separation of powers.

Mary Lou Retton became the star of the Los Angeles Olympics at age 16. The American gymnast won five medals, the most medals won by any United States athlete that year.

Continuing Social Debates

In the years leading to Reagan's election, conservatives gained public support with their stands on social issues as well as economic issues. In the 1980s, conservative policies on social issues made these "hot" issues even hotter.

Civil Rights The federal government's commitment to extend voting rights had given the vote to millions of African Americans who had been denied it for decades. These new voters helped elect an increasing number of African American candidates to local, state, and national offices. In 1983, the cities of Charlotte, North Carolina, Philadelphia, and Chicago elected their first black mayors: Harvey Gantt, Wilson Goode, and Harold Washington, respectively. These cities joined Cleveland, Los Angeles, Detroit, and Atlanta, which had voted African Americans to the mayor's office for the first time in the 1960s and 1970s. In 1989, New York City voters chose African American David Dinkins to be mayor of the nation's most populous city.

Altogether, the number of African American elected officials rose from 4,890 in 1980 to 7,335 ten years later. The vast majority of these officeholders hailed from the Southeast.

In 1983, Reagan signed a bill making the birthday of Martin Luther King, Jr., a national holiday. Despite this symbolic victory, resistance to civil rights initiatives was growing, as critics complained that many policies trampled on the rights of state and local governments. Reagan tried to prevent the extension of the

COMPARING PRIMARY SOURCES

The Legacy of the Civil Rights Movement

Decades after the civil rights movement, Americans disagreed on how much progress had been made.

Analyzing Viewpoints Compare the main arguments in the two quotations below.

Substantial Progress

"Before the civil rights movement, there was a very wide separation between blacks and whites. I don't think the separation is as great today. There has been more speaking out. Blacks now let themselves open up and say how they feel in no uncertain terms. I think there are friendships between blacks and whites that didn't exist before. In spite of everything, I think the racial situation is healthier than it was before. Blacks are no longer invisible."

—Eileen Barth, retired social worker, quoted in Race *by Studs Terkel, 1992*

Little or No Progress

"The country is more segregated today than it was when [Martin Luther] King and [Robert] Kennedy were alive. What Dr. King and Bobby were fighting was segregation and discrimination imposed by law, by the state. . . . All of that has changed. . . . But in the North, everybody knows what's happened in the cities. At universities, there's much more black withdrawal into separate communities. I grew up thinking we were going to have an integrated society, not just an end to official racism."

—Anthony Lewis, New York Times, *April 1993*

LESSON PLAN

Focus Explain that the personable Ronald Reagan was popular with the majority of Americans in large part because he made Americans feel good about themselves and their country. What difficulties became apparent during his second term?

Instruct Discuss the economic, social, and judicial issues that developed during the Reagan era, such as the growing gap between rich and poor, the recession, the defeat of the Equal Rights Amendment, conservative appointments to the Supreme Court, and the extension of the Voting Rights Act of 1965. Did these events help or hurt the conservative cause?

Explain the rapid changes going on in the Soviet Union during this period. Discuss the effects of these changes on Reagan's relationship with Mikhail Gorbachev.

Assess/Reteach How did the problems that emerged during Ronald Reagan's second term affect his standing with the American people? How did those problems affect his legacy?

ACTIVITY

Connecting with Culture

Have students work in pairs or individually to compose a poem, song, or rap that celebrates the bicentennial of the Statue of Liberty or the U.S. Constitution, or the advances in civil rights in the 1980s. Invite students to perform their compositions. **(Musical/Rhythmic)**

CUSTOMIZE FOR ...

Less Proficient Writers

Have students reread the section "Continuing Social Debates" and then make a list of the subheads in the section. After each subhead they should list the conservative response to each issue.

ACTIVITY

Connecting with Government

A President's ability to choose Supreme Court Justices can have long-term effects. Have students research the biographies and judicial histories of the Justices named by Reagan, tracing their votes and influence from the date of their appointments to today. Ask them to evaluate the impact of Reagan's judicial appointments on major decisions made by the Supreme Court. Have students share their findings with the class in an oral presentation or in a poster. **(Verbal/Linguistic; Visual/Spatial)**

From the Archives of

American Heritage®

About the Presidents

With his political identity forged in Barry Goldwater's presidential campaign of 1964, Ronald Reagan (1981–1989) was thought to be far too conservative to be a viable candidate for the presidency. But Reagan's call for a reduced federal role in domestic affairs and his projection of American ideals abroad won him a handy victory in the campaign of 1980. Despite a sharp recession in his first term, Reagan's popularity soared as he won his race for a second term in a landslide. Reagan was widely admired for his optimistic temperament and unwavering patriotism. Yet the true legacy of his presidency was to oversee a substantial shift in public opinion toward the conservative end of the spectrum. Source: Adapted from Henry F. Graff's *The Presidents,* Scribner's, 1996, by the editors of *American Heritage®* magazine.

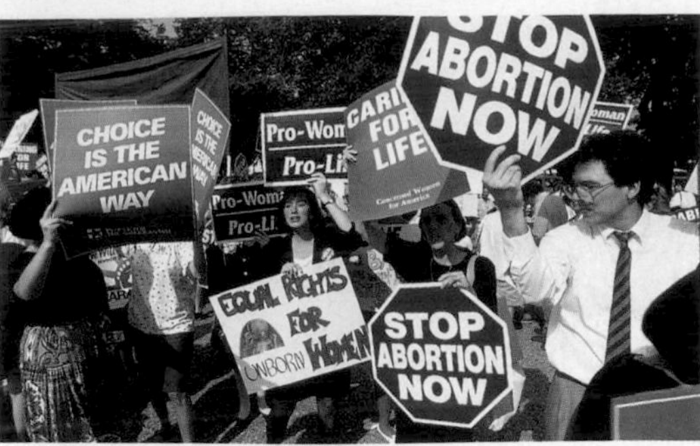

VIEWING HISTORY Pro-choice and anti-abortion activists gathered at this rally. **Determining Relevance** *How did Reagan advance the anti-abortion cause as President?*

Voting Rights Act of 1965, backing off only after intense criticism. He appointed federal judges who were less sympathetic to civil rights goals. The administration also worked to end some affirmative action programs.

The Women's Movement As women gained access to jobs and other opportunities previously denied to them, the women's movement met with a backlash. One sign of this backlash was the defeat in 1982 of the proposed Equal Rights Amendment, which failed to gain the approval of enough state legislatures to be ratified.

Anti-abortion groups took aim at the right to abortion granted in the 1973 *Roe* v. *Wade* Supreme Court decision. Opponents lobbied to halt federal funding of abortions for the poor.

Sexual Orientation The campaign for homosexual rights caused similar polarization. Contributing to the backlash was the spread of acquired immunodeficiency syndrome, known simply as **AIDS.** Most victims of the virus were intravenous drug users and homosexual men. Some people contracted the virus through contaminated blood transfusions. By the late 1980s, the rising costs associated with researching a cure and treating and caring for AIDS patients caused alarm among some Americans. Many people believed the government should promote abstinence as the best way to prevent AIDS, rather than providing controversial information on alternative forms of prevention. Even as AIDS spread into the larger community, the resistance to gay rights grew more vocal.

BIOGRAPHY

Sandra Day O'Connor b. 1930

Born in El Paso, Texas, Sandra Day entered Stanford University in California at age 16 and went on to graduate third in her class at Stanford Law School in 1952. Despite her outstanding record, as a woman she was unable to get a job in a private law firm. She found work as an attorney in a county government office, married, and later opened a private practice in Arizona.

After taking time off to raise her children, she returned to full-time work in 1965, serving in a variety of roles: assistant attorney general, state senator (and the first woman majority leader), and superior court judge. In 1979, Arizona Governor Bruce Babbitt appointed O'Connor to the state appeals court. Reagan elevated her to the Supreme Court two years later.

Conservatives on the Supreme Court Many of these social concerns wound up in the judicial system, just as the courts' temperament began to shift. Reagan's appointees to the federal courts were fairly conservative. In 1981, he selected Arizona judge Sandra Day O'Connor as the nation's first woman Supreme Court justice. In 1986, Reagan chose another conservative, Antonin Scalia, for the Supreme Court and raised conservative Justice William Rehnquist to the post of Chief Justice.

While O'Connor, Scalia, and Rehnquist won Senate confirmation, Reagan's next Supreme Court appointment, conservative judge and former law professor Robert Bork, did not. The Democratic Party had won control of the Senate in the 1986 elections and most Democratic senators did not share Reagan's goal of appointing conservative judges. Liberal groups joined together in 1987 to lobby the Senate to reject Bork's nomination. The nominee whom the Senate finally approved, Anthony Kennedy, was known as a moderate conservative. He joined the Court in 1988.

An Evolving Economy

While many parts of the economy boomed after the recession of 1982, other industries grew slowly or not at all. As a result, prosperity was felt unevenly across the country.

The Farm Crisis America's farmers, who grew more than enough grain to feed Americans and sell excess crops abroad, faced oversupply and falling prices in the 1980s. For a variety of reasons, foreign demand fell and supplies of grain outpaced demand. The price of a bushel of wheat fell from $3.91 in 1980 to $3.39 in 1984, and to $2.42 in 1986;

CAPTION ANSWERS

Viewing History He appointed conservatives to the judiciary.

RESOURCE DIRECTORY

Teaching Resources

Learning with Documents booklet (Visual Learning Activity) *Short-Lived Approval,* p. 72

Technology

RESOURCE PRO® **Biography** *Sandra Day O'Connor,* found on Resource Pro, profiles the first woman appointed to serve on the United States Supreme Court.

RESOURCE PRO® **Critical Thinking Activity** *Recognizing Ideologies: The Bork Nomination,* found on Resource Pro, helps students apply this skill by analyzing the Senate debate about one of Reagan's nominees to the Supreme Court, Robert H. Bork.

a bushel of corn that earned farmers $3.11 in 1980 brought in less than half that much money six years later.

Falling prices hit farmers hard because so many had gone into debt to buy machinery and land when grain prices were high. Only a few years earlier, President Carter's Agriculture Secretary Earl Butz had told them to fill their fields with grain by planting "fencerow to fencerow." Farmers who could not pay their debts risked losing their farms to bankruptcy.

The plight of the family farmer won a lot of sympathy from the public, and members of Congress representing agricultural states sought relief in Washington. The federal government intervened to increase farm income with continued price supports and credit. By 1987, federal spending on agriculture consumed more than $20 billion yearly and supplied 30 percent of America's farm income. Government aid may have protected many farmers from bankruptcy in the 1980s, but it was an expensive and temporary solution that did not address fundamental problems in American agriculture.

Shifts in Manufacturing Several industries with deep roots in the United States lost ground in the 1980s to foreign competition. The recession of 1981–1982 accelerated job losses and factory closings, and many people who lost high-paying manufacturing jobs during the recession were unable to find similar work when the economy picked up. The number of workers in the metal industry, including steel mills, declined from 1,140,000 in December 1980 to 814,000 two years later. While the economy expanded quickly after 1982, the number of metalworking jobs fell further to 728,000 in December 1986. The textile industry also suffered continual job losses.

These losses were part of a historic shift in the United States economy away from manufacturing. In most cases, workers found new jobs in different industries and the parent companies emerged stronger and better able to compete with foreign companies. However, the volume of layoffs and factory closings required difficult adjustments for the workers and cities that were hit hardest, particularly in the Northeast and the Upper Midwest.

Unequal Wealth Wealthy Americans, more than anyone else, flourished under Reagan. The net worth of *Forbes* magazine's 400 richest Americans nearly tripled in the Reagan years. Political analyst Kevin Phillips described this new class:

> "*The truth is that the critical concentration of wealth in the United States was developing at higher levels—decamillionaires, centimillionaires, half-billionaires and billionaires. Garden variety millionaires had become so common that there were about 1.5 million of them by 1989.*"
>
> —Political analyst Kevin Phillips, *New York Times Magazine*, June 24, 1990

By the late 1980s, wealth was more unevenly distributed than at any time since the end of World War II. In terms of current dollars, the average income earned by the top fifth of American households rose 23 percent, from $93,225 in 1980 to $114,912 in 1989. Among the bottom fifth, average household income rose only 4 percent, from $9,075 to $9,433 in the same time period. Many families increased their total income by having both husband and wife

Focus on TECHNOLOGY

The Space Shuttle The first of a new breed of spacecraft took to the sky on April 21, 1981. Unlike the Apollo program rockets that fell to the earth after use, the space shuttle *Columbia* looked and landed like an airplane and could take off again and again to complete multiple missions.

The promising space shuttle program suffered a disastrous setback on January 28, 1986, when the *Challenger* exploded in midair less than two minutes after takeoff. *Challenger*'s crew included Christa McAuliffe, a New Hampshire teacher chosen to teach a class from space. The explosion halted NASA's shuttle program for two years while scientists worked to eliminate future technical problems.

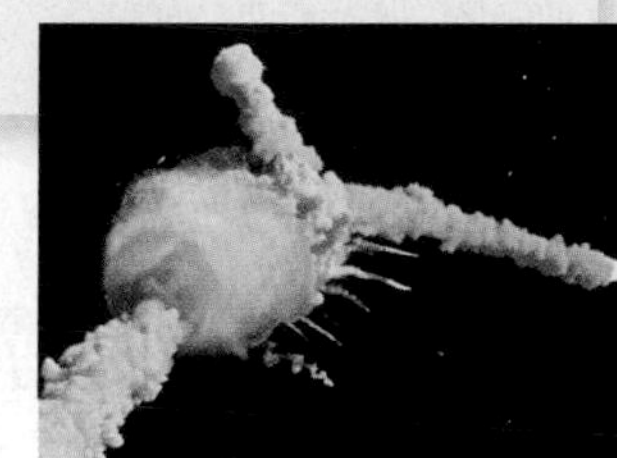

READING CHECK
What changes did the American economy undergo in the 1980s?

ACTIVITY
Connecting with Citizenship

The 1984 presidential election was historic: it included the first woman candidate for a major party and the greatest electoral-vote margin for the victor. Have students discuss and "replay" the election in light of the events of Reagan's second term. Have one group represent the Reagan-Bush campaign team; the other, Mondale-Ferraro. Each group should decide what issues it will emphasize and why. **(Verbal/Linguistic)**

BACKGROUND
Connections to Today

One way the federal government continues to support agriculture is by purchasing farm products and giving them away to feed needy Americans. This practice helps farmers as well as many others in society. For example, through the National School Lunch Program, the government donates beef, chicken, eggs, fruits, vegetables, nuts, and other agricultural produce to some 96,000 schools nationwide. About 15 to 20 percent of the food served in school cafeterias comes from this program. To receive this free food, schools must offer free and reduced-price lunches to children from low-income families. Other programs distribute similar foods to ensure that the elderly, preschool children, pregnant women, and low-income Americans receive adequate nourishment. The government also provides the farm products it buys to community food banks and to the Red Cross for distribution during disasters.

READING CHECK
Farm income declined sharply. Foreign manufacturers became dominant in many traditional industries. American firms endured layoffs and factory closings, but they emerged leaner and more competitive. A wide gap opened between rich and poor.

CUSTOMIZE FOR ...
ESL

Ask students to write the heading *The Farm Crisis* on a piece of paper. Then have them make two columns. One column should be headed *Problems.* There students might list such causes as oversupply, falling prices, and decline in foreign demand. The second column should be headed *Solutions.* There students could list such actions as increased price supports and credit, and increased federal spending on agriculture.

TEST PREPARATION

Have students review the material on this page about shifts in manufacturing and then answer the following question.

Which of the following industries never recovered the jobs it lost during the recession of 1981–1982?

A Financial services
(B) Steel
C Auto manufacturing
D Entertainment

ACTIVITY

Connecting with History and Conflict

Organize students into two pairs of groups for a class debate on Nicaragua and the Iran-Contra affair. One group should support the Reagan administration's Nicaragua policies, and a second group should oppose them. The third and fourth groups should do the same for the Iran-Contra affair. Allow groups time to prepare a one-sentence statement in support of its position for each group member. Then ask students in each pair of groups to alternately present their statements, pro and con, as you list them on the chalkboard. At the end of the debate, poll the class to determine which pair of groups had the most compelling arguments. **(Verbal/ Linguistic)**

BACKGROUND

Global Connections

Nicaragua had been controlled by the wealthy Somoza family for 40 years when the Sandinista National Liberation Front led the overthrow of the government in 1979. The Sandinistas nationalized industry and took land from the rich to give to the peasants. Nicaraguans who were unhappy with some of these reforms and the Sandinistan dictatorship joined with Somoza supporters to fight the Sandinista government. These guerrillas—known as Contras, which means "against"—attacked from bases across the border in Honduras and Costa Rica. Thousands in Nicaragua and neighboring countries died as fighting raged through the 1980s. A negotiated cease-fire in 1990 let Nicaraguans choose their first democratically-elected government.

work outside the home. The wages of individuals, however, declined. The growth in income inequality continued long after Reagan left office and also occurred in other countries over the same period of time.

Reagan's Hands-off Style

Ronald Reagan favored less government regulation of the economy. A decade later, neither party—the Republicans nor the Democrats—would argue with that. Reagan also followed a hands-off style in running the government. He delegated authority to those who worked for him, rather than becoming involved in every decision. Several times this approach led to problems.

The S & L Scandal "Thrift institutions," or savings and loan banks (often called S & Ls) made home mortgage loans to individuals. The Reagan administration, with the help of Democrats in Congress, pressed for the deregulation of S & Ls to permit them to make riskier but more profitable investments.

Officials at some deregulated S & Ls took advantage of the new laws to make huge fortunes for themselves. Many made risky investments in an overheated real estate market. When the market cooled down in the late 1980s, many S & Ls collapsed, taking with them about $2.6 billion in depositors' savings.

Because bank accounts are insured by the federal government, taxpayers had to make up the billions of dollars lost when hundreds of S & Ls failed. A number of banking officials were prosecuted for their role in the scandal and for their efforts to cover it up.

The Iran-Contra Affair In Nicaragua, the Reagan administration sought to undermine the Marxist government that had seized power in 1979. The ruling group, the **Sandinistas,** was named after a Nicaraguan freedom fighter from the 1920s. Reagan feared that the Sandinistas' revolution would spread Marxist upheaval to other Latin American countries.

Working through the Central Intelligence Agency, the United States trained and armed Nicaraguan guerrillas known as **Contras,** from the Spanish word for "counterrevolutionaries." This policy violated laws on American intervention in the affairs of other nations.

Congress discovered these secret missions and in 1984 cut off military aid to the Contras. Some members of the Reagan administration still believed that aid to the Contras was justified. These officials took the profits from secret arms sales to Iran and then sent the profits to the Contras. The arms sales were meant to encourage the release of American hostages held in Lebanon by pro-Iranian terrorists.

When the secret actions became public in the fall of 1986, Oliver North, the marine lieutenant colonel who had made the arrangements, took the blame. The **Iran-Contra affair,** as this scandal came to be called, caused the most serious criticism that the Reagan administration ever faced. The President himself claimed no knowledge of North's operations.

INTERPRETING CHARTS
Soviet leader Mikhail Gorbachev's policy of *glasnost* helped slow the arms race between the United States and the Soviet Union.
Drawing Conclusions *Why do you think arms control agreements were still necessary in the post-Soviet era?*

Arms Control Agreements, 1979–1993

Legislation	Purpose
SALT II (Strategic Arms Limitation Treaty) 1979	Reduced strategic offensive weapons systems, specifically nuclear arms. Set limits on the types and numbers of weapons each nation could build.
INF (Intermediate-Range Nuclear Forces Treaty) 1987	Required both nations to destroy ground-launched and ballistic cruise missiles and their launchers within three years.
START II (Strategic Arms Reduction Treaty) 1993	Signed by the United States and former Soviet republics. Nations reserved the right to inspect former INF missile sites to ensure that no missiles were being manufactured.

The Reagan Legacy

The Iran-Contra affair did not damage Ronald Reagan's personal approval ratings. When he left office in 1989, polls showed that more than 60 percent of the American people gave him high marks for his overall performance.

Foreign Policy Success One reason for the President's continued popularity was the improvement in relations between the United States and the Soviet

CAPTION ANSWERS

Interpreting Charts Sample answer: Because a great many missiles still existed.

RESOURCE DIRECTORY

Teaching Resources

Units 5/6/7 booklet
- Section 3 Quiz, p. 114

Guide to the Essentials
- Section 3 Summary, p. 129

Technology

RESOURCE PRO® **Primary Source Activity** *An Explanation of Iran-Contra,* found on Resource Pro, uses an excerpt from President Reagan's televised address to demonstrate how he defended his involvement in the scandal.

Union during Reagan's second term. Despite his fierce anti-Communist stance, Reagan developed a close relationship with Mikhail Gorbachev, who became the Soviet leader in 1985.

To reform the ailing Soviet system, Gorbachev proposed a program of *glasnost,* a Russian word meaning "political openness." He also initiated *perestroika,* or "restructuring," an economic policy to allow limited free enterprise.

These moves paved the way toward better relations between the United States and the Soviet Union. Reagan and Gorbachev signed the Intermediate-Range Nuclear Forces (INF) Treaty in 1987. The **INF Treaty** provided for the destruction of about 2,500 Soviet and American missiles in Europe.

VIEWING HISTORY Relations between the United States and the Soviet Union warmed during Reagan's second term. Here, Reagan and Gorbachev meet outside St. Basil's Cathedral in Moscow. **Recognizing Cause and Effect** *Why do you think* glasnost *and* perestroika *helped smooth relations between the two countries?*

Domestic Policy Initiatives Another reason for Reagan's popularity was his stated commitment to reducing the size of government. Reagan's policies, however, did not dramatically reduce the Washington bureaucracy. Payments for **entitlements**—programs such as Social Security, Medicare, and Medicaid, which guarantee payments to a particular group of recipients—grew faster than policymakers had expected. Social Security expenditures, for example, skyrocketed as the nation's elderly population continued to rise. The Reagan administration could not restrain the growth of these programs.

Economic turmoil erupted near the end of Reagan's presidency. Investor fears about the huge budget deficits and rising national debt prompted a stock market crash in 1987. Following six weeks of falling prices, the market suffered a huge 22.6 percent drop on October 19. The speculative bubble of the 1980s had burst.

Although the stock market did recover, Reagan's successor, George H. W. Bush, inherited many economic problems. By the end of the decade, the nation found itself in the midst of another recession.

For most Americans, Ronald Reagan's two-term presidency was marked by his vigorous emphasis on restoring national pride, and the force of his own optimistic personality. Reagan's presidency made many Americans feel confident for the first time since the Kennedy years.

Section 3 Assessment

READING COMPREHENSION

1. How did Americans celebrate their patriotism in the 1980s?
2. In what ways did the Reagan administration address ongoing debates on race?
3. How did Reagan's style of governing contribute to the **Iran-Contra affair?**
4. Why did **entitlement** spending have a negative effect on President Reagan's legacy?

CRITICAL THINKING AND WRITING

5. **Analyzing Cause and Effect** Despite some failures, Reagan was a highly popular President. How did Reagan's economic successes and his patriotism affect public opinion?
6. **Defending a Position** In a short essay, explain how the influence of conservatives was felt during the Reagan years, both in social issues and in changes to the Supreme Court.

Take It to the NET

Activity: Writing a Biography Choose one Supreme Court justice appointed by Reagan and write a biography, being sure to include the person's educational background and how he or she changed the Court. Use the links provided in the *America: Pathways to the Present* area of the following Web site for help in completing this activity.
www.phschool.com

Section 3 Assessment

Reading Comprehension

1. 1984 Olympic Games; celebrations of the centennial of the Statue of Liberty and the 200th anniversary of the Constitution.
2. Birthday of Martin Luther King, Jr., was established as a national holiday; tried to prevent the extension of the Voting Rights Act; appointed federal judges who were less sympathetic to civil rights goals; worked to end some affirmative action programs.
3. Reagan's hands-off style enabled other government officials to violate American neutrality laws, acting without the President's knowledge.
4. It contradicted his commitment to reducing the size of the federal government.

Critical Thinking and Writing

5. Sample answer: His ability to arouse patriotism and national confidence secured high opinion ratings even in times of scandal.
6. Essays will vary, but might mention the rise in popularity of televangelists or the promotion of William Rehnquist, a conservative, to the position of Chief Justice of the U.S. Supreme Court.

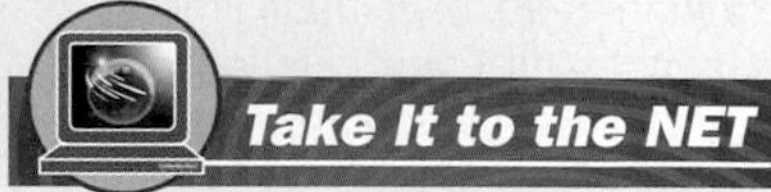

Take It to the NET

Answers will vary. Encourage students to include both personal history and professional accomplishments in their biographical research.

Caption Answers

Viewing History Because these programs meant the Soviet Union was moving away from communism and toward democracy.

Section 4
The George H.W. Bush Presidency

Section Objectives

1. See what challenges George H.W. Bush faced in the 1988 presidential election.
2. Find out how the Cold War came to an end.
3. Learn about the ways in which the United States played a new international role after the Cold War.
4. Observe the effect domestic issues had on Bush's presidency.

Bellringer

Warm-Up Activity Ask students when, in their opinion, the Cold War really ended. What actions and attitudes have changed with the end of the Cold War?

Activating Prior Knowledge Ask students to name some of the causes of the Cold War. Which of these causes are still in dispute today? Which of these causes have been resolved?

Reading Strategy

As students read, have them identify as many cause-and-effect relationships as they can. Have students list these relationships in a chart.

Activity
Connecting with Citizenship

Ask students to design placards or bumper stickers that reflect the spirit and issues of the presidential election campaign of 1988. Tell them that their creations can either promote or attack a candidate and should include a graphic and a catch phrase or slogan that is appropriate to the position taken. You may wish to provide the class with the supplies to create their work full-size and in color. **(Visual/Spatial)**

Section 4

The George H. W. Bush Presidency

READING FOCUS

- What challenges did George Bush face in the 1988 presidential election?
- How did the Cold War come to an end?
- In what ways did the United States play a new international role after the end of the Cold War?
- What effect did domestic issues have on Bush's presidency?

MAIN IDEA

George H. W. Bush achieved notable foreign policy successes, but domestic crises eroded his public support.

KEY TERMS

Strategic Arms Reduction Treaty
Persian Gulf War
downsizing

TAKING NOTES

Copy the web diagram below. As you read, fill in each blank circle with important events that affected George Bush's domestic and foreign policy.

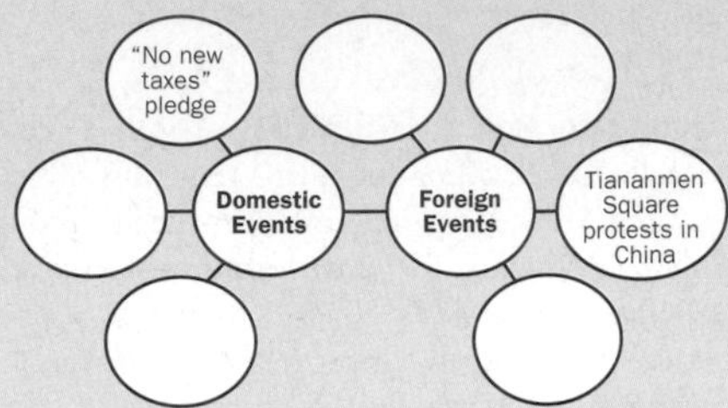

Setting the Scene It is not easy to follow a legendary President. George Bush had the same problem as William Howard Taft, who succeeded Theodore Roosevelt in 1909. So did Harry Truman, who inherited the presidency upon the death of Franklin D. Roosevelt in 1945. Ronald Reagan remained enormously popular as he left office in 1989, and Bush sought to continue the revolution his predecessor had begun. But he lacked Reagan's charismatic appeal and found that it was not always easy to measure up.

George Bush won a solid victory in the 1988 election.

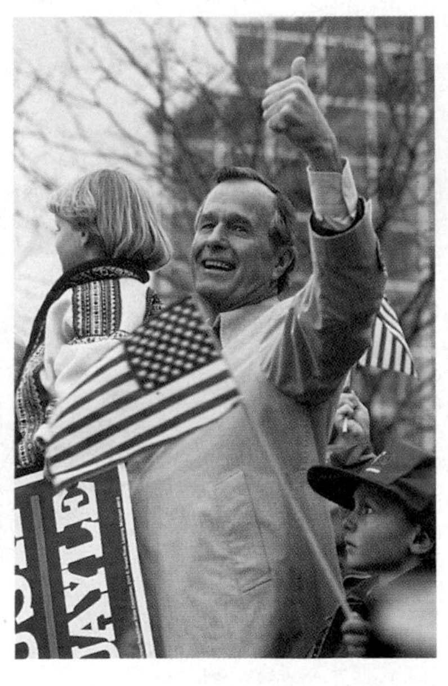

The 1988 Election

The son of a well-to-do Connecticut senator, Bush served in World War II as a bomber pilot in the Pacific and was awarded the Distinguished Flying Cross. After the war, he had a profitable career in the Texas oil industry.

In 1966, he began a long and distinguished political career, serving in many roles: member of Congress from Texas; ambassador to the United Nations under Nixon; chairperson of the Republican National Committee; American envoy to China under President Ford; and head of the Central Intelligence Agency (CIA) until 1977. He was well connected and earned a reputation as a moderate and loyal Republican.

Despite these impressive credentials, Bush lacked the support of conservatives in the Republican Party. Some Republicans, whose hero was Ronald Reagan, questioned Bush's commitment to their cause. They were concerned about his apparent early sympathy for abortion rights, and they never truly forgave him for calling Reagan's economic plans "voodoo economics" during the 1980 primary election campaign. Bush's loyal service as Reagan's Vice President for eight years had failed to ease their fears.

Bush began the 1988 campaign far behind his Democratic opponent, Governor Michael Dukakis of Massachusetts. Dukakis had revived

RESOURCE DIRECTORY

Teaching Resources
Learning Styles Lesson Plans booklet, p. 69
Guided Reading and Review booklet, p. 136

Technology
Section Reading Support Transparencies
Guided Reading Audiotapes (English/Spanish), Ch. 26
Student Edition on Audio CD, Ch. 26
Prentice Hall Presentation Pro CD-ROM, Ch. 26
Companion Web site, www.phschool.com

his state after years of economic distress and promised to bring the "Massachusetts Miracle" to the rest of the nation.

Bush took the offensive in what soon became a nasty contest. One part of his campaign was a pledge that there would be "no new taxes" if he became President. Reagan's popular tax cuts had contributed to the huge budget deficit and national debt. Reagan's successor would be under great pressure to raise taxes in order to reduce the deficit. Yet Bush publicly committed himself to holding the line on taxes.

Bush attacked Dukakis on many issues. He aired ads describing Dukakis as soft on crime and questioning the accuracy of the "Massachusetts Miracle." His campaign challenged Dukakis's environmental record by airing pictures of garbage in the polluted Boston harbor. Bush's attack ads successfully damaged Dukakis, although they apparently alienated some voters. Americans complained that neither candidate addressed the major issues facing the country. Nearly half of all eligible voters stayed home.

Bush won a solid 54 percent of the popular vote and carried 40 states in a 426–111 electoral vote win. But he failed to gain the mandate Reagan had enjoyed, as Democrats still controlled both houses of Congress.

READING CHECK
What strategies did George Bush use in the 1988 presidential election?

The Cold War Ends

Bush's major triumphs came in foreign policy. Even more than Reagan, Bush benefited from the historic changes in the Communist world that were unleashed by Mikhail Gorbachev.

The Soviet leader started a chain reaction that would eventually bring down Europe's "Iron Curtain" and dissolve the Soviet Union. It began with Gorbachev's public statements encouraging Eastern European leaders to adopt *perestroika* and *glasnost.* The suggestion was unthinkable in a region where police states efficiently smothered all opposition. Yet it was enough to give hope and inspiration to anti-Communist movements throughout

MAP SKILLS In the late 1980s the Eastern bloc shattered into a jigsaw puzzle of diverse countries. **Regions** *What kinds of problems do you think might follow the breakup of such a large nation as the Soviet Union?*

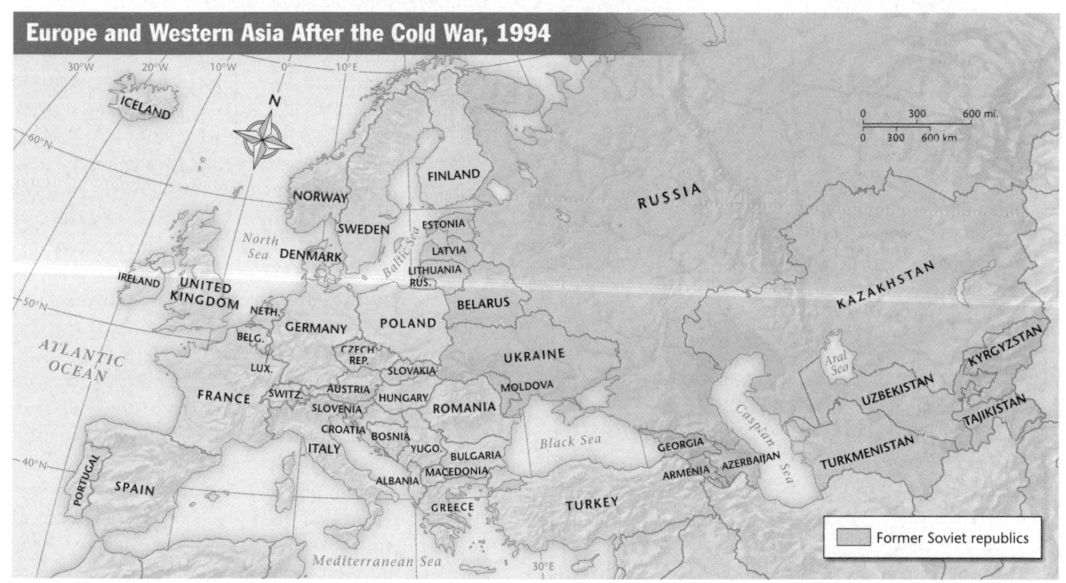

Lesson Plan

Focus Emphasize that it is very difficult to follow a popular President. What challenges did George Bush face in this respect? Explain that Bush found his greatest strength in foreign policy. What major world events took place during the Bush administration?

Instruct Explain that as President, Bush inherited a varied assortment of policies from his popular predecessor. Bush concentrated on foreign policy—where his own background and strengths lay—but also had to deal with economic problems inherited from the Reagan administration. How successful was he domestically and in the sphere of foreign affairs?

Assess/Reteach Ask students to discuss their perception of the legacy of a presidency that is judged to be strong on international affairs, yet weak on domestic affairs.

READING CHECK
Attack advertisements criticizing the record of Governor Michael Dukakis. Bush also promised not to raise taxes.

Test Preparation

Have students reread the two paragraphs under the subheading "The Cold War Ends" and then answer the question below.

What gave hope to anti-Communist movements in Eastern Europe?

A The election of George Bush as President.
B Concessions by many Communist leaders.
C Gorbachev's assumption of leadership of the Soviet Union in 1985.
(D) Gorbachev's public statements about his policies and his encouragement of Eastern European nations to adopt them.

Caption Answers

Map Skills Sample answer: Ethnic conflicts might arise between groups vying for power in the new governments; groups might fight over economic resources.

Activity
Connecting with Government

Have groups of students research one of the countries that experienced upheaval in the years 1988–1992 from the perspective of politics and economics. They should identify and explain reasons for changes in political boundaries resulting from changes in statehood and international conflicts. Ask them to combine their findings in a chart and present it to the class. **(Visual/Spatial)**

From the Archives of
American Heritage®

About the Presidents

George Herbert Walker Bush (1989–1993) reflected in his career some of the important changes that carried the Republican Party far from its roots in the prosperous suburbs of the Northeast and Midwest. Bush was born to privilege, the son of Connecticut senator Prescott Bush, and he was educated at exclusive schools. During World War II, he flew combat missions in the Pacific Theater as a pilot. After receiving his degree from Yale, he settled in Texas, where he launched a career in the freewheeling oil business. He has been a Texan ever since, serving as a congressman from the state and retiring there after his presidency. The years of his public service were also the years when the Republican Party became increasingly southern and western, with its heavy emphasis on libertarian, entrepreneurial economics. Source: Adapted from Henry F. Graff's *The Presidents,* Scribner's, 1996, by the editors of *American Heritage*® magazine.

Eastern Europe that had worked for decades, at great risk, to keep a democratic spirit alive.

Poland In Poland, the stage was set for the downfall of Soviet communism. The story had begun in 1970, when severe food shortages provoked riots in the city of Gdansk. A witness to those riots was a young electrician named Lech Walesa, who worked in the huge Lenin Shipyard at Gdansk. Walesa became involved in anti-Communist union organizing and lost his job after helping to lead a protest in 1976.

When shipyard workers at Gdansk launched a strike in 1980, Walesa climbed over the fence of the facility and joined them, becoming head of a movement that grew with great speed. After two tense weeks, the government gave in to workers' demands for the right to form a free and independent trade union.

Union activity spread throughout Poland, forming an alliance called Solidarity. The Communist government launched a crackdown in 1981, banning Solidarity and jailing its leaders, including Walesa. But support for Solidarity remained alive. In 1983, Walesa, a plain-speaking man with little education, won the Nobel peace prize for his acts of courage.

In 1988, further economic collapse in Poland sparked a new round of protests and strikes. The Communist-led government agreed to meet with Solidarity and together they scheduled free elections for June 1989. In Poland's first free elections in half a century, voters chose as president the electrician from Gdansk, Lech Walesa.

VIEWING HISTORY Berliners from both sides of the city celebrated the fall of the Berlin Wall with joyous, all-night celebrations. **Making Comparisons** *Compare and contrast the roles played by ordinary people in the fall of communism in East Germany and in the Soviet Union.*

The Berlin Wall Falls Throughout Eastern Europe, anti-Communist revolts broke out. Each country had its own stories of courage and its own heroes. In Czechoslovakia, a poet and playwright once persecuted by the Communists, Vaclav Havel, was elected president. Eventually, new regimes took charge in Bulgaria, Hungary, Romania, and Albania. But the most dramatic events of 1989 took place in East Germany.

East Germany's hardline Communist rulers maintained a strong grip on the state, symbolized by the Berlin Wall that divided East Germans from the democratic West. In the summer of 1989, East German tourists visiting Hungary took advantage of newly opened borders there to escape to Austria and West Germany. Their flight embarrassed East German leaders. In East German cities, nonviolent protests pressured the country's dictator, Erich Honecker, to institute reforms and open border crossings. On November 9, the government announced that East Germans could travel freely to West Germany.

East Germans flooded around and over the hated Berlin Wall. Germans scaled it from both sides and stood atop the structure, cheering and chanting and waving signs. They came with sledgehammers and smashed it with glee. The wall, the most potent symbol of the Cold War, had been breached. Within a month, the Communist Party had begun to collapse. A year later, East and West Germany reunified.

Caption Answers

Viewing History In the Soviet Union, leaders like Gorbachev took the initiative in reforming the Communist system, which was also weakened by the coup of August 1991. The leaders in the Republics then attained independence from Moscow. In East Germany, thousands of East Germans pressured their government to act by protesting in the cities and escaping to the West.

Resource Directory

Teaching Resources

Biography, Literature, and Comparing Primary Sources booklet (Biography) *Melissa Rathbun-Nealy,* p. 38

Other Print Resources

American History Block Scheduling Support *The Berlin Wall: Past and Present,* and *The End of the Cold War,* found in The Nation After World War II folder, includes interdisciplinary lesson suggestions and activities for Geography and History, Primary Sources, Biography, and Literature.

Nystrom ***Atlas of Our Country*** *People on the Move,* pp. 34–35

Technology

RESOURCE PRO® **Literature Activity** *Operation Desert Storm,* found on Resource Pro, dramatically illustrates the events surrounding the Allied action in Kuwait with an excerpt from General Norman Schwarzkopf's autobiography, *It Doesn't Take a Hero.*

The Soviet Union Gorbachev hoped to reform the Soviet system while keeping the Communist Party in power, but events slipped beyond his control. In August 1991, conservative Communists in the Soviet Union staged a coup and held Gorbachev captive, hoping to pressure him to resign. The coup quickly collapsed, but the Soviet Union's 15 republics sensed weakness in the central government and began to move toward independence.

Gorbachev resigned the presidency of the Soviet Union on December 25, 1991. One week later the Soviet Union no longer existed. It had been replaced by a loose alliance of former Soviet republics called the Commonwealth of Independent States. Russia's new president, Boris Yeltsin, emerged as the dominant leader in this fragmented land.

Statues of Communist heroes such as Vladimir Lenin (shown above) and Karl Marx were removed from cities across Eastern Europe in the 1990s.

As the Soviet Union disintegrated, Bush continued arms-control talks with Gorbachev. The Soviets and Americans signed a number of pacts that signaled the end of the Cold War. Agreements in 1989 and 1990 limited the buildup of nuclear and chemical weapons. The first **Strategic Arms Reduction Treaty,** known as START I, called for dramatic reductions in the two nations' supplies of long-range nuclear weapons. It was signed in 1991. After the Soviet Union collapsed, Bush continued to negotiate with President Boris Yeltsin of Russia.

"The Cold War is now behind us," Gorbachev had declared. "Let us not wrangle over who won it." But clearly the United States was now the world's lone superpower.

A New International Role

President Bush hoped the world would move smoothly from the hostility of the Cold War to a peaceful "New World Order" under the leadership of the United States and its allies. Instead, conflicts in different regions of the world became the focus of American foreign policy. As the world's sole superpower, the United States needed to respond to crises abroad in a new way.

Tiananmen Square The People's Republic of China occupied much of America's attention in 1989. As Communist governments tottered in Eastern Europe, Chinese students gathered in the capital, Beijing, to march for democracy and reform. In May, protesters occupied Tiananmen Square in the heart of the city, despite official orders to leave. Their numbers soon swelled to more than one million across the city. In Tiananmen Square, they built a "Goddess of Democracy" modeled on the Statue of Liberty.

On June 3, China's leaders ordered the army to attack the protester camps. Hundreds, possibly thousands, of demonstrators died and others quickly scattered in the face of overwhelming military force. The government cracked down on the democracy movement after the attack and many more people were imprisoned and executed.

Bush valued the relationship the United States had with China. Rather than attack China's leaders and risk an international crisis, Bush preferred to negotiate quietly and encourage trade between China and the United States. His nonconfrontational stance upset many people who believed he was indifferent to human rights in China.

Focus on ECONOMICS

China's Transformation Although China's Communist Party held onto power in the 1980s and 1990s, it had long before begun to abandon some of its Communist principles. Under Deng Xiaoping, China moved toward a market-oriented economy based on capitalism and foreign trade. Exports to the United States increased from $4 billion in 1985 to nearly $26 billion in 1992.

ACTIVITY
Connecting with Science and Technology

Ask students to research the size and status of the missile arsenals of the United States and former Soviet Union today. The central question to be addressed is: How many nuclear warheads does each nation now possess, and how has the size of its arsenal changed due to the START initiatives? Have students present their findings in the form of a graph. Ask the class to assess the impact of the Cold War's end on each side's nuclear capability. **(Logical/Mathematical)**

BACKGROUND
Global Connections

The attack on the Tiananmen Square protesters dramatically impacted events in Eastern Europe. For weeks after the massacre, democratic reformers in the satellite nations moved more cautiously, fearing that the Soviet Union might pressure their governments to adopt a "Tiananmen solution." In July 1989, however, Gorbachev advised the Eastern European nations to pursue their own independent solutions to their problems. Emboldened by this statement, hundreds of thousands of Hungarians, East Germans, and Czechs rose up in nonviolent protests against their Communist governments. An estimated one million Latvians, Lithuanians, and Estonians demanded freedom by forming a human chain that linked their capitals. By year's end, all of the Eastern European satellite nations were free of Communist rule.

CUSTOMIZE FOR ...
Gifted and Talented

Ask students to look at the Bush administration and several previous administrations and analyze what makes a President choose to emphasize either foreign or domestic policies. Is the main reason the course of world events? Or are some leaders naturally more interested in either one or the other? Have students illustrate their answers with solid biographical and historical details.

ACTIVITY
Student Portfolio

You may wish to have students add the following to their portfolios. Have students further research aspects of the Gulf War that interest them. Possible topics: media coverage; health questions for veterans; women's participation in military actions; environmental issues; political and cultural characteristics of Iran, Kuwait, or Saudi Arabia; lasting effects of the war. **(Verbal/ Linguistic)**

BACKGROUND
Interdisciplinary

As the Persian Gulf War was ending, Iraqi troops set some 600 oil-well fires and deliberately spilled more than 6 million barrels of oil into the Persian Gulf. The fires spread pollution through the region's air and water. In late 1993 the Geological Society of America found that the Persian Gulf War "caused severe and lasting damage to Kuwait's desert, economic resources, and ecosystems." A 1991 EPA report called the environmental damage "tragic." Marine life in the Gulf still shows toxicity from the oil spills; and wetlands, wildlife, and vegetation around the Persian Gulf will suffer the effects of the war for decades.

The Invasion of Panama Bush enjoyed more support later that year when he acted against the Central American nation of Panama. Bush suspected General Manuel Noriega, Panama's dictator, of smuggling cocaine into the United States. After Noriega declared war on the United States, Bush launched a lightning attack against Panama in December 1989 and quickly won control of the country. Noriega surrendered to American forces on January 3, 1990, and two years later a federal jury in Florida convicted him of drug smuggling. The invasion demonstrated Bush's willingness to act boldly to stop the flow of drugs into the United States.

The Persian Gulf War In August 1990, the Arab nation of Iraq, headed by a brutal dictator, Saddam Hussein, launched a sudden invasion of neighboring Kuwait. Saddam justified the assault by citing centuries-old territorial claims. But in fact he had his sights on Kuwait's substantial oil wealth.

Sounds of an Era

Listen to George Bush's speech and other sounds from the Reagan-Bush era.

Of concern to the Bush administration was the flow of Kuwaiti oil to the West. Bush viewed the protection of those oil reserves as an issue of national security. The administration was also concerned about the security of Saudi Arabia, a key Arab ally in the region, and Saddam's investment in destructive weapons. Bush responded strongly:

> *"There is much in the modern world that is subject to doubts or questions—washed in shades of gray. But not the brutal aggression of Saddam Hussein against a peaceful, sovereign nation and its people. It's black and white. The facts are clear. The choice is unambiguous—right versus wrong."*
>
> —George Bush, 1990

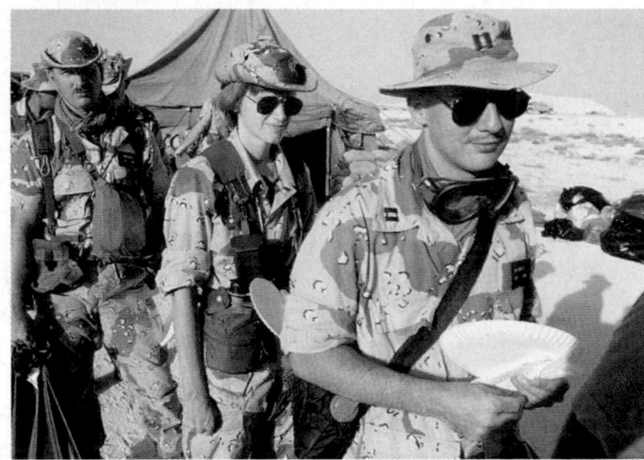

VIEWING HISTORY American soldiers fought a brief, victorious war, aided by the open terrain that provided no shelter for Iraq's armies. **Determining Relevance** *Why did the Bush administration decide to intervene militarily in this regional conflict?*

Americans at first seemed reluctant to get involved in a territorial matter between Arab nations. As the weeks passed, however, rising oil prices and reports of Iraqi atrocities against Kuwaiti civilians drew increasing concern.

Months of diplomatic efforts failed to persuade Saddam to withdraw. Finally, the United States, working through the United Nations, mobilized an alliance of 28 countries to launch the **Persian Gulf War.** It was a limited military operation to drive Iraqi forces out of Kuwait.

To organize military operations, President Bush turned to General Colin Powell. Powell had risen quickly through the ranks of the military. In 1979, at age 42, he had become the Army's youngest brigadier general. He was the first African American to serve as national security advisor. By 1989, he had been named the nation's youngest ever Chairman of the Joint Chiefs of Staff, the top military officer in the nation.

Powell's battle plan was simple. He would use airpower to destroy Iraq's ability to wage war, and then smash the Iraqi forces occupying Kuwait. A series of massive air strikes, known as "Operation Desert Storm," was launched on January 16–17, 1991. UN forces, directed by General Powell and led by Norman Schwarzkopf, liberated Kuwait in just six weeks of war. The allies had lost fewer than 300 soldiers, while tens of thousands of Iraqi troops had died.

Bush opted not to send troops deep into Iraq to oust Saddam, expecting that Saddam's opponents would soon overthrow him. Yet Saddam's opposition

CAPTION ANSWERS

Viewing History The administration saw the protection of American oil reserves as an issue of national security. Also, President Bush perceived the invasion of Kuwait as an act of wanton aggression on the part of Iraq.

RESOURCE DIRECTORY

Teaching Resources

Units 5/6/7 booklet
- Section 4 Quiz, p. 115
- Chapter 26 Test, pp. 116, 119

Guide to the Essentials
- Section 4 Summary, p. 130
- Chapter 26 Test, p. 131

Other Print Resources

Chapter Tests with ExamView® Test Bank CD-ROM, Ch. 26

Technology

Sounds of an Era Audio CD *George Bush,* 1990 recording (time: one minute)

ExamView® Test Bank CD-ROM, Ch. 26

Social Studies Skills Tutor CD-ROM

proved weaker than Bush's advisors had thought, and he remained in power.

Domestic Issues

Bush's leadership during the Persian Gulf War drove his approval rating up to an astounding 89 percent. Yet while his foreign policy generally won him praise, Americans began to believe that Bush did not have a clear plan for handling domestic problems. In the end, this perception helped usher him out of office.

Bush angered many moderates and liberals with his nomination of Clarence Thomas, a conservative black judge, to the Supreme Court in 1991. Thomas faced grilling about his views on civil rights and about charges of past sexual harassment. Thomas won confirmation after stormy televised Senate hearings that ignited public debate on the issue of sexual harassment.

Budget deficits continued to swell during Bush's presidency. Bush countered by slowing spending for social programs. Finally, he agreed to a deficit reduction plan that included new taxes. The tax hike broke Bush's 1988 campaign promise and generated public anger.

Bush's real undoing was a recession that began in the early 1990s. Turmoil in the Persian Gulf led gasoline prices to rise rapidly, creating unexpected costs for businesses and consumers alike. The end of the Cold War enabled the United States to spend less on defense. As a result, firms that supplied planes, ships, and military hardware laid off workers. Companies in several other industries also laid off workers to cut costs in a process called **downsizing.** By 1991, the jobless rate reached 7 percent, the highest level in nearly five years. The recession was felt unevenly across the country. States that relied heavily on defense spending, including California and Connecticut, were hit much harder than others.

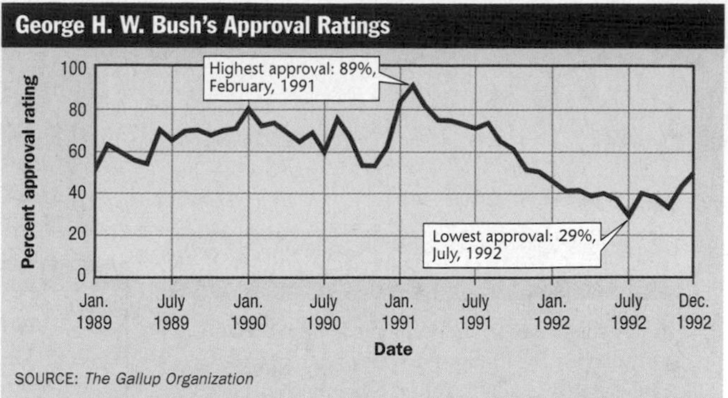

INTERPRETING GRAPHS The percentage of Americans who believed Bush was doing a good job plunged from a high of 89 percent during the Gulf War to only 29 percent 17 months later. **Analyzing Information** *What were Bush's approval ratings in early 1990, before the Gulf War and the recession?*

Section  4 Assessment

READING COMPREHENSION

1. What factors helped George Bush win the 1988 presidential election?
2. List two reasons why Communist regimes in Eastern Europe collapsed in 1989.
3. How did China's Communist government react to democracy protests in 1989?
4. What domestic issues damaged Bush's popularity?

CRITICAL THINKING AND WRITING

5. **Making Comparisons** How was the Persian Gulf War fought differently from the Vietnam War?
6. **Demonstrating Reasoned Judgment** Was it reasonable for Americans to believe that the Cold War would be followed by international peace and cooperation? Why or why not?
7. **Defending a Position** Some people describe George Bush's presidency as Reagan's third term. Explain whether you agree or disagree.

Take It to the NET

Activity: Making a Flowchart What have been the lasting effects of the Persian Gulf War? Research this conflict and create a flowchart of key events in the region before, during, and after the war. Use the links provided in the *America: Pathways to the Present* area at the following Web site for help in completing this activity.
www.phschool.com

Section 4 Assessment

Reading Comprehension

1. His commitment to no new taxes; his attack ads targeting Dukakis's campaign.
2. Sample answer: Gorbachev's leadership; popular protest against the regimes.
3. Cracked down on democracy movement, executing and imprisoning protesters.
4. Nomination of Clarence Thomas; recession; tax hike.

Critical Thinking and Writing

5. Persian Gulf War was fought quickly, with defined goals and a minimum of U.S. casualties.
6. Answers will vary but should be supported with facts from the section.
7. Answers will vary but should include references to the economic and foreign policy goals of the two men.

Take It to the NET

Flowcharts may include the Iraqi military buildup and the invasion of Kuwait, international trade embargoes against Iraq, Iraqi reaction to the initiation of Operation Desert Storm, and "Gulf War Syndrome."

CUSTOMIZE FOR ...

Less Proficient Writers

Ask students to write two headings: *World* and *United States.* Under each heading have them list the major events that took place in each region during the Bush administration.

CAPTION ANSWERS

Interpreting Graphs His approval ratings were between 60 percent and 80 percent.

Chapter 26

Reviewing Key Terms

Students should refer to the definitions of key terms in the chapter to write sentences that show an understanding of the conservative revolution.

Reviewing Main Ideas

16. Sample answer: women's movement; sexual revolution; government spending.
17. They were an active and powerful conservative coalition whose views aligned with Reagan's. They used the technology of television to spread their message and gain support and contributions for their campaign.
18. Taxes were cut.
19. While the tax cuts did contribute to economic recovery, the budget was not balanced during his term.
20. Reagan wanted to confront Communist governments and prevent the spread of communism.
21. Supply-side economics was the antithesis of Keynesian theory; tax cuts were supposed to help business; wealth was unevenly distributed; crisis in some farm and manufacturing industries.
22. Reagan lacked enthusiasm for civil rights and affirmative action. His nomination of conservative justices to the Supreme Court was a reflection of his position on these issues.
23. It encouraged anti-Communist movements throughout Eastern Europe to pursue democracy.
24. He muted official American criticism of the brutal crackdown in Tiananmen Square by the Chinese Communist government. He perhaps felt less obliged to criticize Communist regimes than Reagan had since the Cold War was ending.

Critical Thinking

25. Possible answers: (a) Reagan pressured Communist governments while failing to promote civil rights and affirmative action at home. (b) Bush projected American military force into regional conflicts in Panama and Kuwait. Bush appointed a staunch conservative, Clarence Thomas, to the Supreme Court.

Chapter 26 Review and Assessment

creating a CHAPTER SUMMARY

Copy this chart (right) on a piece of paper and complete it by adding important events and issues that fit each heading. Some entries have been completed for you as examples.

Time Period	Important Events
Evolution of Conservatism (1934–1981)	• American Liberty League is founded to oppose the New Deal. • Barry Goldwater runs for President as a staunch conservative. •
Ronald Reagan's First Term (1981–1985)	
Ronald Reagan's Second Term (1985–1989)	
George H. W. Bush's Administration (1989–1993)	

iTEXT

For additional review and enrichment activities, see the interactive version of *America: Pathways to the Present*, available on the Web and on CD-ROM.

★ Reviewing Key Terms

For each of the terms below, write a sentence explaining how it relates to the presidencies of Ronald Reagan and George Bush.

1. Reagan Democrat
2. New Right
3. televangelism
4. supply-side economics
5. New Federalism
6. Strategic Defense Initiative (SDI)
7. AIDS
8. Sandinista
9. Contra
10. Iran-Contra affair
11. INF Treaty
12. entitlement
13. Strategic Arms Reduction Treaty
14. Persian Gulf War
15. downsizing

★ Reviewing Main Ideas

16. List three conservative criticisms of society in the 1960s and 1970s. (Section 1)
17. How did the New Right help Ronald Reagan win the 1980 presidential election? (Section 1)
18. How did supply-side economics change the federal government's tax policy? (Section 2)
19. Did Reagan's tax cuts achieve all of his economic and budgetary goals? (Section 2)
20. How did Reagan view Communist governments in other countries? (Section 2)
21. What role did Supreme Court appointments have in Reagan's conservative strategy? (Section 3)
22. Describe four economic trends of the 1980s. (Section 3)
23. What was the impact on Eastern Europe of Gorbachev's call for *perestroika* and *glasnost?* (Section 4)
24. How did President Bush change America's foreign policy at the end of the Cold War? (Section 4)

★ Critical Thinking

25. **Recognizing Ideologies** (a) How did conservative beliefs affect Reagan's policies? (b) How did they affect Bush's policies?
26. **Identifying Assumptions** Read the selection from Ronald Reagan's first inaugural speech in Section 2. (a) What words does Reagan use to describe government regulations and taxes? (b) What does his choice of words say about his view of government?
27. **Synthesizing Information** During his first term, Reagan called the Soviet Union an "evil empire." In his second term, he developed a working relationship with Gorbachev. What do you think accounts for this change in strategy?
28. **Understanding Cause and Effect** Was Reagan responsible for all the changes in the American economy in the 1980s? Explain your answer.
29. **Drawing Conclusions** Why did President Bush respond differently to the crisis in Panama than he did to the crisis in China?

Creating a Chapter Summary

Time Period	Important Events
Evolution of Conservatism (1934–1981)	• American Liberty League is founded to oppose the New Deal. • Barry Goldwater runs for President as a staunch conservative. • Formation of the New Right Coalition
Ronald Reagan's First Term (1981–1985)	• Unemployment reaches 40-year high. • Reagan reduces top income tax rate. • United States attacks Libya following terrorist bombing. • Economy recovers from recession.
Ronald Reagan's Second Term (1985–1989)	• Resurgence of patriotism • Farm crisis • Shifts in manufacturing • S & L scandal • Iran-Contra affair
George H.W. Bush's Administration (1989–1993)	• End of the Cold War • Fall of Berlin Wall • Tiananmen Square protests • Defeat of communism in many Eastern European countries • Invasion of Panama • Persian Gulf War

★ Skills Assessment

Analyzing Political Cartoons ▶

30. Analyze the images in the cartoon. (a) Who is the man? (b) What does the ship symbolize? (c) How do you know?
31. (a) Where is the ship headed? (b) What is the man's attitude about the ship's course?
32. Summarize the cartoonist's message.

Interpreting Data

Turn to the Federal Budget Deficit graph in Section 2.

33. During the Reagan years, what happened to the overall course of the budget deficit?
    - **A** It rose steadily.
    - **B** It fell.
    - **C** It increased by about $210 billion.
    - **D** It increased, and then fell back to its original level.
34. What was the major cause of deficit increases during the period shown in the graph?
    - **F** the cost of the Persian Gulf War
    - **G** the Strategic Defense Initiative
    - **H** increased defense spending and tax cuts under Reagan
    - **J** Bush's pledge not to raise taxes
35. **Writing** Do you think the government should be allowed to spend more money in any given year than it earns in revenues from taxes and other sources? Why or why not?

Applying the Chapter Skill: *Analyzing Trends in the Electoral College Map*

36. Review the information on the Skills for Life page. (a) Which regions of the country lost political clout between 1948 and 1980? (b) Did this change affect the outcome of the 1980 presidential election? Explain your answer.

ACTIVITIES

Writing to LEARN

Writing to Compare and Contrast
Is the conservative revolution alive and well today? Write an essay to explain your answer. Include examples of issues from the presidencies of Ronald Reagan and George H. W. Bush that either continue to be debated today or else have faded in significance.

Primary Source CD-ROM

Working With Primary Sources Find additional information on the conservative revolution on the *Exploring Primary Sources in U.S. History CD-ROM* and use the selection(s) provided to complete the Chapter 26 primary source activity located in the *America: Pathways to the Present* area of the following Web site. **www.phschool.com**

Take It to the NET

Chapter Self-Test As a review activity, take the Chapter 26 Self-Test in the *America: Pathways to the Present* area at the Web site listed below. The questions are designed to test your understanding of the chapter content. **www.phschool.com**

26. (a) "Roadblocks" and "punitive," respectively. (b) That it should be smaller and less intrusive.

27. Answers will vary, but will probably focus on the fact that Reagan and Gorbachev got along well together personally, and that Gorbachev was an entirely different kind of Soviet leader, one with whom it was possible to reach meaningful agreements.

28. Possible answer: No. Manufacturing industries would have been hit hard by foreign competition with or without Reagan.

29. Panama was a much weaker nation, and much less valuable as a trading partner, than China. Thus, a strong response by Bush in Panama was not as likely to escalate into a major crisis.

SKILLS ASSESSMENT

30. (a) Ronald Reagan. (b) The U.S. economy. (c) The name "*S.S. Reagonomics*" is printed on the life preserver.

31. (a) Toward an iceberg. (b) He is oblivious to the disaster ahead.

32. Reagan's economic policies are leading the nation toward disaster.

33. C

34. H

35. Answers will vary, but might take into account the long-term burden that paying a deficit places upon a nation.

36. (a) The Northeast lost political clout from 1948 to 1980. (b) This change had no effect on the outcome of the 1980 presidential election because the number of electoral votes remained the same for the states that Carter won.

ANSWERS TO ACTIVITIES

Writing to LEARN

Essays will vary but might mention prominent Republican politicians today, and current conservative causes and movements.

Primary Source CD-ROM

Direct students to the additional primary sources that can be found on the *Exploring Primary Sources in U.S. History CD-ROM.*

Take It to the NET

Additional support materials and activities for Chapter 26 of *America: Pathways to the Present* can be found in the Social Studies area at the Prentice Hall School Web site. **www.phschool.com**

THE RISE OF THE SUNBELT

Focus Point out that until the mid-twentieth century, the South was mainly agricultural. The cities of the Northeast and North Central regions dominated business, banking, and manufacturing.

Instruct Ask students to describe economic and political changes they have observed in their own communities. They may consider:

- **Population** Has the population of the community grown or declined since the 1970s? What factors have caused the change? What effects have population changes had on services such as schools and libraries?
- **Business and industry** Have new firms and factories located in the area? Or have businesses closed or downsized? Has the number of jobs increased? What about service businesses such as supermarkets or video rental stores?
- **Politics** Is the community traditionally Democratic or Republican? What political issues are important in the community?
- **Environment** Have air and water quality improved or declined? Do growing populations put pressure on water supplies and other resources?

Extend The rise of the Sunbelt has had far-reaching ramifications. Have small groups research the growth of recreational attractions in the Sunbelt—e.g., Disney World, new sports franchises—as well as increased sales of sportswear and recreational equipment. What other effects on popular culture or consumer buying habits can they identify?

ANSWERS

1. Jobs were disappearing in the Northeast and Midwest at the same time that employment opportunity was growing in the Sunbelt. Also, people sought warmer weather and opportunities for outdoor recreation in the Sunbelt.

Geography & History

The Rise of the Sunbelt

During the second half of the twentieth century, people and jobs moved on a massive scale from northern portions of the United States to the Sunbelt, a region encompassing states in the South and the Southwest.

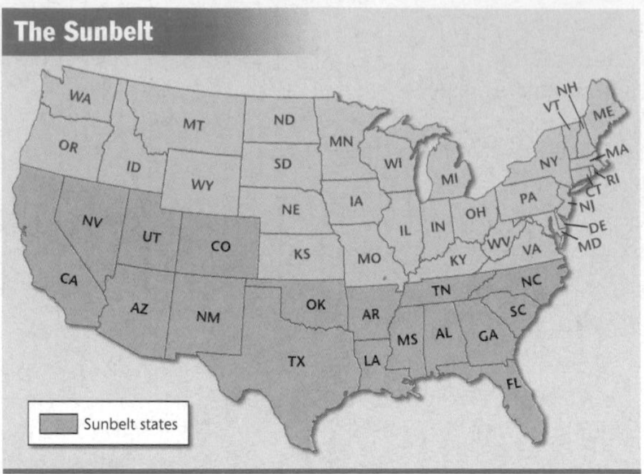

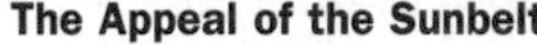

Why People Left
Cold, snowy winters, and older, declining industries made life challenging in the Midwest and the Northeast. In the 1970s and 1980s, many factories in these regions shut down, and jobs moved south or overseas.

The Appeal of the Sunbelt
Many new jobs became available in the Sunbelt. Employers chose to locate in this region because of lower labor and energy costs. Also, some Sunbelt states had lower business taxes. Families and individuals were drawn to the Sunbelt both by abundant jobs and by its warmer climate and opportunities for year-round outdoor recreation.

Geographic Connection

Why did many Americans move from the Northeast and the Midwest to the Sunbelt?

RESOURCE DIRECTORY

Teaching Resources
Geography and History booklet, pp. 20–21

Other Print Resources
Nystrom *Atlas of Our Country* *Regions of Our Country,* pp. 48–67

Technology
Prentice Hall United States History Video Collection™ Volume 20, *Post-War USA*

Sunbelt Development
The Sunbelt offers abundant land for new construction. This mixed office and residential development in southern California illustrates the combination of new employment, housing, and opportunities for outdoor activities that draw people to the Sunbelt.

Reapportionment, 1963–2003

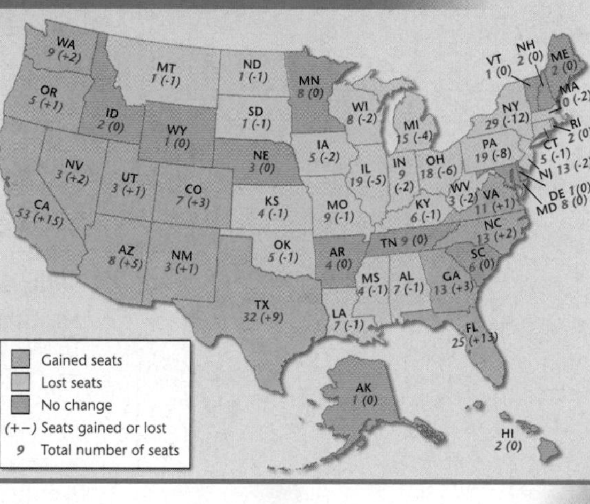

New Political Influence
This map shows changes in congressional representation between 1963 and 2003. States that grew faster than the national average gained seats, while those that grew more slowly or lost population also lost seats. Except in a few older southern states, rapid growth in most of the Sunbelt brought dramatic increases in congressional representation and national political influence. Since 1964, a candidate from the Sunbelt has won every presidential election.

Geographic Connection
How have shifts in population affected political power at the national level? Which states gained the most seats? Which states lost the most seats?

Joining the Major Leagues
Sunbelt cities that once had only minor-league teams have grown so much that they now attract major-league teams, such as the Jacksonville Jaguars.

891

ANSWERS

2. The Sunbelt states have gained greater power at the national level, both in congressional representation and in presidential politics. The biggest gainers were California, Florida, Texas, and Arizona. New York, Pennsylvania, Ohio, Illinois, and Michigan lost the most power.

Chapter 27 Planning Guide
Resource Manager

	CORE INSTRUCTION	READING/SKILLS
Chapter-Level Resources TEKS 24(B)	Teaching Resources • Pacing Charts booklet • Block Scheduling booklet **Resource Pro® CD-ROM,** Ch. 27 **Prentice Hall Presentation Pro CD-ROM,** Ch. 27 **www.phschool.com** • eTeach	**Guided Reading Audiotapes (English/Spanish)** **Student Edition on Audio CD,** Ch. 27 **Social Studies Skills Tutor CD-ROM** **Color Transparencies,** A52, A53, A59, B19, B20, C10, E19, E20, G12, G115
1 Politics in Recent Years **1.** Find out what led to Bill Clinton's election in 1992 and what issues he tackled in his first term. **2.** See why Republicans issued a Contract with America. **3.** Read about the scandals that were debated during Clinton's second term. **4.** Think about the results of the 2000 election and the goals the new President set. **5.** Learn how Americans responded to terrorist attacks in 2001. **TEKS** 6(H), 8(A), 16(A), 20(C), 24(A), 24(H)	Teaching Resources **Units 5/6/7 booklet** • Section 1 Quiz, p. 123	**Guided Reading and Review booklet,** p. 137 **Guide to the Essentials,** p. 132 **Learning with Documents booklet,** pp. 73, 98 **Skills for Life booklet,** p. 36 **Section Reading Support Transparencies**
2 The United States in a New World **1.** Read about political changes that took place in the world in the 1990s. **2.** Find out how the Clinton administration promoted peace abroad. **3.** Describe U.S. relations with China. **4.** Discover the impact of an expanding global economy. **TEKS** 6(G), 8(A), 14(E), 25(D)	Teaching Resources **Units 5/6/7 booklet** • Section 2 Quiz, p. 124 **Learning Styles Lesson Plans booklet,** p. 70	**Guided Reading and Review booklet,** p. 138 **Guide to the Essentials,** p. 133 **Section Reading Support Transparencies**
3 Americans in the New Millennium **1.** Learn about factors that contributed to the growing diversity of the nation's population. **2.** Find out how Americans disagreed about how to make diversity work. **3.** Discover the economic and political impact of the nation's aging population. **4.** Read to find out how the technological revolution at the end of the twentieth century affected American life. **TEKS** 5(A), 6(H), 10(B), 21(C), 22(C), 23(A), 25(D)	Teaching Resources **Units 5/6/7 booklet** • Section 3 Quiz, p. 125 **Learning Styles Lesson Plans booklet,** p. 71	**Guided Reading and Review booklet,** p. 139 **Guide to the Essentials,** p. 134 **Learning with Documents booklet,** p. 39 **Section Reading Support Transparencies**

Enrichment/Pre-AP

Prentice Hall United States History Video Collection™
www.phschool.com
- Section Activities, Virtual Field Trip, Chapter Activities, Current Events Online

Biography, Literature, and Comparing Primary Sources booklet, p. 89
American History Block Scheduling Support
Nystrom *Atlas of Our Country,* pp. 34–35
Sounds of an Era Audio CD
Exploring Primary Sources in U.S. History CD-ROM

Biography, Literature, and Comparing Primary Sources booklet, p. 39
Great Debates booklet, p. 48
American History Block Scheduling Support
Historical Outline Map Book, pp. 72, 74, 75, 76, 78, 79

Biography, Literature, and Comparing Primary Sources booklet, p. 163
American History Block Scheduling Support
Nystrom *Atlas of Our Country,* pp. 36–37
Historical Outline Map Book, p. 82
Exploring Primary Sources in U.S. History CD-ROM
American Pathways Thematic Posters

Assessment

Core Assessment
ExamView® Test Bank, Ch. 27
ExamView® Test Bank CD-ROM, Ch. 27

Standardized Test Preparation
Diagnose and Prescribe
Diagnostic Tests for High School Social Studies Skills

Review and Reteach
Review Book for U.S. History

Practice and Assess
Test-taking Strategies With Transparencies
Test-taking Strategies Posters
Test Prep Book for U.S. History
Alternative Assessment Handbook
Document-Based Assessment

Teaching Resources
Units 5/6/7 booklet
- Section Quizzes, pp. 123–125
- Chapter Tests, pp. 126, 129

www.phschool.com Ch. 27 Self-Test

AmericanHeritage® Resources

From the Archives of American Heritage®, p. 896
AmericanHeritage® My Brush with History™ Videotapes
www.americanheritage.com

Don't miss the exclusive interactive version of this textbook on the Web and on CD-ROM.

Chapter 27 Planning Guide
In Your Classroom

Customize for Individual Needs

Gifted and Talented

Teacher's Edition
- Customize for Gifted and Talented, p. 895

Teaching Resources
- Biography, Literature, and Comparing Primary Sources booklet, pp. 39, 89, 163

Technology
- Exploring Primary Sources in U.S. History CD-ROM *On the Pulse of the Morning, Maya Angelou; Inaugural Address, President George W. Bush*

ESL

Teacher's Edition
- Customize for ESL, p. 907

Teaching Resources
- Guided Reading and Review booklet, pp. 137–139
- Guide to the Essentials (English/Spanish), Chapter 27

Technology
- Student Edition on Audio CD, Chapter 27
- Guided Reading Audiotapes (English/Spanish), Chapter 27
- Section Reading Support Transparencies

Less Proficient Readers

Teacher's Edition
- Customize for Less Proficient Readers, p. 899, 913

Teaching Resources
- Guided Reading and Review booklet, pp. 137–139
- Guide to the Essentials (English/Spanish), Chapter 27

Technology
- Student Edition on Audio CD, Chapter 27
- Guided Reading Audiotapes (English/Spanish), Chapter 27
- Section Reading Support Transparencies

Less Proficient Writers

Teacher's Edition
- Customize for Less Proficient Writers, pp. 899, 913

Teaching Resources
- Guided Reading and Review booklet, pp. 137–139
- Guide to the Essentials (English/Spanish), Chapter 27

Technology
- Student Edition on Audio CD, Chapter 27
- Guided Reading Audiotapes (English/Spanish), Chapter 27
- Section Reading Support Transparencies

Teacher's Edition Index

Chapter 27 – Pacing Suggestions

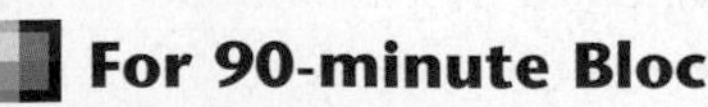

For 90-minute Blocks

- Teach sections 1, 2, and 3 using Transparencies A52, A53, A59, B19, B20, C10, E19, E20, G12, and G115, and the Recent Scholarship notes on pages 907 and 914 for class discussions.

Running Out of Time?

If you are running short on time to cover this chapter, consider the following options:

- Use the Prentice Hall Presentation Pro CD-ROM to create an outline for this chapter.
- Use the Section Summaries for Chapter 27, from **Guide to the Essentials (English/Spanish).**

TEKS Correlation

Chapter-Level	TEKS
	(24) Social studies skills. The student applies critical-thinking skills to organize and use information acquired from a variety of sources, including electronic technology. The student is expected to: **(B)** analyze information by sequencing, categorizing, identifying cause-and-effect relationships, comparing, contrasting, finding the main idea, summarizing, making generalizations and predictions, and drawing inferences and conclusions.
1 Politics in Recent Years	**(6) History.** The student understands the impact of significant national and international decisions and conflicts from World War II and the Cold War to the present on the United States. The student is expected to: **(H)** identify the origins of major domestic and foreign policy issues currently facing the United States. **(8) Geography.** The student uses geographic tools to collect, analyze, and interpret data. The student is expected to: **(A)** create thematic maps, graphs, charts, models, and databases representing various aspects of the United States. **(16) Government.** The student understands the changing relationship among the three branches of the federal government. The student is expected to: **(A)** evaluate the impact of events, including the Gulf of Tonkin Resolution and the War Powers Act, on the relationship between the legislative and executive branches of government. **(20) Culture.** The student understands the relationship between the arts and the times during which they were created. The student is expected to: **(C)** identify examples of American art, music, and literature that transcend American culture and convey universal themes. **(24) Social studies skills.** The student applies critical-thinking skills to organize and use information acquired from a variety of sources, including electronic technology. The student is expected to: **(A)** locate and use primary and secondary sources such as computer software, databases, media and news services, biographies, interviews, and artifacts to acquire information about the United States. **(H)** use appropriate mathematical skills to interpret social studies information such as maps and graphs.
2 The United States in a New World	**(6) History.** The student understands the impact of significant national and international decisions and conflicts from World War II and the Cold War to the present on the United States. The student is expected to: **(G)** analyze the reasons for the Western victory in the Cold War and the challenges of changing relationships among nations. **(8) Geography.** The student uses geographic tools to collect, analyze, and interpret data. The student is expected to: **(A)** create thematic maps, graphs, charts, models, and databases representing various aspects of the United States. **(14) Economics.** The student understands the economic effects of World War II, the Cold War, and increased worldwide competition on contemporary society. The student is expected to: **(E)** describe the dynamic relationship between U.S. international trade policies and the U.S. free enterprise system. **(25) Social studies skills.** The student communicates in written, oral, and visual forms. The student is expected to: **(D)** create written, oral, and visual presentations of social studies information.
3 Americans in the New Millennium	**(5) History.** The student understands significant individuals, events, and issues of the 1920s. The student is expected to: **(A)** analyze causes and effects of significant issues such as immigration, the Red Scare, Prohibition, and the changing role of women. **(6) History.** The student understands the impact of significant national and international decisions and conflicts from World War II and the Cold War to the present on the United States. The student is expected to: **(H)** identify the origins of major domestic and foreign policy issues currently facing the United States. **(10) Geography.** The student understands the effects of migration and immigration on American society. The student is expected to: **(B)** analyze the effects of changing demographic patterns resulting from immigration to the United States. **(21) Culture.** The student understands how people from various groups, including racial, ethnic, and religious groups, adapt to life in the United States and contribute to our national identity. The student is expected to: **(C)** analyze how the contributions of various racial, ethnic, and religious groups have helped to shape the national identity. **(22) Science, technology, and society.** The student understands the impact of science and technology on the economic development of the United States. The student is expected to: **(C)** analyze the impact of technological innovations on the nature of work, the American labor movement, and business. **(23) Science, technology, and society.** The student understands the influence of scientific discoveries and technological innovations on daily life in the United States. The student is expected to: **(A)** analyze how scientific discoveries and technological innovations, including those in transportation and communication, have changed the standard of living in the United States. **(25) Social studies skills.** The student communicates in written, oral, and visual forms. The student is expected to: **(D)** create written, oral, and visual presentations of social studies information.

Chapter 27

Entering a New Era

(1992 to the Present)

Introducing the Chapter

Sweeping changes in world affairs in the early 1990s changed the face of world politics. Although the Cold War was over, these developments offered new challenges to the United States, now the only superpower, and to the President. The United States also faced challenging issues at home, as immigration and an aging population changed the demographics of American society.

Time Line Activity

To provide students with practice in using the time line, ask questions such as these:

1. What organization designed to regulate international commerce was established in 1995? *(The World Trade Organization)*
2. What 1996 act changed the way the government responds to families in need? *(The Welfare Reform Act)*
3. What did NATO do in 1999 in an attempt to keep peace in Kosovo? *(NATO launched airstrikes.)*

Chapter 27 Entering a New Era (1992 to the Present)

This computer-generated portrait combined the characteristics of all the races present in the United States.

American Events

- **1992** Bill Clinton is elected President.
- **1994** The Republicans, running on their "Contract with America," win the 1994 congressional elections.
- **1996** Congress passes the Welfare Reform Act.

Presidential Terms: George H. W. Bush 1989–1993; William J. Clinton 1993–2001

1992 — 1994 — 1996

World Events

- **1994** Nelson Mandela is elected president of South Africa.
- **1995** The World Trade Organization is established.

eTeach

Be sure to check out this month's online discussion with a Master Teacher. Go to **www.phschool.com**.

RESOURCE DIRECTORY

Teaching Resources

Pacing Charts booklet

Block Scheduling booklet, p. 30

Units 5/6/7 booklet

- Chapter Summary, p. 122

Technology

Guided Reading Audiotapes (English/Spanish), Ch. 27

Student Edition on Audio CD, Ch. 27

Prentice Hall United States History Video Collection™ Volume 20, *Post-War USA*

Prentice Hall Presentation Pro CD-ROM, Ch. 27

Resource Pro® CD-ROM

Social Studies Skills Tutor CD-ROM

Companion Web site, www.phschool.com

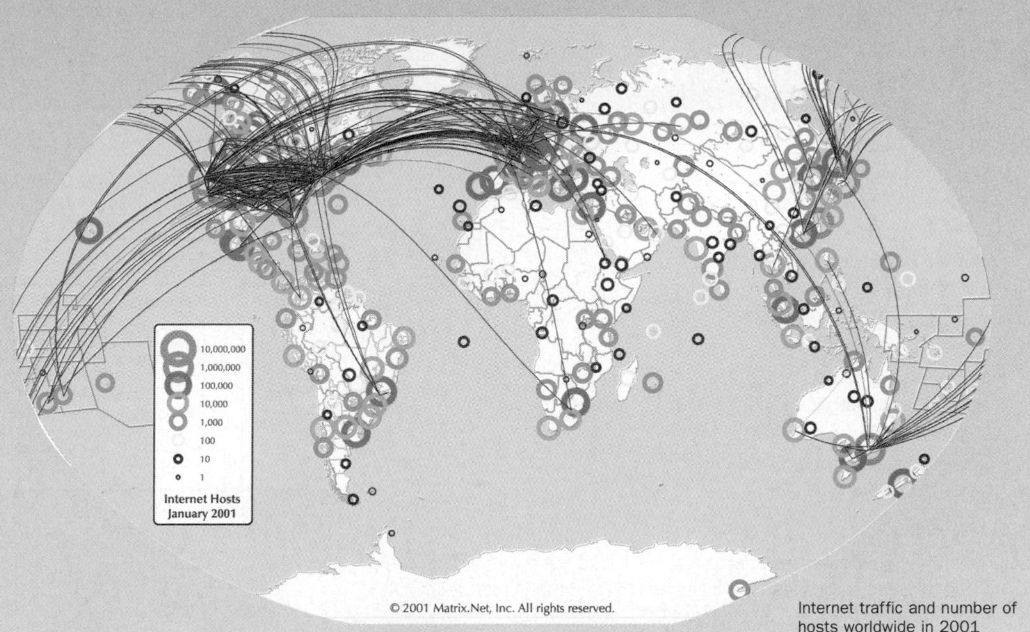

Internet traffic and number of hosts worldwide in 2001

A display of national unity by the United States Congress following the terrorist attacks

1998 The House of Representatives votes to impeach President Clinton.

2000 The Supreme Court's ruling in *Bush* v. *Gore* ends recounts in Florida, leading to George W. Bush's victory in the 2000 presidential election.

2001 Terrorists attack the United States, crashing hijacked planes into the World Trade Center in New York City and the Pentagon in Washington, D.C.

George W. Bush 2001–

1998 • **2000** • **2002**

1998 Voters in Northern Ireland and Ireland approve the Good Friday Accords.

1999 NATO launches airstrikes against Serbia to keep peace in Kosovo.

Entering a New Era, 1992 to the Present

Activating Prior Knowledge Which areas of the world have the most Internet traffic? *(The United States and Europe)*

Previewing What role do you think the Internet has played in international affairs? *(The Internet has made information accessible on a worldwide basis. People have greater access to education, business, and entertainment right from their homes and places of work.)*

BACKGROUND
About the Pictures

1 2 3 4

1. The 1992 presidential race included three major candidates for the first time since 1912: George Bush, Bill Clinton, and Ross Perot.
2. In the 1990s the United States became more diverse than it had ever been in its history.
3. The results of the 2000 presidential election took 36 days and several court battles to decide.
4. In a spontaneous outburst of patriotism, the Congressional members sang "God Bless America." The event was broadcast on live television.

BIBLIOGRAPHY

For the Teacher

Bell, Derrick. ***Faces at the Bottom of the Well: The Permanence of Racism.*** Basic, 1993. (Attitudes toward race revealed through dialogues and myths.)

Glickman, Rose L. ***Daughters of Feminists.*** St. Martin's Press, 1993. (Reports on 50 women raised by feminist mothers.)

Takaki, Ronald. ***A Different Mirror: A History of Multicultural America.*** Little, Brown, 1993. (An attempt to view all American history from a multicultural perspective.)

For the Student

Ashabraner, Brent. ***An Ancient Heritage: The Arab American Minority.*** HarperCollins, 1993. (Personal reflections on the experience of being Arab American.)

Cisneros, Sandra. ***The House on Mango Street.*** Arte Publico, 1989. (A short story collection by a Mexican American writer.)

Santiago, Esmeralda. ***When I Was Puerto Rican.*** Addison-Wesley, 1993.

Smith, Jessie Carney. ***Black Firsts: 2,000 Years of Extraordinary Achievement.*** Visible Ink Press, 1994. (Chronicles the "firsts" among people of color.)

Don't miss the exclusive interactive version of this textbook on the Web and on CD-ROM.

Section 1
Politics in Recent Years

Section Objectives

1. Find out what led to Bill Clinton's election in 1992 and what issues he tackled in his first term.
2. See why Republicans issued a Contract with America.
3. Read about the scandals that were debated during Clinton's second term.
4. Think about the results of the 2000 election and the goals the new President set.
5. Learn how Americans responded to the terrorist attacks in 2001.

Bellringer

Warm-Up Activity Ask students to suppose that they are making a decision about how to vote in the 2000 presidential election. What factors and issues would influence their decision? How would they have voted?

Activating Prior Knowledge Have students list four or five major events they can recall taking place during Bill Clinton's presidency.

Reading Strategy

As students read the section, have them list the actions of government and the private sector to expand economic opportunities to all citizens during the 1990s.

Section 1
Politics in Recent Years

READING FOCUS

- What led to Bill Clinton's election in 1992 and what issues did he tackle during his first term?
- Why did Republicans issue a Contract with America?
- What scandals were debated during Clinton's second term?
- What were the results of the 2000 election, and what goals did the new President set?
- How did Americans respond to the terrorist attacks in 2001?

KEY TERMS

Contract with America
Whitewater affair

TAKING NOTES

As you read, complete the chart below to show the major political issues of the 1990s.

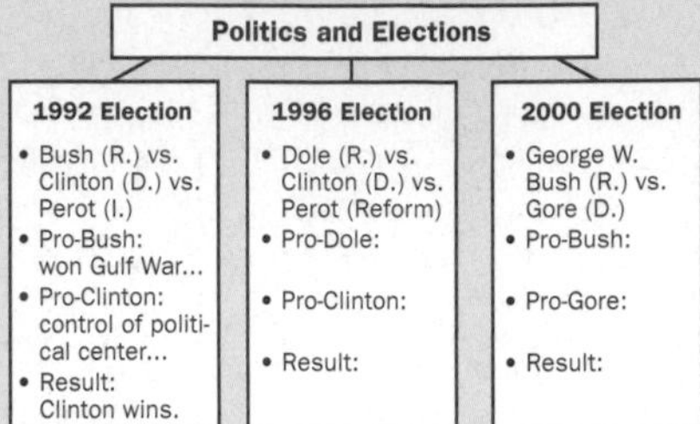

Politics and Elections
1992 Election
• Bush (R.) vs. Clinton (D.) vs. Perot (I.)
• Pro-Bush: won Gulf War...
• Pro-Clinton: control of political center...
• Result: Clinton wins.
1996 Election
• Dole (R.) vs. Clinton (D.) vs. Perot (Reform)
• Pro-Dole:
• Pro-Clinton:
• Result:
2000 Election
• George W. Bush (R.) vs. Gore (D.)
• Pro-Bush:
• Pro-Gore:
• Result:

MAIN IDEA

Bill Clinton's presidency included many low points but it was also marked by great successes. The highs and lows of the Clinton years were followed by the close election of 2000.

Setting the Scene An earnest young man named Bill Clinton reached out and firmly grasped President John F. Kennedy's hand. At just 17, this high school student from a small town in Arkansas was actually shaking hands with the President! Later, the experience contributed to Clinton's decision to pursue a career in politics. In 1993, some three decades after this meeting, Clinton was back in the White House. This time he stayed for eight years, for he had become the forty-second President of the United States.

After meeting President Kennedy at age 17, Bill Clinton decided to pursue a career in politics. Like JFK, Clinton benefited from a media age campaign.

The 1992 Election

The 1992 presidential campaign was a three-way race. Not since 1912, when President Taft faced both Woodrow Wilson and former President Theodore Roosevelt, had a third candidate played such a major role in a presidential election.

The Candidates On the Republican side, President George Bush sought a second term. The Republicans argued that they could best deal with what they charged was a continuing decline in family values. In addition, they hailed President Bush for his role in ending the Cold War and winning the Gulf War. However, the recession of the early 1990s continued, and economic issues dominated the campaign.

Independent candidate H. Ross Perot, a billionaire Texas businessman, entered the race out of frustration over government policies dealing with the budget and the economy. Perot ran as a Washington "outsider." He said that he had no ties to special interest groups and pledged that he would consider the needs of the country as a whole.

The Democrats nominated Arkansas governor Bill Clinton as their candidate. Clinton promised to end the recession and to deal with the nation's other

RESOURCE DIRECTORY

Teaching Resources
Guided Reading and Review booklet, p. 137

Technology
Section Reading Support Transparencies
Guided Reading Audiotapes (English/Spanish), Ch. 27
Student Edition on Audio CD, Ch. 27
Color Transparencies *Historical Maps,* A54
Prentice Hall Presentation Pro CD-ROM, Ch. 27
Companion Web site, www.phschool.com

nagging economic problems. He also pledged to address the federal budget deficit and the problems in the healthcare system.

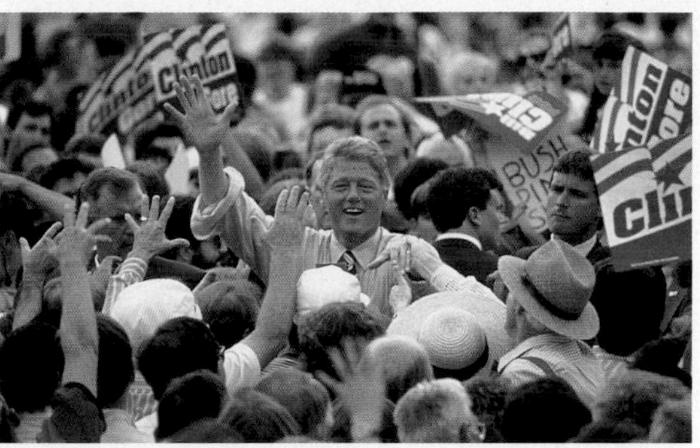

VIEWING HISTORY Even before he ran for President, Bill Clinton had a reputation as a brilliant campaigner. Here, he greets a crowd of supporters during his successful 1992 presidential campaign. **Analyzing Visual Information** *How does this photo illustrate some of the challenges of campaigning for President?*

Campaign Issues Like his hero, President Kennedy, Clinton believed that government was necessary "to make America work again." At the same time, he believed in the need to reduce the size of government to make it more efficient and responsive. Clinton believed he could reconcile both conservative and liberal views. He called himself a "New Democrat," in an effort to shed the traditional stereotype of the "tax-and-spend," big-government Democrat. Clinton's message appealed to Americans who were frustrated at the seemingly endless bickering between Democrats and Republicans in Congress.

Some critics charged that Clinton would say whatever was necessary—regardless of the truth—to win the election. When a woman claimed to have had an affair with Clinton, and produced evidence that seemed to support her story, Clinton denied her charges. In addition, Clinton's statements about how and why he had avoided the draft during the Vietnam War seemed untruthful to some.

Yet these issues of personal character were not strong enough to defeat the hard-working Clinton. His supporters praised his refusal to quit and began calling him the "comeback kid." That nickname also reminded voters that Clinton, at 46, was a full generation younger than the 68-year-old Bush.

On election day, Clinton received 43 percent of the votes, while Bush polled nearly 38 percent. Perot's strong showing of about 19 percent meant that Clinton became President with less than a majority of the popular vote. In the electoral college, Clinton won 370 votes versus 168 for Bush. Perot won no electoral votes.

Clinton's First Term

Bill Clinton began his first term as President in January 1993. He recognized that the voters wanted a change from the politics of the recent past:

> "*Thomas Jefferson believed that to preserve the very foundations of the nation we would need dramatic change from time to time. Well, my fellow Americans, this is our time. Let us embrace it. . . . Today we pledge an end to the era of deadlock and drift, and a new season of American renewal has begun.*"
>
> —Bill Clinton, First Inaugural Address

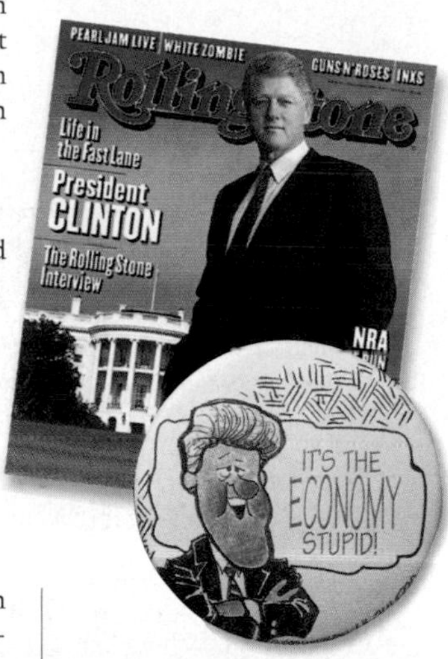

Clinton's charisma and connection to popular culture broadened his appeal as a presidential candidate in 1992. During the campaign, Clinton used the slogan "It's the economy, stupid!" to suggest that he could address the nation's economic issues.

Clinton was buoyed by the fact that Democratic majorities existed in both the House and the Senate. For the first time in more than a decade, the executive and legislative branches would be in the hands of the same political party.

Economic Reform In dealing with the economy, Clinton tried to follow a middle course. He wanted to end the lingering recession by raising spending or cutting taxes. At the same time, he needed to reduce the budget deficit, which meant cutting spending or raising taxes.

Following this course proved more challenging than Clinton had anticipated. Congress did approve Clinton's first budget, but just barely. The House

Lesson Plan

Focus Explain that American voters chose Democrat Bill Clinton after 12 years of Republican Presidents. Two years later, however, they chose a record number of Republican representatives to Congress. Ask students to compare the two parties—where they have moved closer together, and where they still strongly differ.

Instruct Discuss the different attitudes toward the economy shown by the three candidates in the 1992 election. Explain how extreme political differences between a President and Congress—like those after the 1994 midterm elections—can affect the passage of legislation and frustrate political goals. Ask students to think about the role of partisanship in relation to Clinton's impeachment.

Assess/Reteach What impact do students think the Clinton impeachment had on his presidency, and, ultimately, on the country as a whole?

Activity
Connecting with Politics

To help students better understand the issues that decided the 1992 and 1996 presidential campaigns, have them act as spokespersons for the candidates in each of the campaigns. They should create a short "capsule campaign" for each candidate: devise a campaign slogan, list five to eight planks in a platform, and write a press release detailing the candidate's position. In the process, students should explain how participation in the democratic process reflects our national identity. Each campaign manager should present the campaign in class. **(Verbal/Linguistic)**

Customize For ...
Gifted and Talented

Hillary Rodham Clinton's strong and visible role in the Clinton administration made her a controversial figure. Ask students to research the career of Eleanor Roosevelt and prepare for a class discussion on the role each played in her husband's administration. As they prepare, have students consider the question of what the role of the First Lady should be.

Caption Answers

Viewing History It shows the candidates' need to get their message across to millions of people, to sustain energy while campaigning, and to organize large gatherings.

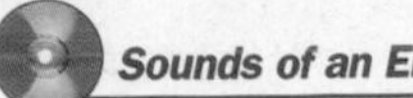

Sounds of an Era

Listen to a campaign speech by Bill Clinton emphasizing the economy and other sounds from recent years.

passed the measure by only two votes, and in the Senate, Vice President Gore had to break a 50-50 tie. To reduce the deficit, the budget included both spending cuts and tax increases. Neither action was well received by the public.

The Battle Over Healthcare When Clinton took office, an estimated 37 million Americans had no health insurance. For years, this number had been rising, as were the costs of healthcare. Many Americans were finding it increasingly difficult to afford medical care. Soon after taking office, Clinton appointed his wife Hillary to head a task force to analyze healthcare and propose reforms.

"This healthcare system of ours is badly broken, and it is time to fix it," Clinton declared to a national TV audience in September 1993. "We must make this our most urgent priority." The proposal he presented to Congress called for the creation of a government-supervised health insurance program that would guarantee affordable coverage to every American.

Although the public at first seemed to favor healthcare reform, Clinton's plea was vigorously opposed by a number of insurance, professional, and small-business groups. Congressional Republicans charged that the program would be expensive for taxpayers, and they attacked it as an example of big government. Democrats too disagreed on how far the program should go. The debate continued for about a year. In the end, Clinton's plan for healthcare reform failed to gain the necessary support in Congress.

The Republicans' Contract With America

The failure of his healthcare plan signaled trouble for the President. During the 1994 midterm elections, Georgia Representative Newt Gingrich called on Republican candidates to endorse what he called a **Contract with America.** This contract was a pledge to scale back the role of the federal government, eliminate some regulations, cut taxes, and balance the budget.

Many voters, feeling that the Democratic-controlled Congress had lost touch with their concerns, responded enthusiastically. In November 1994, voters

COMPARING PRIMARY SOURCES
Regulating Health Maintenance Organizations (HMOs)

During the 1990s, many people debated whether stricter regulations should be placed on HMOs.

Analyzing Viewpoints What concerns do these two editorials raise regarding the regulation of HMOs?

Opposed to Stricter HMO Regulations

"Proponents of [greater regulation of HMOs] say their intention is only to improve a managed care system that's put too much emphasis on finances and not enough emphasis on patient care. . . . However, . . . HMOs have brought revolutionary changes to a health care system that had the exact opposite problem only a few decades ago—too little attention to finances and too much wasteful spending in order to pay for new buildings, equipment, and other dubious expenditures that led to double-digit cost increases."

—*Editorial,* Boston Business Journal, *April 10–16, 1998*

In Favor of Stricter HMO Regulations

"Market discipline of [HMOs] must include legal constraints that enforce remedies for broken contracts and civil injuries. Without the sanction of having to compensate the victims of their wrongdoing, HMOs will continue to cut their expenditures by withholding deserved treatment and paying their managers bonuses for actions that drive down the quality of care. Horror stories . . . will continue, and managed care will never achieve its fundamental purpose—to reduce cost without impairing the quality of care."

—*Editorial by Ronald F. Hoffman and Mark O. Heipler,* The Washington Post, *April 4, 1998*

ACTIVITY
Student Portfolio

You may wish to have students add the following to their portfolios: Maya Angelou wrote and presented the poem "On the Pulse of Morning" at Bill Clinton's inauguration in 1993. Many people were reminded of Robert Frost's reading of his inaugural poem "The Gift Outright" 32 years before at the inauguration of John F. Kennedy. Help students find copies of both poems and ask them to write a brief essay that compares and contrasts them. What differences in attitude or philosophy between the two poets can they identify? How do they differ in their definitions of who is an American? How does each transcend American culture and convey universal themes?

From the Archives of
AmericanHeritage®

About the Presidents

For most of his career Bill Clinton (1992–2001) has been a remarkably successful politician. He successfully campaigned for the Arkansas governor's seat in 1978, becoming the nation's youngest governor in decades. Through much of the 1980s and early 1990s, he won repeated reelection to the office and became a national leader of the Democratic Party. He was elected twice to the presidency, breaking a 12-year Republican run in the office. Yet Clinton's career must also be seen in light of his losses. As a political apprentice, he fought on a number of failed campaigns, most notably that of George McGovern in 1972, and Clinton himself also suffered a stinging loss running for reelection after his first term as governor. In the second term of his presidency scandal engulfed Clinton and the White House, leaving his ultimate legacy in doubt. Source: Adapted from Henry F. Graff's *The Presidents,* Scribner's, 1996, by the editors of *American Heritage®* magazine.

RESOURCE DIRECTORY

Teaching Resources

Biography, Literature, and Comparing Primary Sources booklet (Literature) *The Republican Revolution,* p. 89

Other Print Resources

Nystrom *Atlas of Our Country* *People on the Move,* pp. 34–35

American History Block Scheduling Support *Presidential Power: Changes in the Twentieth Century,* found in The Nation After World War II folder, includes interdisciplinary lesson suggestions and activities for Geography and History, Primary Sources, Biography, and Literature.

Technology

Sounds of an Era Audio CD *Bill Clinton's Democratic Nomination Acceptance Speech,* 1992 recording; *Anti-National Health Care Television Ad*

Exploring Primary Sources in U.S. History CD-ROM *On the Pulse of the Morning, Maya Angelou*

elected Republicans in large numbers, giving them majorities in both houses of Congress for the first time in more than four decades.

Congress Versus the President The first-term Republicans quickly became a potent force in the House. For leadership they looked to Newt Gingrich, who was elected Speaker of the House. There was talk of a new era in American politics in which Congress, not the President, would set the nation's course.

The Republicans in Congress moved swiftly to keep the pledges they had made during the campaign. They demanded that the budget be balanced in seven years and proposed cuts in many social services. Recalling the achievements of the first 100 days of the New Deal in 1933, Gingrich demanded action on these items within the session's first 100 days. In most cases, approval was given.

Many of the bills approved by the House never became law, however. Some were rejected by the Senate, while others were vetoed by Clinton. Even so, Gingrich claimed that he had "changed the whole debate in American politics." That is, Americans were no longer debating whether to cut government and balance the budget, but rather how to do so.

The Government Is Shut Down At the end of 1995, Clinton and Gingrich clashed over the size of budget cuts and the timetable for balancing the budget. When they were unable to compromise, budget allocations expired without reauthorization, leading to the temporary closure of government offices and the disruption of services to millions of Americans. Not until the spring of 1996 did Congress and the President come to an agreement on the budget.

The battle over the budget marked the start of yet another Clinton comeback. Many Americans blamed congressional Republicans for the government shutdown and began to regard them as uncompromising and extreme. By labeling proposed Republican spending cuts as mean-spirited and by presenting himself as one who could make needed reforms, Clinton raised his approval rating in national polls.

Welfare Reform In August 1996, Congress and Clinton agreed on a sweeping reform of the nation's welfare system. Affected were 12.8 million people receiving Aid to Families with Dependent Children (AFDC). The new law eliminated federal guarantees of cash assistance and gave states authority to run their own welfare programs with block grants of federal money. It also established a lifetime limit of five years of aid per family and required most adults to work within two years of receiving aid. The historic policy change reversed six decades of social welfare legislation.

Clinton's Second Term

When the Republicans took control of Congress in 1995, Clinton's chances for reelection seemed slim. The Republican message appeared to have great appeal to voters. In the months that followed, Clinton worked hard to counter that message and to show that he was not a "tax-and-spend liberal."

The 1996 Election The Republican nominee for President in 1996 was Bob Dole, Senate Majority Leader and a respected member of Congress for 35 years. Ross Perot again entered the race, this time as the nominee of the newly created Reform Party.

As the election approached, Clinton successfully maneuvered several popular bills through Congress, including one raising the minimum wage. In addition,

VIEWING HISTORY In an outdoor press conference, Newt Gingrich outlines the accomplishments of the Republicans' Contract with America. **Identifying Central Issues** *How did the Contract change the debate on cutting government spending?*

READING CHECK
What factors led to Clinton's reelection in 1996?

ACTIVITY
Connecting with Government

Engage students in a discussion about the relationship between Congress and the President. Ask students to think about why this relationship is sometimes strained. Have students consider the difficulties of balancing the power between these two branches of government. Prompt them by initiating discussion of recent situations in which the President and Congress were forced to negotiate their differences. **(Verbal/Linguistic)**

BACKGROUND
Biography

Newt Gingrich (b. 1943) rose to become one of America's most powerful politicians, and during his brief reign, he was instrumental in the passage of the conservative manifesto, the Contract with America. Although *Time* magazine named Gingrich Man of the Year in 1995, this controversial figure resigned from his post just four years later. In January 1999 Gingrich left office, following the poor showing of the Republican Party in the 1998 midterm elections. Gingrich was the target of numerous ethics charges. His fellow members of the House imposed a $300,000 fine on him, and opinion polls revealed that he was one of the most unpopular people in the country.

TEST PREPARATION

Have students read the section "The Republicans' Contract with America" and then answer the question below.

What was the most significant change that came about after the 1994 elections?

A There were more Republicans than Democrats in Congress.

B There were more Republicans than Democrats in the Senate.

C This was the first time the Republicans held a majority in both houses in forty years.

(D) All of the above.

CAPTION ANSWERS

Viewing History It changed the debate from whether to cut spending to how to cut spending.

ACTIVITY
Connecting with Economics

Tell students to research details about the economy in 1996. Suggest that students spend time in the library reading newsmagazines that contain articles about the economy. Then ask students to write a brief report explaining how the economy affected the presidential election of 1996. Remind students to consider not only the economic impact on individuals and families, but also the psychological effect. **(Verbal/Linguistic)**

BACKGROUND
Interest in the Election

The election of 1996 failed to arouse interest among the nation's voters. Turnout was the lowest since 1924. One reason for the lack of interest may have been the robust state of the economy. In 1996 the country was at peace, and most Americans were benefiting from the healthy economy. Another factor that led to Clinton's reelection was his weak opponent, Bob Dole. Although Dole had served as a senator for many years, his presidential candidacy revealed him to be inarticulate and out of touch with Americans and their concerns.

Focus on CULTURE

The Oklahoma City Bombing Just after 9 A.M., on April 19, 1995, a bomb exploded outside the Murrah Federal Building in Oklahoma City.

The wreckage from the 9-story building left mounds of rubble and debris. For nearly two weeks, rescue workers searched for trapped bodies. A horrified nation watched with sympathy and waited for some explanation. After the dust had settled, 168 people, 19 of them children from the building's day care center, were dead.

At first, many people suspected that the attack was carried out by a foreign terrorist, but soon investigators discovered that the terrorist came from the United States. The federal government charged Gulf War veteran Timothy McVeigh with the bombing. In 1997, McVeigh was found guilty and sentenced to die. His execution took place in June 2001. McVeigh's execution, however, was only a small part of the healing process for the families and friends of the victims, whose lives were forever changed after the explosion. The Oklahoma City National Memorial now stands as a lasting tribute to the victims and the memory of this devastating act of terrorism.

the economy, which had been an important factor in the 1992 campaign, had become strong. Again, the economy worked in Clinton's favor.

On election day, voters returned Clinton to office with 49 percent of the popular vote. Dole received 41 percent, while Perot dropped off to 8 percent. In the electoral college, Clinton gathered 379 votes to 159 for Dole.

Scandal and the Second Term Charges of scandal in Clinton's first term, which Bob Dole had emphasized in the 1996 campaign, continued into the new administration. In what came to be known as the **Whitewater affair,** Clinton was accused of having taken part in fraudulent loans and land deals in Arkansas years earlier and of having used his influence as then-governor to block an investigation of his business partners. Attorney General Janet Reno appointed a special prosecutor to look into these charges. As a result, some of Clinton's friends and former associates were convicted of various crimes and sentenced to prison. Yet no evidence was found to link the President to any wrongdoing.

Another charge made against Clinton, shortly after his reelection, was that he had accepted illegal campaign donations in return for political favors. A Senate committee found violations of campaign finance laws by members of both political parties, but Clinton was not directly linked to these violations.

Clinton Is Impeached Clinton's sixth year in office, 1998, began with good news: the government had achieved its first budget surplus since 1969. This bright moment was short-lived, however. Later that year, a scandal erupted that engulfed Clinton, leading to only the second impeachment of a President in the nation's history.

The crisis arose when the special prosecutor, Kenneth Starr, who had been looking into the Whitewater affair, began to investigate the relationship between Clinton and a young White House intern, Monica Lewinsky. Under oath in a separate sexual harassment lawsuit, Clinton had denied having sexual relations with the intern. He repeated this denial again to a grand jury convened by Starr in August. Eventually, Clinton admitted to having had an "inappropriate relationship" and to having "misled" his family and the country.

In September, Starr sent a report listing numerous grounds for impeachment to the House of Representatives. This report led to a bitterly partisan debate in the House and throughout the country. Polls showed that while most Americans criticized Clinton's actions, a majority believed that he was doing a good job as President and should not be impeached. On December 19, 1998, however, the full House voted to impeach Clinton on charges of perjury and obstruction of justice. Most Republicans voted yes; most Democrats voted no.

The Senate trial that followed opened on January 7, 1999. Many senators believed that Clinton had committed offenses, but debate centered on whether these offenses qualified as "high crimes and misdemeanors," the constitutional requirement for conviction of a President. On February 12, 1999, the Senate voted to acquit the President.

Support for Clinton throughout the process may have been bolstered by an unprecedented economic boom. The Clinton presidency marked the longest period of economic expansion in American history. As the economy continued to grow, the nation maintained low levels of unemployment and inflation.

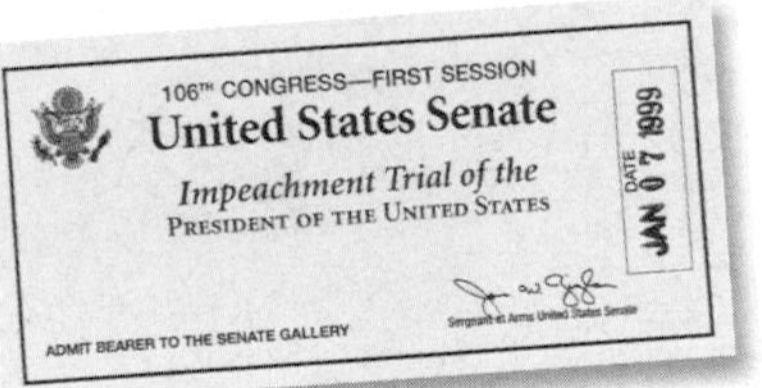

The Senate issued tickets for Bill Clinton's impeachment trial.

RESOURCE DIRECTORY

Teaching Resources

Learning with Documents booklet (Visual Learning Activity) *Campaign Strategies '96,* p. 73

Learning with Documents booklet (Key Documents) *William J. Clinton's Final State of the Union Address,* p. 98

Technology

Color Transparencies *Historical Maps,* A52

RESOURCE PRO® **Critical Thinking Activity** *Drawing Conclusions: Comparing Budget Categories,* found on Resource Pro, helps students apply this skill by analyzing descriptions of President Clinton's 1995–1996 budget.

Sounds of an Era Audio CD *President Clinton on Monica Lewinsky Scandal* (time: 30 seconds); *Al Gore's Conclusion Speech,* 2000 recording

The 2000 Election

The mixture of a strong economy and a scandal-ridden presidency promised a close presidential election in 2000. The nation's prosperity suggested that Vice President Gore, the Democrats' candidate, had a good chance of winning the election. However, some critics believed that he lacked the kind of strong personality that allowed Bill Clinton to rise above scandals and dominate the political center.

During the campaign, Republicans spoke of returning morality and respect to the White House. Leading up to the election, national polls showed that the Republican candidate, Texas Governor George W. Bush (son of former President Bush), was virtually tied with Vice President Gore. Polls also showed that many Americans were not enthusiastic about either candidate.

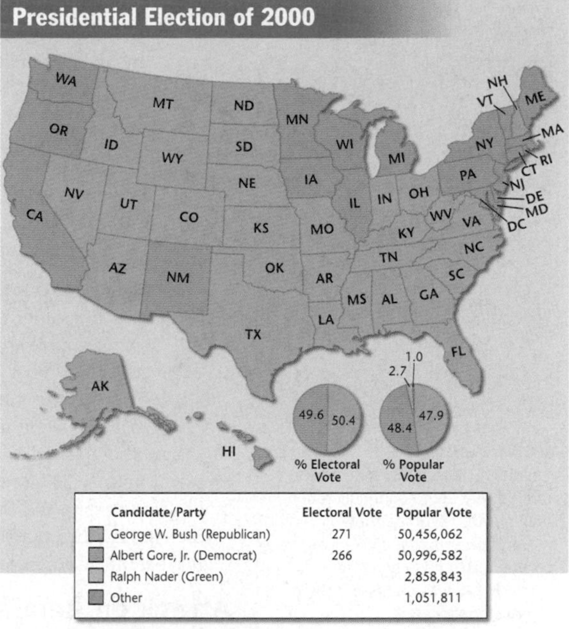

Candidate/Party	Electoral Vote	Popular Vote
George W. Bush (Republican)	271	50,456,062
Albert Gore, Jr. (Democrat)	266	50,996,582
Ralph Nader (Green)		2,858,843
Other		1,051,811

MAP SKILLS The 2000 election was the fourth time in history that the person winning the popular vote failed to win the presidency. **Regions** *Which region(s) in the United States generally supported the Vice President?*

Much of the campaign debate focused on what the government should do with the federal budget surplus. Bush and the Republicans wanted to give much of this money back to the public in the form of a tax cut. Democrats argued that most of Bush's tax cut would only benefit the wealthiest portion of Americans, and that the surplus should instead be used to protect Social Security and pay down the national debt.

On election night, the votes in several states were too close to call; neither candidate had captured the 270 electoral votes needed to win the presidency. One undecided state, Florida, could give either candidate enough electoral votes to win the presidency. By state law a recount of the votes was required, due to the close results. Florida became a battleground for the presidency as lawyers, politicians, and the media swarmed there to monitor the recount.

Democrats and Republicans argued bitterly over how the recount should proceed. Charges were made on both sides that the recounts were not fair or accurate. For 36 days, the nation watched, waited, and argued as the two parties engaged in a variety of court battles.

Eventually, matters reached the U.S. Supreme Court in the case of *Bush* v. *Gore*. Like the nation, the nine justices were sharply divided about how to remedy the election crisis. By a majority of five to four, they issued a ruling that discontinued all recounts in Florida. This ruling effectively secured the presidency for George W. Bush. Although Gore won the national popular vote, Bush won 271 electoral votes to Gore's 266.

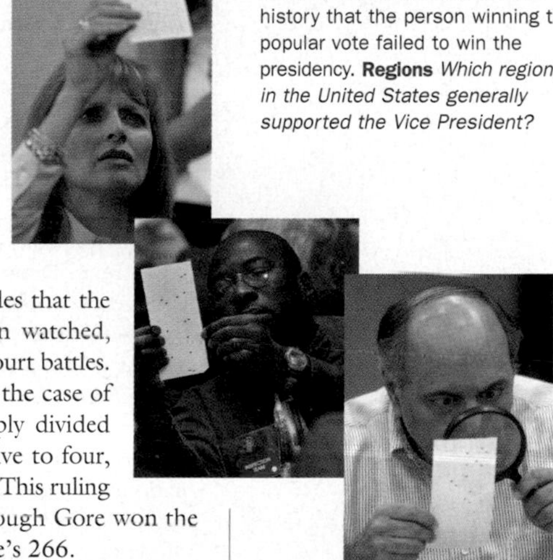

VIEWING HISTORY Election workers in Florida examined ballots to determine voter intentions during the recount that followed the close 2000 election. **Predicting Consequences** *How might the election disputes affect voting practices in the future?*

The George W. Bush Administration

After being sworn in as President in January 2001, George W. Bush faced many challenges. From the outset, he conducted the presidency in a much different style than that of his predecessor.

Change in Presidential Style Analysts described Bush's approach to the presidency as corporate in contrast to Clinton's more laid-back style. Unlike

ACTIVITY
Connecting with Culture

Have students write a short essay about the changing nature of the presidency in relation to media coverage. Tell students to consider whether they think the media should draw the line at a President's personal life. Remind students that in the last 20 or so years, the media has become increasingly aggressive and intrusive in its coverage of public officials. Ask students to examine whether they think the public needs to know the personal details of our elected officials. **(Verbal/ Linguistic)**

BACKGROUND
Impeachment

October 1998 marked only the third time that the House of Representatives has considered impeaching the President. In 1867 a radical Republican Congress passed the Tenure of Office Act, which forbade the President from firing a member of his Cabinet without congressional approval. When President Andrew Johnson dismissed his Secretary of War, the House voted to impeach, but the Senate failed to convict him by one vote.

A century later, a Democratic Congress challenged Richard Nixon over his role in the cover-up of the Watergate break-in. The House Judiciary Committee recommended impeachment on charges of obstruction of justice, abuse of power, and refusal to turn over evidence to Congress. Senior Republicans visited Nixon before the full House was to vote and informed him that he would not win a trial in the Senate. On August 9, 1974, Nixon bowed to the inevitable and resigned from office.

CUSTOMIZE FOR ...
Less Proficient Readers

Have students write two headings: Clinton and Congress. Under each heading, students should list the major goals and issues that concerned each side during Clinton's first term. Ask them to also write an outcome for each issue, noting whether one side prevailed or a compromise was reached.

CAPTION ANSWERS

Map Skills The West Coast, the upper Midwest, and the Northeast.

Viewing History Possible answers include: Legislators may push for uniform voting standards across the country, standards for voting machines may need to be implemented, media outlets that report election results may need to be more restrained.

Activity
Connecting with Government

Engage students in a discussion about the role of personality in presidential elections. Ask students to think about whether a candidate's personality should be a major factor in the election, and if so, how much. Ask students to consider why personality seems to have become increasingly important in modern elections. How does media coverage of an election shape the public's perception of the candidates? What information does the voting public use to draw conclusions about candidates? How does participation in the democratic process reflect our national identity? **(Verbal/ Linguistic)**

Background
A Country United

The terrorist attacks on the U.S. on September 11, 2001, inspired Americans to unite around the core values of American democracy. Democrats and Republicans alike stood behind the President in his quest to defend freedom. People of diverse religions supported Arab Americans who may have been targeted for hate crimes. A kind of pluralism developed among the various institutions—the President, the Congress, and the media—where before there had been animosity and dissent. Perhaps even more importantly, the American people were brought together, united around their shared shock, pain, and sympathy for all who were affected by the tragic events.

VIEWING HISTORY The new President, George W. Bush, walks with his wife Laura on Inauguration Day in 2001. **Synthesizing Information** *(a) What challenges did Bush face upon entering office? (b) What was his approach to these challenges?*

Clinton, Bush was a stickler about being on time to meetings and wearing business clothing in the White House. He kept a strict schedule and preferred to wake up early and leave the office at the end of the workday. Clinton, on the other hand, had often worked long into the night but kept a more casual atmosphere in the White House.

Bush also delegated more responsibility to advisors and staff members. Rather than focus on the tiny details of his administration's policies, Bush preferred to take a broader view, acting as a manager for his Cabinet. In addition, he gave his Vice President, Dick Cheney of Wyoming, an unprecedented role in setting policy.

Bush on Domestic Policy Early in his presidency, Bush focused on a few central issues. In particular, he succeeded in gaining congressional approval of a tax cut based on his campaign proposal. Under this plan, most taxpayers received rebates of $300. Bush argued that by returning money to the taxpayers, he would jumpstart an economy that was beginning to falter.

Bush also pushed for the passage of a major education reform bill. The President's plan called for increased accountability for student performance, flexible funding at the state and local levels, and targeted funds for improving schools and teacher quality through research-based programs and practices. It also proposed to give parents more information about the quality of their children's schools.

Attack on America

On September 11, 2001, Americans reacted with horror when terrorists struck at targets in New York City and Washington, D.C. Using hijacked commercial airplanes as their weapons, the terrorists crashed into both towers of New York's World Trade Center and plowed into part of the Pentagon. A fourth plane crashed in a field near Pittsburgh, Pennsylvania. A total of 266 passengers and crew on the four planes lost their lives.

The attack on the Pentagon took place less than an hour after the first plane hit New York. Damage was contained to a recently renovated section of the building, but fires raged for hours, preventing emergency workers from entering the wreckage. More than 100 people working in the Pentagon were killed.

In New York, the impact of the fully fueled jets caused both towers to burst into flames. Debris rained down on employees evacuating the buildings and on emergency workers rushing to respond to the scene. The fires led to the catastrophic collapse of both 110-story buildings. The fallen structures in turn caused serious damage to other buildings in the World Trade Center complex and the surrounding area. More than 5,000 people were missing after the assault and were presumed dead.

Following the attacks, the Federal Aviation Administration ordered a nationwide "ground stop." This action halted all takeoffs and required airborne planes to land as quickly as possible. Many incoming international flights were diverted to Canada.

On the ground in New York, emergency workers battled fires and began a search-and-rescue operation. Tragically, the speedy response to the disaster had led to the deaths of hundreds of firefighters and police officers who were in and around the buildings when they collapsed.

While no groups or individuals claimed responsibility for the attacks, law-enforcement officials immediately began an investigation into those suspected of carrying out the assaults and the network that supported them. Countries around the world pledged their support in the efforts to hunt down the criminals.

Caption Answers

Viewing History (a) Bush had to make many Americans comfortable with his victory in a hotly debated and controversial election. He needed to define the presidency as his own after eight years of Clinton. (b) He promised to work across party lines and find a center ground on many issues. Bush's presidential style greatly differed from Clinton's, thereby setting the two apart.

Resource Directory

Teaching Resources

Units 5/6/7 booklet
- Section 1 Quiz, p. 123

Guide to the Essentials
- Section 1 Summary, p. 132

Technology

Sounds of an Era Audio CD *George W. Bush Inauguration Speech* (time: one minute)

Exploring Primary Sources in U.S. History CD-ROM *Inaugural Address, President George W. Bush*

In a speech to the nation, President Bush declared, "Whether we bring our enemies to justice or bring justice to our enemies, justice will be done." Bush also named a new Cabinet-level Office of Homeland Security, to be headed by Pennsylvania Governor Tom Ridge.

Within days of the attack, government officials named Saudi dissident Osama bin Laden as "a prime suspect" for masterminding the plot. Bin Laden had been implicated in a series of earlier attacks on U.S. targets, including the U.S. embassies in Kenya and Tanzania and the American ship the USS *Cole*. Bin Laden was believed to be hiding in Afghanistan under the protection of the Taliban, a religious fundamentalist group that ruled Afghanistan. The United States demanded that the Taliban shut down terrorist training camps and turn over bin Laden and other terrorist leaders. The Taliban refused to meet these demands, and as a result, President Bush vowed that they would "pay a price."

On October 7, the United States, along with Great Britain, launched a bombing campaign known as "Operation Enduring Freedom" on Taliban military and communications bases. At the same time, U.S. planes also dropped humanitarian packages of food and supplies for starving Afghan civilians. President Bush made it clear that these bombings were only the beginning of a relentless pursuit to rid the world of terrorism and those who support it.

On the homefront, Americans responded to the tragedy with an outpouring of support for the victims, their families, and the rescue workers at all three sites. Many gave blood or donated money and supplies to relief agencies. The country stood united in its grief, with millions attending vigils and services for the victims. As American citizens struggled to make sense of the terrible events and mourned the losses, a new sense of patriotism and unity swept the nation. Suddenly, American flags appeared on homes, cars, businesses, and public spaces—a symbol of the nation's determination to seek justice, uphold American values, and emerge from adversity strengthened and whole.

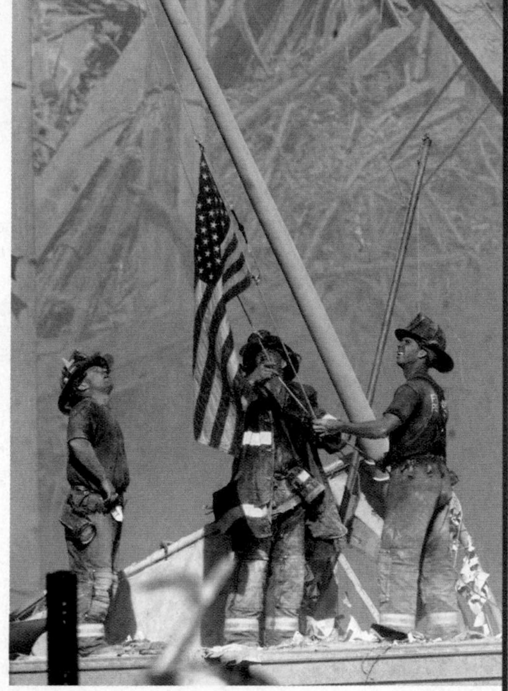

Rescue workers proudly raise the American flag amidst the rubble of the fallen World Trade Center towers.

Section 1 Assessment

READING COMPREHENSION

1. Why did many American voters support Clinton in 1992?
2. What was the Republicans' **Contract with America?**
3. How did scandals such as the **Whitewater affair** and impeachment affect Clinton's presidency?
4. How did the presidential styles of Bill Clinton and George W. Bush differ?
5. What actions did President Bush take following a terrorist attack on America?

CRITICAL THINKING AND WRITING

6. **Recognizing Ideologies** Democrats and Republicans had many bitter confrontations and much partisan debate throughout the 1990s. On what issues did they differ? Why do you think there was a high level of bitterness between the two parties?
7. **Writing a Letter to the Editor** Write a letter to your local newspaper explaining why you think the results of the 2000 election were controversial. Suggest ideas about how to avoid this situation in the future.

Take It to the NET

Activity: Creating a Bar Graph
The economy played a key role in American politics during the 1990s. Research an economic variable, such as the unemployment rate, and plot its performance over the past five years. Use the links provided in the *America: Pathways to the Present* area of the following Web site for help in completing this activity.
www.phschool.com

Section 1 Assessment

Reading Comprehension

1. He promised to end the recession and deal with other economic problems, including the federal budget deficit and a health care system in disarray. Campaigning as a "New Democrat," Clinton appealed to Americans who were frustrated by partisan disagreements in Congress. His youth and energy appealed to voters.
2. A pledge to reduce the role of the federal government, eliminate some regulations, cut taxes, and balance the budget.
3. These scandals did not seem to deter Clinton. His popularity remained high, possibly due in part to the economic boom.
4. Bush's style was more formal and "by the books" than Clinton's laid-back manner. Bush delegated more responsibility to advisors and staff members than Clinton had. Bush also gave his Vice President an unprecedented role in setting policy.
5. He appointed Governor Tom Ridge to head a new Cabinet-level Office of Homeland Security. After giving Taliban leaders the chance to shut down terrorist training camps and turn over terrorists leaders, including bin Laden, to no avail, Bush launched Operation Enduring Freedom.

Critical Thinking and Writing

6. The two parties generally differed on economic issues: balancing the budget, where to cut spending, and the size of government, as well as on the issue of impeachment. Answers describing reasons for the existing bitterness will vary, but should refer to the parties' respective histories, as well as the events of the 1990s.
7. Answers will vary, but should be supported by facts from the section.

Take It to the NET

Answers will vary, but should effectively use either a bar graph or a line graph to track the changes in an economic variable such as unemployment, national income, or government budget.

Predicting Consequences

Focus Students will use the statistics in a table to predict patterns of population growth and median income for three ethnic groups.

Instruct Have students examine the title and headings in the table. Make sure that they understand what the numbers in the Percent Change columns mean. Explain, for example, that the percentage in the 1995 row covers the period from 1990 to 1995. Ask students to compare the percentages for the three ethnic groups and to note any differences among them.

Extend See the Skills for Life Activity in the Resource Directory below.

ANSWERS

Practice the Skill

1. **(a)** It tells the changes in population and in income over time. **(b)** 1980–1995. **(c)** 26.2. **(d)** More than half the families in that group earn less than the median income for the other group.
2. **(a)** Latinos. **(b)** African Americans. **(c)** Latinos.
3. **(a)** The rapid increase in the number of Latino families between 1980 and 1995 reflects the continuing rise in the number of immigrants coming from Latin America after 1965. **(b)** The number of Latino families in the United States is likely to grow at a much faster rate than the number of white or African American families. **(c)** Latino families. **(d)** Sample answer: If the number of Latino families dropped significantly or if the Latino median income stabilized.

Predicting Consequences

Predicting consequences means studying what has happened in the past, and using this knowledge to try to forecast what might happen in the future. Social scientists use this skill to predict trends. They study data from the census and other statistical sources and then relate patterns in the data to historical events. For example, what has the rate of population growth been over recent decades? What does this suggest about the rate of population growth in the next few years? What events have affected this growth? Which groups are likely to grow faster and which groups are likely to grow more slowly? The table at right answers some of these questions.

Change in Number of Families and Median Income,* by Selected Ethnic Groups, 1980–1995

	Year	Number of Families (in thousands)	Percent Change (from preceding census)	Median Income (in dollars)	Percent Change (from preceding census)
White Families	1980	52,710	—	40,561	—
	1990	56,803	+7.8	43,044	+6.1
	1995	58,872	+3.6	42,646	−1.0
African American Families	1980	6,317	—	23,469	—
	1990	7,471	+18.3	24,980	+6.4
	1995	8,055	+7.8	25,970	+4.0
Latino Families	1980	3,235	—	27,251	—
	1990	4,981	+54.0	27,321	+0.3
	1995	6,287	+26.2	24,570	−10.0

* In 1995 dollars. Median income represents the center of the income distribution—exactly half of the families in the group earn more and half earn less than the median income.

SOURCE: *Statistical Abstract of the United States*

LEARN THE SKILL

Use the following steps to predict consequences from a table:

1. **Identify the kinds of information in the table.** Determine what is being measured by the data in the table. Note the time span of the table and the time intervals it shows.
2. **Analyze the rate of change.** Compare the rate, or percent, of change of different ethnic groups at different time periods.
3. **Use your knowledge of history and the trends you have noted in the data to predict future trends.** Determine whether some of the changes and trends you have found in the data were the consequences of particular historical events. In this case, consider the Immigration Act of 1965, which allowed more people from places other than Europe to immigrate to the United States, and the Immigration Act of 1990, which further increased immigration quotas by 40 percent.

PRACTICE THE SKILL

Answer the following questions:

1. **(a)** What does this table tell you about the number of families in various ethnic groups in the United States? **(b)** What periods of time does the table cover? **(c)** By what percentage did the number of Latino families increase between 1990 and 1995? **(d)** What does it mean if one group has a lower median income than another group?
2. **(a)** Which group of families is growing at the fastest rate? **(b)** Which group's median income has grown at the fastest rate? **(c)** Which group seems the most economically vulnerable—that is, which has the least stable median income?
3. **(a)** How might the table illustrate the effects of the 1965 law? **(b)** What consequences might the 1990 law have by the year 2010? **(c)** If an economic recession began early in the twenty-first century, which group's median income would you expect to drop the most? **(d)** What changes in the trends shown on the table would have to take place in order to alter your predictions?

APPLY THE SKILL

See the Chapter Review and Assessment for another opportunity to apply this skill.

RESOURCE DIRECTORY

Teaching Resources
Skills for Life booklet, p. 36

Technology
Social Studies Skills Tutor CD-ROM
Interactive Practice in
- Geographic Literacy
- Critical Thinking and Reading
- Visual Analysis
- Communications

Section

2 The United States in a New World

READING FOCUS

- What political changes took place in the world in the 1990s?
- How did the Clinton administration promote peace abroad?
- Describe U.S. relations with China.
- What was the impact of an expanding global economy?

KEY TERMS

apartheid
economic sanctions
North American Free Trade Agreement (NAFTA)
World Trade Organization (WTO)
multinational corporation

TAKING NOTES

As you read, complete this chart showing the role of the United States in events around the world.

Nation or Region	U.S. Role
Iraq	As part of the United Nations, continued attempts to promote peace in the region. Launched air strikes, implemented economic sanctions, sent inspectors to ensure Iraq's dangerous weapons were destroyed.
Israel	
The Balkans	
China	
North America	

MAIN IDEA

The United States faced new challenges in the post–Cold War world, including the collapse of communism, increased ethnic tensions in several countries, and the expansion of the global economy.

Setting the Scene Witnessing the collapse of communism in the Soviet Union and Eastern Europe, President George H. W. Bush had spoken hopefully of the dawn of a "New World Order" in 1990. By this he had meant a more stable and peaceful world in which "the strong respect the rights of the weak." Many people believed, however, that the world was becoming less stable. While some nations had thrown off repressive governments and become more democratic, others were being torn apart by racial, cultural, or religious tensions. A few observers joked grimly of a "New World Disorder."

Political Changes Worldwide

In the 1980s, communism in the Soviet Union and racial oppression in South Africa had seemed like permanent world problems. For decades they had helped shape American foreign policy. By the late 1990s, however, revolutionary events had changed conditions in these and other nations.

Russia and Eastern Europe As the old Soviet empire crumbled, the United States tried to promote the move toward Western-style democracy in the former Soviet republics. For example, it applauded the election that brought Boris Yeltsin to power as president of Russia.

To help Russia create a free market economy, the international community offered billions in aid, but it was far from enough. Goods remained in short supply and the Russian economy remained unstable. In the fall of 1993, the Russian parliament resisted reforms that Yeltsin argued were necessary. In response, he dissolved the parliament and tightened censorship in a bid to silence his political opponents.

Russian reformers, angry at these curbs on freedom, soon grew angrier. In 1994, Yeltsin ordered troops into Chechnya, a republic that sought independence from Russia. After nearly two years of

VIEWING HISTORY The Russian president, Boris Yeltsin, addresses a crowd in 1993. **Identifying Central Issues** *How did Russia change after the Cold War?*

RESOURCE DIRECTORY

Teaching Resources
Learning Styles Lesson Plans booklet, p. 70
Guided Reading and Review booklet, p. 138

Other Print Resources
Historical Outline Map Book *The World,* p. 71

Section 2 The United States in a New World

SECTION OBJECTIVES

1. Read about political changes that took place in the world in the 1990s.
2. Find out how the Clinton administration promoted peace abroad.
3. Describe U.S. relations with China.
4. Discover the impact of an expanding global economy.

BELLRINGER

Warm-Up Activity Ask students what countries they have heard about in the news in the last few weeks. What problems are making news? Do they involve the United States? What is the responsibility of the United States to those countries?

Activating Prior Knowledge Ask students to state their opinions about the responsibility of the United States to become engaged in international struggles. In their opinion, what constitutes a situation that demands a direct military response from the United States?

READING STRATEGY

Before students read the section, have them sketch a rough outline map of the world. As they read, have them highlight areas of United States involvement and write a brief note explaining the region's connection to the United States. Have them describe the dynamic relationship between U.S. international trade policies and the U.S. free enterprise system.

CAPTION ANSWERS

Viewing History Russia began a move toward Western-style democracy. However, continuing economic problems (despite American aid) created unrest.

Lesson Plan

Focus Explain that for 50 years American foreign policy had been based on Cold War philosophy. Now the nation had to find new ways of dealing with many nations around the world. Ask students how this "new world" offered both hopes and challenges.

Instruct Explain that Americans have a long history of ambivalence about involvement in foreign affairs. Ask students if world events have made such a stand impossible today. How does an isolationist stance affect policies and positions on trade? Discuss the position of the United States as the world's remaining superpower. What are the responsibilities of that position?

Assess/Reteach Ask students to consider the kinds of changes that have resulted from political shifts, an increase in ethnic tensions, a rise in worldwide terrorism, and an increasing emphasis on a global economy.

READING CHECK
The war in Chechnya damaged Boris Yeltsin's political standing. However, a renewal of hostilities in the same region increased the popularity of Vladimir Putin (Yeltsin's successor).

READING CHECK
How did the conflict in Chechnya affect politics in Russia?

fierce fighting, a cease-fire was finally reached, and the Russian troops were withdrawn. With an already ailing economy, charges of government corruption, and thousands of people killed in Chechnya, Yeltsin lost much of his public support.

In 1999, the conflict over Chechnya became the source of great public support for Vladimir Putin, whom Yeltsin had appointed Russia's prime minister. A series of Chechen terrorist attacks in Russia that year prompted Putin to order air raids and a full-scale ground invasion against Chechnya. This act was widely popular in Russia, and political parties that were allied with Putin performed well in that year's parliamentary elections. Yeltsin, in poor health, resigned his post at the end of the year, making Putin the acting president of Russia. In the next presidential election, Russian voters officially elected Putin their new president.

Political changes also continued to occur in Eastern Europe. In the early 1990s, Poland, led by Solidarity hero Lech Walesa, had undertaken bold economic reforms to create a free market. Economic progress was initially slow and many people quickly grew concerned. In 1995, Polish voters elected Aleksander Kwasniewski as president. Despite his Communist background, Kwasniewski continued to push for a free market economy. Eventually the economy began to rebound.

In a clear sign that there was no returning to the past, Poland, Hungary, and the Czech Republic all joined NATO in 1999. NATO held out hope of membership to other former Communist nations in the region if they continued to make progress toward democracy.

F. W. de Klerk and Nelson Mandela shared the 1993 Nobel peace prize for their work in ending apartheid.

South Africa As stunning as the collapse of communism was South Africa's rejection of **apartheid,** the systematic separation of people of different racial backgrounds. South Africa's white minority, which made up only about 15 percent of the population, had long denied equal rights to the black majority. To encourage reform, the United States and other nations had used **economic sanctions,** or trade restrictions and economic measures intended to punish another nation. Finally, in 1990, Prime Minister F. W. de Klerk released anti-apartheid leader Nelson Mandela from jail. Mandela had been held prisoner for 27 years.

Former rivals de Klerk and Mandela worked together to end apartheid. In 1994, South Africa held its first elections in which blacks as well as whites voted. These elections produced a new government, led by a new president, Nelson Mandela, and his anti-apartheid organization, the African National Congress (ANC). Despite fears of civil war, South Africa made a peaceful transition to black majority rule.

From 1996 to 1998, a government-appointed Truth and Reconciliation Commission investigated the brutal crimes of the apartheid era. Its final report, published in 1998, won international praise for addressing wrongdoings on both sides and for continuing the nation's move toward peace.

The Difficult Search for Peace

For the United States, promoting the spread of democracy to new areas was a satisfying challenge. Far less satisfying was the task of trying to stop the terrifying violence that erupted in several different regions of the world. President Clinton had to balance Americans' desire to promote peace with their fear of costly commitments—a fear magnified by memories of the Vietnam War.

One conflict in Africa demonstrated how hard it was to maintain this balance. In the early 1990s, the East African nation of Somalia suffered from a devastating famine, made worse by a civil war. President Bush sent American

RESOURCE DIRECTORY

Other Print Resources

American History Block Scheduling Support *The End of the Cold War,* found in The Nation After World War II folder, includes interdisciplinary lesson suggestions and activities for Geography and History, Primary Sources, Biography, and Literature.

Historical Outline Map Book *Africa,* p. 74; *Europe,* p. 77; *The Middle East,* p. 78

troops to Somalia in 1992 to assist a United Nations (UN) relief effort. The food crisis eased, but Somalia's government remained unable to control the armed groups that ruled the countryside. The following year, after more than a dozen United States soldiers were killed in a battle with Somali rebels, President Clinton recalled the troops without having restored order.

Israel In September 1993, Palestine Liberation Organization (PLO) leader Yasir Arafat and Israeli Prime Minister Yitzhak Rabin signed a historic peace agreement in Washington, D.C. It was an extremely difficult step for both sides. However, as Rabin noted, "Peace is not made with friends. Peace is made with enemies."

President Clinton presided over the signing of the 1993 peace accord between Israel's Yitzhak Rabin (left) and the PLO's Yasir Arafat (right).

The pact provided for Palestinian self-rule in the Gaza Strip (between Israel and the Sinai Peninsula) and in the town of Jericho on the West Bank of the Jordan River. The agreement also set the stage for talks on the status of the rest of the West Bank. Israel had seized these areas in the Six-Day War of 1967. Also in the agreement, the PLO formally recognized Israel's right to exist.

The Middle East peace process had other successes. In 1994, Israel and Jordan signed a treaty ending the state of war that had existed between them. Israel and Syria began talks as well.

Extremists on both sides, meanwhile, tried to destroy the prospects for peace by committing terrorist attacks. In 1995, a Jewish extremist assassinated Prime Minister Rabin.

Benjamin Netanyahu, Israel's next elected prime minister, was more reluctant than Rabin to grant concessions to the Palestinians. Progress toward a peace agreement slowed. In 1999, though, Ehud Barak became prime minister and called for a new commitment to peace talks. The following year, President Clinton invited Barak and Arafat to Camp David in an effort to settle the issues that still divided them. While the two sides had made tremendous progress since their 1993 agreement, they were unable to solve all the remaining issues, such as control of the holy city of Jerusalem.

Hopes for peace then faded rapidly. Violence increased, and Ariel Sharon—a fierce critic of the concessions Israel had made in the search for peace—became Israeli prime minister after a landslide victory over Barak. Violence continued in 2001 as the new Bush administration worked on other ways to keep the peace process alive.

The Balkans The United States played a key role in the peacekeeping process elsewhere as well. One place where peace seemed especially difficult to achieve was Yugoslavia, a nation of several distinct ethnic and religious groups.

READING CHECK
Why did it seem that peacekeeping in the former Yugoslavia would be especially difficult?

Tensions among these groups had remained below the surface for several decades, while a Communist government ruled Yugoslavia. With the collapse of communism, however, these underlying problems erupted, resulting in violent conflict.

Some of the Yugoslav republics, like Bosnia and Croatia, wanted to become independent nations. The republic of Serbia—and its leader, Slobodan Milosevic—wanted to preserve a unified Yugoslavia, dominated by Serbia. A minority of the Bosnians were ethnic Serbs; they, too, opposed independence for Bosnia. Thus, when Bosnia declared its independence in 1991, the Bosnian Serbs took military action. Backed by Serbia, the Bosnian Serbs began a siege of Sarajevo, Bosnia's major city, and carried on a ferocious "ethnic cleansing" campaign to remove

ACTIVITY
Connecting with Geography

Ask students to suppose that they are foreign correspondents for radio or television news. Divide students into groups and assign (or let students choose) one of the regions mentioned in the section. Each group should research recent newspaper and magazine articles about events in its region, then prepare a report to broadcast back to the United States, explaining the situation there. **(Verbal/Linguistic)**

BACKGROUND
A Diverse Nation

"[Africa is] where we came from, it's where civilization started. How can we turn our backs on it?" said George Curry, editor of the African American magazine *Emerge.* He spoke for many African Americans for whom South African history has been painfully relevant. One South African who attracted worldwide admiration was Nelson Mandela (b. 1918). Despite years of imprisonment under apartheid, Mandela emerged as a consummate peacemaker. For working to end apartheid, he shared the 1993 Nobel peace prize with white South African leader F. W. de Klerk. In 1994 Mandela became South Africa's President after a landslide victory in its first democratic, all-race election.

TEST PREPARATION

Have students read the section "South Africa" and then answer the question below.

What was one of the results of South Africa's rejection of apartheid?

A Civil war broke out.
B A dictator was installed.
C Riots broke out, spreading to all major cities.
(D) There was a peaceful transition of power.

ACTIVITY
Connecting with History and Conflict

The futures of nations in crisis or transition often depend greatly on strong leaders. Have students select a leader in one of the countries in the news today and research his or her biography for a short essay or oral report. **(Verbal/Linguistic)**

BACKGROUND
Geography in History

In the 1990s Serb leaders sent troops into the province of Kosovo to crush an independence movement among its ethnic Albanian majority. The poor, mountainous region was the heart of the medieval Serb kingdom that was defeated by the Ottoman Turks in 1389. Although Serbs have become a tiny minority in Kosovo, the province is still home to several historic monasteries and the battlefield where Serbia was defeated. The Muslim Albanians who live in Kosovo do not wish to remain part of Yugoslavia, and thousands were driven from their homes as a result of the fighting.

READING CHECK

NATO used air strikes against Serbia to force Serbia's leader to allow an international peacekeeping force to enter Kosovo.

The Former Yugoslavia, 1998

MAP SKILLS This map shows the regions of Bosnia and Herzegovina controlled by various groups. At right, U.S. soldiers patrol the village of Curenica in Kosovo, as part of a NATO peacekeeping operation. **Regions** *How does the map demonstrate the problems facing the former Yugoslavia?*

non-Serbs from the republic. Millions were forced to flee their homes, and more than 200,000 people were killed in the most brutal violence seen in Europe since World War II.

When Clinton campaigned for President in 1992, he had promised to take strong action in Bosnia. Once in office, however, he hesitated, partly because America's European allies resisted the use of force. Finally, in mid-1995, an American-led NATO bombing campaign pushed the Bosnian Serbs into peace talks. These talks, held in Dayton, Ohio, produced a cease-fire and the commitment to allow foreign peacekeeping troops, including thousands of U.S. troops.

Although these steps toward peace had been taken, none of the underlying problems had gone away. New troubles began in Kosovo, another part of the former Yugoslavia. As in Bosnia, the majority population of Kosovo was not Serbian. Most people living there were ethnic Albanians, and they wanted more self-rule. That demand led to another brutal round of violence, this time between Serbs and ethnic Albanians.

Thousands of ethnic Albanian refugees fled Kosovo in 1998 as the fighting spread. For a time the Kosovo Liberation Army managed to occupy nearly half of Kosovo. The Serbs then took control and began a violent campaign closely resembling their actions in Bosnia.

In 1999, the United States and NATO threatened airstrikes if both sides would not commit to a peace conference. The Kosovar Albanians agreed but the Serbs did not. Acting on its threat, NATO launched a series of airstrikes against Serbia, which forced Serbian leader Milosevic to allow an international peacekeeping force to enter Kosovo. The Albanian refugees were able to return home.

Meanwhile, Serbian opposition to Milosevic was growing. In 2000, voters overwhelmingly rejected Milosevic and declared Vojislav Kostunica their new leader. When Milosevic refused to accept the election results, many Serbs organized a revolt and forced him from power. Reaction around the world was generally positive. Not only Western nations, but also Russia (which had backed Milosevic) welcomed Kostunica as Yugoslavia's new leader. The next year, Milosevic was indicted by an international tribunal for war crimes and taken to the Netherlands to stand trial.

Northern Ireland In Northern Ireland, the United States encouraged renewed efforts in the 1990s to end decades of violence between Protestants and Catholics. In 1996, President Clinton asked former U.S. Senator George Mitchell to lead talks that included representatives of the warring factions and the British and Irish governments.

After months of tense negotiations, Mitchell's efforts paid off. In 1998, all major parties to the peace process signed the Good Friday Accords, agreeing to major reforms in the government of the British province. By large majorities, voters in both Northern Ireland and Ireland later approved the agreement. It stopped short of unifying the two Irelands, which Catholics had desired. Still, it offered the best hope yet for ending the violence.

CAPTION ANSWERS

Map Skills The map shows that, after the dissolution of their strong central government, many groups in the Yugoslav republics competed for political power and control over land.

RESOURCE DIRECTORY

Technology

RESOURCE PRO® Visual Learning Activity *Clinton's Foreign Policy,* found on Resource Pro, uses a cartoon to illustrate the problems that can result from a policy of exclusively supporting one candidate in foreign elections.

Other Print Resources

Historical Outline Map Book *Asia,* p. 75; *East Asia,* p. 76

Iraq After the Gulf War Despite Iraq's defeat in the Persian Gulf War, Iraqi leader Sadaam Hussein continued to oppress opposition groups within the country. He also refused to cooperate fully with UN inspectors sent to Iraq to ensure that the nation destroyed its most dangerous weapons.

President Clinton called for a new government in Iraq, one "committed to peace." UN forces launched several missile and aircraft attacks on Iraq in the 1990s. The United Nations also maintained the economic sanctions it had imposed on Iraq after Iraq's invasion of Kuwait. Over time, however, support for these sanctions began to weaken. By cutting off most of Iraq's trade, it was feared, the sanctions hurt the Iraqi people far more than the Iraqi government. To help deal with this problem, the United Nations set up an "oil-for-food" program, in which Iraq could export small amounts of oil in exchange for food and materials that would help them to grow food. Still, a decade after the Persian Gulf War, UN and U.S. officials were not convinced that any real progress had been made toward a free and peaceful Iraq.

READING CHECK What challenges did the United States face in trying to ensure peace in Iraq?

Afghanistan Afghanistan became a focal point for the United States after the Soviet invasion of that nation in 1979. The Soviets, located on the Afghan border, considered internal agitation there a threat to their own security. The United States responded by boycotting the 1980 Olympic Games in Moscow and withdrawing the SALT II arms control treaty from the American Senate. The campaign proved unsuccessful, and eventually the Soviet Union withdrew. In 1996, a group of Muslim fundamentalists, called the Taliban, seized the Afghan capital of Kabul from the ruling pro-Soviet government. The Taliban sought to set up what their leaders considered a pure Islamic state, banning such things as television and music. The Taliban also provided sanctuary for Osama bin Laden, the wealthy Saudi Arabian businessman exiled from his own country and implicated in the terrorist bombings of September 11, 2001.

Relations With China

While the United States attempted to help the peace process within other nations, it also sought to remain on peaceful terms with China. China's economic growth, combined with its size, made it an increasingly important power in the 1990s. As a result, the United States began working more closely with China on various issues, including trade and regional security. However, underlying tensions between the two nations remained just below the surface.

Probably the greatest source of tension was the issue of Taiwan. China viewed Taiwan as part of China and refused to rule out the use of force to gain control of the island. In particular, China warned Taiwan not to declare its independence from the mainland. The United States, on the other hand, was a major supplier of weapons to Taiwan and opposed any military action by China against Taiwan.

In 1996, as Taiwan was preparing for elections, China held missile tests and military exercises in an effort to frighten Taiwanese voters away from supporting a pro-independence candidate. President Clinton responded by sending warships to the area to show the commitment of the United States to Taiwan. Relations continued to sour in 1999 when NATO warplanes mistakenly bombed the Chinese embassy in Belgrade during its airstrikes on Yugoslavia.

Relations improved later that year, when the United States and China worked on ways to expand China's trade

VIEWING HISTORY In April 1999, the United States and China agreed to expand commercial air service between the two nations. Here, Secretary of State Madeleine Albright shakes hands with Chinese Foreign Minister Tang Jiaxuan after signing the agreement. **Drawing Conclusions** *Why was the United States interested in expanding trade with China?*

ACTIVITY

Connecting with Geography

Tell students to choose one of the areas discussed on this page. Then have students conduct research to find out about the current political climate in the area they have selected. Ask students to present an oral report on their findings. **(Verbal/Linguistic)**

BACKGROUND

Recent Scholarship

In *Making Peace,* former U.S. Senator George Mitchell gives a personal account of his two-year journey to bring peace to Northern Ireland. Mitchell describes the painstaking efforts that were necessary to bring the various factions to the peace table. He recalls the ups and downs of the negotiations and the ongoing outbursts of violence. Nonetheless, all of the parties finally came together to approve the Good Friday peace accord, designed to end the conflict in the war-torn region.

CUSTOMIZE FOR ...

ESL

Ask students to write the names of the following countries on a sheet of paper: Canada, Mexico, Russia, Bosnia, Haiti, Israel, South Africa. After each one, have them write a sentence describing American foreign policy in the mid-1990s related to that country.

CAPTION ANSWERS

Viewing History American policymakers, aware of China's vast size and expanding economy, wished to remain on friendly terms with China's leaders. In spite of underlying tensions, both nations worked to improve and expand relations, including opening up trade.

ACTIVITY
Connecting with Economics

Have students learn more about the eurodollar. Tell students to find newspaper and magazine articles describing European reaction to the euro. Which countries easily accepted the euro and which resisted it? What does a country's response to the eurodollar say about its self-image, its economy, and its willingness to join the European Union? **(Logical/Mathematical)**

BACKGROUND
Trade Blocs

NAFTA is not the only trade bloc in the Western Hemisphere. The Caribbean region has the Association of Caribbean States (ACS), while Argentina's Carlos Menem has worked to create Mercosur, the Southern Common Market, with Argentina's neighbors Brazil, Paraguay, and Uruguay. In the Pacific, ASEAN (Association of Southeast Asian Nations) is emerging as an economic bloc.

READING CHECK

The EEC was established in 1957 to foster trade and economic development. The evolution of this entity into the European Union was an effort to create a European system to coordinate political, monetary, and economic issues.

President George W. Bush consults with National Security Advisor Condoleezza Rice in the Oval Office of the White House.

with other nations. In 2000, President Clinton signed the U.S.-China Relations Act. This act was designed to encourage trade between the two nations by keeping U.S. tariffs on Chinese imports low.

Tensions grew again, however, in April 2001 when a U.S. spy plane and a Chinese fighter plane collided off the coast of China. The incident led to a standoff between the two governments, leaving relations between them strained. The new Bush administration stated, moreover, that the United States would defend Taiwan from military attacks by China, a policy that previous Presidents had not declared openly. China, in turn, warned the United States against sales of advanced weapons to Taiwan.

Trade and the Global Economy

Despite the many political developments of the mid- and late 1990s, the most important development in global terms may have been economic: the continuing growth of world trade. The United States was active in promoting this trend.

READING CHECK
Why did some European nations want to form the European Union?

The European Union In 1957, six European nations had set up the European Economic Community (EEC) to coordinate their economic and trade policies. Over time, other nations had joined them. Meanwhile, member nations agreed to move toward dismantling the tariffs on one another's exports, thereby creating a single market.

In 1993, the EEC nations formed the European Union (EU) to begin coordinating their political and monetary policies as well. The EU, now with more than a dozen members, has a parliament and a council in which all member nations are represented. In the late 1990s, member nations agreed to replace their individual monetary systems gradually with a single new currency called the eurodollar, or euro.

The EU's goal is to create a European economic unit that rivals the size and strength of the American economy. The United States has generally supported Europe's progress toward economic cooperation. As a Clinton administration official stated, "Close partnership between the United States and the European Union is essential to our common agenda of democratic renewal." Today, the EU's largest trading partner is the United States.

NAFTA Meanwhile, the United States sought to encourage greater economic cooperation within the Western Hemisphere. Many economists believed that free

RESOURCE DIRECTORY

Teaching Resources

Biography, Literature, and Comparing Primary Sources booklet (Biography) *Ron Brown,* p. 39

Great Debates booklet (Great Debates) *Building an International Manned Space Station,* p. 48

Other Print Resources

Historical Outline Map Book *Western Hemisphere,* p. 72; *North America,* p. 79

trade would benefit the economy by encouraging foreign investment, reducing prices, raising exports, and improving living standards. In 1992, the United States, Canada, and Mexico signed the **North American Free Trade Agreement (NAFTA),** which called for a gradual removal of trade restrictions among the three nations. NAFTA's main purpose was to stimulate economic growth. The resulting free trade zone created a single market similar to the market of the European Union.

NAFTA aroused tremendous controversy in the United States. Its opponents worried that American factories would move to Mexico, where wages were lower and government regulations (such as environmental controls) were less strict. Its supporters claimed that it would instead create more American jobs by increasing exports to Mexico and Canada.

The U.S. Senate ratified NAFTA, but only after a bruising battle. After NAFTA had been in effect for several years, the government's first study of the agreement revealed it to be only a limited success. The report cited a "modest" increase in United States exports to Mexico and estimated that perhaps 90,000 to 160,000 new, NAFTA-related jobs had been created. Some 128,000 American jobs had disappeared, however. Even with these mixed results, President Clinton and others continued their efforts to expand NAFTA to include other countries in the Western Hemisphere.

GATT and the WTO Clinton's support for NAFTA reflected his foreign policy goal of expanding United States trade throughout the world. As part of this effort, the United States joined many other countries in adopting a revised version of the General Agreement on Tariffs and Trade (GATT) in 1994. The goal of GATT, originally established in 1948, was to reduce tariffs and expand world trade. In 1995, the **World Trade Organization (WTO)** was established to ensure that countries complied with GATT, as well as to negotiate new trade agreements and resolve trade disputes.

The reaction to the WTO was similar to the reaction to NAFTA. Many people supported these efforts to expand world trade, but resistance to these efforts was growing. In late 1999, anti-WTO demonstrators gathered from around the world in Seattle, where the WTO was meeting to plan a new round

Focus on ECONOMICS

Tariffs *Taxes on foreign goods imported into a country.*

The Historical Context In the 1980s and 1990s, a number of governments worked together to reduce tariffs in the hope that expanded trade would stimulate economic growth. These efforts resulted in regional trade agreements, such as NAFTA, and the formation of the World Trade Organization to resolve trade disputes.

The Concept Today Tariffs remain a controversial issue. Some Americans worry that as American tariffs are lowered, jobs will shift from the United States to less-developed nations. Other Americans, in contrast, argue that lower tariffs worldwide will boost American exports and create new jobs.

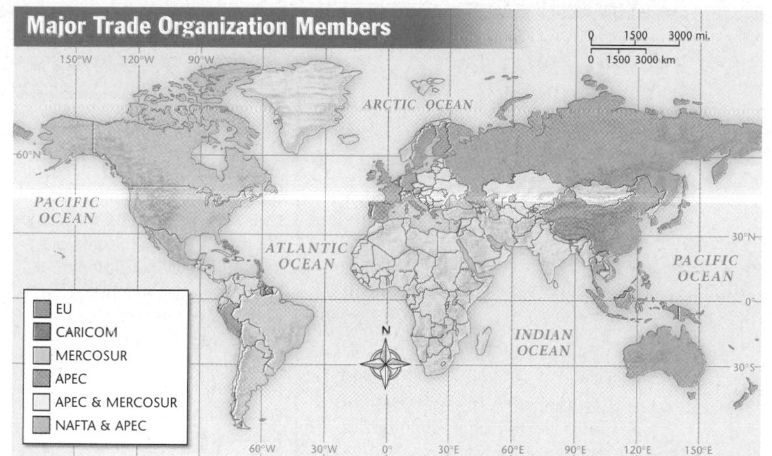

MAP SKILLS Many countries are members of major regional trade organizations including the Caribbean Community and Common Market (CARICOM), the Southern Common Market (MERCOSUR), and the Asia Pacific Economic Cooperation (APEC). **Regions** *(a) How are trade organizations divided geographically? (b) What is the purpose of these organizations?*

ACTIVITY

Connecting with Economics

Tell students to research recent trends in U.S. foreign trade. Have students learn who our trading partners are. Which countries import most to the U.S.? Which countries receive U.S. exports? What products are imported and exported to the U.S.? Have small groups create a visual aid to display the information that they have uncovered. **(Visual/Spatial)**

BACKGROUND

The Fight for Free Trade

Most congressional Democrats did not endorse Clinton's support of NAFTA. In fact, Clinton faced a steep uphill battle in his campaign to pass the free trade bill. While Republicans were largely in favor of free trade, most Democrats opposed it. Clinton won the fight by rallying southern Democrats and Republicans to unite against the rest of the Democrats. Historians call this effort the great *New Democratic* victory of Clinton's first Congress. Although Clinton won the battle, his triumph resulted in his alienation from his own party.

CAPTION ANSWERS

Map Skills (a) They are divided mostly by region. (b) Their purposes vary, but most support economic cooperation, such as the lowering of trade barriers between member nations.

Section 2 Assessment

Reading Comprehension

1. They hoped that economic sanctions might encourage reform.
2. Possible answers: Participating in UN relief efforts in Somalia; U.S. activity in support of resolving the conflict in Kosovo; sponsoring George Mitchell's activities in regard to seeking peace in Northern Ireland.
3. Taiwan: China viewed Taiwan as part of China. On the other hand, the United States was a major supplier of weapons to Taiwan and opposed any military action by China against Taiwan.
4. European Union: To create a European economic unit that rivals that of the American economy. NAFTA: To stimulate economic growth within the Western Hemisphere through the gradual removal of trade restrictions between the United States, Canada, and Mexico. WTO: To ensure that countries complied with GATT and to negotiate new trade agreements and resolve trade disputes.

Critical Thinking and Writing

5. Many Americans believe that these efforts lead to the loss of jobs in the United States as businesses relocate their factories to nations where operating costs are far lower. Some Americans also feel that international trade expansion makes business too powerful, at the expense of workers' rights and the environment.
6. The role of the United States as peacekeeper in nations around the world and the costs involved, and how best to foster economic ties with other nations without harming American interests.
7. Essays will vary, but should be supported with facts from the section.

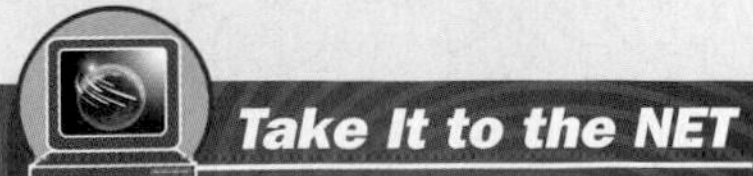

Take It to the NET

Summaries will vary but should present information clearly and accurately and should include quotes and specific facts.

Caption Answers

Viewing History The belief that organizations such as the WTO give big businesses too much control and/or influence over government policies, and that more attention needs to be paid to workers' rights, the environment, and the welfare of developing nations.

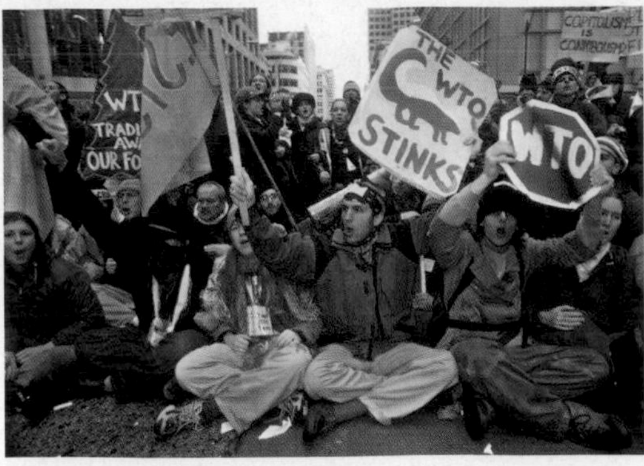

VIEWING HISTORY Anti–World Trade Organization protesters wave signs as they sit on a street in downtown Seattle. **Recognizing Ideologies** *What beliefs led protesters to rally against the WTO?*

of international trade agreements. Made up of different groups, including environmentalists and labor union members, protesters attacked the growing power and influence of giant worldwide corporations. They feared that organizations such as the WTO gave big business too much influence over governments. Speaking out against corporate influence, the protesters called for greater attention to the rights of workers, the welfare of poorer nations, and the global environment.

WTO officials and supporters of free trade believed that the demonstrators were mistaken. Australia's trade minister said that "on both the labor standards and the environment there are very clear and demonstrable benefits that can flow from improved trade and trade liberalization across the world to those sectors—particularly in the developing world."

Rise of Multinationals The debate over the WTO stemmed in part from the growing importance of **multinational corporations,** businesses that operate in more than one country. In the late 1990s, an estimated 37,000 multinational firms operated about 200,000 foreign branches. They accounted for more than $3 trillion in worldwide assets.

Multinationals benefit consumers and workers by providing jobs and products around the world. They also spread advanced technologies and production methods to new countries. Often the jobs they provide help poorer nations obtain better living standards for their people.

On the other hand, multinational firms can greatly influence—not always positively—the culture and politics in the countries in which they operate. Critics complain that the employees of multinationals in poorer countries often receive low wages and endure harsh working conditions. Whatever their advantages and disadvantages, trends suggest that multinationals will become increasingly visible and important in the world economy in the years ahead.

Section 2 Assessment

READING COMPREHENSION

1. Why did the United States impose **economic sanctions** on South Africa during **apartheid?**
2. What steps did the United States take to promote peace around the world?
3. What has been the greatest source of tension between China and the United States?
4. What were the goals of the European Union, **NAFTA,** and the **WTO?**

CRITICAL THINKING AND WRITING

5. **Identifying Central Issues** Why have efforts to reduce tariffs and expand free trade been controversial in the United States?
6. **Drawing Conclusions** What questions did Americans raise about their nation's political and economic role in the post–Cold War era?
7. **Writing to Persuade** Write a brief essay to your senator either in support of or against the expansion of NAFTA to include other countries in the Western Hemisphere.

Take It to the NET

Activity: Writing a Summary
The United States is a member of many global organizations. Select one of these organizations and research its goals and the role the United States plays as a member. Then, prepare a brief "executive summary" on what you've learned. Use the links provided in the *America: Pathways to the Present* area of the following Web site for help in completing this activity.
www.phschool.com

RESOURCE DIRECTORY

Teaching Resources
Units 5/6/7 booklet
- Section 2 Quiz, p. 124

Guide to the Essentials
- Section 2 Summary, p. 133

Technology
Color Transparencies *American Diversity,* G115

Section 3

Americans in the New Millennium

READING FOCUS

- What factors contributed to the growing diversity of the nation's population?
- In what ways did Americans disagree over how to make diversity work?
- What is the economic and political impact of the nation's aging population?
- How did the technological revolution at the end of the twentieth century affect American life?

MAIN IDEA

In the 1990s, the United States sought new ways to create unity out of its ethnic and cultural diversity and to deal with the consequences of an aging population and a technological revolution.

KEY TERMS

bilingual education
multiculturalism
Internet

TAKING NOTES

As you read, complete the flowchart below to show the many changes occurring the United States.

A Rapidly Changing United States

Diverse Population	Aging Population	Technological Revolution
• Causes: changing immigration policy, increased immigration • Effects: ethnically diverse country; new debates over: immigration policy, bilingual education, affirmative action, multiculturalism	• Causes: • Effects:	• Causes: • Effects:

Setting the Scene

The Latin motto of the United States, found on American coins, is *e pluribus unum,* meaning "from many, one." This brief phrase reflects the patterns of the nation's past and the possibilities for its future. The United States was created when 13 separate colonies agreed to form a single union. Since then, people from an astonishing variety of lands have come to the United States and have enriched this nation's culture. That process continues today. Creating unity out of diversity remains one of the nation's greatest challenges and a key to its future.

A Nation of Diversity

In the 1990s, as a result of another wave of immigration, the United States became more diverse than at any time in its history. Close to 80 percent of all legal immigrants during this time came from Asia and Latin America. Earlier in the century, most immigrants had come from various places in Europe. As points of origin shifted away from Europe, Los Angeles began to attract about the same number of immigrants as New York City, which had been the major port of entry a century before.

At the beginning of the twenty-first century, some 30 percent of the nation's people were either African American, Latino, Asian American, or Native American. This expanding diversity meant that the United States was becoming, in the words of writer Ben J. Wattenberg, "the first universal nation."

Changing Immigration Policies Changing immigration policies contributed to the nation's growing diversity. Laws passed in the 1920s had strictly limited immigration and had given preference to immigrants from northern and western Europe. The Immigration Act of 1965, though, eliminated this bias of favoring European immigrants. In 1986, the Immigration Reform and Control Act sought to reduce illegal immigration, in part by forbidding employers to hire illegal aliens. At the same time, however, it permitted illegal aliens who had lived in the United States since 1982 to register to become citizens. The Immigration

This California road sign warns drivers to be on the lookout for undocumented aliens who might have crossed the border from Mexico.

RESOURCE DIRECTORY

Teaching Resources
Learning Styles Lesson Plans booklet, p. 71
Guided Reading and Review booklet, p. 139
Learning with Documents booklet (Primary Source Activity) *Trying to Break the Cycle of Crime,* p. 39

Technology
Section Reading Support Transparencies
Guided Reading Audiotapes (English/Spanish), Ch. 27
Student Edition on Audio CD, Ch. 27
Color Transparencies *American Diversity,* G12
Prentice Hall Presentation Pro CD-ROM, Ch. 27
Companion Web site, www.phschool.com

Section 3
Americans in the New Millennium

Section Objectives

1. Learn about factors that contributed to the growing diversity of the nation's population.
2. Find out how Americans disagreed about how to make diversity work.
3. Discover the economic and political impact of the nation's aging population.
4. Read to find out how the technological revolution at the end of the twentieth century affected American life.

Bellringer

Warm-Up Activity Ask students to take a poll of their classroom. What ethnic and national groups are represented?

Activating Prior Knowledge Ask students what they know about immigration in the United States over the past 150 years. From which countries did most immigrants come in the late nineteenth century? In the early twentieth century? At mid-century? Today?

Reading Strategy

Before students read the section, have them write down the major headings. Then have them make notes under each heading of the main points raised there.

Activity
Connecting with Citizenship

Tell students to write a short essay reflecting on the increasing diversity of the United States. Have students consider the nation's origin as they think about the many different groups who now live here together. Is the current complexion of the United States a reflection of the ideas expressed by the Framers of the Constitution? Is it possible for citizens with different ethnic and religious backgrounds to live together in relative harmony? What are the challenges and the benefits of a diverse population? **(Verbal/Linguistic)**

LESSON PLAN

Focus The face of America was changing in the late 1990s. More Americans were immigrating from places outside Europe, especially from Asia and Latin America. Americans were also growing older. Ask what challenges these changes pose for the United States in the early years of the twenty-first century.

Instruct Explain that, while nearly all Americans are immigrants or descendants of immigrants, it has often been difficult for the newest group to be accepted. Discuss the various ways in which Americans have tried to make diversity work.

Have students discuss their views of the coming decades. For example, how might the "aging of America" affect family relationships?

Assess/Reteach Ask students to consider the ways in which the United States, part of a changing world, is itself changing as it faces the challenges of immigration, an aging population, and new technologies.

ACTIVITY

Connecting with Geography

Divide the class into pairs. Assign each pair of students one of the 50 states. Then direct them to the United States Census Bureau link in the *America: Pathways to the Present* area at the Prentice Hall School Web site, www.phschool.com. Have students pose and answer questions about geographic distributions and patterns of their chosen state as shown on the map database.

INTERPRETING GRAPHS
These graphs show the recent and projected ethnic makeup of the United States. **Analyzing Information** *According to the graphs, which group in the United States will experience the most dramatic rate of growth between 2000 and 2050?*

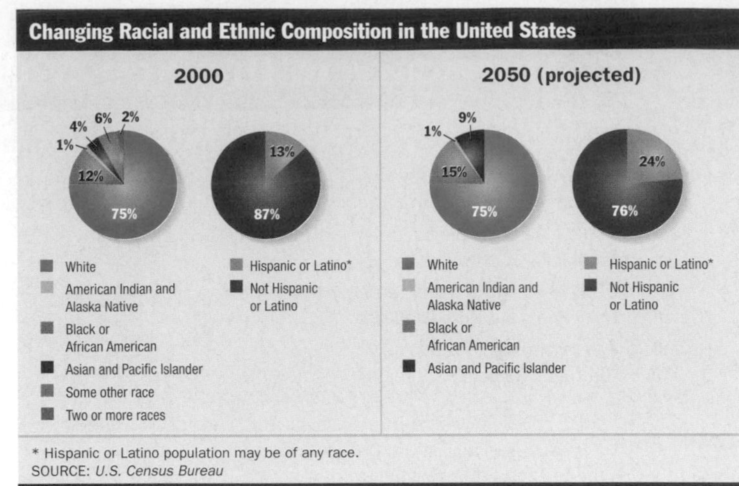

Act of 1990 increased immigration quotas by 40 percent. It also erased restrictions that had denied entrance to many people in the past.

Changing Population Patterns Changes in immigration affected the nation's demographics, or population patterns. While earlier immigrants had settled mainly on the East Coast, many of the new arrivals chose the Sun Belt. (The Sun Belt is the group of states stretching from Florida to California.) Like earlier immigrants, most immigrants of the 1990s settled in urban areas.

In the nation's 100 largest cities in 2000, minorities accounted for 56 percent of the total population, and made up at least half the population in 48 of those cities. African Americans formed a majority of the residents in Detroit, Baltimore, Memphis, and Washington, D.C. Latinos were most heavily concentrated in El Paso, Santa Ana, and Miami. Large numbers of Asian Americans settled in San Francisco.

The most diverse population of all could be found in Los Angeles. Korean, Vietnamese, Cambodian, and Taiwanese newcomers joined established groups of Mexican Americans, African Americans, and European Americans. Like the many nationalities that had crowded into New York City a century earlier, these groups competed for jobs and housing. Similar competition occurred in other cities with large immigrant populations.

Minorities in Politics As minority groups grew in size, they also gained new political power. In 1992, Carol Moseley-Braun, an Illinois Democrat, became the first African American woman to win election to the United States Senate. Also in 1992, Ben Nighthorse Campbell, a Republican from Colorado, became the first Native American to be elected to the United States Senate. Thirty-seven African Americans, 19 Latinos, and 4 Asian Americans took office in the United States House at the start of George W. Bush's presidency.

Making Diversity Work

As American society became more diverse, government, private organizations, and individual citizens all undertook efforts to make diversity work. Some of these efforts aroused controversy.

Focus on CULTURE

Understanding the New Census Data The 2000 Census began a new system for reporting race in the United States. In the 1990 census, respondents could identify their race by choosing one of four racial categories. The 2000 Census expanded these categories to six. The most significant change in 2000, however, was a new set of directions, which allowed respondents to choose more than one racial category by which to identify themselves. In the chart above, the "Two or more races" category represents those respondents who chose to identify themselves in such a way.

Analysts point out that the American system of racial classification has undergone considerable changes in the past. Asian Indians, for example, were included in the white race in 1970, but beginning in 1980, became a part of the Asian and Pacific Islander race. As the nation's racial makeup continues to change, the Census will continue to work to find new and better ways of reporting race.

CAPTION ANSWERS

Interpreting Graphs Hispanic or Latino.

RESOURCE DIRECTORY

Teaching Resources

Biography, Literature, and Comparing Primary Sources booklet (Comparing Primary Sources) *On Immigration Policy,* p. 163

Other Print Resources

Nystrom *Atlas of Our Country* *The Fourth Wave of Immigration,* pp. 36–37

Historical Outline Map Book *Political United States,* p. 82

Technology

Color Transparencies *Historical Maps,* A53, A59; *Fine Art,* E19, E20

Exploring Primary Sources in U.S. History CD-ROM *Texas State Constitution*

RESOURCE PRO® **Biography** *Amy Tan,* found on Resource Pro, profiles the author of the best-selling novel *The Joy Luck Club,* which depicts life in America from the perspective of a group of Chinese American women.

The Debate Over Immigration In the 1990s, as in earlier periods of increased immigration, Americans disagreed over how immigration would affect the nation. Some people warned that immigration would cause the breakdown of American society. Others called immigration the nation's best hope for a prosperous future. In between these two extremes were several other arguments for either restricting or expanding immigration.

People who favored restricting immigration offered these arguments:

1. Immigrants hurt the economy. Because immigrants are willing to work for low wages, some Americans fear they will take jobs away from native-born Americans and drive down the pay of other workers.
2. Immigration services are costly. Some people who favor restricting immigration point to the fact that the federal government sets immigration policy but does not pay for all the services immigrants require. This problem is particularly costly in California, which has more immigrants than any other state.
3. Immigrant groups fragment American society. Some opponents of immigration believe that newer immigrant groups are dividing the United States by staying within their separate ethnic groups rather than adapting to American culture, as previous immigrants did. They fear, for example, that new immigrants will not learn English. **Bilingual education,** in which students are taught in their native language as well as English while their English skills improve, has come under attack. Opponents of bilingual education believe that these programs encourage immigrants to continue using their native language rather than assimilate into the American mainstream.

Those who supported expanded immigration offered their own arguments:

1. Immigrants help, not hurt, the economy. Supporters of immigration point out that immigrants contribute to the economy as consumers, small-business owners, and taxpayers. Immigrants also take jobs few native-born Americans want. They often arrive highly motivated to work, with strong family bonds that promote discipline and high standards.
2. Most immigrants do not receive public assistance. For example, a study in 1997 showed that only 5.7 percent of immigrants received aid to families with dependent children (AFDC), in contrast to 3.9 percent of the native-born population. In addition, most legal immigrants must wait five years before becoming eligible for welfare.
3. Immigration is a good investment for the future. Supporters of immigration claim that it will pay off in future years by expanding both the size of the work force and the number of taxpayers.

Affirmative Action Another heated debate concerned affirmative action. The goal of the first affirmative action policies, introduced by President Johnson in the 1960s, was to improve employment and educational opportunities by giving preference to African Americans and to other minorities and women who had been discriminated against in the past. Some people argued, however, that giving special treatment to some groups was unfair to everyone else.

In 1996, California voters passed Proposition 209, ending affirmative action in state hiring and education. That same year, a federal court struck down an affirmative action admissions program at the University of Texas. The state's attorney general decided not to appeal the ruling to the Supreme Court. His decision reflected growing public doubts about affirmative action across the nation. Among the critics of the policy were some well-known African Americans, including Supreme Court Justice Clarence Thomas.

The courts in recent years have heard a variety of affirmative action cases. The issue remains complex and difficult to decide. Can race be the deciding

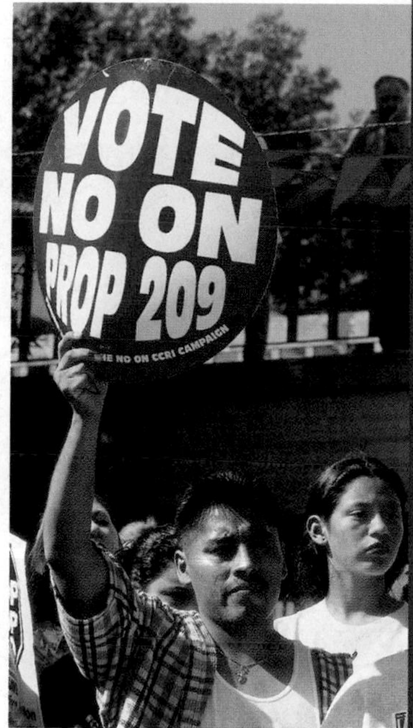

Despite some opposition to Proposition 209, California residents voted to pass the measure that ended affirmative action in government and education.

ACTIVITY
Connecting with Economics

This activity may take place over several class periods: Divide the class into groups of four to six students. Have each group create a poster for use in American schools and travel offices abroad, illustrating and reflecting the diversity of the United States. The goal of the poster should be to present the United States in a global context as a diverse society.

As the students collaborate to create the poster, using markers, collage materials, photographs, etc., they should explore their own ideas about diversity. **(Visual/Spatial)**

BACKGROUND
Art History

Born in Guangdong, China, architect I. M. Pei has helped shape the look of American architecture in the 1980s and 1990s. Buildings like Boston's John F. Kennedy Library incorporate enormous windowed walls that open up the interior to the sky and waterfront. The imaginative Rock and Roll Hall of Fame in Cleveland, Ohio, which opened in 1995, features a glass pyramid and a theater in the shape of a drum. Other notable works by Pei include the Meyerson Symphony Center in Dallas and the Pyramid of the Louvre in Paris.

CUSTOMIZE FOR ...
Less Proficient Readers

Ask students to write a paragraph describing four ways in which the United States was changing in the closing years of the 1990s.

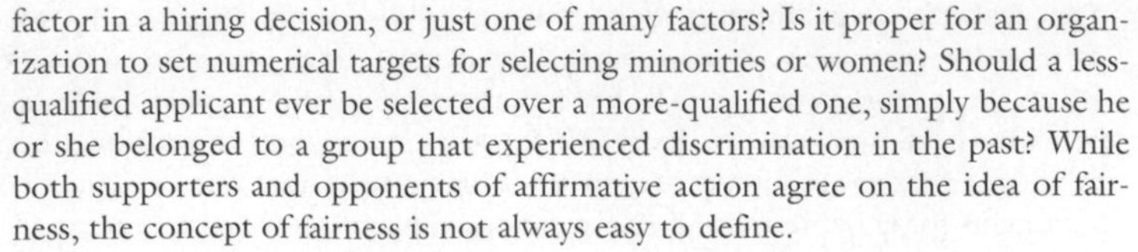

factor in a hiring decision, or just one of many factors? Is it proper for an organization to set numerical targets for selecting minorities or women? Should a less-qualified applicant ever be selected over a more-qualified one, simply because he or she belonged to a group that experienced discrimination in the past? While both supporters and opponents of affirmative action agree on the idea of fairness, the concept of fairness is not always easy to define.

READING CHECK
What issues shaped the debate over affirmative action in recent years?

Multiculturalism Another effort to make diversity work was **multiculturalism,** a movement that called for greater attention to non-European cultures in such areas as education. For example, advocates of multicultural education argued that school textbooks should include more information on the contributions of people from all groups.

Others disapproved of this approach. Professor Arthur M. Schlesinger, Jr., referred to multiculturalism as "ethnic cheerleading." He criticized the use of history to make people feel good about themselves rather than to discover the truth about the past. Other critics worried that extreme versions of multiculturalism could damage the unity of society. They argued that the approach emphasized differences between groups rather than the shared values and experiences of all Americans.

America's Aging Population

As the United States approached the turn of the millennium, its population was older than ever before. Elderly people made up the fastest-growing age group in the country. The number of people 65 years old and over increased nearly elevenfold between 1900 and 1999, while the nation's total population only tripled. In 1999, nearly 13 percent of all Americans were 65 or older, compared to 4 percent in 1900. Advances in medical care increased the average life expectancy of newborns from 47 to 77 years during the 1900s. Clearly, an "aging revolution" was under way.

The "graying of America" had important political and economic effects. Many older Americans advocated passing legislation that prohibited forced retirement at a specific age. In addition, because older Americans were growing in number and living longer, the cost of government programs that served them increased greatly. The Social Security system, for example, faced difficulties because the number of retirees receiving benefits from the program was rising faster than the number of workers paying taxes into it. In 1983, Congress tried to deal with the problem by raising taxes for workers and setting a later age for retirement benefits to begin. Experts warned, however, that more radical steps would have to be taken before the huge baby boom generation begins retiring in the twenty-first century.

In fact, polls showed that many young Americans doubted that the Social Security system would even exist when they reached retirement age. Some of those polled also indicated that they resented paying high taxes to provide benefits for retired persons. Observers suggested that conflict between generations could become another source of tension in American society. Ensuring the long-term health of Social Security remains a difficult but important challenge for the federal government.

VIEWING HISTORY The elderly population of the United States is the fastest-growing segment of American society. Almost all Americans aged 65 and over are insured by Medicare. **Expressing Problems Clearly** *What challenges does the Medicare system face?*

There was similar pressure on the nation's medical system. Medicare, a federal program established during the Great Society of the 1960s, paid for many of the medical expenses of older Americans. As the number of recipients and the price of healthcare rose, however, Medicare costs exploded from $7.5 billion in 1970 to more than $200 billion in the 1990s. As with Social Security, federal

ACTIVITY
Connecting with Culture

Talented authors from many ethnic backgrounds have helped Americans understand and empathize with cultures and heritages different from their own. Ask students to sample works by such contemporary writers as Amy Tan, Esmeralda Santiago, Toni Morrison, Vikram Chandra, and Jamaica Kincaid, and to prepare short essays or oral reports on their reading. In their reports, students should analyze how the contributions of people of various racial, ethnic, and religious groups have helped shape the national identity. **(Verbal/Linguistic)**

BACKGROUND
Recent Scholarship

As the United States became increasingly diverse in the 1990s, some scholars began to stress the need for a more intensive multicultural approach to the American past. In *A Different Mirror: A History of Multicultural America,* Ronald Takaki incorporates a variety of viewpoints—Native American, African, Mexican, Chinese, Japanese, and European, among others—in portraying the groups whose stories together make up the history of the United States. Drawing on folk songs, poems, and memoirs, Takaki describes the experiences of these different ethnic and cultural groups and the reactions they provoked.

READING CHECK
California's Proposition 209, which ended affirmative action in state hiring and education; a federal court striking down an affirmative action admissions program at the University of Texas; growing public doubts about affirmative action.

CAPTION ANSWERS

Viewing History An aging population, rising costs, and political disagreements over how to improve the system.

RESOURCE DIRECTORY

Other Print Resources

American History Block Scheduling Support *Building a Nation: Immigration in the 1980s,* found in The Nation After World War II folder, includes interdisciplinary lesson suggestions and activities for Geography and History, Primary Sources, Biography, and Literature.

Technology

Color Transparencies *Political Cartoons,* B20

lawmakers agreed that long-term changes were needed but disagreed on what those changes should be.

A Technological Revolution

The modern communications revolution began more than a century ago when Samuel Morse developed the telegraph. Since then, communications technology has made major advances with the invention of the telephone, radio, television, and the computer. In the last several decades, the invention of many more ways to store, retrieve, and transmit information has created a new era in communications known as the Information Age.

Communication and Information The centerpiece of the Information Age, of course, is the computer. Between 1984 and 2000, the percentage of American households with a computer jumped from 8 percent to 51 percent.

Originally the size of a room, computers have decreased in size as they have grown in their ability to store and retrieve information. Computers now steer spacecraft, route telephone calls, and assist in all kinds of scientific research.

The **Internet,** a computer network that links millions of people around the world, has revolutionized many areas of American life, from entertainment to education to business. Access to the Internet has spread to schools, businesses, libraries, homes, and even some cafés, where "net-surfing" allows customers to work at computers and drink coffee at the same time. Businesses, seeing the Internet as a way to reach a global audience of millions, have scrambled to set up their own Web sites.

The "New Economy" The United States enjoyed the greatest period of economic expansion in its history during the 1990s, thanks in large part to the technological boom. Investors and entrepreneurs, excited about the opportunities offered by the Internet and other new technologies, created many new businesses and worked on ways to improve old ones. Waves of what came to be called "dot com" companies appeared, each trying to corner a unique market of online business.

The face of business also began to change. New entrepreneurs sported jeans and T-shirts and maintained more casual workplaces. This relaxed style even spread to some older businesses, where workers could enjoy greater benefits, such as more flexible schedules.

How will these changes affect employment? While computers have replaced some human workers, the growth of high-tech industries has created thousands of new jobs. These jobs demand a high level of education and skills. One feature of the new economy is the lack of stable, well-paying jobs for unskilled workers. Education, therefore, has never been as important to economic success as it is now.

Impact on Education Computers and the Internet have become essential parts of American society, but their place in schools is still being determined. An important task for schools will be to find the right balance between traditional teaching and the use of new technology. For many schools, an even bigger challenge will be to find enough money to fund the new and ever-changing technology.

In addition, as the Internet becomes more important as a research tool, students will have to learn how to evaluate the information that is available online. While some of this information is of very high quality, not all of it is reliable.

BIOGRAPHY

Bill Gates
b. 1955

In 1975, Bill Gates envisioned the future of computers and set to work turning that vision into reality. That year, at the age of 19, Gates dropped out of Harvard University to join his high school friend Paul Allen in establishing a new company. During high school, Bill had used his computer knowledge to help create a company that sold traffic data to local governments. In 1975, the two friends first read about a kit computer in *Popular Electronics* magazine. "Paul and I didn't know exactly how it would be used, but we were sure it would change us and the world of computing."

At first, people couldn't make the kit computer do much. Gates and Allen changed that by writing software, or the coded instructions for performing specific tasks, to run on the computer. Their efforts transformed it from a device with limited uses into a general-purpose computer that was similar to (though much less powerful than) those we use today. The company that the two friends started for marketing their software, later named Microsoft, grew to become a giant in the computer industry. Located near Seattle, Washington, where Gates was born, its success made Gates a billionaire by the age of 31.

ACTIVITY
Connecting with Culture

Engage students in a discussion about the cultural effects of the Internet. Suggest that they consider some of the following questions: How does the Internet change the nature of human relationships? What benefits does the Internet offer people? What are some of its drawbacks? Does the Internet bring the world closer by making information accessible to people all around the globe? Or does the Internet serve as an alienating force? **(Verbal/Linguistic)**

BACKGROUND
Protecting Privacy

The ever-increasing role of the Internet has led to an increasing need for Internet security. On October 4, 2001, the Federal Trade Commission chairperson, Timothy J. Muris, announced a pro-consumer Privacy Agenda. Among other things, the agenda provides initiatives for protection from identity theft, increasing enforcement and outreach on children's online privacy, and curbing the dissemination of "spam," chain letters that encourage people to get involved in "get-rich-quick" scams.

CUSTOMIZE FOR ...
Less Proficient Writers

Have students think about the use of communications devices in their own lives. During the course of a day, have them keep track of the number of times they use devices such as the telephone, television, computer, etc. Ask them to write a few sentences describing the importance of each of these devices in their lives.

TEST PREPARATION

Have students read the section on "The New Economy" and then complete the sentence below.

The main idea of this section is that—

A people may now wear T-shirts to work.

(B) a technological boom in the 1990s led to the greatest period of economic expansion in U.S. history.

C many people worked in "dot com" companies in the late 1990s.

D older businesses offered more flexible working environments but demanded more highly skilled workers.

ACTIVITY
Connecting with Geography

Have students find out about Internet access around the world. For example, how many people in Asian or African nations now have Internet access? How does the lack of Internet access affect these people? Then have students make a map of the area they have focused on. Tell students to indicate the countries that have Internet access and those that do not. **(Visual/Spatial)**

BACKGROUND
Interdisciplinary

High-tech wizards have created the Internet and, along with it, the ability to disseminate information quickly. However, even the smartest programmers seem unable to stem the spread of computer viruses. A virus is a code that attaches itself to another code in a computer with the express aim of reproducing itself. Some viruses are created to erase files or lock up the operating system of another computer. Other viruses are less destructive; they can be formed when an infected program is run that was received via e-mail or the Internet. For this reason, it's important to scan for viruses.

READING CHECK

The government has tried to protect the rights of businesses (such as record companies) threatened by new technologies. On the other hand, the government has tried to protect consumers from communications entities deemed to be monopolies (such as Microsoft).

to Tomorrow

What Comes Next?

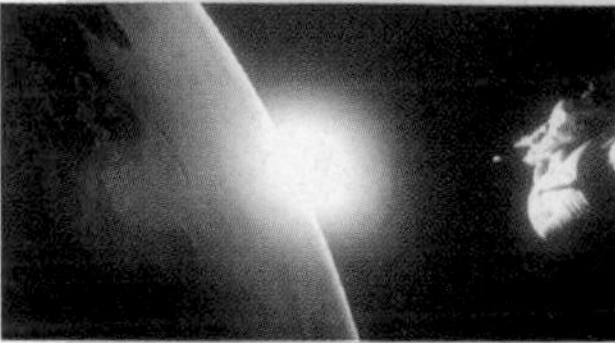

Of course, no one knows for sure what the future holds, but everyone from scientists and politicians to sociologists and historians is talking about what comes next. Surely, the world is bound for another makeover. Think about how much the world has changed since 1900. Who in 1900 could have dreamed of such a thing as the Internet?

Think about the speed of change. The Internet is already evolving as people begin to access it from wireless devices. Experts see a future in which our lives are filled with Internet-enabled appliances, cars, airplanes, and houses.

What exists now that will soon become obsolete? Will we still have a need for books? Most people expect that books aren't going anywhere, but that they will surely change. Businesses are already working on new types of books, into which content can be loaded in the form of digital ink. The covers of such an adaptable book can be customized to fit your hands. Politics will change as well. Experts see world conflicts being resolved through mini-wars, in which powerful peace-oriented nations plan targeted attacks on smaller rogue enemies. The presence of nuclear weapons means that most nations will want to avoid a world war at all costs.

Many Americans contemplate the possibility of time-travel, alternate universes, genetically-engineered people, or replaceable bodies and brains. While many of these ideas are both exciting and frightening, Americans will adapt as they always have to whatever comes next.

? Why do you think the prospect of change is both frightening and exciting for Americans? Explain.

Impact on Foreign Affairs New technologies created both opportunities and challenges for governments around the world. President Clinton claimed that "in the new century, liberty will spread [around the world] by cell phone and cable modem." New communications and information technology encouraged greater ties among people in different nations. Through the Internet, for example, more people around the world than ever before could gain access to the same pools of information.

However, countries in several regions lacked the wealth or infrastructure to become active participants in this global network. In 2001, only about 8 percent of the world population had access to the Internet. By contrast, in the United States nearly 60 percent of the people could go online. As technology changed ever more quickly, fears rose that much of the developing world would be left further and further behind.

Impact on Government The federal government also had to confront domestic issues raised by the Internet and other new technologies. The issue of maintaining privacy was an important concern. Many people worried that the privacy of e-mail conversations or online purchases was not being sufficiently protected.

Another controversial issue concerned ownership rights. One company, Napster, had grown widely popular because its software allowed users to trade song files over the Internet for free. Many record companies and some musicians believed that such sharing of music was illegal because the owners of this music (the record companies and artists) did not make any money when these song files were shared. Not all artists opposed Napster, however. Networks like Napster, some believed, gave consumers access to new music and to little-known musicians who otherwise would have trouble breaking into the industry.

Record companies sued Napster in an effort to halt the trading of copyrighted material on the Internet. A federal judge ruled in favor of the record companies and ordered Napster to stop trading copyrighted material. Other networks not affected by the judge's ruling, though, soon took Napster's place. The debate over whether Napster promoted stealing or sharing was certain to continue.

The government also faced a problem with the giant software company Microsoft. By 1998, Microsoft had become the world's second most valuable company, worth some $200 billion. However, Microsoft's size and success helped make the company controversial. Several competitors argued that Microsoft was trying to drive them out of business.

In 1998, the federal government sued Microsoft for violating the Sherman Antitrust Act of 1890. The government accused Microsoft of using its power to gain a monopoly over the market for software needed to browse the Internet. In 2000, a federal judge ruled that Microsoft was indeed a monopoly and had used unfair business practices, and he ordered that the company be split apart. The following year, an appeals court reversed this order but upheld the judgment

READING CHECK
How has the government reacted to developments in communications technology?

CAPTION ANSWERS

Fast Forward to Tomorrow Answers will vary, but might mention that the rapid pace of change today can, in and of itself, be frightening. The excitement of change can be stimulated by imagining ways in which daily life can be improved by technology.

RESOURCE DIRECTORY

Teaching Resources

Units 5/6/7 booklet
- Section 3 Quiz, p. 125
- Chapter 27 Test, pp. 126, 129

Guide to the Essentials
- Section 3 Summary, p. 134
- Chapter 27 Test, p. 135

Other Print Resources

Chapter Tests with ExamView® Test Bank CD-ROM, Ch. 27

Technology

Color Transparencies *Political Cartoons,* B19; *Time Lines,* C10

ExamView® Test Bank CD-ROM

Social Studies Skills Tutor CD-ROM

that Microsoft had acted improperly. The Justice Department announced later that year that it would abandon its efforts to break up Microsoft.

VIEWING HISTORY This satellite image shows North America at night. **Drawing Inferences** *Study the photograph. What can you infer about population density patterns in the United States?*

Impact on Daily Life The new technologies of the late twentieth century left their mark on Americans' daily lives. Many people kept in touch with friends and family through e-mail as well as (or instead of) through letters or telephone calls. They brought cell phones or hand-held computers along with them on daily errands and vacations. They used the Internet to shop, look for jobs, or to check the weather forecast or sports results. Everything they needed to know about the products they bought, the restaurants where they ate, and the companies in which they invested was only a few "clicks" away.

Some Americans, though, began to wonder whether all of these changes were good. Did people have access to more information than they could use? Had the pace of life grown too fast? Would the United States, like the world as a whole, become divided into two groups: one with access to the new technology and the other too poor to afford it? While modern technology appeared to provide people with greater freedom, could it also be misused to restrict freedom?

Facing the Future

Near the end of his life, Thomas Jefferson wrote, "If a nation expects to be ignorant and free . . . it expects what never was and never will be." Freedom, in other words, does not maintain itself. We must all commit ourselves to its preservation by working to understand and participate in the events around us.

The wealth and power our nation now enjoys might cause some of us to lose sight of this lesson. Yet as changes occur increasingly quickly in the years ahead, bringing advances—and challenges—we can hardly imagine, Jefferson's words could become more true than ever before.

Section 3 Assessment

READING COMPREHENSION

1. What effects did increasing immigration have on the United States?
2. Explain the debate over **bilingual education** and **multiculturalism.**
3. How has the increase in the number of older Americans caused difficulties for the Social Security system?
4. What challenges did the **Internet** pose for the federal government?

CRITICAL THINKING AND WRITING

5. **Drawing Inferences** How can the country's immigration policies affect its economy?
6. **Predicting Consequences** Why is it important for Americans to create unity out of diversity?
7. **Writing to Persuade** Explain how you think schools can best prepare students to take advantage of modern technological innovations like the Internet.

Take It to the NET

Activity: Writing an Editorial
Review current themes and issues regarding bilingual education in the United States. Gather data about existing programs and write an editorial stating whether or not you believe bilingual education is headed in the right direction in America. Use the links provided in the *America: Pathways to the Present* area of the following Web site for help in completing this activity.
www.phschool.com

Section 3 Assessment

Reading Comprehension

1. Minorities made up a much larger part of the population and gained political power; development of bilingual education; it led to debate on how to handle a diverse society.
2. Bilingual education: Supporters believe students should be taught in both their native language and English. Opponents believe this approach prevents these students from learning English and assimilating into American culture. Multiculturalism: Supporters feel that education should fully encompass non-European cultures. Opponents fear that this approach masks the truth about the past, and that extreme multiculturalism could damage the unity of society.
3. The number of retirees receiving benefits from the program was rising faster than the number of workers paying taxes into it.
4. Challenges: maintaining privacy; ownership rights; monopolies.

Critical Thinking and Writing

5. Opponents of expanded immigration claim that large numbers of immigrants require entitlements and compete with native-born workers for jobs. Supporters feel that immigrants benefit society and do not draw off resources.
6. Possible answer: If Americans do not unite, opposing groups could develop hostility toward one another, resulting in political battles or other conflicts.
7. Answers will vary, but should include a discussion of issues of funding, how to teach students to evaluate the validity of Internet sources, and the costs and benefits of other new technologies.

Take It to the NET

Editorials will vary, but should persuade readers with facts gathered about existing programs and predictions about the future of bilingual education in America.

Caption Answers

Viewing History The United States is most densely populated along the East and West coasts, and most populated in the northeast section.

Chapter 27

Reviewing Key Terms

Students should refer to the definitions of key terms in the chapter to write sentences about the important controversies and conflicts facing America and the world during the 1990s and today.

Reviewing Main Ideas

10. Successes: economic reform, balancing the budget, welfare reform. Failures: health care reform, impeachment.
11. Republicans had won a majority in both houses of Congress in the midterm elections, and many backed Gingrich's Contract with America, a conservative plan for cutting the size of government.
12. It took part in the NATO bombing campaigns and committed troops to NATO peacekeeping forces stationed in the area.
13. Supporters said that NAFTA would create new jobs by increasing exports to Canada and Mexico. Opponents argued that manufacturers would move factories to Mexico, resulting in a loss of American jobs.
14. The Immigration Act of 1965 eliminated bias in favor of European immigration, increasing the number of immigrants from Asia, Africa, and Latin America. The 1986 Immigration Reform and Control Act allowed immigrants who had been living in the United States since 1982 to become citizens, and the Immigration Act of 1990 increased immigration quotas.
15. Business: While computers have replaced some human workers, high-tech industries have created a wealth of new jobs and allowed the United States to enjoy a period of vast economic expansion. Stable, well-paying jobs for unskilled workers are in short supply due to the expansion of technology in the workplace. Education: Education is critical for acquiring jobs in an increasingly technological society. In the classroom, the right balance between traditional teaching and the use of technology is still being examined, as is funding and evaluating the information gleaned from the Internet as a research tool. Daily life: facilitating rapid communication between people; shaping

Chapter 27 Review and Assessment

creating a CHAPTER SUMMARY

Copy the web diagram (right) on a separate sheet of paper to summarize international events in recent years.

For additional review and enrichment activities, see the interactive version of *America: Pathways to the Present*, available on the Web and on CD-ROM.

★ Reviewing Key Terms

For each of the terms below, write a sentence explaining how it related to the United States at the end of the twentieth century.

1. Contract with America
2. Whitewater affair
3. apartheid
4. economic sanctions
5. North American Free Trade Agreement
6. World Trade Organization
7. multinational corporation
8. multiculturalism
9. Internet

★ Reviewing Main Ideas

10. What were some domestic successes and failures for Bill Clinton in the 1990s? (Section 1)
11. After the 1994 elections, why did Republicans believe that they had a mandate to reduce the size of the federal government? (Section 1)
12. What role did the United States play in producing cease-fires in Bosnia and Kosovo? (Section 2)
13. Give reasons why some people supported NAFTA and others opposed it. (Section 2)
14. How did government policy contribute to the diversity of the United States? (Section 3)
15. Analyze the impact of recent technological innovations on business, education, and daily life. (Section 3)

★ Critical Thinking

16. **Demonstrating Reasoned Judgment** The United States intervened in some foreign conflicts during the 1990s and launched a war on terrorism in 2001. What do you think should be the role of the United States in future overseas conflicts?
17. **Identifying Assumptions** What arguments might supporters and opponents of affirmative action give in defense of their different positions?
18. **Drawing Inferences** President Clinton gave his speech regarding the need for healthcare reform to a national TV audience in 1993 as a way of rallying public support for reform. What benefits and drawbacks does television offer to Presidents?
19. **Predicting Consequences** Think about how technology affects our daily lives. What changes might take place as a result of technological advances in the next five to ten years?
20. **Synthesizing Information** What various factors and events in the late 1990s helped cause the election of 2000 to be so close?

Creating a Chapter Summary

WTO: An organization to help negotiate trade agreements and resolve trade disputes worldwide
EU: An organization of European countries working to create a single European market
NAFTA: An agreement signed by the United States, Canada, and Mexico removing trade restrictions

The Balkans: With the collapse of communism, ethnic violence erupts.
Israel: Israel and the PLO sign a peace agreement, but hostilities increase again.
Iraq: Iraq still refuses to cooperate with UN inspectors, and some sanctions are still in place.

Russia/Eastern Europe: Elections are held in Russia as it moves toward democracy; in Eastern Europe, countries move toward a free market economy, some joining NATO.
Northern Ireland: The Good Friday peace accords were signed to help halt violence between Protestants and Catholics.
South Africa: The country ends apartheid, and first elections are held.

the way we shop, hunt for jobs, and acquire information.

★ **Skills Assessment**

Analyzing Political Cartoons ▶

21. Read the title of the cartoon. Why do people go on vacations?
22. Examine the scene. (a) What activities do you traditionally associate with a trip to the beach? (b) How is this scene different?
23. What comment is the cartoonist making about 1990s lifestyle?

A '90s VACATION.
CAN YOU HOLD ON? SOMEONE'S ON CALL WAITING.
I BETTER CHECK MY E-MAIL
MOM, YOUR FAX IS COMING IN.
OOPS. THERE GOES MY BEEPER.
IT'S TIME I CHECKED MY VOICE MAIL.

Interpreting Data

Turn to the racial and ethnic composition graphs in Section 3.

24. Which of the following groups made up 12 percent of the United States population in 2000?
    - **A** White
    - **B** Black or African American
    - **C** American Indian and Alaskan Native
    - **D** Asian and Pacific Islander
25. Which of the following groups will more than double its percentage of the United States population by 2050?
    - **F** White
    - **G** Black or African American
    - **H** Asian and Pacific Islander
    - **J** Hispanic or Latino Origin
26. What percentage of the United States population reported that they belonged to one racial category in 2000?
    - **A** 98 percent
    - **B** 6 percent
    - **C** 94 percent
    - **D** 13 percent

Applying the Chapter Skill:
Predicting Consequences

27. Review the steps needed to predict consequences on page 902. Then describe the consequences of the nation's aging population.

ACTIVITIES

Writing to LEARN

Writing a Conclusion
Reread the statement by Thomas Jefferson at the end of Section 3. Describe in your own words how education and freedom are related. Why will education be so important to workers of the twenty-first century?

Primary Source CD-ROM

Working With Primary Sources Find additional information on the United States in recent years on the *Exploring Primary Sources in U.S. History CD-ROM* and use the selection(s) provided to complete the Chapter 27 primary source activity located in the *America: Pathways to the Present* area of the following Web site.
www.phschool.com

Take It to the NET

Chapter Self-Test As a review activity, take the Chapter 27 Self-Test in the *America: Pathways to the Present* area at the Web site listed below. The questions are designed to test your understanding of the chapter content.
www.phschool.com

CRITICAL THINKING

16. Sample answers: The United States, as the world's lone superpower, has an obligation to take on the role of peacekeeper. Or, becoming involved in dangerous situations such as Bosnia or Somalia may be too costly in money and lives.
17. Opponents: Preferential treatment for certain people robs those people of their dignity and self-worth; it is unfair to other groups. Supporters: Gives those who faced discrimination in the past improved employment and educational opportunities.
18. Answers will vary. Benefits might include reaching out to all people. Drawbacks might include appearing unpersuasive if the individual lacks "television appeal."
19. Answers will vary, but should use current technological advancements as a base for speculation and prediction.
20. Possible answers: Clinton's impeachment, the booming economy, political tensions between Democrats and Republicans.

SKILLS ASSESSMENT

21. Relaxation; freedom from work or school.
22. (a) Blankets and towels; coolers; swimming; looking for seashells; sunbathing; making sand castles.
    (b) Instead of engaging in these activities, the family shown is surrounded by portable, mostly business-related, technology, which they are using.
23. Americans no longer know how to relax. The array of communications technology we have created does not free us from work, but enables us to do more of it.
24. B
25. H
26. A
27. Answers will vary, but might involve such predictions as the percentage of Americans who will be 65 or older in 2050.

ANSWERS TO ACTIVITIES

Writing to LEARN

Answers will vary, but should mention that the technological revolution requires advanced education and skills.

Primary Source CD-ROM

Direct students to the additional primary sources that can be found on the *Exploring Primary Sources in U.S. History CD-ROM.*

Take It to the NET

Additional support materials and activities for Chapter 27 of *America: Pathways to the Present* can be found in the Social Studies area at the Prentice Hall School Web site. **www.phschool.com**

Free Enterprise and the American Economy

Focus Remind students that the American economy is based on capitalism—a system in which private individuals or corporations own the money, land, buildings, and equipment that are necessary to run a business. People have individual liberty and the right to own property. They can do whatever they want with their property, provided that they don't harm anyone.

Instruct Have students read the text and examine the photos. What factors affect our economy? What role does the government play in influencing the economy? How has that role changed over the years?

Extend Encourage students to research one era in our economic history, such as the Progressive Era, the Great Depression, the New Deal, or the current Information Age. Suggest that students learn more about the larger forces, such as war and the stock market, that shape the economy.

American Pathways
ECONOMICS

Free Enterprise and the American Economy

In 1776, Scottish economist Adam Smith published *The Wealth of Nations,* a book that promoted capitalism, an economic system based on free enterprise and little government interference. Capitalism has suited independent, industrious, and competitive Americans, who have enjoyed the fruits of a productive economy for two centuries.

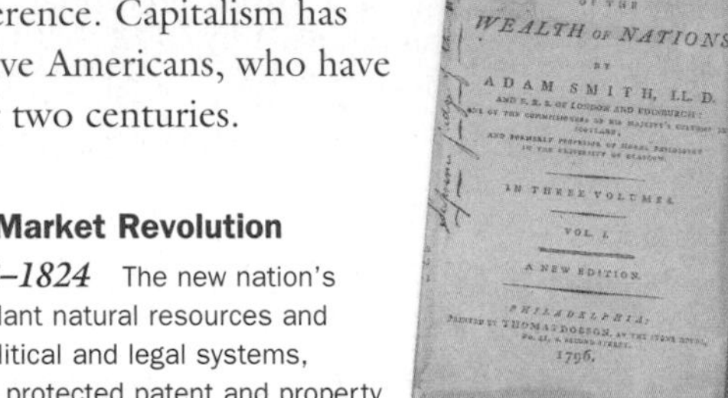
AN INQUIRY INTO THE NATURE AND CAUSES OF THE WEALTH OF NATIONS. BY ADAM SMITH, LL.D.

IN THREE VOLUMES. VOL. I.

A NEW EDITION.

PHILADELPHIA: PRINTED BY THOMAS DOBSON

1796.

1 The Market Revolution

1793–1824 The new nation's abundant natural resources and its political and legal systems, which protected patent and property rights, allowed hard-working Americans to bring about a "market revolution." New, profitable manufacturing enterprises sprang up throughout the Northeast and the Ohio Valley.

Title page of Adam Smith's *The Wealth of Nations* (above right)

2 Nationalism and Sectionalism

1816–1865 In the ongoing power struggle between the federal government and the states, Congress and the Supreme Court worked to strengthen nationalism. The economy, especially the northern industrial economy, expanded. At the same time, slavery was becoming the economic cornerstone of the agricultural South. This issue and other sectional tensions eventually sparked the Civil War.

Currency issued by state-chartered banks and individual companies from the Free Banking Era, 1837–1863 (above)

3 Industrial Expansion and Progressive Reforms

1865–1914 After the Civil War, industry thrived in a free market, with little interference from the government. During the Progressive Era, reformers concerned about low pay and harsh working conditions in the nation's factories pressed government officials to regulate corporations more closely.

An early Ford Motor Company assembly line (above)

RESOURCE DIRECTORY

Teaching Resources

Units 5/6/7 booklet
- American Pathways Activity, pp. 132–133

American Pathways Thematic Posters

Technology

Companion Web site, www.phschool.com

A Consumer Economy

1919–1929 During the 1920s, new products and Americans' power to purchase them grew rapidly, producing a decade of enormous business growth.

The Great Depression and the New Deal

1929–1941 Overproduction and risky investment practices set the stage for economic disaster. On October 29, 1929, stock prices tumbled in what is known as the Great Crash. Investors lost millions of dollars and the economy sank into a devastating Depression. President Franklin D. Roosevelt developed government programs to help American businesses and families recover.

A soup kitchen during the Depression (above)

Postwar Ups and Downs

1944–1987 The national economy finally rebounded with the advent of World War II. Pent-up consumer demand, the GI Bill, and the business shift to peacetime manufacturing helped create a postwar economic boom. In the 1970s and early 1980s, however, the economy sagged.

A 1950s automobile (above)

The Information Age and the Global Economy

1974–Present The personal computer ushered in the Information Age, which, along with increased world trade and corporate multinationalism, created new opportunities and challenges for the American economy.

The New York Stock Exchange located on Wall Street in New York City's financial district (left)

Continuity and Change

1. How does the United States' system of government support free enterprise?
2. What evidence of a typical business cycle can you find in the history of the American economy?

Take It to the NET: Creating a Study Guide
Print and complete the study guide for this topic found in the *America: Pathways to the Present* area of the following Web site. **www.phschool.com**

Take It to the NET

Students can print the American Pathways thematic study guide for this topic at the Prentice Hall School Web site, or you can provide students with copies of the study guide, which is found in the Units 5/6/7 booklet, the American Pathways Activity, pages 132–133. Students should use their texts to fill in a one-sentence description for each event on the study guide. When completed for each of the American Pathways topics, the thematic study guides will aid students in preparing for an end-of-course exam.

Answers

1. The United States system of government supports free enterprise in many ways. The government enforces a system of laws that upholds the rights of private property owners. The government also issues and protects patents and enforces legal contracts.
2. Possible answers: The panics of 1837 and 1839, which had followed a boom in the economy; the Depression of 1893–1897 after the industrial expansion of the Gilded Age; the Great Depression following the boom of the 1920s; the stagflation and recession after the post–World War II boom ended in the 1970s; the 1987 stock market collapse that broke the speculative bubble of the 1980s.

TEST PREPARATION

Use this sample exam to help your students prepare for standardized tests.

Tips for Test Taking

You might want to remind your students of the following:

1. Read the directions carefully.
2. Read each question carefully.
3. For multiple choice questions, try to answer the question before you look at the choices. Read all the choices. Then, eliminate those that are absolutely incorrect.
4. For short answer questions, be sure to answer the question completely if there is more than one part.
5. Answer the easy questions first. Then, go back to the ones that will take more time.
6. Pace yourself. Be sure to set aside enough time for the writing questions.

TEST PREPARATION

Write your answers on a separate sheet of paper.

1. Which one of the following did President Richard Nixon use to try to stop inflation in the United States economy?
   - **A** Veto power over congressional spending
   - **B** Federal Reserve interest rates
   - **C** Federal price, wage, and rent controls
   - **D** Balancing the federal budget

2. What was the purpose of the "southern strategy" of President Richard Nixon?
   - **A** To gain votes from whites opposed to changes in civil rights
   - **B** To allow the Vietnamese to fight the war on their own
   - **C** To control the expansion of suburbs into farmlands
   - **D** To limit the power of Republicans in the eastern states

3. How is President Gerald Ford unique among all of the United States Presidents?
   - **A** He changed political parties as President.
   - **B** He was the only President who also was an athlete.
   - **C** He served as Vice President for two different Presidents.
   - **D** He was the only unelected President.

> **"Our Constitution works. Our great republic is a government of laws, not men."**
>
> *—President Gerald Ford, August 9, 1974*

4. President Ford was speaking about the
   - **A** failure of United States military policy in Vietnam.
   - **B** investigation and resignation of Nixon following the Watergate scandal.
   - **C** need for a comprehensive national energy policy.
   - **D** use of presidential veto power.

5. Which one of the following is a correct statement about the Supreme Court decision in *Regents of the University of California* v. *Bakke*?
   - **A** It extended the scope of the *Brown* v. *Board of Education* decision.
   - **B** It required busing to achieve integration in public schools.
   - **C** It limited the power of the President to spend money on education.
   - **D** It was the first limit on affirmative action programs.

6. Which President was responsible for the Strategic Defense Initiative (SDI)?
   - **A** Gerald Ford
   - **B** Ronald Reagan
   - **C** George H. W. Bush
   - **D** Bill Clinton

922

Diagnose and Prescribe
- Profile student skills with Diagnostic Tests A&B.
- Address student needs with program materials correlated to test questions.

Review and Reteach
- Provide cumulative content review with the Review Book.

Practice and Assess
- Build test-taking skills with Test-taking Strategies With Transparencies.

Use the chart and your knowledge of social studies to answer the following questions.

Year	U.S. Deficit (millions of dollars)
1980	$ 73,835
1982	127,989
1984	185,388
1986	221,245
SOURCE: *Statistical Abstract of the United States, 1995*	

7. The growing deficit during the 1980s was a result of the

A anti-inflationary policies of President Jimmy Carter.

B supply-side economic policies of President Ronald Reagan.

C overseas military activities of President George H. W. Bush.

D limited popularity of President Bill Clinton.

8. President George H. W. Bush used military power to

A break down the Berlin Wall.

B stop a revolution in Grenada.

C force Iraq out of Kuwait.

D end the Communist threat in Vietnam.

9. Which one of the following was a major goal of President Bill Clinton when he was elected in 1992?

A To solve healthcare problems in the United States

B To limit the spending excesses of Congress

C To limit the power of the Republican majority in Congress

D To end United States military involvement overseas

10. Newt Gingrich and the Republican majority in Congress were blamed for which one of the following?

A United States military failure in Somalia

B The negative effects of the NAFTA treaty

C The government shutdown at the end of 1995

D Rising inflation rates in 1997

11. Under President Bill Clinton, the United States experienced the

A highest rate of inflation in the world.

B highest level of unemployment in its history.

C longest period of economic expansion in its history.

D longest period of economic recession in its history.

Writing Practice

12. Describe President Nixon's policies for dealing with the Soviet Union and China.

13. How did the Camp David Accords change the Middle East?

14. Describe two problems the United States faces with the "graying of America."

1. C
2. A
3. D
4. B
5. D
6. B
7. B
8. C
9. A
10. C
11. C
12. Nixon followed a policy of *realpolitik,* or "practical politics," with China, which included laying the groundwork for establishing diplomatic ties, lifting restrictions on travel, and removing an embargo on trade. With the Soviet Union, Nixon agreed to cooperate on space exploration, ease trade limits, and negotiate a weapons pact.
13. Under the Camp David Accords, Israel withdrew from the Sinai Peninsula, and Egypt recognized Israel's existence as a nation. The peace between Egypt and Israel helped to make the Middle East more stabile.
14. Problems include the increased cost of government programs that serve the elderly, such as Social Security and Medicare. There are also concerns about potential intergenerational conflict.

Of Plymouth Plantation 1620–1647
By William Bradford

Focus Have students read the introduction and look up the meanings of the vocabulary words. Then explain that the excerpt offers an eyewitness account of the dramatic events surrounding the Pilgrims' establishment of relations with the Native Americans on Cape Cod.

Instruct Ask your students to review the events that Bradford describes. Why do they think the Pilgrims were first confronted by Native Americans' arrows, and then received peaceful overtures? Ask students to speculate on what might have been going on among the Native Americans that caused this change of attitude. What role did Squanto play in establishing peaceful relations? What role did Massasoit play?

Extend Ask students to research the history of one of the various Native American groups that lived on Cape Cod and in southern New England at the time of the Pilgrims' arrival. For the group they select, ask students to find out about the relationship between that group and European settlers, the background of any key individuals, and the status of that group today—where it is located, how many members it has, how much land it holds, and the group's current economic status.

American Literature
Unit 1

Of Plymouth Plantation 1620–1647
By WILLIAM BRADFORD

William Bradford sailed on the Mayflower *to North America in 1620. One of approximately 100 religious pilgrims to land on present-day Cape Cod in November, he helped establish a colony at Plymouth and served as its governor. Full of adventure, passion, wisdom, and even humor, Bradford's remarkable narrative about this exploration has been called one of the greatest books of the seventeenth century. The following excerpts describe two early encounters with Native Americans. The first occurred less than one month after the* Mayflower*'s landfall, in early December, when an exploring party was camped around present-day Eastham, Massachusetts; the second occurred in the early spring near Plymouth.*

VOCABULARY Before you read the selection, find the meaning of these words in a dictionary:
providence
shallop
skulk

So they rested till about five of the clock in the morning; for the tide, and their purpose to go from thence, made them be stirring betimes. So after prayer they prepared for breakfast, and it being day dawning it was thought best to be carrying things down to the boat. But some said it was not best to carry the arms down, others said they would be the readier, for they had lapped them up in their coats from the dew; but some three or four would not carry theirs till they went themselves. Yet as it fell out, the water being not high enough, they laid them down on the bank side and came up to breakfast.

But presently, all on the sudden, they heard a great and strange cry, which they knew to be the same voices they heard in the night, though they varied their notes; and one of their company being abroad came running in and cried, "Men, Indians! Indians!" And withal, their arrows came flying amongst them. Their men ran with all speed to recover their arms, as by the good providence of God they did. In the meantime, of those that were there ready, two muskets were discharged at them, and two more stood ready in the entrance of their rendezvous but were commanded not to shoot till they could take full aim at them. And the other two charged again with all speed, for there were only four had arms there, and defended the barricado, which was first assaulted. The cry of the Indians was dreadful, especially when they saw their men run out of the rendezvous toward the shallop to recover their arms, the Indians wheeling about upon them. But some running out with coats of mail on, and cutlasses in their hands, they soon got their arms and let fly amongst them and quickly stopped their violence. Yet there was a lusty man, and no less valiant, stood behind a tree within half a musket shot, and let his arrows fly at them; he was seen [to] shoot three arrows, which were all avoided. He stood three shots of a musket, till one taking full aim at him and made the bark or splinters of the tree fly about his ears, after which he gave an extraordinary shriek and away they went, all of them. . . .

Painting of the Pilgrims landing at Plymouth

Thus it pleased God to vanquish their enemies and give them deliverance; and by His special providence so to dispose that not any one of them were either hurt or hit, though their arrows came close by them and on every side [of] them; and sundry of their coats, which hung up in the barricado, were shot through and through. Afterwards they gave God solemn thanks and praise for their deliverance, and gathered up a bundle of their arrows and sent them to England afterward by the master of the ship, and called that place the First Encounter. . . .

Indian Relations

All this while the Indians came skulking about them, and would sometimes show themselves aloof off, but when any approached near them, they would run away; and once they stole away their tools where they had been at work and were gone to dinner. But about the 16th of March, a certain Indian came boldly amongst them and spoke to them in broken English, which they could well understand but marveled at it. At length they understood by discourse with him, that he was not of these parts, but belonged to the eastern parts where some English ships came to fish, with whom he was acquainted and could name sundry of them by their names, amongst whom he had got his language. He became profitable to them in acquainting them with many things concerning the state of the country in the east parts where he lived, which was afterwards profitable unto them; as also of the people here, of their names, number and strength, of their situation and distance from this place, and who was chief amongst them. His name was Samoset. He told them also of another Indian whose name was Squanto, a native of this place, who had been in England and could speak better English than himself.

Being, after some time of entertainment and gifts dismissed, a while after he came again, and five more with him, and they brought again all the tools that were stolen away before, and made way for the coming of their great Sachem, called Massasoit. Who, about four or five days after, came with the chief of his friends and other attendance, with the aforesaid Squanto. With whom, after friendly entertainment and some gifts given him, they made a peace with him (which hath now continued this 24 years) in these terms:

1. That neither he nor any of his should injure or do hurt to any of their people.

2. That if any of his did hurt to any of theirs, he should send the offender, that they might punish him.

3. That if anything were taken away from any of theirs, he should cause it to be restored; and they should do the like to his.

4. If any did unjustly war against him, they would aid him; if any did war against them, he should aid them.

5. He should send to his neighbours confederates to certify them of this, that they might not wrong them, but might be likewise comprised in the conditions of peace.

6. That when their men came to them, they should leave their bows and arrows behind them.

After these things he returned to his place called Sowams, some 40 miles from this place, but Squanto continued with them and was their interpreter and was a special instrument sent of God for their good beyond their expectation. He directed them how to set their corn, where to take fish, and to procure other commodities, and was also their pilot to bring them to unknown places for their profit, and never left them till he died.

Analyzing Literature

Use the passage on these pages to answer the following questions.

1. Whom do the colonists credit and thank for rescuing them from the first Indian attack?
   - **A** Squanto
   - **B** God
   - **C** Sachem
   - **D** Bradford
2. What does this tell you about the *Mayflower* explorers?
   - **A** They have faith in their governor.
   - **B** They are able to rely on all of the natives for support.
   - **C** They trust no one and nothing.
   - **D** They have strong religious faith.
3. **Critical Thinking: Identifying Assumptions** From these two brief excerpts, how would you describe the Native Americans' initial feelings about the new settlers? Why do you suppose the natives feel this way?

American Literature

Analyzing the Document Use this additional question to generate class discussion:

Critical Thinking: Making Comparisons What were the prospects of survival for the Pilgrim settlers before and after they met Squanto? *(Before they met Squanto, they were not likely to survive, because they were in an unfriendly territory, constantly at risk of attack, and unfamiliar with their surroundings. After they met Squanto, their prospects for survival increased dramatically because he brought them peace, and showed them the best ways to raise and gather food in the area.)*

TEST PREPARATION

Have students use the excerpt on these pages to answer the question below.

What was one of the results of the meeting between the Native Americans and the Pilgrims?

- **A** Hostilities broke out.
- **(B)** Terms for peaceful coexistence were negotiated.
- **C** The Native Americans brought the Pilgrims to their village.
- **D** Future European settlements had to be made in another area.

ANSWERS

1. B
2. D
3. Answers might include hostility, fear, and curiosity. Reasons might include the Pilgrims' weapons, different appearance and customs, etc.

April Morning
By Howard Fast

Focus Have students read the introduction and look up the meanings of the vocabulary words. Then explain that the excerpt from Howard Fast's *April Morning* dramatizes the tension of the American Revolution by portraying the war's first battle through the eyes of a fictional young observer.

Instruct Ask students to recall facts about the Battles at Lexington and Concord based on their reading. Then ask them to write a brief summary of the battles, labeled "historical writing." After students have read the selection, ask them to write another brief summary based on their reading, labeled "literary writing." Ask volunteers to read their summaries aloud. Discuss the differences between the two kinds of writing.

Extend Ask students to write the next chapter of *April Morning,* supposing that they are the boy in Fast's book. They should focus on the aftermath of the Battle at Lexington and draw on their knowledge of the events described in the chapter. Have volunteers read their chapters aloud to the class.

April Morning

By HOWARD FAST

The fighting at Lexington and Concord, Massachusetts, on April 19, 1775, marked the beginning of the American Revolution. In the following excerpt from his historical novel April Morning, *Howard Fast captures the sights and sounds of the skirmish at Lexington Green.*

VOCABULARY Before you read the selection, find the meaning of these words in a dictionary:
dissipate
jubilation

When the British saw us, they were on the road past Buckman's [Tavern]. First, there were three officers on horseback. Then two flag-bearers, one carrying the regimental flag and the other bearing the British colors. Then a corps of eight drums. Then rank after rank of the redcoats, stretching back on the road and into the curtain of mist, and emerging from the mist constantly, so that they appeared to be an endless force and an endless number. It was dreamlike and not very believable, and it caused me to turn and look at the houses around the common, to see whether all the rest of what we were, our mothers and sisters and brothers and grandparents, were watching the same thing we watched. My impression was that the houses had appeared by magic, for I could only remember looking around in the darkness and seeing nothing where now all the houses stood—and the houses were dead and silent, every shutter closed and bolted, every door and storm door closed and barred. Never before had I seen the houses like that, not in the worst cold or the worst storms.

And the redcoats did not quicken their pace or slow it, but marched up the road with the same even pace, up to the edge of the common; and when they were there, one of the officers held up his arm—and the drums stopped and the soldiers stopped, the line of soldiers stretching all the way down the road and into the dissipating mist. They were about one hundred and fifty paces from us.

The three officers sat on their horses, studying us. The morning air was cold and clean and sharp, and I could see their faces and the faces of the redcoat soldiers behind them, the black bands of their knapsacks, the glitter of their buckles. Their coats were red as fire, but their light trousers were stained and dirty from the march.

Minuteman statue, Concord, Massachusetts

Then, one of the officers sang out to them, "Fix bayonets!" and all down the line, the bayonets sparkled in the morning sun, and we heard the ring of metal against metal as they were clamped onto the guns. . . .

Then another British officer—I discovered afterward that he was Major Pitcairn—called out orders: "Columns right!" and then, "By the left flank," and, "Drums to the rear!" The drummers stood still and beat their drums, and the redcoats marched past them smartly, wheeling and parading across the common, while the three mounted officers spurred over the grass at a sharp canter, straight across our front and then back, reining in their prancing horses to face us. Meanwhile, the redcoats marched onto the common, the first company wheeling to face us when it was past our front of thirty-three men, the second company repeating the exercise, until they made a wall of red coats across the common, with no more than thirty or forty paces separating us. Even so close, they were unreal; only their guns were real, and their glittering bayonets too—and suddenly, I realized, and I believed that everyone else around me realized, that this was not to be an exercise or a parade or an argument, but something undreamed of and unimagined.

I think the Reverend was beginning to speak when Major Pitcairn drove down on him so that he had to leap aside. My father clutched the Reverend's arm to keep him from falling, and wheeling his horse, Major Pitcairn checked the beast so that it pawed at the air and neighed shrilly. The Reverend was speaking again, but no one heard his words or remembered them. The redcoats were grinning; small, pinched faces under the white wigs—they grinned at us. Leaning over his horse, Major Pitcairn screamed at us:

"Lay down your arms . . . Disperse, do you hear me! Disperse, you lousy peasant scum! Clear the way, do you hear me! Get off the King's green!"

At least, those were the words that I seem to remember. Others remembered differently; but the way he screamed, in his strange London accent, with all the motion and excitement, with his horse rearing and kicking at the Reverend and Father, with the drums beating again and the fixed bayonets glittering in the sunshine, it's a wonder that any of his words remained with us.

Yet for all that, this was a point where everything appeared to happen slowly. Abel Loring clutched my arm and said dryly, "Adam, Adam, Adam." He let go of his gun and it fell to the ground. "Pick it up," I said to him, watching Father, who pulled the Reverend into the protection of his body. Jonas Parker turned to us and cried at us:

"Steady! Steady! Now just hold steady!"

We still stood in our two lines, our guns butt end on the ground or held loosely in our hands. Major Pitcairn spurred his horse and raced between the lines. Somewhere, away from us, a shot sounded. A redcoat soldier raised his musket, leveled it at Father, and fired. My father clutched at his breast, then crumpled to the ground like an empty sack and lay with his face in the grass. I screamed. I was two [persons]. One part of me was screaming; another part of me looked at Father and grasped my gun in aching hands. Then the whole British front burst into a roar of sound and flame and smoke, and our whole world crashed at us, and broke into little pieces that fell around our ears, and came to an end; and the roaring, screaming noise was like the jubilation of the damned.

I ran. I was filled with fear, saturated with it, sick with it. Everyone else was running. The boys were running and the men were running. Our two lines were gone, and now it was only men and boys running in every direction that was away from the British, across the common and away from the British.

British uniform jacket like those worn at Lexington

Analyzing Literature

Use the passage on these pages to answer the following questions.

1. How does the British force at Lexington compare with the colonists' force?
   - **A** The two forces are roughly equal.
   - **B** The colonists' force is much larger.
   - **C** The British force is much larger.
   - **D** The mist makes it impossible to compare the two forces.
2. What does the narrator mean by the use of such words as "dreamlike" and "unreal" to describe the events of that morning?
   - **A** He has not witnessed the events and is only imagining how they must have looked.
   - **B** He has arrived on the scene too late to understand what is happening.
   - **C** He is too young to understand what is happening.
   - **D** He has difficulty believing what is happening.
3. **Critical Thinking: Drawing Conclusions** Based on this account, what do you think caused the fighting at Lexington? Explain your answer.

American Literature

American Literature

Analyzing the Document Use this additional question to generate class discussion:

Critical Thinking: Demonstrating Reasoned Judgment Do you think that the shooting and resulting death that occurred in Lexington were inevitable? *(Answers will vary. Students should point out that the British were provoking the colonists with their show of force and bravado.)*

TEST PREPARATION

Have students use the excerpt on these pages to answer the question below.

On what date did the American Revolution begin?

- **A** April 17, 1775
- **B** April 18, 1775
- **(C)** April 19, 1775
- **D** April 17, 1776

Answers

1. C
2. D
3. The British taunted the colonists; a colonist fired a single shot, and the British retaliated.

Incidents in the Life of a Slave Girl
By Harriet Ann Jacobs

Focus Have students read the introduction and look up the meanings of the vocabulary words. Point out that the autobiography of Harriet Ann Jacobs reveals both the subtle and the blatant abuses that even the kindest slave owners dealt the enslaved.

Instruct Divide the class into two groups and have each group make a list of the hardships described by Harriet Ann Jacobs. Then reconvene as a class and have the groups compare their lists. Use the lists as a basis for discussing the various challenges that African Americans faced in the mid-1800s.

Extend Have students research the daily life of an enslaved person on a southern plantation. Students might use such sources as *Six Women's Slave Narratives* by William Andrews. Then ask pairs of students to prepare a skit that demonstrates the daily life of the person chosen. Discuss with the class what the skit revealed about that person and the history of the times.

American Literature
Unit 2

Incidents in the Life of a Slave Girl

By HARRIET ANN JACOBS

Harriet Ann Jacobs was born into slavery in Edenton, North Carolina, in 1813. Her long and remarkable road to freedom began in 1835, when she and her two young children went into hiding in her hometown. In 1842, Jacobs escaped to New York with her son and daughter. There she made a home for her children and was eventually bought by the Colonization Society and freed in 1852. Shortly afterward she wrote her autobiography, which provides a personal account of what it was like to be enslaved in the 1800s.

VOCABULARY Before you read the selection, find the meaning of these words in a dictionary:
toilsome
bequeath
chattel
defraud

I was born a slave; but I never knew it till six years of happy childhood had passed away. My father was a carpenter, and considered so intelligent and skillful in his trade, that, when buildings out of the common line were to be erected, he was sent for from long distances, to be head workman. On condition of paying his mistress two hundred dollars a year, and supporting himself, he was allowed to work at his trade, and manage his own affairs. His strongest wish was to purchase his children; but, though he several times offered his hard earnings for that purpose, he never succeeded.

I was so fondly shielded that I never dreamed I was a piece of merchandise, trusted to them for safe keeping, and liable to be demanded of them at any moment. . . .

Such were the unusually fortunate circumstances of my early childhood. When I was six years old, my mother died; and then, for the first time, I learned, by the talk around me, that I was a slave. My mother's mistress was the daughter of my grandmother's mistress. She was the foster sister of my mother; they were both nourished at my grandmother's breast. In fact, my mother had been weaned at three months old, that the babe of the mistress might obtain sufficient food. They played together as children; and, when they became women, my mother was a most faithful servant to her white foster sister. On her death-bed her mistress promised that her children should never suffer for any thing; and during her lifetime she kept her word. They all spoke kindly of my dead mother, who had been a slave merely in name, but in nature was noble and womanly. I grieved for her, and my young mind was troubled with the thought who would now take care of me and my little brother. I was told that my home was now to be with her mistress; and I found it a happy one. No toilsome or disagreeable duties were imposed upon me. My mistress was so kind to me that I was always glad to do her bidding, and proud to labor for her as much as my young years would permit. . . .

Antislavery logo linking the women's rights and abolitionist movements

When I was nearly twelve years old, my kind mistress sickened and died. As I saw the cheek grow paler, and the eye more glassy, how earnestly I prayed in my heart that she might live! I loved her; for she had been almost like a mother to me. My prayers were not answered. She died, and they buried her in the little churchyard, where, day after day, my tears fell upon her grave.

I was sent to spend a week with my grandmother. I was now old enough to begin to think of the future; and again and again I asked myself what they would do with me. I felt sure I should never find another mistress so kind as the one who was gone. She had promised my dying mother that her children should never suffer for any thing; and when I remembered that, and recalled her many proofs of attachment to me, I could not help having some hopes that she had left me free. . . .

After a brief period of suspense . . . we learned that she had bequeathed me to her sister's daughter, a child of five years old. So vanished our hopes. My mistress had taught me the precepts of God's Word: "Thou shalt love thy neighbor as thyself." "Whatsoever ye would that men should do unto you, do ye even so unto them." But I was her slave, and I suppose she did not recognize me as her neighbor. I would give much to blot out from my memory that one great wrong. As a child, I loved my mistress; and, looking back on the happy days I spent with her, I try to think with less bitterness of this act of injustice. While I was with her, she taught me to read and spell; and for this privilege, which so rarely falls to the lot of a slave, I bless her memory. . . .

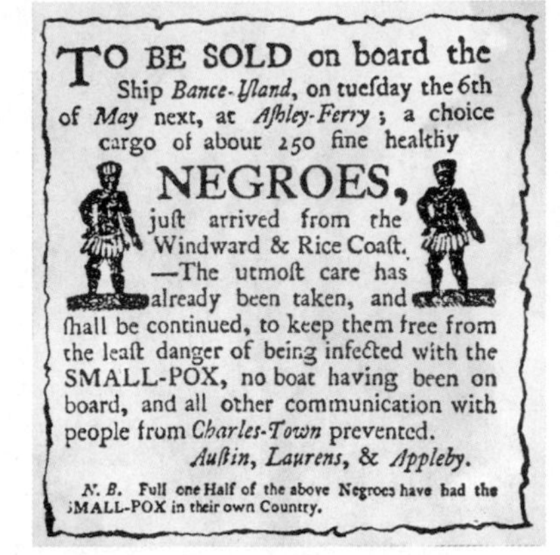

TO BE SOLD on board the Ship Bance-Yland, on tuefday the 6th of May next, at Afhley-Ferry; a choice cargo of about 250 fine healthy
NEGROES,
juft arrived from the Windward & Rice Coaft.
—The utmoft care has already been taken, and fhall be continued, to keep them free from the leaft danger of being infected with the SMALL-POX, no boat having been on board, and all other communication with people from Charles-Town prevented.
Auftin, Laurens, & Appleby.
N. B. Full one Half of the above Negroes have had the SMALL-POX in their own Country.

Slave sale advertisment

My grandmother's mistress had always promised her that, at her death, she should be free; and it was said that in her will she made good the promise. But when the estate was settled, Dr. Flint told the faithful old servant that, under existing circumstances, it was necessary she should be sold.

On the appointed day, the customary advertisement was posted up, proclaiming that there would be a "public sale of negroes, horses, &c." Dr. Flint called to tell my grandmother that he was unwilling to wound her feelings by putting her up at auction, and that he would prefer to dispose of her at private sale. My grandmother saw through his hypocrisy; she understood very well that he was ashamed of the job. She was a very spirited woman, and if he was base enough to sell her, when her mistress intended she should be free, she was determined the public should know it. She had for a long time supplied many families with crackers and preserves; consequently, "Aunt Marthy," as she was called, was generally known, and every body who knew her respected her intelligence and good character. Her long and faithful service in the family was also well known, and the intention of her mistress to leave her free. When the day of sale came, she took her place among the chattels, and at the first call she sprang upon the auction-block. Many voices called out, "Shame! Shame! Who is going to sell *you,* Aunt Marthy? Don't stand there! That is no place for *you.*" Without saying a word, she quietly awaited her fate. No one bid for her. At last, a feeble voice said, "Fifty dollars." It came from a maiden lady, seventy years old, the sister of my grandmother's deceased mistress. She had lived forty years under the same roof with my grandmother; she knew how faithfully she had served her owners, and how cruelly she had been defrauded of her rights; and she resolved to protect her.

Analyzing Literature

Use the passage on these pages to answer the following questions.

1. How does Jacobs learn that she was born a slave?
   - **A** Her mother tells her before she dies.
   - **B** Her father tells her when he purchases her freedom.
   - **C** Others mention it after her mother dies.
   - **D** She is sold at a public auction.
2. Why do people not make bids for Jacobs's grandmother when she is put up for sale at an auction?
   - **A** Dr. Flint tells people that he prefers not to sell her.
   - **B** People disapprove of the selling of human beings.
   - **C** People think she is too old to be a useful worker.
   - **D** People know that her mistress wanted her to be freed upon the mistress's death.
3. **Critical Thinking: Identifying Central Issues** How does the passage show how little control slaves had over their lives?

American Literature

Analyzing the Document Use this additional question to generate class discussion:

Critical Thinking: Predicting Consequences Why would it have been rare for slave owners to educate their slaves? *(Answers will vary, but students may suggest that education could have been a key to a slave's freedom. If slaves were educated, they might have refused to accept the system of slavery that many of them were born into and, as a result, revolted against it.)*

TEST PREPARATION

Have students use the excerpt on these pages to answer the following question.

What skill did Jacobs learn from her mistress?

- **A** Cleaning
- **B** Cooking
- **C** Sewing
- **(D)** Reading

ANSWERS

1. C
2. D
3. Students should point to the passages that describe Jacobs, and later her grandmother, being treated like merchandise that could be sold at any moment.

SLAVERY IN MASSACHUSETTS BY HENRY DAVID THOREAU

Focus Have students read the introduction and look up the meanings of the vocabulary words. Then explain that the excerpt is a speech written to protest the return of two escaped slaves to slavery in the South under terms of the Fugitive Slave Law.

Instruct Ask your students to review the many contrasts Thoreau presents between the intentions of the Founding Fathers—to secure "Liberty and Justice for All" and justifications made in support of slaveholding. Have students list these contrasts. Do they believe Thoreau builds a convincing argument? What points would they add to the list to further demonstrate the contradiction inherent in a country established to preserve freedom that nonetheless sanctions slavery?

Extend Ask students to research the writings and speeches of a prominent abolitionist of the mid-nineteenth century. How did this individual seek to persuade others to support his or her cause? As a class, create a time line that demonstrates major events and major legislation passed in the years 1850–1861 to underscore the growing rift between the North and South.

Slavery in Massachusetts

By HENRY DAVID THOREAU

Henry David Thoreau, remembered most widely today for his nature writings such as Walden, *also had a considerable reputation as an abolitionist speaker. He delivered a version of the speech containing the following excerpt at an "Anti-Slavery Celebration" in Framingham, Massachusetts, on July 4, 1854. The event was a protest against official Independence Day observances.*

Behind Thoreau's anger lay two recent events, both triggered by the Fugitive Slave Law (part of the Compromise of 1850). On April 12, 1851, the Massachusetts state government had returned a fugitive slave named Thomas Sims to his Georgia master. Tensions surrounding the case ran so high that the government had employed 300 armed guards to escort Sims to a ship that sailed before dawn. In the second incident, nine men had been arrested for attempting to rescue another slave, Anthony Burns, from the Boston courthouse where he was held before being returned to his Virginia master.

VOCABULARY Before you read the selection, find the meaning of these words in a dictionary:
humane
incapacity
tribunal
precedent
docket

Three years ago, also, just a week after the authorities of Boston assembled to carry back a perfectly innocent man, and one whom they knew to be innocent, into slavery, the inhabitants of Concord caused the bells to be rung and the cannons to be fired, to celebrate their liberty—and the courage and love of liberty of their ancestors who fought at the bridge. As if *those* three millions had fought for the right to be free themselves, but to hold in slavery three millions others. Now-a-days, men wear a fool's cap, and call it a liberty cap. I do not know but there are some, who, if they were tied to a whipping-post, and could get but one hand free, would use it to ring the bells and fire the cannons, to celebrate *their* liberty. So some of my townsmen took the liberty to ring and fire; that was the extent of their freedom; and when the sound of the bells died away, their liberty died away also; when the powder was all expended, their liberty went off with the smoke.

The joke could be no broader, if the inmates of the prisons were to subscribe for [agree to purchase] all the powder to be used in such salutes, and hire the jailors to do the firing and ringing for them, while they enjoyed it through the grating.

This is what I thought about my neighbors.

Every humane and intelligent inhabitant of Concord, when he or she heard those bells and those cannons, thought not with pride of the events of the 19th of April, 1775, but with shame of the events of the 12th of April, 1851. But now we have half buried that old shame under a new one. . . .

I wish my countrymen to consider, that whatever the human law may be, neither an individual nor a nation can ever commit the least act of injustice against the obscurest individual, without having to pay the penalty for it. A government which deliberately enacts injustice, and persists in it, will at length ever become the laughing-stock of the world.

Much has been said about American slavery, but I think that we do not even yet realize what slavery is. If I were seriously to propose to Congress to make mankind into sausages, I have no doubt that most of the members would smile at my proposition, and if any believed me to be in earnest, they would think that I proposed something much worse than Congress had ever

Henry David Thoreau

done. But if any of them will tell me that to make a man into a sausage would be much worse,—would be any worse, than to make him into a slave,—than it was to enact the Fugitive Slave law, I will accuse him of foolishness, of intellectual incapacity, of making a distinction without a difference. The one is just as reasonable a proposition as the other. . . .

Recent events will be valuable as a criticism on the administration of justice in our midst, or, rather, as showing what are the true resources of justice in any community. It has come to this, that the friends of liberty, the friends of the slave, have shuddered when they have understood that his fate was left to the legal tribunals of the country to be decided. Free men have no faith that justice will be awarded in such a case; the judge may decide this way or that; it is a kind of accident, at best. It is evident that he is not a competent authority in so important a case. It is no time, then, to be judging according to his precedents but to establish a precedent for the future. . . .

It is to some extent fatal to the courts, when the people are compelled to go behind them. I do not wish to believe that the courts were made for fair weather, and for very civil cases merely,—but think of leaving it to any court in the land to decide whether more than three millions of people, in this case, a sixth part of a nation, have a right to be freemen or not! But it has been left to the courts of *justice,* so-called—to the Supreme Court of the land—and, as you all know, recognizing no authority but the Constitution, it has decided that the three millions are, and shall continue to be, slaves. Such judges as these are merely the inspectors of a pick-lock and murderer's tools, to tell him whether they are in working order or not, and there they think that their responsibility ends. There was a prior case on the docket, which they, as judges appointed by God, had no right to skip; which having been justly settled, they would have been saved from this humiliation. It was the case of the murderer himself.

The law will never make men free; it is men who have got to make the law free. They are the lovers of law and order, who observe the law when the government breaks it.

William Lloyd Garrison published Thoreau's speech in his famous antislavery newspaper *The Liberator.*

Analyzing Literature

Use the passage on these pages to answer the following questions.

1. To whom does Thoreau compare his neighbors as they celebrated Independence Day?
   - **A** Supreme Court Justices
   - **B** prison inmates
   - **C** murderers
   - **D** sausage makers
2. Why does he think they are imprisoned—or slaves—themselves?
   - **A** because he believes no one can truly be free while also supporting slavery
   - **B** because the state government has banned all protests against slavery
   - **C** because many of his neighbors have served jail terms
   - **D** because the U.S. Supreme Court has issued a warrant for their arrest
3. **Critical Thinking: Making Comparisons** At the end of this excerpt, Thoreau encourages people to observe a higher law when the government's law is unjust. At what other times in our nation's history have civic leaders encouraged this philosophy? In your opinion, is this philosophy always justified? Why or why not?

American Literature

Analyzing the Document Use this additional question to generate class discussion:

Critical Thinking: Identifying Assumptions What does Thoreau assume when he encourages his listeners to "observe the law when the government breaks it"? *(He assumes that by establishing the Fugitive Slave Law, the government was in effect breaking the law, since the United States was established on principles of freedom for all.)*

TEST PREPARATION

Have students use the excerpt on these pages to answer the question below.

When Thoreau speaks of the events of April 19, 1775, to what is he referring?

- **A** Paul Revere's ride.
- **(B)** The Battles of Lexington and Concord.
- **C** The signing of the Declaration of Independence.
- **D** The end of the War for Independence.

ANSWERS

1. B
2. A
3. Answers will vary, but might mention the 1960s' civil rights movement, labor protests, and others.

Hungry Hearts
By Anzia Yezierska

Focus Have students read the introduction and look up the meanings of the vocabulary words. Explain that throughout American history, a vast difference has existed between the idealized, popular view of the United States and the reality that greets immigrants. Ask students to think about whether the people who painted such glorified pictures of the United States were lying or simply focusing only on some aspects of society and not on others.

Instruct Ask students whether they have undertaken a new experience, such as trying out for a part in a play, attending a new school, or going to a party where they know few people. Ask students to compare their expectations of the experience to the reality. Then ask them to compare those feelings to those described by Anzia Yezierska. How are they similar? How are they different?

Extend Ask students to conduct further research on the immigrant experience, either for Europeans coming through Ellis Island or for Asians coming through Angel Island. Students may choose to concentrate on a period different from that of the selection, such as the present. Have students present the results of their research to the class. Discuss how the experiences described are both similar to and different from those in the selection.

American Literature
Unit 3

Hungry Hearts
By ANZIA YEZIERSKA

Like many other immigrants who flooded into the nation's cities during the late 1800s, Anzia Yezierska and her family came to New York to escape ethnic persecution in their homeland. In her autobiography, Hungry Hearts, *Yezierska describes what it was like to leave her Russian village and begin a new life in the United States.*

VOCABULARY Before you read the selection, find the meaning of these words in a dictionary:
steerage
Cossack
dilapidated
maw

Steerage—dirty bundles—foul odors—seasick humanity—but I saw and heard nothing of the foulness and ugliness around me. I floated in showers of sunshine; visions upon visions of the new world opened before me.

From lips flowed the golden legend of the golden country:

"In America you can say what you feel—you can voice your thoughts in the open streets without fear of a Cossack."

"In America is a home for everybody. The land is your land. Not like in Russia where you feel yourself a stranger in the village where you were born and raised—the village in which your father and grandfather lie buried." . . .

" . . . Everybody can do what he wants with his life in America."

"There are no high or low in America. Even the President holds hands with Gedalyeh Mindel."

"Plenty for all. Learning flows free like milk and honey."

"Learning flows free."

The words painted pictures in my mind. I saw before me free schools, free colleges, free libraries, where I could learn and learn and keep on learning. . . .

"Land! Land!" came the joyous shout.

"America! We're in America!" cried my mother, almost smothering us in her rapture.

All crowded and pushed on deck. They strained and stretched to get the first glimpse of the "golden country," lifting their children on their shoulders that they might see beyond them.

Men fell on their knees to pray. Women hugged their babies and wept. Children danced. Strangers embraced and kissed like old friends. Old men and women had in their eyes a look of young people in love.

Age-old visions sang themselves in me—songs of freedom of an oppressed people.

America!—America! . . .

Between buildings that loomed like mountains, we struggled with our bundles, spreading around us the smell of the steerage. Up Broadway, under the bridge, and through the swarming streets of the ghetto, we followed Gedalyeh Mindel.

I looked about the narrow streets of squeezed-in stores and houses, ragged

Young girl working at a spinning machine, *circa* early 1900s

clothes, dirty bedding oozing out of the windows, ash-cans and garbage-cans cluttering the side-walks. A vague sadness pressed down my heart—the first doubt of America.

"Where are the green fields and open spaces in America?" cried my heart. "Where is the golden country of my dreams?"

A loneliness for the fragrant silence of the woods that lay beyond our mud hut welled up in my heart, a longing for the soft, responsive earth of our village streets. All about me was the hardness of brick and stone, the stinking smells of crowded poverty.

"Here's your house with separate rooms like in a palace." Gedalyeh Mindel flung open the door of a dingy, airless flat.

"Oi weh!" my mother cried in dismay. "Where's the sunshine in America?"

She went to the window and looked out at the blank wall of the next house. "Gottuniu! Like in a grave so dark . . ."

"It ain't so dark, it's only a little shady." Gedalyeh Mindel lighted the gas. "Look only"—he pointed with pride to the dim gaslight. "No candles, no kerosene lamps in America, you turn on a screw and put to it a match and you got it light like with sunshine."

Again the shadow fell over me, again the doubt of America!

In America were rooms without sunlight, rooms to sleep in, to eat in, to cook in, but without sunshine. And Gedalyeh Mindel was happy. Could I be satisfied with just a place to sleep and eat in, and a door to shut people out—to take the place of sunlight? Or would I always need the sunlight to be happy?

And where was there a place in America for me to play? I looked out into the alley below and saw pale-faced children scrambling in the gutter. "Where is America?" cried my heart. . . .

"Heart of mine!" my mother's voice moaned above me. "Father is already gone an hour. You know how they'll squeeze from you a nickel for every minute you're late. Quick only!"

I seized my bread and herring and tumbled down the stairs and out into the street. I ate running, blindly pressing through the hurrying throngs of workers—my haste and fear choking each mouthful.

I felt a strangling in my throat as I neared the sweatshop prison [factory where she worked]; all my nerves screwed together into iron hardness to endure the day's torture.

For an instant I hesitated as I faced the grated window of the old dilapidated building—dirt and decay cried out from every crumbling brick.

In the maw of the shop, raging around me the roar and the clatter, the clatter and the roar, the merciless grind of the pounding machines. Half maddened, half deadened, I struggled to think, to feel, to remember—what am I—who am I—why was I here?

I struggled in vain—bewildered and lost in a whirlpool of noise.

"America—America—where was America? . . ."

Analyzing Literature

Use the passage on these pages to answer the following questions.

1. Which statement best describes Anzia Yezierska's image of the United States before she arrives?
   - **A** It is her homeland.
   - **B** It is a land of freedom for all.
   - **C** It is a crowded and dark country.
   - **D** It is not a place of safety.
2. What is her biggest disappointment about the United States?
   - **A** It reminds her too much of her former home.
   - **B** It has too much open space.
   - **C** It has no jobs.
   - **D** It seems to want her only as a laborer, not as a complete person.
3. **Critical Thinking: Predicting Consequences** In what different ways might immigrants have reacted to disappointments in the United States?

American Literature

American Literature

Analyzing the Document Use this additional question to generate class discussion:

Critical Thinking: Making Comparisons Although Yezierska highlights the differences between her homeland and the United States, were there any similarities? *(Answers will vary, but students may suggest that Yezierska feared for her safety in both places. Also, her life in the United States was restricted by the number of hours she had to work; she points to restrictions in her homeland as well.)*

TEST PREPARATION

Have students use the excerpt on these pages to answer the question below.

Where did Anzia Yezierska work after she came to America?

- **A** On a farm.
- **B** In a tenement.
- **C** She was unable to find work.
- **(D)** In a sweatshop, or factory.

Answers

1. B
2. D
3. Answers will vary, but students may respond that because they had to work so hard in such dingy surroundings, some immigrants may have been depressed about their lives in the United States; others may have thought it worthwhile to remain in America because there were still more opportunities available here than in Europe.

A Farewell to Arms
By Ernest Hemingway

Focus Have students read the introduction and look up the meanings of the vocabulary words. Then explain that in this passage, two World War I ambulance drivers, one American and one Italian, discuss the war. The passage clearly conveys the banality and horror of war.

Instruct Ask students to find words and phrases that convey Frederick Henry's attitude toward the war and his work. In their opinion, is he motivated and energetic, or depressed and apathetic? What might have caused him to arrive at the state of mind demonstrated in the passage? Have students focus on the portion of the text that describes the narrator's perception of the bombardment that takes place in the night. As he describes it, does it seem immediate, or remote? What is his response to the wounded arriving in camp? Is he emotionally engaged with them, or is he detached?

Extend Have students research the history of World War I to learn more about conditions at the time this passage takes place. What battles actually took place in this mountainous region?

A Farewell to Arms

By ERNEST HEMINGWAY

Ernest Hemingway's second novel, A Farewell to Arms, *is set during World War I and focuses on the war efforts in the mountainous region along Italy's northeastern border with present-day Austria and Slovenia, an area referred to in the book as the "Bainsizza." In the excerpt that follows, the main character, American army officer Frederick Henry, an ambulance driver, discusses the war with Gino, a native Italian and fellow driver.*

VOCABULARY Before you read the selection, find the meaning of these words in a dictionary: **quadrilateral** **hallow**

I did not believe in a war in the mountains. I had thought about it a lot, I said. You pinched off one mountain and they pinched off another but when something really started every one had to get down off the mountains.

What were you going to do if you had a mountain frontier? he asked.

I had not worked that out yet, I said, and we both laughed. "But," I said, "in the old days the Austrians were always whipped in the quadrilateral around Verona. They let them come down onto the plain and whipped them there."

"Yes," said Gino. "But those were Frenchmen and you can work out military problems clearly when you are fighting in somebody else's country."

"Yes," I agreed, "when it is your own country you cannot use it so scientifically."

"The Russians did, to trap Napoleon."

"Yes, but they had plenty of country. If you tried to retreat to trap Napoleon in Italy you would find yourself in Brindisi."

"A terrible place," said Gino. "Have you ever been there?"

"Not to stay."

"I am a patriot," Gino said. "But I cannot love Brindisi or Taranto."

"Do you love the Bainsizza?" I asked.

"The soil is sacred," he said. "But I wish it grew more potatoes. You know when we came here we found fields of potatoes the Austrians had planted."

"Has the food really been short?"

"I myself have never had enough to eat but I am a big eater and have not starved. The mess is average. The regiments in the line get pretty good food but those in support don't get so much. Something is wrong somewhere. There should be plenty of food."

"The dogfish are selling it somewhere else."

"Yes, they give the battalions in the front line as much as they can but the ones in back are very short. They have eaten all the Austrians' potatoes and chestnuts from the woods. They ought to feed them better. We are big eaters. I am sure there is plenty of food. It is very bad for the soldiers to be short of food. Have you ever noticed the difference it makes in the way you think?"

"Yes," I said. "It can't win a war but it can lose one."

"We won't talk about losing. There is enough talk about losing. What has been done this summer cannot have been done in vain."

I did not say anything. I was always embarrassed by the words sacred, glorious, and sacrifice and the expression in vain. We had heard them, sometimes standing in the rain almost out of earshot, so that only the shouted words came through, and had read them, on proclamations that were slapped up by billposters

Trench warfare in World War I

over other proclamations, now for a long time, and I had seen nothing sacred, and the things that were glorious had no glory and the sacrifices were like the stockyards at Chicago if nothing was done with the meat except to bury it. There were many words that you could not stand to hear and finally only the names of places had dignity. Certain numbers were the same way and certain dates and these with the names of the places were all you could say and have them mean anything. Abstract words such as glory, honor, courage, or hallow were obscene beside the concrete names of villages, the numbers of roads, the names of rivers, the numbers of regiments and the dates. Gino was a patriot, so he said things that separated us sometimes, but he was also a fine boy and I understood his being a patriot. He was born one. He left with Peduzzi in the car to go back to Gorizia.

It stormed all that day. The wind drove down the rain and everywhere there was standing water and mud. The plaster of the broken houses was gray and wet. Late in the afternoon the rain stopped and from out number two post I saw the bare wet autumn country with clouds over the tops of the hills and the straw screening over the roads wet and dripping. The sun came out once before it went down and shone on the bare woods beyond the ridge. There were many Austrian guns in the woods on that ridge but only a few fired. I watched the sudden round puffs of shrapnel smoke in the sky above a broken farmhouse near where the line was; soft puffs with a yellow white flash in the centre. You saw the flash, then heard the crack, then saw the smoke ball distort and thin in the wind. There were many iron shrapnel balls in the rubble of the houses and on the road beside the broken house where the post was, but they did not shell near the post that afternoon. We loaded two cars and drove down the road that was screened with wet mats and the last of the sun came through in the breaks between the strips of mattings. Before we were out on the clear road behind the hill the sun was down. We went on down the clear road and as it turned a corner into the open and went into the square arched tunnel of matting the rain started again.

The wind rose in the night and at three o'clock in the morning with the rain coming in sheets there was a bombardment and the Croatians came over across the mountain meadows and through patches of woods and into the front line. They fought in the dark in the rain and a counter-attack of scared men from the second line drove them back. There was much shelling and many rockets in the rain and machine-gun and rifle fire all along the line. They did not come again and it was quieter and between the gusts of wind and rain we could hear the sound of a great bombardment far to the north.

The wounded were coming into the post, some were carried on stretchers, some walking and some were brought on the backs of men that came across the field. They were wet to the skin and all were scared. We filled two cars with stretcher cases as they came up from the cellar of the post and as I shut the door of the second car and fastened it I felt the rain on my face turn to snow. The flakes were coming heavy and fast in the rain.

Analyzing Literature

Use the passage on these pages to answer the following questions.

1. What is the narrator's attitude about the war?
   - **A** He is a patriot and defender of his homeland.
   - **B** He is tired and does not believe in the part of the war in which he is fighting.
   - **C** He wants to motivate others to get involved in the war.
   - **D** He is fiercely determined to defeat the enemy.
2. Why might the narrator be embarrassed by Gino's patriotism?
   - **A** He is a shy man who is easily embarrassed by things.
   - **B** Gino is trying to convince him to stay in Italy after the war, and he doesn't want to.
   - **C** His job of handling dead and injured men makes it hard for him to sympathize with Gino.
   - **D** He knows too much about Gino's past to believe him fully.
3. **Critical Thinking: Determining Relevance** Hemingway is known for using simple words and short, descriptive sentences. Do you think this style effectively conveys the feeling of being in a war? Why or why not?

American Literature

American Literature

Analyzing the Document Use this additional question to generate class discussion:

Critical Thinking: Formulating Questions What questions might you ask Frederick Henry to learn more about his attitude toward war? *(How long have you been here? What is your work? How do you feel about your work? What do you think about this war? Do you feel you are helping your country? Do you believe in the cause for which you are fighting?)*

TEST PREPARATION

Have students use the excerpt on these pages to answer the question below.

Which word best describes Frederick Henry's attitude toward war in general?

- **A** Excited
- Ⓑ Disillusioned
- **C** Angry
- **D** Frightened

ANSWERS

1. B
2. C
3. Answers will vary, but might mention a certain starkness, which is a kind of symbolism through which Hemingway conveys his own emotions about war.

Growing Up
By Russell Baker

Focus Have students read the introduction and look up the meanings of the vocabulary words. Then explain that "going on relief" (what today would be called "going on welfare") has often been viewed as shameful in the United States. That is why President Franklin Roosevelt tried so hard to find work for the nation's unemployed, instead of giving them handouts. Some people were not eligible for any of Roosevelt's programs, however, and, like Baker's family, ended up on relief anyway, despite their best efforts.

Instruct Ask students to find evidence of how the Depression affected Baker and his family. What was Baker's attitude toward people who accepted government relief? How might his attitude toward accepting relief have been changed by his experience?

Extend Have students suppose that they are Baker or his mother. Ask them to write a letter to President or Mrs. Roosevelt that Baker or his mother could have written explaining their plight.

American Literature
Unit 4

Growing Up
By RUSSELL BAKER

Single parents rarely have an easy life, and during the Depression their families' very survival was threatened. Because they were the sole caregivers for their children, they could not travel to look for work. Many had no choice but to accept aid from the government. In the following excerpt from his 1982 autobiography, Growing Up, *Russell Baker, a* New York Times *columnist, remembers those difficult days and one trying day in particular.*

VOCABULARY Before you read the selection, find the meaning of these words in a dictionary:
dilapidation
appetizing
edible
incriminating
ostentatious

The paper route earned me three dollars a week, sometimes four, and my mother, in addition to her commissions on magazine sales, also had her monthly check coming from Uncle Willie, but we'd been in Baltimore a year before I knew how desperate things were for her. One Saturday morning she told me she'd need Doris and me to go with her to pick up some food. I had a small wagon she'd bought me to make it easier to move the Sunday papers, and she said I'd better bring it along. The three of us set off eastward, passing the grocery stores we usually shopped at, and kept walking until we came to Fremont Avenue, a grim street of dilapidation and poverty in the heart of East Baltimore.

"This is where we go," she said when we reached the corner of Fremont and Fayette Street. It looked like a grocery, with big plate-glass windows and people lugging out cardboard cartons and bulging bags, but it wasn't. I knew very well what it was.

"Are we going on relief?" I asked her.

"Don't ask questions about things you don't know anything about," she said. "Bring that wagon inside."

I did, and watched with a mixture of shame and greed while men filled it with food. None of it was food I liked. There were huge cans of grapefruit juice, big paper sacks of cornmeal, cellophane bags of rice and prunes. It was hard to believe all this was ours for no money at all, even though none of it was very appetizing. My wonder at this free bounty quickly changed to embarrassment as we headed home with it. Being on relief was a shameful thing. People who accepted the government's handouts were scorned by everyone I knew as idle no-accounts without enough self-respect to pay their own way in the world. I'd often heard my mother say the same thing of families in the neighborhood suspected of being on relief. These, I'd been taught to believe, were people beyond hope. Now we were as low as they were.

Pulling the wagon back toward Lombard Street, with Doris following behind to keep the edible proof of our disgrace from falling off, I knew my mother was far worse off than I'd suspected. She'd never have accepted such shame otherwise. I studied her as she walked along beside me, head high as always, not a bit bowed in disgrace, moving at her usual quick, hurry-up pace. If she'd given up on life, she didn't show it, but on the other hand she was

WORLD'S HIGHEST STANDARD OF LIVING
There's no way like the American Way

Citizens in a Kentucky relief line stand before a billboard promoting the country's high standard of living.

unhappy about something. I dared to mention the dreaded words only once on that trip home.

"Are we on relief now, Mom?"

"Let me worry about that," she said.

What worried me most as we neared home was the possibility we'd be seen with the incriminating food by somebody we knew. There was no mistaking government-surplus food. The grapefruit-juice cans, the prunes and rice, the cornmeal—all were ostentatiously unlabeled, thus advertising themselves as "government handouts." Everybody in the neighborhood could read them easily enough, and our humiliation would be gossiped through every parlor by sundown. I had an inspiration.

"It's hot pulling this wagon," I said. "I'm going to take my sweater off."

It wasn't hot, it was on the cool side, but after removing the sweater I laid it across the groceries in the wagon. It wasn't a very effective cover, but my mother was suddenly affected by the heat too.

"It is warm, isn't it, Buddy?" she said. Removing her topcoat, she draped it over the groceries, providing total concealment.

"You want to take your coat off, Doris?" asked my mother.

"I'm not hot, I'm chilly," Doris said.

It didn't matter. My mother's coat was enough to get us home without being exposed as three of life's failures.

Analyzing Literature

Use the passage on these pages to answer the following questions.

1. What conclusion does Baker draw from his mother's decision to accept government relief?
   - **A** His mother has given up on life.
   - **B** His mother no longer cares what others think of her.
   - **C** His mother wants him to quit his paper route.
   - **D** His mother is desperately poor.
2. Baker places his sweater in the wagon because he is
   - **A** hot.
   - **B** ashamed of the government-surplus food.
   - **C** ashamed of his mother.
   - **D** ashamed of the wagon.
3. **Critical Thinking: Recognizing Ideologies** How might this experience have changed Baker's image of those who accepted government help?

American Literature

Analyzing the Document Use this additional question to generate class discussion:

Critical Thinking: Identifying Assumptions What did Russell Baker assume about people who accepted relief? *(Baker assumed that people on relief were shamefully lazy and didn't want to work to pay their own way. He also assumed that they had given up hope for their lives.)*

TEST PREPARATION

Have students use the excerpt on these pages to answer the question below.

How would the neighbors know that the Bakers were on relief?

- **A** The food had official government labels on it.
- **(B)** The food was not labeled.
- **C** They would have seen them at the store.
- **D** No one would want to buy grapefruit juice, cornmeal, prunes, and rice.

Answers

1. D
2. B
3. Answers should indicate that he probably realized many people who accepted government relief were as hardworking and honest as his own family.

NIGHT
BY ELIE WIESEL

Focus Have students read the introduction and look up the meanings of the vocabulary words. Then remind students that Nazi dictator Adolf Hitler imprisoned millions of European Jews and other "undesirables" in concentration camps as part of his extermination plan. One of these prisoners was Elie Wiesel, who has devoted his life to writing, teaching, and speaking out about the Holocaust.

Instruct Read aloud the first three paragraphs of the selection and point out how Wiesel repeats the word "never" to emphasize his point. Ask students to choose and read aloud the most memorable passages from the selection. Discuss the reasons for their choices.

Extend Have students read *Night* in its entirety, another of Wiesel's works, or another survivor's account of the Holocaust. Ask students to give brief oral reports summarizing their readings. Then lead a discussion on the similarities and differences among the various accounts.

American Literature Unit 5

Night

By ELIE WIESEL

Elie Wiesel, a Hungarian Jew, lost his parents and a sister in the Holocaust. Released from the Buchenwald concentration camp in 1945, he waited ten years before writing of his experiences. Night, *the book he eventually wrote, is one of the most powerful memoirs written by survivors of the Nazi camps. The excerpt below recalls Wiesel's first night in the camp.*

VOCABULARY Before you read the selection, find the meaning of these words in a dictionary:
nocturnal
antechamber
bestial
truncheon
crematory
lucidity
redemption
Talmud

Never shall I forget that night, the first night in camp, which has turned my life into one long night, seven times cursed and seven times sealed. Never shall I forget that smoke. Never shall I forget the little faces of the children, whose bodies I saw turned into wreaths of smoke beneath a silent blue sky.

Never shall I forget those flames which consumed my faith forever.

Never shall I forget that nocturnal silence which deprived me, for all eternity, of the desire to live. Never shall I forget those moments which murdered my God and my soul and turned my dreams to dust. Never shall I forget these things, even if I am condemned to live as long as God Himself. Never.

The barracks we had been made to go into was very long. In the roof were some blue-tinged skylights. The antechamber of Hell must look like this. So many crazed men, so many cries, so much bestial brutality!

There were dozens of prisoners to receive us, truncheons in their hands, striking out anywhere, at anyone, without reason. Orders:

"Strip! Fast! *Los!* Keep only your belts and shoes in your hands. . . ."

We had to throw our clothes at one end of the barracks. There was already a great heap there. New suits and old, torn coats, rags. For us, this was the true equality: nakedness. Shivering with the cold.

Some SS officers moved about in the room, looking for strong men. If they were so keen on strength, perhaps one should try and pass oneself off as sturdy? My father thought the reverse. It was better not to draw attention to oneself. Our fate would then be the same as the others. (Later, we were to learn that he was right. Those who were selected that day were enlisted in the *Sonder-Kommando,* the unit which worked in the crematories. Bela Katz—son of a big tradesman from our town—had arrived at Birkenau with the first transport, a week before us. When he heard of our arrival, he managed to get word to us that, having been chosen for his strength, he had himself put his father's body into the crematory oven.)

Blows continued to rain down.

"To the barber!"

Belt and shoes in hand, I let myself be dragged off to the barbers. They took our hair off with clippers, and shaved off all the hair on our bodies. The same thought buzzed all the time in my head—not to be separated from my father.

Survivors of a Nazi concentration camp

Freed from the hands of the barbers, we began to wander in the crowd, meeting friends and acquaintances. These meetings filled us with joy—yes, joy—"Thank God! You're still alive!"

But others were crying. They used all their remaining strength in weeping. Why had they let themselves be brought here? Why couldn't they have died in their beds? Sobs choked their voices.

Suddenly, someone threw his arms round my neck in an embrace: Yechiel, brother of the rabbi of Sighet. He was sobbing bitterly. I thought he was weeping with joy at still being alive.

"Don't cry, Yechiel," I said. "Don't waste your tears. . . ."

"Not cry? We're on the threshold of death. . . . Soon we shall have crossed over. . . . Don't you understand? How could I not cry?"

Through the blue-tinged skylights I could see the darkness gradually fading. I had ceased to feel fear. And then I was overcome by an inhuman weariness.

Those absent no longer touched even the surface of our memories. We still spoke of them—"Who knows what may have become of them?"—but we had little concern for their fate. We were incapable of thinking of anything at all. Our senses were blunted; everything was blurred as in a fog. It was no longer possible to grasp anything. The instincts of self-preservation, of self-defense, of pride, had all deserted us. In one ultimate moment of lucidity it seemed to me that we were damned souls wandering in the half-world, souls condemned to wander through space till the generations of man came to an end, seeking their redemption, seeking oblivion—without hope of finding it.

Toward five o'clock in the morning, we were driven out of the barracks. The Kapos beat us once more, but I had ceased to feel any pain from their blows. An icy wind enveloped us. We were naked, our shoes and belts in our hands. The command: "Run!" And we ran. After a few minutes of racing, a new barracks.

A barrel of petrol at the entrance. Disinfection. Everyone was soaked in it. Then a hot shower. At high speed. As we came out from the water, we were driven outside. More running. Another barracks, the store. Very long tables. Mountains of prison clothes. On we ran. As we passed, trousers, tunic, shirt, and socks were thrown to us.

Within a few seconds, we had ceased to be men. If the situation had not been tragic, we should have roared with laughter. Such outfits! Meir Katz, a giant, had a child's trousers, and Stern, a thin little chap, a tunic which completely swamped him. We immediately began the necessary exchanges.

I glanced at my father. How he had changed! His eyes had grown dim. I would have liked to speak to him, but I did not know what to say.

The night was gone. The morning star was shining in the sky. I too had become a completely different person. The student of the Talmud, the child that I was, had been consumed in the flames. There remained only a shape that looked like me. A dark flame had entered into my soul and devoured it.

So much had happened within such a few hours that I had lost all sense of time. When had we left our houses? And the ghetto? And the train? Was it only a week? One night—*one single night?*

How long had we been standing like this in the icy wind? An hour? Simply an hour? Sixty minutes?

Surely it was a dream.

Analyzing Literature

Use the passage on these pages to answer the following questions.

1. Prisoners who appear stronger than others are
   - **A** killed immediately.
   - **B** given special privileges.
   - **C** assigned to work in crematories.
   - **D** beaten more severely.
2. The reference to fog on the first night describes the
   - **A** mental confusion of the prisoners.
   - **B** mental confusion of the guards.
   - **C** atmosphere surrounding the camp.
   - **D** atmosphere within the crowded barracks.
3. **Critical Thinking: Drawing Conclusions** Explain what Wiesel means by the sentence, "Surely it was a dream."

American Literature

American Literature

Analyzing the Document Use this additional question to generate class discussion:

Critical Thinking: Formulating Questions What questions might you ask of Elie Wiesel to learn more about his life? *(Questions might include: What sort of work were you forced to do at the concentration camp? How did you survive? Why did you wait ten years to write about your experiences? Do you think that the Holocaust could be repeated today?)*

TEST PREPARATION

Have students use the excerpt on these pages to complete the following sentence.

Elie Wiesel's friend Yechiel was weeping after they left the barber because—

- **A** he no longer had any hair.
- **B** he was still alive.
- **C** he was exhausted.
- **(D)** he knew how close they were to death.

ANSWERS

1. C
2. A
3. Wiesel was probably wondering how this nightmare could really be happening. He had lost all sense of time and everything felt foggy. He might have been asking himself how it was possible that this atrocity was not a dream.

"Letter from Birmingham Jail" By Martin Luther King, Jr.

Focus Have students read the introduction and look up the meanings of the vocabulary words. Then remind students that before the civil rights movement, segregation was widely practiced in the United States, particularly in the South. Ask students to what extent they think racial tension is still evident in our society today, despite the gains made by the civil rights movement.

Instruct Discuss the various peaceful channels for effecting change in American society (e.g., letters to elected officials, petition drives, letters to the editor). What methods for effecting change can Americans turn to if these methods fail? Discuss the various ways that Martin Luther King, Jr., tried to bring about change (speeches, marches, mass protests). Ask students to list Dr. King's justifications for staging the mass protest that resulted in his being jailed.

Extend Ask students to look up articles on Martin Luther King, Jr., and the civil rights movement in issues of *Time, Newsweek,* or other news and popular magazines from the 1960s in the library or on the Internet. What can they learn from these sources about the civil rights movement and about what it was like for both white and African Americans to live during that time? You may wish to have students make photocopies of headlines, photos, and articles for a bulletin board display on civil rights.

American Literature Unit 6

"Letter from Birmingham Jail"

By MARTIN LUTHER KING, JR.

In 1963, the Reverend Martin Luther King, Jr., and the Southern Christian Leadership Conference staged a mass protest in Birmingham, Alabama. King was arrested for his participation in the protest, and from his jail cell he wrote a letter, which is excerpted below. The letter was his answer to eight Birmingham clergymen who had condemned the civil rights demonstration and criticized King as an "outside agitator" coming to stir up trouble in Birmingham.

VOCABULARY Before you read the selection, find the meaning of these words in a dictionary:
deplore
unduly
ominous
complacency
manifest

My Dear Fellow Clergymen:

You deplore the demonstrations taking place in Birmingham. But your statement, I am sorry to say, fails to express a similar concern for the conditions that brought about the demonstrations. . . .

We know through painful experience that freedom is never voluntarily given by the oppressor; it must be demanded by the oppressed. Frankly, I have yet to engage in a direct-action campaign that was "well timed" in the view of those who have not suffered unduly from the disease of segregation. For years now I have heard the word "Wait!" It rings in the ear of every Negro with piercing familiarity. This "Wait!" has almost always meant "Never." We must come to see, with one of our distinguished jurists, that "justice too long delayed is justice denied."

. . . Perhaps it is easy for those who have never felt the stinging darts of segregation to say, "Wait." But when you have seen vicious mobs lynch your mothers and fathers at will and drown your sisters and brothers at whim; when you have seen hate-filled policemen curse, kick, and even kill your black brothers and sisters; when you see the vast majority of your twenty million Negro brothers smothering in an airtight cage of poverty in the midst of an affluent society; when you suddenly find your tongue twisted and your speech stammering as you seek to explain to your six-year-old daughter why she can't go to the public amusement park that has just been advertised on television, and see tears welling up in her eyes when she is told that Funtown is closed to colored children, and see ominous clouds of inferiority beginning to form in her little mental sky, and see her beginning to distort her personality by developing an unconscious bitterness toward white people; . . . then you will understand why we find it difficult to wait. . . .

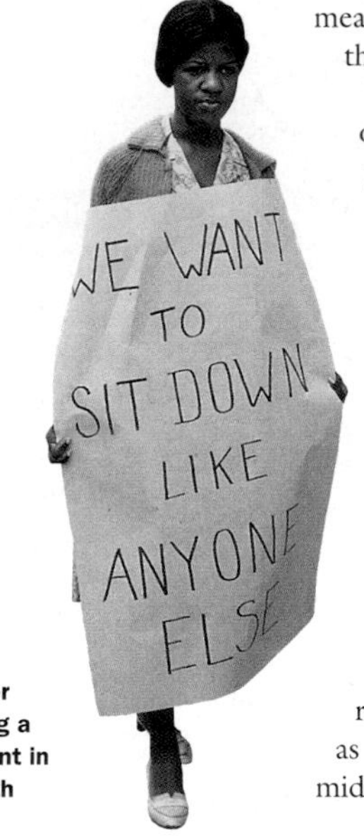

Protester picketing a restaurant in the South

You speak of our activity in Birmingham as extreme. At first I was rather disappointed that fellow clergymen would see my nonviolent efforts as those of an extremist. I began thinking about the fact that I stand in the middle of two opposing forces in the Negro community. One is a force of

As his son looks on, Martin Luther King, Jr., removes a cross that had been burned in front of his home in Atlanta, Georgia, in 1960.

complacency, made up in part of Negroes who, as a result of long years of oppression, are so drained of self-respect and a sense of "somebodiness" that they have adjusted to segregation; and in part of a few middle-class Negroes who, because of a degree of academic and economic security and because in some ways they profit by segregation, have become insensitive to the problems of the masses. The other force is one of bitterness and hatred, and it comes perilously close to advocating violence. It is expressed in the various black nationalist groups that are springing up across the nation, the largest and best-known being Elijah Muhammad's Muslim movement. . . .

I have tried to stand between these two forces, saying that we need emulate neither the "do-nothingism" of the complacent nor the hatred and despair of the black nationalist. For there is the more excellent way of love and nonviolent protest. I am grateful to God that, through the influence of the Negro church, the way of nonviolence became an integral part of our struggle. . . .

Oppressed people cannot remain oppressed forever. The yearning for freedom eventually manifests itself, and that is what has happened to the American Negro. Something within has reminded him of his birthright of freedom, and something without has reminded him that it can be gained.

Analyzing Literature

Use the passage on these pages to answer the following questions.

1. Why, according to King, could African Americans not expect whites to grant them freedom?
   - **A** Those in power never give up power without a struggle.
   - **B** African Americans do not yet deserve full freedom.
   - **C** African Americans are too divided on the issue of segregation.
   - **D** "Do-nothingism" is too common among African Americans.
2. Between which two groups does King see himself as standing?
   - **A** blacks and whites
   - **B** black clergymen and white clergymen
   - **C** blacks who favor him and blacks who favor his enemies
   - **D** blacks who accept segregation and blacks who advocate hatred
3. **Critical Thinking: Expressing Problems Clearly** Restate in your own words the message that "justice too long delayed is justice denied."

American Literature

Analyzing the Document Use this additional question to generate class discussion:

Critical Thinking: Recognizing Cause and Effect What effect did King see in his daughter after he explained that the amusement park was only for white families? *(King saw the first feelings of inferiority and resentment.)*

TEST PREPARATION

Have students use the excerpt on these pages to complete the following sentence.

King criticizes the Birmingham clergy because they—

- **A** advocate the black nationalist movement.
- **B** support direct-action campaigns.
- **Ⓒ** are more concerned with the protests than their underlying causes.
- **D** do not think that African Americans are oppressed.

ANSWERS

1. A
2. D
3. Sample answer: If people have to wait too long to be treated fairly, they are not truly receiving justice.

"Straw into Gold: The Metamorphosis of the Everyday" By Sandra Cisneros

Focus Have students read the introduction and look up the meanings of the vocabulary words. Then point out that in the selection, Sandra Cisneros describes her personal history as influenced by her family, her poverty, and her urban, Latin community. Explain that family, culture, and environment helped shape Cisneros's career as a writer and helped her to discover herself.

Instruct Divide the class into groups and have each group list the various factors that influenced Sandra Cisneros's life. After students share their lists, encourage them to discuss the challenges that the author faced as a female of Mexican descent growing up in 1960s America. Do similar factors influence Hispanic American students today?

Extend Ask volunteers to read aloud Cisneros's descriptions of her family's influence, of herself at age 11, and her accomplishments. Then ask students to write a paragraph about either the influence of their own families, themselves at age 11, or their personal accomplishments.

American Literature Unit 7

"Straw into Gold: The Metamorphosis of the Everyday"

By SANDRA CISNEROS

Recent years have witnessed an explosive growth in the diversity of American literature. Works by women, African Americans, Hispanic Americans, and Asian Americans have been both critical and sales successes, and these works reflect themes as diverse as their authors. One member of the new generation of writers is Sandra Cisneros, who was born in Chicago in 1954. The following selection is taken from her essay "Straw into Gold: The Metamorphosis of the Everyday."

VOCABULARY Before you read the selection, find the meaning of these words in a dictionary:
threshold
taboo
vagabonding
sappy

Sandra Cisneros

I've managed to do a lot of things in my life I didn't think I was capable of and which many others didn't think me capable of either.

Especially because I am a woman, a Latina, an only daughter in a family of six men. My family would've liked to have seen me married long ago. In our culture, men and women don't leave their father's house except by way of marriage. I crossed my father's threshold with nothing carrying me but my own two feet. A woman whom no one came for and no one chased away.

To make matters worse, I had left before any of my six brothers had ventured away from home. I had broken a terrible taboo. Somehow, looking back at photos of myself as a child, I wonder if I was aware of having begun already my own quiet war.

I like to think that somehow my family, my Mexicanness, my poverty all had something to do with shaping me into a writer. I like to think my parents were preparing me all along for my life as an artist even though they didn't know it. From my father I inherited a love of wandering. He was born in Mexico City but as a young man he traveled into the U.S. vagabonding. He eventually was drafted and thus became a citizen. Some of the stories he has told about his first months in the U.S. with little or no English surface in my stories in *The House on Mango Street* as well as others I have in mind to write in the future. From him I inherited a sappy heart. (He still cries when he watches the Mexican soaps [soap operas]—especially if they deal with children who have foresaken their parents.)

My mother was born like me—in Chicago, but of Mexican descent. It would be her tough, streetwise voice that would haunt all my stories and poems. An amazing woman who loves to draw and read books and can sing an opera. A smart cookie. . . .

What would my teachers say if they knew I was a writer? Who would've guessed it? I wasn't a very bright student. I didn't much like school because we moved so much and I was always new and funny-looking. In my fifth-grade report card, I have nothing but an avalanche of C's and D's, but I don't remember being that stupid. I was good at art and I read plenty of library books and Kiki [her brother] laughed at all my jokes. At home I was fine, but at school I never opened my mouth except when the teacher called on me, the first time I'd speak all day.

When I think how I see myself, it would have to be at age eleven. I know I'm thirty-two on the outside, but inside I'm eleven. I'm the girl in the picture with skinny arms and a crumpled shirt and crooked hair. I didn't like school because all they saw was the outside me. School was lots of rules and sitting with your hands folded and being very afraid all the time. I liked looking out the window and thinking. I liked staring at the girl across the way writing her name over and over again in red ink. I wondered why the boy with the dirty collar in front of me didn't have a mama who took better care of him.

I think my mama and papa did the best they could to keep us warm and clean and never hungry. We had birthday and graduation parties and things like that, but there was another hunger that had to be fed. There was a hunger I didn't even have a name for. Was this when I began writing?

In 1966 we moved into a house, a real one, our first real home. This meant we didn't have to change schools and be the new kids on the block every couple of years. We could make friends and not be afraid we'd have to say goodbye to them and start all over. My brothers and the flock of boys they brought home would become important characters eventually for my stories—Louie and his cousins, Meme Ortiz and his dog with two names, one in English and one in Spanish. . . .

This was the period in my life, that slippery age when you are both child and woman and neither, I was to record in *The House on Mango Street.* I was still shy. I was a girl who couldn't come out of her shell.

How was I to know I would be recording and documenting the women who sat their sadness on an elbow and stared out a window? It would be the streets of Chicago I would later record, but from a child's eyes.

I've done all kinds of things I didn't think I could do since then. I've gone to a prestigious university, studied with famous writers, and taken away an MFA [Master of Fine Arts] degree. I've taught poetry in the schools in Illinois and Texas. I've gotten an NEA [National Endowment for the Arts] grant and run away with it as far as my courage would take me. I've seen the bleached and bitter mountains of the Peloponnesus. I've lived on a Greek island. I've been to Venice twice. In Rapallo, I met Ilona once and forever and took her sad heart with me across the south of France and into Spain. . . .

I've moved since Europe to the strange and wonderful country of Texas, land of polaroid-blue skies and big bugs. I met a mayor with my last name. I met famous Chicana/o artists and writers and *politicos* [politicians].

Texas is another chapter in my life. It brought with it the Dobie-Paisano Fellowship, a six-month residency on a 265-acre ranch. But most important Texas brought Mexico back to me.

Sitting at my favorite people-watching spot, the snaky Woolworth's counter across the street from the Alamo, I can't think of anything else I'd rather be than a writer. I've traveled and lectured from Cape Cod to San Francisco, to Spain, Yugoslavia, Greece, Mexico, France, Italy, and finally today to Seguin, Texas. Along the way there is straw for the taking. With a little imagination, it can be spun into gold.

Analyzing Literature

Use the passage on these pages to answer the following questions.

1. How does Cisneros think her family and background affected her as a writer?
   - **A** They shaped the kind of writer she became.
   - **B** She became a writer in order to escape them.
   - **C** They prevented her from becoming a serious writer.
   - **D** They played no role in her career as a writer.
2. Cisneros's teachers would be surprised at her choice of occupation because she
   - **A** always hated writing.
   - **B** was not curious about the world around her.
   - **C** got poor grades and participated little in class.
   - **D** was constantly changing schools.
3. **Critical Thinking: Formulating Questions** In this excerpt, Cisneros refers to accomplishing things she did not expect to accomplish. If you were interviewing Cisneros for a newspaper story on this topic, what questions might you ask her?

American Literature

American Literature

Analyzing the Document Use this additional question to generate class discussion:

Critical Thinking: Making Comparisons How is Sandra Cisneros's adult life different from her childhood? *(Answers will vary, but students may point out that she is no longer poor, has traveled the world, has taught classes, and has accomplished more than she ever dreamed she would.)*

TEST PREPARATION

Have students use the excerpt on these pages to answer the question below.

For what reason was Cisneros, as a Latina, expected to leave her father's house?

- **A** She was expected to stay and take care of the family.
- **(B)** She was expected to leave when she was married.
- **C** She was expected to leave when she had a profession.
- **D** She was expected to leave when her brothers needed her help outside the home.

ANSWERS

1. A
2. C
3. Questions may include: How did your culture affect what you expected to accomplish? How did you accomplish these things despite your expectations? What else would you like to accomplish?

The Pledge of Allegiance and The Iroquois Constitution

Focus Have students read the introductions and look up the meanings of the vocabulary words. Students may be surprised to learn the origin of the Pledge of Allegiance. Point out that the Iroquois Constitution, credited to Native American leader Dekanawidah, existed in oral form until it was finally written down for posterity in the early twentieth century.

Instruct Talk with students about the fact that the Five Nations remained united and strong (even incorporating an additional group in the 1720s) for more than 100 years after the arrival of European settlers. How do students think the Iroquois Constitution helped make this possible? In what ways does the Pledge of Allegiance serve the same function for the people of the United States today?

Eventually, the Six Nation Confederacy fell apart as the Native American groups were overcome. Ask students to apply the adage "United we stand—divided we fall" to that situation.

Assign sections of the Iroquois document to different groups of students. Have them read and discuss their section, then present a summary of it to classmates.

Extend As a class, generate a list that summarizes the proper procedure for conducting Council meetings according to the Iroquois Constitution. Have students research the current method of conducting committee meetings in the U.S. Congress. Then compare the procedures of the Iroquois Council meetings with the procedures used by the U.S. congressional committees.

American Documents

American Documents

Pledge of Allegiance

By FRANCIS BELLAMY

The Pledge of Allegiance first appeared in 1892 in a magazine called The Youth's Companion. *The original Pledge, attributed to Francis Bellamy, stated: "I pledge allegiance to my Flag and the Republic for which it stands; one Nation indivisible with liberty and justice for all." In 1924, "my Flag" was changed to "the Flag of the United States of America." Congress officially recognized the Pledge in 1942 and added the words "under God" in 1954.*

I pledge allegiance to the Flag of the United States of America, and to the Republic for which it stands, one nation under God, indivisible, with liberty and justice for all.

The Iroquois Constitution

By DEKANAWIDAH

VOCABULARY Before you read the selection, find the meaning of these words in a dictionary:
transact
dispatch

The Five (and later Six) Nations Confederacy, which originated sometime between 1390 and 1500, was an alliance of Native American tribes (the Mohawk, Onondaga, Seneca, Oneida, Cayuga, and eventually the Tuscarora) located in present-day upstate New York.

The Iroquois Constitution, generally attributed to a leader named Dekanawidah, lists the decision-making methods and governing principles of this alliance. It contains detailed descriptions of council meeting procedure, war conduct, foreign policy, and trade policy. It also describes many aspects of daily tribal life including ceremonies and rituals connected with religion, birth, adoption, and death. The unity inspired by these laws enabled the Iroquois Confederacy to remain a powerful force in the New World for at least 250 years, until factionalism and war with British and French colonists caused its council fires to be extinguished and its tribes to be dispersed in the late 1700s.

Over time, parts of the Iroquois Constitution's teachings became familiar to scholars of Native American history. But the Constitution itself continued to exist—as it had for hundreds of years—only in oral form. Its knowledge was transmitted from generation to generation, assisted by a collection of wampum belts and strings that helped tribal lords (or "sachems") remember the laws. In the late 1800s, when these belts and strings started to become lost or destroyed, the Six Nations leaders turned to the University of the State of New York and the New York State Museum for help in preserving them. They also began efforts to put their Constitution into written form.

The following excerpts from the beginning of the Iroquois Constitution were first published in 1916 in the New York State Museum Bulletin *by Arthur Caswell Parker, an expert in Native American affairs and an archaeologist at the Peabody Museum (Harvard University) and the New York State Museum. The manuscripts he used originated at the Six Nations Reservation in Ontario, Canada, in 1910. They were compiled and translated by Seth Newhouse, a Mohawk, and corrected by Albert Cusick, a New York Onondaga-Tuscarora.*

The Great Binding Law, Gayanashagowa

1. I am Dekanawidah and with the Five Nations' Confederate Lords I plant the Tree of Great Peace. I plant it in your territory, Adodarhoh, and the Onondaga Nation, in the territory of you who are Firekeepers. I name the tree the Tree of the Great Long Leaves. Under the shade of this Tree of the Great Peace we spread the soft white feathery

down of the globe thistle as seats for you, Adodarhoh, and your cousin Lords. We place you upon those seats, spread soft with the feathery down of the globe thistle, there beneath the shade of the spreading branches of the Tree of Peace. There shall you sit and watch the Council Fire of the Confederacy of the Five Nations, and all the affairs of the Five Nations shall be transacted at this place before you, Adodarhoh, and your cousin Lords, by the Confederate Lords of the Five Nations.

2. Roots have spread out from the Tree of the Great Peace, one to the north, one to the east, one to the south and one to the west. The name of these roots is The Great White Roots and their nature is Peace and Strength. If any man or any nation outside the Five Nations shall obey the laws of the Great Peace and make known their disposition to the Lords of the Confederacy, they may trace the Roots to the Tree and if their minds are clean and they are obedient and promise to obey the wishes of the Confederate Council, they shall be welcomed to take shelter beneath the Tree of the Long Leaves. We place at the top of the Tree of the Long Leaves an Eagle who is able to see afar. If he sees in the distance any evil approaching or any danger threatening he will at once warn the people of the Confederacy.

3. To you Adodarhoh, the Onondaga cousin Lords, I and the other Confederate Lords have entrusted the caretaking and the watching of the Five Nations Council Fire. When there is any business to be transacted and the Confederate Council is not in session, a messenger shall be dispatched either to Adodarhoh, Hononwirehtonh or Skanawatih, Fire Keepers, or to their War Chiefs with a full statement of the case desired to be considered. Then shall Adodarhoh call his cousin (associate) Lords together and consider whether or not the case is of sufficient importance to demand the attention of the Confederate Council. If so, Adodarhoh shall dispatch messengers to summon all the Confederate Lords to assemble beneath the Tree of the Long Leaves. When the Lords are assembled the Council Fire shall be kindled, but not with chestnut wood, and Adodarhoh shall formally open the Council. Then shall Adodarhoh and his cousin Lords, the Fire Keepers, announce the subject for discussion. The Smoke of the Confederate Council Fire shall ever ascend and pierce the sky so that other nations who may be allies may see the Council Fire of the Great Peace. Adodarhoh and his cousin Lords are entrusted with the Keeping of the Council Fire. . . .

More than just items of trade, wampum belts helped Iroquois leaders remember important laws and events.

5. The Council of the Mohawk shall be divided into three parties as follows: Tekarihoken, Ayonhwhathah and Shadekariwade are the first party; Sharenhowaneh, Deyoenhegwenh and Oghrenghrehgowah are the second party, and Dehennakrineh, Aghstawenserenthah and Shoskoharowaneh are the third party. The third party is to listen only to the discussion of the first and second parties and if an error is made or the proceeding is irregular they are to call attention to it, and when the case is right and properly decided by the two parties they shall confirm the decision of the two parties and refer the case to the Seneca Lords for their decision. When the Seneca Lords have decided in accord with the Mohawk Lords, the case or question shall be referred to the Cayuga and Oneida Lords on the opposite side of the house. . . .

7. Whenever the Confederate Lords shall assemble for the purpose of holding a council, the Onondaga Lords shall open it by expressing their gratitude to their cousin Lords and greeting them, and they shall make an address and offer thanks to the earth where men dwell, to the streams of water, the pools, the springs and the lakes, to the maize and the fruits, to the medicinal herbs and trees, to the forest trees for their usefulness, to the animals that serve as food and give their pelts for clothing, to the great winds and the lesser winds, to the Thunderers, to the Sun, the mighty warrior, to the moon, to the messengers of the Creator who reveal his wishes and to the Great Creator who dwells in the heavens above, who gives all the things useful to men, and who is the source and the ruler of health and life.

Then shall the Onondaga Lords declare the council open.

Analyzing Documents

Use the passage on these pages to answer the following questions.

1. Into how many parties was the Council of the Mohawk divided?
   A three
   B four
   C five
   D six
2. What was the function of the third party?
   A to keep the tribal council fire burning
   B to declare the council open
   C to express gratitude to and greet the other lords
   D to monitor the other two parties
3. **Critical Thinking: Making Comparisons** What similarities can you see between the structure of the United States government and the interaction among the three parties of the Council of the Mohawk?

Primary Source CD-ROM Find additional American historical documents on the *Exploring Primary Sources in U.S. History* CD-ROM.

American Documents

Analyzing the Documents Use this additional question to generate class discussion:

Critical Thinking: Recognizing Ideologies Ask students to discuss the respective roles that the Pledge of Allegiance and the excerpt from the Iroquois Constitution were expected to play in maintaining the unity of their respective nations. *(Answers will vary.)*

TEST PREPARATION

Have students use the excerpt from the Iroquois Constitution on these pages to answer the following question.

According to the Iroquois Constitution, which of the following leaders was probably the most powerful?

A Geronimo
B Hononwirehtonh
(C) Dekanawidah
D Skanawatih

ANSWERS

1. A
2. D
3. Answers should cite the Supreme Court's function as a check on the other two government branches.

The Mayflower Compact and An Act for the Gradual Abolition of Slavery

Focus Have students read the introductions and look up the meanings of the vocabulary words. Explain that the first document was created to assert the common vision of the Pilgrims. The second document was created to make Pennsylvania's position on slavery abundantly clear.

Instruct Ask students to recall the reasons the Pilgrims came to America. *(Their primary goal was to secure religious freedom for themselves, in spite of the tremendous odds against them.)* Considering those circumstances, ask students to comment on the importance of a unifying document such as the Mayflower Compact.

As students analyze "An Act for the Gradual Abolition of Slavery," discuss with them the careful way in which its writers formed the analogy between colonists and slaves. Critical to the logic of the document is the strong statement of equality among all people. Ask students to discuss the ways in which this statement echoes the Declaration of Independence.

Extend Have students speculate on what might have happened if the unrest amongst the *Mayflower*'s passengers that inspired the Mayflower Compact had degenerated into a full-blown mutiny, and the settlement at Plymouth had not been established. Then have students research the tenets of the Quaker faith and the geographic areas of the colonies in which large numbers of Quakers settled. Ask students to discuss what role Quaker philosophy might have had in inspiring Pennsylvania's Act for the Gradual Abolition of Slavery.

Answers

1. B
2. B
3. Answers might mention the long boat journey, illness, and the danger of being in a new land with winter approaching.

The Mayflower Compact

VOCABULARY Before you read the selection, find the meaning of these words in a dictionary:
sovereign
covenant

The Mayflower *landed in present-day Cape Cod in 1620. Before coming ashore, several passengers spoke out mutinously, claiming they would not accept command from the expedition's leaders. Faced with this challenge, the pilgrim fathers drafted the document now known as the Mayflower Compact as a way of reasserting shared interests. It was signed by 41 people.*

"In the name of God, Amen. We, whose names are underwritten, the Loyal Subjects of our dread Sovereign Lord, King James, by the Grace of God, of England, France and Ireland, King, Defender of the Faith, e&.

Having undertaken for the Glory of God, and Advancement of the Christian Faith, and the Honour of our King and Country, a voyage to plant the first colony in the northern parts of Virginia; do by these presents, solemnly and mutually in the Presence of God and one of another, covenant and combine ourselves together into a civil Body Politick, for our better Ordering and Preservation, and Furtherance of the Ends aforesaid; And by Virtue hereof to enact, constitute, and frame, such just and equal Laws, Ordinances, Acts, Constitutions and Offices, from time to time, as shall be thought most meet and convenient for the General good of the Colony; unto which we promise all due submission and obedience.

In Witness whereof we have hereunto subscribed our names at Cape Cod the eleventh of November, in the Reign of our Sovereign Lord, King James of England, France and Ireland, the eighteenth, and of Scotland the fifty-fourth. Anno Domini, 1620."

Painting showing the signing of the Mayflower Compact

Analyzing Documents

Use the passage on this page to answer the following questions.

1. Which of the following was a goal of the pilgrims' voyage, according to the document?
   A to bring back wealth to the European patrons of the voyage
   B to advance the Christian faith
   C to conquer the native peoples
   D to seek converts
2. What did the signers of this document promise to do after they had established laws?
   A build shelters
   B submit to and obey the laws
   C notify the king immediately of the laws
   D debate and modify the policies until all present were satisfied
3. **Critical Thinking: Identifying Central Issues** What circumstances of the pilgrims' situation might have made this document necessary? Why do you think some of the passengers were mutinous?

Primary Source CD-ROM Find additional American historical documents on the *Exploring Primary Sources in U.S. History* CD-ROM.

An Act for the Gradual Abolition of Slavery

Pennsylvania, 1780

VOCABULARY Before you read the selection, find the meaning of these words in a dictionary:
abhorrence
fortitude
thraldom

During the Revolutionary War, the British had occupied eastern Pennsylvania from 1777 to 1778. Their mistreatment of the revolutionaries helped galvanize sentiment in the state against oppression of all kinds. As a result, the Quakers and other groups who had long opposed slavery intensified their campaigns for its abolishment. Although many compromises eventually were made with slave owners, the act containing the following excerpt was passed in 1780. It did not immediately free any slaves, but instead prevented people from being "born into" servitude, established upper age limits for releasing young slaves, and

TEST PREPARATION

Have students use the text of the Mayflower Compact to complete the following sentence.

According to the Mayflower Compact itself, the document was written to—

A reinforce loyalty to the King.
B repress rebellion within the group.
C reinforce religious beliefs.
(D) create a common set of laws for the good of the group.

required slave owners to register slaves or free them by default. The act made Pennsylvania the first political entity in the western world to legislate against slavery, and in so doing "to add one more step to universal civilization."

An Act for the gradual abolition of Slavery.

WHEN we contemplate our abhorrence of that condition to which the arms and tyranny of Great Britain were exerted to reduce us; when we look back on the variety of dangers to which we have been exposed, and how miraculously our wants in many instances have been supplied, and our deliverances wrought, when even hope and human fortitude have become unequal to the conflict; we are unavoidably led to a serious and grateful sense of the manifold blessings which we have undeservedly received from the hand of that Being from whom every good and perfect gift cometh. Impressed with these ideas, we conceive that it is our duty, and we rejoice that it is in our power to extend a portion of that freedom to others, which hath been extended to us; and a release from that state of thraldom to which we ourselves were tyrannically doomed, and from which we have now every prospect of being delivered. It is not for us to inquire why, in the creation of mankind, the inhabitants of the several parts of the earth were distinguished by a difference in feature or complexion. It is sufficient to know that all are the work of an Almighty Hand. We find in the distribution of the human species, that the most fertile as well as the most barren parts of the earth are inhabited by men of complexions different from ours, and from each other; from whence we may reasonably, as well as religiously, infer, that He who placed them in their various situations, hath extended equally his care and protection to all, and that it becometh not us to counteract his mercies. We esteem it a peculiar blessing granted to us, that we are enabled this day to add one more step to universal civilization, by removing as much as possible the sorrows of those who have lived in undeserved bondage, and from which, by the assumed authority of the kings of Great Britain, no effectual, legal relief could be obtained. Weaned by a long course of experience from those narrower prejudices and partialities we had imbibed, we find our hearts enlarged with kindness and benevolence towards men of all conditions and nations; and we conceive ourselves at this particular period extraordinarily called upon, by the blessings which we have received, to manifest the sincerity of our profession, and to give a Substantial proof of our gratitude.

And whereas the condition of those persons who have heretofore been denominated Negro and Mulatto slaves, has been attended with circumstances which not only deprived them of the common blessings that they were by nature entitled to, but has cast them into the deepest afflictions, by an unnatural separation and sale of husband and wife from each other and from their children; an injury, the greatness of which can only be conceived by supposing that we were in the same unhappy case. In justice therefore to persons so unhappily circumstanced, and who, having no prospect before them whereon they may rest their sorrows and their hopes, have no reasonable inducement to render their service to society, which they otherwise might; and also, in grateful commemoration of our own happy deliverance from that state of unconditional submission to which we were doomed by the tyranny of Britain.

Be it enacted, and it is hereby enacted, by the representatives of the freemen of the commonwealth of Pennsylvania, in General Assembly met, and by the authority of the same, That all persons, as well Negroes and Mulattoes as others, who shall be born within this state from and after the passing of this act, shall not be deemed and considered as servants for life, or slaves; and that all servitude for life, or slavery of children, in consequence of the slavery of their mothers, in the case of all children born within this state, from and after the passing of this act as aforesaid, shall be, and hereby is utterly taken away, extinguished and for ever abolished. . . .

Analyzing Documents

Use the passage on this page to answer the following questions.

1. Which of the following does this document give as a reason for abolishing slavery in Pennsylvania?
   A Ending slavery would commemorate Pennsylvania's own deliverance from British slavery.
   B Slaves who were separated from their families were a menace to society.
   C Slave owners would profit from abolition because their slaves would become more loyal.
   D Pennsylvania's political leaders were deeply indebted to their slaves.
2. Before the passage of this act, what authority prevented Pennsylvania slaves from obtaining "legal relief"?
   A the United States government
   B the military-industrial state
   C the kings of Britain
   D the British army
3. **Critical Thinking: Identifying Central Issues** If the British had not occupied Pennsylvania and mistreated its residents, do you think this act would have been passed? Choose a passage in the text upon which to base your answer.

Primary Source CD-ROM Find additional American historical documents on the *Exploring Primary Sources in U.S. History* CD-ROM.

Analyzing the Documents Use this additional question to generate class discussion:

Critical Thinking: Making Comparisons In what fundamental way did the Pilgrims at Plymouth differ in their beliefs from those who wrote Pennsylvania's Act for the Gradual Abolition of Slavery? *(The Pilgrims considered themselves to be loyal subjects of the King of England.)*

TEST PREPARATION

Have students use the excerpt from *An Act for the Gradual Abolition of Slavery* to answer the following question.

What is meant by the document's phrase "tyrannically doomed"?

A Frightened of unjust leaders.
(B) Subjected to oppression by brutal, unjust leadership.
C Fated to be oppressed.
D Doomed to be dominated.

ANSWERS

1. A
2. C
3. No. Answers should mention the first two sentences of the document, which clearly connect the institution of slavery with the Pennsylvanians' own mistreatment at the hands of the British.

President Wilson's Address to Congress

Focus Remind students that for more than two years prior to this address, the United States had refrained from active military involvement in the Great War. There was considerable isolationist sentiment in the country. However, America's people, as well as its policymakers, had far more sympathy for the Allies (particularly Great Britain) than for Germany. Thus, when the German Navy resumed unrestricted submarine warfare, it was clear that the time for American passivity had ended.

Instruct Ask students to review the document in search of words and phrases that indicate Wilson's determination, in spite of personal reluctance, to take the step of declaring war on Germany. *(For example: "extraordinary session . . . there are serious, very serious, choices of policy to be made. . . . We must put excited feeling away. Our motive will . . . be . . . the vindication . . . of human right . . . .")* There are many other powerful statements in the document as well. Have students seek them out and read them to the class.

Extend Have students conduct library or Internet research to learn about Wilson's position toward the Great War prior to this speech of April 2, 1917.

President Wilson's Address to Congress

April 2, 1917

VOCABULARY Before you read the selection, find the meaning of these words in a dictionary:
belligerent
proscribe
autocratic
nullify
indemnity
dominion

In a special session of Congress held on April 2, 1917, President Woodrow Wilson delivered this "war message." Four days later, Congress overwhelmingly passed the resolution that brought the United States into World War I.

Gentlemen of the Congress:
I have called the Congress into extraordinary session because there are serious, very serious, choices of policy to be made, and made immediately, which it was neither right nor constitutionally permissible that I should assume the responsibility of making.

On the 3rd of February last I officially laid before you the extraordinary announcement of the Imperial German Government that on and after the 1st day of February it was its purpose to put aside all restraints of law or of humanity and use its submarines to sink every vessel that sought to approach either the ports of Great Britain and Ireland or the western coasts of Europe or any of the ports controlled by the enemies of Germany within the Mediterranean. . . . The new policy has swept every restriction aside. Vessels of every kind, whatever their flag, their character, their cargo, their destination, their errand, have been ruthlessly sent to the bottom without warning and without thought of help or mercy for those on board, the vessels of friendly neutrals along with those of belligerents. Even hospital ships and ships carrying relief to the sorely bereaved and stricken people of Belgium, though the latter were provided with safe-conduct through the proscribed areas by the German Government itself and were distinguished by unmistakable marks of identity, have been sunk with the same reckless lack of compassion or of principle.

I was for a little while unable to believe that such things would in fact be done by any government that had hitherto subscribed to the humane practices of civilized nations. . . . I am not now thinking of the loss of property involved, immense and serious as that is, but only of the wanton and wholesale destruction of the lives of noncombatants, men, women, and children, engaged in pursuits which have always, even in the darkest periods of modern history, been deemed innocent and legitimate. Property can be paid for; the lives of peaceful and innocent people can not be. The present German submarine warfare against commerce is a warfare against mankind.

It is a war against all nations. American ships have been sunk, American lives taken, in ways which it has stirred us very deeply to learn of, but the ships and people of other neutral and friendly nations have been sunk and overwhelmed in the waters in the same way. There has been no discrimination. The challenge is to all mankind. Each nation must decide for itself how it will meet it. The choice we make for ourselves must be made with a moderation of counsel and a temperateness of judgment befitting our character and our motives as a nation. We must put excited feeling away. Our motive will not be revenge or the victorious assertion of the physical might of the nation, but only the

Lifeboat containing survivors from a German submarine attack (above); German submarine off the United States coast (right)

vindication of right, of human right, of which we are only a single champion. . . .

With a profound sense of the solemn and even tragical character of the step I am taking and of the grave responsibilities which it involves, but in unhesitating obedience to what I deem my constitutional duty, I advise that the Congress declare the recent course of the Imperial German Government to be in fact nothing less than war against the Government and people of the United States; that it formally accept the status of belligerent which has thus been thrust upon it, and that it take immediate steps not only to put the country in a more thorough state of defense but also to exert all its power and employ all its resources to bring the Government of the German Empire to terms and end the war. . . .

While we do these things, these deeply momentous things, let us be very clear, and make very clear to all the world what our motives and our objects are. . . . Our object . . . is to vindicate the principles of peace and justice in the life of the world as against selfish and autocratic power and to set up amongst the really free and self-governed peoples of the world such a concert of purpose and of action as will henceforth ensure the observance of those principles. . . .

We have no quarrel with the German people. We have no feeling towards them but one of sympathy and friendship. It was not upon their impulse that their Government acted in entering this war. It was not with their previous knowledge or approval. It was a war determined upon as wars used to be determined upon in the old, unhappy days when peoples were nowhere consulted by their rulers and wars were provoked and waged in the interest of dynasties or of little groups of ambitious men who were accustomed to use their fellow men as pawns and tools. . . .

We are accepting this challenge of hostile purpose because we know that in such a government, following such methods, we can never have a friend; and that in the presence of its organized power, always lying in wait to accomplish we know not what purpose, there can be no assured security for the democratic governments of the world. We are now about to accept gage of battle with this natural foe to liberty and shall, if necessary, spend the whole force of the nation to check and nullify its pretensions and its power. We are glad, now that we see the facts with no veil of false pretence about them, to fight thus for the ultimate peace of the world and for the liberation of its peoples, the German peoples included: for the rights of nations great and small and the privilege of men everywhere to choose their way of life and of obedience. The world must be made safe for democracy. Its peace must be planted upon the tested foundations of political liberty. We have no selfish ends to serve. We desire no conquest, no dominion. We seek no indemnities for ourselves, no material compensation for the sacrifices we shall freely make. We are but one of the champions of the rights of mankind. We shall be satisfied when those rights have been made as secure as the faith and the freedom of nations can make them. . . .

It is a distressing and oppressive duty, gentlemen of the Congress, which I have performed in thus addressing you. There are, it may be, many months of fiery trial and sacrifice ahead of us. It is a fearful thing to lead this great peaceful people into war, into the most terrible and disastrous of all wars, civilization itself seeming to be in the balance. But the right is more precious than peace, and we shall fight for the things which we have always carried nearest our hearts—for democracy, for the right of those who submit to authority to have a voice in their own governments, for the rights and liberties of small nations, for a universal dominion of right by such a concert of free peoples as shall bring peace and safety to all nations and make the world itself at last free. To such a task we can dedicate our lives and our fortunes, everything that we are and everything that we have, with the pride of those who know that the day has come when America is privileged to spend her blood and her might for the principles that gave her birth and happiness and the peace which she has treasured. God helping her, she can do no other.

Analyzing Documents

Use the passage on these pages to answer the following questions.

1. What action by the German government prompted Wilson's speech?
A It sent Wilson a hostile telegram, threatening war.
B It declared war on an ally of the United States.
C It began to sink neutral passenger and medical ships in European waters.
D It sent troops across its border with Austria.

2. Which of the following best expresses Wilson's attitude toward the German people?
A They were at fault for their government's actions.
B They were not to blame for their government's actions.
C They were to be thanked for saving lives with their medical ships.
D They were obligated to help the United States make the world safe for democracy.

3. Critical Thinking: Recognizing Ideologies Wilson was acting out of what he believed to be his "constitutional duty." Do you agree with him that part of our United States constitutional duty is to "make the world safe for democracy"?

Primary Source CD-ROM Find additional American historical documents on the *Exploring Primary Sources in U.S. History* CD-ROM.

American Documents

American Documents

Analyzing the Document Use this additional question to generate class discussion:

Critical Thinking: Identifying Central Issues What did Wilson mean by the phrase "right is more precious than peace"? *(Answers will vary.)*

TEST PREPARATION

Have students use the document on these pages to answer the following question.

Why does Wilson refer to the step he is taking as "tragical"?

A Because its outcome is uncertain.
B Because he was a fighter by nature.
(C) Because he opposes war in principle, and he envisions American casualties and American hardships as a result of his own action.
D Because he is not angry with the German people.

ANSWERS

1. C
2. B
3. Answers will vary.

The Universal Declaration of Human Rights

Focus Have students read the introduction and look up the meanings of the vocabulary words.

Explain to students that this declaration was written soon after the establishment of the United Nations, following the end of World War II.

Instruct This important document has served to assist the United Nations in fulfilling its responsibilities for more than 50 years. Divide the class into small groups. Ask each group to study and discuss one of the articles of the document. Have each group rewrite the article in their own words and be able to state its importance. Hold a classroom discussion in which students compare this document to the Bill of Rights and the Reconstruction Amendments of the U.S. Constitution.

Extend Interested students may continue their examination of this document by seeking out examples in world history over the last 50 years in which the United Nations has intervened in a conflict in order to uphold the tenets of this document.

The Universal Declaration of Human Rights

December 10, 1948

THE UNITED NATIONS

VOCABULARY Before you read the selection, find the meaning of these words in a dictionary:
inalienable
barbarous
advent
aspiration
dignity
sovereignty
incitement
exile

On December 10, 1948, the General Assembly of the United Nations adopted and proclaimed the Universal Declaration of Human Rights. Following this historic act, the Assembly called upon all member countries to publicize the text of the Declaration and "to cause it to be disseminated, displayed, read and expounded principally in schools and other educational institutions, without distinction based on the political status of countries or territories."

The Universal Declaration of Human Rights

PREAMBLE

Whereas recognition of the inherent dignity and of the equal and inalienable rights of all members of the human family is the foundation of freedom, justice and peace in the world,

Whereas disregard and contempt for human rights have resulted in barbarous acts which have outraged the conscience of mankind, and the advent of a world in which human beings shall enjoy freedom of speech and belief and freedom from fear and want has been proclaimed as the highest aspiration of the common people,

Whereas it is essential, if man is not to be compelled to have recourse, as a last resort, to rebellion against tyranny and oppression, that human rights should be protected by the rule of law,

Whereas it is essential to promote the development of friendly relations between nations,

Whereas the peoples of the United Nations have in the Charter reaffirmed their faith in fundamental human rights, in the dignity and worth of the human person and in the equal rights of men and women and have determined to promote social progress and better standards of life in larger freedom,

Whereas Member States have pledged themselves to achieve, in co-operation with the United Nations, the promotion of universal respect for and observance of human rights and fundamental freedoms,

Official emblem of the United Nations, showing a world map centered on the North Pole and surrounded by two olive branches

Whereas a common understanding of these rights and freedoms is of the greatest importance for the full realization of this pledge,

Now, Therefore THE GENERAL ASSEMBLY proclaims THIS UNIVERSAL DECLARATION OF HUMAN RIGHTS as a common standard of achievement for all peoples and all nations, to the end that every individual and every organ of society, keeping this Declaration constantly in mind, shall strive by teaching and education to promote respect for these rights and freedoms and by progressive measures, national and international, to secure their universal and effective recognition and observance, both among the peoples of Member States themselves and among the peoples of territories under their jurisdiction.

Article 1. All human beings are born free and equal in dignity and rights. They are endowed with reason and conscience and should act towards one another in a spirit of brotherhood.

The United Nations building in New York City (above) and the Peace Palace in The Hague, The Netherlands (right), home of the International Court of Justice

Article 2. Everyone is entitled to all the rights and freedoms set forth in this Declaration, without distinction of any kind, such as race, colour, sex, language, religion, political or other opinion, national or social origin, property, birth or other status. Furthermore, no distinction shall be made on the basis of the political, jurisdictional or international status of the country or territory to which a person belongs, whether it be independent, trust, non-self-governing or under any other limitation of sovereignty.

Article 3. Everyone has the right to life, liberty and security of person.

Article 4. No one shall be held in slavery or servitude; slavery and the slave trade shall be prohibited in all their forms.

Article 5. No one shall be subjected to torture or to cruel, inhuman or degrading treatment or punishment.

Article 6. Everyone has the right to recognition everywhere as a person before the law.

Article 7. All are equal before the law and are entitled without any discrimination to equal protection of the law. All are entitled to equal protection against any discrimination in violation of this Declaration and against any incitement to such discrimination.

Article 8. Everyone has the right to an effective remedy by the competent national tribunals for acts violating the fundamental rights granted him by the constitution or by law.

Article 9. No one shall be subjected to arbitrary arrest, detention or exile.

Article 10. Everyone is entitled in full equality to a fair and public hearing by an independent and impartial tribunal, in the determination of his rights and obligations and of any criminal charge against him. . . .

Analyzing Documents

Use the passage on these pages to answer the following questions.

1. According to the document, all humans are born "free and equal" in
   A dignity and rights.
   B religion and political opinion.
   C financial status.
   D national origin.
2. What right does the document provide to individuals for addressing criminal charges against them?
   A They may write a letter to a regional authority in response to the charge.
   B They may take the matter up with a member of their congress.
   C They have the right to remain silent.
   D They are entitled to a fair public hearing by an impartial tribunal.
3. **Critical Thinking: Identifying Assumptions** This document assumes that individuals or nations in conflict should be given impartial hearings. What type of organization is needed to ensure that this occurs? Where is this tribunal conducted?

Primary Source CD-ROM Find additional American historical documents on the *Exploring Primary Sources in U.S. History* CD-ROM.

American Documents

Analyzing the Document Use this additional question to generate class discussion:

Critical Thinking: Making Comparisons Ask students to find portions of the Universal Declaration of Human Rights that echo the Declaration of Independence. *(Answers will vary, but should include Articles 1 and 3.)*

TEST PREPARATION

Have students use the document on these pages to answer the following question.

What is meant by the word "contempt" in the preamble of this document?

Ⓐ Disdain
B Disregard
C Disinclination
D Destruction

ANSWERS

1. A
2. D
3. Answers should mention some sort of world court or tribunal. This court is conducted in The Hague, Netherlands.

Eisenhower's Farewell Address to the Nation

Focus Have students read the introduction and look up the meanings of the vocabulary words.

Explain that President Eisenhower chose to focus his statement on what he viewed as the greatest threat to the world in the years of his presidency: the unbridled growth of communism.

Instruct Eisenhower's speech reflects his position that the threat of communism, though in his opinion insidious and widespread, required a very careful response, one that emphasized negotiation and communication as well as the maintenance of American military strength. Have students isolate portions of the document that present this viewpoint. Eisenhower's speech uses many strong words and phrases to emphasize his points. Have students seek out and discuss some of the most powerful of those statements.

Extend Did subsequent Presidents heed Eisenhower's request for dialogue and negotiation with enemies while maintaining national strength? What Communist nations brought the United States into crisis less than two years after Eisenhower spoke? *(The Soviet Union and Cuba)* In what ways did President Kennedy follow Eisenhower's advice, as given in this speech, following this crisis? *(By negotiating a peaceful solution to the Cuban Missile Crisis while preparing for military action)*

Eisenhower's Farewell Address to the Nation

January 17, 1961

VOCABULARY Before you read the selection, find the meaning of these words in a dictionary:
ideology
atheistic
insidious
indefinite
transitory
provocation

President Dwight D. Eisenhower

Dwight D. Eisenhower served as President of the United States from 1953 to 1961. Previously, he had served as an officer in two world wars, earned the title of "Supreme Commander, Allied Expeditionary Forces" during the invasion of Normandy on D-Day in 1944, and held the presidency of New York's Columbia University for two years. His farewell speech to the nation, given at the height of the Cold War weapons race, contained a famous warning against the buildup of undue power in an American "military-industrial complex" of armed forces leaders and armaments manufacturers. The following excerpts from the speech reveal that this former general also had strong opinions about the proper uses of such military power in the world.

. . . We now stand ten years past the midpoint of a century that has witnessed four major wars among great nations. Three of these involved our own country. Despite these holocausts America is today the strongest, the most influential and most productive nation in the world. Understandably proud of this pre-eminence, we yet realize that America's leadership and prestige depend, not merely upon our unmatched material progress, riches and military strength, but on how we use our power in the interests of world peace and human betterment.

Throughout America's adventure in free government, such basic purposes have been to keep the peace; to foster progress in human achievement, and to enhance liberty, dignity and integrity among peoples and among nations.

To strive for less would be unworthy of a free and religious people.

Any failure traceable to arrogance or our lack of comprehension or readiness to sacrifice would inflict upon us a grievous hurt, both at home and abroad.

Progress toward these noble goals is persistently threatened by the conflict now engulfing the world. It commands our whole attention, absorbs our very beings. We face a hostile ideology global in scope, atheistic in character, ruthless in purpose, and insidious in method. Unhappily the danger it poses promises to be of indefinite duration. To meet it successfully, there is called for, not so much the emotional and transitory sacrifices of crisis, but rather those which enable us to carry forward steadily, surely, and without complaint the burdens of a prolonged and complex struggle—with liberty the stake. Only thus shall we remain, despite every provocation, on our charted course toward permanent peace and human betterment.

Crises there will continue to be. In meeting them, whether foreign or domestic, great or small, there is a recurring temptation to feel that some spectacular and costly action could become the miraculous solution to all current difficulties. A huge increase in the newer elements of our defenses; development of unrealistic programs to cure every ill in agriculture; a dramatic expansion in basic and applied research—these and many other possibilities, each possibly promising in itself, may be suggested as the only way to the road we wish to travel.

But each proposal must be weighed in light of a broader consideration; the need to maintain balance in and among national programs—balance between the private and the public economy, balance between the cost and hoped for advantages—balance between the clearly necessary and the comfortably desirable; balance between our essential requirements as a nation and the duties imposed by the nation upon the individual; balance between the actions of the moment and the national welfare of the future. Good judgment seeks balance and progress; lack of it eventually finds imbalance and frustration.

The record of many decades stands as proof that our people and their Government have, in the main, understood these truths and have responded to them well in the face of threat and stress. . . .

Until the latest of our world conflicts, the United States had no armaments industry. American makers of plowshares could, with time and as required, make swords as well. But now we can no longer risk emergency improvisation of national defense; we have been compelled to create a permanent armaments industry of vast proportions. Added to this, three and a half million men and women are directly engaged in the defense establishment. We annually spend on military security more than the net income of all United States corporations.

This conjunction of an immense military establishment and a large arms industry is new in the American experience. The total influence—economic, political, even spiritual—is felt in every city, every Statehouse, every office of the Federal government. We recognize the imperative need for this development. Yet we must not fail to comprehend its grave implications. Our toil, resources and livelihood are all involved; so is the very structure of our society.

In the councils of government, we must guard against the acquisition of unwarranted influence, whether sought or unsought, by the military-industrial complex. The potential for the disastrous rise of misplaced power exists and will persist.

We must never let the weight of this combination endanger our liberties or democratic processes. We should take nothing for granted. Only an alert and knowledgeable citizenry can compel the proper meshing of the huge industrial and military machinery of defense with our peaceful methods and goals, so that security and liberty may prosper together. . . .

Down the long lane of the history yet to be written America knows that this world of ours, ever growing smaller, must avoid becoming a community of dreadful fear and hate, and be, instead, a proud confederation of mutual trust and respect.

Such a confederation must be one of equals. The weakest must come to the conference table with the same confidence as do we, protected as we are by our moral, economic, and military strength. That table, though scarred by many past frustrations, cannot be abandoned for the certain agony of the battlefield.

Disarmament, with mutual honor and confidence, is a continuing imperative. Together we must learn how to compose differences, not with arms, but with intellect and decent purpose. Because this need is so sharp and apparent I confess that I lay down my official responsibilities in this field with a definite sense of disappointment. As one who has witnessed the horror and the lingering sadness of war—as one who knows that another war could utterly destroy this civilization which has been so slowly and painfully built over thousands of years—I wish I could say tonight that a lasting peace is in sight. . . .

You and I—my fellow citizens—need to be strong in our faith that all nations, under God, will reach the goal of peace with justice. May we be ever unswerving in devotion to principle, confident but humble with power, diligent in pursuit of the Nations' great goals.

To all the peoples of the world, I once more give expression to America's prayerful and continuing aspiration:

We pray that peoples of all faiths, all races, all nations, may have their great human needs satisfied; that those now denied opportunity shall come to enjoy it to the full; that all who yearn for freedom may experience its spiritual blessings; that those who have freedom will understand, also, its heavy responsibilities; that all who are insensitive to the needs of others will learn charity; that the scourges of poverty, disease and ignorance will be made to disappear from the earth, and that, in the goodness of time, all peoples will come to live together in a peace guaranteed by the binding force of mutual respect and love.

Now, on Friday noon, I am to become a private citizen. I am proud to do so. I look forward to it.

Thank you, and good night.

Analyzing Documents

Use the passage on these pages to answer the following questions.

1. For what ends, according to Eisenhower, should the United States use its economic and military strength?
   A fighting terrorism and fascism
   B promoting world peace and human betterment
   C increasing arts and sciences education
   D promoting balance and proper posture
2. To what specific "hostile ideology global in scope, atheistic in character, ruthless in purpose, and insidious in method" was Eisenhower referring in his speech?
   A terrorism
   B secular humanism
   C communism
   D religious fundamentalism
3. **Critical Thinking: Making Comparisons** Does America face any global "hostile ideologies" today? What are they? How are we responding to them?

Primary Source CD-ROM Find additional American historical documents on the *Exploring Primary Sources in U.S. History* CD-ROM.

Analyzing the Document Use this additional question to generate class discussion:

Critical Thinking: Recognizing Ideologies Ask students to summarize Eisenhower's position on disarmament. *(He described disarmament as "a continuing imperative.")*

TEST PREPARATION

Have students use the excerpt on these pages to answer the following question.

How did Eisenhower, former Supreme Commander of the Allied Expeditionary Forces in World War II, feel about armed conflict as he left the presidency?

A He recognized it as an inevitable necessity.
B He urged against it.
C He was opposed to war in any form.
(D) He felt that it was necessary to maintain a strong military, while also pursuing diplomatic solutions to crises.

ANSWERS

1. B
2. C
3. Answers will vary, but might mention terrorism and our war against it.

Address to the Forty-Third UN General Assembly Session

Focus Have students read the introduction and look up the meanings of the vocabulary words.

Explain to students that Gorbachev's extraordinary speech and other actions he took as Soviet General Secretary ultimately led to the "new world order" he envisioned.

Instruct Remind students that when Gorbachev made his speech, the Soviet Union was still united as an enormous nation-state. However, Soviet-bloc nations, such as Poland, Czechoslovakia and others, were very soon to achieve freedom.

In Gorbachev's speech, there are many references to changes in the world itself that he believed reflected changes in the way leaders should manage relations between nations. Ask students if they feel that with this speech, Gorbachev was primarily making observations, or was he seeking to stir the world to action? Was he doing both? Would students consider him an observer, a prophet, an instigator, or all three?

Extend Ask students to compare and contrast Gorbachev's observations about the pervasiveness of global conflict and the emergence "of a mutually connected and integral world." Remind students that when Gorbachev made this speech, the Internet was not available to the general public, and e-mail was not yet widely used. In what ways is Gorbachev's observation even more accurate today than it was when he made it?

Address to the Forty-Third UN General Assembly Session

December 7, 1988

By MIKHAIL GORBACHEV

VOCABULARY Before you read the selection, find the meaning of these words in a dictionary:
ubiquitous
ideological
immutable
prerequisites
infringing
inertia
tenet

On December 7, 1988, Soviet General Secretary Mikhail Gorbachev addressed the United Nations General Assembly. After speaking about the recent changes in the Soviet Union, Gorbachev announced drastic cuts in the Soviet military presence in Eastern Europe and along the Chinese border—a move that ultimately allowed Soviet satellite nations to choose their own paths. In the following excerpts from that speech, Gorbachev reflects on a "new world order" and United States–Soviet relations.

. . . Today we have entered an era when progress will be based on the interests of all mankind. Consciousness of this requires that world policy, too, should be determined by the priority of the values of all mankind.

The history of the past centuries and millennia has been a history of almost ubiquitous wars, and sometimes desperate battles, leading to mutual destruction. They occurred in the clash of social and political interests and national hostility, be it from ideological or religious incompatibility. All that was the case, and even now many still claim that this past—which has not been overcome—is an immutable pattern. However, parallel with the process of wars, hostility, and alienation of peoples and countries, another process, just as objectively conditioned, was in motion and gaining force: The process of the emergence of a mutually connected and integral world.

Further world progress is now possible only through the search for a consensus of all mankind, in movement toward a new world order. We have arrived at a frontier at which controlled spontaneity leads to a dead end. The world community must learn to shape and direct the process in such a way as to preserve civilization, to make it safe for all and more pleasant for normal life. It is a question of cooperation that could be more accurately called "co-creation" and "co-development." The formula of development "at another's expense" is becoming outdated. In light of present realities, genuine progress by infringing upon the rights and liberties of man and peoples, or at the expense of nature, is impossible. . . .

Gorbachev addresses the United Nations.

. . . Behind differences in social structure, in the way of life, and in the preference for certain values, stand interests. There is no getting away from that, but neither is there any getting away from the need to find a balance of interests within an international framework, which has become a condition for survival and progress. As you ponder all this, you come to the conclusion that if we wish to take account of the lessons of the past and the realities of the present, if we must reckon with the objective logic of world development, it is necessary to seek—and to seek jointly—an approach toward improving the international situation and building a new world. If that is so, then it is also worth agreeing on the fundamental and truly universal prerequisites and principles for such activities. It is evident, for example, that force and the threat of force can no longer be, and should not be instruments of foreign policy. . . .

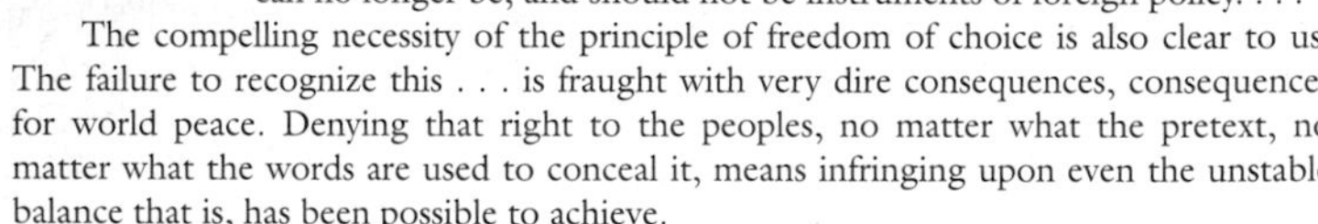

The compelling necessity of the principle of freedom of choice is also clear to us. The failure to recognize this . . . is fraught with very dire consequences, consequences for world peace. Denying that right to the peoples, no matter what the pretext, no matter what the words are used to conceal it, means infringing upon even the unstable balance that is, has been possible to achieve.

Freedom of choice is a universal principle to which there should be no exceptions. We have not come to the conclusion of the immutability of this principle simply through good motives. We have been led to it through impartial analysis of the objective processes of our time. The increasing varieties of social development in different countries are becoming an ever more perceptible feature of these processes. This relates to both the capitalist and socialist systems. The variety of sociopolitical structures which has grown over the last decades from national liberation movements also demonstrates this. This objective fact presupposes respect for other people's views and stands, tolerance, a preparedness to see phenomena that are different as not necessarily bad or hostile, and an ability to learn to live side by side while remaining different and not agreeing with one another on every issue.

. . . We are not giving up our convictions, philosophy, or traditions. Neither are we calling on anyone else to give up theirs. Yet we are not going to shut ourselves up within the range of our values. That would lead to spiritual impoverishment, for it would mean renouncing so powerful a source of development as sharing all the original things created independently by each nation. In the course of such sharing, each should prove the advantages of his own system, his own way of life and values, but not through words or propaganda alone, but through real deeds as well. That is, indeed, an honest struggle of ideology . . .

Finally, being on U.S. soil, but also for other, understandable reasons, I cannot but turn to the subject of our relations with this great country. . . . Relations between the Soviet Union and the United States of America span $5^1/_2$ decades. The world has changed, and so have the nature, role, and place of these relations in world politics. For too long they were built under the banner of confrontation, and sometimes of hostility, either open or concealed. But in the last few years, throughout the world people were able to heave a sigh of relief, thanks to the changes for the better in the substance and atmosphere of the relations between Moscow and Washington.

No one intends to underestimate the serious nature of the disagreements, and the difficulties of the problems which have not been settled. However, we have already graduated from the primary school of instruction in mutual understanding and in searching for solutions in our and in the common interests. The U.S.S.R. and the United States created the biggest nuclear missile arsenals, but after objectively recognizing their responsibility, they were able to be the first to conclude an agreement on the reduction and physical destruction of a proportion of these weapons, which threatened both themselves and everyone else. . . .

We are not inclined to oversimplify the situation in the world. Yes, the tendency toward disarmament has received a strong impetus, and this process is gaining its own momentum, but it has not become irreversible. Yes, the striving to give up confrontation in favor of dialogue and cooperation has made itself strongly felt, but it has by no means secured its position forever in the practice of international relations. Yes, the movement toward a nuclear-free and nonviolent world is capable of fundamentally transforming the political and spiritual face of the planet, but only the very first steps have been taken. Moreover, in certain influential circles, they have been greeted with mistrust, and they are meeting resistance.

The inheritance of inertia of the past are continuing to operate. Profound contradictions and the roots of many conflicts have not disappeared. The fundamental fact remains that the formation of the peaceful period will take place in conditions of the existence and rivalry of various socioeconomic and political systems. However, the meaning of our international efforts, and one of the key tenets of the new thinking, is precisely to impart to this rivalry the quality of sensible competition in conditions of respect for freedom of choice and a balance of interests. In this case it will even become useful and productive from the viewpoint of general world development; otherwise, if the main component remains the arms race, as it has been till now, rivalry will be fatal. Indeed, an ever greater number of people throughout the world, from the man in the street to leaders, are beginning to understand this. . . .

Analyzing Documents

Use the passage on these pages to answer the following questions.

1. Gorbachev did not call for nations to give up their own traditions, but issued a reminder that remaining isolated "within the range" of one's own values would lead to
   A world war.
   B unilateral disarmament.
   C spiritual impoverishment.
   D economic rivalry.
2. According to the speech, what quality should the rivalry between conflicting nations and interests have?
   A fierce and punishing aggression
   B a friendly playfulness
   C sensible competition and respect for freedom of choice
   D the underlying threat of military force
3. **Critical Thinking: Making Comparisons** To what extent have the nations of the world lived up to Gorbachev's ideals since his 1988 speech? Support your claim with historical events from the text.

Primary Source CD-ROM Find additional American historical documents on the *Exploring Primary Sources in U.S. History* CD-ROM.

American Documents

Analyzing the Document Use this additional question to generate class discussion:

Critical Thinking: Identifying Assumptions In his speech, Gorbachev suggested that "Freedom of choice is a universal principle to which there should be no exceptions." Ask students to reflect on how that statement relates to the dissolution of the Soviet bloc that took place under his leadership and in subsequent years? *(Answers will vary.)*

TEST PREPARATION

Have students use the excerpt on these pages to answer the following question.

What is meant by Gorbachev's phrase "controlled spontaneity"?

Ⓐ People should be able to exercise freedom of choice, within limits. Most importantly, the world should be a civilized place.
B People should have fun, and then they should get to work.
C The world should be a place with lots of opportunity for recreation.
D Everyone should be able to enjoy freedom.

ANSWERS

1. C
2. C
3. Answers will vary.

Illustrated Databank

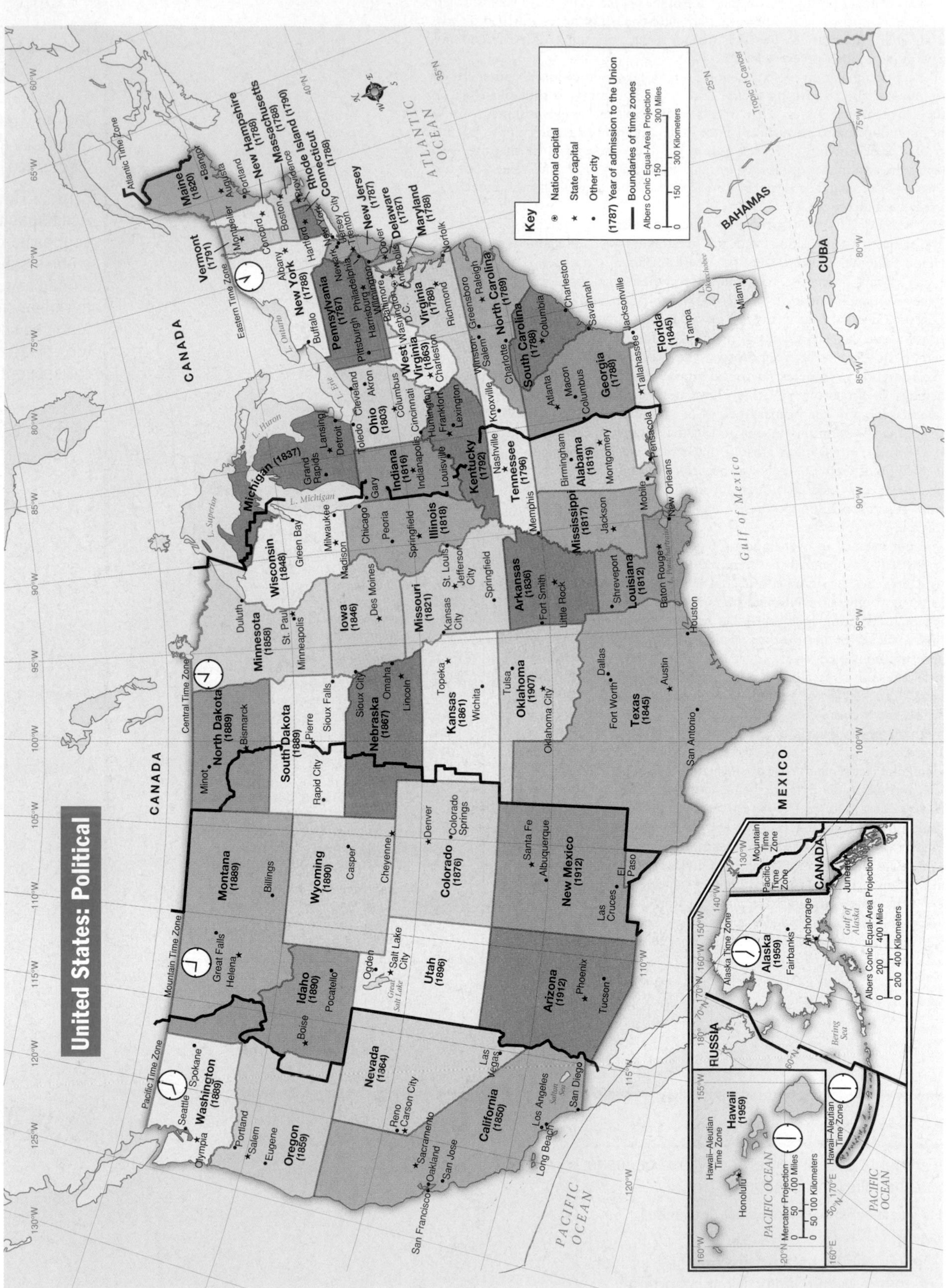

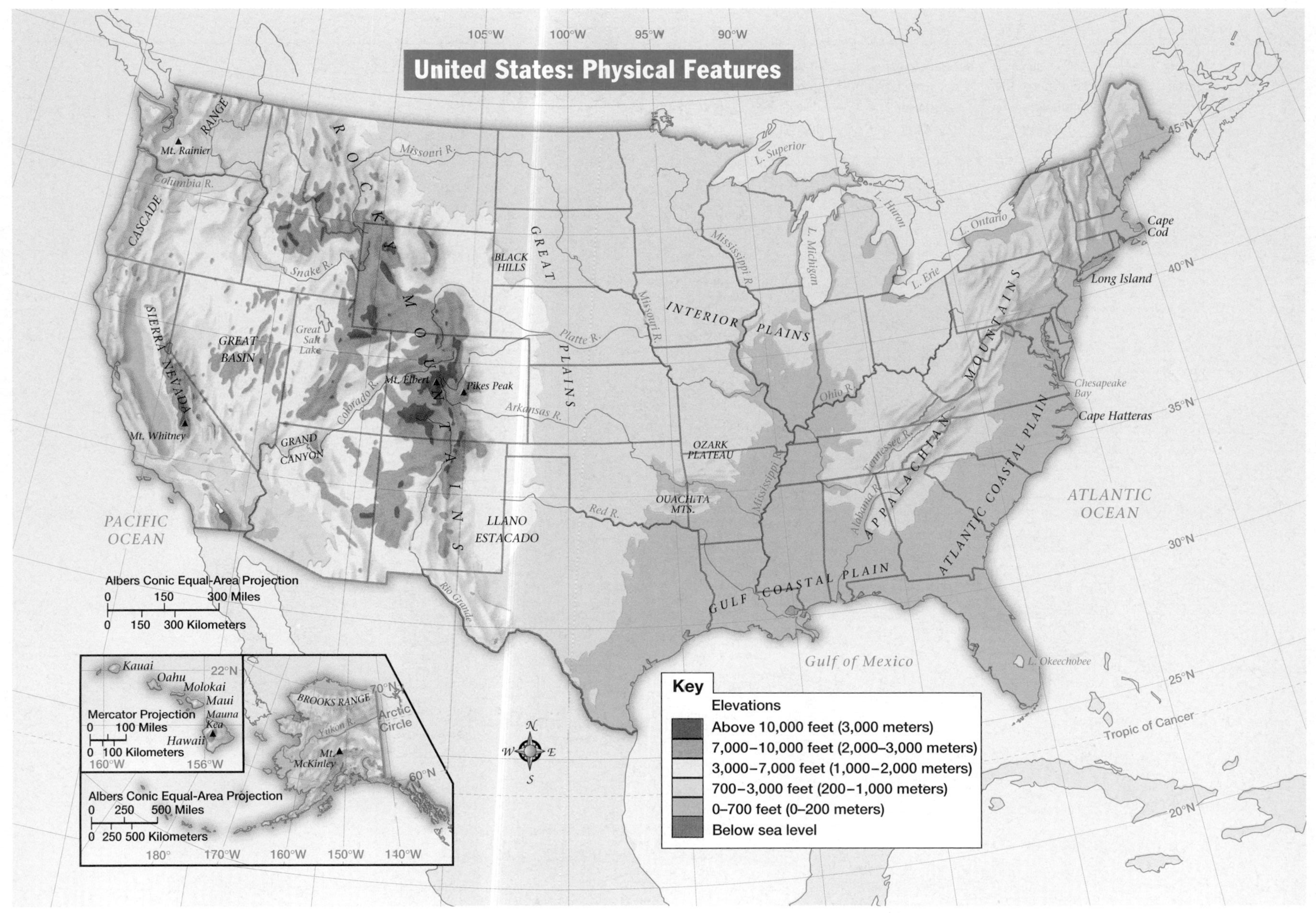

Illustrated Databank

United States: Natural Resources

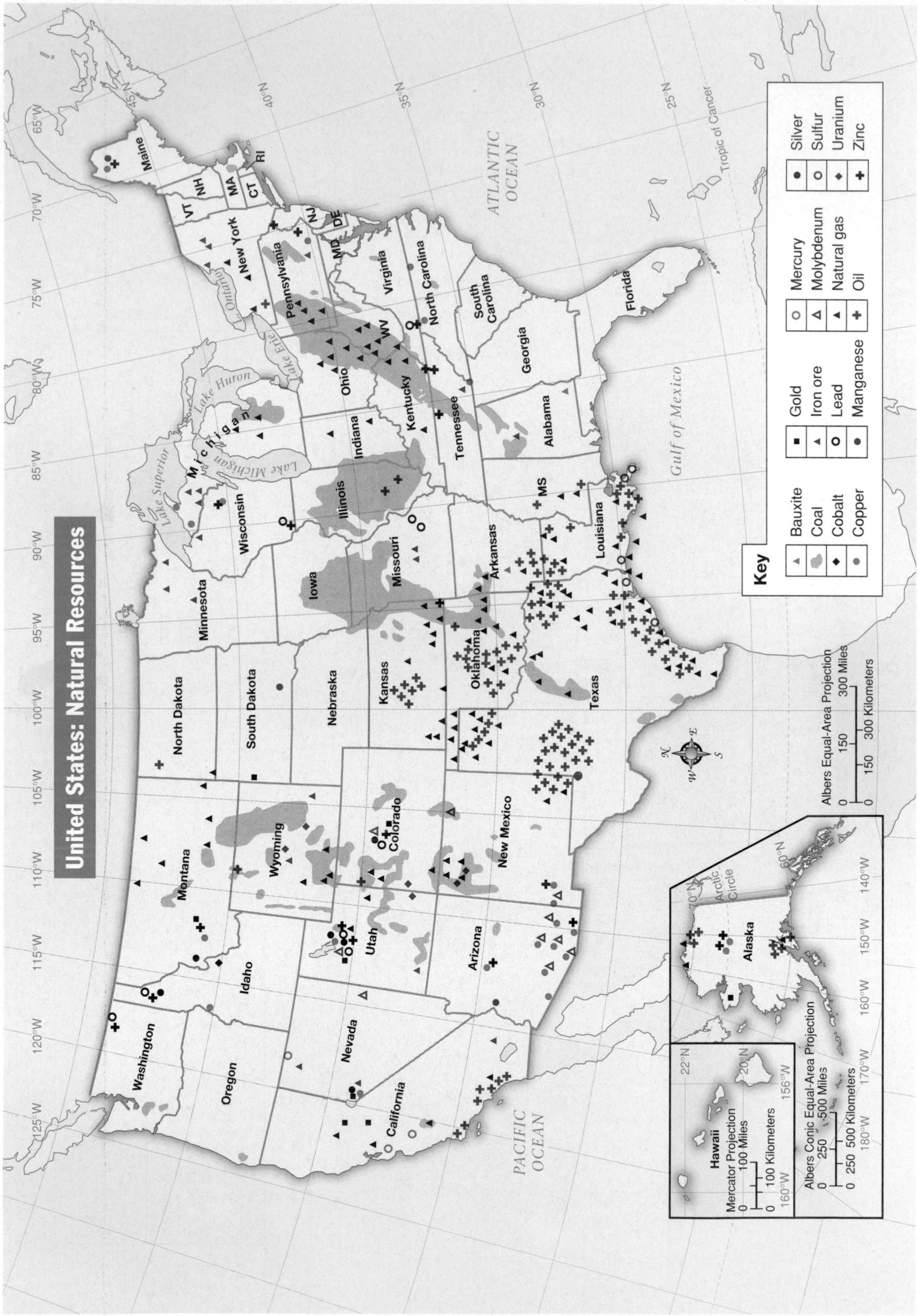

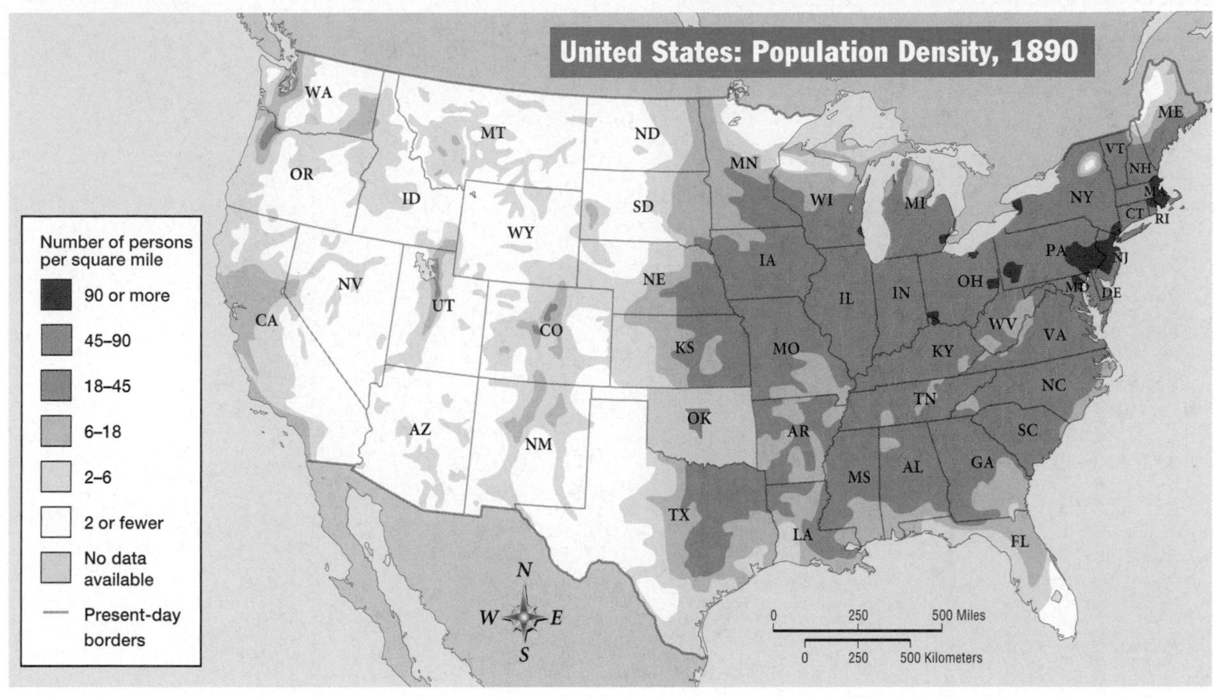

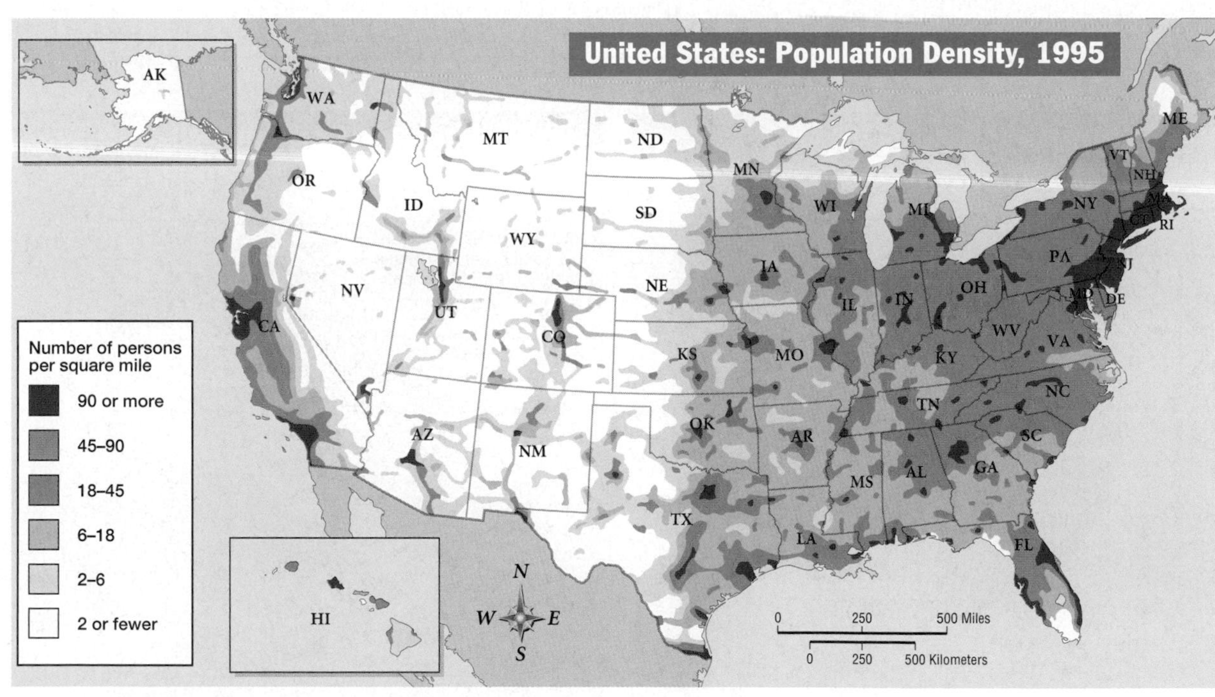

Illustrated Databank

Territorial Expansion From 1763

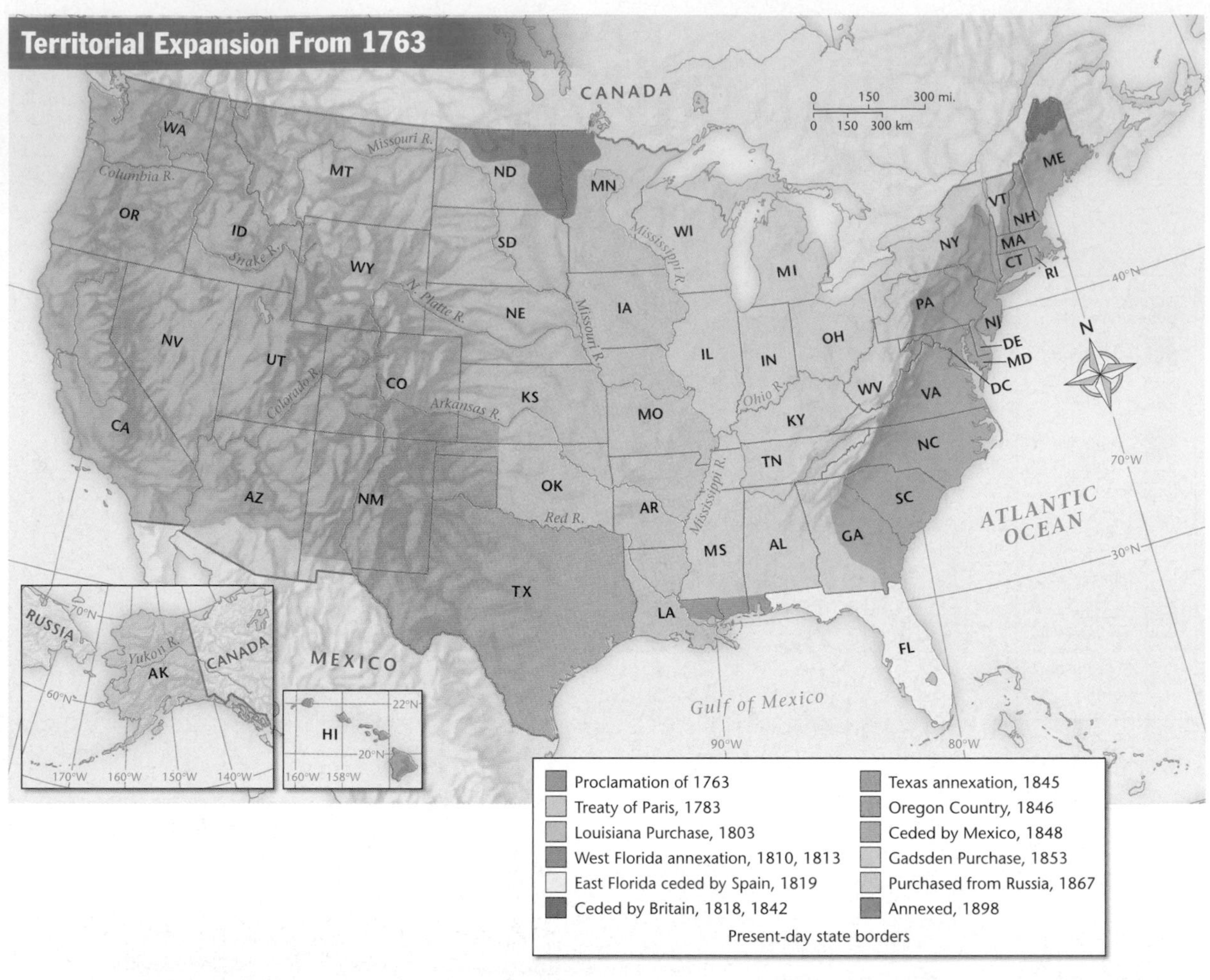

United States Ethnic Groups, 1790

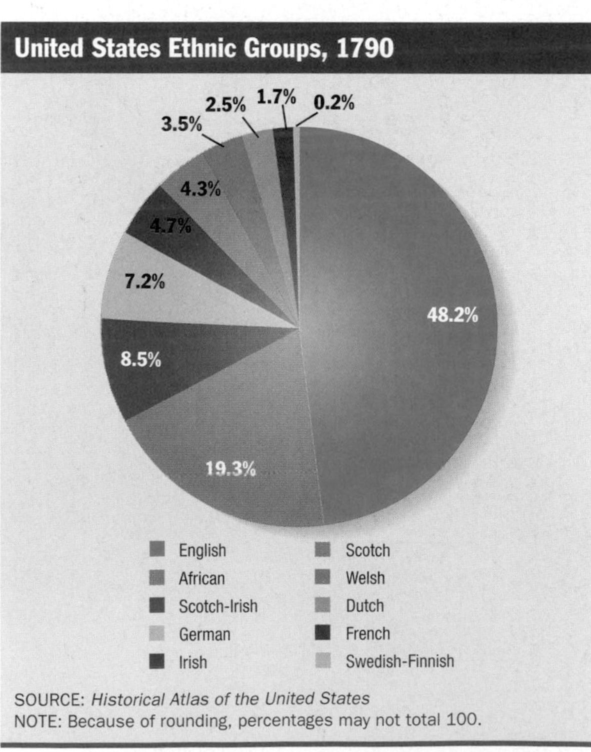

SOURCE: *Historical Atlas of the United States*
NOTE: Because of rounding, percentages may not total 100.

United States Ancestry (Self-Reported), 2000

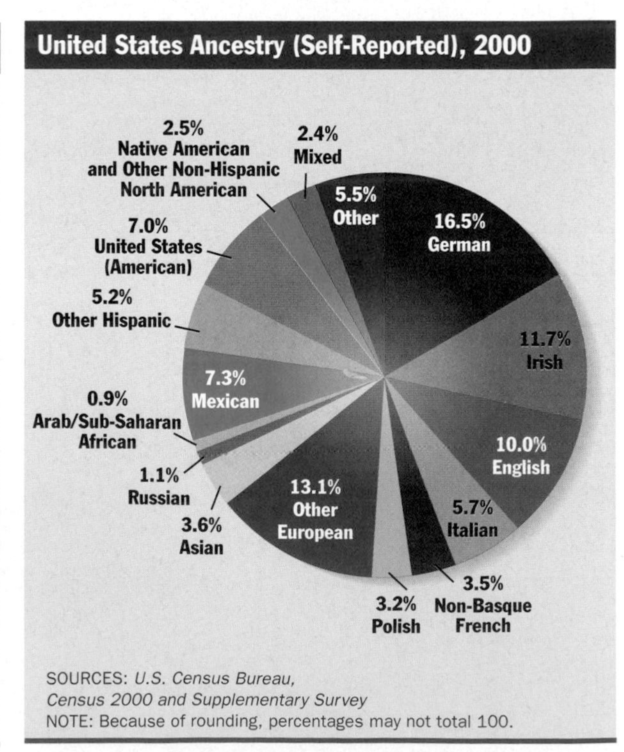

SOURCES: *U.S. Census Bureau, Census 2000 and Supplementary Survey*
NOTE: Because of rounding, percentages may not total 100.

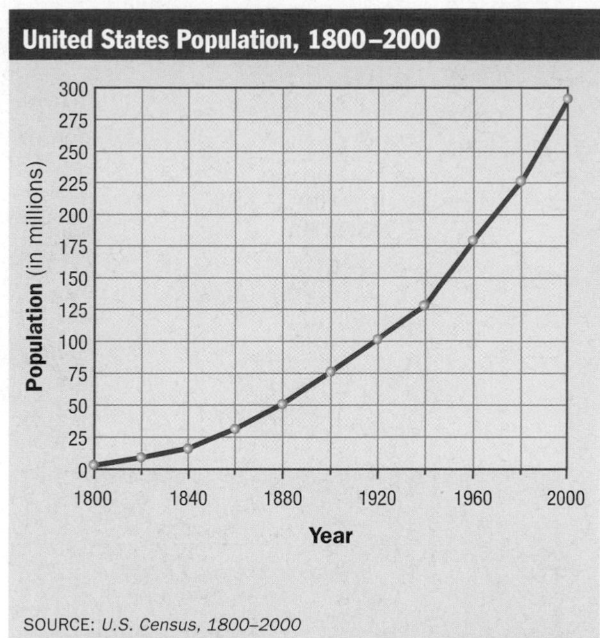
United States Population, 1800–2000
Population (in millions)
300
275
250
225
200
175
150
125
100
75
50
25
0
1800
1840
1880
1920
1960
2000
Year
SOURCE: U.S. Census, 1800–2000

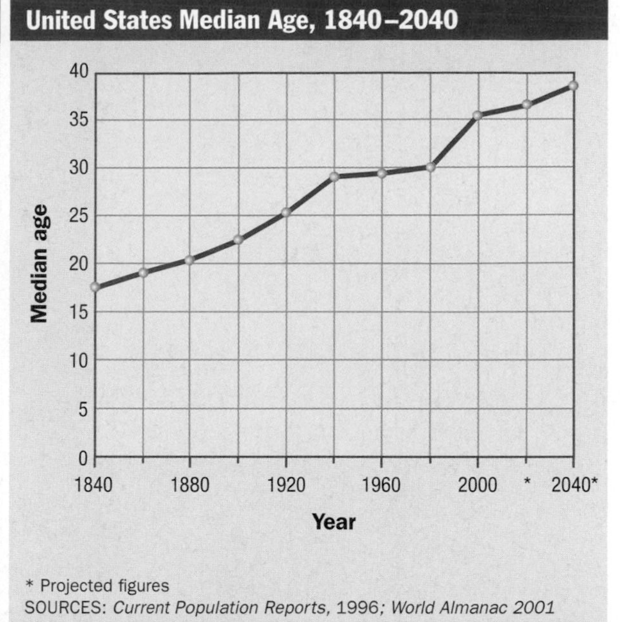
United States Median Age, 1840–2040
Median age
40
35
30
25
20
15
10
5
0
1840
1880
1920
1960
2000
*
2040*
Year
* Projected figures
SOURCES: Current Population Reports, 1996; World Almanac 2001

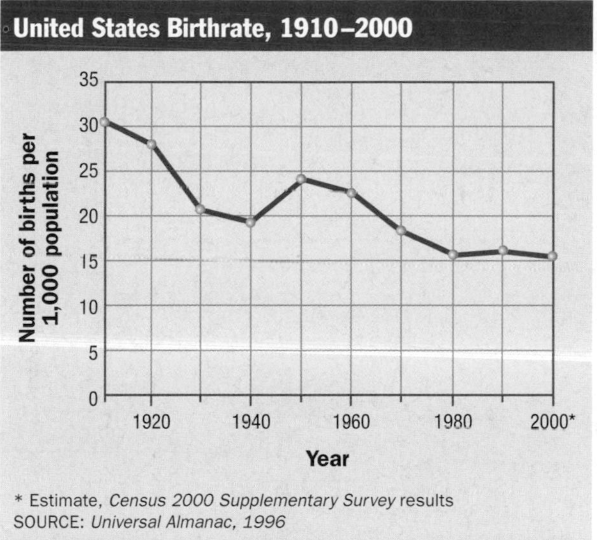
United States Birthrate, 1910–2000
Number of births per 1,000 population
35
30
25
20
15
10
5
0
1920
1940
1960
1980
2000*
Year
* Estimate, Census 2000 Supplementary Survey results
SOURCE: Universal Almanac, 1996

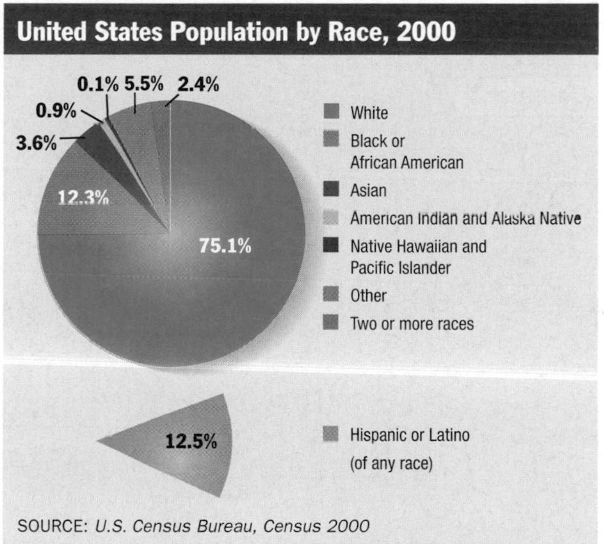
United States Population by Race, 2000
0.1%
5.5%
2.4%
0.9%
3.6%
12.3%
75.1%
White
Black or African American
Asian
American Indian and Alaska Native
Native Hawaiian and Pacific Islander
Other
Two or more races
12.5%
Hispanic or Latino (of any race)
SOURCE: U.S. Census Bureau, Census 2000

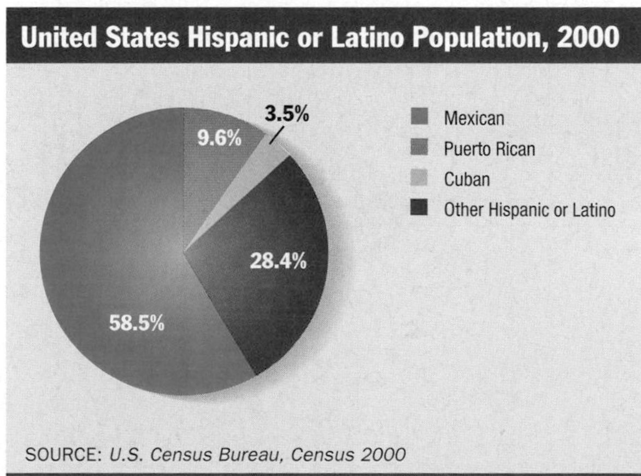
United States Hispanic or Latino Population, 2000
3.5%
9.6%
28.4%
58.5%
Mexican
Puerto Rican
Cuban
Other Hispanic or Latino
SOURCE: U.S. Census Bureau, Census 2000

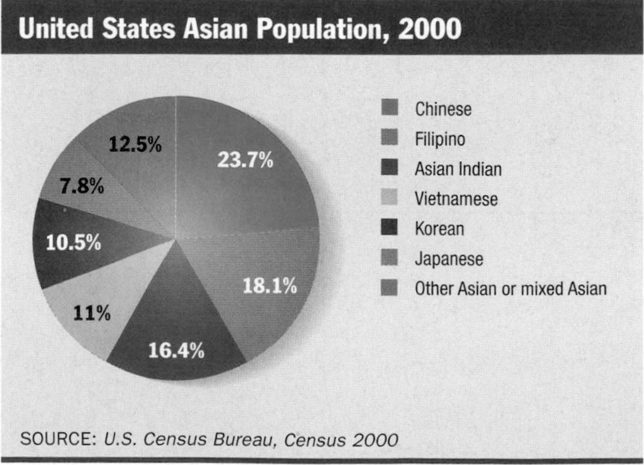
United States Asian Population, 2000
12.5%
23.7%
7.8%
10.5%
11%
16.4%
18.1%
Chinese
Filipino
Asian Indian
Vietnamese
Korean
Japanese
Other Asian or mixed Asian
SOURCE: U.S. Census Bureau, Census 2000

The World: Political

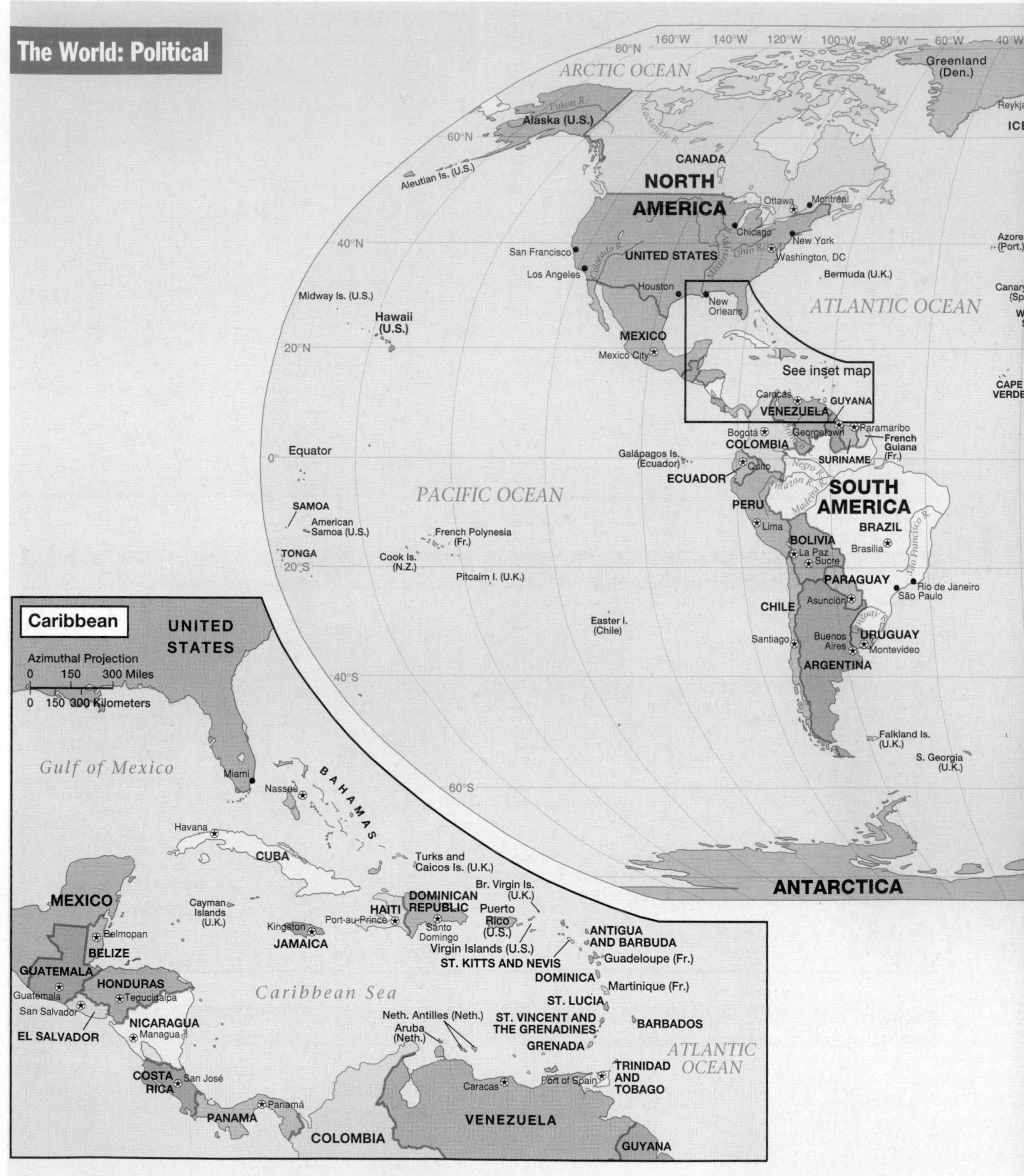

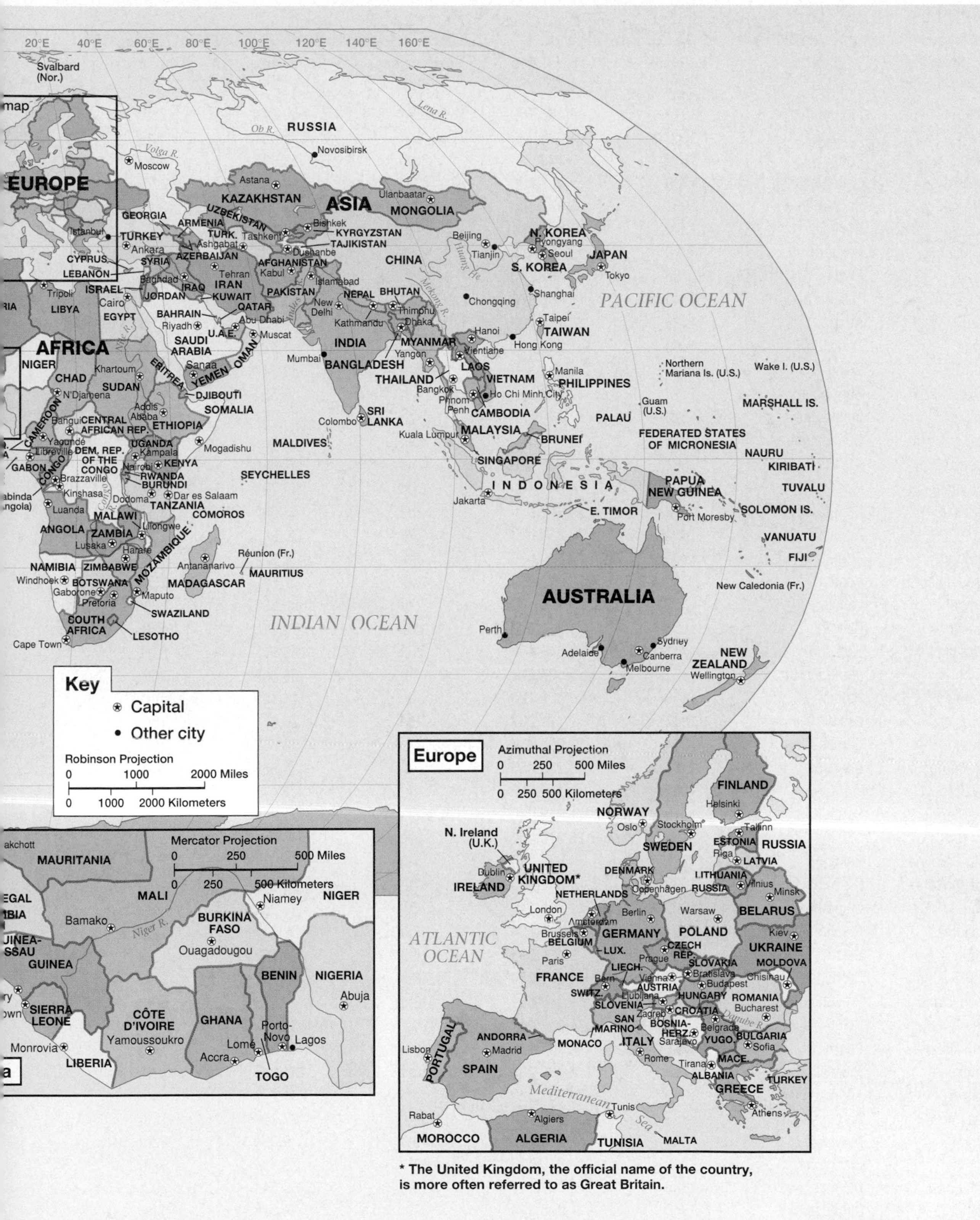

* The United Kingdom, the official name of the country, is more often referred to as Great Britain.

Illustrated Databank

Profile of the Fifty States

State	Capital	Entered Union	Population (2000)	Population Rank	Land Area (Sq. Mi.)	Land Area Rank
Alabama	Montgomery	1819	4,447,100	23rd	50,744	28th
Alaska	Juneau	1959	626,932	48th	571,951	1st
Arizona	Phoenix	1912	5,130,632	20th	113,635	6th
Arkansas	Little Rock	1836	2,673,400	33rd	52,068	27th
California	Sacramento	1850	33,871,648	1st	155,959	3rd
Colorado	Denver	1876	4,301,261	24th	103,718	8th
Connecticut	Hartford	1788	3,405,565	29th	4,845	48th
Delaware	Dover	1787	783,600	45th	1,954	49th
Florida	Tallahassee	1845	15,982,378	4th	53,927	26th
Georgia	Atlanta	1788	8,186,453	10th	57,906	21st
Hawaii	Honolulu	1959	1,211,537	42nd	6,423	47th
Idaho	Boise	1890	1,293,953	39th	82,747	11th
Illinois	Springfield	1818	12,419,293	5th	55,584	24th
Indiana	Indianapolis	1816	6,080,485	14th	35,867	38th
Iowa	Des Moines	1846	2,926,324	30th	55,869	23rd
Kansas	Topeka	1861	2,688,418	32nd	81,815	13th
Kentucky	Frankfort	1792	4,041,769	25th	39,728	36th
Louisiana	Baton Rouge	1812	4,468,976	22nd	43,562	33rd
Maine	Augusta	1820	1,274,923	40th	30,862	39th
Maryland	Annapolis	1788	5,296,486	19th	9,774	42nd
Massachusetts	Boston	1788	6,349,097	13th	7,840	45th
Michigan	Lansing	1837	9,938,444	8th	56,804	22nd
Minnesota	St. Paul	1858	4,919,479	21st	79,610	14th
Mississippi	Jackson	1817	2,844,658	31st	46,907	31st
Missouri	Jefferson City	1821	5,595,211	17th	68,886	18th
Montana	Helena	1889	902,195	44th	145,552	4th
Nebraska	Lincoln	1867	1,711,263	38th	76,872	15th
Nevada	Carson City	1864	1,998,257	35th	109,826	7th
New Hampshire	Concord	1788	1,235,786	41st	8,968	44th
New Jersey	Trenton	1787	8,414,350	9th	7,417	46th
New Mexico	Santa Fe	1912	1,819,046	36th	121,356	5th
New York	Albany	1788	18,976,457	3rd	47,214	30th
North Carolina	Raleigh	1789	8,049,313	11th	48,711	29th
North Dakota	Bismarck	1889	642,200	47th	68,976	17th
Ohio	Columbus	1803	11,353,140	7th	40,948	35th
Oklahoma	Oklahoma City	1907	3,450,654	27th	68,667	19th
Oregon	Salem	1859	3,421,399	28th	95,997	10th
Pennsylvania	Harrisburg	1787	12,281,054	6th	44,817	32nd
Rhode Island	Providence	1790	1,048,319	43rd	1,045	50th
South Carolina	Columbia	1788	4,012,012	26th	30,110	40th
South Dakota	Pierre	1889	754,844	46th	75,885	16th
Tennessee	Nashville	1796	5,689,283	16th	41,217	34th
Texas	Austin	1845	20,851,820	2nd	261,797	2nd
Utah	Salt Lake City	1896	2,233,169	34th	82,144	12th
Vermont	Montpelier	1791	608,827	49th	9,250	43rd
Virginia	Richmond	1788	7,078,515	12th	39,594	37th
Washington	Olympia	1889	5,894,121	15th	66,544	20th
West Virginia	Charleston	1863	1,808,344	37th	24,078	41st
Wisconsin	Madison	1848	5,363,675	18th	54,310	25th
Wyoming	Cheyenne	1890	493,782	50th	97,100	9th

SOURCE: *World Almanac, Census 2000*

Presidents of the United States

1

George Washington
(1732-1799)
Years in Office: 1789–1797
No political party
Elected from: Virginia
Vice President: John Adams

2

John Adams
(1735-1826)
Years in Office: 1797–1801
Federalist
Elected from: Massachusetts
Vice President: Thomas Jefferson

3

Thomas Jefferson
(1743-1826)
Years in Office: 1801–1809
Democratic Republican
Elected from: Virginia
Vice Presidents: Aaron Burr, George Clinton

4

James Madison
(1751-1836)
Years in Office: 1809–1817
Democratic Republican
Elected from: Virginia
Vice Presidents: George Clinton, Elbridge Gerry

5

James Monroe
(1758-1831)
Years in Office: 1817–1825
National Republican
Elected from: Virginia
Vice President: Daniel Tompkins

6

John Quincy Adams
(1767-1848)
Years in Office: 1825–1829
National Republican
Elected from: Massachusetts
Vice President: John Calhoun

7

Andrew Jackson
(1767-1845)
Years in Office: 1829–1837
Democrat
Elected from: Tennessee
Vice Presidents: John Calhoun, Martin Van Buren

8

Martin Van Buren
(1782-1862)
Years in Office: 1837–1841
Democrat
Elected from: New York
Vice President: Richard Johnson

9

William Henry Harrison*
(1773-1841)
Year in Office: 1841
Whig
Elected from: Ohio
Vice President: John Tyler

10

John Tyler
(1790-1862)
Years in Office: 1841–1845
Whig
Elected from: Virginia
Vice President: none

11

James K. Polk
(1795-1849)
Years in Office: 1845–1849
Democrat
Elected from: Tennessee
Vice President: George Dallas

12

Zachary Taylor*
(1784-1850)
Years in Office: 1849–1850
Whig
Elected from: Louisiana
Vice President: Millard Fillmore

13

Millard Fillmore
(1800-1874)
Years in Office: 1850–1853
Whig
Elected from: New York
Vice President: none

14

Franklin Pierce
(1804-1869)
Years in Office: 1853–1857
Democrat
Elected from: New Hampshire
Vice President: William King

15

James Buchanan
(1791-1868)
Years in Office: 1857–1861
Democrat
Elected from: Pennsylvania
Vice President: John Breckinridge

16

Abraham Lincoln**
(1809-1865)
Years in Office: 1861–1865
Republican
Elected from: Illinois
Vice Presidents: Hannibal Hamlin, Andrew Johnson

17 **Andrew Johnson**
(1808-1875)
Years in Office: 1865–1869
Democrat†
Elected from: Tennessee
Vice President: none

18 **Ulysses S. Grant**
(1822-1885)
Years in Office: 1869–1877
Republican
Elected from: Illinois
Vice Presidents: Schuyler Colfax, Henry Wilson

19 **Rutherford B. Hayes**
(1822-1893)
Years in Office: 1877–1881
Republican
Elected from: Ohio
Vice President: William Wheeler

20 **James A. Garfield****
(1831-1881)
Year in Office: 1881
Republican
Elected from: Ohio
Vice President: Chester A. Arthur

21 **Chester A. Arthur**
(1830-1886)
Years in Office: 1881–1885
Republican
Elected from: New York
Vice President: none

22 **Grover Cleveland**
(1837-1908)
Years in Office: 1885–1889
Democrat
Elected from: New York
Vice President: Thomas Hendricks

23 **Benjamin Harrison**
(1833-1901)
Years in Office: 1889–1893
Republican
Elected from: Indiana
Vice President: Levi Morton

24 **Grover Cleveland**
(1837-1908)
Years in Office: 1893–1897
Democrat
Elected from: New York
Vice President: Adlai Stevenson

25 **William McKinley****
(1843-1901)
Years in Office: 1897–1901
Republican
Elected from: Ohio
Vice Presidents: Garret Hobart, Theodore Roosevelt

26 **Theodore Roosevelt**
(1858-1919)
Years in Office: 1901–1909
Republican
Elected from: New York
Vice President: Charles Fairbanks

27 **William Howard Taft**
(1857-1930)
Years in Office: 1909–1913
Republican
Elected from: Ohio
Vice President: James Sherman

28 **Woodrow Wilson**
(1856-1924)
Years in Office: 1913–1921
Democrat
Elected from: New Jersey
Vice President: Thomas Marshall

29 **Warren G. Harding***
(1865-1923)
Years in Office: 1921–1923
Republican
Elected from: Ohio
Vice President: Calvin Coolidge

30 **Calvin Coolidge**
(1872-1933)
Years in Office: 1923–1929
Republican
Elected from: Massachusetts
Vice President: Charles Dawes

31 **Herbert C. Hoover**
(1874-1964)
Years in Office: 1929–1933
Republican
Elected from: New York
Vice President: Charles Curtis

32 **Franklin D. Roosevelt***
(1882-1945)
Years in Office: 1933–1945
Democrat
Elected from: New York
Vice Presidents: John Garner, Henry Wallace, Harry S Truman

33 

Harry S Truman
(1884-1972)
Years in Office: 1945–1953
Democrat
Elected from: Missouri
Vice President: Alben Barkley

34 

Dwight D. Eisenhower
(1890-1969)
Years in Office: 1953–1961
Republican
Elected from: New York
Vice President: Richard M. Nixon

35 

John F. Kennedy**
(1917-1963)
Years in Office: 1961–1963
Democrat
Elected from: Massachusetts
Vice President: Lyndon B. Johnson

36 

Lyndon B. Johnson
(1908-1973)
Years in Office: 1963–1969
Democrat
Elected from: Texas
Vice President: Hubert Humphrey

37 

Richard M. Nixon***
(1913-1994)
Years in Office: 1969–1974
Republican
Elected from: New York
Vice Presidents: Spiro Agnew, Gerald R. Ford

38 

Gerald R. Ford
(1913-)
Years in Office: 1974–1977
Republican
Elected from: Michigan
Vice President: Nelson Rockefeller

39

James E. Carter
(1924-)
Years in Office: 1977–1981
Democrat
Elected from: Georgia
Vice President: Walter F. Mondale

40 

Ronald W. Reagan
(1911-)
Years in Office: 1981–1989
Republican
Elected from: California
Vice President: George H. W. Bush

41 

George H. W. Bush
(1924-)
Years in Office: 1989–1993
Republican
Elected from: Texas
Vice President: J. Danforth Quayle

42 

William J. Clinton
(1946-)
Years in Office: 1993–2001
Democrat
Elected from: Arkansas
Vice President: Albert Gore Jr.

43 

George W. Bush
(1946-)
Years in Office: 2001–
Republican
Elected from: Texas
Vice President: Richard Cheney

* Died in office
** Assassinated
*** Resigned
† Elected Vice President on the coalition Union Party ticket

Illustrated Databank

Key Supreme Court Cases

These pages provide summaries of key Supreme Court rulings over the course of the nation's history. For additional material and links to Supreme Court cases, see the America: Pathways to the Present *companion Web site at* **www.phschool.com**

Baker v. *Carr,* 1962

(14th Amendment) Rapid population growth in Nashville and reluctance of the rural-dominated Tennessee legislature to redraw state legislature districts led Mayor Baker of Nashville to ask for federal court help. The federal district court refused to enter the "political thicket" of redistricting, and the case was appealed. The Court directed a trial to be held in a Tennessee federal court. The case led to the 1964 *Westberry* decision, which created the "one man, one vote" equal representation concept.

Bethel School District #403 v. *Fraser,* 1986

(1st Amendment, freedom of speech) A high school student gave a sexually suggestive political speech at a high school assembly to elect student officers. The school administration strongly disciplined the student, Fraser, who argued that school rules unfairly limited his freedom of political speech. Fraser's view was upheld in Washington State court. The Supreme Court, however, found that "it does not follow . . . that simply because the use of an offensive form of expression [is permitted by] adults making . . . a political point, the same latitude must be permitted to children in a public school."

Bob Jones University v. *United States,* 1983

(14th and 1st amendments) Bob Jones University, a private school, denied admission to applicants in an interracial marriage or who "espouse" interracial marriage or dating. The Internal Revenue Service then denied tax-exempt status to the school because of racial discrimination. The university appealed, claiming that its policy was based on the Bible. The Court upheld the IRS ruling, stating that "Government has a fundamental overriding interest" in ending racial discrimination in education.

Brown v. *Board of Education of Topeka,* 1954

(14th Amendment) Probably no twentieth-century Supreme Court decision so deeply stirred and changed life in the United States as *Brown*. A 10-year-old girl from Topeka, Kansas, was not permitted to attend her neighborhood school because she was an African American. The Court found that segregation itself was a violation of the Equal Protection Clause, commenting that "in the field of public education the doctrine of 'separate but equal' has no place. . . . Segregation is a denial of the equal protection of the laws." The decision overturned *Plessy,* 1896.

City of Philadelphia v. *New Jersey,* 1978

The Court decided that New Jersey may not restrict the importation of solid or liquid waste that originated outside the State. The Commerce Clause protects all objects of interstate trade, including waste. A State may not discriminate against items that are identical except for their origin, and thus may not prohibit out-of-state waste that is no different from domestically produced waste. Although waste disposal is a problem in many locations, States may not constitutionally deal with the problem by erecting a barrier against the movement of interstate trade.

The Civil Rights Cases, 1883

(14th Amendment) The Civil Rights Acts of 1875 included punishments for businesses that practiced discrimination. The Court ruled on a number of cases involving the Acts in 1883, finding that the Constitution, "while prohibiting discrimination by governments, made no provisions . . . for acts of racial discrimination by private individuals." The decision limited the impact of the Equal Protection Clause, giving tacit approval to segregation in the private sector.

Cruzan v. *Director, Missouri Dept. of Health,* 1990

(9th Amendment, right to die) A Missouri woman was in a coma from an automobile accident in 1983. Her family, facing astronomical medical bills and deciding that "her life had ended in 1987," directed the health-care providers to end intravenous feeding. The State of Missouri opposed the family's decision, and the family went to court. The Court ruled that states could require "clear and convincing" evidence that Cruzan would have wanted to die. However, the Court did not require other states to meet the Missouri standard. At a subsequent hearing, "clear and convincing evidence" was presented. The intravenous feeding was ended, and Cruzan died on December 26, 1990.

Dennis v. *United States,* 1951

(1st Amendment) The Smith Act of 1940 made it a crime for any person to work for the violent overthrow of the United States in peacetime or war. Eleven Communist party leaders, including Dennis, had been convicted of violating the Smith Act, and they appealed. The Court upheld the Act. Much modified by later decisions, the Dennis case focused on anti-government speech as an area of controversy.

Dred Scott v. *Sandford*, 1857

(6th Amendment) This decision upheld property rights over human rights by saying that Dred Scott, a slave, could not become a free man just because he had traveled in "free soil" states with his master. A badly divided nation was further fragmented by the decision. "Free soil" federal laws and the Missouri Compromise line of 1820 were held unconstitutional because they deprived a slave owner of the right to his "property" without just compensation. This narrow reading of the Constitution, a landmark case of the Court, was most clearly stated by Chief Justice Roger B. Taney, a states' rights advocate.

Edwards v. *South Carolina*, 1963

(1st Amendment, freedom of speech and assembly) A group of mostly African American civil rights activists held a rally at the South Carolina State Capitol, protesting segregation. A hostile crowd gathered, and the rally leaders were arrested and convicted of "breach of the peace." The Court overturned the convictions, saying, "The Fourteenth Amendment does not permit a State to make criminal the peaceful expression of unpopular views."

Engel v. *Vitale*, 1962

(1st Amendment) The state Board of Regents of New York required the recitation of a 22-word nonsectarian prayer at the beginning of each school day. A group of parents filed suit against the required prayer, claiming it violated their 1st Amendment rights. The Court ruled New York's action unconstitutional, observing, "There can be no doubt that . . . religious beliefs [are] embodied in the Regents' prayer."

Escobedo v. *Illinois*, 1964

(6th Amendment) A person known to Chicago-area police confessed to a murder but had not been provided with a lawyer while under interrogation. The Court's decision in the case extended the "exclusionary rule" to illegal confessions in state court proceedings. Carefully defining an "Escobedo Rule," the Court said, "where . . . the investigation is no longer a general inquiry . . . but has begun to focus on a particular suspect . . . (and where) the suspect has been taken into custody . . . the suspect has requested . . . his lawyer, and the police have not . . . warned him of his right to remain silent, the accused has been denied . . . counsel in violation of the Sixth Amendment."

Everson v. *Board of Education*, 1947

(1st Amendment) In a case known as "the New Jersey School Bus Case," the Court considered New Jersey's use of public funds to operate school buses that carried some students to parochial schools. The Court permitted New Jersey to continue the payments, saying that the aid to children was not governmental support for religion. The decision, however, strongly stated that the wall separating church and state must be kept "high and impregnable." This was a clear incorporation of 1st Amendment limits on states.

Ex parte Milligan, 1866

(Article II) An Indiana man was arrested, treated as a prisoner of war, and imprisoned by a military court during the Civil War under presidential order. He claimed that his right to a fair trial was interfered with and that military courts had no authority outside of "conquered territory." The Court ordered him to be released on the grounds that the Constitution "is a law for rulers and people, equally in war and peace" and covers all people "at all times, and under all circumstances." The Court held that presidential powers in time of war did not extend to creating another court system run by the military.

Furman v. *Georgia*, 1972

(8th Amendment) Three death penalty cases, including *Furman*, raised the issue of racial imbalances in the use of death sentences by state courts. Furman had been sentenced to death in Georgia. Overturning state death penalty laws, the Court noted an "apparent arbitrariness of the use of the sentence." Many states rewrote their death penalty statutes, and these were generally upheld in *Gregg*, 1976.

Gibbons v. *Ogden*, 1824

(Article I, Section 8) This case examined the power of Congress to regulate interstate commerce. Ogden's exclusive New York ferry license gave him the right to operate steamboats to and from New York. Ogden claimed that Gibbons's federal license did not give him landing rights in New York City. Federal and state regulation of commerce conflicted. The Court strengthened the power of the United States to regulate interstate business. Federal controls on television, pipelines, and banking are based on *Gibbons*.

Gideon v. *Wainwright*, 1963

(14th Amendment) Gideon was charged with breaking into a poolroom. He could not afford a lawyer, and Florida refused to provide counsel for trials not involving the death penalty. Gideon defended himself poorly and was sentenced to five years in prison. The Court called for a new trial, arguing that the Due Process Clause of the 14th Amendment applied to the 6th Amendment's guarantee of counsel for all poor persons facing a felony charge. Gideon later was found not guilty with the help of a court-appointed attorney.

Gitlow v. *New York*, 1925

(1st and 14th amendments) For the first time, the Court considered whether the 1st and 14th amendments had influence on state laws. The case, involving "criminal anarchy" under New York law, was the first consideration of what came to be known as the "incorporation" doctrine, under which, it was argued, the provisions of the 1st Amendment were "incorporated" by the 14th Amendment. Although New York law was not overruled in the case, the decision clearly indicated that the Court could make such a ruling. Another important incorporation case is *Powell*, 1932.

Goss v. *Lopez,* 1975

(14th Amendment, Due Process Clause) Ten Ohio students were suspended from their schools without hearings. The students challenged the suspensions, claiming that the absence of a preliminary hearing violated their 14th Amendment right to due process. The Court agreed with the students, holding that "having chosen to extend the right to an education . . . Ohio may not withdraw that right on grounds of misconduct, absent fundamentally fair procedures to determine whether the misconduct has occurred, and must recognize a student's legitimate entitlement to a public education as a property interest that is protected by the Due Process Clause."

Gregg v. *Georgia,* 1976

(8th Amendment) In the 1970s, activists tried to get the death penalty reinstated. Several test cases failed when the Court found the sentence had been motivated by racism, issued arbitrarily, or handed down without due process. The case of Gregg, convicted of murdering two men, was considered to be free from such problems. Finding that his conviction and death sentence were fair and consistent with state law, the Court ruled that Georgia's death penalty did not violate the "cruel and unusual punishment" clause of the 8th Amendment. For the first time, the Court clearly affirmed that "punishment of death does not invariably violate the Constitution."

Griswold v. *Connecticut,* 1965

(14th Amendment) A Connecticut law forbade the use of "any drug, medicinal article, or instrument for the purpose of preventing conception." Griswold, director of Planned Parenthood in New Haven, was arrested for counseling married couples. After conviction, he appealed. The Court overturned the Connecticut law, saying that "various guarantees (of the Constitution) create zones of privacy" and asking, "would we allow the police to search the sacred precincts of marital bedrooms . . . ?" The decision is significant for examining the concept of "unenumerated rights" in the 9th Amendment, later central to *Roe,* 1973.

Hazelwood School District v. *Kuhlmeier,* 1988

(1st Amendment, freedom of speech) In 1983, the principal of Hazelwood East High School in Missouri removed two articles from the upcoming issue of the student newspaper, deeming their content "inappropriate, personal, sensitive, and unsuitable for student readers." Several students sued the school district, claiming that their 1st Amendment right to freedom of expression had been violated. The Court upheld the principal's action, stating that "a school need not tolerate student speech that is inconsistent with its basic educational mission, even though the government could not censor similar speech outside the school." School officials had full control over school-sponsored activities "so long as their actions are reasonably related to legitimate pedagogical concerns. . . ."

Heart of Atlanta Motel, Inc. v. *United States,* 1964

(Article I, Section 8) The Civil Rights Act of 1964 outlawed race discrimination in "public accommodations," including motels that refused rooms to blacks. Although local desegregation appeared to fall outside federal authority, the government argued that it was regulating interstate commerce. The Court agreed, declaring, "The power of Congress to promote interstate commerce also includes the power to regulate the local incidents thereof, including local activities . . . which have a substantial and harmful effect upon that commerce." Racial segregation of private facilities engaged in interstate commerce was found unconstitutional.

In re Gault, 1966

(14th Amendment) Before *Gault,* proceedings against juveniles were generally handled as "family law," not "criminal law," and offenders received few due process rights. Gault was sentenced to six years in state juvenile detention for an alleged obscene phone call. He was not provided counsel and not permitted to confront or cross-examine the key witness. The Court overturned the juvenile proceedings and required that states provide juveniles "some of the due process guarantees of adults," including a right to a phone call, to counsel, to cross-examine, to confront the accuser, and to be advised of the right to silence.

Ingraham v. *Wright,* 1977

(8th Amendment) A majority of the Supreme Court concluded that the 8th Amendment historically protected people convicted of crimes, and does not apply to public school students. If authorized by local law or custom, public schools have the right to administer reasonable discipline, and students do not have a due process right to notice or a hearing before punishment administered in accordance with law or custom.

Johnson v. *Santa Clara Transportation Agency,* 1987

(Discrimination) Under its affirmative action plan, the Transportation Agency in Santa Clara, California, was authorized to "consider as one factor the sex of a qualified applicant" in an effort to combat the significant underrepresentation of women in certain job classifications. When the Agency promoted Diane Joyce, a qualified woman, over Paul Johnson, a qualified man, for the job of road dispatcher, Johnson sued, claiming that the Agency's consideration of the sex of the applicants violated Title VII of the Civil Rights Act of 1964. The Court upheld the Agency's promotion policy, arguing that the affirmative action plan created no "absolute bar" to the advancement of men but rather represented "a moderate, flexible, case-by-case approach to effecting a gradual improvement in the representation of minorities and women . . . in the Agency's work force, and [was] fully consistent with Title VII."

Korematsu v. *United States,* 1944

(5th Amendment) Two months after Japan attacked Pearl Harbor, President Roosevelt ordered the internment of more than 110,000 Japanese Americans living on the West Coast. Although many Japanese Americans were United States citizens, they had to abandon their property and live in primitive camps far from the coast. Korematsu refused to report to an assembly center and was arrested. The Court rejected his appeal, noting that "pressing public necessity [World War II] may sometimes justify the existence of restrictions which curtail the civil rights of a single racial group" but added that "racial antagonism" never can justify such restrictions. The *Korematsu* decision has been widely criticized, particularly since few Americans of German or Italian descent were interned.

Lemon v. *Kurzman,* 1971

(1st Amendment, Establishment Clause) In overturning state laws regarding aid to church-supported schools in this and a similar Rhode Island case, the Court created the *Lemon* test, limiting "excessive government entanglement with religion." The Court noted that any state law about aid to religion must meet three criteria: (1) the purpose of the aid must be clearly secular, not religious; (2) its primary effect must neither advance nor inhibit religion; and (3) it must avoid "excessive entanglement of government with religion."

Mapp v. *Ohio,* 1961

(4th and 14th amendments) Before *Mapp,* the admission of evidence gained by illegal searches was permitted by some state constitutions. Cleveland police raided Mapp's home without a warrant and found obscene materials. She appealed her conviction, saying that the 4th and 14th amendments protected her against improper police behavior. The Court agreed, extending "exclusionary rule" protections to citizens in state courts. The Court said that the prohibition against unreasonable searches would be "meaningless" unless evidence gained in such searches was excluded. The case developed the concept of "incorporation" begun in *Gitlow,* 1925.

Marbury v. *Madison,* 1803

(Article III) Chief Justice Marshall established "judicial review" as a power of the Supreme Court. After his defeat in the 1800 election, President Adams appointed many Federalists to the federal courts, but the commissions were not delivered. New Secretary of State James Madison refused to deliver them. Marbury sued in the Supreme Court. The Court declared a portion of the Judiciary Act of 1789 unconstitutional, thereby establishing the Court's power to find acts of Congress unconstitutional.

Massachusetts v. *Sheppard,* 1984

(4th Amendment) A search in Massachusetts was based on a warrant issued on an improper form. Sheppard argued that the search was illegal and the evidence was inadmissible under *Mapp,* 1961. Massachusetts argued that the police acted in "good faith," believing that the warrant was correct. The Court agreed with Massachusetts, noting that the exclusionary rule should not be applied when the officer conducting the search had acted with the reasonable belief that he was following proper procedures.

McCulloch v. *Maryland,* 1819

(Article I, Section 8) Called the "Bank of the United States" case. A Maryland law required federally chartered banks to use only a special paper to print money, which amounted to a tax. McCulloch, the cashier of the Baltimore branch of the bank, refused to use the paper, claiming that states could not tax the federal government. The Court declared the Maryland law unconstitutional, commenting ". . . the power to tax implies the power to destroy."

Miller v. *California,* 1973

(1st Amendment) In *Miller,* the Court upheld a stringent application of California obscenity law by Newport Beach, California, and attempted to define what is obscene. The "Miller Rule" included three criteria: (1) that the average person would, applying contemporary community standards, find that the work appealed to the prurient interest; (2) that the work depicts or describes, in an offensive way, sexual conduct defined by state law; and (3) that "the work, taken as a whole, lacks serious literary, artistic, political or scientific value. . . ."

Miranda v. *Arizona,* 1966

(5th, 6th, and 14th amendments) Arrested for kidnapping and sexual assault, Miranda signed a confession including a statement that he had "full knowledge" of his legal rights. After conviction, he appealed, claiming that without counsel and without warnings, the confession was illegally obtained. The Court agreed with Miranda that "he must be warned prior to any questioning that he has the right to remain silent, that anything he says can be used against him in a court of law, that he has a right to . . . an attorney and that if he cannot afford an attorney one will be appointed for him. . . ." Although later modified, *Miranda* firmly upheld citizens' rights to a fair trial in state courts.

Mueller v. *Allen,* 1983

(1st and 14th amendments) Minnesota law allowed taxpayers to deduct the costs of tuition, textbooks, and transportation for children in elementary and secondary schools. Several taxpayers sued to prevent parents with children in religious schools from claiming this deduction, arguing that this would constitute state sponsorship of religion. The Court disagreed, ruling that the deduction was not intended to promote religion and was available to all parents with school-age children. The Court argued that a law must have the advancement of religion as its primary purpose to be found unconstitutional.

New Jersey v. *T.L.O.,* 1985

(4th and 14th amendments) After T.L.O., a New Jersey high school student, denied an accusation that she had been smoking in the school lavatory, a vice-principal searched her purse and found cigarettes, marijuana, and evidence that T.L.O. had been involved in marijuana dealing at the school. T.L.O. was then sentenced to probation by a juvenile court, but appealed on the grounds that the evidence against her had been obtained by an "unreasonable" search. The Court rejected T.L.O.'s arguments, stating that the school had a "legitimate need to maintain an environment in which learning can take place," and that to do this "requires some easing of the restrictions to which searches by public authorities are ordinarily subject." The Court thus created a "reasonable suspicion" rule for school searches, a change from the "probable cause" requirement in the wider society.

New York Times v. *United States,* 1971

(1st Amendment) In June 1971, the *New York Times* published the first in a series of secret government documents known as the "Pentagon Papers," which detailed how the United States became involved in the Vietnam War. The Justice Department obtained a court order forbidding the newspaper from printing more documents. The *New York Times* and other newspapers challenged the order. The Court cited the 1st Amendment guarantee of a free press and refused to uphold the ban, noting that the government must prove that publication would harm the nation's security. The decision limited "prior restraint" of the press.

Nix v. *Williams,* 1984

(4th Amendment, illegal evidence) A man was convicted of murdering a 10-year-old girl after he led officers to the body. He had been arrested, but not advised of his rights, in a distant city. During a conversation with a police officer while in transit, Williams agreed that the child should have a proper burial and directed the officer to the body. Later, on appeal, Williams's attorneys argued that the body should not be admitted as evidence because the questioning was illegal. The Court disagreed, observing that search parties were within 2.5 miles of the body. "Evidence otherwise excluded may be admissible when it would have been discovered anyway." The decision was one of several "exceptions to the exclusionary rule" handed down by the Court in the 1980s.

Nixon v. *Fitzgerald,* 1982

In 1968, A. Ernest Fitzgerald, an Air Force management analyst, testified against the government before a congressional subcommittee about cost overruns and problems with the development of an airplane. In 1970, he lost his job in a "reorganization," but he blamed President Nixon's office for firing him in retaliation for his testimony. A long series of official complaints and investigations turned up incriminating evidence against Nixon and two of his aides, including a memo about Fitzgerald recommending that Nixon "let him bleed." Nixon initially took responsibility for the firing at a press conference, but he retracted his admission the next day. Eventually, he offered to settle out of court for a large sum. Fitzgerald persisted, and a final Nixon appeal on the grounds of presidential immunity from prosecution was dismissed by a Federal District Court.

Just as the case seemed about to go to trial, more than ten years after the fact, the Supreme Court intervened. It ruled that a President or former President is entitled to absolute immunity from liability based on his official acts. The President must be able to act forcefully and independently, without fear of liability. Diverting the President's energies with concerns about private lawsuits could impair the effective functioning of government. The President's absolute immunity extends to all acts within the "outer perimeter" of his duties of office, since otherwise he would be required to litigate over the nature of the acts and the scope of his duties in each case. The remedy of impeachment, the vigilant scrutiny of the press, the Congress, and the public, and presidential desire to earn reelection and concern with historical legacy all protect against presidential wrongdoing.

Nixon v. *Shrink Missouri Government PAC,* 2000

In *Buckley* v. *Valeo,* 1976, the Supreme Court had upheld a $1000 limit on contributions by individuals to candidates for federal office. In *Nixon* v. *Shrink Missouri Government PAC,* the Court concluded that large contributions will sometimes create actual corruption, and that voters will inevitably be suspicious of the fairness of a political process that allows wealthy donors to contribute large amounts. The Court concluded that the Missouri contribution limits were appropriate to correct this problem and did not impair the ability of candidates to communicate their messages to the voters and to mount an effective campaign.

Plessy v. *Ferguson,* 1896

(14th Amendment, Equal Protection Clause) A Louisiana law required separate seating for white passengers and black passengers on public railroads. Plessy argued that the policy violated his right to "equal protection of the laws." The Court disagreed, saying that segregation was permissible if facilities were equal. It ruled that the 14th Amendment was "not intended to give Negroes social equality but only political and civil equality. . . ." The Louisiana law was seen as a "reasonable exercise of (state) police power. . . ." This "separate but equal" ruling allowed the segregation of public facilities throughout the South until *Plessy* was overturned by the *Brown* v. *Board of Education* case of 1954.

Powell v. *Alabama,* 1932

(6th Amendment, right to counsel) The case involved the "Scottsboro Boys," seven black men accused of rape. The men were quickly prosecuted without counsel and sentenced to death. The Court overturned the decision, stating that poor people facing the death penalty in state courts must be provided counsel, saying that "there are certain principles of Justice which . . . no [state] may disregard." The case was a step toward incorporating the Bill of Rights into state constitutions.

Printz v. *United States,* 1997

The Supreme Court ruled that the Brady Act's interim provision requiring certain State or local law enforcement agents to perform background checks on prospective handgun purchasers was unconstitutional. Although no provision of the Constitution deals explicitly with federal authority to compel State officials to execute federal law, a review of the Constitution's structure and of prior Supreme Court decisions leads to the conclusion that Congress does not have this power.

Regents of the University of California v. *Bakke,* 1978

(14th Amendment) Under an affirmative action program, the medical school of the University of California at Davis reserved 16 of 100 slots in each class for "disadvantaged citizens." When Bakke, who is white, was not accepted by the school, he claimed racial discrimination in violation of the 14th Amendment. The Court ruled narrowly, requiring Bakke's admission but not overturning affirmative action, preferring to review such questions on a case-by-case basis.

Reno v. *ACLU,* 1997

The Supreme Court ruled that the "indecent transmission" provision and the "patently offensive display" provision of the Communications Decency Act violated the 1st Amendment's freedom of speech. The Internet does not have the special features (such as historical governmental oversight, limited frequencies, and "invasiveness") that have justified allowing greater regulation of content in radio and television.

Reno v. *Condon,* 2000

The Court upheld the federal law that forbids States from selling addresses, telephone numbers, and other information that drivers put on license applications. They agreed with the Federal Government that information, including motor vehicle license information, is an "article of commerce" in the interstate stream of business and therefore is subject to regulation by Congress. The Court emphasized that the statute did not impose on the States any obligation to pass particular laws or policies and thus did not interfere with the States' sovereign functions.

Reynolds v. *Sims,* 1964

Most states have constitutional provisions to reapportion representation in their state legislatures every ten years, based on the U.S. Census. By the 1950s, however, it had become clear that some states were ignoring these laws. The United States was becoming more urban, and one-time rural majorities—now minorities—were holding on to political power at the state level by refusing to reapportion. A complaint was filed by a group of residents, taxpayers, and voters of Jefferson County, Alabama, challenging the apportionment of the Alabama legislature, which was still based on the 1900 federal census. The Court supported the "one person, one vote" formula, and applied it to this case, calling for reapportionment based on current census data.

Roe v. *Wade,* 1973

(9th Amendment) A Texas woman challenged a state law forbidding the artificial termination of a pregnancy, saying that she "had a fundamental right to privacy." The Court upheld a woman's right to choose, noting that the state's "important and legitimate interest in protecting the potentiality of human life" became "compelling" at the end of the first trimester, but that before then "the attending physician, in consultation with his patient, is free to determine, without regulation by the state, that . . . the patient's pregnancy should be terminated." The decision struck down state regulation of abortion in the first three months of pregnancy and was later modified by *Webster,* 1989.

Rostker v. *Goldberg,* 1981

(5th Amendment) In 1980, President Carter reinstated draft registration. For the first time, both sexes were ordered to register. When Congress refused to fund the registration of women, several men sued, arguing that a selective draft violated their due process rights. The Court disagreed, noting that "the purpose of registration was to prepare for draft of combat troops" and that "Congress and the Executive have decided that women should not serve in combat."

Roth v. *United States,* 1957

(1st Amendment) A New York man named Roth operated a business that used the mail to invite people to buy materials considered obscene by postal inspectors. The Court, in its first consideration of censorship of obscenity, created the "prevailing community standards" rule, which required a consideration of the work as a whole. In its decision, the Court defined as obscene that which offends "the average person, applying contemporary community standards."

Schenck v. *United States,* 1919

(1st Amendment) Schenck, a member of an antiwar group, had urged men who were drafted into military service in World War I to resist and to avoid induction. He was charged with violating the Espionage Act of 1917, which outlawed active opposition to the war. The Court limited free speech in time of war, stating that Schenck's words presented a "clear and present danger. . . ." Although later decisions modified this one, the *Schenck* case created a precedent that 1st Amendment rights are not absolute.

973

School District of Abington Township, Pennsylvania v. *Schempp,* 1963

(1st Amendment) Some Pennsylvania parents challenged a state law that required Bible readings each day at school. The Court agreed with the parents, saying that the Establishment Clause and Free Exercise Clause forbade states from engaging in religious activity. The Court ruled that if the purpose and effect of a law "is the advancement or inhibition of religion," it "exceeds the scope of legislative power."

Sheppard v. *Maxwell,* 1966

(14th Amendment) Sam Sheppard was convicted of murdering his wife in a trial sensationalized by the national media. Sheppard appealed, claiming that the pretrial publicity had made it impossible for him to get a fair trial. Rejecting arguments about freedom of the press, the Court overturned the conviction and ordered a new trial. Because of *Sheppard,* judges have issued "gag" orders limiting pretrial publicity.

South Dakota v. *Dole,* 1986

In 1984, Congress voted to withhold five percent of federal highway funds from any state that did not set a minimum drinking age at 21. South Dakota, which would lose money under the new law, challenged the government's right to coerce states to adopt specific policies through funding cuts. The Court ruled that highway funding was not an entitlement, and the national government could impose reasonable conditions upon the states in the interest of the "general welfare." All states that wished to continue to receive full federal highway aid were required to raise the legal age to purchase and consume alcohol to 21 years. In recent years, the threat of spending cuts has become a powerful tool of federal policy.

Tennessee Valley Authority v. *Hiram G. Hill, Jr., et al.,* 1978

The Tellico Dam was nearly completed—and $100 million had been spent on it—when local residents succeeded in halting construction to save a tiny, nearly extinct fish called the snail darter. The fish's only habitat would have been flooded by the dam. The Court found the injunction against the TVA's completion of the nearly finished dam to be proper to prevent violation of the Endangered Species Act. Congress had declared the value of endangered species "incalculable." The Court refused to overrule Congress's judgment. The ruling affirmed the Environmental Protection Agency's power to protect the environment.

Texas v. *Johnson,* 1989

(1st Amendment) To protest national policies, Johnson doused a United States flag with kerosene and burned it outside the 1984 Republican National Convention in Dallas. He was arrested and convicted under a Texas law prohibiting the desecration of the Texas and United States flags. The Court ruled that the Texas law placed an unconstitutional limit on "freedom of expression," noting that ". . . nothing in our precedents suggests that a state may foster its own view of the flag by prohibiting expressive conduct relating to it."

Thompson v. *Oklahoma,* 1988

(8th Amendment, capital punishment) A 15-year-old from Oklahoma was convicted of murder and was sentenced to death at age 16. The Court overturned the death sentence, holding that "[t]he Eighth and Fourteenth Amendments prohibit the execution of a person who was under 16 years of age at the time of his or her offense." A death penalty was deemed cruel and unusual punishment for someone so young.

Tinker v. *Des Moines School District,* 1969

The Court upheld school students' 1st Amendment rights. Because students do not "shed their constitutional rights to freedom of speech or expression at the schoolhouse gate," schools must show a possibility of "substantial disruption" before free speech can be limited at school. Students may express personal opinions as long as they do not materially disrupt classwork, create substantial disorder, or interfere with the rights of others. In this case, the wearing of black armbands was a "silent, passive expression of opinion" without these side effects, and thus constitutionally could not be prohibited by the school.

United States v. *Eichman,* 1990

The Court agreed with the trial courts' rulings that the Flag Protection Act violated the 1st Amendment. Flag-burning constitutes expressive conduct, and thus is entitled to constitutional protection. The Act prevents protesters from using the flag to express their opposition to governmental policies and activities. Although the protesters' ideas may be offensive or disagreeable to many people, the government may not prohibit them from expressing those ideas.

United States v. *Lopez,* 1990

(Article I, Section 8, Commerce Clause) Alfonzo Lopez, a Texas high school student, was convicted of carrying a weapon in a school zone under the Gun-Free School Zones Act of 1990. He appealed his conviction on the basis that the Act, which forbids "any individual knowingly to possess a firearm at a place that [he] knows . . . is a school zone," exceeded Congress's legislative power under the Commerce Clause. The Court agreed that the Act was unconstitutional, stating that to uphold the legislation would "bid fair to convert congressional Commerce Clause authority to a general police power of the sort held only by the States."

United States v. *Nixon,* 1974

President Nixon was widely suspected of participating in the coverup of the Watergate break-in. After journalists discovered that he had recorded all of his conversations in the White House, Congress demanded that Nixon hand over the tapes. The President cited

974

executive privilege, arguing that his office placed him above the law. The Court overruled Nixon and ordered him to surrender the tapes. Limiting executive privilege, it ruled that the President's "generalized interest in confidentiality" was subordinate to "the fundamental demands of due process of law in the fair administration of criminal justice." The tapes implicated Nixon in the coverup and led to his resignation.

Wallace v. *Jaffree,* 1985

(1st Amendment, Establishment Clause) An Alabama law authorized a one-minute period of silence in all public schools "for meditation or voluntary prayer." A group of parents, including Jaffree, challenged the constitutionality of the statute, claiming it violated the Establishment Clause of the 1st Amendment. The Court agreed with Jaffree and struck down the Alabama law, determining that "the State's endorsement . . . of prayer activities at the beginning of each schoolday is not consistent with the established principle that the government must pursue a course of complete neutrality toward religion."

Walz v. *Tax Commission of the City of New York,* 1970

(1st Amendment, Establishment Clause) State and local governments routinely exempt church property from taxes. Walz claimed that such exemptions were a "support of religion." The Court disagreed, noting that such exemptions constituted a "benevolent neutrality" between government and churches, not a support of religion. Governments must avoid taxing churches, because taxation would give government a "control" over religion prohibited by the "wall of separation of church and state" noted in *Everson,* 1947.

Webster v. *Reproductive Health Services,* 1989

(9th Amendment) A 1986 Missouri law stated that (1) life begins at conception; (2) unborn children have rights; (3) public funds could not be used for abortions not necessary to save the life of the mother; and (4) public funds could not be used for abortion counseling. Healthcare providers in Missouri filed suit, challenging the law, claiming that it was in conflict with *Roe,* 1973, and that it intruded into "privacy questions." A 5–4 Court upheld the Missouri law, stating that the people of Missouri, through their legislature, could put limits on the use of public funds. The *Webster* decision narrowed the *Roe* decision.

Weeks v. *United States,* 1914

(4th Amendment) A search without proper warrant was conducted in San Francisco, and the evidence collected was used by a postal inspector to prosecute Weeks. Weeks claimed that the evidence was gained by an illegal search, and thus was inadmissible. The Court agreed, applying for the first time an "exclusionary rule" for illegally gained evidence in federal courts. The decision stated ". . . if letters and private documents can thus be seized and used as evidence . . . his right to be secure against such searches . . . is of no value, and . . . might as well be stricken from the Constitution." See also *Mapp* v. *Ohio,* 1961; *Massachusetts* v. *Sheppard,* 1984; and *Nix* v. *Williams,* 1984.

West Virginia Board of Education v. *Barnette,* 1943

The beliefs of Jehovah's Witnesses forbid them to salute the United States flag. In the patriotic climate of World War II, thousands of children who refused to salute were expelled from public schools. The Court ruled that a compulsory flag salute violated the 1st Amendment's exercise of the religion clause and was therefore unconstitutional. "No official, high or petty, can prescribe what shall be orthodox in politics, nationalism, religion, or other matters of opinion."

Westside Community Schools v. *Mergens,* 1990

(1st Amendment, Establishment Clause) A request by Mergens to form a student Christian religious group at school was denied by an Omaha high school principal. Mergens took legal action, claiming that a 1984 federal law required "equal access" for student religious groups. The Court ordered the school to permit the formation of the club, stating, "a high school does not have to permit any extracurricular activities, but when it does, the school is bound by the Act of 1984. Allowing students to meet on campus and discuss religion is constitutional because it does not amount to a 'State sponsorship of a religion.' "

Wisconsin v. *Yoder,* 1972

(1st Amendment, Free Exercise Clause) Members of the Amish religious sect in Wisconsin objected to sending their children to public schools after the eighth grade, claiming that such exposure of the children to another culture would endanger the group's self-sufficient agrarian lifestyle essential to their religious faith. The Court agreed with the Amish, while noting that the Court must move carefully to weigh the State's "legitimate social concern when faced with religious claim for exemption from generally applicable educational requirements."

975

Glossary

A

abolitionist movement Movement to end slavery (p. 129)
abstinence Refraining from some activity, such as drinking (p. 128)
Adams-Onís Treaty 1819 treaty between the United States and Spain in which Spain ceded Florida to the United States; also called the Transcontinental Treaty (p. 109)
administration Term of office; also the members and agencies of the executive branch as a whole (p. 64)
affirmative action Policy that gives special consideration to women and members of minority groups to make up for past discrimination (p. 854)
Agent Orange An herbicide used as a chemical weapon during the Vietnam War to kill vegetation and expose enemy hiding places (p. 801)
Agricultural Adjustment Administration (AAA) Established in 1933 to raise farm prices through government financial assistance (p. 540)
AIDS Acquired immuno-deficiency syndrome, a virus that killed many people starting in the early 1980s (p. 878)
alien A noncitizen (p. 302)
Alliance for Progress President Kennedy's proposal for cooperation among nations of the Western Hemisphere to meet the basic needs of their people (p. 757)
Allies In World War I, Russia, France, Serbia, and Great Britain; in World War II, the alliance of Great Britain, the United States, the Soviet Union, and other nations (pp. 417, 578)
America First Committee Group formed in 1940 by isolationists to block further aid to Britain (p. 587)
American Expeditionary Force (AEF) Name given to American troops in Europe in World War I (p. 425)
American Indian Movement (AIM) Organization formed in 1968 to help Native Americans (p. 775)
American Liberty League Organization founded in 1934 to oppose the New Deal (p. 547)
amnesty A general pardon for certain crimes (p. 854)
anarchist A radical who opposes all government (p. 251)
annex To join or attach, as in the joining of a new territory to an existing country (pp. 135, 353)
anti-Federalists Opponents of the Constitution during the debate over ratification; opposed to the concept of a strong national government (p. 61)
anti-Semitism Hostility or discrimination toward Jews (p. 609)
apartheid (uh PAHR tayt) The systematic segregation of people of different racial backgrounds (p. 904)
appeasement Policy of giving in to a competitor's demands in order to preserve the peace (p. 573)
apportionment Distribution of seats in a legislative body (p. 748)
arbitration Settlement of a dispute by a person or panel chosen to listen to both sides and come to a decision (p. 358)
armistice A cease-fire or truce (p. 430)
arms race A contest between nations to gain weapons superiority (p. 660)
Articles of Confederation Plan that established, in 1781, a limited national government in the United States, later replaced by the Constitution of the United States (p. 55)
assembly line Manufacturing process in which each worker does one specialized task in the construction of the final product (p. 494)
assimilation Process by which people of one culture merge into and become part of another culture (pp. 266, 321)
Atlantic Charter Agreement signed by President Franklin Roosevelt and Prime Minister Winston Churchill in 1941 outlining the two nations' war aims (p. 600)
autocrat Ruler with unlimited power (p. 418)
autonomy Self-government, with respect to local matters (p. 775)
Axis Powers In World War II, Germany, Italy, and Japan (p. 573)

B

baby boom Dramatic increase in birthrate, especially in the years following World War II (p. 672)
balance of trade Difference in value between imports and exports (p. 25)
banana republic Term used to describe a Central American nation dominated by United States business interests (p. 355)
barrio A Spanish-speaking neighborhood (pp. 455, 625)
barter To trade goods or services without money (p. 6)
Bataan Death March Brutal march of American and Filipino prisoners by Japanese soldiers in 1942 (p. 615)
Battle of Antietam Civil War battle in Maryland in 1862 (p. 165)
Battle of the Bulge World War II battle in which German forces launched a final counterattack in the west (p. 607)
Battle of Chancellorsville Civil War battle in 1863 in Virginia, won by the Confederacy (p. 179)
Battle of Cold Harbor Civil War battle in 1864 in Virginia (p. 187)
Battle of the Coral Sea 1942 World War II battle between American and Japanese aircraft (p. 616)
Battle of Fredericksburg Civil War battle in 1862 in Virginia, won by the Confederacy (p. 179)
Battle of Gettysburg Civil War battle in 1863 in Pennsylvania, won by the Union (p. 180)
Battle of Guadalcanal (gwahd ul kuh NAL) 1942–1943 World War II battle between the United States and Japan (p. 617)

Battle of Iwo Jima 1945 World War II battle between the United States and Japan (p. 619)
Battle of Leyte Gulf 1944 World War II naval battle between the United States and Japan (p. 618)
Battle of Little Bighorn 1876 Sioux victory over army troops led by George Custer (p. 265)
Battle of Midway 1942 World War II battle between the United States and Japan, a turning point in the war in the Pacific (p. 617)
Battle of Okinawa 1945 World War II battle between the United States and Japan (p. 619)
Battle of Shiloh Civil War battle in Tennessee in 1862 (p. 162)
Battle of Spotsylvania Civil War battle in 1864 in Virginia (p. 187)
Battle of the Wilderness Civil War battle in 1864 in Virginia, won by the Confederacy (p. 187)
Battles of Lexington and Concord First battles of the Revolutionary War, on April 19, 1775 (p. 45)
Bay of Pigs invasion Failed invasion of Cuba by a group of anti-Castro forces in 1961 (p. 752)
beatnik In the 1950s, a person who criticized American society as apathetic and conformist (p. 679)
Berlin airlift Operation that moved supplies into West Berlin by American and British planes during a Soviet blockade in 1948–1949 (p. 647)
Berlin Wall Barrier built by the East German government to separate Communist and non-Communist Berlin (p. 754)
Bessemer process A process for making steel more efficiently, patented in 1856 (p. 233)
bicentennial 200th anniversary (p. 850)
bilingual education The teaching of students in their native language, as well as in English (p. 913)
Bill of Rights First ten amendments to the Constitution (p. 62)
bimetallic standard Currency of the United States, prior to 1873, which consisted of gold or silver coins as well as U.S. treasury notes that could be traded in for gold or silver (p. 278)
black codes Laws that restricted freedmen's rights (p. 206)
black nationalism A belief in the separate identity and racial unity of the African American community (p. 723)
black power African American movement seeking unity and self-reliance (p. 724)
Black Tuesday October 29, 1929, the day on which the Great Crash of the stock market began (p. 509)
blacklist List that circulated among employers, beginning in 1947, containing the names of persons who should not be hired (p. 650)
Bland-Allison Act 1878 law that required the federal government to purchase and coin more silver, increasing the money supply and causing inflation (p. 279)
blitzkrieg (BLITS kreeg) Kind of warfare emphasizing rapid and mechanized movement; used by Germany during World War II (p. 576)
blue law Regulation that prohibited certain private activities people considered immoral, such as drinking alcohol on Sundays (p. 292)
bonanza farm Farm controlled by large businesses, managed by professionals, and raising massive quantities of single cash crops (p. 274)
Bonus Army A group of World War I veterans and their families who protested in Washington, D.C., in 1932, demanding immediate payment of a pension bonus that had been promised for 1945 (p. 526)
boomers Settlers who ran in land races to claim land upon the 1889 opening of Indian Territory for settlement (p. 267)
bootlegger Term used to describe a supplier of illegal alcohol during Prohibition (p. 468)
Border States In the Civil War, the states between the North and South: Delaware, Maryland, Kentucky, and Missouri (p. 142)
Boston Massacre Incident on March 5, 1770, in which British soldiers in Boston killed five colonists (p. 43)
boycott Refusal to buy a certain product, or use a certain service (p. 43)
bracero A term used in 1942 to describe Mexican farm laborers brought to the United States (p. 625)
brinkmanship A 1956 term used by Secretary of State John Dulles to describe a policy of risking war in order to protect national interests (p. 660)
Brown* v. *Board of Education of Topeka, Kansas 1954 Supreme Court case in which racial segregation in public schools was outlawed (p. 699)
Bull Moose Party Nickname of the Progressive Party (p. 398)
Burma Road A 700-mile-long highway linking Burma (present day Myanmar) to China (p. 584)
business cycle Periods in which a nation's economy grows, then contracts (p. 509)
buying on margin An option that allows investors to purchase a stock for only a fraction of its price and borrow the rest (p. 500)

C

Camp David Accords 1978 agreement between Israel and Egypt that made a peace treaty between the two nations possible (p. 855)
canister A special type of shell filled with bullets (p. 160)
capital Wealth that can be invested to produce goods and make money (p. 117)
carpet bombing Method of aerial bombing in which large numbers of bombs are dropped over a wide area (p. 605)
carpetbagger Negative nickname for a northern Republican who moved to the South after the Civil War (p. 211)
cartel Loose association of businesses that make the same product (p. 240)
cash and carry World War II policy requiring nations at war to pay cash for all nonmilitary goods and to be

responsible for transporting the goods from the United States (p. 586)

casualty Military term for a person killed, wounded, captured, or missing in action (p. 158)

Central Powers In World War I, Germany and Austria-Hungary (p. 417)

charter Certificate of permission given by a government (p. 17)

checks and balances System in which each of the branches of the federal government can check the actions of the other branches (p. 59)

Chinese Exclusion Act Law passed in 1882 that prohibited Chinese laborers from entering the country, but did not prevent entry of those who had previously established U.S. residence (p. 302)

civil disobedience Nonviolent refusal to obey a law in an effort to change that law (p. 404)

civil rights Citizens' personal liberties guaranteed by law, such as voting rights and equal treatment (p. 207)

Civil Rights Act of 1964 Law that made discrimination illegal in a number of areas, including voting, schools, and jobs (p. 719)

civil service The government's nonelected workers (p. 292)

Civil War War between the Union states of the North and the Confederate states of the South; fought from 1861 to 1865 (p. 156)

Civilian Conservation Corps (CCC) Established by Congress in 1933, this program put more than 2.5 million young men to work restoring and maintaining forests, beaches, and parks (p. 539)

clan Groups of families who are all descended from a common ancestor (p. 5)

Clayton Antitrust Act Law passed in 1914 to strengthen the Sherman Antitrust Act of 1890; specified big business activities that were forbidden (p. 400)

Clean Air Act Law passed in 1970 that aimed to control pollution caused by industrial and auto emissions (p. 784)

Clean Water Act Law passed in 1972 that aimed to control pollution caused by the discharge of industrial and municipal wastewater, and provided for grants to build better sewage-treatment facilities (p. 784)

closed shop Workplace open only to union members (p. 543)

cloture (KLOH chur) In the Senate, a three-fifths vote to limit debate and call for a vote on an issue (p. 719)

coalition Alliance of groups with similar goals (p. 554)

Cold War The competition that developed after World War II between the United States and the Soviet Union for power and influence in the world, lasting until the collapse of the Soviet Union in 1991 (p. 640)

collaboration Close cooperation (p. 578)

collective bargaining Process in which workers negotiate as a group with employers (p. 249)

collective security The principle of mutual military assistance among nations (p. 647)

colony An area of land settled by immigrants who continue to be ruled by their parent country (p. 15)

Columbian Exchange The transatlantic trade of crops, technology, and culture between the Americas and Europe, Africa, and Asia that began in 1492 with Columbus's first voyage to the Americas (p. 11)

communism Official ideology of the Soviet Union, characterized there by complete government ownership of land and property, single-party control of the government, the lack of individual rights, and the call for worldwide revolution (p. 481)

Compromise of 1850 Agreement designed to ease tensions caused by the expansion of slavery into western territories (p. 138)

Compromise of 1877 Agreement in which Democrats agreed to give Rutherford B. Hayes the victory in the presidential election of 1876, and Hayes, in return, agreed to remove the remaining federal troops from southern states (p. 221)

compulsory Required (p. 374)

concentration camp A place where political prisoners are confined, usually under harsh conditions (p. 610)

concession A grant for a piece of land in exchange for a promise to use the land for a specific purpose (p. 366)

Confederate States of America Association of seven seceding southern states, formed in 1861 (p. 143)

conglomerate Corporation made up of three or more unrelated businesses (p. 669)

Congress of Racial Equality (CORE) Organization founded by pacifists in 1942 to promote racial equality through peaceful means (pp. 625, 705)

Congressional Union (CU) Radical organization formed in 1913 and led by Alice Paul that campaigned for a constitutional amendment guaranteeing women's suffrage (p. 406)

conquistador A Spanish conqueror (p. 15)

conscientious objector A person who opposes war on moral or religious grounds (p. 807)

conservationist A person who favors the protection of natural resources (p. 397)

consumer economy An economy that depends on a large amount of spending by consumers (p. 491)

containment American policy of resisting further expansion of communism around the world (p. 641)

Contra Spanish for "counterrevolutionary," a rebel opposed to Nicaragua's Communist government in the 1980s (p. 880)

contraband Items seized from the enemy during wartime (p. 172)

Contract with America Pledge, made by Republican candidates in the 1994 election campaign, to scale back government, eliminate some regulations, cut taxes, and balance the budget (p. 896)

convoy Group of unarmed ships surrounded by a ring of armed naval vessels (p. 426)
Copperhead During the Civil War, an antiwar Northern Democrat (p. 169)
cotton gin Machine that separates the seeds from raw cotton fiber (p. 112)
counterculture Group of young Americans in the 1960s who rejected conventional customs and mainstream culture (p. 777)
craft union A union for laborers devoted to a specific craft (p. 249)
Cross of Gold Speech William Jennings Bryan's 1896 address at the Democratic Convention; one of the most famous speeches in American history (p. 282)
Cuban Missile Crisis 1962 crisis that arose between the United States and the Soviet Union over a Soviet attempt to deploy nuclear missiles in Cuba (p. 754)

D

Dawes Act 1887 law that divided reservation land into private family plots (p. 266)
daylight savings time Turning clocks ahead by one hour for summer (p. 434)
D-Day Code name for the allied invasion of France on June 6, 1944 (p. 606)
death camp In World War II, a German camp created solely for the purpose of mass murder (p. 611)
Declaration of Independence 1776 statement, issued by the Second Continental Congress, explaining why the colonies wanted independence from Britain (p. 46)
***de facto* segregation** Separation caused by social conditions such as poverty (p. 725)
deferment Official postponement, as in a postponement of compulsary military service (p. 808)
deficit spending Paying out more money from the annual federal budget than the government receives in revenues (pp. 550, 828)
deflation A drop in the prices of goods (p. 278)
***de jure* segregation** Racial segregation created by law (p. 725)
demagogue (DEHM uh gawg) A leader who manipulates people with half-truths, deceptive promises and scare tactics (p. 548)
democracy Government by the people (p. 55)
demographics The statistics that describe a population, such as data on race or income (p. 454)
denomination A religious subgroup (p. 114)
department store Large retail establishment that carries a wide variety of goods and sells in large quantities (p. 338)
depression A severe economic downturn marked by a decrease in business activity, widespread unemployment, and falling prices and wages (p. 98)
deregulation The reduction or removal of government controls (p. 853)
détente A relaxation in political tensions between nations (p. 833)
deterrence The policy of making the military power of the United States and its allies so strong that no enemy would attack for fear of retaliation (p. 660)
direct primary Election in which all citizens vote to select nominees for upcoming elections (p. 392)
disarmament Program in which the nations of the world voluntarily give up their weapons (p. 486)
discrimination Unequal treatment of a group of people because of their nationality, race, sex, or religion (p. 133)
dissident A person who criticizes the actions of his or her government (p. 855)
division of labor Way of producing in which different tasks are performed by different persons (p. 245)
dollar diplomacy President Taft's policy of encouraging American investment in foreign economies (p. 370)
domino theory Belief that if one country fell to communism, neighboring countries would likewise fall (p. 792)
dove Nickname for a person who opposes war, as in the Vietnam War (p. 802)
Dow Jones Industrial Average Measure of average of stock prices of major industries (p. 508)
downsizing Laying off workers to cut costs (p. 887)
draft Required military service (p. 167)
dry farming Techniques used to raise crops in areas that receive little rain; water conservation techniques (p. 274)
dumbbell tenement A tenement building that narrowed in the middle, forming air shafts on either side and allowing light and air into the rooms (p. 307)
Dust Bowl Term used to describe the central and southern Great Plains in the 1930s, when the region sustained a period of drought and dust storms (p. 514)

E

economic sanctions Trade restrictions and other economic measures intended to punish another nation (p. 904)
economies of scale Phenomenon that as production increases, the cost of each item produced is often lowered (p. 241)
Emancipation Proclamation A presidential decree by President Lincoln, effective January 1, 1863, that freed slaves in Confederate-held territory (p. 171)
embargo A ban or a restriction on trade (pp. 95, 828)
Enforcement Act of 1870 Passed by Congress to ban the use of terror, force, or bribery to prevent people from voting because of their race (p. 219)
entitlement Government program that guarantees

payments to a particular group, such as the elderly (p. 881)

Environmental Protection Agency (EPA) Government organization formed in 1970 to set and enforce national pollution-control standards (p. 784)

Equal Rights Amendment Proposed constitutional amendment, never ratified, to prohibit discrimination on account of sex (p. 768)

escalation Expansion by stages, as from a local to a national conflict (p. 801)

Exoduster An African American who migrated to the West after the Civil War (p. 260)

F

fascism Political philosophy that emphasizes the importance of the nation or an ethnic group, and the supreme authority of the leader over that of the individual (p. 568)

Federal Reserve System The nation's central banking system, established in 1913 (p. 400)

federal system of government System in which power is shared among state and national authorities (p. 59)

Federal Trade Commission (FTC) 1914 commission established by President Wilson and Congress to enforce the Clayton Act and establish fair-trade laws (p. 400)

Federalists Supporters of the Constitution during the debate over its ratification; favored a strong national government (p. 61)

feminism Theory favoring the political, economic, and social equality of men and women (p. 764)

Fifteenth Amendment Constitutional amendment, ratified in 1870, that guaranteed voting rights to all citizens (p. 210)

filibuster A tactic in which senators prevent a vote on a measure by taking the floor and refusing to stop talking (p. 719)

First Battle of Bull Run First major battle of the Civil War, won by the Confederates in July 1861 (p. 158)

First Continental Congress Assembly of representatives from the colonies that first met in Philadelphia in September 1774 (p. 44)

flapper A 1920s term used to describe a new type of young woman; rebellious, energetic, fun-loving, and bold (p. 452)

Fourteen Points President Wilson's proposal in 1918 for a postwar European peace (p. 437)

Fourteenth Amendment Constitutional amendment, ratified in 1868, to guarantee citizens equal protection under the law (p. 207)

fragmentation bomb A type of bomb that, upon explosion, causes pieces of its thick metal casings to be thrown in all directions (p. 801)

franchise A business that contracts with a large parent company to offer certain goods and services (p. 669)

free enterprise system Economic system characterized by private or corporate ownership of capital goods (p. 117)

free silver The unlimited coining of silver dollars (p. 279)

Freedmen's Bureau Created by Congress in 1865, the first major federal relief agency in the United States (p. 205)

Freedom Ride 1961 event organized by CORE and SNCC in which an interracial group of civil rights activists tested southern states' compliance to the Supreme Court ban of segregation on interstate buses (p. 710)

French and Indian War War from 1754 to 1763 between France, with allied Indian nations, and Britain and its colonists, for control of eastern North America (p. 41)

fundamentalism Set of religious beliefs including traditional Christian ideas about Jesus Christ, the belief that the Bible was inspired by God and does not contain contradictions or errors, and is literally true (p. 470)

G

generation gap A term used to describe the widening difference in values between a younger generation and their parents (p. 806)

Geneva Accords A 1954 international conference in which Vietnam was divided into two nations (p. 793)

Geneva Convention A set of international standards of conduct for treating prisoners of war, established in 1929 (p. 615)

genocide Organized killing of an entire people (p. 431)

Gentlemen's Agreement 1907 agreement between the United States and Japan that restricted Japanese immigration (p. 302)

Gettysburg Address A famous speech by President Lincoln on the meaning of the Civil War, given in November 1863 at the dedication of a national cemetery on the site of the Battle of Gettysburg (p. 185)

ghetto Area in which one ethnic or racial group dominates (p. 300)

Ghost Dance A Native American purification ritual (p. 265)

GI Term used for American soldiers in World War II, derived from the term "Government Issue" (p. 595)

GI Bill of Rights Law passed in 1944 to help returning veterans buy homes and pay for higher education (p. 672)

Gilded Age Term coined by Mark Twain to describe the post-Reconstruction era (p. 290)

graft Use of one's job to gain profit; a major source of income for political machines (p. 309)

grandfather clause Passage in a law that exempts a group of people from obeying the law if they had met certain conditions before the law was passed (p. 333)

Grange, the Established in 1867, this organization helped farmers form cooperatives and pressured state legislators to regulate businesses on which farmers depended (p. 280)

Great Awakening Religious revival in the American colonies during the 1730s and 1740s (p. 32)

Great Crash The collapse of the American stock market in 1929 (p. 509)

Great Depression The most severe economic downturn in the nation's history, which lasted from 1929 to 1941 (p. 511)

Great Plains Vast grassland between the Mississippi River and the Rocky Mountains (p. 261)

Great Society President Lyndon Johnson's proposals for aid to public education voting rights, conservation and beautification projects, medical care for the elderly, and elimination of poverty (p. 745)

Great White Fleet A force of United States Navy ships that undertook a world cruise in 1907 (p. 375)

Greater East Asia Co-Prosperity Sphere As announced in 1940 by Japan's prime minister, the area extending from Manchuria to the Dutch East Indies in which Japan would expand its influence (p. 584)

greenback Name given to the national paper currency created in 1862 (p. 169)

Gross National Product (GNP) Total annual value of goods and services a country produces (p. 493)

guerrilla (guh RIL uh) A soldier who uses surprise raids and hit-and-run tactics (p. 192)

Gulf of Tonkin Resolution 1964 Congressional resolution authorizing President Johnson to take military action in Vietnam (p. 796)

H

Harlem Renaissance African American literary awakening of the 1920s, centered in Harlem (p. 464)

hawk Nickname for a supporter of war, as in the Vietnam War (p. 802)

Hawley-Smoot tariff The highest import tax in history, passed by Congress in 1930 (p. 525)

Haymarket Riot 1886 labor-related violence in Chicago (p. 252)

Head Start A preschool program for children from low-income families that also provides healthcare, nutrition services, and social services (p. 746)

Helsinki Accords Series of agreements on European security made in 1975 (p. 850)

Ho Chi Minh Trail A supply route used to carry troops and supplies from North Vietnam to South Vietnam (p. 802)

holding company Firm that buys up stocks and bonds of smaller companies (p. 394)

Hollywood Ten Group of people in the film industry who were jailed for refusing to answer congressional questions regarding Communist influence in Hollywood (p. 650)

Holocaust Nazi Germany's systematic attempt to murder all European Jews (p. 609)

home rule System that gives cities a limited degree of self-rule (p. 390)

Homestead Act 1862 law that gave 160 acres of land to citizens who met certain conditions (p. 259)

Homestead Strike 1892 strike in Pennsylvania against Carnegie Steel (p. 252)

homesteader One who farmed claims under the Homestead Act (p. 272)

Hooverville Term used to describe a makeshift homeless shelter during the early years of the Great Depression (p. 514)

horizontal consolidation The process of bringing together many firms in the same business to form one large company (p. 241)

House Un-American Activities Committee (HUAC) Established in 1938 to investigate disloyalty in the United States (p. 650)

hundred days Period at the start of Franklin Roosevelt's presidency in 1933, when many New Deal programs were passed by Congress (p. 537)

I

ICBM Intercontinental ballistic missile (p. 661)

immigrant Person who enters a new country to settle (p. 31)

Immigration Act of 1965 Law that ended quotas for individual countries and replaced them with more flexible limits (p. 747)

impeach To charge a public official with wrongdoing in office (pp. 209, 843)

imperialism Policy by a stronger nation to attempt to create an empire by dominating weaker nations economically, politically, culturally, or militarily (p. 352)

incumbent Person currently in office (p. 851)

indentured servant A person who works for another person for a specified period of time, usually seven years, under a contract, in exchange for transportation, food, and shelter (p. 18)

Industrial Revolution Effort, beginning in Britain in the late 1700s, to increase production by using machines powered by sources other than humans or animals (p. 111)

industrial union Union that organizes workers from all crafts in a given industry (p. 251)

industrialization Growth of industry (p. 119)

INF Treaty Intermediate-Range Nuclear Forces, an agreement signed in 1987 by Ronald Reagan and Mikhail Gorbachev that provided for the destruction of about 2,500 Soviet and American missiles in Europe (p. 881)

infrastructure The public property and services that a society uses (p. 215)

initiative A process in which citizens can put a proposed new law directly on the ballot in the next election by collecting voters' signatures on a petition (p. 392)

injunction Court order prohibiting a certain activity (p. 385)

installment plan A payment plan that allows customers to make payments at set intervals over a period of time until the total debt is paid (p. 492)

integration Process of bringing people of different races together (p. 702)

interchangeable parts A system of manufacturing in which all parts are made to an exact standard for easy mass-assembly (p. 112)

interned Confined (p. 626)

Internet A computer network that links millions of people around the world (p. 915)

interracial Between, among, or involving people of different races (p. 705)

Interstate Commerce Act 1887 law passed to regulate railroad and other interstate businesses (p. 281)

Iran-Contra affair Scandal during the Reagan administration involving the use of money from secret Iranian arms sales to support the Nicaraguan Contras (p. 880)

iron curtain Term coined by Winston Churchill to describe the division between Communist and non-Communist life (p. 640)

island-hopping A military strategy used during World War II that involved selectively attacking specific enemy-held islands and bypassing others (p. 618)

isolationism Policy of avoiding political or economic alliances with foreign countries (p. 486)

J

Japanese American Citizens League (JACL) Organization of Japanese Americans working to promote the rights of Asian Americans (p. 774)

Jazz Age Term used to describe the 1920s (p. 462)

Jim Crow Statutes, beginning in the 1890s, that required segregation of public services by race (p. 333)

jingoism A feeling of strong national pride and a desire for an aggressive foreign policy (p. 359)

judicial review Power of federal courts to review state laws and state court decisions to determine if they are constitutional (p. 94)

K

kamikaze (kah mih KAH zee) In World War II, a Japanese suicide plane (p. 618)

Kansas-Nebraska Act 1854 law that called for the creation of these two new territories, and stated that the citizens in each territory should decide whether slavery would be allowed there (p. 139)

Kellogg-Briand Pact Agreement signed in 1928 in which nations agreed not to pose the threat of war against one another (p. 489)

Korean War Conflict over the future of the Korean peninsula, fought between 1950 and 1953 and ending in a stalemate (p. 654)

Kristallnacht The name given to the night of violence on November 9, 1938, when Nazi storm troopers looted and destroyed Jewish homes, businesses, and synagogues and arrested thousands of Jews in Germany and Austria (p. 610)

L

labor union Organization of workers formed to protect the interest of its members (p. 119)

laissez-faire (LES ay FAYR) Doctrine stating that government generally should not interfere in private business (p. 291)

land mine An explosive device planted in the ground (p. 800)

land speculator Person who buys up large areas of land in the hope of selling them later for a profit (p. 259)

Latino Person whose family origins are in Spanish-speaking Latin America (p. 771)

League of Nations International organization formed after World War I that aimed to ensure security and peace for all its members (p. 438)

Lend-Lease Act 1941 law that authorized the President to aid any nation whose defense he believed was vital to American security (p. 588)

Liberty Bond Special war bond sold by the government to support the Allied cause during World War I (p. 432)

Liberty ship A type of large, sturdy merchant ship built in World War II (p. 596)

Limited Test Ban Treaty 1963 treaty in which the United States and the Soviet Union agreed not to test nuclear weapons above the ground (p. 757)

literacy The ability to read and write (p. 321)

long drive Moving of cattle from distant ranges to busy railroad centers that shipped the cattle to market (p. 271)

loose construction Belief that the government can do anything that the Constitution does not prohibit (p. 90)

Lost Generation Group of writers in the 1920s who shared the belief that they were lost in a greedy, materialistic world that lacked moral values, and who often chose to flee to Europe (p. 464)

Louisiana Purchase Purchase by the United States of the Louisiana Territory from France in 1803 (p. 95)

lynching Murder of an accused person by a mob without a lawful trial (p. 334)

M

Magna Carta A "great charter" signed by King John in 1215 that granted certain rights to English nobles and became the foundation for future American ideals of liberty and justice (p. 7)

mail-order catalog Printed material advertising a wide range of goods that can be purchased by mail (p. 339)

Manchurian Incident Situation in 1931, when Japanese troops, claiming that Chinese soldiers had tried to blow up a railway line, took matters in their own hands by capturing several southern Manchurian cities and by continuing to take over the country even after Chinese troops had withdrawn (p. 582)

mandate A public endorsement, expressed to a candidate by voters (p. 737)

Manhattan Project Secret American program during World War II to develop an atomic bomb (p. 620)

manifest destiny Argument that it was the undeniable fate of the United States to expand across North America (p. 135)

manufacturing The making of goods by machinery (p. 116)

Marbury* v. *Madison 1803 Supreme Court case that established the principle of judicial review (p. 94)

March on Washington 1963 civil rights demonstration in Washington, D.C., in which protesters called for "jobs and freedom" (p. 717)

Market Revolution Shift from a home-based, often agricultural, economy to one based on money and the buying and selling of goods (p. 116)

Marshall Plan Program of American economic assistance to Western Europe, announced in 1947 (p. 645)

martial law Emergency rule by military authorities, during which some Bill of Rights guarantees are suspended (p. 170)

mass media Print and broadcast methods of communicating information to large numbers of people (p. 460)

mass production Production of goods in great amounts (p. 234)

Massacre at Wounded Knee 1890 shooting of a group of unarmed Sioux by army troops (p. 265)

Mayflower Compact Agreement in which settlers of Plymouth Colony agreed to obey their government's laws (p. 20)

McCarran-Walter Act Passed by Congress in 1952, this law reaffirmed the quota system that had been established for each country in 1924 (p. 651)

McCarthyism Term used to describe Senator Joseph McCarthy's anti-Communist smear tactics (p. 657)

Medicaid Federal program that provides low-cost health insurance to poor Americans of any age (p. 746)

Medicare Federal program that provides hospital and low-cost medical insurance to most Americans age 65 and older (p. 746)

mercantilism Economic theory that a country should try to get and keep as much bullion, or gold and silver, as possible, by exporting more goods than it imported (p. 25)

Mexican War Conflict between the United States and Mexico from 1846 to 1848, ending with a United States victory (p. 136)

MIA Missing in action (p. 816)

Middle America Term sometimes used to describe mainstream Americans (p. 811)

middle class A new class of merchants, traders, and artisans that arose in Europe in the late Middle Ages; in modern times, the social class between the very wealthy and the lower working class (p. 7)

Middle Passage One leg of the triangular trade; term also used to refer to the forced transport of slaves from Africa to the Americas (p. 28)

migrant farm worker Person who works long hours for low wages moving from farm to farm, often from state to state, to provide the labor needed to plant, cultivate, and harvest crops (p. 772)

migration Movement of people for the purpose of settling in a new place (p. 5)

militarism Policy of aggressively building up a nation's armed forces in preparation for war, as well as giving the military more authority over the government and foreign policy (p. 415)

military-industrial complex The military establishment as it developed links to the corporate and scientific communities, employing 3.5 million Americans by 1960 (p. 656)

Miranda rule Rule that police must inform persons accused of a crime of their legal rights (p. 748)

missionary A person sent out by his or her church to spread religion (p. 16)

Missouri Compromise 1820 agreement calling for the admission of Missouri as a slave state and Maine as a free state, and outlawing slavery in future states to be created north of 36° 30' N latitude (p. 98)

mobilization The readying of troops for war (p. 416)

Modern Republicanism President Eisenhower's approach to government, described as "conservative when it comes to money, liberal when it comes to human beings" (p. 685)

monarch One who rules over a territory, state, or kingdom (p. 7)

monetary policy The federal government's plan for the makeup and quantity of the nation's money supply (p. 278)

money supply The amount of money in the national economy (p. 278)
monopoly Complete control of a product or service (p. 240)
Monroe Doctrine Declaration by President Monroe in 1823 that the United States would oppose efforts by any outside power to control a nation in the Western Hemisphere (p. 121)
Montgomery bus boycott Protest in 1955–1956 by African Americans against racial segregation in the bus system of Montgomery, Alabama (p. 701)
Morrill Land-Grant Act Passed by Congress in 1862, this law distributed millions of acres of western lands to state governments in order to fund state agricultural colleges (p. 259)
muckraker Journalist who uncovers wrongdoing in politics or business (p. 384)
multiculturalism Movement calling for greater attention to non-European cultures in such areas as education (p. 914)
multinational corporation A corporation that operates in more than one country (p. 910)
municipal Relating to a city, as in municipal government (p. 390)
Munn* v. *Illinois 1877 Supreme Court decision that allowed states to regulate certain businesses within their borders (p. 294)

N

napalm (NAY pahm) Highly flammable chemical dropped from U.S. planes in firebombing attacks during the Vietnam War (p. 801)
Nation of Islam Organization, also called the Black Muslims, dedicated to black separation and self-help (p. 722)
National Aeronautics and Space Administration (NASA) Created in 1958 by the United States government as an independent agency for space exploration (p. 686)
National American Woman Suffrage Association (NAWSA) Organization formed in 1890 to continue the pursuit of women's rights, especially the right to vote (p. 405)
National Association for the Advancement of Colored People (NAACP) Organization founded in 1909 to abolish segregation and discrimination, to oppose racism, and to gain civil rights for African Americans (p. 335)
national debt Total amount of money that the federal government borrows and has to pay back (p. 554)
National Defense Education Act 1958 measure designed to improve science and mathematics instruction in schools (p. 686)
National Liberation Front Political arm of the Viet Cong (p. 795)
National Organization for Women (NOW) Organization formed in 1966 to promote the full participation of women in American society (p. 766)
nationalism Devotion to one's nation (p. 353)
nationalization Government takeover and ownership of banks, and the redistribution of their wealth (p. 548)
nativism A policy of favoring native-born Americans over immigrants (pp. 140, 314)
Nazism An extreme form of fascism shaped by Adolf Hitler's fanatical ideas about German nationalism and racial superiority (p. 571)
Neutrality Acts 1939 laws designed to keep the United States out of future wars (p. 586)
New Deal Term used to describe President Franklin Roosevelt's relief, recovery, and reform programs designed to combat the Great Depression (p. 537)
New Federalism President Nixon's call for a new partnership between the federal government and state governments; President Reagan's plan to cut back the role of the federal government while giving more responsibility to state and local governments (pp. 829, 873)
New Frontier President Kennedy's proposals to improve the economy, to assist the poor, and to advance the space program (p. 738)
New Left New political movement of the late 1960s that called for radical changes to fight poverty and racism (p. 806)
New Nationalism Theodore Roosevelt's plan for greater federal regulation of business and workplaces, income and inheritance taxes, and electoral reforms (p. 398)
New Right A political coalition of conservative groups formed in 1980 (p. 867)
Niagara Movement Founded in 1905, a group of African Americans that called for full civil liberties, an end to racial discrimination, and recognition of human brotherhood (p. 325)
Nisei (nee SAY) A Japanese American whose parents were born in Japan (p. 627)
nomadic People who move their homes regularly, usually in search of available food sources (pp. 5, 261)
nonviolent protest A peaceful way of protesting against restrictive policies (p. 706)
North American Free Trade Agreement (NAFTA) Agreement calling for the removal of trade restrictions among the United States, Canada, and Mexico (p. 909)
North Atlantic Treaty Organization (NATO) 1949 alliance of nations that agreed to band together in the event of war and to support and protect each nation involved (p. 647)
Nuclear Regulatory Commission (NRC) Government organization formed in 1974 to oversee the civilian uses of nuclear materials (p. 783)
nullify A state's rejection of a federal law (p. 123)

Nuremberg Trials Series of trials in 1945 conducted by an International Military Tribunal in which former Nazi leaders were charged with crimes against peace, crimes against humanity, and war crimes (p. 613)

O

Office of War Mobilization Federal agency formed to coordinate issues related to war production during World War II (p. 596)

oligopoly A market structure dominated by only a few large, profitable firms (p. 240)

Open Door Policy American approach to China around 1900, favoring open trade relations between China and other nations (p. 364)

Organization of Petroleum Exporting Countries (OPEC) Group of nations that work together to regulate the price and supply of oil (p. 828)

P

Pacific Railway Acts Laws passed in 1862 and 1864 giving large land grants to the Union Pacific and Central Pacific railroads (p. 259)

pardon An official forgiveness of a crime (p. 202)

Paris peace talks Negotiations between the United States and North Vietnam, beginning in 1968 (p. 812)

patent A license that gives an inventor the exclusive right to make, use, or sell an invention for a set period of time (p. 227)

patriotism Love of one's country; the passion which aims to serve one's country, either in defending it from invasion, or in protecting its rights and maintaining its laws and institutions in vigor and purity (p. 49)

Peace Corps Federal program established to send volunteers to help developing nations (p. 758)

Pendleton Civil Service Act 1883 law that created a Civil Service Commission and stated that federal employees could not be required to contribute to campaign funds or be fired for political reasons (p. 293)

penny auction Farm auctions during the Great Depression at which neighbors saved each other's property from foreclosure by bidding low (p. 521)

per capita income Average annual income per person (p. 668)

Persian Gulf War In 1991, a limited military operation to drive Iraqi forces out of Kuwait (p. 886)

philanthropist A person who gives donations to worthy causes (p. 323)

Pickett's Charge Unsuccessful charge by Confederate infantry during the Battle of Gettysburg (p. 182)

piecework System in which workers are paid not by the time worked, but by the number of items they produce (p. 244)

placer mining A mining technique in which miners shoveled loose dirt into boxes and then ran water over the dirt to separate it from gold or silver particles (p. 269)

plantation Large farm on which crops are raised mainly for sale (p. 12)

Platt Amendment An addition to the 1900 Cuban constitution by the American government that gave the United States the right to establish naval bases in Cuba and to intervene in Cuban affairs whenever necessary (p. 362)

Plessy* v. *Ferguson 1896 Supreme Court decision that segregation was legal as long as the separate facilities provided for blacks were equal to those provided to whites (p. 334)

pocket veto Type of veto a chief executive may use after a legislature has adjourned; it is applied when the chief executive does not formally sign or reject a bill within the time period allowed to do so (p. 203)

pogrom Violent massacre of Jews (p. 298)

political machine An unofficial city organization designed to keep a particular party or group in power and usually headed by a single, powerful boss (p. 308)

political party Group of people who seek to win elections and to hold public office in order to control government policies and programs (p. 91)

poll tax A special fee that must be paid before a person can vote (p. 333)

Populist Follower of the People's Party (or Populist Party) formed in 1891 to advocate a larger money supply and other economic reforms (p. 281)

POW Prisoner of war (p. 816)

prejudice An unreasonable, usually unfavorable opinion of another group that is not based on fact (p. 139)

price controls System of pricing determined by the government (p. 433)

productivity The amount of goods and services created in a given period of time (p. 227)

Progressive Era The period from about 1890 to 1920, during which a variety of reforms were enacted at the local, state, and federal levels (p. 383)

prohibition A ban on the manufacture and sale of alcoholic beverages (p. 314)

propaganda Information intended to sway public opinion (p. 418)

Proprietary colony A colony granted by a king or queen to an individual or a group who has full governing rights (p. 22)

public works program Government-funded projects to build public facilities (p. 538)

Pullman Strike 1894 railway workers' strike that spread nationwide (p. 253)

puppet state A supposedly independent country under the control of a powerful neighbor (p. 582)

purge In political terms, the process of removing enemies and undesirable individuals from power (p. 569)
Puritans People who favored the purification of England's Anglican Church (p. 19)
push-pull factors Events and conditions that either force (push) people to move elsewhere or strongly attract (pull) them to do so (p. 258)

Q

quarantine A time of isolation to prevent the spread of a disease (p. 299)
quota A numerical limit (p. 487)

R

racism Belief that differences in character or intelligence are due to one's race; asserting the superiority of one race over another or others (p. 373)
Radical Republicans Group of congressmen from within the Republican Party who believed that the Civil War had been fought over the moral issue of slavery, and insisted that the main goal of Reconstruction should be a total restructuring of society to guarantee blacks true equality (p. 203)
ragtime A type of music featuring melodies with shifting accents over a steady, marching-band beat that originated among black musicians in the South and Midwest in the 1880s (p. 331)
rationing Distribution of goods to consumers in a fixed amount (p. 434)
Reagan Democrat Democratic, blue-collar workers who tended to vote Republican during the 1980s (p. 867)
realpolitik (ray AHL poh lih teek) A German term meaning "practical politics," or foreign policy based on interests rather than moral principles (p. 832)
rebate A partial refund (p. 294)
recall Procedure that permits voters to remove public officials from office before the next election (p. 392)
recession A period of slow business activity (p. 554)
recognition Official acceptance as an independent nation (p. 168)
Reconstruction Program implemented by the federal government between 1865 and 1877 to repair the damage to the South caused by the Civil War and to restore the southern states to the Union (p. 200)
Reconstruction Finance Corporation (RFC) Corporation set up by President Hoover in 1932 to give government credit to a number of institutions, such as large industries and insurance companies (p. 525)
reconversion The social and economic transition from wartime to peacetime (p. 680)
Red Scare Intense fear of communism and other politically radical ideas (p. 482)
referendum Process that allows citizens to approve or reject a law passed by their legislature (p. 392)
religious tolerance Idea that people of different religions should live in peace together (p. 20)
reparations Payment from an enemy for economic injury suffered during a war (p. 439)
republic Government run by the people through their elected representatives (p. 55)
republican virtues Virtues the American people would need to govern themselves, such as self-reliance, industry, frugality, harmony, and the ability to sacrifice individual needs for the good of the community (p. 110)
reservation Federal land set aside for Native Americans (p. 262)
Resistance Movement in France that opposed German occupation during World War II (p. 578)
restrictive covenant Agreement among homeowners not to sell real estate to certain groups of people, such as Jews or African Americans (p. 301)
revenue Income (p. 554)
Revolutionary War American colonists' war of independence from Britain, fought from 1775 to 1783 (p. 45)
rock-and-roll Music popular in the 1950s that grew out of rhythm and blues (p. 678)
Roe* v. *Wade 1973 Supreme Court decision that legalized abortion (p. 768)
Roosevelt Corollary President Theodore Roosevelt's 1904 extension of the Monroe Doctrine in which he asserted the right of the United States to intervene in Latin American nations (p. 368)
rural free delivery (RFD) Beginning in 1896, free delivery offered by the U.S. Post Office to farm families in the rural Midwest (p. 339)
Russian Revolution Collapse of the czar's government in Russia in 1917, after which the Russian monarchy was replaced with a republican government (p. 424)

S

SALT I Strategic Arms Limitation Treaty, a 1972 agreement between the United States and the Soviet Union on limiting nuclear weapons (p. 836)
Sandinista In the 1980s, a member of the ruling Marxist group in Nicaragua (p. 880)
satellite nation A country dominated politically and economically by another nation, especially by the Soviet Union during the Cold War (p. 639)
saturation bombing The dropping of a large concentration of bombs over a certain area (p. 801)
scab Negative term for a worker called in by an employer to replace striking laborers (p. 251)

scalawag Negative nickname for a white southern Republican after the Civil War (p. 211)
Scopes trial 1925 court case argued by Clarence Darrow and William Jennings Bryan in which the issue of teaching evolution in public schools was debated (p. 470)
secede To withdraw formally from membership in a group or organization (p. 123)
Second Great Awakening Religious movement of the early 1800s (p. 114)
Second New Deal Period of legislative activity launched by President Franklin Roosevelt in 1935 (p. 542)
sedition Any speech or action that encourages rebellion (p. 435)
segregation Forced separation, oftentimes by race (p. 333)
Selective Service Act Law passed in 1917 authorizing a draft of young men for military service in World War I (p. 425)
Selective Training and Service Act 1940 law requiring all males aged 21 to 36 to register for military service (p. 594)
self-determination The power to make decisions about one's own future (p. 437)
Seneca Falls Convention The first women's rights convention in United States history, held in 1848 (p. 132)
separation of powers The Constitutional allotting of powers within the federal government among the legislative, executive, and judicial branches (p. 59)
settlement house Community center organized to provide various services to the urban poor (p. 312)
sharecropping System of farming in which a farmer tends some portion of a planter's land and receives a share of the crop at harvest time as payment (p. 213)
shell Device that explodes in the air, or when it hits a solid target (p. 160)
Sherman Antitrust Act Law passed by Congress in 1890 that outlawed any combination of companies that restrained interstate trade or commerce (p. 242)
Sherman Silver Purchase Act Law passed by Congress in 1890 to increase the amount of silver the government was required to purchase every month (p. 279)
siege Tactic in which an enemy is surrounded and starved in order to make it surrender (p. 184)
silent majority Term used by President Nixon to describe Americans who opposed the counterculture (p. 814)
sit-down strike Labor protest in which laborers stop working but refuse to leave the workplace (p. 555)
sit-in Form of protest in which protesters seat themselves and refuse to move (p. 709)
social Darwinism Derived from Darwin's theory of natural selection, the belief that society should do as little as possible to interfere with people's pursuit of success (p. 239)
social gospel movement A social reform movement that developed within religious institutions and sought to apply the teachings of Jesus directly to society (p. 312)
Social Security System System established by the 1935 Social Security Act to provide financial security, in the form of regular payments, to people who cannot support themselves (p. 544)
social welfare program Program designed to ensure a basic standard of living for all citizens (p. 390)
socialism An economic and political philosophy that favors public (or social) instead of private control of property and income (p. 247)
sociology Term coined by philosopher Auguste Comte to describe the study of how people interact with one another in a society (p. 313)
soddie A home whose walls and roof are made from blocks of grass with the thick roots and earth attached (p. 273)
solid South Term used to describe the domination of post–Civil War southern politics by the Democratic Party (p. 220)
sooners In 1889, people who illegally claimed land by sneaking past government officials before the land races began (p. 267)
Southern Christian Leadership Conference (SCLC) Civil rights organization that advocated nonviolent protest; formed in 1957 by Dr. Martin Luther King, Jr., and other leaders (p. 706)
speakeasies Bars that operated illegally during the time of Prohibition (p. 468)
special prosecutor An attorney appointed by the Justice Department to investigate wrongdoing by government officials (p. 843)
speculation The practice of making high-risk investments in hopes of getting a huge return (p. 500)
sphere of influence Area of economic and political control exerted by one nation over another nation or other nations (p. 364)
spiritual A folk hymn (p. 115)
spoils Rewards gained through military victory (p. 438)
Sputnik The first artificial satellite to orbit Earth, launched by the Soviets in 1957 (p. 661)
stagflation Combination of high inflation and high unemployment, with no economic growth (p. 848)
stalemate Situation in which neither side in a conflict is able to gain the advantage (p. 417)
states' rights The powers that the Constitution neither gives to the federal government nor denies to the states (p. 123)
steerage A large open area beneath the ship's deck, often used to house traveling immigrants (p. 298)
stereotype An exaggerated or oversimplified description of reality held by a number of people (p. 275)
Strategic Arms Reduction Treaty Agreement signed in 1991 and known as START, that called for the reduction in the supplies of long-range nuclear weapons in Russia and the United States (p. 885)

Strategic Defense Initiative (SDI) President Reagan's proposed defense system against a Soviet missile attack, popularly known as "Star Wars" (p. 873)
strict construction Belief that the government should not do anything that the Constitution does not specifically say it can do (p. 90)
strike A work stoppage intended to force an employer to meet certain demands, as in the demand for higher wages (p. 119)
Student Nonviolent Coordinating Committee (SNCC) Founded in 1960, a student civil rights organization and an offshoot of the SCLC (p. 707)
subsidy A payment made by the government to encourage the development of certain key industries (p. 291)
suburb Residential community surrounding a city (p. 305)
suffrage The right to vote (p. 132)
supply-side economics Theory that tax reductions will increase investment and thereby encourage business growth (p. 871)
Sussex pledge Pledge by the German government in 1916 that its submarines would warn ships before attacking (p. 423)
sweatshop Factory where employees work long hours at low wages and under poor working conditions (p. 244)

T

Taft-Hartley Act Law passed by Congress in 1947 that allowed the President to declare an 80-day cooling-off period when strikes impacted industries that affected the national interest, and required strikers to return to work while the government conducted a study of the situation (p. 681)
teach-in Special session of lecture and discussion on a controversial topic that often occurred during the Vietnam War era (p. 807)
Teapot Dome scandal Scandal during the Harding administration involving the granting of oil drilling rights on government land in return for money (p. 488)
televangelism The use of television by evangelists to reach millions of people, especially for fund-raising (p. 868)
temperance movement An organized campaign to eliminate alcohol consumption (pp. 128, 314)
tenant farming System of farming in which a person rents land to farm from a planter (p. 214)
tenement A low-cost apartment building that often has poor standards of sanitation, safety, and comfort, and is designed to house as many families as possible (p. 306)
Tennessee Valley Authority (TVA) Federal project to provide inexpensive electric power, flood control, and recreational opportunities to the Tennessee River valley (p. 540)
Tet Offensive 1968 attack by Viet Cong and North Vietnamese forces throughout South Vietnam (p. 803)
Thirteenth Amendment Constitutional amendment, ratified in 1865, abolishing slavery (p. 190)
38th parallel Latitude line that divided North and South Korea at approximately the midpoint of the peninsula (p. 653)
totalitarian A government that exerts total control over the nation and citizens' lives (p. 568)
Trail of Tears The forced movement of Cherokees in 1838 to land west of the Mississippi River (p. 124)
transcendentalism Philosophical movement of the mid-1800s that emphasized spiritual discovery and insight rather than reason (p. 127)
transcontinental railroad Railway extending from coast to coast (p. 230)
transistor A tiny circuit device invented in 1947 that amplifies, controls, and generates electrical signals (p. 670)
triangular trade Trade between the Americas, Europe, and Africa (p. 27)
Truman Doctrine Harry Truman's 1947 speech before a joint session of Congress, calling for the United States to take a leadership role in the world, and declaring that the United States would support nations threatened by communism (p. 642)
trust A group of separate companies that are placed under the control of a single managing board (p. 242)
Turner thesis 1893 theory of Frederick Jackson Turner that claimed the frontier had played a key role in forming the American character (p. 275)
Twenty-first Amendment Constitutional amendment ratified in 1933 to repeal Prohibition (p. 522)
Twenty-fourth Amendment Constitutional amendment ratified in 1964 to outlaw the poll tax (p. 721)

U

U-boat A German submarine (p. 421)
U-2 incident A 1960 incident in which the Soviet military used a guided missile to shoot down an American U-2 spy plane over Soviet territory (p. 661)
Underground Railroad A network of escape routes that provided protection and transportation for slaves fleeing north to freedom (p. 130)
United Farm Workers (UFW) Union created by César Chávez to organize Mexican field hands in the West (p. 773)
United States Constitution Plan of government that describes the different parts of the government and their duties and powers, established in 1787 (p. 57)
utopian community A small society dedicated to perfection in social and political conditions (p. 129)

V

vaudeville A type of variety show that first appeared in the 1870s, often consisting of comic sketches, song-and-dance routines, and magic acts (p. 327)

Versailles Treaty 1919 treaty that ended World War I (p. 439)

vertical consolidation Process of gaining control of the many different businesses that make up all phases of a product's development (p. 241)

vice Immoral or corrupt behavior (p. 315)

victory garden A home vegetable garden created to boost food production during World War II (p. 599)

Viet Cong Communist guerrillas in South Vietnam (p. 795)

Vietminh Common name for the League for Independence of Vietnam (p. 792)

Vietnamization President Nixon's policy of replacing American military forces with those of South Vietnam (p. 813)

vigilante A citizen who takes the law into his or her own hands (p. 435)

Volunteers in Service to America (VISTA) Federal program to send volunteers to help people in poor communities (p. 746)

Voting Rights Act of 1965 Law aimed at reducing the barriers that prevented African Americans from voting, in part by increasing the federal government's authority to register voters (p. 721)

W

Wagner Act Law passed in 1935 that aided unions by legalizing collective bargaining and closed shops, and by establishing the National Labor Relations Board (p. 543)

Wannsee Conference 1942 conference in Germany concerning the plan to murder European Jews (p. 611)

war of attrition A type of war in which one side inflicts continuous losses on the other in order to wear down its strength (p. 159)

War of 1812 War between the United States and Great Britain (p. 96)

War Powers Act 1973 law limiting a President's ability to involve the United States in foreign conflicts without receiving a formal declaration of war from Congress (p. 849)

War Refugee Board (WRB) Federal agency created in 1944 to try to help people threatened with murder by the Nazis (p. 612)

Warren Commission Commission, headed by Chief Justice Earl Warren, that investigated the assassination of President Kennedy (p. 741)

Warsaw ghetto An area of Warsaw sealed off by the Nazis to confine the Jewish population, forcing them into poor, unsanitary conditions (p. 611)

Warsaw Pact Military alliance between the Soviet Union and nations of Eastern Europe, formed in 1955 (p. 648)

Watergate scandal Scandal involving illegal activities that led ultimately to the resignation of President Nixon in 1974 (p. 840)

welfare capitalism An approach to labor relations in which companies meet some of their workers' needs without prompting by unions, thus preventing strikes and keeping productivity high (p. 499)

Whitewater affair Charges that President Clinton had engaged in improper business transactions before becoming President (p. 898)

wiretap A listening device used to intercept telephone information (p. 839)

Woodstock festival 1969 music festival in upstate New York (p. 779)

World Trade Organization (WTO) International organization formed in 1995 to encourage the expansion of world trade (p. 909)

writ of *habeas corpus* Legal protection requiring that a court determine if a person is lawfully imprisoned (p. 171)

Y

yellow journalism Sensational news coverage, emphasizing crime and scandal (p. 329)

Z

zeppelin A German floating airship (p. 429)

Zimmermann note A telegram sent by Germany's foreign secretary in 1917 to Mexican officials proposing an alliance with Mexico and promising U.S. territory if Mexico declared war on the United States (p. 424)

989

Spanish Glossary

A

abolitionist movement/movimiento abolicionista Movimiento para acabar con la esclavitud (pág. 129)

abstinence/abstinencia Acción de abstenerse de alguna actividad, como consumir bebidas alcohólicas (pág. 128)

Adams-Onís Treaty/Tratado Adams-Onís Tratado firmado en 1819 entre los Estados Unidos y España en el que España le cedió la Florida a los Estados Unidos; también se conoce como Tratado Transcontinental (pág. 109)

administration/administración Plazo para ejercer un cargo; también se refiere al conjunto de miembros y entidades de la rama ejecutiva (pág. 64)

affirmative action/discriminación positiva Política que concede consideración especial a las mujeres y a los miembros de grupos minoritarios para compensarlos por discriminaciones pasadas (pág. 854)

Agent Orange/agente naranja Herbicida que se utilizó como arma química durante la Guerra de Vietnam para exterminar la vegetación y poner al descubierto zonas enemigas ocultas (pág. 801)

Agricultural Adjustment Administration (AAA)/Administración de Ajuste Agrícola (AAA) Se estableció en 1933 para elevar los precios de los productos agrícolas a través apoyo económico del gobierno (pág. 540)

AIDS/SIDA Síndrome de inmunodeficiencia adquirida; causado por un virus que ha matado a muchas personas desde principios de la década de 1980 (pág. 878)

alien/extranjero Alguien que no es ciudadano (pág. 302)

Alliance for Progress/Alianza para el Progreso Propuesta del presidente Kennedy para la cooperación entre las naciones del hemisferio occidental con el fin de satisfacer las necesidades básicas de sus habitantes (pág. 757)

Allies/aliados En la Primera Guerra Mundial: Rusia, Francia, Serbia y Gran Bretaña; en la Segunda Guerra Mundial: la alianza de Gran Bretaña, los Estados Unidos de América, la Unión Soviética y otras naciones (págs. 417, 578)

America First Committee/Primer Comité Estadounidense Grupo formado en 1940 por aislacionistas para bloquear la ayuda a Gran Bretaña (pág. 587)

American Expeditionary Force (AEF)/Cuerpo Expedicionario Estadounidense (AEF) Nombre que se le dio a las tropas estadounidenses en Europa durante la Primera Guerra Mundial (pág. 425)

American Indian Movement (AIM)/Movimiento Indio Estadounidense (AIM) Organización formada en 1968 para ayudar a los indígenas (pág. 775)

American Liberty League/Asociación para la Libertad de los Estados Unidos Organización fundada en 1934 en oposición al Nuevo Trato (pág. 547)

amnesty/amnistía Perdón general para ciertos crímenes (pág. 854)

anarchist/anarquista Persona radical que se opone a todo tipo de gobierno (pág. 251)

annex/anexar Incorporar o unir, refiriéndose al caso de la unión de un territorio nuevo a un país determinado (págs. 135, 353)

anti-Federalists/antifederalistas Personas que se oponían a la Constitución durante el debate sobre la ratificación; en contra del concepto de un gobierno nacional sólido (pág. 61)

anti-Semitism/antisemitismo Hostilidad o discriminación hacia los judíos (pág. 609)

apartheid/*apartheid* La discriminación sistemática de personas con diferentes antecedentes raciales (pág. 904)

appeasement/pacificación Política de aceptación de las demandas de un competidor con el fin de preservar la paz (pág. 573)

apportionment/distribución de las asignaciones Distribución de escaños en un cuerpo legislativo (pág. 748)

arbitration/arbitraje Conciliación de una disputa a través de una persona o grupo de expertos que escuchan a ambas partes y toman una decisión (pág. 358)

armistice/armisticio Cese al fuego o tregua (pág. 430)

arms race/carrera armamentista Competencia entre naciones para obtener la superioridad de armamento (pág. 660)

Articles of Confederation/Artículos de la Confederación Plan que estableció en 1781 un gobierno nacional limitado en los Estados Unidos; más tarde fue reemplazado por la Constitución de los Estados Unidos (pág. 55)

assembly line/línea de montaje Proceso de fabricación en el cual cada trabajador realiza una tarea determinada en la construcción del producto final (pág. 494)

assimilation/asimilación Proceso por el cual las personas de una cultura se incorporan y se vuelven parte de otra (págs. 266, 321)

Atlantic Charter/Carta del Atlántico Acuerdo firmado en 1941 por el presidente Franklin Roosevelt y el primer ministro Winston Churchill en el que se resumen los objetivos de guerra de las dos naciones (pág. 600)

autocrat/autócrata Mandatario con poder ilimitado (pág. 418)

autonomy/autonomía Capacidad de un pueblo de gobernarse a sí mismo con respecto a asuntos locales (pág. 775)

Axis Powers/Potencias del Eje En la Segunda Guerra Mundial: Alemania, Italia y Japón (pág. 573)

B

baby boom/*baby boom* Aumento dramático en la tasa de natalidad, sobre todo en los años que siguieron a la Segunda Guerra Mundial (pág. 672)

balance of trade/balanza comercial Diferencia del valor entre las importaciones y las exportaciones (pág. 25)

banana republic/república bananera Término utilizado para describir a una nación centroamericana que esté dominada por los intereses financieros de los Estados Unidos (pág. 355)

***barrio*/barrio** Un vecindario de hispanohablantes (págs. 455, 625)

barter/canjear Comerciar con productos o servicios sin utilizar dinero (pág. 6)

Bataan Death March/Marcha de la muerte de Bataán Marcha brutal de prisioneros norteamericanos y filipinos dirigida por soldados japoneses en 1942 (pág. 615)

Battle of Antietam/Batalla de Antietam Batalla de la Guerra Civil; ocurrió en Maryland en 1862 (pág. 165)

Battle of the Bulge/Batalla de las Ardenas Batalla de la Segunda Guerra Mundial en la que fuerzas alemanas lanzaron un contraataque final en el oeste (pág. 607)

Battle of Chancellorsville/Batalla de Chancellorsville Batalla de la Guerra Civil; tuvo lugar en Virginia, en 1863, y la ganó la Confederación (pág. 179)

Battle of Cold Harbor/Batalla de Cold Harbor Batalla de la Guerra Civil; ocurrió en 1864 en Virginia (pág. 187)

Battle of the Coral Sea/Batalla del Mar del Coral Batalla de la Segunda Guerra Mundial entre aviones norteamericanos y japoneses; tuvo lugar en 1942 (pág. 616)

Battle of Fredericksburg/Batalla de Fredericksburg Batalla de la Guerra Civil; ocurrió en Virginia, en 1862, y la ganó la Confederación (pág. 179)

Battle of Gettysburg/Batalla de Gettysburg Batalla de la Guerra Civil; tuvo lugar en Pennsylvania, en 1863, y la ganó la Unión; representó un momento crucial en la guerra (pág. 180)

Battle of Guadalcanal/Batalla de Guadalcanal Batalla de la Segunda Guerra Mundial que fue librada de 1942 a 1943 entre los Estados Unidos y Japón (pág. 617)

Battle of Iwo Jima/Batalla de Iwo Jima Batalla de la Segunda Guerra Mundial que ocurrió en 1945 entre los Estados Unidos y Japón (pág. 619)

Battle of Leyte Gulf/Batalla del Golfo Leyte Batalla naval de la Segunda Guerra Mundial librada en 1944 entre los Estados Unidos y Japón (pág. 618)

Battle of Little Bighorn/Batalla de Little Bighorn Victoria de la tribu Sioux sobre las tropas armadas dirigidas por George Custer; ocurrió en 1876 (pág. 265)

Battle of Midway/Batalla de Midway Batalla de la Segunda Guerra Mundial librada en 1942 entre los Estados Unidos y Japón; fue un momento crucial en la guerra en el Pacífico (pág. 617)

Battle of Okinawa/Batalla de Okinawa Batalla de la Segunda Guerra Mundial librada en 1945 entre los Estados Unidos y Japón (pág. 619)

Battle of Shiloh/Batalla de Shiloh Batalla de la Guerra Civil; tuvo lugar en Tennessee en 1862 (pág. 162)

Battle of Spotsylvania/Batalla de Spotsylvania Batalla de la Guerra Civil; ocurrió en 1864, en Virginia (pág. 187)

Battle of the Wilderness/Batalla de Wilderness Batalla de la Guerra Civil; tuvo lugar en Virginia, en 1864, y la ganó la Confederación (pág. 187)

Battles of Lexington and Concord/Batallas de Lexington y Concord Primeras batallas de la Guerra Revolucionaria que tuvieron lugar el 19 de abril de 1775 (pág. 45)

Bay of Pigs invasion/Invasión a la Bahía de Cochinos Invasión fallida a Cuba realizada por un grupo de fuerzas anticastristas en 1961 (pág. 752)

beatnik/*beatnik* Persona que, en la década de 1950 criticaba y consideraba a la sociedad estadounidense como indiferente y conformista (pág. 679)

Berlin airlift/puente aéreo de Berlín Operación en la que aviones norteamericanos e ingleses transportaron provisiones a Berlín Occidental durante un bloqueo soviético de 1948 a 1949 (pág. 647)

Berlin Wall/Muro de Berlín Barrera construida por el gobierno de Alemania Oriental para separar la zona comunista de Berlín de la no comunista (pág. 754)

Bessemer process/proceso Bessemer Proceso patentado en 1856 para elaborar acero de manera más eficiente (pág. 233)

bicentennial/bicentenario Fecha en que se cumplen 200 años de un acontecimiento (pág. 850)

bilingual education/educación bilingüe La enseñanza a los estudiantes en su lengua materna y en inglés (pág. 913)

Bill of Rights/Declaración de Derechos Las primeras diez enmiendas a la Constitución (pág. 62)

bimetallic standard/patrón bimetálico Moneda de los Estados Unidos, antes de 1873, que constaba de monedas de oro o de plata, así como de bonos fiscales que podían ser intercambiados por oro o plata (pág. 278)

black codes/*black codes* o códigos negros Leyes que restringían los derechos de los libertos (pág. 206)

black nationalism/nacionalismo negro Creencia en la identidad propia y la unidad racial de la comunidad estadounidense de raza negra (pág. 723)

black power/poder negro Movimiento estadounidense de raza negra que busca la unión y la independencia (pág. 724)

Black Tuesday/Martes Negro El 29 de octubre de 1929, día en que empezó la gran caída de la bolsa de valores (pág. 509)

blacklist/lista negra Lista que a principios de 1947 circulaba entre los empleadores y que contenía los nombres de las personas que no debían ser contratadas (pág. 650)

991

Bland-Allison Act/Ley de Bland-Allison Ley promulgada en 1878 que exigía al gobierno federal comprar y acuñar más plata, lo que aumentó la oferta monetaria y causó inflación (pág. 279)

***blitzkrieg/blitzkrieg* o Guerra Relámpago** Tipo de guerra que enfatiza el movimiento rápido y mecanizado; utilizada por Alemania durante la Segunda Guerra Mundial (pág. 576)

blue law/leyes azules Reglamentos que prohibían ciertas actividades privadas que se consideraban inmorales, como ingerir bebidas alcohólicas los domingos (pág. 292)

bonanza farm/granja "la bonanza" Granja controlada por empresas grandes y manejada por profesionales, en la que se cultivan inmensas cantidades de cosechas que se venden al contado (pág. 274)

Bonus Army/Armados para la Bonificación Un grupo de veteranos de la Primera Guerra Mundial y sus familias que protestaron en Washington, D.C., en 1932, exigiendo el pago inmediato de la bonificación de retiro prometida en 1945 (pág. 526)

boomers/pioneros Colonos que corrían para ganar un pedazo de tierra cuando el territorio indio se abrió para la colonización, en 1889 (pág. 267)

bootlegger/contrabandista de licores Término para describir a un vendedor de alcohol ilegal durante el período de Prohibición (pág. 468)

Border States/Estados fronterizos En la Guerra Civil, los estados entre el norte y el sur: Delaware, Maryland, Kentucky y Missouri (pág. 142)

Boston Massacre/Masacre de Boston Incidente ocurrido el 5 de marzo de 1770 en el que los soldados británicos mataron a cinco colonos (pág. 43)

boycott/boicot Rechazo a comprar un producto determinado o utilizar un servicio determinado (pág. 43)

***bracero*/bracero** Término utilizado en 1942 para describir a los campesinos mexicanos traídos a los Estados Unidos (pág. 625)

brinkmanship/*brinkmanship* Término utilizado en 1956 por el secretario de estado John Dulles para describir la habilidad de llegar al borde de una guerra sin participar en ella, con el fin de proteger los intereses nacionales (pág. 660)

Brown* v. *Board of Education of Topeka, Kansas/Brown* vs. *la Junta de Educación de Topeka, Kansas Caso de la Suprema Corte ocurrido en 1954 en el que se prohibió la discriminación racial en las escuelas públicas (pág. 699)

Bull Moose Party/Partido Bull Moose Sobrenombre del Partido Progresista (pág. 398)

Burma Road/Carretera Birmania Autopista de 700 millas de largo que une Birmania (hoy en día Myanmar) con China (pág. 584)

business cycle/ciclo comercial Períodos en los que la economía de una nación crece y luego disminuye (pág. 509)

buying on margin/compra de valores a crédito Opción que permite a los inversionistas adquirir al contado valores por tan sólo una parte de su precio y pedir un préstamo para el resto (pág. 500)

C

Camp David Accords/Acuerdos de Camp David Convenio firmado en 1978 entre Israel y Egipto que hizo posible un tratado de paz entre las dos naciones (pág. 855)

canister/bote de metralla Tipo especial de recipiente lleno de balas (pág. 160)

capital/capital Riqueza que se puede invertir para producir bienes y hacer dinero (pág. 117)

carpet bombing/bombardeo masivo Método de bombardeo aéreo en el que se arrojan muchas bombas sobre un área extensa (pág. 605)

carpetbagger/norteño en busca de dinero fácil Sobrenombre negativo para referirse a un republicano del norte que se iba al sur después de la Guerra Civil (pág. 211)

cartel/cartel Asociación eventual de empresas que elaboran el mismo producto (pág. 240)

cash and carry/pago al contado y transporte propio Política de la Segunda Guerra Mundial que exigía a las naciones en guerra pagar en efectivo todos aquellos productos que no fueran militares y encargarse de su transporte desde los Estados Unidos (pág. 586)

casualty/baja Término militar para una persona asesinada, herida, capturada o perdida en el campo de batalla (pág. 158)

Central Powers/potencias centrales En la Primera Guerra Mundial: Alemania y Austria-Hungría (pág. 417)

charter/carta Certificado de un permiso dado por el gobierno (pág. 17)

checks and balances/pesos y contrapesos Sistema en el que cada rama del gobierno federal revisa las acciones de las otras ramas (pág. 59)

Chinese Exclusion Act/Ley de Exclusión de los Chinos Ley aprobada en 1882 que prohibía a los trabajadores chinos entrar al país; sin embargo, no impedía la entrada a aquellos que habían establecido con anterioridad su residencia en los Estados Unidos (pág. 302)

civil disobedience/desobediencia civil Rechazo pacífico a obedecer una ley en un esfuerzo por cambiarla (pág. 404)

civil rights/derechos civiles Libertades individuales de los ciudadanos garantizadas por la ley, como el derecho al voto y el mismo trato a todos los habitantes (pág. 207)

Civil Rights Act of 1964/Ley de los Derechos Civiles de 1964 Ley que declaró ilegal la discriminación en un gran número de asuntos, tales como el voto, las escuelas y los empleos (pág. 719)

civil service/administración pública Los trabajadores del gobierno no elegidos (pág. 292)

Civil War/Guerra Civil Guerra entre los estados de la Unión del norte y los estados Confederados del sur que tuvo lugar de 1861 a 1865 (pág. 156)

Civilian Conservation Corps (CCC)/Asociación para la Conservación Civil (CCC) Este programa, establecido por el Congreso en 1933, puso a más de 2.5 millones de jóvenes a trabajar en la restauración y el mantenimiento de bosques, playas y parques (pág. 539)

clan/clan Grupos de familias que descienden de un antepasado común (pág. 5)

Clayton Antitrust Act/Ley Antimonopolista Clayton Ley aprobada en 1914 para fortalecer la Ley Antimonopolista Sherman de 1890; especificaba las actividades que estaban prohibidas en las grandes empresas (pág. 400)

Clean Air Act/Ley de Protección de la Calidad del Aire Ley aprobada en 1970 con el fin de controlar la contaminación causada por la emisión de gases de las industrias y los automóviles (pág. 784)

Clean Water Act/Ley de Protección de la Calidad del Agua Ley aprobada en 1972 con el fin de controlar la contaminación causada por la eliminación de aguas de desecho industriales y municipales, y de otorgar concesiones para construir mejores instalaciones para el tratamiento de aguas negras (pág. 784)

closed shop/obligación de reclutar trabajadores sindicados Lugar de trabajo abierto sólo a miembros del sindicato (pág. 543)

cloture/votación calificada para cerrar el debate En el Senado, el voto de las tres quintas partes para limitar el debate y pedir un voto para un asunto determinado (pág. 719)

coalition/coalición Alianza de grupos con metas similares (pág. 554)

Cold War/Guerra Fría La competencia que se desarrolló después de la Segunda Guerra Mundial entre los Estados Unidos y la Unión Soviética por el poder y la influencia en el mundo; duró hasta la caída de la Unión Soviética en 1991 (pág. 640)

collaboration/colaboración Cooperación cercana (pág. 578)

collective bargaining/acuerdo colectivo Procedimiento en el cual los trabajadores negocian como grupo con los patrones (pág. 249)

collective security/seguridad colectiva El principio de apoyo militar mutuo entre las naciones (pág. 647)

colony/colonia Un área de tierra poblada por inmigrantes que siguen siendo regidos por su país natal (pág. 15)

Columbian Exchange/intercambio colombino El comercio trasatlántico de cosechas, tecnología y cultura entre América y Europa, África y Asia; comenzó en 1492 con el primer viaje de Cristóbal Colón a América (pág. 11)

communism/comunismo Ideología oficial de la Unión Soviética, caracterizada por la posesión total de la tierra y las propiedades por parte del gobierno, el control del gobierno a través de un solo partido, la falta de derechos individuales y la exigencia de una revolución mundial (pág. 481)

Compromise of 1850/Acuerdo de 1850 Acuerdo diseñado para disminuir las tensiones de la expansión de la esclavitud en territorios occidentales (pág. 138)

Compromise of 1877/Acuerdo de 1877 Acuerdo en el que los demócratas acordaron otorgar a Rutherford B. Hayes la victoria en la elección presidencial de 1876, y en el que Hayes acordó, a su vez, retirar las tropas federales de los estados del sur (pág. 221)

compulsory/obligatorio Requerido (pág. 374)

concentration camp/campo de concentración Lugar donde se confinan prisioneros políticos, por lo general bajo condiciones muy severas (pág. 610)

concession/concesión La cesión de un pedazo de tierra a cambio de la promesa de utilizarla para un fin específico (pág. 366)

Confederate States of America/Estados Confederados de América Asociación de siete estados del sur formada en 1861 (pág. 143)

conglomerate/conglomerado Corporación formada por tres o más empresas que no se relacionan entre sí (pág. 669)

Congress of Racial Equality (CORE)/Congreso para la Igualdad Racial (CORE) Organización fundada por pacifistas en 1942 para promover la igualdad racial por medios pacíficos (págs. 625, 705)

Congressional Union (CU)/Unión Congresional (CU) Organización radical formada en 1913 y dirigida por Alice Paul, cuya campaña era en favor de una enmienda constitucional que garantizara el sufragio de las mujeres (pág. 406)

conquistador/conquistador Conquistador español (pág. 15)

conscientious objector/objetor de conciencia Persona que se opone a la guerra por motivos morales o religiosos (pág. 807)

conservationist/conservacionista Persona que apoya la protección de los recursos naturales (pág. 397)

consumer economy/economía de consumo Economía que depende de una gran cantidad de gastos por parte de los consumidores (pág. 491)

containment/contención Política estadounidense que se opone a una mayor expansión del comunismo en el mundo (pág. 641)

Contra/contra Término utilizado en español para referirse a un "contrarrevolucionario", o sea, un rebelde que se oponía al gobierno comunista de Nicaragua en la década de 1980 (pág. 880)

contraband/contrabando Artículos confiscados al enemigo durante el período de guerra (pág. 172)

Contract with America/Contrato con América Garantía ofrecida por los candidatos republicanos en la campaña electoral de 1994 de limitar el gobierno, eliminar algunas leyes, reducir impuestos y equilibrar el presupuesto (pág. 896)

convoy/convoy Grupo de barcos sin armas rodeados por un anillo de buques navales armados (pág. 426)

Copperhead/"cabeza de cobre" Apodo que se les daba durante la Guerra Civil a los demócratas pacifistas del norte (pág. 169)

cotton gin/despepitadora de algodón Máquina para separar las semillas de la fibra de algodón en bruto (pág. 112)

counterculture/contracultura Grupo de jóvenes estadounidenses que en la década de 1960 rechazaban las costumbres convencionales y la cultura tradicional (pág. 777)

craft union/gremio de artesanos Sindicato formado por trabajadores dedicados a un oficio específico (pág. 249)

Cross of Gold Speech/Discurso de la Cruz de Oro Discurso pronunciado en 1896 por William Jennings Bryan en la Asamblea Demócrata; uno de los discursos más famosos de la historia de los Estados Unidos (pág. 282)

Cuban Missile Crisis/crisis de los misiles cubanos Crisis que surgió en 1962 entre los Estados Unidos y la Unión Soviética a raíz de un intento soviético por desplegar misiles nucleares en Cuba (pág. 754)

D

Dawes Act/Ley de Dawes Ley promulgada en 1887 que dividió las reservaciones en lotes familiares privados (pág. 266)

daylight savings time/horario de verano Horario en el que se adelantan los relojes una hora durante el verano (pág. 434)

D-Day/Día D Nombre en clave para referirse a la invasión de los aliados a Francia el 6 de junio de 1944 (pág. 606)

death camp/campo de la muerte Campo alemán creado durante la Segunda Guerra Mundial con el único propósito del asesinato en masa (pág. 611)

Declaration of Independence/Declaración de la Independencia Declaración promulgada en 1776 por el Segundo Congreso Continental, que explica por qué las colonias querían independizarse de Gran Bretaña (pág. 46)

***de facto* segregation/segregación *de facto* o de hecho** Separación causada por condiciones sociales como la pobreza (pág. 725)

deferment/postergación Aplazamiento oficial de un evento, como el servicio militar (pág. 808)

deficit spending/gastos en exceso de los ingresos Cuando se gasta más dinero del presupuesto federal anual en comparación con los ingresos que recibe el gobierno (págs. 550, 828)

deflation/deflación Caída de los precios de los productos (pág. 278)

***de jure* segregation/segregación *de jure* o de ley** Segregación racial creada por ley (pág. 725)

demagogue/demagogo Líder que manipula a las personas con verdades a medias, falsas promesas y tácticas de intimidación (pág. 548)

democracy/democracia Forma de gobierno en que la autoridad reside en el pueblo (pág. 55)

demographics/estadísticas demográficas Estadísticas que describen una población, como los datos sobre la raza o los ingresos (pág. 454)

denomination/grupo religioso Un subgrupo religioso generalmente mayor que una secta (pág. 114)

department store/tienda por departamentos Establecimiento grande que vende al menudeo, ofrece una amplia variedad de productos y vende en grandes cantidades (pág. 338)

depression/depresión Una baja severa en la economía marcada por la disminución en la actividad empresarial, el desempleo general y la caída de precios y salarios (pág. 98)

deregulation/desregulación La reducción o revocación del control del gobierno (pág. 853)

détente/distensión Moderación de las tensiones políticas entre las naciones (pág. 833)

deterrence/disuasión Política de fortalecer el poder militar de los Estados Unidos y de sus aliados a tal grado que el enemigo desista por temor a las represalias (pág. 660)

direct primary/elección primaria directa Elección en la que todos los ciudadanos votan para elegir a los candidatos para las próximas elecciones (pág. 392)

disarmament/desarme Programa en el que las naciones del mundo entregan voluntariamente sus armas (pág. 486)

discrimination/discriminación Trato desigual a un grupo de personas debido a su nacionalidad, raza, sexo o religión (pág. 133)

dissident/disidente Persona que critica las acciones del gobierno (pág. 855)

division of labor/distribución del trabajo Forma de producción en la que diferentes personas realizan diferentes tareas (pág. 245)

dollar diplomacy/diplomacia del dólar Política establecida por el presidente Taft que consiste en estimular la inversión estadounidense en economías extranjeras (pág. 370)

domino theory/teoría del dominó Creencia de que si un país cae en manos del comunismo, los países vecinos también lo hacen (pág. 792)

dove/paloma Sobrenombre para una persona que se opone a la guerra, como en el caso de quienes se oponían a la Guerra de Vietnam (pág. 802)

Dow Jones Industrial Average/promedio industrial Dow Jones Medida promedio de los precios de las acciones de las principales industrias (pág. 508)

downsizing/reducción de personal Despido de empleados para reducir costos (pág. 887)

draft/reclutamiento Servicio militar obligatorio (pág. 167)

dry farming/cultivo seco Técnicas utilizadas para cultivar productos en áreas con poca lluvia; técnicas de conservación del agua (pág. 274)

dumbbell tenement/*dumbbell tenement* Construcción formada por dos edificios cuya separación es muy angosta, lo que produce corrientes de aire en cada lado y permite que entre luz y aire en las habitaciones (pág. 307)

Dust Bowl/tazón de polvo, el Término que describía las grandes praderas del centro y del sur de los Estados Unidos en la década de 1930, cuando la región sufrió un período de sequía y tolvaneras (pág. 514)

E

economic sanctions/sanciones económicas Restricciones comerciales y otras medidas económicas planeadas para castigar a otra nación (pág. 904)

economies of scale/economías de escala Fenómeno en que a medida que aumenta la producción, el costo de cada artículo producido generalmente disminuye (pág. 241)

Emancipation Proclamation/Proclamación de la Emancipación Decreto presidencial del presidente Lincoln que empezó a regir el 1 de enero de 1863, en el que se liberaba a los esclavos del territorio que estaba bajo el poder de los confederados (pág. 171)

embargo/embargo Prohibición o restricción en el comercio (págs. 95, 828)

Enforcement Act of 1870/Ley Contra la Coacción de 1870 Ley aprobada por el Congreso en la que se prohíbe el uso del terror, la fuerza o el soborno para impedir que las personas voten debido a su raza (pág. 219)

entitlement/programa de ayuda social Programa gubernamental que garantiza un pago a un grupo social determinado, por ejemplo, a las personas de la tercera edad (pág. 881)

Environmental Protection Agency (EPA)/Agencia para la Protección Ambiental (EPA) Organización gubernamental formada en 1970 para establecer y hacer cumplir los estándares nacionales de control de contaminantes (pág. 784)

Equal Rights Amendment/Enmienda para la Igualdad de Derechos Enmienda constitucional propuesta, que nunca se ratificó, en la que se prohíbe la discriminación de las personas a causa de su sexo (pág. 768)

escalation/escalamiento Expansión por etapas, por ejemplo, de un conflicto local a uno nacional (pág. 801)

Exoduster/*exoduster* Estadounidense de raza negra que emigró al Oeste después de la Guerra Civil (pág. 260)

F

facism/fascismo Filosofía política que enfatiza la importancia de una nación o grupo étnico, así como la autoridad suprema del líder sobre la del individuo (pág. 568)

Federal Reserve System/sistema de la reserva federal El sistema bancario central de la nación, establecido en 1913 (pág. 400)

federal system of government/sistema federal de gobierno Sistema en el que las autoridades nacionales y estatales comparten el poder (pág. 59)

Federal Trade Commission (FTC)/Comisión Federal de Comercio (FTC) Comisión establecida en 1914 por el presidente Wilson y el Congreso para hacer cumplir el Ley Clayton y establecer leyes para un comercio recíproco (pág. 400)

Federalists/federalistas Partidarios de la Constitución durante el debate sobre su ratificación; en favor de un gobierno nacional sólido (pág. 61)

feminism/feminismo Teoría que apoya la igualdad política, económica y social entre hombres y mujeres (pág. 764)

Fifteenth Amendment/Decimoquinta enmienda Enmienda constitucional, ratificada en 1870, que garantiza a todos los ciudadanos el derecho al voto (pág. 210)

filibuster/obstruccionismo Táctica en la que los senadores obstruyen un voto al tomar la palabra y prolongar excesivamente su discurso (pág. 719)

First Battle of Bull Run/Primera Batalla de Bull Run Primera y más grande batalla de la Guerra Civil, en la que triunfaron los Confederados en julio de 1861 (pág. 158)

First Continental Congress/Primer Congreso Continental Asamblea de representantes de las colonias que se reunieron por primera vez en Filadelfia en septiembre de 1774 (pág. 44)

flapper/*flapper* Término utilizado en la década de 1920 para describir a un nuevo tipo de jovencita; rebelde, llena de energía, amante de las diversiones y atrevida (pág. 452)

Fourteen Points/Propuesta de los Catorce Puntos Propuesta del presidente Wilson en 1918 para lograr la paz europea durante la posguerra (pág. 437)

Fourteenth Amendment/Decimocuarta enmienda Enmienda constitucional, ratificada en 1868, para garantizar a los ciudadanos igualdad en la protección otorgada por la ley (pág. 207)

fragmentation bomb/bomba de fragmentación Un tipo de bomba que al explotar lanza en todas direcciones los fragmentos de su cubierta metálica (pág. 801)

franchise/franquicia Empresa que firma un contrato con una compañía más grande para ofrecer algunos bienes y servicios (pág. 669)

free enterprise system/sistema de libre empresa Sistema económico caracterizado por la propiedad privada o empresarial de los elementos utilizados en la producción (pág. 117)

free silver/acuñación libre de plata Acuñación ilimitada de dólares de plata (pág. 279)

Freedmen's Bureau/Agencia de libertos Primera organización principal de auxilio federal de los Estados Unidos, creada por el Congreso en 1865 (pág. 205)

Freedom Ride/Paseo de la Libertad Evento organizado en 1961 por el CORE y el SNCC, en el que un grupo interracial de activistas de los derechos civiles puso a prueba el acatamiento de los estados del sur a la prohibición de la segregación racial en autobuses interestatales, dictada por la Corte Suprema (pág. 710)

French and Indian War/Guerra francesa e indígena Guerra que tuvo lugar de 1754 a 1763 entre Francia, las naciones indias aliadas, y Gran Bretaña y sus colonizadores, por el control del este de Norteamérica (pág. 41)

fundamentalism/fundamentalismo Conjunto de creencias religiosas, entre ellas, las ideas cristianas tradicionales sobre Jesucristo, la creencia de que la Biblia fue inspirada por Dios y carece de contradicciones o errores y es literalmente verdadera (pág. 470)

G

generation gap/brecha generacional Término que describe la gran diferencia entre los valores de una generación más joven y la de sus padres (pág. 806)

Geneva Accords/Acuerdos de Ginebra Conferencia internacional que tuvo lugar en 1954 y en la que se dividió a Vietnam en dos naciones (pág. 793)

Geneva Convention/Convención de Ginebra Conjunto de normas de conducta internacionales para el trato de los prisioneros de guerra, establecidas en 1929 (pág. 615)

genocide/genocidio Matanza organizada de un pueblo entero (pág. 431)

Gentlemen's Agreement/Pacto de los caballeros Acuerdo firmado en 1907 entre los Estados Unidos y Japón para resstringir la inmigración japonesa (pág. 302)

Gettysburg Address/Discurso de Gettysburg Un discurso famoso que dio el presidente Lincoln en noviembre de 1863 sobre el significado de la Guerra Civil, durante la dedicatoria de un cementerio nacional en la zona donde se libró la Batalla de Gettysburg (pág. 185)

ghetto/*ghetto* Área en la que domina un grupo étnico o racial (pág. 300)

Ghost Dance/Danza de los espíritus Un ritual de purificación realizado por los indígenas estadounidenses (pág. 265)

GI/soldado de infantería Término utilizado para describir a los soldados estadounidenses en la Segunda Guerra Mundial, se deriva del término "Asunto gubernamental" (pág. 595)

GI Bill of Rights/Declaración de los Derechos de los Soldados de Infantería Ley aprobada en 1944 que ayudaba a los veteranos que regresaban a adquirir una casa y costear su educación superior (pág. 672)

Gilded Age/Edad Dorada Término acuñado por Mark Twain para describir la era posterior a la reconstrucción (pág. 290)

graft/corrupción Utilizar el empleo para obtener una ganancia; una de las principales fuentes de ingreso para los aparatos políticos (pág. 309)

grandfather clause/cláusula del abuelo Pasaje que exime a un grupo de personas de obedecer una ley si reunen ciertas condiciones antes de la aprobación de la misma (pág. 333)

Grange, the/ Granja, la Organización establecida en 1867 y también conocida como los Mecenas de la Agricultura; ayudaba a los granjeros a formar cooperativas y presionaba a los legisladores del estado para que regularan las empresas de las que dependían estos campesinos (pág. 280)

Great Awakening/Gran Despertar, el Renacimiento religioso de las colonias norteamericanas durante la década de 1730 y 1740 (pág. 32)

Great Crash/Gran *Crash*, el El derrumbe de la bolsa de valores estadounidense que tuvo lugar en 1929 (pág. 509)

Great Depression/Gran Depresión, la La baja económica más severa en la historia de la nación; duró de 1929 a 1941 (pág. 511)

Great Plains/ Grandes Llanuras, las Llanura de gran tamaño entre el río Mississippi y las montañas Rocosas (pág. 261)

Great Society/Gran Sociedad, la Propuestas del presidente Lyndon Johnson para el apoyo a la educación, el derecho al voto, los proyectos de conservación y embellecimiento, la atención médica para las personas de la tercera edad y la eliminación de la pobreza (pág. 745)

Great White Fleet/Gran Flota Blanca, la Un grupo de barcos de la Marina de los Estados Unidos que realizó una excursión por todo el mundo en 1907 (pág. 375)

Greater East Asia Co-Prosperity Sphere/esfera de prosperidad de Asia Oriental Proclamada en 1940 por el ministro de Japón; área que se extendía de Manchuria a las Indias Orientales Holandesas en las que Japón extendería su influencia (pág. 584)

greenback/papel moneda Nombre que se le da al dinero en forma de billetes creado en 1862 (pág. 169)

Gross National Product (GNP)/Producto Nacional Bruto (GNP) Valor anual total de los bienes y servicios que produce un país (pág. 493)

guerrilla/guerrillero Soldado que utiliza ataques sorpresivos y tácticas que consisten en atacar y huir (pág. 192)

Gulf of Tonkin Resolution/Acuerdo del golfo de Tonkín Resolución del Congreso autorizada en 1964 por el presidente Johnson para emprender una acción militar en Vietnam (pág. 796)

H

Harlem Renaissance/Renacimiento de Harlem Despertar literario estadounidense de raza negra durante la década de 1920, centrado en Harlem (pág. 464)

hawk/halcón Sobrenombre para un partidario de la guerra, como en el caso de los partidarios de la Guerra de Vietnam (pág. 802)

Hawley-Smoot tariff/tarifa Hawley-Smoot El impuesto de importación más alto de la historia, aprobado por el Congreso en 1930 (pág. 525)

Haymarket Riot/disturbios de Haymarket Trifulca laboral violenta que ocurrió en Chicago en 1886 (pág. 252)

Head Start/*Head Start* Un programa preescolar para niños de familias de escasos recursos que también proporciona servicios sociales, de salud y de nutrición (pág. 746)

Helsinki Accords/Acuerdos de Helsinki Serie de acuerdos sobre la seguridad europea firmados en 1975 (pág. 850)

Ho Chi Minh Trail/Sendero de Ho Chi Minh Ruta de abastecimiento que transportaba tropas y provisiones de Vietnam del Norte a Vietnam del Sur (pág. 802)

holding company/compañía tenedora Empresa que compra acciones y títulos de compañías más pequeñas (pág. 394)

Hollywood Ten/el grupo de los diez de Hollywood Grupo de personas de la industria del cine que fueron encarceladas por negarse a responder preguntas del Congreso relacionadas con la influencia comunista en Hollywood (pág. 650)

Holocaust/Holocausto Intento sistemático de la Alemania Nazi de asesinar a todos los judíos europeos (pág. 609)

home rule/autonomía Sistema que le da a las ciudades un grado limitado de gobierno autónomo (pág. 390)

Homestead Act/Ley de Posesión de Tierras Ley promulgada en 1862 que otorgaba 160 acres de tierra a los ciudadanos que reunían ciertas condiciones (pág. 259)

Homestead Strike/Huelga por la Posesión de Tierras Huelga que tuvo lugar en 1892 en Pennsylvania en contra de Carnegie Steel (pág. 252)

homesteader/colono Persona que tramitaba los títulos bajo la ley de posesión de tierras (pág. 272)

Hooverville/*Hooverville* Término que describía un albergue temporal para personas sin hogar durante los primeros años de la Gran Depresión (pág. 514)

horizontal consolidation/integración horizontal El proceso de reunir muchas compañías dentro de la misma empresa para formar una compañía grande (pág. 241)

House Un-American Activities Committee (HUAC)/Comité del Congreso para la Investigación de Actividades Antiestadounidenses (HUAC) Establecido en 1938 para investigar acciones desleales en los Estados Unidos (pág. 650)

hundred days/Cien Días, los Período inicial de la presidencia de Franklin Roosevelt, en 1933, cuando el Congreso aprobó muchos programas del Nuevo Trato (pág. 537)

I

ICBM/ICBM Misil balístico intercontinental (pág. 661)

immigrant/inmigrante Persona que ingresa a un nuevo país para establecerse (pág. 31)

Immigration Act of 1965/Ley de Inmigración de 1965 Ley que eliminó el número fijo de inmigrantes que se podían admitir en los Estados Unidos, provenientes de diferentes países, y los reemplazó con límites más flexibles (pág. 747)

impeach/incapacitación (presidencial) Someter a un funcionario público (generalmente el presidente) a un proceso de incapacitación por un mal desempeño de sus funciones (págs. 209, 843)

imperialism/imperialismo Política practicada por una nación más fuerte en un intento de crear un imperio mediante el dominio económico, político, cultural o militar de las naciones más débiles (pág. 352)

incumbent/titular Funcionario público actual (pág. 851)

indentured servant/siervo obligado por contrato Alguien que trabaja para otra persona por contrato durante un período de tiempo específico, por lo general siete años, a cambio de transporte, alimento y un lugar donde vivir (pág. 18)

Industrial Revolution/Revolución Industrial Esfuerzo que se inició en Gran Bretaña a finales de la década de 1700 para aumentar la producción utilizando máquinas que funcionaban por medios distintos a la fuerza humana o animal (pág. 111)

industrial union/sindicato industrial Sindicato que organiza a los trabajadores de todos los oficios en una industria determinada (pág. 251)

industrialization/industrialización Crecimiento de la industria (pág. 119)

INF Treaty/Tratado INF Acuerdo firmado en 1987 por Ronald Reagan y Mikhail Gorbachev que tenía como objetivo la destrucción de aproximadamente 2,500 misiles soviéticos y estadounidenses en Europa (pág. 881)

997

infrastructure/infraestructura La propiedad pública y los servicios que utiliza una sociedad (pág. 215)

initiative/iniciativa Procedimiento por el cual los ciudadanos pueden someter un ley directamente a votaciòn por elevar una petición pública (pág. 392)

injunction/interdicción Orden judicial que prohíbe la realización de una actividad determinada (pág. 385)

installment plan/pago a plazos Plan de pago a plazos que permite a los clientes realizar pagos en intervalos establecidos durante un período de tiempo hasta cubrir la deuda total (pág. 492)

integration/integración Proceso que reúne a personas de diferentes razas (pág. 702)

interchangeable parts/sistema de partes intercambiables Un sistema de fabricación en el que todas las partes están hechas de acuerdo con un patrón para facilitar el montaje en masa. (pág. 112)

interned/confinado Encerrado (pág. 626)

Internet/Internet Red de computadoras que une a millones de personas alrededor del mundo (pág. 915)

interracial/interracial Que comprende personas de diferentes razas o su participación (pág. 705)

Interstate Commerce Act/Ley de Comercio Interestatal Ley aprobada en 1887 para regular la empresa ferroviaria y otras empresas interestatales (pág. 281)

Iran-contra affair/caso Irán-contras Escándalo durante la administración de Reagan por el uso de dinero obtenido de la venta secreta de armas iraníes para apoyar a los contras nicaragüenses (pág. 880)

iron curtain/cortina de hierro Término acuñado por Winston Churchill para describir la división entre la vida comunista y la no comunista (pág. 640)

island-hopping/estrategia de isla a isla Estrategia militar utilizada durante la Segunda Guerra Mundial que consistía en atacar selectivamente ciertas islas bajo el dominio del enemigo y pasar por alto las demás (pág. 618)

isolationism/aislacionismo Política que consiste en evitar alianzas políticas o económicas con otros países (pág. 486)

J

Japanese American Citizen League (JACL)/Asociación de Ciudadanos Estadounidenses de Origen Japonés (JACL) Organización de estadounidenses de origen japonés que trabajan para promover los derechos de los estadounidenses de origen asiático (pág. 774)

Jazz Age/Época del *jazz* Término para describir la década de 1920 (pág. 462)

Jim Crow/*Jim Crow* Estatutos que, a principios de la década de 1890, exigían la segregación racial en la prestación de los servicios públicos (pág. 333)

jingoism/jingoísmo Sentimiento de orgullo nacional arraigado y deseo de tener una política exterior agresiva (pág. 359)

judicial review/revisión judicial Poder de las cortes federales para revisar las leyes estatales y las decisiones de la corte federal con el fin de determinar si son constitucionales (pág. 94)

K

kamikaze/kamikaze Avión suicida japonés en la Segunda Guerra Mundial (pág. 618)

Kansas-Nebraska Act/Ley Kansas-Nebraska Ley promulgada en 1854 que exigía la creación de estos dos territorios nuevos y les pedía a los ciudadanos que decidieran sobre la esclavitud en su territorio (pág. 139)

Kellogg-Briand Pact/Pacto Kellogg-Briand Acuerdo firmado en 1928 en el que las naciones acordaron no representar una amenaza de guerra entre ellas (pág. 489)

Korean War /Guerra Coreana Conflicto sobre el futuro de la peninsula coreana, luchado entre 1950 y 1953, que llegó a punto muerto (pág. 654)

Kristallnacht/ Kristallnacht Nombre que se le da a la noche violenta del 9 de noviembre de 1938 en Alemania y Austria, cuando milicianos nazis saquearon y atacaron hogares, negocios y sinagogas judías, además de arrestar a miles de judíos (pág. 610)

L

labor union/sindicato laboral Organización de trabajadores formada para proteger los intereses de sus miembros (pág. 119)

laissez-faire/laissez-faire Doctrina que establece que, por lo general, el gobierno no debe interferir en las empresas privadas (pág. 291)

land mine/mina terrestre Dispositivo explosivo enterrado en el suelo (pág. 800)

land speculator/especulador de tierras Persona que compra grandes áreas de tierra con la esperanza de venderlas para obtener una ganancia (pág. 259)

Latino/latino Persona cuyo origen familiar está en la América Latina hispanohablante (pág. 771)

League of Nations/Liga de las Naciones Organización internacional formada después de la Primera Guerra Mundial, cuyo objetivo es asegurar la seguridad y la paz de todos sus miembros (pág. 438)

Lend-Lease Act/Ley de Préstamos y Arriendos Ley promulgada en 1941 que autorizó al Presidente a apoyar a cualquier nación cuya defensa considerara vital para la seguridad de los Estados Unidos (pág. 588)

Liberty Bond/Garantía de libertad Garantía especial de guerra concedida por el gobierno para apoyar la causa de los aliados durante la Primera Guerra Mundial (pág. 432)

Liberty ship/buque "Liberty" Un tipo de barco mercante, grande y fuerte, construido en la Segunda Guerra Mundial (pág. 596)

Limited Test Ban Treaty/Tratado de Prohibición Limitada de Pruebas Nucleares Tratado firmado en 1963, en el que los Estados Unidos y la Unión Soviética acordaron abstenerse de realizar pruebas con armas nucleares en tierra (pág. 757)

literacy/alfabetismo La capacidad de una persona de leer y escribir (pág. 321)

long drive/paseo largo Desplazamiento del ganado de praderas distantes a centros ferroviarios activos que lo transportaban para venderlo (pág. 271)

loose construction/interpretación libre Creencia de que el gobierno puede hacer todo lo que la Constitución no prohíbe (pág. 90)

Lost Generation/Generación Perdida, la Grupo de escritores de la década de 1920 que compartían la idea de que estaban perdidos en un mundo codicioso, materialista y sin valores morales; a menudo decidían huir a Europa (pág. 464)

Louisiana Purchase/Compra de Luisiana Compra del territorio de Louisiana que los Estados Unidos le hicieron a Francia en 1803 (pág. 95)

lynching/linchamiento Asesinato de un acusado, efectuado por una multitud sin que se realice un juicio legal (pág. 334)

M

Magna Carta/Carta Magna Una "gran carta" firmada por el rey Juan en 1215 que concedía algunos derechos a los nobles ingleses y que se convirtió en la base para futuros ideales de libertad y justicia en los Estados Unidos (pág. 7)

mail-order catalog/catálogo de ventas por correo Material impreso que muestra una variedad de productos que se pueden ser adquirir por correo (pág. 339)

Manchurian Incident/incidente de Manchuria Situación en 1931 cuándo las tropas japonesas, que alegaban que los soldados chinos habían tratado de hacer explotar una vía férrea, se hicieron cargo del problema al tomar varias ciudades de Manchuria del sur para después apoderarse del país, incluso después de que las tropas chinas se habían retirado (pág. 582)

mandate/delegación Declaración pública de apoyo que los votantes expresan a un candidato (pág. 737)

Manhattan Project/Proyecto Manhattan Programa estadounidense secreto durante la Segunda Guerra Mundial para desarrollar una bomba atómica (pág. 620)

manifest destiny/destino manifiesto Argumento que establece que los Estados Unidos estaban destinados a expandirse a lo largo de América del Norte (pág. 135)

manufacturing/manufactura La fabricación de productos mediante maquinaria (pág. 116)

Marbury* v. *Madison*/*Marbury* vs. *Madison Caso de la Suprema Corte presentado en 1803 que establecía el principio de la revisión judicial (pág. 94)

March on Washington/Marcha en Washington Manifestación por los derechos civiles realizada en 1963 en Washington, D.C., en la cual los inconformes exigían empleos y libertad (pág. 717)

Market Revolution/revolución del mercado Cambio de una economía basada en el hogar y por lo general agrícola a una economía basada en el dinero, y en la compra y venta de productos (pág. 116)

Marshall Plan/Plan Marshall Programa de apoyo económico estadounidense a Europa Occidental, anunciado en 1947 (pág. 645)

martial law/ley marcial Ley de emergencia dictada por autoridades militares, durante la cual se suspenden algunas garantías de la Declaración de Derechos (pág. 170)

mass media/medios masivos de comunicación Métodos, impresos y transmitidos para difundir información a un gran número de personas (pág. 460)

mass production/producción en masa Fabricación de productos en grandes cantidades (pág. 234)

Massacre at Wounded Knee/masacre en Wounded Knee Tiroteo realizado en 1890 por tropas militares contra un grupo de indigenas Sioux desarmados (pág. 265)

Mayflower Compact/Acuerdo Mayflower Convenio en el que los colonos de Plymouth acordaron acatar las leyes de su gobierno (pág. 20)

McCarran-Walter Act/Ley McCarran-Walter Ley aprobada por el Congreso en 1952 que reafirmó el sistema de cupos que había sido establecido para cada país en 1924 (pág. 651)

McCarthyism/macartismo Término para describir las tácticas de difamación anticomunista del senador Joseph McCarthy (pág. 657)

Medicaid/*Medicaid* Programa federal que proporciona seguro médico a muy bajo costo a estadounidenses de escasos recursos y de cualquier edad (pág. 746)

Medicare/*Medicare* Programa federal que proporciona atención hospitalaria y seguro médico a muy bajo costo a la mayoría de los estadounidenses de 65 años en adelante (pág. 746)

mercantilism/mercantilismo Teoría económica que sostiene que un país debe tratar de adquirir y conservar el mayor número posible de lingotes de oro y plata mediante el aumento de exportaciones en comparación con las importaciones (pág. 25)

Mexican War/Guerra entre México y los Estados Unidos Conflicto entre los Estados Unidos y México que ocurrió de 1846 a 1848 y que terminó con la victoria de los Estados Unidos (pág. 136)

MIA/desaparecido en combate Perdido en el campo de acción (pág. 816)

Middle America/estadounidense promedio Término utilizado a veces para describir la persona estadounidense típica de clase media (pág. 811)

middle class/clase media Una clase nueva de mercaderes, comerciantes y artesanos que surgió a finales de la Edad Media; en nuestros días, la clase social ubicada entre la clase muy acaudalada y la clase obrera (pág. 7)

Middle Passage/el cruce del Atlántico Una parte del comercio triangular; término que también se refiere al transporte forzado de esclavos de África a América (pág. 28)

migrant farm worker/campesino migratorio Persona que trabaja muchas horas a cambio de un salario muy bajo y que va de una granja a otra, generalmente de un estado a otro, para trabajar en las plantaciones (pág. 772)

migration/migración Desplazamiento de personas con el fin de establecerse en otro lugar (pág. 5)

militarism/militarismo Política que consiste en la acumulación agresiva de las fuerzas militares de una nación como preparativo para una guerra, así como en otorgar a los militares más autoridad sobre el gobierno y las políticas extranjeras (pág. 415)

military-industrial complex/complejo militar-industrial El establecimiento militar de 1960 en el que se desarrollaron vínculos con las comunidades empresariales y científicas, y se emplearon 3.5 millones de estadounidenses (pág. 656)

Miranda rule/regla Miranda Regla que establece que la policía debe informar a las personas acusadas de un crimen sobre sus derechos constitucionales (pág. 748)

missionary/misionero Persona que ha sido enviada por su iglesia a difundir su religión (pág. 16)

Missouri Compromise/Concesión de Missouri Acuerdo firmado en 1820 que demanda el reconocimiento de Missouri como un estado esclavista y de Maine como un estado libre, así como la prohibición de la esclavitud en futuros estados que se crearían al norte de la latitud de 36° 30' N (pág. 98)

mobilization/movilización El alistamiento de las tropas para una guerra (pág. 416)

Modern Republicanism/republicanismo moderno Propuesta del presidente Eisenhower al gobierno, descrita como "conservadora cuando se trata de dinero y liberal cuando se trata de seres humanos" (pág. 685)

monarch/monarca Quien gobierna un territorio, estado o reino (pág. 7)

monetary policy/política monetaria Plan del gobierno federal de la composición y la cantidad del suministro nacional de dinero (pág. 278)

money supply/masa monetaria La cantidad de dinero con la que cuenta la economía nacional (pág. 278)

monopoly/monopolio Control total de un producto o servicio (pág. 240)

Monroe Doctrine/Doctrina Monroe Declaración realizada en 1823 por el presidente Monroe que establecía que los Estados Unidos se opondrían a los esfuerzos de cualquier potencia externa por controlar una nación en el hemisferio occidental (pág. 121)

Montgomery bus boycott/boicot a los autobuses Montgomery Protesta realizada por estadounidenses de raza negra de 1955 a 1956 en contra de la segregación racial en el sistema de transporte de Montgomery, Alabama (pág. 701)

Morrill Land-Grant Act/Ley Morill para la Concesión de Tierras Ley aprobada por el Congreso en 1862 que distribuía millones de acres de tierras del occidente del país a los gobiernos estatales para financiar corporaciones agrícolas estatales (pág. 259)

muckraker/descubridor de escándalos Periodista que descubre actos ilícitos en la política o en las empresas (pág. 384)

multiculturalism/multiculturalismo Movimiento que demanda mayor atención a las culturas no europeas en áreas como la educación (pág. 914)

multinational corporation/corporación multinacional Corporación que opera en más de un país (pág. 910)

municipal/municipal Que pertenece a una ciudad, por ejemplo, el gobierno municipal (pág. 390)

Munn* v. *Illinois*/ *Munn* vs. *Illinois Decisión de la Suprema Corte tomada en 1877 que permitía a los estados regular algunas empresas dentro sus límites fronterizos (pág. 294)

N

napalm/*napalm* Substancia química altamente inflamable lanzada por aviones estadounidenses en bombardeos durante la Guerra de Vietnam (pág. 801)

Nation of Islam/Nación del Islam Organización dedicada a la lucha por la separación de la raza negra y el esfuerzo propio; también llamada los Musulmanes Negros (pág. 722)

National Aeronautics and Space Administration (NASA)/Administración Nacional de la Aeronáutica y el Espacio (NASA) Creada en 1958 por el gobierno de los Estados Unidos como una agencia independiente para la exploración del espacio (pág. 686)

National American Woman Suffrage Association (NAWSA)/Asociación Estadounidense para el Sufragio de la Mujer (NAWSA) Organización formada en 1890 para continuar la obtención de los derechos de las mujeres, especialmente el de votar (pág. 405)

National Association for the Advancement of Colored People (NAACP)/Asociación Nacional para el Progreso de las Personas de Color (NAACP) Organización fundada en 1909 para abolir la segregación y discriminación, luchar contra el racismo y lograr que los estadounidenses de raza negra gozaran de derechos civiles (pág. 335)

national debt/deuda nacional Cantidad total de dinero que debe el gobierno federal y que tiene que pagar (pág. 554)

National Defense Education Act/Ley para la Mejoría de la Educación en Defensa de la Nación Medida tomada en 1958 para mejorar la enseñanza de las ciencias y matemáticas en las escuelas (pág. 686)

National Liberation Front/Frente de Liberación Nacional Arma política del Viet Cong (pág. 795)

National Organization for Women (NOW)/Organización Nacional para las Mujeres (NOW) Organización formada en 1966 para fomentar la participación total de las mujeres en la sociedad estadounidense (pág. 766)

nationalism/nacionalismo Devoción por la nación a la que uno pertenece (pág. 353)

nationalization/nacionalización Adquisición por parte del gobierno de instituciones como bancos, con redistribución de sus recursos económicos (pág. 548)

nativism/nativismo Una política que favorece a los nativos de los Estados Unidos frente a los inmigrantes (págs. 140, 314)

Nazism/nazismo Una especie extrema de fascismo delineada por las ideas fanáticas de Adolfo Hitler sobre el nacionalismo alemán y la superioridad racial (pág. 571)

Neutrality Acts/Leyes de Neutralidad Leyes promulgadas en 1939 diseñadas para mantener a los Estados Unidos fuera de futuras guerras (pág. 586)

New Deal/Nuevo Trato Término que describe los programas de apoyo, recuperación y reforma diseñados por el presidente Franklin Roosevelt para combatir la Gran Depresión (pág. 537)

New Federalism/nuevo federalismo Llamado del Presidente Nixon a una asociación nueva entre el gobierno federal y los gobiernos de los estados; plan del Presidente Reagan para reducir el papel del gobierno federal y otorgar más responsabilidad a los gobiernos estatales y locales (págs. 829, 873)

New Frontier/nueva frontera Propuestas del Presidente Kennedy para mejorar la economía, ayudar a los pobres y desarrollar el programa de exploración espacial (pág. 738)

New Left/nueva izquierda Nuevo movimiento político que tuvo lugar a finales de la década de 1960 y que demandaba cambios radicales para combatir la pobreza y el racismo (pág. 806)

New Nationalism/nuevo nacionalismo Plan de Theodore Roosevelt para lograr una mayor regulación federal de las empresas y lugares de trabajo, de los impuestos a las utilidades e impuestos de sucesión, y de las reformas electorales (pág. 398)

New Right/nueva derecha Una coalición política de grupos conservadores formada en 1980 (pág. 867)

Niagara Movement/movimiento Niágara Grupo de estadounidenses de raza negra fundado en 1905, que demandaba libertad civil, eliminación de la discriminación racial y reconocimiento de la hermandad (pág. 325)

Nisei/*Nisei* Estadounidense de origen japonés cuyos padres nacieron en Japón (pág. 627)

nomadic/nómadas Personas que cambian de hogar con regularidad, generalmente en busca de fuentes de alimento disponibles (págs. 5, 261)

nonviolent protest/protesta pacífica Una forma pacífica de protestar en contra de las políticas restrictivas (pág. 706)

North American Free Trade Agreement (NAFTA)/Tratado de Libre Comercio de Norteamérica (TLCN) Acuerdo que demanda la eliminación de las restricciones comerciales entre los Estados Unidos, Canadá y México (pág. 909)

North Atlantic Treaty Organization (NATO)/Organización del Tratado del Atlántico Norte (OTAN) Alianza de naciones que en 1949 acordaron agruparse en caso de guerra, además de apoyar y proteger a cada nación participante (pág. 647)

Nuclear Regulatory Commission (NRC)/Comisión Nuclear Reguladora (NRC) Organización gubernamental formada en 1974 para examinar el uso civil de los materiales nucleares (pág. 783)

nullify/anulación Rechazo de una ley federal por parte del estado (pág. 123)

Nuremberg Trials/Juicios de Nuremberg Serie de juicios realizados en 1945 por un Tribunal Militar Internacional en los que antiguos líderes nazis fueron acusados de crímenes de guerra y crímenes contra la paz y la humanidad (pág. 613)

O

Office of War Mobilization/Oficina de Movilización de Guerra Agencia federal formada para coordinar cuestiones relacionadas con la producción de la guerra durante la Segunda Guerra Mundial (pág. 596)

oligopoly/oligopolio Una estructura de mercado dominada sólo por unas cuantas compañías grandes y lucrativas (pág. 240)

Open Door Policy/política de libre acceso Propuesta que realizó Estados Unidos a China alrededor de 1900 y que apoya las relaciones de libre comercio entre China y otras naciones (pág. 364)

Organization of Petroleum Exporting Countries (OPEC)/Organización de Países Exportadores de Petróleo (OPEP) Grupo de naciones que trabajaron de manera conjunta para regular el precio y el suministro del petróleo (pág. 828)

P

Pacific Railway Acts/Leyes para el Ferrocarril del Pacífico Leyes aprobadas en 1862 y 1864 que otorgaron grandes concesiones de tierra para la

Spanish Glossary

construcción de las vías férreas Union Pacific y Central Pacific (pág. 259)

pardon/perdón Exoneración oficial de un crimen (pág. 202)

Paris peace talks/diálogos de paz de París Negociaciones entre los Estados Unidos y Vietnam del Norte que se iniciaron en 1968 (pág. 812)

patent/patente Licencia expedida a un inventor que le da el derecho exclusivo de fabricar, utilizar o vender su invento durante un período de tiempo establecido (pág. 227)

patriotism/patriotismo Amor por el país al que uno pertenece; pasión que tiene como objetivo servir al propio país, ya sea defendiéndolo de una invasión o protegiendo sus derechos y manteniendo sus leyes e instituciones en vigor y transparencia (pág. 49)

Peace Corps/Cuerpo de Paz Programa federal establecido para enviar voluntarios a auxiliar países en vías de desarrollo (pág. 758)

Pendleton Civil Service Act/Ley Pendleton del Servicio Civil Ley promulgada en 1883 que creó una Comisión de Servicio Civil y estableció que los empleados federales no estaban obligados a contribuir al financiamiento de las campañas ni podían ser despedidos por razones políticas (pág. 293)

penny auction/subasta de a centavo Subastas de granjas durante la Gran Depresión en las que los vecinos salvaban a los demás de perder su propiedad a través de ofertas muy bajas (pág. 521)

per capita income/ingreso per capita Ingreso anual promedio por persona (pág. 668)

Persian Gulf War/Guerra del Golfo Pérsico Operación militar limitada que tuvo lugar en 1991 y cuyo objetivo era sacar a las fuerzas iraquíes de Kuwait (pág. 886)

philanthropist/filántropo Persona que hace donaciones para buenas causas (pág. 323)

Pickett's Charge/ataque de Pickett Ataque fallido de la infantería de los confederados durante la Batalla de Gettysburg (pág. 182)

piecework/trabajo por pieza Sistema en el que el pago de los trabajadores no se basa en el tiempo trabajado sino en el número de artículos que producen (pág. 244)

placer mining/explotación de placeres Técnica minera en la que los mineros echaban en cajas tierra de los placeres y luego le vertían agua para separarla de las partículas de oro o plata (pág. 269)

plantation/plantación Granja de gran extensión en la que se cultivan cosechas principalmente para la venta (pág. 12)

Platt Amendment/enmienda Platt Anexo a la constitución cubana de 1900 realizado por el gobierno estadounidense que le dio a los Estados Unidos el derecho de establecer bases navales en Cuba e intervenir en los asuntos de Cuba cuando fuera necesario (pág. 362)

Plessy* v. *Ferguson*/*Plessy* vs. *Ferguson Decisión tomada en 1896 por la Suprema Corte que consistía en la legalidad de la segregación siempre y cuando las instalaciones asignadas a la gente de color fueran iguales a las asignadas a los de raza blanca (pág. 334)

pocket veto/veto indirecto Tipo de veto que puede utilizar un presidente después de que se haya suspendido una legislatura; se aplica cuando el presidente no firma o rechaza formalmente una propuesta dentro del tiempo permitido (pág. 203)

pogrom/pogrom Masacre de judíos (pág. 298)

political machine/aparato político Organización urbana extraoficial diseñada para mantener un partido o grupo particular en el poder y bajo la dirección de un solo jefe poderoso (pág. 308)

political party/partido político Grupo de personas que buscan ganar las elecciones y tener un puesto público con el fin de controlar las políticas y los programas del gobierno (pág. 91)

poll tax/impuesto sobre el padrón electoral Un gravamen especial que debe ser pagado para que una persona pueda votar (pág. 333)

Populist/populista Seguidor del Partido del Pueblo (o Partido Populista) formado en 1891 para apoyar una oferta monetaria más grande y otras reformas económicas (pág. 281)

POW/prisionero de guerra Prisionero capturado durante una guerra (pág. 816)

prejudice/prejuicio Una opinión irracional y sin fundamentos, por lo general desfavorable, acerca de otro grupo (pág. 139)

price controls/control de precios Sistema determinado por el gobierno para el establecimiento de precios (pág. 433)

productivity/productividad Cantidad de bienes y servicios creada en un período de tiempo (pág. 227)

Progressive Era/período progresista El período entre 1890 y 1920 durante el cual se aprobaron diversas reformas a nivel local, estatal y federal (pág. 383)

prohibition/prohibición Una restricción en la producción y venta de bebidas alcohólicas (pág. 314)

propaganda/propaganda Información orientada a influir en la opinión pública (pág. 418)

Proprietary colony/colonia sujeta a derechos de propiedad Colonia que un rey o reina otorga a un individuo o grupo que tiene todos los derechos de gobernar (pág. 22)

public works program/programa de obras públicas Proyectos financiados por el gobierno para construir instalaciones públicas (pág. 538)

Pullman Strike/huelga Pullman Huelga de los trabajadores ferroviarios que tuvo lugar en 1894 y que se extendió por toda la nación (pág. 253)

puppet state/estado títere Un país supuestamente independiente que se encuentra bajo el control de un vecino poderoso (pág. 582)

Puritan/puritano Personas que favoreción la purificación de la Iglesia Anglicana de Inglaterra (pág. 19)

purge/purga En términos políticos, el proceso de sacar del poder a los enemigos e individuos indeseables (pág. 569)

push-pull factors/factores de expulsión del país de origen y de atracción por otro país Sucesos y condiciones que fuerzan a las personas a irse a otra parte o las atraen fuertemente a hacerlo (pág. 258)

Q

quarantine/cuarentena Período de aislamiento para prevenir la propagación de una enfermedad (pág. 299)

quota/cuota Límite numérico (pág. 487)

R

racism/racismo Creencia en que la raza determina las diferencias de carácter o inteligencia; afirmar la superioridad de una raza sobre otra u otras (pág. 373)

Radical Republicans/republicanos radicales Grupo de congresistas miembros del Partido Republicano que creían que en la Guerra Civil se había luchado por el problema moral de la esclavitud; insistía en que la principal meta de la Reconstrucción debía ser una reestructuración total de la sociedad para garantizar a la gente de color la verdadera igualdad (pág. 203)

ragtime/*ragtime* Tipo de música que se califica de melodias con acentos que cambian contra un ritmo constante, que tuvo su orígen entre los músicos negros en la región central y el sur en el década de 1880 (pág. 331)

rationing/racionamiento Distribución de una cantidad fija de productos a los consumidores (pág. 434)

Reagan Democrat/demócratas Reagan Obreros demócratas que tendían a votar por el partido Republicano durante la década de 1980 (pág. 867)

realpolitik/realpolitik Término alemán que significa "política práctica" o política extranjera basada en los intereses más que en los principios morales (pág. 832)

rebate/reembolso Devolución parcial (pág. 294)

recall/revocación Procedimiento que permite a los votantes destituir a funcionarios públicos de su puesto antes de la siguiente elección (pág. 392)

recession/recesión Período de poco movimiento en el negocio (pág. 554)

recognition/reconocimiento Aceptación oficial como nación independiente (pág. 168)

Reconstruction/Reconstrucción Programa puesto en práctica por el gobierno federal entre 1865 y 1877 para reparar el daño al sur causado por la Guerra Civil y restituir los estados del sur a la Unión (pág. 200)

Reconstruction Finance Corporation (RFC)/Corporación Financiera para la Reconstrucción (RFC) Corporación establecida por el presidente Hoover en 1932, que otorgó crédito público a varias instituciones, entre ellas, industrias grandes, compañías ferroviarias y compañías de seguros (pág. 525)

reconversion/reconversión Transición social y económica de los tiempos de guerra a los tiempos de paz (pág. 680)

Red Scare/amenaza roja Miedo intenso al comunismo y a otras ideas políticamente radicales (pág. 482)

referendum/referéndum Proceso que permite a los ciudadanos aprobar o rechazar una ley aprobada por su legislatura (pág. 392)

religious tolerance/tolerancia religiosa Idea de que las personas de diferentes religiones deben convivir en paz (pág. 20)

reparations/compensaciones Pagos que realiza un enemigo por el daño económico ocasionado durante la guerra (pág. 439)

republic/república Gobierno manejado por el pueblo a través de los representantes elegidos (pág. 55)

republican virtues/virtudes republicanas Virtudes que el pueblo estadounidense necesitaría para gobernarse a sí mismo, tales como confianza en uno mismo, destreza, sobriedad, armonía y capacidad para sacrificar las necesidades individuales por el bien de la comunidad (pág. 110)

reservation/reservación Territorio federal reservado para las tribus de indígenas estadounidenses (pág. 262)

Resistance/Resistencia Movimiento en Francia que se opuso a la ocupación alemana durante la Segunda Guerra Mundial (pág. 578)

restrictive covenant/cláusula de prohibición de competencia Acuerdo entre los dueños de fincas para no vender sus propiedades a ciertos grupos de personas, como judíos o estadounidenses de raza negra (pág. 301)

revenue/ingreso Entrada económica (pág. 554)

Revolutionary War/guerra revolucionaria Guerra de los colonos norteamericanos para independizarse de la Gran Bretaña; tuvo lugar de 1775 a 1783 (pág. 45)

rock-and-roll/*rock-and-roll* Música que surgió del rhythm and blues y que se volvió popular en la década de 1950 (pág. 678)

Roe* v. *Wade*/*Roe* vs. *Wade Decisión tomada en 1973 por la Suprema Corte para legalizar el aborto (pág. 768)

Roosevelt Corollary/Corolario Roosevelt Extensión de la Doctrina Monroe realizada por el presidente Theodore Roosevelt en 1904, en la que hacía valer el derecho de los Estados Unidos de intervenir en las naciones de América Latina (pág. 368)

rural free delivery (RFD)/entrega postal rural gratuita (RFD) En 1896, el Sistema Postal de los Estados

Unidos ofreció entregar el correo de manera gratuita a las familias campesinas en los estados rurales centrales (pág. 339)

Russian Revolution/revolución rusa Colapso del gobierno zarista de Rusia en 1917, después del cual la monarquía rusa fue reemplazada por un gobierno republicano (pág. 424)

S

SALT I/Primer Tratado sobre Limitación de Armas Estratégicas *(SALT I)* Tratado firmado en 1972 entre los Estados Unidos y la Unión Soviética para restringir las armas nucleares (pág. 836)

Sandinista/sandinista En la década de 1980, un miembro del grupo marxista prevaleciente en Nicaragua (pág. 880)

satellite nation/nación satélite Un país dominado política y económicamente por otra nación, sobre todo por la Unión Soviética durante la Guerra Fría (pág. 639)

saturation bombing/bombardeo de saturación El lanzamiento de una gran concentración de bombas sobre un área determinada (pág. 801)

scab/rompehuelgas Término negativo para un obrero que ha sido llamado por un empleador para que reemplace a los trabajadores que están en huelga (pág. 251)

scalawag/caballo piojoso o sureño pro-yanqui Sobrenombre ofensivo utilizado para referirse a un republicano blanco del sur después de la Guerra Civil (pág. 211)

Scopes trial/juicio de Scopes Caso presentado ante los tribunales en 1925 por Clarence Darrow y William Jennings Bryan, en el que se debatía la enseñanza de la evolución en las escuelas públicas (pág. 470)

secede/separarse Dejar de ser miembro formalmente de un grupo u organización (pág. 123)

Second Great Awakening/el Segundo Gran Despertar Movimiento religioso que tuvo lugar a principios del siglo XIX (pág. 114)

Second New Deal/segundo Nuevo Trato Período de actividad legislativa iniciado por el presidente Franklin Roosevelt en 1935 (pág. 542)

sedition/sedición Cualquier discurso o acción que fomente la rebelión (pág. 435)

segregation/segregación Separación forzada, frecuentemente por las diferencias de raza (pág. 333)

Selective Service Act/Ley del Servicio Militar Obligatorio Ley aprobada en 1917 que autoriza el reclutamiento de jóvenes para el servicio militar en la Primera Guerra Mundial (pág. 425)

Selective Training and Service Act/Ley del Servicio y Capacitación Militar Obligatorios Ley promulgada en 1940 que exige que todos los hombres de 21 a 36 años deben realizar el servicio militar (pág. 594)

self-determination/autodeterminación El poder de tomar decisiones sobre el futuro de uno mismo (pág. 437)

Seneca Falls Convention/Convención Seneca Falls La primera convención sobre los derechos de las mujeres en la historia de los Estados Unidos, presidida en 1848 (pág. 132)

separation of powers/división de poderes El reparto constitucional de poderes dentro del gobierno federal entre las ramas legislativa, ejecutiva y judicial (pág. 59)

settlement house/casa del pueblo Centro comunitario organizado para proporcionar varios servicios a las personas de escasos recursos que viven en zonas urbanas (pág. 312)

sharecropping/aparcería Sistema practicado en la agricultura en el que un campesino trabaja un pedazo de tierra del propietario y recibe como pago una parte de la cosecha (pág. 213)

shell/granada Aparato que explota en el aire o cuando golpea un objetivo sólido (pág. 160)

Sherman Antitrust Act/Ley Antimonopolista Sherman Ley aprobada por el Congreso en 1890 que prohibía cualquier combinación de empresas que limitara el intercambio o comercio interestatal (pág. 242)

Sherman Silver Purchase Act/Ley Sherman para la Adquisición de Plata Ley aprobada por el Congreso en 1890 para aumentar la cantidad de plata que el gobierno debía comprar cada mes (pág. 279)

siege/sitio Táctica que consiste en cercar a un enemigo y dejarlo sin alimentos para que se rinda (pág. 184)

silent majority/mayoría silenciosa Término utilizado por el presidente Nixon para describir a los estadounidenses que se oponían a la contracultura (pág. 814)

sit-down strike/huelga de brazos caídos Protesta laboral en la que los trabajadores dejan de trabajar pero se niegan a abandonar el lugar de trabajo (p. 555)

sit-in/sentada Forma de protesta en la que los inconformes se sientan y se niegan a irse (pág. 709)

social Darwinism/darwinismo social Idea que se deriva de la teoría de Darwin de la selección natural; consiste en que la sociedad debe interferir lo menos posible en la búsqueda del éxito de las personas (pág. 239)

social gospel movement/movimiento evangélico social Una reforma social que se desarrolló en las instituciones religiosas y buscó aplicar las enseñanzas de Jesús directamente a la sociedad (pág. 312)

Social Security System/sistema de seguridad social Sistema establecido por el Ley de Seguridad Social de 1935 para proporcionar seguridad económica, a manera de pagos regulares, a quienes no pueden mantenerse por sí mismos (pág. 544)

social welfare program/programa de bienestar social Programa diseñado para asegurar una norma de vida o de subsistencia básica a todos los ciudadanos (pág. 390)

socialism/socialismo Filosofía económica y política que apoya el control público (o social), en lugar del control privado, de la propiedad y los ingresos (pág. 247)

sociology/sociología Término acuñado por el filósofo Auguste Comte para describir el estudio de la forma en que las personas interactúan en una sociedad (pág. 313)

soddie/casa de tepes Casa cuyas paredes y techo están hechas de bloques de pasto compuesto por gruesas raíces y tierra (pág. 273)

solid South/sur sólido Término que describe el dominio del Partido Demócrata sobre las políticas del sur posteriores a la Guerra Civil (pág. 220)

sooners/*sooners* En 1889, personas que exigían ilegalmente un pedazo de tierra escabulléndose de las autoridades antes de que empezaran las carreras por la tierra (pág. 267)

Southern Christian Leadership Conference (SCLC)/Conferencia del Liderazgo Cristiano del Sur (SCLC) Organización de los derechos civiles que apoyaba las protestas pacíficas; formada en 1957 por el Dr. Martin Luther King Jr. y otros líderes (pág. 706)

speakeasies/tabernas clandestinas Bar que operaba ilegalmente durante el período de la Prohibición (pág. 468)

special prosecutor/fiscal especial Un abogado designado por el Departamento de Justicia para investigar actos ilegales de funcionarios públicos (pág. 843)

speculation/especulación Práctica que consiste en hacer inversiones de alto riesgo con la esperanza de obtener una enorme ganancia (pág. 500)

sphere of influence/esfera de influencia Área de control económico y político ejercido por una nación sobre otra u otras (pág. 364)

spiritual/espiritual Himno folklórico (pág. 115)

spoils/botín Ganancias obtenidas en una victoria militar (pág. 438)

Sputnik/Sputnik El primer satélite artificial en entrar en la órbita de la Tierra, lanzado por los soviéticos en 1957 (pág. 661)

stagflation/estanflación Combinación de un alto nivel de inflación y desempleo sin ningún crecimiento económico (pág. 848)

stalemate/estancamiento Situación en la que ninguna de las partes del conflicto logra obtener ventaja (pág. 417)

states' rights/derechos de los estados Los poderes que la Constitución le niega al gobierno y les confiere a los estados (pág. 123)

steerage/entrecubierta Un área abierta muy grande debajo de la cubierta de un barco, por lo general utilizada para alojar inmigrantes (pág. 298)

stereotype/estereotipo Descripción exagerada o demasiado simplificada de la realidad arraigada en ciertas personas (pág. 275)

Strategic Arms Reduction Treaty/Tratado para la Reducción de Armas Estratégicas Acuerdo firmado en 1991 y conocido como START, que demandaba la reducción del suministro de armas nucleares de largo alcance en Rusia y los Estados Unidos (pág. 885)

Strategic Defense Initiative (SDI)/Iniciativa de Defensa Estratégica (SDI) Sistema de defensa propuesto por el presidente Reagan en contra de ataques soviéticos con misiles, popularmente conocido como la "Guerra de las Galaxias" (pág. 873)

strict construction/interpretación estricta Idea de que el gobierno no debe hacer nada que la Constitución no especifique que pueda hacer (pág. 90)

strike/huelga Un paro laboral con el propósito de forzar a los empleadores a cumplir algunas demandas, por ejemplo, un aumento en los salarios (pág. 119)

Student Nonviolent Coordinating Committee (SNCC)/Comité Coordinador Estudiantil Pacifista (SNCC) Organización de los derechos civiles de los estudiantes fundada en 1960, como rama del SCLC (pág. 707)

subsidy/subsidio Un pago realizado por el gobierno para fomentar el desarrollo de ciertas industrias clave (pág. 291)

suburb/área suburbana Comunidad residencial que rodea una ciudad (pág. 305)

suffrage/sufragio El derecho al voto (pág. 132)

supply-side economics/economía de oferta Teoría que establece que la reducción de impuestos aumentará la inversión y, por lo tanto, estimulará el crecimiento de las empresas (pág. 871)

Sussex pledge/promesa Sussex Compromiso adquirido por el gobierno alemán en 1916 de que sus submarinos advertirían a los barcos antes de atacarlos (pág. 423)

sweatshop/fábrica explotadora Fábrica donde los empleados trabajan muchas horas a cambio de salarios muy bajos y en malas condiciones de trabajo (pág. 244)

T

Taft-Hartley Act/Ley Taft-Hartley Ley aprobada por el Congreso en 1947 que permitió al Presidente declarar un período de calma de 80 días cuando las huelgas golpearon las industrias y afectaron los intereses nacionales; asimismo, pedía a los huelguistas que volvieran a su trabajo mientras el gobierno estudiaba la situación (pág. 681)

teach-in/asamblea especial Sesión especial de disertación y discusión sobre un tema controversial utilizada durante la época de la Guerra de Vietnam (pág. 807)

Teapot Dome scandal/escándalo Teapot Dome Escándalo durante la administración de Harding que involucraba la concesión de los derechos de explotación petrolera en el territorio público a cambio de dinero (pág. 488)

televangelism/televangelismo El uso de la televisión por los predicadores para ganarse a millones de personas, especialmente para recaudar dinero (pág. 868)

temperance movement/movimiento de moderación Una campaña organizada para eliminar el consumo de bebidas alcohólicas (págs. 128, 314)

tenant farming/agricultura por arrendamiento Sistema agrícola en el que el propietario de una plantación le arrienda la tierra a un agricultor para que la trabaje (pág. 214)

tenement/casa de vecindad Edificio de apartamentos de bajo costo y por lo regular con normas de sanidad, seguridad y comodidad deficientes; diseñado para alojar el mayor número posible de familias (pág. 306)

Tennessee Valley Authority (TVA)/Autoridad del valle de Tennessee (TVA) Proyecto federal para proporcionar energía eléctrica, control de inundaciones y oportunidades recreativas, a muy bajo precio, al valle del río Tennessee (pág. 540)

Tet Offensive/Ofensiva Tet Ataque realizado en 1968 por el Viet Cong y las fuerzas vietnamitas del Norte a través de Vietnam del Sur (pág. 803)

Thirteenth Amendment/Decimotercera enmienda Enmienda constitucional ratificada en 1865 para abolir la esclavitud (pág. 190)

38th parallel/paralelo 38 Línea de latitud que dividía Corea del Norte y Corea del Sur aproximadamente en el punto céntrico de la península (pág. 653)

totalitarian/totalitario Un gobierno que ejerce un control total sobre la nación y la vida de los ciudadanos (pág. 568)

Trail of Tears/ ruta de las lágrimas El traslado forzado de la tribu Cherokee en 1838 hacia el territorio oeste del río Mississippi (pág. 124)

transcendentalism/trascendentalismo Movimiento filosófico de mediados del siglo XIX que enfatizaba el descubrimiento espiritual y la perspicacia por encima de la razón (pág. 127)

transcontinental railroad/ferrocarril transcontinental Vía férrea que se extiende de costa a costa (pág. 230)

transistor/transistor Circuito diminuto inventado en 1947 que amplifica, controla y genera señales eléctricas (pág. 670)

triangular trade/comercio triangular Comercio entre América, Europa y África (pág. 27)

Truman Doctrine/Doctrina Truman Discurso emitido por Harry Truman en 1947 antes de una sesión conjunta del Congreso, en el que pedía que los Estados Unidos asumieran un papel de liderazgo en el mundo y declaraba que apoyarían a las naciones amenazadas por el comunismo (pág. 642)

trust/consorcio Un grupo de empresas distintas que están bajo el control de un solo consejo administrativo (pág. 242)

Turner thesis/tesis Turner Teoría desarrollada en 1893 por Frederick Jackson Turner, que afirmaba que la región fronteriza había jugado un papel clave en la formación del carácter de los estadounidenses (pág. 275)

Twenty-first Amendment/Vigésima primera enmienda Enmienda constitucional ratificada en 1933 para anular el período de la Prohibición (pág. 522)

Twenty-fourth Amendment/Vigésima cuarta enmienda Enmienda constitucional ratificada en 1964 para prohibir el impuesto sobre el padrón electoral (pág. 721)

U

U-boat/*U-boat* Submarino alemán (pág. 421)

U-2 incident/incidente U-2 Incidente ocurrido en 1960 en el que las fuerzas armadas soviéticas utilizaron un misil guiado para derribar un avión espía U-2 estadounidense que volaba en territorio soviético (pág. 661)

Underground Railroad/vía férrea subterránea Una red de rutas de escape que protegían y transportaban a los esclavos que huían al norte en busca de la libertad (pág. 130)

United Farm Workers (UFW)/Agricultores Unidos (UFW) Sindicato creado por César Chávez para organizar a los agricultores mexicanos en el Oeste (p. 773)

United States Constitution/Constitución de los Estados Unidos Plan de gobierno establecido en 1787 que describe las diferentes partes del gobierno, así como sus deberes y poderes (pág. 57)

utopian community/comunidad utópica Pequeña sociedad que busca la perfección en el ámbito social y político (pág. 129)

V

vaudeville/*vaudeville* Un tipo de teatro de variedades que apareció por primera vez en la década de 1870; generalmente consta de diálogos cómicos, números de música y baile, y actos de magia (pág. 327)

Versailles Treaty/Tratado de Versalles Tratado firmado en 1919 que dio fin a la Primera Guerra Mundial (pág. 439)

vertical consolidation/consolidación vertical Proceso para obtener el control de las diferentes empresas que componen todas las fases del desarrollo de un producto (pág. 241)

vice/vicio Comportamiento inmoral o corrupto (pág. 315)

victory garden/jardín de la victoria Un jardín doméstico de hortalizas creado para apoyar la producción de

1006

alimentos durante la Segunda Guerra Mundial (pág. 599)

Viet Cong/Viet Cong Guerrillas comunistas de Vietnam del Sur (pág. 795)

Vietminh/Vietminh Nombre común de la Liga para la Independencia de Vietnam (pág. 792)

Vietnamization/vietnamización Política del presidente Nixon para reemplazar las fuerzas militares estadounidenses por las de Vietnam del Sur (pág. 813)

vigilante/miembro de un grupo de autodefensa Ciudadano que hace justicia por su propia cuenta (pág. 435)

Volunteers in Service to America (VISTA)/Voluntarios al Servicio de Norteamérica (VISTA) Programa federal que envía voluntarios a las comunidades pobres para brindarles ayuda (pág. 746)

Voting Rights Act of 1965/Ley de Derecho al Voto de 1965 Ley cuyo objetivo era reducir los obstáculos que tenían los estadounidenses de raza negra para votar, mediante el aumento de la autoridad federal para registrar a los votantes (pág. 721)

W

Wagner Act/Ley Wagner Ley aprobada en 1935 para apoyar a los sindicatos mediante la legalización de acuerdos colectivos y el establecimiento del Consejo Nacional para las Relaciones Laborales (pág. 543)

Wannsee Conference/Conferencia Wannsee Conferencia celebrada en 1942 en Alemania, cuyo tema principal era la elaboración del plan para asesinar a los judíos europeos (pág. 611)

war of attrition/guerra por desgaste Tipo de guerra en el que una de las partes causa a la otra continuas pérdidas para mermar su fuerza (pág. 159)

War of 1812/guerra de 1812 Guerra entre los Estados Unidos y Gran Bretaña (pág. 96)

War Powers Act/Ley de Poderes de Guerra Ley promulgada en 1973 que limita la capacidad de un presidente para involucrar a los Estados Unidos en conflictos externos sin recibir una declaración de guerra formal expedida por el Congreso (pág. 849)

War Refugee Board (WRB)/Consejo para los Refugiados de Guerra (WRB) Agencia federal creada en 1944 para ayudar a las personas amenazadas de muerte por los nazis (pág. 612)

Warren Commission/Comisión Warren Comisión encabezada por el presidente de la Corte Suprema, Earl Warren, que investigaba el asesinato del presidente Kennedy (pág. 741)

Warsaw ghetto/ghetto de Varsovia Área de Varsovia cerrada por los nazis para confinar a los judíos y obligarlos a vivir en condiciones malas e insalubres (pág. 611)

Warsaw Pact/Pacto de Varsovia Alianza militar formada en 1955 entre la Unión Soviética y las naciones de Europa Oriental (pág. 648)

Watergate scandal/escándalo de Watergate Escándalo que involucró actividades ilegales que llevaron finalmente a la renuncia del presidente Nixon en 1974 (pág. 840)

welfare capitalism/capitalismo benefactor Una propuesta de relaciones laborales en la cual las empresas cubrían algunas de las necesidades de sus trabajadores sin la presión de los sindicatos, y así prevenían huelgas y mantenían una productividad elevada (p. 499)

Whitewater affair/caso Whitewater Cargos que se le imputaron al presidente Clinton por realizar transacciones empresariales inadecuadas antes de subir a la presidencia (pág. 898)

wiretap/conectador para interceptar líneas telefónicas Un aparato auditivo que se utiliza para interceptar las llamadas telefónicas (pág. 839)

Woodstock festival/festival de Woodstock Festival de música que tuvo lugar en 1969 en la región norte del estado de Nueva York (pág. 779)

World Trade Organization (WTO)/Organización Mundial de Comercio (OMC) Organización internacional formada en 1995 para fomentar la expansión del comercio mundial (pág. 909)

writ of *habeas corpus*/auto de *habeas corpus* Protección legal que exige que una corte determine si una persona debe ser encarcelada o no (pág. 171)

Y

yellow journalism/amarillismo Cobertura de noticias sensacionalistas, centradas en crímenes y escándalos (pág. 329)

Z

zeppelin/zepelín Globo dirigible alemán (pág. 429)

Zimmermann note/nota Zimmermann Telegrama del ministro de Relaciones Exteriores alemán a funcionarios mexicanos, enviado en 1917, que proponía una alianza con México y prometía ceder territorio estadounidense a cambio de una declaración de guerra a los Estados Unidos (pág. 424)

Biographical Dictionary

A

Adams, Abigail First Lady, 1797–1801; as the wife of Patriot John Adams, she urged him to promote women's rights at the beginning of the American Revolution (p. 44)

Adams, John Second President of the United States, 1797–1801; worked to relieve increasing tensions with France; lost reelection bid to Jefferson in 1800 as the country moved away from Federalist policies (p. 91)

Adams, John Quincy Sixth President of the United States, 1825–1829; proposed greater federal involvement in the economy through tariffs and improvements such as roads, bridges, and canals (p. 122)

Addams, Jane Cofounder of Hull House, the first settlement house, in 1889; remained active in social causes through the early 1900s (p. 312)

Agnew, Spiro Vice President under President Richard Nixon until forced to resign in 1973 for crimes committed before taking office; known for his harsh campaign attacks (p. 810)

Anthony, Susan B. Political activist and women's rights leader in the late 1800s (p. 404)

Armstrong, Louis Jazz musician famous for his long trumpet solos and "scat" singing (p. 462)

Arthur, Chester A. Twenty-first President of the United States, 1881–1885; signed 1883 Pendleton Act, which instituted the Civil Service (p. 293)

Askia, Muhammad Ruler of the African empire of Songhai, 1493–1528; promoted Islamic culture (p. 10)

Austin, Stephen Leader of first American group of Texas settlers in 1822 (p. 109)

B

Bakke, Allan Student who won a suit against the University of California in 1978 on the grounds that the affirmative action program had denied him admission (p. 854)

Baldwin, James African American author and spokesperson for the civil rights movement during the 1960s (p. 722)

Banks, Dennis Native American leader in the 1960s and 1970s; helped organize American Indian Movement (AIM) and the 1973 Wounded Knee occupation (p. 775)

Barton, Clara Volunteer known as the "angel of the battlefield" during the Civil War; founded the American Red Cross (p. 175)

Clara Barton

Beecher, Lyman Revivalist during the Second Great Awakening; feared the rise of selfishness in the United States (p. 127)

Begin, Menachem Israeli leader during the 1970s; began the Middle East peace process by reaching the 1978 Camp David Accords with Egypt (p. 855)

Bell, Alexander Graham Inventor; developed the telephone in 1876; one of the founders of American Telephone & Telegraph (AT&T) (p. 230)

Bellamy, Edward Author of the novel *Looking Backward* (1888), which proposed nationalizing trusts to eliminate social problems (p. 384)

Bethune, Mary McLeod African American educator, New Deal worker; founded Bethune Cookman College in the 1920s, advised the National Youth Administration (p. 541)

Beveridge, Albert J. Indiana senator in the early 1900s; saw United States imperialism as a duty owed to "primitive" societies (p. 356)

Booth, John Wilkes Southern actor who assassinated President Abraham Lincoln in 1865 (p. 193)

Breckinridge, John C. Presidential candidate of the southern wing of the Democratic Party in 1860 (p. 142)

Brown, John Abolitionist crusader who massacred proslavery settlers in Kansas before the Civil War; hoped to inspire slave revolt with 1859 attack on Virginia arsenal; executed for treason against the state of Virginia (p. 142)

Bruce, Blanche African American senator from Mississippi during Reconstruction (p. 210)

Bryan, William Jennings Advocate of silver standard and proponent of Democratic and Populist views from the 1890s through the 1910s; Democratic candidate for President in 1896, 1900, and 1908 (p. 282)

Buchanan, James Fifteenth President of the United States, 1857–1861; supported by the South; attempted to moderate fierce disagreement over expansion of slavery (p. 140)

Bush, George H. W. Forty-first President of the United States, 1989–1993; continued Reagan's conservative policies; brought together United Nations coalition to fight the Persian Gulf War (p. 882)

Bush, George W. Forty-third President of the United States, took office in 2001; led efforts to unite world against terrorism (p. 899)

1008

C

Calhoun, John C. Statesman from South Carolina who held many offices in the federal government; supported slavery, cotton exports, states' rights; in 1850 foresaw future conflicts over slavery (p. 138)

Carnegie, Andrew Industrialist who made a fortune in steel in the late 1800s through vertical consolidation; as a philanthropist, he gave away some $350 million (p. 238)

Carson, Rachel Marine biologist, author of *Silent Spring* (1962), which exposed harmful effects of pesticides and inspired concern for the environment (p. 781)

Carter, James Earl, Jr. Thirty-ninth President of the United States, 1977–1981; advocated concern for human rights in foreign policy; assisted in mediating the Camp David Accords (p. 855)

Castro, Fidel Revolutionary leader who took control of Cuba in 1959; ally of Soviet Union through the 1980s (p. 751)

Catt, Carrie Chapman Women's suffrage leader in the early 1900s; helped secure passage of Nineteenth Amendment in 1920; headed National American Woman Suffrage Association (p. 406)

Champlain, Samuel de French explorer who founded the city of Quebec in 1608 (p. 19)

Chávez, César Latino leader from 1962 to his death in 1993; organized the United Farm Workers (UFW) to help migratory farm workers gain better pay and working conditions (p. 772)

Cheney, Richard Vice President under George W. Bush (p. 900)

Chisholm, Shirley New York Representative from 1969–1983; a founder of the National Women's Political Caucus (p. 767)

Churchill, Winston Leader of Great Britain before and during World War II; powerful speechmaker who rallied Allied morale during the war (p. 575)

Clark, William Leader, with Meriwether Lewis, of expedition through the West beginning in 1804; brought back scientific samples, maps, and information on Native Americans (p. 95)

Clay, Henry Statesman from Kentucky; accused by Jackson of giving votes to John Q. Adams in return for post as Secretary of State; endorsed government promotion of economic growth; advocate of Compromise of 1850 (p. 122)

Cleveland, Grover Twenty-second and twenty-fourth President of the United States, 1885–1889, 1893–1897; supported railroad regulation and a return to the gold standard (p. 294)

Clinton, William J. Forty-second President of the United States, 1993–2001; advocated economic and healthcare reform; second President to be impeached (p. 894)

Columbus, Christopher Explorer whose voyage for Spain to North America in 1492 opened the Atlantic World (p. 11)

Coolidge, Calvin Thirtieth President of the United States, 1923–1929; promoted big business and opposed social aid (p. 488)

Coughlin, Father Charles E. "Radio Priest" who supported and then attacked President Franklin Roosevelt's New Deal; prevented by the Catholic Church from broadcasting after he praised Hitler (p. 546)

Coxey, Jacob S. Populist who led Coxey's Army in a march on Washington, D.C., in 1894 to seek government jobs for the unemployed (p. 295)

Custer, George Armstrong General who directed army attacks against Native Americans in the 1870s; commanded army forces killed in 1876 at Little Bighorn in Montana (p. 265)

D

Davis, Jefferson President of the Confederate States of America; ordered attack on Fort Sumter, the first battle of the Civil War (p. 143)

de Tocqueville, Alexis French writer; wrote *Democracy in America* following a visit to the United States in the 1830s (p. 122)

Dewey, George Officer in United States Navy, 1861–1917; led a surprise attack in the Philippines during the Spanish-American War that destroyed the entire Spanish fleet (p. 360)

Diem, Ngo Dinh Leader of South Vietnam, 1954–1963; supported by United States, but not by Vietnamese Buddhist majority; assassinated in 1963 (p. 793)

Dix, Dorothea Advocate of prison reform and of special institutions for the mentally ill in Massachusetts before the Civil War (p. 128)

Dole, Robert Senator from Kansas, 1969–1996; challenged William Clinton for the presidency in 1996 (p. 897)

Douglas, Stephen Illinois senator who introduced the Kansas-Nebraska Act, which allowed new territories to choose their own position on slavery; debated Abraham Lincoln on slavery issues in 1858 (p. 139)

Douglass, Frederick African American abolitionist leader who spoke eloquently for abolition in the United States and Britain before the Civil War (p. 130)

Du Bois, W.E.B. African American scholar and leader in early 1900s; encouraged African Americans to attend colleges to develop leadership skills (p. 325)

Frederick Douglass

Biographical Dictionary

E

Edison, Thomas A. Inventor; developed the light bulb, the phonograph, and hundreds of other inventions in the late 1800s and early 1900s (p. 228)

Ehrlichman, John Advisor on domestic policy to President Richard Nixon; deeply involved in Watergate (p. 827)

Einstein, Albert Physicist who fled Nazi persecution and later encouraged President Roosevelt to develop the atomic bomb (p. 620)

Albert Einstein

Eisenhower, Dwight D. Thirty-fourth President of the United States, 1953–1961; leader of Allied forces in World War II; as President, he promoted business and continued social programs (p. 684)

Ellington, Duke African American musician, bandleader, and composer of the 1920s and 1930s (p. 462)

Ellsberg, Daniel Defense Department official; leaked Pentagon Papers to the *New York Times* in 1971, revealing government lies to public about Vietnam (p. 839)

Emerson, Ralph Waldo Leader in the Transcendental movement; lecturer and writer (p. 127)

Equiano, Olaudah Antislavery activist who wrote an account of his enslavement (p. 28)

F

Father Divine African American minister; his Harlem soup kitchens fed the hungry during the Great Depression (p. 517)

Fillmore, Millard Thirteenth President of the United States, 1850–1853; promoted the Compromise of 1850 to smooth over disagreements about slavery in new territories (p. 965)

Finney, Charles Grandison Revivalist during the Second Great Awakening; emphasized religious conversion and personal choice (p. 127)

Fitzgerald, F. Scott Novelist who depicted the United States and the world during the 1920s in novels such as *The Great Gatsby* (p. 464)

Ford, Gerald R. Thirty-eighth President of the United States, 1974–1977; succeeded and pardoned Nixon; failed to establish strong leadership (p. 846)

Ford, Henry Pioneering auto manufacturer in the early 1900s; made affordable cars for the masses using assembly line and other production techniques (p. 493)

Franklin, Benjamin Colonial inventor, printer, writer, statesman; contributed to the Declaration of Independence and the Constitution (p. 24)

Frémont, John C. Explorer, military officer, and politician; led United States troops in 1846 Bear Flag Revolt when the United States took California from Mexico; ran for President as a Republican in 1856 (p. 136)

Friedan, Betty Feminist author; criticized limited roles for women in her 1963 book *The Feminine Mystique* (p. 766)

G

Garfield, James A. Twentieth President of the United States, 1881; his assassination by a disappointed office seeker led to the reform of the spoils system (p. 293)

Garrison, William Lloyd White leader of radical abolition movement based in Boston; founded *The Liberator* in 1831 to work for an immediate end to slavery (p. 130)

Garvey, Marcus African American leader from 1919 to 1926 who urged African Americans to return to their "motherland" of Africa; provided early inspiration for "black pride" movements (p. 472)

Gates, Bill Founder of Microsoft; revolutionized personal computing, investigated for questionable business practices (p. 915)

George III King of England during the American Revolution (p. 42)

George, Henry Author of *Progress and Poverty* (1879) linking land speculation and poverty; proposed a single tax based on land value (p. 384)

Gingrich, Newt Representative from Georgia, 1979–1998; called on Republican congressional candidates in 1994 elections to endorse "Contract with America" (p. 896)

Goodnight, Charles Texas cattle baron who helped blaze the Goodnight-Loving Trail through the Southwest (p. 272)

Gorbachev, Mikhail Soviet leader whose bold reforms led to the breakup of the Soviet Union in the late 1980s (p. 881)

Gore, Albert A. Senator from Tennessee; Vice President under President William Clinton, 1993–2001 (p. 899)

Graham, Billy Evangelist and presidential advisor; known for leading large-scale crusades, or religious rallies (p. 676)

Grant, Ulysses S. Eighteenth President of the United States, 1869–1877; commander of Union forces who accepted Lee's surrender in 1865 (p. 160)

H

Haldeman, H. R. Chief of Staff under President Richard Nixon; deeply involved in Watergate (p. 827)

Hamilton, Alexander Officer in the War for Independence: delegate to the Constitutional Convention; Federalist and first Secretary of the Treasury (p. 89)

Harding, Warren G. Twenty-ninth President of the United States, 1921–1923; presided over a short administration marked by corruption (p. 480)

Harrington, Michael Author; wrote *The Other America* in 1962, which described areas of poverty in the otherwise prosperous United States (p. 739)

Harrison, Benjamin Twenty-third President of the United States, 1889–1893; signed 1890 Sherman Antitrust Act later used to regulate big business (p. 295)

Harrison, William Henry Ninth President of the United States, 1841; died of pneumonia after only a month in office (p. 125)

Hayes, Rutherford B. Nineteenth President of the United States, 1877–1881; promised to withdraw Union troops from the South in order to end dispute over his election; attacked spoils system (p. 220)

Hearst, William Randolph Newspaper publisher from 1887 until his death in 1951; used "yellow journalism" in the 1890s to stir up sentiment in favor of the Spanish-American War (p. 359)

Hiss, Alger Former State Department official investigated as a possible Communist spy by House Un-American Activities Committee after World War II; convicted of perjury in 1950 (p. 651)

Hitler, Adolf German leader of National Socialist (Nazi) party 1933–1945; rose to power by promoting racist and nationalist views (p. 570)

Ho Chi Minh Leader of the Communist Party in Indochina after World War II; led Vietnamese against the French, then North Vietnamese against the United States in the Vietnam War (p. 792)

Hoover, Herbert Thirty-first President of the United States, 1929–1933; worked to aid Europeans during World War I; responded ineffectively to 1929 stock market crash and Great Depression (p. 498)

Houston, Sam Leader of Texas troops in war for independence from Mexico in 1836; elected first president of independent Texas (p. 110)

Hughes, Langston Writer active during the Harlem Renaissance (p. 465)

Humphrey, Hubert Democratic presidential candidate in 1968; lost narrowly to Nixon in an election bid hurt by support for the Vietnam War and by third-party candidate George Wallace (p. 809)

Hutchinson, Anne Critic of Puritan leadership of Massachusetts Bay Colony; banished for her religious beliefs (p. 21)

I

Isabella Ruler of Spanish Christian kingdoms with Ferdinand in late 1400s; sponsored Columbus's voyage to North America (p. 11)

J

Jackson, Andrew Seventh President of the United States, 1829–1837; supported minimal government and the spoils system; vetoed rechartering of the national bank; pursued harsh policy toward Native Americans (p. 123)

Jackson, Stonewall Confederate general known for his swift strikes against Union forces; earned nickname Stonewall by holding his forces steady under extreme pressure at the First Battle of Manassas (p. 157)

Jefferson, Thomas Third President of the United States, 1801–1809; main author of the Declaration of Independence; a firm believer in the people and decentralized power; reduced the federal government (p. 93)

Thomas Jefferson

Johnson, Andrew Seventeenth President of the United States, 1865–1869; clashed with Radical Republicans on Reconstruction programs; was impeached, then acquitted, in 1868 (p. 203)

Johnson, Lyndon B. Thirty-sixth President of the United States, 1963–1969; expanded social assistance with his Great Society program; increased United States commitment during Vietnam War (p. 744)

Jordan, Barbara Member of Congress from Texas; first African American and woman to represent her state in Congress; gave keynote addresses at 1976 and 1992 Democratic National Conventions (p. 843)

Joseph, Chief Leader of Nez Percé; forced to give up his home by United States army, fled toward Canada; captured in 1877 (p. 263)

K

Kelley, Florence Progressive reformer active from 1886 to 1920; worked in state and federal government for laws on child labor, workplace safety, and consumer protection (p. 386)

Kennedy, John F. Thirty-fifth President of the United States, 1961–1963; seen as youthful and inspiring; known for his firm handling of the Cuban Missile Crisis; assassinated in 1963 (p. 740)

Kennedy, Robert F. Attorney General under his brother, President John Kennedy, in the early 1960s; supported civil rights; assassinated while running for President in 1968 (p. 809)

Keynes, John Maynard British economist who believed that government spending could help a faltering economy; his theories helped shape New Deal legislation (p. 526)

Khomeini, Ayatollah Ruholla Islamic fundamentalist leader of Iran after the 1979 overthrow of the Shah; approved holding of American hostages (p. 856)

Khrushchev, Nikita Soviet leader from 1953 to 1964; opposed President Kennedy in the Cuban Missile Crisis (p. 753)

King, Martin Luther, Jr. African American civil rights leader from the mid-1950s until his assassination in 1968; used nonviolent means such as marches, boycotts, and legal challenges to win civil rights (p. 706)

Kissinger, Henry Secretary of State under Presidents Richard Nixon and Gerald Ford; used *realpolitik* to open relations with China, to end the Vietnam War, and to moderate Middle East conflict (p. 833)

L

Lafayette, Marquis de French officer who assisted American forces in the War for Independence (p. 48)

Dorothea Lange

Lange, Dorothea Photographed migrant farm workers during the Great Depression; inspired government aid programs and Steinbeck's *The Grapes of Wrath* (p. 517)

Lee, Robert E. Brilliant general of Confederate forces during the Civil War (p. 164)

Lenin, Vladimir I. Revolutionary leader in Russia; established a Communist government in 1917 (p. 427)

Levitt, William J. Built new communities in the suburbs after World War II, using mass-production techniques (p. 672)

Lewis, John L. Head of United Mine Workers through World War II; used strikes during the war to win pay raises (p. 597)

Lewis, Meriwether Leader with William Clark of expedition through the West beginning in 1804; brought back scientific samples, maps, and information on Native Americans (p. 95)

Lincoln, Abraham Sixteenth President of the United States, 1861–1865; known for his effective leadership during the Civil War and his Emancipation Proclamation declaring the end of slavery in Confederate-held territory (p. 170)

Lindbergh, Charles A. Aviator who became an international hero when he made the first solo flight across the Atlantic Ocean in 1927 (p. 456)

Lodge, Henry Cabot Massachusetts senator of early 1900s; supported United States imperialism (p. 356)

Long, Huey Louisiana politician in 1930s; suggested redistributing large fortunes by means of grants to families; assassinated in 1935 (p. 549)

M

MacArthur, Douglas United States general during the Great Depression, World War II, and Korean War; forced by Truman to resign in 1951 (p. 655)

Madison, James Fourth President of the United States, 1809–1817; called the Father of the Constitution for his leadership at the Constitutional Convention (p. 57)

Mahan, Alfred T. Author who argued in 1890 that the economic future of the United States rested on new overseas markets protected by a larger navy (p. 355)

Malcolm X African American leader during the 1950s and 1960s; eloquent spokesperson for African American self-sufficiency; assassinated in 1965 (p. 722)

Mann, Horace School reformer and supporter of public education before the Civil War; devised an educational system in Massachusetts later copied by many states (p. 128)

Mao Zedong Leader of Communists who took over China in 1949; remained in power until his death in 1976 (p. 653)

Marshall, George C. Army Chief of Staff during World War II and Secretary of State under President Harry Truman; assisted economic recovery in Europe after World War II and established strong allies for the United States through his Marshall Plan (p. 645)

Marshall, John Chief Justice of the Supreme Court appointed by John Adams; set precedents that established vital powers of the federal courts (p. 94)

Marshall, Thurgood First African American Supreme Court Justice; as a lawyer, won landmark school desegregation case *Brown* v. *Board of Education* in 1954 (p. 699)

McCarthy, Eugene Candidate in the 1968 Democratic presidential race who opposed the Vietnam War; convinced President Lyndon Johnson not to run again through his strong showing in the primaries (p. 809)

McCarthy, Joseph R. Republican senator from Wisconsin in the late 1940s and early 1950s; led a crusade to investigate officials he claimed were Communists; discredited in 1954 (p. 657)

McClellan, George Early Union army leader in the Civil War; careful organizer and planner who moved too slowly for northern politicians; ran against President Abraham Lincoln in the election of 1864 (p. 160)

McKinley, William Twenty-fifth President of the United States, 1897–1901; supported tariffs and a gold standard; expanded the United States by waging the Spanish-American War (p. 296)

McNamara, Robert Secretary of Defense under Presidents Kennedy and Lyndon Johnson; expanded American involvement in Vietnam War (p. 794)

Meade, George G. Union commander at Battle of Gettysburg in 1863; defended the high ground and forced the Confederate army to attack, causing great casualties (p. 181)

Metacom Leader of Pokanokets in Massachusetts; also known by his English name, King Philip; led Native Americans in King Philip's War, 1675–1676 (p. 21)

Mitchell, John Attorney General under President Richard Nixon; deeply involved in Watergate scandal (p. 827)

Monroe, James Fifth President of the United States, 1817–1825; acquired Florida from Spain; declared Monroe Doctrine to keep foreign powers out of the Americas (p. 121)

Morse, Samuel F. B. Artist and inventor; developed telegraph and Morse code in 1844 (p. 229)

Mott, Lucretia Women's rights leader; helped organize first women's convention in Seneca Falls, New York, in 1848 (p. 132)

Mussolini, Benito Italian fascist leader who took power in the 1920s; called Il Duce ("the leader"); known for his brutal policies (p. 570)

N

Nader, Ralph Consumer advocate; published *Unsafe at Any Speed* in 1965 criticizing auto safety and inspiring new safety laws; Green Party candidate for president in the 2000 election (p. 784)

Nimitz, Chester Leader of American naval forces in World War II Battle of Midway, during which several Japanese aircraft carriers were destroyed (p. 617)

Nixon, Richard M. Thirty-seventh President, 1969–1974; known for his foreign policy toward the Soviet Union and China and for illegal acts he committed in the Watergate affair that forced his resignation (p. 835)

O

O'Connor, Sandra Day First woman Supreme Court Justice; appointed by President Reagan in 1981 (p. 878)

Oppenheimer, J. Robert Physicist who led American effort in World War II to develop first atomic bomb (p. 620)

P

Pahlavi, Muhammed Reza Shah, leader of Iran, from 1941 until his overthrow in 1979; supported by the United States; brought modernization to his country along with repression and corruption (p. 856)

Paine, Thomas Author of political pamphlets during 1770s and 1780s; wrote *Common Sense* in 1776 (p. 45)

Parks, Rosa Civil rights worker whose arrest in 1955 touched off the Montgomery bus boycott (p. 701)

Paul, Alice Women's suffrage leader of early 1900s; her Congressional Union used aggressive tactics to push the Nineteenth Amendment (p. 406)

Penn, William English Quaker who founded the colony of Pennsylvania in 1681 (p. 22)

Perkins, Frances Secretary of Labor 1933–1945 under President Franklin Delano Roosevelt; first woman Cabinet member (p. 541)

Pershing, John Leader of the American Expeditionary Forces during World War I (p. 425)

Perot, H. Ross Billionaire businessman who challenged William Clinton and George H. W. Bush for the presidency in 1992; strong opponent of NAFTA (p. 894)

Pierce, Franklin Fourteenth President of the United States, 1853–1857; signed the Kansas-Nebraska Act, which renewed conflicts over slavery in the territories (p. 965)

Polk, James K. Eleventh President of the United States, 1845–1849; led expansion of United States to southwest through war against Mexico (p. 136)

Polo, Marco Venetian traveler to China in the late 1200s; his book about the journey helped make Europeans aware of trade opportunities in eastern Asia (p. 7)

Popé Medicine man who led Pueblos and Apaches against Spanish rule in the Pueblo Revolt of 1680 (p. 16)

Pulitzer, Joseph Early 1900s newspaper publisher; used "yellow journalism" to stir up public sentiment in favor of the Spanish-American War (p. 329)

R

Randolph, A. Philip Civil rights activist from the 1930s to the 1950s; planned the Washington march that pressured President Franklin D. Roosevelt into opening World War II defense jobs to African Americans (p. 624)

Reagan, Ronald Fortieth President of the United States, 1981–1989; popular conservative leader who promoted supply-side economics and created huge budget deficits (p. 870)

Ronald Reagan

Riis, Jacob Reformer who wrote *How the Other Half Lives,* describing the lives of poor immigrants in New York City in the late 1800s (p. 308)

Robinson, Jackie Athlete who in 1947 became the first African American to play baseball in the major leagues (p. 698)

Rockefeller, Nelson Vice President appointed by President Gerald Ford in 1974; the nation's only nonelected Vice President to serve with a nonelected President (p. 847)

Roosevelt, Eleanor First Lady 1933–1945; tireless worker for social causes, including women's rights and civil rights for African Americans and other groups (p. 541)

Roosevelt, Franklin D. Thirty-second President of the United States, 1933–1945; fought the Great Depression through his New Deal social programs; battled Congress over Supreme Court control; proved a strong leader during World War II (p. 539)

Roosevelt, Theodore Twenty-sixth President of the United States, 1901–1909; fought trusts, aided Progressive reforms, built Panama Canal, and increased United States influence overseas (p. 369)

Theodore Roosevelt

Rosenberg, Julius and Ethel Husband and wife convicted and executed in 1953 for passing atomic secrets to the Soviet Union; records opened after the end of the Cold War suggest Julius was guilty, but that Ethel did not take part in espionage (p. 651)

S

Sacco, Nicola Immigrant and anarchist executed, in a highly controversial case, for a 1920 murder at a Massachusetts factory (p. 483)

Sadat, Anwar el- Egyptian leader in the 1970s; began the Middle East peace process by reaching the 1978 Camp David Accords with Israel (p. 855)

Salinger, J. D. Author of 1951 novel *The Catcher in the Rye,* which criticized 1950s conformity (p. 678)

Santa Anna, Antonio López de Mexican dictator who led government and troops in war against Texas; won the battle of the Alamo (p. 109)

Schlafly, Phyllis Conservative activist; led campaign during the 1970s and 1980s to block the Equal Rights Amendment (p. 769)

Seward, William Henry Republican antislavery leader during the 1860s; acquired Alaska in 1867 as Secretary of State (p. 219)

Sherman, William Tecumseh Union general in the Civil War; known for his destructive march from Atlanta to Savannah in 1864 (p. 189)

Sirica, John J. Washington judge who presided over the Watergate investigation in the 1970s; gave tough sentences to convicted participants and ordered President Richard Nixon to release secret tapes (p. 841)

Sitting Bull, Chief Leader of Sioux in clashes with United States Army in Black Hills in 1870s (p. 264)

Slater, Samuel English textile worker who brought the Industrial Revolution to the United States by duplicating British textile machinery from memory (p. 111)

Smith, John Leader of the Jamestown, Virginia, colony in the early 1600s (p. 18)

Smith, Joseph Founder of Church of Jesus Christ of Latter-day Saints, or Mormons, in New York in 1830; killed by a mob in Illinois in 1844 (p. 115)

Spock, Benjamin Pediatrician and author of *The Common Sense Book of Baby and Child Care* (1946), which encourages mothers to stay home with their children rather than work (p. 677)

Stalin, Joseph Leader of the Soviet Union from 1924–1953; worked with Roosevelt and Churchill during World War II but afterward became an aggressive participant in the Cold War (p. 569)

Stanton, Elizabeth Cady Women's rights leader in the 1800s; helped organize first women's convention; wrote the Declaration of Sentiments on women's rights in 1848 (p. 132)

Starr, Ellen Gates Cofounder of Chicago's Hull House, the first settlement house, in 1889 (p. 312)

Steinem, Gloria Journalist, women's rights leader since 1960s; founded *Ms.* magazine in 1972 to cover women's issues (p. 767)

Stevenson, Adlai Senator from Illinois and Democratic candidate for President in 1952 and 1956 against Eisenhower (p. 684)

Stilwell, Joseph World War II general active in the campaign against Japan in Southeast Asia (p. 615)

Stowe, Harriet Beecher Author of the novel *Uncle Tom's Cabin* (1852), which contributed significantly to antisouthern feelings among Northerners before the Civil War (p. 132)

Sumner, Charles Abolitionist and senator from Massachusetts; beaten badly with a cane in the Senate by a southern congressman after making an antislavery speech (p. 140)

T

Taft, William Howard Twenty-seventh President of the United States, 1909–1913; continued Progressive reforms of President Theodore Roosevelt; promoted "dollar diplomacy" to expand foreign investments (p. 370)

Taylor, Zachary Twelfth President of the United States, 1849–1850; Mexican War officer (p. 136)

Thoreau, Henry David Transcendentalist author known for his work *Walden* (1854) and other writings (p. 127)

Travis, William Leader in Texas's bid for independence from Mexico in 1836; died at the Alamo after appealing to the United States for help (p. 109)

Truman, Harry S Thirty-third President of the United States, 1945–1953; authorized use of atomic bomb; signed Marshall Plan to rebuild Europe (p. 638)

Truth, Sojourner Abolitionist and women's rights advocate before the Civil War; as a former slave, she spoke effectively to white audiences on abolition issues (p. 130)

Tubman, Harriet "Conductor" on the Underground Railroad, which helped slaves escape to freedom before the Civil War (p. 131)

Turner, Frederick Jackson Historian who wrote an essay in 1893 emphasizing the western frontier as a powerful force in the formation of the American character (p. 275)

Turner, Nat African American preacher who led a slave revolt in 1831; captured and hanged after the revolt failed (p. 120)

Tweed, William Marcy Boss of the Tammany Hall political machine in New York City; convicted of forgery and larceny in 1873 and died in jail in 1878 (p. 309)

Tyler, John Tenth President of the United States, 1841–1845; accomplished little due to quarrels between Whigs and Jacksonian Democrats (p. 125)

V

Van Buren, Martin Eighth President of the United States, 1837–1841; Jacksonian Democrat; was voted out of office after the Panic of 1837 brought widespread unemployment and poverty (p. 125)

Vance, Cyrus Secretary of State under President Jimmy Carter; invited Israelis and Egyptians to Camp David in 1978 to begin Middle East peace process (p. 855)

Vanzetti, Bartolomeo Immigrant and anarchist executed, in a highly controversial case, for a 1920 murder at a Massachusetts factory (p. 483)

Vesey, Denmark African American who planned 1822 South Carolina slave revolt; captured and hanged after revolt failed (p. 120)

W

Walker, Madam C. J. African American leader and businesswoman in the early 1900s; she spoke out against lynching (p. 336)

Wallace, George C. Third-party candidate for President in 1968; focused his campaign on issues of blue-collar anger in the North and racial tension (p. 811)

Warren, Earl Chief Justice of the United States Supreme Court 1953–1968; investigated President Kennedy's assassination; led in many decisions that protected civil rights, rights of the accused, and right to privacy (p. 749)

Washington, Booker T. African American leader from the late 1800s until his death in 1915; founded Tuskegee Institute in Alabama; encouraged African Americans to learn trades (p. 324)

Booker T. Washington

Washington, George First President of the United States, 1789–1797; led American forces in the War for Independence; set several federal precedents, including the two-term maximum for presidential office (p. 63)

Whitney, Eli Inventor; developed the cotton gin in 1793, which rapidly increased cotton production in the South and led to a greater demand for slave labor (p. 112)

Wilhelm, Kaiser Emperor of Germany during World War I; symbol to the United States of German militarism and severe efficiency (p. 418)

Wilson, Woodrow Twenty-eighth President of the United States, 1913–1921; tried to keep the United States out of World War I; proposed League of Nations (p. 399)

Y

Yeltsin, Boris Leader of Russia in late 1980s and 1990s; took over from Mikhail Gorbachev as reforms continued and Communist Party control ended (p. 903)

York, Alvin American soldier who was awarded the Congressional Medal of Honor for bravery during World War I (p. 431)

Z

Zenger, Peter Colonial printer arrested for libel, his landmark trial established truth as a defense against libel (p. 28)

Index

Note: Entries with a page number followed by a *c* indicate a chart or graph on that page; *go* indicates a graphic organizer; *m* indicates a map; and *p* indicates a picture.

1016

Index

Index

B

Index

Index

Index

D

Index

F

Index

Index

G

Index

Index

J

K

Index

L

Index

M

Index

Index

Index

O

P

Index

Index

Index

Index

Index

1038

Index

U

Index

Index

Index

Acknowledgments

STAFF CREDITS

The people who made up the *America: Pathways to the Present* team—representing editorial, editorial services, design services, market research, online services/multimedia development, product marketing, production services, and publishing processes—are listed below. Bold type denotes core team members.

Leann Davis Alspaugh, Mary Ann Barton, Suzanne Biron, Margaret Broucek, Sarah M. Carroll, Siobhan Costello, Anne Drowns, Alex Crumbley, Deborah Dukeshire, Deborah Feldheim, **Thomas Ferreira, Gabriela Pérez Fiato, Mary Ann Gundersen,** Lance Hatch, Kerri Hoar, Kate House, Katharine Ingram, Nancy Jones, Kevin Keane, Suzanne Klein, Michael Locker, Meredith Mascola, **Constance McCarty,** Anne McLaughlin, Terri Mitchell, Mark O'Malley, Jen Paley, Elizabeth Pearson, Jill Ratzan, Lynn Robbins, **Luess Sampson-Lizotte,** Hope Schuessler, Mark Staloff, Susan Swan, Jerry Thorne, Stacy Tibbetts, Bernadette Walsh, Roberta Warshaw, **Merce Wilczek,** Matthew Wilson, Amy Winchester, Helen Young

COVER IMAGE

Front Cover Vietnam Memorial: Lelia Hendren/Folio, Inc. Flag background: Jim Barber/The StockRep, Inc. **Back Cover** Stone

MAPS

XNR Productions Inc.: 3, 10, 15, 22, 27, 32, 36, 37, 39, 41, 42, 47, 92, 95, 97, 98, 105, 108, 109, 136, 138, 141, 149, 155, 161, 162, 171, 179, 180, 183, 188, 199, 208, 217, 220, 225, 236, 257, 264, 269, 271, 281, 286, 289, 296, 300, 319, 351, 353, 360, 363, 365, 367, 370, 378, 381, 391, 399, 400, 407, 413, 414, 415, 416, 427, 440, 446, 451, 455, 456, 457, 479, 504–505, 507, 515, 529, 535, 540, 541, 567, 569, 572, 577, 583, 588, 593, 601, 603, 606, 612, 616, 635, 641, 646, 654, 659, 667, 673, 691, 693, 697, 700, 711, 735, 737, 752, 754, 763, 789, 791, 793, 802, 811, 813, 825, 863, 869, 883, 890, 891, 899, 906, 909, 960; **Mapping Specialists Limited:** 956, 957, 958, 962–963

ILLUSTRATION

Leann Davis Alspaugh: 865; **argosypublishing.com:** 159, 241, 244, 292, 293, 307, 333, 392, 461, 485, 487, 492, 500, 816, 871, 873, 874, 875, 880; **Kenneth Batelman:** 61, 112, 118, 234, 428–429, 494–495, 510, 753, 756, 800, 836, 854; **Matt Mayerchak & Laura Glassman:** 2-3, 38–39, 104–105, 154–155, 156, 166, 175, 178, 186, 192, 194, 198–199, 200, 206, 212, 218, 221, 222, 224–225, 256–257, 258, 261, 266, 268, 272, 277, 284, 288–289, 318–319, 320, 322, 327, 332, 334, 337, 342, 350–351, 380–381, 382, 389, 396, 403, 412–413, 414, 421, 425, 432, 437, 438, 450–451, 478–479, 506-507, 534–535, 566–567, 592–593, 634–635, 666–667, 672, 696–697, 734–735, 762–763, 790–791, 824–825, 862–863, 892–893; **Jen Paley:** 4, 13, 14, 24, 34, 40, 54, 59, 89, 100, 106, 111, 116, 121, 126, 128, 130, 134, 135, 139, 146, 150, 151, 213, 214, 219, 226, 237, 243, 247, 254, 274, 290, 297, 299, 304, 310, 311, 316, 322, 347, 352, 355, 357, 359, 366, 372, 376, 388, 394, 408, 442, 446, 447, 452, 453, 459, 467, 474, 480, 491, 498, 502, 508, 509, 511, 513, 520, 524, 530, 536, 543, 545, 550, 553, 554, 560, 562, 563, 568, 575, 581, 585, 590, 594, 597, 600, 609, 614, 618, 623, 630, 636, 643, 644, 645, 648, 652, 656, 657, 662, 668, 670, 672, 675, 677, 680, 688, 692, 693, 698, 704, 709, 712, 716, 720, 722, 728, 736, 739, 743, 746, 747, 751, 760, 764, 765, 771, 774, 777, 781, 784, 786, 792, 796, 798, 803, 805, 812, 818, 820, 821, 826, 828, 832, 838, 846, 848, 851, 858, 864, 870, 876, 882, 887, 888, 894, 902, 903, 911, 912, 918, 922, 923, 960, 961, 964; **Hope Schuessler:** 841

PICTURE RESEARCH

Paula Wehde

PHOTOGRAPHY

Front Matter ii T, Courtesy, Andrew Cayton, Ph.D.; **ii TM,** Courtesy, Elisabeth Israels Perry, Ph.D.; **ii BM,** Courtesy, Linda Reed, Ph.D.; **ii B,** Courtesy, Allan M. Winkler, Ph.D.; **iii,** Shelburne Museum

Table of Contents iv T, Dukes County Historical Society/photo by Robert Schellhammer ©1994; **iv B,** The Granger Collection, NY; **v T,** Culver Pictures, Inc.; **v M,** National Museum of American Art, Smithsonian Institution, Washington, D.C., Gift of Mrs. Joseph Harrison, Jr. Art Resource, NY; **v B,** Corbis; **vi TL,** Panama Canal Museum; **vi ML,** Library of Congress; **vi MR,** The Granger Collection, NY; **vi B,** National Archives; **vii BL,** Franklin D. Roosevelt Library; **vii TR,** Corbis; **vii MR,** FDR Library; **vii BR,** Gary Waltz/The Image Works; **viii TL,** The Granger Collection, NY; **viii ML,** Harry S. Truman Presidential Library; **viii BL,** J.R. Eyerman/TimePix; **viii BL inset,** Russ Lappa; **viii BM,** Corbis; **viii BR,** © 1959 Newsweek Inc. All rights reserved. Reprinted by permission.; **ix BL,** Lambert/Hulton/Archive/Getty Images; **ix TR,** Don Uhrbrock *LIFE Magazine* © Time Warner; **ix TM,** Al Freni/*LIFE Magazine* © Time Warner; **ix BM,** David J. Frent; **ix BR,** Guido Rossi/Hulton Archive/Getty Images; **x T,** Steve Northup, © Time Inc. *Time Magazine;* **x M,** David J. Frent; **x B,** Stone; **xi TL,** New Holland Machine Company; **xi BL,** Thomas E. Franklin/Bergen Record/Corbis SABA; **xi TR,** Hulton/Liaison Agency/Getty Images; **xii,** Collection of Ryan Brown; **xiv L,** UPI/Bettmann Archives/Corbis; **xiv R,** Art Resource, NY; **xx T,** Greg E. Mathieson/MAI Photo News Agency, Inc.; **xx M,** Library of Congress; **xx B,** Terry Donnelly/Stone; **xxi T all,** Courtesy of the Federal Reserve Bank of San Francisco; **xxi M,** AP/Wide World Photos; **xxi B,** Brown Brothers; **xxii TL,** Bob Adelman/Magnum Photos, Inc.; **xxii TR,** Hulton/Liaison/Getty Images; **xxii M inset,** Hulton/Archive/Getty Images; **xxii BR,** Time Life Books; **xxiii T,** American Textile History Museum; **xxiii M,** Library of Congress; **xxiii B,** Jewish Hospital/University of Louisville; **xxiv,** Corel Corp.; **xxv all,** Corel Corp.

Unit Openers xi–1, Architect of the Capitol; **152–153,** The Andrew J. Russell Collection, The Oakland Museum of California; **348–349,** Museum of the City of New York; **448–449,** New York Historical Society/Bridgeman Art Library; **564–565,** Corbis; **694–695,** Corbis; **822–823,** Brad Perks

Chapter 1 2 L, Corbis Sygma; **2 R,** The Pilgrim Society; **3 R,** Laurie Minor-Penland, Smithsonian Institution; **3 L,** Courtesy, American Antiquarian Society; **4,** David Gallery, Philadelphia/SuperStock; **5,** Courtesy The Edward E. Ayer Collection, The Newberry Library; **6 T,** Courtesy of the National Museum of the American Indian/Smithsonian Institution; **6 M,** Etowah Indian Mounds Historic Site; **6 B,** Giraudon/Art Resource, NY; **7,** The Granger Collection, NY; **8 T,** Louvre, Paris, France/Art Resource, NY; **8 B,** The Granger Collection, NY; **9,** Photograph by Jeffrey Ploskonka, National Museum of African Art, Eliot Elisofon Archive, Smithsonian Institution; **11,** The Metropolitan Museum of Art, Gift of J. Pierpont Morgan, 1900 (10.18.2); **12,** London Science Museum. Phot G Michael Holford; **14,** The Granger Collection, NY; **16,** Texas Memorial Museum, Austin; **17,** National Maritime Museum; **18,** Fairholt, F.W., Tobacco: It's history, London, 1859 (detail) Arents Collection, The New York Public Library, Astor, Lenox and Tilden Foundations; **19 T,** Library of Congress; **19 B,** Peabody & Essex Museum. Photo by Mark Sexton; **20,** The Pilgrim Society; **21,** Culver Pictures, Inc.; **23,** NC Division of Archives and History; **24 T,** Corbis; **24 B,** The Library Company of Philadelphia; **25,** National Portrait Gallery, London/SuperStock; **26,** Library of Congress; **28,** Royal Albert Memorial Museum, Exeter/Bridgeman Art Library, London/New York; **29,** National Maritime Museum; **30 L,** Courtesy Linda O. King/Coastal Islands Historical Society; **30 R,** H.L. Miller/Stock South/PictureQuest; **33 T,** Library of Congress; **33 B,** Library of Congress; **35,** Steve Kelley/ Copley News Service

Chapter 2 38 L, Shelburne Museum; **38 R,** Corbis; **39,** Library of Congress; **40,** Geoffrey Clements/Corbis; **43 T,** Colonial Williamsburg Foundation; **43 B,** The Granger Collection, NY; **44,** Massachusetts Historical Society; **45,** Corbis; **46,** Tom Stack & Associates; **48,** Emanuel Gottlieb Leutze, The Metropolitan Museum of Art, Gift of John S. Kennedy, 1897; **49,** Private Collection; **53 Declaration of Independence,** Library of Congress; **54,** SuperStock; **56,** Culver Pictures, Inc.; **57,** Independence National Historic Park; **58,** Free Library of Philadelphia; **62 B,** Courtesy, American Antiquarian Society; **62 T,** The Library Company of Philadelphia; **63,** Art Resource, NY; **64,** The Granger Collection, NY; **89 B,** Art Resource, NY; **89 T,** New York Historical Society/The Bridgeman Art Library; **89 M,** Special Collection/Dartmouth College Library; **90,** "An Exciseman" (detail) Atwater Kent Museum; **91,** National Portrait Gallery, Smithsonian Institution, Washington, D.C./Art Resource NY; **93,** ©White House Historical Association/Photo by National Geographic Society; **94,** Missouri Historical Society; **95,** Duke University Archives; **96,** National Portrait Gallery, Smithsonian Institution, Washington, DC #83-7221; **101,** Prentice Hall

Chapter 3 104 L, Library of Congress; **104 R,** Archives Division–Texas State Library; **105 L,** The Granger Collection, NY; **105 R,** Women's Rights Collection, Sophia Smith Archives; **106–107 B,** Panoramic Images; **107 T,** Pearson Education/Prentice Hall College; **109,** San Jacinto Museum of History Association; **110,** Corbis; **111,** Library of Congress; **113 T,** Corbis; **113 B,** The Granger Collection, NY; **114,** The New York Historical Society; **115,** Library of Congress; **116,** Museum of American Folk Art; **117,** Lowell Historical Society; **119,** Library of Congress; **122,** The Metropolitan Museum of Art; **123,** Museum of the City of New York; **124,** Woolaroc Museum, Bartlesville, OK; **125,** The New York Historical Society; **126–127 B,** Corbis; **127 T,** The Granger Collection, NY; **128,** Boston Athenaeum; **129,** Library of Congress; **131,** Sophia Smith Collection, Smith College; **132,** The Granger Collection, NY; **134,** Harper's Weekly ; **135,** Corbis; **136,** The Granger Collection, NY; **137,** American Antiquarian Society; **138,** Library of Congress; **140,** The New York Public Library; **142,** The New York Public Library Prints Division; **143 T,** The Granger Collection, NY; **143 B,** National Geographic Society; **144 L,** State Historical Society of Wisconsin; **144 R,** National Civil War Museum; **147,** The New York Historical Society

Chapter 4 154 R, Greg E. Mathieson/MAI Photo News Agency, Inc.; **154 L,** Artist: Douglas Volk, Minnesota Historical Society; **155,** Brown University Library; **156,** Culver Pictures, Inc.; **157,** Culver Pictures, Inc.; **160 L,** Rick Vargas and Richard Strauss, SI; **160 R,** Collection of David & Kevin Kyle; **161,** Collection of Michael J. McAfee. Courtesy William Gladstone. Photo © Seth Goltzer; **163,** The Collection of Jay P. Altmayer; **164,** Museum of the Confederacy; **165,** Museum of the Confederacy; **166,** Rick Vargas and Richard Strauss, Smithsonian Institution; **168,** John G. Johnson Collection, Philadelphia Museum of Art; **170,** McLellan Lincoln Collection, John Hay Library, Brown University; **172,** Corbis; **173,** Chicago Historical Society; **174,** Culver Pictures, Inc.; **176,** Corbis; **176 inset,** American Antiquarian Society; **178,** Courtesy of Museum of the Confederacy, Richmond, Virginia; **181,** The Granger Collection, NY; **182 TR,** National Archives; **182 BR,** John Bernard Shaw/Corbis Sygma; **182 L,** Philip Jones Griffiths/MP, Zenith Electronics Corporation; **183,** The Beverly R. Robinson Collection, U.S. Naval Academy Museum; **185,** Brown University Library; **186,** The Granger Collection, NY; **189,** The Granger Collection, NY; **190,** The Granger Collection, NY; **191,** Rob Crandall/Folio, Inc.; **192,** Virginia Historical Society; **193,** Anne S.K. Brown Military Collection, Brown University Library, Providence, RI; **195,** Culver Pictures, Inc.

Chapter 5 198 L, The Granger Collection, NY; **198 R,** Library of Congress; **200,** Brown Brothers; **201,** The Granger Collection, NY; **202 B,** Library of Congress; **202 T,** Courtesy of the Museum of the Confederacy/Library of Congress; **204 I,** Collection of William Gladstone; **204 R,** Collection of William Gladstone; **205,** The Granger Collection, NY; The Granger Collection, NY; **208 T,** The Granger Collection, NY; **208 B,** Corbis; **209,** Russ Lappa; **210,** Library of Congress; **211,** Collection of Nancy Gewirz, Antique Textile Resource, Bethesda, Maryland; **212,** Los Angeles County Museum of Art: Acquisition made possible through museum trustees; **213,** The New York Historical Society; **215 T,** Courtesy of the Witte Museum; **215 B,** Library of Congress; **216,** Prentice Hall; **218 inset,** Collection of State Historical Museum/Mississippi Department of Archives and History; **218,** Rutherford B. Hayes Presidential Center; **221,** The Granger Collection, NY; **223,** Library of Congress

Chapter 6 224 L, Library of Congress; **224 R,** Light-Foot Collection; **225,** The Granger Collection, NY; **226,** The Granger Collection, NY; **226 B,** The Granger Collection, NY; **227 T,** Courtesy of the Federal Reserve Bank of San Francisco; **227 B,** Archive Photos; **228 T,** Library of Congress; **228 B,** National Geographic Society; **229,** Hulton Archive/Getty Images; **231,** Index Stock Imagery, Inc.; **231 inset,** The Granger Collection, NY; **232,** The Oakland Museum History Department; **233,** Hulton Archive/Getty Images; **234,** Chicago Historical Society; **235,** Museum of the City of New York; **237,** Corbis; **238,** Museum of American Textile History; **239,** Library of Congress; **240,** Library of Congress; **243,** Brown Brothers; **245,** Putman County Historical Society, Cold Spring, N.Y.; **246 L,** Library of Congress; **246 R,** Library of Congress; **247 L,** Library of Congress; **247 R,** Picture Research Consultants, Inc.; **248 L,** The Granger Collection, NY; **248 R,** Collection of Ralph J. Brunke; **251,** Brown Brothers; **252,** Corbis ; **253,** Brown Brothers; **255,** Library of Congress

Chapter 7 256 L, National Anthropological Archives/Smithsonian Institution; **256 R,** Thomas Moran, Grand Canyon of the Yellowstone, 1872, oil on canvas, The U.S. Department of the Interior Museum, Washington, D.C.; **256 M,** Corbis; **258–259,** Jake Rajs/Stone; **260,** Corbis; **261,** National Museum of American Art, Smithsonian Institution, Washington, D.C. Gift of Mrs. Joseph Harrison, Jr. Art Resource, NY; **263 T,** Library of Congress; **263 B,** Colorado Historical Society; **264–265 B,** National Anthropological Archives/Smithsonian Institution; **265 T,** SuperStock; **267 T,** Cumberland County Historical Society; **267 B,** Cumberland County Historical Society; **268,** California State Library; **270,** Library of Congress; **272,** Amon Carter Museum of Western Art; **273,** Denver Public Library; **275 T,** Buffalo Bill Historical Center, Cody WY; **275 B,** Library of Congress; **276,** Photofest; **279,** American Gold Exchange, Austin, TX; **279,** American Gold Exchange, Austin, TX; **280 T,** Kansas State Historical Society; **280 B,** East

Acknowledgments

Carolina Manuscript Collection, J.Y. Joyner Library, East Carolina University; **282,** Library of Congress; **285,** Library of Congress

Chapter 8 288 M, Division of Political History, Smithsonian Institution; **288 R,** Visions of America; **288 L,** The Granger Collection, NY; **290,** The Granger Collection, NY; **291,** *Puck,* March 10, 1897; **293 T,** Library of Congress; **293 B,** Library of Congress; **295 R,** Collection of David J. Frent and Janice L. Frent; **295 L,** Collection of David J. Frent and Janice L. Frent; **297,** Courtesy George Eastman House; **298 T,** The Museum of the City of New York; **298 BR,** Chermayeff & Geisma; **298 BL,** National Park Service Collection, Gift of Angelo Forgione; **301,** Library of Congress; **302,** California Department of Parks and Recreation, courtesy Fred Wasserman; **303,** El Paso Border Heritage Center; **304,** Brown Brothers; **305 T,** Library of Congress; **305 B,** Library of Congress; **306,** Library of Congress; **308,** Museum of the City of New York, Gift of Joseph Varner Reed; **309,** Thomas Nast; **311,** Library of Congress; **312,** Library of Congress; **313,** California Museum of Photography; **314,** Chermayeff & Geisma; **315,** Corbis; **317,** *Puck,* 1909

Chapter 9 318, Culver Pictures, Inc.; **319 L,** The Kobal Collection; **319 R,** Chicago Historical Society; **319 M, TR,** Wood River Gallery, Mill Valley, California; BR, Wood; **320,** Kansas State Historical Society; **321,** The McGuffy Museum; **322,** Oldest Wooden School House, St. Augustine, Florida; **323,** Sophia Smith Collection; **324,** Brown Brothers; **325,** The New York Public Library; **327 L,** Rick Vargas, Smithsonian Institution; **327 R,** National Baseball Library and Archive, Cooperstown, NY; **328,** Barbara Puorro Galasso/George Eastman House; **329,** Brooklyn Museum; **330,** Corbis; **331,** Fisk University Special Collections; **332,** Corbis; **333,** Mauldin/© 1962 *St. Louis Post-Dispatch;* **335,** The Granger Collection; **336,** Corbis; **337,** Corbis; **338,** Courtesy of The Maytag Company; **339 L,** The Granger Collection, NY; **339 M,** Tony Freeman/PhotoEdit; **339 R,** Bob Daemmrich Photography; **340,** Kansas State Historical Society; **341,** Charles Dana Gibson; **343,** Library of Congress

Chapter 10 350 L, National Portrait gallery, Smithsonian Institution/Art Resource, NY; **350 TR,** New York Historical Society; **350 BR,** Chicago Historical Society; **351 R,** Schalkwijk/New York Historical Society, NY; **351 L,** Courtesy of the U.S. Naval Academy Museum; **352,** Library of Congress; **355,** The Oakland Museum of California; **356,** Library of Congress; **357,** The Granger Collection, NY; **359,** Corbis; **361,** *Puck* magazine 1898; **362 L,** Library of Congress; **362 M,** National Archives; **362 R,** AP/Wide World Photos; **364,** Culver Pictures; **366,** Corbis; **367 BL,** Panama Canal Museum; **367 BR,** Panama Canal Museum; **367 T,** Panama Canal Museum; **368,** Library of Congress; **369,** Theodore Roosevelt Collection Harvard College Library; **372,** The Granger Collection, NY; **374,** Courtesy of the U.S. Naval Academy Museum; **375,** Prentice Hall; **377,** *Puck,* June 29, 1904

Chapter 11 380 L, Sophia Smith College Archives; **380 R,** Texas State Library & Archives Commission; **381,** Dartmouth College College Library, Special Collection; **382,** Brown Brothers; **382 inset,** Courtesy of the Decorative & Industrial Arts Collection of the Chicago Historical Society; **383,** Corbis Sygma; **384,** Culver Pictures, Inc.; **385,** Brown Brothers; **385 inset,** Library of Congress; **386,** Labor Management Documentation Center, Cornell University; **387 T,** Corbis; **387 B,** Corbis; **389,** Corbis; **390–391,** Texas State Library & Archives Commission; **393,** State Historical Society of Wisconsin; **395,** Hulton/Archive/Getty Images; **396,** White House Historical Association; **397,** The Granger Collection, NY; **398 T,** Museum of American Political Life; **398 B,** Theodore Roosevelt Collection Harvard College Library; **401 T,** Bettmann/Corbis; **401 B,** David J.Frent; **402 T,** National Association for the Advancement of Colored People; **402 B,** Schomburg Center for Research in Black Culture; **403,** Courtesy of the Women's Voters of the United States; **404,** Meserve-Kunhardt Collection; **406 T,** Library of Congress; **406 B,** "Vote Yes" suffrage poster/Smithsonian Institution; **409,** Library of Congress

Chapter 12 412 L, Culver Pictures, Inc.; **412 R,** The Granger Collection, NY; **413 R,** Library of Congress; **413 M,** Corbis; **413 L,** Hulton/Archive/Archive Photos; **414,** Hulton/Archive/Archive Photos; **416,** Museum of the City of New York; **417 T,** Collection of Stuart S. Corning, Jr. Photo © Rob Huntley/Lightstream; **417 B,** Bayerisches Hauptstaatsarchiv; **419,** Culver Pictures, Inc.; **421,** The Granger Collection, NY; **422 TL,** Library of Congress; **422 R,** The Granger Collection, NY; **422 BL,** From the publication "My Four Years in Germany"; **423,** National Archives; **424,** Library of Congress; **425,** Library of Congress; **426,** Hulton/Archive/Archive Photos; **427,** Hulton/Archive/Archive Photos; **429,** Russ Lappa; **430 T,** Culver Pictures, Inc.; **430 B,** Corbis; **431,** Brown Brothers; **432,** Library of Congress; **433,** National Archives; **434 B,** Museum of the City of New York; **434 T,** Museum of the City of New York; **435,** Wayne State University, Archives of Labor and Urban Affairs; **436,** Museum of the City of New York; **437,** Super-Stock; **438,** Hulton/Archive/Archive Photos; **443,** Stock Montage

Chapter 13 450 L, *Chicago Daily Tribune;* **450 M,** Corbis; **450 R,** Corbis; **451 L,** John Sloan Sixth Avenue Elevated at Third Street, 1928 (detail). Collection of Whitney Museum of American Art, Purchase 36. 154. Photograph 1998: Whitney Museum of American Art, NY; **451 R,** Superstock; **452,** Corbis; **454,** Brown Brothers; **456,** Culver Pictures, Inc.; **457,** Corbis; **458,** Corbis; **459,** SuperStock; **460,** Culver Pictures, Inc.; **462 T,** Corbis; **462 B,** SuperStock; **463,** Purchased with funds from the Edmunson Art Foundation, Inc. Des Moines Art Center Permanent Collections, 1958.2; **464 L,** Corbis; **464 R,** Beinecke Library, Yale University; **464 M,** Brown Brothers; **465,** Cartier Bresson/Magnum Photos; **467,** The Michael Barson Collection/ Past Perfect. RH/LS; **468,** Library of Congress; **469,** Chicago Historical Society; **470 T,** Corbis; **470 B,** Brown Brothers; **471,** *Chicago Daily Tribune;* **472,** Chermayeff & Geisma; **473 B,** Brown Brothers; **473 T,** Schomburg Center for Black Research; **475,** Historical Society of Wisconsin

Chapter 14 478 L, UPI/Bettmann Archives/Corbis; **478 R,** Calvin Coolidge Memorial Foundation; **479 L,** Gary Waltz/The Image Works; **479 R,** Corbis; **480,** Hulton/Archive/Getty Images; **481,** Hulton/Archive/Getty Images; **482,** The Granger Collection, NY; **484,** Corbis; **486,** Ohio Historical Society; **488,** David J. Frent; **489,** *LIFE* Magazine December 10,1925; **491,** Western Historical Manuscript Collection–Kansas City; **492,** Courtesy of Speigel; **493,** The Granger Collection, NY; **494,** Henry Ford Museum; **495,** The Granger Collection, NY; **496 B,** Schnectady Museum; **496 T,** Hulton /Liaison /Getty Images; **497,** Culver Pictures Inc./PictureQuest; **498,** Culver Pictures Inc.; **499,** Boston Athenaeum; **501,** Corbis; **503,** The Granger Collection, NY

Chapter 15 506 L, Library of Congress; **506 R,** Museum of the City of New York/Hulton/Archive/Getty Images; **507,** Hulton/Archive/Getty Images; **508,** Hulton/Archive/Getty Images; **512,** The Granger Collection, NY; **513,** *Detroit News;* **514,** Museum of the City of New York. Photograph by Bernice Abbott, Federal Arts Project; **516 L,** Library of Congress; **516 R,** Library of Congress; **517,** Library of Congress; **518,** FPG International; **521,** Collection of Ryan Brown; **522,** Culver Pictures, Inc.; **523,** Corbis; **524,** Corbis/Bettmann; **525,** Corbis; **526 L,** Corbis; **526 M,** The White House Photo Office; **526 R,** Karl Gehring/Liaison /Getty Images; **527,** Corbis; **531,** Reprinted from the *Albany Evening News,* 6/7/31 with permission of the *Times Union,* Albany, NY

Chapter 16 534 L, Library of Congress; **534 R,** The Granger Collection, NY; **535 L,** Richard Berenholtz/Corbis Stock Market; **535 R,** The Kobal Collection; **536,** Hoover Presidential Library; **537,** FDR Library; **538 R,** U.S. Forest Service; **538 L,** Library of Congress; **539 T,** Corbis; **539 B,** Corbis; **541,** FDR Library; **542,** Hulton/Archive/Getty Images; **544,** Library of Congress; **545,** The *New Yorker* Collection, 1963, Peter Arno from www.cartoonbank.com. All rights reserved.; **546,** Margaret Bourke-White, *LIFE* Magazine © Time Warner; **547,** Corbis; **548,** ©1935,1963 by the Conde Nast Publications Inc.; **549 T,** Corbis; **549 B,** UPI/Bettman Archives/Corbis; **551,** The Granger Collection, NY; **553,** Corbis; **554,** Corbis; **555,** Library of Congress; **556,** Corbis; **557 L,** Corbis; **557 R,** Corbis; **558,** James Prigoff; **559,** PTC; **561,** Franklin D. Roosevelt Library

Chapter 17 566 R, Hulton/Archive/Getty Images; **566 L,** A.K.G., Berlin/SuperStock; **567,** Sovfoto/Eastfoto; **568,** Holocaust Museum; **570,** Moro Roma; **571 T,** AP/Wide World Photos; **571 M,** Collection of Chester Stott/, ©Rob Huntley/Lightstream; **571 B,** Corbis; **572,** Liaison/Getty Images; **573 T,** Corbis; **573 B,** Corbis; **574,** Estate of Pablo Picasso/Artists Rights Society (ARS), New York/Art Resource, N.Y.; **575,** Corbis; **576,** The Granger Collection, NY; **577,** The Granger Collection, NY; **578 B,** Library of Congress; **578 T,** Corbis; **579,** Corbis; **580,** Admiral Nimitz Museum; **582 T,** Paul Dorsey/TimePix; **582 B,** Corbis; **585,** Corbis; **586,** Brown Brothers; **587,** Corbis; **589,** Bettman/Corbis; **591,** Dr. Seuss

Chapter 18 592 R, The Granger Collection, NY; **592 L,** Jeff Tinsley, Smithsonian Institution; **593 L,** Liaison/Getty Images; **593 R,** Library of Congress; **594,** Collection of Chester H. Stott, ©Rob Huntley/Lightstream; **595 B,** Bill Mauldin; **595 T,** National Archives; **596 inset,** Jeff Tinsley, Smithsonian Institution; **596,** The Bancroft Library, Kaiser Pictorial Collection; **597,** Lawrence Thornton/Hulton/Archive/Getty Images; **598 inset,** National Museum of American History, Smithsonian Institution, Washington D.C.; **598,** H. Armstrong Roberts; **599,** Pearson Education/PH College; **600,** The Granger Collection, NY; **601,** National Archives; **602 T,** U.S. Army; **602 B,** Imperial War Museum; **604,** Liaison/Getty Images; **605,** National Portrait Gallery, Smithsonian Institution, Washington D.C., Art Resource, NY; **607,** Corbis; **608,** U.S. Army; **609,** Hulton/Archive/Getty Images; **610 T,** Courtesy of U.S. Holocaust Memorial Museum Archives; **610 B,** Rijksinstituut voor Oorlogsdocumentatie, courtesy of U.S. Holocaust Memorial Museum Archives; **611 T,** U.S. Holocaust Memorial Museum; **611 M,** U.S. Holocaust Memorial Museum; **611 B,** U.S. Holocaust Memorial Museum ; **612,** U.S. Holocaust Memorial Museum ; **613,** U.S. Holocaust Memorial Museum ; **614,** Liaison/Getty Images; **615,** Liaison/Getty Images; **617,** Keystone/Hulton/Archive/Getty Images; **619,** AP Photo/Joe Rosenthal; **620 B,** The Art Archive; **620 T,** Hulton/Archive/Getty Images; **621,** SuperStock; **623,** Hulton/Archive/Getty Images; **624,** National Portrait Gallery, Gift of the Harmon Foundation/Art Resource, NY; **625 inset,** Collection of Jeff Ikler/ © Huntley,Lightstream; **625,** Library of Congress; **626,** National Archives; **627,** Photri Inc.; **628 T,** Collection of Col. Stuart S. Corning, Jr., © Rob Huntley/Lightstream; **628 B,** Library of Congress; **629,** Ellen Kaiper Collection, Oakland; **631,** *Des Moines Register*

Chapter 19 634 L, Corbis; **634 R,** Hulton/Archive/Getty Images; **636,** U.S. Army; **637,** Harry S. Truman Presidential Library; **638,** Harry S. Truman Presidential Library; **640 T,** The Michael Barson Collection/Past Perfect; **640 B,** UPI/Bettman Archives/Corbis; **641,** Courtesy of the J.N. Ding Darling Foundation; **642,** © 1949 Time, Inc. Reprinted with permission; **644,** American Stock/Hulton/Archive/Getty Images; **645,** AP/Wide World Photos; **646,** Corbis; **647,** AP/Wide World Photos; **649,** GP Putnam's Sons; **650 B,** The Michael Barson Collection/Past Perfect, ©Rob Huntley/Lightstream; **650 T,** The Michael Barson Collection/Past Perfect, © Rob Huntley/Lightstream; **651,** Brown Brothers; **652,** Corbis; **653,** Eastfoto; **655,** Culver Pictures; **657,** *Herblock/Washington Post;* **658 T,** Corbis; **658 B,** The Granger Collection, NY; **660,** Corbis; **661,** © 1959 Newsweek Inc. All rights reserved. Reprinted by permission.; **663,** From *Herblock: A Cartoonist's Life* (Macmillan Publishing, 1993)

Chapter 20 666 L, Van Bucher/Photo Researchers, Inc.; **666 BR,** Harry S. Truman Presidential Library; **666 TR,** Russ Lappa; **667,** Michael Ochs Archive; **668,** Brown Brothers; **669 T,** The McDonald's Corporation; **669 B,** Mike Pattisall; **671 ML,** Russ Lappa; **671 B,** Hulton/Archive/Getty Images; **671 TL,** Russ Lappa; **671 TR,** Corbis Digital Stock; **672,** Dan Weiner, Courtesy Sandra Weiner; **673,** Van Bucher/Photo Researchers, Inc.; **674,** Barson Collection/Hulton/Archive/Getty Images; **675,** J.R. Eyreman/TimePix; **676,** Leo Chopin/Black Star; **677,** Hagley Museum and Library; **678 B,** Corbis; **678 T,** Corbis; **679 T,** Fred W. McDarrah; **679 B,** Courtesey of Ken Lopez-Bookseller; **680,** AP/Wide World Photos; **681 B,** AP/Wide World Photos; **681 T,** Harry S. Truman Library; **682 T,** David J. Frent; **682 B,** Corbis; **683,** Corbis; **684 T,** Division of Political History, Smithsonian Institution; **684 B,** AP/Wide World Photos; **685,** Dwight D. Eisenhower Library; **686,** Corbis; **689,** ©The *New Yorker* Collection, 1954, Robert J. Day from cartoonbank.com. All Rights Reserved.

Chapter 21 696 L, Grey Vieten *LIFE* Magazine © Time Warner; **696 R,** Don Uhrbrock *LIFE* Magazine © Time Warner; **697,** Co Rentmeester *LIFE* Magazine © Time Warner; **698,** The Michael Barson Collection/Past Perfect, © Rob Huntley/Lightstream; **699,** AP/Wide World Photos; **701,** Corbis, **702 B,** AP/Wide World Photos; **702 T,** Dept. of Commerce; **703,** Dr. Hector P. Garcia papers, Special Collections, Texas A&M University-Corpus Christi, Bell library; **704,** Library of Congress; **705,** David J. Frent; **706,** AP/Wide World Photos; **707,** Danny Lyon/Magnum Photos; **708,** Steve Schapiro/Black Star; **709,** Dial Juvenile Books,1968, a Divison of Penguin Books USA, Inc.; **710 L,** Danny Lyons/Magnum Photos; **710 R,** Rapho/Photo Researchers, Inc.; **711,** Corbis ; **713,** Corbis ; **714,** Charles Moore/Black Star; **716,** AP/Wide World Photos; **717,** Danny Lyon/Magnum Photos, Inc.; **718 T,** Bob Adelman/Magnum Photos, Inc.; **718–719 B,** Fred Ward/Black Star; **719 T,** Pullen Library at Georgia State University; **720,** AP/Wide World Photos; **721,** Bob Adelman/Magnum Photos, Inc.; **722,** Corbis ; **723,** Eve Arnold/Magnum Photos, Inc.; **724 B,** Corbis ; **724 T,** Russ Lappa; **726 T,** Joseph Louw *LIFE* Magazine © Time Warner; **726 B,** Bill Eppridge *LIFE* Magazine © Time Warner; **727,** Corbis; **729,** David Horsey/*The Seattle-Post Intelligencer*

Chapter 22 734 L, Hulton/Archive/Getty Images; **734 M,** John F. Kennedy Library; **734 R,** Magnum Photos, Inc.; **735,** Jacques Chenet/Woodfin Camp & Associates; **736,** John F. Kennedy Library; **737,** John F. Kennedy Library; **738,** Bettmann/Corbis; **739,** NASA; **740,** Black Star; **741,** by Dan Farrell/Daily News Pix; **743,** Corbis; **744 B,** Dennis Brack/Black Star; **744 T,** New York Times Pictures; **745 T,** Political Communication Center, The University of Oklahoma; **745 B,** Political Communication Center, The University of Oklahoma; **746,** Estate of Karl Hubenthal; **748 T,** National Archives; **748 B,** AP/Wide World Photos; **749,** Supreme Court Historical Society; **750,** Jacques Chenet/Woodfin Camp & Associates; **751,** AP/Wide World Photos; **752,** AP/Wide World Photos; **753,** Liaison/Getty Images; **754,** John F. Kennedy Library; **755,** New York Times Pictures; **757,** AP/Wide World Photos; **758 L,** Courtesy of The Peace Corps; **758 R,** Courtesy of The Peace Corps; 761, © 1962 Herblock in *The Washington Post*

Chapter 23 762 L, Picture Research Consultants, Inc.; **762 M,** Russ Lappa; **762 R,** Matt Heron/Take Stock; **764,** Radcliffe College Archives, Schlesinger Library; **765,** Al Freni/*LIFE* Magazine © Time Warner; **p 766,** Werner Wolff/Black Star; **768 T,** ©Bettye Lane; **768 M,** Courtesy Lang Communications; **768 B,** C. Gatewood/The Image Works; **769,** Corbis; **771 inset,** David J. Frent; **771,** Matt Heron/Take Stock; **772,** Craig Auerness/Woodfin Camp & Associates; **773,** Michael Nichols/Magnum Photos, Inc.; **774,** Japanese American National

Museum, Gift of K. Patrick and Liby A. Okura; **775,** Rick Smolan/Against All Odds; **776,** Dirck Halstead/*TIME* Magazine; **777 L,** H. Armstrong Roberts; **777 R,** Lambert/Hulton/Archive/Getty Images; **778 T,** Barry Burstein/Corbis; **778 B,** Prentice Hall; **779,** Barry Burstein/Corbis; **780,** Lisa Law/The Image Works; **781,** Alfred Eisenstaedt/*LIFE* Magazine© Time Warner; **782,** Jeff Lepore/Photo Researchers, Inc.; **783 inset,** David J.Frent; **783,** Ken Regan/Camera 5; **785,** Corbis; **787,** Mike Peters

Chapter 24 790 L, Black Star; **790 R,** Hulton/Archive/Getty Images; **791 L,** Stock Boston; **791 R,** David J. Frent; **792,** Russ Lappa; **793,** Bill Mauldin; **794 T,** AP/Wide World Photos; **794 B,** Dennis Brack/Black Star; **795,** Corbis; **796 B,** PhotoDisc, Inc.; **796 T,** PhotoEdit; **798–799,** Jim Pickerell/Black Star; **800,** Larry Burrows/Life; **801,** Corbis; **804,** Courtesy of the Lyndon B. Johnson Presidential Library; **805,** Stock Boston; **807 L,** AP/Wide World Photos; **807 R,** Russ Lappa; **808,** Goffynd/Archive/Getty Images; **809 T,** Philip Jones Griffiths/MP, Zenith Electronics Corporation; **809 B,** Bryson/Corbis Sygma; **810,** Corbis; **812,** Mark Godfrey/The Image Works; **814,** John Filo; **815 L,** Corbis; **815 R,** Thai Khad Chuon/Corbis; **817 B,** Richard Howard/TimePix; **817 T,** AP/Wide World Photos; **819,** From *Herblock on All Fronts* (New American Library, 1980)

Chapter 25 824 M, John T. Barr/Liason/Getty Images; **824 L,** NASA; **824 R,** AP/Wide World Photos; **825 L,** Russ Lappa; **825 R,** Hulton/Liaison/Getty Images; **826,** Rodney E. Mims/Corbis; **827,** Nixon Presidential Materials Project; **829 R,** AP/Wide World Photos; **829 L,** AP/Wide World Photos; **830,** AP/Wide World Photos; **831,** NASA; **832,** Steve Northup, ©Time Inc. *Time Magazine;* **833,** Corbis Sygma; **834 T,** John Dominis *LIFE* Magazine ©Time Warner; **834 B,** Nixon Presidential Materials Project; **835,** Hulton/Archive/Getty Images; **838,** Wayne Stayskal/Tribune Media Service; **839,** Margaret McCullough, Smithsonian Institution, courtesy of the National Archives & Records Administration; **840 B,** TimePix; **840 TL,** Dennis Brack/Black Star; **840 TR,** Richard Ellis/Corbis Sygma; **841 M,** Tony Auth. Reprinted by permission/Tribune Media Services; **841 T,** Mark Godfrey/The Image Works; **841 B,** AP/Wide World Photos; **842,** AP/Wide World Photos; **843,** Dennis Brack/Black Star; **844,** Roland Freeman/Magnum Photos; **845 B,** NASA; **845 T,** NASA Headquarters; **846,** Corbis; **847,** AP/Wide World Photos; **847 inset,** Copyright © 1974 by The New York Times Company; **848,** Russ Lappa; **849,** Gerald Ford Presidential Library; **850,** Joseph Pobereskin Photography; **851,** Jimmy Carter Presidential Library; **852,** Dennis Brack/Black Star; **855,** Jimmy Carter Presidential Library; **856,** Alain Mingam/Liasion/Getty Images; **857,** Peter Marlow/Magnum Photos; **857 inset,** David J.Frent; **859,** Cartoon by Robert Pryor. Courtesy of John Locke Studios, Inc.

Chapter 26 862 L, Corbis Sygma; **862 R,** CNP/Hulton/Archive/Getty Images; **863,** Abbas/Magnum Photos, Inc.; **864,** David J. Frent; **865 TL,** Wendell H. Ford Research Center, University of Kentucky; **865 ML,** Popperfoto/Hulton/Archive/Getty Images; **865 TR,** The Granger Collection, NY; **865 MR,** Sally Anderson Bruce; **865 inset,** Heritage House; **865 BL,** Planned Parenthood; **865 BR,** Russ Lappa; **866,** AP/Wide World Photos; **867 T,** Corbis; **867 B,** John Troha/Black Star; **868,** Les Schofer/Corbis Sygma; **870,** Corbis; **872,** Corbis; **874,** Corbis; **876,** Arthur Grace/Corbis Sygma; **877,** Steve Powell/AllSport; **878 T,** Diana Walker/*Time Magazine;* **878 B,** Zimberhoff/Corbis Sygma; **879,** Bruce Weaver/AP/Wide World Photos; **881,** AP/Wide World Photos; **882,** Atlan/Corbis Sygma; **884,** R. Bossu/Corbis Sygma; **885,** AP/Wide World Photos; **886,** Langevin/Corbis Sygma; **889,** Bob Englehard/*The Hartford Courant*

Chapter 27 892 L, Ira Wyman/Corbis Sygma; **892 R,** ©1993 Time Inc., Reprinted by permission; **893 BL,** Josh Barlow; **893 T,** Matrix.net; **893 BR,** AP Photo/Kenneth Lambert; **894,** John C. Sykes Jr.; **895 T,** Ira Wyman/Corbis Sygma; **895 B,** ©Rolling Stone Inc.; **895 inset,** Smithsonian Institution; **897,** John Harrington/ Black Star; **898,** Terry Ashe/Liaison/Getty images; **899 M,** Corbis Sygma; **899 B,** AP Photo/Wilfred Lee; **899 T,** AP Photo/LM Otero; **900,** Corbis Sygma; **901,** Thomas E. Franklin/*Bergen Record*/Corbis SABA; **903,** Peter Turnley/Corbis; **904,** Corbis; **905,** Les Stone/Corbis Sygma; **906,** AFP Photo; **907,** AFP/Corbis; **908,** AFP/Corbis; **910,** AP/Wide World Photos; **911,** JB Pictures Ltd.; **913,** Kim Kulise/Corbis SABA; **914,** Bob Thomas/Stone; **915,** Corbis Sygma; **916,** Photofest; **917,** Stone; **919,** Mike Smith/Reprinted by permission of United Features Syndicate

American Heritage 102, Francis G. Mayer/Corbis; **103,** Visions of America; **344,** Kansas State Historical Society; **345,** Hulton/Archive/Getty Images; **444,** Hulton/Liaison Agency/Getty Images; **445 T,** Hulton/Liaison Agency/Getty Images; **445 B,** Corbis; **532,** AP/Wide World Photos; **533,** National Baseball Hall of Fame and Museum; **632 B,** U.S. Naval Historical Foundation; **632 T,** U.S. Naval Historical Foundation; **633,** Hulton/Archive/Getty Images; **730 B,** Corbis; **730 T,** Library of Congress; **731,** Corbis; **860 T,** AP/Wide World Photos; **860 B,** Corbis; 861, Prentice Hall

American Pathways 148 BR, Library of Congress; **148 L,** New Holland Machine Company; **148 TR,** Shelburne Museum; **149,** Terry Donnelly/Stone; **196 T,** The Granger Collection, NY; **196 M,** The Granger Collection, NY; **196 B,** Archives of Atlanta Historical Society; **197 L,** AP/Wide World Photos; **197 R,** Brown Brothers; **410 T,** Emanuel Gottlieb Leutze, The Metropolitan Museum of Art, Gift of John S. Kennedy, 1897. (97.34); **410 B,** Greg E. Mathieson/MAI Photo News Agency, Inc.; **411 R,** Hulton/Liaison/Getty Images; **411 BL,** Thomas E. Franklin/*Bergen Record*/Corbis SABA; **411 TL,** Corbis; **476 T,** Yale University Art Gallery, Mabel Brady Garven Collection; **476 MR,** Library of Congress; **476 ML,** The Granger Collection, NY; **476 B,** The Kobal Collection; **477 ML,** Hulton/Archive/Getty Images; **477 T,** Time Life Books; **477 B,** Hulton/Archive/Getty Images; **477 MR,** Corbis; **664 TL,** American Textile History Museum; **664 BL,** The Granger Collection, NY; **664 R,** AT&T Archives; **665 T,** Library of Congress; **665 B,** Jewish Hospital/University of Louisville; **665 M,** Intel Corporation Museum Archives & Collection; **732 B,** Hulton/Liaison/Getty images; **732 T,** The Granger Collection, NY; **732 M,** The Granger Collection, NY; **733 B,** Bob Daemmrich Photography, Inc.; **733 T,** Bob Adelman/Magnum Photos; **920 TR,** Prentice Hall; **920 L (all),** Courtesy of the Federal Reserve Bank of San Francisco; **920 BR,** Ford Motor Company; **921 T,** FPG International; **921 B,** AP/Wide World Photos; **921 M,** Picture Research Consultants

Skills for Life 490, Saturday Evening Post, June 30, 1928, Curtis Archives; **326,** John McCutcheon; **580,** AP/Wide World Photos; **845 B,** NASA; **845 T,** NASA Headquarters

Geography & History 36 L, Skyscan; **36 R,** Pilgrim Hall Museum; **37 B,** Curtis B. Johnson; **37 T,** Corbis; **37 inset,** American Antiquarian Society; **286–287 M,** Russ Lappa; **286–287 B,** Brown Brothers; **287 T,** Corbis; **287 MR,** Corbis; **287 B,** Kansas State Historical Society; **378 T,** Corbis; **378–379 B,** LHSIM/Stone; **379 B,** The Metropolitan Museum of Art; **379 M,** Archive Photos; **379 T,** Corbis; **504,** Brown Brothers; **505 BL,** Walts Postcards; **505 M,** Corbis; **505 TR,** Library of Congress; **505 TL,** Harold Kramer, mapsofpa.com; **505 TL,** Harold Kramer, mapsofpa.com; **505 TL,** Harold Kramer, mapsofpa.com; **505 BR,** Walts Postcards; **690 M,** Josef Scaylea/Corbis; **690 T,** SuperStock; **690 B,** Donovan Marks Photography; **691 B,** Robert Brenner/PhotoEdit; **691 T,** Michael Dwyer/Stock Boston; **788 T,** Ken Regan/Camera 5; **788 B,** Mark Richards/PhotoEdit; **788 M,** NASA/Science Photo Library/Photo Researchers, Inc.; **789 B,** Isaac Hernandez/Mercury Press International; **789 T,** Tom Bean; **789 M,** Tom Brownold; **890 T,** Frank Frisk/GreatLakes photos.com; **890 B,** Spencer Grant/PhotoEdit; **891 BL,** Corbis; **891 BR,** PhotoDisc, Inc; **891 T,** Rancho Santa Margarita

American Literature 924, Library of Congress; **926,** Corbis; **927,** Nichipor Collection, Courtesy of Minuteman National Historic Park. Rob Huntley/Lightstream; **928,** Courtesy, American Antiquarian Society; **929,** The Granger Collection, NY; **930,** The Granger Collection, NY; **931,** The Granger Collection, NY; **932,** Library of Congress; **934,** Corbis; **937,** Margaret Bourke-White, *LIFE* Magazine; **938,** US Holocaust Memorial Museum; **940,** Don Uhrbrock *LIFE* Magazine © Time Warner; **941,** Corbis Bettman; **942,** AP/Wide World Photos

American Documents 945, Peabody & Essex Museum. Photo by Mark Sexton; **946,** The Pilgrim Society; **948 R,** Hulton/Liaison/Getty Images; **948 T,** Hulton/Liaison/Getty Images; **950,** United Nations; **951 R,** United Nations; **951 L,** Impact Visuals Photo & Graphics, Inc.; **952,** White House Historical Association; **954,** AP/Wide World Photos

Illustrated Databank 965–967 (Presidents), 1, 2, 4, 5, 6, 9, 10, 12, 13, 14, 15, 16, 18, 20, 21, 25, 26, 27, 35, Art Resource; 3, 7, 8, 11, 17, 19, 22, 23, 24, 28, 29, 30, 31, 32, 33, 34, 36, 37, 38, 39, 40, 41, 42, White House Historical Association; 43, Corbis Sygma; **967** (seal), White House

Biographical Dictionary 1008, American Antiquarian Society; **1009,** Library of Congress; **1010,** Library of Congress; **1011,** White House Historical Association/Photo by National Geographic Society; **1012,** Library of Congress; **1013,** Corbis; **1014,** Theodore Roosevelt Collection Harvard College Library; **1015,** Brown Brothers

PRIMARY SOURCES BIBLIOGRAPHY

Chapter 1 John Smith: Lankford, John, ed. *Captain John Smith's America: Selections from His Writings.* Harper Torchbooks, Harper and Row, 1967, p. 105; **Mayflower Compact:** Caffrey, Kate. *The Mayflower.* Stein and Day, 1974, p. 340; **Miantonomo:** Cronon, William. *Changes in the Land: Indians, Colonists, and the Ecology of New England.* Hill and Wang, 1983, p. 162; **Olaudah Equiano:** Edwards, Paul, ed. *Equiano's Travels.* Heinemann Educational Books, 1967, p. 32; **Jonathan Edwards:** Kupperman, Karen Ordahl, ed. *Major Problems in American Colonial History: Documents and Essays.* D.C. Heath, 1993, p. 369.

Chapter 2 Henry Wadsworth Longfellow: "Paul Revere's Ride," www.paulreverehouse.org; **Declaration and Resolves of the First Continental Congress:** Commager, Henry Steele, ed. *Documents of American History,* Eighth Edition, Appleton-Century-Crofts, 1968, p. 83; **Patrick Henry:** Commager, Henry Steele, and Richard B. Morris, eds. *The Spirit of 'Seventy-Six: The Story of the American Revolution as Told by Participants.* New York: Bonanza Books, 1983, pp. 108-109; **Thomas Paine, Common Sense:** Curti, Merle, et al., eds. *American Issues: The Social Record,* 4th ed. rev. New York: J.B. Lippincott, 1971, vol. 1, pp. 82, 84; **George Washington:** Commager, Henry Steele, ed. *Documents of American History,* Eighth Edition, Appleton-Century-Crofts, 1968, p. 169; **Thomas Jefferson's First Inaugural Address:** Ravitch, Diane, ed. *The Democracy Reader.* HarperPerennial, 1992, p. 140; **Francis Scott Key:** "The Star-Spangled Banner." www.bcpl.net.

Chapter 3 Morris Birkbeck: Birkbeck, Morris. "Notes on a Journey in America from the Coasts of Virginia to the Territory of Illinois." Philadelphia, 1817, p. 34; **Noah Webster:** Wood, Gordon S. *The Rising Glory of America, 1760–1820.* Northeastern University Press, 1990, p. 169; **The Monroe Doctrine:** Commager, Henry Steele, ed. *Documents of American History, Eighth Edition.* Appleton-Century-Crofts, 1968, pp. 236–237; **Germantown Mennonites:** Commager, p. 37; **Henry David Thoreau:** Walden. Princeton University Press, 1971, p. 326; **William Lloyd Garrison:** Wilentz, Sean, ed. *Major Problems in the Early Republic, 1787–1848.* D. C. Heath, 1992, p. 477; **Elizabeth Cady Stanton:** Stanton, Elizabeth Cady, et al. *History of Woman Suffrage, Vol. 1.* Fowler and Wells, 1889, pp. 58–59; **Sojourner Truth:** Anti-Slavery Bugle, Salem, Ohio, June 21, 1851, 4: p. 81–82; **Lincoln's First Inaugural Address:** Ravitch, Diane, ed. *The Democracy Reader.* HarperPerennial, 1992, p. 165; **Abraham Lincoln:** *Selected Speeches and Writings.* The Library of America, 1992, p. 131; **John Brown:** Oates, Stephen B. *To Purge This Land with Blood: A Biography of John Brown.* Harper Torchbooks, 1970, p. 351; **Augusta, Georgia, newspaper editor:** Holt, Michael F. *The Political Crisis of the 1850's.* John Wiley and Sons, 1978, p. 241.

Chapter 4 Sallie Hunt: B. A. Botkin, ed. *A Civil War Treasury of Tales, Legends and Folklore.* Random House, 1960, p. 21; **Abraham Lincoln:** Ward, Geoffrey C. *The Civil War: An Illustrated History.* Alfred A. Knopf, 1990, p. 110; **Elisha Stockwell:** Murphy, Jim. *The Boys' War.* Clarion Books, 1990, p. 33; **Louis Wigfall:** McPherson, James M. *Battle Cry of Freedom.* Oxford University Press, 1998, p. 430; **Abraham Lincoln:** McPherson, p. 510; **Emancipation Proclamation:** Boorstin, Daniel, ed. *An American Primer.* University of Chicago Press, 1968, p. 431; **Lewis Douglass:** Chang, Ina. *A Separate Battle: Women and the Civil War.* Lodestar Books, 1991, p. 65; **Frederick Douglass:** *Douglass' Monthly,* August, 1863; **Cornelia Hancock:** *South After Gettysburg.* University of Nebraska Press, 1998; **Civil War drummer boy:** Murphy, p. 43; **soldier at Gettysburg:** E. B. Long. *The Civil War Day by Day.* Da Capo Press, 1971, p. 377; **Mary Ann Loughborough:** Gragg, Rod, *The Illustrated Confederate Reader.* Harper and Row, 1989, p.82; **Abraham Lincoln:** *Selected Speeches and Writings.* First Vintage Books, Library of America, p. 450; **R.B. Prescott:** Meltzer, Milton, ed. *Voices from the Civil War.* Thomas Y. Crowell, 1989, pp. 179–181; **Henrietta Lee:** Gragg, p. 88; **Abraham Lincoln:** Lincoln, p. 450.

Chapter 5 Val C. Giles: Lasswell, Mary, and ed., *Rags and Hope: The Memoirs of Val C. Giles,* New York: Coward-McCann, 1961. **Abraham Lincoln:** *Selected Speeches and Writings.* First Vintage Books, Library of America, p. 450; **Charlotte Forten:** "Life on the Sea Islands," *Atlantic Monthly,* Vol. 13 (May and June) 1864, pp. 588–589, 591–594, 666–667; **Black Union Soldier:** Litwack, Leon F. *Been in the Storm So Long, The Aftermath of Slavery.* Vintage Books, 1979, Chapter 7.

Chapter 6 Samuel F.B. Morse: Morse, Edward Lind, ed., *Samuel F.B. Morse, His Letters and Journals,* 2 vols., Houghton Mifflin, 1914, quoted in Ambrose, Stephen and Douglas Brinkley. *Witness to America: An Illustrated Documentary History of the United States from the Revolution to Today.* Harper Collins, 1999, p. 96; **Abram Stevens Hewitt:** *Address Delivered on the Occasion of the Opening of the New York and Brooklyn Bridge, May 24th, 1883,* John Polemus, 1883, quoted in Graebner, William, and Leonard Richards, eds., *The American Record: Images of the Nation's Past,* Vol. 2, Alfred Knopf, 1982, p. 50; **Andrew Carnegie:** "How I Served My Apprenticeship." *Youth's Companion,* April 23, 1896, quoted in Ambrose, pp. 301–305; **Andrew Carnegie:** *The Empire of Business.* Doubleday, 1902, pp. 138–140, quoted in Kirkland, Edward Chase. *Dream and Thought in the Business Community, 1860–1900.* Cornell, 1956, pp. 156–157; **Sadie Frowne:** "The Story of a Sweatshop Girl," *The Independent* 54, September 25, 1902, pp. 2279–2282, quoted in Bailey, Thomas A., and David M. Kennedy. *The American Spirit: United States History as Seen by Contemporaries,* Vol. 2, 8TH ed. D.C. Heath and Company, 1994, pp. 80–85; **Frederick Winslow Taylor:** *The*

Acknowledgments

1046

Principles of Scientific Management. W.W. Norton and Company, 1911, p. 39; **Samuel Gompers:** Letter from *American Federationist,* Vol. 1, September 1894, pp. 150–152, quoted in Hofstadter, Richard, ed., *Great Issues in American History From Reconstruction to the Present Day, 1864–1969,* Vintage Books, 1969, pp. 187–191; **Eugene V. Debs:** *Declaration of Principles, American Railway Union,* 1893, quoted in Salvatore, Nick. *Eugene V. Debs: Citizen and Socialist.* University of Illinois Press, 1982, p. 116; **August Spies:** Kogan, B. R. "The Chicago Haymarket Riot," 1959 (a reproduction of the circular in the Chicago Historical Society collection).

Chapter 7 Mary Clark: Nelson, Paula M. *After the West Was Won: Homesteaders and Town-Builders in Western South Dakota, 1900–1917.* University of Iowa Press, 1986, quoted in Jones, Mary Ellen. *Daily Life on the 19th-Century Frontier.* The Greenwood Press, 1998, p. 187; **death song sung by a Cherokee:** Thomas, David hurst, et al. *The Native Americans: An Illustrated History.* Turner Publishing, 1993, p. 332; **newspaper reporter:** Fite, Gilbert. *The Farmer's Frontier, 1865–1900.* University of New Mexico Press, 1974, p. 205; **diary of a Union Pacific engineer:** Ward, Geoffrey C. *The West: An Illustrated History.* Little, Brown and Company (The West Book Project), 1996, p. 222; **cowboy Charles A. Siringo:** Jones, Mary Ellen. *Daily Life on the 19th-Century Frontier.* The Greenwood Press, 1998, p. 167; **"The Old Chisholm Trail"**: Forbis, William H. *The Old West: The Cowboys.* Time-Life Books, 1973, p. 154; **"Commercial and Financial Chronicle," September 21, 1879:** quoted in Fite, p. 82; **Washington Gladden:** *The Annals of America. Vol. 11, 1884–1894: Agrarianism and Urbanization.* Encyclopedia Britannica, 1968, p. 356.

Chapter 8 Peter Mossini: Coan, Peter M. *Ellis Island Interviews: In Their Own Words.* Facts on File, 1997, p. 45; **Fiorello LaGuardia:** *The Making of an Insurgent.* J. B. Lippincott Co., 1948, pp. 64–65; **Emily Dinwiddie:** "Some Aspects of Italian Housing and Social Conditions in Philadelphia," Charities and the Commons, Vol. 12, 1904, p. 490; **Pedro Martínez:** Hoobler, Dorothy and Thomas Hoobler. *The Mexican American Family Album.* Oxford University Press, 1994, p. 34; **Council of Hygiene and Public Health:** Dolkart, Andrew S. and Ruth Limmer. "The Tenement As History And Housing." Lower East Side Tenement Museum, New York; **Ellen Swallow Richards:** *Conservation by Sanitation; Air and Water Supply; Disposal of Waste.* Wiley, 1911; **Jacob Riis:** *How the Other Half Lives.* Penguin, 1997, p. 6; **Frances Willard:** *Glimpses of Fifty Years: The Autobiography of an American Woman.* H.J. Smith & Co., 1889, pp. 339-341.

Chapter 9 Mary Antin: Levinson, Nancy Smiler. *Turn of the Century: Our Nation One Hundred Years Ago.* Lodestar Books, 1994, pp. 54-55. **Tony Longo:** Loeper, John J. *Going to School in 1876.* Atheneum, 1984, pp. 64-65; **Pauli Murray:** *Proud Shoes.* Harper and Row, 1956, pp. 269–270; **Booker T. Washington:** *Address of Booker T. Washington, principal of the Tuskegee Normal and Industrial Institute, Tuskegee, Alabama, delivered at the opening of the Cotton States and International Exposition, at Atlanta, Ga., September 18, 1895.* Daniel A. P. Murray Pamphlet Collection, Library of Congress, 1894, pp. 7–9; **W.E.B. Du Bois:** Du Bois, W.E.B. *The Negro Problem: A Series of Articles by Representative American Negroes of Today.* J. Pott and Company, 1903, pp. 33-75; **Jack Norworth:** "Take Me Out to the Ball Game." Words by Jack Norworth, music by Albert Von Tilzer. www.geocities.com; **Albon Holsey:** Litwack, Leon F. *Trouble in Mind; Black Southerners in the Age of Jim Crow.* Alfred A. Knopf, 1998; p. 16; **Frederick Howe:** Levinson, p. 95.

Chapter 10 Henry Cabot Lodge: "Our Blundering Foreign Policy," *The Forum,* Vol. 19, March 1895, pp. 14–17, quoted in Hofstadter, Richard, ed., *Great Issues in American History From Reconstruction to the Present Day, 1864–1969,* Vintage Books, 1969, pp. 187–191; **New York Journal Headline:** *New York Journal,* October 10, 1897, quoted in Bailey, Thomas A. and David M. Kennedy. *The American Spirit: United States History as Seen by Contemporaries,* Vol. 2, 8TH ed. D.C. Heath and Company, 1994, pp. 171–172; **William McKinley:** Interview at the White House, November 21, 1899, *Christian Advocate,* January 22, 1903, quoted in Olcott, C.S. *The Life of William McKinley,* Vol. 2, 1916, pp. 110–111, quoted in Bailey, pp. 179–180; **John Hay:** Telegram to U.S. minister in Bogotá. *Foreign Relations of the United States, 1903.* Washington D.C.: Government Printing Office, 1904, p. 146, quoted in Bailey, pp. 190–191; **Theodore Roosevelt:** Hart, Albert Bushnell, and Herbert Ronald Ferleger, eds. *Theodore Roosevelt Cyclopedia.* Roosevelt Memorial Association, 1941, p. 407; **Theodore Roosevelt's Corollary to the Monroe Doctrine:** "Roosevelt's Annual Message, December 5, 1905," quoted in Commager, Henry Steele, ed. *Documents of American History,* vol. 2, Eighth Edition. Appleton-Century Crofts, 1968, p. 34; **Theodore Roosevelt:** Letter to Henry Cabot Lodge, from Morison, Elting E., ed. *The Letters of Theodore Roosevelt,* Vol. 2, Harvard University Press, 1951, quoted in Bailey, pp. 197–198; **Carl Schurz Platform of the Anti-Imperialist League:** "The Policy of Imperialism," Liberty Tracts No. 4, Address by Carl Schurz to Anti-Imperialist Conference in Chicago, October 17, 1899, quoted in Hofstadter, pp. 202–204; **Carl Schurz:** Ibid.; **Bishop Alexander Walters:** "Wisconsin Weekly Advocate," August 17, 1899, quoted in Gatewood, Willard B., Jr. *Black Americans and the White Man's Burden,* 1898–1903. University of Illinois Press, 1975, p. 200; **Walter Hines Page:** "The War With Spain And After," *Atlantic Monthly,* Vol. 81, June 1898, pp. 725–727, quoted in Hofstadter, p. 201.

Chapter 11 Upton Sinclair: *The Jungle.* Doubleday, 1906, pp. 96–97; **Edward Bellamy:** Bellamy, Edward. *Looking Backward.* River City Press, 1888, p. 56; **Jane Addams:** Addams, Jane. "Why Women Should Vote." Ladies Home Journal, Vol. XXVII, January 1910, pp. 21–22; **Rose Schneiderman:** Mitelman, Bonnie. "Rose Schneiderman and the Triangle Shirtwaist Fire." American History Illustrated, July 1981; **Robert M. La Follette:** La Follette, Robert M. *A Personal Narrative of Political Experiences,* 1913, published online at the Library of Congress's American Memory Web site www.lcweb2.loc.gov; **Woodrow Wilson campaign speech:** Wilson, Woodrow. *The New Freedom: A Call for the Emancipation of the Generous Energies of a People.* Double Day, Page and Company, 1913, pp. 163-191, published online at www.1912.history.ohio-state.edu; **Lyman Abbott:** Abbott, Lyman. "Why Women DO Not Wish the Suffrage." The Atlantic Monthly, September 1903, published online at www.theatlantic.com; **Susan B. Anthony:** Sherr, Lynn. *Failure Is Impossible: Susan B. Anthony in Her Own Words.* Times Books, 1995, pp. 110–112.

Chapter 12 Borijove Jevtic: Carey, John. *Eyewitness to History.* Faber and Faber, 1987, p. 443; *The New York Times:* "He Kept Us Out of War." October 21, 1916; **Arthur Zimmermann:** Leckie, Robert. *The Wars of America.* Harper and Row, 1968, p. 628; **Woodrow Wilson:** Cooper, John Milton, Jr. Pivotal Decades: The United States, 1900–1920. W. W. Norton and Company, 1990, p. 265; **Anonymous:** Grist, N R. "A Letter from Camp Devens 1918," *British Medical Journal,* December 22-29, 1979; **Corporal Elmer Sherwood:** Berger, Dorothy and Josef, eds. *Diary of America.* Simon and Schuster, 1957, p. 536; **Henry Ford:** Conot, Robert. *American Odyssey.* William Morrow and Co., 1974, p. 181; Herbert Hoover: "Gospel of the Clean Plate." *Ladies Home Journal,* August 1917, p. 25; **Woodrow Wilson:** Commager, Henry Steele, ed. *Documents of American History,* vol. II, Eighth Edition. Appleton-Century-Crofts, 1968, p. 138; **Alice Lord O'Brian:** *No Glory: Letters from France, 1917–1919.* Airport Publishers, 1936, pp. 8, 141, 152–153.

Chapter 13 Preston Slosson: *The Great Crusade and After, 1914–1928.* Macmillan, 1930, p. 157; **George Gershwin:** Colbert, David, ed. *Eyewitness to America.* Pantheon, 1997, p. 347; **Sinclair Lewis:** *Main Street.* Harcourt, Brace and Company, 1920, p. 265; **Edna St. Vincent Millay:** Allison, Alexander W., et al., eds. *The Norton Anthology of Poetry,* Third Edition. W. W. Norton & Company, 1983, p. 1032; **Langston Hughes:** *I, Too* from SELECTED POEMS OF LANGSTON HUGHES by Langston Hughes. Copyright © 1926 Alfred A. Knopf, Inc. Renewed 1954 Estate of Langston Hughes. Reprinted by permission of Alfred A. Knopf, Inc. **Alice Longworth:** *Crowded Hours: Reminiscences of Alice Roosevelt Longworth.* Charles Scribner's Sons, 1933, p. 324; **Paul Morand:** Colbert, p. 364; **Klansman's Manual:** Marcus, Robert D., and David Burner. *America Firsthand,* Vol. II. St. Martin's Press, 1989, p. 238.

Chapter 14 Warren G. Harding, Boston, May 14, 1920: Schortemeier, Frederick E. *Rededicating America: Life and Recent Speeches of Warren G. Harding.* Bobbs-Merrill, 1920, p. 223; **Warren G. Harding, October 26, 1929:** Russell, Francis. *President Harding: His Life and Times, 1865–1923.* Eyre & Spottiswoode, 1969, pp. 471–472. **Earnest Elmo Calkins:** *Business the Civilizer.* Little, Brown, and Company, 1928, quoted in Marcus, Robert D. and David Burner. *America Firsthand,* Vol. II. St. Martin's Press, 1989, p. 225; **Herbert Hoover, New York City, October 1928:** Birley, Robert, ed. *Speeches and Documents in American History,* Vol. IV. Oxford University Press, p. 89, first published in *The World's Classics,* 1942.

Chapter 15 Gordon Thomas and Max Morgan-Witts: *The Day the Bubble Burst.* Doubleday & Company, 1979, quoted in Cary, John H. and Julius Weinberg, eds. *The Social Fabric: American Life from the Civil War to the Present.* 4th ed. Little, Brown and Company, 1984, p. 299; **Ann Rivington:** "We Live on Relief." *Scribner's Magazine 95,* April 1934, pp. 282–285, quoted in Kutler, Stanley I. *Looking for America: The People's History.* 2nd ed., Vol. 2. W.W. Norton and Company, 1979, pp. 360–361; **Robert Conot:** *American Odyssey.* William Morrow and Company, 1974, p. 283; **Gordon Parks:** *Voices in the Mirror: An Autobiography.* Doubleday, 1990; **Wilson Ledford:** "How I Lived During the Depression." Interview taped and transcribed by Reuben Hiatt, November 7, 1982, quoted in Snell, William R. ed. *Hard Times Remembered: Bradley County and the Great Depression.* Bradley County Historical Society, 1983, pp. 117–121; **Gerald W. Johnson:** "The Average American and the Depression." *Current History,* February 1932; **Kitty McCulloch:** Terkel, Studs. *Hard Times: An Oral History of the Great Depression.* Pantheon Books, 1970; **Harry Haugland:** "The Right to Live." Unpublished, quoted in Kutler, pp. 373–374; **Clarence Lee:** Quoted in *Riding the Rails.* Dirs. Michael Uys and Lexy Lovell, WGBH Educational Foundation, 1998, Transcript; **William Saroyan:** *Inhale and Exhale.* Random House, 1936, p. 81; **"Brother Can You Spare a Dime?":** *Brother, Can You Spare A Dime?* Words by E.Y. Harburg, Music by Jay Gorney. Copyright © 1932 (Renewed) Glocca Morra Music Corp. and Gorney Music Publishing c/o Next Decade Music (ASCAP); **"Happy Days Are Here Again":** *Happy Days Are Here Again* by Milton Ager & Jack Yellin. Copyright © 1929 (Renewed) EMI Robbins Catalog, Inc. c/o EMI Music Publishing, Inc. (ASCAP); **Herbert Hoover:** Myers, William S., ed. *The State Papers and Other Public Writings of Herbert Hoover.* Doubleday, Doran and Company, Inc., Vol. II, 1934, pp. 408–413; **Franklin D. Roosevelt:** *The New York Times,* September 24, 1932; **Roosevelt's First Inaugural Address:** Commager, Henry Steele, ed. *Documents of American History,* vol. 2, Eighth Edition. Appleton-Century-Crofts, 1968, p. 240.

Chapter 16 Harry Hopkins: Dawley, Alan. *Struggles for Justice: Social Responsibility and the Liberal State.* Harvard University Press, 1991, p. 367; testimony by George Dobbin: Federal Writers' Project. *These Are Our Lives.* University of North Carolina Press, 1939; **Roosevelt administration official:** Markowitz, Gerald, and David Rosner, eds. "Slaves of the Depression." Workers' Letters About Life on the Job. Cornell, 1987, p. 154; **Sam T. Mayhew:** Terrill, Tom E., and Jerrold Hirsch, eds. *Such As Us: Southern Voices of the Thirties.* University of North Carolina Press, 1978; **Franklin Roosevelt:** White, Walter. *A Man Called White: The Autobiography of Walter White.* Viking Press, 1948, pp. 179–180; **James Agee:** Agee, James, and Walker Evans. *Let Us Now Praise Famous Men.* Boston: Houghton Mifflin Company, 1941, pp. 118–120; **Walter Reuther:** Madison, Charles A. *American Labor Leaders, Personalities and Forces in the Labor Movement.* Ungar, 1950, p. 382.

Chapter 17 The Party Rally of Honor: *Der Parteitag der Ehre vom 8. bis 14. September 1936.* Zentralverlag der NSDAP, 1936, pp. 170-177; **Nazi Poster:** Hitler, Adolf. *Mein Kampf.* Reynal & Hitchcock, 1940, p. 527; **Alfred Duff Cooper:** Churchill, Winston. *The Gathering Storm.* Vol. 1 of *The Second World War.* Houghton Mifflin, 1948, pp. 291-292. **Winston Churchill:** Baldwin, Hanson W. *The Crucial Years: 1939–1941.* Harper and Row, 1976, p. 127; **Hirota Koki:** Brendon, Piers. *The Dark Valley.* Alfred A. Knopf, 2000, p. 455; **Franklin D. Roosevelt:** Davis, Kenneth S. FDR: *The New Deal Years, 1933–1937.* Random House, 1986, p. 640; **Franklin D. Roosevelt:** Commager, Henry Steele, ed. *Documents of American History,* vol. II, Eighth Edition. Appleton-Century-Crofts, 1968, p. 452.

Chapter 18 Franklin D. Roosevelt: Rosenman, Samuel I., comp. *The Public Papers and Addresses of Franklin D. Roosevelt, 1940 Volume: War—And Aid to Democracies.* MacMillan, 1941, p. 643; **Franklin D. Roosevelt:** Commager, Henry Steele, ed. *Documents of American History,* vol. II, Eighth Edition. Appleton-Century-Crofts, 1968, p. 449; **Franklin D. Roosevelt and Winston S. Churchill:** Curti, Merle, Isidore Starr, and Lewis Paul Todd, eds. *Living American Documents.* Harcourt, 1961, p. 304; **German infantryman:** Carey, John, ed. *Eyewitness to History.* Harvard University Press, 1987, p. 576; **Lieutenant Robert Edlin:** Colbert, Robert, ed. *Eyewitness to America.* Pantheon, 1997, p. 420; **Adolf Hitler:** *Mein Kampf.* Reynal & Hitchcock, 1940, p. 826; **Leon Bass:** *Holocaust and Human Behavior.* Facing History and Ourselves National Foundation, p. 414; **Hiroshima survivor:** Cook, Haruko Taya, and Theodore Cook. *Japan at War: An Oral History.* The New Press, 1992, p. 397; **A. Philip Randolph:** Anderson, Jervis. *A. Philip Randolph.* Harcourt, 1973, p. 249; **Lloyd Brown:** Blum, John Morton. *V Was for Victory: Politics and American Culture During World War II.* Harcourt Brace Jovanovich, 1976, p. 191; **Henry Murakami:** Harris, Mark Jonathan, et al. *The Homefront: America During World War II.* G. P. Putnam's Sons, 1984, p. 113.

Chapter 19 Winston Churchill: *The Annals of America,* vol. 16, 1940–1949: *The Second World War and After.* Encyclopedia Britannica, 1968, p. 367; **Harry Truman:** Commager, Henry Steele, ed. *Documents of American History,* vol. II, Eighth Edition. Appleton-Century-Crofts, 1968, p. 525; **Harry Truman:** "Race for the Superbomb," *The American Experience.* www.pbs.org; **George C. Marshall:** Commager, Henry Steele, ed. *Documents of American History,* vol. II, Eighth Edition. Appleton-Century-Crofts, 1968, p. 532; **Arnold Winter:** Tomedi, Rudy. *No Bugles, No Drums: An Oral History of the Korean War.* John Wiley and Sons, 1993, p. 26; **Tom Clawson:** Tomedi, pp. 147-148; **Douglas MacArthur:** Phillips, Cabell. *The Truman Presidency: The History of a Triumphant Succession.* The Macmillan Company, 1966, p. 348; **Edward R. Murrow:** *See It Now* broadcast, March 29, 1954, published online at www.indiana.edu; **Margaret Chase Smith:** "Declaration of Conscience," Margaret Chase Smith Library, published online at www.mcslibrary.org; **Dwight D. Eisenhower:** Commager, Henry Steele, ed. *Documents of American History,* vol. II, Eighth Edition. Appleton-Century-Crofts, 1968, p. 667.

1047

Chapter 20 Harry Henderson: "The Mass-Produced Suburbs, Part I: How People Live in America's Newest Towns," *Harper's Magazine,* November 1953, Vol. 207, No. 1242, p. 26; **Malvina Reynolds:** *Little Boxes* by Malvina Reynolds. Copyright © 1962 (Renewed) Schroder Music Company (ASCAP); **Geoffrey Perrett:** *A Dream of Greatness: The American People, 1945–1963.* Coward, McCann & Geoghegan, 1979, p. 307; **Betty Friedan:** *The Feminine Mystique.* W.W. Norton & Company, 1963; **Allen Ginsberg:** *Howl* from HOWL & OTHER POEMS by Allen Ginsberg. Copyright © 1956, 1959 by Allen Ginsberg. Reprinted by permission of City Lights Books; **Richard Nixon:** Wicker, Tom. *One of Us: Richard Nixon and the American Dream.* Random House, 1991, p. 98; **Dwight Eisenhower:** Holbo, Paul S., and Robert W. Sellen, eds. *The Eisenhower Era.* Dryden Press, 1974, p. 113.

Chapter 21 Chief Justice Warren: Opinion of the Court in *Brown v. Board of Education of Topeka,* quoted in Commager, Henry Steele, ed. *Documents of American History,* vol. 2, Eighth Edition. Appleton-Century-Crofts, 1968, pp. 607–608; **84th Congress's Southern Manifesto:** from *Congressional Record,* 84th Congress, 2nd session, March 12, 1956, pp. 4515–4516, quoted in Bailey, Thomas A., and David M. Kennedy. *The American Spirit: United States History as Seen by Contemporaries,* Vol. 2, 8th ed. D.C. Heath and Company, 1994, pp. 463–464; **Martin Luther King, Jr.:** Sitkoff, Harvard. *The Struggle for Black Equality: 1954–1980.* Hill and Wang, 1981, p. 50; **Martin Luther King, Jr.:** *Stride Toward Freedom: The Montgomery Story.* Harper and Row, 1958, pp. 53–55; **Elizabeth Eckford:** Bates, Daisy. *The Long Shadow of Little Rock.* David McKay, 1962, quoted in Raskin, Jamin B. *We the Students: Supreme Court Decisions for and about Students.* Congressional Quarterly Press, 2000, p. 178; **Dwight D. Eisenhower:** Address of September 24, 1957, from *Vital Speeches,* vol. 24, October 15, 1957, pp. 11–12, quoted in Bailey, pp. 465–466; **John Lewis:** Morrison, Joan, and Robert K. Morrison. *From Camelot to Kent State: The Sixties Experience in the Words of Those Who Lived It.* Times Books, 1987, pp. 25–26; **W.E.B. DuBois:** Aptheker, Herbert, ed. *Pamphlets and Leaflets* by W.E.B. DuBois. Kraus-Thomason Organization Limited, 1986, p. 116; **Southern Christian Leadership Conference:** Sitkoff, p. 65; **SCLC leaflet:** Sitkoff, p. 59; **Todd Gitlin:** *The Sixties: Years of Hope, Days of Rage.* Bantam Books, 1987, pp. 148–149; **John Lewis:** Hampton, Henry, et al. *Voices of Freedom: An Oral History of the Civil Rights Movement from the 1950's Through the 1980's.* Bantam Books, 1990, p. 58; **James Farmer:** Hampton, p. 78; **James Meredith:** "I'll Know Victory or Defeat," *The Saturday Evening Post,* November 10, 1962, p. 17, quoted in Katz, William Loren. *Eyewitness: The Negro in American History,* 3rd ed. David S. Lake Publishers, 1974, pp. 496–497; **Martin Luther King, Jr.:** "Letter From Birmingham Jail." *Essay Series.* A. J. Muste Memorial Institute, p. 18; **John F. Kennedy:** *Radio and Television Report to the American People on Civil Rights,* June 11, 1963; **Bob Dylan:** *Blowin' In The Wind* by Bob Dylan. Copyright © 1962 (Renewed 1990) Special Rider Music (SESAC); **Martin Luther King, Jr.:** "I Have a Dream." Speech in Washington, D.C., August 1963, quoted in Winkler, Allan M. *The Recent Past: Readings on America Since World War II.* Harper and Row, 1989, p. 275; **Fannie Lou Hamer:** Harley, Sharon, et al. *The African American Experience: A History.* Globe Book Company, 1992, p. 336; **Malcolm X:** *The Autobiography of Malcolm X.* Ballantine Books, 1990, pp. 245–246; **Stokely Carmichael:** Nash, Gary B., et al., eds. *The American People.* Harper and Row, 1986, p. 1001; **Martin Luther King, Jr.:** Kaiser, Charles. *1968 in America: Music, Politics, Chaos, Counterculture, and the Shaping of a Generation.* Weidenfeld and Nicolson, 1988, p. 144; **Barbara Jordan:** Harley, et al., p. 343.

Chapter 22 John F. Kennedy's Inaugural Address: Commager, Henry Steele, ed. *Documents of American History,* 8th ed. Appleton-Century-Crofts, 1968, pp. 668–670; **Kennedy speech at Rice University:** Swenson, Lloyd S., James M. Grimwood, and Charles C. Alexander. *This New Ocean, A History of Project Mercury.* NASA, 1966, frontispiece and p. 470; **Lyndon Johnson:** "Address Before a Joint Session of Congress, November 27, 1963." National Archives and Records Administration, The Lyndon B. Johnson Library and Museum, published online at www.lbjlib.utexas.edu; **John F. Kennedy's Inaugural Address:** Commager, pp. 668–670; **Senator J. William Fulbright:** Schlesinger, Arthur M. *A Thousand Days: John F. Kennedy in the White House.* Houghton Mifflin, 1965, p. 251; **Kennedy:** "Radio and Television Report to the American People on the Soviet Arms Buildup in Cuba, October 22, 1962." John Fitzgerald Kennedy Library, published online at www.jfklibrary.org.

Chapter 23 Helen Reddy: *I Am Woman* by Helen Reddy & Ray Burton. Copyright © 1971 Buggerlugs Music c/o Irving Music (BMI) and Irving Music (BMI); **Phyllis Schlafly:** Nash, Gary B. *The American People: Creating a Nation and a Society.* Harper and Row, 1986, p. 1008; **César Chávez:** Levy, Jacques E. *César Chávez: Autobiography of La Causa.* W. W. Norton, 1975, p. 293; **Onondaga Chief Oren Lyons:** *Voices from Wounded Knee: The People Are Standing Up.* Akwesasne Notes, 1974, p. 96; **Tom Law:** Makower, Joel. *Woodstock: The Oral History.* Doubleday, 1989, p. 333; **Rachel Carson:** *Silent Spring.* Houghton Mifflin, 1962, pp. 2–3; **Rachel Carson:** *Silent Spring.* p. 6; **Lyndon Johnson:** Archer, Jules, *The Incredible Sixties: The Stormy Years That Changed America.* Harcourt Brace Jovanovich, 1986, p. 172; **Ralph Nader:** *Unsafe at Any Speed: The Designed-in Dangers of the American Automobile.* Grossman Publishers, 1972, preface.

Chapter 24 Dwight Eisenhower: Press conference of April 7, 1954. *The Columbia World of Quotations.* Columbia University Press, 1996, no. 18606. **Robert McNamara:** Shapley, Deborah. *Promise and Power: The Life and Times of Robert McNamara.* Little, Brown and Company, 1993, p. 263; **Lyndon B. Johnson:** Kearns, Doris. *Lyndon Johnson and the American Dream.* Harper and Row, 1976, p. 316; **James Webb:** "Heroes of the Vietnam Generation," *The American Enterprise,* September 2000, p. 22; **Letter home from an American soldier:** Edelman, Bernard, ed. *Dear America: Letters Home from Vietnam.* New York Veterans Memorial Commission; **Le Thanh:** Chanoff, David, and Van Toai Doan. *Portrait of the Enemy.* Random House, 1986, pp. 62–63; **Vietnamese peasant:** Trullinger, James Walker, Jr. *Village at War: An Account of Revolution in Vietnam.* Longman, 1980, p. 118; **"Ballad of the Green Berets":** "Ballad of the Green Berets" by Robert L. Moore, Jr. & Barry A. Sadler. Copyright © 1965, 1966 Eastaboga Music (ASCAP); **Private Paul Meadlo:** *The New York Times,* November 25, 1969, p. 16; **Dean Rusk:** *Vietnam: A Television History: The Tet Offensive (1968),* transcript. www.pbs.org; **John McNaughton:** Karnow, Stanley, *Vietnam: A History.* Viking, 1983, p. 479; **Port Huron Statement:** Hayden, Tom. Students for a Democratic Society. Quoted in Winkler, Allan. *The Recent Past: Readings on America Since World War II.* Harper and Row, 1989, pp. 218–219; **Robert F. Kennedy:** Holland, Gini, *A Cultural History of the United States Through the Decades: The 1960s.* Lucent Books, 1999, p. 54; **Lyndon Johnson:** King, Larry L. "LBJ and Vietnam" from *A Sense of History: The Best Writing from the Pages of American Heritage.* American Heritage/Houghton Mifflin Company, 1985, p. 801; **Theodore H. White:** *The Making of the President 1968.* Atheneum, 1969, p. 298; **Richard Nixon:** "Nixon's 'Silent Majority' speech," *Vietnam War History, Speeches, Commentary.* www.geocities.com; **Richard Nixon:** Address to the Nation on the Situation in Southeast Asia. April 30, 1970.

Chapter 25 Richard Nixon: Wicker, Tom. *One of Us: Richard Nixon and the American Dream.* Random House, 1991, p. 9; **Richard Nixon's First Inaugural Address:** *Inaugural Addresses of the Presidents of the United States.* Washington, D.C.: U.S. G.P.O.: for sale by the Supt. of Docs., U.S. G.P.O., 1989; Bartleby.com, 2001. www.bartleby.com/124/. [November 6, 2001]; **Henry Kissinger:** *The White House Years.* Little, Brown and Company, 1979, p. 45; **Richard Nixon, report to Congress, 1970:** *The Memoirs of Richard Nixon.* Grosset & Dunlap, 1978, p. 545; **Richard Nixon:** *Public Papers of the Presidents of the United States: Richard Nixon,* p. 320; **Theodore H. White:** *Breach of Faith.* Atheneum Publishers, Reader's Digest Press, 1975, p. 322; **John J. Sirica:** Bernstein, Carl, and Bob Woodward. *All the President's Men.* Warner Paperback Books, 1975, p. 268; **M. Caldwell Butler:** Burns, James MacGregor. *The Crosswinds of Freedom.* Alfred A. Knopf, 1989, p. 507; **Gerald R. Ford:** *A Time to Heal.* Harper and Row, 1979, pp. 124–125; **Gerald R. Ford:** *A Time to Heal,* pp. 177–178; **Jerald F. terHorst:** P. Goldman, et al. "How Good a President?" October 18, 1976, p. 31; **Jimmy Carter's Inaugural Address:** *Inaugural Addresses of the Presidents of the United States.* Washington, D.C.: U.S. G.P.O.: for sale by the Supt. of Docs., U.S. G.P.O., 1989; Bartleby.com, 2001. www.bartleby.com/124/. [November 6, 2002]; **Cyrus Vance:** *Hard Choices: Critical Years in America's Foreign Policy.* Simon and Schuster, 1983, pp. 228–229; **Kathryn Koob:** *Guest of the Revolution.* Thomas Nelson Publishers, 1982, p. 73.

Chapter 26 Richard Nixon: Cannon, Lou. *Role of a Lifetime.* Simon & Schuster, 1991, p.71; **Ronald Reagan:** Willis, Henry. "Reagan Rejects Debate With Carter." *Eugene Register-Guard,* September 26, 1980, p. 7; **Ronald Reagan:** *Speaking My Mind.* Simon & Schuster, 1989. p. 64; **Ronald Reagan:** "Putting America Back to Work," January 20, 1981. *Vital Speeches of the Day,* Vol. XLVII, No. 9, February 15, 1981; **Kevin Phillips:** "Reagan's America: A Capital Offense." *The New York Times Magazine,* June 24, 1990; **George Bush:** "Open Letter to College Students on the Persian Gulf Crisis," January 9, 1991.

Chapter 27 Bill Clinton's First Inaugural Address: *The New York Times,* January 22, 1993, p. A13.

Skills for Life Christopher Columbus: Phillips, William D. Jr., and Carla Rahn Phillips. *The Worlds of Christopher Columbus.* Cambridge University Press, 1992, p. 111; **Harry Smith:** Smith, G.C. Moore, ed. *The Autobiography of Lieutenant-General Sir Harry Smith.* E.P. Dutton and Company, 1902, p. 200; **Dolley Madison:** Colbert, David, ed. *Eyewitness to America: 500 Years of America in the Words of Those Who Saw It Happen.* Pantheon Books, 1997; **Henry Clay:** *Speech of Mr. Henry Clay, of Kentucky, on the Measures of Compromise.* Jno. T. Towers, 1850, p. 24; **Dr. Samuel McGill:** Barrett, John G. *Sherman's March Through the Carolinas.* The University of North Carolina Press, 1956, p. 95; **William Tecumseh Sherman:** *Memoirs of General William T. Sherman.* Greenwood Press, 1974, pp. 249, 254; **The Railroad Strike:** *The Manufacturer and Builder,* August 1877, p. 170; **Woodrow Wilson:** Appeal for Neutrality, Message to the Senate, August 18, 1914; **Theodore Roosevelt:** *America and the World War.* C. Scribner's Sons, 1915; **Irving N. Fisher:** Grunwald, Lisa, and Stephen J. Adler. *Letters of the Century: America, 1900–1999.* The Dial Press, 1999; **Gordon Parks:** *Voices in the Mirror: An Autobiography.* Doubleday, 1990, p. 35; **Dick Russell:** *Black Genius and the American Experience.* Carroll and Graf, 1998, p. 146; **Herbert Hoover:** *American Ideals Versus the New Deal.* Scribner Press, 1936; **Harry S Truman:** Truman, Margaret, ed. *Where the Buck Stops: The Personal and Private Writings of Harry S. Truman.* Warner Books, 1989, pp. 205–206; **Harry S Truman:** Merrill, Dennis. *Documentary History of the Truman Presidency,* vol. 9. University Publications of America, 1996, pp. 444, 446–447; **Alton R. Lee:** *Truman and Taft-Hartley: A Question of Mandate.* University of Kentucky Press, 1966, pp. 93–95; **John Lewis:** Interview in *Newsweek,* November 28, 1983; **Opponent of ERA:** Boles, Janet K. *The Politics of the Equal Rights Amendment.* Longman, 1979, p.121; **Proponent of Era:** Longwell, Marjorie. "The American Woman—Then and Now," *Delta Kappa Gamma Magazine,* Fall, 1969; **Howard Zinn:** Excerpt from *A People's History of the United States 1492–Present* by Howard Zinn. Copyright © 1980, 1995 by Howard Zinn. Reprinted by permission of HarperCollins Publishers, Inc.; **John M. Dunn:** Excerpt from *The Vietnam War: A History of U.S. Involvement* by John M. Dunn. Copyright © 2001 by Lucent Books, Inc. Reprinted by permission.

SOURCE READINGS ACKNOWLEDGMENTS/LITERATURE

Unit 1 *Of Plymouth Plantation, 1640–1647:* From *Of Plymouth Plantation,*1640–1647 by William Bradford. Ed. Samuel Eliot Morison. New York: Knopf, 1952. ***April Morning:*** From *April Morning* by Howard Fast. Copyright ©1961 by Howard Fast. Copyright renewed 1989. **Unit 2 *Incidents in the Life of a Slave Girl:*** Hariet Ann Jacobs, *Incidents in the Life of a Slave Girl: Written by Herself.* (Cambridge, MA: Harvard University Press, 1987). ***Slavery in Massachusetts:*** Henry David Thoreau. From *The Norton Anthology of American Literature,* Second Edition, Vol. 1. Ed. Nina Baym, et al. New York: W.W. Norton and Company, 1985. **Unit 3 *Hungry Hearts:*** Anzia Yezierska. Permission granted by Ayer Company Publishers. ***A Farewell to Arms:*** Ernest Hemingway. New York: Charles Scribner's Sons, 1957. **Unit 4 *Growing Up:*** From *Growing Up,* by Russell Baker. Copyright © 1982 by Russell Baker. **Unit 5 *Night:*** Excerpt from *NIGHT* by Eli Wiesel, translated by Stella Rodway. Copyright © by MacGibbon & Kee. Copyright renewed © 1988 by the Collins Publishers Group. **Unit 6 "Letter from Birmingham Jail":** Excerpt from *Letter from Birmingham Jail* from WHY WE CAN'T WAIT by Martin Luther King, Jr. Copyright © 1963 Martin Luther King, Jr. Copyright renewed 1991 by Coretta Scott King. Reprinted by arrangement with The Heirs to the Estate of Martin Luther King, Jr. c/o Writer's House, Inc. as agent for the proprietor. **Unit 7 "Straw Into Gold: The Metamorphosis of the Everyday":** Excerpt from *Straw Into Gold: The Metamorphosis of the Everyday* by Sandra Cisneros. Copyright © 1987 by Sandra Cisneros. Reprinted by permission of Susan Bergholz Literary Services, New York. All rights reserved.

SOURCE READINGS ACKNOWLEDGMENTS/DOCUMENTS

The Iroquois Constitution: by Dekanawidah. Published online at The University of Oklahoma Law Center www.law.ou.edu/hist/iroquois.html; **The Mayflower Compact:** Published online at The University of Oklahoma Law Center www.law.ou.edu/hist/mayflow.html; **An Act for the Gradual Abolition of Slavery:** Pennsylvania,1780. Published online at The Avalon Project at the Yale Law School www.yale.edu/lawweb/avalon/states/statutes/pennst01.htm. Spelling updated.; **President Wilson's Address to Congress:** April 2, 1917. Published online at The World War I Document Archive www.lib.byu.edu/~rdh/wwi/1917/wilswarm.html; **The Universal Declaration of Human Rights:** The United Nations. Published online at The United Nations www.un.org/Overview/rights.html; **President Eisenhower's Farewell Address to the Nation:** January 17, 1961. Published online at University of Houston History Department http://vi.uh.edu/pages/buzzmat/ikefarewell.htm; **Mikhail Gorbachev's Address to the Forty-Third UN General Assembly Session:** December 7, 1988. Published online at CNN Interactive www.cnn.com/SPECIALS/cold.war/episodes/23/documents/gorbachev/

Note: Every effort has been made to locate the copyright owner of material used in this textbook. Omissions brought to our attention will be corrected in subsequent editions.

1048